Sporting News BOOKS

BASEBALL REGISTER

2004 EDITION

Major league statistics compiled by STATS, Inc., a News Corporation company, 8130 Lehigh Avenue, Morton Grove, IL 60053. STATS is a trademark of Sports Team Analysis and Tracking Systems, Inc.

Minor league statistics provided by SportsTicker.

ISBN: 0-89204-726-7

10 9 8 7 6 5 4 3 2 1

CONTENTS

EXPLANATION OF FOOTNOTES AND ABBREVIATIONS

Note for statistical comparisons: Player strikes forced the cancellation of games in the 1972 season (10 days missed), the 1981 season (50 days missed), the 1994 season (52 days missed) and the 1995 season (18 games missed).

Positions are listed in descending order of games played; because of limited space, pinch-hitter and pinch-runner are listed in the regular-season section only if a player did not play a defensive position.

*   Led league. For fielding statistics, the player led the league at the position shown.
•   Tied for league lead. For fielding statistics, the player tied for the league lead at the position shown.
†   Led league, but number indicated is total figure for two or more positions.
‡   Tied for league lead, but number indicated is total figure for two or more positions.
§   Led or tied for league lead, but total figure is divided between two different teams.
...   Statistic unavailable, inapplicable, unofficial or mathematically impossible to calculate.
—   Manager statistic inapplicable.

LEAGUES: A.A., Am. Assoc.—American Association. **A.L.**—American. **App., Appal.**—Appalachian. **Ar., Ariz.**—Arizona. **Atl.**—Atlantic. **Cal., Calif.**—California. **Car., Caro.**—Carolina. **CRL**—Cocoa Rookie. **DSL**—Dominican Summer. **East.**—Eastern. **Evan.**—Evangeline. **Fla. St., Florida St., FSL**—Florida State. **GCL**—Gulf Coast. **GSL**—Gulf States. **In.-Am.**—Inter-American. **Int'l., I.L.**—International. **J.P., Jap. Pac., Jp. Pac.**—Japan Pacific. **Jp. Cen., Jp. Cn.**—Japan Central. **Jp. East**—Japan East. **Jp. West**—Japan West. **Mex.**—Mexican. **Mex. Cen.**—Mexican Center. **Mid., Midw.**—Midwest. **Miss.-O.V.**—Mississippi-Ohio Valley. **N.C. St.**—North Carolina State. **N.L.**—National. **North.**—Northern. **N'West, NW**—Northwest. **NYP, NY-P, NY-Penn**—New York-Pennsylvania. **Pac. Coast, PCL**—Pacific Coast. **Pio.**—Pioneer. **S. Atl., SAL**—South Atlantic. **Soph.**—Sophomore. **Sou., South.**—Southern. **Taiw.**—Taiwan. **Tex.**—Texas. **West.**—Western. **W. Car., W. Caro.**—Western Carolinas.

TEAMS: Aguas.—Aguascalientes. **Alb./Colon., Alb./Colonie**—Albany/Colonie. **Ariz.**—Arizona. **Ariz. D-backs**—Arizona League Diamondbacks. **Belling.**—Bellingham. **Birm.**—Birmingham. **Brevard Co.**—Brevard County. **Cant./Akr.**—Canton/Akron. **Ced. Rap.**—Cedar Rapids. **Cent. Ore.**—Central Oregon. **Central Vall.**—Central Valley. **Char., Charl.**—Charleston. **Chatt.**—Chattanooga. **Chiba Lot.**—Chiba Lotte. **Ciu. Juarez**—Ciudad Juarez. **Colo. Spr., Colo. Springs**—Colorado Springs. **Dall./Fort W.**—Dallas/Fort Worth. **Day. Beach.**—Daytona Beach. **Dm., Dom.**—Dominican. **Dom. B. Jays**—Dominican Blue Jays. **Dom. Orioles/WS**—Dominican Orioles/White Sox. **Elizabeth.**—Elizabethton. **Estadio Quis.**—Estadio Quisqueya. **Eve.**—Everett. **Fort Lauder., Fort Laud.**—Fort Lauderdale. **Fukuoka**—Fukuoka Daiei. **GC**—Gulf Coast. **GC Astros-Or.**—Gulf Coast Astros-Orange. **GC Royals-Bl.**—Gulf Coast Royals-Blue. **GC Whi. Sox**—Gulf Coast White Sox. **Grays Har.**—Grays Harbor. **Greens.**—Greensboro. **Greenw.**—Greenwood. **Guana.**—Guanajuato. **H.P.-Thomas.**—High Point-Thomasville. **Hunting.**—Huntington. **Jacksonv.**—Jacksonville. **Johns. City**—Johnson City. **Kane Co.**—Kane County. **Lake Charl.**—Lake Charles. **Matt.**—Mattoon. **M.C., Mex. City**—Mexico City. **Med. Hat**—Medicine Hat. **Monc.**—Monclova. **Niag. F., Niag. Falls**—Niagara Falls. **Okla. City**—Oklahoma City. **Pan. City**—Panama City. **Phoe.**—Phoenix. **Pomp. Beach**—Pompano Beach. **Pres. Lions**—President Lions. **Prin. Will., Prin. William**—Prince William. **Ral./Dur.**—Raleigh/Durham. **Rancho Cuca.**—Rancho Cucamonga. **Rocky Mount.**—Rocky Mountain. **Salt.**—Saltillo. **Salt.-Monc.**—Saltillo-Monclova. **San. Dom., San. Domingo**—Santo Domingo. **San Bern.**—San Bernardino. **San Fran.**—San Francisco. **Schen.**—Schenectady. **Scran./W.B.**—Scranton/Wilkes-Barre. **S.C.**—South Carolina. **S.F. de Mac.**—San Francisco de Macoris. **San Luis Pot.**—San Luis Potosi. **Sonoma Co.**—Sonoma County. **S. Oregon**—Southern Oregon. **Spartan.**—Spartanburg. **St. Cath., St. Cathar.**—St. Catharines. **St. Peters., St. Pete.**—St. Petersburg. **States.**—Statesville. **Stock.**—Stockton. **T.-C., Tri-Cities. Vanc.**—Vancouver. **Ven.**—Venezuelan. **Vent. Co.**—Ventura County. **W. Mich.**—West Michigan. **Win.-Salem, Winst.-Salem**—Winston-Salem. **Wis. Rap., Wis. Rapids**—Wisconsin Rapids. **W.P. Beach**—West Palm Beach. **W.Va.**—West Virginia. **Yuc.**—Yucatan.

STATISTICS: A—assists. **AB**—at-bats. **Avg.**—average (average allowed for pitchers). **BB**—bases on balls. **CG**—complete games. **CS**—caught stealing. **E**—errors. **ER**—earned runs. **ERA**—earned run average. **G**—games. **GDP**—grounded into double play. **GS**—games started. **H**—hits. **HBP**—hit by pitch. **Hld.**—holds. **HR**—home runs. **IBB**—intentional bases on balls. **IP**—innings pitched. **L**—losses. **OBP**—on-base percentage. **OPS**—on-base percentage plus slugging percentage. **Pct.**—winning percentage. **PO**—putouts. **Pos.**—position. **R**—runs. **RBI**—runs batted in. **SB**—stolen bases. **ShO**—shutouts. **SLG**—slugging percentage. **SO**—strikeouts. **Sv.**—saves. **Sv.Opp.**—save opportunities. **W**—wins. **WHIP**—walks plus hits divided by innings pitched. **2B**—doubles. **3B**—triples.

PLAYERS

ABAD, ANDY — OF/1B

PERSONAL: Born August 25, 1972, in Palm Beach, Fla. ... 5-11/196. ... Bats left, throws left. ... Full name: Fausto Andres Abad. ... Junior college: Middle Georgia College.
TRANSACTIONS/CAREER NOTES: Selected by Boston Red Sox organization in 16th round of free-agent draft (June 3, 1993). ... Granted free agency (October 15, 1999). ... Signed by Kintetsu Buffaloes of Japan Pacific League (2000). ... Signed by Oakland Athletics organization (November 15, 2000). ... Granted free agency (October 15, 2001). ... Signed by Florida Marlins organization (November 20, 2001). ... Granted free agency (October 15, 2002). ... Signed by Boston Red Sox as free agent; contract purchased by Boston (September 2, 2003).
2003 GAMES PLAYED BY POSITION (MLB): 1B—7, OF—1.

Year Team (League)	Pos.	G	AB	R	H	2B	3B	HR	RBI	BB	SO	HBP	GDP	SB-CS	Avg.	OBP	SLG	OPS	E	Pct.
1993— GC Red Sox (GCL)	1B-OF	59	230	24	57	9	2	1	28	25	27	2	2	2-2	.248	.322	.317	.639	1	.995
1994— Sarasota (Fla. St.)	1B-OF	111	354	39	102	20	0	2	35	42	58	5	9	2-12	.288	.367	.362	.729	5	.975
1995— Trenton (East.)	OF	89	287	29	69	14	3	4	32	36	58	3	6	5-7	.240	.328	.352	.680	2	.987
— Sarasota (Fla. St.)	1B-OF	18	59	5	17	3	0	0	10	6	13	0	0	4-3	.288	.354	.339	.693	2	.980
1996— Sarasota (Fla. St.)	P-1B-OF	58	202	28	58	15	1	2	41	37	28	3	6	10-3	.287	.402	.401	.803	5	.985
— Trenton (East.)	1B-OF	65	213	33	59	22	1	4	39	33	41	0	4	5-3	.277	.369	.446	.815	1	.997
1997— Trenton (East.)	1B-OF	45	165	37	50	13	0	8	24	33	27	2	2	2-4	.303	.423	.527	.950	3	.986
— Pawtucket (Int'l)	1B-OF	68	227	28	62	7	0	9	32	36	47	2	4	3-2	.273	.376	.423	.799	8	.978
1998— Pawtucket (Int'l)	1B-OF	111	365	71	112	18	1	16	66	68	70	3	7	10-6	.307	.415	.493	.908	5	.994
1999— Pawtucket (Int'l)	1B-OF	102	377	61	112	21	4	15	65	51	50	2	9	7-2	.297	.381	.493	.874	6	.980
2000— Kintetsu (Jp. West.)		61	233	35	72	12	1	8	48	30	18			3-...	.309	...	.472	...	...	...
— Kintetsu (Jp. Pac.)		32	92	7	15	1	0	4	13	9	17			0-...	.163	...	.304	...	...	...
2001— Sacramento (PCL)	OF-1B	124	462	72	139	19	2	19	82	58	67	1	12	4-2	.301	.379	.474	.853	6	.974
— Oakland (A.L.)	1B	1	1	0	0	0	0	0	0	0	0	0	0	0-0	.000	.000	.000	.000	0	1.000
2002— Calgary (PCL)	OF-1B	111	352	50	106	28	2	11	70	57	44	4	7	0-3	.301	.402	.486	.888	3	.991
2003— Pawtucket (Int'l)	1B-OF-DH	134	504	78	153	35	3	13	93	55	67	4	15	0-3	.304	.372	.462	.834	5	.994
— Boston (A.L.)	1B-OF	9	17	1	2	0	0	0	0	2	5	0	1	0-1	.118	.211	.118	.328	1	.973
Major League totals (2 years)		10	18	1	2	0	0	0	0	2	5	0	1	0-1	.111	.200	.111	.311	1	.974

ABBOTT, PAUL — P

PERSONAL: Born September 15, 1967, in Van Nuys, Calif. ... 6-2/203. ... Throws right, bats right. ... Full name: Paul David Abbott. ... High school: Sunny Hills (Fullerton, Calif.).
TRANSACTIONS/CAREER NOTES: Selected by Minnesota Twins organization in third round of free-agent draft (June 3, 1985). ... On Minnesota disabled list (March 28-June 5 and August 14-September 1, 1992). ... Released by Twins (March 2, 1993). ... Signed by Cleveland Indians organization (March 27, 1993). ... On Canton/Akron disabled list (April 8-May 6, 1993). ... Granted free agency (October 15, 1993). ... Signed by Kansas City Royals organization (November 21, 1993). ... On disabled list (March 18-May 25 and June 16-30, 1994). ... Released by Royals (June 30, 1994). ... Signed by Chicago Cubs organization (March 17, 1995). ... Granted free agency (October 16, 1995). ... Signed by San Diego Padres organization (November 29, 1995). ... Granted free agency (October 15, 1996). ... Signed by Seattle Mariners organization (January 10, 1997). ... On Tacoma disabled list (May 23-July 14, 1997). ... On Orlando disabled list (April 2-August 21, 1998); included rehabilitation assignment to Arizona League Mariners (August 19-21). ... Released by Mariners (December 14, 1998). ... Re-signed by Mariners (January 21, 1999). ... On New Haven disabled list (April 9-June 12, 1999). ... On Seattle disabled list (April 1-28, 2001); included rehabilitation assignment to Tacoma (April 23-28). ... On Seattle disabled list (May 6, 2002-remainder of season); included rehabilitation assignment to San Bernardino (June 3-9) and Tacoma (June 10-17). ... Released by Mariners (November 19, 2002). ... Signed by Arizona Diamondbacks as a free agent (February 10, 2003). ... Traded by Diamondbacks to Kansas City Royals for P Aric LeClair (August 8, 2003).
CAREER HITTING: 3-for-9 (.333), 1 R, 1 2B, 0 3B, 0 HR, 0 RBI.

Year League	W	L	Pct.	ERA	WHIP	G	GS	CG	ShO	Hld.	Sv.-Opp.	IP	H	R	ER	HR	BB-IBB	SO	Avg.
1985— Elizabethton (Appal.)	1	5	.167	6.94	1.86	10	10	1	0	...	0-...	35.0	33	32	27	3	32-0	34	.237
1986— Kenosha (Midw.)	6	10	.375	4.50	1.79	25	15	1	0	...	0-...	98.0	102	62	49	13	73-3	73	.267
1987— Kenosha (Midw.)	13	6	.684	3.65	1.41	26	25	1	0	...	0-...	145.1	102	76	59	11	103-0	138	.203
1988— Visalia (Cal.)	11	9	.550	4.18	1.65	28	•28	4	2	...	0-...	172.1	141	95	80	9	*143-5	*205	.222
1989— Orlando (Sou.)	9	3	.750	4.37	1.31	17	17	1	0	...	0-...	90.2	71	48	44	6	48-0	102	.210
1990— Portland (PCL)	5	14	.263	4.56	1.50	23	23	4	1	...	0-...	128.1	110	75	65	9	82-0	129	.230
— Minnesota (A.L.)	0	5	.000	5.97	1.88	7	7	0	0	0	0-0	34.2	37	24	23	0	28-0	25	.282
1991— Portland (PCL)	2	3	.400	3.89	1.45	8	8	1	1	...	0-...	44.0	36	19	19	2	28-0	40	.224
— Minnesota (A.L.)	3	1	.750	4.75	1.56	15	3	0	0	0	0-0	47.1	38	27	25	5	36-1	43	.232
1992— Portland (PCL)	4	1	.800	2.33	1.32	7	7	0	0	...	0-...	46.1	30	13	12	2	31-0	46	.188
— Minnesota (A.L.)	0	0	...	3.27	1.55	6	0	0	0	0	0-0	11.0	12	4	4	1	5-0	13	.279
1993— Cant./Akr. (Eastern)	4	5	.444	4.06	1.33	13	12	1	0	...	0-...	75.1	72	34	34	4	28-2	86	.253
— Cleveland (A.L.)	0	1	.000	6.38	1.64	5	5	0	0	0	0-...	18.1	19	15	13	5	11-1	7	.260
— Charlotte (Int'l)	0	1	.000	6.63	1.68	4	4	0	0	...	0-...	19.0	25	16	14	4	7-0	12	.313
1994— Omaha (Am. Assoc.)	4	1	.800	4.87	1.78	15	10	0	0	...	0-...	57.1	57	32	31	8	45-0	48	.266
1995— Iowa (Am. Assoc.)	7	7	.500	3.67	1.46	46	11	0	0	...	0-...	115.1	104	50	47	12	64-4	*127	.242
1996— Las Vegas (PCL)	4	2	.667	4.18	1.39	28	0	0	0	...	7-...	28.0	27	14	13	4	12-4	37	.260
1997— Tacoma (PCL)	8	4	.667	4.13	1.16	17	14	3	0	...	0-...	93.2	80	48	43	11	29-1	117	.228
— Ariz. Mariners (Ariz.)	0	0	...	0.93	0.72	3	3	0	0	...	0-...	9.2	2	1	1	0	7-0	13	.000
1998— Ariz. Mariners (Ariz.)	0	0	...	0.00	0.33	1	0	0	0	...	0-...	3.0	1	0	0	0	0-0	6	.091
— Tacoma (PCL)	1	0	1.000	1.20	0.93	3	3	0	0	...	0-...	15.0	9	2	2	2	5-0	20	.176
— Seattle (A.L.)	3	1	.750	4.01	1.38	4	4	0	0	0	0-0	24.2	24	11	11	2	10-0	22	.255
1999— Tacoma (PCL)	1	1	.500	6.43	1.79	2	2	0	0	...	0-...	14.0	21	11	10	1	4-0	10	.375
— Seattle (A.L.)	6	2	.750	3.10	1.13	25	7	0	0	3	0-2	72.2	50	31	25	9	32-3	68	.193
2000— Seattle (A.L.)	9	7	.563	4.22	1.36	35	27	0	0	4	0-0	179.0	164	89	84	23	80-4	100	.243
2001— Tacoma (PCL)	0	0	...	0.00	1.25	1	1	0	0	...	0-...	4.0	1	0	0	0	4-0	4	.077
— Seattle (A.L.)	17	4	.810	4.25	1.42	28	27	1	0	0	0-0	163.0	145	79	77	21	87-5	118	.238
2002— Seattle (A.L.)	1	3	.250	11.96	2.28	7	5	0	0	0	0-0	26.1	40	36	35	5	20-0	22	.351
— San Bernardino (Calif.)	0	0	...	0.00	1.00	1	1	0	0	...	0-...	5.0	3	0	0	0	2-0	5	.188
— Tacoma (PCL)	0	1	.000	6.23	1.85	2	2	0	0	...	0-...	8.2	13	10	6	3	3-0	8	.342
2003— Tucson (PCL)	3	4	.429	3.95	1.37	11	8	1	0	...	0-...	54.2	63	29	24	3	12-0	50	.289
— Kansas City (A.L.)	1	2	.333	5.29	1.53	10	8	0	0	0	0-0	47.2	47	29	28	8	26-2	32	.257
Major League totals (10 years)	40	26	.606	4.68	1.46	142	93	1	0	7	0-2	624.2	576	345	325	79	335-16	450	.246

ABERNATHY, BRENT   2B

PERSONAL: Born September 23, 1977, in Atlanta, Ga. ... 6-1/191. ... Bats right, throws right. ... Full name: Michael Brent Abernathy. ... High school: Lovett School (Atlanta, Ga.).

TRANSACTIONS/CAREER NOTES: Selected by Toronto Blue Jays organization in second round of free-agent draft (June 4, 1996); pick received as part of compensation from Florida Marlins for signing of Type B free agent OF Devon White. ... On Syracuse disabled list (June 21-28, 2000). ... Traded by Blue Jays with player to be named later to Tampa Bay Devil Rays for P Steve Trachsel and P Mark Guthrie (July 31, 2000). ... On Durham disabled list (April 15-May 2, 2001). ... Claimed on waivers by Kansas City Royals (April 4, 2003). ... Recalled from Omaha (May 28, 2003). ... Optioned to Omaha (June 20, 2003). ... Recalled from Omaha (June 26, 2003). ... Optioned to Omaha (July 3, 2003). ... Recalled from Omaha (September 29, 2003).

2003 GAMES PLAYED BY POSITION (MLB): 2B—11.

Year	Team (League)	Pos.	G	AB	R	H	2B	3B	HR	RBI	BB	SO	HBP	GDP	SB-CS	Avg.	OBP	SLG	OPS	E	Pct.
1997—Hagerstown (SAL)		2B	99	379	69	117	27	2	1	26	30	32	6	6	22-13	.309	.367	.398	.765	12	.973
1998—Dunedin (Fla. St.)		2B	124	485	85	159	36	1	3	65	44	38	1	11	35-13	.328	.381	.425	.806	16	.973
1999—Knoxville (Sou.)		2B	136	*577	*108	*168	42	1	13	62	55	47	6	11	34-15	.291	.355	.435	.790	16	.976
2000—Syracuse (Int'l)		2B	92	358	47	106	21	2	4	35	26	32	1	7	14-13	.296	.343	.399	.742	11	.973
—Durham (Int'l)		2B	27	91	14	24	6	0	1	15	11	11	4	0	9-2	.264	.351	.363	.714	3	.973
2001—Durham (Int'l)		2B	61	252	45	76	20	0	4	23	16	23	2	3	11-4	.302	.346	.429	.774	9	.969
—Tampa Bay (A.L.)		2B	79	304	43	82	17	1	5	33	27	35	0	3	8-3	.270	.328	.382	.710	7	.981
2002—Tampa Bay (A.L.)		2B-DH	117	463	46	112	18	4	2	40	25	46	6	8	10-4	.242	.288	.311	.599	12	.979
2003—Tampa Bay (A.L.)		2B	2	7	1	0	0	0	0	0	0	0	0	0	1-0	.000	.000	.000	.000	1	.900
—Durham (Int'l)		2B	1	5	0	3	0	0	0	1	0	0	0	0	0-0	.600	.600	.600	1.200	0	.000
—Kansas City (A.L.)		2B	10	27	2	2	0	0	0	0	1	3	0	2	0-0	.074	.107	.074	.181	0	1.000
—Omaha (PCL)		2B-3B-SS	92	368	60	107	22	0	7	40	34	38	4	9	13-7	.291	.354	.408	.761	12	.973
Major League totals (3 years)			208	801	92	196	35	5	7	73	53	84	6	13	19-7	.245	.295	.327	.623	20	.980

ABREU, BOBBY   OF

PERSONAL: Born March 11, 1974, in Aragua, Venezuela. ... 6-0/200. ... Bats left, throws right. ... Full name: Bob Kelly Abreu. ... Name pronounced: ah-BRAY-you.

TRANSACTIONS/CAREER NOTES: Signed as non-drafted free agent by Houston Astros organization (August 21, 1990). ... On Houston disabled list (May 25-July 1, 1997); included rehabilitation assignments to Jackson (June 23-26) and New Orleans (June 27-July 1). ... Selected by Tampa Bay Devil Rays in first round (sixth pick overall) of expansion draft (November 18, 1997). ... Traded by Devil Rays to Philadelphia Phillies for SS Kevin Stocker (November 18, 1997).

2003 GAMES PLAYED BY POSITION (MLB): OF—158.

Year	Team (League)	Pos.	G	AB	R	H	2B	3B	HR	RBI	BB	SO	HBP	GDP	SB-CS	Avg.	OBP	SLG	OPS	E	Pct.
1991—GC Astros (GCL)		SS-OF	56	183	21	55	7	3	0	20	17	27	1	3	10-6	.301	.358	.372	.729	5	.943
1992—Asheville (S. Atl.)		OF	135	480	81	140	21	4	8	48	63	79	3	5	15-11	.292	.375	.402	.777	11	.943
1993—Osceola (Fla. St.)		OF	129	474	62	134	21	17	5	55	51	90	1	8	10-14	.283	.352	.430	.782	8	.961
1994—Jackson (Texas)		OF	118	400	61	121	25	9	16	73	42	81	3	2	12-10	.303	.368	.530	.898	4	.967
1995—Tucson (PCL)		OF-2B	114	415	72	126	24	*17	10	75	67	120	1	6	16-14	.304	.395	.516	.911	7	.970
1996—Tucson (PCL)		OF-DH	132	484	86	138	14	*16	13	68	83	111	2	5	24-18	.285	.391	.461	.851	7	.969
—Houston (N.L.)		OF	15	22	1	5	1	0	0	1	2	3	0	1	0-0	.227	.292	.273	.564	0	1.000
1997—Houston (N.L.)		OF	59	188	22	47	10	2	3	26	21	48	1	0	7-2	.250	.329	.372	.701	2	.978
—Jackson (Texas)		OF	3	12	2	2	1	0	0	0	1	5	0	0	0-0	.167	.231	.250	.481	0	1.000
—New Orleans (A.A.)		OF	47	194	25	52	9	4	2	22	21	49	0	4	7-4	.268	.335	.387	.721	1	.990
1998—Philadelphia (N.L.)		OF	151	497	68	155	29	6	17	74	84	133	0	6	19-10	.312	.409	.497	.906	8	.973
1999—Philadelphia (N.L.)		OF-DH	152	546	118	183	35	•11	20	93	109	113	3	13	27-9	.335	.446	.549	.995	3	.989
2000—Philadelphia (N.L.)		OF	154	576	103	182	42	10	25	79	100	116	1	12	28-8	.316	.416	.554	.970	4	.989
2001—Philadelphia (N.L.)		OF	•162	588	118	170	48	4	31	110	106	137	1	13	36-14	.289	.393	.543	.936	8	.976
2002—Philadelphia (N.L.)		OF	157	572	102	176	*50	6	20	85	104	117	3	11	31-12	.308	.413	.521	.934	5	.983
2003—Philadelphia (N.L.)		OF	158	577	99	173	35	1	20	101	109	126	2	13	22-9	.300	.409	.468	.877	6	.981
Major League totals (8 years)			1008	3566	631	1091	250	40	156	569	635	793	11	69	170-64	.306	.409	.513	.922	36	.982

ACEVEDO, JOSE   P

PERSONAL: Born December 18, 1977, in Santo Domingo, Dominican Republic. ... 6-0/185. ... Throws right, bats right. ... Full name: Jose Omar Acevedo. ... Name pronounced: AH-ceh-vedo.

TRANSACTIONS/CAREER NOTES: Signed as non-drafted free agent by Cincinnati Reds organization (December 7, 1996). ... Recalled from Louisville (July 18, 2003). ... Placed on 15-day disabled list (August 7, 2003).

CAREER HITTING: 5-for-50 (.100), 2 R, 2 2B, 0 3B, 0 HR, 3 RBI.

Year	League	W	L	Pct.	ERA	WHIP	G	GS	CG	ShO	Hld.	Sv.-Opp.	IP	H	R	ER	HR	BB-IBB	SO	Avg.
1997—Char., W.Va. (SAL)		3	3	.500	3.92	1.22	15	8	0	0	...	0-...	57.1	61	29	25	8	9-0	34	.268
1998—Char., W.Va. (SAL)		9	9	.500	3.91	1.32	25	25	2	0	...	0-...	158.2	169	74	69	9	40-0	132	.275
1999—Clinton (Midw.)		8	6	.571	3.77	1.21	24	24	1	1	...	0-...	133.2	119	65	56	14	43-0	136	.236
2000—Dayton (Midw.)		11	5	.688	3.89	1.33	25	23	0	0	...	0-...	141.0	135	74	61	16	53-0	123	.247
2001—Chattanooga (Sou.)		4	4	.500	3.69	1.19	16	11	0	0	...	0-...	78.0	68	34	32	7	25-1	82	.239
—Cincinnati (N.L.)		5	7	.417	5.44	1.41	18	18	0	0	0	0-0	96.0	101	61	58	17	34-2	68	.272
2002—Cincinnati (N.L.)		4	2	.667	7.23	1.69	6	5	0	0	0	0-0	23.2	28	21	19	8	12-0	14	.292
—Louisville (Int'l)		12	7	.632	3.20	1.16	23	23	0	0	...	0-...	154.2	146	61	55	16	34-0	128	.250
2003—Louisville (Int'l)		6	2	.750	3.43	1.26	29	3	0	0	...	0-...	60.1	56	26	23	5	20-1	57	.246
—Cincinnati (N.L.)		2	0	1.000	2.67	0.85	5	4	1	0	0	0-0	27.0	17	8	8	3	6-1	23	.183
Major League totals (3 years)		11	9	.550	5.22	1.35	29	27	1	0	0	0-0	146.2	146	90	85	28	52-3	105	.261

ACEVEDO, JUAN   P

PERSONAL: Born May 5, 1970, in Juarez, Mexico. ... 6-2/245. ... Throws right, bats right. ... Full name: Juan Carlos Acevedo. ... Name pronounced: OSS-uh-vay-doe. ... High school: Dundee-Crown (Carpentersville, Ill.). ... Junior college: Parkland College (Ill.).

TRANSACTIONS/CAREER NOTES: Selected by Colorado Rockies organization in 14th round of free-agent draft (June 1, 1992). ... Traded by Rockies with P Arnold Gooch to New York Mets for P Bret Saberhagen and a player to be named later (July 31, 1995); Rockies acquired P David Swanson to complete deal (August 4, 1995). ... On New York disabled list (March 26-May 9, 1996); included rehabilitation assignment to Norfolk (April 10-May 9). ... Traded by Mets to St. Louis Cardinals for P Rigo Beltran (March 29, 1998). ... On St. Louis disabled list (July 18-August 16, 1998); included rehabilitation assignment to Memphis (August 6-16). ... Traded by Cardinals with two players to be named later to Milwaukee Brewers for 2B Fernando Vina (December 20, 1999); Brewers acquired P Matt Parker and C Eliezer Alfonzo to complete deal (June 13, 2000). ...

On Milwaukee disabled list (April 7-30, 2000); included rehabilitation assignment to Indianapolis (April 25-29). ... Traded by Brewers with P Kane Davis and IF Jose Flores to Rockies for P Mark Leiter, P Mike DeJean and 2B/SS Elvis Pena (April 4, 2001). ... On Colorado disabled list (April 7-22 and April 29-May 24, 2001); included rehabilitation assignments to Colorado Springs (April 17-22 and May 17-24). ... Traded by Rockies to Florida Marlins for IF Josue Espada (August 6, 2001). ... Granted free agency (November 26, 2001). ... Re-signed by Detroit Tigers organization (December 20, 2001). ... Granted free agency (October 28, 2002). ... Signed by New York Yankees organization (January 27, 2003). ... Released by Yankees (June 10, 2003). ... Signed as free agent by Toronto Blue Jays (June 17, 2003). ... Placed on bereavement list (June 30, 2003). ... Given unconditional release (August 9, 2003).

CAREER HITTING: 6-for-65 (.092), 4 R, 2 2B, 0 3B, 0 HR, 0 RBI.

Year League	W	L	Pct.	ERA	WHIP	G	GS	CG	ShO	Hld.	Sv.-Opp.	IP	H	R	ER	HR	BB-IBB	SO	Avg.
1992— Bend (NW)	0	0	...	13.50	2.50	1	0	0	0	...	0-...	2.0	4	3	3	0	1-0	3	.400
—Visalia (Cal.)	3	4	.429	5.43	1.67	12	12	1	0	...	0-...	64.2	75	46	39	2	33-0	37	.301
1993—Central Valley (Cal.)	9	8	.529	4.40	1.49	27	20	1	0	...	0-...	118.2	119	68	58	8	58-0	107	.263
1994—New Haven (East.)	* 17	6	.739	2.37	1.03	26	26	5	2	...	0-...	174.2	142	56	46	16	38-0	161	.219
1995—Colorado (N.L.)	4	6	.400	6.44	1.55	17	11	0	0	1	0-0	65.2	82	53	47	15	20-2	40	.317
—Colo. Springs (PCL)	1	1	.500	6.14	1.70	3	3	0	0	...	0-...	14.2	18	11	10	0	7-0	7	.316
—Norfolk (Int'l)	0	0	...	0.00	0.33	2	2	0	0	...	0-...	3.0	0	0	0	0	1-0	2	.000
1996—Norfolk (Int'l)	4	8	.333	5.96	1.65	19	19	2	1	...	0-...	102.2	116	70	68	15	33-0	83	.289
1997—Norfolk (Int'l)	6	6	.500	3.86	1.24	18	18	1	0	...	0-...	116.2	111	55	50	7	34-1	99	.251
—New York (N.L.)	3	1	.750	3.59	1.55	25	2	0	0	3	0-4	47.2	52	24	19	6	22-2	33	.286
1998—St. Louis (N.L.)	8	3	.727	2.56	1.14	50	9	0	0	3	15-16	98.1	83	30	28	7	29-2	56	.230
—Memphis (PCL)	0	0	...	0.00	0.69	2	2	0	0	...	0-...	8.2	5	0	0	0	1-0	6	.167
1999—St. Louis (N.L.)	6	8	.429	5.89	1.59	50	12	0	0	4	4-6	102.1	115	71	67	17	48-3	52	.291
2000—Milwaukee (N.L.)	3	7	.300	3.81	1.31	62	0	0	0	7	0-2	82.2	77	38	35	11	31-9	51	.246
—Indianapolis (Int'l)	0	0	...	0.00	0.75	2	2	0	0	...	0-...	4.0	3	0	0	0	0-0	4	.200
2001—Colorado (N.L.)	0	2	.000	5.63	1.75	38	0	0	0	3	0-5	32.0	37	24	20	4	19-6	26	.285
—Colo. Springs (PCL)	0	0	...	1.29	1.00	6	0	0	0	...	1-...	7.0	3	2	1	0	4-0	7	.130
—Florida (N.L.)	2	3	.400	2.54	1.66	20	0	0	0	1	0-0	28.1	31	11	8	2	16-3	21	.284
2002—Detroit (A.L.)	1	5	.167	2.65	1.22	65	0	0	0	1	28-35	74.2	68	33	22	4	23-3	43	.246
2003—New York (A.L.)	0	3	.000	7.71	1.71	25	0	0	0	1	6-7	25.2	34	24	22	5	10-3	19	.315
—Toronto (A.L.)	1	2	.333	4.26	2.05	14	0	0	0	1	0-1	12.2	18	8	6	1	8-1	9	.327
American League totals (2 years)	2	10	.167	3.98	1.42	104	0	0	0	5	34-43	113.0	120	65	50	10	41-7	71	.273
National League totals (6 years)	26	30	.464	4.41	1.45	262	34	0	0	22	19-33	457.0	477	251	224	62	185-27	279	.274
Major League totals (8 years)	28	40	.412	4.33	1.44	366	34	0	0	27	53-76	570.0	597	316	274	72	226-34	350	.274

ADAMS, TERRY — P

PERSONAL: Born March 6, 1973, in Mobile, Ala. ... 6-3/220. ... Throws right, bats right. ... Full name: Terry Wayne Adams. ... High school: Mary G. Montgomery (Semmes, Ala.).

TRANSACTIONS/CAREER NOTES: Selected by Chicago Cubs organization in fourth round of free-agent draft (June 3, 1991). ... On disabled list (June 21-September 21, 1993). ... On Chicago disabled list (March 26-May 8 and June 19-July 4, 1999); included rehabilitation assignments to West Tenn (April 30-May 4) and Iowa (May 6-8). ... Traded by Cubs with P Chad Ricketts and a player to be named later to Los Angeles Dodgers for P Ismael Valdes and 2B Eric Young (December 12, 1999); Dodgers acquired P Brian Stephenson to complete deal (December 16, 1999). ... Granted free agency (November 5, 2001). ... Signed by Philadelphia Phillies (January 17, 2002). ... Granted free agency (October 29, 2002). ... Re-signed by Phillies (February 10, 2003). ... Placed on restricted list (May 26, 2003). ... Activated from restricted list (May 27, 2003). ... Placed on 15-day disabled list (August 27, 2003). ... Removed from 15-day disabled list (August 11, 2003).

CAREER HITTING: 4-for-78 (.051), 2 R, 1 2B, 0 3B, 0 HR, 2 RBI.

Year League	W	L	Pct.	ERA	WHIP	G	GS	CG	ShO	Hld.	Sv.-Opp.	IP	H	R	ER	HR	BB-IBB	SO	Avg.
1991— Huntington (Appal.)	0	* 9	.000	5.77	2.24	14	13	0	0	...	0-...	57.2	67	* 56	37	1	62-0	52	.293
1992—Peoria (Midw.)	7	12	.368	4.41	1.46	25	25	3	1	...	0-...	157.0	144	95	77	7	86-0	96	.251
1993—Daytona (Fla. St.)	3	5	.375	4.97	1.71	13	13	0	0	...	0-...	70.2	78	47	39	2	43-0	35	.288
1994—Daytona (Fla. St.)	9	10	.474	4.38	1.58	39	7	0	0	...	7-...	84.1	87	47	41	5	46-3	64	.266
1995—Orlando (Sou.)	2	3	.400	1.43	1.04	37	0	0	0	...	19-...	37.2	23	9	6	2	16-1	26	.177
—Iowa (Am. Assoc.)	0	0	...	0.00	0.79	7	0	0	0	...	5-...	6.1	3	0	0	0	2-0	10	.130
—Chicago (N.L.)	1	1	.500	6.50	1.78	18	0	0	0	0	1-1	18.0	22	15	13	0	10-1	15	.289
1996—Chicago (N.L.)	3	6	.333	2.94	1.32	69	0	0	0	11	4-8	101.0	84	36	33	6	49-6	78	.231
1997—Chicago (N.L.)	2	9	.182	4.62	1.77	74	0	0	0	11	18-22	74.0	91	43	38	3	40-6	64	.306
1998—Chicago (N.L.)	7	7	.500	4.33	1.56	63	0	0	0	13	1-7	72.2	72	39	35	7	41-3	73	.255
—Iowa (PCL)	0	0	...	0.00	1.00	3	0	0	0	...	0-...	4.0	1	1	0	0	3-0	5	.077
1999—West Tenn (Sou.)	0	0	...	16.88	2.63	2	1	0	0	...	0-...	2.2	5	6	5	0	2-0	2	.417
—Chicago (N.L.)	6	3	.667	4.02	1.35	52	0	0	0	3	13-18	65.0	60	33	29	9	28-2	57	.245
2000—Los Angeles (N.L.)	6	9	.400	3.52	1.41	66	0	0	0	15	2-7	84.1	80	42	33	6	39-0	56	.245
2001—Los Angeles (N.L.)	12	8	.600	4.33	1.36	43	22	0	0	4	0-1	166.1	172	84	80	9	54-1	141	.267
2002—Philadelphia (N.L.)	7	9	.438	4.35	1.39	46	19	0	0	12	0-1	136.2	132	76	66	9	58-5	96	.255
2003—Philadelphia (N.L.)	1	4	.200	2.65	1.34	66	0	0	0	16	0-0	68.0	68	22	20	1	23-4	51	.268
Major League totals (9 years)	45	56	.446	3.97	1.43	497	41	0	0	85	39-65	786.0	781	390	347	50	342-28	631	.260

ADKINS, JON — P

PERSONAL: Born August 30, 1977, in Huntington, W.Va. ... 6-0/200. ... Throws right, bats left. ... Full name: Jonathan Scott Adkins. ... High school: Wayne High School (W.V.). ... College: Oklahoma State.

TRANSACTIONS/CAREER NOTES: Selected by Oakland Athletics organization in ninth round of free-agent draft (June 2, 1998). ... Traded by A's to Chicago White Sox for 2B Ray Durham (July 25, 2002). ... Recalled from Charlotte (August 13, 2003). ... Optioned to Charlotte (August 21, 2003). ... Recalled from Charlotte (September 2, 2003).

CAREER HITTING: 0-for-0 (.000), 0 R, 0 2B, 0 3B, 0 HR, 0 RBI.

Year League	W	L	Pct.	ERA	WHIP	G	GS	CG	ShO	Hld.	Sv.-Opp.	IP	H	R	ER	HR	BB-IBB	SO	Avg.
1999— Modesto (Calif.)	9	5	.643	4.76	1.40	26	15	0	0	...	1-...	102.0	113	65	54	6	30-1	93	.275
2000—Ariz. A's (Ariz.)	1	1	.500	3.00	1.20	4	2	0	0	...	0-...	15.0	15	6	5	1	3-0	17	.234
—Sacramento (PCL)	0	1	.000	9.00	1.75	1	1	0	0	...	0-...	4.0	6	4	4	2	1-0	2	.353
—Modesto (Calif.)	5	2	.714	1.81	1.17	9	7	1	0	...	0-...	49.2	41	17	10	1	17-0	38	.225
2001—Midland (Texas)	8	8	.500	4.46	1.33	24	24	1	1	...	0-...	137.1	147	71	68	9	36-1	74	.273
—Sacramento (PCL)	1	0	1.000	4.26	1.97	3	2	0	0	...	0-...	12.2	17	9	6	1	8-0	7	.333
2002—Modesto (Calif.)	0	1	.000	8.10	1.80	1	1	0	0	...	0-...	6.2	11	7	6	0	1-0	4	.379
—Sacramento (PCL)	7	6	.538	6.03	1.77	20	20	0	0	...	0-...	97.0	139	74	65	9	33-0	76	.338
—Charlotte (Int'l)	4	2	.667	3.69	1.27	8	7	1	0	...	0-...	46.1	47	20	19	4	12-0	31	.260
2003—Charlotte (Int'l)	7	8	.467	3.96	1.25	26	19	1	1	...	1-...	122.2	119	65	54	11	34-1	59	.254
—Chicago (A.L.)	0	0	...	4.82	1.61	4	0	0	0	0	0-0	9.1	8	5	5	1	7-0	3	.250
Major League totals (1 year)	0	0	...	4.82	1.61	4	0	0	0	0	0-0	9.1	8	5	5	1	7-0	3	.250

AFFELDT, JEREMY   P

PERSONAL: Born June 6, 1979, in Phoenix, Ariz. ... 6-4/215. ... Throws left, bats left. ... Full name: Jeremy David Affeldt. ... Name pronounced: AFF-felt. ... High school: Northwest Christian (Spokane, Wash.).

TRANSACTIONS/CAREER NOTES: Selected by Kansas City Royals organization in third round of free-agent draft (June 3, 1997). ... On Kansas City disabled list (June 9-August 1, 2002); included rehabilitation assignment to Wichita (July 24-August 1). ... Placed on 15-day disabled list (April 20, 2003). ... Reinstated from 15-day disabled list (May 6, 2003).

CAREER HITTING: 2-for-6 (.333), 0 R, 0 2B, 0 3B, 0 HR, 2 RBI.

Year League	W	L	Pct.	ERA	WHIP	G	GS	CG	ShO	Hld.	Sv.-Opp.	IP	H	R	ER	HR	BB-IBB	SO	Avg.
1997— GC Royals (GCL)	2	0	1.000	4.50	1.38	10	9	0	0	...	0-...	40.0	34	24	20	3	21-0	36	.243
1998— Lansing (Midw.)	0	3	.000	9.53	2.29	6	3	0	0	...	0-...	17.0	27	21	18	1	12-0	8	.355
— GC Royals (GCL)	4	3	.571	2.89	1.32	12	9	0	0	...	0-...	56.0	50	24	18	1	24-0	67	.243
1999—Char., W.Va. (SAL)	7	7	.500	3.83	1.53	27	24	2	1	...	0-...	143.1	140	78	61	4	80-0	111	.261
2000—Wilmington (Caro.)	5	15	.250	4.09	1.47	27	26	0	0	...	0-...	147.1	158	87	67	7	59-0	92	.275
2001—Wichita (Texas)	10	6	.625	3.90	1.37	25	25	0	0	...	0-...	145.1	153	74	63	9	46-0	128	.276
2002—Kansas City (A.L.)	3	4	.429	4.64	1.57	34	7	0	0	1	0-1	77.2	85	41	40	8	37-4	67	.274
— Wichita (Texas)	0	0	...	1.50	0.67	3	3	0	0	...	0-...	6.0	1	1	1	0	3-0	3	.059
2003—Kansas City (A.L.)	7	6	.538	3.93	1.30	36	18	0	0	3	4-4	126.0	126	58	55	12	38-1	98	.261
Major League totals (2 years)	**10**	**10**	**.500**	**4.20**	**1.40**	**70**	**25**	**0**	**0**	**4**	**4-5**	**203.2**	**211**	**99**	**95**	**20**	**75-5**	**165**	**.266**

AINSWORTH, KURT   P

PERSONAL: Born September 9, 1978, in Baton Rouge, La. ... 6-3/192. ... Throws right, bats right. ... Full name: Kurt Harold Ainsworth. ... Name pronounced: ANES-werth. ... High school: Catholic (Baton Rouge, La.). ... College: Louisiana State.

TRANSACTIONS/CAREER NOTES: Selected by San Francisco Giants organization in first round (24th pick overall) of free-agent draft (June 2, 1999). ... On Fresno disabled list (June 16-July 15, 2002). ... Placed on 15-day disabled list by San Francisco (May 31, 2003). ... Sent to Fresno on rehab assignment (June 18, 2003). ... Recalled from Fresno (June 21, 2003). ... Traded by Giants to Baltimore Orioles for P Sidney Ponson (July 31, 2003).

CAREER HITTING: 2-for-28 (.071), 1 R, 1 2B, 0 3B, 0 HR, 0 RBI.

Year League	W	L	Pct.	ERA	WHIP	G	GS	CG	ShO	Hld.	Sv.-Opp.	IP	H	R	ER	HR	BB-IBB	SO	Avg.
1999—Salem-Keizer (NW)	3	3	.500	1.61	1.16	10	10	1	0	...	0-...	44.2	34	18	8	1	18-0	64	.211
2000—Shreveport (Texas)	10	9	.526	3.30	1.27	28	28	0	0	...	0-...	158.0	138	67	58	12	63-3	130	.233
2001—Fresno (PCL)	10	9	.526	5.07	1.30	27	26	0	0	...	0-...	149.0	139	91	84	22	54-1	157	.247
—San Francisco (N.L.)	0	0	...	13.50	2.50	2	0	0	0	0	0-0	2.0	3	3	3	1	2-0	3	.333
2002—Fresno (PCL)	8	6	.571	3.41	1.24	20	19	1	0	...	0-0	116.0	101	49	44	7	43-0	119	.238
—San Francisco (N.L.)	1	2	.333	2.10	1.32	6	4	0	0	0	0-0	25.2	22	7	6	1	12-0	15	.237
2003—San Francisco (N.L.)	5	4	.556	3.82	1.39	11	11	0	0	0	0-0	66.0	66	31	28	7	26-0	48	.262
—Fresno (PCL)	0	0	.000	4.50	2.00	1	1	0	0	...	0-...	2.0	2	1	1	0	2-0	1	.250
—Baltimore (A.L.)	0	1	.000	11.57	3.00	3	0	0	0	0	0-0	2.1	6	3	3	1	1-0	4	.429
American League totals (1 year)	**0**	**1**	**.000**	**11.57**	**3.00**	**3**	**0**	**0**	**0**	**0**	**0-0**	**2.1**	**6**	**3**	**3**	**1**	**1-0**	**4**	**.429**
National League totals (3 years)	**6**	**6**	**.500**	**3.56**	**1.40**	**19**	**15**	**0**	**0**	**0**	**0-0**	**93.2**	**91**	**41**	**37**	**9**	**40-0**	**66**	**.257**
Major League totals (3 years)	**6**	**7**	**.462**	**3.75**	**1.44**	**22**	**15**	**0**	**0**	**0**	**0-0**	**96.0**	**97**	**44**	**40**	**10**	**41-0**	**70**	**.264**

ALFONSECA, ANTONIO   P

PERSONAL: Born April 16, 1972, in La Romana, Dominican Republic. ... 6-5/250. ... Throws right, bats right. ... Name pronounced: al-fon-SAY-kah.

TRANSACTIONS/CAREER NOTES: Signed as non-drafted free agent by Montreal Expos organization (July 3, 1989). ... Selected by Florida Marlins organization from Expos organization in Rule 5 minor league draft (December 13, 1993). ... On disabled list (May 15-June 15, 1995). ... On disabled list (July 12-September 3, 1996). ... On disabled list (May 14-31, 1998). ... Traded by Marlins with P Matt Clement to Chicago Cubs for P Julian Tavarez, P Jose Cueto, P Dontrelle Willis and C Ryan Jorgensen (March 27, 2002). ... On disabled list (March 21, 2003). ... Sent on rehab assignment to Iowa (April 25, 2003). ... Recalled by Chicago from rehab assignment (May 2, 2003). ... Reinstated from 15-day disabled list (May 5, 2003). ... Suspended five games by Major League Baseball (September 5, 2003). ... Reinstated by MLB (September 12, 2003).

CAREER HITTING: 2-for-12 (.167), 0 R, 0 2B, 0 3B, 0 HR, 2 RBI.

Year League	W	L	Pct.	ERA	WHIP	G	GS	CG	ShO	Hld.	Sv.-Opp.	IP	H	R	ER	HR	BB-IBB	SO	Avg.
1990—DSL Expos (DSL)	3	5	.375	3.60	1.53	13	13	1	0	...	0-...	60.0	60	29	24	...	32-...	19	...
1991—GC Expos (GCL)	3	3	.500	3.88	1.39	11	10	0	0	...	0-...	51.0	46	33	22	2	25-0	38	.240
1992—GC Expos (GCL)	3	4	.429	3.68	1.36	12	10	1	1	...	0-...	66.0	55	31	27	0	35-0	62	.233
1993—Jamestown (NYP)	2	2	.500	6.15	1.57	15	4	0	0	...	1-...	33.2	31	26	23	3	22-1	29	.250
1994—Kane County (Midwest)	6	5	.545	4.07	1.15	32	9	0	0	...	0-...	86.1	78	41	39	5	21-1	74	.234
1995—Portland (East.)	9	3	.750	3.64	1.28	19	17	1	0	...	0-...	96.1	81	43	39	6	42-1	75	.229
1996—Charlotte (Int'l)	4	4	.500	5.53	1.51	14	13	0	0	...	1-...	71.2	86	47	44	6	22-0	51	.296
1997—Charlotte (Int'l)	7	2	.778	4.32	1.34	46	0	0	0	...	7-...	58.1	58	34	28	8	20-3	45	.264
—Florida (N.L.)	1	3	.250	4.91	1.19	17	0	0	0	0	0-2	25.2	36	16	14	3	10-3	19	.324
1998—Florida (N.L.)	4	6	.400	4.08	1.53	58	0	0	0	9	8-14	70.2	75	36	32	10	33-9	46	.281
1999—Florida (N.L.)	4	5	.444	3.24	1.39	73	0	0	0	5	21-25	77.2	79	28	28	4	29-6	46	.274
2000—Florida (N.L.)	5	6	.455	4.24	1.51	68	0	0	0	0	* 45-49	70.0	82	35	33	7	24-3	47	.291
2001—Florida (N.L.)	4	4	.500	3.06	1.35	58	0	0	0	0	28-34	61.2	68	24	21	6	15-3	40	.281
2002—Chicago (N.L.)	2	5	.286	4.00	1.47	66	0	0	0	0	19-28	74.1	73	34	33	5	36-3	61	.257
2003—Iowa (PCL)	0	1	.000	4.91	1.91	3	0	0	0	...	0-...	3.2	6	2	2	0	1-0	5	.353
—Chicago (N.L.)	3	1	.750	5.83	1.55	60	0	0	0	0	0-4	66.1	76	43	43	7	27-3	51	.290
Major League totals (7 years)	**23**	**30**	**.434**	**4.11**	**1.49**	**400**	**0**	**0**	**0**	**23**	**121-156**	**446.1**	**489**	**216**	**204**	**42**	**174-30**	**310**	**.282**

ALFONZO, EDGARDO   3B

PERSONAL: Born November 8, 1973, in St. Teresa, Venezuela. ... 5-11/187. ... Bats right, throws right. ... Full name: Edgardo Antonio Alfonzo. ... High school: Cecilio Acosta (Venezuela).

TRANSACTIONS/CAREER NOTES: Signed as non-drafted free agent by New York Mets organization (February 19, 1991). ... On disabled list (August 11, 1995-remainder of season; and May 4-19, 1998). ... On New York disabled list (June 14-July 3, 2001); included rehabilitation assignment to Norfolk (June 30-July 3). ... On disabled list (August 4-24, 2002). ... Granted free agency (October 28, 2002). ... Signed by San Francisco Giants (December 15, 2002).

2003 GAMES PLAYED BY POSITION (MLB): 3B—133, 2B—6.

							BATTING											FIELDING	
Year	Team (League)	Pos.	G	AB	R	H	2B	3B	HR	RBI	BB	SO	HBP	GDP	SB-CS	Avg.	OBP	SLG	OPS	E	Pct.
1991— GC Mets (GCL)	..........2B-3B-SS	54	175	29	58	8	4	0	27	34	12	2	1	6-4	.331	.431	.423	.854	9	.958
1992— St. Lucie (Fla. St.)	2B	4	5	0	0	0	0	0	0	0	0	0	0	0-0	.000	.000	.000	.000	0	1.000
— Pittsfield (NYP)	...............SS	74	* 298	44	* 106	13	5	1	44	18	31	0	6	7-5	.356	.388	.443	.830	* 26	.933
1993— St. Lucie (Fla. St.)	SS	128	494	75	145	18	3	11	86	57	51	5	13	26-16	.294	.366	.409	.775	29	.954
1994— Binghamton (East.)	2B-SS-1B	127	498	89	146	34	2	15	75	64	55	0	9	14-11	.293	.369	.460	.829	27	.958
1995— New York (N.L.)	...............3B-2B-SS	101	335	26	93	13	5	4	41	12	37	1	7	1-1	.278	.301	.382	.683	7	.973
1996— New York (N.L.)	2B-3B-SS	123	368	36	96	15	2	4	40	25	56	0	8	2-0	.261	.304	.345	.649	11	.973
1997— New York (N.L.)	3B-SS-2B	151	518	84	163	27	2	10	72	63	56	5	4	11-6	.315	.391	.432	.823	12	.970
1998— New York (N.L.)	3B-SS	144	557	94	155	28	2	17	78	65	77	3	11	8-3	.278	.355	.427	.782	9	.976
1999— New York (N.L.)	2B	158	628	123	191	41	1	27	108	85	85	3	14	9-2	.304	.385	.502	.886	5	.993
2000— New York (N.L.)	2B-DH	150	544	109	176	40	2	25	94	95	70	5	12	3-2	.324	.425	.542	.967	10	.985
2001— New York (N.L.)	2B	124	457	64	111	22	0	17	49	51	62	5	7	5-0	.243	.322	.403	.725	7	.987
— Norfolk (Int'l)	2B	2	8	0	0	0	0	0	0	0	0	0	1	0-0	.000	.000	.000	.000	0	1.000
2002— New York (N.L.)	3B	135	490	78	151	26	0	16	56	62	55	7	5	6-0	.308	.391	.459	.851	12	.969
2003— San Francisco (N.L.)	.........3B-2B	142	514	56	133	25	2	13	81	58	41	4	14	5-2	.259	.334	.391	.726	11	.968
Major League totals (9 years)		1228	4411	670	1269	237	16	133	619	516	539	33	82	50-16	.288	.363	.439	.802	84	.979

ALLEN, CHAD — OF

PERSONAL: Born February 6, 1975, in Dallas, Texas. ... 6-1/200. ... Bats right, throws right. ... Full name: John Chad Allen. ... High school: Duncanville (Texas). ... College: Texas A&M.

TRANSACTIONS/CAREER NOTES: Selected by Cincinnati Reds organization in 38th round of free-agent draft (June 3, 1993); did not sign. ... Selected by Minnesota Twins organization in fourth round of free-agent draft (June 4, 1996). ... On Salt Lake disabled list (April 11-22, 2000). ... On Minnesota disabled list (June 4-19 and August 15, 2001-remainder of season). ... Granted free agency (October 24, 2001). ... Signed by Baltimore Orioles organization (March 27, 2002). ... Released by Orioles (April 16, 2002). ... Signed by Cleveland Indians organization (May 13, 2002). ... Released by Indians (September 30, 2002). ... Signed by Florida Marlins organization (November 25, 2002). ... Contract purchased by Florida Marlins from Albuquerque (May 18, 2003). ... Optioned to Albuquerque (June 19, 2003). ... Recalled from Albuquerque; sent outright to Albuquerque (August 29, 2003). ... Elected free agency (September 29, 2003).

2003 GAMES PLAYED BY POSITION (MLB): OF—8, DH—1.

							BATTING											FIELDING	
Year	Team (League)	Pos.	G	AB	R	H	2B	3B	HR	RBI	BB	SO	HBP	GDP	SB-CS	Avg.	OBP	SLG	OPS	E	Pct.
1996— Fort Wayne (Midw.)	..........OF	7	21	2	9	0	0	0	2	3	2	0	0	1-1	.429	.480	.429	.909	0	1.000
1997— Fort Myers (FSL)	...............OF	105	401	66	124	18	4	3	45	40	51	2	9	27-15	.309	.373	.397	.770	5	.977
— New Britain (East.)	..........OF	30	115	20	29	9	1	4	18	9	21	0	3	2-0	.252	.304	.452	.756	1	.973
1998— New Britain (East.)	OF	137	504	70	132	31	7	8	82	51	78	6	19	21-9	.262	.334	.399	.733	4	.980
1999— Minnesota (A.L.)	...............OF-DH	137	481	69	133	21	3	10	46	37	89	2	10	14-7	.277	.330	.395	.725	7	.975
2000— Salt Lake (PCL)	...............OF	96	389	71	121	21	5	9	67	31	72	1	13	10-2	.311	.363	.460	.823	1	.993
— Minnesota (A.L.)	OF	15	50	2	15	3	0	0	7	3	14	1	1	0-2	.300	.345	.360	.705	0	1.000
2001— Minnesota (A.L.)	OF-DH	57	175	20	46	13	2	4	20	19	37	0	7	1-2	.263	.333	.429	.762	2	.968
— Edmonton (PCL)	OF	6	22	4	8	2	0	1	1	4	1	1	0	2-0	.364	.481	.591	1.072	0	1.000
2002— Rochester (Int'l)	OF	8	32	1	7	2	1	0	1	0	6	0	2	0-0	.219	.219	.344	.563	0	1.000
— Buffalo (Int'l)	OF	70	279	45	84	20	1	10	62	15	34	2	10	0-1	.301	.340	.487	.828	0	1.000
— Cleveland (A.L.)	OF	5	10	0	1	1	0	0	0	0	2	0	1	0-0	.100	.100	.200	.300	0	1.000
2003— Florida (N.L.)	OF-DH	12	24	2	5	1	1	0	0	0	5	1	1	0-0	.208	.240	.333	.573	0	1.000
— Albuquerque (PCL)	..........OF-DH	91	337	45	109	30	2	8	53	18	48	6	10	11-10	.323	.364	.496	.860	1	.993
American League totals (4 years)		214	716	91	195	38	5	14	73	59	142	3	19	15-11	.272	.329	.398	.727	9	.976
National League totals (1 year)		12	24	2	5	1	1	0	0	0	5	1	1	0-0	.208	.240	.333	.573	0	1.000
Major League totals (5 years)		226	740	93	200	39	6	14	73	59	147	4	20	15-11	.270	.326	.396	.722	9	.977

ALLEN, LUKE — OF

PERSONAL: Born August 4, 1978, in Covington, Ga. ... 6-2/220. ... Bats left, throws right. ... Full name: Lucas G. Allen. ... High school: Newton County (Covington, Ga.).

TRANSACTIONS/CAREER NOTES: Signed as non-drafted free agent by Los Angeles Dodgers organization (August 4, 1996). ... Traded by Dodgers to Colorado Rockies for 2B Jason Romano (January 27, 2003). ... Recalled from Colorado Springs (July 12, 2003). ... Optioned to Colorado Springs (July 18, 2003). ... Recalled from Colorado Springs (September 25, 2003).

							BATTING											FIELDING	
Year	Team (League)	Pos.	G	AB	R	H	2B	3B	HR	RBI	BB	SO	HBP	GDP	SB-CS	Avg.	OBP	SLG	OPS	E	Pct.
1997— Great Falls (Pio.)	...............3B-OF	67	258	50	89	12	6	7	40	19	53	0	3	12-11	.345	.390	.519	.909	22	.868
1998— San Bern. (Calif.)	...............OF	105	399	51	119	25	6	4	46	30	93	3	4	18-11	.298	.349	.421	.770	6	.971
— San Antonio (Texas)	..........OF	23	78	9	26	3	1	3	10	6	16	0	0	1-2	.333	.381	.513	.894	4	.918
1999— San Antonio (Texas)	3B	137	533	90	150	16	12	14	82	44	102	1	8	14-8	.281	.336	.435	.771	53	.851
2000— San Antonio (Texas)	..........3B-1B	90	339	55	90	15	5	7	60	40	71	1	10	14-5	.265	.340	.401	.741	27	.895
2001— Jacksonville (Sou.)	..........OF	125	486	74	141	32	6	16	73	42	111	1	7	13-13	.290	.345	.479	.824	7	.972
— Las Vegas (PCL)	OF	2	9	1	2	1	0	0	0	0	0	0	1	0-0	.222	.222	.333	.556	1	.667
2002— Las Vegas (PCL)	...............OF	137	501	85	165	28	3	12	78	56	77	2	12	4-6	.329	.395	.469	.864	* 9	.969
— Los Angeles (N.L.)	OF	6	7	2	1	1	0	0	0	2	3	0	0	0-0	.143	.333	.286	.619	0	1.000
2003— Colorado (N.L.)		2	2	0	0	0	0	0	0	0	0	0	1	0-0	.000	.000	.000	.000	0	...
— Colo. Springs (PCL)	..........OF-DH	127	438	65	120	21	3	6	45	51	78	0	11	9-12	.274	.346	.377	.723	7	.971
Major League totals (2 years)		8	9	2	1	1	0	0	0	2	3	0	1	0-0	.111	.273	.222	.495	0	1.000

ALMANZA, ARMANDO — P

PERSONAL: Born October 26, 1972, in El Paso, Texas. ... 6-3/240. ... Throws left, bats left. ... Full name: Armando N. Almanza. ... High school: Bel Air (El Paso, Texas). ... Junior college: New Mexico College.

TRANSACTIONS/CAREER NOTES: Selected by St. Louis Cardinals organization in 21st round of free-agent draft (June 3, 1993). ... On disabled list (April 8, 1994-entire season). ... On Memphis disabled list (July 10-21, 1998). ... Traded by Cardinals with P Braden Looper and SS Pablo Ozuna to Florida Marlins for SS Edgar Renteria (December 14, 1998). ... On Calgary disabled list (May 10-June 2, 1999). ... On Florida disabled list (March 30-May 21, 2002); included rehabilitation assignment to Jupiter (May 2-21). ... Placed on 15-day disabled list (August 21, 2003). ... Transferred to 60-day disabled list (September 1, 2003).

CAREER HITTING: 0-for-4 (.000), 0 R, 0 2B, 0 3B, 0 HR, 0 RBI.

Year	League	W	L	Pct.	ERA	WHIP	G	GS	CG	ShO	Hld.	Sv.-Opp.	IP	H	R	ER	HR	BB-IBB	SO	Avg.
1993—Ariz. Cardinals (Ariz.)		4	1	.800	3.21	1.24	20	4	0	0	...	0-...	42.0	38	19	15	2	14-0	56	.236
—Johnson City (App.)		1	1	.500	4.15	2.08	3	3	0	0	...	0-...	4.1	6	2	2	1	3-0	4	.333
1994—Madison (Midw.)											Did not play.									
1995—Savannah (S. Atl.)		3	9	.250	3.92	1.37	20	20	0	0	...	0-...	108.0	108	62	47	13	40-1	72	.255
1996—Peoria (Midw.)		8	6	.571	2.76	1.32	52	1	0	0	...	0-...	62.0	50	27	19	2	32-5	67	.216
1997—Prince William (Caro.)		2	3	.400	1.67	1.08	58	0	0	0	...	* 36-...	64.2	38	18	12	3	32-1	83	.172
1998—Arkansas (Texas)		4	1	.800	3.31	1.38	28	0	0	0	...	8-...	32.2	27	13	12	2	18-0	46	.225
—Memphis (PCL)		3	1	.750	3.03	1.51	31	0	0	0	...	1-...	35.2	35	18	12	1	19-1	45	.246
1999—Calgary (PCL)		2	2	.500	10.90	2.71	15	0	0	0	...	0-...	17.1	29	27	21	3	18-0	20	.363
—Portland (East.)		0	1	.000	3.97	0.79	10	0	0	0	...	3-...	11.1	5	5	5	1	4-0	20	.139
—Florida (N.L.)		0	1	.000	1.72	1.09	14	0	0	0	3	0-0	15.2	8	4	3	1	9-1	20	.154
2000—Florida (N.L.)		4	2	.667	4.86	1.75	67	0	0	0	13	0-4	46.1	38	27	25	3	43-6	46	.228
2001—Florida (N.L.)		2	2	.500	4.83	1.46	52	0	0	0	12	0-2	41.0	34	24	22	8	26-1	45	.230
2002—Jupiter (FSL)		0	0	...	0.00	0.60	6	5	0	0	...	0-...	6.2	1	0	0	0	3-0	6	.050
—Florida (N.L.)		3	2	.600	4.34	1.29	51	0	0	0	12	2-4	45.2	36	22	22	8	23-1	57	.224
2003—Florida (N.L.)		4	5	.444	6.08	1.67	51	0	0	0	6	0-2	50.1	59	37	34	10	25-2	49	.296
Major League totals (5 years)		13	12	.520	4.79	1.51	235	0	0	0	46	2-12	199.0	175	114	106	30	126-11	217	.241

ALMANZAR, CARLOS P

PERSONAL: Born November 6, 1973... 6-2/200. ... Throws right, bats right. ... Full name: Carlos Manuel Almanzar.

TRANSACTIONS/CAREER NOTES: Signed as non-drafted free agent by Toronto Blue Jays organization (December 10, 1990). ... On Knoxville disabled list (May 27-June 3, 1997). ... Traded by Blue Jays with P Woody Williams and OF Peter Tucci to San Diego Padres for P Joey Hamilton (December 13, 1998). ... On San Diego disabled list (April 24-May 27, 1999); included rehabilitation assignment to Las Vegas (May 22-27). ... Traded by Padres to New York Yankees for P David Lee (March 25, 2001). ... Granted free agency (October 15, 2001). ... Signed by Colorado Rockies organization (January 20, 2002). ... Claimed on waivers by Cincinnati Reds (March 30, 2002). ... On Cincinnati disabled list (June 11, 2002-remainder of season); included rehabilitation assignment to Louisville (August 16-September 13).

CAREER HITTING: 0-for-4 (.000), 0 R, 0 2B, 0 3B, 0 HR, 0 RBI.

Year	League	W	L	Pct.	ERA	WHIP	G	GS	CG	ShO	Hld.	Sv.-Opp.	IP	H	R	ER	HR	BB-IBB	SO	Avg.
1991—Dom. B. Jays (DSL)		3	1	.750	2.83	1.34	6	6	1	0	...	0-...	35.0	36	17	11	...	11-...	20	...
1992—Dom. B. Jays (DSL)		10	0	1.000	2.01	1.13	13	11	2	1	...	1-...	67.0	45	26	15	...	31-...	60	...
1993—Dom. B. Jays (DSL)		5	2	.714	3.38	1.33	16	9	0	0	...	2-...	69.1	60	35	26	...	32-...	59	...
1994—Medicine Hat (Pio.)		7	4	.636	2.87	1.19	14	14	0	0	...	0-...	84.2	82	38	27	2	19-0	77	.255
1995—Knoxville (Southern)		3	12	.200	3.99	1.39	35	19	0	0	...	2-...	126.1	144	77	56	10	32-1	93	.287
1996—Knoxville (Southern)		7	8	.467	4.85	1.47	54	0	0	0	...	9-...	94.2	106	58	51	13	33-6	105	.280
1997—Knoxville (Southern)		1	1	.500	4.91	1.36	21	0	0	0	...	8-...	25.2	30	14	14	2	5-1	25	.300
—Syracuse (Int'l)		5	1	.833	1.41	0.75	32	0	0	0	...	3-...	51.0	30	9	8	2	8-0	47	.170
—Toronto (A.L.)		0	1	.000	2.70	0.60	4	0	0	0	...	0-0	3.1	1	1	1	1	1-0	4	.091
1998—Toronto (A.L.)		2	2	.500	5.34	1.47	25	0	0	0	...	0-3	28.2	34	18	17	4	8-2	20	.286
—Syracuse (Int'l)		3	6	.333	2.31	1.13	30	0	0	0	...	10-...	50.2	44	21	13	7	13-2	53	.229
1999—San Diego (N.L.)		0	0	...	7.47	1.69	28	0	0	0	0	0-0	37.1	48	32	31	6	15-2	30	.316
—Las Vegas (PCL)		1	3	.250	9.53	1.76	11	3	0	0	...	0-...	22.2	32	25	24	11	8-1	18	.337
2000—San Diego (N.L.)		4	5	.444	4.39	1.41	62	0	0	0	8	0-3	69.2	73	35	34	12	25-2	56	.266
—Las Vegas (PCL)		0	0	...	4.50	1.50	4	0	0	0	...	0-...	6.0	9	4	3	1	0-0	7	.321
2001—New York (A.L.)		0	1	.000	3.38	1.50	10	0	0	0	...	0-2	10.2	14	4	4	2	2-1	6	.333
—Columbus (Int'l)		2	1	.667	2.43	1.26	35	0	0	0	...	18-...	33.1	36	10	9	2	6-2	26	.279
2002—Louisville (Int'l)		1	0	1.000	2.74	1.13	21	0	0	0	...	11-...	23.0	21	7	7	0	5-0	19	.247
—Cincinnati (N.L.)		0	1	.000	2.31	0.94	8	1	0	0	0	0-0	11.2	6	4	3	0	5-1	7	.158
2003—Louisville (Int'l)		2	2	.500	3.50	1.10	42	0	0	0	...	23-...	46.1	47	19	18	2	3-0	54	.251
American League totals (3 years)		2	4	.333	4.64	1.41	39	0	0	0	0	0-5	42.2	49	23	22	7	11-3	30	.285
National League totals (3 years)		4	6	.400	5.16	1.45	98	1	0	0	8	0-3	118.2	127	71	68	18	45-5	93	.274
Major League totals (6 years)		6	10	.375	5.02	1.44	137	1	0	0	8	0-8	161.1	176	94	90	25	56-8	123	.277

ALMONTE, EDWIN P

PERSONAL: Born December 17, 1976, in Santiago, Dominican Republic. ... 6-3/220. ... Throws right, bats right. ... High school: Seward Park (New York, N.Y.). ... College: St. Francis (N.Y.).

TRANSACTIONS/CAREER NOTES: Selected by Chicago White Sox organization in 26th round of free-agent draft (June 2, 1998). ... Recalled from Charlotte (July 1, 2003). ... Traded by White Sox to New York Mets for IF Roberto Alomar (July 1, 2003). ... Optioned to Norfolk (July 1, 2003). ... Recalled from Norfolk (July 7, 2003). ... Optioned to Norfolk (July 8, 2003). ... Recalled from Norfolk (September 2, 2003).

CAREER HITTING: 0-for-1 (.000), 0 R, 0 2B, 0 3B, 0 HR, 0 RBI.

Year	League	W	L	Pct.	ERA	WHIP	G	GS	CG	ShO	Hld.	Sv.-Opp.	IP	H	R	ER	HR	BB-IBB	SO	Avg.
1998—Ariz. White Sox (Ariz.)		0	0	...	0.93	0.72	5	0	0	0	...	0-...	9.2	6	5	1	0	1-0	8	.171
—Bristol (Appal.)		3	0	1.000	3.38	1.24	8	3	0	0	...	0-...	26.2	29	14	10	3	4-0	26	.271
1999—Burlington (Midw.)		9	12	.429	3.03	1.17	37	5	2	0	...	5-...	115.2	107	48	39	5	28-4	85	.239
2000—Winston-Salem (Caro.)		3	1	.750	3.16	1.12	33	7	0	0	...	2-...	77.0	66	32	27	2	20-0	73	.227
—Birmingham (Sou.)		1	3	.250	4.54	1.36	7	6	0	0	...	0-...	39.2	45	22	20	5	9-0	21	.304
2001—Birmingham (Sou.)		1	4	.200	1.49	1.12	54	0	0	0	...	36-...	66.1	58	16	11	4	16-4	62	.228
2002—Charlotte (Int'l)		2	3	.400	2.24	1.06	50	0	0	0	...	26-...	60.1	52	16	15	6	12-2	56	.236
2003—Charlotte (Int'l)		2	6	.250	6.88	1.74	30	0	0	0	...	14-...	34.0	45	27	26	6	14-4	24	.331
—Norfolk (Int'l)		1	1	.500	2.55	1.25	16	0	0	0	...	6-...	17.2	16	5	5	0	6-0	14	.235
—New York (N.L.)		0	0	...	11.12	2.29	12	0	0	0	2	0-0	11.1	21	15	14	3	5-1	7	.412
Major League totals (1 year)		0	0	...	11.12	2.29	12	0	0	0	2	0-0	11.1	21	15	14	3	5-1	7	.412

ALMONTE, ERICK SS

PERSONAL: Born February 1, 1978, in Santo Domingo, Dominican Republic. ... 6-2/180. ... Bats right, throws right. ... Full name: Erick R. Almonte. ... Name pronounced: al-mon-tay.

TRANSACTIONS/CAREER NOTES: Signed as non-drafted free agent by New York Yankees organization (February 12, 1996). ... On Norwich disabled list (June 14-26, 2001). ... On Columbus disabled list (July 23-August 4, 2001; and April 7-19, 2002). ... Optioned to Columbus by New York (May 13, 2003). ... Recalled by New York from Columbus (July 7, 2003). ... Optioned to Columbus of the International League (July 9, 2003). ... Optioned to Columbus by New York (August 30, 2003). ... Recalled by New York from Columbus (August 30, 2003).

2003 GAMES PLAYED BY POSITION (MLB): SS—31.

Year	Team (League)	Pos.	G	AB	R	H	2B	3B	HR	RBI	BB	SO	HBP	GDP	SB-CS	Avg.	OBP	SLG	OPS	E	Pct.
1996—Dom. Yankees (DSL)		3B	58	216	37	61	7	0	8	36	15	30	...		3-...	.282	...	.426	...	36	.848
1997—GC Yankees (GCL)		3B	52	180	32	51	4	4	3	31	21	27	...	5	8-2	.283	.355	.400	.755	18	.890
1998—Greensboro (S. Atl.)		SS	120	450	53	94	13	0	6	33	29	121	3	17	6-2	.209	.260	.278	.538	47	.911
1999—Tampa (Fla. St.)		SS	61	230	36	59	8	2	5	25	18	49	2	6	3-1	.257	.313	.374	.687	20	.938
—GC Yankees (GCL)		SS	9	30	5	9	2	0	2	9	3	10	0	1	1-0	.300	.343	.567	.910	2	.931
2000—Norwich (East.)		SS	131	454	56	123	18	4	15	77	35	129	3	3	12-2	.271	.326	.427	.753	*33	.943
2001—Columbus (Int'l)		SS	97	345	55	99	19	3	12	55	44	90	2	7	4-5	.287	.369	.464	.833	*27	.936
—Norwich (East.)		SS	3	12	2	3	0	0	0	0	1	6	0	0	1-0	.250	.308	.250	.558	1	.900
—New York (East.)		SS-DH	8	4	0	2	1	0	0	0	0	1	0	0	2-0	.500	.500	.750	1.250	1	.875
2002—Columbus (Int'l)		SS	66	221	25	52	10	1	9	28	15	60	0	2	2-1	.235	.282	.412	.693	18	.937
—Norwich (East.)		SS-3B	53	187	28	45	7	0	8	33	30	59	0	6	10-2	.241	.342	.406	.749	8	.963
2003—GC Yankees (GCL)		3B-SS	6	21	4	6	0	0	0	0	5	9	0	0	0-0	.286	.423	.286	.709	3	.769
—Columbus (Int'l)		SS-3B-DH	48	179	26	43	11	1	4	26	17	46	1	5	4-3	.240	.310	.380	.690	9	.960
—New York (A.L.)		SS	31	100	17	26	6	0	1	11	8	24	1	3	1-0	.260	.321	.350	.671	12	.906
Major League totals (2 years)			39	104	17	28	7	0	1	11	8	25	1	3	3-0	.269	.327	.365	.693	13	.904

ALMONTE, HECTOR — P

PERSONAL: Born October 17, 1975, in Santo Domingo, Dominican Republic. ... 6-2/190. ... Throws right, bats right. ... Full name: Hector Radhames Almonte. ... High school: Liceo Jose Marti (Santo Domingo, Dominican Republic).

TRANSACTIONS/CAREER NOTES: Signed as non-drafted free agent by Florida Marlins organization (February 9, 1993). ... Elected free agency (July 7, 2003). ... Signed by Montreal Expos (July 10, 2003).

CAREER HITTING: 0-for-1 (.000), 0 R, 0 2B, 0 3B, 0 HR, 0 RBI.

Year	League	W	L	Pct.	ERA	WHIP	G	GS	CG	ShO	Hld.	Sv.-Opp.	IP	H	R	ER	HR	BB-IBB	SO	Avg.
1993—Dom. Marlins (DSL)		1	6	.143	4.79	1.56	13	7	1	0	...	1-...	56.1	59	39	30	...	29-...	20	...
1994—Dom. Marlins (DSL)		3	5	.375	4.34	1.62	20	4	0	0	...	0-...	58.0	68	40	28	...	26-...	26	...
1995—Dom. Marlins (DSL)		1	2	.333	4.26	1.23	20	1	0	0	...	9-...	31.2	28	17	15	...	11-...	27	...
1996—Dom. Marlins (DSL)		0	0	...	0.00	0.60	2	0	0	0	...	0-...	1.2	0	0	0	...	1-...	2	...
1997—GC Marlins (GCL)		2	0	1.000	0.76	0.76	8	0	0	0	...	3-...	23.2	12	3	2	0	6-0	25	.150
—Kane County (Midwest)		0	1	.000	3.86	1.21	8	1	0	0	...	1-...	14.0	11	6	6	1	6-0	10	.224
1998—Kane County (Midwest)		1	5	.167	3.95	1.62	43	0	0	0	...	21-...	43.1	51	22	19	5	19-0	51	.287
1999—Portland (East.)		1	4	.200	2.84	1.53	47	0	0	0	...	23-...	44.1	42	14	14	1	26-3	42	.255
—Florida (N.L.)		0	2	.000	4.20	1.73	15	0	0	0	2	0-0	15.0	20	7	7	1	6-2	8	.339
2000—Calgary (PCL)		0	4	.000	11.17	2.33	18	0	0	0	...	3-...	19.1	36	24	24	7	9-0	16	.409
—Brevard County (FSL)		1	1	.500	2.35	1.04	8	2	0	0	...	0-...	15.1	11	6	4	2	5-0	16	.208
—Portland (East.)		0	1	.000	3.60	1.80	4	0	0	0	...	3-...	5.0	5	2	2	1	4-0	6	.238
—GC Marlins (GCL)		0	0	...	4.50	2.00	1	1	0	0	...	0-...	2.0	3	1	1	0	1-0	2	.429
2001—Calgary (PCL)		0	0	...	8.39	2.07	18	0	0	0	...	0-...	24.2	36	29	23	6	15-0	21	.340
2002—Yomiuri (Jp. Cen.)		0	0	...	1.50	0.96	...	0	0	0	...	1-...	24.0	16	4	4	...	7-0	18	...
2003—Boston (A.L.)		0	1	.000	8.22	2.09	7	0	0	0	0	0-0	7.2	9	7	7	1	7-1	6	.310
—Montreal (N.L.)		1	1	.500	6.83	1.76	28	0	0	0	0	0-1	29.0	34	22	22	4	17-2	26	.291
American League totals (1 year)		0	1	.000	8.22	2.09	7	0	0	0	0	0-0	7.2	9	7	7	1	7-1	6	.310
National League totals (2 years)		1	3	.250	5.93	1.75	43	0	0	0	2	0-1	44.0	54	29	29	5	23-4	34	.307
Major League totals (2 years)		1	4	.200	6.27	1.80	50	0	0	0	2	0-1	51.2	63	36	36	6	30-5	40	.307

ALOMAR, ROBERTO — 2B

PERSONAL: Born February 5, 1968, in Ponce, Puerto Rico. ... 6-0/185. ... Bats both, throws right. ... Full name: Roberto Velazquez Alomar. ... Name pronounced: AL-loh-mar.

TRANSACTIONS/CAREER NOTES: Signed as non-drafted free agent by San Diego Padres organization (February 16, 1985). ... Traded by Padres with OF Joe Carter to Toronto Blue Jays for 1B Fred McGriff and SS Tony Fernandez (December 5, 1990). ... On suspended list (May 23-24, 1995). ... Granted free agency (October 30, 1995). ... Signed by Baltimore Orioles (December 21, 1995). ... On suspended list (April 1-7, 1997). ... On disabled list (July 30-August 26, 1997; and July 19-August 4, 1998). ... Granted free agency (October 26, 1998). ... Signed by Cleveland Indians (December 1, 1998). ... Traded by Indians with P Mike Bacsik and OF Danny Peoples to New York Mets for OF Matt Lawton, OF Alex Escobar, P Jerrod Riggan and two players to be named later (December 11, 2001); Indians acquired P Billy Traber and 1B Earl Snyder to complete deal (December 13, 2001). ... Traded by Mets to Chicago White Sox for P Edwin Almonte (July 1, 2003).

2003 GAMES PLAYED BY POSITION (MLB): 2B—139.

Year	Team (League)	Pos.	G	AB	R	H	2B	3B	HR	RBI	BB	SO	HBP	GDP	SB-CS	Avg.	OBP	SLG	OPS	E	Pct.
1985—Char., S.C. (SAL)		2B-SS	*137	*546	89	160	14	3	0	54	61	73	0	9	36-19	.293	.362	.330	.691	‡36	.947
1986—Reno (Calif.)		2B	90	356	53	123	16	4	4	49	32	38	3	7	14-8	*.346	.397	.447	.844	18	.963
1987—Wichita (Texas)		2B-SS	130	536	88	171	41	4	12	68	49	74	2	9	43-15	.319	.374	.478	.851	‡36	.932
1988—Las Vegas (PCL)		2B	9	37	5	10	1	0	2	14	1	4	0	0	3-0	.270	.282	.459	.742	1	.981
—San Diego (N.L.)		2B	143	545	84	145	24	6	9	41	47	83	3	15	24-6	.266	.328	.382	.709	16	.980
1989—San Diego (N.L.)		2B	158	623	82	184	27	1	7	56	53	76	1	10	42-17	.295	.347	.376	.723	*28	.967
1990—San Diego (N.L.)		2B-SS	147	586	80	168	27	5	6	60	48	72	2	16	24-7	.287	.340	.381	.721	‡19	.974
1991—Toronto (A.L.)		2B	161	637	88	188	41	11	9	69	57	86	4	5	53-11	.295	.354	.436	.791	15	.981
1992—Toronto (A.L.)		2B-DH	152	571	105	177	27	8	8	76	87	52	5	8	49-9	.310	.405	.427	.832	5	.993
1993—Toronto (A.L.)		2B	153	589	109	192	35	6	17	93	80	67	5	13	55-15	.326	.408	.492	.900	14	.980
1994—Toronto (A.L.)		2B	107	392	78	120	25	4	8	38	51	41	2	14	19-8	.306	.386	.452	.838	4	.991
1995—Toronto (A.L.)		2B	130	517	71	155	24	7	13	66	47	45	0	16	30-3	.300	.354	.449	.803	4	.993
1996—Baltimore (A.L.)		2B-DH	153	588	132	193	43	4	22	94	90	65	1	14	17-6	.328	.411	.527	.938	11	.985
1997—Baltimore (A.L.)		2B-DH	112	412	64	137	23	2	14	60	40	43	3	10	9-3	.333	.390	.500	.890	6	.988
1998—Baltimore (A.L.)		2B-DH	147	588	86	166	36	1	14	56	59	70	2	11	18-5	.282	.347	.418	.765	11	.985
1999—Cleveland (A.L.)		2B-DH	159	563	*138	182	40	3	24	120	99	96	7	13	37-6	.323	.422	.533	.955	6	.992
2000—Cleveland (A.L.)		2B	155	610	111	189	40	2	19	89	64	82	6	19	39-4	.310	.378	.475	.853	15	.980
2001—Cleveland (A.L.)		2B	157	575	113	193	34	12	20	100	80	71	4	9	30-6	.336	.415	.541	.956	5	.993
2002—New York (N.L.)		2B	149	590	73	157	24	4	11	53	57	83	1	12	16-4	.266	.331	.376	.708	11	.983
2003—New York (N.L.)		2B	73	263	34	69	17	1	2	22	29	40	2	8	6-0	.262	.336	.357	.693	6	.981
—Chicago (A.L.)		2B	67	253	42	64	11	1	3	17	30	37	1	9	6-2	.253	.336	.340	.670	3	.990
American League totals (12 years)			1653	6295	1137	1956	379	61	171	878	784	755	40	141	362-78	.311	.386	.472	.858	99	.987
National League totals (5 years)			670	2607	353	723	119	17	35	232	234	354	9	61	112-34	.277	.337	.376	.713	80	.976
Major League totals (16 years)			2323	8902	1490	2679	498	78	206	1110	1018	1109	49	202	474-112	.301	.372	.444	.816	179	.984

ALOMAR JR., SANDY   C

PERSONAL: Born June 18, 1966, in Salinas, Puerto Rico. ... 6-5/235. ... Bats right, throws right. ... Full name: Santos Alomar Jr.. ... Name pronounced: AL-uh-mar. ... High school: Luis Munoz Rivera (Salinas, Puerto Rico).

TRANSACTIONS/CAREER NOTES: Signed as non-drafted free agent by San Diego Padres organization (October 21, 1983). ... Traded by Padres with OF Chris James and 3B Carlos Baerga to Cleveland Indians for OF Joe Carter (December 6, 1989). ... On Cleveland disabled list (May 15-June 17 and July 29, 1991-remainder of season); included rehabilitation assignments to Colorado Springs (June 8-17 and August 9-12). ... On disabled list (May 2-18, 1992). ... On suspended list (July 29-August 2, 1992). ... On Cleveland disabled list (May 1-August 7, 1993); included rehabilitation assignment to Charlotte, S.C. (July 22-August 7). ... On disabled list (April 24-May 11, 1994). ... On Cleveland disabled list (April 19-June 29, 1995); included rehabilitation assignment to Canton/Akron (June 22-29). ... On Cleveland disabled list (May 11-September 6, 1999); included rehabilitation assignments to Akron (July 5-19 and September 3-6) and Buffalo (August 10-27). ... Granted free agency (October 27, 2000). ... Signed by Chicago White Sox (December 18, 2000). ... On disabled list (August 8-September 18, 2001). ... On Chicago disabled list (June 13-July 1, 2002); included rehabilitation assignment to Charlotte (June 28-July 1). ... Traded by White Sox to Colorado Rockies for P Enemencio Pacheco (July 29, 2002). ... Granted free agency (October 31, 2002). ... Signed by White Sox (December 20, 2002). ... Placed on 15-day disabled list (May 31, 2003). ... Sent to Charlotte on rehab assignment (June 16, 2003). ... Recalled from rehab assignment; reinstated from 15-day disabled list (June 23, 2003).

2003 GAMES PLAYED BY POSITION (MLB): C—75.

										BATTING										FIELDING	
Year Team (League)	Pos.	G	AB	R	H	2B	3B	HR	RBI	BB	SO	HBP	GDP	SB-CS	Avg.	OBP	SLG	OPS		E	Pct.
1984—Spokane (N'west)	C-1B	59	219	13	47	5	0	0	21	13	20	1	7	3-0	.215	.260	.237	.497		8 ‡	.985
1985—Char., S.C. (SAL)	C-OF	100	352	38	73	7	0	3	43	31	30	3	9	3-1	.207	.276	.253	.529		18	.979
1986—Beaumont (Texas)	C	100	346	36	83	15	1	4	27	15	35	1	2-6		.240	.271	.324	.595		* 18	.969
1987—Wichita (Texas)	C	103	375	50	115	19	1	8	65	21	37	5	12	1-5	.307	.346	.427	.772		* 15	.978
1988—Las Vegas (PCL)	C-OF	93	337	59	100	9	5	16	71	28	35	4	11	1-1	.297	.354	.496	.849		‡ 14	.978
— San Diego (N.L.)		1	1	0	0	0	0	0	0	0	1	0	0	0-0	.000	.000	.000	.000		...	.000
1989—Las Vegas (PCL)	C-OF	131	* 523	88	160	33	8	13	101	42	58	2	23	3-1	.306	.358	.474	.832		12	.984
— San Diego (N.L.)	C	7	19	1	4	1	0	1	6	3	3	0	1	0-0	.211	.318	.421	.739		0	1.000
1990—Cleveland (A.L.)	C	132	445	60	129	26	2	9	66	25	46	2	10	4-1	.290	.326	.418	.744		* 14	.981
1991—Cleveland (A.L.)	DH-C	51	184	10	40	9	0	0	7	8	24	4	4	0-4	.217	.264	.266	.530		4	.987
— Colo. Springs (PCL)	C	12	35	5	14	2	0	1	10	5	0	0	0	0-0	.400	.463	.543	1.006		1	.833
1992—Cleveland (A.L.)	C-DH	89	299	22	75	16	0	2	26	13	32	5	7	3-3	.251	.293	.324	.618		2	.996
1993—Cleveland (A.L.)	C	64	215	24	58	7	1	6	32	11	28	6	3	3-1	.270	.318	.395	.713		6	.984
— Charlotte (Int'l)	C	12	44	8	16	5	0	1	8	5	8	1	1	0-0	.364	.440	.545	.985		0	1.000
1994—Cleveland (A.L.)	C	80	292	44	84	15	1	14	43	25	31	2	7	8-4	.288	.347	.490	.837		2	.996
1995—Cant./Akr. (Eastern)	C-DH	6	15	3	6	1	0	0	1	1	1	0	1	0-0	.400	.438	.467	.904		1	.958
— Cleveland (A.L.)	C	66	203	32	61	6	0	10	35	7	26	3	8	3-1	.300	.332	.478	.810		2	.995
1996—Cleveland (A.L.)	C-1B	127	418	53	110	23	0	11	50	19	42	3	20	1-0	.263	.299	.397	.696		9	.988
1997—Cleveland (A.L.)	C-DH	125	451	63	146	37	0	21	83	19	48	3	16	0-2	.324	.354	.545	.900		* 12	.985
1998—Cleveland (A.L.)	C-DH	117	409	45	96	26	2	6	44	18	45	3	15	0-3	.235	.270	.352	.622		6	.992
1999—Cleveland (A.L.)	C-DH	37	137	19	42	13	0	6	25	4	23	0	1	0-1	.307	.322	.533	.855		7	.974
— Akron (East.)	DH-C	10	29	8	9	0	0	1	6	3	2	0	0	1-0	.310	.353	.414	.767		1	.929
— Buffalo (Int'l)	C	10	33	9	9	2	1	2	10	6	3	1	1	0-0	.273	.400	.576	.976		3	.921
2000—Cleveland (A.L.)	C-DH	97	356	44	103	16	2	7	42	16	41	4	9	2-2	.289	.324	.404	.728		8	.993
2001—Chicago (A.L.)	C	70	220	17	54	8	1	4	21	12	17	2	6	1-2	.245	.288	.345	.634		4	.990
2002—Chicago (A.L.)	C	51	167	21	48	10	1	7	25	5	14	1	5	0-0	.287	.309	.485	.794		2	.994
— Charlotte (Int'l)	C	3	8	0	1	0	0	0	0	0	0	0	1	0-0	.125	.125	.125	.250		0	1.000
— Colorado (N.L.)	C	38	116	8	31	4	0	0	12	4	19	0	6	0-0	.267	.292	.302	.593		0	1.000
2003—Charlotte (Int'l)	C-DH	5	15	2	4	0	0	0	1	1	1	0	2	0-0	.267	.313	.267	.579		0	1.000
— Chicago (A.L.)	C	75	194	22	52	12	0	5	26	4	17	0	4	0-0	.268	.281	.407	.689		1	.997
American League totals (14 years)		1181	3990	476	1098	224	10	108	525	186	434	38	115	25-24	.275	.311	.418	.729		79	.989
National League totals (3 years)		46	136	9	35	5	0	1	18	7	23	0	7	0-0	.257	.294	.316	.610		0	1.000
Major League totals (16 years)		1227	4126	485	1133	229	10	109	543	193	457	38	122	25-24	.275	.311	.414	.725		79	.989

ALOU, MOISES   OF

PERSONAL: Born July 3, 1966, in Atlanta, Ga. ... 6-3/220. ... Bats right, throws right. ... Full name: Moises Rojas Alou. ... Name pronounced: MOY-zes ah-LOO. ... High school: C.E.E. (Santo Domingo, Dominican Republic). ... Junior college: Canada College (Calif.).

TRANSACTIONS/CAREER NOTES: Selected by Pittsburgh Pirates organization in first round (second pick overall) of free-agent draft (January 14, 1986). ... Traded by Pirates to Montreal Expos (August 16, 1990), completing deal in which Expos traded P Zane Smith to Pirates for P Scott Ruskin, SS Willie Greene and a player to be named later (August 8, 1990). ... On Montreal disabled list (March 19, 1991-entire season; July 7-27, 1992; September 18, 1993-remainder of season; August 18-September 5 and September 11, 1995-remainder of season). ... On disabled list (August 23-27, 1996). ... Granted free agency (December 7, 1996). ... Signed by Florida Marlins (December 12, 1996). ... Traded by Marlins to Houston Astros for P Oscar Henriquez, P Manuel Barrios and a player to be named later (November 11, 1997); Marlins acquired P Mark Johnson to complete deal (December 16, 1997). ... On disabled list (April 3, 1999-entire season; April 27-May 14, 2000; and March 29-April 16, 2001). ... Granted free agency (November 5, 2001). ... Signed by Chicago Cubs (December 19, 2001). ... On Chicago disabled list (March 31-April 15, 2002); included rehabilitation assignment to Daytona (April 10-15).

2003 GAMES PLAYED BY POSITION (MLB): OF—142, DH—9.

										BATTING										FIELDING	
Year Team (League)	Pos.	G	AB	R	H	2B	3B	HR	RBI	BB	SO	HBP	GDP	SB-CS	Avg.	OBP	SLG	OPS		E	Pct.
1986—Watertown (NYP)	OF	69	254	30	60	9	* 8	6	35	22	72	1	5	14-8	.236	.300	.406	.705		7	.952
1987—Macon (S. Atl.)	OF	4	8	1	1	0	0	0	0	2	4	0	0	0-0	.125	.300	.125	.425		0	1.000
— Watertown (NYP)	OF	39	117	20	25	6	2	4	8	16	36	4	0	6-3	.214	.324	.402	.725		2	.957
1988—Augusta (S. Atl.)	OF	105	358	58	112	23	5	7	62	51	84	5	5	24-12	.313	.399	.464	.863		9	.962
1989—Salem (Caro.)	OF	86	321	50	97	29	2	14	53	35	69	3	6	12-5	.302	.374	.536	.910		10	.947
— Harrisburg (East.)	OF	54	205	36	60	5	2	3	19	17	38	0	1	8-4	.293	.344	.380	.724		2	.978
1990—Harrisburg (East.)	OF	36	132	19	39	12	2	3	22	16	21	1	5	7-4	.295	.373	.485	.858		1	.990
— Buffalo (A.A.)	OF	75	271	38	74	4	6	5	31	30	43	2	8	9-4	.273	.345	.387	.733		8	.957
— Pittsburgh (N.L.)	OF	2	5	0	1	0	0	0	0	0	0	0	1	0-0	.200	.200	.200	.400		0	1.000
— Indianapolis (A.A.)	OF	15	55	6	12	1	0	0	6	3	7	0	0	4-3	.218	.254	.236	.491		0	1.000
— Montreal (N.L.)	OF	14	15	4	3	0	1	0	0	3	3	0	0	0-0	.200	.200	.333	.533		0	1.000
1991—Montreal (N.L.)							Did not play.														
1992—Montreal (N.L.)	OF	115	341	53	96	28	2	9	56	25	46	1	5	16-2	.282	.328	.455	.783		4	.978
1993—Montreal (N.L.)	OF	136	482	70	138	29	6	18	85	38	53	5	9	17-6	.286	.340	.483	.824		4	.985
1994—Montreal (N.L.)	OF	107	422	81	143	31	5	22	78	42	63	2	7	7-6	.339	.397	.592	.989		3	.986
1995—Montreal (N.L.)	OF	93	344	48	94	22	0	14	58	29	56	9	9	4-3	.273	.342	.459	.801		3	.981
1996—Montreal (N.L.)	OF	143	540	87	152	28	2	21	96	49	83	2	15	9-4	.281	.339	.457	.797		3	.989

– 11 –

Year	Team (League)	Pos.	G	AB	R	H	2B	3B	HR	RBI	BB	SO	HBP	GDP	SB-CS	Avg.	OBP	SLG	OPS	E	Pct.
1997—	Florida (N.L.)	OF	150	538	88	157	29	5	23	115	70	85	4	13	9-5	.292	.373	.493	.866	3	.988
1998—	Houston (N.L.)	OF-DH	159	584	104	182	34	5	38	124	84	87	5	14	11-3	.312	.399	.582	.981	5	.980
1999—	Houston (N.L.)									Did not play.											
2000—	Houston (N.L.)	OF-DH	126	454	82	161	28	2	30	114	52	45	2	*21	3-3	.355	.416	.623	1.039	6	.970
2001—	Houston (N.L.)	OF-DH	136	513	79	170	31	1	27	108	57	57	3	18	5-1	.331	.396	.554	.949	2	.991
2002—	Daytona (Fla. St.)	OF	2	8	0	5	1	0	0	2	1	1	0	0	0-0	.625	.667	.750	1.417	0	1.000
—	Chicago (N.L.)	OF-DH	132	484	50	133	23	1	15	61	47	61	0	15	8-0	.275	.337	.419	.757	2	.991
2003—	Chicago (N.L.)	OF-DH	151	565	83	158	35	1	22	91	63	67	7	16	3-1	.280	.357	.462	.819	6	.972
	Major League totals (12 years)		1464	5287	829	1588	318	31	239	986	556	706	40	143	92-34	.300	.367	.508	.875	41	.983

ALVAREZ, JUAN   P

PERSONAL: Born August 9, 1973, in Coral Gables, Fla. ... 6-0/184. ... Throws left, bats left. ... Full name: Juan M. Alvarez. ... High school: Coral Gables (Fla.). ... College: St. Thomas (Fla.).

TRANSACTIONS/CAREER NOTES: Signed as non-drafted free agent by California Angels organization (July 25, 1995). ... Angels franchise renamed Anaheim Angels for 1997 season. ... Granted free agency (October 15, 2001). ... Signed by Texas Rangers organization (December 6, 2001). ... Released by Rangers (November 18, 2002). ... Signed by Florida Marlins (May 6, 2003). ... Optioned to Albuquerque (June 4, 2003). ... Recalled from Albuquerque (September 26, 2003).

CAREER HITTING: 0-for-0 (.000), 0 R, 0 2B, 0 3B, 0 HR, 0 RBI.

Year	League	W	L	Pct.	ERA	WHIP	G	GS	CG	ShO	Hld.	Sv.-Opp.	IP	H	R	ER	HR	BB-IBB	SO	Avg.
1995—	Boise (NW)	0	0	...	0.77	1.20	9	0	0	0	...	0-...	11.2	12	1	1	0	2-0	11	.273
1996—	Cedar Rapids (Midw.)	1	2	.333	3.40	1.51	40	0	0	0	...	3-...	53.0	50	25	20	0	30-1	53	.254
1997—	Lake Elsinore (Calif.)	4	2	.667	1.40	0.90	27	0	0	0	...	3-...	51.1	33	9	8	2	13-2	46	.188
—	Midland (Texas)	4	1	.800	8.27	2.30	24	0	0	0	...	0-...	37.0	63	42	34	5	22-1	27	.364
1998—	Midland (Texas)	3	4	.429	4.30	1.33	40	0	0	0	...	12-...	46.0	40	26	22	5	21-3	41	.234
—	Vancouver (PCL)	1	1	.500	5.02	1.53	18	0	0	0	...	0-...	14.1	14	9	8	2	8-0	12	.264
1999—	Erie (East.)	1	2	.333	2.05	0.85	23	0	0	0	...	4-...	30.2	20	14	7	4	6-0	22	.182
—	Edmonton (PCL)	0	3	.000	3.49	1.34	27	0	0	0	...	0-...	28.1	30	13	11	2	8-0	25	.268
—	Anaheim (A.L.)	0	1	.000	3.00	1.67	8	0	0	0	1	0-0	3.0	1	1	1	0	4-0	4	.111
2000—	Edmonton (PCL)	3	1	.750	2.82	1.28	44	0	0	0	...	0-...	38.1	30	12	12	3	19-1	27	.222
—	Anaheim (A.L.)	0	0	...	13.50	3.50	11	0	0	0	0	0-0	6.0	14	9	9	3	7-1	2	.467
2001—	Salt Lake (PCL)	2	2	.500	4.95	1.41	48	1	0	0	...	0-...	67.1	68	42	37	13	27-0	44	.265
2002—	Tulsa (Texas)	0	0	...	0.00	0.60	2	0	0	0	...	0-...	1.2	1	0	0	0	0-0	0	.143
—	Oklahoma (PCL)	0	0	...	3.63	1.62	15	0	0	0	...	1-...	17.1	19	7	7	1	9-1	13	.292
—	Texas (A.L.)	0	4	.000	4.76	1.41	52	0	0	0	10	0-3	39.2	35	22	21	7	21-0	30	.241
2003—	Florida (N.L.)	0	0	...	3.09	1.37	9	0	0	0	0	0-0	11.2	8	4	4	2	8-1	6	.216
—	Albuquerque (PCL)	3	2	.600	5.88	1.79	51	0	0	0	...	0-...	52.0	69	38	34	9	24-1	43	.329
	American League totals (3 years)	0	5	.000	5.73	1.68	71	0	0	0	11	0-3	48.2	50	32	31	10	32-1	36	.272
	National League totals (1 year)	0	0	...	3.09	1.37	9	0	0	0	0	0-0	11.2	8	4	4	2	8-1	6	.216
	Major League totals (4 years)	0	5	.000	5.22	1.62	80	0	0	0	11	0-3	60.1	58	36	35	12	40-2	42	.262

ALVAREZ, VICTOR   P

PERSONAL: Born November 8, 1976, in Culiacan, Mexico. ... 5-10/150. ... Throws left, bats left. ... Full name: Victor Aurelio Alvarez. ... Name pronounced: AL-vuh-rez.

TRANSACTIONS/CAREER NOTES: Signed as non-drafted free agent by Los Angeles Dodgers organization (May 16, 1997). ... Loaned by Dodgers organization to Mexico City Reds, Mexican League (March 18-October 28, 1998; and April 2-June 12, 2000). ... Recalled from Las Vegas (June 6, 2003). ... Optioned to Las Vegas by Los Angeles (August 30, 2003).

CAREER HITTING: 0-for-2 (.000), 0 R, 0 2B, 0 3B, 0 HR, 0 RBI.

Year	League	W	L	Pct.	ERA	WHIP	G	GS	CG	ShO	Hld.	Sv.-Opp.	IP	H	R	ER	HR	BB-IBB	SO	Avg.
1997—	Dom. Dodgers (DSL)	2	0	1.000	0.90	0.90	3	0	0	0	...	1-...	10.0	4	1	1	...	5-...	18	...
—	Great Falls (Pio.)	4	1	.800	3.35	1.37	12	8	0	0	...	0-...	48.1	49	30	18	0	17-0	50	.261
1998—	Mex. City Reds (Mx.)	3	4	.429	3.62	1.78	22	12	0	0	...	2-...	79.2	93	39	32	2	49-...	36	...
1999—	Vero Beach (FSL)	4	4	.500	1.97	0.99	12	12	1	0	...	0-...	73.0	56	21	16	4	16-0	57	.215
—	San Antonio (Texas)	4	3	.571	3.67	1.21	9	9	0	0	...	0-...	56.1	58	27	23	5	10-0	43	.266
2000—	Mex. City Reds (Mx.)	0	2	.000	6.33	2.06	7	6	0	0	...	0-...	21.1	30	15	15	0	14-...	14	...
—	San Antonio (Texas)	0	3	.000	3.91	1.53	11	8	0	0	...	0-...	48.1	44	27	21	3	30-1	43	.254
—	Vero Beach (FSL)	1	1	.500	5.16	1.24	4	4	0	0	...	0-...	22.2	17	14	13	6	11-0	20	.205
2001—	Jacksonville (Sou.)	2	0	1.000	1.20	0.76	8	8	0	0	...	0-...	45.0	27	6	6	1	7-0	40	.176
—	Las Vegas (PCL)	7	4	.636	4.27	1.32	20	20	0	0	...	0-...	118.0	115	63	56	12	41-0	94	.256
2002—	Las Vegas (PCL)	10	7	.588	4.70	1.39	34	15	0	0	...	3-...	122.2	132	69	64	11	39-1	106	.278
—	Los Angeles (N.L.)	0	1	.000	4.35	1.06	4	1	0	0	0	0-0	10.1	9	5	5	1	2-0	7	.237
2003—	Los Angeles (N.L.)	0	1	.000	12.71	2.65	5	0	0	0	0	0-0	5.2	9	8	8	1	6-0	3	.391
—	Las Vegas (PCL)	4	4	.500	2.70	1.07	22	7	0	0	...	1-...	63.1	53	25	19	2	15-0	47	.225
	Major League totals (2 years)	0	2	.000	7.31	1.63	9	1	0	0	0	0-0	16.0	18	13	13	2	8-0	10	.295

ALVAREZ, WILSON   P

PERSONAL: Born March 24, 1970, in Maracaibo, Venezuela. ... 6-1/255. ... Throws left, bats left. ... Full name: Wilson Eduardo Alvarez.

TRANSACTIONS/CAREER NOTES: Signed as non-drafted free agent by Texas Rangers organization (September 23, 1986). ... Traded by Rangers with IF Scott Fletcher and OF Sammy Sosa to Chicago White Sox for OF Harold Baines and IF Fred Manrique (July 29, 1989). ... Traded by White Sox with P Danny Darwin and P Roberto Hernandez to San Francisco Giants for SS Michael Caruso, OF Brian Manning, P Lorenzo Barcelo, P Keith Foulke, P Bobby Howry and P Ken Vining (July 31, 1997). ... Granted free agency (November 1, 1997). ... Signed by Tampa Bay Devil Rays (December 3, 1997). ... On Tampa Bay disabled list (May 21-July 6, 1998); included rehabilitation assignments to Gulf Coast Devil Rays (June 26-29), St. Petersburg (June 30-July 4) and Durham (July 5-6). ... On disabled list (April 12-29 and July 24-August 8, 1999). ... On Tampa Bay disabled list (March 25, 2000-entire season); included rehabilitation assignment to St. Petersburg (April 15). ... On Tampa Bay disabled list (March 23, 2001-entire season); included rehabilitation assignments to Orlando (June 9-18 and July 29-August 13) and Durham (June 19-July 3 and August 14-27). ... On Tampa Bay disabled list (April 15-May 31 and July 15-August 5, 2002); included rehabilitation assignment to Orlando (May 19-31). ... Released by Devil Rays (September 30, 2002). ... Signed by Los Angeles Dodgers organization (January 16, 2003). ... Recalled from Las Vegas (June 7, 2003).

CAREER HITTING: 8-for-62 (.129), 2 R, 0 2B, 0 3B, 0 HR, 1 RBI.

Year League	W	L	Pct.	ERA	WHIP	G	GS	CG	ShO	Hld.	Sv.-Opp.	IP	H	R	ER	HR	BB-IBB	SO	Avg.
1987— Gastonia (S. Atl.)	1	5	.167	6.47	1.94	8	6	0	0	...	0-...	32.0	39	24	23	5	23-0	19	.312
— GC Rangers (GCL)	2	5	.286	5.24	1.39	10	10	0	0	...	0-...	44.2	41	29	26	6	21-0	46	.246
1988— Gastonia (S. Atl.)	4	11	.267	2.98	1.28	23	23	1	0	...	0-...	127.0	113	63	42	5	49-1	134	.233
— Oklahoma City (A.A.)	1	1	.500	3.78	1.38	5	3	0	0	...	0-...	16.2	17	8	7	2	6-0	9	.274
1989— Charlotte (Fla. St.)	7	4	.636	2.11	1.10	13	13	3	2	...	0-...	81.0	68	29	19	2	21-0	51	.227
— Tulsa (Texas)	2	2	.500	2.06	1.17	7	7	1	1	...	0-...	48.0	40	14	11	1	16-3	29	.227
— Texas (A.L.)	0	1	.000	...	...	1	1	0	0	0	0-0	.0	3	3	3	2	2-0	0	1.000
— Birmingham (Sou.)	2	1	.667	3.03	1.35	6	6	0	0	...	0-...	35.2	32	12	12	2	16-0	18	.246
1990— Vancouver (PCL)	7	7	.500	6.00	1.89	17	15	1	0	...	0-...	75.0	91	54	50	7	51-0	35	.314
— Birmingham (Sou.)	5	1	.833	4.27	1.49	7	7	1	0	...	0-...	46.1	44	24	22	5	25-0	36	.246
1991— Birmingham (Sou.)	10	6	.625	1.83	1.20	23	23	3	2	...	0-...	152.1	109	46	31	6	74-0	165	.200
— Chicago (A.L.)	3	2	.600	3.51	1.35	10	9	2	1	0	0-0	56.1	47	26	22	9	29-0	32	.230
1992— Chicago (A.L.)	5	3	.625	5.20	1.67	34	9	0	0	3	1-1	100.1	103	64	58	12	65-2	66	.272
1993— Chicago (A.L.)	15	8	.652	2.95	1.24	31	31	1	1	0	0-0	207.2	168	78	68	14	* 122-8	155	.230
— Nashville (A.A.)	0	1	.000	2.84	1.42	1	1	0	0	...	0-...	6.1	7	7	2	0	2-0	8	.241
1994— Chicago (A.L.)	12	8	.600	3.45	1.29	24	24	2	1	0	0-0	161.2	147	72	62	16	62-1	108	.241
1995— Chicago (A.L.)	8	11	.421	4.32	1.51	29	29	3	0	0	0-0	175.0	171	96	84	21	93-4	118	.258
1996— Chicago (A.L.)	15	10	.600	4.22	1.44	35	35	0	0	0	0-0	217.1	216	106	102	21	97-3	181	.258
1997— Chicago (A.L.)	9	8	.529	3.03	1.24	22	22	2	1	0	0-0	145.2	126	61	49	9	55-1	110	.232
— San Francisco (N.L.)	4	3	.571	4.48	1.36	11	11	0	0	0	0-0	66.1	54	36	33	9	36-3	69	.224
1998— Tampa Bay (A.L.)	6	14	.300	4.73	1.39	25	25	0	0	0	0-0	142.2	130	78	75	18	68-0	107	.239
— GC Devil Rays (GCL)	0	0	...	0.00	1.00	1	1	0	0	...	0-...	3.0	2	0	0	0	1-0	4	.200
— St. Pete. (FSL)	0	1	.000	27.00	4.20	1	1	0	0	...	0-...	1.2	5	5	5	1	2-0	2	.500
— Durham (Int'l)	0	0	...	3.86	1.29	1	1	0	0	...	0-...	4.2	4	2	2	0	2-0	6	.235
1999— Tampa Bay (A.L.)	9	9	.500	4.22	1.49	28	28	1	0	0	0-0	160.0	159	92	75	22	79-1	128	.260
2000— St. Pete. (FSL)	0	0	...	0.00	0.00	1	1	0	0	...	0-...	4.0	0	0	0	0	0-0	2	.000
2001— Orlando (Sou.)	1	3	.250	4.43	1.48	5	5	0	0	...	0-...	20.1	24	10	10	2	6-0	18	.286
— Durham (Int'l)	1	1	.500	3.00	1.44	4	4	0	0	...	0-...	18.0	20	8	6	2	6-0	16	.282
2002— Tampa Bay (A.L.)	2	3	.400	5.28	1.55	23	10	0	0	2	1-1	75.0	80	47	44	13	36-3	56	.272
— Orlando (Sou.)	1	0	1.000	1.10	1.00	2	2	0	0	...	0-...	8.0	6	1	1	0	2-0	7	.222
2003— Las Vegas (PCL)	5	1	.833	1.34	0.89	8	8	0	0	...	0-...	47.0	36	9	7	1	6-0	33	.216
— Los Angeles (N.L.)	6	2	.750	2.37	1.08	21	12	1	1	1	1-1	95.0	80	27	25	5	23-1	82	.231
American League totals (11 years)	**84**	**77**	**.522**	**4.01**	**1.43**	**262**	**223**	**11**	**4**	**5**	**2-2**	**1441.2**	**1350**	**723**	**642**	**157**	**708-23**	**1061**	**.249**
National League totals (2 years)	**10**	**5**	**.667**	**3.24**	**1.20**	**32**	**23**	**1**	**1**	**1**	**1-1**	**161.1**	**134**	**63**	**58**	**14**	**59-4**	**151**	**.228**
Major League totals (13 years)	**94**	**82**	**.534**	**3.93**	**1.40**	**294**	**246**	**12**	**5**	**6**	**3-3**	**1603.0**	**1484**	**786**	**700**	**171**	**767-27**	**1212**	**.247**

AMEZAGA, ALFREDO — SS/2B

PERSONAL: Born January 16, 1978, in Obregon, Mexico. ... 5-10/165. ... Bats both, throws right. ... Name pronounced: ah-mezz-ah-guh. ... High school: Miami Senior (Miami). ... Junior college: St. Petersburg College (Fla.).
TRANSACTIONS/CAREER NOTES: Selected by Anaheim Angels organization in 13th round of free-agent draft (June 2, 1999). ... On Arkansas disabled list (April 21-May 4, 2001). ... Recalled by Anaheim (July 25, 2003).
2003 GAMES PLAYED BY POSITION (MLB): SS—24, 3B—13, DH—1.

									BATTING									FIELDING	
Year — Team (League)	Pos.	G	AB	R	H	2B	3B	HR	RBI	BB	SO	HBP	GDP	SB-CS	Avg.	OBP	SLG	OPS	E	Pct.
1999— Butte (Pio.)	2B-SS	8	34	11	10	2	0	0	5	5	5	1	0	6-2	.294	.400	.353	.753	0	1.000
— Boise (NW)	2B-SS	48	205	52	66	6	4	2	29	23	29	5	7	14-3	.322	.402	.420	.821	12	.953
2000— Lake Elsinore (Calif.)	2B-SS	108	420	90	117	13	4	4	44	63	70	4	4	73-21	.279	.374	.357	.731	22	.961
2001— Arkansas (Texas)	SS	70	285	50	89	10	5	4	21	22	55	4	0	24-15	.312	.370	.425	.794	13	.964
— Salt Lake (PCL)	SS	49	200	28	50	5	4	1	16	14	45	3	2	9-6	.250	.307	.330	.637	11	.954
2002— Salt Lake (PCL)	SS-2B	128	518	77	130	25	7	6	51	45	100	8	15	23-14	.251	.317	.361	.678	‡ 24	.962
— Anaheim (A.L.)	SS-DH	12	13	3	7	2	0	0	2	0	1	0	1	1-0	.538	.538	.692	1.231	0	1.000
2003— Salt Lake (PCL)	SS-2B-DH	75	317	55	110	20	5	3	45	20	39	4	3	14-8	.347	.391	.470	.861	7	.982
— Anaheim (A.L.)	SS-3B-DH	37	105	15	22	3	2	2	7	9	23	1	2	2-2	.210	.278	.333	.612	5	.962
Major League totals (2 years)		**49**	**118**	**18**	**29**	**5**	**2**	**2**	**9**	**9**	**24**	**1**	**3**	**3-2**	**.246**	**.305**	**.373**	**.678**	**5**	**.967**

ANDERSON, BRIAN — P

PERSONAL: Born April 26, 1972, in Portsmouth, Va. ... 6-1/185. ... Throws left, bats right. ... Full name: Brian James Anderson. ... High school: Geneva (Ohio). ... College: Wright State.
TRANSACTIONS/CAREER NOTES: Selected by California Angels organization in first round (third pick overall) of free-agent draft (June 3, 1993). ... On California disabled list (May 7-June 7, 1994); included rehabilitation assignment to Lake Elsinore (May 27-June 7). ... On California disabled list (May 6-June 20, 1995); included rehabilitation assignment to Lake Elsinore (June 4-20). ... Traded by Angels to Cleveland Indians for P Jason Grimsley and P Pep Harris (February 15, 1996). ... On Cleveland disabled list (July 5-August 12, 1997); included rehabilitation assignment to Buffalo (August 3-13). ... Selected by Arizona Diamondbacks in first round (second pick overall) of expansion draft (November 18, 1997). ... On Arizona disabled list (April 12-May 2 and June 3-July 1, 2001); included rehabilitation assignments to Tucson (April 27-May 2 and June 26-27). ... Granted free agency (October 28, 2002). ... Signed by Indians (December 23, 2002). ... Traded by Indians to Kansas City Royals for two minor league players and cash (August 25, 2003).
CAREER HITTING: 35-for-254 (.138), 15 R, 5 2B, 3 3B, 1 HR, 10 RBI.

Year League	W	L	Pct.	ERA	WHIP	G	GS	CG	ShO	Hld.	Sv.-Opp.	IP	H	R	ER	HR	BB-IBB	SO	Avg.
1993— Midland (Texas)	0	1	.000	3.38	1.50	2	2	0	0	...	0-...	10.2	16	5	4	2	0-0	9	.340
— Vancouver (PCL)	0	1	.000	12.38	2.38	2	2	0	0	...	0-...	8.0	13	12	11	3	6-0	2	.394
— California (A.L.)	0	0	...	3.97	1.15	4	1	0	0	0	0-0	11.1	11	5	5	1	2-0	4	.256
1994— California (A.L.)	7	5	.583	5.22	1.45	18	18	0	0	0	0-0	101.2	120	63	59	13	27-0	47	.300
— Lake Elsinore (Calif.)	0	1	.000	3.00	0.50	2	2	0	0	...	0-...	12.0	6	4	4	1	0-0	9	.146
1995— California (A.L.)	6	8	.429	5.87	1.40	18	17	0	0	0	0-0	99.2	110	66	65	24	30-2	45	.282
— Lake Elsinore (Calif.)	1	1	.500	1.93	0.79	3	3	0	0	...	0-...	14.0	10	3	3	0	1-0	13	.204
1996— Buffalo (A.A.)	11	5	.688	3.59	1.20	19	19	2	0	...	0-...	128.0	125	57	51	14	28-0	85	.253
— Cleveland (A.L.)	3	1	.750	4.91	1.40	10	9	0	0	1	0-0	51.1	58	29	28	9	14-1	21	.296
1997— Buffalo (A.A.)	7	1	.875	3.05	1.09	15	15	1	1	...	0-...	85.2	78	33	29	13	15-0	60	.238
— Cleveland (A.L.)	4	2	.667	4.69	1.38	8	8	0	0	0	0-0	48.0	55	28	25	7	11-0	22	.301
1998— Arizona (N.L.)	12	13	.480	4.33	1.18	32	32	2	1	0	0-0	208.0	221	109	100	*39	24-2	95	.274
1999— Arizona (N.L.)	8	2	.800	4.57	1.32	31	19	2	1	1	1-2	130.0	144	69	66	18	28-3	75	.279
— Tucson (PCL)	0	0	...	5.40	1.50	2	2	0	0	...	0-...	6.2	9	5	4	1	1-0	8	.333

Year — League	W	L	Pct.	ERA	WHIP	G	GS	CG	ShO	Hld.	Sv.-Opp.	IP	H	R	ER	HR	BB-IBB	SO	Avg.
2000— Arizona (N.L.)	11	7	.611	4.05	1.24	33	32	2	0	0	0-0	213.1	226	101	96	38	39-7	104	.275
2001— Arizona (N.L.)	4	9	.308	5.20	1.40	29	22	1	0	0	0-1	133.1	156	93	77	25	30-2	55	.295
— Tucson (PCL)	1	0	1.000	1.50	0.75	2	2	0	0	...	0-...	12.0	7	2	2	0	2-0	8	.167
2002— Arizona (N.L.)	6	11	.353	4.79	1.32	35	24	0	0	1	0-0	156.0	174	86	83	23	32-3	81	.284
2003— Cleveland (A.L.)	9	10	.474	3.71	1.31	25	24	0	0	0	0-0	148.0	162	88	61	21	32-3	72	.282
— Kansas City (A.L.)	5	1	.833	3.99	1.23	7	7	2	1	0	0-0	49.2	50	22	22	6	11-0	15	.272
American League totals (6 years)	34	27	.557	4.68	1.36	90	84	3	1	1	0-0	509.2	566	301	265	81	127-6	226	.287
National League totals (5 years)	41	42	.494	4.52	1.28	160	129	7	2	2	1-3	840.2	921	458	422	143	153-17	410	.280
Major League totals (11 years)	75	69	.521	4.58	1.31	250	213	10	3	3	1-3	1350.1	1487	759	687	224	280-23	636	.283

ANDERSON, GARRET   OF

PERSONAL: Born June 30, 1972, in Los Angeles, Calif. ... 6-3/225. ... Bats left, throws left. ... Full name: Garret Joseph Anderson. ... High school: John F. Kennedy (Granada Hills, Calif.).

TRANSACTIONS/CAREER NOTES: Selected by California Angels organization in fourth round of free-agent draft (June 4, 1990). ... Angels franchise renamed Anaheim Angels for 1997 season.

2003 GAMES PLAYED BY POSITION (MLB): OF—144, DH—15.

Year — Team (League)	Pos.	G	AB	R	H	2B	3B	HR	RBI	BB	SO	HBP	GDP	SB-CS	Avg.	OBP	SLG	OPS	E	Pct.
1990— Ariz. Angels (Ariz.)	OF	32	127	5	27	2	0	0	14	2	24	2	3	3-0	.213	.231	.228	.460	2	.965
— Boise (NW)	OF	25	83	11	21	3	1	1	8	4	18	0	3	0-1	.253	.284	.349	.633	2	.950
1991— Quad City (Midw.)	OF	105	392	40	102	22	2	2	42	20	89	0	16	5-6	.260	.295	.342	.637	10	.943
1992— Palm Springs (Calif.)	OF	81	322	46	104	15	2	1	62	21	61	1	9	1-1	.323	.366	.391	.758	6	.959
— Midland (Texas)	OF	39	146	16	40	5	0	2	19	9	30	0	8	2-1	.274	.316	.349	.665	1	.986
1993— Vancouver (PCL)	OF-1B	124	467	57	137	34	4	4	71	31	95	0	15	3-4	.293	.334	.409	.743	2	.991
1994— Vancouver (PCL)	OF-DH-1B	123	505	75	162	42	6	12	102	28	93	1	7	3-3	.321	.356	.499	.855	2	.990
— California (A.L.)	OF	5	13	0	5	0	0	0	1	0	2	0	0	0-0	.385	.385	.385	.769	0	1.000
1995— California (A.L.)	OF-DH	106	374	50	120	19	1	16	69	19	65	1	8	6-2	.321	.352	.505	.857	5	.978
— Vancouver (PCL)	OF-DH	14	61	9	19	7	0	0	12	5	14	0	3	0-0	.311	.364	.426	.790	1	.957
1996— California (A.L.)	OF-DH	150	607	79	173	33	2	12	72	27	84	0	22	7-9	.285	.314	.405	.719	7	.979
1997— Anaheim (A.L.)	OF-DH	154	624	76	189	36	3	8	92	30	70	2	20	10-4	.303	.334	.409	.743	3	.992
1998— Anaheim (A.L.)	OF	156	622	62	183	41	7	15	79	29	80	1	13	8-3	.294	.325	.455	.780	6	.983
1999— Anaheim (A.L.)	OF-DH	157	620	88	188	36	2	21	80	34	81	0	15	3-4	.303	.336	.469	.806	3	.993
2000— Anaheim (A.L.)	OF-DH-1B	159	647	92	185	40	3	35	117	24	87	0	21	7-6	.286	.307	.519	.827	4	.990
2001— Anaheim (A.L.)	OF-DH	161	672	83	194	39	2	28	123	27	100	0	12	13-6	.289	.314	.478	.792	2	.994
2002— Anaheim (A.L.)	OF-DH	158	638	93	195	• 56	3	29	123	30	80	0	11	6-4	.306	.332	.539	.871	2	.994
2003— Anaheim (A.L.)	OF-DH	159	638	80	201	•49	4	29	116	31	83	0	15	6-3	.315	.345	.541	.885	1	.997
Major League totals (10 years)		1365	5455	703	1633	349	27	193	872	251	732	4	137	66-41	.299	.328	.479	.807	33	.989

ANDERSON, JASON   P

PERSONAL: Born June 9, 1979, in Danville, Ill. ... 6-0/170. ... Throws right, bats left. ... Full name: Jason R. Anderson. ... College: Illinois.

TRANSACTIONS/CAREER NOTES: Selected by New York Yankees in 10th round of free-agent draft (June 5, 2000). ... Traded by Yankees with P Ryan Bicondoa and P Anderson Garcia to New York Mets for P Armando Benitez (July 18, 2003).

CAREER HITTING: 0-for-0 (.000), 0 R, 0 2B, 0 3B, 0 HR, 0 RBI.

Year — League	W	L	Pct.	ERA	WHIP	G	GS	CG	ShO	Hld.	Sv.-Opp.	IP	H	R	ER	HR	BB-IBB	SO	Avg.
2000— Staten Island (NY-P)	6	5	.545	4.03	1.36	15	15	0	0	...	0-...	80.1	84	41	36	1	25-0	73	.273
2001— Greensboro (S. Atl.)	7	9	.438	3.76	1.34	23	19	1	0	...	1-...	124.1	127	68	52	9	40-1	101	.267
— Staten Island (NY-P)	5	1	.833	1.70	0.92	7	7	0	0	...	0-...	47.2	32	9	9	2	12-0	56	.190
2002— Tampa (FSL)	4	2	.667	4.07	1.23	12	3	0	0	...	1-...	24.1	27	13	11	2	3-0	22	.281
— Norwich (East.)	1	1	.500	0.93	0.98	16	0	0	0	...	2-...	19.1	14	2	2	1	5-1	21	.212
— Columbus (Int'l)	5	1	.833	3.15	1.08	26	0	0	0	...	7-...	34.1	26	13	12	3	11-0	28	.211
2003— Columbus (Int'l)	0	0	.000	0.00	0.65	6	0	0	0	...	3-...	7.2	3	0	0	0	2-0	13	.115
— New York (A.L.)	1	0	1.000	4.79	1.79	22	0	0	0	0	0-0	20.2	23	13	11	3	14-4	9	.280
— Norfolk (Int'l)	1	3	.250	2.70	1.07	10	5	0	0	...	4-...	23.1	18	8	7	3	7-0	9	.214
— New York (N.L.)	0	0	...	5.06	1.41	6	0	0	0	0	0-0	10.2	10	6	6	2	5-1	7	.256
American League totals (1 year)	1	0	1.000	4.79	1.79	22	0	0	0	0	0-0	20.2	23	13	11	3	14-4	9	.280
National League totals (1 year)	0	0	...	5.06	1.41	6	0	0	0	0	0-0	10.2	10	6	6	2	5-1	7	.256
Major League totals (1 year)	1	0	1.000	4.88	1.66	28	0	0	0	0	0-0	31.1	33	19	17	5	19-5	16	.273

ANDERSON, JIMMY   P

PERSONAL: Born January 22, 1976, in Portsmouth, Va. ... 6-1/226. ... Throws left, bats left. ... Full name: James Drew Anderson. ... High school: Western Branch (Chesapeake, Va.).

TRANSACTIONS/CAREER NOTES: Selected by Pittsburgh Pirates organization in ninth round of free-agent draft (June 2, 1994). ... On disabled list (July 5-12, 1998). ... Released by Pirates (December 16, 2002). ... Signed by Cincinnati Reds organization (January 15, 2003). ... Sent outright to Louisville (April 23, 2003). ... Recalled from Louisville (June 16, 2003). ... Designated for assignment (June 27, 2003). ... Sent outright to Louisville (July 1, 2003). ... Elected free agency (July 1, 2003). ... Contract purchased by Cincinnati from Louisville (July 5, 2003) .

CAREER HITTING: 23-for-169 (.136), 11 R, 3 2B, 0 3B, 0 HR, 6 RBI.

Year — League	W	L	Pct.	ERA	WHIP	G	GS	CG	ShO	Hld.	Sv.-Opp.	IP	H	R	ER	HR	BB-IBB	SO	Avg.
1994— GC Pirates (GCL)	5	1	.833	1.60	1.10	10	10	0	0	...	0-...	56.1	35	21	10	1	27-0	66	.177
1995— Augusta (S. Atl.)	4	2	.667	1.53	1.07	14	14	0	0	...	0-...	76.2	51	15	13	1	31-0	75	.190
— Lynchburg (Carolina)	1	5	.167	4.13	1.47	10	9	0	0	...	0-...	52.1	56	29	24	1	21-1	32	.280
1996— Lynchburg (Carolina)	5	3	.625	1.93	1.10	11	11	1	1	...	0-...	65.1	51	25	14	2	21-0	56	.211
— Carolina (Sou.)	8	5	.615	3.34	1.40	17	16	0	0	...	0-...	97.0	92	40	36	3	44-3	79	.253
1997— Carolina (Sou.)	2	1	.667	1.46	1.01	4	4	0	0	...	0-...	24.2	16	6	4	1	9-0	23	.184
— Calgary (PCL)	7	6	.538	5.68	1.83	21	21	0	0	...	0-...	103.0	124	78	65	9	64-3	71	.305
1998— Nashville (PCL)	9	10	.474	5.02	1.75	35	17	0	0	...	0-...	123.2	144	87	69	8	72-6	63	.301
1999— Nashville (PCL)	11	2	.846	3.84	1.45	21	21	1	0	...	0-...	133.2	153	67	57	5	41-0	93	.289
— Pittsburgh (N.L.)	2	1	.667	3.99	1.40	13	4	0	0	0	0-0	29.1	25	15	13	2	16-2	13	.234
2000— Pittsburgh (N.L.)	5	11	.313	5.25	1.58	27	26	1	0	0	0-0	144.0	169	94	84	13	58-2	73	.294
— Nashville (PCL)	0	0	...	4.15	1.69	2	2	0	0	...	0-...	13.0	18	6	6	0	4-0	7	.360
— Altoona (East.)	1	0	1.000	0.00	0.89	1	1	0	0	...	0-...	9.0	7	1	0	0	1-0	6	.212

– 14 –

Year	League	W	L	Pct.	ERA	WHIP	G	GS	CG	ShO	Hld.	Sv.-Opp.	IP	H	R	ER	HR	BB-IBB	SO	Avg.
2001—Pittsburgh (N.L.)		9	17	.346	5.10	1.53	34	34	1	0	0	0-0	206.1	232	123	117	15	83-14	89	.287
2002—Pittsburgh (N.L.)		8	13	.381	5.44	1.64	28	25	1	0	0	0-0	140.2	167	91	85	20	63-5	47	.299
2003—Louisville (Int'l)		6	1	.857	3.12	1.24	9	9	0	0	...	0-...	60.2	61	26	21	2	14-0	30	.265
—Cincinnati (N.L.)		1	5	.167	8.84	1.91	8	7	0	0	0	0-0	38.2	60	39	38	8	14-1	13	.359
—Fresno (PCL)		1	4	.200	6.44	1.85	8	8	0	0	0	0-...	43.1	65	36	31	3	15-0	17	.351
Major League totals (5 years)		25	47	.347	5.43	1.59	110	96	3	0	0	0-0	559.0	653	362	337	58	234-24	235	.295

ANDERSON, MARLON — 2B

PERSONAL: Born January 6, 1974, in Montgomery, Ala. ... 5-11/200. ... Bats left, throws right. ... Full name: Marlon Ordell Anderson. ... High school: Prattville (Ala.). ... College: South Alabama.

TRANSACTIONS/CAREER NOTES: Selected by Philadelphia Phillies organization in second round of free-agent draft (June 1, 1995); choice received from St. Louis Cardinals as part of compensation for Cardinals signing Type A free-agent P Danny Jackson. ... Granted free agency (December 21, 2002). ... Signed by Tampa Bay Devil Rays (January 16, 2003). ... Suspended by Major League Baseball (July 29, 2003). ... Reinstated by MLB (August 1, 2003).

2003 GAMES PLAYED BY POSITION (MLB): 2B—134, DH—4, OF—3.

Year	Team (League)	Pos.	G	AB	R	H	2B	3B	HR	RBI	BB	SO	HBP	GDP	SB-CS	Avg.	OBP	SLG	OPS	E	Pct.
1995—Batavia (NY-Penn)		2B	* 74	* 312	52	92	13	4	3	40	15	20	4	2	22-8	.295	.331	.391	.722	14	.965
1996—Clearwater (FSL)		2B	60	257	37	70	10	3	2	22	14	18	2	4	26-1	.272	.315	.358	.673	16	.958
—Reading (East.)		2B	75	314	38	86	14	3	3	28	26	44	1	5	17-9	.274	.330	.366	.697	18	.957
1997—Reading (East.)		2B	137	* 553	88	147	18	6	10	62	42	77	10	8	27-15	.266	.328	.374	.703	* 29	.961
1998—Scran./W.B. (I.L.)		2B	136	575	104	* 176	32	* 14	16	86	28	77	7	11	24-12	.306	.343	.494	.837	* 28	.959
—Philadelphia (N.L.)		2B	17	43	4	14	3	0	1	4	1	6	0	0	2-0	.326	.333	.465	.798	1	.978
1999—Philadelphia (N.L.)		2B	129	452	48	114	26	4	5	54	24	61	2	6	13-2	.252	.292	.361	.652	11	.979
2000—Scran./W.B. (I.L.)		2B	103	397	57	121	18	8	8	53	39	43	5	2	24-10	.305	.370	.451	.821	• 14	.969
—Philadelphia (N.L.)		2B	41	162	10	37	8	1	1	15	12	22	0	5	2-2	.228	.282	.309	.590	2	.989
2001—Philadelphia (N.L.)		2B	147	522	69	153	30	2	11	61	35	74	2	12	8-5	.293	.337	.421	.758	12	.982
2002—Philadelphia (N.L.)		2B	145	539	64	139	30	6	8	48	42	71	5	16	5-1	.258	.315	.380	.696	* 20	.970
2003—Tampa Bay (A.L.)		2B-DH-OF	145	482	59	130	27	3	6	67	41	60	3	6	19-3	.270	.328	.376	.703	15	.973
American League totals (1 year)			145	482	59	130	27	3	6	67	41	60	3	6	19-3	.270	.328	.376	.703	15	.973
National League totals (5 years)			479	1718	195	457	97	13	26	182	114	234	9	39	30-10	.266	.313	.383	.696	46	.978
Major League totals (6 years)			624	2200	254	587	124	16	32	249	155	294	12	45	49-13	.267	.316	.381	.698	61	.977

ANDERSON, MATT — P

PERSONAL: Born August 17, 1976, in Louisville, Ky. ... 6-4/200. ... Throws right, bats right. ... Full name: Matthew Jason Anderson. ... High school: St. Xavier (Louisville, Ky.). ... College: Rice.

TRANSACTIONS/CAREER NOTES: Selected by Detroit Tigers organization in first round (first pick overall) of free-agent draft (June 3, 1997). ... On disabled list (April 27-May 18 and May 19-September 20, 2002). ... Optioned to Toledo (May 7, 2003). ... Recalled from Toledo (September 2, 2003).

CAREER HITTING: 0-for-0 (.000), 0 R, 0 2B, 0 3B, 0 HR, 0 RBI.

Year	League	W	L	Pct.	ERA	WHIP	G	GS	CG	ShO	Hld.	Sv.-Opp.	IP	H	R	ER	HR	BB-IBB	SO	Avg.
1998—Lakeland (Fla. St.)		1	0	1.000	0.69	1.00	17	0	0	0	...	3-...	26.0	18	4	2	0	8-0	34	.186
—Jacksonville (Sou.)		1	0	1.000	0.60	0.80	13	0	0	0	...	10-...	15.0	7	1	1	1	5-0	11	.143
—Detroit (A.L.)		5	1	.833	3.27	1.57	42	0	0	0	6	0-4	44.0	38	16	16	3	31-4	44	.250
1999—Detroit (A.L.)		2	1	.667	5.68	1.79	37	0	0	0	3	0-2	38.0	33	27	24	8	35-1	32	.232
—Toledo (Int'l)		0	4	.000	6.39	1.66	24	4	0	0	...	5-...	38.0	32	27	27	9	31-0	35	.229
2000—Detroit (A.L.)		3	2	.600	4.72	1.43	69	0	0	0	9	1-1	74.1	61	44	39	8	45-4	71	.228
2001—Detroit (A.L.)		3	1	.750	4.82	1.32	62	0	0	0	9	22-24	56.0	56	33	30	2	18-4	52	.257
2002—Detroit (A.L.)		2	1	.667	9.00	2.27	12	0	0	0	0	0-2	11.0	17	13	11	1	8-1	8	.378
2003—Toledo (Int'l)		1	3	.250	3.79	1.53	23	5	0	0	...	3-...	38.0	50	23	16	4	8-1	31	.314
—Detroit (A.L.)		0	1	.000	5.40	1.46	23	0	0	0	4	3-4	23.1	25	17	14	5	9-1	13	.272
Major League totals (6 years)		15	7	.682	4.89	1.52	245	0	0	0	31	26-37	246.2	230	150	134	27	146-15	220	.251

APPIER, KEVIN — P

PERSONAL: Born December 6, 1967, in Lancaster, Calif. ... 6-2/215. ... Throws right, bats right. ... Full name: Robert Kevin Appier. ... Name pronounced: APE-ee-er. ... High school: Antelope Valley (Lancaster, Calif.). ... College: Fresno State.

TRANSACTIONS/CAREER NOTES: Selected by Kansas City Royals organization in first round (ninth pick overall) of free-agent draft (June 2, 1987). ... On disabled list (July 26-August 12, 1995). ... On Kansas City disabled list (March 20-September 1, 1998); included rehabilitation assignments to Gulf Coast Royals (July 16-21), Lansing (July 22-26), Wichita (July 27-30) and Omaha (July 31-August 27). ... Traded by Royals to Oakland Athletics for P Blake Stein, P Jeff D'Amico, and P Brad Rigby (July 31, 1999). ... On disabled list (April 25-May 13, 2000). ... Granted free agency (October 31, 2000). ... Signed by New York Mets (December 11, 2000). ... Traded by Mets to Anaheim Angels for 1B Mo Vaughn (December 27, 2001). ... Placed on 15-day disabled list (April 20, 2003). ... Reinstated from 15-day disabled list (May 7, 2003). ... Released by Angels (July 30, 2003). ... Signed by Kansas City Royals as free agent (August 6, 2003). ... Placed on 15-day disabled list (August 26, 2003). ... Transferred to 60-day disabled list (September 2, 2003).

CAREER HITTING: 8-for-83 (.096), 4 R, 0 2B, 0 3B, 0 HR, 4 RBI.

Year	League	W	L	Pct.	ERA	WHIP	G	GS	CG	ShO	Hld.	Sv.-Opp.	IP	H	R	ER	HR	BB-IBB	SO	Avg.
1987—Eugene (NW)		5	2	.714	3.04	1.43	15	• 15	0	0	...	0-...	77.0	81	43	26	2	29-0	72	.263
1988—Baseball City (FSL)		10	9	.526	2.75	1.17	24	24	1	0	...	0-...	147.1	134	58	45	1	39-5	112	.244
—Memphis (Sou.)		2	0	1.000	1.83	0.92	3	3	0	0	...	0-...	19.2	11	5	4	0	7-0	18	.164
1989—Omaha (Am. Assoc.)		8	8	.500	3.95	1.32	22	22	3	2	...	0-...	139.0	141	70	61	6	42-1	109	.259
—Kansas City (A.L.)		1	4	.200	9.14	2.12	6	5	0	0	0	0-0	21.2	34	22	22	3	12-1	10	.374
1990—Omaha (Am. Assoc.)		2	1	1.000	1.50	1.00	3	3	0	0	...	0-...	18.0	15	3	3	0	3-0	17	.231
—Kansas City (A.L.)		12	8	.600	2.76	1.25	32	24	3	3	0	0-0	185.2	179	67	57	13	54-2	127	.252
1991—Kansas City (A.L.)		13	10	.565	3.42	1.28	34	31	6	3	1	0-0	207.2	205	97	79	13	61-3	158	.255
1992—Kansas City (A.L.)		15	8	.652	2.46	1.13	30	30	3	0	0	0-0	208.1	167	59	57	10	68-5	150	.217
1993—Kansas City (A.L.)		18	8	.692	2.56	1.11	34	34	5	1	0	0-0	238.2	183	74	68	8	81-3	186	.212
1994—Kansas City (A.L.)		7	6	.538	3.83	1.29	23	23	1	0	0	0-0	155.0	137	68	66	11	63-7	145	.240
1995—Kansas City (A.L.)		15	10	.600	3.89	1.21	31	31	4	1	0	0-0	201.1	163	90	87	14	80-1	185	.221
1996—Kansas City (A.L.)		14	11	.560	3.62	1.26	32	32	5	1	0	0-0	211.1	192	87	85	17	75-2	207	.245

Year	League	W	L	Pct.	ERA	WHIP	G	GS	CG	ShO	Hld.	Sv.-Opp.	IP	H	R	ER	HR	BB-IBB	SO	Avg.
1997—	Kansas City (A.L.)	9	13	.409	3.40	1.23	34	34	4	1	0	0-0	235.2	215	96	89	24	74-2	196	.243
1998—	GC Royals (GCL)	0	1	.000	2.70	1.20	1	1	0	0	...	0-...	3.1	3	3	1	0	1-0	2	.214
	—Lansing (Midw.)	0	0	...	2.25	1.00	1	1	0	0	...	0-...	4.0	4	1	1	0	0-0	5	.267
	—Wichita (Texas)	0	1	.000	6.00	1.67	1	1	0	0	...	0-...	6.0	8	4	4	1	2-0	1	.348
	—Omaha (PCL)	3	2	.600	7.03	1.66	6	6	0	0	...	0-...	32.0	41	25	25	7	12-1	22	.301
	—Kansas City (A.L.)	1	2	.333	7.80	1.73	3	3	0	0	0	0-0	15.0	21	13	13	3	5-1	9	.339
1999—	Kansas City (A.L.)	9	9	.500	4.87	1.45	22	22	1	0	0	0-0	140.1	153	81	76	18	51-3	78	.279
	—Oakland (A.L.)	7	5	.583	5.77	1.60	12	12	0	0	0	0-0	68.2	77	50	44	9	33-1	53	.280
2000—	Oakland (A.L.)	15	11	.577	4.52	1.55	31	31	1	1	0	0-0	195.1	200	109	98	23	* 102-10	129	.262
2001—	New York (N.L.)	11	10	.524	3.57	1.19	33	33	1	1	0	0-0	206.2	181	89	82	22	64-4	172	.237
2002—	Anaheim (A.L.)	14	12	.538	3.92	1.35	32	32	0	0	0	0-0	188.1	191	89	82	15	64-2	132	.267
2003—	Anaheim (A.L.)	7	7	.500	5.63	1.52	19	19	0	0	0	0-0	92.2	105	60	58	17	36-4	50	.279
	—Kansas City (A.L.)	1	2	.333	4.26	1.16	4	4	0	0	0	0-0	19.0	15	9	9	4	7-0	5	.217
	American League totals (14 years)	158	126	.556	3.74	1.30	379	367	33	11	1	0-0	2384.2	2237	1071	990	210	866-47	1820	.248
	National League totals (1 year)	11	10	.524	3.57	1.19	33	33	1	1	0	0-0	206.2	181	89	82	22	64-4	172	.237
	Major League totals (15 years)	169	136	.554	3.72	1.29	412	400	34	12	1	0-0	2591.1	2418	1160	1072	232	930-51	1992	.247

ARMAS, TONY — P

PERSONAL: Born April 29, 1978, in Puerto Piritu, Venezuela. ... 6-3/225. ... Throws right, bats right. ... Full name: Antonio Jose Armas. ... Name pronounced: ar-MUS.

TRANSACTIONS/CAREER NOTES: Signed as non-drafted free agent by New York Yankees organization (August 16, 1994). ... Traded by Yankees with a player to be named later to Boston Red Sox for C Mike Stanley and SS Randy Brown (August 13, 1997); Red Sox acquired P Jim Mecir to complete deal (September 29, 1997). ... Traded by Red Sox to Montreal Expos (December 18, 1997), completing deal in which Red Sox traded P Carl Pavano and a player to be named later to Expos for P Pedro Martinez (November 18, 1997). ... On Montreal disabled list (April 1-28 and July 19-September 6, 2000); included rehabilitation assignments to Jupiter (April 22-28) and Ottawa (August 27-September 4). ... On disabled list (July 27-August 19, 2002). ... Placed on 15-day disabled list (April 21, 2003). ... Transferred to Emergency disabled list (July 10, 2003).

CAREER HITTING: 16-for-141 (.113), 4 R, 1 2B, 1 3B, 0 HR, 7 RBI.

Year	League	W	L	Pct.	ERA	WHIP	G	GS	CG	ShO	Hld.	Sv.-Opp.	IP	H	R	ER	HR	BB-IBB	SO	Avg.
1995—	GC Yankees (GCL)	0	1	.000	0.64	1.29	5	4	0	0	...	0-...	14.0	12	9	1	1	6-0	13	.226
1996—	Oneonta (N.Y.-Penn)	1	1	.500	5.74	1.60	3	3	0	0	...	0-...	15.2	14	12	10	1	11-0	14	.230
	—GC Yankees (GCL)	4	1	.800	3.15	1.18	8	7	0	0	...	1-...	45.2	41	18	16	1	13-0	45	.236
1997—	Greensboro (S. Atl.)	5	2	.714	1.05	0.95	9	9	2	1	...	0-...	51.2	36	13	6	3	13-0	64	.190
	—Tampa (FSL)	3	1	.750	3.33	1.28	9	9	0	0	...	0-...	46.0	43	23	17	1	16-3	26	.257
	—Sarasota (Fla. St.)	2	1	.667	6.62	1.70	3	3	0	0	...	0-...	17.2	18	13	13	2	12-0	9	.281
1998—	Jupiter (FSL)	12	8	.600	2.88	1.30	27	27	1	1	...	0-...	153.1	140	63	49	11	59-0	136	.244
1999—	Harrisburg (Eastern)	9	7	.563	2.89	1.19	24	24	2	1	...	0-...	149.2	123	62	48	10	55-0	106	.226
	—Montreal (N.L.)	0	1	.000	1.50	1.67	1	1	0	0	0	0-0	6.0	8	4	1	0	2-1	2	.320
2000—	Jupiter (FSL)	0	0	...	0.00	0.86	1	1	0	0	...	0-...	4.2	4	0	0	0	4-0	8	.222
	—Ottawa (Int'l)	1	2	.333	3.79	1.37	4	4	0	0	...	0-...	19.0	22	11	8	3	4-0	12	.286
	—Montreal (N.L.)	7	9	.438	4.36	1.31	17	17	0	0	0	0-0	95.0	74	49	46	10	50-2	59	.218
2001—	Montreal (N.L.)	9	14	.391	4.03	1.38	34	34	0	0	0	0-0	196.2	180	101	88	18	91-6	176	.247
2002—	Montreal (N.L.)	12	12	.500	4.44	1.38	29	29	0	0	0	0-0	164.1	149	87	81	22	78-12	131	.243
2003—	Montreal (N.L.)	2	1	.667	2.61	1.06	5	5	0	0	0	0-0	31.0	25	9	9	4	8-0	23	.225
	Major League totals (5 years)	30	37	.448	4.11	1.35	86	86	0	0	0	0-0	493.0	436	250	225	54	229-21	391	.240

ARROYO, BRONSON — P

PERSONAL: Born February 24, 1977, in Key West, Fla. ... 6-5/190. ... Throws right, bats right. ... Full name: Bronson Anthony Arroyo. ... Name pronounced: ah-ROY-yoh. ... High school: Hernando (Fla.).

TRANSACTIONS/CAREER NOTES: Selected by Pittsburgh Pirates organization in third round of free-agent draft (June 1, 1995). ... On suspended list (May 29-June 1, 1996). ... On disabled list (May 18-June 7 and June 18-July 4, 1998). ... Claimed on waivers by Boston Red Sox (February 4, 2003). ... Contract purchased by Boston from Pawtucket (August 22, 2003).

CAREER HITTING: 4-for-48 (.083), 2 R, 2 2B, 0 3B, 0 HR, 1 RBI.

Year	League	W	L	Pct.	ERA	WHIP	G	GS	CG	ShO	Hld.	Sv.-Opp.	IP	H	R	ER	HR	BB-IBB	SO	Avg.
1995—	GC Pirates (GCL)	5	4	.556	4.26	1.32	13	9	0	0	...	1-...	61.1	72	39	29	4	9-0	48	.277
1996—	Augusta (S. Atl.)	8	6	.571	3.52	1.17	26	26	0	0	...	0-...	135.2	123	64	53	11	36-0	107	.242
1997—	Lynchburg (Carolina)	• 12	4	.750	3.31	1.17	24	24	3	1	...	0-...	160.1	154	69	59	17	33-0	121	.250
1998—	Carolina (Sou.)	9	8	.529	5.46	1.65	23	22	1	0	...	0-...	127.0	158	91	77	18	51-0	90	.310
1999—	Altoona (East.)	• 15	4	.789	3.65	1.47	25	25	2	1	...	0-...	153.0	167	73	62	15	58-1	100	.280
	—Nashville (PCL)	0	2	.000	10.38	2.46	3	3	0	0	...	0-...	13.0	22	15	15	1	10-0	11	.367
2000—	Nashville (PCL)	8	2	.800	3.65	1.21	13	13	1	0	...	0-...	88.2	82	43	36	7	25-3	52	.251
	—Pittsburgh (N.L.)	2	6	.250	6.40	1.73	20	12	0	0	0	0-0	71.2	88	61	51	10	36-6	50	.302
	—Lynchburg (Carolina)	0	0	...	3.86	1.43	1	1	0	0	...	0-...	7.0	8	3	3	0	2-0	3	.267
2001—	Pittsburgh (N.L.)	5	7	.417	5.09	1.51	24	13	1	0	2	0-0	88.1	99	54	50	12	34-6	39	.289
	—Nashville (PCL)	6	2	.750	3.93	1.18	9	9	2	0	...	0-...	66.1	63	32	29	6	15-1	49	.247
2002—	Nashville (PCL)	8	6	.571	2.96	1.08	22	21	• 3	• 2	...	0-...	143.0	126	57	47	10	28-1	116	.236
	—Pittsburgh (N.L.)	2	1	.667	4.00	1.67	9	4	0	0	1	0-0	27.0	30	14	12	1	15-3	22	.283
2003—	Pawtucket (Int'l)	12	6	.667	3.43	1.14	24	24	1	1	...	0-...	149.2	148	66	57	9	23-0	155	.252
	—Boston (A.L.)	0	0	...	2.08	0.81	6	0	0	0	0	1-1	17.1	10	5	4	0	4-2	14	.164
	American League totals (1 year)	0	0	...	2.08	0.81	6	0	0	0	0	1-1	17.1	10	5	4	0	4-2	14	.164
	National League totals (3 years)	9	14	.391	5.44	1.61	53	29	1	0	3	0-0	187.0	217	129	113	23	85-15	111	.294
	Major League totals (4 years)	9	14	.391	5.15	1.55	59	29	1	0	3	1-1	204.1	227	134	117	23	89-17	125	.284

ASENCIO, MIGUEL — P

PERSONAL: Born September 29, 1980, in Villa Mella, Dominican Republic. ... 6-2/190. ... Throws right, bats right. ... Full name: Miguel Depaula Asencio. ... Name pronounced: ah-SEN-see-oh. ... High school: Liceo Tiro Al Blanco (La Victoria, Dominican Republic).

TRANSACTIONS/CAREER NOTES: Signed as non-drafted free agent by Philadelphia Phillies organization (March 2, 1998). ... Selected by Kansas City in Rule 5 draft (December 13, 2001). ... Placed on the 15-day disabled list (May 16, 2003). ... Transferred to Emergency disabled list (June 15, 2003). ... Sent on rehab assignment by Kansas City (August 18, 2003). ... Recalled from minor league rehab assignment (September 5, 2003).

CAREER HITTING: 0-for-2 (.000), 0 R, 0 2B, 0 3B, 0 HR, 0 RBI.

Year League	W	L	Pct.	ERA	WHIP	G	GS	CG	ShO	Hld.	Sv.-Opp.	IP	H	R	ER	HR	BB-IBB	SO	Avg.
1998— Dom. Phillies (DSL)	0	2	.000	6.55	2.32	11	4	0	0	...	0-...	22.0	39	29	16	...	12-...	7	...
1999— GC Phillies (GCL)	1	4	.200	5.97	1.78	9	5	0	0	...	0-...	28.2	35	24	19	1	16-0	14	.304
2000— Clearwater (Fla. St.)	2	1	.667	2.73	1.18	5	5	0	0	...	0-...	33.0	22	10	10	2	17-0	24	.191
— Batavia (N.Y.-Penn)	2	2	.500	4.99	1.24	7	7	1	0	...	0-...	39.2	32	23	22	3	17-0	28	.224
2001— Clearwater (Fla. St.)	12	5	.706	2.84	1.25	28	21	2	1	...	0-...	155.1	124	62	49	7	70-1	123	.218
2002— Kansas City (A.L.)	4	7	.364	5.11	1.62	31	21	0	0	0	0-0	123.1	136	73	70	17	64-2	58	.282
2003— Kansas City (A.L.)	2	1	.667	5.21	1.55	8	8	1	0	0	0-0	48.1	54	29	28	4	21-0	27	.295
— Arizona Royals (Ariz.)	0	0	.000	2.84	1.89	3	3	0	0	...	0-...	6.1	11	3	2	0	1-0	3	.367
— Wichita (Texas)	0	0	.000	0.00	0.50	1	1	0	0	...	0-...	4.0	1	0	0	0	1-0	3	.077
Major League totals (2 years)	6	8	.429	5.14	1.60	39	29	1	0	0	0-0	171.2	190	102	98	21	85-2	85	.286

ASHBY, ANDY — P

PERSONAL: Born July 11, 1967, in Kansas City, Mo. ... 6-1/202. ... Throws right, bats right. ... Full name: Andrew Jason Ashby. ... High school: Park Hill (Kansas City, Mo.). ... Junior college: Crowder College (Mo.).

TRANSACTIONS/CAREER NOTES: Signed as non-drafted free agent by Philadelphia Phillies organization (May 4, 1986). ... On Spartanburg disabled list (April 7-July 10, 1988). ... On Spartanburg disabled list (April 6-26, 1989). ... On Philadelphia disabled list (April 27-August 11, 1992); included rehabilitation assignments to Scranton/Wilkes-Barre (July 8-August 2 and August 6-10). ... Selected by Colorado Rockies in first round (25th pick overall) of expansion draft (November 17, 1992). ... Traded by Rockies to San Diego Padres (July 27, 1993), completing deal in which Padres traded P Bruce Hurst and P Greg W. Harris to Rockies for C Brad Ausmus, P Doug Bochtler and a player to be named later (July 26, 1993). ... On disabled list (June 6-22, June 29-July 15 and July 27-September 1, 1996; May 20-June 15, 1997; and June 7-24, 1999). ... Traded by Padres to Phillies for P Carlton Loewer, P Steve Montgomery and P Adam Eaton (November 10, 1999). ... On Philadelphia disabled list (June 12-27, 2000). ... Traded by Phillies to Atlanta Braves for P Bruce Chen and P Jimmy Osting (July 12, 2000). ... Granted free agency (November 1, 2000). ... Signed by Los Angeles Dodgers (December 6, 2000). ... On disabled list (April 16, 2001-remainder of season).

CAREER HITTING: 70-for-521 (.134), 26 R, 13 2B, 0 3B, 1 HR, 26 RBI.

Year League	W	L	Pct.	ERA	WHIP	G	GS	CG	ShO	Hld.	Sv.-Opp.	IP	H	R	ER	HR	BB-IBB	SO	Avg.
1986— Bend (NW)	1	2	.333	4.95	1.50	16	6	0	0	...	2-...	60.0	56	40	33	3	34-1	45	...
1987— Spartanburg (SAL)	4	6	.400	5.60	1.73	13	13	1	0	...	0-...	64.1	73	45	40	8	38-2	52	.284
— Utica (N.Y.-Penn)	3	7	.300	4.05	1.53	13	13	0	0	...	0-...	60.0	56	38	27	3	36-3	51	.250
1988— Spartanburg (SAL)	1	1	.500	2.70	1.20	3	3	0	0	...	0-...	16.2	13	7	5	0	7-0	16	.213
— Batavia (N.Y.-Penn)	3	1	.750	1.61	0.92	6	6	2	1	...	0-...	44.2	25	11	8	3	16-0	32	.161
1989— Spartanburg (SAL)	5	9	.357	2.87	1.35	17	17	3	1	...	0-...	106.2	95	48	34	8	49-0	100	.234
— Clearwater (Fla. St.)	1	4	.200	1.24	1.12	6	6	2	1	...	0-...	43.2	28	9	6	0	21-0	44	.185
1990— Reading (East.)	10	7	.588	3.42	1.30	23	23	4	1	...	0-...	139.2	134	65	53	3	48-0	94	.253
1991— Scran./W.B. (I.L.)	11	11	.500	3.46	1.26	26	26	•6	•3	...	0-...	161.1	144	78	62	12	60-2	113	.235
— Philadelphia (N.L.)	1	5	.167	6.00	1.43	8	8	0	0	0	0-0	42.0	41	28	28	5	19-0	26	.256
1992— Philadelphia (N.L.)	1	3	.250	7.54	1.70	10	8	0	0	0	0-0	37.0	42	31	31	6	21-0	24	.290
— Scran./W.B. (I.L.)	0	3	.000	3.00	1.12	7	7	1	0	...	0-...	33.0	23	13	11	4	14-0	18	.202
1993— Colorado (N.L.)	0	4	.000	8.50	2.24	20	9	0	0	0	1-1	54.0	89	54	51	5	32-4	33	.377
— Colo. Springs (PCL)	4	2	.667	4.10	1.37	7	6	1	0	...	0-...	41.2	45	25	19	2	12-0	35	.276
— San Diego (N.L.)	3	6	.333	5.48	1.49	12	12	0	0	0	0-0	69.0	79	46	42	14	24-1	44	.295
1994— San Diego (N.L.)	6	11	.353	3.40	1.14	24	24	4	0	0	0-0	164.1	145	75	62	16	43-12	121	.233
1995— San Diego (N.L.)	12	10	.545	2.94	1.26	31	•31	2	2	0	0-0	192.2	180	79	63	17	62-3	150	.253
1996— San Diego (N.L.)	9	5	.643	3.23	1.20	24	24	1	0	0	0-0	150.2	147	60	54	17	34-1	85	.259
1997— San Diego (N.L.)	9	11	.450	4.13	1.28	30	30	2	0	0	0-0	200.2	207	108	92	17	49-2	144	.266
1998— San Diego (N.L.)	17	9	.654	3.34	1.24	33	33	5	1	0	0-0	226.2	223	90	84	23	58-8	151	.259
1999— San Diego (N.L.)	14	10	.583	3.80	1.25	31	31	4	*3	0	0-0	206.0	204	95	87	26	54-4	132	.258
2000— Philadelphia (N.L.)	4	7	.364	5.68	1.49	16	16	1	0	0	0-0	101.1	113	75	64	17	38-5	51	.288
— Atlanta (N.L.)	8	6	.571	4.13	1.29	15	15	2	1	0	0-0	98.0	103	49	45	12	23-4	55	.271
2001— Los Angeles (N.L.)	2	0	1.000	3.86	1.29	2	2	0	0	0	0-0	11.2	14	5	5	2	1-0	7	.292
2002— Los Angeles (N.L.)	9	13	.409	3.91	1.34	30	30	0	0	0	0-0	181.2	179	85	79	20	65-3	107	.261
2003— Los Angeles (N.L.)	3	10	.231	5.18	1.47	21	12	0	0	0	0-0	73.0	90	42	42	8	17-2	41	.311
Major League totals (13 years)	98	110	.471	4.13	1.32	307	285	21	7	0	1-1	1808.2	1856	922	829	205	540-49	1171	.268

ASTACIO, PEDRO — P

PERSONAL: Born November 28, 1969, in Hato Mayor, Dominican Republic. ... 6-2/210. ... Throws right, bats right. ... Full name: Pedro Julio Astacio. ... Name pronounced: ah-STAH-see-oh. ... High school: Pilar Rondon (Dominican Republic).

TRANSACTIONS/CAREER NOTES: Signed as non-drafted free agent by Los Angeles Dodgers organization (November 21, 1987). ... On Albuquerque disabled list (April 26-May 21, 1992). ... Traded by Dodgers to Colorado Rockies for 2B Eric Young (August 19, 1997). ... Traded by Rockies to Houston Astros for P Scott Elarton and a player to be named later (July 31, 2001). ... On Houston disabled list (August 29, 2001-remainder of season). ... Granted free agency (November 8, 2001). ... Signed by New York Mets (January 16, 2002). ... On New York disabled list (March 21-April 24, 2003); included rehabilitation assignment to St. Lucie (April 3, 2003). ... Reinstated from the 15-day disabled list (April 24, 2003). ... Recalled by New York from St. Lucie rehab assignment (April 24, 2003). ... Placed on 15-day disabled list, retroactive to May 22 (May 29, 2003). ... Transferred to Emergency disabled list (June 13, 2003). ... Transferred from the 15-day to 60-day disabled list (July 3, 2003).

CAREER HITTING: 84-for-635 (.132), 28 R, 8 2B, 1 3B, 0 HR, 27 RBI.

Year League	W	L	Pct.	ERA	WHIP	G	GS	CG	ShO	Hld.	Sv.-Opp.	IP	H	R	ER	HR	BB-IBB	SO	Avg.
1988— Dom. Dodgers (DSL)	4	2	.667	2.08	1.28	8	7	1	...	...	0-...	47.2	43	21	11	...	18-...	20	...
1989— GC Dodgers (GCL)	7	3	.700	3.17	1.16	12	12	1	•1	...	0-...	76.2	77	30	27	3	12-0	52	.258
1990— Vero Beach (FSL)	1	5	.167	6.32	1.64	8	8	0	0	...	0-...	47.0	54	39	33	3	23-0	41	.286
— Yakima (NW)	2	0	1.000	1.74	0.63	3	3	0	0	...	0-...	20.2	9	8	4	0	4-0	22	.123
— Bakersfield (Calif.)	5	2	.714	2.77	1.17	10	7	1	0	...	0-...	52.0	46	22	16	2	15-1	34	.238
1991— Vero Beach (FSL)	5	3	.625	1.67	0.88	9	9	3	1	...	0-...	59.1	44	19	11	0	8-0	45	.209
— San Antonio (Texas)	4	11	.267	4.78	1.60	19	19	2	1	...	0-...	113.0	142	67	60	9	39-3	62	.318
1992— Albuquerque (PCL)	6	6	.500	5.47	1.61	24	15	1	0	...	0-...	98.2	115	68	60	8	44-1	66	.293
— Los Angeles (N.L.)	5	5	.500	1.98	1.22	11	11	4	4	0	0-0	82.0	80	23	18	1	20-4	43	.255
1993— Los Angeles (N.L.)	14	9	.609	3.57	1.25	31	31	3	2	0	0-0	186.1	165	80	74	14	68-5	122	.239
1994— Los Angeles (N.L.)	6	8	.429	4.29	1.27	23	23	3	1	0	0-0	149.0	142	77	71	18	47-4	108	.252
1995— Los Angeles (N.L.)	7	8	.467	4.24	1.27	48	11	1	1	2	0-1	104.0	103	54	49	12	29-5	80	.261
1996— Los Angeles (N.L.)	9	8	.529	3.44	1.29	35	32	0	0	0	0-0	211.2	207	86	81	18	67-9	130	.261
1997— Los Angeles (N.L.)	7	9	.438	4.13	1.29	26	24	2	1	0	0-0	153.2	151	75	70	15	47-0	115	.256
— Colorado (N.L.)	5	1	.833	4.25	1.29	7	7	0	0	0	0-0	48.2	49	23	23	9	14-0	51	.262
1998— Colorado (N.L.)	13	14	.481	6.23	1.52	35	34	0	0	0	0-0	209.1	245	*160	*145	*39	74-0	170	.294
1999— Colorado (N.L.)	17	11	.607	5.04	1.44	34	34	7	0	0	0-0	232.0	258	140	130	*38	75-6	210	.285
2000— Colorado (N.L.)	12	9	.571	5.27	1.50	32	32	3	0	0	0-0	196.1	217	119	115	32	77-5	193	.281

Year League	W	L	Pct.	ERA	WHIP	G	GS	CG	ShO	Hld.	Sv.-Opp.	IP	H	R	ER	HR	BB-IBB	SO	Avg.
2001— Colorado (N.L.)	6	13	.316	5.49	1.43	22	22	4	1	0	0-0	141.0	151	91	86	21	50-3	125	.276
— Houston (N.L.)	2	1	.667	3.14	1.19	4	4	0	0	0	0-0	28.2	30	10	10	1	4-0	19	.280
2002— New York (N.L.)	12	11	.522	4.79	1.33	31	31	3	1	0	0-0	191.2	192	106	102	* 32	63-5	152	.262
2003— St. Lucie (Fla. St.)	0	2	.000	2.08	1.04	4	4	0	0	...	0-...	17.1	15	6	4	0	3-0	15	.231
— New York (N.L.)	3	2	.600	7.36	1.77	7	7	0	0	0	0-0	36.2	47	30	30	8	18-1	20	.311
Major League totals (12 years)	118	109	.520	4.58	1.36	346	303	30	11	2	0-1	1971.0	2037	1073	1004	258	653-47	1538	.269

ATKINS, GARRETT   3B

PERSONAL: Born December 12, 1979, in Orange, Calif. ... 6-3/210. ... Bats right, throws right. ... Full name: Garrett Bernard Atkins. ... High school: University (Irvine, CA). ... College: UCLA.

TRANSACTIONS/CAREER NOTES: Selected by Colorado Rockies in fifth round of free-agent draft (June 5, 2000).

2003 GAMES PLAYED BY POSITION (MLB): 3B—19.

Year Team (League)	Pos.	G	AB	R	H	2B	3B	HR	RBI	BB	SO	HBP	GDP	SB-CS	Avg.	OBP	SLG	OPS	E	Pct.
2000— Portland (NW)	1B-3B	69	251	34	76	12	0	7	47	45	48	2	3	2-0	.303	.411	.434	.846	6	.983
2001— Salem (Caro.)	1B-3B	135	465	70	151	43	5	5	67	74	98	8	8	6-4	.325	.421	.471	.892	7	.995
2002— Carolina (Sou.)	3B-1B	128	510	71	138	27	3	12	61	59	77	2	12	6-6	.271	.345	.406	.751	19	.940
2003— Colo. Springs (PCL) 3B-DH-1B		118	439	80	140	30	1	13	67	45	52	3	9	2-4	.319	.382	.481	.863	20	.942
— Colorado (N.L.)	3B	25	69	6	11	2	0	0	4	3	14	1	1	0-0	.159	.205	.188	.394	6	.850
Major League totals (1 year)		25	69	6	11	2	0	0	4	3	14	1	1	0-0	.159	.205	.188	.394	6	.850

AURILIA, RICH   SS

PERSONAL: Born September 2, 1971, in Brooklyn, N.Y. ... 6-1/185. ... Bats right, throws right. ... Full name: Richard Santo Aurilia. ... Name pronounced: uh-REEL-yuh. ... High school: Xaverian (Brooklyn, N.Y.). ... College: St. John's.

TRANSACTIONS/CAREER NOTES: Selected by Texas Rangers organization in 24th round of free-agent draft (June 1, 1992). ... On disabled list (April 9-16, 1993). ... Traded by Rangers with IF/OF Desi Wilson to San Francisco Giants for P John Burkett (December 24, 1994). ... On San Francisco disabled list (September 24, 1996-remainder of season). ... On disabled list (July 4-20, 1998; and May 20-June 4, 2002). ... Placed on 15-day disabled list (August 4, 2003). ... Removed from 15-day disabled list (August 19, 2003).

2003 GAMES PLAYED BY POSITION (MLB): SS—123, DH—1.

Year Team (League)	Pos.	G	AB	R	H	2B	3B	HR	RBI	BB	SO	HBP	GDP	SB-CS	Avg.	OBP	SLG	OPS	E	Pct.
1992— Butte (Pio.)	SS	59	202	37	68	11	3	3	30	42	18	0	2	13-9	.337	.447	.465	.913	14	.943
1993— Charlotte (Fla. St.)	SS	122	440	80	136	16	5	5	56	75	57	3	9	15-18	.309	.408	.402	.810	24	.964
1994— Tulsa (Texas)	SS	129	458	67	107	18	6	12	57	53	74	4	8	10-13	.234	.315	.378	.693	24	.962
1995— Shreveport (Texas)	SS	64	226	29	74	17	1	4	42	27	26	1	8	10-3	.327	.398	.465	.863	14	.962
— Phoenix (PCL)	SS	71	258	42	72	12	0	5	34	35	29	0	4	2-2	.279	.361	.384	.745	9	.975
— San Francisco (N.L.)	SS	9	19	4	9	3	0	2	4	1	2	0	1	1-0	.474	.476	.947	1.424	0	1.000
1996— Phoenix (PCL)	SS-2B	7	30	9	13	7	0	0	4	2	3	0	1	1-1	.433	.469	.667	1.135	1	.972
— San Francisco (N.L.)	SS-2B	105	318	27	76	7	1	3	26	25	52	1	1	4-1	.239	.295	.296	.590	10	.975
1997— San Francisco (N.L.)	SS	46	102	16	28	8	0	5	19	8	15	0	3	1-1	.275	.321	.500	.821	3	.979
— Phoenix (PCL)	SS	8	34	9	10	2	0	1	5	5	4	0	1	2-1	.294	.385	.441	.826	0	1.000
1998— San Francisco (N.L.)	SS	122	413	54	110	27	2	9	49	31	62	2	3	3-3	.266	.319	.407	.726	10	.979
1999— San Francisco (N.L.)	SS	152	558	68	157	23	1	22	80	43	71	5	16	2-3	.281	.336	.444	.780	* 28	.957
2000— San Francisco (N.L.)	SS	141	509	67	138	24	2	20	79	54	90	0	15	1-2	.271	.339	.444	.783	21	.967
2001— San Francisco (N.L.)	SS	156	636	114	* 206	37	5	37	97	47	83	0	14	1-3	.324	.369	.572	.941	17	.975
2002— San Francisco (N.L.)	SS	133	538	76	138	35	2	15	61	37	90	4	15	1-2	.257	.305	.413	.718	11	.980
2003— San Francisco (N.L.)	SS-DH	129	505	65	140	26	1	13	58	36	82	1	18	2-2	.277	.325	.410	.735	13	.974
Major League totals (9 years)		993	3598	491	1002	190	14	126	473	282	547	13	86	16-17	.278	.331	.444	.775	113	.972

AUSMUS, BRAD   C

PERSONAL: Born April 14, 1969, in New Haven, Conn. ... 5-11/200. ... Bats right, throws right. ... Full name: Bradley David Ausmus. ... Name pronounced: AHHS-muss. ... High school: Cheshire (Conn.). ... College: Dartmouth.

TRANSACTIONS/CAREER NOTES: Selected by New York Yankees organization in 48th round of free-agent draft (June 2, 1987). ... Selected by Colorado Rockies in third round (54th pick overall) of expansion draft (November 17, 1992). ... Traded by Rockies with P Doug Bochtler and a player to be named later to San Diego Padres for P Bruce Hurst and P Greg W. Harris (July 26, 1993). ... Padres acquired P Andy Ashby to complete deal (July 27, 1993). ... Traded by Padres with SS Andujar Cedeno and P Russ Spear to Detroit Tigers for C John Flaherty and SS Chris Gomez (June 18, 1996). ... On Detroit suspended list (September 4-5, 1996). ... Traded by Tigers with P Jose Lima, P C.J. Nitkowski, P Trever Miller and IF Daryle Ward to Houston Astros for OF Brian L. Hunter, IF Orlando Miller, P Doug Brocail, P Todd Jones and cash (December 10, 1996). ... Traded by Astros with P C.J. Nitkowski to Tigers for C Paul Bako, P Dean Crow, P Mark Persails, P Brian Powell, and 3B Carlos Villalobos (January 14, 1999). ... Traded by Tigers with P Doug Brocail and P Nelson Cruz to Astros for C Mitch Meluskey, P Chris Holt and OF Roger Cedeno (December 11, 2000).

2003 GAMES PLAYED BY POSITION (MLB): C—143.

Year Team (League)	Pos.	G	AB	R	H	2B	3B	HR	RBI	BB	SO	HBP	GDP	SB-CS	Avg.	OBP	SLG	OPS	E	Pct.
1988— GC Yankees (GCL)	C	43	133	22	34	2	0	0	15	11	25	2	4	5-2	.256	.320	.271	.590	9	.979
— Oneonta (NYP)	C	2	4	0	1	0	0	0	0	0	2	0	1	0-0	.250	.250	.250	.500	0	—
1989— Oneonta (NYP)	3B-C	52	165	29	43	6	0	1	18	22	28	0	2	6-4	.261	.348	.315	.663	7	.984
1990— Prince Will. (Car.)	C	107	364	46	86	12	2	0	27	32	73	3	7	2-8	.236	.303	.280	.583	5	.993
1991— Prince Will. (Car.)	C	63	230	28	70	14	3	2	30	24	37	0	2	17-6	.304	.366	.417	.783	5	.990
— Alb./Colon. (East.)	C	67	229	36	61	9	2	1	29	27	36	1	8	14-3	.266	.345	.336	.681	4	.992
1992— Alb./Colon. (East.)	C	5	18	0	3	0	1	0	1	2	3	0	1	2-1	.167	.250	.278	.528	1	.970
— Columbus (Int'l)	C-OF	111	364	48	88	14	3	2	35	40	56	1	14	19-5	.242	.317	.313	.630	9	.988
1993— Colo. Springs (PCL)	C	76	241	31	65	10	4	2	33	27	41	1	6	10-6	.270	.342	.369	.711	6	.987
— San Diego (N.L.)	C	49	160	18	41	8	1	5	12	6	28	0	2	2-0	.256	.283	.413	.696	8	.975
1994— San Diego (N.L.)	C-1B	101	327	45	82	12	1	7	24	30	63	1	8	5-1	.251	.314	.358	.672	6	.991
1995— San Diego (N.L.)	C-1B	103	328	44	96	16	4	5	34	31	56	2	6	16-5	.293	.353	.412	.765	6	.992
1996— San Diego (N.L.)	C	50	149	16	27	4	0	1	13	13	27	3	4	1-4	.181	.261	.228	.489	6	.982
— Detroit (A.L.)	C	75	226	30	56	12	0	4	22	26	45	2	4	3-4	.248	.328	.354	.682	4	.992
1997— Houston (N.L.)	C	130	425	45	113	25	1	4	44	38	78	3	14	14-6	.266	.326	.358	.684	7	.992
1998— Houston (N.L.)	C	128	412	62	111	10	4	6	45	53	60	3	18	10-3	.269	.356	.357	.713	7	.992
1999— Detroit (A.L.)	C	127	458	62	126	25	6	9	54	51	71	14	11	12-9	.275	.365	.415	.779	2	.998

Year	Team (League)	Pos.	G	AB	R	H	2B	3B	HR	RBI	BB	SO	HBP	GDP	SB-CS	Avg.	OBP	SLG	OPS	E	Pct.
2000—	Detroit (A.L.) C-2B-3B-1B		150	523	75	139	25	3	7	51	69	79	6	19	11-5	.266	.357	.365	.722	8	.992
2001—	Houston (N.L.)	C	128	422	45	98	23	4	5	34	30	64	1	13	4-1	.232	.284	.341	.625	3	.997
2002—	Houston (N.L.)	C	130	447	57	115	19	3	6	50	38	71	6	*30	2-3	.257	.322	.353	.675	3	.997
2003—	Houston (N.L.)	C	143	450	43	103	12	2	4	47	46	66	4	8	5-3	.229	.303	.291	.594	3	.997
	American League totals (3 years)		352	1207	167	321	62	9	20	127	146	195	22	34	26-18	.266	.354	.382	.736	14	.994
	National League totals (9 years)		962	3120	375	786	129	20	43	303	285	513	23	97	59-26	.252	.317	.347	.664	50	.993
	Major League totals (11 years)		1314	4327	542	1107	191	29	63	430	431	708	45	131	85-44	.256	.328	.357	.685	64	.993

AUSTIN, JEFF   P

PERSONAL: Born October 19, 1976, in San Bernardino, Calif. ... 6-0/185. ... Throws right, bats right. ... Full name: Jeffrey Wellington Austin. ... High school: Kingwood (Texas). ... College: Stanford.

TRANSACTIONS/CAREER NOTES: Selected by Montreal Expos organization in 10th round of free-agent draft (June 1, 1995); did not sign. ... Selected by Kansas City Royals organization in first round (fourth pick overall) of free-agent draft (June 2, 1998). ... Traded by Royals with P Brian Shackelford to Cincinnati Reds for OF Alan Moye and 3B Damaso Espino (March 6, 2003). ... Recalled by Cincinnati from Louisville (April 20, 2003). ... Optioned to Louisville of the International League by Cincinnati (May 28, 2003). ... Recalled by Cincinnati from Louisville (September 15, 2003).

CAREER HITTING: 1-for-8 (.125), 0 R, 0 2B, 0 3B, 0 HR, 0 RBI.

Year	League	W	L	Pct.	ERA	WHIP	G	GS	CG	ShO	Hld.	Sv.-Opp.	IP	H	R	ER	HR	BB-IBB	SO	Avg.
1999—	Wilmington (Caro.)	7	2	.778	3.77	1.31	18	18	0	0	...	0-...	112.1	108	52	47	10	39-0	97	.255
	— Wichita (Texas)	3	1	.750	4.46	1.49	6	6	0	0	...	0-...	34.1	40	19	17	1	11-1	21	.284
2000—	Wichita (Texas)	2	2	.500	2.93	0.86	6	6	1	0	...	0-...	43.0	33	16	14	3	4-0	31	.210
	— Omaha (PCL)	7	9	.438	4.48	1.46	23	19	1	1	...	0-...	126.2	150	85	63	16	35-1	57	.299
2001—	Omaha (PCL)	3	7	.300	6.88	1.64	28	8	0	0	...	2-...	70.2	89	56	54	14	27-1	55	.314
	— Kansas City (A.L.)	0	0	...	5.54	1.58	21	0	0	0	1	0-0	26.0	27	17	16	4	14-2	27	.273
2002—	Kansas City (A.L.)	0	0	...	4.91	1.82	10	0	0	0	0	0-0	11.0	14	6	6	0	6-1	6	.318
	— Omaha (PCL)	4	0	1.000	3.27	1.32	39	0	0	0	0	2-...	52.1	54	24	19	2	15-2	44	.263
2003—	Cincinnati (N.L.)	2	3	.400	8.58	1.73	7	7	0	0	0	0-0	28.1	28	27	27	9	21-0	22	.255
	— Louisville (Int'l)	4	2	.667	4.34	1.42	9	9	0	0	...	0-...	45.2	46	24	22	5	19-0	37	.266
	American League totals (2 years)	0	0	...	5.35	1.65	31	0	0	0	1	0-0	37.0	41	23	22	4	20-3	33	.287
	National League totals (1 year)	2	3	.400	8.58	1.73	7	7	0	0	0	0-0	28.1	28	27	27	9	21-0	22	.255
	Major League totals (3 years)	2	3	.400	6.75	1.68	38	7	0	0	1	0-0	65.1	69	50	49	13	41-3	55	.273

AVERY, STEVE   P

PERSONAL: Born April 14, 1970, in Taylor, Mich. ... 6-4/205. ... Throws left, bats left. ... Full name: Steven Thomas Avery. ... Name pronounced: AY-virr-ee. ... High school: John F. Kennedy (Taylor, Mich.).

TRANSACTIONS/CAREER NOTES: Selected by Atlanta Braves organization in first round (third pick overall) of free-agent draft (June 1, 1988). ... On Atlanta disabled list (July 13-September 2, 1996); included rehabilitation assignment to Greenville (August 12-18). ... Granted free agency (October 31, 1996). ... Signed by Boston Red Sox (January 22, 1997). ... On Boston disabled list (May 4-July 5, 1997); included rehabilitation assignments to Sarasota (June 12-25) and Gulf Coast Red Sox (June 25-July 5). ... Granted free agency (October 28, 1998). ... Signed by Cincinnati Reds (December 21, 1998). ... On disabled list (July 24, 1999-remainder of season). ... Granted free agency (October 29, 1999). ... Signed by Braves organization (February 22, 2000). ... On Richmond disabled list (July 27-September 6, 2000). ... Granted free agency (October 18, 2000). ... Re-signed by Braves organization (January 26, 2001). ... Released by Braves (March 30, 2001). ... Signed by Detroit Tigers organization (January 23, 2003). ... Contract purchased by Detroit from Toledo (May 9, 2003). ... Optioned to Toledo by Detroit (July 26, 2003). ... Recalled by Detroit from Toledo; sent outright to Toledo (August 1, 2003).

CAREER HITTING: 76-for-437 (.174), 35 R, 14 2B, 4 3B, 4 HR, 32 RBI.

Year	League	W	L	Pct.	ERA	WHIP	G	GS	CG	ShO	Hld.	Sv.-Opp.	IP	H	R	ER	HR	BB-IBB	SO	Avg.
1988—	Pulaski (Appal.)	7	1	.875	1.50	0.86	10	10	3	•2	...	0-...	66.0	38	16	11	2	19-0	80	.167
1989—	Durham (Caro.)	6	4	.600	1.45	0.91	13	13	3	1	...	0-...	86.2	59	22	14	5	20-1	90	.190
	— Greenville (Sou.)	6	3	.667	2.77	1.21	13	13	1	0	...	0-...	84.1	68	32	26	3	34-0	75	.226
1990—	Richmond (Int'l)	5	5	.500	3.39	1.29	13	13	3	0	...	0-...	82.1	85	35	31	7	21-0	69	.272
	— Atlanta (N.L.)	3	11	.214	5.64	1.68	21	20	1	1	0	0-0	99.0	121	79	62	7	45-2	75	.302
1991—	Atlanta (N.L.)	18	8	.692	3.38	1.21	35	35	3	1	0	0-0	210.1	189	89	79	21	65-0	137	.240
1992—	Atlanta (N.L.)	11	11	.500	3.20	1.23	35	•35	2	2	0	0-0	233.2	216	95	83	14	71-3	129	.246
1993—	Atlanta (N.L.)	18	6	.750	2.94	1.16	35	35	3	1	0	0-0	223.1	216	81	73	14	43-5	125	.261
1994—	Atlanta (N.L.)	8	3	.727	4.04	1.20	24	24	1	0	0	0-0	151.2	127	71	68	15	55-4	122	.227
1995—	Atlanta (N.L.)	7	13	.350	4.67	1.25	29	29	3	1	0	0-0	173.1	165	92	90	22	52-4	141	.252
1996—	Atlanta (N.L.)	7	10	.412	4.47	1.42	24	23	1	0	0	0-0	131.0	146	70	65	10	40-8	86	.285
	— Greenville (Sou.)	0	0	...	0.00	0.00	1	1	0	0	...	0-...	.2	0	0	0	0	0-0	0	.000
1997—	Boston (A.L.)	6	7	.462	6.42	1.82	22	18	0	0	1	0-0	96.2	127	76	69	15	49-0	51	.320
	— Sarasota (Fla. St.)	0	0	...	0.00	1.00	1	1	0	0	...	0-...	3.0	2	0	0	0	1-0	3	.200
	— GC Red Sox (GCL)	0	0	...	1.50	0.83	1	1	0	0	...	0-...	6.0	5	3	1	1	0-0	8	.200
	— Pawtucket (Int'l)	1	0	1.000	0.00	0.80	1	1	0	0	...	0-...	5.0	1	0	0	0	3-0	1	.063
1998—	Boston (A.L.)	10	7	.588	5.02	1.55	34	23	0	0	1	0-1	123.2	128	74	69	14	64-0	57	.269
	— Pawtucket (Int'l)	0	2	.000	5.56	1.59	3	3	0	0	...	0-...	11.1	9	9	7	2	9-0	6	.237
1999—	Cincinnati (N.L.)	6	7	.462	5.16	1.59	19	19	0	0	0	0-0	96.0	75	62	55	11	78-0	51	.222
2000—	Greenville (Sou.)	0	5	.000	8.69	2.24	6	6	0	0	0	0-...	29.0	43	32	28	6	22-1	17	.361
	— Macon (S. Atl.)	0	1	.000	1.50	1.17	2	2	0	0	...	0-...	6.0	6	5	1	2	1-0	7	.250
	— Myrtle Beach (Caro.)	3	3	.500	1.53	1.38	7	7	1	0	...	0-...	47.0	40	11	8	2	25-0	32	.240
	— Richmond (Int'l)	1	3	.250	9.43	1.90	4	4	0	0	...	0-...	21.0	23	25	22	3	17-0	8	.287
2003—	Detroit (A.L.)	2	0	1.000	5.63	1.63	19	0	0	0	1	0-1	16.0	19	11	10	5	7-1	6	.302
	— Toledo (Int'l)	1	4	.200	3.15	1.37	22	2	0	0	...	0-...	34.1	37	16	12	6	10-3	14	.285
	American League totals (3 years)	18	14	.563	5.64	1.67	75	41	0	0	3	0-2	236.1	274	161	148	34	120-1	114	.293
	National League totals (8 years)	78	69	.531	3.93	1.29	222	220	14	6	0	0-0	1318.1	1255	639	575	114	449-26	866	.253
	Major League totals (11 years)	96	83	.536	4.19	1.35	297	261	14	6	3	0-2	1554.2	1529	800	723	148	569-27	980	.259

AYALA, LUIS   P

PERSONAL: Born January 12, 1978, in Los Mochis, Mexico. ... 6-2/170. ... Throws right, bats right. ... Full name: Luis Ignacio Ayala. ... Name pronounced: eye-YA-lah.
TRANSACTIONS/CAREER NOTES: Signed by Saltillo, Mexican League (1997). ... Contract purchased by Colorado Rockies organization from Saltillo (October 14, 1999). ... Loaned by Rockies to Saltillo, Mexican League (April 13, 2000-entire season). ... Contract sold by Rockies to Saltillo, Mexican League (May 15, 2001). ... Contract purchased by Montreal Expos from Saltillo (August 13, 2002). ... Granted free agency (October 15, 2002). ... Signed by Arizona Diamondbacks organization (October 23, 2002). ... Selected by Expos from Diamondbacks organization in Rule 5 major league draft (December 16, 2002). ... Placed on 15-day disabled list (June 22, 2003). ... Sent on rehab assignment to Gulf Coast League Expos by Montreal (July 14, 2003). ... Recall from GCL Expos rehab assignment by Montreal (July 21, 2003).
CAREER HITTING: 0-for-1 (.000), 0 R, 0 2B, 0 3B, 0 HR, 0 RBI.

Year League	W	L	Pct.	ERA	WHIP	G	GS	CG	ShO	Hld.	Sv.-Opp.	IP	H	R	ER	HR	BB-IBB	SO	Avg.
2001— Salem (Caro.)	0	1	.000	4.05	1.80	13	0	0	0	...	7-...	13.1	19	10	6	0	5-0	10	.358
2002— Ottawa (Int'l)	0	0	...	3.52	1.43	6	0	0	0	...	0-...	7.2	7	3	3	1	4-0	6	.250
2003— GC Expos (GCL)	0	0	.000	0.00	1.09	2	2	0	0	...	0-...	3.2	2	0	0	0	2-0	2	.154
— Montreal (N.L.)	10	3	.769	2.92	1.10	65	0	0	0	19	5-8	71.0	65	27	23	8	13-3	46	.244
Major League totals (1 year)	10	3	.769	2.92	1.10	65	0	0	0	19	5-8	71.0	65	27	23	8	13-3	46	.244

AYBAR, MANNY   P

PERSONAL: Born May 4, 1972, in Bani, Dominican Republic. ... 6-1/177. ... Throws right, bats right. ... Full name: Manuel Antonio Aybar. ... Name pronounced: EYE-bar.

TRANSACTIONS/CAREER NOTES: Signed as non-drafted free agent by St. Louis Cardinals organization (October 21, 1991). ... Traded by Cardinals with P Jose Jimenez, P Rick Croushore and IF Brent Butler to Colorado Rockies for P Darryl Kile, P Dave Veres and P Luther Hackman (November 16, 1999). ... Traded by Rockies to Cincinnati Reds for P Gabe White (April 7, 2000). ... On Cincinnati disabled list (July 2-24, 2000); included rehabilitation assignment to Louisville (July 8-23). ... Traded by Reds to Florida Marlins for P Jorge Cordova (July 26, 2000). ... Traded by Marlins to Chicago Cubs for P Oswaldo Mairena (March 30, 2001). ... Traded by Cubs with a player to be named later to Tampa Bay Devil Rays for 1B Fred McGriff (July 27, 2001); Devil Rays acquired SS Jason Smith to complete deal (August 5, 2001). ... Granted free agency (October 12, 2001). ... Signed by San Francisco Giants (February 2, 2002). ... On San Francisco disabled list (August 15-September 1, 2002); included rehabilitation assignment to Fresno (August 27-September 1). ... Granted free agency (December 21, 2002). ... Signed by Arizona Diamondbacks organization (January 24, 2003). ... Contract purchased by San Francisco from Fresno (May 19, 2003). ... Designated for assignment by San Francisco (May 28, 2003). ... Sent outright to Fresno by San Francisco (June 2, 2003).

CAREER HITTING: 13-for-70 (.186), 6 R, 0 2B, 0 3B, 1 HR, 5 RBI.

Year League	W	L	Pct.	ERA	WHIP	G	GS	CG	ShO	Hld.	Sv.-Opp.	IP	H	R	ER	HR	BB-IBB	SO	Avg.
1992— Dom. Cardinals (DSL)	1	0	1.000	0.00	1.33	55	0	0	0	...	0-...	3.0	1	0	0	...	3-...	1	...
1993— Dom. Cardinals (DSL)	4	4	.500	3.15	1.22	13	11	1	0	...	0-...	71.1	54	33	25	...	33-...	66	...
1994— Ariz. Cardinals (Ariz.)	6	1	.857	2.12	1.08	13	13	1	0	...	0-...	72.1	69	25	17	0	9-0	79	.250
1995— Savannah (S. Atl.)	3	8	.273	3.04	1.05	18	18	2	1	...	0-...	112.2	82	46	38	8	36-0	99	.199
— St. Pete. (FSL)	2	5	.286	3.35	1.20	9	9	0	0	...	0-...	48.1	42	27	18	4	16-0	43	.228
1996— Arkansas (Texas)	8	6	.571	3.05	1.27	20	20	0	0	...	0-...	121.0	120	53	41	10	34-0	83	.259
— Louisville (A.A.)	2	2	.500	3.23	1.08	5	5	0	0	...	0-...	30.2	26	12	11	1	7-0	25	.226
1997— St. Louis (N.L.)	5	8	.385	3.48	1.28	22	22	3	•2	...	0-...	137.0	131	60	53	10	45-2	114	.250
— St. Louis (N.L.)	2	4	.333	4.24	1.40	12	12	0	0	0	0-0	68.0	66	33	32	8	29-0	41	.263
1998— St. Louis (N.L.)	6	6	.500	5.98	1.62	20	14	0	0	0	0-0	81.1	90	58	54	6	42-1	57	.281
— Memphis (PCL)	10	0	1.000	2.60	0.95	13	13	0	0	...	0-...	83.0	62	24	24	7	17-0	63	.207
1999— St. Louis (N.L.)	4	5	.444	5.47	1.44	65	1	0	0	12	3-5	97.0	104	67	59	13	36-3	74	.272
2000— Colorado (N.L.)	0	1	.000	16.20	3.00	1	0	0	0	0	0-0	1.2	5	3	3	1	0-0	0	.500
— Cincinnati (N.L.)	1	1	.500	4.83	1.45	32	0	0	0	1	0-...	50.1	51	31	27	7	22-2	31	.262
— Louisville (Int'l)	0	2	.000	13.50	3.00	3	2	0	0	...	0-...	6.2	10	10	10	0	10-0	1	.345
— Florida (N.L.)	1	0	1.000	2.63	1.13	21	0	0	0	0	0-1	27.1	18	8	8	3	13-1	14	.184
2001— Chicago (N.L.)	2	1	.667	6.35	1.99	17	1	0	0	2	0-0	22.2	28	19	16	5	17-0	16	.304
— Iowa (PCL)	1	2	.333	5.02	1.35	8	7	1	1	...	0-...	43.0	42	26	24	8	16-1	32	.251
— Durham (Int'l)	1	3	.250	5.68	1.55	11	3	0	0	...	0-...	31.2	40	25	20	5	9-0	29	.320
2002— Fresno (PCL)	1	4	.200	3.75	1.27	45	0	0	0	...	24-...	50.1	46	24	21	6	18-1	53	.244
— San Francisco (N.L.)	1	0	1.000	2.51	1.33	15	0	0	0	1	0-0	14.1	16	6	4	1	3-2	11	.271
2003— San Francisco (N.L.)	0	0	...	6.00	2.33	3	0	0	0	0	0-0	3.0	4	2	2	1	3-0	2	.333
— Fresno (PCL)	2	4	.333	4.08	1.36	52	0	0	0	...	17-...	57.1	55	27	26	7	23-0	45	.253
Major League totals (7 years)	17	18	.486	5.05	1.50	186	28	0	0	16	3-6	365.2	382	227	205	45	165-9	246	.269

BACKE, BRANDON   P

PERSONAL: Born April 5, 1978, in Galveston, Texas. ... 6-0/188. ... Throws right, bats right. ... Full name: Brandon Allen Backe. ... Name pronounced: back-EE. ... High school: Ball (Galveston, Texas). ... Junior college: Galveston (Texas) Community College.

TRANSACTIONS/CAREER NOTES: Selected by Tampa Bay Devil Rays organization in 18th round of free-agent draft (June 2, 1998). ... On Bakersfield disabled list (April 5-19, 2001). ... Optioned to Durham of the International League by Tampa Bay (May 27, 2003). ... Recalled by Tampa Bay from Durham (May 16, 2003). ... Recalled by Tampa Bay from Durham (June 18, 2003).

CAREER HITTING: 0-for-0 (.000), 1 R, 0 2B, 0 3B, 0 HR, 0 RBI.

Year League	W	L	Pct.	ERA	WHIP	G	GS	CG	ShO	Hld.	Sv.-Opp.	IP	H	R	ER	HR	BB-IBB	SO	Avg.
2001— Char., S.C. (SAL)	2	1	.667	2.92	0.97	16	0	0	0	...	7-...	24.2	17	8	8	2	7-1	20	.200
— Bakersfield (Calif.)	1	0	1.000	1.09	0.85	17	0	0	0	...	3-...	24.2	13	7	3	1	8-0	33	.149
— Orlando (Sou.)	1	0	1.000	5.73	1.41	14	0	0	0	...	0-...	22.0	20	14	14	1	11-0	20	.253
2002— Orlando (Sou.)	4	6	.400	4.68	1.39	20	14	•3	1	...	2-...	92.1	91	58	48	9	37-1	45	.256
— Tampa Bay (A.L.)	0	0	...	6.92	1.69	9	0	0	0	0	0-0	13.0	15	10	10	3	7-0	6	.288
2003— Durham (Int'l)	2	1	.667	4.64	1.39	16	2	0	0	...	0-...	33.0	33	21	17	1	13-0	27	.250
— Tampa Bay (A.L.)	1	1	.500	5.44	1.46	28	0	0	0	5	0-0	44.2	40	28	27	6	25-1	36	.247
Major League totals (2 years)	1	1	.500	5.77	1.51	37	0	0	0	5	0-0	57.2	55	38	37	9	32-1	42	.257

BACSIK, MIKE   P

PERSONAL: Born November 11, 1977, in Dallas, Texas. ... 6-3/190. ... Throws left, bats left. ... Full name: Michael J. Bacsik. ... High school: Duncanville (Texas).

TRANSACTIONS/CAREER NOTES: Selected by Cleveland Indians organization in 18th round of free-agent draft (June 4, 1996). ... Traded by Indians with 2B Roberto Alomar and OF Danny Peoples to New York Mets for OF Matt Lawton, OF Alex Escobar, P Jerrod Riggan and two players to be named later (December 11, 2001); Indians acquired P Billy Traber and 1B Earl Snyder to complete deal (December 13, 2001). ... Recalled from Norfolk of the International League by New York Mets (May 31, 2003). ... Optioned to Norfolk by New York (June 26, 2003). ... Recalled from Norfolk by New York; sent outright to Norfolk (August 20, 2003).

CAREER HITTING: 2-for-21 (.095), 0 R, 1 2B, 0 3B, 0 HR, 2 RBI.

Year League	W	L	Pct.	ERA	WHIP	G	GS	CG	ShO	Hld.	Sv.-Opp.	IP	H	R	ER	HR	BB-IBB	SO	Avg.
1996— Burlington (Appal.)	4	2	.667	2.20	0.90	13	13	1	0	...	0-...	69.2	49	23	17	3	14-0	61	.189
1997— Columbus (S. Atl.)	4	14	.222	5.44	1.51	28	28	0	0	...	0-...	139.0	163	94	84	16	47-1	100	.293
1998— Kinston (Caro.)	10	9	.526	2.88	1.11	27	27	1	0	...	0-...	165.2	147	64	53	17	37-3	128	.239
1999— Akron (East.)	11	11	.500	4.64	1.41	26	26	1	0	...	0-...	149.1	164	84	77	24	47-0	84	.281
2000— Kinston (Caro.)	3	6	.333	4.57	1.23	11	11	0	0	...	0-...	65.0	72	36	33	4	8-0	56	.281
— Akron (East.)	7	1	.875	2.78	1.07	11	11	1	1	...	0-...	71.1	61	23	22	3	15-0	44	.231
— Buffalo (Int'l)	0	3	.000	5.59	1.31	5	5	0	0	...	0-...	29.0	31	20	18	7	7-0	9	.270
2001— Buffalo (Int'l)	12	5	.706	3.26	1.15	21	20	2	0	...	0-...	121.1	115	47	44	13	25-0	81	.244
— Akron (East.)	1	1	.500	1.98	0.88	4	4	1	1	...	0-...	27.1	21	7	6	2	3-0	19	.208
— Cleveland (A.L.)	0	0	...	9.00	1.78	3	0	0	0	0	0-0	9.0	13	10	9	0	3-1	4	.325

Year League	W	L	Pct.	ERA	WHIP	G	GS	CG	ShO	Hld.	Sv.-Opp.	IP	H	R	ER	HR	BB-IBB	SO	Avg.
2002— Norfolk (Int'l)	5	5	.500	3.74	1.47	25	14	1	1	...	0-...	108.1	134	48	45	13	25-0	75	.312
— New York (N.L.)	3	2	.600	4.37	1.47	11	9	1	0	0	0-0	55.2	63	29	27	8	19-3	30	.289
2003— New York (N.L.)	1	2	.333	10.19	2.04	5	3	0	0	0	0-0	17.2	28	21	20	5	8-0	12	.368
— Norfolk (Int'l)	2	9	.182	4.97	1.39	22	21	0	0	...	0-...	117.2	129	70	65	13	34-1	62	.288
American League totals (1 year)	0	0	...	9.00	1.78	3	0	0	0	0	0-0	9.0	13	10	9	0	3-1	4	.325
National League totals (2 years)	4	4	.500	5.77	1.61	16	12	1	0	0	0-0	73.1	91	50	47	13	27-3	42	.310
Major League totals (3 years)	4	4	.500	6.12	1.63	19	12	1	0	0	0-0	82.1	104	60	56	13	30-4	46	.311

BAERGA, CARLOS — 2B/3B

PERSONAL: Born November 4, 1968, in San Juan, Puerto Rico. ... 5-11/215. ... Bats both, throws right. ... Full name: Carlos Obed Baerga. ... Name pronounced: by-AIR-ga. ... High school: Barbara Ann Rooshart (Rio Piedras, Puerto Rico).

TRANSACTIONS/CAREER NOTES: Signed as non-drafted free agent by San Diego Padres organization (November 4, 1985). ... Traded by Padres with C Sandy Alomar and OF Chris James to Cleveland Indians for OF Joe Carter (December 6, 1989). ... Traded by Indians with IF Alvaro Espinoza to New York Mets for IF Jose Vizcaino and IF Jeff Kent (July 29, 1996). ... Granted free agency (October 26, 1998). ... Signed by St. Louis Cardinals (January 27, 1999). ... Released by Cardinals (March 17, 1999). ... Signed by Cincinnati Reds organization (March 23, 1999). ... Released by Reds (June 4, 1999). ... Signed by San Diego Padres organization (June 6, 1999). ... Traded by Padres to Indians for cash (August 16, 1999). ... Granted free agency (October 29, 1999). ... Signed by Tampa Bay Devil Rays organization (February 24, 2000). ... Contract voided (March 21, 2000). ... Signed by Seattle Mariners organization (January 19, 2001). ... Released by Mariners (March 30, 2001). ... Signed by Samsung, Korean League (April 2001). ... Signed by Long Island, Atlantic League (April 19, 2001). ... Signed by Boston Red Sox organization (December 18, 2001). ... On disabled list (July 2-26, 2002). ... Granted free agency (October 29, 2002). ... Signed by Arizona Diamondbacks organization (January 31, 2003).

2003 GAMES PLAYED BY POSITION (MLB): 1B—19, 2B—15, DH—6, 3B—5.

Year Team (League)	Pos.	G	AB	R	H	2B	3B	HR	RBI	BB	SO	HBP	GDP	SB-CS	Avg.	OBP	SLG	OPS	E	Pct.
1986— Char., S.C. (SAL)	2B-SS	111	378	57	102	14	4	7	41	26	60	5	4	6-1	.270	.321	.384	.705	27	.943
1987— Char., S.C. (SAL)	2B-SS	134	515	83	157	23	•9	7	50	38	107	12	10	26-21	.305	.365	.425	.790	§ 36	.943
1988— Wichita (Texas)	2B-SS	122	444	67	121	28	1	12	65	31	83	9	8	4-4	.273	.331	.421	.752	33	.943
1989— Las Vegas (PCL)	3B	132	520	63	143	28	2	10	74	30	98	6	10	6-6	.275	.319	.394	.713	* 32	.916
1990— Cleveland (A.L.) 2B-3B-SS	108	312	46	81	17	2	7	47	16	57	4	4	0-2	.260	.300	.394	.694	17	.935
— Colo. Springs (PCL)	3B	12	50	11	19	2	1	1	11	5	4	0	4	1-0	.380	.436	.520	.956	4	.925
1991— Cleveland (A.L.) 2B-3B-SS	158	593	80	171	28	2	11	69	48	74	6	12	3-2	.288	.346	.398	.744	27	.959
1992— Cleveland (A.L.)	2B-DH	161	657	92	205	32	1	20	105	35	76	13	15	10-2	.312	.354	.455	.809	19	.979
1993— Cleveland (A.L.)	2B-DH	154	624	105	200	28	6	21	114	34	68	6	17	15-4	.321	.355	.486	.840	17	.979
1994— Cleveland (A.L.)	2B-DH	103	442	81	139	32	2	19	80	10	45	6	10	8-2	.314	.333	.525	.858	* 15	.971
1995— Cleveland (A.L.)	2B-DH	135	557	87	175	28	2	15	90	35	31	3	15	11-2	.314	.355	.452	.807	19	.973
1996— Cleveland (A.L.)	2B	100	424	54	113	25	6	10	55	16	25	7	15	1-1	.267	.302	.396	.698	15	.971
— New York (N.L.)	1B-3B-2B	26	83	5	16	3	0	2	11	5	2	2	8	0-0	.193	.253	.301	.554	4	.966
1997— New York (N.L.)	2B	133	467	53	131	25	1	9	52	20	54	3	13	2-6	.281	.311	.396	.707	14	.978
1998— New York (N.L.)	2B	147	511	46	136	27	1	7	53	24	55	6	21	0-1	.266	.303	.364	.667	9	.986
1999— Indianapolis (Int'l) 3B-2B-1B-D	52	221	32	64	10	0	3	27	10	18	1	11	2-1	.290	.321	.376	.696	6	.975
— Las Vegas (PCL)	3B-2B	21	91	15	26	7	0	2	9	9	5	1	2	0-0	.286	.356	.429	.785	5	.919
— San Diego (N.L.) 2B-3B-1B-D	33	80	6	20	1	0	2	5	6	14	2	2	1-0	.250	.318	.338	.656	2	.962
— Cleveland (A.L.) 3B-2B-DH	22	57	4	13	0	0	1	5	4	10	0	3	1-1	.228	.274	.281	.555	1	.976
2000—										Did not play.									
2001— Samsung (Korean)	...	120	18	33	...	4	17	10	12	...	...	...-...	.275	...	...	...	...	
— Long Island (Atl.)	53	203	38	64	9	3	9	44	18	24	...	3-...	.315	...	.522	...	...	
2002— Boston (A.L.) DH-2B-3B	73	182	17	52	11	0	2	19	7	20	2	6	6-0	.286	.316	.379	.695	1	.983
2003— Arizona (N.L.) 1-2-DH-3	105	207	31	71	13	0	4	39	18	20	2	6	1-1	.343	.396	.464	.859	3	.986
American League totals (9 years)		1014	3848	566	1149	201	15	106	584	205	406	47	97	55-16	.299	.338	.441	.779	131	.971
National League totals (5 years)		444	1348	141	374	69	2	24	160	73	145	15	50	4-8	.277	.318	.385	.703	32	.981
Major League totals (12 years)		1458	5196	707	1523	270	17	130	744	278	551	62	147	59-24	.293	.333	.427	.759	163	.973

BAEZ, DANYS — P

PERSONAL: Born September 10, 1977, in Pinar del Rio, Cuba. ... 6-3/225. ... Throws right, bats right. ... Name pronounced: DAN-ees BUY-ez.

TRANSACTIONS/CAREER NOTES: Signed as non-drafted free agent by Cleveland Indians organization (November 5, 1999). ... On Buffalo disabled list (June 19-July 4, 2000; and June 4-29, 2001).

CAREER HITTING: 0-for-3 (.000), 0 R, 0 2B, 0 3B, 0 HR, 0 RBI.

Year League	W	L	Pct.	ERA	WHIP	G	GS	CG	ShO	Hld.	Sv.-Opp.	IP	H	R	ER	HR	BB-IBB	SO	Avg.
2000— Kinston (Caro.)	2	2	.500	4.71	1.31	9	9	0	0	...	0-...	49.2	45	29	26	5	20-0	56	.236
— Akron (East.)	4	9	.308	3.68	1.27	18	18	0	0	...	0-...	102.2	98	46	42	6	32-0	77	.259
2001— Buffalo (Int'l)	2	0	1.000	3.20	1.07	16	0	0	0	...	3-...	25.1	18	9	9	2	9-0	30	.200
— Akron (East.)	0	0	...	0.00	0.50	1	0	0	0	...	0-...	2.0	1	0	0	0	0-0	2	.143
— Cleveland (A.L.)	5	3	.625	2.50	1.07	43	0	0	0	14	0-1	50.1	34	22	14	5	20-4	52	.191
2002— Cleveland (A.L.)	10	11	.476	4.41	1.46	39	26	1	0	0	6-8	165.1	160	84	81	14	82-5	130	.256
2003— Cleveland (A.L.)	2	9	.182	3.81	1.16	73	0	0	0	5	25-35	75.2	65	36	32	9	23-0	66	.229
Major League totals (3 years)	17	23	.425	3.92	1.32	155	26	1	0	19	31-44	291.1	259	142	127	28	125-9	248	.238

BAGWELL, JEFF — 1B

PERSONAL: Born May 27, 1968, in Boston, Mass. ... 6-0/215. ... Bats right, throws right. ... Full name: Jeffrey Robert Bagwell. ... Name pronounced: BAG-well. ... High school: Xavier (Middletown, Conn.). ... College: Hartford.

TRANSACTIONS/CAREER NOTES: Selected by Boston Red Sox organization in fourth round of free-agent draft (June 5, 1989). ... Traded by Red Sox to Houston Astros for P Larry Andersen (August 31, 1990). ... On Houston disabled list (July 31-September 1, 1995; included rehabilitation assignment to Jackson (August 28-September 1). ... On disabled list (May 13-28, 1998).

2003 GAMES PLAYED BY POSITION (MLB): 1B—158.

Year	Team (League)	Pos.	G	AB	R	H	2B	3B	HR	RBI	BB	SO	HBP	GDP	SB-CS	Avg.	OBP	SLG	OPS	E	Pct.
1989— GC Red Sox (GCL)	2B-3B	5	19	3	6	1	0	0	3	3	0	0	1		0-0	.316	.409	.368	.778	2	.875
— Winter Haven (FSL)	2B-3B-1B	64	210	27	65	13	2	2	19	22	25	3	7	1-1	.310	.381	.419	.800	12	.931
1990— New Britain (East.)	3B	136	481	63	*160	•34	7	4	61	73	57	7	15	5-7	.333	.423	.457	.881	34	.914
1991— Houston (N.L.)	1B	156	554	79	163	26	4	15	82	75	116	*13	12	7-4	.294	.387	.437	.824	12	.991
1992— Houston (N.L.)	1B	•162	586	87	160	34	6	18	96	84	97	12	17	10-6	.273	.368	.444	.812	7	.995
1993— Houston (N.L.)	1B	142	535	76	171	37	4	20	88	62	73	3	20	13-4	.320	.388	.516	.903	9	.993
1994— Houston (N.L.)	1B-OF	110	400	*104	147	32	2	39	*116	65	65	4	12	15-4	.368	.451	*.750	1.201	§9	.991
1995— Houston (N.L.)	1B	114	448	88	130	29	0	21	87	79	102	6	9	12-5	.290	.399	.496	.894	7	.994
— Jackson (Texas)	1B-DH	4	12	0	2	0	0	0	0	3	2	1	0	0-0	.167	.375	.167	.542	0	1.000
1996— Houston (N.L.)	1B	*162	568	111	179	*48	2	31	120	135	114	10	15	21-7	.315	.451	.570	1.021	*16	.989
1997— Houston (N.L.)	1B-DH	•162	566	109	162	40	2	43	135	127	122	16	10	31-10	.286	.425	.592	1.017	11	.993
1998— Houston (N.L.)	1B	147	540	124	164	33	1	34	111	109	90	7	14	19-7	.304	.424	.557	.981	7	.995
1999— Houston (N.L.)	1B-DH	•162	562	*143	171	35	0	42	126	*149	127	11	18	30-11	.304	.454	.591	1.045	8	.994
2000— Houston (N.L.)	1B-DH	159	590	*152	183	37	1	47	132	107	116	15	19	9-6	.310	.424	.615	1.039	9	.994
2001— Houston (N.L.)	1B	161	600	126	173	43	4	39	130	106	135	6	20	11-3	.288	.397	.568	.966	12	.992
2002— Houston (N.L.)	1B-DH	158	571	94	166	33	2	31	98	101	130	10	16	7-3	.291	.401	.518	.919	7	.995
2003— Houston (N.L.)	1B	160	605	109	168	28	2	39	100	88	119	6	25	11-4	.278	.373	.524	.897	9	.994
Major League totals (13 years)			1955	7125	1402	2137	455	30	419	1421	1287	1406	119	207	196-74	.300	.411	.549	.959	123	.993

BAKO, PAUL   C

PERSONAL: Born June 20, 1972, in Lafayette, La. ... 6-2/215. ... Bats left, throws right. ... Full name: Gabor Paul II Bako. ... Name pronounced: BAH-koh. ... High school: Lafayette (La.). ... College: Southwestern Louisiana.

TRANSACTIONS/CAREER NOTES: Selected by Cincinnati Reds organization in fifth round of free-agent draft (June 3, 1993). ... Traded by Reds with P Donne Wall to Detroit Tigers for OF Melvin Nieves (November 11, 1997). ... Traded by Tigers with P Dean Crow, P Mark Persails, P Brian Powell and 3B Carlos Villalobos to Houston Astros for C Brad Ausmus and P C.J. Nitkowski (January 14, 1999). ... Traded by Astros to Florida Marlins for a player to be named to later (April 11, 2000); Astros acquired cash to complete deal (October 10, 2000). ... Claimed on waivers by Atlanta Braves (July 21, 2000). ... Traded by Braves with P Jose Cabrera to Milwaukee Brewers for C Henry Blanco (March 20, 2002). ... On disabled list (June 9-24, 2002). ... Traded by Brewers to Chicago Cubs for a player to be named later (November 26, 2002).
2003 GAMES PLAYED BY POSITION (MLB): C—69.

Year	Team (League)	Pos.	G	AB	R	H	2B	3B	HR	RBI	BB	SO	HBP	GDP	SB-CS	Avg.	OBP	SLG	OPS	E	Pct.
1993— Billings (Pio.)	C-1B	57	194	34	61	11	0	4	30	22	37	1	5	5-1	.314	.382	.433	.815	6	.984
1994— Win.-Salem (Car.)	C	90	289	29	59	9	1	3	26	35	81	4	6	2-2	.204	.299	.273	.572	15	.977
1995— Win.-Salem (Car.)	C	82	249	29	71	11	2	7	27	42	66	1	6	3-1	.285	.389	.430	.819	6	.989
1996— Chattanooga (Sou.)	C	110	360	53	106	27	0	8	48	48	93	5	5	1-0	.294	.381	.436	.817	13	.984
1997— Indianapolis (A.A.)	C	104	321	34	78	14	1	6	43	34	81	2	7	0-5	.243	.316	.368	.683	6	.991
1998— Toledo (Int'l)	C	13	48	5	14	3	1	1	6	1	13	0	1	0-0	.292	.300	.458	.758	1	.988
— Detroit (A.L.)	C	96	305	23	83	12	1	3	30	23	82	0	3	1-1	.272	.319	.348	.667	6	.989
1999— New Orleans (PCL)	C	12	47	2	9	3	1	1	4	1	11	0	1	0-0	.191	.208	.362	.570	1	.984
— Houston (N.L.)	C	73	215	16	55	14	1	2	17	26	57	0	4	1-1	.256	.332	.358	.690	6	.988
2000— Houston (N.L.)	C	1	2	0	0	0	0	0	0	0	1	0	0	0-0	.000	.000	.000	.000	0	1.000
— Florida (N.L.)	C	56	161	10	39	6	1	0	14	22	48	1	4	0-0	.242	.335	.292	.627	3	.991
— Atlanta (N.L.)	C-1B	24	58	8	11	4	0	2	6	5	15	0	2	0-0	.190	.254	.362	.616	1	.992
2001— Atlanta (N.L.)	C	61	137	19	29	10	1	2	15	20	34	0	3	1-0	.212	.312	.343	.655	3	.991
2002— Milwaukee (N.L.)	C	87	234	24	55	8	1	4	20	20	46	0	4	0-2	.235	.295	.329	.624	4	.991
2003— Chicago (N.L.)	C	70	188	19	43	13	3	0	17	22	47	1	2	0-1	.229	.311	.330	.641	6	.987
American League totals (1 year)		96	305	23	83	12	1	3	30	23	82	0	3	1-1	.272	.319	.348	.667	6	.989
National League totals (5 years)		372	995	96	232	55	7	10	89	115	248	2	19	2-4	.233	.312	.333	.645	23	.990
Major League totals (6 years)		468	1300	119	315	67	8	13	119	138	330	2	22	3-5	.242	.314	.336	.650	29	.990

BALDELLI, ROCCO   OF

PERSONAL: Born September 25, 1981, in Woonsocket, R.I. ... 6-4/190. ... Bats right, throws right. ... Full name: Rocco Daniel Baldelli. ... High school: Bishop Hendrickson (Warwick, R.I.).

TRANSACTIONS/CAREER NOTES: Selected by Tampa Bay Devil Rays organization in first round (sixth pick overall) of free-agent draft (June 5, 2000).
2003 GAMES PLAYED BY POSITION (MLB): OF—154, DH—2.

Year	Team (League)	Pos.	G	AB	R	H	2B	3B	HR	RBI	BB	SO	HBP	GDP	SB-CS	Avg.	OBP	SLG	OPS	E	Pct.
2000— Princeton (Appal.)	OF-3B	60	232	33	50	9	2	3	25	12	56	5	3	11-3	.216	.269	.310	.579	4	.966
2001— Char., S.C. (SAL)	OF	113	406	58	101	23	6	8	55	23	89	11	7	25-9	.249	.303	.394	.697	9	.964
2002— Bakersfield (Calif.)	OF	77	312	63	104	19	1	14	51	18	63	7	2	21-6	.333	.382	.535	.917	3	.975
— Orlando (South.)	OF	17	70	10	26	3	1	2	13	5	11	2	1	3-2	.371	.413	.529	.941	1	.967
— Durham (Int'l)	OF	23	96	13	28	6	1	3	7	0	23	0	1	2-5	.292	.292	.469	.760	0	1.000
2003— Tampa Bay (A.L.)	OF-DH	156	637	89	184	32	8	11	78	30	128	8	10	27-10	.289	.326	.416	.742	5	.989
Major League totals (1 year)		156	637	89	184	32	8	11	78	30	128	8	10	27-10	.289	.326	.416	.742	5	.989

BALDWIN, JAMES   P

PERSONAL: Born July 15, 1971, in Southern Pines, N.C. ... 6-3/235. ... Throws right, bats right. ... Full name: James J. Baldwin Jr.. ... High school: Pinecrest (Southern Pines, N.C.).

TRANSACTIONS/CAREER NOTES: Selected by Chicago White Sox organization in fourth round of free-agent draft (June 4, 1990). ... On disabled list (August 3-19, 1994). ... On Chicago disabled list (March 23-April 21, 2001); included rehabilitation assignment to Charlotte (April 11-17). ... Traded by White Sox to Los Angeles Dodgers for P Onan Masaoka, P Gary Majewski and OF Jeff Barry (July 26, 2001). ... Granted free agency (November 5, 2001). ... Signed by Seattle Mariners (February 1, 2002). ... Granted free agency (October 29, 2002). ... Signed by Kansas City Royals organization (January 23, 2003). ... Released by Royals (2003). ... Signed by Minnesota Twins to a minor league contract and assigned to Rochester of the International League (June 10, 2003). ... Contract purchased by Minnesota Twins from Rochester (July 9, 2003). ... Sent outright to Rochester (August 15, 2003). ... Refused minor league assignment; became free agent (August 17, 2003).
CAREER HITTING: 4-for-41 (.098), 1 R, 1 2B, 1 3B, 0 HR, 2 RBI.

Year League	W	L	Pct.	ERA	WHIP	G	GS	CG	ShO	Hld.	Sv.-Opp.	IP	H	R	ER	HR	BB-IBB	SO	Avg.
1990— GC White Sox (GCL)	1	6	.143	4.10	1.34	9	7	0	0	...	0-...	37.1	32	29	17	1	18-0	32	.225
1991— GC White Sox (GCL)	3	1	.750	2.12	0.94	6	6	0	0	...	0-...	34.0	16	8	8	0	16-0	48	.140
— Utica (N.Y.-Penn)	1	4	.200	5.30	1.79	7	7	1	0	...	0-...	37.1	40	26	22	0	27-0	23	.267
1992— South Bend (Mid.)	9	5	.643	2.42	1.18	21	21	1	1	...	0-...	137.2	118	53	37	6	45-0	137	.228
— Sarasota (Fla. St.)	1	2	.333	2.87	1.01	6	6	1	0	...	0-...	37.2	31	13	12	2	7-0	39	.225
1993— Birmingham (Sou.)	8	5	.615	2.25	1.14	17	17	•4	0	...	0-...	120.0	94	48	30	6	43-0	107	.219
— Nashville (A.A.)	5	4	.556	2.61	1.14	10	10	1	0	...	0-...	69.0	43	21	20	5	36-0	61	.180
1994— Nashville (A.A.)	12	6	.667	3.72	1.40	26	26	2	0	...	0-...	162.0	144	75	67	14	83-1	*156	.237
1995— Chicago (A.L.)	0	1	.000	12.89	2.80	6	4	0	0	0	0-0	14.2	32	22	21	6	9-1	10	.444
— Nashville (A.A.)	5	9	.357	5.85	1.72	18	18	0	0	...	0-...	95.1	120	76	62	* 27	44-1	89	.302
1996— Nashville (A.A.)	1	1	.500	0.64	0.64	2	2	1	0	...	0-...	14.0	5	1	1	0	4-0	15	.116
— Chicago (A.L.)	11	6	.647	4.42	1.33	28	28	0	0	0	0-0	169.0	168	88	83	24	57-3	127	.257
1997— Chicago (A.L.)	12	•15	.444	5.27	1.44	32	32	1	0	0	0-0	200.0	205	128	117	19	83-3	140	.262
1998— Chicago (A.L.)	13	6	.684	5.32	1.48	37	24	1	0	0	0-1	159.0	176	103	94	18	60-2	108	.278
1999— Chicago (A.L.)	12	13	.480	5.10	1.51	35	33	1	0	0	0-0	199.1	219	119	113	34	81-1	123	.278
2000— Chicago (A.L.)	14	7	.667	4.65	1.37	29	28	2	1	0	0-0	178.0	185	96	92	34	59-3	116	.272
2001— Charlotte (Int'l)	1	0	1.000	5.25	1.17	2	2	0	0	...	0-...	12.0	12	7	7	2	2-0	11	.273
— Chicago (A.L.)	7	5	.583	4.61	1.54	17	16	2	1	0	0-0	95.2	109	56	49	15	38-0	42	.286
— Los Angeles (N.L.)	3	6	.333	4.20	1.35	12	12	0	0	0	0-0	79.1	82	39	37	10	25-1	53	.274
2002— Seattle (A.L.)	7	10	.412	5.28	1.52	30	23	0	0	0	0-0	150.0	179	95	88	26	49-2	88	.298
2003— Omaha (PCL)	3	2	.600	4.08	1.32	8	8	0	0	...	0-...	46.1	48	25	21	3	13-0	24	.265
— Rochester (Int'l)	0	2	.000	2.43	0.94	5	5	0	0	...	0-...	29.2	25	11	8	2	3-0	18	.225
— Minnesota (A.L.)	0	1	.000	5.40	1.67	10	0	0	0	1	1-2	15.0	21	10	9	6	4-1	7	.333
American League totals (9 years)	76	64	.543	5.08	1.47	224	188	7	2	1	1-3	1180.2	1294	717	666	182	440-16	761	.278
National League totals (1 year)	3	6	.333	4.20	1.35	12	12	0	0	0	0-0	79.1	82	39	37	10	25-1	53	.274
Major League totals (9 years)	79	70	.530	5.02	1.46	236	200	7	2	1	1-3	1260.0	1376	756	703	192	465-17	814	.278

BALE, JOHN   P

PERSONAL: Born May 22, 1974, in Cheverly, Md. ... 6-4/205. ... Throws left, bats left. ... Full name: John Robert Bale. ... High school: Crestview (Fla.). ... College: Southern Mississippi.

TRANSACTIONS/CAREER NOTES: Selected by St. Louis Cardinals organization in 12th round of free-agent draft (June 2, 1994); did not sign. ... Selected by Toronto Blue Jays organization in fifth round of free-agent draft (June 4, 1996). ... On Syracuse disabled list (May 4-19 and June 29-July 20, 2000). ... Traded by Blue Jays to Baltimore Orioles for C Jayson Werth (December 11, 2000). ... On Rochester disabled list (June 11-July 16, 2001). ... Traded by Orioles to New York Mets for OF Gary Matthews Jr. (April 3, 2002). ... On Norfolk disabled list (April 26-May 10 and May 28, 2002-remainder of season). ... Granted free agency (October 15, 2002). ... Contract purchased by Cincinnati Reds from Louisville of the International League (July 30, 2003). ... Contract purchased by Cincinnati from Louisville (July 30, 2003).

CAREER HITTING: 2-for-17 (.118), 0 R, 0 2B, 0 3B, 0 HR, 0 RBI.

Year League	W	L	Pct.	ERA	WHIP	G	GS	CG	ShO	Hld.	Sv.-Opp.	IP	H	R	ER	HR	BB-IBB	SO	Avg.
1996— St. Catharines (NYP)	3	2	.600	4.86	1.50	8	8	0	0	...	0-...	33.1	39	21	18	2	11-0	35	.289
1997— Hagerstown (S. Atl.)	7	7	.500	4.30	1.38	25	25	0	0	...	0-...	140.1	130	83	67	11	63-1	155	.244
1998— Dunedin (Fla. St.)	4	5	.444	4.64	1.38	24	9	0	0	...	4-...	66.0	68	39	34	5	23-1	78	.267
— Knoxville (Sou.)	0	0	...	6.75	0.75	3	0	0	0	...	0-...	1.1	1	1	1	1	0-0	0	.200
1999— Knoxville (Sou.)	2	2	.500	3.75	1.28	33	4	0	0	...	1-...	62.1	64	32	26	7	16-1	91	.258
— Syracuse (Int'l)	0	3	.000	3.97	1.15	6	4	0	0	...	0-...	22.2	16	14	10	1	10-0	10	.208
— Toronto (A.L.)	0	0	...	13.50	2.00	1	0	0	0	0	0-0	2.0	2	3	3	1	2-0	4	.250
2000— Syracuse (Int'l)	3	4	.429	3.19	1.38	21	12	0	0	...	0-...	79.0	68	35	28	4	41-0	70	.234
— Toronto (A.L.)	0	0	...	14.73	2.18	2	0	0	0	0	0-0	3.2	5	7	6	1	3-0	6	.313
2001— Rochester (Int'l)	1	1	.500	2.05	1.17	9	7	0	0	...	0-...	30.2	31	8	7	1	5-0	41	.263
— Baltimore (A.L.)	1	0	1.000	3.04	1.31	14	0	0	0	2	0-0	26.2	18	14	9	2	17-0	21	.194
— GC Orioles (GCL)	0	0	...	2.25	0.75	2	2	0	0	...	0-...	4.0	1	1	1	0	2-0	7	.091
2002— Norfolk (Int'l)	2	2	.500	3.54	1.04	12	0	0	0	...	0-...	28.0	22	11	11	2	7-0	27	.220
2003— Norfolk (Int'l)	0	1	.000	3.29	1.02	8	0	0	0	...	0-...	13.2	11	5	5	0	3-0	15	.220
— Louisville (Int'l)	4	1	.800	3.30	1.12	26	2	0	0	...	4-...	43.2	36	17	16	1	13-0	43	.221
— Cincinnati (N.L.)	1	2	.333	4.47	1.34	10	9	0	0	0	0-0	46.1	50	24	23	7	12-2	37	.281
American League totals (3 years)	1	0	1.000	5.01	1.45	17	0	0	0	2	0-0	32.1	25	24	18	4	22-0	31	.214
National League totals (1 year)	1	2	.333	4.47	1.34	10	9	0	0	0	0-0	46.1	50	24	23	7	12-2	37	.281
Major League totals (4 years)	2	2	.500	4.69	1.39	27	9	0	0	2	0-0	78.2	75	48	41	11	34-2	68	.254

BALFOUR, GRANT   P

PERSONAL: Born December 30, 1977, in Sydney, Australia. ... 6-2/185. ... Throws right, bats right. ... Full name: Grant Robert Balfour. ... High school: William Clarke College (Kellyville, New South Wales, Australia).

TRANSACTIONS/CAREER NOTES: Signed as non-drafted free agent by Minnesota Twins organization (January 19, 1997). ... On New Britain disabled list (April 6-26, 2001). ... Recalled from Rochester by Minnesota (July 3, 2003). ... Optioned to Rochester by Minnesota (July 17, 2003). ... Called up by Minnesota from Rochester (August 15, 2003).

CAREER HITTING: 0-for-0 (.000), 0 R, 0 2B, 0 3B, 0 HR, 0 RBI.

Year League	W	L	Pct.	ERA	WHIP	G	GS	CG	ShO	Hld.	Sv.-Opp.	IP	H	R	ER	HR	BB-IBB	SO	Avg.
1997— GC Twins (GCL)	2	4	.333	3.76	1.39	13	12	0	0	...	0-...	67.0	* 73	31	28	1	20-0	43	.292
1998— Elizabethton (Appal.)	* 7	2	.778	3.36	1.25	13	13	0	0	...	0-...	77.2	70	36	29	7	27-0	75	.240
1999— Quad City (Midw.)	8	5	.615	3.53	1.12	19	14	0	0	...	0-...	91.2	66	39	36	7	37-0	95	.204
2000— Fort Myers (Fla. St.)	8	5	.615	4.25	1.40	35	10	0	0	...	6-...	89.0	91	46	42	8	34-2	90	.263
2001— New Britain (East.)	2	1	.667	1.08	0.96	35	0	0	0	...	13-...	50.0	26	6	6	1	22-2	72	.149
— Minnesota (A.L.)	0	0	...	13.50	2.25	2	0	0	0	0	0-0	2.2	3	4	4	2	3-0	2	.333
— Edmonton (PCL)	2	2	.500	5.51	1.71	11	0	0	0	...	0-...	16.1	18	11	10	2	10-1	17	.305
2002— Edmonton (PCL)	2	4	.333	4.16	1.26	58	0	0	0	...	8-...	71.1	60	34	33	3	30-1	88	.231
2003— Rochester (Int'l)	5	2	.714	2.41	0.90	21	11	0	0	...	5-...	71.0	48	21	19	6	16-0	87	.188
— Minnesota (A.L.)	1	0	1.000	4.15	1.42	17	1	0	0	1	0-1	26.0	23	12	12	4	14-2	30	.235
Major League totals (2 years)	1	0	1.000	5.02	1.50	19	1	0	0	1	0-1	28.2	26	16	16	6	17-2	32	.243

BANKS, BRIAN — OF/1B

PERSONAL: Born September 28, 1970, in Mesa, Ariz. ... 6-3/218. ... Bats both, throws right. ... Full name: Brian Glen Banks. ... High school: Mountain View (Mesa, Ariz.). ... College: Brigham Young.

TRANSACTIONS/CAREER NOTES: Selected by Milwaukee Brewers organization in second round of free-agent draft (June 3, 1993); pick received as part of compensation for Seattle Mariners signing Type A free-agent P Chris Bosio. ... Released by Brewers (March 28, 2000). ... Signed by Fukuoka Daiei Hawks of Japan Pacific League (2000). ... Signed by Chicago Cubs organization (December 13, 2000). ... Released by Cubs (May 2, 2001). ... Signed by Florida Marlins organization (May 6, 2001). ... On Calgary disabled list (July 22-August 4, 2001). ... Granted free agency (October 15, 2001). ... Re-signed by Marlins organization (November 14, 2001).

2003 GAMES PLAYED BY POSITION (MLB): OF—33, 1B—12, DH—1.

Year	Team (League)	Pos.	G	AB	R	H	2B	3B	HR	RBI	BB	SO	HBP	GDP	SB-CS	Avg.	OBP	SLG	OPS	E	Pct.
1993—Helena (Pio.)		OF	12	48	8	19	1	1	2	8	11	8	0	2	1-2	.396	.500	.583	1.083	1	.962
—Beloit (Midw.)		OF	38	147	21	36	5	1	4	19	7	34	1	1	1-2	.245	.284	.374	.658	1	.980
1994—Beloit (Midw.)		3B-1B-OF	65	237	41	71	13	1	9	47	29	40	2	3	11-1	.300	.375	.477	.852	2	.985
—Stockton (Calif.)		OF	67	246	29	58	9	1	4	28	38	46	2	8	3-8	.236	.340	.329	.670	4	.966
1995—El Paso (Texas)		3B-1B-OF	128	441	81	136	* 39	10	12	78	* 81	113	3	10	9-9	.308	.413	.524	.937	10	.962
1996—New Orleans (A.A.)		OF-3B-DH-C	137	487	71	132	29	7	16	64	66	105	2	6	17-8	.271	.356	.458	.814	8	.972
—Milwaukee (A.L.)		OF-1B	4	7	2	4	2	0	1	2	1	2	0	0	0-0	.571	.625	1.286	1.911	0	1.000
1997—Tucson (PCL)		OF-C-DH	98	378	53	112	26	3	10	63	35	83	1	6	7-3	.296	.353	.460	.814	3	.986
—Milwaukee (A.L.)		OF-1B-3B-D	28	68	9	14	1	0	1	8	6	17	0	1	0-1	.206	.267	.265	.531	2	.949
1998—Louisville (Int'l)		OF-D-C-1-3	85	299	58	87	18	1	21	66	52	72	2	5	14-3	.291	.397	.569	.966	6	.979
—Milwaukee (A.L.)		C-1B-3B-OF	24	24	3	7	2	0	1	5	4	7	0	0	0-0	.292	.393	.500	.893	1	.929
1999—Milwaukee (N.L.)		1B-C-OF	105	219	34	53	7	1	5	22	25	59	0	2	6-1	.242	.317	.352	.669	5	.988
—Louisville (Int'l)		1B-OF-C	6	24	3	5	2	1	1	6	2	5	0	0	0-0	.208	.259	.500	.759	1	.968
2000—Fukuoka (Jp. West.)			48	157	23	42	6	0	7	29	26	28	...	...	3-...	.268	...	.439	...	...	...
—Fukuoka (Jp. Pac.)			32	74	6	11	2	0	0	4	8	23	...	...	0-...	.149	...	.176	...	...	...
2001—Iowa (PCL)		OF-1B	17	39	2	7	2	0	1	4	4	11	0	2	0-0	.179	.256	.308	.564	0	1.000
—Calgary (PCL)		1B-OF-C	101	357	70	104	27	4	23	63	32	97	3	5	5-4	.291	.352	.583	.935	8	.988
2002—Calgary (PCL)		1B-OF-C-3B	130	439	90	136	38	3	19	89	73	77	6	6	10-5	.310	.410	.540	.949	9	.988
—Florida (N.L.)		OF-1B	20	28	3	9	1	0	1	4	1	6	0	0	0-0	.321	.345	.464	.809	1	.923
2003—Florida (N.L.)		OF-1B-DH	92	149	14	35	6	2	4	23	25	38	2	4	2-1	.235	.348	.383	.731	1	.991
American League totals (2 years)			32	75	11	18	3	0	2	10	7	19	0	1	0-1	.240	.301	.360	.661	2	.964
National League totals (4 years)			241	420	54	104	16	3	11	54	55	110	2	6	8-2	.248	.335	.379	.713	8	.985
Major League totals (6 years)			273	495	65	122	19	3	13	64	62	129	2	7	8-3	.246	.330	.376	.706	10	.983

BARAJAS, ROD — C

PERSONAL: Born September 5, 1975, in Ontario, Calif. ... 6-2/220. ... Bats right, throws right. ... Full name: Rodrigo Richard Barajas. ... Name pronounced: bar-AH-hoss. ... High school: Sante Fe Springs (Calif.). ... Junior college: Cerritos College (Calif.).

TRANSACTIONS/CAREER NOTES: Signed as non-drafted free agent by Arizona Diamondbacks organization (January 23, 1996). ... Loaned by Diamondbacks to Visalia, Oakland Athletics organization (April 5-June 16, 1996). ... On disabled list (April 7-28, 2003). ... Sent on rehab assignment by Arizona to Tucson (April 24, 2003). ... Reinstated from the 15-day disabled list; recalled by Arizona from Tucson rehab assignment (April 28, 2003). ... Placed on the 15-day disabled (July 5, 2003). ... Sent to Lancaster on rehab assignment by Arizona (July 20, 2003). ... Recalled from Tucson rehab assignment by Arizona; reinstated from 15-day disabled list (July 23, 2003).

2003 GAMES PLAYED BY POSITION (MLB): C—79.

Year	Team (League)	Pos.	G	AB	R	H	2B	3B	HR	RBI	BB	SO	HBP	GDP	SB-CS	Avg.	OBP	SLG	OPS	E	Pct.
1996—Visalia (Calif.)		C	27	74	6	12	3	0	0	8	7	21	1	3	0-0	.162	.244	.203	.447	0	1.000
—Lethbridge (Pio.)		C-1B	51	175	47	59	9	3	10	50	12	24	2	6	2-1	.337	.378	.594	.973	5	.986
1997—High Desert (Calif.)		C-1B	57	199	24	53	11	0	7	30	8	41	1	7	0-2	.266	.297	.427	.724	3	.993
1998—High Desert (Calif.)		C	113	442	67	134	26	0	23	81	25	81	7	13	1-1	.303	.345	.518	.863	14	.983
1999—El Paso (Texas)		C-DH-1B	127	510	77	162	41	2	14	95	24	73	8	8	2-0	.318	.354	.488	.842	‡ 14	.985
—Arizona (N.L.)		C	5	16	3	4	1	0	1	3	1	1	0	0	0-0	.250	.294	.500	.794	0	1.000
2000—Tucson (PCL)		C-1B-3B	110	416	43	94	25	0	13	75	14	65	5	13	4-3	.226	.253	.380	.633	§ 14	.980
—Arizona (N.L.)		C	5	13	1	3	0	0	1	3	0	4	0	0	0-0	.231	.231	.462	.692	0	1.000
2001—Arizona (N.L.)		C	51	106	9	17	3	0	3	9	4	26	0	0	0-0	.160	.191	.274	.464	1	.995
—Tucson (PCL)		1B-C-3B	45	162	23	52	13	0	9	32	9	23	3	2	3-1	.321	.366	.568	.934	3	.990
2002—Arizona (N.L.)		C	70	154	12	36	10	0	3	23	10	25	3	4	1-0	.234	.288	.357	.645	1	.997
—Tucson (PCL)		C-1B	5	16	2	7	1	0	1	1	1	2	0	0	0-0	.438	.471	.688	1.158	0	1.000
2003—Tucson (PCL)		C-DH	4	16	3	7	1	0	1	4	1	1	0	0	0-0	.438	.471	.688	1.158	0	1.000
—Lancaster (Calif.)		C-DH	3	12	2	5	0	0	0	3	1	2	0	0	0-0	.417	.462	.417	.878	0	1.000
—Arizona (N.L.)		C	80	220	19	48	15	0	3	28	14	43	1	6	0-0	.218	.265	.327	.592	0	1.000
Major League totals (5 years)			211	509	44	108	29	0	11	66	29	99	4	10	1-0	.212	.257	.334	.591	2	.998

BARD, JOSH — C

PERSONAL: Born March 30, 1978, in Ithaca, N.Y. ... 6-3/215. ... Bats both, throws right. ... Full name: Joshua David Bard. ... Name pronounced: baahrd. ... High school: Cherry Creek (Englewood, Colo.). ... College: Texas Tech.

TRANSACTIONS/CAREER NOTES: Selected by Minnesota Twins organization in 35th round of free-agent draft (June 4, 1996); did not sign. ... Selected by Colorado Rockies organization in third round of free-agent draft (June 2, 1999). ... Traded by Rockies with OF Jody Gerut to Cleveland Indians for OF Jacob Cruz (June 2, 2001). ... Optioned to Buffalo by Cleveland (June 27, 2003). ... Recalled by Cleveland from Buffalo (August 9, 2003).

2003 GAMES PLAYED BY POSITION (MLB): C—87, DH—1.

Year	Team (League)	Pos.	G	AB	R	H	2B	3B	HR	RBI	BB	SO	HBP	GDP	SB-CS	Avg.	OBP	SLG	OPS	E	Pct.
2000—Salem (Caro.)		C	93	309	40	88	17	0	2	25	32	33	1	6	3-1	.285	.352	.359	.711	10	.987
—Colo. Springs (PCL)		C	4	17	0	4	0	0	1	0	1	2	0	0	0-0	.235	.235	.235	.471	1	.923
2001—Carolina (Sou.)		C	35	124	14	32	13	0	1	24	19	23	1	1	0-1	.258	.359	.387	.746	2	.993
—Akron (East.)		C	51	194	26	54	11	0	4	25	16	27	2	4	0-0	.278	.338	.397	.735	4	.986
—Mahoning Valley (NY-P)		C	13	44	7	12	4	0	2	8	6	2	1	1	0-1	.273	.373	.500	.873	3	.769
—Buffalo (Int'l)		DH	1	4	0	0	0	0	0	0	0	1	0	0	0-0	.000	.000	.000	.000	...	...
2002—Buffalo (Int'l)		C	94	344	36	102	26	2	6	53	20	45	0	13	0-0	.297	.332	.436	.768	* 11	.984
—Cleveland (A.L.)		C	24	90	9	20	5	0	3	12	4	13	0	6	0-0	.222	.255	.378	.633	5	.991
2003—Buffalo (Int'l)		C-DH	35	115	14	38	7	0	5	21	14	17	1	5	1-2	.330	.408	.522	.929	1	.995
—Cleveland (A.L.)		C-DH	91	303	25	74	13	1	8	36	22	53	0	9	0-2	.244	.293	.373	.666	5	.991
Major League totals (2 years)			115	393	34	94	18	1	11	48	26	66	0	15	0-2	.239	.284	.374	.658	7	.990

BARMES, CLINT   SS

PERSONAL: Born March 6, 1979, in Vincennes, Ind. ... 6-0/175. ... Bats right, throws right. ... Full name: Clint Harold Barmes. ... College: Indiana State.
TRANSACTIONS/CAREER NOTES: Selected by Colorado Rockies in 10th round of free-agent draft (June 5, 2000).
2003 GAMES PLAYED BY POSITION (MLB): SS—12.

Year Team (League)	Pos.	G	AB	R	H	2B	3B	HR	RBI	BB	SO	HBP	GDP	SB-CS	Avg.	OBP	SLG	OPS	E	Pct.
2000— Portland (NW)	SS-OF	45	181	37	51	6	4	2	16	18	28	5	1	12-9	.282	.361	.392	.753	12	.934
—Asheville (S. Atl.)	2B-SS-3B-OF	19	81	11	14	4	0	0	4	10	13	1	3	4-1	.173	.269	.222	.491	2	.977
2001—Asheville (S. Atl.)	SS	74	285	40	74	14	1	5	24	17	37	7	6	21-7	.260	.314	.368	.683	22	.943
—Salem (Caro.)	SS	38	121	17	30	3	3	0	9	15	20	4	5	4-1	.248	.350	.322	.672	13	.934
2002—Carolina (Sou.)	SS	103	438	62	119	23	2	15	60	31	72	9	3	15-11	.272	.329	.436	.765	33	.940
2003—Colo. Springs (PCL)	SS-2B	136	493	63	136	35	1	7	54	22	63	9	9	12-7	.276	.316	.394	.709	29	.951
—Colorado (N.L.)	SS	12	25	2	8	2	0	0	2	0	10	2	0	0-0	.320	.357	.400	.757	2	.958
Major League totals (1 year)		12	25	2	8	2	0	0	2	0	10	2	0	0-0	.320	.357	.400	.757	2	.958

BARNES, LARRY   1B

PERSONAL: Born July 23, 1974, in Bakersfield, Calif. ... 6-1/195. ... Bats left, throws left. ... Full name: Larry Richard Barnes. ... High school: Bakersfield (Calif.). ... College: Fresno State.
TRANSACTIONS/CAREER NOTES: Selected by Florida Marlins organization in 69th round of free-agent draft (June 3, 1993); did not sign. ... Signed as non-drafted free agent by California Angels organization (June 6, 1995). ... Angels franchise renamed Anaheim Angels for 1997 season. ... On disabled list (September 1, 1999-remainder of season). ... On disabled list (July 26-August 9, 2000). ... On Salt Lake disabled list (May 12-24, 2001). ... Contract purchased by Los Angeles (May 6, 2003). ... Optioned to Las Vegas by Los Angeles (May 21, 2003). ... Recalled by Los Angeles from Las Vegas (June 23, 2003). ... Designated for assignemnt by Los Angeles (September 1, 2003). ... Sent outright to Las Vegas (September 4, 2003).
2003 GAMES PLAYED BY POSITION (MLB): 1B—8, OF—2, DH—1.

Year Team (League)	Pos.	G	AB	R	H	2B	3B	HR	RBI	BB	SO	HBP	GDP	SB-CS	Avg.	OBP	SLG	OPS	E	Pct.
1995— Ariz. Angels (Ariz.)	1B	• 56	197	• 42	61	8	3	3	• 37	27	42	5	1	12-5	.310	.403	.426	.829	7	.987
1996—Cedar Rap. (Midw.)	1B-DH-OF-C	131	489	84	155	• 36	5	* 27	* 112	58	101	6	8	9-6	.317	.392	.577	.968	11	.990
1997—Lake Elsinore (Calif.)	1B-OF	115	446	68	128	32	2	13	71	43	84	5	6	3-4	.287	.353	.455	.808	8	.993
1998—Lake Elsinore (Calif.)	1B	51	183	30	45	11	2	7	33	22	49	1	3	2-0	.246	.330	.443	.773	6	.987
—Midland (Texas)	1B-DH-OF	69	245	29	67	16	4	6	35	28	54	1	5	4-2	.273	.348	.445	.793	7	.988
1999—Erie (East.)	1B-DH	130	497	73	142	25	9	20	100	49	99	5	7	14-3	.286	.346	.493	.839	9	.992
2000—Edmonton (PCL)	1B-OF	103	397	56	102	22	11	7	54	48	81	0	4	3-6	.257	.335	.421	.755	3	.996
2001—Salt Lake (PCL)	1B-OF	100	404	78	117	21	8	18	73	29	90	1	6	6-1	.290	.337	.515	.852	7	.991
—Anaheim (A.L.)	1B-OF	16	40	2	4	0	0	1	2	1	9	0	1	0-0	.100	.122	.175	.297	0	1.000
2002—Salt Lake (PCL)	1B-OF	114	452	71	142	29	11	20	95	28	90	4	11	8-1	.314	.354	.560	.913	8	.990
2003—Los Angeles (N.L.)	1B-OF-DH	30	38	2	8	2	0	0	2	1	9	0	0	0-0	.211	.231	.263	.494	0	1.000
—Las Vegas (PCL)	1B-OF	82	302	43	83	20	3	15	57	23	61	2	3	4-1	.275	.326	.510	.836	8	.988
American League totals (1 year)		16	40	2	4	0	0	1	2	1	9	0	1	0-0	.100	.122	.175	.297	0	1.000
National League totals (1 year)		30	38	2	8	2	0	0	2	1	9	0	0	0-0	.211	.231	.263	.494	0	1.000
Major League totals (2 years)		46	78	4	12	2	0	1	4	2	18	0	1	0-0	.154	.175	.218	.393	0	1.000

BARRETT, MICHAEL   C

PERSONAL: Born October 22, 1976, in Atlanta, Ga. ... 6-2/200. ... Bats right, throws right. ... Full name: Michael Patrick Barrett. ... High school: Pace Academy (Atlanta).
TRANSACTIONS/CAREER NOTES: Selected by Montreal Expos organization in first round (28th pick overall) of free-agent draft (June 1, 1995). ... On Montreal disabled list (June 24-July 11, 1999); included rehabilitation assignment to Ottawa (July 9-10). ... Placed on the 15-day disabled list, retroactive to July 27 (July 29, 2003). ... Removed from 15-day disabled list (September 10, 2003).
2003 GAMES PLAYED BY POSITION (MLB): C—68.

Year Team (League)	Pos.	G	AB	R	H	2B	3B	HR	RBI	BB	SO	HBP	GDP	SB-CS	Avg.	OBP	SLG	OPS	E	Pct.
1995—GC Expos (GCL)	3B-SS	50	183	22	57	13	4	0	19	15	19	0	1	7-6	.311	.362	.426	.788	25	.893
—Vermont (NYP)	SS	3	10	0	1	0	0	0	1	1	1	0	0	0-0	.100	.167	.100	.267	0	1.000
1996—Delmarva (S. Atl.)	C-DH-3B	129	474	57	113	29	4	4	62	18	42	9	9	5-11	.238	.277	.342	.618	15	.978
1997—W.P. Beach (FSL)	C-DH	119	423	52	120	30	0	8	61	36	49	5	11	7-4	.284	.340	.411	.751	13	.982
1998—Harrisburg (East.)	C-3B-DH	120	453	78	145	32	2	19	87	27	43	2	16	7-6	.320	.358	.525	.883	12	.981
—Montreal (N.L.)	3B-C	8	23	3	7	2	0	1	2	3	6	1	0	0-0	.304	.407	.522	.929	3	.912
1999—Montreal (N.L.)	3B-C-SS	126	433	53	127	32	3	8	52	32	39	3	18	0-2	.293	.345	.436	.782	14	.973
—Ottawa (Int'l)	3B	2	7	1	3	0	0	0	2	1	0	0	0	0-1	.429	.500	.429	.929	1	.800
2000—Ottawa (Int'l)	3B-C	31	120	21	43	7	0	2	19	13	10	2	5	1-0	.358	.430	.467	.896	5	.945
—Montreal (N.L.)	3B-C	89	271	28	58	15	1	1	22	23	35	1	7	0-1	.214	.277	.288	.565	15	.949
2001—Montreal (N.L.)	C	132	472	42	118	33	2	6	38	25	54	2	14	2-1	.250	.289	.367	.655	7	.993
2002—Montreal (N.L.)	C-1B	117	376	41	99	20	1	12	49	40	65	1	14	6-3	.263	.332	.418	.749	9	.989
2003—Edmonton (PCL)	C	2	6	2	2	1	0	0	0	0	2	0	0	1-0	.333	.333	.500	.833	0	1.000
—Montreal (N.L.)	C	70	226	33	47	9	2	10	30	21	37	2	6	0-0	.208	.280	.398	.678	1	.998
Major League totals (6 years)		542	1801	200	456	111	9	38	193	144	236	10	59	8-7	.253	.310	.388	.698	49	.984

BATISTA, MIGUEL   P

PERSONAL: Born February 19, 1971, in Santo Domingo, Dominican Republic. ... 6-1/197. ... Throws right, bats right. ... Full name: Miguel Jerez Batista. ... Name pronounced: bah-TEESE-tah. ... High school: Nuevo Horizondes (San Pedro de Macoris, Dominican Republic).
TRANSACTIONS/CAREER NOTES: Signed as non-drafted free agent by Montreal Expos organization (February 29, 1988). ... Selected by Pittsburgh Pirates from Expos organization in Rule 5 major league draft (December 9, 1991). ... Returned to Expos organization (April 23, 1992). ... On disabled list (April 14-30 and May 7, 1994-remainder of season). ... Released by Expos (November 18, 1994). ... Signed by Florida Marlins organization (December 9, 1994). ... Claimed on waivers by Chicago Cubs (December 17, 1996). ... Traded by Cubs to Expos for OF Henry Rodriguez (December 12, 1997). ... On Montreal disabled list (July 16-August 10, 1999); included rehabilitation assignment to Ottawa (July 30-August 8). ... Traded by Expos to Kansas City Royals for P Brad Rigby (April 25, 2000). ... Granted free agency (October 2, 2000). ... Signed by Arizona Diamondbacks organization (November 3, 2000). ... Placed on suspended list by MLB (May 23, 2003).
CAREER HITTING: 21-for-219 (.096), 16 R, 4 2B, 0 3B, 2 HR, 5 RBI.

Year League	W	L	Pct.	ERA	WHIP	G	GS	CG	ShO	Hld.	Sv.-Opp.	IP	H	R	ER	HR	BB-IBB	SO	Avg.
1988—											Did not play.								
1989— DSL Expos (DSL)	1	7	.125	4.24	1.56	13	11	0	0	...	0-...	68.0	56	46	32	...	50-...	60	...
1990— GC Expos (GCL)	4	3	.571	2.06	1.27	9	6	0	0	...	0-...	39.1	33	16	9	0	17-0	21	.226
— Rockford (Midwest)	0	1	.000	8.76	1.70	3	2	0	0	...	0-...	12.1	16	13	12	2	5-0	7	.302
1991— Rockford (Midwest)	11	5	.688	4.04	1.37	23	23	2	1	...	0-...	133.2	126	74	60	1	57-0	90	.245
1992— Pittsburgh (N.L.)	0	0	...	9.00	3.50	1	0	0	0	0	0-0	2.0	4	2	2	1	3-0	1	.400
— W.P. Beach (FSL)	7	7	.500	3.79	1.36	24	24	1	0	...	0-...	135.1	130	69	57	3	54-1	92	.251
1993— Harrisburg (Eastern)	13	5	.722	4.34	1.60	26	26	0	0	...	0-...	141.0	139	79	68	11	86-0	91	.263
1994— Harrisburg (Eastern)	0	1	.000	2.38	1.50	3	3	0	0	...	0-...	11.1	8	3	3	0	9-0	5	.200
1995— Charlotte (Int'l)	6	12	.333	4.80	1.53	34	18	0	0	...	0-...	116.1	118	79	62	11	60-2	58	.260
1996— Charlotte (Int'l)	4	3	.571	5.38	1.71	47	2	0	0	...	4-...	77.0	93	57	46	4	39-0	56	.303
— Florida (N.L.)	0	0	...	5.56	1.41	9	0	0	0	0	0-0	11.1	9	8	7	0	7-2	6	.231
1997— Iowa (Am. Assoc.)	9	4	.692	4.20	1.27	31	14	2	• 2	...	0-...	122.0	117	60	57	19	38-1	95	.252
— Chicago (N.L.)	0	5	.000	5.70	1.65	11	6	0	0	0	0-0	36.1	36	24	23	4	24-2	27	.267
1998— Montreal (N.L.)	3	5	.375	3.80	1.53	56	13	0	0	3	0-0	135.0	141	66	57	12	65-7	92	.274
1999— Montreal (N.L.)	8	7	.533	4.88	1.51	39	17	2	1	0	1-1	134.2	146	88	73	10	58-2	95	.280
— Ottawa (Int'l)	0	1	.000	2.25	0.88	3	3	0	0	...	0-...	8.0	3	2	2	1	4-0	7	.115
2000— Montreal (N.L.)	0	1	.000	14.04	2.64	4	0	0	0	0	0-2	8.1	19	14	13	2	3-0	7	.452
— Kansas City (A.L.)	2	6	.250	7.74	1.75	14	9	0	0	0	0-0	57.0	66	54	49	17	34-2	30	.292
— Omaha (PCL)	2	2	.500	6.04	1.48	18	1	0	0	...	3-...	28.1	35	20	19	6	7-0	27	.302
2001— Arizona (N.L.)	11	8	.579	3.36	1.24	48	18	0	0	4	0-0	139.1	113	57	52	13	60-2	90	.226
2002— Arizona (N.L.)	8	9	.471	4.29	1.31	36	29	1	0	2	0-0	184.2	172	99	88	12	70-3	112	.245
2003— Arizona (N.L.)	10	9	.526	3.54	1.33	36	29	2	1	0	0-0	193.1	197	85	76	13	60-3	142	.267
American League totals (1 year)	2	6	.250	7.74	1.75	14	9	0	0	0	0-0	57.0	66	54	49	17	34-2	30	.292
National League totals (9 years)	40	44	.476	4.16	1.40	240	112	5	2	9	1-3	845.0	837	443	391	67	350-21	572	.262
Major League totals (9 years)	42	50	.457	4.39	1.43	254	121	5	2	9	1-3	902.0	903	497	440	84	384-23	602	.264

BATISTA, TONY — 3B

PERSONAL: Born December 9, 1973, in Puerto Plata, Dominican Republic. ... 6-0/208. ... Bats right, throws right. ... Full name: Leocadio Francisco Batista. ... Name pronounced: bah-TEESE-tah.

TRANSACTIONS/CAREER NOTES: Signed as non-drafted free agent by Oakland Athletics organization (February 8, 1991). ... On Tacoma disabled list (July 29, 1993-remainder of season). ... On Oakland disabled list (August 27-September 12, 1997); included rehabilitation assignment to Edmonton (September 11-12). ... Selected by Arizona Diamondbacks in first round (27th pick overall) of expansion draft (November 18, 1997). ... Traded by Diamondbacks with P John Frascatore to Toronto Blue Jays for P Dan Plesac (June 12, 1999). ... Claimed on waivers by Baltimore Orioles (June 25, 2001).

2003 GAMES PLAYED BY POSITION (MLB): 3B—154, DH—7.

Year Team (League)	Pos.	G	AB	R	H	2B	3B	HR	RBI	BB	SO	HBP	GDP	SB-CS	Avg.	OBP	SLG	OPS	E	Pct.
1991— Dom. Athletics (DSL)		46	166	16	31	5	1	2	15	23	16			4-...	.187		.265			
1992— Ariz. A's (Ariz.)	2B-SS-OF	45	167	32	41	6	2	0	22	15	29	2	4	1-0	.246	.315	.305	.621	8	.960
1993— Ariz. A's (Ariz.)	2B-3B-SS	24	104	21	34	6	2	2	17	6	14	0	1	6-2	.327	.357	.481	.838	3	.967
— Tacoma (PCL)	OF	4	12	1	2	1	0	0	1	1	4	1	0	0-0	.167	.286	.250	.536	0	1.000
1994— Modesto (Calif.)	2B-SS	119	466	91	131	26	3	17	68	54	108	4	10	7-7	.281	.359	.459	.819	30	.949
1995— Huntsville (Sou.)	SS-2B	120	419	55	107	23	1	16	61	29	98	2	8	7-8	.255	.305	.430	.734	29	.949
1996— Edmonton (PCL)	SS	57	205	33	66	17	4	8	40	15	30	2	8	2-1	.322	.372	.561	.933	8	.973
— Oakland (A.L.) 2B-3B-S-D		74	238	38	71	10	2	6	25	19	49	1	2	7-3	.298	.350	.433	.783	5	.983
1997— Oakland (A.L.) S-3B-2B-D		68	188	22	38	10	1	4	18	14	31	2	8	2-2	.202	.265	.330	.594	8	.971
— Edmonton (PCL)	SS-DH	33	124	25	39	10	1	3	21	17	18	1	4	2-2	.315	.396	.484	.880	6	.952
1998— Arizona (N.L.)	2B-SS-3B	106	293	46	80	16	1	18	41	18	52	3	7	1-1	.273	.318	.519	.836	6	.963
1999— Arizona (N.L.)	SS	44	144	16	37	5	0	5	21	16	17	2	1	2-0	.257	.335	.396	.731	4	.979
— Toronto (A.L.)	SS	57	205	33	66	17	4	8	40	15	30	2	8	2-1	.322	.372	.561	.933	8	.973
— Toronto (A.L.)	SS	98	375	61	107	25	1	26	79	22	79	4	11	2-0	.285	.328	.565	.893	12	.975
2000— Toronto (A.L.)	3B	154	620	96	163	32	2	41	114	35	121	6	15	5-4	.263	.307	.519	.827	17	.963
2001— Toronto (A.L.)	3B	72	271	29	56	11	1	13	45	13	66	4	2	0-1	.207	.251	.399	.649	10	.953
— Baltimore (A.L.) DH-3B-SS		84	308	41	82	16	5	12	42	19	47	0	7	5-1	.266	.305	.468	.773	6	.965
2002— Baltimore (A.L.)	3B-DH	161	615	90	150	36	1	31	87	50	107	11	13	5-4	.244	.309	.457	.766	16	.962
2003— Baltimore (A.L.)	3B-DH	161	631	76	148	20	1	26	99	28	102	5	20	4-3	.235	.270	.393	.663	20	.950
American League totals (7 years)		872	3246	453	815	160	14	159	509	200	602	33	78	30-18	.251	.299	.456	.755	94	.965
National League totals (2 years)		150	437	62	117	21	1	23	62	34	69	5	8	3-1	.268	.324	.478	.802	10	.981
Major League totals (8 years)		1022	3683	515	932	181	15	182	571	234	671	38	86	33-19	.253	.302	.459	.760	104	.968

BAUER, RICK — P

PERSONAL: Born January 10, 1977, in Garden Grove, Calif. ... 6-6/218. ... Throws right, bats right. ... Full name: Richard Edward Bauer. ... Name pronounced: BOW-er. ... High school: Centennial (Meridian, Idaho). ... Junior college: Treasure Valley (Ore.) Community College.

TRANSACTIONS/CAREER NOTES: Selected by Baltimore Orioles organization in fifth round of free-agent draft (June 3, 1997). ... Optioned to Ottawa by Baltimore (June 14, 2003). ... Recalled by Baltimore from Ottawa (July 3, 2003). ... Optioned to Ottawa of the International League by Baltimore (July 10, 2003). ... Recalled by Baltimore from Ottawa (August 12, 2003).

CAREER HITTING: 0-for-0 (.000), 0 R, 0 2B, 0 3B, 0 HR, 0 RBI.

Year League	W	L	Pct.	ERA	WHIP	G	GS	CG	ShO	Hld.	Sv.-Opp.	IP	H	R	ER	HR	BB-IBB	SO	Avg.
1997— Bluefield (Appal.)	8	3	.727	2.86	1.08	13	13	0	0	...	0-...	72.1	58	31	23	1	20-0	67	.218
— Delmarva (S. Atl.)	0	0	...	0.00	0.50	1	0	0	0	...	1-...	2.0	0	0	0	0	1-0	2	.000
1998— Delmarva (S. Atl.)	5	8	.385	4.73	1.45	22	22	1	1	...	0-...	118.0	127	69	62	11	44-0	81	.285
1999— Frederick (Caro.)	10	9	.526	4.56	1.40	26	26	• 4	0	...	0-...	152.0	159	85	77	17	54-2	123	.273
2000— Bowie (East.)	6	8	.429	5.30	1.50	26	23	1	0	...	1-...	129.0	154	89	76	16	39-1	87	.293
— Frederick (Caro.)	0	1	.000	5.21	1.37	3	3	0	0	...	0-...	19.0	20	13	11	1	6-0	15	.278
2001— Bowie (East.)	2	6	.250	3.54	1.02	9	9	2	0	...	0-...	61.0	52	27	24	8	10-0	34	.227
— Rochester (Int'l)	10	4	.714	3.89	1.30	19	18	1	1	...	0-...	113.1	119	63	49	10	28-0	89	.263
— Baltimore (A.L.)	0	5	.000	4.64	1.33	6	6	0	0	0	0-0	33.0	35	22	17	7	9-0	16	.265
2002— Baltimore (A.L.)	6	7	.462	3.98	1.43	56	1	0	0	12	1-5	83.2	84	41	37	12	36-4	45	.265
— Rochester (Int'l)	0	1	.000	6.75	1.50	1	1	0	0	...	0-...	4.0	4	4	3	2	2-0	1	.267
2003— Ottawa (Int'l)	3	1	.750	2.45	1.20	7	7	0	0	...	0-...	36.2	31	10	10	1	13-0	21	.235
— Baltimore (A.L.)	0	0	...	4.55	1.34	35	0	0	0	3	0-1	61.1	58	36	31	5	24-3	43	.256
Major League totals (3 years)	6	12	.333	4.30	1.38	97	7	0	0	15	1-6	178.0	177	99	85	24	69-7	104	.263

BAUTISTA, DANNY — OF

PERSONAL: Born May 24, 1972, in Santo Domingo, Dominican Republic. ... 5-11/225. ... Bats right, throws right. ... Full name: Daniel Bautista. ... Name pronounced: BAW-tee-sta.

TRANSACTIONS/CAREER NOTES: Signed as non-drafted free agent by Detroit Tigers organization (June 24, 1989). ... On disabled list (May 24-July 10, 1991). ... On Toledo disabled list (June 8-July 31, 1994). ... Traded by Tigers to Atlanta Braves for OF Anton French (May 31, 1996). ... On Atlanta disabled list (June 28, 1996-remainder of season). ... On Atlanta disabled list (March 23-April 23, 1997); included rehabilitation assignment to Richmond (April 18-23). ... On Atlanta disabled list (April 17-May 7 and August 25-September 17, 1998); included rehabilitation assignment to Greenville (May 5-7). ... Released by Braves (April 2, 1999). ... Signed by Florida Marlins organization (April 8, 1999). ... On Calgary disabled list (June 1-8, 1999). ... Traded by Marlins to Arizona Diamondbacks for IF Andy Fox (June 10, 2000). ... Granted free agency (November 8, 2001). ... Re-signed by Diamondbacks (December 19, 2001). ... On disabled list (May 23, 2002-remainder of season). ... Placed on 15-day disabled list (June 19, 2003). ... Sent to Tucson on rehab assignment by Arizona (July 7, 2003). ... Recalled from Tucson rehab assingment; reinstated from 15-day disabled list (July 23, 2003).

2003 GAMES PLAYED BY POSITION (MLB): OF—79.

										BATTING										FIELDING	
Year	Team (League)	Pos.	G	AB	R	H	2B	3B	HR	RBI	BB	SO	HBP	GDP	SB-CS	Avg.	OBP	SLG	OPS	E	Pct.
1989—										Did not play.											
1990—	Bristol (Appal.)	OF	27	95	9	26	3	0	2	12	8	21	0	1	2-3	.274	.330	.368	.699	0	1.000
1991—	Fayetteville (SAL)	OF	69	234	21	45	6	4	1	30	21	65	1	8	7-7	.192	.259	.265	.524	4	.973
1992—	Fayetteville (SAL)	OF	121	453	59	122	22	0	5	52	29	76	5	9	18-20	.269	.319	.351	.670	6	.974
1993—	London (East.)	OF	117	424	55	121	21	1	6	48	32	69	2	8	28-12	.285	.334	.382	.716	3	.989
	—Detroit (A.L.)	OF-DH	17	61	6	19	3	0	1	9	1	10	0	1	3-1	.311	.317	.410	.727	0	1.000
1994—	Detroit (A.L.)	OF-DH	31	99	12	23	4	1	4	15	3	18	0	3	1-2	.232	.255	.414	.669	0	1.000
	—Toledo (Int'l)	OF	27	98	7	25	7	0	2	14	6	23	0	2	2-3	.255	.292	.388	.680	1	.982
1995—	Detroit (A.L.)	OF	89	271	28	55	9	0	7	27	12	68	0	6	4-1	.203	.237	.314	.550	2	.988
	—Toledo (Int'l)	OF	18	58	6	14	3	0	0	4	1	10	3	1	1-2	.241	.290	.293	.583	2	.943
1996—	Detroit (A.L.)	OF-DH	25	64	12	16	2	0	2	8	9	15	0	1	1-2	.250	.342	.375	.717	1	.974
	—Atlanta (N.L.)	OF	17	20	1	3	0	0	0	1	2	5	1	3	0-0	.150	.261	.150	.411	0	1.000
1997—	Richmond (Int'l)	OF-DH	46	170	28	48	10	3	2	28	19	30	1	9	1-0	.282	.356	.412	.768	0	1.000
	—Atlanta (N.L.)	OF	64	103	14	25	3	2	3	9	5	24	1	3	2-0	.243	.282	.398	.680	1	.984
1998—	Atlanta (N.L.)	OF-DH	82	144	17	36	11	0	3	17	7	21	0	4	1-0	.250	.281	.389	.670	2	.959
	—Greenville (Sou.)	OF	2	6	1	2	0	0	1	2	1	1	0	0	0-0	.333	.429	.833	1.262	0	1.000
1999—	Calgary (PCL)	OF-DH	38	135	25	43	8	1	8	28	11	18	1	1	3-3	.319	.374	.570	.945	3	.969
	—Florida (N.L.)	OF	70	205	32	59	10	1	5	24	4	30	1	5	3-0	.288	.303	.420	.723	3	.979
2000—	Florida (N.L.)	OF	44	89	9	17	4	0	4	12	5	20	0	1	1-0	.191	.234	.371	.605	1	.980
	—Arizona (N.L.)	OF	87	262	45	83	16	7	7	47	20	30	3	10	5-2	.317	.366	.511	.877	2	.987
2001—	Arizona (N.L.)	OF	100	222	26	67	11	2	5	26	14	31	1	7	3-2	.302	.346	.437	.783	0	1.000
2002—	Arizona (N.L.)	OF	40	154	22	50	5	2	6	23	11	21	0	4	4-2	.325	.367	.500	.867	1	.985
2003—	El Paso (Texas)	OF	2	7	1	1	0	0	0	1	1	2	0	0	0-0	.143	.250	.143	.393	0	1.000
	—Tucson (PCL)	OF	8	24	4	9	1	1	1	4	2	2	0	2	1-1	.375	.423	.625	1.048	0	1.000
	—Arizona (N.L.)	OF	88	284	29	78	16	3	4	36	21	50	4	7	3-2	.275	.330	.394	.724	5	.961
	American League totals (4 years)		162	495	58	113	18	1	14	59	25	111	0	11	9-6	.228	.265	.354	.618	3	.990
	National League totals (8 years)		592	1483	195	418	76	17	37	195	89	232	11	44	22-8	.282	.325	.431	.755	15	.980
	Major League totals (11 years)		754	1978	253	531	94	18	51	254	114	343	11	55	31-14	.268	.310	.412	.721	18	.983

BAY, JASON — OF

PERSONAL: Born September 20, 1978, in Trail, British Columbia. ... 6-2/200. ... Bats right, throws right. ... Full name: Jason Raymond Bay. ... High school: J. Lloyd Crowe Secondary (Trail, B.C.). ... College: Gonzaga.

TRANSACTIONS/CAREER NOTES: Selected by Montreal Expos in 22nd round of free-agent draft (June 5, 2000). ... Traded by Expos with P Jim Serrano to New York Mets for SS Lou Collier (March 27, 2002). ... Traded by Mets with P Bobby M. Jones and P Josh Reynolds to San Diego Padres for P Steve Reed and P Jason Middlebrook (July 31, 2002). ... Traded by Padres with P Oliver Perez and a player to be named to Pittsburgh Pirates for OF Brian Giles (August 27, 2003).

2003 GAMES PLAYED BY POSITION (MLB): OF—29.

										BATTING										FIELDING	
Year	Team (League)	Pos.	G	AB	R	H	2B	3B	HR	RBI	BB	SO	HBP	GDP	SB-CS	Avg.	OBP	SLG	OPS	E	Pct.
2000—	Vermont (NYP)	OF	35	135	17	41	5	0	2	12	11	25	1	2	17-4	.304	.358	.385	.743	0	1.000
2001—	Jupiter (FSL)	OF-2B	38	123	12	24	4	1	1	10	18	26	2	4	10-3	.195	.306	.268	.574	3	.963
	—Clinton (Midw.)	OF	87	318	67	115	20	4	13	61	48	62	4	4	15-2	.362	.449	.572	1.021	3	.984
2002—	St. Lucie (Fla. St.)	OF	69	261	48	71	12	2	9	54	34	54	5	4	22-2	.272	.363	.437	.800	6	.950
	—Binghamton (East.)	OF	34	107	17	31	4	2	4	19	15	23	3	2	13-3	.290	.383	.477	.859	2	.956
	—Mobile (Sou.)	OF	23	81	16	25	5	2	4	12	13	22	1	0	4-2	.309	.411	.568	.978	0	1.000
2003—	San Diego (N.L.)	OF	3	8	2	2	1	0	1	2	1	1	1	0	0-0	.250	.400	.750	1.150	0	1.000
	—Portland (PCL)	OF	91	307	64	93	11	1	20	59	55	71	5	3	23-4	.303	.410	.541	.951	1	.995
	—Pittsburgh (N.L.)	OF	27	79	13	23	6	1	3	12	18	28	0	0	3-1	.291	.423	.506	.929	1	.976
	Major League totals (1 year)		30	87	15	25	7	1	4	14	19	29	1	0	3-1	.287	.421	.529	.949	1	.980

BECK, ROD — P

PERSONAL: Born August 3, 1968, in Burbank, Calif. ... 6-1/235. ... Throws right, bats right. ... Full name: Rodney Roy Beck. ... High school: Grant (Van Nuys, Calif.).

TRANSACTIONS/CAREER NOTES: Selected by Oakland Athletics organization in 13th round of free-agent draft (June 2, 1986). ... Traded by A's to San Francisco Giants for P Charlie Corbell (March 23, 1988). ... On disabled list (April 6-30, 1994). ... Granted free agency (October 27, 1997). ... Signed by Chicago Cubs (January 15, 1998). ... On Chicago disabled list (May 17-July 21, 1999); included rehabilitation assignment to Iowa (July 17-21). ... Traded by Cubs to Boston Red Sox for P Mark Guthrie and a player to named later (August 31, 1999); Cubs acquired 3B Cole Liniak to complete deal (September 1, 1999). ... On Boston disabled list (March 18-June 13 and July 3-22, 2000); included rehabilitation assignment to Pawtucket (June 2-13). ... Granted free agency (November 5, 2001). ... Signed by Cubs organization (January 2, 2003). ... Released by Cubs (2003). ... Signed by San Diego Padres (June 1, 2003).

CAREER HITTING: 4-for-19 (.211), 0 R, 0 2B, 0 3B, 0 HR, 1 RBI.

Year	League	W	L	Pct.	ERA	WHIP	G	GS	CG	ShO	Hld.	Sv.-Opp.	IP	H	R	ER	HR	BB-IBB	SO	Avg.
1986—	Medford (N'west)	1	3	.250	5.23	1.78	13	6	0	0	...	1-...	32.2	47	25	19	4	11-1	21	...
1987—	Medford (N'west)	5	8	.385	5.18	1.43	17	12	2	0	...	0-...	92.0	106	74	53	5	26-0	69	.270
1988—	Clinton (Midw.)	12	7	.632	3.00	1.15	28	23	5	1	...	0-...	177.0	177	68	59	11	27-2	123	.263
1989—	San Jose (Calif.)	11	2	.846	2.40	1.20	13	13	4	0	...	0-...	97.1	91	29	26	5	26-0	88	.245
	—Shreveport (Texas)	7	3	.700	3.55	1.25	16	14	4	1	...	0-...	99.0	108	45	39	6	16-3	74	.275
1990—	Shreveport (Texas)	10	3	.769	2.23	1.10	14	14	2	1	...	0-...	93.0	85	26	23	4	17-1	71	.248
	—Phoenix (PCL)	4	7	.364	4.93	1.54	12	12	2	0	...	0-...	76.2	100	51	42	8	18-1	43	.313

– 27 –

B

Year	League	W	L	Pct.	ERA	WHIP	G	GS	CG	ShO	Hld.	Sv.-Opp.	IP	H	R	ER	HR	BB-IBB	SO	Avg.
1991—Phoenix (PCL)		4	3	.571	2.02	0.97	23	5	3	0	...	6-...	71.1	56	18	16	3	13-2	35	.216
—San Francisco (N.L.)		1	1	.500	3.78	1.26	31	0	0	0	1	1-1	52.1	53	22	22	4	13-2	38	.273
1992—San Francisco (N.L.)		3	3	.500	1.76	0.84	65	0	0	0	4	17-23	92.0	62	20	18	4	15-2	87	.190
1993—San Francisco (N.L.)		3	1	.750	2.16	0.88	76	0	0	0	0	48-52	79.1	57	20	19	11	13-4	86	.201
1994—San Francisco (N.L.)		2	4	.333	2.77	1.27	48	0	0	0	0	28-28	48.2	49	17	15	10	13-2	39	.261
1995—San Francisco (N.L.)		5	6	.455	4.45	1.38	60	0	0	0	0	33-43	58.2	60	31	29	7	21-3	42	.267
1996—San Francisco (N.L.)		0	9	.000	3.34	1.06	63	0	0	0	0	35-42	62.0	56	23	23	9	10-2	48	.238
1997—San Francisco (N.L.)		7	4	.636	3.47	1.07	73	0	0	0	1	37-45	70.0	67	31	27	7	8-2	53	.249
1998—Chicago (N.L.)		3	4	.429	3.02	1.32	81	0	0	0	1	51-58	80.1	86	33	27	11	20-4	81	.269
1999—Chicago (N.L.)		2	4	.333	7.80	1.80	31	0	0	0	1	7-11	30.0	41	26	26	5	13-3	13	.331
—Iowa (PCL)		0	0	...	0.00	0.50	2	0	0	0	...	0-...	2.0	1	0	0	0	0-0	2	.143
—Boston (A.L.)		0	1	.000	1.93	1.00	12	0	0	0	2	3-4	14.0	9	3	3	0	5-0	12	.184
2000—Pawtucket (Int'l)		1	0	1.000	0.00	0.67	3	0	0	0	...	0-...	6.0	4	0	0	0	0-0	7	.182
—Boston (A.L.)		3	0	1.000	3.10	1.13	34	0	0	0	7	0-3	40.2	34	15	14	2	12-1	35	.222
2001—Boston (A.L.)		6	4	.600	3.90	1.30	68	0	0	0	15	6-11	80.2	77	42	35	15	28-6	63	.252
2002—												Did not play.								
2003—Iowa (PCL)		1	1	.500	0.59	1.04	21	0	0	0	...	4-...	30.2	25	3	2	2	7-0	26	.227
—San Diego (N.L.)		3	2	.600	1.78	1.02	36	0	0	0	1	20-20	35.1	25	7	7	4	11-2	32	.197
American League totals (3 years)		9	5	.643	3.46	1.22	114	0	0	0	24	9-18	135.1	120	60	52	17	45-7	110	.236
National League totals (10 years)		29	38	.433	3.15	1.14	564	0	0	0	9	277-323	608.2	556	230	213	72	137-26	519	.242
Major League totals (12 years)		38	43	.469	3.21	1.15	678	0	0	0	33	286-341	744.0	676	290	265	89	182-33	629	.241

BECKETT, JOSH — P

PERSONAL: Born May 15, 1980, in Spring, Texas. ... 6-5/218. ... Throws right, bats right. ... Full name: Joshua Patrick Beckett. ... High school: Spring (Texas).

TRANSACTIONS/CAREER NOTES: Selected by Florida Marlins organization in first round (second pick overall) of free-agent draft (June 2, 1999). ... On Brevard County disabled list (April 17-May 30 and August 16-September 11, 2000). ... On Florida disabled list (April 29-May 14, June 5-July 16 and August 23-September 11, 2002); included rehabilitation assignments to Gulf Coast Marlins (July 6-11) and Jupiter (July 12-16). ... Placed on 15-day disabled list by Florida (May 8, 2003). ... Sent on rehab assignment to Jupiter by Florida (June 18, 2003). ... Recalled from Carolina rehab assignment; reinstated from 15-day disabled list (July 1, 2003).

CAREER HITTING: 10-for-84 (.119), 4 R, 4 2B, 0 3B, 0 HR, 3 RBI.

Year	League	W	L	Pct.	ERA	WHIP	G	GS	CG	ShO	Hld.	Sv.-Opp.	IP	H	R	ER	HR	BB-IBB	SO	Avg.
2000—Kane County (Midwest)		2	3	.400	2.12	1.01	13	12	0	0	...	0-...	59.1	45	18	14	4	15-0	61	.214
2001—Brevard County (FSL)		6	0	1.000	1.23	0.72	13	12	0	0	...	0-...	65.2	32	13	9	0	15-0	101	.145
—Portland (East.)		8	1	.889	1.82	0.93	13	13	0	0	...	0-...	74.1	50	16	15	8	19-0	102	.191
—Florida (N.L.)		2	2	.500	1.50	1.04	4	4	0	0	0	0-0	24.0	14	9	4	3	11-0	24	.161
2002—Florida (N.L.)		6	7	.462	4.10	1.27	23	21	0	0	0	0-0	107.2	93	56	49	13	44-2	113	.232
—GC Marlins (GCL)		0	0	...	4.50	1.50	1	1	0	0	...	0-...	4.0	5	2	2	0	1-0	7	.294
—Jupiter (FSL)		1	0	1.000	0.00	0.83	1	1	0	0	...	0-...	6.0	4	0	0	0	1-0	12	.174
2003—Jupiter (FSL)		0	0	...	0.00	0.67	1	1	0	0	...	0-...	3.0	2	0	0	0	0-0	5	.182
—Carolina (Sou.)		0	0	...	4.50	1.00	1	1	0	0	...	0-...	4.0	4	2	2	1	0-0	7	.267
—Florida (N.L.)		9	8	.529	3.04	1.32	24	23	0	0	0	0-0	142.0	132	54	48	9	56-4	152	.246
Major League totals (3 years)		17	17	.500	3.32	1.28	51	48	0	0	0	0-0	273.2	239	119	101	25	111-6	289	.233

BEIMEL, JOE — P

PERSONAL: Born April 19, 1977, in St. Marys, Pa. ... 6-3/220. ... Throws left, bats left. ... Full name: Joseph Ronald Beimel. ... Name pronounced: BYE-muhl. ... High school: St. Mary's Area (St. Mary's, Pa.). ... College: Duquesne.

TRANSACTIONS/CAREER NOTES: Selected by Pittsburgh Pirates organization in 18th round of free-agent draft (June 3, 1998).

CAREER HITTING: 10-for-41 (.244), 3 R, 1 2B, 0 3B, 0 HR, 1 RBI.

Year	League	W	L	Pct.	ERA	WHIP	G	GS	CG	ShO	Hld.	Sv.-Opp.	IP	H	R	ER	HR	BB-IBB	SO	Avg.
1998—Erie (N.Y.-Penn)		1	4	.200	6.32	1.66	17	6	0	0	...	0-...	47.0	56	39	33	6	22-0	37	.296
1999—Hickory (S. Atl.)		5	11	.313	4.43	1.45	29	22	0	0	...	0-...	130.0	146	81	64	12	43-0	102	.289
2000—Lynchburg (Carolina)		10	6	.625	3.36	1.28	18	18	2	1	...	0-...	120.2	111	49	45	6	44-1	82	.247
—Altoona (East.)		1	6	.143	4.16	1.48	10	10	1	0	...	0-...	62.2	72	38	29	8	21-0	28	.288
2001—Pittsburgh (N.L.)		7	11	.389	5.23	1.56	42	15	0	0	0	0-0	115.1	131	72	67	12	49-4	58	.290
2002—Pittsburgh (N.L.)		2	5	.286	4.64	1.56	53	8	0	0	5	0-1	85.1	88	49	44	9	45-12	53	.267
2003—Pittsburgh (N.L.)		1	3	.250	5.05	1.64	69	0	0	0	12	0-5	62.1	69	35	35	7	33-6	42	.299
Major League totals (3 years)		10	19	.345	5.00	1.58	164	23	0	0	17	0-6	263.0	288	156	146	28	127-22	153	.284

BELISLE, MATT — P

PERSONAL: Born June 6, 1980, in McCallum, Texas. ... 6-3/195. ... Throws right, bats both. ... Full name: Matthew Thomas Belisle. ... High school: McCallum (Austin, Texas).

TRANSACTIONS/CAREER NOTES: Selected by Atlanta Braves organization in second round of free-agent draft (June 2, 1998). ... On disabled list (April 6, 2001-entire season). ... Recalled by Atlanta from Richmond; claimed off waivers by Cincinnati Reds (August 14, 2003). ... Called up by Cincinnati from Louisville (September 7, 2003).

CAREER HITTING: 0-for-1 (.000), 0 R, 0 2B, 0 3B, 0 HR, 0 RBI.

Year	League	W	L	Pct.	ERA	WHIP	G	GS	CG	ShO	Hld.	Sv.-Opp.	IP	H	R	ER	HR	BB-IBB	SO	Avg.
1999—Danville (Appal.)		2	5	.286	4.67	1.53	14	14	0	0	...	0-...	71.1	86	50	37	3	23-0	60	.291
2000—Myrtle Beach (Caro.)		3	4	.429	3.43	1.06	12	12	0	0	...	0-...	78.2	72	32	30	5	11-0	71	.246
—Macon (S. Atl.)		9	5	.643	2.37	0.95	15	15	1	0	...	0-...	102.1	79	37	27	7	18-0	97	.216
2001—												Did not play.								
2002—Greenville (Sou.)		5	9	.357	4.35	1.26	26	26	1	0	...	0-...	159.1	162	91	77	18	39-1	123	.261
2003—Greenville (Sou.)		6	8	.429	3.52	1.36	21	21	1	0	...	0-...	125.1	128	59	49	5	42-2	94	.272
—Richmond (Int'l)		1	1	.500	2.25	0.85	3	3	0	0	...	0-...	20.0	17	6	5	1	0-0	10	.230
—Louisville (Int'l)		1	3	.250	3.81	1.38	4	4	0	0	...	0-...	26.0	31	15	11	2	5-0	15	.304
—Cincinnati (N.L.)		1	1	.500	5.19	1.38	6	0	0	0	0	0-1	8.2	10	5	5	1	2-0	6	.303
Major League totals (1 year)		1	1	.500	5.19	1.38	6	0	0	0	0	0-1	8.2	10	5	5	1	2-0	6	.303

BELL, DAVID — 3B

PERSONAL: Born September 14, 1972, in Cincinnati, Ohio. ... 5-10/195. ... Bats right, throws right. ... Full name: David Michael Bell. ... High school: Moeller (Cincinnati).

TRANSACTIONS/CAREER NOTES: Selected by Cleveland Indians organization in seventh round of free-agent draft (June 4, 1990). ... Traded by Indians with C Pepe McNeal and P Rick Heiserman to St. Louis Cardinals for P Ken Hill (July 27, 1995). ... On St. Louis disabled list (April 29-June 30, 1997); included rehabilitation assignments to

B

Arkansas (June 10-19) and Louisville (June 20-26). ... Claimed on waivers by Indians (April 14, 1998). ... Traded by Indians to Seattle Mariners for 2B Joey Cora (August 31, 1998). ... Granted free agency (November 7, 2001). ... Re-signed by Mariners (December 19, 2001). ... Traded by Mariners to San Francisco Giants for SS Desi Relaford and cash (January 25, 2002). ... Granted free agency (October 31, 2002). ... Signed by Philadelphia Phillies (November 24, 2002). ... Placed on 15-day disabled list (July 11, 2003). ... Removed from 15-day disabled list (September 23, 2003).

2003 GAMES PLAYED BY POSITION (MLB): 3B—85, 2B—3.

										BATTING									FIELDING	
Year Team (League)	Pos.	G	AB	R	H	2B	3B	HR	RBI	BB	SO	HBP	GDP	SB-CS	Avg.	OBP	SLG	OPS	E	Pct.
1990— GC Indians (GCL)	3B	30	111	18	29	5	1	0	13	10	8	4	5	1-1	.261	.341	.324	.666	7	.919
— Burlington (Appal.)	3B	12	42	4	7	1	1	0	2	2	5	1	1	2-1	.167	.217	.238	.455	3	.921
1991— Columbus (S. Atl.)	3B	136	491	47	113	24	1	5	63	37	50	5	22	3-2	.230	.287	.314	.601	31	.920
1992— Kinston (Caro.)	3B	123	464	52	117	17	2	6	47	54	66	1	13	2-4	.252	.327	.336	.663	20	.946
1993— Cant./Akr. (Eastern)	3B-2B-SS	129	483	69	141	20	2	9	60	43	54	3	12	3-4	.292	.350	.398	.747	21	.950
1994— Charlotte (Int'l)	3B-SS-2B	134	481	66	141	17	4	18	88	41	54	9	9	2-5	.293	.355	.457	.812	20	.956
1995— Buffalo (A.A.)	3B-SS-2B	70	254	34	69	11	1	8	34	22	37	4	4	0-3	.272	.336	.417	.753	11	.952
— Cleveland (A.L.)	3B	2	2	0	0	0	0	0	0	0	0	0	0	0-0	.000	.000	.000	.000	0	1.000
— Louisville (A.A.)	2B	18	76	9	21	3	1	1	9	2	10	3	2	4-0	.276	.321	.382	.703	1	.989
— St. Louis (N.L.)	2B-3B	39	144	13	36	7	2	2	19	4	25	2	0	1-2	.250	.278	.368	.646	7	.964
1996— St. Louis (N.L.)	3B-2B-SS	62	145	12	31	6	0	1	9	10	22	1	3	1-1	.214	.268	.276	.543	5	.969
— Louisville (A.A.)	2B-3B-SS	42	136	9	24	5	1	0	7	7	15	0	4	1-2	.176	.217	.228	.445	5	.973
1997— St. Louis (N.L.)	3B-2B-SS	66	142	9	30	7	2	1	12	10	28	0	2	1-0	.211	.261	.310	.571	8	.949
— Arkansas (Texas)	3B-2B	9	32	3	7	2	0	1	3	2	2	0	1	1-0	.219	.265	.375	.640	1	.947
— Louisville (A.A.)	2B-3B-SS-DH	6	22	3	5	0	0	1	4	0	6	1	0	0-0	.227	.250	.364	.614	1	.941
1998— St. Louis (N.L.)	3B-2B	4	9	0	2	1	0	0	0	0	3	0	0	0-0	.222	.222	.333	.556	0	1.000
— Cleveland (A.L.)	2-3-SS-1	107	340	37	89	21	2	10	41	22	54	2	8	0-4	.262	.306	.424	.730	9	.983
— Seattle (A.L.)	2-3-1-OF	21	80	11	26	8	0	0	8	5	8	0	3	0-0	.325	.365	.425	.790	1	.991
1999— Seattle (A.L.)	2B-1B-SS	157	597	92	160	31	2	21	78	58	90	2	7	7-4	.268	.331	.432	.763	17	.978
2000— Seattle (A.L.)	3-2-1-S-D	133	454	57	112	24	2	11	47	42	66	6	11	2-3	.247	.316	.381	.697	15	.963
2001— Seattle (A.L.)	3B-1B	135	470	62	122	28	0	15	64	28	59	3	8	2-1	.260	.303	.415	.718	14	.962
2002— San Francisco (N.L.)	3-2-SS-1	154	552	82	144	29	2	20	73	54	80	9	18	1-2	.261	.333	.429	.762	12	.971
2003— Philadelphia (N.L.)	3B-2B	85	297	32	58	14	0	4	37	41	40	4	7	0-0	.195	.296	.283	.579	8	.968
American League totals (5 years)		555	1943	259	509	112	6	57	238	155	277	13	37	11-12	.262	.318	.414	.731	56	.974
National League totals (6 years)		410	1289	148	301	64	6	28	150	119	198	16	30	4-5	.234	.303	.358	.660	40	.966
Major League totals (9 years)		965	3232	407	810	176	12	85	388	274	475	29	67	15-17	.251	.312	.391	.703	96	.971

BELL, JAY — 2B

PERSONAL: Born December 11, 1965, in Eglin AFB, Fla. ... 6-0/184. ... Bats right, throws right. ... Full name: Jay Stuart Bell. ... High school: Tate (Gonzalez, Fla.).

TRANSACTIONS/CAREER NOTES: Selected by Minnesota Twins organization in first round (eighth pick overall) of free-agent draft (June 4, 1984). ... Traded by Twins with P Curt Wardle, OF Jim Weaver and a player to be named later to Cleveland Indians for P Bert Blyleven (August 1, 1985); Indians acquired P Rich Yett to complete deal (September 17, 1985). ... Traded by Indians to Pittsburgh Pirates for SS Felix Fermin (March 25, 1989). ... Traded by Pirates with 1B/3B Jeff King to Kansas City Royals for 3B Joe Randa, P Jeff Granger, P Jeff Martin and P Jeff Wallace (December 13, 1996). ... Granted free agency (November 4, 1997). ... Signed by Arizona Diamondbacks (November 17, 1997). ... On Arizona disabled list (March 28-July 19, 2002); included rehabilitation assignments to Tucson (April 29-May 6) and Lancaster (July 9-19). ... Granted free agency (October 29, 2002). ... Signed by New York Mets organization (February 11, 2003). ... Placed on the 15-day disabled list (May 22, 2003). ... Reinstated from 15-day disabled list (June 6, 2003).

2003 GAMES PLAYED BY POSITION (MLB): 2B—14, 3B—14, 1B—13, SS—12, DH—1.

										BATTING									FIELDING	
Year Team (League)	Pos.	G	AB	R	H	2B	3B	HR	RBI	BB	SO	HBP	GDP	SB-CS	Avg.	OBP	SLG	OPS	E	Pct.
1984— Elizabethton (App.)	SS	66	245	43	54	12	1	6	30	42	50	1	5	4-2	.220	.334	.351	.686	25	.929
1985— Visalia (Calif.)	SS	106	376	56	106	16	6	9	59	41	73	4	6	10-6	.282	.353	.428	.781	53	.905
— Waterbury (East.)	SS	29	114	13	34	11	2	1	14	9	16	0	3	3-3	.298	.350	.456	.806	6	.952
1986— Waterbury (East.)	SS	138	494	86	137	28	4	7	74	87	65	0	7	10-9	.277	.378	.393	.771	* 45	.927
— Cleveland (A.L.)	2B-DH	5	14	3	5	2	0	1	4	2	3	0	0	0-0	.357	.438	.714	1.152	2	.778
1987— Buffalo (A.A.)	2B-SS	110	362	71	94	15	4	17	60	70	84	2	3	6-5	.260	.380	.464	.844	‡ 30	.946
— Cleveland (A.L.)	SS	38	125	14	27	9	1	2	13	8	31	1	0	2-0	.216	.269	.352	.621	9	.947
1988— Cleveland (A.L.)	SS-DH	73	211	23	46	5	1	2	21	21	53	1	3	4-2	.218	.289	.280	.569	10	.965
— Colo. Springs (PCL)	SS	49	181	35	50	12	2	7	24	26	27	1	8	3-1	.276	.368	.481	.849	18	.935
1989— Pittsburgh (N.L.)	SS	78	271	33	70	13	3	2	27	19	47	1	9	5-3	.258	.307	.351	.658	10	.968
— Buffalo (A.A.)	3B-SS	86	298	49	85	15	3	10	54	38	55	3	6	12-5	.285	.370	.456	.826	16	.954
1990— Pittsburgh (N.L.)	SS	159	583	93	148	28	7	7	52	65	109	3	14	10-6	.254	.329	.362	.691	22	.970
1991— Pittsburgh (N.L.)	SS	157	608	96	164	32	8	16	67	52	99	4	15	10-6	.270	.330	.428	.757	* 24	.968
1992— Pittsburgh (N.L.)	SS	159	632	87	167	36	6	9	55	55	103	4	12	7-5	.264	.326	.383	.709	22	.973
1993— Pittsburgh (N.L.)	SS	154	604	102	187	32	9	9	51	77	122	6	16	16-10	.310	.392	.437	.830	11	.986
1994— Pittsburgh (N.L.)	SS	110	424	68	117	35	4	9	45	49	82	3	15	2-0	.276	.353	.441	.794	15	.973
1995— Pittsburgh (N.L.)	SS-3B	138	530	79	139	28	4	13	55	55	110	4	13	2-5	.262	.336	.404	.739	14	.978
1996— Pittsburgh (N.L.)	SS	151	527	65	132	29	3	13	71	54	108	5	10	6-4	.250	.323	.391	.714	10	.986
1997— Kansas City (A.L.)	SS-3B	153	573	89	167	28	3	21	92	71	101	4	13	10-6	.291	.368	.461	.829	10	.985
1998— Arizona (N.L.)	SS-2B	155	549	79	138	29	5	20	67	81	129	7	14	3-5	.251	.353	.432	.785	19	.972
1999— Arizona (N.L.)	2B-DH-SS	151	589	132	170	32	6	38	112	82	132	4	9	7-4	.289	.374	.557	.931	‡ 22	.982
2000— Arizona (N.L.)	2B-DH	149	565	87	151	30	6	18	68	70	88	3	7	7-3	.267	.348	.437	.786	8	.988
2001— Arizona (N.L.)	2B-3B-DH	129	428	59	106	24	1	13	46	65	79	4	9	0-1	.248	.349	.400	.749	7	.983
2002— Tucson (PCL)	3B	7	22	4	5	3	0	0	2	4	1	0	1	0-0	.227	.346	.364	.710	2	.833
— Lancaster (Calif.)	SS	7	20	4	4	1	0	1	7	4	6	0	1	0-0	.200	.333	.400	.733	0	1.000
— Arizona (N.L.)	3-1-2-SS	32	49	3	8	1	0	2	11	5	9	1	2	0-0	.163	.250	.306	.556	0	1.000
2003— New York (N.L.)	2-3-1-S-D	72	116	11	21	1	0	0	3	22	38	2	4	0-0	.181	.319	.190	.509	5	.961
American League totals (4 years)		269	923	129	245	44	5	26	130	102	188	6	16	16-8	.265	.339	.408	.747	31	.973
National League totals (14 years)		1794	6475	994	1718	350	62	169	730	751	1255	51	149	75-52	.265	.344	.417	.761	189	.976
Major League totals (18 years)		2063	7398	1123	1963	394	67	195	860	853	1443	57	165	91-60	.265	.343	.416	.759	220	.976

BELL, ROB — P

PERSONAL: Born January 17, 1977, in Newburgh, N.Y. ... 6-5/225. ... Throws right, bats right. ... Full name: Robert Allen Bell. ... High school: Marlboro (N.Y.) Central.

TRANSACTIONS/CAREER NOTES: Selected by Atlanta Braves organization in third round of free-agent draft (June 1, 1995). ... Traded by Braves with OF Michael Tucker and P Denny Neagle to Cincinnati Reds for 2B Bret Boone and P Mike Remlinger (November 10, 1998). ... On Chattanooga disabled list (April 20-July 20, 1999). ... Traded by

Reds to Texas Rangers for OF Ruben Mateo and 3B Edwin Encarnacion (June 15, 2001). ... Released by Rangers (March 12, 2003). ... Signed by Tampa Bay Devil Rays organization (March 17, 2003). ... Contract purchased by Tampa Bay from Durham (June 14, 2003). ... Recalled by Tampa Bay from Durham of the International League (July 4, 2003).

CAREER HITTING: 4-for-55 (.073), 1 R, 1 2B, 0 3B, 0 HR, 0 RBI.

Year League	W	L	Pct.	ERA	WHIP	G	GS	CG	ShO	Hld.	Sv.-Opp.	IP	H	R	ER	HR	BB-IBB	SO	Avg.
1995— GC Braves (GCL)	1	6	.143	6.88	1.53	10	8	0	0	...	0-...	34.0	38	29	26	2	14-0	33	.279
1996— Eugene (NW)	5	6	.455	5.11	1.46	16	*16	0	0	...	0-...	81.0	89	49	46	5	29-1	74	.282
1997— Macon (S. Atl.)	•14	7	.667	3.68	1.26	27	27	1	0	...	0-...	146.2	144	72	60	15	41-1	140	.258
1998— Danville (Caro.)	7	9	.438	3.28	1.21	28	•28	2	0	...	0-...	*178.1	169	79	65	8	46-0	*197	.252
1999— Chattanooga (Sou.)	3	6	.333	3.13	1.28	12	12	2	1	...	0-...	72.0	75	30	25	7	17-0	68	.276
— GC Reds (GCL)	0	0	...	1.13	0.38	2	2	0	0	...	0-...	8.0	3	1	1	0	0-0	11	.120
2000— Cincinnati (N.L.)	7	8	.467	5.00	1.45	26	26	1	0	0	0-0	140.1	130	84	78	32	73-6	112	.243
— Louisville (Int'l)	4	0	1.000	3.73	1.17	6	6	0	0	...	0-...	41.0	35	18	17	6	13-0	47	.224
2001— Cincinnati (N.L.)	0	5	.000	5.48	1.42	9	9	0	0	0	0-0	44.1	46	28	27	9	17-1	33	.275
— Louisville (Int'l)	2	2	.500	3.33	1.33	5	4	0	0	...	0-...	27.0	32	10	10	4	4-0	26	.288
— Texas (A.L.)	5	5	.500	7.18	1.68	18	18	0	0	0	0-0	105.1	130	87	84	23	47-0	64	.310
2002— Oklahoma (PCL)	5	0	1.000	4.06	1.26	12	11	2	•2	...	0-...	75.1	70	36	34	10	25-0	55	.247
— Texas (A.L.)	4	3	.571	6.22	1.57	17	15	0	0	0	0-0	94.0	113	69	65	16	35-0	70	.296
— Tulsa (Texas)	1	0	1.000	0.00	0.50	1	1	0	0	...	0-...	8.0	4	0	0	0	0-0	5	.154
2003— Durham (Int'l)	6	4	.600	4.02	1.21	12	12	0	0	...	0-...	71.2	72	33	32	10	15-1	48	.260
— Tampa Bay (A.L.)	5	4	.556	5.52	1.41	19	18	0	0	0	0-0	101.0	103	64	62	15	39-1	44	.263
American League totals (3 years)	14	12	.538	6.32	1.55	54	51	0	0	0	0-0	300.1	346	220	211	54	121-1	178	.290
National League totals (2 years)	7	13	.350	5.12	1.44	35	35	1	0	0	0-0	184.2	176	112	105	41	90-7	145	.251
Major League totals (4 years)	21	25	.457	5.86	1.51	89	86	1	0	0	0-0	485.0	522	332	316	95	211-8	323	.275

BELLHORN, MARK   2B/3B

PERSONAL: Born August 23, 1974, in Boston, Mass. ... 6-1/205. ... Bats both, throws right. ... Full name: Mark Christian Bellhorn. ... High school: Oviedo (Fla.). ... College: Auburn.

TRANSACTIONS/CAREER NOTES: Selected by Oakland Athletics organization in second round of free agent draft (June 1, 1995). ... On Vancouver disabled list (April 8-July 29, 1999). ... On Sacramento disabled list (May 12-24, 2000). ... Traded by A's to Chicago Cubs for IF Adam Morrissey (November 2, 2001). ... Traded to Colorado by Chicago Cubs to Colorado for IF Jose Hernandez (June 20, 2003). ... Placed on 15-day disabled list (August 1, 2003). ... Sent to Colorado Springs on rehab assignment by Colorado (August 7, 2003). ... Recalled from minor league rehab assignment; removed from 15-day disabled list (August 23, 2003).

2003 GAMES PLAYED BY POSITION (MLB): 3B—57, 2B—20, SS—6, OF—5, 1B—1.

Year Team (League)	Pos.	G	AB	R	H	2B	3B	HR	RBI	BB	SO	HBP	GDP	SB-CS	Avg.	OBP	SLG	OPS	E	Pct.
1995— Modesto (Calif.)	SS	56	229	35	59	12	0	6	31	27	52	4	9	5-2	.258	.346	.389	.735	21	.927
1996— Huntsville (Sou.)	IF	131	468	84	117	24	5	10	71	73	124	4	7	19-2	.250	.353	.387	.740	32	.945
1997— Edmonton (PCL)	2B-SS-3B-D	70	241	54	79	18	3	11	46	64	59	2	4	6-6	.328	.472	.564	1.037	13	.957
— Oakland (A.L.)	3B-2B-DH-S	68	224	33	51	9	1	6	19	32	70	0	1	7-1	.228	.324	.357	.681	9	.956
1998— Edmonton (PCL)	3-2-DH-S-1	87	309	57	77	20	4	10	44	62	90	6	8	6-2	.249	.384	.437	.820	11	.965
— Oakland (A.L.)	3B-SS-D-2	11	12	1	1	1	0	0	1	3	4	1	0	2-0	.083	.313	.167	.479	0	1.000
1999— Ariz. A's (Ariz.)	2B-DH	12	43	11	10	3	0	0	5	11	9	0	1	0-0	.233	.389	.302	.691	0	1.000
— Midland (Texas)	2B	17	57	12	17	3	0	2	8	11	13	0	2	1-0	.298	.412	.456	.868	2	.973
2000— Sacramento (PCL)	3-2-SS-1	117	436	*111	116	17	11	24	73	*94	121	5	5	20-5	.266	.399	.521	.920	15	.956
— Oakland (A.L.)	2B-3B-SS	9	13	2	2	0	0	0	0	2	6	0	0	0-0	.154	.267	.154	.421	0	1.000
2001— Sacramento (PCL)	OF-2B-SS-3B	43	156	30	42	6	0	12	36	22	60	4	0	3-0	.269	.370	.538	.908	2	.985
— Oakland (A.L.)	2-3-S-D-O	38	74	11	10	1	2	1	4	7	37	0	1	0-0	.135	.210	.243	.453	5	.932
2002— Chicago (N.L.)	2-3-1-S-O	146	445	86	115	24	4	27	56	76	144	6	6	7-5	.258	.374	.512	.886	11	.947
2003— Chicago (N.L.)	3B	51	139	15	29	7	1	2	22	29	46	1	2	3-3	.209	.341	.317	.658	6	.938
— Colo. Springs (PCL)	3B-2B	16	54	11	21	5	1	4	16	11	10	0	0	2-0	.389	.485	.741	1.226	1	.981
— Colorado (N.L.)	2-3-S-O-1	48	110	12	26	3	0	0	4	21	32	2	1	2-3	.236	.368	.264	.632	3	.974
American League totals (4 years)		126	323	47	64	11	3	7	24	44	117	1	2	9-1	.198	.296	.316	.612	14	.952
National League totals (2 years)		245	694	113	170	34	5	29	82	126	222	9	9	12-11	.245	.366	.434	.800	20	.971
Major League totals (6 years)		371	1017	160	234	45	8	36	106	170	339	10	11	21-12	.230	.345	.396	.741	34	.966

BELLIARD, RONNIE   2B

PERSONAL: Born April 7, 1975, in Bronx, N.Y. ... 5-8/197. ... Bats right, throws right. ... Full name: Ronald Belliard. ... Name pronounced: BELL-ee-yard. ... High school: Central (Miami).

TRANSACTIONS/CAREER NOTES: Selected by Milwaukee Brewers organization in eighth round of free-agent draft (June 2, 1994). ... On disabled list (August 8-September 30, 2001). ... Granted free agency (December 21, 2002). ... Placed on 15-day disabled list by Colorado (June 2, 2003). ... Sent to Colorado Springs on rehab assignment by Colorado (June 17, 2003). ... Recalled by Colorado from Colorado Springs rehab assignment; reinstated from 15-day disabled list (June 23, 2003).

2003 GAMES PLAYED BY POSITION (MLB): 2B—113.

Year Team (League)	Pos.	G	AB	R	H	2B	3B	HR	RBI	BB	SO	HBP	GDP	SB-CS	Avg.	OBP	SLG	OPS	E	Pct.
1994— Ariz. Brewers (Ariz.)	2B-3B-SS	39	143	32	42	7	3	0	27	14	25	3	3	7-0	.294	.366	.385	.751	12	.935
1995— Beloit (Midw.)	2B-3B	130	461	76	137	28	5	13	76	36	67	7	10	16-12	.297	.356	.464	.821	‡26	.956
1996— El Paso (Texas)	2B-DH	109	416	73	116	20	8	3	57	60	51	4	11	26-10	.279	.373	.387	.760	16	.972
1997— Tucson (PCL)	2B-SS	118	443	80	125	35	4	4	55	61	69	11	13	10-7	.282	.379	.406	.785	‡26	.959
1998— Louisville (Int'l)	2B-SS	133	507	*114	163	36	7	14	73	69	77	8	17	33-12	.321	.408	.503	.911	14	.979
— Milwaukee (N.L.)	2B	8	5	1	1	0	0	0	0	0	0	0	0	0-0	.200	.200	.200	.400	0	...
1999— Louisville (Int'l)	2B	29	108	14	26	4	0	1	8	14	13	1	3	12-2	.241	.331	.306	.636	3	.975
— Milwaukee (N.L.)	2B-3B-SS	124	457	60	135	29	4	8	58	64	59	0	16	4-5	.295	.379	.429	.808	13	.978
2000— Milwaukee (N.L.)	2B	152	571	83	150	30	9	8	54	82	84	3	12	7-5	.263	.354	.389	.743	*19	.976
2001— Milwaukee (N.L.)	2B	101	364	69	96	30	3	11	36	35	65	5	5	5-2	.264	.335	.453	.788	5	.990
2002— Milwaukee (N.L.)	2B-3B	104	289	30	61	13	0	3	26	18	46	1	9	2-3	.211	.257	.287	.544	10	.963
2003— Colo. Springs (PCL)	2B	6	19	2	5	1	0	0	0	0	1	0	0	0-0	.263	.263	.316	.579	0	1.000
— Colorado (N.L.)	2B	116	447	73	124	31	2	8	50	49	71	2	7	7-2	.277	.351	.409	.760	15	.973
Major League totals (6 years)		605	2133	316	567	133	18	38	224	248	325	11	49	25-17	.266	.343	.398	.741	62	.977

BELTRAN, CARLOS   OF

PERSONAL: Born April 24, 1977, in Manati, Puerto Rico. ... 6-1/190. ... Bats both, throws right. ... Full name: Carlos Ivan Beltran. ... Name pronounced: BELL-tron. ... High school: Fernando Callejas (Manati, Puerto Rico).

TRANSACTIONS/CAREER NOTES: Selected by Kansas City Royals organization in second round of free-agent draft (June 1, 1995). ... On Kansas City disabled list (July 4-September 4, 2000); included rehabilitation assignments to Gulf Coast Royals (August 21-24), Wilmington (August 25-30) and Omaha (August 31-September 4). ... On Kansas City disabled list (March 21-April 18, 2003); included rehabilitation assignment to Wichita. ... Reinstated from the 15-day disabled list; recalled by Kansas City from Wichita (April 18, 2003).

2003 GAMES PLAYED BY POSITION (MLB): OF—130, DH—8.

Year	Team (League)	Pos.	G	AB	R	H	2B	3B	HR	RBI	BB	SO	HBP	GDP	SB-CS	Avg.	OBP	SLG	OPS	E	Pct.
1995— GC Royals (GCL)		OF	52	180	29	50	9	0	0	23	13	30	3	1	5-3	.278	.332	.328	.659	2	.977
1996— Lansing (Midw.)		OF	11	42	3	6	2	0	0	0	1	11	0	0	1-0	.143	.163	.190	.353	2	.938
— Spokane (N'west)		OF	59	215	29	58	8	3	7	29	31	65	0	4	10-2	.270	.359	.433	.791	7	.938
1997— Wilmington (Caro.)		OF	120	419	57	96	15	4	11	46	46	96	4	10	17-7	.229	.311	.363	.673	8	.968
1998— Wilmington (Caro.)		OF	52	192	32	53	14	0	5	32	25	39	2	2	11-7	.276	.364	.427	.791	2	.983
— Wichita (Texas)		OF	47	182	50	64	13	3	14	44	23	30	1	4	7-1	.352	.427	.687	1.114	4	.960
— Kansas City (A.L.)		OF	14	58	12	16	5	3	0	7	3	12	1	2	3-0	.276	.317	.466	.783	1	.978
1999— Kansas City (A.L.)		OF-DH	156	663	112	194	27	7	22	108	46	123	4	17	27-8	.293	.337	.454	.791	* 12	.972
2000— Kansas City (A.L.)		OF-DH	98	372	49	92	15	4	7	44	35	69	0	12	13-0	.247	.309	.366	.675	6	.975
— GC Royals (GCL)		DH	1	4	3	2	1	0	1	1	1	0	0	0	0-0	.500	.600	1.500	2.100	...	...
— Wilmington (Caro.)		OF	3	13	2	4	0	1	2	6	0	5	0	0	0-0	.308	.308	.923	1.231	0	1.000
— Omaha (PCL)		OF	5	18	4	6	1	0	2	2	3	3	1	0	1-0	.333	.455	.722	1.177	0	1.000
2001— Kansas City (A.L.)		OF-DH	155	617	106	189	32	12	24	101	52	120	5	7	31-1	.306	.362	.514	.876	5	.988
2002— Kansas City (A.L.)		OF-DH	• 162	637	114	174	44	7	29	105	71	135	4	12	35-7	.273	.346	.501	.847	7	.983
2003— Wichita (Texas)		OF-DH	3	9	3	3	2	0	0	1	2	3	0	0	1-0	.333	.455	.556	1.010	0	1.000
— Kansas City (A.L.)		OF-DH	141	521	102	160	14	10	26	100	72	81	2	8	41-4	.307	.389	.522	.911	5	.987
Major League totals (6 years)			726	2868	495	825	137	43	108	465	279	540	16	58	150-20	.288	.350	.478	.829	36	.981

BELTRE, ADRIAN   3B

PERSONAL: Born April 7, 1979, in Santo Domingo, Dominican Republic. ... 5-11/170. ... Bats right, throws right. ... Full name: Adrian Perez Beltre. ... Name pronounced: BELL-tray. ... High school: Liceo Maximo Gomez (Santo Domingo, Dominican Republic).

TRANSACTIONS/CAREER NOTES: Signed as non-drafted free agent by Los Angeles Dodgers (July 7, 1994). ... On San Bernardino disabled list (June 25-July 2, 1996). ... On Albuquerque disabled list (April 23-May 1 and May 12-19, 1998). ... On disabled list (May 28-June 17, 2000). ... On Los Angeles disabled list (March 23-May 12, 2001); included rehabilitation assignments to Vero Beach (May 6-9) and Las Vegas (May 10-12).

2003 GAMES PLAYED BY POSITION (MLB): 3B—157, SS—1.

Year	Team (League)	Pos.	G	AB	R	H	2B	3B	HR	RBI	BB	SO	HBP	GDP	SB-CS	Avg.	OBP	SLG	OPS	E	Pct.
1995— Dom. Dodgers (DSL)		3B	62	218	56	67	15	3	8	40	54	26	...	...	2-1	.307	...	.514	...	19	.920
1996— Savannah (S. Atl.)		3B-2B	68	244	48	75	14	3	16	59	35	46	7	7	4-3	.307	.406	.586	.992	19	.912
— San Bern. (Calif.)		3B-DH	63	238	40	62	13	1	10	40	19	44	5	3	3-4	.261	.322	.450	.772	7	.953
1997— Vero Beach (FSL)		3B-OF	123	435	95	138	24	2	* 26	* 104	67	66	6	9	25-9	.317	.407	.561	.967	37	.895
1998— San Antonio (Texas)		3B-SS	64	246	49	79	21	2	13	56	39	37	2	3	20-4	.321	.411	.581	.992	17	.910
— Los Angeles (N.L.)		3B-SS	77	195	18	42	9	0	7	22	14	37	3	4	3-1	.215	.278	.369	.648	13	.926
1999— Los Angeles (N.L.)		3B	152	538	84	148	27	5	15	67	61	105	6	4	18-7	.275	.352	.428	.780	• 29	.932
2000— Los Angeles (N.L.)		3B-SS	138	510	71	148	30	2	20	85	56	80	2	13	12-5	.290	.360	.475	.835	23	.944
2001— Vero Beach (FSL)		3B	3	9	0	4	1	0	0	1	2	1	1	0	0-0	.444	.583	.556	1.139	0	1.000
— Las Vegas (PCL)		3B	2	5	2	3	1	0	1	2	2	0	0	0	0-0	.600	.714	1.400	2.114	1	.833
— Los Angeles (N.L.)		3B-SS	126	475	59	126	22	4	13	60	28	82	5	9	13-4	.265	.310	.411	.720	16	.953
2002— Los Angeles (N.L.)		3B	159	587	70	151	26	5	21	75	37	96	4	17	7-5	.257	.303	.426	.729	20	.954
2003— Los Angeles (N.L.)		3B-SS	158	559	50	134	30	2	23	80	37	103	5	13	2-2	.240	.290	.424	.714	19	.957
Major League totals (6 years)			810	2864	352	749	144	18	99	389	233	503	25	60	55-24	.262	.320	.428	.748	120	.946

BENARD, MARVIN   OF

PERSONAL: Born January 20, 1970, in Mina Rosita, Nicaragua. ... 5-9/191. ... Bats left, throws left. ... Full name: Marvin Larry Benard. ... Name pronounced: buh-NARD. ... High school: Bell (Bell Gardens, Calif.). ... College: Lewis-Clark (Idaho) State.

TRANSACTIONS/CAREER NOTES: Selected by Philadelphia Phillies organization in 20th round of free-agent draft (June 4, 1990); did not sign. ... Selected by San Francisco Giants organization in 50th round of free-agent draft (June 1, 1992). ... On disabled list (April 17-28, 1993). ... On disabled list (July 2-September 1, 2002). ... Placed on 15-day disabled list (May 5, 2003). ... Sent on rehab assignment to Fresno (May 11, 2003). ... Recalled from rehab assignment by San Francisco (May 13, 2003). ... Activated from the 15-day disabled list (May 28, 2003). ... Placed on 15-day disabled list (June 16, 2003). ... Sent to Fresno on rehab assignment by San Francisco (July 31, 2003). ... Recalled by San Francisco from Fresno rehab assignment (August 5, 2003). ... Reinstated from 15-day disabled list (August 8, 2003). ... Sent on rehab assignment by San Francisco (August 19, 2003). ... Recalled from minor league rehab assignment; removed from 15-day disabled list (September 1, 2003).

2003 GAMES PLAYED BY POSITION (MLB): OF—21.

Year	Team (League)	Pos.	G	AB	R	H	2B	3B	HR	RBI	BB	SO	HBP	GDP	SB-CS	Avg.	OBP	SLG	OPS	E	Pct.
1992— Everett (N'west)		OF	64	161	31	38	10	2	1	17	24	39	6	1	17-3	.236	.356	.342	.698	3	.970
1993— Clinton (Midw.)		OF	112	349	68	105	14	2	5	50	56	66	4	1	42-10	.301	.403	.395	.799	5	.974
1994— Shreveport (Texas)		OF	125	454	66	143	32	3	4	48	31	58	4	14	24-13	.315	.361	.425	.786	* 12	.958
1995— Phoenix (PCL)		OF-DH	111	378	70	115	14	6	6	32	50	66	5	2	10-13	.304	.390	.421	.811	8	.959
— San Francisco (N.L.)		OF	13	34	5	13	2	0	1	4	1	7	0	1	1-0	.382	.400	.529	.929	0	1.000
1996— Phoenix (PCL)		OF	4	19	2	7	0	0	0	4	2	2	0	0	1-0	.368	.429	.368	.797	0	1.000
— San Francisco (N.L.)		OF	135	488	89	121	17	4	5	27	59	84	4	8	25-11	.248	.330	.330	.663	5	.984
1997— San Francisco (N.L.)		OF-DH	84	114	13	26	4	0	1	13	13	29	2	2	3-1	.228	.315	.289	.605	1	.967
— Phoenix (PCL)		OF	17	60	14	20	5	0	0	5	11	9	1	3	4-3	.333	.444	.417	.861	1	.966
1998— San Francisco (N.L.)		OF-DH	121	286	41	92	21	1	3	36	34	39	2	3	11-4	.322	.396	.434	.830	2	.982
1999— San Francisco (N.L.)		OF	149	562	100	163	36	5	16	64	55	97	6	5	27-14	.290	.359	.457	.816	4	.988
2000— San Francisco (N.L.)		OF	149	560	102	147	27	6	12	55	63	97	6	4	22-7	.263	.342	.396	.739	1	.997
2001— San Francisco (N.L.)		OF	129	392	70	104	19	2	15	44	29	66	4	3	10-5	.265	.320	.439	.759	8	.965
2002— San Francisco (N.L.)		OF	65	123	16	34	9	2	1	13	7	26	1	1	5-1	.276	.321	.407	.727	0	1.000
2003— San Jose (Calif.)		OF-DH	3	9	2	2	0	0	0	0	0	2	1	0	0-0	.222	.300	.222	.522	0	1.000
— Fresno (PCL)		OF	14	50	8	11	3	0	1	8	1	4	1	2	2-0	.220	.250	.340	.590	1	.967
— San Francisco (N.L.)		OF	46	71	5	14	3	1	0	4	4	9	0	3	1-0	.197	.237	.268	.504	0	1.000
Major League totals (9 years)			891	2630	441	714	138	21	54	260	265	454	25	32	105-43	.271	.343	.402	.744	21	.986

B

BENES, ALAN — P

PERSONAL: Born January 21, 1972, in Evansville, Ind. ... 6-5/240. ... Throws right, bats right. ... Full name: Alan Paul Benes. ... Name pronounced: BEN-ess. ... High school: Lake Forest (Ill.). ... College: Creighton.

TRANSACTIONS/CAREER NOTES: Selected by San Diego Padres organization in 49th round of free-agent draft (June 4, 1990); did not sign. ... Selected by St. Louis Cardinals organization in first round (16th pick overall) of free-agent draft (June 3, 1993). ... On Louisville disabled list (May 3-August 9, 1995). ... On disabled list (July 31, 1997-remainder of season; and March 22, 1998-entire season). ... On St. Louis disabled list (March 26-September 5, 1999); included rehabilitation assignments to Arkansas (August 5-10 and August 26-30), Potomac (August 11-15 and August 31-September 3) and Memphis (August 16-25 and September 4-5). ... Granted free agency (December 21, 2001). ... Signed by Chicago Cubs organization (January 16, 2002). ... On Iowa disabled list (May 7-14, 2002). ... Recalled by Chicago from Iowa (April 16, 2003). ... Traded by Cubs to Texas Rangers for a player to be named later (May 9, 2003). ... Assigned to Oklahoma of the Pacific Coast League by Texas Rangers (May 29, 2003). ... Sent outright to Oklahoma by Texas (June 2, 2003).

CAREER HITTING: 22-for-139 (.158), 6 R, 6 2B, 0 3B, 0 HR, 8 RBI.

Year League	W	L	Pct.	ERA	WHIP	G	GS	CG	ShO	Hld.	Sv.-Opp.	IP	H	R	ER	HR	BB-IBB	SO	Avg.
1993—Glens Falls (NYP)	0	4	.000	3.65	1.43	7	7	0	0	...	0-...	37.0	39	20	15	2	14-0	29	.269
1994—Savannah (S. Atl.)	2	0	1.000	1.48	1.15	4	4	0	0	...	0-...	24.1	21	5	4	1	7-0	24	.241
—St. Pete. (FSL)	7	1	.875	1.61	0.89	11	11	0	0	...	0-...	78.1	55	18	14	0	15-0	69	.197
—Arkansas (Texas)	7	2	.778	2.98	0.96	13	13	1	0	...	0-...	87.2	58	38	29	8	26-0	75	.188
—Louisville (A.A.)	1	0	1.000	2.93	0.91	2	2	1	0	...	0-...	15.1	10	5	5	1	4-0	16	.175
1995—Louisville (A.A.)	4	2	.667	2.41	0.91	11	11	2	1	...	0-...	56.0	37	16	15	5	14-1	54	.185
—St. Louis (N.L.)	1	2	.333	8.44	1.75	3	3	0	0	0	0-0	16.0	24	15	15	2	4-0	20	.343
1996—St. Louis (N.L.)	13	10	.565	4.90	1.46	34	32	3	1	0	0-0	191.0	192	120	104	27	87-3	131	.266
1997—St. Louis (N.L.)	9	9	.500	2.89	1.21	23	23	2	0	0	0-0	161.2	128	60	52	13	68-3	160	.219
1998—St. Louis (N.L.)										Did not play.									
1999—Arkansas (Texas)	0	0		6.23	1.62	2	2	0	0	...	0-...	4.1	6	3	3	0	1-0	0	.333
—Potomac (Caro.)	0	0		1.80	1.00	2	2	0	0	...	0-...	5.0	1	1	1	0	4-0	2	.077
—Memphis (PCL)	0	1	.000	3.18	1.76	3	3	0	0	...	0-...	5.2	8	3	2	0	2-0	3	.348
—St. Louis (N.L.)	0	0		0.00	1.00	2	0	0	0	0	0-0	2.0	2	0	0	0	0-0	2	.286
2000—Memphis (PCL)	1	2	.333	5.95	1.68	9	8	0	0	...	0-...	39.1	45	31	26	7	21-0	26	.288
—St. Louis (N.L.)	2	2	.500	5.67	1.67	30	0	0	0	2	0-1	46.0	54	33	29	7	23-2	26	.290
2001—Memphis (PCL)	7	6	.538	3.55	1.51	25	25	1	0	...	0-...	142.0	164	71	56	13	51-1	96	.288
—St. Louis (N.L.)	2	0	1.000	7.36	1.77	9	1	0	0	0	0-0	14.2	14	12	12	5	12-0	10	.250
2002—Iowa (PCL)	10	9	.526	5.65	1.62	28	19	0	0	...	0-...	113.0	130	79	71	17	53-0	85	.293
—Chicago (N.L.)	2	2	.500	4.35	1.37	7	7	0	0	0	0-0	39.1	42	22	19	3	12-1	32	.276
2003—Chicago (N.L.)	0	0		2.16	1.68	3	0	0	0	0	1-1	8.1	8	2	2	0	6-0	9	.267
—Texas (A.L.)	0	3	.000	11.40	2.47	4	4	0	0	0	0-0	15.0	29	20	19	2	8-0	11	.414
—Iowa (PCL)	7	7	.500	5.37	1.52	19	17	2	0	...	0-...	114.0	129	74	68	13	44-1	81	.294
American League totals (1 year)	0	3	.000	11.40	2.47	4	4	0	0	0	0-0	15.0	29	20	19	2	8-0	11	.414
National League totals (8 years)	29	25	.537	4.38	1.41	111	66	5	1	2	1-2	479.0	464	264	233	57	212-9	390	.257
Major League totals (8 years)	29	28	.509	4.59	1.44	115	70	5	1	2	1-2	494.0	493	284	252	59	220-9	401	.263

BENITEZ, ARMANDO — P

PERSONAL: Born November 3, 1972, in Ramon Santana, Dominican Republic. ... 6-4/229. ... Throws right, bats right. ... Full name: Armando German Benitez. ... Name pronounced: buh-NEE-tezz.

TRANSACTIONS/CAREER NOTES: Signed as non-drafted free agent by Baltimore Orioles organization (April 1, 1990). ... On Baltimore disabled list (April 20-August 26, 1996); included rehabilitation assignments to Bowie (May 17-19) and Gulf Coast Orioles (August 13-26). ... On suspended list (May 20-28, 1998). ... Traded by Orioles to New York Mets for C Charles Johnson (December 1, 1998). ... Traded by Mets to New York Yankees for P Jason Anderson, P Ryan Bicondoa and P Anderson Garcia (July 18, 2003). ... Traded by Yankees to Seattle Mariners for P Jeff Nelson (August 6, 2003).

CAREER HITTING: 0-for-7 (.000), 0 R, 0 2B, 0 3B, 0 HR, 2 RBI.

Year League	W	L	Pct.	ERA	WHIP	G	GS	CG	ShO	Hld.	Sv.-Opp.	IP	H	R	ER	HR	BB-IBB	SO	Avg.
1990—Dom. Orioles/W.S. (DSL)	3	1	.750	2.72	1.37	19	0	0	0	...	8-...	43.0	39	23	13	...	20-...	34	...
1991—GC Orioles (GCL)	3	2	.600	2.72	1.27	14	3	0	0	...	0-...	36.1	35	16	11	2	11-0	33	.252
1992—Bluefield (Appal.)	1	2	.333	4.31	1.85	25	0	0	0	...	5-...	31.1	35	31	15	1	23-0	37	.276
1993—Albany (S. Atl.)	5	1	.833	1.52	0.94	40	0	0	0	...	14-...	53.1	31	10	9	2	19-0	83	.168
—Frederick (Caro.)	3	0	1.000	0.66	0.80	12	0	0	0	...	4-...	13.2	7	1	1	0	4-0	29	.149
1994—Bowie (East.)	8	4	.667	3.14	1.12	53	0	0	0	...	16-...	71.2	41	29	25	6	39-0	106	.160
—Baltimore (A.L.)	0	0		0.90	1.20	3	0	0	0	0	0-0	10.0	8	1	1	0	4-0	14	.216
1995—Baltimore (A.L.)	1	5	.167	5.66	1.55	44	0	0	0	6	2-5	47.2	37	33	30	8	37-2	56	.213
—Rochester (Int'l)	2	2	.500	1.25	0.78	17	0	0	0	...	8-...	21.2	10	4	3	2	7-0	37	.135
1996—Baltimore (A.L.)	1	0	1.000	3.77	0.91	18	0	0	0	1	4-5	14.1	7	6	6	2	6-0	20	.143
—Bowie (East.)	0	0		4.50	1.17	4	4	0	0	...	0-...	6.0	7	3	3	0	0-0	8	.304
—GC Orioles (GCL)	1	0	1.000	0.00	0.50	1	0	0	0	...	0-...	2.0	1	0	0	0	0-0	5	.143
—Rochester (Int'l)	0	0		2.25	1.00	2	0	0	0	...	0-...	4.0	3	1	1	1	1-0	5	.188
1997—Baltimore (A.L.)	4	5	.444	2.45	1.25	71	0	0	0	20	9-10	73.1	49	22	20	7	43-5	106	.194
1998—Baltimore (A.L.)	5	6	.455	3.82	1.27	71	0	0	0	3	22-26	68.1	48	29	29	10	39-2	87	.199
1999—New York (N.L.)	4	3	.571	1.85	1.04	77	0	0	0	17	22-28	78.0	40	17	16	4	41-4	128	.148
2000—New York (N.L.)	4	4	.500	2.61	1.01	76	0	0	0	0	41-46	76.0	39	24	22	10	38-2	106	.148
2001—New York (N.L.)	6	4	.600	3.77	1.30	73	0	0	0	0	43-46	76.1	59	32	32	12	40-6	93	.214
2002—New York (N.L.)	1	0	1.000	2.27	1.05	62	0	0	0	0	33-37	67.1	46	20	17	8	25-0	79	.190
2003—New York (N.L.)	3	3	.500	3.10	1.32	45	0	0	0	0	21-28	49.1	41	18	17	5	24-1	50	.223
—New York (A.L.)	1	1	.500	1.93	1.50	9	0	0	0	0	0-0	9.1	8	4	2	0	6-1	10	.235
—Seattle (A.L.)	0	0		3.14	1.47	15	0	0	0	1	0-1	14.1	10	5	5	1	11-1	15	.189
American League totals (6 years)	12	17	.414	3.53	1.32	231	0	0	0	35	37-47	237.1	167	100	93	28	146-11	308	.198
National League totals (5 years)	18	14	.563	2.70	1.13	333	0	0	0	17	160-185	347.0	225	111	104	39	168-13	456	.182
Major League totals (10 years)	30	31	.492	3.03	1.21	564	0	0	0	52	197-232	584.1	392	211	197	67	314-24	764	.188

BENNETT, GARY — C

PERSONAL: Born April 17, 1972, in Waukegan, Ill. ... 6-0/208. ... Bats right, throws right. ... Full name: Gary David Bennett. ... High school: Waukegan East (Ill.).

TRANSACTIONS/CAREER NOTES: Selected by Philadelphia Phillies organization in 11th round of free-agent draft (June 4, 1990). ... On Clearwater disabled list (September 5-15, 1993). ... Granted free agency (October 8, 1996). ... Signed by Boston Red Sox organization (February 10, 1997). ... Granted free agency (October 15, 1997). ... Signed by Phillies organization (December 27, 1997). ... On Scranton/Wilkes-Barre disabled list (June 23-July 4, 2000). ... Traded by Phillies to New York Mets for C Todd Pratt (July 23, 2001). ... Traded by Mets to Colorado Rockies for a player to be named later (August 24, 2001); Mets acquired OF Ender Chavez to complete deal (December 27, 2001).

... Granted free agency (December 21, 2002). ... Signed by San Diego Padres (December 23, 2002). ... Placed on 15-day disabled list (April 17, 2003). ... Reinstated from the 15-day disabled list (May 23, 2003). ... Sent outright to Portland by San Diego (September 29, 2003).

2003 GAMES PLAYED BY POSITION (MLB): C—91.

Year	Team (League)	Pos.	G	AB	R	H	2B	3B	HR	RBI	BB	SO	HBP	GDP	SB-CS	Avg.	OBP	SLG	OPS	E	Pct.
1990—	Martinsville (App.)	C	16	52	3	14	2	1	0	10	4	15	0	0	0-1	.269	.316	.346	.662	3	.965
1991—	Martinsville (App.)	C	41	136	15	32	7	0	1	16	17	26	5	5	0-1	.235	.340	.309	.648	2	.994
1992—	Batavia (NY-Penn)	C	47	146	22	30	2	0	0	12	15	27	2	2	2-1	.205	.288	.219	.508	2	.994
1993—	Spartanburg (SAL)	C	42	126	18	32	4	1	0	15	12	22	1	2	0-2	.254	.321	.302	.623	2	.992
—Clearwater (FSL)		C	17	55	5	18	0	1	0	6	3	10	1	0	0-1	.327	.373	.382	.755	0	1.000
1994—	Clearwater (FSL)	C	19	55	6	13	3	0	0	10	8	6	0	1	0-0	.236	.328	.291	.619	1	.991
—Reading (East.)		C	63	208	13	48	9	0	3	22	14	26	0	6	0-1	.231	.276	.317	.593	2	.995
1995—	Reading (East.)	C-DH	86	271	27	64	11	0	4	40	22	36	3	12	0-0	.236	.299	.321	.620	4	.994
—Scran./W.B. (I.L.)		C	7	20	1	3	0	0	0	1	2	2	0	0	0-0	.150	.227	.150	.377	0	1.000
—Philadelphia (N.L.)			1	1	0	0	0	0	0	0	0	1	0	0	0-0	.000	.000	.000	.000	...	...
1996—	Scran./W.B. (I.L.)	C	91	286	37	71	15	1	8	37	24	43	3	10	1-0	.248	.310	.392	.702	7	.988
—Philadelphia (N.L.)		C	6	16	0	4	0	0	0	1	2	6	0	0	0-0	.250	.333	.250	.583	0	1.000
1997—	Pawtucket (Int'l)	C-1B	71	224	16	48	7	1	4	22	18	39	2	10	1-1	.214	.278	.308	.586	8	.986
1998—	Scran./W.B. (I.L.)	C-DH-1B	86	282	33	72	18	0	10	40	25	41	2	6	0-0	.255	.316	.426	.742	1	.998
—Philadelphia (N.L.)		C	9	31	4	9	0	0	0	3	5	5	0	1	0-0	.290	.378	.290	.669	0	1.000
1999—	Philadelphia (N.L.)	C	36	88	7	24	4	0	1	21	4	11	0	7	0-0	.273	.298	.352	.650	4	.971
2000—	Scran./W.B. (I.L.)	C	92	317	47	97	24	0	12	52	40	44	7	9	1-0	.306	.393	.495	.889	2	.996
—Philadelphia (N.L.)		C	31	74	8	18	5	0	2	5	13	15	2	0	0-0	.243	.371	.392	.763	1	.995
2001—	Philadelphia (N.L.)	C	26	75	8	16	3	1	1	6	9	19	0	1	0-0	.213	.294	.320	.614	2	.987
—New York (N.L.)			1	1	0	1	0	0	0	0	0	0	0	0	0-0	1.000	1.000	1.000	2.000	...	...
—Norfolk (Int'l)		C-3B	20	67	7	20	5	0	2	14	4	12	1	0	0-0	.299	.342	.463	.805	0	1.000
—Colorado (N.L.)		C	19	55	7	15	3	0	1	4	3	5	1	0	0-0	.273	.317	.382	.698	0	1.000
2002—	Colorado (N.L.)	C	90	291	26	77	10	2	4	26	15	45	6	10	1-3	.265	.314	.354	.668	1	.992
2003—	San Diego (N.L.)	C	96	307	26	73	15	0	2	42	24	48	2	8	3-0	.238	.296	.306	.602	2	.996
Major League totals (8 years)			315	939	86	237	40	3	11	108	75	155	11	27	4-3	.252	.313	.337	.650	13	.992

BENOIT, JOAQUIN — P

PERSONAL: Born July 26, 1977, in Santiago, Dominican Republic. ... 6-3/205. ... Throws right, bats right. ... Full name: Joaquin Antonio Benoit. ... Name pronounced: ben-WUH.

TRANSACTIONS/CAREER NOTES: Signed as non-drafted free agent by Texas Rangers organization (May 20, 1996). ... On disabled list (May 2-June 21, 2000). ... Recalled by Texas from Oklahoma (May 2, 2003). ... Placed on 15-day disabled list by Texas (June 1, 2003). ... Sent on rehab assignment to Oklahoma by Texas (June 17, 2003). ... Recalled from Texas rehab assignment; reinstated from 15-day disabled list (June 22, 2003).

CAREER HITTING: 0-for-2 (.000), 0 R, 0 2B, 0 3B, 0 HR, 0 RBI.

Year	League	W	L	Pct.	ERA	WHIP	G	GS	CG	ShO	Hld.	Sv.-Opp.	IP	H	R	ER	HR	BB-IBB	SO	Avg.
1996—	Dom. Rangers (DSL)	6	5	.545	2.28	1.15	14	13	2	1	...	0-...	75.0	63	26	19	0	23-...	63	...
1997—	GC Rangers (GCL)	3	3	.500	2.05	1.16	10	10	1	0	...	0-...	44.0	40	14	10	0	11-0	38	.244
1998—	Savannah (S. Atl.)	4	3	.571	3.83	1.21	15	1	0	0	...	0-...	80.0	79	41	34	8	18-0	68	.252
1999—	Charlotte (Fla. St.)	7	4	.636	5.31	1.59	22	22	0	0	...	0-...	105.0	117	67	62	5	50-0	83	.283
2000—	Tulsa (Texas)	4	4	.500	3.83	1.25	16	16	0	0	...	0-...	82.1	73	40	35	6	30-0	72	.237
2001—	Tulsa (Texas)	1	0	1.000	3.32	1.34	4	4	0	0	...	0-...	21.2	23	8	8	1	6-0	23	.264
—Oklahoma (PCL)		9	5	.643	4.19	1.42	24	24	1	1	...	0-...	131.0	113	63	61	14	73-0	142	.234
—Texas (A.L.)		0	0	...	10.80	2.20	1	1	0	0	0	0-0	5.0	8	6	6	3	3-0	4	.364
2002—	Oklahoma (PCL)	8	4	.667	3.56	1.13	16	16	0	0	...	0-...	98.2	74	42	39	8	37-0	103	.204
—Texas (A.L.)		4	5	.444	5.31	1.76	17	13	0	0	1-1		84.2	91	51	50	6	58-2	59	.272
—Charlotte (Fla. St.)		0	0	...	0.00	0.80	1	1	0	0	...	0-...	5.0	1	0	0	0	3-0	8	.059
2003—	Oklahoma (PCL)	2	1	.667	3.82	1.18	6	6	0	0	...	0-...	33.0	28	17	14	3	11-0	31	.231
—Texas (A.L.)		8	5	.615	5.49	1.43	25	17	0	0	0	0-0	105.0	99	67	64	23	51-0	87	.246
Major League totals (3 years)		12	10	.545	5.55	1.59	43	31	0	0	0	1-1	194.2	198	124	120	32	112-2	150	.261

BENSON, KRIS — P

PERSONAL: Born November 7, 1974, in Superior, Wis. ... 6-4/195. ... Throws right, bats right. ... Full name: Kristin James Benson. ... High school: Spayberry (Marietta, Ga.). ... College: Clemson.

TRANSACTIONS/CAREER NOTES: Selected by Pittsburgh Pirates organization in first round (first pick overall) of free-agent draft (June 2, 1996). ... On disabled list (March 31, 2001-entire season). ... On Pittsburgh disabled list (March 22-May 13, 2002); included rehabilitation assignments to Nashville (April 4-19 and April 27-May 7) and Altoona (May 8-13). ... Placed on 15-day disabled list (July 28, 2003). ... Transferred to Emergency disabled list (August 8, 2003).

CAREER HITTING: 23-for-200 (.115), 15 R, 6 2B, 0 3B, 0 HR, 9 RBI.

Year	League	W	L	Pct.	ERA	WHIP	G	GS	CG	ShO	Hld.	Sv.-Opp.	IP	H	R	ER	HR	BB-IBB	SO	Avg.
1997—	Lynchburg (Carolina)	5	2	.714	2.58	1.04	10	10	0	0	...	0-...	59.1	49	20	17	1	13-0	72	.221
—Carolina (Sou.)		3	5	.375	4.98	1.65	14	14	0	0	...	0-...	68.2	81	49	38	11	32-1	66	.289
1998—	Nashville (PCL)	8	10	.444	5.37	1.36	28	28	1	1	...	0-...	156.0	162	102	93	26	50-5	129	.260
1999—	Pittsburgh (N.L.)	11	14	.440	4.07	1.36	31	31	2	0	0	0-0	196.2	184	105	89	16	83-5	139	.249
2000—	Pittsburgh (N.L.)	10	12	.455	3.85	1.34	32	32	2	1	0	0-0	217.2	206	104	93	24	86-5	184	.249
2001—	Pittsburgh (N.L.)										Did not play.									
2002—	Nashville (PCL)	0	2	.000	1.53	0.91	4	4	0	0	...	0-...	17.2	8	4	3	1	8-0	25	.133
—Altoona (East.)		1	0	1.000	1.29	0.71	1	1	0	0	...	0-...	7.0	5	1	1	1	0-0	7	.208
—Pittsburgh (N.L.)		9	6	.600	4.70	1.55	25	25	0	0	0	0-0	130.1	152	76	68	18	50-8	79	.295
2003—	Pittsburgh (N.L.)	5	9	.357	4.97	1.55	18	18	0	0	0	0-0	105.0	127	67	58	14	36-4	68	.295
Major League totals (4 years)		35	41	.461	4.27	1.42	106	106	4	1	0	0-0	649.2	669	352	308	72	255-22	470	.266

BERE, JASON — P

PERSONAL: Born May 26, 1971, in Cambridge, Mass. ... 6-3/225. ... Throws right, bats right. ... Full name: Jason Phillip Bere. ... Name pronounced: bur-A. ... High school: Wilmington (Mass.). ... Junior college: Middlesex (Mass.) Community College.

TRANSACTIONS/CAREER NOTES: Selected by Chicago White Sox organization in 36th round of free-agent draft (June 4, 1990). ... On Chicago disabled list (August 5-20, 1995); included rehabilitation assignment to South Bend (August 13-18). ... On Chicago disabled list (April 22-September 3 and September 14, 1996-remainder of season); included rehabilitation assignments to Nashville (May 14-19 and August 27-28), Gulf Coast White Sox (August 5-10), Hickory (August 10-16) and Birmingham (August 16-

B

27). ... On Chicago disabled list (March 31-August 19, 1997); included rehabilitation assignments to Gulf Coast White Sox (July 2-7), Hickory (July 12), Birmingham (July 17-22) and Nashville (July 29-August 14). ... Released by White Sox (July 16, 1998). ... Signed by Cincinnati Reds organization (July 21, 1998). ... On Cincinnati disabled list (June 16-August 4, 1999); included rehabilitation assignment to Indianapolis (July 11-August 4). ... Released by Reds (August 4, 1999). ... Signed by Milwaukee Brewers organization (August 12, 1999). ... Granted free agency (November 1, 1999). ... Re-signed by Brewers (November 19, 1999). ... Traded by Brewers with P Bob Wickman and P Steve Woodard to Cleveland Indians for 1B/OF Richie Sexson, P Paul Rigdon, P Kane Davis and a player to be named later (July 28, 2000); Brewers acquired 2B Marcos Scutaro to complete deal (August 30, 2000). ... Granted free agency (October 31, 2000). ... Signed by Chicago Cubs (December 18, 2000). ... On Chicago disabled list (June 27-August 31 and September 6, 2002-remainder of season); included rehabilitation assignment to Iowa (August 25-26). ... Granted free agency (October 28, 2002). ... Signed by Indians (December 19, 2002). ... On disabled list (March 27-April 30, 2003). ... Sent on rehab assignment to Buffalo by Cleveland (May 1, 2003). ... Placed on the 15-day disabled list by Cleveland (May 28, 2003). ... Reinstated from the 15-day disabled list (May 22, 2003). ... Transferred to Emergency disabled list (May 30, 2003).

CAREER HITTING: 30-for-161 (.186), 9 R, 6 2B, 1 3B, 0 HR, 5 RBI.

Year League	W	L	Pct.	ERA	WHIP	G	GS	CG	ShO	Hld.	Sv.-Opp.	IP	H	R	ER	HR	BB-IBB	SO	Avg.
1990— GC White Sox (GCL)	0	4	.000	2.37	1.18	16	2	0	0	...	1-...	38.0	26	19	10	1	19-0	41	.187
1991— South Bend (Mid.)	9	12	.429	2.87	1.33	27	27	2	1	...	0-...	163.0	116	66	52	8	* 100-0	158	.204
1992— Sarasota (Fla. St.)	7	2	.778	2.41	1.02	18	18	1	1	...	0-...	116.0	84	35	31	3	34-3	106	* .202
—Birmingham (Sou.)	4	4	.500	3.00	1.19	8	8	4	2	...	0-...	54.0	44	22	18	1	20-1	45	.229
—Vancouver (PCL)	0	0	...	0.00	2.00	1	1	0	0	...	0-...	1.0	2	0	0	0	0-0	2	.400
1993— Nashville (A.A.)	5	1	.833	2.37	1.24	8	8	0	0	...	0-...	49.1	36	19	13	1	25-1	52	.206
—Chicago (A.L.)	12	5	.706	3.47	1.33	24	24	1	0	0	0-0	142.2	109	60	55	12	81-0	129	.210
1994— Chicago (A.L.)	12	2	*.857	3.81	1.40	24	24	0	0	0	0-0	141.1	119	65	60	17	80-0	127	.229
1995— Chicago (A.L.)	8	• 15	.348	7.19	1.87	27	27	1	0	0	0-0	137.2	151	120	110	21	106-6	110	.273
—Nashville (A.A.)	1	0	1.000	3.38	1.50	1	1	0	0	...	0-...	5.1	6	2	2	0	2-0	7	.273
1996— Chicago (A.L.)	0	1	.000	10.26	2.64	5	5	0	0	0	0-0	16.2	26	19	19	3	18-1	19	.356
—Nashville (A.A.)	0	0	...	1.42	1.03	3	3	0	0	...	0-...	12.2	9	2	2	1	4-0	15	.205
—GC White Sox (GCL)	0	1	.000	6.00	1.33	1	1	0	0	...	0-...	3.0	3	2	2	0	1-0	3	.231
—Hickory (S. Atl.)	1	0	1.000	0.00	0.60	1	1	0	0	...	0-...	5.0	3	0	0	0	0-0	5	.167
—Birmingham (Sou.)	0	0	...	4.15	1.85	1	1	0	0	...	0-...	4.1	4	2	2	2	4-0	5	.235
1997— GC White Sox (GCL)	0	0	...	0.00	0.40	2	2	0	0	...	0-...	5.0	2	0	0	0	0-0	5	.125
—Hickory (S. Atl.)	0	0	...	6.00	1.33	1	1	0	0	...	0-...	3.0	4	2	2	0	2-0	2	.308
—Birmingham (Sou.)	0	1	.000	7.71	1.43	2	2	0	0	...	0-...	7.0	8	7	6	2	2-0	7	.308
—Nashville (A.A.)	1	1	.500	5.59	1.55	4	4	0	0	...	0-...	19.1	23	13	12	2	7-0	13	.295
—Chicago (A.L.)	4	2	.667	4.71	1.29	6	6	0	0	0	0-0	28.2	20	15	15	4	17-0	21	.198
1998— Chicago (A.L.)	3	7	.300	6.45	1.86	18	15	0	0	0	0-0	83.2	98	71	60	14	58-0	53	.293
—Cincinnati (N.L.)	3	2	.600	4.12	1.35	9	7	0	0	0	0-0	43.2	39	20	20	3	20-0	31	.242
1999— Cincinnati (N.L.)	3	0	1.000	6.85	2.22	12	10	0	0	0	0-0	43.1	56	37	33	6	40-3	28	.326
—Indianapolis (Int'l)	0	2	.000	10.19	2.49	5	4	0	0	...	0-...	17.2	25	20	20	3	19-0	8	.338
—Louisville (Int'l)	2	1	.667	2.08	1.12	5	5	0	0	...	0-...	26.0	21	8	6	0	8-0	27	.233
—Milwaukee (N.L.)	2	0	1.000	4.63	1.41	5	4	0	0	0	0-0	23.1	23	15	12	3	10-0	19	.256
2000— Milwaukee (N.L.)	6	7	.462	4.93	1.55	20	20	0	0	0	0-0	115.0	115	66	63	19	63-7	98	.264
—Cleveland (A.L.)	6	3	.667	6.63	1.67	11	11	0	0	0	0-0	54.1	65	41	40	6	26-0	44	.297
2001— Chicago (N.L.)	11	11	.500	4.31	1.32	32	32	2	0	0	0-0	188.0	171	99	90	24	77-7	175	.241
2002— Chicago (N.L.)	1	10	.091	5.67	1.47	16	16	0	0	0	0-0	85.2	98	63	54	13	28-1	65	.290
—Iowa (PCL)	1	0	1.000	1.80	1.00	1	1	0	0	...	0-...	5.0	2	1	1	0	3-0	3	.118
2003— Lake County (S. Atl.)	0	0	...	6.75	1.75	1	1	0	0	...	0-...	4.0	7	3	3	1	0-0	1	.389
—Buffalo (Int'l)	1	0	1.000	0.61	0.82	3	3	0	0	...	0-...	14.2	9	1	1	0	3-1	17	.180
—Cleveland (A.L.)	0	0	...	4.05	1.05	2	2	0	0	0	0-0	6.2	5	3	3	0	2-0	1	.208
American League totals (8 years)	45	35	.563	5.32	1.60	117	114	2	0	0	0-0	612.0	593	394	362	77	388-7	504	.254
National League totals (5 years)	26	30	.464	4.91	1.48	94	89	2	0	0	0-0	499.0	502	300	272	68	238-18	416	.263
Major League totals (11 years)	71	65	.522	5.14	1.55	211	203	4	0	0	0-0	1111.0	1095	694	634	145	626-25	920	.258

BERG, DAVE   IF

PERSONAL: Born September 3, 1970, in Roseville, Calif. ... 5-11/185. ... Bats right, throws right. ... Full name: David Scott Berg. ... High school: Roseville (Calif.). ... College: Miami (Fla.).

TRANSACTIONS/CAREER NOTES: Selected by California Angels organization in 32nd round of free-agent draft (June 4, 1990); did not sign. ... Selected by Florida Marlins organization in 38th round of free-agent draft (June 3, 1993). ... On Florida disabled list (April 2-25, 2000); included rehabilitation assignment to Brevard County (April 22-25). ... Granted free agency (December 21, 2001). ... Signed by Toronto Blue Jays organization (January 12, 2002). ... Placed on 15-day disabled list (June 28, 2003). ... Sent to Syracuse on rehab assignment by Toronto (July 23, 2003). ... Activated from the 15-day disabled list (July 28, 2003).

2003 GAMES PLAYED BY POSITION (MLB): 2B—24, 3B—17, DH—7, OF—6, 1B—2, SS—1.

Year Team (League)	Pos.	G	AB	R	H	2B	3B	HR	RBI	BB	SO	HBP	GDP	SB-CS	Avg.	OBP	SLG	OPS	E	Pct.
1993— Elmira (N.Y.-Penn)	2B-3B-OF	75	281	37	74	13	1	4	28	34	37	8	8	7-4	.263	.356	.359	.715	20	.925
1994— Kane Co. (Midw.)	2B-3B	121	437	80	117	27	8	9	53	54	80	8	10	8-6	.268	.354	.428	.782	17	.948
1995— Brevard County (FSL)	2B-3B-SS	114	382	71	114	18	1	3	39	68	61	8	5	9-4	.298	.407	.374	.781	26	.951
1996— Portland (East.)	3B-SS	109	414	64	125	28	5	9	73	42	60	5	10	17-7	.302	.368	.459	.827	26	.951
1997— Charlotte (Int'l)	2B-3B-SS	117	424	76	125	26	6	9	47	55	71	3	13	16-7	.295	.377	.448	.825	22	.954
1998— Florida (N.L.)	2B-3B-SS	81	182	18	57	11	0	2	21	26	46	0	1	3-0	.313	.393	.407	.800	7	.969
1999— Florida (N.L.)	SS-2-3-OF	109	304	42	87	18	1	3	25	27	59	2	7	2-2	.286	.348	.382	.730	8	.974
2000— Brevard County (FSL)	2B-3B-SS	3	11	2	3	0	0	0	2	1	3	1	1	0-1	.273	.385	.273	.657	0	1.000
—Florida (N.L.)	SS-3B-2B	82	210	23	53	14	1	1	21	25	46	5	5	3-0	.252	.340	.343	.683	6	.964
2001— Florida (N.L.)	2B-3B-SS	82	215	26	52	12	1	4	16	14	39	2	3	0-1	.242	.292	.363	.655	8	.961
2002— Toronto (A.L.)	2-3-S-0-1-D	109	374	42	101	26	2	4	39	26	57	5	6	0-2	.270	.322	.382	.704	10	.974
2003— Syracuse (Int'l)	2B-3B-DH	6	20	3	5	1	0	0	0	1	2	1	0	0-0	.250	.318	.300	.618	0	1.000
—Toronto (A.L.)	2-3-D-0-1-S	61	161	26	41	6	1	4	18	11	34	0	7	0-1	.255	.301	.379	.679	5	.966
American League totals (2 years)		170	535	68	142	32	3	8	57	37	91	5	13	0-3	.265	.316	.381	.697	15	.972
National League totals (4 years)		354	911	109	249	55	3	10	83	92	190	9	16	8-3	.273	.343	.373	.716	31	.968
Major League totals (6 years)		524	1446	177	391	87	6	18	140	129	281	14	29	8-6	.270	.333	.376	.709	46	.969

BERGER, BRANDON   OF

PERSONAL: Born February 21, 1975, in Covington, Ky. ... 5-11/205. ... Bats right, throws right. ... Full name: Brandon Charles Berger. ... High school: Beechwood (Fort Mitchell, Ky.). ... College: Eastern Kentucky.

TRANSACTIONS/CAREER NOTES: Selected by Kansas City Royals organization in 14th round of free-agent draft (June 4, 1996). ... Optioned to Omaha by Kansas City Royals (May 6, 2003). ... Recalled by Kansas City from Omaha (September 29, 2003).

2003 GAMES PLAYED BY POSITION (MLB): OF—11, DH—1.

Year— Team (League)	Pos.	G	AB	R	H	2B	3B	HR	RBI	BB	SO	HBP	GDP	SB-CS	Avg.	OBP	SLG	OPS	E	Pct.
1996— Spokane (N'west)	OF	71	283	46	87	12	1	13	58	31	64	2	7	17-5	.307	.376	.495	.871	4	.967
1997— Lansing (Midw.)	OF	107	393	64	115	22	6	12	73	42	79	7	8	13-1	.293	.368	.471	.838	3	.979
1998— Wilmington (Caro.)	P-OF	110	338	53	75	18	3	8	50	53	94	5	11	13-3	.222	.332	.364	.696	2	.983
1999— Wilmington (Caro.)	OF	119	450	73	132	27	4	16	73	45	93	8	3	29-7	.293	.363	.478	.841	5	.964
2000— Wichita (Texas)	OF	27	86	9	14	2	0	3	8	7	27	2	2	6-1	.163	.240	.291	.530	0	1.000
— Wilmington (Caro.)	OF	102	379	63	108	18	4	15	71	40	71	17	8	12-4	.285	.376	.472	.848	3	.983
2001— Wichita (Texas)	OF	120	454	98	140	28	3	* 40	118	43	91	14	9	14-6	.308	.383	.648	1.031	4	.971
— Kansas City (A.L.)	OF-DH	16	16	4	5	1	1	2	2	2	2	0	0	0-0	.313	.389	.875	1.264	0	1.000
2002— Omaha (PCL)	OF-1B	68	261	34	76	16	1	13	47	25	43	5	4	11-2	.291	.363	.510	.873	3	.975
— Kansas City (A.L.) OF-DH-1B		51	134	16	27	5	1	6	17	8	32	2	2	1-0	.201	.255	.388	.643	0	1.000
2003— Kansas City (A.L.)	OF-DH-1B	13	32	3	7	0	0	0	3	5	4	0	0	0-0	.219	.324	.219	.543	0	1.000
— Omaha (PCL)	OF-DH-1B	62	226	43	61	16	3	12	53	31	58	6	5	6-1	.270	.367	.527	.894	4	.966
Major League totals (3 years)		70	182	23	39	6	2	8	22	15	38	2	2	1-0	.214	.280	.401	.681	0	1.000

BERKMAN, LANCE   OF

PERSONAL: Born February 10, 1976, in Waco, Texas. ... 6-1/220. ... Bats both, throws left. ... Full name: William Lance Berkman. ... High school: Canyon (New Braunfels, Texas). ... College: Rice.

TRANSACTIONS/CAREER NOTES: Selected by Houston Astros organization in first round (16th pick overall) of free-agent draft (June 3, 1997). ... On New Orleans disabled list (April 13-May 14, 1999).

2003 GAMES PLAYED BY POSITION (MLB): OF—153.

Year— Team (League)	Pos.	G	AB	R	H	2B	3B	HR	RBI	BB	SO	HBP	GDP	SB-CS	Avg.	OBP	SLG	OPS	E	Pct.
1997— Kissimmee (Fla. St.)	OF-DH	53	184	31	54	10	0	12	35	37	38	2	2	2-1	.293	.417	.543	.961	0	1.000
1998— Jackson (Texas)	OF-DH	122	425	82	130	34	0	24	89	85	82	4	12	6-4	.306	.424	.555	.979	4	.980
— New Orleans (PCL)	OF	17	59	14	16	4	0	6	13	12	16	2	1	0-0	.271	.411	.644	1.055	0	1.000
1999— New Orleans (PCL)	OF-1B	64	226	42	73	20	0	8	49	39	47	0	10	7-1	.323	.419	.518	.937	4	.972
— Houston (N.L.)	OF-1B	34	93	10	22	2	0	4	15	12	21	0	2	5-1	.237	.321	.387	.708	2	.956
2000— New Orleans (PCL)	OF-1B	31	112	18	37	4	2	6	27	31	20	1	7	4-4	.330	.479	.563	1.042	2	.982
— Houston (N.L.)	OF-1B	114	353	76	105	28	1	21	67	56	73	1	6	6-2	.297	.388	.561	.949	6	.968
2001— Houston (N.L.)	OF	156	577	110	191	* 55	5	34	126	92	121	13	8	7-9	.331	.430	.620	1.051	6	.981
2002— Houston (N.L.)	OF	158	578	106	169	35	2	42	* 128	107	118	4	10	8-4	.292	.405	.578	.982	7	.977
2003— Houston (N.L.)	OF	153	538	110	155	35	6	25	93	107	108	9	10	5-3	.288	.412	.515	.927	3	.989
Major League totals (5 years)		615	2139	412	642	155	14	126	429	374	441	27	36	31-19	.300	.407	.562	.970	24	.979

BERNERO, ADAM   P

PERSONAL: Born November 28, 1976, in Los Gatos, Calif. ... 6-4/210. ... Throws right, bats right. ... Full name: Adam Gino Bernero. ... Name pronounced: bur-NAIR-o. ... High school: John F. Kennedy (Sacramento, Calif.). ... College: Armstrong Atlantic State (Ga.).

TRANSACTIONS/CAREER NOTES: Signed as non-drafted free agent by Detroit Tigers organization (May 21, 1999). ... On Jacksonville disabled list (April 10-28, 2000). ... On Toledo disabled list (June 18-July 4, 2001). ... Traded by Detroit to Colorado Rockies for C Ben Petrick (July 13, 2003). ... Contract purchased by Colorado from Colorado Springs (July 17, 2003).

CAREER HITTING: 0-for-10 (.000), 1 R, 0 2B, 0 3B, 0 HR, 0 RBI.

Year— League	W	L	Pct.	ERA	WHIP	G	GS	CG	ShO	Hld.	Sv.-Opp.	IP	H	R	ER	HR	BB-IBB	SO	Avg.
1999— West. Mich. (Mid.)	8	4	.667	2.54	1.02	15	15	2	1	...	0-...	95.2	75	36	27	8	23-0	80	.210
2000— Jacksonville (Sou.)	2	5	.286	2.79	1.27	10	10	0	0	...	0-...	61.1	54	26	19	6	24-0	46	.237
— Toledo (Int'l)	3	1	.750	2.47	0.93	7	7	1	1	...	0-...	47.1	34	16	13	5	10-0	37	.201
— Detroit (A.L.)	0	1	.000	4.19	1.34	12	4	0	0	1	0-0	34.1	33	18	16	3	13-1	20	.270
2001— Toledo (Int'l)	6	11	.353	5.13	1.61	26	25	1	0	...	0-...	140.1	172	90	80	13	54-0	99	.303
— Detroit (A.L.)	0	0	...	7.30	1.38	5	0	0	0	0	0-0	12.1	13	13	10	4	4-0	8	.260
2002— Toledo (Int'l)	2	2	.500	1.58	1.04	9	9	2	1	...	0-...	57.0	46	13	10	2	13-0	49	.223
— Detroit (A.L.)	4	7	.364	6.20	1.56	28	11	0	0	0	0-0	101.2	128	74	70	17	31-1	69	.309
2003— Toledo (Int'l)	1	12	.077	6.08	1.44	18	17	0	0	0	0-0	100.2	104	68	68	14	41-0	54	.267
— Colorado (N.L.)	0	2	.000	5.23	1.41	31	0	0	0	5	0-2	32.2	33	22	19	5	13-1	26	.266
American League totals (4 years)	5	20	.200	5.93	1.47	63	32	0	0	1	0-0	249.0	278	173	164	38	89-2	151	.285
National League totals (1 year)	0	2	.000	5.23	1.41	31	0	0	0	5	0-2	32.2	33	22	19	5	13-1	26	.266
Major League totals (4 years)	5	22	.185	5.85	1.47	94	32	0	0	6	0-2	281.2	311	195	183	43	102-3	177	.283

BERROA, ANGEL   SS

PERSONAL: Born January 27, 1978, in Santo Domingo, Dominican Republic. ... 6-0/175. ... Bats right, throws right. ... Full name: Angel Maria Berroa.

TRANSACTIONS/CAREER NOTES: Signed as non-drafted free agent by Oakland Athletics organization (August 14, 1997). ... Traded by Athletics with C A.J. Hinch and cash to Kansas City Royals as part of three-way deal in which Kansas City Royals received P Roberto Hernandez from Tampa Devil Rays, A's received P Cory Lidle from Devil Rays and OF Johnny Damon, IF Mark Ellis and player to be named from Royals and Devil Rays received OF Ben Grieve and a player to be named or cash from A's (January 8, 2001). ... On Omaha disabled list (April 15-June 9, 2002).

2003 GAMES PLAYED BY POSITION (MLB): SS—158.

Year— Team (League)	Pos.	G	AB	R	H	2B	3B	HR	RBI	BB	SO	HBP	GDP	SB-CS	Avg.	OBP	SLG	OPS	E	Pct.
1998— Dom. Athletics (DSL)		58	196	51	48	7	4	8	37	25	37	...	...	4-...	.245	...	.444	...	...	...
1999— Ariz. A's (Ariz.) 2B-3B-SS-OF		46	169	42	49	11	4	2	24	16	26	7	1	11-4	.290	.371	.438	.809	18	.925
— Midland (Texas)	SS	4	17	3	1	1	0	0	0	0	2	0	0	0-0	.059	.059	.118	.176	2	.889
2000— Visalia (Calif.)	SS	129	429	61	119	25	6	10	63	30	70	10	10	11-9	.277	.337	.434	.770	* 54	.909
2001— Wilmington (Caro.)	SS	51	199	43	63	18	4	6	25	9	41	14	7	10-6	.317	.382	.538	.920	17	.933
— Wichita (Texas)	SS	80	304	63	90	20	4	8	42	17	55	22	6	15-6	.296	.373	.467	.840	13	.965
— Kansas City (A.L.)	SS	15	53	8	16	2	0	0	4	3	10	0	2	2-0	.302	.339	.340	.679	3	.953
2002— Omaha (PCL)	SS	77	297	37	64	11	4	8	35	15	84	11	5	6-4	.215	.277	.360	.637	16	.950
— Kansas City (A.L.)	SS	20	75	8	17	7	1	0	5	7	10	1	1	3-0	.227	.301	.347	.648	4	.964
2003— Kansas City (A.L.)	SS	158	567	92	163	28	7	17	73	29	100	18	13	21-5	.287	.338	.451	.789	24	.968
Major League totals (3 years)		193	695	108	196	37	8	17	82	39	120	19	16	26-5	.282	.334	.432	.765	31	.967

BETANCOURT, RAFAEL　　　　　　　　　　P

PERSONAL: Born April 29, 1975, in Cumana, Venezuela. ... 6-2/176. ... Throws right, bats right. ... Full name: Rafael Jose Betancourt. ... High school: A.J.S. (Cumana, Venezuela). ... College: Isaac Newton College (VZ).

TRANSACTIONS/CAREER NOTES: Signed as non-drafted free agent by Boston Red Sox organization (September 13, 1993). ... On Trenton disabled list (May 5-June 29 and August 27-September 3, 1998). ... On Sarasota disabled list (April 8-23, 1999). ... Released by Red Sox (November 18, 1999). ... Signed by Boston Red Sox organization (December 13, 2000). ... On disabled list (May 18, 2001-remainder of season). ... Granted free agency (October 15, 2001). ... Signed by Milwaukee Brewers organization (February 6, 2003). ... Contract purchased by Cleveland from Buffalo of the International League (July 12, 2003).

CAREER HITTING: 0-for-0 (.000), 0 R, 0 2B, 0 3B, 0 HR, 0 RBI.

Year League	W	L	Pct.	ERA	WHIP	G	GS	CG	ShO	Hld.	Sv.-Opp.	IP	H	R	ER	HR	BB-IBB	SO	Avg.
1997— Michigan (Midw.)	0	3	.000	1.95	0.87	27	0	0	0	...	11-...	32.1	26	9	7	2	2-0	52	.213
1998— GC Red Sox (GCL)	0	2	.000	7.20	1.40	4	3	0	0	...	0-...	5.0	6	5	4	1	1-0	4	.300
— Sarasota (Fla. St.)	3	1	.750	3.54	1.00	20	0	0	0	...	2-...	28.0	22	12	11	2	6-0	33	.212
— Trenton (East.)	0	0	...	6.75	1.29	7	0	0	0	...	0-...	9.1	9	7	7	0	3-0	9	.237
1999— Sarasota (Fla. St.)	0	0	...	0.00	0.86	6	0	0	0	...	4-...	7.0	5	0	0	0	1-0	6	.208
— Trenton (East.)	6	2	.750	3.62	1.10	39	0	0	0	...	13-...	54.2	50	24	22	7	10-0	57	.248
2001— Trenton (East.)	0	1	.000	5.63	1.29	16	0	0	0	...	4-...	24.0	28	16	15	0	3-0	27	.295
2003— Akron (East.)	0	0	...	1.39	1.01	31	0	0	0	...	16-...	45.1	33	10	7	0	13-2	75	.195
— Buffalo (Int'l)	0	0	...	4.05	1.20	4	0	0	0	...	1-...	6.2	6	3	3	1	2-0	6	.240
— Cleveland (A.L.)	2	2	.500	2.13	1.05	33	0	0	0	4	1-3	38.0	27	11	9	5	13-2	36	.196
Major League totals (1 year)	**2**	**2**	**.500**	**2.13**	**1.05**	**33**	**0**	**0**	**0**	**4**	**1-3**	**38.0**	**27**	**11**	**9**	**5**	**13-2**	**36**	**.196**

BIDDLE, ROCKY　　　　　　　　　　P

PERSONAL: Born May 21, 1976, in Las Vegas, Nev. ... 6-3/230. ... Throws right, bats right. ... Full name: Lee Francis Biddle. ... High school: Temple City (Calif.). ... College: Long Beach State.

TRANSACTIONS/CAREER NOTES: Selected by Chicago White Sox organization in supplemental round ("sandwich" pick between first and second round, 51st pick overall) of free-agent draft (June 3, 1997); pick received as compensation for failure to sign 1996 first-round pick P Bobby Seay. ... On disabled list (April 9, 1999-entire season). ... On disabled list (September 21, 2001-remainder of season); included rehabilitation assignment to Charlotte (April 25-May 3). ... Traded by White Sox with P Orlando Hernandez, 3B/OF Jeff Liefer and cash to Montreal Expos for P Bartolo Colon and 2B/SS Jorge Nunez (January 15, 2003).

CAREER HITTING: 0-for-2 (.000), 0 R, 0 2B, 0 3B, 0 HR, 0 RBI.

Year League	W	L	Pct.	ERA	WHIP	G	GS	CG	ShO	Hld.	Sv.-Opp.	IP	H	R	ER	HR	BB-IBB	SO	Avg.
1997— Hickory (S. Atl.)	0	1	.000	4.64	1.50	13	0	0	0	...	1-...	21.1	22	18	11	2	10-0	25	.265
1998— Winston-Salem (Caro.)	4	5	.444	4.57	1.66	16	16	0	0	...	0-...	82.2	92	55	42	7	45-0	72	.280
— Ariz. White Sox (Ariz.)	1	0	1.000	3.94	1.44	5	2	0	0	...	0-...	16.0	15	9	7	2	8-0	18	.242
1999— Winston-Salem (Caro.)										Did not play.									
2000— Birmingham (Sou.)	11	6	.647	3.08	1.31	23	23	2	2	...	0-...	146.1	138	63	50	10	54-0	118	.250
— Chicago (A.L.)	1	2	.333	8.34	1.72	4	4	0	0	0	0-0	22.2	31	25	21	5	8-0	7	.326
2001— Chicago (A.L.)	7	8	.467	5.39	1.47	30	21	0	0	1	0-3	128.2	137	87	77	16	52-3	85	.272
2002— Charlotte (Int'l)	0	0	...	1.29	0.71	2	2	0	0	...	0-...	7.0	4	1	1	0	1-0	9	.160
— Chicago (A.L.)	3	4	.429	4.06	1.43	44	7	0	0	4	1-3	77.2	72	42	35	13	39-4	64	.245
2003— Montreal (N.L.)	5	8	.385	4.65	1.55	73	0	0	0	4	34-41	71.2	71	43	37	10	40-5	54	.254
American League totals (3 years)	**11**	**14**	**.440**	**5.23**	**1.48**	**78**	**32**	**0**	**0**	**5**	**1-6**	**229.0**	**240**	**154**	**133**	**34**	**99-7**	**156**	**.269**
National League totals (1 year)	**5**	**8**	**.385**	**4.65**	**1.55**	**73**	**0**	**0**	**0**	**4**	**34-41**	**71.2**	**71**	**43**	**37**	**10**	**40-5**	**54**	**.254**
Major League totals (4 years)	**16**	**22**	**.421**	**5.09**	**1.50**	**151**	**32**	**0**	**0**	**9**	**35-47**	**300.2**	**311**	**197**	**170**	**44**	**139-12**	**210**	**.265**

BIERBRODT, NICK　　　　　　　　　　P

PERSONAL: Born May 16, 1978, in Tarzana, Calif. ... 6-5/214. ... Throws left, bats left. ... Full name: Nicholas Raymond Bierbrodt. ... Name pronounced: BEER-brot. ... High school: Millikan (Long Beach, Calif.).

TRANSACTIONS/CAREER NOTES: Selected by Arizona Diamondbacks organization in first round (30th pick overall) of free-agent draft (June 4, 1996). ... On Tucson disabled list (May 4-July 8 and July 23-28, 2000). ... On Arizona disabled list (March 23-April 19, 2001); included rehabilitation assignment to Tucson (May 1-19). ... Traded by Diamondbacks with OF Jason Conti to Tampa Bay Devil Rays for P Albie Lopez and C Mike Difelice (July 25, 2001). ... On disabled list (June 7, 2002-remainder of season). ... Placed on suspended list by BOC (May 2, 2003). ... Reinstated from suspended list by BOC (May 5, 2003). ... Sent outright to Buffalo of the Independent League (July 9, 2003). ... Designated for assignment by Cleveland (June 7, 2003). ... Claimed off waivers by Tampa Bay from Cleveland (June 11, 2003). ... Designated for assignment by Cleveland (July 6, 2003). ... Sent outright to Buffalo by Cleveland (July 9, 2003).

CAREER HITTING: 4-for-6 (.667), 3 R, 1 2B, 0 3B, 0 HR, 0 RBI.

Year League	W	L	Pct.	ERA	WHIP	G	GS	CG	ShO	Hld.	Sv.-Opp.	IP	H	R	ER	HR	BB-IBB	SO	Avg.
1996— Ariz. D'backs (Ariz.)	1	1	.500	1.66	1.00	8	8	0	0	...	0-...	38.0	25	9	7	1	13-0	46	.188
— Lethbridge (Pio.)	2	0	1.000	0.50	0.94	3	3	0	0	...	0-...	18.0	12	4	1	0	5-0	23	.185
1997— South Bend (Mid.)	2	4	.333	4.04	1.51	15	15	0	0	...	0-...	75.2	77	43	34	4	37-0	64	.266
1998— High Desert (Calif.)	8	7	.533	3.40	1.43	24	23	1	0	...	0-...	129.2	122	66	49	7	64-0	88	.254
1999— El Paso (Texas)	5	6	.455	4.62	1.51	14	14	2	•1	...	0-...	76.0	78	45	39	3	37-0	55	.266
— Tucson (PCL)	1	4	.200	7.27	2.01	11	11	0	0	...	0-...	43.1	57	42	35	9	30-0	43	.324
2000— Tucson (PCL)	2	1	.667	4.82	1.45	4	3	0	0	...	0-...	18.2	13	10	10	3	14-0	11	.203
— Ariz. D'backs (Ariz.)	0	0	...	4.50	1.13	4	3	0	0	...	0-...	8.0	4	4	4	0	5-0	10	.143
— El Paso (Texas)	1	3	.250	7.13	1.73	7	7	0	0	...	0-...	35.1	37	30	28	1	24-0	36	.272
2001— El Paso (Texas)	2	1	.667	1.37	0.97	4	4	0	0	...	0-...	19.2	13	3	3	1	6-0	18	.186
— Tucson (PCL)	4	1	.800	2.18	1.26	7	6	0	0	...	0-...	45.1	48	15	11	0	9-1	56	.281
— Arizona (N.L.)	2	2	.500	8.22	1.78	5	5	0	0	0	0-0	23.0	29	21	21	6	12-0	17	.305
— Tampa Bay (A.L.)	3	4	.429	4.55	1.60	11	11	0	0	0	0-0	61.1	71	38	31	11	27-1	56	.285
2002— Char., S.C. (SAL)	0	0	...	3.60	1.40	1	1	0	0	...	0-...	5.0	5	4	2	0	2-0	2	.238
2003— Tampa Bay (A.L.)	0	2	.000	9.68	2.32	13	5	0	0	0	0-0	35.1	59	41	38	9	23-3	20	.379
— Cleveland (A.L.)	0	0	...	6.75	1.13	5	0	0	0	0	0-0	8.0	5	6	6	0	4-0	9	.185
— Buffalo (Int'l)	2	2	.500	3.00	1.48	16	1	0	0	...	0-...	27.0	22	10	9	1	18-2	31	.222
American League totals (2 years)	**3**	**6**	**.333**	**6.45**	**1.81**	**29**	**16**	**0**	**0**	**0**	**0-0**	**104.2**	**135**	**85**	**75**	**20**	**54-4**	**85**	**.312**
National League totals (1 year)	**2**	**2**	**.500**	**8.22**	**1.78**	**5**	**5**	**0**	**0**	**0**	**0-0**	**23.0**	**29**	**21**	**21**	**6**	**12-0**	**17**	**.305**
Major League totals (2 years)	**5**	**8**	**.385**	**6.77**	**1.80**	**34**	**21**	**0**	**0**	**0**	**0-0**	**127.2**	**164**	**106**	**96**	**26**	**66-4**	**102**	**.311**

BIGBIE, LARRY　　　　　　　　　　OF

PERSONAL: Born November 4, 1977, in Hobart, Ind. ... 6-4/215. ... Bats left, throws left. ... Full name: Larry Robert Bigbie. ... High school: Hobart (Ind.). ... College: Ball State.

TRANSACTIONS/CAREER NOTES: Selected by Baltimore Orioles organization in first round (21st pick overall) of free-agent draft (June 2, 1999); pick received from Texas Rangers as part of compensation for Type A free agent 1B Rafael Palmeiro. ... On Frederick disabled list (April 22-29, 2000). ... On Bowie disabled list (July 28, 2000-remainder of season). ... On Rochester disabled list (July 5-25, 2002). ... Recalled from Ottawa by Baltimore (April 23, 2003). ... Placed on the 15-day disabled list (May 22, 2003). ... Sent on rehab assignment to Bowie by Baltimore (June 10, 2003). ... Recalled by Baltimore from Ottawa (June 15, 2003). ... Sent to Ottawa by Baltimore on rehab assignment (June 21, 2003). ... Recalled by Baltimore from Ottawa rehab assignment (June 22, 2003). ... Recalled from GCL rehab assignment by Baltimore (July 15, 2003). ... Recalled from Ottawa rehab assignment; reinstated from 15-day disabled list (July 27, 2003).

2003 GAMES PLAYED BY POSITION (MLB): OF—80.

										BATTING									FIELDING	
Year	Team (League)	Pos.	G	AB	R	H	2B	3B	HR	RBI	BB	SO	HBP	GDP	SB-CS	Avg.	OBP	SLG	OPS	E	Pct.
1999— Bluefield (Appal.)	OF	8	30	3	8	0	0	0	4	3	8	1	1	1-3	.267	.343	.267	.610	0	1.000
— Delmarva (S. Atl.)	OF	43	165	18	46	7	3	2	27	29	42	0	4	3-1	.279	.381	.394	.775	3	.950
2000— Frederick (Carolina)	OF	55	201	33	59	11	0	2	28	23	34	0	3	7-3	.294	.360	.378	.738	3	.975
— Bowie (East.)	OF	31	112	11	27	6	0	0	5	11	28	0	3	3-0	.241	.309	.295	.604	0	1.000
2001— Bowie (East.)	OF	71	262	41	77	13	3	8	33	40	54	0	5	10-7	.294	.386	.458	.844	4	.972
— Baltimore (A.L.)	OF	47	131	15	30	6	0	2	11	17	42	0	2	4-1	.229	.318	.321	.638	0	1.000
— Rochester (Int'l)	OF	10	42	5	13	4	0	1	2	3	8	0	0	1-1	.310	.356	.476	.832	0	1.000
2002— Rochester (Int'l)	OF	98	348	42	105	23	2	2	35	35	79	1	9	7-3	.302	.363	.397	.760	2	.990
— Baltimore (A.L.)	OF	16	34	1	6	1	0	0	3	1	11	0	1	1-0	.176	.194	.206	.400	0	1.000
2003— GC Orioles (GCL)	OF	2	6	1	2	1	0	0	0	0	1	0	0	0-0	.333	.333	.500	.833	0	1.000
— Ottawa (Int'l)	OF-DH	30	117	23	41	14	4	3	21	14	31	1	1	0-0	.350	.421	.615	1.036	1	.974
— Baltimore (A.L.)	OF	83	287	43	87	15	1	9	31	29	60	0	2	7-1	.303	.365	.456	.821	1	.994
Major League totals (3 years)		146	452	59	123	22	1	11	45	47	113	0	5	12-2	.272	.339	.398	.737	1	.996

BIGGIO, CRAIG   OF

PERSONAL: Born December 14, 1965, in Smithtown, N.Y. ... 5-11/185. ... Bats right, throws right. ... Full name: Craig Alan Biggio. ... Name pronounced: BIDG-ee-oh. ... High school: Kings Park (N.Y.). ... College: Seton Hall.

TRANSACTIONS/CAREER NOTES: Selected by Houston Astros organization in first round (22nd pick overall) of free-agent draft (June 2, 1987). ... Granted free agency (October 31, 1995). ... Re-signed by Astros (December 14, 1995). ... On disabled list (August 2, 2000-remainder of season).

2003 GAMES PLAYED BY POSITION (MLB): OF—150.

										BATTING									FIELDING	
Year	Team (League)	Pos.	G	AB	R	H	2B	3B	HR	RBI	BB	SO	HBP	GDP	SB-CS	Avg.	OBP	SLG	OPS	E	Pct.
1987— Asheville (S. Atl.)	C-OF	64	216	59	81	17	2	9	49	39	33	2	5	31-10	.375	.471	.597	1.068	2	.995
1988— Tucson (PCL)	C-OF	77	281	60	90	21	4	3	41	40	39	3	2	19-4	.320	.408	.456	.863	6	.983
— Houston (N.L.)	C	50	123	14	26	6	1	3	5	7	29	0	1	6-1	.211	.254	.350	.603	3	.991
1989— Houston (N.L.)	C-OF	134	443	64	114	21	2	13	60	49	64	6	7	21-3	.257	.336	.402	.738	9	.989
1990— Houston (N.L.)	C-OF	150	555	53	153	24	2	4	42	53	79	3	11	25-11	.276	.342	.348	.689	13	.982
1991— Houston (N.L.)	2B-C-OF	149	546	79	161	23	4	4	46	53	71	2	2	19-6	.295	.358	.374	.731	11	.989
1992— Houston (N.L.)	2B	• 162	613	96	170	32	3	6	39	94	95	7	5	38-15	.277	.378	.369	.747	12	.984
1993— Houston (N.L.)	2B	155	610	98	175	41	5	21	64	77	93	10	10	15-17	.287	.373	.474	.847	14	.982
1994— Houston (N.L.)	2B	114	437	88	139	* 44	5	6	56	62	58	8	5	* 39-4	.318	.411	.483	.893	7	.984
1995— Houston (N.L.)	2B	141	553	* 123	167	30	2	22	77	80	85	*22	6	33-8	.302	.406	.483	.889	10	.986
1996— Houston (N.L.)	2B	• 162	605	113	174	24	4	15	75	75	72	*27	10	25-7	.288	.386	.415	.801	10	.988
1997— Houston (N.L.)	2B-DH	• 162	619	* 146	191	37	8	22	81	84	107	*34	0	47-10	.309	.415	.501	.916	18	.979
1998— Houston (N.L.)	2B-DH	160	646	123	210	* 51	2	20	88	64	113	23	10	50-8	.325	.403	.503	.906	15	.980
1999— Houston (N.L.)	2B-OF-DH	160	639	123	188	* 56	0	16	73	88	107	11	5	28-14	.294	.386	.457	.843	12	.985
2000— Houston (N.L.)	2B	101	377	67	101	13	5	8	35	61	73	16	10	12-2	.268	.388	.393	.780	6	.987
2001— Houston (N.L.)	2B-DH	155	617	118	180	35	3	20	70	66	100	*28	11	7-4	.292	.382	.455	.838	11	.988
2002— Houston (N.L.)	2B-OF	145	577	96	146	36	3	15	58	50	111	17	15	16-2	.253	.330	.404	.734	8	.988
2003— Houston (N.L.)	OF	153	628	102	166	44	2	15	62	57	116	*27	4	8-4	.264	.350	.412	.763	1	.997
Major League totals (16 years)		2253	8588	1503	2461	517	51	210	931	1020	1373	241	112	389-116	.287	.375	.432	.807	160	.986

BLAKE, CASEY   3B

PERSONAL: Born August 23, 1973, in Des Moines, Iowa. ... 6-2/210. ... Bats right, throws right. ... Full name: William Casey Blake. ... High school: Indianola (Iowa). ... College: Wichita State.

TRANSACTIONS/CAREER NOTES: Selected by Philadelphia Phillies organization in 11th round of free-agent draft (June 1, 1992); did not sign. ... Selected by New York Yankees organization in 45th round of free-agent draft (June 1, 1995); did not sign. ... Selected by Toronto Blue Jays organization in seventh round of free-agent draft (June 4, 1996). ... Claimed on waivers by Minnesota Twins (May 23, 2000). ... On Salt Lake disabled list (June 28-July 7, 2000). ... Claimed on waivers by Baltimore Orioles (September 21, 2001). ... Claimed on waivers by Twins (October 12, 2001). ... Released by Twins (October 14, 2002). ... Signed by Cleveland Indians organization (December 18, 2002).

2003 GAMES PLAYED BY POSITION (MLB): 3B—140, 1B—31.

										BATTING									FIELDING	
Year	Team (League)	Pos.	G	AB	R	H	2B	3B	HR	RBI	BB	SO	HBP	GDP	SB-CS	Avg.	OBP	SLG	OPS	E	Pct.
1996— Hagerstown (SAL)	3B-1B-OF	48	172	29	43	13	1	2	18	11	40	7	3	5-3	.250	.318	.372	.690	12	.906
1997— Dunedin (Fla. St.)	3B-SS	129	449	56	107	21	0	7	39	48	91	6	5	19-9	.238	.319	.332	.651	‡ 39	.895
1998— Dunedin (Fla. St.)	3B	88	340	62	119	28	3	11	65	30	81	9	5	9-6	.350	.409	.547	.956	16	.939
— Knoxville (Sou.)	3B	45	172	44	64	15	4	7	38	22	25	2	6	10-0	.372	.442	.628	1.070	11	.913
1999— Syracuse (Int'l)	3B-SS-DH	110	387	69	95	16	2	22	75	61	82	7	10	9-5	.245	.357	.468	.824	10	.963
— Toronto (A.L.)	3B	14	39	6	10	2	0	1	1	2	7	0	1	0-0	.256	.293	.385	.677	0	1.000
— St. Catharines (NYP)	3B	1	3	0	2	0	0	0	0	1	0	0	0	0-0	.667	.750	.667	1.417	0	1.000
2000— Syracuse (Int'l)	3B-SS	30	106	10	23	6	1	2	7	8	23	3	2	0-3	.217	.291	.349	.640	2	.971
— Salt Lake (PCL)	3B-SS-1B	80	293	59	93	22	2	12	52	39	59	6	4	7-2	.317	.406	.529	.935	14	.934
— Minnesota (A.L.)	3B-DH-1B	7	16	1	3	2	0	0	1	3	7	1	1	0-0	.188	.333	.313	.646	0	1.000
2001— Edmonton (PCL)	3-1-2-S-OF	94	375	64	116	24	6	10	49	34	66	6	11	14-3	.309	.376	.485	.861	11	.961
— Minnesota (A.L.)	3B-DH-1B	13	22	1	7	1	0	0	2	3	8	0	0	1-0	.318	.400	.364	.764	1	.955
— Baltimore (A.L.)	1B-DH	6	15	2	2	0	0	1	2	1	4	0	0	2-0	.133	.188	.333	.521	1	.967
2002— Edmonton (PCL)	3-2-1-OF	126	482	87	149	25	3	19	58	54	78	6	11	24-9	.309	.383	.492	.874	12	.969
— Minnesota (A.L.)	3B-1B-DH	9	20	2	4	1	0	0	1	2	7	0	0	0-0	.200	.273	.250	.523	2	.920
2003— Cleveland (A.L.)	3B-1B	152	557	80	143	35	0	17	67	38	109	10	11	7-9	.257	.312	.411	.723	19	.965
Major League totals (5 years)		201	669	92	169	41	0	19	74	49	142	11	13	10-9	.253	.310	.399	.709	23	.965

B

BLALOCK, HANK — 3B

PERSONAL: Born November 21, 1980, in San Diego, Calif. ... 6-1/192. ... Bats left, throws right. ... Full name: Hank Joe Blalock. ... Name pronounced: BLAY-lock. ... High school: Rancho Bernardo (San Diego).

TRANSACTIONS/CAREER NOTES: Selected by Texas Rangers organization in third round of free-agent draft (June 2, 1999). ... On Oklahoma disabled list (June 10-17, 2002).

2003 GAMES PLAYED BY POSITION (MLB): 3B—141, 2B—4.

Year	Team (League)	Pos.	G	AB	R	H	2B	3B	HR	RBI	BB	SO	HBP	GDP	SB-CS	Avg.	OBP	SLG	OPS	E	Pct.
1999—	GC Rangers (GCL)	3B	51	191	34	69	17	6	3	38	25	23	1	7	3-2	.361	.428	.560	.988	12	.914
—Savannah (S. Atl.)		3B	7	25	3	6	1	0	1	2	1	3	1	0	0-0	.240	.286	.400	.686	5	.762
2000—Savannah (S. Atl.)		3B	139	512	66	153	32	2	10	77	62	53	5	13	31-8	.299	.373	.428	.801	20	.942
2001—Tulsa (Texas)		3B	68	272	50	89	18	4	11	61	39	38	2	5	3-3	.327	.413	.544	.957	8	.953
—Charlotte (Fla. St.)		3B	63	237	46	90	19	1	7	47	26	31	1	6	7-4	.380	.437	.557	.994	7	.963
2002—Texas (A.L.)		3B	49	147	16	31	8	0	3	17	20	43	1	2	0-0	.211	.306	.327	.632	6	.943
—Oklahoma (PCL)		3B-2B	95	387	63	119	32	1	8	62	34	61	1	9	2-1	.307	.363	.457	.821	16	.938
2003—Texas (A.L.)		3B-2B	143	567	89	170	33	3	29	90	44	97	1	16	2-3	.300	.350	.522	.872	16	.957
Major League totals (2 years)			192	714	105	201	41	3	32	107	64	140	2	18	2-3	.282	.340	.482	.822	22	.954

BLANCO, HENRY — C

PERSONAL: Born August 29, 1971, in Caracas, Venezuela. ... 5-11/224. ... Bats right, throws right. ... Full name: Henry Ramon Blanco. ... Name pronounced: BLAHN-ko. ... High school: Antonio Jose de Sucre (Venezuela).

TRANSACTIONS/CAREER NOTES: Signed as non-drafted free agent by Los Angeles Dodgers organization (November 12, 1989). ... On disabled list (June 16-25, 1993). ... On Los Angeles disabled list (March 22-July 29, 1998); included rehabilitation assignment to San Bernardino (May 19-27). ... Granted free agency (October 15, 1998). ... Signed by Colorado Rockies organization (December 18, 1998). ... Traded by Rockies with P Jamey Wright to Milwaukee Brewers as part of three-way deal in which Rockies received 3B Jeff Cirillo, P Scott Karl and cash from Brewers, Oakland Athletics received P Justin Miller and cash from Rockies and Brewers received P Jimmy Haynes from A's (December 13, 1999). ... On Milwaukee disabled list (April 14-May 2, 2000); included rehabilitation assignment to Indianapolis (April 30-May 2). ... Traded by Brewers to Atlanta Braves for C Paul Bako and P Jose Cabrera (March 20, 2002). ... On disabled list (August 12-27, 2002).

2003 GAMES PLAYED BY POSITION (MLB): C—52.

Year	Team (League)	Pos.	G	AB	R	H	2B	3B	HR	RBI	BB	SO	HBP	GDP	SB-CS	Avg.	OBP	SLG	OPS	E	Pct.
1990—GC Dodgers (GCL)		3B	60	178	23	39	8	0	1	19	26	41	1	6	7-2	.219	.316	.281	.597	11	.941
1991—Vero Beach (FSL)		3B-SS	5	7	0	1	0	0	0	0	2	0	0	0	0-0	.143	.333	.143	.476	0	1.000
—Great Falls (Pio.)		3B-1B	62	216	35	55	7	1	5	28	27	39	1	5	3-6	.255	.336	.366	.702	8	.960
1992—Bakersfield (Calif.)		3B	124	401	42	94	21	2	5	52	51	91	9	10	10-6	.234	.328	.334	.662	14	.959
1993—San Antonio (Texas)		3B-1B-SS	117	374	33	73	19	1	10	42	29	80	4	7	3-3	.195	.260	.332	.591	16	.952
1994—San Antonio (Texas)		3B-1B-P	* 132	405	36	93	23	2	6	38	53	67	2	12	6-6	.230	.320	.341	.660	21	.924
1995—San Antonio (Texas)		3B-C	88	302	37	77	18	4	12	48	29	52	4	4	1-1	.255	.328	.460	.789	11	.964
—Albuquerque (PCL)		3B-1B-OF	29	97	11	22	4	1	2	13	10	23	0	3	0-0	.227	.294	.351	.644	2	.988
1996—San Antonio (Texas)		C-3B	92	307	39	82	14	1	5	40	28	38	0	8	2-3	.267	.324	.368	.692	‡ 13	.979
—Albuquerque (PCL)		C	2	6	1	1	0	0	0	0	0	3	0	0	0-0	.167	.167	.167	.333	0	1.000
1997—Albuquerque (PCL)		C-1B-D-O	91	294	38	92	20	1	6	47	37	63	1	7	7-4	.313	.388	.449	.837	3	.996
—Los Angeles (N.L.)		3B-1B	3	5	1	2	0	0	1	1	0	1	0	0	0-0	.400	.400	1.000	1.400	0	1.000
1998—San Bern. (Calif.)		C-DH	7	19	5	6	1	0	2	3	4	6	0	2	1-0	.316	.435	.684	1.119	0	1.000
—Albuquerque (PCL)		C-DH	48	134	19	36	11	0	4	23	22	27	0	5	2-0	.269	.367	.440	.807	4	.985
1999—Colo. Springs (PCL)		C	15	57	8	19	4	0	3	12	1	12	0	1	0-1	.333	.339	.561	.900	1	.990
—Colorado (N.L.)		C-OF	88	263	30	61	12	3	6	28	34	38	1	4	1-1	.232	.320	.369	.689	5	.992
2000—Milwaukee (N.L.)		C	93	284	29	67	24	0	7	31	36	60	0	9	0-3	.236	.318	.394	.712	5	.991
—Indianapolis (Int'l)		DH	1	3	1	1	1	0	0	0	1	0	0	1	0-0	.333	.500	.667	1.167	...	...
2001—Milwaukee (N.L.)		C	104	314	33	66	18	3	6	31	34	72	2	10	3-1	.210	.290	.344	.634	6	.992
2002—Atlanta (N.L.)		C	81	221	17	45	9	1	6	22	20	51	1	5	0-2	.204	.267	.335	.602	3	.993
2003—Atlanta (N.L.)		C	55	151	11	30	8	0	1	13	10	21	1	3	0-0	.199	.252	.272	.523	1	.996
Major League totals (6 years)			424	1238	121	271	71	7	27	126	134	243	5	31	4-7	.219	.295	.353	.648	20	.992

BLAND, NATE — P

PERSONAL: Born December 27, 1974, in Birmingham, Ala. ... 6-5/190. ... Throws left, bats left. ... Full name: Nathan Garrett Bland. ... High school: Mountain Brook High (Birmingham, AL).

TRANSACTIONS/CAREER NOTES: Selected by Los Angeles Dodgers organization in fourth round of free-agent draft (June 9, 1993). ... Granted free agency (October 15, 1999). ... Re-signed by Dodgers (December 17, 1999). ... On disabled list (April 8-September 22, 1999). ... Released by Dodgers (March 31, 2000). ... Signed by Sioux City of the independent Northern League (June 2000). ... Signed by San Diego Padres organization as a free agent (October 29, 2000). ... Released by Padres (March 26, 2001). ... Signed by Chico of the independent Western League (June 2002). ... Contract purchased by New York Mets (July 16, 2002). ... Granted free agency (October 15, 2002). ... Re-signed by Mets (October 22, 2002). ... Selected by Houston Astros from Mets in Rule 5 minor league draft (December 16, 2002).

CAREER HITTING: 0-for-0 (.000), 0 R, 0 2B, 0 3B, 0 HR, 0 RBI.

Year	League	W	L	Pct.	ERA	WHIP	G	GS	CG	ShO	Hld.	Sv.-Opp.	IP	H	R	ER	HR	BB-IBB	SO	Avg.
1993—Yakima (NW)		4	6	.400	2.84	1.29	16	13	0	0	...	0-...	63.1	53	34	20	2	29-1	43	.219
1994—Great Falls (Pio.)		0	0	...	0.96	0.96	2	1	0	0	...	0-...	9.1	6	2	1	0	3-0	12	.188
—Bakersfield (Calif.)		2	6	.250	5.36	1.69	12	9	0	0	...	0-...	50.1	58	31	30	10	27-0	19	.294
1995—Bakersfield (Calif.)		4	9	.308	5.22	1.72	27	23	0	0	...	0-...	122.1	155	89	71	13	55-0	46	.311
1996—Savannah (S. Atl.)		1	0	1.000	1.63	1.23	5	5	0	0	...	0-...	27.2	24	8	5	0	10-0	24	.233
—Vero Beach (FSL)		10	4	.714	3.09	1.40	17	17	0	0	...	0-...	96.0	99	42	33	3	35-0	69	.268
1997—San Antonio (Texas)		3	2	.600	7.02	1.73	10	8	0	0	...	0-...	41.0	47	34	32	5	24-0	30	.296
—Vero Beach (FSL)		7	7	.500	3.38	1.49	17	14	0	0	...	0-...	82.2	85	35	31	7	38-0	67	.275
1998—San Antonio (Texas)		4	2	.667	2.78	1.54	26	0	0	0	...	0-...	45.1	56	21	14	0	14-0	34	.303
1999—												Did not play.								
2002—Binghamton (Eastern)		4	2	.667	2.55	0.97	15	0	0	0	...	0-...	24.2	16	9	7	0	8-3	19	.182
2003—Houston (N.L.)		1	2	.333	5.75	1.67	22	0	0	0	3	0-1	20.1	22	13	13	3	12-2	18	.286
—New Orleans (PCL)		0	1	.000	2.84	1.26	17	0	0	0	...	1-...	19.0	15	6	6	1	9-1	23	.217
Major League totals (1 year)		1	2	.333	5.75	1.67	22	0	0	0	3	0-1	20.1	22	13	13	3	12-2	18	.286

BLOOMQUIST, WILLIE — IF/OF

PERSONAL: Born November 27, 1977, in Bremerton, Wash. ... 5-11/185. ... Bats right, throws right. ... Full name: William Paul Bloomquist. ... High school: South Kitsap (Port Orchard, Wash.). ... College: Arizona State.

TRANSACTIONS/CAREER NOTES: Selected by Seattle Mariners organization in eighth round of free-agent draft (June 4, 1996); did not sign. ... Selected by Mariners organization in third round of free-agent draft (June 2, 1999). ... On Lancaster disabled list (August 6, 2000-remainder of season). ... On Tacoma disabled list (April 22-May 3 and June 6-18, 2002).

2003 GAMES PLAYED BY POSITION (MLB): 3B—37, SS—18, DH—12, OF—11, 2B—7, 1B—3.

										BATTING									FIELDING	
Year	Team (League)	Pos.	G	AB	R	H	2B	3B	HR	RBI	BB	SO	HBP	GDP	SB-CS	Avg.	OBP	SLG	OPS	E	Pct.
1999— Everett (N'west)		2B-OF	42	178	35	51	10	3	2	27	22	25	1	1	17-5	.287	.366	.410	.776	7	.954
2000— Lancaster (Calif.)		2B-SS	64	256	63	97	19	6	2	51	37	27	0	3	22-12	.379	.456	.523	.979	12	.961
—Tacoma (PCL)		2B	51	191	17	43	5	1	1	23	7	28	0	3	5-0	.225	.249	.277	.526	3	.987
2001— San Antonio (Texas)		2B-SS	123	491	59	125	23	2	0	28	28	55	1	11	34-9	.255	.294	.310	.603	24	.959
2002— Tacoma (PCL)		OF-2-3-SS	104	337	47	91	14	3	6	47	29	44	3	5	20-10	.270	.331	.383	.713	12	.961
—Seattle (A.L.)		OF-2B-DH	12	33	11	15	4	0	0	7	5	2	0	0	3-1	.455	.526	.576	1.102	0	1.000
2003— Seattle (A.L.)		3-S-D-O-2-1	89	196	30	49	7	2	1	14	19	39	1	6	4-1	.250	.317	.321	.638	4	.975
Major League totals (2 years)			101	229	41	64	11	2	1	21	24	41	1	6	7-2	.279	.348	.358	.706	4	.979

BLUM, GEOFF — IF/OF

PERSONAL: Born April 26, 1973, in Redwood City, Calif. ... 6-3/200. ... Bats both, throws right. ... Full name: Geoffrey Edward Blum. ... Name pronounced: bluhm. ... High school: Chino (Calif.). ... College: UC-Berkeley.

TRANSACTIONS/CAREER NOTES: Selected by Montreal Expos organization in seventh round of free-agent draft (June 2, 1994). ... On Ottawa disabled list (May 21-June 15, 1999). ... Traded by Expos to Houston Astros for 3B Chris Truby (March 12, 2002).

2003 GAMES PLAYED BY POSITION (MLB): 3B—83, 2B—25, SS—11, 1B—6, OF—2.

										BATTING									FIELDING	
Year	Team (League)	Pos.	G	AB	R	H	2B	3B	HR	RBI	BB	SO	HBP	GDP	SB-CS	Avg.	OBP	SLG	OPS	E	Pct.
1994— Vermont (NYP)		SS	63	241	48	83	15	1	3	38	33	21	3	4	5-5	.344	.428	.452	.880	15	.948
1995— W.P. Beach (FSL)		2B-3B-SS	125	457	54	120	20	2	1	62	34	61	3	12	6-5	.263	.313	.322	.635	18	.963
1996— Harrisburg (East.)			120	396	47	95	22	2	1	41	59	51	3	11	6-7	.240	.341	.313	.654	9	.984
1997— Ottawa (Int'l)		2B-3B-SS	118	407	59	101	21	2	3	35	52	73	3	6	14-6	.248	.333	.332	.665	17	.969
1998— Ottawa (Int'l)		2B	8	23	1	4	0	0	0	1	3	6	0	0	0-0	.174	.269	.174	.443	0	1.000
—GC Expos (GCL)		2B	5	18	0	3	1	1	0	1	1	4	0	0	0-0	.167	.211	.333	.544	0	1.000
—Jupiter (FSL)		2B	17	58	13	16	6	0	0	5	13	14	1	0	1-0	.276	.411	.379	.790	2	.976
—Harrisburg (East.)		2-3-SS-1	39	139	25	43	12	3	6	21	17	24	4	3	2-1	.309	.400	.568	.968	2	.986
1999— Ottawa (Int'l)		SS-2-1-3-D	77	268	43	71	14	1	10	37	37	39	2	5	6-1	.265	.350	.437	.787	12	.965
—Montreal (N.L.)		SS-2B	45	133	21	32	7	2	8	18	17	25	0	3	1-0	.241	.327	.504	.830	10	.929
2000— Montreal (N.L.)		3-SS-2-1	124	343	40	97	20	2	11	45	26	60	3	4	1-4	.283	.335	.449	.784	9	.974
2001— Montreal (N.L.)		3-0-2-1-S	148	453	57	107	25	0	9	50	43	94	10	12	9-5	.236	.313	.351	.664	8	.980
2002— Houston (N.L.)		3-0-S-2-1	130	368	45	104	20	4	10	52	49	70	1	8	2-0	.283	.367	.440	.807	8	.972
2003— Houston (N.L.)		3-2-S-1-O	123	420	51	110	19	0	10	52	20	50	2	15	0-0	.262	.295	.379	.674	7	.975
Major League totals (5 years)			570	1717	214	450	91	8	48	217	155	299	16	42	13-9	.262	.326	.408	.734	42	.971

BOCACHICA, HIRAM — 2B/OF

PERSONAL: Born March 4, 1976, in Ponce, Puerto Rico. ... 5-11/185. ... Bats right, throws right. ... Full name: Hiram Colon Bocachica. ... Name pronounced: hear-ram bow-ka-cheeka. ... High school: Rexville (Bayamon, Puerto Rico).

TRANSACTIONS/CAREER NOTES: Selected by Montreal Expos organization in first round (21st pick overall) of free-agent draft (June 2, 1994). ... On West Palm Beach disabled list (May 16-July 12, 1996). ... On Harrisburg disabled list (June 15-18, 1997). ... On Harrisburg disabled list (June 18-25, 1997). ... Traded by Expos with P Carlos Perez and SS Mark Grudzielanek to Los Angeles Dodgers for 2B Wilton Guerrero, P Ted Lilly, OF Peter Bergeron and 1B Jonathan Tucker (July 31, 1998). ... On San Antonio suspended list (August 16-19, 1999). ... On Albuquerque disabled list (May 23-June 2, 2000). ... On disabled list (July 9-26, 2001). ... Traded by Dodgers to Detroit Tigers for P Tom Farmer and a player to be named later (July 25, 2002); Dodgers acquired P Jason Frasor to complete deal (September 18, 2002). ... Designated for assignment by Tigers (April 18, 2003). ... Sent outright to Toledo (April 24, 2003).

2003 GAMES PLAYED BY POSITION (MLB): OF—6.

										BATTING									FIELDING	
Year	Team (League)	Pos.	G	AB	R	H	2B	3B	HR	RBI	BB	SO	HBP	GDP	SB-CS	Avg.	OBP	SLG	OPS	E	Pct.
1994— GC Expos (GCL)		SS	43	168	31	47	9	0	5	16	15	42	2	1	11-4	.280	.346	.423	.769	23	.896
1995— Albany (S. Atl.)		2B-SS	96	380	65	108	20	10	2	30	52	78	8	4	47-17	.284	.381	.405	.786	‡ 58	.881
1996— W.P. Beach (FSL)		DH-SS	71	267	50	90	17	5	2	26	34	47	6	6	21-3	.337	.419	.461	.880	24	.833
—GC Expos (GCL)		DH	9	32	11	8	3	0	0	2	5	3	1	0	2-1	.250	.368	.344	.712	...	...
1997— Harrisburg (East.)		SS-2B-DH	119	443	82	123	19	3	11	35	41	98	13	3	29-12	.278	.354	.409	.763	32	.909
1998— Harrisburg (East.)		OF-DH	80	296	39	78	18	4	4	27	21	61	11	1	20-8	.264	.334	.392	.726	10	.946
—Ottawa (Int'l)		OF	12	41	5	8	3	1	0	5	6	14	1	1	2-0	.195	.313	.317	.630	0	1.000
—Albuquerque (PCL)		OF	26	101	16	24	7	1	4	16	13	24	6	1	5-3	.238	.358	.446	.804	2	.976
1999— San Antonio (Texas)		2B-DH	123	477	84	139	22	10	11	60	60	71	13	6	30-15	.291	.382	.449	.831	31	.946
2000— Albuquerque (PCL)		2B	124	482	99	155	38	4	23	84	40	100	15	7	10-14	.322	.390	.560	.950	23	.963
—Los Angeles (N.L.)		2B	8	10	2	3	0	0	0	0	0	2	0	0	0-0	.300	.300	.300	.600	0	1.000
2001— Los Angeles (N.L.)		2B-OF-3B	75	133	15	31	11	1	2	9	9	33	1	1	4-1	.233	.287	.376	.663	7	.919
2002— Los Angeles (N.L.)		OF-DH	49	65	12	14	3	0	4	9	5	19	0	1	1-1	.215	.271	.446	.718	1	.960
—Detroit (A.L.)		OF-2B-DH	34	103	14	23	4	0	4	8	5	22	0	2	2-2	.223	.259	.379	.638	2	.969
2003— Detroit (A.L.)		OF	6	22	1	1	1	0	0	0	0	7	0	0	0-0	.045	.045	.091	.136	0	1.000
—Toledo (Int'l)		OF-2-3-DH	95	322	48	78	19	3	12	37	24	57	10	5	11-6	.242	.313	.432	.745	11	.954
American League totals (2 years)			40	125	15	24	5	0	4	8	5	29	0	2	2-2	.192	.223	.328	.551	2	.974
National League totals (3 years)			132	208	29	48	14	1	6	18	14	54	1	2	5-2	.231	.283	.394	.677	8	.935
Major League totals (4 years)			172	333	44	72	19	1	10	26	19	83	1	4	7-4	.216	.261	.369	.630	10	.950

BOEHRINGER, BRIAN — P

PERSONAL: Born January 8, 1970, in St. Louis, Mo. ... 6-2/192. ... Throws right, bats both. ... Full name: Brian Edward Boehringer. ... Name pronounced: BOH-ring-uhr. ... High school: Northwest (House Springs, Mo.). ... College: UNLV.

TRANSACTIONS/CAREER NOTES: Selected by Houston Astros organization in 10th round of free-agent draft (June 4, 1990); did not sign. ... Selected by Chicago White Sox organization in fourth round of free-agent draft (June 3, 1991). ... On Utica disabled list (June 29-August 25, 1991). ... On disabled list (June 24-August 25, 1992). ... Traded by White Sox to New York Yankees for P Paul Assenmacher (March 21, 1994). ... On New York disabled list (May 27-August 19, 1997); included rehabilitation assignments to Gulf Coast Yankees (August 10-12) and Tampa (August 13-19). ... Selected by Tampa Bay Devil Rays in second round (30th pick overall) of expansion draft (November 18, 1997). ... Traded by Devil Rays with SS Andy Sheets to San Diego Padres for C John Flaherty (November 18, 1997). ... On disabled list (August 14, 1999-remainder of season). ... On San Diego disabled list (April 21-May 24 and July 4, 2000-remainder of season); included rehabilitation assignment to Rancho Cucamonga (May 17-24). ... Granted free agency (October 25, 2000). ... Signed by Yankees organization (December 14, 2000). ... Traded by Yankees to San Francisco Giants for C Bobby Estalella and P Joe Smith (July 5, 2001). ... Granted free agency (December 21, 2001). ... Signed by Pittsburgh Pirates organization (January 25, 2002). ... Granted free agency (October 28, 2002). ... Re-signed by Pirates (December 12, 2002).

CAREER HITTING: 2-for-30 (.067), 0 R, 1 2B, 0 3B, 0 HR, 2 RBI.

Year	League	W	L	Pct.	ERA	WHIP	G	GS	CG	ShO	Hld.	Sv.-Opp.	IP	H	R	ER	HR	BB-IBB	SO	Avg.
1991—	GC White Sox (GCL)	1	1	.500	6.57	1.54	5	1	0	0	...	0-...	12.1	14	9	9	1	5-0	10	.292
—	Utica (N.Y.-Penn)	1	1	.500	2.37	1.16	4	4	0	0	...	0-...	19.0	14	8	5	0	8-0	19	.206
1992—	South Bend (Mid.)	6	7	.462	4.38	1.47	15	15	2	0	...	0-...	86.1	87	52	42	5	40-0	59	.264
1993—	Sarasota (Fla. St.)	10	4	.714	2.80	1.29	18	17	3	0	...	0-...	119.0	103	47	37	2	51-2	92	.237
—	Birmingham (Sou.)	2	1	.667	3.54	1.35	7	7	1	0	...	0-...	40.2	41	20	16	3	14-0	29	.265
1994—	Alb./Colon. (East.)	10	11	.476	3.62	1.29	27	27	5	1	...	0-...	171.2	165	85	69	10	57-1	145	.256
1995—	New York (A.L.)	0	3	.000	13.75	2.60	7	3	0	0	0	0-1	17.2	24	27	27	5	22-1	10	.320
—	Columbus (Int'l)	8	6	.571	2.77	1.27	17	17	3	0	...	0-...	104.0	101	39	32	6	31-1	58	.254
1996—	Columbus (Int'l)	11	7	.611	4.00	1.38	25	25	3	1	...	0-...	153.0	155	79	68	13	56-1	132	.263
—	New York (A.L.)	2	4	.333	5.44	1.45	15	3	0	0	4	0-1	46.1	46	28	28	6	21-2	37	.260
1997—	New York (A.L.)	3	2	.600	2.63	1.48	34	0	0	0	5	0-3	48.0	39	16	14	4	32-6	53	.225
—	GC Yankees (GCL)	0	0	...	0.00	0.50	1	1	0	0	...	0-...	2.0	1	0	0	0	0-0	2	.143
—	Tampa (FSL)	0	1	.000	5.00	1.56	3	3	0	0	...	0-...	9.0	9	5	5	1	5-0	8	.265
1998—	San Diego (N.L.)	5	2	.714	4.36	1.57	56	1	0	0	7	0-1	76.1	75	38	37	10	45-4	67	.257
1999—	San Diego (N.L.)	6	5	.545	3.24	1.40	33	11	0	0	3	0-2	94.1	97	38	34	10	35-4	64	.267
2000—	San Diego (N.L.)	0	3	.000	5.74	1.79	7	3	0	0	0	0-1	15.2	18	15	10	4	10-0	9	.286
—	Rancho Cuca. (Calif.)	0	2	.000	5.40	1.80	4	2	0	0	...	0-...	5.0	8	3	3	0	1-0	5	.381
2001—	New York (A.L.)	0	1	.000	3.12	1.36	22	0	0	0	1	1-1	34.2	35	15	12	3	12-0	33	.255
—	San Francisco (N.L.)	0	3	.000	4.19	1.43	29	0	0	0	2	1-1	34.1	32	20	16	4	17-5	27	.239
2002—	Pittsburgh (N.L.)	4	4	.500	3.39	1.23	70	0	0	0	28	1-6	79.2	65	30	30	5	33-6	65	.229
2003—	Pittsburgh (N.L.)	5	4	.556	5.49	1.51	62	0	0	0	15	0-3	62.1	64	39	38	11	30-3	47	.267
American League totals (4 years)		5	10	.333	4.97	1.57	78	6	0	0	10	1-6	146.2	144	86	81	18	87-9	133	.256
National League totals (6 years)		20	21	.488	4.09	1.44	257	15	0	0	55	2-14	362.2	351	180	165	44	170-22	279	.255
Major League totals (9 years)		25	31	.446	4.35	1.48	335	21	0	0	65	3-20	509.1	495	266	246	62	257-31	412	.255

BONDERMAN, JEREMY — P

PERSONAL: Born October 28, 1982, in Kennewick, Wash. ... 6-2/210. ... Throws right, bats right. ... Full name: Jeremy Allen Bonderman. ... High school: Pasco High (Washington).

TRANSACTIONS/CAREER NOTES: Selected by Oakland A's in first round of free-agent draft (June 2001); pick received as compensation for New York Mets' signing of P Kevin Appier. ... Traded by A's to Detroit Tigers to complete an earlier trade (August 22, 2002).

CAREER HITTING: 0-for-2 (.000), 0 R, 0 2B, 0 3B, 0 HR, 0 RBI.

Year	League	W	L	Pct.	ERA	WHIP	G	GS	CG	ShO	Hld.	Sv.-Opp.	IP	H	R	ER	HR	BB-IBB	SO	Avg.
2002—	Modesto (Calif.)	9	8	.529	3.61	1.27	25	25	1	0	...	0-...	144.2	129	77	58	15	55-1	160	.233
—	Lakeland (Fla. St.)	0	1	.000	6.00	1.25	2	2	1	0	...	0-...	12.0	11	8	8	3	4-0	10	.262
2003—	Detroit (A.L.)	6	19	.240	5.56	1.55	33	28	0	0	0	0-0	162.0	193	118	100	23	58-2	108	.294
Major League totals (1 year)		6	19	.240	5.56	1.55	33	28	0	0	0	0-0	162.0	193	118	100	23	58-2	108	.294

BONDS, BARRY — OF

PERSONAL: Born July 24, 1964, in Riverside, Calif. ... 6-2/228. ... Bats left, throws left. ... Full name: Barry Lamar Bonds. ... High school: Serra (San Mateo, Calif.). ... College: Arizona State.

TRANSACTIONS/CAREER NOTES: Selected by San Francisco Giants organization in second round of free-agent draft (June 7, 1982); did not sign. ... Selected by Pittsburgh Pirates organization in first round (sixth pick overall) of free-agent draft (June 3, 1985). ... On disabled list (June 15-July 4, 1992). ... Granted free agency (October 26, 1992). ... Signed by Giants (December 8, 1992). ... On suspended list (August 14-16, 1998). ... On disabled list (April 18-June 9, 1999). ... Granted free agency (November 5, 2001). ... Re-signed by Giants (January 17, 2002). ... Placed on bereavement list (August 14, 2003). ... Reinstated from bereavement list (August 19, 2003). ... Placed on bereavement list (August 24, 2003). ... Reinstated from bereavement list (August 30, 2003).

2003 GAMES PLAYED BY POSITION (MLB): OF—123, DH—6.

Year	Team (League)	Pos.	G	AB	R	H	2B	3B	HR	RBI	BB	SO	HBP	GDP	SB-CS	Avg.	OBP	SLG	OPS	E	Pct.
1985—	Prince Will. (Car.)	OF	71	254	49	76	16	4	13	37	37	52	0	3	15-3	.299	.383	.547	.930	5	.976
1986—	Hawaii (PCL)	OF	44	148	30	46	7	2	7	37	33	31	2	1	16-5	.311	.435	.527	.963	2	.983
—	Pittsburgh (N.L.)	OF	113	413	72	92	26	3	16	48	65	102	2	4	36-7	.223	.330	.416	.746	5	.983
1987—	Pittsburgh (N.L.)	OF	150	551	99	144	34	9	25	59	54	88	3	4	32-10	.261	.329	.492	.821	5	.986
1988—	Pittsburgh (N.L.)	OF	144	538	97	152	30	5	24	58	72	82	2	3	17-11	.283	.368	.491	.859	6	.980
1989—	Pittsburgh (N.L.)	OF	159	580	96	144	34	6	19	58	93	93	1	9	32-10	.248	.351	.426	.777	6	.984
1990—	Pittsburgh (N.L.)	OF	151	519	104	156	32	3	33	114	93	83	3	8	52-13	.301	.406	*.565	.970	6	.983
1991—	Pittsburgh (N.L.)	OF	153	510	95	149	28	5	25	116	107	73	4	8	43-13	.292	*.410	.514	.924	3	.991
1992—	Pittsburgh (N.L.)	OF	140	473	*109	147	36	5	34	103	*127	69	5	9	39-8	.311	*.456	*.624	1.080	3	.991
1993—	San Francisco (N.L.)	OF	159	539	129	181	38	4	*46	*123	126	79	2	11	29-12	.336	*.458	*.677	1.136	5	.984
1994—	San Francisco (N.L.)	OF	112	391	89	122	18	1	37	81	*74	43	6	3	29-9	.312	.426	.647	1.073	3	.986
1995—	San Francisco (N.L.)	OF	*144	506	109	149	30	7	33	104	*120	83	5	12	31-10	.294	*.431	.577	1.009	6	.980
1996—	San Francisco (N.L.)	OF	158	517	122	159	27	3	42	129	*151	76	1	11	40-7	.308	.461	.615	1.076	6	.980
1997—	San Francisco (N.L.)	OF	159	532	123	155	26	5	40	101	*145	87	8	13	37-8	.291	.446	.585	1.031	5	.984
1998—	San Francisco (N.L.)	OF	156	552	120	167	44	7	37	122	130	92	8	15	28-12	.303	.438	.609	1.047	5	.984
1999—	San Francisco (N.L.)	OF-DH	102	355	91	93	20	2	34	83	73	62	3	6	15-2	.262	.389	.617	1.006	3	.984
2000—	San Francisco (N.L.)	OF	143	480	129	147	28	4	49	106	*117	77	3	6	11-3	.306	.440	.688	1.127	3	.989
2001—	San Francisco (N.L.)	OF-DH	153	476	129	156	32	2	*73	137	*177	93	9	5	13-3	.328	*.515	*.863	1.379	6	.977
2002—	San Francisco (N.L.)	OF-DH	143	403	117	149	31	2	46	110	*198	47	9	4	9-2	*.370	*.582	*.799	1.381	8	.968
2003—	San Francisco (N.L.)	OF-DH	130	390	111	133	22	1	45	90	*148	58	10	7	7-0	.341	*.529	*.749	1.278	2	.992
Major League totals (18 years)			2569	8725	1941	2595	536	74	658	1742	2070	1387	84	138	500-140	.297	.433	.602	1.035	86	.984

BONG, JUNG   P

PERSONAL: Born July 15, 1980, in Seoul, South Korea. ... 6-3/175. ... Throws left, bats left. ... Full name: Jung Kuen Bong.

TRANSACTIONS/CAREER NOTES: Signed as non-drafted free agent by Atlanta Braves organization (November 6, 1997). ... Optioned to Richmond by Atlanta (August 13, 2003). ... Recalled from Richmond by Atlanta (August 28, 2003).

CAREER HITTING: 0-for-7 (.000), 0 R, 0 2B, 0 3B, 0 HR, 0 RBI.

Year	League	W	L	Pct.	ERA	WHIP	G	GS	CG	ShO	Hld.	Sv.-Opp.	IP	H	R	ER	HR	BB-IBB	SO	Avg.
1998— GC Braves (GCL)		1	1	.500	1.49	0.93	11	10	0	0	...	0-...	48.1	31	9	8	2	14-0	56	.195
1999— Macon (S. Atl.)		6	5	.545	3.98	1.48	26	20	0	0	...	1-...	108.2	111	61	48	8	50-0	100	.266
2000— Macon (S. Atl.)		7	7	.500	4.23	1.46	20	19	0	0	...	0-...	112.2	119	65	53	4	45-0	90	.275
— Myrtle Beach (Caro.)		3	1	.750	2.18	0.97	7	6	0	0	...	0-...	41.1	33	14	10	1	7-0	37	.220
2001— Myrtle Beach (Caro.)		13	9	.591	3.00	1.18	28	• 28	0	0	...	0-...	168.0	151	67	56	7	47-0	145	.245
2002— Greenville (Sou.)		7	8	.467	3.25	1.48	27	17	0	0	...	2-...	122.0	136	59	44	6	45-1	107	.286
— Atlanta (N.L.)		0	1	.000	7.50	1.67	1	1	0	0	0	0-0	6.0	8	5	5	0	2-0	4	.320
2003— Richmond (Int'l)		1	2	.333	5.56	1.24	3	3	0	0	...	0-...	11.1	11	7	7	1	3-0	15	.239
— Atlanta (N.L.)		6	2	.750	5.05	1.53	44	0	0	0	2	1-3	57.0	56	32	32	8	31-6	47	.267
Major League totals (2 years)		**6**	**3**	**.667**	**5.29**	**1.54**	**45**	**1**	**0**	**0**	**2**	**1-3**	**63.0**	**64**	**37**	**37**	**8**	**33-6**	**51**	**.272**

BOONE, AARON   3B

PERSONAL: Born March 9, 1973, in La Mesa, Calif. ... 6-2/200. ... Bats right, throws right. ... Full name: Aaron John Boone. ... High school: Villa Park (Calif.). ... College: USC.

TRANSACTIONS/CAREER NOTES: Selected by California Angels organization in 43rd round of free-agent draft (June 3, 1991); did not sign. ... Selected by Cincinnati Reds organization in third round of free-agent draft (June 2, 1994). ... On disabled list (July 10, 2000-remainder of season). ... On Cincinnati disabled list (May 15-June 15, August 15-September 1 and September 24, 2001-remainder of season); included rehabilitation assignment to Louisville (June 14-15). ... Traded by Cincinnati Reds to New York Yankees for P Brandon Claussen, P Charlie Manning and cash (July 31, 2003).

2003 GAMES PLAYED BY POSITION (MLB): 3B—137, 2B—19, SS—5.

Year	Team (League)	Pos.	G	AB	R	H	2B	3B	HR	RBI	BB	SO	HBP	GDP	SB-CS	Avg.	OBP	SLG	OPS	E	Pct.
1994— Billings (Pio.)	3B-1B	67	256	48	70	15	5	7	55	36	35	3	7	6-3	.273	.362	.453	.815	18	.924
1995— Chattanooga (Sou.)	3B	23	66	6	15	3	0	0	3	5	12	0	5	2-0	.227	.274	.273	.547	6	.875
— Win.-Salem (Car.)	3B	108	395	61	103	19	1	14	50	43	77	9	4	11-7	.261	.345	.420	.765	21	.940
1996— Chattanooga (Sou.)	3B-SS-DH	136	* 548	86	158	* 44	7	17	95	38	77	5	5	21-10	.288	.338	.487	.825	22	.945
1997— Indianapolis (A.A.)	3B-SS-2B	131	476	79	138	30	4	22	75	40	81	1	11	12-4	.290	.344	.508	.853	24	.941
— Cincinnati (N.L.)	3B-2B	16	49	5	12	1	0	0	5	2	5	0	1	1-0	.245	.275	.265	.540	3	.917
1998— Cincinnati (N.L.)	3B-2B-SS	58	181	24	51	13	2	2	28	15	36	5	3	6-1	.282	.350	.409	.759	8	.944
— Indianapolis (Int'l)	3B	87	332	56	80	18	1	7	38	31	71	8	6	17-5	.241	.316	.364	.680	19	.943
1999— Cincinnati (N.L.)	3B-SS	139	472	56	132	26	5	14	72	30	79	8	6	17-6	.280	.330	.445	.775	15	.958
— Indianapolis (Int'l)	3B-2B-SS	11	41	6	14	2	1	0	7	3	4	2	1	2-2	.341	.388	.439	.827	3	.930
2000— Cincinnati (N.L.)	3B-SS	84	291	44	83	18	0	12	43	24	52	10	5	6-1	.285	.356	.471	.826	8	.965
2001— Cincinnati (N.L.)	3B	103	381	54	112	26	2	14	62	29	71	8	9	6-3	.294	.351	.483	.834	19	.936
— Louisville (Int'l)	3B	1	4	0	1	0	0	0	0	0	0	0	0	0-0	.250	.250	.250	.500	0	1.000
2002— Cincinnati (N.L.)	3B-SS	• 162	606	83	146	38	2	26	87	56	111	10	9	32-8	.241	.314	.439	.753	22	.956
2003— Cincinnati (N.L.)	3B-2B-SS	106	403	61	110	19	3	18	65	35	74	5	6	15-3	.273	.339	.469	.808	17	.956
— New York (A.L.)	3B	54	189	31	48	13	0	6	31	11	30	3	7	8-0	.254	.302	.418	.720	6	.961
American League totals (1 year)		**54**	**189**	**31**	**48**	**13**	**0**	**6**	**31**	**11**	**30**	**3**	**7**	**8-0**	**.254**	**.302**	**.418**	**.720**	**6**	**.961**
National League totals (7 years)		**668**	**2383**	**327**	**646**	**141**	**14**	**86**	**362**	**191**	**428**	**46**	**39**	**83-22**	**.271**	**.334**	**.450**	**.785**	**92**	**.953**
Major League totals (7 years)		**722**	**2572**	**358**	**694**	**154**	**14**	**92**	**393**	**202**	**458**	**49**	**46**	**91-22**	**.270**	**.332**	**.448**	**.780**	**98**	**.953**

BOONE, BRET   2B

PERSONAL: Born April 6, 1969, in El Cajon, Calif. ... 5-10/190. ... Bats right, throws right. ... Full name: Bret Robert Boone. ... High school: El Dorado (Yorba Linda, Calif.). ... College: USC.

TRANSACTIONS/CAREER NOTES: Selected by Minnesota Twins organization in 28th round of free-agent draft (June 2, 1987); did not sign. ... Selected by Seattle Mariners organization in fifth round of free-agent draft (June 4, 1990). ... Traded by Mariners with P Erik Hanson to Cincinnati Reds for P Bobby Ayala and C Dan Wilson (November 2, 1993). ... On disabled list (April 1-16, 1996). ... Traded by Reds with P Mike Remlinger to Atlanta Braves for P Denny Neagle, OF Michael Tucker and P Rob Bell (November 10, 1998). ... Traded by Braves with OF/1B Ryan Klesko and P Jason Shiell to San Diego Padres for 2B Quilvio Veras, 1B Wally Joyner and OF Reggie Sanders (December 22, 1999). ... On disabled list (August 27, 2000-remainder of season). ... Granted free agency (October 31, 2000). ... Signed by Mariners (December 22, 2000). ... Granted free agency (November 5, 2001). ... Re-signed by Mariners (January 17, 2002).

2003 GAMES PLAYED BY POSITION (MLB): 2B—158.

Year	Team (League)	Pos.	G	AB	R	H	2B	3B	HR	RBI	BB	SO	HBP	GDP	SB-CS	Avg.	OBP	SLG	OPS	E	Pct.
1990— Peninsula (Caro.)	2B	74	255	42	68	13	2	8	38	47	57	1	1	5-2	.267	.383	.427	.810	19	.951
1991— Jacksonville (Sou.)	2B-3B	• 139	475	64	121	18	1	19	75	72	123	6	21	9-9	.255	.357	.417	.774	21	.970
1992— Calgary (PCL)	2B-SS	118	439	73	138	26	5	13	73	60	88	5	12	17-12	.314	.398	.485	.883	10	.984
— Seattle (A.L.)	2B-3B	33	129	15	25	4	0	4	15	4	34	1	4	1-1	.194	.224	.318	.542	6	.966
1993— Calgary (PCL)	2B	71	274	48	91	18	3	8	56	28	58	1	7	3-8	.332	.388	.507	.896	8	.976
— Seattle (A.L.)	2B-DH	76	271	31	68	12	2	12	38	17	52	4	6	2-3	.251	.301	.443	.743	3	.991
1994— Cincinnati (N.L.)	2B-3B	108	381	59	122	25	2	12	68	24	74	8	10	3-4	.320	.368	.491	.858	12	.975
1995— Cincinnati (N.L.)	2B	138	513	63	137	34	2	15	68	41	84	6	14	5-1	.267	.326	.429	.755	4	.994
1996— Cincinnati (N.L.)	2B	142	520	56	121	21	3	12	69	31	100	3	9	3-2	.233	.275	.354	.629	6	.991
1997— Cincinnati (N.L.)	2B	139	443	40	99	25	1	7	46	45	101	4	11	5-5	.223	.298	.332	.630	2	.994
— Indianapolis (A.A.)	2B	3	7	1	2	1	0	0	1	2	2	0	0	1-0	.286	.444	.429	.873	0	1.000
1998— Cincinnati (N.L.)	2B	157	583	76	155	38	1	24	95	48	104	4	23	6-4	.266	.324	.458	.782	9	.988
1999— Atlanta (N.L.)	2B	152	608	102	153	38	1	20	63	47	112	5	11	14-9	.252	.310	.416	.726	13	.982
2000— San Diego (N.L.)	2B	127	463	61	116	18	2	19	74	50	97	5	11	8-4	.251	.326	.421	.747	15	.977
2001— Seattle (A.L.)	2B-DH	158	623	118	206	37	3	37	* 141	40	110	9	11	5-5	.331	.372	.578	.950	10	.986
2002— Seattle (A.L.)	2B-DH	155	608	88	169	34	3	24	107	53	102	6	11	12-5	.278	.339	.462	.801	7	.989
2003— Seattle (A.L.)	2B	159	622	111	183	35	5	35	117	68	125	7	17	16-3	.294	.366	.535	.902	7	.990
American League totals (5 years)		**581**	**2253**	**363**	**651**	**122**	**13**	**112**	**418**	**182**	**423**	**27**	**49**	**36-17**	**.289**	**.345**	**.504**	**.849**	**33**	**.987**
National League totals (7 years)		**963**	**3511**	**457**	**903**	**199**	**12**	**109**	**483**	**286**	**672**	**35**	**89**	**44-29**	**.257**	**.316**	**.414**	**.730**	**61**	**.987**
Major League totals (12 years)		**1544**	**5764**	**820**	**1554**	**321**	**25**	**221**	**901**	**468**	**1095**	**62**	**138**	**80-46**	**.270**	**.328**	**.449**	**.777**	**94**	**.987**

B

BOOTCHECK, CHRIS — P

PERSONAL: Born October 24, 1978, in LaPorte, Ind. ... 6-5/200. ... Throws right, bats right. ... Full name: Christopher Brandon Bootcheck. ... High school: La Porte (Ind.). ... College: Auburn.

TRANSACTIONS/CAREER NOTES: Selected by Anaheim Angels in first round (20th pick overall) of free-agent draft (June 5, 2000).

CAREER HITTING: 0-for-0 (.000), 0 R, 0 2B, 0 3B, 0 HR, 0 RBI.

Year	League	W	L	Pct.	ERA	WHIP	G	GS	CG	ShO	Hld.	Sv.-Opp.	IP	H	R	ER	HR	BB-IBB	SO	Avg.
2001—	Rancho Cuca. (Calif.)	8	4	.667	3.93	1.23	15	14	1	0	...	0-...	87.0	84	45	38	11	23-0	86	.251
—	Arkansas (Texas)	3	3	.500	5.45	1.38	6	6	1	0	...	0-...	36.1	39	25	22	3	11-0	22	.265
2002—	Arkansas (Texas)	8	7	.533	4.81	1.42	19	19	3	0	...	0-...	116.0	130	68	62	11	35-0	90	.277
—	Salt Lake (PCL)	4	3	.571	3.88	1.38	9	9	1	1	...	0-...	58.0	64	29	25	5	16-0	38	.283
2003—	Salt Lake (PCL)	8	9	.471	4.25	1.38	28	26	3	0	...	0-...	171.1	194	103	81	19	43-1	82	.290
—	Anaheim (A.L.)	0	1	.000	9.58	2.13	4	1	0	0	0	0-0	10.1	16	13	11	5	6-0	7	.340
Major League totals (1 year)		0	1	.000	9.58	2.13	4	1	0	0	0	0-0	10.1	16	13	11	5	6-0	7	.340

BORBON, PEDRO — P

PERSONAL: Born November 15, 1967, in Mao, Dominican Republic. ... 6-1/230. ... Throws left, bats left. ... Full name: Pedro Felix Borbon. ... High school: DeWitt Clinton (Sioux, N.J.). ... Junior college: Ranger College (Texas).

TRANSACTIONS/CAREER NOTES: Selected by Milwaukee Brewers organization in 35th round of free-agent draft (June 3, 1985); did not sign. ... Selected by Los Angeles Dodgers organization in secondary phase of free-agent draft (January 14, 1986); did not sign. ... Signed as non-drafted free agent by Chicago White Sox organization (June 4, 1988). ... Released by White Sox (April 1, 1989). ... Signed by Atlanta Braves organization (August 25, 1989). ... On Atlanta disabled list (April 8-26 and August 23, 1996-remainder of season); included rehabilitation assignment to Greenville (April 23-26). ... On disabled list (March 30, 1997-entire season). ... On Atlanta disabled list (March 29, 1998-entire season); included rehabilitation assignments to Macon (June 4-7), Greenville (June 9-July 5 and July 9-14) and Richmond (July 16-August 31 and September 1-8). ... Granted free agency (October 1, 1998). ... Signed by Dodgers organization (December 30, 1998). ... Traded by Dodgers with OF Raul Mondesi to Toronto Blue Jays for OF Shawn Green and 2B Jorge Nunez (November 8, 1999). ... Traded by Blue Jays to Houston Astros for a player to be named later (May 15, 2002). ... Granted free agency (October 28, 2002). ... Signed by Dodgers organization (January 13, 2003). ... Released by Dodgers (March 13, 2003). ... Signed as free agent by St. Louis Cardinals (July 28, 2003). ... Sent to Louisville by St. Louis (August 17, 2003). ... Recalled by St. Louis from Memphis; released by St. Louis (September 9, 2003).

CAREER HITTING: 1-for-7 (.143), 0 R, 0 2B, 0 3B, 0 HR, 0 RBI.

Year	League	W	L	Pct.	ERA	WHIP	G	GS	CG	ShO	Hld.	Sv.-Opp.	IP	H	R	ER	HR	BB-IBB	SO	Avg.
1988—	GC White Sox (GCL)	5	3	.625	2.41	0.92	16	11	1	1		1-...	74.2	52	28	20	1	17-0	67	.190
1989—											Did not play.									
1990—	Burlington (Midw.)	11	3	.786	1.47	0.98	14	14	6	2	...	0-...	97.2	73	25	16	3	23-0	76	.206
—	Durham (Caro.)	4	5	.444	5.43	1.45	11	11	0	0	...	0-...	61.1	73	40	37	8	16-0	37	.299
1991—	Durham (Caro.)	4	3	.571	2.27	1.32	37	6	1	0	...	5-...	91.0	85	40	23	2	35-2	79	.249
—	Greenville (Sou.)	0	1	.000	2.79	1.14	4	4	0	0	...	0-...	29.0	23	12	9	1	10-0	22	.217
1992—	Greenville (Sou.)	8	2	.800	3.06	1.22	39	10	0	0	...	3-...	94.0	73	36	32	6	42-1	79	.218
—	Atlanta (N.L.)	0	1	.000	6.75	2.25	2	0	0	0	0	0-0	1.1	2	1	1	0	1-1	1	.333
1993—	Richmond (Int'l)	5	5	.500	4.23	1.47	52	0	0	0	...	1-...	76.2	71	40	36	7	42-9	95	.247
—	Atlanta (N.L.)	0	0	...	21.60	3.60	3	0	0	0	0	0-0	1.2	3	4	4	0	3-0	2	.429
1994—	Richmond (Int'l)	3	4	.429	2.79	1.33	59	0	0	0	...	4-...	80.2	66	29	25	3	41-5	82	.228
1995—	Atlanta (N.L.)	2	2	.500	3.09	1.44	41	0	0	0	6	2-4	32.0	29	12	11	2	17-4	33	.240
1996—	Atlanta (N.L.)	3	0	1.000	2.75	0.92	43	0	0	0	4	1-1	36.0	26	12	11	1	7-0	31	.203
—	Greenville (Sou.)	0	0	...	0.00	0.00	1	0	0	0	...	0-...	1.0	0	0	0	0	0-0	0	.000
1997—	Atlanta (N.L.)											Did not play.									
1998—	Macon (S. Atl.)	0	0	...	9.00	1.67	3	0	0	0	...	0-...	3.0	4	3	3	1	1-0	3	.308
—	Greenville (Sou.)	0	2	.000	4.74	1.84	16	0	0	0	...	0-...	19.0	21	14	10	2	14-0	10	.288
—	Richmond (Int'l)	0	1	.000	5.70	1.56	20	0	0	0	...	0-...	23.2	29	17	15	1	8-0	15	.302
1999—	Los Angeles (N.L.)	4	3	.571	4.09	1.34	70	0	0	0	15	1-2	50.2	39	23	23	5	29-1	33	.209
2000—	Toronto (A.L.)	1	1	.500	6.48	1.99	59	0	0	0	12	1-1	41.2	45	37	30	5	38-5	29	.280
2001—	Toronto (A.L.)	2	4	.333	3.71	1.13	71	0	0	0	13	0-5	53.1	48	24	22	8	12-3	45	.244
2002—	Toronto (A.L.)	1	2	.333	4.97	1.42	16	0	0	0	1	0-2	12.2	12	8	7	3	6-3	11	.231
—	Houston (N.L.)	3	2	.600	5.50	1.59	56	0	0	0	16	1-3	37.2	41	24	23	7	19-5	39	.287
2003—	St. Louis (N.L.)	0	1	.000	20.25	4.00	7	0	0	0	1	0-0	4.0	14	9	9	2	2-2	5	.560
—	Memphis (PCL)	0	1	.000	3.12	0.70	7	0	0	0	...	1-...	8.2	6	3	3	1	0-0	6	.200
American League totals (3 years)		4	7	.364	4.93	1.50	146	0	0	0	26	1-8	107.2	105	69	59	16	56-11	85	.256
National League totals (7 years)		12	9	.571	4.52	1.42	222	0	0	0	42	5-10	163.1	154	85	82	17	78-13	139	.250
Major League totals (9 years)		16	16	.500	4.68	1.45	368	0	0	0	68	6-18	271.0	259	154	141	33	134-24	224	.252

BORCHARD, JOE — OF

PERSONAL: Born November 25, 1978, in Panorama City, Calif. ... 6-5/220. ... Bats both, throws right. ... Full name: Joseph Edward Borchard. ... Name pronounced: BORE-churd. ... High school: Camarillo (Calif.). ... College: Stanford.

TRANSACTIONS/CAREER NOTES: Selected by Baltimore Orioles organization in 20th round of free-agent draft (June 3, 1997); did not sign. ... Selected by Chicago White Sox organization in first round (12th pick overall) of free-agent draft (June 5, 2000). ... On Charlotte disabled list (April 4-22, 2002). ... Recalled by Chicago from Charlotte (May 23, 2003). ... Optioned to Charlotte of the International League (June 9, 2003). ... Recalled by Chicago from Charlotte (September 29, 2003).

2003 GAMES PLAYED BY POSITION (MLB): OF—16.

Year	Team (League)	Pos.	G	AB	R	H	2B	3B	HR	RBI	BB	SO	HBP	GDP	SB-CS	Avg.	OBP	SLG	OPS	E	Pct.
2000—	Ariz. White Sox (Ariz.)	OF	7	29	3	12	4	0	0	8	4	4	0	0	0-0	.414	.485	.552	1.037	0	1.000
—	Win.-Salem (Car.)	OF	14	52	7	15	3	0	2	7	6	9	2	0	0-0	.288	.377	.462	.839	0	1.000
—	Birmingham (Sou.)	OF	6	22	3	5	0	1	0	3	3	8	0	1	0-0	.227	.308	.318	.626	1	.875
2001—	Birmingham (Sou.)	OF	133	515	95	152	27	1	27	98	67	158	10	13	5-4	.295	.384	.509	.892	12	.964
2002—	Win.-Salem (Car.)	OF	2	3	1	0	0	0	0	0	6	0	0	0	0-0	.000	.667	.000	.667	0	1.000
—	Charlotte (Int'l)	OF	117	438	62	119	35	2	20	59	49	139	4	11	2-4	.272	.349	.498	.847	3	.990
—	Chicago (A.L.)	OF	16	36	5	8	0	0	2	5	1	14	0	0	0-0	.222	.243	.389	.632	0	1.000
2003—	Chicago (A.L.)	OF	16	49	5	9	1	0	1	5	5	18	0	0	0-1	.184	.246	.265	.511	0	1.000
—	Charlotte (Int'l)	OF	114	435	62	110	20	2	13	53	27	103	8	14	2-4	.253	.307	.398	.705	5	.985
Major League totals (2 years)			32	85	10	17	1	0	3	10	6	32	0	0	0-1	.200	.245	.318	.562	0	1.000

BORDERS, PAT   C

PERSONAL: Born May 14, 1963, in Columbus, Ohio. ... 6-2/200. ... Bats right, throws right. ... Full name: Patrick Lance Borders. ... High school: Lake Wales (Fla.).

TRANSACTIONS/CAREER NOTES: Selected by Toronto Blue Jays organization in sixth round of free-agent draft (June 7, 1982). ... On Toronto disabled list (July 5-August 19, 1988); included rehabilitation assignment to Syracuse (July 30-August 19). ... Granted free agency (October 21, 1994). ... Signed by Kansas City Royals (April 10, 1995). ... Traded by Royals to Houston Astros for a player to be named later (August 12, 1995); Royals acquired P Rick Huisman to complete deal (August 17, 1995). ... On Houston suspended list (September 8-14, 1995). ... Granted free agency (November 6, 1995). ... Signed by St. Louis Cardinals organization (January 10, 1996). ... Traded by Cardinals to California Angels for P Ben VanRyn (June 15, 1996). ... Traded by Angels to Chicago White Sox for P Robert Ellis (July 27, 1996). ... Granted free agency (November 8, 1996). ... Signed by Cleveland Indians organization (December 13, 1996). ... Granted free agency (November 7, 1997). ... Re-signed by Indians organization (December 17, 1997). ... Granted free agency (November 3, 1998). ... Re-signed by Indians organization (February 26, 1999). ... Released by Indians (August 30, 1999). ... Signed by Blue Jays (August 31, 1999). ... Granted free agency (November 11, 1999). ... Signed by Tampa Bay Devil Rays (January 27, 2000). ... Contract sold by Devil Rays to Seattle Mariners organization (August 27, 2001). ... Granted free agency (November 7, 2001). ... Signed by Texas Rangers organization (February 2, 2002). ... Released by Rangers (April 2, 2002). ... Signed by Mariners organization (April 8, 2002). ... Granted free agency (November 4, 2002). ... Re-signed by Mariners organization (December 7, 2002). ... Recalled by Seattle from Tacoma (May 31, 2003). ... Optioned to Tacoma by Seattle (June 16, 2003). ... Optioned to Tacoma of the Pacific Coast League by Seattle (July 5, 2003). ... Recalled by Seattle from Tacoma (July 25, 2003). ... Sent to Tacoma by Seattle (August 15, 2003). ... Recalled from Tacoma by Seattle (August 31, 2003).

2003 GAMES PLAYED BY POSITION (MLB): C—7, 3B—2, DH—1.

								BATTING												FIELDING	
Year	Team (League)	Pos.	G	AB	R	H	2B	3B	HR	RBI	BB	SO	HBP	GDP	SB-CS	Avg.	OBP	SLG	OPS	E	Pct.
1982— Medicine Hat (Pio.)		3B	61	217	30	66	12	2	5	33	24	52	2	...	1-2	.304	.377	.447	.824	* 25	.826
1983— Florence (S. Atl.)		3B	131	457	62	125	31	4	5	54	46	116	1	...	4-1	.274	.341	.392	.732	* 41	.881
1984— Florence (S. Atl.)		3B-1B-OF	131	467	69	129	32	5	12	85	56	109	1	6	3-4	.276	.353	.443	.796	25	.967
1985— Kinston (Caro.)		1B	127	460	43	120	16	1	10	60	45	116	1	11	6-5	.261	.327	.365	.692	* 20	.978
1986— Florence (S. Atl.)		C-OF	16	40	8	15	7	0	3	9	2	9	0	0	0-0	.375	.405	.775	1.180	0	1.000
— Knoxville (Sou.)		C-1B	12	34	3	12	1	0	2	5	1	6	0	2	0-3	.353	.371	.559	.930	3	.943
— Kinston (Caro.)		C-1B-OF	49	174	24	57	10	0	6	26	10	42	1	5	0-0	.328	.366	.489	.854	7	.971
1987— Dunedin (Fla. St.)		1B	3	11	0	4	0	0	0	1	0	3	0	0	0-0	.364	.364	.364	.727	0	1.000
— Knoxville (Sou.)		3B-C	94	349	44	102	14	1	11	51	20	56	2	13	2-5	.292	.332	.433	.764	12	.976
1988— Toronto (A.L.) 2B-3B-DH-C			56	154	15	42	6	3	5	21	3	24	0	5	0-0	.273	.285	.448	.733	7	.970
— Syracuse (Int'l)		C	35	120	11	29	8	0	3	14	16	22	0	1	0-0	.242	.326	.383	.709	3	.991
1989— Toronto (A.L.)		DH-C	94	241	22	62	11	1	3	29	11	45	1	7	2-1	.257	.290	.349	.639	6	.980
1990— Toronto (A.L.)		DH-C	125	346	36	99	24	2	15	49	18	57	0	17	0-1	.286	.319	.497	.816	4	.993
1991— Toronto (A.L.)		C	105	291	22	71	17	0	5	36	11	45	1	8	0-0	.244	.271	.354	.625	4	.993
1992— Toronto (A.L.)		C	138	480	47	116	26	2	13	53	33	75	2	11	1-1	.242	.290	.385	.676	8	.991
1993— Toronto (A.L.)		C	138	488	38	124	30	0	9	55	20	66	2	18	2-2	.254	.285	.371	.656	* 13	.986
1994— Toronto (A.L.)		C	85	295	24	73	13	1	3	26	15	50	0	1	1-1	.247	.284	.329	.613	8	.988
1995— Kansas City (A.L.)		C-DH	52	143	14	33	8	1	4	13	7	22	0	1	0-0	.231	.267	.385	.651	0	1.000
— Houston (N.L.)		C	11	35	1	4	0	0	0	0	2	7	0	2	0-0	.114	.162	.114	.276	1	.987
1996— St. Louis (N.L.)		C-1B	26	69	3	22	3	0	0	4	1	14	0	1	0-1	.319	.329	.362	.691	3	.977
— California (A.L.)		C	19	57	6	13	3	0	2	8	3	11	0	1	0-1	.228	.267	.386	.653	2	.984
— Chicago (A.L.)		C-DH	31	94	6	26	1	0	3	6	5	18	0	2	0-0	.277	.313	.383	.696	3	.982
1997— Cleveland (A.L.)		C	55	159	17	47	7	1	4	15	9	27	2	5	0-2	.296	.341	.428	.769	0	1.000
1998— Cleveland (A.L.)		C-3B	54	160	12	38	6	0	0	8	6	40	2	3	0-2	.238	.289	.275	.564	6	.974
1999— Buffalo (Int'l)		C-DH	55	198	17	47	7	0	5	23	12	31	3	5	0-1	.237	.290	.348	.638	5	.986
— Cleveland (A.L.)		C-3B	6	20	2	6	0	1	0	3	0	3	0	0	0-1	.300	.300	.400	.700	2	.943
— Toronto (A.L.)		DH-C	6	14	1	3	0	0	1	3	1	2	0	0	0-0	.214	.267	.429	.695	0	1.000
2000— Durham (Int'l)		C-1B	96	348	44	95	16	0	12	55	20	66	1	8	7-2	.273	.311	.422	.733	3	.995
2001— Durham (Int'l)		C-1B	87	313	26	74	15	1	2	28	16	61	2	14	3-2	.236	.278	.310	.588	4	.989
— Tacoma (PCL)		C	3	11	2	3	0	0	1	2	1	1	1	1	0-0	.273	.385	.545	.930	0	1.000
— Seattle (A.L.)		C	5	6	1	3	0	0	0	0	0	1	0	0	0-0	.500	.500	.500	1.000	1	.923
2002— Tacoma (PCL)		C-3B-1B	92	317	42	84	16	1	12	27	11	47	0	6	3-2	.265	.289	.435	.724	5	.992
— Seattle (A.L.)		DH-C	4	4	0	2	1	0	0	1	0	1	0	0	0-0	.500	.500	.750	1.250	0	1.000
2003— Tacoma (PCL)		C-3B-1B	79	293	36	92	27	1	12	51	20	54	4	12	1-2	.314	.363	.536	.898	6	.987
— Seattle (A.L.)		C-3B-DH	12	14	1	2	1	0	0	1	1	5	0	0	0-0	.143	.200	.214	.414	0	1.000
American League totals (15 years)			985	2966	264	760	154	12	67	325	147	492	10	85	6-12	.256	.292	.384	.676	66	.988
National League totals (2 years)			37	104	4	26	3	0	0	4	3	21	0	3	0-1	.250	.271	.279	.550	4	.980
Major League totals (15 years)			1022	3070	268	786	157	12	67	329	150	513	10	88	6-13	.256	.291	.380	.672	70	.987

BORDICK, MIKE   SS

PERSONAL: Born July 21, 1965, in Marquette, Mich. ... 5-11/174. ... Bats right, throws right. ... Full name: Michael Todd Bordick. ... Name pronounced: BOR-dick. ... High school: Hampden (Maine) Academy. ... College: Maine.

TRANSACTIONS/CAREER NOTES: Signed as non-drafted free agent by Oakland Athletics organization (July 10, 1986). ... On Tacoma disabled list (April 14-May 13, 1991). ... On Oakland disabled list (May 8-27, 1995); included rehabilitation assignment to Modesto (May 23-26). ... Granted free agency (December 7, 1996). ... Signed by Baltimore Orioles (December 13, 1996). ... Traded by Orioles to New York Mets for OF Melvin Mora, 3B Mike Kinkade, P Lesli Brea and P Pat Gorman (July 28, 2000). ... Granted free agency (October 27, 2000). ... Signed by Orioles (December 20, 2000). ... On Baltimore disabled list (June 14, 2001-remainder of season); included rehabilitation assignments to Bowie (August 2-3) and Delmarva (August 4-10). ... On disabled list (July 16-August 17, 2002). ... Granted free agency (October 31, 2002). ... Signed by Toronto Blue Jays (December 20, 2002).

2003 GAMES PLAYED BY POSITION (MLB): SS—69, 3B—22, 2B—13, DH—1.

								BATTING												FIELDING	
Year	Team (League)	Pos.	G	AB	R	H	2B	3B	HR	RBI	BB	SO	HBP	GDP	SB-CS	Avg.	OBP	SLG	OPS	E	Pct.
1986— Medford (N'west)		SS	46	187	30	48	3	1	0	19	40	21	1	5	6-0	.257	.389	.283	.672	18	.921
1987— Modesto (Calif.)		SS	133	497	73	133	17	0	3	75	87	92	5	13	8-8	.268	.377	.320	.697	17	* .968
1988— Huntsville (Sou.) 2B-3B-SS			132	481	48	130	13	2	0	28	87	50	4	11	7-9	.270	.384	.306	.690	24	.965
1989— Tacoma (PCL) 2B-3B-SS			136	487	55	117	17	1	1	43	58	51	7	14	4-9	.240	.329	.285	.614	33	.954
1990— Oakland (A.L.) 2B-3B-SS			25	14	0	1	0	0	0	0	1	4	0	0	0-0	.071	.133	.071	.205	0	1.000
— Tacoma (PCL)		2B-SS	111	348	49	79	16	1	2	30	46	40	3	6	3-0	.227	.321	.296	.617	16	‡ .973
1991— Tacoma (PCL)		SS	26	81	15	22	4	1	2	14	17	10	1	0	0-1	.272	.404	.420	.824	3	.974
— Oakland (A.L.) 2B-3B-SS			90	235	21	56	5	1	0	21	14	37	3	3	3-4	.238	.289	.268	.557	11	.970
1992— Oakland (A.L.)		2B-SS	154	504	62	151	19	4	3	48	40	59	9	10	12-6	.300	.358	.371	.729	16	.979
1993— Oakland (A.L.)		SS-2B	159	546	60	136	21	2	3	48	60	58	11	9	10-10	.249	.332	.311	.644	13	.982
1994— Oakland (A.L.)		SS-2B	114	391	38	99	18	4	2	37	38	44	3	9	7-2	.253	.320	.335	.655	14	.973
1995— Oakland (A.L.)		SS-DH	126	428	46	113	13	0	8	44	35	45	5	8	11-3	.264	.325	.350	.675	10	.983
— Modesto (Calif.)		SS	1	2	0	0	0	0	0	0	0	1	0	0	0-1	.000	.333	.000	.333	0	1.000

B

Year	Team (League)	Pos.	G	AB	R	H	2B	3B	HR	RBI	BB	SO	HBP	GDP	SB-CS	Avg.	OBP	SLG	OPS	E	Pct.
1996— Oakland (A.L.)	SS	155	525	46	126	18	4	5	54	52	59	1	8	5-6	.240	.307	.318	.625	16	.979
1997— Baltimore (A.L.)	SS	153	509	55	120	19	1	7	46	33	66	2	23	0-2	.236	.283	.318	.601	13	.980
1998— Baltimore (A.L.)	SS	151	465	59	121	29	1	13	51	39	65	10	13	6-7	.260	.328	.411	.739	7	.990
1999— Baltimore (A.L.)	SS	160	631	93	175	35	7	10	77	54	102	5	25	14-4	.277	.334	.403	.737	9	.989
2000— Baltimore (A.L.)	SS	100	391	70	116	22	1	16	59	34	71	1	12	6-5	.297	.350	.481	.831	9	.979
— New York (N.L.)	SS	56	192	18	50	8	0	4	21	15	28	2	4	3-1	.260	.321	.365	.685	7	.968
2001— Baltimore (A.L.)	SS	58	229	32	57	13	0	7	30	17	36	6	4	9-3	.249	.314	.397	.711	6	.977
— Bowie (East.)	DH	1	4	0	1	0	0	0	0	0	1	0	0	0-0	.250	.250	.250	.500	...	...
— Delmarva (S. Atl.)	SS	3	8	0	0	0	0	0	1	2	1	0	0	0-0	.000	.200	.000	.200	0	...
2002— Baltimore (A.L.)	SS	117	367	37	85	19	3	8	36	35	63	3	9	7-4	.232	.302	.365	.667	1	.998
2003— Toronto (A.L.)	S-3-2-DH	102	343	39	94	18	2	5	54	33	60	2	8	3-1	.274	.340	.382	.722	5	.988
American League totals (14 years)		1664	5578	658	1450	249	30	87	605	485	772	61	141	93-57	.260	.323	.362	.685	130	.983
National League totals (1 year)		56	192	18	50	8	0	4	21	15	28	2	4	3-1	.260	.321	.365	.685	7	.968
Major League totals (14 years)		1720	5770	676	1500	257	30	91	626	500	800	63	145	96-58	.260	.323	.362	.685	137	.982

BORLAND, TOBY — P

PERSONAL: Born May 29, 1969, in Quitman, La. ... 6-6/210. ... Throws right, bats right. ... Full name: Toby Shawn Borland. ... High school: Quitman (La.).

TRANSACTIONS/CAREER NOTES: Selected by Philadelphia Phillies organization in 27th round of free-agent draft (June 2, 1987). ... On Philadelphia disabled list (June 14-July 8, 1995); included rehabilitation assignment to Scranton/Wilkes-Barre (June 22-July 8). ... Traded by Phillies with P Ricardo Jordan to New York Mets for 1B Rico Brogna (November 27, 1996). ... Traded by Mets to Boston Red Sox for P Rick Trlicek (May 12, 1997). ... Granted free agency (October 15, 1997). ... Signed by Cincinnati Reds organization (November 27, 1997). ... Released by Reds (March 5, 1998). ... Signed by Phillies organization (March 6, 1998). ... Released by Phillies (July 6, 1998). ... Signed by Florida Marlins organization (July 14, 1998). ... Granted free agency (October 15, 1998). ... Signed by Anaheim Angels organization (November 23, 1998). ... On Edmonton disabled list (June 1, 1999-remainder of season). ... Granted free agency (October 15, 1999). ... Re-signed by Angels organization (January 25, 2000). ... On Edmonton disabled list (April 7-July 25, 2000). ... Granted free agency (October 18, 2000). ... Re-signed by Angels organization (November 27, 2000). ... On Salt Lake disabled list (August 29, 2001-remainder of season). ... Granted free agency (October 8, 2001). ... Signed by Marlins organization (November 20, 2001). ... Contract purchased by Florida from Albuquerque (April 28, 2003). ... Placed on the 15-day disabled list by Florida (May 15, 2003). ... Transferred to Emergency disabled list (June 23, 2003).

CAREER HITTING: 1-for-12 (.083), 1 R, 0 2B, 0 3B, 0 HR, 2 RBI.

Year	League	W	L	Pct.	ERA	WHIP	G	GS	CG	ShO	Hld.	Sv.-Opp.	IP	H	R	ER	HR	BB-IBB	SO	Avg.
1988— Martinsville (App.)		2	3	.400	4.04	1.45	34	0	0	0	...	*12-...	49.0	42	26	22	1	29-1	43	.233
1989— Spartanburg (SAL)		4	5	.444	2.97	1.46	47	0	0	0	...	9-...	66.2	62	29	22	3	35-1	48	.248
1990— Clearwater (Fla. St.)		1	2	.333	2.26	1.32	44	0	0	0	...	5-...	59.2	44	21	15	1	35-4	44	.209
— Reading (East.)		4	1	.800	1.44	1.08	14	0	0	0	...	0-...	25.0	16	6	4	1	11-1	26	.186
1991— Reading (East.)		8	3	.727	2.70	1.62	59	0	0	0	...	•24-...	76.2	68	31	23	2	56-5	72	.232
1992— Scran./W.B. (I.L.)		0	1	.000	7.24	1.87	27	0	0	0	...	1-...	27.1	25	23	22	2	26-3	25	.253
— Reading (East.)		2	4	.333	3.43	1.69	32	0	0	0	...	5-...	42.0	39	23	16	2	32-3	45	.244
1993— Reading (East.)		2	2	.500	2.52	1.08	44	0	0	0	...	13-...	53.2	38	17	15	2	20-1	74	.194
— Scran./W.B. (I.L.)		2	4	.333	5.76	1.72	26	0	0	0	...	1-...	29.2	31	20	19	4	20-3	26	.273
1994— Scran./W.B. (I.L.)		4	1	.800	1.68	1.06	27	1	0	0	...	4-...	53.2	36	12	10	2	21-7	61	.191
— Philadelphia (N.L.)		1	0	1.000	2.36	1.31	24	0	0	0	0	1-1	34.1	31	10	9	1	14-3	26	.248
1995— Philadelphia (N.L.)		1	3	.250	3.77	1.59	50	0	0	0	11	6-9	74.0	81	37	31	3	37-7	59	.277
— Scran./W.B. (I.L.)		0	0	...	0.00	0.97	8	0	0	0	...	1-...	11.1	5	0	0	0	6-1	15	.128
1996— Philadelphia (N.L.)		7	3	.700	4.07	1.39	69	0	0	0	10	0-2	90.2	83	51	41	9	43-3	76	.239
1997— New York (N.L.)		0	1	1.000	6.08	1.88	13	0	0	0	1	1-2	13.1	11	9	9	1	14-0	7	.240
— Boston (A.L.)		0	0	...	13.50	3.90	3	0	0	0	...	0-0	3.1	6	5	5	1	7-0	1	.400
— Pawtucket (Int'l)		2	0	1.000	3.99	1.58	28	2	0	0	...	2-...	47.1	50	22	21	5	25-3	46	.269
1998— Reading (East.)		1	3	.250	9.64	2.46	8	0	0	0	...	3-...	9.1	18	12	10	4	5-0	13	.400
— Scran./W.B. (I.L.)		0	2	.000	5.68	1.34	13	0	0	0	...	5-...	12.2	14	8	8	1	3-0	15	.298
— Philadelphia (N.L.)		0	0	...	5.00	1.44	6	0	0	0	...	0-0	9.0	8	5	5	1	5-0	9	.242
— Charlotte (Int'l)		3	0	1.000	2.70	1.47	19	0	0	0	...	0-...	36.2	33	12	11	3	21-1	26	.244
1999— Edmonton (PCL)		2	1	.667	7.00	2.00	21	0	0	0	...	0-...	27.0	31	24	21	5	23-2	34	.292
2000— Erie (East.)		1	3	.250	4.50	1.58	9	1	0	0	...	1-...	12.0	12	8	6	0	7-0	12	.250
2001— Salt Lake (PCL)		7	3	.700	2.30	1.10	45	1	0	0	...	0-...	74.1	53	25	19	2	29-0	92	.198
— Anaheim (A.L.)		0	1	.000	10.80	2.70	2	0	0	0	0	0-1	3.1	8	5	4	1	1-0	9	.471
2002— Calgary (PCL)		5	2	.714	2.96	1.21	56	0	0	0	...	14-...	70.0	55	24	23	2	30-3	75	.216
— Florida (N.L.)		1	0	1.000	5.27	1.39	15	0	0	0	1	0-0	13.2	14	8	8	3	5-0	11	.269
2003— Albuquerque (PCL)		1	1	.500	3.72	1.24	9	0	0	0	...	3-...	9.2	6	5	4	1	6-0	12	.176
— Florida (N.L.)		0	0	...	1.86	1.14	7	0	0	0	...	3-...	9.2	3	3	2	0	8-1	4	.097
American League totals (2 years)		0	1	.000	12.15	3.30	5	0	0	0	...	0-1	6.2	14	10	9	2	8-0	1	.438
National League totals (7 years)		10	7	.588	3.86	1.46	184	0	0	0	23	8-14	244.2	231	123	105	18	126-14	192	.248
Major League totals (8 years)		10	8	.556	4.08	1.51	189	0	0	0	23	8-15	251.1	245	133	114	20	134-14	193	.254

BOROWSKI, JOE — P

PERSONAL: Born May 4, 1971, in Bayonne, N.J. ... 6-2/225. ... Throws right, bats right. ... Full name: Joseph Thomas Borowski. ... Name pronounced: bor-OW-ski. ... High school: Marist (Bayonne, N.J.). ... College: Rutgers.

TRANSACTIONS/CAREER NOTES: Selected by Chicago White Sox organization in 32nd round of free-agent draft (June 5, 1989). ... Traded by White Sox to Baltimore Orioles for IF Pete Rose Jr. (March 21, 1991). ... Traded by Orioles with P Rachaad Stewart to Atlanta Braves for P Kent Mercker (December 17, 1995). ... Claimed on waivers by New York Yankees (September 15, 1997). ... On New York disabled list (August 24-September 8, 1998). ... Claimed on waivers by Milwaukee Brewers (December 4, 1998). ... Granted free agency (October 15, 1999). ... Signed by Cincinnati Reds organization (November 9, 1999). ... Released by Reds (April 14, 2000). ... Signed by Newark, Atlantic League (2000). ... Signed by Monterrey, Mexican League (2000). ... Signed by Chicago Cubs organization (December 11, 2000). ... Granted free agency (October 10, 2001). ... Re-signed by Cubs organization (November 20, 2001).

CAREER HITTING: 2-for-9 (.222), 1 R, 0 2B, 0 3B, 0 HR, 0 RBI.

Year	League	W	L	Pct.	ERA	WHIP	G	GS	CG	ShO	Hld.	Sv.-Opp.	IP	H	R	ER	HR	BB-IBB	SO	Avg.
1990— GC White Sox (GCL)		2	•8	.200	5.58	1.61	12	11	0	0	...	0-...	61.1	74	*47	*38	3	25-0	67	.289
1991— Kane County (Midwest)		7	2	.778	2.56	1.27	49	0	0	0	...	13-...	81.0	60	26	23	2	43-2	76	.207
1992— Frederick (Caro.)		5	6	.455	3.70	1.51	48	0	0	0	...	10-...	80.1	71	40	33	3	50-3	85	.238
1993— Frederick (Caro.)		1	1	.500	3.61	1.57	42	2	0	0	...	11-...	62.1	61	30	25	5	37-0	70	.258
— Bowie (East.)		3	0	1.000	0.00	1.25	9	0	0	0	...	0-...	17.2	11	0	0	1	11-3	17	.180
1994— Bowie (East.)		3	4	.429	1.91	1.21	49	0	0	0	...	14-...	66.0	52	14	14	3	28-3	73	.213

Year	League	W	L	Pct.	ERA	WHIP	G	GS	CG	ShO	Hld.	Sv.-Opp.	IP	H	R	ER	HR	BB-IBB	SO	Avg.
1995— Rochester (Int'l)		1	3	.250	4.04	1.40	28	0	0	0	...	6-...	35.2	32	16	16	3	18-2	32	.256
— Bowie (East.)		2	2	.500	3.92	1.11	16	0	0	0	...	7-...	20.2	16	9	9	2	7-1	32	.211
— Baltimore (A.L.)		0	0	...	1.23	1.23	6	0	0	0	0	0-0	7.1	5	1	1	0	4-0	3	.192
1996— Richmond (Int'l)		1	5	.167	3.71	1.35	34	0	0	0	...	7-...	53.1	42	25	22	4	30-1	40	.226
— Atlanta (N.L.)		2	4	.333	4.85	1.77	22	0	0	0	1	0-0	26.0	33	15	14	4	13-4	15	.324
1997— Atlanta (N.L.)		2	2	.500	3.75	1.79	20	0	0	0	2	0-0	24.0	27	11	10	2	16-4	6	.287
— Richmond (Int'l)		1	2	.333	3.58	1.35	21	0	0	0	...	2-...	37.2	32	16	15	3	19-2	34	.234
— New York (A.L.)		0	1	.000	9.00	3.00	1	0	0	0	0	0-0	2.0	2	2	2	0	4-1	2	.250
1998— Columbus (Int'l)		3	3	.500	2.93	1.43	45	0	0	0	...	4-...	73.2	66	25	24	6	39-1	67	.243
— New York (A.L.)		1	0	1.000	6.52	1.55	8	0	0	0	0	0-0	9.2	11	7	7	0	4-0	7	.289
1999— Louisville (Int'l)		6	2	.750	5.46	1.55	58	0	0	0	...	4-...	89.0	94	59	54	7	44-3	70	.275
2000— Newark (Atl.)		6	3	.667	5.50	1.62	28	0	0	0	...	0-...	37.2	44	23	23	...	17-...	39	...
— Monterrey (Mex.)		4	2	.667	3.19	1.16	12	5	0	0	...	1-...	42.1	31	15	15	5	18-...	44	...
2001— Iowa (PCL)		8	7	.533	2.62	1.03	39	12	1	1	...	1-...	110.0	87	35	32	10	26-3	131	.216
— Chicago (N.L.)		0	1	.000	32.40	5.40	1	1	0	0	0	0-0	1.2	6	6	6	1	3-0	1	.667
2002— Chicago (N.L.)		4	4	.500	2.73	1.18	73	0	0	0	12	2-6	95.2	84	31	29	10	29-6	97	.239
2003— Chicago (N.L.)		2	2	.500	2.63	1.05	68	0	0	0	1	33-37	68.1	53	23	20	5	19-1	66	.207
American League totals (3 years)		1	1	.500	4.74	1.58	15	0	0	0	0	0-0	19.0	18	10	10	0	12-1	12	.250
National League totals (5 years)		10	13	.435	3.30	1.31	184	1	0	0	16	35-43	215.2	203	86	79	22	80-15	185	.250
Major League totals (7 years)		11	14	.440	3.41	1.33	199	1	0	0	16	35-43	234.2	221	96	89	22	92-16	197	.250

BOTTALICO, RICKY P

PERSONAL: Born August 26, 1969, in New Britain, Conn. ... 6-0/222. ... Throws right, bats left. ... Full name: Richard Paul Bottalico. ... Name pronounced: bo-TAL-e-koh. ... High school: South Catholic (Hartford, Conn.). ... College: Central Connecticut State.

TRANSACTIONS/CAREER NOTES: Signed as non-drafted free agent by Philadelphia Phillies organization (July 21, 1991). ... On Philadelphia disabled list (April 24-July 1, 1998); included rehabilitation assignment to Scranton/Wilkes-Barre (June 6-July 1). ... On suspended list (August 25-28, 1998). ... Traded by Phillies with P Garrett Stephenson to St. Louis Cardinals for OF Ron Gant, P Jeff Brantley and P Cliff Politte (November 19, 1998). ... Granted free agency (December 21, 1999). ... Signed by Kansas City Royals (January 27, 2000). ... Granted free agency (November 4, 2000). ... Signed by Phillies (December 15, 2000). ... On Philadelphia disabled list (June 29-July 20, 2001); included rehabilitation assignment to Reading (July 13-20). ... Granted free agency (November 5, 2001). ... Re-signed by Phillies (January 8, 2002). ... On disabled list (June 23, 2002-remainder of season). ... Granted free agency (October 30, 2002). ... Signed by Arizona Diamondbacks organization (January 30, 2003). ... Contract purchased by Arizona from Tucson (June 23, 2003). ... Designated for assignment (June 30, 2003). ... Sent outright to Tucson by Arizona (July 2, 2003). ... Elected free agency (September 30, 2003).

CAREER HITTING: 2-for-15 (.133), 1 R, 2 2B, 0 3B, 0 HR, 1 RBI.

Year	League	W	L	Pct.	ERA	WHIP	G	GS	CG	ShO	Hld.	Sv.-Opp.	IP	H	R	ER	HR	BB-IBB	SO	Avg.
1991— Martinsville (App.)		3	2	.600	4.09	1.36	7	6	2	•1	...	0-...	33.0	32	20	15	2	13-0	38	.248
— Spartanburg (SAL)		2	0	1.000	0.00	0.40	2	2	0	0	...	0-...	15.0	4	0	0	0	2-0	11	.082
1992— Spartanburg (SAL)		5	10	.333	2.41	1.25	42	11	1	0	...	13-...	119.2	94	41	32	6	56-0	118	.216
1993— Clearwater (Fla. St.)		1	0	1.000	2.75	1.22	13	0	0	0	...	4-...	19.2	19	6	6	0	5-0	19	.257
— Reading (East.)		3	3	.500	2.25	1.24	49	0	0	0	...	20-...	72.0	63	22	18	4	26-3	65	.236
1994— Scran./W.B. (I.L.)		3	1	.750	8.87	2.42	19	0	0	0	...	3-...	22.1	32	27	22	4	22-2	22	.327
— Reading (East.)		2	2	.500	2.53	0.91	38	0	0	0	...	22-...	42.2	29	13	12	6	10-0	51	.190
— Philadelphia (N.L.)		0	0	...	0.00	1.33	3	0	0	0	0	0-...	3.0	3	0	0	0	1-0	3	.250
1995— Philadelphia (N.L.)		5	3	.625	2.46	1.05	62	0	0	0	*20	1-5	87.2	50	25	24	7	42-3	87	.167
1996— Philadelphia (N.L.)		4	5	.444	3.19	1.03	61	0	0	0	...	34-38	67.2	47	24	24	6	23-2	74	.197
1997— Philadelphia (N.L.)		2	5	.286	3.65	1.49	69	0	0	0	...	34-41	74.0	68	31	30	7	42-4	89	.245
1998— Philadelphia (N.L.)		1	5	.167	6.44	1.82	39	0	0	0	3	6-7	43.1	54	31	31	7	25-5	27	.305
— Scran./W.B. (I.L.)		0	1	.000	2.92	1.38	10	5	0	0	...	1-...	12.1	8	4	4	1	9-0	4	.190
1999— St. Louis (N.L.)		3	7	.300	4.91	1.80	68	0	0	0	8	20-28	73.1	83	45	40	8	49-1	66	.284
2000— Kansas City (A.L.)		9	6	.600	4.83	1.46	62	0	0	0	1	16-23	72.2	65	40	39	12	41-3	56	.239
2001— Philadelphia (N.L.)		3	4	.429	3.90	1.24	66	0	0	0	22	3-7	67.0	58	31	29	11	25-2	57	.241
— Reading (East.)		0	1	.000	1.80	0.80	3	3	0	0	...	0-...	5.0	3	2	1	1	1-0	5	.167
2002— Philadelphia (N.L.)		0	3	.000	4.61	1.68	30	0	0	0	15	0-1	27.1	33	16	14	3	13-2	24	.300
2003— Arizona (N.L.)		1	0	1.000	5.40	3.00	2	0	0	0	1	0-0	1.2	3	1	1	0	2-1	2	.375
— Tucson (PCL)		2	2	.500	3.68	1.40	31	0	0	0	...	0-...	39.1	39	24	16	4	16-1	28	.258
American League totals (1 year)		9	6	.600	4.83	1.46	62	0	0	0	1	16-23	72.2	65	40	39	12	41-3	56	.239
National League totals (9 years)		19	32	.373	3.90	1.40	400	0	0	0	69	98-127	445.0	399	204	193	49	222-20	429	.241
Major League totals (10 years)		28	38	.424	4.03	1.40	462	0	0	0	70	114-150	517.2	464	244	232	61	263-23	485	.241

BOWEN, ROB C

PERSONAL: Born February 24, 1981, in Bedford, Texas. ... 6-3/225. ... Bats both, throws right. ... Full name: Robert McClure Bowen. ... High school: Homestead (Fort Wayne, Ind.).

TRANSACTIONS/CAREER NOTES: Selected by Minnesota Twins organization in second round of free-agent draft (June 2, 1999). ... Recalled from Rochester by Minnesota (August 20, 2003).

2003 GAMES PLAYED BY POSITION (MLB): C—7.

Year	Team (League)	Pos.	G	AB	R	H	2B	3B	HR	RBI	BB	SO	HBP	GDP	SB-CS	Avg.	OBP	SLG	OPS	E	Pct.
1999— GC Twins (GCL)		C	29	77	10	20	4	0	0	11	20	15	0	0	2-2	.260	.400	.312	.712	8	.959
2000— Elizabethton (App.)		C	21	73	17	21	3	0	4	19	11	18	0	0	0-0	.288	.381	.493	.874	3	.983
2001— Quad City (Midw.)		C	106	385	47	98	18	2	18	70	37	112	2	11	4-0	.255	.321	.452	.773	6	.993
2002— Fort Myers (FSL)		C-1B	100	342	52	63	12	1	10	49	38	69	5	12	1-0	.184	.272	.313	.585	12	.981
— Quad City (Midw.)		C	5	21	1	4	1	0	0	2	2	4	0	0	0-0	.190	.261	.238	.499	0	1.000
2003— New Britain (East.)		C	42	134	17	41	13	0	1	16	13	24	2	0	0-0	.306	.376	.425	.801	2	.992
— Rochester (Int'l)		C-DH	30	105	14	27	7	0	6	17	11	25	1	3	0-0	.257	.333	.495	.829	1	.995
— Minnesota (A.L.)		C	7	10	0	1	0	0	0	1	0	4	0	1	0-0	.100	.091	.100	.191	1	.944
Major League totals (1 year)			7	10	0	1	0	0	0	1	0	4	0	1	0-0	.100	.091	.100	.191	1	.944

BOWIE, MICAH P

PERSONAL: Born November 10, 1974, in Webster, Texas. ... 6-4/203. ... Throws left, bats left. ... Full name: Micah Andrew Bowie. ... Name pronounced: bu-ee. ... High school: Kingwood (Texas).

TRANSACTIONS/CAREER NOTES: Signed as non-drafted free agent by Atlanta Braves organization (July 15, 1993). ... On Durham disabled list (July 4, 1996-remainder of season). ... On Richmond disabled list (May 18-June 10, 1999). ... Traded by Braves with P Ruben Quevado and a player to be named later to Chicago Cubs for P Terry Mulholland and SS Jose Hernandez (July 31, 1999); Cubs acquired P Joey Nation to complete deal (August 24, 1999). ... Released by Cubs (November 27, 2000). ... Signed by Oakland Athletics organization (December 20, 2000). ... Placed on the 15-day disabled list (May 26, 2003). ... Cleared waivers and sent outright to Sacramento of the Pacific Coast League by Oakland (May 1, 2003). ... Contract purchased by Oakland from Sacramento (May 11, 2003). ... Placed on the 15-day disabled list (May 23, 2003). ... Sent on rehab assignment by Oakland (August 18, 2003). ... Recalled from minor league rehab assignment (September 1, 2003). ... Transferred to 60-day disabled list (September 14, 2003).

CAREER HITTING: 3-for-14 (.214), 0 R, 0 2B, 0 3B, 0 HR, 3 RBI.

Year League	W	L	Pct.	ERA	WHIP	G	GS	CG	ShO	Hld.	Sv.-Opp.	IP	H	R	ER	HR	BB-IBB	SO	Avg.
1994— GC Braves (GCL)	0	3	.000	3.03	1.08	6	5	0	0	...	0-...	29.2	27	14	10	1	5-0	35	.233
— Danville (Appal.)	3	1	.750	3.58	1.26	7	5	0	0	...	0-...	32.2	28	16	13	4	13-1	38	.233
1995— Macon (S. Atl.)	4	1	.800	2.28	0.72	5	5	0	0	...	0-...	27.2	9	8	7	1	11-0	36	.100
— Durham (Caro.)	4	11	.267	3.59	1.38	23	23	1	0	...	0-...	130.1	119	65	52	8	61-3	91	.250
1996— Durham (Caro.)	3	6	.333	3.66	1.33	13	13	0	0	...	0-...	66.1	55	29	27	4	33-0	65	.235
1997— Durham (Caro.)	2	2	.500	3.66	1.42	9	6	0	0	...	0-...	39.1	29	16	16	2	27-0	44	.210
— Greenville (Sou.)	3	2	.600	3.50	1.37	8	7	0	0	...	0-...	43.2	34	19	17	3	26-1	41	.211
1998— Greenville (Sou.)	11	6	.647	3.48	1.20	30	•29	1	0	...	0-...	163.0	132	73	63	12	64-0	160	.221
1999— Richmond (Int'l)	4	4	.500	2.96	1.08	13	13	0	0	...	0-...	73.0	65	24	24	4	14-0	82	.241
— Atlanta (N.L.)	0	1	.000	13.50	3.00	3	0	0	0	0	0-0	4.0	8	6	6	1	4-0	2	.421
— Chicago (N.L.)	2	6	.250	9.96	2.19	11	11	0	0	0	0-0	47.0	73	54	52	8	30-2	39	.358
2000— Iowa (PCL)	1	7	.125	7.94	1.99	9	9	0	0	...	0-...	45.1	59	44	40	9	31-3	35	.321
— West Tenn. (Sou.)	7	6	.538	3.45	1.18	18	18	1	1	...	0-...	117.1	91	47	45	6	48-1	106	.216
2001— Sacramento (PCL)	6	8	.429	5.04	1.44	38	10	1	1	...	3-...	116.0	123	68	65	13	44-1	102	.272
2002— Sacramento (PCL)	3	2	.600	3.13	1.17	46	0	0	0	...	4-...	54.2	40	21	19	2	24-2	64	.201
— Oakland (A.L.)	2	0	1.000	1.50	1.67	13	0	0	0	3	0-0	12.0	12	2	2	1	8-1	8	.261
2003— Oakland (A.L.)	0	1	.000	7.56	1.80	6	0	0	0	0	0-0	8.1	13	7	7	1	2-0	4	.361
— Modesto (Calif.)	0	0	...	0.00	0.00	2	2	0	0	...	0-...	2.0	0	0	0	0	0-0	3	.000
— Sacramento (PCL)	0	0	...	0.00	0.75	5	0	0	0	...	2-...	4.0	2	1	0	0	1-0	3	.133
American League totals (2 years)	2	1	.667	3.98	1.72	19	0	0	0	3	0-0	20.1	25	9	9	2	10-1	12	.265
National League totals (1 year)	2	7	.222	10.24	2.25	14	11	0	0	0	0-0	51.0	81	60	58	9	34-2	41	.363
Major League totals (3 years)	4	8	.333	8.45	2.10	33	11	0	0	3	0-0	71.1	106	69	67	11	44-3	53	.348

BOWLES, BRIAN   P

PERSONAL: Born August 18, 1976, in Manhattan Beach, Calif. ... 6-5/220. ... Throws right, bats right. ... Full name: Brian Christopher Bowles. ... High school: Peninsula (Manhattan Beach, Calif.). ... College: UC-San Diego.

TRANSACTIONS/CAREER NOTES: Selected by Toronto Blue Jays organization in 50th round of free-agent draft (June 2, 1994). ... Recalled by Toronto from Syracuse (May 6, 1999). ... Optioned to Syracuse of the International League by Toronto (May 22, 2003). ... Optioned to Syracuse by Toronto (August 22, 2003). ... Recalled by Toronto from Syracuse (September 2, 2003).

CAREER HITTING: 0-for-0 (.000), 0 R, 0 2B, 0 3B, 0 HR, 0 RBI.

Year League	W	L	Pct.	ERA	WHIP	G	GS	CG	ShO	Hld.	Sv.-Opp.	IP	H	R	ER	HR	BB-IBB	SO	Avg.
1995— GC Blue Jays (GCL)	0	1	.000	2.40	1.40	8	0	0	0	...	0-...	15.0	18	12	4	2	3-0	11	.277
1996— Medicine Hat (Pio.)	2	2	.500	6.35	1.87	24	0	0	0	...	1-...	39.2	53	35	28	5	21-1	29	.325
1997— Hagerstown (S. Atl.)	1	0	1.000	6.97	1.84	4	0	0	0	...	0-...	10.1	14	10	8	2	5-0	9	.333
— Dunedin (Fla. St.)	0	2	.000	7.53	1.88	7	1	0	0	...	0-...	14.1	20	14	12	2	7-1	9	.333
— St. Catharines (NYP)	5	8	.385	5.03	1.41	16	16	0	0	...	0-...	78.2	76	53	44	6	35-0	64	.252
1998— Dunedin (Fla. St.)	1	2	.333	3.33	1.78	9	2	1	0	...	0-...	27.0	32	13	10	2	16-0	17	.299
— Hagerstown (S. Atl.)	2	4	.333	4.52	1.45	31	4	0	0	...	0-...	67.2	80	41	34	4	18-1	48	.292
1999— Hagerstown (S. Atl.)	6	2	.750	3.97	1.41	48	1	0	0	...	3-...	79.1	73	41	35	4	39-3	80	.246
2000— Tennessee (Sou.)	4	4	.500	2.98	1.22	49	0	0	0	...	0-...	81.2	64	31	27	1	36-1	72	.218
2001— Syracuse (Int'l)	3	5	.375	2.91	1.29	66	0	0	0	...	6-...	77.1	56	30	25	3	44-4	81	.199
— Toronto (A.L.)	0	0	...	0.00	1.36	2	0	0	0	0	0-0	3.2	4	0	0	0	1-0	4	.286
2002— Syracuse (Int'l)	4	7	.364	3.36	1.32	59	0	0	0	...	14-...	59.0	46	24	22	4	32-5	53	.216
— Toronto (A.L.)	2	1	.667	4.05	1.35	17	0	0	0	1	0-1	20.0	13	11	9	0	14-1	19	.183
2003— Syracuse (Int'l)	2	3	.400	2.66	1.44	41	0	0	0	...	14-...	47.1	47	23	14	1	21-3	32	.257
— Toronto (A.L.)	0	0	...	2.57	1.43	5	0	0	0	0	0-0	7.0	8	4	2	1	2-0	2	.267
Major League totals (3 years)	2	1	.667	3.23	1.37	24	0	0	0	1	0-1	30.2	25	15	11	1	17-1	25	.217

BOYD, JASON   P

PERSONAL: Born February 23, 1973, in St. Clair, Ill. ... 6-3/180. ... Throws right, bats right. ... Full name: Jason Pernell Boyd. ... High school: Edwardsville (Ill.). ... Junior college: John A. Logan College (Ill.).

TRANSACTIONS/CAREER NOTES: Selected by Philadelphia Phillies organization in eighth round of free-agent draft (June 2, 1994). ... Selected by Arizona Diamondbacks in first round (23rd pick overall) of expansion draft (November 18, 1997). ... On disabled list (May 22, 1998-remainder of season). ... Traded by Diamondbacks to Pittsburgh Pirates (August 25, 1999); completing deal in which Pirates traded 2B Tony Womack to Diamondbacks for P Paul Weichard and a player to be named later (February 26, 1999). ... Claimed on waivers by Milwaukee Brewers (March 29, 2000). ... Claimed on waivers by Philadelphia Phillies (March 31, 2000). ... On Philadelphia disabled list (March 25-May 4 and June 15-August 15, 2000); included rehabilitation assignments to Clearwater (April 7-15 and July 28-31) and Scranton (April 16-19, April 26-May 2 and August 1-15). ... Granted free agency (October 15, 2001). ... Signed by San Diego Padres organization (December 6, 2001). ... Released by Padres (August 4, 2002). ... Signed by Boston Red Sox organization (August 16, 2002). ... Granted free agency (October 15, 2002). ... Contract purchased by Cleveland from Buffalo (May 4, 2003). ... Suspended by Major League Baseball (June 27, 2003). ... Reinstated by MLB (June 30, 2003). ... Placed on 15-day disabled list by Cleveland (August 16, 2003). ... Removed from 15-day disabled list (September 1, 2003).

CAREER HITTING: 0-for-1 (.000), 0 R, 0 2B, 0 3B, 0 HR, 0 RBI.

Year League	W	L	Pct.	ERA	WHIP	G	GS	CG	ShO	Hld.	Sv.-Opp.	IP	H	R	ER	HR	BB-IBB	SO	Avg.
1994— Martinsville (App.)	3	7	.300	4.17	1.41	14	13	1	0	...	0-...	69.0	65	46	32	6	32-0	45	.242
1995— Piedmont (S. Atl.)	6	8	.429	3.58	1.29	26	24	1	0	...	0-...	151.0	151	77	60	8	44-0	129	.259
1996— Clearwater (Fla. St.)	11	8	.579	3.90	1.29	26	26	2	0	...	0-...	161.2	160	75	70	12	49-1	120	.261
1997— Reading (East.)	10	6	.625	4.82	1.53	48	7	0	0	...	0-...	115.2	113	65	62	16	64-7	98	.259
1998— Tucson (PCL)	2	2	.500	6.23	1.94	15	0	0	0	...	0-...	21.2	28	22	15	4	14-1	13	.298
1999— Tucson (PCL)	6	5	.545	4.52	1.36	44	0	0	0	...	5-...	75.2	76	42	38	6	27-2	60	.263
— Nashville (PCL)	0	0	...	0.00	0.43	5	0	0	0	...	0-...	4.2	2	0	0	0	0-0	2	.143
— Pittsburgh (N.L.)	0	0	...	3.38	1.31	4	0	0	0	0	0-0	5.1	5	2	2	0	2-0	4	.250
2000— Clearwater (Fla. St.)	1	0	1.000	2.38	1.32	6	3	0	0	...	0-...	11.1	11	4	3	0	4-0	12	.250
— Scran./W.B. (I.L.)	1	0	1.000	1.72	1.40	11	2	0	0	...	0-...	15.2	8	3	3	0	14-0	10	.157
— Philadelphia (N.L.)	0	1	.000	6.55	1.83	30	0	0	0	2	0-1	34.1	39	28	25	2	24-4	32	.293

Year	League	W	L	Pct.	ERA	WHIP	G	GS	CG	ShO	Hld.	Sv.-Opp.	IP	H	R	ER	HR	BB-IBB	SO	Avg.
2001— Scran./W.B. (I.L.)		2	7	.222	1.97	1.11	52	0	0	0	...	12-...	59.1	44	17	13	4	22-1	66	.205
2002— Portland (PCL)		0	1	.000	1.04	1.00	19	0	0	0	...	4-...	26.0	19	4	3	2	7-0	22	.216
— San Diego (N.L.)		1	0	1.000	7.94	1.69	23	0	0	0	4	0-3	28.1	33	29	25	6	15-1	18	.300
— Pawtucket (Int'l)		1	0	1.000	3.94	1.38	9	0	0	0	...	1-...	16.0	13	7	7	3	9-0	15	.213
2003— Buffalo (Int'l)		1	0	1.000	1.23	0.95	9	0	0	0	...	3-...	14.2	12	3	2	0	2-0	14	.222
— Cleveland (A.L.)		3	1	.750	4.30	1.22	44	0	0	0	8	0-1	52.1	38	25	25	4	26-1	31	.200
American League totals (1 year)		3	1	.750	4.30	1.22	44	0	0	0	8	0-1	52.1	38	25	25	4	26-1	31	.200
National League totals (3 years)		1	1	.500	6.88	1.74	57	0	0	0	6	0-4	68.0	77	59	52	8	41-5	54	.293
Major League totals (4 years)		4	2	.667	5.76	1.51	101	0	0	0	14	0-5	120.1	115	84	77	12	67-6	85	.254

BRADFORD, CHAD — P

PERSONAL: Born September 14, 1974, in Jackson, Miss. ... 6-5/203. ... Throws right, bats right. ... Full name: Chadwick Lee Bradford. ... High school: Byram (Jackson, Miss.). ... College: Southern Mississippi.

TRANSACTIONS/CAREER NOTES: Selected by Chicago White Sox organization in 13th round of free-agent draft (June 4, 1996). ... On Charlotte disabled list (June 28-July 5, 2000). ... Traded by White Sox to Oakland Athletics for a player to be named later (December 7, 2000); White Sox acquired C Miguel Olivo to complete deal (December 13, 2000).

CAREER HITTING: 0-for-0 (.000), 0 R, 0 2B, 0 3B, 0 HR, 0 RBI.

Year	League	W	L	Pct.	ERA	WHIP	G	GS	CG	ShO	Hld.	Sv.-Opp.	IP	H	R	ER	HR	BB-IBB	SO	Avg.
1996— Hickory (S. Atl.)		0	2	.000	0.90	0.93	28	0	0	0	...	18-...	30.0	21	7	3	1	7-1	27	.194
1997— Winston-Salem (Caro.)		3	7	.300	3.95	1.39	46	0	0	0	...	15-...	54.2	51	30	24	2	25-5	43	.239
1998— Birmingham (Sou.)		1	1	.500	2.60	1.21	10	0	0	0	...	1-...	17.1	13	6	5	2	8-0	14	.203
— Calgary (PCL)		4	1	.800	1.94	1.20	29	0	0	0	...	0-...	51.0	50	12	11	3	11-2	27	.260
— Chicago (A.L.)		2	1	.667	3.23	1.11	29	0	0	0	9	1-3	30.2	27	16	11	0	7-0	11	.229
1999— Charlotte (Int'l)		9	3	.750	1.94	1.05	47	0	0	0	...	5-...	74.1	63	19	16	2	15-0	56	.231
— Chicago (A.L.)		0	0	...	19.64	3.82	3	0	0	0	0	0-0	3.2	9	8	8	1	5-0	0	.474
2000— Charlotte (Int'l)		2	4	.333	1.51	0.93	55	0	0	0	...	10-...	53.2	38	18	9	2	12-1	42	.200
— Chicago (A.L.)		1	0	1.000	1.98	1.02	12	0	0	0	2	0-0	13.2	13	4	3	0	1-1	9	.255
2001— Sacramento (PCL)		0	0	...	0.38	0.72	12	0	0	0	...	2-...	23.2	15	2	1	0	2-0	24	.181
— Oakland (A.L.)		2	1	.667	2.70	1.28	35	0	0	0	4	1-4	36.2	41	12	11	6	6-0	34	.281
2002— Oakland (A.L.)		4	2	.667	3.11	1.15	75	0	0	0	24	2-5	75.1	73	29	26	2	14-5	56	.253
2003— Oakland (A.L.)		7	4	.636	3.04	1.26	72	0	0	0	23	2-5	77.0	67	28	26	7	30-•9	62	.236
Major League totals (6 years)		16	8	.667	3.23	1.24	226	0	0	0	62	6-17	237.0	230	97	85	16	63-15	172	.254

BRADLEY, MILTON — OF

PERSONAL: Born April 15, 1978, in Harbor City, Calif. ... 6-0/190. ... Bats both, throws right. ... Full name: Milton Obelle Bradley. ... High school: Polytechnic (Long Beach, Calif.).

TRANSACTIONS/CAREER NOTES: Selected by Montreal Expos organization in second round of free-agent draft (June 4, 1996). ... On disabled list (June 14-25, 1999). ... Traded by Expos to Cleveland Indians for P Zach Day (July 31, 2001). ... On Cleveland disabled list (May 2-June 4 and August 14-30, 2002); included rehabilitation assignments to Buffalo (May 28-June 4) and Akron (August 27-30). ... Placed on the 15-day disabled list by Cleveland (April 23, 2003). ... Reinstated from 15-day disabled list (May 8, 2003). ... Placed on 15-day disabled list by Cleveland (August 10, 2003). ... Placed on 15-day disabled list by Cleveland (August 15, 2003).

2003 GAMES PLAYED BY POSITION (MLB): OF—93, DH—8.

Year	Team (League)	Pos.	G	AB	R	H	2B	3B	HR	RBI	BB	SO	HBP	GDP	SB-CS	Avg.	OBP	SLG	OPS	E	Pct.
1996— GC Expos (GCL)		OF	32	112	18	27	7	1	1	12	13	15	1	2	7-4	.241	.320	.348	.669	3	.949
1997— Vermont (NYP)		OF	50	200	29	60	7	5	3	30	17	34	0	6	7-7	.300	.352	.430	.782	4	.967
— GC Expos (GCL)		OF	9	25	6	5	2	0	1	2	4	4	1	0	2-2	.200	.333	.400	.733	1	.938
1998— Cape Fear (S. Atl.)		OF	75	281	54	85	21	4	6	50	23	57	4	7	13-8	.302	.360	.470	.830	3	.968
— Jupiter (FSL)		OF	67	261	55	75	14	1	5	34	30	42	5	3	17-9	.287	.369	.406	.775	1	.993
1999— Harrisburg (East.)		OF	87	346	62	114	22	5	12	50	33	61	3	5	14-10	.329	.391	.526	.917	5	.971
2000— Ottawa (Int'l)		OF	88	342	58	104	20	1	6	29	45	56	1	5	10-15	.304	.385	.421	.806	3	.987
— Montreal (N.L.)		OF	42	154	20	34	8	1	2	15	14	32	1	3	2-1	.221	.288	.325	.613	2	.979
2001— Montreal (N.L.)		OF	67	220	19	49	16	3	1	19	19	62	1	6	7-4	.223	.288	.336	.624	2	.988
— Ottawa (Int'l)		OF	35	136	21	37	7	2	2	13	23	30	2	3	14-1	.272	.383	.397	.780	3	.966
— Buffalo (Int'l)		OF	30	114	18	29	3	0	5	15	19	31	0	0	9-2	.254	.361	.412	.773	0	1.000
— Cleveland (A.L.)		OF-DH	10	18	3	4	1	0	0	0	2	3	0	1	1-1	.222	.300	.278	.578	1	.929
2002— Cleveland (A.L.)		OF-DH	98	325	48	81	18	3	9	38	32	58	0	12	6-3	.249	.317	.406	.723	4	.982
— Buffalo (Int'l)		OF	6	23	3	6	0	0	0	3	3	5	0	0	2-1	.261	.321	.261	.582	0	1.000
— Akron (East.)		OF	3	11	1	3	1	0	0	1	1	1	0	0	0-1	.273	.333	.364	.697	0	1.000
2003— Cleveland (A.L.)		OF-DH	101	377	61	121	34	2	10	56	64	73	5	10	17-7	.321	.421	.501	.923	2	.992
American League totals (3 years)			209	720	112	206	53	5	19	94	98	134	5	23	24-11	.286	.373	.453	.826	7	.986
National League totals (2 years)			109	374	39	83	24	4	3	34	33	94	2	9	9-5	.222	.288	.332	.619	4	.984
Major League totals (4 years)			318	1094	151	289	77	9	22	128	131	228	7	32	33-16	.264	.345	.411	.756	11	.985

BRAGG, DARREN — OF

PERSONAL: Born September 7, 1969, in Waterbury, Conn. ... 5-9/180. ... Bats left, throws right. ... Full name: Darren William Bragg. ... High school: Taft (Watertown, Conn.). ... College: Georgia Tech.

TRANSACTIONS/CAREER NOTES: Selected by Seattle Mariners organization in 22nd round of free-agent draft (June 30, 1991). ... Traded by Mariners to Boston Red Sox for P Jamie Moyer (July 30, 1996). ... Granted free agency (December 21, 1998). ... Signed by St. Louis Cardinals (January 12, 1999). ... On disabled list (August 3, 1999-remainder of season). ... Released by Cardinals (December 16, 1999). ... Signed by Colorado Rockies (February 1, 2000). ... Released by Rockies (July 24, 2000). ... Signed by New York Mets organization (January 9, 2001). ... Claimed on waivers by New York Yankees (June 12, 2001). ... Granted free agency (October 9, 2001). ... Signed by Mets organization (January 15, 2002). ... Released by Mets (April 2, 2002). ... Signed by Atlanta Braves organization (April 2, 2002). ... Granted free agency (October 30, 2002). ... Re-signed by Braves (March 29, 2003).

2003 GAMES PLAYED BY POSITION (MLB): OF—78.

Year	Team (League)	Pos.	G	AB	R	H	2B	3B	HR	RBI	BB	SO	HBP	GDP	SB-CS	Avg.	OBP	SLG	OPS	E	Pct.
1991—Peninsula (Caro.)	2B-OF	69	237	42	53	14	0	3	29	66	72	2	8	21-9	.224	.395	.321	.716	4	.978
1992—Peninsula (Caro.)	OF	135	428	* 83	117	29	5	9	58	* 105	76	5	8	44-19	.273	.418	.428	.846	4	.986
1993—Jacksonville (Sou.)	P	131	451	74	119	26	3	11	46	81	82	7	12	19-11	.264	.382	.408	.790	10	.970
1994—Calgary (PCL)	OF	126	500	112	175	33	6	17	85	68	72	6	11	28-12	.350	.430	.542	.972	7	.980
—Seattle (A.L.)	DH-OF	8	19	4	3	1	0	0	2	2	5	0	0	0-0	.158	.238	.211	.449	0	1.000
1995—Seattle (A.L.)	OF-DH	52	145	20	34	5	1	3	12	18	37	4	2	9-0	.234	.331	.345	.676	1	.989
—Tacoma (PCL)	OF-DH	53	212	24	65	13	3	4	31	23	39	0	3	10-3	.307	.373	.453	.826	4	.968
1996—Seattle (A.L.)	OF	69	195	36	53	12	1	7	25	33	35	2	2	8-5	.272	.376	.451	.827	1	.992
—Tacoma (PCL)	OF	20	71	17	20	8	0	3	8	14	14	2	1	1-0	.282	.414	.521	.935	0	1.000
—Boston (A.L.)	OF	58	222	38	56	14	1	3	22	36	39	2	3	6-4	.252	.357	.365	.722	2	.986
1997—Boston (A.L.)	OF-3B	153	513	65	132	35	2	9	57	61	102	3	16	10-6	.257	.337	.386	.723	5	.987
1998—Boston (A.L.)	OF-DH	129	409	51	114	29	3	8	57	42	99	6	16	5-3	.279	.351	.423	.774	1	.996
1999—St. Louis (N.L.)	OF	93	273	38	71	12	1	6	26	44	67	3	5	3-0	.260	.369	.377	.746	3	.982
2000—Colorado (N.L.)	OF	71	149	16	33	7	1	3	21	17	41	0	3	4-1	.221	.296	.342	.638	0	1.000
2001—Norfolk (Int'l)	OF	32	99	22	33	4	0	4	7	23	22	2	1	5-2	.333	.468	.495	.963	0	1.000
—New York (N.L.)	OF	18	57	4	15	6	0	0	5	4	23	1	0	3-2	.263	.323	.368	.691	0	1.000
—New York (A.L.)	OF	5	4	1	1	1	0	0	0	0	1	0	0	0-0	.250	.250	.500	.750	0	1.000
—Columbus (Int'l)	OF	53	199	30	58	11	2	7	21	27	51	1	4	3-2	.291	.379	.472	.851	0	1.000
2002—Richmond (Int'l)	OF	22	75	15	22	5	0	1	8	20	15	0	0	4-2	.293	.442	.400	.842	0	1.000
—Atlanta (N.L.)	OF-DH	109	212	34	57	15	2	3	15	24	52	2	4	5-2	.269	.347	.401	.748	3	.971
2003—Atlanta (N.L.)	OF	104	162	21	39	5	1	0	9	13	38	2	1	2-1	.241	.305	.284	.589	1	.988
American League totals (6 years)		474	1507	215	393	97	8	30	175	192	318	17	39	38-18	.261	.347	.395	.743	10	.990
National League totals (5 years)		395	853	113	215	45	5	12	76	102	221	8	13	17-6	.252	.336	.359	.695	7	.983
Major League totals (10 years)		869	2360	328	608	142	13	42	251	294	539	25	52	55-24	.258	.343	.382	.726	17	.988

BRANYAN, RUSSELL   3B

PERSONAL: Born December 19, 1975, in Warner Robins, Ga. ... 6-3/195. ... Bats left, throws right. ... Full name: Russell Oles Branyan. ... Name pronounced: BRAN-yen. ... High school: Stratford Academy (Warner Robins, Ga.).

TRANSACTIONS/CAREER NOTES: Selected by Cleveland Indians organization in seventh round of free-agent draft (June 2, 1994). ... On Akron disabled list (April 23-May 11 and May 16-August 15, 1998). ... Traded by Indians to Cincinnati Reds for OF Ben Broussard (June 7, 2002). ... On disabled list (March 18, 2003). ... Sent on rehab assignment to Louisville (April 17, 2003). ... Recalled from Louisville rehab assignment by Cincinnati (May 5, 2003). ... Reinstated from the 15-day disabled list (May 29, 2003). ... Placed on 15-day disabled list (August 13, 2003). ... Sent on rehab assignment by Cincinnati (August 25, 2003). ... Recalled from minor league rehab assignment (August 27, 2003). ... Removed from 15-day disabled list (August 28, 2003).

2003 GAMES PLAYED BY POSITION (MLB): 3B—20, OF—17, 1B—14, DH—1.

Year	Team (League)	Pos.	G	AB	R	H	2B	3B	HR	RBI	BB	SO	HBP	GDP	SB-CS	Avg.	OBP	SLG	OPS	E	Pct.
1994—Burlington (Appal.)	3B	55	171	21	36	10	0	5	13	25	64	4	3	4-2	.211	.323	.357	.680	21	.851
1995—Columbus (S. Atl.)	3B	76	277	46	71	8	6	19	55	27	120	3	6	1-1	.256	.326	.534	.860	26	.856
1996—Columbus (S. Atl.)	3B-DH	130	482	102	129	20	4	* 40	* 106	62	166	5	4	7-4	.268	.355	.575	.930	44	.885
1997—Kinston (Caro.)	3B-DH	83	297	59	86	26	2	27	75	52	94	5	9	3-1	.290	.398	.663	1.062	21	.897
—Akron (East.)	3B-DH	41	137	26	32	4	0	12	30	28	56	2	1	0-0	.234	.369	.526	.895	11	.921
1998—Akron (East.)	3B-DH	43	163	35	48	11	3	16	46	35	58	0	2	1-1	.294	.417	.693	1.110	7	.932
—Cleveland (A.L.)	3B	1	4	0	0	0	0	0	0	0	2	0	0	0-0	.000	.000	.000	.000	0	1.000
1999—Buffalo (Int'l)	3B	109	395	51	82	11	1	30	67	52	187	4	5	8-3	.208	.305	.468	.773	23	.921
—Cleveland (A.L.)	3B-DH	11	38	4	8	2	0	1	6	3	19	1	0	0-0	.211	.286	.342	.628	1	.960
2000—Buffalo (Int'l)	3B	64	229	46	56	9	2	21	60	28	93	2	2	1-1	.245	.330	.576	.906	9	.942
—Cleveland (A.L.)	OF-DH-3B	67	193	32	46	7	2	16	38	22	76	4	2	0-0	.238	.327	.544	.871	3	.954
2001—Cleveland (A.L.)	3B-OF-DH	113	315	48	73	16	2	20	54	38	132	3	2	1-1	.232	.316	.486	.802	14	.931
2002—Cleveland (A.L.)	3B-DH	50	161	16	33	4	0	8	17	17	65	0	3	1-2	.205	.278	.379	.657	2	.976
—Cincinnati (N.L.)	OF-1B-3B-DH	84	217	34	53	9	1	16	39	34	86	2	2	3-1	.244	.349	.516	.865	6	.977
2003—Louisville (Int'l)	DH-OF-3B-1B	14	49	5	16	5	0	1	3	9	15	1	0	0-0	.327	.441	.490	.930	1	.968
—Cincinnati (N.L.)	3-OF-1-DH	74	176	22	38	12	0	9	26	27	69	1	1	0-0	.216	.322	.438	.759	3	.985
American League totals (5 years)		242	711	100	160	29	4	45	115	80	294	8	7	2-3	.225	.307	.467	.774	20	.947
National League totals (2 years)		158	393	56	91	21	1	25	65	61	155	3	3	3-1	.232	.337	.481	.818	9	.980
Major League totals (6 years)		400	1104	156	251	50	5	70	180	141	449	11	10	5-4	.227	.318	.472	.790	29	.965

BRAZELTON, DEWON   P

PERSONAL: Born June 16, 1980, in Tullahoma, Tenn. ... 6-4/214. ... Throws right, bats right. ... Full name: Dewon Cortez Brazelton. ... Name pronounced: de-wan bra-zel-ton. ... College: Middle Tennessee State.

TRANSACTIONS/CAREER NOTES: Selected by Tampa Bay Devil Rays organization in first round (third pick overall) of free-agent draft (June 1, 2001). ... Recalled by Tampa Bay from Durham (May 3, 2003). ... Optioned to Bakersfield by Tampa Bay (June 25, 2003). ... Recalled by Tampa Bay from Orlando (September 19, 2003).

CAREER HITTING: 0-for-1 (.000), 0 R, 0 2B, 0 3B, 0 HR, 0 RBI.

Year	League	W	L	Pct.	ERA	WHIP	G	GS	CG	ShO	Hld.	Sv.-Opp.	IP	H	R	ER	HR	BB-IBB	SO	Avg.
2002—Orlando (Sou.)	5	9	.357	3.33	1.34	26	26	1	0	...	0-...	146.0	129	69	54	7	67-1	109	.241
—Durham (Int'l)	1	0	1.000	0.00	1.20	1	1	0	0	...	0-...	5.0	5	0	0	0	1-0	6	.263
—Tampa Bay (A.L.)	0	1	.000	4.85	1.38	2	2	0	0	0	0-0	13.0	12	7	7	3	6-0	5	.279
2003—Durham (Int'l)	2	2	.500	4.21	1.32	5	5	0	0	...	0-...	25.2	23	14	12	1	11-0	18	.235
—Tampa Bay (A.L.)	1	6	.143	6.89	1.66	10	10	0	0	0	0-0	48.1	57	49	37	9	23-1	24	.292
—Bakersfield (Calif.)	1	5	.167	5.26	1.63	9	9	0	0	0	0-0	49.2	62	33	29	4	19-0	42	.298
—Orlando (Sou.)	2	0	1.000	2.53	1.50	2	2	0	0	...	0-...	10.2	8	6	3	0	8-0	5	.200
Major League totals (2 years)	1	7	.125	6.46	1.60	12	12	0	0	0	0-0	61.1	69	56	44	12	29-1	29	.290

BROHAWN, TROY   P

PERSONAL: Born January 14, 1973, in Cambridge, Md. ... 6-1/190. ... Throws left, bats left. ... Full name: Michael Troy Brohawn. ... Name pronounced: BRO-hon. ... High school: Cambridge South Dorchester (Cambridge, Md.). ... College: Nebraska.

TRANSACTIONS/CAREER NOTES: Selected by San Francisco Giants organization in fourth round of free-agent draft (June 2, 1994). ... Traded by Giants to Arizona Diamondbacks (December 21, 1998), completing deal in which Diamondbacks traded P Felix Rodriguez to Giants for future considerations (December 8, 1998). ... On Tucson disabled list (April 24-August 30, 1999). ... On Arizona disabled list (August 31, 1999-remainder of season). ... On Tucson disabled list (April 6-July 31, 2000). ... Released by Diamondbacks (March 27, 2002). ... Signed by Giants organization (March 28, 2002). ... Granted free agency (October 15, 2002). ... Signed by Los Angeles Dodgers organization (March 21, 2003). ... Placed on 15-day disabled list by Los Angeles (May 13, 2003). ... Transferred to Emergency disabled list (June 4, 2003).

CAREER HITTING: 1-for-2 (.500), 0 R, 0 2B, 0 3B, 0 HR, 0 RBI.

B

Year	League	W	L	Pct.	ERA	WHIP	G	GS	CG	ShO	Hld.	Sv.-Opp.	IP	H	R	ER	HR	BB-IBB	SO	Avg.
1994— San Jose (Calif.)		0	2	.000	7.02	1.92	4	4	0	0	...	0-...	16.2	27	15	13	2	5-0	13	.375
1995— San Jose (Calif.)		7	3	.700	1.65	0.99	11	10	0	0	...	0-...	65.1	45	14	12	4	20-0	57	.202
1996— Shreveport (Texas)		9	10	.474	4.60	1.35	28	28	0	0	...	0-...	156.2	163	99	80	30	49-0	82	.270
1997— Shreveport (Texas)		13	5	.722	2.56	1.25	26	26	1	•1	...	0-...	169.0	148	57	48	10	64-0	98	.238
1998— Fresno (PCL)		10	8	.556	5.25	1.48	30	19	0	0	...	0-...	121.2	144	75	71	18	36-1	87	.304
1999— Tucson (PCL)		1	0	1.000	3.29	1.83	3	2	0	0	...	0-...	13.2	22	8	5	1	3-0	12	.361
2000— Ariz. D'backs (Ariz.)		0	0	...	0.00	1.50	3	3	0	0	...	0-...	4.0	5	1	0	0	1-0	6	.333
— Tucson (PCL)		0	0	...	3.78	1.38	11	1	0	0	...	0-...	16.2	18	7	7	5	5-0	16	.295
2001— Tucson (PCL)		0	0	...	0.00	0.60	2	0	0	0	...	0-...	3.1	1	0	0	0	1-0	4	.083
— Arizona (N.L.)		2	3	.400	4.93	1.58	59	0	0	0	10	1-3	49.1	55	27	27	5	23-2	30	.289
2002— Fresno (PCL)		3	3	.500	3.65	1.33	56	0	0	0	...	1-...	69.0	71	31	28	7	21-2	55	.262
— San Francisco (N.L.)		0	1	.000	6.35	1.06	11	0	0	0	3	0-0	5.2	5	4	4	1	1-0	3	.227
2003— Las Vegas (PCL)		1	0	1.000	4.50	0.75	1	0	0	0	...	0-...	4.0	3	2	2	1	0-0	1	.200
— Los Angeles (N.L.)		2	0	1.000	3.86	1.20	12	0	0	0	1	0-0	11.2	10	6	5	2	4-0	13	.227
Major League totals (3 years)		4	4	.500	4.86	1.47	82	0	0	0	14	1-3	66.2	70	37	36	8	28-2	46	.273

BROUSSARD, BEN — 1B/OF

PERSONAL: Born September 24, 1976, in Beaumont, Texas. ... 6-2/220. ... Bats left, throws left. ... Full name: Benjamin Isaac Broussard. ... Name pronounced: brew-SARD. ... College: McNeese State.

TRANSACTIONS/CAREER NOTES: Selected by Cincinnati Reds organization in second round of free-agent draft (June 2, 1999). ... On disabled list (May 10-June 26, 2000). ... On Chattanooga disabled list (May 22-29, 2001). ... Traded by Reds to Cleveland Indians for 3B Russell Branyan (June 7, 2002). ... On Cleveland disabled list (March 21-April 6, 2003); included rehabilitation assignment to Buffalo (April 4-6). ... Recalled by Cleveland from Buffalo (May 13, 2003).

2003 GAMES PLAYED BY POSITION (MLB): 1B—114.

Year	Team (League)	Pos.	G	AB	R	H	2B	3B	HR	RBI	BB	SO	HBP	GDP	SB-CS	Avg.	OBP	SLG	OPS	E	Pct.
1999— Billings (Pio.)	1B-OF	38	145	39	59	11	2	14	48	34	30	4	0	1-0	.407	.527	.800	1.327	5	.963
— Clinton (Midw.)	1B-OF	5	20	8	11	4	1	2	6	3	4	0	0	0-0	.550	.609	1.150	1.759	2	.926
— Chattanooga (Sou.)	1B-OF	35	127	26	27	5	0	8	21	11	41	3	0	1-0	.213	.291	.441	.732	2	.987
2000— Chattanooga (Sou.)	1B-OF	87	286	64	73	8	4	14	51	72	78	6	6	15-2	.255	.413	.458	.871	10	.958
2001— Mudville California (Calif.)	1B	30	102	14	25	5	0	5	21	16	31	4	2	0-0	.245	.360	.441	.801	2	.992
— Chattanooga (Sou.)	1B-OF	100	353	81	113	27	0	23	69	61	69	8	5	10-3	.320	.428	.592	1.020	8	.990
2002— Louisville (Int'l)	1B	57	187	31	51	14	1	11	30	31	50	9	4	4-1	.273	.396	.535	.930	2	.995
— Buffalo (Int'l)	OF-1B	42	153	30	37	8	0	5	21	24	30	3	1	0-0	.242	.354	.392	.746	3	.975
— Cleveland (A.L.)	OF-1B-DH	39	112	10	27	4	0	4	9	7	25	1	3	0-0	.241	.292	.384	.676	2	.974
2003— Buffalo (Int'l)	1B-DH	32	120	17	30	2	1	3	15	9	29	1	1	3-0	.250	.303	.358	.661	2	.990
— Cleveland (A.L.)	1B	116	386	53	96	21	3	16	55	32	75	5	6	5-2	.249	.312	.443	.755	9	.991
Major League totals (2 years)		155	498	63	123	25	3	20	64	39	100	6	9	5-2	.247	.308	.430	.737	11	.990

BROWER, JIM — P

PERSONAL: Born December 29, 1972, in Edina, Minn. ... 6-3/215. ... Throws right, bats right. ... Full name: James Robert Brower. ... Name pronounced: BROW-er. ... High school: Minnetonka (Minn.). ... College: Minnesota.

TRANSACTIONS/CAREER NOTES: Selected by Texas Rangers organization in sixth round of free-agent draft (June 2, 1994). ... Released by Rangers (April 15, 1998). ... Signed by Cleveland Indians organization (April 18, 1998). ... Granted free agency (October 16, 1998). ... Re-signed by Indians organization (January 4, 1999). ... Traded by Indians with P Robert Pugmire to Cincinnati Reds for C Eddie Taubensee (November 16, 2000). ... Traded by Reds to Montreal Expos for P Bruce Chen (June 14, 2002). ... Traded by Expos with a player to be named later to San Francisco Giants for P Livan Hernandez, 3B/C Edwards Guzman and cash (March 24, 2003); Giants acquired P Matt Blank to complete deal (April 30, 2003).

CAREER HITTING: 11-for-55 (.200), 8 R, 1 2B, 0 3B, 0 HR, 4 RBI.

Year	League	W	L	Pct.	ERA	WHIP	G	GS	CG	ShO	Hld.	Sv.-Opp.	IP	H	R	ER	HR	BB-IBB	SO	Avg.
1994— Hudson Valley (NYP)		2	1	.667	3.20	1.02	4	4	1	0	...	0-...	19.2	14	10	7	0	6-0	15	.189
— Char., S.C. (SAL)		7	3	.700	1.72	0.99	12	12	3	2	...	0-...	78.2	52	18	15	2	26-1	84	.186
1995— Charlotte (Fla. St.)		7	10	.412	3.89	1.34	27	27	2	1	...	0-...	173.2	170	93	75	16	62-1	110	.256
1996— Charlotte (Fla. St.)		9	8	.529	3.79	1.30	23	21	2	0	...	0-...	145.0	148	67	61	11	40-0	86	.267
— Tulsa (Texas)		3	2	.600	3.78	1.35	5	5	1	1	...	0-...	33.1	35	16	14	4	10-0	16	.273
1997— Tulsa (Texas)		5	12	.294	5.21	1.41	23	23	1	0	...	0-...	140.0	156	99	81	13	42-1	103	.286
— Oklahoma City (A.A.)		2	1	.667	7.23	2.04	4	3	0	0	...	0-...	18.2	30	17	15	3	8-0	7	.370
1998— Akron (East.)		13	5	.722	3.01	1.16	23	23	2	2	...	0-...	155.2	142	60	52	9	38-0	91	.246
1999— Buffalo (Int'l)		11	11	.500	4.73	1.39	27	27	0	0	...	0-...	160.0	164	101	84	23	59-6	76	.270
— Cleveland (A.L.)		3	1	.750	4.56	1.44	9	2	0	0	0	0-0	25.2	27	13	13	8	10-1	18	.270
2000— Buffalo (Int'l)		9	4	.692	3.11	1.21	16	15	1	0	...	0-...	101.1	99	41	35	7	24-1	68	.253
— Cleveland (A.L.)		2	3	.400	6.24	1.79	17	11	0	0	0	0-0	62.0	80	45	43	11	31-1	32	.309
2001— Louisville (Int'l)		1	0	1.000	4.09	1.27	2	2	0	0	...	0-...	11.0	12	5	5	1	2-0	11	.273
— Cincinnati (N.L.)		7	10	.412	3.97	1.38	46	10	0	0	2	1-2	129.1	119	65	57	17	60-5	94	.247
2002— Cincinnati (N.L.)		2	0	1.000	3.89	1.22	22	0	0	0	0	0-0	39.1	38	18	17	2	10-1	24	.260
— Montreal (N.L.)		1	2	.333	4.83	1.49	30	0	0	0	6	0-1	41.0	39	22	22	5	22-1	33	.245
2003— San Francisco (N.L.)		8	5	.615	3.96	1.29	51	5	0	0	2	2-3	100.0	90	48	44	8	39-2	65	.249
American League totals (2 years)		5	4	.556	5.75	1.69	26	13	0	0	0	0-0	87.2	107	58	56	19	41-2	50	.298
National League totals (3 years)		18	17	.514	4.07	1.35	149	15	0	0	10	3-6	309.2	286	153	140	32	131-9	216	.249
Major League totals (5 years)		23	21	.523	4.44	1.42	175	28	0	0	10	3-6	397.1	393	211	196	51	172-11	266	.261

BROWN, ADRIAN — OF

PERSONAL: Born February 7, 1974, in Summitt, Miss. ... 6-0/200. ... Bats both, throws right. ... Full name: Adrian Demond Brown. ... High school: McComb (Miss.).

TRANSACTIONS/CAREER NOTES: Selected by Pittsburgh Pirates organization in 48th round of free-agent draft (June 1, 1992). ... Loaned by Pirates organization to Lethbridge of Pioneer League (June 11-September 19, 1993). ... On Pittsburgh disabled list (June 13-July 4 and July 6-August 7, 2000); included rehabilitation assignments to Altoona (July 2-4) and Nashville (July 30-August 7). ... On Pittsburgh disabled list (April 17, 2001-remainder of season); included rehabilitation assignments to Altoona (May 7-15), Lynchburg (August 28-September 2) and Williamsport (September 3-13). ... Released by Pirates (October 10, 2002). ... Signed by Tampa Bay Devil Rays organization (November 6, 2002). ... Selected by Boston Red Sox from Devil Rays organization in Rule 5 major league draft (December 16, 2002). ... Returned to Devil Rays (March 26, 2003). ... Devil Rays declined to take him back; outrighted to Pawtucket (March 28, 2003). ... Contract purchased by Boston from Pawtucket (September 12, 2003).

2003 GAMES PLAYED BY POSITION (MLB): OF—9.

Year	Team (League)	Pos.	G	AB	R	H	2B	3B	HR	RBI	BB	SO	HBP	GDP	SB-CS	Avg.	OBP	SLG	OPS	E	Pct.
							BATTING													FIELDING	
1992— GC Pirates (GCL)	1B-OF	39	121	11	31	2	2	0	12	0	12	2	3	8-4	.256	.268	.306	.574	1	.985
1993— Lethbridge (Pio.)	OF	69	282	47	75	12	*9	3	27	17	34	5	8	22-7	.266	.319	.404	.723	1	.992
1994— Augusta (S. Atl.)	OF	79	308	41	80	17	1	1	18	14	38	0	2	19-12	.260	.292	.331	.623	2	.984
1995— Augusta (S. Atl.)	OF	76	287	64	86	15	4	4	31	33	23	1	2	25-14	.300	.372	.422	.793	7	.950
— Lynchburg (Caro.)	OF	54	215	30	52	5	2	1	14	12	20	1	3	11-6	.242	.284	.298	.582	2	.983
1996— Lynchburg (Caro.)	OF	52	215	39	69	9	3	4	25	14	24	2	1	18-9	.321	.368	.447	.814	2	.981
— Carolina (Sou.)	OF	84	341	48	101	11	3	3	25	25	40	1	4	27-11	.296	.345	.372	.718	2	.990
1997— Carolina (Sou.)	OF	37	145	29	44	4	4	2	15	18	12	2	1	9-5	.303	.388	.428	.815	3	.956
— Pittsburgh (N.L.)	OF	48	147	17	28	6	0	1	10	13	18	4	3	8-4	.190	.273	.252	.524	1	.987
— Calgary (PCL)	OF	62	248	53	79	10	1	1	19	27	38	0	9	20-4	.319	.383	.379	.762	1	.993
1998— Nashville (PCL)	OF	85	311	58	90	12	5	3	27	28	38	0	7	25-7	.289	.346	.389	.735	5	.977
— Pittsburgh (N.L.)	OF	41	152	20	43	4	1	0	5	9	18	0	3	4-0	.283	.323	.322	.645	2	.987
1999— Pittsburgh (N.L.)	OF	116	226	34	61	5	2	4	17	30	39	1	5	5-3	.270	.364	.363	.727	4	.966
— Nashville (PCL)	OF	17	56	10	18	3	1	0	4	11	8	0	0	6-1	.321	.433	.411	.844	1	.969
2000— Pittsburgh (N.L.)	OF	104	308	64	97	18	3	4	28	29	34	0	1	13-1	.315	.373	.432	.805	4	.976
— Altoona (East.)	OF	2	5	1	0	0	0	0	0	3	1	0	0	0-0	.000	.375	.000	.375	0	1.000
— Nashville (PCL)	OF	8	26	3	6	1	0	0	2	2	4	1	0	3-0	.231	.310	.269	.580	0	1.000
2001— Pittsburgh (N.L.)	OF	8	31	3	6	0	0	1	2	3	3	0	1	2-1	.194	.265	.290	.555	0	1.000
— Altoona (East.)	DH	7	30	7	10	1	1	0	1	1	7	0	0	1-2	.333	.344	.433	.777	...	...
— Lynchburg (Caro.)	DH	4	18	2	6	0	0	0	1	1	3	1	0	2-0	.333	.400	.333	.733	...	...
— Will. (NYP)	DH	4	18	4	6	0	1	0	4	1	2	0	0	2-0	.333	.368	.444	.813	...	...
2002— Pittsburgh (N.L.)	OF	91	208	20	45	10	2	1	21	19	34	1	5	10-6	.216	.284	.298	.582	3	.974
— Nashville (PCL)	OF	51	184	36	62	7	1	3	16	23	18	0	3	22-6	.337	.409	.435	.843	2	.975
2003— Pawtucket (Int'l)	OF-DH	122	482	81	136	16	3	5	32	48	81	0	10	34-11	.282	.347	.359	.706	5	.983
— Boston (A.L.)	OF	9	15	2	3	0	0	0	1	1	4	0	0	2-0	.200	.250	.200	.450	0	1.000
American League totals (1 year)		9	15	2	3	0	0	0	1	1	4	0	0	2-0	.200	.250	.200	.450	0	1.000
National League totals (6 years)		408	1072	158	280	43	8	11	83	106	146	6	18	42-15	.261	.330	.347	.677	14	.976
Major League totals (7 years)		417	1087	160	283	43	8	11	84	107	150	6	18	44-15	.260	.329	.345	.674	14	.976

BROWN, DEE — OF

PERSONAL: Born March 27, 1978, in Bronx, N.Y. ... 6-0/225. ... Bats left, throws right. ... Full name: Dermal Bram Brown. ... High school: Marlboro (N.Y.) Central.

TRANSACTIONS/CAREER NOTES: Selected by Kansas City Royals organization in first round (14th pick overall) of free-agent draft (June 2, 1996). ... On Kansas City disabled list (June 17-July 27, 2001); included rehabilitation assignment to Omaha (July 12-27). ... Placed on the 15-day disabled list (May 28, 2003). ... Sent to Arizona League on rehab assignment (July 2, 2003). ... Recalled by Kansas City from Omaha; reinstated from 15-day disabled list (July 19, 2003).

2003 GAMES PLAYED BY POSITION (MLB): OF—33, DH—11.

Year	Team (League)	Pos.	G	AB	R	H	2B	3B	HR	RBI	BB	SO	HBP	GDP	SB-CS	Avg.	OBP	SLG	OPS	E	Pct.
							BATTING													FIELDING	
1996— GC Royals (GCL)	DH	7	20	1	1	1	0	0	1	0	6	1	0	0-2	.050	.095	.100	.195	...	...
1997— Spokane (N'west)	OF	73	298	67	97	20	6	13	*73	38	65	2	5	17-4	.326	.404	.564	.968	7	.921
1998— Wilmington (Caro.)	OF	128	442	64	114	30	2	10	58	53	115	7	12	26-10	.258	.347	.403	.749	13	.908
— Kansas City (A.L.)	DH-OF	5	3	2	0	0	0	0	0	0	1	0	0	0-0	.000	.000	.000	.000	0	1.000
1999— Wilmington (Caro.)	OF-DH	61	221	49	68	10	2	13	46	44	56	4	10	20-7	.308	.431	.548	.979	2	.979
— Wichita (Texas)	OF	65	235	58	83	14	3	12	56	35	41	3	2	10-8	.353	.440	.591	1.031	5	.958
— Kansas City (A.L.)	OF-DH	12	25	1	2	0	0	0	0	2	7	0	0	0-0	.080	.148	.080	.228	1	.929
2000— Omaha (PCL)	OF	125	479	76	129	25	6	23	70	37	112	3	14	20-3	.269	.324	.491	.814	7	.966
— Kansas City (A.L.)	OF	15	25	4	4	1	0	0	4	3	9	0	0	0-0	.160	.250	.200	.450	0	1.000
2001— Kansas City (A.L.)	OF-DH	106	380	39	93	19	0	7	40	22	81	1	12	5-3	.245	.286	.350	.636	2	.988
— Omaha (PCL)	OF	10	37	5	11	0	0	2	6	3	5	1	3	0-0	.297	.357	.459	.817	1	.950
2002— Omaha (PCL)	OF	121	458	66	126	23	1	17	75	44	111	6	12	10-4	.275	.344	.441	.785	5	.968
— Kansas City (A.L.)	OF-DH	16	51	5	12	3	1	1	7	4	20	0	0	0-0	.235	.291	.392	.683	1	.923
2003— Arizona Royals (Ariz.)	OF	2	7	4	5	2	0	0	3	0	2	1	0	0-0	.714	.750	1.000	1.750	0	1.000
— Omaha (PCL)	OF-DH	12	47	6	13	2	0	2	9	4	9	1	2	1-0	.277	.340	.447	.786	1	.955
— Kansas City (A.L.)	OF-DH	50	132	16	30	7	0	2	14	8	37	2	0	1-1	.227	.280	.326	.605	1	.985
Major League totals (6 years)		204	616	67	141	30	1	10	65	39	155	3	12	6-4	.229	.277	.330	.606	5	.981

BROWN, KEVIN — P

PERSONAL: Born March 14, 1965, in McIntyre, Ga. ... 6-4/200. ... Throws right, bats right. ... Full name: James Kevin Brown. ... High school: Wilkinson County (Irwinton, Ga.). ... College: Georgia Tech.

TRANSACTIONS/CAREER NOTES: Selected by Texas Rangers organization in first round (fourth pick overall) of free-agent draft (June 2, 1986). ... On disabled list (August 14-29, 1990 and March 27-April 11, 1993). ... Granted free agency (October 15, 1994). ... Signed by Baltimore Orioles (April 9, 1995). ... On disabled list (June 23-July 17, 1995). ... Granted free agency (November 3, 1995). ... Signed by Florida Marlins (December 22, 1995). ... On disabled list (May 13-28, 1996). ... Traded to San Diego Padres for P Rafael Medina, P Steve Hoff and 1B Derrek Lee (December 15, 1997). ... Granted free agency (October 26, 1998). ... Signed by Los Angeles Dodgers (December 12, 1998). ... On disabled list (April 9-25, 2000; March 24-April 10, May 30-June 24 and July 16-August 28, 2001). ... On Los Angeles disabled list (April 14-30 and May 27-August 15, 2002); included rehabilitation assignment to Las Vegas (August 3-15). ... Placed on 15-day disabled list (July 4, 2003). ... Reinstated from 15-day disabled list (July 19, 2003).

CAREER HITTING: 63-for-493 (.128), 20 R, 9 2B, 0 3B, 2 HR, 29 RBI.

Year	League	W	L	Pct.	ERA	WHIP	G	GS	CG	ShO	Hld.	Sv.-Opp.	IP	H	R	ER	HR	BB-IBB	SO	Avg.
1986— GC Rangers (GCL)	0	0	...	6.00	1.50	3	0	0	0	...	0-...	6.0	7	4	4	0	2-0	1	.292
— Tulsa (Texas)	0	0	...	4.50	1.40	3	2	0	0	...	0-...	10.0	9	7	5	0	5-0	10	.220
— Texas (A.L.)	1	0	1.000	3.60	1.20	1	1	0	0	0	0-0	5.0	6	2	2	0	0-0	4	.316
1987— Tulsa (Texas)	1	4	.200	7.29	1.69	8	8	0	0	...	0-...	42.0	53	36	34	3	18-1	26	.308
— Oklahoma City (A.A.)	0	5	.000	10.73	2.01	5	5	0	0	...	0-...	24.1	32	32	29	2	17-0	9	.311
— Charlotte (Fla. St.)	0	2	.000	2.72	1.38	6	6	1	0	...	0-...	36.1	33	14	11	1	17-0	21	.248
1988— Tulsa (Texas)	12	10	.545	3.51	1.35	26	26	5	0	...	0-...	174.1	174	94	68	5	61-1	118	.261
— Texas (A.L.)	1	1	.500	4.24	1.76	4	4	1	0	0	0-0	23.1	33	15	11	2	8-0	12	.330
1989— Texas (A.L.)	12	9	.571	3.35	1.24	28	28	7	0	0	0-0	191.0	167	81	71	10	70-2	104	.234
1990— Texas (A.L.)	12	10	.545	3.60	1.31	26	26	6	2	0	0-0	180.0	175	84	72	13	60-3	88	.257
1991— Texas (A.L.)	9	12	.429	4.40	1.53	33	33	0	0	0	0-0	210.2	233	116	103	17	90-5	96	.284
1992— Texas (A.L.)	•21	11	.656	3.32	1.27	35	35	11	1	0	0-0	*265.2	*262	117	98	11	76-2	173	.260

Year	League	W	L	Pct.	ERA	WHIP	G	GS	CG	ShO	Hld.	Sv.-Opp.	IP	H	R	ER	HR	BB-IBB	SO	Avg.
1993— Texas (A.L.)		15	12	.556	3.59	1.30	34	34	12	3	0	0-0	233.0	228	105	93	14	74-5	142	.252
1994— Texas (A.L.)		7	9	.438	4.82	1.58	26	•25	3	0	0	0-0	170.0	*218	109	91	18	50-3	123	.314
1995— Baltimore (A.L.)		10	9	.526	3.60	1.18	26	26	3	1	0	0-0	172.1	155	73	69	10	48-1	117	.241
1996— Florida (N.L.)		17	11	.607	*1.89	0.94	32	32	5	*3	0	0-0	233.0	187	60	49	8	33-2	159	.220
1997— Florida (N.L.)		16	8	.667	2.69	1.18	33	33	6	2	0	0-0	237.1	214	77	71	10	66-7	205	.240
1998— San Diego (N.L.)		18	7	.720	2.38	1.07	36	•35	7	3	1	0-0	257.0	225	77	68	8	49-4	257	.235
1999— Los Angeles (N.L.)		18	9	.667	3.00	1.07	35	•35	5	1	0	0-0	252.1	210	99	84	19	59-1	221	.222
2000— Los Angeles (N.L.)		13	6	.684	*2.58	0.99	33	33	5	1	0	0-0	230.0	181	76	66	21	47-1	216	*.213
2001— Los Angeles (N.L.)		10	4	.714	2.65	1.14	20	19	1	0	0	0-0	115.2	94	41	34	8	38-2	104	.224
2002— Los Angeles (N.L.)		3	4	.429	4.81	1.43	17	10	0	0	1	0-0	63.2	68	36	34	9	23-1	58	.274
— Las Vegas (PCL)		1	0	1.000	1.86	0.93	2	2	0	0	...	0-...	9.2	6	2	2	0	3-0	7	.182
2003— Los Angeles (N.L.)		14	9	.609	2.39	1.14	32	32	0	0	0	0-0	211.0	184	67	56	11	56-2	185	.236
American League totals (9 years)		**88**	**73**	**.547**	**3.78**	**1.35**	**213**	**212**	**43**	**7**	**0**	**0-0**	**1451.0**	**1477**	**702**	**610**	**95**	**476-21**	**859**	**.264**
National League totals (8 years)		**109**	**58**	**.653**	**2.60**	**1.08**	**238**	**229**	**29**	**10**	**2**	**0-0**	**1600.0**	**1363**	**533**	**462**	**94**	**371-20**	**1405**	**.230**
Major League totals (17 years)		**197**	**131**	**.601**	**3.16**	**1.21**	**451**	**441**	**72**	**17**	**2**	**0-0**	**3051.0**	**2840**	**1235**	**1072**	**189**	**847-41**	**2264**	**.246**

BRUNTLETT, ERIC — SS/2B/OF

PERSONAL: Born March 29, 1978, in Lafayette, Ind. ... 6-0/200. ... Bats right, throws right. ... Full name: Eric Kevin Bruntlett. ... High school: Harrison High (Evansville, Indiana). ... College: Stanford.

TRANSACTIONS/CAREER NOTES: Selected by Houston Astros in ninth round of free-agent draft (June 5, 2000).

2003 GAMES PLAYED BY POSITION (MLB): SS—10, 2B—9, OF—2, 3B—1.

Year	Team (League)	Pos.	G	AB	R	H	2B	3B	HR	RBI	BB	SO	HBP	GDP	SB-CS	Avg.	OBP	SLG	OPS	E	Pct.
2000— Martinsville (App.)	SS-OF	50	172	40	47	11	4	1	21	30	22	11	2	14-1	.273	.413	.401	.814	12	.944
2001— Round Rock (Texas)	SS	123	503	84	134	23	3	3	40	50	76	8	7	23-7	.266	.340	.342	.682	23	.956
— New Orleans (PCL)	SS	5	16	3	2	0	0	0	1	2	1	0	1	0-0	.125	.222	.125	.347	0	1.000
2002— New Orleans (PCL)	SS-2B	18	68	9	14	3	0	0	1	10	10	0	3	1-1	.206	.308	.250	.558	6	.941
— Round Rock (Texas)	SS-2B	116	464	81	123	21	2	2	48	56	61	10	17	35-12	.265	.351	.332	.683	19	.966
2003— New Orleans (PCL) SS-2B-OF		84	324	48	84	10	0	2	27	35	51	3	3	9-4	.259	.332	.309	.641	13	.967
— Houston (N.L.)	S-2-OF-3	31	54	3	14	3	0	1	4	0	10	0	1	0-0	.259	.255	.370	.625	1	.981
Major League totals (1 year)		**31**	**54**	**3**	**14**	**3**	**0**	**1**	**4**	**0**	**10**	**0**	**1**	**0-0**	**.259**	**.255**	**.370**	**.625**	**1**	**.981**

BUCHANAN, BRIAN — OF

PERSONAL: Born July 21, 1973, in Miami, Fla. ... 6-4/230. ... Bats right, throws right. ... Full name: Brian James Buchanan. ... High school: Fairfax (Va.). ... College: Virginia.

TRANSACTIONS/CAREER NOTES: Selected by New York Yankees organization in first round (24th pick overall) of free-agent draft (June 2, 1994). ... On disabled list (April 29, 1995-remainder of season). ... Traded by Yankees with P Eric Milton, P Danny Mota, SS Cristian Guzman and cash to Minnesota Twins for 2B Chuck Knoblauch (February 6, 1998). ... On disabled list (July 18-27 and July 29-August 9, 1999). ... On disabled list (June 29-July 14, 2001). ... On Minnesota disabled list (April 7-19, 2002); included rehabilitation assignment to Edmonton (April 18-19). ... Traded by Twins to San Diego Padres for SS Jason Bartlett (July 12, 2002).

2003 GAMES PLAYED BY POSITION (MLB): OF—43, 1B—24, DH—5.

Year	Team (League)	Pos.	G	AB	R	H	2B	3B	HR	RBI	BB	SO	HBP	GDP	SB-CS	Avg.	OBP	SLG	OPS	E	Pct.
1994— Oneonta (NYP)	OF	50	177	28	40	9	2	4	26	24	53	6	2	5-3	.226	.335	.367	.702	0	1.000
1995— Greensboro (S. Atl.)	OF	23	96	19	29	3	0	3	12	9	17	1	1	7-1	.302	.368	.427	.795	1	.970
1996— Tampa (Fla. St.)	OF	131	526	65	137	22	4	10	58	37	108	10	14	23-8	.260	.321	.375	.695	6	.969
1997— Norwich (East.)	OF	116	470	75	145	25	2	10	69	32	85	11	11	11-9	.309	.362	.434	.796	8	.962
— Columbus (Int'l)	OF	18	61	8	17	1	0	4	7	4	11	3	3	2-1	.279	.348	.492	.840	1	.947
1998— Salt Lake (PCL)	OF	133	500	74	139	29	3	17	82	36	90	9	7	14-2	.278	.337	.450	.787	8	.969
1999— Salt Lake (PCL)	OF	107	391	67	116	24	1	10	60	28	85	9	14	11-2	.297	.355	.440	.795	4	.980
2000— Salt Lake (PCL)	OF-1B	95	364	82	108	20	1	27	103	41	75	3	16	5-1	.297	.363	.580	.942	4	.980
— Minnesota (A.L.)	OF-DH	30	82	10	19	3	0	1	8	8	22	1	3	0-2	.232	.301	.305	.606	0	1.000
2001— Minnesota (A.L.)	OF-DH	69	197	28	54	12	0	10	32	19	58	2	2	1-1	.274	.342	.487	.830	2	.973
2002— Minnesota (A.L.)	OF-DH	44	135	19	34	5	1	5	15	6	33	2	4	2-1	.252	.294	.415	.709	0	1.000
— Edmonton (PCL)	OF	1	3	0	0	0	0	0	0	0	0	0	0	0-0	.000	.000	.000	.000	0	1.000
— San Diego (N.L.)	1B-OF	48	92	12	27	5	0	6	13	9	26	1	2	0-1	.293	.363	.543	.906	1	.990
2003— San Diego (N.L.) OF-1B-DH		115	198	29	52	10	2	8	29	24	51	3	8	6-2	.263	.346	.455	.801	2	.990
American League totals (3 years)		**143**	**414**	**57**	**107**	**20**	**1**	**16**	**55**	**33**	**113**	**5**	**9**	**3-4**	**.258**	**.319**	**.428**	**.746**	**2**	**.987**
National League totals (2 years)		**163**	**290**	**41**	**79**	**15**	**2**	**14**	**42**	**33**	**77**	**4**	**10**	**6-3**	**.272**	**.352**	**.483**	**.834**	**3**	**.990**
Major League totals (4 years)		**306**	**704**	**98**	**186**	**35**	**3**	**30**	**97**	**66**	**190**	**9**	**19**	**9-7**	**.264**	**.332**	**.450**	**.783**	**5**	**.989**

BUDZINSKI, MARK — OF

PERSONAL: Born August 26, 1973, in Baltimore, Md. ... 6-2/180. ... Bats left, throws left. ... Full name: Mark Joseph Budzinski. ... College: Richmond.

TRANSACTIONS/CAREER NOTES: Selected by Cleveland Indians in 21st round of free-agent draft (June 1995). ... Granted free agency (October 15, 2001). ... Signed by Chicago Cubs as a free agent (November 23, 2001). ... Granted free agency (October 15, 2002). ... Signed by Milwaukee Brewers as a free agent (November 25, 2002). ... Traded by Brewers to Cincinnati Reds for cash (June 6, 2003).

2003 GAMES PLAYED BY POSITION (MLB): OF—1.

Year	Team (League)	Pos.	G	AB	R	H	2B	3B	HR	RBI	BB	SO	HBP	GDP	SB-CS	Avg.	OBP	SLG	OPS	E	Pct.
1995— Watertown (NYP)	OF	70	253	50	64	12	8	3	25	52	49	8	3	15-5	.253	.394	.399	.793	5	.959
1996— Columbus (S. Atl.)	OF	74	260	42	68	12	4	3	38	59	68	4	5	12-3	.262	.404	.373	.777	2	.985
1997— Kinston (Caro.)	OF	68	241	43	69	13	3	7	39	48	61	1	3	6-4	.286	.407	.452	.859	2	.984
1998— Akron (East.)	OF	127	478	68	125	21	5	10	62	50	125	1	9	12-8	.262	.331	.389	.721	3	.989
1999— Akron (East.)	OF	86	297	58	84	17	6	6	46	48	63	5	3	9-4	.283	.391	.441	.833	2	.989
— Buffalo (Int'l)	OF	47	133	24	38	7	3	2	17	22	36	0	3	4-2	.286	.387	.429	.816	0	1.000
2000— Akron (East.)	OF	18	71	7	17	2	0	1	5	6	20	1	0	3-2	.239	.308	.310	.618	0	1.000
— Buffalo (Int'l)	OF	118	427	68	124	21	7	6	37	49	81	1	2	12-4	.290	.365	.415	.779	2	.991
2001— Buffalo (Int'l)	OF	122	438	69	112	26	4	2	39	28	125	7	4	13-4	.256	.308	.347	.655	0	1.000
2002— Iowa (PCL)	OF	12	32	6	9	2	1	0	4	3	5	0	0	1-0	.281	.343	.406	.749	0	1.000
— West Tenn. (Sou.)	OF	114	427	68	127	19	6	4	36	51	85	5	4	21-7	.297	.377	.398	.775	3	.987
2003— Indianapolis (Int'l)	OF	46	159	27	43	7	1	1	12	16	39	1	0	7-2	.270	.339	.346	.685	0	1.000
— Cincinnati (N.L.)	OF	4	7	0	0	0	0	0	0	0	4	0	0	0-0	.000	.000	.000	.000	0	1.000
— Louisville (Int'l)	OF-DH	74	259	53	71	15	3	1	15	37	56	3	1	10-4	.274	.370	.367	.737	2	.987
Major League totals (1 year)		**4**	**7**	**0**	**0**	**0**	**0**	**0**	**0**	**0**	**4**	**0**	**0**	**0-0**	**.000**	**.000**	**.000**	**.000**	**0**	**1.000**

B

BUEHRLE, MARK   P

PERSONAL: Born March 23, 1979, in St. Charles, Mo. ... 6-2/200. ... Throws left, bats left. ... Full name: Mark Anthony Buehrle. ... Name pronounced: BURR-lee. ... High school: Francis Howell North (St. Charles, Mo.). ... Junior college: Jefferson College (Mo.).
TRANSACTIONS/CAREER NOTES: Selected by Chicago White Sox organization in 38th round of free-agent draft (June 2, 1998). '
CAREER HITTING: 2-for-15 (.133), 1 R, 0 2B, 0 3B, 0 HR, 1 RBI.

Year League	W	L	Pct.	ERA	WHIP	G	GS	CG	ShO	Hld.	Sv.-Opp.	IP	H	R	ER	HR	BB-IBB	SO	Avg.
1999— Burlington (Midw.)	7	4	.636	4.10	1.23	20	14	1	1	...	3-...	98.2	105	49	45	8	16-1	91	.271
2000— Birmingham (Sou.)	8	4	.667	2.28	0.94	16	16	1	1	...	0-...	118.2	95	37	30	8	17-0	68	.222
— Chicago (A.L.)	4	1	.800	4.21	1.44	28	3	0	0	3	0-2	51.1	55	27	24	5	19-1	37	.272
2001— Chicago (A.L.)	16	8	.667	3.29	1.07	32	32	4	2	0	0-0	221.1	188	89	81	24	48-2	126	.230
2002— Chicago (A.L.)	19	12	.613	3.58	1.24	34	34	5	2	0	0-0	239.0	236	102	95	25	61-7	134	.260
2003— Chicago (A.L.)	14	14	.500	4.14	1.35	35	35	2	0	0	0-0	230.1	250	124	106	22	61-2	119	.278
Major League totals (4 years)	53	35	.602	3.71	1.24	129	104	11	4	3	0-2	742.0	729	342	306	76	189-12	416	.258

BUKVICH, RYAN   P

PERSONAL: Born May 13, 1978, in Naperville, Ill. ... 6-2/250. ... Throws right, bats right. ... Full name: Ryan Adrien Bukvich. ... Name pronounced: BUCK-vich. ... High school: Northwest Rankin (Brandon, Miss.). ... College: Mississippi.
TRANSACTIONS/CAREER NOTES: Selected by Kansas City Royals organization in 11th round of free-agent draft (June 5, 2000). ... Optioned to Omaha by Kansas City Royals (May 6, 2003). ... Recalled by Kansas City from Omaha (June 20, 2003). ... Optioned to Omaha by Kansas City (June 26, 2003). ... Recalled by Kansas City from Omaha (September 29, 2003).
CAREER HITTING: 0-for-0 (.000), 0 R, 0 2B, 0 3B, 0 HR, 0 RBI.

Year League	W	L	Pct.	ERA	WHIP	G	GS	CG	ShO	Hld.	Sv.-Opp.	IP	H	R	ER	HR	BB-IBB	SO	Avg.
2000— Spokane (N'west)	2	0	1.000	0.64	1.00	10	0	0	0	...	2-...	14.0	5	1	1	0	9-0	15	.111
— Char., W.Va. (SAL)	0	0	...	1.88	0.91	11	0	0	0	...	4-...	14.1	6	3	3	0	7-0	17	.128
— Wilmington (Caro.)	0	1	.000	18.00	4.00	2	0	0	0	...	0-...	2.0	3	4	4	0	5-2	3	.375
2001— Wilmington (Caro.)	0	1	.000	1.72	1.25	37	0	0	0	...	13-...	57.2	41	16	11	1	31-0	80	.193
— Wichita (Texas)	0	0	...	3.75	0.92	7	0	0	0	...	0-...	12.0	9	6	5	2	2-0	14	.200
2002— Wichita (Texas)	1	1	.500	1.31	0.93	23	0	0	0	...	8-...	34.1	17	8	5	0	15-1	47	.145
— Omaha (PCL)	1	0	1.000	0.00	0.80	12	0	0	0	...	8-...	13.2	4	0	0	0	7-0	17	.093
— Kansas City (A.L.)	1	0	1.000	6.12	1.80	26	0	0	0	5	0-1	25.0	26	19	17	2	19-3	20	.277
2003— Kansas City (A.L.)	1	0	1.000	9.58	2.03	9	0	0	0	0	0-0	10.1	12	11	11	2	9-0	8	.293
— Omaha (PCL)	1	2	.333	4.91	1.75	34	0	0	0	...	5-...	36.2	39	21	20	2	25-0	44	.273
Major League totals (2 years)	2	0	1.000	7.13	1.87	35	0	0	0	5	0-1	35.1	38	30	28	4	28-3	28	.281

BULLINGER, KIRK   P

PERSONAL: Born October 28, 1969, in New Orleans, La. ... 6-2/170. ... Throws right, bats right. ... Full name: Kirk Matthew Bullinger. ... High school: Archbishop Rummel (Metairie, La.). ... College: Southeastern Louisiana.
TRANSACTIONS/CAREER NOTES: Selected by St. Louis Cardinals in 32nd round of free-agent draft (June 1, 1992). ... Traded by Cardinals organization with OF DaRond Stovall and P Bryan Eversgerd to Montreal Expos organization for P Ken Hill (April 5, 1995). ... On Ottawa disabled list (April 9-July 3, 1998); included rehabilitation assignment to Gulf Coast Expos (June 26-July 3). ... Granted free agency (October 15, 1998). ... Signed by Boston Red Sox organization (December 14, 1998). ... On Pawtucket disabled list (August 6-18, 1999). ... Granted free agency (October 4, 1999). ... Signed by Philadelphia Phillies organization (January 29, 2000). ... On Philadelphia disabled list (April 11-June 20, 2000); included rehabilitation assignments to Reading (May 6-8 and May 13-18) and Gulf Coast Phillies (June 19-20). ... Granted free agency (October 2, 2000). ... Granted free agency (October 15, 2001). ... Granted free agency (October 15, 2002). ... Signed by Houston Astros as free agent; contract purchased by Houston (September 2, 2003).
CAREER HITTING: 0-for-1 (.000), 0 R, 0 2B, 0 3B, 0 HR, 0 RBI.

Year League	W	L	Pct.	ERA	WHIP	G	GS	CG	ShO	Hld.	Sv.-Opp.	IP	H	R	ER	HR	BB-IBB	SO	Avg.
1992— Hamilton (NYP)	2	2	.500	1.11	0.80	35	0	0	0	...	2-...	48.2	24	7	6	0	15-4	61	.140
1993— Springfield (Mid.)	1	3	.250	2.28	0.92	50	0	0	0	...	* 33-...	51.1	26	19	13	5	21-1	72	.144
1994— St. Pete. (FSL)	2	0	1.000	1.17	1.06	39	0	0	0	...	6-...	53.2	37	16	7	0	20-5	50	.191
1995— Harrisburg (Eastern)	5	3	.625	2.42	1.28	56	0	0	0	...	7-...	67.0	61	22	18	4	25-5	42	.242
1996— Ottawa (Int'l)	2	1	.667	3.52	1.24	10	0	0	0	...	0-...	15.1	10	6	6	3	9-1	9	.189
— Harrisburg (Eastern)	3	4	.429	1.97	1.40	47	0	0	0	...	22-...	45.2	46	16	10	5	18-3	29	.271
1997— Harrisburg (Eastern)	3	0	1.000	2.67	1.04	21	0	0	0	...	6-...	27.0	22	9	8	4	6-0	21	.224
— W.P. Beach (FSL)	2	0	1.000	0.00	0.82	2	0	0	0	...	0-...	3.2	3	0	0	0	0-0	7	.200
— Ottawa (Int'l)	3	4	.429	1.71	0.85	22	0	0	0	...	5-...	31.2	17	7	6	0	10-0	15	.160
1998— GC Expos (GCL)	0	0	...	0.00	0.50	2	2	0	0	...	0-...	4.0	2	0	0	0	0-0	7	.143
— Jupiter (FSL)	0	0	...	5.40	1.10	8	0	0	0	...	0-...	10.0	9	7	6	1	2-0	12	.225
— Ottawa (Int'l)	1	0	1.000	1.06	1.29	13	0	0	0	...	3-...	17.0	16	2	2	0	6-1	7	.246
— Montreal (N.L.)	1	0	1.000	9.00	2.00	8	0	0	0	0	0-1	7.0	14	8	7	1	0-0	2	.400
1999— Trenton (East.)	1	1	.500	0.53	0.65	17	0	0	0	...	10-...	17.0	6	2	1	0	5-1	16	.111
— Pawtucket (Int'l)	0	2	.000	2.39	1.33	35	0	0	0	...	15-...	37.2	37	14	10	3	13-4	27	.259
— Boston (A.L.)	0	0	...	4.50	2.00	4	0	0	0	2	0-0	2.0	2	1	1	0	2-0	0	.286
2000— Philadelphia (N.L.)	0	0	...	5.40	1.20	3	0	0	0	1	0-0	3.1	4	2	2	0	0-0	4	.308
— Scran./W.B. (I.L.)	0	1	.000	0.72	1.16	26	0	0	0	...	12-...	25.0	19	4	2	0	10-2	16	.224
— Reading (East.)	0	0	...	0.00	1.33	2	1	0	0	...	0-...	3.0	3	0	0	0	1-0	1	.300
— GC Phillies (GCL)	0	0	...	0.00	0.00	1	1	0	0	...	0-...	1.0	0	0	0	0	0-0	1	.000
2001— Akron (East.)	0	1	.000	4.91	1.64	3	0	0	0	...	1-...	3.2	5	2	2	0	1-1	4	.357
— Charlotte (Int'l)	0	3	.000	3.58	1.29	36	1	0	0	...	5-...	50.1	44	23	20	5	21-6	34	.247
2002— New Orleans (PCL)	4	1	.800	2.75	0.96	55	1	0	0	...	4-...	75.1	61	25	23	6	11-4	46	.223
2003— New Orleans (PCL)	3	3	.500	1.94	1.08	55	0	0	0	...	20-...	65.0	56	18	14	3	14-4	46	.230
— Houston (N.L.)	0	0	...	6.75	1.00	7	0	0	0	1	0-0	8.0	7	6	6	2	1-0	5	.219
American League totals (1 year)	0	0	...	4.50	2.00	4	0	0	0	2	0-0	2.0	2	1	1	0	2-0	0	.286
National League totals (3 years)	1	0	1.000	7.36	1.42	18	0	0	0	2	0-1	18.1	25	16	15	3	1-0	11	.313
Major League totals (4 years)	1	0	1.000	7.08	1.48	22	0	0	0	4	0-1	20.1	27	17	16	3	3-0	11	.310

BUMP, NATE   P

PERSONAL: Born July 24, 1976, in Towanda, Pa. ... 6-2/185. ... Throws right, bats right. ... Full name: Nathan Louis Bump. ... College: Penn State.
TRANSACTIONS/CAREER NOTES: Selected by San Francisco Giants organization in first round (25th pick overall) of free-agent draft (June 2, 1998). ... Traded by Giants with P Jason Grilli to Florida Marlins for P Livan Hernandez (July 24, 1999). ... Recalled by Florida from Albuquerque (June 28, 2003).
CAREER HITTING: 0-for-0 (.000), 0 R, 0 2B, 0 3B, 0 HR, 0 RBI.

Year— League	W	L	Pct.	ERA	WHIP	G	GS	CG	ShO	Hld.	Sv.-Opp.	IP	H	R	ER	HR	BB-IBB	SO	Avg.
1998— Salem-Keizer (NW)	0	0	...	0.00	1.00	2	2	0	0	...	0-...	8.0	5	0	0	0	3-0	8	.192
— San Jose (Calif.)	6	1	.857	1.75	0.99	11	11	0	0	...	0-...	61.2	37	13	12	2	24-0	61	.175
1999— Shreveport (Texas)	4	10	.286	3.31	1.27	17	17	1	1	...	0-...	92.1	85	40	34	9	32-0	59	.242
— Portland (East.)	2	6	.250	6.07	1.60	8	8	0	0	...	0-...	43.0	57	38	29	3	12-0	33	.311
2000— Portland (East.)	8	9	.471	4.57	1.46	26	26	3	1	...	0-...	149.2	169	85	76	16	49-1	98	.287
2001— Portland (East.)	4	5	.444	5.27	1.19	11	8	0	0	...	0-...	54.2	55	41	32	10	10-0	41	.259
2002— Portland (East.)	7	6	.538	3.38	1.09	20	20	3	0	...	0-...	127.2	110	56	48	5	29-0	81	.227
2003— Albuquerque (PCL)	6	5	.545	4.43	1.32	15	15	0	0	...	0-...	85.1	89	48	42	4	24-1	52	.267
— Florida (N.L.)	4	0	1.000	4.71	1.49	32	0	0	0	6	0-0	36.1	34	21	19	3	20-0	17	.248
Major League totals (1 year)	**4**	**0**	**1.000**	**4.71**	**1.49**	**32**	**0**	**0**	**0**	**6**	**0-0**	**36.1**	**34**	**21**	**19**	**3**	**20-0**	**17**	**.248**

BURBA, DAVE   P

PERSONAL: Born July 7, 1966, in Dayton, Ohio. ... 6-4/240. ... Throws right, bats right. ... Full name: David Allen Burba. ... Name pronounced: BUR-ba. ... High school: Kenton Ridge (Springfield, Ohio). ... College: Ohio State.

TRANSACTIONS/CAREER NOTES: Selected by Seattle Mariners organization in second round of free-agent draft (June 2, 1987). ... Traded by Mariners with P Bill Swift and P Mike Jackson to San Francisco Giants for OF Kevin Mitchell and P Mike Remlinger (December 11, 1991). ... Traded by Giants with OF Darren Lewis and P Mark Portugal to Cincinnati Reds for OF Deion Sanders, P John Roper, P Ricky Pickett, P Scott Service and IF Dave McCarty (July 21, 1995). ... On disabled list (August 7-27, 1997). ... Traded by Reds to Cleveland Indians for 1B Sean Casey (March 30, 1998). ... Granted free agency (November 6, 2001). ... Signed by Texas Rangers (December 19, 2001). ... Released by Rangers (July 29, 2002). ... Signed by Indians organization (August 7, 2002). ... Granted free agency (November 4, 2002). ... Re-signed by Indians organization (January 8, 2003). ... Released by Indians (2003). ... Signed by Milwaukee Brewers organization as a free agent (May 4, 2003). ... Contract purchased by Milwaukee from Indianapolis (June 27, 2003).

CAREER HITTING: 26-for-190 (.137), 10 R, 1 2B, 0 3B, 3 HR, 12 RBI.

Year— League	W	L	Pct.	ERA	WHIP	G	GS	CG	ShO	Hld.	Sv.-Opp.	IP	H	R	ER	HR	BB-IBB	SO	Avg.
1987— Bellingham (N'west)	3	1	.750	1.93	0.99	5	5	0	0	...	0-...	23.1	20	10	5	0	3-0	24	.213
— Salinas (Calif.)	1	6	.143	4.61	1.50	9	9	0	0	...	0-...	54.2	53	31	28	3	29-0	46	.252
1988— San Bernardino (Calif.)	5	7	.417	2.68	1.40	20	20	0	0	...	0-...	114.0	106	41	34	4	54-1	102	.252
1989— Williamsport (Eastern)	11	7	.611	3.16	1.23	25	25	5	1	...	0-...	156.2	138	69	55	7	55-0	89	.236
1990— Calgary (PCL)	10	6	.625	4.67	1.49	31	18	1	0	...	2-...	113.2	124	64	59	11	45-0	47	.282
— Seattle (A.L.)	0	0	...	4.50	1.25	6	0	0	0	0	0-0	8.0	8	6	4	0	2-0	4	.267
1991— Seattle (A.L.)	2	2	.500	3.68	1.31	22	2	0	0	0	1-1	36.2	34	16	15	6	14-3	16	.245
— Calgary (PCL)	6	4	.600	3.53	1.53	23	9	0	0	...	4-...	71.1	82	35	28	4	27-0	42	.294
1992— San Francisco (N.L.)	2	7	.222	4.97	1.57	23	11	0	0	0	0-0	70.2	80	43	39	4	31-2	47	.287
— Phoenix (PCL)	5	5	.500	4.72	1.48	13	13	0	0	...	0-...	74.1	86	40	39	5	24-2	44	.295
1993— San Francisco (N.L.)	10	3	.769	4.25	1.38	54	5	0	0	10	0-0	95.1	95	49	45	14	37-5	88	.265
1994— San Francisco (N.L.)	3	6	.333	4.38	1.41	57	0	0	0	11	0-3	74.0	59	39	36	5	45-3	84	.221
1995— San Francisco (N.L.)	4	2	.667	4.98	1.45	37	0	0	0	5	0-1	43.1	38	26	24	5	25-2	46	.235
— Cincinnati (N.L.)	6	2	.750	3.27	1.23	15	9	1	1	0	0-0	63.1	52	24	23	4	26-1	50	.223
1996— Cincinnati (N.L.)	11	13	.458	3.83	1.42	34	33	0	0	0	0-0	195.0	179	96	83	18	97-9	148	.244
1997— Cincinnati (N.L.)	11	10	.524	4.73	1.44	30	27	2	0	0	0-0	160.0	157	88	84	22	73-10	131	.255
1998— Cleveland (A.L.)	15	10	.600	4.11	1.37	32	31	0	0	0	0-0	203.2	210	100	93	30	69-4	132	.269
1999— Cleveland (A.L.)	15	9	.625	4.25	1.40	34	34	1	0	0	0-0	220.0	211	113	104	30	96-3	174	.254
2000— Cleveland (A.L.)	16	6	.727	4.47	1.52	32	32	0	0	0	0-0	191.1	199	99	95	19	91-2	180	.267
2001— Cleveland (A.L.)	10	10	.500	6.21	1.61	32	27	1	0	0	0-0	150.2	188	112	104	16	54-2	118	.306
2002— Texas (A.L.)	4	5	.444	5.42	1.48	23	18	1	0	0	0-1	111.1	125	71	67	13	40-3	70	.279
— Akron (East.)	0	0	...	0.00	0.64	1	1	0	0	...	0-...	4.2	2	0	0	0	1-0	1	.133
— Cleveland (A.L.)	1	0	1.000	4.50	1.38	12	3	0	0	1	0-1	34.0	30	20	17	3	17-0	25	.236
2003— Buffalo (Int'l)	1	3	.250	2.05	1.05	4	4	0	0	...	0-...	22.0	18	6	5	2	5-0	10	.228
— Indianapolis (Int'l)	5	4	.556	5.33	1.60	10	9	0	0	...	0-...	50.2	65	37	30	4	16-0	34	.316
— Milwaukee (N.L.)	1	1	.500	3.53	1.41	17	2	0	0	0	0-0	43.1	42	19	17	5	19-2	35	.250
American League totals (7 years)	**63**	**42**	**.600**	**4.70**	**1.45**	**193**	**147**	**3**	**0**	**1**	**1-3**	**955.2**	**1005**	**537**	**499**	**117**	**383-17**	**719**	**.270**
National League totals (7 years)	**48**	**44**	**.522**	**4.24**	**1.42**	**267**	**87**	**3**	**1**	**26**	**0-4**	**745.0**	**702**	**384**	**351**	**77**	**353-34**	**629**	**.249**
Major League totals (14 years)	**111**	**86**	**.563**	**4.50**	**1.44**	**460**	**234**	**6**	**1**	**27**	**1-7**	**1700.2**	**1707**	**921**	**850**	**194**	**736-51**	**1348**	**.261**

BURKE, JAMIE   C/IF

PERSONAL: Born September 24, 1971, in Roseburg, Ore. ... 6-0/195. ... Bats right, throws right. ... Full name: James Eugene Burke. ... High school: Roseburg (Ore.). ... College: Oregon State.

TRANSACTIONS/CAREER NOTES: Selected by California Angels organization in ninth round of free-agent draft (June 3, 1993). ... On Salt Lake disabled list (August 26, 2002-remainder of season). ... Granted free agency (October 15, 2002). ... Signed by Chicago White Sox organization (January 27, 2003). ... Contract purchased by Chicago from Charlotte (August 8, 2003). ... Optioned to Charlotte by Chicago (August 11, 2003). ... Recalled from Charlotte by Chicago (August 31, 2003).

2003 GAMES PLAYED BY POSITION (MLB): C—4, DH—1, 1B—1.

Year— Team (League)	Pos.	G	AB	R	H	2B	3B	HR	RBI	BB	SO	HBP	GDP	SB-CS	Avg.	OBP	SLG	OPS	E	Pct.
1993— Boise (NW)	3B	66	226	32	68	11	1	1	30	39	28	5	4	2-3	.301	.412	.372	.783	18	.873
1994— Cedar Rap. (Midw.)	3B-1B	127	469	57	124	24	1	1	47	40	64	12	15	6-8	.264	.333	.326	.659	22	.973
1995— Lake Elsinore (Calif.)	3B-1B	106	365	47	100	15	6	2	56	32	53	9	12	6-4	.274	.344	.364	.708	22	.949
1996— Midland (Texas)	3-C-1-OF	45	144	24	46	8	2	2	16	20	22	2	1	1-1	.319	.410	.444	.854	5	.968
— Vancouver (PCL)	3B-C-OF	41	156	12	39	5	0	1	14	7	18	1	5	2-1	.250	.283	.301	.584	5	.952
1997— Midland (Texas)	3-C-1-OF	116	428	77	141	44	3	6	72	40	46	8	12	2-3	.329	.395	.488	.883	27	.956
— Vancouver (PCL)	3B-C	8	27	4	8	1	0	0	3	3	2	1	1	0-0	.296	.387	.333	.720	3	.923
1998— Vancouver (PCL)	3B-C-1B	61	162	16	35	6	0	2	14	13	25	6	7	0-1	.216	.295	.290	.585	5	.985
— Midland (Texas)	3B	12	41	7	10	1	0	0	4	7	4	0	4	0-0	.244	.354	.268	.622	3	.870
1999— Edmonton (PCL) 2-3-P-C-1		46	149	24	50	9	0	3	16	23	18	3	2	0-1	.336	.434	.456	.891	5	.958
2000— Edmonton (PCL)	2B-3B-C	75	263	25	63	12	0	0	17	19	42	5	5	1-1	.240	.301	.285	.586	6	.980
2001— Salt Lake (PCL)	C-3-1-OF	61	215	25	47	10	2	0	27	19	28	5	1	1-0	.219	.292	.293	.585	5	.988
— Anaheim (A.L.)	C-DH-1B	9	5	1	1	0	0	0	0	0	2	0	0	0-0	.200	.200	.200	.400	0	1.000
2002— Salt Lake (PCL)	C-3B-1B	88	316	47	96	12	4	8	44	20	37	4	9	1-3	.304	.350	.443	.793	13	.974
2003— Charlotte (Int'l)	C-DH-1-3	94	323	47	104	13	0	6	50	20	39	4	9	1-1	.322	.363	.418	.781	6	.990
— Chicago (A.L.)	C-DH-1B	6	8	0	3	0	0	0	2	0	0	0	0	0-0	.375	.375	.375	.750	0	1.000
Major League totals (2 years)		**15**	**13**	**1**	**4**	**0**	**0**	**0**	**2**	**0**	**2**	**0**	**0**	**0-0**	**.308**	**.308**	**.308**	**.615**	**0**	**1.000**

B

BURKETT, JOHN   P

PERSONAL: Born November 28, 1964, in New Brighton, Pa. ... 6-3/215. ... Throws right, bats right. ... Full name: John David Burkett. ... Name pronounced: BURK-it. ... High school: Beaver (Pa.).

TRANSACTIONS/CAREER NOTES: Selected by San Francisco Giants organization in sixth round of free-agent draft (June 6, 1983). ... Traded by Giants to Texas Rangers for IF Rich Aurilia and OF Desi Wilson (December 22, 1994). ... Granted free agency (April 7, 1995). ... Signed by Florida Marlins (April 9, 1995). ... Traded by Marlins to Texas Rangers for P Ryan Dempster and a player to be named later (August 8, 1996); Marlins acquired P Rick Helling to complete deal (September 3, 1996). ... On Texas disabled list (August 6-31, 1997); included rehabilitation assignment to Oklahoma City (August 26). ... On Texas disabled list (April 21-May 9, 1999); included rehabilitation assignment to Tulsa (May 1-9). ... Granted free agency (November 1, 1999). ... Signed by Tampa Bay Devil Rays organization (January 17, 2000). ... Released by Devil Rays (March 29, 2000). ... Signed by Atlanta Braves (April 2, 2000). ... Granted free agency (October 31, 2000). ... Re-signed by Braves (December 20, 2000). ... Granted free agency (November 6, 2001). ... Signed by Boston Red Sox (December 20, 2001). ... On Boston disabled list (March 21-April 19, 2002); included rehabilitation assignment to Pawtucket (April 14-19).

CAREER HITTING: 50-for-540 (.093), 22 R, 6 2B, 0 3B, 0 HR, 18 RBI.

Year	League	W	L	Pct.	ERA	WHIP	G	GS	CG	ShO	Hld.	Sv.-Opp.	IP	H	R	ER	HR	BB-IBB	SO	Avg.
1983— Great Falls (Pio.)		2	6	.250	6.26	2.05	13	9	0	0	...	0-...	50.1	73	44	35	1	30-2	38	...
1984— Clinton (Midw.)		7	6	.538	4.33	1.31	20	20	2	0	...	0-...	126.2	128	81	61	5	38-1	83	.257
1985— Fresno (Calif.)		7	4	.636	2.87	1.31	20	20	1	1	...	0-...	109.2	98	43	35	3	46-0	72	...
1986— Shreveport (Texas)		10	6	.625	2.66	1.10	22	21	4	2	...	0-...	128.2	99	46	38	7	42-0	73	.214
— Fresno (Calif.)		0	3	.000	5.47	1.70	4	4	0	0	...	0-...	24.2	34	19	15	2	8-0	14	.318
1987— Shreveport (Texas)		• 14	8	.636	3.34	1.32	27	27	6	1	...	0-...	* 177.2	181	75	66	11	53-2	126	.263
— San Francisco (N.L.)		0	0	...	4.50	1.67	3	0	0	0	0	0-0	6.0	7	4	3	2	3-0	5	.304
1988— Phoenix (PCL)		5	11	.313	5.21	1.67	21	21	0	0	0	0-0	114.0	141	79	66	7	49-3	74	.308
— Shreveport (Texas)		5	1	.833	2.13	1.01	7	7	2	1	0	0-0	50.2	33	15	12	3	18-1	34	.190
1989— Phoenix (PCL)		10	11	.476	5.05	1.53	28	• 28	2	1	...	0- 28	167.2	197	111	94	19	59-3	105	.296
1990— Phoenix (PCL)		2	1	.667	2.74	0.91	3	3	2	1	...	0-...	23.0	18	8	7	2	3-0	9	.220
— San Francisco (N.L.)		14	7	.667	3.79	1.28	33	32	2	0	0	1-1	204.0	201	92	86	18	61-7	118	.257
1991— San Francisco (N.L.)		12	11	.522	4.18	1.37	36	34	3	1	1	0-0	206.2	223	103	96	19	60-2	131	.277
1992— San Francisco (N.L.)		13	9	.591	3.84	1.26	32	32	3	1	0	0-0	189.2	194	96	81	13	45-6	107	.264
1993— San Francisco (N.L.)		• 22	7	.759	3.65	1.14	34	34	2	1	0	0-0	231.2	224	100	94	18	40-4	145	.255
1994— San Francisco (N.L.)		6	8	.429	3.62	1.33	25	25	0	0	0	0-0	159.1	176	72	64	14	36-7	85	.286
1995— Florida (N.L.)		14	14	.500	4.30	1.41	30	30	4	0	0	0-0	188.1	208	95	90	22	57-5	126	.282
1996— Florida (N.L.)		6	10	.375	4.32	1.27	24	24	1	0	0	0-0	154.0	154	84	74	15	42-2	108	.263
— Texas (A.L.)		5	2	.714	4.06	1.33	10	10	1	1	0	0-0	68.2	75	33	31	4	16-2	47	.280
1997— Texas (A.L.)		9	12	.429	4.56	1.43	30	30	2	0	0	0-0	189.1	240	106	96	20	30-1	139	.307
— Oklahoma City (A.A.)		1	0	1.000	3.60	1.60	1	1	0	0	...	0-...	5.0	6	2	2	1	2-0	3	.286
1998— Texas (A.L.)		9	13	.409	5.68	1.42	32	32	0	0	0	0-0	195.0	230	131	* 123	19	46-1	131	.292
1999— Texas (A.L.)		9	8	.529	5.62	1.56	30	25	0	0	0	0-0	147.1	184	95	92	18	46-1	96	.307
— Tulsa (Texas)		0	1	.000	2.70	1.50	2	2	0	0	...	0-...	6.2	7	5	2	0	3-0	3	.241
2000— Atlanta (N.L.)		10	6	.625	4.89	1.59	31	22	0	0	0	0-1	134.1	162	79	73	13	51-2	110	.303
2001— Atlanta (N.L.)		12	12	.500	3.04	1.17	34	34	1	1	0	0-0	219.1	187	83	74	17	70-13	187	.230
2002— Pawtucket (Int'l)		0	1	.000	11.57	2.14	1	1	0	0	...	0-...	2.1	4	3	3	0	1-0	2	.400
— Boston (A.L.)		13	8	.619	4.53	1.44	29	29	1	1	0	0-0	173.0	199	93	87	25	50-5	124	.287
2003— Boston (A.L.)		12	9	.571	5.15	1.37	32	30	1	0	0	0-0	181.2	202	108	104	20	47-1	107	.281
American League totals (6 years)		57	52	.523	5.02	1.43	163	156	5	2	0	0-0	955.0	1130	566	533	106	235-11	644	.294
National League totals (10 years)		109	84	.565	3.91	1.30	282	267	16	4	1	1-2	1693.1	1736	808	735	151	465-48	1122	.267
Major League totals (15 years)		166	136	.550	4.31	1.35	445	423	21	6	1	1-2	2648.1	2866	1374	1268	257	700-59	1766	.277

BURKHART, MORGAN   1B

PERSONAL: Born January 29, 1972, in St. Louis, Mo. ... 5-11/225. ... Bats both, throws left. ... High school: Hazelwood West (Hazelwood, Mo.). ... College: Central Missouri State.

TRANSACTIONS/CAREER NOTES: Signed by Richmond, Frontier League (1995). ... Contract sold by Richmond to Boston Red Sox organization (October 21, 1998). ... Released by Red Sox (October 9, 2001). ... Played in Japan (2002). ... Signed by Kansas City Royals as a free agent (November 20, 2002). ... Contract purchased by Kansas City from Omaha (June 20, 2003). ... Designated for assignment by Kansas City (July 3, 2003). ... Sent outright to Omaha by Kansas City (July 7, 2003).

2003 GAMES PLAYED BY POSITION (MLB): DH—2, 1B—2.

Year	Team (League)	Pos.	G	AB	R	H	2B	3B	HR	RBI	BB	SO	HBP	GDP	SB-CS	Avg.	OBP	SLG	OPS	E	Pct.
1995— Richmond (Fron.)		1B	70	282	58	* 93	* 28	1	9	* 70	41	24	7	5	16-7	.330	.418	.532	.950	...	...
1996— Richmond (Fron.)		1B	74	266	60	95	* 27	1	17	64	49	24	14	3	22-4	.357	.472	.658	1.130	...	...
1997— Richmond (Fron.)		1B	80	285	* 76	92	22	0	* 24	74	73	47	8	6	8-4	.323	.466	.653	1.119	...	...
1998— Richmond (Fron.)		1B	80	280	* 97	113	16	1	* 36	* 98	85	38	13	6	13-1	.404	.557	.854	1.410	...	...
1999— Sarasota (Fla. St.)		1B	68	245	56	89	18	0	* 23	67	37	33	6	4	5-2	.363	.447	.718	1.166	4	.992
— Trenton (East.)		1B	66	239	40	55	14	1	12	41	31	43	10	2	3-0	.230	.339	.448	.787	3	.987
2000— Pawtucket (Int'l)		1B-OF	105	353	59	90	17	1	23	77	69	89	12	6	0-0	.255	.392	.504	.896	4	.993
— Boston (A.L.)		DH-1B-OF	25	73	16	21	3	0	4	18	17	25	4	1	0-0	.288	.442	.493	.935	1	.964
2001— Pawtucket (Int'l)		1B-OF	120	412	64	111	19	1	25	62	68	113	8	4	1-0	.269	.382	.502	.884	7	.992
— Boston (A.L.)		DH-1B	11	33	3	6	1	0	1	4	1	11	0	1	0-0	.182	.206	.303	.509	0	1.000
2003— Kansas City (A.L.)		DH-1B	6	15	1	3	0	0	0	1	1	2	0	0	0-0	.200	.250	.200	.450	0	1.000
— Omaha (PCL)		1B-DH	104	382	54	96	18	0	17	57	50	67	17	5	2-0	.251	.361	.432	.793	3	.997
Major League totals (3 years)			42	121	20	30	4	0	5	23	19	38	4	2	0-0	.248	.366	.405	.770	1	.986

BURKS, ELLIS   DH/OF

PERSONAL: Born September 11, 1964, in Vicksburg, Miss. ... 6-2/205. ... Bats right, throws right. ... Full name: Ellis Rena Burks. ... High school: Everman (Texas). ... Junior college: Ranger College (Texas).

TRANSACTIONS/CAREER NOTES: Selected by Boston Red Sox organization in first round (20th pick overall) of free-agent draft (January 11, 1983). ... On disabled list (March 26-April 12, 1988). ... On Boston disabled list (June 15-August 1, 1989); included rehabilitation assignment to Pawtucket (July 26-August 1). ... On disabled list (June 25, 1992-remainder of season). ... Granted free agency (December 19, 1992). ... Signed by Chicago White Sox (January 4, 1993). ... Granted free agency (October 27, 1993). ... Signed by Colorado Rockies (November 30, 1993). ... On Colorado disabled list (May 18-July 31, 1994); included rehabilitation assignment to Colorado Springs (July 18-

20). ... On Colorado disabled list (April 17-May 5, 1995); included rehabilitation assignment to Colorado Springs (April 25-May 5). ... On disabled list (June 28-July 29, 1997). ... Traded by Rockies to San Francisco Giants for OF Darryl Hamilton, P James Stoops and a player to be named later (July 31, 1998); Rockies acquired P Jason Brester to complete deal (August 17, 1998). ... Granted free agency (November 2, 1998). ... Re-signed by Giants (November 13, 1998). ... On disabled list (June 9-26, 1999; and May 9-24, 2000). ... Granted free agency (October 30, 2000). ... Signed by Cleveland Indians (November 19, 2000). ... On disabled list (July 16-August 1, 2001). ... Placed on the 15-day disabled list, retroactive to June 8 (June 10, 2003). ... Transferred to Emergency disabled list (June 22, 2003).

2003 GAMES PLAYED BY POSITION (MLB): DH—51, OF—2.

Year	Team (League)	Pos.	G	AB	R	H	2B	3B	HR	RBI	BB	SO	HBP	GDP	SB-CS	Avg.	OBP	SLG	OPS	E	Pct.
1983— Elmira (N.Y.-Penn)		OF	53	174	30	42	9	0	2	23	17	43	1	...	9-0	.241	.313	.328	.640	2	.979
1984— Winter Haven (FSL)		OF	112	375	52	96	15	4	6	43	42	68	5	8	29-8	.256	.337	.365	.703	5	.977
1985— New Britain (East.)		OF	133	476	66	121	25	7	10	61	42	85	3	5	17-14	.254	.316	.399	.715	8	.975
1986— New Britain (East.)		OF	124	462	70	126	20	3	14	55	44	75	2	4	31-9	.273	.337	.420	.757	5	.985
1987— Pawtucket (Int'l)		OF	11	40	11	9	3	1	3	6	7	7	0	1	1-0	.225	.340	.575	.915	0	1.000
— Boston (A.L.)		DH-OF	133	558	94	152	30	2	20	59	41	98	2	1	27-6	.272	.324	.441	.765	4	.988
1988— Boston (A.L.)		DH-OF	144	540	93	159	37	5	18	92	62	89	3	8	25-9	.294	.367	.481	.848	9	.977
1989— Boston (A.L.)		DH-OF	97	399	73	121	19	6	12	61	36	52	5	8	21-5	.303	.365	.471	.836	6	.977
— Pawtucket (Int'l)		OF	5	21	4	3	1	0	0	0	2	3	0	2	0-0	.143	.217	.190	.408	0	1.000
1990— Boston (A.L.)		DH-OF	152	588	89	174	33	8	21	89	48	82	1	18	9-11	.296	.349	.486	.835	2	.994
1991— Boston (A.L.)		DH-OF	130	474	56	119	33	3	14	56	39	81	6	7	6-11	.251	.314	.422	.736	2	.993
1992— Boston (A.L.)		OF-DH	66	235	35	60	8	3	8	30	25	48	1	5	5-2	.255	.327	.417	.744	2	.984
1993— Chicago (A.L.)		OF	146	499	75	137	24	4	17	74	60	97	4	11	6-9	.275	.352	.441	.793	6	.982
1994— Colorado (N.L.)		OF	42	149	33	48	8	3	13	24	16	39	0	3	3-1	.322	.388	.678	1.066	3	.964
— Colo. Springs (PCL)		OF	2	8	4	4	1	0	1	2	2	1	0	1	0-0	.500	.600	1.000	1.600	0	1.000
1995— Colo. Springs (PCL)		OF-DH	8	29	9	9	2	1	2	6	4	8	0	1	0-0	.310	.394	.655	1.049	0	1.000
— Colorado (N.L.)		OF	103	278	41	74	10	6	14	49	39	72	2	7	7-3	.266	.359	.496	.856	5	.970
1996— Colorado (N.L.)		OF	156	613	*142	211	45	8	40	128	61	114	6	19	32-6	.344	.408	*.639	1.047	5	.983
1997— Colorado (N.L.)		OF	119	424	91	123	19	2	32	82	47	75	3	17	7-2	.290	.363	.571	.934	4	.982
1998— Colorado (N.L.)		OF	100	357	54	102	22	5	16	54	39	80	2	10	3-7	.286	.355	.510	.865	5	.975
— San Francisco (N.L.)		OF	42	147	22	45	6	1	5	22	19	31	3	2	8-1	.306	.387	.463	.850	1	.989
1999— San Francisco (N.L.)		OF-DH	120	390	73	110	19	0	31	96	69	86	6	11	7-5	.282	.394	.569	.964	2	.991
2000— San Francisco (N.L.)		OF-DH	122	393	74	135	21	5	24	96	56	49	1	10	5-1	.344	.419	.606	1.025	4	.982
2001— Cleveland (A.L.)		DH-OF	124	439	83	123	29	1	28	74	62	85	5	16	5-1	.280	.369	.542	.911	0	1.000
2002— Cleveland (A.L.)		DH-OF	138	518	92	156	28	0	32	91	44	108	6	13	2-3	.301	.362	.541	.903	0	1.000
2003— Cleveland (A.L.)		DH-OF	55	198	27	52	11	1	6	28	27	46	3	4	1-1	.263	.360	.419	.779	0	1.000
American League totals (10 years)			1185	4448	717	1253	252	33	176	654	444	786	36	91	107-58	.282	.349	.472	.821	31	.985
National League totals (7 years)			804	2751	530	848	150	30	175	551	346	546	23	79	72-26	.308	.387	.575	.962	29	.980
Major League totals (17 years)			1989	7199	1247	2101	402	63	351	1205	790	1332	59	170	179-84	.292	.364	.511	.875	60	.983

BURNETT, A.J.　　　　　P

PERSONAL: Born January 3, 1977, in North Little Rock, Ark. ... 6-4/232. ... Throws right, bats right. ... Full name: Allan James Burnett. ... High school: Central Arkansas Christian (North Little Rock, Ark.).

TRANSACTIONS/CAREER NOTES: Selected by New York Mets organization in eighth round of free-agent draft (June 1, 1995). ... Traded by Mets with P Jesus Sanchez and OF Robert Stratton to Florida Marlins for P Al Leiter and 2B Ralph Milliard (February 6, 1998). ... On Florida disabled list (March 17-July 20, 2000); included rehabilitation assignments to Brevard County (July 4-14) and Calgary (July 15-20). ... On Florida disabled list (March 23-May 7, 2001); included rehabilitation assignment to Brevard County (April 24-May 1). ... On disabled list (August 19-September 14, 2002). ... Placed on 15-day disabled list (April 26, 2003). ... Transferred to Emergency disabled list (May 6, 2003).

CAREER HITTING: 20-for-156 (.128), 5 R, 4 2B, 1 3B, 2 HR, 6 RBI.

Year	League	W	L	Pct.	ERA	WHIP	G	GS	CG	ShO	Hld.	Sv.-Opp.	IP	H	R	ER	HR	BB-IBB	SO	Avg.
1995— GC Mets (GCL)		2	3	.400	4.28	1.49	9	8	1	0	...	0-...	33.2	27	16	16	2	23-0	26	.231
1996— Kingsport (Appal.)		4	0	1.000	3.88	1.47	12	12	0	0	...	0-...	58.0	31	26	25	2	*54-0	68	.171
1997— GC Mets (GCL)		0	1	.000	3.18	1.41	3	2	0	0	...	0-...	11.1	8	8	4	0	8-0	15	.182
— Pittsfield (NYP)		3	1	.750	4.70	1.43	20	9	0	0	...	0-...	44.0	28	26	23	3	35-0	48	.188
1998— Kane County (Midwest)		10	4	.714	1.97	1.00	20	20	0	0	...	0-...	119.0	74	27	26	3	45-0	186	.179
1999— Portland (East.)		6	12	.333	5.52	1.68	26	23	0	0	...	0-...	120.2	132	91	74	15	71-0	121	.281
— Florida (N.L.)		4	2	.667	3.48	1.50	7	7	0	0	0	0-0	41.1	37	23	16	3	25-2	33	.242
2000— Brevard County (FSL)		0	0	...	3.68	1.36	2	2	0	0	...	0-...	7.1	4	3	3	0	6-0	6	.160
— Calgary (PCL)		0	0	...	0.00	0.60	1	1	0	0	...	0-...	5.0	0	0	0	0	3-0	6	.000
— Florida (N.L.)		3	7	.300	4.79	1.50	13	13	0	0	0	0-0	82.2	80	46	44	8	44-3	57	.259
2001— Brevard County (FSL)		0	0	...	1.93	0.86	2	2	0	0	...	0-...	9.1	4	2	2	0	4-0	10	.129
— Florida (N.L.)		11	12	.478	4.05	1.32	27	27	2	1	0	0-0	173.1	145	82	78	20	83-3	128	.231
2002— Florida (N.L.)		12	9	.571	3.30	1.19	31	29	7	*5	0	0-1	204.1	153	84	75	12	90-5	203	.209
2003— Florida (N.L.)		0	2	.000	4.70	1.57	4	4	0	0	0	0-0	23.0	18	13	12	2	18-2	21	.217
Major League totals (5 years)		30	32	.484	3.86	1.32	82	80	9	6	0	0-1	524.2	433	248	225	45	260-15	442	.227

BURNITZ, JEROMY　　　　　OF

PERSONAL: Born April 15, 1969, in Westminster, Calif. ... 6-0/213. ... Bats left, throws right. ... Full name: Jeromy Neal Burnitz. ... Name pronounced: ber-NITS. ... High school: Conroe (Texas). ... College: Oklahoma State.

TRANSACTIONS/CAREER NOTES: Selected by Milwaukee Brewers organization in 24th round of free-agent draft (June 2, 1987); did not sign. ... Selected by New York Mets organization in first round (17th pick overall) of free-agent draft (June 4, 1990). ... On disabled list (August 23-September 18, 1992). ... On Norfolk suspended list (August 11-13, 1994). ... Traded by Mets with P Joe Roa to Cleveland Indians for P Paul Byrd, P Jerry DiPoto, P Dave Mlicki and a player to be named later (November 18, 1994); Mets acquired 2B Jesus Azuaje to complete deal (December 6, 1994). ... Traded by Indians to Milwaukee Brewers for 3B/1B Kevin Seitzer (August 31, 1996). ... On disabled list (July 18-August 20, 1999). ... Traded by Brewers to Mets as part of three-way deal in which Mets traded P Glendon Rusch to Brewers, Colorado Rockies traded 1B/OF Ross Gload and P Craig House to Mets, Brewers traded P Jeff D'Amico, IF Lou Collier, OF/1B Mark Sweeney and cash to Mets, Mets traded 1B/3B Todd Zeile, OF Benny Agbayani, IF/OF Lenny Harris and cash to Rockies and Rockies traded OF Alex Ochoa to Brewers (January 21, 2002). ... Placed on 15-day disabled list (April 23, 2003). ... Sent on rehab assignment to Binghamton (May 20, 2003). ... Recalled by New York from Binghamton; reinstated from 15-day disabled list (May 23, 2003). ... Traded by New York Mets to Los Angeles for INF Victor Diaz, P Joselo Diaz, and P Kole Strayhorn (July 14, 2003).

2003 GAMES PLAYED BY POSITION (MLB): OF—125.

Year	Team (League)	Pos.	G	AB	R	H	2B	3B	HR	RBI	BB	SO	HBP	GDP	SB-CS	Avg.	OBP	SLG	OPS	E	Pct.
1990— Pittsfield (NYP)		OF	51	173	37	52	6	5	6	22	45	39	3	3	12-5	.301 *	.444	.497	.942	0	1.000
— St. Lucie (Fla. St.)		OF	11	32	6	5	1	0	0	3	7	12	4	0	1-0	.156	.372	.188	.560	0	1.000
1991— Williamsport (East.)		OF	135	457	80	103	16	•10	*31	•85	*104	127	4	7	31-13	.225	.368	.508	.876	•11	.958
1992— Tidewater (Int'l)		OF	121	445	56	108	21	3	8	40	33	84	3	7	30-7	.243	.298	.357	.655	8	.967
1993— Norfolk (Int'l)		OF	65	255	33	58	15	3	8	44	25	53	2	6	10-7	.227	.298	.404	.702	1	.993
— New York (N.L.)		OF	86	263	49	64	10	6	13	38	38	66	1	2	3-6	.243	.339	.475	.814	4	.977
1994— New York (N.L.)		OF	45	143	26	34	4	0	3	15	23	45	1	2	1-1	.238	.347	.329	.676	2	.970
— Norfolk (Int'l)		OF-DH	85	314	58	75	15	5	14	49	49	82	1	0	18-6	.239	.340	.452	.792	4	.979
1995— Buffalo (A.A.)		OF	128	443	72	126	26	7	19	*85	50	83	3	6	13-5	.284	.359	.503	.862	5	.981
— Cleveland (A.L.)		OF-DH	9	7	4	4	1	0	0	0	0	0	0	0	0-0	.571	.571	.714	1.286	0	1.000
1996— Cleveland (A.L.)		OF-DH	71	128	30	36	10	0	7	26	25	31	2	3	2-1	.281	.406	.523	.930	0	1.000
— Milwaukee (A.L.)		OF	23	72	8	17	4	0	2	14	8	16	2	1	2-0	.236	.321	.375	.696	1	.975
1997— Milwaukee (A.L.)		OF	153	494	85	139	37	8	27	85	75	111	5	8	20-13	.281	.382	.553	.934	7	.975
1998— Milwaukee (N.L.)		OF	161	609	92	160	28	1	38	125	70	158	4	9	7-4	.263	.339	.499	.838	9	.972
1999— Milwaukee (N.L.)		OF-DH	130	467	87	126	33	2	33	103	91	124	16	11	7-3	.270	.402	.561	.963	5	.982
2000— Milwaukee (N.L.)		OF-DH	161	564	91	131	29	2	31	98	99	121	14	12	6-4	.232	.356	.456	.811	7	.979
2001— Milwaukee (N.L.)		OF	154	562	104	141	32	4	34	100	80	150	5	8	0-4	.251	.347	.504	.851	6	.981
2002— New York (N.L.)		OF-DH	154	479	65	103	15	0	19	54	58	135	10	11	10-7	.215	.311	.365	.677	9	.966
2003— Binghamton (East.)		OF	3	13	1	3	0	0	1	3	0	4	0	0	1-0	.231	.231	.462	.692	0	1.000
— New York (N.L.)		OF	65	234	38	64	18	0	18	45	21	55	4	4	1-4	.274	.344	.581	.925	2	.986
— Los Angeles (N.L.)		OF	61	230	25	47	4	0	13	32	14	57	1	1	4-0	.204	.252	.391	.643	5	.946
American League totals (3 years)			256	701	127	196	52	8	36	125	108	158	9	12	24-14	.280	.382	.531	.912	8	.978
National League totals (8 years)			1017	3551	577	870	173	15	202	610	494	911	56	60	39-33	.245	.344	.473	.816	49	.975
Major League totals (11 years)			1273	4252	704	1066	225	23	238	735	602	1069	65	72	63-47	.251	.350	.482	.832	57	.976

BURRELL, PAT — OF

PERSONAL: Born October 10, 1976, in Eureka Springs, Ark. ... 6-4/222. ... Bats right, throws right. ... Full name: Patrick Brian Burrell. ... Name pronounced: BURL. ... High school: Bellarmine Prep (San Jose, Calif.). ... College: Miami (Fla.).
TRANSACTIONS/CAREER NOTES: Selected by Boston Red Sox organization in 43rd round of free-agent draft (June 1, 1995); did not sign. ... Selected by Philadelphia Phillies organization in first round (first pick overall) of free-agent draft (June 2, 1998).
2003 GAMES PLAYED BY POSITION (MLB): OF—140, DH—2.

Year	Team (League)	Pos.	G	AB	R	H	2B	3B	HR	RBI	BB	SO	HBP	GDP	SB-CS	Avg.	OBP	SLG	OPS	E	Pct.
1998— Clearwater (FSL)		1B	37	132	29	40	7	1	7	30	27	22	0	3	2-0	.303	.416	.530	.946	1	.995
1999— Reading (East.)		1B-OF	117	417	84	139	28	6	28	90	79	103	0	13	3-1	.333	.438	.631	1.068	12	.985
— Scran./W.B. (I.L.)		1B-OF	10	33	4	5	0	0	1	4	4	8	1	0	0-1	.152	.263	.242	.506	0	1.000
2000— Scran./W.B. (I.L.)		OF-1B	40	143	31	42	15	1	4	25	32	36	0	1	1-1	.294	.420	.497	.917	2	.987
— Philadelphia (N.L.)		1B-OF-DH	111	408	57	106	27	1	18	79	63	139	1	5	0-0	.260	.359	.463	.822	8	.986
2001— Philadelphia (N.L.)		OF-DH	155	539	70	139	29	2	27	89	70	162	5	12	2-1	.258	.346	.469	.816	7	.972
2002— Philadelphia (N.L.)		OF	157	586	96	165	39	2	37	116	89	153	3	16	1-0	.282	.376	.544	.920	6	.979
2003— Philadelphia (N.L.)		OF-DH	146	522	57	109	31	4	21	64	72	142	4	18	0-0	.209	.309	.404	.713	6	.976
Major League totals (4 years)			569	2055	280	519	126	9	103	348	294	596	13	51	3-1	.253	.348	.473	.821	27	.980

BURROUGHS, SEAN — 3B/2B

PERSONAL: Born September 12, 1980, in Atlanta, Ga. ... 6-2/200. ... Bats left, throws right. ... Full name: Sean Patrick Burroughs. ... High school: Wilson (Long Beach, Calif.).
TRANSACTIONS/CAREER NOTES: Selected by San Diego Padres organization in first round (ninth pick overall) of free-agent draft (June 2, 1998). ... On San Diego disabled list (May 29-July 15, 2002); included rehabilitation assignment to Portland (June 28-July 15). ... On Portland disabled list (August 4-11, 2002).
2003 GAMES PLAYED BY POSITION (MLB): 3B—137.

Year	Team (League)	Pos.	G	AB	R	H	2B	3B	HR	RBI	BB	SO	HBP	GDP	SB-CS	Avg.	OBP	SLG	OPS	E	Pct.
1999— Fort Wayne (Midw.)		3B	122	426	65	153	30	3	5	80	74	59	14	10	17-15	.359	.464	.479	.943	37	.898
— Rancho Cuca. (Calif.)		3B	6	23	3	10	3	0	1	5	3	3	1	1	0-1	.435	.519	.696	1.214	6	1.000
2000— Mobile (Sou.)		3B	108	392	46	114	29	4	2	42	58	45	3	10	6-8	.291	.383	.401	.783	16	.947
2001— Portland (PCL)		3B	104	394	60	127	28	1	9	55	37	54	4	13	9-2	.322	.386	.467	.853	10	.964
2002— San Diego (N.L.)		3B-2B	63	192	18	52	5	1	1	11	12	30	1	6	2-0	.271	.317	.323	.640	8	.949
— Portland (PCL)		2B-3B	50	179	29	54	16	2	2	23	21	16	3	5	1-0	.302	.380	.447	.827	6	.969
2003— San Diego (N.L.)		3B	146	517	62	148	27	6	7	58	44	75	11	13	7-2	.286	.352	.402	.755	12	.966
Major League totals (2 years)			209	709	80	200	32	7	8	69	56	105	12	19	9-2	.282	.343	.381	.724	20	.961

BUTLER, BRENT — 2B/SS

PERSONAL: Born February 11, 1978, in Laurinburg, N.C. ... 6-0/180. ... Bats right, throws right. ... Full name: Justin Brent Butler. ... High school: Scotland County (Laurinburg, N.C.).
TRANSACTIONS/CAREER NOTES: Selected by St. Louis Cardinals organization in third round of free-agent draft (June 2, 1996). ... On disabled list (June 21-June 28, 1998). ... Traded by Cardinals with P Jose Jimenez, P Manny Aybar and P Rick Croushore to Colorado Rockies for P Darryl Kile, P Dave Veres and P Luther Hackman (November 16, 1999). ... On Colorado Springs disabled list (August 29-September 12, 2000). ... On Colorado Springs disabled list (April 17-28, 2002). ... Designated for assignment (June 23, 2003). ... Sent outright to Colorado Springs by Colorado (June 27, 2003).
2003 GAMES PLAYED BY POSITION (MLB): 2B—20, 3B—8, SS—4.

Year	Team (League)	Pos.	G	AB	R	H	2B	3B	HR	RBI	BB	SO	HBP	GDP	SB-CS	Avg.	OBP	SLG	OPS	E	Pct.
1996— Johnson City (App.)		SS	62	248	45	*85	21	1	8	50	25	29	2	11	8-1	.343	.404	.532	.937	12	.945
1997— Peoria (Midw.)		SS	129	480	81	147	37	2	15	71	63	69	4	9	6-4	.306	.388	.485	.873	35	.942
1998— Prince Will. (Car.)		S-3-2-DH	126	475	63	136	27	2	11	76	39	74	9	12	3-4	.286	.347	.421	.768	29	.945
1999— Arkansas (Texas)		SS-3B-2B	•139	528	68	142	21	1	13	64	26	47	6	16	0-4	.269	.308	.386	.694	17	.968
2000— Colo. Springs (PCL)		2B-SS	122	438	73	128	35	1	8	54	44	46	4	15	1-3	.292	.356	.432	.787	16	.971
2001— Colo. Springs (PCL)		2B-SS-3B	65	272	51	91	20	3	7	38	15	26	4	13	4-2	.335	.375	.507	.883	5	.982
— Colorado (N.L.)		2B-SS-3B	53	119	17	29	7	1	1	14	7	7	1	4	1-1	.244	.287	.345	.631	5	.960
2002— Colorado (N.L.)		2B-3B-SS	113	344	55	89	18	4	9	42	10	40	5	6	2-6	.259	.287	.413	.699	9	.975
— Colo. Springs (PCL)		SS-2B	24	105	20	35	9	1	2	17	6	12	1	3	0-0	.333	.375	.495	.870	4	.982
2003— Colorado (N.L.)		2B-3B-SS	37	90	13	19	3	1	1	4	7	13	1	2	1-0	.211	.276	.300	.576	3	.971
— Colo. Springs (PCL)		2-1-DH-SS	54	205	37	68	19	1	6	27	19	20	4	7	0-1	.332	.399	.522	.921	5	.982
Major League totals (3 years)			203	553	85	137	28	6	11	60	24	60	7	12	4-7	.248	.285	.380	.664	17	.971

BYNUM, MIKE   P

PERSONAL: Born March 20, 1978, in Tampa, Fla. ... 6-4/200. ... Throws left, bats left. ... Full name: Michael Alan Bynum. ... Name pronounced: BI-num. ... College: North Carolina.

TRANSACTIONS/CAREER NOTES: Selected by San Diego Padres organization in first round (19th pick overall) of free-agent draft (June 2, 1999). ... On Mobile disabled list (April 4-May 31 and June 4-17, 2002). ... Recalled by San Diego from Portland of the Pacific Coast League (May 1, 2003). ... Optioned to Portland by San Diego (May 18, 2003). ... Recalled by San Diego from Portland (September 2, 2003).

CAREER HITTING: 3-for-18 (.167), 0 R, 0 2B, 0 3B, 0 HR, 0 RBI.

Year	League	W	L	Pct.	ERA	WHIP	G	GS	CG	ShO	Hld.	Sv.-Opp.	IP	H	R	ER	HR	BB-IBB	SO	Avg.
1999—	Idaho Falls (Pioneer)	1	0	1.000	0.00	0.65	5	3	0	0	...	0-...	17.0	7	0	0	0	4-0	21	.127
—	Rancho Cuca. (Calif.)	3	1	.750	3.29	1.12	7	7	0	0	...	0-...	38.1	35	17	14	1	8-0	44	.238
2000—	Rancho Cuca. (Calif.)	9	6	.600	3.00	1.21	21	21	0	0	...	0-...	126.0	101	55	42	4	51-0	129	.224
—	Mobile (Sou.)	3	1	.750	2.91	1.38	6	6	0	0	...	0-...	34.0	31	12	11	2	16-0	27	.252
2001—	Mobile (Sou.)	2	7	.222	5.02	1.48	16	15	0	0	...	0-...	84.1	90	53	47	14	35-0	69	.279
2002—	Mobile (Sou.)	4	0	1.000	0.82	0.73	6	5	0	0	...	0-...	33.0	17	5	3	0	7-0	29	.150
—	Portland (PCL)	3	2	.600	3.51	1.05	7	7	0	0	...	0-...	41.0	36	19	16	6	7-0	35	.235
—	San Diego (N.L.)	1	0	1.000	5.27	1.76	14	3	0	0	0	0-0	27.1	33	16	16	3	15-2	17	.308
2003—	Portland (PCL)	7	12	.368	4.81	1.52	24	23	0	0	...	0-...	125.1	130	76	67	11	60-2	106	.271
—	San Diego (N.L.)	1	4	.200	8.75	1.64	13	5	0	0	0	0-0	36.0	44	35	35	14	15-0	35	.297
Major League totals (2 years)		2	4	.333	7.25	1.69	27	8	0	0	0	0-0	63.1	77	51	51	17	30-2	52	.302

BYRD, MARLON   OF

PERSONAL: Born August 30, 1977, in Boynton Beach, Fla. ... 6-0/230. ... Bats right, throws right. ... Full name: Marlon Jerrard Byrd. ... High school: Sprayberry (Marietta, Ga.). ... Junior college: Georgia Perimeter College.

TRANSACTIONS/CAREER NOTES: Selected by Philadelphia Phillies organization in 10th round of free-agent draft (June 2, 1999). ... On disabled list (April 14, 2003). ... Sent to Reading by Philadelphia for rehab assignment (April 23, 2003). ... Recalled by Philadelphia from Reading rehab assignment; reinstated from 15-day disabled list (April 29, 2003).

2003 GAMES PLAYED BY POSITION (MLB): OF—131.

Year	Team (League)	Pos.	G	AB	R	H	2B	3B	HR	RBI	BB	SO	HBP	GDP	SB-CS	Avg.	OBP	SLG	OPS	E	Pct.
1999—Batavia (NY-Penn)		OF	65	243	40	72	7	6	13	50	28	70	5	3	8-2	.296	.376	.535	.911	7	.926
2000—Piedmont (S. Atl.)		OF	133	515	104	159	29 *	13	17	93	51	110	10	7	41-5	.309	.379	.515	.893	4	.980
2001—Reading (East.)		OF	137	510	108	161	22	8	28	89	52	93	11	7	32-5	.316	.386	.555	.941	2	.994
2002—Scran./W.B. (I.L.)		OF	136	538	* 103	160	37	4	15	63	46	98	11	5	15-1	.297	.362	.476	.838	8	.975
—Philadelphia (N.L.)		OF	10	35	2	8	2	0	1	1	1	8	0	0	0-2	.229	.250	.371	.621	0	1.000
2003—Scran./W.B. (I.L.)		OF	1	4	1	3	1	0	0	0	0	1	0	0	0-0	.750	.750	1.000	1.750	0	1.000
—Reading (East.)		OF	3	16	3	5	0	0	1	3	0	3	0	1	0-0	.313	.313	.500	.813	1	.800
—Philadelphia (N.L.)		OF	135	495	86	150	28	4	7	45	44	94	7	8	11-1	.303	.366	.418	.784	5	.984
Major League totals (2 years)			145	530	88	158	30	4	8	46	45	102	7	8	11-3	.298	.359	.415	.774	5	.984

BYRD, PAUL   P

PERSONAL: Born December 3, 1970... 6-1/185. ... Throws right, bats right. ... Full name: Paul Gregory Byrd. ... High school: St. Xavier (Louisville, Ky.).

TRANSACTIONS/CAREER NOTES: Selected by Cincinnati Reds organization in 13th round of free-agent draft (June 1, 1988); did not sign. ... Selected by Cleveland Indians organization in fourth round of free-agent draft (June 3, 1991). ... On disabled list (August 12, 1992-remainder of season). ... On disabled list (May 23-July 24, 1993). ... Traded by Indians with P Dave Mlicki, P Jerry DiPoto and a player to be named later to New York Mets for OF Jeromy Burnitz and P Joe Roa (November 18, 1994); Mets acquired 2B Jesus Azuaje to complete deal (December 6, 1994). ... On Norfolk disabled list (June 1-19, 1995). ... On New York disabled list (March 22-June 9, 1996); included rehabilitation assignment to Norfolk (May 27-June 9). ... Traded by Mets with a player to be named later to Atlanta Braves for P Greg McMichael (November 25, 1996); Braves acquired P Andy Zwirchitz to complete deal (May 25, 1997). ... On Richmond disabled list (June 3-July 2, 1998). ... Claimed on waivers by Philadelphia Phillies (August 14, 1998). ... On Philadelphia disabled list (July 27, 2000-remainder of season). ... Granted free agency (October 12, 2000). ... Re-signed by Phillies organization (January 29, 2001). ... Traded by Phillies to Kansas City Royals for P Jose Santiago (June 5, 2001). ... On Kansas City disabled list (September 22, 2001-remainder of season). ... Granted free agency (December 21, 2001). ... Re-signed by Royals (January 10, 2002). ... Granted free agency (October 28, 2002). ... Signed by Braves (December 17, 2002). ... On Atlanta disabled list (March 21, 2003-entire season); included rehabilitation assignment to Greenville (April 5-6).

CAREER HITTING: 16-for-111 (.144), 9 R, 0 2B, 0 3B, 0 HR, 6 RBI.

Year	League	W	L	Pct.	ERA	WHIP	G	GS	CG	ShO	Hld.	Sv.-Opp.	IP	H	R	ER	HR	BB-IBB	SO	Avg.
1991—Kinston (Caro.)		4	3	.571	3.16	1.21	14	11	0	0	...	0-...	62.2	40	27	22	7	36-0	62	.181
1992—Cant./Akr. (Eastern)		14	6	.700	3.01	1.29	24	24	4	0	...	0-...	152.1	122	68	51	4	75-2	118	.216
1993—Charlotte (Int'l)		7	4	.636	3.89	1.36	14	14	1	1	...	0-...	81.0	80	43	35	9	30-0	54	.257
—Cant./Akr. (Eastern)		0	0	...	3.60	1.00	2	1	0	0	...	0-...	10.0	7	4	4	1	3-0	8	.189
1994—Cant./Akr. (Eastern)		5	9	.357	3.81	1.34	21	20	4	1	...	0-...	139.1	135	70	59	10	52-3	106	.255
—Charlotte (Int'l)		2	2	.500	3.93	1.20	9	4	0	0	...	1-...	36.2	33	19	16	5	11-1	15	.250
1995—Norfolk (Int'l)		3	5	.375	2.79	1.06	22	10	1	0	...	6-...	87.0	71	29	27	6	21-0	61	.227
—New York (N.L.)		2	0	1.000	2.05	1.14	17	0	0	0	3	0-0	22.0	18	6	5	1	7-1	26	.222
1996—Norfolk (Int'l)		2	0	1.000	3.52	1.04	5	0	0	0	...	1-...	7.2	4	3	3	0	4-1	8	.148
—New York (N.L.)		1	2	.333	4.24	1.48	38	0	0	0	3	0-2	46.2	48	22	22	7	21-4	31	.265
1997—Atlanta (N.L.)		4	4	.500	5.26	1.42	31	4	0	0	1	0-...	53.0	47	34	31	6	28-4	37	.235
—Richmond (Int'l)		2	1	.667	3.18	0.88	3	3	0	0	...	0-...	17.0	14	6	6	2	1-0	14	.230
1998—Richmond (Int'l)		5	5	.500	3.69	1.25	17	17	2	0	...	0-...	102.1	92	44	42	9	36-2	84	.241
—Atlanta (N.L.)		0	0	...	13.50	2.50	1	0	0	0	0	0-...	2.0	4	3	3	0	1-0	1	.400
—Philadelphia (N.L.)		5	2	.714	2.29	1.05	8	8	2	1	0	0-...	55.0	41	16	14	6	17-1	38	.204
1999—Philadelphia (N.L.)		15	11	.577	4.60	1.38	32	32	1	0	0	0-...	199.2	205	119	102	34	70-2	106	.265
2000—Philadelphia (N.L.)		2	9	.182	6.51	1.49	17	15	0	0	0	0-...	83.0	89	67	60	17	35-2	53	.271
—Scran./W.B. (I.L.)		2	0	1.000	1.73	1.00	3	3	2	0	...	0-...	26.0	20	6	5	2	6-0	10	.215
2001—Clearwater (Fla. St.)		0	3	.000	3.42	1.23	4	4	0	0	...	0-...	23.2	24	10	9	1	5-0	17	.267
—Scran./W.B. (I.L.)		1	3	.250	3.65	1.11	5	5	0	0	...	0-...	37.0	34	18	15	4	7-0	35	.239
—Philadelphia (N.L.)		0	1	.000	8.10	1.40	3	1	0	0	0	0-...	10.0	10	9	9	1	4-0	3	.278
—Kansas City (A.L.)		6	6	.500	4.05	1.41	16	15	1	0	0	0-...	93.1	110	45	42	11	22-1	49	.298
2002—Kansas City (A.L.)		17	11	.607	3.90	1.15	33	33	* 7	2	0	0-...	228.1	224	111	99	36	38-1	129	.256
2003—Greenville (Sou.)		0	0	...	8.31	2.10	1	1	0	0	...	0-...	4.1	8	6	4	1	1-0	3	.364
American League totals (2 years)		23	17	.575	3.95	1.22	49	48	8	2	0	0-0	321.2	334	156	141	47	60-2	178	.268
National League totals (7 years)		29	29	.500	4.70	1.37	147	60	3	1	7	0-2	471.1	462	276	246	72	183-14	295	.255
Major League totals (8 years)		52	46	.531	4.39	1.31	196	108	11	3	7	0-2	793.0	796	432	387	119	243-16	473	.260

B

BYRNES, ERIC — OF

PERSONAL: Born February 16, 1976, in Redwood City, Calif. ... 6-2/210. ... Bats right, throws right. ... Full name: Eric James Byrnes. ... Name pronounced: burns. ... High school: St. Francis (Mountain View, Calif.). ... College: UCLA.

TRANSACTIONS/CAREER NOTES: Selected by Oakland Athletics organization in eighth round of free-agent draft (June 2, 1998).

2003 GAMES PLAYED BY POSITION (MLB): OF—117, DH—2.

Year	Team (League)	Pos.	G	AB	R	H	2B	3B	HR	RBI	BB	SO	HBP	GDP	SB-CS	Avg.	OBP	SLG	OPS	E	Pct.
1998— S. Oregon (N'west)	OF	42	169	36	53	10	2	7	31	16	16	2	3	6-1	.314	.378	.521	.898	1	.986
— Visalia (Calif.)	OF	29	108	26	46	9	2	4	21	18	15	1	2	11-1	.426	.504	.657	1.161	3	.952
1999— Modesto (Calif.)	OF	96	365	86	123	28	1	6	66	58	37	9	14	28-8	.337	.433	.468	.901	6	.960
— Midland (Texas)	OF	43	164	25	39	14	0	1	22	17	32	3	5	6-3	.238	.316	.341	.657	5	.923
2000— Midland (Texas)	OF	67	259	49	78	25	2	5	37	43	38	1	5	21-11	.301	.395	.471	.866	2	.980
— Sacramento (PCL)	OF	67	243	55	81	23	1	9	47	31	30	2	3	12-5	.333	.410	.547	.957	2	.980
— Oakland (A.L.)	OF-DH	10	10	5	3	0	0	0	0	0	1	1	0	2-1	.300	.364	.300	.664	0	1.000
2001— Sacramento (PCL)	OF	100	415	81	120	23	2	20	51	33	66	5	10	25-3	.289	.343	.499	.842	5	.973
— Oakland (A.L.)	OF-DH	19	38	9	9	1	0	3	5	4	6	1	0	1-0	.237	.326	.500	.826	1	.933
2002— Sacramento (PCL)	OF	31	119	16	31	7	0	4	16	7	15	0	2	5-1	.261	.302	.420	.722	2	.971
— Oakland (A.L.)	OF-DH	90	94	24	23	4	2	3	11	4	17	3	3	3-0	.245	.291	.426	.717	1	.982
2003— Oakland (A.L.)	OF-DH	121	414	64	109	27	9	12	51	42	71	2	3	10-2	.263	.333	.459	.792	2	.991
Major League totals (4 years)		240	556	102	144	32	11	18	67	50	95	7	6	16-3	.259	.326	.453	.779	4	.986

CABRERA, JOLBERT — IF/OF

PERSONAL: Born December 8, 1972, in Cartagena, Colombia. ... 6-1/195. ... Bats right, throws right. ... Full name: Jolbert Alexis Cabrera. ... Name pronounced: HOLE-bert kah-brair-RAH. ... High school: Confenalco (Cartagena, Colombia).

TRANSACTIONS/CAREER NOTES: Signed as non-drafted free agent by Montreal Expos organization (July 3, 1990). ... Loaned by Expos organization to San Bernardino, California League (July 27-September 1, 1994). ... Granted free agency (October 17, 1997). ... Signed by Cleveland Indians organization (January 19, 1998). ... On Cleveland disabled list (March 28-May 2, 2002); included rehabilitation assignment to Buffalo (April 25-May 2). ... Traded by Indians to Los Angeles Dodgers for P Lance Caraccioli (July 22, 2002).

2003 GAMES PLAYED BY POSITION (MLB): OF—63, 2B—59, SS—9, 1B—8, 3B—5.

Year	Team (League)	Pos.	G	AB	R	H	2B	3B	HR	RBI	BB	SO	HBP	GDP	SB-CS	Avg.	OBP	SLG	OPS	E	Pct.
1990— Dom. Expos (DSL)	SS	29	115	31	36	3	2	0	12	14	10			14-...	.313	...	.374	...	...	...
1991— Sumter (S. Atl.)	SS	101	324	33	66	4	0	1	20	19	62	4	5	10-11	.204	.255	.225	.480	28	.934
1992— Albany (S. Atl.)	SS	118	377	44	86	9	2	0	23	34	77	1	8	22-11	.228	.294	.263	.556	35	.927
1993— Burlington (Midw.)	SS	128	507	62	129	24	2	0	38	39	93	7	13	31-11	.254	.314	.310	.624	* 36	.929
1994— W.P. Beach (FSL)	SS	83	266	32	54	4	0	0	13	14	48	8	4	7-10	.203	.264	.218	.482	26	.933
— San Bern. (Calif.)	SS	30	109	14	27	5	1	0	11	14	24	0	1	2-2	.248	.328	.312	.640	7	.950
— Harrisburg (East.)	SS	3	2	0	0	0	0	0	0	0	1	0	0	0-0	.000	.000	.000	.000	0	1.000
1995— W.P. Beach (FSL)	2B-3B-SS	103	357	62	102	23	2	1	25	38	61	8	3	19-12	.286	.364	.370	.733	29	.938
— Harrisburg (East.)	SS	9	35	4	10	2	0	0	1	1	3	0	1	3-1	.286	.306	.343	.648	2	.935
1996— Harrisburg (East.)	3B-SS-OF	107	354	40	85	18	2	3	29	23	63	1	9	10-5	.240	.285	.328	.613	25	.951
1997— Harrisburg (East.)	2B-SS-OF	48	171	28	43	9	0	2	11	28	28	1	4	5-4	.251	.360	.339	.699	9	.951
— Ottawa (Int'l)	2-3-SS-OF	68	191	28	54	10	4	0	12	11	31	0	5	15-5	.283	.320	.377	.697	7	.962
1998— Cleveland (A.L.)	SS	1	2	0	0	0	0	0	0	0	1	0	0	0-0	.000	.000	.000	.000	0	1.000
— Buffalo (Int'l)	2B-SS-OF	129	494	94	157	24	1	10	45	68	71	13	10	25-15	.318	.412	.431	.844	27	.956
1999— Cleveland (A.L.)	OF-2B-DH	30	37	6	7	1	0	0	0	1	8	1	1	3-0	.189	.231	.216	.447	1	.968
— Buffalo (Int'l)	OF-SS-2-3	71	279	44	74	13	4	0	27	26	43	2	8	20-4	.265	.327	.341	.667	6	.975
2000— Buffalo (Int'l)	OF-SS-2B	20	74	18	25	6	1	3	11	5	8	1	0	2-1	.338	.383	.568	.950	0	1.000
— Cleveland (A.L.)	OF-2-S-D	100	175	27	44	3	1	2	15	8	15	2	1	6-4	.251	.290	.314	.605	1	.993
2001— Cleveland (A.L.)	0-2-3-S-D	141	287	50	75	16	3	1	38	16	41	6	4	10-4	.261	.312	.348	.660	6	.973
2002— Buffalo (Int'l)	OF-S-3-1-2	23	91	16	26	5	0	0	7	9	10	1	3	4-2	.286	.353	.341	.694	0	1.000
— Cleveland (A.L.)	OF-2B-DH	38	72	5	8	1	0	0	7	5	13	1	3	1-1	.111	.177	.125	.302	0	1.000
— Las Vegas (PCL)	OF-3-S-2	27	102	22	35	8	1	2	11	14	18	1	3	2-3	.343	.417	.500	.917	2	.969
— Los Angeles (N.L.)	OF-3B-2B	10	12	3	4	1	0	0	1	2	2	0	0	0-0	.333	.429	.417	.845	0	1.000
2003— Los Angeles (N.L.)	0-2-S-1-3	128	347	43	98	32	2	6	37	17	62	10	10	6-4	.282	.332	.438	.770	5	.984
American League totals (5 years)		310	573	88	134	21	4	3	60	30	78	10	9	20-9	.234	.282	.300	.582	8	.983
National League totals (2 years)		138	359	46	102	33	2	6	38	19	64	10	10	6-4	.284	.335	.437	.772	5	.984
Major League totals (6 years)		448	932	134	236	54	6	9	98	49	142	20	19	26-13	.253	.303	.353	.656	13	.983

CABRERA, MIGUEL — 3B/OF

PERSONAL: Born April 18, 1983, in Maracay, Venezuela. ... 6-2/185. ... Bats right, throws right. ... Full name: Jose Miguel Torres Cabrera.

TRANSACTIONS/CAREER NOTES: Signed by Florida Marlins organization as a non-drafted free agent (July 2, 1999).

2003 GAMES PLAYED BY POSITION (MLB): OF—55, 3B—34.

Year	Team (League)	Pos.	G	AB	R	H	2B	3B	HR	RBI	BB	SO	HBP	GDP	SB-CS	Avg.	OBP	SLG	OPS	E	Pct.
2000— GC Marlins (GCL)	SS	57	219	38	57	10	2	2	22	23	46	6	7	1-0	.260	.344	.352	.696	13	.950
— Utica (N.Y.-Penn)	SS-2B-3B	8	32	3	8	2	0	0	6	2	6	0	0	0-0	.250	.294	.313	.607	4	.902
2001— Kane Co. (Midw.)	SS-3B	110	422	61	113	19	4	7	66	37	76	2	10	3-0	.268	.328	.382	.709	32	.931
2002— Jupiter (FSL)	3B-SS	124	489	77	134	43	1	9	75	38	85	9	19	10-1	.274	.333	.421	.754	17	.941
2003— Carolina (Sou.)	3B-OF-DH	69	266	46	97	29	3	10	59	31	49	2	8	9-4	.365	.429	.609	1.038	15	.950
— Florida (N.L.)	OF-3B	87	314	39	84	21	3	12	62	25	84	2	12	0-2	.268	.325	.468	.793	4	.978
Major League totals (1 year)		87	314	39	84	21	3	12	62	25	84	2	12	0-2	.268	.325	.468	.793	4	.978

CABRERA, ORLANDO — SS

PERSONAL: Born November 2, 1974, in Cartagena, Colombia. ... 5-9/180. ... Bats right, throws right. ... Full name: Orlando Luis Cabrera. ... Name pronounced: kah-BRAIR-rah.

TRANSACTIONS/CAREER NOTES: Signed as non-drafted free agent by Montreal Expos organization (June 1, 1993). ... On disabled list (August 9, 1999-remainder of season). ... On Montreal disabled list (July 15-August 15, 2000); included rehabilitation assignment to Ottawa (August 12-15).

2003 GAMES PLAYED BY POSITION (MLB): SS—162.

Year	Team (League)	Pos.	G	AB	R	H	2B	3B	HR	RBI	BB	SO	HBP	GDP	SB-CS	Avg.	OBP	SLG	OPS	E	Pct.
1993— Dom. Expos (DSL)	IF	38	122	24	42	6	1	1	17	18	11	...	...	14-...	.344	...	.434	...	3	.982
1994— GC Expos (GCL)	2B-SS-OF	22	73	13	23	4	1	0	11	5	8	0	2	6-0	.315	.359	.397	.756	4	.941
1995— Vermont (NYP)	2B-SS	65	248	37	70	12	5	3	33	16	28	1	3	15-8	.282	.323	.407	.731	17	.950
— W.P. Beach (FSL)	SS	3	5	0	1	0	0	0	0	0	1	0	0	0-0	.200	.200	.200	.400	1	.833
1996— Delmarva (S. Atl.)	2B-SS	134	512	86	129	28	4	14	65	54	63	5	4	51-18	.252	.327	.404	.731	27	.953
1997— W.P. Beach (FSL)	SS-DH-2B	69	279	56	77	19	2	5	26	27	33	0	1	32-12	.276	.340	.412	.752	20	.927
— Harrisburg (East.)	SS-2B	35	133	34	41	13	2	5	20	15	18	0	0	7-2	.308	.378	.549	.927	5	.966
— Ottawa (Int'l)	SS-2B	31	122	17	32	5	2	2	14	7	16	2	0	8-1	.262	.306	.385	.691	3	.979
— Montreal (N.L.)	SS-2B	16	18	4	4	0	0	0	2	1	3	0	1	1-2	.222	.263	.222	.485	1	.963
1998— Ottawa (Int'l)	SS-2B	66	272	31	63	9	4	0	26	28	27	0	8	19-9	.232	.298	.294	.592	12	.963
— Montreal (N.L.)	SS-2B	79	261	44	73	16	5	3	22	18	27	0	6	6-2	.280	.325	.414	.739	7	.978
1999— Montreal (N.L.)	SS	104	382	48	97	23	5	8	39	18	38	3	9	2-2	.254	.293	.403	.696	10	.979
2000— Montreal (N.L.)	SS-2B	125	422	47	100	25	1	13	55	25	28	1	12	4-4	.237	.279	.393	.673	10	.981
— Ottawa (Int'l)	SS	2	6	1	4	0	0	0	0	1	0	1	0	1-0	.667	.750	.667	1.417	0	1.000
2001— Montreal (N.L.)	SS	• 162	626	64	173	41	6	14	96	43	54	4	15	19-7	.276	.324	.428	.752	11	.986
2002— Montreal (N.L.)	SS	153	563	64	148	43	1	7	56	48	53	2	16	25-7	.263	.321	.380	.701	* 29	.962
2003— Montreal (N.L.)	SS	•162	626	95	186	47	2	17	80	52	64	1	18	24-2	.297	.347	.460	.807	18	.975
Major League totals (7 years)		801	2898	366	781	195	20	62	350	205	267	11	77	81-26	.269	.318	.415	.732	86	.976

CAIRO, MIGUEL   2B

PERSONAL: Born May 4, 1974, in Anaco, Venezuela. ... 6-1/208. ... Bats right, throws right. ... Full name: Miguel Jesus Cairo. ... Name pronounced: KI-row. ... High school: Escuela Anaco (Anaco, Venezuela).

TRANSACTIONS/CAREER NOTES: Signed as non-drafted free agent by Los Angeles Dodgers organization (September 20, 1990). ... Traded by Dodgers with 3B Willis Otanez to Seattle Mariners for 3B Mike Blowers (November 29, 1995). ... Traded by Mariners with P Bill Risley to Toronto Blue Jays for P Edwin Hurtado and P Paul Menhart (December 18, 1995). ... Traded by Blue Jays to Chicago Cubs for P Jason Stevenson (November 20, 1996). ... Selected by Tampa Bay Devil Rays in first round (eighth pick overall) of expansion draft (November 18, 1997). ... On Tampa Bay disabled list (April 24-May 17 and July 26-August 11, 1999); included rehabilitation assignments to Orlando (May 14-17) and St. Petersburg (August 7-11). ... Released by Devil Rays (November 27, 2000). ... Signed by Oakland Athletics organization (January 7, 2001). ... Traded by A's to Chicago Cubs for 3B/1B Eric Hinske (March 28, 2001). ... Claimed on waivers by St. Louis Cardinals (August 10, 2001). ... Placed on 15-day disabled list (June 19, 2003). ... Sent to Memphis on rehab assignment by St. Louis (July 25, 2003). ... Recalled from Memphis rehab assignment; reinstated from 15-day disabled list (July 29, 2003).

2003 GAMES PLAYED BY POSITION (MLB): 2B—40, OF—27, 3B—12, SS—7, 1B—3.

Year	Team (League)	Pos.	G	AB	R	H	2B	3B	HR	RBI	BB	SO	HBP	GDP	SB-CS	Avg.	OBP	SLG	OPS	E	Pct.
1991— Dom. Dodgers (DSL)	IF	57	203	16	45	5	1	0	17	0	17	...	...	8-...	.222	...	.256	...	...	...
1992— GC Dodgers (GCL)	3B-SS	21	76	10	23	5	2	0	9	2	6	2	1	1-0	.303	.333	.421	.754	4	.953
— Vero Beach (FSL)	2B-3B	36	125	7	28	0	0	0	7	11	12	0	3	5-3	.224	.285	.224	.509	10	.935
1993— Vero Beach (FSL)	2B-3B-SS	90	346	50	109	10	1	1	23	28	22	7	2	23-16	.315	.378	.358	.736	18	.959
1994— Bakersfield (Calif.)	2B-SS	133	533	76	155	23	4	2	48	34	37	6	9	44-23	.291	.338	.360	.698	28	.958
1995— San Antonio (Texas)	2B-SS-DH	107	435	53	121	20	1	1	41	26	31	5	6	33-16	.278	.323	.336	.659	23	.958
1996— Syracuse (Int'l)	2B-3B-SS	120	465	71	129	14	4	3	48	26	44	8	5	27-9	.277	.323	.344	.667	23	.955
— Toronto (A.L.)	2B	9	27	5	6	2	0	0	1	2	9	1	1	0-0	.222	.300	.296	.596	0	1.000
1997— Iowa (Am. Assoc.)	2B-SS	135	* 569	82	159	35	4	5	46	24	54	6	9	* 40-15	.279	.314	.381	.695	20	.969
— Chicago (N.L.)	2B-SS	16	29	7	7	1	0	0	1	2	3	1	0	0-0	.241	.313	.276	.588	0	1.000
1998— Tampa Bay (A.L.)	2B-DH	150	515	49	138	26	5	5	46	24	44	6	9	19-8	.268	.307	.367	.674	16	.978
1999— Tampa Bay (A.L.)	2B-DH	120	465	61	137	15	5	3	36	24	46	7	13	22-7	.295	.335	.368	.703	9	.986
— Orlando (South.)	2B	3	13	1	5	2	0	0	1	0	1	0	0	0-1	.385	.385	.538	.923	0	1.000
— St. Pete. (FSL)	2B	3	13	2	5	0	0	0	0	1	2	0	0	1-1	.385	.429	.385	.813	1	.958
2000— Tampa Bay (A.L.)	2B-DH	119	375	49	98	18	2	1	34	29	34	2	7	28-7	.261	.314	.328	.642	9	.983
2001— Iowa (PCL)	2B-SS-3B	34	123	22	37	7	1	3	14	8	11	1	3	3-4	.301	.348	.447	.796	3	.978
— Chicago (N.L.)	3B-2B-SS	66	123	20	35	3	1	2	9	16	21	0	3	2-1	.285	.364	.374	.738	7	.917
— St. Louis (N.L.)	O-2-3-S-1	27	33	5	11	5	0	1	7	2	2	0	1	0-0	.333	.371	.576	.947	1	.929
2002— St. Louis (N.L.)	O-2-3-S-1-D	108	184	28	46	9	2	2	23	13	36	3	5	1-1	.250	.307	.353	.660	4	.963
2003— Memphis (PCL)	2B-DH	3	13	2	3	1	0	0	0	0	3	0	0	0-0	.231	.231	.308	.538	0	1.000
— St. Louis (N.L.)	2-O-3-S-1	92	261	41	64	15	2	5	32	13	30	6	6	4-1	.245	.289	.375	.665	6	.972
American League totals (4 years)		398	1382	164	379	61	12	9	117	79	133	16	30	69-22	.274	.318	.355	.674	34	.982
National League totals (4 years)		309	630	101	163	33	5	10	72	46	92	10	15	7-3	.259	.315	.375	.689	18	.961
Major League totals (8 years)		707	2012	265	542	94	17	19	189	125	225	26	45	76-25	.269	.317	.361	.678	52	.978

CALERO, KIKO   P

PERSONAL: Born January 9, 1975, in Santurce, Puerto Rico. ... 6-1/180. ... Throws right, bats right. ... Full name: Enrique Nomar Calero. ... High school: University Gardens (P.R.). ... College: St. Thomas (Fla.).

TRANSACTIONS/CAREER NOTES: Selected by Kansas City Royals organization in 27th round of free-agent draft (June 1996). ... Minor league contract with Royals expired (October 15, 2002). .. Signed by St. Louis Cardinals organization as a free agent (December 3, 2002).

CAREER HITTING: 1-for-4 (.250), 1 R, 0 2B, 0 3B, 0 HR, 1 RBI.

Year	League	W	L	Pct.	ERA	WHIP	G	GS	CG	ShO	Hld.	Sv.-Opp.	IP	H	R	ER	HR	BB-IBB	SO	Avg.
1996— Spokane (N'west)	4	2	.667	2.52	1.27	17	11	0	0	...	1-...	75.0	77	34	21	5	18-0	61	.265
1997— Wichita (Texas)	11	9	.550	4.44	1.28	23	22	2	0	...	0-...	127.2	120	78	63	15	44-0	100	.248
1998— Lansing (Midw.)	1	0	1.000	3.78	1.56	4	4	0	0	...	0-...	16.2	19	7	7	1	7-0	10	.284
— Wichita (Texas)	1	0	1.000	9.64	2.07	3	3	0	0	...	0-...	14.0	23	16	15	2	6-0	5	.359
— Wilmington (Caro.)	7	3	.700	2.86	1.28	17	17	0	0	...	0-...	97.2	74	33	31	7	51-1	90	.213
1999— Wichita (Texas)	9	3	.750	4.11	1.55	26	23	1	1	...	1-...	129.1	143	67	59	14	57-3	92	.279
2000— Wichita (Texas)	10	7	.588	3.63	1.35	28	25	0	0	...	0-...	153.2	141	74	62	16	66-2	130	.251
2001— Wichita (Texas)	14	5	.737	3.33	1.29	27	19	0	0	...	0-...	124.1	110	57	46	10	51-1	94	.237
2002— Wichita (Texas)	1	0	1.000	2.25	0.94	5	2	0	0	...	0-...	16.0	10	5	4	2	5-0	15	.172
— Omaha (PCL)	7	7	.500	3.44	1.17	20	18	0	0	...	0-...	125.2	112	52	48	11	35-1	109	.244
2003— St. Louis (N.L.)	1	1	.500	2.82	1.28	26	1	0	0	1	1-4	38.1	29	12	12	5	20-2	51	.212
Major League totals (1 year)	1	1	.500	2.82	1.28	26	1	0	0	1	1-4	38.1	29	12	12	5	20-2	51	.212

C

CALLAWAY, MICKEY   P

PERSONAL: Born May 13, 1975, in Memphis, Tenn. ... 6-2/205. ... Throws right, bats right. ... Full name: Michael C. Callaway. ... High school: Germantown (Tenn.). ... College: Mississippi.

TRANSACTIONS/CAREER NOTES: Selected by Tampa Bay Devil Rays organization in seventh round of free-agent draft (June 4, 1996). ... Loaned Devil Rays to Orlando, Seattle Mariners organization (April 2-July 21, 1998). ... On Tampa Bay disabled list (June 19-July 6, 1999). ... On disabled list (May 22-June 5, 2000). ... Traded by Devil Rays to Anaheim Angels for SS/2B Wilmy Caceres (December 17, 2001). ... On Salt Lake disabled list (May 25-June 11 and June 15-July 28, 2002). ... Placed on the 15-day disabled list by Anaheim (June 6, 2003). ... Sent to Salt Lake by Anaheim on rehab assignment (June 24, 2003). ... Recalled from Salt Lake rehab assignment; reinstated from 15-day disabled list (July 23, 2003). ... Designated for assignment by Anaheim (July 28, 2003). ... Given unconditional release (July 29, 2003). ... Signed by Texas Rangers organization (August 7, 2003). ... Contract purchased by Texas from Oklahoma (August 30, 2003).

CAREER HITTING: 2-for-3 (.667), 0 R, 0 2B, 0 3B, 0 HR, 1 RBI.

Year	League	W	L	Pct.	ERA	WHIP	G	GS	CG	ShO	Hld.	Sv.-Opp.	IP	H	R	ER	HR	BB-IBB	SO	Avg.
1996— Butte (Pio.)		6	2	.750	3.71	1.51	16	11	0	0	...	0-...	63.0	70	37	26	5	25-0	57	.288
1997— St. Pete. (FSL)		11	7	.611	3.22	1.18	28	•28	3	0	...	0-...	170.2	162	74	61	9	39-0	109	.250
1998— Orlando (Sou.)		5	6	.455	4.42	1.64	18	17	0	0	...	0-...	89.2	103	56	44	8	44-0	57	.289
— Durham (Int'l)		5	3	.625	4.53	1.38	9	8	0	0	...	0-...	47.2	49	27	24	6	17-0	19	.258
1999— Orlando (Sou.)		1	1	.500	4.50	1.70	2	2	0	0	...	0-...	10.0	15	6	5	1	2-0	7	.357
— Durham (Int'l)		7	1	.875	4.20	1.40	15	15	0	0	...	0-...	81.1	86	45	38	5	28-0	56	.277
— Tampa Bay (A.L.)		1	2	.333	7.45	2.28	5	4	0	0	0	0-0	19.1	30	20	16	2	14-1	11	.357
2000— Durham (Int'l)		11	6	.647	5.29	1.71	26	20	0	0	...	0-...	117.1	151	88	69	11	50-2	64	.313
2001— Durham (Int'l)		11	7	.611	3.07	1.20	29	21	2	1	...	0-...	129.0	131	50	44	9	24-0	81	.265
— Tampa Bay (A.L.)		0	0	...	7.20	1.00	2	0	0	0	0	0-0	5.0	3	4	4	2	2-0	2	.167
2002— Salt Lake (PCL)		9	2	.818	1.68	1.11	17	14	1	0	...	0-...	91.1	79	26	17	7	22-0	75	.229
— Anaheim (A.L.)		2	1	.667	4.19	1.22	6	6	0	0	0	0-0	34.1	31	20	16	4	11-0	23	.235
2003— Salt Lake (PCL)		1	0	1.000	2.95	1.31	7	4	0	0	...	0-...	21.1	22	8	7	1	6-0	10	.286
— Anaheim (A.L.)		1	4	.200	6.81	1.90	17	4	0	0	0	0-0	38.1	57	32	29	7	16-1	22	.345
— Oklahoma (PCL)		2	0	1.000	1.59	1.24	4	4	0	0	...	0-...	17.0	16	6	3	0	5-0	9	.254
— Texas (A.L.)		0	3	.000	6.45	1.57	6	3	0	0	0	0-0	22.1	27	18	16	0	8-0	19	.314
Major League totals (4 years)		4	10	.286	6.11	1.67	36	17	0	0	0	0-0	119.1	148	94	81	15	51-2	77	.305

CALLOWAY, RON   OF

PERSONAL: Born September 4, 1976, in San Jose, Calif. ... 6-1/210. ... Bats left, throws left. ... Full name: Ronald Isiah Calloway. ... High school: James Lick (San Jose, Calif.). ... Junior college: Canada College (Calif.).

TRANSACTIONS/CAREER NOTES: Selected by Arizona Diamondbacks organization in eighth round of free-agent draft (June 3, 1997). ... Traded by Diamondbacks to Montreal Expos (July 5, 1999), completing deal in which Expos traded C John Pachot to Diamondbacks for future considerations (May 21, 1999).

2003 GAMES PLAYED BY POSITION (MLB): OF—97.

Year	Team (League)	Pos.	G	AB	R	H	2B	3B	HR	RBI	BB	SO	HBP	GDP	SB-CS	Avg.	OBP	SLG	OPS	E	Pct.
1997— Lethbridge (Pio.)		OF	43	148	23	37	5	0	0	9	14	29	3	4	5-8	.250	.323	.284	.607	3	.954
— South Bend (Mid.)		OF	9	25	3	7	1	0	0	1	2	8	0	1	1-0	.280	.333	.320	.653	2	.846
1998— High Desert (Calif.)		OF	44	156	30	44	8	2	3	27	12	38	2	3	2-4	.282	.337	.417	.754	4	.946
— South Bend (Mid.)		OF	69	251	29	66	12	2	3	33	25	50	2	3	7-5	.263	.331	.363	.694	6	.944
1999— High Desert (Calif.)		OF	60	196	41	62	14	1	3	23	30	34	2	3	22-7	.316	.412	.444	.856	3	.962
— El Paso (Texas)		OF	11	32	4	7	0	0	0	1	7	7	0	0	1-2	.219	.359	.219	.578	0	1.000
— Jupiter (FSL)		OF	54	211	30	57	8	4	3	25	15	45	2	9	5-6	.270	.325	.389	.713	0	1.000
2000— Jupiter (FSL)		OF	135	530	78	147	24	6	6	65	55	89	4	13	34-14	.277	.346	.379	.725	2	.994
2001— Harrisburg (East.)		OF	74	279	48	92	22	4	9	47	24	46	3	2	25-7	.330	.385	.534	.919	4	.969
— Ottawa (Int'l)		OF	61	239	27	63	12	0	10	35	16	64	6	4	11-1	.264	.323	.439	.763	5	.959
2002— Ottawa (Int'l)		OF	128	447	72	118	21	5	14	60	44	89	6	18	16-12	.264	.335	.427	.762	3	.983
2003— Montreal (N.L.)		OF	126	340	36	81	17	1	9	52	20	80	2	13	9-2	.238	.282	.374	.656	3	.983
Major League totals (1 year)			126	340	36	81	17	1	9	52	20	80	2	13	9-2	.238	.282	.374	.656	3	.983

CAMERON, MIKE   OF

PERSONAL: Born January 8, 1973, in LaGrange, Ga. ... 6-2/200. ... Bats right, throws right. ... Full name: Michael Terrance Cameron. ... High school: La Grange (Ga.).

TRANSACTIONS/CAREER NOTES: Selected by Chicago White Sox organization in 18th round of free-agent draft (June 3, 1991). ... Traded by White Sox to Cincinnati Reds for 1B/3B Paul Konerko (November 11, 1998). ... Traded by Reds with P Brett Tomko, IF Antonio Perez and P Jake Meyer to Seattle Mariners for OF Ken Griffey Jr. (February 10, 2000).

2003 GAMES PLAYED BY POSITION (MLB): OF—147.

Year	Team (League)	Pos.	G	AB	R	H	2B	3B	HR	RBI	BB	SO	HBP	GDP	SB-CS	Avg.	OBP	SLG	OPS	E	Pct.
1991— GC Whi. Sox (GCL)		OF	44	136	20	30	3	0	0	11	17	29	4	3	13-2	.221	.325	.243	.567	3	.951
1992— Utica (N.Y.-Penn)		OF	26	87	15	24	1	4	2	12	11	26	0	0	3-7	.276	.354	.448	.802	0	1.000
— South Bend (Mid.)		OF	35	114	19	26	8	1	1	9	10	37	4	0	2-3	.228	.310	.342	.652	3	.957
1993— South Bend (Mid.)		OF	122	411	52	98	14	5	0	30	27	101	6	8	19-10	.238	.292	.297	.589	4	.985
1994— Prince Will. (Car.)		OF	131	468	86	116	15	* 17	6	48	60	101	8	6	22-10	.248	.343	.391	.734	6	.979
1995— Birmingham (Sou.)		OF	107	350	64	87	20	5	11	60	54	104	6	9	21-12	.249	.355	.429	.784	4	.985
— Chicago (A.L.)		OF	28	38	4	7	2	0	1	2	3	15	0	0	0-0	.184	.244	.316	.560	0	1.000
1996— Birmingham (Sou.)		OF-DH	123	473	* 120	142	34	12	28	77	71	117	12	5	* 39-15	.300	.402	.600	1.002	7	.973
— Chicago (A.L.)		OF-DH	11	11	1	1	0	0	0	0	1	3	0	0	0-1	.091	.167	.091	.258	0	1.000
1997— Nashville (A.A.)		OF-DH	30	120	21	33	7	3	6	17	18	31	3	1	4-2	.275	.378	.533	.911	1	.985
— Chicago (A.L.)		OF-DH	116	379	63	98	18	3	14	55	55	105	5	5	23-2	.259	.356	.433	.789	5	.985
1998— Chicago (A.L.)		OF	141	396	53	83	16	5	8	43	37	101	6	6	27-11	.210	.285	.336	.621	4	.988
1999— Cincinnati (N.L.)		OF	146	542	93	139	34	9	21	66	80	145	6	4	38-12	.256	.357	.469	.825	8	.979
2000— Seattle (A.L.)		OF	155	543	96	145	28	4	19	78	78	133	9	10	24-7	.267	.365	.438	.803	6	.985
2001— Seattle (A.L.)		OF-DH	150	540	99	144	35	5	25	110	69	155	10	13	34-5	.267	.353	.480	.832	6	.988
2002— Seattle (A.L.)		OF-DH	158	545	84	130	26	5	25	80	79	176	7	8	31-8	.239	.340	.442	.782	5	.988
2003— Seattle (A.L.)		OF	147	534	74	135	31	5	18	76	70	137	5	13	17-7	.253	.344	.431	.774	4	.992
American League totals (8 years)			906	2986	474	743	151	27	110	444	392	825	42	58	156-41	.249	.341	.428	.769	30	.988
National League totals (1 year)			146	542	93	139	34	9	21	66	80	145	6	4	38-12	.256	.357	.469	.825	8	.979
Major League totals (9 years)			1052	3528	567	882	185	36	131	510	472	970	48	62	194-53	.250	.343	.434	.777	38	.987

CAPUANO, CHRIS   P

PERSONAL: Born August 19, 1978, in Springfield, Mass. ... 6-3/210. ... Throws left, bats left. ... Full name: Christopher Frank Capuano. ... Name pronounced: cap-u-ON-o. ... High school: Cathedral (West Springfield, Mass.). ... College: Duke.

TRANSACTIONS/CAREER NOTES: Selected by Arizona Diamondbacks organization in eighth round of free-agent draft (June 1999). ... On disabled list (May 6 through remainder of 2002 season).

CAREER HITTING: 0-for-8 (.000), 0 R, 0 2B, 0 3B, 0 HR, 0 RBI.

Year League	W	L	Pct.	ERA	WHIP	G	GS	CG	ShO	Hld.	Sv.-Opp.	IP	H	R	ER	HR	BB-IBB	SO	Avg.
2000— South Bend (Mid.)	10	4	.714	2.21	1.11	18	18	0	0	...	0-...	101.2	68	35	25	2	45-0	105	.193
2001— El Paso (Texas)	10	11	.476	5.31	1.63	28	28	2	2	...	0-...	159.1	184	109	94	13	75-0	167	.290
2002— Tucson (PCL)	4	1	.800	2.72	1.13	6	6	0	0	...	0-...	36.1	30	12	11	1	11-0	29	.227
2003— Tucson (PCL)	9	5	.643	3.34	1.23	23	23	0	0	...	0-...	142.2	133	66	53	9	43-2	108	.250
— Arizona (N.L.)	2	4	.333	4.64	1.15	9	5	0	0	1	0-0	33.0	27	19	17	3	11-1	23	.233
Major League totals (1 year)	2	4	.333	4.64	1.15	9	5	0	0	1	0-0	33.0	27	19	17	3	11-1	23	.233

CARPENTER, CHRIS   P

PERSONAL: Born April 27, 1975... 6-6/215. ... Throws right, bats right. ... Full name: Christopher John Carpenter. ... High school: Trinity (Manchester, N.H.).

TRANSACTIONS/CAREER NOTES: Selected by Toronto Blue Jays organization in first round (15th pick overall) of free-agent draft (June 3, 1993). ... On Toronto disabled list (June 3-28, 1999); included rehabilitation assignment to St. Catharines (June 23-28). ... On Toronto disabled list (April 2-20, April 22-June 21 and August 14, 2002-remainder of season); included rehabilitation assignments to Tennessee (May 23-June 12) and Syracuse (June 13-18). ... Released by Blue Jays (October 9, 2002). ... Signed by St. Louis Cardinals (December 13, 2002). ... On disabled list (entire 2003 season). ... Sent to Palm Beach on rehab assignment by St. Louis (June 16, 2003). ... Recalled from Tennessee rehab assignment (July 15, 2003). ... Reinstated from Emergency disabled list (September 30, 2003).

CAREER HITTING: 2-for-11 (.182), 1 R, 0 2B, 0 3B, 0 HR, 0 RBI.

Year League	W	L	Pct.	ERA	WHIP	G	GS	CG	ShO	Hld.	Sv.-Opp.	IP	H	R	ER	HR	BB-IBB	SO	Avg.
1994— Medicine Hat (Pio.)	6	3	.667	2.76	1.36	15	15	0	0	...	0-...	84.2	76	40	26	3	39-0	80	.243
1995— Dunedin (Fla. St.)	3	5	.375	2.17	1.34	15	15	0	0	...	0-...	99.1	83	29	24	3	50-0	56	.229
— Knoxville (Sou.)	3	7	.300	5.18	1.59	12	12	0	0	...	0-...	64.1	71	47	37	3	31-1	53	.284
1996— Knoxville (Sou.)	7	9	.438	3.94	1.47	28	28	1	0	...	0-...	171.1	161	94	75	13	91-4	150	.250
1997— Syracuse (Int'l)	4	9	.308	4.50	1.38	19	19	3	2	...	0-...	120.0	113	64	60	16	53-0	97	.257
— Toronto (A.L.)	3	7	.300	5.09	1.78	14	13	1	1	0	0-0	81.1	108	55	46	7	37-0	55	.325
1998— Toronto (A.L.)	12	7	.632	4.37	1.36	33	24	1	1	0	0-0	175.0	177	97	85	18	61-1	136	.265
1999— Toronto (A.L.)	9	8	.529	4.38	1.50	24	24	4	1	0	0-0	150.0	177	81	73	16	48-1	106	.294
— St. Catharines (NYP)	0	0	...	4.50	1.50	1	1	0	0	...	0-...	4.0	5	2	2	0	1-0	6	.294
2000— Toronto (A.L.)	10	12	.455	6.26	1.64	34	27	2	0	0	0-0	175.1	204	*130	*122	30	83-1	113	.290
2001— Toronto (A.L.)	11	11	.500	4.09	1.41	34	34	3	2	0	0-0	215.2	229	112	98	29	75-5	157	.274
2002— Tennessee (Sou.)	0	1	.000	8.20	1.82	5	5	0	0	...	0-...	18.2	26	18	17	5	8-0	9	.338
— Toronto (A.L.)	4	5	.444	5.28	1.58	13	13	1	0	0	0-0	73.1	89	45	43	11	27-0	45	.306
— Syracuse (Int'l)	0	1	.000	4.50	1.67	1	1	0	0	...	0-...	6.0	8	3	3	1	2-0	6	.320
2003— Memphis (PCL)...............	0	0	...	5.40	1.60	3	3	0	0	...	0-0	8.1	11	5	5	0	2-0	4	.333
— Tennessee (Sou.)	0	1	.000	13.50	2.70	1	1	0	0	...	0-0	3.1	7	5	5	1	2-0	2	.438
Major League totals (6 years)	49	50	.495	4.83	1.51	152	135	12	5	0	0-0	870.2	984	520	467	111	331-8	612	.287

CARRARA, GIOVANNI   P

PERSONAL: Born March 4, 1968, in Anzoategui, Venezuela. ... 6-2/235. ... Throws right, bats right. ... Full name: Giovanni Jimenez Carrara. ... Name pronounced: ka-rah-rah.

TRANSACTIONS/CAREER NOTES: Signed as non-drafted free agent by Toronto Blue Jays organization (January 23, 1990). ... Claimed on waivers by Cincinnati Reds (July 3, 1996). ... Granted free agency (October 15, 1996). ... Signed by Baltimore Orioles organization (November 12, 1996). ... Released by Orioles (May 14, 1997). ... Signed by Reds organization (May 17, 1997). ... Granted free agency (September 11, 1997). ... Played for Seibu Lions of Japan Pacific League (1998). ... Signed by Reds organization (December 23, 1998). ... Granted free agency (October 15, 1999). ... Signed by Colorado Rockies organization (December 1, 1999). ... On Colorado disabled list (May 29-June 21, 2000). ... On Colorado disabled list (August 3-September 4, 2000); included rehabilitation assignment to Colorado Springs (August 29-September 4). ... Granted free agency (October 4, 2000). ... Signed by Los Angeles Dodgers organization (January 4, 2001). ... On disabled list (August 11-September 1, 2002). ... Released by Dodgers (March 26, 2003). ... Signed by Seattle Mariners (March 28, 2003). ... Sent outright to Tacoma by Seattle (June 19, 2003).

CAREER HITTING: 3-for-28 (.107), 2 R, 0 2B, 0 3B, 0 HR, 0 RBI.

Year League	W	L	Pct.	ERA	WHIP	G	GS	CG	ShO	Hld.	Sv.-Opp.	IP	H	R	ER	HR	BB-IBB	SO	Avg.
1990— Dom. B. Jays (DSL)	2	2	.500	2.62	1.35	15	14	4	0	...	0-...	86.0	88	31	25	...	28-...	55	...
1991— St. Catharines (NYP)	5	2	.714	1.71	0.97	15	13	2	•2	...	0-...	89.2	66	26	17	5	21-0	83	.200
1992— Dunedin (Fla. St.)	0	1	.000	4.63	1.41	5	4	0	0	...	0-...	23.1	22	13	12	1	11-0	16	.250
— Myrtle Beach (SAL)	11	7	.611	3.14	1.22	22	16	1	1	...	0-...	100.1	86	40	35	12	36-0	100	.231
1993— Dunedin (Fla. St.)	6	11	.353	3.45	1.39	27	24	1	0	...	0-...	140.2	136	69	54	14	59-0	108	.258
1994— Knoxville (Sou.)	13	7	.650	3.89	1.32	26	26	1	0	...	0-...	164.1	158	85	71	16	59-0	96	.251
1995— Syracuse (Int'l)	7	7	.500	3.96	1.31	21	21	0	0	...	0-...	131.2	116	72	58	11	56-2	81	.232
— Toronto (A.L.)	2	4	.333	7.21	1.83	12	7	1	0	0	0-0	48.2	64	46	39	10	25-1	27	.322
1996— Toronto (A.L.)	0	1	.000	11.40	2.33	11	0	0	0	0	0-1	15.0	23	19	19	5	12-2	10	.359
— Syracuse (Int'l)	4	4	.500	3.58	1.30	9	6	1	0	...	0-...	37.2	37	16	15	2	12-1	28	.253
— Indianapolis (A.A.)	4	0	1.000	0.76	0.71	9	6	1	1	...	1-...	47.2	25	6	4	2	9-0	45	.152
— Cincinnati (N.L.)	1	0	1.000	5.87	1.91	8	0	0	0	...	0-0	23.0	31	17	15	6	13-1	13	.323
1997— Rochester (Int'l)	4	2	.667	4.44	1.31	8	8	1	0	...	0-...	46.2	45	23	23	4	16-0	48	.259
— Indianapolis (A.A.)	12	5	.706	3.51	1.34	19	18	2	0	...	0-...	120.2	111	50	47	12	51-3	105	.247
— Cincinnati (N.L.)	0	1	.000	7.84	1.94	2	2	0	0	0	0-0	10.1	14	9	9	4	6-1	5	.333
1998— Seibu (Jp. East.)	2	0	1.000	4.50	1.13	4	0	0	0	...	0-...	8.0	8	4	4	...	1-...	8	...
— Seibu (Jap. Pac.)	1	2	.333	4.91	1.47	33	5	0	0	...	1-...	73.1	68	44	40	...	40-...	50	...
1999— Indianapolis (Int'l)	12	7	.632	3.47	1.28	39	21	2	1	...	0-...	158.0	144	68	61	20	58-3	114	.240
2000— Colo. Springs (PCL)	7	2	.778	3.26	1.23	18	15	0	0	...	0-...	96.2	89	39	35	8	30-1	89	.245
— Colorado (N.L.)	0	1	.000	12.83	2.40	8	0	0	0	0	0-1	13.1	21	19	19	5	11-2	15	.356
2001— Las Vegas (PCL)	1	2	.333	3.10	1.24	6	6	0	0	...	0-...	29.0	27	10	10	5	9-0	35	.248
— Los Angeles (N.L.)	6	1	.857	3.16	1.14	47	3	0	0	9	0-3	85.1	73	30	30	12	24-3	70	.231
2002— Los Angeles (N.L.)	6	3	.667	3.28	1.27	63	1	0	0	14	1-6	90.2	83	34	33	14	32-4	56	.243
2003— Seattle (A.L.)	2	0	1.000	6.83	1.86	23	0	0	0	4	0-0	29.0	40	22	22	6	14-0	13	.333
— Tacoma (PCL)	1	1	.500	4.23	1.34	18	0	0	0	...	5-...	27.2	28	14	13	2	9-0	27	.264
American League totals (3 years)	4	5	.444	7.77	1.92	46	7	1	0	4	0-1	92.2	127	87	80	21	51-3	50	.332
National League totals (5 years)	13	6	.684	4.28	1.38	128	11	0	0	23	1-10	222.2	222	109	106	41	86-11	159	.260
Major League totals (7 years)	17	11	.607	5.31	1.54	174	18	1	0	27	1-11	315.1	349	196	186	62	137-14	209	.282

C

CARRASCO, D.J.   P

PERSONAL: Born April 12, 1977, in Safford, Ariz. ... 6-1/215. ... Throws right, bats right. ... Full name: Daniel Carrasco. ... Junior college: Pima (Ari.) Community College.
TRANSACTIONS/CAREER NOTES: Selected by Baltimore Orioles in 26th round of free-agent draft (June 1997). ... Released by Orioles (June 14, 1998). ... Signed by Cleveland Indians organization (June 18, 1998). ... Released by Indians (1998). ... Signed by Pittsburgh Pirates organization (March 29, 1999). ... Selected by Kansas City Royals organization in Rule 5 draft (December 16, 2002).
CAREER HITTING: 0-for-2 (.000), 0 R, 0 2B, 0 3B, 0 HR, 0 RBI.

Year	League	W	L	Pct.	ERA	WHIP	G	GS	CG	ShO	Hld.	Sv.-Opp.	IP	H	R	ER	HR	BB-IBB	SO	Avg.
1998—	Watertown (NYP)	1	1	.500	5.40	1.58	13	1	0	0	...	2-...	31.2	36	23	19	3	14-0	38	.281
1999—	Williamsport (NYP)	4	2	.667	2.96	1.28	18	4	0	0	...	0-...	51.2	43	20	17	2	23-0	49	.236
	— Lynchburg (Carolina)	0	1	.000	6.35	2.12	2	0	0	0	...	0-...	5.2	9	8	4	0	3-0	4	.360
2000—	Hickory (S. Atl.)	5	4	.556	1.34	1.36	27	0	0	0	...	6-...	40.1	35	10	6	0	20-1	40	.236
	— Lynchburg (Carolina)	1	0	1.000	3.48	1.55	8	0	0	0	...	2-...	10.1	8	5	4	1	8-0	10	.222
	— Altoona (East.)	1	1	.500	8.36	2.07	9	0	0	0	...	0-...	14.0	16	14	13	0	13-0	10	.296
2001—	Lynchburg (Carolina)	4	0	1.000	1.50	0.89	22	0	0	0	...	7-...	36.0	18	7	6	0	14-1	40	.145
	— Altoona (East.)	2	2	.500	4.14	1.59	27	1	0	0	...	1-...	37.0	34	22	17	2	25-2	35	.239
2002—	Lynchburg (Carolina)	4	4	.500	1.61	0.96	55	0	0	0	...	29-...	72.2	52	18	13	1	18-1	83	.205
2003—	Kansas City (A.L.)	6	5	.545	4.82	1.52	50	2	0	0	6	2-5	80.1	82	44	43	8	40-4	57	.271
	Major League totals (1 year)	6	5	.545	4.82	1.52	50	2	0	0	6	2-5	80.1	82	44	43	8	40-4	57	.271

CARRASCO, HECTOR   P

PERSONAL: Born October 22, 1969, in San Pedro de Macoris, Dominican Republic. ... 6-2/220. ... Throws right, bats right. ... Full name: Hector Pacheco Pipo Carrasco. ... Name pronounced: kuh-RASS-koh. ... High school: Liceo Mattias Mella (San Pedro de Macoris, Dominican Republic).
TRANSACTIONS/CAREER NOTES: Signed as non-drafted free agent by New York Mets organization (March 20, 1988). ... Released by Mets (January 6, 1992). ... Signed by Houston Astros organization (January 21, 1992). ... Traded by Astros with P Brian Griffiths to Florida Marlins for P Tom Edens (November 17, 1992). ... Traded by Marlins to Cincinnati Reds (September 10, 1993), completing deal in which Reds traded P Chris Hammond to Marlins for 3B Gary Scott and a player to be named later (March 27, 1993). ... On disabled list (May 12-June 1, 1994). ... Traded by Reds with P Scott Service to Kansas City Royals for OF Jon Nunnally and IF/OF Chris Stynes (July 15, 1997). ... Selected by Arizona Diamondbacks in second round (49th pick overall) of expansion draft (November 18, 1997). ... Claimed on waivers by Minnesota Twins (April 3, 1998). ... On Minnesota disabled list (April 3-June 25, 1999); included rehabilitation assignments to Fort Myers (June 16-17) and Salt Lake (June 18-25). ... Traded by Twins to Boston Red Sox for OF Lew Ford (September 10, 2000). ... Granted free agency (November 1, 2000). ... Signed by Toronto Blue Jays organization (January 9, 2001). ... Released by Blue Jays (March 28, 2001). ... Signed by Twins organization (March 31, 2001). ... Granted free agency (October 19, 2001). ... Signed by Texas Rangers organization (January 18, 2002). ... On Oklahoma disabled list (April 4-30, 2002). ... Signed by Baltimore Orioles organization as a minor league free agent (March 1, 2003). ... Contract purchased by Baltimore from Ottawa (June 29, 2003).
CAREER HITTING: 1-for-18 (.056), 0 R, 0 2B, 0 3B, 0 HR, 0 RBI.

Year	League	W	L	Pct.	ERA	WHIP	G	GS	CG	ShO	Hld.	Sv.-Opp.	IP	H	R	ER	HR	BB-IBB	SO	Avg.
1988—	GC Mets (GCL)	0	2	.000	4.17	1.36	14	2	0	0	...	0-...	36.2	37	29	17	0	13-0	21	.248
1989—	Kingsport (Appal.)	1	6	.143	5.74	1.93	12	10	0	0	...	0-...	53.1	69	49	34	6	34-1	55	.314
1990—	Kingsport (Appal.)	0	0		4.05	1.35	3	1	0	0	...	0-...	6.2	8	3	3	1	1-0	5	.308
1991—	Pittsfield (NYP)	0	1	.000	5.40	1.97	12	1	0	0	...	1-...	23.1	25	17	14	1	21-0	20	.263
1992—	Asheville (S. Atl.)	5	5	.500	2.99	1.44	49	0	0	0	...	8-...	78.1	66	30	26	5	47-6	67	.237
1993—	Kane County (Midwest)	6	12	.333	4.11	1.54	28	* 28	0	0	...	0-...	149.0	153	90	68	11	76-6	127	.266
1994—	Cincinnati (N.L.)	5	6	.455	2.24	1.28	45	0	0	0	3	6-8	56.1	42	17	14	3	30-1	41	.210
1995—	Cincinnati (N.L.)	2	7	.222	4.12	1.51	64	0	0	0	11	5-9	87.1	86	45	40	1	46-5	64	.257
1996—	Cincinnati (N.L.)	4	3	.571	3.75	1.39	56	0	0	0	15	0-2	74.1	58	37	31	6	45-5	59	.214
	— Indianapolis (A.A.)	0	1	.000	2.14	1.48	13	2	0	0	...	0-...	21.0	18	7	5	1	13-1	17	.222
1997—	Indianapolis (A.A.)	0	0		6.23	1.85	3	0	0	0	...	1-...	4.1	5	3	3	1	3-0	4	.294
	— Cincinnati (N.L.)	1	2	.333	3.68	1.48	38	0	0	0	5	0-0	51.1	51	25	21	3	25-2	46	.250
	— Kansas City (A.L.)	1	6	.143	5.45	1.30	28	0	0	0	3	0-2	34.2	29	21	21	4	16-3	30	.227
1998—	Minnesota (A.L.)	4	2	.667	4.38	1.72	63	0	0	0	10	1-2	61.2	75	30	30	4	31-1	46	.304
1999—	Fort Myers (Fla. St.)	0	0		4.50	1.50	1	1	0	0	...	0-...	2.0	2	1	1	0	1-0	1	.286
	— Salt Lake (PCL)	1	0	1.000	0.00	0.92	3	0	0	0	...	1-...	4.1	3	0	0	0	1-0	3	.188
	— Minnesota (A.L.)	2	3	.400	4.96	1.35	39	0	0	0	7	1-2	49.0	48	29	27	3	18-0	35	.261
2000—	Minnesota (A.L.)	4	3	.571	4.25	1.50	61	0	0	0	7	1-5	72.0	75	38	34	6	33-0	57	.271
	— Boston (A.L.)	1	1	.500	9.45	3.00	8	1	0	0	1	0-1	6.2	15	8	7	2	5-1	7	.469
2001—	Minnesota (A.L.)	4	3	.571	4.64	1.45	56	0	0	0	8	1-2	73.2	77	40	38	8	30-3	70	.277
2002—	......										Did not play.									
2003—	Ottawa (Int'l)	4	2	.667	2.22	1.16	33	0	0	0	...	4-...	44.2	32	11	11	2	20-2	47	.208
	— Baltimore (A.L.)	2	6	.250	4.93	1.57	40	0	0	0	8	1-3	38.1	40	22	21	5	20-3	27	.270
	American League totals (6 years)	18	24	.429	4.77	1.52	295	1	0	0	37	5-17	336.0	359	188	178	32	153-11	272	.277
	National League totals (4 years)	12	18	.400	3.54	1.42	203	0	0	0	34	11-19	269.1	237	124	106	13	146-13	210	.235
	Major League totals (9 years)	30	42	.417	4.22	1.48	498	1	0	0	71	16-36	605.1	596	312	284	45	299-24	482	.259

CARROLL, JAMEY   IF

PERSONAL: Born February 18, 1974, in Evansville, Ind. ... 5-9/175. ... Bats right, throws right. ... Full name: Jamey Blake Carroll. ... High school: Castle (Newburgh, Ind.). ... College: Evansville.
TRANSACTIONS/CAREER NOTES: Selected by Montreal Expos organization in 14th round of free-agent draft (June 4, 1996).
2003 GAMES PLAYED BY POSITION (MLB): 3B—67, SS—14, 2B—11, DH—1.

Year	Team (League)	Pos.	G	AB	R	H	2B	3B	HR	RBI	BB	SO	HBP	GDP	SB-CS	Avg.	OBP	SLG	OPS	E	Pct.
1996—	Vermont (NYP)	SS-2B-3B	54	203	40	56	6	1	0	17	29	25	0	1	16-11	.276	.363	.315	.679	9	.960
1997—	W.P. Beach (FSL)	SS-2B	121	407	56	99	19	1	0	38	43	48	4	4	17-11	.243	.319	.295	.614	22	.951
1998—	Jupiter (FSL)	2B-SS	55	222	40	58	5	0	0	14	24	26	5	2	11-4	.261	.345	.284	.629	6	.977
	— Harrisburg (East.)	2B-SS	75	261	43	66	11	3	0	20	41	29	5	4	11-5	.253	.365	.318	.683	17	.953
1999—	Harrisburg (East.)	2B-SS	141	561	78	164	34	5	5	63	48	58	5	13	21-10	.292	.351	.398	.749	14	.979
2000—	Ottawa (Int'l)	2B-3B-SS	91	349	53	97	17	2	2	23	33	32	2	9	6-3	.278	.342	.355	.697	13	.967
	— Harrisburg (East.)	3B-SS-2B	45	169	23	49	5	3	0	18	12	13	0	6	8-2	.290	.335	.355	.690	6	.960
2001—	Ottawa (Int'l)	2B-SS-3B	83	267	26	64	8	2	0	16	18	41	2	8	5-5	.240	.292	.285	.576	9	.972
2002—	Harrisburg (East.)	2B	9	9	1	4	0	0	1	3	3	0	0	0	0-0	.444	.583	.444	1.028	0	1.000
	— Ottawa (Int'l)	3B-SS-2B	117	421	57	118	19	2	8	49	37	39	3	8	6-10	.280	.342	.392	.734	7	.983
	— Montreal (N.L.)	3B-SS-2B	16	71	16	22	5	3	1	6	4	12	0	1	1-0	.310	.347	.507	.854	4	.925
2003—	Montreal (N.L.)	3-S-2-D	105	227	31	59	10	1	1	10	19	39	3	10	5-2	.260	.323	.326	.649	5	.976
	Major League totals (2 years)		121	298	47	81	15	4	2	16	23	51	3	11	6-2	.272	.328	.369	.697	9	.966

CARTER, LANCE   P

PERSONAL: Born December 18, 1974, in Bradenton, Fla. ... 6-1/190. ... Throws right, bats right. ... Full name: Lance David Carter. ... High school: Manatee (Bradenton, Fla.). ... Junior college: Manatee College (Fla.).

TRANSACTIONS/CAREER NOTES: Selected by Kansas City Royals organization in 21st round of free-agent draft (June 21, 1994). ... On disabled list (June 12-September 15, 1997). ... On Omaha disabled list (August 7-September 12, 2000). ... Granted free agency (October 10, 2000). ... Signed by Tampa Bay Devil Rays organization (January 22, 2002). ... On Durham disabled list (May 14-23, 2002).

CAREER HITTING: 0-for-0 (.000), 0 R, 0 2B, 0 3B, 0 HR, 0 RBI.

Year	League	W	L	Pct.	ERA	WHIP	G	GS	CG	ShO	Hld.	Sv.-Opp.	IP	H	R	ER	HR	BB-IBB	SO	Avg.
1994— Eugene (NW)		1	0	1.000	5.47	1.56	8	7	0	0	...	0-...	26.1	26	17	16	2	15-0	23	.265
— GC Royals (GCL)		3	0	1.000	0.29	0.71	5	5	0	0	...	0-...	31.0	19	1	1	1	3-0	36	.179
1995— Springfield (Mid.)		9	5	.643	3.99	1.26	27	24	1	1	...	0-...	137.2	151	77	61	14	22-0	118	.276
1996— Wilmington (Caro.)		3	6	.333	6.34	1.50	16	12	0	0	...	0-...	65.1	81	50	46	8	17-2	49	.298
1997— Kingsport (Appal.)											Did not play.									
1998— Lansing (Midw.)		3	1	.750	0.67	1.07	15	2	0	0	...	2-...	40.1	34	6	3	0	9-1	37	.231
— Wilmington (Caro.)		1	4	.200	3.29	1.23	28	1	0	0	...	5-...	52.0	50	21	19	5	14-1	61	.262
1999— Wichita (Texas)		5	2	.714	0.78	1.09	44	0	0	0	...	13-...	69.2	49	10	6	1	27-5	77	.195
— Kansas City (A.L.)		0	1	.000	5.06	1.13	6	0	0	0	0	0-0	5.1	3	3	3	2	3-0	3	.167
2000— Omaha (PCL)		2	8	.200	4.95	1.39	34	6	0	0	...	5-...	76.1	88	46	42	13	18-1	51	.295
2001—											Did not play.									
2002— Durham (Int'l)		12	2	.857	2.80	0.93	33	18	2	1	...	1-...	132.0	111	43	41	15	12-0	90	.230
— Tampa Bay (A.L.)		2	0	1.000	1.33	0.98	8	0	0	0	0	2-2	20.1	15	3	3	2	5-1	14	.203
2003— Tampa Bay (A.L.)		7	5	.583	4.33	1.15	62	0	0	0	2	26-33	79.0	72	39	38	12	19-6	47	.242
Major League totals (3 years)		**9**	**6**	**.600**	**3.78**	**1.12**	**76**	**0**	**0**	**0**	**2**	**28-35**	**104.2**	**90**	**45**	**44**	**16**	**27-7**	**64**	**.231**

CASEY, SEAN   1B

PERSONAL: Born July 2, 1974, in Willingboro, N.J. ... 6-4/225. ... Bats left, throws right. ... Full name: Sean Thomas Casey. ... Name pronounced: KAY-see. ... High school: Upper St. Clair (Pittsburgh). ... College: Richmond.

TRANSACTIONS/CAREER NOTES: Selected by Cleveland Indians organization in second round of free-agent draft (June 1, 1995). ... On disabled list (July 23-September 23, 1996). ... On Akron disabled list (April 4-June 8, 1997). ... Traded by Indians to Cincinnati Reds for P Dave Burba (March 30, 1998). ... On Cincinnati disabled list (April 2-May 5, 1998); included rehabilitation assignment to Indianapolis (April 30-May 5). ... On disabled list (April 2-19, 2000). ... On Cincinnati disabled list (July 23-August 9 and September 10, 2002-remainder of season); included rehabilitation assignment to Louisville (August 7-9). ... Suspended by Major League Baseball (July 2, 2003). ... Reinstated (July 4, 2003).

2003 GAMES PLAYED BY POSITION (MLB): 1B—144.

Year	Team (League)	Pos.	G	AB	R	H	2B	3B	HR	RBI	BB	SO	HBP	GDP	SB-CS	Avg.	OBP	SLG	OPS	E	Pct.
1995— Watertown (NYP)		1B	55	207	26	68	18	0	2	37	18	21	1	6	3-0	.329	.380	.444	.824	3	.985
1996— Kinston (Caro.)		1B-DH	92	344	62	114	31	3	12	57	36	47	6	5	1-1	.331	.402	.544	.946	6	.991
1997— Akron (East.)		1B-DH	62	241	38	93	19	1	10	66	23	34	5	5	0-1	.386	.448	.598	1.046	5	.988
— Buffalo (A.A.)		DH-1B	20	72	12	26	7	0	5	18	9	11	1	0	0-0	.361	.439	.667	1.106	0	1.000
— Cleveland (A.L.)		1B	6	10	1	2	0	0	0	1	1	2	1	0	0-0	.200	.333	.200	.533	0	1.000
1998— Cincinnati (N.L.)		1B	96	302	44	82	21	1	7	52	43	45	3	11	1-1	.272	.365	.417	.782	4	.994
— Indianapolis (Int'l)		1B-DH	27	95	14	31	8	1	1	13	14	10	1	0	0-0	.326	.418	.463	.881	2	.991
1999— Cincinnati (N.L.)		1B	151	594	103	197	42	3	25	99	61	88	9	15	0-2	.332	.399	.539	.938	6	.995
2000— Cincinnati (N.L.)		1B	133	480	69	151	33	2	20	85	52	80	7	16	1-0	.315	.385	.517	.902	6	.995
2001— Cincinnati (N.L.)		1B-DH	145	533	69	165	40	0	13	89	43	63	9	16	3-1	.310	.369	.458	.827	7	.994
2002— Cincinnati (N.L.)		1B-DH	120	425	56	111	25	0	6	42	43	47	5	11	2-1	.261	.334	.362	.696	7	.993
— Louisville (Int'l)		DH	2	8	2	4	0	0	1	3	1	0	0	0	0-0	.500	.556	.875	1.431	...	...
2003— Cincinnati (N.L.)		1B	147	573	71	167	19	3	14	80	51	58	2	19	4-0	.291	.350	.408	.758	6	.996
American League totals (1 year)			6	10	1	2	0	0	0	1	1	2	1	0	0-0	.200	.333	.200	.533	0	1.000
National League totals (6 years)			792	2907	412	873	180	9	85	447	293	381	35	88	11-5	.300	.369	.456	.825	36	.995
Major League totals (7 years)			798	2917	413	875	180	9	85	448	294	383	36	88	11-5	.300	.369	.455	.824	36	.995

CASH, KEVIN   C

PERSONAL: Born December 6, 1977, in Tampa, Fla. ... 6-0/185. ... Bats right, throws right. ... Full name: Kevin Forrest Cash. ... College: Florida State.

TRANSACTIONS/CAREER NOTES: Signed as non-drafted free agent by Toronto Blue Jays organization (August 7, 1999). ... Recalled by Toronto from Syracuse (August 11, 2003).

2003 GAMES PLAYED BY POSITION (MLB): C—34.

Year	Team (League)	Pos.	G	AB	R	H	2B	3B	HR	RBI	BB	SO	HBP	GDP	SB-CS	Avg.	OBP	SLG	OPS	E	Pct.
2000— Hagerstown (SAL)		C	59	196	28	48	10	1	10	27	22	54	1	7	5-3	.245	.323	.459	.782	10	.974
2001— Dunedin (Fla. St.)		C	105	371	55	105	27	0	12	66	43	80	8	11	4-3	.283	.369	.453	.822	12	.979
2002— Syracuse (Int'l)		C	67	236	27	52	18	0	10	26	25	72	2	3	0-1	.220	.299	.424	.723	4	.989
— Tennessee (Sou.)		C-DH-3B	55	213	38	59	15	1	8	44	36	44	1	4	5-2	.277	.381	.469	.850	4	.983
— Toronto (A.L.)		C	7	14	1	2	0	0	0	0	1	4	0	1	0-0	.143	.200	.143	.343	1	.968
2003— Syracuse (Int'l)		C-DH-3B	93	326	37	88	28	2	8	37	29	81	2	14	1-0	.270	.331	.442	.772	1	.998
— Toronto (A.L.)		C	34	106	10	15	3	0	1	8	4	22	1	6	0-0	.142	.179	.198	.377	1	.995
Major League totals (2 years)			41	120	11	17	3	0	1	8	5	26	1	7	0-0	.142	.181	.192	.373	2	.991

CASTILLA, VINNY   3B

PERSONAL: Born July 4, 1967, in Oaxaca, Mexico. ... 6-1/205. ... Bats right, throws right. ... Full name: Vinicio Soria Castilla. ... Name pronounced: cas-TEE-yah. ... High school: Instituto Carlos Gracida (Oaxaca, Mexico). ... College: Benito Suarez (Mexico).

TRANSACTIONS/CAREER NOTES: Signed as non-drafted free agent by Saltillo, Mexican League (1987). ... Contract sold by Saltillo to Atlanta Braves organization (March 19, 1990). ... Selected by Colorado Rockies in second round (40th pick overall) of expansion draft (November 17, 1992). ... On disabled list (May 20-June 4, 1993). ... Traded by Rockies to Tampa Bay Devil Rays for P Rolando Arrojo and IF Aaron Ledesma (December 13, 1999). ... On Tampa Bay disabled list (March 25-April 11, June 14-July 3 and July 30-September 4, 2000); included rehabilitation assignment to Durham (July 1-3). ... Released by Devil Rays (May 10, 2001). ... Signed by Houston Astros (May 15, 2001). ... Granted free agency (November 6, 2001). ... Signed by Braves (December 11, 2001).

2003 GAMES PLAYED BY POSITION (MLB): 3B—147.

Year	Team (League)	Pos.	G	AB	R	H	2B	3B	HR	RBI	BB	SO	HBP	GDP	SB-CS	Avg.	OBP	SLG	OPS	E	Pct.
									BATTING											FIELDING	
1987— Saltillo (Mex.)	3B	13	27	0	5	2	0	0	1	0	5	...	...	0-0	.185		.259		1	.976
1988— Salt.-Monc. (Mex.)	SS	50	124	22	30	2	2	5	18	8	29	...	...	1-4	.242	...	.411	...	13	.924
1989— Saltillo (Mex.)	3B-SS	128	462	70	142	25	13	10	58	33	70	...	...	11-12	.307	...	.483	...	34	.950
1990— Sumter (S. Atl.)	SS	93	339	47	91	15	2	9	53	28	54	8	8	2-5	.268	.334	.404	.738	23	.952
— Greenville (Sou.)	SS	46	170	20	40	5	1	4	16	13	23	2	7	4-4	.235	.296	.347	.643	7	.971
1991— Greenville (Sou.)	SS	66	259	34	70	17	3	7	44	9	35	2	4	0-1	.270	.296	.440	.736	11	.965
— Richmond (Int'l)	SS	67	240	25	54	7	4	7	36	14	32	3	4	1-1	.225	.271	.375	.646	12	.962
— Atlanta (N.L.)	SS	12	5	1	1	0	0	0	0	0	2	0	0	0-0	.200	.200	.200	.400	0	1.000
1992— Richmond (Int'l)	SS	127	449	49	113	29	1	7	44	21	68	4	19	1-2	.252	.288	.367	.655	* 31	.944
— Atlanta (N.L.)	3B-SS	9	16	1	4	1	0	0	1	1	4	1	0	0-0	.250	.333	.313	.646	1	.933
1993— Colorado (N.L.)	SS	105	337	36	86	9	7	9	30	13	45	2	10	2-5	.255	.283	.404	.686	11	.975
1994— Colorado (N.L.)	SS-2-3-1	52	130	16	43	11	1	3	18	7	23	0	3	2-1	.331	.357	.500	.857	2	.986
— Colo. Springs (PCL)	3B-2B-SS	22	78	13	19	6	1	1	11	7	11	1	6	0-0	.244	.303	.385	.688	3	.964
1995— Colorado (N.L.)	3B-SS	139	527	82	163	34	2	32	90	30	87	4	15	2-8	.309	.347	.564	.911	15	.959
1996— Colorado (N.L.)	3B	160	629	97	191	34	0	40	113	35	88	5	20	7-2	.304	.343	.548	.892	20	.960
1997— Colorado (N.L.)	3B	159	612	94	186	25	2	40	113	44	108	8	17	2-4	.304	.356	.547	.904	21	.954
1998— Colorado (N.L.)	3B-SS	•162	645	108	206	28	4	46	144	40	89	6	24	5-9	.319	.362	.589	.951	13	.970
1999— Colorado (N.L.)	3B	158	615	83	169	24	1	33	102	53	75	1	15	2-3	.275	.331	.478	.809	19	.954
2000— Tampa Bay (A.L.)	3B	85	331	22	73	9	1	6	42	14	41	3	9	1-2	.221	.254	.308	.562	8	.967
— Durham (Int'l)	3B	2	8	1	3	1	0	1	3	0	1	0	0	0-0	.375	.375	.875	1.250	0	1.000
2001— Tampa Bay (A.L.)	3B	24	93	7	20	6	0	2	9	3	22	1	3	0-0	.215	.247	.344	.592	5	.934
— Houston (N.L.)	3B-SS	122	445	62	120	28	1	23	82	32	86	3	19	1-4	.270	.320	.492	.812	12	.963
2002— Atlanta (N.L.)	3B	143	543	56	126	23	2	12	61	22	69	7	22	4-1	.232	.268	.348	.616	6	.982
2003— Atlanta (N.L.)	3B	147	542	65	150	28	3	22	76	26	86	3	22	1-2	.277	.310	.461	.771	19	.955
American League totals (2 years)		109	424	29	93	15	1	8	51	17	63	4	12	1-2	.219	.253	.316	.569	13	.959
National League totals (12 years)		1368	5046	701	1445	245	23	260	830	303	762	40	167	28-39	.286	.329	.499	.827	139	.964
Major League totals (13 years)		1477	5470	730	1538	260	24	268	881	320	825	44	179	29-41	.281	.323	.484	.807	152	.964

CASTILLO, ALBERTO C

PERSONAL: Born February 10, 1970, in San Juan de la Maguana, Dominican Republic. ... 6-0/200. ... Bats right, throws right. ... Full name: Alberto Terrero Castillo. ... Name pronounced: cas-TEE-oh. ... High school: Mercedes Maria Mateo (Dominican Republic).

TRANSACTIONS/CAREER NOTES: Signed as non-drafted free agent by New York Mets organization (April 15, 1987). ... On disabled list (July 3, 1992-remainder of season; and June 1-July 13, 1994). ... On suspended list (August 27-29, 1994). ... Granted free agency (October 15, 1998). ... Signed by Philadelphia Phillies organization (November 5, 1998). ... Selected by St. Louis Cardinals from Phillies organization in Rule 5 major league draft (December 14, 1998). ... Traded by Cardinals with P Lance Painter and P Matt DeWitt to Toronto Blue Jays for P Pat Hentgen and P Paul Spoljaric (November 11, 1999). ... Released by Blue Jays (December 12, 2001). ... Signed by New York Yankees organization (December 21, 2001). ... Released by Yankees (October 10, 2002). ... Signed by San Francisco Giants (January 22, 2003).

2003 GAMES PLAYED BY POSITION (MLB): C—10.

Year	Team (League)	Pos.	G	AB	R	H	2B	3B	HR	RBI	BB	SO	HBP	GDP	SB-CS	Avg.	OBP	SLG	OPS	E	Pct.
									BATTING											FIELDING	
1987— Kingsport (Appal.)	C	7	9	1	1	0	0	0	0	5	5	0	1	1-0	.111	.429	.111	.540	0	1.000
1988— GC Mets (GCL)	C	22	68	7	18	4	0	0	10	4	4	2	3	2-0	.265	.312	.324	.635	1	.993
— Kingsport (Appal.)	C	24	75	7	22	3	0	1	14	15	14	0	1	0-1	.293	.407	.373	.780	5	.973
1989— Kingsport (Appal.)	C-1B	27	74	15	19	4	0	3	12	11	14	1	2	2-1	.257	.360	.432	.793	1	.994
— Pittsfield (NYP)	C	34	123	13	29	8	0	1	13	7	26	1	3	2-0	.236	.278	.325	.603	2	.991
1990— Columbia (S. Atl.)	C	30	103	8	24	4	3	1	14	10	21	0	2	1-1	.233	.296	.359	.655	5	.977
— Pittsfield (NYP)	C-1B-OF	58	187	19	41	8	1	4	24	26	35	5	7	3-3	.219	.327	.337	.664	9	.982
— St. Lucie (Fla. St.)	C	3	11	4	4	0	0	1	3	1	1	0	2	0-0	.364	.417	.636	1.053	0	1.000
1991— Columbia (S. Atl.)	C	90	267	35	74	20	3	3	47	43	44	5	6	6-6	.277	.382	.408	.790	15	.982
1992— St. Lucie (Fla. St.)	C	60	162	11	33	6	0	3	17	16	37	2	4	0-0	.204	.280	.296	.577	12	.967
1993— St. Lucie (Fla. St.)	C	105	333	37	86	21	0	5	42	28	46	3	5	0-2	.258	.315	.366	.682	12	.983
1994— Binghamton (East.)	C-1B	90	315	33	78	14	0	7	42	41	46	0	11	1-3	.248	.333	.359	.692	6	.991
1995— Norfolk (Int'l)	C-DH	69	217	23	58	13	1	4	31	26	32	1	6	2-3	.267	.346	.392	.737	7	.987
— New York (N.L.)	C	13	29	2	3	0	0	0	0	3	9	1	0	1-0	.103	.212	.103	.316	2	.974
1996— New York (N.L.)	C	6	11	1	4	0	0	0	0	0	4	0	0	0-0	.364	.364	.364	.727	0	1.000
— Norfolk (Int'l)	C	113	341	34	71	12	1	11	39	39	67	4	3	2-2	.208	.295	.346	.641	8	.990
1997— New York (N.L.)	C	35	59	3	12	1	0	0	7	9	16	0	3	0-1	.203	.304	.220	.525	2	.987
— Norfolk (Int'l)	C-OF	34	83	4	18	1	0	1	8	17	16	0	3	1-0	.217	.347	.265	.612	7	.968
1998— New York (N.L.)	C-DH	38	83	13	17	4	0	2	7	9	17	1	1	0-2	.205	.290	.325	.616	2	.990
— Norfolk (Int'l)	C-OF	21	49	4	9	2	0	1	6	11	12	0	0	0-0	.184	.333	.286	.619	1	.991
1999— St. Louis (N.L.)	C	93	255	21	67	9	0	4	31	24	48	2	6	0-0	.263	.326	.341	.667	5	.991
2000— Toronto (A.L.)	C	66	185	14	39	7	0	1	16	21	36	0	3	0-0	.211	.287	.265	.552	3	.993
2001— Toronto (A.L.)	C	66	131	9	26	4	0	1	4	7	30	3	2	1-1	.198	.255	.252	.507	4	.989
2002— New York (A.L.)	C	15	37	3	5	1	1	0	4	1	12	0	2	0-0	.135	.158	.216	.374	1	.990
— Columbus (Int'l)	C	30	91	7	25	7	0	0	8	9	8	2	3	1-0	.275	.350	.352	.701	4	.983
2003— Fresno (PCL)	C	12	34	2	8	1	0	0	7	8	8	0	1	0-0	.235	.381	.265	.646	0	1.000
— San Francisco (N.L.)	C	11	15	2	3	1	0	0	4	0	5	0	0	0-0	.200	.200	.467	.667	1	.975
American League totals (3 years)		147	353	26	70	12	1	2	24	29	78	3	7	1-1	.198	.263	.255	.518	8	.991
National League totals (6 years)		196	452	42	106	14	0	7	49	45	99	4	10	1-3	.235	.306	.312	.618	12	.989
Major League totals (9 years)		343	805	68	176	26	1	9	73	74	177	7	17	2-4	.219	.287	.287	.574	20	.990

CASTILLO, LUIS 2B

PERSONAL: Born September 12, 1975, in San Pedro de Macoris, Dominican Republic. ... 5-11/190. ... Bats both, throws right. ... Full name: Luis Antonio Castillo. ... Name pronounced: ca-STEE-yo. ... High school: Colegio San Benito Abad (San Pedro de Macoris, Dominican Republic). ... College: San Benito Abad (D.R.).

TRANSACTIONS/CAREER NOTES: Signed as non-drafted free agent by Florida Marlins organization (August 19, 1992). ... On disabled list (July 20-September 11, 1995). ... On Florida disabled list (May 7-22, 1997). ... On Florida disabled list (April 16-May 5, 2000); included rehabilitation assignment to Calgary (April 28-May 5).

2003 GAMES PLAYED BY POSITION (MLB): 2B—152.

Year	Team (League)	Pos.	G	AB	R	H	2B	3B	HR	RBI	BB	SO	HBP	GDP	SB-CS	Avg.	OBP	SLG	OPS	E	Pct.
1993— Dom. Marlins (DSL)	IF	69	266	48	75	7	1	4	31	36	22	...	...	21-...	.282	...	.361	...	20	.943
1994— GC Marlins (GCL)	2B-SS	57	216	49	57	8	0	0	16	37	36	1	1	31-12	.264	.371	.301	.672	9	.972
1995— Kane Co. (Midw.)	2B	89	340	71	111	4	4	0	23	55	50	0	1	41-18	.326	.419	.362	.781	17	.962
1996— Portland (East.)	2B	109	420	83	133	15	7	1	35	66	68	2	2	* 51-28	.317	.411	.393	.804	14	.975
— Florida (N.L.)	2B	41	164	26	43	2	1	1	8	14	46	0	0	17-4	.262	.320	.305	.625	3	.986
1997— Florida (N.L.)	2B	75	263	27	63	8	0	0	8	27	53	0	6	16-10	.240	.310	.270	.580	9	.971
— Charlotte (Int'l)	2B	37	130	25	46	5	0	0	5	16	22	0	2	8-6	.354	.425	.392	.817	5	.970
1998— Charlotte (Int'l)	2B	100	381	74	109	11	2	0	15	75	68	0	6	41-15	.286	.403	.325	.728	16	.970
— Florida (N.L.)	2B	44	153	21	31	3	2	1	10	22	33	1	1	3-0	.203	.307	.268	.575	7	.970
1999— Florida (N.L.)	2B	128	487	76	147	23	4	0	28	67	85	0	3	50-17	.302	.384	.366	.750	15	.976
2000— Florida (N.L.)	2B	136	539	101	180	17	3	2	17	78	86	0	11	* 62-22	.334	.418	.388	.806	11	.983
— Calgary (PCL)	2B	4	13	4	4	1	1	0	0	4	2	0	0	1-0	.308	.471	.538	1.009	1	.944
2001— Florida (N.L.)	2B	134	537	76	141	16	10	2	45	67	90	1	6	33-16	.263	.344	.344	.685	* 13	.980
2002— Florida (N.L.)	2B	146	606	86	185	18	5	2	39	55	76	2	7	* 48-15	.305	.364	.361	.726	13	.981
2003— Florida (N.L.)	2B	152	595	99	187	19	6	6	39	63	60	2	7	21-19	.314	.381	.397	.778	10	.986
Major League totals (8 years)		856	3344	512	977	106	31	14	194	393	529	6	41	250-103	.292	.367	.355	.722	81	.980

CASTRO, JUAN   SS/2B

PERSONAL: Born June 20, 1972... 5-11/195. ... Bats right, throws right. ... Full name: Juan Gabriel Castro. ... High school: CBTIS 43 (Los Mochis, Mexico).
TRANSACTIONS/CAREER NOTES: Signed as non-drafted free agent by Los Angeles Dodgers organization (June 13, 1991). ... On Los Angeles disabled list (June 5-August 1, 1997). ... Traded by Dodgers to Cincinnati Reds for a player to be named later and cash (April 1, 2000); Dodgers acquired P Kenny Lutz to complete deal (June 8, 2000). ... On Cincinnati disabled list (March 27-June 1, 2002); included rehabilitation assignments to Louisville (April 10-11 and May 27-June 1). ... On Cincinnati disabled list (March 25-April 14, 2003); included rehabilitation assignment to Louisville (April 3-14).
2003 GAMES PLAYED BY POSITION (MLB): 2B—56, 3B—30, SS—24, 1B—1.

Year	Team (League)	Pos.	G	AB	R	H	2B	3B	HR	RBI	BB	SO	HBP	GDP	SB-CS	Avg.	OBP	SLG	OPS	E	Pct.
1991— Great Falls (Pio.)	2B-SS	60	217	36	60	4	2	1	27	33	31	0	2	7-6	.276	.369	.327	.696	21	.921
1992— Bakersfield (Calif.)	SS	113	446	56	116	15	4	4	42	37	64	1	7	14-11	.260	.314	.339	.652	38	.928
1993— San Antonio (Texas)	2B-SS	118	424	55	117	23	8	7	41	30	40	2	14	12-11	.276	.325	.417	.742	28	.945
1994— San Antonio (Texas)	SS	123	445	55	128	25	4	4	44	31	66	1	9	4-7	.288	.334	.389	.723	29	.951
1995— Albuquerque (PCL)	SS-2B	104	341	51	91	18	4	3	43	20	42	0	11	4-4	.267	.307	.370	.677	14	.973
— Los Angeles (N.L.)	3B-SS	11	4	0	1	0	0	0	0	1	1	0	0	0-0	.250	.400	.250	.650	0	1.000
1996— Albuquerque (PCL) 3B-SS-2B		17	56	12	21	4	2	1	8	6	7	1	0	1-1	.375	.444	.571	1.016	2	.962
— Los Angeles (N.L.) SS-3-2-OF		70	132	16	26	5	3	0	5	10	27	0	3	1-0	.197	.254	.280	.534	3	.979
1997— Los Angeles (N.L.)	SS-2B-3B	40	75	3	11	3	1	0	4	7	20	0	2	0-0	.147	.220	.213	.433	1	.990
— Albuquerque (PCL)	SS	27	101	11	31	5	2	2	11	4	20	0	5	1-0	.307	.327	.455	.783	9	.928
1998— Los Angeles (N.L.)	SS-2B-3B	89	220	25	43	7	0	2	14	15	37	0	5	0-0	.195	.245	.255	.499	10	.965
1999— Albuquerque (PCL)	SS-3-2-D	116	423	52	116	25	4	7	51	34	70	0	14	2-3	.274	.325	.402	.727	19	.956
— Los Angeles (N.L.)	2B-SS	2	1	0	0	0	0	0	0	0	1	0	0	0-0	.000	.000	.000	.000	0	1.000
2000— Louisville (Int'l)	SS-2B-3B	19	60	9	19	5	1	2	10	12	12	0	3	0-1	.317	.425	.533	.958	4	.956
— Cincinnati (N.L.)	SS-2B-3B	82	224	20	54	12	2	4	23	14	33	0	9	0-2	.241	.283	.366	.649	2	.993
2001— Cincinnati (N.L.)	SS-2-3-1	96	242	27	54	10	0	3	13	13	50	0	9	0-0	.223	.261	.302	.562	8	.970
2002— Louisville (Int'l)	SS-2B	5	17	2	3	0	0	0	2	1	3	0	0	0-0	.176	.222	.176	.399	1	.962
— Cincinnati (N.L.)	SS-2-3-1	54	82	5	18	3	0	2	11	7	18	0	0	0-0	.220	.278	.329	.607	3	.971
2003— Louisville (Int'l)	SS	9	32	3	7	0	0	1	5	2	3	0	2	0-1	.219	.257	.313	.570	2	.950
— Cincinnati (N.L.)	2-3-SS-1	113	320	28	81	14	1	9	33	18	58	0	7	2-3	.253	.290	.388	.678	5	.987
Major League totals (9 years)		557	1300	124	288	54	7	20	103	85	245	0	35	3-5	.222	.267	.320	.587	32	.980

CASTRO, RAMON   C

PERSONAL: Born March 1, 1976, in Vega Baja, Puerto Rico. ... 6-3/235. ... Bats right, throws right. ... Full name: Ramon Abraham Castro. ... Name pronounced: RA-mon. ... High school: Lino P. Rivera (Vega Baja, Puerto Rico).
TRANSACTIONS/CAREER NOTES: Selected by Houston Astros organization in first round (17th pick overall) of free-agent draft (June 2, 1994). ... On Jackson disabled list (April 27-May 15, 1998). ... Traded by Astros to Florida Marlins for P Jay Powell and C Scott Makarewicz (July 6, 1998). ... On Calgary disabled list (April 20-May 5, 2000). ... On disabled list (May 17-June 8, 2002).
2003 GAMES PLAYED BY POSITION (MLB): C—18, DH—1.

Year	Team (League)	Pos.	G	AB	R	H	2B	3B	HR	RBI	BB	SO	HBP	GDP	SB-CS	Avg.	OBP	SLG	OPS	E	Pct.
1994— GC Astros (GCL)	C	37	123	17	34	7	0	3	14	17	14	2	4	5-5	.276	.373	.407	.780	4	.983
1995— Kissimmee (Fla. St.)	C	36	120	6	25	5	0	0	8	6	21	1	1	0-0	.208	.250	.250	.500	7	.967
— Auburn (NY-Penn)	C	63	224	40	67	17	0	9	49	24	27	0	6	0-1	.299	.358	.496	.854	2	.994
1996— Quad City (Midw.)	C	96	314	38	78	15	0	7	43	31	61	2	12	2-0	.248	.317	.363	.680	10	.987
1997— Kissimmee (Fla. St.)	C	115	410	53	115	22	1	8	65	53	73	2	17	1-0	.280	.357	.398	.755	6	.992
1998— Jackson (Texas)	C	48	168	27	43	6	0	8	25	13	31	4	3	0-1	.256	.324	.435	.759	10	.974
— Portland (East.)	C	31	88	9	22	3	0	3	11	8	21	0	3	0-0	.250	.306	.386	.692	5	.946
1999— Calgary (PCL)	C-DH	97	349	43	90	22	0	15	61	24	64	2	11	0-0	.258	.307	.450	.757	7	.989
— Florida (N.L.)	C	24	67	4	12	4	0	2	4	10	14	0	1	0-0	.179	.282	.328	.610	1	.992
2000— Calgary (PCL)	C	67	218	44	73	22	0	14	45	16	38	0	5	0-0	.335	.380	.628	1.009	4	.990
— Florida (N.L.)	C	50	138	10	33	4	0	2	14	16	36	1	1	0-0	.239	.318	.312	.630	6	.980
2001— Florida (N.L.)	C	7	11	0	2	0	0	0	1	1	1	0	0	0-0	.182	.250	.182	.432	0	1.000
— Calgary (PCL)	C	108	390	81	131	33	0	27	90	38	74	1	11	1-1	.336	.393	.628	1.021	7	.989
2002— Florida (N.L.)	C-DH	54	101	11	24	4	0	6	18	14	24	0	4	0-0	.238	.322	.455	.777	0	1.000
2003— Florida (N.L.)	C-DH	40	53	6	15	2	0	5	8	4	11	0	0	0-0	.283	.333	.604	.937	1	.982
Major League totals (5 years)		175	370	31	86	14	0	15	45	45	86	1	6	0-0	.232	.313	.392	.705	8	.988

CATALANOTTO, FRANK   OF/IF

PERSONAL: Born April 27, 1974, in Smithtown, N.Y. ... 5-11/195. ... Bats left, throws right. ... Full name: Frank John Catalanotto. ... Name pronounced: ca-tal-a-NAH-tow. ... High school: Smithtown (N.Y.) East. ... College: C.W. Post (N.Y.).

TRANSACTIONS/CAREER NOTES: Selected by Detroit Tigers organization in 10th round of free-agent draft (June 1, 1992). ... Selected by Oakland Athletics from Tigers organization in Rule 5 major league draft (December 9, 1996). ... Returned to Tigers organization (March 21, 1997). ... On Toledo disabled list (June 18-25, 1998). ... Traded by Tigers with P Justin Thompson, P Francisco Cordero, OF Gabe Kapler, C Bill Haselman and P Alan Webb to Texas Rangers for OF Juan Gonzalez, P Danny Patterson and C Gregg Zaun (November 2, 1999). ... On Texas disabled list (April 22-May 15, 2000); included rehabilitation assignment to Oklahoma (May 12-15). ... On Texas disabled list (May 11-June 28 and August 17, 2002-remainder of season); included rehabilitation assignment to Tulsa (June 24-28). ... Granted free agency (December 21, 2002). ... Signed by Toronto Blue Jays (December 30, 2002).

2003 GAMES PLAYED BY POSITION (MLB): OF—100, DH—21, 1B—5.

Year Team (League)	Pos.	G	AB	R	H	2B	3B	HR	RBI	BB	SO	HBP	GDP	SB-CS	Avg.	OBP	SLG	OPS	E	Pct.
1992—Bristol (Appal.)	2B	21	50	6	10	2	0	0	4	8	8	0	0	0-1	.200	.310	.240	.550	2	.875
1993—Bristol (Appal.)	2B	55	199	37	61	9	5	3	22	15	19	3	3	3-6	.307	.364	.447	.811	10	.957
1994—Fayetteville (SAL)	2B	119	458	72	149	24	8	3	56	37	54	3	4	4-5	.325	.379	.432	.811	15	.973
1995—Jacksonville (Sou.)	2B	134	491	66	111	19	5	8	48	49	56	9	9	13-8	.226	.306	.334	.640	18	.974
1996—Jacksonville (Sou.)	2B	132	497	105	148	34	6	17	67	74	69	11	8	15-14	.298	.398	.493	.891	•22	.968
1997—Toledo (Int'l)	2-3-OF-D	134	500	75	150	32	3	16	68	47	80	10	9	12-11	.300	.368	.472	.840	18	.966
—Detroit (A.L.)	2B-DH	13	26	2	8	2	0	0	3	3	7	0	0	0-0	.308	.379	.385	.764	0	1.000
1998—Detroit (A.L.)	2-DH-1-3	89	213	23	60	13	2	6	25	12	39	4	4	3-2	.282	.325	.446	.771	3	.989
—Toledo (Int'l)	1B-2B-DH	28	105	20	35	6	3	4	28	14	21	7	2	0-0	.333	.438	.562	.999	2	.989
1999—Detroit (A.L.)	2-1-3-DH	100	286	41	79	19	0	11	35	15	49	9	5	3-4	.276	.327	.458	.785	5	.986
2000—Texas (A.L.)	2-DH-1-OF	103	282	55	82	13	2	10	42	33	36	6	5	6-2	.291	.375	.457	.832	9	.969
—Oklahoma (PCL)	2B-OF	3	11	2	3	0	0	0	1	0	4	1	0	0-0	.273	.333	.273	.606	0	1.000
2001—Texas (A.L.)	O-2-3-D-1	133	463	77	153	31	5	11	54	39	55	8	5	15-5	.330	.391	.490	.882	4	.985
2002—Texas (A.L.)	OF-2-1	68	212	42	57	16	6	3	23	25	27	8	3	9-5	.269	.364	.443	.808	2	.990
—Tulsa (Texas)	1B-2B-OF	4	16	1	2	0	1	0	3	1	1	1	3	0-0	.125	.222	.250	.472	0	1.000
2003—Toronto (A.L.)	OF-DH-1B	133	489	83	146	34	6	13	59	35	62	6	9	2-2	.299	.351	.472	.823	3	.983
Major League totals (7 years)		639	1971	323	585	128	21	54	241	162	275	41	31	38-20	.297	.359	.465	.825	26	.983

CEDENO, ROGER   OF

PERSONAL: Born August 16, 1974, in Valencia, Venezuela. ... 6-1/205. ... Bats both, throws right. ... Full name: Roger Leandro Cedeno. ... Name pronounced: sid-AIN-yo.

TRANSACTIONS/CAREER NOTES: Signed as non-drafted free agent by Los Angeles Dodgers organization (March 28, 1991). ... On disabled list (June 27-July 14, 1994). ... On Los Angeles disabled list (March 25-April 17 and August 25, 1997-remainder of season); included rehabilitation assignment to Albuquerque (April 17-21). ... On Los Angeles disabled list (March 22-April 24, 1998); included rehabilitation assignment to Vero Beach (April 16-24). ... Traded by Dodgers with C Charles Johnson to New York Mets for C Todd Hundley and P Arnold Gooch (December 1, 1998). ... Traded by Mets with P Octavio Dotel and P Kyle Kessel to Houston Astros for P Mike Hampton and OF Derek Bell (December 23, 1999). ... On Houston disabled list (May 26-August 18, 2000); included rehabilitation assignment to New Orleans (August 10-18). ... Traded by Astros with C Mitch Meluskey and P Chris Holt to Detroit Tigers for C Brad Ausmus, P Doug Brocail and P Nelson Cruz (December 11, 2000). ... Granted free agency (November 5, 2001). ... Signed by Mets (December 17, 2001).

2003 GAMES PLAYED BY POSITION (MLB): OF—128.

Year Team (League)	Pos.	G	AB	R	H	2B	3B	HR	RBI	BB	SO	HBP	GDP	SB-CS	Avg.	OBP	SLG	OPS	E	Pct.
1991—Dom. Dodgers (DSL)	OF	58	209	25	50	1	1	0	7	0	0	...	...	26-13	.239	...	.254	...	...	...
1992—Great Falls (Pio.)	OF	69	256	60	81	6	5	2	27	51	53	2	4	*40-9	.316	.431	.402	.833	8	.937
1993—San Antonio (Texas)	OF	122	465	70	134	12	8	4	30	45	90	1	5	28-20	.288	.352	.374	.726	9	.961
—Albuquerque (PCL)	OF	6	18	1	4	1	1	0	4	3	3	0	0	0-1	.222	.333	.389	.722	1	.923
1994—Albuquerque (PCL)	OF	104	383	84	123	18	5	4	49	51	57	0	4	30-13	.321	.395	.426	.820	8	.962
1995—Albuquerque (PCL)	OF-DH	99	367	67	112	19	9	2	44	53	56	2	5	23-18	.305	.393	.422	.815	3	.985
—Los Angeles (N.L.)	OF	40	42	4	10	2	0	0	3	3	10	0	1	1-0	.238	.283	.286	.568	1	.977
1996—Los Angeles (N.L.)	OF	86	211	26	52	11	1	2	18	24	47	1	0	5-1	.246	.326	.336	.663	2	.983
—Albuquerque (PCL)	OF	33	125	16	28	2	3	1	10	15	22	0	1	6-5	.224	.307	.312	.619	0	1.000
1997—Albuquerque (PCL)	OF	29	113	21	40	4	4	2	9	22	16	1	1	5-5	.354	.463	.513	.977	2	.964
—Los Angeles (N.L.)	OF	80	194	31	53	10	2	3	17	25	44	3	1	9-1	.273	.362	.392	.753	2	.987
1998—Vero Beach (FSL)	OF	6	21	5	9	0	1	1	6	5	5	0	2	1-0	.429	.538	.667	1.205	1	.933
—Los Angeles (N.L.)	OF	105	240	33	58	11	1	2	17	27	57	0	1	8-2	.242	.317	.321	.638	2	.978
1999—New York (N.L.)	OF-2B	155	453	90	142	23	4	4	36	60	100	3	5	66-17	.313	.396	.408	.804	3	.989
2000—Houston (N.L.)	OF	74	259	54	73	2	5	6	26	43	47	0	6	25-11	.282	.383	.398	.781	3	.978
—New Orleans (PCL)	OF	6	20	2	7	0	1	0	3	2	5	0	0	1-1	.350	.391	.450	.841	0	1.000
2001—Detroit (A.L.)	OF-DH	131	523	79	153	14	11	6	48	36	83	2	5	55-15	.293	.337	.396	.733	12	.953
2002—New York (N.L.)	OF	149	511	65	133	19	2	7	41	42	92	2	10	25-4	.260	.318	.346	.664	8	.966
2003—New York (N.L.)	OF	148	484	70	129	25	4	7	37	38	86	1	8	14-9	.267	.320	.378	.698	3	.987
American League totals (1 year)		131	523	79	153	14	11	6	48	36	83	2	5	55-15	.293	.337	.396	.733	12	.953
National League totals (8 years)		837	2394	373	650	103	19	31	195	262	483	10	32	153-45	.272	.344	.369	.714	24	.981
Major League totals (9 years)		968	2917	452	803	117	30	37	243	298	566	12	37	208-60	.275	.343	.374	.717	36	.977

CEPICKY, MATT   OF

PERSONAL: Born November 10, 1977, in St. Louis, Mo. ... 6-2/225. ... Bats left, throws right. ... Full name: Matthew William Cepicky. ... Name pronounced: suh-PICK-ee. ... High school: Vianney (Kirkwood, Mo.). ... College: Southwest Missouri State.

TRANSACTIONS/CAREER NOTES: Selected by Montreal Expos organization in fourth round of free-agent draft (June 2, 1999). ... Recalled from Edmonton by Montreal (July 12, 2003). ... Optioned to Edmonton by Montreal (July 21, 2003). ... Recalled by Montreal from Edmonton (September 12, 2003).

2003 GAMES PLAYED BY POSITION (MLB): OF—4.

Year Team (League)	Pos.	G	AB	R	H	2B	3B	HR	RBI	BB	SO	HBP	GDP	SB-CS	Avg.	OBP	SLG	OPS	E	Pct.
1999—Vermont (NYP)	OF	74	323	50	99	15	5	12	53	20	49	1	6	10-9	.307	.349	.495	.844	1	.986
2000—Jupiter (FSL)	OF	131	*536	61	160	32	7	6	88	24	64	2	9	32-13	.299	.328	.412	.740	4	.983
2001—Harrisburg (East.)	OF	122	459	59	121	23	8	15	77	21	97	2	6	5-12	.264	.296	.447	.743	3	.986
2002—Harrisburg (East.)	OF	109	419	54	116	25	2	16	76	33	94	2	14	7-1	.277	.327	.461	.788	2	.988
—Montreal (N.L.)	OF	32	74	7	16	3	0	3	15	4	21	0	0	0-0	.216	.256	.378	.635	0	1.000
2003—Montreal (N.L.)	OF	5	8	0	2	1	0	0	0	0	2	0	0	0-0	.250	.250	.375	.625	0	1.000
—Edmonton (PCL)	OF-DH-1B	122	442	61	133	23	4	7	64	31	82	4	12	7-2	.301	.349	.419	.767	11	.948
Major League totals (2 years)		37	82	7	18	4	0	3	15	4	23	0	0	0-0	.220	.256	.378	.634	0	1.000

CERDA, JAIME   P

PERSONAL: Born October 26, 1978, in Fresno, Calif. ... 6-0/175. ... Throws left, bats left. ... Full name: Jaime M. Cerda. ... Name pronounced: SER-da. ... Junior college: Fresno City (Calif.) Community College.

TRANSACTIONS/CAREER NOTES: Selected by New York Mets organization in 23rd round of free-agent draft (June 2, 1998). ... On disabled list (June 18, 1999-entire season). ... Optioned to Norfolk by New York Mets (April 30, 2003). ... Recalled by New York from Norfolk (May 12, 2003). ... Optioned to Norfolk by New York (May 27, 2003). ... Recalled by New York from Norfolk (June 29, 2003). ... Optioned to Norfolk by New York (July 12, 2003). ... Recalled by New York from Norfolk of the International League (July 28, 2003). ... Optioned to Norfolk by New York (August 23, 2003). ... Recalled by New York from Norfolk (September 2, 2003).

CAREER HITTING: 0-for-2 (.000), 0 R, 0 2B, 0 3B, 0 HR, 0 RBI.

Year League	W	L	Pct.	ERA	WHIP	G	GS	CG	ShO	Hld.	Sv.-Opp.	IP	H	R	ER	HR	BB-IBB	SO	Avg.
1999—										Did not play.									
2000— Pittsfield (NYP)	4	1	.800	0.57	0.83	20	1	0	0	...	5-...	47.0	33	6	3	0	6-1	51	.198
2001— St. Lucie (Fla. St.)	2	1	.667	0.97	0.93	28	0	0	0	...	6-...	55.2	40	8	6	3	12-0	53	.204
— Binghamton (Eastern)	1	0	1.000	3.10	1.13	12	0	0	0	...	3-...	20.1	17	7	7	1	6-0	22	.233
— Norfolk (Int'l)	0	0	...	3.86	0.86	3	0	0	0	...	0-...	4.2	2	2	2	0	2-0	4	.125
2002— Binghamton (Eastern)	5	1	.833	2.27	0.98	14	0	0	0	...	0-...	31.2	21	8	8	0	10-0	33	.193
— Norfolk (Int'l)	0	0	...	0.43	0.81	12	0	0	0	...	1-...	21.0	10	2	1	0	7-1	17	.143
— New York (N.L.)	0	0	...	2.45	1.40	32	0	0	0	4	0-0	25.2	22	7	7	0	14-0	21	.232
2003— Norfolk (Int'l)	3	0	1.000	1.67	1.21	22	0	0	0	...	0-...	32.1	29	7	6	3	10-1	35	.246
— New York (N.L.)	1	1	.500	5.85	1.61	27	0	0	0	2	0-1	32.1	32	21	21	4	20-1	19	.267
Major League totals (2 years)	**1**	**1**	**.500**	**4.34**	**1.52**	**59**	**0**	**0**	**0**	**6**	**0-1**	**58.0**	**54**	**28**	**28**	**4**	**34-1**	**40**	**.251**

CERROS, JUAN   P

PERSONAL: Born September 25, 1976, in Monterrey, Mexico. ... 6-1/200. ... Throws right, bats right. ... Full name: R. Juan Cerros.

TRANSACTIONS/CAREER NOTES: Signed by Reynosa of the Mexican League (March 20, 1996). ... Contract purchased by New York Mets from Reynosa (March 28, 1999). ... Selected by Cincinnati Reds from Mets organization in Rule 5 draft (December 2002).

CAREER HITTING: 0-for-0 (.000), 0 R, 0 2B, 0 3B, 0 HR, 0 RBI.

Year League	W	L	Pct.	ERA	WHIP	G	GS	CG	ShO	Hld.	Sv.-Opp.	IP	H	R	ER	HR	BB-IBB	SO	Avg.
1999— St. Lucie (Fla. St.)	2	0	1.000	0.00	1.17	5	0	0	0	...	0-...	7.2	5	1	0	0	4-0	6	.185
2000— Binghamton (Eastern)	10	4	.714	3.50	1.35	50	2	0	0	...	3-...	74.2	71	33	29	8	30-1	52	.245
2001— Binghamton (Eastern)	1	2	.333	4.91	1.69	13	0	0	0	...	0-...	18.1	24	10	10	2	7-0	14	.304
— Norfolk (Int'l)	1	3	.250	3.95	1.53	38	1	0	0	...	1-...	57.0	65	33	25	5	22-3	32	.291
2002— Binghamton (Eastern)	0	0	...	0.00	0.00	3	0	0	0	...	0-...	3.0	0	0	0	0	0-0	3	.000
— Norfolk (Int'l)	1	3	.250	3.35	1.35	25	3	0	0	...	2-...	37.2	40	21	14	2	11-0	23	.261
2003— Louisville (Int'l)	0	0	...	4.50	1.50	4	0	0	0	...	0-...	4.0	6	2	2	0	0-0	1	.353
— Cincinnati (N.L.)	0	0	...	4.85	1.23	11	0	0	0	0	0-0	13.0	11	7	7	1	5-2	9	.224
Major League totals (1 year)	**0**	**0**	**...**	**4.85**	**1.23**	**11**	**0**	**0**	**0**	**0**	**0-0**	**13.0**	**11**	**7**	**7**	**1**	**5-2**	**9**	**.224**

CHACON, SHAWN   P

PERSONAL: Born December 23, 1977, in Anchorage, Alaska. ... 6-3/212. ... Throws right, bats right. ... Full name: Shawn Anthony Chacon. ... Name pronounced: chah-CONE. ... High school: Greeley (Colo.) Central.

TRANSACTIONS/CAREER NOTES: Selected by Colorado Rockies organization in third round of free-agent draft (June 4, 1996). ... On Colorado disabled list (May 10-June 6, 2002); included rehabilitation assignment to Colorado Springs (May 29-June 6). ... Placed on 15-day disabled list by Colorado (June 30, 2003). ... Sent to Colorado Springs on rehab assignment by Colorado (July 13, 2003). ... Recalled from Colorado Springs rehab assignment; reinstated from 15-day disabled list (July 19, 2003). ... Placed on 15-day disabled list (August 18, 2003).

CAREER HITTING: 20-for-128 (.156), 9 R, 3 2B, 0 3B, 1 HR, 8 RBI.

Year League	W	L	Pct.	ERA	WHIP	G	GS	CG	ShO	Hld.	Sv.-Opp.	IP	H	R	ER	HR	BB-IBB	SO	Avg.
1996— Ariz. Rockies (Ariz.)	1	2	.333	1.60	1.08	11	11	1	0	...	0-...	56.1	46	17	10	1	15-0	64	.209
— Portland (NW)	0	2	.000	6.86	1.68	4	4	0	0	...	0-...	19.2	24	18	15	2	9-0	17	.293
1997— Asheville (S. Atl.)	11	7	.611	3.89	1.35	28	27	1	0	...	0-...	162.0	155	80	70	13	63-1	149	.252
1998— Salem (Caro.)	0	4	.000	5.30	1.50	12	12	0	0	...	0-...	56.0	53	35	33	5	31-0	54	.245
1999— Salem (Caro.)	5	5	.500	4.13	1.43	12	12	0	0	...	0-...	72.0	69	44	33	3	34-0	66	.250
2000— Carolina (Sou.)	10	10	.500	3.16	1.36	27	•27	4	*3	...	0-...	173.2	151	71	61	10	*85-1	*172	.236
2001— Colo. Springs (PCL)	2	0	1.000	2.25	1.04	4	4	0	0	...	0-...	24.0	18	6	6	3	7-0	28	.207
— Colorado (N.L.)	6	10	.375	5.06	1.53	27	27	0	0	0	0-0	160.0	157	96	90	26	87-10	134	.260
2002— Colorado (N.L.)	5	11	.313	5.73	1.53	21	21	0	0	0	0-0	119.1	122	84	76	25	60-3	67	.263
— Colo. Springs (PCL)	2	0	1.000	4.79	1.60	4	4	0	0	...	0-...	20.2	23	12	11	3	10-0	15	.291
2003— Colo. Springs (PCL)	0	0	...	6.00	1.67	1	1	0	0	...	0-...	3.0	5	2	2	1	0-0	2	.385
— Colorado (N.L.)	11	8	.579	4.60	1.33	23	23	0	0	0	0-0	137.0	124	73	70	12	58-4	93	.243
Major League totals (3 years)	**22**	**29**	**.431**	**5.10**	**1.46**	**71**	**71**	**0**	**0**	**0**	**0-0**	**416.1**	**403**	**253**	**236**	**63**	**205-17**	**294**	**.255**

CHAMBLEE, JIM   2B/SS

PERSONAL: Born May 6, 1975, in Denton, Texas. ... 6-4/186. ... Bats right, throws right. ... Full name: James Nathaniel Chamblee. ... High school: Denton High (Texas). ... Junior college: Odessa College (Texas).

TRANSACTIONS/CAREER NOTES: Selected by Boston Red Sox organization in 12th round of free-agent draft (June 1, 1995). ... Granted free agency (October 15, 2001). ... Granted free agency (October 15, 2002). ... Signed by Cincinnati Reds (December 18, 2002). ... Designated for assignment by Cincinnati (August 23, 2003). ... Sent outright to Louisville by Cincinnati (August 27, 2003).

2003 GAMES PLAYED BY POSITION (MLB): 3B—1.

Year Team (League)	Pos.	G	AB	R	H	2B	3B	HR	RBI	BB	SO	HBP	GDP	SB-CS	Avg.	OBP	SLG	OPS	E	Pct.
1995— Utica (N.Y.-Penn)	SS	62	200	36	51	9	1	2	16	23	45	6	5	9-7	.255	.348	.340	.688	30	.892
1996— Michigan (Midw.) SS-OF-3B-P	100	303	31	66	15	2	1	39	16	75	7	1	2-2	.218	.270	.290	.560	27	.935
1997— Michigan (Midw.)	2B-SS	133	487	112	146	29	5	22	73	53	107	17	8	18-4	.300	.384	.515	.900	27	.955
1998— Trenton (East.)	2B-SS-OF	136	489	71	118	33	3	17	65	62	144	16	2	9-5	.241	.349	.425	.769	16	.974
1999— Pawtucket (Int'l)	2B-3B-1B	127	464	84	127	21	3	24	88	43	126	13	4	5-3	.274	.350	.487	.837	18	.966
2000— Pawtucket (Int'l)	OF	127	407	72	105	26	4	17	56	50	129	7	4	8-3	.258	.348	.467	.814	3	.987
2001— Pawtucket (Int'l)	2B-OF	103	378	40	91	22	0	10	32	31	104	6	4	8-5	.241	.308	.378	.686	8	.981
— New Orleans (PCL) 2-3-1-S-O	11	35	3	9	2	0	1	4	4	13	1	1	0-0	.257	.350	.400	.750	1	.981

Year	Team (League)	Pos.	G	AB	R	H	2B	3B	HR	RBI	BB	SO	HBP	GDP	SB-CS	Avg.	OBP	SLG	OPS	E	Pct.
2002— Memphis (PCL)	2B-1B-OF	5	10	1	1	0	0	0	1	1	4	0	0	0-0	.100	.182	.100	.282	0	1.000
— New Haven (East.)	3-1-OF-2	122	434	77	119	32	3	17	72	48	92	8	5	8-2	.274	.355	.479	.834	23	.953
2003— Chattanooga (Sou.)	3-OF-1-D	28	102	16	34	7	0	4	16	9	27	5	1	3-1	.333	.414	.520	.933	1	.988
— Cincinnati (N.L.)	3B	2	2	0	0	0	0	0	0	0	2	0	0	0-0	.000	.000	.000	.000	0	...
— Louisville (Int'l)	3-1-2-O-D	85	263	31	75	13	4	5	35	29	59	5	6	2-0	.285	.366	.422	.788	4	.989
Major League totals (1 year)		2	2	0	0	0	0	0	0	0	2	0	0	0-0	.000	.000	.000	.000	0	...

CHAPMAN, TRAVIS   3B

PERSONAL: Born June 5, 1978, in Jacksonville, Fla. ... 6-2/185. ... Bats right, throws right. ... Full name: Travis A. Chapman. ... High school: Bishop Kenny High (Jacksonville, Fla.). ... College: Mississippi State.

TRANSACTIONS/CAREER NOTES: Selected by Philadelphia Phillies organization in 17th round of free-agent draft (June 5, 2000). ... Selected by Cleveland Indians from Phillies organization in Rule 5 major league draft (December 16, 2002). ... Traded by Indians to Detroit Tigers for cash (December 16, 2002). ... Returned to Phillies (March 26, 2003). ... Contract purchased by Philadelphia from Scranton (September 2, 2003).

2003 GAMES PLAYED BY POSITION (MLB): 3B—1.

Year	Team (League)	Pos.	G	AB	R	H	2B	3B	HR	RBI	BB	SO	HBP	GDP	SB-CS	Avg.	OBP	SLG	OPS	E	Pct.
2000— GC Phillies (GCL)	3B	9	32	3	6	3	1	0	5	4	4	2	0	0-1	.188	.308	.344	.651	1	.967
— Batavia (NY-Penn)	3B	49	174	23	55	10	2	1	28	12	24	7	1	0-1	.316	.379	.414	.793	9	.938
2001— Clearwater (FSL)	3B	96	329	39	101	22	0	4	50	44	39	11	12	3-1	.307	.400	.410	.810	12	.953
— Reading (East.)	3B	7	22	3	4	0	0	1	3	0	5	2	0	0-0	.182	.250	.318	.568	0	1.000
2002— Reading (East.)	3B-1B	136	478	64	144	35	1	15	76	54	77	19	11	3-1	.301	.388	.473	.861	19	.951
2003— Scran./W.B. (I.L.)	3B-DH	134	478	62	130	36	0	12	82	44	97	15	12	2-2	.272	.348	.423	.771	12	.962
— Philadelphia (N.L.)	3B	1	1	0	0	0	0	0	0	0	0	0	0	0-0	.000	.000	.000	.000	0	...
Major League totals (1 year)		1	1	0	0	0	0	0	0	0	0	0	0	0-0	.000	.000	.000	.000	0	...

CHAVEZ, ENDY   OF

PERSONAL: Born February 7, 1978, in Valencia, Venezuela. ... 5-9/170. ... Bats left, throws left. ... Full name: Endy DeJesus Chavez. ... Name pronounced: shah-VEZ. ... High school: Liceo Bataila Carabobo (Venezuela).

TRANSACTIONS/CAREER NOTES: Signed as non-drafted free agent by New York Mets organization (April 29, 1996). ... Selected by Kansas City Royals from Mets organization in Rule 5 major league draft (December 11, 2000). ... Returned to Mets organization (March 30, 2001). ... Traded by Mets to Royals for OF Michael Curry (March 30, 2001). ... Claimed on waivers by Detroit Tigers (December 20, 2001). ... Claimed on waivers by Mets (February 1, 2002). ... Claimed on waivers by Montreal Expos (February 22, 2002).

2003 GAMES PLAYED BY POSITION (MLB): OF—135.

Year	Team (League)	Pos.	G	AB	R	H	2B	3B	HR	RBI	BB	SO	HBP	GDP	SB-CS	Avg.	OBP	SLG	OPS	E	Pct.
1996— Dom. Mets (DSL)	OF	48	164	42	58	11	1	7	29	22	16	...	...	3-...	.354	...	.561	...	3	.963
1997— GC Mets (GCL)	OF	33	119	26	33	6	3	0	15	20	10	0	2	1-2	.277	.379	.378	.757	2	.967
— Kingsport (Appal.)	OF	19	73	16	22	4	0	0	4	13	10	0	2	5-2	.301	.407	.356	.763	2	.957
1998— Kingsport (Appal.)	OF	33	114	26	33	8	4	0	16	17	17	0	1	10-5	.289	.373	.430	.803	2	.941
1999— Capital City (SAL)	OF	73	253	40	64	8	1	0	15	34	36	0	3	20-12	.253	.340	.292	.633	5	.967
— St. Lucie (Fla. St.)	OF	45	183	33	57	8	3	2	18	22	22	0	5	9-3	.311	.383	.421	.804	2	.980
2000— St. Lucie (Fla. St.)	OF	111	433	84	129	20	2	1	43	47	48	0	3	38-16	.298	.364	.360	.725	5	.980
2001— Wichita (Texas)	OF	43	168	27	50	6	1	1	13	16	13	0	1	11-6	.298	.353	.363	.716	1	.990
— Kansas City (A.L.)	OF	29	77	4	16	2	0	0	5	3	8	0	3	0-2	.208	.238	.234	.471	0	1.000
— Omaha (PCL)	OF	23	104	18	35	6	0	0	4	0	13	0	1	4-3	.337	.333	.394	.728	0	1.000
2002— Ottawa (Int'l)	OF	103	405	67	139	28	5	4	41	33	37	0	8	21-13	.343	.392	.467	.858	4	.985
— Montreal (N.L.)	OF	36	125	20	37	8	5	1	9	5	16	0	0	3-5	.296	.321	.464	.785	1	.989
2003— Montreal (N.L.)	OF	141	483	66	121	25	5	5	47	31	59	0	7	18-7	.251	.294	.354	.648	3	.990
American League totals (1 year)		29	77	4	16	2	0	0	5	3	8	0	3	0-2	.208	.238	.234	.471	0	1.000
National League totals (2 years)		177	608	86	158	33	10	6	56	36	75	0	7	21-12	.260	.299	.377	.676	4	.990
Major League totals (3 years)		206	685	90	174	35	10	6	61	39	83	0	10	21-14	.254	.293	.361	.653	4	.991

CHAVEZ, ERIC   3B

PERSONAL: Born December 7, 1977, in Los Angeles, Calif. ... 6-1/206. ... Bats left, throws right. ... Full name: Eric Cesar Chavez. ... Name pronounced: shah-VEZ. ... High school: Mount Carmel (San Diego).

TRANSACTIONS/CAREER NOTES: Selected by Oakland Athletics organization in first round (10th pick overall) of free-agent draft (June 2, 1996). ... On Oakland disabled list (August 21-September 19, 1999); included rehabilitation assignment to Vancouver (September 14-19).

2003 GAMES PLAYED BY POSITION (MLB): 3B—154.

Year	Team (League)	Pos.	G	AB	R	H	2B	3B	HR	RBI	BB	SO	HBP	GDP	SB-CS	Avg.	OBP	SLG	OPS	E	Pct.
1997— Visalia (Calif.)	3B-DH	134	520	61	141	30	3	18	100	37	91	2	20	13-7	.271	.321	.444	.765	* 32	.917
1998— Huntsville (Sou.)	3B-DH	88	335	66	110	27	1	22	86	42	61	1	6	12-4	.328	.402	.612	1.014	14	.935
— Edmonton (PCL)	3B-DH	47	194	38	63	18	0	11	40	12	32	1	4	2-3	.325	.364	.588	.951	7	.935
— Oakland (A.L.)	3B	16	45	6	14	4	1	0	6	3	5	0	1	1-1	.311	.354	.444	.799	0	1.000
1999— Oakland (A.L.)	3B-DH-SS	115	356	47	88	21	2	13	50	46	56	0	7	1-1	.247	.333	.427	.760	9	.961
2000— Oakland (A.L.)	3B-SS-DH	153	501	89	139	23	4	26	86	62	94	1	9	2-2	.277	.355	.495	.850	18	.951
2001— Oakland (A.L.)	3-S-D-1	151	552	91	159	43	0	32	114	41	99	4	7	8-2	.288	.338	.540	.878	12	.972
2002— Oakland (A.L.)	3B-DH-OF	153	585	87	161	31	3	34	109	65	119	1	8	8-3	.275	.348	.513	.860	17	.961
2003— Oakland (A.L.)	3B	156	588	94	166	39	5	29	101	62	89	1	14	8-3	.282	.350	.514	.864	14	.971
Major League totals (6 years)		744	2627	414	727	161	15	134	466	279	462	7	46	28-12	.277	.346	.502	.848	70	.965

CHAVEZ, RAUL   C

PERSONAL: Born March 18, 1973, in Valencia, Venezuela. ... 5-11/210. ... Bats right, throws right. ... Full name: Raul Alexander Chavez.

TRANSACTIONS/CAREER NOTES: Signed as non-drafted free agent by Houston Astros organization (January 10, 1990). ... Traded by Astros with P Dave Veres to Montreal Expos for 3B Sean Berry (December 20, 1995). ... Traded by Expos to Seattle Mariners for OF Robert Perez (May 8, 1998). ... Granted free agency (October 15, 1999). ... Signed by Astros organization (January 5, 2000). ... On disabled list (August 10-19, 2001). ... Sent outright to New Orleans by Houston (April 17, 2003). ... Contract purchased by Houston from New Orleans (August 21, 2003).

2003 GAMES PLAYED BY POSITION (MLB): C—16.

Year Team (League)	Pos.	G	AB	R	H	2B	3B	HR	RBI	BB	SO	HBP	GDP	SB-CS	Avg.	OBP	SLG	OPS	E	Pct.
1990— GC Astros (GCL) ...2B-3B-SS		48	155	23	50	8	1	0	23	7	12	2	7	5-3	.323	.358	.387	.745	9	.954
1991— Burlington (Midw.) ...3B-SS		114	420	54	108	17	0	3	41	25	65	10	13	1-4	.257	.312	.319	.631	41	.914
1992— Asheville (S. Atl.)	C	95	348	37	99	22	1	2	40	16	39	4	11	1-0	.284	.320	.371	.691	13	.976
1993— Osceola (Fla. St.)	C	58	197	13	45	5	1	0	16	8	19	1	12	1-1	.228	.261	.264	.525	5	.986
1994— Jackson (Texas)	C	89	251	17	55	7	0	1	22	17	41	2	5	1-0	.219	.273	.259	.532	9	.986
1995— Jackson (Texas)	C	58	188	16	54	8	0	4	25	8	17	3	7	0-4	.287	.323	.394	.717	5	.987
— Tucson (PCL)	C	32	103	14	27	5	0	0	10	8	13	2	7	0-1	.262	.325	.311	.635	5	.980
1996— Ottawa (Int'l)	C	60	198	15	49	10	0	2	24	11	31	1	7	0-2	.247	.290	.328	.619	4	.990
— Montreal (N.L.)	C	4	5	1	1	0	0	0	0	1	1	0	1	1-0	.200	.333	.200	.533	0	1.000
1997— Ottawa (Int'l)	C-DH	92	310	31	76	17	0	4	46	18	42	4	9	1-3	.245	.293	.339	.631	* 15	.978
— Montreal (N.L.)	C	13	26	0	7	0	0	0	2	0	5	0	0	1-0	.269	.259	.269	.528	0	1.000
1998— Ottawa (Int'l)	C	11	31	2	7	0	0	0	1	5	5	0	1	0-0	.226	.333	.226	.559	0	1.000
— Tacoma (PCL)	C-DH	76	233	27	52	6	0	4	34	22	41	4	7	1-2	.223	.294	.300	.595	6	.990
— Seattle (A.L.)	C	1	1	0	0	0	0	0	0	0	0	0	0	0-0	.000	.000	.000	.000	0	1.000
1999— Tacoma (PCL)	C-D-2-3-S-1	102	354	39	95	20	1	3	40	28	63	6	11	1-3	.268	.331	.356	.687	10	.987
2000— New Orleans (PCL)	C	99	303	31	74	13	0	2	36	34	44	4	12	3-0	.244	.325	.307	.632	8	.987
— Houston (N.L.)	C	14	43	3	11	2	0	1	5	3	6	0	5	0-0	.256	.298	.372	.670	1	.986
2001— New Orleans (PCL)	C-3B-1B	85	278	38	84	17	0	8	40	19	34	7	9	1-1	.302	.361	.450	.810	5	.992
2002— New Orleans (PCL)	C	111	373	24	85	10	0	3	36	21	50	7	11	3-4	.228	.278	.279	.557	7	.991
— Houston (N.L.)	C	2	4	1	1	1	0	0	0	1	0	0	0	0-0	.250	.500	.500	1.000	0	1.000
2003— New Orleans (PCL)	C-3B-DH	101	355	47	97	28	1	6	47	13	43	11	11	0-2	.273	.315	.408	.724	11	.977
— Houston (N.L.)	C	19	37	5	10	1	1	1	4	1	6	0	3	0-0	.270	.289	.432	.722	0	1.000
American League totals (1 year)		1	1	0	0	0	0	0	0	0	0	0	0	0-0	.000	.000	.000	.000	0	1.000
National League totals (5 years)		52	115	10	30	4	1	2	11	6	18	1	9	2-0	.261	.298	.365	.664	1	.995
Major League totals (6 years)		53	116	10	30	4	1	2	11	6	18	1	9	2-0	.259	.296	.362	.658	1	.995

CHEN, BRUCE   P

PERSONAL: Born June 19, 1977, in Panama City, Panama. ... 6-2/210. ... Throws left, bats left. ... Full name: Bruce Kastulo Chen. ... High school: Instituto Panamericano (Panama). ... College: Institute of Panama.

TRANSACTIONS/CAREER NOTES: Signed as non-drafted free agent by Atlanta Braves organization (July 1, 1993). ... Traded by Braves with P Jimmy Osting to Philadelphia Phillies for P Andy Ashby (July 12, 2000). ... Traded by Phillies with P Adam Walker to New York Mets for P Turk Wendell and P Dennis Cook (July 27, 2001). ... Traded by Mets with P Dicky Gonzalez and SS/2B Luis Figueroa to Montreal Expos for P Scott Strickland, OF Matt Watson and P Philip Seibel (April 5, 2002). ... Traded by Expos to Cincinnati Reds for P Jim Brower (June 14, 2002). ... Released by Reds (March 10, 2003). ... Signed by Houston Astros organization (March 14, 2003). ... Designated for assignment by Houston (May 3, 2003). ... Claimed off waivers by Boston (May 7, 2003). ... Recalled from Pawtucket by Boston (May 9, 2003). ... Designated for assignment by Boston Red Sox (May 30, 2003). ... Sent outright to Pawtucket by Boston (June 4, 2003).

CAREER HITTING: 13-for-111 (.117), 4 R, 1 2B, 0 3B, 0 HR, 3 RBI.

Year League	W	L	Pct.	ERA	WHIP	G	GS	CG	ShO	Hld.	Sv.-Opp.	IP	H	R	ER	HR	BB-IBB	SO	Avg.
1994— GC Braves (GCL)	1	4	.200	3.80	1.05	9	7	0	0	...	1-...	42.2	42	21	18	2	3-0	26	.244
1995— Danville (Appal.)	4	4	.500	3.97	1.38	14	13	1	0	...	0-...	70.1	78	42	31	3	19-1	56	.276
1996— Eugene (NW)	4	1	.800	2.27	1.04	11	8	0	0	...	0-...	35.2	23	13	9	1	14-0	55	.173
1997— Macon (S. Atl.)	12	7	.632	3.51	1.12	28	28	1	1	...	0-...	146.1	120	67	57	* 19	44-0	* 182	.222
1998— Greenville (Sou.)	13	7	.650	3.29	1.11	24	23	1	0	...	0-...	139.1	106	57	51	12	48-0	164	.209
— Richmond (Int'l)	2	1	.667	1.88	1.50	4	4	0	0	...	0-...	24.0	17	5	5	1	19-0	29	.205
— Atlanta (N.L.)	2	0	1.000	3.98	1.57	4	4	0	0	0	0-0	20.1	23	9	9	3	9-1	17	.288
1999— Richmond (Int'l)	6	3	.667	3.81	1.27	14	14	0	0	...	0-...	78.0	73	36	33	10	26-0	90	.251
— Atlanta (N.L.)	2	2	.500	5.47	1.27	16	7	0	0	0	0-0	51.0	38	32	31	11	27-3	45	.208
2000— Atlanta (N.L.)	4	0	1.000	2.50	1.36	22	0	0	0	0	0-0	39.2	35	15	11	4	19-2	32	.232
— Richmond (Int'l)	1	0	1.000	0.00	1.00	1	1	0	0	...	0-...	6.0	5	0	0	0	1-0	6	.238
— Philadelphia (N.L.)	3	4	.429	3.63	1.14	15	15	0	0	0	0-0	94.1	81	39	38	14	27-2	80	.232
2001— Philadelphia (N.L.)	4	5	.444	5.00	1.40	16	16	0	0	0	0-0	86.1	90	53	48	19	31-4	79	.262
— Reading (East.)	1	0	1.000	0.00	0.50	1	1	0	0	...	0-...	6.0	3	0	0	0	0-0	7	.136
— Scran./W.B. (I.L.)	1	0	1.000	3.86	1.02	3	3	0	0	...	0-...	18.2	14	8	8	2	5-0	14	.212
— New York (N.L.)	3	2	.600	4.68	1.41	11	11	0	0	0	0-0	59.2	56	37	31	10	28-0	47	.255
2002— New York (N.L.)	0	0	...	0.00	1.50	1	0	0	0	0	0-0	.2	1	0	0	0	0-0	0	.333
— Montreal (N.L.)	2	3	.400	6.99	1.88	15	5	0	0	0	0-0	37.1	47	29	29	9	23-3	43	.303
— Cincinnati (N.L.)	0	2	.000	4.31	1.44	39	1	0	0	4	0-0	39.2	37	24	19	7	20-2	37	.243
2003— Houston (N.L.)	0	0	...	6.00	1.83	11	0	0	0	1	0-0	12.0	14	8	8	2	8-1	8	.311
— Boston (A.L.)	0	1	.000	5.11	1.14	5	2	0	0	0	0-0	12.1	12	8	7	4	2-0	12	.255
— Pawtucket (Int'l)	5	5	.500	4.24	1.12	16	15	1	1	...	1-...	85.0	80	44	40	12	15-1	73	.244
American League totals (1 year)	0	1	.000	5.11	1.14	5	2	0	0	0	0-0	12.1	12	8	7	4	2-0	12	.255
National League totals (6 years)	20	18	.526	4.57	1.39	150	59	0	0	5	0-0	441.0	422	246	224	79	192-18	388	.251
Major League totals (6 years)	20	19	.513	4.59	1.39	155	61	0	0	5	0-0	453.1	434	254	231	83	194-18	400	.251

CHEN, CHIN-FENG   OF

PERSONAL: Born October 28, 1977, in Tainan City, Taiwan. ... 6-1/189. ... Bats right, throws right.

TRANSACTIONS/CAREER NOTES: Signed as non-drafted free agent by Los Angeles Dodgers organization (January 5, 1999). ... Recalled by Los Angeles from Las Vegas (July 11, 2003). ... Optioned to Las Vegas by Los Angeles (July 17, 2003).

Year Team (League)	Pos.	G	AB	R	H	2B	3B	HR	RBI	BB	SO	HBP	GDP	SB-CS	Avg.	OBP	SLG	OPS	E	Pct.
1999— San Bern. (Calif.)	OF	131	510	98	161	22	10	31	• 123	75	129	5	7	31-7	.316	.404	.580	.984	6	.971
2000— San Antonio (Texas)	OF	133	516	66	143	27	3	6	67	61	131	3	7	23-15	.277	.355	.376	.731	3	.988
2001— Vero Beach (FSL)	OF	62	235	38	63	15	3	5	41	28	56	6	3	2-0	.268	.359	.421	.781	0	1.000
— Jacksonville (Sou.)	OF	66	224	47	70	16	2	17	50	41	65	2	7	5-4	.313	.422	.629	1.051	3	.966
2002— Las Vegas (PCL)	1B-OF	137	511	90	145	26	4	26	84	58	160	0	19	6-0	.284	.352	.503	.855	11	.988
— Los Angeles (N.L.)	OF	3	5	1	0	0	0	0	0	1	3	0	0	0-0	.000	.167	.000	.167	0	1.000
2003— Los Angeles (N.L.)		1	1	0	0	0	0	0	0	0	0	0	0	0-0	.000	.000	.000	.000	0	...
— Las Vegas (PCL)	OF-1B-DH	133	474	84	133	30	5	26	86	59	106	2	15	6-4	.281	.360	.530	.889	11	.963
Major League totals (2 years)		4	6	1	0	0	0	0	0	1	3	0	0	0-0	.000	.143	.000	.143	0	1.000

C

CHOATE, RANDY · P

PERSONAL: Born September 5, 1975, in San Antonio, Texas. ... 6-2/190. ... Throws left, bats left. ... Full name: Randol Doyol Choate. ... Name pronounced: chote. ... High school: Winston Churchill (San Antonio). ... College: Florida State.

TRANSACTIONS/CAREER NOTES: Selected by New York Yankees organization in fifth round of free-agent draft (June 3, 1997). ... Recalled by New York Yankees from Columbus (April 19, 2003). ... Optioned to Columbus by New York (May 14, 2003). ... Recalled by New York from Columbus (September 29, 2003).

CAREER HITTING: 0-for-4 (.000), 0 R, 0 2B, 0 3B, 0 HR, 0 RBI.

Year League	W	L	Pct.	ERA	WHIP	G	GS	CG	ShO	Hld.	Sv.-Opp.	IP	H	R	ER	HR	BB-IBB	SO	Avg.
1997— Oneonta (N.Y.-Penn)	5	1	.833	1.73	0.98	10	10	0	0	...	0-...	62.1	49	12	12	1	12-1	61	.216
1998— Tampa (FSL)	1	8	.111	5.27	1.50	13	13	0	0	...	0-...	70.0	83	57	41	6	22-2	55	.290
— Greensboro (S. Atl.)	1	5	.167	3.00	1.36	8	8	1	0	...	0-...	39.0	46	21	13	1	7-0	32	.293
1999— Tampa (FSL)	2	2	.500	4.50	1.50	47	0	0	0	...	1-...	50.0	51	25	25	4	24-5	62	.263
2000— Columbus (Int'l)	2	0	1.000	2.04	1.36	33	0	0	0	...	1-...	35.1	34	8	8	2	14-3	37	.254
— New York (A.L.)	0	0	.000	4.76	1.29	22	0	0	0	2	0-0	17.0	14	10	9	3	8-0	12	.215
2001— New York (A.L.)	3	1	.750	3.35	1.26	37	0	0	0	3	0-0	48.1	34	21	18	0	27-2	35	.202
— Columbus (Int'l)	1	1	.500	2.08	2.31	4	0	0	0	...		4.1	7	1	1	0	3-0	4	.389
2002— Columbus (Int'l)	3	2	.600	1.72	1.09	31	0	0	0	...	1-...	36.2	25	8	7	0	15-1	32	.189
— New York (A.L.)	0	0	...	6.04	1.48	18	0	0	0	0	0-0	22.1	18	18	15	1	15-0	17	.217
2003— New York (A.L.)	0	0	...	7.36	2.18	5	0	0	0	0	0-0	3.2	7	3	3	0	1-0	0	.467
— Columbus (Int'l)	3	5	.375	3.91	1.39	54	3	0	0	...	1-...	71.1	75	35	31	4	24-3	56	.271
Major League totals (4 years)	3	2	.600	4.43	1.36	82	0	0	0	5	0-0	91.1	73	52	45	4	51-2	64	.221

CHOI, HEE SEOP · 1B

PERSONAL: Born March 16, 1979, in Chun-Nam, South Korea. ... 6-5/240. ... Bats left, throws left. ... Name pronounced: hee sop choy. ... High school: Kwang-Ju Jae (Kwang-Ju, Korea). ... College: Korea University.

TRANSACTIONS/CAREER NOTES: Signed as non-drafted free agent by Chicago Cubs organization (March 8, 1999). ... On disabled list (May 24-June 17 and June 25-August 3, 2001). ... Placed on the 15-day disabled list (June 8, 2003). ... Sent to Iowa for rehab assignment by Chicago (June 23, 2003). ... Recalled from Iowa by Chicago; reinstated from 15-day disabled list by Chicago (June 30, 2003). ... Optioned to Iowa by Chicago (August 17, 2003). ... Recalled by Chicago from Iowa (September 2, 2003).

2003 GAMES PLAYED BY POSITION (MLB): 1B—69.

								BATTING												FIELDING	
Year Team (League)	Pos.	G	AB	R	H	2B	3B	HR	RBI	BB	SO	HBP	GDP	SB-CS	Avg.	OBP	SLG	OPS	E	Pct.
1999— Lansing (Midw.)	1B	79	290	71	93	18	6	18	70	50	68	2	8	2-1	.321	.422	.610	1.032	18	.976
2000— Daytona (Fla. St.)	1B	96	345	60	102	25	6	15	70	37	78	6	7	4-1	.296	.369	.533	.902	4	.995
— West Tenn (Sou.)	1B	36	122	25	37	9	0	10	25	25	38	0	5	3-1	.303	.419	.623	1.042	1	.997
2001— Iowa (PCL)	1B	77	266	38	61	11	0	13	45	34	67	0	5	5-1	.229	.313	.417	.730	3	.995
2002— Iowa (PCL)	1B	135	478	94	137	24	3	26	97	*95	119	6	6	3-2	.287	.406	.513	.919	12	.991
— Chicago (N.L.)	1B	24	50	6	9	1	0	2	4	7	15	0	2	0-0	.180	.281	.320	.601	2	.983
2003— Iowa (PCL)	1B	18	66	12	17	4	1	6	16	9	19	1	2	0-1	.258	.351	.621	.972	0	1.000
— Chicago (N.L.)	1B	80	202	31	44	17	0	8	28	37	71	4	2	1-1	.218	.350	.421	.771	5	.991
Major League totals (2 years)		104	252	37	53	18	0	10	32	44	86	4	4	1-1	.210	.337	.401	.737	7	.990

CHRISTENSON, RYAN · OF

PERSONAL: Born March 28, 1974, in Redlands, Calif. ... 6-0/190. ... Bats right, throws right. ... Full name: Ryan Alan Christenson. ... High school: Apple Valley (Calif.). ... College: Pepperdine.

TRANSACTIONS/CAREER NOTES: Selected by Oakland Athletics organization in 10th round of free-agent draft (June 1, 1995). ... On Sacramento disabled list (May 20-June 9, 2001). ... Traded by A's to Arizona Diamondbacks for OF Rob Ryan (June 19, 2001). ... Selected by Milwaukee Brewers from Diamondbacks organization in Rule 5 major league draft (December 13, 2001). ... On Indianapolis disabled list (June 24-August 14, 2002). ... Released by Brewers (October 15, 2002). ... Signed by Texas Rangers organization (January 16, 2003). ... Contract purchased by Texas Rangers (April 16, 2003). ... Sent outright to Oklahoma of the Pacific Coast League (June 7, 2003). ... Contract purchased by Texas from Oklahoma (September 1, 2003).

2003 GAMES PLAYED BY POSITION (MLB): OF—59.

								BATTING											FIELDING	
Year Team (League)	Pos.	G	AB	R	H	2B	3B	HR	RBI	BB	SO	HBP	GDP	SB-CS	Avg.	OBP	SLG	OPS	E	Pct.
1995— S. Oregon (N'west)	OF	49	158	14	30	4	1	1	16	22	33	0	3	5-5	.190	.286	.247	.533	2	.954
1996— S. Oregon (N'west)	OF	36	136	31	39	11	0	5	21	19	21	1	3	8-6	.287	.376	.478	.854	4	.954
— W. Mich. (Mid.)	3B-OF	33	122	21	38	2	2	2	18	13	22	4	2	2-4	.311	.387	.410	.797	3	.956
1997— Visalia (Calif.)	OF	83	308	69	90	18	8	13	54	70	72	2	4	20-11	.292	.425	.529	.954	3	.982
— Huntsville (Sou.)	OF	29	120	39	44	9	3	2	18	24	23	0	3	5-4	.367	.469	.542	1.011	1	.988
— Edmonton (PCL)	OF	16	49	12	14	2	2	2	5	11	11	2	1	2-0	.286	.435	.531	.966	0	1.000
1998— Edmonton (PCL)	OF	22	88	17	23	6	1	1	7	15	24	0	1	4-1	.261	.365	.386	.752	0	1.000
— Oakland (A.L.)	OF	117	370	56	95	22	2	5	40	36	106	1	1	5-6	.257	.321	.368	.689	5	.983
1999— Oakland (A.L.)	OF-DH	106	268	41	56	12	1	4	24	38	58	1	6	7-5	.209	.305	.366	.611	7	.978
— Vancouver (PCL)	OF	33	128	30	44	8	1	1	16	22	21	0	4	7-2	.344	.440	.445	.885	2	.978
2000— Oakland (A.L.)	OF	121	129	31	32	2	2	4	18	19	33	1	1	1-2	.248	.349	.388	.737	5	.951
2001— Oakland (A.L.)	OF-DH	7	4	1	0	0	0	0	0	0	1	0	0	0-0	.000	.000	.000	.000	0	1.000
— Sacramento (PCL)	OF	19	70	7	12	4	0	1	3	4	13	0	1	2-0	.171	.216	.271	.488	0	1.000
— Arizona (N.L.)	OF	19	4	3	1	1	0	0	1	1	1	0	0	1-0	.250	.400	.500	.900	0	1.000
— Tucson (PCL)	OF	57	215	32	62	17	0	6	27	23	43	0	4	5-2	.288	.353	.451	.804	7	.950
2002— Indianapolis (Int'l)	OF	67	260	38	66	17	2	5	30	18	28	2	5	11-5	.254	.306	.392	.698	0	1.000
— Ariz. Brewers (Ariz.)	OF	4	10	1	4	2	0	0	2	0	2	0	0	0-0	.400	.364	.600	.964	0	1.000
— Milwaukee (N.L.)	OF	22	58	5	9	4	0	1	3	5	13	0	1	0-0	.155	.222	.276	.498	0	1.000
2003— Oklahoma (PCL)	OF	52	195	30	61	15	1	5	24	28	45	1	6	11-1	.313	.400	.477	.877	0	1.000
— Texas (A.L.)	OF	60	165	22	29	7	0	2	16	15	44	3	3	2-2	.176	.255	.255	.510	0	1.000
American League totals (5 years)		411	936	151	212	43	5	15	98	108	242	6	11	15-15	.226	.308	.331	.639	17	.978
National League totals (2 years)		41	62	8	10	5	0	1	4	6	14	0	1	1-0	.161	.235	.290	.526	0	1.000
Major League totals (6 years)		452	998	159	222	48	5	16	102	114	256	6	12	16-15	.222	.303	.329	.632	17	.979

CHRISTIANSEN, JASON · P

PERSONAL: Born September 21, 1969, in Omaha, Neb. ... 6-5/241. ... Throws left, bats right. ... Full name: Jason Samuel Christiansen. ... High school: Elkhorn (Neb.). ... Junior college: Iowa Western College.

TRANSACTIONS/CAREER NOTES: Signed as non-drafted free agent by Pittsburgh Pirates organization (July 5, 1991). ... On Calgary disabled list (August 12-September 5, 1996). ... On Pittsburgh disabled list (March 31-June 19, 1997). ... On Pittsburgh disabled list (May 7-28, July 29-August 21 and August 24-September 23, 1999); included rehabilitation assignments to Altoona (May 22-28) and Nashville (August 16-21). ... Traded by Pirates to St. Louis Cardinals for SS Jack Wilson (July 30, 2000). ... On St. Louis disabled list (March 23-May 7, 2001); included rehabilitation assignment to Memphis (April 17-May 7). ... Traded by Cardinals to San Francisco Giants for P Kevin Joseph and a player to be named later or cash (July 31, 2001). ... Granted free agency (November 6, 2001). ... Re-signed by Giants (December 5, 2001). ... On disabled list (April 16, 2002-remainder of season). ... On San Francisco disabled list (March 25, 2003); included rehabilitation assignment to San Jose (April 9). ... Recalled by San Francisco from Fresno (April 13, 2003). ... Recalled from Fresno rehab assignment by San Francisco; reinstated from 15-day disabled list (June 3, 2003).

CAREER HITTING: 1-for-10 (.100), 0 R, 0 2B, 0 3B, 0 HR, 1 RBI.

Year League	W	L	Pct.	ERA	WHIP	G	GS	CG	ShO	Hld.	Sv.-Opp.	IP	H	R	ER	HR	BB-IBB	SO	Avg.
1991— GC Pirates (GCL)	1	0	1.000	0.00	0.63	6	0	0	0	...	1-...	8.0	4	0	0	0	1-0	8	.143
— Welland (N.Y.-Penn)	0	1	.000	2.53	1.27	8	1	0	0	...	0-...	21.1	15	9	6	1	12-1	17	.208
1992— Augusta (S. Atl.)	1	0	1.000	1.80	1.00	10	0	0	0	...	2-...	20.0	12	4	4	0	8-0	21	.194
— Salem (Caro.)	3	1	.750	3.24	1.38	38	0	0	0	...	2-...	50.0	47	20	18	7	22-2	59	.254
1993— Salem (Caro.)	1	1	.500	3.15	1.01	57	0	0	0	...	4-...	71.1	48	30	25	5	24-2	70	.190
— Carolina (Sou.)	0	0	...	0.00	1.50	2	0	0	0	...	0-...	2.2	3	0	0	0	1-0	2	.273
1994— Carolina (Sou.)	2	1	.667	2.09	1.14	28	0	0	0	...	2-...	38.2	30	10	9	2	14-1	43	.216
— Buffalo (A.A.)	3	1	.750	2.41	1.04	33	0	0	0	...	0-...	33.2	19	9	9	3	16-0	39	.168
1995— Pittsburgh (N.L.)	1	3	.250	4.15	1.47	63	0	0	0	12	0-4	56.1	49	28	26	5	34-9	53	.234
1996— Pittsburgh (N.L.)	3	3	.500	6.70	1.69	33	0	0	0	2	0-2	44.1	56	34	33	7	19-2	38	.311
— Calgary (PCL)	1	0	1.000	3.27	0.91	2	2	0	0	...	0-...	11.0	9	4	4	1	1-0	10	.237
1997— Pittsburgh (N.L.)	0	1	.000	4.20	1.47	8	1	0	0	...	1-...	15.0	17	7	7	1	5-0	25	.293
— Pittsburgh (N.L.)	3	0	1.000	2.94	1.60	39	0	0	0	8	0-2	33.2	37	11	11	2	17-3	37	.274
1998— Pittsburgh (N.L.)	3	3	.500	2.51	1.21	60	• 0	0	0	15	6-10	64.2	51	22	18	2	27-7	71	.216
1999— Pittsburgh (N.L.)	2	3	.400	4.06	1.27	39	0	0	0	7	3-5	37.2	26	17	17	2	22-4	35	.197
— Altoona (East.)	0	0	...	0.00	0.67	2	1	0	0	...	0-...	3.0	1	0	0	0	1-0	2	.100
— Nashville (PCL)	0	0	...	0.00	0.00	2	0	0	0	...	0-...	2.0	0	0	0	0	0-0	1	.000
2000— Pittsburgh (N.L.)	2	8	.200	4.97	1.39	44	0	0	0	13	1-3	38.0	28	22	21	2	25-4	41	.207
— St. Louis (N.L.)	1	0	1.000	5.40	1.50	21	0	0	0	9	0-1	10.0	13	7	6	1	2-1	12	.317
2001— Memphis (PCL)	0	0	...	2.25	1.13	7	1	0	0	...	0-...	8.0	9	2	2	0	0-0	9	.281
— St. Louis (N.L.)	1	1	.500	4.66	1.29	30	0	0	0	4	3-3	19.1	15	10	10	4	10-1	19	.211
— San Francisco (N.L.)	1	0	1.000	1.59	1.12	25	0	0	0	7	0-1	17.0	14	3	3	1	5-0	12	.241
2002— San Francisco (N.L.)	0	1	.000	5.40	1.60	6	0	0	0	1	0-0	5.0	6	3	3	1	2-0	1	.316
2003— San Jose (Calif.)	0	0	...	1.93	1.71	5	1	0	0	...	0-...	4.2	5	1	1	0	3-0	2	.313
— Fresno (PCL)	0	0	...	5.40	1.20	4	1	0	0	...	0-...	5.0	5	3	3	0	1-0	2	.263
— San Francisco (N.L.)	0	0	...	5.19	1.38	40	0	0	0	7	0-1	26.0	25	15	15	3	11-0	22	.243
Major League totals (9 years)	**17**	**22**	**.436**	**4.17**	**1.40**	**400**	**0**	**0**	**0**	**84**	**13-32**	**352.0**	**320**	**172**	**163**	**30**	**174-31**	**341**	**.243**

CHULK, VINNIE — P

PERSONAL: Born December 19, 1978, in Miami, Fla. ... 6-2/195. ... Throws right, bats right. ... Full name: Charles Vincent Chulk. ... College: St. Thomas (Fla.).
TRANSACTIONS/CAREER NOTES: Selected by Toronto Blue Jays in 12th round of free-agent draft (June 2001).
CAREER HITTING: 0-for-0 (.000), 0 R, 0 2B, 0 3B, 0 HR, 0 RBI.

Year League	W	L	Pct.	ERA	WHIP	G	GS	CG	ShO	Hld.	Sv.-Opp.	IP	H	R	ER	HR	BB-IBB	SO	Avg.
2000— Medicine Hat (Pio.)	2	4	.333	3.80	1.38	14	13	0	0	...	0-...	68.2	75	36	29	5	20-0	51	.277
2001— Syracuse (Int'l)	1	0	1.000	1.50	1.50	5	0	0	0	...	0-...	6.0	5	1	1	0	4-0	3	.238
— Dunedin (Fla. St.)	1	2	.333	3.12	1.47	16	1	0	0	...	1-...	34.2	38	16	12	2	13-1	50	.271
— Tennessee (Sou.)	2	5	.286	3.14	0.98	24	1	0	0	...	2-...	43.0	34	15	15	5	8-1	43	.227
2002— Tennessee (Sou.)	13	5	.722	2.96	1.22	25	24	0	0	...	1-...	152.0	133	55	50	12	53-0	108	.236
— Syracuse (Int'l)	0	1	.000	5.79	2.57	2	1	0	0	...	0-...	4.2	6	6	3	0	6-0	2	.316
2003— Syracuse (Int'l)	8	10	.444	4.22	1.37	23	21	1	0	...	0-...	119.1	118	70	56	14	46-0	90	.256
— Toronto (A.L.)	0	0	...	5.06	1.69	3	0	0	0	0	0-1	5.1	6	3	3	0	3-0	2	.273
Major League totals (1 year)	**0**	**0**	**...**	**5.06**	**1.69**	**3**	**0**	**0**	**0**	**0**	**0-1**	**5.1**	**6**	**3**	**3**	**0**	**3-0**	**2**	**.273**

CINTRON, ALEX — SS

PERSONAL: Born December 17, 1978, in Humacao, Puerto Rico. ... 6-2/199. ... Bats both, throws right. ... Full name: Alexander Cintron. ... Name pronounced: SIN-tron. ... High school: Mech-Tech (Caguas, Puerto Rico).
TRANSACTIONS/CAREER NOTES: Selected by Arizona Diamondbacks organization in 36th round of free-agent draft (June 3, 1997). ... On Tucson disabled list (April 30-May 8, 2001). ... Recalled by Arizona from Tucson (May 7, 2003).
2003 GAMES PLAYED BY POSITION (MLB): SS—93, 3B—16, 2B—9.

Year Team (League)	Pos.	G	AB	R	H	2B	3B	HR	RBI	BB	SO	HBP	GDP	SB-CS	Avg.	OBP	SLG	OPS	E	Pct.
1997— Ariz. D'backs (Ariz.)	SS	43	152	23	30	6	1	0	20	21	32	2	3	1-4	.197	.301	.250	.551	15	.931
— Lethbridge (Pio.)	SS	1	3	0	1	0	0	0	0	0	1	0	0	0-0	.333	.333	.333	.667	1	.857
1998— Lethbridge (Pio.)	SS	67	258	41	68	11	4	3	34	20	32	2	8	8-4	.264	.319	.372	.691	27	.921
1999— High Desert (Calif.)	SS	128	499	78	153	25	4	3	64	19	65	3	14	15-8	.307	.333	.391	.724	28	.950
2000— El Paso (Texas)	SS	125	522	83	157	30	6	4	59	29	56	2	22	9-9	.301	.336	.404	.740	32	.950
2001— Tucson (PCL)	SS-2B	107	425	53	124	24	3	3	35	15	48	2	12	9-6	.292	.315	.384	.698	‡ 32	.936
— Arizona (N.L.)	SS	8	7	0	2	0	1	0	0	0	0	0	0	0-0	.286	.286	.571	.857	0	1.000
2002— Tucson (PCL)	SS-2B	85	351	53	113	22	3	4	26	11	33	2	8	9-5	.322	.345	.436	.781	14	.960
— Arizona (N.L.)	2B-3B-SS	38	75	11	16	6	0	0	4	12	13	0	2	0-0	.213	.322	.293	.615	1	.989
2003— Tucson (PCL)	SS-2B	26	107	21	42	11	2	2	21	8	6	0	0	1-0	.393	.435	.589	1.024	4	.970
— Arizona (N.L.)	SS-3B-2B	117	448	70	142	26	6	13	51	29	33	2	7	2-3	.317	.359	.489	.848	11	.976
Major League totals (3 years)		**163**	**530**	**81**	**160**	**32**	**7**	**13**	**55**	**41**	**46**	**2**	**9**	**2-3**	**.302**	**.352**	**.462**	**.815**	**12**	**.978**

CIRILLO, JEFF — 3B

PERSONAL: Born September 23, 1969, in Pasadena, Calif. ... 6-1/200. ... Bats right, throws right. ... Full name: Jeffrey Howard Cirillo. ... Name pronounced: suh-RILL-oh. ... High school: Providence (Burbank, Calif.). ... College: USC.
TRANSACTIONS/CAREER NOTES: Selected by Chicago Cubs organization in 37th round of free-agent draft (June 2, 1987); did not sign. ... Selected by Milwaukee Brewers organization in 11th round of free-agent draft (June 3, 1991). ... On New Orleans disabled list (July 22-August 6, 1993). ... Traded by Brewers with P Scott Karl and cash to Colorado Rockies as part of three-way deal in which Brewers received P Jamey Wright and C Henry Blanco from Rockies, Oakland Athletics received P Justin Miller and cash from Rockies and Brewers received P Jimmy Haynes from A's (December 13, 1999). ... On Colorado disabled list (April 27-May 13, 2001); included rehabilitation assignment to Colorado Springs (May 12-13). ... Traded by Rockies to Seattle Mariners for P Jose Paniagua, P Dennis Stark and P Brian Fuentes (December 15, 2001). ... Placed on 15-day disabled list (July 24, 2003). ... Sent to Arizona League Mariners on rehab assignment by Seattle (July 29, 2003). ... Recalled from Arizona League Mariners rehab assignment (August 17, 2003). ... Removed from 15-day disabled list (August 19, 2003).
2003 GAMES PLAYED BY POSITION (MLB): 3B—85, DH—1, 1B—1.

									BATTING											FIELDING	
Year	Team (League)	Pos.	G	AB	R	H	2B	3B	HR	RBI	BB	SO	HBP	GDP	SB-CS	Avg.	OBP	SLG	OPS	E	Pct.
1991—	Helena (Pio.)	3B-OF	• 70	286	60	100	16	2	10	51	31	28	4	11	3-1	.350	.418	.524	.942	15	.921
1992—	Stockton (Calif.)	3B	7	27	2	6	1	0	0	5	2	0	2	2	0-0	.222	.323	.259	.582	0	1.000
	— Beloit (Midw.)	2B-3B	126	444	65	135	27	3	9	71	84	85	6	7	21-12	.304	.417	.439	.856	26	.942
1993—	El Paso (Texas)	2B-3B	67	249	53	85	16	2	9	41	26	37	5	5	2-3	.341	.410	.530	.940	9	.962
	— New Orleans (A.A.)	3B-2B-SS	58	215	31	63	13	2	3	32	29	33	3	7	2-1	.293	.385	.414	.799	5	.974
1994—	New Orleans (A.A.)	3-2-SS-DH	61	236	45	73	18	2	10	46	28	39	2	9	4-0	.309	.386	.530	.915	8	.963
	— Milwaukee (A.L.)	3B-2B	39	126	17	30	9	0	3	12	11	16	2	4	0-1	.238	.309	.381	.690	3	.965
1995—	Milwaukee (A.L.)	3-2-1-SS	125	328	57	91	19	4	9	39	47	42	4	8	7-2	.277	.371	.442	.813	15	.958
1996—	Milwaukee (A.L.)	3-DH-1-2	158	566	101	184	46	5	15	83	58	69	7	14	4-9	.325	.391	.504	.894	‡ 18	.963
1997—	Milwaukee (A.L.)	3B-DH	154	580	74	167	46	2	10	82	60	74	14	13	4-3	.288	.367	.426	.793	17	.963
1998—	Milwaukee (N.L.)	3B-1B	156	604	97	194	31	1	14	68	79	88	4	*26	10-4	.321	.402	.445	.847	11	.979
1999—	Milwaukee (N.L.)	3B	157	607	98	198	35	1	15	88	75	83	5	15	7-4	.326	.401	.461	.862	15	.967
2000—	Colorado (N.L.)	3B	157	598	111	195	53	2	11	115	67	72	6	19	3-4	.326	.392	.477	.869	15	.964
2001—	Colorado (N.L.)	3B	138	528	72	165	26	4	17	83	43	63	5	15	12-2	.313	.364	.473	.838	7	.982
	— Colo. Springs (PCL)		1	4	2	3	1	0	0	3	1	0	0	0	0-0	.750	.800	1.000	1.800	0	1.000
2002—	Seattle (A.L.)	3B-1B	146	485	51	121	20	0	6	54	31	67	9	12	8-4	.249	.301	.328	.629	9	.976
2003—	Ariz. Mariners (Ariz.)	DH-3B	6	20	2	6	0	0	0	0	4	1	1	1	0-1	.300	.440	.300	.740	0	1.000
	— Inland Empire (Calif.)	3B-DH	5	15	1	3	1	0	0	1	3	1	0	1	0-0	.200	.333	.267	.600	1	.833
	— Tacoma (PCL)	3B-DH	5	17	7	6	3	0	2	6	3	3	1	0	0-0	.353	.476	.882	1.359	0	1.000
	— Seattle (A.L.)	3B-DH-1B	87	258	24	53	11	0	2	23	24	32	5	6	1-1	.205	.284	.271	.555	4	.978
	American League totals (6 years)		709	2343	324	646	151	11	45	293	231	300	41	57	24-20	.276	.348	.407	.755	66	.964
	National League totals (4 years)		608	2337	378	752	145	8	57	354	264	306	20	75	32-14	.322	.391	.464	.855	48	.973
	Major League totals (10 years)		1317	4680	702	1398	296	19	102	647	495	606	61	132	56-34	.299	.369	.435	.805	114	.968

C

CLARK, BRADY   OF

PERSONAL: Born April 18, 1973, in Portland, Ore. ... 6-2/195. ... Bats right, throws right. ... Full name: Brady William Clark. ... High school: Sunset (Beaverton, Ore.). ... College: San Diego.

TRANSACTIONS/CAREER NOTES: Signed as non-drafted free agent by Cincinnati Reds organization (January 13, 1996). ... Released by Reds (April 10, 1996). ... Re-signed by Reds organization (February 15, 1997). ... On Louisville disabled list (June 20-July 11 and August 22-29, 2002). ... Traded by Reds to New York Mets (September 9, 2002), completing deal in which Reds traded P Pedro Feliciano, OF Elvin Andujar and two players to be named later to Mets for P Shawn Estes (August 15, 2002). Mets acquired OF Raul Gonzalez as partial completion (August 20, 2002). ... Claimed on waivers by Milwaukee Brewers (January 21, 2003). ... On Milwaukee disabled list (March 21-April 15, 2003); included rehabilitation assignment to Indianapolis (April 3-15).

2003 GAMES PLAYED BY POSITION (MLB): OF—105.

									BATTING											FIELDING	
Year	Team (League)	Pos.	G	AB	R	H	2B	3B	HR	RBI	BB	SO	HBP	GDP	SB-CS	Avg.	OBP	SLG	OPS	E	Pct.
1997—	Burlington (Midw.)	OF	126	459	108	149	29	7	11	63	76	71	4	10	31-18	.325	.423	.490	.913	4	.986
1998—	Chattanooga (Sou.)	OF	64	222	41	60	13	1	2	16	31	34	4	11	12-4	.270	.370	.365	.735	1	.993
1999—	Chattanooga (Sou.)	OF-3B	* 138	506	103	165	37	4	17	75	89	58	2	6	25-17	.326	.425	.516	.941	5	.981
2000—	Louisville (Int'l)	OF	132	487	90	148	* 41	6	16	79	72	51	9	14	12-8	.304	.397	.511	.908	6	.981
	— Cincinnati (N.L.)	OF	11	11	1	3	1	0	0	2	0	2	0	0	0-0	.273	.273	.364	.636	0	1.000
2001—	Louisville (Int'l)	OF	49	167	24	44	5	1	2	18	18	17	6	5	6-2	.263	.354	.341	.695	2	.981
	— Cincinnati (N.L.)	OF-DH	89	129	22	34	3	0	6	18	22	16	1	6	4-1	.264	.373	.426	.799	1	.981
2002—	Cincinnati (N.L.)	OF	51	66	6	10	3	0	0	9	6	9	1	2	1-2	.152	.233	.197	.430	1	.938
	— Louisville (Int'l)	OF-3B	25	109	17	33	7	0	1	17	3	9	2	3	0-2	.303	.328	.394	.722	3	.955
	— New York (N.L.)	OF	10	12	3	5	1	0	0	1	1	2	0	0	0-0	.417	.462	.500	.962	0	1.000
2003—	Indianapolis (Int'l)	OF-DH	9	34	4	9	3	0	0	3	2	6	0	3	1-0	.265	.306	.353	.658	0	1.000
	— Milwaukee (N.L.)	OF	128	315	33	86	21	1	6	40	21	40	9	12	13-2	.273	.330	.403	.733	5	.973
	Major League totals (4 years)		289	533	65	138	29	1	12	70	50	69	11	20	18-5	.259	.331	.385	.715	7	.973

CLARK, HOWIE   OF

PERSONAL: Born February 13, 1974, in San Diego, Calif. ... 5-10/191. ... Bats left, throws right. ... Full name: Howard Roddy Clark. ... High school: Huntington Beach (Calif.).

TRANSACTIONS/CAREER NOTES: Selected by Baltimore Orioles organization in 27th round of free-agent draft (June 1, 1992). ... Granted free agency (October 15, 1999). ... Re-signed by Orioles organization (December 4, 1999). ... Granted free agency (October 15, 2000). ... Signed by Yucatan, Mexican League (April 2001). ... Signed by Chico, Western League (August 2001). ... Signed by Orioles organization (October 8, 2001). ... Granted free agency (October 15, 2002). ... Signed by Toronto Blue Jays organization (November 5, 2002). ... Recalled by Toronto from Syracuse of the International League (May 26, 2003). ... Optioned to Syracuse by Toronto (June 25, 2003). ... Recalled by Toronto from Syracuse (July 1, 2003). ... Optioned to Syracuse by Toronto (July 27, 2003). ... Recalled by Toronto from Syracuse (September 2, 2003).

2003 GAMES PLAYED BY POSITION (MLB): 3B—13, DH—7, OF—5, 2B—3, 1B—2, SS—1.

									BATTING											FIELDING	
Year	Team (League)	Pos.	G	AB	R	H	2B	3B	HR	RBI	BB	SO	HBP	GDP	SB-CS	Avg.	OBP	SLG	OPS	E	Pct.
1992—	GC Orioles (GCL)	2B-3B-1B	43	138	12	33	7	1	0	6	12	21	2	2	1-2	.239	.309	.304	.614	7	.948
1993—	Albany (S. Atl.)	2B	7	17	2	4	0	0	0	1	0	3	0	1	1-0	.235	.235	.235	.471	2	.833
	— Bluefield (Appal.)	2B-OF-1B	58	180	29	53	10	1	3	30	26	34	4	4	2-2	.294	.388	.411	.799	10	.900
1994—	Albany (S. Atl.)	1B-2B	108	353	56	95	22	7	2	47	51	58	7	7	5-4	.269	.371	.388	.759	14	.978
	— Frederick (Carolina)	2B	2	7	1	1	1	0	0	0	0	2	0	1	0-0	.143	.143	.286	.429	0	1.000
1995—	High Desert (Calif.)	3-2-0-S-C-1	109	329	50	85	20	2	5	40	32	51	4	4	12-6	.258	.329	.377	.706	21	.920
1996—	Bowie (East.)	2-0-3-S-C-1	127	449	55	122	29	3	4	52	59	54	2	8	2-8	.272	.354	.376	.730	14	.975
1997—	Bowie (East.)	3B-2B-1B	105	314	39	90	16	0	9	37	32	38	1	5	2-2	.287	.351	.424	.775	20	.909
1998—	Bowie (East.)	OF-2-1-3	88	276	37	79	16	0	9	45	29	42	3	7	1-1	.286	.359	.442	.801	6	.954
	— Rochester (Int'l)	1B-2B-3B	30	95	13	22	4	1	3	8	9	11	0	2	1-2	.232	.298	.389	.688	2	.983
1999—	Bowie (East.)	2B-1B-OF-C	39	126	17	37	6	0	2	12	10	12	3	0	2-0	.294	.360	.389	.749	0	1.000
	— Rochester (Int'l)	OF-2-3-1	79	279	33	82	19	4	6	28	34	24	1	8	1-2	.294	.370	.455	.825	2	.988
2000—	Bowie (East.)	OF-1B	13	53	11	18	6	0	1	9	3	6	1	1	0-0	.340	.379	.509	.889	0	1.000
	— Rochester (Int'l)	2-OF-3-1	54	189	25	54	10	0	3	21	26	14	1	4	3-1	.286	.373	.386	.760	5	.966
2001—	Yucatan (Mex.)		121	493	68	164	42	7	5	64	43	47	...	...	5-4	.333	...	.477	...	2	.993
	— Chico (West.)		4	15	3	8	0	1	0	1	1	1	...	...	0-...	.533	...	.667	...	...	...
2002—	Rochester (Int'l)	OF-1-2-3	108	418	57	129	21	4	7	43	41	28	2	11	3-4	.309	.369	.428	.797	8	.976
	— Baltimore (A.L.)	DH-OF-1B	14	53	3	16	5	0	0	4	3	6	2	5	0-0	.302	.362	.396	.758	0	1.000
2003—	Syracuse (Int'l)	2-0-1-D-3	66	252	29	65	14	1	4	30	21	20	3	3	1-0	.258	.316	.369	.685	9	.970
	— Toronto (A.L.)	3-D-0-2-1-S	38	70	9	25	3	1	0	7	3	6	2	3	0-1	.357	.400	.429	.829	2	.959
	Major League totals (2 years)		52	123	12	41	8	1	0	11	6	12	4	8	0-1	.333	.383	.415	.798	2	.970

CLARK, JERMAINE — 2B

PERSONAL: Born September 29, 1976, in Berkeley, Calif. ... 5-10/175. ... Bats left, throws right. ... Full name: Jermaine Marcel Clark. ... High school: Will C. Wood (Vavaville, Calif.). ... College: San Francisco.

TRANSACTIONS/CAREER NOTES: Selected by Seattle Mariners organzation in fifth round of free-agent draft (June 3, 1997). ... Selected by Detroit Tigers from Mariners organization in Rule 5 major-league draft (December 11, 2000). ... Returned to Mariners (April 19, 2001). ... On Tacoma disabled list (June 5-17, 2001). ... On Tacoma disabled list (May 18-28, 2002). ... Traded by Mariners with P Derrick Van Dusen to Texas Rangers for P Ismael Valdes (August 18, 2002). ... Designated for assignment by Texas (April 26, 2003). ... Claimed on waivers by San Diego Padres (April 30, 2003). ... Recalled by San Diego from Portland of the Pacific Coast League (May 26, 2003). ... Sent outright to Portland by San Diego (May 30, 2003). ... Called up by Texas from Oklahoma (September 6, 2003).

2003 GAMES PLAYED BY POSITION (MLB): OF—18, 2B—7, DH—2.

Year	Team (League)	Pos.	G	AB	R	H	2B	3B	HR	RBI	BB	SO	HBP	GDP	SB-CS	Avg.	OBP	SLG	OPS	E	Pct.
1997— Everett (N'west)	2B-3B	59	199	42	67	13	2	3	29	34	31	3	1	22-3	.337	.437	.467	.904	9	.957
1998— Wisconsin (Midw.)	2B-OF	123	448	81	145	24	* 13	6	55	57	64	2	3	40-14	.324	.402	.475	.877	14	.970
1999— Lancaster (Calif.)	2B	126	502	* 112	158	27	8	6	61	58	80	2	10	33-15	.315	.386	.436	.822	10	.983
2000— New Haven (East.)	2B	133	447	80	131	23	9	2	44	87	69	14	7	38-8	.293	.421	.398	.819	13	.977
2001— Detroit (A.L.)	DH	3	0	1	0	0	0	0	0	0	0	0	0	0-0	...	...	...	...	...	...
— Tacoma (PCL)	2B	74	216	35	54	7	3	1	26	27	39	3	6	13-2	.250	.340	.324	.664	6	.980
2002— Tacoma (PCL)	2B-SS	108	368	47	98	14	4	6	36	62	59	2	3	29-14	.266	.370	.375	.745	8	.982
— Oklahoma (PCL)	2B-OF	13	57	13	17	2	1	1	4	7	11	0	0	6-2	.298	.375	.421	.796	1	.982
2003— San Diego (N.L.)	OF	1	2	0	0	0	0	0	1	0	1	0	0	0-1	.000	.000	.000	.000	0	1.000
— Portland (PCL)	OF-2-S-3	50	160	27	40	2	2	4	10	22	24	1	1	14-3	.250	.342	.363	.705	4	.968
— Oklahoma (PCL)	OF-2B	49	171	24	38	6	4	6	24	16	26	1	3	11-1	.222	.291	.409	.700	2	.981
— Texas (A.L.)	OF-2B-DH	24	46	2	8	2	0	0	6	6	4	0	1	2-1	.174	.264	.217	.482	0	1.000
American League totals (2 years)		27	46	3	8	2	0	0	6	6	4	0	1	2-1	.174	.264	.217	.482	0	1.000
National League totals (1 year)		1	2	0	0	0	0	0	1	0	1	0	0	0-1	.000	.000	.000	.000	0	1.000
Major League totals (2 years)		28	48	3	8	2	0	0	7	6	5	0	1	2-2	.167	.250	.208	.458	0	1.000

CLARK, TONY — 1B/DH

PERSONAL: Born June 15, 1972, in Newton, Kan. ... 6-7/245. ... Bats both, throws right. ... Full name: Anthony Christopher Clark. ... High school: Valhalla (El Cajon, Calif.), then Christian (El Cajon, Calif.). ... College: San Diego State.

TRANSACTIONS/CAREER NOTES: Selected by Detroit Tigers organization in first round (second pick overall) of free-agent draft (June 4, 1990). ... On Niagara Falls temporarily inactive list (June 17, 1991-remainder of season; and August 17, 1992-remainder of season). ... On disabled list (August 24, 1993-remainder of season). ... On Detroit disabled list (May 26-June 10, 1999); included rehabilitation assignment to Toledo (June 8-10). ... On Detroit disabled list (May 13-June 12, July 15-September 1 and September 19, 2000-remainder of season); included rehabilitation assignments to Toledo (June 9-12 and August 28-September 1). ... Claimed on waivers by Boston Red Sox (November 20, 2001). ... Granted free agency (October 30, 2002). ... Signed by New York Mets organization (February 20, 2003).

2003 GAMES PLAYED BY POSITION (MLB): 1B—80, OF—1.

Year	Team (League)	Pos.	G	AB	R	H	2B	3B	HR	RBI	BB	SO	HBP	GDP	SB-CS	Avg.	OBP	SLG	OPS	E	Pct.
1990— Bristol (Appal.)	OF	25	73	2	12	2	0	1	8	6	28	1	0	0-0	.164	.238	.233	.470	0	1.000
1991— Niagara Falls (NYP)									Did not play.											
1992— Niagara Falls (NYP)	OF	27	85	12	26	9	0	5	17	9	34	0	0	1-0	.306	.372	.588	.961	0	1.000
1993— Lakeland (Fla. St.)	OF	36	117	14	31	4	1	1	22	18	32	0	1	0-1	.265	.358	.342	.700	2	.944
1994— Trenton (East.)	DH-1B	107	394	50	110	25	0	21	86	40	113	1	9	0-4	.279	.346	.503	.848	• 13	.977
— Toledo (Int'l)	1B-DH	25	92	10	24	4	0	2	13	12	25	0	1	2-0	.261	.340	.370	.709	0	1.000
1995— Toledo (Int'l)	1B-DH	110	405	50	98	17	2	14	63	52	129	3	8	0-2	.242	.330	.398	.728	* 13	.981
— Detroit (A.L.)	1B	27	101	10	24	5	1	3	11	8	30	0	2	0-0	.238	.294	.396	.690	4	.985
1996— Toledo (Int'l)	1B-DH	55	194	42	58	7	1	14	36	31	58	0	3	1-1	.299	.396	.562	.957	3	.993
— Detroit (A.L.)	1B-DH	100	376	56	94	14	0	27	72	29	127	0	7	0-0	.250	.299	.503	.802	6	.993
1997— Detroit (A.L.)	1B-DH	159	580	105	160	28	3	32	117	93	144	3	11	1-3	.276	.376	.500	.876	10	.993
1998— Detroit (A.L.)	1B-DH	157	602	84	175	37	0	34	103	63	128	3	16	3-3	.291	.358	.522	.880	13	.991
1999— Detroit (A.L.)	1B-DH	143	536	74	150	29	0	31	99	64	133	6	14	2-1	.280	.361	.507	.869	10	.992
— Toledo (Int'l)	1B	1	3	0	0	0	0	0	0	1	1	0	0	0-0	.000	.250	.000	.250	0	1.000
2000— Detroit (A.L.)	1B-DH	60	208	32	57	14	0	13	37	24	51	0	10	0-0	.274	.349	.529	.878	4	.993
— Toledo (Int'l)	1B	6	22	1	2	1	0	1	2	1	1	0	0	0-0	.091	.130	.273	.403	0	1.000
2001— Detroit (A.L.)	1B-DH	126	428	67	123	29	3	16	75	62	108	1	14	0-1	.287	.374	.481	.856	3	.996
2002— Boston (A.L.)	1B-DH	90	275	25	57	12	1	3	29	21	57	1	11	0-0	.207	.265	.291	.556	6	.992
2003— St. Lucie (Fla. St.)	1B	1	4	0	1	0	0	0	0	0	1	0	0	0-0	.250	.250	.250	.500	1	1.000
— New York (N.L.)	1B-OF	125	254	29	59	13	0	16	43	24	73	1	8	0-0	.232	.300	.472	.772	4	.992
American League totals (8 years)		862	3106	453	840	168	8	159	543	364	778	14	85	6-9	.270	.347	.483	.830	56	.992
National League totals (1 year)		125	254	29	59	13	0	16	43	24	73	1	8	0-0	.232	.300	.472	.772	4	.992
Major League totals (9 years)		987	3360	482	899	181	8	175	586	388	851	15	93	6-9	.268	.344	.482	.826	60	.992

CLAUSSEN, BRANDON — P

PERSONAL: Born May 1, 1979, in Rapid City, S.D. ... 6-2/175. ... Throws left, bats right. ... Full name: Brandon Allen Falkerson Claussen. ... Name pronounced: CLAW-sin. ... High school: Goddard (Roswell, N.M.). ... Junior college: Howard College (Texas).

TRANSACTIONS/CAREER NOTES: Selected by New York Yankees organization in 34th round of free-agent draft (June 2, 1998). ... On Columbus disabled list (June 18, 2002-remainder of season). ... Recalled by New York from Columbus (June 28, 2003). ... Optioned to Columbus by New York (July 2, 2003). ... Traded by New York Yankees to Cincinnati Reds for 3B Aaron Boone (July 31, 2003). ... Called up by Cincinnati from Louisville (September 15, 2003).

CAREER HITTING: 1-for-4 (.250), 0 R, 0 2B, 0 3B, 0 HR, 1 RBI.

Year	League	W	L	Pct.	ERA	WHIP	G	GS	CG	ShO	Hld.	Sv.-Opp.	IP	H	R	ER	HR	BB-IBB	SO	Avg.
1999— GC Yankees (GCL)		0	1	.000	3.18	0.79	2	2	0	0	...	0-...	11.1	7	4	4	2	2-0	16	.175
— Staten Island (NY-P)		6	4	.600	3.38	1.14	12	12	1	0	...	0-...	72.0	70	30	27	4	12-2	89	.253
— Greensboro (S. Atl.)		0	1	.000	10.50	1.67	1	1	1	0	...	0-...	6.0	8	7	7	1	2-0	5	.296
2000— Greensboro (S. Atl.)		8	5	.615	4.05	1.38	17	17	1	0	...	0-...	97.2	91	49	44	9	44-0	98	.251
— Tampa (FSL)		2	5	.286	3.10	1.26	9	9	1	1	...	0-...	52.1	49	24	18	1	17-0	44	.245
2001— Tampa (FSL)		5	2	.714	2.73	1.07	8	8	0	0	...	0-...	56.0	47	21	17	2	13-0	69	.224
— Norwich (East.)		9	2	.818	2.13	1.19	21	21	1	1	...	0-...	131.0	101	42	31	6	55-0	151	.210
2002— Columbus (Int'l)		2	8	.200	3.28	1.40	15	15	0	0	...	0-...	93.1	85	47	34	4	46-3	73	.242
2003— Tampa (FSL)		2	0	1.000	1.64	0.86	4	4	0	0	...	0-...	22.0	16	5	4	0	3-0	26	.198
— New York (A.L.)		1	0	1.000	1.42	1.42	1	1	0	0	0	0-0	6.1	8	2	1	1	1-0	5	.296
— Columbus (Int'l)		2	1	.667	2.75	1.03	11	11	1	0	...	0-...	68.2	53	28	21	4	18-0	39	.213
— Louisville (Int'l)		0	1	.000	7.47	1.47	3	3	0	0	...	0-...	15.2	17	13	13	3	6-0	16	.293
Major League totals (1 year)		1	0	1.000	1.42	1.42	1	1	0	0	0	0-0	6.1	8	2	1	1	1-0	5	.296

C

CLAYTON, ROYCE   SS

PERSONAL: Born January 2, 1970, in Burbank, Calif. ... 6-0/185. ... Bats right, throws right. ... Full name: Royce Spencer Clayton. ... High school: St. Bernard (Playa del Ray, Calif.).

TRANSACTIONS/CAREER NOTES: Selected by San Francisco Giants organization in first round (15th pick overall) of free-agent draft (June 1, 1988); pick received as compensation for Cincinnati Reds signing Type B free-agent OF Eddie Milner. ... Traded by Giants with a player to be named later to St. Louis Cardinals for P Allen Watson, P Rich DeLucia and P Doug Creek (December 14, 1995); Cardinals acquired 2B Chris Wimmer to complete deal (January 16, 1996). ... On St. Louis disabled list (June 24-July 9, 1998). ... Traded by Cardinals with P Todd Stottlemyre to Texas Rangers for P Darren Oliver, 3B Fernando Tatis and a player to be named later (July 31, 1998); Cardinals acquired OF Mark Little to complete deal (August 9, 1998). ... Granted free agency (October 23, 1998). ... Re-signed by Rangers (December 2, 1998). ... On Texas disabled list (May 1-21, 1999); included rehabilitation assignment to Oklahoma (May 18-21). ... Traded by Rangers to Chicago White Sox for P Aaron Myette and P Brian Schmack (December 14, 2000). ... Released by White Sox (September 8, 2002). ... Signed by Milwaukee Brewers (December 11, 2002).

2003 GAMES PLAYED BY POSITION (MLB): SS—141.

Year	Team (League)	Pos.	G	AB	R	H	2B	3B	HR	RBI	BB	SO	HBP	GDP	SB-CS	Avg.	OBP	SLG	OPS	E	Pct.
1988—	Everett (N'west)	SS	60	212	35	55	4	0	3	29	27	54	3	8	10-4	.259	.348	.321	.669	35	.873
1989—	Clinton (Midw.)	SS	104	385	39	91	13	3	0	24	39	101	4	6	28-16	.236	.309	.286	.595	31	.943
	— San Jose (Calif.)	SS	28	92	5	11	2	0	0	4	13	27	1	5	10-1	.120	.236	.141	.377	8	.939
1990—	San Jose (Calif.)	SS	123	460	80	123	15	10	7	71	68	98	4	13	33-15	.267	.364	.389	.753	37	.938
1991—	Shreveport (Texas)	SS	126	485	84	136	22	8	5	68	61	104	3	7	36-10	.280	.361	.390	.751	29	.950
	— San Francisco (N.L.)	SS	9	26	0	3	1	0	0	2	1	6	0	1	0-0	.115	.148	.154	.302	3	.880
1992—	San Francisco (N.L.)	SS-3B	98	321	31	72	7	4	4	24	26	63	0	11	8-4	.224	.281	.308	.589	11	.973
	— Phoenix (PCL)	SS	48	192	30	46	6	2	3	18	17	25	0	8	15-6	.240	.300	.339	.639	7	.971
1993—	San Francisco (N.L.)	SS	153	549	54	155	21	5	6	70	38	91	5	16	11-10	.282	.331	.372	.702	27	.963
1994—	San Francisco (N.L.)	SS	108	385	38	91	14	6	3	30	30	74	3	7	23-3	.236	.295	.327	.623	14	.973
1995—	San Francisco (N.L.)	SS	138	509	56	124	29	3	5	58	38	109	3	7	24-9	.244	.298	.342	.640	20	.969
1996—	St. Louis (N.L.)	SS	129	491	64	136	20	4	6	35	33	89	1	13	33-15	.277	.321	.371	.692	15	.972
1997—	St. Louis (N.L.)	SS	154	576	75	153	39	5	9	61	33	109	3	19	30-10	.266	.302	.398	.704	19	.973
1998—	St. Louis (N.L.)	SS	90	355	59	83	19	1	4	29	40	51	2	10	19-6	.234	.313	.327	.640	13	.970
	— Texas (A.L.)	SS	52	186	30	53	12	1	5	24	13	32	1	6	5-5	.285	.330	.441	.771	7	.972
1999—	Texas (A.L.)	SS	133	465	69	134	21	5	14	52	39	100	4	6	8-6	.288	.346	.445	.792	* 25	.961
	— Oklahoma (PCL)	SS	2	7	1	1	0	0	0	1	3	3	0	0	0-0	.143	.400	.143	.543	0	1.000
2000—	Texas (A.L.)	SS	148	513	70	124	21	5	14	54	42	92	3	21	11-7	.242	.301	.384	.685	16	.977
2001—	Chicago (A.L.)	SS	135	433	62	114	21	4	9	60	33	72	3	16	10-7	.263	.315	.393	.708	7	.988
2002—	Chicago (A.L.)	SS	112	342	51	86	14	2	7	35	20	67	3	7	5-1	.251	.295	.365	.661	5	.989
2003—	Milwaukee (N.L.)	SS	146	483	49	110	16	1	11	39	49	92	3	25	5-2	.228	.301	.333	.634	14	.977
	American League totals (5 years)		580	1939	282	511	89	17	49	225	147	363	14	56	39-26	.264	.317	.403	.720	60	.977
	National League totals (9 years)		1025	3695	426	927	166	29	48	348	288	684	20	109	153-59	.251	.306	.350	.657	136	.971
	Major League totals (13 years)		1605	5634	708	1438	255	46	97	573	435	1047	34	165	192-85	.255	.310	.368	.678	196	.973

CLEMENS, ROGER   P

PERSONAL: Born August 4, 1962, in Dayton, Ohio. ... 6-4/238. ... Throws right, bats right. ... Full name: William Roger Clemens. ... High school: Spring Woods (Houston). ... College: Texas.

TRANSACTIONS/CAREER NOTES: Selected by New York Mets organization in 12th round of free-agent draft (June 8, 1981); did not sign. ... Selected by Boston Red Sox organization in first round (19th pick overall) of free-agent draft (June 6, 1983). ... On disabled list (July 8-August 3 and August 21, 1985-remainder of season). ... On suspended list (April 26-May 3, 1991). ... On Boston disabled list (June 19-July 16, 1993); included rehabilitation assignment to Pawtucket (July 11-16). ... On Boston disabled list (April 16-June 2, 1995); included rehabilitation assignments to Sarasota (May 25-28) and Pawtucket (May 28-June 2). ... Granted free agency (November 5, 1996). ... Signed by Toronto Blue Jays (December 13, 1996). ... Traded by Blue Jays to New York Yankees for P David Wells, P Graeme Lloyd and 2B Homer Bush (February 18, 1999). ... On disabled list (April 28-May 21, 1999; and June 15-July 2, 2000). ... On New York disabled list (July 13-August 7, 2002); included rehabilitation assignments to Tampa (July 27-31) and Norwich (August 1-7). ... Granted free agency (October 31, 2002). ... Re-signed by Yankees (December 30, 2002).

CAREER HITTING: 4-for-20 (.200), 2 R, 2 2B, 0 3B, 0 HR, 1 RBI.

Year	League	W	L	Pct.	ERA	WHIP	G	GS	CG	ShO	Hld.	Sv.-Opp.	IP	H	R	ER	HR	BB-IBB	SO	Avg.
1983—	Winter Haven (FSL)	3	1	.750	1.24	0.76	4	4	3	1	...	0-...	29.0	22	4	4	0	0-0	36	...
	— New Britain (East.)	4	1	.800	1.38	0.83	7	7	1	1	...	0-...	52.0	31	8	8	1	12-0	59	...
1984—	Pawtucket (Int'l)	2	3	.400	1.93	1.14	7	6	3	1	...	0-...	46.2	39	12	10	3	14-0	50	.228
	— Boston (A.L.)	9	4	.692	4.32	1.31	21	20	5	1	0	0-0	133.1	146	67	64	13	29-3	126	.271
1985—	Boston (A.L.)	7	5	.583	3.29	1.22	15	15	3	1	0	0-0	98.1	83	38	36	5	37-0	74	.228
1986—	Boston (A.L.)	* 24	4	* .857	* 2.48	0.97	33	33	10	1	0	0-0	254.0	179	77	70	21	67-0	238	*.195
1987—	Boston (A.L.)	● 20	9	.690	2.97	1.18	36	36	* 18	* 7	0	0-0	281.2	248	100	93	19	83-4	256	.235
1988—	Boston (A.L.)	18	12	.600	2.93	1.06	35	35	● 14	* 8	0	0-0	264.0	217	93	86	17	62-4	* 291	.220
1989—	Boston (A.L.)	17	11	.607	3.13	1.22	35	35	8	3	0	0-0	253.1	215	101	88	20	93-5	230	.231
1990—	Boston (A.L.)	21	6	.778	* 1.93	1.08	31	31	7	● 4	0	0-0	228.1	193	59	49	7	54-3	209	.228
1991—	Boston (A.L.)	18	10	.643	*2.62	1.05	35	● 35	13	* 4	0	0-0	* 271.1	219	93	79	15	65-12	* 241	.221
1992—	Boston (A.L.)	18	11	.621	*2.41	1.07	32	32	11	* 5	0	0-0	246.2	203	80	66	11	62-5	208	.224
1993—	Boston (A.L.)	11	14	.440	4.46	1.26	29	29	2	1	0	0-0	191.2	175	99	95	17	67-4	160	.244
	— Pawtucket (Int'l)	0	0	...	0.00	1.36	1	1	0	0	0	0-...	3.2	1	0	0	0	4-0	8	.091
1994—	Boston (A.L.)	9	7	.563	2.85	1.14	24	24	3	1	0	0-0	170.2	124	62	54	15	71-1	168	*.204
1995—	Sarasota (Fla. St.)	0	0	...	0.00	0.50	1	1	0	0	0	0-...	4.0	0	0	0	0	2-0	7	.000
	— Pawtucket (Int'l)	0	0	...	0.00	0.80	1	1	0	0	0	0-...	5.0	1	0	0	0	3-0	5	.063
	— Boston (A.L.)	10	5	.667	4.18	1.44	23	23	0	0	0	0-0	140.0	141	70	65	15	60-0	132	.259
1996—	Boston (A.L.)	10	13	.435	3.63	1.33	34	34	6	2	0	0-0	242.2	216	106	98	19	106-2	* 257	.237
1997—	Toronto (A.L.)	* 21	7	.750	*2.05	1.03	34	34	● 9	● 3	0	0-0	● 264.0	204	65	60	9	68-1	* 292	.213
1998—	Toronto (A.L.)	● 20	6	.769	*2.65	1.10	33	33	5	3	0	0-0	234.2	169	78	69	11	88-0	* 271	*.198
1999—	New York (A.L.)	14	10	.583	4.60	1.47	30	30	1	1	0	0-0	187.2	185	101	96	20	90-0	163	.261
2000—	New York (A.L.)	13	8	.619	3.70	1.31	32	32	1	0	0	0-0	204.1	184	96	84	26	84-0	188	.236
2001—	New York (A.L.)	20	3	*.870	3.51	1.26	33	33	0	0	0	0-0	220.1	205	94	86	19	72-1	213	.246
2002—	New York (A.L.)	13	6	.684	4.35	1.31	29	29	0	0	0	0-0	180.0	172	94	87	18	63-6	192	.250
	— Tampa (FSL)	1	0	1.000	5.40	1.40	1	1	0	0	0	0-...	5.0	5	3	3	1	2-0	6	.263
	— Norwich (East.)	0	1	.000	1.29	0.71	1	1	0	0	0	0-...	7.0	5	1	1	0	0-0	7	.200
2003—	New York (A.L.)	17	9	.654	3.91	1.21	33	33	1	1	0	0-0	211.2	199	99	92	24	58-1	190	.247
	Major League totals (20 years)	310	160	.660	3.19	1.18	607	606	117	46	0	0-0	4278.2	3677	1672	1517	321	1379-52	4099	.231

CLEMENT, MATT — P

PERSONAL: Born August 12, 1974, in Butler, Pa. ... 6-3/210. ... Throws right, bats right. ... Full name: Matthew Paul Clement. ... Name pronounced: klah-MENT. ... High school: Butler (Pa.).

TRANSACTIONS/CAREER NOTES: Selected by San Diego Padres organization in third round of free-agent draft (June 3, 1993). ... Traded by Padres with OF Eric Owens and P Omar Ortiz to Florida Marlins for OF Mark Kotsay and OF Cesar Crespo (March 28, 2001). ... Traded by Marlins with P Antonio Alfonseca to Chicago Cubs for P Julian Tavarez, P Jose Cueto, P Dontrelle Willis and C Ryan Jorgensen (March 27, 2002).

CAREER HITTING: 24-for-287 (.084), 19 R, 4 2B, 1 3B, 0 HR, 10 RBI.

Year League	W	L	Pct.	ERA	WHIP	G	GS	CG	ShO	Hld.	Sv.-Opp.	IP	H	R	ER	HR	BB-IBB	SO	Avg.
1994— Spokane (N'west)	1	1	.500	6.14	2.59	2	2	0	0	...	0-...	7.1	8	7	5	0	11-0	4	.296
— Ariz. Padres (Ariz.)	•8	5	.615	4.43	1.22	13	13	0	0	...	0-...	67.0	65	38	33	0	17-0	76	.248
1995— Rancho Cuca. (Calif.)	3	4	.429	4.24	1.92	12	12	0	0	...	0-...	57.1	61	37	27	1	49-0	33	.295
— Idaho Falls (Pioneer)	6	3	.667	4.33	1.27	14	14	0	0	...	0-...	81.0	61	53	39	3	42-0	65	.214
1996— Clinton (Midw.)	8	3	.727	2.80	1.22	16	16	1	•1	...	0-...	96.1	66	31	30	3	52-0	109	.191
— Rancho Cuca. (Calif.)	4	5	.444	5.59	1.54	11	11	0	0	...	0-...	56.1	61	40	35	8	26-0	75	.280
1997— Rancho Cuca. (Calif.)	6	3	.667	1.60	1.04	14	14	2	1	...	0-...	101.0	74	30	18	3	31-1	109	.202
— Mobile (Sou.)	6	5	.545	2.56	1.31	13	13	1	1	...	0-...	88.0	83	37	25	4	32-0	92	.249
1998— Las Vegas (PCL)	10	9	.526	3.98	1.41	27	27	1	0	...	0-...	171.2	157	94	76	12	85-2	*160	.245
— San Diego (N.L.)	2	0	1.000	4.61	1.61	4	2	0	0	0	0-0	13.2	15	8	7	0	7-1	13	.283
1999— San Diego (N.L.)	10	12	.455	4.48	1.53	31	31	0	0	0	0-0	180.2	190	106	90	18	86-2	135	.273
2000— San Diego (N.L.)	13	17	.433	5.14	1.56	34	34	0	0	0	0-0	205.0	194	131	117	22	*125-4	170	.248
2001— Florida (N.L.)	9	10	.474	5.05	1.52	31	31	0	0	0	0-0	169.1	172	102	95	15	85-2	134	.267
2002— Chicago (N.L.)	12	11	.522	3.60	1.20	32	32	3	2	0	0-0	205.0	162	84	82	18	85-7	215	.215
2003— Chicago (N.L.)	14	12	.538	4.11	1.23	32	32	2	1	0	0-0	201.2	169	100	92	22	79-2	171	.227
Major League totals (6 years)	60	62	.492	4.46	1.40	164	162	5	3	0	0-0	975.1	902	531	483	95	467-18	838	.246

COLBRUNN, GREG — 1B

PERSONAL: Born July 26, 1969, in Fontana, Calif. ... 6-0/215. ... Bats right, throws right. ... Full name: Gregory Joseph Colbrunn. ... Name pronounced: COAL-brun. ... High school: Fontana (Calif.).

TRANSACTIONS/CAREER NOTES: Selected by Montreal Expos organization in sixth round of free-agent draft (June 2, 1987). ... On disabled list (April 10, 1991-entire season). ... On Indianapolis disabled list (April 9-May 5, 1992). ... On Montreal disabled list (August 2-18, 1992); included rehabilitation assignment to Indianapolis (August 13-18). ... On Montreal disabled list (April 5-21, 1993); included rehabilitation assignment to West Palm Beach (April 9-20). ... On Montreal disabled list (July 12, 1993-remainder of season); included rehabilitation assignment to Ottawa (July 27-August 2). ... Claimed on waivers by Florida Marlins (October 7, 1993). ... On Florida disabled list (April 9-May 27, and July 15-30, 1994); included rehabilitation assignments to Brevard County (May 12-18 and July 28-30) and Edmonton (May 18-27). ... On Florida disabled list (July 24-August 8, 1996). ... Granted free agency (December 20, 1996). ... Signed by Minnesota Twins organization (January 24, 1997). ... Traded by Twins to Atlanta Braves for a player to be named later (August 14, 1997); Twins acquired OF Marc Lewis to complete deal (October 1, 1997). ... Granted free agency (October 23, 1997). ... Signed by Colorado Rockies organization (December 23, 1997). ... Traded by Rockies to Braves for P David Cortes, P Mike Porzio and a player to be named later (July 30, 1998); Rockies acquired P Anthony Briggs to complete deal (September 9, 1998). ... Granted free agency (October 23, 1998). ... Signed by Arizona Diamondbacks (November 17, 1998). ... On Arizona disabled list (June 6-25 and June 27-August 17, 2001); included rehabilitation assignment to Tucson (August 10-17). ... On Arizona disabled list (March 22-April 10 and July 18-August 2, 2002); included rehabilitation assignment to Tucson (April 4-10). ... Granted free agency (October 28, 2002). ... Signed by Seattle Mariners (January 3, 2003). ... Placed on the 15-day disabled list, retroactive to June 23 (July 9, 2003). ... Placed on the 15-day disabled list by Seattle, retroactive to June 9 (July 4, 2003). ... Sent to Tacoma on rehab assignment by Seattle (June 20, 2003). ... Recalled from Tacoma rehab assignment (June 24, 2003). ... Recalled from Everett by Seattle; reinstated from 15-day disabled list (June 28, 2003). ... Placed on 15-day disabled list (July 3, 2003).

2003 GAMES PLAYED BY POSITION (MLB): 1B—14, DH—4.

Year Team (League)	Pos.	G	AB	R	H	2B	3B	HR	RBI	BB	SO	HBP	GDP	SB-CS	Avg.	OBP	SLG	OPS	E	Pct.
1988— Rockford (Midwest)	C	115	417	55	111	18	2	7	46	22	60	11	5	5-3	.266	.318	.369	.687	15	.978
1989— W.P. Beach (FSL)	C	59	228	20	54	8	0	0	25	6	29	2	5	3-1	.237	.261	.272	.532	5	.988
— Jacksonville (Sou.)	C	55	178	21	49	11	1	3	18	13	33	2	9	0-1	.275	.330	.399	.729	4	.988
1990— Jacksonville (Sou.)	C	125	458	57	138	29	1	13	76	38	78	6	8	1-2	.301	.358	.454	.812	15	.981
1991—					Did not play.															
1992— Indianapolis (A.A.)	1B	57	216	32	66	19	1	11	48	7	41	3	7	1-0	.306	.333	.556	.889	4	.992
— Montreal (N.L.)	1B	52	168	12	45	8	0	2	18	6	34	2	1	3-2	.268	.294	.351	.646	3	.992
1993— W.P. Beach (FSL)	1B	8	31	6	12	2	1	1	5	4	1	0	2	0-0	.387	.457	.613	1.070	1	.988
— Montreal (N.L.)	1B	70	153	15	39	9	0	4	23	6	33	1	1	4-2	.255	.282	.392	.674	2	.995
— Ottawa (Int'l)	1B	6	22	4	6	1	0	0	8	1	2	0	1	1-0	.273	.292	.318	.610	0	1.000
1994— Florida (N.L.)	1B	47	155	17	47	10	0	6	31	9	27	2	3	1-1	.303	.345	.484	.829	4	.988
— Brevard County (FSL)	DH-1B	7	11	3	6	2	0	1	2	1	0	0	0	0-0	.545	.583	1.000	1.583	1	.944
— Edmonton (PCL)	1B-DH	7	17	2	4	0	0	1	2	0	1	1	1	0-0	.235	.278	.412	.690	1	.967
1995— Florida (N.L.)	1B	138	528	70	146	22	1	23	89	22	69	6	15	11-3	.277	.311	.453	.763	5	.996
1996— Florida (N.L.)	1B	141	511	60	146	26	2	16	69	25	76	14	22	4-5	.286	.333	.438	.772	6	.995
1997— Minnesota (A.L.)	1B-DH	70	217	24	61	14	0	5	26	8	38	1	7	1-2	.281	.307	.415	.722	6	.988
— Atlanta (N.L.)	1B-DH	28	54	3	15	3	0	2	9	2	11	1	1	0-0	.278	.316	.444	.760	1	.984
1998— Colorado (N.L.)	1-OF-3-C	62	122	12	38	8	2	2	13	8	23	1	1	3-3	.311	.359	.459	.818	2	.992
— Atlanta (N.L.)	1B-OF	28	44	6	13	3	0	1	10	2	11	3	0	1-0	.295	.367	.432	.799	0	1.000
1999— Arizona (N.L.)	1B-3B-DH	67	135	20	44	5	3	5	24	12	23	4	3	1-1	.326	.392	.519	.911	1	.996
2000— Arizona (N.L.)	1B-DH-3B	116	329	48	103	22	1	15	57	43	45	10	13	0-1	.313	.405	.523	.928	8	.989
2001— Arizona (N.L.)	1B-3B	59	97	12	28	8	0	4	18	9	14	4	5	0-0	.289	.373	.495	.868	3	.968
— Tucson (PCL)	1B	5	13	1	5	1	0	0	4	2	0	0	1	0-0	.385	.467	.462	.928	0	1.000
2002— Tucson (PCL)	1B	6	25	6	9	3	0	2	7	3	3	0	1	0-0	.360	.429	.720	1.149	1	.960
— Arizona (N.L.)	1B-3B-DH	72	171	30	57	16	2	10	27	13	19	0	5	0-0	.333	.378	.626	1.004	2	.993
2003— Tacoma (PCL)	DH-1B	3	11	3	3	0	0	1	2	1	1	0	0	0-0	.273	.333	.545	.879	0	1.000
— Everett (N'west)	DH	1	3	0	2	1	0	0	0	1	0	0	0	0-0	.667	.750	1.000	1.750	0	1.000
— Seattle (A.L.)	1B-DH	22	58	7	16	1	1	3	7	4	16	0	3	0-1	.276	.323	.483	.805	1	.989
American League totals (2 years)		92	275	31	77	15	1	8	33	12	54	1	10	1-3	.280	.310	.429	.739	7	.988
National League totals (11 years)		880	2467	305	721	140	11	90	388	157	385	48	70	28-18	.292	.343	.467	.811	37	.993
Major League totals (12 years)		972	2742	336	798	155	12	98	421	169	439	49	80	29-21	.291	.340	.464	.804	44	.992

COLLIER, LOU — IF/OF

PERSONAL: Born August 21, 1973, in Chicago, Ill. ... 5-10/191. ... Bats right, throws right. ... Full name: Louis Keith Collier. ... High school: Vocational (Chicago). ... Junior college: Triton College (Ill.).

TRANSACTIONS/CAREER NOTES: Selected by Pittsburgh Pirates organization in 31st round of free-agent draft (June 1, 1992). ... On Pittsburgh disabled list (May 22-June 7, 1998); included rehabilitation assignment to Lynchburg (June 3-7). ... Claimed on waivers by Milwaukee Brewers (December 18, 1998). ... On Indianapolis disabled list (April 27-July 7, 2000). ... Traded by Brewers to New York Mets as part of three-way deal in which Mets traded P Glendon Rusch to Brewers, Colorado Rockies traded 1B/OF Ross Gload and P Craig House to Mets, Brewers traded P Jeff D'Amico, OF Jeromy Burnitz, OF/1B Mark Sweeney and cash to Mets, Mets traded 1B/3B Todd Zeile, OF Benny Agbayani, IF/OF Lenny Harris and cash to Rockies and Rockies traded OF Alex Ochoa to Brewers (January 21, 2002). ... Traded by Mets to Montreal Expos for P Jimmy Serrano and OF Jason Bay (March 26, 2002). ... Released by Expos (September 30, 2002). ... Signed by Red Sox as a free agent (March 21, 2003).

2003 GAMES PLAYED BY POSITION (MLB): 3B—2, OF—2.

Year	Team (League)	Pos.	G	AB	R	H	2B	3B	HR	RBI	BB	SO	HBP	GDP	SB-CS	Avg.	OBP	SLG	OPS	E	Pct.
1993— Welland (NYP)		SS	50	201	35	61	6	2	1	19	12	31	5	2	8-7	.303	.356	.368	.724	27	.887
1994— Augusta (S. Atl.)		SS	85	318	48	89	17	4	7	40	25	53	8	4	32-10	.280	.345	.425	.769	34	.915
— Salem (Caro.)		SS	43	158	25	42	4	1	6	16	15	29	6	4	5-8	.266	.348	.418	.766	11	.946
1995— Lynchburg (Caro.)		SS	114	399	68	110	19	3	4	38	51	60	7	13	31-11	.276	.365	.368	.734	35	.937
1996— Carolina (Sou.)		SS-DH	119	443	76	124	20	3	3	49	48	73	7	11	29-9	.280	.355	.359	.714	30	.943
1997— Calgary (PCL)		SS-2B-DH	112	397	65	131	31	5	1	48	37	47	6	13	12-7	.330	.393	.441	.834	34	.937
— Pittsburgh (N.L.)		SS	18	37	3	5	0	0	0	3	1	11	0	1	1-0	.135	.158	.135	.293	0	1.000
1998— Pittsburgh (N.L.)		SS	110	334	30	82	13	6	2	34	31	70	6	8	2-2	.246	.316	.338	.655	18	.960
— Lynchburg (Caro.)		SS	5	18	4	3	2	0	0	0	2	0	1	0	2-0	.167	.286	.278	.563	4	.840
1999— Milwaukee (N.L.)		SS-OF-3-2	74	135	18	35	9	0	2	21	14	32	0	2	3-2	.259	.325	.370	.695	5	.951
— Louisville (Int'l)		3B-SS-OF	27	91	25	35	10	0	4	11	15	14	1	2	6-3	.385	.472	.626	1.099	3	.962
2000— Indianapolis (Int'l)		OF-2B-3B	17	56	7	14	4	1	0	12	11	9	1	1	2-2	.250	.371	.357	.729	3	.933
— Huntsville (Sou.)		3-OF-2-S	50	172	29	46	4	2	2	29	30	44	1	5	7-3	.267	.374	.349	.723	8	.929
— Milwaukee (N.L.)		OF-3B	14	32	9	7	1	0	1	2	6	4	0	1	0-0	.219	.333	.344	.677	0	1.000
2001— Indianapolis (Int'l)		OF-2B-3B	86	312	48	90	17	2	14	36	24	64	7	6	9-3	.288	.350	.490	.840	6	.976
— Milwaukee (N.L.)		OF-3B-DH	50	127	19	32	8	1	2	14	17	30	1	0	5-1	.252	.340	.378	.718	4	.948
2002— Montreal (N.L.)		OF-2B-3B	13	11	3	1	1	0	0	0	1	3	1	0	0-0	.091	.231	.182	.413	0	1.000
— Ottawa (Int'l)		O-3-2-S-1	89	307	48	97	26	6	6	52	37	69	6	9	5-2	.316	.394	.498	.893	14	.932
2003— Boston (A.L.)		3B-OF	4	1	0	0	0	0	0	0	0	0	0	0	0-1	.000	.000	.000	.000	0	1.000
— Pawtucket (Int'l)		O-S-D-3-1	103	392	58	115	19	4	14	69	32	94	8	13	8-7	.293	.354	.469	.823	7	.971
American League totals (1 year)			4	1	0	0	0	0	0	0	0	0	0	0	0-1	.000	.000	.000	.000	0	1.000
National League totals (6 years)			279	676	82	162	32	7	7	74	70	150	8	12	11-5	.240	.314	.339	.653	27	.962
Major League totals (7 years)			283	677	82	162	32	7	7	74	70	150	8	12	11-6	.239	.314	.338	.652	27	.962

COLOME, JESUS — P

PERSONAL: Born December 23, 1977, in San Pedro de Macoris, Dominican Republic. ... 6-4/205. ... Throws right, bats right. ... Full name: Jesus Colome De La Cruz. ... Name pronounced: hay-soos cal-um-ay.

TRANSACTIONS/CAREER NOTES: Signed as non-drafted free agent by Oakland Athletics organization (September 29, 1996). ... Traded by A's with player to be named to Tampa Bay Devil Rays for P Jim Mecir and P Todd Belitz (July 28, 2000). ... On Durham disabled list (April 5-May 20, 2001).

CAREER HITTING: 0-for-0 (.000), 0 R, 0 2B, 0 3B, 0 HR, 0 RBI.

Year	League	W	L	Pct.	ERA	WHIP	G	GS	CG	ShO	Hld.	Sv.-Opp.	IP	H	R	ER	HR	BB-IBB	SO	Avg.
1997— Dominican Athletics (DSL)		9	3	.750	2.70	1.06	18	7	3	0	...	0-...	90.0	73	33	27	...	22-...	55	...
1998— Ariz. A's (Ariz.)		2	5	.286	3.18	1.11	12	11	0	0	...	0-...	56.2	47	27	20	1	16-0	62	.228
1999— Modesto (Calif.)		8	4	.667	3.36	1.44	31	22	0	0	...	1-...	128.2	125	63	48	6	60-2	127	.256
2000— Midland (Texas)		9	4	.692	3.59	1.35	20	20	0	0	...	0-...	110.1	99	62	44	10	50-0	95	.239
— Orlando (Sou.)		1	2	.333	6.75	1.70	3	3	0	0	...	0-...	14.2	18	12	11	2	7-0	9	.290
2001— Durham (Int'l)		0	3	.000	6.23	1.62	13	0	0	0	...	0-...	17.1	22	13	12	1	6-0	18	.319
— Tampa Bay (A.L.)		2	3	.400	3.33	1.27	30	0	0	0	6	0-0	48.2	37	22	18	8	25-4	31	.208
2002— Tampa Bay (A.L.)		2	7	.222	8.27	2.15	32	0	0	0	3	0-5	41.1	56	41	38	6	33-5	33	.341
— Durham (Int'l)		2	2	.500	2.17	1.07	18	0	0	0	...	1-...	29.0	18	8	7	1	13-0	30	.176
2003— Tampa Bay (A.L.)		3	7	.300	4.50	1.55	54	0	0	0	11	2-8	74.0	69	37	37	9	46-5	69	.247
Major League totals (3 years)		7	17	.292	5.10	1.62	116	0	0	0	20	2-13	164.0	162	100	93	23	104-14	133	.261

COLON, BARTOLO — P

PERSONAL: Born May 24, 1973, in Altamira, Dominican Republic. ... 5-11/240. ... Throws right, bats right. ... Name pronounced: bar-TOE-loh ko-LONE.

TRANSACTIONS/CAREER NOTES: Signed as non-drafted free agent by Cleveland Indians organization (June 26, 1993). ... On Canton/Akron disabled list (May 30-July 24, 1996). ... On Cleveland disabled list (April 16-May 12, 2000). ... On suspended list (July 28-August 2, 2001). ... Traded by Indians with future considerations to Montreal Expos for 1B Lee Stevens, SS Brandon Phillips, P Cliff Lee and OF Grady Sizemore (June 27, 2002); Expos acquired P Tim Drew to complete deal (June 28, 2002). ... Traded by Expos with 2B/SS Jorge Nunez to Chicago White Sox for P Orlando Hernandez, P Rocky Biddle, 3B/OF Jeff Liefer and cash (January 15, 2003). ... Suspended by Major League Baseball (May 21, 2003). ... Reinstated (May 27, 2003).

CAREER HITTING: 9-for-73 (.123), 1 R, 0 2B, 0 3B, 0 HR, 4 RBI.

Year	League	W	L	Pct.	ERA	WHIP	G	GS	CG	ShO	Hld.	Sv.-Opp.	IP	H	R	ER	HR	BB-IBB	SO	Avg.
1993— Santiago (DSL)		6	1	.857	2.59	1.17	11	10	2	1	...	1-...	66.0	44	24	19	...	33-...	48	...
1994— Burlington (Appal.)		7	4	.636	3.14	1.36	12	12	0	0	...	0-...	66.0	46	32	23	3	44-0	84	.192
1995— Kinston (Caro.)		13	3	.813	1.96	1.01	21	21	0	0	...	0-...	128.2	91	31	28	8	39-0	* 152	.202
1996— Cant./Akr. (Eastern)		2	2	.500	1.74	1.11	13	12	0	0	...	0-...	62.0	44	17	12	2	25-0	56	.196
— Buffalo (A.A.)		0	0	...	6.00	1.60	8	0	0	0	...	0-...	15.0	16	10	10	2	8-0	19	.271
1997— Cleveland (A.L.)		4	7	.364	5.65	1.62	19	17	1	0	0	0-0	94.0	107	66	59	12	45-1	66	.286
— Buffalo (A.A.)		7	1	.875	2.22	1.20	10	10	1	1	...	0-...	56.2	45	15	14	4	23-0	54	.221
1998— Cleveland (A.L.)		14	9	.609	3.71	1.39	31	31	6	2	0	0-0	204.0	205	91	84	15	79-5	158	.260
1999— Cleveland (A.L.)		18	5	.783	3.95	1.27	32	32	1	1	0	0-0	205.0	185	97	90	24	76-5	161	.242
2000— Cleveland (A.L.)		15	8	.652	3.88	1.39	30	30	2	1	0	0-0	188.0	163	86	81	21	98-4	212	.233
— Buffalo (Int'l)		1	0	1.000	1.80	1.20	1	1	0	0	...	0-...	5.0	6	1	1	0	0-0	4	.286
2001— Cleveland (A.L.)		14	12	.538	4.09	1.39	34	34	1	0	0	0-0	222.1	220	106	101	26	90-2	201	.261
2002— Cleveland (A.L.)		10	4	.714	2.55	1.26	16	16	4	2	0	0-0	116.1	104	37	33	11	31-1	75	.245
— Montreal (N.L.)		10	4	.714	3.31	1.32	17	17	4	1	0	0-0	117.0	115	48	43	9	39-4	74	.259
2003— Chicago (A.L.)		15	13	.536	3.87	1.20	34	34	•9	1	0	0-0	242.0	223	107	104	30	67-3	173	.248
American League totals (7 years)		90	58	.608	3.91	1.33	196	194	24	6	0	0-0	1271.2	1207	590	552	139	486-21	1046	.252
National League totals (1 year)		10	4	.714	3.31	1.32	17	17	4	1	0	0-0	117.0	115	48	43	9	39-4	74	.259
Major League totals (7 years)		100	62	.617	3.86	1.33	213	211	28	7	0	0-0	1388.2	1322	638	595	148	525-25	1120	.252

COLYER, STEVE — P

PERSONAL: Born February 22, 1979, in St. Louis, Mo. ... 6-4/205. ... Throws left, bats left. ... Full name: Stephen Edward Colyer. ... Name pronounced: call-yer. ... High school: Fort Zumwalt South (O'Fallon, Mo.). ... Junior college: Meramec College (Mo.).

TRANSACTIONS/CAREER NOTES: Selected by Los Angeles Dodgers organization in supplemental round ("sandwich pick" between second and third round) of free-agent draft (June 3, 1997); pick received as part of compensation for St. Louis Cardinals signing Type C free agent 2B Delino DeShields. ... Recalled by Los Angeles from Las Vegas (May 13, 2003). ... Optioned to Las Vegas of the Pacific Coast League by Los Angeles (May 29, 2003). ... Recalled by Los Angeles from Las Vegas (July 6, 2003). ... Optioned to Las Vegas by Los Angeles (July 23, 2003). ... Recalled from Las Vegas by Los Angeles (September 1, 2003).

CAREER HITTING: 0-for-0 (.000), 0 R, 0 2B, 0 3B, 0 HR, 0 RBI.

Year — League	W	L	Pct.	ERA	WHIP	G	GS	CG	ShO	Hld.	Sv.-Opp.	IP	H	R	ER	HR	BB-IBB	SO	Avg.
1998— Yakima (NW)	2	2	.500	4.96	1.65	15	12	0	0	...	0-...	65.1	72	46	36	2	36-0	75	.277
1999— San Bernardino (Calif.)	7	9	.438	4.70	1.59	27	25	1	0	...	0-...	145.2	145	82	76	12	86-0	131	.269
2000— Vero Beach (FSL)	5	7	.417	5.76	1.73	26	18	1	0	...	0-...	95.1	97	74	61	9	68-0	80	.272
2001— Vero Beach (FSL)	4	8	.333	3.96	1.48	24	24	0	0	...	0-...	120.1	101	62	53	16	77-0	118	.234
2002— Jacksonville (Sou.)	5	4	.556	3.45	1.44	59	0	0	0	...	21-...	62.2	50	29	24	6	40-3	68	.214
2003— Las Vegas (PCL)	2	3	.400	3.21	1.38	44	0	0	0	...	23-...	47.2	44	18	17	1	22-0	50	.243
— Los Angeles (N.L.)	0	0	...	2.75	1.58	13	0	0	0	0	0-0	19.2	22	6	6	0	9-0	16	.297
Major League totals (1 year)	**0**	**0**	**...**	**2.75**	**1.58**	**13**	**0**	**0**	**0**	**0**	**0-0**	**19.2**	**22**	**6**	**6**	**0**	**9-0**	**16**	**.297**

CONDREY, CLAY — P

PERSONAL: Born November 19, 1975, in Beaumont, Texas. ... 6-3/195. ... Throws right, bats right. ... Full name: Clayton Lee Condrey. ... Name pronounced: con-DREE. ... High school: Navasota (Texas). ... College: McNeese State.

TRANSACTIONS/CAREER NOTES: Signed as non-drafted free agent by San Diego Padres organization (June 29, 1998). ... Placed on the 15-day disabled list (May 13, 2003). ... Sent to Portland on rehab assignment by San Diego (June 30, 2003). ... Recalled from Portland rehab assignment; activated from the 15-day disabled list by San Diego (July 7, 2003). ... Optioned by San Diego to Portland (July 7, 2003). ... Recalled by San Diego from Portland; sent outright to Portland (September 4, 2003).

CAREER HITTING: 2-for-16 (.125), 1 R, 0 2B, 0 3B, 0 HR, 0 RBI.

Year — League	W	L	Pct.	ERA	WHIP	G	GS	CG	ShO	Hld.	Sv.-Opp.	IP	H	R	ER	HR	BB-IBB	SO	Avg.
1998— Ariz. Padres (Ariz.)	0	1	.000	3.38	2.06	5	0	0	0	...	0-...	5.1	6	4	2	0	5-1	4	.286
— Idaho Falls (Pioneer)	2	1	.667	2.55	1.42	18	0	0	0	...	5-...	24.2	31	12	7	2	4-0	19	.298
1999— Rancho Cuca. (Calif.)	0	0	...	3.68	0.95	6	0	0	0	...	0-...	7.1	4	3	3	1	3-0	9	.154
— Fort Wayne (Midw.)	2	3	.400	3.78	1.24	42	0	0	0	...	20-...	47.2	40	24	20	5	19-4	47	.221
2000— Rancho Cuca. (Calif.)	1	1	.500	3.48	1.21	18	0	0	0	...	4-...	20.2	18	9	8	1	7-0	21	.240
— Mobile (Sou.)	2	2	.500	5.36	1.40	35	0	0	0	...	6-...	43.2	41	27	26	4	20-0	25	.248
2001— Mobile (Sou.)	2	2	.500	4.54	1.43	27	0	0	0	...	12-...	33.2	33	23	17	1	15-4	21	.268
— Portland (PCL)	1	3	.250	4.75	1.43	39	0	0	0	...	2-...	53.0	63	37	28	7	13-1	45	.304
2002— Portland (PCL)	10	4	.714	3.50	1.26	25	23	0	0	...	0-...	133.2	128	55	52	12	40-1	73	.257
— San Diego (N.L.)	1	2	.333	1.69	1.05	9	3	0	0	3	0-0	26.2	20	7	5	1	8-1	16	.217
2003— San Diego (N.L.)	1	2	.333	8.47	1.88	9	6	0	0	0	0-0	34.0	43	32	32	7	21-4	25	.305
— Portland (PCL)	3	3	.500	4.14	1.21	11	11	0	0	...	0-...	63.0	64	34	29	7	12-0	46	.263
Major League totals (2 years)	**2**	**4**	**.333**	**5.49**	**1.52**	**18**	**9**	**0**	**0**	**3**	**0-0**	**60.2**	**63**	**39**	**37**	**8**	**29-5**	**41**	**.270**

CONE, DAVID — P

PERSONAL: Born January 2, 1963, in Kansas City, Mo. ... 6-1/200. ... Throws right, bats left. ... Full name: David Brian Cone. ... High school: Rockhurst (Kansas City, Mo.).

TRANSACTIONS/CAREER NOTES: Selected by Kansas City Royals organization in third round of free-agent draft (June 8, 1981). ... On disabled list (April 8, 1983-entire season). ... Traded by Royals with C Chris Jelic to New York Mets for C Ed Hearn, P Rick Anderson and P Mauro Gozzo (March 27, 1987). ... On New York disabled list (May 28-August 14, 1987); included rehabilitation assignment to Tidewater (July 30-August 14). ... Traded by Mets to Toronto Blue Jays for IF Jeff Kent and a player to be named later (August 27, 1992); Mets acquired OF Ryan Thompson to complete deal (September 1, 1992). ... Granted free agency (October 30, 1992). ... Signed by Royals (December 8, 1992). ... Traded by Royals to Blue Jays for P David Sinnes, IF Chris Stynes and IF Tony Medrano (April 6, 1995). ... Traded by Blue Jays to New York Yankees for P Marty Janzen, P Jason Jarvis and P Mike Gordon (July 28, 1995). ... Granted free agency (November 3, 1995). ... Re-signed by Yankees (December 21, 1995). ... On New York disabled list (May 3-September 2, 1996); included rehabilitation assignment to Norwich (August 21-September 1). ... On disabled list (August 18-September 20, 1997). ... Granted free agency (November 5, 1998). ... Re-signed by Yankees (November 11, 1998). ... Granted free agency (November 3, 1999). ... Re-signed by Yankees (December 6, 1999). ... Granted free agency (November 7, 2000). ... Signed by Boston Red Sox (January 11, 2001). ... On Boston disabled list (March 21-May 14, 2001); included rehabilitation assignment to Sarasota (May 12-14). ... Granted free agency (November 6, 2001). ... Signed by Mets organization (February 13, 2003). ... Placed on 15-day disabled list (April 23, 2003). ... Sent on rehab assignment to St. Lucie by New York (May 11, 2003). ... Activated from the 15-day disabled list by New York Mets; sent to Port St. Lucie for rehab assignment (May 27, 2003). ... Recalled by New York from rehab assignment (May 31, 2003).

CAREER HITTING: 64-for-412 (.155), 28 R, 9 2B, 0 3B, 0 HR, 22 RBI.

Year — League	W	L	Pct.	ERA	WHIP	G	GS	CG	ShO	Hld.	Sv.-Opp.	IP	H	R	ER	HR	BB-IBB	SO	Avg.
1981— GC Royals-Bl. (GCL)	6	4	.600	2.55	1.27	14	12	0	0	...	0-...	67.0	52	24	19	0	33-1	45	...
1982— Char., S.C. (SAL)	9	2	.818	2.06	1.25	16	16	1	1	...	0-...	104.2	84	38	24	4	47-0	87	...
— Fort Myers (Fla. St.)	7	1	.875	2.12	1.12	10	9	6	1	...	0-...	72.1	56	21	17	1	25-0	57	...
1983— Jacksonville (Sou.)										Did not play.									
1984— Memphis (Sou.)	8	12	.400	4.28	1.54	29	29	9	1	...	0-...	178.2	162	103	85	9	114-1	110	.242
1985— Omaha (Am. Assoc.)	9	15	.375	4.65	1.58	28	27	5	1	...	0-...	158.2	157	90	82	13	* 93-3	115	.263
1986— Omaha (Am. Assoc.)	8	4	.667	2.79	1.20	39	2	2	0	...	14-...	71.0	60	23	22	3	25-4	63	.231
— Kansas City (A.L.)	0	0	...	5.56	1.85	11	0	0	0	0	0-0	22.2	29	14	14	2	13-1	21	.309
1987— New York (N.L.)	5	6	.455	3.71	1.32	21	13	1	0	2	1-1	99.1	87	46	41	11	44-1	68	.239
— Tidewater (Int'l)	0	1	.000	5.73	1.45	3	3	0	0	...	0-...	11.0	10	8	7	1	6-0	7	.233
1988— New York (N.L.)	20	3	* .870	2.22	1.12	35	28	8	4	1	0-0	231.1	178	67	57	10	80-7	213	.213
1989— New York (N.L.)	14	8	.636	3.52	1.17	34	33	7	2	0	0-0	219.2	183	92	86	20	74-6	190	.223
1990— New York (N.L.)	14	10	.583	3.23	1.14	31	30	6	2	0	0-0	211.2	177	84	76	21	65-1	* 233	.223
1991— New York (N.L.)	14	14	.500	3.29	1.19	34	34	5	2	0	0-0	232.2	204	95	85	13	73-2	* 241	.235
1992— New York (N.L.)	13	7	.650	2.88	1.24	27	27	7	• 5	0	0-0	196.2	162	75	63	12	* 82-5	214	.223
— Toronto (A.L.)	4	3	.571	2.55	1.28	8	7	0	0	0	0-0	53.0	39	16	15	3	29-2	47	.207
1993— Kansas City (A.L.)	11	14	.440	3.33	1.26	34	34	6	1	0	0-0	254.0	205	102	94	20	114-2	191	.223
1994— Kansas City (A.L.)	16	5	.762	2.94	1.07	23	23	4	3	0	0-0	171.2	130	60	56	15	54-0	132	.209
1995— Toronto (A.L.)	9	6	.600	3.38	1.18	17	17	5	2	0	0-0	130.1	113	53	49	12	41-2	102	.232
— New York (A.L.)	9	2	.818	3.82	1.30	13	13	1	0	0	0-0	† 99.0	82	42	42	12	47-0	89	.223
1996— New York (A.L.)	7	2	.778	2.88	1.17	11	11	1	0	0	0-0	72.0	50	25	23	3	34-0	71	.198
— Norwich (East.)	0	0	...	0.90	1.00	2	2	0	0	...	0-...	10.0	9	3	1	1	1-0	13	.243
1997— New York (A.L.)	12	6	.667	2.82	1.24	29	29	1	0	0	0-0	195.0	155	67	61	17	86-2	222	.218
1998— New York (A.L.)	• 20	7	.741	3.55	1.18	31	31	3	0	0	0-0	207.2	186	89	82	20	59-1	209	.237

Year League	W	L	Pct.	ERA	WHIP	G	GS	CG	ShO	Hld.	Sv.-Opp.	IP	H	R	ER	HR	BB-IBB	SO	Avg.
1999— New York (A.L.)	12	9	.571	3.44	1.31	31	31	1	1	0	0-0	193.1	164	84	74	21	90-2	177	.229
2000— New York (A.L.)	4	14	.222	6.91	1.77	30	29	0	0	0	0-0	155.0	192	124	119	25	82-3	120	.306
2001— Sarasota (Fla. St.)	0	0	...	0.00	0.50	1	1	0	0	...	0-...	4.0	2	0	0	0	0-0	6	.143
— Boston (A.L.)	9	7	.563	4.31	1.51	25	25	0	0	0	0-0	135.2	148	74	65	17	57-4	115	.275
2002—										Did not play.									
2003— St. Lucie (Fla. St.)	0	1	.000	2.84	1.03	3	3	0	0	...	0-...	12.2	10	4	4	1	3-0	6	.213
— New York (N.L.)	1	3	.250	6.50	1.83	5	4	0	0	0	0-0	18.0	20	13	13	4	13-1	13	.282
American League totals (11 years)	113	75	.601	3.70	1.30	263	250	22	7	0	0-0	1689.1	1493	750	694	167	706-19	1496	.237
National League totals (7 years)	81	51	.614	3.13	1.19	187	169	34	15	3	1-1	1209.1	1011	472	421	91	431-23	1172	.226
Major League totals (17 years)	194	126	.606	3.46	1.26	450	419	56	22	3	1-1	2898.2	2504	1222	1115	258	1137-42	2668	.232

CONINE, JEFF — 1B/OF

PERSONAL: Born June 27, 1966, in Tacoma, Wash. ... 6-1/220. ... Bats right, throws right. ... Full name: Jeffrey Guy Conine. ... Name pronounced: COH-nine. ... High school: Eisenhower (Rialto, Calif.). ... College: UCLA.

TRANSACTIONS/CAREER NOTES: Selected by Kansas City Royals organization in 58th round of free-agent draft (June 2, 1987). ... On disabled list (June 28, 1991-remainder of season). ... Selected by Florida Marlins in first round (22nd pick overall) of expansion draft (November 17, 1992). ... Traded by Marlins to Royals for P Blaine Mull (November 20, 1997). ... On Kansas City disabled list (March 25-May 5 and July 27-August 19, 1998); included rehabilitation assignment to Omaha (August 17-19). ... Traded by Royals to Baltimore Orioles for P Chris Fussell (April 2, 1999). ... Granted free agency (November 5, 1999). ... Re-signed by Orioles (December 15, 1999). ... On disabled list (June 15-August 7, 2002). ... Traded by Baltimore to Florida for P Denny Bautista and P Don Levinski (August 31, 2003).

2003 GAMES PLAYED BY POSITION (MLB): 1B—118, OF—33, 3B—1.

Year Team (League)	Pos.	G	AB	R	H	2B	3B	HR	RBI	BB	SO	HBP	GDP	SB-CS	Avg.	OBP	SLG	OPS	E	Pct.
1988—Baseball City (FSL)	3B-1B	118	415	63	113	23	9	10	59	46	77	0	6	26-12	.272	.342	.443	.785	22	.970
1989—Baseball City (FSL)	1B	113	425	68	116	12	7	14	60	40	91	3	14	32-13	.273	.338	.433	.771	18	.980
1990—Memphis (Sou.)	3B-1B	137	487	89	156	37	8	15	95	94	88	1	10	21-6	.320	.425	.522	.947	‡ 22	.983
—Kansas City (A.L.)	1B	9	20	3	5	2	0	0	2	2	5	0	1	0-0	.250	.318	.350	.668	1	.977
1991—Omaha (A.A.)	1B-OF	51	171	23	44	9	1	3	15	26	39	1	3	0-6	.257	.359	.374	.733	7	.984
1992—Omaha (A.A.)	1B-OF	110	397	69	120	24	5	20	72	54	67	2	6	4-5	.302	.383	.539	.922	6	.993
—Kansas City (A.L.)	OF-1B	28	91	10	23	5	2	0	9	8	23	0	1	0-0	.253	.313	.352	.665	0	1.000
1993—Florida (N.L.)	OF-1B	* 162	595	75	174	24	3	12	79	52	135	5	14	2-2	.292	.351	.403	.754	2	.995
1994—Florida (N.L.)	OF-1B	115	451	60	144	27	6	18	82	40	92	1	8	1-2	.319	.373	.525	.898	6	.986
1995—Florida (N.L.)	OF-1B	133	483	72	146	26	2	25	105	66	94	1	13	2-0	.302	.379	.520	.899	6	.981
1996—Florida (N.L.)	OF-1B	157	597	84	175	32	2	26	95	62	121	4	17	1-4	.293	.360	.484	.844	8	.985
1997—Florida (N.L.)	1B-OF	151	405	46	98	13	1	17	61	57	89	2	11	2-0	.242	.337	.405	.742	8	.992
1998—Kansas City (A.L.)	OF-1B-DH	93	309	30	79	26	0	8	43	26	68	2	8	3-0	.256	.312	.417	.729	1	.996
—Omaha (PCL)	DH-OF	2	9	0	0	0	0	0	0	0	3	0	0	0-0	.000	.000	.000	.000	0	1.000
1999—Baltimore (A.L.)	1-D-0-3	139	444	54	129	31	1	13	75	30	40	3	12	0-3	.291	.335	.453	.787	7	.992
2000—Baltimore (A.L.)	3-1-0-D	119	409	53	116	20	2	13	46	36	53	2	14	4-3	.284	.341	.438	.779	15	.969
2001—Baltimore (A.L.)	1-OF-3-D	139	524	75	163	23	2	14	97	64	75	5	12	12-8	.311	.386	.443	.829	4	.995
2002—Baltimore (A.L.)	1B-DH-OF	116	451	44	123	26	4	15	63	25	66	2	10	8-0	.273	.307	.448	.755	10	.990
2003—Baltimore (A.L.)	1B-OF-3B	124	493	75	143	33	3	15	80	37	60	5	14	5-0	.290	.338	.460	.799	9	.992
—Florida (N.L.)	OF	25	84	13	20	3	0	5	15	13	10	0	2	0-0	.238	.337	.452	.789	0	1.000
American League totals (8 years)		767	2741	344	781	166	14	78	415	228	390	19	72	32-14	.285	.339	.441	.780	47	.990
National League totals (6 years)		743	2615	350	757	125	14	103	437	290	541	13	65	8-8	.289	.359	.466	.825	30	.989
Major League totals (13 years)		1510	5356	694	1538	291	28	181	852	518	931	32	137	40-22	.287	.349	.453	.802	77	.990

C

CONTI, JASON — OF

PERSONAL: Born January 27, 1975, in Pittsburgh, Pa. ... 5-11/175. ... Bats left, throws right. ... Full name: Stanley Jason Conti. ... Name pronounced: CON-tie. ... High school: Seneca Valley (Harmony, Pa.). ... College: Pittsburgh.

TRANSACTIONS/CAREER NOTES: Selected by Arizona Diamondbacks organization in 32nd round of free-agent draft (June 4, 1996). ... Loaned by Diamondbacks to Tulsa, Texas Rangers organization (April 1-September 14, 1998). ... Traded by Diamondbacks with P Nick Bierbrodt to Tampa Bay Devil Rays for P Albie Lopez and C Mike Difelice (July 25, 2001). ... Traded by Devil Rays to Milwaukee Brewers for C Javier Valentin (March 24, 2003). ... Contract purchased by Milwaukee from Indianapolis (August 19, 2003). ... Sent outright to Indianapolis by Milwaukee (August 22, 2003). ... Contract purchased by Milwaukee from Indianapolis (August 29, 2003).

2003 GAMES PLAYED BY POSITION (MLB): OF—20.

Year Team (League)	Pos.	G	AB	R	H	2B	3B	HR	RBI	BB	SO	HBP	GDP	SB-CS	Avg.	OBP	SLG	OPS	E	Pct.
1996—Lethbridge (Pio.)	OF	63	226	63	83	15	1	4	49	30	29	6	3	30-7	.367	.449	.496	.945	4	.955
1997—South Bend (Mid.)	OF	117	458	78	142	22	10	3	43	45	99	11	10	30-18	.310	.383	.421	.804	5	.981
—High Desert (Calif.)	OF	14	59	15	21	5	1	2	8	10	12	1	0	1-2	.356	.457	.576	1.033	5	.853
1998—Tulsa (Texas)	OF	130	530	* 125	167	31	12	15	67	63	96	9	5	19-13	.315	.396	.504	.899	5	.976
1999—Tucson (PCL)	OF	133	520	100	151	23	8	9	57	55	89	5	8	22-7	.290	.360	.417	.777	8	.974
2000—Tucson (PCL)	OF	93	383	75	117	20	5	11	57	23	57	5	8	11-3	.305	.349	.470	.819	10	.950
—Arizona (N.L.)	OF	47	91	11	21	4	3	1	15	7	30	1	2	3-0	.231	.293	.374	.667	1	.983
2001—Tucson (PCL)	OF	92	362	68	120	23	6	9	52	33	54	12	2	2-5	.331	.402	.503	.905	2	.991
—Arizona (N.L.)	OF	5	4	1	1	0	0	0	0	1	2	0	0	0-0	.250	.400	.250	.650	0	
—Durham (Int'l)	OF	38	157	24	48	12	0	5	18	9	31	1	0	3-1	.306	.347	.478	.825	1	.987
2002—Tampa Bay (A.L.)	OF	78	222	26	57	15	2	3	21	18	55	1	5	4-2	.257	.315	.383	.698	6	.966
2003—Indianapolis (Int'l)	OF-DH	121	456	57	113	17	3	10	40	24	120	8	6	13-8	.248	.295	.364	.659	7	.976
—Milwaukee (N.L.)	OF	30	48	3	11	2	0	2	7	2	18	0	1	0-1	.229	.255	.396	.651	3	.909
American League totals (1 year)		78	222	26	57	15	2	3	21	18	55	1	5	4-2	.257	.315	.383	.698	6	.966
National League totals (3 years)		82	143	15	33	6	3	3	22	10	50	1	3	3-1	.231	.284	.378	.661	4	.956
Major League totals (4 years)		160	365	41	90	21	5	6	43	28	105	2	8	7-3	.247	.303	.381	.684	10	.963

CONTRERAS, JOSE — P

PERSONAL: Born December 6, 1971, in Havana, Cuba. ... 6-4/224. ... Throws right, bats right.

TRANSACTIONS/CAREER NOTES: Signed by New York Yankees as a non-drafted free agent (February 6, 2003). ... Optioned to Columbus by New York Yankees (April 19, 2003). ... Recalled by New York from Trenton (May 20, 2003). ... Placed on 15-day disabled list (June 7, 2003). ... Sent to Tampa on rehab assignment by New York (August 11, 2003). ... Recalled from minor league rehab assignment (August 22, 2003). ... Removed from 15-day disabled list (August 24, 2003). ... Optioned to Columbus by New York (August 30, 2003). ... Recalled by New York from Columbus (September 1, 2003).

CAREER HITTING: 0-for-3 (.000), 0 R, 0 2B, 0 3B, 0 HR, 0 RBI.

Year	League	W	L	Pct.	ERA	WHIP	G	GS	CG	ShO	Hld.	Sv.-Opp.	IP	H	R	ER	HR	BB-IBB	SO	Avg.
2003—Columbus (Int'l)		2	0	1.000	1.20	0.80	3	3	0	0	...	0-...	15.0	10	2	2	1	2-0	18	.189
—Trenton (East.)		0	0	...	0.00	1.80	1	1	0	0	...	0-...	1.2	1	0	0	0	2-0	3	.167
—Tampa (FSL)		0	0	...	4.50	1.75	1	1	0	0	...	0-...	4.0	4	2	2	0	3-0	5	.286
—Staten Island (NY-P)		0	0	...	0.00	0.29	1	1	0	0	...	0-...	7.0	2	0	0	0	0-0	15	.087
—New York (A.L.)		7	2	.778	3.30	1.15	18	9	0	0	1	0-1	71.0	52	27	26	4	30-1	72	.202
Major League totals (1 year)		7	2	.778	3.30	1.15	18	9	0	0	1	0-1	71.0	52	27	26	4	30-1	72	.202

COOK, AARON — P

PERSONAL: Born February 8, 1979, in Ft. Campbell, Ky. ... 6-3/205. ... Throws right, bats right. ... Full name: Aaron Lane Cook. ... High school: Hamilton (Ohio).

TRANSACTIONS/CAREER NOTES: Selected by Colorado Rockies organization in second round of free-agent draft (June 3, 1997). ... Recalled by Colorado from Colorado Springs (July 4, 2003). ... Optioned to Colorado Springs of the Pacific Coast League by Colorado (July 5, 2003).

CAREER HITTING: 6-for-40 (.150), 3 R, 0 2B, 0 3B, 0 HR, 4 RBI.

Year	League	W	L	Pct.	ERA	WHIP	G	GS	CG	ShO	Hld.	Sv.-Opp.	IP	H	R	ER	HR	BB-IBB	SO	Avg.
1997—Ariz. Rockies (Ariz.)		1	3	.250	3.13	1.41	9	8	0	0	...	0-...	46.0	48	27	16	1	17-0	35	.261
1998—Portland (NW)		5	8	.385	4.88	1.59	15	15	•1	0	...	0-...	79.1	87	50	43	8	39-0	38	.275
1999—Asheville (S. Atl.)		4	12	.250	6.44	1.64	25	25	2	0	...	0-...	121.2	157	•99	87	17	42-0	73	.310
2000—Asheville (S. Atl.)		10	7	.588	2.96	1.07	21	21	4	•2	...	0-...	142.2	130	54	47	10	23-0	118	.241
—Salem (Caro.)		1	6	.143	5.44	1.49	7	7	1	0	...	0-...	43.0	52	33	26	4	12-0	37	.297
2001—Salem (Caro.)		11	11	.500	3.08	1.26	27	27	0	0	...	0-...	155.0	157	73	53	4	38-0	122	.263
2002—Carolina (Sou.)		7	2	.778	1.42	0.97	14	14	2	2	...	0-...	95.0	73	24	15	4	19-0	58	.213
—Colo. Springs (PCL)		4	4	.500	3.78	1.32	10	10	1	0	...	0-...	64.1	67	40	27	6	18-0	32	.264
—Colorado (N.L.)		2	1	.667	4.54	1.51	9	5	0	0	1	0-0	35.2	41	18	18	4	13-0	14	.295
2003—Colo. Springs (PCL)		1	1	.500	2.25	0.88	2	2	1	0	...	0-...	16.0	10	4	4	2	4-0	12	.175
—Colorado (N.L.)		4	6	.400	6.02	1.75	43	16	1	0	1	0-0	124.0	160	89	83	8	57-7	43	.317
Major League totals (2 years)		6	7	.462	5.69	1.70	52	21	1	0	2	0-0	159.2	201	107	101	12	70-7	57	.313

COOMER, RON — 1B

PERSONAL: Born November 18, 1966, in Chicago, Ill. ... 6-0/215. ... Bats right, throws right. ... Full name: Ronald Bryan Coomer. ... High school: Lockport (Ill.). ... Junior college: Taft College.

TRANSACTIONS/CAREER NOTES: Selected by Oakland Athletics organization in 14th round of free-agent draft (June 2, 1987). ... Released by A's (August 1, 1990). ... Signed by Chicago White Sox organization (March 18, 1991). ... On disabled list (June 5-19, 1992). ... On Birmingham disabled list (June 12-21, 1993). ... Traded by White Sox to Los Angeles Dodgers for P Isidro Martinez (December 27, 1993). ... Traded by Dodgers with P Greg Hansell, P Jose Parra and a player to be named later to Minnesota Twins for P Kevin Tapani and P Mark Guthrie (July 31, 1995); Twins acquired OF Chris Latham to complete deal (October 30, 1995). ... Granted free agency (December 21, 2000). ... Signed by Chicago Cubs (January 10, 2001). ... On Chicago disabled list (April 3-25, 2001); included rehabilitation assignment to Iowa (April 21-25). ... Granted free agency (November 7, 2001). ... Signed by New York Yankees organization (January 25, 2002). ... Granted free agency (October 29, 2002). ... Signed by Los Angeles Dodgers organization (January 30, 2003). ... Placed on 15-day disabled list (July 8, 2003). ... Sent to Vero Beach on rehab assignment by Los Angeles (July 30, 2003).

2003 GAMES PLAYED BY POSITION (MLB): 1B—24, 3B—11, DH—4.

Year	Team (League)	Pos.	G	AB	R	H	2B	3B	HR	RBI	BB	SO	HBP	GDP	SB-CS	Avg.	OBP	SLG	OPS	E	Pct.
1987—Medford (N'west)	3B-1B	45	168	23	58	10	2	1	26	19	22	0	...	1-1	.345	.410	.446	.856	11	.923
1988—Modesto (Calif.)	3B-1B	131	495	67	138	23	2	17	85	60	88	3	...	2-6	.279	.357	.436	.793	16	.920
1989—Madison (Mid.)	3B-1B	61	216	28	69	15	0	4	28	30	34	0	...	0-1	.319	.401	.444	.845	6	.956
1990—Huntsville (Sou.)	2B-3B-1B	66	194	22	43	7	0	3	27	21	40	1	5	3-1	.222	.297	.304	.601	11	.965
1991—Birmingham (Sou.)	3B-1B	137	505	*81	129	27	5	13	76	59	78	1	21	0-3	.255	.330	.406	.736	§26	.938
1992—Vancouver (PCL)	3B	86	262	29	62	10	0	9	40	16	36	0	14	3-0	.237	.277	.378	.654	13	.927
1993—Birmingham (Sou.)	3B-1B	69	262	44	85	18	0	13	50	15	43	0	8	1-1	.324	.358	.542	.900	11	.931
—Nashville (A.A.)	3B	59	211	34	66	19	0	13	51	10	29	1	5	1-2	.313	.342	.588	.930	16	.895
1994—Albuquerque (PCL)	3B-DH-2B	127	535	89	181	34	6	22	*123	26	62	2	12	4-3	.338	.367	.548	.914	19	.952
1995—Albuquerque (PCL)	3B-1B-DH	85	323	54	104	23	2	16	76	18	28	2	16	5-2	.322	.357	.554	.912	9	.979
—Minnesota (A.L.)	1-3-D-OF	37	101	15	26	3	1	5	19	9	11	1	0	0-1	.257	.324	.455	.780	2	.988
1996—Minnesota (A.L.)	1-OF-3-D	95	233	34	69	12	1	12	41	17	24	0	10	3-0	.296	.340	.511	.851	4	.988
1997—Minnesota (A.L.)	3-1-OF-D	140	523	63	156	30	2	13	85	22	91	0	11	3-0	.298	.324	.438	.761	11	.969
1998—Minnesota (A.L.)	3-1-OF-D	137	529	54	146	22	1	15	72	18	72	0	*22	2-2	.276	.295	.406	.702	6	.990
1999—Minnesota (A.L.)	1-3-D-OF	127	467	53	123	25	1	16	65	30	69	1	16	2-1	.263	.307	.424	.731	6	.991
2000—Minnesota (A.L.)	1B-DH-3B	140	544	64	147	29	4	16	82	36	50	4	25	2-0	.270	.317	.415	.733	5	.995
2001—Chicago (N.L.)	3B-1B-DH	111	349	25	91	19	1	8	53	29	70	2	23	0-0	.261	.316	.390	.706	7	.977
—Iowa (PCL)		4	12	0	4	0	0	0	0	1	3	0	0	0-0	.333	.385	.333	.718	0	1.000
2002—New York (A.L.)	3B-DH-1B	55	148	14	39	7	0	3	17	6	23	0	8	0-0	.264	.290	.372	.662	0	.941
2003—Vero Beach (FSL)	3B-1B	3	10	1	5	1	0	0	2	0	1	0	0	0-0	.500	.455	.600	1.055	0	1.000
—Los Angeles (N.L.)	1B-3B-DH	69	125	11	30	4	0	4	15	10	19	1	7	0-0	.240	.299	.368	.667	0	1.000
American League totals (7 years)		731	2545	297	706	128	7	80	381	138	340	6	101	13-7	.277	.313	.428	.741	41	.988
National League totals (2 years)		180	474	36	121	23	1	12	68	39	89	3	30	0-0	.255	.312	.384	.696	7	.984
Major League totals (9 years)		911	3019	333	827	151	8	92	449	177	429	9	131	13-7	.274	.313	.421	.734	48	.987

CORA, ALEX — 2B/SS

PERSONAL: Born October 18, 1975, in Caguas, Puerto Rico. ... 6-0/180. ... Bats left, throws right. ... Full name: Jose Alexander Cora. ... High school: Bautista (Caguas, Puerto Rico). ... College: Miami (Fla.).

TRANSACTIONS/CAREER NOTES: Selected by Los Angeles Dodgers organization in third round of free-agent draft (June 4, 1996). ... On Los Angeles disabled list (March 25-June 27, 1999); included rehabilitation assignment to Albuquerque (June 8-27).

2003 GAMES PLAYED BY POSITION (MLB): 2B—141, SS—15.

Year	Team (League)	Pos.	G	AB	R	H	2B	3B	HR	RBI	BB	SO	HBP	GDP	SB-CS	Avg.	OBP	SLG	OPS	E	Pct.
1996—Vero Beach (FSL)	SS-OF	61	214	26	55	5	4	0	26	12	36	3	1	5-5	.257	.306	.318	.623	16	.940
1997—San Antonio (Texas)	SS	127	448	52	105	20	4	3	48	25	60	3	17	12-9	.234	.279	.317	.596	20	.968
1998—Albuquerque (PCL)	2B-SS	81	299	42	79	17	5	5	45	15	38	3	1	10-7	.264	.303	.405	.708	18	.957
—Los Angeles (N.L.)	SS-2B	29	33	1	4	0	1	0	0	2	8	1	0	0-0	.121	.194	.182	.376	2	.965
1999—Albuquerque (PCL)	SS-2B-DH	80	302	51	93	11	7	4	37	12	37	8	8	9-5	.308	.348	.430	.778	12	.968
—Los Angeles (N.L.)	SS-2B	11	30	2	5	1	0	0	3	0	4	1	1	0-0	.167	.194	.200	.394	2	.943
2000—Albuquerque (PCL)	SS	30	110	18	41	8	3	0	20	7	10	2	1	5-3	.373	.417	.500	.917	7	.959
—Los Angeles (N.L.)	SS-2B	109	353	39	84	18	6	4	32	26	53	7	6	4-1	.238	.302	.357	.658	12	.973
2001—Los Angeles (N.L.)	SS-2B	134	405	38	88	18	3	4	29	31	58	8	16	0-2	.217	.285	.306	.591	20	.962
2002—Los Angeles (N.L.)	SS-2B	115	258	37	75	14	4	5	28	26	38	7	2	7-2	.291	.371	.434	.805	7	.977
2003—Los Angeles (N.L.)	2B-SS	148	477	39	119	24	3	4	34	16	59	10	5	4-2	.249	.287	.338	.625	15	.979
Major League totals (6 years)		546	1556	156	375	75	17	17	126	101	220	34	31	15-7	.241	.301	.344	.644	58	.972

C

CORCORAN, ROY   P

PERSONAL: Born May 11, 1980, in Baton Rouge, La. ... 5-10/170. ... Throws right, bats right. ... Full name: Roy Elliot Corcoran. ... High school: Silliman Institute (Clinton, Louisiana). ... College: Louisiana State.
TRANSACTIONS/CAREER NOTES: Signed by Montreal Expos as an undrafted free agent (2001).
CAREER HITTING: 0-for-1 (.000), 0 R, 0 2B, 0 3B, 0 HR, 0 RBI.

Year League	W	L	Pct.	ERA	WHIP	G	GS	CG	ShO	Hld.	Sv.-Opp.	IP	H	R	ER	HR	BB-IBB	SO	Avg.
2001— Jupiter (FSL)	0	0	...	0.00	1.00	1	0	0	0	...	0-...	2.0	0	0	0	0	2-0	0	.000
— GC Expos (GCL)	2	0	1.000	1.56	0.81	13	0	0	0	...	2-...	17.1	12	4	3	2	2-0	21	.185
2002— Clinton (Midw.)	3	4	.429	4.16	1.33	48	1	0	0	...	11-...	80.0	82	51	37	5	24-1	106	.253
2003— Brevard County (FSL)	5	3	.625	1.91	0.91	28	0	0	0	...	12-...	33.0	19	8	7	1	11-1	35	.171
— Harrisburg (Eastern)	1	1	.500	0.38	0.89	14	0	0	0	...	3-...	23.2	14	4	1	0	7-1	26	.167
— Montreal (N.L.)	0	0	...	1.23	1.36	5	0	0	0	0	0-0	7.1	7	2	1	0	3-0	2	.250
— Edmonton (PCL)	0	0	...	0.00	0.00	2	0	0	0	0	0-...	2.0	0	0	0	0	0-0	1	.000
Major League totals (1 year)	0	0	...	1.23	1.36	5	0	0	0	0	0-0	7.1	7	2	1	0	3-0	2	.250

CORDERO, CHAD   P

PERSONAL: Born March 18, 1982, in Upland, Calif. ... 6-0/195. ... Throws right, bats right. ... Full name: Chad P. Cordero. ... College: Cal State Fullerton.
TRANSACTIONS/CAREER NOTES: Selected by Montreal Expos in first round (20th pick overall) of free-agent draft (June 3, 2003).
CAREER HITTING: 0-for-0 (.000), 0 R, 0 2B, 0 3B, 0 HR, 0 RBI.

Year League	W	L	Pct.	ERA	WHIP	G	GS	CG	ShO	Hld.	Sv.-Opp.	IP	H	R	ER	HR	BB-IBB	SO	Avg.
2003— Brevard County (FSL)	1	1	.500	2.05	1.03	19	0	0	0	...	6-...	26.1	17	8	6	1	10-0	17	.198
— Montreal (N.L.)	1	0	1.000	1.64	0.64	12	0	0	0	1	1-1	11.0	4	2	2	1	3-1	12	.111
Major League totals (1 year)	1	0	1.000	1.64	0.64	12	0	0	0	1	1-1	11.0	4	2	2	1	3-1	12	.111

CORDERO, FRANCISCO   P

PERSONAL: Born May 11, 1975, in Santo Domingo, Dominican Republic. ... 6-2/200. ... Throws right, bats right. ... Full name: Francisco Javier Cordero. ... Name pronounced: cor-DAIR-oh. ... High school: Colegió Luz de Arroyo Hondo (Dominican Republic).
TRANSACTIONS/CAREER NOTES: Signed as non-drafted free agent by Detroit Tigers organization (June 18, 1994). ... On Jamestown disabled list (June 28, 1996-remainder of season). ... On Jacksonville disabled list (May 22-June 18 and June 26, 1998-remainder of season). ... Traded by Tigers with P Justin Thompson, OF Gabe Kapler, C Bill Haselman, 2B Frank Catalanotto and P Alan Webb to Texas Rangers for OF Juan Gonzalez, P Danny Patterson and C Gregg Zaun (November 2, 1999). ... On Texas disabled list (March 23-June 19 and June 26, 2001-remainder of season); included rehabilitation assignment to Oklahoma (May 21-June 19). ... On Texas disabled list (June 25-July 27, 2002); included rehabilitation assignment to Oklahoma (July 20-27).
CAREER HITTING: 0-for-1 (.000), 0 R, 0 2B, 0 3B, 0 HR, 0 RBI.

Year League	W	L	Pct.	ERA	WHIP	G	GS	CG	ShO	Hld.	Sv.-Opp.	IP	H	R	ER	HR	BB-IBB	SO	Avg.
1994— Dominican Tigers (DSL)	4	3	.571	3.90	1.53	12	12	0	0	...	0-...	60.0	65	47	26	...	27-...	36	...
1995— Fayetteville (S. Atl.)	0	3	.000	6.30	1.90	4	4	0	0	...	0-...	20.0	26	16	14	1	12-0	19	.342
— Jamestown (NYP)	4	7	.364	5.22	1.51	15	14	0	0	...	0-...	88.0	96	62	51	3	37-0	54	.282
1996— Fayetteville (S. Atl.)	0	0	...	2.57	1.14	2	1	0	0	...	0-...	7.0	2	2	2	0	6-0	7	.095
— Jamestown (NYP)	0	0	...	0.82	0.64	2	2	0	0	...	0-...	11.0	5	1	1	0	2-0	10	.135
1997— West. Mich. (Mid.)	6	1	.857	0.99	0.94	50	0	0	0	...	* 35-...	54.1	36	13	6	2	15-2	67	.193
1998— Jacksonville (Sou.)	1	1	.500	4.86	1.68	17	0	0	0	...	8-...	16.2	19	12	9	1	9-0	18	.284
— Lakeland (Fla. St.)	0	0	...	...	...	1	0	0	0	...	0-...	...	1	0	0	0	0-0	1	1.000
1999— Jacksonville (Sou.)	4	1	.800	1.38	1.09	47	0	0	0	...	* 27-...	52.1	35	9	8	3	22-0	58	.183
— Detroit (A.L.)	2	2	.500	3.32	1.95	20	0	0	0	6	0-0	19.0	19	7	7	2	18-2	19	.284
2000— Texas (A.L.)	1	2	.333	5.35	1.75	56	0	0	0	4	0-3	77.1	87	51	46	11	48-3	49	.285
— Oklahoma (PCL)	0	0	...	4.15	2.31	3	0	0	0	...	1-...	4.1	7	3	2	0	3-0	5	.350
2001— Oklahoma (PCL)	0	1	.000	0.59	0.72	12	0	0	0	...	6-...	15.1	8	2	1	0	3-0	20	.148
— Texas (A.L.)	0	1	.000	3.86	2.14	3	0	0	0	1	0-0	2.1	3	1	1	0	2-1	3	.300
2002— Texas (A.L.)	2	0	1.000	1.79	1.01	39	0	0	0	1	10-12	45.1	33	12	9	2	13-1	41	.204
— Oklahoma (PCL)	0	2	.000	5.84	1.78	11	1	0	0	...	2-...	12.1	15	14	8	2	7-1	21	.278
2003— Texas (A.L.)	5	8	.385	2.94	1.31	73	0	0	0	18	15-25	82.2	70	33	27	4	38-6	90	.230
Major League totals (5 years)	10	13	.435	3.57	1.46	191	0	0	0	30	25-40	226.2	212	104	90	19	119-13	200	.250

CORDERO, WIL   1B/OF

PERSONAL: Born October 3, 1971, in Mayaguez, Puerto Rico. ... 6-2/215. ... Bats right, throws right. ... Full name: Wilfredo Nieva Cordero. ... Name pronounced: cor-DARE-oh. ... High school: Centro de Servicios Education de Mayaguez (Puerto Rico).
TRANSACTIONS/CAREER NOTES: Signed as non-drafted free agent by Montreal Expos organization (May 24, 1988). ... On Indianapolis disabled list (August 1, 1991-remainder of season; and May 12-June 11 and July 7-20, 1992). ... Traded by Expos with P Bryan Eversgerd to Boston Red Sox for P Rheal Cormier, 1B Ryan McGuire and P Shayne Bennett (January 10, 1996). ... On Boston disabled list (May 21-August 12, 1996); included rehabilitation assignments to Gulf Coast Red Sox (July 23-27) and Pawtucket (July 27-August 6). ... Released by Red Sox (September 28, 1997). ... Signed by Chicago White Sox (March 23, 1998). ... Granted free agency (November 3, 1998). ... Signed by Cleveland Indians (February 3, 1999). ... On Cleveland disabled list (June 9-September 8, 1999); included rehabilitation assignment to Akron (September 3-8). ... Granted free agency (October 29, 1999). ... Signed by Pittsburgh Pirates (December 14, 1999). ... Traded by Pirates to Indians for OF Alex Ramirez and IF Enrique Wilson (July 28, 2000). ... On suspended list (September 19-23, 2000). ... On disabled list (June 11-26, 2001). ... Released by Indians (April 29, 2002). ... Signed by Expos (May 12, 2002). ... On Montreal disabled list (August 1-16, 2002). ... Granted free agency (October 28, 2002). ... Re-signed by Expos (December 7, 2002).
2003 GAMES PLAYED BY POSITION (MLB): 1B—123, DH—2, OF—1.

Year Team (League)	Pos.	G	AB	R	H	2B	3B	HR	RBI	BB	SO	HBP	GDP	SB-CS	Avg.	OBP	SLG	OPS	E	Pct.
1988— Jamestown (NYP)	SS	52	190	18	49	3	6	2	22	15	44	4	2	3-3	.258	.322	.305	.628	31	.886
1989— W.P. Beach (FSL)	SS	78	289	37	80	12	2	6	29	33	58	3	6	2-5	.277	.355	.394	.749	29	.922
— Jacksonville (Sou.)	SS	39	121	9	26	6	1	3	17	12	33	0	3	1-2	.215	.284	.355	.639	7	.957
1990— Jacksonville (Sou.)	SS	131	444	63	104	18	4	7	40	56	122	5	5	9-4	.234	.326	.340	.666	41	.928
1991— Indianapolis (A.A.)	SS	98	360	48	94	16	4	11	52	26	89	3	4	9-3	.261	.315	.419	.734	27	.943
1992— Indianapolis (A.A.)	SS	52	204	32	64	11	1	6	27	24	54	0	7	6-7	.314	.384	.466	.850	12	.948
— Montreal (N.L.)	SS-2B	45	126	17	38	4	1	2	8	9	31	1	3	0-0	.302	.353	.397	.750	8	.947
1993— Montreal (N.L.)	SS-3B	138	475	56	118	32	2	10	58	34	60	7	12	12-3	.248	.308	.387	.695	36	.937
1994— Montreal (N.L.)	SS	110	415	65	122	30	3	15	63	41	62	6	8	16-3	.294	.363	.489	.853	22	.952
1995— Montreal (N.L.)	SS-OF	131	514	64	147	35	2	10	49	36	88	9	11	9-5	.286	.341	.420	.761	22	.953

Year	Team (League)	Pos.	G	AB	R	H	2B	3B	HR	RBI	BB	SO	HBP	GDP	SB-CS	Avg.	OBP	SLG	OPS	E	Pct.
1996— Boston (A.L.) 2B-DH-1B		59	198	29	57	14	0	3	37	11	31	2	8	2-1	.288	.330	.404	.734	10	.950
— GC Red Sox (GCL)	DH-2B	3	10	1	3	0	0	1	3	0	2	0	1	0-0	.300	.273	.600	.873	0	1.000
— Pawtucket (Int'l)	2B-DH	4	10	2	3	1	0	1	2	2	3	0	1	0-0	.300	.417	.700	1.117	0	1.000
1997— Boston (A.L.)	OF-DH-2B	140	570	82	160	26	3	18	72	31	122	4	11	1-3	.281	.320	.432	.752	2	.992
1998— Birmingham (Sou.)	1B-DH	11	35	6	10	2	0	2	11	7	3	0	1	0-0	.286	.405	.514	.919	1	.989
— Chicago (A.L.)	1B-OF	96	341	58	91	18	2	13	49	22	66	3	7	2-1	.267	.314	.446	.759	3	.991
1999— Cleveland (A.L.)	OF-DH	54	194	35	58	15	0	8	32	15	37	6	7	2-0	.299	.364	.500	.864	1	.981
— Akron (East.)	OF-DH	3	11	2	4	2	0	0	0	0	3	1	1	0-0	.364	.417	.545	.962	0	...
2000— Pittsburgh (N.L.)	OF-DH	89	348	46	98	24	3	16	51	25	58	4	11	1-2	.282	.336	.506	.842	2	.983
— Cleveland (A.L.)	OF	38	148	18	39	11	2	0	17	7	18	3	7	0-0	.264	.310	.365	.675	0	1.000
2001— Cleveland (A.L.)	OF-1B-DH	89	268	30	67	11	1	4	21	22	50	4	8	0-0	.250	.313	.343	.656	2	.992
2002— Cleveland (A.L.)	OF-1B	6	18	1	4	0	0	0	1	0	3	0	1	0-0	.222	.222	.222	.444	0	1.000
— Montreal (N.L.)	OF-1B-DH	66	143	21	39	9	0	6	29	17	26	2	3	2-0	.273	.349	.462	.811	2	.983
2003— Montreal (N.L.)	1B-DH-OF	130	436	57	121	27	0	16	71	49	90	4	11	1-1	.278	.354	.450	.803	5	.996
American League totals (7 years)		482	1737	253	476	95	8	46	229	108	327	22	49	7-5	.274	.322	.417	.740	22	.987
National League totals (7 years)		709	2457	326	683	161	11	75	329	211	415	33	59	41-14	.278	.341	.444	.785	97	.968
Major League totals (12 years)		1191	4194	579	1159	256	19	121	558	319	742	55	108	48-19	.276	.333	.433	.766	119	.974

CORDOVA, MARTY — OF

PERSONAL: Born July 10, 1969, in Las Vegas, Nev. ... 6-0/213. ... Bats right, throws right. ... Full name: Martin Keevin Cordova. ... Name pronounced: core-DOE-vuh. ... High school: Bishop Gorman (Las Vegas). ... Junior college: Orange Coast College (Calif.).
TRANSACTIONS/CAREER NOTES: Selected by San Diego Padres organization in eighth round of free-agent draft (June 2, 1987); did not sign. ... Selected by Minnesota Twins organization in 10th round of free-agent draft (June 5, 1989). ... On Visalia disabled list (April 12-May 20, 1991). ... On Salt Lake disabled list (April 17-May 11, 1994). ... On Minnesota disabled list (April 11-May 26, 1997); included rehabilitation assignment to Salt Lake (May 20-26). ... On disabled list (April 27-May 12, 1998). ... Granted free agency (October 7, 1999). ... Signed by Boston Red Sox organization (January 19, 2000). ... Released by Red Sox (March 26, 2000). ... Signed by Toronto Blue Jays organization (March 27, 2000). ... Granted free agency (October 4, 2000). ... Signed by Cleveland Indians organization (December 20, 2000). ... Granted free agency (November 5, 2001). ... Signed by Baltimore Orioles (December 6, 2001). ... On disabled list (March 31-April 12, 2002). ... Placed on the 15-day disabled list (April 23, 2003). ... Transferred to Emergency Disabled List (May 19, 2003).
2003 GAMES PLAYED BY POSITION (MLB): DH—5, OF—4.

Year	Team (League)	Pos.	G	AB	R	H	2B	3B	HR	RBI	BB	SO	HBP	GDP	SB-CS	Avg.	OBP	SLG	OPS	E	Pct.
1989— Elizabethton (App.)	3B-OF	38	148	32	42	2	3	8	29	14	29	3	7	2-1	.284	.358	.500	.858	4	.789
1990— Kenosha (Midw.)	OF	81	269	35	58	7	5	7	25	28	73	5	5	6-3	.216	.300	.357	.657	5	.948
1991— Visalia (Calif.)	OF	71	189	31	40	6	1	7	19	17	46	2	3	2-3	.212	.284	.365	.649	5	.923
1992— Visalia (Calif.)	OF	134	513	103	175	31	6	*28	*131	76	99	9	20	13-5	.341	.431	.589	1.020	3	.984
1993— Nashville (Sou.)	OF	138	508	83	127	30	5	19	77	64	153	13	10	10-5	.250	.347	.441	.788	2	.991
1994— Salt Lake (PCL)	OF-DH	103	385	69	138	25	4	19	66	39	63	8	9	17-6	.358	.426	.592	1.018	8	.962
1995— Minnesota (A.L.)	OF	137	512	81	142	27	4	24	84	52	111	10	10	20-7	.277	.352	.486	.839	5	.986
1996— Minnesota (A.L.)	OF	145	569	97	176	46	1	16	111	53	96	8	18	11-5	.309	.371	.478	.849	3	.991
1997— Minnesota (A.L.)	OF-DH	103	378	44	93	18	4	15	51	30	92	3	13	5-3	.246	.305	.434	.739	2	.991
— Salt Lake (PCL)	DH-OF	6	24	5	9	4	0	1	4	2	3	0	0	1-0	.375	.423	.667	1.090	1	.750
1998— Minnesota (A.L.)	OF-DH	119	438	52	111	20	2	10	69	50	103	5	14	3-6	.253	.333	.377	.709	6	.978
1999— Minnesota (A.L.)	OF-DH	124	425	62	121	28	3	14	70	48	96	9	22	13-4	.285	.365	.464	.828	3	.927
2000— Toronto (A.L.)	OF-DH	62	200	23	49	7	0	4	18	18	35	3	6	3-2	.245	.317	.340	.657	1	.982
2001— Cleveland (A.L.)	OF-DH	122	409	61	123	20	2	20	69	23	81	8	9	0-3	.301	.348	.506	.855	2	.990
2002— Baltimore (A.L.)	OF-DH	131	458	55	116	25	2	18	64	47	111	3	17	1-6	.253	.325	.434	.759	4	.971
2003— Baltimore (A.L.)	DH-OF	9	30	5	7	1	0	1	4	8	5	1	1	1-0	.233	.410	.367	.777	0	1.000
Major League totals (9 years)		952	3419	480	938	192	18	122	540	329	730	50	110	57-36	.274	.344	.448	.792	26	.984

COREY, MARK — P

PERSONAL: Born November 16, 1974, in Coudersport, Pa. ... 6-3/220. ... Throws right, bats right. ... Full name: Mark Franklin Corey. ... High school: Austin Area (Austin, Pa.). ... College: Edinboro (Pa.).
TRANSACTIONS/CAREER NOTES: Selected by Cincinnati Reds organization in fourth round of free-agent draft (June 1, 1995). ... On disabled list (June 12, 1996-entire season). ... Traded by Reds to New York Mets for IF Ralph Millard (February 4, 1999). ... On New York disabled list (June 27-July 12, 2002); included rehabilitation assignment to Norfolk (July 5-12). ... Traded by Mets with OF Jay Payton and OF Robert Stratton to Colorado Rockies for P John Thomson and OF Mark Little (July 31, 2002). ... Granted free agency (October 15, 2002). ... Signed by Pittsburgh Pirates as a minor league free agent (December 25, 2002).
CAREER HITTING: 0-for-2 (.000), 0 R, 0 2B, 0 3B, 0 HR, 0 RBI.

Year	League	W	L	Pct.	ERA	WHIP	G	GS	CG	ShO	Hld.	Sv.-Opp.	IP	H	R	ER	HR	BB-IBB	SO	Avg.
1995— Princeton (Appal.)	1	1	.500	3.68	1.23	4	3	0	0	...	0-...	14.2	12	7	6	1	6-0	8	.218
1996—											Did not play.								
1997— Char., W.Va. (SAL)	8	13	.381	4.57	1.55	26	26	1	0	...	0-...	136.0	169	87	69	7	42-3	97	.311
1998— Burlington (Midw.)	12	6	.667	2.44	1.15	20	20	•6	•2	...	0-...	140.0	125	55	38	9	36-0	109	.236
— Chattanooga (Sou.)	0	4	.000	8.20	1.82	6	6	1	0	...	0-...	26.1	32	25	24	6	16-1	26	.302
— Indianapolis (Int'l)	0	1	.000	4.50	1.17	1	1	1	0	...	0-...	6.0	4	3	3	1	3-0	2	.200
1999— Binghamton (Eastern)	7	13	.350	5.40	1.54	29	27	0	0	...	0-...	155.0	175	108	93	18	64-0	111	.282
2000— Binghamton (Eastern)	0	0	...	1.05	1.01	14	2	0	0	...	0-...	25.2	15	5	3	0	11-0	19	.170
— Norfolk (Int'l)	3	7	.300	6.79	1.71	20	11	0	0	...	1-...	63.2	80	52	48	11	29-1	43	.307
2001— Binghamton (Eastern)	1	2	.333	1.80	1.00	25	0	0	0	...	17-...	35.0	23	10	7	1	12-0	50	.189
— Norfolk (Int'l)	8	2	.800	1.47	1.25	28	0	0	0	...	10-...	36.2	24	7	6	1	22-0	42	.197
— New York (N.L.)	0	0	...	16.20	4.80	2	0	0	0	...	0-0	1.2	5	3	3	0	3-1	3	.500
2002— Norfolk (Int'l)	3	1	.750	1.03	0.80	25	0	0	0	...	7-...	26.1	14	3	3	1	7-1	37	.157
— New York (N.L.)	0	3	.000	4.50	1.80	12	0	0	0	...	0-0	10.0	10	7	5	2	8-1	9	.250
— St. Lucie (Fla. St.)	0	0	...	0.00	0.00	1	0	0	0	...	0-...	2.0	0	0	0	0	0-0	3	.000
— Colorado (N.L.)	0	0	...	12.00	2.50	14	0	0	0	1	0-0	12.0	22	16	16	7	8-1	12	.440
2003— Nashville (PCL)	1	3	.250	4.34	1.20	46	0	0	0	...	30-...	45.2	37	23	22	5	18-2	63	.214
— Pittsburgh (N.L.)	1	2	.333	5.34	1.32	22	0	0	0	4	0-0	30.1	29	19	18	2	11-1	27	.252
Major League totals (3 years)	1	5	.167	7.00	1.78	50	0	0	0	5	0-0	54.0	66	45	42	11	30-4	51	.300

CORMIER, RHEAL   P

PERSONAL: Born April 23, 1967, in Moncton, New Brunswick. ... 5-10/195. ... Throws left, bats left. ... Full name: Rheal Paul Cormier. ... Name pronounced: ree-AL cor-MEE-ay. ... High school: Polyvalente Louis J. Robichaud. ... Junior college: Rhode Island Community College.

TRANSACTIONS/CAREER NOTES: Selected by St. Louis Cardinals organization in sixth round of free-agent draft (June 6, 1988). ... On Louisville disabled list (April 10-29, 1991). ... On disabled list (August 12-September 7, 1993). ... On St. Louis disabled list (April 28-May 13 and May 21-August 3, 1994); included rehabilitation assignments to Arkansas (July 7-18) and Louisville (July 18-30). ... Traded by Cardinals with OF Mark Whiten to Boston Red Sox for 3B Scott Cooper, P Cory Bailey and a player to be named later (April 8, 1995). ... Traded by Red Sox with 1B Ryan McGuire and P Shayne Bennett to Montreal Expos for SS Wil Cordero and P Bryan Eversgerd (Jauary 10, 1996). ... On disabled list (August 26-September 10, 1996). ... Granted free agency (October 30, 1997). ... Signed by Cleveland Indians organization (December 18, 1997). ... On Buffalo disabled list (April 9-June 2, 1998). ... On Akron disabled list (June 18, 1998-remainder of season). ... Granted free agency (October 15, 1998). ... Signed by Red Sox organization (January 5, 1999). ... On suspended list (May 7-10, 1999). ... Granted free agency (November 1, 2000). ... Signed by Philadelphia Phillies (November 29, 2000). ... On Philadelphia disabled list (August 10-29, 2001); included rehabilitation assignment to Reading (August 27-29).

CAREER HITTING: 36-for-190 (.189), 15 R, 4 2B, 1 3B, 0 HR, 12 RBI.

Year	League	W	L	Pct.	ERA	WHIP	G	GS	CG	ShO	Hld.	Sv.-Opp.	IP	H	R	ER	HR	BB-IBB	SO	Avg.
1989—	St. Pete. (FSL)	12	7	.632	2.23	1.03	26	26	4	1	...	0-...	169.2	141	63	42	9	33-2	122	.225
1990—	Arkansas (Texas)	5	• 12	.294	5.04	1.34	22	21	3	1	...	0-...	121.1	133	81	68	9	30-2	102	.273
	Louisville (A.A.)	1	1	.500	2.25	0.88	4	4	0	0	...	0-...	24.0	18	8	6	1	3-0	9	.202
1991—	Louisville (A.A.)	7	9	.438	4.23	1.34	21	21	3	* 3	...	0-...	127.2	140	64	60	5	31-1	74	.286
	St. Louis (N.L.)	4	5	.444	4.12	1.21	11	10	2	0	0	0-0	67.2	74	35	31	5	8-1	38	.277
1992—	St. Louis (N.L.)	10	10	.500	3.68	1.22	31	30	3	0	0	0-...	186.0	194	83	76	15	33-2	117	.269
	Louisville (A.A.)	0	1	.000	6.75	2.00	1	1	0	0	...	0-...	4.0	8	4	3	0	0-0	1	.400
1993—	St. Louis (N.L.)	7	6	.538	4.33	1.31	38	21	1	0	0	0-...	145.1	163	80	70	18	27-3	75	.284
1994—	St. Louis (N.L.)	3	2	.600	5.45	1.18	7	7	0	0	0	0-...	39.2	40	24	24	6	7-0	26	.256
	Arkansas (Texas)	1	0	1.000	1.93	0.96	2	2	0	0	...	0-...	9.1	9	2	2	0	0-0	11	.257
	Louisville (A.A.)	1	2	.333	4.50	1.32	3	3	1	0	...	0-...	22.0	21	11	11	3	8-1	13	.250
1995—	Boston (A.L.)	7	5	.583	4.07	1.41	48	12	0	0	9	0-2	115.0	131	60	52	12	31-2	69	.294
1996—	Montreal (N.L.)	7	10	.412	4.17	1.29	33	27	1	1	0	0-0	159.2	165	80	74	16	41-3	100	.269
1997—	Montreal (N.L.)	0	1	.000	33.75	3.75	1	1	0	0	0	0-0	1.1	4	5	5	1	1-0	0	.500
1998—	Akron (East.)	0	0	...	6.52	1.76	3	3	0	0	...	0-...	9.2	15	7	7	3	2-0	6	.366
1999—	Boston (A.L.)	2	0	1.000	3.69	1.25	60	0	0	0	15	0-3	63.1	61	34	26	4	18-2	39	.246
2000—	Boston (A.L.)	3	3	.500	4.61	1.33	64	0	0	0	9	0-2	68.1	74	40	35	7	17-2	43	.275
2001—	Philadelphia (N.L.)	5	6	.455	4.21	1.29	60	0	0	0	12	1-6	51.1	49	26	24	5	17-4	37	.247
	Reading (East.)	0	0	...	0.00	0.50	1	1	0	0	...	0-...	2.0	0	0	0	0	1-0	2	.000
2002—	Philadelphia (N.L.)	5	6	.455	5.25	1.55	54	0	0	0	9	0-3	60.0	61	38	35	6	32-6	49	.266
2003—	Philadelphia (N.L.)	8	0	1.000	1.70	0.93	65	0	0	0	14	1-4	84.2	54	18	16	4	25-2	67	.182
American League totals (3 years)		12	8	.600	4.12	1.35	172	12	0	0	33	0-7	246.2	266	134	113	23	66-6	151	.276
National League totals (9 years)		49	46	.516	4.02	1.25	300	96	7	1	35	2-13	795.2	804	389	355	76	191-21	509	.263
Major League totals (12 years)		61	54	.530	4.04	1.27	472	108	7	1	68	2-20	1042.1	1070	523	468	99	257-27	660	.266

CORNEJO, NATE   P

PERSONAL: Born September 24, 1979, in Wellington, Kan. ... 6-5/245. ... Throws right, bats right. ... Full name: Nathan J. Cornejo. ... Name pronounced: cor-NAY-ho. ... High school: Wellington (Kan.).

TRANSACTIONS/CAREER NOTES: Selected by Detroit Tigers organization in supplemental round ("sandwich pick" between first and second round, 34th pick overall) of free-agent draft (June 2, 1998); pick received as part of compensation for Arizona Diamondbacks signing Type A free-agent P Willie Blair.

CAREER HITTING: 0-for-4 (.000), 0 R, 0 2B, 0 3B, 0 HR, 0 RBI.

Year	League	W	L	Pct.	ERA	WHIP	G	GS	CG	ShO	Hld.	Sv.-Opp.	IP	H	R	ER	HR	BB-IBB	SO	Avg.
1998—	GC Tigers (GCL)	1	0	1.000	1.26	0.98	5	0	0	0	...	1-...	14.1	12	2	2	0	2-0	9	.218
1999—	West. Mich. (Mid.)	9	11	.450	3.71	1.37	28	• 28	4	1	...	0-...	174.2	173	87	72	4	67-0	125	.265
2000—	Lakeland (Fla. St.)	5	5	.500	3.04	1.27	12	12	1	0	...	0-...	77.0	67	37	26	4	31-0	60	.234
	Jacksonville (Sou.)	5	7	.417	4.61	1.46	16	16	0	0	...	0-...	91.2	91	52	47	6	43-1	60	.271
2001—	Erie (East.)	12	3	.800	2.68	1.19	19	19	3	1	...	0-...	124.1	107	47	37	12	41-0	105	.229
	Toledo (Int'l)	4	0	1.000	2.12	1.04	4	4	0	0	...	0-...	29.2	24	8	7	1	7-0	22	.229
	Detroit (A.L.)	4	4	.500	7.38	2.13	10	10	0	0	0	0-0	42.2	63	38	35	10	28-4	22	.344
2002—	Toledo (Int'l)	9	8	.529	4.42	1.47	21	20	1	0	...	0-...	132.1	163	72	65	11	31-1	86	.307
	Detroit (A.L.)	1	5	.167	5.04	1.62	9	9	1	0	0	0-0	50.0	63	33	28	6	18-0	23	.303
2003—	Detroit (A.L.)	6	17	.261	4.67	1.51	32	32	2	0	0	0-0	194.2	236	111	101	18	58-8	46	.307
Major League totals (3 years)		11	26	.297	5.14	1.62	51	51	3	0	0	0-0	287.1	362	182	164	34	104-12	91	.312

CORREIA, KEVIN   P

PERSONAL: Born August 24, 1980, in San Diego, Calif. ... 6-3/200. ... Throws right, bats right. ... Full name: Kevin John Correia. ... College: Cal-Poly SLO.

TRANSACTIONS/CAREER NOTES: Selected by San Francisco Giants organization in fourth round of free-agent draft (June 2002).

CAREER HITTING: 2-for-13 (.154), 1 R, 0 2B, 0 3B, 0 HR, 2 RBI.

Year	League	W	L	Pct.	ERA	WHIP	G	GS	CG	ShO	Hld.	Sv.-Opp.	IP	H	R	ER	HR	BB-IBB	SO	Avg.
2002—	Salem-Keizer (NW)	2	2	.500	4.54	1.35	10	8	0	0	...	0-...	37.2	37	20	19	1	14-0	31	.257
2003—	Norwich (East.)	6	6	.500	3.65	1.27	16	14	0	0	...	0-...	86.1	80	38	35	3	30-0	73	.248
	Fresno (PCL)	1	0	1.000	2.84	0.95	3	3	0	0	...	0-...	19.0	16	8	6	3	2-0	23	.222
	San Francisco (N.L.)	3	1	.750	3.66	1.50	10	7	0	0	0	0-0	39.1	41	16	16	6	18-1	28	.275
Major League totals (1 year)		3	1	.750	3.66	1.50	10	7	0	0	0	0-0	39.1	41	16	16	6	18-1	28	.275

CORTES, DAVID   P

PERSONAL: Born October 15, 1973, in Mexicali, Mexico. ... 5-11/195. ... Throws right, bats right. ... Full name: David C. Cortes. ... Name pronounced: cor-tez. ... High school: Central Union (Calif.). ... Junior college: Imperial Valley College (Calif.).

TRANSACTIONS/CAREER NOTES: Signed as non-drafted free agent by Atlanta Braves organization (July 13, 1996). ... On disabled list (June 4-July 5, 1998). ... Traded by Braves with P Mike Porzio to Colorado Rockies for 1B Greg Colbrunn (July 30, 1998). ... Traded by Rockies to Braves for a player to be named later (August 19, 1998); Rockies acquired P Anthony Briggs to complete deal (September 8, 1998). ... On Richmond disabled list (April 8-15, 1999). ... On disabled list (April 2, 2000-remainder of season). ... On Richmond disabled list (April 5-May 17, 2001). ... Released by Braves (March 28, 2002). ... Signed with Mexican League. ... Signed by Arizona Diamondbacks as a free agent (August 24, 2002). ... Signed by Cleveland Indians.

CAREER HITTING: 0-for-0 (.000), 0 R, 0 2B, 0 3B, 0 HR, 0 RBI.

Year League	W	L	Pct.	ERA	WHIP	G	GS	CG	ShO	Hld.	Sv.-Opp.	IP	H	R	ER	HR	BB-IBB	SO	Avg.
1996— Eugene (NW)	2	1	.667	0.73	0.77	15	0	0	0	...	4-...	24.2	13	2	2	0	6-0	33	.148
1997— Macon (S. Atl.)	3	0	1.000	0.57	0.64	27	0	0	0	...	15-...	31.1	16	3	2	0	4-0	32	.152
— Durham (Caro.)	2	0	1.000	2.33	1.03	19	0	0	0	...	8-...	19.1	15	5	5	1	5-0	16	.214
— Greenville (Sou.)	0	1	.000	1.80	1.00	3	0	0	0	...	0-...	5.0	4	1	1	1	1-0	7	.211
1998— Richmond (Int'l)	3	3	.500	2.82	1.14	29	0	0	0	...	4-...	44.2	37	15	14	2	14-3	46	.227
— Colo. Springs (PCL)	1	0	1.000	7.71	2.29	6	0	0	0	...	0-...	7.0	14	6	6	0	2-0	5	.400
1999— Richmond (Int'l)	2	3	.400	3.35	1.40	47	0	0	0	...	22-...	45.2	50	19	17	2	14-5	42	.276
— Atlanta (N.L.)	0	0	...	4.91	1.91	4	0	0	0	0	0-0	3.2	3	3	2	0	4-0	2	.214
2000— Atlanta (N.L.)										Did not play.									
2001— Myrtle Beach (Caro.)	0	2	.000	5.91	1.50	9	0	0	0	...	2-...	10.2	11	7	7	2	5-0	9	.256
— Greenville (Sou.)	0	3	.000	8.15	1.70	14	0	0	0	...	0-...	17.2	19	18	16	2	11-2	10	.264
— Macon (S. Atl.)	1	0	1.000	7.11	1.50	10	0	0	0	...	0-...	12.2	14	11	10	1	5-0	8	.259
2002— Tucson (PCL)	0	0	...	0.00	0.75	3	0	0	0	...	0-...	4.0	3	0	0	0	0-0	1	.188
2003— Cleveland (A.L.)	0	0	...	12.00	2.67	2	0	0	0	0	0-0	3.0	8	5	4	1	0-0	1	.471
— Buffalo (Int'l)	1	0	1.000	2.70	0.60	5	0	0	0	...	1-...	6.2	4	3	2	1	0-0	9	.154
American League totals (1 year)	0	0	...	12.00	2.67	2	0	0	0	0	0-0	3.0	8	5	4	1	0-0	1	.471
National League totals (1 year)	0	0	...	4.91	1.91	4	0	0	0	0	0-0	3.2	3	3	2	0	4-0	2	.214
Major League totals (2 years)	0	0	...	8.10	2.25	6	0	0	0	0	0-0	6.2	11	8	6	1	4-0	3	.355

COTA, HUMBERTO — C

PERSONAL: Born February 7, 1979, in San Luis Rio Colorado, Mexico. ... 6-0/210. ... Bats right, throws right. ... Full name: Humberto Figueroa Cota. ... Name pronounced: KOH-ta. ... High school: Preparatoria Abierta.

TRANSACTIONS/CAREER NOTES: Signed as non-drafted free agent by Atlanta Braves organization (December 22, 1995). ... Loaned by Braves organization to Mexico City Tigres, Mexican League (June 23-September 23, 1996); did not play. ... Released by Braves (January 27, 1997). ... Signed by Tampa Bay Devil Rays organization (May 22, 1997). ... Traded by Devil Rays with C Joe Oliver to Pittsburgh Pirates for OF Jose Guillen and P Jeff Sparks (July 23, 1999). ... On Nashville disabled list (April 18-26, 2001). ... Recalled from Nashville by Pittsburgh (June 29, 2003). ... Optioned to Nashville of the Pacific Coast League by Pittsburgh (July 7, 2003). ... Recalled by Pittsburgh from Nashville (July 21, 2003). ... Optioned to Nashville by Pittsburgh (August 19, 2003). ... Recalled from Nashville by Pittsburgh (September 15, 2003).

2003 GAMES PLAYED BY POSITION (MLB): C—4.

Year — Team (League)	Pos.	G	AB	R	H	2B	3B	HR	RBI	BB	SO	HBP	GDP	SB-CS	Avg.	OBP	SLG	OPS	E	Pct.
1996— M.C. Tigers (Mex.)										Did not play.										
1997— GC Devil Rays (GCL)	C	44	133	14	32	6	1	2	20	17	27	3	1	3-1	.241	.333	.346	.679	5	.985
— Hudson Valley (NYP)	C	3	9	0	2	0	0	0	2	0	1	0	0	0-0	.222	.222	.222	.444	0	1.000
1998— Princeton (Appal.)	C	67	245	48	76	13	4	15	61	32	59	6	3	4-4	.310	.399	.580	.978	• 12	.973
1999— Char., S.C. (SAL)	C-1B	85	336	42	94	21	1	9	61	20	51	2	9	1-1	.280	.320	.429	.748	7	.986
— Hickory (S. Atl.)	C	37	133	28	36	11	2	2	20	21	20	0	0	3-1	.271	.365	.429	.794	2	.992
2000— Altoona (East.)	C-1B	112	429	49	112	20	1	8	44	21	80	3	8	6-4	.261	.297	.368	.665	* 17	.973
2001— Nashville (PCL)	C	111	377	61	112	22	2	14	72	25	74	8	8	7-2	.297	.351	.477	.829	8	.986
— Pittsburgh (N.L.)	C	7	9	0	2	0	0	0	1	0	5	0	0	0-0	.222	.222	.222	.444	0	1.000
2002— Nashville (PCL)	C-1B	118	404	51	108	27	1	9	54	31	106	5	11	5-8	.267	.321	.406	.727	4	.994
— Pittsburgh (N.L.)	C	7	17	2	5	1	0	0	1	1	4	0	0	0-0	.294	.333	.353	.686	0	1.000
2003— Pittsburgh (N.L.)	C	10	16	1	4	1	0	0	1	1	5	0	0	0-0	.250	.294	.313	.607	0	1.000
— Nashville (PCL)	C-DH	62	200	23	41	9	0	8	27	20	59	2	4	2-0	.205	.284	.370	.654	0	1.000
Major League totals (3 years)		24	42	3	11	2	0	0	2	2	14	0	0	0-0	.262	.295	.310	.605	0	1.000

COTTS, NEAL — P

PERSONAL: Born March 25, 1980, in Belleville, Ill. ... 6-2/200. ... Throws left, bats left. ... Full name: Neal James Cotts. ... High school: Lebanon (Ill). ... College: Illinois State.

TRANSACTIONS/CAREER NOTES: Selected by Oakland A's organization in second round of free-agent draft (June 5, 2001). ... Traded by Oakland to Chicago White Sox as the player to be named later in deal that sent P Keith Foulke, P Joe Valentine and C Mark Johnson to A's (December 17, 2002).

CAREER HITTING: 0-for-0 (.000), 0 R, 0 2B, 0 3B, 0 HR, 0 RBI.

Year League	W	L	Pct.	ERA	WHIP	G	GS	CG	ShO	Hld.	Sv.-Opp.	IP	H	R	ER	HR	BB-IBB	SO	Avg.
2001— Vancouver (NW)	1	0	1.000	3.09	1.17	9	7	0	0	...	0-...	35.0	28	14	12	2	13-0	44	.215
— Visalia (Calif.)	3	2	.600	2.32	1.35	7	7	0	0	...	0-...	31.0	27	14	8	0	15-0	34	.225
2002— Modesto (Calif.)	12	6	.667	4.12	1.53	28	28	0	0	...	0-...	137.2	123	72	63	5	87-0	178	.239
2003— Chicago (A.L.)	1	1	.500	8.10	2.40	4	4	0	0	0	0-0	13.1	15	12	12	1	17-0	10	.294
— Birmingham (Sou.)	9	7	.563	2.16	1.14	21	21	0	0	...	0-...	108.1	67	32	26	2	56-1	133	.178
Major League totals (1 year)	1	1	.500	8.10	2.40	4	4	0	0	0	0-0	13.1	15	12	12	1	17-0	10	.294

COUNSELL, CRAIG — IF

PERSONAL: Born August 21, 1970, in South Bend, Ind. ... 6-0/184. ... Bats left, throws right. ... Full name: Craig John Counsell. ... High school: Whitefish Bay (Milwaukee). ... College: Notre Dame.

TRANSACTIONS/CAREER NOTES: Selected by Colorado Rockies organization in 11th round of free-agent draft (June 1, 1992). ... On disabled list (April 7-May 13, July 30-August 6 and August 7-27, 1994). ... On disabled list (May 1-July 15 and July 18-September 3, 1996). ... Traded by Rockies to Florida Marlins for P Mark Hutton (July 27, 1997). ... On disabled list (August 4, 1998-remainder of season). ... Traded by Marlins to Los Angeles Dodgers for a player to be named later (June 15, 1999); Marlins acquired P Ryan Moskau to complete deal (July 15, 1999). ... Released by Dodgers (March 15, 2000). ... Signed by Arizona Diamondbacks organization (March 20, 2000). ... On disabled list (August 9, 2002-remainder of season). ... Placed on 15-day disabled list (May 7, 2003). ... Transferred to Emergency disabled list (May 18, 2003). ... Sent to Tucson on rehab assignment by Arizona (July 2, 2003). ... Recalled from Tucson rehab assignment; reinstated from Emergency disabled list (July 7, 2003). ... Activated from the 15-day disabled list by Arizona (July 7, 2003).

2003 GAMES PLAYED BY POSITION (MLB): 3B—57, SS—26, 2B—10, 1B—2.

Year — Team (League)	Pos.	G	AB	R	H	2B	3B	HR	RBI	BB	SO	HBP	GDP	SB-CS	Avg.	OBP	SLG	OPS	E	Pct.
1992— Bend (NW)	2B-SS	18	61	11	15	6	1	0	8	9	10	1	2	1-2	.246	.352	.377	.729	2	.967
1993— Central Valley (Cal.)	SS	131	471	79	132	26	3	5	59	95	68	3	8	14-8	.280	.401	.380	.781	35	.944
1994— New Haven (East.)	2B-SS	83	300	47	84	20	1	5	37	37	32	5	6	4-1	.280	.366	.403	.770	27	.931
1995— Colo. Springs (PCL)	SS	118	399	60	112	22	6	5	53	34	47	2	12	10-2	.281	.336	.404	.739	30	.950
— Colorado (N.L.)	SS	3	1	0	0	0	0	0	0	1	0	0	0	0-0	.000	.500	.000	.500	0	1.000
1996— Colo. Springs (PCL) 2B-3B-SS		25	75	17	18	3	0	2	10	24	7	0	2	4-3	.240	.424	.360	.784	4	.961
1997— Colo. Springs (PCL)	2B-SS	96	376	77	126	31	6	5	63	45	38	6	6	12-2	.335	.409	.489	.898	9	.981
— Colorado (N.L.)		1	0	0	0	0	0	0	0	0	0	0	0	0-0	.000	...	...	...	0	...
— Florida (N.L.)	2B	51	164	20	49	9	2	1	16	18	17	3	5	1-1	.299	.376	.396	.773	3	.989

Year	Team (League)	Pos.	G	AB	R	H	2B	3B	HR	RBI	BB	SO	HBP	GDP	SB-CS	Avg.	OBP	SLG	OPS	E	Pct.
1998— Florida (N.L.)	2B	107	335	43	84	19	5	4	40	51	47	4	5	3-0	.251	.355	.373	.729	5	.991
1999— Florida (N.L.)	2B	37	66	4	10	1	0	0	2	5	10	0	1	0-0	.152	.211	.167	.378	1	.980
— Los Angeles (N.L.)	2B-SS	50	108	20	28	6	0	0	9	9	14	0	1	1-0	.259	.311	.315	.626	1	.993
2000— Tucson (PCL)	2B-3B-SS	50	198	45	69	14	3	3	27	22	20	1	1	4-1	.348	.413	.495	.908	4	.981
— Arizona (N.L.)	2B-3B-SS	67	152	23	48	8	1	2	11	20	18	2	4	3-3	.316	.400	.421	.821	6	.957
2001— Arizona (N.L.)	SS-2-3-1	141	458	76	126	22	3	4	38	61	76	2	9	6-8	.275	.359	.362	.721	8	.985
2002— Arizona (N.L.)	3B-SS-2B	112	436	63	123	22	1	2	51	45	52	1	10	7-5	.282	.348	.351	.699	8	.979
2003— Tucson (PCL)	2B-SS-3B	5	23	8	10	2	0	0	2	1	3	0	0	0-0	.435	.458	.522	.980	1	.963
— Arizona (N.L.)	3-SS-2-1	89	303	40	71	6	3	3	21	41	32	2	4	11-4	.234	.328	.304	.631	3	.989
Major League totals (8 years)		658	2023	289	539	93	15	16	188	251	266	14	39	32-21	.266	.349	.351	.700	35	.985

CRAWFORD, CARL — OF

PERSONAL: Born August 5, 1981, in Houston, Texas. ... 6-2/219. ... Bats left, throws left. ... Full name: Carl Demonte Crawford. ... High school: Jefferson Davis (Houston).

TRANSACTIONS/CAREER NOTES: Selected by Tampa Bay Devil Rays organization in second round of free-agent draft (June 2, 1999). ... On Durham disabled list (May 21-30, 2002). ... Suspended by Major League Baseball (July 19, 2003). ... Reinstated (July 22, 2003).

2003 GAMES PLAYED BY POSITION (MLB): OF—146, DH—1.

Year	Team (League)	Pos.	G	AB	R	H	2B	3B	HR	RBI	BB	SO	HBP	GDP	SB-CS	Avg.	OBP	SLG	OPS	E	Pct.
1999— Princeton (Appal.)	OF	60	260	62	83	14	4	0	25	13	47	1	5	17-2	.319	.350	.404	.754	8	.934
2000— Char., S.C. (SAL)	OF	135	564	99	170	21	11	6	57	32	102	3	1	55-9	.301	.342	.410	.751	8	.968
2001— Orlando (South.)	OF	132	537	64	147	24	3	4	51	36	90	4	3	36-20	.274	.323	.352	.675	6	.981
2002— Durham (Int'l)	OF	85	353	59	105	17	9	7	52	20	69	2	5	26-8	.297	.335	.456	.791	1	.994
— Tampa Bay (A.L.)	OF	63	259	23	67	11	6	2	30	9	41	3	0	9-5	.259	.290	.371	.661	1	.994
2003— Tampa Bay (A.L.)	OF-DH	151	630	80	177	18	9	5	54	26	102	1	5	*55-10	.281	.309	.362	.671	3	.992
Major League totals (2 years)		214	889	103	244	29	15	7	84	35	143	4	5	64-15	.274	.304	.364	.668	4	.992

CREDE, JOE — 3B

PERSONAL: Born April 26, 1978, in Jefferson City, Mo. ... 6-2/195. ... Bats right, throws right. ... Full name: Joseph Crede. ... Name pronounced: CREE-dee. ... High school: Fatima (Westphalia, Mo.).

TRANSACTIONS/CAREER NOTES: Selected by Chicago White Sox organization in fifth round of free-agent draft (June 2, 1996). ... On Birmingham disabled list (July 2, 1999-remainder of season).

2003 GAMES PLAYED BY POSITION (MLB): 3B—151.

Year	Team (League)	Pos.	G	AB	R	H	2B	3B	HR	RBI	BB	SO	HBP	GDP	SB-CS	Avg.	OBP	SLG	OPS	E	Pct.
1996— GC Whi. Sox (GCL)	3B	56	221	30	66	17	1	4	32	9	41	2	8	1-1	.299	.326	.439	.765	* 25	.857
1997— Hickory (S. Atl.)	3B	113	402	45	109	25	0	5	62	24	83	5	6	3-1	.271	.319	.371	.689	33	.905
1998— Win.-Salem (Car.)	3B	* 137	492	•92	155	32	3	20	* 88	53	98	12	10	9-7	.315	.387	.514	.902	* 30	.929
1999— Birmingham (Sou.)	3B	74	291	37	73	14	1	4	42	22	47	1	15	2-6	.251	.303	.347	.650	20	.910
2000— Birmingham (Sou.)	3B	138	533	84	* 163	35	0	21	94	56	111	15	18	3-4	.306	.384	.490	.874	19	.942
— Chicago (A.L.)	3B-DH	7	14	2	5	1	0	0	3	0	3	0	0	0-0	.357	.333	.429	.762	1	.933
2001— Charlotte (Int'l)	3B	124	463	67	128	34	1	17	65	46	88	7	5	2-1	.276	.349	.464	.813	20	.946
— Chicago (A.L.)	3B	17	50	1	11	1	1	0	7	3	11	1	1	1-0	.220	.273	.280	.553	0	1.000
2002— Charlotte (Int'l)	3B	95	359	57	112	21	0	24	65	26	48	4	8	0-1	.312	.359	.571	.930	15	.944
— Chicago (A.L.)	3B	53	200	28	57	10	0	12	35	8	40	0	1	0-2	.285	.311	.515	.826	8	.938
2003— Chicago (A.L.)	3B	151	536	68	140	31	2	19	75	32	75	6	11	1-1	.261	.308	.433	.741	14	.964
Major League totals (4 years)		228	800	99	213	43	3	31	120	43	129	7	13	2-3	.266	.307	.444	.751	23	.959

CREEK, DOUG — P

PERSONAL: Born March 1, 1969, in Winchester, Va. ... 6-0/227. ... Throws left, bats left. ... Full name: Paul Douglas Creek. ... High school: Martinsburg (W.Va.). ... College: Georgia Tech.

TRANSACTIONS/CAREER NOTES: Selected by California Angels organization in fifth round of free-agent draft (June 4, 1990); did not sign. ... Selected by St. Louis Cardinals organization in seventh round of free-agent draft (June 3, 1991). ... On Arkansas disabled list (April 10-May 21, 1992; July 25-August 1, 1993; and June 25-July 10, 1994). ... Traded by Cardinals with P Allen Watson and P Rich DeLucia to San Francisco Giants for SS Royce Clayton and a player to be named later (December 14, 1995). ... Cardinals acquired 2B Chris Wimmer to complete deal (January 16, 1996). ... Contract purchased by Chicago White Sox from Giants organization (November 7, 1997). ... Contract sold by White Sox to Hanshin Tigers of Japan Central League (December 4, 1997). ... Signed by Chicago Cubs organization (January 29, 1999). ... Released by Cubs (September 13, 1999). ... Signed by Tampa Bay Devil Rays organization (February 1, 2000). ... On Durham disabled list (April 6-25, 2000). ... Traded by Devil Rays to Seattle Mariners for cash considerations (July 24, 2002). ... Released by Mariners (October 15, 2002). ... Signed by Toronto Blue Jays organization (October 29, 2002). ... Transferred to Emergency disabled list (June 2, 2003). ... Reinstated from Emergency disabled list (September 29, 2003).

CAREER HITTING: 1-for-5 (.200), 1 R, 0 2B, 0 3B, 0 HR, 0 RBI.

Year	League	W	L	Pct.	ERA	WHIP	G	GS	CG	ShO	Hld.	Sv.-Opp.	IP	H	R	ER	HR	BB-IBB	SO	Avg.
1991— Hamilton (NYP)	3	2	.600	5.12	1.47	7	6	0	0	...	0-...	38.2	39	22	22	2	18-0	45	.269
— Savannah (S. Atl.)	2	1	.667	4.45	1.45	5	5	0	0	...	0-...	28.1	24	14	14	2	17-0	32	.245
1992— Springfield (Mid.)	4	1	.800	2.58	1.17	6	6	0	0	...	0-...	38.1	32	11	11	4	13-1	43	.227
— St. Pete. (FSL)	5	4	.556	2.82	1.28	13	13	0	0	...	0-...	73.1	57	31	23	5	37-1	63	.221
1993— Arkansas (Texas)	11	10	.524	4.02	1.29	25	25	1	1	...	0-...	147.2	142	75	66	15	48-1	128	.254
— Louisville (A.A.)	0	0	...	3.21	1.36	2	2	0	0	...	0-...	14.0	10	5	5	0	9-0	9	.208
1994— Louisville (A.A.)	1	4	.200	8.54	2.28	7	7	0	0	...	0-...	26.1	37	26	25	2	23-0	16	.349
— Arkansas (Texas)	3	10	.231	4.40	1.43	17	17	0	0	...	0-...	92.0	96	54	45	8	36-0	65	.274
1995— Louisville (A.A.)	3	2	.600	3.23	1.34	26	0	0	0	...	0-...	30.2	20	12	11	1	21-0	29	.182
— Arkansas (Texas)	4	2	.667	2.88	1.17	26	0	0	0	...	1-...	34.1	24	12	11	4	16-2	50	.198
— St. Louis (N.L.)	0	0	...	0.00	0.75	6	0	0	0	0	0-0	6.2	2	0	0	0	3-0	10	.095
1996— San Francisco (N.L.)	0	2	.000	6.52	1.59	63	0	0	0	7	0-1	48.1	45	41	35	11	32-2	38	.243
1997— Phoenix (PCL)	8	6	.571	4.93	1.59	25	23	2	1	...	0-...	129.2	140	76	71	15	66-0	* 137	.276
— San Francisco (N.L.)	1	2	.333	6.75	1.95	3	3	0	0	0	0-0	13.1	12	12	10	1	14-0	14	.240
1998— Hanshin (Jp. West.)	9	1	.900	2.16	1.29	17	16	2	0	...	0-...	100.0	77	28	24	0	52-...	101	...
— Hanshin (Jp. Cn.)	0	4	.000	5.65	1.67	7	6	0	0	...	0-...	28.2	23	21	18	0	25-...	24	...
1999— Iowa (PCL)	7	3	.700	3.79	1.36	25	20	0	0	...	1-...	130.2	116	66	55	20	62-0	140	.241
— Chicago (N.L.)	0	0	...	10.50	2.33	3	0	0	0	0	0-0	6.0	6	7	7	1	8-1	6	.261

C

Year League	W	L	Pct.	ERA	WHIP	G	GS	CG	ShO	Hld.	Sv.-Opp.	IP	H	R	ER	HR	BB-IBB	SO	Avg.
2000— Durham (Int'l)	0	0	...	1.96	1.31	10	1	0	0	...	0-...	18.1	10	5	4	1	14-0	22	.152
— Tampa Bay (A.L.)	1	3	.250	4.60	1.45	45	0	0	0	2	1-3	60.2	49	33	31	10	39-3	73	.224
2001—Tampa Bay (A.L.)	2	5	.286	4.31	1.60	66	0	0	0	15	0-3	62.2	51	34	30	7	49-5	66	.230
2002—Tampa Bay (A.L.)	2	1	.667	6.27	1.61	29	0	0	0	4	0-2	37.1	39	27	26	8	21-1	37	.264
— Seattle (A.L.)	1	1	.500	4.91	1.75	23	0	0	0	1	0-0	18.1	18	10	10	2	14-1	19	.257
2003—Toronto (A.L.)	0	0	...	3.29	1.90	21	0	0	0	2	0-1	13.2	14	6	5	2	12-3	11	.264
American League totals (4 years)	6	10	.375	4.76	1.59	184	0	0	0	24	1-9	192.2	171	110	102	29	135-13	206	.240
National League totals (4 years)	1	4	.200	6.30	1.64	75	3	0	0	7	0-1	74.1	65	60	52	13	57-3	68	.233
Major League totals (8 years)	7	14	.333	5.19	1.60	259	3	0	0	31	1-10	267.0	236	170	154	42	192-16	274	.238

CRESSEND, JACK — P

PERSONAL: Born May 13, 1975, in New Orleans, La. ... 6-1/195. ... Throws right, bats right. ... Full name: John Baptiste Cressend. ... High school: Mandeville (La.). ... College: Tulane.

TRANSACTIONS/CAREER NOTES: Signed as non-drafted free agent by Boston Red Sox organization (July 24, 1996). ... Claimed on waivers by Minnesota Twins (April 22, 1999). ... On Minnesota disabled list (June 8-September 30, 2002); included rehabilitation assignments to Gulf Coast Twins (August 9-21) and Fort Myers (August 22-September 1). ... Claimed on waivers by Cleveland Indians (October 17, 2002). ... Contract purchased from Buffalo by Cleveland (June 25, 2003).

CAREER HITTING: 0-for-0 (.000), 0 R, 0 2B, 0 3B, 0 HR, 0 RBI.

Year League	W	L	Pct.	ERA	WHIP	G	GS	CG	ShO	Hld.	Sv.-Opp.	IP	H	R	ER	HR	BB-IBB	SO	Avg.
1996—Lowell (NY-Penn)	3	2	.600	2.36	1.18	9	8	0	0	...	0-...	45.2	37	15	12	0	17-1	57	.226
1997—Sarasota (Fla. St.)	8	11	.421	3.80	1.32	28	25	2	1	...	0-...	165.2	163	98	70	15	56-1	149	.252
1998—Trenton (East.)	10	11	.476	4.34	1.49	29	29	1	1	...	0-...	149.1	168	86	72	13	55-0	130	.293
1999—Trenton (East.)	1	0	1.000	7.20	1.73	3	3	0	0	...	0-...	15.0	19	12	12	3	7-0	11	.302
—New Britain (East.)	7	10	.412	4.34	1.39	25	24	2	* 2	...	0-...	145.0	152	79	70	10	50-0	125	.269
2000—Salt Lake (PCL)	4	4	.500	3.44	1.46	54	1	0	0	...	8-...	86.1	87	40	33	3	39-4	87	.261
—Minnesota (A.L.)	0	0	...	5.27	1.90	11	0	0	0	0	0-0	13.2	20	8	8	0	6-0	6	.364
2001—Edmonton (PCL)	2	2	.500	3.50	1.44	12	0	0	0	...	1-...	18.0	19	12	7	2	7-2	9	.284
—Minnesota (A.L.)	3	2	.600	3.67	1.17	44	0	0	0	5	0-2	56.1	50	24	23	6	16-0	40	.237
2002—Minnesota (A.L.)	0	1	.000	5.91	1.84	23	0	0	0	0	0-0	32.0	40	25	21	6	19-4	22	.305
—GC Twins (GCL)	0	0	...	7.11	1.74	3	3	0	0	...	0-...	6.1	10	7	5	0	1-0	8	.357
—Fort Myers (Fla. St.)	1	0	1.000	3.60	1.20	3	1	0	0	...	0-...	5.0	4	2	2	0	2-0	5	.211
2003—Kinston (Caro.)	0	1	.000	12.46	2.08	2	0	0	0	...	0-...	4.1	9	6	6	1	0-0	4	.429
—Akron (East.)	2	0	1.000	0.00	1.06	8	0	0	0	...	1-...	16.0	15	4	0	0	2-0	10	.234
—Buffalo (Int'l)	1	0	1.000	1.23	0.89	8	0	0	0	...	0-...	14.2	7	2	2	0	6-0	12	.149
—Cleveland (A.L.)	2	1	.667	2.51	1.14	33	0	0	0	5	0-1	43.0	40	12	12	1	9-1	28	.252
Major League totals (4 years)	5	4	.556	3.97	1.38	111	0	0	0	10	0-3	145.0	150	69	64	13	50-5	96	.270

CRISP, COCO — OF

PERSONAL: Born November 1, 1979, in Los Angeles, Calif. ... 6-0/185. ... Bats both, throws right. ... Full name: Covelli Loyce Crisp. ... Junior college: Los Angeles Pierce College.

TRANSACTIONS/CAREER NOTES: Selected by St. Louis Cardinals organization in seventh round of free-agent draft (June 2, 1999). ... Traded by Cardinals to Cleveland Indians (August 6, 2002), completing deal in which Cardinals traded 1B Luis Garcia and a player to be named later for P Chuck Finley (July 19, 2002). ... Recalled from Buffalo of the International League by Cleveland (June 10, 2003). ... Recalled from Buffalo by Cleveland (June 10, 2003).

2003 GAMES PLAYED BY POSITION (MLB): OF—90, DH—7.

Year Team (League)	Pos.	G	AB	R	H	2B	3B	HR	RBI	BB	SO	HBP	GDP	SB-CS	Avg.	OBP	SLG	OPS	E	Pct.
1999—Johnson City (App.)	2B	65	229	55	59	5	4	3	22	44	41	2	0	27-5	.258	.379	.354	.733	24	.912
2000—New Jersey (NYP)	OF-2B	36	134	18	32	5	0	0	14	11	22	1	1	25-3	.239	.301	.276	.577	2	.972
—Peoria (Midw.)	OF	27	98	14	27	9	0	0	7	16	15	0	1	7-3	.276	.377	.367	.745	0	1.000
2001—Potomac Carolina (Caro.)	OF	139	530	80	162	23	3	11	47	52	64	1	8	39-21	.306	.368	.423	.791	6	.975
2002—New Haven (East.)	OF	89	355	61	107	16	1	9	47	36	56	0	6	26-10	.301	.365	.428	.793	3	.985
—Akron (East.)	OF	7	32	9	13	1	0	1	4	3	3	0	4	4-0	.406	.457	.531	.988	0	1.000
—Cleveland (A.L.)	OF	32	127	16	33	9	2	1	9	11	19	0	0	4-1	.260	.314	.386	.700	1	.988
—Buffalo (Int'l)	OF	4	21	3	5	1	0	0	2	0	2	0	2	1-0	.238	.238	.286	.524	0	1.000
2003—Buffalo (Int'l)	OF	56	225	42	81	19	6	1	24	26	24	5	5	20-8	.360	.434	.511	.945	3	.982
—Cleveland (A.L.)	OF-DH	99	414	55	110	15	6	3	27	23	51	0	4	15-9	.266	.302	.353	.655	1	.995
Major League totals (2 years)		131	541	71	143	24	8	4	36	34	70	0	4	19-10	.264	.305	.360	.666	2	.993

CROMER, TRIPP — IF

PERSONAL: Born November 21, 1967, in Lake City, S.C. ... 6-2/165. ... Bats right, throws right. ... Full name: Roy Bunyan Cromer. ... High school: Lake City (S.C.). ... College: South Carolina.

TRANSACTIONS/CAREER NOTES: Selected by St. Louis Cardinals organization in third round of free-agent draft (June 5, 1989). ... On Arkansas disabled list (May 14-26, 1992). ... On Louisville disabled list (April 30-May 28 and July 5-August 3, 1993). ... On disabled list (May 20-27, 1996). ... Claimed on waivers by Los Angeles Dodgers (October 10, 1996). ... On disabled list (July 31, 1997-remainder of season). ... On Los Angeles disabled list (March 12-July 17 and July 31-September 1, 1998); included rehabilitation assignment to Albuquerque (June 16-26 and July 9-17) and San Bernardino (August 27-September 1). ... On Los Angeles disabled list (July 5-September 1, 1999); included rehabilitation assignments to Albuquerque (July 21-27) and San Bernardino (August 27-September 1). ... Granted free agency (November 24, 1999). ... Signed by Houston Astros organization (December 21, 1999). ... On Houston disabled list (August 25, 2000-remainder of season). ... Granted free agency (October 12, 2000). ... Re-signed by Astros organization (January 17, 2002). ... On New Orleans disabled list (May 1-20 and June 10-July 11, 2002). ... Granted free agency (October 15, 2002). ... Contract purchased by Houston from New Orleans of the Pacific Coast League (May 26, 2003). ... Designated for assignment by Houston Astros (May 28, 2003). ... Sent outright to New Orleans by Houston (May 30, 2003).

2003 GAMES PLAYED BY POSITION (MLB): 2B—1.

Year Team (League)	Pos.	G	AB	R	H	2B	3B	HR	RBI	BB	SO	HBP	GDP	SB-CS	Avg.	OBP	SLG	OPS	E	Pct.
1989—Hamilton (NYP)	SS	35	137	18	36	6	3	0	6	17	30	1	5	4-4	.263	.346	.350	.697	11	.932
1990—St. Pete. (FSL)	SS	121	408	53	88	12	5	5	38	46	78	5	11	7-12	.216	.300	.306	.606	32	.944
1991—St. Pete. (FSL)	SS	43	137	11	28	3	1	0	10	9	17	1	8	0-0	.204	.257	.241	.498	3	.986
—Arkansas (Texas)	SS	73	227	28	52	12	1	1	18	15	37	3	7	0-1	.229	.282	.304	.586	10	.969
1992—Arkansas (Texas)	SS	110	339	30	81	16	6	7	29	22	82	4	9	4-6	.239	.292	.383	.675	18	.962
—Louisville (A.A.)	SS	6	25	5	5	1	1	1	7	1	6	0	0	0-0	.200	.222	.440	.662	0	1.000
1993—Louisville (A.A.)	SS	85	309	39	85	8	4	11	33	15	60	2	10	1-3	.275	.313	.434	.747	12	.969
—St. Louis (N.L.)	SS	10	23	1	2	0	0	0	0	1	6	0	0	0-0	.087	.125	.087	.212	3	.912

C

Year Team (League)	Pos.	G	AB	R	H	2B	3B	HR	RBI	BB	SO	HBP	GDP	SB-CS	Avg.	OBP	SLG	OPS	E	Pct.
1994— Louisville (A.A.)	SS	124	419	53	115	23	9	9	50	33	85	3	12	5-6	.274	.330	.437	.767	12	.978
— St. Louis (N.L.)	SS	2	0	1	0	0	0	0	0	0	0	0	0	0-0	...	.000	...	...	1	.000
1995— St. Louis (N.L.)	SS-2B	105	345	36	78	19	0	5	18	14	66	4	14	0-0	.226	.261	.325	.586	17	.961
1996— Louisville (A.A.)	SS-2B	80	244	28	55	4	4	4	25	22	47	2	12	3-1	.225	.294	.324	.617	5	.986
1997— Albuquerque (PCL)	SS	43	140	25	45	8	6	5	24	14	34	1	0	4-1	.321	.380	.571	.951	6	.966
— Los Angeles (N.L.)	2B-SS-3B	28	86	8	25	3	0	4	20	6	16	0	2	0-1	.291	.333	.465	.798	3	.973
1998— Albuquerque (PCL)	SS-DH	12	30	3	10	1	0	2	5	1	5	0	0	0-1	.333	.344	.567	.910	1	.952
— Los Angeles (N.L.)		6	6	1	1	0	0	1	1	0	2	0	0	0-0	.167	.167	.667	.833	...	...
— San Bern. (Calif.)	2B-DH	4	15	3	6	1	0	2	6	0	2	0	0	0-0	.400	.400	.867	1.267	0	1.000
1999— Los Angeles (N.L.)	2-S-3-0-1	33	52	5	10	0	0	2	8	5	10	0	4	0-0	.192	.263	.308	.571	0	1.000
— Albuquerque (PCL)	2B-SS-1B	5	15	1	4	2	0	0	1	1	3	1	0	0-1	.267	.353	.400	.753	0	1.000
— San Bern. (Calif.)	2-3-SS-1	4	18	3	9	3	0	1	8	0	3	0	0	0-0	.500	.500	.833	1.333	0	1.000
2000— New Orleans (PCL)	2-3-SS-1	66	224	21	48	7	3	4	24	17	47	0	4	1-0	.214	.267	.326	.593	7	.972
— Houston (N.L.)	3B-2B-SS	9	8	2	1	0	0	0	0	1	1	0	0	0-0	.125	.222	.125	.347	1	.667
2001—										Did not play.										
2002— New Orleans (PCL)	1-2-SS-3	77	265	31	68	13	2	7	26	9	42	4	9	0-0	.257	.289	.400	.689	6	.987
2003— Houston (N.L.)	2B	3	4	0	1	0	1	0	1	0	0	0	0	0-0	.250	.250	.750	1.000	0	1.000
— New Orleans (PCL)	2-3-DH-1	84	242	29	61	15	3	4	36	17	41	2	5	0-0	.252	.303	.388	.691	5	.982
Major League totals (8 years)		196	524	54	118	22	1	12	48	27	101	4	20	0-1	.225	.266	.340	.605	25	.961

CROSBY, BOBBY — SS

PERSONAL: Born January 12, 1980, in Lakewood, Calif. ... 6-3/195. ... Bats right, throws right. ... Full name: Robert Edward Crosby. ... High school: La Quinta (Westminster, Calif.). ... College: Cal State Long Beach.

TRANSACTIONS/CAREER NOTES: Selected by Anaheim Angels organization in 34th round of free-agent draft (June 2, 1998); did not sign. ... Selected by Oakland A's organization in first round (25th pick overall) of free-agent draft (June 5, 2001).

2003 GAMES PLAYED BY POSITION (MLB): SS—9, DH—2.

Year Team (League)	Pos.	G	AB	R	H	2B	3B	HR	RBI	BB	SO	HBP	GDP	SB-CS	Avg.	OBP	SLG	OPS	E	Pct.
2001— Modesto (Calif.)	SS	11	38	7	15	5	0	1	3	3	8	0	1	0-0	.395	.439	.605	1.044	4	.889
2002— Modesto (Calif.)	SS	73	280	47	86	17	2	2	38	33	43	7	5	5-0	.307	.393	.404	.796	19	.938
— Midland (Texas)	SS	59	228	31	64	16	0	7	31	19	41	0	9	9-2	.281	.335	.443	.778	13	.952
2003— Sacramento (PCL)	SS-DH	127	465	86	143	32	6	22	90	63	110	7	16	24-4	.308	.395	.544	.939	15	.973
— Oakland (A.L.)	SS-DH	11	12	1	0	0	0	0	0	1	5	1	0	0-0	.000	.143	.000	.143	2	.889
Major League totals (1 year)		11	12	1	0	0	0	0	0	1	5	1	0	0-0	.000	.143	.000	.143	2	.889

CROSBY, BUBBA — OF

PERSONAL: Born August 11, 1976, in Houston, Texas. ... 5-11/185. ... Bats left, throws left. ... Full name: Richard Stephen Crosby. ... High school: Bellaire (Texas). ... College: Rice.

TRANSACTIONS/CAREER NOTES: Selected by Los Angeles Dodgers organization in first round (23rd pick overall) in free-agent draft (June 2, 1998).

2003 GAMES PLAYED BY POSITION (MLB): OF—1.

Year Team (League)	Pos.	G	AB	R	H	2B	3B	HR	RBI	BB	SO	HBP	GDP	SB-CS	Avg.	OBP	SLG	OPS	E	Pct.
1998— San Bern. (Calif.)	OF	56	199	25	43	9	2	0	14	17	38	0	3	3-5	.216	.274	.281	.555	1	.990
1999— San Bern. (Calif.)	OF	96	371	53	110	21	3	1	37	42	71	6	6	19-8	.296	.376	.377	.754	5	.975
2000— Vero Beach (FSL)	OF	73	274	50	73	13	8	8	51	31	41	7	9	27-10	.266	.355	.460	.814	4	.969
— San Bern. (Calif.)		3	12	2	3	0	0	0	2	0	4	0	1	1-0	.250	.250	.250	.500	0	...
2001— Las Vegas (PCL)	OF	13	42	5	9	2	1	0	5	1	8	0	0	1-1	.214	.233	.310	.542	0	1.000
— Jacksonville (Sou.)	OF	107	384	68	116	22	5	6	47	37	60	8	7	22-6	.302	.369	.432	.802	3	.985
2002— Las Vegas (PCL)	OF	73	279	26	73	12	1	9	36	19	47	2	3	3-1	.262	.312	.409	.721	2	.989
— Jacksonville (Sou.)	OF	38	150	14	39	6	2	2	20	11	23	2	2	7-3	.260	.317	.367	.684	0	1.000
2003— Las Vegas (PCL)	OF-DH	76	277	57	100	24	8	12	57	25	47	3	6	8-0	.361	.410	.635	1.046	1	.991
— Los Angeles (N.L.)	OF	9	12	0	1	0	0	0	1	0	3	0	0	0-0	.083	.083	.083	.167	1	1.000
— Columbus (Int'l)	OF	16	63	9	19	2	1	2	8	6	12	1	0	3-0	.302	.366	.460	.827	0	1.000
Major League totals (1 year)		9	12	0	1	0	0	0	1	0	3	0	0	0-0	.083	.083	.083	.167	1	.667

CRUDALE, MIKE — P

PERSONAL: Born January 3, 1977, in San Diego, Calif. ... 6-0/220. ... Throws right, bats right. ... Full name: Michael Christopher Crudale. ... Name pronounced: CREW-dale. ... High school: Monte Vista (Danville, Calif.). ... College: Santa Clara.

TRANSACTIONS/CAREER NOTES: Selected by St. Louis Cardinals organization in 24th round of free-agent draft (June 2, 1999). ... Recalled by St. Louis from Memphis (May 2, 2003). ... Optioned to Memphis by St. Louis (June 3, 2003). ... Recalled from Memphis by St. Louis (July 22, 2003). ... Optioned to Memphis of the Pacific Coast League (July 28, 2003). ... Recalled by St. Louis from Memphis (August 27, 2003). ... Traded by St. Louis to Milwaukee Brewers for P Mike DeJean (August 27, 2003). ... Called up by Milwaukee from Indianapolis (September 2, 2003).

CAREER HITTING: 0-for-2 (.000), 0 R, 0 2B, 0 3B, 0 HR, 0 RBI.

Year League	W	L	Pct.	ERA	WHIP	G	GS	CG	ShO	Hld.	Sv.-Opp.	IP	H	R	ER	HR	BB-IBB	SO	Avg.
1999— Johnson City (App.)	0	1	.000	3.27	1.30	24	0	0	0	...	1-...	33.0	29	15	12	1	14-0	36	.230
2000— Peoria (Midw.)	6	1	.857	2.31	1.11	38	0	0	0	...	5-...	50.2	40	17	13	2	16-3	45	.216
— Potomac (Caro.)	2	4	.333	4.56	1.64	21	0	0	0	...	2-...	25.2	31	17	13	3	11-1	28	.298
2001— New Haven (East.)	4	9	.308	3.25	1.22	62	0	0	0	...	9-...	80.1	76	42	29	7	22-4	85	.244
2002— Memphis (PCL)	1	0	1.000	1.84	1.02	13	0	0	0	...	7-...	14.2	10	3	3	1	5-1	16	.192
— St. Louis (N.L.)	3	0	1.000	1.88	1.08	49	1	0	0	6	0-1	52.2	43	11	11	3	14-2	47	.228
2003— St. Louis (N.L.)	0	1	.000	2.38	2.03	13	0	0	0	1	0-1	11.1	11	5	3	1	12-1	6	.250
— Memphis (PCL)	5	5	.500	5.52	1.53	32	0	0	0	...	6-...	29.1	34	19	18	7	11-1	23	.285
— Indianapolis (Int'l)	0	0	...	0.00	0.50	2	0	0	0	...	0-...	2.0	1	0	0	0	0-0	1	.143
— Milwaukee (N.L.)	0	0	...	2.89	0.75	9	0	0		3	0-0	9.1	1	3	3	0	6-0	7	.036
Major League totals (2 years)	3	1	.750	2.09	1.19	71	1	0	0	10	0-2	73.1	55	19	17	4	32-3	60	.211

CRUZ, DEIVI   SS

PERSONAL: Born November 6, 1972, in Nizao de Bani, Dominican Republic. ... 6-0/207. ... Bats right, throws right. ... Full name: Deivi Garcia Cruz. ... Name pronounced: DAY-vee. ... High school: Liceo Aliro Paulino Nizao (Dominican Republic).

TRANSACTIONS/CAREER NOTES: Signed as non-drafted free agent by San Francisco Giants organization (April 23, 1993). ... Selected by Los Angeles Dodgers from Giants organization in Rule 5 major league draft (December 9, 1996). ... Traded by Dodgers with OF Juan Hernaiz to Detroit Tigers for 2B Jeff Berblinger (December 9, 1996). ... On Detroit disabled list (March 20-April 27, 1998); included rehabilitation assignments to Lakeland (April 21-23) and Toledo (April 24-27). ... On Detroit disabled list (June 8-July 18, 2001); included rehabilitation assignment to Erie (July 14-18). ... Granted free agency (December 21, 2001). ... Signed by San Diego Padres (January 30, 2002). ... Granted free agency (October 29, 2002). ... Signed by Baltimore Orioles (December 15, 2002).

2003 GAMES PLAYED BY POSITION (MLB): SS—147, DH—5.

										BATTING									FIELDING	
Year	Team (League)	Pos.	G	AB	R	H	2B	3B	HR	RBI	BB	SO	HBP	GDP	SB-CS	Avg.	OBP	SLG	OPS	E	Pct.
1993— Ariz. Giants (Ariz.)		3B-SS-1B	28	82	8	28	3	0	0	15	4	5	0	3	3-0	.341	.368	.378	.746	2	.972
1994— Ariz. Giants (Ariz.)		3B-SS	18	53	10	16	8	0	0	5	5	3	1	1	0-1	.302	.367	.453	.819	1	.980
1995— Burlington (Midw.)		2B-3B-SS	16	58	2	8	1	0	1	9	4	7	0	1	1-1	.138	.194	.207	.400	2	.969
— Bellingham (N'west)		2B-3B	62	223	32	66	17	0	3	28	19	21	0	5	6-3	.296	.348	.413	.761	10	.947
1996— Burlington (Midw.)		SS-3B	127	517	72	152	27	2	9	64	35	49	4	20	12-5	.294	.342	.406	.748	13	.979
1997— Detroit (A.L.)		SS	147	436	35	105	26	0	2	40	14	55	0	9	3-6	.241	.263	.314	.577	13	.979
1998— Lakeland (Fla. St.)		SS	2	9	0	0	0	0	0	1	0	1	0	0	0-0	.000	.000	.000	.000	0	1.000
— Toledo (Int'l)		SS	2	9	1	1	1	0	0	2	2	3	0	0	0-0	.111	.273	.222	.495	0	1.000
— Detroit (A.L.)		SS	135	454	52	118	23	3	5	45	13	55	3	11	3-4	.260	.284	.355	.639	11	.983
1999— Detroit (A.L.)		SS	155	518	64	147	35	0	13	58	12	57	4	10	1-4	.284	.302	.427	.729	12	.983
2000— Detroit (A.L.)		SS	156	583	68	176	46	5	10	82	13	43	4	25	1-4	.302	.318	.449	.767	13	.982
2001— Detroit (A.L.)		SS-3B	110	414	39	106	28	1	7	52	17	46	4	13	4-1	.256	.291	.379	.670	17	.964
— Erie (East.)		SS-3B	4	12	2	5	1	0	1	3	0	0	0	0	1-0	.417	.417	.750	1.167	1	.929
2002— San Diego (N.L.)		SS-1B	151	514	49	135	28	2	7	47	22	58	3	20	2-3	.263	.294	.366	.660	15	.973
2003— Baltimore (A.L.)		SS-DH	152	548	61	137	24	2	14	65	13	49	2	13	1-2	.250	.269	.378	.647	16	.975
American League totals (6 years)			855	2953	319	789	181	11	51	342	82	305	17	81	13-21	.267	.289	.388	.677	82	.979
National League totals (1 year)			151	514	49	135	28	2	7	47	22	58	3	20	2-3	.263	.294	.366	.660	15	.973
Major League totals (7 years)			1006	3467	368	924	209	13	58	389	104	363	20	101	15-24	.267	.290	.384	.674	97	.978

CRUZ, ENRIQUE   3B

PERSONAL: Born November 21, 1981, in Santo Domingo, Dominican Republic. ... 6-1/180. ... Bats right, throws right. ... Full name: Enrique Manuel Cruz.

TRANSACTIONS/CAREER NOTES: Signed as non-drafted free agent by New York Mets organization (August 5, 1998). ... Selected by Milwaukee Brewers from Mets organization in Rule 5 major league draft (December 16, 2002). ... Contract purchased by Milwaukee (June 6, 2003).

2003 GAMES PLAYED BY POSITION (MLB): SS—13, 2B—6, 3B—2.

										BATTING									FIELDING	
Year	Team (League)	Pos.	G	AB	R	H	2B	3B	HR	RBI	BB	SO	HBP	GDP	SB-CS	Avg.	OBP	SLG	OPS	E	Pct.
1999— GC Mets (GCL)		SS-3B	54	183	34	56	14	2	4	24	28	41	1	3	0-3	.306	.399	.470	.869	16	.926
2000— Capital City (SAL)		SS-3B-C	49	157	19	29	12	0	1	12	25	44	1	1	1-3	.185	.299	.280	.579	19	.912
— Kingsport (Appal.)		3B-SS-2B	63	223	35	56	14	0	9	39	26	56	3	3	19-7	.251	.335	.435	.770	21	.913
2001— Capital City (SAL)		3B-SS	124	438	60	110	20	2	9	59	59	106	6	7	33-7	.251	.346	.368	.713	30	.922
2002— St. Lucie (Fla. St.)		3B-SS	124	467	69	136	21	2	6	45	32	76	2	15	33-16	.291	.336	.383	.719	33	.919
2003— Milwaukee (N.L.)		SS-2B-3B	60	71	6	6	1	0	0	2	4	30	1	2	0-0	.085	.145	.099	.243	1	.976
Major League totals (1 year)			60	71	6	6	1	0	0	2	4	30	1	2	0-0	.085	.145	.099	.243	1	.976

CRUZ, JOSE   OF

PERSONAL: Born April 19, 1974, in Arroyo, Puerto Rico. ... 6-0/210. ... Bats both, throws right. ... Full name: Jose L. Cruz Jr.. ... High school: Bellaire (Houston). ... College: Rice.

TRANSACTIONS/CAREER NOTES: Selected by Atlanta Braves organization in 15th round of free-agent draft (June 1, 1992); did not sign. ... Selected by Seattle Mariners organization in first round (third pick overall) of free-agent draft (June 1, 1995). ... Traded by Mariners to Toronto Blue Jays for P Mike Timlin and P Paul Spoljaric (July 31, 1997). ... On Toronto disabled list (June 24-July 9, 1999); included rehabilitation assignment to Syracuse (July 5-9). ... On disabled list (May 6-21, 2001; and August 10-September 15, 2002). ... Granted free agency (December 20, 2002). ... Signed by San Francisco Giants (January 28, 2003). ... Option declined by Giants (October 22, 2003).

2003 GAMES PLAYED BY POSITION (MLB): OF—158.

										BATTING									FIELDING	
Year	Team (League)	Pos.	G	AB	R	H	2B	3B	HR	RBI	BB	SO	HBP	GDP	SB-CS	Avg.	OBP	SLG	OPS	E	Pct.
1995— Everett (N'west)		OF	3	11	6	5	0	0	0	2	3	3	0	0	1-0	.455	.571	.455	1.026	0	1.000
— Riverside (Calif.)		OF	35	144	34	37	7	1	7	29	24	50	0	1	3-1	.257	.359	.465	.824	3	.961
1996— Lancaster (Calif.)		OF-DH	53	203	38	66	17	1	6	43	39	33	0	4	7-1	.325	.423	.507	.931	1	.986
— Port City (Sou.)		OF-DH	47	181	39	51	10	2	3	31	27	38	0	8	5-0	.282	.373	.409	.782	1	.990
— Tacoma (PCL)		OF	22	76	15	18	1	2	6	15	18	12	0	2	1-1	.237	.383	.539	.922	0	1.000
1997— Tacoma (PCL)		OF-DH	50	190	33	51	16	2	6	30	34	44	1	4	3-0	.268	.382	.468	.851	0	1.000
— Seattle (A.L.)		OF	49	183	28	49	12	1	12	34	13	45	0	3	1-0	.268	.315	.541	.856	3	.966
— Toronto (A.L.)		OF	55	212	31	49	7	0	14	34	28	72	0	2	6-2	.231	.316	.462	.778	2	.981
1998— Toronto (A.L.)		OF	105	352	55	89	14	3	11	42	57	99	0	0	11-4	.253	.354	.403	.757	4	.984
— Syracuse (Int'l)		OF	40	141	29	42	14	1	7	23	32	32	0	2	8-4	.298	.425	.560	.986	1	.991
1999— Toronto (A.L.)		OF	106	349	63	84	19	3	14	45	64	91	0	6	14-4	.241	.358	.433	.791	3	.990
— Syracuse (Int'l)		OF-DH	31	103	17	19	3	1	3	14	28	20	0	3	5-0	.184	.356	.320	.676	0	1.000
2000— Toronto (A.L.)		OF	• 162	603	91	146	32	5	31	76	71	129	2	11	15-5	.242	.323	.466	.789	3	.993
2001— Toronto (A.L.)		OF-DH	146	577	92	158	38	4	34	88	45	138	1	8	32-5	.274	.326	.530	.857	3	.990
2002— Toronto (A.L.)		OF-DH	124	466	64	114	26	5	18	70	51	106	0	8	7-1	.245	.317	.438	.754	2	.992
2003— San Francisco (N.L.)		OF	158	539	90	135	26	1	20	68	102	121	0	14	5-8	.250	.366	.414	.779	2	.994
American League totals (6 years)			747	2742	424	689	148	21	134	389	329	680	3	38	86-21	.251	.330	.467	.797	20	.988
National League totals (1 year)			158	539	90	135	26	1	20	68	102	121	0	14	5-8	.250	.366	.414	.779	2	.994
Major League totals (7 years)			905	3281	514	824	174	22	154	457	431	801	3	52	91-29	.251	.336	.458	.795	22	.989

CRUZ, JUAN   P

PERSONAL: Born October 15, 1978, in Bonao, Dominican Republic. ... 6-2/165. ... Throws right, bats right. ... Full name: Juan Carlos Cruz.

TRANSACTIONS/CAREER NOTES: Signed as non-drafted free agent by Chicago Cubs organization (July 4, 1997). ... On disabled list (August 10-25, 2002). ... Optioned to Iowa by Chicago Cubs (June 3, 2003). ... Recalled by Chicago from Iowa (June 26, 2003). ... Optioned to Iowa by Chicago (July 4, 2003). ... Recalled from Iowa by Chicago (August 31, 2003).

CAREER HITTING: 7-for-42 (.167), 1 R, 0 2B, 1 3B, 0 HR, 2 RBI.

Year League	W	L	Pct.	ERA	WHIP	G	GS	CG	ShO	Hld.	Sv.-Opp.	IP	H	R	ER	HR	BB-IBB	SO	Avg.
1998—Ariz. Cubs (Ariz.)	2	4	.333	6.10	1.81	12	6	0	0	...	0-...	41.1	61	48	28	2	14-0	36	.326
1999—Eugene (NW)	5	6	.455	5.94	1.62	15	15	0	0	...	0-...	80.1	97	59	53	11	33-0	65	.297
2000—Lansing (Midw.)	5	5	.500	3.28	1.41	17	17	2	1	...	0-...	96.0	75	50	35	6	60-0	106	.215
—Daytona (Fla. St.)	3	0	1.000	3.25	1.08	8	7	1	0	...	0-...	44.1	30	22	16	5	18-0	54	.186
2001—West Tenn (Sou.)	9	6	.600	4.01	1.38	23	23	0	0	...	0-...	121.1	107	56	54	6	60-0	137	.238
—Chicago (N.L.)	3	1	.750	3.22	1.28	8	8	0	0	0	0-0	44.2	40	16	16	4	17-1	39	.244
2002—Chicago (N.L.)	3	11	.214	3.98	1.47	45	9	0	0	3	1-4	97.1	84	56	43	11	59-4	81	.241
2003—Iowa (PCL)	4	0	1.000	1.95	0.95	9	9	0	0	...	0-...	50.2	37	12	11	1	11-0	47	.207
—Chicago (N.L.)	2	7	.222	6.05	1.54	25	6	0	0	1	0-1	61.0	66	44	41	7	28-0	65	.275
Major League totals (3 years)	8	19	.296	4.43	1.45	78	23	0	0	4	1-5	203.0	190	116	100	22	104-5	185	.252

CRUZ, NELSON · P

PERSONAL: Born September 13, 1972, in Puerto Plata, Dominican Republic. ... 6-1/185. ... Throws right, bats right. ... High school: Liceo Jose Castellanos (Puerto Plata, Dominican Republic).

TRANSACTIONS/CAREER NOTES: Signed as non-drafted free agent by Montreal Expos organization (July 5, 1989). ... Released by Expos (March 27, 1992). ... Signed by Chicago White Sox organization (December 10, 1994). ... Granted free agency (October 15, 1998). ... Signed by Detroit Tigers (November 19, 1998). ... On Toledo disabled list (May 7-24, 2000). ... Traded by Tigers with C Brad Ausmus and P Doug Brocail to Houston Astros for C Mitch Meluskey, P Chris Holt and OF Roger Cedeno (December 11, 2000). ... On Houston disabled list (April 19-May 4, 2002); included rehabilitation assignment to New Orleans (April 22-May 3). ... Traded by Astros to Colorado Rockies for OF Victor Hall (December 16, 2002). ... Placed on the 15-day disabled list (May 17, 2003). ... Reinstated from 15-day disabled list (June 6, 2003). ... Placed on 15-day disabled list by Colorado (July 10, 2003). ... Sent on rehab assignment by Colorado (August 17, 2003). ... Recalled from minor league rehab assignment; removed from 15-day disabled list; sent outright to Colorado Springs (September 5, 2003).

CAREER HITTING: 3-for-33 (.091), 1 R, 1 2B, 0 3B, 0 HR, 2 RBI.

Year League	W	L	Pct.	ERA	WHIP	G	GS	CG	ShO	Hld.	Sv.-Opp.	IP	H	R	ER	HR	BB-IBB	SO	Avg.
1990—DSL Expos (DSL)	9	2	.818	2.62	1.43	16	16	0	0	...	0-...	103.0	105	49	30	...	42-...	83	
1991—GC Expos (GCL)	2	4	.333	2.40	1.21	12	8	1	1	...	0-...	48.2	40	18	13	1	19-0	34	.220
1992—										Did not play.									
1993—										Did not play.									
1994—										Did not play.									
1995—Bristol (Appal.)	0	0	...	9.00	2.00	1	0	0	0	...	0-...	1.0	2	1	1	0	0-0	0	.500
—Hickory (S. Atl.)	2	7	.222	2.70	1.20	44	0	0	0	...	9-...	66.2	65	31	20	6	15-2	68	.248
—Prince William (Caro.)	2	1	.667	0.47	0.93	9	0	0	0	...	1-...	19.1	12	1	1	1	6-0	15	.179
1996—Birmingham (Sou.)	6	6	.500	3.20	1.28	37	18	2	1	...	1-...	149.0	150	65	53	10	41-2	142	.265
1997—Nashville (A.A.)	11	7	.611	5.11	1.38	21	20	1	0	...	0-...	123.1	139	75	70	20	31-0	93	.285
—Chicago (A.L.)	0	2	.000	6.49	1.44	19	0	0	0	6	0-0	26.1	29	19	19	6	9-1	23	.274
1998—Calgary (PCL)	10	6	.625	5.33	1.57	35	18	2	1	...	0-...	126.2	159	85	75	18	40-1	101	.310
1999—Toledo (Int'l)	7	1	.875	2.73	1.09	10	10	4	•2	...	0-...	62.2	47	20	19	5	21-0	41	.212
—Detroit (A.L.)	2	5	.286	5.67	1.46	29	6	0	0	4	0-0	66.2	74	44	42	11	23-1	46	.281
2000—Toledo (Int'l)	2	4	.333	4.82	1.36	11	10	0	0	...	0-...	52.1	54	37	28	9	17-0	39	.262
—Detroit (A.L.)	5	2	.714	3.07	1.27	27	0	0	0	2	0-1	41.0	39	14	14	4	13-3	34	.253
2001—Houston (N.L.)	3	3	.500	4.15	1.17	66	0	0	0	10	2-4	82.1	72	41	38	11	24-4	75	.237
2002—Houston (N.L.)	2	6	.250	4.48	1.52	43	5	0	0	1	0-2	78.1	90	44	39	12	29-4	61	.285
—New Orleans (PCL)	0	1	.000	4.50	1.00	6	0	0	0	...	1-...	8.0	4	4	4	2	4-0	8	.148
2003—Colorado (N.L.)	3	5	.375	7.21	1.42	20	7	0	0	2	0-1	53.2	65	43	43	15	11-2	38	.301
—Colo. Springs (PCL)	1	2	.333	7.20	1.80	4	4	0	0	...	0-...	15.0	24	18	12	3	3-0	10	.369
American League totals (3 years)	7	9	.438	5.04	1.40	75	6	0	0	12	0-1	134.0	142	77	75	21	45-5	103	.272
National League totals (3 years)	8	14	.364	5.04	1.36	129	12	0	0	13	2-7	214.1	227	128	120	38	64-10	174	.272
Major League totals (6 years)	15	23	.395	5.04	1.37	204	18	0	0	25	2-8	348.1	369	205	195	59	109-15	277	.272

CUDDYER, MICHAEL · 3B/OF

PERSONAL: Born March 27, 1979, in Norfolk, Va. ... 6-2/225. ... Bats right, throws right. ... Full name: Michael Brent Cuddyer. ... Name pronounced: cuh-DIE-er. ... High school: Great Bridge (Chesapeake, Va.).

TRANSACTIONS/CAREER NOTES: Selected by Minnesota Twins organization in first round (ninth pick overall) of free-agent draft (June 3, 1997). ... On Edmonton disabled list (April 27-May 10, 2002). ... Optioned to Rochester by Minnesota (May 9, 2003). ... Recalled by Minnesota from Rochester (August 31, 2003).

2003 GAMES PLAYED BY POSITION (MLB): OF—18, 3B—7, 1B—5, DH—2, 2B—1.

								BATTING											FIELDING	
Year Team (League)	Pos.	G	AB	R	H	2B	3B	HR	RBI	BB	SO	HBP	GDP	SB-CS	Avg.	OBP	SLG	OPS	E	Pct.
1998—Fort Wayne (Midw.)	2B-SS	129	497	82	137	37	7	12	81	61	107	10	13	16-7	.276	.364	.451	.814	‡61	.907
1999—Fort Myers (FSL)	3B	130	466	87	139	24	4	16	82	•76	91	10	20	14-4	.298	.403	.470	.873	28	.921
2000—New Britain (East.)	3B	138	490	72	129	30	8	6	61	55	93	12	16	5-4	.263	.351	.394	.745	*34	.903
2001—New Britain (East.)	3B-1B-OF	141	509	95	153	36	3	30	87	75	106	6	6	5-9	.301	.395	.560	.955	28	.963
—Minnesota (A.L.)	1B-3B-DH	8	18	1	4	2	0	0	1	2	6	0	1	1-0	.222	.300	.333	.633	1	.975
2002—Edmonton (PCL)	OF-1B-3B	86	330	70	102	16	9	20	53	36	79	3	9	12-7	.309	.379	.594	.973	7	.971
—Minnesota (A.L.)	OF-3-1-D	41	112	12	29	7	0	4	13	8	30	1	3	2-0	.259	.311	.429	.740	1	.990
2003—GC Twins (GCL)	DH-OF	2	5	1	4	0	0	1	3	1	0	1	0	0-1	.800	.857	1.400	2.257	0	1.000
—Rochester (Int'l)	O-2-D-3-1	53	186	25	57	17	0	3	34	25	49	1	4	5-4	.306	.381	.446	.827	1	.993
—Minnesota (A.L.)	O-3-1-D-2	35	102	14	25	1	3	4	8	12	19	0	6	1-1	.245	.325	.431	.756	1	.985
Major League totals (3 years)		84	232	27	58	10	3	8	22	22	55	1	10	4-1	.250	.316	.422	.739	3	.985

CUNNANE, WILL · P

PERSONAL: Born April 24, 1974, in Suffern, N.Y. ... 6-1/200. ... Throws right, bats right. ... Full name: William Joseph Cunnane. ... Name pronounced: COO-nayn. ... High school: Clarkstown North (New City, N.Y.).

TRANSACTIONS/CAREER NOTES: Signed as non-drafted free agent by Florida Marlins organization (August 18, 1992). ... On Portland disabled list (August 7-23, 1996). ... Selected by San Diego Padres from Marlins organization in Rule 5 major league draft (December 9, 1996). ... On San Diego disabled list (March 29-June 21, 1998); included rehabilitation assignment to Las Vegas (June 9-21). ... Traded by Padres to Milwaukee Brewers for OF Chad Green (December 20, 2000), completing deal in which Brewers traded SS Santiago Perez and a player to be named later or cash to San Diego Padres for P Brandon Kolb (December 1, 2000). ... Granted free agency (October 8, 2001). ... Signed by Chicago Cubs organization (December 17, 2001). ... Granted free agency (December 21, 2002). ... Signed by Atlanta Braves as a free agent (2003).

CAREER HITTING: 7-for-35 (.200), 6 R, 1 2B, 1 3B, 0 HR, 4 RBI.

Year	League	W	L	Pct.	ERA	WHIP	G	GS	CG	ShO	Hld.	Sv.-Opp.	IP	H	R	ER	HR	BB-IBB	SO	Avg.
1993— GC Marlins (GCL)		3	3	.500	2.70	1.25	16	9	0	0	...	2-...	66.2	75	32	20	1	8-0	64	.269
1994— Kane County (Midwest)		11	3	.786	1.43	0.96	32	16	5	* 4	...	1-...	138.2	110	27	22	2	23-4	106	.217
1995— Portland (East.)		9	2	.818	3.67	1.31	21	21	1	1	...	0-...	117.2	120	48	48	10	34-1	83	.264
1996— Portland (East.)		10	12	.455	3.74	1.23	25	25	4	0	...	0-...	151.2	156	73	63	15	30-6	101	.263
1997— San Diego (N.L.)		6	3	.667	5.81	1.78	54	8	0	0	4	0-2	91.1	114	69	59	11	49-3	79	.305
1998— Las Vegas (PCL)		1	2	.333	5.25	1.78	33	0	0	0	...	4-...	36.0	45	26	21	1	19-4	30	.310
— San Diego (N.L.)		0	0	...	6.00	1.67	3	0	0	0	0	0-0	3.0	4	2	2	1	1-1	1	.308
1999— Las Vegas (PCL)		2	1	.667	0.98	1.25	28	0	0	0	...	11-...	36.2	30	5	4	0	16-2	54	.214
— San Diego (N.L.)		2	1	.667	5.23	1.48	24	0	0	0	5	0-0	31.0	34	19	18	8	12-3	22	.293
2000— San Diego (N.L.)		1	1	.500	4.23	1.46	27	3	0	0	1	0-0	38.1	35	21	18	2	21-0	34	.241
— Las Vegas (PCL)		7	4	.636	3.98	1.25	17	17	1	1	...	0-...	97.1	96	46	43	7	26-0	97	.257
2001— Milwaukee (N.L.)		0	3	.000	5.40	1.70	31	1	0	0	1	0-0	51.2	66	34	31	6	22-6	37	.320
— Indianapolis (Int'l)		0	1	.000	3.86	1.33	7	3	0	0	...	1-...	23.1	25	10	10	2	6-1	25	.278
2002— Iowa (PCL)		4	1	.800	2.20	1.22	43	0	0	0	...	2-...	73.2	67	23	18	3	23-3	69	.245
— Chicago (N.L.)		1	1	.500	5.47	1.52	16	0	0	0	1	0-1	26.1	27	16	16	5	13-1	30	.270
2003— Iowa (PCL)		0	1	.000	2.20	1.53	12	0	0	0	...	0-...	16.1	17	5	4	0	8-3	16	.274
— Richmond (Int'l)		1	0	1.000	0.00	0.62	15	0	0	0	...	2-...	21.0	11	2	0	0	2-0	19	.159
— Atlanta (N.L.)		2	2	.500	2.70	1.00	20	0	0	0	5	3-3	20.0	14	6	6	2	6-2	20	.189
Major League totals (7 years)		12	11	.522	5.16	1.60	175	12	0	0	17	3-6	261.2	294	167	150	35	124-16	223	.286

CUST, JACK — OF

PERSONAL: Born January 16, 1979, in Flemington, N.J. ... 6-1/225. ... Bats left, throws right. ... Full name: John Joseph Cust. ... High school: Immaculata (Somerville, N.J.).
TRANSACTIONS/CAREER NOTES: Selected by Arizona Diamondbacks organization in first round (30th pick overall) of free-agent draft (June 3, 1997). ... Traded by Diamondbacks with C J.D. Closser to Colorado Rockies for P Mike Myers (January 7, 2002). ... Traded by Rockies to Baltimore Orioles for OF/1B Chris Richard (March 11, 2003).
2003 GAMES PLAYED BY POSITION (MLB): DH—23, OF—1.

										BATTING										FIELDING	
Year	Team (League)	Pos.	G	AB	R	H	2B	3B	HR	RBI	BB	SO	HBP	GDP	SB-CS	Avg.	OBP	SLG	OPS	E	Pct.
1997— Ariz. D'backs (Ariz.)		OF	35	121	26	37	11	1	3	33	31	39	0	4	2-0	.306	.447	.488	.935	5	.902
1998— South Bend (Mid.)		OF	16	62	5	15	3	0	0	4	5	20	0	0	0-1	.242	.294	.290	.584	4	.975
— Lethbridge (Pio.)		OF	73	223	75	77	20	2	11	56	86	71	4	3	15-8	.345	.530	.601	1.131	0	1.000
1999— High Desert (Calif.)		OF	125	455	107	152	42	3	32	112	96	145	2	5	1-4	.334	.450	.651	1.100	12	.922
2000— El Paso (Texas)		OF	129	447	100	131	32	6	20	75	117	150	2	10	12-9	.293	.440	.526	.966	11	.944
2001— Tucson (PCL)		OF	135	442	81	123	24	2	27	79	102	160	5	10	6-3	.278	.415	.525	.940	* 11	.948
— Arizona (N.L.)		OF	3	2	0	1	0	0	0	0	1	0	0	0	0-0	.500	.667	.500	1.167	0	...
2002— Colo. Springs (PCL)		OF	105	359	74	95	24	0	23	55	83	121	5	5	6-3	.265	.407	.524	.930	6	.961
— Colorado (N.L.)		OF	35	65	8	11	2	0	1	8	12	32	0	3	0-1	.169	.295	.246	.541	1	.960
2003— Ottawa (Int'l)		OF-DH	97	333	55	95	18	1	9	58	80	94	0	9	5-2	.285	.422	.426	.848	3	.978
— Baltimore (A.L.)		DH-OF	27	73	7	19	7	0	4	11	10	25	1	0	0-0	.260	.357	.521	.878	0	1.000
American League totals (1 year)			27	73	7	19	7	0	4	11	10	25	1	0	0-0	.260	.357	.521	.878	0	1.000
National League totals (2 years)			38	67	8	12	2	0	1	8	13	32	0	3	0-1	.179	.309	.254	.562	1	.960
Major League totals (3 years)			65	140	15	31	9	0	5	19	23	57	1	3	0-1	.221	.333	.393	.726	1	.964

DAAL, OMAR — P

PERSONAL: Born March 1, 1972, in Maracaibo, Venezuela. ... 6-3/193. ... Throws left, bats left. ... Full name: Omar Jose Daal. ... Name pronounced: DOLL. ... High school: Valencia (Venezuela) Superior.
TRANSACTIONS/CAREER NOTES: Signed as non-drafted free agent by Los Angeles Dodgers organization (August 24, 1990). ... Traded by Dodgers to Montreal Expos for P Rick Clelland (December 14, 1995). ... Claimed on waivers by Toronto Blue Jays (July 25, 1997). ... Selected by Arizona Diamondbacks in second round (31st pick overall) of expansion draft (November 18, 1997). ... On Arizona disabled list (June 22-July 11, 1998); included rehabilitation assignment to Tucson (July 9-11). ... Traded by Diamondbacks with OF Travis Lee, P Vicente Padilla and P Nelson Figueroa to Philadelphia Phillies for P Curt Schilling (July 26, 2000). ... Traded by Phillies to Dodgers for P Eric Junge and P Jesus Cordero (November 9, 2001). ... Granted free agency (October 28, 2002). ... Signed by Baltimore Orioles (January 3, 2003). ... Placed on 15-day disabled list by Baltimore (June 28, 2003). ... Sent on minor league rehab assignment (September 1, 2003). ... Recalled from minor league rehab assignment (September 5, 2003). ... Removed from 15-day disabled list (September 10, 2003).
CAREER HITTING: 53-for-270 (.196), 23 R, 8 2B, 0 3B, 2 HR, 21 RBI.

Year	League	W	L	Pct.	ERA	WHIP	G	GS	CG	ShO	Hld.	Sv.-Opp.	IP	H	R	ER	HR	BB-IBB	SO	Avg.
1990— Dom. Dodgers (DSL)		3	6	.333	1.18	0.98	17	13	6	0	...	2-...	91.2	61	29	12	...	29-...	91	...
1991— Dom. Dodgers (DSL)		7	2	.778	1.16	0.67	13	13	0	0	...	0-...	93.0	30	17	12	...	32-...	81	...
1992— San Antonio (Texas)		2	6	.250	5.02	1.62	35	5	0	0	...	5-...	57.1	60	39	32	3	33-1	52	.284
— Albuquerque (PCL)		0	2	.000	7.84	2.42	12	0	0	0	...	0-...	10.1	14	9	9	1	11-1	9	.341
1993— Albuquerque (PCL)		1	1	.500	3.38	1.50	6	0	0	0	...	2-...	5.1	5	2	2	1	3-1	2	.250
— Los Angeles (N.L.)		2	3	.400	5.09	1.61	47	0	0	0	7	0-1	35.1	36	20	20	5	21-3	19	.277
1994— Albuquerque (PCL)		4	2	.667	5.19	1.56	11	5	0	0	...	1-...	34.2	38	20	20	6	16-0	28	.297
— Los Angeles (N.L.)		0	0	...	3.29	1.24	24	0	0	0	3	0-0	13.2	12	5	5	1	5-0	9	.245
1995— Albuquerque (PCL)		2	3	.400	4.05	1.54	17	9	0	0	...	1-...	53.1	56	28	24	3	26-2	46	.273
— Los Angeles (N.L.)		4	0	1.000	7.20	2.20	28	0	0	0	4	0-1	20.0	29	16	16	1	15-4	11	.354
1996— Montreal (N.L.)		4	5	.444	4.02	1.27	64	6	0	0	9	0-0	87.1	74	40	39	10	37-3	82	.228
1997— Montreal (N.L.)		1	2	.333	9.79	2.08	33	0	0	0	3	1-3	30.1	48	35	33	4	15-3	16	.378
— Ottawa (Int'l)		0	1	.000	5.63	1.38	2	2	0	0	...	0-...	8.0	10	6	5	1	1-0	9	.286
— Toronto (A.L.)		1	1	.500	4.00	1.48	9	3	0	0	0	0-0	27.0	34	13	12	3	6-0	28	.304
— Syracuse (Int'l)		3	0	1.000	0.53	0.82	5	5	1	1	...	0-...	34.0	18	2	2	0	10-0	29	.154
1998— Arizona (N.L.)		8	12	.400	2.88	1.21	33	23	3	1	1	0-0	162.2	146	60	52	12	51-3	132	.245
— Tucson (PCL)		0	0	...	3.00	1.33	1	1	0	0	...	0-...	3.0	3	2	1	0	1-0	4	.250
1999— Arizona (N.L.)		16	9	.640	3.65	1.24	32	32	2	1	0	0-0	214.2	188	92	87	21	79-3	148	.236
2000— Arizona (N.L.)		2	10	.167	7.22	1.76	20	16	0	0	0	0-0	96.0	127	88	77	17	42-11	45	.315
— Philadelphia (N.L.)		2	† 9	.182	4.69	1.56	12	12	0	0	0	0-0	71.0	81	40	37	9	30-0	51	.290
2001— Philadelphia (N.L.)		13	7	.650	4.46	1.37	32	32	0	0	0	0-0	185.2	199	100	92	26	56-3	107	.273
2002— Los Angeles (N.L.)		11	9	.550	3.90	1.21	39	23	0	0	1	0-0	161.1	142	73	70	20	54-3	105	.239
2003— Bowie (East.)		0	0	...	12.00	2.33	1	1	0	0	...	0-...	3.0	5	4	4	1	2-0	2	.385
— Baltimore (A.L.)		4	11	.267	6.34	1.75	19	17	0	0	1	0-0	93.2	134	69	66	11	30-1	53	.343
American League totals (2 years)		5	12	.294	5.82	1.69	28	20	0	0	1	0-0	120.2	168	82	78	14	36-1	81	.334
National League totals (10 years)		63	66	.488	4.41	1.38	364	144	5	2	28	1-9	1078.0	1082	569	528	126	405-36	725	.263
Major League totals (11 years)		68	78	.466	4.55	1.41	392	164	5	2	29	1-9	1198.2	1250	651	606	140	441-37	806	.271

D

D'AMICO, JEFF P

PERSONAL: Born December 27, 1975... 6-7/250. ... Throws right, bats right. ... Full name: Jeffrey Charles D'Amico. ... High school: Northeast (St. Petersburg, Fla.).

TRANSACTIONS/CAREER NOTES: Selected by Milwaukee Brewers organization in first round (23rd pick overall) of free-agent draft (June 3, 1993). ... On disabled list (June 24, 1994-entire season). ... On Milwaukee disabled list (July 28-September 2, 1997; and January 14, 1998-entire season). ... On Milwaukee disabled list (March 29-September 25, 1999); included rehabilitation assignments to Beloit (July 6-15), Huntsville (July 16-21) and Louisville (August 12-25). ... On Milwaukee disabled list (June 6-30, 2000). ... On Milwaukee disabled list (April 23-September 1, 2001); included rehabilitation assignments to Beloit (June 6-11 and August 29-31) and Huntsville (June 12). ... Traded by Brewers to New York Mets as part of three-way deal in which Mets traded P Glendon Rusch to Brewers, Colorado Rockies traded 1B/OF Ross Gload and P Craig House to Mets, Brewers traded OF Jeromy Burnitz, IF Lou Collier, OF/1B Mark Sweeney and cash to Mets, Mets traded 1B/3B Todd Zeile, OF Benny Agbayani, IF/OF Lenny Harris and cash to Rockies and Rockies traded OF Alex Ochoa to Brewers (January 21, 2002). ... Granted free agency (October 28, 2002). ... Signed by Pittsburgh Pirates organization (January 17, 2003).

CAREER HITTING: 15-for-148 (.101), 7 R, 2 2B, 1 3B, 2 HR, 5 RBI.

Year League	W	L	Pct.	ERA	WHIP	G	GS	CG	ShO	Hld.	Sv.-Opp.	IP	H	R	ER	HR	BB-IBB	SO	Avg.
1994—Ariz. Brewers (Ariz.)										Did not play.									
1995—Beloit (Midw.)	13	3	.813	2.39	1.01	21	20	3	1	...	0-...	132.0	102	40	35	7	31-2	119	.211
1996—El Paso (Texas)	5	4	.556	3.19	1.06	13	13	3	0	...	0-...	96.0	89	42	34	10	13-0	76	.241
—Milwaukee (A.L.)	6	6	.500	5.44	1.38	17	17	0	0	0	0-0	86.0	88	53	52	21	31-0	53	.267
1997—Milwaukee (A.L.)	9	7	.563	4.71	1.34	23	23	1	1	0	0-0	135.2	139	81	71	25	43-2	94	.264
—Beloit (Midw.)	0	0	...	0.00	0.33	1	1	0	0	...	0-...	3.0	0	0	0	0	1-0	7	.000
1998—Milwaukee (A.L.)										Did not play.									
1999—Beloit (Midw.)	1	0	1.000	0.00	1.00	2	2	0	0	...	0-...	8.0	7	0	0	0	1-0	6	.233
—Huntsville (Sou.)	0	0	...	36.00	3.50	1	1	0	0	...	0-...	2.0	6	8	8	3	1-0	2	.500
—Louisville (Int'l)	0	0	...	13.50	2.40	1	1	0	0	...	0-...	3.1	6	5	5	0	2-0	1	.400
—Milwaukee (N.L.)	0	0	...	0.00	1.00	1	0	0	0	0	0-0	1.0	1	0	0	0	0-0	1	.250
2000—Indianapolis (Int'l)	1	1	.500	3.16	1.15	6	6	0	0	...	0-...	31.1	25	11	11	6	11-0	20	.219
—Milwaukee (N.L.)	12	7	.632	2.66	1.16	23	23	1	1	0	0-0	162.1	143	55	48	14	46-5	101	.238
2001—Milwaukee (N.L.)	2	4	.333	6.08	1.61	10	10	0	0	0	0-0	47.1	60	42	32	11	16-4	32	.306
—Beloit (Midw.)	0	0	...	5.40	1.44	2	2	0	0	...	0-...	8.1	11	6	5	1	1-0	6	.306
—Huntsville (Sou.)	1	0	1.000	2.57	0.71	1	1	0	0	...	0-...	7.0	3	2	2	2	2-0	5	.130
2002—New York (N.L.)	6	10	.375	4.94	1.30	29	22	1	1	0	0-0	145.2	152	84	80	20	37-8	101	.267
2003—Pittsburgh (N.L.)	9	*16	.360	4.77	1.40	29	29	2	1	0	0-0	175.1	204	104	93	23	42-6	100	.291
American League totals (2 years)	15	13	.536	4.99	1.36	40	40	1	1	0	0-0	221.2	227	134	123	46	74-2	147	.265
National League totals (5 years)	29	37	.439	4.28	1.32	92	84	4	3	0	0-0	531.2	560	285	253	68	141-23	335	.270
Major League totals (7 years)	44	50	.468	4.49	1.33	132	124	5	4	0	0-0	753.1	787	419	376	114	215-25	482	.269

DAMON, JOHNNY OF

PERSONAL: Born November 5, 1973, in Fort Riley, Kan. ... 6-2/190. ... Bats left, throws left. ... Full name: Johnny David Damon. ... Name pronounced: DAY-mun. ... High school: Dr. Phillips (Orlando).

TRANSACTIONS/CAREER NOTES: Selected by Kansas City Royals organization in supplemental round ("sandwich pick" between first and second round, 35th pick overall) of free-agent draft (June 1, 1992). ... On suspended list (September 5-7, 1997). ... Traded by Royals with IF Mark Ellis and a player to be named later to Oakland Athletics as part of three-way deal in which Royals received P Roberto Hernandez from Tampa Bay Devil Rays, A's received P Cory Lidle from Devil Rays, Royals received C A.J. Hinch, IF Angel Berroa and cash from A's and Devil Rays received OF Ben Grieve and a player to be named later or cash from A's (January 8, 2001). ... Granted free agency (November 5, 2001). ... Signed by Boston Red Sox (December 21, 2001).

2003 GAMES PLAYED BY POSITION (MLB): OF—144, DH—1.

Year Team (League)	Pos.	G	AB	R	H	2B	3B	HR	RBI	BB	SO	HBP	GDP	SB-CS	Avg.	OBP	SLG	OPS	E	Pct.
1992—GC Royals (GCL)	OF	50	192	*58	67	12	*9	4	24	31	21	4	1	33-6	.349	.449	.568	1.017	1	.988
—Baseball City (FSL)	OF	1	1	0	0	0	0	0	0	0	0	0	0	0-0	.000	.000	.000	.000	0	...
1993—Rockford (Midwest)	OF	127	511	82	148	25	*13	5	52	52	83	6	4	59-18	.290	.360	.419	.779	6	.977
1994—Wilmington (Caro.)	OF	119	472	96	149	25	13	6	75	62	55	8	4	44-9	.316	.399	.462	.861	3	.989
1995—Wichita (Texas)	OF-DH	111	423	83	145	15	9	16	54	67	35	2	3	26-15	.343	*.434	.534	.968	5	.984
—Kansas City (A.L.)	OF	47	188	32	53	11	5	3	23	12	22	1	2	7-0	.282	.324	.441	.765	1	.991
1996—Kansas City (A.L.)	OF-DH	145	517	61	140	22	5	6	50	31	64	3	4	25-5	.271	.313	.368	.680	6	.983
1997—Kansas City (A.L.)	OF-DH	146	472	70	130	12	8	8	48	42	70	3	3	16-10	.275	.338	.386	.723	4	.988
1998—Kansas City (A.L.)	OF	161	642	104	178	30	10	18	66	58	84	4	4	26-12	.277	.339	.439	.779	4	.990
1999—Kansas City (A.L.)	OF-DH	145	583	101	179	39	9	14	77	67	50	3	13	36-6	.307	.379	.477	.856	4	.987
2000—Kansas City (A.L.)	OF-DH	159	655	*136	214	42	10	16	88	65	60	1	7	*46-9	.327	.382	.495	.877	5	.986
2001—Oakland (A.L.)	OF	155	644	108	165	34	4	9	49	61	70	5	7	27-12	.256	.324	.363	.687	3	.991
2002—Boston (A.L.)	OF-DH	154	623	118	178	34	*11	14	63	65	70	6	4	31-6	.286	.356	.443	.799	1	.997
2003—Boston (A.L.)	OF-DH	145	608	103	166	32	6	12	67	68	74	2	5	30-6	.273	.345	.405	.750	1	.997
Major League totals (9 years)		1257	4932	833	1403	256	68	100	531	469	564	28	49	244-66	.284	.347	.425	.772	29	.990

DARENSBOURG, VIC P

PERSONAL: Born November 13, 1970, in Los Angeles, Calif. ... 5-8/170. ... Throws left, bats left. ... Full name: Victor Anthony Darensbourg. ... Name pronounced: darensberg. ... High school: Westchester (Los Angeles). ... College: Lewis-Clark (Idaho) State.

TRANSACTIONS/CAREER NOTES: Signed as non-drafted free agent by Florida Marlins organization (June 11, 1992). ... On disabled list entire 1995 season. ... On Portland disabled list (April 4-15, 1996). ... On disabled list (April 25-June 21 and July 29-September 6, 1997). ... On disabled list (August 20-September 17, 2001). ... Granted free agency (October 15, 2002). ... Re-signed by Marlins (late 2002). ... Traded by Marlins with C Charles Johnson, OF Preston Wilson and 2B Pablo Ozuna to Colorado Rockies for P Mike Hampton, OF Juan Pierre and cash (November 16, 2002). ... Released by Rockies (2003). ... Signed by Montreal Expos as a free agent (July 28, 2003).

CAREER HITTING: 2-for-18 (.111), 0 R, 0 2B, 0 3B, 0 HR, 0 RBI.

Year League	W	L	Pct.	ERA	WHIP	G	GS	CG	ShO	Hld.	Sv.-Opp.	IP	H	R	ER	HR	BB-IBB	SO	Avg.
1992—GC Marlins (GCL)	2	1	.667	0.64	0.93	8	4	0	0	...	2-...	42.0	28	5	3	1	11-2	37	.190
1993—Kane County (Midwest)	9	1	.900	2.14	1.21	46	0	0	0	...	16-...	71.1	58	17	17	3	28-3	89	.221
—High Desert (Calif.)	0	0	...	0.00	0.00	1	0	0	0	...	0-...	1.0	0	0	0	0	0-0	1	.000
1994—Portland (East.)	10	7	.588	3.81	1.38	35	21	1	1	...	4-...	149.0	146	76	63	18	60-3	103	.264
1995—Florida (N.L.)										Did not play.									
1996—Brevard County (FSL)	0	0	...	0.00	0.67	2	0	0	0	...	0-...	3.0	1	0	0	0	1-0	5	.111
—Charlotte (Int'l)	1	5	.167	3.69	1.47	47	0	0	0	...	7-...	63.1	61	30	26	7	32-3	66	.253
1997—Charlotte (Int'l)	4	2	.667	4.38	1.50	27	0	0	0	...	2-...	24.2	22	12	12	4	15-3	21	.242
1998—Florida (N.L.)	0	7	.000	3.68	1.15	59	0	0	0	13	1-2	71.0	52	29	29	5	30-6	74	.207

Year League	W	L	Pct.	ERA	WHIP	G	GS	CG	ShO	Hld.	Sv.-Opp.	IP	H	R	ER	HR	BB-IBB	SO	Avg.
1999— Florida (N.L.)	0	1	.000	8.83	2.05	56	0	0	0	10	0-1	34.2	50	36	34	3	21-1	16	.340
— Calgary (PCL)	0	0	...	4.63	1.11	9	0	0	0	...	1-...	11.2	13	6	6	0	0-0	12	.289
2000— Florida (N.L.)	5	3	.625	4.06	1.44	56	0	0	0	3	0-1	62.0	61	32	28	7	28-1	59	.260
2001— Florida (N.L.)	1	2	.333	4.25	1.27	58	0	0	0	11	1-3	48.2	52	24	23	4	10-6	33	.277
2002— Florida (N.L.)	1	2	.333	6.14	1.80	42	0	0	0	3	0-0	48.1	61	34	33	10	26-4	33	.305
2003— Colorado (N.L.)	0	0	...	0.00	1.71	3	0	0	0	0	0-0	2.1	4	1	0	0	0-0	0	.333
— Colo. Springs (PCL)	2	2	.500	3.57	1.28	20	0	0	0	...	0-...	22.2	24	13	9	1	5-1	15	.273
— Edmonton (PCL)	1	1	.500	1.98	1.39	11	0	0	0	...	0-...	13.2	12	3	3	0	7-0	11	.235
— Montreal (N.L.)	0	0	...	10.80	2.10	6	0	0	0	0	0-0	6.2	13	8	8	2	1-0	4	.406
Major League totals (6 years)	7	15	.318	5.10	1.49	280	0	0	0	40	2-7	273.2	293	164	155	31	116-18	219	.275

DAUBACH, BRIAN — 1B/DH

PERSONAL: Born February 11, 1972, in Belleville, Ill. ... 6-1/230. ... Bats left, throws right. ... Full name: Brian Michael Daubach. ... Name pronounced: DAW-back. ... High school: Belleville (Ill.) West.

TRANSACTIONS/CAREER NOTES: Selected by New York Mets organization in 17th round of free-agent draft (June 4, 1990). ... Granted free agency (October 15, 1996). ... Signed by Florida Marlins organization (November 7, 1996). ... Granted free agency (October 17, 1997). ... Re-signed by Marlins organization (January 6, 1998). ... Released by Marlins (November 19, 1998). ... Signed by Boston Red Sox organization (December 18, 1998). ... On Boston disabled list (August 15-September 2, 2001); included rehabilitation assignments to Pawtucket (August 29-30) and Lowell (August 31-September 1). ... Granted free agency (December 21, 2002). ... Signed by Chicago White Sox organization (January 27, 2003).

2003 GAMES PLAYED BY POSITION (MLB): 1B—45, DH—15, OF—12.

Year Team (League)	Pos.	G	AB	R	H	2B	3B	HR	RBI	BB	SO	HBP	GDP	SB-CS	Avg.	OBP	SLG	OPS	E	Pct.
1990— GC Mets (GCL)	1B	45	152	26	41	8	4	1	19	22	41	2	2	2-1	.270	.363	.395	.758	1	.976
1991— Kingsport (Appal.)	1B	65	218	30	53	9	1	7	42	33	64	6	1	1-3	.243	.355	.390	.745	9	.986
1992— Pittsfield (NYP)	1B	72	260	26	63	15	2	2	40	30	61	3	5	4-0	.242	.323	.338	.662	12	.982
1993— Capital City (SAL)	1B-OF	102	379	50	106	19	3	7	72	52	84	5	14	6-1	.280	.368	.401	.769	5	.989
1994— St. Lucie (Fla. St.)	1B	129	450	52	123	30	2	6	74	58	120	5	3	14-9	.273	.360	.389	.749	12	.991
1995— Binghamton (East.)	3B-1B	135	469	61	115	25	2	10	72	51	104	7	5	6-2	.245	.324	.371	.695	10	.992
— Norfolk (Int'l)	1B	2	7	0	0	0	0	0	0	1	0	0	0	0-0	.000	.125	.000	.125	0	1.000
1996— Binghamton (East.)	3B-1B	122	436	80	129	24	1	22	76	74	103	7	8	7-9	.296	.403	.507	.910	11	.991
— Norfolk (Int'l)	1B	17	54	7	11	2	0	0	6	6	14	0	1	1-1	.204	.279	.241	.519	0	1.000
1997— Charlotte (Int'l)	1B	136	461	66	128	40	2	21	93	65	126	6	7	1-8	.278	.367	.510	.877	8	.991
1998— Charlotte (Int'l)	1B-OF	140	497	102	157	* 45	4	* 35	* 124	80	114	15	15	9-3	.316	.421	.634	1.055	3	.992
— Florida (N.L.)	1B	10	15	0	3	1	0	0	3	1	5	1	0	0-0	.200	.294	.267	.561	0	1.000
1999— Boston (A.L.)	1-D-OF-3	110	381	61	112	33	3	21	73	36	92	3	5	0-1	.294	.360	.562	.921	8	.983
— Pawtucket (Int'l)	DH-1B-OF	9	31	4	9	2	0	1	6	6	8	2	0	0-0	.290	.436	.452	.888	1	.971
2000— Boston (A.L.)	1-D-OF-3	142	495	55	123	32	2	21	76	44	130	6	6	1-1	.248	.315	.448	.764	3	.996
2001— Boston (A.L.)	1B-OF	122	407	54	107	28	3	22	71	53	108	5	10	1-0	.263	.350	.509	.859	11	.988
— Pawtucket (Int'l)	DH	1	4	0	1	0	0	0	0	0	2	0	0	0-0	.250	.250	.250	.500	...	...
— Lowell (NY-Penn)	1B	1	2	0	0	0	0	0	0	1	1	0	0	0-0	.000	.333	.000	.333	0	1.000
2002— Boston (A.L.) 1B-OF-DH		137	444	62	118	24	2	20	78	51	126	7	10	2-1	.266	.348	.464	.812	5	.991
2003— Chicago (A.L.) 1B-D-DH		95	183	26	42	11	0	6	21	34	54	1	3	1-0	.230	.352	.388	.740	2	.993
American League totals (5 years)		606	1910	258	502	128	10	90	319	218	510	22	34	5-3	.263	.343	.482	.824	29	.990
National League totals (1 year)		10	15	0	3	1	0	0	3	1	5	1	0	0-0	.200	.294	.267	.561	0	1.000
Major League totals (6 years)		616	1925	258	505	129	10	90	322	219	515	23	34	5-3	.262	.342	.480	.822	29	.990

DaVANON, JEFF — OF

PERSONAL: Born December 8, 1973, in San Diego, Calif. ... 6-0/185. ... Bats both, throws right. ... Full name: Jeffrey Graham DaVanon. ... Name pronounced: duh-VAN-un. ... High school: Bellaire (Texas). ... College: San Diego State.

TRANSACTIONS/CAREER NOTES: Selected by Oakland Athletics organization in 26th round of free-agent draft (June 1, 1995). ... Traded by Athletics with P Elvin Nina and OF Nathan Haynes to Anaheim Angels for P Omar Olivares and 2B Randy Velarde (July 29, 1999). ... On disabled list (March 20, 2000-entire season). ... On Salt Lake disabled list (April 14-21, 2001). ... On Salt Lake disabled list (May 25-August 23 and August 29, 2002-remainder of season).

2003 GAMES PLAYED BY POSITION (MLB): OF—115, DH—1.

Year Team (League)	Pos.	G	AB	R	H	2B	3B	HR	RBI	BB	SO	HBP	GDP	SB-CS	Avg.	OBP	SLG	OPS	E	Pct.
1995— S. Oregon (N'west)	OF	57	167	29	42	6	2	1	17	34	49	0	1	6-5	.251	.376	.329	.706	8	.864
1996— W. Mich. (Mid.)	2B-1B-OF	89	289	43	70	13	4	2	33	49	66	1	6	5-7	.242	.353	.336	.689	2	.976
1997— Visalia (Calif.)	OF	119	408	70	104	17	3	6	38	81	101	0	7	23-14	.255	.377	.355	.732	10	.948
1998— Modesto (Calif.)	OF	84	301	66	101	17	4	5	60	59	69	1	4	33-10	.336	.439	.468	.907	13	.902
1999— Midland (Texas)	OF-DH	100	374	87	128	29	11	11	60	53	68	4	6	18-10	.342	.424	.567	.991	7	.960
— Edmonton (PCL)	OF-DH	34	132	35	43	8	3	6	19	20	27	1	1	11-4	.326	.416	.568	.984	0	1.000
— Anaheim (A.L.)	OF-DH	7	20	4	4	0	1	1	4	2	7	0	0	0-1	.200	.273	.450	.723	0	1.000
2000— Anaheim (A.L.)										Did not play.										
2001— Salt Lake (PCL)	OF	69	256	46	80	19	8	10	48	32	57	3	4	8-3	.313	.390	.566	.956	1	.992
— Anaheim (A.L.)	OF-DH	40	88	7	17	2	1	5	9	11	29	0	1	1-3	.193	.280	.409	.689	1	.980
2002— Salt Lake (PCL)	OF	16	30	3	5	3	0	1	4	2	6	0	0	1-0	.167	.219	.367	.585	0	1.000
— Ariz. Angels (Ariz.)	OF	25	100	21	33	10	1	5	18	17	24	1	1	5-3	.330	.429	.600	1.029	2	.962
— Ariz. Angels (Ariz.)	OF	5	15	5	10	6	1	0	4	5	2	0	0	2-0	.667	.714	1.200	1.914	0	1.000
2003— Salt Lake (PCL)	OF-DH	16	60	11	18	4	1	2	14	9	9	1	1	4-1	.300	.400	.500	.900	2	.933
— Anaheim (A.L.)	OF-DH	123	330	56	93	16	1	12	43	42	59	1	6	17-5	.282	.360	.445	.805	4	.983
Major League totals (4 years)		186	468	70	119	21	3	19	60	57	101	1	7	19-9	.254	.333	.434	.766	5	.983

DAVIS, BEN — C

PERSONAL: Born March 10, 1977, in Chester, Pa. ... 6-4/225. ... Bats both, throws right. ... Full name: Mark Christopher Davis. ... High school: Malvern (Pa.) Prep.

TRANSACTIONS/CAREER NOTES: Selected by San Diego Padres organization in first round (second pick overall) of free-agent draft (June 3, 1995). ... On San Diego disabled list (August 13-September 1, 2000). ... Traded by Padres for with P Wascar Serrano and SS Alex Arias to Seattle Mariners for P Brett Tomko, C Tom Lampkin and SS Ramon Vazquez (December 11, 2001).

2003 GAMES PLAYED BY POSITION (MLB): C—73, DH—1.

Year Team (League)	Pos.	G	AB	R	H	2B	3B	HR	RBI	BB	SO	HBP	GDP	SB-CS	Avg.	OBP	SLG	OPS	FIELDING E	Pct.
1995— Idaho Falls (Pio.)	C	52	197	36	55	8	3	5	46	17	36	1	3	0-0	.279	.338	.426	.764	6	.985
1996— Rancho Cuca. (Calif.)	C-DH	98	353	35	71	10	1	6	41	31	89	0	8	1-1	.201	.264	.286	.550	9	.987
1997— Rancho Cuca. (Calif.)	C-DH-1B	122	474	67	132	30	1	17	76	28	107	2	11	3-1	.278	.320	.454	.773	14	.987
1998— Mobile (Sou.)	C-DH	116	433	65	124	29	2	14	75	42	60	6	11	4-2	.286	.352	.460	.812	6	.994
— San Diego (N.L.)	C	1	1	0	0	0	0	0	0	0	0	0	0	0-0	.000	.000	.000	.000	0	1.000
1999— Las Vegas (PCL)	C	58	201	27	62	18	1	7	44	24	41	2	5	4-1	.308	.384	.512	.897	4	.992
— San Diego (N.L.)	C	76	266	29	65	14	1	5	30	25	70	0	9	2-1	.244	.307	.361	.668	7	.986
2000— San Diego (N.L.)	C-DH	43	130	12	29	6	0	3	14	14	35	0	2	1-1	.223	.297	.338	.635	1	.996
— Las Vegas (PCL)	C	59	221	38	58	16	1	7	40	38	43	1	5	5-2	.262	.373	.439	.812	7	.986
2001— San Diego (N.L.)	C-1B	138	448	56	107	20	0	11	57	66	112	4	13	4-4	.239	.337	.357	.694	9	.990
2002— Seattle (A.L.)	C-1B	80	228	24	59	10	1	7	43	18	58	2	6	1-1	.259	.313	.404	.717	1	.998
2003— Seattle (A.L.)	C-DH	80	246	25	58	18	0	6	42	18	61	0	5	0-0	.236	.284	.382	.666	4	.991
American League totals (2 years)		160	474	49	117	28	1	13	85	36	119	2	11	1-1	.247	.298	.392	.690	5	.994
National League totals (4 years)		258	845	97	201	40	1	19	101	105	217	4	24	7-6	.238	.322	.355	.677	17	.990
Major League totals (6 years)		418	1319	146	318	68	2	32	186	141	336	6	35	8-7	.241	.313	.368	.682	22	.991

DAVIS, DOUG — P

PERSONAL: Born September 21, 1975, in Sacramento, Calif. ... 6-4/190. ... Throws left, bats right. ... Full name: Douglas P. Davis. ... High school: Northgate (Walnut Creek, Calif.). ... Junior college: San Francisco (Calif.) Community College.

TRANSACTIONS/CAREER NOTES: Selected by Texas Rangers organization in 10th round of free-agent draft (June 4, 1996). ... On Oklahoma disabled list (July 24, 2002-remainder of season). ... Contract purchased by Texas from Oklahoma (April 26, 2003). ... Designated for assignment by Texas (April 27, 2003). ... Claimed on waivers by Toronto Blue Jays (April 30, 2003). ... Elected free agency (July 11, 2003). ... Signed by Milwaukee Brewers (July 13, 2003).

CAREER HITTING: 2-for-24 (.083), 0 R, 0 2B, 0 3B, 0 HR, 0 RBI.

Year League	W	L	Pct.	ERA	WHIP	G	GS	CG	ShO	Hld.	Sv.-Opp.	IP	H	R	ER	HR	BB-IBB	SO	Avg.
1996— GC Rangers (GCL)	3	1	.750	1.90	1.27	8	7	0	0	...	0-...	42.2	28	13	9	0	26-1	49	.193
1997— GC Rangers (GCL)	3	1	.750	1.71	1.38	4	4	0	0	...	0-...	21.0	14	5	4	0	15-0	27	.200
— Charlotte (Fla. St.)	5	3	.625	3.10	1.26	9	8	1	0	...	0-...	49.1	29	19	17	2	33-1	52	.175
1998— Charlotte (Fla. St.)	11	7	.611	3.24	1.31	27	27	1	1	...	0-...	155.1	129	69	56	8	74-0	* 173	.225
1999— Tulsa (Texas)	4	4	.500	2.42	1.21	12	12	1	0	...	0-...	74.1	65	26	20	9	24-0	79	.235
— Oklahoma (PCL)	7	0	1.000	3.00	1.38	13	11	0	0	...	0-...	78.0	77	27	26	4	31-0	74	.263
— Texas (A.L.)	0	0	...	33.75	4.50	2	0	0	0	0	0-0	2.2	12	10	10	3	0-0	3	.600
2000— Oklahoma (PCL)	8	3	.727	2.84	1.38	12	12	2	0	...	0-...	69.2	62	32	22	8	34-1	53	.248
— Texas (A.L.)	7	6	.538	5.38	1.69	30	13	1	0	2	0-3	98.2	109	61	59	14	58-3	66	.288
2001— Texas (A.L.)	11	10	.524	4.45	1.55	30	30	1	0	0	0-0	186.0	220	103	92	14	69-1	115	.295
— Oklahoma (PCL)	2	0	1.000	2.87	0.89	2	2	0	0	...	0-...	15.2	10	5	5	1	4-0	14	.189
2002— Texas (A.L.)	3	5	.375	4.98	1.49	10	10	1	1	0	0-...	59.2	67	36	33	7	22-0	28	.290
— Oklahoma (PCL)	4	3	.571	4.99	1.32	9	9	0	0	...	0-...	61.1	70	38	34	7	11-0	48	.290
2003— Oklahoma (PCL)	3	0	1.000	3.25	1.08	4	4	0	0	...	0-...	27.2	29	10	10	3	1-0	18	.271
— Texas (A.L.)	0	0	...	12.00	2.67	1	1	0	0	0	0-0	3.0	4	4	4	2	4-0	2	.308
— Toronto (A.L.)	4	6	.400	5.00	1.78	12	11	0	0	0	0-0	54.0	70	33	30	6	26-1	25	.318
— Huntsville (Sou.)	1	0	1.000	3.00	1.33	1	1	0	0	...	0-...	6.0	5	2	2	0	3-0	6	.217
— Indianapolis (Int'l)	1	2	.333	4.15	1.24	5	5	0	0	...	0-...	34.2	33	16	16	2	10-0	19	.250
— Milwaukee (N.L.)	3	2	.600	2.58	1.34	8	8	1	0	0	0-0	52.1	49	18	15	8	21-0	35	.247
American League totals (5 years)	25	27	.481	5.08	1.64	85	65	3	1	2	0-3	404.0	482	247	228	46	179-5	239	.300
National League totals (1 year)	3	2	.600	2.58	1.34	8	8	1	0	0	0-0	52.1	49	18	15	8	21-0	35	.247
Major League totals (5 years)	28	29	.491	4.79	1.60	93	73	4	1	2	0-3	456.1	531	265	243	54	200-5	274	.294

DAVIS, J.J. — OF

PERSONAL: Born October 25, 1978, in Glendora, Calif. ... 6-5/240. ... Bats right, throws right. ... Full name: Jerry C. Davis. ... High school: Baldwin Park (Calif.).

TRANSACTIONS/CAREER NOTES: Selected by Pittsburgh Pirates organization in first round (eighth pick overall) of free-agent draft (June 3, 1997). ... On Altoona disabled list (June 22-August 23, 2001). ... On Altoona disabled list (April 9-May 13, 2002). ... Recalled by Pittsburgh from Nashville (August 19, 2003). ... Optioned to Nashville by Pittsburgh (August 29, 2003). ... Recalled by Pittsburgh from Nashville (September 13, 2003).

2003 GAMES PLAYED BY POSITION (MLB): OF—10.

Year Team (League)	Pos.	G	AB	R	H	2B	3B	HR	RBI	BB	SO	HBP	GDP	SB-CS	Avg.	OBP	SLG	OPS	FIELDING E	Pct.
1997— GC Pirates (GCL)	OF	45	165	19	42	10	2	1	18	14	44	2	4	0-0	.255	.315	.358	.673	0	1.000
— Erie (N.Y.-Penn)	DH	4	13	1	1	0	0	0	0	0	4	0	0	0-0	.077	.077	.077	.154	...	...
1998— Augusta (S. Atl.)	OF	30	106	11	21	6	0	4	11	3	24	0	4	1-1	.198	.220	.368	.588	3	.923
— Erie (N.Y.-Penn)	OF	52	196	25	53	12	2	8	39	20	54	2	3	4-1	.270	.341	.474	.815	7	.932
1999— Hickory (S. Atl.)	OF	86	317	58	84	26	1	19	65	44	99	4	3	2-5	.265	.360	.533	.893	4	.950
2000— Lynchburg (Caro.)	OF	130	485	77	118	36	1	20	80	52	171	4	11	9-4	.243	.319	.445	.765	18	.925
2001— Altoona (East.)	OF	67	228	21	57	13	3	4	26	21	79	2	1	2-5	.250	.317	.386	.703	0	1.000
— GC Pirates (GCL)	OF	4	17	3	8	1	0	2	6	1	2	0	1	0-0	.471	.500	.882	1.382	1	.667
2002— Altoona (East.)	OF	101	348	51	100	17	3	20	62	33	101	3	3	7-4	.287	.351	.526	.877	6	.971
— Pittsburgh (N.L.)	OF	9	10	1	1	0	0	0	0	0	4	1	1	0-0	.100	.182	.100	.282	0	1.000
2003— Nashville (PCL)	OF-DH	122	426	68	121	29	4	26	67	35	85	4	11	23-6	.284	.342	.554	.896	9	.964
— Pittsburgh (N.L.)	OF	19	35	1	7	0	1	1	4	3	13	0	0	0-1	.200	.263	.286	.549	0	1.000
Major League totals (2 years)		28	45	2	8	0	1	1	4	3	17	1	1	0-1	.178	.245	.244	.489	0	1.000

DAVIS, JASON — P

PERSONAL: Born May 8, 1980, in Chattanooga, Tenn. ... 6-6/210. ... Throws right, bats right. ... Full name: Jason Thomas Davis. ... College: Cleveland State.

TRANSACTIONS/CAREER NOTES: Selected by Cleveland Indians organization in 21st round of free-agent draft (June 5, 1999).

CAREER HITTING: 0-for-2 (.000), 0 R, 0 2B, 0 3B, 0 HR, 0 RBI.

Year League	W	L	Pct.	ERA	WHIP	G	GS	CG	ShO	Hld.	Sv.-Opp.	IP	H	R	ER	HR	BB-IBB	SO	Avg.
2000— Burlington (Appal.)	4	4	.500	4.40	1.42	10	10	0	0	...	0-...	45.0	48	27	22	5	16-0	35	.276
2001— Columbus (S. Atl.)	14	6	.700	2.70	1.24	27	27	1	1	...	0-...	160.0	147	72	48	9	51-1	115	.243
2002— Kinston (Caro.)	3	6	.333	4.15	1.38	17	17	1	1	...	0-...	99.2	107	64	46	7	31-2	68	.272
— Akron (East.)	6	2	.750	3.51	1.34	10	10	0	0	...	0-...	59.0	63	26	23	2	16-0	45	.278
— Cleveland (A.L.)	1	0	1.000	1.84	1.09	3	2	0	0	0	0-0	14.2	12	3	3	1	4-0	11	.218
2003— Cleveland (A.L.)	8	11	.421	4.68	1.32	27	27	1	0	0	0-0	165.1	172	101	86	25	47-4	85	.273
Major League totals (2 years)	9	11	.450	4.45	1.31	30	29	1	0	0	0-0	180.0	184	104	89	26	51-4	96	.268

DAWKINS, GOOKIE   SS

PERSONAL: Born May 12, 1979, in Newberry, S.C. ... 6-1/186. ... Bats right, throws right. ... Full name: Travis Sentell Dawkins. ... High school: Newberry (S.C.).

TRANSACTIONS/CAREER NOTES: Selected by Cincinnati Reds organization in second round of free-agent draft (June 3, 1997). ... On Louisville disabled list (August 1-8, 2000). ... On disabled list (April 5-12 and April 28-May 9, 2001). ... Claimed on waivers by Los Angeles Dodgers (March 17, 2003). ... Acquired by the Kansas City Royals from Los Angeles Dodgers for P Scott Mullen and SS Victor Rodriguez (July 6, 2003).

2003 GAMES PLAYED BY POSITION (MLB): 2B—3.

Year Team (League)	Pos.	G	AB	R	H	2B	3B	HR	RBI	BB	SO	HBP	GDP	SB-CS	Avg.	OBP	SLG	OPS	FIELDING E	Pct.
1997— Billings (Pio.)	SS	70	253	47	61	5	0	4	37	30	38	0	6	16-6	.241	.315	.308	.623	34	.908
1998— Burlington (Midw.)	SS	102	367	52	97	7	6	1	30	37	60	1	10	37-10	.264	.332	.324	.656	36	.925
1999— Rockford (Midwest)	SS	76	305	56	83	10	6	8	32	35	38	0	5	38-13	.272	.346	.423	.769	17	.950
— Chattanooga (Sou.)	SS	32	129	24	47	7	0	2	13	14	17	0	5	15-5	.364	.427	.465	.892	3	.979
— Cincinnati (N.L.)	SS	7	7	1	1	0	0	0	0	0	4	1	0	0-0	.143	.250	.143	.393	0	1.000
2000— Chattanooga (Sou.)	SS-2B	95	368	54	85	20	6	6	31	40	71	3	3	22-10	.231	.310	.367	.677	19	.962
— Cincinnati (N.L.)	SS	14	41	5	9	2	0	0	3	2	7	0	3	0-0	.220	.256	.268	.524	2	.965
2001— Chattanooga (Sou.)	SS	104	394	59	89	16	3	8	40	32	88	2	9	14-4	.226	.285	.343	.628	16	.964
2002— Cincinnati (N.L.)	SS-2B	31	48	2	6	2	0	0	0	6	21	0	1	2-1	.125	.222	.167	.389	4	.927
— Chattanooga (Sou.)	SS-2B	40	155	21	42	10	1	1	12	25	28	0	8	5-5	.271	.372	.368	.740	6	.968
— Louisville (Int'l)	SS-2B	47	167	14	42	5	2	0	8	12	34	1	4	2-3	.251	.302	.305	.608	4	.983
2003— Las Vegas (PCL)	SS	32	115	5	19	5	1	0	12	9	26	0	1	3-1	.165	.224	.226	.450	10	.928
— Jacksonville (Sou.)	SS	35	113	12	30	6	0	4	20	10	12	2	2	3-2	.265	.333	.425	.758	7	.953
— Kansas City (A.L.)	2B	3	2	0	0	0	0	0	0	1	2	0	0	0-0	.000	.333	.000	.333	0	1.000
— Omaha (PCL)	SS-3B	33	112	18	29	6	0	2	18	7	24	1	5	2-3	.259	.303	.366	.669	3	.981
American League totals (1 year)		3	2	0	0	0	0	0	0	1	2	0	0	0-0	.000	.333	.000	.333	0	1.000
National League totals (3 years)		52	96	8	16	4	0	0	3	8	32	1	4	2-1	.167	.238	.208	.446	6	.949
Major League totals (4 years)		55	98	8	16	4	0	0	3	9	34	1	4	2-1	.163	.241	.204	.445	6	.952

DAWLEY, JOE   P

PERSONAL: Born September 19, 1971, in Riverside, Calif. ... 6-4/205. ... Throws right, bats right. ... Full name: Joseph Thomas Dawley. ... Junior college: Riverside City (Calif.).

TRANSACTIONS/CAREER NOTES: Selected by Baltimore Orioles organization in 28th round of free-agent draft (June 1, 1992). ... Released by Orioles (July 9, 1995). ... Signed by Palm Springs, Western League (July 1995). ... Signed by Chico, Western League (May 1997). ... Signed by Atlanta Braves organization (September 19, 1998). ... Granted free agency (October 15, 1999). ... Re-signed by Braves organization (November 9, 1999). ... On disabled list (April 6, 2000-entire season). ... Granted free agency (October 15, 2000). ... Re-signed by Braves organization (November 1, 2000). ... Recalled by Atlanta from Richmond (May 7, 2003). ... Optioned to Richmond by Atlanta (May 17, 2003). ... Recalled from Richmond by Atlanta (August 28, 2003). ... Designated for assignment (August 30, 2003). ... Sent outright to Richmond (September 9, 2003).

CAREER HITTING: 0-for-1 (.000), 0 R, 0 2B, 0 3B, 0 HR, 0 RBI.

Year League	W	L	Pct.	ERA	WHIP	G	GS	CG	ShO	Hld.	Sv.-Opp.	IP	H	R	ER	HR	BB-IBB	SO	Avg.
1993— Bluefield (Appal.)	3	1	.750	3.52	1.57	20	0	0	0	...	3-...	30.2	34	20	12	1	14-3	30	.272
1994— Bluefield (Appal.)	1	2	.333	5.70	1.61	11	2	0	0	...	2-...	23.2	20	18	15	2	18-0	18	.222
— Albany (S. Atl.)	0	0	...	6.14	1.91	5	0	0	0	...	0-...	7.1	7	6	5	0	7-1	4	.250
1995— Frederick (Caro.)	1	2	.333	6.34	1.93	24	0	0	0	...	1-...	32.2	41	28	23	4	22-1	29	.301
— Palm Springs (West.)	1	0	1.000	3.86	1.32	15	0	0	0	...	0-...	28.0	28	14	12	2	9-0	20	.241
1996— Palm Springs (West.)	2	1	.667	1.59	1.29	27	0	0	0	...	4-...	34.0	26	14	6	3	18-1	29	.205
1997— Chico (West.)	1	4	.200	4.39	1.46	41	0	0	0	...	14-...	41.0	42	24	20	2	18-2	51	.256
1998— Chico (West.)	2	4	.333	3.35	1.63	45	0	0	0	...	26-...	43.0	43	22	16	2	27-2	36	.261
1999— Greenville (Sou.)	5	3	.625	4.03	1.23	26	11	0	0	...	0-...	91.2	76	54	41	5	37-3	89	.224
— Richmond (Int'l)	0	3	.000	5.18	1.38	7	7	1	0	...	0-...	40.0	43	26	23	5	12-0	31	.274
2000—										Did not play.									
2001— Myrtle Beach (Caro.)	1	0	1.000	1.80	0.40	5	0	0	0	...	0-...	10.0	4	2	2	0	0-0	16	.118
— Richmond (Int'l)	1	0	1.000	2.84	0.63	3	0	0	0	...	0-...	6.1	3	2	2	1	1-0	5	.143
— Greenville (Sou.)	7	5	.583	3.04	1.11	22	21	1	0	...	0-...	127.1	95	50	43	15	46-0	130	.207
2002— Richmond (Int'l)	9	7	.563	2.63	1.06	24	23	1	1	...	0-...	140.1	113	44	41	10	36-0	136	.220
— Atlanta (N.L.)	0	0	...	0.00	0.00	1	0	0	0	0	0-0	.1	0	0	0	0	0-0	1	.000
2003— Atlanta (N.L.)	0	0	...	18.00	2.57	5	0	0	0	0	0-0	7.0	15	14	14	3	3-0	8	.405
— Richmond (Int'l)	3	5	.375	3.34	1.24	46	4	0	0	...	23-...	56.2	47	25	21	4	23-1	73	.221
Major League totals (2 years)	0	0	...	17.18	2.45	6	0	0	0	0	0-0	7.1	15	14	14	3	3-0	9	.395

DAY, ZACH   P

PERSONAL: Born June 15, 1978, in Cincinnati, Ohio. ... 6-4/210. ... Throws right, bats right. ... Full name: Stephen Zachary Day. ... High school: La Salle (Cincinnati). ... College: Cincinnati.

TRANSACTIONS/CAREER NOTES: Selected by New York Yankees organization in fifth round of free-agent draft (June 4, 1996). ... Traded by Yankees to Cleveland Indians with P Jake Westbrook (July 24, 2000), completing deal in which Indians traded OF David Justice to Yankees for OF Ricky Ledee and two players to be named later (June 29, 2000). ... Traded by Indians to Montreal Expos for OF Milton Bradley (July 31, 2001). ... Placed on the 15-day disabled list, retroactive to May 29 (May 30, 2003). ... Sent on rehab assignment to Gulf Coast League Expos by Montreal (July 16, 2003). ... Recalled from Brevard County rehab assignment by Montreal (July 22, 2003).

CAREER HITTING: 3-for-53 (.057), 3 R, 0 2B, 0 3B, 0 HR, 2 RBI.

Year League	W	L	Pct.	ERA	WHIP	G	GS	CG	ShO	Hld.	Sv.-Opp.	IP	H	R	ER	HR	BB-IBB	SO	Avg.
1996— GC Yankees (GCL)	5	2	.714	5.61	1.31	7	5	0	0	...	0-...	33.2	41	26	21	3	3-0	23	.311
1997— Oneonta (N.Y.-Penn)	7	2	.778	2.15	1.14	14	14	0	0	...	0-...	92.0	82	26	22	2	23-0	92	.240
1998— Tampa (FSL)	5	8	.385	5.49	1.74	18	17	0	0	...	0-...	100.0	142	89	61	5	32-4	69	.326
— Greensboro (S. Atl.)	1	2	.333	2.75	1.14	7	6	1	0	...	0-...	36.0	35	22	11	1	6-0	37	.245
1999— GC Yankees (GCL)	1	1	.500	3.78	1.44	5	4	0	0	...	0-...	16.2	20	10	7	1	4-0	17	.290
— Greensboro (S. Atl.)	0	1	.000	2.25	1.88	2	2	0	0	...	0-...	8.0	14	11	2	0	1-0	4	.359
2000— Greensboro (S. Atl.)	9	3	.750	1.90	1.21	13	13	1	1	...	0-...	85.1	72	29	18	6	31-0	101	.232
— Tampa (FSL)	2	4	.333	4.19	1.40	7	7	0	0	...	0-...	34.1	33	22	16	2	15-1	36	.246
— Akron (East.)	4	2	.667	3.52	1.28	8	8	0	0	...	0-...	46.0	38	20	18	1	21-0	43	.232
2001— Akron (East.)	9	10	.474	3.10	1.23	22	22	2	0	...	0-...	136.2	123	57	47	8	45-1	94	.237
— Buffalo (Int'l)	1	0	1.000	1.50	0.67	1	1	0	0	...	0-...	6.0	3	1	1	0	1-0	4	.143
— Ottawa (Int'l)	2	2	.500	7.43	1.78	6	5	0	0	...	0-...	26.2	38	23	22	2	8-0	15	.349
2002— Ottawa (Int'l)	5	6	.455	3.50	1.21	17	16	1	0	...	0-...	90.0	77	38	35	5	32-0	68	.231
— Montreal (N.L.)	4	1	.800	3.62	1.15	19	2	0	0	2	1-2	37.1	28	18	15	3	15-2	25	.207

D

Year League	W	L	Pct.	ERA	WHIP	G	GS	CG	ShO	Hld.	Sv.-Opp.	IP	H	R	ER	HR	BB-IBB	SO	Avg.
2003— GC Expos (GCL)	0	0	...	3.86	1.71	1	1	0	0	...	0-...	2.1	3	3	1	0	1-0	3	.300
— Brevard County (FSL)	0	0	...	1.69	0.75	1	1	0	0	...	0-...	5.1	3	1	1	0	1-0	3	.167
— Montreal (N.L.)	9	8	.529	4.18	1.45	23	23	1	1	0	0-0	131.1	132	64	61	8	59-3	61	.262
Major League totals (2 years)	13	9	.591	4.06	1.39	42	25	1	1	2	1-2	168.2	160	82	76	11	74-5	86	.250

DEAGO, ROGER   P

PERSONAL: Born June 21, 1977, in Monagrillo, Panama. ... 5-10/180. ... Throws left, bats right. ... Full name: Roger I. Villarreal Deago.
TRANSACTIONS/CAREER NOTES: Signed by San Diego Padres organization as a non-drafted free agent (October 29, 2002).
CAREER HITTING: 0-for-4 (.000), 0 R, 0 2B, 0 3B, 0 HR, 0 RBI.

Year League	W	L	Pct.	ERA	WHIP	G	GS	CG	ShO	Hld.	Sv.-Opp.	IP	H	R	ER	HR	BB-IBB	SO	Avg.
2003— San Diego (N.L.)	0	1	.000	7.84	1.84	2	2	0	0	0	0-0	10.1	11	9	9	0	8-0	10	.282
— Mobile (Sou.)	8	7	.533	4.03	1.50	26	20	0	0	...	0-...	118.1	127	64	53	9	51-1	109	.281
Major League totals (1 year)	0	1	.000	7.84	1.84	2	2	0	0	0	0-0	10.1	11	9	9	0	8-0	10	.282

DeHART, RICK   P

PERSONAL: Born March 21, 1970, in Topeka, Kan. ... 6-1/180. ... Throws left, bats left. ... Full name: Rick Allen DeHart. ... High school: Seaman (Topeka, Kan.). ... College: Washburn University.
TRANSACTIONS/CAREER NOTES: Signed as non-drafted free agent by Montreal Expos organization (March 24, 1992). ... Loaned by Expos organization to San Bernardino, California League (April 4-May 27, 1993). ... Re-signed by Expos organization (April 8, 1999). ... Contract sold by Expos to Hiroshima Toyo Carp of the Japan Central League (June 11, 1999). ... Signed by Los Angeles Dodgers organization (December 17, 1999). ... On Albuquerque disabled list (April 6-September 11, 2000). ... Granted free agency (October 18, 2000). ... Granted free agency (October 15, 2002). ... Contract purchased by Kansas City from Omaha (May 28, 2003). ... Designated for assignment by Kansas City (June 10, 2003).
CAREER HITTING: 0-for-3 (.000), 0 R, 0 2B, 0 3B, 0 HR, 0 RBI.

Year League	W	L	Pct.	ERA	WHIP	G	GS	CG	ShO	Hld.	Sv.-Opp.	IP	H	R	ER	HR	BB-IBB	SO	Avg.
1992— Albany (S. Atl.)	9	6	.600	2.46	1.12	38	10	1	1	...	3-...	117.0	91	42	32	11	40-1	133	.216
1993— San Bernardino (Calif.)	4	3	.571	3.04	1.52	9	9	0	0	...	0-...	53.1	56	26	18	4	25-0	44	.269
— Harrisburg (Eastern)	2	4	.333	7.68	1.88	12	7	0	0	...	0-...	34.0	45	31	29	5	19-0	18	.324
— W.P. Beach (FSL)	1	3	.250	3.00	1.40	7	7	1	1	...	0-...	42.0	42	14	14	0	17-0	33	.271
1994— W.P. Beach (FSL)	9	7	.563	3.37	1.22	30	20	3	2	...	0-...	136.1	132	61	51	12	34-0	68	.254
1995— Harrisburg (Eastern)	6	7	.462	4.84	1.43	35	12	0	0	...	0-...	93.0	94	62	50	13	39-3	64	.259
1996— Harrisburg (Eastern)	1	2	.333	2.68	1.49	30	2	0	0	...	1-...	43.2	46	19	13	4	19-0	30	.269
1997— Ottawa (Int'l)	0	4	.000	4.00	1.30	43	0	0	0	...	2-...	63.0	60	33	28	6	22-2	57	.255
— Montreal (N.L.)	2	1	.667	5.52	1.60	23	0	0	0	1	0-1	29.1	33	21	18	7	14-4	29	.291
1998— Montreal (N.L.)	0	0	...	4.82	1.68	26	0	0	0	4	1-2	28.0	34	22	15	3	13-1	14	.291
— Ottawa (Int'l)	7	1	.875	3.23	1.19	38	0	0	0	...	4-...	53.0	46	19	19	5	17-2	48	.230
1999— Ottawa (Int'l)	2	4	.333	4.78	1.67	15	2	0	0	...	0-...	26.1	33	19	14	4	11-1	22	.297
— Montreal (N.L.)	0	0	...	21.60	5.40	3	0	0	0	1	0-0	1.2	6	4	4	2	3-1	1	.545
— Hiroshima (Jp. Cn.)	0	1	.000	8.53	2.84	6	1	0	0	...		6.1	13	8	6	0	5-...	3	...
2000—											Did not play.								
2001— Wilmington (Caro.)	0	1	.000	1.59	1.41	5	0	0	0	...	...-1	5.2	5	2	1	0	3-1	2	.250
— Wichita (Texas)	2	2	.500	6.56	1.59	13	0	0	0	...	0-...	23.1	30	20	17	3	7-0	16	.303
2002— Omaha (PCL)	1	0	1.000	3.90	1.32	49	0	0	0	...	1-...	57.2	55	25	25	4	21-2	46	.247
2003— Kansas City (A.L.)	0	2	.000	13.50	2.50	4	0	0	0	0	0-0	4.0	8	6	6	1	2-0	1	.421
— Omaha (PCL)	1	3	.250	4.82	1.61	25	0	0	0	...	1-...	28.0	38	15	15	1	7-2	17	.333
American League totals (1 year)	0	2	.000	13.50	2.50	4	0	0	0	0	0-0	4.0	8	6	6	1	2-0	1	.421
National League totals (3 years)	2	1	.667	5.64	1.75	52	0	0	0	6	1-3	59.0	73	47	37	12	30-6	44	.303
Major League totals (4 years)	2	3	.400	6.14	1.79	56	0	0	0	6	1-3	63.0	81	53	43	13	32-6	45	.312

DeJEAN, MIKE   P

PERSONAL: Born September 28, 1970, in Baton Rouge, La. ... 6-4/217. ... Throws right, bats right. ... Full name: Michel Dwain DeJean. ... Name pronounced: DAY-zhan. ... High school: Walker (La.). ... College: Livingston University (Ala.).
TRANSACTIONS/CAREER NOTES: Selected by New York Yankees organization in 24th round of free-agent draft (June 1, 1992). ... On disabled list (June 4-July 21 and July 26, 1993-remainder of season). ... Traded by Yankees with a player to be named later to Colorado Rockies for C Joe Girardi (November 20, 1995); Rockies acquired P Steve Shoemaker to complete deal (December 6, 1995). ... On Colorado disabled list (July 18-August 8, 1997); included rehabilitation assignment to New Haven (July 30-August 8). ... On disabled list (September 2, 1998-remainder of season). ... On Colorado disabled list (August 14-September 1, 1999); included rehabilitation assignment to Colorado Springs (August 30-September 1). ... On Colorado disabled list (March 29-April 28 and July 25-August 15, 2000); included rehabilitation assignment to Colorado Springs (April 6-28 and August 10-13). ... Traded by Rockies with P Mark Leiter and 2B/SS Elvis Pena to Milwaukee Brewers for P Juan Acevedo, P Kane Davis and IF Jose Flores (April 4, 2001). ... Traded by Milwaukee Brewers to St. Louis Cardinals for two players to be named (August 22, 2003). Brewers later acquire P Mike Crudale and P John Novinsky to complete deal (September 10, 2003).
CAREER HITTING: 1-for-16 (.063), 0 R, 1 2B, 0 3B, 0 HR, 0 RBI.

Year League	W	L	Pct.	ERA	WHIP	G	GS	CG	ShO	Hld.	Sv.-Opp.	IP	H	R	ER	HR	BB-IBB	SO	Avg.
1992— Oneonta (N.Y.-Penn)	0	1	...	0.44	0.73	20	0	0	0	...	16-...	20.2	12	3	1	1	3-0	20	.160
1993— Greensboro (S. Atl.)	2	3	.400	5.00	1.67	20	0	0	0	...	9-...	18.0	22	12	10	1	8-2	16	.286
1994— Tampa (FSL)	0	2	.000	2.38	1.53	34	0	0	0	...	16-...	34.0	39	15	9	1	13-0	22	.283
— Albany (East.)	0	2	.000	4.38	1.50	16	0	0	0	...	4-...	24.2	22	14	12	1	15-3	13	.250
1995— Norwich (East.)	5	5	.500	2.99	1.17	59	0	0	0	...	20-...	78.1	58	29	26	5	34-2	57	.208
1996— Colo. Springs (PCL)	0	2	.000	5.13	1.81	30	0	0	0	...	1-...	40.1	52	24	23	3	21-3	31	.319
— New Haven (East.)	0	0	...	3.22	1.25	16	0	0	0	...	11-...	22.1	20	9	8	0	8-0	12	.247
1997— Colo. Springs (PCL)	0	1	.000	5.40	2.40	10	0	0	0	...	4-...	10.0	17	6	6	0	7-1	9	.405
— Colorado (N.L.)	5	0	1.000	3.99	1.45	55	0	0	0	13	2-4	67.2	74	34	30	4	24-2	38	.280
— New Haven (East.)	0	1	.000	6.00	1.67	2	0	0	0	...	0-...	3.0	3	2	2	0	2-0	2	.273
1998— Colorado (N.L.)	3	1	.750	3.03	1.37	59	1	0	0	11	2-3	74.1	78	29	25	4	24-1	27	.265
1999— Colorado (N.L.)	2	4	.333	8.41	1.89	56	0	0	0	9	0-4	61.0	83	61	57	13	32-8	31	.335
— Colo. Springs (PCL)	0	0	...	0.00	1.00	1	0	0	0	...	0-...	1.0	1	0	0	0	0-0	0	.333
2000— Colo. Springs (PCL)	1	1	.500	2.51	1.33	12	0	0	0	...	5-...	14.1	15	4	4	0	4-0	12	.283
— Colorado (N.L.)	4	4	.500	4.89	1.58	54	0	0	0	7	0-4	53.1	54	31	29	4	30-6	34	.269
2001— Milwaukee (N.L.)	4	2	.667	2.77	1.35	75	0	0	0	8	2-4	84.1	75	31	26	4	39-7	68	.236
2002— Milwaukee (N.L.)	1	5	.167	3.12	1.40	68	0	0	0	0	27-30	75.0	66	28	26	7	39-8	65	.241
2003— Milwaukee (N.L.)	4	7	.364	4.87	1.48	58	0	0	0	5	18-26	64.2	69	38	35	12	27-7	58	.271
— St. Louis (N.L.)	1	1	.500	4.00	1.61	18	0	0	0	5	1-1	18.0	17	8	8	1	12-0	13	.262
Major League totals (7 years)	24	24	.500	4.26	1.49	443	1	0	0	58	52-76	498.1	516	260	236	54	227-39	334	.271

D

DeJESUS, DAVID — OF

PERSONAL: Born December 20, 1979, in Brooklyn, N.Y. ... 6-0/175. ... Bats left, throws left. ... Full name: David Christopher DeJesus. ... High school: Manalapan (N.J.). ... College: Rutgers.

TRANSACTIONS/CAREER NOTES: Selected by Kansas City Royals organization in fourth round of free-agent draft (June 5, 2000).

2003 GAMES PLAYED BY POSITION (MLB): OF—9.

											BATTING								FIELDING	
Year Team (League)	Pos.	G	AB	R	H	2B	3B	HR	RBI	BB	SO	HBP	GDP	SB-CS	Avg.	OBP	SLG	OPS	E	Pct.
2001—										Did not play.										
2002—Wilmington (Caro.)	OF	87	334	69	99	22	6	4	41	48	42	13	8	15-6	.296	.400	.434	.834	1	.994
—Wichita (Texas)	OF	25	79	7	20	5	2	2	15	8	10	5	3	3-1	.253	.347	.443	.790	1	.976
2003—Wichita (Texas)	OF	17	71	14	24	4	0	2	10	9	8	2	3	1-3	.338	.422	.479	.901	1	.980
—Omaha (PCL)	OF-DH	59	215	49	64	16	3	5	23	34	30	9	9	8-4	.298	.412	.470	.881	0	1.000
—Kansas City (A.L.)	OF	12	7	0	2	0	1	0	1	1	2	1	0	0-0	.286	.444	.571	1.016	0	1.000
Major League totals (1 year)		12	7	0	2	0	1	0	1	1	2	1	0	0-0	.286	.444	.571	1.016	0	1.000

DELGADO, CARLOS — 1B

PERSONAL: Born June 25, 1972, in Aguadilla, Puerto Rico. ... 6-3/230. ... Bats left, throws right. ... Full name: Carlos Juan Delgado. ... Name pronounced: del-GAH-doh. ... High school: Jose de Diego (Aguadilla, Puerto Rico).

TRANSACTIONS/CAREER NOTES: Signed as non-drafted free agent by Toronto Blue Jays organization (October 9, 1988). ... On Toronto disabled list (March 15-April 24, 1998); included rehabilitation assignments to Dunedin (April 17-19) and Syracuse (April 20-24). ... On disabled list (August 9-25, 2002).

2003 GAMES PLAYED BY POSITION (MLB): 1B—147, DH—14.

											BATTING								FIELDING	
Year Team (League)	Pos.	G	AB	R	H	2B	3B	HR	RBI	BB	SO	HBP	GDP	SB-CS	Avg.	OBP	SLG	OPS	E	Pct.
1989—St. Catharines (NYP)	C	31	89	9	16	5	0	0	11	23	39	0	4	0-0	.180	.345	.236	.581	2	.974
1990—St. Catharines (NYP)	C	67	228	30	64	13	0	6	39	35	65	5	2	2-7	.281	.382	.417	.799	7	.987
1991—Myrtle Beach (SAL)	C	132	441	72	126	18	2	18	70	75	97	8	7	9-10	.286	.396	.458	.854	19	.976
—Syracuse (Int'l)	C	1	3	0	0	0	0	0	0	0	2	0	0	0-0	.000	.000	.000	.000	0	1.000
1992—Dunedin (Fla. St.)	C	133	485	83	* 157	* 30	2	* 30	* 100	59	91	6	8	2-5	.324	* .402	.579	.982	11	.986
1993—Knoxville (Sou.)	C	140	468	91	142	28	0	* 25	* 102	* 102	98	6	11	10-3	.303	* .430	.524	.954	* 14	.983
—Toronto (A.L.)	DH-C	2	1	0	0	0	0	0	0	1	0	0	0	0-0	.000	.500	.000	.500	0	1.000
1994—Toronto (A.L.)	OF-C	43	130	17	28	2	0	9	24	25	46	3	5	1-1	.215	.352	.438	.791	2	.967
—Syracuse (Int'l)	DH-C-1B	85	307	52	98	11	0	19	58	42	58	3	3	1-0	.319	.404	.541	.945	7	.974
1995—Toronto (A.L.) OF-DH-1B		37	91	7	15	3	0	3	11	6	26	0	1	0-0	.165	.212	.297	.509	0	1.000
—Syracuse (Int'l)	1B-OF	91	333	59	106	23	4	22	74	45	78	5	8	0-4	.318	.403	.610	1.013	4	.995
1996—Toronto (A.L.)	DH-1B	138	488	68	132	28	2	25	92	58	139	9	13	0-0	.270	.353	.490	.843	4	.983
1997—Toronto (A.L.)	1B-DH	153	519	79	136	42	3	30	91	64	133	8	6	0-3	.262	.350	.528	.878	12	.988
1998—Dunedin (Fla. St.)	DH-1B	4	16	4	5	1	0	2	7	2	4	0	1	0-0	.313	.389	.750	1.139	0	1.000
—Syracuse (Int'l)	1B	2	7	4	4	2	0	1	6	2	0	0	0	0-0	.571	.667	1.286	1.952	0	1.000
—Toronto (A.L.)	1B-DH	142	530	94	155	43	1	38	115	73	139	11	8	3-0	.292	.385	.592	.978	10	.992
1999—Toronto (A.L.)	1B-DH	152	573	113	156	39	0	44	134	86	141	15	11	1-1	.272	.377	.571	.948	* 14	.990
2000—Toronto (A.L.)	1B	•162	569	115	196	* 57	1	41	137	123	104	•15	12	0-1	.344	.470	.664	1.134	13	.991
2001—Toronto (A.L.)	1B	•162	574	102	160	31	1	39	102	111	136	16	9	3-0	.279	.408	.540	.948	9	.994
2002—Toronto (A.L.)	1B-DH	143	505	103	140	34	2	33	108	102	126	13	8	1-0	.277	.406	.549	.955	12	.991
2003—Toronto (A.L.)	1B-DH	161	570	117	172	38	1	42	*145	109	137	19	9	0-0	.302	.426	.593	*1.019	10	.993
Major League totals (11 years)		1295	4550	815	1290	317	11	304	959	758	1127	109	82	9-6	.284	.395	.558	.953	86	.991

DELGADO, WILSON — SS/2B

PERSONAL: Born July 15, 1972, in San Cristobal, Dominican Republic. ... 5-11/165. ... Bats both, throws right. ... Full name: Wilson Duran Delgado. ... Name pronounced: del-GAH-doh.

TRANSACTIONS/CAREER NOTES: Signed as non-drafted free agent by Seattle Mariners organization (October 29, 1992). ... Traded by Mariners with P Shawn Estes to San Francisco Giants for P Salomon Torres (May 21, 1995). ... Traded by Giants to New York Yankees for SS Juan Melo (March 23, 2000). ... Traded by Yankees to Kansas City Royals for SS Nick Ortiz (August 11, 2000). ... Granted free agency (October 9, 2001). ... Signed by St. Louis Cardinals organization (December 23, 2001). ... On Memphis disabled list (June 12-July 29, 2002). ... Sent outright to Memphis of the Pacific Coast League by St. Louis (July 29, 2003). ... Traded by St. Louis to Anaheim for cash considerations (August 31, 2003). ... Contract purchased by Anaheim (September 1, 2003).

2003 GAMES PLAYED BY POSITION (MLB): 3B—20, SS—20, 2B—13.

											BATTING								FIELDING	
Year Team (League)	Pos.	G	AB	R	H	2B	3B	HR	RBI	BB	SO	HBP	GDP	SB-CS	Avg.	OBP	SLG	OPS	E	Pct.
1993—Dom. Mariners (DSL)	IF	60	171	19	50	8	0	0	26	34	25			5-...	.292	...	.339	...	16	.938
1994—Ariz. Mariners (Ariz.)	2B-SS	39	149	30	56	5	4	0	10	15	24	1	2	13-5	.376	.436	.463	.899	10	.945
—Appleton (Midwest)	SS	9	31	2	6	0	0	0	0	0	8	0	2	0-0	.194	.194	.194	.387	1	.967
1995—Port City (Sou.)	SS	13	41	3	8	4	0	0	1	6	8	0	1	0-0	.195	.298	.293	.591	5	.917
—Wisconsin (Midw.)	SS	19	70	13	17	3	0	0	7	3	15	0	5	3-0	.243	.274	.286	.560	6	.940
—Burlington (Midw.)	SS	93	365	52	113	20	3	5	37	32	57	2	7	9-9	.310	.368	.422	.789	19	.956
—San Jose (Calif.)	SS	1	2	1	0	0	0	0	0	0	0	0	0	0-0	.000	.000	.000	.000	0	1.000
1996—San Jose (Calif.)	SS	121	462	59	124	19	6	2	54	48	89	2	8	8-2	.268	.337	.348	.686	24	.957
—Phoenix (PCL)	SS	12	43	1	6	0	1	0	1	3	7	0	1	0-1	.140	.196	.186	.382	2	.975
—San Francisco (N.L.)	SS	6	22	3	8	0	0	0	2	1	5	2	0	1-0	.364	.440	.364	.804	1	.960
1997—San Francisco (N.L.)	2B-SS	8	7	1	1	1	0	0	0	0	2	0	0	0-0	.143	.143	.286	.429	1	1.000
—Phoenix (PCL)	SS-2B	119	416	47	120	22	4	9	59	24	70	1	9	9-3	.288	.326	.425	.751	18	.969
1998—Fresno (PCL)	SS	127	512	87	142	22	2	12	63	52	92	3	6	9-5	.277	.345	.398	.743	23	.963
—San Francisco (N.L.)	SS	10	12	1	2	1	0	0	1	1	3	0	0	0-0	.167	.231	.250	.481	0	1.000
1999—Fresno (PCL) SS-2B-DH		57	213	28	64	10	3	1	33	18	35	0	8	4-2	.300	.355	.390	.745	15	.944
—San Francisco (N.L.)	SS	35	71	7	18	2	1	0	3	5	9	1	2	1-0	.254	.312	.310	.622	5	.942
2000—New York (A.L.)	2B-SS-3B	31	45	6	11	1	0	1	4	5	9	0	1	1-0	.244	.314	.333	.647	3	.952
—Kansas City (A.L.)	2B-SS-3B	33	83	15	22	1	0	0	7	6	17	0	1	1-1	.265	.311	.277	.588	1	.993
2001—Omaha (PCL) 2B-3B-SS		76	255	24	63	11	2	4	30	16	43	1	10	8-3	.247	.293	.353	.646	11	.963
—Kansas City (A.L.) SS-3B-2B		14	25	1	3	0	0	0	1	3	4	0	1	0-0	.120	.214	.120	.334	0	1.000

Year	Team (League)	Pos.	G	AB	R	H	2B	3B	HR	RBI	BB	SO	HBP	GDP	SB-CS	Avg.	OBP	SLG	OPS	E	Pct.
2002— Memphis (PCL)		SS	98	365	31	95	19	2	7	35	23	54	3	6	2-5	.260	.309	.381	.689	10	.977
— St. Louis (N.L.)		SS	12	20	2	4	2	0	2	5	0	5	0	0	0-0	.200	.200	.600	.800	0	1.000
2003— St. Louis (N.L.) 2B-3B-SS			43	77	8	13	3	0	0	3	3	10	1	4	0-0	.169	.207	.208	.415	1	.983
— Memphis (PCL)		SS-2B	26	86	11	20	2	0	2	12	10	15	0	2	2-1	.233	.313	.326	.638	1	.991
— Anaheim (A.L.) 3B-SS-2B			19	50	4	16	0	0	0	4	8	8	0	1	0-0	.320	.414	.320	.734	3	.951
American League totals (3 years)			97	203	26	52	2	0	1	16	22	44	0	4	2-1	.256	.326	.281	.607	7	.975
National League totals (6 years)			114	209	22	46	9	1	2	14	10	35	4	6	2-0	.220	.268	.301	.569	7	.965
Major League totals (8 years)			211	412	48	98	11	1	3	30	32	79	4	10	4-1	.238	.297	.291	.588	14	.971

DELLUCCI, DAVID — OF

PERSONAL: Born October 31, 1973, in Baton Rouge, La. ... 5-11/189. ... Bats left, throws left. ... Full name: David Michael Dellucci. ... Name pronounced: duh-LOO-chee. ... High school: Catholic (Baton Rouge, La.). ... College: Mississippi.

TRANSACTIONS/CAREER NOTES: Selected by Baltimore Orioles organization in 10th round of free agent draft (June 1, 1995). ... Selected by Arizona Diamondbacks in second round (45th pick overall) of expansion draft (November 18, 1997). ... On disabled list (July 25, 1999-remainder of season). ... On Tucson disabled list (May 8-July 26, 2000). ... On Arizona disabled list (May 3-24, 2002); included rehabilitation assignment to Tucson (May 20-24). ... Placed on 15-day disabled list (June 2, 2003). ... Reinstated from 15-day disabled list (June 17, 2003). ... Traded by Diamondbacks to New York Yankees for OF Raul Mondesi (July 29, 2003). ... Placed on 15-day disabled list (August 28, 2003). ... Removed from 15-day disabled list (September 27, 2003).

2003 GAMES PLAYED BY POSITION (MLB): OF—71, DH—2.

Year	Team (League)	Pos.	G	AB	R	H	2B	3B	HR	RBI	BB	SO	HBP	GDP	SB-CS	Avg.	OBP	SLG	OPS	E	Pct.
1995— Bluefield (Appal.)		OF	20	69	11	23	5	1	2	12	6	7	1	1	3-1	.333	.390	.522	.911	2	.846
— Frederick (Carolina)		OF	28	96	16	27	3	0	1	10	12	10	3	3	1-2	.281	.378	.344	.722	1	.966
1996— Frederick (Carolina)		OF	59	185	33	60	11	1	4	28	38	34	0	2	5-6	.324	.438	.459	.897	3	.972
— Bowie (East.)		OF	66	251	27	73	14	1	2	33	28	56	1	4	2-7	.291	.363	.378	.741	3	.972
1997— Bowie (East.)		OF-DH	107	385	71	126	29	3	20	55	58	69	5	6	11-4	.327	.421	.574	.995	1	.994
— Baltimore (A.L.)		OF-DH	17	27	3	6	1	0	1	3	4	7	1	2	0-0	.222	.344	.370	.714	0	1.000
1998— Tucson (PCL)		OF	17	72	17	22	4	3	1	11	5	8	0	2	4-0	.306	.346	.486	.832	0	1.000
— Arizona (N.L.)		OF	124	416	43	108	19	*12	5	51	33	103	3	6	3-5	.260	.318	.399	.717	3	.987
1999— Arizona (N.L.)		OF-DH	63	109	27	43	7	1	1	15	11	24	3	3	2-0	.394	.463	.505	.968	0	1.000
2000— Arizona (N.L.)		OF	34	50	2	15	3	0	0	2	4	9	0	1	0-2	.300	.352	.360	.712	0	1.000
— Tucson (PCL)		OF	33	122	16	28	6	3	3	17	13	15	0	0	4-0	.230	.301	.402	.703	2	.966
— Ariz. D'backs (Ariz.)		OF	2	6	0	2	1	0	0	2	0	1	0	0	0-0	.333	.333	.500	.833	0	...
— South Bend (Mid.)		OF	2	5	3	1	1	0	0	1	2	0	0	0	0-1	.200	.375	.400	.775	0	1.000
2001— Arizona (N.L.)		OF	115	217	28	60	10	2	10	40	22	52	2	2	2-1	.276	.349	.479	.828	1	.989
2002— Arizona (N.L.)		OF-DH	97	229	34	56	11	2	7	29	28	55	1	7	2-4	.245	.326	.402	.727	3	.967
— Tucson (PCL)		OF	4	15	2	2	1	0	0	1	2	4	0	0	0-0	.133	.235	.200	.435	0	1.000
2003— Arizona (N.L.)		OF	70	165	18	40	11	3	2	19	19	45	3	4	9-0	.242	.328	.382	.710	2	.976
— New York (A.L.)		OF-DH	21	51	8	9	1	0	1	4	4	13	2	2	3-0	.176	.263	.255	.518	0	1.000
American League totals (2 years)			38	78	11	15	2	0	2	7	8	20	3	4	3-0	.192	.292	.295	.587	0	1.000
National League totals (6 years)			503	1186	152	322	61	20	25	156	117	288	12	23	18-12	.272	.341	.420	.761	9	.984
Major League totals (7 years)			541	1264	163	337	63	20	27	163	125	308	15	27	21-12	.267	.338	.412	.750	9	.985

DE LOS SANTOS, VALERIO — P

PERSONAL: Born October 6, 1972, in Las Matas, Dominican Republic. ... 6-2/218. ... Throws left, bats left. ... Full name: Valerio Lorenzo de los Santos.

TRANSACTIONS/CAREER NOTES: Signed as non-drafted free agent by Milwaukee Brewers organization (January 26, 1993). ... On El Paso disabled list (April-May 4, 1998). ... On Milwaukee disabled list (April 29-September 23, 1999). ... On disabled list (April 4, 2001-remainder of season). ... Placed on 15-day disabled list (April 27, 2003). ... Activated from the 15-day disabled list by Milwaukee (May 27, 2003). ... Traded by Milwaukee Brewers to Philadelphia Phillies for a player to be named (September 2, 2003).

CAREER HITTING: 0-for-9 (.000), 0 R, 0 2B, 0 3B, 0 HR, 0 RBI.

Year	League	W	L	Pct.	ERA	WHIP	G	GS	CG	ShO	Hld.	Sv.-Opp.	IP	H	R	ER	HR	BB-IBB	SO	Avg.
1993— Dom. Brewers (DSL)		1	7	.125	6.50	2.01	19	6	1	0	...	0-...	63.2	91	57	46	...	37-...	39	...
1994— Dom. Brewers (DSL)		7	6	.538	3.69	1.38	17	•16	1	1	...	0-...	90.1	90	52	37	...	35-...	50	...
1995— Ariz. Brewers (Ariz.)		4	6	.400	2.20	1.13	14	12	0	0	...	0-...	82.0	*81	34	20	3	12-2	57	.258
1996— Beloit (Midw.)		10	8	.556	3.55	1.35	33	23	•5	•1	...	4-...	164.2	164	83	65	11	59-4	137	.257
1997— El Paso (Texas)		6	10	.375	5.75	1.61	26	16	1	0	...	2-...	114.1	146	83	73	6	38-2	61	.314
1998— El Paso (Texas)		6	2	.750	3.92	1.59	42	4	0	0	...	10-...	66.2	81	34	29	2	25-1	62	.299
— Milwaukee (N.L.)		0	0	...	2.91	0.60	13	0	0	0	0	0-0	21.2	11	7	7	4	2-0	18	.151
— Louisville (Int'l)		0	0	...	3.60	0.80	5	0	0	0	0	0-...	5.0	4	2	2	0	0-0	5	.211
1999— Milwaukee (N.L.)		0	1	.000	6.48	2.28	7	0	0	0	0	0-0	8.1	12	6	6	1	7-0	5	.343
2000— Milwaukee (N.L.)		2	3	.400	5.13	1.43	66	2	0	0	9	0-1	73.2	72	43	42	15	33-7	70	.254
2001— Milwaukee (N.L.)		0	0	...	9.00	2.00	1	0	0	0	0	0-0	1.0	1	1	1	0	1-0	1	.250
2002— Indianapolis (Int'l)		1	0	1.000	0.00	1.00	2	0	0	0	0	0-...	2.0	1	0	0	0	1-0	5	.143
— Milwaukee (N.L.)		2	3	.400	3.12	1.18	51	0	0	0	7	0-0	57.2	42	21	20	4	26-3	38	.211
2003— Milwaukee (N.L.)		3	3	.500	4.13	1.25	45	0	0	0	11	1-4	48.0	38	24	22	8	22-0	35	.225
— Philadelphia (N.L.)		1	0	1.000	9.00	2.50	6	0	0	0	0	0-0	4.0	7	7	4	0	3-0	4	.389
Major League totals (6 years)		8	10	.444	4.28	1.29	189	2	0	0	27	1-5	214.1	183	109	102	32	94-10	171	.234

DEMPSTER, RYAN — P

PERSONAL: Born May 3, 1977, in Sechelt, British Columbia. ... 6-3/215. ... Throws right, bats right. ... Full name: Ryan Scott Dempster. ... High school: Elphinstone (Gibsons, B.C.).

TRANSACTIONS/CAREER NOTES: Selected by Texas Rangers organization in third round of free-agent draft (June 1, 1995). ... Traded by Rangers with a player to be named later to Florida Marlins for P John Burkett (August 8, 1996); Marlins acquired P Rick Helling to complete deal (September 3, 1996). ... Traded by Marlins to Cincinnati Reds for OF Juan Encarnacion, OF/2B Wilton Guerrero and P Ryan Snare (July 11, 2002). ... Placed on 15-day disabled list (July 31, 2003). ... Sent to Louisville on rehab assignment by Cincinnati (May 27, 2003). ... Placed on 15-day disabled list (May 15, 2003). ... Recalled by Cincinnati from Louisville rehab assignment (June 2, 2003). ... Reinstated from 15-day disabled list (June 7, 2003). ... Placed on 15-day disabled list (July 29, 2003). ... Transferred to Emergency disabled list (August 7, 2003).

CAREER HITTING: 23-for-296 (.078), 12 R, 5 2B, 1 3B, 0 HR, 7 RBI.

Year	League	W	L	Pct.	ERA	WHIP	G	GS	CG	ShO	Hld.	Sv.-Opp.	IP	H	R	ER	HR	BB-IBB	SO	Avg.
1995— GC Rangers (GCL)		3	1	.750	2.36	1.49	8	6	1	0	...	0-...	34.1	34	21	9	1	17-0	37	.254
— Hudson Valley (NYP)		1	0	1.000	3.18	1.41	1	1	0	0	...	0-...	5.2	7	2	2	0	1-0	6	.318
1996— Char., S.C. (SAL)		7	11	.389	3.30	1.23	23	23	2	0	...	0-...	144.1	120	71	53	13	58-1	141	.229
— Kane County (Midwest)		2	1	.667	2.73	1.37	4	4	1	1	...	0-...	26.1	18	10	8	0	18-0	16	.202
1997— Brevard County (FSL)		10	9	.526	4.90	1.43	28	26	2	1	...	0-...	165.1	190	100	90	8	46-1	131	.290
1998— Portland (East.)		4	3	.571	3.22	1.10	7	7	0	0	...	0-...	44.2	34	20	16	8	15-0	33	.214
— Florida (N.L.)		1	5	.167	7.08	2.01	14	11	0	0	0	0-1	54.2	72	47	43	6	38-1	35	.336
— Charlotte (Int'l)		3	1	.750	3.27	1.36	5	5	1	0	...	0-...	33.0	33	14	12	4	12-1	24	.270
1999— Calgary (PCL)		1	1	.500	4.99	1.30	5	5	0	0	...	0-...	30.2	30	17	17	6	10-1	29	.252
— Florida (N.L.)		7	8	.467	4.71	1.63	25	25	0	0	0	0-0	147.0	146	77	77	21	93-2	126	.262
2000— Florida (N.L.)		14	10	.583	3.66	1.36	33	33	2	1	0	0-0	226.1	210	102	92	30	97-7	209	.243
2001— Florida (N.L.)		15	12	.556	4.94	1.56	34	34	2	1	0	0-0	211.1	218	123	116	21	* 112-5	171	.269
2002— Florida (N.L.)		5	8	.385	4.79	1.50	18	18	3	0	0	0-0	120.1	126	66	64	12	55-1	87	.281
— Cincinnati (N.L.)		5	5	.500	6.19	1.58	15	15	1	0	0	0-0	88.2	102	61	† 61	16	38-1	66	.293
2003— Louisville (Int'l)		1	1	.500	3.29	1.17	2	2	1	0	...	0-...	13.2	13	5	5	1	3-0	9	.255
— Cincinnati (N.L.)		3	7	.300	6.54	1.76	22	20	0	0	0	0-0	115.2	134	89	84	14	70-4	84	.293
Major League totals (6 years)		50	55	.476	5.01	1.57	161	156	8	2	0	0-1	964.0	1008	565	537	120	503-21	778	.273

DePASTINO, JOE   C

PERSONAL: Born September 4, 1973, in Philadelphia, Pa. ... 6-2/210. ... Bats right, throws right. ... Full name: Joseph Bernard DePastino. ... High school: Riverview (Fla.).
TRANSACTIONS/CAREER NOTES: Selected by Boston Red Sox organization in seventh round of free-agent draft (June 1992). ... Signed by Baltimore Orioles organization as a six-year minor league free agent (December 3, 1999). ... Signed by Houston Astros organization as a six-year minor league free agent (August 7, 2000). ... Signed by New York Mets organization as a six-year minor league free agent (January 3, 2001).
2003 GAMES PLAYED BY POSITION (MLB): C—1.

Year	Team (League)	Pos.	G	AB	R	H	2B	3B	HR	RBI	BB	SO	HBP	GDP	SB-CS	Avg.	OBP	SLG	OPS	E	Pct.
1992— GC Red Sox (GCL)		1B-OF-3B	40	157	13	41	6	1	1	16	7	25	3	7	1-1	.261	.302	.331	.633	2	.994
1993— Utica (N.Y.-Penn)		3B-1B	62	221	28	56	9	1	2	32	16	51	4	4	3-2	.253	.309	.330	.639	13	.958
1994— Utica (N.Y.-Penn)		1B-C-3B-OF	51	172	23	46	11	1	5	31	22	41	3	1	5-2	.267	.357	.430	.787	7	.977
1995— Michigan (Midw.)		C-1B	98	325	47	90	20	4	10	53	30	70	8	5	3-3	.277	.348	.455	.803	5	.992
1996— Sarasota (Fla. St.)		C-1B	97	344	35	90	16	2	6	44	29	71	3	7	2-3	.262	.321	.372	.693	11	.980
1997— Trenton (East.)		C	79	276	51	70	14	1	17	55	32	63	7	10	1-2	.254	.345	.496	.841	6	.988
1998— Trenton (East.)		C-1B	73	275	34	81	16	0	10	43	28	51	1	4	3-0	.295	.359	.462	.821	6	.988
— Pawtucket (Int'l)		C	9	33	1	8	1	0	0	4	0	8	1	1	1-1	.242	.265	.273	.537	0	1.000
— GC Red Sox (GCL)		C	6	17	2	5	1	1	1	1	5	3	0	0	0-0	.294	.455	.647	1.102	0	1.000
1999— Pawtucket (Int'l)		C-1B	77	257	35	65	13	0	13	52	27	40	1	4	1-1	.253	.324	.455	.779	4	.992
— Trenton (East.)		C	6	23	5	5	1	0	2	5	3	3	1	2	1-0	.217	.333	.522	.855	0	1.000
2000— Rochester (Int'l)		C	20	71	7	18	3	0	0	5	8	16	1	1	1-1	.254	.338	.296	.633	1	.993
— Bowie (East.)		C-1B	19	65	11	14	6	0	2	9	6	13	0	4	0-0	.215	.282	.400	.682	0	1.000
— Round Rock (Texas)		C	5	18	3	8	0	1	2	4	0	2	0	0	0-1	.444	.444	.889	1.333	0	1.000
2002— Norfolk (Int'l)		C	70	248	24	74	15	3	5	27	12	47	3	10	4-0	.298	.338	.444	.782	5	.988
2003— New York (N.L.)		C	2	2	0	0	0	0	0	0	0	1	0	0	0-0	.000	.000	.000	.000	0	1.000
— Norfolk (Int'l)		C-DH-1B	84	277	26	74	16	0	2	22	20	51	2	8	2-1	.267	.320	.347	.667	3	.995
Major League totals (1 year)			2	2	0	0	0	0	0	0	0	1	0	0	0-0	.000	.000	.000	.000	0	1.000

DePAULA, JORGE   P

PERSONAL: Born November 10, 1978, in Sabana Grande, Dominican Republic. ... 6-1/160. ... Throws right, bats right.
TRANSACTIONS/CAREER NOTES: Signed by Colorado Rockies organization as a non-drafted free agent (January 13, 1997). ... Traded by Rockies to New York Yankees as the player to be named later in trade for P Craig Dingman (April 20, 2001).
CAREER HITTING: 0-for-0 (.000), 0 R, 0 2B, 0 3B, 0 HR, 0 RBI.

Year	League	W	L	Pct.	ERA	WHIP	G	GS	CG	ShO	Hld.	Sv.-Opp.	IP	H	R	ER	HR	BB-IBB	SO	Avg.
1998— Ariz. Rockies (Ariz.)		5	5	.500	3.81	1.33	17	9	0	0	...	2-...	54.1	54	30	23	1	18-1	62	.252
1999— Portland (East.)		6	6	.500	6.01	1.64	16	16	0	0	...	0-...	85.1	97	67	57	8	43-0	77	.290
2000— Asheville (S. Atl.)		8	13	.381	4.70	1.37	28	27	1	1	...	0-...	155.0	151	90	81	16	62-0	187	.260
2001— Asheville (S. Atl.)		1	1	.500	3.78	1.26	3	3	0	0	...	0-...	16.2	19	13	7	3	6-0	26	.268
— Greensboro (S. Atl.)		6	1	.857	2.75	1.01	8	8	0	0	...	0-...	55.2	35	19	17	2	21-0	67	.179
— Tampa (FSL)		9	5	.643	3.58	1.42	16	13	0	0	...	0-...	83.0	65	43	33	3	53-2	77	.212
2002— Norwich (East.)		14	6	.700	3.45	1.10	27	26	6	1	...	0-...	175.0	141	74	67	11	52-0	152	.221
2003— Columbus (Int'l)		10	11	.476	4.35	1.34	27	27	3	2	...	0-...	167.2	168	90	81	22	57-2	125	.262
— New York (A.L.)		0	0	...	0.79	0.35	4	1	0	0	0	0-0	11.1	3	1	1	1	1-0	7	.083
Major League totals (1 year)		0	0	...	0.79	0.35	4	1	0	0	0	0-0	11.1	3	1	1	1	1-0	7	.083

DeROSA, MARK   IF

PERSONAL: Born February 26, 1975, in Passaic, N.J. ... 6-1/205. ... Bats right, throws right. ... Full name: Mark Thomas DeRosa. ... High school: Bergen Catholic (Oradell, N.J.). ... College: Pennsylvania.
TRANSACTIONS/CAREER NOTES: Selected by Atlanta Braves organization in seventh round of free-agent draft (June 4, 1996). ... On Atlanta disabled list (May 18-July 17, 2002); included rehabilitation assignment to Richmond (June 28-July 8) and Myrtle Beach (July 9-17).
2003 GAMES PLAYED BY POSITION (MLB): 2B—29, 3B—25, SS—20, DH—2, OF—2, 1B—1.

Year	Team (League)	Pos.	G	AB	R	H	2B	3B	HR	RBI	BB	SO	HBP	GDP	SB-CS	Avg.	OBP	SLG	OPS	E	Pct.
1996— Eugene (Northwest)		SS	70	255	43	66	13	1	2	28	38	48	5	10	3-4	.259	.363	.341	.705	24	.921
1997— Durham (Caro.)		SS	92	346	51	93	11	3	8	37	25	73	10	12	6-8	.269	.332	.387	.720	21	.948
1998— Greenville (Sou.)		SS	125	461	67	123	26	2	8	49	60	57	5	18	7-13	.267	.356	.384	.740	20	.964
— Atlanta (N.L.)		SS	5	3	2	1	0	0	0	0	0	1	0	0	0-0	.333	.333	.333	.667	0	1.000
1999— Richmond (Int'l)		SS-DH	105	364	41	99	16	2	1	40	21	49	5	5	7-6	.272	.317	.335	.652	20	.951
— Atlanta (N.L.)		SS	7	8	0	0	0	0	0	0	0	2	0	0	0-0	.000	.000	.000	.000	0	1.000
2000— Richmond (Int'l)		SS-2B-3B	101	370	62	108	22	3	3	35	38	36	3	13	13-4	.292	.359	.392	.751	19	.958
— Atlanta (N.L.)		SS	22	13	9	4	1	0	0	3	2	1	0	0	0-0	.308	.400	.385	.785	0	1.000
2001— Richmond (Int'l)		SS-3B-2B	49	186	31	55	18	0	2	17	17	22	1	6	7-3	.296	.351	.425	.776	4	.978
— Atlanta (N.L.)		S-2-D-3-O	66	164	27	47	8	0	3	20	12	19	5	3	2-1	.287	.350	.390	.740	7	.966

Year	Team (League)	Pos.	G	AB	R	H	2B	3B	HR	RBI	BB	SO	HBP	GDP	SB-CS	Avg.	OBP	SLG	OPS	E	Pct.
2002—Atlanta (N.L.)	2-S-OF-3	72	212	24	63	9	2	5	23	12	24	3	5	2-3	.297	.339	.429	.768	6	.976
—Richmond (Int'l)	2B-SS	16	55	9	14	3	0	0	6	5	2	2	4	2-0	.255	.339	.309	.648	3	.952
—Myrtle Beach (Caro.)	2B	2	7	0	0	0	0	0	0	1	1	0	0	0-0	.000	.125	.000	.125	1	.889
2003—Atlanta (N.L.)	2-3-S-D-O-1	103	266	40	70	14	0	6	22	16	49	5	6	1-0	.263	.316	.383	.699	6	.976
Major League totals (6 years)		275	666	102	185	32	2	14	68	42	96	13	14	5-4	.278	.330	.395	.725	19	.974

DESSENS, ELMER — P

PERSONAL: Born January 13, 1972, in Hermosillo, Mexico. ... 5-10/198. ... Throws right, bats right. ... Full name: Elmer Dessens Jusaino Dessens. ... Name pronounced: duh-SENZ. ... High school: Carrera Technica (Hermosillo, Mexico).

TRANSACTIONS/CAREER NOTES: Signed as non-drafted free agent by Pittsburgh Pirates organization (January 27, 1993). ... Loaned by Pirates organization to Mexico City Red Devils, Mexican League for 1993 and 1994 seasons; returned to Pirates organization for 1995 season. ... Loaned by Pirates organization to Red Devils (May 7, 1996). ... Returned to Pirates organization (June 21, 1996). ... On Pittsburgh disabled list (July 31-September 10, 1996); included rehabilitation assignment to Carolina (August 16-September 10). ... Loaned by Pirates to Red Devils (March 27-September 5, 1997). ... On Pittsburgh disabled list (April 8-24, 1998); included rehabilitation assignment to Nashville (April 21-24). ... Released by Pirates (March 31, 1999). ... Played for Yomiuri Giants of Japan Central League (1999). ... Signed by Cincinnati Reds organization (December 15, 1999). ... On disabled list (August 2-27, 2002). ... Traded by Reds with cash to Arizona Diamondbacks as part of four-team trade in which Diamondbacks sent 1B Erubiel Durazo to Oakland Athletics, A's sent a player to be named later to Toronto Blue Jays and Blue Jays sent SS Felipe Lopez to Reds (December 15, 2002); Blue Jays acquired P Jason Arnold to complete deal (December 16, 2002).

CAREER HITTING: 35-for-201 (.174), 12 R, 2 2B, 1 3B, 0 HR, 16 RBI.

Year	League	W	L	Pct.	ERA	WHIP	G	GS	CG	ShO	Hld.	Sv.-Opp.	IP	H	R	ER	HR	BB-IBB	SO	Avg.
1993—M.C. Red Devils (Mex.)	3	1	.750	2.35	1.17	14	0	0	0	...	2-...	30.2	31	8	8	2	5-...	16	...
1994—M.C. Red Devils (Mex.)	11	4	.733	2.04	1.20	37	15	4	1	...	3-...	127.2	121	37	29	5	32-...	51	...
1995—Carolina (Sou.)	*15	8	.652	2.49	1.26	27	27	1	0	...	0-...	152.0	170	62	42	10	21-3	68	.284
1996—Calgary (PCL)	2	2	.500	3.15	1.60	6	6	0	0	...	0-...	34.1	40	14	12	5	15-1	15	.305
—M.C. Red Devils (Mex.)	7	0	1.000	1.26	1.08	7	7	1	0	...	0-...	50.0	44	12	7	1	10-...	17	...
—Pittsburgh (N.L.)	0	2	.000	8.28	1.76	15	3	0	0	3	0-0	25.0	40	23	23	2	4-0	13	.385
—Carolina (Sou.)	0	1	.000	5.40	1.63	5	1	0	0	...	0-0	11.2	15	8	7	1	4-0	7	.300
1997—M.C. Red Devils (Mex.)	*16	5	.762	3.56	1.30	26	25	3	1	...	0-...	159.1	156	73	63	1	51-...	61	...
—Pittsburgh (N.L.)	0	0	...	0.00	0.60	3	0	0	0	0	0-0	3.1	2	0	0	0	0-0	2	.167
1998—Pittsburgh (N.L.)	2	6	.250	5.67	1.54	43	5	0	0	6	0-1	74.2	90	50	47	10	25-2	43	.300
—Nashville (PCL)	3	1	.750	3.30	1.27	6	5	0	0	...	0-...	30.0	32	12	11	2	6-1	13	.274
1999—Yomiuri (Jp. East.)	4	3	.571	2.08	0.96	15	14	2	...	...	0-...	95.0	67	26	22	...	24-...	58	...
—Yomiuri (Jp. Cen.)	0	1	.000	3.86	1.71	8	0	0	0	...	0-...	16.1	24	7	7	...	4-...	6	...
2000—Louisville (Int'l)	2	0	1.000	3.18	1.37	4	4	0	0	...	0-...	22.2	24	10	8	1	7-0	14	.270
—Cincinnati (N.L.)	11	5	.688	4.28	1.45	40	16	1	0	1	1-1	147.1	170	73	70	10	43-7	85	.296
2001—Cincinnati (N.L.)	10	14	.417	4.48	1.35	34	34	1	1	0	0-0	205.0	221	103	102	32	56-1	128	.279
2002—Cincinnati (N.L.)	7	8	.467	3.03	1.25	30	30	0	0	0	0-0	178.0	173	70	60	24	49-8	93	.257
2003—Arizona (N.L.)	8	8	.500	5.07	1.53	34	30	0	0	0	0-0	175.2	212	107	99	22	57-6	113	.299
Major League totals (7 years)	38	43	.469	4.46	1.41	199	118	2	1	10	1-2	809.0	908	426	401	100	234-24	477	.287

DIAZ, EINAR — C

PERSONAL: Born December 28, 1972, in Chiriqui, Panama. ... 5-10/195. ... Bats right, throws right. ... Full name: Einar Antonio Diaz. ... Name pronounced: AY-een-ar.

TRANSACTIONS/CAREER NOTES: Signed as non-drafted free agent by Cleveland Indians organization (October 5, 1990). ... On Cleveland disabled list (August 23-September 30, 2002); included rehabilitation assignment to Mahoning Valley (September 2-6). ... Traded by Indians with P Ryan Drese to Texas Rangers for 1B Travis Hafner and P Aaron Myette (December 6, 2002).

2003 GAMES PLAYED BY POSITION (MLB): C—101.

Year	Team (League)	Pos.	G	AB	R	H	2B	3B	HR	RBI	BB	SO	HBP	GDP	SB-CS	Avg.	OBP	SLG	OPS	E	Pct.
1991—Dom. Inds. (DSL)		62	239	35	67	6	3	1	29	14	5	...	...	10-...	.280	...	.343	...		
1992—Burlington (Appal.)	3B-SS	52	178	19	37	3	0	1	14	20	9	3	4	2-3	.208	.296	.242	.537	7	.959
1993—Burlington (Appal.)	3B-C	60	231	40	69	15	3	5	33	8	7	4	5	7-3	.299	.328	.455	.782	‡10	.974
—Columbus (S. Atl.)	C	1	5	0	0	0	0	0	0	0	1	0	1	0-0	.000	.000	.000	...	0	1.000
1994—Columbus (S. Atl.)	3B-C	120	491	67	137	23	2	16	71	17	34	21	18	4-4	.279	.330	.432	.762	9	.991
1995—Kinston (Caro.)	C-3B-DH	104	373	46	98	21	0	6	43	12	29	8	6	3-6	.263	.297	.367	.665	7	.991
1996—Cant./Akr. (Eastern)	C-3B	104	395	47	111	26	2	3	35	12	22	9	11	3-2	.281	.317	.380	.696	‡15	.983
—Cleveland (A.L.)	C	4	1	0	0	0	0	0	0	0	0	0	0	0-0	.000	.000	.000	.000	0	1.000
1997—Buffalo (A.A.)	C-3B	109	336	40	86	18	2	3	31	18	34	5	12	2-6	.256	.302	.348	.650	‡19	.974
—Cleveland (A.L.)	C	5	7	1	1	1	0	0	1	0	2	0	0	0-0	.143	.143	.286	.429	1	.955
1998—Buffalo (Int'l)	C	115	415	62	130	21	3	8	63	21	33	6	8	3-3	.313	.354	.436	.790	*12	.986
—Cleveland (A.L.)	C	17	48	8	11	1	0	2	9	3	2	2	2	0-0	.229	.286	.375	.661	3	.973
1999—Cleveland (A.L.)	C	119	392	43	110	21	1	3	32	23	41	5	10	11-4	.281	.328	.362	.690	10	.988
2000—Cleveland (A.L.)	C-3B	75	250	29	68	14	2	4	25	11	29	8	7	4-2	.272	.323	.392	.715	4	.994
2001—Cleveland (A.L.)	C-2B	134	437	54	121	34	1	4	56	17	44	16	11	1-2	.277	.328	.387	.714	8	.992
2002—Cleveland (A.L.)	C	102	320	34	66	19	0	2	16	17	27	6	13	0-1	.206	.258	.284	.542	8	.989
2003—Texas (A.L.)	C	101	334	30	86	14	1	4	35	9	32	10	12	3-1	.257	.294	.341	.635	8	.989
Major League totals (8 years)		557	1789	199	463	104	5	19	174	80	177	47	55	19-10	.259	.306	.354	.661	42	.990

DIAZ, MATT — OF

PERSONAL: Born March 3, 1978, in Portland, Ore. ... 6-1/206. ... Bats right, throws right. ... Full name: Matthew E. Diaz. ... High school: Sante Fe (Fla.). ... College: Florida State.

TRANSACTIONS/CAREER NOTES: Selected by Tampa Bay Devil Rays organization in 17th round of free-agent draft (June 1999).

2003 GAMES PLAYED BY POSITION (MLB): DH—2, OF—1.

Year	Team (League)	Pos.	G	AB	R	H	2B	3B	HR	RBI	BB	SO	HBP	GDP	SB-CS	Avg.	OBP	SLG	OPS	E	Pct.
1999—Hudson Valley (NYP)	OF	54	208	22	51	15	2	1	20	6	43	6	5	6-2	.245	.284	.351	.635	3	.972
2000—St. Pete. (FSL)	OF	106	392	37	106	21	3	6	53	11	54	11	21	2-3	.270	.305	.385	.691	10	.957
2001—Bakersfield (Calif.)	OF	131	524	79	172	40	2	17	81	24	73	14	11	11-5	.328	.370	.510	.880	10	.961
2002—Orlando (South.)	OF-1B	122	449	71	123	28	1	10	50	34	72	10	11	31-9	.274	.337	.408	.744	3	.994
2003—Orlando (South.)	OF	60	227	32	87	21	0	5	41	19	24	8	7	9-5	.383	.444	.542	.985	1	.994
—Tampa Bay (A.L.)	DH-OF	4	9	2	1	0	0	0	0	1	3	0	0	0-0	.111	.200	.111	.311	1	.857
—Durham (Int'l)	OF-DH	67	253	35	83	18	3	8	45	16	45	8	8	6-2	.328	.382	.518	.900	1	.993
Major League totals (1 year)		4	9	2	1	0	0	0	0	1	3	0	0	0-0	.111	.200	.111	.311	1	.857

DICKEY, R.A.   P

PERSONAL: Born October 29, 1974, in Nashville, Tenn. ... 6-3/205. ... Throws right, bats right. ... Full name: Robert Alan Dickey. ... High school: Montgomery Bell Academy (Nashville, Tenn.). ... College: Tennessee.

TRANSACTIONS/CAREER NOTES: Selected by Detroit Tigers organization in 10th round of free-agent draft (June 3, 1993); did not sign. ... Selected by Texas Rangers organization in first round (18th pick overall) of free-agent draft (June 4, 1996). ... On disabled list (May 11, 1997-remainder of season). ... Contract purchased by Texas Rangers (April 15, 2003). ... Optioned to Oklahoma by Texas (June 19, 2003). ... Recalled by Texas from Oklahoma (June 30, 2003).

CAREER HITTING: 1-for-1 (1.000), 0 R, 0 2B, 0 3B, 0 HR, 0 RBI.

Year League	W	L	Pct.	ERA	WHIP	G	GS	CG	ShO	Hld.	Sv.-Opp.	IP	H	R	ER	HR	BB-IBB	SO	Avg.
1997— Charlotte (Fla. St.)	1	4	.200	6.94	1.80	8	6	0	0	...	0-...	35.0	51	32	27	8	12-1	32	.340
1998— Charlotte (Fla. St.)	1	5	.167	3.30	1.33	57	0	0	0	...	* 38-...	60.0	58	31	22	9	22-3	53	.249
1999— Tulsa (Texas)	6	7	.462	4.55	1.53	35	11	0	0	...	10-...	95.0	105	60	48	13	40-1	59	.282
— Oklahoma (PCL)	2	2	.500	4.37	1.32	6	2	0	0	...	0-...	22.2	23	12	11	1	7-1	17	.261
2000— Oklahoma (PCL)	8	9	.471	4.49	1.47	30	23	2	0	...	1-...	158.1	167	83	79	13	65-1	85	.281
2001— Oklahoma (PCL)	11	7	.611	3.75	1.28	24	24	3	0	...	0-...	163.0	164	77	68	14	45-1	120	.262
— Texas (A.L.)	0	1	.000	6.75	1.67	4	0	0	0	0	0-0	12.0	13	9	9	3	7-1	4	.283
2002— Oklahoma (PCL)	8	7	.533	4.09	1.45	37	19	1	0	...	0-...	154.0	176	81	70	8	47-5	109	.295
2003— Oklahoma (PCL)	1	1	.500	1.20	1.13	3	2	0	0	...	0-...	15.0	14	3	2	1	3-0	4	.259
— Texas (A.L.)	9	8	.529	5.09	1.48	38	13	1	1	3	1-1	116.2	135	68	66	16	38-5	94	.292
Major League totals (2 years)	9	9	.500	5.25	1.50	42	13	1	1	3	1-1	128.2	148	77	75	19	45-6	98	.291

DiFELICE, MIKE   C

PERSONAL: Born May 28, 1969, in Philadelphia, Pa. ... 6-2/205. ... Bats right, throws right. ... Full name: Michael William DiFelice. ... Name pronounced: DEE-fah-lease. ... High school: Bearden (Knoxville, Tenn.). ... College: Tennessee.

TRANSACTIONS/CAREER NOTES: Selected by St. Louis Cardinals organization in 11th round of free-agent draft (June 3, 1991). ... Selected by Tampa Bay Devil Rays in first round (20th pick overall) of expansion draft (November 18, 1997). ... Traded by Devil Rays to Arizona Diamondbacks for OF Jason Conti and P Nick Bierbrodt (July 25, 2001). ... Released by Diamondbacks (September 4, 2001). ... Signed by Cardinals (November 20, 2001). ... Granted free agency (November 1, 2002). ... Signed by Kansas City Royals (January 9, 2003). ... Suspended by Major League Baseball for two games and fined an undisclosed amount (August 25, 2003). ... Reinstated (September 6, 2003).

2003 GAMES PLAYED BY POSITION (MLB): C—58, DH—2.

										BATTING										FIELDING	
Year Team (League)	Pos.	G	AB	R	H	2B	3B	HR	RBI	BB	SO	HBP	GDP	SB-CS	Avg.	OBP	SLG	OPS		E	Pct.
1991— Hamilton (NYP)	C	43	157	10	33	5	0	4	15	9	40	1	3	1-5	.210	.257	.318	.576		9	.974
1992— Hamilton (NYP)	C-1B	18	58	11	20	3	0	2	9	4	7	1	0	2-0	.345	.397	.500	.897		5	.969
— St. Pete. (FSL)	C	17	53	0	12	3	0	0	4	3	11	0	3	0-0	.226	.259	.283	.542		2	.977
1993— Springfield (Midw.)	C	8	20	5	7	1	0	0	3	2	3	1	0	0-1	.350	.435	.400	.835		0	1.000
— St. Pete. (FSL)	C	30	97	5	22	2	0	0	8	11	13	1	4	1-0	.227	.306	.247	.554		7	.964
1994— Arkansas (Texas)	C	71	200	19	50	11	2	2	15	12	48	2	9	0-1	.250	.296	.355	.651		6	.987
1995— Arkansas (Texas)	C	62	176	14	47	10	1	1	24	23	29	3	13	0-2	.267	.360	.352	.712		6	.984
— Louisville (A.A.)	C	21	63	8	17	4	0	0	3	5	11	0	4	1-0	.270	.324	.333	.657		2	.984
1996— Louisville (A.A.)	C	79	246	25	70	13	0	9	33	20	43	1	15	0-3	.285	.338	.447	.785		8	.984
— St. Louis (N.L.)	C	4	7	0	2	1	0	0	2	0	1	0	0	0-0	.286	.286	.429	.714		0	1.000
1997— Arkansas (Texas)	C	1	3	0	1	1	0	0	0	1	0	0	0	0-0	.333	.500	.667	1.167		0	1.000
— St. Louis (N.L.)	C-1B	93	260	16	62	10	1	4	30	19	61	3	11	1-1	.238	.297	.331	.628		6	.991
— Louisville (A.A.)	C	1	4	1	1	0	0	1	1	0	1	0	0	0-0	.250	.250	1.000	1.250		0	1.000
1998— Tampa Bay (A.L.)	C	84	248	17	57	12	3	3	23	15	56	1	12	0-0	.230	.277	.339	.613		4	.993
1999— Tampa Bay (A.L.)	C	51	179	21	55	11	0	6	27	8	23	3	1	0-0	.307	.346	.469	.815		5	.987
2000— Tampa Bay (A.L.)	C	60	204	23	49	13	1	6	19	12	40	0	8	0-0	.240	.280	.402	.682		8	.980
2001— Tampa Bay (A.L.)	C	48	149	13	31	5	1	2	9	8	39	3	3	1-1	.208	.259	.295	.555		6	.982
— Arizona (N.L.)	C	12	21	1	1	0	0	0	1	0	10	1	0	0-0	.048	.091	.048	.139		1	.982
— Tucson (PCL)	C-1B	7	26	6	9	0	0	1	2	3	6	0	2	0-0	.346	.414	.462	.875		3	.940
2002— St. Louis (N.L.)	C	70	174	17	40	11	0	4	19	17	42	1	4	0-0	.230	.297	.362	.660		3	.991
2003— Kansas City (A.L.)	C-DH	62	189	29	48	16	1	3	25	9	30	4	6	1-0	.254	.299	.397	.696		2	.994
American League totals (5 years)		305	969	103	240	57	6	20	103	52	188	11	30	2-1	.248	.291	.381	.672		25	.987
National League totals (4 years)		179	462	34	105	22	1	8	52	36	114	5	15	1-1	.227	.290	.331	.619		10	.991
Major League totals (8 years)		484	1431	137	345	79	7	28	155	88	302	16	45	3-2	.241	.290	.365	.655		35	.989

DOMINGUEZ, JUAN   P

PERSONAL: Born May 18, 1980, in Ensanchez Ramirez, Dominican Republic. ... 6-2/180. ... Throws right, bats right. ... Full name: Juan Ramon Dominguez.

TRANSACTIONS/CAREER NOTES: Signed by Texas Rangers as an undrafted free agent (December 26, 1999).

CAREER HITTING: 0-for-0 (.000), 0 R, 0 2B, 0 3B, 0 HR, 0 RBI.

Year League	W	L	Pct.	ERA	WHIP	G	GS	CG	ShO	Hld.	Sv.-Opp.	IP	H	R	ER	HR	BB-IBB	SO	Avg.
2001— GC Rangers (GCL)	4	2	.667	4.01	1.17	11	9	1	1	...	0-...	58.1	56	29	26	4	12-0	55	.250
— Charlotte (Int'l)	1	0	1.000	3.60	1.00	2	0	0	0	...	0-...	5.0	4	2	2	1	1-0	5	.235
2002— Savannah (S. Atl.)	1	3	.250	2.16	1.07	16	9	0	0	...	1-...	66.2	50	23	16	4	21-1	70	.209
2003— Stockton (Calif.)	4	0	1.000	2.84	1.12	16	9	0	0	...	1-...	63.1	55	27	20	3	16-0	72	.226
— Oklahoma (PCL)	1	0	1.000	3.50	1.00	3	3	0	0	...	0-...	18.0	15	7	7	1	3-0	14	.227
— Frisco (Texas)	5	0	1.000	2.60	1.01	9	9	0	0	...	0-...	55.1	35	17	16	2	21-0	54	.178
— Texas (A.L.)	0	2	.000	7.16	1.71	6	3	0	0	0	0-0	16.1	16	14	13	5	12-0	13	.271
Major League totals (1 year)	0	2	.000	7.16	1.71	6	3	0	0	0	0-0	16.1	16	14	13	5	12-0	13	.271

DONNELLY, BRENDAN   P

PERSONAL: Born July 4, 1971, in Washington, District of Columbia. ... 6-3/240. ... Throws right, bats right. ... Full name: Brendan Kevin Donnelly. ... High school: Sandia (Albuquerque, N.M.). ... Junior college: Mesa (Ari.) Community College.

TRANSACTIONS/CAREER NOTES: Selected by Chicago White Sox organization in 27th round of free-agent draft (June 1, 1992). ... Released by White Sox (April 16, 1993). ... Signed by Chicago Cubs organization (June 16, 1993). ... Released by Cubs (March 29, 1994). ... Signed by Ohio Valley, Frontier League (July 1994). ... Signed by Cincinnati Reds organization (March 4, 1995). ... Granted free agency (October 16, 1998). ... Signed by Reds organization (March 15, 1999). ... Released by Reds (April 3, 1999). ... Signed by Nashua, Atlantic League (May 1999). ... Sold by Nashua to Tampa Bay Devil Rays organization (May 15, 1999). ... Released by Devil Rays (August 12, 1999). ... Signed by Pittsburgh Pirates organization (August 18, 1999). ... Released by Pirates (August 25, 1999). ... Signed by Toronto Blue Jays organization (August 26, 1999). ...

Released by Blue Jays (July 28, 2000). ... Signed by Cubs organization (August 10, 2000). ... Granted free agency (October 15, 2000). ... Signed by Anaheim Angels organization (January 9, 2001).

CAREER HITTING: 0-for-0 (.000), 0 R, 0 2B, 0 3B, 0 HR, 0 RBI.

Year League	W	L	Pct.	ERA	WHIP	G	GS	CG	ShO	Hld.	Sv.-Opp.	IP	H	R	ER	HR	BB-IBB	SO	Avg.
1992— GC White Sox (GCL)	0	3	.000	3.67	1.49	9	7	0	0	...	1-...	41.2	41	25	17	0	21-0	31	.256
1993— Geneva (N.Y.-Penn)	4	0	1.000	6.28	1.58	21	3	0	0	...	1-...	43.0	39	34	30	4	29-0	29	.242
1994— Ohio Valley (Fron.)	1	1	.500	2.57	1.21	10	0	0	0	...	0-...	14.0	13	5	4	1	4-0	20	.250
1995— Char., W.Va. (SAL)	1	1	.500	1.19	0.69	24	0	0	0	...	12-...	30.1	14	4	4	0	7-1	33	.139
— Winston-Salem (Caro.)	1	2	.333	1.02	0.96	23	0	0	0	...	2-...	35.1	20	6	4	1	14-2	32	.167
— Indianapolis (A.A.)	1	1	.500	23.63	3.38	3	0	0	0	...	0-...	2.2	7	8	7	2	2-0	1	.500
1996— Chattanooga (Sou.)	1	2	.333	5.52	1.50	22	0	0	0	...	0-...	29.1	27	21	18	4	17-2	22	.237
1997— Chattanooga (Sou.)	6	4	.600	3.27	1.31	62	0	0	0	...	6-...	82.2	71	43	30	6	37-4	64	.228
1998— Chattanooga (Sou.)	2	5	.286	2.98	1.48	38	0	0	0	...	13-...	45.1	43	16	15	4	24-5	47	.247
— Indianapolis (Int'l)	4	1	.800	2.65	1.21	19	1	0	0	...	0-...	37.1	29	16	11	3	16-3	39	.212
1999— Nashua (Atl.)	0	0	...	3.00	1.33	3	0	0	0	...	0-...	3.0	1	1	1	...	3-...	4	...
— Durham (Int'l)	5	5	.500	3.05	1.15	37	1	0	0	...	2-...	62.0	53	23	21	5	18-1	61	.240
— Altoona (East.)	0	0	...	7.71	2.57	2	0	0	0	...	1-...	2.1	4	2	2	0	2-0	0	.571
— Syracuse (Int'l)	0	1	.000	2.89	1.29	5	0	0	0	...	0-...	9.1	8	4	3	1	4-1	9	.242
2000— Syracuse (Int'l)	4	6	.400	5.48	1.73	37	0	0	0	...	0-...	42.2	47	34	26	5	27-2	34	.278
— Iowa (PCL)	0	3	.000	7.56	1.86	9	0	0	0	...	1-...	16.2	25	19	14	3	6-1	14	.338
2001— Arkansas (Texas)	4	1	.800	2.48	1.17	27	0	0	0	...	12-...	29.0	21	8	8	2	13-1	37	.200
— Salt Lake (PCL)	5	1	.833	2.40	1.11	29	0	0	0	...	1-...	41.1	38	11	11	4	8-0	50	.245
2002— Salt Lake (PCL)	4	0	1.000	3.48	1.13	25	0	0	0	...	6-...	33.2	27	13	13	5	11-0	42	.213
— Anaheim (A.L.)	1	1	.500	2.17	1.03	46	0	0	0	13	1-3	49.2	32	13	12	2	19-3	54	.184
2003— Anaheim (A.L.)	2	2	.500	1.58	1.07	63	0	0	0	*29	3-5	74.0	55	14	13	2	24-1	79	.200
Major League totals (2 years)	**3**	**3**	**.500**	**1.82**	**1.05**	**109**	**0**	**0**	**0**	**42**	**4-8**	**123.2**	**87**	**27**	**25**	**4**	**43-4**	**133**	**.194**

DOTEL, OCTAVIO   P

PERSONAL: Born November 25, 1973, in Santo Domingo, Dominican Republic. ... 6-0/200. ... Throws right, bats right. ... Full name: Octavio Eduardo Dotel. ... Name pronounced: OC-tay-vee-oh dough-TEL. ... High school: Liceo Eansino Afuera (Dominican Republic).

TRANSACTIONS/CAREER NOTES: Signed as non-drafted free agent by New York Mets organization (March 20, 1993). ... On disabled list (July 18-August 16, 1996). ... On Binghamton disabled list (June 3-24, 1997). ... On Norfolk disabled list (May 7-17, 1999). ... Traded by Mets with OF Roger Cedeno and P Kyle Kessel to Houston Astros for P Mike Hampton and OF Derek Bell (December 23, 1999).

CAREER HITTING: 5-for-74 (.068), 3 R, 0 2B, 0 3B, 0 HR, 1 RBI.

Year League	W	L	Pct.	ERA	WHIP	G	GS	CG	ShO	Hld.	Sv.-Opp.	IP	H	R	ER	HR	BB-IBB	SO	Avg.
1993— Dom. Mets (DSL)	6	2	.750	4.10	1.42	15	11	0	0	...	0-...	59.1	46	30	27	...	38-...	48	...
1994— Dom. Mets (DSL)	5	0	1.000	4.32	1.41	15	14	1	0	...	0-...	81.1	84	53	39	...	31-...	95	...
1995— GC Mets (GCL)	• 7	4	.636	2.18	0.87	13	12	2	0	...	0-...	* 74.1	48	23	18	0	17-1	* 86	.178
— St. Lucie (Fla. St.)	1	0	1.000	5.63	1.75	3	0	0	0	...	0-...	8.0	10	5	5	1	4-0	9	.323
1996— Capital City (S. Atl.)	11	3	.786	3.59	1.20	22	19	0	0	...	0-...	115.1	89	49	46	7	49-0	142	.212
1997— St. Lucie (Fla. St.)	5	2	.714	2.52	1.34	9	8	1	1	...	0-...	50.0	44	18	14	2	23-0	39	.235
— Binghamton (Eastern)	3	4	.429	5.98	1.87	12	12	0	0	...	0-...	55.2	66	50	37	5	38-1	40	.293
— GC Mets (GCL)	0	0	...	0.96	1.18	3	2	0	0	...	1-...	9.1	9	1	1	0	2-0	7	.250
1998— Binghamton (Eastern)	4	2	.667	1.97	0.95	10	10	2	1	...	0-...	68.2	41	19	15	4	24-1	82	.175
— Norfolk (Int'l)	8	6	.571	3.45	1.26	17	16	1	0	...	0-...	99.0	82	47	38	9	43-1	118	.221
1999— Norfolk (Int'l)	5	2	.714	3.84	1.22	13	13	1	0	...	0-...	70.1	52	33	30	9	34-1	90	.204
— New York (N.L.)	8	3	.727	5.38	1.38	19	14	0	0	...	0-0	85.1	69	52	51	12	49-1	85	.226
2000— Houston (N.L.)	3	7	.300	5.40	1.50	50	16	0	0	0	16-23	125.0	127	80	75	26	61-3	142	.265
2001— Houston (N.L.)	7	5	.583	2.66	1.20	61	4	0	0	14	2-4	105.0	79	35	31	5	47-2	145	.205
2002— Houston (N.L.)	6	4	.600	1.85	0.87	83	0	0	0	31	6-10	97.1	58	21	20	7	27-2	118	.173
2003— Houston (N.L.)	6	4	.600	2.48	0.97	76	0	0	0	*33	4-6	87.0	53	25	24	9	31-2	97	.172
Major League totals (5 years)	**30**	**23**	**.566**	**3.62**	**1.20**	**289**	**34**	**0**	**0**	**78**	**28-43**	**499.2**	**386**	**213**	**201**	**59**	**215-10**	**587**	**.213**

DOUGLASS, SEAN   P

PERSONAL: Born April 28, 1979, in Lancaster, Calif. ... 6-6/218. ... Throws right, bats right. ... Full name: Sean R. Douglass. ... High school: Antelope Valley (Lancaster, Calif.).
TRANSACTIONS/CAREER NOTES: Selected by Baltimore Orioles organization in second round of free-agent draft (June 3, 1997). ... Called up by Baltimore from Ottawa (September 9, 2003).

CAREER HITTING: 0-for-0 (.000), 0 R, 0 2B, 0 3B, 0 HR, 0 RBI.

Year League	W	L	Pct.	ERA	WHIP	G	GS	CG	ShO	Hld.	Sv.-Opp.	IP	H	R	ER	HR	BB-IBB	SO	Avg.
1997— GC Orioles (GCL)	1	3	.250	6.11	1.64	9	1	0	0	...	0-...	17.2	20	14	12	2	9-0	10	.308
1998— Bluefield (Appal.)	2	2	.500	3.23	1.11	10	0	0	0	...	0-...	53.0	45	20	19	6	14-0	62	.231
1999— Frederick (Caro.)	5	6	.455	3.32	1.63	16	16	1	0	...	0-...	97.2	101	48	36	9	58-0	161	.267
2000— Bowie (East.)	9	8	.529	4.02	1.31	27	27	2	0	...	0-...	159.0	174	88	71	17	34-1	105	.284
2001— Rochester (Int'l)	8	9	.471	3.49	1.36	27	27	0	0	...	0-...	162.1	160	79	63	13	61-0	156	.252
— Baltimore (A.L.)	2	1	.667	5.31	1.57	4	4	0	0	0	0-0	20.1	21	12	12	3	11-0	17	.259
2002— Rochester (Int'l)	4	6	.400	4.73	1.52	14	13	0	0	...	0-...	66.2	66	39	35	4	35-0	71	.256
— Baltimore (A.L.)	0	5	.000	6.08	1.74	15	8	0	0	0	0-0	53.1	58	41	36	10	35-2	44	.283
2003— Ottawa (Int'l)	10	8	.556	3.40	1.40	27	27	0	0	...	0-...	143.0	142	67	54	6	58-4	118	.256
— Baltimore (A.L.)	0	0	...	13.50	2.50	3	0	0	0	0	0-0	8.0	14	12	12	2	6-0	3	.378
Major League totals (3 years)	**2**	**6**	**.250**	**6.61**	**1.78**	**22**	**12**	**0**	**0**	**0**	**0-0**	**81.2**	**93**	**65**	**60**	**15**	**52-2**	**64**	**.288**

DOWNS, SCOTT   P

PERSONAL: Born March 17, 1976, in Louisville, Ky. ... 6-2/190. ... Throws left, bats left. ... Full name: Scott Jeremy Downs. ... High school: Pleasure Ridge Park (Louisville, Ky.). ... College: Kentucky.
TRANSACTIONS/CAREER NOTES: Selected by Chicago Cubs organization in third round of free-agent draft (June 3, 1997). ... Traded by Cubs to Minnesota Twins (November 3, 1998), completing deal in which Twins traded P Mike Morgan to Cubs for cash and a player to be named later (August 25, 1998). ... Traded by Twins with P Rick Aguilera to Cubs for P Kyle Lohse and P Jason Ryan (May 21, 1999). ... Traded by Cubs to Montreal Expos for OF Rondell White (July 31, 2000). ... On Montreal disabled list (August 9, 2000-remainder of season). ... On disabled list (March 23, 2001-entire season). ... On Montreal disabled list (March 27-June 10, 2002; included rehabilitation assignment to Brevard (May 16-June 1) and Ottawa (June 1-June 10). ... On Ottawa disabled list (August 4-September 3, 2002). ... Optioned to Ottawa by Montreal (August 20, 2003). ... Designated for assignment (September 2, 2003). ... Sent outright to Edmonton by Montreal (September 4, 2003).
CAREER HITTING: 2-for-29 (.069), 2 R, 0 2B, 0 3B, 0 HR, 1 RBI.

Year	League	W	L	Pct.	ERA	WHIP	G	GS	CG	ShO	Hld.	Sv.-Opp.	IP	H	R	ER	HR	BB-IBB	SO	Avg.
1997— Williamsport (NYP)		0	2	.000	2.74	0.96	5	5	0	0	...	0-...	23.0	15	11	7	0	7-0	28	.181
— Rockford (Midwest)		3	0	1.000	1.25	0.69	5	5	0	0	...	0-...	36.0	17	5	5	1	8-0	43	.144
1998— Daytona (Fla. St.)		8	9	.471	3.90	1.45	27	27	2	0	...	0-...	161.2	179	83	70	12	55-0	117	.280
1999— New Britain (East.)		0	0	...	8.69	2.19	6	3	0	0	...	0-...	19.2	33	21	19	5	10-1	22	.375
— Fort Myers (Fla. St.)		0	1	.000	0.00	1.34	2	2	0	0	...	0-...	9.2	7	3	0	0	6-0	9	.184
— Daytona (Fla. St.)		5	0	1.000	1.88	1.08	7	7	1	1	...	0-...	48.0	41	12	10	2	11-0	41	.237
— West Tenn (Sou.)		8	1	.889	1.35	1.05	13	12	1	0	...	0-...	80.0	56	13	12	2	28-0	101	.194
2000— Chicago (N.L.)		4	3	.571	5.17	1.64	18	18	0	0	0	0-0	94.0	117	59	54	13	37-1	63	.310
— Montreal (N.L.)		0	0	...	9.00	2.67	1	1	0	0	0	0-0	3.0	5	3	3	0	3-0	0	.385
2001— Montreal (N.L.)												Did not play.								
2002— Brevard County (FSL)		0	0	...	3.00	1.00	7	0	0	0	...	1-...	9.0	7	3	3	0	2-0	7	.206
— Ottawa (Int'l)		2	1	.667	5.79	1.46	17	0	0	0	...	0-...	23.1	31	21	15	6	3-0	15	.320
2003— Montreal (N.L.)		0	1	.000	15.00	2.67	1	1	0	0	0	0-0	3.0	5	5	5	2	3-2	4	.357
— Edmonton (PCL)		8	9	.471	4.29	1.30	21	21	3	0	...	0-...	121.2	119	67	58	13	39-0	54	.263
Major League totals (2 years)		4	4	.500	5.58	1.70	20	20	0	0	0	0-0	100.0	127	67	62	15	43-3	67	.314

DREIFORT, DARREN   P

PERSONAL: Born May 3, 1972, in Wichita, Kan. ... 6-2/211. ... Throws right, bats right. ... Full name: Darren John Dreifort. ... Name pronounced: DRY-fort. ... High school: Wichita (Kan.) Heights. ... College: Wichita State.

TRANSACTIONS/CAREER NOTES: Selected by New York Mets organization in 11th round of free-agent draft (June 4, 1990); did not sign. ... Selected by Los Angeles Dodgers organization in first round (second pick overall) of free-agent draft (June 3, 1993). ... On San Antonio disabled list (July 7-28, 1994). ... On Albuquerque disabled list (August 27, 1994-remainder of season). ... On disabled list (April 23, 1995-entire season). ... On Los Angeles disabled list (March 25-May 16, 1996); included rehabilitation assignment to Albuquerque (April 18-May 15). ... On Los Angeles disabled list (May 12-June 17, 1997); included rehabilitation assignment to Albuquerque (June 11-17). ... Granted free agency (October 30, 2000). ... Re-signed by Dodgers (December 11, 2000). ... On disabled list (June 30, 2001-remainder of season; and March 19, 2002-entire season). ... Placed on 15-day disabled list (May 29, 2003). ... Transferred to Emergency disabled list (July 3, 2003).

CAREER HITTING: 44-for-238 (.185), 26 R, 10 2B, 0 3B, 6 HR, 23 RBI.

Year	League	W	L	Pct.	ERA	WHIP	G	GS	CG	ShO	Hld.	Sv.-Opp.	IP	H	R	ER	HR	BB-IBB	SO	Avg.
1994— Los Angeles (N.L.)		0	5	.000	6.21	2.07	27	0	0	0	3	6-9	29.0	45	21	20	0	15-3	22	.357
— San Antonio (Texas)		3	1	.750	2.80	1.39	8	8	0	0	...	0-...	35.1	36	14	11	0	13-0	32	.261
— Albuquerque (PCL)		1	0	1.000	5.68	1.74	1	1	0	0	...	0-...	6.1	8	4	4	1	3-0	3	.348
1995— Los Angeles (N.L.)												Did not play.								
1996— Albuquerque (PCL)		5	6	.455	4.17	1.62	18	18	0	0	...	0-...	86.1	88	49	40	6	52-3	75	.272
— Los Angeles (N.L.)		1	4	.200	4.94	1.48	19	0	0	0	1	0-2	23.2	23	13	13	2	12-4	24	.256
1997— Los Angeles (N.L.)		5	2	.714	2.86	1.25	48	0	0	0	9	4-7	63.0	45	21	20	3	34-2	63	.202
— Albuquerque (PCL)		0	0	...	1.59	0.53	2	2	0	0	...	0-...	5.2	2	1	1	1	1-0	3	.111
1998— Los Angeles (N.L.)		8	12	.400	4.00	1.27	32	26	1	1	0	0-0	180.0	171	84	80	12	57-2	168	.256
1999— Los Angeles (N.L.)		13	13	.500	4.79	1.42	30	29	1	1	0	0-0	178.2	177	105	95	20	76-2	140	.260
2000— Los Angeles (N.L.)		12	9	.571	4.16	1.36	32	32	1	1	0	0-0	192.2	175	105	89	31	87-1	164	.238
2001— Los Angeles (N.L.)		4	7	.364	5.13	1.44	16	16	0	0	0	0-0	94.2	89	62	54	11	47-0	91	.251
2002— Los Angeles (N.L.)												Did not play.								
2003— Los Angeles (N.L.)		4	4	.500	4.03	1.38	10	10	0	0	0	0-0	60.1	58	29	27	6	25-0	67	.250
Major League totals (8 years)		47	56	.456	4.36	1.38	214	113	3	3	13	10-18	822.0	783	440	398	85	353-14	739	.252

DRESE, RYAN   P

PERSONAL: Born April 5, 1976, in San Francisco, Calif. ... 6-3/220. ... Throws right, bats right. ... Full name: Ryan Thomas Drese. ... Name pronounced: drees. ... High school: Bishop O'Dowd (Oakland). ... College: UC-Berkeley.

TRANSACTIONS/CAREER NOTES: Selected by Oakland Athletics organization in fifth round of free-agent draft (June 2, 1994); did not sign. ... Selected by Cleveland Indians organization in fifth round of free-agent draft (June 2, 1998). ... On disabled list (April 10-June 20, 2000). ... Traded by Indians with C Einar Diaz to Texas Rangers for 1B Travis Hafner and P Aaron Myette (December 6, 2002). ... Optioned to Oklahoma by Texas (May 9, 2003). ... Recalled by Texas from Oklahoma (July 16, 2003). ... Optioned to Oklahoma by Texas (July 21, 2003). ... Recalled by Texas from Oklahoma (September 1, 2003).

CAREER HITTING: 0-for-3 (.000), 0 R, 0 2B, 0 3B, 0 HR, 0 RBI.

Year	League	W	L	Pct.	ERA	WHIP	G	GS	CG	ShO	Hld.	Sv.-Opp.	IP	H	R	ER	HR	BB-IBB	SO	Avg.
1998— Watertown (NYP)		2	5	.286	4.07	1.29	9	9	0	0	...	0-...	42.0	40	21	19	1	14-0	40	.250
1999— Kinston (Caro.)		5	4	.556	4.93	1.41	15	15	1	0	...	0-...	69.1	46	47	38	2	52-0	81	.189
— Mahoning Valley (NY-P)		0	2	.000	2.65	0.88	5	5	0	0	...	0-...	17.0	8	6	5	1	7-0	26	.143
— Columbia (S. Atl.)		0	2	.000	4.50	1.08	2	2	0	0	...	0-...	12.0	9	6	6	2	4-0	15	.200
2000— Kinston (Caro.)		0	1	.000	3.86	1.29	1	1	0	0	...	0-...	2.1	2	1	1	0	1-0	4	.286
2001— Akron (East.)		5	7	.417	3.35	1.08	14	13	1	1	...	0-...	86.0	64	34	32	4	29-0	73	.215
— Buffalo (Int'l)		5	1	.833	4.01	1.27	11	10	0	0	...	0-...	60.2	60	28	27	7	17-0	52	.262
— Cleveland (A.L.)		1	2	.333	3.44	1.28	9	4	0	0	0	0-0	36.2	32	15	14	2	15-2	24	.242
2002— Cleveland (A.L.)		10	9	.526	6.55	1.73	26	26	1	0	0	0-0	137.1	176	104	100	15	62-1	102	.317
— Buffalo (Int'l)		1	0	1.000	1.64	0.91	3	3	0	0	...	0-...	22.0	16	4	4	1	4-0	16	.200
2003— Frisco (Texas)		1	1	.500	4.00	1.11	2	2	0	0	...	0-...	9.0	10	4	4	1	0-0	8	.278
— Oklahoma (PCL)		8	6	.571	4.65	1.49	20	20	0	0	...	0-...	122.0	143	70	63	8	39-1	68	.300
— Texas (A.L.)		2	4	.333	6.85	1.85	11	8	0	0	1	0-0	46.0	61	42	35	8	24-1	26	.314
Major League totals (3 years)		13	15	.464	6.10	1.68	46	38	1	0	1	0-0	220.0	269	161	149	25	101-4	152	.305

DREW, J.D.   OF

PERSONAL: Born November 20, 1975, in Valdosta, Ga. ... 6-1/200. ... Bats left, throws right. ... Full name: David Jonathan Drew. ... High school: Lowndes County (Hahira, Ga.). ... College: Florida State.

TRANSACTIONS/CAREER NOTES: Selected by San Francisco Giants organization in 20th round of free-agent draft (June 2, 1994); did not sign. ... Selected by Philadelphia Phillies organization in first round (second pick overall) of free-agent draft (June 3, 1997); did not sign. ... Selected by St. Louis Cardinals organization in first round (fifth pick overall) of free-agent draft (June 2, 1998). ... On Arkansas disabled list (July 21-August 6, 1998). ... On St. Louis disabled list (May 16-June 17, 1999); included rehabilitation assignment to Memphis (May 28-June 17). ... On disabled list (July 8-27, 2000). ... On St. Louis disabled list (June 18-July 31, 2001); included rehabilitation assignment to Peoria (July 26-31). ... On disabled list (June 28-July 13, 2002). ... On St. Louis disabled list (March 21-April 20, 2003); included rehabilitation assignment to Palm Beach (April 5). ... Recalled from the 15-day disabled list; reinstated from the 15-day disabled list (April 20, 2003). ... Placed on 15-day disabled list (August 16, 2003). ... Removed from 15-day disabled list (September 1, 2003).

2003 GAMES PLAYED BY POSITION (MLB): OF—75.

D

Year Team (League)	Pos.	G	AB	R	H	2B	3B	HR	RBI	BB	SO	HBP	GDP	SB-CS	Avg.	OBP	SLG	OPS	E	Pct.
1997— St. Paul (Nor.)		44	170	51	58	6	1	18	50	30	40	2	1	5-3	.341	.443	.706	1.149	...	...
1998— St. Paul (Nor.)		30	114	27	44	11	2	9	33	21	32	6	2	8-1	.386	.504	.754	1.258	...	...
— Arkansas (Texas)	OF	19	67	18	22	3	1	5	11	13	15	1	0	2-1	.328	.444	.627	1.071	1	.980
— Memphis (PCL)	OF	26	79	15	25	8	1	2	13	22	18	1	1	1-3	.316	.471	.519	.990	2	.966
— St. Louis (N.L.)	OF	14	36	9	15	3	1	5	13	4	10	0	4	0-0	.417	.463	.972	1.436	0	1.000
1999— St. Louis (N.L.)	OF	104	368	72	89	16	6	13	39	50	77	6	4	19-3	.242	.340	.424	.763	7	.972
— Memphis (PCL)	OF	25	87	11	26	5	1	2	15	8	20	2	0	6-1	.299	.371	.448	.819	0	1.000
2000— St. Louis (N.L.)	OF	135	407	73	120	17	2	18	57	67	99	6	3	17-9	.295	.401	.479	.880	9	.966
2001— St. Louis (N.L.)	OF	109	375	80	121	18	5	27	73	57	75	4	6	13-3	.323	.414	.613	1.027	6	.973
— Peoria (Midw.)	OF	3	11	3	6	2	0	0	0	1	0	0	1	0-0	.545	.583	.727	1.311	0	1.000
2002— St. Louis (N.L.)	OF	135	424	61	107	19	1	18	56	57	104	8	4	8-2	.252	.349	.429	.778	3	.987
2003— W.P. Beach (FSL)	OF-DH	8	19	4	7	0	0	1	3	7	4	1	0	0-0	.368	.556	.526	1.082	0	1.000
— St. Louis (N.L.)	OF	100	287	60	83	13	3	15	42	36	48	3	6	2-2	.289	.374	.512	.886	1	.994
Major League totals (6 years)		597	1897	355	535	86	18	96	280	271	413	27	27	59-19	.282	.377	.498	.875	26	.977

DREW, TIM — P

PERSONAL: Born August 31, 1978, in Valdosta, Ga. ... 6-1/200. ... Throws right, bats right. ... Full name: Timothy Andrew Drew. ... High school: Lowndes County (Hahira, Ga.).

TRANSACTIONS/CAREER NOTES: Selected by Cleveland Indians organization in first round (28th pick overall) of free-agent draft (June 3, 1997). ... On Buffalo disabled list (June 18-26, 2001). ... Traded by Indians to Montreal Expos (June 28, 2002), completing deal in which Indians traded P Bartolo Colon with future considerations to Expos for 1B Lee Stevens, SS Brandon Phillips, P Cliff Lee and OF Grady Sizemore (June 27, 2002). ... Contract purchased by Montreal from Edmonton (June 26, 2003). ... Sent outright to Edmonton by Montreal (July 26, 2003).

CAREER HITTING: 0-for-5 (.000), 0 R, 0 HR, 0 RBI.

Year League	W	L	Pct.	ERA	WHIP	G	GS	CG	ShO	Hld.	Sv.-Opp.	IP	H	R	ER	HR	BB-IBB	SO	Avg.
1997— Burlington (Appal.)	0	1	.000	6.17	1.71	4	4	0	0	...	0-...	11.2	16	15	8	0	4-0	14	.302
— Watertown (NYP)	0	0	...	1.93	1.50	1	1	0	0	...	0-...	4.2	4	1	1	0	3-0	9	.235
1998— Columbus (S. Atl.)	4	3	.571	3.79	1.32	13	13	0	0	...	0-...	71.1	68	43	30	5	26-0	64	.247
— Kinston (Caro.)	3	8	.273	5.20	1.51	15	15	0	0	...	0-...	90.0	105	58	52	9	31-1	67	.302
1999— Kinston (Caro.)	* 13	5	.722	3.73	1.27	28	* 28	2	0	...	0-...	169.0	154	79	70	12	60-0	125	.243
2000— Akron (East.)	3	2	.600	2.42	1.08	9	9	0	0	...	0-...	52.0	41	19	14	1	15-0	22	.217
— Cleveland (A.L.)	1	0	1.000	10.00	2.78	3	3	0	0	...	0-0	9.0	17	12	10	1	8-0	5	.425
— Buffalo (Int'l)	7	8	.467	5.87	1.61	16	16	2	0	...	0-...	95.0	122	69	62	12	31-0	53	.312
2001— Cleveland (A.L.)	0	2	.000	7.97	1.91	8	6	0	0	0	0-0	35.0	51	39	31	9	16-0	15	.340
— Buffalo (Int'l)	8	6	.571	3.92	1.31	18	18	1	1	...	0-...	108.0	115	54	47	13	27-1	75	.268
2002— Akron (East.)	8	4	.667	3.27	1.24	15	15	2	2	...	0-...	96.1	96	43	35	6	23-1	43	.261
— Ottawa (Int'l)	6	3	.667	2.87	1.19	13	13	0	0	...	0-...	† 84.2	77	31	27	5	24-2	29	.248
— Montreal (N.L.)	1	0	1.000	2.81	0.88	7	1	0	0	1	2-3	16.0	12	8	5	1	2-0	10	.200
2003— Montreal (N.L.)	0	2	.000	12.46	2.31	6	1	0	0	0	0-0	8.2	12	12	12	3	8-1	3	.343
— Edmonton (PCL)	5	9	.357	7.23	1.75	27	15	0	0	...	2-...	93.1	128	80	75	10	35-2	54	.334
American League totals (2 years)	1	2	.333	8.39	2.09	11	9	0	0	0	0-0	44.0	68	51	41	10	24-0	20	.358
National League totals (2 years)	1	2	.333	6.20	1.38	13	2	0	0	1	2-3	24.2	24	20	17	4	10-1	13	.253
Major League totals (4 years)	2	4	.333	7.60	1.83	24	11	0	0	1	2-3	68.2	92	71	58	14	34-1	33	.323

DRISKILL, TRAVIS — P

PERSONAL: Born August 1, 1971, in Omaha, Neb. ... 6-0/215. ... Throws right, bats right. ... Full name: Travis Corey Driskill. ... High school: L.C. Anderson (Austin, Texas). ... College: Texas Tech.

TRANSACTIONS/CAREER NOTES: Selected by Houston Astros organization in 76th round of free-agent draft (June 4, 1990); did not sign. ... Selected by Cleveland Indians organization in fourth round of free-agent draft (June 3, 1993). ... Contract sold by Indians to Yakult Swallows of Japanese Central League (January 6, 1998). ... Signed by Indians organization (August 3, 1998). ... Granted free agency (October 15, 1999). ... Signed by Astros organization (January 3, 2000). ... Granted free agency (October 15, 2001). ... Signed by Baltimore Orioles organization (November 16, 2001). ... Contract purchased by Baltimore from Ottawa (May 8, 2003). ... Optioned to Ottawa by Baltimore (August 12, 2003). ... Recalled from Ottawa by Baltimore; sent outright to Ottawa (August 22, 2003).

CAREER HITTING: 0-for-4 (.000), 1 R, 0 2B, 0 3B, 0 HR, 0 RBI.

Year League	W	L	Pct.	ERA	WHIP	G	GS	CG	ShO	Hld.	Sv.-Opp.	IP	H	R	ER	HR	BB-IBB	SO	Avg.
1993— Watertown (NYP)	5	4	.556	4.14	1.32	21	8	0	0	...	3-...	63.0	62	38	29	4	21-0	53	.257
1994— Columbus (S. Atl.)	5	5	.500	2.52	1.26	62	0	0	0	...	35-...	64.1	51	25	18	2	30-4	88	.223
1995— Kinston (Caro.)	0	2	.000	2.74	0.96	15	0	0	0	...	0-...	23.0	17	7	7	2	5-1	24	.210
— Cant./Akr. (Eastern)	3	4	.429	4.66	1.40	33	0	0	0	...	4-...	46.1	46	24	24	3	19-1	39	.258
1996— Cant./Akr. (Eastern)	13	7	.650	3.61	1.35	29	24	4	2	...	0-...	172.0	169	89	69	8	63-0	148	.258
1997— Buffalo (A.A.)	8	7	.533	4.65	1.49	29	24	1	0	...	0-...	147.0	159	86	76	22	60-0	102	.277
1998— Yakult (Jp. East.)	1	6	.143	6.08	1.63	12	5	0	0	...	0-...	40.0	46	29	27	...	19-...	25	...
— Yakult (Jp. Cen.)	0	1	.000	4.80	1.80	7	3	0	0	...	0-...	15.0	21	9	8	...	6-...	7	...
— Akron (East.)	3	0	1.000	3.42	1.29	5	4	0	0	...	0-...	26.1	27	12	10	4	7-0	16	.270
— Buffalo (Int'l)	0	0	...	9.00	1.67	1	1	0	0	...	0-...	6.0	9	6	6	0	1-0	5	.333
1999— Buffalo (Int'l)	9	8	.529	4.83	1.35	31	18	0	0	...	0-...	132.1	146	78	71	21	32-2	90	.285
2000— New Orleans (PCL)	12	11	.522	4.01	1.37	28	28	2	1	...	0-...	* 179.1	201	101	80	15	45-0	113	.282
2001— New Orleans (PCL)	11	5	.688	3.78	1.16	28	28	1	0	...	0-...	* 178.2	175	83	75	21	33-2	145	.255
2002— Rochester (Int'l)	2	2	.500	1.64	0.82	4	4	1	1	...	0-...	22.0	17	8	4	1	1-0	15	.202
— Baltimore (A.L.)	8	8	.500	4.95	1.49	29	19	0	0	0	0-0	132.2	150	78	73	21	48-1	78	.284
2003— Baltimore (A.L.)	3	5	.375	6.00	1.48	20	0	0	0	0	1-1	48.0	62	35	32	8	9-2	33	.310
— Ottawa (Int'l)	4	0	1.000	2.84	1.03	9	9	0	0	...	0-...	50.2	46	17	16	8	6-0	36	.238
Major League totals (2 years)	11	13	.458	5.23	1.49	49	19	0	0	0	1-1	180.2	212	113	105	29	57-3	111	.291

DuBOSE, ERIC — P

PERSONAL: Born May 15, 1976, in Bradenton, Fla. ... 6-3/233. ... Throws left, bats left. ... Full name: Eric Ladell DuBose. ... Name pronounced: dew-BOWES. ... High school: Patrician Academy (Butler, Ala.). ... College: Mississippi State.

TRANSACTIONS/CAREER NOTES: Selected by Oakland Athletics organization in first round (21st pick overall) of free-agent draft (June 3, 1997); pick received as compensation for Baltimore Orioles signing SS Mike Bordick. ... On Midland disabled list (June 18-July 23, 1999). ... On Midland disabled list (April 14-June 13, 2000). ... Claimed on waivers by Cleveland Indians (September 8, 2000). ... Claimed on waivers by Detroit Tigers (September 22, 2000). ... Released by Tigers (March 31, 2001). ... Signed by

D

Baltimore Orioles organization (February 4, 2002). ... On Rochester disabled list (April 4-May 1, 2002). ... Optioned to Ottawa by Baltimore (May 4, 2003). ... Recalled by Baltimore from Ottawa (May 4, 2003). ... Recalled by Baltimore from Ottawa (July 22, 2003).

CAREER HITTING: 0-for-0 (.000), 0 R, 0 2B, 0 3B, 0 HR, 0 RBI.

Year — League	W	L	Pct.	ERA	WHIP	G	GS	CG	ShO	Hld.	Sv.-Opp.	IP	H	R	ER	HR	BB-IBB	SO	Avg.
1997— S. Oregon (N'west)	1	0	1.000	0.00	1.10	3	1	0	0	...	0-...	10.0	5	0	0	0	6-0	15	.152
—Visalia (Calif.)	1	3	.250	7.04	1.85	10	9	0	0	...	0-...	38.1	43	37	30	4	28-0	39	.270
1998— Visalia (Calif.)	6	1	.857	3.38	1.13	17	10	0	0	...	1-...	72.0	56	34	27	5	25-0	85	.212
—Huntsville (Sou.)	7	6	.538	2.70	1.44	14	14	1	1	...	0-...	83.1	86	37	25	2	34-1	66	.273
1999— Midland (Texas)	4	2	.667	5.49	1.73	21	14	0	0	...	1-...	77.0	89	57	47	10	44-1	68	.293
2000— Midland (Texas)	5	1	.833	4.13	1.52	18	0	0	0	...	0-...	28.1	25	16	13	1	18-2	20	.227
—Visalia (Calif.)	0	1	.000	1.69	1.22	5	0	0	0	...	1-...	10.2	8	2	2	0	5-1	12	.200
2001—										Did not play.									
2002— Rochester (Int'l)	0	0	...	27.00	9.00	1	0	0	0	...	0-...	.1	1	2	1	0	2-0	0	.333
—Bowie (East.)	5	3	.625	2.51	1.04	41	0	0	0	...	3-...	64.2	46	21	18	2	21-0	66	.198
—Baltimore (A.L.)	0	0	...	3.00	1.33	4	0	0	0	0	0-0	6.0	7	2	2	1	1-0	4	.304
2003— Ottawa (Int'l)	9	5	.643	3.39	1.28	19	19	0	0	...	0-...	114.0	112	49	43	7	34-2	107	.261
—Baltimore (A.L.)	3	6	.333	3.79	1.15	17	10	1	0	1	0-1	73.2	60	33	31	6	25-2	44	.222
Major League totals (2 years)	**3**	**6**	**.333**	**3.73**	**1.17**	**21**	**10**	**1**	**0**	**1**	**0-1**	**79.2**	**67**	**35**	**33**	**7**	**26-2**	**48**	**.229**

DUCHSCHERER, JUSTIN   P

PERSONAL: Born November 19, 1977, in Aberdeen, S.D. ... 6-3/190. ... Throws right, bats right. ... Full name: Justin Craig Duchscherer. ... Name pronounced: DUKE-sher. ... High school: Coronado (Lubbock, Texas).

TRANSACTIONS/CAREER NOTES: Selected by Boston Red Sox organization in eighth round of free-agent draft (June 4, 1996). ... Traded by Red Sox to Texas Rangers for C Doug Mirabelli (June 12, 2001). ... Traded by Rangers to Oakland Athletics for P Luis Vizcaino (March 18, 2002). ... On Sacramento disabled list (April 27-June 30 and August 5, 2002-remainder of season). ... Called up by Oakland from Sacramento (September 8, 2003).

CAREER HITTING: 0-for-0 (.000), 0 R, 0 2B, 0 3B, 0 HR, 0 RBI.

Year — League	W	L	Pct.	ERA	WHIP	G	GS	CG	ShO	Hld.	Sv.-Opp.	IP	H	R	ER	HR	BB-IBB	SO	Avg.
1996— GC Red Sox (GCL)	0	2	.000	3.13	1.21	13	8	0	0	...	1-...	54.2	52	26	19	0	14-0	45	.249
1997— GC Red Sox (GCL)	2	3	.400	1.81	1.14	10	8	0	0	...	0-...	44.2	34	18	9	0	17-0	59	.204
—Michigan (Midw.)	1	1	.500	5.63	1.50	4	4	0	0	...	0-...	24.0	26	17	15	1	10-0	19	.274
1998— Michigan (Midw.)	7	12	.368	4.79	1.49	30	26	0	0	...	0-...	142.2	166	87	76	9	47-3	106	.298
1999— Augusta (S. Atl.)	4	0	1.000	0.22	0.71	6	6	0	0	...	0-...	41.0	21	1	1	0	8-0	39	.148
—Sarasota (Fla. St.)	7	7	.500	4.49	1.17	20	18	0	0	...	0-...	112.1	101	62	56	14	30-0	105	.237
2000— Trenton (East.)	7	9	.438	3.39	1.18	24	24	2	2	...	0-...	143.1	134	59	54	7	35-1	126	.246
2001— Trenton (East.)	6	3	.667	2.44	0.86	12	12	1	1	...	0-...	73.2	49	25	20	6	14-1	69	.179
—Tulsa (Texas)	4	0	1.000	2.08	1.13	6	6	1	0	...	0-...	43.1	39	14	10	3	10-0	55	.242
—Texas (A.L.)	1	1	.500	12.27	1.91	5	2	0	0	0	0-0	14.2	24	20	20	5	4-0	11	.353
—Oklahoma (PCL)	3	3	.500	2.84	1.14	7	7	1	1	...	0-...	50.2	48	20	16	6	10-0	52	.255
2002— Sacramento (PCL)	2	4	.333	5.57	1.43	14	11	0	0	...	0-...	63.0	73	45	39	7	17-0	52	.283
2003— Sacramento (PCL)	14	2	.875	3.25	1.09	24	23	0	0	...	0-...	155.0	151	59	56	12	18-0	117	.254
—Oakland (A.L.)	1	1	.500	3.31	1.22	4	3	0	0	0	0-0	16.1	17	7	6	1	3-0	15	.262
Major League totals (2 years)	**2**	**2**	**.500**	**7.55**	**1.55**	**9**	**5**	**0**	**0**	**0**	**0-0**	**31.0**	**41**	**27**	**26**	**6**	**7-0**	**26**	**.308**

DUCKWORTH, BRANDON   P

PERSONAL: Born January 23, 1976, in Salt Lake City, Utah. ... 6-2/195. ... Throws right, bats right. ... Full name: Brandon J. Duckworth. ... High school: Kearns (Utah). ... College: Cal State Fullerton.

TRANSACTIONS/CAREER NOTES: Selected by Toronto Blue Jays organization in 30th round of free-agent draft (June 1, 1995); did not sign. ... Selected by Arizona Diamondbacks organization in 61st round of free-agent draft (June 4, 1996); did not sign. ... Signed by Philadelphia Phillies organization as non-drafted free agent (August 13, 1997). ... On Philadelphia disabled list (April 21, 2003); included rehabilitation assignment to Clearwater (April 6). ... Recalled by Philadelphia from Reading rehab assignment (April 20, 2003). ... Optioned to Scranton by Philadelphia (May 7, 2003). ... Recalled by Philadelphia from Scranton of the International League (May 17, 2003). ... Recalled by Philadelphia from Scranton (August 27, 2003). ... Optioned to Scranton by Philadelphia (August 31, 2003). ... Recalled by Philadelphia from Scranton (September 2, 2003).

CAREER HITTING: 19-for-97 (.196), 5 R, 2 2B, 0 3B, 0 HR, 7 RBI.

Year — League	W	L	Pct.	ERA	WHIP	G	GS	CG	ShO	Hld.	Sv.-Opp.	IP	H	R	ER	HR	BB-IBB	SO	Avg.
1998— Piedmont (S. Atl.)	9	8	.529	2.80	0.95	21	21	• 5	• 3	...	0-...	147.2	116	58	46	10	24-0	119	.215
—Clearwater (Fla. St.)	6	2	.750	3.74	1.62	9	9	1	1	...	0-...	53.0	64	25	22	2	22-0	46	.306
1999— Clearwater (Fla. St.)	11	5	.688	4.84	1.55	27	17	0	0	...	1-...	132.0	164	84	71	13	40-0	101	.301
2000— Reading (East.)	13	7	.650	3.16	1.19	27	27	1	0	...	0-...	165.0	145	70	58	17	52-0	* 178	.233
2001— Scran./W.B. (I.L.)	* 13	2	.867	2.63	1.07	22	20	2	1	...	0-...	147.0	122	46	43	14	36-2	150	.228
—Philadelphia (N.L.)	3	2	.600	3.52	1.25	11	11	0	0	0	0-0	69.0	57	29	27	2	29-5	40	.234
2002— Philadelphia (N.L.)	8	9	.471	5.41	1.45	30	29	0	0	0	0-...	163.0	167	103	98	26	69-5	167	.261
2003— Clearwater (Fla. St.)	0	0	...	1.00	0.56	2	2	0	0	...	0-...	9.0	3	1	1	1	2-0	11	.100
—Reading (East.)	0	0	...	4.50	0.50	1	1	0	0	...	0-...	2.0	1	1	1	1	0-0	2	.143
—Scran./W.B. (I.L.)	2	1	.667	3.38	1.34	3	3	0	0	...	0-...	18.2	21	11	7	3	4-0	14	.280
—Philadelphia (N.L.)	4	7	.364	4.94	1.53	24	18	0	0	0	0-0	93.0	98	58	51	12	44-3	68	.272
Major League totals (3 years)	**15**	**18**	**.455**	**4.87**	**1.43**	**65**	**58**	**0**	**0**	**0**	**0-0**	**325.0**	**322**	**190**	**176**	**40**	**142-13**	**275**	**.259**

DUNCAN, JEFF   OF

PERSONAL: Born December 9, 1978, in Harvey, Ill. ... 6-2/188. ... Bats left, throws left. ... Full name: Jeffrey Matthew Duncan. ... High school: Lemont (Ill.). ... College: Arizona State.

TRANSACTIONS/CAREER NOTES: Selected by New York Mets organization in seventh round of free-agent draft (June 5, 2000).

2003 GAMES PLAYED BY POSITION (MLB): OF—52.

Year— Team (League)	Pos.	G	AB	R	H	2B	3B	HR	RBI	BATTING BB	SO	HBP	GDP	SB-CS	Avg.	OBP	SLG	OPS	FIELDING E	Pct.
2000— Pittsfield (NYP)	OF	53	186	39	45	3	5	2	13	34	46	4	1	20-3	.242	.371	.344	.715	1	.990
2001— Capital City (SAL)	OF	88	318	49	69	16	8	3	23	46	97	3	2	41-3	.217	.320	.346	.666	6	.959
2002— St. Lucie (Fla. St.)	OF	29	102	20	35	5	0	2	10	24	15	1	4	10-1	.343	.472	.451	.923	2	.967
—Capital City (SAL)	OF	40	150	33	59	13	3	4	17	18	34	3	1	15-3	.393	.468	.600	1.068	4	.882
2003— Binghamton (East.)	OF	76	278	49	80	11	5	4	23	36	59	5	0	24-10	.288	.376	.406	.782	2	.987
—Norfolk (Int'l)	OF	4	15	2	4	1	0	2	4	1	7	0	0	1-0	.267	.313	.733	1.046	0	1.000
—New York (N.L.)	OF	56	139	13	27	0	2	1	10	17	41	2	1	4-2	.194	.291	.245	.536	0	1.000
Major League totals (1 year)		**56**	**139**	**13**	**27**	**0**	**2**	**1**	**10**	**17**	**41**	**2**	**1**	**4-2**	**.194**	**.291**	**.245**	**.536**	**0**	**1.000**

D

DUNN, ADAM — OF

PERSONAL: Born November 9, 1979, in Houston, Texas. ... 6-6/240. ... Bats left, throws right. ... Full name: Adam Troy Dunn. ... High school: New Caney (Texas).
TRANSACTIONS/CAREER NOTES: Selected by Cincinnati Reds organization in second round of free-agent draft (June 2, 1998). ... On Clinton disabled list (June 8-25, 2000). ... Suspended by Major League Baseball (June 20, 2003). ... Reinstated (June 22, 2003). ... Placed on 15-day disabled list (August 16, 2003).
2003 GAMES PLAYED BY POSITION (MLB): OF—102, 1B—19, DH—2.

									BATTING										FIELDING	
Year	Team (League)	Pos.	G	AB	R	H	2B	3B	HR	RBI	BB	SO	HBP	GDP	SB-CS	Avg.	OBP	SLG	OPS	E	Pct.
1998—	Billings (Pio.)	OF	34	125	26	36	3	1	4	13	22	33	3	3	4-2	.288	.404	.424	.828	6	.860
1999—	Rockford (Midwest)	OF	93	313	62	96	16	2	11	44	46	64	10	6	21-9	.307	.409	.476	.885	8	.918
2000—	Dayton (Midw.)	OF	122	420	101	118	29	1	16	79	100	101	12	10	24-5	.281 *	.428	.469	.897	9	.958
2001—	Chattanooga (Sou.)	OF	39	140	30	48	9	0	12	31	24	31	3	1	6-3	.343	.449	.664	1.113	3	.961
—	Louisville (Int'l)	OF	55	210	44	69	13	0	20	53	38	51	5	1	5-1	.329	.441	.676	1.117	5	.954
—	Cincinnati (N.L.)	OF	66	244	54	64	18	1	19	43	38	74	4	4	4-2	.262	.371	.578	.948	2	.986
2002—	Cincinnati (N.L.)	OF-1B-DH	158	535	84	133	28	2	26	71	128	170	9	8	19-9	.249	.400	.454	.854	15	.975
2003—	Cincinnati (N.L.)	OF-1B-DH	116	381	70	82	12	1	27	57	74	126	10	4	8-2	.215	.354	.465	.819	11	.965
	Major League totals (3 years)		340	1160	208	279	58	4	72	171	240	370	23	16	31-13	.241	.379	.484	.863	28	.974

DURAZO, ERUBIEL — 1B

PERSONAL: Born January 23, 1975, in Hermosillo, Mexico. ... 6-3/240. ... Bats left, throws left. ... Full name: Erubiel Durazo Cardenas Durazo. ... Name pronounced: eh-ROO-bee-el du-RAH-zo. ... High school: Amphitheater (Tucson, Ariz.). ... Junior college: Pima (Ari.) Community College.
TRANSACTIONS/CAREER NOTES: Signed by Monterrey, Mexican League (1997). ... Contract sold by Monterrey to Arizona Diamondbacks organization (December 16, 1998). ... On Arizona disabled list (May 30-June 24, June 27-July 13 and August 20, 2000-remainder of season); included rehabilitation assignments to Tucson (June 20-24 and July 8-9) and Arizona League Diamondbacks (July 9-13). ... On Arizona disabled list (August 15-September 1, 2001); included rehabilitation assignment to Tucson (August 28-September 1). ... On Arizona disabled list (March 22-May 16 and June 30-July 27, 2002); included rehabilitation assignments to Tucson (May 10-16) and El Paso (July 20-27). ... Traded by Diamondbacks to Oakland Athletics as part of four-team trade in which A's sent a player to be named later to Toronto Blue Jays, Blue Jays sent SS Felipe Lopez to Cincinnati Reds and Reds traded P Elmer Dessens and cash to Diamondbacks (December 15, 2002); Blue Jays acquired P Jason Arnold to complete deal (December 16, 2002).
2003 GAMES PLAYED BY POSITION (MLB): DH—121, 1B—33.

									BATTING										FIELDING	
Year	Team (League)	Pos.	G	AB	R	H	2B	3B	HR	RBI	BB	SO	HBP	GDP	SB-CS	Avg.	OBP	SLG	OPS	E	Pct.
1997—	Monterrey (Mex.)	1B-OF	110	358	47	101	21	10	8	61	52	43	...	...	3-7	.282	...	.464	...	3	.994
1998—	Monterrey (Mex.)	1B-OF	119	420	84	147	32	2	19	98	99	71	...	...	4-3	.350	...	.571	...	0	1.000
1999—	El Paso (Texas)	1B	64	226	53	91	18	3	14	55	44	37	2	5	2-1	.403	.498	.695	1.193	10	.982
—	Tucson (PCL)	1B-DH	30	118	27	48	7	0	10	28	14	18	1	0	1-0	.407	.470	.720	1.190	1	.996
—	Arizona (N.L.)	1B	52	155	31	51	4	2	11	30	26	43	1	1	1-1	.329	.422	.594	1.015	0	1.000
2000—	Arizona (N.L.)	1B	67	196	35	52	11	0	8	33	34	43	1	3	1-0	.265	.373	.444	.817	5	.989
—	Tucson (PCL)	1B	13	43	9	18	6	0	3	10	6	7	0	0	0-0	.419	.490	.767	1.257	3	.957
—	Ariz. D'backs (Ariz.)	1B	2	5	2	3	0	0	1	2	1	0	0	0	0-0	.600	.667	1.200	1.867	0	1.000
2001—	Arizona (N.L.)	1B-DH-OF	92	175	34	47	11	0	12	38	28	49	2	1	0-0	.269	.372	.537	.909	2	.993
—	Tucson (PCL)	1B	3	11	3	3	0	0	1	1	1	3	0	0	0-0	.273	.333	.545	.879	0	1.000
2002—	Arizona (N.L.)	1B-DH-OF	76	222	46	58	12	2	16	48	49	60	2	1	0-1	.261	.395	.500	.944	7	.984
—	El Paso (Texas)	1B	5	14	5	7	3	0	2	7	4	1	0	1	0-0	.500	.611	1.143	1.754	0	1.000
2003—	Oakland (A.L.)	DH-1B	154	537	92	139	29	0	21	77	100	105	2	11	1-1	.259	.374	.430	.804	6	.981
	American League totals (1 year)		154	537	92	139	29	0	21	77	100	105	2	11	1-1	.259	.374	.430	.804	6	.981
	National League totals (4 years)		287	748	146	208	38	4	47	149	137	195	6	6	2-2	.278	.390	.528	.918	14	.991
	Major League totals (5 years)		441	1285	238	347	67	4	68	226	237	300	8	17	3-7	.270	.383	.487	.870	20	.989

DURBIN, CHAD — P

PERSONAL: Born December 3, 1977, in Spring Valley, Ill. ... 6-2/200. ... Throws right, bats right. ... Full name: Chad Griffin Durbin. ... High school: Woodlawn (Shreveport, La.).
TRANSACTIONS/CAREER NOTES: Selected by Kansas City Royals organization in third round of free-agent draft (June 4, 1996). ... On Omaha disabled list (April 17-August 12, 2002). ... On Wichita disabled list (August 22, 2002-remainder of season). ... Granted free agency (December 21, 2002). ... Signed by Cleveland Indians as free agent; contract purchased by Cleveland (September 1, 2003).
CAREER HITTING: 0-for-1 (.000), 0 R, 0 2B, 0 3B, 0 HR, 0 RBI.

Year	League	W	L	Pct.	ERA	WHIP	G	GS	CG	ShO	Hld.	Sv.-Opp.	IP	H	R	ER	HR	BB-IBB	SO	Avg.
1996—	GC Royals (GCL)	3	1	.600	4.26	1.33	11	8	1	1	...	0-...	44.1	34	22	21	3	25-0	43	.213
1997—	Lansing (Midw.)	5	8	.385	4.79	1.45	26	26	0	0	...	0-...	144.2	157	85	77	15	53-0	116	.277
1998—	Wilmington (Caro.)	10	7	.588	2.93	1.25	26	26	0	0	...	0-...	147.2	126	57	48	10	59-3	162	.231
1999—	Wichita (Texas)	8	10	.444	4.64	1.29	28	27	1	• 1	...	0-...	157.0	154	88	81	20	49-1	122	.258
—	Kansas City (A.L.)	0	0		0.00	0.86	1	0	0	0	0	0-0	2.1	1	0	0	0	1-0	3	.125
2000—	Kansas City (A.L.)	2	5	.286	8.21	1.85	16	16	0	0	0	0-...	72.1	91	71	66	14	43-1	37	.301
—	Omaha (PCL)	4	4	.500	4.46	1.33	12	12	0	0	0	0-...	72.2	75	37	36	10	22-0	53	.269
2001—	Omaha (PCL)	2	2	.500	3.33	1.04	5	5	0	0	0	0-...	27.0	22	11	10	4	6-0	35	.216
—	Kansas City (A.L.)	9	16	.360	4.93	1.45	29	29	0	0	0	0-0	179.0	201	109	98	26	58-0	95	.288
2002—	Kansas City (A.L.)	0	1	.000	11.88	2.04	2	2	0	0	0	0-...	8.1	13	11	11	3	4-0	5	.342
—	Omaha (PCL)	0	1	.000	10.80	2.40	1	1	0	0	0	0-...	1.2	4	2	2	0	0-0	2	.444
—	GC Royals (GCL)	0	0		0.00	0.83	3	3	0	0	0	0-...	6.0	4	0	0	0	0-0	5	.200
—	Wichita (Texas)	0	0		5.06	1.69	3	1	0	0	0	0-...	5.1	5	4	3	1	4-0	6	.238
2003—	Mahoning Valley (NY-P)	1	1	.500	2.25	1.00	2	2	0	0	0	0-...	12.0	9	4	3	1	3-0	8	.220
—	Akron (East.)	2	0	1.000	1.50	0.67	3	3	0	0	0	0-...	12.0	7	2	2	1	1-0	11	.163
—	Buffalo (Int'l)	3	6	.333	4.60	1.14	10	10	1	0	0	0-...	58.2	51	30	30	9	16-0	64	.233
—	Cleveland (A.L.)	0	1	.000	7.27	2.42	3	1	0	0	0	0-0	8.2	18	12	7	2	3-0	8	.429
	Major League totals (5 years)	11	23	.324	6.05	1.60	51	48	2	0	0	0-0	270.2	324	203	182	45	109-1	148	.298

DURHAM, RAY — 2B

PERSONAL: Born November 30, 1971, in Charlotte, N.C. ... 5-8/180. ... Bats both, throws right. ... High school: Harding (Charlotte).
TRANSACTIONS/CAREER NOTES: Selected by Chicago White Sox organization in fifth round of free-agent draft (June 4, 1990). ... On Utica suspended list (April 1-May 22, 1992). ... On Sarasota disabled list (June 16-July 9, 1992). ... Traded by White Sox to Oakland Athletics for P Jon Adkins (July 25, 2002). ... Granted free agency (November 1, 2002). ... Signed by San Francisco Giants (December 7, 2002). ... Placed on 15-day disabled list by San Francisco (May 11, 2003). ... Activated from the 15-day disabled list (May 26, 2003). ... Placed on 15-day disabled list (August 7, 2003). ... Removed from 15-day disabled list (September 1, 2003).
2003 GAMES PLAYED BY POSITION (MLB): 2B—105.

									BATTING										FIELDING	
Year	Team (League)	Pos.	G	AB	R	H	2B	3B	HR	RBI	BB	SO	HBP	GDP	SB-CS	Avg.	OBP	SLG	OPS	E	Pct.
1990—	GC Whi. Sox (GCL)	2B-SS	35	116	18	32	3	3	0	13	15	36	4	0	23-9	.276	.375	.353	.728	15	.907
1991—	Utica (N.Y.-Penn)	2B	39	142	29	36	2	7	0	17	25	44	2	0	12-1	.254	.371	.366	.737	12	.928
—	GC Whi. Sox (GCL)	2B	6	23	3	7	1	0	0	4	3	5	0	0	5-1	.304	.385	.348	.732	0	1.000
1992—	Sarasota (Fla. St.)	2B	57	202	37	55	6	3	0	7	32	36	10	2	28-8	.272	.398	.332	.729	10	.945
—	GC Whi. Sox (GCL)	2B	5	13	3	7	2	0	0	2	3	1	0	0	1-0	.538	.625	.692	1.317	0	1.000
1993—	Birmingham (Sou.)	2B	137	528	83	143	22 *	10	3	37	42	100	14	5	39-* 25	.271	.338	.367	.705	* 30	.945

D

Year	Team (League)	Pos.	G	AB	R	H	2B	3B	HR	RBI	BB	SO	HBP	GDP	SB-CS	Avg.	OBP	SLG	OPS	E	Pct.
1994—Nashville (A.A.)	2B	133	527	89	156	33	•12	16	66	46	91	12	5	34-11	.296	.363	.495	.859	*19	.973
1995—Chicago (A.L.)	2B-DH	125	471	68	121	27	6	7	51	31	83	6	8	18-5	.257	.309	.384	.693	15	.973
1996—Chicago (A.L.)	2B-DH	156	557	79	153	33	5	10	65	58	95	10	6	30-4	.275	.350	.406	.755	11	.984
1997—Chicago (A.L.)	2B-DH	155	634	106	172	27	5	11	53	61	96	6	14	33-16	.271	.337	.382	.719	*18	.974
1998—Chicago (A.L.)	2B	158	635	126	181	35	8	19	67	73	105	6	5	36-9	.285	.363	.455	.818	18	.976
1999—Chicago (A.L.)	2B-DH	153	612	109	181	30	8	13	60	73	105	4	9	34-11	.296	.373	.435	.808	19	.974
2000—Chicago (A.L.)	2B	151	614	121	172	35	9	17	75	75	105	7	13	25-13	.280	.361	.450	.810	15	.980
2001—Chicago (A.L.)	2B-DH	152	611	104	163	42	10	20	65	64	110	4	10	23-10	.267	.337	.466	.804	10	.986
2002—Chicago (A.L.)	2B	96	345	71	103	20	2	9	48	49	59	5	13	20-5	.299	.390	.446	.836	15	.968
—Oakland (A.L.)	DH-2B	54	219	43	60	14	4	6	22	24	34	2	2	6-2	.274	.350	.457	.806	2	.967
2003—San Francisco (N.L.)	2B	110	410	61	117	30	5	8	33	50	82	3	4	7-7	.285	.366	.441	.807	5	.990
American League totals (8 years)		1200	4698	827	1306	263	57	112	506	508	792	50	80	225-75	.278	.352	.430	.782	123	.977
National League totals (1 year)		110	410	61	117	30	5	8	33	50	82	3	4	7-7	.285	.366	.441	.807	5	.990
Major League totals (9 years)		1310	5108	888	1423	293	62	120	539	558	874	53	84	232-82	.279	.353	.431	.784	128	.978

DUROCHER, JAYSON   P

PERSONAL: Born August 18, 1974, in Hartford, Conn. ... 6-3/229. ... Throws right, bats right. ... Full name: Jayson Paul Durocher. ... Name pronounced: der-o-sher. ... High school: Horizon (Scottsdale, Ariz.).

TRANSACTIONS/CAREER NOTES: Selected by Montreal Expos organization in ninth round of free-agent draft (June 3, 1993). ... Selected by Chicago White Sox from Expos organization in Rule 5 major league draft (December 9, 1996). ... Returned by White Sox to Expos organization (March 31, 1997). ... On disabled list (April 3-20, 1997). ... On Harrisburg disabled list (April 3-May 21, 1998). ... Granted free agency (October 15, 1999). ... Signed by San Diego Padres organization (November 22, 1999). ... Granted free agency (October 18, 2000). ... Signed by Texas Rangers organization (November 13, 2000). ... On disabled list (July 4-15, 2001). ... Granted free agency (October 15, 2001). ... Signed by Milwaukee Brewers organization (November 20, 2001). ... On Indianapolis disabled list (May 23-30, 2002). ... On disabled list (March 21, 2003). ... Sent on rehab assignment to Indianapolis by Milwaukee (May 13, 2003). ... Activated from the 15-day disabled list by Milwaukee (May 27, 2003). ... Placed on 15-day disabled list (June 14, 2003). ... Recalled from Indianapolis on rehab assignment by Milwaukee (August 18, 2003). ... Reinstated from 15-day disabled list (September 29, 2003).

CAREER HITTING: 0-for-2 (.000), 0 R, 0 2B, 0 3B, 0 HR, 0 RBI.

Year	League	W	L	Pct.	ERA	WHIP	G	GS	CG	ShO	Hld.	Sv.-Opp.	IP	H	R	ER	HR	BB-IBB	SO	Avg.
1993—GC Expos (GCL)	2	3	.400	3.46	1.15	7	7	3	2	...	0-...	39.0	32	23	15	0	13-0	21	.242
1994—Vermont (NY-P)	•9	2	.818	3.09	1.37	15	•15	•3	1	...	0-...	•99.0	92	40	34	0	44-1	74	.247
1995—Albany (S. Atl.)	3	7	.300	3.91	1.32	24	22	1	0	...	0-...	122.0	105	67	53	5	56-1	88	.234
1996—W.P. Beach (FSL)	7	6	.538	3.34	1.25	23	23	1	1	...	0-...	129.1	118	65	48	5	44-0	101	.236
1997—W.P. Beach (FSL)	6	4	.600	3.83	1.41	25	17	0	0	...	0-...	87.0	84	58	37	6	39-0	71	.250
1998—Jupiter (FSL)	2	1	.667	4.21	1.51	23	0	0	0	...	5-...	36.1	47	21	17	3	8-0	27	.313
—Harrisburg (Eastern)	0	1	.000	3.97	1.41	10	0	0	0	...	1-...	11.1	10	8	5	0	6-0	12	.250
1999—Harrisburg (Eastern)	1	3	.250	3.48	1.33	29	1	0	0	...	4-...	51.2	44	29	20	5	25-1	36	.233
—Ottawa (Int'l)	1	3	.250	1.51	1.04	17	0	0	0	...	4-...	35.2	17	12	6	2	20-2	22	.140
2000—Las Vegas (PCL)	3	5	.375	4.95	1.73	31	0	0	0	...	7-...	40.0	44	25	22	2	25-3	38	.284
—Mobile (Sou.)	1	1	.500	2.08	1.25	27	0	0	0	...	14-...	30.1	26	7	7	4	12-1	43	.228
2001—Tulsa (Texas)	0	0	...	0.00	0.82	3	0	0	0	...	0-...	3.2	0	0	0	0	3-0	4	.000
—Oklahoma (PCL)	4	1	.800	4.99	1.44	31	0	0	0	...	6-...	39.2	34	25	22	5	23-1	52	.231
2002—Indianapolis (Int'l)	1	0	1.000	2.73	1.29	20	0	0	0	...	6-...	26.1	19	9	8	3	15-0	39	.194
—Milwaukee (N.L.)	1	1	.500	1.88	1.00	39	0	0	0	3	0-1	48.0	27	13	10	3	21-2	44	.164
2003—Milwaukee (N.L.)	2	0	1.000	11.05	1.50	6	0	0	0	0	0-0	7.1	9	9	9	4	2-0	7	.300
—Ariz. Brewers (Ariz.)	0	0	...	0.00	0.00	2	2	0	0	0	0-...	2.0	0	0	0	0	0-0	3	.000
—Indianapolis (Int'l)	0	0	...	2.57	1.14	7	3	0	0	0	0-...	7.0	7	2	2	0	1-0	9	.241
Major League totals (2 years)		3	1	.750	3.09	1.07	45	0	0	0	3	0-1	55.1	36	22	19	7	23-2	51	.185

DURRINGTON, TRENT   2B

PERSONAL: Born August 27, 1975, in Sydney, Australia. ... 5-10/188. ... Bats right, throws right. ... Full name: Trent John Durrington. ... High school: The Southport School (Australia).

TRANSACTIONS/CAREER NOTES: Signed as non-drafted free agent by California Angels organization (April 22, 1994). ... Angels franchise renamed Anaheim Angels for 1997 season. ... On Edmonton disabled list (May 25-August 29, 2000). ... Released by Angels (August 29, 2000). ... Granted free agency (October 15, 2002). ... Signed by Anaheim Angels; contract purchased by Anaheim (August 20, 2003).

2003 GAMES PLAYED BY POSITION (MLB): 2B—5, 3B—4, DH—2, OF—1.

Year	Team (League)	Pos.	G	AB	R	H	2B	3B	HR	RBI	BB	SO	HBP	GDP	SB-CS	Avg.	OBP	SLG	OPS	E	Pct.
1994—Ariz. Angels (Ariz.)	2B-SS	16	52	13	14	3	0	1	2	11	16	1	1	5-1	.269	.406	.385	.791	5	.907
1995—Boise (NW)	2B-SS	50	140	23	24	4	1	3	19	17	35	2	4	2-0	.171	.267	.279	.546	8	.959
1996—Boise (NW)	2B-3B-SS	40	154	38	43	7	2	1	19	31	32	13	4	•24-5	.279	.439	.351	.790	12	.946
—Cedar Rap. (Midw.)	2B	25	76	12	19	1	0	0	4	33	20	2	2	15-2	.250	.482	.263	.745	3	.969
1997—Lake Elsinore (Calif.)	2B-3B-OF	123	409	80	101	21	3	3	36	51	90	11	8	52-18	.247	.344	.335	.679	17	.969
1998—Midland (Texas)		112	351	62	79	10	1	1	30	50	74	17	5	24-12	.225	.346	.268	.614	13	.971
1999—Erie (East.)	2B	107	396	84	114	26	1	3	34	52	66	9	4	59-16	.288	.379	.381	.760	14	.974
—Anaheim (A.L.)	2B-DH	43	122	14	22	2	0	0	2	9	28	0	1	4-3	.180	.237	.197	.433	6	.966
2000—Edmonton (PCL)	2B-SS	28	105	19	23	4	1	3	14	16	25	1	3	8-6	.219	.325	.362	.687	2	.986
—Anaheim (A.L.)	2B	4	3	0	0	0	0	0	0	0	0	0	1	0-0	.000	.000	.000	.000	0	1.000
2001—Salt Lake (PCL)	2-OF-3-S	39	122	20	40	11	4	3	21	11	24	2	3	7-4	.328	.387	.557	.944	4	.960
—Arkansas (Texas)	2-SS-3-OF	51	182	37	53	12	0	10	35	26	47	7	2	22-2	.291	.398	.522	.920	10	.949
—Las Vegas (PCL)	2B	22	55	10	12	4	1	1	2	8	19	1	0	3-1	.218	.328	.382	.710	2	.973
2002—Arkansas (Texas)	C-2-O-3-S	107	382	59	94	18	4	9	47	39	71	11	3	25-14	.246	.328	.385	.713	14	.969
—Salt Lake (PCL)	OF-2-3-C	19	68	6	14	3	1	3	10	3	15	2	4	2-1	.206	.260	.412	.672	1	.984
2003—Salt Lake (PCL)	2-3-1-D-O-C	117	447	81	136	27	5	7	54	61	75	6	6	35-8	.304	.390	.434	.824	10	.980
—Anaheim (A.L.)	2-3-D-O	12	14	5	2	0	0	0	1	3	0	0	0	1-1	.143	.294	.143	.437	0	1.000
Major League totals (3 years)		59	139	19	24	2	0	0	3	12	28	0	2	5-4	.173	.238	.187	.425	6	.968

DYE, JERMAINE   OF

PERSONAL: Born January 28, 1974, in Vacaville, Calif. ... 6-5/220. ... Bats right, throws right. ... Full name: Jermaine Terrell Dye. ... Name pronounced: ger-MAIN. ... High school: Will C. Wood (Vacaville, Calif.). ... Junior college: Consumnes River (Calif.) Community College.

TRANSACTIONS/CAREER NOTES: Selected by Atlanta Braves organization in 17th round of free-agent draft (June 3, 1993). ... On disabled list (July 13-August 9, 1995). ... Traded by Braves with P Jamie Walker to Kansas City Royals for OF Michael Tucker and IF Keith Lockhart (March 27, 1997). ... On Kansas City disabled list (April 17-May 3, 1997); included rehabilitation assignment to Omaha (May 1-3). ... On Kansas City disabled list (July 10-August 13, 1997); included rehabilitation assignment to Omaha (July 27-August 13). ... On Kansas City disabled list (March 23-May 8 and September 1, 1998-remainder of season); included rehabilitation assignment to Omaha (April 21-May 8). ... Traded by Royals to Colorado Rockies for SS Neifi Perez (July 25, 2001). ... Traded by Rockies to Oakland Athletics for OF Mario Encarnacion, 2B/SS Jose Ortiz and P Todd Belitz (July 25, 2001). ... On Oakland disabled list (March 22-April 26, 2002); included rehabilitation assignments to Sacramento (April 16-23) and Modesto (April 23-26). ... Placed on the 15-day disabled list by Oakland (April 25, 2003). ... Sent to Sacramento on rehab assignment by Oakland (May 25, 2003). ... Recalled by Oakland from Sacramento; reinstated from 15-day disabled list (May 30, 2003). ... Placed on 15-day disabled list, retroactive to July 7 (July 8, 2003). ... Sent on minor league rehab assignment by Oakland (August 24, 2003). ... Recalled from minor league rehab assignment; removed from 15-day disabled list (September 1, 2003).

2003 GAMES PLAYED BY POSITION (MLB): OF—61, DH—3.

Year	Team (League)	Pos.	G	AB	R	H	2B	3B	HR	RBI	BB	SO	HBP	GDP	SB-CS	Avg.	OBP	SLG	OPS	E	Pct.
1993—GC Braves (GCL)	3B-OF	31	124	17	43	14	0	0	27	5	13	5	5	5-0	.347	.393	.460	.852	3	.948
—Danville (Appal.)	OF	25	94	6	26	6	1	2	12	8	10	0	2	19-1	.277	.327	.426	.752	2	.963
1994—Macon (S. Atl.)	OF	135	506	73	151	*41	1	15	98	33	82	8	10	19-10	.298	.346	.472	.818	9	.969
1995—Greenville (Sou.)	OF	104	403	50	115	26	4	15	71	27	74	1	9	4-8	.285	.329	.481	.810	5	.981
1996—Richmond (Int'l)	OF	36	142	25	33	7	1	6	19	5	25	1	3	3-0	.232	.264	.423	.686	4	.955
—Atlanta (N.L.)	OF	98	292	32	82	16	0	12	37	8	67	3	11	1-4	.281	.304	.459	.763	8	.950
1997—Kansas City (A.L.)	OF	75	263	26	62	14	0	7	22	17	51	1	6	2-1	.236	.284	.369	.653	6	.966
—Omaha (A.A.)	OF-DH	39	144	21	44	6	0	10	25	9	25	1	3	0-2	.306	.348	.556	.904	0	1.000
1998—Omaha (PCL)	OF-1B-DH	41	157	29	47	6	0	12	35	19	29	1	8	7-0	.299	.374	.567	.941	1	.992
—Kansas City (A.L.)	OF	60	214	24	50	5	1	5	23	11	46	1	8	2-2	.234	.270	.336	.606	2	.987
1999—Kansas City (A.L.)	OF-DH	158	608	96	179	44	8	27	119	58	119	1	17	2-3	.294	.354	.526	.880	6	.984
2000—Kansas City (A.L.)	OF-DH	157	601	107	193	41	2	33	118	69	99	3	12	0-1	.321	.390	.561	.951	7	.976
2001—Kansas City (A.L.)	OF-DH	97	367	50	100	14	0	13	47	30	68	6	2	7-1	.272	.333	.417	.749	3	.984
—Oakland (A.L.)	OF	61	232	41	69	17	1	13	59	27	44	1	6	2-0	.297	.366	.547	.913	3	.971
2002—Sacramento (PCL)	DH	4	16	3	3	2	0	0	1	2	2	0	1	0-0	.188	.278	.313	.590	...	...
—Modesto (Calif.)	OF	2	8	1	4	3	0	0	2	0	0	0	0	0-0	.500	.500	.875	1.375	0	1.000
—Oakland (A.L.)	OF-DH	131	488	74	123	27	1	24	86	52	108	10	15	2-0	.252	.333	.459	.792	5	.972
2003—Sacramento (PCL)	DH-OF	13	49	9	14	2	0	2	9	11	11	0	1	0-0	.286	.417	.449	.866	0	1.000
—Oakland (A.L.)	OF-DH	65	221	28	38	6	0	4	20	25	42	3	11	1-0	.172	.261	.253	.514	0	1.000
American League totals (7 years)		804	2994	446	814	168	13	126	494	289	577	26	77	18-8	.272	.337	.463	.800	32	.980
National League totals (1 year)		98	292	32	82	16	0	12	37	8	67	3	11	1-4	.281	.304	.459	.763	8	.950
Major League totals (8 years)		902	3286	478	896	184	13	138	531	297	644	29	88	19-12	.273	.335	.463	.797	40	.977

EASLEY, DAMION — 2B

PERSONAL: Born November 11, 1969, in New York, N.Y. ... 5-11/190. ... Bats right, throws right. ... Full name: Jacinto Damion Easley. ... High school: Lakewood (Calif.). ... Junior college: Long Beach (Calif.) Community College.

TRANSACTIONS/CAREER NOTES: Selected by California Angels organization in 30th round of free-agent draft (June 1, 1988). ... On disabled list (June 19-July 4 and July 28, 1993-remainder of season; and May 30-June 17, 1994). ... On California disabled list (April 1-May 10, 1996); included rehabilitation assignment to Vancouver (April 30-May 10). ... Traded by Angels to Detroit Tigers for P Greg Gohr (July 31, 1996). ... On Detroit disabled list (April 10-25 and May 9-June 2, 2000); included rehabilitation assignments to Toledo (April 24-25 and May 29-June 2). ... On Detroit disabled list (April 17-June 1, 2002) included rehabilitation assignment to Toledo (May 23-June 1). ... Released by Tigers (March 28, 2003). ... Signed by Tampa Bay Devil Rays (April 2, 2003). ... Given unconditional release (June 4, 2003).

2003 GAMES PLAYED BY POSITION (MLB): 3B—23, DH—8, 2B—4.

Year	Team (League)	Pos.	G	AB	R	H	2B	3B	HR	RBI	BB	SO	HBP	GDP	SB-CS	Avg.	OBP	SLG	OPS	E	Pct.
1989—Bend (NW)	2B	36	131	34	39	5	1	4	21	25	21	4	1	9-4	.298	.425	.443	.868	22	.863
1990—Quad City (Midw.)	SS	103	365	59	100	19	3	10	56	41	60	8	8	25-8	.274	.358	.425	.783	41	.893
1991—Midland (Texas)	SS	127	452	73	115	24	5	6	57	58	67	7	12	23-9	.254	.347	.369	.716	*47	.924
1992—Edmonton (PCL)	SS-3B	108	429	61	124	18	3	3	44	31	44	5	13	26-10	.289	.340	.366	.706	30	.943
—California (A.L.)	3B-SS	47	151	14	39	5	0	1	12	8	26	3	2	9-5	.258	.307	.311	.618	5	.964
1993—California (A.L.)	2B-3B-DH	73	230	33	72	13	2	2	22	28	35	3	5	6-6	.313	.392	.413	.805	6	.978
1994—California (A.L.)	3B-2B	88	316	41	68	16	1	6	30	29	48	4	8	4-5	.215	.288	.329	.617	7	.977
1995—California (A.L.)	2B-SS	114	357	35	77	14	2	4	35	32	47	6	11	5-2	.216	.288	.300	.588	10	.979
1996—Vancouver (PCL)	SS-2B-3B	12	48	13	15	2	1	2	8	9	6	1	0	4-1	.313	.424	.521	.945	2	.958
—Midland (Texas)	3B-SS	4	14	1	6	2	0	0	2	0	0	0	0	1-0	.429	.429	.571	1.000	1	.944
—California (A.L.)	S-2-3-D-O	28	45	4	7	1	0	2	7	6	12	0	0	0-0	.156	.255	.311	.566	3	.954
—Detroit (A.L.)	2-SS-3-D	21	67	10	23	1	0	2	10	4	13	1	0	3-1	.343	.384	.448	.831	3	.958
1997—Detroit (A.L.)	2B-SS-DH	151	527	97	139	37	3	22	72	68	102	16	18	28-13	.264	.362	.471	.833	12	.982
1998—Detroit (A.L.)	2B-SS-DH	153	594	84	161	38	2	27	100	39	112	16	8	15-5	.271	.332	.478	.810	12	.985
1999—Detroit (A.L.)	2B-SS	151	549	83	146	30	1	20	65	51	124	19	15	11-3	.266	.346	.434	.779	8	.990
2000—Detroit (A.L.)	2B	126	464	76	120	27	2	14	58	55	79	11	11	13-4	.259	.350	.416	.766	6	.990
—Toledo (Int'l)	2B	4	13	3	3	1	0	1	4	4	2	2	0	0-0	.231	.474	.538	1.012	0	1.000
2001—Detroit (A.L.)	2B-SS	154	585	77	146	27	7	11	65	52	90	13	10	10-5	.250	.323	.376	.699	14	.982
2002—Detroit (A.L.)	2B-DH	85	304	29	68	14	1	8	30	27	43	11	4	1-3	.224	.307	.355	.663	9	.980
—Toledo (Int'l)	2B	8	26	5	3	1	0	0	0	5	0	1	1	0-2	.115	.281	.154	.435	2	.949
2003—Tampa Bay (A.L.)	3B-DH-2B	36	107	8	20	3	1	1	7	2	18	0	3	0-0	.187	.202	.262	.464	4	.935
Major League totals (12 years)		1227	4296	591	1086	226	22	120	513	401	749	103	95	105-52	.253	.329	.399	.729	99	.982

EATON, ADAM — P

PERSONAL: Born November 23, 1977, in Seattle, Wash. ... 6-2/190. ... Throws right, bats right. ... Full name: Adam Thomas Eaton. ... High school: Snohomish (Wash.).

TRANSACTIONS/CAREER NOTES: Selected by Philadelphia Phillies organization in first round (11th pick overall) of free-agent draft (June 4, 1996). ... Traded by Phillies with P Carlton Loewer and P Steve Montgomery to San Diego Padres for P Andy Ashby (November 10, 1999). ... On disabled list (July 6, 2001-remainder of season). ... On San Diego disabled list (March 27-September 1, 2002); included rehabilitation assignments to Lake Elsinore (August 7-21) and Portland (August 22-29). ... Placed on 15-day disabled list (May 5, 2003). ... Reinstated from the 15-day disabled list (May 20, 2003).

CAREER HITTING: 27-for-141 (.191), 13 R, 6 2B, 0 3B, 2 HR, 9 RBI.

Year	League	W	L	Pct.	ERA	WHIP	G	GS	CG	ShO	Hld.	Sv.-Opp.	IP	H	R	ER	HR	BB-IBB	SO	Avg.
1997—Piedmont (S. Atl.)	5	6	.455	4.16	1.56	14	14	0	0	...	0-...	71.1	81	38	33	2	30-0	57	.287
1998—Clearwater (Fla. St.)	9	8	.529	4.44	1.51	24	23	1	0	...	0-...	131.2	152	68	65	9	47-1	89	.293
1999—Clearwater (Fla. St.)	5	5	.500	3.91	1.52	13	13	0	0	...	0-...	69.0	81	39	30	2	24-0	50	.293
—Reading (East.)	5	4	.556	2.92	1.14	12	12	2	0	...	0-...	77.0	60	30	25	9	28-1	67	.214
—Scran./W.B. (I.L.)	1	1	.500	3.00	1.10	3	3	0	0	...	0-...	21.0	17	10	7	1	6-0	10	.224
2000—Mobile (Sou.)	4	1	.800	2.68	1.14	10	10	1	1	...	0-...	57.0	47	20	17	3	18-0	58	.219
—San Diego (N.L.)	7	4	.636	4.13	1.44	22	22	0	0	0	0-0	135.0	134	63	62	14	61-3	90	.260
2001—San Diego (N.L.)	8	5	.615	4.27	1.27	17	17	2	0	0	0-0	116.2	108	61	56	20	40-3	109	.241
2002—Lake Elsinore (Calif.)	0	0	...	2.70	0.98	3	3	0	0	...	0-...	13.1	10	7	4	0	3-0	19	.196
—Portland (PCL)	1	1	.500	2.92	0.97	2	2	0	0	...	0-...	12.1	9	9	4	3	3-0	6	.200
—San Diego (N.L.)	1	1	.500	5.40	1.35	6	6	0	0	0	0-0	33.1	38	20	20	5	17-0	25	.235
2003—San Diego (N.L.)	9	12	.429	4.08	1.32	31	31	1	0	0	0-0	183.0	173	91	83	20	68-6	146	.246
Major League totals (4 years)	25	22	.532	4.25	1.34	76	76	3	0	0	0-0	468.0	443	235	221	59	186-12	370	.248

ECKENSTAHLER, ERIC   P

PERSONAL: Born December 17, 1976, in Waukegan, Ill. ... 6-7/220. ... Throws left, bats left. ... Full name: Eric Ryan Eckenstahler. ... High school: Antioch (Lindenhurst, Ill.). ... College: Illinois State.

TRANSACTIONS/CAREER NOTES: Selected by Houston Astros organization in 35th round of free-agent draft (June 1, 1995); did not sign. ... Selected by New York Yankees organization in 36th round of free-agent draft (June 2, 1998); did not sign. ... Selected by Detroit Tigers organization in 32nd round of free-agent draft (June 2, 1999). ... Recalled from Toledo (July 26, 2003). ... Optioned to Toledo (August 24, 2003). ... Recalled from Toledo (September 2, 2003).

CAREER HITTING: 0-for-0 (.000), 0 R, 0 2B, 0 3B, 0 HR, 0 RBI.

Year League	W	L	Pct.	ERA	WHIP	G	GS	CG	ShO	Hld.	Sv.-Opp.	IP	H	R	ER	HR	BB-IBB	SO	Avg.
2000— West. Mich. (Mid.)	0	2	.000	5.79	1.71	10	3	0	0	...	1-...	18.2	21	15	12	4	11-0	22	.280
— Oneonta (N.Y.-Penn)	0	0	...	1.64	0.91	8	0	0	0	...	0-...	11.0	7	3	2	0	3-0	13	.175
2001— Lakeland (Fla. St.)	1	0	1.000	1.50	0.83	4	0	0	0	...	1-...	6.0	3	1	1	0	2-0	7	.158
— Erie (East.)	4	2	.667	3.90	1.48	46	0	0	0	...	4-...	64.2	65	32	28	7	31-4	73	.257
2002— Toledo (Int'l)	2	4	.333	4.43	1.37	52	0	0	0	...	0-...	67.0	57	37	33	8	35-1	69	.234
— Detroit (A.L.)	1	0	1.000	5.63	2.00	7	0	0	0	0	0-0	8.0	14	5	5	1	2-0	13	.378
2003— Toledo (Int'l)	3	6	.333	3.16	1.34	39	0	0	0	...	0-...	42.2	32	21	15	2	25-3	40	.213
— Detroit (A.L.)	0	0	...	2.87	1.53	20	0	0	0	4	0-0	15.2	9	6	5	0	15-1	12	.167
Major League totals (2 years)	1	0	1.000	3.80	1.69	27	0	0	0	4	0-0	23.2	23	11	10	1	17-1	25	.253

ECKSTEIN, DAVID   SS

PERSONAL: Born January 20, 1975, in Sanford, Fla. ... 5-7/165. ... Bats right, throws right. ... Full name: David Mark Eckstein. ... Name pronounced: eck-STYNE. ... High school: Seminole (Sanford, Fla.). ... College: Florida.

TRANSACTIONS/CAREER NOTES: Selected by Boston Red Sox organization in 19th round of free-agent draft (June 3, 1997). ... Claimed on waivers by Anaheim Angels (August 16, 2000). ... Placed on 15-day disabled list by Anaheim (August 20, 2003). ... Removed from 15-day disabled list (September 9, 2003).

2003 GAMES PLAYED BY POSITION (MLB): SS—116, DH—3.

Year Team (League)	Pos.	G	AB	R	H	2B	3B	HR	RBI	BB	SO	HBP	GDP	SB-CS	Avg.	OBP	SLG	OPS	E	Pct.
1997— Lowell (NY-Penn)	2B	68	249	43	75	11	4	4	39	33	29	12	2	21-5	.301	.407	.426	.832	9	.971
1998— Sarasota (Fla. St.)	2B-SS	135	503	99	154	29	4	3	58	87	51	22	8	45-16	.306	.428	.398	.826	8	.986
1999— Trenton (East.)	2B	131	483	109	151	22	5	6	52	89	48	25	6	32-13	.313	.440	.416	.856	9	.985
2000— Pawtucket (Int'l)	2B-SS	119	422	77	104	20	0	1	31	60	45	20	8	11-8	.246	.364	.301	.665	4	.992
— Edmonton (PCL)	2B	15	52	17	18	8	0	3	8	9	1	5	0	5-3	.346	.485	.673	1.158	0	1.000
2001— Anaheim (A.L.)	SS-2B-DH	153	582	82	166	26	2	4	41	43	60	*21	11	29-4	.285	.355	.357	.712	18	.969
2002— Anaheim (A.L.)	SS-DH	152	608	107	178	22	6	8	63	45	44	*27	11	21-13	.293	.363	.388	.752	14	.977
2003— Anaheim (A.L.)	SS-DH	120	452	59	114	22	1	3	31	36	45	15	9	16-5	.252	.325	.325	.651	8	.984
Major League totals (3 years)		425	1642	248	458	70	9	15	135	124	149	63	27	66-22	.279	.350	.360	.710	40	.976

EDMONDS, JIM   OF

PERSONAL: Born June 27, 1970, in Fullerton, Calif. ... 6-1/212. ... Bats left, throws left. ... Full name: James Patrick Edmonds. ... Name pronounced: ED-muns. ... High school: Diamond Bar (Calif.).

TRANSACTIONS/CAREER NOTES: Selected by California Angels organization in seventh round of free-agent draft (June 1, 1988). ... On disabled list (June 19-September 2, 1989; April 10-May 7 and May 23, 1991-remainder of season). ... On Vancouver disabled list (June 29-July 19, 1993). ... On California disabled list (May 26-June 10 and June 12-July 18, 1996); included rehabilitation assignment to Lake Elsinore (July 13-18). ... Angels franchise renamed Anaheim Angels for 1997 season. ... On disabled list (August 1-16, 1997). ... On Anaheim disabled list (March 30-August 2, 1999): included rehabilitation assignment to Lake Elsinore (July 26-August 2). ... Traded by Angels to St. Louis Cardinals for 2B/SS Adam Kennedy and P Kent Bottenfield (March 23, 2000). ... On disabled list (June 1-16, 2002).

2003 GAMES PLAYED BY POSITION (MLB): OF—129, DH—2.

Year Team (League)	Pos.	G	AB	R	H	2B	3B	HR	RBI	BB	SO	HBP	GDP	SB-CS	Avg.	OBP	SLG	OPS	E	Pct.
1988— Bend (NW)	OF	35	122	23	27	4	0	0	13	20	44	0	2	4-0	.221	.329	.254	.583	1	.984
1989— Quad City (Midw.)	OF	31	92	11	24	4	0	1	4	7	34	0	3	1-0	.261	.313	.337	.650	3	.942
1990— Palm Springs (Calif.)	OF	91	314	36	92	18	6	3	56	27	75	2	10	5-2	.293	.351	.417	.768	10	.954
1991— Palm Springs (Calif.)	P	60	187	28	55	15	1	2	27	40	57	0	2	2-2	.294	.417	.417	.834	0	1.000
1992— Midland (Texas)	OF	70	246	42	77	15	2	8	32	41	83	1	8	3-4	.313	.413	.488	.901	5	.967
— Edmonton (PCL)	OF	50	194	37	58	15	2	6	36	14	55	0	2	3-1	.299	.343	.490	.833	1	.988
1993— Vancouver (PCL)	OF	95	356	59	112	28	4	9	74	41	81	0	5	6-8	.315	.382	.492	.873	3	.983
— California (A.L.)	OF	18	61	5	15	4	1	0	4	2	16	0	1	0-2	.246	.270	.344	.614	1	.981
1994— California (A.L.)	OF-1B	94	289	35	79	13	1	5	37	30	72	1	3	4-2	.273	.343	.377	.720	3	.991
1995— California (A.L.)	OF	141	558	120	162	30	4	33	107	51	130	5	10	1-4	.290	.352	.536	.888	1	.998
1996— California (A.L.)	OF-DH	114	431	73	131	28	3	27	66	46	101	4	8	4-0	.304	.375	.571	.946	1	.997
— Lake Elsinore (Calif.)	OF	5	15	4	6	2	0	1	4	1	1	1	0	0-0	.400	.471	.733	1.204	0	1.000
1997— Anaheim (A.L.)	OF-1B-DH	133	502	82	146	27	0	26	80	60	80	4	8	5-7	.291	.368	.500	.868	5	.988
1998— Anaheim (A.L.)	OF	154	599	115	184	42	1	25	91	57	114	1	16	7-5	.307	.368	.506	.874	5	.988
1999— Lake Elsinore (Calif.)	DH	5	19	4	8	2	0	0	3	4	2	0	0	2-0	.421	.522	.526	1.048	0	...
— Anaheim (A.L.)	OF-DH-1B	55	204	34	51	17	2	5	23	28	45	0	3	5-4	.250	.339	.426	.766	1	.993
2000— St. Louis (N.L.)	OF-1B	152	525	129	155	25	0	42	108	103	167	6	5	10-3	.295	.411	.583	.994	4	.990
2001— St. Louis (N.L.)	OF-1B	150	500	95	150	38	1	30	110	93	136	4	8	5-5	.304	.410	.564	.974	6	.983
2002— St. Louis (N.L.)	OF	144	476	96	148	31	2	28	83	86	134	8	9	4-3	.311	.420	.561	.981	5	.986
2003— St. Louis (N.L.)	OF-DH	137	447	89	123	32	2	39	89	77	127	4	11	1-3	.275	.385	.617	1.002	5	.986
American League totals (7 years)		709	2644	464	768	161	12	121	408	274	558	15	49	26-24	.290	.359	.498	.856	17	.992
National League totals (4 years)		583	1948	409	578	126	5	139	390	359	564	22	33	20-14	.297	.407	.581	.988	20	.986
Major League totals (11 years)		1292	4592	873	1346	287	17	260	798	633	1122	37	82	46-38	.293	.380	.533	.913	37	.989

EDWARDS, MIKE   OF

PERSONAL: Born November 24, 1976, in Goshen, N.Y. ... 6-1/185. ... Bats right, throws right. ... Full name: Michael Donald Edwards. ... High school: Mechanicsburg, Pa.

TRANSACTIONS/CAREER NOTES: Selected by Cleveland Indians organization in ninth round of free-agent draft (June 1, 1995). ... Granted free agency (October 15, 2001); signed by Cincinnati Reds organization (November 8, 2001). ... Granted free agency (October 15, 2002); signed by Oakland A's organization (November 8, 2002).

2003 GAMES PLAYED BY POSITION (MLB): DH—2, OF—2.

E

Year	Team (League)	Pos.	G	AB	R	H	2B	3B	HR	RBI	BB	SO	HBP	GDP	SB-CS	Avg.	OBP	SLG	OPS	E	Pct.
1995—	Burlington (Appal.)	SS	43	130	20	22	2	0	0	5	17	35	2	2	5-2	.169	.275	.185	.460	18	.897
1996—	Burlington (Appal.)	3B-SS	58	206	31	58	13	1	1	17	37	26	3	4	5-4	.282	.394	.369	.763	13	.901
1997—	Burlington (Appal.) 3-1-SS-OF		60	236	50	68	16	2	4	41	38	53	1	2	10-5	.288	.386	.424	.810	21	.903
1998—	Columbus (S. Atl.)	3B-1B	124	497	82	146	34	4	8	81	66	95	3	13	16-6	.294	.379	.427	.805	31	.910
1999—	Kinston (Caro.)	3B	133	456	76	132	25	4	16	89	93	117	9	12	8-3	.289	.413	.467	.880	28	.910
2000—	Akron (East.)	3B	136	481	72	142	25	2	11	63	68	86	5	9	7-3	.295	.386	.424	.810	20	.943
2001—	Mahoning Valley (NY-P)	3B	20	71	19	26	5	0	6	24	12	7	1	0	0-1	.366	.464	.690	1.154	1	.960
—	Akron (East.)	1B-3B	29	111	21	37	7	3	6	24	13	26	0	3	0-0	.333	.403	.613	1.016	4	.978
—	Buffalo (Int'l)	1B	3	9	1	2	0	0	0	1	1	3	0	1	0-0	.222	.300	.222	.522	0	1.000
2002—	Chattanooga (Sou.) ...	OF-1B-3B	119	424	57	130	19	2	11	60	41	57	10	19	9-11	.307	.377	.439	.816	10	.981
—	Louisville (Int'l)	OF-1B	15	57	7	23	5	1	2	8	6	9	0	1	0-0	.404	.460	.632	1.092	1	.976
2003—	Sacramento (PCL)	O-D-3-SS	125	436	78	130	23	4	14	95	60	78	6	17	5-2	.298	.387	.466	.853	3	.984
—	Oakland (A.L.)	DH-OF	4	4	0	1	0	0	0	0	2	1	0	0	0-0	.250	.500	.250	.750	0	...
Major League totals (1 year)			4	4	0	1	0	0	0	0	2	1	0	0	0-0	.250	.500	.250	.750	0	...

EISCHEN, JOEY   P

PERSONAL: Born May 25, 1970, in West Covina, Calif. ... 6-0/215. ... Throws left, bats left. ... Full name: Joseph Raymond Eischen. ... Name pronounced: EYE-shen. ... High school: West Covina (Calif.). ... Junior college: Pasadena (Calif.) Community College.

TRANSACTIONS/CAREER NOTES: Selected by Chicago White Sox organization in fifth round of free-agent draft (June 1, 1988); did not sign. ... Selected by Texas Rangers in fourth round of free-agent draft (June 5, 1989). ... Traded by Rangers with P Jonathan Hurst and a player to be named later to Montreal Expos for P Oil Can Boyd (July 21, 1991); Expos acquired P Travis Buckley to complete deal (September 1, 1991). ... Traded by Expos with OF Roberto Kelly to Los Angeles Dodgers for OF Henry Rodriguez and IF Jeff Treadway (May 23, 1995). ... Traded by Dodgers with P John Cummings to Detroit Tigers for OF Chad Curtis (July 31, 1996). ... Traded by Tigers with P Cam Smith to San Diego Padres for C Brian Johnson and P Willie Blair (December 17, 1996). ... Traded by Padres to Cincinnati Reds for a player to be named later (March 16, 1997); Padres acquired IF Ray Brown to complete deal (March 19, 1997). ... On Cincinnati disabled list (March 25-April 26 and April 29-July 18, 1997); included rehabilitation assignment to Indianapolis (April 13-26). ... Granted free agency (December 21, 1997). ... Signed by New York Yankees organization (February 3, 1998). ... Released by Yankees (March 11, 1998). ... Signed by Reds (March 19, 1998). ... Released by Reds (March 12, 1999). ... Signed by Arizona Diamondbacks organization (March 18, 1999). ... Released by Diamondbacks (July 1, 1999). ... Signed by Adirondack, Northern League (July 1999). ... Signed by Cleveland Indians organization (December 3, 1999). ... Released by Indians (April 29, 2000). ... Signed by Adirondack, Northern League (May 2000). ... Signed by Expos organization (July 12, 2000). ... Granted free agency (October 12, 2001). ... Re-signed by Expos organization (October 22, 2001).

CAREER HITTING: 2-for-20 (.100), 2 R, 1 2B, 0 3B, 0 HR, 0 RBI.

Year	League	W	L	Pct.	ERA	WHIP	G	GS	CG	ShO	Hld.	Sv.-Opp.	IP	H	R	ER	HR	BB-IBB	SO	Avg.
1989—	Butte (Pio.)	3	7	.300	5.30	1.67	12	12	0	0	...	0-...	52.2	50	45	31	4	38-0	57	.246
1990—	Gastonia (S. Atl.)	3	7	.300	2.70	1.24	17	14	0	0	...	0-...	73.1	51	36	22	0	40-0	69	.195
1991—	Charlotte (Fla. St.)	4	10	.286	3.41	1.42	18	18	1	0	...	0-...	108.1	99	59	41	5	55-1	80	.249
—	W.P. Beach (FSL)	4	2	.667	5.17	1.54	8	8	1	0	...	0-...	38.1	35	† 27	22	3	24-0	26	.238
1992—	W.P. Beach (FSL)	9	8	.529	3.08	1.24	27	26	3	2	...	0-...	169.2	128	68	58	5	* 83-2	167	.211
1993—	Harrisburg (Eastern)	* 14	4	.778	3.62	1.53	20	20	0	0	...	0-...	119.1	122	62	48	11	60-0	110	.265
—	Ottawa (Int'l)	2	2	.500	3.54	1.20	6	6	0	0	...	0-...	40.2	34	18	16	3	15-0	29	.230
1994—	Ottawa (Int'l)	2	6	.250	4.94	1.52	48	2	0	0	...	2-...	62.0	54	38	34	7	40-4	57	.238
—	Montreal (N.L.)	0	0	...	54.00	6.00	1	0	0	0	0	0-0	.2	4	4	4	0	0-0	1	.667
1995—	Ottawa (Int'l)	2	1	.667	1.72	1.09	11	0	0	0	...	0-...	15.2	9	4	3	0	8-1	13	.173
—	Los Angeles (N.L.)	0	0	...	3.10	1.48	17	0	0	0	1	0-...	20.1	19	9	7	1	11-1	15	.232
—	Albuquerque (PCL)	3	0	1.000	0.00	0.67	13	0	0	0	...	2-...	16.1	8	0	0	0	3-0	14	.145
1996—	Los Angeles (N.L.)	0	1	.000	4.78	1.57	28	0	0	0	1	0-0	43.1	48	25	23	4	20-4	36	.282
—	Detroit (A.L.)	1	1	.500	3.24	1.64	24	0	0	0	1	0-2	25.0	27	11	9	3	14-3	15	.284
1997—	Indianapolis (A.A.)	1	0	1.000	1.27	1.27	26	5	0	0	...	2-...	42.2	41	7	6	1	13-1	26	.261
—	Cincinnati (N.L.)	0	0	...	6.75	2.25	1	0	0	0	0	0-0	1.1	2	2	1	0	1-0	2	.333
1998—	Indianapolis (Int'l)	2	5	.286	4.54	1.39	61	0	0	0	...	2-...	73.1	73	42	37	9	29-3	60	.258
1999—	Tucson (PCL)	1	3	.250	9.07	2.14	27	1	0	0	...	1-...	41.2	63	47	42	7	26-3	36	.350
—	Adirondack (Nor.)	4	2	.667	1.31	1.31	7	7	1	0	...	0-...	48.0	52	22	20	1	11-...	49	...
2000—	Buffalo (Int'l)	0	0	...	40.50	6.00	1	0	0	0	...	0-...	.2	4	3	3	0	0-0	0	.667
—	Adirondack (Nor.)	7	1	.875	1.80	1.22	10	10	0	0	...	0-...	65.0	55	25	13	...	24-...	57	...
—	Ottawa (Int'l)	0	4	.000	3.64	1.30	10	9	0	0	...	0-...	59.1	55	31	24	8	22-0	34	.250
2001—	Ottawa (Int'l)	2	3	.400	2.24	1.01	34	1	0	0	...	7-...	52.1	42	16	13	6	11-0	54	.220
—	Montreal (N.L.)	0	1	.000	4.85	1.52	24	0	0	0	2	0-2	29.2	29	17	16	4	16-1	19	.257
2002—	Ottawa (Int'l)	1	0	1.000	0.00	0.79	11	0	0	0	...	4-...	14.0	8	4	0	0	3-0	15	.167
—	Montreal (N.L.)	6	1	.857	1.34	1.14	59	0	0	0	11	2-3	53.2	43	11	8	1	18-5	51	.224
2003—	Montreal (N.L.)	2	2	.500	3.06	1.32	70	0	0	0	15	1-4	53.0	57	27	18	7	13-1	40	.282
American League totals (1 year)		1	1	.500	3.24	1.64	24	0	0	0	1	0-2	25.0	27	11	9	3	14-3	15	.284
National League totals (7 years)		8	5	.615	3.43	1.39	200	0	0	0	30	3-9	202.0	202	95	77	17	79-12	164	.262
Major League totals (7 years)		9	6	.600	3.41	1.42	224	0	0	0	31	3-11	227.0	229	106	86	20	93-15	179	.264

ELARTON, SCOTT   P

PERSONAL: Born February 23, 1976, in Lamar, Colo. ... 6-8/240. ... Throws right, bats right. ... Full name: Vincent Scott Elarton. ... High school: Lamar (Colo.).

TRANSACTIONS/CAREER NOTES: Selected by Houston Astros organization in first round (25th pick overall) of free-agent draft (June 2, 1994). ... On Houston disabled list (March 29-April 23, 2000); included rehabilitation assignments to New Orleans (April 6-11) and Round Rock (April 18). ... On Houston disabled list (July 17-31, 2001). ... Traded by Astros with a player to be named later to Colorado Rockies for P Pedro Astacio (July 31, 2001). ... On Colorado disabled list (July 31-September 4, 2001); included rehabilitation assignment to Colorado Springs (August 29-September 4). ... On disabled list (March 8, 2002-entire season). ... Granted free agency (December 21, 2002). ... Re-signed by Rockies (December 22, 2002). ... Optioned to Colorado Springs by Colorado; reinstated from 15-day disabled list and recalled by Colorado (April 30, 2003). ... On Colorado disabled list (March 26, 2003); included rehabilitation assignment to Colorado Springs (April 4). ... Optioned to Colorado Springs (May 1, 2003). ... Recalled from rehab assignment by Colorado (May 23, 2003). ... Optioned to Colorado Springs (June 27, 2003). ... Recalled by Colorado from Colorado Springs (September 5, 2003).

CAREER HITTING: 19-for-148 (.128), 10 R, 2 2B, 0 3B, 0 HR, 3 RBI.

Year	League	W	L	Pct.	ERA	WHIP	G	GS	CG	ShO	Hld.	Sv.-Opp.	IP	H	R	ER	HR	BB-IBB	SO	Avg.
1994—	GC Astros (GCL)	4	0	1.000	0.00	0.50	5	5	0	0	...	0-...	28.0	9	0	0	0	5-0	28	.103
—	Quad City (Midw.)	4	1	.800	3.29	1.10	9	9	0	0	...	0-...	54.2	42	23	20	4	18-0	42	.213
1995—	Quad City (Midw.)	13	7	.650	4.45	1.47	26	26	0	0	...	0-...	149.2	149	86	74	12	71-2	112	.259
1996—	Kissimmee (Fla. St.)	12	7	.632	2.92	1.21	27	27	3	1	...	0-...	172.1	154	67	56	13	54-0	130	.241
1997—	Jackson (Texas)	7	4	.636	3.24	1.13	20	20	2	0	...	0-...	133.1	103	57	48	4	47-3	141	.210
—	New Orleans (A.A.)	4	4	.500	5.33	1.26	9	9	0	0	...	0-...	54.0	51	36	32	5	17-1	50	.249

E

Year League	W	L	Pct.	ERA	WHIP	G	GS	CG	ShO	Hld.	Sv.-Opp.	IP	H	R	ER	HR	BB-IBB	SO	Avg.
1998— New Orleans (PCL)	9	4	.692	4.01	1.22	14	14	2	1	...	0-...	92.0	71	42	41	6	41-3	100	.212
— Houston (N.L.)	2	1	.667	3.32	1.05	28	2	0	0	2	2-3	57.0	40	21	21	5	20-0	56	.196
1999— Houston (N.L.)	9	5	.643	3.48	1.24	42	15	0	0	5	1-4	124.0	111	55	48	8	43-0	121	.238
2000— New Orleans (PCL)	1	0	1.000	0.75	0.58	2	2	0	0	...	0-...	12.0	3	1	1	0	4-0	12	.081
— Round Rock (Texas)	1	0	1.000	2.84	1.11	1	1	0	0	...	0-...	6.1	7	2	2	1	0-0	7	.280
— Houston (N.L.)	17	7	.708	4.81	1.46	30	30	2	0	0	0-0	192.2	198	117	103	29	84-1	131	.263
2001— Houston (N.L.)	4	8	.333	7.14	1.60	20	20	0	0	0	0-0	109.2	126	88	87	26	49-1	76	.290
— Colo. Springs (PCL)	0	1	.000	7.04	1.83	2	2	0	0	...	0-...	7.2	14	6	6	2	0-0	8	.378
— Colorado (N.L.)	0	2	.000	6.65	1.30	4	4	0	0	0	0-0	23.0	20	17	17	8	10-1	11	.233
2002— Colorado (N.L.)										Did not play.									
2003— Colo. Springs (PCL)	6	8	.429	5.31	1.56	20	20	0	0	0	0-0	118.2	146	81	70	15	39-1	92	.298
— Colorado (N.L.)	4	4	.500	6.27	1.80	11	10	0	0	0	0-0	51.2	73	46	36	13	20-3	20	.329
Major League totals (5 years)	36	27	.571	5.03	1.42	135	81	2	0	7	3-7	558.0	568	344	312	89	226-6	415	.262

ELDER, DAVE — P

PERSONAL: Born September 23, 1975, in Atlanta, Ga. ... 6-0/180. ... Throws right, bats right. ... Full name: David Matthew Elder. ... High school: Booker T. Washington (Pensacola, Fla.). ... College: Georgia Tech.

TRANSACTIONS/CAREER NOTES: Selected by Texas Rangers organization in fourth round of free-agent draft (June 3, 1997). ... On disabled list (April 7, 1998-entire season). ... On Charlotte disabled list (May 8-19, 1999). ... Traded by Rangers to Cleveland Indians for P John Rocker (December 18, 2001). ... Transferred from the 15-day to 60-day disabled list (June 11, 2003). ... Contract purchased by Cleveland from Buffalo of the International League (May 1, 2003). ... Placed on 15-day disabled list by Cleveland (May 12, 2003). ... Transferred to Emergency disabled list (June 11, 2003).

CAREER HITTING: 0-for-0 (.000), 0 R, 0 2B, 0 3B, 0 HR, 0 RBI.

Year League	W	L	Pct.	ERA	WHIP	G	GS	CG	ShO	Hld.	Sv.-Opp.	IP	H	R	ER	HR	BB-IBB	SO	Avg.
1997— Pulaski (Appal.)	2	2	.500	1.95	0.93	20	0	0	0	...	6-...	32.1	18	8	7	2	12-0	57	.157
1998— Pulaski (Appal.)										Did not play.									
1999— Charlotte (Fla. St.)	4	2	.667	2.84	1.31	24	1	0	0	...	4-...	44.1	33	15	14	2	25-0	42	.213
— Tulsa (Texas)	1	0	1.000	8.10	2.10	3	0	0	0	...	0-...	6.2	8	7	6	0	6-1	7	.308
2000— Tulsa (Texas)	7	6	.538	4.94	1.79	33	21	0	0	...	3-...	116.2	121	80	64	9	* 88-0	104	.267
2001— Tulsa (Texas)	4	6	.400	3.00	1.49	13	13	0	0	...	0-...	72.0	64	28	24	1	43-0	78	.246
— Oklahoma (PCL)	5	4	.556	4.99	1.68	15	8	0	0	...	0-...	57.2	54	36	32	4	43-0	56	.249
2002— Akron (East.)	2	1	.667	2.00	1.03	23	1	0	0	...	9-...	36.0	19	8	8	1	18-2	42	.154
— Buffalo (Int'l)	3	1	.750	2.65	1.35	22	1	0	0	...	5-...	34.0	32	11	10	1	14-0	42	.248
— Cleveland (A.L.)	0	2	.000	3.13	1.39	15	0	0	0	3	0-0	23.0	18	10	8	1	14-3	23	.220
2003— Buffalo (Int'l)	0	0	...	0.00	0.87	8	0	0	0	...	6-...	12.2	5	0	0	0	6-0	17	.122
— Cleveland (A.L.)	1	1	.500	19.29	3.86	4	0	0	0	0	0-1	2.1	5	5	5	2	4-0	3	.417
Major League totals (2 years)	1	3	.250	4.62	1.62	19	0	0	0	3	0-1	25.1	23	15	13	3	18-3	26	.245

ELDRED, CAL — P

PERSONAL: Born November 24, 1967, in Cedar Rapids, Iowa. ... 6-4/235. ... Throws right, bats right. ... Full name: Calvin John Eldred. ... Name pronounced: EL-dred. ... High school: Urbana (Iowa) Community. ... College: Iowa.

TRANSACTIONS/CAREER NOTES: Selected by Milwaukee Brewers organization in first round (17th pick overall) of free-agent draft (June 5, 1989). ... On disabled list (May 15, 1995-remainder of season). ... On Milwaukee disabled list (March 29-July 14, 1996); included rehabilitation assignment to New Orleans (June 10-July 9). ... On disabled list (July 26, 1998-remainder of season). ... On Milwaukee disabled list (March 29-April 20 and July 2-August 15, 1999); included rehabilitation assignments to Huntsville (April 8-17) and Louisville (April 18-20 and July 31-August 15). ... Traded by Brewers with SS Jose Valentin to Chicago White Sox for P Jaime Navarro and P John Snyder (January 12, 2000). ... On Chicago disabled list (July 15-September 27, 2000); included rehabilitation assignment to Charlotte (August 29-September 22). ... Granted free agency (November 8, 2000). ... Re-signed by White Sox (December 7, 2000). ... On disabled list (April 12, 2001-remainder of season). ... Granted free agency (November 7, 2001). ... Signed by St. Louis Cardinals organization (December 18, 2002).

CAREER HITTING: 8-for-65 (.123), 7 R, 2 2B, 0 3B, 0 HR, 4 RBI.

Year League	W	L	Pct.	ERA	WHIP	G	GS	CG	ShO	Hld.	Sv.-Opp.	IP	H	R	ER	HR	BB-IBB	SO	Avg.
1989— Beloit (Midw.)	2	1	.667	2.30	1.09	5	5	0	0	...	0-...	31.1	23	10	8	0	11-1	32	.202
1990— Stockton (Calif.)	4	2	.667	1.62	1.00	7	7	3	1	...	0-...	50.0	31	12	9	2	19-0	75	.177
— El Paso (Texas)	5	4	.556	4.49	1.57	19	19	0	0	...	0-...	110.1	126	61	55	9	47-0	93	.293
1991— Denver (Am. Assoc.)	13	9	.591	3.75	1.32	29	* 29	3	1	...	0-...	* 185.0	161	82	77	13	84-2	* 168	.239
— Milwaukee (A.L.)	2	0	1.000	4.50	1.63	3	3	0	0	0	0-0	16.0	20	9	8	2	6-0	10	.299
1992— Denver (Am. Assoc.)	10	6	.625	3.00	1.16	19	19	4	1	...	0-...	141.0	122	49	47	9	42-0	99	.237
— Milwaukee (A.L.)	11	2	.846	1.79	0.99	14	14	2	1	0	0-0	100.1	76	21	20	4	23-0	62	.207
1993— Milwaukee (A.L.)	16	16	.500	4.01	1.25	36	• 36	8	1	0	0-0	* 258.0	232	120	115	32	91-5	180	.239
1994— Milwaukee (A.L.)	11	11	.500	4.68	1.35	25	• 25	6	0	0	0-0	179.0	158	96	93	23	84-0	98	.236
1995— Milwaukee (A.L.)	1	1	.500	3.42	1.44	4	4	0	0	0	0-0	23.2	24	10	9	4	10-0	18	.261
1996— New Orleans (A.A.)	2	2	.500	3.34	1.27	6	6	0	0	...	0-...	32.1	24	12	12	2	17-0	30	.205
— Milwaukee (A.L.)	4	4	.500	4.46	1.42	15	15	0	0	0	0-0	84.2	82	43	42	8	38-0	50	.259
1997— Milwaukee (N.L.)	13	• 15	.464	4.99	1.47	34	34	1	1	0	0-0	202.0	207	118	112	31	89-0	122	.266
1998— Milwaukee (N.L.)	4	8	.333	4.80	1.64	23	23	0	0	0	0-0	133.0	157	82	71	14	61-3	86	.297
1999— Huntsville (Sou.)	0	1	1.000	7.50	1.33	2	2	1	0	...	0-...	12.0	13	10	10	2	3-0	10	.260
— Louisville (Int'l)	0	1	.000	5.30	1.55	4	4	0	0	...	0-...	18.2	19	12	11	4	10-0	21	.250
— Milwaukee (N.L.)	2	8	.200	7.79	1.79	20	15	0	0	0	0-0	82.0	101	75	71	19	46-0	60	.297
2000— Chicago (A.L.)	10	2	.833	4.58	1.45	20	20	2	1	0	0-0	112.0	103	61	57	12	59-0	97	.243
— Charlotte (Int'l)	0	1	.000	7.20	0.80	2	2	0	0	...	0-...	5.0	4	4	4	2	0-0	1	.211
2001— Chicago (A.L.)	0	1	.000	13.50	2.50	2	2	0	0	0	0-0	6.0	12	9	9	1	3-1	6	.429
2002—										Did not play.									
2003— St. Louis (N.L.)	7	4	.636	3.74	1.38	62	0	0	0	11	8-14	67.1	62	32	28	9	31-4	67	.248
American League totals (9 years)	68	52	.567	4.26	1.34	153	153	19	4	0	0-0	981.2	914	487	465	117	403-6	643	.246
National League totals (3 years)	13	20	.394	5.42	1.62	105	38	0	0	11	8-14	282.1	320	189	170	42	138-7	213	.286
Major League totals (12 years)	81	72	.529	4.52	1.40	258	191	19	4	11	8-14	1264.0	1234	676	635	159	541-13	856	.256

ELLIS, MARK — 2B

PERSONAL: Born June 6, 1977, in Rapid City, S.D. ... 5-11/180. ... Bats right, throws right. ... Full name: Mark William Ellis. ... High school: Stevens (Rapid City, S.D.). ... College: Florida.

TRANSACTIONS/CAREER NOTES: Selected by Kansas City Royals organization in ninth round of free-agent draft (June 2, 1999). ... Traded by Royals with OF Johnny Damon and player to be named later to Oakland Athletics as part of three-way deal in which Royals received P Roberto Hernandez from Tampa Bay Devil Rays, A's received P Cory

E

Lidle from Devil Rays, Royals received C A.J. Hinch, IF Angel Berroa and cash from A's and Devil Rays received OF Ben Grieve and player to be named later or cash from A's (January 8, 2001). ... On Sacramento disabled list (May 12-29, 2002).

2003 GAMES PLAYED BY POSITION (MLB): 2B—153.

Year	Team (League)	Pos.	G	AB	R	H	2B	3B	HR	RBI	BB	SO	HBP	GDP	SB-CS	Avg.	OBP	SLG	OPS	E	Pct.
1999—	Spokane (N'west)	SS	71	281	67	92	14	0	7	47	47	40	3	1	21-7	.327	.424	.452	.876	16	.958
2000—	Wilmington (Caro.)	2B-SS	132	484	83	* 146	27	4	6	62	78	72	7	11	25-7	.302	.404	.411	.815	‡ 31	.954
—	Wichita (Texas)	2B	7	22	4	7	1	0	0	4	5	5	0	0	1-0	.318	.444	.364	.808	0	1.000
2001—	Sacramento (PCL)	SS	132	472	71	129	38	0	10	53	54	78	5	13	21-7	.273	.351	.417	.768	19	.968
2002—	Sacramento (PCL)	SS	21	84	14	25	10	1	0	5	6	13	4	1	4-0	.298	.372	.440	.813	3	.974
—	Oakland (A.L.)	2-S-3-D	98	345	58	94	16	4	6	35	44	54	4	3	4-2	.272	.359	.394	.753	11	.976
2003—	Oakland (A.L.)	2B	154	553	78	137	31	5	9	52	48	94	7	7	6-2	.248	.313	.371	.684	14	.982
	Major League totals (2 years)		252	898	136	231	47	9	15	87	92	148	11	10	10-4	.257	.331	.380	.711	25	.980

ELLIS, ROBERT   P

PERSONAL: Born December 15, 1970, in Baton Rouge, La. ... 6-5/220. ... Throws right, bats right. ... Full name: Robert Randolph Ellis. ... High school: Belaire (Baton Rouge, La.). ... Junior college: Panola College (Texas).

TRANSACTIONS/CAREER NOTES: Selected by Chicago White Sox organization in third round of free-agent draft (June 4, 1990). ... On South Bend disabled list (May 20-July 1, 1992). ... On disabled list (July 25, 1994-remainder of season; and May 17, 1995-remainder of season). ... Traded by White Sox to California Angels for C Pat Borders (July 27, 1996). ... Angels franchise renamed Anaheim Angels for 1997 season. ... Granted free agency (October 15, 1997). ... Signed by Detroit Tigers organization (November 10, 1997). ... Released by Tigers (March 3, 1998). ... Signed by Milwaukee Brewers organization (March 4, 1998). ... On Louisville disabled list (May 23-30, 1998). ... Granted free agency (October 16, 1998). ... Signed by Houston Astros organization (January 15, 1999). ... Granted free agency (October 15, 1999). ... Signed by Toronto Blue Jays organization (January 6, 2000). ... Released by Blue Jays (May 23, 2000). ... Signed by Monterrey, Mexican League (June 2000). ... Signed by Arizona Diamondbacks organization (October 10, 2000). ... On Arizona disabled list (July 23-September 25, 2001); included rehabilitation assignment to Tucson (August 4-16). ... Granted free agency (December 21, 2001). ... Signed by Los Angeles Dodgers organization (January 14, 2002). ... Released by Dodgers (October 7, 2002). ... Signed by Texas Rangers organization (November 13, 2002). ... Contract purchased by Texas Rangers from Oklahoma (July 22, 2003). ... Sent outright to Oklahoma by Texas (August 18, 2003).

CAREER HITTING: 4-for-26 (.154), 2 R, 0 2B, 0 3B, 0 HR, 1 RBI.

Year	League	W	L	Pct.	ERA	WHIP	G	GS	CG	ShO	Hld.	Sv.-Opp.	IP	H	R	ER	HR	BB-IBB	SO	Avg.
1991—	Utica (N.Y.-Penn)	3	• 9	.250	4.62	1.68	15	15	1	1	...	0-...	87.2	86	* 66	45	4	61-0	66	.262
1992—	South Bend (Mid.)	6	5	.545	2.34	1.02	18	18	1	1	...	0-...	123.0	90	46	32	3	35-0	97	.206
—	GC White Sox (GCL)	1	0	1.000	10.80	2.20	1	1	0	0	...	0-...	5.0	10	6	6	0	1-0	4	.435
1993—	Sarasota (Fla. St.)	7	8	.467	2.51	1.08	15	15	* 8	2	...	0-...	104.0	81	37	29	3	31-1	79	.217
—	Birmingham (Sou.)	6	3	.667	3.10	1.09	12	12	2	1	...	0-...	81.1	68	33	28	2	21-0	77	.220
1994—	Nashville (A.A.)	4	10	.286	6.09	1.72	19	19	1	0	...	0-...	105.0	126	77	71	9	55-1	76	.304
1995—	Nashville (A.A.)	1	1	.500	2.18	1.26	4	4	0	0	...	0-...	20.2	16	7	5	2	10-0	9	.219
1996—	Nashville (A.A.)	3	8	.273	6.01	1.75	19	13	1	0	...	0-...	70.1	78	49	47	6	45-3	35	.292
—	Birmingham (Sou.)	0	1	.000	11.05	1.91	2	2	0	0	...	0-...	7.1	9	9	9	1	8-0	8	.240
—	Vancouver (PCL)	2	3	.400	3.25	1.31	7	7	1	0	...	0-...	44.1	30	19	16	2	28-0	29	.195
—	California (A.L.)	0	0	...	0.00	0.80	3	0	0	0	0	0-0	5.0	0	0	0	0	4-0	5	.000
1997—	Vancouver (PCL)	9	10	.474	5.92	1.80	29	23	3	0	...	0-...	149.0	185	108	98	15	83-1	70	.310
1998—	Louisville (Int'l)	10	10	.500	5.63	1.66	30	28	0	0	...	0-...	150.1	171	103	94	21	78-1	79	.286
1999—	New Orleans (PCL)	7	12	.368	5.43	1.46	27	27	1	0	...	0-...	155.2	176	106	94	20	51-1	105	.283
2000—	Syracuse (Int'l)	1	1	.500	4.50	1.78	16	0	0	0	...	2-...	18.0	17	10	9	2	15-1	18	.262
—	Monterrey (Mex.)	8	5	.615	3.51	1.19	15	14	3	0	...	0-...	92.1	78	39	36	8	32-...	70	...
2001—	Tucson (PCL)	1	1	.500	3.08	1.14	5	5	0	0	...	0-...	26.1	25	12	9	2	5-0	13	.250
—	Arizona (N.L.)	6	5	.545	5.77	1.52	19	17	0	0	0	0-0	92.0	106	61	59	12	34-2	41	.293
2002—	Las Vegas (PCL)	9	7	.563	4.17	1.34	29	• 28	1	0	...	0-...	172.2	195	100	80	17	37-0	110	.284
—	Los Angeles (N.L.)	0	1	.000	10.13	2.25	3	0	0	0	0	0-0	2.2	6	3	3	1	0-0	0	.545
2003—	Texas (A.L.)	1	1	.500	8.35	1.96	4	4	0	0	0	0-0	18.1	26	17	17	7	10-0	8	.342
—	Oklahoma (PCL)	3	10	.231	4.94	1.38	27	15	2	0	...	3-...	118.1	128	68	65	12	35-3	49	.279
	American League totals (2 years)	1	1	.500	6.56	1.71	7	4	0	0	0	0-0	23.1	26	17	17	7	14-0	13	.286
	National League totals (2 years)	6	6	.500	5.89	1.54	22	17	0	0	0	0-0	94.2	112	64	62	13	34-2	41	.299
	Major League totals (4 years)	7	7	.500	6.03	1.58	29	21	0	0	0	0-0	118.0	138	81	79	20	48-2	54	.296

ELLISON, JASON   OF

PERSONAL: Born April 4, 1978, in Quincy, Calif. ... 5-10/180. ... Bats right, throws right. ... Full name: Jason Jerome Ellison. ... High school: South Kitsap High (Port Orchar, Wash.). ... College: Lewis-Clark (Idaho) State.

TRANSACTIONS/CAREER NOTES: Selected by San Francisco Giants organization in 22nd round of free-agent draft (June 5, 2000). ... Recalled by San Francisco from Fresno (May 9, 2003). ... Optioned to Fresno by San Francisco (May 19, 2003). ... Recalled by San Francisco from Fresno (September 29, 2003).

2003 GAMES PLAYED BY POSITION (MLB): OF—4.

Year	Team (League)	Pos.	G	AB	R	H	2B	3B	HR	RBI	BB	SO	HBP	GDP	SB-CS	Avg.	OBP	SLG	OPS	E	Pct.
2000—	Salem-Keizer (NW)	OF	74	300	67	90	15	2	0	28	29	45	7	1	13-7	.300	.374	.363	.737	4	.976
2001—	Hagerstown (SAL)	OF	130	494	95	144	38	3	8	55	71	68	10	6	19-15	.291	.388	.429	.817	5	.984
2002—	San Jose (Calif.)	OF	81	322	40	87	13	0	5	40	25	37	2	10	9-9	.270	.325	.357	.682	4	.980
—	Fresno (PCL)	OF	49	196	31	61	8	1	3	8	21	28	4	4	16-3	.311	.389	.408	.797	1	.992
2003—	San Francisco (N.L.)	OF	7	10	1	1	0	0	0	0	0	1	0	0	0-0	.100	.100	.100	.200	0	1.000
—	Fresno (PCL)	OF-DH	119	461	74	136	22	4	6	39	39	52	6	7	21-13	.295	.356	.399	.755	9	.974
	Major League totals (1 year)		7	10	1	1	0	0	0	0	0	1	0	0	0-0	.100	.100	.100	.200	0	1.000

EMBREE, ALAN   P

PERSONAL: Born January 23, 1970, in The Dalles, Ore. ... 6-2/190. ... Throws left, bats left. ... Full name: Alan Duane Embree. ... Name pronounced: EMM-bree. ... High school: Prairie (Vancouver, Wash.).

TRANSACTIONS/CAREER NOTES: Selected by Cleveland Indians organization in fifth round of free-agent draft (June 5, 1989). ... On Cleveland disabled list (April 1-June 2 and June 2, 1993-remainder of season); included rehabilitation assignment to Canton/Akron (June 2-15). ... On Cleveland disabled list (August 1-September 7, 1996); included rehabilitation assignment to Buffalo (August 6-September 4). ... Traded by Indians with OF Kenny Lofton to Atlanta Braves for OF Marquis Grissom and OF Dave Justice (March 25, 1997). ... Traded by Braves to Arizona Diamondbacks for P Russ Springer (June 23, 1998). ... Traded by Diamondbacks to San Francisco Giants for OF Dante Powell (November 10, 1998). ... On San Francisco disabled list (May 23-June 12, 2001); included rehabilitation assignment to Fresno (May 28-June 12). ... Traded by Giants to Chicago White Sox for P Derek Hasselhoff (June 29, 2001). ... Granted free agency (November 6, 2001). ... Signed by San Diego Padres (January 3, 2002). ... Traded by Padres with P Andy Shibilo to Boston Red Sox for P Brad Baker and P Dan Giese (June 26, 2002). ... On Boston disabled list (July 14-29, 2002). ... Sent on rehab assignment to Sarasota by Boston Red Sox (April 26, 2003). ... Reinstated from the 15-day disabled list by Boston (April 29, 2003).

CAREER HITTING: 0-for-2 (.000), 0 R, 0 2B, 0 3B, 0 HR, 0 RBI.

Year — League	W	L	Pct.	ERA	WHIP	G	GS	CG	ShO	Hld.	Sv.-Opp.	IP	H	R	ER	HR	BB-IBB	SO	Avg.
1990— Burlington (Appal.)	4	4	.500	2.64	1.43	15	•15	0	0	...	0-...	81.2	87	36	24	3	30-0	58	.274
1991— Columbus (S. Atl.)	10	8	.556	3.59	1.31	27	26	3	1	...	0-...	155.1	126	80	62	4	77-1	137	.224
1992— Kinston (Caro.)	10	5	.667	3.30	1.20	15	15	1	0	...	0-...	101.0	89	48	37	10	32-0	115	.234
— Cant./Akr. (Eastern)	7	2	.778	2.28	1.13	12	12	0	0	...	0-...	79.0	61	24	20	2	28-1	56	.216
— Cleveland (A.L.)	0	2	.000	7.00	1.50	4	4	0	0	0	0-0	18.0	19	14	14	3	8-0	12	.271
1993— Cant./Akr. (Eastern)	0	0	...	3.38	1.13	1	1	0	0	...	0-...	5.1	3	2	2	0	3-0	4	.176
1994— Cant./Akr. (Eastern)	9	•16	.360	5.50	1.57	30	27	2	1	...	0-...	157.0	183	106	96	15	64-3	81	.294
1995— Buffalo (A.A.)	3	4	.429	0.89	1.23	30	0	0	0	...	5-...	40.2	31	10	4	0	19-2	56	.211
— Cleveland (A.L.)	3	2	.600	5.11	1.58	23	0	0	0	6	1-1	24.2	23	16	14	2	16-0	23	.253
1996— Cleveland (A.L.)	1	1	.500	6.39	1.65	24	0	0	0	1	0-0	31.0	30	26	22	10	21-3	33	.259
— Buffalo (A.A.)	4	1	.800	3.93	1.17	20	0	0	0	...	5-...	34.1	26	16	15	1	14-0	46	.210
1997— Atlanta (N.L.)	3	1	.750	2.54	1.22	66	0	0	0	16	0-0	46.0	36	13	13	1	20-2	45	.221
1998— Atlanta (N.L.)	1	0	1.000	4.34	1.77	20	0	0	0	6	0-1	18.2	23	14	9	2	10-0	19	.307
— Arizona (N.L.)	3	2	.600	4.11	1.31	35	0	0	0	6	1-2	35.0	33	18	16	5	13-0	24	.248
1999— San Francisco (N.L.)	3	2	.600	3.38	1.16	68	0	0	0	22	0-3	58.2	42	22	22	6	26-2	53	.200
2000— San Francisco (N.L.)	3	5	.375	4.95	1.45	63	0	0	0	9	2-5	60.0	62	34	33	4	25-2	49	.274
2001— San Francisco (N.L.)	0	2	.000	11.25	2.20	22	0	0	0	0	0-1	20.0	34	26	25	7	10-2	25	.374
— Fresno (PCL)	1	0	1.000	1.13	0.75	7	0	0	0	...	1-...	8.0	5	3	1	0	1-0	6	.179
— Chicago (A.L.)	1	2	.333	5.03	1.12	39	0	0	0	9	0-2	34.0	31	21	19	7	7-0	34	.242
2002— San Diego (N.L.)	3	4	.429	1.26	1.12	36	0	0	0	10	0-2	28.2	23	7	4	2	9-2	38	.211
— Boston (A.L.)	1	2	.333	2.97	1.05	32	0	0	0	8	2-5	33.1	24	12	11	4	11-1	43	.203
2003— Sarasota (Fla. St.)	0	0	...	13.50	3.00	1	1	0	0	...	0-...	.2	2	1	1	0	0-0	2	.500
— Boston (A.L.)	4	1	.800	4.25	1.18	65	0	0	0	14	1-2	55.0	49	26	26	5	16-3	45	.241
American League totals (6 years)	10	10	.500	4.87	1.30	187	4	0	0	38	4-10	196.0	176	115	106	31	79-7	190	.242
National League totals (6 years)	16	16	.500	4.08	1.37	310	0	0	0	69	3-14	267.0	253	134	121	27	113-10	253	.251
Major League totals (10 years)	26	26	.500	4.41	1.34	497	4	0	0	107	7-24	463.0	429	249	227	58	192-17	443	.248

ENCARNACION, JUAN   OF

PERSONAL: Born March 8, 1976, in Las Matas de Farfan, Dominican Republic. ... 6-3/215. ... Bats right, throws right. ... Full name: Juan de Dios Encarnacion. ... Name pronounced: en-car-NAH-see-own. ... High school: Liceo Mercedes Maria Mateo (Las Matas de Faran, Dominican Republic).

TRANSACTIONS/CAREER NOTES: Signed as non-drafted free agent by Detroit Tigers organization (December 27, 1992). ... On Detroit disabled list (March 20-April 29, 1998); included rehabilitation assignment to Lakeland (April 24-29). ... On suspended list (May 27-29, 2000). ... Traded by Tigers with P Luis Pineda to Cincinnati Reds for OF Dmitri Young (December 11, 2001). ... Traded by Reds with OF/2B Wilton Guerrero and P Ryan Snare to Florida Marlins for P Ryan Dempster (July 11, 2002).

2003 GAMES PLAYED BY POSITION (MLB): OF—155.

									BATTING										FIELDING	
Year — Team (League)	Pos.	G	AB	R	H	2B	3B	HR	RBI	BB	SO	HBP	GDP	SB-CS	Avg.	OBP	SLG	OPS	E	Pct.
1993— Dom. Tigers (DSL)	OF	72	251	36	63	13	4	13	49	15	65	...	...	6-...	.251	...	.490	...	17	.879
1994— Bristol (Appal.)	OF	54	197	16	49	7	1	4	31	13	54	5	2	9-2	.249	.310	.355	.666	3	.968
— Fayetteville (SAL)	OF	24	83	6	16	1	1	1	4	8	36	1	2	1-1	.193	.272	.265	.537	2	.920
— Lakeland (Fla. St.)	OF	3	6	1	2	0	0	0	0	0	3	1	0	0-0	.333	.429	.333	.762	0	...
1995— Fayetteville (SAL)	OF	124	457	62	129	31	7	16	72	30	113	8	10	30-6	.282	.336	.486	.822	7	.956
1996— Lakeland (Fla. St.)	OF	131	499	54	120	31	2	15	58	24	104	12	10	11-5	.240	.290	.401	.691	6	.976
1997— Jacksonville (Sou.)	OF-DH	131	493	91	159	31	4	26	90	43	86	19	8	17-3	.323	.394	.560	.954	3	.987
— Detroit (A.L.)	OF	11	33	3	7	1	1	1	5	3	12	2	1	3-1	.212	.316	.394	.710	0	1.000
1998— Lakeland (Fla. St.)	OF	4	16	4	4	0	1	0	4	2	4	1	0	4-0	.250	.368	.375	.743	0	1.000
— Toledo (Int'l)	OF-DH	92	356	55	102	17	3	8	41	29	85	10	9	24-4	.287	.353	.419	.772	5	.973
— Detroit (A.L.)	OF-DH	40	164	30	54	9	4	7	21	7	31	1	2	7-4	.329	.354	.561	.915	1	.985
1999— Detroit (A.L.)	OF	132	509	62	130	30	6	19	74	14	113	9	12	33-12	.255	.287	.450	.736	9	.968
2000— Detroit (A.L.)	OF	141	547	75	158	25	6	14	72	29	90	7	15	16-4	.289	.330	.433	.764	5	.987
2001— Detroit (A.L.)	OF-DH	120	417	52	101	19	7	12	52	25	93	6	9	9-5	.242	.292	.408	.700	6	.977
2002— Cincinnati (N.L.)	OF	83	321	43	89	11	2	16	51	26	63	1	7	9-4	.277	.330	.474	.804	5	.977
— Florida (N.L.)	OF	69	263	34	69	11	3	8	34	20	50	3	11	12-5	.262	.317	.418	.735	1	.993
2003— Florida (N.L.)	OF	156	601	80	162	37	6	19	94	37	82	4	17	19-8	.270	.313	.446	.759	0	1.000
American League totals (5 years)		444	1670	222	450	84	24	53	224	78	339	25	39	68-26	.269	.310	.444	.753	21	.979
National League totals (2 years)		308	1185	157	320	59	11	43	179	83	195	8	35	40-17	.270	.319	.447	.766	6	.991
Major League totals (7 years)		752	2855	379	770	143	35	96	403	161	534	33	74	108-43	.270	.313	.445	.759	27	.984

ENSBERG, MORGAN   3B

PERSONAL: Born August 26, 1975, in Hermosa Beach, Calif. ... 6-2/220. ... Bats right, throws right. ... Full name: Morgan Paul Ensberg. ... High school: Redondo Union (Redondo Beach, Calif.). ... College: USC.

TRANSACTIONS/CAREER NOTES: Selected by Houston Astros organization in ninth round of free-agent draft (June 2, 1998). ... On disabled list (June 22-August 10, 2001).

2003 GAMES PLAYED BY POSITION (MLB): 3B—111, DH—1.

									BATTING										FIELDING	
Year — Team (League)	Pos.	G	AB	R	H	2B	3B	HR	RBI	BB	SO	HBP	GDP	SB-CS	Avg.	OBP	SLG	OPS	E	Pct.
1998— Auburn (NY-Penn)	3B-SS	59	196	39	45	10	1	5	31	46	51	6	5	15-3	.230	.388	.367	.755	11	.927
1999— Kissimmee (Fla. St.)	3B-SS-1B	123	427	72	102	25	2	15	69	68	90	9	9	17-6	.239	.353	.412	.765	35	.900
2000— Round Rock (Texas)	3B	137	483	95	145	34	0	28	90	92	107	9	15	9-12	.300	.416	.545	.960	24	.942
— Houston (N.L.)	3B	4	7	0	2	0	0	0	0	0	1	0	0	0-0	.286	.286	.286	.571	1	.667
2001— New Orleans (PCL)	3B-SS	87	316	65	98	20	0	23	61	45	60	3	12	6-3	.310	.397	.592	.989	17	.929
2002— Houston (N.L.)	3B	49	132	14	32	7	2	3	19	18	25	3	8	2-0	.242	.346	.394	.740	8	.929
— New Orleans (PCL)	3B-1B	83	292	50	84	12	3	7	37	50	56	7	9	9-5	.288	.401	.421	.822	19	.926
2003— Houston (N.L.)	3B-DH	127	385	69	112	15	1	25	60	48	60	6	10	7-2	.291	.377	.530	.907	9	.967
Major League totals (3 years)		180	524	83	146	22	3	28	79	66	86	9	18	9-2	.279	.368	.492	.861	18	.953

E

ERSTAD, DARIN — OF

PERSONAL: Born June 4, 1974, in Jamestown, N.D. ... 6-2/210. ... Bats left, throws left. ... Full name: Darin Charles Erstad. ... Name pronounced: ER-stad. ... High school: Jamestown (N.D.). ... College: Nebraska.

TRANSACTIONS/CAREER NOTES: Selected by New York Mets organization in 13th round of free-agent draft (June 1, 1992); did not sign. ... Selected by California Angels organization in first round (first pick overall) of free-agent draft (June 1, 1995). ... Angels franchise renamed Anaheim Angels for 1997 season. ... On disabled list (August 4-19, 1998; and August 11-26, 1999). ... Placed on the 15-day disabled list (April 20, 2003). ... Sent to Salt Lake on rehab assignment (May 31, 2003). ... Recalled from Salt Lake rehab assignment (June 9, 2003). ... Placed on 15-day disabled list (August 7, 2003).

2003 GAMES PLAYED BY POSITION (MLB): OF—66.

										BATTING									FIELDING	
Year	Team (League)	Pos.	G	AB	R	H	2B	3B	HR	RBI	BB	SO	HBP	GDP	SB-CS	Avg.	OBP	SLG	OPS	E	Pct.
1995— Ariz. Angels (Ariz.)		OF	4	18	2	10	1	0	0	1	1	1	0	0	1-0	.556	.579	.611	1.190	0	1.000
— Lake Elsinore (Calif.)		OF	25	113	24	41	7	2	5	24	6	22	0	2	3-0	.363	.392	.593	.985	1	.985
1996— Vancouver (PCL)		OF-1B-DH	85	351	63	107	22	5	6	41	44	53	3	5	11-6	.305	.385	.447	.832	1	.995
— California (A.L.)		OF	57	208	34	59	5	1	4	20	17	29	0	3	3-3	.284	.333	.375	.708	3	.976
1997— Anaheim (A.L.)		1B-DH-OF	139	539	99	161	34	4	16	77	51	86	4	5	23-8	.299	.360	.466	.826	11	.990
1998— Anaheim (A.L.)		OF-1B-DH	133	537	84	159	39	3	19	82	43	77	6	2	20-6	.296	.353	.486	.839	3	.995
1999— Anaheim (A.L.)		1B-DH-OF	142	585	84	148	22	5	13	53	47	101	1	16	13-7	.253	.308	.374	.683	1	.999
2000— Anaheim (A.L.)		OF-DH-1B	157	* 676	121	* 240	39	6	25	100	64	82	1	8	28-8	.355	.409	.541	.951	3	.992
2001— Anaheim (A.L.)		OF-1B-DH	157	631	89	163	35	1	9	63	62	113	10	8	24-10	.258	.331	.360	.691	1	.998
2002— Anaheim (A.L.)		OF-1B-DH	150	625	99	177	28	4	10	73	27	67	2	9	23-3	.283	.313	.389	.702	1	.998
2003— Salt Lake (PCL)		OF	7	27	6	11	0	0	0	4	2	1	0	0	1-0	.407	.448	.407	.856	0	1.000
— Anaheim (A.L.)		OF	67	258	35	65	7	1	4	17	18	40	4	8	9-1	.252	.309	.333	.642	0	1.000
Major League totals (8 years)			1002	4059	645	1172	209	25	100	485	329	595	28	59	143-46	.289	.344	.426	.770	23	.995

ESCALONA, FELIX — SS

PERSONAL: Born March 12, 1979, in Puerto Cabello, Venezuela. ... 6-0/190. ... Bats right, throws right. ... Full name: Felix Eduardo Escalona.

TRANSACTIONS/CAREER NOTES: Signed as non-drafted free agent by Houston Astros organization (October 2, 1995). ... Selected by San Francisco Giants from Astros organization in Rule 5 major league draft (December 13, 2001). ... Claimed on waivers by Tampa Bay Devil Rays (March 27, 2002). ... Recalled by Tampa Bay from Orlando (April 24, 2003). ... Optioned to Orlando by Tampa Bay (May 3, 2003). ... Recalled by Tampa Bay from Orlando (May 9, 2003). ... Optioned to Bowie of the International League by Baltimore (May 19, 2003). ... Claimed by Tampa Bay off waivers from Baltimore (May 19, 2003). ... Recalled by Baltimore from Ottawa (September 29, 2003).

2003 GAMES PLAYED BY POSITION (MLB): SS—8, 2B—1, 3B—1.

										BATTING									FIELDING	
Year	Team (League)	Pos.	G	AB	R	H	2B	3B	HR	RBI	BB	SO	HBP	GDP	SB-CS	Avg.	OBP	SLG	OPS	E	Pct.
1996— GC Astros (GCL)		2B-3B	28	75	8	11	2	0	1	9	8	31	4	0	1-2	.147	.261	.213	.475	6	.924
1997— GC Astros (GCL)		2B	51	189	27	39	9	0	1	9	20	49	3	1	11-3	.206	.292	.270	.562	7	.969
— Kissimmee (Fla. St.)		2B	3	9	6	2	0	0	0	0	1	2	3	0	0-0	.222	.462	.222	.684	3	.833
1998— Kissimmee (Fla. St.)		3B	3	4	0	0	0	0	0	0	0	1	0	0	0-0	.000	.000	.000	.000	0	1.000
— Auburn (NY-Penn)		2B-3B-SS	51	149	22	31	5	0	1	17	11	33	6	4	4-2	.208	.282	.262	.544	14	.933
1999— Michigan (Midw.)		2B-3B-SS	116	396	78	114	29	4	6	47	29	60	17	4	7-7	.288	.360	.427	.786	21	.935
2000— Michigan (Midw.)		2B-SS	64	251	42	65	14	1	6	35	22	49	4	4	7-0	.259	.326	.394	.721	14	.953
— Kissimmee (Fla. St.)		2B-3B-SS	42	143	19	36	5	1	0	8	9	21	6	3	5-3	.252	.321	.301	.621	7	.955
2001— Lexington (S. Atl.)		2B-SS	130	536	92	155	42	2	16	64	30	85	16	8	46-12	.289	.342	.465	.807	23	.963
2002— Tampa Bay (A.L.)		S-2-3-D	59	157	17	34	8	2	0	9	3	44	7	2	7-2	.217	.262	.293	.555	11	.949
2003— Orlando (South.)		S-2-3-D	22	90	11	22	7	0	1	8	5	14	5	3	0-0	.244	.320	.356	.676	11	.896
— Tampa Bay (A.L.)		SS-2B-3B	10	27	2	5	2	0	0	2	2	6	0	0	1-0	.185	.241	.259	.501	0	1.000
— Bowie (East.)		2B	1	3	0	1	0	0	0	0	0	1	0	0	0-0	.333	.333	.333	.667	0	1.000
— Ottawa (Int'l)		2B-SS	9	30	5	7	2	0	0	5	1	5	2	0	2-0	.233	.303	.300	.603	2	.950
Major League totals (2 years)			69	184	19	39	10	2	0	11	5	50	7	2	8-2	.212	.259	.288	.547	11	.957

ESCOBAR, ALEX — OF

PERSONAL: Born September 6, 1978, in Valencia, Venezuela. ... 6-1/190. ... Bats right, throws right. ... Full name: Alexander Jose Escobar. ... Name pronounced: ess-COE-bar. ... High school: El Santuario (Valencia, Venezuela).

TRANSACTIONS/CAREER NOTES: Signed as non-drafted free agent by New York Mets organization (July 1, 1995). ... On St. Lucie disabled list (April 14-June 21 and July 8, 1999-remainder of season). ... Traded by Mets with OF Matt Lawton, P Jerrod Riggan and two players to be named later to Cleveland Indians for 2B Roberto Alomar, P Mike Bacsik and OF Danny Peoples (December 11, 2001); Indians acquired P Billy Traber and 1B Earl Snyder to complete deal (December 13, 2001). ... On disabled list (March 30, 2002-entire season). ... Recalled by Cleveland from Buffalo (August 15, 2003).

2003 GAMES PLAYED BY POSITION (MLB): OF—25.

										BATTING									FIELDING	
Year	Team (League)	Pos.	G	AB	R	H	2B	3B	HR	RBI	BB	SO	HBP	GDP	SB-CS	Avg.	OBP	SLG	OPS	E	Pct.
1996— GC Mets (GCL)		SS-OF	24	75	15	27	4	0	0	10	4	9	3	0	7-1	.360	.410	.413	.823	3	.936
1997— Kingsport (Appal.)		OF	10	36	6	7	3	0	0	3	3	8	0	3	1-0	.194	.250	.278	.528	2	.905
— GC Mets (GCL)		OF	26	73	12	18	4	1	1	11	10	17	1	1	0-0	.247	.341	.370	.711	1	.966
1998— Capital City (SAL)		OF	112	416	90	129	23	5	27	91	54	133	5	1	49-7	.310	.393	.584	.977	12	.941
1999— GC Mets (GCL)		OF	2	8	1	3	2	0	0	1	1	2	0	0	0-0	.375	.444	.625	1.069	0	1.000
— St. Lucie (Fla. St.)		OF	1	3	1	2	0	0	1	3	1	1	0	0	1-1	.667	.600	1.667	2.267	0	1.000
2000— Binghamton (East.)		OF	122	437	79	126	25	7	16	67	57	114	7	8	24-5	.288	.375	.487	.863	5	.983
2001— Norfolk (Int'l)		OF	111	397	55	106	21	4	12	52	35	146	3	10	18-3	.267	.327	.431	.758	5	.980
— New York (N.L.)		OF	18	50	3	10	1	0	3	8	3	19	0	1	1-0	.200	.245	.400	.645	2	.935
2002— Cleveland (A.L.)							Did not play.														
2003— Buffalo (Int'l)		OF-DH	118	439	63	110	21	2	24	78	24	133	1	7	8-3	.251	.296	.472	.768	5	.975
— Cleveland (A.L.)		OF	28	99	16	27	2	0	5	14	7	33	1	0	1-0	.273	.324	.444	.769	2	.969
American League totals (1 year)			28	99	16	27	2	0	5	14	7	33	1	0	1-0	.273	.324	.444	.769	2	.969
National League totals (1 year)			18	50	3	10	1	0	3	8	3	19	0	1	1-0	.200	.245	.400	.645	2	.935
Major League totals (2 years)			46	149	19	37	3	0	8	22	10	52	1	1	2-0	.248	.298	.430	.728	4	.958

ESCOBAR, KELVIM — P

PERSONAL: Born April 11, 1976, in La Guaria, Venezuela. ... 6-1/210. ... Throws right, bats right. ... Full name: Kelvim Jose Escobar.

TRANSACTIONS/CAREER NOTES: Signed as non-drafted free agent by Toronto Blue Jays organization (July 9, 1992). ... On Toronto disabled list (April 16-May 6, 1998); included rehabilitation assignment to Syracuse (May 2-6).

CAREER HITTING: 1-for-14 (.071), 1 R, 0 2B, 0 3B, 0 HR, 1 RBI.

Year League	W	L	Pct.	ERA	WHIP	G	GS	CG	ShO	Hld.	Sv.-Opp.	IP	H	R	ER	HR	BB-IBB	SO	Avg.
1993— Dom. B. Jays (DSL)	2	1	.667	4.13	1.81	8	7	0	0	...	0-...	32.2	34	17	15	...	25-...	31	...
1994— GC Blue Jays (GCL)	4	4	.500	2.35	1.14	11	10	1	0	...	1-...	65.0	56	23	17	0	18-0	64	.237
1995— Dom. B. Jays (DSL)	0	1	.000	1.72	1.21	3	2	0	0	...	0-...	15.2	14	3	3	...	5-...	20	...
— Medicine Hat (Pio.)	3	3	.500	5.71	1.43	14	14	1	• 1	...	0-...	69.1	66	47	44	6	33-0	75	.253
1996— Dunedin (Fla. St.)	9	5	.643	2.69	1.21	18	18	1	0	...	0-...	110.1	101	44	33	5	33-0	113	.240
— Knoxville (Sou.)	3	4	.429	5.33	1.57	10	10	0	0	...	0-...	54.0	61	36	32	7	24-0	44	.288
1997— Dunedin (Fla. St.)	0	1	.000	3.75	1.58	3	2	0	0	...	0-...	12.0	16	9	5	0	3-0	16	.327
— Knoxville (Sou.)	2	1	.667	3.70	1.48	5	5	1	0	...	0-...	24.1	20	13	10	1	16-0	31	.222
— Toronto (A.L.)	3	2	.600	2.90	1.52	27	0	0	0	1	14-17	31.0	28	12	10	1	19-2	36	.237
1998— Toronto (A.L.)	7	3	.700	3.73	1.34	22	10	0	0	5	0-1	79.2	72	37	33	5	35-0	72	.238
— Syracuse (Int'l)	2	2	.500	3.77	1.26	13	10	0	0	...	1-...	59.2	51	26	25	7	24-0	64	.229
1999— Toronto (A.L.)	14	11	.560	5.69	1.63	33	30	1	0	0	0-0	174.0	203	118	110	19	81-2	129	.293
2000— Toronto (A.L.)	10	15	.400	5.35	1.51	43	24	3	1	3	2-3	180.0	186	118	107	26	85-3	142	.267
2001— Toronto (A.L.)	6	8	.429	3.50	1.15	59	11	1	1	13	0-0	126.0	93	51	49	8	52-5	121	.204
2002— Toronto (A.L.)	5	7	.417	4.27	1.53	76	0	0	0	0	38-46	78.0	75	39	37	10	44-6	85	.246
2003— Toronto (A.L.)	13	9	.591	4.29	1.48	41	26	1	1	0	4-5	180.1	189	94	86	15	78-3	159	.270
Major League totals (7 years)	58	55	.513	4.58	1.46	301	101	6	3	22	58-72	849.0	846	469	432	84	394-21	744	.259

ESTALELLA, BOBBY   C

PERSONAL: Born August 23, 1974, in Hialeah, Fla. ... 6-1/225. ... Bats right, throws right. ... Full name: Robert M. Estalella. ... Name pronounced: ES-ta-LAY-yuh. ... High school: Cooper City (Fla.). ... Junior college: Miami-Dade South Community College.

TRANSACTIONS/CAREER NOTES: Selected by Philadelphia Phillies organization in 23rd round of free-agent draft (June 1, 1992). ... On Philadelphia disabled list (March 27-April 29, 1999); included rehabilitation assignments to Clearwater (April 9-17) and to Scranton/Wilkes-Barre (April 19-29). ... Traded by Phillies to San Francisco Giants for P Chris Brock (December 12, 1999). ... Traded by Giants with P Joe Smith to New York Yankees for P Brian Boehringer (July 5, 2001). ... Released by Yankees (March 27, 2002). ... Signed by Colorado Rockies organization (March 31, 2002). ... On Colorado disabled list (July 8, 2002-remainder of season). ... Placed on 15-day disabled list by Colorado (August 15, 2003). ... Transferred to 60-day disabled list (August 28, 2003).

2003 GAMES PLAYED BY POSITION (MLB): C—46.

Year Team (League)	Pos.	G	AB	R	H	2B	3B	HR	RBI	BB	SO	HBP	GDP	SB-CS	Avg.	OBP	SLG	OPS	E	Pct.
1993— Martinsville (App.)	C	35	122	14	36	11	0	3	19	14	24	2	6	0-1	.295	.377	.459	.836	6	.975
— Clearwater (FSL)	C	11	35	4	8	0	0	0	4	2	3	0	1	0-0	.229	.270	.229	.499	0	1.000
1994— Spartanburg (SAL)	C	86	299	34	65	19	1	9	41	31	85	1	5	0-1	.217	.290	.378	.667	10	.985
— Clearwater (FSL)	C	13	46	3	12	1	0	2	9	3	17	0	1	0-0	.261	.300	.413	.713	1	.990
1995— Clearwater (FSL)	C	117	404	61	105	24	1	15	58	56	76	2	12	0-3	.260	.350	.436	.785	11	.987
— Reading (East.)	C	10	34	5	8	1	0	2	9	4	7	1	1	0-0	.235	.333	.441	.775	1	.986
1996— Reading (East.)	C	111	365	48	89	14	2	23	72	67	104	5	7	2-4	.244	.365	.482	.847	14	.984
— Scran./W.B. (I.L.)	C	11	36	7	9	3	0	3	8	5	10	0	1	0-0	.250	.341	.583	.925	2	.968
— Philadelphia (N.L.)	C	7	17	5	6	0	0	2	4	1	6	0	0	1-0	.353	.389	.706	1.095	0	1.000
1997— Scran./W.B. (I.L.)	C-DH	123	433	63	101	32	0	16	65	56	109	9	14	3-0	.233	.332	.418	.750	13	.986
— Philadelphia (N.L.)	C	13	29	9	10	1	0	4	9	7	7	0	2	0-0	.345	.472	.793	1.265	0	1.000
1998— Scran./W.B. (I.L.)	C-DH	76	242	49	68	14	1	17	49	66	49	2	13	0-0	.281	.436	.558	.994	5	.990
— Philadelphia (N.L.)	C	47	165	16	31	6	1	8	20	13	49	1	4	0-0	.188	.247	.382	.629	4	.980
1999— Clearwater (FSL)	C-DH	8	26	3	11	3	0	1	8	3	3	0	0	0-0	.423	.483	.654	1.137	1	.976
— Scran./W.B. (I.L.)	C-DH	110	386	58	89	23	2	15	62	55	100	5	12	4-1	.231	.330	.417	.747	5	.993
— Philadelphia (N.L.)	C	9	18	2	3	0	0	0	1	4	7	0	0	0-1	.167	.318	.167	.485	1	.976
2000— San Francisco (N.L.)	C	106	299	45	70	22	3	14	53	57	92	2	4	3-0	.234	.357	.468	.826	5	.993
2001— San Francisco (N.L.)	C	29	93	11	19	5	1	3	10	11	28	1	2	0-0	.204	.295	.376	.672	0	1.000
— Fresno (PCL)	C-1B	6	22	3	7	1	0	1	4	1	9	0	1	0-0	.318	.348	.500	.848	0	1.000
— Columbus (Int'l)	C-1B	48	171	26	44	10	1	10	38	21	45	2	7	0-2	.257	.340	.503	.843	2	.993
— New York (A.L.)	C	3	4	1	0	0	0	0	0	1	2	1	0	0-0	.000	.333	.000	.333	0	1.000
2002— Colo. Springs (PCL)	C	23	79	16	23	9	0	6	20	11	20	0	0	0-0	.291	.374	.633	1.007	1	.995
— Colorado (N.L.)	C	38	112	17	23	8	0	8	25	14	33	0	1	0-1	.205	.285	.491	.776	1	.995
2003— Colorado (N.L.)	C	46	140	17	28	7	0	7	21	19	55	1	4	2-0	.200	.294	.400	.694	4	.985
American League totals (1 year)		3	4	1	0	0	0	0	0	1	2	1	0	0-0	.000	.333	.000	.333	0	1.000
National League totals (8 years)		295	873	122	190	49	5	46	143	126	277	5	17	6-2	.218	.316	.443	.759	15	.992
Major League totals (8 years)		298	877	123	190	49	5	46	143	127	279	6	17	6-2	.217	.316	.441	.757	15	.992

ESTES, SHAWN   P

PERSONAL: Born February 18, 1973, in San Bernardino, Calif. ... 6-2/200. ... Throws left, bats right. ... Full name: Aaron Shawn Estes. ... Name pronounced: ES-tus. ... High school: Douglas (Minden, Nev.).

TRANSACTIONS/CAREER NOTES: Selected by Seattle Mariners organization in first round (11th pick overall) of free-agent draft (June 3, 1991). ... On disabled list (August 19, 1993-remainder of season). ... On Appleton disabled list (April 8-July 19 and July 25-August 15, 1994). ... Traded by Mariners with IF Wilson Delgado to San Francisco Giants for P Salomon Torres (May 21, 1995). ... On disabled list (March 23-April 6, 1997). ... On San Francisco disabled list (July 11-September 4, 1998); included rehabilitation assignments to Bakersfield (August 26-29) and Fresno (August 30-September 4). ... On San Francisco disabled list (March 29-April 17, 2000); included rehabilitation assignments to Fresno (April 7-12) and San Jose (April 13-17). ... On disabled list (May 9-24 and August 23, 2001-remainder of season). ... Traded by Giants to New York Mets for OF Tsuyoshi Shinjo and SS Desi Relaford (December 16, 2001). ... Traded by Mets with cash to Cincinnati Reds for P Pedro Feliciano, OF Elvin Andujar and two players to be named later (August 15, 2002); Mets acquired OF Raul Gonzalez (August 20, 2002) and OF Brady Clark to complete deal (September 9, 2002). ... Granted free agency (October 28, 2002). ... Signed by Chicago Cubs (December 20, 2002).

CAREER HITTING: 58-for-387 (.150), 34 R, 11 2B, 0 3B, 4 HR, 26 RBI.

Year League	W	L	Pct.	ERA	WHIP	G	GS	CG	ShO	Hld.	Sv.-Opp.	IP	H	R	ER	HR	BB-IBB	SO	Avg.
1991— Bellingham (N'west)	1	3	.250	6.88	2.41	9	9	0	0	...	0-...	34.0	27	33	26	2	55-0	35	.218
1992— Bellingham (N'west)	3	3	.500	4.32	1.68	15	15	0	0	...	0-...	77.0	84	55	37	6	45-0	77	.279
1993— Appleton (Midw.)	5	9	.357	7.24	1.92	19	18	0	0	...	0-...	83.1	108	85	67	3	52-1	65	.305
1994— Ariz. Mariners (Ariz.)	0	3	.000	3.15	1.10	5	5	0	0	...	0-...	20.0	16	9	7	0	6-0	31	.205
— Appleton (Midw.)	0	2	.000	4.58	1.83	5	4	0	0	...	0-...	19.2	19	13	10	1	17-0	28	.271
1995— Wisconsin (Midw.)	0	0	...	0.90	1.00	2	2	0	0	...	0-...	10.0	5	1	1	0	5-0	11	.156
— Burlington (Midw.)	0	0	...	4.11	1.63	4	4	0	0	...	0-...	15.1	13	8	7	2	12-0	22	.224
— San Jose (Calif.)	5	2	.714	2.17	0.99	9	8	0	0	...	0-...	49.2	32	13	12	1	17-0	61	.188
— Shreveport (Texas)	2	0	1.000	2.01	1.07	4	4	0	0	...	0-...	22.1	14	5	5	1	10-0	18	.184
— San Francisco (N.L.)	0	3	.000	6.75	1.21	3	3	0	0	0	0-0	17.1	16	14	13	2	5-0	14	.229

E

Year	League	W	L	Pct.	ERA	WHIP	G	GS	CG	ShO	Hld.	Sv.-Opp.	IP	H	R	ER	HR	BB-IBB	SO	Avg.
1996— Phoenix (PCL)		9	3	.750	3.43	1.18	18	18	0	0	...	0-...	110.1	92	43	42	7	38-1	95	.228
— San Francisco (N.L.)		3	5	.375	3.60	1.46	11	11	0	0	0	0-0	70.0	63	30	28	3	39-3	60	.243
1997— San Francisco (N.L.)		19	5	.792	3.18	1.30	32	32	3	2	0	0-0	201.0	162	80	71	12	* 100-2	181	.223
1998— San Francisco (N.L.)		7	12	.368	5.06	1.54	25	25	1	1	0	0-0	149.1	150	89	84	14	80-6	136	.269
— Bakersfield (Calif.)		0	0	...	0.00	0.92	1	1	0	0	...	0-...	4.1	3	0	0	0	1-0	5	.188
— Fresno (PCL)		1	0	1.000	1.80	1.20	1	1	0	0	...	0-...	5.0	3	1	1	1	3-0	6	.188
1999— San Francisco (N.L.)		11	11	.500	4.92	1.58	32	32	1	1	0	0-0	203.0	209	121	111	21	112-2	159	.268
2000— Fresno (PCL)		0	1	.000	9.00	2.33	1	1	0	0	...	0-...	3.0	5	9	3	2	2-0	2	.294
— San Jose (Calif.)		1	0	1.000	0.00	0.43	1	1	0	0	...	0-...	7.0	2	0	0	0	1-0	11	.095
— San Francisco (N.L.)		15	6	.714	4.26	1.59	30	30	4	2	0	0-0	190.1	194	99	90	11	108-1	136	.275
2001— San Francisco (N.L.)		9	8	.529	4.02	1.43	27	27	0	0	0	0-0	159.0	151	78	71	11	77-7	109	.253
2002— New York (N.L.)		4	9	.308	4.55	1.50	23	23	1	1	0	0-0	132.2	133	70	67	12	66-9	92	.267
— Cincinnati (N.L.)		1	3	.250	7.71	1.96	6	6	0	0	0	0-0	28.0	38	24	24	1	16-0	17	.345
2003— Chicago (N.L.)		8	11	.421	5.73	1.74	29	28	1	1	0	0-0	152.1	182	113	97	20	83-1	103	.305
Major League totals (9 years)		77	73	.513	4.53	1.52	218	217	11	8	0	0-0	1303.0	1298	718	656	107	687-31	1007	.265

ESTRADA, JOHNNY — C

PERSONAL: Born June 27, 1976, in Hayward, Calif. ... 5-11/209. ... Bats both, throws right. ... Full name: Johnny P. Estrada. ... High school: Roosevelt (Fresno, Calif.). ... Junior college: College of the Sequoias (Calif.).

TRANSACTIONS/CAREER NOTES: Selected by Houston Astros organization in 71st round of free-agent draft (June 2, 1994); did not sign. ... Selected by Phiadelphia Phillies organization in 17th round of free-agent draft (June 3, 1997). ... Traded by Phillies to Atlanta Braves for P Kevin Millwood (December 20, 2002). ... Recalled by Atlanta from Richmond (April 20, 2003). ... Optioned to Richmond by Atlanta (April 29, 2003). ... Recalled from Richmond by Atlanta (August 31, 2003).

2003 GAMES PLAYED BY POSITION (MLB): C—14.

										BATTING									FIELDING	
Year	Team (League)	Pos.	G	AB	R	H	2B	3B	HR	RBI	BB	SO	HBP	GDP	SB-CS	Avg.	OBP	SLG	OPS	E	Pct.
1997— Batavia (NY-Penn)		C-1B	58	223	28	70	17	2	6	43	9	15	1	9	0-0	.314	.336	.489	.825	0	1.000
1998— Piedmont (S. Atl.)		C	77	303	33	94	14	2	7	44	6	19	5	11	0-1	.310	.331	.439	.770	6	.990
— Clearwater (FSL)		C	37	117	8	26	8	0	0	13	5	7	0	2	0-0	.222	.250	.291	.541	5	.979
1999— Clearwater (FSL)		C	98	346	35	96	15	0	9	52	14	26	2	12	1-0	.277	.303	.399	.702	5	.989
2000— Reading (East.)		C	95	356	42	105	18	0	12	42	10	20	4	8	1-0	.295	.322	.447	.768	7	.990
2001— Scran./W.B. (I.L.)		C	32	131	13	38	13	0	0	16	5	6	1	5	0-0	.290	.319	.389	.708	0	1.000
— Philadelphia (N.L.)		C	89	298	26	68	15	0	8	37	16	32	4	15	0-0	.228	.273	.359	.632	4	.993
2002— Scran./W.B. (I.L.)		C	118	434	49	121	27	0	11	67	26	53	5	19	1-0	.279	.322	.417	.739	4	.995
— Philadelphia (N.L.)		C	10	17	0	2	1	0	0	2	2	2	0	0	0-0	.118	.211	.176	.387	0	1.000
2003— Richmond (Int'l)		C-DH	106	354	40	116	29	0	10	66	30	30	12	11	0-0	.328	.393	.494	.887	4	.994
— Atlanta (N.L.)		C	16	36	2	11	0	0	0	2	0	3	3	1	0-0	.306	.359	.306	.665	0	1.000
Major League totals (3 years)			115	351	28	81	16	0	8	41	18	37	7	16	0-0	.231	.279	.345	.624	4	.994

ESTRELLA, LEO — P

PERSONAL: Born February 20, 1975, in Puerto Plata, Dominican Republic. ... 6-1/185. ... Throws right, bats right. ... Full name: Leoncio Ramirez Estrella. ... Name pronounced: LE-ON-cio es-TRAY-yah. ... High school: Liceo Padre Las Casas (Puerto Plata, Dominican Republic).

TRANSACTIONS/CAREER NOTES: Signed as non-drafted free agent by New York Mets organization (October 12, 1993). ... On Capital City disabled list (April 10-24, 1998). ... Traded by Mets to Toronto Blue Jays for IF/OF Tony Phillips (July 31, 1998). ... Traded by Blue Jays with P Clayton Andrews to Cincinnati Reds for P Steve Parris (November 22, 2000). ... Claimed on waivers by New York Mets (June 14, 2001). ... Claimed on waivers by Reds (July 17, 2001). ... Granted free agency (October 15, 2001). ... Signed by Milwaukee Brewers organization (January 17, 2003). ... Contract purchased by Milwaukee from Indianapolis (April 29, 2003). ... Sent outright to Indianapolis by Milwaukee (August 20, 2003).

CAREER HITTING: 0-for-0 (.000), 0 R, 0 2B, 0 3B, 0 HR, 0 RBI.

Year	League	W	L	Pct.	ERA	WHIP	G	GS	CG	ShO	Hld.	Sv.-Opp.	IP	H	R	ER	HR	BB-IBB	SO	Avg.
1994— Dom. Mets (DSL)		5	0	1.000	3.47	1.79	30	0	0	0	...	3-...	36.1	33	28	14	...	32-...	20	
1995— Dom. Mets (DSL)		2	4	.333	5.44	1.72	12	8	0	0	...	0-...	43.0	61	37	26	...	13-...	32	
1996— Kingsport (Appal.)		6	3	.667	3.88	1.34	15	7	1	0	...	0-...	58.0	54	32	25	3	24-0	52	.248
1997— Pittsfield (NYP)		7	6	.538	3.03	1.28	15	15	0	0	...	0-...	92.0	91	48	31	0	27-0	55	.253
1998— Capital City (S. Atl.)		10	8	.556	3.93	1.20	20	20	3	0	...	0-...	119.0	120	66	52	10	23-0	97	.261
— Hagerstown (S. Atl.)		1	3	.250	4.50	1.57	5	5	0	0	...	0-...	30.0	34	19	15	0	13-1	27	.304
1999— Dunedin (Fla. St.)		14	7	.667	3.21	1.27	27	24	2	• 2	...	0-...	168.0	166	74	60	11	47-0	116	.267
2000— Tennessee (Sou.)		5	5	.500	3.67	1.29	13	13	3	2	...	0-...	76.0	68	36	31	6	30-1	63	.246
— Syracuse (Int'l)		5	4	.556	4.01	1.20	15	15	3	1	...	0-...	89.2	68	42	40	8	40-0	48	.215
— Toronto (A.L.)		0	0	...	5.79	1.93	2	0	0	0	0	0-0	4.2	9	3	3	1	0-0	3	.450
2001— Chattanooga (Sou.)		0	1	.000	3.68	1.16	3	3	0	0	...	0-...	14.2	13	6	6	0	4-0	14	.241
— Louisville (Int'l)		1	1	.500	4.88	1.50	34	5	0	0	...	1-...	62.2	67	36	34	8	27-0	37	.277
— Norfolk (Int'l)		2	0	1.000	3.12	1.79	8	1	0	0	...	0-...	17.1	23	7	6	1	8-0	10	.354
2002— West Tenn (Sou.)		2	2	.500	3.28	1.26	10	3	0	0	...	0-...	24.2	23	13	9	0	8-0	18	.250
— Iowa (PCL)		0	0	...	5.91	1.59	8	0	0	0	...	1-...	10.2	10	8	7	0	7-0	9	.238
— New Haven (East.)		2	2	.500	4.81	1.68	14	5	0	0	...	0-...	39.1	46	30	21	4	20-0	23	.289
2003— Indianapolis (Int'l)		1	0	1.000	1.20	1.00	7	0	0	0	...	0-...	15.0	9	2	2	1	6-0	12	.170
— Milwaukee (N.L.)		7	3	.700	4.36	1.45	58	0	0	0	9	3-8	66.0	75	32	32	10	21-5	25	.290
American League totals (1 year)		0	0	...	5.79	1.93	2	0	0	0	0	0-0	4.2	9	3	3	1	0-0	3	.450
National League totals (1 year)		7	3	.700	4.36	1.45	58	0	0	0	9	3-8	66.0	75	32	32	10	21-5	25	.290
Major League totals (2 years)		7	3	.700	4.46	1.49	60	0	0	0	9	3-8	70.2	84	35	35	11	21-5	28	.301

ETHERTON, SETH — P

PERSONAL: Born October 17, 1976, in Laguna Beach, Calif. ... 6-1/200. ... Throws right, bats right. ... Full name: Seth Michael Etherton. ... High school: Dana Hills (Dana Point, Calif.). ... College: USC.

TRANSACTIONS/CAREER NOTES: Selected by St. Louis Cardinals organization in ninth-round of free-agent draft (June 3, 1997); did not sign. ... Selected by Anaheim Angels organization in first round (18th pick overall) of free-agent draft (June 2, 1998). ... On Anaheim disabled list (August 5, 2000-remainder of season) ... Traded by Angels to Cincinnati Reds for SS Wilmy Caceres (December 10, 2000). ... On disabled list (March 22, 2001-entire season). ... On Cincinnati disabled list (March 21-July 11 and July 23, 2002-remainder of season); included rehabilitation assignment to Dayton (May 17-20), Chattanooga (May 21-June 6) and Louisville (June 13-July 9). ... Claimed on waivers by New York Yankees (July 11, 2002). ... Waiver claim voided by commissioner's office (July 23, 2002). ... Called up from Louisville by Cincinnati (August 16, 2003).

CAREER HITTING: 1-for-9 (.111), 1 R, 0 2B, 0 3B, 0 HR, 0 RBI.

Year League	W	L	Pct.	ERA	WHIP	G	GS	CG	ShO	Hld.	Sv.-Opp.	IP	H	R	ER	HR	BB-IBB	SO	Avg.
1998— Midland (Texas)	1	5	.167	6.14	1.43	9	7	1	0	...	0-...	48.1	57	36	33	9	12-0	35	.295
1999— Erie (East.)	10	10	.500	3.27	1.17	24	24	4	1	...	0-...	167.2	153	72	61	14	43-0	153	.241
— Edmonton (PCL)	0	2	.000	5.48	1.45	4	4	0	0	...	0-...	21.1	25	13	13	7	6-0	19	.291
2000— Edmonton (PCL)	3	2	.600	4.01	1.35	9	9	0	0	...	0-...	58.1	60	30	26	6	19-0	50	.264
— Anaheim (A.L.)	5	1	.833	5.52	1.49	11	11	0	0	0	0-0	60.1	68	38	37	16	22-0	32	.278
2001— Cincinnati (N.L.)										Did not play.									
2002— Dayton (Midw.)	0	0	...	0.00	1.00	1	1	0	0	...	0-...	1.0	1	0	0	0	0-0	2	.250
— Chattanooga (Sou.)	0	1	.000	0.96	0.75	3	3	0	0	...	0-...	9.1	5	1	1	0	2-0	4	.167
— Louisville (Int'l)	0	1	.000	8.22	1.76	5	5	0	0	...	0-...	15.1	21	16	14	4	6-0	10	.328
— Norwich (East.)	0	0	...	0.00	1.00	1	1	0	0	...	0-...	2.0	1	1	0	0	1-0	2	.143
2003— Louisville (Int'l)	7	7	.500	4.31	1.38	21	21	2	1	...	0-...	123.1	144	62	59	11	26-1	69	.297
— Cincinnati (N.L.)	2	4	.333	6.90	1.80	7	7	0	0	0	0-0	30.0	39	23	23	4	15-1	17	.322
American League totals (1 year)	5	1	.833	5.52	1.49	11	11	0	0	0	0-0	60.1	68	38	37	16	22-0	32	.278
National League totals (1 year)	2	4	.333	6.90	1.80	7	7	0	0	0	0-0	30.0	39	23	23	4	15-1	17	.322
Major League totals (2 years)	7	5	.583	5.98	1.59	18	18	0	0	0	0-0	90.1	107	61	60	20	37-1	49	.292

EVERETT, ADAM   SS

PERSONAL: Born February 2, 1977, in Austell, Ga. ... 6-0/160. ... Bats right, throws right. ... Full name: Jeffrey Adam Everett. ... High school: Harrison (Kennesaw, Ga.). ... College: South Carolina.

TRANSACTIONS/CAREER NOTES: Selected by Boston Red Sox organization in first round (12th pick overall) of free-agent draft (June 2, 1998). ... Traded by Red Sox with P Greg Miller to Houston Astros for OF Carl Everett (December 14, 1999). ... Recalled by Houston from New Orleans (May 2, 2003).

2003 GAMES PLAYED BY POSITION (MLB): SS—128.

										BATTING									FIELDING	
Year Team (League)	Pos.	G	AB	R	H	2B	3B	HR	RBI	BB	SO	HBP	GDP	SB-CS	Avg.	OBP	SLG	OPS	E	Pct.
1998— Lowell (NY-Penn)	SS	21	71	11	21	6	2	0	9	11	13	3	2	2-1	.296	.407	.437	.844	9	.918
1999— Trenton (East.)	SS	98	338	56	89	11	0	10	44	41	64	10	3	21-5	.263	.356	.385	.741	18	.959
2000— New Orleans (PCL)	SS	126	453	82	111	25	2	5	37	75	100	11	6	13-4	.245	.363	.342	.705	25	.959
2001— New Orleans (PCL)	SS	114	441	69	110	20	8	5	40	39	74	16	4	24-5	.249	.330	.365	.695	24	.956
— Houston (N.L.)	SS	9	3	1	0	0	0	0	0	0	1	0	0	1-0	.000	.000	.000	.000	2	.667
2002— Houston (N.L.)	SS	40	88	11	17	3	0	0	4	12	19	1	1	3-0	.193	.297	.227	.524	5	.962
— New Orleans (PCL)	SS	88	345	51	95	16	7	2	25	24	59	6	3	12-3	.275	.331	.380	.710	7	.984
2003— New Orleans (PCL)	SS-2B	25	100	23	25	6	1	1	9	7	16	1	1	3-1	.250	.306	.360	.666	2	.982
— Houston (N.L.)	SS	128	387	51	99	18	3	8	51	28	66	9	7	8-1	.256	.320	.380	.700	17	.970
Major League totals (3 years)		177	478	63	116	21	3	8	55	40	86	10	8	12-1	.243	.314	.349	.663	24	.966

EVERETT, CARL   OF

PERSONAL: Born June 3, 1971, in Tampa, Fla. ... 6-0/215. ... Bats both, throws right. ... Full name: Carl Edward Everett. ... High school: Hillsborough (Tampa).

TRANSACTIONS/CAREER NOTES: Selected by New York Yankees organization in first round (10th pick overall) of free-agent draft (June 4, 1990). ... On Fort Lauderdale disabled list (July 7-August 15, 1992). ... Selected by Florida Marlins in second round (27th pick overall) of expansion draft (November 17, 1992). ... On High Desert disabled list (April 8-13, 1993). ... On Florida disabled list (July 23-August 10, 1994). ... On Edmonton suspended list (August 29, 1994-remainder of season). ... Traded by Marlins to New York Mets for 2B Quilvio Veras (November 29, 1994). ... On disabled list (April 12-27, 1996). ... Traded by Mets to Houston Astros for P John Hudek (December 22, 1997). ... On disabled list (July 16-August 6, 1999). ... Traded by Astros to Boston Red Sox for SS Adam Everett and P Greg Miller (December 14, 1999). ... On suspended list (July 24-August 5, 2000; and March 29-30, 2001). ... On Boston disabled list (June 22-July 28, 2001); included rehabilitation assignments to Sarasota (July 21-24) and Gulf Coast Red Sox (July 25-28). ... Traded by Red Sox to Texas Rangers for P Darren Oliver (December 13, 2001). ... On Texas disabled list (May 5-21 and June 3-July 2, 2002); included rehabilitation assignment to Charlotte (May 19-21). ... Traded by Rangers to Chicago White Sox for two or three minor league players to be named (July 1, 2003); Rangers acquired P Frankie Francisco, P Josh Rupe and OF Anthony Webster to complete deal (July 25, 2003).

2003 GAMES PLAYED BY POSITION (MLB): OF—140, DH—4.

										BATTING									FIELDING	
Year Team (League)	Pos.	G	AB	R	H	2B	3B	HR	RBI	BB	SO	HBP	GDP	SB-CS	Avg.	OBP	SLG	OPS	E	Pct.
1990— GC Yankees (GCL)	OF	48	185	28	48	8	5	1	14	15	38	6	1	15-2	.259	.333	.373	.706	5	.932
1991— Greensboro (S. Atl.)	OF	123	468	96	127	18	0	4	40	57	122	23	1	28-19	.271	.376	.335	.711	7	.974
1992— Fort Laud. (FSL)	OF	46	183	30	42	8	2	2	9	12	40	4	1	11-3	.230	.291	.328	.619	3	.975
— Prince Will. (Car.)	OF	6	22	7	7	0	0	4	9	5	7	0	0	1-0	.318	.444	.864	1.308	0	1.000
1993— High Desert (Calif.)	OF	59	253	48	73	12	6	10	52	22	73	6	3	24-9	.289	.358	.502	.860	2	.985
— Florida (N.L.)	OF	11	19	0	2	0	0	0	0	1	9	0	0	1-0	.105	.150	.105	.255	1	.857
— Edmonton (PCL)	OF	35	136	28	42	13	4	6	16	19	45	2	1	12-1	.309	.401	.596	.997	2	.976
1994— Edmonton (PCL)	OF-DH	78	321	63	108	17	2	11	47	19	65	4	7	16-13	.336	.380	.505	.884	2	.989
— Florida (N.L.)	OF	16	51	7	11	1	0	2	6	3	15	0	0	4-0	.216	.259	.363	.612	0	1.000
1995— New York (N.L.)	OF	79	289	48	75	13	1	12	54	39	67	2	11	2-5	.260	.352	.436	.788	3	.981
— Norfolk (Int'l)	OF-SS-DH	67	260	52	78	16	4	6	35	20	47	4	2	12-6	.300	.358	.462	.819	0	1.000
1996— New York (N.L.)	OF	101	192	29	46	8	1	1	16	21	53	4	6	6-0	.240	.326	.307	.633	7	.935
1997— New York (N.L.)	OF	142	443	58	110	28	3	14	57	32	102	7	3	17-9	.248	.308	.420	.728	7	.971
1998— Houston (N.L.)	OF	133	467	72	138	34	4	15	76	44	102	3	11	14-12	.296	.359	.482	.840	4	.987
1999— Houston (N.L.)	OF-DH	123	464	86	151	33	3	25	108	50	94	11	5	27-7	.325	.398	.571	.969	6	.975
2000— Boston (A.L.)	OF-DH	137	496	82	149	32	4	34	108	52	113	8	4	11-4	.300	.373	.587	.959	6	.980
2001— Boston (A.L.)	OF-DH	102	409	61	105	24	4	14	58	27	104	13	3	9-2	.257	.323	.438	.761	5	.974
— Sarasota (Fla. St.)	DH	2	7	0	3	0	0	0	0	2	0	0	0	0-0	.429	.556	.429	.984	...	...
— GC Red Sox (GCL)	OF	3	10	2	2	0	0	2	2	1	3	0	0	0-0	.200	.273	.800	1.073	0	1.000
2002— Texas (A.L.)	OF-DH	105	374	47	100	16	0	16	62	33	77	6	7	2-3	.267	.333	.439	.772	5	.969
— Charlotte (Fla. St.)	OF	1	4	1	2	0	0	1	0	1	0	1	0	0-0	.500	.500	1.500	1.500	0	1.000
2003— Texas (A.L.)	OF-DH	74	270	53	74	13	3	18	51	31	48	5	2	4-1	.274	.356	.544	.900	2	.986
— Chicago (A.L.)	OF-DH	73	256	40	77	14	0	10	41	22	36	10	5	4-3	.301	.377	.473	.850	2	.987
American League totals (4 years)		491	1805	283	505	99	11	92	320	165	378	42	21	30-13	.280	.352	.500	.851	20	.975
National League totals (7 years)		605	1925	300	533	117	12	69	317	190	442	27	34	71-33	.277	.348	.458	.806	28	.975
Major League totals (11 years)		1096	3730	583	1038	216	23	161	637	355	820	69	55	101-46	.278	.350	.478	.828	48	.977

EYRE, SCOTT   P

PERSONAL: Born May 30, 1972, in Inglewood, Calif. ... 6-1/210. ... Throws left, bats left. ... Full name: Scott Alan Eyre. ... Name pronounced: AIR. ... High school: Cyprus (Magna, Utah). ... Junior college: Southern Idaho College.

TRANSACTIONS/CAREER NOTES: Selected by Texas Rangers organization in ninth round of free-agent draft (June 3, 1991). ... Traded by Rangers to Chicago White Sox for SS Esteban Beltre (March 28, 1994). ... On disabled list (April 8-27, 1994). ... On Prince William disabled list (April 6-September 7, 1995). ... On Charlotte disabled list (June 2-13, 1999). ... On Chicago disabled list (August 31-September 26, 1999); included rehabilitation assignment to Charlotte (September 8-26). ... Traded by White Sox to Toronto Blue Jays for P Gary Glover (November 7, 2000). ... Claimed on waivers by San Francisco Giants (August 8, 2002).

CAREER HITTING: 2-for-7 (.286), 0 R, 0 2B, 0 3B, 0 HR, 0 RBI.

Year League	W	L	Pct.	ERA	WHIP	G	GS	CG	ShO	Hld.	Sv.-Opp.	IP	H	R	ER	HR	BB-IBB	SO	Avg.
1992— Butte (Pio.)	7	3	.700	2.90	1.36	15	14	2	1	...	0-...	80.2	71	30	26	6	39-0	94	.241
1993— Char., S.C. (SAL)	11	7	.611	3.45	1.21	26	26	0	0	...	0-...	143.2	115	74	55	6	59-1	154	.220
1994— South Bend (Mid.)	8	4	.667	3.47	1.30	19	18	2	0	...	0-...	111.2	108	56	43	7	37-0	111	.248
1995— GC White Sox (GCL)	0	2	.000	2.30	1.02	9	9	0	0	...	0-...	27.1	16	7	7	0	12-0	40	.174
1996— Birmingham (Sou.)	12	7	.632	4.38	1.57	27	27	0	0	...	0-...	158.1	170	90	77	12	79-3	137	.277
1997— Birmingham (Sou.)	• 13	5	.722	3.84	1.30	22	22	0	0	...	0-...	126.2	110	61	54	14	55-2	127	.231
— Chicago (A.L.)	4	4	.500	5.04	1.53	11	11	0	0	0	0-0	60.2	62	36	34	11	31-1	36	.267
1998— Chicago (A.L.)	3	8	.273	5.38	1.66	33	17	0	0	0	0-0	107.0	114	78	64	24	64-0	73	.271
1999— Charlotte (Int'l)	6	4	.600	3.82	1.43	12	11	0	0	...	0-...	68.1	75	32	29	3	23-1	63	.284
— Chicago (A.L.)	1	1	.500	7.56	2.12	21	0	0	0	1	0-0	25.0	38	22	21	6	15-2	17	.339
2000— Chicago (A.L.)	1	1	.500	6.63	2.16	13	1	0	0	0	0-0	19.0	29	15	14	3	12-0	16	.372
— Charlotte (Int'l)	3	2	.600	3.00	1.10	47	0	0	0	...	12-...	48.0	33	18	16	1	20-3	46	.200
2001— Syracuse (Int'l)	4	6	.400	3.18	1.17	62	2	0	0	...	0-...	79.1	67	30	28	8	26-4	96	.224
— Toronto (A.L.)	1	2	.333	3.45	1.40	17	0	0	0	3	2-3	15.2	15	6	6	1	7-2	16	.263
2002— Toronto (A.L.)	2	4	.333	4.97	1.55	49	3	0	0	12	0-1	63.1	69	37	35	4	29-7	51	.278
— San Francisco (N.L.)	0	0	...	1.59	1.59	21	0	0	0	6	0-0	11.1	11	4	2	0	7-1	7	.256
2003— San Francisco (N.L.)	2	1	.667	3.32	1.51	74	0	0	0	20	1-3	57.0	60	23	21	4	26-0	35	.268
American League totals (6 years)	**12**	**20**	**.375**	**5.39**	**1.67**	**144**	**32**	**0**	**0**	**16**	**2-4**	**290.2**	**327**	**194**	**174**	**49**	**158-12**	**209**	**.285**
National League totals (2 years)	**2**	**1**	**.667**	**3.03**	**1.52**	**95**	**0**	**0**	**0**	**26**	**1-3**	**68.1**	**71**	**27**	**23**	**4**	**33-1**	**42**	**.266**
Major League totals (7 years)	**14**	**21**	**.400**	**4.94**	**1.64**	**239**	**32**	**0**	**0**	**42**	**3-7**	**359.0**	**398**	**221**	**197**	**53**	**191-13**	**251**	**.281**

FARNSWORTH, KYLE   P

PERSONAL: Born April 14, 1976, in Wichita, Kan. ... 6-4/235. ... Throws right, bats right. ... Full name: Kyle Lynn Farnsworth. ... High school: Milton (Alpharetta, Ga.). ... Junior college: Abraham Baldwin College (Ga.).

TRANSACTIONS/CAREER NOTES: Selected by Chicago Cubs organization in 47th round of free-agent draft (June 2, 1994). ... On Chicago disabled list (April 10-June 4, 2002); included rehabilitation assignment to Iowa (May 31-June 3). ... Suspended by Major League Baseball (June 26, 2003). ... Reinstated (June 28, 2003).

CAREER HITTING: 4-for-53 (.075), 3 R, 1 2B, 0 3B, 0 HR, 3 RBI.

Year League	W	L	Pct.	ERA	WHIP	G	GS	CG	ShO	Hld.	Sv.-Opp.	IP	H	R	ER	HR	BB-IBB	SO	Avg.
1995— GC Cubs (GCL)	3	2	.600	0.87	1.06	16	0	0	0	...	1-...	31.0	22	8	3	0	11-0	18	.214
1996— Rockford (Midwest)	9	6	.600	3.70	1.40	20	20	1	0	...	0-...	112.0	122	62	46	7	35-0	82	.274
1997— Daytona (Fla. St.)	10	10	.500	4.09	1.44	27	27	2	0	...	0-...	156.1	178	91	71	13	47-1	105	.286
1998— West Tenn (Sou.)	8	2	.800	2.77	1.12	13	13	0	0	...	0-...	81.1	70	32	25	6	21-0	73	.231
— Iowa (PCL)	5	9	.357	6.93	1.61	18	18	0	0	...	0-...	102.2	129	88	79	18	36-0	79	.309
1999— Iowa (PCL)	2	2	.500	3.20	1.19	6	6	0	0	...	0-...	39.1	38	16	14	5	9-0	29	.262
— Chicago (N.L.)	5	9	.357	5.05	1.48	27	21	1	1	0	0-0	130.0	140	80	73	28	52-1	70	.271
2000— Chicago (N.L.)	2	9	.182	6.43	1.82	46	5	0	0	6	1-6	77.0	90	58	55	14	50-8	74	.291
— Iowa (PCL)	0	2	.000	3.20	1.66	22	0	0	0	...	9-...	25.1	24	10	9	1	18-2	22	.250
2001— Chicago (N.L.)	4	6	.400	2.74	1.15	76	0	0	0	24	2-3	82.0	65	26	25	8	29-2	107	.213
2002— Chicago (N.L.)	4	6	.400	7.33	1.65	45	0	0	0	6	1-7	46.2	53	47	38	9	24-7	46	.293
— Iowa (PCL)	0	1	.000	6.00	1.00	2	0	0	0	...	0-...	3.0	3	2	2	1	0-0	2	.273
2003— Chicago (N.L.)	3	2	.600	3.30	1.17	77	0	0	0	19	0-3	76.1	53	31	28	6	36-1	92	.196
Major League totals (5 years)	**18**	**32**	**.360**	**4.78**	**1.44**	**271**	**26**	**1**	**1**	**55**	**4-19**	**412.0**	**401**	**242**	**219**	**65**	**191-19**	**389**	**.253**

FASSERO, JEFF   P

PERSONAL: Born January 5, 1963, in Springfield, Ill. ... 6-1/200. ... Throws left, bats left. ... Full name: Jeffrey Joseph Fassero. ... Name pronounced: fuh-SAIR-oh. ... High school: Griffin (Springfield, Ill.). ... College: Mississippi.

TRANSACTIONS/CAREER NOTES: Selected by St. Louis Cardinals organization in 22nd round of free-agent draft (June 4, 1984). ... Selected by Chicago White Sox organization from Cardinals organization in Rule 5 minor league draft (December 5, 1989). ... Released by White Sox (April 3, 1990). ... Signed by Cleveland Indians organization (April 9, 1990). ... Granted free agency (October 15, 1990). ... Signed by Montreal Expos organization (January 3, 1991). ... On disabled list (July 24-August 11, 1994). ... Traded by Expos with P Alex Pacheco to Seattle Mariners for C Chris Widger, P Trey Moore and P Matt Wagner (October 29, 1996). ... On disabled list (March 22-April 12, 1998). ... Traded by Mariners to Texas Rangers for a player to be named later (August 27, 1999); Mariners acquired OF Adrian Myers to complete deal (September 22, 1999). ... Granted free agency (October 28, 1999). ... Signed by Boston Red Sox (December 22, 1999). ... On disabled list (June 19-July 5, 2000). ... Granted free agency (November 1, 2000). ... Signed by Chicago Cubs (December 8, 2000). ... Traded by Cubs with cash to Cardinals for two players to be named later (August 24, 2002); Cubs acquired P Jason Karnuth and P Jared Blasdell to complete deal (September 24, 2002). ... Granted free agency (November 1, 2002). ... Re-signed by Cardinals (December 6, 2002). ... Suspended by Major League Baseball (May 2, 2003). ... Reinstated (May 4, 2003).

CAREER HITTING: 18-for-238 (.076), 16 R, 2 2B, 1 3B, 0 HR, 5 RBI.

Year League	W	L	Pct.	ERA	WHIP	G	GS	CG	ShO	Hld.	Sv.-Opp.	IP	H	R	ER	HR	BB-IBB	SO	Avg.
1984— Johnson City (App.)	4	5	.364	4.59	1.56	13	11	2	0	...	1-...	66.2	65	42	34	2	39-0	59	.261
1985— Springfield (Mid.)	4	8	.333	4.01	1.43	29	15	1	0	...	1-...	119.0	125	78	53	11	45-3	65	.262
1986— St. Pete. (FSL)	13	7	.650	2.45	1.20	26	• 26	6	1	...	0-...	* 176.0	156	63	48	5	56-4	112	.239
1987— Arkansas (Texas)	10	7	.588	4.10	1.55	28	27	2	1	...	0-...	151.1	168	90	69	16	67-7	118	.283
1988— Arkansas (Texas)	5	5	.500	3.58	1.77	70	1	0	0	...	17-...	78.0	97	48	31	1	41-13	72	.301
1989— Louisville (A.A.)	3	10	.231	5.22	1.63	22	19	0	0	...	0-...	112.0	136	79	65	13	47-1	73	.302
— Arkansas (Texas)	4	1	.800	1.64	1.00	6	6	2	1	...	0-...	44.0	32	11	8	1	12-0	38	.200
1990— Cant./Akr. (Eastern)	5	4	.556	2.80	1.40	61	0	0	0	...	6-...	64.1	66	24	20	5	24-6	61	.263
1991— Indianapolis (A.A.)	3	0	1.000	1.47	0.98	18	0	0	0	...	4-...	18.1	11	3	3	1	7-3	12	.177
— Montreal (N.L.)	2	5	.286	2.44	1.01	51	0	0	0	7	8-11	55.1	39	17	15	1	17-1	42	.196
1992— Montreal (N.L.)	8	7	.533	2.84	1.34	70	0	0	0	12	1-7	85.2	81	35	27	4	34-6	63	.249
1993— Montreal (N.L.)	12	5	.706	2.29	1.16	56	15	1	0	6	1-3	149.2	119	50	38	7	54-0	140	.216
1994— Montreal (N.L.)	8	6	.571	2.99	1.15	21	21	1	0	0	0-0	138.2	119	54	46	13	40-4	119	.229
1995— Montreal (N.L.)	13	14	.481	4.33	1.49	30	30	1	0	0	0-0	189.0	207	102	91	15	74-3	164	.283
1996— Montreal (N.L.)	15	11	.577	3.30	1.17	34	34	5	1	0	0-0	231.2	217	95	85	20	55-3	222	.244
1997— Seattle (A.L.)	16	9	.640	3.61	1.32	35	• 35	2	1	0	0-0	234.1	226	108	94	21	84-6	189	.249
1998— Seattle (A.L.)	13	12	.520	3.97	1.29	32	32	7	0	0	0-0	224.2	223	115	99	33	66-2	176	.259
1999— Seattle (A.L.)	4	14	.222	7.38	1.88	30	24	0	0	2	0-0	139.0	188	121	114	34	73-3	101	.321
— Texas (A.L.)	1	0	1.000	5.71	1.73	7	3	0	0	0	0-0	17.1	20	12	11	1	10-0	13	.286

F

Year League	W	L	Pct.	ERA	WHIP	G	GS	CG	ShO	Hld.	Sv.-Opp.	IP	H	R	ER	HR	BB-IBB	SO	Avg.
2000— Boston (A.L.)	8	8	.500	4.78	1.56	38	23	0	0	5	0-0	130.0	153	72	69	16	50-2	97	.296
2001— Chicago (N.L.)	4	4	.500	3.42	1.21	82	0	0	0	25	12-17	73.2	66	31	28	6	23-5	79	.235
2002— Chicago (N.L.)	5	6	.455	6.18	1.71	57	0	0	0	6	0-1	51.0	65	37	35	5	22-5	44	.313
— St. Louis (N.L.)	3	0	1.000	3.00	1.17	16	0	0	0	7	0-2	18.0	16	6	6	4	5-0	12	.232
2003— St. Louis (N.L.)	1	7	.125	5.68	1.64	62	6	0	0	11	3-6	77.2	93	51	49	17	34-4	55	.296
American League totals (4 years)	42	43	.494	4.67	1.47	142	117	9	1	7	0-0	745.1	810	430	387	105	283-13	576	.276
National League totals (9 years)	71	65	.522	3.53	1.29	479	106	8	1	74	25-47	1070.1	1022	478	420	89	358-31	940	.250
Major League totals (13 years)	113	108	.511	4.00	1.36	621	223	17	2	81	25-47	1815.2	1832	908	807	194	641-44	1516	.261

FEBLES, CARLOS — 2B

PERSONAL: Born May 24, 1976, in El Seybo, Dominican Republic. ... 5-11/185. ... Bats right, throws right. ... Full name: Carlos Manuel Febles. ... Name pronounced: FAY-bless. ... High school: Sagrado Corazon de Jesus (Dominican Republic).

TRANSACTIONS/CAREER NOTES: Signed as non-drafted free agent by Kansas City Royals (November 2, 1993). ... On disabled list (August 24-September 17, 1999). ... On Kansas City disabled list (June 5-July 18 and August 14-September 2, 2000); included rehabilitation assignments to Gulf Coast Royals (June 29-30), Wichita (July 1-4) and Omaha (July 10-18). ... On Kansas City disabled list (April 20-June 8, 2001); included rehabilitation assignment to Omaha (June 4-8). ... Placed on the 15-day disabled list (May 28, 2003). ... Reinstated from disabled list (June 15, 2003). ... Activated from 15-day disabled list (July 4, 2003). ... Designated for assignment (August 12, 2003). ... Sent outright to Omaha (August 20, 2003).

2003 GAMES PLAYED BY POSITION (MLB): 2B—67, DH—4, SS—1.

										BATTING									FIELDING	
Year	Team (League)	Pos.	G	AB	R	H	2B	3B	HR	RBI	BB	SO	HBP	GDP	SB-CS	Avg.	OBP	SLG	OPS	E	Pct.
1994— Dom. Royals (DSL)		2B	56	184	38	61	9	3	2	37	38	27	...	...	12-...	.332	...	.446	...	16	.934
1995— GC Royals (GCL)		2B	54	188	40	53	13	5	3	20	26	30	4	5	16-8	.282	.381	.452	.833	12	.948
1996— Lansing (Midw.)		2B-SS	102	363	84	107	23	5	5	43	66	64	11	8	30-14	.295	.414	.427	.841	19	.963
1997— Wilmington (Caro.)		2B	122	438	78	104	27	6	3	29	51	95	12	13	49-11	.237	.333	.347	.680	* 23	.961
1998— Wichita (Texas)		2B	126	432	110	141	28	9	14	52	80	70	11	6	* 51-16	.326	.441	.530	.971	19	.968
— Kansas City (A.L.)		2B	11	25	5	10	1	2	0	2	4	7	0	0	2-1	.400	.483	.600	1.083	0	1.000
1999— Kansas City (A.L.)		2B	123	453	71	116	22	9	10	53	47	91	9	16	20-4	.256	.334	.411	.747	14	.979
2000— Kansas City (A.L.)		2B	100	339	59	87	12	1	2	29	36	48	10	10	17-6	.257	.345	.316	.660	10	.978
— GC Royals (GCL)		2B	1	3	0	1	1	0	0	0	1	0	0	0	1-0	.333	.500	.667	1.167	0	1.000
— Wichita (Texas)		2B	4	15	2	2	0	0	0	1	2	4	1	0	2-0	.133	.263	.133	.396	0	1.000
— Omaha (PCL)		2B	11	42	6	9	4	0	1	5	7	10	1	2	3-3	.214	.340	.381	.721	1	.983
2001— Kansas City (A.L.)		2B	79	292	45	69	9	2	8	25	22	58	1	7	5-2	.236	.291	.363	.654	7	.981
— Omaha (PCL)		2B	25	98	23	33	7	1	2	9	9	14	4	0	6-2	.337	.414	.490	.904	0	1.000
2002— Kansas City (A.L.)		2B-SS	119	351	44	86	16	4	4	26	41	63	7	8	16-5	.245	.336	.348	.683	15	.971
— Omaha (PCL)		2B	13	54	10	12	2	1	1	5	4	5	1	1	2-1	.222	.283	.352	.635	1	.982
2003— Kansas City (A.L.) 2B-DH-SS			74	196	31	46	5	0	0	11	13	30	5	8	8-2	.235	.299	.260	.559	3	.989
— Omaha (PCL)		2B-SS	9	32	7	10	4	0	0	6	3	6	1	0	0-0	.313	.389	.438	.826	1	.974
Major League totals (6 years)			506	1656	255	414	65	18	24	146	163	297	32	49	68-20	.250	.328	.354	.683	49	.979

FELICIANO, PEDRO — P

PERSONAL: Born August 25, 1976, in Rio Piedras, Puerto Rico. ... 5-10/185. ... Throws left, bats left. ... Full name: Pedro Juan Feliciano. ... High school: Jose S. Alegria (Dorado, Puerto Rico).

TRANSACTIONS/CAREER NOTES: Selected by Los Angeles Dodgers organization in 31st round of free-agent draft (June 1, 1995). ... On disabled list (April 8, 1999-entire season). ... Granted free agency (October 15, 2001). ... Signed by Cincinnati Reds organization (November 19, 2001). ... Traded by Reds with OF Elvin Andujar and two players to be named later to New York Mets for P Shawn Estes and cash (August 15, 2002); Mets acquired OF Raul Gonzalez (August 20, 2002) and OF Brady Clark to complete deal (September 9, 2002). ... Claimed on waivers by Detroit Tigers (October 11, 2002). ... Released by Tigers (December 16, 2002). ... Signed by Mets organization (January 13, 2003). ... Contract purchased by New York Mets (May 22, 2003).

CAREER HITTING: 0-for-3 (.000), 0 R, 0 2B, 0 3B, 0 HR, 0 RBI.

Year League	W	L	Pct.	ERA	WHIP	G	GS	CG	ShO	Hld.	Sv.-Opp.	IP	H	R	ER	HR	BB-IBB	SO	Avg.
1995— Great Falls (Pio.)	0	0	...	13.50	2.85	6	0	0	0	...	0-...	6.2	12	12	10	0	7-1	9	.333
1996— Great Falls (Pio.)	2	3	.400	5.71	1.85	22	1	0	0	...	3-...	41.0	50	36	26	1	26-2	39	.291
1997— Savannah (S. Atl.)	3	7	.300	2.64	1.22	36	9	1	0	...	4-...	105.2	90	45	31	11	39-0	94	.230
— Vero Beach (FSL)	0	0	...	4.50	1.50	1	0	0	0	...	0-...	2.0	3	1	1	1	0-0	1	.429
1998— Vero Beach (FSL)	2	5	.286	4.61	1.43	22	10	0	0	...	2-...	68.1	68	44	35	8	30-1	51	.255
1999—										Did not play.									
2000— Vero Beach (FSL)	4	5	.444	3.82	1.63	25	2	0	0	...	0-...	61.1	76	31	26	4	24-1	48	.303
— San Antonio (Texas)	0	0	...	1.93	1.18	9	0	0	0	...	2-...	9.1	7	2	2	0	4-1	11	.226
— Albuquerque (PCL)	0	0	...	18.00	4.00	1	0	0	0	...	0-...	1.0	3	3	2	2	1-0	2	.375
2001— Jacksonville (Sou.)	5	4	.556	1.94	0.86	54	0	0	0	...	17-...	60.1	41	14	13	3	11-1	55	.194
— Las Vegas (PCL)	0	1	.000	7.27	2.42	6	0	0	0	...	0-...	8.2	16	11	7	2	5-1	5	.390
2002— Chattanooga (Sou.)	2	1	.667	2.56	1.14	28	0	0	0	...	4-...	38.2	33	14	11	1	11-1	26	.234
— Louisville (Int'l)	1	1	.500	3.04	1.46	20	0	0	0	...	0-...	26.2	35	10	9	3	4-0	19	.327
— Norfolk (Int'l)	0	0	...	7.00	1.67	5	0	0	0	...	2-...	9.0	14	7	7	1	1-0	11	.359
— New York (N.L.)	0	0	...	7.50	1.67	6	0	0	0	0	0-0	6.0	9	5	5	0	1-0	4	.360
2003— Norfolk (Int'l)	3	2	.600	3.97	1.15	15	0	0	0	...	1-...	22.2	20	10	10	3	6-1	18	.238
— New York (N.L.)	0	0	...	3.35	1.51	23	0	0	0	0	0-0	48.1	52	21	18	5	21-3	43	.269
Major League totals (2 years)	0	0	...	3.81	1.53	29	0	0	0	0	0-0	54.1	61	26	23	5	22-3	47	.280

FELIZ, PEDRO — 3B

PERSONAL: Born April 27, 1977, in Azua, Dominican Republic. ... 6-1/205. ... Bats right, throws right. ... Full name: Pedro Julio Feliz. ... High school: Augustine de Chequer (Dominican Republic).

TRANSACTIONS/CAREER NOTES: Signed as non-drafted free agent by San Francisco Giants organization (February 7, 1994).

2003 GAMES PLAYED BY POSITION (MLB): 3B—49, OF—15, 1B—12.

F

Year Team (League)	Pos.	G	AB	R	H	2B	3B	HR	RBI	BB	SO	HBP	GDP	SB-CS	Avg.	OBP	SLG	OPS	E	Pct.
1994— Ariz. Giants (Ariz.)	3B	38	119	7	23	0	0	0	3	2	20	2	3	2-3	.193	.220	.193	.413	5	.953
1995— Bellingham (N'west)	3B-1B	43	113	14	31	2	1	0	16	7	33	0	2	1-1	.274	.311	.310	.621	2	.971
1996— Burlington (Midw.)	3B	93	321	36	85	12	2	5	36	18	65	1	11	5-2	.265	.303	.361	.665	17	.937
1997— Bakersfield (Calif.)	3B	135	515	59	140	25	4	14	56	23	90	7	15	5-7	.272	.310	.417	.728	23	.950
1998— Shreveport (Texas)	3B	100	364	39	96	23	2	12	50	9	62	2	15	0-1	.264	.282	.437	.719	22	.926
— Fresno (PCL)	3B	3	7	1	3	1	0	1	3	1	0	0	1	0-0	.429	.500	1.500	1.500	0	1.000
1999— Shreveport (Texas)	3B	131	491	52	124	24	6	13	77	19	90	3	18	4-2	.253	.282	.405	.687	27	.934
2000— Fresno (PCL)	3B-SS	128	503	85	150	34	2	33	105	30	94	2	18	1-1	.298	.337	.571	.908	‡ 24	.939
— San Francisco (N.L.)	3B	8	7	1	2	0	0	0	0	0	1	0	0	0-0	.286	.286	.286	.571	0	...
2001— San Francisco (N.L.)	3B-DH	94	220	23	50	9	1	7	22	10	50	2	5	2-1	.227	.264	.373	.637	12	.908
2002— San Francisco (N.L.)	3B-SS-OF	67	146	14	37	4	1	2	13	6	27	0	2	0-0	.253	.281	.336	.617	3	.966
2003— San Francisco (N.L.)	3B-OF-1B	95	235	31	58	9	3	16	48	10	53	1	7	2-2	.247	.278	.515	.793	4	.982
Major League totals (4 years)		264	608	69	147	22	5	25	83	26	131	3	14	4-3	.242	.274	.418	.691	19	.957

FERNANDEZ, JARED — P

PERSONAL: Born February 2, 1972, in Salt Lake City, Utah. ... 6-1/225. ... Throws right, bats right. ... Full name: Jared Wade Fernandez. ... High school: Kearns (Utah). ... College: Fresno State.

TRANSACTIONS/CAREER NOTES: Signed as non-drafted free agent by Boston Red Sox organization (June 23, 1994). ... On disabled list (July 30, 2000-remainder of season). ... Granted free agency (October 15, 2000). ... Signed by Cincinnati Reds organization (December 15, 2000). ... Released by Reds (December 15, 2002). ... Signed by Houston Astros organization (December 20, 2002). ... Recalled by Astros from New Orleans (July 31, 2003). ... Contract purchased by Houston from New Orleans (August 1, 2003). ... Optioned to New Orleans by Houston (August 31, 2003). ... Recalled by Houston (September 1, 2003).

CAREER HITTING: 2-for-21 (.095), 3 R, 0 2B, 0 3B, 0 HR, 1 RBI.

Year League	W	L	Pct.	ERA	WHIP	G	GS	CG	ShO	Hld.	Sv.-Opp.	IP	H	R	ER	HR	BB-IBB	SO	Avg.
1994— Utica (N.Y.-Penn)	1	1	.500	3.60	1.70	21	1	0	0	...	4-...	30.0	43	18	12	4	8-2	24	.316
1995— Utica (N.Y.-Penn)	3	2	.600	1.89	1.03	5	5	1	0	...	0-...	38.0	30	11	8	2	9-1	23	.219
— Trenton (East.)	5	4	.556	3.90	1.37	11	10	1	0	...	0-...	67.0	64	32	29	4	28-1	40	.253
1996— Trenton (East.)	9	9	.500	5.08	1.50	30	* 29	3	0	...	0-...	179.0	185	* 115	* 101	19	83-5	94	.268
1997— Trenton (East.)	4	6	.400	5.41	1.68	21	16	1	0	...	0-...	121.1	138	90	73	12	66-0	73	.282
— Pawtucket (Int'l)	0	3	.000	5.79	1.71	11	11	0	0	...	0-...	60.2	76	45	39	7	28-1	33	.311
1998— Trenton (East.)	3	7	.300	5.25	1.55	36	7	0	0	...	1-...	118.1	132	80	69	8	51-3	70	.286
— Pawtucket (Int'l)	1	1	.500	4.74	1.34	5	2	0	0	...	0-...	24.2	26	16	13	5	7-0	15	.274
1999— Trenton (East.)	3	0	1.000	3.38	1.39	7	0	0	0	...	1-...	18.2	18	9	7	4	8-0	10	.250
— Pawtucket (Int'l)	12	9	.571	4.25	1.29	27	20	3	0	...	0-...	163.0	172	88	77	20	39-0	76	.273
2000— Pawtucket (Int'l)	10	4	.714	3.02	1.23	31	9	2	0	...	4-...	113.1	103	51	38	10	36-0	65	.248
2001— Louisville (Int'l)	10	9	.526	4.13	1.39	33	28	4	1	...	0-...	* 196.1	* 218	105	90	24	54-0	118	.281
— Cincinnati (N.L.)	0	1	.000	4.38	1.54	5	2	0	0	0	0-0	12.1	13	9	6	1	6-0	5	.265
2002— Louisville (Int'l)	12	5	.706	3.93	1.42	26	18	1	0	...	1-...	128.1	151	63	56	14	31-1	80	.294
— Cincinnati (N.L.)	1	3	.250	4.44	1.64	14	8	0	0	0	0-0	50.2	59	31	25	5	24-1	36	.294
2003— New Orleans (PCL)	7	10	.412	3.81	1.29	26	23	2	0	...	0-...	156.0	164	73	66	16	37-1	51	.270
— Houston (N.L.)	3	3	.500	3.99	1.28	12	6	0	0	0	0-0	38.1	37	17	17	2	12-2	19	.259
Major League totals (3 years)	4	7	.364	4.26	1.49	31	16	0	0	0	0-0	101.1	109	57	48	8	42-3	60	.277

FERRARI, ANTHONY — P

PERSONAL: Born June 22, 1978, in San Francisco, Calif. ... 5-9/165. ... Throws left, bats left. ... Full name: Anthony Michael Ferrari. ... College: Lewis-Clark (Idaho) State.

TRANSACTIONS/CAREER NOTES: Drafted by Montreal Expos in 44th round of free-agent draft (June 5, 2000).

CAREER HITTING: 0-for-0 (.000), 0 R, 0 2B, 0 3B, 0 HR, 0 RBI.

Year League	W	L	Pct.	ERA	WHIP	G	GS	CG	ShO	Hld.	Sv.-Opp.	IP	H	R	ER	HR	BB-IBB	SO	Avg.
2000— Vermont (NY-P)	2	2	.500	1.71	0.97	25	0	0	0	...	5-...	47.1	31	14	9	2	15-0	37	.186
2001— Jupiter (FSL)	2	3	.400	0.79	0.94	51	0	0	0	...	21-...	56.2	36	11	5	1	17-0	45	.180
2002— Harrisburg (Eastern)	7	4	.636	4.06	1.50	44	0	0	0	...	6-...	75.1	79	35	34	2	34-1	53	.270
2003— Harrisburg (Eastern)	2	0	1.000	0.56	1.19	14	0	0	0	...	5-...	16.0	13	1	1	0	6-1	9	.224
— Montreal (N.L.)	0	0	...	6.75	2.25	4	0	0	0	1	0-0	4.0	4	3	3	1	5-1	1	.267
— Edmonton (PCL)	5	2	.714	4.89	1.63	28	0	0	0	...	0-...	49.2	63	29	27	3	18-4	17	.317
Major League totals (1 year)	0	0	...	6.75	2.25	4	0	0	0	1	0-0	4.0	4	3	3	1	5-1	1	.267

FETTERS, MIKE — P

PERSONAL: Born December 19, 1964, in Van Nuys, Calif. ... 6-4/230. ... Throws right, bats right. ... Full name: Michael Lee Fetters. ... High school: Iolani (Honolulu, Hawaii). ... College: Pepperdine.

TRANSACTIONS/CAREER NOTES: Selected by Los Angeles Dodgers organization in 22nd round of free-agent draft (June 6, 1983); did not sign. ... Selected by California Angels organization in supplemental round ("sandwich pick" between first and second round, 27th pick overall) of free-agent draft (June 2, 1986); pick received as compensation for Baltimore Orioles signing Type A free-agent OF/IF Juan Beniquez. ... Traded by Angels with P Glenn Carter to Milwaukee Brewers for P Chuck Crim (December 10, 1991). ... On disabled list (March 3-19, 1992; and May 25-June 9, 1995). ... On Milwaukee disabled list (April 4-May 5, 1997); included rehabilitation assignment to Tucson (April 30-May 5). ... Traded by Brewers with P Ben McDonald and P Ron Villone to Cleveland Indians for OF Marquis Grissom and P Jeff Juden (December 8, 1997). ... Traded by Indians to Oakland Athletics for P Steve Karsay (December 8, 1997). ... On Oakland disabled list (April 6-26, 1998). ... Traded by A's to Anaheim Angels for a player to be named later and cash (August 10, 1998). ... Granted free agency (October 26, 1998). ... Signed by Baltimore Orioles organization (February 4, 1999). ... On Baltimore disabled list (June 7-September 1, 1999); included rehabilitation assignment to Rochester (August 23-31). ... Granted free agency (November 1, 1999). ... Signed by Dodgers organization (December 15, 1999). ... On disabled list (May 4-26, 2000). ... On suspended list (July 21-22, 2000). ... On Los Angeles disabled list (June 20-July 5, 2001). ... Traded by Dodgers with P Adrian Burnside to Pittsburgh Pirates for P Terry Mulholland (July 31, 2001). ... Traded by Pirates to Arizona Diamondbacks for P Duaner Sanchez (July 6, 2002). ... Granted free agency (November 11, 2002). ... Signed by Minnesota Twins organization (January 27, 2003).

CAREER HITTING: 0-for-0 (.000), 0 R, 0 2B, 0 3B, 0 HR, 0 RBI.

Year League	W	L	Pct.	ERA	WHIP	G	GS	CG	ShO	Hld.	Sv.-Opp.	IP	H	R	ER	HR	BB-IBB	SO	Avg.
1986— Salem (NW)	4	2	.667	3.38	1.54	12	12	1	0	...	0-...	72.0	60	39	27	4	51-0	72	...
1987— Palm Springs (Calif.)	9	7	.563	3.57	1.54	19	19	2	0	...	0-...	116.0	106	62	46	2	73-0	105	.247
1988— Midland (Texas)	8	8	.500	5.92	1.61	20	20	2	0	...	0-...	114.0	116	78	75	10	67-3	101	.262
— Edmonton (PCL)	2	0	1.000	1.93	1.29	2	2	1	0	...	0-...	14.0	8	3	3	0	10-0	11	.170
1989— Edmonton (PCL)	12	8	.600	3.80	1.38	26	26	•6	2	...	0-...	168.0	160	80	71	11	72-2	* 144	.257
— California (A.L.)	0	0	...	8.10	1.80	1	1	0	0	...	0-0	3.1	5	4	3	1	1-0	4	.333

F

Year	League	W	L	Pct.	ERA	WHIP	G	GS	CG	ShO	Hld.	Sv.-Opp.	IP	H	R	ER	HR	BB-IBB	SO	Avg.
1990— Edmonton (PCL)		1	1	.500	0.99	1.28	5	5	1	1	...	0-...	27.1	22	9	3	0	13-0	26	.218
— California (A.L.)		1	1	.500	4.12	1.43	26	2	0	0	1	1-1	67.2	77	33	31	9	20-0	35	.287
1991— Edmonton (PCL)		2	7	.222	4.87	1.49	11	11	1	0	...	0-...	61.0	65	39	33	5	26-0	43	.279
— California (A.L.)		2	5	.286	4.84	1.81	19	4	0	0	0	0-1	44.2	53	29	24	4	28-2	24	.305
1992— Milwaukee (A.L.)		5	1	.833	1.87	0.99	50	0	0	0	8	2-5	62.2	38	15	13	3	24-2	43	.185
1993— Milwaukee (A.L.)		3	3	.500	3.34	1.37	45	0	0	0	8	0-0	59.1	59	29	22	4	22-4	23	.278
1994— Milwaukee (A.L.)		1	4	.200	2.54	1.48	42	0	0	0	3	17-20	46.0	41	16	13	0	27-5	31	.243
1995— Milwaukee (A.L.)		0	3	.000	3.38	1.73	40	0	0	0	2	22-27	34.2	40	16	13	3	20-4	33	.286
1996— Milwaukee (A.L.)		3	3	.500	3.38	1.48	61	0	0	0	1	32-38	61.1	65	28	23	4	26-4	53	.274
1997— Tucson (PCL)		0	0	...	10.80	1.20	2	0	0	0	...	0-...	1.2	1	2	2	0	1-0	0	.167
— Milwaukee (A.L.)		1	5	.167	3.45	1.35	51	0	0	0	11	6-11	70.1	62	30	27	4	33-3	62	.244
1998— Oakland (A.L.)		1	6	.143	3.99	1.46	48	0	0	0	10	5-8	47.1	48	26	21	3	21-2	34	.258
— Anaheim (A.L.)		1	2	.333	5.56	1.59	12	0	0	0	1	0-1	11.1	14	8	7	2	4-0	9	.304
1999— Baltimore (A.L.)		1	0	1.000	5.81	1.84	27	0	0	0	2	0-3	31.0	35	23	20	5	22-2	22	.278
— Rochester (Int'l)		0	0	...	0.00	0.55	4	0	0	0	...	0-...	3.2	0	0	0	0	2-0	6	.000
2000— Los Angeles (N.L.)		6	2	.750	3.24	1.20	51	0	0	0	11	5-7	50.0	35	18	18	7	25-2	40	.205
2001— Los Angeles (N.L.)		2	1	.667	6.07	1.55	34	0	0	0	14	1-3	29.2	33	23	20	6	13-0	26	.273
— Pittsburgh (N.L.)		1	1	.500	4.58	1.64	20	0	0	0	0	8-9	17.2	16	9	9	1	13-1	11	.235
2002— Pittsburgh (N.L.)		1	0	1.000	3.26	1.42	32	0	0	0	11	0-1	30.1	25	13	11	3	18-1	29	.219
— Arizona (N.L.)		2	3	.400	5.11	1.91	33	0	0	0	5	0-1	24.2	28	18	14	1	19-5	24	.292
2003— Minnesota (A.L.)		0	0	...	0.00	0.50	5	0	0	0	0	0-0	6.0	2	0	0	0	1-0	1	.100
American League totals (12 years)		19	33	.365	3.58	1.44	427	6	0	0	47	85-115	545.2	539	257	217	42	249-28	374	.263
National League totals (3 years)		12	7	.632	4.25	1.48	170	0	0	0	41	14-21	152.1	137	81	72	18	88-9	130	.240
Major League totals (15 years)		31	40	.437	3.73	1.45	597	6	0	0	88	99-136	698.0	676	338	289	60	337-37	504	.258

FICK, ROBERT — 1B/OF

PERSONAL: Born March 15, 1974, in Torrance, Calif. ... 6-1/205. ... Bats left, throws right. ... Full name: Robert Charles Fick. ... High school: Newbury Park (Calif.). ... College: Cal State Northridge.

TRANSACTIONS/CAREER NOTES: Selected by Oakland Athletics organization in 45th round of free-agent draft (June 1, 1992); did not sign. ... Selected by Detroit Tigers organization in 43rd round of free-agent draft (June 1, 1995); did not sign. ... Selected by Tigers organization in fifth round of free-agent draft (June 4, 1996). ... On Detroit disabled list (March 31-September 7, 1999); included rehabilitation assignments to Gulf Coast Tigers (August 18-20), West Michigan (August 21-23) and Toledo (August 24-September 6). ... On suspended list (May 23-26, 2000). ... On Detroit disabled list (July 6-September 1, 2000); included rehabilitation assignment to Toledo (August 13-September 1). ... On suspended list (September 22-27, 2001). ... Granted free agency (December 21, 2002). ... Signed by Atlanta Braves organization (January 6, 2003). ... Placed on 15-day disabled list (April 13, 2003). ... Reinstated from 15-day disabled list (April 29, 2003).

2003 GAMES PLAYED BY POSITION (MLB): 1B—115.

Year	Team (League)	Pos.	G	AB	R	H	2B	3B	HR	RBI	BB	SO	HBP	GDP	SB-CS	Avg.	OBP	SLG	OPS	E	Pct.
1996— Jamestown (NYP)		C	43	133	18	33	6	1	1	14	12	25	0	4	3-1	.248	.306	.316	.622	3	.982
1997— W. Mich. (Mid.)		3B-C-1B	122	463	100	* 158	* 50	3	16	90	75	74	1	10	13-4	.341	.429	.566	.994	12	.989
1998— Jacksonville (Sou.)		C-1B-OF	130	515	101	164	• 47	6	18	114	71	83	6	8	8-4	.318	.401	.538	.939	9	.985
— Detroit (A.L.)		C-DH-1B	7	22	6	8	1	0	3	7	2	7	0	1	1-0	.364	.417	.818	1.235	1	.966
1999— GC Tigers (GCL)		DH-C-1B	3	9	2	3	1	0	0	2	2	0	0	0	1-0	.333	.455	.444	.899	0	1.000
— W. Mich. (Mid.)		DH-C-1B	3	11	2	3	0	0	0	0	2	1	0	0	1-0	.273	.385	.273	.657	2	.913
— Toledo (Int'l)		1-C-DH-3	14	48	11	15	0	1	2	8	8	5	1	0	1-0	.313	.414	.479	.893	5	.944
— Detroit (A.L.)		DH-C	15	41	6	9	0	0	3	10	7	6	0	1	1-0	.220	.327	.439	.766	0	1.000
2000— Detroit (A.L.)		1B-C-DH	66	163	18	41	7	2	3	22	22	39	1	4	2-1	.252	.340	.374	.715	5	.983
— Toledo (Int'l)		1B	17	68	5	10	5	0	1	7	6	13	0	0	1-0	.147	.234	.265	.498	0	1.000
2001— Detroit (A.L.)		C-1-D-O	124	401	62	109	21	2	19	61	39	62	4	10	0-3	.272	.339	.476	.816	7	.989
2002— Detroit (A.L.)		OF-DH	148	556	66	150	36	2	17	63	46	90	7	17	0-1	.270	.331	.433	.764	* 12	.963
2003— Atlanta (N.L.)		1B	126	409	52	110	26	1	11	80	42	47	2	9	1-0	.269	.335	.418	.753	14	.987
American League totals (5 years)			360	1183	158	317	65	6	45	163	116	204	12	33	4-5	.268	.336	.447	.784	25	.981
National League totals (1 year)			126	409	52	110	26	1	11	80	42	47	2	9	1-0	.269	.335	.418	.753	14	.987
Major League totals (6 years)			486	1592	210	427	91	7	56	243	158	251	14	42	5-5	.268	.336	.440	.776	39	.984

FIELD, NATE — P

PERSONAL: Born December 11, 1975, in Denver, Colo. ... 6-2/200. ... Throws right, bats right. ... Full name: Nathan Patrick Field. ... College: Fort Hays State (Kan.).

TRANSACTIONS/CAREER NOTES: Signed as non-drafted free agent by Montreal Expos organization (June 11, 1998). ... Released by Expos (March 29, 2000). ... Signed by Sioux City, Northern League (May 2000). ... Contract purchased by Kansas City Royals organization from Sioux City (June 29, 2000). ... Claimed on waivers by New York Yankees (June 12, 2002). ... On Columbus disabled list (July 30-August 11, 2002). ... Granted free agency (October 15, 2002). ... Contract purchased by Kansas City from Omaha (June 10, 2003). ... Optioned to Omaha by Kansas City (June 15, 2003). ... Recalled from Omaha by Kansas City (August 6, 2003). ... Optioned to Omaha by Kansas City (August 8, 2003). ... Recalled by Kansas City from Omaha (August 31, 2003).

CAREER HITTING: 0-for-0 (.000), 0 R, 0 2B, 0 3B, 0 HR, 0 RBI.

Year	League	W	L	Pct.	ERA	WHIP	G	GS	CG	ShO	Hld.	Sv.-Opp.	IP	H	R	ER	HR	BB-IBB	SO	Avg.
1998— Vermont (NY-P)		3	1	.750	3.09	1.23	25	0	0	0	...	2-...	35.0	32	16	12	1	11-0	39	.237
1999— Cape Fear (S. Atl.)		4	8	.333	5.40	1.49	42	0	0	0	...	2-...	65.0	75	49	39	8	22-2	55	.282
— Ottawa (Int'l)		0	0	...	3.00	2.67	2	0	0	0	...	0-...	3.0	4	1	1	0	4-0	4	.333
2000— Sioux City (Nor.)		3	0	1.000	1.93	1.37	11	0	0	0	...	0-...	23.1	17	10	5	...	15-...	19	...
— Char., W.Va. (SAL)		1	2	.333	2.23	1.18	17	0	0	0	...	0-...	36.1	28	10	9	2	15-0	31	.215
2001— Wichita (Texas)		4	2	.667	1.48	1.08	52	0	0	0	...	19-...	73.0	61	16	12	3	18-3	67	.222
2002— Omaha (PCL)		0	1	.000	3.31	1.84	18	0	0	0	...	7-...	16.1	22	10	6	0	8-0	13	.301
— Kansas City (A.L.)		0	0	...	9.00	2.20	5	0	0	0	0	0-0	5.0	8	5	5	2	3-1	3	.364
2003— Wichita (Texas)		2	1	.667	6.75	1.73	21	0	0	0	...	0-...	38.2	46	30	29	6	21-1	25	.305
— Omaha (PCL)		1	0	1.000	3.60	1.40	15	0	0	0	...	3-...	20.0	20	9	8	2	8-1	20	.256
— Omaha (PCL)		2	2	.500	3.18	0.84	19	0	0	0	...	4-...	22.2	15	8	8	4	4-0	17	.188
— Kansas City (A.L.)		1	1	.500	4.15	1.52	19	0	0	0	2	0-0	21.2	19	10	10	3	14-1	19	.235
Major League totals (2 years)		1	1	.500	5.06	1.65	24	0	0	0	2	0-0	26.2	27	15	15	5	17-2	22	.262

FIGGINS, CHONE — 2B/OF

PERSONAL: Born January 22, 1978, in Leary, Ga. ... 5-7/160. ... Bats both, throws right. ... Full name: Desmond DeChone Figgins. ... Name pronounced: shawn. ... High school: Brandon (Fla.).

TRANSACTIONS/CAREER NOTES: Selected by Colorado Rockies organization in fourth round of free-agent draft (June 3, 1997). ... Traded by Rockies to Anaheim Angels for OF Kimera Bartee (July 13, 2001). ... Optioned to Salt Lake by Anaheim (April 22, 2003). ... Recalled by Anaheim (May 24, 2003). ... Optioned to Salt Lake (June 6, 2003). ... Recalled by Anaheim (June 27, 2003).

2003 GAMES PLAYED BY POSITION (MLB): OF—47, 2B—14, SS—8, DH—3.

Year	Team (League)	Pos.	G	AB	R	H	2B	3B	HR	RBI	BB	SO	HBP	GDP	SB-CS	Avg.	OBP	SLG	OPS	E	Pct.
1997—Ariz. Rockies (Ariz.)		SS	54	214	41	60	5	6	1	23	35	51	3	2	30-12	.280	.386	.374	.760	40	.865
1998—Portland (NW)		SS	69	269	41	76	9	3	1	26	24	56	2	3	25-4	.283	.345	.349	.694	16	.947
1999—Salem (Caro.)		SS	123	444	65	106	12	3	0	22	41	86	3	5	27-13	.239	.306	.279	.585	45	.925
2000—Salem (Caro.)		2B	134	522	92	145	26	14	3	48	67	107	1	7	37-19	.278	.358	.398	.756	28	.955
2001—Carolina (Sou.)		2B-SS	86	332	41	73	14	5	2	25	40	73	2	0	27-8	.220	.306	.310	.616	16	.963
—Arkansas (Texas)		2B-SS-3B	39	138	21	37	12	2	0	12	14	26	0	0	7-2	.268	.329	.384	.713	10	.945
2002—Salt Lake (PCL)		2B-SS	125	511	100	156	25	18	7	62	53	83	0	0	39-8	.305	.364	.466	.830	‡23	.964
—Anaheim (A.L.)		2B	15	12	6	2	1	0	0	1	0	5	0	1	2-1	.167	.167	.250	.417	1	.941
2003—Salt Lake (PCL)		2-S-OF-3	68	285	55	89	14	15	4	30	29	36	3	4	16-6	.312	.379	.509	.888	17	.949
—Anaheim (A.L.)		OF-2-S-D	71	240	34	71	9	4	0	27	20	38	0	1	13-7	.296	.345	.367	.711	3	.985
Major League totals (2 years)			86	252	40	73	10	4	0	28	20	43	0	2	15-8	.290	.337	.361	.698	4	.981

FIGUEROA, NELSON   P

PERSONAL: Born May 18, 1974, in Brooklyn, N.Y. ... 6-1/170. ... Throws right, bats right. ... Full name: Nelson Walter Figueroa. ... Name pronounced: fig-uh-ROE-uh. ... High school: Abraham Lincoln (Brooklyn, N.Y.). ... College: Brandeis (Mass.).

TRANSACTIONS/CAREER NOTES: Selected by New York Mets organization in 30th round of free-agent draft (June 1, 1995). ... Traded by Mets with OF Bernard Gilkey and cash to Arizona Diamondbacks for P Willie Blair, C Jorge Fabregas and cash considerations (July 31, 1998). ... On Tucson disabled list (June 12-23 and July 6-30, 1999). ... Traded by Diamondbacks with OF Travis Lee, P Omar Daal and P Vicente Padilla to Philadelphia Phillies for P Curt Schilling (July 26, 2000). ... Claimed on waivers by Milwaukee Brewers (April 3, 2002). ... On Milwaukee disabled list (May 8-21, 2002). ... Released by Brewers (October 11, 2002). ... Signed by Pittsburgh Pirates organization as a minor league free agent (January 13, 2003).

CAREER HITTING: 9-for-49 (.184), 5 R, 1 2B, 0 3B, 0 HR, 4 RBI.

Year	League	W	L	Pct.	ERA	WHIP	G	GS	CG	ShO	Hld.	Sv.-Opp.	IP	H	R	ER	HR	BB-IBB	SO	Avg.
1995—Kingsport (Appal.)		7	3	.700	3.07	1.03	12	12	2	*2	...	0-...	76.1	57	31	26	3	22-1	79	.210
1996—Capital City (S. Atl.)		14	7	.667	2.04	0.96	26	25	*8	*4	...	0-...	*185.1	119	55	42	10	58-1	*200	.181
1997—Binghamton (Eastern)		5	11	.313	4.34	1.43	33	22	0	0	...	0-...	143.0	137	76	69	14	68-1	116	.257
1998—Binghamton (Eastern)		12	3	.800	4.66	1.43	21	21	3	2	...	0-...	123.2	133	73	64	19	44-2	116	.275
—Tucson (PCL)		2	2	.500	3.70	1.50	7	7	0	0	...	0-...	41.1	46	22	17	8	16-1	29	.288
1999—Tucson (PCL)		11	6	.647	3.94	1.32	24	21	1	1	...	0-...	128.0	128	59	56	16	41-0	106	.261
—Ariz. D'backs (Ariz.)		0	1	.000	0.00	1.00	1	1	0	0	...	0-...	3.0	3	1	0	0	0-0	2	.273
2000—Tucson (PCL)		9	4	.692	2.81	1.15	17	16	1	0	...	0-...	112.0	101	41	35	9	28-2	78	.239
—Arizona (N.L.)		0	1	.000	7.47	1.40	3	3	0	0	0	0-0	15.2	17	13	13	4	5-0	7	.283
—Scran./W.B. (I.L.)		4	3	.571	3.78	1.22	8	8	1	0	...	0-...	50.0	50	28	21	9	11-0	35	.259
2001—Scran./W.B. (I.L.)		4	2	.667	2.47	1.05	13	12	3	0	...	0-...	87.1	74	33	24	6	18-2	74	.224
—Philadelphia (N.L.)		4	5	.444	3.94	1.48	19	13	0	0	0	0-0	89.0	95	40	39	8	37-3	61	.275
2002—Milwaukee (N.L.)		1	7	.125	5.03	1.43	30	11	0	0	1	0-0	93.0	96	59	52	18	37-6	51	.270
—Indianapolis (Int'l)		5	0	1.000	3.63	1.31	6	6	0	0	...	0-...	39.2	39	18	16	2	13-0	25	.253
2003—Nashville (PCL)		12	5	.706	2.97	1.20	23	23	3	1	...	0-...	151.1	144	54	50	11	37-5	121	.251
—Pittsburgh (N.L.)		2	1	.667	3.31	1.16	12	3	0	0	0	0-0	35.1	28	13	13	8	13-2	23	.220
Major League totals (4 years)		7	14	.333	4.52	1.41	64	30	0	0	1	0-0	233.0	236	125	117	38	92-11	142	.266

FIKAC, JEREMY   P

PERSONAL: Born April 8, 1975, in Shiner, Texas. ... 6-2/185. ... Throws right, bats right. ... Full name: Jeremy Joseph Fikac. ... Name pronounced: FEE-kotch. ... High school: Somerville (Texas). ... College: Southwest Texas State.

TRANSACTIONS/CAREER NOTES: Selected by San Diego Padres organization in 19th round of free-agent draft (June 2, 1998). ... Traded by Padres to Oakland Athletics for a player to be named later (January 2, 2003). ... Optioned to Sacramento (May 11, 2003). ... Recalled by Oakland (September 14, 2003).

CAREER HITTING: 0-for-2 (.000), 0 R, 0 2B, 0 3B, 0 HR, 0 RBI.

Year	League	W	L	Pct.	ERA	WHIP	G	GS	CG	ShO	Hld.	Sv.-Opp.	IP	H	R	ER	HR	BB-IBB	SO	Avg.
1998—Idaho Falls (Pioneer)		2	0	1.000	2.25	0.95	12	0	0	0	...	1-...	20.0	11	6	5	0	8-1	19	.153
1999—Rancho Cuca. (Calif.)		8	3	.727	5.08	1.61	40	6	0	0	...	0-...	85.0	94	50	48	7	43-0	75	.283
2000—Rancho Cuca. (Calif.)		5	3	.625	1.80	0.93	61	0	0	0	...	20-...	75.0	46	19	15	2	24-0	101	.174
2001—Mobile (Sou.)		6	0	1.000	1.97	1.08	53	0	0	0	...	18-...	68.2	54	16	15	3	20-4	75	.219
—Portland (PCL)		0	0	...	3.00	1.00	1	0	0	0	...	0-...	3.0	3	1	1	0	0-0	3	.250
—San Diego (N.L.)		2	0	1.000	1.37	0.76	23	0	0	0	6	0-2	26.1	15	6	4	2	5-1	19	.165
2002—San Diego (N.L.)		4	7	.364	5.48	1.57	65	0	0	0	12	0-6	69.0	74	50	42	13	34-8	66	.267
—Mobile (Sou.)		1	0	1.000	3.00	1.67	3	0	0	0	...	1-...	3.0	5	1	1	0	0-0	0	.455
2003—Sacramento (PCL)		3	3	.500	2.25	0.95	42	0	0	0	...	4-...	56.0	40	19	14	4	13-1	50	.197
—Oakland (A.L.)		0	1	.000	4.50	1.56	14	0	0	0	2	0-0	16.0	14	8	8	4	11-1	9	.246
American League totals (1 year)		0	1	.000	4.50	1.56	14	0	0	0	2	0-0	16.0	14	8	8	4	11-1	9	.246
National League totals (2 years)		6	7	.462	4.34	1.34	88	0	0	0	18	0-8	95.1	89	56	46	15	39-9	85	.242
Major League totals (3 years)		6	8	.429	4.37	1.37	102	0	0	0	20	0-8	111.1	103	64	54	19	50-10	94	.242

FINLEY, STEVE   OF

PERSONAL: Born March 12, 1965, in Union City, Tenn. ... 6-2/194. ... Bats left, throws left. ... Full name: Steven Allen Finley. ... High school: Paducah (Ky.) Tilghman. ... College: Southern Illinois.

TRANSACTIONS/CAREER NOTES: Selected by Atlanta Braves organization in 11th round of free-agent draft (June 2, 1986); did not sign. ... Selected by Baltimore Orioles organization in 13th round of free-agent draft (June 2, 1987). ... On Baltimore disabled list (April 4-22, 1989). ... On Baltimore disabled list (July 29-September 1, 1989); included rehabilitation assignment to Hagerstown (August 21-23). ... Traded by Orioles with P Pete Harnisch and P Curt Schilling to Houston Astros for 1B Glenn Davis (January 10, 1991). ... On disabled list (April 25-May 14, 1993). ... On Houston disabled list (June 13-July 3, 1994); included rehabilitation assignment to Jackson (June 28-July 3). ... Traded by Astros with 3B Ken Caminiti, SS Andujar Cedeno, 1B Roberto Petagine, P Brian Williams and a player to be named later to San Diego Padres for OF Phil Plantier, C Derek Bell, P Pedro Martinez, P Doug Brocail, IF Craig Shipley and SS Ricky Gutierrez (December 28, 1994); Padres acquired P Sean Fesh to complete deal (May 1, 1995). ... On San Diego disabled list (April 20-May 6, 1997); included rehabilitation assignment to Rancho Cucamonga (April 25-May 6). ... Granted free agency (October 26, 1998). ... Signed by Arizona Diamondbacks (December 18, 1998). ... Granted free agency (October 29, 2002). ... Re-signed by Diamondbacks (December 7, 2002).

2003 GAMES PLAYED BY POSITION (MLB): OF—140.

Year	Team (League)	Pos.	G	AB	R	H	2B	3B	HR	RBI	BB	SO	HBP	GDP	SB-CS	Avg.	OBP	SLG	OPS	E	Pct.
											BATTING									FIELDING	
1987— Newark (NY-Penn)	OF	54	222	40	65	13	2	3	33	22	24	2	4	26-5	.293	.359	.410	.769	4	.970	
— Hagerstown (Car.)	OF	15	65	9	22	3	2	1	5	1	6	0	2	7-2	.338	.348	.492	.841	0	1.000	
1988— Hagerstown (Car.)	OF	8	28	2	6	2	0	0	3	4	3	0	2	4-0	.214	.313	.286	.598	0	1.000	
— Charlotte (Sou.)	OF	10	40	7	12	4	2	1	6	4	3	1	1	2-0	.300	.378	.575	.953	0	1.000	
— Rochester (Int'l)	OF	120	456	61	*143	19	7	5	54	28	55	0	4	20-11	*.314	.352	.419	.771	*12	.962	
1989— Baltimore (A.L.)	DH-OF	81	217	35	54	5	2	2	25	15	30	1	3	17-3	.249	.298	.318	.616	2	.986	
— Rochester (Int'l)	OF	7	25	2	4	0	0	0	2	1	5	0	0	3-0	.160	.192	.160	.352	0	1.000	
— Hagerstown (East.)	OF	11	48	11	20	3	1	0	7	4	3	0	0	4-0	.417	.453	.521	.974	3	.925	
1990— Baltimore (A.L.)	DH-OF	142	464	46	119	16	4	3	37	32	53	2	8	22-9	.256	.304	.328	.632	7	.977	
1991— Houston (N.L.)	OF	159	596	84	170	28	10	8	54	42	65	2	8	34-18	.285	.331	.406	.737	5	.985	
1992— Houston (N.L.)	OF	•162	607	84	177	29	13	5	55	58	63	3	10	44-9	.292	.354	.407	.762	3	.993	
1993— Houston (N.L.)	OF	142	545	69	145	15	*13	8	44	28	65	3	8	19-6	.266	.304	.385	.689	4	.988	
1994— Houston (N.L.)	OF	94	373	64	103	16	5	11	33	28	52	2	3	13-7	.276	.329	.434	.764	4	.982	
— Jackson (Texas)	OF-DH	5	13	3	4	0	0	0	0	4	0	0	0	1-0	.308	.471	.308	.778	0	1.000	
1995— San Diego (N.L.)	OF	139	562	104	167	23	8	10	44	59	62	3	8	36-12	.297	.366	.420	.786	7	.977	
1996— San Diego (N.L.)	OF	161	655	126	195	45	9	30	95	56	87	4	20	22-8	.298	.354	.531	.885	7	.982	
1997— San Diego (N.L.)	OF	143	560	101	146	26	5	28	92	43	92	3	10	15-3	.261	.313	.475	.788	4	.989	
— Mobile (Sou.)	DH	1	4	1	2	0	0	1	2	1	2	0	0	0-0	.500	.600	1.250	1.850	...	...	
— Rancho Cuca. (Calif.)	DH-0	4	14	3	4	0	0	2	3	3	2	1	0	1-0	.286	.444	.714	1.159	0	...	
1998— San Diego (N.L.)	OF	159	619	92	154	40	6	14	67	45	103	3	9	12-3	.249	.301	.401	.702	7	.981	
1999— Arizona (N.L.)	OF-DH	156	590	100	156	32	10	34	103	63	94	3	4	8-4	.264	.336	.525	.861	2	.995	
2000— Arizona (N.L.)	OF-DH	152	539	100	151	27	5	35	96	65	87	8	9	12-6	.280	.361	.544	.904	3	.992	
2001— Arizona (N.L.)	OF	140	495	66	136	27	4	14	73	47	67	1	8	11-7	.275	.337	.430	.767	2	.994	
2002— Arizona (N.L.)	OF	150	505	82	145	24	4	25	89	65	73	3	10	16-4	.287	.370	.499	.869	2	.994	
2003— Arizona (N.L.)	OF	147	516	82	148	24	•10	22	70	57	94	6	6	15-8	.287	.363	.500	.863	5	.982	
American League totals (2 years)		223	681	81	173	21	6	5	62	47	83	3	11	39-12	.254	.302	.325	.627	9	.980	
National League totals (13 years)		1904	7162	1154	1993	356	102	244	915	656	1004	44	113	257-95	.278	.340	.459	.799	55	.988	
Major League totals (15 years)		2127	7843	1235	2166	377	108	249	977	703	1087	47	124	296-107	.276	.337	.447	.784	64	.987	

FIORE, TONY — P

PERSONAL: Born October 12, 1971, in Oak Park, Ill. ... 6-4/220. ... Throws right, bats right. ... Full name: Anthony James Fiore. ... High school: Holy Cross (River Grove, Ill.). ... Junior college: Triton College (Ill.).

TRANSACTIONS/CAREER NOTES: Selected by Philadelphia Phillies organization in 28th round of free-agent draft (June 1, 1992). ... On disabled list (April 2-20, 1995). ... Granted free agency (October 15, 1998). ... Re-signed by Phillies organization (November 28, 1998). ... Released by Phillies (May 19, 1999). ... Signed by Minnesota Twins organization (June 3, 1999). ... Granted free agency (October 15, 1999). ... Signed by Tampa Bay Devil Rays organization (January 14, 2000). ... On suspended list (September 22-24, 2000). ... Released by Devil Rays (May 25, 2001). ... Signed by Twins organization (May 30, 2001). ... Optioned to Rochester (June 17, 2003). ... Designated for assignment by Minnesota (July 20, 2003). ... Sent outright to Rochester (July 23, 2003).

CAREER HITTING: 0-for-4 (.000). ... 0 R, 0 2B, 0 3B, 0 HR, 0 RBI.

Year	League	W	L	Pct.	ERA	WHIP	G	GS	CG	ShO	Hld.	Sv.-Opp.	IP	H	R	ER	HR	BB-IBB	SO	Avg.
1992— Martinsville (App.)	2	3	.400	4.18	1.95	17	2	0	0	...	0-...	32.1	32	20	15	0	31-1	30	.258
1993— Batavia (N.Y.-Penn)	2	•8	.200	3.05	1.25	16	•16	1	0	...	0-...	97.1	82	51	33	1	40-0	55	.228
1994— Spartanburg (SAL)	12	13	.480	4.10	1.43	28	•28	*9	1	...	0-...	166.2	162	94	76	10	77-1	113	.257
1995— Clearwater (Fla. St.)	6	2	.750	3.71	1.62	24	10	0	0	...	0-...	70.1	70	41	29	4	44-2	45	.260
1996— Clearwater (Fla. St.)	8	4	.667	3.16	1.23	22	22	3	1	...	0-...	128.0	102	61	45	4	56-1	80	.217
— Reading (East.)	1	2	.333	4.35	1.61	5	5	0	0	...	0-...	31.0	32	21	15	2	18-0	19	.254
1997— Reading (East.)	8	3	.727	3.01	1.23	17	16	0	0	...	0-...	104.2	89	47	35	6	40-0	64	.237
— Scran./W.B. (I.L.)	3	5	.375	3.86	1.42	9	9	1	0	...	0-...	60.2	60	34	26	3	26-1	56	.252
1998— Scran./W.B. (I.L.)	4	7	.364	4.45	1.52	41	7	0	0	...	1-...	95.0	92	53	47	4	52-1	71	.256
1999— Scran./W.B. (I.L.)	0	0	...	6.64	2.11	13	0	0	0	...	0-...	20.1	28	19	15	0	15-1	13	.326
— Salt Lake (PCL)	2	1	.667	3.47	1.52	40	0	0	0	...	19-...	46.2	45	21	18	1	26-3	38	.260
2000— Durham (Int'l)	8	5	.615	2.28	1.33	53	1	0	0	...	8-...	75.0	62	22	19	3	38-6	39	.230
— Tampa Bay (A.L.)	1	1	.500	8.40	2.00	11	0	0	0	0	0-1	15.0	21	16	14	3	9-2	8	.333
2001— Tampa Bay (A.L.)	0	0	...	5.40	1.50	3	0	0	0	0	0-0	3.1	4	2	2	0	1-0	3	.308
— Edmonton (PCL)	5	0	1.000	3.68	1.36	32	6	0	0	0	1-...	80.2	85	35	33	4	25-0	58	.272
— Minnesota (A.L.)	0	1	.000	5.68	1.11	4	0	0	0	0	0-0	6.1	5	4	4	0	2-0	5	.208
2002— Edmonton (PCL)	2	0	1.000	4.15	1.31	2	2	0	0	0	1-...	13.0	15	6	6	2	2-0	6	.294
— Minnesota (A.L.)	10	3	.769	3.16	1.29	48	2	0	0	5	0-0	91.0	74	32	32	10	43-4	55	.224
2003— Minnesota (A.L.)	1	1	.500	5.50	1.47	21	0	0	0	0	0-0	36.0	32	25	22	5	21-1	23	.242
— Rochester (Int'l)	5	6	.455	3.95	1.20	16	11	2	0	...	1-...	84.1	80	43	37	5	21-2	48	.248
Major League totals (4 years)	12	6	.667	4.39	1.40	87	2	0	0	5	0-1	151.2	136	79	74	18	76-7	94	.242

FLAHERTY, JOHN — C

PERSONAL: Born October 21, 1967, in New York, N.Y. ... 6-1/200. ... Bats right, throws right. ... Full name: John Timothy Flaherty. ... High school: St. Joseph's Regional (Montvale, N.J.). ... College: George Washington.

TRANSACTIONS/CAREER NOTES: Selected by Boston Red Sox organization in 25th round of free-agent draft (June 1, 1988). ... Traded by Red Sox to Detroit Tigers for C Rich Rowland (April 1, 1994). ... Traded by Tigers with SS Chris Gomez to San Diego Padres for C Brad Ausmus, SS Andujar Cedeno and P Russ Spear (June 18, 1996). ... Traded by Padres to Tampa Bay Devil Rays for P Brian Boehringer and IF Andy Sheets (November 18, 1997). ... On Tampa Bay disabled list (May 26-June 20, 1998); included rehabilitation assignment to Durham (June 14-20). ... Granted free agency (October 28, 2002). ... Signed by New York Yankees organization (January 16, 2003).

2003 GAMES PLAYED BY POSITION (MLB): C—40.

Year	Team (League)	Pos.	G	AB	R	H	2B	3B	HR	RBI	BB	SO	HBP	GDP	SB-CS	Avg.	OBP	SLG	OPS	E	Pct.
											BATTING									FIELDING	
1988— Elmira (N.Y.-Penn)	C	46	162	17	38	3	0	3	16	12	23	2	5	2-1	.235	.294	.309	.602	7	.975	
1989— Winter Haven (FSL)	C-1B	95	334	31	87	14	2	4	28	20	44	3	19	1-0	.260	.306	.350	.657	9	.979	
1990— Pawtucket (Int'l)	3B-C	99	317	35	72	18	0	4	32	24	43	2	11	1-1	.227	.284	.322	.606	10	.983	
— Lynchburg (Caro.)	C	1	4	0	0	0	0	0	1	0	1	0	0	0-0	.000	.000	.000	.000	0	1.000	
1991— New Britain (East.)	C	67	225	27	65	9	0	3	18	31	22	1	5	0-2	.289	.375	.369	.743	9	.977	
— Pawtucket (Int'l)	C	45	156	18	29	7	0	3	13	15	14	0	1	0-1	.186	.254	.288	.546	•9	.970	
1992— Boston (A.L.)	C	35	66	3	13	2	0	0	2	3	7	0	0	0-0	.197	.229	.227	.456	2	.982	
— Pawtucket (Int'l)	C	31	104	11	26	3	0	0	7	5	8	1	6	0-0	.250	.291	.279	.570	4	.978	

F

Year	Team (League)	Pos.	G	AB	R	H	2B	3B	HR	RBI	BB	SO	HBP	GDP	SB-CS	Avg.	OBP	SLG	OPS	E	Pct.
1993—Pawtucket (Int'l)		C	105	365	29	99	22	0	6	35	26	41	5	9	0-2	.271	.327	.381	.707	10	.986
—Boston (A.L.)		C	13	25	3	3	2	0	0	2	2	6	1	0	0-0	.120	.214	.200	.414	0	1.000
1994—Toledo (Int'l)		C-DH	44	151	20	39	10	2	7	17	6	21	0	1	3-1	.258	.285	.490	.775	2	.984
—Detroit (A.L.)		C-DH	34	40	2	6	1	0	0	4	1	11	0	1	0-1	.150	.167	.175	.342	0	1.000
1995—Detroit (A.L.)		C	112	354	39	86	22	1	11	40	18	47	3	8	0-0	.243	.284	.404	.688	* 11	.982
1996—Detroit (A.L.)		C	47	152	18	38	12	0	4	23	8	25	1	5	1-0	.250	.290	.408	.698	5	.981
—San Diego (N.L.)		C	72	264	22	80	12	0	9	41	9	36	2	8	2-3	.303	.327	.451	.778	5	.990
1997—San Diego (N.L.)		C	129	439	38	120	21	1	9	46	33	62	0	11	4-4	.273	.323	.387	.710	11	.987
1998—Tampa Bay (A.L.)		C	91	304	21	63	11	0	3	24	22	46	1	9	0-5	.207	.261	.273	.534	4	.993
—Durham (Int'l)		DH-C	6	23	1	3	1	0	0	2	1	5	0	1	0-0	.130	.160	.174	.334	0	1.000
1999—Tampa Bay (A.L.)		C-DH	117	446	53	124	19	0	14	71	19	64	6	14	0-2	.278	.310	.415	.725	6	.993
2000—Tampa Bay (A.L.)		C	109	394	36	103	15	0	10	39	20	57	0	11	0-0	.261	.296	.376	.671	5	.993
2001—Tampa Bay (A.L.)		C	78	248	20	59	17	1	4	29	10	33	1	9	1-0	.238	.269	.363	.632	7	.986
2002—Tampa Bay (A.L.)		C	76	281	27	73	20	0	4	33	15	50	1	6	2-2	.260	.296	.374	.669	4	.992
2003—New York (A.L.)		C	40	105	16	28	8	0	4	14	4	19	1	6	0-0	.267	.297	.457	.754	2	.991
American League totals (11 years)			752	2415	238	596	129	2	54	281	122	365	15	69	4-10	.247	.284	.369	.653	46	.990
National League totals (2 years)			201	703	60	200	33	1	18	87	42	98	2	19	6-7	.284	.324	.411	.736	16	.988
Major League totals (12 years)			953	3118	298	796	162	3	72	368	164	463	17	88	10-17	.255	.293	.378	.672	62	.989

FLOYD, CLIFF — OF

PERSONAL: Born December 5, 1972, in Chicago, Ill. ... 6-4/230. ... Bats left, throws right. ... Full name: Cornelius Clifford Floyd. ... High school: Thornwood (South Holland, Ill.).

TRANSACTIONS/CAREER NOTES: Selected by Montreal Expos organization in first round (14th pick overall) of free-agent draft (June 3, 1991). ... On disabled list (May 16-September 11, 1995). ... Traded by Expos to Florida Marlins for OF Joe Orsulak and P Dustin Hermanson (March 26, 1997). ... On Florida disabled list (May 9-24 and June 21-September 1, 1997); included rehabilitation assigment to Charlotte (July 20-September 1). ... On Florida disabled list (March 30-April 27 and June 20-September 7, 1999); included rehabilitation assigment to Calgary (August 28-September 7). ... On disabled list (July 29-August 29, 2000). ... Traded by Marlins with P Claudio Vargas, OF/2B Wilton Guerrero, cash considerations and a player to be named later to Expos for P Carl Pavano, P Graeme Lloyd, IF Mike Mordecai and P Justin Wayne (July 11, 2002); Expos acquired P Don Levinski to complete deal (August 5, 2002). ... Traded by Expos to Boston Red Sox for P Seung Song, P Sun-Woo Kim and a player to be named later (July 30, 2002). ... Granted free agency (October 28, 2002). ... Signed by New York Mets (December 20, 2002). ... Placed on 15-day disabled list (August 19, 2003). ... Transferred to 60-day disabled list (September 2, 2003).

2003 GAMES PLAYED BY POSITION (MLB): OF—95, DH—9.

Year	Team (League)	Pos.	G	AB	R	H	2B	3B	HR	RBI	BB	SO	HBP	GDP	SB-CS	Avg.	OBP	SLG	OPS	E	Pct.
1991—GC Expos (GCL)		1B	56	214	35	56	9	3	6	30	19	37	5	3	13-3	.262	.335	.416	.751	15	.970
1992—Albany (S. Atl.)		1B-OF	134	516	83	157	24	* 16	16	* 97	45	75	9	4	32-11	.304	.368	.506	.874	17	.964
—W.P. Beach (FSL)		OF	1	4	0	0	0	0	0	0	1	0	0	0	0-0	.000	.000	.000	.000	0	1.000
1993—Harrisburg (East.)		1B-OF	101	380	82	125	17	4	• 26	* 101	54	71	5	8	31-10	.329	.417	.600	1.017	19	.969
—Ottawa (Int'l)		1B	32	125	12	30	2	2	2	18	16	34	1	1	2-2	.240	.329	.336	.665	5	.983
—Montreal (N.L.)		1B	10	31	3	7	0	0	1	2	0	9	0	0	0-0	.226	.226	.323	.548	1	1.000
1994—Montreal (N.L.)		1B-OF	100	334	43	94	19	4	4	41	24	63	3	3	10-3	.281	.332	.398	.731	6	.990
1995—Montreal (N.L.)		1B-OF	29	69	6	9	1	0	1	8	7	22	1	1	3-0	.130	.221	.188	.409	3	.981
1996—Ottawa (Int'l)		OF-3B-DH	20	76	7	23	3	1	1	8	7	20	1	0	2-2	.303	.369	.408	.777	2	.951
—Montreal (N.L.)		OF-1B	117	227	29	55	15	4	6	26	30	52	5	3	7-1	.242	.340	.423	.763	5	.957
1997—Florida (N.L.)		OF-1B	61	137	23	32	9	1	6	19	24	33	2	3	6-2	.234	.354	.445	.799	3	.971
—Charlotte (Int'l)		OF-1B	39	131	27	48	10	0	9	33	10	29	1	3	7-2	.366	.415	.649	1.064	1	.988
1998—Florida (N.L.)		OF-DH	153	588	85	166	45	3	22	90	47	112	3	10	27-14	.282	.337	.481	.818	7	.974
1999—Florida (N.L.)		OF-DH	69	251	37	76	19	1	11	49	30	47	2	8	5-6	.303	.379	.518	.897	6	.952
—Calgary (PCL)		OF	9	31	6	12	1	0	3	8	2	8	0	0	0-1	.387	.424	.710	1.134	0	1.000
2000—Florida (N.L.)		OF-DH	121	420	75	126	30	0	22	91	50	82	8	4	24-3	.300	.378	.529	.906	9	.951
2001—Florida (N.L.)		OF-DH	149	555	123	176	44	4	31	103	59	101	10	9	18-3	.317	.390	.578	.968	8	.972
2002—Florida (N.L.)		OF-DH	84	296	49	85	20	0	18	57	58	68	7	0	10-5	.287	.414	.537	.952	3	.983
—Montreal (N.L.)		OF	15	53	7	11	2	0	3	4	3	10	1	0	1-0	.208	.263	.415	.678	1	.941
—Boston (A.L.)		OF-DH	47	171	30	54	21	0	7	18	15	28	2	6	4-0	.316	.374	.561	.935	1	.977
2003—New York (N.L.)		OF-DH	108	365	57	106	25	2	18	68	51	66	3	10	3-0	.290	.376	.518	.894	5	.971
American League totals (1 year)			47	171	30	54	21	0	7	18	15	28	2	6	4-0	.316	.374	.561	.935	1	.977
National League totals (11 years)			1016	3326	537	943	229	19	143	558	383	665	45	51	114-37	.284	.362	.493	.855	56	.976
Major League totals (11 years)			1063	3497	567	997	250	19	150	576	398	693	47	57	118-37	.285	.363	.496	.859	57	.976

FOGG, JOSH — P

PERSONAL: Born December 13, 1976, in Lynn, Mass. ... 6-0/202. ... Throws right, bats right. ... Full name: Joshua Smith Fogg. ... High school: Cadinal Gibbons (Fort Lauderdale, Fla.). ... College: Florida.

TRANSACTIONS/CAREER NOTES: Selected by Chicago White Sox organization in third round of free-agent draft (June 2, 1998). ... Traded by White Sox with P Kip Wells and P Sean Lowe to Pittsburgh Pirates for P Todd Ritchie and C Lee Evans (December 13, 2001). ... Placed on 15-day disabled list (April 21, 2003). ... Transferred from Pittsburgh to Nashville on rehab assignment (May 16, 2003). ... Activated from the 15-day disabled list (May 26, 2003).

CAREER HITTING: 15-for-100 (.150), 6 R, 0 2B, 0 3B, 0 HR, 2 RBI.

Year	League	W	L	Pct.	ERA	WHIP	G	GS	CG	ShO	Hld.	Sv.-Opp.	IP	H	R	ER	HR	BB-IBB	SO	Avg.
1998—Ariz. White Sox (Ariz.)		1	0	1.000	0.00	0.25	2	0	0	0	...	0-...	4.0	0	0	0	0	1-0	5	.000
—Hickory (S. Atl.)		1	3	.250	2.18	1.19	8	8	0	0	...	0-...	41.1	36	17	10	4	13-0	29	.228
—Winston-Salem (Caro.)		0	1	.000	0.00	2.00	1	0	0	0	...	0-...	1.0	2	2	0	0	0-0	2	.333
1999—Winston-Salem (Caro.)		10	5	.667	2.96	1.22	17	17	1	1	...	0-...	103.1	93	44	34	3	33-0	109	.235
—Birmingham (Sou.)		3	2	.600	5.89	1.53	10	10	0	0	...	0-...	55.0	66	37	36	8	18-0	40	.296
2000—Birmingham (Sou.)		11	7	.611	4.35	1.22	27	27	2	0	...	0-...	192.1	190	68	55	7	44-2	136	.261
2001—Charlotte (Int'l)		4	7	.364	4.79	1.39	40	16	0	0	...	4-...	114.2	129	68	61	19	30-1	89	.283
—Chicago (A.L.)		0	0	...	2.03	0.98	11	0	0	0	...	0-0	13.1	10	3	3	0	3-1	17	.208
2002—Pittsburgh (N.L.)		12	12	.500	4.35	1.38	33	33	0	0	...	0-0	194.1	199	102	94	28	69-12	113	.267
2003—Nashville (PCL)		0	1	.000	5.40	1.30	2	2	0	0	...	0-...	10.0	12	6	6	1	1-0	7	.324
—Pittsburgh (N.L.)		10	9	.526	5.26	1.45	26	26	1	0	...	0-0	142.0	166	90	83	22	40-0	71	.293
American League totals (1 year)		0	0	...	2.03	0.98	11	0	0	0	...	0-0	13.1	10	3	3	0	3-1	17	.208
National League totals (2 years)		22	21	.512	4.74	1.41	59	59	1	0	...	0-0	336.1	365	192	177	50	109-12	184	.278
Major League totals (3 years)		22	21	.512	4.63	1.39	70	59	1	0	2	0-0	349.2	375	195	180	50	112-13	201	.276

FOPPERT, JESSE   P

PERSONAL: Born July 10, 1980, in Reading, Pa. ... 6-6/210. ... Throws right, bats right. ... Full name: Jesse W. Foppert. ... College: San Francisco.
TRANSACTIONS/CAREER NOTES: Selected by San Francisco Giants organization in second round of free-agent draft (June 5, 2001). ... Optioned to Fresno by San Francisco (July 10, 2003). ... Placed on 15-day disabled list (August 21, 2003).
CAREER HITTING: 3-for-37 (.081), 3 R, 1 2B, 1 3B, 0 HR, 1 RBI.

Year	League	W	L	Pct.	ERA	WHIP	G	GS	CG	ShO	Hld.	Sv.-Opp.	IP	H	R	ER	HR	BB-IBB	SO	Avg.
2001— Salem-Keizer (NW)		8	1	.889	1.93	0.83	14	14	0	0	...	0-...	70.0	35	18	15	7	23-0	88	.150
2002— Shreveport (Texas)		3	3	.500	2.79	1.06	11	11	1	0	...	0-...	61.1	44	22	19	3	21-0	74	.199
— Fresno (PCL)		3	6	.333	3.99	1.34	14	14	0	0	...	0-...	79.0	71	37	35	12	35-0	109	.244
2003— Fresno (PCL)		0	0	...	1.80	0.60	1	1	0	0	...	0-...	5.0	3	1	1	0	0-0	9	.167
— San Jose (Calif.)		0	1	.000	9.00	1.67	1	1	0	0	...	0-...	3.0	5	3	3	0	0-0	3	.385
— San Francisco (N.L.)		8	9	.471	5.03	1.55	23	21	0	0	1	0-0	111.0	103	69	62	16	69-4	101	.249
Major League totals (1 year)		8	9	.471	5.03	1.55	23	21	0	0	1	0-0	111.0	103	69	62	16	69-4	101	.249

FORD, LEW   OF

PERSONAL: Born August 12, 1976, in Beaumont, Texas. ... 6-0/190. ... Bats right, throws right. ... Full name: Jon Lewis Ford. ... High school: Port Neches-Groves High (Texarkana, Texas). ... College: Dallas Baptist (Texas).
TRANSACTIONS/CAREER NOTES: Selected by Boston Red Sox organization in 12th round of free-agent draft (June 2, 1999). ... Traded by Red Sox to Minnesota Twins for P Hector Carrasco (September 10, 2000). ... Recalled from Rochester of the International League (May 28, 2003). ... Placed on 15-day disabled list by Minnesota (July 14, 2003). ... Sent on rehab assignment by Minnesota (August 21, 2003). ... Recalled from minor league rehab assignment; removed from 15-day disabled list (September 2, 2003).
2003 GAMES PLAYED BY POSITION (MLB): OF—25, DH—4.

Year	Team (League)	Pos.	G	AB	R	H	2B	3B	HR	RBI	BB	SO	HBP	GDP	SB-CS	Avg.	OBP	SLG	OPS	E	Pct.
1999— Lowell (NY-Penn)	OF	62	250	48	70	17	4	7	34	19	35	5	6	15-2	.280	.339	.464	.803	1	.993
2000— Augusta (S. Atl.)	OF	126	514	122	162	35	11	9	74	52	83	12	12	52-4	.315	.390	.479	.868	2	.994
2001— Fort Myers (FSL)	OF	67	265	42	79	15	2	2	24	21	30	12	3	19-9	.298	.373	.392	.766	1	.993
— New Britain (East.)	OF	62	252	30	55	9	3	7	25	20	35	6	4	5-5	.218	.289	.361	.650	3	.974
2002— New Britain (East.)	OF	93	373	81	116	27	2	15	51	49	47	8	5	17-5	.311	.401	.515	.916	3	.986
— Edmonton (PCL)	OF	47	193	40	64	11	2	5	24	13	21	6	2	11-1	.332	.390	.487	.877	5	.964
2003— Rochester (Int'l)	OF-DH	53	211	33	64	18	2	3	31	10	28	8	1	4-5	.303	.357	.450	.807	1	.990
— Minnesota (A.L.)	OF-DH	34	73	16	24	7	1	3	15	8	9	1	1	2-0	.329	.402	.575	.978	3	.923
Major League totals (1 year)		34	73	16	24	7	1	3	15	8	9	1	1	2-0	.329	.402	.575	.978	3	.923

FORD, MATT   P

PERSONAL: Born April 8, 1981, in Plantation, Fla. ... 6-1/170. ... Throws left, bats both. ... Full name: Matthew Lee Ford.
TRANSACTIONS/CAREER NOTES: Selected by Toronto Blue Jays in third round of free-agent draft (June 1999). ... Selected by Milwaukee Brewers from Toronto in Rule 5 draft (December 16, 2002).
CAREER HITTING: 1-for-7 (.143), 0 R, 1 2B, 0 3B, 0 HR, 1 RBI.

Year	League	W	L	Pct.	ERA	WHIP	G	GS	CG	ShO	Hld.	Sv.-Opp.	IP	H	R	ER	HR	BB-IBB	SO	Avg.
1999— Medicine Hat (Pio.)		4	0	1.000	2.05	1.12	13	7	0	0	...	0-...	48.1	31	11	11	0	23-0	68	.182
2000— Hagerstown (S. Atl.)		5	3	.625	3.87	1.40	18	14	1	0	...	0-...	83.2	81	42	36	5	36-0	86	.261
2001— Dunedin (Fla. St.)		2	7	.222	5.85	1.73	13	12	0	0	...	0-...	60.0	67	41	39	8	37-0	48	.294
— Char., W.Va. (SAL)		4	4	.500	2.42	1.19	11	11	1	0	...	0-...	70.2	62	28	19	2	22-0	69	.237
2002— Dunedin (Fla. St.)		9	5	.643	2.37	1.25	21	18	0	0	...	0-...	114.0	100	43	30	7	42-0	85	.240
2003— Milwaukee (N.L.)		0	3	.000	4.33	1.53	25	4	0	0	1	0-0	43.2	46	23	21	5	21-0	26	.264
Major League totals (1 year)		0	3	.000	4.33	1.53	25	4	0	0	1	0-0	43.2	46	23	21	5	21-0	26	.264

FORDYCE, BROOK   C

PERSONAL: Born May 7, 1970, in New London, Conn. ... 6-0/194. ... Bats right, throws right. ... Full name: Brook Alexander Fordyce. ... Name pronounced: four-DICE. ... High school: St. Bernard (Uncasville, Conn.).
TRANSACTIONS/CAREER NOTES: Selected by New York Mets organization in third round of free-agent draft (June 5, 1989). ... On disabled list (June 19-July 2 and July 18-August 30, 1994). ... On suspended list (August 30-September 1, 1994). ... Claimed on waivers by Cleveland Indians (May 15, 1995). ... Granted free agency (October 16, 1995). ... Signed by Cincinnati Reds organization (December 7, 1995). ... On disabled list (July 16-August 5, 1997); included rehabilitation assignment to Indianapolis (July 21-August 5). ... On Cincinnati disabled list (July 13-August 12, 1998); included rehabilitation assignment to Indianapolis (August 4-12). ... Traded by Reds to Chicago White Sox for P Jake Meyer (March 25, 1999). ... On Chicago disabled list (March 25-May 23, 2000); included rehabilitation assignment to Charlotte (May 5-23). ... Traded by White Sox with P Miguel Felix, P Juan Figueroa and P Jason Lakman to Baltimore Orioles for C Charles Johnson and DH Harold Baines (July 29, 2000).
2003 GAMES PLAYED BY POSITION (MLB): C—107.

Year	Team (League)	Pos.	G	AB	R	H	2B	3B	HR	RBI	BB	SO	HBP	GDP	SB-CS	Avg.	OBP	SLG	OPS	E	Pct.
1989— Kingsport (Appal.)	3B-C-OF	69	226	45	74	15	0	9	38	30	26	1	3	10-6	.327	.405	.513	.919	4	.988
1990— Columbia (S. Atl.)	C	104	372	45	117	29	1	10	54	39	42	0	18	4-1	.315	.378	.478	.856	15	.977
1991— St. Lucie (Fla. St.)	C	115	406	42	97	19	3	7	55	37	50	4	7	4-5	.239	.305	.352	.657	13	.982
1992— Binghamton (East.)	C	118	425	59	118	30	0	11	61	37	78	4	13	1-2	.278	.337	.426	.763	3	.996
1993— Norfolk (Int'l)	C	116	409	33	106	21	2	2	41	26	62	5	10	2-2	.259	.307	.335	.642	8	.990
1994— Norfolk (Int'l)	C-DH	66	229	26	60	13	3	3	32	19	26	1	9	1-0	.262	.320	.384	.704	7	.981
1995— New York (N.L.)	C	4	2	1	1	1	0	0	0	1	0	0	0	0-0	.500	.667	1.000	1.667	...	...
— Buffalo (A.A.)	C-OF-DH	58	176	18	44	13	0	9	9	14	20	2	2	1-0	.250	.313	.324	.636	3	.991
1996— Indianapolis (A.A.)	C-DH-1B	107	374	48	103	20	3	16	64	25	56	1	5	2-1	.275	.319	.473	.793	4	.994
— Cincinnati (N.L.)	C	4	7	0	2	1	0	0	1	3	1	0	0	0-0	.286	.500	.429	.929	0	1.000
1997— Cincinnati (N.L.)	C-DH	47	96	7	20	5	0	1	8	8	15	0	0	2-0	.208	.267	.292	.558	3	.983
— Indianapolis (Int'l)	C-DH	12	47	7	11	2	0	2	6	5	6	1	3	1-1	.234	.321	.404	.725	0	1.000
1998— Cincinnati (N.L.)	C	57	146	8	37	9	0	3	14	11	28	0	2	0-1	.253	.306	.377	.682	7	.978
— Indianapolis (Int'l)	C	6	24	4	6	1	0	2	3	1	2	0	1	0-0	.250	.280	.542	.822	0	1.000
1999— Chicago (A.L.)	C	105	333	36	99	25	1	9	49	21	48	3	5	2-0	.297	.343	.459	.802	8	.987
2000— Charlotte (Int'l)	C	17	67	9	16	5	0	2	12	8	13	0	2	0-1	.239	.316	.403	.719	0	1.000
— Chicago (A.L.)	C	40	125	18	34	7	1	5	21	6	23	2	1	0-0	.272	.313	.464	.777	4	.988
— Baltimore (A.L.)	C	53	177	23	57	11	0	9	28	11	27	2	3	0-0	.322	.361	.537	.898	4	.988

F

Year Team (League)	Pos.	G	AB	R	H	2B	3B	HR	RBI	BB	SO	HBP	GDP	SB-CS	Avg.	OBP	SLG	OPS	FIELDING E	Pct.
2001—Baltimore (A.L.)	C	95	292	30	61	18	0	5	19	21	56	3	7	1-2	.209	.268	.322	.590	10	.983
2002—Baltimore (A.L.)	C	56	130	7	30	8	0	1	8	9	19	4	5	1-0	.231	.301	.315	.616	4	.986
2003—Baltimore (A.L.)	C	108	348	28	95	12	2	6	31	19	44	1	10	2-3	.273	.311	.371	.682	3	.996
American League totals (5 years)		457	1405	142	376	81	4	35	156	87	217	15	31	6-5	.268	.315	.406	.721	29	.989
National League totals (4 years)		112	251	16	60	16	0	4	23	23	44	0	2	2-1	.239	.302	.351	.652	10	.980
Major League totals (9 years)		569	1656	158	436	97	4	39	179	110	261	15	33	8-6	.263	.313	.397	.710	39	.988

FOSSUM, CASEY   P

PERSONAL: Born January 6, 1978, in Cherry Hill, N.J. ... 6-1/165. ... Throws left, bats both. ... Full name: Casey Paul Fossum. ... High school: Midway (Waco, Texas). ... College: Texas A&M.

TRANSACTIONS/CAREER NOTES: Selected by Arizona Diamondbacks organization in sixth round of free-agent draft (June 4, 1996); did not sign. ... Selected by Boston Red Sox organization as "sandwich pick" between first and second round of free-agent draft (June 2, 1999); pick received as part of compensation for Arizona Diamondbacks signing Type A free agent P Greg Swindell. ... Placed on 15-day disabled list (June 8, 2003). ... Sent to Portland on rehab assignment (July 4, 2003). ... Reinstated from 15-day disabled list (July 17, 2003). ... Optioned to Pawtucket (July 28, 2003). ... Recalled by Boston (August 8, 2003). ... Optioned to Pawtucket (August 22, 2003). ... Recalled by Boston (September 1, 2003).

CAREER HITTING: 0-for-0 (.000), 0 R, 0 2B, 0 3B, 0 HR, 0 RBI.

Year League	W	L	Pct.	ERA	WHIP	G	GS	CG	ShO	Hld.	Sv.-Opp.	IP	H	R	ER	HR	BB-IBB	SO	Avg.
1999—Lowell (NY-Penn)	0	1	.000	1.26	0.77	5	5	0	0	...	0-...	14.1	6	2	2	1	5-0	16	.122
2000—Sarasota (Fla. St.)	9	10	.474	3.44	1.23	27	27	3	* 3	...	0-...	149.1	147	71	57	7	36-0	143	.257
2001—Trenton (East.)	3	7	.300	2.83	1.10	20	20	0	0	...	0-...	117.2	102	47	37	5	28-0	130	.231
—Boston (A.L.)	3	2	.600	4.87	1.44	13	7	0	0	0	0-0	44.1	44	26	24	4	20-1	26	.259
2002—Boston (A.L.)	5	4	.556	3.46	1.34	43	12	0	0	3	1-1	106.2	113	56	41	12	30-0	101	.268
—Pawtucket (Int'l)	0	3	.000	3.96	1.60	5	3	1	0	...	0-...	25.0	34	15	11	1	6-0	28	.337
2003—Portland (East.)	0	1	.000	6.75	2.00	3	2	0	0	...	0-...	4.0	5	3	3	1	3-0	7	.294
—Pawtucket (Int'l)	1	0	1.000	3.46	1.23	5	4	0	0	...	1-...	13.0	11	5	5	1	5-0	14	.234
—Boston (A.L.)	6	5	.545	5.47	1.47	19	14	0	0	0	1-1	79.0	82	55	48	9	34-0	63	.270
Major League totals (3 years)	14	11	.560	4.42	1.40	75	33	0	0	3	2-2	230.0	239	137	113	25	84-1	190	.267

FOSTER, JOHN   P

PERSONAL: Born May 17, 1978, in Stockton, Calif. ... 6-0/200. ... Throws left, bats left. ... Full name: John Norman Foster. ... College: Lewis-Clark (Idaho) State.

TRANSACTIONS/CAREER NOTES: Selected by Atlanta Braves organization in 25th round of free-agent draft (June 2, 1999). ... On Atlanta disabled list (August 18, 2002-remainder of season); included rehabilitation assignment to Richmond (August 28-September 3). ... Traded by Braves with 3B Wes Helms to Milwaukee Brewers for P Ray King (December 16, 2002). ... Assigned to Indianapolis by Milwaukee (May 25, 2003). ... Recalled from Indianapolis (June 20, 2003). ... Optioned to Indianapolis (July 6, 2003). ... Recalled from Indianapolis (September 29, 2003).

CAREER HITTING: 0-for-0 (.000), 0 R, 0 2B, 0 3B, 0 HR, 0 RBI.

Year League	W	L	Pct.	ERA	WHIP	G	GS	CG	ShO	Hld.	Sv.-Opp.	IP	H	R	ER	HR	BB-IBB	SO	Avg.
1999—Danville (Appal.)	4	1	.800	1.38	0.87	18	0	0	0	...	1-...	39.0	28	10	6	0	6-0	36	.207
2000—Myrtle Beach (Caro.)	2	1	.667	1.85	1.27	38	0	0	0	...	3-...	48.2	48	13	10	2	14-4	46	.264
2001—Greenville (Sou.)	8	7	.533	3.01	1.51	50	0	0	0	...	7-...	68.2	71	30	23	6	33-7	63	.280
2002—Richmond (Int'l)	8	4	.667	4.21	1.53	55	0	0	0	...	8-...	62.0	67	30	29	5	28-8	48	.276
—Atlanta (N.L.)	1	0	1.000	10.80	2.40	5	0	0	0	0	0-0	5.0	6	6	6	3	6-0	6	.286
2003—Milwaukee (N.L.)	2	0	1.000	4.71	1.81	23	0	0	0	3	0-2	21.0	30	11	11	5	8-2	16	.341
—Indianapolis (Int'l)	2	2	.500	3.70	1.38	27	0	0	0	...	0-...	41.1	44	21	17	4	13-1	37	.272
Major League totals (2 years)	3	0	1.000	5.88	1.92	28	0	0	0	3	0-2	26.0	36	17	17	8	14-2	22	.330

FOULKE, KEITH   P

PERSONAL: Born October 19, 1972, in Ellsworth AFB, S.D. ... 6-0/210. ... Throws right, bats right. ... Full name: Keith Charles Foulke. ... Name pronounced: FOLK. ... High school: Hargrove (Huffman, Texas). ... College: Lewis-Clark (Idaho) State.

TRANSACTIONS/CAREER NOTES: Selected by San Francisco Giants organization in ninth round of free-agent draft (June 2, 1994). ... Traded by Giants with SS Mike Caruso, OF Brian Manning, P Lorenzo Barcelo, P Bobby Howry and P Ken Vining to Chicago White Sox for P Wilson Alvarez, P Danny Darwin and P Roberto Hernandez (July 31, 1997). ... On disabled list (August 28, 1998-remainder of season). ... On suspended list (May 5-7, 2000). ... Traded by White Sox with C Mark Johnson, P Joe Valentine and cash to Oakland Athletics for P Billy Koch and two players to be named later (December 3, 2002); White Sox acquired P Neal Cotts and OF Daylon Holt to complete deal (December 16, 2002).

CAREER HITTING: 2-for-16 (.125), 0 R, 0 2B, 0 3B, 0 HR, 0 RBI.

Year League	W	L	Pct.	ERA	WHIP	G	GS	CG	ShO	Hld.	Sv.-Opp.	IP	H	R	ER	HR	BB-IBB	SO	Avg.
1994—Everett (Northwest)	2	0	1.000	0.93	1.03	4	4	0	0	...	0-...	19.1	17	4	2	0	3-0	22	.233
1995—San Jose (Calif.)	13	6	.684	3.50	1.12	28	26	2	1	...	0-...	177.1	166	85	69	16	32-0	168	.247
1996—Shreveport (Texas)	12	7	.632	2.76	1.01	27	27	4	2	...	0-...	* 182.2	149	61	56	16	35-0	129	.225
1997—Phoenix (PCL)	5	4	.556	4.50	1.24	12	12	0	0	...	0-...	76.0	79	38	38	11	15-0	54	.270
—San Francisco (N.L.)	1	5	.167	8.26	1.75	11	8	0	0	0	0-1	44.2	60	41	41	9	18-1	33	.324
—Nashville (A.A.)	0	0	...	5.79	1.71	1	1	0	0	...	0-...	4.2	8	3	3	1	0-0	4	.400
—Chicago (A.L.)	3	0	1.000	3.45	1.15	16	0	0	0	5	3-5	28.2	28	11	11	4	5-1	21	.255
1998—Chicago (A.L.)	3	2	.600	4.13	1.09	54	0	0	0	13	1-2	65.1	51	31	30	9	20-3	57	.213
1999—Chicago (A.L.)	3	3	.500	2.22	0.88	67	0	0	0	22	9-13	105.1	72	28	26	11	21-4	123	.188
2000—Chicago (A.L.)	3	1	.750	2.97	1.00	72	0	0	0	3	34-39	88.0	66	31	29	9	22-2	91	.207
2001—Chicago (A.L.)	4	9	.308	2.33	0.98	72	0	0	0	0	42-45	81.0	57	21	21	3	22-1	75	.199
2002—Chicago (A.L.)	2	4	.333	2.90	1.00	65	0	0	0	8	11-14	77.2	65	26	25	7	13-2	58	.225
2003—Oakland (A.L.)	9	1	.900	2.08	0.89	72	0	0	0	0	*43-48	86.2	57	21	20	10	20-2	88	.184
American League totals (7 years)	27	20	.574	2.74	0.97	418	0	0	0	51	143-166	532.2	396	169	162	53	123-15	513	.204
National League totals (1 year)	1	5	.167	8.26	1.75	11	8	0	0	0	0-1	44.2	60	41	41	9	18-1	33	.324
Major League totals (7 years)	28	25	.528	3.16	1.03	429	8	0	0	51	143-167	577.1	456	210	203	62	141-16	546	.215

FOX, ANDY   IF

PERSONAL: Born January 12, 1971, in Sacramento, Calif. ... 6-4/202. ... Bats left, throws right. ... Full name: Andrew Junipero Fox. ... High school: Christian Brothers (Sacramento).

TRANSACTIONS/CAREER NOTES: Selected by New York Yankees organization in second round of free-agent draft (June 5, 1989). ... On disabled list (June 11-21, 1991; April 9-22, 1992 and June 10-August 1, 1993). ... On Columbus disabled list (August 5-19, 1997). ... Traded by Yankees to Arizona Diamondbacks for P Marty Janzen and P Todd Erdos (March 8, 1998). ... On disabled list (August 28-September 11, 1999). ... On Arizona disabled list (March 23-April 17, 2000); included rehabilitation assignments to El

F

Paso (April 10-14) and Tucson (April 15-17). ... Traded by Diamondbacks to Florida Marlins for OF Danny Bautista (June 9, 2000). ... On Florida disabled list (April 11-July 12, 2001); included rehabilitation assignments to Calgary (June 5-15 and July 2-9).

2003 GAMES PLAYED BY POSITION (MLB): 2B—15, SS—9, 3B—5, 1B—2, OF—2.

Year	Team (League)	Pos.	G	AB	R	H	2B	3B	HR	RBI	BATTING BB	SO	HBP	GDP	SB-CS	Avg.	OBP	SLG	OPS	FIELDING E	Pct.
1989— GC Yankees (GCL)		3B	40	141	26	35	9	2	3	25	31	29	2	1	6-1	.248	.386	.404	.791	10	.920
1990— Greensboro (S. Atl.)		3B	134	455	68	99	19	4	9	55	92	132	4	14	26-5	.218	.353	.336	.689	* 45	.880
1991— Prince Will. (Car.)		3B	126	417	60	96	22	2	10	46	81	104	6	7	15-13	.230	.357	.365	.721	* 29	.920
1992— Prince Will. (Car.)		3B-SS	125	473	75	113	18	3	7	42	54	81	6	7	28-14	.239	.325	.334	.659	27	.937
1993— Alb./Colon. (East.)		3B	65	236	44	65	16	1	3	24	32	54	0	1	12-6	.275	.362	.390	.752	19	.917
1994— Alb./Colon. (East.)		3B-SS-2B	121	472	75	105	20	3	11	43	62	102	2	4	22-13	.222	.315	.347	.662	‡ 34	.916
1995— Norwich (East.)		SS	44	175	23	36	3	5	5	17	19	36	0	3	8-1	.206	.282	.366	.648	9	.958
— Columbus (Int'l)		3-S-OF-2	82	302	61	105	16	6	9	37	43	41	4	5	22-4	.348	.432	.530	.962	9	.970
1996— New York (A.L.)		2-3-S-D-O	113	189	26	37	4	0	3	13	20	28	1	2	11-3	.196	.276	.265	.541	12	.955
1997— Columbus (Int'l)		3-2-S-D-O	95	318	66	87	11	4	6	33	54	64	1	5	28-11	.274	.380	.390	.770	14	.959
— New York (A.L.)		3-2-S-D-O	22	31	13	7	1	0	0	1	7	9	0	1	2-1	.226	.368	.258	.626	1	.980
1998— Arizona (N.L.)		2-0-3-1	139	502	67	139	21	6	9	44	43	97	18	2	14-7	.277	.355	.396	.751	8	.984
1999— Arizona (N.L.)		SS-3B	99	274	34	70	12	2	6	33	33	61	9	4	4-1	.255	.351	.380	.731	14	.955
2000— El Paso (Texas)		3B-SS-OF	4	15	3	6	2	0	0	4	2	2	0	0	1-1	.400	.471	.533	1.004	2	.714
— Tucson (PCL)		2B-3B-SS	3	13	1	3	0	1	0	3	0	1	0	1	0-1	.231	.231	.385	.615	1	.917
— Arizona (N.L.)		3B-OF-1B	31	86	10	18	4	0	1	10	4	16	0	1	2-1	.209	.244	.291	.535	2	.962
— Florida (N.L.)		S-O-3-2	69	164	19	40	4	2	3	10	18	37	3	1	8-3	.244	.330	.348	.677	11	.938
2001— Florida (N.L.)		S-3-2-0	54	81	8	15	0	1	3	7	15	17	2	2	1-0	.185	.327	.321	.648	3	.957
— Calgary (PCL)		2-S-0-3-1	11	42	10	18	2	1	2	8	3	2	1	1	1-1	.429	.478	.667	1.145	1	.971
2002— Florida (N.L.)		S-2-3-0	133	435	55	109	14	5	4	41	49	94	10	9	31-7	.251	.338	.333	.671	18	.966
2003— Florida (N.L.)		2-S-3-1-0	70	108	12	21	5	1	0	8	7	29	4	2	1-2	.194	.269	.259	.528	4	.950
American League totals (2 years)			135	220	39	44	5	0	3	14	27	37	1	3	13-4	.200	.290	.264	.554	13	.959
National League totals (6 years)			595	1650	205	412	60	17	26	153	169	351	46	21	61-21	.250	.335	.354	.689	60	.965
Major League totals (8 years)			730	1870	244	456	65	17	29	167	196	388	47	24	74-25	.244	.330	.343	.673	73	.964

FOX, CHAD — P

PERSONAL: Born September 3, 1970, in Houston, Texas. ... 6-3/190. ... Throws right, bats right. ... Full name: Chad Douglas Fox. ... High school: Westfield (Houston). ... College: Tarleton State (Texas).

TRANSACTIONS/CAREER NOTES: Selected by Cincinnati Reds organization in 23rd round of free-agent draft (June 1, 1992). ... Traded by Reds with a player to be named later to Atlanta Braves for OF Mike Kelly (January 9, 1996); Braves acquired P Ray King to complete deal (June 11, 1996). ... On disabled list (July 16-September 3, 1996). ... Traded by Braves to Milwaukee Brewers for OF Gerald Williams (December 11, 1997). ... On Milwaukee disabled list (May 11-June 30, 1998); included rehabilitation assignment to Beloit (June 25-July 1). ... On disabled list (April 21, 1999-remainder of season; and March 28, 2000-entire season). ... On Milwaukee disabled list (March 30-May 31 and June 8, 2002-remainder of season); included rehabilitation assignment to Huntsville (May 25-31). ... Released by Brewers (October 15, 2002). ... Signed by Boston Red Sox (December 24, 2002). ... Placed on the 15-day disabled list (April 28, 2003). ... Sent on rehab assignment to Sarasota (June 17, 2003). ... Recalled from Sarasota rehab assignment; reinstated from 15-day disabled list (June 29, 2003). ... Released by Boston Red Sox (July 30, 2003). ... Signed by Florida Marlins as a free agent (August 8, 2003).

CAREER HITTING: 0-for-7 (.000). ... 0 R, 0 2B, 0 3B, 0 HR, 0 RBI.

Year— League	W	L	Pct.	ERA	WHIP	G	GS	CG	ShO	Hld.	Sv.-Opp.	IP	H	R	ER	HR	BB-IBB	SO	Avg.
1992— Princeton (Appal.)	4	2	.667	4.74	1.80	15	8	0	0	...	0-...	49.1	55	43	26	2	34-1	37	.275
1993— Char., W.Va. (SAL)	9	12	.429	5.37	1.73	27	26	0	0	...	0-...	135.2	138	100	81	7	97-0	81	.268
1994— Winston-Salem (Caro.)	12	5	.706	3.86	1.38	25	25	1	0	...	0-...	156.1	121	77	67	18	* 94-0	137	.216
1995— Chattanooga (Sou.)	4	5	.444	5.06	1.60	20	17	0	0	...	0-...	80.0	76	49	45	2	52-1	56	.250
1996— Richmond (Int'l)	3	10	.231	4.73	1.50	18	18	1	0	...	0-...	93.1	91	57	49	9	49-1	87	.261
1997— Richmond (Int'l)	1	0	1.000	3.70	1.56	13	0	0	0	...	0-...	24.1	24	10	10	1	14-0	25	.273
— Atlanta (N.L.)	0	1	.000	3.29	1.46	30	0	0	0	7	0-1	27.1	24	12	10	4	16-0	28	.231
1998— Milwaukee (N.L.)	1	4	.200	3.95	1.33	49	0	0	0	20	0-2	57.0	56	27	25	4	20-0	64	.260
— Beloit (Midw.)	0	1	.000	4.50	0.50	2	1	0	0	...	0-...	6.0	1	1	1	0	0-0	3	.167
1999— Milwaukee (N.L.)	0	0	...	10.80	2.25	6	0	0	0	1	0-0	6.2	11	8	8	1	4-0	12	.355
2000— Milwaukee (N.L.)											Did not play.								
2001— Indianapolis (Int'l)	3	0	1.000	1.50	1.17	4	0	0	0	...	0-...	6.0	4	1	1	0	3-0	8	.190
— Milwaukee (N.L.)	5	2	.714	1.89	1.20	65	0	0	0	20	2-4	66.2	44	16	14	6	36-7	80	.181
2002— Huntsville (Sou.)	0	1	.000	0.00	1.31	3	0	0	0	...	0-...	5.1	5	1	0	0	2-0	7	.263
— Milwaukee (N.L.)	1	0	1.000	5.79	2.36	3	0	0	0	0	0-0	4.2	6	3	3	0	5-1	3	.316
2003— Sarasota (Fla. St.)	0	0	...	4.50	1.50	2	0	0	0	...	0-...	2.0	2	1	1	0	1-0	1	.250
— Pawtucket (Int'l)	0	0	...	13.50	3.00	1	0	0	0	...	0-...	1.1	3	3	2	1	1-0	2	.500
— Portland (East.)	0	0	...	0.00	2.25	1	0	0	0	...	0-...	1.1	1	0	0	0	2-0	2	.200
— Boston (A.L.)	1	2	.333	4.50	2.00	17	0	0	0	0	3-5	18.0	19	10	9	2	17-2	19	.264
— Albuquerque (PCL)	0	0	...	3.86	2.14	3	0	0	0	...	0-...	2.1	4	1	1	0	1-0	5	.364
— Florida (N.L.)	2	1	.667	2.13	1.18	21	0	0	0	7	0-0	25.1	16	6	6	1	14-2	27	.190
American League totals (1 year)	1	2	.333	4.50	2.00	17	0	0	0	0	3-5	18.0	19	10	9	2	17-2	19	.264
National League totals (6 years)	9	8	.529	3.17	1.34	174	0	0	0	55	2-7	187.2	157	72	66	16	95-10	214	.226
Major League totals (6 years)	10	10	.500	3.28	1.40	191	0	0	0	55	5-12	205.2	176	82	75	18	112-12	233	.229

FRANCO, JOHN — P

PERSONAL: Born September 17, 1960, in Brooklyn, N.Y. ... 5-10/185. ... Throws left, bats left. ... Full name: John Anthony Franco. ... High school: Lafayette (Brooklyn, N.Y.). ... College: St. John's.

TRANSACTIONS/CAREER NOTES: Selected by Los Angeles Dodgers organization in fifth round of free-agent draft (June 8, 1981). ... Traded by Dodgers with P Brett Wise to Cincinnati Reds for IF Rafael Landestoy (May 9, 1983). ... Traded by Reds with OF Don Brown to New York Mets for P Randy Myers and P Kip Gross (December 6, 1989). ... On disabled list (June 30-August 1 and August 26, 1992-remainder of season; April 17-May 7 and August 3-26, 1993). ... Granted free agency (October 18, 1994). ... Re-signed by Mets (April 5, 1995). ... On New York disabled list (July 3-September 4, 1999); included rehabilitation assignment to Binghamton (September 3-4). ... Granted free agency (October 31, 2000). ... Re-signed by Mets (November 25, 2000). ... On disabled list (March 21, 2002-entire season). ... On disabled list (March 28, 2003). ... Sent on rehab assignment to St. Lucie (May 12, 2003). ... Recalled from rehab assignment by New York (May 30, 2003).

CAREER HITTING: 3-for-34 (.088). 2 R, 0 2B, 0 3B, 0 HR, 1 RBI.

F

Year League	W	L	Pct.	ERA	WHIP	G	GS	CG	ShO	Hld.	Sv.-Opp.	IP	H	R	ER	HR	BB-IBB	SO	Avg.
1981— Vero Beach (FSL)	7	4	.636	3.53	1.51	13	11	3	0	...	0-...	79.0	78	41	31	1	41-2	60	...
1982— Albuquerque (PCL)	1	2	.333	7.24	2.05	5	5	0	0	...	0-...	27.1	41	22	22	3	15-1	24	...
— San Antonio (Texas)	10	5	.667	4.96	1.74	17	17	3	0	...	0-...	105.1	137	70	58	11	46-1	76	...
1983— Albuquerque (PCL)	0	0	...	5.40	1.40	11	0	0	0	...	0-...	15.0	10	11	9	3	11-2	8	...
— Indianapolis (A.A.)	6	10	.375	4.85	1.65	23	18	2	0	...	2-...	115.0	148	69	62	10	42-3	54	...
1984— Wichita (Am. Assoc.)	1	0	1.000	5.79	1.29	6	0	0	0	...	0-...	9.1	8	6	6	1	4-0	11	.235
— Cincinnati (N.L.)	6	2	.750	2.61	1.39	54	0	0	0	1	4-9	79.1	74	28	23	3	36-4	55	.256
1985— Cincinnati (N.L.)	12	3	.800	2.18	1.24	67	0	0	0	11	12-15	99.0	83	27	24	5	40-8	61	.234
1986— Cincinnati (N.L.)	6	6	.500	2.94	1.33	74	0	0	0	1	29-38	101.0	90	40	33	7	44-12	84	.243
1987— Cincinnati (N.L.)	8	5	.615	2.52	1.26	68	0	0	0	0	32-41	82.0	76	26	23	6	27-6	61	.245
1988— Cincinnati (N.L.)	6	6	.500	1.57	1.01	70	0	0	0	0	* 39-42	86.0	60	18	15	3	27-3	46	.198
1989— Cincinnati (N.L.)	4	8	.333	3.12	1.40	60	0	0	0	0	32-39	80.2	77	35	28	3	36-8	60	.258
1990— New York (N.L.)	5	3	.625	2.53	1.29	55	0	0	0	0	* 33-39	67.2	66	22	19	4	21-2	56	.252
1991— New York (N.L.)	5	9	.357	2.93	1.43	52	0	0	0	0	30-35	55.1	61	27	18	2	18-4	45	.271
1992— New York (N.L.)	6	2	.750	1.64	1.06	31	0	0	0	0	15-17	33.0	24	6	6	1	11-2	20	.209
1993— New York (N.L.)	4	3	.571	5.20	1.79	35	0	0	0	0	10-17	36.1	46	24	21	6	19-3	29	.313
1994— New York (N.L.)	1	4	.200	2.70	1.32	47	0	0	0	0	* 30-36	50.0	47	20	15	2	19-0	42	.244
1995— New York (N.L.)	5	3	.625	2.44	1.26	48	0	0	0	0	29-36	51.2	48	17	14	4	17-2	41	.251
1996— New York (N.L.)	4	3	.571	1.83	1.39	51	0	0	0	0	28-36	54.0	54	15	11	2	21-0	48	.260
1997— New York (N.L.)	5	3	.625	2.55	1.15	59	0	0	0	0	36-42	60.0	49	18	17	3	20-2	53	.226
1998— New York (N.L.)	0	8	.000	3.62	1.47	61	0	0	0	0	38-46	64.2	66	28	26	4	29-7	59	.267
1999— New York (N.L.)	0	2	.000	2.88	1.45	46	0	0	0	1	19-21	40.2	40	14	13	1	19-1	41	.255
— Binghamton (Eastern)	0	0	...	0.00	0.00	1	1	0	0	...	0-...	1.1	0	0	0	0	0-0	1	.000
2000— New York (N.L.)	5	4	.556	3.40	1.29	62	0	0	0	20	4-4	55.2	46	24	21	6	26-6	56	.221
2001— New York (N.L.)	6	2	.750	4.05	1.39	58	0	0	0	17	2-7	53.1	55	25	24	8	19-2	50	.264
2002— New York (N.L.)											Did not play.								
2003— St. Lucie (Fla. St.)	0	1	.000	6.23	1.62	4	3	0	0	...	0-...	4.1	6	3	3	1	1-0	5	.316
— Norfolk (Int'l)	0	0	...	0.00	1.20	2	0	0	0	...	0-...	1.2	1	0	0	0	1-0	2	.167
— New York (N.L.)	0	3	.000	2.62	1.40	38	0	0	0	4	2-3	34.1	35	11	10	5	13-2	16	.265
Major League totals (19 years)	88	79	.527	2.74	1.32	1036	0	0	0	55	424-523	1184.2	1097	425	361	75	462-74	923	.247

FRANCO, JULIO 1B/DH

PERSONAL: Born August 23, 1958, in San Pedro de Macoris, Dominican Republic. ... 6-1/188. ... Bats right, throws right. ... Full name: Julio Cesar Franco. ... High school: Divine Providence (San Pedro de Macoris, Dominican Republic).

TRANSACTIONS/CAREER NOTES: Signed as non-drafted free agent by Philadelphia Phillies organization (June 23, 1978). ... Traded by Phillies with 2B Manny Trillo, OF George Vukovich, P Jay Baller and C Jerry Willard to Cleveland Indians for OF Von Hayes (December 9, 1982). ... On disabled list (July 13-August 8, 1987). ... Traded by Indians to Texas Rangers for 1B Pete O'Brien, OF Oddibe McDowell and 2B Jerry Browne (December 6, 1988). ... On disabled list (March 28-April 19, May 4-June 1 and July 9, 1992-remainder of season). ... Granted free agency (October 27, 1993). ... Signed by Chicago White Sox (December 15, 1993). ... Granted free agency (October 21, 1994). ... Signed by Chiba Lotte Marines of Japan Pacific League (December 28, 1994). ... Signed by Indians (December 7, 1995). ... On disabled list (July 7-25 and August 4-30, 1996). ... Released by Indians (August 13, 1997). ... Signed by Milwaukee Brewers (August 13, 1997). ... Granted free agency (October 28, 1997). ... Played for Chiba Lotte Marines of Japan Pacific League (1998). ... Signed by Tampa Bay Devil Rays organization (February 19, 1999). ... Loaned by Devil Rays organization to Mexico City Tigres, Mexican League (March 29-September 18, 1999). ... Granted free agency (October 13, 1999). ... Contract purchased by Atlanta Braves organization from Mexico City, Mexican League (August 31, 2001). ... Granted free agency (November 5, 2001). ... Re-signed by Braves organization (December 17, 2001). ... Granted free agency (October 28, 2002). ... Re-signed by Braves organization (December 20, 2002). ... Placed on 15-day disabled list by Atlanta (August 18, 2003). ... Removed from 15-day disabled list (September 1, 2003).

2003 GAMES PLAYED BY POSITION (MLB): 1B—75.

		BATTING																	FIELDING	
Year Team (League)	Pos.	G	AB	R	H	2B	3B	HR	RBI	BB	SO	HBP	GDP	SB-CS	Avg.	OBP	SLG	OPS	E	Pct.
1978— Butte (Pio.)	SS	47	141	34	43	5	2	3	28	17	30	1	...	4-3	.305	.381	.433	.814	25	.781
1979— Cen. Oregon (NWL)	SS	• 71	299	57	* 98	15	5	• 10	45	24	59	3	...	22-9	.328	.381	.512	.893	31	.921
1980— Peninsula (Caro.)	SS	• 140	* 555	105	178	25	6	11	* 99	33	66	8	...	44-12	.321	.361	.447	.808	42	.934
1981— Reading (East.)	SS	* 139	* 532	70	160	17	3	8	74	52	60	5	...	27-14	.301	.365	.389	.754	30	.958
1982— Okla. City (A.A.)	3B-SS	120	463	80	139	19	5	21	66	39	56	3	...	33-11	.300	.357	.499	.856	‡ 42	.930
— Philadelphia (N.L.)	3B-SS	16	29	3	8	1	0	0	3	2	4	0	1	0-2	.276	.323	.310	.633	0	1.000
1983— Cleveland (A.L.)	SS	149	560	68	153	24	8	8	80	27	50	2	21	32-12	.273	.306	.388	.693	28	.961
1984— Cleveland (A.L.)	SS-DH	160	* 658	82	188	22	5	3	79	43	68	6	23	19-10	.286	.331	.348	.679	* 36	.955
1985— Cleveland (A.L.)	2B-SS-DH	160	636	97	183	33	4	6	90	54	74	4	26	13-9	.288	.343	.381	.723	‡ 36	.950
1986— Cleveland (A.L.)	2B-SS-DH	149	599	80	183	30	5	10	74	32	66	0	*28	10-7	.306	.338	.422	.760	19	.972
1987— Cleveland (A.L.)	2B-SS-DH	128	495	86	158	24	3	8	52	57	56	3	23	32-9	.319	.389	.428	.818	18	.964
1988— Cleveland (A.L.)	2B-DH	152	613	88	186	23	6	10	54	56	72	2	17	25-11	.303	.361	.409	.771	14	.982
1989— Texas (A.L.)	2B-DH	150	548	80	173	31	5	13	92	66	69	1	*27	21-3	.316	.386	.462	.848	13	.980
1990— Texas (A.L.)	2B-DH	157	582	96	172	27	1	11	69	82	83	2	12	31-10	.296	.383	.402	.785	• 19	.975
1991— Texas (A.L.)	2B	146	589	108	201	27	3	15	78	65	78	3	13	36-9	*.341	.408	.474	.882	14	.979
1992— Texas (A.L.)	DH-2B-OF	35	107	19	25	7	0	2	8	15	17	0	3	1-1	.234	.328	.355	.683	3	.927
1993— Texas (A.L.)	DH	144	532	85	154	31	3	14	84	62	95	1	16	9-3	.289	.360	.438	.798	...	...
1994— Chicago (A.L.)	DH-1B	112	433	72	138	19	2	20	98	62	75	5	14	8-1	.319	.406	.510	.916	3	.969
1995— Chiba Lotte (Jap. Pac.)	1B	127	474	60	145	25	3	10	58	...	...	...	...	11-...	.306	...	.435	...	...	...
1996— Cleveland (A.L.)	1B-DH	112	432	72	139	20	1	14	76	61	82	3	14	8-8	.322	.407	.470	.877	9	.990
1997— Cleveland (A.L.)	DH-2B-1B	78	289	46	82	13	1	3	25	38	75	0	13	8-5	.284	.367	.367	.734	3	.983
— Milwaukee (A.L.)	DH-1B	42	141	22	34	3	0	4	19	31	41	1	4	7-1	.241	.373	.348	.720	1	.992
1998— Chiba Lotte (Jap. Pac.)		131	487	78	141	27	2	18	77	...	...	...	...	7-...	.290	...	.464	...	...	...
1999— Tigres (Mex.)	1B	93	326	90	138	22	6	14	77	80	44	...	...	9-1	.423	...	.656	...	2	.993
— Tampa Bay (A.L.)	1B	1	1	0	0	0	0	0	0	0	1	0	0	0-0	.000	.000	.000	.000	0	1.000
2000— Samsung (Korean)		132	477	...	156	...	...	22	110	...	...	...	...	...-...	.327	...	...	...	...	...
2001— Tigres (Mex.)	DH-1B-OF	110	407	90	* 178	34	5	18	90	50	56	...	...	15-6	.437	...	.678	...	5	.991
— Atlanta (N.L.)	1B	25	90	13	27	4	0	3	11	10	20	1	3	0-0	.300	.376	.444	.821	1	.995
2002— Atlanta (N.L.)	1B-DH	125	338	51	96	13	1	6	30	39	75	1	13	5-1	.284	.357	.382	.739	8	.990
2003— Atlanta (N.L.)	1B	103	197	28	58	12	2	5	31	25	43	0	8	0-1	.294	.372	.452	.824	1	.998
American League totals (15 years)		1875	7215	1101	2169	334	47	141	978	751	1002	33	254	260-99	.301	.366	.419	.785	216	.972
National League totals (4 years)		269	654	95	189	30	3	14	75	76	142	2	25	5-4	.289	.363	.408	.771	10	.993
Major League totals (19 years)		2144	7869	1196	2358	364	50	155	1053	827	1144	35	279	265-103	.300	.366	.418	.783	226	.975

FRANCO, MATT — IF/OF

PERSONAL: Born August 19, 1969, in Santa Monica, Calif. ... 6-1/210. ... Bats left, throws right. ... Full name: Matthew Neil Franco. ... High school: Westlake (Calif.).

TRANSACTIONS/CAREER NOTES: Selected by Chicago Cubs organization in seventh round of free-agent draft (June 2, 1987). ... On disabled list (May 6-13, 1994). ... Traded by Cubs to New York Mets organization for a player to be named later (April 8, 1996); Cubs acquired P Chris DeWitt to complete deal (June 11, 1996). ... On Norfolk disabled list (April 8-11, 1996). ... Granted free agency (October 15, 1996). ... Re-signed by Mets organization (November 21, 1996). ... On New York disabled list (June 29-July 14, 1998); included rehabilitation assignment to Norfolk (July 9-14). ... Granted free agency (December 21, 2000). ... Re-signed by Mets organization (February 1, 2001). ... Granted free agency (October 15, 2001). ... Signed by Atlanta Braves organization (November 8, 2001).

2003 GAMES PLAYED BY POSITION (MLB): 1B—15, DH—3, OF—3.

Year	Team (League)	Pos.	G	AB	R	H	2B	3B	HR	RBI	BB	SO	HBP	GDP	SB-CS	Avg.	OBP	SLG	OPS	E	Pct.
1987— Wytheville (App.)		2B-3B-1B	62	202	25	50	10	1	1	21	26	41	0	3	4-1	.248	.333	.322	.655	23	.888
1988— Wytheville (App.)		3B-1B	20	79	14	31	9	1	0	16	7	5	0	2	0-1	.392	.442	.532	.974	6	.902
— Geneva (NY-Penn)		3B-1B	44	164	19	42	2	0	3	21	19	13	0	7	2-0	.256	.332	.323	.655	14	.943
1989— Char., W.Va. (SAL)			109	377	42	102	16	1	5	48	57	40	0	10	2-2	.271	.363	.358	.721	22	.932
— Peoria (Midw.)		3B	16	58	4	13	4	0	0	9	5	5	1	1	0-1	.224	.292	.293	.585	6	.878
1990— Peoria (Midw.)		3B-1B	123	443	52	125	* 33	2	6	65	43	39	1	19	4-4	.282	.346	.406	.752	18	.980
1991— Win.-Salem (Car.)		3B-SS-1B	104	307	47	66	12	1	4	41	46	42	2	6	4-1	.215	.316	.300	.615	11	.986
1992— Charlotte (Sou.)		3B-1B-OF	108	343	35	97	18	3	2	31	26	46	1	4	3-3	.283	.332	.370	.703	13	.961
1993— Orlando (South.)		1B-3B	68	237	31	75	20	1	7	37	29	30	2	2	3-6	.316	.393	.498	.890	4	.992
— Iowa (Am. Assoc.)		1-OF-2-P	62	199	24	58	17	4	5	29	16	30	1	6	4-1	.291	.342	.492	.835	2	.996
1994— Iowa (Am. Assoc.)		1-D-3-O	128	437	63	121	32	4	11	71	52	66	2	7	3-3	.277	.353	.444	.797	7	.993
1995— Iowa (Am. Assoc.)		3-1-D-P-C	121	455	51	128	28	5	6	58	37	44	0	11	1-1	.281	.331	.404	.736	19	.960
— Chicago (N.L.)		2B-3B-1B	16	17	3	5	1	0	0	1	0	4	0	0	0-0	.294	.294	.353	.647	0	1.000
1996— Norfolk (Int'l)		3B-1B-1B-DH	133	508	74	* 164	* 40	2	7	81	36	55	3	10	5-2	.323	.365	.451	.816	22	.962
— New York (N.L.)		3B-1B	14	31	3	6	1	0	1	2	1	5	1	0	0-0	.194	.235	.323	.558	3	.900
1997— Norfolk (Int'l)		OF-D-1-3	7	26	5	7	2	0	0	0	2	2	1	0	0-0	.269	.345	.346	.691	0	1.000
— New York (N.L.)		3-1-D-O	112	163	21	45	5	0	5	21	13	23	0	4	1-0	.276	.330	.399	.728	4	.966
1998— New York (N.L.)		3-O-1-D	103	161	20	44	7	2	1	13	23	26	1	8	0-1	.273	.366	.360	.726	1	.991
— Norfolk (Int'l)		3B-OF-1B	5	19	2	7	1	0	0	1	3	1	0	1	2-0	.368	.455	.421	.876	2	.909
1999— New York (N.L.)		1-O-3-D-P	122	132	18	31	5	0	4	21	28	21	0	9	0-0	.235	.366	.364	.730	1	.987
2000— New York (N.L.)		1-3-O-D-2	101	134	9	32	4	0	2	14	21	22	0	3	0-0	.239	.340	.313	.653	4	.969
— Norfolk (Int'l)		3B-OF-1B	14	51	3	7	1	0	0	1	3	10	0	0	0-0	.137	.185	.157	.342	2	.933
2001— Norfolk (Int'l)		3B-1B-OF	124	433	49	106	25	1	8	47	52	72	2	16	5-2	.245	.325	.363	.688	14	.973
2002— Richmond (Int'l)		1B-3B	47	173	24	50	11	0	6	28	14	19	3	6	1-0	.289	.349	.457	.806	2	.993
— Atlanta (N.L.)		1B-OF	81	205	25	65	15	4	6	30	27	31	0	5	1-0	.317	.395	.517	.912	4	.990
2003— Atlanta (N.L.)		1B-DH-OF	112	134	11	33	5	0	3	15	11	26	0	4	0-1	.246	.299	.351	.650	3	.977
Major League totals (8 years)			661	977	110	261	43	6	22	117	124	158	2	34	2-2	.267	.349	.391	.740	20	.980

FRANKLIN, RYAN — P

PERSONAL: Born March 5, 1973, in Fort Smith, Ark. ... 6-3/180. ... Throws right, bats right. ... Full name: Ryan Ray Franklin. ... High school: Spiro (Okla.). ... Junior college: Seminole College (Okla.).

TRANSACTIONS/CAREER NOTES: Selected by Toronto Blue Jays organization in 25th round of free-agent draft (June 3, 1991); did not sign. ... Selected by Seattle Mariners organization in 23rd round of free-agent draft (June 1, 1992). ... On Seattle disabled list (June 28-July 15, 2002); included rehabilitation assignment to Everett (July 10-15).

CAREER HITTING: 1-for-4 (.250), 1 R, 0 2B, 0 3B, 0 HR, 0 RBI.

Year	League	W	L	Pct.	ERA	WHIP	G	GS	CG	ShO	Hld.	Sv.-Opp.	IP	H	R	ER	HR	BB-IBB	SO	Avg.
1993— Bellingham (N'west)		5	3	.625	2.92	1.34	15	14	1	1	...	0-...	74.0	72	38	24	2	27-0	55	.250
1994— Appleton (Midw.)		9	6	.600	3.13	1.08	18	18	5	1	...	0-...	118.0	105	60	41	6	23-0	102	.234
— Riverside (Calif.)		4	2	.667	3.06	1.12	8	8	1	1	...	0-...	61.2	61	26	21	5	8-0	35	.249
— Calgary (PCL)		0	0	...	7.94	1.76	1	1	0	0	...	0-...	5.2	9	6	5	2	1-0	2	.333
1995— Port City (Sou.)		6	10	.375	4.32	1.34	31	20	1	1	...	0-...	146.0	153	84	70	13	43-4	102	.274
1996— Port City (Sou.)		6	12	.333	4.01	1.23	28	27	2	0	...	0-...	182.0	186	99	81	23	37-0	127	.265
1997— Memphis (Sou.)		4	2	.667	3.03	0.99	11	8	2	• 2	...	0-...	59.1	45	22	20	4	14-1	49	.208
— Tacoma (PCL)		5	5	.500	4.18	1.34	14	14	0	0	...	0-...	90.1	97	48	42	11	24-1	59	.281
1998— Tacoma (PCL)		5	6	.455	4.51	1.41	34	16	1	0	...	1-...	127.2	148	75	64	18	32-2	90	.292
1999— Tacoma (PCL)		6	9	.400	4.71	1.29	29	19	2	1	...	2-...	135.2	142	81	71	17	33-1	94	.270
— Seattle (A.L.)		0	0	...	4.76	1.59	6	0	0	0	1	0-0	11.1	10	6	6	2	8-1	6	.238
2000— Tacoma (PCL)		11	5	.688	3.90	1.11	31	22	4	0	...	0-...	164.0	147	85	71	28	35-1	142	.240
2001— Seattle (A.L.)		5	1	.833	3.56	1.28	38	0	0	0	5	0-1	78.1	76	32	31	13	24-4	60	.250
— Tacoma (PCL)		0	0	...	0.00	0.55	1	0	0	0	...	0-...	3.2	2	0	0	0	0-0	3	.167
2002— Seattle (A.L.)		7	5	.583	4.02	1.17	41	12	0	0	3	0-1	118.2	117	60	53	14	22-1	65	.255
— Everett (Northwest)		0	0	...	0.00	0.75	1	1	0	0	...	0-...	2.2	2	1	0	0	0-0	1	.200
2003— Seattle (A.L.)		11	13	.458	3.57	1.23	32	32	2	1	0	0-0	212.0	199	93	84	•34	61-3	99	.251
Major League totals (4 years)		23	19	.548	3.73	1.23	117	44	2	1	9	0-2	420.1	402	193	174	63	115-9	230	.252

FRANKLIN, WAYNE — P

PERSONAL: Born March 9, 1974, in Wilmington, Del. ... 6-2/211. ... Throws left, bats left. ... Full name: Gary Wayne Franklin. ... High school: Northeast (Md.). ... College: Maryland-Baltimore County.

TRANSACTIONS/CAREER NOTES: Selected by Los Angeles Dodgers organization in 36th round of free-agent draft (June 4, 1996). ... Selected by Houston Astros organization from Dodgers organization in Rule 5 minor league draft (December 14, 1998). ... Traded by Astros to Milwaukee Brewers (September 3, 2002), as partial completion of deal in which Brewers traded IF Mark Loretta to Astros for two players to be named later (August 31, 2002); Brewers acquired 2B Keith Ginter to complete deal (September 5, 2002).

CAREER HITTING: 10-for-67 (.149), 1 R, 1 2B, 0 3B, 0 HR, 3 RBI.

Year	League	W	L	Pct.	ERA	WHIP	G	GS	CG	ShO	Hld.	Sv.-Opp.	IP	H	R	ER	HR	BB-IBB	SO	Avg.
1996— Yakima (NW)		1	0	1.000	2.52	1.76	20	0	0	0	...	1-...	25.0	32	10	7	2	12-3	22	.311
1997— Savannah (S. Atl.)		5	3	.625	3.18	1.39	28	7	1	0	...	0-...	82.0	79	41	29	10	35-0	58	.246
— San Bernardino (Calif.)		0	0	...	0.00	1.00	1	0	0	0	...	0-...	2.0	2	0	0	0	0-0	1	.286
1998— Vero Beach (FSL)		9	3	.750	3.53	1.23	48	0	0	0	...	10-...	86.2	81	43	34	7	26-0	78	.243
1999— Kissimmee (Fla. St.)		3	0	1.000	1.53	0.96	12	0	0	0	...	1-...	17.2	11	4	3	0	6-0	22	.180
— Jackson (Texas)		3	1	.750	1.61	0.93	46	0	0	0	...	20-...	50.1	31	11	9	3	16-3	40	.178
2000— New Orleans (PCL)		3	3	.500	3.63	1.57	48	0	0	0	...	4-...	44.2	51	29	18	4	19-3	37	.279
— Houston (N.L.)		0	0	...	5.48	1.69	25	0	0	0	8	0-0	21.1	24	14	13	2	12-1	21	.282

F

Year League	W	L	Pct.	ERA	WHIP	G	GS	CG	ShO	Hld.	Sv.-Opp.	IP	H	R	ER	HR	BB-IBB	SO	Avg.
2001— Houston (N.L.)	0	0		6.75	2.17	11	0	0	0	1	0-0	12.0	17	9	9	4	9-0	9	.333
— New Orleans (PCL)	2	1	.667	3.81	1.31	41	0	0	0		0-...	49.2	47	28	21	6	18-2	51	.244
2002— New Orleans (PCL)	13	9	.591	3.12	1.18	29	27	1	0		0-...	179.0	153	68	62	14	59-2	* 141	.235
— Milwaukee (N.L.)	2	1	.667	2.63	1.38	4	4	0	0	0	0-...	24.0	16	8	7	1	17-1	17	.188
2003— Milwaukee (N.L.)	10	13	.435	5.50	1.52	36	34	1	1	0	0-0	194.2	201	*129	•119	*36	94-2	116	.268
Major League totals (4 years)	12	14	.462	5.29	1.55	76	38	1	1	9	0-0	252.0	258	160	148	43	132-4	163	.265

FREEL, RYAN   OF

PERSONAL: Born March 8, 1976, in Jacksonville, Fla. ... 5-10/178. ... Bats right, throws right. ... Full name: Ryan Paul Freel. ... High school: Englewood (Jacksonville). ... Junior college: Tallahassee (Fla.) Community College.

TRANSACTIONS/CAREER NOTES: Selected by St. Louis Cardinals organization in 14th round of free-agent draft (June 2, 1994); did not sign. ... Selected by Toronto Blue Jays organization in 10th round of free-agent draft (June 1, 1995). ... On Dunedin disabled list (July 2-18 and July 23-30, 1997). ... On Syracuse disabled list (May 10, 1999-remainder of season). ... On Tennessee disabled list (April 10-May 3 and May 10-21, 2000). ... On Durham disabled list (June 16-25, 2002). ... Granted free agency (October 15, 2002). ... Signed by Cincinnati Reds organization (November 19, 2002). ... Contract purchased by Cincinnati from Louisville (April 20, 2003). ... Optioned to Louisville by Cincinnati (May 6, 2003). ... Recalled by Cincinnati from Louisville (May 22, 2003). ... Placed on the 15-day disabled list, retroactive to May 28. (May 29, 2003). ... Reinstated from 15-day disabled list; designated for assignment by Cincinnati (July 4, 2003). ... Optioned to Louisville by Cincinnati (July 9, 2003). ... Recalled by Cincinnati from Louisville (July 31, 2003). ... Optioned to Louisville by Cincinnati (August 6, 2003). ... Recalled from Louisville by Cincinnati (August 20, 2003).

2003 GAMES PLAYED BY POSITION (MLB): OF—24, 2B—11, 3B—2.

Year Team (League)	Pos.	G	AB	R	H	2B	3B	HR	RBI	BB	SO	HBP	GDP	SB-CS	Avg.	OBP	SLG	OPS	E	Pct.
1995— St. Catharines (NYP)	2B	65	243	30	68	10	5	3	29	22	49	7	3	12-7	.280	.350	.399	.749	* 19	.940
1996— Dunedin (Fla. St.)	2B-3B	104	381	64	97	23	3	4	41	33	76	5	4	19-15	.255	.321	.362	.683	20	.959
1997— Knoxville (Sou.)	SS	33	94	18	19	1	1	0	4	19	13	2	3	5-3	.202	.348	.234	.582	13	.913
— Dunedin (Fla. St.)	2-3-S-O	61	181	42	51	8	2	3	17	46	28	9	3	24-5	.282	.447	.398	.845	18	.910
1998— Knoxville (Sou.)	2B-SS-3B	66	252	47	72	17	3	4	36	33	32	1	3	18-9	.286	.366	.425	.790	3	.982
— Syracuse (Int'l)	2B-OF	37	118	19	27	4	0	2	12	26	16	4	3	9-4	.229	.377	.314	.691	3	.962
1999— Knoxville (Sou.)	OF	11	46	9	13	5	1	1	9	8	4	0	0	4-2	.283	.382	.500	.882	0	1.000
— Syracuse (Int'l)	OF-SS	20	77	15	23	3	2	1	11	8	13	4	3	10-3	.299	.393	.429	.822	1	.976
2000— Dunedin (Fla. St.)	OF	4	18	7	9	1	0	3	6	0	1	0	0	0-0	.500	.500	1.056	1.556	0	1.000
— Tennessee (Sou.)	OF-2B	12	44	11	13	3	1	0	8	8	6	1	3	2-3	.295	.400	.409	.809	0	1.000
— Syracuse (Int'l)	2-OF-3-S	80	283	62	81	14	5	10	30	35	44	9	3	30-7	.286	.380	.477	.857	9	.957
2001— Toronto (A.L.)	OF	9	22	1	6	1	0	0	3	1	4	1	0	2-1	.273	.333	.318	.652	1	.969
— Syracuse (Int'l)	OF-2-3-S	85	319	60	83	21	3	5	33	42	42	7	8	22-9	.260	.357	.392	.749	9	.959
2002— Durham (Int'l)	2B-OF	119	448	65	117	27	4	8	48	38	51	14	10	37-10	.261	.337	.393	.730	7	.981
2003— Louisville (Int'l)	2B-S-3-D	54	215	38	59	11	1	3	12	21	32	0	2	25-6	.274	.336	.377	.713	2	.990
— Cincinnati (N.L.)	OF-2B-3B	43	137	23	39	6	1	4	12	9	13	4	2	9-4	.285	.344	.431	.775	1	.990
American League totals (1 year)		9	22	1	6	1	0	0	3	1	4	1	0	2-1	.273	.333	.318	.652	1	.969
National League totals (1 year)		43	137	23	39	6	1	4	12	9	13	4	2	9-4	.285	.344	.431	.775	1	.990
Major League totals (2 years)		52	159	24	45	7	1	4	15	10	17	5	2	11-5	.283	.343	.415	.758	2	.984

FUENTES, BRIAN   P

PERSONAL: Born August 9, 1975, in Merced, Calif. ... 6-4/220. ... Throws left, bats left. ... Full name: Brian Christopher Fuentes. ... Name pronounced: foo-WHEN-tayz. ... High school: Merced (Calif.). ... Junior college: Merced College (Calif.).

TRANSACTIONS/CAREER NOTES: Selected by Seattle Mariners organization in 25th round of free-agent draft (June 1, 1995). ... On disabled list (April 2-20, 1998). ... On disabled list (June 9-August 22, 1999). ... On Tacoma disabled list (August 26, 2001-remainder of season). ... Traded by Mariners with P Jose Paniagua and P Dennis Stark to Colorado Rockies for 3B Jeff Cirillo (December 15, 2001).

CAREER HITTING: 0-for-1 (.000), 0 R, 0 2B, 0 3B, 0 HR, 0 RBI.

Year League	W	L	Pct.	ERA	WHIP	G	GS	CG	ShO	Hld.	Sv.-Opp.	IP	H	R	ER	HR	BB-IBB	SO	Avg.
1996— Everett (Northwest)	0	1	.000	4.39	1.35	13	2	0	0	...	0-...	26.2	23	14	13	2	13-0	26	.230
1997— Wisconsin (Midw.)	6	7	.462	3.56	1.21	22	22	0	0	...	0-...	118.2	84	52	47	6	59-0	153	.203
1998— Lancaster (Calif.)	7	7	.500	4.17	1.70	24	22	0	0	...	0-...	118.2	121	73	55	8	81-0	137	.273
1999— New Haven (East.)	3	3	.500	4.95	1.65	15	14	0	0	...	0-...	60.0	53	36	33	5	46-0	66	.255
2000— New Haven (East.)	7	12	.368	4.51	1.41	26	26	1	0	...	0-...	139.2	127	80	70	7	70-0	152	.246
2001— Tacoma (PCL)	3	2	.600	2.94	1.15	35	0	0	0	...	6-...	52.0	35	19	17	4	25-0	70	.206
— Seattle (A.L.)	1	1	.500	4.63	1.20	10	0	0	0	1	0-1	11.2	6	6	6	2	8-0	10	.171
2002— Colo. Springs (PCL)	3	3	.500	3.70	1.56	41	0	0	0	...	1-...	48.2	44	25	20	0	32-1	61	.246
— Colorado (N.L.)	2	0	1.000	4.73	1.43	31	0	0	0	0	0-0	26.2	25	14	14	4	13-0	38	.250
2003— Colorado (N.L.)	3	3	.500	2.75	1.30	75	0	0	0	19	4-6	75.1	64	24	23	7	34-2	82	.231
American League totals (1 year)	1	1	.500	4.63	1.20	10	0	0	0	1	0-1	11.2	6	6	6	2	8-0	10	.171
National League totals (2 years)	5	3	.625	3.26	1.33	106	0	0	0	19	4-6	102.0	89	38	37	11	47-2	120	.236
Major League totals (3 years)	6	4	.600	3.40	1.32	116	0	0	0	20	4-7	113.2	95	44	43	13	55-2	130	.231

FULLMER, BRAD   DH/1B

PERSONAL: Born January 17, 1975, in Chatsworth, Calif. ... 6-0/220. ... Bats left, throws right. ... Full name: Bradley Ryan Fullmer. ... High school: Montclair Prep (Van Nuys, Calif.).

TRANSACTIONS/CAREER NOTES: Selected by Montreal Expos organization in second round of free-agent draft (June 3, 1993). ... On disabled list (June 20, 1994-entire season). ... Traded by Expos to Toronto Blue Jays as part of three-way deal in which Blue Jays sent 1B/DH David Segui and cash to Texas Rangers and Rangers sent 1B Lee Stevens to Expos (March 16, 2000). ... Traded by Blue Jays to Anaheim Angels for P Brian Cooper (January 17, 2002). ... Granted free agency (December 21, 2002). ... Re-signed by Angels (January 6, 2003). ... Placed on 15-day disabled list by Anaheim (June 27, 2003). ... Transferred to 60-day disabled list (September 1, 2003).

2003 GAMES PLAYED BY POSITION (MLB): DH—41, 1B—19.

Year Team (League)	Pos.	G	AB	R	H	2B	3B	HR	RBI	BB	SO	HBP	GDP	SB-CS	Avg.	OBP	SLG	OPS	E	Pct.
1994—								Did not play.												
1995— Albany (S. Atl.)	3B-1B	123	468	69	• 151	38	4	8	67	36	33	17	9	10-10	.323	.387	.472	.859	30	.918
1996— W.P. Beach (FSL)	1B-OF	102	380	52	115	29	1	5	63	32	43	11	9	4-6	.303	.367	.424	.790	7	.967
— Harrisburg (East.)	1B	24	98	11	27	4	1	4	14	3	8	2	3	0-0	.276	.311	.459	.770	2	.957
1997— Harrisburg (East.) 1	1B-OF-DH	94	357	60	111	24	2	19	62	30	25	7	11	6-4	.311	.372	.549	.921	6	.990
— Ottawa (Int'l)	1B-DH-OF	24	91	13	27	7	0	3	17	3	10	2	3	1-1	.297	.317	.473	.789	1	.995
— Montreal (N.L.)	1B-OF	19	40	4	12	2	0	3	8	2	7	1	0	0-0	.300	.349	.575	.924	2	.966

Year Team (League)	Pos.	G	AB	R	H	2B	3B	HR	RBI	BB	SO	HBP	GDP	SB-CS	Avg.	OBP	SLG	OPS	E	Pct.
1998— Montreal (N.L.)	1B	140	505	58	138	44	2	13	73	39	70	2	12	6-6	.273	.327	.446	.773	* 17	.985
1999— Montreal (N.L.)	1B	100	347	38	96	34	2	9	47	22	35	2	14	2-3	.277	.321	.464	.785	7	.991
— Ottawa (Int'l)	1B-DH	39	142	31	45	9	0	11	32	12	16	3	5	2-2	.317	.380	.613	.992	2	.990
2000— Toronto (A.L.)	DH-1B	133	482	76	142	29	1	32	104	30	68	6	14	3-1	.295	.340	.558	.898	0	1.000
2001— Toronto (A.L.)	DH-1B	146	522	71	143	31	2	18	83	38	88	6	13	5-2	.274	.326	.444	.771	0	1.000
2002— Anaheim (A.L.)	DH-1B	130	429	75	124	35	6	19	59	32	44	15	7	10-3	.289	.357	.531	.888	1	.995
2003— Anaheim (A.L.)	DH-1B	63	206	32	63	9	2	9	35	26	31	2	4	5-4	.306	.387	.500	.887	0	1.000
American League totals (4 years)		472	1639	254	472	104	11	78	281	126	231	29	38	23-10	.288	.346	.508	.854	1	.997
National League totals (3 years)		259	892	100	246	80	4	25	128	63	112	5	26	8-9	.276	.326	.459	.784	26	.987
Major League totals (7 years)		731	2531	354	718	184	15	103	409	189	343	34	64	31-19	.284	.339	.490	.829	27	.988

FULTZ, AARON — P

PERSONAL: Born September 4, 1973, in Memphis, Tenn. ... 6-0/200. ... Throws left, bats left. ... Full name: Richard Aaron Fultz. ... High school: Munford (Tenn.). ... Junior college: North Florida College.

TRANSACTIONS/CAREER NOTES: Selected by San Francisco Giants organization in sixth round of free-agent draft (June 1, 1992). ... Traded by Giants with SS Andres Duncan and P Greg Brummett to Minnesota Twins for P Jim Deshaies (August 28, 1993). ... Released by Twins (April 1, 1996). ... Signed by Giants organization (April 4, 1996). ... Granted free agency (October 16, 1998). ... Re-signed by Giants organization (October 23, 1998). ... Granted free agency (December 21, 2002). ... Signed by Texas Rangers (December 31, 2002). ... Placed on 15-day disabled list by Texas (June 23, 2003). ... Sent to Oklahoma on rehab assignment (July 6, 2003). ... Reinstated from 15-day disabled list (July 11, 2003).

CAREER HITTING: 4-for-12 (.333), 1 R, 0 2B, 0 3B, 0 HR, 0 RBI.

Year League	W	L	Pct.	ERA	WHIP	G	GS	CG	ShO	Hld.	Sv.-Opp.	IP	H	R	ER	HR	BB-IBB	SO	Avg.
1992— Ariz. Giants (Ariz.)	3	2	.600	2.13	1.24	14	•14	0	0	...	0-...	67.2	51	24	16	0	33-0	72	.213
1993— Clinton (Midw.)	14	8	.636	3.41	1.32	26	25	2	1	...	0-...	148.0	132	63	56	8	64-2	144	.239
— Fort Wayne (Midw.)	0	0	...	9.00	2.50	1	1	0	0	...	0-...	4.0	10	4	4	0	0-0	3	.476
1994— Fort Myers (Fla. St.)	9	10	.474	4.33	1.50	28	28	3	0	...	0-...	168.1	193	95	* 81	9	60-5	132	.289
1995— Fort Myers (Fla. St.)	3	6	.333	3.25	1.28	21	21	2	2	...	0-...	122.0	115	52	44	10	41-1	127	.250
— New Britain (East.)	0	2	.000	6.60	1.33	3	3	0	0	...	0-...	15.0	11	12	11	1	9-0	12	.208
1996— San Jose (Calif.)	9	5	.643	3.96	1.48	36	12	0	0	...	1-...	104.2	101	52	46	7	54-2	103	.262
1997— Shreveport (Texas)	6	3	.667	2.83	1.20	49	0	0	0	...	1-...	70.0	65	30	22	6	19-0	60	.247
1998— Shreveport (Texas)	5	7	.417	3.77	1.40	54	0	0	0	...	15-...	62.0	58	40	26	4	29-10	61	.252
— Fresno (PCL)	0	0	...	5.06	1.50	10	0	0	0	...	0-...	16.0	22	10	9	2	2-1	13	.333
1999— Fresno (PCL)	9	8	.529	4.98	1.40	37	20	1	0	...	0-...	137.1	141	87	76	32	51-1	151	.266
2000— San Francisco (N.L.)	5	2	.714	4.67	1.37	58	0	0	0	7	1-3	69.1	67	38	36	8	28-0	62	.263
2001— San Francisco (N.L.)	3	1	.750	4.56	1.28	66	0	0	0	12	1-2	71.0	70	40	36	9	21-3	67	.259
2002— San Francisco (N.L.)	2	2	.500	4.79	1.60	43	0	0	0	4	0-1	41.1	47	22	22	4	19-3	31	.294
— Fresno (PCL)	1	3	.250	3.18	1.28	17	0	0	0	...	4-...	22.2	18	8	8	1	11-2	22	.222
2003— Oklahoma (PCL)	0	0	...	27.00	3.00	1	0	0	0	...	0-...	1.0	2	3	3	2	1-0	2	.400
— Frisco (Texas)	0	0	...	9.00	2.00	1	0	0	0	...	0-...	1.0	2	1	1	0	0-0	3	.333
— Texas (A.L.)	1	3	.250	5.21	1.51	64	0	0	0	19	0-0	67.1	75	43	39	9	27-7	53	.287
American League totals (1 year)	1	3	.250	5.21	1.51	64	0	0	0	19	0-0	67.1	75	43	39	9	27-7	53	.287
National League totals (3 years)	10	5	.667	4.66	1.39	167	0	0	0	23	2-6	181.2	184	100	94	21	68-6	160	.269
Major League totals (4 years)	11	8	.579	4.81	1.42	231	0	0	0	42	2-6	249.0	259	143	133	30	95-13	213	.274

FURCAL, RAFAEL — SS

PERSONAL: Born October 24, 1977, in Loma de Cabrera, Dominican Republic. ... 5-10/165. ... Bats both, throws right. ... Full name: Rafael Antoni Furcal. ... Name pronounced: fur-CALL. ... High school: Jose Cabrera (Loma De Cabrera, Dominican Republic).

TRANSACTIONS/CAREER NOTES: Signed as non-drafted free agent by Atlanta Braves organization (November 9, 1996). ... On Atlanta disabled list (June 13-29, 2000). ... On disabled list (July 7, 2001-remainder of season).

2003 GAMES PLAYED BY POSITION (MLB): SS—155.

Year Team (League)	Pos.	G	AB	R	H	2B	3B	HR	RBI	BB	SO	HBP	GDP	SB-CS	Avg.	OBP	SLG	OPS	E	Pct.
1997— GC Braves (GCL)	2B-OF	50	190	31	49	5	4	1	9	20	21	2	1	15-2	.258	.335	.342	.677	10	.961
1998— Danville (Appal.)	2B	66	268	56	88	15	4	0	23	36	29	3	2	* 60-15	.328	.412	.414	.827	14	.965
1999— Macon (S. Atl.)	SS	83	335	73	113	15	1	1	29	41	36	5	4	* 73-22	.337	.417	.397	.814	30	.912
— Myrtle Beach (Caro.)	SS	43	184	32	54	9	3	0	12	14	42	0	3	23-8	.293	* .343	.375	.718	4	.975
2000— Greenville (Sou.)	SS	3	10	1	2	0	0	1	3	1	0	0	0	0-0	.200	.273	.500	.773	1	.889
— Atlanta (N.L.)	SS-2B	131	455	87	134	20	4	4	37	73	80	3	2	40-14	.295	.394	.382	.776	24	.958
2001— Atlanta (N.L.)	SS	79	324	39	89	19	0	4	30	24	56	1	5	22-6	.275	.321	.370	.691	11	.970
2002— Atlanta (N.L.)	SS-2B	154	636	95	175	31	8	8	47	43	114	3	8	27-15	.275	.323	.387	.710	27	.964
2003— Atlanta (N.L.)	SS	156	664	130	194	35	•10	15	61	60	76	3	1	25-2	.292	.352	.443	.794	31	.959
Major League totals (4 years)		520	2079	351	592	105	22	31	175	200	326	10	16	114-37	.285	.348	.401	.749	93	.962

GAGNE, ERIC — P

PERSONAL: Born January 7, 1976, in Montreal, Quebec. ... 6-2/195. ... Throws right, bats right. ... Full name: Eric Serge Gagne. ... Name pronounced: gahn-yay. ... High school: Polyvalente Edouard Montpetit (Montreal). ... Junior college: Seminole College (Okla.).

TRANSACTIONS/CAREER NOTES: Signed as non-drafted free agent by Los Angeles Dodgers organization (July 26, 1995). ... On disabled list entire 1997 season. ... On San Antonio suspended list (April 26-29, 1999).

CAREER HITTING: 12-for-83 (.145), 5 R, 2 2B, 1 3B, 1 HR, 3 RBI.

Year League	W	L	Pct.	ERA	WHIP	G	GS	CG	ShO	Hld.	Sv.-Opp.	IP	H	R	ER	HR	BB-IBB	SO	Avg.
1996— Savannah (S. Atl.)	7	6	.538	3.28	1.19	23	21	1	1	...	0-...	115.1	94	48	42	11	43-1	131	.221
1997—						Did not play.													
1998— Vero Beach (FSL)	9	7	.563	3.74	1.19	25	25	3	1	...	0-...	139.2	118	69	58	16	48-0	144	.225
1999— San Antonio (Texas)	12	4	.750	2.63	1.11	26	26	0	0	...	0-...	167.2	122	55	49	17	64-0	185	.201
— Los Angeles (N.L.)	1	1	.500	2.10	1.10	5	5	0	0	0	0-0	30.0	18	8	7	3	15-0	30	.175
2000— Albuquerque (PCL)	5	1	.833	3.88	1.28	9	9	0	0	...	0-...	55.2	56	30	24	8	15-0	59	.260
— Los Angeles (N.L.)	4	6	.400	5.15	1.64	20	19	0	0	0	0-0	101.1	106	62	58	20	60-1	79	.270
2001— Los Angeles (N.L.)	6	7	.462	4.75	1.25	33	24	0	0	0	0-0	151.2	144	90	80	24	46-1	130	.251
— Las Vegas (PCL)	3	0	1.000	1.52	0.97	4	4	0	0	...	0-...	23.2	15	4	4	2	8-0	31	.195
2002— Los Angeles (N.L.)	4	1	.800	1.97	0.86	77	0	0	0	1	52-56	82.1	55	18	18	6	16-4	114	.189
2003— Los Angeles (N.L.)	2	3	.400	1.20	0.69	77	0	0	0	0	*55-55	82.1	37	12	11	2	20-2	137	.133
Major League totals (5 years)	17	18	.486	3.50	1.15	212	48	0	0	1	107-111	447.2	360	190	174	55	157-8	490	.220

G

GALARRAGA, ANDRES — 1B

PERSONAL: Born June 18, 1961, in Caracas, Venezuela. ... 6-3/265. ... Bats right, throws right. ... Full name: Andres Jose Galarraga. ... Name pronounced: ON-dress Gahl-la-RAH-ga. ... High school: Enrique Felmi (Caracas, Venezuela).

TRANSACTIONS/CAREER NOTES: Signed as non-drafted free agent by Montreal Expos organization (January 19, 1979). ... On disabled list (July 10-August 19 and August 20-September 4, 1986; and May 26-July 4, 1991). ... Traded by Expos to St. Louis Cardinals for P Ken Hill (November 25, 1991). ... On St. Louis disabled list (April 8-May 22, 1992); included rehabilitation assignment to Louisville (May 13-22). ... Granted free agency (October 27, 1992). ... Signed by Colorado Rockies (November 16, 1992). ... On disabled list (May 10-27 and July 25-August 21, 1993). ... Granted free agency (October 25, 1993). ... Re-signed by Rockies (December 6, 1993). ... On disabled list (July 29, 1994-remainder of season). ... On suspended list (August 3-5, 1997). ... Granted free agency (October 27, 1997). ... Signed by Atlanta Braves (November 20, 1997). ... On suspended list (September 2-5, 1998). ... On Atlanta disabled list (April 3, 1999-entire season). ... On suspended list (September 7-10, 2000). ... Granted free agency (October 30, 2000). ... Signed by Texas Rangers (December 8, 2000). ... Traded by Rangers to San Francisco Giants for P Erasma Ramirez, IF Chris Magruder and P Todd Ozias (July 24, 2001). ... Granted free agency (November 7, 2001). ... Signed by Expos (March 7, 2002). ... On disabled list (May 3-26, 2002). ... Granted free agency (October 28, 2002). ... Signed by Giants organization (January 29, 2003).

2003 GAMES PLAYED BY POSITION (MLB): 1B—69, DH—2.

Year Team (League)	Pos.	G	AB	R	H	2B	3B	HR	RBI	BB	SO	HBP	GDP	SB-CS	Avg.	OBP	SLG	OPS	E	Pct.
1979— W.P. Beach (FSL)	1B	7	23	3	3	0	0	0	1	2	11	1	...	0-0	.130	.231	.130	.361	0	1.000
—Calgary (Pio.)	3B-C-1B	42	112	14	24	3	1	4	16	9	42	5	...	1-1	.214	.299	.366	.665	5	.977
1980— Calgary (Pio.)	3-C-1-OF	59	190	27	50	11	4	4	22	7	55	5	...	3-0	.263	.307	.426	.733	21	.942
1981— Jamestown (NYP)	3-C-1-OF	47	154	24	40	5	4	6	26	15	44	4	...	0-0	.260	.339	.461	.800	0	1.000
1982— W.P. Beach (FSL)	1B-OF	105	338	39	95	20	2	14	51	34	77	9	...	2-1	.281	.360	.476	.837	9	.982
1983— W.P. Beach (FSL)	3B-1B-OF	104	401	55	116	18	3	10	66	33	68	7	...	7-5	.289	.353	.424	.777	13	.986
1984— Jacksonville (Sou.)	1B	143	533	81	154	28	4	27	87	59	122	9	10	2-8	.289	.367	.548	.875	16	.986
1985— Indianapolis (A.A.)	1B-OF	121	439	* 75	118	15	8	25	87	45	103	7	12	3-0	.269	.344	.510	.854	14	.986
—Montreal (N.L.)	1B	24	75	9	14	1	0	2	4	3	18	1	0	1-2	.187	.228	.280	.508	1	.995
1986— Montreal (N.L.)	1B	105	321	39	87	13	0	10	42	30	79	3	8	6-5	.271	.338	.405	.743	4	.995
1987— Montreal (N.L.)	1B	147	551	72	168	40	3	13	90	41	127	*10	11	7-10	.305	.361	.459	.821	10	.993
1988— Montreal (N.L.)	1B	157	609	99	* 184	* 42	8	29	92	39	*153	10	12	13-4	.302	.352	.540	.893	15	.991
1989— Montreal (N.L.)	1B	152	572	76	147	30	1	23	85	48	*158	*13	12	12-5	.257	.327	.434	.761	11	.992
1990— Montreal (N.L.)	1B	155	579	65	148	29	0	20	87	40	*169	4	14	10-1	.256	.306	.409	.715	10	.993
1991— Montreal (N.L.)	1B	107	375	34	82	13	2	9	33	23	86	2	6	5-6	.219	.268	.336	.604	9	.991
1992— St. Louis (N.L.)	1B	95	325	38	79	14	2	10	39	11	69	8	8	5-4	.243	.282	.391	.673	8	.991
—Louisville (A.A.)	1B	11	34	3	6	0	1	2	3	0	8	1	0	1-0	.176	.200	.412	.612	2	.971
1993— Colorado (N.L.)	1B	120	470	71	174	35	4	22	98	24	73	6	9	2-4	*.370	.403	.602	1.005	11	.990
1994— Colorado (N.L.)	1B	103	417	77	133	21	0	31	85	19	93	8	10	8-3	.319	.356	.592	.949	8	.992
1995— Colorado (N.L.)	1B	143	554	89	155	29	3	31	106	32	*146	13	14	12-2	.280	.331	.511	.842	* 13	.991
1996— Colorado (N.L.)	1B-3B	159	626	119	190	39	3	* 47	* 150	40	157	17	16	18-8	.304	.357	.601	.958	14	.992
1997— Colorado (N.L.)	1B	154	600	120	191	31	3	41	* 140	54	141	17	16	15-8	.318	.389	.585	.974	* 15	.991
1998— Atlanta (N.L.)	1B-DH	153	555	103	169	27	1	44	121	63	146	25	8	7-6	.305	.397	.595	.991	11	.992
1999— Atlanta (N.L.)						Did not play.														
2000— Atlanta (N.L.)	1B-DH	141	494	67	149	25	1	28	100	36	126	17	15	3-5	.302	.369	.526	.895	14	.988
2001— Texas (A.L.)	DH-1B	72	243	33	57	16	0	10	34	18	68	9	9	1-0	.235	.310	.424	.734	1	.995
—San Francisco (N.L.)	1B	49	156	17	45	12	1	7	35	13	49	3	3	0-3	.288	.351	.513	.863	5	.984
2002— Montreal (N.L.)	1B	104	292	30	76	12	0	9	40	30	81	9	8	2-2	.260	.344	.394	.738	13	.981
2003— San Francisco (N.L.)	1B-DH	110	272	36	82	15	0	12	42	19	61	2	9	1-3	.301	.352	.489	.841	3	.994
American League totals (1 year)		72	243	33	57	16	0	10	34	18	68	9	9	1-0	.235	.310	.424	.734	1	.995
National League totals (18 years)		2178	7843	1161	2273	428	32	388	1389	565	1932	168	169	127-81	.290	.348	.501	.849	175	.991
Major League totals (18 years)		2250	8086	1194	2330	444	32	398	1423	583	2000	177	178	128-81	.288	.347	.499	.846	176	.991

GALLO, MIKE — P

PERSONAL: Born April 2, 1977, in Long Beach, Calif. ... 6-0/175. ... Throws left, bats left. ... Full name: Michael Dwain Gallo. ... College: Long Beach State.

TRANSACTIONS/CAREER NOTES: Selected by Houston Astros organization in fifth round of free-agent draft (June 1999).

CAREER HITTING: 0-for-2 (.000), 0 R, 0 2B, 0 3B, 0 HR, 0 RBI.

Year League	W	L	Pct.	ERA	WHIP	G	GS	CG	ShO	Hld.	Sv.-Opp.	IP	H	R	ER	HR	BB-IBB	SO	Avg.
1999— Auburn (N.Y.-Penn)	1	0	1.000	1.23	1.36	3	3	0	0	...	0-...	14.2	13	4	2	0	7-0	11	.232
—Michigan (Midw.)	2	3	.400	5.85	1.65	12	12	0	0	...	0-...	60.0	76	47	39	6	23-0	32	.315
2000— Michigan (Midw.)	8	3	.727	4.86	1.44	24	13	0	0	...	0-...	90.2	104	58	49	6	27-1	56	.285
2001— Michigan (Midw.)	9	2	.818	3.84	1.21	44	0	0	0	...	4-...	84.1	83	38	36	4	19-1	67	.252
2002— Lexington (S. Atl.)	4	4	.500	1.83	1.08	42	2	0	0	...	8-...	88.1	69	29	18	6	26-4	93	.211
—Round Rock (Texas)	0	0	...	6.75	0.75	1	0	0	0	...	0-...	1.1	1	1	1	1	0-0	0	.200
2003— Round Rock (Texas)	1	1	.500	1.37	1.17	17	0	0	0	...	2-...	19.2	17	3	3	1	6-2	22	.246
—New Orleans (PCL)	3	0	1.000	2.08	0.92	16	0	0	0	...	0-...	17.1	13	4	4	0	3-0	11	.217
—Houston (N.L.)	1	0	1.000	3.00	1.27	32	0	0	0	6	0-1	30.0	28	10	10	3	10-2	16	.267
Major League totals (1 year)	1	0	1.000	3.00	1.27	32	0	0	0	6	0-1	30.0	28	10	10	3	10-2	16	.267

GANT, RON — OF

PERSONAL: Born March 2, 1965, in Victoria, Texas. ... 6-0/195. ... Bats right, throws right. ... Full name: Ronald Edwin Gant. ... High school: Victoria (Texas).

TRANSACTIONS/CAREER NOTES: Selected by Atlanta Braves organization in fourth round of free-agent draft (June 6, 1983). ... On suspended list (July 31, 1991). ... Released by Braves (March 15, 1994). ... Signed by Cincinnati Reds (June 21, 1994). ... On disabled list (June 21, 1994-remainder of season). ... On suspended list (September 11-15, 1995). ... Granted free agency (October 30, 1995). ... Signed by St. Louis Cardinals (December 23, 1995). ... On disabled list (May 11-June 14, 1996; and June 21-July 11, 1998). ... Traded by Cardinals with P Jeff Brantley and P Cliff Politte to Philadelphia Phillies for P Ricky Bottalico and P Garrett Stephenson (November 19, 1998). ... Traded by Phillies to Anaheim Angels for P Kent Bottenfield (July 30, 2000). ... Granted free agency (October 30, 2000). ... Signed by Colorado Rockies (December 10, 2000). ... Traded by Rockies to Oakland Athletics for OF Robin Jennings (July 3, 2001). ... Granted free agency (November 5, 2001). ... Signed by San Diego Padres organization (January 18, 2002). ... On disabled list (April 24-May 21, 2002). ... Granted free agency (October 28, 2002). ... Signed by A's organization (February 21, 2003). ... Designated for assignment by Oakland (May 29, 2003). ... Given unconditional release by Oakland (June 4, 2003).

2003 GAMES PLAYED BY POSITION (MLB): OF—9, DH—6.

G

Year	Team (League)	Pos.	G	AB	R	H	2B	3B	HR	RBI	BB	SO	HBP	GDP	SB-CS	Avg.	OBP	SLG	OPS	E	Pct.
1983— GC Braves (GCL)	SS	56	193	32	45	2	2	1	14	41	34	0	...	4-6	.233	.366	.280	.646	22	.902
1984— Anderson (S. Atl.)	2B	105	359	44	85	14	6	3	38	29	65	1	6	13-5	.237	.291	.334	.625	31	.943
1985— Sumter (S. Atl.)	2B-SS-OF	102	305	46	78	14	4	7	37	33	59	2	8	19-10	.256	.332	.397	.729	10	.973
1986— Durham (Caro.)	2B	137	512	108	142	31	10	* 26	102	78	85	3	12	35-9	.277	.372	.529	.902	26	.960
1987— Greenville (Sou.)	2B	140	527	78	130	27	3	14	82	59	91	2	8	24-4	.247	.321	.389	.710	21	* .973
— Atlanta (N.L.)	2B	21	83	9	22	4	0	2	9	1	11	0	3	4-2	.265	.271	.386	.656	3	.972
1988— Richmond (Int'l)	2B	12	45	3	14	2	2	0	4	2	10	0	0	1-1	.311	.333	.444	.778	5	.900
— Atlanta (N.L.)	2B-3B	146	563	85	146	28	8	19	60	46	118	3	7	19-10	.259	.317	.439	.755	‡17	.959
1989— Atlanta (N.L.)	3B-OF	75	260	26	46	8	3	9	25	20	63	1	0	9-6	.177	.237	.335	.571	17	.911
— Sumter (S. Atl.)	OF	12	39	13	15	4	1	1	5	11	3	0	0	4-2	.385	.520	.615	1.135	2	.909
— Richmond (Int'l)	3B-OF	63	225	42	59	13	2	1	27	29	42	0	6	6-2	.262	.345	.484	.830	5	.962
1990— Atlanta (N.L.)	OF	152	575	107	174	34	3	32	84	50	86	1	8	33-16	.303	.357	.539	.896	8	.978
1991— Atlanta (N.L.)	OF	154	561	101	141	35	3	32	105	71	104	5	6	34-15	.251	.338	.496	.834	6	.983
1992— Atlanta (N.L.)	OF	153	544	74	141	22	6	17	80	45	101	7	10	32-10	.259	.321	.415	.736	4	.986
1993— Atlanta (N.L.)	OF	157	606	113	166	27	4	36	117	67	117	2	14	26-9	.274	.345	.510	.854	* 11	.962
1994— Cincinnati (N.L.)								Did not play.												
1995— Cincinnati (N.L.)	OF	119	410	79	113	19	4	29	88	74	108	3	11	23-8	.276	.386	.554	.940	3	.985
1996— St. Louis (N.L.)	OF	122	419	74	103	14	2	30	82	73	98	3	9	13-4	.246	.359	.504	.862	5	.978
1997— St. Louis (N.L.)	OF-DH	139	502	68	115	21	4	17	62	58	162	1	2	14-6	.229	.310	.388	.698	6	.977
1998— St. Louis (N.L.)	OF	121	383	60	92	17	1	26	67	51	92	2	6	8-0	.240	.331	.493	.825	5	.971
1999— Philadelphia (N.L.)	OF-DH	138	516	107	134	27	5	17	77	85	112	1	6	13-3	.260	.364	.430	.794	2	.993
2000— Philadelphia (N.L.)	OF	89	343	54	87	16	2	20	38	36	73	1	7	5-4	.254	.324	.487	.811	6	.968
— Anaheim (A.L.)	OF-DH	34	82	15	19	3	1	6	16	20	18	0	0	1-2	.232	.379	.512	.891	1	.977
2001— Colorado (N.L.)	OF	59	171	31	44	8	2	8	22	24	56	0	0	3-1	.257	.345	.468	.813	3	.965
— Oakland (A.L.)	DH-OF	34	81	15	21	5	1	2	13	11	24	0	0	2-0	.259	.344	.420	.764	0	1.000
2002— San Diego (N.L.)	OF-DH	102	309	58	81	14	1	18	59	36	59	2	8	4-6	.262	.338	.489	.827	3	.980
2003— Oakland (A.L.)	OF-DH	17	41	4	6	0	0	1	4	2	9	0	1	0-0	.146	.182	.220	.401	0	1.000
American League totals (3 years)		85	204	34	46	8	2	9	33	33	51	0	1	3-2	.225	.329	.417	.746	1	.982
National League totals (15 years)		1747	6245	1046	1605	294	48	312	975	737	1360	32	97	240-100	.257	.336	.469	.805	113	.971
Major League totals (16 years)		1832	6449	1080	1651	302	50	321	1008	770	1411	32	98	243-102	.256	.336	.468	.803	114	.971

GARCIA, DANNY   2B

PERSONAL: Born April 12, 1980, in Riverside, Calif. ... 6-1/174. ... Bats right, throws right. ... Full name: Daniel Joseph Garcia. ... High school: J.W. North. ... College: Pepperdine.
TRANSACTIONS/CAREER NOTES: Selected by New York Mets organization in fifth round of free-agent draft (June 5, 2001).
2003 GAMES PLAYED BY POSITION (MLB): 2B—17, OF—1.

Year	Team (League)	Pos.	G	AB	R	H	2B	3B	HR	RBI	BB	SO	HBP	GDP	SB-CS	Avg.	OBP	SLG	OPS	E	Pct.
2001— Brooklyn (NY-P)	2B	15	56	10	18	2	0	1	6	4	10	2	0	3-2	.321	.387	.411	.798	3	.952
— Capital City (SAL)	2B-OF	30	103	25	31	12	1	2	16	15	18	6	0	7-3	.301	.409	.495	.905	11	.927
2002— St. Lucie (Fla. St.)	2B-SS-OF	122	432	69	118	34	5	4	52	53	77	15	9	13-6	.273	.369	.403	.772	21	.963
2003— Binghamton (East.)	2B-DH	32	117	22	39	12	1	3	22	10	20	3	2	2-2	.333	.391	.530	.921	4	.967
— Norfolk (Int'l)	2B-DH	101	388	45	102	23	3	4	54	22	60	9	3	11-1	.263	.313	.369	.681	13	.972
— New York (N.L.)	2B-OF	19	56	5	12	2	0	2	6	2	11	3	2	0-0	.214	.274	.357	.631	4	.950
Major League totals (1 year)		19	56	5	12	2	0	2	6	2	11	3	2	0-0	.214	.274	.357	.631	4	.950

GARCIA, FREDDY   P

PERSONAL: Born June 10, 1976, in Caracas, Venezuela. ... 6-4/240. ... Throws right, bats right. ... Full name: Freddy Antonio Garcia.
TRANSACTIONS/CAREER NOTES: Signed as non-drafted free agent by Houston Astros organization (October 21, 1993). ... Traded by Astros with SS Carlos Guillen and a player to be named later to Seattle Mariners for P Randy Johnson (July 31, 1998); Mariners acquired P John Halama to complete deal (October 1, 1998). ... On Seattle disabled list (April 22-July 7, 2000); included rehabilitation assignments to Tacoma (June 15-20) and Everett (June 21-July 7).
CAREER HITTING: 7-for-25 (.280), 0 R, 1 2B, 0 3B, 0 HR, 2 RBI.

Year	League	W	L	Pct.	ERA	WHIP	G	GS	CG	ShO	Hld.	Sv.-Opp.	IP	H	R	ER	HR	BB-IBB	SO	Avg.
1994— Dom. Astros (DSL)	4	6	.400	5.29	1.39	16	15	0	0	...	0-...	85.0	80	61	50	...	38-...	68	...
1995— GC Astros (GCL)	6	3	.667	4.47	1.27	11	11	0	0	...	0-...	58.1	60	32	29	2	14-0	58	.261
1996— Quad City (Midw.)	5	4	.556	·3.12	1.38	13	13	0	0	...	0-...	60.2	57	27	21	3	27-0	50	.247
1997— Kissimmee (Fla. St.)	10	8	.556	2.56	1.20	27	27	5	• 2	...	0-...	179.0	165	63	51	6	49-3	131	.242
1998— Jackson (Texas)	6	7	.462	3.24	1.27	19	19	2	0	...	0-...	119.1	94	48	43	8	58-0	115	.215
— New Orleans (PCL)	1	0	1.000	3.14	1.05	2	2	0	0	...	0-...	14.1	14	5	5	2	1-0	13	.255
— Tacoma (PCL)	3	1	.750	3.86	1.32	5	5	0	0	...	0-...	32.2	30	14	14	6	13-0	30	.246
1999— Seattle (A.L.)	17	8	.680	4.07	1.47	33	33	2	1	0	0-0	201.1	205	96	91	18	90-4	170	.263
2000— Seattle (A.L.)	9	5	.643	3.91	1.42	21	20	0	0	0	0-0	124.1	112	62	54	16	64-4	79	.241
— Everett (Northwest)	0	0	...	4.50	1.30	2	2	0	0	...	0-...	10.0	11	5	5	1	2-0	15	.262
— Tacoma (PCL)	1	0	1.000	2.57	1.00	1	1	0	0	...	0-...	7.0	5	2	2	2	2-0	11	.208
2001— Seattle (A.L.)	18	6	.750	*3.05	1.12	34	34	4	3	0	0-0	* 238.2	199	88	81	16	69-6	163	*.225
2002— Seattle (A.L.)	16	10	.615	4.39	1.30	34	34	1	0	0	0-0	223.2	227	110	109	30	63-3	181	.260
2003— Seattle (A.L.)	12	14	.462	4.51	1.33	33	33	1	0	0	0-0	201.1	196	109	101	31	71-2	144	.255
Major League totals (5 years)	72	43	.626	3.97	1.31	155	154	8	4	0	0-0	989.1	939	465	436	111	357-19	737	.249

GARCIA, JESSE   SS/2B

PERSONAL: Born September 24, 1973, in Corpus Christi, Texas. ... 5-10/171. ... Bats right, throws right. ... Full name: Jesus Jesse Garcia. ... High school: Robstown (Texas). ... Junior college: Lee College (Texas).
TRANSACTIONS/CAREER NOTES: Selected by Baltimore Orioles organization in 26th round of free-agent draft (June 3, 1993). ... On disabled list (June 19, 1994-entire season). ... Granted free agency (December 21, 1998). ... Re-signed by Orioles organization (December 21, 1998). ... On Rochester disabled list (May 25-July 18, 1999). ... Traded by Orioles for Atlanta Braves for IF Steve Sisco (December 18, 2000). ... Granted free agency (December 21, 2002). ... Re-signed by Braves (March 20, 2003).
2003 GAMES PLAYED BY POSITION (MLB): 2B—6, SS—3, 3B—2.

Year Team (League)	Pos.	G	AB	R	H	2B	3B	HR	RBI	BB	SO	HBP	GDP	SB-CS	Avg.	OBP	SLG	OPS	E	Pct.
1993— GC Orioles (GCL) 2B-3B-SS		48	156	20	37	4	0	0	16	21	32	1	1	14-6	.237	.326	.263	.589	14	.934
1994— Bluefield (Appl.)							Did not play.													
1995— Frederick (Carolina)	2B	124	365	52	82	11	3	3	27	49	75	9	5	5-10	.225	.329	.296	.625	28	.952
1996— High Desert (Calif.)	2B-SS	137	459	94	122	21	5	10	66	57	81	8	7	25-7	.266	.354	.399	.753	§ 22	.968
1997— Bowie (East.) 2B-3B-SS	*	141	437	52	103	18	1	5	42	38	71	6	9	7-7	.236	.304	.316	.620	13	.981
1998— Bowie (East.)	2B-SS-OF	86	258	46	73	13	1	2	20	34	37	1	3	12-3	.283	.369	.364	.733	9	.973
— Rochester (Int'l)	2B	44	160	20	47	6	4	0	18	7	22	3	3	7-5	.294	.329	.381	.711	8	.969
1999— Baltimore (A.L.)	S-2-3-D	17	29	6	6	0	0	2	2	2	3	0	1	0-0	.207	.258	.414	.672	0	1.000
— Rochester (Int'l)	SS-2B	62	220	25	56	10	2	2	23	11	21	0	5	9-6	.255	.289	.345	.634	15	.944
2000— Baltimore (A.L.)	2B-SS	14	17	2	1	0	0	0	0	2	2	0	0	0-0	.059	.158	.059	.217	0	1.000
— Rochester (Int'l) SS-2B-3B		106	372	44	90	12	2	1	23	27	60	4	8	9-4	.242	.300	.293	.593	18	.963
2001— Richmond (Int'l) SS-2B-3B		105	375	50	100	23	3	2	22	22	54	4	9	18-6	.267	.313	.357	.671	20	.955
— Atlanta (N.L.)	2B-SS	22	5	3	1	0	0	0	0	0	1	0	0	6-2	.200	.200	.200	.400	0	1.000
2002— Richmond (Int'l) 2-S-3-OF		58	230	29	69	12	1	6	17	16	32	2	5	9-5	.300	.349	.439	.789	9	.966
— Atlanta (N.L.)	2B-SS-OF	39	61	6	12	1	0	0	5	0	14	0	1	0-1	.197	.197	.213	.410	1	.989
2003— Richmond (Int'l) S-2-0-3-D		110	425	45	130	17	3	2	30	12	50	4	9	29-9	.306	.329	.374	.703	18	.956
— Atlanta (N.L.)	2B-SS-3B	13	10	6	4	0	1	0	2	0	1	0	0	0-1	.400	.400	.600	1.000	0	1.000
American League totals (2 years)		31	46	8	7	0	0	2	2	4	5	0	1	0-0	.152	.220	.283	.503	0	1.000
National League totals (3 years)		74	76	15	17	1	1	0	7	0	16	0	1	6-4	.224	.224	.263	.487	1	.991
Major League totals (5 years)		105	122	23	24	1	1	2	9	4	21	0	2	6-4	.197	.222	.270	.493	1	.994

GARCIA, KARIM — OF

PERSONAL: Born October 29, 1975, in Ciudad Obregon, Mexico. ... 6-0/195. ... Bats left, throws left. ... Full name: Gustavo Karim Garcia. ... Name pronounced: ka-REEM. ... High school: Preparatoria Abierta (Ciudad Obregon, Mexico).

TRANSACTIONS/CAREER NOTES: Signed as non-drafted free agent by Los Angeles Dodgers organization (July 16, 1992). ... On Los Angeles disabled list (September 1, 1997-remainder of season). ... Selected by Arizona Diamondbacks in first round (ninth pick overall) of expansion draft (November 18, 1997). ... Traded by Diamondbacks to Detroit Tigers for OF Luis Gonzalez (December 28, 1998). ... Traded by Tigers to Baltimore Orioles for future considerations (June 12, 2000). ... On suspended list (September 1-4, 2000). ... Released by Orioles (October 17, 2000). ... Signed by Cleveland Indians organization (December 22, 2000). ... Released by Indians (March 27, 2002). ... Signed by New York Yankees organization (April 2, 2002). ... Released by Yankees (July 2, 2002). ... Signed by Indians organization (July 12, 2002). ... Placed on disabled list (May 8, 2003); recalled (June 21). ... Traded by Indians with P Dan Miceli to New York Yankees for a player to be named later (June 25, 2003).

2003 GAMES PLAYED BY POSITION (MLB): OF—73, DH—2.

Year Team (League)	Pos.	G	AB	R	H	2B	3B	HR	RBI	BB	SO	HBP	GDP	SB-CS	Avg.	OBP	SLG	OPS	E	Pct.
1993— Bakersfield (Calif.)	OF	123	460	61	111	20	9	19	54	37	109	2	5	5-3	.241	.299	.448	.747	* 13	.940
1994— Vero Beach (FSL)	OF	121	452	72	120	28	10	* 21	84	37	112	1	7	8-3	.265	.319	.511	.830	5	.980
1995— Albuquerque (PCL)	OF-DH	124	474	88	151	26	10	20	• 91	38	102	0	12	12-6	.319	.369	.542	.912	* 14	.932
— Los Angeles (N.L.)	OF	13	20	1	4	0	0	0	0	0	4	0	0	0-0	.200	.200	.200	.400	0	1.000
1996— Albuquerque (PCL)	OF-DH	84	327	54	97	17	10	13	58	29	67	1	9	6-4	.297	.353	.529	.882	13	.921
— San Antonio (Texas)	OF	35	129	21	32	6	1	5	22	9	38	0	1	1-1	.248	.297	.426	.723	2	.971
— Los Angeles (N.L.)	OF	1	1	0	0	0	0	0	0	0	1	0	0	0-0	.000	.000	.000	.000	0	...
1997— Albuquerque (PCL)	OF-DH	71	262	53	80	17	6	20	66	23	70	0	4	11-5	.305	.361	.645	1.006	5	.952
— Los Angeles (N.L.)	OF	15	39	5	5	0	0	1	8	6	14	0	0	0-0	.128	.239	.205	.444	0	1.000
1998— Arizona (N.L.)	OF	113	333	39	74	10	8	9	43	18	78	0	6	5-4	.222	.260	.381	.641	5	.975
— Tucson (PCL)	OF	27	106	21	33	4	2	10	27	15	24	0	2	5-1	.311	.393	.670	1.063	3	.958
1999— Detroit (A.L.)	OF-DH	96	288	38	69	10	3	14	32	20	67	0	2	2-4	.240	.288	.441	.729	7	.958
2000— Detroit (A.L.)	OF-DH	8	17	1	3	0	0	0	0	0	4	0	1	0-0	.176	.176	.176	.353	0	1.000
— Toledo (Int'l)	OF	40	155	31	46	6	2	15	38	11	32	3	4	2-1	.297	.349	.652	1.000	4	.956
— Rochester (Int'l)	OF	76	270	38	75	17	1	13	54	34	70	2	7	3-3	.278	.358	.493	.851	3	.977
— Baltimore (A.L.)	DH-OF	16	18	0	0	0	0	0	0	0	6	0	0	0-0	.000	.000	.000	.000	0	1.000
2001— Buffalo (Int'l)	OF-1B	125	462	73	122	16	4	31	85	44	106	1	9	4-4	.264	.326	.517	.843	7	.973
— Cleveland (A.L.)	OF-1B	20	45	8	14	3	0	5	9	3	13	1	1	0-0	.311	.360	.711	1.071	2	.917
2002— Columbus (Int'l)	OF-1B	74	288	44	78	16	3	12	49	20	48	0	2	1-5	.271	.316	.472	.788	2	.987
— New York (A.L.)	OF	2	5	1	1	0	0	0	0	0	1	0	0	0-0	.200	.200	.200	.400	0	1.000
— Buffalo (Int'l)	OF	23	91	16	36	7	2	3	22	9	14	0	1	0-1	.396	.450	.615	1.065	0	1.000
— Cleveland (A.L.)	OF	51	197	29	59	8	0	16	52	6	40	0	6	0-3	.299	.317	.584	.901	1	.990
2003— Cleveland (A.L.)	OF-DH	24	93	8	18	1	0	5	14	5	20	1	4	0-0	.194	.238	.366	.603	4	.905
— Buffalo (Int'l)	OF-DH	14	60	6	16	6	0	0	7	2	17	0	1	2-1	.267	.290	.367	.657	0	1.000
— New York (A.L.)	OF-DH	52	151	17	46	5	0	6	21	9	32	0	4	0-2	.305	.342	.457	.799	2	.981
American League totals (5 years)		261	812	102	210	27	3	46	128	43	183	2	18	2-9	.259	.295	.469	.764	16	.964
National League totals (4 years)		142	393	45	83	10	8	10	51	24	97	0	6	5-4	.211	.254	.354	.608	5	.977
Major League totals (9 years)		403	1205	147	293	37	11	56	179	67	280	2	24	7-13	.243	.282	.432	.713	21	.969

G

GARCIA, REYNALDO — P

PERSONAL: Born April 15, 1974, in Mayua, Dominican Republic. ... 6-3/170. ... Throws right, bats right.

TRANSACTIONS/CAREER NOTES: Signed as non-drafted free agent by Texas Rangers organization (December 16, 1996). ... Recalled by Texas from Oklahoma (May 29, 2003). ... Optioned to Oklahoma (June 8, 2003). ... Recalled from Oklahoma (September 1, 2003).

CAREER HITTING: 0-for-0 (.000), 0 R, 0 2B, 0 3B, 0 HR, 0 RBI.

Year League	W	L	Pct.	ERA	WHIP	G	GS	CG	ShO	Hld.	Sv.-Opp.	IP	H	R	ER	HR	BB-IBB	SO	Avg.
1997— Dom. Rangers (DSL)	1	3	.250	6.81	1.65	16	1	0	0		5-...	37.0	39	34	28	...	22-...	27	
1998— Dom. Rangers (DSL)	3	8	.273	4.56	1.58	13	13	1	...		0-...	73.0	88	50	37	...	27-...	36	
1999— GC Rangers (GCL)	4	4	.500	3.23	1.27	12	11	0	0		0-...	64.0	55	30	23	3	26-0	42	.233
2000— Savannah (S. Atl.)	6	7	.462	2.69	1.24	49	2	1	0		14-...	97.0	87	37	29	6	33-1	82	.238
2001— Charlotte (Fla. St.)	5	10	.333	3.56	1.31	35	16	0	0		4-...	116.1	107	62	46	7	45-3	111	.247
2002— Tulsa (Texas)	5	1	.833	3.69	1.36	18	9	0	0		0-...	68.1	63	36	28	11	30-1	54	.246
— Oklahoma (PCL)	2	2	.500	2.84	1.17	25	0	0	0		4-...	31.2	23	12	10	2	14-1	33	.198
— Texas (A.L.)	0	0	...	31.50	4.00	3	0	0	0	0	0-0	2.0	7	7	7	3	1-0	2	.538
2003— Oklahoma (PCL)	4	3	.571	3.69	1.36	39	3	0	0		9-...	61.0	64	27	25	3	19-1	64	.255
— Texas (A.L.)	0	0	...	9.00	1.83	17	0	0	0	1	0-0	18.0	19	18	18	6	14-0	15	.275
Major League totals (2 years)	0	0	...	11.25	2.05	20	0	0	0	1	0-0	20.0	26	25	25	9	15-0	17	.317

GARCIA, ROSMAN — P

PERSONAL: Born January 3, 1979, in Maracay, Venezuela. ... 6-2/160. ... Throws right, bats right. ... Full name: Rosman J. Garcia.

TRANSACTIONS/CAREER NOTES: Signed by New York Yankees organization as a non-drafted free agent (February 15, 1996). ... Traded by Yankees to Texas Rangers with P Randy Flores as the player to be named later in deal that sent IF Randy Velarde from Texas to New York (October 11, 2001).

CAREER HITTING: 0-for-0 (.000), 0 R, 0 2B, 0 3B, 0 HR, 0 RBI.

Year	League	W	L	Pct.	ERA	WHIP	G	GS	CG	ShO	Hld.	Sv.-Opp.	IP	H	R	ER	HR	BB-IBB	SO	Avg.
1998—GC Yankees (GCL)		4	3	.571	2.55	1.18	12	12	0	0	...	0-...	67.0	70	38	19	1	9-0	47	.260
1999—Greensboro (S. Atl.)		2	3	.400	6.38	1.89	9	9	0	0	...	0-...	42.1	60	33	30	4	20-0	31	.331
—Staten Island (NY-P)		2	6	.250	4.26	1.44	18	10	0	0	...	1-...	69.2	86	40	33	3	14-2	40	.301
2000—Greensboro (S. Atl.)		6	6	.500	4.57	1.44	23	15	1	0	...	0-...	104.1	115	67	53	12	35-0	73	.280
—Tampa (FSL)		0	2	.000	5.50	1.22	4	3	0	0	...	1-...	18.0	18	13	11	1	4-0	6	.265
2001—Norwich (East.)		1	0	1.000	0.00	1.17	1	1	0	0	...	0-...	6.0	5	4	0	0	2-0	6	.200
—Tampa (FSL)		2	6	.250	3.47	1.31	26	7	0	0	...	1-...	59.2	56	30	23	2	22-6	42	.243
2002—Tulsa (Texas)		8	5	.615	3.01	1.43	53	0	0	0	...	6-...	74.2	75	34	25	1	32-9	38	.270
2003—Oklahoma (PCL)		1	2	.333	1.91	0.92	17	2	0	0	...	10-...	28.1	20	7	6	1	6-0	21	.196
—Texas (A.L.)		1	2	.333	6.02	1.86	46	0	0	0	7	0-2	46.1	63	33	31	4	23-0	25	.320
Major League totals (1 year)		1	2	.333	6.02	1.86	46	0	0	0	7	0-2	46.1	63	33	31	4	23-0	25	.320

GARCIAPARRA, NOMAR — SS

PERSONAL: Born July 23, 1973, in Whittier, Calif. ... 6-0/190. ... Bats right, throws right. ... Full name: Anthony Nomar Garciaparra. ... Name pronounced: no-mar GARCIA-par-uh. ... High school: St. John Bosco (Bellflower, Calif.). ... College: Georgia Tech.

TRANSACTIONS/CAREER NOTES: Selected by Milwaukee Brewers organization in fifth round of free-agent draft (June 3, 1991); did not sign. ... Selected by Boston Red Sox organization in first round (12th pick overall) of free-agent draft (June 2, 1994). ... On Pawtucket disabled list (April 4-15 and April 19-July 11, 1996). ... On disabled list (May 9-28, 1998; and May 12-27, 2000). ... On Boston disabled list (March 21-July 29 and August 27, 2001-remainder of season); included rehabilitation assignment to Pawtucket (July 24-29).

2003 GAMES PLAYED BY POSITION (MLB): SS—156.

Year	Team (League)	Pos.	G	AB	R	H	2B	3B	HR	RBI	BB	SO	HBP	GDP	SB-CS	Avg.	OBP	SLG	OPS	E	Pct.
1994—Sarasota (Fla. St.)	SS	28	105	20	31	8	1	1	16	10	6	1	2	5-2	.295	.356	.419	.775	3	.974
1995—Trenton (East.)	SS	125	513	77	137	20	8	8	47	50	42	8	10	35-12	.267	.338	.384	.722	23	.963
1996—Pawtucket (Int'l)	SS	43	172	40	59	15	2	16	46	14	21	1	6	3-1	.343	.387	.733	1.120	5	.973
—GC Red Sox (GCL)	SS	5	14	4	4	2	1	0	5	1	0	1	1	0-0	.286	.375	.571	.946	1	.950
—Boston (A.L.)	SS-2B-DH	24	87	11	21	2	3	4	16	4	14	0	0	5-0	.241	.272	.471	.743	1	.989
1997—Boston (A.L.)	SS	153	*684	122	*209	44	*11	30	98	35	92	6	9	22-9	.306	.342	.534	.875	21	.971
1998—Boston (A.L.)	SS	143	604	111	195	37	8	35	122	33	62	8	20	12-6	.323	.362	.584	.946	25	.962
1999—Boston (A.L.)	SS	135	532	103	190	42	4	27	104	51	39	8	11	14-3	*.357	.418	.603	1.022	17	.972
2000—Boston (A.L.)	SS-DH	140	529	104	197	51	3	21	96	61	50	2	8	5-2	*.372	.434	.599	1.033	18	.971
2001—Pawtucket (Int'l)	SS	4	16	3	7	2	0	1	4	1	2	1	0	0-0	.438	.500	.750	1.250	1	.941
—Boston (A.L.)	SS	21	83	13	24	3	0	4	8	7	9	1	1	0-1	.289	.352	.470	.822	3	.968
2002—Boston (A.L.)	SS	156	635	101	197	•56	5	24	120	41	63	6	17	5-2	.310	.352	.528	.880	*25	.965
2003—Boston (A.L.)	SS	156	658	120	198	37	13	28	105	39	61	11	10	19-5	.301	.345	.524	.870	20	.971
Major League totals (8 years)		928	3812	685	1231	272	47	173	669	271	390	42	76	82-28	.323	.370	.555	.925	130	.969

GARLAND, JON — P

PERSONAL: Born September 27, 1979, in Valencia, Calif. ... 6-6/205. ... Throws right, bats right. ... Full name: Jon Steven Garland. ... High school: John F. Kennedy (Granada Hills, Calif.).

TRANSACTIONS/CAREER NOTES: Selected by Chicago Cubs organization in first round (10th pick overall) of free-agent draft (June 3, 1997). ... Traded by Cubs to Chicago White Sox for P Matt Karchner (July 29, 1998). ... On Chicago disabled list (August 19-September 3, 2000); included rehabilitation assignment to Birmingham (August 30-September 3).

CAREER HITTING: 0-for-6 (.000), 0 R, 0 2B, 0 3B, 0 HR, 0 RBI.

Year	League	W	L	Pct.	ERA	WHIP	G	GS	CG	ShO	Hld.	Sv.-Opp.	IP	H	R	ER	HR	BB-IBB	SO	Avg.
1997—Ariz. Cubs (Ariz.)		3	2	.600	2.70	1.18	10	7	0	0	...	0-...	40.0	37	14	12	3	10-0	39	.247
1998—Rockford (Midwest)		4	7	.364	5.03	1.57	19	19	1	0	...	0-...	107.1	124	69	60	11	45-0	70	.301
—Hickory (S. Atl.)		1	4	.200	5.40	1.84	5	5	0	0	...	0-...	26.2	36	20	16	2	13-0	19	.333
1999—Winston-Salem (Caro.)		5	7	.417	3.33	1.24	19	19	2	1	...	0-...	119.0	109	57	44	7	39-2	84	.244
—Birmingham (Sou.)		3	1	.750	4.38	1.46	7	7	0	0	...	0-...	39.0	39	22	19	4	18-0	27	.258
2000—Charlotte (Int'l)		9	2	.818	2.26	1.26	16	16	2	1	...	0-...	103.2	99	28	26	3	32-2	63	.251
—Chicago (A.L.)		4	8	.333	6.46	1.75	15	13	0	0	1	0-0	69.2	82	55	50	10	40-0	42	.292
—Birmingham (Sou.)		0	0	...	0.00	0.83	1	1	0	0	...	0-...	6.0	4	0	0	0	1-0	10	.200
2001—Charlotte (Int'l)		0	3	.000	2.73	1.27	5	5	1	0	...	0-...	33.0	31	10	10	1	11-1	26	.261
—Chicago (A.L.)		6	7	.462	3.69	1.52	35	16	0	0	2	1-1	117.0	123	59	48	16	55-2	61	.277
2002—Chicago (A.L.)		12	12	.500	4.58	1.41	33	33	1	1	0	0-0	192.2	188	109	98	23	83-1	112	.258
2003—Chicago (A.L.)		12	13	.480	4.51	1.37	32	32	0	0	0	0-0	191.2	188	103	96	28	74-1	108	.260
Major League totals (4 years)		34	40	.459	4.60	1.46	115	94	1	1	3	1-1	571.0	581	326	292	77	252-4	323	.267

GAUDIN, CHAD — P

PERSONAL: Born March 24, 1983, in New Orleans, La. ... 5-11/165. ... Throws right, bats right. ... Full name: Chad Edward Gaudin. ... High school: Crescent City (Calif.).

TRANSACTIONS/CAREER NOTES: Selected by Tampa Bay Devil Rays organization in 34th round of free-agent draft (June 5, 2001).

CAREER HITTING: 0-for-0 (.000), 0 R, 0 2B, 0 3B, 0 HR, 0 RBI.

Year	League	W	L	Pct.	ERA	WHIP	G	GS	CG	ShO	Hld.	Sv.-Opp.	IP	H	R	ER	HR	BB-IBB	SO	Avg.
2002—Char., S.C. (SAL)		4	6	.400	2.26	1.20	26	17	0	0	...	1-...	119.1	106	43	30	5	37-0	106	.244
2003—Bakersfield (Calif.)		5	3	.625	2.13	1.07	14	14	1	0	...	0-...	80.1	63	23	19	2	23-0	70	.214
—Orlando (Sou.)		2	0	1.000	0.47	0.58	3	3	1	1	...	0-...	19.0	8	1	1	0	3-0	23	.131
—Tampa Bay (A.L.)		2	0	1.000	3.60	1.33	15	3	0	0	0	0-0	40.0	37	18	16	4	16-0	23	.240
Major League totals (1 year)		2	0	1.000	3.60	1.33	15	3	0	0	0	0-0	40.0	37	18	16	4	16-0	23	.240

G

GEARY, GEOFF   P

PERSONAL: Born August 26, 1976, in Buffalo, N.Y. ... 6-0/170. ... Throws right, bats right. ... Full name: Geoffrey Michael Geary. ... High school: Grossmont (El Cajon, Calif.). ... College: Oklahoma.

TRANSACTIONS/CAREER NOTES: Selected by Milwaukee Brewers organization in 41st round of free-agent draft (June 1997); did not sign. ... Selected by Philadelphia Phillies organization in 15th round of free-agent draft (June 1998).

CAREER HITTING: 0-for-0 (.000), 0 R, 0 2B, 0 3B, 0 HR, 0 RBI.

Year League	W	L	Pct.	ERA	WHIP	G	GS	CG	ShO	Hld.	Sv.-Opp.	IP	H	R	ER	HR	BB-IBB	SO	Avg.
1998— Batavia (N.Y.-Penn)	9	1	.900	1.60	0.97	16	15	1	1	...	0-...	95.1	78	20	17	6	14-0	101	.222
1999— Clearwater (Fla. St.)	10	5	.667	3.95	1.48	24	19	2	0	...	0-...	139.0	175	77	61	11	31-1	77	.310
2000— Reading (East.)	7	6	.538	4.11	1.26	22	22	1	0	...	0-...	129.1	141	66	59	15	22-0	112	.272
2001— Reading (East.)	9	7	.563	3.61	1.09	29	13	0	0	...	2-...	112.1	101	48	45	14	21-3	88	.245
— Scran./W.B. (I.L.)	0	3	.000	6.95	1.86	7	3	0	0	...	0-...	22.0	35	17	17	2	6-1	21	.376
2002— Scran./W.B. (I.L.)	4	2	.667	3.03	1.39	38	8	0	0	...	1-...	101.0	108	46	34	9	32-1	82	.277
2003— Scran./W.B. (I.L.)	9	4	.692	2.16	0.98	46	3	0	0	...	5-...	87.2	73	26	21	3	13-1	80	.229
— Philadelphia (N.L.)	0	0	...	4.50	1.83	5	0	0	0	0	0-0	6.0	8	3	3	0	3-0	3	.333
Major League totals (1 year)	**0**	**0**	**...**	**4.50**	**1.83**	**5**	**0**	**0**	**0**	**0**	**0-0**	**6.0**	**8**	**3**	**3**	**0**	**3-0**	**3**	**.333**

GEORGE, CHRIS   P

PERSONAL: Born September 16, 1979, in Houston, Texas. ... 6-2/200. ... Throws left, bats left. ... Full name: Christopher Coleman George. ... High school: Klein (Texas).

TRANSACTIONS/CAREER NOTES: Selected by Kansas City Royals organization as "sandwich pick" between first and second round of free-agent draft (June 2, 1998); pick received as part of compensation for Arizona Diamondbacks signing Type A free agent IF Jay Bell. ... On Kansas City disabled list (May 18-June 18, 2002); included rehabilitation assignment to Omaha (May 30-June 18). ... Optioned to Omaha by Kansas City (July 11, 2003). ... Recalled by Kansas City from Omaha (September 29, 2003).

CAREER HITTING: 1-for-1 (1.000), 0 R, 0 2B, 0 3B, 0 HR, 1 RBI.

Year League	W	L	Pct.	ERA	WHIP	G	GS	CG	ShO	Hld.	Sv.-Opp.	IP	H	R	ER	HR	BB-IBB	SO	Avg.
1998— GC Royals (GCL)	0	1	.000	2.87	1.15	5	4	0	0	...	0-...	15.2	14	9	5	1	4-0	10	.233
1999— Wilmington (Caro.)	9	7	.563	3.60	1.34	27	27	0	0	...	0-...	145.0	142	65	58	8	53-0	142	.257
2000— Wichita (Texas)	8	5	.615	3.14	1.47	18	18	0	0	...	0-...	97.1	92	41	34	5	51-1	80	.253
— Omaha (PCL)	3	2	.600	4.84	1.50	8	8	0	0	...	0-...	44.2	47	29	24	8	20-0	27	.273
2001— Omaha (PCL)	11	3	.786	3.53	1.31	20	20	0	0	...	0-...	117.1	103	54	46	14	51-0	84	.237
— Kansas City (A.L.)	4	8	.333	5.59	1.36	13	13	1	0	0	0-0	74.0	83	48	46	14	18-0	32	.288
2002— Kansas City (A.L.)	6	12	.333	5.87	1.65	22	21	1	0	...	0-...	127.1	145	86	83	15	65-0	94	.287
— Kansas City (A.L.)	0	4	.000	5.60	1.65	6	6	0	0	0	0-0	27.1	37	17	17	2	8-0	13	.325
2003— Kansas City (A.L.)	9	6	.600	7.11	1.75	18	18	0	0	0	0-0	93.2	120	75	74	22	44-2	39	.309
— Omaha (PCL)	3	5	.375	7.29	1.71	10	10	0	0	...	0-...	54.1	71	49	44	8	22-0	28	.314
Major League totals (3 years)	**13**	**18**	**.419**	**6.32**	**1.59**	**37**	**37**	**1**	**0**	**0**	**0-0**	**195.0**	**240**	**140**	**137**	**38**	**70-2**	**84**	**.304**

GERMAN, ESTEBAN   2B

PERSONAL: Born January 26, 1978, in Santo Domingo, Dominican Republic. ... 5-9/165. ... Bats right, throws right. ... Full name: Esteban German German Guridi. ... Name pronounced: her-MAHN.

TRANSACTIONS/CAREER NOTES: Signed as non-drafted free agent by Oakland Athletics organization (July 4, 1996). ... Recalled by Oakland from Sacramento (July 24, 2003). ... Optioned to Sacramento by Oakland (July 27, 2003). ... Recalled by Oakland from Sacramento (September 14, 2003).

2003 GAMES PLAYED BY POSITION (MLB): 2B—5.

Year Team (League)	Pos.	G	AB	R	H	2B	3B	HR	RBI	BB	SO	HBP	GDP	SB-CS	Avg.	OBP	SLG	OPS	E	Pct.
									BATTING										**FIELDING**	
1997— Dom. Athletics (DSL)		69	249	69	79	17	1	2	29	73	30	...	...	58-...	.317	...	.418	...	...	...
1998— Dom. Athletics (DSL)		10	32	9	10	1	1	0	4	7	2	...	...	4-...	.313	...	.406	...	...	...
— Ariz. A's (Ariz.)	2B	• 55	202	* 52	62	3	* 10	2	28	33	43	4	1	* 40-8	.307	.413	.450	.863	* 13	.940
1999— Modesto (Calif.)	2B	128	501	107	156	16	12	4	52	* 102	128	5	3	40-16	.311	.428	.415	.843	* 38	.932
2000— Midland (Texas)	2B	24	75	13	16	1	0	1	6	18	21	2	1	5-3	.213	.379	.267	.646	5	.951
— Visalia (Calif.)	2B-SS	109	428	82	113	14	10	2	35	61	86	5	4	* 78-8	.264	.361	.357	.718	‡ 25	.953
2001— Midland (Texas)	2B	92	335	79	95	20	3	6	30	63	66	12	6	31-11	.284	.415	.415	.830	16	.963
— Sacramento (PCL)	2B	38	150	40	56	8	0	4	14	18	20	6	4	17-2	.373	.457	.507	.964	7	.962
2002— Sacramento (PCL)	2B	121	458	72	126	16	4	2	43	78	66	8	7	26-14	.275	.390	.341	.730	8	.986
— Oakland (A.L.)	2B	9	35	4	7	0	0	0	0	4	11	1	0	1-0	.200	.300	.200	.500	1	.978
2003— Sacramento (PCL)	2B	115	467	86	143	20	8	3	51	56	64	2	17	32-8	.306	.379	.403	.781	13	.976
— Oakland (A.L.)	2B	5	4	0	1	0	0	0	1	0	1	0	1	0-0	.250	.250	.250	.500	0	1.000
Major League totals (2 years)		**14**	**39**	**4**	**8**	**0**	**0**	**0**	**1**	**4**	**12**	**1**	**1**	**1-0**	**.205**	**.295**	**.205**	**.501**	**1**	**.982**

GERMAN, FRANKLYN   P

PERSONAL: Born January 20, 1980, in San Cristobal, Dominican Republic. ... 6-7/270. ... Throws right, bats right. ... Full name: Franklyn Miguel German. ... Name pronounced: her-MAHN.

TRANSACTIONS/CAREER NOTES: Signed as non-drafted free agent by Oakland Athletics organization (July 2, 1996). ... Traded by A's to Detroit Tigers with 1B Carlos Pena and a player to be named later as part of three-way deal in which New York Yankees acquired P Jeff Weaver from Tigers and A's acquired P Ted Lilly, OF John-Ford Griffin and P Jason Arnold from Yankees (July 5, 2002); Tigers acquired P Jeremy Bonderman to complete deal (August 22, 2002).

CAREER HITTING: 0-for-0 (.000), 0 R, 0 2B, 0 3B, 0 HR, 0 RBI.

Year League	W	L	Pct.	ERA	WHIP	G	GS	CG	ShO	Hld.	Sv.-Opp.	IP	H	R	ER	HR	BB-IBB	SO	Avg.
1997— Dominican Athletics (DSL)	8	3	.727	2.33	1.09	13	13	5	...	...	0-...	89.0	66	33	23	...	31-...	80	...
1998— Ariz. A's (Ariz.)	2	1	.667	6.13	1.60	14	12	0	0	...	0-...	54.1	69	43	37	5	18-0	48	.317
1999— S. Oregon (N'west)	3	5	.375	5.99	1.82	15	15	0	0	...	0-...	73.2	89	52	49	10	45-1	58	.306
2000— Modesto (Calif.)	5	5	.500	5.50	1.74	17	14	0	0	...	0-...	72.0	88	55	44	4	37-0	52	.307
— Vancouver (NW)	1	0	1.000	1.77	1.13	9	2	0	0	...	0-...	20.1	13	4	4	0	10-0	20	.173
2001— Visalia (Calif.)	2	4	.333	3.98	1.55	53	0	0	0	...	19-...	63.1	67	34	28	7	31-1	93	.262
2002— Midland (Texas)	1	1	.500	3.05	1.33	37	0	0	0	...	16-...	41.1	28	14	14	0	27-2	59	.194
— Toledo (Int'l)	1	1	.500	1.59	0.97	23	0	0	0	...	13-...	22.2	15	4	4	0	7-0	31	.188
— Detroit (A.L.)	1	0	1.000	0.00	0.75	7	0	0	0	1	1-1	6.2	3	0	0	0	2-1	6	.150
2003— Toledo (Int'l)	1	4	.200	2.45	1.02	24	0	0	0	...	4-...	29.1	21	9	8	2	9-1	32	.212
— Detroit (A.L.)	2	4	.333	6.04	2.06	45	0	0	0	4	5-7	44.2	47	32	30	5	45-3	41	.260
Major League totals (2 years)	**3**	**4**	**.429**	**5.26**	**1.89**	**52**	**0**	**0**	**0**	**5**	**6-8**	**51.1**	**50**	**32**	**30**	**5**	**47-4**	**47**	**.260**

G

GERUT, JODY — OF

PERSONAL: Born September 18, 1977, in Elmhurst, Ill. ... 6-0/190. ... Bats left, throws left. ... Full name: Joseph Gerut. ... Name pronounced: GARE-et. ... High school: Willowbrook (Ill.). ... College: Stanford.
TRANSACTIONS/CAREER NOTES: Selected by Colorado Rockies organization in second round of free-agent draft (June 2, 1998). ... Traded by Rockies with C Josh Bard to Cleveland Indians for OF Jacob Cruz (June 1, 2001).
2003 GAMES PLAYED BY POSITION (MLB): OF—113, DH—11.

Year Team (League)	Pos.	G	AB	R	H	2B	3B	HR	RBI	BB	SO	HBP	GDP	SB-CS	Avg.	OBP	SLG	OPS	E	Pct.
1999— Salem (Caro.)	OF	133	499	80	144	33	11	11	63	61	65	3	10	25-12	.289	.367	.465	.832	7	.970
2000— Carolina (Sou.)	OF	109	362	48	103	32	3	3	57	76	54	2	9	18-11	.285	.405	.414	.819	4	.977
2001—								Did not play.												
2002— Akron (East.)	OF	65	256	44	72	15	2	9	39	34	30	1	7	17-8	.281	.368	.461	.829	3	.979
— Buffalo (Int'l)	OF	55	183	31	59	7	2	1	21	23	20	1	6	3-5	.322	.401	.399	.800	1	.993
2003— Buffalo (Int'l)	OF-DH	17	65	13	18	5	0	5	19	11	11	0	1	4-0	.277	.377	.585	.961	0	1.000
— Cleveland (A.L.)	OF-DH	127	480	66	134	33	2	22	75	35	70	7	13	4-5	.279	.336	.494	.830	4	.984
Major League totals (1 year)		127	480	66	134	33	2	22	75	35	70	7	13	4-5	.279	.336	.494	.830	4	.984

GIAMBI, JASON — 1B

PERSONAL: Born January 8, 1971, in West Covina, Calif. ... 6-3/230. ... Bats left, throws right. ... Full name: Jason Gilbert Giambi. ... Name pronounced: gee-OM-bee. ... High school: South Hills (West Covina, Calif.). ... College: Long Beach State.
TRANSACTIONS/CAREER NOTES: Selected by Milwaukee Brewers organization in 43rd round of free-agent draft (June 5, 1989); did not sign. ... Selected by Oakland Athletics organization in second round of free-agent draft (June 1, 1992). ... On disabled list (July 27-August 28, 1993). ... On Huntsville disabled list (April 7-14, 1994). ... Granted free agency (November 5, 2001). ... Signed by New York Yankees (December 18, 2001).
2003 GAMES PLAYED BY POSITION (MLB): 1B—85, DH—69.

Year Team (League)	Pos.	G	AB	R	H	2B	3B	HR	RBI	BB	SO	HBP	GDP	SB-CS	Avg.	OBP	SLG	OPS	E	Pct.
1992— S. Oregon (N'west)	3B	13	41	9	13	3	0	3	13	9	6	0	0	1-1	.317	.440	.610	1.050	1	.962
1993— Modesto (Calif.)	3B	89	313	72	91	16	2	12	60	73	47	10	12	2-3	.291	.436	.470	.906	19	.911
1994— Huntsville (Sou.)	3B-1B	56	193	31	43	9	0	6	30	27	31	2	8	0-0	.223	.319	.363	.681	11	.945
— Tacoma (PCL)	3B-SS	52	176	28	56	20	0	4	38	25	32	0	1	1-0	.318	.388	.500	.888	8	.949
1995— Edmonton (PCL)	3B-DH-1B	55	190	34	65	26	1	3	41	34	26	2	4	0-0	.342	.441	.537	.978	9	.938
— Oakland (A.L.)	3B-1B-DH	54	176	27	45	7	0	6	25	28	31	3	4	2-1	.256	.364	.398	.761	4	.984
1996— Oakland (A.L.)	1-0-3-D	140	536	84	156	40	1	20	79	51	95	5	15	0-1	.291	.355	.481	.836	11	.982
1997— Oakland (A.L.)	OF-1B-DH	142	519	66	152	41	2	20	81	55	89	6	11	0-1	.293	.362	.495	.857	7	.987
1998— Oakland (A.L.)	1B-DH	153	562	92	166	28	0	27	110	81	102	5	16	2-2	.295	.384	.489	.873	* 14	.990
1999— Oakland (A.L.)	1B-DH-3B	158	575	115	181	36	1	33	123	105	106	7	11	1-1	.315	.422	.553	.975	7	.995
2000— Oakland (A.L.)	1B-DH	152	510	108	170	29	1	43	137	* 137	96	9	9	2-0	.333	*.476	.647	1.123	6	.995
2001— Oakland (A.L.)	1B-DH	154	520	109	178	* 47	2	38	120	* 129	83	13	17	2-0	.342	*.477	*.660	1.137	11	.992
2002— New York (A.L.)	1B-DH	155	560	120	176	34	1	41	122	109	112	15	18	2-2	.314	.435	.598	1.034	4	.995
2003— New York (A.L.)	1B-DH	156	535	97	134	25	0	41	107	* 129	*140	*21	9	2-1	.250	.412	.527	.939	4	.995
Major League totals (9 years)		1264	4493	818	1358	287	8	269	904	824	854	84	110	13-9	.302	.415	.549	.964	68	.992

GIAMBI, JEREMY — 1B/OF

PERSONAL: Born September 30, 1974, in San Jose, Calif. ... 5-11/216. ... Bats left, throws left. ... Full name: Jeremy Dean Giambi. ... Name pronounced: gee-OM-bee. ... High school: South Hills (West Covina, Calif.). ... College: Cal State Fullerton.
TRANSACTIONS/CAREER NOTES: Selected by Detroit Tigers organization in 44th round of free-agent draft (June 1, 1995); did not sign. ... Selected by Kansas City Royals organization in sixth round of free-agent draft (June 4, 1996). ... On Omaha disabled list (July 12-August 2, 1998). ... On Kansas City disabled list (March 27-May 15, 1999); included rehabilitation assignment to Omaha (April 28-May 15). ... Traded by Royals to Oakland Athletics for P Brett Laxton (February 18, 2000). ... On Oakland disabled list (August 22-September 8, 2000); included rehabilitation assignment to Sacramento (May 25-June 9). ... Traded by A's to Philadelphia Phillies for OF/3B John Mabry (May 22, 2002). ... Traded by Phillies to Boston Red Sox for P Josh Hancock (December 15, 2002). ... Placed on 15-day disabled list by Boston Red Sox (June 22, 2003). ... Sent to Pawtucket on rehab assignment (July 2, 2003). ... Recalled from Pawtucket rehab assignment; reinstated from 15-day disabled list (July 17, 2003). ... Placed on 15-day disabled list (August 2, 2003).
2003 GAMES PLAYED BY POSITION (MLB): DH—30, OF—11.

Year Team (League)	Pos.	G	AB	R	H	2B	3B	HR	RBI	BB	SO	HBP	GDP	SB-CS	Avg.	OBP	SLG	OPS	E	Pct.
1996— Spokane (N'west)	OF	67	231	* 58	63	17	0	6	39	* 61	32	8	5	22-5	.273	.440	.424	.864	* 11	.901
1997— Lansing (Midw.)	OF	31	116	33	39	11	1	5	21	23	16	2	1	5-1	.336	.451	.578	1.028	0	1.000
— Wichita (Texas)	1B-OF	74	268	50	86	15	1	11	52	44	47	6	7	4-4	.321	.422	.507	.930	3	.975
1998— Omaha (PCL)	1B-OF	96	325	68	121	21	2	20	66	57	64	6	4	8-5	.372	.469	.634	1.103	3	.975
— Kansas City (A.L.)	OF-DH	18	58	6	13	4	0	2	8	11	9	0	3	0-1	.224	.343	.397	.739	0	1.000
1999— Omaha (PCL)	OF-1B-DH	35	127	31	44	5	1	12	28	31	30	1	2	1-1	.346	.472	.685	1.157	2	.988
— Kansas City (A.L.)	DH-1B-OF	90	288	34	82	13	1	3	34	40	67	3	7	0-0	.285	.373	.368	.741	2	.991
2000— Sacramento (PCL)	OF-1B	8	31	8	11	2	0	2	8	8	7	0	1	1-1	.355	.487	.613	1.100	1	.960
— Oakland (A.L.)	OF-DH-1B	104	260	42	66	10	2	10	50	32	61	3	7	0-0	.254	.338	.423	.761	3	.980
2001— Oakland (A.L.)	DH-OF-1B	124	371	64	105	26	0	12	57	63	83	4	13	0-1	.283	.391	.460	.841	5	.962
— Sacramento (PCL)	OF	9	27	1	9	1	0	0	1	1	6	0	1	0-0	.333	.357	.370	.728	0	1.000
2002— Oakland (A.L.)	OF-DH	42	157	26	43	7	0	8	17	27	40	3	4	0-0	.274	.390	.471	.862	1	.984
— Philadelphia (N.L.)	1B-OF-DH	82	156	32	38	10	0	12	28	52	54	1	1	0-1	.244	.435	.538	.974	4	.981
2003— Pawtucket (Int'l)	DH	10	35	6	8	4	0	1	4	7	15	0	0	0-0	.229	.357	.429	.786	0	.000
— Boston (A.L.)	DH-OF	50	127	15	25	5	0	5	15	26	42	2	3	1-0	.197	.342	.354	.696	1	.944
American League totals (6 years)		428	1261	187	334	65	3	40	181	199	302	15	37	1-2	.265	.369	.416	.785	12	.980
National League totals (1 year)		82	156	32	38	10	0	12	28	52	54	1	1	0-1	.244	.435	.538	.974	4	.981
Major League totals (6 years)		510	1417	219	372	75	3	52	209	251	356	16	38	1-3	.263	.377	.430	.807	16	.980

GIBBONS, JAY — OF/1B

PERSONAL: Born March 2, 1977, in Rochester, Mich. ... 6-0/193. ... Bats left, throws left. ... Full name: Jay Jonathon Gibbons. ... High school: Mayfair (Lakewood, Calif.). ... College: Cal State Los Angeles.

G

TRANSACTIONS/CAREER NOTES: Selected by Toronto Blue Jays organization in 14th round of free-agent draft (June 4, 1998). ... Selected by Baltimore Orioles from Blue Jays organization in Rule 5 major league draft (December 11, 2000). ... On disabled list (August 5, 2001-remainder of season).

2003 GAMES PLAYED BY POSITION (MLB): OF—144, 1B—13, DH—5.

Year Team (League)	Pos.	G	AB	R	H	2B	3B	HR	RBI	BB	SO	HBP	GDP	SB-CS	Avg.	OBP	SLG	OPS	E	Pct.
1998— Medicine Hat (Pio.)	1B	73	290	66	* 115	* 29	1	* 19	* 98	37	25	3	7	2-1	.397	.457	.700	1.157	6	.983
1999— Hagerstown (SAL)	1B-OF	71	292	53	89	20	2	16	69	32	56	1	12	3-0	.305	.370	.551	.921	6	.975
— Dunedin (Fla. St.)	1B	60	212	34	66	14	0	9	39	25	38	0	4	2-1	.311	.382	.505	.887	5	.991
2000— Tennessee (Sou.)	1B-OF	132	474	85	152	38	1	19	75	61	67	10	10	3-1	.321	.404	.525	.929	8	.991
2001— Baltimore (A.L.) DH-OF-1B	73	225	27	53	10	0	15	36	17	39	4	7	0-1	.236	.301	.480	.781	0	1.000
2002— Baltimore (A.L.) OF-1B-DH	136	490	71	121	29	1	28	69	45	66	2	9	1-3	.247	.311	.482	.792	2	.995
2003— Baltimore (A.L.) OF-1B-DH	160	625	80	173	39	2	23	100	49	89	3	12	0-1	.277	.330	.456	.786	6	.985
Major League totals (3 years)		369	1340	178	347	78	3	66	205	111	194	9	28	1-5	.259	.318	.469	.787	8	.991

GIL, BENJI   IF

PERSONAL: Born October 6, 1972, in Tijuana, Mexico. ... 6-2/210. ... Bats right, throws right. ... Full name: Romar Benjamin Gil. ... Name pronounced: GILL. ... High school: Castle Park (Chula Vista, Calif.).

TRANSACTIONS/CAREER NOTES: Selected by Texas Rangers organization in first round (19th pick overall) of free-agent draft (June 3, 1991). ... On Texas disabled list (March 22-May 22, 1996); included rehabilitation assigments to Charlotte (May 2-17) and Oklahoma City (May 17-21). ... Traded by Rangers to Chicago White Sox for P Al Levine and P Larry Thomas (December 19, 1997). ... On disabled list (August 12-20, 1998). ... Selected by Florida Marlins organization from White Sox organization in Rule 5 minor league draft (December 15, 1998). ... Granted free agency (October 15, 1999). ... Signed by Anaheim Angels organization (February 1, 2000). ... On Anaheim disabled list (April 5-May 30, 2002); included rehabilitation assignment to Salt Lake (May 24-30). ... Designated for assignment by Anaheim (August 9, 2003). ... Released by Anaheim (August 18, 2003). ... Signed to minor league contract by Cleveland Indians organization (August 24, 2003).

2003 GAMES PLAYED BY POSITION (MLB): 2B—28, SS—20, 1B—5, 3B—4, DH—2.

Year Team (League)	Pos.	G	AB	R	H	2B	3B	HR	RBI	BB	SO	HBP	GDP	SB-CS	Avg.	OBP	SLG	OPS	E	Pct.
1991— Butte (Pio.)	SS	32	129	25	37	4	3	2	15	14	36	0	0	9-3	.287	.354	.411	.765	14	.914
1992— Gastonia (S. Atl.)	SS	132	482	75	132	21	1	9	55	50	106	3	16	26-13	.274	.343	.378	.721	45	.931
1993— Texas (A.L.)	SS	22	57	3	7	0	0	0	2	5	22	0	0	1-2	.123	.194	.123	.316	5	.954
— Tulsa (Texas)	SS	101	342	45	94	9	1	17	59	35	89	7	9	20-12	.275	.351	.456	.808	19	.959
1994— Okla. City (A.A.)	SS	* 139	487	62	121	20	6	10	55	33	120	4	9	14-8	.248	.298	.376	.674	* 37	.944
1995— Texas (A.L.)	SS	130	415	36	91	20	3	9	46	26	147	1	5	2-4	.219	.266	.347	.613	17	.974
1996— Charlotte (Fla. St.)	SS-DH	11	31	2	8	6	0	1	7	3	7	0	0	0-0	.258	.324	.548	.872	2	.931
— Okla. City (A.A.)	SS	84	292	32	65	15	1	6	28	21	90	2	10	4-6	.223	.277	.342	.619	21	.949
— Texas (A.L.)	SS	5	5	0	2	0	0	0	1	1	1	0	0	0-1	.400	.500	.400	.900	1	.923
1997— Texas (A.L.)	SS-DH	110	317	35	71	13	2	5	31	17	96	1	3	1-2	.224	.263	.325	.587	19	.963
1998— Calgary (PCL) ....SS-DH-OF	128	460	80	114	24	5	14	69	41	90	4	9	11-4	.248	.311	.413	.724	30	.941
1999— Calgary (PCL) ....SS-OF	116	412	74	115	29	1	17	64	27	101	7	5	17-5	.279	.332	.478	.810	29	.944
2000— Anaheim (A.L.) S-2-D-1	110	301	28	72	14	1	6	23	30	59	5	7	10-6	.239	.317	.352	.669	18	.961
2001— Anaheim (A.L.) S-2-1-D-O	104	260	33	77	15	4	8	39	14	57	0	6	3-4	.296	.330	.477	.807	14	.961
2002— Anaheim (A.L.) 2-S-D-1	61	130	11	37	8	1	3	20	5	33	0	0	2-1	.285	.307	.431	.737	4	.955
— Salt Lake (PCL)	2B-SS-1B	6	24	4	10	5	1	2	6	1	4	0	0	0-2	.417	.440	.958	1.398	1	.969
2003— Anaheim (A.L.) 2-S-1-3-D	62	125	12	24	5	1	1	9	4	33	0	5	5-1	.192	.214	.272	.486	6	.967
— Buffalo (Int'l) 2-1-3-S-D	9	36	4	5	1	0	2	6	0	10	0	1	0-0	.139	.139	.333	.472	1	.976
Major League totals (8 years)		604	1610	158	381	75	12	32	171	102	448	7	26	24-21	.237	.283	.358	.641	84	.966

GIL, GERONIMO   C

PERSONAL: Born August 7, 1975, in Oaxaca, Mexico. ... 6-2/227. ... Bats right, throws right. ... Name pronounced: heel.

TRANSACTIONS/CAREER NOTES: Signed by Mexico City Red Devils, Mexican League (1993). ... Contract sold by Mexico City to Los Angeles Dodgers organization (February 15, 1996). ... Traded by Dodgers with P Kris Foster to Baltimore Orioles for P Mike Trombley (July 31, 2001). ... Optioned to Ottawa by Baltimore (July 20, 2003). ... Recalled by Baltimore from Ottawa (September 9, 2003).

2003 GAMES PLAYED BY POSITION (MLB): C—53.

Year Team (League)	Pos.	G	AB	R	H	2B	3B	HR	RBI	BB	SO	HBP	GDP	SB-CS	Avg.	OBP	SLG	OPS	E	Pct.
1993— M.C. R. Dev. (Mex.)	DH	1	1	0	0	0	0	0	0	0	1	...	...	0-0	.000	...	.000	...	...	...
1994—							Did not play.													
1995— M.C. R. Dev. (Mex.)	OF	4	7	1	2	0	0	0	0	0	1	...	...	0-0	.286	...	.286	...	0	1.000
1996— Savannah (S. Atl.)	C	79	276	29	67	13	1	7	38	8	69	5	4	0-2	.243	.274	.373	.647	10	.983
1997— Vero Beach (FSL)	C	66	213	30	53	13	1	6	24	15	41	4	5	3-0	.249	.310	.404	.714	13	.975
1998— San Antonio (Texas)	C-1B-OF	75	241	27	70	17	3	6	29	15	43	0	8	2-1	.290	.329	.461	.790	9	.972
1999— San Antonio (Texas)	3-C-1-OF	106	343	47	97	26	1	15	59	49	58	2	15	2-0	.283	.372	.496	.867	9	.986
2000— San Antonio (Texas)	3-C-1-OF	100	352	42	100	19	1	11	58	33	65	6	8	3-2	.284	.351	.438	.789	8	.988
— Albuquerque (PCL)	3B-C-OF	15	50	9	19	5	0	2	22	5	8	0	1	0-1	.380	.421	.600	1.021	3	.959
2001— Las Vegas (PCL)	C-1B-SS	82	281	40	83	15	0	9	40	16	56	2	9	0-1	.295	.334	.445	.779	3	.995
— Rochester (Int'l)	C	23	82	7	22	6	1	2	14	0	23	1	1	0-0	.268	.271	.439	.710	3	.986
— Baltimore (A.L.)	C	17	58	3	17	2	0	0	6	5	7	2	1	0-0	.293	.369	.328	.697	2	.985
2002— Baltimore (A.L.)	C	125	422	33	98	19	0	12	45	21	88	1	17	2-2	.232	.270	.363	.632	4	.995
2003— Ottawa (Int'l)	C-DH-1B	36	134	15	47	10	0	1	17	7	28	2	2	0-3	.351	.386	.448	.834	2	.992
— Baltimore (A.L.)	C	54	169	22	40	4	0	3	16	12	34	3	2	0-0	.237	.299	.314	.613	6	.984
Major League totals (3 years)		196	649	58	155	25	0	15	67	38	129	6	20	2-2	.239	.287	.347	.633	12	.991

GILES, BRIAN   OF

PERSONAL: Born January 20, 1971, in El Cajon, Calif. ... 5-10/205. ... Bats left, throws left. ... Full name: Brian Stephen Giles. ... Name pronounced: JYLES. ... High school: Granite Hills (El Cajon, Calif.).

TRANSACTIONS/CAREER NOTES: Selected by Cleveland Indians organization in 17th round of free-agent draft (June 5, 1989). ... On Canton/Akron disabled list (May 15-July 7, 1992). ... On Cleveland disabled list (June 1-July 7, 1998); included rehabilitation assignment to Buffalo (June 23-July 7). ... Traded by Indians to Pittsburgh Pirates for P Ricardo Rincon (November 18, 1998). ... On disabled list (April 11, 2003). ... Reinstated from 15-day disabled list (May 7, 2003). ... Traded by Pittsburgh Pirates to San Diego Padres for P Oliver Perez, OF Jason Bay and a player to be named (August 26, 2003).

2003 GAMES PLAYED BY POSITION (MLB): OF—134.

G

Year — Team (League)	Pos.	G	AB	R	H	2B	3B	HR	RBI	BB	SO	HBP	GDP	SB-CS	Avg.	OBP	SLG	OPS	E	Pct.
1989— Burlington (Appal.)	OF	36	129	18	40	7	0	0	20	11	19	1	0	6-3	.310	.366	.364	.731	1	.982
1990— Watertown (NYP)	OF	70	246	44	71	15	2	1	23	48	23	0	3	11-8	.289	.403	.378	.781	1	.991
1991— Kinston (Caro.)	OF	125	394	71	122	14	0	4	47	68	70	2	5	19-7	.310	.411	.376	.787	5	.975
1992— Cant./Akr. (Eastern)	OF	23	74	6	16	4	0	0	3	10	10	0	4	3-1	.216	.310	.270	.580	0	1.000
— Kinston (Caro.)	OF	42	140	28	37	5	1	3	18	30	21	1	5	3-5	.264	.398	.379	.776	1	.987
1993— Cant./Akr. (Eastern)	OF	123	425	64	139	17	6	6	64	57	43	4	9	18-12	.327	.409	.438	.847	5	.974
1994— Charlotte (Int'l)	OF	128	434	74	136	18	3	16	58	55	61	2	5	8-5	.313	.390	.479	.869	4	.984
1995— Buffalo (A.A.)	OF-DH	123	413	67	128	18	•8	15	67	54	40	8	9	7-3	.310	.395	.501	.896	5	.981
— Cleveland (A.L.)	OF-DH	6	9	6	5	0	0	1	3	0	1	0	0	0-0	.556	.556	.889	1.444	0	1.000
1996— Buffalo (A.A.)	OF	83	318	65	100	17	6	20	64	42	29	2	4	1-0	.314	.395	.594	.989	2	.986
— Cleveland (A.L.)	DH-OF	51	121	26	43	14	1	5	27	19	13	0	6	3-0	.355	.434	.612	1.045	0	1.000
1997— Cleveland (A.L.)	OF-DH	130	377	62	101	15	3	17	61	63	50	1	10	13-3	.268	.368	.459	.827	6	.972
1998— Cleveland (A.L.)	OF-DH	112	350	56	94	19	0	16	66	73	75	3	7	10-5	.269	.396	.460	.856	5	.978
— Buffalo (Int'l)	OF-DH	13	46	5	11	2	0	2	7	6	8	0	2	0-0	.239	.327	.413	.740	1	.947
1999— Pittsburgh (N.L.)	OF-DH	141	521	109	164	33	3	39	115	95	80	3	14	6-2	.315	.418	.614	1.032	3	.990
2000— Pittsburgh (N.L.)	OF	156	559	111	176	37	7	35	123	114	69	7	15	6-0	.315	.432	.594	1.026	6	.982
2001— Pittsburgh (N.L.)	OF	160	576	116	178	37	7	37	95	90	67	4	10	13-6	.309	.404	.590	.994	10	.969
2002— Pittsburgh (N.L.)	OF	153	497	95	148	37	5	38	103	135	74	7	10	15-6	.298	.450	.622	1.072	7	.973
2003— Pittsburgh (N.L.)	OF	105	388	70	116	30	4	16	70	85	48	6	8	0-3	.299	.430	.521	.951	2	.992
— San Diego (N.L.)	OF	29	104	23	31	4	2	4	18	20	10	2	4	4-0	.298	.414	.490	.904	2	.966
American League totals (4 years)		299	857	150	243	48	4	39	157	155	139	4	23	26-8	.284	.391	.485	.876	11	.976
National League totals (5 years)		744	2645	524	813	178	28	169	524	539	348	29	61	44-17	.307	.426	.588	1.013	30	.980
Major League totals (9 years)		1043	3502	674	1056	226	32	208	681	694	487	33	84	70-25	.302	.417	.563	.980	41	.979

GILES, MARCUS · 2B

PERSONAL: Born May 18, 1978, in San Diego, Calif. ... 5-8/180. ... Bats right, throws right. ... Full name: Marcus William Giles. ... Name pronounced: JYLES. ... High school: Granite Hills (Calif.). ... Junior college: Grossmont College (Calif.).

TRANSACTIONS/CAREER NOTES: Selected by Atlanta Braves organization in 53rd round of free-agent draft (June 4, 1996). ... On Atlanta disabled list (May 29-July 16, 2002); included rehabilitation assignment to Richmond (June 28-July 16).

2003 GAMES PLAYED BY POSITION (MLB): 2B—139.

Year — Team (League)	Pos.	G	AB	R	H	2B	3B	HR	RBI	BB	SO	HBP	GDP	SB-CS	Avg.	OBP	SLG	OPS	E	Pct.
1997— Danville (Appal.)	2B	55	207	53	72	13	3	8	45	32	47	3	4	5-2	.348	.437	.556	.992	7	.962
1998— Macon (S. Atl.)	2B	135	505	*111	166	38	3	*37	*108	*85	103	10	15	12-5	.329	.433	.636	1.068	25	.954
1999— Myrtle Beach (Caro.)	2B	126	497	80	*162	*40	4	13	73	54	89	4	9	9-6	.326	.393	.513	.906	8	.985
2000— Greenville (Sou.)	2B	132	458	73	133	28	2	17	62	72	71	2	11	25-5	.290	.388	.472	.860	18	.973
2001— Richmond (Int'l)	2-S-3-O	67	252	48	84	19	1	6	44	22	48	2	4	13-5	.333	.387	.488	.875	8	.975
— Atlanta (N.L.)	2B	68	244	36	64	10	2	9	31	28	37	0	8	2-5	.262	.338	.430	.769	6	.978
2002— Atlanta (N.L.)	2B-3B	68	213	27	49	10	1	8	23	25	41	2	5	1-1	.230	.315	.399	.714	8	.972
— Richmond (Int'l)	2B-3B	31	115	25	37	6	0	3	16	13	15	0	1	3-0	.322	.385	.452	.837	3	.970
2003— Atlanta (N.L.)	2B	145	551	101	174	49	2	21	69	59	80	11	7	14-4	.316	.390	.526	.917	14	.982
Major League totals (3 years)		281	1008	164	287	69	5	38	123	112	158	13	20	17-10	.285	.362	.476	.838	28	.979

GILFILLAN, JASON · P

PERSONAL: Born August 31, 1976, in Shelby, N.C. ... 6-5/220. ... Throws right, bats right. ... Full name: Jason Edward Gilfillan. ... High school: Blacksburg (S.C.). ... Junior college: Limestone College (S.C.).

TRANSACTIONS/CAREER NOTES: Selected by Kansas City Royals organization in 12th round of free-agent draft (June 3, 1997).

CAREER HITTING: 0-for-0 (.000), 0 R, 0 2B, 0 3B, 0 HR, 0 RBI.

Year — League	W	L	Pct.	ERA	WHIP	G	GS	CG	ShO	Hld.	Sv.-Opp.	IP	H	R	ER	HR	BB-IBB	SO	Avg.
1997— Spokane (N'west)	2	1	.667	5.06	2.00	16	0	0	0	...	0-...	16.0	16	13	9	0	16-1	22	.250
1998— GC Royals (GCL)	1	1	.500	8.00	1.56	7	6	0	0	...	0-...	9.0	10	8	8	1	4-0	6	.270
— Spokane (N'west)	0	0	...	4.91	1.77	6	0	0	0	...	0-...	7.1	7	5	4	0	6-0	8	.259
1999— Char., W.Va. (SAL)	0	1	.000	14.66	2.40	8	0	0	0	...	0-...	11.2	22	21	19	2	6-0	9	.373
— Spokane (N'west)	4	1	.800	5.71	1.53	25	0	0	0	...	1-...	34.2	31	23	22	6	22-0	37	.246
2000— Char., W.Va. (SAL)	1	2	.333	4.20	1.47	30	0	0	0	...	7-...	45.0	45	24	21	3	21-0	44	.259
— Wilmington (Caro.)	3	1	.750	1.76	1.70	12	0	0	0	...	1-...	15.1	13	6	3	0	13-1	20	.217
— Omaha (PCL)	0	0	...	0.00	1.00	1	0	0	0	...	0-...	1.0	0	0	0	0	1-0	2	.000
2001— Wilmington (Caro.)	4	1	.800	0.98	0.95	33	0	0	0	...	9-...	55.0	35	8	6	0	17-1	68	.179
— Wichita (Texas)	0	0	...	6.23	2.08	11	0	0	0	...	0-...	17.1	23	13	12	0	13-2	13	.311
2002— Wichita (Texas)	2	2	.500	2.63	1.65	21	1	0	0	...	0-...	37.2	35	16	11	2	27-5	31	.250
— Omaha (PCL)	2	2	.500	3.69	1.18	33	0	0	0	...	4-...	39.0	32	16	16	5	14-0	28	.232
2003— Kansas City (A.L.)	2	0	1.000	7.71	1.96	13	0	0	0	1	0-1	16.1	22	14	14	3	10-1	12	.310
— Omaha (PCL)	6	0	1.000	2.05	1.10	35	0	0	0	...	7-...	52.2	46	14	12	4	12-0	33	.240
Major League totals (1 year)	2	0	1.000	7.71	1.96	13	0	0	0	1	0-1	16.1	22	14	14	3	10-1	12	.310

G

GINTER, KEITH · 2B/3B

PERSONAL: Born May 5, 1976, in Norwalk, Calif. ... 5-10/195. ... Bats right, throws right. ... Full name: Keith Michael Ginter. ... Name pronounced: GHIN-ter. ... High school: Fullerton Union (Fullerton, Calif.). ... College: Texas Tech.

TRANSACTIONS/CAREER NOTES: Selected by Houston Astros organization in 10th round of free-agent draft (June 2, 1998). ... Traded by Astros to Milwaukee Brewers (September 5, 2002), completing deal in which Brewers traded IF Mark Loretta to Astros for two players to be named later (August 31, 2002); Brewers acquired P Wayne Franklin as partial completion (September 3, 2002).

2003 GAMES PLAYED BY POSITION (MLB): 2B—53, 3B—40, SS—2, OF—2.

Year	Team (League)	Pos.	G	AB	R	H	2B	3B	HR	RBI	BB	SO	HBP	GDP	SB-CS	Avg.	OBP	SLG	OPS	E	Pct.
1998— Auburn (NY-Penn)	2B	71	241	• 55	76	22	1	8	41	* 60	68	7	1	10-7	.315	.461	.515	.976	8	.971
1999— Kissimmee (Fla. St.)	2B	103	376	66	99	15	4	13	46	61	90	12	7	9-10	.263	.381	.428	.810	21	.959
— Jackson (Texas)	2B	9	34	9	13	1	0	1	6	4	6	2	0	0-0	.382	.463	.500	.963	2	.956
2000— Round Rock (Texas)	2B	125	462	108	154	30	3	26	92	82	127	24	9	24-11	.333	.457	.580	1.037	17	.972
— Houston (N.L.)	2B	5	8	3	2	0	0	1	3	1	3	0	0	0-0	.250	.300	.625	.925	0	1.000
2001— New Orleans (PCL)	2B-OF-3B	132	457	76	123	31	5	16	70	61	147	23	6	8-6	.269	.380	.464	.844	12	.975
— Houston (N.L.)		1	1	0	0	0	0	0	0	0	0	0	0	0-0	.000	.000	.000	.000	...	...
2002— New Orleans (PCL)	2B-3B-OF	121	435	70	115	28	1	12	54	56	97	12	7	3-4	.264	.362	.416	.778	22	.952
— Houston (N.L.)	3B-SS	7	5	1	1	1	0	0	0	2	1	1	0	0-0	.200	.500	.400	.900	1	.909
— Milwaukee (N.L.)	3B	21	76	6	18	8	0	1	8	15	14	0	0	0-0	.237	.363	.382	.744	2	.961
2003— Milwaukee (N.L.)	2-3-S-O	127	358	51	92	15	2	14	44	37	87	17	8	1-1	.257	.352	.427	.779	8	.975
Major League totals (4 years)		161	448	61	113	24	2	16	55	55	105	18	8	1-1	.252	.354	.422	.776	11	.972

GINTER, MATT   P

PERSONAL: Born December 24, 1977, in Winchester, Ky. ... 6-1/220. ... Throws right, bats right. ... Full name: Matthew Shane Ginter. ... High school: George Rogers Clark (Winchester, Ky.). ... College: Mississippi State.

TRANSACTIONS/CAREER NOTES: Selected by New York Yankees organization in 17th round of free-agent draft (June 4, 1996); did not sign. ... Selected by Chicago White Sox organization in first round (22nd pick overall) of free-agent draft (June 2, 1999); pick received from New York Mets as compensation for signing Type A free agent 3B Robin Ventura. ... Recalled by Chicago from Charlotte (July 27, 2003). ... Optioned to Charlotte by Chicago (August 8, 2003). ... Recalled by Chicago from Charlotte (September 29, 2003).

CAREER HITTING: 0-for-0 (.000), 0 R, 0 2B, 0 3B, 0 HR, 0 RBI.

Year	League	W	L	Pct.	ERA	WHIP	G	GS	CG	ShO	Hld.	Sv.-Opp.	IP	H	R	ER	HR	BB-IBB	SO	Avg.
1999— Ariz. White Sox (Ariz.)	1	0	1.000	3.24	0.96	3	0	0	0	...	1-...	8.1	5	4	3	0	3-0	10	.172
— Burlington (Midw.)	4	2	.667	4.05	1.43	9	9	0	0	...	0-...	40.0	38	20	18	3	19-0	29	.253
2000— Birmingham (Sou.)	11	8	.579	2.25	1.19	27	26	0	0	...	0-...	179.2	153	72	45	6	60-2	126	.233
— Chicago (A.L.)	1	0	1.000	13.50	2.68	7	0	0	0	0	0-1	9.1	18	14	14	5	7-0	6	.409
2001— Charlotte (Int'l)	2	3	.400	2.59	1.13	22	10	0	0	0	0-...	76.1	62	26	22	3	24-4	67	.219
— Chicago (A.L.)	1	0	1.000	5.22	1.21	20	0	0	0	0	0-0	39.2	34	23	23	2	14-2	24	.238
2002— Charlotte (Int'l)	1	0	1.000	3.94	1.88	13	0	0	0	0	0-...	16.0	20	8	7	3	10-1	9	.313
— Chicago (A.L.)	1	0	1.000	4.47	1.47	33	0	0	0	0	1-1	54.1	59	34	27	6	21-0	37	.278
2003— Chicago (A.L.)	0	0	...	13.50	0.90	3	0	0	0	0	0-0	3.1	2	5	5	1	1-0	0	.182
— Charlotte (Int'l)	3	5	.375	3.03	1.29	49	0	0	0	0	14-...	68.1	66	27	23	2	22-3	52	.249
Major League totals (4 years)	3	0	1.000	5.82	1.46	63	0	0	0	0	1-2	106.2	113	76	69	14	43-2	67	.276

GIPSON, CHARLES   OF/IF

PERSONAL: Born December 16, 1972, in Orange, Calif. ... 6-0/195. ... Bats right, throws right. ... Full name: Charles Wells Gipson. ... High school: Loara (Anaheim, Calif.). ... Junior college: Cypress College (Calif.).

TRANSACTIONS/CAREER NOTES: Selected by Seattle Mariners organization in 63rd round of free-agent draft (June 3, 1991). ... On disabled list (May 4-19, 1993). ... On Seattle disabled list (July 11-September 1, 1999); included rehabilitation assignments to New Haven (August 14-21) and Everett (August 22-September 1). ... Granted free agency (December 21, 2002). ... Signed by Chicago Cubs organization (January 21, 2003). ... Released by Cubs (2003). ... Signed by New York Yankees as a free agent (April 17, 2003). ... Elected free agency (September 29, 2003).

2003 GAMES PLAYED BY POSITION (MLB): OF—8, DH—3.

Year	Team (League)	Pos.	G	AB	R	H	2B	3B	HR	RBI	BB	SO	HBP	GDP	SB-CS	Avg.	OBP	SLG	OPS	E	Pct.
1992— Ariz. Mariners (Ariz.)	SS	39	124	30	39	2	0	0	14	13	19	6	0	11-5	.315	.403	.331	.734	• 23	.876
1993— Appleton (Midwest)	2B-SS-OF	109	348	53	89	13	1	0	20	61	76	27	3	21-15	.256	.405	.299	.704	28	.933
1994— Riverside (Calif.)	OF	128	481	* 102	141	12	3	1	41	76	67	12	8	34-15	.293	.401	.337	.738	9	.972
1995— Port City (Sou.)	2B-OF	112	391	36	87	11	2	0	29	30	66	8	13	10-12	.223	.291	.261	.552	6	.977
1996— Port City (Sou.)	SS-OF	119	407	54	109	12	3	1	30	41	62	7	9	15-15	.268	.345	.319	.664	15	.961
1997— Memphis (Sou.)	2-3-S-O	88	320	56	79	9	4	1	28	34	71	13	4	31-6	.247	.342	.309	.652	23	.939
— Tacoma (PCL)	2-3-S-O	11	35	5	11	2	0	0	5	4	3	1	0	0-1	.314	.400	.371	.771	3	.912
1998— Seattle (A.L.)	OF-3B-DH	44	51	11	12	1	0	0	2	5	9	1	1	2-1	.235	.316	.255	.571	2	.957
— Tacoma (PCL)	2-3-S-O	75	278	39	67	16	2	0	11	27	50	6	17	14-11	.241	.322	.313	.634	11	.954
1999— Seattle (A.L.)	O-3-D-2-S	55	80	16	18	5	2	0	9	6	13	1	2	3-4	.225	.287	.338	.625	3	.967
— Tacoma (PCL)	S-O-3-2-D	47	174	26	52	6	3	0	21	14	24	3	5	18-4	.299	.361	.368	.729	9	.940
— New Haven (East.)	2-3-S-D-O	5	18	2	0	0	0	0	0	3	2	0	0	1-0	.000	.143	.000	.143	1	.944
— Everett (N'west)	SS	1	2	0	1	0	1	0	1	2	0	0	0	1-0	.500	.750	1.500	2.250	0	1.000
2000— Seattle (A.L.)	0-3-S-D	59	29	7	9	1	1	0	3	4	9	0	0	2-3	.310	.394	.414	.808	0	1.000
— Tacoma (PCL)	0-3-S-2	67	214	27	53	6	6	1	22	31	38	3	7	16-7	.248	.347	.346	.692	6	.971
2001— Seattle (A.L.)	O-D-3-S-2	94	64	16	14	2	2	0	5	4	20	2	2	1-1	.219	.282	.313	.594	2	.972
2002— Seattle (A.L.)	OF-3B-DH	79	72	22	17	5	2	0	8	9	14	1	3	4-0	.236	.329	.361	.690	2	.972
2003— New York (A.L.)	OF-DH	18	10	3	2	0	0	0	2	1	2	0	0	2-1	.200	.273	.200	.473	0	1.000
— Columbus (Int'l)	OF-3B-2B	31	120	17	33	6	1	0	5	9	18	5	1	5-6	.275	.351	.342	.692	3	.972
Major League totals (6 years)		349	306	75	72	14	7	0	29	29	67	5	8	14-10	.235	.311	.327	.638	9	.972

GIRARDI, JOE   C

PERSONAL: Born October 14, 1964, in Peoria, Ill. ... 5-11/200. ... Bats right, throws right. ... Full name: Joseph Elliott Girardi. ... Name pronounced: jeh-RAR-dee. ... High school: Spalding Institute (Peoria, Ill.). ... College: Northwestern.

TRANSACTIONS/CAREER NOTES: Selected by Chicago Cubs organization in fifth round of free-agent draft (June 2, 1986). ... On disabled list (August 27, 1986-remainder of season; and August 7, 1988-remainder of season). ... On Chicago disabled list (April 17-August 6, 1991); included rehabilitation assignment to Iowa (July 23-August 6). ... Selected by Colorado Rockies in first round (19th pick overall) of expansion draft (November 17, 1992). ... On Colorado disabled list (June 5-August 11, 1993); included rehabilitation assignment to Colorado Springs (August 1-11). ... On disabled list (July 11-26, 1994). ... Traded by Rockies to New York Yankees for P Mike DeJean and a player to be named later (November 20, 1995); Rockies acquired P Steve Shoemaker to complete deal (December 6, 1995). ... Granted free agency (November 5, 1996). ... Re-signed by Yankees (December 3, 1996). ... Granted free agency (November 5, 1999). ... Signed by Cubs (December 15, 1999). ... On disabled list (July 17-August 1, 2002). ... Granted free agency (October 28, 2002). ... Signed by St. Louis Cardinals (December 18, 2002). ... On disabled list (March 21, 2003). ... Transferred to Emergency disabled list (May 13, 2003). ... Activated from the 60-day disabled list; recalled from Tennessee rehab assignment (June 10, 2003). ... Placed on 15-day disabled list (June 30, 2003). ... Sent to Memphis on rehab assignment (July 29, 2003). ... Recalled from Memphis (August 7, 2003). ... Sent to Memphis on rehab assignment (August 11, 2003). ... Recalled from Memphis rehab assignment (August 30, 2003). ... Removed from 15-day disabled list (September 1, 2003).

2003 GAMES PLAYED BY POSITION (MLB): C—13.

G

Year	Team (League)	Pos.	G	AB	R	H	2B	3B	HR	RBI	BB	SO	HBP	GDP	SB-CS	Avg.	OBP	SLG	OPS	E	Pct.
1986— Peoria (Midw.)	C	68	230	36	71	13	1	3	28	17	36	3	8	6-3	.309	.360	.413	.773	5	.989
1987— Win.-Salem (Car.)	C	99	364	51	102	9	8	8	46	33	64	2	11	9-2	.280	.343	.415	.757	18	.973
1988— Pittsfield (East.)	C-OF	104	357	44	97	14	1	7	41	29	51	3	10	7-4	.272	.330	.375	.705	6 ‡	.989
1989— Chicago (N.L.)	C	59	157	15	39	10	0	1	14	11	26	2	4	2-1	.248	.304	.331	.635	7	.981
— Iowa (Am. Assoc.)	C	32	110	12	27	4	2	2	11	5	19	0	0	3-1	.245	.278	.373	.651	1	.995
1990— Chicago (N.L.)	C	133	419	36	113	24	2	1	38	17	50	3	13	8-3	.270	.300	.344	.644	11	.985
1991— Chicago (N.L.)	C	21	47	3	9	2	0	0	6	6	6	0	0	0-0	.191	.283	.234	.517	3	.972
— Iowa (Am. Assoc.)	C	12	36	3	8	1	0	0	4	4	8	0	0	2-0	.222	.300	.250	.550	3	.957
1992— Chicago (N.L.)	C	91	270	19	73	3	1	1	12	19	38	1	8	0-2	.270	.320	.300	.620	4	.991
1993— Colorado (N.L.)	C	86	310	35	90	14	5	3	31	24	41	3	6	6-6	.290	.346	.397	.743	6	.989
— Colo. Springs (PCL)	C	8	31	6	15	1	1	1	6	0	3	0	0	1-0	.484	.484	.677	1.161	1	.977
1994— Colorado (N.L.)	C	93	330	47	91	9	4	4	34	21	48	2	13	3-3	.276	.321	.364	.685	5	.992
1995— Colorado (N.L.)	C	125	462	63	121	17	2	8	55	29	76	2	15	3-3	.262	.308	.359	.667	10	.988
1996— New York (A.L.)	C-DH	124	422	55	124	22	3	2	45	30	55	5	11	13-4	.294	.346	.374	.720	3	.996
1997— New York (A.L.)	C	112	398	38	105	23	1	1	50	26	53	2	15	2-3	.264	.311	.334	.645	5	.994
1998— New York (A.L.)	C	78	254	31	70	11	4	3	31	14	38	2	10	2-4	.276	.317	.386	.703	3	.995
1999— New York (A.L.)	C	65	209	23	50	16	1	2	27	10	26	0	16	3-1	.239	.271	.354	.626	8	.984
2000— Chicago (N.L.)	C	106	363	47	101	15	1	6	40	32	61	3	12	1-0	.278	.339	.375	.714	5	.993
2001— Chicago (N.L.)	C	78	229	22	58	10	1	3	25	21	50	0	2	0-1	.253	.315	.345	.660	0	1.000
2002— Chicago (N.L.)	C	90	234	19	53	10	1	1	13	16	35	0	10	1-0	.226	.275	.291	.565	6	.990
2003— Peoria (Midw.)	C-DH	3	9	0	1	0	0	0	1	0	2	1	0	0-0	.111	.200	.111	.311	0	1.000
— Tennessee (Sou.)	C	3	10	0	4	0	0	0	1	0	1	0	1	0-1	.400	.455	.400	.855	0	1.000
— Memphis (PCL)	C	18	65	3	19	1	0	0	4	5	6	1	4	0-0	.292	.352	.308	.660	0	1.000
— St. Louis (N.L.)	C	16	23	1	3	0	0	0	1	3	4	0	2	0-0	.130	.231	.130	.361	1	.958
American League totals (4 years)		379	1283	147	349	72	9	8	153	80	172	9	52	20-12	.272	.317	.361	.678	19	.993
National League totals (11 years)		898	2844	307	751	114	17	28	269	199	435	16	85	24-19	.264	.314	.346	.660	58	.989
Major League totals (15 years)		1277	4127	454	1100	186	26	36	422	279	607	25	137	44-31	.267	.315	.350	.666	77	.991

GLANVILLE, DOUG — OF

PERSONAL: Born August 25, 1970, in Hackensack, N.J. ... 6-2/174. ... Bats right, throws right. ... Full name: Douglas Metunwa Glanville. ... High school: Teaneck (N.J.). ... College: Pennsylvania.

TRANSACTIONS/CAREER NOTES: Selected by Chicago Cubs organization in first round (12th pick overall) of free-agent draft (June 3, 1991). ... Traded by Cubs to Philadelphia Phillies for 2B Mickey Morandini (December 23, 1997). ... Granted free agency (October 29, 2002). ... Signed by Texas Rangers (December 18, 2002). ... Placed on the 15-day disabled list (April 15, 2003). ... Traded by Rangers to Chicago Cubs for OF Jason Fransz and cash (July 30, 2003).

2003 GAMES PLAYED BY POSITION (MLB): OF—70.

Year	Team (League)	Pos.	G	AB	R	H	2B	3B	HR	RBI	BB	SO	HBP	GDP	SB-CS	Avg.	OBP	SLG	OPS	E	Pct.
1991— Geneva (NY-Penn)	OF	36	152	29	46	8	0	2	12	11	25	1	1	17-3	.303	.352	.395	.746	0	1.000
1992— Win.-Salem (Car.)	OF	120	485	72	125	18	4	4	36	40	78	4	6	32-9	.258	.318	.336	.654	7	.978
1993— Daytona (Fla. St.)	OF	61	239	47	70	10	1	2	21	28	24	3	2	18-15	.293	.374	.368	.742	7	.950
— Orlando (South.)	OF	73	296	42	78	14	4	9	40	12	41	2	1	15-7	.264	.292	.429	.721	5	.972
1994— Orlando (South.)	OF	130	483	53	127	22	2	5	52	24	49	5	7	26-20	.263	.301	.348	.648	3	.991
1995— Iowa (Am. Assoc.)	OF-DH	112	419	48	113	16	2	4	37	16	64	3	4	13-9	.270	.299	.346	.645	4	.982
1996— Iowa (Am. Assoc.)	OF-DH	90	373	53	115	23	3	3	34	12	35	2	2	15-10	.308	.331	.410	.741	3	.987
— Chicago (N.L.)	OF	49	83	10	20	5	1	1	10	3	11	0	0	2-0	.241	.264	.361	.626	1	.973
1997— Chicago (N.L.)	OF	146	474	79	142	22	5	4	35	24	46	1	9	19-11	.300	.333	.392	.726	3	.989
1998— Philadelphia (N.L.)	OF	158	*678	106	189	28	7	8	49	42	89	6	7	23-6	.279	.325	.376	.701	2	.995
1999— Philadelphia (N.L.)	OF	150	628	101	204	38	6	11	73	48	82	6	9	34-2	.325	.376	.457	.833	8	.980
2000— Philadelphia (N.L.)	OF	154	637	89	175	27	6	8	52	31	76	2	11	31-8	.275	.307	.374	.681	4	.990
2001— Philadelphia (N.L.)	OF	153	634	74	166	24	3	14	55	19	91	4	7	28-6	.262	.285	.375	.660	4	.991
2002— Philadelphia (N.L.)	OF	138	422	49	105	16	3	6	29	25	57	2	5	19-2	.249	.292	.344	.636	0	1.000
2003— Oklahoma (PCL)	OF-DH	9	37	4	6	0	0	0	3	2	3	1	1	1-0	.162	.225	.162	.387	0	1.000
— Frisco (Texas)	OF	4	15	2	2	0	0	0	0	1	4	0	0	0-0	.133	.188	.133	.321	1	.875
— Texas (A.L.)	OF	52	195	22	53	5	0	4	14	6	25	0	2	4-0	.272	.294	.359	.653	0	1.000
— Chicago (N.L.)	OF	28	51	2	12	0	0	1	2	2	4	0	0	0-1	.235	.259	.294	.553	0	1.000
American League totals (1 year)		52	195	22	53	5	0	4	14	6	25	0	2	4-0	.272	.294	.359	.653	0	1.000
National League totals (8 years)		976	3607	510	1013	160	31	53	305	194	456	21	48	156-36	.281	.319	.386	.705	22	.990
Major League totals (8 years)		1028	3802	532	1066	165	31	57	319	200	481	21	50	160-36	.280	.318	.385	.703	22	.990

GLAUS, TROY — 3B

PERSONAL: Born August 3, 1976, in Tarzana, Calif. ... 6-5/240. ... Bats right, throws right. ... Full name: Troy Edward Glaus. ... Name pronounced: gloss. ... High school: Carlsbad (Calif.). ... College: UCLA.

TRANSACTIONS/CAREER NOTES: Selected by San Diego Padres organization in second round of free-agent draft (June 2, 1994); did not sign. ... Selected by Anaheim Angels organization in first round (third pick overall) of free-agent draft (June 3, 1997). ... Placed on 15-day disabled list (July 22, 2003). ... Sent to Rancho Cucamonga on rehab assigment (August 5, 2003). ... Recalled from Rancho Cucamonga rehab assignment (August 11, 2003).

2003 GAMES PLAYED BY POSITION (MLB): 3B—87, DH—4.

Year	Team (League)	Pos.	G	AB	R	H	2B	3B	HR	RBI	BB	SO	HBP	GDP	SB-CS	Avg.	OBP	SLG	OPS	E	Pct.
1998— Midland (Texas)	3B	50	188	51	58	11	2	19	51	39	51	2	4	4-2	.309	.430	.691	1.122	11	.925
— Vancouver (PCL)	3B	59	219	33	67	16	0	16	42	21	55	3	1	3-2	.306	.374	.598	.973	13	.932
— Anaheim (A.L.)	3B	48	165	19	36	9	0	1	23	15	51	0	3	1-0	.218	.280	.291	.571	7	.941
1999— Anaheim (A.L.)	3B-DH	154	551	85	132	29	0	29	79	71	143	6	9	5-1	.240	.331	.450	.781	19	.954
2000— Anaheim (A.L.)	3B-SS-DH	159	563	120	160	37	1	*47	102	112	163	2	14	14-11	.284	.404	.604	1.008	‡33	.934
2001— Anaheim (A.L.)	3B-SS-DH	161	588	100	147	38	2	41	108	107	158	6	10	10-3	.250	.367	.531	.898	19	.954
2002— Anaheim (A.L.)	3B-SS	156	569	99	142	24	1	30	111	88	144	6	12	10-3	.250	.352	.453	.805	20	.950
2003— Anaheim (A.L.)	3B-DH	91	319	53	79	17	2	16	50	46	73	1	8	7-2	.248	.343	.464	.807	16	.923
— Rancho Cuca. (Calif.)	DH	2	6	1	2	0	0	0	1	3	2	0	0	0-0	.333	.556	.333	.889	0	.000
Major League totals (6 years)		769	2755	476	696	154	6	164	473	439	732	21	62	47-20	.253	.357	.491	.849	114	.944

G

GLAVINE, MIKE — 1B

PERSONAL: Born January 24, 1973, in Concord, Mass. ... 6-3/210. ... Bats left, throws left. ... Full name: Michael Patrick Glavine. ... High school: Memorial (Billerica, Mass,). ... College: Northeastern (Mass.).

TRANSACTIONS/CAREER NOTES: Selected by Cleveland Indians organization in 22nd round of free-agent draft (June 1995).

2003 GAMES PLAYED BY POSITION (MLB): 1B—3.

Year Team (League)	Pos.	G	AB	R	H	2B	3B	HR	RBI	BB	SO	HBP	GDP	SB-CS	Avg.	OBP	SLG	OPS	FIELDING E	Pct.
1995— Burlington (Appal.)	1B	46	155	28	38	10	0	11	28	22	37	1	0	1-0	.245	.339	.523	.861	3	.990
1996— Columbus (S. Atl.)	1B	38	119	17	33	5	0	6	16	28	33	1	2	0-0	.277	.416	.471	.887	1	.958
1997— Columbus (S. Atl.)	1B	114	397	62	95	16	0	28	75	80	127	3	9	0-1	.239	.370	.491	.861	6	.991
1998— Kinston (Caro.)	1B	125	398	61	87	23	1	22	76	73	117	5	4	1-4	.219	.342	.447	.790	6	.993
1999— Greenville (Sou.)	OF-1B	107	305	47	82	24	0	17	52	49	65	1	3	0-3	.269	.370	.515	.885	5	.991
2000— Greenville (Sou.)	1B-OF	128	423	37	99	26	0	11	81	36	83	5	8	1-1	.234	.297	.374	.671	5	.995
2001— Richmond (Int'l)	1B	23	44	1	6	2	0	0	4	6	11	0	1	0-0	.136	.235	.182	.417	1	.950
2003— Norfolk (Int'l)	1B-DH-OF	79	169	15	45	11	0	5	17	25	36	0	4	0-0	.266	.357	.420	.777	2	.990
— New York (N.L.)	1B	6	7	0	1	0	0	0	0	0	2	0	0	0-0	.143	.143	.143	.286	0	1.000
Major League totals (1 year)		6	7	0	1	0	0	0	0	0	2	0	0	0-0	.143	.143	.143	.286	0	1.000

GLAVINE, TOM — P

PERSONAL: Born March 25, 1966, in Concord, Mass. ... 6-0/185. ... Throws left, bats left. ... Full name: Thomas Michael Glavine. ... Name pronounced: GLA-vin. ... High school: Billerica (Mass.).

TRANSACTIONS/CAREER NOTES: Selected by Atlanta Braves organization in second round of free-agent draft (June 4, 1984). ... Granted free agency (October 28, 2002). ... Signed by New York Mets (December 5, 2002).

CAREER HITTING: 199-for-1077 (.185), 75 R, 21 2B, 2 3B, 1 HR, 72 RBI.

Year League	W	L	Pct.	ERA	WHIP	G	GS	CG	ShO	Hld.	Sv.-Opp.	IP	H	R	ER	HR	BB-IBB	SO	Avg.
1984— GC Braves (GCL)	2	3	.400	3.34	1.30	8	7	0	0	...	0-...	32.1	29	17	12	0	13-0	34	.236
1985— Sumter (S. Atl.)	9	6	.600	* 2.35	1.11	26	26	2	1	...	0-...	168.2	114	58	44	6	73-0	174	.193
1986— Greenville (Sou.)	11	6	.647	3.41	1.37	22	22	2	1	...	0-...	145.1	129	62	55	14	70-3	114	.237
— Richmond (Int'l)	1	5	.167	5.63	1.68	7	7	1	1	...	0-...	40.0	40	29	25	4	27-0	12	.260
1987— Richmond (Int'l)	6	12	.333	3.35	1.32	22	22	4	1	...	0-...	150.1	142	70	56	15	56-3	91	.248
— Atlanta (N.L.)	2	4	.333	5.54	1.75	9	9	0	0	0	0-0	50.1	55	34	31	5	33-4	20	.279
1988— Atlanta (N.L.)	7	* 17	.292	4.56	1.35	34	34	1	0	0	0-0	195.1	201	111	99	12	63-7	84	.270
1989— Atlanta (N.L.)	14	8	.636	3.68	1.14	29	29	6	4	0	0-0	186.0	172	88	76	20	40-3	90	.243
1990— Atlanta (N.L.)	10	12	.455	4.28	1.45	33	33	1	0	0	0-0	214.1	232	111	102	18	78-10	129	.281
1991— Atlanta (N.L.)	• 20	11	.645	2.55	1.09	34	34	• 9	1	0	0-0	246.2	201	83	70	17	69-6	192	.222
1992— Atlanta (N.L.)	• 20	8	.714	2.76	1.19	33	33	7	• 5	0	0-0	225.0	197	81	69	6	70-7	129	.235
1993— Atlanta (N.L.)	• 22	6	.786	3.20	1.36	36	• 36	4	2	0	0-0	239.1	236	91	85	16	90-7	120	.259
1994— Atlanta (N.L.)	13	9	.591	3.97	1.47	25	25	2	0	0	0-0	165.1	173	76	73	10	70-10	140	.268
1995— Atlanta (N.L.)	16	7	.696	3.08	1.25	29	29	3	1	0	0-0	198.2	182	76	68	9	66-0	127	.242
1996— Atlanta (N.L.)	15	10	.600	2.98	1.30	36	* 36	1	0	0	0-0	235.1	222	91	78	14	85-7	181	.249
1997— Atlanta (N.L.)	14	7	.667	2.96	1.15	33	33	5	2	0	0-0	240.0	197	86	79	20	79-9	152	.226
1998— Atlanta (N.L.)	* 20	6	.769	2.47	1.20	33	33	4	3	0	0-0	229.1	202	67	63	13	74-2	157	.238
1999— Atlanta (N.L.)	14	11	.560	4.12	1.46	35	• 35	2	0	0	0-0	234.0	* 259	115	107	18	83-14	138	.287
2000— Atlanta (N.L.)	* 21	9	.700	3.40	1.19	35	• 35	4	2	0	0-0	241.0	222	101	91	24	65-6	152	.244
2001— Atlanta (N.L.)	16	7	.696	3.57	1.41	35	• 35	1	1	0	0-0	219.1	213	92	87	24	97-10	116	.261
2002— Atlanta (N.L.)	18	11	.621	2.96	1.28	36	* 36	2	1	0	0-0	224.2	210	85	74	21	78-8	127	.252
2003— New York (N.L.)	9	14	.391	4.52	1.48	32	32	0	0	0	0-0	183.1	205	94	92	21	66-7	82	.288
Major League totals (17 years)	251	157	.615	3.43	1.30	537	537	52	22	0	0-0	3528.0	3379	1482	1344	268	1206-117	2136	.254

GLOVER, GARY — P

PERSONAL: Born December 3, 1976, in Cleveland, Ohio. ... 6-5/205. ... Throws right, bats right. ... Full name: John Gary Glover. ... High school: Deland (Fla.).

TRANSACTIONS/CAREER NOTES: Selected by Toronto Blue Jays organization in 15th round of free-agent draft (June 2, 1994). ... On disabled list (August 10-September 8, 1994). ... Traded by Blue Jays to Chicago White Sox for P Scott Eyre (November 7, 2000). ... Traded by White Sox with P Scott Dunn and P Tim Bittner to Anaheim Angels for P Scott Schoeneweis and P Doug Nickle (July 30, 2003).

CAREER HITTING: 0-for-1 (.000), 0 R, 0 2B, 0 3B, 0 HR, 0 RBI.

Year League	W	L	Pct.	ERA	WHIP	G	GS	CG	ShO	Hld.	Sv.-Opp.	IP	H	R	ER	HR	BB-IBB	SO	Avg.
1994— GC Blue Jays (GCL)	0	0	...	47.25	6.00	2	0	0	0	...	0-...	1.1	4	8	7	1	4-0	2	.500
1995— GC Blue Jays (GCL)	3	7	.300	4.91	1.41	12	10	2	0	...	0-...	62.1	62	48	34	4	26-0	46	.264
1996— Medicine Hat (Pio.)	3	* 12	.200	7.75	1.77	15	• 15	* 2	0	...	0-...	83.2	* 119	* 94	* 72	14	29-1	54	.322
1997— Hagerstown (S. Atl.)	6	* 17	.261	3.73	1.28	28	28	3	0	...	0-...	173.2	165	94	72	9	58-1	155	.245
1998— Knoxville (Sou.)	0	5	.000	6.75	1.85	8	8	0	0	...	0-...	37.1	41	36	28	2	28-0	14	.277
— Dunedin (Fla. St.)	7	6	.538	4.28	1.40	19	18	0	0	...	0-...	109.1	117	66	52	8	36-0	88	.270
1999— Knoxville (Sou.)	8	2	.800	3.56	1.13	13	13	1	0	...	0-...	86.0	70	39	34	5	27-0	77	.224
— Syracuse (Int'l)	4	6	.400	5.19	1.68	14	14	0	0	...	0-...	76.1	93	50	44	10	35-0	57	.301
— Toronto (A.L.)	0	0	...	0.00	1.00	1	0	0	0	0	0-0	1.0	0	0	0	0	1-0	0	.000
2000— Syracuse (Int'l)	9	9	.500	5.02	1.46	27	27	1	0	...	0-...	166.2	181	104	93	21	62-0	119	.274
2001— Chicago (A.L.)	5	5	.500	4.93	1.30	46	11	0	0	7	0-1	100.1	98	61	55	16	32-3	63	.252
— Charlotte (Int'l)	2	1	.667	1.88	0.68	6	6	1	1	...	0-...	38.1	21	8	8	3	5-0	29	.158
2002— Chicago (A.L.)	7	8	.467	5.20	1.36	41	22	0	0	2	1-1	138.1	136	86	80	21	52-1	70	.253
2003— Chicago (A.L.)	1	0	1.000	4.54	1.60	24	0	0	0	1	0-0	35.2	43	18	18	3	14-2	23	.305
— Anaheim (A.L.)	1	0	1.000	5.00	1.56	18	0	0	0	0	0-0	27.0	34	15	15	3	8-1	14	.315
Major League totals (4 years)	14	13	.519	5.00	1.38	130	33	0	0	10	1-2	302.0	311	180	168	43	107-7	170	.264

GOBBLE, JIMMY — P

PERSONAL: Born July 19, 1981, in Bristol, Tenn. ... 6-3/190. ... Throws left, bats left. ... Full name: Billy James Gobble. ... High school: John S. Battle (Bristol, Va.).

TRANSACTIONS/CAREER NOTES: Selected by Kansas City Royals organization in first round (43rd pick overall) of free-agent draft (June 2, 1999). ... Recalled by Kansas City from Wichita (August 2, 2003). ... Optioned to Omaha by Kansas City (August 30, 2003). ... Recalled by Kansas City from Omaha (September 2, 2003).

CAREER HITTING: 0-for-0 (.000), 0 R, 0 2B, 0 3B, 0 HR, 0 RBI.

Year League	W	L	Pct.	ERA	WHIP	G	GS	CG	ShO	Hld.	Sv.-Opp.	IP	H	R	ER	HR	BB-IBB	SO	Avg.
1999—GC Royals (GCL)	0	0	...	2.70	1.65	4	1	0	0	...	0-...	6.2	6	3	2	0	5-0	8	.222
2000—Char., W.Va. (SAL)	12	10	.545	3.66	1.23	25	25	3	2	...	0-...	145.0	144	75	59	10	34-0	115	.256
2001—Wilmington (Caro.)	10	6	.625	2.55	1.03	27	27	0	0	...	0-...	162.1	134	58	46	8	33-3	154	.226
2002—Wichita (Texas)	5	7	.417	3.38	1.30	13	13	0	0	...	0-...	69.1	71	29	26	3	19-2	52	.267
2003—Wichita (Texas)	12	8	.600	3.19	1.27	22	22	2	1	...	0-...	132.2	128	57	47	11	40-1	100	.254
—Kansas City (A.L.)	4	5	.444	4.61	1.35	9	9	0	0	0	0-0	52.2	56	32	27	8	15-0	31	.271
Major League totals (1 year)	4	5	.444	4.61	1.35	9	9	0	0	0	0-0	52.2	56	32	27	8	15-0	31	.271

GOMES, JONNY   OF

PERSONAL: Born November 22, 1980, in Petaluma, Calif. ... 6-1/205. ... Bats right, throws right. ... Full name: Jonny Johnson Gomes. ... Junior college: Santa Rosa College (Calif.).
TRANSACTIONS/CAREER NOTES: Selected by Tampa Bay Devil Raysn in 18th round of free-agent draft (June 2001).
2003 GAMES PLAYED BY POSITION (MLB): DH—8.

Year Team (League)	Pos.	G	AB	R	H	2B	3B	HR	RBI	BB	SO	HBP	GDP	SB-CS	Avg.	OBP	SLG	OPS	E	Pct.
2001—Princeton (Appal.)	OF	62	206	58	60	11	2	16	44	33	73	26	1	15-4	.291	.442	.597	1.039	7	.936
2002—Bakersfield (Calif.)	OF	134	446	102	124	24	9	30	72	91	173	31	4	15-3	.278	.432	.574	1.006	7	.961
2003—Bakersfield (Calif.)	DH-OF-1B	105	401	67	108	26	2	9	55	41	88	9	9	2-4	.269	.350	.411	.761	5	.948
—Orlando (South.)	OF-DH	120	442	68	110	28	3	17	56	53	148	16	5	23-2	.249	.348	.441	.789	4	.977
—Durham (Int'l)	OF-DH	5	19	2	6	2	1	0	1	2	5	2	0	0-0	.316	.435	.526	.961	0	1.000
—Tampa Bay (A.L.)	DH	8	15	1	2	1	0	0	0	0	6	1	0	0-0	.133	.188	.200	.388	0	...
Major League totals (1 year)		8	15	1	2	1	0	0	0	0	6	1	0	0-0	.133	.188	.200	.388	0	...

GOMEZ, ALEXIS   OF

PERSONAL: Born August 6, 1980... 6-2/180. ... Bats left, throws left. ... Full name: Alexis De Jesus Gomez. ... High school: Liceo General Jose Cabrera (Loma de Cabrera, Dominican Republic).
TRANSACTIONS/CAREER NOTES: Signed as non-drafted free agent by Kansas City Royals organization (February 21, 1997). ... On Wichita disabled list (April 29-May 10, 2002). ... Recalled by Kansas City from Omaha (September 29, 2003).

Year Team (League)	Pos.	G	AB	R	H	2B	3B	HR	RBI	BB	SO	HBP	GDP	SB-CS	Avg.	OBP	SLG	OPS	E	Pct.
1997—Dom. Royals (DSL)		64	248	51	87	12	9	0	42	33	52	...	...	9-...	.351	...	.472	...	...	...
1998—Dom. Royals (DSL)		67	233	51	66	11	3	1	34	50	46	...	...	17-...	.283	...	.369	...	...	...
1999—GC Royals (GCL)	OF	56	214	44	59	12	1	5	31	32	48	1	1	13-5	.276	.371	.411	.782	2	.986
2000—Wilmington (Caro.)	OF	121	461	63	117	13	4	1	33	45	121	2	8	21-10	.254	.322	.306	.628	14	.950
2001—Wilmington (Caro.)	OF	48	169	29	51	8	2	1	9	11	43	1	4	7-3	.302	.348	.391	.739	5	.957
—Wichita (Texas)	OF	83	342	55	96	15	6	4	34	27	70	4	4	16-10	.281	.337	.395	.732	6	.971
2002—Wichita (Texas)	OF	114	461	72	136	21	8	14	75	45	84	3	9	36-24	.295	.359	.466	.825	• 8	.967
—Kansas City (A.L.)	OF	5	10	0	2	0	0	0	0	0	2	0	0	0-0	.200	.200	.200	.400	0	1.000
2003—Omaha (PCL)	OF	121	457	49	123	23	8	8	58	27	92	1	12	4-5	.269	.307	.407	.714	9	.970
Major League totals (1 year)		5	10	0	2	0	0	0	0	0	2	0	0	0-0	.200	.200	.200	.400	0	1.000

GOMEZ, CHRIS   SS

PERSONAL: Born June 16, 1971, in Los Angeles, Calif. ... 6-1/190. ... Bats right, throws right. ... Full name: Christopher Cory Gomez. ... High school: Lakewood (Calif.). ... College: Long Beach State.
TRANSACTIONS/CAREER NOTES: Selected by California Angels organization in 37th round of free-agent draft (June 5, 1989); did not sign. ... Selected by Detroit Tigers organization in third round of free-agent draft (June 1, 1992). ... Traded by Tigers with C John Flaherty to San Diego Padres for C Brad Ausmus, SS Andujar Cedeno and P Russ Spear (June 18, 1996). ... On San Diego disabled list (June 2-July 31, 1999); included rehabilitation assignment to Las Vegas (July 15-30). ... On disabled list (June 22, 2000-remainder of season). ... Released by Padres (June 22, 2001). ... Signed by Tampa Bay Devil Rays organization (June 27, 2001). ... Granted free agency (November 5, 2001). ... Re-signed by Devil Rays (December 7, 2001). ... Signed by Devil Rays (September 30, 2002). ... Signed by Minnesota Twins organization (January 2, 2003).
2003 GAMES PLAYED BY POSITION (MLB): 2B—23, 3B—18, SS—17, DH—1.

Year Team (League)	Pos.	G	AB	R	H	2B	3B	HR	RBI	BB	SO	HBP	GDP	SB-CS	Avg.	OBP	SLG	OPS	E	Pct.
1992—London (East.)	SS	64	220	20	59	13	2	1	19	20	34	3	11	1-3	.268	.337	.359	.697	14	.951
1993—Toledo (Int'l)	SS	87	277	29	68	12	2	0	20	23	37	3	4	6-2	.245	.308	.303	.611	16	.961
—Detroit (A.L.)	SS-2B-DH	46	128	11	32	7	1	0	11	9	17	1	2	2-2	.250	.304	.320	.625	5	.974
1994—Detroit (A.L.)	SS-2B	84	296	32	76	19	0	8	53	33	64	3	8	5-3	.257	.336	.402	.738	8	.978
1995—Detroit (A.L.)	SS-2B-DH	123	431	49	96	20	2	11	50	41	96	3	13	4-1	.223	.292	.355	.647	15	.974
1996—Detroit (A.L.)	SS	48	128	21	31	5	0	1	16	18	20	1	5	1-1	.242	.340	.305	.645	6	.970
—San Diego (N.L.)	SS	89	328	32	86	16	1	3	29	39	64	6	11	2-2	.262	.349	.345	.694	13	.967
1997—San Diego (N.L.)	SS	150	522	62	132	19	2	5	54	53	114	5	16	5-8	.253	.326	.326	.652	15	.978
1998—San Diego (N.L.)	SS	145	449	55	120	32	3	4	39	51	87	5	11	1-3	.267	.346	.379	.725	12	.980
1999—San Diego (N.L.)	SS	76	234	20	59	8	1	1	15	27	49	1	6	1-2	.252	.331	.308	.638	12	.961
—Las Vegas (PCL)	SS	10	27	3	9	1	0	0	4	2	6	1	1	0-0	.333	.400	.370	.770	2	.933
2000—San Diego (N.L.)	SS-2B	33	54	4	12	0	0	0	3	7	5	0	1	0-0	.222	.306	.222	.529	5	.933
2001—San Diego (N.L.)	SS-2B	40	112	6	21	3	0	0	7	9	14	0	5	1-0	.188	.244	.214	.458	6	.948
—Portland (PCL)	SS-2B	11	40	5	12	3	0	1	5	2	4	0	1	1-0	.300	.333	.450	.783	2	.959
—Durham (Int'l)	SS	23	93	16	28	5	1	4	17	11	5	0	5	1-1	.301	.375	.505	.880	2	.978
—Tampa Bay (A.L.)	SS	58	189	31	57	16	0	8	36	8	24	2	4	3-0	.302	.332	.513	.845	7	.968
2002—Tampa Bay (A.L.)	SS	130	461	51	122	31	3	10	46	21	58	7	8	1-3	.265	.305	.410	.715	12	.980
2003—Minnesota (A.L.)	2-3-S-D	58	175	14	44	9	3	1	15	7	13	0	10	2-1	.251	.279	.354	.633	3	.982
American League totals (7 years)		547	1808	209	458	107	9	39	227	137	292	17	50	18-11	.253	.310	.387	.697	56	.976
National League totals (6 years)		533	1699	179	430	78	7	13	147	186	333	17	50	10-15	.253	.331	.330	.661	63	.971
Major League totals (11 years)		1080	3507	388	888	185	16	52	374	323	625	34	100	28-26	.253	.320	.360	.680	119	.973

GONZALEZ, ALEX   SS

PERSONAL: Born February 15, 1977, in Cagua, Venezuela. ... 6-0/200. ... Bats right, throws right. ... Full name: Alexander Gonzalez. ... High school: Liceo Ramon Bastidas (Venezuela).

G

TRANSACTIONS/CAREER NOTES: Signed as non-drafted free agent by Florida Marlins organization (April 18, 1994). ... On Kane County disabled list (April 5-August 17, 1996). ... On Portland disabled list (September 7, 1996-remainder of season). ... On Florida disabled list (July 28-September 1, 2000); included rehabilitation assignment to Brevard County (August 26-31). ... On Florida disabled list (May 19, 2002-remainder of season); included rehabilitation assignments to Gulf Coast Marlins (July 3-5 and July 15-19).
2003 GAMES PLAYED BY POSITION (MLB): SS—150.

Year Team (League)	Pos.	G	AB	R	H	2B	3B	HR	RBI	BB	SO	HBP	GDP	SB-CS	Avg.	OBP	SLG	OPS	E	Pct.
1994— Dom. Marlins (DSL)	SS	54	239	30	54	7	3	3	31	15	36	...	...	4-...	.226	...	.318	...	34	.914
1995— Brevard County (FSL)	SS	17	59	6	12	2	1	0	8	1	14	1	2	1-1	.203	.230	.271	.501	8	.906
— GC Marlins (GCL)	SS	53	187	30	55	7	4	2	30	19	27	2	2	11-2	.294	.358	.406	.765	17	.932
1996— GC Marlins (GCL)	SS	10	41	6	16	3	0	0	6	2	4	0	1	1-0	.390	.419	.463	.882	5	.898
— Kane Co. (Midw.)	SS	4	10	2	2	0	0	0	0	2	4	1	1	0-0	.200	.385	.200	.585	1	1.000
— Portland (East.)	SS	11	34	4	8	0	1	0	1	2	10	1	2	0-0	.235	.297	.294	.591	7	.887
1997— Portland (East.)	SS	133	449	69	114	16	4	19	65	27	83	7	7	4-7	.254	.305	.434	.739	37	.943
1998— Charlotte (Int'l)	SS	108	422	71	117	20	10	10	51	28	80	6	6	4-7	.277	.330	.443	.773	20	.960
— Florida (N.L.)	SS	25	86	11	13	2	0	3	7	9	30	1	2	0-0	.151	.240	.279	.519	2	.978
1999— Florida (N.L.)	SS	136	560	81	155	28	8	14	59	15	113	12	13	3-5	.277	.308	.430	.739	27	.955
2000— Florida (N.L.)	SS	109	385	35	77	17	4	7	42	13	77	2	7	7-1	.200	.229	.319	.548	19	.957
— Brevard County (FSL)	SS	4	17	1	2	0	0	0	2	1	3	0	0	1-0	.118	.167	.118	.284	0	1.000
2001— Florida (N.L.)	SS-C	145	515	57	129	36	1	9	48	30	107	10	13	2-2	.250	.303	.377	.680	26	.960
2002— Florida (N.L.)	SS	42	151	15	34	7	1	2	18	12	32	4	2	3-1	.225	.296	.325	.620	3	.984
— GC Marlins (GCL)	SS	5	12	0	2	1	0	0	1	0	5	0	1	0-0	.167	.154	.250	.404	1	.923
2003— Florida (N.L.)	SS	150	528	52	135	33	6	18	77	33	106	13	8	0-4	.256	.313	.443	.756	16	.976
Major League totals (6 years)		607	2225	251	543	123	20	53	251	112	465	42	45	15-13	.244	.291	.389	.680	93	.965

GONZALEZ, ALEX S. SS

PERSONAL: Born April 8, 1973, in Miami, Fla. ... 6-0/200. ... Bats right, throws right. ... Full name: Alexander Scott Gonzalez. ... High school: Miami Killian.
TRANSACTIONS/CAREER NOTES: Selected by Toronto Blue Jays organization in 14th round of free-agent draft (June 3, 1991). ... On Toronto disabled list (April 29-May 27, 1994); included rehabilitation assignment to Syracuse (May 14-27). ... On disabled list (August 13-September 14, 1997; and May 17, 1999-remainder of season). ... On Toronto disabled list (July 7-22, 2000); included rehabilitation assignment to Syracuse (July 21). ... Granted free agency (October 30, 2000). ... Re-signed by Blue Jays (December 10, 2000). ... Traded by Blue Jays to Chicago Cubs for P Felix Heredia and a player to be named later (December 10, 2001); Blue Jays acquired IF James Deschaine to complete deal (December 13, 2001). ... On disabled list (May 10-25, 2002).
2003 GAMES PLAYED BY POSITION (MLB): SS—150.

Year Team (League)	Pos.	G	AB	R	H	2B	3B	HR	RBI	BB	SO	HBP	GDP	SB-CS	Avg.	OBP	SLG	OPS	E	Pct.
1991— GC Jays (GCL)	SS	53	191	29	40	5	4	0	10	12	41	3	1	7-2	.209	.267	.277	.544	21	.915
1992— Myrtle Beach (SAL)	SS	134	535	83	145	22	9	10	62	38	119	3	9	26-14	.271	.322	.402	.724	48	.932
1993— Knoxville (Sou.)	SS	* 142	561	* 93	162	29	7	16	69	39	110	6	9	38-13	.289	.339	.451	.790	30	.956
1994— Toronto (A.L.)	SS	15	53	7	8	3	1	0	1	4	17	1	2	3-0	.151	.224	.245	.469	6	.918
— Syracuse (Int'l)	SS-DH	110	437	69	124	22	4	12	57	53	92	1	9	23-6	.284	.361	.435	.796	* 31	.943
1995— Toronto (A.L.)	SS-3B-DH	111	367	51	89	19	4	10	42	44	114	1	7	4-4	.243	.322	.398	.720	19	.954
1996— Toronto (A.L.)	SS	147	527	64	124	30	5	14	64	45	127	5	12	16-6	.235	.300	.391	.691	21	.973
1997— Toronto (A.L.)	SS	126	426	46	102	23	2	12	35	34	94	5	9	15-6	.239	.302	.387	.689	8	.986
1998— Toronto (A.L.)	SS	158	568	70	136	28	1	13	51	28	121	6	13	21-6	.239	.281	.361	.642	17	.976
1999— Toronto (A.L.)	SS-DH	38	154	22	45	13	0	2	12	16	23	3	4	4-2	.292	.370	.416	.786	4	.980
2000— Toronto (A.L.)	SS	141	527	68	133	31	2	15	69	43	113	4	14	4-4	.252	.313	.404	.717	16	.975
— Syracuse (Int'l)	SS	1	5	0	0	0	0	0	0	0	2	0	0	0-0	.000	.000	.000	.000	0	1.000
2001— Toronto (A.L.)	SS	154	636	79	161	25	5	17	76	43	149	7	16	18-11	.253	.303	.388	.692	10	.987
2002— Chicago (N.L.)	SS	142	513	58	127	27	5	18	61	46	136	3	11	5-3	.248	.312	.425	.737	21	.965
2003— Chicago (N.L.)	SS	152	536	71	122	37	0	20	59	47	123	6	17	3-3	.228	.295	.409	.704	10	.984
American League totals (8 years)		890	3258	407	798	172	20	83	350	257	758	32	77	85-39	.245	.304	.386	.691	101	.975
National League totals (2 years)		294	1049	129	249	64	5	38	120	93	259	9	28	8-6	.237	.303	.417	.720	31	.975
Major League totals (10 years)		1184	4307	536	1047	236	25	121	470	350	1017	41	105	93-45	.243	.304	.394	.698	132	.975

GONZALEZ, EDGAR P

PERSONAL: Born February 23, 1983, in Monterrey, Mexico. ... 6-0/215. ... Throws right, bats right. ... Full name: Edgar Gerardo Gonzalez.
TRANSACTIONS/CAREER NOTES: Signed by Arizona Diamondbacks organization as a non-drafted free agent (April 18, 2000). ... Did not report and was placed on suspended list for 2000 and 2001 seasons. ... Contract purchased by Arizona from Tucson (May 30, 2003). ... Optioned to Tucson (June 8, 2003). ... Recalled by Arizona (September 1, 2003).
CAREER HITTING: 1-for-4 (.250), 1 R, 0 2B, 0 3B, 0 HR, 0 RBI.

Year League	W	L	Pct.	ERA	WHIP	G	GS	CG	ShO	Hld.	Sv.-Opp.	IP	H	R	ER	HR	BB-IBB	SO	Avg.
2001—										Did not play.									
2002— Lancaster (Calif.)	3	0	1.000	0.78	1.17	4	4	0	0	...	0-...	23.0	24	7	2	1	3-0	21	.264
— South Bend (Mid.)	11	8	.579	2.91	1.16	23	23	4	2	...	0-...	151.1	141	66	49	4	34-0	110	.246
2003— El Paso (Texas)	2	2	.500	3.50	1.42	6	6	0	0	...	0-...	36.0	40	18	14	1	11-0	30	.282
— Tucson (PCL)	8	7	.533	3.75	1.19	20	19	1	0	...	0-...	129.2	126	65	54	4	28-0	69	.255
— Arizona (N.L.)	2	1	.667	4.91	1.91	9	2	0	0	0	0-1	18.1	28	10	10	3	7-2	14	.368
Major League totals (1 year)	2	1	.667	4.91	1.91	9	2	0	0	0	0-1	18.1	28	10	10	3	7-2	14	.368

GONZALEZ, JEREMI P

PERSONAL: Born January 8, 1975, in Maracaibo, Venezuela. ... 6-0/220. ... Throws right, bats right. ... Full name: Geremis Segundo Gonzalez. ... High school: Colegro La Chinita (Maracaibo, Venezuela).
TRANSACTIONS/CAREER NOTES: Signed as non-drafted free agent by Chicago Cubs organization (October 21, 1991). ... On disabled list (July 6-August 10, 1996). ... On disabled list (July 25, 1998-remainder of season). ... On Chicago disabled list (April 1, 1999-entire season); included rehabilitation assignments to Dayton (April 16-22), West Tenn (April 26-May 8) and Iowa (May 12-18 and May 29-31). ... On Chicago disabled list (March 28, 2000-remainder of season); included rehabilitation assignments to Arizona Cubs (July 19-August 7) and Lansing (August 7-8). ... Released by Cubs (March 13, 2001). ... Signed by Texas Rangers organization (December 18, 2001). ... Granted free agency (October 15, 2002). ... Signed by Tampa Bay Devil Rays organization (November 21, 2002).
CAREER HITTING: 10-for-78 (.128), 1 R, 1 2B, 0 3B, 0 HR, 3 RBI.

G

Year League	W	L	Pct.	ERA	WHIP	G	GS	CG	ShO	Hld.	Sv.-Opp.	IP	H	R	ER	HR	BB-IBB	SO	Avg.
1992— Ariz. Cubs (Ariz.)	0	5	.000	7.80	1.93	14	7	0	0	...	0-...	45.0	65	59	39	0	22-0	39	.325
1993— Huntington (Appal.)	3	9	.250	6.25	1.77	12	12	1	0	...	0-...	67.2	82	59	47	6	38-0	42	.300
1994— Peoria (Midw.)	1	7	.125	5.55	1.65	13	13	1	0	...	0-...	71.1	86	53	44	4	32-0	39	.306
— Williamsport (NYP)	4	6	.400	4.24	1.39	16	12	1	1	...	1-...	80.2	83	46	38	6	29-0	64	.266
1995— Rockford (Midwest)	4	4	.500	5.10	1.39	12	12	1	0	...	0-...	65.1	63	43	37	4	28-0	36	.247
— Daytona (Fla. St.)	5	1	.833	1.22	1.06	19	2	0	0	...	4-...	44.1	34	15	6	0	13-1	30	.211
1996— Orlando (Sou.)	6	3	.667	3.34	1.27	17	14	0	0	...	0-...	97.0	95	39	36	6	28-1	85	.250
1997— Iowa (Am. Assoc.)	2	2	.500	3.48	1.10	10	10	1	1	...	0-...	62.0	47	27	24	8	21-0	58	.209
— Chicago (N.L.)	11	9	.550	4.25	1.35	23	23	1	1	0	0-0	144.0	126	73	68	16	69-5	93	.236
1998— Chicago (N.L.)	7	7	.500	5.32	1.50	20	20	1	1	0	0-0	110.0	124	72	65	13	41-5	70	.281
1999— Daytona (Fla. St.)	0	0	...	0.00	0.43	2	2	0	0	...	0-...	4.2	2	0	0	0	0-0	4	.125
— West Tenn (Sou.)	0	0	...	1.74	1.55	3	3	0	0	...	0-...	10.1	7	2	2	0	9-0	12	.200
— Iowa (PCL)	0	1	.000	4.50	1.60	3	3	0	0	...	0-...	10.0	10	8	5	1	6-0	10	.270
2000— Ariz. Cubs (Ariz.)	0	1	.000	2.70	1.00	4	4	0	0	...	0-...	10.0	8	3	3	0	2-0	15	.211
— Lansing (Midw.)	0	0	...	0.00	0.00	1	1	0	0	...	0-...	.2	0	0	0	0	0-0	2	.000
2001—											Did not play.								
2002— Oklahoma (PCL)	6	5	.545	3.33	1.36	46	5	0	0	...	14-...	92.0	86	40	34	8	39-5	93	.249
2003— Durham (Int'l)	1	0	1.000	2.53	0.94	7	6	0	0	...	0-...	32.0	24	11	9	2	6-0	33	.202
— Tampa Bay (A.L.)	6	11	.353	3.91	1.28	25	25	2	0	0	0-0	156.1	131	71	68	18	69-1	97	.228
American League totals (1 year)	6	11	.353	3.91	1.28	25	25	2	0	0	0-0	156.1	131	71	68	18	69-1	97	.228
National League totals (2 years)	18	16	.529	4.71	1.42	43	43	2	2	0	0-0	254.0	250	145	133	29	110-10	163	.256
Major League totals (3 years)	24	27	.471	4.41	1.36	68	68	4	2	0	0-0	410.1	381	216	201	47	179-11	260	.246

GONZALEZ, JUAN — OF

PERSONAL: Born October 16, 1969, in Vega Baja, Puerto Rico. ... 6-3/220. ... Bats right, throws right. ... Full name: Juan Alberto Gonzalez. ... High school: Vega Baja (Puerto Rico).

TRANSACTIONS/CAREER NOTES: Signed as non-drafted free agent by Texas Rangers organization (May 30, 1986). ... On disabled list (April 27-June 17, 1988; March 30-April 26, 1991; April 16-June 1 and July 27-August 16, 1995; May 8-June 1, 1996; and March 24-May 2, 1997). ... Traded by Rangers with P Danny Patterson and C Gregg Zaun to Detroit Tigers for P Justin Thompson, P Francisco Cordero, OF Gabe Kapler, C Bill Haselman, 2B Frank Catalanotto and P Alan Webb (November 2, 1999). ... On disabled list (July 8-26, 2000). ... Granted free agency (November 1, 2000). ... Signed by Cleveland Indians (January 9, 2001). ... Granted free agency (November 5, 2001). ... Signed by Rangers (January 8, 2002). ... On disabled list (April 9-May 17 and July 31, 2002-remainder of season). ... Placed on 15-day disabled list (July 20, 2003). ... Transferred to 60-day disabled list (September 7, 2003).

2003 GAMES PLAYED BY POSITION (MLB): OF—57, DH—24.

									BATTING									FIELDING	
Year Team (League)	Pos.	G	AB	R	H	2B	3B	HR	RBI	BB	SO	HBP	GDP	SB-CS	Avg.	OBP	SLG	OPS	E	Pct.
1986— GC Rangers (GCL)	OF	60	* 233	24	56	4	1	0	36	21	57	1	9	7-5	.240	.302	.266	.568	• 6	.941
1987— Gastonia (S. Atl.)	OF	127	509	69	135	21	2	14	74	30	92	5	14	9-4	.265	.310	.397	.707	12	.953
1988— Charlotte (Fla. St.)	OF	77	277	25	71	14	3	8	43	25	64	4	7	5-2	.256	.325	.415	.740	4	.973
1989— Tulsa (Texas)	OF	133	502	73	147	30	7	21	85	31	98	9	8	1-8	.293	.342	.506	.848	9	.972
— Texas (A.L.)	OF	24	60	6	9	3	0	1	7	6	17	0	0	0-0	.150	.227	.250	.477	2	.964
1990— Okla. City (A.A.)	OF	128	496	78	128	29	4	* 29	* 101	32	109	1	11	2-2	.258	.300	.508	.808	8	.966
— Texas (A.L.)	DH-OF	25	90	11	26	7	1	4	12	2	18	2	2	0-1	.289	.316	.522	.838	0	1.000
1991— Texas (A.L.)	DH-OF	142	545	78	144	34	1	27	102	42	118	5	10	4-4	.264	.321	.479	.800	6	.981
1992— Texas (A.L.)	OF-DH	155	584	77	152	24	2	* 43	109	35	143	5	16	0-1	.260	.304	.529	.833	10	.975
1993— Texas (A.L.)	OF-DH	140	536	105	166	33	1	* 46	118	37	99	13	12	4-1	.310	.368	*.632	1.000	4	.985
1994— Texas (A.L.)	OF	107	422	57	116	18	4	19	85	30	66	7	18	6-4	.275	.330	.472	.802	2	.991
1995— Texas (A.L.)	DH-OF	90	352	57	104	20	2	27	82	17	66	0	15	0-0	.295	.324	.594	.917	0	1.000
1996— Texas (A.L.)	OF-DH	134	541	89	170	33	2	47	144	45	82	3	10	2-0	.314	.368	.643	1.011	2	.988
1997— Texas (A.L.)	DH-OF	133	533	87	158	24	3	42	131	33	107	3	12	0-0	.296	.335	.589	.924	4	.971
1998— Texas (A.L.)	OF-DH	154	606	110	193	* 50	2	45	* 157	46	126	6	20	2-1	.318	.366	.630	.997	4	.982
1999— Texas (A.L.)	OF-DH	144	562	114	183	36	1	39	128	51	105	4	10	3-3	.326	.378	.601	.980	4	.983
2000— Detroit (A.L.)	OF-DH	115	461	69	133	30	2	22	67	32	84	2	13	1-2	.289	.337	.505	.842	1	.992
2001— Cleveland (A.L.)	OF-DH	140	532	97	173	34	1	35	140	41	94	6	18	1-0	.325	.370	.590	.960	3	.987
2002— Texas (A.L.)	OF-DH	70	277	38	78	21	1	8	35	17	56	1	11	2-0	.282	.324	.451	.776	1	.992
2003— Texas (A.L.)	OF-DH	82	327	49	96	17	1	24	70	14	73	4	10	1-1	.294	.329	.572	.901	0	1.000
Major League totals (15 years)		1655	6428	1044	1901	384	24	429	1387	448	1254	61	181	26-18	.296	.344	.563	.907	43	.984

GONZALEZ, LUIS — OF

PERSONAL: Born September 3, 1967, in Tampa, Fla. ... 6-2/200. ... Bats left, throws right. ... Full name: Luis Emilio Gonzalez. ... High school: Jefferson (Tampa). ... College: South Alabama.

TRANSACTIONS/CAREER NOTES: Selected by Houston Astros organization in fourth round of free-agent draft (June 1, 1988). ... On disabled list (May 26-July 5, 1989 and August 29-September 13, 1991). ... On Houston disabled list (July 21-August 5, 1992). ... Traded by Astros with C Scott Servais to Chicago Cubs for C Rick Wilkins (June 28, 1995). ... Granted free agency (December 7, 1996). ... Signed by Astros (December 19, 1996). ... Granted free agency (October 28, 1997). ... Signed by Detroit Tigers (December 9, 1997). ... Traded by Tigers to Arizona Diamondbacks for OF Karim Garcia (December 28, 1998).

2003 GAMES PLAYED BY POSITION (MLB): OF—154.

									BATTING									FIELDING	
Year Team (League)	Pos.	G	AB	R	H	2B	3B	HR	RBI	BB	SO	HBP	GDP	SB-CS	Avg.	OBP	SLG	OPS	E	Pct.
1988— Asheville (S. Atl.)	3B	31	115	13	29	7	1	2	14	12	17	2	4	2-2	.252	.333	.383	.716	6	.931
— Auburn (NY-Penn)	3B-SS-1B	39	157	32	49	10	3	5	27	12	19	1	1	2-0	.312	.354	.510	.864	13	.902
1989— Osceola (Fla. St.)	DH	86	287	46	82	16	7	6	38	37	49	4	3	2-1	.286	.370	.453	.823	...	.000
1990— Columbus (Sou.)	3B-1B	138	495	86	131	30	6	• 24	89	54	100	6	6	27-9	.265	.337	.495	.832	23	.980
— Houston (N.L.)	3B-1B	12	21	1	4	2	0	0	0	2	5	0	0	0-0	.190	.261	.286	.547	0	1.000
1991— Houston (N.L.)	OF	137	473	51	120	28	9	13	69	40	101	8	9	10-7	.254	.320	.433	.753	5	.984
1992— Houston (N.L.)	OF	122	387	40	94	19	3	10	55	24	52	2	6	7-7	.243	.289	.385	.674	2	.993
— Tucson (PCL)	OF	13	44	11	19	4	2	1	9	5	7	1	0	4-1	.432	.490	.682	1.172	1	.963
1993— Houston (N.L.)	OF	154	540	82	162	34	3	15	72	47	83	10	9	20-9	.300	.361	.457	.818	8	.978
1994— Houston (N.L.)	OF	112	392	57	107	29	4	8	67	49	57	3	10	15-13	.273	.353	.429	.782	2	.991
1995— Houston (N.L.)	OF	56	209	35	54	10	4	6	35	18	30	3	8	1-3	.258	.322	.431	.753	2	.980
— Chicago (N.L.)	OF	77	262	34	76	19	4	7	34	39	33	3	6	5-5	.290	.384	.473	.858	4	.978
1996— Chicago (N.L.)	OF-1B	146	483	70	131	30	4	15	79	61	49	4	13	9-6	.271	.354	.443	.797	3	.988

G

Year Team (League)	Pos.	G	AB	R	H	2B	3B	HR	RBI	BB	SO	HBP	GDP	SB-CS	Avg.	OBP	SLG	OPS	E	Pct.
1997— Houston (N.L.)	OF-1B	152	550	78	142	31	2	10	68	71	67	5	12	10-7	.258	.345	.376	.722	5	.982
1998— Detroit (A.L.)	OF-DH	154	547	84	146	35	5	23	71	57	62	8	9	12-7	.267	.340	.475	.816	3	.988
1999— Arizona (N.L.)	OF-DH	153	614	112	*206	45	4	26	111	66	63	7	13	9-5	.336	.403	.549	.952	5	.983
2000— Arizona (N.L.)	OF	•162	618	106	192	47	2	31	114	78	85	12	12	2-4	.311	.392	.544	.935	3	.990
2001— Arizona (N.L.)	OF	•162	609	128	198	36	7	57	142	100	83	14	14	1-1	.325	.429	.688	1.117	0	1.000
2002— Arizona (N.L.)	OF	148	524	90	151	19	3	28	103	97	76	5	12	9-2	.288	.400	.496	.896	4	.985
2003— Arizona (N.L.)	OF	156	579	92	176	46	4	26	104	94	67	3	19	5-3	.304	.402	.532	.934	5	.989
American League totals (1 year)		154	547	84	146	35	5	23	71	57	62	8	9	12-7	.267	.340	.475	.816	3	.988
National League totals (13 years)		1749	6261	976	1813	395	53	252	1053	786	851	79	145	103-72	.290	.372	.490	.862	46	.987
Major League totals (14 years)		1903	6808	1060	1959	430	58	275	1124	843	913	87	154	115-79	.288	.370	.489	.859	49	.987

GONZALEZ, MIKE — P

PERSONAL: Born May 23, 1978, in Corpus Christi, Texas. ... 6-2/213. ... Throws left, bats right. ... Full name: Michael Vela Gonzalez. ... High school: Harvest Christian Academy (Pasadena, Texas). ... Junior college: San Jacinto College (Texas).

TRANSACTIONS/CAREER NOTES: Selected by Pittsburgh Pirates organization in 30th round of free-agent draft (June 3, 1997). ... On disabled list (April 7-June 19 and June 22-24, 2000). ... On Lynchburg disabled list (April 5-19, 2001). ... On Altoona disabled list (June 5-August 10, 2002). ... Traded by Pirates with P Scott Sauerbeck to Boston Red Sox for P Brandon Lyon and P Anastacio Martinez (July 22, 2003). ... Traded by Red Sox with INF Freddy Sanchez to Pirates for P Jeff Suppan, P Brandon Lyon and P Anastacio Martinez (July 31, 2003).

CAREER HITTING: 0-for-0 (.000), 0 R, 0 2B, 0 3B, 0 HR, 0 RBI.

Year League	W	L	Pct.	ERA	WHIP	G	GS	CG	ShO	Hld.	Sv.-Opp.	IP	H	R	ER	HR	BB-IBB	SO	Avg.
1997— GC Pirates (GCL)	2	0	1.000	2.48	1.00	7	3	0	0	...	0-...	29.0	21	9	8	0	8-0	33	.200
—Augusta (S. Atl.)	1	1	.500	1.86	0.98	4	3	0	0	...	0-...	19.1	11	5	4	1	8-0	22	.164
1998— Lynchburg (Carolina)	0	3	.000	6.67	1.87	7	7	0	0	...	0-...	28.1	40	21	21	5	13-0	22	.331
—Augusta (S. Atl.)	4	2	.667	2.84	1.36	11	9	0	0	...	0-...	50.2	43	24	16	2	26-0	72	.231
1999— Lynchburg (Carolina)	10	4	.714	4.02	1.44	20	20	0	0	...	0-...	112.0	98	55	50	10	63-0	119	.240
—Altoona (East.)	2	3	.400	8.10	1.99	7	5	0	0	...	0-...	26.2	34	25	24	4	19-0	31	.312
2000— GC Pirates (GCL)	1	0	1.000	4.50	2.00	2	1	0	0	...	0-...	6.0	8	6	3	1	4-0	7	.267
—Lynchburg (Carolina)	4	3	.571	4.66	1.63	12	10	0	0	...	0-...	56.0	57	34	29	6	34-0	53	.269
2001— Lynchburg (Carolina)	2	2	.500	2.93	1.14	14	2	0	0	...	0-...	30.2	28	14	10	3	7-1	32	.241
—Altoona (East.)	5	4	.556	3.71	1.34	14	14	1	1	...	0-...	87.1	81	38	36	5	36-0	66	.251
2002— GC Pirates (GCL)	2	0	1.000	0.00	0.60	2	2	0	0	...	0-...	13.1	5	1	0	0	3-0	14	.114
—Altoona (East.)	8	4	.667	3.80	1.45	16	16	0	0	...	0-...	85.1	77	38	36	4	47-2	82	.244
2003— Lynchburg (Carolina)	0	1	.000	5.14	1.71	5	5	0	0	...	0-...	7.0	7	9	4	0	5-0	9	.269
—Altoona (East.)	0	0	...	1.23	0.82	5	0	0	0	...	0-...	7.1	4	1	1	1	2-0	10	.154
—Pawtucket (Int'l)	0	0	...	0.00	1.80	2	0	0	0	...	1-...	1.2	2	0	0	0	1-0	2	.286
—Nashville (PCL)	0	0	...	4.50	1.30	7	0	0	0	...	2-...	10.0	9	5	5	0	4-1	10	.231
—Pittsburgh (N.L.)	0	1	.000	7.56	1.56	16	0	0	0	3	0-0	8.1	7	7	7	4	6-0	6	.233
Major League totals (1 year)	0	1	.000	7.56	1.56	16	0	0	0	3	0-0	8.1	7	7	7	4	6-0	6	.233

GONZALEZ, RAUL — OF

PERSONAL: Born December 27, 1973, in Santurce, Puerto Rico. ... 5-9/190. ... Bats right, throws right. ... Full name: Victor Raul Gonzalez. ... High school: Gilberto Concepcion (Carolina, Puerto Rico).

TRANSACTIONS/CAREER NOTES: Selected by Kansas City Royals organization in 17th round free-agent draft (June 4, 1990). ... On disabled list (April 28-September 19, 1996). ... Granted free agency (October 17, 1997). ... Re-signed by Royals organization (November 27, 1997). ... Granted free agency (October 16, 1998). ... Signed by Boston Red Sox organization (November 18, 1998). ... Granted free agency (October 15, 1999). ... Signed by Chicago Cubs organization (November 18, 1999). ... On Iowa disabled list (July 8-26 and August 2-September 5, 2000). ... Granted free agency (October 18, 2000). ... Signed by Cincinnati Reds organization (December 21, 2000). ... Traded by Reds to New York Mets (August 20, 2002), as partial completion of deal in which Mets traded P Shawn Estes and cash to Reds for P Pedro Feliciano, OF Elvin Andujar and two players to be named later (August 15, 2002); Mets acquired OF Brady Clark to complete deal (September 9, 2002).

2003 GAMES PLAYED BY POSITION (MLB): OF—88.

Year Team (League)	Pos.	G	AB	R	H	2B	3B	HR	RBI	BB	SO	HBP	GDP	SB-CS	Avg.	OBP	SLG	OPS	E	Pct.
1991— GC Royals (GCL)	OF	47	160	24	47	5	3	0	17	19	21	0	4	3-4	.294	.365	.363	.727	4	.941
1992— Appleton (Midwest)	OF	119	449	82	115	32	1	9	51	57	58	2	4	13-5	.256	.339	.392	.731	5	.981
1993— Wilmington (Caro.)	OF	127	461	59	124	30	3	11	55	54	58	4	8	13-5	.269	.348	.419	.767	8	.969
1994— Wilmington (Caro.)	OF	115	414	60	108	19	8	9	51	45	50	2	8	0-4	.261	.333	.411	.744	10	.941
1995— Wichita (Texas)	OF	22	79	14	23	3	2	2	11	8	13	0	1	4-0	.291	.356	.456	.812	2	.957
— Wilmington (Caro.)	OF	86	308	36	90	19	3	11	49	14	34	2	3	6-4	.292	.320	.481	.801	5	.966
1996— Wichita (Texas)	OF	23	84	17	24	5	1	1	9	5	12	1	3	1-2	.286	.333	.405	.738	1	.969
1997— Wichita (Texas)	OF	129	452	66	129	30	4	13	74	36	52	2	12	12-8	.285	.335	.456	.791	*14	.969
1998— Wichita (Texas)	OF	118	455	84	148	31	1	17	86	58	53	2	15	12-8	.325	.401	.510	.911	9	.957
1999— Trenton (East.)	OF	127	505	80	*169	33	4	18	103	51	71	3	14	12-3	.335	.394	.523	.917	2	.993
2000— Iowa (PCL)	OF	69	241	35	64	13	1	4	33	21	20	2	6	5-5	.266	.328	.378	.706	3	.974
— Chicago (N.L.)	OF	3	2	0	0	0	0	0	0	0	2	0	0	0-0	.000	.000	.000	.000	0	...
2001— Louisville (Int'l)	OF	*142	539	*90	*161	*39	1	11	66	64	70	1	20	6-8	.299	.371	.436	.807	9	.973
— Cincinnati (N.L.)	OF	11	14	0	3	0	0	0	0	1	3	0	0	0-0	.214	.267	.214	.481	0	1.000
2002— Louisville (Int'l)	OF	114	432	91	144	27	2	13	69	61	59	4	15	9-8	.333	*.416	.495	.911	8	.970
— Cincinnati (N.L.)	OF	10	23	4	6	1	0	0	1	2	5	0	1	2-0	.261	.320	.304	.624	0	1.000
— New York (N.L.)	OF	30	81	9	21	2	0	3	11	4	17	0	2	2-2	.259	.291	.395	.686	0	1.000
2003— Norfolk (Int'l)	OF-DH	32	120	18	43	3	1	3	19	16	23	0	3	5-2	.358	.431	.475	.906	0	1.000
— New York (N.L.)	OF	107	217	28	50	12	2	2	21	27	34	1	8	3-0	.230	.317	.332	.649	1	.993
Major League totals (4 years)		161	337	41	80	15	2	5	33	34	61	1	11	7-2	.237	.307	.338	.646	1	.995

GONZALEZ, WIKI — C

PERSONAL: Born May 17, 1974, in Aragua, Venezuela. ... 5-11/203. ... Bats right, throws right. ... Full name: Wiklenman Vicente Gonzalez. ... Name pronounced: WICK-ee.

TRANSACTIONS/CAREER NOTES: Signed as non-drafted free agent by Pittsburgh Pirates organization (February 12, 1992). ... Selected by San Diego Padres organization from Pirates organization in Rule 5 minor league draft (December 9, 1996). ... Granted free agency (October 16, 1998). ... Re-signed by Padres organization (October 23, 1998). ... On Mobile disabled list (May 24-June 6, 1999). ... On San Diego disabled list (June 3-July 3, 2001); included rehabilitation assignment to Lake Elsinore (June 28-July 3). ... On San Diego disabled list (April 5-May 15 and July 18-August 24, 2002); included rehabilitation assignment to Lake Elsinore (August 5-21). ... Sent outright to Portland (May 17, 2003).

2003 GAMES PLAYED BY POSITION (MLB): C—23, P—1.

Year— Team (League)	Pos.	G	AB	R	H	2B	3B	HR	RBI	BB	SO	HBP	GDP	SB-CS	Avg.	OBP	SLG	OPS	E	Pct.
1992— Dom. Pirates (DSL)	C	63	190	20	48	6	1	3	33	22	12	...	...	4-...	.253	...	.342	...	9	.969
1993— Dom. Pirates (DSL)	IF-C	69	244	47	73	10	3	7	47	40	15	...	...	24-...	.299	...	.451	...	8	.986
1994— GC Pirates (GCL)	C-1B	41	143	25	48	8	2	4	26	13	13	3	3	2-4	.336	.400	.503	.903	12	.961
1995— Augusta (S. Atl.)	C	84	278	41	67	17	0	3	36	26	32	2	7	5-4	.241	.305	.335	.640	6	.985
1996— Augusta (S. Atl.)	C	118	419	52	106	21	3	4	62	58	41	7	14	4-6	.253	.350	.346	.696	* 23	.976
1997— Rancho Cuca. (Calif.)	C	33	110	18	33	9	1	5	26	7	25	0	1	1-1	.300	.339	.536	.875	2	.985
— Mobile (Sou.)	C	47	143	15	39	7	1	4	25	10	12	2	5	1-1	.273	.327	.420	.747	3	.989
1998— Rancho Cuca. (Calif.)	C	75	292	51	84	24	2	10	59	26	54	2	6	0-0	.288	.346	.486	.832	3	.993
— Mobile (Sou.)	C	22	67	20	26	9	0	4	26	14	4	2	1	0-0	.388	.494	.701	1.196	0	1.000
1999— Mobile (Sou.)	C-DH	61	225	38	76	16	2	10	49	29	28	7	8	0-0	.338	.424	.560	.984	7	.982
— Las Vegas (PCL)	C-DH	24	92	13	25	6	0	6	12	5	10	3	3	0-0	.272	.330	.533	.863	3	.984
— San Diego (N.L.)	C	30	83	7	21	2	1	3	12	1	8	1	5	0-0	.253	.271	.410	.680	1	.992
2000— San Diego (N.L.)	C	95	284	25	66	15	1	5	30	30	31	3	5	1-2	.232	.311	.345	.656	5	.991
2001— San Diego (N.L.)	C-DH	64	160	16	44	6	0	8	27	11	28	4	3	2-0	.275	.335	.463	.798	3	.989
— Lake Elsinore (Calif.)	C	4	13	1	2	0	0	0	1	2	4	0	0	0-0	.154	.250	.154	.404	1	.973
2002— San Diego (N.L.)	C	56	164	16	36	8	1	1	20	27	24	1	10	0-0	.220	.330	.299	.629	6	.985
— Lake Elsinore (Calif.)	C	19	53	10	18	8	0	1	6	12	3	4	2	0-0	.340	.486	.547	1.033	2	.983
2003— San Diego (N.L.)	C-P	24	65	1	13	5	0	0	10	5	13	1	3	0-0	.200	.264	.277	.541	1	.993
— Portland (PCL)	C-DH	44	149	17	42	8	1	4	20	21	12	3	5	1-0	.282	.379	.430	.809	4	.987
Major League totals (5 years)		269	756	65	180	36	3	17	99	74	104	10	26	3-2	.238	.312	.361	.674	16	.989

GOOD, ANDREW — P

PERSONAL: Born September 19, 1979, in San Diego, Calif. ... 6-1/209. ... Throws right, bats right. :.. Full name: Andrew Richard Good. ... High school: Rochester (Rochester Hills, Mich.).

TRANSACTIONS/CAREER NOTES: Selected by Arizona Diamondbacks organization in eighth round of free-agent draft (June 2, 1998). ... On disabled list (April 6 through remainder of 2000 season).

CAREER HITTING: 2-for-16 (.125), 0 R, 0 2B, 0 3B, 0 HR, 1 RBI.

Year— League	W	L	Pct.	ERA	WHIP	G	GS	CG	ShO	Hld.	Sv.-Opp.	IP	H	R	ER	HR	BB-IBB	SO	Avg.
1998— Ariz. D'backs (Ariz.)	1	3	.250	4.28	1.57	9	8	0	0	...	0-...	33.2	46	25	16	1	7-0	25	.324
— South Bend (Mid.)	0	1	.000	3.00	1.33	2	0	0	0	...	0-...	6.0	7	4	2	0	1-0	6	.280
1999— South Bend (Mid.)	11	10	.524	4.10	1.31	27	27	0	0	...	0-...	153.2	160	80	70	9	42-0	146	.267
2000—										Did not play.									
2001— Lancaster (Calif.)	8	6	.571	4.80	1.33	19	18	0	0	...	0-...	101.1	108	63	54	12	27-0	104	.267
— El Paso (Texas)	2	3	.400	5.88	1.75	10	9	0	0	...	0-...	56.2	79	44	37	2	20-0	46	.324
2002— El Paso (Texas)	13	6	.684	3.54	1.10	28	27	2	1	...	0-...	178.0	170	89	70	21	26-0	127	.248
2003— Arizona (N.L.)	4	2	.667	5.29	1.36	16	10	0	0	1	0-0	66.1	74	42	39	15	16-3	42	.281
— Tucson (PCL)	4	4	.500	5.00	1.44	11	11	0	0	...	0-...	63.0	78	36	35	12	13-0	45	.300
Major League totals (1 year)	4	2	.667	5.29	1.36	16	10	0	0	1	0-0	66.1	74	42	39	15	16-3	42	.281

GOODWIN, TOM — OF

PERSONAL: Born July 27, 1968, in Fresno, Calif. ... 6-0/185. ... Bats left, throws right. ... Full name: Thomas Jones Goodwin. ... High school: Central (Fresno, Calif.). ... College: Fresno State.

TRANSACTIONS/CAREER NOTES: Selected by Pittsburgh Pirates organization in sixth round of free-agent draft (June 2, 1986); did not sign. ... Selected by Los Angeles Dodgers organization in first round (22nd pick overall) of free-agent draft (June 5, 1989). ... Claimed on waivers by Kansas City Royals (January 6, 1994). ... Traded by Royals to Texas Rangers for 3B Dean Palmer (July 25, 1997). ... On Texas disabled list (June 11-27 and June 28-August 6, 1999); included rehabilitation assignment to Charlotte (August 2-6). ... Granted free agency (October 28, 1999). ... Signed by Colorado Rockies (December 9, 1999). ... Traded by Rockies with cash to Dodgers for OF Todd Hollandsworth, OF Kevin Gibbs and P Randey Dorame (July 31, 2000). ... On Los Angeles disabled list (July 21-August 9, 2001); included rehabilitation assignment to Wilmington (S. Atl.) (July 7-9). ... Released by Dodgers (April 8, 2002). ... Signed by San Francisco Giants organization (April 17, 2002). ... Granted free agency (November 6, 2003). ... Signed by Chicago Cubs organization (January 16, 2003).

2003 GAMES PLAYED BY POSITION (MLB): OF—57.

Year— Team (League)	Pos.	G	AB	R	H	2B	3B	HR	RBI	BB	SO	HBP	GDP	SB-CS	Avg.	OBP	SLG	OPS	E	Pct.
1989— Great Falls (Pio.)	OF	63	240	* 55	74	12	3	2	33	28	30	2	3	* 60-8	.308	.382	.408	.791	1	.986
1990— Bakersfield (Calif.)	OF	32	134	24	39	6	2	0	13	11	22	0	0	22-4	.291	.345	.366	.710	0	1.000
— San Antonio (Texas)	OF	102	428	76	119	15	4	0	28	38	72	1	3	* 60-11	.278	.336	.332	.668	3	.989
1991— Albuquerque (PCL)	OF	132	509	84	139	19	4	1	45	59	83	2	5	48-* 22	.273	.349	.332	.681	3	.990
— Los Angeles (N.L.)	OF	16	7	3	1	0	0	0	0	0	0	0	0	1-1	.143	.143	.143	.286	0	1.000
1992— Albuquerque (PCL)	OF	82	319	48	96	10	4	2	28	37	47	1	3	27-10	.301	.372	.376	.748	1	.995
— Los Angeles (N.L.)	OF	57	73	15	17	1	1	0	3	6	10	0	0	7-3	.233	.291	.274	.565	0	1.000
1993— Los Angeles (N.L.)	OF	30	17	6	5	1	0	0	1	1	4	0	1	1-2	.294	.333	.353	.686	0	1.000
— Albuquerque (PCL)	OF	85	289	48	75	5	5	1	28	30	51	2	1	21-5	.260	.329	.322	.651	2	.986
1994— Kansas City (A.L.)	DH-OF	2	2	0	0	0	0	0	0	0	1	0	0	0-0	.000	.000	.000	.000	0	1.000
— Omaha (A.A.)	OF	113	429	67	132	17	7	2	34	23	60	4	1	* 50-* 20	.308	.346	.394	.740	2	.993
1995— Kansas City (A.L.)	OF-DH	133	480	72	138	16	3	4	28	38	72	5	7	50-18	.288	.346	.358	.704	3	.990
1996— Kansas City (A.L.)	OF-DH	143	524	80	148	14	4	1	35	39	79	2	3	66-22	.282	.334	.330	.664	5	.984
1997— Kansas City (A.L.)	OF	97	367	51	100	13	4	2	22	19	51	2	5	34-10	.272	.311	.346	.657	1	.996
— Texas (A.L.)	OF	53	207	39	49	13	2	0	17	25	37	1	2	16-6	.237	.319	.319	.638	2	.986
1998— Texas (A.L.)	OF-DH	154	520	102	151	13	3	2	33	73	90	2	2	38-20	.290	.378	.338	.716	3	.992
1999— Texas (A.L.)	OF	109	405	63	105	12	6	3	33	40	61	0	7	39-11	.259	.324	.341	.664	3	.989
— Charlotte (Fla. St.)	OF	3	11	2	4	1	0	0	0	1	4	0	0	0-0	.364	.417	.455	.871	0	1.000
2000— Colorado (N.L.)	OF	91	317	65	86	8	8	5	47	50	76	1	3	39-7	.271	.368	.394	.763	3	.986
— Los Angeles (N.L.)	OF	56	211	29	53	3	1	1	11	18	41	0	4	16-3	.251	.310	.289	.599	1	.994
2001— Los Angeles (N.L.)	OF	105	286	51	66	8	5	4	22	23	58	0	3	22-8	.231	.286	.336	.622	1	.994
— Wilmington (S. Atl.)	OF	2	5	2	2	0	1	0	1	1	0	0	0	0-0	.400	.429	.800	1.229	0	1.000
2002— Fresno (PCL)	OF	17	62	11	14	3	1	0	7	8	8	0	1	3-2	.226	.314	.306	.621	0	1.000
— San Francisco (N.L.)	OF	78	154	23	40	5	2	1	17	14	25	0	3	16-2	.260	.321	.338	.659	1	.990
2003— Chicago (N.L.)	OF	87	171	26	49	10	0	1	12	11	33	0	3	19-5	.287	.328	.363	.690	0	1.000
American League totals (6 years)		691	2505	407	691	81	22	12	168	234	391	12	26	243-87	.276	.339	.340	.679	17	.990
National League totals (7 years)		520	1236	218	317	36	17	12	113	123	247	1	17	121-31	.256	.323	.342	.665	5	.993
Major League totals (13 years)		1211	3741	625	1008	117	39	24	281	357	638	13	43	364-118	.269	.334	.341	.675	22	.991

G

GORDON, TOM   P

PERSONAL: Born November 18, 1967, in Sebring, Fla. ... 5-10/190. ... Throws right, bats right. ... Full name: Thomas Gordon. ... High school: Avon Park (Fla.).

TRANSACTIONS/CAREER NOTES: Selected by Kansas City Royals organization in sixth round of free-agent draft (June 2, 1986). ... On disabled list (August 12-September 1, 1992; and May 8-24, 1995). ... Granted free agency (October 30, 1995). ... Signed by Boston Red Sox (December 21, 1995). ... On Boston disabled list (April 18-May 10 and June 12-September 27, 1999); included rehabilitation assignments to Trenton (September 11-13) and Augusta (September 14-25). ... On disabled list (April 2, 2000-entire season). ... Granted free agency (November 1, 2000). ... Signed by Chicago Cubs (December 14, 2000). ... On Chicago disabled list (March 23-May 1, 2001); included rehabilitation assignments to Daytona (April 23-27) and Iowa (April 28-May 1). ... On Chicago disabled list (March 28-July 2, 2002); included rehabilitation assignments to Daytona (June 21-27) and Iowa (June 28-July 1). ... Traded by Cubs to Houston Astros for P Russ Rohlicek and two players to be named later (August 22, 2002); Cubs acquired P Travis Anderson and P Mike Nannini to complete deal (September 11, 2002). ... Granted free agency (October 29, 2002). ... Signed by Chicago White Sox (January 20, 2003).

CAREER HITTING: 0-for-1 (.000), 0 R, 0 2B, 0 3B, 0 HR, 0 RBI.

Year League	W	L	Pct.	ERA	WHIP	G	GS	CG	ShO	Hld.	Sv.-Opp.	IP	H	R	ER	HR	BB-IBB	SO	Avg.
1986— GC Royals (GCL)	3	1	.750	1.02	1.23	9	7	2	1	...	0-...	44.0	31	12	5	0	23-1	47	.194
— Omaha (Am. Assoc.)	0	0	...	47.25	6.00	1	0	0	0	...	0-...	1.1	6	7	7	0	2-0	3	.600
1987— Eugene (NW)	•9	0	•1.000	2.86	1.31	15	13	0	0	...	1-...	72.1	48	33	23	2	47-0	91	.183
— Fort Myers (Fla. St.)	1	0	1.000	2.63	1.61	3	3	0	0	...	0-...	13.2	5	4	4	0	17-0	11	.122
1988— Appleton (Midw.)	7	5	.583	2.06	0.95	17	17	5	1	...	0-...	118.0	69	30	27	3	43-1	*172	.163
— Memphis (Sou.)	6	0	1.000	0.38	0.70	6	6	2	2	...	0-...	47.1	16	3	2	1	17-0	62	.103
— Omaha (Am. Assoc.)	3	0	1.000	1.33	1.28	3	3	0	0	...	0-...	20.1	11	3	3	0	15-0	29	.157
— Kansas City (A.L.)	0	2	.000	5.17	1.47	5	2	0	0	2	0-0	15.2	16	9	9	1	7-0	18	.267
1989— Kansas City (A.L.)	17	9	.654	3.64	1.28	49	16	1	1	3	1-7	163.0	122	67	66	10	86-4	153	.210
1990— Kansas City (A.L.)	12	11	.522	3.73	1.49	32	32	6	1	0	0-0	195.1	192	99	81	17	99-1	175	.258
1991— Kansas City (A.L.)	9	14	.391	3.87	1.37	45	14	1	0	4	1-4	158.0	129	76	68	16	87-6	167	.221
1992— Kansas City (A.L.)	6	10	.375	4.59	1.45	40	11	0	0	0	0-2	117.2	116	67	60	9	55-4	98	.258
1993— Kansas City (A.L.)	12	6	.667	3.58	1.30	48	14	2	0	2	1-6	155.2	125	65	62	11	77-5	143	.223
1994— Kansas City (A.L.)	11	7	.611	4.35	1.44	24	24	0	0	0	0-0	155.1	136	79	75	15	87-3	126	.237
1995— Kansas City (A.L.)	12	12	.500	4.43	1.55	31	31	2	0	0	0-0	189.0	204	110	93	12	89-4	119	.279
1996— Boston (A.L.)	12	9	.571	5.59	1.64	34	34	4	1	0	0-0	215.2	249	143	*134	28	105-5	171	.293
1997— Boston (A.L.)	6	10	.375	3.74	1.28	42	25	2	1	0	11-13	182.2	155	85	76	10	78-1	159	.226
1998— Boston (A.L.)	7	4	.636	2.72	1.01	73	0	0	0	0	*46-47	79.1	55	24	24	2	25-1	78	.191
1999— Boston (A.L.)	0	2	.000	5.60	1.64	21	0	0	0	1	11-13	17.2	17	11	11	2	12-2	24	.246
2000— Boston (A.L.)										Did not play.									
2001— Daytona (Fla. St.)	0	0	...	0.00	0.00	2	2	0	0	...	0-...	2.0	0	0	0	0	0-0	3	.000
— Iowa (PCL)	0	0	...	0.00	1.00	2	0	0	0	...	0-...	2.0	1	0	0	0	1-0	2	.167
— Chicago (N.L.)	1	2	.333	3.38	1.06	47	0	0	0	9	27-31	45.1	32	18	17	4	16-1	67	.188
2002— Daytona (Fla. St.)	0	0	...	3.38	1.13	2	2	0	0	...	0-...	2.2	1	1	1	0	2-0	3	.100
— Iowa (PCL)	0	0	...	16.20	2.40	2	0	0	0	...	1-...	1.2	1	4	3	0	3-0	0	.167
— Chicago (N.L.)	1	1	.500	3.42	1.56	19	0	0	0	2	0-0	23.2	27	12	9	1	10-1	31	.293
— Houston (N.L.)	0	2	.000	3.32	1.11	15	0	0	0	4	0-0	19.0	15	7	7	2	6-2	17	.217
2003— Chicago (A.L.)	7	6	.538	3.16	1.19	66	0	0	0	7	12-17	74.0	57	29	26	4	31-3	91	.213
American League totals (13 years)	111	102	.521	4.11	1.40	510	203	18	4	19	83-109	1719.0	1573	864	785	137	838-39	1522	.243
National League totals (2 years)	2	5	.286	3.38	1.20	81	0	0	0	6	27-31	88.0	74	37	33	7	32-4	115	.224
Major League totals (15 years)	113	107	.514	4.07	1.39	591	203	18	4	25	110-140	1807.0	1647	901	818	144	870-43	1637	.242

GRABOW, JOHN   P

PERSONAL: Born November 4, 1978, in Arcadia, Calif. ... 6-2/185. ... Throws left, bats left. ... Full name: John William Grabow. ... High school: San Gabriel (Calif.).

TRANSACTIONS/CAREER NOTES: Selected by Pittsburgh Pirates organization in third round of free-agent draft (June 3, 1997). ... On disabled list (June 20-July 6, 2000). ... On Altoona disabled list (May 20-June 25 and July 17-26, 2001).

CAREER HITTING: 0-for-0 (.000), 0 R, 0 2B, 0 3B, 0 HR, 0 RBI.

Year League	W	L	Pct.	ERA	WHIP	G	GS	CG	ShO	Hld.	Sv.-Opp.	IP	H	R	ER	HR	BB-IBB	SO	Avg.
1997— GC Pirates (GCL)	2	7	.222	4.57	1.57	11	8	0	0	...	0-...	45.1	57	32	23	0	14-0	28	.305
1998— Augusta (S. Atl.)	6	3	.667	5.78	1.65	17	16	0	0	...	0-...	71.2	84	59	46	7	34-0	67	.294
1999— Hickory (S. Atl.)	9	10	.474	3.80	1.18	26	26	0	0	...	0-...	156.1	152	82	66	16	32-0	164	.249
2000— Altoona (East.)	8	7	.533	4.33	1.44	24	24	1	0	...	0-...	145.1	145	81	70	10	65-0	109	.259
2001— GC Pirates (GCL)	0	1	.000	3.75	1.25	6	6	0	0	...	0-...	12.0	11	6	5	1	4-0	9	.244
— Lynchburg (Carolina)	1	3	.250	6.38	1.85	7	7	0	0	...	0-...	36.2	42	30	26	3	26-0	35	.294
— Altoona (East.)	2	5	.286	3.38	1.36	10	10	0	0	...	0-...	50.2	30	23	19	1	39-0	42	.175
2002— Altoona (East.)	8	13	.381	5.47	1.56	28	27	1	1	...	0-...	146.1	181	94	89	10	47-0	97	.308
2003— Altoona (East.)	6	1	.857	3.36	1.28	24	9	0	0	...	1-...	83.0	87	34	31	9	19-2	73	.281
— Nashville (PCL)	0	2	.000	4.74	1.54	17	0	0	0	...	0-...	24.2	31	17	13	0	7-2	26	.298
— Pittsburgh (N.L.)	0	0	...	3.60	1.20	5	0	0	0	0	0-0	5.0	6	3	2	0	0-0	9	.273
Major League totals (1 year)	0	0	...	3.60	1.20	5	0	0	0	0	0-0	5.0	6	3	2	0	0-0	9	.273

GRABOWSKI, JASON   3B/OF

PERSONAL: Born May 24, 1976, in New Haven, Conn. ... 6-3/200. ... Bats left, throws right. ... Full name: Jason William Grabowski. ... High school: The Morgan School (Clinton, Conn.). ... College: Connecticut.

TRANSACTIONS/CAREER NOTES: Selected by New York Yankees organization in 17th round of free-agent draft (June 2, 1994); did not sign. ... Selected by Texas Rangers organization in second round of free-agent draft (June 3, 1997). ... Claimed on waivers by Seattle Mariners (December 18, 2000). ... On disabled list (June 22-July 2, 2001). ... Selected by Oakland Athletics from Mariners organization in Rule 5 major league draft (December 13, 2001). ... On Sacramento disabled list (April 18-May 29 and June 29-July 19, 2002).

2003 GAMES PLAYED BY POSITION (MLB): OF—3, 3B—1, DH—1.

Year Team (League)	Pos.	G	AB	R	H	2B	3B	HR	RBI	BB	SO	HBP	GDP	SB-CS	Avg.	OBP	SLG	OPS	E	Pct.
1997— Pulaski (Appal.)	C	50	174	36	51	14	0	4	24	40	32	0	2	6-1	.293	.423	.443	.866	8	.982
1998— Savannah (S. Atl.)	C-1B	104	352	63	95	13	6	14	52	57	93	1	7	16-9	.270	.372	.460	.832	6	.990
1999— Charlotte (Fla. St.)	3B-1B	123	434	68	136	31	6	12	87	65	66	5	8	13-10	.313	.407	.495	.903	21	.917
— Tulsa (Texas)	DH	2	6	1	1	0	0	0	0	2	2	0	0	0-0	.167	.375	.167	.542	...	...
2000— Tulsa (Texas)	3B	135	493	93	135	33	5	19	90	88	106	4	12	8-7	.274	.383	.477	.860	*40	.898
2001— Tacoma (PCL)	3-0-1-S	114	394	60	117	32	3	9	58	61	94	2	8	7-4	.297	.390	.462	.852	21	.942
2002— Sacramento (PCL)	OF-C-3	73	265	50	78	22	3	12	52	39	56	1	6	6-4	.294	.387	.536	.923	8	.962
— Oakland (A.L.)	OF	4	8	3	3	1	1	0	1	3	1	0	0	0-0	.375	.545	.750	1.295	0	1.000
2003— Ariz. A's (Ariz.)	DH	2	6	1	2	1	0	1	3	0	0	0	0	0-0	.333	.556	.500	1.056	0	.000
— Sacramento (PCL)	0-D-C-1-S	67	250	44	73	13	2	9	40	31	46	0	6	7-2	.292	.364	.468	.832	5	.969
— Oakland (A.L.)	OF-3B-DH	8	8	0	0	0	0	0	0	1	5	0	0	0-0	.000	.111	.000	.111	0	1.000
Major League totals (2 years)		12	16	3	3	1	1	0	1	4	6	0	0	0-0	.188	.350	.375	.725	0	1.000

G

GRACE, MARK — 1B

PERSONAL: Born June 28, 1964, in Winston-Salem, N.C. ... 6-2/200. ... Bats left, throws left. ... Full name: Mark Eugene Grace. ... High school: Tustin (Calif.). ... College: San Diego State.

TRANSACTIONS/CAREER NOTES: Selected by Minnesota Twins organization in 15th round of free-agent draft (January 17, 1984); did not sign. ... Selected by Chicago Cubs organization in 24th round of free-agent draft (June 3, 1985). ... On disabled list (June 5-23, 1989). ... Granted free agency (October 15, 1994). ... Re-signed by Cubs (April 7, 1995). ... Granted free agency (November 3, 1995). ... Re-signed by Cubs (December 19, 1995). ... On disabled list (June 11-28, 1996; April 4-19, 1997; and May 11-31, 2000). ... Granted free agency (October 30, 2000). ... Signed by Arizona Diamondbacks (December 8, 2000). ... Granted free agency (November 1, 2002). ... Re-signed by Diamondbacks (December 21, 2002).

2003 GAMES PLAYED BY POSITION (MLB): 1B—39, DH—1.

Year — Team (League)	Pos.	G	AB	R	H	2B	3B	HR	RBI	BB	SO	HBP	GDP	SB-CS	Avg.	OBP	SLG	OPS	E	Pct.
1986— Peoria (Midw.)	1B-OF	126	465	81	159	30	4	15	95	60	28	4	11	6-5	* .342	.417	.520	.937	13	.989
1987— Pittsfield (East.)	1B	123	453	81	151	29	8	17	* 101	48	24	2	3	5-5	.333	.394	.545	.939	6	* .995
1988— Iowa (Am. Assoc.)	1B	21	67	11	17	4	0	0	14	13	4	0	0	1-0	.254	.361	.313	.675	1	.995
—Chicago (N.L.)	1B	134	486	65	144	23	4	7	57	60	43	0	12	3-3	.296	.371	.403	.774	• 17	.987
1989— Chicago (N.L.)	1B	142	510	74	160	28	3	13	79	80	42	0	13	14-7	.314	.405	.457	.862	6	.996
1990— Chicago (N.L.)	1B	157	589	72	182	32	1	9	82	59	54	5	10	15-6	.309	.372	.413	.785	12	.992
1991— Chicago (N.L.)	1B	160	* 619	87	169	28	5	8	58	70	53	3	6	3-4	.273	.346	.373	.719	8	.995
1992— Chicago (N.L.)	1B	158	603	72	185	37	5	9	79	72	36	4	14	6-1	.307	.380	.430	.809	4	.998
1993— Chicago (N.L.)	1B	155	594	86	193	39	4	14	98	71	32	1	*25	8-4	.325	.393	.475	.867	5	.997
1994— Chicago (N.L.)	1B	106	403	55	120	23	3	6	44	48	41	0	10	0-1	.298	.370	.414	.784	7	.993
1995— Chicago (N.L.)	1B	143	552	97	180	* 51	3	16	92	65	46	2	10	6-2	.326	.395	.516	.911	7	.995
1996— Chicago (N.L.)	1B	142	547	88	181	39	1	9	75	62	41	1	18	2-3	.331	.396	.455	.851	4	.997
1997— Chicago (N.L.)	1B	151	555	87	177	32	5	13	78	88	45	2	18	2-4	.319	.409	.465	.874	6	.995
1998— Chicago (N.L.)	1B	158	595	92	184	39	3	17	89	93	56	3	17	4-7	.309	.401	.471	.872	8	.994
1999— Chicago (N.L.)	1B	161	593	107	183	44	5	16	91	83	44	2	14	3-4	.309	.390	.481	.870	8	.994
2000— Chicago (N.L.)	1B	143	510	75	143	41	1	11	82	95	28	6	7	1-2	.280	.394	.429	.824	4	.997
2001— Arizona (N.L.)	1B	145	476	66	142	31	2	15	78	67	36	4	7	1-0	.298	.386	.466	.852	5	.995
2002— Arizona (N.L.)	1B	124	298	43	75	19	0	7	48	46	30	1	5	2-0	.252	.351	.386	.736	7	.990
2003— Arizona (N.L.)	1B-DH	66	135	13	27	5	0	3	16	16	15	0	6	0-0	.200	.279	.304	.583	2	.993
Major League totals (16 years)		2245	8065	1179	2445	511	45	173	1146	1075	642	34	192	70-48	.303	.383	.442	.825	110	.995

GRAFFANINO, TONY — SS/2B

PERSONAL: Born June 6, 1972, in Amityville, N.Y. ... 6-1/190. ... Bats right, throws right. ... Full name: Anthony Joseph Graffanino. ... Name pronounced: graf-a-NEEN-oh. ... High school: East Islip (Islip Terrace, N.Y.).

TRANSACTIONS/CAREER NOTES: Selected by Atlanta Braves organization in 10th round of free-agent draft (June 4, 1990). ... On disabled list (July 3, 1995-remainder of season). ... Released by Braves (April 2, 1999). ... Signed by Tampa Bay Devil Rays organization (April 9, 1999). ... Traded by Devil Rays to Chicago White Sox for P Tanyon Sturtze (May 31, 2000). ... On disabled list (August 26-September 30, 2002).

2003 GAMES PLAYED BY POSITION (MLB): SS—36, 2B—29, 3B—20, DH—3, 1B—2.

Year — Team (League)	Pos.	G	AB	R	H	2B	3B	HR	RBI	BB	SO	HBP	GDP	SB-CS	Avg.	OBP	SLG	OPS	E	Pct.
1990— Pulaski (Appal.)	SS	42	131	23	27	5	1	0	11	26	17	2	3	6-3	.206	.344	.260	.603	24	.873
1991— Idaho Falls (Pio.)	SS	66	274	53	95	16	4	4	56	27	37	3	2	19-4	.347	.408	.478	.887	* 29	.912
1992— Macon (S. Atl.)	2B	112	400	50	96	15	5	10	31	50	84	8	6	9-6	.240	.333	.378	.711	17	.961
1993— Durham (Caro.)	2B	123	459	78	126	30	5	15	69	45	78	4	10	24-11	.275	.342	.460	.801	15	.968
1994— Greenville (Sou.)	2B-DH	124	440	66	132	28	3	7	52	50	53	2	8	29-7	.300	.372	.425	.797	14	.976
1995— Richmond (Int'l)	2B	50	179	20	34	6	0	4	17	15	49	1	4	2-2	.190	.254	.291	.544	4	.983
1996— Richmond (Int'l)	2B	96	353	57	100	29	2	7	33	34	72	3	3	11-7	.283	.350	.436	.787	10	.977
—Atlanta (N.L.)	2B	22	46	7	8	1	1	0	2	4	13	1	0	0-0	.174	.250	.239	.489	2	.969
1997— Atlanta (N.L.)	2-3-SS-1	104	186	33	48	9	1	8	20	26	46	1	3	6-4	.258	.344	.446	.790	5	.982
1998— Atlanta (N.L.)	2B-SS-3B	105	289	32	61	14	1	5	22	24	68	2	7	1-4	.211	.275	.318	.594	11	.971
1999— Durham (Int'l)	2B-DH-3B	87	345	66	108	25	6	9	58	37	46	3	9	16-9	.313	.379	.499	.878	1	.998
—Tampa Bay (A.L.)	2-SS-3-D	39	130	20	41	9	4	2	19	9	22	1	1	3-2	.315	.364	.492	.857	5	.973
2000— Tampa Bay (A.L.)	2B-3B-SS	13	20	8	6	1	0	0	1	1	2	1	1	0-0	.300	.364	.350	.714	0	1.000
—Durham (Int'l)	SS-2-3-1	10	35	9	10	3	0	2	6	7	8	0	0	2-0	.286	.405	.543	.948	0	1.000
—Chicago (A.L.)	SS-2-3-D	57	148	25	40	5	1	2	16	21	25	1	1	7-4	.270	.363	.358	.721	6	.968
2001— Chicago (A.L.)	3-2-S-D-O-1	74	145	23	44	9	0	2	15	16	29	1	4	4-1	.303	.370	.407	.777	7	.957
2002— Chicago (A.L.)	3B-2B-SS	70	229	35	60	12	4	6	31	22	38	2	2	2-1	.262	.329	.428	.757	10	.953
2003— Chicago (A.L.)	S-2-3-D-1	90	250	51	65	15	3	7	23	24	37	3	1	8-0	.260	.331	.428	.759	8	.972
American League totals (5 years)		343	922	162	256	51	12	19	105	93	153	9	10	24-8	.278	.347	.421	.768	36	.966
National League totals (3 years)		231	521	72	117	24	3	13	44	54	127	4	10	7-8	.225	.299	.357	.656	18	.975
Major League totals (8 years)		574	1443	234	373	75	15	32	149	147	280	13	20	31-16	.258	.330	.398	.727	54	.970

GRAVES, DANNY — P

PERSONAL: Born August 7, 1973, in Saigon, Vietnam. ... 6-0/185. ... Throws right, bats right. ... Full name: Daniel Peter Graves. ... High school: Brandon (Fla.). ... College: Miami (Fla.).

TRANSACTIONS/CAREER NOTES: Selected by Cleveland Indians organization in fourth round of free-agent draft (June 2, 1994). ... Traded by Indians with P Jim Crowell, P Scott Winchester and IF Damian Jackson to Cincinnati Reds for P John Smiley and IF Jeff Branson (July 31, 1997).

CAREER HITTING: 8-for-76 (.105), 5 R, 0 2B, 0 3B, 2 HR, 3 RBI.

Year — League	W	L	Pct.	ERA	WHIP	G	GS	CG	ShO	Hld.	Sv.-Opp.	IP	H	R	ER	HR	BB-IBB	SO	Avg.
1995— Kinston (Caro.)	3	1	.750	0.82	0.95	38	0	0	0	...	21-...	44.0	30	11	4	0	12-2	46	.183
—Cant./Akr. (Eastern)	1	0	1.000	0.00	0.51	17	0	0	0	...	10-...	23.1	10	1	0	0	2-0	11	.133
—Buffalo (A.A.)	0	0	...	3.00	2.00	3	0	0	0	...	0-...	3.0	5	4	1	0	1-0	2	.333
1996— Buffalo (A.A.)	4	3	.571	1.48	1.03	43	0	0	0	...	19-...	79.0	57	14	13	1	24-2	46	.208
—Cleveland (A.L.)	2	0	1.000	4.55	1.31	15	0	0	0	0	0-1	29.2	29	18	15	2	10-0	22	.246
1997— Buffalo (A.A.)	2	3	.400	4.19	1.30	19	3	0	0	...	2-...	43.0	45	21	20	3	11-0	21	.276
—Cleveland (A.L.)	0	0	...	4.76	2.12	5	0	0	0	0	0-0	11.1	15	8	6	2	9-0	4	.326
—Indianapolis (A.A.)	1	0	1.000	3.09	1.03	11	0	0	0	...	5-...	11.2	7	4	4	1	5-0	5	.184
—Cincinnati (N.L.)	0	0	...	6.14	2.52	14	0	0	0	1	0-0	14.2	26	14	10	0	11-1	7	.413

G

Year	League	W	L	Pct.	ERA	WHIP	G	GS	CG	ShO	Hld.	Sv.-Opp.	IP	H	R	ER	HR	BB-IBB	SO	Avg.
1998— Indianapolis (Int'l)		1	0	1.000	1.93	1.29	13	0	0	0	...	0-...	14.0	15	3	3	0	3-0	11	.273
— Cincinnati (N.L.)		2	1	.667	3.32	1.28	62	0	0	0	6	8-8	81.1	76	31	30	6	28-4	44	.252
1999— Cincinnati (N.L.)		8	7	.533	3.08	1.25	75	0	0	0	0	27-36	111.0	90	42	38	0	49-4	69	.227
2000— Cincinnati (N.L.)		10	5	.667	2.56	1.35	66	0	0	0	0	30-35	91.1	81	31	26	8	42-7	53	.243
2001— Cincinnati (N.L.)		6	5	.545	4.15	1.26	66	0	0	0	0	32-39	80.1	83	41	37	7	18-6	49	.268
2002— Cincinnati (N.L.)		7	3	.700	3.19	1.26	68	4	0	0	0	32-39	98.2	99	37	35	7	25-9	58	.264
2003— Cincinnati (N.L.)		4	15	.211	5.33	1.45	30	26	2	1	0	2-2	169.0	204	108	100	30	41-6	60	.298
American League totals (2 years)		2	0	1.000	4.61	1.54	20	0	0	0	0	0-1	41.0	44	26	21	4	19-0	26	.268
National League totals (7 years)		37	36	.507	3.84	1.35	377	30	2	1	7	131-159	646.1	659	304	276	68	214-37	340	.268
Major League totals (8 years)		39	36	.520	3.89	1.36	397	30	2	1	7	131-160	687.1	703	330	297	72	233-37	366	.268

GREEN, SHAWN   OF

PERSONAL: Born November 10, 1972, in Des Plaines, Ill. ... 6-4/200. ... Bats left, throws left. ... Full name: Shawn David Green. ... High school: Tustin (Calif.).

TRANSACTIONS/CAREER NOTES: Selected by Toronto Blue Jays organization in first round (16th pick overall) of free-agent draft (June 3, 1991); pick received as compensation for San Francisco Giants signing Type A free-agent P Bud Black. ... On disabled list (June 30-July 23, 1992). ... On Knoxville disabled list (June 11-July 24, 1993). ... Traded by Blue Jays with 2B Jorge Nunez to Los Angeles Dodgers for OF Raul Mondesi and P Pedro Borbon (November 8, 1999).

2003 GAMES PLAYED BY POSITION (MLB): OF—157, DH—2.

Year	Team (League)	Pos.	G	AB	R	H	2B	3B	HR	RBI	BB	SO	HBP	GDP	SB-CS	Avg.	OBP	SLG	OPS	E	Pct.
1992— Dunedin (Fla. St.)		OF	114	417	44	114	21	3	1	49	28	66	4	9	22-9	.273	.319	.345	.665	5	.974
1993— Knoxville (Sou.)		OF	99	360	40	102	14	2	4	34	26	72	5	6	4-9	.283	.339	.367	.706	8	.956
— Toronto (A.L.)		OF-DH	3	6	0	0	0	0	0	0	0	1	0	0	0-0	.000	.000	.000	.000	0	1.000
1994— Syracuse (Int'l)		OF-DH	109	433	82	149	27	3	13	61	40	54	4	5	19-7	.344	.401	.510	.912	1	.996
— Toronto (A.L.)		OF	14	33	1	3	1	0	0	1	1	8	0	1	1-0	.091	.118	.121	.239	0	1.000
1995— Toronto (A.L.)		OF	121	379	52	109	31	4	15	54	20	68	3	4	1-2	.288	.326	.509	.835	6	.973
1996— Toronto (A.L.)		OF-DH	132	422	52	118	32	3	11	45	33	75	8	9	5-1	.280	.342	.448	.790	2	.992
1997— Toronto (A.L.)		OF-DH	135	429	57	123	22	4	16	53	36	99	1	4	14-3	.287	.340	.469	.809	3	.984
1998— Toronto (A.L.)		OF	158	630	106	175	33	4	35	100	50	142	5	6	35-12	.278	.334	.510	.844	7	.979
1999— Toronto (A.L.)		OF	153	614	134	190	* 45	0	42	123	66	117	11	13	20-7	.309	.384	.588	.972	1	.997
2000— Los Angeles (N.L.)		OF	• 162	610	98	164	44	4	24	99	90	121	8	18	24-5	.269	.367	.472	.839	6	.980
2001— Los Angeles (N.L.)		OF-1B	161	619	121	184	31	4	49	125	72	107	5	10	20-4	.297	.372	.598	.970	6	.982
2002— Los Angeles (N.L.)		OF-1B	158	582	110	166	31	1	42	114	93	112	5	26	8-5	.285	.385	.558	.944	2	.994
2003— Los Angeles (N.L.)		OF-DH	160	611	84	171	49	2	19	85	68	112	6	18	6-2	.280	.355	.460	.814	5	.982
American League totals (7 years)			716	2513	402	718	164	15	119	376	206	510	28	37	76-25	.286	.344	.505	.849	19	.986
National League totals (4 years)			641	2422	413	685	155	11	134	423	323	452	24	72	58-16	.283	.370	.522	.892	19	.985
Major League totals (11 years)			1357	4935	815	1403	319	26	253	799	529	962	52	109	134-41	.284	.357	.513	.870	38	.985

GREENE, KHALIL   SS

PERSONAL: Born October 21, 1979, in Butler, Pa. ... 5-11/210. ... Bats right, throws right. ... Full name: Khalil Thabit Greene. ... High school: Key West (Fla.). ... College: Clemson.

TRANSACTIONS/CAREER NOTES: Selected by San Diego Padres organization in first round (13th pick overall) of free-agent draft (June 2002).

2003 GAMES PLAYED BY POSITION (MLB): SS—20.

Year	Team (League)	Pos.	G	AB	R	H	2B	3B	HR	RBI	BB	SO	HBP	GDP	SB-CS	Avg.	OBP	SLG	OPS	E	Pct.
2002— Eugene (Northwest)		SS	10	37	5	10	1	0	0	6	5	6	3	1	0-0	.270	.400	.297	.697	3	.900
— Lake Elsinore (Calif.)		SS-3B-2B	46	183	33	58	9	1	9	32	12	33	4	7	0-0	.317	.368	.525	.893	9	.947
2003— Mobile (Sou.)		SS-SH	59	229	20	63	17	2	3	20	16	55	2	7	2-3	.275	.327	.406	.733	9	.949
— Portland (PCL)		SS	76	319	42	92	19	0	10	47	20	52	11	3	5-4	.288	.346	.442	.788	11	.967
— San Diego (N.L.)		SS	20	65	8	14	4	1	2	6	4	19	1	3	0-1	.215	.271	.400	.671	3	.963
Major League totals (1 year)			20	65	8	14	4	1	2	6	4	19	1	3	0-1	.215	.271	.400	.671	3	.963

GREENE, TODD   C/DH

PERSONAL: Born May 8, 1971, in Augusta, Ga. ... 5-10/208. ... Bats right, throws right. ... Full name: Todd Anthony Greene. ... High school: Evans (Ga.). ... College: Georgia Southern.

TRANSACTIONS/CAREER NOTES: Selected by Atlanta Braves organization in 27th round of free-agent draft (June 5, 1989); did not sign. ... Selected by California Angels organization in 12th round of free-agent draft (June 3, 1993). ... On Vancouver disabled list (April 11-May 25, 1996). ... Angels franchise renamed Anaheim Angels for 1997 season. ... On Anaheim disabled list (August 20, 1997-remainder of season). ... On Anaheim disabled list (March 19-August 5, 1998); included rehabilitation assignments to Lake Elsinore (April 14-May 16, May 21 and May 27-31) and Vancouver (May 17-20, May 22-26, June 1-2 and July 17-August 5). ... On suspended list (May 13-16, 1999). ... Released by Angels (March 29, 2000). ... Signed by Toronto Blue Jays organization (April 10, 2000). ... On Toronto disabled list (June 7-23, 2000); included rehabilitation assignment to Dunedin (June 20-22). ... Released by Blue Jays (March 28, 2001). ... Signed by New York Yankees organization (April 5, 2001). ... Released by Yankees (March 26, 2002). ... Signed by Los Angeles Dodgers organization (April 2, 2002). ... Released by Dodgers (May 15, 2002). ... Signed by Texas Rangers (May 16, 2002). ... Placed on 15-day disabled list (April 30, 2003). ... Sent to Frisco on rehab assignment (May 12, 2003). ... Reinstated from 15-day disabled list (May 15, 2003).

2003 GAMES PLAYED BY POSITION (MLB): C—51, DH—3, 1B—2.

Year	Team (League)	Pos.	G	AB	R	H	2B	3B	HR	RBI	BB	SO	HBP	GDP	SB-CS	Avg.	OBP	SLG	OPS	E	Pct.
1993— Boise (NW)		OF	• 76	* 305	55	82	15	3	* 15	* 71	34	44	9	3	4-3	.269	.356	.485	.841	3	.979
1994— Lake Elsinore (Calif.)		C-1B-OF	133	524	98	158	39	2	35	124	64	96	4	12	10-3	.302	.378	.584	.962	15	.979
1995— Midland (Texas)		C-DH	82	318	59	104	19	1	26	57	17	55	5	6	3-5	.327	.365	.638	1.004	3	.992
— Vancouver (PCL)		C-DH	43	168	28	42	3	1	14	35	11	36	4	3	1-0	.250	.308	.530	.838	1	.995
1996— Vancouver (PCL)		C-DH	60	223	27	68	18	0	5	33	16	36	1	6	0-2	.305	.347	.453	.800	3	.988
— California (A.L.)		C-DH	29	79	9	15	1	0	2	9	4	11	1	4	2-0	.190	.238	.278	.517	0	1.000
1997— Anaheim (A.L.)		C-DH	34	124	24	36	6	0	9	24	7	25	0	1	2-0	.290	.328	.556	.885	1	1.000
— Vancouver (PCL)		C-DH-1-OF	64	260	51	92	22	0	25	75	20	31	5	6	5-1	.354	.408	.727	1.135	3	.992
1998— Lake Elsinore (Calif.)		DH-1B	12	44	9	10	2	0	1	6	4	7	0	1	0-0	.227	.286	.341	.627	2	.833
— Vancouver (PCL)		DH-1-C-OF	30	108	16	30	12	0	7	20	12	17	3	2	1-0	.278	.360	.583	.943	1	.990
— Anaheim (A.L.)		OF-DH-1B	29	71	3	18	4	0	1	7	2	20	0	0	0-0	.254	.274	.352	.626	0	1.000
1999— Anaheim (A.L.)		DH-OF-C	97	321	36	78	20	0	14	42	12	63	3	8	1-4	.243	.275	.436	.711	2	.980
— Edmonton (PCL)		OF-DH	19	74	10	18	6	0	5	14	0	12	1	1	0-0	.243	.253	.527	.780	0	1.000

G

Year— Team (League)	Pos.	G	AB	R	H	2B	3B	HR	RBI	BB	SO	HBP	GDP	SB-CS	Avg.	OBP	SLG	OPS	E	Pct.
2000— Syracuse (Int'l)	OF-C	24	91	14	27	3	0	7	14	6	16	0	3	1-0	.297	.337	.560	.897	1	.970
— Toronto (A.L.)	DH-C-OF	34	85	11	20	2	0	5	10	5	18	0	4	0-0	.235	.278	.435	.713	0	1.000
— Dunedin (Fla. St.)	OF	5	20	2	4	1	0	1	4	2	4	1	0	0-0	.200	.304	.400	.704	0	1.000
2001— Columbus (Int'l)	C-OF	34	131	16	33	8	0	6	17	4	19	1	3	3-2	.252	.279	.450	.730	4	.982
— New York (A.L.)	C-DH	35	96	9	20	4	0	1	11	3	21	1	3	0-0	.208	.240	.281	.521	0	1.000
2002— Las Vegas (PCL)	C-1B-OF	32	125	27	44	12	0	11	41	3	21	3	5	0-0	.352	.373	.712	1.085	2	.989
— Texas (A.L.)	C-1-DH-OF	42	112	15	30	5	0	10	19	2	23	1	4	0-0	.268	.282	.580	.862	3	.985
— Oklahoma (PCL)	C-OF-1B	39	152	21	46	9	0	6	29	9	27	1	2	2-0	.303	.339	.480	.820	2	.991
2003— Frisco (Texas)	C-1B	3	9	3	3	0	0	2	4	2	2	0	1	0-0	.333	.455	1.000	1.455	0	1.000
— Texas (A.L.)	C-DH-1B	62	205	25	47	10	1	10	20	2	47	2	2	0-0	.229	.243	.434	.677	4	.988
Major League totals (8 years)		362	1093	132	264	52	1	52	142	37	228	8	26	5-4	.242	.270	.434	.704	9	.992

GREGG, KEVIN — P

PERSONAL: Born June 20, 1978, in Corvallis, Ore. ... 6-6/220. ... Throws right, bats right. ... Full name: Kevin Marschall Gregg. ... High school: Corvallis (Ore.).

TRANSACTIONS/CAREER NOTES: Selected by Oakland Athletics organization in 15th round of free-agent draft (June 4, 1996). ... On Sacramento disabled list (June 17-24 and June 29-July 11, 2002). ... Granted free agency (October 15, 2002). ... Signed by Anaheim Angels as a free agent (November 21, 2002).

CAREER HITTING: 0-for-0 (.000), 0 R, 0 2B, 0 3B, 0 HR, 0 RBI.

Year— League	W	L	Pct.	ERA	WHIP	G	GS	CG	ShO	Hld.	Sv.-Opp.	IP	H	R	ER	HR	BB-IBB	SO	Avg.
1996— Ariz. A's (Ariz.)	3	3	.500	3.10	1.25	11	9	0	0	...	0-...	40.2	30	14	14	1	21-0	48	.208
1997— Visalia (Calif.)	6	8	.429	5.70	1.65	25	24	0	0	...	0-...	115.1	116	81	73	8	74-0	136	.258
1998— Modesto (Calif.)	8	7	.533	3.81	1.49	30	24	0	0	...	1-...	144.0	139	72	61	7	76-2	141	.254
1999— Midland (Texas)	4	7	.364	3.74	1.16	16	16	2	0	...	0-...	91.1	75	45	38	7	31-1	66	.221
— Vancouver (NW)	1	0	1.000	3.60	1.60	1	1	0	0	...	0-...	5.0	6	2	2	0	2-0	4	.316
— Visalia (Calif.)	4	4	.500	3.80	1.30	13	11	1	1	...	1-...	64.0	60	34	27	3	23-0	48	.249
2000— Midland (Texas)	5	14	.263	6.40	1.73	28	27	0	0	...	0-...	140.2	171	120	100	18	73-0	97	.304
2001— Midland (Texas)	5	5	.500	4.54	1.57	44	1	0	0	...	1-...	81.1	88	48	41	5	40-4	72	.274
2002— Midland (Texas)	3	3	.500	4.30	1.30	11	4	0	0	...	0-...	37.2	31	20	18	3	18-0	45	.221
— Visalia (Calif.)	2	1	.667	2.08	0.98	3	3	0	0	...	0-...	17.1	8	5	4	0	9-0	11	.140
— Sacramento (PCL)	2	5	.286	7.52	1.79	16	8	0	0	...	0-...	58.2	82	56	49	7	23-0	45	.332
2003— Arkansas (Texas)	4	3	.571	3.53	1.19	15	11	2	0	...	0-...	66.1	60	29	26	2	19-0	60	.241
— Salt Lake (PCL)	7	4	.636	4.03	1.18	15	15	0	0	...	0-...	91.2	90	47	41	10	18-0	75	.256
— Anaheim (A.L.)	2	0	1.000	3.28	1.05	5	3	0	0	0	0-0	24.2	18	9	9	3	8-0	14	.205
Major League totals (1 year)	2	0	1.000	3.28	1.05	5	3	0	0	0	0-0	24.2	18	9	9	3	8-0	14	.205

GREGORIO, TOM — C

PERSONAL: Born May 5, 1977, in Brooklyn, N.Y. ... 6-2/215. ... Bats right, throws right. ... Full name: Thomas Andrew Gregorio. ... High school: Tottenville (Staten Island, N.Y.). ... College: Troy State.

TRANSACTIONS/CAREER NOTES: Selected by Anaheim Angels organization in 27th round of free-agent draft (June 2, 1999).

2003 GAMES PLAYED BY POSITION (MLB): C—12.

Year— Team (League)	Pos.	G	AB	R	H	2B	3B	HR	RBI	BB	SO	HBP	GDP	SB-CS	Avg.	OBP	SLG	OPS	E	Pct.
1999— Boise (NW)	C	52	186	29	55	10	1	5	36	11	33	2	3	0-1	.296	.338	.441	.779	5	.987
2000— Cedar Rap. (Midw.)	C	106	379	46	93	17	0	6	41	35	79	7	13	2-1	.245	.319	.338	.657	15	.979
2001— Ariz. Angels (Ariz.)	C	4	11	1	3	0	0	0	1	3	2	0	0	0-0	.273	.429	.273	.701	1	.955
— Arkansas (Texas)	C	45	157	15	30	10	0	1	23	7	37	4	3	0-0	.191	.243	.274	.516	3	.989
2002— Arkansas (Texas)	C	56	188	18	47	10	1	3	15	9	33	2	3	2-0	.250	.291	.362	.653	6	.977
— Salt Lake (PCL)	C	15	51	7	13	4	0	1	3	2	14	2	1	0-1	.255	.309	.392	.701	0	1.000
2003— Salt Lake (PCL)	C-DH	54	181	26	40	10	0	5	24	14	44	4	1	0-0	.221	.290	.359	.649	0	1.000
— Anaheim (A.L.)	C	12	19	1	3	0	0	0	2	1	8	1	0	0-0	.158	.238	.158	.396	1	.979
Major League totals (1 year)		12	19	1	3	0	0	0	2	1	8	1	0	0-0	.158	.238	.158	.396	1	.979

GRIEVE, BEN — OF

PERSONAL: Born May 4, 1976, in Arlington, Texas. ... 6-4/216. ... Bats left, throws right. ... Full name: Benjamin Grieve. ... Name pronounced: greev. ... High school: James W. Martin (Arlington, Texas).

TRANSACTIONS/CAREER NOTES: Selected by Oakland Athletics organization in first round (second pick overall) of free-agent draft (June 2, 1994). ... Traded by A's with a player to be named later or cash to Tampa Bay Devil Rays as part of three-way deal in which Kansas City Royals received P Roberto Hernandez from Devil Rays, A's received P Cory Lidle from Devil Rays, A's received OF Johnny Damon, IF Mark Ellis and a player to be named later from Royals and Royals received C A.J. Hinch, IF Angel Berroa and cash from A's (January 8, 2001). ... Placed on 15-day disabled list by Tampa Bay (April 18, 2003). ... Reinstated from the 15-day disabled list (May 22, 2003). ... Placed on 15-day disabled list (July 18, 2003). ... Transferred to Emergency disabled list (August 5, 2003).

2003 GAMES PLAYED BY POSITION (MLB): DH—37, OF—10.

Year— Team (League)	Pos.	G	AB	R	H	2B	3B	HR	RBI	BB	SO	HBP	GDP	SB-CS	Avg.	OBP	SLG	OPS	E	Pct.
1994— S. Oregon (N'west)	OF	72	252	44	83	13	0	7	50	51	48	10	6	2-2	.329	.456	.464	.920	6	.959
1995— W. Mich. (Mid.)	OF	102	371	53	97	16	1	4	62	60	75	4	8	11-3	.261	.371	.342	.713	8	.942
— Modesto (Calif.)	OF	28	107	17	28	5	0	2	14	14	15	0	3	2-0	.262	.341	.364	.706	2	.951
1996— Modesto (Calif.)	OF-DH	72	281	61	100	20	1	11	51	38	52	1	5	8-7	.356	.430	.552	.982	5	.956
— Huntsville (Sou.)	OF-DH	63	232	34	55	8	1	8	32	35	53	2	3	0-3	.237	.338	.384	.722	4	.953
1997— Huntsville (Sou.)	OF-DH	100	372	100	122	29	2	24	108	81	75	9	8	5-1	.328	.455	.610	1.065	•8	.961
— Edmonton (PCL)	OF	27	108	27	46	11	1	7	28	12	16	1	4	0-1	.426	.484	.741	1.224	2	.964
— Oakland (A.L.)	OF	24	93	12	29	6	0	3	24	13	25	1	1	0-0	.312	.402	.473	.875	0	1.000
1998— Oakland (A.L.)	OF-DH	155	583	94	168	41	2	18	89	85	123	9	18	2-2	.288	.386	.458	.844	2	.993
1999— Oakland (A.L.)	OF-DH	148	486	80	129	21	0	28	86	63	108	8	17	4-0	.265	.358	.481	.840	3	.988
2000— Oakland (A.L.)	OF-DH	158	594	92	166	40	1	27	104	73	130	3	*32	3-0	.279	.359	.487	.845	3	.988
2001— Tampa Bay (A.L.)	OF-DH	154	542	72	143	30	2	11	72	87	159	8	13	7-1	.264	.372	.387	.760	4	.984
2002— Tampa Bay (A.L.)	OF-DH	136	482	62	121	30	0	19	64	69	121	8	15	8-2	.251	.353	.432	.784	3	.988
2003— Tampa Bay (A.L.)	DH-OF	55	165	28	38	7	0	4	17	32	41	6	3	0-0	.230	.371	.345	.716	1	.947
Major League totals (7 years)		830	2945	440	794	175	5	110	456	422	707	43	99	24-5	.270	.368	.444	.812	16	.988

G

GRIFFEY JR., KEN — OF

PERSONAL: Born November 21, 1969, in Donora, Pa. ... 6-3/205. ... Bats left, throws left. ... Full name: George Kenneth Griffey Jr.. ... High school: Moeller (Cincinnati).

TRANSACTIONS/CAREER NOTES: Selected by Seattle Mariners organization in first round (first pick overall) of free-agent draft (June 2, 1987). ... On San Bernardino disabled list (June 9-August 15, 1988). ... On disabled list (July 24-August 20, 1989; June 9-25, 1992; and June 20-July 13, 1996). ... On Seattle disabled list (May 27-August 15, 1995); included rehabilitation assignment to Tacoma (August 13-15). ... Traded by Mariners to Cincinnati Reds for P Brett Tomko, OF Mike Cameron, IF Antonio Perez and P Jake Meyer (February 10, 2000). ... On disabled list (April 29-June 15, 2001; and April 7-May 24 and June 24-July 22, 2002). ... On disabled list (April 6, 2003). ... Reinstated from 15-day disabled list (May 13, 2003). ... Placed on 15-day disabled list (July 18, 2003). ... Transferred to Emergency disabled list (July 19, 2003).

2003 GAMES PLAYED BY POSITION (MLB): OF—43, DH—3.

											BATTING								FIELDING	
Year	Team (League)	Pos.	G	AB	R	H	2B	3B	HR	RBI	BB	SO	HBP	GDP	SB-CS	Avg.	OBP	SLG	OPS	E	Pct.
1987— Bellingham (N'west)		OF	54	182	43	57	9	1	14	40	44	42	0	2	13-6	.313	.445	.604	1.049	1	* .992
1988— San Bern. (Calif.)		OF	58	219	50	74	13	3	11	42	34	39	2	3	32-9	.338	.431	.575	1.007	2	.987
— Vermont (East.)		OF	17	61	10	17	5	1	2	10	5	12	2	3	4-2	.279	.353	.492	.845	1	.977
1989— Seattle (A.L.)		DH-OF	127	455	61	120	23	0	16	61	44	83	2	4	16-7	.264	.329	.420	.748	• 10	.969
1990— Seattle (A.L.)		OF	155	597	91	179	28	7	22	80	63	81	2	12	16-11	.300	.366	.481	.847	7	.980
1991— Seattle (A.L.)		DH-OF	154	548	76	179	42	1	22	100	71	82	1	10	18-6	.327	.399	.527	.926	4	.989
1992— Seattle (A.L.)		OF-DH	142	565	83	174	39	4	27	103	44	67	5	15	10-5	.308	.361	.535	.896	1	.987
1993— Seattle (A.L.)	OF-DH-1B	156	582	113	180	38	3	45	109	96	91	6	14	17-9	.309	.408	.617	1.025	3	.991
1994— Seattle (A.L.)		OF-DH	111	433	94	140	24	4	* 40	90	56	73	2	9	11-3	.323	.402	.674	1.076	4	.983
1995— Seattle (A.L.)		OF-DH	72	260	52	67	7	0	17	42	52	53	0	4	4-2	.258	.379	.481	.860	2	.990
— Tacoma (PCL)		DH	1	3	0	0	0	0	0	0	0	1	0	0	0-0	.000	.000	.000	.000	...	...
1996— Seattle (A.L.)		OF-DH	140	545	125	165	26	2	49	140	78	104	7	7	16-1	.303	.392	.628	1.020	4	.990
1997— Seattle (A.L.)		OF-DH	157	608	* 125	185	34	3	* 56	* 147	76	121	8	12	15-4	.304	.382	*.646	1.028	6	.985
1998— Seattle (A.L.)	OF-DH-1B	161	633	120	180	33	4	* 56	146	76	121	7	14	20-5	.284	.365	.611	.977	5	.988
1999— Seattle (A.L.)		OF-DH	160	606	123	173	26	3	* 48	134	91	108	7	8	24-7	.285	.384	.576	.960	9	.978
2000— Cincinnati (N.L.)		OF	145	520	100	141	22	3	40	118	94	117	9	7	6-4	.271	.387	.556	.942	5	.987
2001— Cincinnati (N.L.)		OF-DH	111	364	57	104	20	2	22	65	44	72	4	8	2-0	.286	.365	.533	.898	3	.985
2002— Cincinnati (N.L.)		OF	70	197	17	52	8	0	8	23	28	39	3	6	1-2	.264	.358	.426	.784	3	.971
2003— Cincinnati (N.L.)		OF-DH	53	166	34	41	12	1	13	26	27	44	6	3	1-0	.247	.370	.566	.936	1	.989
American League totals (11 years)			1535	5832	1063	1742	320	30	398	1152	747	984	47	109	167-60	.299	.380	.569	.948	55	.986
National League totals (4 years)			379	1247	208	338	62	6	83	232	193	272	22	24	10-6	.271	.374	.530	.904	12	.985
Major League totals (15 years)			1914	7079	1271	2080	382	36	481	1384	940	1256	69	133	177-66	.294	.379	.562	.940	67	.985

GRIFFITHS, JEREMY — P

PERSONAL: Born March 22, 1978, in Fairview, Ohio. ... 6-6/240. ... Throws right, bats right. ... Full name: Jeremy Richard Griffiths. ... High school: Avon Lake (Ohio). ... College: Toledo.

TRANSACTIONS/CAREER NOTES: Selected by New York Mets organization in third round of free-agent draft (June 1999).

CAREER HITTING: 0-for-9 (.000), 0 R, 0 2B, 0 3B, 0 HR, 0 RBI.

Year	League	W	L	Pct.	ERA	WHIP	G	GS	CG	ShO	Hld.	Sv.-Opp.	IP	H	R	ER	HR	BB-IBB	SO	Avg.
1999— Kingsport (Appal.)		3	5	.375	3.30	1.36	14	14	1	0	...	0-...	76.1	68	40	28	6	36-1	74	.243
2000— Capital City (S. Atl.)		7	12	.368	4.34	1.24	26	26	0	0	...	0-...	128.2	120	78	62	12	39-0	138	.242
2001— St. Lucie (Fla. St.)		7	8	.467	3.75	1.22	23	20	2	0	...	0-...	132.0	126	63	55	9	35-1	95	.253
— Binghamton (Eastern)		2	0	1.000	0.69	0.92	2	2	1	0	...	0-...	13.0	8	3	1	0	4-0	12	.174
2002— Binghamton (Eastern)		8	6	.571	3.89	1.38	27	26	2	0	...	0-...	152.2	157	75	66	12	54-0	126	.272
2003— Norfolk (Int'l)		7	6	.538	2.74	1.04	21	19	1	0	...	1-...	115.0	94	43	35	6	26-0	78	.224
— New York (N.L.)		1	4	.200	7.02	1.85	9	6	0	0	0	0-0	41.0	57	34	32	5	19-2	25	.328
Major League totals (1 year)		1	4	.200	7.02	1.85	9	6	0	0	0	0-0	41.0	57	34	32	5	19-2	25	.328

GRIMSLEY, JASON — P

PERSONAL: Born August 7, 1967, in Cleveland, Texas. ... 6-3/205. ... Throws right, bats right. ... Full name: Jason Alan Grimsley. ... High school: Tarkington (Cleveland, Texas).

TRANSACTIONS/CAREER NOTES: Selected by Philadelphia Phillies organization in 10th round of free-agent draft (June 3, 1985). ... On Clearwater disabled list (April 8-May 10, 1988). ... On Philadelphia disabled list (June 6-August 22, 1991); included rehabilitation assignments to Scranton/Wilkes-Barre (June 15-30 and August 7-21). ... Traded by Phillies to Houston Astros for P Curt Schilling (April 2, 1992). ... On disabled list (May 14-June 14, 1992). ... Released by Astros (March 30, 1993). ... Signed by Cleveland Indians organization (April 7, 1993). ... On Charlotte disabled list (April 15-26, 1993). ... Traded by Indians with P Pep Harris to California Angels for P Brian Anderson (February 15, 1996). ... On Charlotte disabled list (April 15-26, 1996). ... Signed by Detroit Tigers organization (January 17, 1996). ... Released by Tigers (March 20, 1997). ... Signed by Milwaukee Brewers (April 3, 1997). ... Traded by Brewers to Kansas City Royals for P Jamie Brewington (July 29, 1997). ... Granted free agency (October 15, 1997). ... Signed by Indians organization (January 8, 1998). ... Granted free agency (October 15, 1998). ... Signed by New York Yankees organization (January 26, 1999). ... On suspended list (August 11-15, 1999). ... Released by Yankees (November 20, 2000). ... Signed by Royals (January 19, 2001). ... On Kansas City disabled list (June 4-22, 2002); included rehabilitation assignment to Wichita (June 20-22).

CAREER HITTING: 4-for-39 (.103), 3 R, 0 2B, 0 3B, 0 HR, 2 RBI.

Year	League	W	L	Pct.	ERA	WHIP	G	GS	CG	ShO	Hld.	Sv.-Opp.	IP	H	R	ER	HR	BB-IBB	SO	Avg.
1985— Bend (NW)		0	0	.000	13.50	3.26	6	1	0	0	...	0-...	11.1	12	21	17	0	25-0	10	.261
1986— Utica (N.Y.-Penn)		1	• 10	.091	6.40	2.16	14	14	3	0	...	0-...	64.2	63	61	46	3	* 77-0	46	.251
1987— Spartanburg (SAL)		7	4	.636	3.16	1.28	23	9	3	0	...	0-...	88.1	59	48	31	4	54-2	98	.190
1988— Clearwater (Fla. St.)		4	7	.364	3.73	1.15	16	15	2	0	...	0-...	101.1	80	48	42	2	37-1	90	.217
— Reading (East.)		1	3	.250	7.17	1.55	5	4	0	0	...	0-...	21.1	20	19	17	1	13-1	14	.247
1989— Reading (East.)		11	5	.579	2.98	1.34	26	26	8	2	...	0-...	172.0	121	65	57	13	* 109-4	134	.202
— Philadelphia (N.L.)		1	3	.250	5.89	2.07	4	4	0	0	0	0-0	18.1	19	13	12	2	19-1	7	.268
1990— Scran./W.B. (I.L.)		8	5	.615	3.93	1.47	22	22	0	0	...	0-...	128.1	111	68	56	7	78-1	99	.236
— Philadelphia (N.L.)		3	2	.600	3.30	1.57	11	11	0	0	0	0-0	57.1	47	21	21	1	43-0	41	.227
1991— Philadelphia (N.L.)		1	7	.125	4.87	1.56	12	12	0	0	0	0-0	61.0	54	34	33	4	41-3	42	.242
— Scran./W.B. (I.L.)		2	3	.400	4.35	1.65	9	9	0	0	...	0-...	51.2	48	28	25	3	37-2	43	.254
1992— Tucson (PCL)		8	7	.533	5.05	1.66	26	20	0	0	...	0-...	124.2	152	79	70	4	55-0	90	.308
1993— Charlotte (Int'l)		6	6	.500	3.39	1.38	28	19	3	1	...	0-...	135.1	138	64	51	10	49-1	102	.263
— Cleveland (A.L.)		3	4	.429	5.31	1.70	10	6	0	0	1	0-0	42.1	52	26	25	3	20-1	27	.302
1994— Charlotte (Int'l)		7	0	1.000	3.42	1.06	10	10	2	0	...	0-...	71.0	58	36	27	10	17-0	60	.218
— Cleveland (A.L.)		5	2	.714	4.57	1.51	14	13	1	0	0	0-0	82.2	91	47	42	7	34-1	59	.283
1995— Cleveland (A.L.)		0	0	...	6.09	2.03	15	2	0	0	...	1-1	34.0	37	24	23	4	32-1	25	.289
— Buffalo (A.A.)		5	3	.625	2.91	1.18	10	10	2	0	...	0-...	68.0	61	26	22	4	19-0	40	.236
1996— Vancouver (PCL)		2	0	1.000	1.20	0.73	2	2	1	0	...	0-...	15.0	8	2	2	0	3-0	11	.163
— California (A.L.)		5	7	.417	6.84	1.72	35	20	2	1	...	0-0	130.1	150	110	99	7	74-5	82	.286
1997— Tucson (PCL)		5	10	.333	5.70	1.63	36	10	0	0	...	4-...	85.1	96	70	54	0	43-2	65	.278
— Omaha (Am. Assoc.)		1	5	.167	6.68	2.10	7	6	0	0	...	0-...	31.0	36	26	23	3	29-0	22	.293

G

Year— League	W	L	Pct.	ERA	WHIP	G	GS	CG	ShO	Hld.	Sv.-Opp.	IP	H	R	ER	HR	BB-IBB	SO	Avg.
1998— Buffalo (Int'l)	6	3	.667	3.76	1.50	52	0	0	0	...	0-...	88.2	76	40	37	10	57-3	68	.234
1999— New York (A.L.)	7	2	.778	3.60	1.41	55	0	0	0	8	1-4	75.0	66	39	30	7	40-5	49	.231
2000— New York (A.L.)	3	2	.600	5.04	1.47	63	4	0	0	4	1-4	96.1	100	58	54	10	42-1	53	.268
2001— Kansas City (A.L.)	1	5	.167	3.02	1.23	73	0	0	0	26	0-7	80.1	71	32	27	8	28-5	61	.241
2002— Kansas City (A.L.)	4	7	.364	3.91	1.42	70	0	0	0	13	1-3	71.1	64	32	31	4	37-8	59	.236
— Wichita (Texas)	0	0	...	9.00	2.00	1	1	0	0	...	0-...	1.0	1	1	1	0	1-0	0	.250
2003— Kansas City (A.L.)	2	6	.250	5.16	1.65	76	0	0	0	28	0-7	75.0	88	47	43	6	36-5	58	.299
American League totals (9 years)	30	35	.462	4.90	1.55	411	45	3	1	80	4-26	687.1	719	415	374	63	343-32	473	.270
National League totals (3 years)	5	12	.294	4.35	1.63	27	27	0	0	0	0-0	136.2	120	68	66	7	103-4	90	.240
Major League totals (12 years)	35	47	.427	4.81	1.56	438	72	3	1	80	4-26	824.0	839	483	440	70	446-36	563	.265

GRISSOM, MARQUIS — OF

PERSONAL: Born April 17, 1967, in Atlanta, Ga. ... 5-11/180. ... Bats right, throws right. ... Full name: Marquis Deon Grissom. ... Name pronounced: mar-KEESE. ... High school: Lakeshore (College Park, Ga.). ... College: Florida A&M.

TRANSACTIONS/CAREER NOTES: Selected by Montreal Expos organization in third round of free-agent draft (June 1, 1988). ... On Montreal disabled list (May 29-June 30, 1990); included rehabilitation assignment to Indianapolis (June 25-30). ... Traded by Expos to Atlanta Braves for OF Roberto Kelly, OF Tony Tarasco and P Esteban Yan (April 6, 1995). ... Traded by Braves with OF Dave Justice to Cleveland Indians for OF Kenny Lofton and P Alan Embree (March 25, 1997). ... On disabled list (April 22-May 5, 1997). ... Traded by Indians with P Jeff Juden to Milwaukee Brewers for P Ben McDonald, P Mike Fetters and P Ron Villone (December 8, 1997). ... Traded by Brewers with a player to be named later to Los Angeles Dodgers for OF Devon White (February 25, 2001); Dodgers acquired P Rudy Lugo to complete deal (June 1, 2001). ... On suspended list (July 18-24, 2001). ... Granted free agency (October 28, 2002). ... Signed by San Francisco Giants (December 7, 2002).

2003 GAMES PLAYED BY POSITION (MLB): OF—148.

Year— Team (League)	Pos.	G	AB	R	H	2B	3B	HR	RBI	BB	SO	HBP	GDP	SB-CS	Avg.	OBP	SLG	OPS	E	Pct.
1988— Jamestown (NYP)	OF	74	* 291	* 69	94	14	7	8	39	35	39	2	2	23-7	.323	.393	.502	.895	3	.978
1989— Jacksonville (Sou.)	OF	78	278	43	83	15	4	3	31	24	31	7	1	24-6	.299	.365	.414	.779	3	.980
— Indianapolis (A.A.)	OF	49	187	28	52	10	4	2	21	14	23	0	2	16-4	.278	.327	.406	.733	0	1.000
— Montreal (N.L.)	OF	26	74	16	19	2	0	1	2	12	21	0	1	1-0	.257	.360	.324	.685	2	.943
1990— Montreal (N.L.)	OF	98	288	42	74	14	2	3	29	27	40	0	3	22-2	.257	.320	.351	.670	3	.988
— Indianapolis (A.A.)	OF	5	22	3	4	0	0	2	3	0	5	0	0	1-0	.182	.182	.455	.636	0	1.000
1991— Montreal (N.L.)	OF	148	558	73	149	23	9	6	39	34	89	1	8	* 76-17	.267	.310	.373	.683	6	.984
1992— Montreal (N.L.)	OF	159	* 653	99	180	39	6	14	66	42	81	5	12	* 78-13	.276	.322	.418	.741	7	.983
1993— Montreal (N.L.)	OF	157	630	104	188	27	2	19	95	52	76	3	9	53-10	.298	.351	.438	.789	7	.984
1994— Montreal (N.L.)	OF	110	475	96	137	25	4	11	45	41	66	1	10	36-6	.288	.344	.427	.771	5	.985
1995— Atlanta (N.L.)	OF	139	551	80	142	23	3	12	42	47	61	3	8	29-9	.258	.317	.376	.693	2	.994
1996— Atlanta (N.L.)	OF	158	671	106	207	32	10	23	74	41	73	3	12	28-11	.308	.349	.489	.838	1	.997
1997— Cleveland (A.L.)	OF	144	558	74	146	27	6	12	66	43	89	6	12	22-13	.262	.317	.396	.713	3	.992
1998— Milwaukee (N.L.)	OF	142	542	57	147	28	1	10	60	24	78	2	12	13-8	.271	.304	.382	.685	3	.991
1999— Milwaukee (N.L.)	OF	154	603	92	161	27	1	20	83	49	109	0	12	24-6	.267	.320	.415	.734	5	.987
2000— Milwaukee (N.L.)	OF	146	595	67	145	18	2	14	62	39	99	0	9	20-10	.244	.288	.351	.640	3	.992
2001— Los Angeles (N.L.)	OF-DH	135	448	56	99	17	1	21	60	16	107	2	12	7-5	.221	.250	.404	.654	0	1.000
2002— Los Angeles (N.L.)	OF	111	343	57	95	21	4	17	60	22	68	2	6	5-1	.277	.321	.510	.831	4	.978
2003— San Francisco (N.L.)	OF	149	587	82	176	33	3	20	79	20	82	2	14	11-3	.300	.322	.468	.790	8	.977
American League totals (1 year)		144	558	74	146	27	6	12	66	43	89	6	12	22-13	.262	.317	.396	.713	3	.992
National League totals (14 years)		1832	7018	1027	1919	329	48	191	796	466	1050	24	128	403-101	.273	.319	.416	.734	55	.987
Major League totals (15 years)		1976	7576	1101	2065	356	54	203	862	509	1139	30	140	425-114	.273	.319	.414	.733	58	.987

GROOM, BUDDY — P

PERSONAL: Born July 10, 1965, in Dallas, Texas. ... 6-2/201. ... Throws left, bats left. ... Full name: Wedsel Gary Groom. ... High school: Red Oak (Texas). ... College: Mary Hardin-Baylor.

TRANSACTIONS/CAREER NOTES: Selected by Chicago White Sox organization in 12th round of free-agent draft (June 2, 1987). ... Selected by Detroit Tigers organization from White Sox organization in Rule 5 minor league draft (December 3, 1990). ... Traded by Tigers to Florida Marlins for a player to be named later (August 7, 1995); Tigers acquired P Mike Myers to complete deal (August 9, 1995). ... Granted free agency (October 16, 1995). ... Signed by Oakland Athletics organization (November 27, 1995). ... Granted free agency (November 1, 1999). ... Signed by Baltimore Orioles (December 21, 1999).

CAREER HITTING: 0-for-0 (.000), 0 R, 0 2B, 0 3B, 0 HR, 0 RBI.

Year— League	W	L	Pct.	ERA	WHIP	G	GS	CG	ShO	Hld.	Sv.-Opp.	IP	H	R	ER	HR	BB-IBB	SO	Avg.
1987— GC White Sox (GCL)	1	0	1.000	0.75	1.17	4	1	0	0	...	1-...	12.0	12	1	1	0	2-0	8	.273
— Daytona Beach (FSL)	7	2	.778	3.59	1.37	11	10	2	0	...	0-...	67.2	60	30	27	4	33-1	29	.236
1988— Tampa (FSL)	13	10	.565	2.54	1.19	27	27	8	0	...	0-...	* 195.0	181	69	55	7	51-1	118	.247
1989— Birmingham (Sou.)	13	8	.619	4.52	1.49	26	26	3	1	...	0-...	167.1	172	101	84	13	78-1	94	.270
1990— Birmingham (Sou.)	6	8	.429	5.07	1.59	20	20	0	0	...	0-...	115.1	135	81	65	10	48-1	66	.290
1991— Toledo (Int'l)	2	5	.286	4.32	1.33	24	6	0	0	...	1-...	75.0	75	39	36	7	25-2	49	.264
— London (East.)	7	1	.875	3.48	1.22	11	7	0	0	...	0-...	51.2	51	20	20	7	12-1	39	.248
1992— Toledo (Int'l)	7	7	.500	2.80	1.14	16	16	1	0	...	0-...	109.1	102	41	34	8	23-1	71	.248
— Detroit (A.L.)	0	5	.000	5.82	1.81	12	7	0	0	0	1-2	38.2	48	28	25	4	22-4	15	.320
1993— Toledo (Int'l)	9	3	.750	2.74	1.25	16	15	0	0	...	0-...	102.0	98	34	31	5	30-1	78	.254
— Detroit (A.L.)	0	2	.000	6.14	1.66	19	3	0	0	1	0-0	36.2	48	25	25	4	13-5	15	.322
1994— Toledo (Int'l)	0	0	...	2.25	0.50	5	0	0	0	...	0-...	4.0	2	1	1	0	0-0	6	.154
— Detroit (A.L.)	0	1	.000	3.94	1.38	40	0	0	0	11	1-1	32.0	31	14	14	4	13-2	27	.256
1995— Detroit (A.L.)	1	3	.250	7.52	1.99	23	4	0	0	0	1-3	40.2	55	35	34	6	26-4	23	.322
— Toledo (Int'l)	2	3	.400	1.91	1.06	6	5	1	0	...	0-...	33.0	31	14	7	4	4-0	24	.244
— Florida (N.L.)	1	2	.333	7.20	2.13	14	0	0	0	0	0-0	15.0	26	12	12	2	6-0	12	.400
1996— Oakland (A.L.)	5	0	1.000	3.84	1.54	72	1	0	0	10	2-4	77.1	85	37	33	8	34-3	57	.281
1997— Oakland (A.L.)	2	2	.500	5.15	1.53	78	0	0	0	12	3-5	64.2	75	38	37	9	24-1	45	.292
1998— Oakland (A.L.)	3	1	.750	4.24	1.43	75	0	0	0	16	0-6	57.1	62	30	27	4	20-1	36	.274
1999— Oakland (A.L.)	3	2	.600	5.09	1.43	76	0	0	0	*27	0-3	46.0	48	29	26	1	18-5	32	.274
2000— Baltimore (A.L.)	6	3	.667	4.85	1.42	70	0	0	0	27	4-11	59.1	63	37	32	5	21-2	44	.275
2001— Baltimore (A.L.)	1	4	.200	3.55	1.11	70	0	0	0	16	11-13	66.0	64	28	26	4	9-0	54	.252
2002— Baltimore (A.L.)	3	2	.600	1.60	0.90	70	0	0	0	19	2-4	62.0	44	11	11	4	12-3	48	.196
2003— Baltimore (A.L.)	1	3	.250	5.36	1.59	60	0	0	0	16	1-3	45.1	58	27	27	7	14-2	34	.309
American League totals (12 years)	25	28	.472	4.56	1.45	665	15	0	0	155	26-55	626.0	681	339	317	60	226-32	430	.278
National League totals (1 year)	1	2	.333	7.20	2.13	14	0	0	0	0	0-0	15.0	26	12	12	2	6-0	12	.400
Major League totals (12 years)	26	30	.464	4.62	1.46	679	15	0	0	155	26-55	641.0	707	351	329	62	232-32	442	.282

G

GRUDZIELANEK, MARK — 2B

PERSONAL: Born June 30, 1970, in Milwaukee, Wis. ... 6-1/190. ... Bats right, throws right. ... Full name: Mark James Grudzielanek. ... Name pronounced: grud-zuh-LAN-nick. ... High school: J.M. Hanks (El Paso, Texas). ... Junior college: Trinidad State College (Colo.).

TRANSACTIONS/CAREER NOTES: Selected by New York Mets organization in 17th round of free-agent draft (June 5, 1989); did not sign. ... Selected by Montreal Expos organization in 11th round of free-agent draft (June 3, 1991). ... On disabled list (July 13-August 9, 1993 and May 12-19, 1994). ... Traded by Expos with P Carlos Perez and OF Hiram Bocachica to Los Angeles Dodgers for 2B Wilton Guerrero, P Ted Lilly, OF Peter Bergeron and 1B Jonathan Tucker (July 31, 1998). ... On Los Angeles disabled list (June 12-July 6, 1999); included rehabilitation assignment to San Bernadino (July 2-6). ... On disabled list (June 12-28, 2001). ... Traded by Dodgers with 1B Eric Karros and cash to Chicago Cubs for C Todd Hundley and OF Chad Hermansen (December 4, 2002). ... Placed on 15-day disabled list (August 3, 2003). ... Sent on minor league rehab assignment (August 29, 2003). ... Recalled from minor league rehab assignment; removed from 15-day disabled list (September 2, 2003).

2003 GAMES PLAYED BY POSITION (MLB): 2B—121.

Year Team (League)	Pos.	G	AB	R	H	2B	3B	HR	RBI	BB	SO	HBP	GDP	SB-CS	Avg.	OBP	SLG	OPS	E	Pct.
1991— Jamestown (NYP)	SS	72	275	44	72	9	3	2	32	18	43	3	6	14-4	.262	.311	.338	.649	23	.933
1992— Rockford (Midwest)	SS	128	496	64	122	12	5	5	54	22	59	5	10	25-4	.246	.285	.321	.605	41	.919
1993— W.P. Beach (FSL)	2-3-SS-OF	86	300	41	80	11	6	1	34	14	42	7	6	17-10	.267	.315	.353	.668	13	.949
1994— Harrisburg (East.)	3B-SS	122	488	92	157	• 37	3	11	66	43	66	8	15	32-10	.322	.382	.477	.860	23	.958
1995— Montreal (N.L.)	SS-3B-2B	78	269	27	66	12	2	1	20	14	47	7	7	8-3	.245	.300	.316	.616	10	.967
— Ottawa (Int'l)	SS	49	181	26	54	9	1	1	22	10	17	4	6	12-1	.298	.342	.376	.717	14	.939
1996— Montreal (N.L.)	SS	153	657	99	201	34	4	6	49	26	83	9	10	33-7	.306	.340	.397	.737	27	.959
1997— Montreal (N.L.)	SS	156	* 649	76	177	* 54	3	4	51	23	76	10	13	25-9	.273	.307	.384	.690	* 32	.955
1998— Montreal (N.L.)	SS	105	396	51	109	15	1	8	41	21	50	9	11	11-5	.275	.323	.379	.702	23	.950
— Los Angeles (N.L.)	SS	51	193	11	51	6	0	2	21	5	23	2	7	7-0	.264	.286	.326	.612	† 10	.962
1999— Los Angeles (N.L.)	SS	123	488	72	159	23	5	7	46	31	65	10	13	6-6	.326	.376	.436	.812	13	.973
— San Bern. (Calif.)	SS	4	16	2	4	0	0	0	0	0	1	0	1	0-2	.250	.250	.250	.500	0	1.000
2000— Los Angeles (N.L.)	2B-SS	148	617	101	172	35	6	7	49	45	81	9	16	12-3	.279	.335	.389	.724	17	.976
2001— Los Angeles (N.L.)	2B	133	539	83	146	21	3	13	55	28	83	11	9	4-4	.271	.317	.393	.711	10	.984
2002— Los Angeles (N.L.)	2B-DH	150	536	56	145	23	0	9	50	22	89	3	17	4-1	.271	.301	.364	.665	7	.989
2003— Iowa (PCL)	2B-DH	2	10	1	5	0	0	0	1	1	1	0	0	0-0	.500	.545	.500	1.045	0	1.000
— Chicago (N.L.)	2B	121	481	73	151	38	1	3	38	30	64	11	12	6-2	.314	.366	.416	.782	8	.986
Major League totals (9 years)		1218	4825	649	1377	261	25	60	420	245	661	81	115	116-40	.285	.329	.387	.716	157	.971

GRYBOSKI, KEVIN — P

PERSONAL: Born November 15, 1973, in Wilkes-Barre, Pa. ... 6-5/235. ... Throws right, bats right. ... Full name: Kevin John Gryboski. ... Name pronounced: gri-BOS-ski. ... College: Wilkes University (Pa.).

TRANSACTIONS/CAREER NOTES: Selected by Seattle Mariners organization in 16th round of free-agent draft (June 1, 1995). ... On disabled list (May 11-June 14 and July 31-August 12, 1997). ... On Lancaster disabled list (May 3-10, 1998). ... On Tacoma disabled list (July 24-31, 2000). ... Traded by Mariners to Atlanta Braves for P Elvis Perez (January 18, 2002). ... On Atlanta disabled list (July 24-August 20, 2002); included rehabilitation assignment to Macon (August 16-20). ... Placed on 15-day disabled list (August 28, 2003). ... Removed from 15-day disabled list (September 20, 2003).

CAREER HITTING: 0-for-1 (.000), 0 R, 0 2B, 0 3B, 0 HR, 0 RBI.

Year League	W	L	Pct.	ERA	WHIP	G	GS	CG	ShO	Hld.	Sv.-Opp.	IP	H	R	ER	HR	BB-IBB	SO	Avg.
1995— Everett (Northwest)	1	5	.167	3.50	1.25	25	0	0	0	...	2-...	36.0	27	18	14	2	18-2	25	.206
1996— Wisconsin (Midw.)	10	5	.667	4.74	1.50	32	21	3	0	...	1-...	138.2	146	90	73	7	62-2	100	.270
1997— Lancaster (Calif.)	0	7	.000	9.89	2.06	21	15	0	0	...	0-...	67.1	113	82	74	13	26-0	41	.383
1998— Lancaster (Calif.)	5	5	.500	2.65	1.25	37	3	0	0	...	8-...	85.0	75	35	25	4	31-1	73	.240
— Orlando (Sou.)	0	0	...	9.00	1.80	2	0	0	0	...	0-...	5.0	8	5	5	1	1-0	4	.364
1999— New Haven (East.)	2	5	.286	2.89	1.40	47	0	0	0	...	10-...	62.1	67	27	20	5	20-4	41	.283
2000— New Haven (East.)	2	2	.500	2.50	1.28	16	0	0	0	...	9-...	18.0	15	5	5	0	8-1	20	.231
— Tacoma (PCL)	2	2	.500	4.83	1.66	31	0	0	0	...	0-...	41.0	45	23	22	3	23-4	35	.288
2001— Tacoma (PCL)	2	5	.286	3.90	1.38	58	0	0	0	...	22-...	60.0	64	29	26	8	19-2	50	.277
2002— Richmond (Int'l)	1	0	1.000	1.29	1.14	7	0	0	0	...	3-...	7.0	7	1	1	0	1-0	5	.250
— Atlanta (N.L.)	2	1	.667	3.48	1.68	57	0	0	0	11	0-2	51.2	50	20	20	6	37-5	33	.256
— Macon (S. Atl.)	0	0	...	0.00	1.00	2	1	0	0	...	0-...	2.0	1	0	0	0	1-0	2	.167
2003— Atlanta (N.L.)	6	4	.600	3.86	1.51	64	0	0	0	12	0-4	44.1	44	22	19	3	23-6	32	.272
Major League totals (2 years)	8	5	.615	3.66	1.60	121	0	0	0	23	0-6	96.0	94	42	39	9	60-11	65	.263

GUARDADO, EDDIE — P

PERSONAL: Born October 2, 1970, in Stockton, Calif. ... 6-0/194. ... Throws left, bats right. ... Full name: Edward Adrian Guardado. ... Name pronounced: gwar-DAH-doe. ... High school: Franklin (Stockton, Calif.). ... Junior college: San Joaquin Delta College (Calif.).

TRANSACTIONS/CAREER NOTES: Selected by Minnesota Twins organization in 21st round of free-agent draft (June 4, 1990). ... On Minnesota disabled list (May 22-June 28, 1999); included rehabilitation assignment to New Britain (June 22-28). ... On disabled list (June 5-20, 2001).

CAREER HITTING: 0-for-0 (.000), 0 R, 0 2B, 0 3B, 0 HR, 0 RBI.

Year League	W	L	Pct.	ERA	WHIP	G	GS	CG	ShO	Hld.	Sv.-Opp.	IP	H	R	ER	HR	BB-IBB	SO	Avg.
1991— Elizabethton (Appal.)	8	4	.667	1.86	1.07	14	13	3	• 1	...	0-...	92.0	67	30	19	5	31-0	* 106	.199
1992— Kenosha (Midw.)	5	10	.333	4.37	1.35	18	18	2	1	...	0-...	101.0	106	57	49	5	30-0	103	.274
— Visalia (Calif.)	7	0	1.000	1.64	1.16	7	7	1	1	...	0-...	49.1	47	13	9	1	10-0	39	.258
1993— Nashville (Sou.)	4	0	1.000	1.24	0.96	10	10	2	2	...	0-...	65.1	53	10	9	1	10-0	57	.221
— Minnesota (A.L.)	3	8	.273	6.18	1.68	19	16	0	0	0	0-0	94.2	123	68	65	13	36-2	46	.319
1994— Salt Lake (PCL)	12	7	.632	4.83	1.47	24	24	2	0	...	0-...	151.0	171	90	81	23	51-0	87	.290
— Minnesota (A.L.)	0	2	.000	8.47	1.76	4	4	0	0	0	0-0	17.0	26	16	16	3	4-0	8	.351
1995— Minnesota (A.L.)	4	9	.308	5.12	1.58	51	5	0	0	5	2-5	91.1	99	54	52	13	45-2	71	.277
1996— Minnesota (A.L.)	6	5	.545	5.25	1.28	*83	0	0	0	18	4-7	73.2	61	45	43	12	33-4	74	.228
1997— Minnesota (A.L.)	0	4	.000	3.91	1.49	69	0	0	0	13	1-1	46.0	45	23	20	7	17-2	54	.251
1998— Minnesota (A.L.)	3	1	.750	4.52	1.43	79	0	0	0	16	0-4	65.2	66	34	33	10	28-6	53	.265
1999— Minnesota (A.L.)	5	5	.286	4.50	1.29	63	0	0	0	15	2-4	48.0	37	24	24	6	25-4	50	.222
— New Britain (East.)	0	0	...	1.93	0.64	3	0	0	0	...	0-...	4.2	3	1	1	0	0-0	5	.176
2000— Minnesota (A.L.)	7	4	.636	3.94	1.30	70	0	0	0	8	9-11	61.2	55	27	27	14	25-3	52	.238
2001— Minnesota (A.L.)	7	3	.700	3.51	1.05	67	0	0	0	14	12-14	66.2	47	27	26	6	23-4	67	.197
2002— Minnesota (A.L.)	1	3	.250	2.93	1.05	68	0	0	0	0	* 45-51	67.2	53	22	22	9	18-2	70	.215
2003— Minnesota (A.L.)	3	5	.375	2.89	0.98	66	0	0	0		41-45	65.1	50	22	21	7	14-2	60	.207
Major League totals (11 years)	36	47	.434	4.50	1.33	639	25	0	0	89	116-142	697.2	662	362	349	99	268-31	605	.252

G

GUERRERO, VLADIMIR — OF

PERSONAL: Born February 9, 1976, in Nizao Bani, Dominican Republic. ... 6-3/220. ... Bats right, throws right. ... Full name: Vladimir Alvino Guerrero. ... Name pronounced: guh-RAR-oh.

TRANSACTIONS/CAREER NOTES: Signed as non-drafted free agent by Montreal Expos organization (March 1, 1993). ... On Montreal disabled list (March 30-May 2, June 5-21 and July 12-27, 1997); included rehabilitation assignment to West Palm Beach (April 29-May 2). ... On suspended list (March 30-April 3, 2003). ... Placed on 15-day disabled list (June 5, 2003). ... Sent to Brevard County on rehab assignment (July 17, 2003). ... Recalled from Brevard County rehab assignment; reinstated from 15-day disabled list (July 21, 2003).

2003 GAMES PLAYED BY POSITION (MLB): OF—112.

Year— Team (League)	Pos.	G	AB	R	H	2B	3B	HR	RBI	BB	SO	HBP	GDP	SB-CS	Avg.	OBP	SLG	OPS	E	Pct.
1993— Dom. Expos (DSL)	P	34	105	19	35	4	0	1	14	8	13	...	...	4-...	.333	...	.400	...	5	.943
1994— Dom. Expos (DSL)	OF	25	92	34	39	11	0	12	35	21	6	...	...	5-...	.424	...	.935	...	2	.957
— GC Expos (GCL)	OF	37	137	24	43	13	3	5	25	11	18	2	0	0-7	.314	.366	.562	.928	1	.986
1995— Albany (S. Atl.)	OF	110	421	77	140	21	10	16	63	30	45	7	8	12-7	.333	.383	.544	.927	11	.953
1996— W.P. Beach (FSL)	OF	20	80	16	29	8	0	5	18	3	10	1	1	2-2	.363	.388	.650	1.038	3	.917
— Harrisburg (East.)	OF	118	417	84	150	32	8	19	78	51	42	9	8	17-10	.360	.438	.612	1.050	8	.961
— Montreal (N.L.)	OF	9	27	2	5	0	0	1	1	0	3	0	1	0-0	.185	.185	.296	.481	0	1.000
1997— W.P. Beach (FSL)	OF	3	10	0	4	2	0	0	2	1	0	0	1	1-0	.400	.455	.600	1.055	0	1.000
— Montreal (N.L.)	OF	90	325	44	98	22	2	11	40	19	39	7	11	3-4	.302	.350	.483	.833	* 12	.929
1998— Montreal (N.L.)	OF	159	623	108	202	37	7	38	109	42	95	7	15	11-9	.324	.371	.589	.960	* 17	.951
1999— Montreal (N.L.)	OF	160	610	102	193	37	5	42	131	55	62	7	18	14-7	.316	.378	.600	.978	* 19	.948
2000— Montreal (N.L.)	OF-DH	154	571	101	197	28	11	44	123	58	74	8	15	9-10	.345	.410	.664	1.074	* 10	.969
2001— Montreal (N.L.)	OF	159	599	107	184	45	4	34	108	60	88	9	*24	37-16	.307	.377	.566	.943	12	.965
2002— Montreal (N.L.)	OF	161	614	106	* 206	37	2	39	111	84	70	6	20	40-* 20	.336	.417	.593	1.010	* 10	.969
2003— Brevard County (FSL)	OF-DH	3	6	2	3	0	0	1	1	0	1	0	0	0-0	.500	.571	1.000	1.571	0	1.000
— Montreal (N.L.)	OF	112	394	71	130	20	3	25	79	63	53	6	18	9-5	.330	.426	.586	1.012	7	.970
Major League totals (8 years)		1004	3763	641	1215	226	34	234	702	381	484	50	122	123-71	.323	.390	.588	.978	87	.959

GUIEL, AARON — OF

PERSONAL: Born October 5, 1972, in Vancouver, British Columbia. ... 5-10/200. ... Bats left, throws right. ... Full name: Aaron Colin Guiel. ... Name pronounced: GUY-el. ... High school: Woodlands Senior (B.C.). ... Junior college: Kwantlen College (B.C.).

TRANSACTIONS/CAREER NOTES: Selected by California Angels organization in 21st round of free-agent draft (June 1, 1992). ... Traded by Angels to San Diego Padres for C Angelo Encarnacion (August 25, 1997). ... Granted free agency (October 15, 1999). ... Signed by Oakland Athletics organization (March 18, 2000). ... Released by A's (March 30, 2000). ... Signed by Oaxaca of Mexican League (April 2000). ... Signed by Kansas City Royals organization (June 13, 2000). ... Granted free agency (October 15, 2001). ... Re-signed by Royals organization (October 31, 2001).

2003 GAMES PLAYED BY POSITION (MLB): OF—89, DH—2.

Year— Team (League)	Pos.	G	AB	R	H	2B	3B	HR	RBI	BB	SO	HBP	GDP	SB-CS	Avg.	OBP	SLG	OPS	E	Pct.
1993— Boise (NW)	2B-OF	35	104	24	31	6	4	2	12	26	21	4	1	3-0	.298	.455	.490	.946	12	.874
1994— Cedar Rap. (Midw.)	2B	127	454	84	122	30	1	18	82	64	93	6	7	21-7	.269	.364	.458	.822	32	.944
1995— Lake Elsinore (Calif.)	2B	113	409	73	110	25	7	7	58	69	96	7	7	7-6	.269	.380	.416	.796	22	.958
1996— Midland (Texas)	3B-2B-OF	129	439	72	118	29	7	10	48	56	71	10	6	11-7	.269	.364	.435	.799	28	.933
1997— Midland (Texas)	OF-3B-2B	116	419	91	138	37	7	22	85	59	94	18	9	14-10	.329	.431	.609	1.039	8	.953
— Mobile (Sou.)	OF	8	26	9	10	2	0	1	9	5	4	1	0	1-0	.385	.500	.577	1.077	0	1.000
1998— Ariz. Padres (Ariz.)	OF	8	16	8	8	3	1	1	6	5	5	3	0	1-1	.500	.667	1.000	1.667	0	1.000
— Las Vegas (PCL)	OF-3B	60	183	33	57	15	4	5	31	28	51	4	4	5-1	.311	.410	.519	.929	4	.947
1999— Las Vegas (PCL)	OF	84	257	46	63	25	2	12	39	44	86	5	6	5-4	.245	.362	.498	.861	5	.944
2000— Oaxaca (Mex.)		56	192	55	70	11	1	22	62	52	35	...	...	7-5	.365	...	.776	...	4	...
— Omaha (PCL)	OF	73	258	47	74	15	2	13	40	35	54	8	3	6-0	.287	.389	.512	.900	4	.977
2001— Omaha (PCL)	OF	121	442	78	118	27	3	21	73	51	92	13	12	6-4	.267	.355	.484	.840	6	.973
2002— Omaha (PCL)	OF	61	215	44	76	11	1	9	50	29	34	8	4	8-1	.353	.443	.540	.983	3	.977
— Kansas City (A.L.)	OF-DH	70	240	30	56	13	0	4	38	19	61	4	3	1-5	.233	.296	.338	.633	6	.952
2003— Omaha (PCL)	OF	52	190	38	53	9	2	8	30	33	43	9	3	3-0	.279	.408	.474	.881	5	.962
— Kansas City (A.L.)	OF-DH	99	354	63	98	30	0	15	52	27	63	13	3	3-5	.277	.346	.489	.835	3	.985
Major League totals (2 years)		169	594	93	154	43	0	19	90	46	124	17	6	4-10	.259	.326	.428	.753	9	.972

GUILLEN, CARLOS — SS

PERSONAL: Born September 30, 1975, in Maracay, Venezuela. ... 6-1/205. ... Bats both, throws right. ... Full name: Carlos Alfonso Guillen. ... Name pronounced: GEY-un.

TRANSACTIONS/CAREER NOTES: Signed as non-drafted free agent by Houston Astros organization (September 19, 1992). ... On disabled list (June 1, 1994-entire season). ... On disabled list (May 2, 1996-remainder of season). ... Traded by Astros with P Freddy Garcia and a player to be named later to Seattle Mariners for P Randy Johnson (July 31, 1998); Mariners acquired P John Halama to complete deal (October 1, 1998). ... On disabled list (April 7, 1999-remainder of season). ... On Seattle disabled list (April 13-28, 2000); included rehabilitation assignment to Tacoma (April 22-28). ... Placed on 15-day disabled list (July 29, 2003). ... Sent on rehab assignment by Seattle (August 18, 2003). ... Recalled from minor league rehab assignment; removed from 15-day disabled list (August 23, 2003).

2003 GAMES PLAYED BY POSITION (MLB): SS—76, 3B—32, DH—1.

Year— Team (League)	Pos.	G	AB	R	H	2B	3B	HR	RBI	BB	SO	HBP	GDP	SB-CS	Avg.	OBP	SLG	OPS	E	Pct.
1993— Dom. Astros (DSL)	IF	18	56	12	14	4	2	0	8	8	12	...	...	0-...	.250	...	.393	...	2	.956
1994—										Did not play.										
1995— GC Astros (GCL)		30	105	17	31	4	2	2	15	9	17	1	0	17-1	.295	.350	.429	.779	...	...
1996— Quad City (Midw.)	SS	29	112	23	37	7	1	3	17	16	25	0	1	13-6	.330	.405	.491	.896	9	.929
1997— Jackson (Texas)	SS-DH	115	390	47	99	16	1	10	39	38	78	2	9	6-5	.254	.322	.377	.699	35	.932
— New Orleans (A.A.)	SS	3	13	3	4	1	0	0	0	0	4	0	0	0-0	.308	.308	.385	.692	0	1.000
1998— New Orleans (PCL)	SS	100	374	67	109	18	4	12	51	31	61	5	5	3-4	.291	.350	.457	.807	26	.943
— Tacoma (PCL)	2B	24	92	8	21	1	1	1	4	9	17	0	1	1-2	.228	.297	.293	.591	2	.982
— Seattle (A.L.)	2B	10	39	9	13	1	1	0	5	3	9	0	0	2-0	.333	.381	.410	.791	0	1.000
1999— Seattle (A.L.)	SS-2B	5	19	2	3	0	0	1	3	1	6	0	1	0-0	.158	.200	.316	.516	1	.964
2000— Seattle (A.L.)	3B-SS	90	288	45	74	15	2	7	42	28	53	2	6	1-3	.257	.324	.396	.720	21	.921
— Tacoma (PCL)	3B-SS	24	87	19	26	4	1	2	11	12	17	1	3	4-1	.299	.386	.437	.823	6	.926
2001— Seattle (A.L.)	SS-DH	140	456	72	118	21	4	5	53	53	89	1	9	4-1	.259	.333	.355	.689	10	.980
2002— Seattle (A.L.)	SS-DH	134	475	73	124	24	6	9	56	46	91	1	8	4-5	.261	.326	.394	.719	18	.965
2003— Tacoma (PCL)	3B-DH	4	14	2	5	1	0	2	4	0	1	1	2	0-0	.357	.400	.857	1.257	0	1.000
— Seattle (A.L.)	SS-3B-DH	109	388	63	107	19	3	7	52	52	64	1	12	4-4	.276	.359	.394	.753	14	.963
Major League totals (6 years)		488	1665	264	439	80	16	29	211	183	312	5	36	15-13	.264	.335	.383	.718	64	.963

G

GUILLEN, JOSE — OF

PERSONAL: Born May 17, 1976, in San Cristobal, Dominican Republic. ... 5-11/190. ... Bats right, throws right. ... Full name: Jose Manuel Guillen. ... Name pronounced: GHEE-yen.

TRANSACTIONS/CAREER NOTES: Signed as non-drafted free agent by Pittsburgh Pirates organization (August 19, 1992). ... Traded by Pirates with P Jeff Sparks to Tampa Bay Devil Rays for C Joe Oliver and C Humberto Cota (July 23, 1999). ... On Durham disabled list (July 23-30, 1999). ... On Tampa Bay disabled list (March 28-April 12, 2000). ... On Tampa Bay disabled list (May 17-June 24 and June 25-July 30, 2001); included rehabilitation assignments to Durham (June 10-24 and July 14-30). ... On Durham disabled list (August 7-24, 2001). ... Released by Devil Rays (November 27, 2001). ... Signed by Arizona Diamondbacks (December 18, 2001). ... Released by Diamondbacks (July 22, 2002). ... Signed by Colorado Rockies organization (July 29, 2002). ... Released by Rockies (August 1, 2002). ... Signed by Cincinnati Reds organization (August 20, 2002). ... Released by Reds (March 12, 2003). ... Re-signed by Reds organization (March 13, 2003). ... Traded by Cincinnati to Oakland A's for P Aaron Harang, PJoe Valentine, and P Jeff Bruksch (July 30, 2003). ... Suspended by American League (September 4, 2003). ... Reinstated (September 6, 2003).

2003 GAMES PLAYED BY POSITION (MLB): OF—122, DH—1.

Year — Team (League)	Pos.	G	AB	R	H	2B	3B	HR	RBI	BB	SO	HBP	GDP	SB-CS	Avg.	OBP	SLG	OPS	E	Pct.
1993— Dom. Pirates (DSL)	OF	63	234	39	53	3	4	11	41	21	55	...	...	10-	.226	...	.415	...	7	.947
1994— GC Pirates (GCL)	OF	30	110	17	29	4	1	4	11	7	15	6	0	2-1	.264	.341	.427	.769	2	.970
1995— Erie (N.Y.-Penn)	OF	66	258	41	81	17	1	* 12	46	10	44	12	5	1-5	.314	.367	.527	.894	13	.900
— Augusta (S. Atl.)	OF	10	34	6	8	1	1	2	6	2	9	2	0	0-0	.235	.316	.500	.816	0	1.000
1996— Lynchburg (Caro.)	OF-DH	136	* 528	78	* 170	30	0	• 21	94	20	73	13	16	24-13	.322	.357	.498	.855	* 13	.949
1997— Pittsburgh (N.L.)	OF	143	498	58	133	20	5	14	70	17	88	8	16	1-2	.267	.300	.412	.712	9	.963
1998— Pittsburgh (N.L.)	OF	153	573	60	153	38	2	14	84	21	100	6	7	3-5	.267	.298	.414	.712	10	.968
1999— Pittsburgh (N.L.)	OF	40	120	18	32	6	0	1	18	10	21	0	7	1-0	.267	.321	.342	.662	3	.952
— Nashville (PCL)	OF-DH	35	132	28	44	10	0	5	22	8	21	2	4	0-1	.333	.378	.523	.900	4	.939
— Durham (Int'l)	OF	9	34	8	13	1	0	3	12	7	7	0	2	0-1	.382	.476	.676	1.153	0	1.000
— Tampa Bay (A.L.)	OF	47	168	24	41	10	0	2	13	10	36	7	9	0-0	.244	.312	.339	.651	3	.966
2000— Durham (Int'l)	OF	19	78	20	33	8	2	9	31	8	11	1	2	0-1	.423	.477	.923	1.400	3	.912
— Tampa Bay (A.L.)	OF	105	316	40	80	16	5	10	41	18	65	13	6	3-1	.253	.320	.430	.750	4	.978
2001— Tampa Bay (A.L.)	OF-DH	41	135	14	37	5	0	3	11	6	26	3	2	2-3	.274	.317	.378	.695	3	.969
— Durham (Int'l)	OF	33	119	18	35	9	0	7	29	3	28	0	3	0-0	.294	.306	.546	.853	1	.982
2002— Arizona (N.L.)	OF-DH	54	131	13	30	4	0	4	15	7	25	2	7	3-4	.229	.277	.351	.628	0	1.000
— Colo. Springs (PCL)	OF	5	17	2	7	3	0	0	5	1	2	1	1	0-1	.412	.474	.588	1.062	0	1.000
— Louisville (Int'l)	OF	8	29	4	9	4	0	2	8	0	5	0	1	0-0	.310	.310	.655	.966	0	1.000
— Cincinnati (N.L.)	OF	31	109	12	27	3	0	4	16	7	18	1	6	1-1	.248	.299	.385	.684	1	.979
2003— Louisville (Int'l)	OF	4	15	4	5	1	0	0	3	1	3	0	1	1-0	.333	.353	.400	.753	0	1.000
— Cincinnati (N.L.)	OF	91	315	52	106	21	1	23	63	17	63	9	8	1-3	.337	.385	.629	1.013	8	.957
— Oakland (A.L.)	OF-DH	45	170	25	45	7	1	8	23	7	32	5	8	0-0	.265	.311	.459	.770	4	.942
American League totals (4 years)		238	789	103	203	38	6	23	88	41	159	28	25	5-4	.257	.316	.408	.724	14	.968
National League totals (5 years)		512	1746	213	481	92	8	60	266	79	315	26	51	10-15	.275	.315	.440	.755	31	.966
Major League totals (7 years)		750	2535	316	684	130	14	83	354	120	474	54	76	15-19	.270	.315	.430	.745	45	.966

GUTHRIE, MARK — P

PERSONAL: Born September 22, 1965, in Buffalo, N.Y. ... 6-4/215. ... Throws left, bats right. ... Full name: Mark Andrew Guthrie. ... High school: Venice (Fla.). ... College: Louisiana State.

TRANSACTIONS/CAREER NOTES: Selected by St. Louis Cardinals organization in fourth round of free-agent draft (June 2, 1986); did not sign. ... Selected by Minnesota Twins organization in seventh round of free-agent draft (June 2, 1987). ... On disabled list (May 29, 1993-remainder of season). ... Traded by Twins with P Kevin Tapani to Los Angeles Dodgers for 1B/3B Ron Coomer, P Greg Hansell, P Jose Parra and a player to be named later (July 31, 1995); Twins acquired OF Chris Latham to complete deal (October 30, 1995). ... Granted free agency (October 29, 1996). ... Re-signed by Dodgers (November 6, 1996). ... Granted free agency (October 26, 1998). ... Signed by Boston Red Sox (December 19, 1998). ... On Boston disabled list (July 5-24, 1999); included rehabilitation assignment to Pawtucket (July 22-23). ... Traded by Red Sox with a player to named later to Chicago Cubs for P Rod Beck (August 31, 1999); Cubs acquired 3B Cole Liniak to complete deal (September 1, 1999). ... Traded by Cubs to Tampa Bay Devil Rays for OF Dave Martinez (May 12, 2000). ... Traded by Devil Rays with P Steve Trachsel to Toronto Blue Jays for 2B Brent Abernathy and a player to be named later (July 31, 2000). ... Granted free agency (October 31, 2000). ... Signed by Oakland Athletics (January 5, 2001). ... Traded by A's with P Tyler Yates to New York Mets for OF David Justice (December 14, 2001). ... Granted free agency (October 29, 2002). ... Signed by Cubs (January 20, 2003).

CAREER HITTING: 1-for-14 (.071), 0 R, 0 2B, 0 3B, 0 HR, 0 RBI.

Year — League	W	L	Pct.	ERA	WHIP	G	GS	CG	ShO	Hld.	Sv.-Opp.	IP	H	R	ER	HR	BB-IBB	SO	Avg.
1987— Visalia (Calif.)	2	1	.667	4.50	1.25	4	1	0	0	...	0-...	12.0	10	7	6	0	5-1	9	.244
1988— Visalia (Calif.)	12	9	.571	3.31	1.49	25	25	4	1	...	0-...	171.1	169	81	63	6	86-1	182	.262
1989— Orlando (Sou.)	8	3	.727	1.97	1.18	14	14	0	0	...	0-...	96.0	75	32	21	4	38-0	103	.222
— Portland (PCL)	3	4	.429	3.65	1.38	7	7	1	0	...	0-...	44.1	45	21	18	4	16-0	35	.266
— Minnesota (A.L.)	2	4	.333	4.55	1.52	13	8	0	0	0	0-0	57.1	66	32	29	7	21-1	38	.292
1990— Minnesota (A.L.)	7	9	.438	3.79	1.33	24	21	3	1	0	0-0	144.2	154	65	61	8	39-3	101	.276
— Portland (PCL)	1	3	.250	2.98	1.39	9	8	1	0	...	0-...	42.1	47	19	14	1	12-0	39	.284
1991— Minnesota (A.L.)	7	5	.583	4.32	1.60	41	12	0	0	5	2-2	98.0	116	52	47	11	41-2	72	.303
1992— Minnesota (A.L.)	2	3	.400	2.88	1.09	54	0	0	0	19	5-7	75.0	59	27	24	7	23-7	76	.215
1993— Minnesota (A.L.)	2	1	.667	4.71	1.71	22	0	0	0	8	0-1	21.0	20	11	11	2	16-2	15	.250
1994— Minnesota (A.L.)	4	2	.667	6.14	1.62	50	2	0	0	12	1-3	51.1	65	43	35	8	18-2	38	.316
1995— Minnesota (A.L.)	5	3	.625	4.46	1.49	36	0	0	0	10	0-2	42.1	47	22	21	5	16-3	48	.290
— Los Angeles (N.L.)	0	2	.000	3.66	1.42	24	0	0	0	5	0-0	19.2	19	11	8	1	9-2	19	.241
1996— Los Angeles (N.L.)	2	3	.400	2.22	1.19	66	0	0	0	12	1-3	73.0	65	21	18	3	22-2	56	.240
1997— Los Angeles (N.L.)	1	4	.200	5.32	1.46	62	0	0	0	13	1-4	69.1	71	44	41	12	30-6	42	.272
1998— Los Angeles (N.L.)	2	1	.667	3.50	1.48	53	0	0	0	8	0-1	54.0	56	26	21	3	24-1	45	.267
1999— Boston (A.L.)	1	1	.500	5.83	1.51	46	0	0	0	12	2-2	46.1	50	32	30	9	20-3	36	.275
— Pawtucket (Int'l)	0	0	...	0.00	0.00	1	1	0	0	...	0-...	1.0	0	0	0	0	0-0	1	.000
— Chicago (N.L.)	0	2	.000	3.65	0.89	11	0	0	0	2	0-0	12.1	7	6	5	1	4-2	9	.171
2000— Chicago (N.L.)	2	3	.400	4.82	1.45	19	0	0	0	3	0-0	18.2	17	11	10	1	10-4	17	.258
— Tampa Bay (A.L.)	1	1	.500	4.50	1.59	34	0	0	0	4	0-3	32.0	33	18	16	4	18-5	26	.262
— Toronto (A.L.)	0	2	.000	4.79	1.40	23	0	0	0	3	0-1	20.2	20	12	11	3	9-0	20	.263
2001— Oakland (A.L.)	6	2	.750	4.47	1.32	54	0	0	0	12	1-3	52.1	49	29	26	7	20-1	52	.249
2002— New York (N.L.)	5	3	.625	2.44	1.13	68	0	0	0	17	1-2	48.0	35	13	13	3	19-3	44	.201
2003— Chicago (N.L.)	2	3	.400	2.74	1.45	65	0	0	0	10	0-1	42.2	40	14	13	6	22-4	24	.260
American League totals (10 years)	37	33	.529	4.37	1.44	397	43	3	1	85	11-24	641.0	679	343	311	71	241-29	522	.276
National League totals (8 years)	14	21	.400	3.44	1.33	368	0	0	0	70	3-11	337.2	310	146	129	30	140-24	256	.248
Major League totals (15 years)	51	54	.486	4.05	1.40	765	43	3	1	155	14-35	978.2	989	489	440	101	381-53	778	.266

G

GUTIERREZ, RICKY — IF

PERSONAL: Born May 23, 1970, in Miami, Fla. ... 6-1/190. ... Bats right, throws right. ... Full name: Ricardo Gutierrez. ... Name pronounced: goo-tee-AIR-ezz. ... High school: American (Hialeah, Fla.).

TRANSACTIONS/CAREER NOTES: Selected by Baltimore Orioles organization in supplemental round ("sandwich pick" between first and second round, 28th pick overall) of free-agent draft (June 1, 1988); pick received as compensation for Orioles failing to sign 1987 No. 1 pick P Brad DuVall. ... Traded by Orioles to San Diego Padres (September 4, 1992), completing deal in which Padres traded P Craig Lefferts to Orioles for P Erik Schullstrom and a player to be named later (August 31, 1992). ... Traded by Padres with OF Phil Plantier, OF Derek Bell, P Pedro Martinez, P Doug Brocail and IF Craig Shipley to Houston Astros for 3B Ken Caminiti, OF Steve Finley, SS Andujar Cedeno, 1B Robert Petagine, P Brian Williams and a player to be named later (December 28, 1994); Padres acquired P Sean Fesh to complete deal (May 1, 1995). ... On Houston disabled list (March 31-May 6, 1997); included rehabilitation assignment to New Orleans (April 29-May 6). ... On Houston disabled list (April 28-June 7 and July 10-August 9, 1999); included rehabilitation assignments to Jackson (June 3-7) and New Orleans (August 5-9). ... Granted free agency (October 28, 1999). ... Signed by Chicago Cubs (December 20, 1999). ... On Chicago disabled list (May 25-June 23, 2000); included rehabilitation assignment to Daytona (June 19-23). ... Granted free agency (November 5, 2001). ... Signed by Cleveland Indians (December 19, 2001). ... On disabled list (June 14-July 2 and August 15, 2002-remainder of season). ... On disabled list (March 29, 2003). ... Sent on rehab assignment to Buffalo (June 5, 2003). ... Recalled from Buffalo rehab assignment (June 24, 2003). ... Reinstated from Emergency disabled list (June 24, 2003). ... Placed on 15-day disabled list (July 13, 2003). ... Transferred to Emergency disabled list (August 10, 2003).

2003 GAMES PLAYED BY POSITION (MLB): SS—9, 3B—7.

Year	Team (League)	Pos.	G	AB	R	H	2B	3B	HR	RBI	BB	SO	HBP	GDP	SB-CS	Avg.	OBP	SLG	OPS	E	Pct.
1988—Bluefield (Appal.)		SS	62	208	35	51	8	2	2	19	44	40	5	4	5-3	.245	.383	.332	.715	34	.890
1989—Frederick (Carolina)		SS	127	456	48	106	16	2	3	41	39	89	3	12	15-10	.232	.294	.296	.590	34	.943
1990—Frederick (Carolina)		SS	112	425	54	117	16	4	1	46	38	59	6	11	12-6	.275	.341	.339	.680	26	.948
—Hagerstown (East.)		SS	20	64	4	15	0	1	0	6	3	8	0	2	2-0	.234	.265	.266	.530	4	.944
1991—Hagerstown (East.)		SS	84	292	47	69	6	4	0	30	57	52	2	8	11-0	.236	.363	.284	.647	22	.941
—Rochester (Int'l)		3B-SS	49	157	23	48	5	3	0	15	24	27	0	3	4-1	.306	.396	.376	.771	8	.960
1992—Rochester (Int'l)		2B-SS	125	431	54	109	9	3	0	41	53	77	0	12	14-12	.253	.331	.288	.619	15	.973
—Las Vegas (PCL)		SS	3	6	0	1	0	0	0	1	1	3	0	0	0-0	.167	.250	.167	.417	0	1.000
1993—Las Vegas (PCL)		2B-SS	5	24	4	10	4	0	0	4	0	4	0	0	4-0	.417	.417	.583	1.000	2	.926
—San Diego (N.L.)		SS-2-OF-3	133	438	76	110	10	5	5	26	50	97	5	7	4-3	.251	.334	.331	.665	14	.973
1994—San Diego (N.L.)		SS-2B	90	275	27	66	11	2	1	28	32	54	2	8	2-6	.240	.321	.305	.626	22	.931
1995—Houston (N.L.)		SS-3B	52	156	22	43	6	0	0	12	10	33	1	4	5-0	.276	.321	.314	.636	8	.956
—Tucson (PCL)		SS-DH	64	236	46	71	12	4	1	26	28	28	3	6	9-7	.301	.379	.398	.777	6	.977
1996—Houston (N.L.)		SS-3B-2B	89	218	28	62	8	1	1	15	23	42	3	4	6-1	.284	.359	.344	.703	12	.951
1997—New Orleans (A.A.)		SS	7	27	2	5	1	0	0	4	2	4	0	1	0-1	.185	.233	.222	.456	1	.971
—Houston (N.L.)		SS-3B-2B	102	303	33	79	14	4	3	34	21	50	3	17	5-2	.261	.315	.363	.678	8	.974
1998—Houston (N.L.)		SS	141	491	55	128	24	3	2	46	54	84	6	20	13-7	.261	.337	.334	.671	15	.976
1999—Houston (N.L.)		SS-3B	85	268	33	70	7	5	1	25	37	45	2	9	2-5	.261	.354	.336	.690	9	.971
—Jackson (Texas)		SS-DH	4	12	4	4	1	0	0	1	4	3	0	0	0-1	.333	.500	.417	.917	0	1.000
—New Orleans (PCL)		SS	4	14	0	3	0	0	0	1	2	3	0	2	0-0	.214	.313	.214	.527	3	.875
2000—Chicago (N.L.)		SS	125	449	73	124	19	2	11	56	66	58	7	10	8-2	.276	.375	.401	.775	7	.986
—Daytona (Fla. St.)		SS	4	10	0	4	1	0	0	1	2	2	0	1	1-0	.400	.500	.500	1.000	3	.727
2001—Chicago (N.L.)		SS	147	528	76	153	23	3	10	66	40	56	10	13	4-3	.290	.345	.402	.746	16	.971
2002—Cleveland (A.L.)		2B-DH	94	353	38	97	13	0	4	38	20	48	7	14	0-1	.275	.325	.346	.671	11	.976
2003—Buffalo (Int'l)		3-SS-2-DH	16	65	8	19	2	1	0	5	4	5	1	2	4-1	.292	.338	.354	.692	0	1.000
—Cleveland (A.L.)		SS-3B	16	50	2	13	3	0	0	3	3	5	1	1	0-0	.260	.309	.320	.629	3	.942
American League totals (2 years)			110	403	40	110	16	0	4	41	23	53	8	15	0-1	.273	.323	.342	.666	14	.972
National League totals (9 years)			964	3126	423	835	122	25	34	308	333	519	39	92	49-29	.267	.342	.355	.697	111	.969
Major League totals (11 years)			1074	3529	463	945	138	25	38	349	356	572	47	107	49-30	.268	.340	.353	.694	125	.969

GUZMAN, CRISTIAN — SS

PERSONAL: Born March 21, 1978, in Santo Domingo, Dominican Republic. ... 6-0/195. ... Bats both, throws right. ... Full name: Christian Antonio Guzman. ... Name pronounced: GOOZ-mahn.

TRANSACTIONS/CAREER NOTES: Signed as non-drafted free agent by New York Yankees organization (August 24, 1994). ... Traded by Yankees with P Eric Milton, P Danny Mota, OF Brian Buchanan and cash to Minnesota Twins for 2B Chuck Knoblauch (February 6, 1998). ... On disabled list (May 27-June 11, 1999). ... On suspended list (September 10-13, 1999). ... On Minnesota disabled list (July 13-August 17, 2001); included rehabilitation assignment to Gulf Coast Twins (August 13-17).

2003 GAMES PLAYED BY POSITION (MLB): SS—141.

Year	Team (League)	Pos.	G	AB	R	H	2B	3B	HR	RBI	BB	SO	HBP	GDP	SB-CS	Avg.	OBP	SLG	OPS	E	Pct.
1995—Dom. Yankees (DSL)		SS	46	160	24	43	6	5	3	20	12	23	...	...	11-...	.269	...	.425	...	13	.935
1996—GC Yankees (GCL)		SS	42	170	37	50	8	2	1	21	10	31	3	2	7-6	.294	.341	.382	.723	20	.890
1997—Greensboro (S. Atl.)		SS	124	495	68	135	21	4	4	52	17	105	10	3	23-12	.273	.309	.356	.665	37	.936
—Tampa (Fla. St.)		SS	4	14	4	4	0	0	0	1	1	1	0	0	0-1	.286	.333	.286	.619	2	.889
1998—New Britain (East.)		SS	• 140	566	68	157	29	5	1	40	21	111	1	13	23-14	.277	.304	.352	.655	* 32	.952
1999—Minnesota (A.L.)		SS	131	420	47	95	12	3	1	26	22	90	3	5	9-7	.226	.267	.276	.543	24	.959
2000—Minnesota (A.L.)		SS-DH	`156	631	89	156	25	* 20	8	54	46	101	2	5	28-10	.247	.299	.388	.687	22	.969
2001—Minnesota (A.L.)		SS	118	493	80	149	28	* 14	10	51	21	78	5	6	25-8	.302	.337	.477	.814	* 21	.959
—GC Twins (GCL)		SS	5	16	4	4	0	1	0	0	2	4	1	1	0-1	.250	.368	.375	.743	0	1.000
2002—Minnesota (A.L.)		SS-DH	148	623	80	170	31	6	9	59	17	79	2	12	12-13	.273	.292	.385	.677	12	.981
2003—Minnesota (A.L.)		SS	143	534	78	143	15	*14	3	53	30	79	5	4	18-9	.268	.311	.365	.676	11	.980
Major League totals (5 years)			696	2701	374	713	111	57	31	243	136	427	17	32	92-47	.264	.302	.382	.683	90	.969

GUZMAN, EDWARDS — 3B/C

PERSONAL: Born September 11, 1976, in Bayamon, Puerto Rico. ... 5-11/204. ... Bats left, throws right. ... Name pronounced: gooz-MAHN. ... High school: Emilio Delgado (Corozal, Puerto Rico). ... College: Inter American (P.R.).

TRANSACTIONS/CAREER NOTES: Selected by San Francisco Giants organization in 50th round of free-agent draft (June 1, 1995). ... On Fresno disabled list (June 12-23, 1999). ... On Fresno disabled list (May 24-June 1, 2002). ... Traded by Giants with P Livan Hernandez and cash to Montreal Expos for P Jim Brower and a player to be named later (March 24, 2003); Giants acquired P Matt Blank to complete deal (April 30, 2003).

2003 GAMES PLAYED BY POSITION (MLB): 3B—28, 1B—13, C—4, DH—3.

G

Year	Team (League)	Pos.	G	AB	R	H	2B	3B	HR	RBI	BB	SO	HBP	GDP	SB-CS	Avg.	OBP	SLG	OPS	E	Pct.
1996— San Jose (Calif.)	3B-OF	106	367	41	99	19	5	1	40	39	60	5	6	3-5	.270	.344	.357	.701	25	.919
1997— Shreveport (Texas)	3B	118	380	52	108	15	4	3	42	33	57	1	6	3-1	.284	.341	.368	.709	19	.935
1998— Fresno (PCL)	3B-C	102	325	50	99	17	0	9	48	24	47	3	4	1-0	.305	.357	.440	.797	14	.938
1999— Fresno (PCL)	3-C-1-DH	90	358	48	98	13	0	7	48	17	50	3	11	6-5	.274	.309	.369	.678	26	.941
— San Francisco (N.L.)	3B-C	14	15	0	0	0	0	0	0	0	4	0	0	0-0	.000	.000	.000	.000	0	1.000
2000— Fresno (PCL)	2-C-3-0-1	115	421	52	118	24	1	6	52	17	43	5	17	1-5	.280	.314	.385	.699	18	.963
2001— Fresno (PCL)	C-3-2-1	18	72	13	26	3	2	0	11	4	3	0	1	0-1	.361	.395	.458	.853	0	1.000
— San Francisco (N.L.)	C-3-1-2-OF	61	115	8	28	6	0	3	7	5	16	0	2	0-0	.243	.273	.374	.647	3	.980
2002— Fresno (PCL) C-3-1-2-OF	112	390	45	116	22	0	5	55	16	26	0	16	1-3	.297	.324	.392	.716	9	.984
2003— Edmonton (PCL)	C-1-2-3	55	213	26	75	12	1	3	27	8	18	0	6	5-1	.352	.372	.460	.832	6	.984
— Montreal (N.L.)	3-1-C-DH	52	146	15	35	5	0	1	14	5	17	0	6	0-0	.240	.263	.295	.558	4	.972
Major League totals (3 years)		127	276	23	63	11	0	4	21	10	37	0	8	0-0	.228	.253	.312	.565	7	.977

HACKMAN, LUTHER   P

PERSONAL: Born October 10, 1974, in Columbus, Miss. ... 6-4/195. ... Throws right, bats right. ... Full name: Luther Gean Hackman. ... High school: Columbus (Miss.).
TRANSACTIONS/CAREER NOTES: Selected by Colorado Rockies organization in sixth round of free-agent draft (June 2, 1994). ... On disabled list (June 1-July 10, 1996). ... Traded by Rockies with P Darryl Kile and P Dave Veres to St. Louis Cardinals for P Jose Jimenez, P Manny Aybar, P Rick Croushore and SS Brent Butler (November 16, 1999). ... On Memphis disabled list (June 3-July 4, 2000). ... On St. Louis disabled list (March 23-May 9, 2001); included rehabilitation assignment to New Haven (May 1-9). ... Traded by Cardinals with a player to be named later to San Diego Padres for P Brett Tomko (December 15, 2002); Padres acquired P Mike Wodnicki to complete deal (December 16, 2002). ... Sent outright to Portland by San Diego (September 29, 2003).
CAREER HITTING: 2-for-24 (.083), 1 R, 0 2B, 0 3B, 0 HR, 0 RBI.

Year	League	W	L	Pct.	ERA	WHIP	G	GS	CG	ShO	Hld.	Sv.-Opp.	IP	H	R	ER	HR	BB-IBB	SO	Avg.
1994—Ariz. Rockies (Ariz.)	1	3	.250	2.10	1.19	12	12	0	0	...	0-...	55.2	50	21	13	1	16-0	63	.230
1995—Asheville (S. Atl.)	11	11	.500	4.64	1.38	28	28	2	0	...	0-...	165.0	162	* 95	* 85	11	65-0	108	.259
1996—Salem (Caro.)	5	7	.417	4.24	1.47	21	21	1	0	...	0-...	110.1	93	60	52	2	69-1	83	.233
1997—New Haven (East.)	0	6	.000	7.82	1.82	10	10	0	0	...	0-...	50.2	58	49	44	11	34-1	34	.297
—Salem (Caro.)	1	4	.200	5.80	1.69	15	15	2	0	...	0-...	80.2	99	60	52	14	37-0	59	.301
1998—New Haven (East.)	3	12	.200	5.44	1.60	28	23	1	0	...	0-...	139.0	169	• 102	84	18	54-1	90	.301
1999—Carolina (Sou.)	4	3	.571	4.04	1.30	11	10	0	0	...	0-...	62.1	53	33	28	4	28-0	50	.225
—Colo. Springs (PCL)	7	6	.538	3.74	1.49	15	15	1	1	...	0-...	101.0	106	49	42	7	44-2	88	.273
—Colorado (N.L.)	1	2	.333	10.69	2.38	5	3	0	0	0	0-0	16.0	26	19	19	5	12-0	10	.371
2000—Memphis (PCL)	8	9	.471	4.74	1.42	21	21	0	0	...	0-...	119.2	134	71	63	11	36-1	66	.283
—St. Louis (N.L.)	0	0	...	10.13	3.00	1	0	0	0	0	0-0	2.2	4	3	3	0	4-1	0	.400
2001—New Haven (East.)	0	0	...	2.25	0.75	3	1	0	0	...	0-...	4.0	2	2	1	0	1-0	5	.154
—Memphis (PCL)	0	2	.000	2.78	0.97	16	0	0	0	...	0-...	22.2	21	7	7	2	1-0	12	.253
—St. Louis (N.L.)	1	2	.333	4.29	1.18	35	0	0	0	5	1-3	35.2	28	18	17	7	14-0	24	.212
2002—St. Louis (N.L.)	5	4	.556	4.11	1.59	43	6	0	0	1	0-1	81.0	90	42	37	7	39-3	46	.287
2003—San Diego (N.L.)	2	2	.500	5.17	1.49	65	0	0	0	11	0-2	76.2	78	51	44	7	36-2	48	.261
Major League totals (5 years)	9	10	.474	5.09	1.56	149	9	0	0	17	1-6	212.0	226	133	120	26	105-6	128	.274

HAFNER, TRAVIS   1B

PERSONAL: Born June 3, 1977, in Jamestown, N.D. ... 6-3/240. ... Bats left, throws right. ... Full name: Travis Lee Hafner. ... Name pronounced: HAF-ner. ... Junior college: Cowley County College (Kan.).
TRANSACTIONS/CAREER NOTES: Selected by Texas Rangers organization in 31st round of free-agent draft (June 4, 1996). ... On disabled list (August 6-22, 2000). ... On disabled list (April 5-May 11, 2001). ... Traded by Rangers with P Aaron Myette to Cleveland Indians for C Einar Diaz and P Ryan Drese (December 6, 2002).
2003 GAMES PLAYED BY POSITION (MLB): DH—43, 1B—42.

Year	Team (League)	Pos.	G	AB	R	H	2B	3B	HR	RBI	BB	SO	HBP	GDP	SB-CS	Avg.	OBP	SLG	OPS	E	Pct.
1997— GC Rangers (GCL)	1B-OF	55	189	38	54	14	0	5	24	24	45	3	3	7-2	.286	.375	.439	.814	3	.991
1998— Savannah (S. Atl.)	3B-1B-OF	123	405	62	96	15	4	16	84	68	139	6	8	7-3	.237	.351	.412	.764	12	.980
1999— Savannah (S. Atl.)	3B-1B	134	480	94	140	30	4	• 28	* 111	67	151	11	11	5-4	.292	.387	.546	.933	15	.984
2000— Charlotte (Fla. St.)	1B-3B	122	436	90	151	34	4	22	109	67	86	18	9	0-4	.346	* .447	.580	1.027	13	.978
2001— Tulsa (Texas)	1B	88	323	59	91	25	0	20	74	59	82	4	10	3-1	.282	.396	.545	.941	5	.993
2002— Oklahoma (PCL)	1B	110	401	79	137	22	1	21	77	79	76	12	9	2-1	.342	* .463	.559	1.022	4	.993
— Texas (A.L.)	DH-1B	23	62	6	15	4	1	1	6	8	15	0	0	0-1	.242	.329	.387	.716	1	.909
2003— Buffalo (Int'l)	1B-DH	29	100	15	27	4	0	2	10	25	26	1	2	2-1	.270	.421	.370	.791	3	.986
— Cleveland (A.L.)	DH-1B	91	291	35	74	19	3	14	40	22	81	10	5	2-1	.254	.327	.485	.812	6	.985
Major League totals (2 years)		114	353	41	89	23	4	15	46	30	96	10	7	2-2	.252	.327	.467	.795	7	.983

HAIRSTON JR., JERRY   2B

PERSONAL: Born May 29, 1976, in Naperville, Ill. ... 5-10/185. ... Bats right, throws right. ... Full name: Jerry Wayne Hairston Jr.. ... High school: Naperville (Ill.) North. ... College: Southern Illinois.
TRANSACTIONS/CAREER NOTES: Selected by Baltimore Orioles organization in 42nd round of free-agent draft (June 1, 1995); did not sign. ... Selected by Orioles organization in 11th round of free-agent draft (June 3, 1997). ... On Rochester disabled list (May 16-July 4, 2000). ... Placed on the 15-day disabled list (May 21, 2003). ... Transferred to Emergency disabled list (June 29, 2003). ... Sent on minor league rehab assignment (August 26, 2003). ... Recalled from rehab assignment; removed from 60-day disabled list (September 4, 2003).
2003 GAMES PLAYED BY POSITION (MLB): 2B—48, DH—9.

Year	Team (League)	Pos.	G	AB	R	H	2B	3B	HR	RBI	BB	SO	HBP	GDP	SB-CS	Avg.	OBP	SLG	OPS	E	Pct.
1997— Bluefield (Appal.)	SS	59	221	44	73	13	4	2	36	21	29	10	4	13-9	.330	.409	.452	.862	14	.949
1998— Frederick (Carolina)	2B-SS	80	293	56	83	22	3	5	33	28	32	12	4	13-7	.283	.366	.430	.796	24	.943
— Bowie (East.)	2B-SS	55	221	42	72	12	3	5	37	20	25	5	5	6-4	.326	.393	.475	.868	5	.980
— Baltimore (A.L.)	2B	6	7	2	0	0	0	0	0	0	1	0	0	0-0	.000	.000	.000	.000	2	.750
1999— Rochester (Int'l)	2B-SS	107	413	65	120	24	5	7	48	30	50	19	9	19-10	.291	.363	.424	.787	16	.968
— Baltimore (A.L.)	2B	50	175	26	47	12	1	4	17	11	24	3	2	9-4	.269	.323	.417	.740	0	1.000
2000— Baltimore (A.L.)	2B	49	180	27	46	5	0	5	19	21	22	6	8	8-5	.256	.353	.367	.719	5	.981
— Rochester (Int'l)	2B-SS	58	201	43	59	15	1	4	21	29	32	5	2	6-4	.294	.392	.438	.830	11	.963
— GC Orioles (GCL)	2B	4	10	3	3	2	0	0	3	3	2	1	0	4-0	.300	.500	.500	1.000	0	1.000
— Frederick (Carolina)	2B	2	8	1	3	2	0	0	1	1	0	0	0	0-0	.375	.444	.625	1.069	0	1.000

H

Year Team (League)	Pos.	G	AB	R	H	2B	3B	HR	RBI	BB	SO	HBP	GDP	SB-CS	Avg.	OBP	SLG	OPS	E	Pct.
2001— Baltimore (A.L.)	2B	159	532	63	124	25	5	8	47	44	73	13	12	29-11	.233	.305	.344	.649	19	.976
2002— Baltimore (A.L.)	2B	122	426	55	114	25	3	5	32	34	55	7	5	21-6	.268	.329	.376	.705	11	.982
2003— Bowie (East.)	2B-DH	6	20	4	6	1	0	1	2	1	4	2	0	0-0	.300	.391	.500	.891	1	.941
—Aberdeen (NY-P)	2B-DH	2	3	2	1	0	0	0	0	3	0	0	0	1-0	.333	.667	.333	1.000	0	1.000
—Baltimore (A.L.)	2B-DH	58	218	25	59	12	2	2	21	23	25	6	8	14-5	.271	.353	.372	.725	5	.980
Major League totals (6 years)		444	1538	198	390	79	11	24	136	133	200	35	35	81-31	.254	.325	.366	.691	42	.981

HALAMA, JOHN   P

PERSONAL: Born February 22, 1972, in Brooklyn, N.Y. ... 6-5/215. ... Throws left, bats left. ... Full name: John Thadeuz Halama. ... Name pronounced: ha-LA-ma. ... High school: Bishop Ford (Brooklyn, N.Y.). ... College: St. Francis (N.Y.).

TRANSACTIONS/CAREER NOTES: Selected by Houston Astros organization in 23rd round of free-agent draft (June 3, 1994). ... On New Orleans disabled list (July 2-August 6, 1998). ... Traded by Astros to Seattle Mariners (October 1, 1998), completing deal in which Mariners traded P Randy Johnson to Astros for SS Carlos Guillen, P Freddy Garcia and a player to be named later (July 31, 1998). ... Granted free agency (December 21, 2002). ... Signed by Oakland Athletics (January 17, 2003).

CAREER HITTING: 2-for-18 (.111), 2 R, 1 2B, 0 3B, 0 HR, 0 RBI.

Year League	W	L	Pct.	ERA	WHIP	G	GS	CG	ShO	Hld.	Sv.-Opp.	IP	H	R	ER	HR	BB-IBB	SO	Avg.
1994— Auburn (N.Y.-Penn)	4	1	.800	1.29	0.82	6	3	0	0	...	1-...	28.0	18	5	4	1	5-0	27	.180
—Quad City (Midw.)	3	4	.429	4.56	1.58	9	9	1	1	...	0-...	51.1	63	31	26	2	18-1	37	.317
1995— Quad City (Midw.)	1	2	.333	2.02	1.12	55	0	0	0	...	2-...	62.1	48	16	14	7	22-1	56	.225
1996— Jackson (Texas)	9	10	.474	3.21	1.29	27	27	0	0	...	0-...	162.2	151	77	58	10	59-0	110	.248
1997— New Orleans (A.A.)	13	3	.813	2.58	1.06	26	24	1	0	...	0-...	171.0	150	57	49	9	32-1	126	.238
1998— Houston (N.L.)	1	1	.500	5.85	1.55	6	6	0	0	0	0-0	32.1	37	21	21	0	13-0	21	.296
—New Orleans (PCL)	12	3	.800	3.20	1.11	17	17	4	1	...	0-...	121.0	118	48	43	11	16-1	86	.255
1999— Seattle (A.L.)	11	10	.524	4.22	1.39	38	24	1	1	1	0-0	179.0	193	88	84	20	56-3	105	.282
2000— Seattle (A.L.)	14	9	.609	5.08	1.57	30	30	1	1	0	0-0	166.2	206	108	94	19	56-0	87	.308
2001— Seattle (A.L.)	10	7	.588	4.73	1.43	31	17	0	0	1	0-0	110.1	132	69	58	18	26-0	50	.296
—Tacoma (PCL)	2	0	1.000	0.47	0.47	3	3	1	1	...	0-...	19.0	9	2	1	1	0-0	22	.138
2002— Seattle (A.L.)	6	5	.545	3.56	1.44	31	10	0	0	0	0-0	101.0	112	45	40	9	33-5	70	.281
—Tacoma (PCL)	0	1	.000	6.14	1.36	2	2	0	0	...	0-...	14.2	19	11	10	0	1-1	9	.322
2003— Oakland (A.L.)	3	5	.375	4.22	1.41	35	13	0	0	3	0-0	108.2	117	68	51	18	36-2	51	.268
American League totals (5 years)	44	36	.550	4.42	1.45	165	94	2	2	5	0-0	665.2	760	378	327	84	207-10	363	.289
National League totals (1 year)	1	1	.500	5.85	1.55	6	6	0	0	0	0-0	32.1	37	21	21	0	13-0	21	.296
Major League totals (6 years)	45	37	.549	4.49	1.46	171	100	2	2	5	0-0	698.0	797	399	348	84	220-10	384	.289

HALL, BILL   SS

PERSONAL: Born December 28, 1979, in Nettleton, Miss. ... 6-0/198. ... Bats right, throws right. ... Full name: William Hall. ... High school: Nettleton (Miss.).

TRANSACTIONS/CAREER NOTES: Selected by Milwaukee Brewers organization in sixth round of free-agent draft (June 2, 1998).

2003 GAMES PLAYED BY POSITION (MLB): 2B—18, SS—18, 3B—1.

Year Team (League)	Pos.	G	AB	R	H	2B	3B	HR	RBI	BB	SO	HBP	GDP	SB-CS	Avg.	OBP	SLG	OPS	E	Pct.
1998— Helena (Pio.)	SS	29	85	11	15	3	0	0	5	9	27	1	2	5-5	.176	.263	.212	.475	16	.876
1999— Ogden (Pio.)	SS	69	280	41	81	15	2	6	31	15	61	2	6	19-8	.289	.329	.421	.750	* 38	.894
2000— Beloit (Midw.)	SS	130	470	57	123	30	6	3	41	18	127	1	12	10-11	.262	.287	.370	.658	* 40	.939
2001— High Desert (Calif.)	SS	89	346	61	105	21	6	15	51	22	78	3	3	18-9	.303	.348	.529	.876	30	.929
—Huntsville (Sou.)	SS	41	160	14	41	8	1	3	14	5	46	0	5	5-3	.256	.279	.375	.654	15	.925
2002— Indianapolis (Int'l)	SS	134	465	35	106	20	1	4	31	25	105	4	12	17-10	.228	.272	.301	.573	* 41	.934
—Milwaukee (N.L.)	SS-3B	19	36	3	7	1	1	1	5	3	13	0	1	0-1	.194	.256	.361	.618	2	.951
2003— Indianapolis (Int'l)	2B-SS-OF	89	354	57	100	25	2	5	32	27	79	1	7	10-11	.282	.335	.407	.742	19	.957
—Milwaukee (N.L.)	2B-SS-3B	52	142	23	37	9	2	5	20	7	28	1	5	1-2	.261	.298	.458	.756	9	.948
Major League totals (2 years)		71	178	26	44	10	3	6	25	10	41	1	6	1-3	.247	.289	.438	.728	11	.949

HALL, JOSH   P

PERSONAL: Born December 16, 1980, in Lynchburg, Va. ... 6-2/190. ... Throws right, bats right. ... Full name: Joshua Alan Hall. ... High school: E.C. Glass (Lynchburg, Va.).

TRANSACTIONS/CAREER NOTES: Selected by Cincinnati Reds organization in seventh round of free-agent draft (June 2, 1998). ... On disabled list (June 16, 1999-entire season). ... Recalled by Cincinnati from Chattanooga (August 2, 2003). ... Optioned to Chattanooga by Cincinnati (August 3, 2003). ... Recalled by Cincinnati from Chattanooga (September 6, 2003).

CAREER HITTING: 1-for-6 (.167), 2 R, 0 2B, 0 3B, 0 HR, 0 RBI.

Year League	W	L	Pct.	ERA	WHIP	G	GS	CG	ShO	Hld.	Sv.-Opp.	IP	H	R	ER	HR	BB-IBB	SO	Avg.
1998— Billings (Pio.)	5	4	.556	5.00	1.51	14	14	1	0	...	0-...	81.0	89	53	45	6	33-0	50	.276
1999—										Did not play.									
2000— GC Reds (GCL)	0	5	.000	10.57	2.54	6	6	0	0	...	0-...	15.1	26	25	18	2	13-0	20	.371
2001— Dayton (Midw.)	11	5	.688	2.65	1.18	22	22	2	0	...	0-...	132.1	117	52	39	4	39-1	122	.232
2002— Stockton (Calif.)	4	0	1.000	2.27	1.01	7	7	1	0	...	0-...	43.2	31	13	11	1	13-0	51	.194
—Chattanooga (Sou.)	7	8	.467	3.75	1.44	22	22	1	0	...	0-...	132.0	140	75	55	7	50-0	116	.276
2003— Chattanooga (Sou.)	8	10	.444	3.47	1.34	26	25	2	0	...	0-...	153.0	152	73	59	9	53-1	114	.260
—Cincinnati (N.L.)	0	2	.000	6.57	1.95	6	5	0	0	0	0-0	24.2	33	22	18	4	15-1	18	.314
Major League totals (1 year)	0	2	.000	6.57	1.95	6	5	0	0	0	0-0	24.2	33	22	18	4	15-1	18	.314

HALL, TOBY   C

PERSONAL: Born October 21, 1975, in Tacoma, Wash. ... 6-3/240. ... Bats right, throws right. ... Full name: Toby Jason Hall. ... High school: El Dorado (Placentia, Calif.). ... College: UNLV.

TRANSACTIONS/CAREER NOTES: Selected by Tampa Bay Devil Rays organization in ninth round of free-agent draft (June 3, 1997).

2003 GAMES PLAYED BY POSITION (MLB): C—130.

H

Year Team (League)	Pos.	G	AB	R	H	2B	3B	HR	RBI	BATTING BB	SO	HBP	GDP	SB-CS	Avg.	OBP	SLG	OPS	FIELDING E	Pct.
1997— Hudson Valley (NYP)	C	55	200	25	50	3	0	1	27	13	33	1	3	0-0	.250	.295	.280	.575	3	.989
1998— Char., S.C. (SAL)	C	105	377	59	121	25	1	6	50	39	32	5	15	3-7	.321	.386	.440	.827	18	.979
1999— Orlando (South.)	C	46	173	20	44	7	0	9	34	4	10	1	7	1-1	.254	.269	.451	.720	4	.986
—St. Pete. (FSL)	C	56	212	24	63	13	1	4	36	17	9	2	7	0-2	.297	.350	.425	.775	4	.980
2000— Orlando (South.)	C	68	271	37	93	14	0	9	50	17	24	1	6	3-2	.343	.378	.494	.872	7	.984
— Durham (Int'l)	C	47	184	21	56	15	0	7	35	3	19	2	9	0-0	.304	.314	.500	.814	2	.993
— Tampa Bay (A.L.)	C	4	12	1	2	0	0	1	1	1	0	0	0	0-0	.167	.231	.417	.647	0	1.000
2001— Durham (Int'l)	C	94	373	59	125	28	1	19	72	29	22	3	15	1-3	.335	.385	.568	.953	6	.987
— Tampa Bay (A.L.)	C	49	188	28	56	16	0	4	30	4	16	3	5	2-2	.298	.321	.447	.768	5	.986
2002— Tampa Bay (A.L.)	C	85	330	37	85	19	1	6	42	17	27	1	14	0-1	.258	.293	.376	.669	6	.989
— Durham (Int'l)	C	22	92	13	32	4	0	2	20	3	10	4	3	0-0	.348	.382	.457	.839	1	.993
2003— Tampa Bay (A.L.)	C	130	463	50	117	23	0	12	47	23	40	7	14	0-1	.253	.295	.380	.675	9	.988
Major League totals (4 years)		268	993	116	260	58	1	23	120	45	83	11	33	2-4	.262	.299	.392	.690	20	.988

HALLADAY, ROY   P

PERSONAL: Born May 14, 1977, in Denver, Colo. ... 6-6/230. ... Throws right, bats right. ... Full name: Harry Leroy Halladay. ... Name pronounced: HAL-luh-day. ... High school: Arvada (Colo.) West.

TRANSACTIONS/CAREER NOTES: Selected by Toronto Blue Jays organization in first round (17th pick overall) of free-agent draft (June 1, 1995). ... On Syracuse disabled list (May 15-June 17, 1998). ... On Tennessee disabled list (May 16-23, 2001).

CAREER HITTING: 1-for-18 (.056), 2 R, 0 2B, 0 3B, 0 HR, 0 RBI.

Year League	W	L	Pct.	ERA	WHIP	G	GS	CG	ShO	Hld.	Sv.-Opp.	IP	H	R	ER	HR	BB-IBB	SO	Avg.
1995— GC Blue Jays (GCL)	3	5	.375	3.40	1.01	10	8	0	0	...	0-...	50.1	35	25	19	4	16-0	48	.190
1996— Dunedin (Fla. St.)	15	7	.682	2.73	1.24	27	27	2	•2	...	0-...	164.2	158	75	50	7	46-0	109	.251
1997— Knoxville (Sou.)	2	3	.400	5.40	1.55	7	7	0	0	...	0-...	36.2	46	26	22	4	11-0	30	.305
— Syracuse (Int'l)	7	10	.412	4.58	1.47	22	22	2	2	...	0-...	125.2	132	74	64	13	53-1	64	.276
1998— Syracuse (Int'l)	9	5	.643	3.79	1.38	21	21	1	1	...	0-...	116.1	107	52	49	11	53-3	71	.244
— Toronto (A.L.)	1	0	1.000	1.93	0.79	2	2	1	0	0	0-0	14.0	9	4	3	2	2-0	13	.176
1999— Toronto (A.L.)	8	7	.533	3.92	1.57	36	18	1	1	2	1-1	149.1	156	76	65	19	79-1	82	.270
2000— Toronto (A.L.)	4	7	.364	10.64	2.20	19	13	0	0	0	0-0	67.2	107	87	80	14	42-0	44	.357
— Syracuse (Int'l)	2	3	.400	5.50	1.44	11	11	3	0	...	0-...	73.2	85	46	45	10	21-0	38	.290
2001— Dunedin (Fla. St.)	0	1	.000	3.97	1.37	13	0	0	0	...	2-...	22.2	28	12	10	1	3-0	15	.304
— Tennessee (Sou.)	2	1	.667	2.12	0.91	5	5	3	0	...	0-...	34.0	25	9	8	2	6-0	29	.202
— Syracuse (Int'l)	1	0	1.000	3.21	0.86	2	2	0	0	...	0-...	14.0	12	5	5	2	0-0	13	.222
— Toronto (A.L.)	5	3	.625	3.16	1.16	17	16	1	1	0	0-0	105.1	97	41	37	3	25-0	96	.241
2002— Toronto (A.L.)	19	7	.731	2.93	1.19	34	34	2	1	0	0-0	* 239.1	223	93	78	10	62-6	168	.244
2003— Toronto (A.L.)	*22	7	.759	3.25	1.07	36	*36	•9	•2	0	0-0	*266.0	*253	111	96	26	32-1	204	.247
Major League totals (6 years)	59	31	.656	3.84	1.29	144	119	14	5	2	1-1	841.2	845	412	359	74	242-8	607	.258

HALTER, SHANE   IF

PERSONAL: Born November 8, 1969, in LaPlata, Md. ... 6-0/195. ... Bats right, throws right. ... Full name: Shane David Halter. ... High school: Hooks (Texas). ... College: Texas.

TRANSACTIONS/CAREER NOTES: Selected by Cincinnati Reds organization in 16th round of free-agent draft (June 4, 1990); did not sign. ... Selected by Kansas City Royals organization in fifth round of free-agent draft (June 3, 1991). ... Loaned by Royals organization to Charlotte, Florida Marlins organization (April 11-May 7, 1996). ... Traded by Royals to New York Mets for OF Jonathan Guzman (March 23, 1999). ... Claimed on waivers by Detroit Tigers (March 13, 2000).

2003 GAMES PLAYED BY POSITION (MLB): 3B—50, SS—27, 2B—24, 1B—12, DH—4, OF—2.

Year Team (League)	Pos.	G	AB	R	H	2B	3B	HR	RBI	BATTING BB	SO	HBP	GDP	SB-CS	Avg.	OBP	SLG	OPS	FIELDING E	Pct.
1991— Eugene (Northwest)	SS	64	236	41	55	9	1	1	18	49	60	3	3	12-6	.233	.370	.292	.663	21	.928
1992— Appleton (Midwest)	SS	80	313	50	83	22	3	3	33	41	54	1	4	21-6	.265	.349	.383	.733	16	.959
— Baseball City (FSL)	SS	44	117	11	28	1	0	1	14	24	31	0	4	5-5	.239	.359	.274	.632	6	.969
1993— Wilmington (Caro.)	SS	54	211	44	63	8	5	5	32	27	55	2	3	5-4	.299	.377	.455	.832	15	.939
— Memphis (Sou.)	SS	81	306	50	79	7	0	4	20	30	74	2	3	4-7	.258	.326	.320	.646	16	.959
1994— Memphis (Sou.)	SS	129	494	61	111	23	1	6	35	39	102	3	10	10-14	.225	.282	.312	.594	29	.950
1995— Omaha (A.A.)	SS-2B	124	392	42	90	19	3	8	39	40	97	0	6	2-3	.230	.300	.355	.655	19	.968
1996— Omaha (A.A.) O-3-SS-2	93	299	43	77	24	0	3	33	31	49	2	6	7-2	.258	.330	.368	.698	13	.940
— Charlotte (Int'l) O-2-3-D-1	16	41	3	12	1	0	0	4	2	8	0	0	0-0	.293	.311	.317	.628	1	.962
1997— Omaha (A.A.) 3-OF-2-S	14	49	10	13	1	1	2	9	6	10	1	1	0-0	.265	.345	.449	.794	2	.947
— Kansas City (A.L.) O-2-3-S-D	74	123	16	34	5	1	2	10	10	28	2	1	4-3	.276	.341	.382	.723	1	.990
1998— Kansas City (A.L.) ...S-O-3-2-P-1	86	204	17	45	12	0	2	13	12	38	1	3	2-5	.221	.265	.309	.574	10	.964
— Omaha (PCL) S-2-1-3-O	22	97	15	30	6	1	1	13	6	15	0	2	4-1	.309	.350	.423	.772	3	.973
1999— Norfolk (Int'l) S-0-2-3-C	127	474	77	130	23	3	6	35	60	90	0	10	19-17	.274	.354	.371	.725	20	.955
— New York (N.L.) ....OF-SS	7	0	0	0	0	0	0	0	0	0	0	0	0-0	...	...	...	...	0	...
2000— Detroit (A.L.) 3-1-S-2-0-C-P	105	238	26	62	12	2	3	27	14	49	1	5	5-2	.261	.302	.366	.668	8	.979
2001— Detroit (A.L.) 3-S-1-DH	136	450	53	128	32	7	12	65	37	100	7	14	3-3	.284	.344	.467	.811	26	.955
2002— Detroit (A.L.) S-3-0-2-D-1	122	410	46	98	22	6	10	39	39	92	4	12	0-4	.239	.309	.395	.704	21	.980
2003— Detroit (A.L.) 3-S-2-1-D-0	114	360	33	78	5	2	12	30	27	77	0	11	2-3	.217	.269	.342	.611	9	.980
American League totals (6 years)		637	1785	191	445	88	18	41	184	139	384	15	46	16-20	.249	.306	.388	.694	75	.967
National League totals (1 year)		7	0	0	0	0	0	0	0	0	0	0	0	0-0	...	...	...	...	0	...
Major League totals (7 years)		644	1785	191	445	88	18	41	184	139	384	15	46	16-20	.249	.306	.388	.694	75	.967

HAMILTON, JOEY   P

PERSONAL: Born September 9, 1970, in Statesboro, Ga. ... 6-4/240. ... Throws right, bats right. ... Full name: Johns Joseph Hamilton. ... High school: Statesboro (Ga.). ... College: Georgia Southern.

TRANSACTIONS/CAREER NOTES: Selected by Baltimore Orioles organization in 28th round of free-agent draft (June 1, 1988); did not sign. ... Selected by San Diego Padres organization in first round (eighth pick overall) of free-agent draft (June 3, 1991). ... On Rancho Cucamonga disabled list (April 5-20, 1993). ... On disabled list (April 24-May 17, 1997). ... Traded by Padres to Toronto Blue Jays for P Woody Williams, P Carlos Almanzar and OF Peter Tucci (December 13, 1998). ... On Toronto disabled list (April 14-May 24, 1999); included rehabilitation assignment to Syracuse (May 10-24). ... On Toronto disabled list (March 21-August 19, 2000); included rehabilitation assignment to Syracuse (July 17-August 15). ... Released by Blue Jays (August 3, 2001). ... Signed by Cincinnati Reds organization (August 17, 2001). ... Granted free agency (November 5, 2001). ... Re-signed by Reds organization (January 7, 2002). ... On Cincinnati disabled list (May 7-22 and July 8-August 6, 2002); included rehabilitation assignment to

Louisville (July 24-August 6). ... Granted free agency (October 30, 2002). ... Signed by St. Louis Cardinals (January 6, 2003). ... Released by Cardinals (March 26, 2003). ... Signed by Reds organization (April 11, 2003). ... Contract purchased from Louisville by Cincinnati (May 28, 2003). ... Sent outright to Louisville by Cincinnati (June 6, 2003).

CAREER HITTING: 43-for-339 (.127), 19 R, 8 2B, 1 3B, 4 HR, 22 RBI.

Year	League	W	L	Pct.	ERA	WHIP	G	GS	CG	ShO	Hld.	Sv.-Opp.	IP	H	R	ER	HR	BB-IBB	SO	Avg.
1992—	Char., S.C. (SAL)	2	2	.500	3.38	1.18	7	7	0	0	...	0-...	34.2	37	24	13	2	4-0	35	.261
	— High Desert (Calif.)	4	3	.571	2.74	1.30	9	8	0	0	...	0-...	49.1	46	20	15	0	18-0	43	.245
	— Wichita (Texas)	3	0	1.000	2.86	1.27	6	6	0	0	...	0-...	34.2	33	12	11	2	11-1	26	.258
1993—	Rancho Cuca. (Calif.)	1	0	1.000	4.09	1.18	2	2	0	0	...	0-...	11.0	11	5	5	0	2-0	6	.244
	— Wichita (Texas)	4	9	.308	3.97	1.51	15	15	0	0	...	0-...	90.2	101	55	40	3	36-2	50	.277
	— Las Vegas (PCL)	3	2	.600	4.40	1.51	8	8	0	0	...	0-...	47.0	49	25	23	0	22-1	33	.266
1994—	Las Vegas (PCL)	3	5	.375	2.73	1.53	9	9	1	1	...	0-...	59.1	69	25	18	2	22-0	32	.297
	— San Diego (N.L.)	9	6	.600	2.98	1.17	16	16	1	1	0	0-0	108.2	98	40	36	7	29-3	61	.241
1995—	San Diego (N.L.)	6	9	.400	3.08	1.20	31	30	2	2	0	0-0	204.1	189	89	70	17	56-5	123	.246
1996—	San Diego (N.L.)	15	9	.625	4.17	1.37	34	33	3	1	1	0-0	211.2	206	100	98	19	83-3	184	.256
1997—	San Diego (N.L.)	12	7	.632	4.25	1.39	31	29	1	0	0	0-0	192.2	199	100	91	22	69-2	124	.271
1998—	San Diego (N.L.)	13	13	.500	4.27	1.50	34	34	0	0	0	0-0	217.1	220	113	103	15	* 106-10	147	.267
1999—	Toronto (A.L.)	7	8	.467	6.52	1.60	22	18	0	0	1	0-0	98.0	118	73	71	13	39-0	56	.298
	— Syracuse (Int'l)	0	1	.000	5.11	1.62	3	3	0	0	...	0-...	12.1	15	8	7	2	5-0	9	.313
2000—	Syracuse (Int'l)	3	2	.600	3.66	1.35	6	6	1	0	...	0-...	39.1	41	18	16	1	12-0	17	.281
	— Toronto (A.L.)	2	1	.667	3.55	1.21	6	6	0	0	0	0-0	33.0	28	13	13	3	12-0	15	.233
2001—	Toronto (A.L.)	5	8	.385	5.89	1.70	22	22	0	0	0	0-0	122.1	170	88	80	17	38-1	82	.339
	— Louisville (Int'l)	1	0	1.000	5.40	1.00	1	1	0	0	...	0-...	5.0	4	3	3	1	1-0	1	.222
	— Cincinnati (Int'l)	1	2	.333	6.23	1.67	4	4	0	0	0	0-0	17.1	23	12	12	3	6-0	10	.320
2002—	Cincinnati (N.L.)	4	10	.286	5.27	1.49	39	17	0	0	4	1-2	124.2	136	78	73	11	50-2	85	.279
	— Louisville (Int'l)	1	0	1.000	2.57	1.14	3	3	0	0	...	0-...	14.0	10	4	4	2	6-0	10	.196
2003—	Cincinnati (N.L.)	0	0	...	12.66	2.44	3	0	0	0	0	0-0	10.2	21	15	15	3	5-0	7	.404
	— Louisville (Int'l)	8	3	.727	3.23	1.40	33	8	0	0	0	1-...	86.1	103	38	31	5	18-1	45	.306
American League totals (3 years)		14	17	.452	5.83	1.60	50	46	0	0	1	0-0	253.1	316	174	164	33	89-1	153	.311
National League totals (8 years)		60	56	.517	4.12	1.38	192	163	7	4	5	1-2	1087.1	1092	547	498	97	404-25	741	.263
Major League totals (10 years)		74	73	.503	4.44	1.42	242	209	7	4	6	1-2	1340.2	1408	721	662	130	493-26	894	.273

HAMMOCK, ROBBY — C/OF

PERSONAL: Born May 13, 1977, in Macon, Ga. ... 5-11/180. ... Bats right, throws right. ... Full name: Robert Wade Hammock. ... Name pronounced: HAM-uk. ... High school: South Cobb (Dacula, Ga.). ... College: Georgia.

TRANSACTIONS/CAREER NOTES: Selected by Arizona Diamondbacks organization in 23rd round of free-agent draft (June 2, 1998). ... On disabled list (July 27-August 23, 2000).

2003 GAMES PLAYED BY POSITION (MLB): C—36, OF—17, 3B—16, DH—1.

Year	Team (League)	Pos.	G	AB	R	H	2B	3B	HR	RBI	BB	SO	HBP	GDP	SB-CS	Avg.	OBP	SLG	OPS	E	Pct.
1998—	Lethbridge (Pio.)	C-3B	62	227	46	65	14	2	10	56	28	34	2	3	5-4	.286	.367	.498	.865	4	.990
1999—	High Desert (Calif.)	C-3B-OF	114	379	80	126	20	7	9	72	47	63	2	8	3-6	.332	.403	.493	.897	18	.975
2000—	High Desert (Calif.)	C-1B	40	136	25	48	15	1	3	23	27	24	1	5	3-3	.353	.453	.544	.999	11	.962
	— El Paso (Texas)	C-3B-OF	45	140	22	35	5	1	1	15	11	25	1	1	1-2	.250	.305	.321	.627	2	.990
2001—	South Bend (Mid.)	C-OF	34	125	16	31	3	2	2	14	14	21	0	2	5-6	.248	.324	.352	.676	2	.988
	— El Paso (Texas)	3-1-OF-C	26	74	6	12	5	0	0	4	7	18	0	1	2-2	.162	.235	.230	.464	5	.948
	— Lancaster (Calif.)	O-C-3-1-2	45	190	33	59	11	3	4	36	16	42	7	6	3-2	.311	.378	.463	.841	7	.966
2002—	El Paso (Texas)	C-OF-3B	122	441	68	128	28	4	11	73	43	68	8	14	5-4	.290	.358	.447	.805	8	.986
2003—	Tucson (PCL)	C-OF-1-3	33	116	14	31	6	2	2	17	11	24	0	2	1-0	.267	.321	.405	.726	5	.972
	— Arizona (N.L.)	C-OF-3-D	65	195	30	55	10	2	8	28	17	44	2	5	3-2	.282	.343	.477	.820	7	.980
Major League totals (1 year)			65	195	30	55	10	2	8	28	17	44	2	5	3-2	.282	.343	.477	.820	7	.980

HAMMOND, CHRIS — P

PERSONAL: Born January 21, 1966, in Atlanta, Ga. ... 6-1/190. ... Throws left, bats left. ... Full name: Chris Andrew Hammond. ... High school: Vestavia Hills (Birmingham, Ala.). ... Junior college: Gulf Coast (Fla.) Community College.

TRANSACTIONS/CAREER NOTES: Selected by Cincinnati Reds organization in sixth round of free-agent draft (January 14, 1986). ... On disabled list (July 27-September 1, 1991). ... Traded by Reds to Florida Marlins for 3B Gary Scott and a player to be named later (March 27, 1993); Reds acquired P Hector Carrasco to complete deal (September 10, 1993). ... On Florida disabled list (June 11-August 3, 1994); included rehabilitation assignments to Portland (June 24-25) and Brevard County (July 25-30). ... On Florida disabled list (April 16-May 13 and August 3-19, 1995); included rehabilitation assignments to Brevard County (May 4-9) and Charlotte (May 9-13). ... On Florida disabled list (June 9-July 14, 1996); included rehabilitation assignments to Brevard County (July 1-5) and Charlotte (July 5-14). ... Granted free agency (October 4, 1996). ... Signed by Boston Red Sox (December 17, 1996). ... On disabled list (June 30, 1997-remainder of season). ... Granted free agency (October 30, 1997). ... Signed by Kansas City Royals organization (January 12, 1998). ... Released by Royals (March 23, 1998). ... Signed by Marlins organization (March 27, 1998). ... Released by Marlins (June 2, 1998). ... Signed by Cleveland Indians organization (March 30, 2001). ... Released by Indians (July 3, 2001). ... Signed by Atlanta Braves organization (July 17, 2001). ... Granted free agency (October 15, 2001). ... Re-signed by Braves organization (November 19, 2001). ... On suspended list (September 13-16, 2002). ... Granted free agency (October 28, 2002). ... Signed by New York Yankees (December 12, 2002).

CAREER HITTING: 48-for-235 (.204), 30 R, 7 2B, 1 3B, 4 HR, 14 RBI.

Year	League	W	L	Pct.	ERA	WHIP	G	GS	CG	ShO	Hld.	Sv.-Opp.	IP	H	R	ER	HR	BB-IBB	SO	Avg.
1986—	GC Reds (GCL)	3	2	.600	2.81	1.06	7	7	1	0	...	0-...	41.2	27	21	13	0	17-1	53	.172
	— Tampa (FSL)	0	2	.000	3.32	1.75	5	5	0	0	...	0-...	21.2	25	8	8	0	13-1	5	.291
1987—	Tampa (FSL)	11	11	.500	3.55	1.38	25	24	6	0	...	0-...	170.0	174	81	67	10	60-1	126	.258
1988—	Chattanooga (Sou.)	* 16	5	.762	* 1.72	1.12	26	26	4	2	...	0-...	182.2	127	48	35	2	77-3	127	.193
1989—	Nashville (A.A.)	11	7	.611	3.38	1.53	24	24	3	1	...	0-...	157.1	144	69	59	7	96-1	142	.245
1990—	Nashville (A.A.)	* 15	1	* .938	* 2.17	1.21	24	24	5	* 3	...	0-...	149.0	118	43	36	7	63-1	* 149	.219
	— Cincinnati (N.L.)	0	2	.000	6.35	2.21	3	3	0	0	...	0-...	11.1	13	9	8	2	12-1	4	.302
1991—	Cincinnati (N.L.)	7	7	.500	4.06	1.40	20	18	0	0	0	0-0	99.2	92	51	45	4	48-3	50	.250
1992—	Cincinnati (N.L.)	7	10	.412	4.21	1.38	28	26	0	0	0	0-0	147.1	149	75	69	13	55-6	79	.266
1993—	Florida (N.L.)	11	12	.478	4.66	1.43	32	32	1	0	0	0-0	191.0	207	106	99	18	66-2	108	.277
1994—	Florida (N.L.)	4	4	.500	3.07	1.39	13	13	1	1	0	0-0	73.1	79	30	25	5	23-1	40	.281
	— Portland (East.)	0	0	...	0.00	0.00	1	1	0	0	...	0-...	5.0	0	0	0	0	0-0	2	.000
	— Brevard County (FSL)	0	0	...	1.23	0.95	2	2	0	0	...	0-...	7.1	4	3	1	0	3-0	5	.160

H

Year	League	W	L	Pct.	ERA	WHIP	G	GS	CG	ShO	Hld.	Sv.-Opp.	IP	H	R	ER	HR	BB-IBB	SO	Avg.
1995— Brevard County (FSL)		0	0	...	0.00	0.75	1	1	0	0	...	0-...	4.0	3	1	0	0	0-0	4	.200
— Charlotte (Int'l)		0	0	...	0.00	1.25	1	1	0	0	...	0-...	4.0	3	1	0	0	2-0	3	.176
— Florida (N.L.)		9	6	.600	3.80	1.27	25	24	3	2	0	0-0	161.0	157	73	68	17	47-2	126	.256
1996— Florida (N.L.)		5	8	.385	6.56	1.62	38	9	0	0	5	0-0	81.0	104	65	59	14	27-3	50	.315
— Brevard County (FSL)		0	0	...	0.00	0.75	1	1	0	0	...	0-...	4.0	3	0	0	0	0-0	8	.214
— Charlotte (Int'l)		1	0	1.000	7.20	1.00	1	1	0	0	...	0-...	5.0	5	4	4	0	0-0	3	.250
1997— Boston (A.L.)		3	4	.429	5.92	1.65	29	8	0	0	4	1-2	65.1	81	45	43	5	27-4	48	.310
1998— Charlotte (Int'l)		1	3	.250	4.82	1.75	5	5	0	0	...	0-...	28.0	35	17	15	2	14-2	22	.315
— Florida (N.L.)		0	2	.000	6.59	2.05	3	3	0	0	...	0-...	13.2	20	11	10	3	8-0	8	.357
1999—											Did not play.									
2000—											Did not play.									
2001— Buffalo (Int'l)		7	3	.700	3.31	1.41	28	4	0	0	...	0-...	51.2	53	22	19	5	20-1	54	.261
— Richmond (Int'l)		3	1	.750	2.35	1.17	21	0	0	0	...	1-...	30.2	32	9	8	0	4-0	29	.281
2002— Atlanta (N.L.)		7	2	.778	0.95	1.11	63	0	0	0	17	0-2	76.0	53	15	8	1	31-9	63	.195
2003— New York (N.L.)		3	2	.600	2.86	1.21	62	0	0	0	17	1-4	63.0	65	23	20	5	11-0	45	.270
American League totals (2 years)		6	6	.500	4.42	1.43	91	8	0	0	21	2-6	128.1	146	68	63	10	38-4	93	.291
National League totals (9 years)		50	53	.485	4.12	1.39	225	128	5	3	22	0-2	854.1	874	435	391	77	317-27	528	.267
Major League totals (11 years)		56	59	.487	4.16	1.40	316	136	5	3	43	2-8	982.2	1020	503	454	87	355-31	621	.270

HAMMONDS, JEFFREY · OF

PERSONAL: Born March 5, 1971, in Scotch Plains, N.J. ... 6-0/207. ... Bats right, throws right. ... Full name: Jeffrey Bryan Hammonds. ... High school: Scotch Plains (N.J.)-Fanwood. ... College: Stanford.

TRANSACTIONS/CAREER NOTES: Selected by Toronto Blue Jays organization in ninth round of free-agent draft (June 5, 1989); did not sign. ... Selected by Baltimore Orioles organization in first round (fourth pick overall) of free-agent draft (June 1, 1992). ... On Rochester disabled list (May 17-28, 1993). ... On Baltimore disabled list (August 8-September 1 and September 28, 1993-remainder of season); included rehabilitation assignment to Bowie (August 28-September 1). ... On Baltimore disabled list (May 4-June 16, 1994; July 18-September 3, 1995; and August 17-September 22, 1996). ... On Baltimore disabled list (June 3-July 15, 1998); included rehabilitation assignment to Bowie (July 9-11). ... Traded by Orioles to Cincinnati Reds for 3B/OF Willie Greene (August 10, 1998). ... Traded by Reds with P Stan Belinda to Colorado Rockies for OF Dante Bichette and cash (October 30, 1999). ... On disabled list (April 4-22, 2000). ... Granted free agency (October 27, 2000). ... Signed by Milwaukee Brewers (December 22, 2000). ... On Milwaukee disabled list (June 7, 2001-remainder of season); included rehabilitation assignment to Arizona League Brewers (July 15-18). ... On disabled list (April 15, 2003). ... Given unconditional release by Milwaukee (June 4, 2003). ... Signed as a free agent by San Francisco Giants (July 1, 2003).

2003 GAMES PLAYED BY POSITION (MLB): OF—40.

Year	Team (League)	Pos.	G	AB	R	H	2B	3B	HR	RBI	BB	SO	HBP	GDP	SB-CS	Avg.	OBP	SLG	OPS	E	Pct.
1992— Hagerstown (East.)										Did not play.											
1993— Bowie (East.)	OF	24	92	13	26	3	0	3	10	9	18	2	1	4-3	.283	.356	.413	.769	0	1.000
— Rochester (Int'l)	OF	36	151	25	47	9	1	5	23	5	27	2	1	6-3	.311	.338	.483	.821	0	1.000
— Baltimore (A.L.)	OF-DH	33	105	10	32	8	0	3	19	2	16	0	3	4-0	.305	.312	.467	.779	2	.961
1994— Baltimore (A.L.)	OF	68	250	45	74	18	2	8	31	17	39	2	3	5-0	.296	.339	.480	.819	6	.962
1995— Baltimore (A.L.)	OF-DH	57	178	18	43	9	1	4	23	9	30	1	3	4-2	.242	.279	.371	.650	1	.989
— Bowie (East.)	OF-DH	9	31	7	12	3	1	1	11	10	7	0	0	3-0	.387	.524	.645	1.169	1	.923
1996— Baltimore (A.L.)	OF-DH	71	248	38	56	10	1	9	27	23	53	4	7	3-3	.226	.301	.383	.684	3	.980
— Rochester (Int'l)	OF-DH	34	125	24	34	4	2	3	19	19	19	1	2	3-1	.272	.365	.408	.773	1	.987
1997— Baltimore (A.L.)	OF-DH	118	397	71	105	19	3	21	55	32	73	3	6	15-1	.264	.323	.486	.809	5	.980
1998— Baltimore (A.L.)	OF-DH	63	171	36	46	12	1	6	28	26	38	3	2	7-2	.269	.369	.456	.826	2	.980
— Bowie (East.)	OF	3	6	4	2	0	0	0	0	2	2	1	0	3-1	.333	.556	.333	.889	0	1.000
— Cincinnati (N.L.)	OF	26	86	14	26	4	1	0	11	13	18	0	1	1-1	.302	.390	.372	.762	1	.985
1999— Cincinnati (N.L.)	OF	123	262	43	73	13	0	17	41	27	64	1	4	3-6	.279	.347	.523	.870	0	1.000
2000— Colorado (N.L.)	OF	122	454	94	152	24	2	20	106	44	83	5	11	14-7	.335	.395	.529	.924	2	.980
2001— Milwaukee (N.L.)	OF	49	174	20	43	11	1	6	21	14	42	4	2	5-3	.247	.314	.425	.740	2	.982
— Ariz. Brewers (Ariz.)	OF	1	3	0	1	0	0	0	0	0	0	0	0	0-0	.333	.333	.333	.667	0	...
2002— Milwaukee (N.L.)	OF	128	448	47	115	26	5	9	41	52	86	2	13	4-5	.257	.332	.397	.729	2	.992
2003— Milwaukee (N.L.)	OF	10	38	2	6	2	0	1	3	3	7	0	2	0-0	.158	.220	.289	.509	0	1.000
— Ariz. Giants (Ariz.)	OF	4	10	4	5	1	1	3	6	1	1	0	2	0-0	.500	.545	1.700	2.245	0	1.000
— Fresno (PCL)	OF-DH	11	36	7	12	1	0	2	2	3	3	0	1	1-0	.333	.385	.528	.912	0	1.000
— San Francisco (N.L.)	OF	36	94	20	26	10	0	3	10	13	21	1	1	1-0	.277	.370	.479	.849	0	1.000
American League totals (6 years)		410	1349	218	356	76	8	51	183	109	249	13	24	38-8	.264	.322	.446	.767	19	.976
National League totals (6 years)		494	1556	240	441	90	9	56	233	166	321	13	33	28-22	.283	.354	.461	.815	7	.992
Major League totals (11 years)		904	2905	458	797	166	17	107	416	275	570	26	57	66-30	.274	.339	.454	.793	26	.984

HAMPTON, MIKE · P

PERSONAL: Born September 9, 1972, in Brooksville, Fla. ... 5-10/180. ... Throws left, bats right. ... Full name: Michael William Hampton. ... High school: Crystal River (Fla.).

TRANSACTIONS/CAREER NOTES: Selected by Seattle Mariners organization in sixth round of free-agent draft (June 4, 1990). ... Traded by Mariners with OF Mike Felder to Houston Astros for OF Eric Anthony (December 10, 1993). ... On disabled list (May 15-June 13, 1995; June 16-July 4, 1998). ... Traded by Astros with OF Derek Bell to New York Mets for OF Roger Cedeno, P Octavio Dotel and P Kyle Kessel (December 23, 1999). ... Granted free agency (November 4, 2000). ... Signed by Colorado Rockies (December 9, 2000). ... On suspended list (October 3-8, 2001). ... Traded by Rockies with OF Juan Pierre and cash to Florida Marlins for C Charles Johnson, P Vic Darensbourg, OF Preston Wilson and 2B Pablo Ozuna (November 16, 2002). ... Traded by Marlins with cash to Atlanta Braves for P Tim Spooneybarger and P Ryan Baker (November 18, 2002). ... Placed on 15-day disabled list (March 21-29, 2003). ... Reinstated from 15-day disabled list (April 19, 2003).

CAREER HITTING: 142-for-575 (.247), 77 R, 15 2B, 5 3B, 12 HR, 60 RBI.

Year	League	W	L	Pct.	ERA	WHIP	G	GS	CG	ShO	Hld.	Sv.-Opp.	IP	H	R	ER	HR	BB-IBB	SO	Avg.
1990— Ariz. Mariners (Ariz.)		• 7	2	.778	2.66	1.43	14	• 13	0	0	...	0-...	64.1	52	32	19	0	40-0	59	.213
1991— San Bernardino (Calif.)		1	7	.125	5.25	1.60	18	15	1	1	...	0-...	73.2	71	58	43	3	47-1	57	.249
— Bellingham (N'west)		5	2	.714	1.58	1.02	9	9	0	0	...	0-...	57.0	32	15	10	0	26-0	65	.162
1992— San Bernardino (Calif.)		13	8	.619	3.12	1.35	25	25	6	• 2	...	0-...	170.0	163	75	59	8	66-1	132	.255
— Jacksonville (Sou.)		0	1	.000	4.35	1.35	2	2	1	0	...	0-...	10.1	13	5	5	0	1-0	6	.317
1993— Seattle (A.L.)		1	3	.250	9.53	2.65	13	3	0	0	2	1-1	17.0	28	20	18	3	17-3	8	.368
— Jacksonville (Sou.)		6	4	.600	3.71	1.19	15	14	1	0	...	0-...	87.1	71	43	36	3	33-1	84	.225
1994— Houston (N.L.)		2	1	.667	3.70	1.50	44	0	0	0	10	0-1	41.1	46	19	17	4	16-1	24	.282
1995— Houston (N.L.)		9	8	.529	3.35	1.26	24	24	0	0	0	0-0	150.2	141	73	56	13	49-3	115	.247
1996— Houston (N.L.)		10	10	.500	3.59	1.40	27	27	2	1	0	0-0	160.1	175	79	64	12	49-1	101	.280
1997— Houston (N.L.)		15	10	.600	3.83	1.32	34	34	7	2	0	0-0	223.0	217	105	95	16	77-2	139	.257

H

– 160 –

Year	League	W	L	Pct.	ERA	WHIP	G	GS	CG	ShO	Hld.	Sv.-Opp.	IP	H	R	ER	HR	BB-IBB	SO	Avg.
1998— Houston (N.L.)		11	7	.611	3.36	1.46	32	32	1	1	0	0-0	211.2	227	92	79	18	81-1	137	.278
1999— Houston (N.L.)		* 22	4	*.846	2.90	1.28	34	34	3	2	0	0-0	239.0	206	86	77	12	101-2	177	.241
2000— New York (N.L.)		15	10	.600	3.14	1.35	33	33	3	1	0	0-0	217.2	194	89	76	10	99-5	151	.241
2001— Colorado (N.L.)		14	13	.519	5.41	1.58	32	32	2	1	0	0-0	203.0	236	138	122	31	85-7	122	.296
2002— Colorado (N.L.)		7	15	.318	6.15	1.79	30	30	0	0	0	0-0	178.2	228	* 135	122	24	91-4	74	.313
2003— Atlanta (N.L.)		14	8	.636	3.84	1.39	31	31	1	0	0	0-0	190.0	186	91	81	14	78-4	110	.255
American League totals (1 year)		1	3	.250	9.53	2.65	13	3	0	0	2	1-1	17.0	28	20	18	3	17-3	8	.368
National League totals (10 years)		119	86	.580	3.91	1.42	321	277	19	8	10	0-1	1815.1	1856	907	789	154	726-30	1150	.268
Major League totals (11 years)		120	89	.574	3.96	1.43	334	280	19	8	12	1-2	1832.1	1884	927	807	157	743-33	1158	.269

HANCOCK, JOSH   P

PERSONAL: Born April 11, 1978, in Cleveland, Miss. ... 6-3/217. ... Throws right, bats right. ... Full name: Joshua Morgan Hancock. ... High school: Vestavia Hills (Ala.). ... College: Auburn.

TRANSACTIONS/CAREER NOTES: Selected by Boston Red Sox organization in fifth round of free-agent draft (June 2, 1998). ... On disabled list (July 18-30 and August 26, 2001-remainder of season). ... On Trenton disabled list (June 4-July 3, 2002). ... Traded by Red Sox to Philadelphia Phillies for 1B/OF Jeremy Giambi (December 15, 2002). ... Called up by Philadelphia from Scranton (September 2, 2003).

CAREER HITTING: 0-for-0 (.000), 0 R, 0 2B, 0 3B, 0 HR, 0 RBI.

Year	League	W	L	Pct.	ERA	WHIP	G	GS	CG	ShO	Hld.	Sv.-Opp.	IP	H	R	ER	HR	BB-IBB	SO	Avg.
1998— GC Red Sox (GCL)		1	1	.500	3.38	0.90	5	1	0	0	...	0-...	13.1	9	5	5	1	3-0	21	.196
— Lowell (NY-Penn)		0	1	.000	2.25	2.25	1	1	0	0	...	0-...	4.0	5	2	1	0	4-0	4	.333
1999— Augusta (S. Atl.)		6	8	.429	3.80	1.43	25	25	0	0	...	0-...	139.2	154	79	59	12	46-0	106	.279
2000— Sarasota (Fla. St.)		5	10	.333	4.45	1.40	26	24	1	0	...	0-...	143.2	164	89	71	9	37-0	95	.286
2001— Trenton (East.)		8	6	.571	3.65	1.34	24	24	0	0	...	0-...	130.2	138	60	53	8	37-0	119	.273
2002— Trenton (East.)		3	4	.429	3.61	1.18	15	14	2	0	...	1-...	84.2	82	40	34	9	18-0	69	.250
— Pawtucket (Int'l)		4	2	.667	3.45	1.47	8	8	0	0	...	0-...	44.1	39	20	17	2	26-0	29	.235
— Boston (A.L.)		0	1	.000	3.68	0.95	3	1	0	0	0	0-0	7.1	5	3	3	1	2-0	6	.200
2003— Scran./W.B. (I.L.)		10	9	.526	3.86	1.16	28	27	2	2	...	0-...	165.2	147	78	71	14	46-1	122	.238
— Philadelphia (N.L.)		0	0	...	3.00	0.67	2	0	0	0	0	0-0	3.0	2	1	1	0	0-0	4	.182
American League totals (1 year)		0	1	.000	3.68	0.95	3	1	0	0	0	0-0	7.1	5	3	3	1	2-0	6	.200
National League totals (1 year)		0	0	...	3.00	0.67	2	0	0	0	0	0-0	3.0	2	1	1	0	0-0	4	.182
Major League totals (2 years)		0	1	.000	3.48	0.87	5	1	0	0	0	0-0	10.1	7	4	4	1	2-0	10	.194

HANSEN, DAVE   1B/3B

PERSONAL: Born November 24, 1968, in Long Beach, Calif. ... 6-0/195. ... Bats left, throws right. ... Full name: David Andrew Hansen. ... High school: Rowland (Long Beach, Calif.).

TRANSACTIONS/CAREER NOTES: Selected by Los Angeles Dodgers organization in second round of free-agent draft (June 2, 1986). ... On disabled list (May 9-28, 1994). ... Granted free agency (November 27, 1996). ... Signed by Chicago Cubs organization (January 22, 1997). ... Granted free agency (October 27, 1997). ... Signed by Hanshin Tigers of Japan Central League (November 7, 1997). ... Signed by Dodgers (January 11, 1999). ... On Los Angeles disabled list (March 23-April 26, 2001); included rehabilitation assignment to Vero Beach (April 21-27). ... Granted free agency (October 29, 2002). ... Signed by San Diego Padres (December 10, 2002).

2003 GAMES PLAYED BY POSITION (MLB): 1B—20, 3B—11, DH—3, 2B—1.

Year	Team (League)	Pos.	G	AB	R	H	2B	3B	HR	RBI	BB	SO	HBP	GDP	SB-CS	Avg.	OBP	SLG	OPS	E	Pct.
1986— Great Falls (Pio.)	2B-3B-C-OF	61	204	39	61	7	3	1	36	27	28	0	6	9-3	.299	.381	.377	.758	7	.901
1987— Bakersfield (Calif.)	3B-OF	132	432	68	113	22	1	3	38	65	61	4	11	4-2	.262	.363	.338	.701	‡ 45	.860
1988— Vero Beach (Calif.)	3B	135	512	68	* 149	* 28	6	7	* 81	56	46	4	9	2-2	.291	.360	.410	.770	18	* .953
1989— San Antonio (Texas)	3B	121	464	72	138	21	4	6	52	50	44	2	18	3-2	.297	.365	.399	.763	16	* .949
— Albuquerque (PCL)	3B	6	30	6	8	1	0	2	10	2	3	0	1	0-0	.267	.313	.500	.813	3	.786
1990— Albuquerque (PCL)	3B-SS-OF	135	487	90	154	20	3	11	92	* 90	54	3	12	9-4	.316	.419	.437	.857	26	‡ .926
— Los Angeles (N.L.)	3B	5	7	0	1	0	0	0	1	0	3	0	0	0-0	.143	.143	.143	.286	1	.500
1991— Albuquerque (PCL)	3B-SS	68	254	42	77	11	1	5	40	49	33	0	7	4-3	.303	.406	.413	.820	6	.966
— Los Angeles (N.L.)	3B-SS	53	56	3	15	4	0	1	5	2	12	0	2	1-0	.268	.293	.393	.686	0	1.000
1992— Los Angeles (N.L.)	3B	132	341	30	73	11	0	6	22	34	49	1	9	0-2	.214	.286	.299	.585	8	.968
1993— Los Angeles (N.L.)	3B	84	105	13	38	3	0	4	30	21	13	0	0	0-1	.362	.465	.505	.969	3	.927
1994— Los Angeles (N.L.)	3B	40	44	3	15	3	0	0	5	5	5	0	0	0-0	.341	.408	.409	.817	1	.857
1995— Los Angeles (N.L.)	3B	100	181	19	52	10	0	1	14	28	28	1	4	0-0	.287	.384	.359	.743	7	.933
1996— Los Angeles (N.L.)	3B-1B	80	104	7	23	1	0	0	6	11	22	0	4	0-0	.221	.293	.231	.524	1	.988
1997— Chicago (N.L.)	3B-1B-2B	90	151	19	47	8	2	3	21	31	32	1	0	1-2	.311	.429	.450	.880	7	.929
1998— Hanshin (Jp. Cn.)	3B	121	400	42	101	13	1	11	55	42	89	...	...	0-...	.253	...	.373	...	...	...
1999— Los Angeles (N.L.)	1-3-D-OF	100	107	14	27	8	1	2	17	26	20	2	2	0-0	.252	.404	.402	.806	3	.962
2000— Los Angeles (N.L.)	3-1-D-OF	102	121	18	35	6	2	8	26	26	32	0	3	0-1	.289	.415	.570	.985	2	.973
2001— Vero Beach (FSL)	3B	3	9	1	0	0	0	0	1	2	0	0	0	0-0	.000	.100	.000	.100	0	1.000
— Los Angeles (N.L.)	1-3-S-DH	92	140	13	33	10	0	2	20	32	29	0	3	0-1	.236	.371	.350	.721	6	.973
2002— Los Angeles (N.L.)	1-3-DH	96	120	15	35	6	0	2	17	14	22	0	2	1-0	.292	.363	.392	.755	2	.980
2003— San Diego (N.L.)	1-3-DH-2	110	135	13	33	4	1	2	15	23	25	1	4	1-0	.244	.358	.333	.692	1	.993
Major League totals (13 years)		1084	1612	167	427	74	6	31	199	253	292	6	33	4-7	.265	.365	.376	.740	42	.966

HARANG, AARON   P

PERSONAL: Born May 9, 1978, in San Diego, Calif. ... 6-7/240. ... Throws right, bats right. ... Full name: Aaron Michael Harang. ... Name pronounced: ha-RANG. ... High school: Patrick Henry (San Diego). ... College: San Diego State.

TRANSACTIONS/CAREER NOTES: Selected by Texas Rangers organization in sixth round of free-agent draft (June 2, 1999). ... Traded by Rangers with P Ryan Cullen to Oakland Athletics for 2B Randy Velarde (December 12, 2000). ... Recalled from Sacramento of the Pacific Coast League by Oakland (May 24, 2003). ... Optioned to Sacramento by Oakland (July 16, 2003). ... Traded by Oakland Athletics to Cincinnati Reds for OF Jose Guillen (July 30, 2003). ... Recalled by Cincinnati from Louisville (August 9, 2003).

CAREER HITTING: 1-for-21 (.048), 0 R, 0 2B, 0 3B, 0 HR, 0 RBI.

Year — League	W	L	Pct.	ERA	WHIP	G	GS	CG	ShO	Hld.	Sv.-Opp.	IP	H	R	ER	HR	BB-IBB	SO	Avg.
1999— Pulaski (Appal.)	9	2	.818	2.30	1.03	16	10	1	1	...	1-...	78.1	64	22	20	5	17-1	87	.226
2000— Charlotte (Fla. St.)	13	5	.722	3.32	1.13	28	27	3	2	...	0-...	157.0	128	68	58	10	50-0	136	.220
2001— Midland (Texas)	10	8	.556	4.14	1.40	27	27	0	0	...	0-...	150.0	173	81	69	9	37-1	112	.285
2002— Midland (Texas)	2	0	1.000	1.08	1.14	3	3	0	0	...	0-...	16.2	12	3	2	0	7-0	21	.218
— Sacramento (PCL)	3	3	.500	3.26	1.29	8	8	0	0	...	0-...	38.2	41	17	14	0	9-0	39	.301
— Oakland (A.L.)	5	4	.556	4.83	1.57	16	15	0	0	0	0-0	78.1	78	44	42	7	45-2	64	.261
2003— Oakland (A.L.)	1	3	.250	5.34	1.65	7	6	0	0	0	0-0	30.1	41	19	18	5	9-0	16	.331
— Sacramento (PCL)	8	2	.800	2.71	1.13	12	12	0	0	...	0-...	69.2	62	24	21	5	17-0	60	.234
— Louisville (Int'l)	0	1	.000	15.00	2.33	1	1	0	0	...	0-...	3.0	5	5	5	1	2-0	4	.357
— Cincinnati (N.L.)	4	3	.571	5.28	1.26	9	9	0	0	0	0-0	46.0	48	28	27	6	10-0	26	.271
American League totals (2 years)	6	7	.462	4.97	1.59	23	21	0	0	0	0-0	108.2	119	63	60	12	54-2	80	.281
National League totals (1 year)	4	3	.571	5.28	1.26	9	9	0	0	0	0-0	46.0	48	28	27	6	10-0	26	.271
Major League totals (2 years)	10	10	.500	5.06	1.49	32	30	0	0	0	0-0	154.2	167	91	87	18	64-2	106	.278

HARDEN, RICH — P

PERSONAL: Born November 30, 1981, in Victoria, British Columbia. ... 6-1/180. ... Throws right, bats left. ... Full name: James Richard Harden. ... High school: Claremont Secondary (Victoria, B.C.). ... Junior college: Central Arizona College.

TRANSACTIONS/CAREER NOTES: Selected by Seattle Mariners organization in 38th round of free-agent draft (June 2, 1999); did not sign. ... Selected by Oakland A's organization in 17th round of free-agent draft (June 5, 2001).

CAREER HITTING: 0-for-0 (.000), 0 R, 0 2B, 0 3B, 0 HR, 0 RBI.

Year — League	W	L	Pct.	ERA	WHIP	G	GS	CG	ShO	Hld.	Sv.-Opp.	IP	H	R	ER	HR	BB-IBB	SO	Avg.
2001— Vancouver (NW)	2	4	.333	3.39	1.14	18	14	0	0	...	0-...	74.1	47	29	28	3	38-0	100	.179
2002— Visalia (Calif.)	4	3	.571	2.93	1.08	12	12	1	0	...	0-...	67.2	49	27	22	4	24-0	85	.201
— Midland (Texas)	8	3	.727	2.95	1.39	16	16	1	0	...	0-...	85.1	67	33	28	2	52-1	102	.217
2003— Midland (Texas)	2	0	1.000	0.00	0.00	2	2	0	0	...	0-...	13.0	0	0	0	0	0-0	17	.000
— Sacramento (PCL)	9	4	.692	3.15	1.21	16	14	0	0	...	0-...	88.2	72	34	31	6	35-0	91	.226
— Oakland (A.L.)	5	4	.556	4.46	1.50	15	13	0	0	0	0-0	74.2	72	38	37	5	40-1	67	.259
Major League totals (1 year)	5	4	.556	4.46	1.50	15	13	0	0	0	0-0	74.2	72	38	37	5	40-1	67	.259

HAREN, DANNY — P

PERSONAL: Born September 17, 1980, in Monterey Park, Calif. ... 6-5/220. ... Throws right, bats right. ... Full name: Daniel John Haren. ... College: Pepperdine.

TRANSACTIONS/CAREER NOTES: Selected by St. Louis Cardinals organization in second round of free-agent draft (June 5, 2001).

CAREER HITTING: 2-for-25 (.080), 0 R, 2 2B, 0 3B, 0 HR, 1 RBI.

Year — League	W	L	Pct.	ERA	WHIP	G	GS	CG	ShO	Hld.	Sv.-Opp.	IP	H	R	ER	HR	BB-IBB	SO	Avg.
2001— New Jersey (NYP)	3	3	.500	3.10	1.05	12	8	0	0	...	1-...	52.1	47	22	18	6	8-0	57	.239
2002— Peoria (Midw.)	7	3	.700	1.95	0.99	14	14	1	0	...	0-...	101.2	89	32	22	6	12-0	89	.234
— Potomac (Caro.)	3	6	.333	3.62	1.18	14	14	1	0	...	0-...	92.0	90	43	37	8	19-2	82	.252
2003— Tennessee (Sou.)	6	0	1.000	0.82	0.76	8	8	0	0	...	0-...	55.0	36	8	5	2	6-0	49	.181
— Memphis (PCL)	2	1	.667	4.93	1.27	8	8	0	0	...	0-...	45.2	50	25	25	6	8-1	35	.272
— St. Louis (N.L.)	3	7	.300	5.08	1.46	14	14	0	0	0	0-0	72.2	84	44	41	9	22-0	43	.293
Major League totals (1 year)	3	7	.300	5.08	1.46	14	14	0	0	0	0-0	72.2	84	44	41	9	22-0	43	.293

HARPER, TRAVIS — P

PERSONAL: Born May 21, 1976, in Harrisonburg, Va. ... 6-4/192. ... Throws right, bats right. ... Full name: Travis Boyd Harper. ... High school: Circleville (W. Va.). ... College: James Madison (Va.).

TRANSACTIONS/CAREER NOTES: Selected by New York Mets organization in 14th round of free-agent draft (June 2, 1994); did not sign. ... Selected by Boston Red Sox organization in third round of free-agent draft (June 3, 1997). ... Contract with Red Sox voided due to pre-existing injury (October 29, 1997). ... Signed by Tampa Bay Devil Rays organization (June 29, 1998).

CAREER HITTING: 0-for-0 (.000), 0 R, 0 2B, 0 3B, 0 HR, 0 RBI.

Year — League	W	L	Pct.	ERA	WHIP	G	GS	CG	ShO	Hld.	Sv.-Opp.	IP	H	R	ER	HR	BB-IBB	SO	Avg.
1998— Hudson Valley (NYP)	6	2	.750	1.92	1.03	13	10	0	0	...	0-...	56.1	38	14	12	2	20-0	81	.192
1999— St. Pete. (FSL)	5	4	.556	3.43	1.29	14	14	0	0	...	0-...	81.1	82	36	31	4	23-0	79	.265
— Orlando (Sou.)	6	3	.667	5.38	1.38	14	14	1	1	...	0-...	72.0	73	45	43	10	26-0	68	.263
2000— Orlando (Sou.)	3	1	.750	2.63	1.17	9	9	0	0	...	0-...	51.1	49	19	15	1	11-0	33	.255
— Durham (Int'l)	7	4	.636	4.24	1.19	17	17	0	0	...	0-...	104.0	98	53	49	15	26-1	48	.246
— Tampa Bay (A.L.)	1	2	.333	4.78	1.41	6	5	1	1	0	0-0	32.0	30	17	17	5	15-0	14	.244
2001— Tampa Bay (A.L.)	0	2	.000	7.71	2.57	2	2	0	0	0	0-0	7.0	15	11	6	5	3-0	2	.455
— Durham (Int'l)	12	6	.667	3.70	1.14	25	25	1	1	...	0-...	155.2	140	70	64	25	38-0	115	.241
2002— Durham (Int'l)	1	2	.333	6.98	1.76	4	4	0	0	...	0-...	19.1	31	15	15	5	3-0	17	.383
— Tampa Bay (A.L.)	5	9	.357	5.46	1.49	37	7	0	0	3	1-2	85.2	101	54	52	14	27-3	60	.289
2003— Tampa Bay (A.L.)	4	8	.333	3.77	1.26	61	0	0	0	15	1-6	93.0	86	45	39	9	31-8	64	.251
Major League totals (4 years)	10	21	.323	4.71	1.42	106	14	1	1	18	2-8	217.2	232	127	114	33	76-11	140	.274

HARRIS, LENNY — IF/OF

PERSONAL: Born October 28, 1964, in Miami, Fla. ... 5-10/220. ... Bats left, throws right. ... Full name: Leonard Anthony Harris. ... High school: Jackson (Miami). ... Junior college: Miami-Dade Community College.

TRANSACTIONS/CAREER NOTES: Selected by Cincinnati Reds organization in fifth round of free-agent draft (June 6, 1983). ... Loaned by Reds organization to Glens Falls, Detroit Tigers organization (May 6-28, 1988). ... Traded by Reds with OF Kal Daniels to Los Angeles Dodgers for P Tim Leary and SS Mariano Duncan (July 18, 1989). ... Granted free agency (October 8, 1993). ... Signed by Reds (December 1, 1993). ... Granted free agency (October 31, 1996). ... Re-signed by Reds (November 13, 1996). ... Traded by Reds to New York Mets for P John Hudek (July 3, 1998). ... Granted free agency (October 27, 1998). ... Signed by Colorado Rockies (November 9, 1998). ... Traded by Rockies to Arizona Diamondbacks for IF Belvani Martinez (August 31, 1999). ... Traded by Diamondbacks to Mets for P Bill Pulsipher (June 2, 2000). ... Granted free agency (October 28, 2002). ... Signed by Chicago Cubs organization (January 8, 2003). ... Given unconditional release (August 2, 2003). ... Signed by Florida Marlins; contract purchased by Florida (August 22, 2003).

2003 GAMES PLAYED BY POSITION (MLB): 3B—35, OF—6, 1B—2.

H

Year	Team (League)	Pos.	G	AB	R	H	2B	3B	HR	RBI	BB	SO	HBP	GDP	SB-CS	Avg.	OBP	SLG	OPS	E	Pct.
1983— Billings (Pio.)	3B	56	224	37	63	8	1	1	26	13	35	1	...	7-1	.281	.322	.339	.661	22	.854
1984— Cedar Rap. (Midw.)	3B	132	468	52	115	15	3	6	53	42	59	3	14	31-10	.246	.308	.329	.637	*34	.903
1985— Tampa (Fla. St.)	3B	132	499	66	129	11	8	3	51	37	57	1	9	15-8	.259	.307	.331	.638	*35	.913
1986— Vermont (East.)	3B-SS	119	450	68	114	17	2	10	52	29	38	6	9	36-10	.253	.303	.367	.670	‡28	.924
1987— Nashville (A.A.)	3B-SS	120	403	45	100	12	3	2	31	27	43	5	10	30-12	.248	.302	.308	.610	34	.908
1988— Nashville (A.A.)	2B-3B-SS	107	422	46	117	20	2	0	35	22	36	0	13	*45-*22	.277	.313	.334	.647	‡25	.947
— Glens Falls (East.)	2B	17	65	9	22	5	1	1	7	9	6	0	1	6-2	.338	.419	.492	.911	5	.947
— Cincinnati (N.L.)	2B-3B	16	43	7	16	1	0	0	8	5	4	0	0	4-1	.372	.420	.395	.815	1	.979
1989— Nashville (A.A.)	2B	8	34	6	9	2	0	3	6	0	5	0	0	0-2	.265	.265	.588	.853	0	1.000
— Cincinnati (N.L.)	2B-3B-SS	61	188	17	42	4	0	2	11	9	20	1	5	10-6	.223	.263	.277	.539	13	.946
— Los Angeles (N.L.)	2-3-S-OF	54	147	19	37	6	1	1	15	11	13	1	9	4-3	.252	.308	.327	.635	2	.978
1990— Los Angeles (N.L.)	2-3-S-OF	137	431	61	131	16	4	2	29	29	31	1	8	31-10	.304	.348	.374	.722	11	.969
1991— Los Angeles (N.L.)	2-3-S-OF	145	429	59	123	16	1	3	38	37	32	5	16	12-3	.287	.349	.350	.698	20	.949
1992— Los Angeles (N.L.)	2-3-OF-S	135	347	28	94	11	0	0	30	24	24	1	10	19-7	.271	.318	.303	.621	27	.943
1993— Los Angeles (N.L.)	2-3-S-OF	107	160	20	38	6	1	2	11	15	15	0	4	3-1	.238	.303	.325	.628	3	.982
1994— Cincinnati (N.L.)	3-1-OF-2	66	100	13	31	3	1	0	14	5	13	0	0	7-2	.310	.340	.360	.700	6	.903
1995— Cincinnati (N.L.)	3-1-OF-2	101	197	32	41	8	3	2	16	14	20	0	6	10-1	.208	.259	.310	.569	4	.982
1996— Cincinnati (N.L.)	OF-3-1-2	125	302	33	86	17	2	5	32	21	31	1	3	14-6	.285	.330	.404	.734	6	.978
1997— Cincinnati (N.L.)	OF-2-3-1	120	238	32	65	13	1	3	28	18	18	2	10	4-3	.273	.327	.374	.701	3	.983
1998— Cincinnati (N.L.)	OF-P-DH	57	122	12	36	8	0	0	10	8	9	1	8	1-3	.295	.338	.361	.699	3	.929
— New York (N.L.)	OF-3-2-1	75	168	18	39	7	0	6	17	9	12	1	5	5-2	.232	.272	.381	.653	2	.980
1999— Colorado (N.L.)	2-OF-3-D	91	158	15	47	12	0	0	13	6	6	0	7	1-1	.297	.323	.373	.697	9	.926
— Arizona (N.L.)	3B-OF	19	29	2	11	1	0	1	7	0	1	0	0	1-0	.379	.367	.517	.884	0	1.000
2000— Arizona (N.L.)	3B-OF	36	85	9	16	1	1	1	13	3	5	0	3	5-0	.188	.209	.259	.468	4	.909
— New York (N.L.)	3-0-1-2-D	76	138	22	42	6	3	3	13	17	17	0	4	8-1	.304	.381	.457	.837	11	.904
2001— New York (N.L.)	3-0-1-D-2	110	135	12	30	5	1	0	9	8	9	0	3	3-2	.222	.266	.274	.540	3	.943
2002— Milwaukee (N.L.)	OF-3-1-D	122	197	23	60	8	2	3	17	14	17	2	4	4-1	.305	.355	.411	.766	0	1.000
2003— Chicago (N.L.)	2B	75	131	11	24	3	0	1	7	13	20	0	1	1-0	.183	.255	.229	.484	3	.953
— Albuquerque (PCL)	1B-3B-DH	8	24	3	4	1	0	0	1	4	3	0	1	0-0	.167	.286	.208	.494	1	.979
— Florida (N.L.)	OF	13	14	3	4	0	0	0	1	3	1	0	1	0-0	.286	.412	.286	.697	0	1.000
Major League totals (16 years)		1741	3759	448	1013	152	21	35	339	269	318	16	107	131-53	.269	.319	.349	.668	131	.958

HARRIS, WILLIE   2B/OF

PERSONAL: Born June 22, 1978, in Cairo, Ga. ... 5-9/175. ... Bats left, throws right. ... Full name: William Charles Harris. ... High school: Cairo (Ga.). ... College: Kennesaw State.

TRANSACTIONS/CAREER NOTES: Selected by Pittsburgh Pirates organization in 28th round of free-agent draft (June 4, 1996); did not sign. ... Selected by Baltimore Orioles organization in 24th round of free-agent draft (June 2, 1999). ... Traded by Orioles to Chicago White Sox for OF Chris Singleton (January 29, 2002). ... Recalled by Chicago from Charlotte (May 2, 2003). ... Placed on 15-day disabled list (May 22, 2003). ... Sent to Charlotte on a rehab assignment (June 10, 2003). ... Recalled from Charlotte rehab assignment; reinstated from 15-day disabled list (June 16, 2003). ... Activated by Chicago White Sox from the 15-day disabled list (July 5, 2003).

2003 GAMES PLAYED BY POSITION (MLB): OF—61, 2B—12.

Year	Team (League)	Pos.	G	AB	R	H	2B	3B	HR	RBI	BB	SO	HBP	GDP	SB-CS	Avg.	OBP	SLG	OPS	E	Pct.
1999— Bluefield (Appal.)	2B	5	22	3	6	1	0	0	3	4	2	0	1	1-0	.273	.370	.318	.689	1	.966
— Delmarva (S. Atl.)	2B-OF	66	272	42	72	13	3	2	32	20	41	1	4	11-11	.265	.313	.357	.670	11	.965
2000— Delmarva (S. Atl.)	2B-SS-OF	133	474	106	130	27	10	6	60	89	89	9	3	38-15	.274	.396	.411	.807	19	.968
2001— Bowie (East.)	2B-OF	133	525	83	160	27	4	9	49	46	71	5	6	54-16	.305	.364	.423	.787	14	.974
— Baltimore (A.L.)	OF	9	24	3	3	1	0	0	0	0	7	0	0	0-0	.125	.125	.167	.292	0	1.000
2002— Charlotte (Int'l)	2B-OF	89	360	54	102	16	5	5	33	33	61	2	4	32-14	.283	.345	.397	.742	6	.986
— Chicago (A.L.)	2B-OF	49	163	14	38	4	0	2	12	9	21	0	3	8-0	.233	.270	.294	.565	3	.986
2003— Charlotte (Int'l)	2B-OF	28	100	22	38	6	1	6	13	17	20	0	0	9-3	.380	.470	.640	1.110	0	1.000
— Chicago (A.L.)	OF-2B	79	137	19	28	3	1	0	5	10	28	0	1	12-2	.204	.259	.241	.499	2	.984
Major League totals (3 years)		137	324	36	69	8	1	2	17	19	56	0	4	20-2	.213	.255	.262	.517	5	.986

HART, BO   2B

PERSONAL: Born September 27, 1976, in Creswell, Ore. ... 5-11/170. ... Bats right, throws right. ... Full name: Bodhi J. Hart. ... College: Gonzaga.

TRANSACTIONS/CAREER NOTES: Selected by St. Louis Cardinals organization in 33rd round of free-agent draft (June 1999).

2003 GAMES PLAYED BY POSITION (MLB): 2B—69, SS—3.

Year	Team (League)	Pos.	G	AB	R	H	2B	3B	HR	RBI	BB	SO	HBP	GDP	SB-CS	Avg.	OBP	SLG	OPS	E	Pct.
1999— New Jersey (NYP)	SS-2B	50	163	23	30	3	3	3	15	10	38	12	1	4-2	.184	.281	.294	.576	9	.957
2000— Potomac Carolina (Caro.) ...	2B-OF	75	273	42	70	25	4	0	20	23	42	13	2	9-6	.256	.342	.377	.719	13	.955
2001— Potomac Carolina (Caro.) ..	2B-3B-OF	81	279	48	85	23	3	5	34	17	69	15	3	16-7	.305	.375	.462	.837	6	.985
2002— New Haven (East.)	2B-SS	104	405	61	101	17	6	4	39	43	82	12	6	14-7	.249	.348	.351	.698	7	.985
2003— Memphis (PCL)	2-3-S-DH	67	266	30	79	14	2	7	31	15	55	0	2	4-2	.297	.331	.444	.775	7	.973
— St. Louis (N.L.)	2B-SS	77	296	46	82	13	5	4	28	12	64	6	3	3-1	.277	.317	.395	.713	4	.989
Major League totals (1 year)		77	296	46	82	13	5	4	28	12	64	6	3	3-1	.277	.317	.395	.713	4	.989

HART, JASON   1B

PERSONAL: Born September 5, 1977... 6-4/240. ... Bats right, throws right. ... Full name: Jason Wyatt Hart. ... High school: Fair Grove (Mo.).

TRANSACTIONS/CAREER NOTES: Selected by Oakland Athletics organization in fifth round of free-agent draft (June 2, 1998). ... Traded by A's with P Mario Ramos, C Gerald Laird and OF Ryan Ludwick to Texas Rangers for 1B Carlos Pena and P Mike Venafro (January 14, 2002). ... Recalled by Texas from Oklahoma (September 30, 2003).

Year	Team (League)	Pos.	G	AB	R	H	2B	3B	HR	RBI	BB	SO	HBP	GDP	SB-CS	Avg.	OBP	SLG	OPS	E	Pct.
1998— S. Oregon (N'west)	3B-1B	•75	295	58	76	19	1	*20	69	36	67	3	9	0-1	.258	.336	.532	.868	*12	.982
1999— Modesto (Calif.)	1B	135	*550	96	168	*48	2	19	•123	56	105	4	18	2-5	.305	.370	.504	.873	13	.989
2000— Midland (Texas)	1B	135	*546	98	*178	44	3	30	*121	67	112	6	18	4-0	.326	.401	.582	.983	11	.991
— Sacramento (PCL)	1B	5	18	4	5	1	0	1	4	3	7	0	0	0-0	.278	.381	.500	.881	0	1.000
2001— Sacramento (PCL)	1B	134	494	71	122	26	1	19	75	57	102	4	11	3-3	.247	.325	.419	.744	•15	.988
2002— Sacramento (PCL)	OF-1B	134	514	78	135	32	1	25	83	68	122	8	14	1-0	.263	.356	.475	.831	8	.987
— Texas (A.L.)	OF-1B	10	15	2	4	3	0	0	0	2	7	0	0	0-0	.267	.353	.467	.820	0	1.000
2003— Oklahoma (PCL).................	1B-OF-DH	137	512	65	129	22	0	21	82	54	106	5	12	2-1	.252	.325	.418	.743	4	.997
Major League totals (1 year)		10	15	2	4	3	0	0	0	2	7	0	0	0-0	.267	.353	.467	.820	0	1.000

H

HARVEY, KEN   1B

PERSONAL: Born March 1, 1978, in Los Angeles, Calif. ... 6-2/240. ... Bats right, throws right. ... Full name: Kenneth Eugene Harvey. ... High school: Beverly Hills (Calif.). ... College: Nebraska.

TRANSACTIONS/CAREER NOTES: Selected by Kansas City Royals organization in fifth round of free-agent draft (June 2, 1999).

2003 GAMES PLAYED BY POSITION (MLB): 1B—99, DH—32.

										BATTING									FIELDING	
Year Team (League)	Pos.	G	AB	R	H	2B	3B	HR	RBI	BB	SO	HBP	GDP	SB-CS	Avg.	OBP	SLG	OPS	E	Pct.
1999— Spokane (N'west)	1B	56	204	49	81	17	0	8	41	23	30	8	3	7-1	.397	.477	.598	1.075	5	.984
2000— Wilmington (Caro.)	1B	46	164	20	55	10	0	4	25	14	29	7	4	0-2	.335	.411	.470	.880	3	.983
2001— Wilmington (Caro.)	1B	35	137	22	52	9	1	6	27	13	21	6	5	3-1	.380	.455	.591	1.046	3	.984
— Wichita (Texas)	1B-OF	79	314	54	106	20	3	9	63	18	60	4	12	3-0	.338	.372	.506	.878	5	.990
— Kansas City (A.L.)	1B-DH	4	12	1	3	1	0	0	2	0	4	0	...	0-1	.250	.250	.333	.583	0	1.000
2002— Omaha (PCL)	1B	128	488	75	135	30	1	20	75	42	87	8	22	8-3	.277	.342	.465	.807	* 15	.984
2003— Kansas City (A.L.)	1B-DH	135	485	50	129	30	0	13	64	29	94	5	15	2-3	.266	.313	.408	.721	11	.988
Major League totals (2 years)		139	497	51	132	31	0	13	66	29	98	5	15	2-4	.266	.311	.406	.718	11	.988

HARVILLE, CHAD   P

PERSONAL: Born September 16, 1976, in Selmer, Tenn. ... 5-9/185. ... Throws right, bats right. ... Full name: Chad Ashley Harville. ... High school: Hardin County (Savannah, Tenn.). ... College: Memphis.

TRANSACTIONS/CAREER NOTES: Selected by Oakland Athletics organization in second round of free-agent draft (June 3, 1997). ... On Oakland disabled list (March 31-June 9, 2001); included rehabilitation assignments to Visalia (June 3-5) and Modesto (June 5-9). ... On Sacramento disabled list (May 20-August 7, 2002). ... Contract purchased by Oakland from Sacramento (August 1, 2003).

CAREER HITTING: 0-for-0 (.000), 0 R, 0 2B, 0 3B, 0 HR, 0 RBI.

Year League	W	L	Pct.	ERA	WHIP	G	GS	CG	ShO	Hld.	Sv.-Opp.	IP	H	R	ER	HR	BB-IBB	SO	Avg.
1997— S. Oregon (N'west)	1	0	1.000	0.00	1.20	3	0	0	0	...	0-...	5.0	3	0	0	0	3-0	6	.176
— Visalia (Calif.)	0	0	...	5.79	2.04	14	0	0	0	...	0-...	18.2	25	14	12	2	13-1	24	.325
1998— Visalia (Calif.)	4	3	.571	3.00	1.30	24	7	0	0	...	4-...	69.0	59	25	23	0	31-0	76	.230
— Huntsville (Sou.)	0	0	...	2.45	1.30	12	0	0	0	...	8-...	14.2	6	4	4	0	13-1	24	.122
1999— Midland (Texas)	2	0	1.000	2.01	0.99	17	0	0	0	...	7-...	22.1	13	6	5	1	9-0	35	.165
— Vancouver (PCL)	1	0	1.000	1.75	1.36	22	0	0	0	...	11-...	25.2	24	5	5	0	11-1	36	.240
— Oakland (A.L.)	0	2	.000	6.91	1.95	15	0	0	0	0	0-0	14.1	18	11	11	2	10-1	15	.310
2000— Sacramento (PCL)	5	3	.625	4.50	1.38	53	0	0	0	...	9-...	64.0	53	35	32	8	35-0	77	.222
2001— Modesto (Calif.)	0	0	...	3.00	0.67	2	1	0	0	...	0-...	3.0	2	2	1	0	0-0	3	.182
— Visalia (Calif.)	0	0	...	0.00	1.00	1	1	0	0	...	0-...	3.0	3	0	0	0	0-0	3	.250
— Sacramento (PCL)	5	2	.714	3.98	1.16	33	0	0	0	...	8-...	40.2	35	20	18	5	12-0	55	.230
— Oakland (A.L.)	0	0	...	0.00	0.67	3	0	0	0	1	0-0	3.0	2	0	0	0	0-0	2	.182
2002— Sacramento (PCL)	1	2	.333	5.40	1.50	24	0	0	0	...	5-...	30.0	32	19	18	5	13-1	26	.274
2003— Sacramento (PCL)	3	5	.375	2.05	1.11	48	0	0	0	...	18-...	57.0	42	16	13	5	21-2	57	.202
— Oakland (A.L.)	1	0	1.000	5.82	1.94	21	0	0	0	0	1-1	21.2	25	15	14	3	17-1	18	.294
Major League totals (3 years)	1	2	.333	5.77	1.85	39	0	0	0	1	1-1	39.0	45	26	25	5	27-2	35	.292

HASEGAWA, SHIGETOSHI   P

PERSONAL: Born August 1, 1968, in Kobe, Japan. ... 5-11/180. ... Throws right, bats right. ... Name pronounced: shig-eh-toe-shi hoss-eh-gawa. ... College: Ritsumeikan University (Japan).

TRANSACTIONS/CAREER NOTES: Played for Orix Blue Wave of Japan Pacific League (1991-96). ... Signed as non-drafted free agent by Anaheim Angels (January 9, 1997). ... On Anaheim disabled list (May 20-June 29, 2001); included rehabilitation assignment to Rancho Cucamonga (June 25-29). ... Granted free agency (December 21, 2001). ... Signed by Seattle Mariners (January 23, 2002).

CAREER HITTING: 0-for-1 (.000), 0 R, 0 2B, 0 3B, 0 HR, 0 RBI.

Year League	W	L	Pct.	ERA	WHIP	G	GS	CG	ShO	Hld.	Sv.-Opp.	IP	H	R	ER	HR	BB-IBB	SO	Avg.
1991— Orix (Jap. Pac.)	12	9	.571	3.55	1.26	28	25	11	3	...	1-...	185.0	184	76	73	...	50-...	111	...
1992— Orix (Jap. Pac.)	6	8	.429	3.27	1.32	24	19	4	0	...	1-...	143.1	138	60	52	...	51-...	86	...
1993— Orix (Jap. Pac.)	12	6	.667	2.71	1.22	23	22	9	3	...	0-...	159.2	146	61	48	...	48-...	86	...
1994— Orix (Jap. Pac.)	11	9	.550	3.11	1.38	25	22	8	3	...	1-...	156.1	169	61	54	...	46-...	86	...
1995— Orix (Jap. Pac.)	12	7	.632	2.89	1.27	24	23	9	4	...	0-...	171.0	167	62	55	...	51-...	91	...
1996— Orix (Jap. Pac.)	4	6	.400	5.34	1.70	18	16	2	0	...	1-...	87.2	109	60	52	...	40-...	55	...
1997— Anaheim (A.L.)	3	7	.300	3.93	1.41	50	7	0	0	3	0-1	116.2	118	60	51	14	46-6	83	.269
1998— Anaheim (A.L.)	8	3	.727	3.14	1.21	61	0	0	0	10	5-7	97.1	86	37	34	14	32-2	73	.241
1999— Anaheim (A.L.)	4	6	.400	4.91	1.48	64	1	0	0	6	2-5	77.0	80	45	42	14	34-2	44	.276
2000— Anaheim (A.L.)	10	5	.667	3.48	1.44	66	0	0	0	19	9-18	95.2	100	42	37	11	38-6	59	.276
2001— Anaheim (A.L.)	5	6	.455	4.04	1.29	46	0	0	0	12	0-6	55.2	52	28	25	5	20-5	41	.248
— Rancho Cuca. (Calif.)	0	0	...	0.00	1.50	2	2	0	0	...	0-...	2.0	3	1	0	0	0-0	1	.375
2002— Seattle (A.L.)	8	3	.727	3.20	1.28	53	0	0	0	8	1-5	70.1	60	26	25	4	30-8	39	.238
2003— Seattle (A.L.)	2	4	.333	1.48	1.10	63	0	0	0	12	16-17	73.0	62	12	12	5	18-3	32	.235
Major League totals (7 years)	40	34	.541	3.47	1.32	403	8	0	0	70	33-59	585.2	558	250	226	67	218-32	371	.256

HASELMAN, BILL   C

PERSONAL: Born May 25, 1966, in Long Branch, N.J. ... 6-3/225. ... Bats right, throws right. ... Full name: William Joseph Haselman. ... Name pronounced: HASS-el-man. ... High school: Saratoga (Calif.). ... College: UCLA.

TRANSACTIONS/CAREER NOTES: Selected by Texas Rangers organization in first round (23rd pick overall) of free-agent draft (June 2, 1987); pick received as compensation for New York Yankees signing Type A free-agent OF Gary Ward. ... On Oklahoma City disabled list (March 28-May 4, 1992). ... Claimed on waivers by Seattle Mariners (May 29, 1992). ... On suspended list (July 22-25, 1993). ... Granted free agency (October 15, 1994). ... Signed by Boston Red Sox (November 7, 1994). ... On Boston disabled list (June 30-August 8, 1997); included rehabilitation assignment to Gulf Coast Red Sox (July 29-August 1) and Trenton (August 1-8). ... Traded by Red Sox with P Aaron Sele and P Mark Brandenburg to Rangers for C Jim Leyritz and OF Damon Buford (November 6, 1997). ... Granted free agency (October 23, 1998). ... Signed by Detroit Tigers (December 14, 1998). ... Traded by Tigers with P Justin Thompson, P Francisco Cordero, OF Gabe Kapler, 2B Frank Catalanotto and P Alan Webb to Rangers for OF Juan Gonzalez, P Danny Patterson and C Gregg Zaun (November 2, 1999). ... On Texas disabled list (March 31-June 22, 2001); included rehabilitation assignment to Oklahoma (June 13-22). ... Granted free agency (October 30, 2002). ... Signed by Tigers organization (December 19, 2002). ... Released by Tigers (March 28, 2003). ... Signed by Boston Red Sox as free agent; contract purchased by Boston (September 1, 2003).

2003 GAMES PLAYED BY POSITION (MLB): DH—2, C—2.

Year Team (League)	Pos.	G	AB	R	H	2B	3B	HR	RBI	BB	SO	HBP	GDP	SB-CS	Avg.	OBP	SLG	OPS	E	Pct.
1987— Gastonia (S. Atl.)	C	61	235	35	72	13	1	8	33	19	46	1	3	1-2	.306	.359	.472	.832	2	.933
1988— Charlotte (Fla. St.)	C	122	453	56	111	17	2	10	54	45	99	3	10	8-5	.245	.316	.358	.674	6	.979
1989— Tulsa (Texas)	C	107	352	38	95	17	2	7	36	40	88	3	7	5-10	.270	.348	.389	.737	9	.984
1990— Tulsa (Texas)	3-C-1-OF	120	430	68	137	39	2	18	80	43	96	6	11	3-7	.319	.386	.544	.930	‡ 20	.976
— Texas (A.L.)	DH-C	7	13	0	2	0	0	0	3	1	5	0	0	0-0	.154	.214	.154	.368	0	1.000
1991— Okla. City (A.A.)	3-C-1-OF	126	442	57	113	22	2	9	60	61	89	1	14	10-6	.256	.344	.376	.720	11	.986
1992— Okla. City (A.A.)	OF-C	17	58	8	14	5	0	1	9	13	12	0	2	1-0	.241	.380	.379	.760	3	.945
— Calgary (PCL)	C-OF	88	302	49	77	14	2	19	53	41	89	2	9	3-3	.255	.345	.503	.848	6	.977
— Seattle (A.L.)	C-OF	8	19	1	5	0	0	0	0	0	7	0	1	0-0	.263	.263	.263	.526	0	1.000
1993— Seattle (A.L.)	C-DH-OF	58	137	21	35	8	0	5	16	12	19	1	5	2-1	.255	.316	.423	.739	2	.992
1994— Seattle (A.L.)	C-DH-OF	38	83	11	16	7	1	1	8	3	11	1	2	1-0	.193	.230	.337	.567	3	.982
— Calgary (PCL)	C-DH-1B	44	163	44	54	10	1	15	46	30	33	1	5	1-0	.331	.436	.669	1.105	5	.979
1995— Boston (A.L.)	C-DH-3-1	64	152	22	37	6	1	5	23	17	30	2	4	0-2	.243	.322	.395	.717	3	.989
1996— Boston (A.L.)	C-DH-1B	77	237	33	65	13	1	8	34	19	52	1	13	4-2	.274	.331	.439	.770	3	.994
1997— Boston (A.L.)	C	67	212	22	50	15	0	6	26	15	44	2	8	0-2	.236	.290	.392	.682	7	.983
— GC Red Sox (GCL)	DH	4	16	2	2	0	0	0	1	0	1	0	0	1-0	.125	.125	.125	.250	...	...
— Trenton (East.)	C-DH	7	26	3	6	1	0	2	3	2	2	0	0	0-0	.231	.286	.500	.786	0	1.000
1998— Texas (A.L.)	C-DH	40	105	11	33	6	0	6	17	3	17	0	2	0-0	.314	.327	.543	.870	1	.995
1999— Detroit (A.L.)	C-DH	48	143	13	39	8	0	4	14	10	26	1	4	2-0	.273	.320	.413	.733	1	.996
2000— Texas (A.L.)	C	62	193	23	53	18	0	6	26	15	36	1	1	0-1	.275	.329	.461	.790	4	.989
2001— Oklahoma (PCL)	C	8	28	2	4	0	0	0	1	1	10	1	3	0-0	.143	.194	.143	.336	1	.957
— Texas (A.L.)	C	47	130	12	37	6	0	3	25	8	27	1	5	0-1	.285	.331	.400	.731	0	1.000
2002— Texas (A.L.)	C-DH	69	179	16	44	7	0	3	18	11	25	2	6	0-0	.246	.297	.335	.632	3	.991
2003— Pawtucket (Int'l)	C-DH	79	280	37	63	6	0	6	24	9	46	0	15	1-1	.225	.247	.311	.558	6	.989
— Boston (A.L.)	DH-C	4	3	0	0	0	0	0	0	0	1	0	0	0-0	.000	.000	.000	.000	0	1.000
Major League totals (13 years)		589	1606	185	416	94	3	47	210	114	300	11	51	9-9	.259	.311	.409	.720	27	.991

HATTEBERG, SCOTT — 1B

PERSONAL: Born December 14, 1969, in Salem, Ore. ... 6-1/210. ... Bats left, throws right. ... Full name: Scott Allen Hatteberg. ... Name pronounced: HATT-eh-berg. ... High school: Eisenhower (Yakima, Wash.). ... College: Washington State.

TRANSACTIONS/CAREER NOTES: Selected by Philadelphia Phillies organization in 12th round of free-agent draft (June 1, 1988); did not sign. ... Selected by Boston Red Sox organization in supplemental round ("sandwich pick" between first and second round, 43rd pick overall) of free-agent draft (June 3, 1991); pick received as part of compensation for Kansas City signing Type A free-agent P Mike Boddicker. ... On disabled list (July 27-August 3, 1992). ... On Boston disabled list (April 15-May 7 and May 17-August 16, 1999); included rehabilitation assignments to Pawtucket (May 4-7 and August 3-13), Gulf Coast Red Sox (July 24-31) and Sarasota (August 1-2). ... Traded by Red Sox to Colorado Rockies for 2B Pokey Reese (December 19, 2001). ... Granted free agency (December 21, 2001). ... Signed by Oakland Athletics (January 2, 2002). ... Contract purchased by Oakland Athletics from Sacramento (July 24, 2003).

2003 GAMES PLAYED BY POSITION (MLB): 1B—128, DH—15.

Year Team (League)	Pos.	G	AB	R	H	2B	3B	HR	RBI	BB	SO	HBP	GDP	SB-CS	Avg.	OBP	SLG	OPS	E	Pct.
1991— Winter Haven (FSL)	C	56	191	21	53	7	3	1	25	22	22	0	6	1-2	.277	.349	.361	.710	5	.983
— Lynchburg (Caro.)	C	8	25	4	5	1	0	0	2	7	6	0	0	0-0	.200	.375	.240	.615	0	1.000
1992— New Britain (East.)	C	103	297	28	69	13	2	1	30	41	49	2	6	1-3	.232	.327	.300	.626	11	.979
1993— New Britain (East.)	C	68	227	35	63	10	2	7	28	42	38	1	6	1-3	.278	.393	.432	.824	10	.978
— Pawtucket (Int'l)	C	18	53	6	10	0	0	1	2	6	12	1	5	0-0	.189	.283	.245	.529	5	.964
1994— New Britain (East.)	C	20	68	6	18	4	1	1	9	7	9	0	2	0-2	.265	.329	.397	.726	1	.993
— Pawtucket (Int'l)	C	78	238	26	56	14	0	7	19	32	49	3	14	2-1	.235	.332	.382	.714	7	.986
1995— Pawtucket (Int'l)	C-DH	85	251	36	68	15	1	7	27	40	39	4	8	2-0	.271	.376	.422	.798	• 8	.984
— Boston (A.L.)	C	2	2	1	1	0	0	0	0	0	0	0	1	0-0	.500	.500	.500	1.000	0	1.000
1996— Pawtucket (Int'l)	C-DH	90	287	52	77	16	0	12	49	58	66	2	6	1-1	.268	.391	.449	.841	6	.990
— Boston (A.L.)	C	10	11	3	2	1	0	0	3	2	0	0	2	0-0	.182	.357	.273	.630	0	1.000
1997— Boston (A.L.)	C-DH	114	350	46	97	23	1	10	44	40	70	2	11	0-1	.277	.354	.434	.788	11	.983
1998— Boston (A.L.)	C	112	359	46	99	23	1	12	43	43	58	5	11	0-0	.276	.359	.446	.804	5	.993
1999— Boston (A.L.)	C-DH	30	80	12	22	5	0	1	11	18	14	1	2	0-0	.275	.410	.375	.785	1	.993
— Pawtucket (Int'l)	C-DH	10	34	3	6	2	0	0	4	4	6	0	2	0-0	.176	.263	.235	.498	0	1.000
— GC Red Sox (GCL)	C-DH	6	15	4	6	2	0	1	6	7	1	0	1	0-0	.400	.591	.733	1.324	0	1.000
— Sarasota (Fla. St.)	C	1	1	0	1	0	0	0	1	0	0	1	0	0-0	1.000	1.000	1.000	2.000	0	1.000
2000— Boston (A.L.)	C-DH-3B	92	230	21	61	15	0	8	36	38	39	0	8	0-1	.265	.367	.435	.801	6	.981
2001— Boston (A.L.)	C-DH	94	278	34	68	19	0	3	25	33	26	4	7	1-1	.245	.332	.345	.678	4	.992
2002— Oakland (A.L.)	1B-DH	136	492	58	138	22	4	15	61	68	56	6	8	0-0	.280	.374	.433	.807	5	.994
2003— Oakland (A.L.)	1B-DH	147	541	63	137	34	0	12	61	66	53	9	14	0-1	.253	.342	.383	.725	10	.992
Major League totals (9 years)		737	2343	284	625	142	6	61	281	309	318	27	64	1-4	.267	.357	.411	.768	42	.991

HAWKINS, LATROY — P

PERSONAL: Born December 21, 1972, in Gary, Ind. ... 6-5/214. ... Throws right, bats right. ... High school: West Side (Gary, Ind.).

TRANSACTIONS/CAREER NOTES: Selected by Minnesota Twins organization in seventh round of free-agent draft (June 3, 1991).

CAREER HITTING: 0-for-5 (.000), 0 R, 0 2B, 0 3B, 0 HR, 0 RBI.

Year League	W	L	Pct.	ERA	WHIP	G	GS	CG	ShO	Hld.	Sv.-Opp.	IP	H	R	ER	HR	BB-IBB	SO	Avg.
1991— GC Twins (GCL)	4	3	.571	4.75	1.60	11	11	0	0	...	0-...	55.0	62	34	29	2	26-0	47	.281
1992— GC Twins (GCL)	3	2	.600	3.22	1.27	6	6	1	0	...	0-...	36.1	36	19	13	1	10-0	35	.243
— Elizabethton (Appal.)	0	1	.000	3.38	1.20	5	5	1	0	...	0-...	26.2	21	12	10	2	11-0	36	.224
1993— Fort Wayne (Midw.)	• 15	5	.750	2.06	0.96	26	23	4	• 3	...	0-...	157.1	110	53	36	6	41-0	* 179	.195
1994— Fort Myers (Fla. St.)	4	0	1.000	2.33	0.98	6	6	1	1	...	0-...	38.2	32	10	10	1	6-0	36	.224
— Nashville (Sou.)	9	2	.818	2.33	1.06	11	11	1	0	...	0-...	73.1	50	23	19	2	28-0	53	.191
— Salt Lake (PCL)	5	4	.556	4.08	1.53	12	12	1	0	...	0-...	81.2	92	42	37	8	33-0	37	.296
1995— Minnesota (A.L.)	2	3	.400	8.67	1.89	6	6	1	0	0	0-0	27.0	39	29	26	3	12-0	9	.339
— Salt Lake (PCL)	9	7	.563	3.55	1.32	22	22	4	1	...	0-...	144.1	150	63	57	7	40-1	74	.271
1996— Minnesota (A.L.)	1	1	.500	8.20	1.94	7	6	0	0	0-0	0-0	26.1	42	24	24	8	9-0	24	.372
— Salt Lake (PCL)	9	8	.529	3.92	1.23	20	20	4	1	...	0-...	137.2	138	66	60	11	31-3	99	.263
1997— Salt Lake (PCL)	9	4	.692	5.45	1.53	14	13	2	1	...	0-...	76.0	100	53	46	4	16-1	53	.311
— Minnesota (A.L.)	6	12	.333	5.84	1.75	20	20	0	0	0	0-0	103.1	134	71	67	19	47-0	58	.317

H

Year	League	W	L	Pct.	ERA	WHIP	G	GS	CG	ShO	Hld.	Sv.-Opp.	IP	H	R	ER	HR	BB-IBB	SO	Avg.
1998— Minnesota (A.L.)		7	14	.333	5.25	1.51	33	33	0	0	0	0-0	190.1	227	126	111	27	61-1	105	.299
1999— Minnesota (A.L.)		10	14	.417	6.66	1.71	33	33	1	0	0	0-0	174.1	238	* 136	* 129	29	60-2	103	.323
2000— Minnesota (A.L.)		2	5	.286	3.39	1.33	66	0	0	0	7	14-14	87.2	85	34	33	7	32-1	59	.256
2001— Minnesota (A.L.)		1	5	.167	5.96	1.91	62	0	0	0	1	28-37	51.1	59	34	34	3	39-3	36	.291
2002— Minnesota (A.L.)		6	0	1.000	2.13	0.97	65	0	0	0	13	0-3	80.1	63	23	19	5	15-1	63	.217
2003— Minnesota (A.L.)		9	3	.750	1.86	1.09	74	0	0	0	28	2-8	77.1	69	20	16	4	15-1	75	.239
Major League totals (9 years)		**44**	**57**	**.436**	**5.05**	**1.52**	**366**	**98**	**2**	**0**	**49**	**44-62**	**818.0**	**956**	**497**	**459**	**105**	**290-9**	**532**	**.293**

HAYNES, JIMMY   P

PERSONAL: Born September 5, 1972, in LaGrange, Ga. ... 6-4/219. ... Throws right, bats right. ... Full name: Jimmy Wayne Haynes. ... High school: Troup (La Grange, Ga.).

TRANSACTIONS/CAREER NOTES: Selected by Baltimore Orioles organization in seventh round of free-agent draft (June 3, 1991). ... Traded by Orioles with a player to be named later to Oakland Athletics for OF Geronimo Berroa (June 27, 1997); A's acquired P Mark Seaver to complete deal (September 2, 1997). ... Traded by A's to Milwaukee Brewers as part of three-way deal in which A's received P Justin Miller and cash from Colorado Rockies, Brewers received P Jamey Wright and C Henry Blanco from Rockies and Rockies received 3B Jeff Cirillo, P Scott Karl and cash from Brewers (December 13, 1999). ... On disabled list (August 24-September 26, 2001). ... Granted free agency (December 21, 2001). ... Signed by Cincinnati Reds organization (January 11, 2002). ... Granted free agency (October 31, 2002). ... Re-signed by Reds (December 6, 2002). ... Placed on 15-day disabled list (April 18, 2003). ... Recalled from Louisville rehab assignment (May 9, 2003). ... Sent on rehab assignment to Dayton (May 16, 2003). ... Activated from 15-day disabled list (May 26, 2003). ... Recalled from Dayton; reinstated from the 15-day disabled list (May 27, 2003). ... Placed on 15-day disabled list (August 4, 2003). ... Transferred to 60-day disabled list (September 3, 2003).

CAREER HITTING: 32-for-209 (.153), 16 R, 9 2B, 0 3B, 0 HR, 13 RBI.

Year	League	W	L	Pct.	ERA	WHIP	G	GS	CG	ShO	Hld.	Sv.-Opp.	IP	H	R	ER	HR	BB-IBB	SO	Avg.
1991— GC Orioles (GCL)		3	2	.600	1.60	1.05	14	8	1	0	...	2-...	62.0	44	27	11	0	21-0	67	.190
1992— Kane County (Midwest)		7	11	.389	2.56	1.22	24	24	4	0	...	0-...	144.0	131	66	41	2	45-0	141	.236
1993— Frederick (Caro.)		12	8	.600	3.03	1.16	27	27	2	1	...	0-...	172.1	139	73	58	13	61-1	174	.217
1994— Bowie (East.)		13	8	.619	2.90	1.15	25	25	5	1	...	0-...	173.2	154	67	56	16	46-1	* 177	.236
— Rochester (Int'l)		1	0	1.000	6.75	1.95	3	3	0	0	...	0-...	13.1	20	12	10	3	6-0	14	.333
1995— Rochester (Int'l)		• 12	8	.600	3.29	1.26	26	25	3	1	...	0-...	167.0	162	77	61	16	49-0	* 140	.257
— Baltimore (A.L.)		2	1	.667	2.25	0.96	4	3	0	0	0	0-0	24.0	11	6	6	2	12-1	22	.136
1996— Baltimore (A.L.)		3	6	.333	8.29	2.02	26	11	0	0	0	1-1	89.0	122	84	82	14	58-1	65	.333
— Rochester (Int'l)		1	1	.500	5.65	1.71	5	5	0	0	...	0-...	28.2	31	19	18	5	18-0	24	.279
1997— Rochester (Int'l)		5	4	.556	3.44	1.41	16	16	2	1	...	0-...	102.0	89	49	39	9	55-0	113	.239
— Edmonton (PCL)		0	2	.000	4.85	1.58	5	5	0	0	...	0-...	29.2	36	22	16	4	11-0	24	.298
— Oakland (A.L.)		3	6	.333	4.42	1.55	13	13	0	0	0	0-0	73.1	74	38	36	7	40-1	65	.262
1998— Oakland (A.L.)		11	9	.550	5.09	1.63	33	33	1	1	0	0-0	194.1	229	124	110	25	88-4	134	.295
1999— Oakland (A.L.)		7	12	.368	6.34	1.68	30	25	0	0	0	0-0	142.0	158	112	100	21	80-3	93	.282
2000— Milwaukee (N.L.)		12	13	.480	5.33	1.65	33	33	0	0	0	0-0	199.1	228	128	118	21	100-7	88	.295
2001— Milwaukee (N.L.)		8	17	.320	4.85	1.51	31	29	0	0	0	0-0	172.2	182	98	93	20	78-17	112	.279
2002— Cincinnati (N.L.)		15	10	.600	4.12	1.48	34	34	0	0	0	0-0	196.2	210	97	90	21	81-4	126	.278
2003— Dayton (Midw.)		1	0	1.000	0.00	0.57	1	1	0	0	...	0-...	7.0	2	1	0	0	2-0	6	.091
— Louisville (Int'l)		1	1	.500	2.53	1.22	2	2	0	0	...	0-...	10.2	10	4	3	1	3-0	7	.244
— Cincinnati (N.L.)		2	12	.143	6.30	1.86	18	18	1	0	0	0-0	94.1	118	74	66	14	57-3	49	.311
American League totals (5 years)		**26**	**34**	**.433**	**5.75**	**1.67**	**106**	**85**	**1**	**1**	**0**	**1-1**	**522.2**	**594**	**364**	**334**	**69**	**278-10**	**379**	**.289**
National League totals (4 years)		**37**	**52**	**.416**	**4.98**	**1.59**	**116**	**114**	**1**	**0**	**0**	**0-0**	**663.0**	**738**	**397**	**367**	**76**	**316-31**	**375**	**.288**
Major League totals (9 years)		**63**	**86**	**.423**	**5.32**	**1.62**	**222**	**199**	**2**	**1**	**0**	**1-1**	**1185.2**	**1332**	**761**	**701**	**145**	**594-41**	**754**	**.288**

HEBSON, BRYAN   P

PERSONAL: Born March 12, 1976, in Columbus, Ga. ... 6-5/210. ... Throws right, bats right. ... Full name: Bryan McCall Hebson. ... High school: Central (Phenix, Ala.). ... College: Auburn.

TRANSACTIONS/CAREER NOTES: Selected by Montreal Expos organization in first round of free-agent draft (June 3, 1997); pick received as compensation for loss of free-agent P Mel Rojas.

CAREER HITTING: 0-for-0 (.000), 0 R, 0 2B, 0 3B, 0 HR, 0 RBI.

Year	League	W	L	Pct.	ERA	WHIP	G	GS	CG	ShO	Hld.	Sv.-Opp.	IP	H	R	ER	HR	BB-IBB	SO	Avg.
1998— GC Expos (GCL)		2	0	1.000	0.53	1.00	4	4	0	0	...	0-...	17.0	10	1	1	0	7-0	16	.175
— Cape Fear (S. Atl.)		4	5	.444	4.71	1.38	16	16	0	0	...	0-...	72.2	71	42	38	8	29-0	57	.255
1999— Cape Fear (S. Atl.)		0	1	.000	2.67	1.16	6	6	0	0	...	0-...	33.2	22	13	10	2	17-0	34	.183
— Jupiter (FSL)		7	6	.538	2.00	1.07	17	16	0	0	...	0-...	103.1	85	33	23	5	26-0	79	.225
2000— Harrisburg (Eastern)		7	15	.318	4.57	1.41	29	29	3	1	...	0-...	171.1	175	102	87	23	66-2	90	.264
2001— Harrisburg (Eastern)		2	8	.200	4.44	1.29	26	8	2	0	...	0-...	75.0	78	40	37	12	19-0	54	.272
2002— Harrisburg (Eastern)		10	1	.909	1.72	0.89	38	3	0	0	...	7-...	94.1	60	20	18	5	24-2	75	.182
— Ottawa (Int'l)		1	0	1.000	4.82	1.18	5	0	0	0	...	0-...	9.1	8	5	5	0	3-0	11	.222
2003— Edmonton (PCL)		6	0	1.000	4.36	1.52	30	0	0	0	...	6-...	43.1	44	23	21	3	22-1	44	.260
— Montreal (N.L.)		0	0	...	13.50	2.50	2	0	0	0	0	0-0	2.0	4	3	3	1	1-0	1	.444
— Pawtucket (Int'l)		2	1	.667	2.73	0.87	18	0	0	0	...	0-...	26.1	17	9	8	4	6-0	22	.177
Major League totals (1 year)		**0**	**0**	**...**	**13.50**	**2.50**	**2**	**0**	**0**	**0**	**0**	**0-0**	**2.0**	**4**	**3**	**3**	**1**	**1-0**	**1**	**.444**

HEILMAN, AARON   P

PERSONAL: Born November 12, 1978, in Logansport, Ind. ... 6-5/220. ... Throws right, bats right. ... Full name: Aaron Michael Heilman. ... High school: Logansport (Ind.). ... College: Notre Dame.

TRANSACTIONS/CAREER NOTES: Selected by Minnesota Twins organization in 31st round of free-agent draft (June 5, 2000); did not sign. ... Selected by New York Mets organization in first round (18th pick overall) of free-agent draft (June 5, 2001).

CAREER HITTING: 1-for-22 (.045), 1 R, 0 2B, 0 3B, 0 HR, 1 RBI.

Year	League	W	L	Pct.	ERA	WHIP	G	GS	CG	ShO	Hld.	Sv.-Opp.	IP	H	R	ER	HR	BB-IBB	SO	Avg.
2001— St. Lucie (Fla. St.)		0	1	.000	2.35	1.02	7	7	0	0	...	0-...	38.1	26	11	10	0	13-0	39	.190
2002— Binghamton (Eastern)		4	4	.500	3.82	1.17	17	17	0	0	...	0-...	96.2	85	43	41	7	28-2	97	.237
— Norfolk (Int'l)		2	3	.400	3.28	1.18	10	7	0	0	...	0-...	49.1	42	18	18	3	16-1	35	.240
2003— Norfolk (Int'l)		6	4	.600	3.24	1.39	16	16	0	0	...	0-...	94.1	99	37	34	5	32-0	71	.274
— New York (N.L.)		2	7	.222	6.75	1.84	14	13	0	0	0	0-0	65.1	79	53	49	13	41-2	51	.300
Major League totals (1 year)		**2**	**7**	**.222**	**6.75**	**1.84**	**14**	**13**	**0**	**0**	**0**	**0-0**	**65.1**	**79**	**53**	**49**	**13**	**41-2**	**51**	**.300**

HELLING, RICK   P

PERSONAL: Born December 15, 1970, in Devils Lake, N.D. ... 6-3/241. ... Throws right, bats right. ... Full name: Ricky Allen Helling. ... High school: Lakota (Fargo, N.D.), then Shanley (Fargo, N.D.). ... College: Stanford.

TRANSACTIONS/CAREER NOTES: Selected by New York Mets organization in 50th round of free-agent draft (June 4, 1990); did not sign. ... Selected by Texas Rangers organization in first round (22nd pick overall) of free-agent draft (June 1, 1992). ... Traded by Rangers to Florida Marlins (September 3, 1996), completing deal in which Marlins traded P John Burkett to Rangers for P Ryan Dempster and a player to be named later (August 8, 1996). ... Traded by Marlins to Rangers for P Ed Vosberg (August 12, 1997). ... Granted free agency (December 21, 2001). ... Signed by Arizona Diamondbacks (January 19, 2002). ... On Arizona disabled list (July 16-August 7, 2002); included rehabilitation assignment to Tucson (August 2-7). ... Granted free agency (October 28, 2002). ... Signed by Baltimore Orioles organization (February 11, 2003). ... Designated for assignment by Baltimore (August 15, 2003). ... Released by Baltimore (August 18, 2003). ... Signed by Florida Marlins (August 22, 2003).

CAREER HITTING: 6-for-88 (.068), 4 R, 1 2B, 0 3B, 0 HR, 1 RBI.

Year	League	W	L	Pct.	ERA	WHIP	G	GS	CG	ShO	Hld.	Sv.-Opp.	IP	H	R	ER	HR	BB-IBB	SO	Avg.
1992—	Charlotte (Fla. St.)	1	1	.500	2.29	0.86	3	3	0	0	...	0-...	19.2	13	5	5	1	4-0	20	.181
1993—	Tulsa (Texas)	12	8	.600	3.60	1.11	26	26	2	• 2	...	0-...	177.1	150	76	71	14	46-1	* 188	.227
—	Oklahoma City (A.A.)	1	1	.500	1.64	0.73	2	2	1	0	...	0-...	11.0	5	3	2	0	3-0	17	.135
1994—	Texas (A.L.)	3	2	.600	5.88	1.54	9	9	1	1	0	0-0	52.0	62	34	34	14	18-0	25	.295
—	Oklahoma City (A.A.)	4	12	.250	5.78	1.48	20	20	2	0	...	0-...	132.1	153	93	85	17	43-2	85	.294
1995—	Texas (A.L.)	0	2	.000	6.57	2.03	3	3	0	0	0	0-0	12.1	17	11	9	2	8-0	5	.340
—	Oklahoma City (A.A.)	4	8	.333	5.33	1.58	20	20	3	0	...	0-...	109.2	132	73	65	13	41-1	80	.304
1996—	Oklahoma City (A.A.)	12	4	.750	2.96	1.16	23	22	2	1	...	0-...	140.0	124	54	46	10	38-1	157	.238
—	Texas (A.L.)	1	2	.333	7.52	1.57	6	2	0	0	1	0-0	20.1	23	17	17	7	9-0	16	.280
—	Florida (N.L.)	2	1	.667	1.95	0.76	5	4	0	0	0	0-0	27.2	14	6	6	2	7-0	26	.143
1997—	Florida (N.L.)	2	6	.250	4.38	1.43	31	8	0	0	6	0-1	76.0	61	38	37	12	48-2	53	.232
—	Texas (A.L.)	3	3	.500	4.58	1.24	10	8	0	0	0	0-0	55.0	47	29	28	5	21-0	46	.235
1998—	Texas (A.L.)	• 20	7	.741	4.41	1.33	33	33	4	2	0	0-0	216.1	209	109	106	27	78-6	164	.253
1999—	Texas (A.L.)	13	11	.542	4.84	1.43	35	* 35	3	0	0	0-0	219.1	228	127	118	* 41	85-5	131	.272
2000—	Texas (A.L.)	16	13	.552	4.48	1.43	35	* 35	0	0	0	0-0	217.0	212	122	108	29	99-2	146	.252
2001—	Texas (A.L.)	12	11	.522	5.17	1.48	34	34	2	1	0	0-0	215.2	* 256	* 134	* 124	* 38	63-2	154	.297
2002—	Arizona (N.L.)	10	12	.455	4.51	1.30	30	30	0	0	0	0-0	175.2	180	94	88	31	48-6	120	.264
—	Tucson (PCL)	1	0	1.000	1.29	0.71	1	1	0	0	...	0-...	7.0	4	1	1	0	1-0	7	.167
2003—	Baltimore (A.L.)	7	8	.467	5.71	1.41	24	24	0	0	0	0-0	138.2	156	90	88	30	40-0	86	.286
—	Florida (N.L.)	1	0	1.000	0.55	0.98	11	0	0	0	1	0-0	16.1	11	1	1	1	5-0	12	.193
American League totals (9 years)		75	59	.560	4.96	1.42	189	183	10	4	1	0-0	1146.2	1210	673	632	193	421-15	773	.272
National League totals (4 years)		15	19	.441	4.02	1.26	77	42	0	0	7	0-1	295.2	266	139	132	46	108-8	211	.242
Major League totals (10 years)		90	78	.536	4.77	1.39	266	225	10	4	8	0-1	1442.1	1476	812	764	239	529-23	984	.266

HELMS, WES   3B

PERSONAL: Born May 12, 1976, in Gastonia, N.C. ... 6-4/230. ... Bats right, throws right. ... Full name: Wesley Ray Helms. ... High school: Ashbrook (Gastonia, N.C.).

TRANSACTIONS/CAREER NOTES: Selected by Atlanta Braves organization in 10th round of free-agent draft (June 2, 1994). ... On Atlanta disabled list (April 3-July 15 and September 5, 1999-remainder of season); included rehabilitation assignment to Gulf Coast Braves (June 22-July 11). ... On Greenville disabled list (August 15-September 4, 1999). ... On disabled list (August 10-September 10, 2002). ... Traded by Braves with P John Foster to Milwaukee Brewers for P Ray King (December 16, 2002). ... Sent on rehab assignment to Indianapolis (August 20, 2003). ... Recalled from rehab assignment; removed from 15-day disabled list (August 22, 2003).

2003 GAMES PLAYED BY POSITION (MLB): 3B—130.

Year	Team (League)	Pos.	G	AB	R	H	2B	3B	HR	RBI	BB	SO	HBP	GDP	SB-CS	Avg.	OBP	SLG	OPS	E	Pct.
1994—	GC Braves (GCL)	3B	56	184	22	49	15	1	4	29	22	36	4	3	6-1	.266	.355	.424	.779	20	.875
1995—	Macon (S. Atl.)	3B	136	* 539	89	149	32	1	11	85	50	107	10	8	2-2	.276	.347	.401	.748	40	.900
1996—	Durham (Caro.)	3B	67	258	40	83	19	2	13	54	12	51	7	7	1-1	.322	.367	.562	.929	15	.920
—	Greenville (Sou.)	3B	64	231	24	59	13	2	4	22	13	48	4	6	2-1	.255	.306	.381	.687	12	.924
1997—	Richmond (Int'l)	3B	32	110	11	21	4	0	3	15	10	34	5	4	1-1	.191	.286	.309	.595	9	.902
—	Greenville (Sou.)	3B	86	314	50	93	14	1	11	44	33	50	6	14	3-4	.296	.371	.452	.823	11	.950
1998—	Richmond (Int'l)	3B-DH	125	451	56	124	27	1	13	75	35	103	13	11	6-2	.275	.342	.426	.768	15	.952
—	Atlanta (N.L.)	3B	7	13	2	4	1	0	1	2	0	4	0	0	0-0	.308	.308	.615	.923	1	.750
1999—	GC Braves (GCL)	DH-1B	9	33	1	15	2	0	0	10	5	4	1	1	0-1	.455	.538	.515	1.054	0	1.000
—	Greenville (Sou.)	1B	30	113	15	34	6	0	8	26	7	34	1	3	1-0	.301	.347	.566	.913	4	.984
2000—	Richmond (Int'l)	3B	136	539	74	155	27	7	20	88	27	92	6	10	0-6	.288	.325	.475	.800	23	.933
—	Atlanta (N.L.)	3B	5	5	0	1	0	0	0	0	0	2	0	0	0-0	.200	.200	.200	.400	1	.833
2001—	Atlanta (N.L.)	1B-3B-OF	100	216	28	48	10	3	10	36	21	56	1	3	1-1	.222	.293	.435	.728	4	.992
2002—	Atlanta (N.L.)	1B-3B-OF	85	210	20	51	16	0	6	22	11	57	3	5	1-1	.243	.283	.405	.687	5	.986
2003—	Indianapolis (Int'l)	3B	2	5	0	2	0	0	0	0	1	1	0	0	0-0	.400	.500	.400	.900	0	1.000
—	Milwaukee (N.L.)	3B	134	476	56	124	21	0	23	67	43	131	10	10	0-1	.261	.330	.450	.780	19	.945
Major League totals (5 years)			332	920	106	228	48	3	40	127	75	250	14	18	2-3	.248	.310	.437	.747	30	.975

HELTON, TODD   1B

PERSONAL: Born August 20, 1973, in Knoxville, Tenn. ... 6-2/204. ... Bats left, throws left. ... Full name: Todd Lynn Helton. ... High school: Knoxville (Tenn.) Central. ... College: Tennessee.

TRANSACTIONS/CAREER NOTES: Selected by San Diego Padres organization in second round of free-agent draft (June 1, 1992); did not sign. ... Selected by Colorado Rockies organization in first round (eighth pick overall) of free-agent draft (June 3, 1995). ... On New Haven disabled list (June 15-24, 1996).

2003 GAMES PLAYED BY POSITION (MLB): 1B—159.

Year	Team (League)	Pos.	G	AB	R	H	2B	3B	HR	RBI	BB	SO	HBP	GDP	SB-CS	Avg.	OBP	SLG	OPS	E	Pct.
1995—	Asheville (S. Atl.)	DH-1B	54	201	24	51	11	1	1	15	25	32	1	7	1-1	.254	.339	.333	.673	4	.990
1996—	New Haven (East.)	1B-DH	93	319	46	106	24	2	7	51	51	37	1	8	2-5	.332	.425	.486	.911	5	.994
—	Colo. Springs (PCL)	1B-OF	21	71	13	25	4	1	2	13	11	12	0	3	0-0	.352	.439	.521	.960	2	.988
1997—	Colo. Springs (PCL)	1B-OF-DH	99	392	87	138	31	2	16	88	61	68	0	10	3-1	.352	.434	.564	.997	9	.987
—	Colorado (N.L.)	OF-1B	35	93	13	26	2	1	5	11	8	11	0	1	0-1	.280	.337	.484	.821	0	1.000
1998—	Colorado (N.L.)	1B	152	530	78	167	37	1	25	97	53	54	6	15	3-3	.315	.380	.530	.911	7	.995
1999—	Colorado (N.L.)	1B	159	578	114	185	39	5	35	113	68	77	6	14	7-6	.320	.395	.587	.981	9	.993
2000—	Colorado (N.L.)	1B	160	580	138	* 216	* 59	2	42	* 147	103	61	4	12	5-3	* .372	* .463	.698	1.162	7	.995
2001—	Colorado (N.L.)	1B	159	587	132	197	54	2	49	146	98	104	5	14	7-5	.336	.432	.685	1.116	2	.999
2002—	Colorado (N.L.)	1B	156	553	107	182	39	4	30	109	99	91	5	10	5-1	.329	.429	.577	1.006	7	.995
2003—	Colorado (N.L.)	1B	160	583	135	209	49	5	33	117	111	72	2	19	0-4	.358	.458	.630	1.088	11	.993
Major League totals (7 years)			981	3504	717	1182	279	20	219	740	540	470	28	85	27-23	.337	.425	.616	1.041	43	.995

H

PERSONAL: Born December 25, 1958, in Chicago, Ill. ... 5-10/190. ... Bats right, throws left. ... Full name: Rickey Lee Henderson. ... High school: Technical (Oakland).

TRANSACTIONS/CAREER NOTES: Selected by Oakland Athletics organization in fourth round of free-agent draft (June 8, 1976). ... Traded by A's with P Bert Bradley and cash to New York Yankees for OF Stan Javier, P Jay Howell, P Jose Rijo, P Eric Plunk and P Tim Birtsas (December 5, 1984). ... On New York disabled list (March 30-April 22, 1985); included rehabilitation assignment to Fort Lauderdale (April 19-22). ... On disabled list (June 5-29 and July 26-September 1, 1987). ... Traded by Yankees to A's for P Greg Cadaret, P Eric Plunk and OF Luis Polonia (June 21, 1989). ... Granted free agency (November 13, 1989). ... Re-signed by A's (November 28, 1989). ... On disabled list (April 12-27, 1991; May 28-June 17 and June 30-July 16, 1992). ... Traded by A's to Toronto Blue Jays for P Steve Karsay and a player to be named later (July 31, 1993); A's acquired OF Jose Herrera to complete deal (August 6, 1993). ... Granted free agency (October 29, 1993). ... Signed by A's (December 17, 1993). ... On disabled list (May 11-27, 1994). ... Granted free agency (October 30, 1995). ... Signed by San Diego Padres (December 29, 1995). ... On San Diago disabled list (May 9-24, 1997). ... Traded by Padres to Anaheim Angels for P Ryan Hancock, P Stevenson Agosto and a player to be named later (August 13, 1997); Padres acquired 3B George Arias to complete deal (August 19, 1997). ... Granted free agency (October 27, 1997). ... Signed by A's (January 22, 1998). ... Granted free agency (October 26, 1998). ... Signed by New York Mets (December 16, 1998). ... On disabled list (May 3-22, 1999). ... Released by Mets (May 13, 2000). ... Signed by Seattle Mariners (May 19, 2000). ... Granted free agency (November 3, 2000). ... Signed by Padres organization (March 19, 2001). ... Granted free agency (November 5, 2001). ... Signed by Boston Red Sox organization (February 13, 2002). ... Granted free agency (October 29, 2002). ... Signed by Los Angeles Dodgers as free agent (July 14, 2003).

2003 GAMES PLAYED BY POSITION (MLB): OF—18.

										BATTING									FIELDING	
Year Team (League)	Pos.	G	AB	R	H	2B	3B	HR	RBI	BB	SO	HBP	GDP	SB-CS	Avg.	OBP	SLG	OPS	E	Pct.
1976— Boise (NW)	OF	46	140	34	47	13	2	3	23	33	32	2	...	29-7	.336	.463	.521	.985	* 12	.895
1977— Modesto (Calif.)	OF	134	481	120	166	18	4	11	69	104	67	7	...	* 95-* 22	.345	.466	.468	.934	* 20	.936
1978— Jersey City (East.)	OF	133	455	81	141	14	4	0	34	83	67	3	...	* 81-* 28	.310	.417	.358	.775	7	.979
1979— Ogden (PCL)	OF	71	259	66	80	11	8	3	26	53	41	3	...	44-9	.309	.430	.448	.878	6	.963
— Oakland (A.L.)	OF	89	351	49	96	13	3	1	26	34	39	2	4	33-11	.274	.338	.336	.675	6	.973
1980— Oakland (A.L.)	DH-OF	158	591	111	179	22	4	9	53	117	54	5	6	* 100-* 26	.303	.420	.399	.820	7	.984
1981— Oakland (A.L.)	OF	108	423	* 89	* 135	18	7	6	35	64	68	2	7	* 56-* 22	.319	.408	.437	.845	7	.984
1982— Oakland (A.L.)	DH-OF	149	536	119	143	24	4	10	51	* 116	94	2	5	* 130-* 42	.267	.398	.382	.780	9	.977
1983— Oakland (A.L.)	DH-OF	145	513	105	150	25	7	9	48	* 103	80	4	11	* 108-* 19	.292	.414	.421	.835	3	.992
1984— Oakland (A.L.)	OF	142	502	113	147	27	4	16	58	86	81	5	7	* 66-18	.293	.399	.458	.857	11	.969
1985— Fort Laud. (FSL)	OF	3	6	5	1	0	1	0	3	5	2	0	0	1-1	.167	.545	.500	1.045	0	1.000
— New York (A.L.)	DH-OF	143	547	* 146	172	28	5	24	72	99	65	3	8	* 80-10	.314	.419	.516	.934	9	.980
1986— New York (A.L.)	DH-OF	153	608	* 130	160	31	5	28	74	89	81	2	12	* 87-* 18	.263	.358	.469	.827	6	.986
1987— New York (A.L.)	OF	95	358	78	104	17	3	17	37	80	52	2	10	41-8	.291	.423	.497	.920	4	.980
1988— New York (A.L.)	DH-OF	140	554	118	169	30	2	6	50	82	54	3	4	* 93-13	.305	.394	.399	.793	12	.965
1989— New York (A.L.)	OF	65	235	41	58	13	1	3	22	56	29	1	0	25-8	.247	.392	.344	.741	1	.993
— Oakland (A.L.)	DH-OF	85	306	† 72	90	13	2	9	35	† 70	39	2	8	† 52-6	.294	.425	.438	.863	3	.985
1990— Oakland (A.L.)	DH-OF	136	489	* 119	159	33	3	28	61	97	60	4	13	* 65-10	.325	* .439	.577	1.016	5	.983
1991— Oakland (A.L.)	DH-OF	134	470	105	126	17	1	18	57	98	73	7	7	* 58-18	.268	.400	.423	.823	8	.970
1992— Oakland (A.L.)	OF-DH	117	396	77	112	18	3	15	46	95	56	6	5	48-11	.283	.426	.457	.883	4	.984
1993— Oakland (A.L.)	OF-DH	90	318	77	104	19	1	17	47	85	46	2	8	31-6	.327	.469	.553	1.023	5	.974
— Toronto (A.L.)	OF	44	163	37	35	3	1	4	12	35	19	2	1	22-2	.215	.356	.319	.675	2	.955
1994— Oakland (A.L.)	OF-DH	87	296	66	77	13	0	6	20	72	45	5	0	22-7	.260	.411	.365	.776	4	.977
1995— Oakland (A.L.)	OF-DH	112	407	67	122	31	1	9	54	72	66	4	8	32-10	.300	.407	.447	.855	2	.988
1996— San Diego (N.L.)	OF	148	465	110	112	17	2	9	29	125	90	10	5	37-15	.241	.410	.344	.754	6	.975
1997— San Diego (N.L.)	OF-DH	88	288	63	79	11	0	6	27	71	62	4	7	29-4	.274	.422	.375	.797	7	.959
— Anaheim (A.L.)	DH-OF	32	115	21	21	3	0	2	7	26	23	2	3	16-4	.183	.343	.261	.604	0	1.000
1998— Oakland (A.L.)	OF	152	542	101	128	16	1	14	57	* 118	114	5	5	* 66-13	.236	.376	.347	.723	4	.988
1999— New York (N.L.)	OF-DH	121	438	89	138	30	0	12	42	82	82	2	4	37-14	.315	.423	.466	.889	2	.988
2000— New York (N.L.)	OF	31	96	17	21	1	0	0	2	25	20	2	2	5-2	.219	.387	.229	.616	2	.946
— Seattle (A.L.)	OF-DH	92	324	58	77	13	2	4	30	63	55	2	9	31-9	.238	.362	.327	.689	3	.984
2001— Portland (PCL)	OF	9	40	5	11	3	0	0	2	1	9	0	1	1-0	.275	.293	.350	.643	1	.933
— San Diego (N.L.)	OF-DH	123	379	70	86	17	3	8	42	81	84	3	8	25-7	.227	.366	.351	.717	3	.982
2002— Boston (A.L.)	OF-DH	72	179	40	40	6	1	5	16	38	47	4	3	8-2	.223	.369	.352	.721	5	.946
2003— Los Angeles (N.L.)	OF	30	72	7	15	1	0	2	5	11	16	1	0	3-0	.208	.321	.306	.627	1	.955
American League totals (21 years)		2540	9223	1939	2604	433	61	260	968	1795	1340	76	146	1270-293	.282	.401	.427	.828	120	.980
National League totals (6 years)		541	1738	356	451	77	5	37	147	395	354	22	26	136-42	.259	.401	.373	.774	21	.974
Major League totals (25 years)		3081	10961	2295	3055	510	66	297	1115	2190	1694	98	172	1406-335	.279	.401	.419	.820	141	.979

HENDRICKSON, MARK   P

PERSONAL: Born June 23, 1974, in Mount Vernon, Wash. ... 6-9/230. ... Throws left, bats left. ... Full name: Mark Allan Hendrickson. ... College: Washington State.

TRANSACTIONS/CAREER NOTES: Selected by Toronto Blue Jays organization in 20th round of free-agent draft (June 3, 1997). ... On Syracuse disabled list (June 18-July 12, 2002). ... Optioned to Syracuse of the International League (July 9, 2003). ... Recalled from Dunedin by Toronto (July 21, 2003).

CAREER HITTING: 1-for-4 (.250), 1 R, 0 2B, 0 3B, 1 HR, 1 RBI.

Year League	W	L	Pct.	ERA	WHIP	G	GS	CG	ShO	Hld.	Sv.-Opp.	IP	H	R	ER	HR	BB-IBB	SO	Avg.
1998— Dunedin (Fla. St.)	4	3	.571	2.37	1.42	16	5	0	0	...	1-...	49.1	44	16	13	2	26-1	38	.249
1999— Knoxville (Sou.)	2	7	.222	6.63	1.69	12	11	0	0	...	0-...	55.2	73	46	41	4	21-0	39	.319
2000— Tennessee (Sou.)	3	1	.750	3.63	1.11	6	6	0	0	...	0-...	39.2	32	17	16	5	12-0	29	.216
— Dunedin (Fla. St.)	2	2	.500	5.61	1.79	12	12	1	0	...	0-...	51.1	63	34	32	7	29-0	38	.315
2001— Syracuse (Int'l)	2	9	.182	4.66	1.34	38	6	0	0	...	0-...	73.1	80	43	38	13	18-1	33	.274
2002— Syracuse (Int'l)	7	5	.583	3.52	1.22	19	14	0	0	...	0-...	92.0	90	38	36	12	22-0	68	.254
— Toronto (A.L.)	3	0	1.000	2.45	1.01	16	4	0	0	1	0-1	36.2	25	11	10	1	12-3	21	.202
2003— Syracuse (Int'l)	0	0	...	4.50	1.50	1	1	0	0	...	0-...	6.0	8	4	3	1	1-0	5	.333
— Dunedin (Fla. St.)	1	0	1.000	1.59	1.59	1	1	0	0	...	0-...	5.2	5	2	1	0	4-0	3	.227
— Toronto (A.L.)	9	9	.500	5.51	1.56	30	30	1	1	0	0-0	158.1	207	111	97	24	40-3	76	.317
Major League totals (2 years)	12	9	.571	4.94	1.46	46	34	1	1	1	0-1	195.0	232	122	107	25	52-6	97	.298

HENSON, DREW   3B

H

PERSONAL: Born February 13, 1980, in San Diego, Calif. ... 6-5/220. ... Bats right, throws right. ... Full name: Drew Daniel Henson. ... High school: Brighton (Mich.).

TRANSACTIONS/CAREER NOTES: Selected by New York Yankees organization in third round of free-agent draft (June 2, 1998). ... Traded by Yankees with OF Jackson Melian, P Ed Yarnall and P Brian Reith to Cincinnati Reds for P Denny Neagle and OF Mike Frank (July 12, 2000). ... Traded by Reds with OF Michael Coleman to Yankees for OF Wily Mo Pena (March 20, 2001). ... Called up by New York Yankees from Columbus (September 5, 2003).

2003 GAMES PLAYED BY POSITION (MLB): 3B—3.

Year	Team (League)	Pos.	G	AB	R	H	2B	3B	HR	RBI	BB	SO	HBP	GDP	SB-CS	Avg.	OBP	SLG	OPS	E	Pct.
1998—	GC Yankees (GCL)	3B	10	38	5	12	3	0	1	2	3	9	0	1	0-0	.316	.366	.474	.840	2	.951
1999—	Tampa (Fla. St.)	3B	69	254	37	71	12	0	13	37	26	71	1	6	3-1	.280	.345	.480	.825	17	.864
2000—	Tampa (Fla. St.)	3B	5	21	4	7	2	0	1	1	1	7	0	0	0-1	.333	.364	.571	.935	0	1.000
	—Norwich (East.)	3B	59	223	39	64	9	2	7	39	20	75	1	6	0-5	.287	.347	.439	.786	9	.917
	—Chattanooga (Sou.)	3B	16	64	7	11	8	0	1	9	4	25	0	2	2-0	.172	.221	.344	.564	3	.933
2001—	Tampa (Fla. St.)	3B	5	14	2	2	0	0	1	3	2	7	2	0	1-0	.143	.316	.357	.673	1	.929
	—Norwich (East.)	3B	5	19	2	7	1	0	0	2	1	4	1	1	0-1	.368	.429	.421	.850	3	.842
	—Columbus (Int'l)	3B	71	270	29	60	6	0	11	38	10	85	0	8	2-1	.222	.249	.367	.616	16	.912
2002—	Columbus (Int'l)	3B	128	471	68	113	30	4	18	65	37	151	6	11	2-1	.240	.301	.435	.736	* 35	.893
	—New York (A.L.)	DH	3	1	1	0	0	0	0	0	0	0	0	0	0-0	.000	.000	.000	.000	...	...
2003—	Columbus (Int'l)	3B-DH	133	483	60	113	40	2	14	78	32	122	11	8	8-4	.234	.291	.412	.703	28	.918
	—New York (A.L.)	3B	5	8	2	1	0	0	0	0	0	2	0	0	0-0	.125	.125	.125	.250	0	1.000
	Major League totals (2 years)		8	9	3	1	0	0	0	0	0	3	0	0	0-0	.111	.111	.111	.222	0	1.000

HENTGEN, PAT — P

PERSONAL: Born November 13, 1968, in Detroit, Mich. ... 6-2/195. ... Throws right, bats right. ... Full name: Patrick George Hentgen. ... Name pronounced: HENT-gen. ... High school: Fraser (Mich.).

TRANSACTIONS/CAREER NOTES: Selected by Toronto Blue Jays organization in fifth round of free-agent draft (June 2, 1986). ... On Toronto disabled list (August 13-September 29, 1992); included rehabilitation assignment to Syracuse (September 1-8). ... Traded by Blue Jays with P Paul Spoljaric to St. Louis Cardinals for P Lance Painter, C Alberto Castillo and P Matt DeWitt (November 11, 1999). ... Granted free agency (October 31, 2000). ... Signed by Baltimore Orioles (December 19, 2000). ... On disabled list (May 17, 2001-remainder of season). ... On Baltimore disabled list (March 31-September 8, 2002); included rehabilitation assignments to Gulf Coast Orioles (August 5-9), Delmarva (August 10-15), Aberdeen (August 16-27 and September), Bowie (August 28-September 1) and Frederick (September 3).

CAREER HITTING: 9-for-83 (.108), 4 R, 0 2B, 0 3B, 0 HR, 0 RBI.

Year	League	W	L	Pct.	ERA	WHIP	G	GS	CG	ShO	Hld.	Sv.-Opp.	IP	H	R	ER	HR	BB-IBB	SO	Avg.
1986—	St. Catharines (NYP)	0	4	.000	4.50	1.70	13	11	0	0	...	1-...	40.0	38	27	20	3	30-1	30	.244
1987—	Myrtle Beach (SAL)	11	5	.688	2.35	1.09	32	* 31	2	2	...	0-...	* 188.0	145	62	49	5	60-0	131	.214
1988—	Dunedin (Fla. St.)	3	12	.200	3.45	1.35	31	* 30	0	0	...	0-...	151.1	139	80	58	10	65-1	125	.243
1989—	Dunedin (Fla. St.)	9	8	.529	2.68	1.28	29	28	0	0	...	0-...	151.1	123	53	45	5	71-1	148	.225
1990—	Knoxville (Sou.)	9	5	.643	3.05	1.23	28	26	0	0	...	0-...	153.1	121	57	52	10	68-0	142	.218
1991—	Syracuse (Int'l)	8	9	.471	4.47	1.38	31	• 28	1	0	...	0-...	171.0	146	91	85	17	* 90-1	* 155	.234
	—Toronto (A.L.)	0	0		2.45	1.09	3	1	0	0	0	0-0	7.1	5	2	2	1	3-0	3	.208
1992—	Toronto (A.L.)	5	2	.714	5.36	1.61	28	2	0	0	1	0-1	50.1	49	30	30	7	32-5	39	.254
	—Syracuse (Int'l)	1	2	.333	2.66	1.13	4	4	0	0	...	0-...	20.1	15	6	6	1	8-0	17	.211
1993—	Toronto (A.L.)	19	9	.679	3.87	1.34	34	32	3	0	0	0-0	216.1	215	103	93	27	74-0	122	.258
1994—	Toronto (A.L.)	13	8	.619	3.40	1.24	24	24	6	3	0	0-0	174.2	158	74	66	21	59-1	147	.240
1995—	Toronto (A.L.)	10	14	.417	5.11	1.62	30	30	2	0	0	0-0	200.2	* 236	* 129	* 114	24	90-6	135	.290
1996—	Toronto (A.L.)	20	10	.667	3.22	1.25	35	35	* 10	• 3	0	0-0	* 265.2	238	105	95	24	94-3	177	.241
1997—	Toronto (A.L.)	15	10	.600	3.68	1.23	35	• 35	• 9	• 3	0	0-0	• 264.0	253	116	108	31	71-2	160	.254
1998—	Toronto (A.L.)	12	11	.522	5.17	1.56	29	29	0	0	0	0-0	177.2	208	109	102	28	69-1	94	.293
1999—	Toronto (A.L.)	11	12	.478	4.79	1.46	34	34	1	0	0	0-0	199.0	225	115	106	32	65-1	118	.286
2000—	St. Louis (N.L.)	15	12	.556	4.72	1.50	33	33	1	1	0	0-0	194.1	202	107	102	24	89-4	118	.276
2001—	Baltimore (A.L.)	2	3	.400	3.47	1.12	9	9	1	0	0	0-0	62.1	51	25	24	7	19-3	33	.221
2002—	GC Orioles (GCL)	0	0	...	0.00	0.67	1	1	0	0	0	0-...	3.0	2	0	0	0	0-0	3	.182
	—Delmarva (S. Atl.)	0	1	.000	1.80	1.00	1	1	0	0	0	0-...	5.0	4	1	1	0	1-0	4	.235
	—Aberdeen (NY-P)	1	1	.500	3.09	1.37	2	2	0	0	0	0-...	11.2	16	8	4	1	0-0	10	.314
	—Bowie (East.)	0	0	...	1.50	1.17	1	1	0	0	0	0-...	6.0	5	2	1	1	2-0	3	.227
	—Frederick (Caro.)	1	0	1.000	2.57	1.00	1	1	1	0	0	0-...	7.0	5	2	2	0	2-0	5	.208
	—Baltimore (A.L.)	0	4	.000	7.77	1.86	4	4	0	0	0	0-0	22.0	31	20	19	6	10-0	11	.337
2003—	Baltimore (A.L.)	7	8	.467	4.09	1.29	28	22	1	0	0	1-1	160.2	150	74	73	25	58-1	100	.247
	American League totals (12 years)	114	91	.556	4.16	1.37	293	257	33	9	1	1-2	1800.2	1819	902	832	229	644-23	1139	.262
	National League totals (1 year)	15	12	.556	4.72	1.50	33	33	1	1	0	0-0	194.1	202	107	102	24	89-4	118	.276
	Major League totals (13 years)	129	103	.556	4.21	1.38	326	290	34	10	1	1-2	1995.0	2021	1009	934	253	733-27	1257	.264

HEREDIA, FELIX — P

PERSONAL: Born June 18, 1975, in Barahona, Dominican Republic. ... 6-0/180. ... Throws left, bats left. ... Full name: Felix Perez Heredia. ... Name pronounced: heh-RAY-dee-ah. ... High school: Escuela Dominical (Barahona, Dominican Republic).

TRANSACTIONS/CAREER NOTES: Signed as non-drafted free agent by Florida Marlins organization (November 22, 1992). ... Traded by Marlins with P Steve Hoff to Chicago Cubs for 3B Kevin Orie, P Todd Noel and P Justin Speier (July 31, 1998). ... On disabled list (August 21-September 5 and September 18-October 3, 2001). ... Traded by Cubs with a player to be named later to Toronto Blue Jays for SS Alex Gonzalez (December 10, 2001); Blue Jays acquired IF James Deschaine to complete deal (December 13, 2001). ... Granted free agency (October 28, 2002). ... Signed by Cincinnati Reds organization (January 7, 2003). ... Claimed off waivers by New York Yankees from Cincinnati (August 25, 2003).

CAREER HITTING: 4-for-15 (.267), 0 R, 0 2B, 0 3B, 0 HR, 1 RBI.

Year	League	W	L	Pct.	ERA	WHIP	G	GS	CG	ShO	Hld.	Sv.-Opp.	IP	H	R	ER	HR	BB-IBB	SO	Avg.
1993—	GC Marlins (GCL)	5	1	.833	2.47	0.98	12	• 12	0	0	...	0-...	62.0	50	18	17	0	11-0	53	.234
1994—	Kane County (Midwest)	4	5	.444	5.69	1.47	24	8	1	0	...	3-...	68.0	86	55	43	7	14-0	65	.305
1995—	Brevard County (FSL)	6	4	.600	3.57	1.43	34	8	0	0	...	1-...	95.2	101	52	38	6	36-1	76	.271
1996—	Portland (East.)	8	1	.889	1.50	1.05	55	0	0	0	...	5-...	60.0	48	11	10	3	15-2	42	.223
	—Florida (N.L.)	1	1	.500	4.32	1.86	21	0	0	0	2	0-0	16.2	21	8	8	1	10-1	10	.313
1997—	Florida (N.L.)	5	3	.625	4.29	1.46	56	0	0	0	7	0-1	56.2	53	30	27	3	30-1	54	.243
1998—	Florida (N.L.)	0	3	.000	5.49	1.71	41	2	0	0	9	2-3	41.0	38	30	25	1	32-2	38	.241
	—Chicago (N.L.)	3	0	1.000	4.08	1.42	30	0	0	0	8	0-2	17.2	19	9	8	1	6-1	16	.279
1999—	Chicago (N.L.)	3	1	.750	4.85	1.56	69	0	0	0	12	1-7	52.0	56	35	28	7	25-2	50	.272
2000—	Chicago (N.L.)	7	3	.700	4.76	1.35	74	0	0	0	12	0-2	52.0	56	31	31	6	33-4	52	.220
2001—	Chicago (N.L.)	2	2	.500	6.17	1.74	48	0	0	0	8	0-3	35.0	45	27	24	6	19-1	28	.315
2002—	Toronto (A.L.)	1	2	.333	5.41	1.47	53	0	0	0	7	0-2	52.1	51	29	21	5	26-3	31	.256
2003—	Cincinnati (N.L.)	5	2	.714	3.00	1.24	57	0	0	0	7	1-4	72.0	61	27	24	9	28-5	41	.228
	—New York (A.L.)	0	1	.000	1.20	1.20	12	0	0	0	1	0-1	15.0	13	5	2	1	5-2	4	.228
	American League totals (2 years)	1	3	.250	3.07	1.41	65	0	0	0	8	0-3	67.1	64	34	23	6	31-5	35	.250
	National League totals (7 years)	26	15	.634	4.50	1.48	396	2	0	0	65	6-25	349.2	339	197	175	34	180-17	289	.254
	Major League totals (8 years)	27	18	.600	4.27	1.47	461	2	0	0	73	6-28	417.0	403	231	198	40	211-22	324	.253

H

HERGES, MATT   P

PERSONAL: Born April 1, 1970, in Champaign, Ill. ... 6-0/205. ... Throws right, bats left. ... Full name: Matthew Tyler Herges. ... Name pronounced: hur-JISS. ... High school: Centennial (Champaign, Ill.). ... College: Illinois State.

TRANSACTIONS/CAREER NOTES: Signed as non-drafted free agent by Los Angeles Dodgers organization (June 13, 1992). ... Granted free agency (October 15, 1998). ... Re-signed by Dodgers organization (January 1, 1999). ... Traded by Dodgers with IF Jorge Nunez to Montreal Expos for P Guillermo Mota and OF Wilkin Ruan (March 24, 2002). ... Traded by Expos to Pittsburgh Pirates for P Chris Young and P Jon Searles (December 20, 2002). ... Released by Pirates (March 26, 2003). ... Signed as a free agent by San Diego Padres organization (April 11, 2003). ... Traded by Padres to San Francisco Giants for P Clay Hensley and a player to be named or cash (July 13, 2003).

CAREER HITTING: 6-for-27 (.222), 0 R, 0 2B, 0 3B, 0 HR, 1 RBI.

Year League	W	L	Pct.	ERA	WHIP	G	GS	CG	ShO	Hld.	Sv.-Opp.	IP	H	R	ER	HR	BB-IBB	SO	Avg.
1992— Yakima (NW)	2	3	.400	3.22	1.28	27	0	0	0	...	9-...	44.2	33	21	16	2	24-1	57	.199
1993— Bakersfield (Calif.)	2	6	.250	3.69	1.39	51	0	0	0	...	2-...	90.1	70	49	37	6	56-6	84	.214
1994— Vero Beach (FSL)	8	9	.471	3.32	1.33	48	3	1	0	...	3-...	111.0	115	45	41	8	33-3	61	.268
1995— San Antonio (Texas)	0	3	.000	4.88	1.81	19	0	0	0	...	8-...	27.2	34	16	15	2	16-1	18	.306
— San Bernardino (Calif.)	5	2	.714	3.66	1.41	22	2	0	0	...	1-...	51.2	58	29	21	3	15-0	35	.275
1996— San Antonio (Texas)	3	2	.600	2.71	1.34	30	6	0	0	...	3-...	83.0	83	38	25	3	28-0	45	.261
— Albuquerque (PCL)	4	1	.800	2.60	1.36	10	4	2	1	...	0-...	34.2	33	11	10	2	14-0	15	.270
1997— Albuquerque (PCL)	0	8	.000	8.89	1.95	31	12	0	0	...	0-...	85.0	120	92	84	13	46-1	61	.340
— San Antonio (Texas)	0	1	.000	8.80	2.09	4	3	0	0	...	0-...	15.1	22	15	15	2	10-0	12	.355
1998— Albuquerque (PCL)	3	5	.375	5.71	1.72	34	8	0	0	...	0-...	88.1	115	64	56	9	37-1	75	.325
— San Antonio (Texas)	0	0	...	0.00	0.83	3	0	0	0	...	0-...	6.0	3	0	0	0	2-0	3	.158
1999— Albuquerque (PCL)	8	3	.727	4.73	1.39	21	21	2	0	...	0-...	131.1	135	82	69	17	47-0	88	.272
— Los Angeles (N.L.)	0	2	.000	4.07	1.32	17	0	0	0	1	0-2	24.1	24	13	11	5	8-0	18	.255
2000— Los Angeles (N.L.)	11	3	.786	3.17	1.27	59	4	0	0	4	1-3	110.2	100	43	39	7	40-5	75	.249
2001— Los Angeles (N.L.)	9	8	.529	3.44	1.44	75	0	0	0	15	1-8	99.1	97	39	38	8	46-12	76	.259
2002— Montreal (N.L.)	2	5	.286	4.04	1.64	62	0	0	0	9	6-14	64.2	80	33	29	10	26-8	50	.305
2003— Portland (PCL)	0	0	...	1.80	0.60	4	0	0	0	...	0-...	5.0	1	1	1	0	2-0	5	.063
— San Diego (N.L.)	2	2	.500	2.86	1.36	40	0	0	0	4	3-5	44.0	40	16	14	2	20-2	40	.244
— San Francisco (N.L.)	1	0	1.000	2.31	1.06	27	0	0	0	5	0-1	35.0	28	11	9	1	9-0	28	.219
Major League totals (5 years)	25	20	.556	3.33	1.37	280	4	0	0	38	11-33	378.0	369	155	140	33	149-27	287	.259

HERMANSEN, CHAD   OF

PERSONAL: Born September 10, 1977, in Salt Lake City, Utah. ... 6-2/192. ... Bats right, throws right. ... Full name: Chad Bruce Hermansen. ... High school: Green Valley (Henderson, Nev.).

TRANSACTIONS/CAREER NOTES: Selected by Pittsburgh Pirates organization in first round (10th pick overall) of free-agent draft (June 1, 1995). ... On Pittsburgh disabled list (March 27-May 10, 2002); included rehabilitation assignment to Nashville (April 22-May 11). ... Traded by Pirates to Chicago Cubs for OF Darren Lewis (July 31, 2002). ... Traded by Cubs with C Todd Hundley to Los Angeles Dodgers for 1B Eric Karros, 2B Mark Grudzielanek and cash (December 4, 2002). ... On disabled list (March 30, 2003). ... Sent on rehab assignment by Los Angeles to Vero Beach (April 28, 2003). ... Recalled from rehab assignment by Los Angeles from Vero Beach (May 16, 2003). ... Sent outright to Las Vegas by Los Angeles (May 16, 2003). ... Contract purchased by Los Angeles from Las Vegas (July 7, 2003). ... Designated for assignment (July 19, 2003). ... Sent outright to Las Vegas by Los Angeles (July 23, 2003). ... Contract purchased by Los Angeles from Las Vegas (September 2, 2003).

2003 GAMES PLAYED BY POSITION (MLB): OF—6.

Year Team (League)	Pos.	G	AB	R	H	2B	3B	HR	RBI	BB	SO	HBP	GDP	SB-CS	Avg.	OBP	SLG	OPS	E	Pct.
1995— GC Pirates (GCL)	SS	24	92	14	28	10	1	3	17	9	19	0	2	0-0	.304	.363	.533	.895	10	.884
— Erie (N.Y.-Penn)	SS	44	165	30	45	8	3	6	25	18	39	4	6	4-2	.273	.354	.467	.821	30	.839
1996— Augusta (S. Atl.)	SS-DH	62	226	41	57	11	3	14	41	38	65	8	1	11-3	.252	.377	.513	.891	25	.892
— Lynchburg (Caro.)	SS-DH	66	251	40	69	11	3	10	46	29	56	3	8	5-1	.275	.352	.462	.814	28	.897
1997— Carolina (Sou.)	OF-S-2-D	129	487	87	134	31	4	20	70	69	136	10	3	18-6	.275	.373	.478	.851	§ 39	.891
1998— Nashville (PCL)	OF-2B	126	458	81	118	26	5	28	78	50	152	4	3	21-4	.258	.334	.520	.854	14	.942
1999— Nashville (PCL)	OF	125	496	89	134	27	3	32	97	35	119	4	9	19-9	.270	.321	.530	.851	3	.989
— Pittsburgh (N.L.)	OF	19	60	5	14	3	0	1	1	7	19	1	0	2-2	.233	.324	.333	.657	0	1.000
2000— Pittsburgh (N.L.)	OF	33	108	12	20	4	1	2	8	6	37	0	3	0-0	.185	.226	.296	.522	1	.979
— Nashville (PCL)	OF	78	294	47	66	12	1	11	38	25	89	9	2	16-4	.224	.304	.384	.688	4	.975
2001— Nashville (PCL)	OF	123	447	75	110	22	6	19	64	41	154	5	5	22-5	.246	.315	.478	.751	4	.984
— Pittsburgh (N.L.)	OF	22	55	5	9	1	0	2	5	1	18	0	0	0-1	.164	.179	.291	.469	0	1.000
2002— Nashville (PCL)	OF	16	56	11	11	2	0	4	9	8	23	2	0	1-0	.196	.318	.446	.765	0	1.000
— Pittsburgh (N.L.)	OF	65	194	22	40	11	1	7	15	17	68	1	1	7-5	.206	.272	.381	.654	2	.982
— Chicago (N.L.)	OF	35	43	3	9	3	0	1	3	5	14	0	0	0-0	.209	.292	.349	.641	2	.895
2003— Vero Beach (FSL)	OF-DH	17	63	12	15	4	0	1	7	6	7	0	0	0-1	.238	.296	.349	.645	1	.952
— Las Vegas (PCL)	OF-DH-1B	68	235	43	83	15	1	9	31	19	38	2	4	4-1	.353	.405	.540	.945	1	.989
— Los Angeles (N.L.)	OF	11	25	2	4	1	0	0	2	2	9	0	0	0-0	.160	.222	.200	.422	0	1.000
Major League totals (5 years)		185	485	49	96	23	2	13	34	38	165	2	4	9-8	.198	.258	.334	.592	5	.980

HERMANSON, DUSTIN   P

PERSONAL: Born December 21, 1972, in Springfield, Ohio. ... 6-2/200. ... Throws right, bats right. ... Full name: Dustin Michael Hermanson. ... High school: Kenton Ridge (Springfield, Ohio). ... College: Kent State.

TRANSACTIONS/CAREER NOTES: Selected by Pittsburgh Pirates organization in 39th round of free-agent draft (June 3, 1991); did not sign. ... Selected by San Diego Padres organization in first round (third pick overall) of free-agent draft (June 2, 1994). ... Traded by Padres to Florida Marlins for 2B Quilvio Veras (November 21, 1996). ... Traded by Marlins with OF Joe Orsulak to Montreal Expos for OF/1B Cliff Floyd (March 26, 1997). ... On disabled list (May 15-30, 1998). ... Traded by Expos with P Steve Kline to St. Louis Cardinals for 3B Fernando Tatis and P Britt Reames (December 14, 2000). ... Traded by Cardinals to Boston Red Sox for OF Rick Asadoorian, 1B Luis Garcia and P Dustin Brisson (December 15, 2001). ... On Boston disabled list (April 4-July 20 and July 21-August 22, 2002); included rehabiliation assignments to Pawtucket (July 13-20 and August 14-20) and Gulf Coast Red Sox (August 9-13). ... Granted free agency (November 1, 2002). ... Signed by Cardinals (January 20, 2003). ... Designated for assignment (June 18, 2003). ... Given unconditional release (June 26, 2003). ... Signed by San Francisco Giants (July 11, 2003).

CAREER HITTING: 27-for-292 (.092), 12 R, 5 2B, 0 3B, 2 HR, 9 RBI.

H

Year — League	W	L	Pct.	ERA	WHIP	G	GS	CG	ShO	Hld.	Sv.-Opp.	IP	H	R	ER	HR	BB-IBB	SO	Avg.
1994— Wichita (Texas)	1	0	1.000	0.43	0.90	16	0	0	0	...	8-...	21.0	13	1	1	0	6-2	30	.176
— Las Vegas (PCL)	0	0	...	6.14	1.50	7	0	0	0	...	3-...	7.1	6	5	5	1	5-0	6	.222
1995— Las Vegas (PCL)	0	1	.000	3.50	1.78	31	0	0	0	...	11-...	36.0	35	23	14	5	29-0	42	.245
— San Diego (N.L.)	3	1	.750	6.82	1.80	26	0	0	0	1	0-0	31.2	35	26	24	8	22-1	19	.280
1996— Las Vegas (PCL)	1	4	.200	3.13	1.48	42	0	0	0	...	21-...	46.0	41	20	16	3	27-7	54	.229
— San Diego (N.L.)	1	0	1.000	8.56	1.61	8	0	0	0	0	0-0	13.2	18	15	13	3	4-0	11	.340
1997— Montreal (N.L.)	8	8	.500	3.69	1.26	32	28	1	1	0	0-0	158.1	134	68	65	15	66-2	136	.234
1998— Montreal (N.L.)	14	11	.560	3.13	1.17	32	30	1	0	1	0-0	187.0	163	80	65	21	56-3	154	.234
1999— Montreal (N.L.)	9	14	.391	4.20	1.36	34	34	0	0	0	0-0	216.1	225	110	101	20	69-4	145	.271
2000— Montreal (N.L.)	12	14	.462	4.77	1.52	38	30	2	1	1	4-7	198.0	226	128	105	26	75-5	94	.290
2001— St. Louis (N.L.)	14	13	.519	4.45	1.39	33	33	0	0	0	0-0	192.1	195	106	95	34	73-3	123	.264
2002— Boston (A.L.)	1	1	.500	7.77	1.91	12	1	0	0	2	0-1	22.0	35	19	19	3	7-0	13	.354
— Pawtucket (Int'l)	0	1	.000	2.63	1.17	5	3	0	0	...	0-...	13.2	9	5	4	0	7-0	11	.191
— GC Red Sox (GCL)	0	0	...	9.00	2.50	1	1	0	0	...	0-...	2.0	5	3	2	0	0-0	1	.500
2003— St. Louis (N.L.)	1	2	.333	5.46	1.65	23	0	0	0	1	1-6	29.2	35	18	18	4	14-2	12	.315
— Fresno (PCL)	0	1	.000	4.85	1.23	4	4	0	0	...	0-...	26.0	29	16	14	2	3-1	17	.290
— San Francisco (N.L.)	2	1	.667	3.00	1.15	9	6	0	0	0	0-0	39.0	35	14	13	5	10-2	27	.238
American League totals (1 year)	1	1	.500	7.77	1.91	12	1	0	0	2	0-1	22.0	35	19	19	3	7-0	13	.354
National League totals (8 years)	64	64	.500	4.21	1.36	235	161	4	2	4	5-13	1066.0	1066	565	499	136	389-22	721	.263
Major League totals (9 years)	65	65	.500	4.28	1.38	247	162	4	2	6	5-14	1088.0	1101	584	518	139	396-22	734	.265

HERNANDEZ, CARLOS   P

PERSONAL: Born April 22, 1980... 5-10/185. ... Throws left, bats both. ... Full name: Carlos E. Hernandez.

TRANSACTIONS/CAREER NOTES: Signed as non-drafted free agent by Houston Astros organization (April 23, 1997). ... On Houston disabled list (July 2-August 18, 2002); included rehabilitation assignments to New Orleans (August 2-4) and Round Rock (August 5-18). ... On disabled list (March 29, 2003-entire season).

CAREER HITTING: 7-for-40 (.175), 3 R, 0 2B, 0 3B, 0 HR, 1 RBI.

Year — League	W	L	Pct.	ERA	WHIP	G	GS	CG	ShO	Hld.	Sv.-Opp.	IP	H	R	ER	HR	BB-IBB	SO	Avg.
1997— VSL Astros (VSL)	5	1	.833	2.54	1.48	22	0	0	0	...	3-...	46.0	47	20	13	...	21-...	53	...
1998— Dom. Astros (DSL)	2	0	1.000	1.46	1.14	17	0	0	0	...	9-...	24.2	16	4	4	...	12-...	33	...
1999— Martinsville (App.)	5	1	.833	1.79	1.07	13	9	0	0	...	0-...	55.1	36	21	11	2	23-0	82	.184
2000— Michigan (Midw.)	6	6	.500	3.82	1.40	22	22	2	1	...	0-...	110.2	92	57	47	8	63-0	115	.225
2001— Round Rock (Texas)	12	3	.800	3.69	1.32	24	23	0	0	...	0-...	139.0	115	60	57	11	69-0	167	.228
— Houston (N.L.)	1	0	1.000	1.02	1.02	3	3	0	0	0	0-0	17.2	11	2	2	1	7-0	17	.177
2002— Houston (N.L.)	7	5	.583	4.38	1.56	23	21	0	0	0	0-0	111.0	112	56	54	11	61-5	93	.261
— New Orleans (PCL)	0	0	...	0.00	0.67	1	1	0	0	...	0-...	3.0	1	0	0	0	1-0	2	.100
— Round Rock (Texas)	0	0	...	4.15	0.92	2	2	0	0	...	0-...	8.2	4	4	4	1	4-0	10	.138
2003— Houston (N.L.)											Did not play.								
Major League totals (2 years)	8	5	.615	3.92	1.48	26	24	0	0	0	0-0	128.2	123	58	56	12	68-5	110	.251

HERNANDEZ, JOSE   SS

PERSONAL: Born July 14, 1969, in Vega Alta, Puerto Rico. ... 6-1/188. ... Bats right, throws right. ... Full name: Jose Antonio Hernandez. ... Name pronounced: her-NAN-dezz. ... High school: Maestro Ladi (Vega Alta, Puerto Rico). ... College: Interamericana University.

TRANSACTIONS/CAREER NOTES: Signed as non-drafted free agent by Texas Rangers organization (January 13, 1987). ... Claimed on waivers by Cleveland Indians (April 3, 1992). ... Traded by Indians to Chicago Cubs for P Heathcliff Slocumb (June 1, 1993). ... Traded by Cubs with P Terry Mulholland to Atlanta Braves for P Micah Bowie, P Ruben Quevado and a player to be named later (July 31, 1999); Cubs acquired P Joey Nation to complete deal (August 24, 1999). ... Granted free agency (November 5, 1999). ... Signed by Milwaukee Brewers (December 16, 1999). ... On Milwaukee disabled list (August 10-September 1, 2000); included rehabilitation assignment to Indianapolis (August 29-31). ... Granted free agency (October 28, 2002). ... Signed by Colorado Rockies (January 24, 2003). ... Traded by Rockies to Chicago Cubs for IF Mark Bellhorn (June 20, 2003). ... Traded by Cubs with P Matt Bruback and a player to be named later to Pittsburgh Pirates for 3B Aramis Ramirez, OF Kenny Lofton and cash considerations (July 23, 2003).

2003 GAMES PLAYED BY POSITION (MLB): 3B—75, SS—74, OF—2, 2B—1, 1B—1.

Year — Team (League)	Pos.	G	AB	R	H	2B	3B	HR	RBI	BB	SO	HBP	GDP	SB-CS	Avg.	OBP	SLG	OPS	E	Pct.
1987— GC Rangers (GCL)	SS	24	52	5	9	1	1	0	2	9	25	1	1	2-1	.173	.306	.231	.537	5	.932
1988— GC Rangers (GCL)		55	162	19	26	7	1	1	13	12	36	0	5	4-1	.160	.217	.235	.452	8	.958
1989— Gastonia (S. Atl.)	2-3-S-OF	91	215	35	47	7	6	1	16	33	67	0	3	9-2	.219	.323	.321	.644	17	.941
1990— Charlotte (Fla. St.)	SS-OF	121	388	43	99	14	7	1	44	50	122	4	8	11-8	.255	.345	.335	.680	25	.958
1991— Tulsa (Texas)	SS	91	301	36	72	17	4	1	20	26	75	1	6	4-3	.239	.298	.332	.630	15	.968
— Okla. City (A.A.)	SS	14	46	6	14	1	1	1	3	4	10	0	1	0-0	.304	.353	.435	.788	3	.962
— Texas (A.L.)	3B-SS	45	98	8	18	2	1	0	4	3	31	0	2	0-1	.184	.208	.224	.432	4	.976
1992— Cant./Akr. (Eastern)	SS	130	404	56	103	16	4	3	46	37	108	5	...	7-2	.255	.315	.337	.652	* 40	.932
— Cleveland (A.L.)	SS	3	4	0	0	0	0	0	0	0	2	0	0	0-0	.000	.000	.000	.000	1	.857
1993— Cant./Akr. (Eastern)	SS-3B	45	150	19	30	6	0	2	17	10	39	1	3	9-2	.200	.250	.280	.530	7	.968
— Orlando (South.)	SS	71	263	42	80	8	3	8	33	20	60	0	5	8-4	.304	.352	.449	.801	14	.961
— Iowa (Am. Assoc.)	SS	6	24	3	6	1	0	0	3	0	2	1	1	0-0	.250	.280	.292	.572	1	.976
1994— Chicago (N.L.)	3-S-2-OF	56	132	18	32	2	3	1	9	8	29	1	4	2-2	.242	.291	.326	.617	4	.971
1995— Chicago (N.L.)	S-2-3	93	245	37	60	11	4	13	40	13	69	0	8	1-0	.245	.281	.482	.762	9	.971
1996— Chicago (N.L.)	S-3-2-OF	131	331	52	80	14	1	10	41	24	97	1	10	4-0	.242	.293	.381	.674	20	.952
1997— Chicago (N.L.)	3-S-2-0-D-1	121	183	33	50	8	5	7	26	14	42	0	5	2-5	.273	.323	.486	.810	8	.955
1998— Chicago (N.L.)	3-O-S-1-2	149	488	76	124	23	7	23	75	40	140	1	12	4-6	.254	.311	.471	.782	13	.970
1999— Chicago (N.L.)	SS-OF-1B	99	342	57	93	12	2	15	43	40	101	5	5	7-2	.272	.357	.450	.807	11	.973
— Atlanta (N.L.)	SS-1B-OF	48	166	22	42	8	0	4	19	12	44	0	5	4-1	.253	.302	.373	.675	6	.966
2000— Milwaukee (N.L.)	3B-SS-OF	124	446	51	109	22	1	11	59	41	125	6	12	3-7	.244	.315	.372	.687	19	.955
— Indianapolis (Int'l)	3B	2	9	2	3	0	0	2	3	1	3	0	0	0-0	.333	.400	1.000	1.400	0	1.000
2001— Milwaukee (N.L.)	SS-OF	152	542	67	135	26	2	25	78	39	*185	2	9	5-4	.249	.300	.443	.743	18	.972
2002— Milwaukee (N.L.)	SS	152	525	72	151	24	2	24	73	52	*188	4	19	3-5	.288	.356	.478	.834	19	.973
2003— Colorado (N.L.)	SS-1B	69	257	33	61	6	1	8	27	27	95	0	6	1-1	.237	.308	.362	.670	5	.984
— Chicago (N.L.)	3-S-OF-2	23	69	6	13	3	1	2	9	3	26	0	1	0-0	.188	.222	.348	.570	1	.977
— Pittsburgh (N.L.)	3B	58	193	19	43	9	1	3	21	16	56	1	9	1-0	.223	.282	.326	.608	8	.955
American League totals (2 years)		48	102	8	18	2	1	0	4	3	33	0	2	0-1	.176	.200	.216	.416	5	.971
National League totals (10 years)		1275	3919	543	993	168	30	146	520	329	1197	21	105	37-33	.253	.313	.423	.736	141	.968
Major League totals (12 years)		1323	4021	551	1011	170	31	146	524	332	1230	21	107	37-34	.251	.310	.418	.728	146	.968

H

HERNANDEZ, LIVAN   P

PERSONAL: Born February 20, 1975, in Villa Clara, Cuba. ... 6-2/240. ... Throws right, bats right. ... Full name: Eisler Livan Hernandez. ... Name pronounced: lee-VAHN her-NAN-dezz.

TRANSACTIONS/CAREER NOTES: Signed as non-drafted free agent by Florida Marlins orgaization (January 13, 1996). ... Traded by Marlins to San Francisco Giants for P Jason Grilli and P Nathan Bump (July 24, 1999). ... Traded by Giants with 3B/C Edwards Guzman and cash to Montreal Expos for P Jim Brower and a player to be named later (March 24, 2003); Giants acquired P Matt Blank to complete deal (April 30, 2003).

CAREER HITTING: 113-for-483 (.234), 33 R, 19 2B, 1 3B, 4 HR, 45 RBI.

Year	League	W	L	Pct.	ERA	WHIP	G	GS	CG	ShO	Hld.	Sv.-Opp.	IP	H	R	ER	HR	BB-IBB	SO	Avg.
1996—	Charlotte (Int'l)	2	4	.333	5.14	1.94	10	10	0	0	...	0-...	49.0	61	32	28	3	34-1	45	.308
	Portland (East.)	9	2	.818	4.34	1.23	15	15	0	0	...	0-...	93.1	81	48	45	14	34-1	95	.238
	Florida (N.L.)	0	0	...	0.00	1.67	1	0	0	0	0	0-...	3.0	3	0	0	0	2-0	2	.273
1997—	Charlotte (Int'l)	5	3	.625	3.98	1.40	14	14	0	0	...	0-...	81.1	76	39	36	5	38-2	58	.247
	Florida (N.L.)	9	3	.750	3.18	1.24	17	17	0	0	0	0-0	96.1	81	39	34	5	38-1	72	.229
	Portland (East.)	0	0	...	2.25	2.25	1	1	0	0	...	0-...	4.0	2	1	1	0	7-0	2	.154
1998—	Florida (N.L.)	10	12	.455	4.72	1.57	33	33	9	0	0	0-0	234.1	* 265	133	123	37	104-8	162	.289
1999—	Florida (N.L.)	5	9	.357	4.76	1.59	20	20	2	0	0	0-0	136.0	161	78	72	17	55-3	97	.294
	San Francisco (N.L.)	3	3	.500	4.38	1.37	10	10	0	0	0	0-0	63.2	66	32	31	6	21-2	47	.267
2000—	San Francisco (N.L.)	17	11	.607	3.75	1.36	33	33	5	2	0	0-0	240.0	* 254	114	100	22	73-3	165	.273
2001—	San Francisco (N.L.)	13	15	.464	5.24	1.55	34	34	2	0	0	0-0	226.2	* 266	* 143	* 132	24	85-7	138	.297
2002—	San Francisco (N.L.)	12	• 16	.429	4.38	1.41	33	33	5	3	0	0-0	216.0	233	113	105	19	71-5	134	.283
2003—	Montreal (N.L.)	15	10	.600	3.20	1.21	33	33	*8	0	0	0-0	*233.1	225	92	83	27	57-3	178	.253
	Major League totals (8 years)	84	79	.515	4.22	1.42	214	213	31	5	0	0-0	1449.1	1554	744	680	157	506-32	995	.277

HERNANDEZ, MICHEL   C

PERSONAL: Born August 12, 1978, in La Habana, Cuba. ... 6-0/208. ... Bats right, throws right.

TRANSACTIONS/CAREER NOTES: Signed by New York Yankees organization as a non-drafted free agent (May 11, 1998).

2003 GAMES PLAYED BY POSITION (MLB): C—5.

Year	Team (League)	Pos.	G	AB	R	H	2B	3B	HR	RBI	BB	SO	HBP	GDP	SB-CS	Avg.	OBP	SLG	OPS	E	Pct.
1998—	Oneonta (NYP)	C	61	205	29	52	8	2	0	24	20	19	0	10	4-4	.254	.319	.312	.631	9	.981
1999—	Tampa (Fla. St.)	C	82	281	26	69	10	1	2	23	18	49	3	8	2-2	.246	.296	.310	.606	7	.989
2000—	Norwich (East.)	C	21	66	7	14	2	0	0	4	4	13	0	1	1-0	.212	.254	.242	.496	4	.975
	Tampa (Fla. St.)	C	75	231	17	51	12	0	1	28	29	23	3	4	3-4	.221	.312	.286	.598	7	.988
2001—	GC Yankees (GCL)	C	2	5	0	0	0	0	0	0	0	1	1	1	0-0	.000	.167	.000	.167	0	1.000
	Norwich (East.)	C	51	128	10	29	6	0	2	10	10	20	2	5	1-0	.227	.291	.320	.611	7	.981
2002—	Norwich (East.)	C	20	61	11	19	6	0	1	12	5	6	0	2	0-1	.311	.358	.459	.817	2	.981
	Columbus (S. Atl.)	C	41	121	11	34	5	1	1	12	8	13	2	5	1-3	.281	.336	.364	.700	8	.966
2003—	Columbus (Int'l)	C-DH	89	282	39	79	14	0	4	30	37	35	3	9	0-2	.280	.367	.372	.740	4	.993
	New York (A.L.)	C	5	4	0	1	0	0	0	0	1	1	0	0	0-0	.250	.400	.250	.650	0	1.000
	Major League totals (1 year)		5	4	0	1	0	0	0	0	1	1	0	0	0-0	.250	.400	.250	.650	0	1.000

HERNANDEZ, ORLANDO   P

PERSONAL: Born October 11, 1969... 6-2/220. ... Throws right, bats right. ... Full name: Orlando P. Hernandez.

TRANSACTIONS/CAREER NOTES: Signed as non-drafted free agent by New York Yankees (March 23, 1998). ... On New York disabled list (July 18-August 6, 2000); included rehabilitation assignment to Tampa (August 1-3). ... On New York disabled list (June 1-August 21, 2001); included rehabilitation assignments to Tampa (August 6-16) and Staten Island (August 17-20). ... On New York disabled list (May 16-June 27, 2002); included rehabilitation assignment to Columbus (June 22-27). ... On suspended list (July 21-28, 2002). ... Traded by Yankees to Chicago White Sox for P Antonio Osuna and P Delvis Lantigua (January 15, 2003). ... Traded by White Sox with P Rocky Biddle, 3B/OF Jeff Liefer and cash to Montreal Expos for P Bartolo Colon and 2B/SS Jorge Nunez (January 15, 2003). ... On disabled list (March 21, 2003). ... Sent on rehab assignment to Brevard County by Montreal (April 28, 2003). ... Recalled by Montreal from Brevard County rehab assignment (May 10, 2003). ... Transferred to Emergency disabled list (July 4, 2003).

CAREER HITTING: 1-for-19 (.053), 1 R, 0 2B, 0 3B, 0 HR, 0 RBI.

Year	League	W	L	Pct.	ERA	WHIP	G	GS	CG	ShO	Hld.	Sv.-Opp.	IP	H	R	ER	HR	BB-IBB	SO	Avg.
1998—	Tampa (FSL)	1	1	.500	1.00	0.67	2	2	0	0	...	0-...	9.0	3	2	1	0	3-0	15	.100
	Columbus (Int'l)	6	0	1.000	3.83	1.37	7	7	0	0	...	0-...	42.1	41	19	18	2	17-0	59	.261
	New York (A.L.)	12	4	.750	3.13	1.17	21	21	3	1	0	0-0	141.0	113	53	49	11	52-1	131	.222
1999—	New York (A.L.)	17	9	.654	4.12	1.28	33	33	2	1	0	0-0	214.1	187	108	98	24	87-2	157	.233
2000—	New York (A.L.)	12	13	.480	4.51	1.21	29	29	3	0	0	0-0	195.2	186	104	98	34	51-2	141	.247
	Tampa (FSL)	0	0	...	0.00	0.50	1	0	0	0	0	0-...	4.0	1	0	0	0	1-0	5	.077
2001—	New York (A.L.)	4	7	.364	4.85	1.39	17	16	0	0	0	0-0	94.2	90	51	51	19	42-1	77	.248
	Tampa (FSL)	0	0	...	0.00	1.00	2	2	0	0	0	0-...	7.0	6	2	0	0	1-0	8	.214
	Staten Island (NY-P)	1	0	1.000	0.00	0.50	1	1	0	0	0	0-...	6.0	2	0	0	0	1-0	11	.100
2002—	New York (A.L.)	8	5	.615	3.64	1.14	24	22	0	0	1	1-1	146.0	131	63	59	17	36-2	113	.236
	Columbus (Int'l)	1	0	1.000	1.59	1.41	1	1	0	0	0	0-...	5.2	7	2	1	0	1-0	5	.280
2003—	Brevard Co. (Fla. St.)	0	1	.000	10.80	1.80	2	2	0	0	0	0-0	5.0	5	6	6	0	4-0	7	.250
	Major League totals (5 years)	53	38	.582	4.04	1.23	124	121	8	2	1	1-1	791.2	707	379	355	105	268-8	619	.237

HERNANDEZ, RAMON   C

PERSONAL: Born May 20, 1976, in Caracas, Venezuela. ... 6-0/210. ... Bats right, throws right. ... Full name: Ramon Jose Hernandez. ... Name pronounced: ruh-MOWN.

TRANSACTIONS/CAREER NOTES: Signed as non-drafted free agent by Oakland Athletics organization (February 18, 1994). ... On Oakland disabled list (July 26-August 27, 1999); included rehabilitation assignment to Vancouver (August 13-27).

2003 GAMES PLAYED BY POSITION (MLB): C—139.

Year	Team (League)	Pos.	G	AB	R	H	2B	3B	HR	RBI	BB	SO	HBP	GDP	SB-CS	Avg.	OBP	SLG	OPS	E	Pct.
1994—	Dom. Athletics (DSL)	C	42	134	24	33	2	0	2	18	18	10	...	...	1-5	.246	...	.306	...	2	.991
1995—	Ariz. A's (Ariz.)	3B-C-1B	48	143	37	52	9	6	4	• 37	* 39	16	8	3	6-2	.364	.510	.594	1.105	12	.972
1996—	W. Mich. (Mid.)	C-DH-1B	123	447	62	114	26	2	12	68	69	62	4	22	2-3	.255	.355	.403	.758	§ 20	.980
1997—	Visalia (Calif.)	C-DH-1B	86	332	57	120	21	2	15	85	35	47	9	5	2-4	.361	* .427	.572	.999	‡ 16	.976
	Huntsville (Sou.)	C-D-1-3	44	161	27	31	3	0	4	24	18	23	3	8	0-0	.193	.281	.286	.567	1	.997

H

Year	Team (League)	Pos.	G	AB	R	H	2B	3B	HR	RBI	BB	SO	HBP	GDP	SB-CS	Avg.	OBP	SLG	OPS	E	Pct.
1998— Huntsville (Sou.)	DH-C-1B	127	479	83	142	24	1	15	98	57	61	19	15	4-5	.296	.389	.445	.833	11	.981
1999— Vancouver (PCL)	C-3B-1B	77	291	38	76	11	3	13	55	23	37	7	13	1-2	.261	.326	.454	.780	5	.987
— Oakland (A.L.)	C	40	136	13	38	7	0	3	21	18	11	1	5	1-0	.279	.363	.397	.760	6	.980
2000— Oakland (A.L.)	C	143	419	52	101	19	0	14	62	38	64	7	14	1-0	.241	.311	.387	.698	* 13	.984
2001— Oakland (A.L.)	C-1B	136	453	55	115	25	0	15	60	37	68	6	10	1-1	.254	.316	.408	.724	12	.988
2002— Oakland (A.L.)	C	136	403	51	94	20	0	7	42	43	64	5	11	0-0	.233	.313	.335	.648	7	.992
2003— Oakland (A.L.)	C	140	483	70	132	24	1	21	78	33	79	12	14	0-0	.273	.331	.458	.789	8	.991
Major League totals (5 years)		595	1894	241	480	95	1	60	263	169	286	31	54	3-1	.253	.322	.400	.721	46	.988

HERNANDEZ, ROBERTO   P

PERSONAL: Born November 11, 1964, in Santurce, Puerto Rico. ... 6-4/250. ... Throws right, bats right. ... Full name: Roberto Manuel Hernandez. ... Name pronounced: her-NAN-dezz. ... High school: New Hampton (N.H.) Prep. ... College: South Carolina.

TRANSACTIONS/CAREER NOTES: Selected by California Angels organization in first round (16th pick overall) of free-agent draft (June 2, 1986); pick received as compensation for Baltimore Orioles signing Type A free-agent OF/IF Juan Beniquez. ... On disabled list (May 6-21 and June 4-August 14, 1987). ... Traded by Angels with OF Mark Doran to Chicago White Sox organization for OF Mark Davis (August 2, 1989). ... On Vancouver disabled list (May 17-August 10, 1991). ... Traded by White Sox with P Wilson Alvarez and P Danny Darwin to San Francisco Giants for SS Mike Caruso, OF Brian Manning, P Lorenzo Barcelo, P Keith Foulke, P Bobby Howry and P Ken Vining (July 31, 1997). ... Granted free agency (October 30, 1997). ... Signed by Tampa Bay Devil Rays (November 18, 1997). ... Traded by Devil Rays to Kansas City Royals as part of three-way deal in which Devil Rays received OF Ben Grieve and a player to be named later or cash from the Oakland Athletics, A's received P Cory Lidle from Devil Rays, A's received OF Johnny Damon, IF Mark Ellis and a player to be named later from Royals and Royals received C A.J. Hinch, IF Angel Berroa and cash from A's (January 8, 2001). ... On Kansas City disabled list (March 22-May 2, 2002); included rehabilitation assignment to Omaha (April 4-8). ... Granted free agency (October 28, 2002). ... Signed by Atlanta Braves (January 22, 2003). ... Placed on 15-day disabled list by Atlanta (June 12, 2003). ... Reinstated from 15-day disabled list (June 27, 2003). ... Sent on rehab assignment by Atlanta (August 18, 2003). ... Recalled from minor league rehab assignment; removed from 15-day disabled list (September 2, 2003).

CAREER HITTING: 1-for-2 (.500), 0 R, 0 2B, 0 3B, 0 HR, 0 RBI.

Year	League	W	L	Pct.	ERA	WHIP	G	GS	CG	ShO	Hld.	Sv.-Opp.	IP	H	R	ER	HR	BB-IBB	SO	Avg.
1986— Salem (NW)	2	2	.500	4.58	1.80	10	10	0	0	...	0-...	55.0	57	37	28	3	42-1	38	...
1987— Quad City (Midw.)	2	3	.400	6.86	1.71	7	6	0	0	...	1-...	21.0	24	21	16	2	12-0	21	.273
1988— Quad City (Midw.)	9	10	.474	3.17	1.24	24	24	6	1	...	0-...	164.2	157	70	58	8	48-0	114	.248
— Midland (Texas)	0	2	.000	6.57	1.95	3	3	0	0	...	0-...	12.1	16	13	9	0	8-0	7	.320
1989— Midland (Texas)	2	7	.222	6.89	1.94	12	12	0	0	...	0-...	64.0	94	57	49	4	30-0	42	.352
— Palm Springs (Calif.)	1	4	.200	4.64	1.52	7	7	0	0	...	0-...	42.2	49	27	22	2	16-0	33	.295
— South Bend (Mid.)	1	1	.500	3.33	1.07	4	4	0	0	...	0-...	24.1	19	9	9	1	7-0	17	.221
1990— Birmingham (Sou.)	8	5	.615	3.67	1.35	17	17	1	0	...	0-...	108.0	103	57	44	6	43-2	62	.251
— Vancouver (PCL)	3	5	.375	2.84	1.25	11	11	3	1	...	0-...	79.1	73	33	25	4	26-0	49	.247
1991— Vancouver (PCL)	4	1	.800	3.22	1.43	7	7	0	0	...	0-...	44.2	41	17	16	2	23-0	40	.241
— GC White Sox (GCL)	0	0	...	0.00	0.33	1	1	0	0	...	0-...	6.0	2	0	0	0	0-0	7	.111
— Birmingham (Sou.)	2	1	.667	1.99	0.75	4	4	0	0	...	0-...	22.2	11	5	5	2	6-0	25	.145
— Chicago (A.L.)	1	0	1.000	7.80	1.67	9	3	0	0	0	0-0	15.0	18	15	13	1	7-0	6	.290
1992— Chicago (A.L.)	7	3	.700	1.65	0.92	43	0	0	0	6	12-16	71.0	45	15	13	4	20-1	68	.180
— Vancouver (PCL)	3	3	.500	2.61	1.16	9	0	0	0	...	2-...	20.2	13	9	6	0	11-1	23	.176
1993— Chicago (A.L.)	3	4	.429	2.29	1.09	70	0	0	0	...	38-44	78.2	66	21	20	6	20-1	71	.228
1994— Chicago (A.L.)	4	4	.500	4.91	1.32	45	0	0	0	...	14-20	47.2	44	29	26	5	19-1	50	.238
1995— Chicago (A.L.)	3	7	.300	3.92	1.53	60	0	0	0	...	32-42	59.2	63	30	26	9	28-4	84	.266
1996— Chicago (A.L.)	6	5	.545	1.91	1.22	72	0	0	0	...	38-46	84.2	65	21	18	2	38-5	85	.208
1997— Chicago (A.L.)	5	1	.833	2.44	1.29	46	0	0	0	0	27-31	48.0	38	15	13	5	24-4	47	.216
— San Francisco (N.L.)	5	2	.714	2.48	1.32	28	0	0	0	9	4-8	32.2	29	9	9	2	14-1	35	.238
1998— Tampa Bay (A.L.)	2	6	.250	4.04	1.35	67	0	0	0	...	26-35	71.1	55	33	32	5	41-4	55	.212
1999— Tampa Bay (A.L.)	2	3	.400	3.07	1.38	72	0	0	0	...	43-47	73.1	68	27	25	1	33-1	69	.245
2000— Tampa Bay (A.L.)	4	7	.364	3.19	1.35	68	0	0	0	1	32-40	73.1	76	33	26	9	23-1	61	.272
2001— Kansas City (A.L.)	5	6	.455	4.12	1.40	63	0	0	0	...	28-34	67.2	69	34	31	7	26-3	46	.266
2002— Omaha (PCL)	0	0	...	0.00	1.50	2	0	0	0	...	0-...	2.0	0	1	0	0	3-0	3	.000
— Kansas City (A.L.)	1	3	.250	4.33	1.42	53	0	0	0	...	26-33	52.0	62	29	25	6	12-2	39	.300
2003— Richmond (Int'l)	1	1	.500	9.45	2.25	6	0	0	0	...	0-...	6.2	11	9	7	0	4-0	5	.333
— Atlanta (N.L.)	5	3	.625	4.35	1.73	66	0	0	0	19	0-4	60.0	61	36	29	10	43-7	45	.263
American League totals (12 years)	43	49	.467	3.25	1.29	668	3	0	0	7	316-388	742.1	669	302	268	60	291-27	681	.239
National League totals (2 years)	10	5	.667	3.69	1.59	94	0	0	0	28	4-12	92.2	90	45	38	12	57-8	80	.254
Major League totals (13 years)	53	54	.495	3.30	1.33	762	3	0	0	35	320-400	835.0	759	347	306	72	348-35	761	.241

HERNANDEZ, RUNELVYS   P

PERSONAL: Born April 27, 1978, in Santo Domingo, Dominican Republic. ... 6-1/205. ... Throws right, bats right. ... Full name: Runelvys Antonio Hernandez.

TRANSACTIONS/CAREER NOTES: Signed as non-drafted free agent by Kansas City Royals organization (December 16, 1997). ... Placed on the 15-day disabled list, retroactive to May 17 (May 27, 2003). ... Sent to Omaha on rehab assignment (June 1, 2003). ... Recalled from Omaha rehab assignment (June 4, 2003). ... Sent on rehab assignment to Wichita (June 20, 2003). ... Recalled from Wichita rehab assignment; reinstated from 15-day disabled list (July 11, 2003). ... Placed on 15-day disabled list; transferred to 60-day disabled list (August 26, 2003).

CAREER HITTING: 0-for-0 (.000), 0 R, 0 2B, 0 3B, 0 HR, 0 RBI.

Year	League	W	L	Pct.	ERA	WHIP	G	GS	CG	ShO	Hld.	Sv.-Opp.	IP	H	R	ER	HR	BB-IBB	SO	Avg.
1998— Dom. Royals (DSL)	0	2	.000	5.34	1.88	19	2	0	0	...	0-...	32.0	31	26	19	...	29-...	27	...
1999— Dom. Royals (DSL)	2	2	.500	3.09	1.25	16	2	0	0	...	5-...	32.0	23	19	11	...	17-...	36	...
2000— Dom. Royals (DSL)	7	3	.700	2.25	1.04	14	10	0	0	...	1-...	72.0	57	25	18	...	18-...	70	...
2001— Burlington (Midw.)	7	5	.583	3.40	1.22	17	17	0	0	...	0-...	100.2	94	46	38	5	29-0	100	.241
2002— Wilmington (Caro.)	1	1	.500	3.75	1.08	2	2	0	0	...	0-...	12.0	12	6	5	0	1-0	9	.273
— Wichita (Texas)	8	3	.727	2.71	1.13	16	14	2	0	...	0-...	106.1	96	38	32	3	24-1	86	.249
— Kansas City (A.L.)	4	4	.500	4.36	1.36	12	12	0	0	0	0-0	74.1	79	36	36	8	22-0	45	.273
2003— Omaha (PCL)	1	0	1.000	1.80	1.00	1	1	0	0	...	0-...	5.0	3	1	1	0	2-0	5	.176
— Wichita (Texas)	0	2	.000	3.86	1.50	2	2	0	0	...	0-...	9.1	9	4	4	0	5-0	5	.257
— Kansas City (A.L.)	7	5	.583	4.61	1.35	16	16	0	0	0	0-0	91.2	87	51	47	9	37-0	48	.249
Major League totals (2 years)	11	9	.550	4.50	1.36	28	28	0	0	0	0-0	166.0	166	87	83	17	59-0	93	.260

H

HERRERA, ALEX   P

PERSONAL: Born November 5, 1976, in Maracaibo, Venezuela. ... 5-11/200. ... Throws left, bats left. ... Full name: Alexander J. Herrera. ... Name pronounced: her-AIR-ah.

TRANSACTIONS/CAREER NOTES: Signed as non-drafted free agent by Cleveland Indians organization (July 4, 1997).

CAREER HITTING: 0-for-0 (.000), 0 R, 0 2B, 0 3B, 0 HR, 0 RBI.

Year	League	W	L	Pct.	ERA	WHIP	G	GS	CG	ShO	Hld.	Sv.-Opp.	IP	H	R	ER	HR	BB-IBB	SO	Avg.
1998—	Guacara 2 (VSL)	7	4	.636	2.30	1.17	18	11	0	0	...	3-...	74.1	70	34	19	...	17-...	68	...
1999—	San Felipe (VSL)	3	2	.600	1.28	1.10	16	9	0	0	...	5-...	56.1	42	19	8	...	20-...	74	...
2000—	Columbus (S. Atl.)	4	3	.571	3.43	1.48	20	0	0	0	...	0-...	42.0	41	25	16	1	21-1	41	.263
	— Kinston (Caro.)	0	1	.000	2.32	1.52	17	0	0	0	...	1-...	31.0	28	11	8	1	19-0	40	.243
	— Akron (East.)	0	0	...	0.00	2.25	2	0	0	0	...	0-...	1.1	2	1	0	0	1-0	1	.400
2001—	Kinston (Caro.)	4	0	1.000	0.60	0.91	28	0	0	0	...	3-...	59.2	36	6	4	1	18-0	83	.171
	— Akron (East.)	3	0	1.000	2.83	1.15	15	0	0	0	...	2-...	28.2	24	9	9	1	9-0	22	.229
2002—	Akron (East.)	0	2	.000	3.38	1.26	30	0	0	0	...	5-...	61.1	47	24	23	8	30-1	65	.212
	— Cleveland (A.L.)	0	0	...	0.00	0.75	5	0	0	0	0	0-0	5.1	3	0	0	0	1-0	5	.158
	— Buffalo (Int'l)	0	1	.000	11.57	2.57	5	0	0	0	...	0-...	7.0	10	9	9	0	8-0	5	.345
2003—	Cleveland (A.L.)	0	0	...	9.00	2.14	10	0	0	0	1	0-0	7.0	7	7	7	3	8-1	6	.250
	— Buffalo (Int'l)	4	6	.400	5.30	1.71	34	0	0	0	...	1-...	56.0	51	40	33	9	45-1	46	.241
	Major League totals (2 years)	0	0	...	5.11	1.54	15	0	0	0	1	0-0	12.1	10	7	7	3	9-1	11	.213

HESSMAN, MIKE   IF/OF

PERSONAL: Born March 5, 1978, in Fountain Valley, Calif. ... 6-5/215. ... Bats right, throws right. ... Full name: Michael Steven Hessman. ... High school: Mater Dei (Santa Ana, Calif.).

TRANSACTIONS/CAREER NOTES: Selected by Atlanta Braves organization in 15th round of free-agent draft (June 4, 1996).

2003 GAMES PLAYED BY POSITION (MLB): OF—8, 1B—4, 3B—3.

Year	Team (League)	Pos.	G	AB	R	H	2B	3B	HR	RBI	BB	SO	HBP	GDP	SB-CS	Avg.	OBP	SLG	OPS	E	Pct.
1996—	GC Braves (GCL)	3B-1B-OF	53	190	13	41	10	1	1	15	12	41	4	0	1-1	.216	.277	.295	.571	11	.949
1997—	Macon (S. Atl.)	3B	122	459	69	108	25	0	21	74	41	167	6	6	0-2	.235	.305	.427	.732	29	.899
1998—	Danville (Caro.)	3B	118	445	47	89	21	0	20	63	30	172	6	6	3-3	.200	.259	.382	.641	18	.934
1999—	Myrtle Beach (Caro.)	3B-SS	103	365	62	90	25	0	23	54	47	135	11	3	0-3	.247	.347	.504	.852	13	.946
2000—	Greenville (Sou.)	3B	127	437	52	80	23	1	19	50	37	178	8	9	3-1	.183	.258	.371	.629	23	.926
2001—	Greenville (Sou.)	3B-OF-1B	129	478	66	110	23	2	26	80	39	124	7	5	2-4	.230	.298	.450	.748	27	.927
2002—	Richmond (Int'l)	3B-1B	134	484	67	127	28	1	26	77	34	107	10	13	1-5	.262	.321	.486	.807	18	.955
2003—	Danville (Appal.)	OF-DH	5	15	1	1	0	0	0	2	2	2	1	0	0-0	.067	.200	.067	.267	0	1.000
	— Richmond (Int'l)	1-OF-3-D	96	359	47	89	15	3	16	52	24	87	4	6	3-1	.248	.296	.440	.736	5	.990
	— Atlanta (N.L.)	OF-1B-3B	19	21	2	6	2	0	2	3	5	6	0	2	0-0	.286	.423	.667	1.090	1	.974
	Major League totals (1 year)		19	21	2	6	2	0	2	3	5	6	0	2	0-0	.286	.423	.667	1.090	1	.974

HIDALGO, RICHARD   OF

PERSONAL: Born July 2, 1975, in Caracas, Venezuela. ... 6-3/220. ... Bats right, throws right. ... Full name: Richard Jose Hidalgo. ... Name pronounced: HUH-dahl-go.

TRANSACTIONS/CAREER NOTES: Signed as non-drafted free agent by Houston Astros organization (July 2, 1991). ... On Houston disabled list (May 30-July 21, 1998); included rehabilitation assignment to New Orleans (July 11-21). ... On disabled list (August 9, 1999-remainder of season). ... On disabled list (August 23-September 9, 2002).

2003 GAMES PLAYED BY POSITION (MLB): OF—137, DH—1.

Year	Team (League)	Pos.	G	AB	R	H	2B	3B	HR	RBI	BB	SO	HBP	GDP	SB-CS	Avg.	OBP	SLG	OPS	E	Pct.
1992—	GC Astros (GCL)	OF	51	184	20	57	7	3	1	27	13	27	3	1	14-5	.310	.360	.397	.756	0	1.000
1993—	Asheville (S. Atl.)	OF	111	403	49	109	23	3	10	55	30	76	4	3	21-13	.270	.324	.417	.740	6	.974
1994—	Quad City (Midw.)	OF	124	476	68	139	* 47	6	12	76	23	80	7	6	12-12	.292	.331	.492	.823	11	.953
1995—	Jackson (Texas)	OF	133	489	59	130	28	6	14	59	32	76	2	11	8-9	.266	.309	.434	.743	5	.981
1996—	Jackson (Texas)	OF-DH	130	513	66	151	34	2	14	78	29	55	11	24	11-7	.294	.341	.450	.791	6	.981
1997—	New Orleans (A.A.)	OF-DH	134	526	74	147	* 37	5	11	78	35	57	8	16	6-10	.279	.330	.432	.761	9	.968
	— Houston (N.L.)	OF	19	62	8	19	5	0	2	6	4	18	1	0	1-0	.306	.358	.484	.842	0	1.000
1998—	Houston (N.L.)	OF	74	211	31	64	15	0	7	35	17	37	2	5	3-3	.303	.355	.474	.829	3	.978
	— New Orleans (PCL)	OF	10	24	0	4	2	0	0	1	3	2	0	3	0-0	.167	.259	.250	.509	0	1.000
1999—	Houston (N.L.)	OF	108	383	49	87	25	2	15	56	56	73	4	5	8-5	.227	.328	.420	.748	2	.993
2000—	Houston (N.L.)	OF	153	558	118	175	42	3	44	122	56	110	21	13	13-6	.314	.391	.636	1.028	7	.984
2001—	Houston (N.L.)	OF	146	512	70	141	29	3	19	80	54	107	16	15	3-5	.275	.356	.455	.811	3	.991
2002—	Houston (N.L.)	OF	114	388	54	91	17	4	15	48	43	85	6	13	6-2	.235	.319	.474	.734	1	.995
2003—	Houston (N.L.)	OF-DH	141	514	91	159	43	4	28	88	58	104	8	10	9-7	.309	.385	.572	.957	4	.987
	Major League totals (7 years)		755	2628	421	736	176	16	130	435	288	534	58	61	43-28	.280	.359	.508	.867	20	.988

HIGGINSON, BOBBY   OF

PERSONAL: Born August 18, 1970, in Philadelphia, Pa. ... 5-11/195. ... Bats left, throws right. ... Full name: Robert Leigh Higginson. ... High school: Frankford (Philadelphia). ... College: Temple.

TRANSACTIONS/CAREER NOTES: Selected by Detroit Tigers organization in 12th round of free-agent draft (June 1, 1992). ... On Detroit disabled list (May 11-June 7, 1996); included rehabilitation assignment to Toledo (June 4-7). ... On disabled list (June 15-26, 1997). ... On suspended list (September 26, 1997). ... On disabled list (July 24-August 24, 1999). ... On suspended list (May 10-16, 2000). ... On disabled list (May 20-June 5, 2001; and June 9-July 11, 2002). ... Placed on 15-day disabled list (June 29, 2003). ... Reinstated from 15-day disabled list (July 25, 2003). ... Suspended by Major League Baseball for two games (August 18, 2003). ... Reinstated (September 4, 2003). ... Suspended by Major League Baseball for two games (September 23, 2003). ... Reinstated (September 25, 2003).

2003 GAMES PLAYED BY POSITION (MLB): OF—118, DH—8.

Year	Team (League)	Pos.	G	AB	R	H	2B	3B	HR	RBI	BB	SO	HBP	GDP	SB-CS	Avg.	OBP	SLG	OPS	E	Pct.
1992—	Niagara Falls (NYP)	OF	70	232	35	68	17	4	2	37	33	44	1	4	12-8	.293	.383	.427	.810	2	.983
1993—	Lakeland (Fla. St.)	OF	61	223	42	67	11	7	3	25	40	31	1	6	8-3	.300	.406	.453	.859	2	.979
	— London (East.)	OF	63	224	25	69	15	4	4	35	19	37	0	6	3-4	.308	.358	.464	.822	2	.982
1994—	Toledo (Int'l)	OF	137	476	81	131	28	3	23	67	46	99	5	9	16-8	.275	.343	.492	.835	8	.973
1995—	Detroit (A.L.)	OF-DH	131	410	61	92	17	5	14	43	62	107	5	5	6-4	.224	.329	.393	.721	4	.985
1996—	Detroit (A.L.)	OF-DH	130	440	75	141	35	0	26	81	65	66	1	7	6-3	.320	.404	.577	.982	9	.963
	— Toledo (Int'l)	OF	3	13	4	4	0	0	1	0	3	0	1	0	0-0	.308	.438	.462	.899	0	1.000

H

Year	Team (League)	Pos.	G	AB	R	H	2B	3B	HR	RBI	BB	SO	HBP	GDP	SB-CS	Avg.	OBP	SLG	OPS	E	Pct.
														BATTING						FIELDING	
1997—Detroit (A.L.)	OF-DH	146	546	94	163	30	5	27	101	70	85	3	10	12-7	.299	.379	.520	.899	9	.972
1998—Detroit (A.L.)	OF-DH	157	612	92	174	37	4	25	85	63	101	6	16	3-3	.284	.355	.480	.835	6	.982
1999—Detroit (A.L.)	OF-DH	107	377	51	90	18	0	12	46	64	66	2	2	4-6	.239	.351	.382	.733	3	.983
2000—Detroit (A.L.)	OF-DH	154	597	104	179	44	4	30	102	74	99	2	5	15-3	.300	.377	.538	.915	7	.979
2001—Detroit (A.L.)	OF-DH	147	541	84	150	28	6	17	71	80	65	2	8	20-12	.277	.367	.445	.813	8	.976
2002—Detroit (A.L.)	OF-DH	119	444	50	125	24	3	10	63	41	45	6	8	12-5	.282	.345	.417	.762	7	.973
2003—Detroit (A.L.)	OF-DH	130	469	61	110	13	4	14	52	59	73	3	12	8-8	.235	.320	.369	.689	5	.981
Major League totals (9 years)		1221	4436	672	1224	246	31	175	644	578	707	30	73	86-51	.276	.360	.464	.823	58	.977

HILL, BOBBY   2B

PERSONAL: Born April 3, 1978, in San Jose, Calif. ... 5-10/190. ... Bats both, throws right. ... Full name: William Robert Hill. ... High school: Leland (Calif.). ... College: Miami (Fla.).

TRANSACTIONS/CAREER NOTES: Selected by California Angels organization in fifth round of free-agent draft (June 4, 1996); did not sign. ... Selected by Chicago White Sox organization in second round of free-agent draft (June 2, 1999); did not sign. ... Selected by Chicago Cubs organization in second round of free-agent draft (June 5, 2000). ... Played with Newark, Atlantic League (2000). ... On West Tenn disabled list (May 4-19 and June 13-August 8, 2001). ... Traded to Pittsburgh Pirates to complete an earlier trade; optioned to Nashville (August 15, 2003).

2003 GAMES PLAYED BY POSITION (MLB): 2B—3.

Year	Team (League)	Pos.	G	AB	R	H	2B	3B	HR	RBI	BB	SO	HBP	GDP	SB-CS	Avg.	OBP	SLG	OPS	E	Pct.
2000—Newark (Atl.)	SS	132	481	109	157	22	9	13	82	101	57	4	...	81-15	.326	.442	.491	.933	38	...
2001—West Tenn (Sou.)	2B-SS	57	209	30	63	8	1	3	21	32	39	2	7	20-8	.301	.396	.392	.788	6	.973
—Ariz. Cubs (Ariz.)	2B	3	9	1	2	0	0	0	1	2	3	0	0	1-0	.222	.364	.222	.586	0	1.000
2002—Iowa (PCL)	2B	92	354	80	99	23	3	8	39	49	66	11	7	29-5	.280	.382	.429	.812	6	.986
—Chicago (N.L.)	2B-SS	59	190	26	48	7	2	4	20	17	42	4	0	6-1	.253	.327	.374	.701	3	.986
2003—Chicago (N.L.)	2B	5	4	0	1	0	0	0	0	1	2	0	1	0-0	.250	.400	.250	.650	0	1.000
—Iowa (PCL)	2B-3B	92	361	53	104	23	4	6	40	37	65	8	5	8-7	.288	.365	.424	.789	11	.973
—Nashville (PCL)	2B-DH	17	66	5	11	2	1	1	4	8	8	0	2	1-2	.167	.257	.273	.529	0	1.000
—Pittsburgh (N.L.)	2B	1	3	1	1	0	0	0	0	1	0	0	0	0-0	.333	.500	.333	.833	0	1.000
Major League totals (2 years)		65	197	27	50	7	2	4	20	19	44	4	1	6-1	.254	.332	.371	.702	3	.986

HILL, JEREMY   P

PERSONAL: Born August 8, 1977, in Dallas, Texas. ... 5-11/200. ... Throws right, bats right. ... Full name: Jeremy Dee Hill. ... High school: W.T. White (Dallas).

TRANSACTIONS/CAREER NOTES: Selected by Kansas City Royals organization in fifth round of free-agent draft (June 4, 1996). ... Traded by Royals to New York Mets for P Graeme Lloyd (July 28, 2003).

CAREER HITTING: 0-for-0 (.000), 0 R, 0 2B, 0 3B, 0 HR, 0 RBI.

Year	League	W	L	Pct.	ERA	WHIP	G	GS	CG	ShO	Hld.	Sv.-Opp.	IP	H	R	ER	HR	BB-IBB	SO	Avg.
2001—Burlington (Midw.)	0	2	.000	1.51	0.99	40	0	0	0	...	12-...	47.2	22	11	8	2	25-0	66	.138
—Wilmington (Caro.)	4	0	1.000	0.73	1.46	9	0	0	0	...	2-...	12.1	10	2	1	0	8-1	13	.233
2002—Wichita (Texas)	4	7	.364	2.36	1.22	56	0	0	0	...	19-...	76.1	61	26	20	4	32-5	80	.221
—Kansas City (A.L.)	0	1	.000	3.86	1.71	10	0	0	0	0	0-0	9.1	8	4	4	1	8-1	7	.235
2003—Kansas City (A.L.)	0	0	...	0.00	1.00	1	0	0	0	0	0-0	1.0	1	0	0	0	0-0	0	.250
—Omaha (PCL)	1	3	.250	7.81	2.08	26	1	0	0	...	1-...	40.1	42	38	35	5	42-0	41	.275
—Wichita (Texas)	0	0	...	0.00	1.50	2	0	0	0	...	0-...	2.0	0	1	0	0	3-0	3	.000
—Binghamton (Eastern)	0	2	.000	10.38	2.23	11	0	0	0	...	0-...	13.0	14	15	15	3	15-2	10	.269
Major League totals (2 years)	0	1	.000	3.48	1.65	11	0	0	0	0	0-0	10.1	9	4	4	1	8-1	7	.237

HILL, KOYIE   C

PERSONAL: Born March 9, 1979, in Tulsa, Okla. ... 6-0/190. ... Bats both, throws right. ... Full name: Koyie Dolan Hill. ... Name pronounced: koy. ... High school: Eisenhower High (Lawton, OK). ... College: Wichita State.

TRANSACTIONS/CAREER NOTES: Selected by Los Angeles Dodgers organization in fourth round of free-agent draft (June 5, 2000).

Year	Team (League)	Pos.	G	AB	R	H	2B	3B	HR	RBI	BB	SO	HBP	GDP	SB-CS	Avg.	OBP	SLG	OPS	E	Pct.
2000—Yakima (N'west)	3B-C-2B	64	251	26	65	13	1	2	29	25	47	0	7	0-7	.259	.324	.343	.666	8	.941
2001—Wilmington (Caro.)	C	134	498	65	150	20	2	8	79	49	82	7	7	21-12	.301	.368	.398	.766	18	.977
2002—Jacksonville (Sou.)	C	130	468	67	127	25	1	11	64	76	88	0	14	5-3	.271	.368	.400	.768	17	.981
2003—Jacksonville (Sou.)	C-DH	25	101	9	23	7	0	0	7	6	19	0	3	2-1	.228	.271	.297	.568	2	.989
—Las Vegas (PCL)	C-DH-1B	85	312	48	98	18	0	3	36	15	39	1	7	5-0	.314	.345	.401	.746	9	.982
—Los Angeles (N.L.)	C	3	3	0	1	1	0	0	0	0	2	0	0	0-0	.333	.333	.667	1.000	0	...
Major League totals (1 year)		3	3	0	1	1	0	0	0	0	2	0	0	0-0	.333	.333	.667	1.000	0	...

HILLENBRAND, SHEA   1B/3B

PERSONAL: Born July 27, 1975, in Mesa, Ariz. ... 6-1/211. ... Bats right, throws right. ... Full name: Shea Matthew Hillenbrand. ... Name pronounced: SHAY. ... High school: Mountain View (Mesa, Ariz.). ... Junior college: Mesa (Ari.) Community College.

TRANSACTIONS/CAREER NOTES: Selected by Boston Red Sox organization in 10th round of free-agent draft (June 4, 1996). ... On Trenton disabled list (July 5-August 31, 1999). ... On Boston disabled list (August 31, 1999-remainder of season). ... Granted free agency (December 21, 1999). ... Re-signed by Red Sox organization (January 29, 2000). ... Traded by Red Sox to Arizona Diamondbacks for P Byung-Hyun Kim (May 29, 2003). ... Placed on 15-day disabled list (June 9, 2003). ... Sent to Tucson for rehab assignment (June 26, 2003). ... Reinstated from 15-day disabled list (June 29, 2003). ... Recalled from Tucson rehab assignment (June 30, 2003).

2003 GAMES PLAYED BY POSITION (MLB): 1B—84, 3B—63, DH—2.

Year	Team (League)	Pos.	G	AB	R	H	2B	3B	HR	RBI	BB	SO	HBP	GDP	SB-CS	Avg.	OBP	SLG	OPS	E	Pct.
1996—Lowell (NY-Penn)	3B-SS-1B	72	279	33	88	18	2	2	38	18	32	8	6	4-3	.315	.371	.416	.787	‡ 33	.938
1997—Michigan (Midw.)	3B-1B	64	224	28	65	13	3	3	39	4	20	1	2	1-3	.290	.315	.415	.730	8	.950
—Sarasota (Fla. St.)	3B-1B	57	220	25	65	12	0	2	28	7	29	2	4	9-8	.295	.320	.377	.698	20	.926
1998—Michigan (Midw.)	3B-C-1B	129	498	80	174	33	4	19	93	19	49	10	11	13-7	.349	.383	.546	.929	14	.982
1999—Trenton (East.)	C	69	282	41	73	15	0	7	36	14	27	3	6	6-5	.259	.298	.387	.685	5	.987
2000—Trenton (East.)	1B-3B	135	529	77	* 171	35	3	11	79	19	39	8	15	3-3	.323	.355	.463	.818	15	.979

H

Year	Team (League)	Pos.	G	AB	R	H	2B	3B	HR	RBI	BB	SO	HBP	GDP	SB-CS	Avg.	OBP	SLG	OPS	E	Pct.
								BATTING												FIELDING	
2001—Boston (A.L.) 3B-1B-DH			139	468	52	123	20	2	12	49	13	61	7	12	3-4	.263	.291	.391	.682	18	.950
2002—Boston (A.L.)	3B		156	634	94	186	43	4	18	83	25	95	12	18	4-2	.293	.330	.459	.789	* 23	.943
2003—Boston (A.L.) 3B-1B-DH			49	185	20	56	17	0	3	38	7	26	4	9	1-0	.303	.335	.443	.778	3	.989
—Tucson (PCL) 3B-1B			3	10	0	3	1	0	0	1	0	1	0	0	0-0	.300	.300	.400	.700	0	1.000
—Arizona (N.L.) 1B-3B			85	330	40	88	18	1	17	59	17	44	2	13	0-0	.267	.302	.482	.784	12	.978
American League totals (3 years)			344	1287	166	365	80	6	33	170	45	182	23	39	8-6	.284	.317	.432	.749	44	.958
National League totals (1 year)			85	330	40	88	18	1	17	59	17	44	2	13	0-0	.267	.302	.482	.784	12	.978
Major League totals (3 years)			429	1617	206	453	98	7	50	229	62	226	25	52	8-6	.280	.314	.442	.756	56	.965

HINCH, A.J.   C

PERSONAL: Born May 15, 1974, in Waverly, Iowa. ... 6-1/200. ... Bats right, throws right. ... Full name: Andrew Jay Hinch. ... High school: Midwest City (Okla.). ... College: Stanford.

TRANSACTIONS/CAREER NOTES: Selected by Chicago White Sox organization in second round of free-agent draft (June 2, 1992); did not sign. ... Selected by Minnesota Twins organization in third round of free-agent draft (June 1, 1995); did not sign. ... Selected by Oakland Athletics organization in third round of free-agent draft (June 4, 1996). ... On Modesto suspended list (June 7-9, 1997). ... Traded by A's with IF Angel Berroa and cash to Kansas City Royals as part of three-way deal in which Royals received P Roberto Hernandez from Tampa Bay Devil Rays, A's received P Cory Lidle from Devil Rays, A's received OF Johnny Damon, IF Mark Ellis and a player to be named later from Royals and Devil Rays received OF Ben Grieve and a player to be named later or cash from A's (January 8, 2001). ... Released by Royals (October 15, 2002). ... Signed by Cleveland Indians organization (December 23, 2002). ... Traded by Indians to Detroit Tigers for a player to be named later (March 30, 2003). ... Contract purchased from Toledo (June 18, 2003). ... Placed on 15-day disabled list (July 18, 2003). ... Reinstated from 15-day disabled list (August 3, 2003). ... Placed on 15-day disabled list; recalled from Toledo (August 6, 2003) ... Sent on minor league rehab assignment (August 24, 2003). ... Recalled from minor league rehab assignment; removed from 15-day disabled list (September 1, 2003).

2003 GAMES PLAYED BY POSITION (MLB): C—27.

Year	Team (League)	Pos.	G	AB	R	H	2B	3B	HR	RBI	BB	SO	HBP	GDP	SB-CS	Avg.	OBP	SLG	OPS	E	Pct.
								BATTING												FIELDING	
1997—Modesto (Calif.)	C-DH-1B		95	333	70	103	25	3	20	73	42	68	11	9	8-3	.309	.400	.583	.983	3	.996
—Edmonton (PCL)	C-DH-OF		39	125	23	47	7	0	4	24	20	13	3	7	2-0	.376	.473	.528	1.001	3	.986
1998—Oakland (A.L.)	C		120	337	34	78	10	0	9	35	30	89	4	6	3-0	.231	.296	.341	.638	• 9	.986
1999—Oakland (A.L.)	C		76	205	26	44	4	1	7	24	11	41	2	4	6-2	.215	.260	.346	.607	5	.987
—Vancouver (PCL)	C		15	61	9	23	3	0	2	7	3	12	1	0	1-1	.377	.415	.525	.940	1	.989
2000—Sacramento (PCL)	C-1B		109	417	65	111	23	2	6	47	45	67	7	8	5-5	.266	.344	.374	.718	4	.994
—Oakland (A.L.)	C-DH		6	8	1	2	0	0	0	0	1	1	0	0	0-0	.250	.333	.250	.583	1	.900
2001—Kansas City (A.L.)	C-DH		45	121	10	19	3	0	6	15	8	26	3	5	1-1	.157	.226	.331	.556	3	.987
—Omaha (PCL)	C-OF		45	168	28	54	14	0	10	33	11	33	1	5	1-0	.321	.365	.583	.948	1	.995
2002—Kansas City (A.L.)	C		72	197	25	49	7	1	7	27	18	35	3	2	3-3	.249	.321	.401	.722	4	.989
2003—Toledo (Int'l)	C-D-1-3		55	185	20	48	15	1	4	23	13	38	4	2	0-1	.259	.320	.416	.736	3	.991
—Detroit (A.L.)	C		27	74	7	15	3	1	3	11	3	18	2	3	0-0	.203	.247	.392	.639	2	.983
Major League totals (6 years)			346	942	103	207	27	3	32	112	71	210	14	20	13-6	.220	.281	.357	.638	24	.987

HINSKE, ERIC   3B

PERSONAL: Born August 5, 1977, in Menasha, Wis. ... 6-2/225. ... Bats left, throws right. ... Full name: Eric Scott Hinske. ... Name pronounced: hin-SKEE. ... High school: Menasha (Wisc.). ... College: Arkansas.

TRANSACTIONS/CAREER NOTES: Selected by Chicago Cubs organization in 17th round of free-agent draft (June 2, 1998). ... Traded by Cubs to Oakland Athletics for 2B Miguel Cairo (March 28, 2001). ... On disabled list (May 1-12, 2001). ... Traded by A's with P Justin Miller to Toronto Blue Jays for P Billy Koch (December 7, 2001). ... Placed on 15-day disabled list (May 24, 2003). ... Sent to Syracuse on rehab assignment (June 24, 2003). ... Recalled from Syracuse rehab assignment; reinstated from 15-day disabled list (June 26, 2003).

2003 GAMES PLAYED BY POSITION (MLB): 3B—124.

Year	Team (League)	Pos.	G	AB	R	H	2B	3B	HR	RBI	BB	SO	HBP	GDP	SB-CS	Avg.	OBP	SLG	OPS	E	Pct.
								BATTING												FIELDING	
1998—Will. (NYP)	1B		68	248	46	74	20	0	9	57	35	61	2	2	19-3	.298	.384	.488	.872	2	.997
—Rockford (Midwest)	1B		6	20	8	9	4	0	1	4	5	6	0	0	1-0	.450	.538	.800	1.338	0	1.000
1999—Daytona (Fla. St.)	3B-1B-OF		130	445	76	132	28	6	19	79	62	90	5	5	16-10	.297	.385	.515	.900	22	.965
—Iowa (PCL)	3B-1B		4	15	3	4	0	1	1	2	1	4	0	0	0-0	.267	.313	.600	.913	1	.952
2000—West Tenn (Sou.)	3B-1B-OF		131	436	76	113	21	9	20	73	78	133	3	7	14-5	.259	.373	.486	.859	28	.916
2001—Sacramento (PCL)	3B-2B		121	436	71	123	27	1	25	79	54	113	10	6	20-7	.282	.373	.521	.893	17	.941
2002—Toronto (A.L.)	3B		151	566	99	158	38	2	24	84	77	138	2	12	13-1	.279	.365	.481	.845	20	.946
2003—Syracuse (Int'l)	3B		2	8	2	4	1	0	1	2	0	0	0	0	0-0	.500	.500	1.000	1.500	0	1.000
—Toronto (A.L.)	3B		124	449	74	109	45	3	12	63	59	104	1	11	12-2	.243	.329	.437	.765	22	.930
Major League totals (2 years)			275	1015	173	267	83	5	36	147	136	242	3	23	25-3	.263	.349	.461	.810	42	.939

HITCHCOCK, STERLING   P

PERSONAL: Born April 29, 1971, in Fayetteville, N.C. ... 6-0/200. ... Throws left, bats left. ... Full name: Sterling Alex Hitchcock. ... High school: Armwood (Seffner, Fla.).

TRANSACTIONS/CAREER NOTES: Selected by New York Yankees organization in ninth round of free-agent draft (June 5, 1989). ... On disabled list (June 26-August 14, 1991). ... On Columbus disabled list (May 23-July 21, 1993). ... Traded by Yankees with 3B Russ Davis to Seattle Mariners for 1B Tino Martinez, P Jeff Nelson and P Jim Mecir (December 7, 1995). ... Traded by Mariners to San Diego Padres for P Scott Sanders (December 6, 1996). ... On disabled list (June 6-July 3, 1997; and May 27, 2000-remainder of season). ... On San Diego disabled list (March 27-July 4, 2001); included rehabilitation assignments to Lake Elsinore (April 5-27 and June 14-18) and Portland (June 19-July 4). ... Traded by Padres to Yankees for P Brett Jodie and OF Darren Blakely (July 30, 2001). ... Granted free agency (November 6, 2001). ... Re-signed by Yankees (December 19, 2001). ... On New York disabled list (March 22-May 8 and June 28-July 18, 2002); included rehabilitation assignments to Tampa (April 25-29), Columbus (April 30-May 8) and Gulf Coast Yankees (July 25-28). ... Traded by Yankees to St. Louis Cardinals for P Justin Pope, and P Ben Julianel (August 22, 2003).

CAREER HITTING: 19-for-203 (.094), 14 R, 0 2B, 0 3B, 0 HR, 5 RBI.

Year	League	W	L	Pct.	ERA	WHIP	G	GS	CG	ShO	Hld.	Sv.-Opp.	IP	H	R	ER	HR	BB-IBB	SO	Avg.
1989—GC Yankees (GCL)		* 9	1	.900	1.64	0.98	13	• 13	0	0	...	0-...	76.2	48	16	14	1	27-0	* 98	.182
1990—Greensboro (S. Atl.)		12	12	.500	2.91	1.05	27	27	6	* 5	...	0-...	173.1	122	68	56	7	60-1	* 171	.197
1991—Prince William (Caro.)		7	7	.500	2.64	1.15	19	19	2	0	...	0-...	119.1	111	49	35	2	26-0	101	.239
1992—Alb./Colon. (East.)		6	9	.400	2.58	1.08	24	24	1	0	...	0-...	146.2	116	51	42	6	42-0	* 155	.213
—New York (A.L.)		0	2	.000	8.31	2.23	3	3	0	0	0	0-0	13.0	23	12	12	2	6-0	6	.377
1993—Columbus (Int'l)		3	5	.375	4.81	1.41	16	16	0	0	...	0-...	76.2	80	43	41	8	28-0	85	.267
—Oneonta (N.Y.-Penn)		0	0	...	0.00	1.00	1	0	0	0	...	0-...	1.0	0	0	0	0	0-0	0	.000
—New York (A.L.)		1	2	.333	4.65	1.48	6	6	0	0	0	0-0	31.0	32	18	16	4	14-1	26	.271

H

Year League	W	L	Pct.	ERA	WHIP	G	GS	CG	ShO	Hld.	Sv.-Opp.	IP	H	R	ER	HR	BB-IBB	SO	Avg.
1994— New York (A.L.)	4	1	.800	4.20	1.56	23	5	1	0	3	2-2	49.1	48	24	23	3	29-1	37	.265
—Columbus (Int'l)	3	4	.429	4.32	1.42	10	9	1	0	...	0-...	50.0	53	30	24	4	18-0	47	.265
—Alb./Colon. (East.)	1	0	1.000	1.80	0.80	1	1	0	0	...	0-...	5.0	4	1	1	0	0-0	7	.235
1995— New York (A.L.)	11	10	.524	4.70	1.32	27	27	4	1	0	0-0	168.1	155	91	88	22	68-1	121	.245
1996— Seattle (A.L.)	13	9	.591	5.35	1.62	35	35	0	0	0	0-0	196.2	245	131	117	27	73-4	132	.309
1997— San Diego (N.L.)	10	11	.476	5.20	1.41	32	28	1	0	0	0-0	161.0	172	102	93	24	55-2	106	.276
1998— San Diego (N.L.)	9	7	.563	3.93	1.23	39	27	2	1	3	1-2	176.1	169	83	77	29	48-2	158	.251
1999— San Diego (N.L.)	12	14	.462	4.11	1.35	33	33	1	0	0	0-0	205.2	202	99	94	29	76-6	194	.254
2000— San Diego (N.L.)	1	6	.143	4.93	1.45	11	11	0	0	0	0-0	65.2	69	38	36	12	26-1	61	.267
2001— Lake Elsinore (Calif.)	0	2	.000	4.10	1.29	6	6	0	0	...	0-...	26.1	33	18	12	3	1-0	31	.292
—Portland (PCL)	2	0	1.000	3.71	1.29	3	3	0	0	...	0-...	17.0	20	7	7	1	2-0	11	.308
—San Diego (N.L.)	2	1	.667	3.32	1.32	3	3	0	0	0	0-0	19.0	22	9	7	1	3-0	15	.275
—New York (A.L.)	4	4	.500	6.49	1.66	10	9	1	0	0	0-0	51.1	67	37	37	5	18-0	28	.315
2002— Tampa (FSL)	0	0	...	1.50	0.50	1	1	0	0	...	0-...	6.0	3	1	1	0	0-0	3	.150
—Columbus (Int'l)	0	0	...	13.50	3.00	2	2	0	0	...	0-...	7.1	19	11	11	2	3-0	3	.487
—New York (A.L.)	1	2	.333	5.49	1.83	20	2	0	0	0	0-0	39.1	57	29	24	4	15-3	31	.326
—GC Yankees (GCL)	0	0	...	0.00	0.00	2	2	0	0	...	0-...	3.0	0	0	0	0	0-0	6	.000
2003— New York (A.L.)	1	3	.250	5.44	1.51	27	1	0	0	2	0-0	49.2	57	33	30	6	18-3	36	.285
—St. Louis (N.L.)	5	1	.833	3.79	1.26	8	6	0	0	0	0-0	38.0	34	17	16	8	14-1	32	.238
American League totals (8 years)	**35**	**33**	**.515**	**5.22**	**1.55**	**151**	**88**	**6**	**1**	**5**	**2-2**	**598.2**	**684**	**375**	**347**	**73**	**241-13**	**417**	**.288**
National League totals (6 years)	**39**	**40**	**.494**	**4.37**	**1.34**	**126**	**108**	**4**	**1**	**3**	**1-2**	**665.2**	**668**	**348**	**323**	**103**	**222-12**	**566**	**.260**
Major League totals (12 years)	**74**	**73**	**.503**	**4.77**	**1.44**	**277**	**196**	**10**	**2**	**8**	**3-4**	**1264.1**	**1352**	**723**	**670**	**176**	**463-25**	**983**	**.273**

HOCKING, DENNY   IF

PERSONAL: Born April 2, 1970, in Torrance, Calif. ... 5-10/187. ... Bats both, throws right. ... Full name: Dennis Lee Hocking. ... Name pronounced: HAWK-ing. ... High school: West Torrance (Calif.). ... Junior college: El Camino (Calif.) Community College.

TRANSACTIONS/CAREER NOTES: Selected by Minnesota Twins organization in 52nd round of free-agent draft (June 5, 1989). ... On Nashville disabled list (April 8-29, 1993). ... On Minnesota disabled list (March 22-April 30, May 30-June 29 and July 31-September 8, 1996); included rehabilitation assignments to Salt Lake (April 4-30, June 21-29 and August 24-September 8). ... Placed on the 15-day disabled list (April 22, 2003). ... Reinstated from 15-day disabled list (May 9, 2003).

2003 GAMES PLAYED BY POSITION (MLB): 2B—26, 3B—24, SS—17, 1B—10, OF—8, DH—2.

										BATTING									FIELDING	
Year Team (League)	Pos.	G	AB	R	H	2B	3B	HR	RBI	BB	SO	HBP	GDP	SB-CS	Avg.	OBP	SLG	OPS	E	Pct.
1990— Elizabethton (App.) 2B-3B-SS		54	201	45	59	6	2	6	30	40	26	6	6	14-4	.294	.422	.433	.855	20	.928
1991— Kenosha (Midw.)	SS	125	432	72	110	17	8	2	36	77	69	6	6	22-10	.255	.372	.345	.717	42	.923
1992— Visalia (Calif.)	SS	135	*550	117	*182	34	9	7	81	72	77	8	7	38-18	.331	.415	.464	.878	38	.947
1993— Nashville (Sou.)	SS	107	409	54	109	9	4	8	50	34	66	4	12	15-5	.267	.327	.367	.694	30	.937
—Minnesota (A.L.)	SS-2B	15	36	7	5	1	0	0	0	6	8	0	1	1-0	.139	.262	.167	.429	1	.977
1994— Salt Lake (PCL)	SS	112	394	61	110	14	6	5	57	28	57	2	6	13-7	.279	.327	.383	.710	26	.949
—Minnesota (A.L.)	SS	11	31	3	10	3	0	0	2	0	4	0	1	2-0	.323	.323	.419	.742	1	1.000
1995— Salt Lake (PCL) SS-2B-DH		117	397	51	112	24	2	8	75	25	41	2	10	12-8	.282	.324	.413	.737	20	.966
—Minnesota (A.L.)	SS	9	25	4	5	0	0	0	3	2	2	0	1	1-0	.200	.259	.360	.619	1	.971
1996— Salt Lake (PCL) S-0-D-2-3-1		37	130	18	36	6	2	3	22	10	17	2	4	2-2	.277	.333	.423	.756	3	.976
—Minnesota (A.L.) O-S-2-D-1		49	127	16	25	6	0	1	10	8	24	0	3	3-3	.197	.243	.268	.510	1	.987
1997— Minnesota (A.L.) S-3-0-2-D-1		115	253	28	65	12	4	2	25	18	51	1	6	3-5	.257	.308	.360	.667	4	.985
1998— Minnesota (A.L.) 2-S-0-3-D-1		110	198	32	40	6	1	3	15	16	44	0	2	2-1	.202	.259	.288	.547	4	.982
1999— Minnesota (A.L.) S-2-0-3-1		136	386	47	103	18	2	7	41	22	54	3	10	11-7	.267	.307	.378	.685	3	.992
2000— Minnesota (A.L.) 0-2-3-S-1-D		134	373	52	111	24	4	4	47	48	77	0	2	7-5	.298	.373	.416	.789	5	.985
2001— Minnesota (A.L.) S-2-0-1-D-3		112	327	34	82	16	2	3	25	29	67	2	7	6-1	.251	.315	.339	.654	5	.984
2002— Minnesota (A.L.) 2-S-3-1-O		102	260	28	65	13	0	2	25	24	44	1	3	0-2	.250	.310	.323	.633	10	.968
2003— Minnesota (A.L.) 2-3-S-1-O-D		83	188	22	45	10	2	3	22	15	37	0	3	0-1	.239	.291	.362	.653	3	.988
Major League totals (11 years)		**876**	**2204**	**273**	**556**	**109**	**17**	**25**	**215**	**188**	**412**	**7**	**39**	**36-25**	**.252**	**.310**	**.351**	**.661**	**37**	**.984**

HODGES, TREY   P

PERSONAL: Born June 29, 1978, in Houston, Texas. ... 6-3/187. ... Throws right, bats right. ... Full name: Trey Alan Hodges.

TRANSACTIONS/CAREER NOTES: Selected by Atlanta Braves organization in 17th round of free-agent draft (June 5, 2000). ... Placed on the 15-day disabled list, retroactive to July 27 (July 28, 2003). ... Reinstated from 15-day disabled list (August 13, 2003).

CAREER HITTING: 0-for-8 (.000), 0 R, 0 2B, 0 3B, 0 HR, 0 RBI.

Year League	W	L	Pct.	ERA	WHIP	G	GS	CG	ShO	Hld.	Sv.-Opp.	IP	H	R	ER	HR	BB-IBB	SO	Avg.
2000— Jamestown (NYP)	0	2	.000	5.95	1.73	13	2	0	0	...	0-...	19.2	22	14	13	3	12-0	13	.278
2001— Myrtle Beach (Caro.)	*15	8	.652	2.76	1.01	26	26	1	0	...	0-...	*173.0	156	64	53	13	18-0	139	.237
2002— Richmond (Int'l)	*15	9	.625	3.19	1.24	28	28	1	1	...	0-...	172.1	158	66	61	9	56-1	116	.247
—Atlanta (N.L.)	2	0	1.000	5.40	1.54	4	0	0	0	0	0-0	11.2	16	7	7	2	2-0	6	.348
2003— Atlanta (N.L.)	3	3	.500	4.66	1.52	52	1	0	0	4	0-2	65.2	69	38	34	11	31-7	66	.268
Major League totals (2 years)	**5**	**3**	**.625**	**4.77**	**1.53**	**56**	**1**	**0**	**0**	**4**	**0-2**	**77.1**	**85**	**45**	**41**	**13**	**33-7**	**72**	**.281**

HOFFMAN, TREVOR   P

PERSONAL: Born October 13, 1967, in Bellflower, Calif. ... 6-0/205. ... Throws right, bats right. ... Full name: Trevor William Hoffman. ... High school: Savanna (Anaheim). ... College: Arizona.

TRANSACTIONS/CAREER NOTES: Selected by Cincinnati Reds organization in 11th round of free-agent draft (June 5, 1989). ... Selected by Florida Marlins in first round (eighth pick overall) of expansion draft (November 17, 1992). ... Traded by Marlins with P Jose Martinez and P Andres Berumen to San Diego Padres for 3B Gary Sheffield and P Rich Rodriguez (June 24, 1993). ... On disabled list (March 25, 2003). ... Sent on minor league rehab assignment (August 23, 2003). ... Recalled from minor league rehab assignment; removed from 60-day disabled list (September 2, 2003).

CAREER HITTING: 4-for-33 (.121), 1 R, 2 2B, 0 3B, 0 HR, 5 RBI.

H

Year	League	W	L	Pct.	ERA	WHIP	G	GS	CG	ShO	Hld.	Sv.-Opp.	IP	H	R	ER	HR	BB-IBB	SO	Avg.
1991— Cedar Rapids (Midw.)		1	1	.500	1.87	1.04	27	0	0	0	...	12-...	33.2	22	8	7	0	13-0	52	.188
—Chattanooga (Sou.)		1	0	1.000	1.93	1.21	14	0	0	0	...	8-...	14.0	10	4	3	0	7-0	23	.192
1992— Chattanooga (Sou.)		3	0	1.000	1.52	1.11	6	6	0	0	...	0-...	29.2	22	6	5	1	11-1	31	.212
—Nashville (A.A.)		4	6	.400	4.27	1.36	42	5	0	0	...	6-...	65.1	57	32	31	6	32-3	63	.234
1993— Florida (N.L.)		2	2	.500	3.28	1.21	28	0	0	0	8	2-3	35.2	24	13	13	5	19-7	26	.185
—San Diego (N.L.)		2	4	.333	4.31	1.40	39	0	0	0	7	3-5	54.1	56	30	26	5	20-6	53	.264
1994— San Diego (N.L.)		4	4	.500	2.57	1.05	47	0	0	0	1	20-23	56.0	39	16	16	4	20-6	68	.193
1995— San Diego (N.L.)		7	4	.636	3.88	1.16	55	0	0	0	0	31-38	53.1	48	25	23	10	14-3	52	.235
1996— San Diego (N.L.)		9	5	.643	2.25	0.92	70	0	0	0	0	42-49	88.0	50	23	22	6	31-5	111	.161
1997— San Diego (N.L.)		6	4	.600	2.66	1.02	70	0	0	0	0	37-44	81.1	59	25	24	9	24-4	111	.200
1998— San Diego (N.L.)		4	2	.667	1.48	0.85	66	0	0	0	0	* 53-54	73.0	41	12	12	2	21-2	86	.165
1999— San Diego (N.L.)		2	3	.400	2.14	0.94	64	0	0	0	0	40-43	67.1	48	23	16	5	15-2	73	.197
2000— San Diego (N.L.)		4	7	.364	2.99	0.00	70	0	0	0	0	43-50	72.1	61	29	24	7	11-4	85	.224
2001— San Diego (N.L.)		3	4	.429	3.43	1.14	62	0	0	0	0	43-46	60.1	48	25	23	10	21-2	63	.216
2002— San Diego (N.L.)		2	5	.286	2.73	1.18	61	0	0	0	0	38-41	59.1	52	20	18	2	18-2	69	.234
2003— Lake Elsinore (Calif.)		0	0	...	0.00	0.67	3	0	0	0	...	0-...	3.0	2	0	0	0	0-0	4	.182
—San Diego (N.L.)		0	0	...	2.00	1.11	9	0	0	0	0	0-0	9.0	7	2	2	1	3-0	11	.212
Major League totals (11 years)		45	44	.506	2.78	1.06	641	0	0	0	16	352-396	710.0	533	243	219	66	217-43	808	.205

HOLLANDSWORTH, TODD — OF

PERSONAL: Born April 20, 1973, in Dayton, Ohio. ... 6-2/225. ... Bats left, throws left. ... Full name: Todd Mathew Hollandsworth. ... Name pronounced: HAHL-enz-worth. ... High school: Newport (Bellevue, Wash.).

TRANSACTIONS/CAREER NOTES: Selected by Los Angeles Dodgers organization in third round of free-agent draft (June 3, 1991); pick received as part of compensation for Kansas City Royals signing Type B free-agent OF/DH Kirk Gibson. ... On Los Angeles disabled list (May 3-July 7 and August 9-September 12, 1995); included rehabilitation assignments to San Bernardino (June 6-7) and Albuquerque (June 27-July 7). ... On Los Angeles disabled list (August 2-16 and August 17-September 6, 1997); included rehabilitation assignment to San Bernardino (August 15-17). ... On disabled list (June 5, 1998-remainder of season). ... On Los Angeles disabled list (April 3-23 and June 4-19, 1999); included rehabilitation assignments to San Bernardino (April 20-23 and June 18-19). ... Traded by Dodgers with OF Kevin Gibbs and P Randey Dorame to Colorado Rockies for OF Tom Goodwin and cash (July 31, 2000). ... Granted free agency (October 27, 2000). ... Re-signed by Rockies (November 16, 2000). ... On disabled list (May 12, 2001-remainder of season). ... Traded by Rockies with P Dennys Reyes to Texas Rangers for OF Gabe Kapler and 2B Jason Romano (July 31, 2002). ... On Texas disabled list (August 4-20, 2002). ... Granted free agency (October 28, 2002). ... Signed by Florida Marlins (January 8, 2003). ... Placed on 15-day disabled list (August 21, 2003). ... Removed from 15-day disabled list (September 1, 2003).

2003 GAMES PLAYED BY POSITION (MLB): OF—64, DH—1.

										BATTING										FIELDING	
Year	Team (League)	Pos.	G	AB	R	H	2B	3B	HR	RBI	BB	SO	HBP	GDP	SB-CS	Avg.	OBP	SLG	OPS	E	Pct.
1991— GC Dodgers (GCL)		OF	6	16	1	5	0	0	0	0	0	0	0	1	0-0	.313	.313	.313	.625	0	1.000
—Yakima (N'west)		OF	56	203	34	48	5	1	8	33	27	57	4	2	11-1	.236	.338	.389	.727	7	.939
1992— Bakersfield (Calif.)		OF	119	430	70	111	23	5	13	58	50	113	3	6	27-13	.258	.338	.426	.764	6	.975
1993— San Antonio (Texas)		OF	126	474	57	119	24	9	17	63	29	101	5	7	24-12	.251	.298	.447	.746	12	.956
1994— Albuquerque (PCL)		OF	132	505	80	144	31	5	19	91	46	96	0	15	15-9	.285	.343	.479	.822	13	.949
1995— Los Angeles (N.L.)		OF	41	103	16	24	2	0	5	13	10	29	1	1	2-1	.233	.304	.398	.702	4	.938
—San Bern. (Calif.)		OF	1	2	0	1	0	0	0	0	0	1	0	0	0-1	.500	.500	.500	1.000	0	...
—Albuquerque (PCL)		OF	10	38	9	9	2	0	2	4	6	8	1	1	1-0	.237	.356	.447	.803	0	1.000
1996— Los Angeles (N.L.)		OF	149	478	64	139	26	4	12	59	41	93	2	2	21-6	.291	.348	.437	.785	5	.978
1997— Los Angeles (N.L.)		OF	106	296	39	73	20	2	4	31	17	60	0	8	5-5	.247	.286	.368	.654	3	.984
—Albuquerque (PCL)		OF	13	56	13	24	4	3	1	14	4	4	0	0	2-3	.429	.467	.661	1.127	0	1.000
—San Bern. (Calif.)		OF	2	8	1	2	0	1	0	2	1	2	0	0	0-0	.250	.333	.500	.833	0	1.000
1998— Los Angeles (N.L.)		OF	55	175	23	47	6	4	3	20	9	42	1	2	4-3	.269	.308	.400	.708	4	.957
1999— San Bern. (Calif.)		OF	4	13	3	5	2	0	0	3	2	4	1	1	0-1	.385	.500	.538	1.038	0	1.000
—Los Angeles (N.L.)		OF-1B	92	261	39	74	12	2	9	32	24	61	1	2	5-2	.284	.345	.448	.793	3	.987
2000— Los Angeles (N.L.)		OF	81	261	42	61	12	0	8	24	30	61	1	4	11-4	.234	.314	.372	.686	2	.987
—Colorado (N.L.)		OF	56	167	39	54	8	0	11	23	11	38	0	4	7-3	.323	.365	.569	.934	1	.987
2001— Colorado (N.L.)		OF	33	117	21	43	15	1	6	19	8	20	0	1	5-0	.368	.408	.667	1.075	1	.981
2002— Colorado (N.L.)		OF	95	298	39	88	21	1	11	48	26	71	1	8	7-8	.295	.352	.483	.835	4	.973
—Texas (A.L.)		OF	39	132	16	34	6	0	5	19	14	27	0	0	1-0	.258	.327	.417	.743	0	1.000
2003— Florida (N.L.)		OF-DH	93	228	32	58	23	3	3	20	22	55	0	2	2-3	.254	.317	.421	.739	2	.983
American League totals (1 year)			39	132	16	34	6	0	5	19	14	27	0	0	1-0	.258	.327	.417	.743	0	1.000
National League totals (9 years)			801	2384	354	661	145	17	72	289	198	530	7	34	69-35	.277	.333	.443	.776	29	.979
Major League totals (9 years)			840	2516	370	695	151	17	77	308	212	557	7	34	70-35	.276	.333	.442	.774	29	.980

HOLMES, DARREN — P

PERSONAL: Born April 25, 1966, in Asheville, N.C. ... 6-0/202. ... Throws right, bats right. ... Full name: Darren Lee Holmes. ... High school: T.C. Roberson (Asheville, N.C.).

TRANSACTIONS/CAREER NOTES: Selected by Los Angeles Dodgers organization in 16th round of free-agent draft (June 4, 1984). ... On disabled list (June 5, 1986-remainder of season). ... Loaned by Dodgers organization to San Luis Potosi, Mexican League (1988). ... Traded by Dodgers to Milwaukee Brewers for C Bert Heffernan (December 20, 1990). ... On Milwaukee disabled list (July 3-18, 1991); included rehabilitation assignment to Beloit (July 13-18). ... Selected by Colorado Rockies in first round (fifth pick overall) of expansion draft (November 17, 1992). ... On Colorado disabled list (May 30-June 24 and July 21-August 11, 1994); included rehabilitation assignments to Asheville (June 14-19) and Colorado Springs (June 20). ... On disabled list (April 30-May 15, 1997). ... Granted free agency (October 27, 1997). ... Signed by New York Yankees (December 22, 1997). ... On New York disabled list (July 30-September 4, 1998); included rehabilitation assignment to Tampa (August 31-September 4). ... Traded by Yankees with cash to Arizona Diamondbacks for C Izzy Molina and P Ben Ford (March 30, 1999). ... On Arizona disabled list (June 24-July 15 and July 18-August 11, 1999); included rehabilitation assignments to Arizona League Diamondbacks (August 3-8) and Tucson (August 9-11). ... Released by Diamondbacks (April 28, 2000). ... Signed by St. Louis Cardinals organization (May 4, 2000). ... Traded by Cardinals to Baltimore Orioles for future considerations (June 28, 2000). ... Released by Orioles (July 19, 2000). ... Signed by Diamondbacks organization (August 11, 2000). ... Granted free agency (October 13, 2000). ... Signed by Atlanta Braves organization (January 28, 2002). ... On disabled list (July 7-27, 2002). ... Granted free agency (November 4, 2002). ... Re-signed by Braves (December 7, 2002). ... Placed on 15-day disabled list (May 2, 2003). ... Reinstated from 15-day disabled list (May 17, 2003). ... Placed on 15-day disabled list (August 6, 2003). ... Removed from 15-day disabled list (September 12, 2003).

CAREER HITTING: 3-for-28 (.107), 2 R, 0 2B, 0 3B, 1 HR, 2 RBI.

H

Year	League	W	L	Pct.	ERA	WHIP	G	GS	CG	ShO	Hld.	Sv.-Opp.	IP	H	R	ER	HR	BB-IBB	SO	Avg.
1984— Great Falls (Pio.)		2	5	.286	6.65	1.86	18	6	1	0	...	0-...	44.2	53	41	33	5	30-1	29	...
1985— Vero Beach (FSL)		4	3	.571	3.11	1.45	33	0	0	0	...	2-...	63.2	57	31	22	0	35-2	46	.245
1986— Vero Beach (FSL)		3	6	.333	2.92	1.45	11	10	0	0	...	0-...	64.2	55	30	21	0	39-2	59	.226
1987— Vero Beach (FSL)		6	4	.600	4.52	1.65	19	19	1	0	...	0-...	99.2	111	60	50	4	53-0	46	.284
1988— San Luis Potosi (Mex.)		9	9	.500	4.64	1.74	23	23	7	1	...	0-...	139.2	151	88	72	5	92-...	110	...
1989— San Antonio (Texas)		5	8	.385	3.83	1.32	17	16	3	2	...	1-...	110.1	102	59	47	5	44-2	81	.244
— Albuquerque (PCL)		1	4	.200	7.45	1.76	9	8	0	0	...	0-...	38.2	50	32	32	8	18-1	31	.318
1990— Albuquerque (PCL)		12	2	* .857	3.11	1.26	56	0	0	0	...	13-...	92.2	78	34	32	3	39-2	99	.228
— Los Angeles (N.L.)		0	1	.000	5.19	1.50	14	0	0	0	0	0-0	17.1	15	10	10	1	11-3	19	.238
1991— Denver (Am. Assoc.)		0	0	...	9.00	3.00	1	0	0	0	...	0-...	1.0	1	1	1	0	2-0	2	.250
— Milwaukee (A.L.)		1	4	.200	4.72	1.53	40	0	0	0	3	3-6	76.1	90	43	40	6	27-1	59	.295
— Beloit (Midw.)		0	0	...	0.00	0.00	2	0	0	0	...	2-...	2.0	0	0	0	0	0-0	3	.000
1992— Denver (Am. Assoc.)		0	0	...	1.38	0.62	12	0	0	0	...	7-...	13.0	7	2	2	1	1-0	12	.152
— Milwaukee (A.L.)		4	4	.500	2.55	1.09	41	0	0	0	2	6-8	42.1	35	12	12	1	11-4	31	.224
1993— Colorado (N.L.)		3	3	.500	4.05	1.14	62	0	0	0	2	25-29	66.2	56	31	30	6	20-1	60	.222
— Colo. Springs (PCL)		1	0	1.000	0.00	0.23	3	2	0	0	...	0-...	8.2	1	1	0	0	1-0	9	.036
1994— Colorado (N.L.)		0	3	.000	6.35	2.08	29	0	0	0	3	3-8	28.1	35	25	20	5	24-4	33	.313
— Colo. Springs (PCL)		0	1	.000	8.22	1.83	4	2	0	0	...	0-...	7.2	11	7	7	1	3-0	12	.324
— Asheville (S. Atl.)		0	0	...	0.00	0.33	2	1	0	0	...	0-...	3.0	1	0	0	0	0-0	7	.100
1995— Colorado (N.L.)		6	1	.857	3.24	1.31	68	0	0	0	13	14-18	66.2	59	26	24	3	28-3	61	.237
1996— Colorado (N.L.)		5	4	.556	3.97	1.38	62	0	0	0	7	1-8	77.0	78	41	34	8	28-2	73	.260
1997— Colorado (N.L.)		9	2	.818	5.34	1.67	42	6	0	0	5	3-4	89.1	113	58	53	12	36-3	70	.314
1998— New York (A.L.)		0	3	.000	3.33	1.31	34	0	0	0	2	2-3	51.1	53	19	19	4	14-3	31	.270
— Tampa (FSL)		0	1	.000	4.50	2.00	2	1	0	0	...	0-...	2.0	4	2	1	0	0-0	6	.364
1999— Arizona (N.L.)		4	3	.571	3.70	1.54	44	0	0	0	4	0-2	48.2	50	21	20	3	25-8	35	.262
— Ariz. D'backs (Ariz.)		0	0	...	0.00	0.38	2	2	0	0	...	0-...	2.2	1	0	0	0	0-0	4	.111
— Tucson (PCL)		0	0	...	0.00	1.00	1	1	0	0	...	0-...	1.0	0	0	0	0	1-0	0	.000
2000— Arizona (N.L.)		0	0	...	8.53	2.05	8	0	0	0	1	1-1	6.1	12	6	6	1	1-0	5	.414
— Tucson (PCL)		1	1	.500	2.08	1.85	3	0	0	0	...	1-...	4.1	4	1	1	0	4-1	2	.250
— St. Louis (N.L.)		0	1	.000	9.72	1.80	5	0	0	0	0	0-1	8.1	12	9	9	2	3-0	5	.364
— Memphis (PCL)		0	0	...	2.45	0.89	9	0	0	0	...	0-...	14.2	10	4	4	0	3-0	8	.204
— Baltimore (A.L.)		0	0	...	25.07	3.86	5	0	0	0	0	0-0	4.2	13	13	13	3	5-0	6	.481
2001—												Did not play.								
2002— Atlanta (N.L.)		2	2	.500	1.81	0.97	55	0	0	0	7	1-2	54.2	41	12	11	3	12-4	47	.210
2003— Atlanta (N.L.)		1	2	.333	4.29	1.38	48	0	0	0	11	0-1	42.0	47	22	20	5	11-0	46	.280
American League totals (4 years)		5	11	.313	4.33	1.42	120	0	0	0	7	11-17	174.2	191	87	84	14	57-8	127	.279
National League totals (10 years)		30	22	.577	4.22	1.42	437	6	0	0	53	48-74	505.1	518	261	237	49	199-28	454	.265
Major League totals (13 years)		35	33	.515	4.25	1.42	557	6	0	0	60	59-91	680.0	709	348	321	63	256-36	581	.269

HOUSE, J.R.   C

PERSONAL: Born November 11, 1979, in Charleston, W.Va. ... 5-10/202. ... Bats right, throws right. ... Full name: James Rodger House. ... High school: Seabreeze (Daytona Beach, Fla.).

TRANSACTIONS/CAREER NOTES: Selected by Pittsburgh Pirates organization in fifth round of free-agent draft (June 2, 1999). ... On disabled list (April 24-May 1 and May 8-22, 2001). ... On Altoona disabled list (April 19-August 9, 2002). ... Called up by Pittsburgh from Nashville (September 15, 2003).

										BATTING								FIELDING	
Year	Team (League)	Pos.	G	AB	R	H	2B	3B	HR	RBI	BB	SO	HBP	GDP	SB-CS	Avg.	OBP	SLG	OPS	E	Pct.
1999— GC Pirates (GCL)	1B-3B	33	113	13	37	9	3	5	23	11	23	2	1	1-0	.327	.394	.593	.987	3	.987
— Will. (NYP)	C-1B	26	100	11	30	6	0	1	13	9	21	0	2	0-1	.300	.358	.390	.748	3	.985
— Hickory (S. Atl.)	3B-OF	4	11	1	3	0	0	0	0	0	3	0	0	0-0	.273	.273	.273	.545	0	...
2000— Hickory (S. Atl.)	C-1B	110	420	78	146	29	1	23	90	46	91	6	7	1-2	.348	.414	.586	.000	8	.990
2001— Altoona (East.)	C-1B	112	426	51	110	25	1	11	56	37	103	5	12	1-1	.258	.323	.399	.722	7	.991
2002— GC Pirates (GCL)	C-1B	5	16	3	5	2	0	1	2	3	1	0	0	0-0	.313	.421	.625	1.046	0	1.000
— Altoona (East.)	C	30	91	9	24	6	0	2	11	13	21	0	4	0-0	.264	.349	.396	.745	1	.994
2003— GC Pirates (GCL)	DH-C	20	65	16	26	9	0	4	23	12	5	1	1	0-0	.400	.476	.723	1.199	1	.984
— Altoona (East.)	C-DH	20	63	12	21	6	0	2	11	5	11	0	4	0-0	.333	.382	.524	.906	1	.983
— Pittsburgh (N.L.)		1	1	0	1	0	0	0	0	0	0	0	0	0-0	1.000	1.000	1.000	2.000	0	...
Major League totals (1 year)		1	1	0	1	0	0	0	0	0	0	0	0	0-0	1.000	1.000	1.000	2.000	0	...

HOUSTON, TYLER   3B

PERSONAL: Born January 17, 1971, in Long Beach, Calif. ... 6-1/218. ... Bats left, throws right. ... Full name: Tyler Sam Houston. ... High school: Valley (Las Vegas).

TRANSACTIONS/CAREER NOTES: Selected by Atlanta Braves organization in first round (second pick overall) of free-agent draft (June 5, 1989). ... On Greenville disabled list (June 25-July 5, 1993). ... Traded by Braves to Chicago Cubs for P Ismael Villegas (June 27, 1996). ... On Chicago disabled list (May 3-19, 1997); included rehabilitation assignment to Iowa (May 14-19, 1997). ... On Chicago disabled list (June 11-July 11, 1997); included rehabilitation assignment to Rockford (July 9-11). ... On suspended list (September 16, 1997). ... On disabled list (May 26-June 24, 1998). ... Traded by Cubs to Cleveland Indians for P Richard Negrette (August 31, 1999). ... Granted free agency (December 21, 1999). ... Signed by Milwaukee Brewers (January 17, 2000). ... On disabled list (May 19-June 2, 2000). ... On Milwaukee disabled list (July 14-September 1 and September 8, 2001-remainder of season); included rehabilitation assignment to Beloit (August 29-September 1). ... Traded by Brewers with a player to be named later to Los Angeles Dodgers for P Ben Diggins and P Shane Nance (July 23, 2002); Dodgers acquired P Brian Mallette to complete deal (October 16, 2002). ... Granted free agency (October 28, 2002). ... Signed by Philadelphia Phillies (January 15, 2003). ... Placed on 15-day disabled list (May 14, 2003). ... Sent on rehab assignment to Scranton (July 5, 2003). ... Recalled from Scranton rehab assignment; reinstated from 15-day disabled list (July 12, 2003). ... Designated for assignment (August 30, 2003). ... Released by Philadelphia (September 7, 2003).

2003 GAMES PLAYED BY POSITION (MLB): 3B—21, 1B—1.

										BATTING								FIELDING	
Year	Team (League)	Pos.	G	AB	R	H	2B	3B	HR	RBI	BB	SO	HBP	GDP	SB-CS	Avg.	OBP	SLG	OPS	E	Pct.
1989— Idaho Falls (Pio.)	C	50	176	30	43	11	0	4	24	25	41	1	4	4-0	.244	.342	.375	.717	5	.970
1990— Sumter (S. Atl.)	C	117	442	58	93	14	3	13	56	49	101	2	15	6-2	.210	.288	.344	.632	* 18	.968
1991— Macon (S. Atl.)	C	107	351	41	81	16	3	8	47	39	70	1	8	10-2	.231	.307	.362	.669	10	.985
1992— Durham (Caro.)	C-3B-1B	117	402	39	91	17	1	7	38	20	89	1	5	5-6	.226	.262	.326	.588	15	.974
1993— Greenville (Sou.)	C-OF	84	262	27	73	14	1	5	33	13	50	2	12	5-3	.279	.313	.397	.710	9	.980
— Richmond (Int'l)	C	13	36	4	5	1	1	1	3	1	8	0	1	0-0	.139	.162	.306	.468	3	.959
1994— Richmond (Int'l)	1-C-D-O	97	312	33	76	15	2	4	33	16	44	0	12	3-3	.244	.276	.343	.619	7	.990
1995— Richmond (Int'l)	1-C-O-3-D	103	349	41	89	10	3	12	42	18	62	4	6	3-5	.255	.298	.404	.702	11	.983

H

Year	Team (League)	Pos.	G	AB	R	H	2B	3B	HR	RBI	BB	SO	HBP	GDP	SB-CS	Avg.	OBP	SLG	OPS	E	Pct.
1996—	Atlanta (N.L.)	1B-OF	33	27	3	6	2	1	1	8	1	9	0	1	0-0	.222	.250	.481	.731	0	1.000
—	Chicago (N.L.)	C-3-2-1	46	115	18	39	7	0	2	19	8	18	0	4	3-2	.339	.382	.452	.834	3	.982
1997—	Chicago (N.L.)	C-3-1-2-S	72	196	15	51	10	0	2	28	9	35	0	4	1-0	.260	.290	.342	.632	5	.984
—	Iowa (Am. Assoc.)	3B-DH-C	6	23	0	5	2	0	0	4	0	2	0	0	0-0	.217	.217	.304	.522	2	.882
—	Rockford (Midwest)	3B-C	2	6	1	3	1	0	0	1	0	0	0	0	0-0	.500	.500	.667	1.167	0	1.000
1998—	Chicago (N.L.)	C-3B-1B	95	255	26	65	7	1	9	33	13	53	0	6	2-2	.255	.290	.396	.686	5	.990
1999—	Chicago (N.L.)	3-C-1-OF	100	249	26	58	9	1	9	27	28	67	0	7	1-1	.233	.309	.386	.695	17	.921
—	Cleveland (A.L.)	3B-C	13	27	2	4	1	0	1	3	3	11	0	0	0-0	.148	.233	.296	.530	0	1.000
2000—	Milwaukee (N.L.)	1B-OF	101	284	30	71	15	0	18	43	17	72	0	13	2-1	.250	.292	.493	.785	13	.974
2001—	Milwaukee (N.L.)	3B-1B	75	235	36	68	7	0	12	38	18	62	1	3	0-0	.289	.343	.472	.815	10	.934
—	Beloit (Midw.)	3B	1	3	0	0	0	0	0	0	0	1	0	0	0-0	.000	.000	.000	.000	1	.500
2002—	Milwaukee (N.L.)	3B-1B	76	255	25	77	15	2	7	33	14	41	4	4	1-0	.302	.347	.459	.806	8	.949
—	Los Angeles (N.L.)	1B-3B	35	65	9	13	5	1	0	7	2	21	0	5	0-0	.200	.224	.308	.532	3	.972
2003—	Scran./W.B. (I.L.)	DH-1B-3B	6	23	2	4	1	1	0	0	1	1	0	0	0-0	.174	.208	.304	.513	0	1.000
—	Philadelphia (N.L.)	3B-1B	54	97	7	27	6	0	2	14	6	19	0	2	0-0	.278	.320	.402	.722	3	.943
American League totals (1 year)			13	27	2	4	1	0	1	3	3	11	0	0	0-0	.148	.233	.296	.530	0	1.000
National League totals (8 years)			687	1778	195	475	83	6	62	250	116	397	5	49	10-6	.267	.313	.425	.738	67	.969
Major League totals (8 years)			700	1805	197	479	84	6	63	253	119	408	5	49	10-6	.265	.312	.423	.735	67	.969

HOWARD, BEN P

PERSONAL: Born January 15, 1979, in Danville, Ill. ... 6-2/190. ... Throws right, bats right. ... Full name: Benjamin Richard Howard. ... High school: Jackson-Central Merry (Jackson, Tenn.).

TRANSACTIONS/CAREER NOTES: Selected by San Diego Padres organization in second round of free-agent draft (June 3, 1997). ... On Portland disabled list (June 19-August 18, 2002). ... Recalled from Portland by San Diego (August 26, 2003).

CAREER HITTING: 1-for-15 (.067), 1 R, 0 2B, 0 3B, 0 HR, 0 RBI.

Year	League	W	L	Pct.	ERA	WHIP	G	GS	CG	ShO	Hld.	Sv.-Opp.	IP	H	R	ER	HR	BB-IBB	SO	Avg.
1997—	Ariz. Padres (Ariz.)	1	4	.200	7.45	2.15	13	12	0	0	...	0-...	54.1	54	53	* 45	3	* 63-0	59	.255
1998—	Idaho Falls (Pioneer)	4	5	.444	6.03	2.24	15	15	0	0	...	0-...	68.2	67	61	46	2	* 87-0	79	.260
1999—	Fort Wayne (Midw.)	6	10	.375	4.73	1.61	28	28	0	0	...	0-...	144.2	123	100	76	17	* 110-0	131	.226
2000—	Rancho Cuca. (Calif.)	5	11	.313	6.37	1.85	32	19	0	0	...	0-...	107.1	88	87	76	8	* 111-1	150	.227
2001—	Lake Elsinore (Calif.)	8	2	.800	2.83	1.16	18	18	0	0	...	0-...	101.2	86	37	32	4	52-0	107	.229
—	Mobile (Sou.)	2	0	1.000	2.40	1.07	7	5	0	0	...	0-...	30.0	17	9	8	3	15-0	29	.167
2002—	Mobile (Sou.)	3	1	.750	2.18	1.27	6	6	0	0	...	0-...	33.0	26	10	8	2	16-0	30	.222
—	San Diego (N.L.)	0	1	.000	9.28	2.53	3	2	0	0	0	0-0	10.2	13	11	11	4	14-1	10	.302
—	Portland (PCL)	0	4	.000	6.20	1.38	11	7	0	0	...	0-...	45.0	47	34	31	10	15-0	25	.266
2003—	Portland (PCL)	7	9	.438	4.55	1.28	22	22	0	0	...	0-...	130.2	118	69	66	17	49-0	68	.243
—	San Diego (N.L.)	1	3	.250	3.63	1.33	6	6	0	0	0	0-0	34.2	31	17	14	10	15-1	24	.235
Major League totals (2 years)		1	4	.200	4.96	1.61	9	8	0	0	0	0-0	45.1	44	28	25	14	29-2	34	.251

HOWRY, BOB P

PERSONAL: Born August 4, 1973, in Phoenix, Ariz. ... 6-5/220. ... Throws right, bats left. ... Full name: Bobby Dean Howry. ... Name pronounced: HOW-ree. ... High school: Deer Valley (Phoenix). ... College: McNeese State.

TRANSACTIONS/CAREER NOTES: Selected by San Francisco Giants organization in fifth round of free-agent draft (June 2, 1994). ... Traded by Giants with SS Mike Caruso, OF Brian Manning, P Keith Foulke, P Lorenzo Barcelo and P Ken Vining to Chicago White Sox for P Wilson Alvarez, P Danny Darwin and P Roberto Hernandez (July 31, 1997). ... On suspended list (April 28-May 30, 2000). ... Traded by White Sox to Boston Red Sox for P Franklin Francisco and P Byeong An (July 31, 2002). ... Optioned to Pawtucket by Boston Red Sox (April 15, 2003). ... Recalled from Pawtucket (August 22, 2003). ... Placed on 60-day disabled list (August 22, 2003).

CAREER HITTING: 0-for-0 (.000), 0 R, 0 2B, 0 3B, 0 HR, 0 RBI.

Year	League	W	L	Pct.	ERA	WHIP	G	GS	CG	ShO	Hld.	Sv.-Opp.	IP	H	R	ER	HR	BB-IBB	SO	Avg.
1994—	Everett (Northwest)	0	4	.000	4.74	2.05	5	5	0	0	...	0-...	19.0	29	15	10	3	10-2	16	.341
—	Clinton (Midw.)	1	3	.250	4.20	1.56	9	8	0	0	...	0-...	49.1	61	29	23	1	16-0	22	.316
1995—	San Jose (Calif.)	12	10	.545	3.54	1.36	27	25	1	0	...	0-...	165.1	171	79	65	6	54-0	107	.277
1996—	Shreveport (Texas)	12	10	.545	4.65	1.40	27	27	0	0	...	0-...	156.2	163	90	81	17	56-3	57	.269
1997—	Shreveport (Texas)	6	3	.667	4.91	1.44	48	0	0	0	...	* 22-...	55.0	58	35	30	6	21-0	43	.270
—	Birmingham (Sou.)	0	0	...	2.84	1.50	12	0	0	0	...	0-...	12.2	16	4	4	1	3-0	3	.314
1998—	Calgary (PCL)	1	2	.333	3.41	1.11	23	0	0	0	...	5-...	31.2	25	12	12	2	10-3	22	.216
—	Chicago (A.L.)	0	3	.000	3.15	1.03	44	0	0	0	19	9-11	54.1	37	20	19	7	19-2	51	.194
1999—	Chicago (A.L.)	5	3	.625	3.59	1.42	69	0	0	0	1	28-34	67.2	58	34	27	8	38-3	80	.229
2000—	Chicago (A.L.)	2	4	.333	3.17	1.17	65	0	0	0	14	7-12	71.0	54	26	25	6	29-2	60	.216
2001—	Chicago (A.L.)	4	5	.444	4.69	1.46	69	0	0	0	21	5-11	78.2	85	41	41	11	30-9	64	.279
2002—	Chicago (A.L.)	2	2	.500	3.91	1.22	47	0	0	0	10	0-0	50.2	45	22	22	7	17-2	31	.245
—	Boston (A.L.)	1	3	.250	5.00	1.44	20	0	0	0	5	0-1	18.0	22	15	10	2	4-2	14	.306
2003—	Boston (A.L.)	0	0	...	12.46	3.23	4	0	0	0	0	0-1	4.1	11	6	6	1	3-1	4	.478
—	Pawtucket (Int'l)	2	0	1.000	1.06	0.88	13	0	0	0	...	0-...	17.0	14	2	2	1	1-0	10	.215
Major League totals (6 years)		14	20	.412	3.92	1.31	318	0	0	0	70	49-70	344.2	312	164	150	42	140-21	304	.244

HUBBARD, TRENIDAD OF

PERSONAL: Born May 11, 1966, in Chicago, Ill. ... 5-9/203. ... Bats right, throws right. ... Full name: Trenidad Aviel Hubbard. ... High school: South Shore (Chicago). ... College: Southern University.

TRANSACTIONS/CAREER NOTES: Selected by Houston Astros organization in 12th round of free-agent draft (June 2, 1986). ... Granted free agency (October 15, 1992). ... Signed by Colorado Rockies organization (October 30, 1992). ... On disabled list (June 15-24, 1993). ... Granted free agency (October 15, 1993). ... Re-signed by Rockies organization (December 3, 1993). ... Granted free agency (October 15, 1994). ... Re-signed by Rockies organization (November 14, 1994). ... Claimed on waivers by San Francisco Giants (August 21, 1996). ... On San Francisco disabled list (September 13, 1996-remainder of season). ... Traded by Giants to Cleveland Indians for P Joe Roa (December 16, 1996), completing deal in which Indians traded IF Jeff Kent, IF Jose Vizcaino, P Julian Tavarez and a player to be named later to Giants for 3B Matt Williams and a player to be named later (November 13, 1996). ... Granted free agency (October 8, 1997). ... Signed by Los Angeles Dodgers (December 3, 1997). ... On Los Angeles disabled list (May 14-June 22, 1998; included rehabilitation assignment to Albuquerque (June 9-22). ... Granted free agency (January 19, 2000). ... Signed by Atlanta Braves organization (January 20, 2000). ... Traded by Braves with P Luis Rivera and C Fernando Rivera to Baltimore Orioles for OF B.J. Surhoff and P Gabe Molina (July 31, 2000). ... Released by Orioles (October 5, 2000). ... Signed by Toronto Blue Jays organization (December 21, 2000). ... Released by Blue Jays (March 17, 2001). ... Signed by Kansas

H

City Royals organization (March 23, 2001). ... Released by Royals (May 23, 2001). ... Signed by Chicago Cubs organization (July 4, 2001). ... Released by Cubs (September 10, 2001). ... Signed by San Diego Padres organization (February 24, 2002). ... Released by Padres (September 4, 2002). ... Signed by Chicago Cubs (February 19, 2003).

2003 GAMES PLAYED BY POSITION (MLB): OF—4.

											BATTING									FIELDING	
Year	Team (League)	Pos.	G	AB	R	H	2B	3B	HR	RBI	BB	SO	HBP	GDP	SB-CS	Avg.	OBP	SLG	OPS	E	Pct.
1986— Auburn (NY-Penn)		2B-OF	70	242	42	75	12	1	1	32	28	42	1	2	35-5	.310	.381	.380	.761	18	.931
1987— Asheville (S. Atl.)		P	101	284	39	67	8	1	1	35	28	42	0	4	28-13	.236	.298	.282	.579	14	.943
1988— Osceola (Fla. St.)		C	130	446	68	116	15	11	3	65	61	72	3	10	44-18	.260	.351	.363	.714	12	.972
1989— Columbus (Sou.)		2B-3B-C-O	104	348	55	92	7	8	3	37	43	53	2	8	28-6	.264	.347	.356	.703	15	.967
—Tucson (PCL)		3B-C-OF	21	50	3	11	2	0	0	2	1	10	1	2	3-3	.220	.250	.260	.510	1	.967
1990— Columbus (Sou.)		2-3-C-OF	95	335	39	84	14	4	4	35	32	51	3	7	17-8	.251	.320	.352	.672	11	.968
—Tucson (PCL)		2B-3B-C	12	27	5	6	2	2	0	2	3	6	0	1	1-1	.222	.300	.444	.744	3	.933
1991— Jackson (Texas)		P	126	455	78	135	21	3	2	41	65	81	9	3	39-17	.297	.394	.369	.763	21	.968
—Tucson (PCL)		2B	2	4	0	0	0	0	0	0	0	0	0	0	0-0	.000	.000	.000	.000	0	1.000
1992— Tucson (PCL)		2B-3B	115	420	69	130	16	4	2	33	45	68	4	7	34-10	.310	.380	.381	.761	18	.970
1993— Colo. Springs (PCL)		OF-2B	117	439	83	138	24	8	7	56	47	57	6	4	33-•18	.314	.387	.453	.841	6	.975
1994— Colo. Springs (PCL)		OF	79	320	78	116	22	5	8	38	44	40	2	7	28-10	.363	.441	.538	.979	7	.964
—Colorado (N.L.)		OF	18	25	3	7	1	1	1	3	3	4	0	1	0-0	.280	.357	.520	.877	0	1.000
1995— Colo. Springs (PCL)		OF	123	480	* 102	163	29	7	12	66	61	59	5	2	* 37-14	.340	.416	.504	.920	6	.980
—Colorado (N.L.)		OF	24	58	13	18	4	0	3	9	8	6	0	2	2-1	.310	.394	.534	.928	0	1.000
1996— Colorado (N.L.)		OF	45	60	12	13	5	1	1	12	9	22	1	1	2-0	.217	.329	.383	.712	0	1.000
—Colo. Springs (PCL)		OF-2-3-C	50	188	41	59	15	5	6	16	28	14	2	4	6-8	.314	.406	.543	.949	4	.973
—San Francisco (N.L.)		OF	10	29	3	6	0	1	1	2	2	5	0	2	0-0	.207	.258	.379	.637	0	1.000
1997— Buffalo (A.A.)		OF-3B-DH	103	375	71	117	22	1	16	60	57	52	3	10	26-10	.312	* .401	.504	.905	2	.992
—Cleveland (A.L.)		P	7	12	3	3	1	0	0	0	1	3	0	0	2-0	.250	.308	.333	.641	0	1.000
1998— Los Angeles (N.L.)		OF-3B	94	208	29	62	9	1	7	18	18	46	3	5	9-5	.298	.358	.452	.810	1	.991
—Albuquerque (PCL)		OF-DH	11	30	6	9	0	0	3	5	5	5	1	1	2-1	.300	.417	.600	1.017	0	1.000
1999— Albuquerque (PCL)		OF-DH	32	123	24	41	8	2	5	24	16	27	0	4	16-3	.333	.401	.553	.954	2	.974
—Los Angeles (N.L.)		OF-2B-C	82	105	23	33	5	0	1	13	13	24	0	2	4-3	.314	.387	.390	.777	1	.981
2000— Atlanta (N.L.)		OF	61	81	15	15	2	1	1	6	11	20	1	1	2-1	.185	.290	.272	.562	0	1.000
—Baltimore (A.L.)		OF-DH	31	27	3	5	0	1	0	0	0	3	0	2	2-1	.185	.185	.259	.444	1	.929
2001— Omaha (PCL)		OF	49	175	35	50	9	1	10	28	30	34	2	1	8-5	.286	.392	.520	.912	0	1.000
—Kansas City (A.L.)		OF	5	12	2	3	0	1	0	0	0	2	0	0	0-0	.250	.250	.417	.667	0	1.000
—Iowa (PCL)		OF-3B	49	171	38	54	11	3	6	31	37	27	2	4	17-5	.316	.439	.520	.959	1	.989
2002— San Diego (N.L.)		O-3-2-DH	89	129	16	27	5	0	1	7	14	28	0	3	9-6	.209	.285	.271	.556	2	.970
—Portland (PCL)		OF	8	29	9	11	2	0	3	6	2	3	0	...	2-2	.379	.406	.759	1.165	0	1.000
2003— Chicago (N.L.)		OF	10	16	2	4	1	0	0	2	4	3	1	0	1-0	.250	.429	.313	.741	0	1.000
—Iowa (PCL)		OF-3B-DH	91	348	65	111	16	2	5	27	47	29	5	13	24-7	.319	.405	.420	.825	6	.972
American League totals (3 years)			43	51	8	11	1	2	0	0	1	8	0	2	4-1	.216	.231	.314	.544	1	.947
National League totals (8 years)			433	711	116	185	32	5	16	72	82	158	6	17	29-16	.260	.340	.387	.726	4	.989
Major League totals (10 years)			476	762	124	196	33	7	16	72	83	166	6	19	33-17	.257	.333	.382	.715	5	.986

HUCKABY, KEN   C

PERSONAL: Born January 27, 1971, in San Leandro, Calif. ... 6-1/205. ... Bats right, throws right. ... Full name: Kenneth Paul Huckaby. ... Name pronounced: HUCK-a-be. ... High school: Manteca (Calif.). ... Junior college: San Joaquin Delta College (Calif.).

TRANSACTIONS/CAREER NOTES: Selected by Los Angeles Dodgers organization in 22nd round of free-agent draft (June 3, 1991). ... On disabled list (May 26-June 5 and July 2-21, 1992). ... On San Antonio disabled list (May 4-13, 1994). ... Granted free agency (October 15, 1997). ... Signed by Seattle Mariners organization (December 3, 1997). ... On Tacoma disabled list (April 7-May 3, 1998). ... Released by Mariners (June 13, 1998). ... Signed by New York Yankees organization (June 28, 1998). ... Granted free agency (October 16, 1998). ... Signed by Arizona Diamondbacks organization (January 22, 1999). ... Granted free agency (October 15, 1999). ... Re-signed by Diamondbacks organization (November 15, 1999). ... Granted free agency (October 18, 2000). ... Re-signed by Diamondbacks organization (November 2, 2000). ... Released by Diamondbacks (October 29, 2001). ... Signed by Toronto Blue Jays organization (February 10, 2002). ... Contract purchased by Toronto from Syracuse (June 2, 2003). ... Sent outright to Syracuse (June 12, 2003). ... Elected free agency (September 29, 2003).

2003 GAMES PLAYED BY POSITION (MLB): C—4.

											BATTING									FIELDING	
Year	Team (League)	Pos.	G	AB	R	H	2B	3B	HR	RBI	BB	SO	HBP	GDP	SB-CS	Avg.	OBP	SLG	OPS	E	Pct.
1991— Great Falls (Pio.)		C	57	213	39	55	16	0	3	37	17	38	4	4	3-2	.258	.321	.376	.696	* 12	.977
1992— Vero Beach (FSL)		C	73	261	14	63	9	0	0	21	7	42	1	5	1-1	.241	.262	.276	.538	9	.982
1993— Vero Beach (FSL)		C	79	281	22	75	14	1	4	41	11	35	2	3	2-1	.267	.297	.367	.664	12	.980
—San Antonio (Texas)		C	28	82	4	18	1	0	0	5	2	7	2	0	0-0	.220	.253	.232	.485	4	.978
1994— San Antonio (Texas)		C	11	41	3	11	1	0	1	9	1	1	0	1	1-0	.268	.286	.366	.652	6	.931
—Bakersfield (Calif.)		C	77	270	29	81	18	1	2	30	10	37	2	7	2-3	.300	.329	.396	.725	10	.986
1995— Albuquerque (PCL)		C-1B	89	278	30	90	16	2	1	40	12	26	4	16	3-1	.324	.359	.406	.766	16	.973
1996— Albuquerque (PCL)		C	103	287	37	79	16	2	3	41	17	35	2	10	0-0	.275	.319	.376	.696	6	.990
1997— Albuquerque (PCL)		C-DH	69	201	14	40	5	1	0	18	9	36	0	5	1-0	.199	.231	.234	.465	10	.975
1998— Tacoma (PCL)		C-1B	16	49	4	11	2	0	0	1	5	6	0	2	0-0	.224	.296	.265	.562	0	1.000
—Columbus (Int'l)		C	36	101	13	21	3	1	1	10	11	14	0	3	0-2	.208	.286	.287	.573	5	.978
1999— Tucson (PCL)		C-3-DH-1	107	355	44	107	20	1	2	42	13	33	2	11	0-0	.301	.325	.380	.706	10	.987
2000— Tucson (PCL)		C-3-OF-1	76	243	31	67	11	1	4	33	10	30	2	10	2-2	.276	.306	.379	.685	8	.982
2001— El Paso (Texas)		1B-C	30	104	14	36	4	0	2	14	3	16	3	3	0-0	.346	.368	.442	.811	4	.989
—Tucson (PCL)		C-1-3-2	78	262	31	76	15	1	2	34	7	62	2	3	1-3	.290	.313	.378	.690	14	.972
—Arizona (N.L.)		C	1	1	0	0	0	0	0	0	0	1	0	0	0-0	.000	.000	.000	.000	0	1.000
2002— Syracuse (Int'l)		C-1B	21	81	7	22	2	0	0	9	2	15	0	6	0-2	.272	.286	.296	.582	3	.981
—Toronto (A.L.)		C	88	273	29	67	6	1	3	22	9	44	0	10	0-0	.245	.270	.308	.577	6	.989
2003— Toronto (A.L.)		C	5	11	1	2	1	0	0	2	0	2	0	0	0-0	.182	.182	.273	.455	0	1.000
—Syracuse (Int'l)		C-1-DH-3	75	267	24	78	14	0	3	25	15	30	0	11	1-1	.292	.326	.378	.705	7	.987
American League totals (2 years)			93	284	30	69	7	1	3	24	9	46	0	10	0-0	.243	.266	.304	.573	6	.989
National League totals (1 year)			1	1	0	0	0	0	0	0	0	1	0	0	0-0	.000	.000	.000	.000	0	1.000
Major League totals (3 years)			94	285	30	69	7	1	3	24	9	47	0	10	0-0	.242	.265	.305	.571	6	.989

H

HUDSON, ORLANDO — 2B

PERSONAL: Born December 12, 1977, in Darlington, S.C. ... 6-0/185. ... Bats both, throws right. ... Full name: Orlando Thill Hudson. ... High school: Darlington (S.C.). ... College: Spartanburg Methodist (S.C.).

TRANSACTIONS/CAREER NOTES: Selected by Toronto Blue Jays organization in 43rd round of free-agent draft (June 3, 1997).

2003 GAMES PLAYED BY POSITION (MLB): 2B—139.

Year Team (League)	Pos.	G	AB	R	H	2B	3B	HR	RBI	BB	SO	HBP	GDP	SB-CS	Avg.	OBP	SLG	OPS	E	Pct.
1998— Medicine Hat (Pio.)	2B	65	242	50	71	18	1	8	42	22	36	7	3	6-5	.293	.366	.475	.842	13	.959
1999— Hagerstown (SAL) ...	2B-3B-OF	132	513	66	137	36	6	7	74	42	85	2	10	8-6	.267	.322	.402	.724	21	.946
2000— Dunedin (Fla. St.)	2B-3B-SS	96	358	54	102	16	2	7	48	37	42	2	15	9-5	.285	.354	.399	.754	19	.941
— Tennessee (Sou.)	3B	39	134	17	32	4	3	2	15	15	18	2	3	3-2	.239	.320	.358	.678	11	.921
2001— Tennessee (Sou.)	2B-3B	84	306	51	94	22	8	4	52	37	42	3	12	8-3	.307	.385	.471	.856	8	.979
— Syracuse (Int'l)	2B-3B	55	194	31	59	14	3	4	27	23	34	2	1	11-3	.304	.378	.469	.847	4	.986
2002— Syracuse (Int'l)	2B	100	417	63	127	27	3	10	37	35	54	4	14	8-5	.305	.363	.456	.819	10	.982
— Toronto (A.L.)	2B	54	192	20	53	10	5	4	23	11	27	2	6	0-1	.276	.319	.443	.762	4	.986
2003— Toronto (A.L.)	2B	142	474	54	127	21	6	9	57	39	87	5	13	5-4	.268	.328	.395	.723	12	.984
Major League totals (2 years)		196	666	74	180	31	11	13	80	50	114	7	19	5-5	.270	.326	.408	.734	16	.985

HUDSON, TIM — P

PERSONAL: Born July 14, 1975, in Columbus, Ga. ... 6-1/164. ... Throws right, bats right. ... Full name: Timothy Adam Hudson. ... High school: Glenwood (Phenix City, Ala.). ... College: Auburn.

TRANSACTIONS/CAREER NOTES: Selected by Oakland Athletics organization in sixth-round of free-agent draft (June 3, 1997).

CAREER HITTING: 3-for-23 (.130), 2 R, 1 2B, 0 3B, 0 HR, 1 RBI.

Year League	W	L	Pct.	ERA	WHIP	G	GS	CG	ShO	Hld.	Sv.-Opp.	IP	H	R	ER	HR	BB-IBB	SO	Avg.
1997— S. Oregon (N'west)	3	1	.750	2.51	0.94	8	4	0	0	...	0-...	28.2	12	8	8	0	15-2	37	.128
1998— Modesto (Calif.)	4	0	1.000	1.67	0.98	8	5	0	0	...	0-...	37.2	19	10	7	0	18-0	48	.148
— Huntsville (Sou.)	10	9	.526	4.54	1.54	22	22	2	0	...	0-...	134.2	136	84	68	13	71-2	104	.270
1999— Midland (Texas)	3	0	1.000	0.50	0.67	3	3	0	0	...	0-...	18.0	9	1	1	0	3-0	18	.153
— Vancouver (PCL)	4	0	1.000	2.20	1.20	8	8	0	0	...	0-...	49.0	38	16	12	2	21-0	61	.212
— Oakland (A.L.)	11	2	.846	3.23	1.34	21	21	1	0	0	0-0	136.1	121	56	49	8	62-2	132	.237
2000— Oakland (A.L.)	• 20	6	.769	4.14	1.24	32	32	2	2	0	0-0	202.1	169	100	93	24	82-5	169	.227
2001— Oakland (A.L.)	18	9	.667	3.37	1.22	35	• 35	3	0	0	0-0	235.0	216	100	88	20	71-5	181	.245
2002— Oakland (A.L.)	15	9	.625	2.98	1.25	34	34	2	2	0	0-0	238.1	237	87	79	19	62-9	152	.263
2003— Oakland (A.L.)	16	7	.696	2.70	1.08	34	34	3	•2	0	0-0	240.0	197	84	72	15	61-•9	162	.223
Major League totals (5 years)	80	33	.708	3.26	1.21	156	156	13	6	0	0-0	1052.0	940	427	381	86	338-30	796	.239

HUFF, AUBREY — OF/1B

PERSONAL: Born December 20, 1976, in Marion, Ohio. ... 6-4/231. ... Bats left, throws right. ... Full name: Aubrey Lewis Huff. ... High school: Brewer (Fort Worth, Texas). ... College: Miami (Fla.).

TRANSACTIONS/CAREER NOTES: Selected by Tampa Bay Devil Rays organization in fifth round of free-agent draft (June 2, 1998). ... On Durham disabled list (April 4-24, 2002).

2003 GAMES PLAYED BY POSITION (MLB): OF—102, DH—33, 1B—22, 3B—8.

Year Team (League)	Pos.	G	AB	R	H	2B	3B	HR	RBI	BB	SO	HBP	GDP	SB-CS	Avg.	OBP	SLG	OPS	E	Pct.
1998— Char., S.C. (SAL)	3B	69	265	38	85	19	1	13	54	24	40	0	5	3-1	.321	.371	.547	.918	8	.957
1999— Orlando (South.)	3B	133	491	85	148	40	3	22	78	64	77	4	14	2-3	.301	.385	.530	.915	29	.958
2000— Durham (Int'l)	3B-1B	108	408	73	129	36	3	20	76	51	72	2	15	2-3	.316	.394	.566	.960	21	.915
— Tampa Bay (A.L.)	3B	39	122	12	35	7	0	4	14	5	18	1	6	0-0	.287	.318	.443	.760	5	.939
2001— Durham (Int'l)	3B	17	66	14	19	6	0	3	10	5	7	0	3	0-0	.288	.338	.515	.853	4	.929
— Tampa Bay (A.L.)	3B-DH-1B	111	411	42	102	25	1	8	45	23	72	0	18	1-3	.248	.288	.372	.660	20	.940
2002— Durham (Int'l)	1B	32	126	18	41	9	0	3	20	12	13	1	4	0-0	.325	.386	.468	.854	0	1.000
— Tampa Bay (A.L.)	DH-1B-3B	113	454	67	142	25	0	23	59	37	55	1	17	4-1	.313	.364	.520	.884	8	.981
2003— Tampa Bay (A.L.)	O-D-1-3	162	636	91	198	47	3	34	107	53	80	8	19	2-3	.311	.367	.555	.922	9	.977
Major League totals (4 years)		425	1623	212	477	104	4	69	225	118	225	10	60	7-7	.294	.343	.490	.834	42	.966

HUMMEL, TIM — IF

PERSONAL: Born November 18, 1978, in Goshen, N.Y. ... 6-2/195. ... Bats right, throws right. ... Full name: Timothy Robert Hummel. ... High school: Burke (Montgomery, N.Y.). ... College: Old Dominion.

TRANSACTIONS/CAREER NOTES: Selected by San Diego Padres organization in fifth round of free-agent draft (June 3, 1997); did not sign. ... Selected by Chicago White Sox organization in second round of free-agent draft (June 5, 2000). ... Claimed off waivers by Cincinnati Reds as compensation for trade of P Scott Sullivan (August 27, 2002).

2003 GAMES PLAYED BY POSITION (MLB): 3B—20, SS—2, 2B—1.

Year Team (League)	Pos.	G	AB	R	H	2B	3B	HR	RBI	BB	SO	HBP	GDP	SB-CS	Avg.	OBP	SLG	OPS	E	Pct.
2000— Burlington (Appal.)	SS	39	144	22	47	9	1	1	21	21	20	1	2	8-3	.326	.411	.424	.834	5	.964
— Win.-Salem (Car.)	3B-SS	27	98	15	32	7	0	1	9	13	12	2	4	1-1	.327	.416	.429	.845	8	.912
2001— Birmingham (Sou.)	2B-SS-3B	134	524	83	152	33	6	7	63	62	69	5	12	14-3	.290	.364	.416	.780	26	.958
2002— Charlotte (Int'l)	SS-2-3-1	142	523	55	136	33	0	4	41	51	95	10	7	6-5	.260	.332	.346	.678	12	.981
2003— Charlotte (Int'l)	3-S-2-D	128	476	72	135	25	3	15	80	46	83	5	10	9-3	.284	.350	.443	.794	13	.960
— Cincinnati (N.L.)	3B-SS-2B	26	84	9	19	5	0	2	10	8	13	0	1	0-0	.226	.290	.357	.647	5	.912
Major League totals (1 year)		26	84	9	19	5	0	2	10	8	13	0	1	0-0	.226	.290	.357	.647	5	.912

HUNDLEY, TODD — C

PERSONAL: Born May 27, 1969, in Martinsville, Va. ... 5-11/200. ... Bats both, throws right. ... Full name: Todd Randolph Hundley. ... High school: William Fremd (Palatine, Ill.).

TRANSACTIONS/CAREER NOTES: Selected by New York Mets organization in second round of free-agent draft (June 2, 1987); pick received as compensation for Baltimore Orioles signing Type B free-agent 3B/1B Ray Knight. ... On Tidewater disabled list (June 29-July 6, 1991). ... On disabled list (July 23, 1995-remainder of season). ... On New

H

York disabled list (March 21-July 11 and August 28-September 12, 1998); included rehabilitation assignments to St. Lucie (June 24-July 6 and July 9), Gulf Coast Mets (July 7-8) and Norfolk (July 10-11 and August 31-September 8). ... Traded by Mets with P Arnold Gooch to Los Angeles Dodgers for C Charles Johnson and OF Roger Cedeno (December 1, 1998). ... On suspended list (July 22-24, 1999). ... On Los Angeles disabled list (May 31-June 26 and July 9-27, 2000); included rehabilitation assignment to Albuquerque (June 23-26). ... Granted free agency (October 27, 2000). ... Signed by Chicago Cubs (December 13, 2000). ... On Chicago disabled list (June 19-July 26, 2001); included rehabilitation assignment to West Tenn (June 29-July 2) and Iowa (July 7-25). ... On Chicago disabled list (May 6-29, 2002); included rehabilitation assignment to Iowa (May 25-28). ... Traded by Cubs with OF Chad Hermansen to Dodgers for 1B Eric Karros, 2B Mark Grudzielanek and cash (December 4, 2002). ... Placed on 15-day disabled list by Los Angeles (May 3, 2003). ... Transferred to Emergency disabled list (July 14, 2003). ... Sent on minor league rehab assignment (August 23, 2003). ... Recalled from minor league rehab assignment; removed from 60-day disabled list (September 1, 2003).

2003 GAMES PLAYED BY POSITION (MLB): C—10.

Year Team (League)	Pos.	G	AB	R	H	2B	3B	HR	RBI	BB	SO	HBP	GDP	SB-CS	Avg.	OBP	SLG	OPS	E	Pct.
1987— Little Falls (NYP)	C	34	103	12	15	4	0	1	10	12	27	3	2	0-0	.146	.254	.214	.468	7	.967
1988— Little Falls (NYP)	C	52	176	23	33	8	0	2	18	16	31	4	2	1-1	.188	.269	.267	.536	8	.980
— St. Lucie (Fla. St.)	C	1	1	0	0	0	0	0	0	2	1	0	0	0-0	.000	.667	.000	.667	1	.800
1989— Columbia (S. Atl.)	C-OF	125	439	67	118	23	4	11	66	54	67	8	20	6-3	.269	.356	.415	.770	13	.986
1990— Jackson (Texas)	3B-C	81	279	27	74	12	2	1	35	34	44	1	5	5-3	.265	.344	.333	.677	9	.984
— New York (N.L.)	C	36	67	8	14	6	0	0	2	6	18	0	1	0-0	.209	.274	.299	.572	2	.988
1991— Tidewater (Int'l)	C-1B	125	454	62	124	24	4	14	66	51	95	2	12	1-2	.273	.344	.436	.780	§ 9	.986
— New York (N.L.)	C	21	60	5	8	0	1	1	7	6	14	1	3	0-0	.133	.221	.217	.437	0	1.000
1992— New York (N.L.)	C	123	358	32	75	17	0	7	32	19	76	4	8	3-0	.209	.256	.356	.572	3	.996
1993— New York (N.L.)	C	130	417	40	95	17	2	11	53	23	62	2	10	1-1	.228	.269	.357	.626	8	.988
1994— New York (N.L.)	C	91	291	45	69	10	1	16	42	25	73	3	2	2-1	.237	.303	.443	.746	5	.990
1995— New York (N.L.)	C	90	275	39	77	11	0	15	51	42	64	5	4	1-0	.280	.382	.484	.865	7	.987
1996— New York (N.L.)	C	153	540	85	140	32	1	41	112	79	146	5	9	1-3	.259	.356	.550	.906	8	.992
1997— New York (N.L.)	C-DH	132	417	78	114	21	2	30	86	83	116	3	10	2-3	.273	.394	.549	.943	10	.987
1998— St. Lucie (Fla. St.)	OF-DH	12	42	4	9	2	0	1	6	12	8	0	1	0-1	.214	.389	.333	.722	2	.900
— GC Mets (GCL)	OF	1	2	0	0	0	0	0	0	2	1	0	0	0-0	.000	.500	.000	.500	0	1.000
— Norfolk (Int'l)	OF-DH-C	10	30	9	13	1	0	4	15	14	10	0	0	0-0	.433	.614	.867	1.480	1	.960
— New York (N.L.)	OF-C	53	124	8	20	4	0	3	12	16	55	1	0	1-1	.161	.261	.266	.527	5	.928
1999— Los Angeles (N.L.)	C	114	376	49	78	14	0	24	55	44	113	4	5	3-0	.207	.295	.436	.731	* 16	.979
2000— Los Angeles (N.L.)	C-DH	90	299	49	85	16	0	24	70	45	69	2	5	0-1	.284	.375	.579	.954	* 13	.979
— Albuquerque (PCL)	C	3	9	2	5	0	0	1	5	1	0	0	1	0-0	.556	.600	.889	1.489	0	1.000
2001— Chicago (N.L.)	C	79	246	23	46	10	0	12	31	25	89	3	7	0-0	.187	.268	.374	.642	4	.993
— West Tenn (Sou.)	C	4	12	1	4	2	0	0	1	1	3	0	0	0-0	.333	.385	.500	.885	0	1.000
— Iowa (PCL)	C	15	51	7	10	1	0	3	8	4	23	1	1	0-0	.196	.263	.392	.655	0	1.000
2002— Chicago (N.L.)	C-DH	92	266	32	56	8	0	16	35	32	80	3	6	0-0	.211	.301	.421	.722	11	.984
— Iowa (PCL)	C	3	9	1	2	0	0	1	4	1	2	0	0	0-0	.222	.300	.556	.856	0	1.000
2003— Vero Beach (FSL)	DH-C	7	24	2	2	0	0	0	1	3	5	1	0	0-0	.083	.214	.083	.298	0	1.000
— Los Angeles (N.L.)	C	21	33	2	6	1	0	2	11	8	13	0	0	0-1	.182	.341	.394	.735	1	.981
Major League totals (14 years)		1225	3769	495	883	167	7	202	599	453	988	34	71	14-11	.234	.320	.443	.763	93	.987

HUNTER, BRIAN L.   OF

PERSONAL: Born March 25, 1971, in Portland, Ore. ... 6-3/180. ... Bats right, throws right. ... Full name: Brian Lee Hunter. ... High school: Fort Vancouver (Vancouver, Wash.).

TRANSACTIONS/CAREER NOTES: Selected by Houston Astros organization in second round of free-agent draft (June 5, 1989); pick received as part of compensation for Texas Rangers signing Type A free-agent P Nolan Ryan. ... On Houston disabled list (July 5-23, 1995); included rehabilitation assignment to Jackson (May 21-23). ... On Houston disabled list (June 29-July 27, 1996); included rehabilitation assignment to Tucson (June 23-27). ... Traded by Astros with IF Orlando Miller, P Doug Brocail, P Todd Jones and cash to Detroit Tigers for C Brad Ausmus, P Jose Lima, P C.J. Nitkowski, P Trever Miller and IF Daryle Ward (December 10, 1996). ... Traded by Tigers to Seattle Mariners for two players to be named later (April 29, 1999); Tigers acquired P Andrew Vanhekken (June 27, 1999) and OF Jerry Amador (August 26, 1999) to complete deal. ... On Seattle disabled list (July 12-27, 1999). ... Released by Mariners (March 27, 2000). ... Signed by Colorado Rockies (March 31, 2000). ... Traded by Rockies from Cincinnati Reds for P Robert Averette (August 6, 2000). ... On suspended list (August 14-17, 2000). ... Released by Reds (November 27, 2000). ... Signed by Philadelphia Phillies (January 10, 2001). ... On Philadelphia disabled list (April 4-22, 2001); included rehabilitation assignment to Scranton/Wilkes-Barre (April 20-22). ... Granted free agency (November 5, 2001). ... Signed by Astros (December 3, 2001). ... On Houston disabled list (July 14-August 20, 2002); included rehabilitation assignment to New Orleans (August 14-20). ... Given unconditional release (July 28, 2003).

2003 GAMES PLAYED BY POSITION (MLB): OF—32.

Year Team (League)	Pos.	G	AB	R	H	2B	3B	HR	RBI	BB	SO	HBP	GDP	SB-CS	Avg.	OBP	SLG	OPS	E	Pct.
1989— GC Astros (GCL)	OF	51	206	15	35	2	0	0	13	7	42	1	1	12-6	.170	.201	.180	.381	2	.980
1990— Asheville (S. Atl.)	OF	127	444	84	111	14	6	0	16	60	72	8	3	45-13	.250	.349	.309	.657	11	.955
1991— Osceola (Fla. St.)	OF	118	392	51	94	15	3	1	30	45	75	1	6	32-9	.240	.316	.301	.617	9	.966
1992— Osceola (Fla. St.)	OF	131	489	62	146	18	9	1	62	31	76	5	7	39-19	.299	.344	.378	.722	9	.971
1993— Jackson (Texas)	OF	133	523	84	154	22	5	10	52	34	85	1	11	* 35-18	.294	.338	.413	.751	* 14	.953
1994— Tucson (PCL)	OF-DH	128	513	* 113	* 191	28	4	10	51	52	52	5	11	* 49-14	.372	.432	.520	.953	5	.981
— Houston (N.L.)	OF	6	24	2	6	1	0	0	0	1	6	0	0	2-1	.250	.280	.292	.572	1	.938
1995— Tucson (PCL)	OF	38	155	28	51	5	1	1	16	17	13	0	1	11-3	.329	.395	.394	.789	0	1.000
— Houston (N.L.)	OF	78	321	52	97	14	5	2	28	21	52	2	2	24-7	.302	.346	.396	.741	9	.955
— Jackson (Texas)	OF	2	6	1	3	0	0	0	0	1	0	0	1	0-0	.500	.571	.500	1.071	0	1.000
1996— Houston (N.L.)	OF	132	526	74	145	27	2	5	35	17	92	2	6	35-9	.276	.297	.363	.660	• 12	.960
— Tucson (PCL)	OF	3	14	3	5	0	1	0	1	0	2	0	0	3-0	.357	.333	.500	.833	0	1.000
1997— Detroit (A.L.)	OF	• 162	658	112	177	29	7	4	45	66	121	1	13	* 74-18	.269	.334	.353	.687	4	.990
1998— Detroit (A.L.)	OF	142	595	67	151	29	3	4	36	36	94	2	8	42-12	.254	.298	.309	.631	5	.988
1999— Detroit (A.L.)	OF	18	55	8	13	2	1	0	0	5	11	1	0	0-3	.236	.311	.309	.621	0	1.000
— Seattle (A.L.)	OF	121	484	71	112	11	5	4	34	32	80	1	8	† 44-5	.231	.277	.300	.576	4	.985
2000— Colorado (N.L.)	OF	72	200	36	55	4	1	1	13	21	31	1	2	15-3	.275	.347	.320	.667	2	.981
— Cincinnati (N.L.)	OF	32	40	11	9	1	0	1	0	6	9	0	1	5-0	.225	.319	.250	.569	1	.971
2001— Philadelphia (N.L.)	OF-DH	83	145	22	40	6	0	2	16	16	25	0	3	14-3	.276	.344	.359	.702	0	1.000
— Scran./W.B. (I.L.)	OF	2	9	1	1	0	0	0	0	1	3	0	0	0-0	.111	.200	.111	.311	1	.833
2002— Houston (N.L.)	OF	98	201	32	54	9	3	3	20	16	39	2	1	5-0	.269	.329	.423	.752	0	1.000
— New Orleans (PCL)	OF	5	19	4	3	0	1	0	2	2	7	0	1	2-0	.158	.238	.263	.501	0	1.000
2003— Houston (N.L.)	OF	56	98	13	23	6	1	0	13	6	21	1	1	0-0	.235	.278	.316	.594	2	.944
American League totals (3 years)		443	1792	258	453	71	16	12	115	139	306	5	29	160-38	.253	.306	.330	.637	13	.989
National League totals (7 years)		557	1555	242	429	75	12	13	126	104	275	8	17	100-23	.276	.321	.365	.686	27	.970
Major League totals (10 years)		1000	3347	500	882	146	28	25	241	243	581	13	46	260-61	.264	.313	.346	.660	40	.980

H

HUNTER, TORII   OF

PERSONAL: Born July 18, 1975, in Pine Bluff, Ark. ... 6-2/210. ... Bats right, throws right. ... Full name: Torii Kedar Hunter. ... High school: Pine Bluff (Ark.).

TRANSACTIONS/CAREER NOTES: Selected by Minnesota Twins organization in first round (20th pick overall) of free-agent draft (June 3, 1993); pick recieved as part of compensation for Cincinnati Reds signing Type A free-agent P John Smiley. ... On New Britain disabled list (April 4-May 10, 1996). ... On Salt Lake disabled list (July 28-August 11, 1998). ... On disabled list (April 6-21, 2001). ... On suspended list (July 20-23, 2002).

2003 GAMES PLAYED BY POSITION (MLB): OF—151, DH—3.

									BATTING											FIELDING	
Year	Team (League)	Pos.	G	AB	R	H	2B	3B	HR	RBI	BB	SO	HBP	GDP	SB-CS	Avg.	OBP	SLG	OPS		E	Pct.
1993—	GC Twins (GCL)	OF	28	100	6	19	3	0	0	8	4	23	9	1	4-2	.190	.283	.220	.503	•	6	.895
1994—	Fort Wayne (Midw.)	OF	91	335	57	98	17	1	10	50	25	80	10	5	8-10	.293	.358	.439	.796		7	.971
1995—	Fort Myers (FSL)	OF	113	391	64	96	15	2	7	36	38	77	12	8	7-4	.246	.330	.348	.678		7	.973
1996—	Fort Myers (FSL)	OF	4	16	1	3	0	0	0	1	2	5	0	0	1-1	.188	.278	.188	.465		0	1.000
	New Britain (East.)	OF	99	342	49	90	20	3	7	33	28	60	7	7	7-7	.263	.331	.401	.731		4	.982
1997—	New Britain (East.)	OF-DH	127	471	57	109	22	2	8	56	47	94	3	6	8-8	.231	.305	.338	.642		7	.974
	Minnesota (A.L.)		1	0	0	0	0	0	0	0	0	0	0	0	0-0	...	.000	...	...		...	...
1998—	New Britain (East.)	OF	82	308	42	87	24	3	6	32	19	64	4	2	11-9	.282	.329	.438	.768		2	.989
	Minnesota (A.L.)	OF	6	17	0	4	1	0	0	2	2	6	0	1	0-1	.235	.316	.294	.610		0	1.000
	Salt Lake (PCL)	OF-DH	26	92	15	31	7	0	4	20	1	13	1	3	2-2	.337	.347	.543	.891		2	.966
1999—	Minnesota (A.L.)	OF	135	384	52	98	17	2	9	35	26	72	6	9	10-6	.255	.309	.380	.689		1	.997
2000—	Minnesota (A.L.)	OF	99	336	44	94	14	7	5	44	18	68	2	13	4-3	.280	.318	.408	.726		3	.989
	Salt Lake (PCL)		55	209	58	77	17	2	18	61	11	28	3	4	11-3	.368	.403	.727	1.130		3	.973
2001—	Minnesota (A.L.)	OF	148	564	82	147	32	5	27	92	29	125	8	12	9-6	.261	.306	.479	.784		4	.992
2002—	Minnesota (A.L.)	OF-DH	148	561	89	162	37	4	29	94	35	118	5	17	23-8	.289	.334	.524	.859		3	.990
2003—	Minnesota (A.L.)	OF-DH	154	581	83	145	31	4	26	102	50	106	5	15	6-7	.250	.312	.451	.762		4	.991
	Major League totals (7 years)		691	2443	350	650	132	22	96	369	160	495	26	67	52-31	.266	.316	.456	.772		15	.992

HYZDU, ADAM   OF

PERSONAL: Born December 6, 1971, in San Jose, Calif. ... 6-2/220. ... Bats right, throws right. ... Full name: Adam David Hyzdu. ... Name pronounced: HIGHS-doo. ... High school: Moeller (Cincinnati).

TRANSACTIONS/CAREER NOTES: Selected by San Francisco Giants organization in first round (15th pick overall) of free-agent draft (June 4, 1990); pick received as compensation for Houston Astros signing Type B free-agent IF Ken Oberkfell. ... Selected by Cincinnati Reds from Giants organization in Rule 5 major league draft (December 13, 1993). ... Released by Reds (March 23, 1996). ... Signed by Boston Red Sox organization (April 26, 1996). ... Signed by Arizona Diamondbacks organization (January 2, 1998). ... Loaned by Diamondbacks organization to Monterrey, Mexican League (April 7-May 17, 1998). ... On disabled list (June 30-August 23, 1998). ... Granted free agency (October 15, 1998). ... Signed by Pittsburgh Pirates organization (May 10, 1999). ... Granted free agency (October 15, 1999). ... Re-signed by Pirates organization (October 30, 1999). ... Granted free agency (October 18, 2000). ... Re-signed by Pirates organization (October 24, 2000). ... Optioned to Nashville (May 7, 2003). ... Recalled from Nashville (May 22, 2003). ... Elected free agency (September 29, 2003).

2003 GAMES PLAYED BY POSITION (MLB): OF—34.

									BATTING											FIELDING	
Year	Team (League)	Pos.	G	AB	R	H	2B	3B	HR	RBI	BB	SO	HBP	GDP	SB-CS	Avg.	OBP	SLG	OPS		E	Pct.
1990—	Everett (N'west)	OF	69	253	31	62	16	1	6	34	28	78	2	4	2-4	.245	.319	.387	.707		5	.963
1991—	Clinton (Midw.)	OF	124	410	47	96	13	5	5	50	64	131	3	10	4-5	.234	.340	.327	.667		9	.955
1992—	San Jose (Calif.)	OF	128	457	60	127	25	5	9	60	55	134	1	6	10-5	.278	.351	.414	.765		5	.976
1993—	San Jose (Calif.)	OF	44	165	35	48	11	3	13	38	29	53	0	3	1-1	.291	.393	.630	1.023		3	.963
	Shreveport (Texas)	OF	86	302	30	61	17	0	6	25	20	82	1	5	0-5	.202	.253	.318	.571		4	.973
1994—	Chattanooga (Sou.)	OF-DH-1B	38	133	17	35	10	0	3	9	8	21	1	1	0-2	.263	.310	.406	.716		4	.949
	Win.-Salem (Car.)	OF-DH	55	210	30	58	11	1	15	39	18	33	2	3	1-5	.276	.336	.552	.889		4	.945
	Indianapolis (A.A.)	OF	12	25	3	3	2	0	0	3	1	5	0	0	0-0	.120	.143	.200	.343		1	.917
1995—	Chattanooga (Sou.)	OF	102	312	55	82	14	1	13	48	45	56	4	4	3-2	.263	.362	.439	.801		1	.995
1996—	Trenton (East.)	OF-DH-C	109	374	71	126	24	3	25	80	56	75	2	7	1-8	.337	.424	.618	1.042		3	.980
1997—	Pawtucket (Int'l)	OF-DH	119	413	77	114	21	1	23	84	72	113	4	6	10-6	.276	.387	.499	.886		4	.978
1998—	Monterrey (Mex.)	OF	29	110	20	36	3	0	5	22	14	17	...	...	7-1	.327	...	.491	...		0	1.000
	Tucson (PCL)	OF-DH-P	34	100	21	34	7	1	4	14	15	23	0	2	0-1	.340	.419	.550	.969		1	.974
1999—	Pawtucket (Int'l)	OF-DH	12	35	4	8	0	0	1	6	4	13	0	1	0-0	.229	.308	.314	.622		0	1.000
	Altoona (East.)	OF-1-3-D	91	345	64	109	26	2	24	78	40	62	3	2	8-4	.316	.392	.612	1.003		11	.965
	Nashville (PCL)	OF	14	44	6	11	1	0	5	13	4	11	0	2	0-0	.250	.313	.614	.926		0	1.000
2000—	Altoona (East.)	OF-1B	* 142	514	• 96	149	39	2	* 31	* 106	94	102	8	6	3-7	.290	.405	.554	.960		1	.996
	Pittsburgh (N.L.)	OF	12	18	2	7	2	0	1	4	0	4	0	0	0-0	.389	.389	.667	1.056		0	1.000
2001—	Nashville (PCL)	OF-1B-3B	69	261	38	76	17	2	11	39	17	68	0	3	1-3	.291	.332	.498	.830		1	.994
	Pittsburgh (N.L.)	OF-1B	51	72	7	15	1	0	5	9	4	18	1	1	0-1	.208	.260	.431	.690		0	1.000
2002—	Nashville (PCL)	OF-1B	65	243	33	59	17	0	10	50	29	59	0	4	1-2	.243	.318	.436	.754		3	.980
	Pittsburgh (N.L.)	OF-1B	59	155	24	36	6	0	11	34	21	44	1	1	0-0	.232	.324	.484	.808		0	1.000
2003—	Pittsburgh (N.L.)	OF	51	63	16	13	5	0	1	8	10	21	1	2	0-0	.206	.320	.333	.653		0	1.000
	Nashville (PCL)	OF-1B	40	135	22	38	10	1	6	18	18	28	1	2	2-2	.281	.365	.504	.869		2	.981
	Major League totals (4 years)		173	308	49	71	14	0	18	55	35	87	3	4	0-1	.231	.312	.451	.764		0	1.000

IBANEZ, RAUL   OF

PERSONAL: Born June 2, 1972, in Manhattan, N.Y. ... 6-2/200. ... Bats left, throws right. ... Full name: Raul Javier Ibanez. ... Name pronounced: ee-BON-yez. ... High school: Sunset (Miami). ... Junior college: Miami-Dade South Community College.

TRANSACTIONS/CAREER NOTES: Selected by Seattle Mariners organization in 36th round of free-agent draft (June 1, 1992). ... On disabled list (June 4-July 16, 1994). ... On Seattle disabled list (March 30-June 29, 1998); included rehabilitation assignment to Tacoma (May 30-June 28). ... On Tacoma disabled list (July 7-14, 1998). ... On Seattle disabled list (May 18-June 3, 1999); included rehabilitation assignment to Tacoma (May 26-June 3). ... On Seattle disabled list (August 7-22, 2000); included rehabilitation assignment to Tacoma (August 11-22). ... Granted free agency (December 21, 2000). ... Signed by Kansas City Royals organization (January 22, 2001).

2003 GAMES PLAYED BY POSITION (MLB): OF—131, 1B—22, DH—12.

Year	Team (League)	Pos.	G	AB	R	H	2B	3B	HR	RBI	BB	SO	HBP	GDP	SB-CS	Avg.	OBP	SLG	OPS	E	Pct.
								BATTING												FIELDING	
1992—Ariz. Mariners (Ariz.)	C-1B-OF	33	120	25	37	8	2	1	16	9	18	2	3	1-2	.308	.366	.433	.800	4	.931
1993—Appleton (Midwest)	C-1B-OF	52	157	26	43	9	0	5	21	24	31	1	2	0-2	.274	.370	.427	.796	2	.980
—Bellingham (N'west)	C	43	134	16	38	5	2	0	15	21	23	0	0	0-3	.284	.378	.351	.729	1	.993
1994—Appleton (Midwest)	C-1B-OF	91	327	55	102	30	3	7	59	32	37	2	3	10-5	.312	.375	.486	.861	10	.971
1995—Riverside (Calif.)	C-1B	95	361	59	120	23	9	20	108	41	49	2	7	4-3	.332	.395	.612	1.007	12	.977
1996—Tacoma (PCL)	OF-1B-DH	111	405	59	115	20	3	11	47	44	56	2	4	7-7	.284	.353	.430	.783	11	.951
—Port City (Sou.)	O-D-C-1	19	76	12	28	8	1	1	13	8	7	0	1	3-2	.368	.424	.539	.963	4	.905
—Seattle (A.L.)	DH	4	5	0	0	0	0	0	0	0	1	1	0	0-0	.000	.167	.000	.167	0	...
1997—Tacoma (PCL)	OF	111	438	84	133	30	5	15	84	32	75	1	12	7-5	.304	.349	.498	.847	5	.976
—Seattle (A.L.)	OF-DH	11	26	3	4	0	1	1	4	0	6	0	0	0-0	.154	.154	.346	.500	0	1.000
1998—Tacoma (PCL)	OF-DH	52	190	24	41	8	1	6	25	24	47	0	3	1-1	.216	.301	.363	.664	1	.988
—Seattle (A.L.)	OF-1B-DH	37	98	12	25	7	1	2	12	5	22	0	4	0-0	.255	.291	.408	.699	1	.991
1999—Seattle (A.L.)	O-1-D-C	87	209	23	54	7	0	9	27	17	32	0	4	5-1	.258	.313	.421	.734	3	.988
—Tacoma (PCL)	OF-DH-1B	8	31	6	11	1	0	3	5	1	7	0	0	1-0	.355	.375	.677	1.052	0	1.000
2000—Seattle (A.L.)	OF-DH-1B	92	140	21	32	8	0	2	15	14	25	1	1	2-0	.229	.301	.329	.630	2	.980
—Tacoma (PCL)	OF	10	40	3	10	4	0	0	6	1	3	0	0	0-0	.250	.268	.350	.618	0	1.000
2001—Kansas City (A.L.)	O-D-1-3	104	279	44	78	11	5	13	54	32	51	0	6	0-2	.280	.353	.495	.847	5	.962
—Omaha (PCL)	OF-SS	8	27	3	4	1	0	2	5	1	10	0	0	0-0	.148	.179	.407	.586	1	.857
2002—Kansas City (A.L.)	OF-1B-DH	137	497	70	146	37	6	24	103	40	76	2	11	5-3	.294	.346	.537	.883	3	.994
2003—Kansas City (A.L.)	OF-1B-DH	157	608	95	179	33	5	18	90	49	81	3	10	8-4	.294	.345	.454	.799	4	.991
Major League totals (8 years)		629	1862	268	518	103	18	69	305	157	294	7	36	20-10	.278	.334	.464	.798	18	.988

INFANTE, OMAR — SS

PERSONAL: Born December 26, 1981, in Puerto la Cruz, Venezuela. ... 6-0/176. ... Bats right, throws right. ... Full name: Omar R. Infante. ... Name pronounced: in-fahn-TAY.
TRANSACTIONS/CAREER NOTES: Signed as non-drafted free agent by Detroit Tigers organization (April 28, 1999).
2003 GAMES PLAYED BY POSITION (MLB): SS—63, 3B—4, 2B—2.

Year	Team (League)	Pos.	G	AB	R	H	2B	3B	HR	RBI	BB	SO	HBP	GDP	SB-CS	Avg.	OBP	SLG	OPS	E	Pct.
								BATTING												FIELDING	
1999—GC Tigers (GCL)	SS	25	97	11	26	4	0	0	7	4	11	0	1	4-0	.268	.294	.309	.603	8	.932
2000—Lakeland (Fla. St.)	SS	79	259	35	71	11	0	2	24	20	29	1	4	11-5	.274	.324	.340	.664	19	.951
—W. Mich. (Mid.)	SS	12	48	7	11	0	0	0	5	5	7	2	2	1-0	.229	.327	.229	.556	1	.983
2001—Erie (East.)	SS	132	540	86	163	21	4	2	62	46	87	2	9	27-12	.302	.355	.367	.721	27	.955
2002—Toledo (Int'l)	SS	120	436	49	117	16	8	4	51	28	49	0	5	19-15	.268	.309	.369	.678	26	.959
—Detroit (A.L.)	SS-2B	18	72	4	24	3	0	1	6	3	10	0	0	0-1	.333	.360	.417	.777	5	.945
2003—Toledo (Int'l)	SS	64	224	28	50	10	0	2	18	22	32	3	3	22-4	.223	.299	.295	.593	18	.942
—Detroit (A.L.)	SS-3B-2B	69	221	24	49	6	1	0	8	18	37	0	1	6-3	.222	.278	.258	.536	14	.961
Major League totals (2 years)		87	293	28	73	9	1	1	14	21	47	0	1	6-4	.249	.297	.297	.594	19	.958

INGE, BRANDON — C

PERSONAL: Born May 19, 1977, in Lynchburg, Va. ... 5-11/195. ... Bats right, throws right. ... Full name: Charles Brandon Inge. ... Name pronounced: inj. ... High school: Brookville (Lynchburg, Va.). ... College: Virginia Commonwealth.
TRANSACTIONS/CAREER NOTES: Selected by Detroit Tigers organization in second round of free-agent draft (June 2, 1998). ... On Detroit disabled list (June 25-August 6, 2001); included rehabilitation assignments to Gulf Coast Tigers (July 25-29), West Michigan (July 30-August 2) and Toledo (August 3-6). ... On Detroit disabled list (May 12-May 27, 2002); included rehabilitation assignment to Toledo (May 17-27). ... Optioned to Toledo by Detroit (June 17, 2003).
2003 GAMES PLAYED BY POSITION (MLB): C—104.

Year	Team (League)	Pos.	G	AB	R	H	2B	3B	HR	RBI	BB	SO	HBP	GDP	SB-CS	Avg.	OBP	SLG	OPS	E	Pct.
								BATTING												FIELDING	
1998—Jamestown (NYP)	C	51	191	24	44	10	1	8	29	17	53	6	4	8-8	.230	.312	.419	.730	6	.981
1999—W. Mich. (Mid.)	C	100	352	54	86	25	2	9	46	39	87	3	7	15-3	.244	.320	.403	.723	8	.990
2000—Jacksonville (Sou.)	C-OF	78	298	39	77	25	1	6	53	26	73	0	10	10-3	.258	.313	.409	.722	5	.990
—Toledo (Int'l)	C	55	190	24	42	9	3	5	20	15	51	1	5	2-1	.221	.280	.379	.659	3	.991
2001—Detroit (A.L.)	C	79	189	13	34	11	0	0	15	9	41	0	2	1-4	.180	.215	.238	.453	4	.989
—GC Tigers (GCL)	C	3	10	1	1	0	0	1	2	2	2	0	0	0-0	.100	.250	.400	.650	1	1.000
—W. Mich. (Mid.)	C	4	16	3	3	1	0	0	2	2	5	1	0	0-0	.188	.316	.250	.566	0	1.000
—Toledo (Int'l)	C	27	90	11	26	11	1	2	15	7	24	1	2	1-0	.289	.337	.500	.837	2	.989
2002—Toledo (Int'l)	C	21	65	10	17	2	4	3	13	11	16	2	2	1-3	.262	.380	.554	.934	1	.978
—Detroit (A.L.)	C-DH	95	321	27	65	15	3	7	24	24	101	4	7	1-3	.202	.266	.333	.599	1	.998
2003—Toledo (Int'l)	C-DH	39	142	15	39	9	0	5	15	11	23	0	6	3-1	.275	.327	.444	.770	0	1.000
—Detroit (A.L.)	C	104	330	32	67	15	3	8	30	24	79	5	8	4-4	.203	.265	.339	.605	2	.996
Major League totals (3 years)		278	840	72	166	41	6	15	69	57	221	9	17	6-11	.198	.254	.314	.569	7	.995

ISHII, KAZUHISA — P

PERSONAL: Born September 9, 1973, in Chiba, Japan. ... 6-0/200. ... Throws left, bats left. ... Name pronounced: kaz-u-heesa ee-shee-ee.
TRANSACTIONS/CAREER NOTES: Played with Yakult Swallows of Japan Central League (1992-2001). ... Signed as non-drafted free agent by Los Angeles Dodgers (February 8, 2002). ... On disabled list (September 9, 2002-remainder of season). ... Removed from 15-day disabled list (August 30, 2003).
CAREER HITTING: 6-for-84 (.071), 2 R, 0 2B, 1 3B, 0 HR, 2 RBI.

Year	League	W	L	Pct.	ERA	WHIP	G	GS	CG	ShO	Hld.	Sv.-Opp.	IP	H	R	ER	HR	BB-IBB	SO	Avg.
1992—Yakult (Jp. Cen.)		0	0	...	4.18	1.43	12	...	0	0	...	0-...	28.0	23	13	13	4	17-...	22	...
1993—Yakult (Jp. Cen.)		3	1	.750	4.70	1.45	19	...	1	0	...	0-...	59.1	48	32	31	8	38-...	66	...
1994—Yakult (Jp. Cen.)		7	5	.583	4.08	1.56	54	...	2	2	...	0-...	108.0	92	56	49	11	77-...	98	...
1995—Yakult (Jp. Cen.)		13	4	.765	2.76	1.24	26	...	3	0	...	1-...	153.0	112	49	47	14	77-...	159	...
1996—Yakult (Jp. Cen.)		1	5	.167	5.23	1.61	8	...	0	0	...	0-...	31.0	28	19	18	6	22-...	26	...
1997—Yakult (Jp. Cen.)		10	4	.714	1.91	1.05	18	...	2	2	...	0-...	117.2	73	28	25	5	50-...	120	...
1998—Yakult (Jp. Cen.)		14	6	.700	3.30	1.29	28	...	6	0	...	0-...	196.1	149	78	72	12	105-...	241	...
1999—Yakult (Jp. Cen.)		8	6	.571	4.80	1.46	23	...	2	1	...	0-...	133.0	123	75	71	16	71-...	162	...
2000—Yakult (Jp. Cen.)		10	9	.526	2.61	1.15	29	...	3	1	...	0-...	183.0	137	54	53	15	73-...	210	...
2001—Yakult (Jp. Cen.)		12	6	.667	3.39	1.19	27	...	0	0	...	0-...	175.0	135	74	66	18	73-...	173	...
2002—Los Angeles (N.L.)		14	10	.583	4.27	1.58	28	28	0	0	0	0-0	154.0	137	82	73	20	* 106-3	143	.240
2003—Los Angeles (N.L.)		9	7	.563	3.86	1.56	27	27	0	0	0	0-0	147.0	129	72	63	16	101-4	140	.238
Major League totals (2 years)		23	17	.575	4.07	1.57	55	55	0	0	0	0-0	301.0	266	154	136	36	207-7	283	.239

ISRINGHAUSEN, JASON   P

PERSONAL: Born September 7, 1972, in Brighton, Ill. ... 6-3/230. ... Throws right, bats right. ... Full name: Jason Derek Isringhausen. ... Name pronounced: IS-ring-how-zin. ... High school: Southwestern (Brighton, Ill.). ... Junior college: Lewis & Clark (Ill.) Community College.

TRANSACTIONS/CAREER NOTES: Selected by New York Mets organization in 44th round of free-agent draft (June 3, 1991). ... On disabled list (August 13-September 1, 1996). ... On disabled list (March 24-August 27, 1997); included rehabilitation assignments to Norfolk (April 6-11 and August 22-27), Gulf Coast Mets (August 6-11) and St. Lucie (August 11-22). ... On disabled list (March 21, 1998-entire season). ... Traded by Mets with P Greg McMichael to Oakland Athletics for P Billy Taylor (July 31, 1999). ... Granted free agency (November 5, 2001). ... Signed by St. Louis Cardinals (December 11, 2001). ... On disabled list (March 21, 2003). ... Sent to Tennessee on rehab assignment (June 5, 2003). ... Activated from 15-day disabled list; recalled from Tennessee rehab assignment (June 10, 2003).

CAREER HITTING: 20-for-99 (.202), 10 R, 4 2B, 1 3B, 2 HR, 14 RBI.

Year League	W	L	Pct.	ERA	WHIP	G	GS	CG	ShO	Hld.	Sv.-Opp.	IP	H	R	ER	HR	BB-IBB	SO	Avg.
1992— GC Mets (GCL)	2	4	.333	4.34	1.48	6	6	0	0	...	0-...	29.0	26	19	14	0	17-1	25	.230
— Kingsport (Appal.)	4	1	.800	3.25	1.22	7	6	1	1	...	0-...	36.0	32	22	13	2	12-1	24	.222
1993— Pittsfield (NYP)	7	4	.636	3.29	1.06	15	15	2	0	...	0-...	90.1	68	45	33	7	28-0	* 104	.204
1994— St. Lucie (Fla. St.)	6	4	.600	2.23	1.02	14	14	• 6	• 3	...	0-...	101.0	76	31	25	2	27-2	59	.211
— Binghamton (Eastern)	5	4	.556	3.02	1.09	14	14	2	0	...	0-...	92.1	78	35	31	6	23-0	69	.234
1995— Binghamton (Eastern)	2	1	.667	2.85	0.93	6	6	1	0	...	0-...	41.0	26	15	13	1	12-0	59	.174
— Norfolk (Int'l)	9	1	.900	1.55	1.01	12	12	3	* 3	...	0-...	87.0	64	17	15	2	24-0	75	.203
— New York (N.L.)	9	2	.818	2.81	1.28	14	14	1	0	0	0-0	93.0	88	29	29	6	31-2	55	.254
1996— New York (N.L.)	6	14	.300	4.77	1.53	27	27	2	1	0	0-0	171.2	190	103	91	13	73-5	114	.284
1997— Norfolk (Int'l)	0	2	.000	4.05	1.40	3	3	0	0	...	0-...	20.0	20	10	9	4	8-0	17	.267
— GC Mets (GCL)	1	0	1.000	1.93	0.64	1	0	0	0	...	0-...	4.2	2	1	1	0	1-0	7	.125
— St. Lucie (Fla. St.)	1	0	1.000	0.00	1.08	2	2	0	0	...	0-...	12.0	8	1	0	0	5-0	15	.190
— New York (N.L.)	2	2	.500	7.58	2.09	6	6	0	0	0	0-0	29.2	40	27	25	3	22-0	25	.336
1998— New York (N.L.)										Did not play.									
1999— Norfolk (Int'l)	3	1	.750	2.29	1.04	12	8	0	0	...	0-...	51.0	33	18	13	4	20-0	51	.182
— New York (N.L.)	1	3	.250	6.41	1.65	13	5	0	0	0	1-1	39.1	43	29	28	7	22-2	31	.279
— Oakland (A.L.)	0	1	.000	2.13	1.30	20	0	0	0	8	8-9	25.1	21	6	6	2	12-2	20	.223
2000— Oakland (A.L.)	6	4	.600	3.78	1.43	66	0	0	0	0	33-40	69.0	67	34	29	6	32-5	57	.252
2001— Oakland (A.L.)	4	3	.571	2.65	1.08	65	0	0	0	0	34-43	71.1	54	24	21	5	23-5	74	.203
2002— St. Louis (N.L.)	3	2	.600	2.48	0.98	60	0	0	0	0	32-37	65.1	46	22	18	0	18-1	68	.199
2003— Tennessee (Sou.)	0	0	...	0.00	0.50	2	2	0	0	...	0-...	2.0	1	0	0	0	0-0	3	.143
— St. Louis (N.L.)	0	1	.000	2.36	1.17	40	0	0	0	1	22-25	42.0	31	14	11	2	18-1	41	.200
American League totals (3 years)	10	8	.556	3.04	1.26	151	0	0	0	0	75-91	165.2	142	64	56	13	67-12	151	.227
National League totals (6 years)	21	24	.467	4.12	1.41	160	52	3	1	1	55-63	441.0	438	224	202	31	184-11	334	.262
Major League totals (8 years)	31	32	.492	3.83	1.37	311	52	3	1	1	130-154	606.2	580	288	258	44	251-23	485	.252

IZTURIS, CESAR   SS

PERSONAL: Born February 10, 1980, in Barquisimeto, Venezuela. ... 5-9/175. ... Bats both, throws right. ... Full name: Cesar D. Izturis. ... Name pronounced: IS-tur-is.

TRANSACTIONS/CAREER NOTES: Signed as non-drafted free agent by Toronto Blue Jays organization (July 11, 1996). ... Traded by Blue Jays with P Paul Quantrill to Los Angeles Dodgers for P Luke Prokopec and P Chad Ricketts (December 13, 2001).

2003 GAMES PLAYED BY POSITION (MLB): SS—158.

Year Team (League)	Pos.	G	AB	R	H	2B	3B	HR	RBI	BB	SO	HBP	GDP	SB-CS	Avg.	OBP	SLG	OPS	E	Pct.
1997— St. Catharines (NYP)	2B-SS	70	231	32	44	3	0	1	11	15	27	1	3	6-3	.190	.241	.216	.457	16	.951
1998— Hagerstown (SAL)	2B-3B-SS	130	413	56	108	13	1	1	38	20	43	2	5	20-9	.262	.297	.305	.603	29	.952
1999— Dunedin (Fla. St.)	2B-3B-SS	131	536	77	165	28	12	3	77	22	58	6	9	32-16	.308	.337	.422	.758	21	.969
2000— Syracuse (Int'l)	SS	132	435	54	95	16	5	0	27	20	44	1	5	21-11	.218	.253	.278	.531	12	.981
2001— Syracuse (Int'l)	SS-2B	87	342	32	100	16	3	2	35	10	22	1	4	24-9	.292	.310	.374	.684	16	.962
— Toronto (A.L.)	2B-SS	46	134	19	36	6	2	2	9	2	15	0	0	8-1	.269	.279	.388	.667	3	.985
2002— Los Angeles (N.L.)	SS-2B-DH	135	439	43	102	24	2	1	31	14	39	0	12	7-7	.232	.253	.303	.556	10	.979
2003— Los Angeles (N.L.)	SS	158	558	47	140	21	6	1	40	25	70	0	8	10-5	.251	.282	.315	.597	16	.977
American League totals (1 year)		46	134	19	36	6	2	2	9	2	15	0	0	8-1	.269	.279	.388	.667	3	.985
National League totals (2 years)		293	997	90	242	45	8	2	71	39	109	0	20	17-12	.243	.269	.310	.579	26	.978
Major League totals (3 years)		339	1131	109	278	51	10	4	80	41	124	0	20	25-13	.246	.270	.319	.590	29	.979

JACKSON, DAMIAN   IF/OF

PERSONAL: Born August 16, 1973, in Los Angeles, Calif. ... 5-11/185. ... Bats right, throws right. ... Full name: Damian Jacques Jackson. ... High school: Ygnacio Valley (Concord, Calif.). ... Junior college: Laney College (Calif.).

TRANSACTIONS/CAREER NOTES: Selected by Cleveland Indians organization in 44th round of free-agent draft (June 3, 1991). ... Traded by Indians with P Danny Graves, P Jim Crowell and P Scott Winchester to Cincinnati Reds for P John Smiley and IF Jeff Branson (July 31, 1997). ... Traded by Reds with OF Reggie Sanders and P Josh Harris to San Diego Padres for OF Greg Vaughn and OF/1B Mark Sweeney (February 2, 1999). ... On San Diego disabled list (May 13-June 22, 2001); included rehabilitation assignment to Portland (June 18-21). ... Traded by Padres with C Matt Walbeck to Detroit Tigers for C Javier Cardona and OF Rich Gomez (March 24, 2002). ... On disabled list (April 7-22, 2002). ... Released by Tigers (November 20, 2002). ... Signed by Boston Red Sox (December 18, 2002).

2003 GAMES PLAYED BY POSITION (MLB): 2B—38, OF—38, SS—18, DH—9, 3B—3, 1B—2.

Year Team (League)	Pos.	G	AB	R	H	2B	3B	HR	RBI	BB	SO	HBP	GDP	SB-CS	Avg.	OBP	SLG	OPS	E	Pct.
1992— Burlington (Appal.)	SS	62	226	32	56	12	1	0	23	32	31	6	1	29-5	.248	.352	.310	.662	23	.933
1993— Columbus (S. Atl.)	SS	108	350	70	94	19	3	6	45	41	61	5	1	26-7	.269	.353	.391	.744	52	.908
1994— Cant./Akr. (Eastern)	SS-OF	138	531	85	143	29	5	5	60	60	121	5	8	37-16	.269	.346	.371	.717	‡ 54	.927
1995— Cant./Akr. (Eastern)	SS-OF	131	484	67	120	20	2	3	34	65	103	9	6	40-22	.248	.348	.316	.664	* 36	.939
1996— Buffalo (A.A.)	SS	133	452	77	116	15	1	12	49	48	78	7	7	24-7	.257	.333	.374	.707	29	.954
— Cleveland (A.L.)	SS	5	10	2	3	2	0	0	1	1	4	0	0	0-0	.300	.364	.500	.864	0	1.000
1997— Buffalo (A.A.)	SS-2B-OF	73	266	51	78	12	0	4	13	37	45	3	2	20-8	.293	.383	.383	.767	23	.942
— Cleveland (A.L.)	SS-2B	8	9	2	1	0	0	0	0	0	1	1	0	1-0	.111	.200	.111	.311	0	1.000
— Indianapolis (A.A.)	2B-SS	19	71	12	19	6	1	0	7	10	17	1	1	4-1	.268	.361	.380	.742	5	.949
— Cincinnati (N.L.)	SS-2B	12	27	6	6	2	1	1	2	4	7	0	0	1-1	.222	.323	.481	.804	1	.971
1998— Cincinnati (N.L.)	SS-OF	13	38	4	12	5	0	0	7	6	4	0	1	2-0	.316	.400	.447	.847	1	.976
— Indianapolis (Int'l)	SS-OF	131	517	102	135	36	10	6	49	62	125	10	2	25-10	.261	.349	.404	.753	‡ 44	.938
1999— San Diego (N.L.)	SS-2B-OF	133	388	56	87	20	3	9	39	53	105	3	2	34-10	.224	.320	.356	.676	26	.948

Year	Team (League)	Pos.	G	AB	R	H	2B	3B	HR	RBI	BB	SO	HBP	GDP	SB-CS	Avg.	OBP	SLG	OPS	E	Pct.
2000— San Diego (N.L.)	..............SS-2B-OF		138	470	68	120	27	6	6	37	62	108	3	7	28-6	.255	.345	.377	.721	25	.960
2001— San Diego (N.L.)	..............2B-SS-OF		122	440	67	106	21	6	4	38	44	128	6	6	23-6	.241	.316	.343	.660	8	.986
— Portland (PCL)	....	SS	3	10	4	3	3	0	0	0	3	1	0	0	0-1	.300	.462	.600	1.062	0	1.000
2002— Detroit (A.L.)	..................2-S-O-D-3		81	245	31	63	20	1	1	25	21	36	3	3	12-3	.257	.320	.359	.679	8	.972
2003— Boston (A.L.)	..................2-0-S-D-3-1		109	161	34	42	7	0	1	13	8	28	0	4	16-8	.261	.294	.323	.617	9	.951
American League totals (4 years)			203	425	69	109	29	1	2	39	30	69	4	7	29-11	.256	.309	.344	.652	17	.966
National League totals (5 years)			418	1363	201	331	75	15	20	123	169	352	12	16	88-23	.243	.330	.364	.694	61	.966
Major League totals (8 years)			621	1788	270	440	104	16	22	162	199	421	16	23	117-34	.246	.325	.359	.684	78	.966

JACKSON, EDWIN   P

PERSONAL: Born September 9, 1983, in Neu-Ulm, West Germany. ... 6-3/190. ... Throws right, bats right. ... High school: Shaw (Columbus, Ga.).

TRANSACTIONS/CAREER NOTES: Selected by Los Angeles Dodgers organization in sixth round of free-agent draft (June 5, 2001).

CAREER HITTING: 0-for-6 (.000), 0 R, 0 2B, 0 3B, 0 HR, 0 RBI.

Year	League	W	L	Pct.	ERA	WHIP	G	GS	CG	ShO	Hld.	Sv.-Opp.	IP	H	R	ER	HR	BB-IBB	SO	Avg.
2001— GC Dodgers (GCL)	....	2	1	.667	2.45	1.50	12	2	0	0	...	0-...	22.0	14	12	6	1	19-0	23	.173
2002— South Georgia (S. Atl.)	......	5	2	.714	1.98	1.07	19	19	0	0	...	0-...	104.2	79	34	23	2	33-0	85	.206
2003— Jacksonville (Sou.)	....	7	7	.500	3.70	1.17	27	27	0	0	...	0-...	148.1	121	68	61	9	53-0	157	.220
— Los Angeles (N.L.)	....	2	1	.667	2.45	1.27	4	3	0	0	0	0-0	22.0	17	6	6	2	11-1	19	.221
Major League totals (1 year)		2	1	.667	2.45	1.27	4	3	0	0	0	0-0	22.0	17	6	6	2	11-1	19	.221

JARVIS, KEVIN   P

PERSONAL: Born August 1, 1969, in Lexington, Ky. ... 6-2/200. ... Throws right, bats left. ... Full name: Kevin Thomas Jarvis. ... High school: Tates Creek (Lexington, Ky.). ... College: Wake Forest.

TRANSACTIONS/CAREER NOTES: Selected by Cincinnati Reds organization in 21st round of free-agent draft (June 3, 1991). ... Claimed on waivers by Detroit Tigers (May 2, 1997). ... Claimed on waivers by Minnesota Twins (May 9, 1997). ... Claimed on waivers by Tigers (June 17, 1997). ... On Detroit disabled list (June 25-July 14, 1997); included rehabilitation assignment to Toledo (July 4-14). ... Released by Tigers (December 12, 1997). ... Signed by Chunichi Dragons of the Japan Central League (January 23, 1998). ... Signed by Reds organization (August 27, 1998). ... Released by Reds (September 9, 1998). ... Signed by Oakland Athletics organization (January 4, 1999). ... On Oakland disabled list (April 19-June 4, 1999); included rehabilitation assignment to Modesto (May 28-June 4). ... Granted free agency (October 8, 1999). ... Signed by Colorado Rockies organization (December 1, 1999). ... On Colorado disabled list (July 28-September 1, 2000); included rehabilitation assignment to Colorado Springs (August 12-September 1). ... Granted free agency (December 21, 2000). ... Signed by San Diego Padres (January 5, 2001). ... On San Diego disabled list (April 18-May 5, May 10-June 27 and July 12, 2002-remainder of season); included rehabilitation assignments to Mobile (June 17-22) and Lake Elsinore (June 23-25). ... Placed on disabled list (March 26, 2003). ... Transferred to the Emergency disabled list (May 16, 2003). ... Contract purchased by San Diego (May 29, 2003). ... Recalled from Lake Elsinore rehab assignment (June 13, 2003). ... Activated from the 60-day disabled list by San Diego (July 3, 2003).

CAREER HITTING: 30-for-188 (.160), 19 R, 6 2B, 0 3B, 1 HR, 14 RBI.

Year	League	W	L	Pct.	ERA	WHIP	G	GS	CG	ShO	Hld.	Sv.-Opp.	IP	H	R	ER	HR	BB-IBB	SO	Avg.
1991— Princeton (Appal.)	....	5	6	.455	2.42	1.19	13	13	4	• 1	...	0-...	85.2	73	34	23	6	29-3	79	.220
1992— Cedar Rapids (Midw.)	....	0	0	...	0.00	1.00	1	0	0	0	...	0-...	1.0	1	0	0	0	0-0	0	.333
— Char., W.Va. (SAL)	....	6	8	.429	3.11	1.20	28	18	2	1	...	0-...	133.0	123	59	46	3	37-1	131	.244
1993— Winston-Salem (Caro.)	....	8	7	.533	3.41	1.25	21	20	2	1	...	0-...	145.0	133	68	55	13	48-2	101	.241
— Chattanooga (Sou.)	....	3	1	.750	1.69	0.99	7	3	2	0	...	0-...	37.1	26	7	7	0	11-0	18	.203
1994— Cincinnati (N.L.)	....	1	1	.500	7.13	1.53	6	3	0	0	0	0-0	17.2	22	14	14	4	5-0	10	.301
— Indianapolis (A.A.)	....	10	2	.833	3.54	1.28	21	20	2	0	0	0-0	132.1	136	55	52	13	34-2	90	.261
1995— Indianapolis (A.A.)	....	4	2	.667	4.45	1.32	10	10	2	1	...	0-...	60.2	62	33	30	2	18-1	37	.256
— Cincinnati (N.L.)	....	3	4	.429	5.70	1.56	19	11	1	1	0	0-0	79.0	91	56	50	13	32-2	33	.292
1996— Indianapolis (A.A.)	....	4	3	.571	5.06	1.34	8	8	0	0	...	0-...	42.2	45	27	24	3	12-0	32	.263
— Cincinnati (N.L.)	....	8	9	.471	5.98	1.62	24	20	2	1	0	0-0	120.1	152	93	80	17	43-5	63	.305
1997— Cincinnati (N.L.)	....	0	1	.000	10.13	2.10	9	0	0	0	1	1-1	13.1	21	16	15	4	7-0	12	.344
— Minnesota (A.L.)	....	0	0	...	12.46	2.38	6	2	0	0	0	0-...	13.0	23	18	18	4	8-0	9	.371
— Detroit (A.L.)	....	0	3	.000	5.40	1.66	17	3	0	0	0	0-...	41.2	55	28	25	9	14-0	27	.318
— Toledo (Int'l)	....	0	1	.000	6.75	1.38	2	2	0	0	...	0-...	8.0	7	6	6	0	4-0	5	.226
1998— Chunichi (Jp. Cn.)	....	1	2	.333	4.41	1.41	4	3	0	0	...	0-...	16.1	18	8	8	...	5-...	7	...
— Indianapolis (Int'l)	....	1	0	1.000	9.00	1.57	2	2	0	0	...	0-...	7.0	10	7	7	3	1-0	5	.323
1999— Oakland (A.L.)	....	0	1	.000	11.57	2.43	4	1	0	0	0	0-0	14.0	28	19	18	6	6-0	11	.418
— Modesto (Calif.)	....	0	0	...	1.29	0.71	2	2	0	0	...	0-...	7.0	4	1	1	0	1-0	10	.167
— Vancouver (PCL)	....	10	2	.833	3.41	1.32	17	16	2	1	...	0-...	103.0	110	47	39	14	26-0	64	.270
2000— Colo. Springs (PCL)	....	3	2	.600	0.69	0.79	7	7	0	0	...	0-...	39.0	18	6	3	1	13-0	18	.138
— Colorado (N.L.)	....	3	4	.429	5.95	1.49	24	19	0	0	0	0-0	115.0	138	83	76	26	33-3	60	.300
2001— San Diego (N.L.)	....	12	11	.522	4.79	1.23	32	32	1	1	0	0-0	193.1	189	107	103	•37	49-4	133	.254
2002— San Diego (N.L.)	....	2	4	.333	4.37	1.31	7	7	0	0	0	0-0	35.0	36	19	17	5	10-1	24	.269
— Mobile (Sou.)	....	0	0	...	0.00	0.67	1	1	0	0	...	0-...	3.0	2	0	0	0	0-0	3	.182
— Lake Elsinore (Calif.)	....	1	0	1.000	0.00	0.60	1	1	0	0	...	0-...	5.0	2	0	0	0	1-0	1	.133
2003— Lake Elsinore (Calif.)	....	2	1	.667	4.09	1.00	3	3	0	0	...	0-...	22.0	18	11	10	1	4-0	19	.222
— San Diego (N.L.)	....	4	8	.333	5.87	1.58	16	16	0	0	0	0-0	92.0	113	65	60	15	32-5	49	.304
American League totals (2 years)		0	4	.000	8.00	1.95	27	6	0	0	0	0-0	68.2	106	65	61	19	28-0	47	.351
National League totals (8 years)		33	42	.440	5.61	1.46	137	108	4	3	0	1-1	665.2	762	453	415	121	211-20	384	.287
Major League totals (9 years)		33	46	.418	5.83	1.51	164	114	4	3	0	1-1	734.1	868	518	476	140	239-20	431	.294

JENKINS, GEOFF   OF

PERSONAL: Born July 21, 1974, in Olympia, Wash. ... 6-1/213. ... Bats left, throws right. ... Full name: Geoff Scott Jenkins. ... High school: Cordova Senior (Rancho Cordova, Calif.). ... College: USC.

TRANSACTIONS/CAREER NOTES: Selected by Milwaukee Brewers organization in first round (ninth pick overall) of free-agent draft (June 1, 1995). ... On El Paso disabled list (May 8-July 23, 1996). ... On disabled list (July 4-August 11, 1997). ... On disabled list (May 7-29, 2000). ... On Milwaukee disabled list (May 2-19 and July 29-August 28, 2001); included rehabilitation assignment to Beloit (August 27-28). ... On disabled list (June 18, 2002-remainder of season). ... On Milwaukee disabled list (March 21-April 9, 2003); included rehabilitation assignment to Huntsville (April 3-9). ... Placed on 15-day disabled list (August 29, 2003). ... Reinstated from 15-day disabled list (September 29, 2003).

2003 GAMES PLAYED BY POSITION (MLB): OF—123, DH—1.

Year	Team (League)	Pos.	G	AB	R	H	2B	3B	HR	RBI	BB	SO	HBP	GDP	SB-CS	Avg.	OBP	SLG	OPS	E	Pct.
											BATTING									**FIELDING**	
1995— Helena (Pio.)	OF	7	28	2	9	0	1	0	9	3	11	0	0	0-2	.321	.375	.393	.768	0	1.000
— Stockton (Calif.)	OF	13	47	13	12	2	0	3	12	10	12	0	0	2-0	.255	.373	.489	.862	2	.895
— El Paso (Texas)	OF	22	79	12	22	4	2	1	13	8	23	0	1	3-1	.278	.341	.418	.759	7	.857
1996— El Paso (Texas)	DH	22	77	17	22	5	4	1	11	12	21	2	2	1-2	.286	.391	.494	.885	...	...
— Stockton (Calif.)	DH-OF	37	138	27	48	8	4	3	25	20	32	3	3	3-3	.348	.433	.529	.962	0	1.000
1997— Tucson (PCL)	SS-OF	93	347	44	82	24	3	10	56	33	87	3	7	0-2	.236	.308	.409	.717	5	.961
1998— Louisville (Int'l)	OF	55	215	38	71	10	4	7	52	14	39	5	6	1-1	.330	.381	.512	.893	2	.979
— Milwaukee (N.L.)	OF	84	262	33	60	12	1	9	28	20	61	2	7	1-3	.229	.288	.385	.673	4	.968
1999— Milwaukee (N.L.)	OF	135	447	70	140	43	3	21	82	35	87	7	10	5-1	.313	.371	.564	.935	7	.974
2000— Milwaukee (N.L.)	OF	135	512	100	155	36	4	34	94	33	135	15	9	11-1	.303	.360	.588	.948	7	.975
2001— Milwaukee (N.L.)	OF	105	397	60	105	21	1	20	63	36	120	8	11	4-2	.264	.334	.474	.808	3	.986
— Beloit (Midw.)	OF	1	3	1	1	1	0	0	1	1	1	0	0	0-0	.333	.500	.667	1.167	0	...
2002— Milwaukee (N.L.)	OF	67	243	35	59	17	1	10	29	22	60	6	8	1-2	.243	.320	.444	.764	1	.992
2003— Huntsville (Sou.)	OF	6	20	6	5	0	0	2	3	1	7	0	0	1-0	.250	.286	.550	.836	0	1.000
— Milwaukee (N.L.)	OF-DH	124	487	81	144	30	2	28	95	58	120	6	12	0-0	.296	.375	.538	.913	1	1.000
Major League totals (6 years)		650	2348	379	663	159	12	122	391	204	583	44	57	22-9	.282	.349	.516	.865	22	.983

JENNINGS, JASON — P

PERSONAL: Born July 17, 1978, in Dallas, Texas. ... 6-2/245. ... Throws right, bats left. ... Full name: Jason Ryan Jennings. ... High school: Dr. Ralph H. Poteet (Mesquite, Texas). ... College: Baylor.

TRANSACTIONS/CAREER NOTES: Selected by Colorado Rockies organization in first round (16th pick overall) of free-agent draft (June 2, 1999).

CAREER HITTING: 35-for-131 (.267), 11 R, 8 2B, 0 3B, 1 HR, 16 RBI.

Year	League	W	L	Pct.	ERA	WHIP	G	GS	CG	ShO	Hld.	Sv.-Opp.	IP	H	R	ER	HR	BB-IBB	SO	Avg.
1999— Portland (NW)	1	0	1.000	1.00	0.78	2	2	0	0	...	0-...	9.0	5	1	1	0	2-0	11	.161
— Asheville (S. Atl.)	2	2	.500	3.70	1.08	12	12	0	0	...	0-...	58.1	55	27	24	3	8-0	69	.247
2000— Salem (Caro.)	7	10	.412	3.47	1.18	22	22	3	1	...	0-...	150.1	136	66	58	6	42-0	133	.234
— Carolina (Sou.)	1	3	.250	3.44	1.17	6	6	0	0	...	0-...	36.2	32	19	14	4	11-0	33	.234
2001— Carolina (Sou.)	2	0	1.000	2.88	1.32	4	4	0	0	...	0-...	25.0	25	9	8	1	8-0	24	.258
— Colo. Springs (PCL)	7	8	.467	4.72	1.41	22	22	4	0	...	0-...	131.2	145	80	69	9	41-0	110	.281
— Colorado (N.L.)	4	1	.800	4.58	1.55	7	7	1	1	0	0-0	39.1	42	21	20	2	19-0	26	.276
2002— Colorado (N.L.)	16	8	.667	4.52	1.46	32	32	0	0	0	0-0	185.1	201	102	93	26	70-2	127	.280
2003— Colorado (N.L.)	12	13	.480	5.11	1.65	32	32	1	0	0	0-0	181.1	212	115	103	20	88-7	119	.299
Major League totals (3 years)	32	22	.593	4.79	1.56	71	71	2	1	0	0-0	406.0	455	238	216	48	177-9	272	.288

JENSEN, RYAN — P

PERSONAL: Born September 17, 1975, in Salt Lake City, Utah. ... 6-0/205. ... Throws right, bats right. ... Full name: Larry Ryan Jensen. ... High school: Cottonwood (Salt Lake City). ... College: Southern Utah.

TRANSACTIONS/CAREER NOTES: Selected by San Francisco Giants organization in eighth round of free-agent draft (June 4, 1996). ... On disabled list (June 21-30, 1999). ... On disabled list (April 10, 2003). ... Sent on rehab assignment to Fresno (April 19, 2003). ... Recalled from 15-day disabled list; reinstated from 15-day disabled list (May 9, 2003). ... Recalled from Fresno (September 29, 2003).

CAREER HITTING: 10-for-73 (.137), 5 R, 2 2B, 0 3B, 0 HR, 6 RBI.

Year	League	W	L	Pct.	ERA	WHIP	G	GS	CG	ShO	Hld.	Sv.-Opp.	IP	H	R	ER	HR	BB-IBB	SO	Avg.
1996— Bellingham (N'west)	2	4	.333	4.98	1.55	13	11	0	0	...	0-...	47.0	35	30	26	4	38-0	31	.208
1997— Bakersfield (Calif.)	0	0	...	13.50	2.25	1	1	0	0	...	0-...	1.1	3	2	2	1	0-0	2	.500
— Salem-Keizer (NW)	7	3	.700	5.15	1.48	16	•16	0	0	...	0-...	80.1	87	55	46	•10	32-0	67	.278
1998— Bakersfield (Calif.)	11	12	.478	3.37	1.32	29	27	0	0	...	0-...	168.1	162	89	63	14	61-3	164	.249
— Fresno (PCL)	0	0	...	4.76	1.41	2	1	0	0	...	0-...	5.2	4	5	3	2	4-0	6	.190
1999— Fresno (PCL)	11	10	.524	5.12	1.46	27	27	0	0	...	0-...	156.1	160	96	89	17	68-1	150	.266
2000— Fresno (PCL)	5	8	.385	5.79	1.70	26	26	1	0	...	0-...	135.1	167	106	87	18	63-0	114	.305
2001— Fresno (PCL)	11	2	.846	3.48	1.24	20	17	1	1	...	0-...	106.0	97	43	41	11	34-0	95	.242
— San Francisco (N.L.)	1	2	.333	4.25	1.63	10	7	0	0	0	0-0	42.1	44	21	20	5	25-0	26	.268
2002— San Francisco (N.L.)	13	8	.619	4.51	1.45	32	30	1	0	0	0-0	171.2	183	93	86	21	66-4	105	.278
2003— San Francisco (N.L.)	0	0	...	10.80	1.95	6	2	0	0	0	0-0	13.1	21	16	16	6	5-0	3	.404
— Fresno (PCL)	1	10	.091	5.30	1.45	27	18	0	0	...	0-...	103.2	114	70	61	14	36-2	50	.285
Major League totals (3 years)	14	10	.583	4.83	1.51	48	39	1	0	0	0-0	227.1	248	130	122	32	96-4	134	.284

JETER, DEREK — SS

PERSONAL: Born June 26, 1974, in Pequannock, N.J. ... 6-3/195. ... Bats right, throws right. ... Full name: Derek Sanderson Jeter. ... Name pronounced: JEE-ter. ... High school: Central (Kalamazoo, Mich.).

TRANSACTIONS/CAREER NOTES: Selected by New York Yankees organization in first round (sixth pick overall) of free-agent draft (June 1, 1992). ... On New York disabled list (June 3-19, 1998); included rehabilitation assignment to Columbus (June 18-19). ... On New York disabled list (May 12-27, 2000); included rehabilitation assignment to Tampa (May 26-27). ... On disabled list (March 23-April 7, 2001). ... On disabled list (April 1-May 14, 2003).

2003 GAMES PLAYED BY POSITION (MLB): SS—118.

Year	Team (League)	Pos.	G	AB	R	H	2B	3B	HR	RBI	BB	SO	HBP	GDP	SB-CS	Avg.	OBP	SLG	OPS	E	Pct.
											BATTING									**FIELDING**	
1992— GC Yankees (GCL)	SS	47	173	19	35	10	0	3	25	19	36	5	4	2-2	.202	.296	.312	.609	12	.943
— Greensboro (S. Atl.)	SS	11	37	4	9	0	0	1	4	7	16	1	0	0-1	.243	.378	.324	.702	9	.813
1993— Greensboro (S. Atl.)	SS	128	515	85	152	14	11	5	71	56	95	11	9	18-9	.295	.374	.394	.768	56	.889
1994— Tampa (Fla. St.)	SS	69	292	61	96	13	8	0	39	23	30	3	4	28-2	.329	.380	.428	.808	12	.961
— Alb./Colon. (East.)	SS	34	122	17	46	7	2	2	13	15	16	1	3	12-2	.377	.446	.516	.962	6	.961
— Columbus (Int'l)	SS	35	126	25	44	7	1	3	16	20	15	1	6	10-4	.349	.439	.492	.931	7	.955
1995— Columbus (Int'l)	SS	123	486	* 96	154	27	9	2	45	61	56	4	9	20-12	.317	.394	.422	.816	* 29	.953
— New York (A.L.)	SS	15	48	5	12	4	1	0	7	3	11	0	0	0-0	.250	.294	.375	.669	2	.962
1996— New York (A.L.)	SS	157	582	104	183	25	6	10	78	48	102	9	13	14-7	.314	.370	.430	.800	22	.969
1997— New York (A.L.)	SS	159	654	116	190	31	7	10	70	74	125	10	14	23-12	.291	.370	.405	.775	18	.975
1998— New York (A.L.)	SS	149	626	* 127	203	25	8	19	84	57	119	5	13	30-6	.324	.384	.481	.864	9	.986
— Columbus (Int'l)	SS	1	5	2	2	2	0	0	0	0	0	0	0	0-0	.400	.400	.800	1.200	1	.875
1999— New York (A.L.)	SS	158	627	134	* 219	37	9	24	102	91	116	12	12	19-8	.349	.438	.552	.989	14	.978

Year Team (League)	Pos.	G	AB	R	H	2B	3B	HR	RBI	BB	SO	HBP	GDP	SB-CS	Avg.	OBP	SLG	OPS	E	Pct.
2000— New York (A.L.)	SS	148	593	119	201	31	4	15	73	68	99	12	14	22-4	.339	.416	.481	.896	24	.961
— Tampa (Fla. St.)	SS	1	3	2	2	1	0	0	0	0	0	0	0	0-0	.667	.667	1.000	1.667	0	1.000
2001— New York (A.L.)	SS	150	614	110	191	35	3	21	74	56	99	10	13	27-3	.311	.377	.480	.858	15	.974
2002— New York (A.L.)	SS-DH	157	644	124	191	26	0	18	75	73	114	7	14	32-3	.297	.373	.421	.794	14	.977
2003— Trenton (East.)	SS	5	18	2	8	1	1	0	5	3	0	1	0	0-0	.444	.545	.611	1.157	1	.957
— New York (A.L.)	SS	119	482	87	156	25	3	10	52	43	88	13	10	11-5	.324	.393	.450	.844	14	.968
Major League totals (9 years)		1212	4870	926	1546	239	41	127	615	513	873	78	103	178-48	.317	.389	.462	.851	132	.973

JIMENEZ, D'ANGELO — IF

PERSONAL: Born December 21, 1977, in Santo Domingo, Dominican Republic. ... 6-0/195. ... Bats both, throws right. ... Name pronounced: he-MEN-ez.

TRANSACTIONS/CAREER NOTES: Signed as non-drafted free agent by New York Yankees organization (August 1, 1994). ... On Columbus disabled list (August 6-19, 1999). ... On New York disabled list (March 23-August 24, 2000); included rehabilitation assignments to Gulf Coast Yankees (July 26-31), Tampa (August 1-14) and Columbus (August 15-24). ... Traded by Yankees to San Diego Padres for P Jay Witasick (June 23, 2001). ... Traded by Padres to Chicago White Sox for OF Alex Fernandez and C Humberto Quintero (July 12, 2002). ... Traded by White Sox to Cincinnati Reds for P Scott Dunn (July 6, 2003).

2003 GAMES PLAYED BY POSITION (MLB): 2B—141, 3B—4.

Year Team (League)	Pos.	G	AB	R	H	2B	3B	HR	RBI	BB	SO	HBP	GDP	SB-CS	Avg.	OBP	SLG	OPS	E	Pct.
1995— GC Yankees (GCL)	SS	57	214	41	60	14	* 8	2	28	23	31	1	4	6-3	.280	.347	.449	.796	21	.927
1996— Greensboro (S. Atl.)	SS	138	* 537	68	131	25	5	6	48	56	113	3	7	15-17	.244	.317	.343	.660	* 50	.922
1997— Tampa (Fla. St.)	SS	94	352	52	99	14	6	6	48	50	50	2	3	8-14	.281	.368	.406	.775	21	.953
— Columbus (Int'l)	SS	2	7	1	1	0	0	0	1	0	1	0	1	0-0	.143	.125	.143	.268	2	.833
1998— Norwich (East.)	SS	40	152	21	41	6	2	2	21	25	26	2	3	5-5	.270	.378	.375	.753	12	.938
— Columbus (Int'l)	2B-SS	91	344	55	88	19	4	8	51	46	67	1	7	6-6	.256	.341	.404	.745	26	.946
1999— Columbus (Int'l) SS-3B-2B		126	526	97	172	32	5	15	88	59	75	1	8	26-14	.327	.392	.492	.884	26	.957
— New York (A.L.)	3B-2B	7	20	3	8	2	0	0	4	3	4	0	0	0-0	.400	.478	.500	.978	0	1.000
2000— GC Yankees (GCL)	2B-SS	4	10	2	1	0	0	0	0	5	1	0	0	0-0	.100	.400	.100	.500	2	.900
— Tampa (Fla. St.)	SS-2B	12	41	8	8	1	1	1	2	8	7	0	1	0-0	.195	.320	.341	.661	7	.875
— Columbus (Int'l) 2B-3B-SS		21	73	11	17	3	1	1	5	7	12	1	2	2-0	.233	.309	.342	.651	4	.944
2001— Columbus (Int'l) 2B-SS-SS		56	214	33	56	11	1	5	19	24	31	1	2	5-6	.262	.333	.393	.726	7	.965
— San Diego (N.L.)	SS	86	308	45	85	19	0	3	33	39	68	0	9	2-3	.276	.355	.367	.722	21	.948
2002— San Diego (N.L.)	2B-3B	87	321	39	77	11	4	3	33	34	63	0	10	4-2	.240	.311	.327	.638	12	.968
— Charlotte (Int'l)	2B	42	157	24	44	11	1	6	18	24	14	0	2	6-2	.280	.372	.478	.849	6	.966
— Chicago (A.L.) 2B-SS-3B		27	108	22	31	4	3	1	11	16	10	1	1	2-1	.287	.384	.407	.791	2	.985
2003— Chicago (A.L.) 2B-3B		73	271	35	69	11	5	7	26	32	46	0	3	4-3	.255	.332	.410	.742	9	.970
— Cincinnati (N.L.)	2B-3B	73	290	34	84	13	2	7	31	34	43	2	4	7-4	.290	.365	.421	.785	4	.990
American League totals (3 years)		107	399	60	108	17	8	8	41	51	60	1	4	6-4	.271	.354	.414	.768	11	.976
National League totals (3 years)		246	919	118	246	43	6	13	97	107	174	2	23	13-9	.268	.343	.370	.713	37	.968
Major League totals (4 years)		353	1318	178	354	60	14	21	138	158	234	3	27	19-13	.269	.346	.383	.729	48	.970

JIMENEZ, JOSE — P

PERSONAL: Born July 7, 1973, in San Pedro de Macoris, Dominican Republic. ... 6-3/230. ... Throws right, bats right. ... Full name: Jose Antena Jimenez. ... Name pronounced: he-MEN-ez.

TRANSACTIONS/CAREER NOTES: Signed as non-drafted free agent by St. Louis Cardinals organization (October 21, 1991). ... Traded by Cardinals with P Manny Aybar, P Rick Croushore and SS Brent Butler to Colorado Rockies for P Darryl Kile, P Dave Veres and P Luther Hackman (November 16, 1999). ... On disabled list (July 8-23 and August 20-September 17, 2001). ... Elected free agency (September 30, 2003).

CAREER HITTING: 10-for-81 (.123), 8 R, 0 2B, 1 3B, 0 HR, 4 RBI.

Year League	W	L	Pct.	ERA	WHIP	G	GS	CG	ShO	Hld.	Sv.-Opp.	IP	H	R	ER	HR	BB-IBB	SO	Avg.
1992— Dom. Cardinals (DSL)	3	2	.600	6.10	1.87	18	2	0	0	...	0-...	48.2	68	43	33	...	23-...	21	...
1993— Dom. Cardinals (DSL)	3	5	.375	3.51	1.70	12	12	0	0	...	0-...	56.1	61	47	22	...	35-...	30	...
1994— Dom. Cardinals (DSL)	3	9	.250	2.77	1.23	19	9	0	0	...	3-...	68.1	54	43	21	...	30-...	54	...
1995— Johnson City (App.)	5	7	.417	3.49	1.17	14	• 14	1	1	...	0-...	* 90.1	81	48	35	3	25-0	85	.234
1996— Peoria (Midw.)	12	9	.571	2.92	1.22	28	27	3	1	...	0-...	172.1	158	75	56	6	53-0	129	.245
1997— Prince William (Caro.)	9	7	.563	3.09	1.17	24	24	2	0	...	0-...	145.2	128	73	50	12	42-2	81	.231
1998— Arkansas (Texas)	* 15	6	.714	3.11	1.25	26	26	1	• 1	...	0-...	* 179.2	156	71	62	9	68-1	88	.239
— St. Louis (N.L.)	3	0	1.000	2.95	1.41	4	3	0	0	0	0-0	21.1	22	8	7	0	8-0	12	.262
1999— St. Louis (N.L.)	5	14	.263	5.85	1.50	29	28	2	2	0	0-1	163.0	173	114	106	16	71-2	113	.275
— Memphis (PCL)	2	2	.500	3.04	1.46	4	4	0	0	0	0-...	26.2	30	10	9	0	9-0	18	.303
2000— Colorado (N.L.)	5	2	.714	3.18	1.29	72	0	0	0	2	24-30	70.2	63	27	25	4	28-6	44	.239
2001— Colorado (N.L.)	6	1	.857	4.09	1.42	56	0	0	0	0	17-22	55.0	56	27	25	6	22-4	37	.264
2002— Colorado (N.L.)	2	10	.167	3.56	1.19	74	0	0	0	0	41-47	73.1	76	34	29	7	11-4	47	.265
2003— Colorado (N.L.)	2	10	.167	5.22	1.66	63	7	0	0	2	20-23	101.2	137	62	59	7	32-5	45	.322
Major League totals (6 years)	23	37	.383	4.66	1.44	298	38	2	2	4	102-123	485.0	527	272	251	40	172-21	298	.277

JOHNSON, ADAM — P

PERSONAL: Born July 12, 1979, in San Jose, Calif. ... 6-2/210. ... Throws right, bats right. ... Full name: Adam Bryant Johnson. ... High school: Torrey Pines (Del Mar, Calif.). ... College: Cal State Fullerton.

TRANSACTIONS/CAREER NOTES: Selected by Minnesota Twins organization in first round (second pick overall) of free-agent draft (June 5, 2000).

CAREER HITTING: 0-for-2 (.000), 0 R, 0 2B, 0 3B, 0 HR, 0 RBI.

Year League	W	L	Pct.	ERA	WHIP	G	GS	CG	ShO	Hld.	Sv.-Opp.	IP	H	R	ER	HR	BB-IBB	SO	Avg.
2000— Fort Myers (Fla. St.)	5	4	.556	2.47	0.94	13	12	1	1	...	0-...	69.1	45	24	19	2	20-1	92	.186
2001— New Britain (East.)	5	6	.455	3.82	1.27	18	18	0	0	...	0-...	113.0	105	53	48	10	39-2	110	.248
— Minnesota (A.L.)	1	2	.333	8.28	1.80	7	4	0	0	0	0-0	25.0	32	25	23	6	13-0	17	.323
— Edmonton (PCL)	1	1	.500	5.70	1.23	4	4	0	0	0	0-...	23.2	19	15	15	0	10-0	25	.226
2002— Edmonton (PCL)	13	8	.619	5.47	1.57	27	27	1	1	...	0-...	151.1	182	96	92	25	55-0	112	.304
2003— Rochester (Int'l)	6	11	.353	5.35	1.54	28	17	1	0	...	0-...	114.1	128	73	68	7	48-2	78	.292
— Minnesota (A.L.)	0	1	.000	47.25	6.75	2	0	0	0	0	0-0	1.1	8	8	7	1	1-0	0	.667
Major League totals (2 years)	1	3	.250	10.25	2.05	9	4	0	0	0	0-0	26.1	40	33	30	7	14-0	17	.360

JOHNSON, CHARLES   C

PERSONAL: Born July 20, 1971, in Fort Pierce, Fla. ... 6-3/250. ... Bats right, throws right. ... Full name: Charles Edward Johnson. ... High school: Westwood (Fort Pierce, Fla.). ... College: Miami (Fla.).

TRANSACTIONS/CAREER NOTES: Selected by Montreal Expos organization in first round (10th pick overall) of free-agent draft (June 5, 1989); did not sign. ... Selected by Florida Marlins organization in first round (28th pick overall) of free-agent draft (June 1, 1992). ... On Florida disabled list (August 9-September 1, 1995); included rehabilitation assignment to Portland (August 30-September 1). ... On disabled list (July 28-September 1, 1996). ... Traded by Marlins with OF Gary Sheffield, 3B Bobby Bonilla, OF Jim Eisenreich and P Manuel Barrios to Los Angeles Dodgers for C Mike Piazza and 3B Todd Zeile (May 15, 1998). ... Traded by Dodgers with OF Roger Cedeno to New York Mets for C Todd Hundley and P Arnold Gooch; then traded by Mets to Baltimore Orioles for P Armando Benitez (December 1, 1998). ... Traded by Orioles with DH Harold Baines to Chicago White Sox for C Brook Fordyce, P Miguel Felix, P Juan Figueroa and P Jason Lakman (July 29, 2000). ... Granted free agency (October 30, 2000). ... Signed by Marlins (December 18, 2000). ... On Florida disabled list (March 26-April 8 and July 28-August 16, 2002); included rehabilitation assignment to Jupiter (August 13-16). ... Traded by Marlins with P Vic Darensbourg, OF Preston Wilson and 2B Pablo Ozuna to Colorado Rockies for P Mike Hampton, OF Juan Pierre and cash (November 16, 2002).

2003 GAMES PLAYED BY POSITION (MLB): C—107.

										BATTING									FIELDING	
Year Team (League)	Pos.	G	AB	R	H	2B	3B	HR	RBI	BB	SO	HBP	GDP	SB-CS	Avg.	OBP	SLG	OPS	E	Pct.
1993— Kane Co. (Midw.)	C	• 135	488	74	134	29	5	19	* 94	62	111	2	12	9-1	.275	.356	.471	.827	12	.988
1994— Portland (East.)	C-DH	132	443	64	117	29	1	* 28	80	* 74	97	3	14	4-5	.264	.371	.524	.895	7	.991
— Florida (N.L.)	C	4	11	5	5	1	0	1	4	1	4	0	1	0-0	.455	.462	.818	1.280	0	1.000
1995— Florida (N.L.)	C	97	315	40	79	15	1	11	39	46	71	4	11	0-2	.251	.351	.410	.761	6	.992
— Portland (East.)	C	2	7	0	0	0	0	0	0	1	3	0	0	0-0	.000	.125	.000	.125	1	.958
1996— Florida (N.L.)	C	120	386	34	84	13	1	13	37	40	91	2	20	1-0	.218	.292	.358	.649	4	.995
1997— Florida (N.L.)	C	124	416	43	104	26	1	19	63	60	109	3	13	0-2	.250	.347	.454	.802	0	1.000
1998— Florida (N.L.)	C	31	113	13	25	5	0	7	23	16	30	0	3	0-1	.221	.315	.451	.767	2	.990
— Los Angeles (N.L.)	C	102	346	31	75	13	0	12	35	29	99	1	9	0-1	.217	.279	.358	.638	6	.992
1999— Baltimore (A.L.)	C	135	426	58	107	19	1	16	54	55	107	4	13	0-0	.251	.340	.413	.753	5	.994
2000— Baltimore (A.L.)	C-DH	84	286	52	84	16	0	21	55	32	69	0	8	2-0	.294	.364	.570	.934	3	.994
— Chicago (A.L.)	C	44	135	24	44	8	0	10	36	20	37	1	0	0-0	.326	.411	.607	1.019	3	.987
2001— Florida (N.L.)	C	128	451	51	117	32	0	18	75	38	133	4	9	0-0	.259	.321	.450	.771	4	.996
2002— Florida (N.L.)	C	83	244	18	53	19	0	6	36	31	61	0	10	0-0	.217	.301	.369	.670	3	.994
— Jupiter (FSL)	C	5	16	5	7	0	0	3	9	2	4	0	0	0-0	.438	.500	1.000	1.500	0	1.000
2003— Colorado (N.L.)	C	108	356	49	82	20	0	20	61	49	84	1	8	1-3	.230	.320	.455	.775	4	.993
American League totals (2 years)		263	847	134	235	43	1	47	145	107	213	5	21	2-0	.277	.360	.497	.857	11	.993
National League totals (8 years)		797	2638	284	624	144	3	107	373	310	682	15	83	2-9	.237	.318	.415	.733	29	.995
Major League totals (10 years)		1060	3485	418	859	187	4	154	518	417	895	20	104	4-9	.246	.328	.435	.763	40	.994

JOHNSON, GARY   OF

PERSONAL: Born October 29, 1975, in Palo Alto, Calif. ... 6-3/210. ... Bats left, throws left. ... Full name: Gerald Clyde Johnson. ... High school: Menlo School (Atherton, Calif.). ... College: Brigham Young.

TRANSACTIONS/CAREER NOTES: Selected by Anaheim Angels organization in 19th round of free-agent draft (June 2, 1999).

2003 GAMES PLAYED BY POSITION (MLB): OF—4.

										BATTING									FIELDING	
Year Team (League)	Pos.	G	AB	R	H	2B	3B	HR	RBI	BB	SO	HBP	GDP	SB-CS	Avg.	OBP	SLG	OPS	E	Pct.
1999— Boise (NW)	OF	71	264	56	83	17	1	2	48	34	44	2	6	6-2	.314	.393	.409	.802	5	.957
2000— Lake Elsinore (Calif.)	OF	70	266	56	90	20	2	13	62	41	59	4	6	13-6	.338	.427	.575	1.002	6	.948
— Erie (East.)	OF	71	258	44	74	10	4	10	56	35	63	3	4	4-4	.287	.377	.473	.850	2	.980
2001— Arkansas (Texas)	OF	128	466	63	114	24	2	11	72	60	93	7	8	8-7	.245	.336	.376	.712	2	.989
2002— Salt Lake (PCL)	OF	40	143	30	38	9	3	5	35	15	49	3	3	1-1	.266	.341	.476	.817	0	1.000
2003— Anaheim (A.L.)	OF	5	8	1	3	1	0	0	0	1	1	0	0	0-1	.375	.444	.500	.944	0	1.000
— Salt Lake (PCL)	OF-DH	121	447	65	114	23	7	12	74	61	112	4	5	4-2	.255	.346	.418	.764	3	.985
Major League totals (1 year)		5	8	1	3	1	0	0	0	1	1	0	0	0-1	.375	.444	.500	.944	0	1.000

JOHNSON, JASON   P

PERSONAL: Born October 27, 1973, in Santa Barbara, Calif. ... 6-6/217. ... Throws right, bats right. ... Full name: Jason Michael Johnson. ... High school: Conner (Hebron, Ky.).

TRANSACTIONS/CAREER NOTES: Signed as non-drafted free agent by Pittsburgh Pirates organization (July 21, 1992). ... Selected by Tampa Bay Devil Rays in first round (14th pick overall) of expansion draft (November 18, 1997). ... On Tampa Bay disabled list (July 4, 1998-remainder of season). ... Traded by Devil Rays to Baltimore Orioles for OF Danny Clyburn and a player to be named later (March 29, 1999); Devil Rays acquired SS Bolivar Voquez to complete deal (April 22, 1999). ... On Baltimore disabled list (April 25-June 7 and July 23-August 9, 2002); included rehabilitation assignment to Bowie (June 1-7).

CAREER HITTING: 2-for-19 (.105), 1 R, 0 2B, 0 3B, 0 HR, 0 RBI.

Year League	W	L	Pct.	ERA	WHIP	G	GS	CG	ShO	Hld.	Sv.-Opp.	IP	H	R	ER	HR	BB-IBB	SO	Avg.
1992— GC Pirates (GCL)	2	0	1.000	3.68	1.64	5	0	0	0	...	0-...	7.1	6	3	3	0	6-0	3	.240
1993— GC Pirates (GCL)	1	4	.200	2.33	1.15	9	9	0	0	...	0-...	54.0	48	22	14	0	14-0	39	.243
— Welland (N.Y.-Penn)	1	5	.167	4.63	1.20	6	6	1	0	...	0-...	35.0	33	24	18	0	9-0	19	.243
1994— Augusta (S. Atl.)	2	12	.143	4.03	1.47	20	19	1	0	...	0-...	102.2	119	67	46	5	32-0	69	.285
1995— Augusta (S. Atl.)	3	5	.375	4.36	1.38	11	11	1	0	...	0-...	53.2	57	32	26	2	17-0	42	.271
— Lynchburg (Carolina)	1	2	.333	2.05	1.27	5	4	0	0	...	0-...	22.0	23	6	5	9	5-0	9	.109
1996— Lynchburg (Carolina)	1	4	.200	6.50	1.53	15	5	0	0	...	0-...	44.1	56	37	32	6	12-0	27	.303
— Augusta (S. Atl.)	4	4	.500	3.11	1.27	14	14	1	1	...	0-...	84.0	82	40	29	2	25-0	83	.256
1997— Lynchburg (Carolina)	8	4	.667	3.71	1.29	17	17	0	0	...	0-...	99.1	98	43	41	4	30-1	92	.266
— Carolina (Sou.)	3	3	.500	4.08	1.26	9	9	1	0	...	0-...	57.1	56	31	26	6	16-0	63	.249
— Pittsburgh (N.L.)	0	0	...	6.00	1.83	3	0	0	0	0	0-0	6.0	10	4	4	2	1-0	3	.385
1998— Durham (Int'l)	1	0	1.000	2.92	0.65	2	2	0	0	0	0-...	12.1	6	4	4	2	2-0	14	.143
— Tampa Bay (A.L.)	2	5	.286	5.70	1.68	13	13	0	0	0	0-0	60.0	74	38	38	9	27-0	36	.306
1999— Rochester (Int'l)	4	2	.667	3.65	1.40	8	8	0	0	0	0-0	44.1	35	19	18	6	27-0	47	.212
— Baltimore (A.L.)	8	7	.533	5.46	1.52	22	21	0	0	0	0-0	115.1	120	74	70	16	55-0	71	.273
2000— Rochester (Int'l)	3	1	.750	1.47	0.96	8	8	1	1	0	0-0	55.0	32	12	9	2	21-0	56	.170
— Baltimore (A.L.)	1	10	.091	7.02	1.67	25	13	0	0	2	0-0	107.2	119	95	84	21	61-2	79	.287
2001— Baltimore (A.L.)	10	12	.455	4.09	1.38	32	32	2	0	0	0-0	196.0	194	109	89	28	77-3	114	.257
2002— Baltimore (A.L.)	5	14	.263	4.59	1.39	22	22	1	0	0	0-0	131.1	141	68	67	19	41-2	97	.276
— Bowie (East.)	1	0	1.000	0.00	1.00	1	1	0	0	0	0-...	5.0	4	0	0	0	1-0	6	.211
2003— Baltimore (A.L.)	10	10	.500	4.18	1.56	32	32	0	0	0	0-0	189.2	216	100	88	22	80-8	118	.283
American League totals (6 years)	36	58	.383	4.91	1.51	146	133	3	0	2	0-0	800.0	864	484	436	115	341-15	515	.274
National League totals (1 year)	0	0	...	6.00	1.83	3	0	0	0	0	0-0	6.0	10	4	4	2	1-0	3	.400
Major League totals (7 years)	36	58	.383	4.91	1.51	149	133	3	0	2	0-0	806.0	874	488	440	117	342-15	518	.275

JOHNSON, JONATHAN — P

PERSONAL: Born July 16, 1974, in LaGrange, Ga. ... 6-0/180. ... Throws right, bats right. ... Full name: Jonathan Kent Johnson. ... High school: Forest (Ocala, Fla.). ... College: Florida State.

TRANSACTIONS/CAREER NOTES: Selected by Texas Rangers organization in first round (seventh pick overall) of free-agent draft (June 1, 1995). ... On Oklahoma disabled list (May 1-17, 1998; and May 13-July 5, 1999). ... Traded by Rangers to Arizona Diamondback for cash considerations (April 27, 2001). ... On Tucson disabled list (July 21, 2001-remainder of season). ... Granted free agency (October 15, 2001). ... Re-signed by Diamondbacks organization (December 26, 2001). ... On Tucson disabled list (May 15-June 4, 2002). ... Released by Diamondbacks (June 30, 2002). ... Signed by San Diego Padres organization (July 18, 2002). ... Released by Padres (October 7, 2002). ... Signed by Houston Astros organization (November 1, 2002). ... Contract purchased by Houston from New Orleans of the Pacific Coast League (May 28, 2003). ... Designated for assignment (June 17, 2003). ... Sent outright to New Orleans (June 18, 2003).

CAREER HITTING: 0-for-4 (.000), 0 R, 0 2B, 0 3B, 0 HR, 0 RBI.

Year	League	W	L	Pct.	ERA	WHIP	G	GS	CG	ShO	Hld.	Sv.-Opp.	IP	H	R	ER	HR	BB-IBB	SO	Avg.
1995—	Charlotte (Fla. St.)	1	5	.167	2.70	1.15	8	7	1	0	...	0-...	43.1	34	14	13	2	16-0	25	.214
1996—	Tulsa (Texas)	* 13	10	.565	3.56	1.24	26	25	* 6	0	...	0-...	174.1	176	86	69	15	41-1	97	.262
—	Oklahoma City (A.A.)	1	0	1.000	0.00	0.33	1	1	1	1	...	0-...	9.0	2	0	0	0	1-0	6	.071
1997—	Oklahoma City (A.A.)	1	8	.111	7.29	1.93	13	12	1	0	...	1-...	58.0	83	54	47	6	29-3	33	.343
—	Tulsa (Texas)	5	4	.556	3.52	1.19	10	10	4	0	...	0-...	71.2	70	35	28	3	15-0	47	.254
1998—	Oklahoma (PCL)	6	6	.500	4.90	1.26	19	18	1	0	...	1-...	112.0	109	66	61	15	32-0	94	.255
—	Charlotte (Fla. St.)	0	2	.000	4.63	1.20	3	3	0	0	...	0-...	11.2	10	6	6	2	4-0	11	.227
—	Texas (A.L.)	0	0	...	8.31	2.31	1	1	0	0	0	0-0	4.1	5	4	4	0	5-0	3	.313
1999—	Oklahoma (PCL)	8	4	.667	6.25	1.68	21	8	0	0	...	2-...	67.2	91	53	47	9	23-0	38	.327
—	GC Rangers (GCL)	0	0	...	1.80	0.60	1	1	0	0	...	0-...	5.0	3	1	1	0	0-0	5	.167
—	Tulsa (Texas)	0	0	...	9.53	2.12	1	1	0	0	...	0-...	5.2	12	6	6	3	0-0	4	.462
—	Texas (A.L.)	0	0	...	15.00	3.67	1	0	0	0	0	0-0	3.0	9	5	5	0	2-0	3	.529
2000—	Oklahoma (PCL)	4	7	.364	5.08	1.43	36	2	0	0	...	5-...	56.2	55	38	32	8	26-2	63	.257
—	Texas (A.L.)	1	1	.500	6.21	1.83	15	0	0	0	0	0-0	29.0	34	23	20	3	19-2	23	.291
2001—	Texas (A.L.)	0	0	...	9.58	1.94	5	0	0	0	0	0-0	10.1	13	11	11	2	7-1	11	.317
—	Tucson (PCL)	4	4	.500	5.25	1.43	15	12	0	0	...	0-...	73.2	63	48	43	7	42-0	51	.229
2002—	El Paso (Texas)	0	1	.000	5.56	1.50	3	1	0	0	...	0-...	11.1	14	7	7	1	3-0	9	.304
—	Tucson (PCL)	0	3	.000	9.41	1.71	14	5	0	0	...	0-...	36.1	48	41	38	6	14-0	27	.320
—	Portland (PCL)	0	0	...	2.41	0.86	12	0	0	0	...	1-...	18.2	14	5	5	2	2-0	17	.215
—	San Diego (N.L.)	1	2	.333	4.11	1.30	16	0	0	0	1	0-0	15.1	15	8	7	2	5-1	21	.250
2003—	Houston (N.L.)	0	1	.000	5.87	2.28	4	3	0	0	0	0-0	15.1	20	11	10	2	15-3	7	.323
—	New Orleans (PCL)	5	4	.556	3.92	1.29	13	13	1	0	...	0-...	78.0	74	38	34	4	27-0	62	.247
American League totals (4 years)		1	1	.500	7.71	2.01	22	1	0	0	0	0-0	46.2	61	43	40	5	33-3	40	.319
National League totals (2 years)		1	3	.250	4.99	1.79	20	3	0	0	1	0-0	30.2	35	19	17	4	20-4	28	.287
Major League totals (6 years)		2	4	.333	6.63	1.93	42	4	0	0	1	0-0	77.1	96	62	57	9	53-7	68	.307

JOHNSON, MARK — C

PERSONAL: Born September 12, 1975, in Wheat Ridge, Colo. ... 6-0/200. ... Bats left, throws right. ... Full name: Mark Landon Johnson. ... High school: Warner Robins (Ga.).

TRANSACTIONS/CAREER NOTES: Selected by Chicago White Sox organization in first round (26th pick overall) of free-agent draft (June 2, 1994). ... Traded by White Sox with P Keith Foulke, P Joe Valentine and cash to Oakland Athletics for P Billy Koch and two players to be named later (December 3, 2002); White Sox acquired P Neal Cotts and OF Daylon Holt to complete deal (December 16, 2002).

2003 GAMES PLAYED BY POSITION (MLB): C—13.

										BATTING									FIELDING	
Year	Team (League)	Pos.	G	AB	R	H	2B	3B	HR	RBI	BB	SO	HBP	GDP	SB-CS	Avg.	OBP	SLG	OPS	E	Pct.
1994—	GC Whi. Sox (GCL)	C	32	87	10	21	5	0	0	14	14	15	3	0	1-1	.241	.365	.299	.664	3	.986
1995—	Hickory (S. Atl.)	C	107	319	31	58	9	0	2	17	59	52	3	4	3-5	.182	.313	.229	.542	11	.986
1996—	South Bend (Mid.)	C	67	214	29	55	14	3	2	27	39	25	1	8	3-3	.257	.368	.379	.747	9	.980
—	Prince Will. (Car.)	C	18	58	9	14	3	0	0	3	13	6	1	0	0-0	.241	.389	.293	.682	1	.992
1997—	Win.-Salem (Car.)	C	120	375	59	95	27	4	4	46	* 106	85	5	7	4-2	.253	* .420	.379	.798	11	.989
1998—	Birmingham (Sou.)	C-1B	117	382	68	108	17	3	9	59	* 105	72	6	5	0-1	.283	.443	.414	.857	8	.990
—	Chicago (A.L.)	C	7	23	2	2	0	2	0	1	1	8	0	0	0-0	.087	.125	.261	.386	0	1.000
1999—	Chicago (A.L.)	C-DH	73	207	27	47	11	0	4	16	36	58	2	2	3-1	.227	.344	.338	.682	3	.993
2000—	Chicago (A.L.)	C-DH	75	213	29	48	11	0	3	23	27	40	1	3	3-2	.225	.315	.319	.635	4	.992
2001—	Charlotte (Int'l)	C-1B	55	196	24	53	5	2	4	24	29	34	0	4	2-1	.270	.363	.378	.740	4	.991
—	Chicago (A.L.)	C	61	173	21	43	6	1	5	18	23	31	2	5	2-1	.249	.338	.382	.720	3	.992
2002—	Chicago (A.L.)	C	86	263	34	55	8	1	4	18	30	52	3	4	0-0	.209	.287	.293	.590	3	.994
2003—	Sacramento (PCL)	C-DH	51	162	28	37	11	1	3	30	35	23	3	2	0-0	.228	.369	.364	.734	3	.992
—	Oakland (A.L.)	C	13	27	3	3	1	0	0	3	3	4	1	0	0-0	.111	.219	.148	.367	0	1.000
Major League totals (6 years)			315	906	113	198	37	4	16	79	120	193	9	14	8-4	.219	.314	.321	.635	13	.993

JOHNSON, NICK — 1B

PERSONAL: Born September 19, 1978, in Sacramento, Calif. ... 6-3/195. ... Bats left, throws left. ... Full name: Nicholas Robert Johnson. ... High school: McClatchy (Sacramento).

TRANSACTIONS/CAREER NOTES: Selected by New York Yankees organization in third round of free-agent draft (June 4, 1996). ... On disabled list (April 2, 2000-entire season). ... On Columbus disabled list (May 18-June 3, 2001). ... On New York disabled list (August 8-September 3, 2002); included rehabilitation assignment to Columbus (August 31-September 3). ... Placed on the 15-day disabled list (May 16, 2003). ... Sent to Columbus on rehab assignment (July 18, 2003). ... Recalled from Columbus rehab assignment; reinstated from 15-day disabled list (July 25, 2003).

2003 GAMES PLAYED BY POSITION (MLB): 1B—60, DH—34.

										BATTING									FIELDING	
Year	Team (League)	Pos.	G	AB	R	H	2B	3B	HR	RBI	BB	SO	HBP	GDP	SB-CS	Avg.	OBP	SLG	OPS	E	Pct.
1996—	GC Yankees (GCL)	1B	47	157	31	45	11	1	2	33	30	35	9	5	0-0	.287	* .422	.408	.830	3	.991
1997—	Greensboro (S. Atl.)	1B	127	433	77	118	23	1	16	75	76	99	18	5	16-3	.273	.398	.441	.839	16	.987
1998—	Tampa (Fla. St.)	1B	92	303	69	96	14	1	17	58	68	76	19	5	1-4	.317	* .466	.538	1.004	12	.986
1999—	Norwich (East.)	1B	132	420	* 114	145	33	5	14	87	* 123	88	37	9	8-6	.345	.525	.548	1.073	* 20	.983
2000—	New York (A.L.)								Did not play.												
2001—	Columbus (Int'l)	1B	110	359	68	92	20	0	18	49	81	105	14	6	9-2	.256	.407	.462	.870	• 10	.989
—	New York (A.L.)	1B-DH	23	67	6	13	2	0	2	8	7	15	4	3	0-0	.194	.308	.313	.621	0	1.000
2002—	New York (A.L.)	1B-DH-OF	129	378	56	92	15	0	15	58	48	98	12	11	1-3	.243	.347	.402	.749	7	.988
—	Columbus (Int'l)	1B	3	11	1	1	0	0	0	0	1	4	0	1	0-0	.091	.167	.091	.258	0	1.000
2003—	Columbus (Int'l)	1B-DH	3	10	1	5	2	0	1	3	2	2	0	0	0-0	.500	.583	1.000	1.583	1	.952
—	Trenton (East.)	1B	4	12	3	5	1	0	1	1	5	0	1	1	0-0	.417	.611	.500	1.111	0	1.000
—	New York (A.L.)	1B-DH	96	324	60	92	19	0	14	47	70	57	8	9	5-2	.284	.422	.472	.894	5	.991
Major League totals (3 years)			248	769	122	197	36	0	31	113	125	170	24	23	6-5	.256	.376	.424	.800	12	.990

J

JOHNSON, RANDY — P

PERSONAL: Born September 10, 1963, in Walnut Creek, Calif. ... 6-10/231. ... Throws left, bats right. ... Full name: Randall David Johnson. ... High school: Livermore (Calif.). ... College: USC.

TRANSACTIONS/CAREER NOTES: Selected by Atlanta Braves organization in third round of free-agent draft (June 7, 1982); did not sign. ... Selected by Montreal Expos organization in second round of free-agent draft (June 3, 1985). ... Traded by Expos with P Brian Holman and P Gene Harris to Seattle Mariners for P Mark Langston and a player to be named later (May 25, 1989); Expos acquired P Mike Campbell to complete deal (July 31, 1989). ... On disabled list (June 11-27, 1992). ... On Seattle disabled list (May 15-August 6 and August 27, 1996-remainder of season); included rehabilitation assignment to Everett (August 3-6). ... On suspended list (April 24-27, 1998). ... Traded by Mariners to Houston Astros for SS Carlos Guillen, P Freddy Garcia and a player to be named later (July 31, 1998); Mariners acquired P John Halama to complete deal (October 1, 1998). ... Granted free agency (October 28, 1998). ... Signed by Arizona Diamondbacks (December 10, 1998). ... Placed on 15-day disabled list by Arizona (April 12, 2003). ... Reinstated from the 15-day disabled list (April 27, 2003). ... Transferred to Emergency disabled list (June 23, 2003). ... Sent to Tucson on rehab assignment by Arizona (July 5, 2003). ... Recalled from Lancaster rehab assignment; reinstated from Emergency disabled list (July 20, 2003).

CAREER HITTING: 57-for-440 (.130), 16 R, 10 2B, 0 3B, 1 HR, 29 RBI.

Year	League	W	L	Pct.	ERA	WHIP	G	GS	CG	ShO	Hld.	Sv.-Opp.	IP	H	R	ER	HR	BB-IBB	SO	Avg.
1985—	Jamestown (NYP)	0	3	.000	5.93	1.94	8	8	0	0	...	0-...	27.1	29	22	18	2	24-0	21	.287
1986—	W.P. Beach (FSL)	8	7	.533	3.16	1.53	26	• 26	2	1	...	0-...	119.2	89	49	42	3	* 94-0	133	.211
1987—	Jacksonville (Sou.)	11	8	.579	3.73	1.63	25	24	0	0	...	0-...	140.0	100	63	58	10	128-0	* 163	.204
1988—	Indianapolis (A.A.)	8	7	.533	3.26	1.39	20	19	0	0	...	0-...	113.1	85	52	41	6	72-0	111	.209
—	Montreal (N.L.)	3	0	1.000	2.42	1.15	4	4	1	0	0	0-0	26.0	23	8	7	3	7-0	25	.225
1989—	Montreal (N.L.)	0	4	.000	6.67	1.85	7	6	0	0	0	0-0	29.2	29	25	22	2	26-1	26	.264
—	Indianapolis (A.A.)	1	1	.500	2.00	1.22	3	3	0	0	...	0-...	18.0	13	5	4	0	9-0	17	.194
—	Seattle (A.L.)	7	9	.438	4.40	1.44	22	22	2	0	0	0-0	131.0	118	75	64	11	70-1	104	.244
1990—	Seattle (A.L.)	14	11	.560	3.65	1.34	33	33	5	2	0	0-0	219.2	174	103	89	26	* 120-2	194	.216
1991—	Seattle (A.L.)	13	10	.565	3.98	1.50	33	33	2	1	0	0-0	201.1	151	96	89	15	* 152-0	228	.213
1992—	Seattle (A.L.)	12	14	.462	3.77	1.42	31	31	6	2	0	0-0	210.1	154	104	88	13	* 144-1	* 241	.206
1993—	Seattle (A.L.)	19	8	.704	3.24	1.11	35	34	10	3	0	1-1	255.1	185	97	92	22	99-1	* 308	.203
1994—	Seattle (A.L.)	13	6	.684	3.19	1.19	23	23	* 9	* 4	0	0-0	172.0	132	65	61	14	72-2	* 204	.216
1995—	Seattle (A.L.)	18	2	*.900	*2.48	1.05	30	30	6	3	0	0-0	214.1	159	65	59	12	65-1	* 294	.201
1996—	Seattle (A.L.)	5	0	1.000	3.67	1.19	14	8	0	0	0	1-2	61.1	48	27	25	8	25-0	85	.213
—	Everett (Northwest)	0	0	...	0.00	0.00	1	1	0	0	...	0-...	2.0	0	0	0	0	0-0	5	.000
1997—	Seattle (A.L.)	20	4	*.833	*2.28	1.05	30	29	5	2	0	0-0	213.0	147	60	54	20	77-2	291	*.194
1998—	Seattle (A.L.)	9	10	.474	4.33	1.29	23	23	6	2	0	0-0	160.0	146	90	77	19	60-0	213	.240
—	Houston (N.L.)	10	1	.909	1.28	0.98	11	11	4	4	0	0-0	84.1	57	12	12	4	26-1	116	.191
1999—	Arizona (N.L.)	17	9	.654	2.48	1.02	35	* 35	* 12	2	0	0-0	* 271.2	207	86	75	30	70-3	* 364	.208
2000—	Arizona (N.L.)	19	7	.731	2.64	1.12	35	* 35	* 8	• 3	0	0-0	248.2	202	89	73	23	76-1	* 347	.224
2001—	Arizona (N.L.)	21	6	*.778	*2.49	1.01	35	34	3	2	0	0-0	249.2	181	74	69	19	71-2	* 372	.203
2002—	Arizona (N.L.)	* 24	5	*.828	*2.32	1.03	35	35	* 8	4	0	0-0	* 260.0	197	78	67	26	71-1	* 334	*.208
2003—	Tucson (PCL)	0	0	...	0.00	0.00	1	1	0	0	...	0-...	4.0	0	0	0	0	0-0	4	.000
—	El Paso (Texas)	0	0	...	0.00	1.00	1	1	0	0	...	0-...	4.0	3	2	0	0	1-0	5	.231
—	Lancaster (Calif.)	0	1	.000	6.00	1.83	1	1	0	0	...	0-...	6.0	11	5	4	1	0-0	6	.367
—	Arizona (N.L.)	6	8	.429	4.26	1.33	18	18	1	1	0	0-0	114.0	125	61	54	16	27-3	125	.280
American League totals (10 years)		130	74	.637	3.42	1.25	274	266	51	19	0	2-3	1838.1	1414	782	698	160	884-10	2162	.212
National League totals (8 years)		100	40	.714	2.66	1.09	180	178	37	16	0	0-0	1284.0	1021	433	379	123	374-12	1709	.218
Major League totals (16 years)		230	114	.669	3.10	1.18	454	444	88	35	0	2-3	3122.1	2435	1215	1077	283	1258-22	3871	.215

JOHNSON, REED — OF

PERSONAL: Born December 8, 1976, in Riverside, Calif. ... 5-10/180. ... Bats right, throws right. ... Full name: Reed Cameron Johnson. ... High school: Temecula Valley (Temecula, Calif.). ... College: Cal State Fullerton.

TRANSACTIONS/CAREER NOTES: Selected by Toronto Blue Jays organization in 17th round of free-agent draft (June 2, 1999). ... On Syracuse disabled list (April 4-June 8 and August 8, 2002-remainder of season). ... Contract purchased Toronto from Syracuse (April 16, 2003). ... Optioned to Syracuse by Toronto (April 21, 2003). ... Recalled from Syracuse by Toronto (May 16, 2003).

2003 GAMES PLAYED BY POSITION (MLB): OF—111, DH—2.

									BATTING										FIELDING	
Year	Team (League)	Pos.	G	AB	R	H	2B	3B	HR	RBI	BB	SO	HBP	GDP	SB-CS	Avg.	OBP	SLG	OPS	E	Pct.
1999—	St. Catharines (NYP)	OF	60	191	24	46	8	2	2	23	24	31	2	4	5-5	.241	.326	.335	.661	3	.976
2000—	Hagerstown (SAL)	OF	95	324	66	94	24	5	8	70	62	49	14	9	14-2	.290	.422	.469	.891	1	.995
—	Dunedin (Fla. St.)	OF	36	133	26	42	9	2	4	28	14	27	11	1	3-2	.316	.416	.504	.920	2	.975
2001—	Tennessee (Sou.)	OF	136	554	104	174	29	4	13	74	45	79	18	11	42-12	.314	.383	.451	.834	4	.983
2002—	Dunedin (Fla. St.)	OF	8	33	7	9	3	0	0	6	3	3	2	0	0-1	.273	.368	.364	.732	0	1.000
—	Syracuse (Int'l)	OF	44	159	27	37	8	3	2	10	12	23	8	1	1-4	.233	.317	.358	.675	1	.991
2003—	Syracuse (Int'l)	OF	26	101	14	33	4	1	2	16	3	13	5	2	3-1	.327	.369	.446	.815	0	1.000
—	Toronto (A.L.)	OF-DH	114	412	79	121	21	2	10	52	20	67	20	10	5-3	.294	.353	.427	.780	4	.977
Major League totals (1 year)			114	412	79	121	21	2	10	52	20	67	20	10	5-3	.294	.353	.427	.780	4	.977

JOHNSON, RONTREZ — OF

PERSONAL: Born December 8, 1976, in Marshall, Texas. ... 5-10/165. ... Bats right, throws right. ... Full name: Rontrez DeMon Johnson. ... High school: Marshall (Texas).

TRANSACTIONS/CAREER NOTES: Selected by Boston Red Sox organization in 16th round of free-agent draft (June 1, 1995). ... Granted free agency (October 15, 2001). ... Signed by Kansas City Royals organization (November 29, 2001). ... Selected by Oakland Athletics from Royals organization in Rule 5 major league draft (December 16, 2002). ... Returned to Royals (March 14, 2003). ... Returned to Oklahoma by Kansas City (April 18, 2003).

2003 GAMES PLAYED BY POSITION (MLB): OF—6, DH—2.

									BATTING										FIELDING	
Year	Team (League)	Pos.	G	AB	R	H	2B	3B	HR	RBI	BB	SO	HBP	GDP	SB-CS	Avg.	OBP	SLG	OPS	E	Pct.
1995—	GC Red Sox (GCL)	OF	52	193	37	49	4	2	0	11	30	30	1	1	25-5	.254	.356	.295	.651	4	.960
1996—	GC Red Sox (GCL)	OF	28	85	20	25	6	0	0	9	17	11	0	2	6-2	.294	.412	.365	.776	0	1.000
—	Lowell (NY-Penn)	OF	35	135	27	30	4	0	4	12	21	30	0	2	7-3	.222	.323	.341	.664	4	.947
1997—	Michigan (Midw.)	OF	118	411	87	99	10	6	5	40	65	96	9	2	29-12	.241	.355	.331	.685	7	.975
1998—	Michigan (Midw.)	OF	85	306	65	83	15	5	5	32	66	46	4	4	24-8	.271	.402	.402	.804	3	.983
1999—	Sarasota (Fla. St.)	OF	132	494	97	148	30	4	8	59	74	63	8	7	18-14	.300	.395	.425	.820	8	.975
2000—	Trenton (East.)	OF	134	524	83	141	21	2	6	53	55	73	6	12	30-19	.269	.343	.351	.694	8	.979
2001—	Trenton (East.)	OF	73	255	48	72	15	1	10	31	22	40	9	4	17-7	.282	.356	.467	.823	6	.964
—	Pawtucket (Int'l)	OF	44	187	32	56	16	3	4	22	10	35	7	7	8-4	.299	.358	.481	.839	1	.989
2002—	Omaha (PCL)	OF	109	403	71	121	27	4	9	53	50	51	19	6	31-11	.300	.397	.454	.852	6	.979
2003—	Kansas City (A.L.)	OF-DH	8	3	3	1	0	0	0	0	0	2	0	0	0-0	.333	.333	.333	.667	1	.000
—	Oklahoma (PCL)	OF	70	241	35	54	10	3	5	20	19	29	7	1	14-6	.224	.296	.353	.649	3	.981
—	Richmond (Int'l)	OF	31	81	8	14	1	0	0	5	8	15	2	2	3-1	.173	.261	.185	.446	0	1.000
Major League totals (1 year)			8	3	3	1	0	0	0	0	0	2	0	0	0-0	.333	.333	.333	.667	1	.000

J

JONES, ANDRUW — OF

PERSONAL: Born April 23, 1977, in Willemstad, Curacao. ... 6-1/210. ... Bats right, throws right. ... Full name: Andruw Rudolf Jones. ... High school: St. Paulus (Willemstad, Curacao).

TRANSACTIONS/CAREER NOTES: Signed as non-drafted free agent by Atlanta Braves organization (July 1, 1993).

2003 GAMES PLAYED BY POSITION (MLB): OF—155.

Year Team (League)	Pos.	G	AB	R	H	2B	3B	HR	RBI	BB	SO	HBP	GDP	SB-CS	Avg.	OBP	SLG	OPS	E	Pct.
1994— GC Braves (GCL)	OF	27	95	22	21	5	1	2	10	16	19	2	3	5-2	.221	.345	.358	.703	3	.968
— Danville (Appal.)	OF	36	143	20	48	9	2	1	16	9	25	3	0	16-9	.336	.385	.448	.832	2	.977
1995— Macon (S. Atl.)	OF	• 139	537	* 104	149	41	5	25	100	70	122	16	9	* 56-11	.277	.372	.512	.884	4	.988
1996— Durham (Caro.)	OF	66	243	65	76	14	3	17	43	42	54	3	5	16-4	.313	.419	.605	1.024	7	.963
— Greenville (Sou.)	OF	38	157	39	58	10	1	12	37	17	34	1	3	12-4	.369	.432	.675	1.107	1	.993
— Richmond (Int'l)	OF	12	45	11	17	3	1	5	12	1	9	0	0	2-2	.378	.391	.822	1.214	1	.972
— Atlanta (N.L.)	OF	31	106	11	23	7	1	5	13	7	29	0	1	3-0	.217	.265	.443	.709	2	.975
1997— Atlanta (N.L.)	OF	153	399	60	92	18	1	18	70	56	107	4	11	20-11	.231	.329	.416	.745	7	.977
1998— Atlanta (N.L.)	OF	159	582	89	158	33	8	31	90	40	129	4	10	27-4	.271	.321	.515	.836	2	.995
1999— Atlanta (N.L.)	OF	• 162	592	97	163	35	5	26	84	76	103	9	12	24-12	.275	.365	.483	.848	10	.981
2000— Atlanta (N.L.)	OF	161	* 656	122	199	36	6	36	104	59	100	9	12	21-6	.303	.366	.541	.907	2	.996
2001— Atlanta (N.L.)	OF	161	625	104	157	25	2	34	104	56	142	3	10	11-4	.251	.312	.461	.772	6	.987
2002— Atlanta (N.L.)	OF-DH	154	560	91	148	34	0	35	94	83	135	10	14	8-3	.264	.366	.513	.878	3	.993
2003— Atlanta (N.L.)	OF	156	595	101	165	28	2	36	116	53	125	5	18	4-3	.277	.338	.513	.851	3	.993
Major League totals (8 years)		1137	4115	675	1105	216	25	221	675	430	870	44	88	118-43	.269	.341	.494	.836	35	.989

JONES, CHIPPER — OF

PERSONAL: Born April 24, 1972, in DeLand, Fla. ... 6-4/220. ... Bats both, throws right. ... Full name: Larry Wayne Jones. ... High school: The Bolles School (Jacksonville).

TRANSACTIONS/CAREER NOTES: Selected by Atlanta Braves organization in first round (first pick overall) of free-agent draft (June 4, 1990). ... On disabled list (March 20, 1994-entire season; and March 22-April 16, 1996).

2003 GAMES PLAYED BY POSITION (MLB): OF—149, DH—1.

Year Team (League)	Pos.	G	AB	R	H	2B	3B	HR	RBI	BB	SO	HBP	GDP	SB-CS	Avg.	OBP	SLG	OPS	E	Pct.
1990— GC Braves (GCL)	SS	44	140	20	32	1	1	1	18	14	25	6	3	5-3	.229	.321	.271	.592	18	.919
1991— Macon (S. Atl.)	SS	136	473	* 104	154	24	11	15	98	69	70	3	6	40-11	.326	.407	.518	.925	56	.919
1992— Durham (Caro.)	SS	70	264	43	73	22	1	4	31	31	34	2	5	10-8	.277	.353	.413	.766	14	.956
— Greenville (Sou.)	SS	67	266	43	92	17	11	9	42	11	32	0	5	14-1	.346	.367	.594	.961	18	.945
1993— Richmond (Int'l)	SS	139	536	* 97	* 174	31	* 12	13	89	57	70	1	8	23-7	.325	.387	.500	.887	* 43	.931
— Atlanta (N.L.)	SS	8	3	2	2	1	0	0	0	1	1	0	0	0-0	.667	.750	1.000	1.750	0	1.000
1994— Atlanta (N.L.)						Did not play.														
1995— Atlanta (N.L.)	3B-OF	140	524	87	139	22	3	23	86	73	99	0	10	8-4	.265	.353	.450	.803	25	.935
1996— Atlanta (N.L.)	3B-SS-OF	157	598	114	185	32	5	30	110	87	88	0	14	14-1	.309	.393	.530	.923	17	.958
1997— Atlanta (N.L.)	3B-OF	157	597	100	176	41	3	21	111	76	88	0	19	20-5	.295	.371	.479	.850	15	.956
1998— Atlanta (N.L.)	3B	160	601	123	188	29	5	34	107	96	93	1	17	16-6	.313	.404	.547	.951	12	.971
1999— Atlanta (N.L.)	3B-SS	157	567	116	181	41	1	45	110	126	94	2	20	25-3	.319	.441	.633	1.074	17	.951
2000— Atlanta (N.L.)	3B-SS	156	579	118	180	38	1	36	111	95	64	2	14	14-7	.311	.404	.566	.970	25	.941
2001— Atlanta (N.L.)	3B-OF-DH	159	572	113	189	33	5	38	102	98	82	2	13	9-10	.330	.427	.605	1.032	18	.947
2002— Atlanta (N.L.)	OF	158	548	90	179	35	1	26	100	107	89	2	18	8-2	.327	.435	.536	.972	7	.975
2003— Atlanta (N.L.)	OF-DH	153	555	103	169	33	2	27	106	94	83	1	10	2-2	.305	.402	.517	.920	7	.968
Major League totals (10 years)		1405	5144	966	1588	305	26	280	943	853	781	10	135	116-40	.309	.404	.541	.946	143	.955

JONES, GREG — P

PERSONAL: Born November 15, 1976, in Clearwater, Fla. ... 6-2/195. ... Throws right, bats right. ... Full name: Greg Alan Jones. ... High school: Seminole, Fla. ... College: Pasco Hernando (Fla.).

TRANSACTIONS/CAREER NOTES: Selected by Anaheim Angels organization in 42nd round of free-agent draft (June 4, 1996).

CAREER HITTING: 0-for-0 (.000), 0 R, 0 2B, 0 3B, 0 HR, 0 RBI.

Year League	W	L	Pct.	ERA	WHIP	G	GS	CG	ShO	Hld.	Sv.-Opp.	IP	H	R	ER	HR	BB-IBB	SO	Avg.
1997— Boise (NW)	2	2	.500	3.62	1.45	21	4	0	0	...	2-...	37.1	35	19	15	1	19-1	39	.243
1998— Boise (NW)	0	0	.000	4.93	1.44	22	0	0	0	...	1-...	34.2	37	22	19	3	13-0	28	.278
1999— Cedar Rapids (Midw.)	2	4	.333	3.83	1.25	34	0	0	0	...	13-...	40.0	37	18	17	5	13-2	41	.247
2000— Lake Elsinore (Calif.)	0	0	...	4.08	1.64	16	0	0	0	...	3-...	17.2	19	9	8	0	10-3	12	.284
— Edmonton (PCL)	2	2	.500	7.65	2.13	25	0	0	0	...	1-...	42.1	57	42	36	5	33-1	21	.324
— Erie (East.)	0	2	.000	5.40	1.53	11	0	0	0	...	2-...	15.0	19	9	9	1	4-0	7	.306
2001— Rancho Cuca. (Calif.)	1	3	.250	4.23	1.30	6	6	0	0	...	0-...	27.2	25	15	13	2	11-0	27	.238
— Ariz. Angels (Ariz.)	0	0	...	0.00	2.50	2	2	0	0	...	0-...	2.0	3	0	0	0	2-0	2	.375
2002— Salt Lake (PCL)	7	4	.636	4.31	1.44	39	0	0	0	...	2-...	62.2	68	35	30	5	22-0	55	.273
2003— Salt Lake (PCL)	2	3	.400	4.40	0.96	33	0	0	0	...	4-...	47.0	36	24	23	4	9-0	56	.207
— Anaheim (A.L.)	0	0	...	4.88	1.55	18	0	0	0	2	0-0	27.2	29	15	15	3	14-0	28	.261
Major League totals (1 year)	0	0	...	4.88	1.55	18	0	0	0	2	0-0	27.2	29	15	15	3	14-0	28	.261

JONES, JACQUE — OF

PERSONAL: Born April 25, 1975, in San Diego, Calif. ... 5-10/200. ... Bats left, throws left. ... Full name: Jacque Dewayne Jones. ... High school: San Diego High. ... College: USC.

TRANSACTIONS/CAREER NOTES: Selected by Minnesota Twins organization in second round of free-agent draft (June 2, 1996). ... Placed on the 15-day disabled list by Minnesota (July 1, 2003). ... Reinstated from 15-day disabled list (July 17, 2003).

2003 GAMES PLAYED BY POSITION (MLB): OF—101, DH—29.

Year Team (League)	Pos.	G	AB	R	H	2B	3B	HR	RBI	BB	SO	HBP	GDP	SB-CS	Avg.	OBP	SLG	OPS	E	Pct.
1996— Fort Myers (FSL)	OF	1	3	0	2	1	0	0	1	0	0	0	0	0-1	.667	.667	1.000	1.667	0	...
1997— Fort Myers (FSL)	OF	131	539	84	* 160	33	6	15	82	33	110	3	9	24-12	.297	.340	.464	.804	7	.979
1998— New Britain (East.)	OF-DH	134	518	78	155	39	3	21	85	37	134	4	4	18-11	.299	.349	.508	.856	10	.968
1999— Salt Lake (PCL)	OF	52	198	32	59	13	2	4	26	9	36	0	5	9-2	.298	.325	.444	.770	2	.987
— Minnesota (A.L.)	OF	95	322	54	93	24	2	9	44	17	63	4	7	3-4	.289	.329	.460	.789	5	.980
2000— Minnesota (A.L.)	OF	154	523	66	149	26	5	19	76	26	111	0	17	7-5	.285	.319	.463	.781	2	.994
2001— Minnesota (A.L.)	OF-DH	149	475	57	131	25	0	14	49	39	92	3	10	12-9	.276	.335	.417	.751	5	.983
2002— Minnesota (A.L.)	OF-DH	149	577	96	173	37	2	27	85	37	129	2	8	6-7	.300	.341	.511	.852	5	.986
2003— Minnesota (A.L.)	OF-DH	136	517	76	157	33	1	16	69	21	105	4	10	13-1	.304	.333	.464	.797	5	.977
Major League totals (5 years)		683	2414	349	703	145	10	85	323	140	500	13	52	41-26	.291	.332	.465	.797	22	.985

JONES, JASON — OF/1B

PERSONAL: Born October 17, 1976, in Marietta, Ga. ... 6-3/210. ... Bats both, throws right. ... Full name: Jason D. Jones. ... College: Kennesaw State.

TRANSACTIONS/CAREER NOTES: Selected by Texas Rangers organization in 13th round of free-agent draft (June 1999).

2003 GAMES PLAYED BY POSITION (MLB): OF—27, DH—6, 1B—3.

Year Team (League)	Pos.	G	AB	R	H	2B	3B	HR	RBI	BB	SO	HBP	GDP	SB-CS	Avg.	OBP	SLG	OPS	E	Pct.
1999— Pulaski (Appal.)	1B-OF	69	262	65	93	24	1	11	58	33	55	7	5	1-2	.355	.433	.580	1.013	12	.980
2000— Savannah (S. Atl.)	1B-OF	132	466	59	125	34	6	9	61	65	97	4	14	9-5	.268	.359	.425	.784	9	.990
2001— Tulsa (Texas)	1B	30	107	8	23	6	0	2	8	3	17	1	4	0-0	.215	.243	.327	.570	3	.988
— Charlotte (Int'l)	1B-OF	102	375	50	106	26	2	15	81	56	48	1	12	1-3	.283	.374	.483	.857	12	.988
2002— Tulsa (Texas)	1B-OF	136	471	82	139	33	2	13	75	87	97	0	12	12-7	.295	.401	.456	.858	22	.983
2003— Oklahoma (PCL)	OF-DH-1B	100	375	52	108	29	0	9	55	50	80	2	8	7-2	.288	.374	.437	.811	2	.990
— Texas (A.L.)	OF-DH-1B	40	107	11	23	6	0	3	11	10	21	3	1	0-1	.215	.298	.355	.653	1	.979
Major League totals (1 year)		40	107	11	23	6	0	3	11	10	21	3	1	0-1	.215	.298	.355	.653	1	.979

JONES, TODD — P

PERSONAL: Born April 24, 1968, in Marietta, Ga. ... 6-3/230. ... Throws right, bats both. ... Full name: Todd Barton Jones. ... High school: Osborne (Ga.). ... College: Jacksonville State.

TRANSACTIONS/CAREER NOTES: Selected by New York Mets organization in 41st round of free-agent draft (June 2, 1986); did not sign. ... Selected by Houston Astros organization in supplemental round ("sandwich pick" between first and second round, 27th pick overall) of free-agent draft (June 5, 1989); pick received as part of compensation for Texas Rangers signing Type A free-agent P Nolan Ryan. ... On suspended list (September 14-16, 1993). ... On Houston disabled list (July 19-August 12 and August 18-September 12, 1996); included rehabilitation assignment to Tucson (August 9-12). ... Traded by Astros with OF Brian Hunter, IF Orlando Miller, P Doug Brocail and cash to Detroit Tigers for C Brad Ausmus, P Jose Lima, P C.J. Nitkowski, P Trever Miller and IF Daryle Ward (December 10, 1996). ... Traded by Tigers to Minnesota Twins for P Mark Redman (July 28, 2001). ... Granted free agency (November 5, 2001). ... Signed by Colorado Rockies (January 15, 2002). ... Designated for assignment by Colorado (June 27, 2003). ... Given unconditional release (June 30, 2003). ... Signed with Boston as free agent (July 2, 2003). ... Optioned to Pawtucket (August 29, 2003). ... Called up from Pawtucket (September 2, 2003).

CAREER HITTING: 3-for-16 (.188), 1 R, 1 2B, 0 3B, 0 HR, 0 RBI.

Year League	W	L	Pct.	ERA	WHIP	G	GS	CG	ShO	Hld.	Sv.-Opp.	IP	H	R	ER	HR	BB-IBB	SO	Avg.
1989— Auburn (N.Y.-Penn)	2	3	.400	5.44	1.79	11	9	1	0	...	0-...	49.2	47	39	30	2	42-1	71	.240
1990— Osceola (Florida St.)	12	10	.545	3.51	1.54	27	• 27	1	0	...	0-...	151.1	124	81	59	2	* 109-1	106	.223
1991— Osceola (Florida St.)	4	4	.500	4.35	1.44	14	14	0	0	...	0-...	72.1	69	38	35	2	35-0	51	.256
— Jackson (Texas)	4	3	.571	4.88	1.63	10	10	0	0	...	0-...	55.1	51	37	30	1	39-1	37	.241
1992— Jackson (Texas)	3	7	.300	3.14	1.45	61	0	0	0	...	25-...	66.0	52	28	23	3	44-3	60	.213
— Tucson (PCL)	0	1	.000	4.50	2.75	3	0	0	0	...	0-...	4.0	1	2	2	0	10-1	4	.077
1993— Tucson (PCL)	4	2	.667	4.44	1.64	41	0	0	0	...	12-...	48.2	49	26	24	5	31-2	45	.265
— Houston (N.L.)	1	2	.333	3.13	1.15	27	0	0	0	6	2-3	37.1	28	14	13	4	15-2	25	.214
1994— Houston (N.L.)	5	2	.714	2.72	1.07	48	0	0	0	8	5-9	72.2	52	23	22	3	26-4	63	.202
1995— Houston (N.L.)	6	5	.545	3.07	1.41	68	0	0	0	8	15-20	99.2	89	38	34	8	52-17	96	.237
1996— Houston (N.L.)	6	3	.667	4.40	1.62	51	0	0	0	1	17-23	57.1	61	30	28	5	32-6	44	.274
— Tucson (PCL)	0	0	...	0.00	1.50	1	0	0	0	...	0-...	2.0	1	1	0	0	2-0	0	.200
1997— Detroit (A.L.)	5	4	.556	3.09	1.36	68	0	0	0	5	31-36	70.0	60	29	24	3	35-2	70	.231
1998— Detroit (A.L.)	1	4	.200	4.97	1.48	65	0	0	0	0	28-32	63.1	58	38	35	7	36-4	57	.243
1999— Detroit (A.L.)	4	4	.500	3.80	1.49	65	0	0	0	0	30-35	66.1	64	30	28	7	35-1	64	.259
2000— Detroit (A.L.)	2	4	.333	3.52	1.44	67	0	0	0	0	• 42-46	64.0	67	28	25	6	25-1	67	.276
2001— Detroit (A.L.)	4	5	.444	4.62	1.68	45	0	0	0	3	11-17	48.2	60	31	25	6	22-1	39	.303
— Minnesota (A.L.)	1	0	1.000	3.26	1.76	24	0	0	0	7	2-4	19.1	27	8	7	3	7-0	15	.333
2002— Colorado (N.L.)	1	4	.200	4.70	1.36	79	0	0	0	30	1-3	82.1	84	43	43	10	28-3	73	.269
2003— Colorado (N.L.)	1	4	.200	8.24	2.01	33	1	0	0	3	0-5	39.1	61	39	36	8	18-0	28	.361
— Boston (A.L.)	2	1	.667	5.52	1.53	26	0	0	0	1	0-0	29.1	32	19	18	2	13-2	31	.269
American League totals (6 years)	19	22	.463	4.04	1.50	360	0	0	0	16	144-170	361.0	368	183	162	34	173-11	343	.266
National League totals (6 years)	20	20	.500	4.08	1.40	306	1	0	0	56	40-63	388.2	375	187	176	38	171-32	329	.256
Major League totals (11 years)	39	42	.481	4.06	1.45	666	1	0	0	72	184-233	749.2	743	370	338	72	344-43	672	.261

JORDAN, BRIAN — OF

PERSONAL: Born March 29, 1967, in Baltimore, Md. ... 6-1/205. ... Bats right, throws right. ... Full name: Brian O'Neal Jordan. ... High school: Milford (Baltimore). ... College: Richmond.

TRANSACTIONS/CAREER NOTES: Selected by Cleveland Indians organization in 20th round of free-agent draft (June 3, 1985); did not sign. ... Selected by St. Louis Cardinals organization in supplemental round ("sandwich pick" between first and second round, 30th pick overall) of free-agent draft (June 1, 1988); pick received as part of compensation for New York Yankees signing Type A free-agent 1B/OF Jack Clark. ... On disabled list (May 1-8 and June 3-10, 1991). ... On temporarily inactive list (July 3, 1991-remainder of season). ... On St. Louis disabled list (May 23-June 22, 1992); included rehabilitation assignment to Louisville (June 10-22). ... On Louisville disabled list (June 7-14, 1993). ... On disabled list (July 10, 1994-remainder of season; and March 31-April 15, 1996). ... On St. Louis disabled list (May 6-June 13, June 26-August 10 and August 25, 1997-remainder of season); included rehabilitation assignment to Louisville (June 5-13). ... Granted free agency (October 22, 1998). ... Signed by Atlanta Braves (November 23, 1998). ... On disabled list (April 4-19, 2000). ... Traded by Braves with P Odalis Perez and P Andrew Brown to Los Angeles Dodgers for OF Gary Sheffield (January 15, 2002). ... On disabled list (August 17-September 1, 2002). ... Placed on 15-day disabled list (June 25, 2003). ... Transferred to Emergency list (July 14, 2003).

2003 GAMES PLAYED BY POSITION (MLB): OF—62, DH—2.

Year Team (League)	Pos.	G	AB	R	H	2B	3B	HR	RBI	BB	SO	HBP	GDP	SB-CS	Avg.	OBP	SLG	OPS	E	Pct.
1988— Hamilton (NYP)	OF	19	71	12	22	3	1	4	12	6	15	3	0	3-3	.310	.388	.549	.937	1	.971
1989— St. Pete. (FSL)	OF	11	43	7	15	4	1	2	11	0	8	2	1	0-2	.349	.378	.628	1.006	0	1.000
1990— Arkansas (Texas)	OF	16	50	4	8	1	0	0	0	0	11	1	1	0-0	.160	.176	.180	.356	2	.933
— St. Pete. (FSL)	OF	9	30	3	5	0	1	0	1	2	11	0	0	0-2	.167	.219	.233	.452	0	1.000
1991— Louisville (A.A.)	OF	61	212	35	56	11	4	4	24	17	41	8	5	10-4	.264	.342	.410	.752	2	.987
1992— St. Louis (N.L.)	OF	55	193	17	40	9	4	5	22	10	48	1	6	7-2	.207	.250	.373	.623	1	.991
— Louisville (A.A.)	OF	43	155	23	45	3	1	4	16	8	21	4	1	13-2	.290	.337	.400	.737	1	.989
1993— St. Louis (N.L.)	OF	67	223	33	69	10	6	10	44	12	35	4	6	6-6	.309	.351	.543	.894	4	.973
— Louisville	OF	38	144	24	54	13	2	5	35	16	17	3	3	9-4	.375	.442	.597	1.040	0	1.000
1994— St. Louis (N.L.)	OF-1B	53	178	14	46	8	2	5	15	16	40	1	6	4-3	.258	.320	.410	.730	1	.991
1995— St. Louis (N.L.)	OF	131	490	83	145	20	4	22	81	22	79	11	5	24-9	.296	.339	.488	.827	1	.996
1996— St. Louis (N.L.)	OF-1B	140	513	82	159	36	1	17	104	29	84	7	6	22-5	.310	.349	.483	.833	2	.994
1997— St. Louis (N.L.)	OF	47	145	17	34	5	0	0	10	10	21	6	4	6-1	.234	.311	.269	.580	1	1.000
— Louisville (A.A.)	OF-DH	6	20	1	3	0	0	0	2	1	2	1	0	0-1	.150	.227	.150	.377	0	1.000
1998— St. Louis (N.L.)	OF-DH-3B	150	564	100	178	34	7	25	91	40	66	9	18	17-5	.316	.368	.534	.902	9	.970
1999— Atlanta (N.L.)	OF	153	576	100	163	28	4	23	115	51	81	9	9	13-8	.283	.346	.465	.811	3	.990
2000— Atlanta (N.L.)	OF	133	489	71	129	26	0	17	77	38	80	5	12	10-2	.264	.320	.421	.742	3	.990
2001— Atlanta (N.L.)	OF-DH	148	560	82	165	32	3	25	97	31	88	6	18	3-2	.295	.334	.469	.830	3	.991
2002— Los Angeles (N.L.)	OF-DH	128	471	65	134	27	3	18	80	34	86	6	10	2-2	.285	.338	.469	.807	4	.982
2003— Los Angeles (N.L.)	OF-DH	66	224	28	67	9	0	6	28	23	30	4	3	1-1	.299	.372	.420	.791	1	.990
Major League totals (12 years)		1271	4626	692	1329	244	34	173	764	316	738	69	103	115-46	.287	.339	.467	.806	32	.988

JOSE, FELIX   OF

PERSONAL: Born May 8, 1965, in Santo Domingo, Dominican Republic. ... 6-1/220. ... Bats both, throws right. ... Full name: Domingo Felix Jose. ... High school: Eldo Foreda Reyez de Munoz (Santo Domingo, Dominican Republic).

TRANSACTIONS/CAREER NOTES: Signed as non-drafted free agent by Oakland Athletics organization (January 3, 1984). ... Traded by A's with 3B Stan Royer and P Daryl Green to St. Louis Cardinals for OF Willie McGee (August 29, 1990). ... On St. Louis disabled list (March 28-April 29, 1992); included rehabilitation assignments to Louisville (April 17-22) and St. Petersburg (April 22-29). ... Traded by Cardinals with IF/OF Craig Wilson to Kansas City Royals for 3B Gregg Jefferies and OF Ed Gerald (February 12, 1993). ... On Kansas City disabled list (March 25-April 15, 1994); included rehabilitation assignment to Memphis (April 7-13). ... Granted free agency (December 12, 1994). ... Re-signed by Royals organization (April 19, 1995). ... Released by Royals (May 14, 1995). ... Signed by Chicago Cubs organization (May 24, 1995). ... Released by Cubs (June 1, 1995). ... Signed by Boston Red Sox organization (February 15, 1996). ... On Pawtucket disabled list (April 4-20, 1996). ... Released by Red Sox (May 12, 1996). ... Signed by Toronto Blue Jays organization (May 24, 1996). ... Granted free agency (October 15, 1996). ... Signed by New York Yankees organization (April 2, 2000). ... On New York disabled list (April 30-May 30, 2000); included rehabilitation assignment to Columbus (May 19-29). ... Granted free agency (October 2, 2000). ... Contract purchased by Arizona Diamondbacks organization from Mexico City Reds, Mexican League (September 4, 2002).

2003 GAMES PLAYED BY POSITION (MLB): DH—1, OF—1.

Year Team (League)	Pos.	G	AB	R	H	2B	3B	HR	RBI	BB	SO	HBP	GDP	SB-CS	Avg.	OBP	SLG	OPS	E	Pct.
1984— Idaho Falls (Pio.)	OF	45	152	16	33	6	0	1	18	18	37	1	4	5-1	.217	.301	.276	.577	1	.982
1985— Madison (Midw.)	OF	117	409	46	89	13	3	3	33	32	82	5	8	6-6	.218	.281	.286	.567	12	.942
1986— Modesto (Calif.)	OF	127	516	77	147	22	8	14	77	36	89	2	5	14-9	.285	.333	.440	.773	14	.942
1987— Huntsville (Sou.)	OF	91	296	29	67	11	1	5	42	28	61	2	11	9-3	.226	.295	.321	.616	8	.945
1988— Tacoma (PCL)	OF	134	508	72	161	29	5	12	83	53	75	1	10	16-8	.317	.380	.465	.844	8	.971
— Oakland (A.L.)	OF	8	6	2	2	1	0	0	1	0	1	0	0	1-0	.333	.333	.500	.833	0	1.000
1989— Oakland (A.L.)	OF	20	57	3	11	2	0	0	5	4	13	0	2	0-1	.193	.246	.228	.474	1	.974
— Tacoma (PCL)	OF	104	387	59	111	26	0	14	63	41	82	3	14	11-7	.287	.358	.463	.820	* 10	.951
1990— Oakland (A.L.)	DH-OF	101	341	42	90	12	0	8	39	16	65	5	8	8-2	.264	.306	.370	.675	5	.977
— St. Louis (N.L.)	OF	25	85	12	23	4	1	3	13	8	16	0	1	4-4	.271	.333	.447	.780	0	1.000
1991— St. Louis (N.L.)	OF	154	568	69	173	40	6	8	77	50	113	2	12	20-12	.305	.360	.438	.798	3	.990
1992— Louisville (A.A.)	OF	2	7	0	1	0	0	0	0	1	0	0	0	0-0	.143	.250	.143	.393	0	1.000
— St. Pete. (FSL)	OF	6	18	2	8	1	1	0	2	1	2	0	0	1-0	.444	.474	.611	1.085	0	1.000
— St. Louis (N.L.)	OF	131	509	62	150	22	3	14	75	40	100	1	9	28-12	.295	.347	.432	.779	6	.979
1993— Kansas City (A.L.)	OF-DH	149	499	64	126	24	3	6	43	36	95	1	5	31-13	.253	.303	.349	.652	7	.972
1994— Memphis (Sou.)	OF	6	21	3	7	2	0	0	6	5	6	0	0	1-1	.333	.462	.429	.890	0	1.000
— Kansas City (A.L.)	OF	99	366	56	111	28	1	11	55	35	75	0	9	10-12	.303	.362	.475	.838	4	.980
1995— Kansas City (A.L.)	OF	9	30	2	4	1	0	0	1	2	9	0	1	0-0	.133	.188	.167	.354	0	1.000
— Iowa (Am. Assoc.)	OF-DH	10	37	2	5	3	0	0	1	1	6	1	1	0-0	.135	.179	.216	.396	0	1.000
1996— Pawtucket (Int'l)	DH-OF	11	32	3	7	3	0	2	5	3	10	0	0	0-0	.219	.286	.500	.786	1	.889
— Syracuse (Int'l)	DH-OF	88	327	47	84	14	2	16	61	32	63	0	9	3-0	.257	.321	.459	.780	1	.923
1997— Monc.-Tab. (Mex.)	OF	92	308	54	83	16	1	10	41	61	60	...	...	8-5	.269	...	.425	...	2	.977
1998— Nashua (Atl.)	OF-DH	98	327	72	112	19	1	26	86	78	55	2	12	8-9	.343	.469	.645	1.115	3	.975
1999— Lobbe (Korean)	...		462	93	151	...	...	36	122	...	...	...	...	12-...	.327	...	...	...	...	...
2000— Columbus (Int'l)	OF	59	210	31	65	17	2	11	38	23	60	1	7	4-3	.310	.379	.567	.945	1	.970
— New York (A.L.)	OF-DH	20	29	4	7	0	0	1	5	2	9	0	1	0-1	.241	.281	.345	.626	1	.929
2002— M.C. R. Dev. (Mex.)	OF	85	324	88	124	21	2	27	102	62	56	...	...	4-1	.383	...	.710	...	2	.969
— Arizona (N.L.)	OF	13	19	5	5	0	0	2	4	4	8	0	1	0-0	.263	.360	.579	.939	1	1.000
2003— Arizona (N.L.)	DH-OF	18	18	1	6	1	0	1	6	6	3	0	1	0-0	.333	.500	.556	1.056	0	...
American League totals (7 years)		406	1328	173	351	68	4	26	149	95	267	6	26	50-29	.264	.315	.380	.695	18	.976
National League totals (5 years)		341	1199	149	357	67	10	28	175	108	240	3	24	52-28	.298	.355	.440	.795	9	.986
Major League totals (11 years)		747	2527	322	708	135	14	54	324	203	507	9	50	102-57	.280	.334	.409	.743	27	.980

JOURNELL, JIMMY   P

PERSONAL: Born December 29, 1977, in Springfield, Ohio. ... 6-4/205. ... Throws right, bats right. ... Full name: James Richard Journell. ... Name pronounced: JUR-nell. ... High school: Springfield North (Springfield, Ohio). ... College: Illinois.

TRANSACTIONS/CAREER NOTES: Selected by St. Louis Cardinals organization in fourth round of free-agent draft (June 2, 1999). ... On New Haven disabled list (April 15-29, 2002). ... On Memphis disabled list (July 3-August 6, 2002). ... Recalled by St. Louis from Memphis (June 27, 2003). ... Optioned to Memphis by St. Louis (June 30, 2003). ... Recalled by St. Louis from Memphis (August 11, 2003). ... Placed on 15-day disabled list (August 23, 2003). ... Removed from 15-day disabled list (September 6, 2003).

CAREER HITTING: 0-for-0 (.000), 0 R, 0 2B, 0 3B, 0 HR, 0 RBI.

Year League	W	L	Pct.	ERA	WHIP	G	GS	CG	ShO	Hld.	Sv.-Opp.	IP	H	R	ER	HR	BB-IBB	SO	Avg.
2000— New Jersey (NYP)	1	0	1.000	1.97	1.13	13	1	0	0	...	0-...	32.0	12	12	7	0	24-0	39	.111
2001— Potomac (Caro.)	14	6	.700	2.50	1.08	26	26	0	0	...	0-...	151.0	121	54	42	8	42-0	156	.220
— New Haven (East.)	1	0	1.000	0.00	0.43	1	1	1	1	...	0-...	7.0	0	0	0	0	3-0	6	.000
2002— New Haven (East.)	3	3	.500	2.70	1.02	10	10	2	0	...	0-...	66.2	50	22	20	3	18-0	66	.206
— Memphis (PCL)	2	4	.333	3.68	1.53	7	7	0	0	...	0-...	36.2	38	16	15	3	18-0	32	.264
2003— Memphis (PCL)	6	6	.500	3.92	1.44	40	7	0	0	...	5-...	78.0	80	38	34	3	32-2	70	.268
— St. Louis (N.L.)	0	0	...	6.00	2.33	7	0	0	0	0	0-0	9.0	10	7	6	0	11-0	8	.278
Major League totals (1 year)	0	0	...	6.00	2.33	7	0	0	0	0	0-0	9.0	10	7	6	0	11-0	8	.278

JULIO, JORGE — P

PERSONAL: Born March 3, 1979, in Caracas, Venezuela. ... 6-1/223. ... Throws right, bats right. ... Full name: Jorge Dandys Julio. ... High school: Fundacion Bolivariana (Caracas, Venezuela).

TRANSACTIONS/CAREER NOTES: Signed as non-drafted free agent by Montreal Expos organization (February 14, 1996). ... Traded by Expos to Baltimore Orioles for 3B Ryan Minor (December 22, 2000).

CAREER HITTING: 0-for-0 (.000), 0 R, 0 2B, 0 3B, 0 HR, 0 RBI.

Year League	W	L	Pct.	ERA	WHIP	G	GS	CG	ShO	Hld.	Sv.-Opp.	IP	H	R	ER	HR	BB-IBB	SO	Avg.
1996— DSL Expos (DSL)	1	1	.500	6.06	1.47	10	0	0	0	...	0-...	16.1	13	12	11	0	11-...	21	...
1997— GC Expos (GCL)	5	6	.455	3.58	1.41	15	8	0	0	...	1-...	55.1	57	25	22	0	21-0	42	.256
— W.P. Beach (FSL)	0	0	...	...	...	1	0	0	0	...	0-...	.0	2	1	1	0	0-0	0	1.000
1998— Vermont (NY-P)	3	1	.750	2.57	1.07	7	7	0	0	...	0-...	42.0	30	12	12	1	15-0	52	.196
— Cape Fear (S. Atl.)	2	2	.500	5.68	1.42	6	6	0	0	...	0-...	31.2	33	20	20	4	12-0	20	.260
1999— Jupiter (FSL)	4	8	.333	3.92	1.31	23	22	0	0	...	0-...	114.2	116	62	50	6	34-0	80	.260
2000— Jupiter (FSL)	2	10	.167	5.90	1.61	21	15	0	0	...	1-...	79.1	93	60	52	4	35-0	67	.292
2001— Bowie (East.)	0	0	...	0.73	0.57	12	0	0	0	...	7-...	12.1	5	1	1	0	2-1	14	.125
— Baltimore (A.L.)	1	1	.500	3.80	1.59	18	0	0	0	3	0-1	21.1	25	13	9	2	9-0	22	.287
— Rochester (Int'l)	1	2	.333	3.74	1.34	34	0	0	0	...	12-...	43.1	39	27	18	4	19-3	48	.242
2002— Baltimore (A.L.)	5	6	.455	1.99	1.21	67	0	0	0	1	25-31	68.0	55	22	15	5	27-3	55	.213
2003— Baltimore (A.L.)	0	7	.000	4.38	1.52	64	0	0	0	2	36-44	61.2	60	36	30	10	34-4	52	.256
Major League totals (3 years)	6	14	.300	3.22	1.39	149	0	0	0	6	61-76	151.0	140	71	54	17	70-7	129	.242

JUNGE, ERIC — P

PERSONAL: Born January 5, 1977, in Manhasset, N.Y. ... 6-5/215. ... Throws right, bats right. ... Full name: Eric Debari Junge. ... Name pronounced: young. ... High school: Rye (N.Y.). ... College: Bucknell.

TRANSACTIONS/CAREER NOTES: Selected by Los Angeles Dodgers organization in 11th round of free-agent draft (June 2, 1999). ... Traded with P Jesus Cordero to Philadelphia Phillies for P Omar Daal (November 9, 2001).

CAREER HITTING: 0-for-3 (.000), 0 R, 0 2B, 0 3B, 0 HR, 0 RBI.

Year League	W	L	Pct.	ERA	WHIP	G	GS	CG	ShO	Hld.	Sv.-Opp.	IP	H	R	ER	HR	BB-IBB	SO	Avg.
1999— Yakima (NW)	5	7	.417	5.82	1.57	15	15	0	0	...	0-...	82.0	98	60	53	10	31-0	55	.303
2000— San Bernardino (Calif.)	8	1	.889	3.36	1.34	29	24	0	0	...	1-...	158.0	159	69	59	8	53-0	116	.267
2001— Jacksonville (Sou.)	10	11	.476	3.46	1.21	27	27	1	1	...	0-...	164.0	143	72	63	19	56-2	116	.249
2002— Scran./W.B. (I.L.)	12	6	.667	3.54	1.31	29	• 29	1	0	...	0-...	180.2	170	77	71	16	67-1	126	.249
— Philadelphia (N.L.)	2	0	1.000	1.42	1.50	4	1	0	0	...	0-0	12.2	14	3	2	0	5-0	11	.286
2003— Philadelphia (N.L.)	0	0	...	3.52	0.78	6	0	0	0	0	0-0	7.2	5	3	3	1	1-0	5	.185
— Scran./W.B. (I.L.)	1	0	1.000	3.06	1.15	10	8	0	0	...	0-...	47.0	38	20	16	2	16-1	42	.216
Major League totals (2 years)	2	0	1.000	2.21	1.23	10	1	0	0	0	0-0	20.1	19	6	5	1	6-0	16	.250

KAPLER, GABE — OF

PERSONAL: Born August 31, 1975, in Hollywood, Calif. ... 6-2/208. ... Bats right, throws right. ... Full name: Gabriel Stefan Kapler. ... Name pronounced: CAP-ler. ... High school: Taft (Woodland Hills, Calif.). ... Junior college: Moorpark College (Calif.).

TRANSACTIONS/CAREER NOTES: Selected by Detroit Tigers organization in 57th round of free-agent draft (June 1, 1995). ... Traded by Tigers with P Justin Thompson, P Francisco Cordero, C Bill Haselman, 2B Frank Catalanotto and P Alan Webb to Texas Rangers for OF Juan Gonzalez, P Danny Patterson and C Gregg Zaun (November 2, 1999). ... On Texas disabled list (May 4-June 9, 2000); included rehabilitation assignments to Oklahoma (May 20-24) and Tulsa (June 5-9). ... On Texas disabled list (March 23-April 22, 2001); included rehabilitation assignment to Tulsa (April 17-22). ... On Texas disabled list (June 24-July 16, 2002); included rehabilitation assignment to Oklahoma (July 11-16). ... Traded by Rangers with 2B Jason Romano to Colorado Rockies for OF Todd Hollandsworth and P Dennys Reyes (July 31, 2002). ... Optioned to Colorado Springs (June 4, 2003). ... Designated for assignment (June 17, 2003). ... Sent outright to Colorado Springs (June 18, 2003). ... Contract purchased by Boston Red Sox from Portland (June 28, 2003).

2003 GAMES PLAYED BY POSITION (MLB): OF—90, DH—1, 1B—1.

Year Team (League)	Pos.	G	AB	R	H	2B	3B	HR	RBI	BB	SO	HBP	GDP	SB-CS	Avg.	OBP	SLG	OPS	E	Pct.
1995—Jamestown (NYP)	OF	63	236	38	68	19	4	4	34	23	37	2	4	1-2	.288	.351	.453	.804	9	.926
1996—Fayetteville (SAL)	3B-OF	138	524	81	* 157	* 45	0	26	99	62	73	7	6	14-4	.300	.378	.534	.912	7	.968
1997—Lakeland (Fla. St.)	OF	137	519	87	153	* 40	6	19	87	54	68	5	8	8-6	.295	.361	.505	.865	6	.978
1998—Jacksonville (Sou.)	1B-OF	• 139	547	* 113	* 176	• 47	6	* 28	* 146	66	93	5	6	6-4	.322	.393	.583	.976	5	.984
—Detroit (A.L.)	OF-DH	7	25	3	5	0	1	0	0	1	4	0	0	0-0	.200	.231	.280	.511	0	1.000
1999—Detroit (A.L.)	OF-DH	130	416	60	102	22	4	18	49	42	74	2	7	11-5	.245	.315	.447	.762	6	.981
—Toledo (Int'l)	OF	14	54	11	17	6	2	3	14	9	10	0	0	0-1	.315	.400	.667	1.067	0	1.000
2000—Texas (A.L.)	OF	116	444	59	134	32	1	14	66	42	57	0	12	8-4	.302	.360	.473	.833	• 10	.969
—Oklahoma (PCL)	OF	3	9	3	3	0	0	0	0	3	2	0	0	0-0	.333	.500	.333	.833	0	1.000
—Tulsa (Texas)	OF	3	12	3	7	0	0	1	4	1	2	0	0	0-0	.583	.615	.833	1.449	0	1.000
2001—Tulsa (Texas)	OF	5	15	2	5	1	0	0	0	6	1	0	0	0-1	.333	.524	.400	.924	0	1.000
—Texas (A.L.)	OF-DH	134	483	77	129	29	1	17	72	61	70	3	10	23-6	.267	.348	.437	.785	1	.997
2002—Texas (A.L.)	OF-DH-1B	72	196	25	51	12	1	0	17	8	30	0	3	5-2	.260	.285	.332	.617	3	1.000
—Oklahoma (PCL)	OF	5	17	6	8	2	0	1	5	3	2	0	0	1-0	.471	.550	.765	1.315	0	1.000
—Colorado (N.L.)	OF	40	119	12	37	4	3	2	17	8	23	1	2	6-2	.311	.359	.445	.805	0	1.000
2003—Colorado (N.L.)	OF	39	67	10	15	3	0	0	4	8	18	0	3	2-0	.224	.307	.254	.560	1	.970
—Colo. Springs (PCL)	OF	13	35	5	6	2	1	0	2	8	10	1	0	4-0	.171	.333	.286	.619	1	.955
—Lowell (NY-Penn)	OF	1	3	2	2	0	0	0	1	0	1	0	1	1-0	.667	.750	.667	1.417	0	1.000
—Portland (East.)	1B-OF	1	3	1	1	1	0	0	0	0	1	0	0	0-0	.333	.333	.667	1.000	0	1.000
—Boston (A.L.)	OF-DH-1B	68	158	29	46	11	1	4	23	14	23	0	5	4-2	.291	.349	.449	.798	6	.934
American League totals (6 years)		527	1722	253	467	106	9	53	227	168	258	5	37	53-19	.271	.335	.434	.770	26	.979
National League totals (2 years)		79	186	22	52	6	3	2	21	16	41	1	5	8-2	.280	.340	.376	.716	1	.990
Major League totals (6 years)		606	1908	275	519	112	12	55	248	184	299	6	42	61-21	.272	.335	.430	.765	27	.979

KARROS, ERIC   1B

PERSONAL: Born November 4, 1967, in Hackensack, N.J. ... 6-4/220. ... Bats right, throws right. ... Full name: Eric Peter Karros. ... Name pronounced: CARE-ose. ... High school: Patrick Henry (San Diego). ... College: UCLA.

TRANSACTIONS/CAREER NOTES: Selected by Los Angeles Dodgers organization in sixth round of free-agent draft (June 1, 1988). ... On Los Angeles disabled list (March 29-April 24, 1998); included rehabilitation assignment to San Bernardino (April 19-25). ... On disabled list (May 22-June 15, 2001). ... Traded by Dodgers with 2B Mark Grudzielanek and cash to Chicago Cubs for C Todd Hundley and OF Chad Hermansen (December 4, 2002).

2003 GAMES PLAYED BY POSITION (MLB): 1B—97.

Year Team (League)	Pos.	G	AB	R	H	2B	3B	HR	RBI	BB	SO	HBP	GDP	SB-CS	Avg.	OBP	SLG	OPS	E	Pct.
1988— Great Falls (Pio.)	3B-1B	66	268	68	98	12	1	12	55	32	35	3	7	8-2	.366	.433	.552	.985	§19	.966
1989— Bakersfield (Calif.)	3B-1B	*142	545	86	*165	*40	1	15	86	63	99	2	15	18-7	.303	.375	.462	.837	19	.986
1990— San Antonio (Texas)	1B	•131	509	91	*179	*45	2	18	78	57	79	6	18	8-10	*.352	.419	.554	.973	8	*.994
1991— Albuquerque (PCL)	3B-1B	132	488	88	154	33	8	22	101	58	80	6	6	3-2	.316	.391	.551	.943	11	.991
— Los Angeles (N.L.)	1B	14	14	0	1	1	0	0	1	1	6	0	0	0-0	.071	.133	.143	.276	0	1.000
1992— Los Angeles (N.L.)	1B	149	545	63	140	30	1	20	88	37	103	2	15	2-4	.257	.304	.426	.730	9	.993
1993— Los Angeles (N.L.)	1B	158	619	74	153	27	2	23	80	34	82	2	17	0-1	.247	.287	.409	.696	12	.992
1994— Los Angeles (N.L.)	1B	111	406	51	108	21	1	14	46	29	53	2	13	2-0	.266	.310	.426	.736	•9	.991
1995— Los Angeles (N.L.)	1B	143	551	83	164	29	3	32	105	61	115	4	14	4-4	.298	.369	.535	.905	7	.995
1996— Los Angeles (N.L.)	1B	154	608	84	158	29	1	34	111	53	121	1	*27	8-0	.260	.316	.479	.795	15	.990
1997— Los Angeles (N.L.)	1B	•162	628	86	167	28	0	31	104	61	116	2	10	15-7	.266	.329	.459	.787	11	.992
1998— San Bern. (Calif.)	1B	4	15	3	4	1	0	0	1	0	2	0	1	0-0	.267	.267	.333	.600	0	1.000
— Los Angeles (N.L.)	1B-DH	139	507	59	150	20	1	23	87	47	93	3	7	7-2	.296	.355	.475	.830	12	.991
1999— Los Angeles (N.L.)	1B	153	578	74	176	40	0	34	112	53	119	2	18	8-5	.304	.362	.550	.912	13	.991
2000— Los Angeles (N.L.)	1B-DH	155	584	84	146	29	0	31	106	63	122	4	18	4-3	.250	.321	.459	.780	7	.995
2001— Los Angeles (N.L.)	1B	121	438	42	103	22	0	15	63	41	101	3	15	3-1	.235	.303	.388	.691	4	.996
2002— Los Angeles (N.L.)	1B	142	524	52	142	26	1	13	73	37	74	6	11	4-2	.271	.323	.399	.722	4	.997
2003— Chicago (N.L.)	1B	114	336	37	96	16	1	12	40	28	46	0	14	1-1	.286	.340	.446	.786	6	.992
Major League totals (13 years)		1715	6338	789	1704	318	11	282	1016	545	1151	31	179	58-30	.269	.326	.456	.782	109	.993

KARSAY, STEVE   P

PERSONAL: Born March 24, 1972... 6-3/215. ... Throws right, bats right. ... Full name: Stefan Andrew Karsay. ... Name pronounced: CAR-say. ... High school: Christ the King (Queens, N.Y.).

TRANSACTIONS/CAREER NOTES: Selected by Toronto Blue Jays organization in first round (22nd pick overall) of free-agent draft (June 4, 1990). ... On Knoxville disabled list (July 3-16, 1993). ... Traded by Blue Jays with a player to be named later to Oakland Athletics for OF Rickey Henderson (July 31, 1993); A's acquired OF Jose Herrera to complete deal (August 6, 1993). ... On disabled list (April 26, 1994-remainder of season; April 24, 1995-entire season; and August 6, 1997-remainder of season). ... Traded by A's to Cleveland Indians for P Mike Fetters (December 8, 1997). ... On Buffalo disabled list (May 14-25 and June 12-July 15, 1998). ... On disabled list (July 2-26 and August 25-September 22, 1999). ... Traded by Indians with P Steve Reed to Atlanta Braves for P John Rocker and 3B Troy Cameron (June 22, 2001). ... Granted free agency (November 5, 2001). ... Signed by New York Yankees (December 7, 2001). ... On disabled list (March 21, 2003-entire season).

CAREER HITTING: 0-for-4 (.000), 1 R, 0 2B, 0 3B, 0 HR, 0 RBI.

Year League	W	L	Pct.	ERA	WHIP	G	GS	CG	ShO	Hld.	Sv.-Opp.	IP	H	R	ER	HR	BB-IBB	SO	Avg.
1990— St. Catharines (NYP)	1	1	.500	0.79	1.01	5	5	0	0	...	0-...	22.2	11	4	2	0	12-0	25	.141
1991— Myrtle Beach (SAL)	4	9	.308	3.58	1.30	20	20	1	0	...	0-...	110.2	96	58	44	7	48-0	100	.240
1992— Dunedin (Fla. St.)	6	3	.667	2.73	0.99	16	16	3	2	...	0-...	85.2	56	32	26	6	29-0	87	.187
1993— Knoxville (Sou.)	8	4	.667	3.38	1.25	19	18	1	0	...	0-...	104.0	98	42	39	9	32-1	100	.251
— Huntsville (Sou.)	0	0	...	5.14	1.14	2	2	0	0	...	0-...	14.0	13	8	8	2	3-0	22	.254
— Oakland (A.L.)	3	3	.500	4.04	1.33	8	8	0	0	0	0-0	49.0	49	23	22	4	16-1	33	.258
1994— Oakland (A.L.)	1	1	.500	2.57	1.21	4	4	1	0	0	0-0	28.0	26	8	8	1	8-0	15	.252
1995— Oakland (A.L.)											Did not play.								
1996— Modesto (Calif.)	0	1	.000	2.65	1.06	14	14	0	0	...	0-...	34.0	35	16	10	2	1-0	31	.255
1997— Oakland (A.L.)	3	12	.200	5.77	1.61	24	24	0	0	0	0-...	132.2	166	92	85	20	47-3	92	.304
1998— Buffalo (Int'l)	6	4	.600	3.76	1.32	16	14	0	0	...	0-...	79.0	89	39	33	5	15-0	63	.276
— Cleveland (A.L.)	0	2	.000	5.92	1.52	11	1	0	0	2	0-0	24.1	31	16	16	3	6-1	13	.310
1999— Cleveland (A.L.)	10	2	.833	2.97	1.28	50	3	0	0	9	1-3	78.2	71	29	26	6	30-3	68	.247
2000— Cleveland (A.L.)	5	9	.357	3.76	1.36	72	0	0	0	11	20-29	76.2	79	33	32	5	25-4	66	.266
2001— Cleveland (A.L.)	0	1	.000	1.25	0.85	31	0	0	0	8	1-1	43.1	29	6	6	1	8-2	44	.188
— Atlanta (N.L.)	3	4	.429	3.43	1.37	43	0	0	0	4	7-11	44.2	44	21	17	4	17-8	39	.265
2002— New York (A.L.)	6	4	.600	3.26	1.32	78	0	0	0	14	12-16	88.1	87	33	32	7	30-14	65	.258
2003—											Did not play.								
American League totals (8 years)	28	34	.452	3.92	1.36	278	40	1	0	44	34-49	521.0	538	240	227	47	170-28	396	.267
National League totals (1 year)	3	4	.429	3.43	1.37	43	0	0	0	4	7-11	44.2	44	21	17	4	17-8	39	.265
Major League totals (8 years)	31	38	.449	3.88	1.36	321	40	1	0	48	41-60	565.2	582	261	244	51	187-36	435	.267

KATA, MATT   IF

PERSONAL: Born March 14, 1978, in Avon Lakes, Ohio. ... 6-1/185. ... Bats both, throws right. ... Full name: Matthew John Kata. ... Name pronounced: KATE-a. ... High school: St. Ignatius (Cleveland). ... College: Vanderbilt.

TRANSACTIONS/CAREER NOTES: Selected by Arizona Diamondbacks organization in ninth round of free-agent draft (June 1999).

2003 GAMES PLAYED BY POSITION (MLB): 2B—52, 3B—23, SS—6.

Year Team (League)	Pos.	G	AB	R	H	2B	3B	HR	RBI	BB	SO	HBP	GDP	SB-CS	Avg.	OBP	SLG	OPS	E	Pct.
1999— South Bend (Mid.)	SS	78	318	40	83	14	5	3	33	28	46	4	5	5-6	.261	.328	.365	.692	22	.937
2000— South Bend (Mid.)	SS-2B-OF	133	521	82	133	22	9	6	59	52	58	6	10	38-12	.255	.327	.367	.694	39	.937
2001— Lancaster (Calif.)	2B-SS	119	494	80	146	19	6	10	54	41	79	5	4	30-8	.296	.355	.419	.774	29	.952
— El Paso (Texas)	2B	4	16	4	7	2	0	0	4	2	2	0	0	1-1	.438	.500	.563	1.063	0	1.000
2002— El Paso (Texas)	2B-SS-3B	136	578	95	172	33	9	11	57	37	79	4	6	12-7	.298	.341	.443	.784	18	.972
2003— Tucson (PCL)	2B-SS	48	201	31	58	13	5	3	25	9	29	3	1	2-3	.289	.327	.448	.775	10	.958
— Arizona (N.L.)	2B-3B-SS	78	288	42	74	16	5	7	29	25	53	1	4	3-2	.257	.315	.420	.736	4	.987
Major League totals (1 year)		78	288	42	74	16	5	7	29	25	53	1	4	3-2	.257	.315	.420	.736	4	.987

K

KEARNS, AUSTIN — OF

PERSONAL: Born May 20, 1980, in Lexington, Ky. ... 6-3/220. ... Bats right, throws right. ... Full name: Austin Ryan Kearns. ... High school: Lafayette (Lexington, Ky.).

TRANSACTIONS/CAREER NOTES: Selected by Cincinnati Reds organization in first round (seventh pick overall) of free-agent draft (June 2, 1998). ... On Chattanooga disabled list (May 27-August 13, 2001). ... On Cincinnati disabled list (August 27, 2002-remainder of season). ... Placed on 15-day disabled list (July 9, 2003). ... Sent to Chattanooga on rehab assignment (August 4, 2003). ... Recalled from Chattanooga rehab assignment (August 7, 2003). ... Transferred to 60-day disabled list (August 18, 2003).

2003 GAMES PLAYED BY POSITION (MLB): OF—80.

Year Team (League)	Pos.	G	AB	R	H	2B	3B	HR	RBI	BB	SO	HBP	GDP	SB-CS	Avg.	OBP	SLG	OPS	E	Pct.
1998— Billings (Pio.)	OF	30	108	17	34	9	0	1	14	23	22	1	4	1-1	.315	.433	.426	.859	4	.905
1999— Rockford (Midwest)	OF	124	426	72	110	36	5	13	48	50	120	9	9	21-8	.258	.346	.458	.804	13	.939
2000— Dayton (Midw.)	OF	* 136	484	* 110	148	37	2	* 27	* 104	90	93	7	14	18-5	.306	.415	.558	.973	12	.955
2001— Chattanooga (Sou.)	OF	59	205	30	55	11	2	6	36	26	43	6	4	7-5	.268	.364	.429	.793	2	.979
— GC Reds (GCL)	OF	6	17	2	3	2	0	0	4	2	7	0	0	0-0	.176	.227	.294	.521	0	1.000
2002— Chattanooga (Sou.)	OF	12	41	10	11	2	0	5	13	9	9	3	0	1-0	.268	.434	.683	1.117	0	1.000
— Cincinnati (N.L.)	OF	107	372	66	117	24	3	13	56	54	81	6	11	6-3	.315	.407	.500	.907	4	.983
— Louisville (Int'l)	OF	1	4	3	3	2	0	0	2	1	0	0	0	0-0	.750	.800	1.250	2.050	0	1.000
2003— Cincinnati (N.L.)	OF	82	292	39	77	11	0	15	58	41	68	5	7	5-2	.264	.364	.455	.819	2	.990
— Chattanooga (Sou.)	OF	3	5	2	1	0	0	0	1	2	2	1	0	0-0	.200	.500	.200	.700	0	1.000
Major League totals (2 years)		189	664	105	194	35	3	28	114	95	149	11	18	11-5	.292	.388	.480	.869	6	.986

KEISLER, RANDY — P

PERSONAL: Born February 24, 1976, in Richards, Texas. ... 6-3/190. ... Throws left, bats left. ... Full name: Randy Dean Keisler. ... Name pronounced: keyz-lur. ... High school: Navasota (Texas), then Palmer (Texas). ... College: Louisiana State.

TRANSACTIONS/CAREER NOTES: Selected by Cleveland Indians organization in 40th round of free-agent draft (June 1, 1995); did not sign. ... Selected by Indians organization in 57th round of free-agent draft (June 4, 1996); did not sign. ... Selected by New York Yankees organization in second round of free-agent draft (June 2, 1998). ... On disabled list (March 31, 2002-entire season). ... Released by Yankees (February 5, 2003). ... Signed by San Diego Padres organization (February 16, 2003). ... Contract purchased by San Diego from Portland (May 16, 2003). ... Sent to Portland (May 29, 2003). ... Elected free agency (June 5, 2003).

CAREER HITTING: 0-for-4 (.000), 0 R, 0 2B, 0 3B, 0 HR, 0 RBI.

Year League	W	L	Pct.	ERA	WHIP	G	GS	CG	ShO	Hld.	Sv.-Opp.	IP	H	R	ER	HR	BB-IBB	SO	Avg.
1998— Oneonta (N.Y.-Penn)	1	1	.500	7.45	2.17	6	2	0	0	...	1-...	9.2	14	10	8	0	7-1	11	.341
1999— Greensboro (S. Atl.)	1	1	.500	2.38	0.97	4	4	0	0	...	0-...	22.2	12	6	6	1	10-0	42	.150
— Tampa (FSL)	10	3	.769	3.30	1.19	15	15	1	0	...	0-...	90.0	67	43	33	2	40-0	77	.204
— Norwich (East.)	3	4	.429	4.57	1.43	8	8	0	0	...	0-...	43.1	45	24	22	2	17-0	33	.273
2000— Norwich (East.)	6	2	.750	2.60	1.33	11	11	1	0	...	0-...	72.2	63	29	21	4	34-1	70	.227
— Columbus (Int'l)	8	3	.727	3.02	1.29	17	17	1	1	...	0-...	113.1	104	44	38	9	42-1	86	.244
— New York (A.L.)	1	0	1.000	11.81	2.25	4	1	0	0	0	0-0	10.2	16	14	14	1	8-0	6	.364
2001— Columbus (Int'l)	5	7	.417	5.18	1.54	18	18	3	1	...	0-...	97.1	111	67	56	10	39-0	88	.284
— New York (A.L.)	1	2	.333	6.22	1.70	10	10	0	0	0	0-0	50.2	52	36	35	12	34-0	36	.259
2002— New York (A.L.)										Did not play.									
2003— Portland (PCL)	5	1	.833	2.61	1.09	8	6	0	0	...	0-...	41.1	33	12	12	6	12-0	24	.216
— San Diego (N.L.)	0	1	.000	12.00	2.33	2	2	0	0	0	0-0	6.0	7	9	8	3	7-0	5	.292
— Oklahoma (PCL)	0	2	.000	8.53	2.05	5	2	0	0	...	0-...	12.2	21	13	12	0	5-0	9	.389
— New Orleans (PCL)	2	3	.400	4.28	1.53	9	9	0	0	...	0-...	48.1	53	24	23	3	21-2	27	.290
American League totals (2 years)	2	2	.500	7.19	1.79	14	11	0	0	0	0-0	61.1	68	50	49	13	42-0	42	.278
National League totals (1 year)	0	1	.000	12.00	2.33	2	2	0	0	0	0-0	6.0	7	9	8	3	7-0	5	.292
Major League totals (3 years)	2	3	.400	7.62	1.84	16	13	0	0	0	0-0	67.1	75	59	57	16	49-0	47	.279

KELTON, DAVID — OF/3B

PERSONAL: Born December 17, 1979, in Dothan, Ala. ... 6-3/205. ... Bats right, throws right. ... Full name: David Wayne Kelton. ... High school: LaGrange High (La Grange, Ga.).

TRANSACTIONS/CAREER NOTES: Selected by Chicago Cubs organization in second round of free-agent draft (June 2, 1998). ... On disabled list (June 16, 2001-remainder of season). ... On West Tenn disabled list (April 4-13, 2002).

2003 GAMES PLAYED BY POSITION (MLB): OF—2.

Year Team (League)	Pos.	G	AB	R	H	2B	3B	HR	RBI	BB	SO	HBP	GDP	SB-CS	Avg.	OBP	SLG	OPS	E	Pct.
1998— Ariz. Cubs (Ariz.)	3B	50	181	39	48	7	5	6	29	23	58	2	2	16-3	.265	.353	.459	.811	15	.891
1999— Lansing (Midw.)	3B-SS	124	509	75	137	17	4	13	68	39	121	2	11	22-9	.269	.322	.395	.717	32	.893
2000— Daytona (Fla. St.)	3B	132	523	75	140	30	7	18	84	38	120	2	9	7-8	.268	.317	.455	.772	26	.896
2001— West Tenn (Sou.)	3B	58	224	33	70	9	4	12	45	24	55	1	1	1-3	.313	.378	.549	.928	15	.883
2002— West Tenn (Sou.)	1B-3B-OF	129	498	68	130	28	6	20	79	52	129	2	10	12-6	.261	.332	.462	.793	13	.988
2003— Iowa (PCL)	OF-3-D-1	121	442	62	119	24	3	16	67	46	115	2	7	8-2	.269	.338	.446	.784	15	.936
— Chicago (N.L.)	OF	10	12	1	2	1	0	0	1	0	5	0	0	0-0	.167	.167	.250	.417	0	1.000
Major League totals (1 year)		10	12	1	2	1	0	0	1	0	5	0	0	0-0	.167	.167	.250	.417	0	1.000

KENDALL, JASON — C

PERSONAL: Born June 26, 1974, in San Diego, Calif. ... 6-0/197. ... Bats right, throws right. ... Full name: Jason Daniel Kendall. ... High school: Torrance (Calif.).

TRANSACTIONS/CAREER NOTES: Selected by Pittsburgh Pirates organization in first round (23rd pick overall) of free-agent draft (June 1, 1992). ... On suspended list (July 21-23, 1998). ... On disabled list (July 5, 1999-remainder of season). ... On suspended list (September 19-20, 2001). ... Denied appeal of three-game suspension for his role in a June 13 bench-clearing brawl against Tampa Bay (July 28, 2003). ... Reinstated from suspension (August 1, 2003).

2003 GAMES PLAYED BY POSITION (MLB): C—146.

Year Team (League)	Pos.	G	AB	R	H	2B	3B	HR	RBI	BB	SO	HBP	GDP	SB-CS	Avg.	OBP	SLG	OPS	E	Pct.
1992— GC Pirates (GCL)	C	33	111	7	29	2	0	0	10	8	9	2	3	2-2	.261	.317	.279	.596	5	.978
1993— Augusta (S. Atl.)	C	102	366	43	101	17	4	1	40	22	30	7	17	8-5	.276	.325	.352	.677	20	.964
1994— Salem (Caro.)	C	101	371	68	118	19	2	7	66	47	21	13	15	14-3	.318	.406	.437	.843	9	.980
— Carolina (Sou.)	C	13	47	6	11	2	0	0	6	2	3	2	0	0-0	.234	.294	.277	.571	2	.969

Year	Team (League)	Pos.	G	AB	R	H	2B	3B	HR	RBI	BB	SO	HBP	GDP	SB-CS	Avg.	OBP	SLG	OPS	E	Pct.
1995—Carolina (Sou.)	C	117	429	87	140	26	1	8	71	56	22	14	10	10-7	.326	.414	.448	.862	8	.989
1996—Pittsburgh (N.L.)	C	130	414	54	124	23	5	3	42	35	30	15	7	5-2	.300	.372	.401	.773	* 18	.980
1997—Pittsburgh (N.L.)	C	144	486	71	143	36	4	8	49	49	53	31	11	18-6	.294	.391	.434	.825	11	.990
1998—Pittsburgh (N.L.)	C	149	535	95	175	36	3	12	75	51	51	*31	6	26-5	.327	.411	.473	.884	9	.992
1999—Pittsburgh (N.L.)	C	78	280	61	93	20	3	8	41	38	32	12	8	22-3	.332	.428	.511	.939	7	.988
2000—Pittsburgh (N.L.)	C	152	579	112	185	33	6	14	58	79	79	15	13	22-12	.320	.412	.470	.882	10	.991
2001—Pittsburgh (N.L.)	C-OF	157	606	84	161	22	2	10	53	44	48	20	18	13-14	.266	.335	.358	.693	17	.980
2002—Pittsburgh (N.L.)	C	145	545	59	154	25	3	3	44	49	29	9	11	15-8	.283	.350	.356	.706	9	.990
2003—Pittsburgh (N.L.)	C	150	587	84	191	29	3	6	58	49	40	25	9	8-7	.325	.399	.416	.815	10	.989
Major League totals (8 years)		1105	4032	620	1226	224	29	64	420	394	362	158	83	129-57	.304	.385	.422	.807	91	.988

KENNEDY, ADAM — 2B

PERSONAL: Born January 10, 1976, in Riverside, Calif. ... 6-1/185. ... Bats left, throws right. ... Full name: Adam Thomas Kennedy. ... High school: J.W. North (Riverside, Calif.). ... College: Cal State Northridge.

TRANSACTIONS/CAREER NOTES: Selected by St. Louis Cardinals organization in first round (20th pick overall) of free-agent draft (June 3, 1997). ... On Memphis disabled list (June 9-19, 1999). ... Traded by Cardinals with P Kent Bottenfield to Anaheim Angels for OF Jim Edmonds (March 23, 2000). ... On Anaheim disabled list (March 23-April 13, 2001); included rehabilitation assignment to Rancho Cucamonga (April 9-13). ... On disabled list (April 7-22, 2003). ... Optioned to Rancho Cucamonga for rehab assignment (April 18, 2003). ... Reinstated from the 15-day disabled list (April 22, 2003).

2003 GAMES PLAYED BY POSITION (MLB): 2B—140, DH—1.

Year	Team (League)	Pos.	G	AB	R	H	2B	3B	HR	RBI	BB	SO	HBP	GDP	SB-CS	Avg.	OBP	SLG	OPS	E	Pct.
1997—New Jersey (NYP)	SS	29	114	20	39	6	3	0	19	13	10	2	3	9-1	.342	.412	.447	.860	7	.951
—Prince Will. (Car.)	SS	35	154	24	48	9	3	1	27	6	17	2	3	4-3	.312	.346	.429	.774	10	.939
1998—Prince Will. (Car.)	2B-SS	17	69	9	18	6	0	0	7	5	12	0	1	5-2	.261	.307	.348	.654	5	.938
—Arkansas (Texas)	2B-SS	52	205	35	57	11	2	6	24	8	21	2	4	6-2	.278	.307	.439	.746	15	.940
—Memphis (PCL)	2B-SS	74	305	36	93	22	7	4	41	12	42	1	3	15-4	.305	.331	.462	.794	10	.972
1999—Memphis (PCL) 2-S-O-3-D		91	367	69	120	22	4	10	63	29	36	4	7	20-6	.327	.378	.490	.868	18	.953
—St. Louis (N.L.)	2B	33	102	12	26	10	1	1	16	3	8	2	1	0-1	.255	.284	.402	.686	4	.971
2000—Anaheim (A.L.)	2B	156	598	82	159	33	11	9	72	28	73	3	10	22-8	.266	.300	.403	.703	* 19	.976
2001—Rancho Cuca. (Calif.)	2B	3	8	3	3	2	0	0	1	2	1	1	0	3-0	.375	.545	.625	1.170	0	1.000
—Anaheim (A.L.)	2B-DH	137	478	48	129	25	3	6	40	27	71	11	7	12-7	.270	.318	.372	.690	10	.984
2002—Anaheim (A.L.)	2B-DH-OF	144	474	65	148	32	6	7	52	19	80	7	5	17-4	.312	.345	.449	.795	11	.983
2003—Rancho Cuca. (Calif.)	2B	3	11	3	3	1	0	1	1	0	2	1	0	0-0	.273	.333	.636	.970	1	.923
—Anaheim (A.L.)	2B-DH	143	449	71	121	17	1	13	49	45	73	9	7	22-9	.269	.344	.399	.743	6	.990
American League totals (4 years)		580	1999	266	557	107	21	35	213	119	297	30	29	73-28	.279	.325	.406	.731	46	.983
National League totals (1 year)		33	102	12	26	10	1	1	16	3	8	2	1	0-1	.255	.284	.402	.686	4	.971
Major League totals (5 years)		613	2101	278	583	117	22	36	229	122	305	32	30	73-29	.277	.323	.406	.729	50	.982

KENNEDY, JOE — P

PERSONAL: Born May 24, 1979, in La Mesa, Calif. ... 6-4/237. ... Throws left, bats right. ... Full name: Joseph Darley Kennedy. ... High school: El Cajon Valley (El Cajon, Calif.). ... Junior college: Grossmont College (Calif.).

TRANSACTIONS/CAREER NOTES: Selected by Tampa Bay Devil Rays organization in eighth round of free-agent draft (June 2, 1998). ... On suspended list (July 12-19, 2002). ... Placed on 15-day disabled list (June 1, 2003). ... Sent to Orlando on rehab assignment (June 29, 2003). ... Recalled from Durham rehab assignment; reinstated from the 15-day disabled list (July 9, 2003).

CAREER HITTING: 4-for-11 (.364), 2 R, 0 2B, 0 3B, 0 HR, 1 RBI.

Year	Team (League)	W	L	Pct.	ERA	WHIP	G	GS	CG	ShO	Hld.	Sv.-Opp.	IP	H	R	ER	HR	BB-IBB	SO	Avg.
1998—Princeton (Appal.)	6	4	.600	3.74	1.37	13	13	0	0	...	0-...	67.1	66	37	28	5	26-0	44	.264
1999—Hudson Valley (NYP)	6	5	.545	2.65	1.09	16	* 16	1	1	...	0-...	* 95.0	78	33	28	2	26-0	* 101	.227
2000—Char., S.C. (SAL)	11	6	.647	3.30	1.11	22	22	3	2	...	0-...	136.1	122	59	50	6	29-1	142	.242
2001—Orlando (Sou.)	4	0	1.000	0.19	0.68	7	7	0	0	...	0-...	47.0	29	3	1	0	3-0	52	.178
—Durham (Int'l)	2	0	1.000	2.42	1.19	4	4	0	0	...	0-...	26.0	22	8	7	2	9-0	23	.227
—Tampa Bay (A.L.)	7	8	.467	4.44	1.33	20	20	0	0	0	0-0	117.2	122	63	58	16	34-0	78	.269
2002—Tampa Bay (A.L.)	8	11	.421	4.53	1.32	30	30	5	1	0	0-0	196.2	204	114	99	23	55-0	109	.269
2003—Orlando (Sou.)	0	0		8.10	2.10	1	1	0	0	...	0-...	3.1	6	3	3	0	1-0	3	.400
—Durham (Int'l)	1	0	1.000	1.42	0.95	1	1	0	0	...	0-...	6.1	6	1	1	0	0-0	4	.250
—Tampa Bay (A.L.)	3	12	.200	6.13	1.60	32	22	1	1	1	1-2	133.2	167	101	91	19	47-1	77	.303
Major League totals (3 years)	18	31	.367	4.98	1.40	82	72	6	2	1	1-2	448.0	493	278	248	58	136-1	264	.279

KENT, JEFF — 2B

PERSONAL: Born March 7, 1968, in Bellflower, Calif. ... 6-1/215. ... Bats right, throws right. ... Full name: Jeffrey Frank Kent. ... High school: Edison (Huntington Beach, Calif.). ... College: UC-Berkeley.

TRANSACTIONS/CAREER NOTES: Selected by Toronto Blue Jays organization in 20th round of free-agent draft (June 5, 1989). ... Traded by Blue Jays with a player to be named later to New York Mets for P David Cone (August 27, 1992); Mets acquired OF Ryan Thompson to complete deal (September 1, 1992). ... On disabled list (July 6-21, 1995). ... Traded by New York Mets with IF Jose Vizcaino to Cleveland Indians for 2B Carlos Baerga and IF Alvaro Espinoza (July 29, 1996). ... Traded by Indians with IF Jose Vizcaino, P Julian Tavarez and a player to be named later to San Francisco Giants for 3B Matt Williams and a player to be named later (November 13, 1996); Indians traded P Joe Roa to Giants for OF Trenidad Hubbard to complete deal (December 16, 1996). ... On suspended list (August 22-25, 1997). ... On disabled list (June 10-July 10, 1998; August 3-21, 1999; March 21-April 6, 2002). ... Granted free agency (October 29, 2002). ... Signed by Houston Astros (December 18, 2002). ... Placed on 15-day disabled list (June 19, 2003). ... Sent to Round Rock on rehab assignment (July 11, 2003). ... Recalled from rehab assignment; reinstated from 15-day disabled list (July 16, 2003). ... Suspended by Major League Baseball (August 6, 2003). ... Reinstated by MLB (August 9, 2003).

2003 GAMES PLAYED BY POSITION (MLB): 2B—128.

Year	Team (League)	Pos.	G	AB	R	H	2B	3B	HR	RBI	BB	SO	HBP	GDP	SB-CS	Avg.	OBP	SLG	OPS	E	Pct.
1989—St. Catharines (NYP)	3B-SS	73	268	34	60	14	1	* 13	37	33	81	6	2	5-1	.224	.318	.429	.747	29	.906
1990—Dunedin (Fla. St.)	2B	132	447	72	124	32	2	16	60	53	98	6	4	17-7	.277	.360	.465	.825	15	.978
1991—Knoxville (Sou.)	2B	* 139	445	68	114	* 34	1	2	61	80	104	10	3	25-6	.256	.379	.351	.730	* 29	.957
1992—Toronto (A.L.)	3B-2B-1B	65	192	36	46	13	1	8	35	20	47	6	3	2-1	.240	.324	.443	.767	11	.941
—New York (N.L.)	2B-3B-SS	37	113	16	27	8	1	3	15	7	29	1	2	0-2	.239	.289	.407	.696	3	.981
1993—New York (N.L.) 2B-3B-SS		140	496	65	134	24	0	21	80	30	88	8	11	4-4	.270	.320	.446	.765	‡ 22	.965

K

| | BATTING | | | | | | | | | | | | | | | | | | FIELDING | |
Year Team (League)	Pos.	G	AB	R	H	2B	3B	HR	RBI	BB	SO	HBP	GDP	SB-CS	Avg.	OBP	SLG	OPS	E	Pct.
1994— New York (N.L.)	2B	107	415	53	121	24	5	14	68	23	84	10	7	1-4	.292	.341	.475	.816	•14	.976
1995— New York (N.L.)	2B	125	472	65	131	22	3	20	65	29	89	8	9	3-3	.278	.327	.464	.791	10	.984
1996— New York (N.L.)	3B	89	335	45	97	20	1	9	39	21	56	1	7	4-3	.290	.331	.436	.766	21	.925
—Cleveland (A.L.)	1-2-3-D	39	102	16	27	7	0	3	16	10	22	1	1	2-1	.265	.328	.422	.749	1	.994
1997— San Francisco (N.L.)	2B-1B	155	580	90	145	38	2	29	121	48	133	13	14	11-3	.250	.316	.472	.789	16	.981
1998— San Francisco (N.L.)	2B-1B	137	526	94	156	37	3	31	128	48	110	9	16	9-4	.297	.359	.555	.914	‡20	.972
1999— San Francisco (N.L.)	2B-1B	138	511	86	148	40	2	23	101	61	112	5	12	13-6	.290	.366	.511	.877	10	.984
2000— San Francisco (N.L.)	2B-1B	159	587	114	196	41	7	33	125	90	107	9	17	12-9	.334	.424	.596	1.021	12	.985
2001— San Francisco (N.L.)	2B-1B	159	607	84	181	49	6	22	106	65	96	11	11	7-6	.298	.369	.507	.877	11	.987
2002— San Francisco (N.L.)	2B-1B	152	623	102	195	42	2	37	108	52	101	4	20	5-1	.313	.368	.565	.933	16	.979
2003— Round Rock (Texas)	2B-DH	3	10	1	3	0	0	1	6	1	1	0	1	0-1	.300	.333	.600	.933	1	.875
—Houston (N.L.)	2B	130	505	77	150	39	1	22	93	39	85	5	13	6-2	.297	.351	.509	.860	11	.983
American League totals (2 years)		104	294	52	73	20	1	11	51	30	69	7	4	4-2	.248	.325	.435	.761	12	.966
National League totals (12 years)		1528	5770	891	1681	384	33	264	1049	513	1090	84	139	75-47	.291	.354	.507	.860	166	.978
Major League totals (12 years)		1632	6064	943	1754	404	34	275	1100	543	1159	91	143	79-49	.289	.352	.503	.856	178	.977

KERSHNER, JASON   P

PERSONAL: Born December 19, 1976, in Scottsdale, Ariz. ... 6-2/165. ... Throws left, bats left. ... Full name: Jason Ashley Kershner. ... High school: Saguaro (Scottsdale, Ariz.).

TRANSACTIONS/CAREER NOTES: Selected by Philadelphia Philles organization in 12th round of free-agent draft (June 1, 1995). ... Granted free agency (October 15, 2001). ... Signed by San Diego Padres organization (November 20, 2001). ... Claimed on waivers by Toronto Blue Jays (August 30, 2002).

CAREER HITTING: 0-for-0 (.000), 0 R, 0 2B, 0 3B, 0 HR, 0 RBI.

Year League	W	L	Pct.	ERA	WHIP	G	GS	CG	ShO	Hld.	Sv.-Opp.	IP	H	R	ER	HR	BB-IBB	SO	Avg.
1995— Martinsville (App.)	4	2	.667	5.14	1.52	13	13	0	0	...	0-...	63.0	67	42	36	10	29-0	64	.277
1996— Piedmont (S. Atl.)	11	9	.550	3.75	1.27	28	28	2	1	...	0-...	168.0	154	81	70	12	59-0	156	.244
1997— Clearwater (Fla. St.)	5	10	.333	3.90	1.35	22	16	0	0	...	1-...	99.1	113	49	43	9	21-0	51	.293
1998— Clearwater (Fla. St.)	3	3	.500	4.01	1.41	41	8	0	0	...	3-...	94.1	108	57	42	8	25-0	65	.292
1999— Reading (East.)	4	4	.500	5.73	1.50	57	2	0	0	...	8-...	92.2	99	67	59	14	40-3	86	.277
2000— Reading (East.)	9	2	.818	3.63	1.26	27	19	0	0	...	1-...	119.0	125	49	48	15	25-0	80	.269
—Clearwater (Fla. St.)	1	0	1.000	0.64	0.86	2	2	0	0	...	0-...	14.0	7	1	1	1	5-0	15	.149
2001— Reading (East.)	5	9	.357	4.80	1.40	26	19	0	0	...	0-...	123.2	147	75	66	18	26-1	70	.302
—Scran./W.B. (I.L.)	1	1	.500	3.60	1.00	6	1	0	0	...	0-...	15.0	12	8	6	3	3-0	1	.207
2002— Portland (PCL)	7	2	.778	3.03	1.06	31	12	0	0	...	0-...	86.0	65	30	29	8	26-0	83	.215
—San Diego (N.L.)	0	1	.000	5.79	1.34	15	0	0	0	0	0-0	18.2	15	14	12	2	10-0	11	.217
—Toronto (A.L.)	0	0	...	1.69	1.69	10	0	0	0	1	1-2	5.1	5	2	1	1	4-1	7	.227
2003— Syracuse (Int'l)	6	1	.857	2.36	1.12	24	0	0	0	...	0-...	45.2	42	15	12	1	9-1	30	.255
—Toronto (A.L.)	3	3	.500	3.17	1.07	40	0	0	0	7	0-1	54.0	43	21	19	5	15-2	32	.217
American League totals (2 years)	3	3	.500	3.03	1.13	50	0	0	0	8	1-3	59.1	48	23	20	6	19-3	39	.218
National League totals (1 year)	0	1	.000	5.79	1.34	15	0	0	0	0	0-0	18.2	15	14	12	2	10-0	11	.217
Major League totals (2 years)	3	4	.429	3.69	1.18	65	0	0	0	8	1-3	78.0	63	37	32	8	29-3	50	.218

KIDA, MASAO   P

PERSONAL: Born September 12, 1968, in Tokyo, Japan. ... 6-3/210. ... Throws right, bats right. ... Name pronounced: muh-SOW KEY-duh.

TRANSACTIONS/CAREER NOTES: Played with Yomiuri Giants (1989-97) and Orix Blue Wave (1998) of Japan League. ... Signed as non-drafted free agent by Detroit Tigers (December 16, 1998). ... On Detroit disabled list (June 30-July 28, 1999; included rehabilitation assignment to Toledo (July 14-28). ... Contract sold by Tigers to Orix of Japan Pacific League (June 8, 2000). ... Optioned to minors by Los Angeles (August 16, 2003). ... Recalled by Los Angeles from Las Vegas (September 2, 2003).

CAREER HITTING: 1-for-4 (.250), 0 R, 0 2B, 0 3B, 0 HR, 0 RBI.

Year League	W	L	Pct.	ERA	WHIP	G	GS	CG	ShO	Hld.	Sv.-Opp.	IP	H	R	ER	HR	BB-IBB	SO	Avg.
1988— Miami (Florida St.)	7	*17	.292	3.99	1.30	27	27	9	1	...	0-...	162.1	149	88	72	9	62-3	100	...
1989— Yomiuri (Jp. Cen.)	2	1	.667	4.62	1.49	8	4	1	0	...	0-...	37.0	41	19	19	...	14-...	26	...
1990— Yomiuri (Jp. Cen.)	12	8	.600	2.71	0.99	32	17	13	1	...	0-...	182.2	130	56	55	...	51-...	182	...
1991— Yomiuri (Jp. Cen.)	4	7	.364	6.44	1.63	19	5	2	0	...	1-...	50.1	51	41	36	...	31-...	44	...
1992— Yomiuri (Jp. Cen.)	3	6	.333	4.53	1.48	29	11	2	1	...	0-...	93.1	103	48	47	...	35-...	87	...
1993— Yomiuri (Jp. Cen.)	7	7	.500	3.35	1.28	35	17	1	1	...	2-...	131.2	129	50	49	...	40-...	97	...
1994— Yomiuri (Jp. Cen.)	6	8	.429	4.93	1.40	28	13	1	0	...	1-...	87.2	86	52	48	...	37-...	61	...
1995— Yomiuri (Jp. Cen.)	7	9	.438	3.40	1.22	40	12	2	0	...	0-...	121.2	117	49	46	...	31-...	97	...
1996— Yomiuri (Jp. Cen.)	7	9	.438	3.78	1.25	33	16	3	2	...	2-...	123.2	121	53	52	...	34-...	99	...
1997— Yomiuri (Jp. Cen.)	2	2	.500	1.99	1.39	39	0	0	0	...	7-...	49.2	47	13	11	...	22-...	53	...
1998— Orix (Jap. Pac.)	4	7	.364	4.62	1.37	36	13	1	0	...	16-...	97.1	97	54	50	...	36-...	74	...
1999— Detroit (A.L.)	1	0	1.000	6.26	1.59	49	0	0	0	4	1-1	64.2	73	48	45	6	30-3	50	.289
—Toledo (Int'l)	0	0	...	3.18	1.24	3	0	0	0	...	0-...	5.2	6	2	2	2	1-0	4	.273
2000— Toledo (Int'l)	2	1	.667	2.16	1.00	21	0	0	0	...	7-...	25.0	21	6	6	3	4-1	26	.233
—Detroit (A.L.)	0	0	...	10.13	1.88	2	0	0	0	0	0-0	2.2	5	3	3	1	0-0	0	.385
2002—										Did not play.									
2003— Las Vegas (PCL)	2	4	.333	5.02	1.33	21	12	0	0	...	1-...	84.1	89	53	47	9	23-1	57	.271
—Los Angeles (N.L.)	0	1	.000	3.00	1.50	3	2	0	0	0	0-0	12.0	15	5	4	0	3-0	8	.300
American League totals (2 years)	1	0	1.000	6.42	1.60	51	0	0	0	4	1-1	67.1	78	51	48	7	30-3	50	.293
National League totals (1 year)	0	1	.000	3.00	1.50	3	2	0	0	0	0-0	12.0	15	5	4	0	3-0	8	.300
Major League totals (3 years)	1	1	.500	5.90	1.59	54	2	0	0	4	1-1	79.1	93	56	52	7	33-3	58	.294

KIELTY, BOBBY   OF

PERSONAL: Born August 5, 1976, in Fontana, Calif. ... 6-1/225. ... Bats both, throws right. ... Full name: Robert Michael Kielty. ... Name pronounced: kell-tee. ... High school: Canyon Springs (Moreno Valley, Calif.). ... College: Mississippi.

TRANSACTIONS/CAREER NOTES: Signed as non-drafted free agent by Minnesota Twins organization (February 16, 1999). ... On disabled list (May 21-June 24 and August 25-September 3, 1999). ... On Edmonton disabled list (May 4-18, 2001). ... Traded by Twins to Toronto Blue Jays for OF Shannon Stewart (July 16, 2003).

2003 GAMES PLAYED BY POSITION (MLB): OF—96, DH—32, 1B—3.

Year Team (League)	Pos.	G	AB	R	H	2B	3B	HR	RBI	BB	SO	HBP	GDP	SB-CS	Avg.	OBP	SLG	OPS	E	Pct.
1999— Quad City (Midw.)	OF	69	245	52	72	13	1	13	43	43	56	3	7	12-3	.294	.401	.514	.916	3	.977
2000— New Britain (East.)	OF	129	451	79	118	30	3	14	65	98	109	5	16	6-4	.262	.396	.435	.831	3	.988
— Salt Lake (PCL)	OF	9	33	8	8	4	0	0	2	7	10	0	0	0-0	.242	.375	.364	.739	1	.957
2001— Edmonton (PCL)	OF	94	341	58	98	25	2	12	50	53	76	6	11	5-0	.287	.391	.478	.869	2	.991
— Minnesota (A.L.)	OF-DH	37	104	8	26	8	0	2	14	8	25	1	2	3-0	.250	.297	.385	.681	3	.956
2002— Edmonton (PCL)	OF	2	7	0	3	1	0	0	0	1	1	0	1	0-0	.429	.500	.571	1.071	0	1.000
— Minnesota (A.L.)	OF-DH-1B	112	289	49	84	14	3	12	46	52	66	5	4	4-1	.291	.405	.484	.890	0	1.000
2003— Minnesota (A.L.)	OF-DH	75	238	40	60	13	0	9	32	42	56	3	5	6-2	.252	.370	.420	.790	2	.972
— Toronto (A.L.)	OF-1B	62	189	31	44	13	1	4	25	29	36	4	6	2-1	.233	.342	.376	.718	1	.991
Major League totals (3 years)		286	820	128	214	48	4	27	117	131	183	13	17	15-4	.261	.367	.428	.795	6	.986

KIESCHNICK, BROOKS · P/OF

PERSONAL: Born June 6, 1972, in Robstown, Texas. ... 6-4/230. ... Bats left, throws right. ... Full name: Michael Brooks Kieschnick. ... Name pronounced: KEESH-nick. ... High school: Mary Carroll (Corpus Christi, Texas). ... College: Texas.

TRANSACTIONS/CAREER NOTES: Selected by Chicago Cubs organization in first round (10th pick overall) of free-agent draft (June 3, 1993). ... Selected by Tampa Bay Devil Rays in third round (64th pick overall) of expansion draft (November 18, 1997). ... On Durham disabled list (April 16-August 2, 1998). ... Loaned by Devil Rays organization to Edmonton, Anaheim Angels organization (May 24-September 20, 1999). ... Granted free agency (October 15, 1999). ... Signed by Cincinnati Reds organization (November 16, 1999). ... Granted free agency (October 3, 2000). ... Signed by Colorado Rockies organization (December 1, 2000). ... On Colorado disabled list (May 13-28, 2001); included rehabilitation assignment to Colorado Springs (May 19-28). ... Granted free agency (October 8, 2001). ... Signed by Cleveland Indians organization (February 1, 2002). ... Signed by Chicago White Sox organization (May 16, 2002). ... On Charlotte disabled list (June 13-22, 2002). ... Granted free agency (October 15, 2002). ... Signed by Milwaukee Brewers organization (November 8, 2002).

2003 GAMES PLAYED BY POSITION (MLB): P—42, OF—3.

Year Team (League)	Pos.	G	AB	R	H	2B	3B	HR	RBI	BB	SO	HBP	GDP	SB-CS	Avg.	OBP	SLG	OPS	E	Pct.
1993— GC Cubs (GCL)	OF	3	9	0	2	1	0	0	0	0	1	0	0	0-0	.222	.222	.333	.555	0	1.000
— Daytona (Fla. St.)	OF	6	22	1	4	2	0	0	2	1	4	0	1	0-1	.182	.217	.273	.490	0	1.000
— Orlando (South.)	OF	25	91	12	31	8	0	2	10	7	19	0	1	1-2	.341	.388	.495	.883	3	.885
1994— Orlando (South.)	3B-1B-OF	126	468	57	132	25	3	14	55	33	78	4	10	3-5	.282	.332	.438	.770	6	.978
1995— Iowa (Am. Assoc.)	OF-DH-1B	138	505	61	*149	30	1	*23	73	58	91	4	11	2-3	.295	.370	.495	.865	2	.990
1996— Chicago (N.L.)	OF	25	29	6	10	2	0	1	6	3	8	0	0	0-0	.345	.406	.517	.923	1	.833
— Iowa (Am. Assoc.)	1B-OF-DH	117	441	47	114	20	1	18	64	37	108	0	8	0-1	.259	.315	.431	.746	8	.985
1997— Iowa (Am. Assoc.)	1-OF-D-3	97	360	57	93	21	0	21	66	36	89	1	8	0-2	.258	.323	.492	.815	8	.987
— Chicago (N.L.)	OF	39	90	9	18	2	0	4	12	12	21	0	2	1-0	.200	.294	.356	.650	2	.952
1998— Durham (Int'l)	OF-1B	7	23	4	3	1	0	1	2	4	8	0	2	0-1	.130	.259	.304	.563	1	.955
— St. Pete. (FSL)	OF-DH	28	105	15	26	6	0	5	18	11	18	0	4	0-0	.248	.316	.448	.764	3	.889
— GC Devil Rays (GCL)	DH-1B	4	12	4	6	1	0	2	8	1	0	0	0	0-0	.500	.538	1.083	1.621	0	1.000
1999— Durham (Int'l)	DH-OF	23	75	6	15	5	0	1	5	5	14	0	3	0-0	.200	.250	.307	.557	0	1.000
— Edmonton (PCL)	D-1-O-3	77	296	54	93	20	3	23	73	19	60	2	5	0-1	.314	.357	.635	.992	5	.982
2000— Louisville (Int'l)	OF-1B	113	440	68	122	35	0	25	90	38	107	1	10	2-1	.277	.335	.527	.862	5	.990
— Cincinnati (N.L.)	1B	14	12	0	0	0	0	0	0	1	5	0	0	0-0	.000	.077	.000	.077	0	1.000
2001— Colo. Springs (PCL)	OF-1B	71	252	44	74	9	3	13	45	24	72	2	7	3-2	.294	.360	.508	.868	2	.982
— Colorado (N.L.)	OF-1B	35	42	5	10	2	1	3	9	3	13	0	1	0-0	.238	.289	.548	.837	2	.833
2002— Charlotte (Int'l)	OF	69	189	32	52	11	0	13	40	14	46	0	4	0-0	.275	.320	.540	.860	0	1.000
2003— Indianapolis (Int'l)	P-DH	11	10	0	0	0	0	0	0	1	4	0	0	0-0	.000	.091	.000	.091	1	.750
— Milwaukee (N.L.)	OF	70	70	12	21	1	0	7	12	6	13	0	2	0-0	.300	.355	.614	.969	1	.955
Major League totals (5 years)		183	243	32	59	7	1	15	39	25	60	0	5	1-0	.243	.313	.465	.778	6	.909

RECORD AS PITCHER

Year League	W	L	Pct.	ERA	WHIP	G	GS	CG	ShO	Hld.	Sv.-Opp.	IP	H	R	ER	HR	BB-IBB	SO	Avg.
1999— Durham (Int'l)	0	0	...	0.00	1.00	1	0	0	0	...	0-...	2.0	1	0	0	0	1-0	1	.125
2001— Colo. Springs (PCL)	0	0	...	18.00	3.00	1	0	0	0	...	0-...	1.0	3	2	2	0	0-0	1	.500
2002— Charlotte (Int'l)	0	1	.000	2.59	1.28	25	0	0	0	...	0-...	31.1	30	9	9	1	10-1	30	.252
2003— Milwaukee (N.L.)	1	1	.500	5.26	1.49	42	0	0	0	2	0-0	53.0	66	32	31	5	13-4	39	.299
Major League totals (1 year)	1	1	.500	5.26	1.49	42	0	0	0	2	0-0	53.0	66	32	31	5	13-4	39	.299

KIM, BYUNG-HYUN · P

PERSONAL: Born January 19, 1979, in Gwangju, South Korea. ... 5-9/180. ... Throws right, bats right. ... Name pronounced: bee-yung hee-yun. ... High school: Kwang-ju (Korea). ... College: Sungkyunkwan (South Korea).

TRANSACTIONS/CAREER NOTES: Signed as non-drafted free agent by Arizona Diamondbacks organization (February 19, 1999). ... On Arizona disabled list (July 28-September 7, 2000). ... Placed on 15-day disabled list (April 30, 2003). ... Sent to Tucson on rehab assignment (May 11, 2003). ... Recalled by Arizona from rehab assignment (May 23, 2003). ... Traded by Arizona to Boston Red Sox for IF Shea Hillenbrand (May 30, 2003).

CAREER HITTING: 6-for-32 (.188), 0 R, 1 2B, 0 3B, 0 HR, 3 RBI.

Year League	W	L	Pct.	ERA	WHIP	G	GS	CG	ShO	Hld.	Sv.-Opp.	IP	H	R	ER	HR	BB-IBB	SO	Avg.
1999— El Paso (Texas)	2	0	1.000	2.11	0.70	10	0	0	0	...	0-...	21.1	6	5	5	0	9-0	32	.092
— Tucson (PCL)	4	0	1.000	2.40	1.20	11	3	0	0	...	1-...	30.0	21	9	8	2	15-1	40	.196
— Arizona (N.L.)	1	2	.333	4.61	1.46	25	0	0	0	3	1-4	27.1	20	15	14	2	20-2	31	.211
— Ariz. D'backs (Ariz.)	0	0	...	0.00	1.00	1	1	0	0	...	0-...	2.0	1	0	0	0	1-0	2	.167
2000— Arizona (N.L.)	6	6	.500	4.46	1.39	61	0	0	0	5	14-20	70.2	52	39	35	9	46-5	111	.200
— Tucson (PCL)	0	0	...	0.00	0.60	2	2	0	0	...	0-...	8.1	1	0	0	0	4-0	13	.042
2001— Arizona (N.L.)	5	6	.455	2.94	1.04	78	0	0	0	11	19-23	98.0	58	32	32	10	44-3	113	.173
2002— Arizona (N.L.)	8	3	.727	2.04	1.07	72	0	0	0	0	36-42	84.0	64	20	19	5	26-2	92	.208
2003— Tucson (PCL)	1	1	.500	2.55	1.02	3	3	0	0	...	0-...	17.2	17	5	5	2	1-0	8	.270
— Arizona (N.L.)	1	5	.167	3.56	1.14	7	7	0	0	0	0-0	43.0	34	17	17	6	15-0	33	.214
— Boston (A.L.)	8	5	.615	3.18	1.11	49	5	0	0	1	16-19	79.1	70	38	28	6	18-3	69	.230
American League totals (1 year)	8	5	.615	3.18	1.11	49	5	0	0	1	16-19	79.1	70	38	28	6	18-3	69	.230
National League totals (5 years)	21	22	.488	3.26	1.17	243	8	0	0	19	70-89	323.0	228	123	117	32	151-12	380	.197
Major League totals (5 years)	29	27	.518	3.24	1.16	292	13	0	0	20	86-108	402.1	298	161	145	38	169-15	449	.204

K

KIM, SUN-WOO　　　　　　　　　P

PERSONAL: Born September 4, 1977, in Inchon, South Korea. ... 6-1/185. ... Throws right, bats right. ... College: Korea University.

TRANSACTIONS/CAREER NOTES: Signed as non-drafted free agent by Boston Red Sox organization (November 21, 1997). ... Traded by Red Sox with P Seung Song and a player to be named later to Montreal Expos for OF Cliff Floyd (July 30, 2002).

CAREER HITTING: 2-for-11 (.182), 2 R, 0 2B, 0 3B, 0 HR, 0 RBI.

Year	League	W	L	Pct.	ERA	WHIP	G	GS	CG	ShO	Hld.	Sv.-Opp.	IP	H	R	ER	HR	BB-IBB	SO	Avg.
1998—	Sarasota (Fla. St.)	12	8	.600	4.82	1.30	26	24	•5	0	...	0-...	153.0	159	88	82	18	40-1	132	.264
1999—	Trenton (East.)	9	8	.529	4.89	1.37	26	26	1	1	...	0-...	149.0	160	86	81	16	44-2	130	.275
2000—	Pawtucket (Int'l)	11	7	.611	6.03	1.58	26	25	0	0	...	0-...	134.1	170	98	90	17	42-1	116	.309
2001—	Pawtucket (Int'l)	6	7	.462	5.36	1.35	19	14	0	0	...	0-...	89.0	93	55	53	10	27-1	79	.272
	— Boston (A.L.)	0	2	.000	5.83	1.80	20	2	0	0	1	0-0	41.2	54	27	27	1	21-5	27	.312
2002—	Pawtucket (Int'l)	4	2	.667	3.18	1.10	8	8	1	0	...	0-...	45.1	34	18	16	4	16-0	37	.206
	— Boston (A.L.)	2	0	1.000	7.45	1.41	15	2	0	0	2	0-0	29.0	34	24	24	5	7-0	18	.288
	— Ottawa (Int'l)	3	0	1.000	1.24	1.03	7	7	1	1	...	0-...	43.2	29	11	6	2	16-0	28	.195
	— Montreal (N.L.)	1	0	1.000	0.89	1.23	4	3	0	0	0	0-0	20.1	18	2	2	0	7-2	11	.250
2003—	Montreal (N.L.)	0	1	.000	8.36	2.29	4	3	0	0	0	0-0	14.0	24	13	13	6	8-0	5	.407
	— Edmonton (PCL)	10	8	.556	5.03	1.51	22	22	3	2	...	0-...	132.1	147	83	74	18	53-1	83	.281
American League totals (2 years)		2	2	.500	6.50	1.64	35	4	0	0	3	0-0	70.2	88	51	51	6	28-5	45	.302
National League totals (2 years)		1	1	.500	3.93	1.66	8	6	0	0	0	0-0	34.1	42	15	15	6	15-2	16	.321
Major League totals (3 years)		3	3	.500	5.66	1.65	43	10	0	0	3	0-0	105.0	130	66	66	12	43-7	61	.308

KING, RAY　　　　　　　　　P

PERSONAL: Born January 15, 1974, in Chicago, Ill. ... 6-1/247. ... Throws left, bats left. ... Full name: Raymond Keith King. ... High school: Ripley (Tenn.). ... College: Lambuth (Tenn.).

TRANSACTIONS/CAREER NOTES: Selected by Cincinnati Reds organization in eighth round of free-agent draft (June 1, 1995). ... Loaned by Reds organization to Macon, Atlanta Braves organization (March 22-June 11, 1996). ... Traded by Reds to Braves (June 11, 1996), completing deal in which Braves traded OF Mike Kelly to Reds for P Chad Fox and a player to be named later (January 9, 1996). ... Traded by Braves to Chicago Cubs for P Jon Ratliff (January 20, 1998). ... Traded by Cubs to Milwaukee Brewers for P Doug Johnston (April 14, 2000). ... On Milwaukee disabled list (April 5-19, 2002); included rehabilitation assignment to Indianapolis (April 17-18). ... Traded by Brewers to Atlanta Braves for 3B Wes Helms and P John Foster (December 16, 2002).

CAREER HITTING: 0-for-3 (.000), 0 R, 0 2B, 0 3B, 0 HR, 0 RBI.

Year	League	W	L	Pct.	ERA	WHIP	G	GS	CG	ShO	Hld.	Sv.-Opp.	IP	H	R	ER	HR	BB-IBB	SO	Avg.
1995—	Billings (Pio.)	3	0	1.000	1.67	1.07	28	0	0	0	...	5-...	43.0	31	11	8	1	15-3	43	.204
1996—	Macon (S. Atl.)	3	5	.375	2.80	1.17	18	10	1	0	...	0-...	70.2	63	34	22	4	20-0	63	.237
	— Durham (Caro.)	3	6	.333	4.46	1.44	14	14	2	0	...	0-...	82.2	104	54	41	3	15-2	52	.308
1997—	Greenville (Sou.)	5	5	.500	6.85	1.66	12	9	0	0	...	0-...	65.2	85	53	50	9	24-2	42	.304
	— Durham (Sou.)	6	9	.400	5.40	1.60	24	6	0	0	...	3-...	71.2	89	54	43	6	26-4	60	.300
1998—	West Tenn (Sou.)	1	2	.333	2.43	1.11	25	0	0	0	...	3-...	29.2	23	9	8	1	10-0	26	.213
	— Iowa (PCL)	1	3	.250	5.01	1.58	37	0	0	0	...	2-...	32.1	36	20	18	4	15-1	26	.283
1999—	Iowa (PCL)	4	4	.500	1.88	1.23	37	0	0	0	...	2-...	43.0	31	11	9	1	22-3	41	.200
	— Chicago (N.L.)	0	0	...	5.91	1.97	10	0	0	0	2	0-0	10.2	11	8	7	2	10-0	5	.289
2000—	Iowa (PCL)	1	0	1.000	0.00	0.75	1	0	0	0	...	0-...	1.1	1	0	0	0	0-0	1	.200
	— Indianapolis (Int'l)	0	3	.000	3.51	1.48	29	0	0	0	...	1-...	25.2	26	15	10	1	12-0	20	.271
	— Milwaukee (N.L.)	3	2	.600	1.26	0.98	36	0	0	0	5	0-1	28.2	18	7	4	1	10-1	19	.180
2001—	Milwaukee (N.L.)	0	4	.000	3.60	1.35	82	0	0	0	18	1-4	55.0	49	22	22	5	25-7	49	.241
2002—	Milwaukee (N.L.)	3	2	.600	3.05	1.31	76	0	0	0	18	0-1	65.0	61	24	22	5	24-6	50	.255
	— Indianapolis (Int'l)	0	0	...	0.00	2.00	1	1	0	0	...	0-...	1.0	1	0	0	0	1-0	1	.333
2003—	Atlanta (N.L.)	3	4	.429	3.51	1.24	80	0	0	0	18	0-1	59.0	46	30	23	3	27-2	43	.213
Major League totals (5 years)		9	12	.429	3.22	1.29	284	0	0	0	58	1-7	218.1	185	91	78	16	96-16	166	.232

KINGSALE, GENE　　　　　　　　　OF

PERSONAL: Born August 20, 1976, in Oranjestad, Aruba. ... 6-3/190. ... Bats both, throws right. ... Full name: Eugene Humphrey Kingsale. ... Name pronounced: KING-sale. ... High school: John F. Kennedy Technical School (Oranjestad, Aruba).

TRANSACTIONS/CAREER NOTES: Signed as non-drafted free agent by Baltimore Orioles organization (June 19, 1993). ... On Frederick disabled list (May 29-August 31, 1996). ... On Bowie disabled list (April 8-August 8, 1997). ... On Baltimore disabled list (March 29-August 27, 2000); included rehabilitation assignments Gulf Coast Orioles (August 8-18), Frederick (August 19-25) and Bowie (August 26-27). ... Claimed on waivers by Seattle Mariners (July 10, 2001). ... Claimed on waivers by San Diego Padres (June 14, 2002). ... Traded by Padres to Detroit Tigers for C Mike Rivera (November 15, 2002). ... Elected free agency (September 29, 2003).

2003 GAMES PLAYED BY POSITION (MLB): OF—30, DH—4.

										BATTING										FIELDING	
Year	Team (League)	Pos.	G	AB	R	H	2B	3B	HR	RBI	BB	SO	HBP	GDP	SB-CS	Avg.	OBP	SLG	OPS		E	Pct.
1994—	GC Orioles (GCL)	2B-OF	50	168	26	52	2	3	0	9	18	24	2	1	15-8	.310	.381	.357	.738		3	.971
1995—	Bluefield (Appal.)	OF	47	171	45	54	11	2	0	16	27	31	5	0	20-8	.316	.420	.404	.823		*11	.899
1996—	Frederick (Carolina)	OF	49	166	26	45	6	4	0	9	19	32	6	1	23-4	.271	.363	.355	.718		4	.962
	— Baltimore (A.L.)	OF	3	0	0	0	0	0	0	0	0	0	0	0	0-0	...	.000	...	...		0	1.000
1997—	Bowie (East.)	OF	13	46	8	19	6	0	0	4	5	4	1	2	5-1	.413	.481	.543	1.024		1	.958
	— GC Orioles (GCL)	OF	6	17	2	5	0	0	0	2	2	1	1	0	1-0	.294	.400	.294	.694		1	.941
1998—	Bowie (East.)	OF	111	427	69	112	11	5	1	34	48	79	12	6	29-12	.262	.350	.319	.669		6	.980
	— Rochester (Int'l)	OF-DH	18	55	3	12	1	1	0	2	4	8	1	3	3-3	.218	.283	.273	.556		0	1.000
	— Baltimore (A.L.)	OF-DH	11	2	1	0	0	0	0	0	0	1	0	0	0-0	.000	.000	.000	.000		0	1.000
1999—	Bowie (East.)	OF	67	268	43	63	11	4	3	23	33	46	1	4	13-7	.235	.319	.340	.659		4	.978
	— Rochester (Int'l)	OF	48	191	31	59	9	0	2	20	13	23	3	2	10-9	.309	.361	.387	.748		3	.975
	— Baltimore (A.L.)	OF-DH	28	85	9	21	2	0	0	7	5	13	2	3	1-3	.247	.301	.271	.572		1	.980
2000—	GC Orioles (GCL)	OF	5	16	7	5	0	0	0	4	4	0	0	0	2-0	.313	.429	.313	.741		0	1.000
	— Frederick (Carolina)	OF	6	25	8	11	3	0	1	3	1	6	0	0	2-0	.440	.462	.680	1.142		0	1.000
	— Bowie (East.)	OF	3	11	5	4	2	0	1	5	3	0	0	0	1-0	.364	.500	.818	1.318		0	1.000
	— Rochester (Int'l)	OF	2	10	2	4	1	0	0	1	0	1	0	0	1-1	.400	.400	.500	.900		0	1.000
	— Baltimore (A.L.)	OF-DH	26	88	13	21	2	1	0	9	2	14	0	4	1-2	.239	.253	.284	.537		3	.954
2001—	Rochester (Int'l)	OF	64	244	31	49	12	2	0	15	26	44	2	6	16-2	.201	.283	.266	.549		5	.965
	— Baltimore (A.L.)	OF	3	4	0	0	0	0	0	0	0	2	0	0	1-1	.000	.000	.000	.000		0	1.000
	— Tacoma (PCL)	OF	51	215	30	63	14	4	3	24	8	25	3	1	12-4	.293	.327	.437	.765		3	.976
	— Seattle (A.L.)	OF	10	15	4	5	0	0	0	1	2	1	1	0	2-0	.333	.444	.333	.778		0	1.000

Year Team (League)	Pos.	G	AB	R	H	2B	3B	HR	RBI	BB	SO	HBP	GDP	SB-CS	Avg.	OBP	SLG	OPS	E	Pct.
2002— Tacoma (PCL)	OF	49	188	25	49	15	3	6	26	15	30	1	6	10-3	.261	.317	.468	.785	0	1.000
— Seattle (A.L.)	OF	2	3	0	2	0	0	0	0	0	0	0	1	0-0	.667	.667	.667	1.333	0	1.000
— San Diego (N.L.)	OF	89	216	27	60	10	3	2	28	20	47	3	5	9-2	.278	.346	.380	.725	2	.985
2003— Detroit (A.L.)	OF-DH	39	120	11	25	3	1	1	8	10	17	0	2	1-3	.208	.265	.275	.540	1	.985
— Toledo (Int'l)	OF	46	160	19	39	6	5	0	12	11	24	2	2	9-5	.244	.297	.344	.641	0	1.000
American League totals (7 years)		122	317	38	74	7	2	1	25	19	49	3	11	6-9	.233	.280	.278	.557	5	.975
National League totals (1 year)		89	216	27	60	10	3	2	28	20	47	3	5	9-2	.278	.346	.380	.725	2	.985
Major League totals (7 years)		211	533	65	134	17	5	3	53	39	96	6	16	15-11	.251	.307	.319	.626	7	.979

KINKADE, MIKE   OF/1B

PERSONAL: Born May 6, 1973, in Livonia, Mich. ... 6-1/210. ... Bats right, throws right. ... Full name: Michael A. Kinkade. ... Name pronounced: kin-KADE. ... High school: Tigard (Ore.). ... College: Washington State.

TRANSACTIONS/CAREER NOTES: Selected by Milwaukee Brewers organization in ninth round of free-agent draft (June 1, 1995). ... On Louisville disabled list (April 20-May 14, 1998). ... Traded by Brewers to New York Mets for P Bill Pulsipher (July 31, 1998). ... Traded by Mets with OF Melvin Mora, P Leslie Brea and P Pat Gorman to Baltimore Orioles for SS Mike Bordick (July 28, 2000). ... On disabled list (August 24-September 18 and October 3, 2001-remainder of season). ... Released by Orioles (November 19, 2001). ... Signed by Los Angeles Dodgers organization (January 10, 2002). ... On Las Vegas disabled list (May 17-June 4 and June 16-23, 2002).

2003 GAMES PLAYED BY POSITION (MLB): OF—36, 1B—13, 3B—2, DH—1.

Year Team (League)	Pos.	G	AB	R	H	2B	3B	HR	RBI	BB	SO	HBP	GDP	SB-CS	Avg.	OBP	SLG	OPS	E	Pct.
1995— Helena (Pio.)	3B-C-1B	69	266	76	94	19	1	4	39	43	38	10	6	26-9	.353	.452	.477	.930	10	.974
1996— Beloit (Midw.)	3B-C-1B	• 135	499	* 104	151	33	4	15	100	47	69	32	10	23-12	.303	.394	.475	.869	39	.922
1997— El Paso (Texas)	3B-DH	125	468	•112	* 180	35	12	12	* 109	52	66	13	13	17-4	.385	* .455	.588	1.042	* 60	.845
1998— Louisville (Int'l) 3B-1B-DH		80	291	57	90	24	6	7	46	36	52	6	7	10-2	.309	.394	.505	.899	15	.953
— Norfolk (Int'l)	3B-1B	30	125	12	35	5	0	1	18	3	24	5	5	6-1	.280	.319	.344	.663	5	.949
— New York (N.L.)	3B	3	2	0	0	0	0	0	0	0	0	0	0	0-0	.000	.000	.000	.000	0	...
1999— New York (N.L.)	OF-3-C-1	28	46	3	9	2	1	2	6	3	9	2	1	1-0	.196	.275	.413	.688	0	1.000
— Norfolk (Int'l)	3-C-1-OF	84	312	53	96	20	2	7	49	21	31	5	9	7-1	.308	.359	.452	.811	10	.967
2000— Binghamton (East.)	C-3B-OF	90	317	66	116	24	3	10	67	35	39	9	6	18-7	.366	.440	.555	.995	9	.985
— New York (N.L.)	OF	2	2	0	0	0	0	0	0	0	1	0	0	0-0	.000	.000	.000	.000	0	...
— Bowie (East.)	C-3B	8	27	4	7	1	0	3	5	3	7	2	2	0-0	.259	.375	.630	1.005	0	1.000
— Rochester (Int'l)	C-1B-3B	15	55	10	20	5	0	1	10	11	11	1	0	0-1	.364	.471	.509	.980	4	.953
— Baltimore (A.L.)	DH-1B	3	7	0	3	1	0	0	1	0	0	1	0	0-0	.429	.500	.571	1.071	0	1.000
2001— Baltimore (A.L.) O-3-D-1-C		61	160	19	44	5	0	4	16	14	31	3	8	2-1	.275	.345	.381	.726	2	.977
2002— Las Vegas (PCL)	O-3-1-C	74	287	63	98	22	6	11	50	29	49	19	9	6-2	.341	.433	.575	1.008	5	.976
— Los Angeles (N.L.)	1B-OF	37	50	7	19	5	0	2	11	4	10	6	2	1-0	.380	.483	.600	1.083	0	1.000
2003— Los Angeles (N.L.)	O-1-3-D	88	162	25	35	7	0	5	14	13	38	16	8	1-3	.216	.335	.352	.687	4	.966
American League totals (2 years)		64	167	19	47	6	0	4	17	14	31	4	8	2-1	.281	.351	.389	.741	2	.977
National League totals (5 years)		158	262	37	63	14	1	9	31	20	58	24	11	3-3	.240	.350	.405	.754	4	.978
Major League totals (6 years)		222	429	56	110	20	1	13	48	34	89	28	19	5-4	.256	.350	.399	.749	6	.978

KINNEY, MATT   P

PERSONAL: Born December 16, 1976, in Bangor, Maine. ... 6-5/225. ... Throws right, bats right. ... Full name: Matthew John Kinney. ... High school: Bangor (Maine).

TRANSACTIONS/CAREER NOTES: Selected by Boston Red Sox organization in sixth round of free-agent draft (June 1, 1995). ... Traded by Red Sox with P Joe Thomas and OF John Barnes to Minnesota Twins for P Greg Swindell and 1B Orlando Merced (July 31, 1998). ... On New Britain disabled list (June 7-August 16, 1999). ... On disabled list (April 23-May 3, 2001). ... On Minnesota disabled list (June 30-August 19, 2002); included rehabilitation assignments to Gulf Coast Twins (July 27-August 10), Fort Myers (August 11-13) and New Britain (August 14-19). ... Traded by Twins with C Javier Valentin to Milwaukee Brewers for P Matt Yeatman and P Gerard Oakes (November 15, 2002).

CAREER HITTING: 2-for-57 (.035), 3 R, 1 2B, 0 3B, 0 HR, 0 RBI.

Year League	W	L	Pct.	ERA	WHIP	G	GS	CG	ShO	Hld.	Sv.-Opp.	IP	H	R	ER	HR	BB-IBB	SO	Avg.
1995— GC Red Sox (GCL)	1	3	.250	2.93	1.41	8	2	0	0	...	2-...	27.2	29	13	9	0	10-0	11	.279
1996— Lowell (NY-Penn)	3	9	.250	2.68	1.28	15	• 15	0	0	...	0-...	87.1	68	51	26	0	44-2	72	.207
1997— Michigan (Midw.)	8	5	.615	3.53	1.46	22	22	2	1	...	0-...	117.1	93	59	46	4	78-2	123	.217
1998— Sarasota (Fla. St.)	9	6	.600	4.01	1.52	22	20	0	1	...	1-...	121.1	109	70	54	5	* 75-3	96	.241
— Fort Myers (Fla. St.)	3	2	.600	3.13	1.31	7	7	0	0	...	0-...	37.1	31	18	13	0	† 18-0	39	.220
1999— New Britain (East.)	4	7	.364	7.12	1.73	14	13	0	0	...	0-...	60.2	69	54	48	8	36-0	50	.289
— GC Twins (GCL)	0	1	.000	4.76	1.59	3	3	0	0	...	0-...	5.2	6	4	3	0	3-0	8	.286
2000— New Britain (East.)	6	1	.857	2.71	1.26	15	15	0	0	...	0-...	86.1	74	31	26	7	35-0	93	.231
— Salt Lake (PCL)	5	2	.714	4.25	1.24	9	9	0	0	...	0-...	55.0	42	26	26	5	26-0	59	.211
— Minnesota (A.L.)	2	2	.500	5.10	1.56	8	8	0	0	0	0-0	42.1	41	26	24	7	25-1	24	.261
2001— Edmonton (PCL)	6	11	.353	5.07	1.56	29	• 29	2	0	...	0-...	161.2	178	101	91	25	74-0	146	.280
2002— Edmonton (PCL)	2	1	.667	8.89	1.68	5	5	0	0	...	0-...	27.1	42	27	27	9	4-0	21	.350
— Minnesota (A.L.)	2	7	.222	4.64	1.68	14	12	0	0	0	0-0	66.0	78	39	34	13	33-0	45	.295
— GC Twins (GCL)	0	0	...	3.00	1.00	2	2	0	0	...	0-...	6.0	2	2	2	1	4-0	7	.100
— Fort Myers (Fla. St.)	0	0	...	0.00	1.40	1	1	0	0	...	0-...	5.0	4	2	0	0	3-0	5	.222
— New Britain (East.)	0	0	...	6.75	1.25	1	1	0	0	...	0-...	4.0	4	4	3	1	1-0	3	.250
2003— Milwaukee (N.L.)	10	13	.435	5.19	1.47	33	31	1	0	0	0-0	190.2	201	121	110	27	80-4	152	.272
American League totals (2 years)	4	9	.308	4.82	1.63	22	20	0	0	0	0-0	108.1	119	65	58	20	58-1	69	.283
National League totals (1 year)	10	13	.435	5.19	1.47	33	31	1	0	0	0-0	190.2	201	121	110	27	80-4	152	.272
Major League totals (3 years)	14	22	.389	5.06	1.53	55	51	1	0	0	0-0	299.0	320	186	168	47	138-5	221	.276

KLASSEN, DANNY   SS/2B

PERSONAL: Born September 22, 1975, in Leamington, Ontario. ... 6-0/190. ... Bats right, throws right. ... Full name: Daniel Victor Klassen. ... Name pronounced: CLAUS-en. ... High school: John Carroll (Fort Pierce, Fla.).

TRANSACTIONS/CAREER NOTES: Selected by Milwaukee Brewers organization in second round of free-agent draft (June 3, 1993). ... On disabled list (April 7-June 23, 1995 and April 11-22, 1996). ... Selected by Arizona Diamondbacks in second round (37th pick overall) of expansion draft (November 18, 1997). ... On Tucson disabled list (August 13-September 8, 1998; and June 11-August 26, 1999). ... On Arizona disabled list (July 8-September 1, 2000). ... On Arizona disabled list (April 3, 2001-entire season); included rehabilitation assignment to Tucson (June 18-30). ... On Arizona disabled list (April 10-May 3, 2002); included rehabilitation assignment to El Paso (April 12-May 1). ... Granted free agency (October 15, 2002). ... Signed by Detroit Tigers (January 10, 2003).

2003 GAMES PLAYED BY POSITION (MLB): 3B—13, 2B—4, SS—3.

Year	Team (League)	Pos.	G	AB	R	H	2B	3B	HR	RBI	BB	SO	HBP	GDP	SB-CS	Avg.	OBP	SLG	OPS	E	Pct.
1993—Ariz. Brewers (Ariz.)	SS		38	117	26	26	5	0	2	20	24	28	8	2	14-3	.222	.379	.316	.695	12	.922
—Helena (Pio.)	SS		18	45	8	9	1	0	0	3	7	11	2	2	2-1	.200	.333	.222	.556	7	.905
1994—Beloit (Midw.)	SS		133	458	61	119	20	3	6	54	58	123	12	3	28-14	.260	.356	.356	.712	40	.927
1995—Beloit (Midw.)	3B-SS		59	218	27	60	15	2	2	25	16	43	4	4	12-4	.275	.332	.390	.722	18	.920
1996—Stockton (Calif.)	SS		118	432	58	116	22	4	2	46	34	77	10	12	14-8	.269	.335	.352	.687	* 33	.944
1997—El Paso (Texas)	SS		135	519	112	172	30	6	14	81	48	104	10	13	16-9	.331	.396	.493	.889	* 50	.920
1998—Tucson (PCL)	2B-SS		73	281	47	82	25	2	10	47	19	54	6	11	6-2	.292	.344	.502	.846	8	.976
—Arizona (N.L.)	2B		29	108	12	21	2	1	3	8	9	33	1	5	1-1	.194	.263	.315	.578	5	.964
1999—Tucson (PCL)	SS-DH-2B		64	245	38	66	16	3	6	33	20	51	1	5	5-3	.269	.325	.433	.757	9	.969
—Ariz. D'backs (Ariz.)	SS		6	17	2	4	1	0	0	1	1	4	0	1	0-0	.235	.278	.294	.572	1	.962
—Arizona (N.L.)			1	1	0	1	0	0	0	0	0	0	0	0	0-0	1.000	1.000	1.000	2.000	...	...
2000—Arizona (N.L.)	3B-SS		29	76	13	18	3	0	2	8	8	24	1	0	1-1	.237	.318	.355	.673	2	.966
—Tucson (PCL)	SS-2B-3B		28	97	25	31	7	2	2	14	19	23	1	2	1-2	.320	.436	.495	.931	8	.946
2001—Tucson (PCL)	3B-2B-SS		7	18	5	4	0	0	1	3	2	3	1	0	0-0	.222	.333	.389	.722	1	.952
2002—Arizona (N.L.)	3B-SS		4	3	0	1	0	0	0	0	0	1	0	0	0-0	.333	.333	.333	.667	0	1.000
—El Paso (Texas)	SS-3B-2B		18	65	11	15	4	0	2	7	7	24	0	2	0-0	.231	.306	.385	.690	7	.923
—Tucson (PCL)	SS-3B-2B		103	361	41	83	20	5	2	42	22	106	4	7	6-1	.230	.277	.330	.606	11	.974
2003—Toledo (Int'l)	S-2-D-3		112	407	63	100	19	4	11	48	28	110	7	5	12-5	.246	.303	.393	.696	22	.960
—Detroit (A.L.)	3B-2B-SS		22	73	9	18	3	1	1	7	4	26	0	1	0-1	.247	.286	.356	.642	3	.964
American League totals (1 year)			22	73	9	18	3	1	1	7	4	26	0	1	0-1	.247	.286	.356	.642	3	.964
National League totals (4 years)			63	188	25	41	5	1	5	16	17	58	2	5	2-2	.218	.290	.335	.625	7	.965
Major League totals (5 years)			85	261	34	59	8	2	6	23	21	84	2	6	2-3	.226	.289	.341	.630	10	.964

KLESKO, RYAN — 1B/OF

PERSONAL: Born June 12, 1971, in Westminster, Calif. ... 6-3/220. ... Bats left, throws left. ... Full name: Ryan Anthony Klesko. ... High school: Westminster (Calif.).
TRANSACTIONS/CAREER NOTES: Selected by Atlanta Braves organization in fifth round of free-agent draft (June 5, 1989). ... On Atlanta disabled list (May 3-18, 1995); included rehabilitation assignment to Greenville (May 13-17). ... Traded by Braves with 2B Bret Boone and P Jason Shiell to San Diego Padres for 2B Quilvio Veras, 1B Wally Joyner and OF Reggie Sanders (December 22, 1999). ... Placed on 15-day disabled list (September 6, 2003). ... Reinstated from 15-day disabled list (September 29, 2003).
2003 GAMES PLAYED BY POSITION (MLB): 1B—111, DH—1.

Year	Team (League)	Pos.	G	AB	R	H	2B	3B	HR	RBI	BB	SO	HBP	GDP	SB-CS	Avg.	OBP	SLG	OPS	E	Pct.
1989—GC Braves (GCL)	DH		17	57	14	23	5	4	1	16	6	6	0	2	4-3	.404	.453	.684	1.137	...	...
—Sumter (S. Atl.)	1B		25	90	17	26	6	0	1	12	11	14	0	5	1-0	.289	.363	.389	.752	4	.979
1990—Sumter (S. Atl.)	1B		63	231	41	85	15	1	10	38	31	30	1	6	13-1	.368	.437	.571	1.008	14	.978
—Durham (Caro.)	1B		77	292	40	80	16	1	7	47	32	53	2	8	10-5	.274	.343	.408	.751	13	.976
1991—Greenville (Sou.)	1B		126	419	64	122	22	3	14	67	75	60	6	5	14-17	.291	.404	.458	.862	* 17	.985
1992—Richmond (Int'l)	1B		123	418	63	105	22	2	17	59	41	72	4	14	3-5	.251	.323	.435	.758	* 11	.989
—Atlanta (N.L.)	1B		13	14	0	0	0	0	0	1	0	5	1	0	0-0	.000	.067	.000	.067	0	1.000
1993—Richmond (Int'l)	1B-OF		98	343	59	94	14	2	22	74	47	69	2	8	4-3	.274	.361	.519	.880	12	.981
—Atlanta (N.L.)	1B-OF		22	17	3	6	1	0	2	5	3	4	0	0	0-0	.353	.450	.765	1.215	0	1.000
1994—Atlanta (N.L.)	OF-1B		92	245	42	68	13	3	17	47	26	48	1	8	1-0	.278	.344	.563	.907	7	.929
1995—Atlanta (N.L.)	OF-1B		107	329	48	102	25	2	23	70	47	72	2	8	5-4	.310	.396	.608	1.004	8	.944
—Greenville (Sou.)	DH-OF		4	13	1	3	0	0	1	4	2	1	0	1	0-0	.231	.333	.462	.795	0	1.000
1996—Atlanta (N.L.)	OF-1B		153	528	90	149	21	4	34	93	68	129	2	10	6-3	.282	.364	.530	.894	5	.977
1997—Atlanta (N.L.)	OF-1B		143	467	67	122	23	6	24	84	48	130	4	12	4-4	.261	.334	.490	.824	6	.977
1998—Atlanta (N.L.)	OF-1B		129	427	69	117	29	1	18	70	56	66	3	9	5-3	.274	.359	.473	.832	2	.990
1999—Atlanta (N.L.)	1B-OF-DH		133	404	55	120	28	2	21	80	53	69	2	6	5-2	.297	.376	.532	.908	6	.990
2000—San Diego (N.L.)	1B-OF		145	494	88	140	33	2	26	92	91	81	1	10	23-7	.283	.393	.516	.909	9	.992
2001—San Diego (N.L.)	1B		146	538	105	154	34	6	30	113	88	89	3	16	23-4	.286	.384	.539	.923	11	.991
2002—San Diego (N.L.)	1B-OF-DH		146	540	90	162	39	1	29	95	76	86	4	7	6-4	.300	.388	.537	.925	7	.993
2003—San Diego (N.L.)	1B-DH		121	397	47	100	18	0	21	67	65	83	3	11	2-5	.252	.354	.456	.810	6	.994
Major League totals (12 years)			1350	4400	704	1240	264	27	245	817	621	862	26	97	80-34	.282	.370	.521	.891	67	.989

KLINE, STEVE — P

PERSONAL: Born August 22, 1972, in Sunbury, Pa. ... 6-1/215. ... Throws left, bats both. ... Full name: Steven James Kline. ... High school: Lewisburg (Pa.). ... College: West Virginia.
TRANSACTIONS/CAREER NOTES: Selected by Cleveland Indians organization in eighth round of free-agent draft (June 3, 1993). ... On disabled list (May 23-August 5, 1995). ... On temporarily inactive list (April 5-20, 1996). ... Traded by Indians to Montreal Expos for P Jeff Juden (July 31, 1997). ... On disabled list (April 11-27, 1999). ... Traded by Expos with P Dustin Hermanson to St. Louis Cardinals for 3B Fernando Tatis and P Britt Reames (December 14, 2000). ... On St. Louis disabled list (April 29-May 31, 2002); included rehabilitation assignments to Peoria (May 24-28) and New Haven (May 29-31).
CAREER HITTING: 2-for-13 (.154), 0 R, 1 2B, 0 3B, 0 HR, 2 RBI.

Year	League	W	L	Pct.	ERA	WHIP	G	GS	CG	ShO	Hld.	Sv.-Opp.	IP	H	R	ER	HR	BB-IBB	SO	Avg.
1993—Burlington (Appal.)		1	1	.500	4.91	1.77	2	1	0	0	...	0-...	7.1	11	4	4	0	2-1	4	.355
—Watertown (NYP)		5	4	.556	3.19	1.13	13	13	2	1	...	0-...	79.0	77	36	28	3	12-0	45	.248
1994—Columbus (S. Atl.)		* 18	5	.783	3.01	1.14	28	* 28	2	1	...	0-...	* 185.2	175	67	62	14	36-0	* 174	.251
1995—Cant./Akr. (Eastern)		2	3	.400	2.42	1.30	14	14	0	0	...	0-...	89.1	86	34	24	6	30-3	45	.252
1996—Cant./Akr. (Eastern)		8	12	.400	5.46	1.52	25	24	0	0	...	0-...	146.2	168	98	89	16	55-2	107	.288
1997—Cleveland (A.L.)		3	1	.750	5.81	2.09	20	1	0	0	4	0-2	26.1	42	19	17	6	13-1	17	.365
—Buffalo (A.A.)		3	3	.500	4.03	1.29	20	4	0	0	...	1-...	51.1	53	26	23	4	13-1	41	.265
—Montreal (N.L.)		1	3	.250	6.15	1.56	26	0	0	0	1	0-1	26.1	31	18	18	4	10-3	20	.307
1998—Ottawa (Int'l)		0	0	...	0.00	0.38	2	0	0	0	...	0-...	2.2	1	0	0	0	0-0	1	.125
—Montreal (N.L.)		3	6	.333	2.76	1.44	78	0	0	0	18	1-2	71.2	62	25	22	4	41-7	76	.228
1999—Montreal (N.L.)		7	4	.636	3.75	1.28	82	0	0	0	16	0-2	69.2	56	32	29	8	33-6	69	.218
2000—Montreal (N.L.)		1	5	.167	3.50	1.40	83	0	0	0	12	14-18	82.1	88	36	32	8	27-2	64	.278
2001—St. Louis (N.L.)		3	3	.500	1.80	1.09	89	0	0	0	17	9-10	75.0	53	16	15	3	29-7	54	.203
2002—St. Louis (N.L.)		2	1	.667	3.39	1.29	66	0	0	0	21	6-8	58.1	54	23	22	3	21-2	41	.251
—Peoria (Midw.)		0	0	...	0.00	0.86	2	1	0	0	...	0-...	2.1	1	0	0	0	1-0	5	.111
—New Haven (East.)		0	0	...	0.00	0.50	1	1	0	0	...	0-...	2.0	0	0	0	0	1-0	2	.000
2003—St. Louis (N.L.)		5	5	.500	3.82	1.35	78	0	0	0	18	3-7	63.2	56	29	27	6	30-5	31	.237
American League totals (1 year)		3	1	.750	5.81	2.09	20	1	0	0	4	0-2	26.1	42	19	17	6	13-1	17	.365
National League totals (7 years)		22	27	.449	3.32	1.32	502	0	0	0	103	33-48	447.0	400	179	165	35	191-32	355	.241
Major League totals (7 years)		25	28	.472	3.46	1.36	522	0	0	0	107	33-50	473.1	442	198	182	41	204-33	372	.249

KNOTT, ERIC   P

PERSONAL: Born September 23, 1974, in Harvey, Ill. ... 6-1/188. ... Throws left, bats left. ... Full name: Eric James Knott. ... High school: Sebring (Fla.). ... College: Stetson.

TRANSACTIONS/CAREER NOTES: Selected by Arizona Diamondbacks organization in 24th round of free-agent draft (June 4. 1996). ... On Tucson disabled list (May 23-June 12, 2000). ... Released by Diamondbacks (June 12, 2000). ... Signed by Chiba Lotte Marines of Japan Pacific League (2000). ... Signed by Diamondbacks (November 25, 2000). ... On Tucson disabled list (April 5-12, 2001). ... Granted free agency (December 21, 2001). ... Signed by Montreal Expos organization (Januay 23, 2003).

CAREER HITTING: 0-for-6 (.000), 0 R, 0 2B, 0 3B, 0 HR, 0 RBI.

Year League	W	L	Pct.	ERA	WHIP	G	GS	CG	ShO	Hld.	Sv.-Opp.	IP	H	R	ER	HR	BB-IBB	SO	Avg.
1997— Lethbridge (Pio.)	0	4	.000	2.87	1.06	21	3	0	0	...	3-...	47.0	41	21	15	4	9-1	62	.224
1998— High Desert (Calif.)	12	7	.632	4.52	1.42	28	22	1	0	...	0-...	143.1	175	84	72	16	28-1	96	.302
1999— El Paso (Texas)	7	11	.389	4.57	1.49	27	27	* 3	0	...	0-...	161.1	* 198	95	82	11	42-0	83	.302
2000— Tucson (PCL)	3	2	.600	6.35	1.69	11	7	0	0	...	0-...	39.2	59	30	28	6	8-0	21	.355
— Chiba (Jp. East.)	1	1	.500	4.09	1.27	5	5	0	0	...	0-...	22.0	22	12	10	...	6-...	17	...
— Chiba Lotte (Jap. Pac.)	1	1	.500	11.02	2.08	5	5	0	0	...	0-...	16.1	22	20	20	...	12-...	6	...
2001— El Paso (Texas)	4	1	.800	3.12	1.42	17	0	0	0	...	0-...	26.0	29	13	9	2	8-2	20	.276
— Tucson (PCL)	6	2	.750	3.80	1.23	25	8	0	0	...	1-...	73.1	82	34	31	6	8-1	43	.285
— Arizona (N.L.)	0	1	.000	1.93	1.71	3	1	0	0	0	0-0	4.2	8	9	1	0	0-0	4	.348
2002— Tucson (PCL)	8	10	.444	4.86	1.41	31	23	1	1	...	1-...	150.0	188	91	81	12	23-1	96	.306
2003— Montreal (N.L.)	1	2	.333	5.12	1.50	13	1	0	0	0	0-0	19.1	23	12	11	2	6-0	17	.295
— Edmonton (PCL)	6	5	.545	4.32	1.49	24	10	1	1	...	0-...	77.0	102	40	37	6	13-4	38	.315
Major League totals (2 years)	1	3	.250	4.50	1.54	16	2	0	0	0	0-0	24.0	31	21	12	2	6-0	21	.307

KNOTTS, GARY   P

PERSONAL: Born February 12, 1977, in Decatur, Ala. ... 6-4/230. ... Throws right, bats right. ... Full name: Gary Everett Knotts. ... High school: Brewer (Somerville, Ala.). ... Junior college: Northwest Alabama Community College.

TRANSACTIONS/CAREER NOTES: Selected by Florida Marlins organization in 11th round of free agent draft (June 1, 1995). ... Granted free agency (December 21, 1999). ... Re-signed by Marlins organization (December 22, 1999). ... On Calgary disabled list (August 21, 2001-remainder of season). ... Traded by Marlins with P Nate Robertson and P Rob Henkel to Detroit Tigers for P Mark Redman and P Jerrod Fuell (January 11, 2003).

CAREER HITTING: 1-for-4 (.250), 0 R, 0 2B, 0 3B, 0 HR, 0 RBI.

Year League	W	L	Pct.	ERA	WHIP	G	GS	CG	ShO	Hld.	Sv.-Opp.	IP	H	R	ER	HR	BB-IBB	SO	Avg.
1996— GC Marlins (GCL)	4	2	.667	2.04	0.91	12	9	1	1	...	0-...	57.1	35	16	13	0	17-0	48	.175
1997— Kane County (Midwest)	1	5	.167	13.05	2.50	7	7	0	0	...	0-...	20.0	33	34	29	2	17-0	19	.363
— Utica (N.Y.-Penn)	3	5	.375	3.62	1.39	12	12	1	0	...	0-...	69.2	70	34	28	3	27-1	65	.263
1998— Kane County (Midwest)	8	8	.500	3.87	1.33	27	27	3	0	...	0-...	158.1	144	84	68	11	66-1	148	.240
1999— Brevard County (FSL)	9	6	.600	4.60	1.38	16	16	3	2	...	0-...	94.0	101	52	48	7	29-0	65	.280
— Portland (East.)	6	3	.667	3.75	1.37	12	12	1	1	...	0-...	81.2	79	39	34	12	33-0	63	.255
2000— Portland (East.)	9	8	.529	4.66	1.43	27	27	2	0	...	0-...	156.1	161	102	81	15	63-1	113	.264
2001— Calgary (PCL)	6	7	.462	5.46	1.51	21	21	1	1	...	0-...	118.2	136	77	72	16	43-0	104	.285
— Florida (N.L.)	0	1	.000	6.00	1.33	2	1	0	0	0	0-0	6.0	7	4	4	1	1-0	9	.280
2002— Florida (N.L.)	3	1	.750	4.40	1.21	28	0	0	0	5	0-1	30.2	21	15	15	6	16-0	21	.193
— Calgary (PCL)	5	3	.625	4.25	1.60	42	0	0	0	...	3-...	53.0	53	29	25	4	32-2	44	.269
2003— Toledo (Int'l)	4	6	.400	5.13	1.59	13	13	0	0	...	0-...	79.0	98	54	45	15	28-3	63	.304
— Detroit (A.L.)	3	8	.273	6.04	1.66	20	18	0	0	0	0-0	95.1	111	70	64	14	47-0	51	.288
American League totals (1 year)	3	8	.273	6.04	1.66	20	18	0	0	0	0-0	95.1	111	70	64	14	47-0	51	.288
National League totals (2 years)	3	2	.600	4.66	1.23	30	1	0	0	5	0-1	36.2	28	19	19	7	17-0	30	.209
Major League totals (3 years)	6	10	.375	5.66	1.54	50	19	0	0	5	0-1	132.0	139	89	83	21	64-0	81	.267

KOCH, BILLY   P

PERSONAL: Born December 14, 1974, in Rockville Center, N.Y. ... 6-3/215. ... Throws right, bats right. ... Full name: William Christopher Koch. ... Name pronounced: COTCH. ... High school: West Babylon (N.Y.). ... College: Clemson.

TRANSACTIONS/CAREER NOTES: Selected by Toronto Blue Jays organization in first round (fourth pick overall) of free-agent draft (June 4, 1996). ... On disabled list (April 14, 1997-remainder of season). ... Traded by Blue Jays to Oakland Athletics for P Justin Miller and 3B Eric Hinske (December 7, 2001). ... Traded by A's with two players to be named later to Chicago White Sox for P Keith Foulke, C Mark Johnson, P Joe Valentine and cash (December 3, 2002; White Sox acquired P Neal Cotts and OF Daylon Holt to complete deal (December 16, 2002). ... Placed on 15-day disabled list (August 12, 2003). ... Sent on minor league rehab assignment (August 25, 2003). ... Recalled from minor league rehab assignment; removed from 15-day disabled list (September 2, 2003).

CAREER HITTING: 0-for-2 (.000), 0 R, 0 2B, 0 3B, 0 HR, 0 RBI.

Year League	W	L	Pct.	ERA	WHIP	G	GS	CG	ShO	Hld.	Sv.-Opp.	IP	H	R	ER	HR	BB-IBB	SO	Avg.
1997— Dunedin (Fla. St.)	0	1	.000	2.49	1.38	3	3	0	0	...	0-...	21.2	27	10	6	1	3-0	20	.325
1998— Dunedin (Fla. St.)	• 14	7	.667	3.75	1.29	25	25	0	0	...	0-...	124.2	120	65	52	8	41-0	108	.252
— Syracuse (Int'l)	0	1	.000	14.29	2.47	2	2	0	0	...	0-...	5.2	9	9	9	1	5-0	9	.360
1999— Syracuse (Int'l)	3	0	1.000	3.86	1.44	5	5	0	0	...	0-...	25.2	27	11	11	3	10-0	22	.276
— Toronto (A.L.)	0	5	.000	3.39	1.34	56	0	0	0	0	31-35	63.2	55	26	24	5	30-5	57	.235
2000— Toronto (A.L.)	9	3	.750	2.63	1.22	68	0	0	0	0	33-38	78.2	78	28	23	6	18-4	60	.258
2001— Toronto (A.L.)	2	5	.286	4.80	1.47	69	0	0	0	0	36-44	69.1	69	39	37	7	33-7	55	.265
2002— Oakland (A.L.)	11	4	.733	3.27	1.27	84	0	0	0	0	44-50	93.2	73	38	34	7	46-6	93	.214
2003— Charlotte (Int'l)	0	1	.000	4.91	2.18	4	0	0	0	0	0-...	3.2	5	2	2	0	3-0	2	.313
— Chicago (A.L.)	5	5	.500	5.77	1.64	55	0	0	0	1	11-15	53.0	59	36	34	10	28-1	42	.281
Major League totals (5 years)	27	22	.551	3.82	1.36	332	0	* 0	0	1	155-182	358.1	334	167	152	35	155-23	307	.248

KOLB, DANNY   P

PERSONAL: Born March 29, 1975, in Sterling, Ill. ... 6-4/215. ... Throws right, bats right. ... Full name: Danny Lee Kolb. ... High school: Walnut (Ill.). ... College: Illinois State.

TRANSACTIONS/CAREER NOTES: Selected by Minnesota Twins organization in 17th round of free-agent draft (June 3, 1993); did not sign. ... Selected by Texas Rangers organization in sixth round of free-agent draft (June 3, 1995). ... On Texas disabled list (October 3, 1999-remainder of season). ... On Texas disabled list (May 29, 2000-remainder of season). ... On Texas disabled list (March 23-July 11, 2001; included rehabilitation assignments to Charlotte (June 11-July 3) and Tulsa (July 4-10). ... On Texas disabled list (March 28-July 16, 2002; included rehabilitation assignments to Charlotte (June 25-July 1) and Tulsa (July 2-16). ... Released by Rangers (March 26, 2003). ... Signed by Milwaukee Brewers (April 3, 2003).

CAREER HITTING: 0-for-0 (.000), 0 R, 0 2B, 0 3B, 0 HR, 0 RBI.

Year	League	W	L	Pct.	ERA	WHIP	G	GS	CG	ShO	Hld.	Sv.-Opp.	IP	H	R	ER	HR	BB-IBB	SO	Avg.
1995— GC Rangers (GCL)		1	7	.125	2.21	1.25	12	11	0	0	...	0-...	53.0	38	22	13	0	28-0	46	.204
1996— Char., S.C. (SAL)		8	6	.571	2.57	1.11	20	20	4	2	...	0-...	126.0	80	50	36	5	60-2	127	.181
— Charlotte (Fla. St.)		2	2	.500	4.26	1.37	6	6	0	0	...	0-...	38.0	38	18	18	1	14-0	28	.260
— Tulsa (Texas)		1	0	1.000	0.77	1.11	2	2	0	0	...	0-...	11.2	5	1	1	0	8-0	7	.139
1997— Charlotte (Fla. St.)		4	10	.286	4.87	1.56	24	23	3	0	...	0-...	133.0	146	91	72	10	62-1	83	.282
— Tulsa (Texas)		0	2	.000	4.76	1.59	2	2	0	0	...	0-...	11.1	7	7	6	1	11-0	6	.179
1998— Tulsa (Texas)		12	11	.522	4.82	1.62	28	28	2	0	...	0-...	162.1	187	104	87	11	76-1	83	.293
— Oklahoma (PCL)		0	0	...	0.00	2.00	1	0	0	0	...	0-...	1.0	1	0	0	0	1-0	0	.250
1999— Tulsa (Texas)		1	2	.333	2.79	1.45	7	7	1	1	...	0-...	38.2	38	16	12	0	18-0	32	.260
— Oklahoma (PCL)		5	3	.625	5.10	1.68	11	8	0	0	...	0-...	60.0	74	35	34	4	27-0	21	.320
— Texas (A.L.)		2	1	.667	4.65	1.55	16	0	0	0	0	0-0	31.0	33	18	16	2	15-0	15	.268
2000— Oklahoma (PCL)		4	1	.800	0.98	1.04	13	0	0	0	...	4-...	18.1	11	6	2	0	8-1	18	.175
— Texas (A.L.)		0	0	...	67.50	10.50	1	0	0	0	0	0-...	.2	5	5	5	0	2-0	0	.833
2001— Charlotte (Fla. St.)		1	2	.333	3.86	1.23	7	3	0	0	...	0-...	18.2	21	8	8	1	2-0	16	.276
— Tulsa (Texas)		1	0	1.000	0.00	0.50	1	0	0	0	...	0-...	2.0	0	0	0	0	1-0	0	.000
— Oklahoma (PCL)		0	1	.000	1.42	0.89	12	0	0	0	...	3-...	19.0	13	3	3	1	4-0	21	.188
— Texas (A.L.)		0	0	...	4.70	1.63	17	0	0	0	7	0-0	15.1	15	8	8	2	10-1	15	.259
2002— Charlotte (Fla. St.)		1	0	1.000	1.50	1.50	4	0	0	0	...	0-...	6.0	5	1	1	0	4-0	2	.227
— Tulsa (Texas)		0	1	.000	2.16	1.44	5	1	0	0	...	0-...	8.1	9	2	2	0	3-0	4	.290
— Texas (A.L.)		3	6	.333	4.22	1.53	34	0	0	0	2	1-4	32.0	27	17	15	1	22-2	20	.227
2003— Indianapolis (Int'l)		0	1	.000	1.37	0.99	26	0	0	0	...	4-...	39.1	26	10	6	1	13-0	46	.183
— Milwaukee (N.L.)		1	2	.333	1.96	1.28	37	0	0	0	4	21-23	41.1	34	10	9	2	19-3	39	.221
American League totals (4 years)		5	7	.417	5.01	1.63	68	0	0	0	9	1-4	79.0	80	48	44	5	49-3	50	.261
National League totals (1 year)		1	2	.333	1.96	1.28	37	0	0	0	4	21-23	41.1	34	10	9	2	19-3	39	.221
Major League totals (5 years)		6	9	.400	3.96	1.51	105	0	0	0	13	22-27	120.1	114	58	53	7	68-6	89	.248

KONERKO, PAUL — 1B

PERSONAL: Born March 5, 1976, in Providence, R.I. ... 6-2/215. ... Bats right, throws right. ... Full name: Paul Henry Konerko. ... Name pronounced: kone-err-coe. ... High school: Chaparral (Scottsdale, Ariz.).

TRANSACTIONS/CAREER NOTES: Selected by Los Angeles Dodgers organization in first round (13th pick overall) of free-agent draft (June 2, 1994). ... Traded by Dodgers with P Dennis Reyes to Cincinnati Reds for P Jeff Shaw (July 4, 1998). ... Traded by Reds to Chicago White Sox for OF Mike Cameron (November 11, 1998).

2003 GAMES PLAYED BY POSITION (MLB): 1B—119, DH—14.

										BATTING										FIELDING	
Year	Team (League)	Pos.	G	AB	R	H	2B	3B	HR	RBI	BB	SO	HBP	GDP	SB-CS	Avg.	OBP	SLG	OPS	E	Pct.
1994— Yakima (N'west)		DH-C	67	257	25	74	15	2	6	* 58	36	52	6	6	1-0	.288	.379	.432	.811	5	.984
1995— San Bern. (Calif.)		DH-C	118	448	7	124	21	1	19	77	59	88	4	12	3-1	.277	.362	.455	.817	11	.985
1996— San Antonio (Texas)		1B-DH	133	470	78	141	23	2	29	86	72	85	8	7	1-3	.300	.397	.543	.939	14	.989
— Albuquerque (PCL)		1B	4	14	2	6	0	0	1	2	1	2	0	0	0-1	.429	.467	.643	1.110	0	1.000
1997— Albuquerque (PCL)		3-1-D-2	130	483	97	156	31	1	* 37	* 127	64	61	8	16	2-3	.323	.407	.621	1.028	24	.952
— Los Angeles (N.L.)		3B-1B	6	7	0	1	0	0	0	1	0	1	2	0	1	0-0	.143	.250	.143	.393	0	1.000
1998— Los Angeles (N.L.)		1-3-O-D	49	144	14	31	1	0	4	16	10	30	2	5	0-1	.215	.272	.306	.578	2	.991
— Albuquerque (PCL)		OF-1B-3B	24	87	16	33	10	0	6	26	11	12	0	3	0-0	.379	.436	.701	1.137	3	.985
— Cincinnati (N.L.)		3B-1B-OF	26	73	7	16	3	0	3	13	6	10	1	5	0-0	.219	.284	.384	.668	0	1.000
— Indianapolis (Int'l)		3B	39	150	25	49	8	0	8	39	19	18	2	8	1-0	.327	.402	.540	.942	4	.957
1999— Chicago (A.L.)		1B-DH-3B	142	513	71	151	31	4	24	81	45	68	2	19	1-0	.294	.352	.511	.862	4	.995
2000— Chicago (A.L.)		1B-3B-DH	143	524	84	156	31	1	21	97	47	72	10	22	1-0	.298	.363	.481	.844	11	.990
2001— Chicago (A.L.)		1B-DH	156	582	92	164	35	0	32	99	54	89	9	17	1-0	.282	.349	.507	.856	8	.994
2002— Chicago (A.L.)		1B-DH	151	570	81	173	30	0	27	104	44	72	9	17	0-0	.304	.359	.498	.857	8	.993
2003— Chicago (A.L.)		1B-DH	137	444	49	104	19	0	18	65	43	50	4	*28	0-0	.234	.305	.399	.704	2	.998
American League totals (5 years)			729	2633	377	748	146	5	122	446	233	351	34	103	3-0	.284	.347	.482	.829	33	.994
National League totals (2 years)			81	224	21	48	4	0	7	29	17	42	3	11	0-1	.214	.275	.326	.601	2	.993
Major League totals (7 years)			810	2857	398	796	150	5	129	475	250	393	37	114	3-1	.279	.342	.470	.812	35	.994

KOONCE, GRAHAM — 1B

PERSONAL: Born May 15, 1975, in El Cajon, Calif. ... 6-4/225. ... Bats left, throws left. ... Full name: Graham CLinton Koonce. ... High school: Julian (Calif.). ... College: UCLA.

TRANSACTIONS/CAREER NOTES: Selected by Detroit Tigers organization in 60th round of free-agent draft (June 3, 1993). ... Released by Tigers (March 26, 1997); signed by Tri-City of the independent Western League (May 1998); signed by Chico of the independent Western League (May 1998); signed by San Diego Padres organization (December 5, 1998). ... Selected from San Diego by Oakland A's in Rule 5 draft (December 13, 2001).

2003 GAMES PLAYED BY POSITION (MLB): 1B—5.

										BATTING										FIELDING	
Year	Team (League)	Pos.	G	AB	R	H	2B	3B	HR	RBI	BB	SO	HBP	GDP	SB-CS	Avg.	OBP	SLG	OPS	E	Pct.
1994— Bristol (Appal.)		1B-OF	43	115	14	25	4	0	0	15	28	22	3	6	3-0	.217	.376	.252	.628	8	.975
1995— Jamestown (NYP)		1B	73	289	37	81	16	1	3	34	35	63	2	1	8-3	.280	.361	.374	.735	12	.985
1996— Fayetteville (SAL)		1B-OF	133	486	61	116	22	3	8	59	58	97	5	9	7-7	.239	.324	.346	.669	9	.993
1997— Tri-City (West.)		1B-OF-3B	89	286	46	82	15	3	3	34	67	55	3	5	13-6	.287	.422	.392	.814	9	.988
1998— Chico (West.)		1B-OF	69	242	50	80	15	0	10	41	38	41	3	6	0-0	.331	.426	.517	.943	7	.986
1999— Rancho Cuca. (Calif.)		1B	132	474	76	135	16	1	19	79	76	110	11	12	4-1	.285	.392	.443	.835	17	.986
2000— Rancho Cuca. (Calif.)		1B	137	475	92	140	40	3	18	93	107	105	4	4	0-0	.295	.425	.505	.931	18	.984
2001— Mobile (Sou.)		1B-OF	109	320	52	85	18	0	13	48	89	83	4	3	0-0	.266	.429	.444	.873	3	.994
— Portland (NW)		1B	6	14	5	3	1	0	1	2	5	6	0	1	0-0	.214	.421	.500	.921	0	1.000
2002— Midland (Texas)		1B	140	470	86	129	28	0	24	96	133	117	10	10	2-0	.274	.440	.487	.927	14	.987
2003— Sacramento (PCL)		1B-DH	138	480	82	133	23	1	34	115	98	119	11	11	0-0	.277	.403	.544	.944	4	.995
— Oakland (A.L.)		1B	6	8	0	1	1	0	0	0	0	6	0	0	0-0	.125	.125	.250	.375	0	1.000
Major League totals (1 year)			6	8	0	1	1	0	0	0	0	6	0	0	0-0	.125	.125	.250	.375	0	1.000

KOPLOVE, MIKE — P

PERSONAL: Born August 30, 1976, in Philadelphia, Pa. ... 5-10/178. ... Throws right, bats right. ... Full name: Michael Paul Koplove. ... Name pronounced: COP-luv. ... High school: Chestnut Hill Academy (Philadelphia). ... College: Delaware.

TRANSACTIONS/CAREER NOTES: Selected by Arizona Diamondbacks organization in 29th round of free-agent draft (June 2, 1998). ... On El Paso disabled list (April 7-29, 2001). ... Activated from the 15-day disabled list (July 3, 2003). ... Placed on the 15-day disabled list, retroactive to May 28 (May 30, 2003). ... Reinstated from 15-day disabled list (June 13, 2003). ... Placed on 15-day disabled list (June 19, 2003). ... Sent to Tucson on rehab assignment (July 26, 2003). ... Recalled from Tucson rehab assignment (August 5, 2003). ... Transferred to 60-day disabled list (September 1, 2003).

CAREER HITTING: 0-for-2 (.000), 0 R, 0 2B, 0 3B, 0 HR, 0 RBI.

Year— League	W	L	Pct.	ERA	WHIP	G	GS	CG	ShO	Hld.	Sv.-Opp.	IP	H	R	ER	HR	BB-IBB	SO	Avg.
1998— Ariz. D'backs (Ariz.)	0	0	...	9.00	1.50	2	0	0	0	...	0-...	4.0	4	4	4	0	2-0	5	.250
— Lethbridge (Pio.)	1	2	.333	3.54	0.93	12	1	0	0	...	2-...	28.0	23	12	11	2	3-0	22	.217
1999— South Bend (Mid.)	5	2	.714	2.04	1.18	45	45	0	0	...	7-...	84.0	70	23	19	5	29-0	98	.227
2000— High Desert (Calif.)	2	0	1.000	1.42	0.95	20	0	0	0	...	8-...	25.1	14	4	4	0	10-0	31	.163
— El Paso (Texas)	4	3	.571	4.46	1.41	35	0	0	0	...	6-...	40.1	38	28	20	2	19-1	47	.225
2001— El Paso (Texas)	3	2	.600	2.66	1.43	34	0	0	0	...	4-...	44.0	44	18	13	3	19-3	43	.263
— Tucson (PCL)	4	1	.800	2.82	1.21	17	0	0	0	...	9-...	22.1	17	7	7	1	10-1	22	.207
— Arizona (N.L.)	0	1	.000	3.60	1.70	9	0	0	0	1	0-0	10.0	8	7	4	1	9-1	14	.211
2002— Tucson (PCL)	1	2	.333	1.17	0.82	23	0	0	0	...	3-...	30.2	21	5	4	1	4-0	31	.196
— Arizona (N.L.)	6	1	.857	3.36	1.14	55	0	0	0	10	0-0	61.2	47	24	23	2	23-4	46	.213
2003— Arizona (N.L.)	3	0	1.000	2.15	1.09	31	0	0	0	5	0-1	37.2	31	11	9	3	10-1	27	.225
— Tucson (PCL)	0	1	.000	13.50	2.63	3	0	0	0	...	1-...	2.2	4	4	4	1	3-0	2	.333
Major League totals (3 years)	**9**	**2**	**.818**	**2.96**	**1.17**	**95**	**0**	**0**	**0**	**16**	**0-1**	**109.1**	**86**	**42**	**36**	**6**	**42-6**	**87**	**.217**

KOSKIE, COREY   3B

PERSONAL: Born June 28, 1973, in Anola, Manitoba. ... 6-3/220. ... Bats left, throws right. ... Full name: Cordel Leonard Koskie. ... Name pronounced: KOSS-key. ... High school: Springfield Collegiate (Oakbank, Man.). ... College: University of Manitoba.

TRANSACTIONS/CAREER NOTES: Selected by Minnesota Twins organization in 26th round of free-agent draft (June 2, 1994). ... On disabled list (May 10-28 and June 25-July 4, 1996). ... On disabled list (May 8-24, 2002). ... Placed on 15-day disabled list (July 12, 2003). ... Reinstated from 15-day disabled list (August 4, 2003).

2003 GAMES PLAYED BY POSITION (MLB): 3B—131.

Year— Team (League)	Pos.	G	AB	R	H	2B	3B	HR	RBI	BB	SO	HBP	GDP	SB-CS	Avg.	OBP	SLG	OPS	E	Pct.
1994— Elizabethton (App.)	3B	34	107	13	25	2	1	3	10	18	27	2	3	0-0	.234	.354	.355	.709	8	.930
1995— Fort Wayne (Midw.)	3B	123	462	64	143	37	5	16	78	38	79	9	10	2-4	.310	.370	.515	.885	36	.900
1996— Fort Myers (FSL)	3B	95	338	43	88	19	4	9	55	40	76	1	4	1-1	.260	.338	.420	.758	19	.926
1997— New Britain (East.)	3B-DH	131	437	88	125	26	6	23	79	90	106	7	13	9-5	.286	.414	.531	.945	22	.933
1998— Salt Lake (PCL)	3B-DH	135	505	91	152	32	5	26	105	51	104	8	17	15-7	.301	.368	.539	.906	23	.935
— Minnesota (A.L.)	3B	11	29	2	4	0	0	1	2	2	10	0	0	0-0	.138	.194	.241	.435	1	.941
1999— Minnesota (A.L.) 3B-OF-DH		117	342	42	106	21	0	11	58	40	72	5	6	4-4	.310	.387	.468	.855	8	.962
2000— Minnesota (A.L.)	3B-DH	146	474	79	142	32	4	9	65	77	104	4	11	5-4	.300	.400	.441	.841	12	.966
2001— Minnesota (A.L.)	3B-DH	153	562	100	155	37	2	26	103	68	110	12	16	27-6	.276	.362	.488	.850	15	.964
2002— Minnesota (A.L.)	3B-DH	140	490	71	131	37	3	15	69	72	127	9	14	10-11	.267	.368	.447	.815	12	.969
2003— Minnesota (A.L.)	3B	131	469	76	137	29	2	14	69	77	113	7	5	11-5	.292	.393	.452	.845	9	.973
Major League totals (6 years)		**698**	**2366**	**370**	**675**	**156**	**11**	**76**	**366**	**336**	**544**	**37**	**52**	**57-30**	**.285**	**.379**	**.457**	**.836**	**57**	**.967**

KOTSAY, MARK   OF

PERSONAL: Born December 2, 1975, in Whittier, Calif. ... 6-0/201. ... Bats left, throws left. ... Full name: Mark Steven Kotsay. ... Name pronounced: KAH-tsay. ... High school: Santa Fe Springs (Calif.). ... College: Cal State Fullerton.

TRANSACTIONS/CAREER NOTES: Selected by Florida Marlins organization in first round (ninth pick overall) of free-agent draft (June 4, 1996). ... Traded by Marlins with OF Cesar Crespo to San Diego Padres for OF Eric Owens, P Matt Clement and P Omar Ortiz (March 28, 2001). ... On disabled list (April 16-May 1, 2001). ... Placed on the 15-day disabled list (May 19, 2003). ... Reinstated from 15-day disabled list (June 5, 2003).

2003 GAMES PLAYED BY POSITION (MLB): OF—126.

Year— Team (League)	Pos.	G	AB	R	H	2B	3B	HR	RBI	BB	SO	HBP	GDP	SB-CS	Avg.	OBP	SLG	OPS	E	Pct.
1996— Kane Co. (Midw.)	OF	17	60	16	17	5	0	2	8	16	8	1	3	3-0	.283	.436	.467	.903	0	1.000
1997— Portland (East.)	OF-DH	114	438	103	134	27	2	20	77	75	65	0	16	17-5	.306	.405	.514	.919	2	.992
— Florida (N.L.)	OF	14	52	5	10	1	0	4	4	7	0	1	3-0	.192	.250	.250	.500	0	1.000
1998— Florida (N.L.)	OF-1B	154	578	72	161	25	7	11	68	34	61	1	17	10-5	.279	.318	.403	.721	6	.984
1999— Florida (N.L.)	OF-1B	148	495	57	134	23	9	8	50	29	50	0	11	7-6	.271	.306	.402	.708	5	.987
2000— Florida (N.L.)	OF-1B	152	530	87	158	31	5	12	57	42	46	0	17	19-9	.298	.347	.443	.791	3	.990
2001— San Diego (N.L.)	OF	119	406	67	118	29	1	10	58	48	58	2	11	13-5	.291	.366	.411	.807	4	.986
2002— San Diego (N.L.)	OF	153	578	82	169	27	7	17	61	59	89	3	10	11-9	.292	.359	.452	.810	4	.989
2003— San Diego (N.L.)	OF	128	482	64	128	28	4	7	38	56	82	1	8	6-3	.266	.343	.384	.726	3	.991
Major League totals (7 years)		**868**	**3121**	**434**	**878**	**164**	**34**	**65**	**336**	**272**	**393**	**7**	**75**	**69-37**	**.281**	**.338**	**.418**	**.756**	**25**	**.988**

KREUTER, CHAD   C

PERSONAL: Born August 26, 1964, in Greenbrae, Calif. ... 6-2/200. ... Bats both, throws right. ... Full name: Chadden Michael Kreuter. ... Name pronounced: CREW-ter. ... High school: Redwood (Calif.). ... College: Pepperdine.

TRANSACTIONS/CAREER NOTES: Selected by Texas Rangers organization in fifth round of free-agent draft (June 3, 1985). ... Granted free agency (October 15, 1991). ... Signed by Detroit Tigers organization (January 2, 1992). ... Granted free agency (December 23, 1994). ... Signed by Seattle Mariners (April 8, 1995). ... On Seattle disabled list (June 19-July 6, 1995). ... On Tacoma disabled list (August 4-25, 1995). ... Granted free agency (October 16, 1995). ... Signed by Chicago White Sox organization (December 11, 1995). ... On disabled list (July 20, 1996-remainder of season). ... Granted free agency (October 14, 1996). ... Re-signed by White Sox organization (January 29, 1997). ... Traded by White Sox with OF Tony Phillips to Anaheim Angels for P Chuck McElroy and C Jorge Fabregas (May 18, 1997). ... Granted free agency (November 7, 1997). ... Signed by White Sox (December 10, 1997). ... Traded by White Sox to Angels for cash considerations (September 18, 1998). ... Granted free agency (October 26, 1998). ... Signed by Kansas City Royals (December 15, 1998). ... Granted free agency (October 29, 1999). ... Signed by Los Angeles Dodgers organization (January 20, 2000). ... On disabled list (June 25-July 12, 2002). ... Granted free agency (November 11, 2002). ... Signed by Rangers organization (January 7, 2003). ... Released by Rangers (April 28, 2003).

2003 GAMES PLAYED BY POSITION (MLB): C—7.

Year	Team (League)	Pos.	G	AB	R	H	2B	3B	HR	RBI	BB	SO	HBP	GDP	SB-CS	Avg.	OBP	SLG	OPS	E	Pct.
1985— Burlington (Midw.)	C	69	199	25	53	9	0	4	26	38	48	1	4	3-2	.266	.382	.372	.754	8	.980
1986— Salem (Caro.)	3B-C-OF	125	387	55	85	21	2	6	49	67	82	3	14	5-5	.220	.336	.331	.667	‡ 21	.972
1987— Charlotte (Fla. St.)	3B-C-OF	85	281	36	61	18	1	9	40	31	32	1	5	1-1	.217	.296	.384	.681	8	.982
1988— Tulsa (Texas)	C	108	358	46	95	24	6	3	51	55	66	2	12	2-2	.265	.362	.391	.753	• 13	.981
— Texas (A.L.)	C	16	51	3	14	2	1	1	5	7	13	0	1	0-0	.275	.362	.412	.774	1	.990
1989— Texas (A.L.)	C	87	158	16	24	3	0	5	9	27	40	0	4	0-1	.152	.274	.266	.540	4	.992
— Okla. City (A.A.)	C	26	87	10	22	3	0	0	6	13	11	0	2	1-1	.253	.347	.287	.634	2	.988
1990— Texas (A.L.)	C	22	22	2	1	1	0	0	2	8	9	0	0	0-0	.045	.290	.091	.381	1	.977
— Okla. City (A.A.)	C	92	291	41	65	17	1	7	35	52	80	2	8	0-3	.223	.345	.361	.706	10	.984
1991— Texas (A.L.)	C	3	4	0	0	0	0	0	0	0	1	0	0	0-0	.000	.000	.000	.000	0	1.000
— Okla. City (A.A.)	C	24	70	14	19	6	0	1	12	18	16	0	4	2-0	.271	.416	.400	.816	7	.960
— Tulsa (Texas)	C	42	128	23	30	5	1	2	10	29	23	1	3	1-0	.234	.380	.336	.716	4	.987
1992— Detroit (A.L.)	C-DH	67	190	22	48	9	0	2	16	20	38	0	8	0-1	.253	.321	.332	.652	5	.983
1993— Detroit (A.L.)	C-DH-1B	119	374	59	107	23	3	15	51	49	92	3	5	2-1	.286	.371	.484	.855	7	.988
1994— Detroit (A.L.)	C-1B-OF	65	170	17	38	8	0	1	19	28	36	0	3	0-1	.224	.327	.288	.615	4	.987
1995— Seattle (A.L.)	C	26	75	12	17	5	0	1	8	5	22	2	0	0-0	.227	.293	.333	.626	4	.976
— Tacoma (PCL)	C-DH	15	48	6	14	5	0	1	11	8	11	0	3	0-0	.292	.393	.458	.851	1	.988
1996— Chicago (A.L.)	C-1B-DH	46	114	14	25	8	0	3	18	13	29	2	2	0-0	.219	.308	.368	.676	2	.990
1997— Chicago (A.L.)	C-1B	19	37	6	8	2	1	1	3	8	9	0	0	0-1	.216	.356	.405	.761	2	.969
— Anaheim (A.L.)	C-DH	70	218	19	51	7	1	4	18	21	57	0	7	0-2	.234	.301	.330	.632	3	.994
1998— Chicago (A.L.)	C	93	245	26	62	9	1	2	33	32	45	3	8	1-0	.253	.345	.322	.668	7	.985
— Anaheim (A.L.)	C	3	7	1	1	1	0	0	0	1	4	0	0	0-0	.143	.250	.286	.536	† 2	.882
1999— Kansas City (A.L.)	C-DH	107	324	31	73	15	0	5	35	34	65	6	16	0-0	.225	.309	.318	.627	3	.994
2000— Los Angeles (N.L.)	C	80	212	32	56	13	0	6	28	54	48	2	6	1-0	.264	.416	.410	.827	3	.994
2001— Los Angeles (N.L.)	C-DH	73	191	21	41	11	1	6	17	41	52	1	5	0-0	.215	.355	.377	.732	0	1.000
2002— Los Angeles (N.L.)	C	41	95	8	25	5	0	2	12	10	31	1	3	1-0	.263	.333	.379	.712	3	.986
2003— Texas (A.L.)	C	7	18	0	2	1	0	0	0	3	2	0	0	0-0	.111	.238	.167	.405	0	1.000
American League totals (13 years)		750	2007	228	471	94	7	40	217	256	462	16	54	3-7	.235	.324	.348	.672	45	.988
National League totals (3 years)		194	498	61	122	29	1	14	57	105	131	4	14	2-0	.245	.378	.392	.770	6	.995
Major League totals (16 years)		944	2505	289	593	123	8	54	274	361	593	20	68	5-7	.237	.335	.357	.692	51	.990

L

LACKEY, JOHN   P

PERSONAL: Born October 23, 1978, in Abilene, Texas. ... 6-6/235. ... Throws right, bats right. ... Full name: John Derran Lackey. ... High school: Abilene (Texas). ... Junior college: Grayson County (Texas) Community College.
TRANSACTIONS/CAREER NOTES: Selected by Anaheim Angels organization in second round of free-agent draft (June 2, 1999).
CAREER HITTING: 0-for-3 (.000), 0 R, 0 2B, 0 3B, 0 HR, 0 RBI.

Year	League	W	L	Pct.	ERA	WHIP	G	GS	CG	ShO	Hld.	Sv.-Opp.	IP	H	R	ER	HR	BB-IBB	SO	Avg.
1999— Boise (NW)	6	2	.750	4.98	1.61	15	15	1	0	...	0-...	81.1	81	59	45	7	50-1	77	.264
2000— Cedar Rapids (Midw.)	3	2	.600	2.08	0.82	5	5	0	0	...	0-...	30.1	20	7	7	1	5-0	21	.185
— Lake Elsinore (Calif.)	6	6	.500	3.40	1.35	15	15	2	• 1	...	0-...	100.2	94	56	38	9	42-0	74	.249
— Erie (East.)	6	1	.857	3.30	1.17	8	8	2	0	...	0-...	57.1	58	23	21	6	9-0	43	.260
2001— Arkansas (Texas)	9	7	.563	3.46	1.06	18	18	3	2	...	0-...	127.1	106	55	49	11	29-0	94	.227
— Salt Lake (PCL)	3	4	.429	6.71	1.58	10	10	1	0	...	0-...	57.2	75	44	43	5	16-0	42	.322
2002— Salt Lake (PCL)	8	2	.800	2.57	1.15	16	16	2	1	...	0-...	101.2	89	35	29	5	28-0	82	.235
— Anaheim (A.L.)	9	4	.692	3.66	1.35	18	18	1	0	0	0-0	108.1	113	52	44	10	33-0	69	.267
2003— Anaheim (A.L.)	10	16	.385	4.63	1.42	33	33	2	•2	0	0-0	204.0	223	117	105	31	66-4	151	.278
Major League totals (2 years)	19	20	.487	4.29	1.39	51	51	3	2	0	0-0	312.1	336	169	149	41	99-4	220	.274

LaFOREST, PETE   C

PERSONAL: Born January 17, 1978, in Hull, Quebec. ... 6-2/208. ... Bats left, throws right. ... Full name: Pierre-Luc LaForest. ... High school: Gatineau (Que.).
TRANSACTIONS/CAREER NOTES: Selected by Montreal Expos organization in 16th round of free-agent draft (June 1, 1995). ... Contract voided by Commissioner's Office (August 15, 1995). ... Signed by Tampa Bay Devil Rays (May 10, 1997).
2003 GAMES PLAYED BY POSITION (MLB): DH—12, C—4.

Year	Team (League)	Pos.	G	AB	R	H	2B	3B	HR	RBI	BB	SO	HBP	GDP	SB-CS	Avg.	OBP	SLG	OPS	E	Pct.
1995— GC Expos (GCL)	3B	2	6	1	0	0	0	0	0	2	4	0	0	0-0	.000	.250	.000	.250	0	...
1996—					Did not play.															
1997— GC Devil Rays (GCL)	3B	34	107	21	28	7	2	3	21	10	18	1	1	4-3	.262	.328	.449	.776	7	.909
1998— Princeton (Appal.)	3B	25	91	18	25	7	1	2	14	12	18	1	0	4-1	.275	.365	.440	.805	7	.870
1999— Char., S.C. (SAL)	3B-2B	125	445	64	114	21	3	13	53	55	97	5	11	9-3	.256	.343	.404	.747	37	.893
2000— St. Pete. (FSL)	C	129	474	85	128	28	7	14	70	56	108	6	4	2-4	.270	.351	.447	.798	10	.974
2001— Orlando (South.)	C	7	21	3	2	0	0	1	1	5	9	0	0	0-0	.095	.269	.238	.507	2	.968
2002— Orlando (South.)	C-1B	106	359	57	97	18	1	20	64	60	94	2	4	9-6	.270	.374	.493	.867	13	.977
— Durham (Int'l)	C	17	66	7	17	3	0	3	15	3	28	0	1	0-1	.258	.290	.439	.729	5	.950
2003— Orlando (South.)	DH-C-3B	21	72	9	18	8	0	3	15	16	17	1	1	0-0	.250	.385	.486	.871	1	.981
— Durham (Int'l)	C-DH	61	201	40	54	14	2	14	38	36	56	2	2	2-1	.269	.382	.567	.949	3	.990
— Tampa Bay (A.L.)	DH-C	19	48	0	8	2	0	0	6	1	14	1	1	0-0	.167	.196	.208	.404	0	1.000
Major League totals (1 year)		19	48	0	8	2	0	0	6	1	14	1	1	0-0	.167	.196	.208	.404	0	1.000

LAIRD, GERALD   C

PERSONAL: Born November 13, 1979, in Westminster, Calif. ... 6-2/195. ... Bats right, throws right. ... Full name: Gerald Lee Laird. ... High school: La Quinta High (Westminster,Calif.). ... Junior college: Cypress College (Calif.).
TRANSACTIONS/CAREER NOTES: Selected by Oakland Athletics organization in second round of free-agent draft (June 2, 1998). ... Traded by A's with P Mario Ramos, 1B Jason Hart and OF Ryan Ludwick to Texas Rangers for P Mike Venafro and 1B Carlos Pena (January 14, 2002). ... Recalled by Texas from Oklahoma (April 30, 2003). ... Optioned to Oklahoma by Texas (May 15, 2003). ... Recalled by Texas from Oklahoma (September 2, 2003).
2003 GAMES PLAYED BY POSITION (MLB): C—16.

Year	Team (League)	Pos.	G	AB	R	H	2B	3B	HR	RBI	BB	SO	HBP	GDP	SB-CS	Avg.	OBP	SLG	OPS	E	Pct.
1999— S. Oregon (N'west)	C	60	228	45	65	7	2	2	39	28	43	2	4	10-5	.285	.361	.360	.721	11	.972
2000— Ariz. A's (Ariz.)	C	14	50	10	15	2	1	0	9	6	7	1	3	2-0	.300	.379	.380	.759	0	1.000
—Visalia (Calif.)	C	33	103	14	25	3	0	0	13	14	27	1	3	7-2	.243	.333	.272	.605	8	.969
2001— Modesto (Calif.) C-0-1-2-3-S		119	443	71	113	13	5	5	46	48	101	10	9	10-9	.255	.337	.341	.678	18	.976
2002— Tulsa (Texas)	C-OF	123	442	70	122	21	4	11	67	45	95	5	14	8-6	.276	.343	.416	.759	8	.988
2003— Oklahoma (PCL)	C-DH	99	338	50	88	20	5	9	42	37	61	7	7	9-3	.260	.344	.429	.773	11	.983
—Texas (A.L.)	C	19	44	9	12	2	1	1	4	5	11	1	2	0-0	.273	.360	.432	.792	1	.986
Major League totals (1 year)		19	44	9	12	2	1	1	4	5	11	1	2	0-0	.273	.360	.432	.792	1	.986

LAKER, TIM   C

PERSONAL: Born November 27, 1969, in Encino, Calif. ... 6-3/225. ... Bats right, throws right. ... Full name: Timothy John Laker. ... High school: Simi Valley (Calif.). ... Junior college: Oxnard College (Calif.).

TRANSACTIONS/CAREER NOTES: Selected by Kansas City Royals organization in 49th round of free-agent draft (June 2, 1987); did not sign. ... Selected by Montreal Expos organization in sixth round of free-agent draft (June 1, 1988). ... On Ottawa disabled list (April 30-May 14, 1993). ... On disabled list (March 29, 1996-entire season). ... Claimed on waivers by Baltimore Orioles (March 25, 1997). ... On Rochester disabled list (June 5-16, 1997). ... Granted free agency (October 15, 1997). ... Signed by Tampa Bay Devil Rays (December 19, 1997). ... Released by Devil Rays (June 26, 1998). ... Signed by Pittsburgh Pirates organization (July 9, 1998). ... Released by Pirates (December 18, 1998). ... Signed by Los Angeles Dodgers organization (January 11, 1999). ... Traded by Dodgers to Pirates for a player to be named later (March 26, 1999). ... On Nashville suspended list (August 23-26, 1999). ... Granted free agency (October 14, 1999). ... Re-signed by Pirates organization (December 20, 1999). ... Granted free agency (October 18, 2000). ... Signed by Cleveland Indians organization (December 20, 2000). ... Released by Indians (March 1, 2002). ... Re-signed by Indians organization (March 5, 2002). ... On Buffalo disabled list (April 4-May 23, 2002).

2003 GAMES PLAYED BY POSITION (MLB): C—50, DH—2.

Year	Team (League)	Pos.	G	AB	R	H	2B	3B	HR	RBI	BB	SO	HBP	GDP	SB-CS	Avg.	OBP	SLG	OPS	E	Pct.
1988—Jamestown (NYP)	C-OF	47	152	14	34	9	0	0	17	8	30	0	4	2-1	.224	.261	.283	.544	2	.992
1989—Rockford (Midwest)	C	14	48	4	11	1	1	0	4	3	6	0	1	1-0	.229	.275	.292	.566	4	.960
—Jamestown (NYP)	C	58	216	25	48	9	1	2	24	16	40	2	4	8-4	.222	.278	.301	.579	8	.984
1990—Rockford (Midwest)	C-OF	120	425	46	94	18	3	7	57	32	83	1	9	7-2	.221	.273	.327	.600	‡18	.981
—W.P. Beach (FSL)	C	2	3	0	0	0	0	0	0	0	1	0	0	0-0	.000	.000	.000	.000	0	1.000
1991—W.P. Beach (FSL)	C	100	333	35	77	15	2	5	33	22	51	2	9	10-1	.231	.280	.333	.613	* 14	.979
—Harrisburg (East.)	C	11	35	4	10	1	0	1	5	2	5	1	1	0-1	.286	.342	.400	.742	3	.959
1992—Harrisburg (East.)	C	117	409	55	99	19	3	15	68	39	89	5	10	3-1	.242	.312	.413	.725	* 14	.980
—Montreal (N.L.)	C	28	46	8	10	3	0	0	4	2	14	0	1	1-1	.217	.250	.283	.533	1	.991
1993—Montreal (N.L.)	C	43	86	3	17	2	1	0	7	2	16	1	2	2-0	.198	.222	.244	.466	2	.987
—Ottawa (Int'l)	C-1B	56	204	26	47	10	0	4	23	21	41	1	10	3-2	.230	.304	.338	.642	§11	.972
1994—Ottawa (Int'l)	C-DH	118	424	68	131	32	2	12	71	47	96	3	10	11-6	.309	.381	.479	.860	• 11	.985
1995—Montreal (N.L.)	C	64	141	17	33	8	1	3	20	14	38	1	5	0-1	.234	.306	.369	.675	7	.977
1996—Montreal (N.L.)									Did not play.											
1997—Rochester (Int'l)	DH-C	79	290	45	75	11	1	11	37	34	49	5	4	1-2	.259	.342	.417	.760	6	.980
—Baltimore (A.L.)	C	7	14	0	0	0	0	0	1	2	9	0	0	0-0	.000	.118	.000	.118	1	.966
1998—Durham (Int'l)	C-DH	40	134	36	32	7	0	11	26	28	32	1	4	1-1	.239	.372	.537	.909	2	.991
—Tampa Bay (A.L.)	C-DH	3	5	1	1	0	0	0	0	1	1	0	0	0-1	.200	.333	.200	.533	0	1.000
—Nashville (PCL)	C-1B-DH	44	152	30	54	16	1	11	34	21	26	3	6	1-0	.355	.441	.691	1.131	4	.987
—Pittsburgh (N.L.)	1B-C	14	24	2	9	1	0	1	2	1	3	0	1	0-0	.375	.385	.542	.926	0	1.000
1999—Nashville (PCL)	C-1-D-3	112	405	48	109	29	3	12	65	29	68	4	10	3-0	.269	.322	.444	.766	§15	.981
—Pittsburgh (N.L.)	C	6	9	0	3	0	0	0	0	0	2	0	0	0-0	.333	.333	.333	.667	0	1.000
2000—Nashville (PCL)	C-1B-3B	121	421	70	104	28	4	19	75	54	73	1	9	5-0	.247	.329	.468	.796	‡12	.984
2001—Buffalo (Int'l)	C-1B	86	320	45	79	13	0	20	57	28	53	4	10	2-1	.247	.314	.475	.789	6	.990
—Cleveland (A.L.)	C	16	33	5	6	0	0	1	5	6	8	0	1	0-0	.182	.308	.273	.580	1	.988
2002—Columbus (S. Atl.)	C	11	38	5	11	1	0	2	13	10	6	1	0	0-0	.289	.440	.474	.914	0	1.000
—Buffalo (Int'l)	C-1B	62	216	23	49	10	0	4	28	21	52	3	9	2-0	.227	.303	.329	.632	3	.992
2003—Cleveland (A.L.)	C-DH	52	162	17	39	11	0	3	21	9	38	0	4	2-2	.241	.281	.364	.645	5	.983
American League totals (4 years)		78	214	23	46	11	0	4	27	18	56	0	5	2-3	.215	.275	.322	.597	7	.983
National League totals (5 years)		155	306	30	72	14	2	4	33	19	73	2	9	3-2	.235	.282	.333	.615	10	.984
Major League totals (8 years)		233	520	53	118	25	2	8	60	37	129	2	14	5-5	.227	.279	.329	.608	17	.983

LAMB, MIKE   3B

PERSONAL: Born August 9, 1975, in West Covina, Calif. ... 6-1/195. ... Bats left, throws right. ... Full name: Michael Robert Lamb. ... High school: Bishop Amat (La Puente, Calif.). ... College: Cal State Fullerton.

TRANSACTIONS/CAREER NOTES: Selected by Texas Rangers organization in seventh round of free-agent draft (June 3, 1997).

2003 GAMES PLAYED BY POSITION (MLB): DH—6, 1B—5, OF—2, 3B—1.

Year	Team (League)	Pos.	G	AB	R	H	2B	3B	HR	RBI	BB	SO	HBP	GDP	SB-CS	Avg.	OBP	SLG	OPS	E	Pct.
1997—Pulaski (Appal.)	3B	60	233	59	78	19	3	9	47	31	18	4	5	7-2	.335	.412	.558	.970	25	.862
1998—Charlotte (Fla. St.)	3B-1B	135	536	83	162	35	3	9	93	45	63	4	10	18-7	.302	.356	.429	.785	31	.933
1999—Tulsa (Texas)	3B-C	137	* 544	98	* 176	* 51	5	21	100	53	65	7	11	4-3	.324	.386	.551	.937	28	.930
—Oklahoma (PCL)	3B	2	2	0	1	0	0	0	0	1	0	1	0	0-1	.500	.750	.500	1.250	0	...
2000—Oklahoma (PCL)	3B	14	55	8	14	5	1	2	5	5	6	0	5	2-1	.255	.317	.491	.808	7	.806
—Texas (A.L.)	3B-DH	138	493	65	137	25	2	6	47	34	60	4	10	0-2	.278	.328	.373	.702	• 33	.913
2001—Oklahoma (PCL)	3B	69	273	35	81	19	3	8	40	13	31	3	8	0-2	.297	.331	.476	.807	15	.908
—Texas (A.L.)	3B	76	284	42	87	18	0	4	35	14	27	5	6	2-1	.306	.348	.412	.760	18	.914
2002—Oklahoma (PCL)	C-3B	6	28	3	11	1	0	0	4	1	4	0	1	0-0	.393	.414	.429	.842	3	.893
—Texas (A.L.)	1-D-0-3-C-2	115	314	54	89	13	0	9	33	33	48	3	7	0-0	.283	.354	.411	.765	9	.980
2003—Texas (A.L.)	D-1-0-3	28	38	3	5	0	0	0	2	2	7	1	1	1-0	.132	.190	.132	.322	0	1.000
—Oklahoma (PCL) 3B-1B-DH		73	274	45	79	19	4	9	46	42	45	2	4	1-1	.288	.383	.485	.869	11	.953
Major League totals (4 years)		357	1129	164	318	56	2	19	117	83	142	13	24	3-3	.282	.336	.385	.721	60	.943

L

LANE, JASON — OF

PERSONAL: Born December 22, 1976, in Santa Rosa, Calif. ... 6-2/215. ... Bats right, throws left. ... Full name: Jason Dean Lane. ... High school: Santa Rosa (Calif.). ... College: USC.

TRANSACTIONS/CAREER NOTES: Selected by Houston Astros organization in sixth round of free-agent draft (June 2, 1999).

2003 GAMES PLAYED BY POSITION (MLB): OF—10.

										BATTING									FIELDING	
Year	Team (League)	Pos.	G	AB	R	H	2B	3B	HR	RBI	BB	SO	HBP	GDP	SB-CS	Avg.	OBP	SLG	OPS	E	Pct.
1999— Auburn (NY-Penn)	P-1B	74	283	46	79	18	5	13	* 59	38	46	3	2	6-4	.279	.366	.516	.882	9	.986
2000— Michigan (Midw.)	1B-OF	133	511	98	153	38	0	23	• 104	62	91	8	9	20-7	.299	.375	.509	.884	5	.986
2001— Round Rock (Texas)	OF	137	526	* 103	166	36	2	38	* 124	61	98	21	6	14-2	.316	.407	.608	1.016	2	.992
2002— New Orleans (PCL)	OF-1B	111	426	65	116	36	2	15	83	31	90	7	6	13-3	.272	.328	.472	.799	2	.993
— Houston (N.L.)	OF	44	69	12	20	3	1	4	10	10	12	0	0	1-1	.290	.375	.536	.911	1	.980
2003— New Orleans (PCL)	OF-DH-1B	71	248	37	74	17	0	7	39	30	26	3	6	2-1	.298	.374	.452	.826	4	.976
— Houston (N.L.)	OF	18	27	5	8	2	0	4	10	0	2	0	0	0-0	.296	.296	.815	1.111	0	1.000
Major League totals (2 years)		62	96	17	28	5	1	8	20	10	14	0	0	1-1	.292	.355	.615	.970	1	.983

LANGERHANS, RYAN — OF

PERSONAL: Born February 20, 1980, in San Antonio, Texas. ... 6-3/195. ... Bats left, throws left. ... Full name: Ryan David Langerhans. ... Name pronounced: lahn-ger-hahns. ... High school: Round Rock (Texas).

TRANSACTIONS/CAREER NOTES: Selected by Atlanta Braves organization in third round of free-agent draft (June 2, 1998). ... On Greenville disabled list (May 24-June 17, 2002). ... Called up by Atlanta from Richmond (September 2, 2003).

2003 GAMES PLAYED BY POSITION (MLB): OF—14.

										BATTING									FIELDING	
Year	Team (League)	Pos.	G	AB	R	H	2B	3B	HR	RBI	BB	SO	HBP	GDP	SB-CS	Avg.	OBP	SLG	OPS	E	Pct.
1998— GC Braves (GCL)	OF	43	148	15	41	10	4	2	19	19	38	0	0	2-5	.277	.357	.439	.796	2	.975
1999— Macon (S. Atl.)	OF	121	448	66	120	30	1	9	49	52	99	7	8	19-11	.268	.352	.400	.751	5	.977
2000— Myrtle Beach (Caro.)	OF	116	392	55	83	14	7	6	37	32	104	9	3	25-11	.212	.286	.329	.615	6	.961
2001— Myrtle Beach (Caro.)	OF	125	450	66	186	30	3	7	48	55	104	8	6	22-13	.413	.485	.540	1.025	7	.972
2002— Greenville (Sou.)	OF	109	391	57	98	23	2	9	62	68	83	6	9	10-5	.251	.366	.389	.755	2	.992
— Atlanta (N.L.)	OF	1	1	0	0	0	0	0	0	0	0	0	0	0-0	.000	.000	.000	.000	0	...
2003— Greenville (Sou.)	OF	94	336	42	85	23	2	6	38	46	85	3	6	10-10	.253	.348	.387	.735	2	.991
— Richmond (Int'l)	OF	38	132	13	37	10	2	4	11	11	29	1	2	2-1	.280	.338	.477	.815	4	.949
— Atlanta (N.L.)	OF	16	15	2	4	0	0	0	0	0	6	0	1	0-0	.267	.267	.267	.533	0	1.000
Major League totals (2 years)		17	16	2	4	0	0	0	0	0	6	0	1	0-0	.250	.250	.250	.500	0	1.000

LARKIN, BARRY — SS

PERSONAL: Born April 28, 1964, in Cincinnati, Ohio. ... 6-0/185. ... Bats right, throws right. ... Full name: Barry Louis Larkin. ... High school: Moeller (Cincinnati). ... College: Michigan.

TRANSACTIONS/CAREER NOTES: Selected by Cincinnati Reds organization in second round of free-agent draft (June 7, 1982); did not sign. ... Selected by Reds organization in first round (fourth pick overall) of free-agent draft (June 3, 1985). ... On disabled list (April 13-May 2, 1987). ... On Cincinnati disabled list (July 11-September 1, 1989); included rehabilitation assignment to Nashville (August 27-September 1). ... On disabled list (May 18-June 4, 1991; April 19-May 8, 1992; and August 5, 1993-remainder of season). ... On disabled list (June 17-August 2 and September 1, 1997-remainder of season; March 12-April 7, 1998; April 22-May16, 2000; May 17-June 15 and June 29, 2001-remainder of season). ... On disabled list (April 11, 2003). ... Reinstated from 15-day disabled list (May 6, 2003). ... Placed on 15-day disabled list (May 22, 2003). ... Reinstated from 15-day disabled list (June 13, 2003). ... Activated from the 15-day disabled list (July 3, 2003). ... Placed on 15-day disabled list (August 23, 2003).

2003 GAMES PLAYED BY POSITION (MLB): SS—60.

										BATTING									FIELDING	
Year	Team (League)	Pos.	G	AB	R	H	2B	3B	HR	RBI	BB	SO	HBP	GDP	SB-CS	Avg.	OBP	SLG	OPS	E	Pct.
1985— Vermont (East.)	SS	72	255	42	68	13	2	1	31	23	21	3	13	12-1	.267	.331	.345	.676	17	.942
1986— Denver (A.A.)	2B-SS	103	413	67	136	31	10	10	51	31	43	2	1	19-6	.329	.373	.525	.898	18	.962
— Cincinnati (N.L.)	2B-SS	41	159	27	45	4	3	3	19	9	21	0	2	8-0	.283	.320	.403	.722	4	.978
1987— Cincinnati (N.L.)	SS	125	439	64	107	16	2	12	43	36	52	5	8	21-6	.244	.306	.371	.678	19	.965
1988— Cincinnati (N.L.)	SS	151	588	91	174	32	5	12	56	41	24	8	7	40-7	.296	.347	.429	.776	• 29	.960
1989— Cincinnati (N.L.)	SS	97	325	47	111	14	4	4	36	20	23	2	7	10-5	.342	.375	.446	.821	10	.976
— Nashville (A.A.)	SS	2	5	2	5	1	0	0	0	0	0	0	0	0-0	1.000	1.000	1.200	2.200	0	1.000
1990— Cincinnati (N.L.)	SS	158	614	85	185	25	6	7	67	49	49	7	14	30-5	.301	.358	.396	.753	17	.977
1991— Cincinnati (N.L.)	SS	123	464	88	140	27	4	20	69	55	64	3	7	24-6	.302	.378	.506	.884	15	.976
1992— Cincinnati (N.L.)	SS	140	533	76	162	32	6	12	78	63	58	4	13	15-4	.304	.377	.454	.831	11	.983
1993— Cincinnati (N.L.)	SS	100	384	57	121	20	3	8	51	51	33	1	13	14-1	.315	.394	.445	.839	16	.965
1994— Cincinnati (N.L.)	SS	110	427	78	119	23	5	9	52	64	58	0	6	26-2	.279	.369	.419	.788	10	.980
1995— Cincinnati (N.L.)	SS	131	496	98	158	29	6	15	66	61	49	3	6	51-5	.319	.394	.492	.886	11	.980
1996— Cincinnati (N.L.)	SS	152	517	117	154	32	4	33	89	96	52	7	20	36-10	.298	.410	.567	.977	17	.975
1997— Cincinnati (N.L.)	SS-DH	73	224	34	71	17	3	4	20	47	24	3	3	14-3	.317	.440	.473	.913	5	.980
1998— Cincinnati (N.L.)	SS	145	538	93	166	34	10	17	72	79	69	2	12	26-3	.309	.397	.504	.901	12	.979
1999— Cincinnati (N.L.)	SS	161	583	108	171	30	4	12	75	93	57	2	12	30-8	.293	.390	.420	.810	14	.978
2000— Cincinnati (N.L.)	SS-DH	102	396	71	124	26	5	11	41	48	31	1	10	14-6	.313	.389	.487	.876	11	.973
2001— Cincinnati (N.L.)	SS	45	156	29	40	12	0	2	17	27	25	2	2	3-2	.256	.373	.372	.745	9	.951
2002— Cincinnati (N.L.)	SS	145	507	72	124	37	2	7	47	44	57	3	13	13-4	.245	.305	.367	.672	12	.979
2003— Cincinnati (N.L.)	SS	70	241	39	68	16	1	2	18	22	32	1	7	2-0	.282	.345	.382	.726	9	.962
Major League totals (18 years)		2069	7591	1274	2240	426	73	190	916	905	778	54	162	377-77	.295	.371	.446	.817	231	.974

LaROCCA, GREG — IF

PERSONAL: Born November 10, 1972, in Oswego, N.Y. ... 5-11/185. ... Bats right, throws right. ... Full name: Gregory Mark LaRocca. ... High school: West (Manchester, N.H.). ... College: Massachusetts.

TRANSACTIONS/CAREER NOTES: Selected by San Diego Padres organization in 10th round of free-agent draft (June 2, 1994). ... On disabled list (April 22, 1999-remainder of season). ... Released by Padres (March 28, 2001). ... Signed by Cleveland Indians organization (May 7, 2001). ... On Buffalo disabled list (June 13-21, 2002). ... Contract purchased by Cleveland; optioned to Buffalo (September 3, 2003). ... Called up from Buffalo (September 13, 2003).

2003 GAMES PLAYED BY POSITION (MLB): 3B—2, DH—1.

Year	Team (League)	Pos.	G	AB	R	H	2B	3B	HR	RBI	BB	SO	HBP	GDP	SB-CS	Avg.	OBP	SLG	OPS	E	Pct.
1994— Spokane (N'west)	2B-SS	42	158	20	46	9	2	0	14	14	18	2	4	7-2	.291	.356	.373	.730	8	.961
— Rancho Cuca. (Calif.)	SS	28	85	7	14	5	1	1	8	7	11	2	2	3-1	.165	.242	.282	.524	10	.921
1995— Rancho Cuca. (Calif.)	2B-3B-SS	125	466	77	150	36	5	8	74	44	77	12	13	15-4	.322	.393	.472	.865	36	.931
— Memphis (Sou.)	SS	2	7	0	1	0	0	0	0	0	1	0	1	0-1	.143	.143	.143	.286	1	.889
1996— Memphis (Sou.)	2B-SS	128	445	66	122	22	5	6	42	51	58	10	9	5-9	.274	.358	.387	.745	24	.955
1997— Mobile (Sou.)	2B-3B-SS	76	300	44	80	16	2	3	31	26	46	8	4	8-3	.267	.336	.363	.700	4	.988
1998— Las Vegas (PCL) 2-3-SS-OF	95	304	55	94	22	5	8	39	19	48	12	3	7-4	.309	.371	.493	.864	12	.953
1999— Las Vegas (PCL)	2B-3B-SS	14	51	3	14	2	0	0	2	2	10	4	3	2-2	.275	.345	.314	.659	3	.939
2000— Las Vegas (PCL) .... * 137	3-2-S-OF		482	90	142	* 42	7	9	80	54	62	12	9	13-4	.295	.378	.467	.845	25	.940
— San Diego (N.L.) 3B-SS-2B	13	27	1	6	2	0	0	2	1	4	0	1	0-0	.222	.250	.296	.546	2	.917
2001— Akron (East.) SS-3B-2B	31	104	16	33	9	0	3	19	18	11	2	1	0-2	.317	.421	.490	.911	8	.942
— Buffalo (Int'l) 3B-SS-2B	61	216	39	67	12	1	12	37	12	35	6	4	2-1	.310	.362	.542	.903	6	.967
2002— Buffalo (Int'l) 3-2-OF-SS	107	382	70	112	28	2	7	41	48	48	23	4	17-4	.293	.402	.432	.834	10	.966
— Cleveland (A.L.) 3B-2B-DH	21	52	12	14	3	1	0	4	6	6	2	1	1-0	.269	.367	.365	.732	6	.838
2003— Buffalo (Int'l) 3-D-2-1-C	132	500	63	145	33	2	10	68	40	53	6	5	5-3	.290	.346	.424	.770	22	.941
— Cleveland (A.L.)	3B-DH	5	9	3	3	1	0	0	0	1	1	0	0	0-0	.333	.400	.444	.844	0	1.000
American League totals (2 years)		26	61	15	17	4	1	0	4	7	7	2	1	1-0	.279	.371	.377	.748	6	.860
National League totals (1 year)		13	27	1	6	2	0	0	2	1	4	0	1	0-0	.222	.250	.296	.546	2	.917
Major League totals (3 years)		39	88	16	23	6	1	0	6	8	11	2	2	1-0	.261	.337	.352	.689	8	.881

LARSON, BRANDON — 3B

PERSONAL: Born May 24, 1976, in San Angelo, Texas. ... 6-0/210. ... Bats right, throws right. ... Full name: Brandon John Larson. ... High school: Holmes (San Antonio, Texas). ... College: Louisiana State.

TRANSACTIONS/CAREER NOTES: Selected by Pittsburgh Pirates organization in 46th round of free-agent draft (June 2, 1994); did not sign. ... Selected by Pittsburgh Pirates organization in 38th round of free-agent draft (June 1, 1995); did not sign. ... Selected by San Francisco Giants organization in 44th round of free-agent draft (June 4, 1996); did not sign. ... Selected by Cincinnati Reds organization in first round (14th pick overall) of free-agent draft (June 3, 1997). ... On Chattanooga disabled list (June 13-18, 1999). ... On Cincinnati disabled list (August 16-August 31 and September 4, 2002-remainder of season); included rehabilitation assignment to Louisville (August 28-31). ... Optioned to Louisville (April 19, 2003). ... Recalled from Louisville (July 17, 2003). ... Optioned to Louisville (July 26, 2003). ... Sent outright to Louisville (July 31, 2003). ... Recalled from Louisville (August 6, 2003). ... Placed on 15-day disabled list (August 18, 2003). ... Transferred to 60-day disabled list (September 2, 2003).

2003 GAMES PLAYED BY POSITION (MLB): 3B—24, OF—3.

Year	Team (League)	Pos.	G	AB	R	H	2B	3B	HR	RBI	BB	SO	HBP	GDP	SB-CS	Avg.	OBP	SLG	OPS	E	Pct.
1997— Chattanooga (Sou.)	SS	11	41	4	11	5	1	0	6	1	10	0	1	0-0	.268	.279	.439	.718	5	.891
1998— Burlington (Midw.)	3B	18	68	5	15	3	0	2	9	4	16	0	1	2-1	.221	.264	.353	.617	0	1.000
1999— Rockford (Midwest)	3B	69	250	38	75	18	1	13	52	25	67	3	7	12-2	.300	.367	.536	.903	18	.912
— Chattanooga (Sou.)	3B	43	172	28	49	10	0	12	42	10	51	3	3	4-5	.285	.332	.552	.884	15	.885
2000— Chattanooga (Sou.)	3B	111	427	61	116	26	0	20	64	31	122	8	8	15-5	.272	.330	.473	.804	24	.917
— Louisville (Int'l)	3B	17	63	11	18	7	1	2	4	4	16	0	1	0-0	.286	.328	.524	.852	4	.929
2001— Louisville (Int'l) 3B-SS-1B	115	424	61	108	22	2	14	55	24	123	12	15	5-6	.255	.312	.415	.727	20	.949
— Cincinnati (N.L.)	3B	14	33	2	4	2	0	0	1	2	10	0	1	0-0	.121	.171	.182	.353	2	.939
2002— Louisville (Int'l)	3B-OF	80	297	47	101	20	1	25	66	24	70	3	5	1-1	.340	.393	.667	1.059	17	.917
— Cincinnati (N.L.) OF-3B-1B	23	51	8	14	2	0	4	13	6	10	1	1	1-0	.275	.362	.549	.911	0	1.000
2003— Louisville (Int'l) 3B-1B-OF	72	282	51	91	19	2	20	74	28	70	2	7	3-0	.323	.384	.617	1.001	16	.936
— Cincinnati (N.L.)	3B-OF	32	89	6	9	1	0	1	9	13	31	0	2	2-2	.101	.212	.146	.358	4	.950
Major League totals (3 years)		69	173	16	27	5	0	5	23	21	51	1	4	3-2	.156	.249	.272	.520	6	.958

LaRUE, JASON — C

PERSONAL: Born March 19, 1974, in Houston, Texas. ... 5-11/200. ... Bats right, throws right. ... Full name: Michael Jason LaRue. ... Name pronounced: la-ROO. ... High school: Spring Valley (Spring Branch, Texas). ... College: Dallas Baptist (Texas).

TRANSACTIONS/CAREER NOTES: Selected by Cincinnati Reds organization in fifth round of free-agent draft (June 1, 1995). ... On disabled list (June 30-September 13, 1996). ... On disabled list (September 23, 2002-remainder of season).

2003 GAMES PLAYED BY POSITION (MLB): C—114, 1B—1, OF—1.

Year	Team (League)	Pos.	G	AB	R	H	2B	3B	HR	RBI	BB	SO	HBP	GDP	SB-CS	Avg.	OBP	SLG	OPS	E	Pct.
1995— Billings (Pio.)	C	58	183	35	50	8	1	5	31	16	28	12	2	3-5	.273	.366	.410	.776	8	.980
1996— Char., W.Va. (SAL)	C-1B	37	123	17	26	8	0	2	14	11	28	2	2	3-0	.211	.287	.325	.612	6	.979
1997— Char., W.Va. (SAL)	3-C-1-OF	132	473	78	149	50	3	8	81	47	90	5	8	14-4	.315	.377	.484	.861	19	.977
1998— Chattanooga (Sou.)	3B-C-1B	105	386	71	141	39	8	14	82	40	60	10	13	4-3	.365	.429	.617	1.046	10	.985
— Indianapolis (Int'l)	C	15	51	5	12	4	0	0	5	4	8	0	2	0-1	.235	.286	.314	.599	0	1.000
1999— Indianapolis (Int'l)	C-DH	70	263	42	66	12	2	12	37	15	52	4	13	0-3	.251	.299	.449	.748	7	.984
— Cincinnati (N.L.)	C	36	90	12	19	7	0	3	10	11	32	2	4	4-1	.211	.311	.389	.700	2	.990
2000— Louisville (Int'l)	C	82	307	54	78	22	1	14	48	22	52	8	4	3-2	.254	.320	.469	.790	8	.984
— Cincinnati (N.L.)	C	31	98	12	23	3	0	5	12	5	19	4	1	0-0	.235	.299	.418	.717	2	.991
2001— Cincinnati (N.L.) C-3-OF-1	121	364	39	86	21	2	12	43	27	106	9	11	3-3	.236	.303	.404	.707	7	.990
2002— Cincinnati (N.L.)	C	113	353	42	88	17	1	12	52	27	117	13	3	1-2	.249	.324	.405	.729	4	.994
2003— Cincinnati (N.L.)	C-1B-OF	118	379	52	87	23	1	16	50	33	111	20	9	3-3	.230	.321	.422	.743	11	.985
Major League totals (5 years)		419	1284	157	303	71	4	48	167	103	385	48	38	11-9	.236	.315	.410	.724	26	.990

LATHAM, CHRIS — OF

PERSONAL: Born May 26, 1973, in Coeur D'Alene, Idaho. ... 6-0/200. ... Bats both, throws right. ... Full name: Christopher Joseph Latham. ... Name pronounced: LAY-thum. ... High school: Basic Technical (Las Vegas).

TRANSACTIONS/CAREER NOTES: Selected by Los Angeles Dodgers organization in 11th round of free-agent draft (June 3, 1991). ... Traded by Dodgers to Minnesota Twins (October 30, 1995), completing deal in which Twins traded P Mark Guthrie and P Kevin Tapani to Dodgers for 1B/3B Ron Coomer, P Greg Hansell, P Jose Parra and a player to be named later (July 31, 1995). ... On disabled list (August 30-September 9, 1996). ... Traded by Twins to Colorado Rockies for P Scott Randall (December 7, 1999). ... Granted free agency (October 18, 2000). ... Signed by Toronto Blue Jays organization (December 2, 2000). ... Claimed on waivers by New York Mets (March 27, 2002). ... On Norfolk disabled list (May 1-8, 2002). ... Released by Mets (October 2, 2002). ... Signed by New York Yankees (December 4, 2002). ... Designated for assignment (April 21, 2003). ... Given unconditional release (April 24, 2003).

2003 GAMES PLAYED BY POSITION (MLB): OF—2, DH—1.

Year	Team (League)	Pos.	G	AB	R	H	2B	3B	HR	RBI	BB	SO	HBP	GDP	SB-CS	Avg.	OBP	SLG	OPS	E	Pct.
1991— GC Dodgers (GCL)		2B	43	109	17	26	2	1	0	11	16	45	0	0	14-4	.239	.333	.275	.609	10	.917
1992— Great Falls (Pio.)		2B	17	37	8	12	2	0	0	3	8	8	0	0	1-1	.324	.444	.378	.823	6	.872
— GC Dodgers (GCL)		2B-3B-SS	14	48	4	11	2	0	0	2	5	17	0	0	2-3	.229	.296	.271	.567	1	.976
1993— Yakima (N'west)		OF	54	192	46	50	2	*6	4	17	39	53	1	2	25-9	.260	.388	.396	.784	6	.936
— Bakersfield (Calif.)		OF	6	27	1	5	1	0	0	3	4	5	0	2	2-2	.185	.290	.222	.513	1	.923
1994— Bakersfield (Calif.)		OF	52	191	29	41	5	2	2	15	28	49	2	2	28-7	.215	.321	.293	.614	7	.929
— Yakima (N'west)		OF	71	288	*69	*98	19	*8	5	32	55	66	2	1	33-20	.340	.449	.514	.963	4	.974
1995— Vero Beach (FSL)		OF	71	259	53	74	13	4	6	39	56	54	2	2	42-11	.286	.413	.436	.849	7	.949
— San Antonio (Texas)		OF	58	214	38	64	14	5	9	37	33	59	2	2	11-11	.299	.386	.537	.933	4	.972
— Albuquerque (PCL)		OF	5	18	2	3	0	1	0	3	1	4	0	0	1-0	.167	.200	.278	.478	0	1.000
1996— Salt Lake (PCL)		OF-DH	115	376	59	103	16	6	9	50	36	91	2	5	26-9	.274	.338	.420	.758	9	.964
1997— Salt Lake (PCL)		OF	118	492	78	152	22	5	8	58	58	110	4	8	21-19	.309	.386	.423	.809	11	.961
— Minnesota (A.L.)		OF	15	22	4	4	1	0	0	1	0	8	0	0	0-0	.182	.182	.227	.409	1	.917
1998— Salt Lake (PCL)		OF-DH	97	377	81	122	21	4	11	51	56	99	1	5	29-5	.324	.412	.488	.901	9	.959
— Minnesota (A.L.)		OF	34	94	14	15	1	0	1	5	13	36	0	0	4-2	.160	.262	.202	.464	2	.972
1999— Minnesota (A.L.)		OF	14	22	1	2	0	0	0	3	0	13	0	0	0-0	.091	.083	.091	.174	0	1.000
— Salt Lake (PCL)		OF	94	382	93	123	24	8	15	51	54	95	1	5	18-13	.322	.405	.545	.950	6	.978
2000— Colo. Springs (PCL)		OF	126	339	76	83	16	6	7	49	71	105	2	8	29-7	.245	.373	.389	.763	7	.971
2001— Syracuse (Int'l)		OF	79	288	57	80	20	9	13	54	51	90	1	6	14-11	.278	.382	.545	.927	6	.965
— Toronto (A.L.)		OF	43	73	12	20	3	1	2	10	10	28	1	1	4-1	.274	.369	.425	.794	0	1.000
2002— Norfolk (Int'l)		OF	117	405	60	94	22	6	6	43	62	103	4	6	26-9	.232	.338	.360	.698	7	.974
2003— New York (A.L.)		OF-DH	4	2	3	2	0	0	0	0	0	0	0	0	1-0	1.000	1.000	1.000	2.000	0	1.000
Major League totals (5 years)			110	213	34	43	5	1	3	19	23	85	1	1	9-3	.202	.280	.277	.557	3	.980

LAWRENCE, BRIAN   P

PERSONAL: Born May 14, 1976, in Fort Collins, Colo. ... 6-0/195. ... Throws right, bats right. ... Full name: Brian Michael Lawrence. ... High school: Carthage (Texas). ... College: Northwestern State (La.).

TRANSACTIONS/CAREER NOTES: Selected by San Diego Padres organization in 17th round of free-agent draft (June 2, 1998).

CAREER HITTING: 24-for-156 (.154), 8 R, 6 2B, 0 3B, 1 HR, 14 RBI.

Year	League	W	L	Pct.	ERA	WHIP	G	GS	CG	ShO	Hld.	Sv.-Opp.	IP	H	R	ER	HR	BB-IBB	SO	Avg.
1998— Idaho Falls (Pioneer)	3	0	1.000	2.45	1.23	4	4	2	•1	...	0-...	22.0	22	7	6	1	5-0	21	.262
— Clinton (Midw.)	5	3	.625	2.80	0.00	12	12	2	0	...	0-...	80.1	67	34	25	5	13-0	79	.221
1999— Rancho Cuca. (Calif.)	12	8	.600	3.39	1.19	27	27	4	3	...	0-...	175.1	178	72	66	6	30-1	166	.265
2000— Mobile (Sou.)	7	6	.538	2.42	1.00	21	21	0	0	...	0-...	126.2	99	40	34	6	28-0	119	.217
— Las Vegas (PCL)	4	0	1.000	1.93	1.18	8	8	0	0	...	0-...	46.2	48	13	10	6	7-0	46	.264
2001— Portland (PCL)	1	3	.250	3.80	1.31	9	8	0	0	...	1-...	45.0	42	22	19	3	17-2	42	.239
— San Diego (N.L.)	5	5	.500	3.45	1.23	27	15	1	0	0	0-0	114.2	107	53	44	10	34-5	84	.244
2002— San Diego (N.L.)	12	12	.500	3.69	1.34	35	31	2	2	1	0-0	210.0	230	97	86	16	52-6	149	.281
2003— San Diego (N.L.)	10	15	.400	4.19	1.25	33	33	1	0	0	0-0	210.2	206	106	98	27	57-8	116	.258
Major League totals (3 years)	27	32	.458	3.83	1.28	95	79	4	2	1	0-0	535.1	543	256	228	53	143-19	349	.264

LAWTON, MATT   OF

PERSONAL: Born November 3, 1971, in Gulfport, Miss. ... 5-10/195. ... Bats left, throws right. ... Full name: Matthew Lawton III. ... Name pronounced: LAW-ton. ... High school: Harrison Central (Gulfport, Miss.). ... Junior college: Mississippi Gulf Coast College.

TRANSACTIONS/CAREER NOTES: Selected by Minnesota Twins organization in 13th round of free-agent draft (June 3, 1991). ... On Minnesota disabled list (June 9-July 18, 1999); included rehabilitation assignments to Fort Myers (July 12-16) and Gulf Coast Twins (July 17-18). ... Traded by Twins to New York Mets for P Rick Reed (July 30, 2001). ... Traded by Mets with OF Alex Escobar, P Jerrod Riggan and two players to be named later to Cleveland Indians for 2B Roberto Alomar, P Mike Bacsik and OF Danny Peoples (December 11, 2001); Indians acquired P Billy Traber and 1B Earl Snyder to complete deal (December 13, 2001). ... On Cleveland disabled list (July 12-July 27 and September 4, 2002-remainder of season); included rehabilitation assignment to Akron (July 23-27). ... Placed on the 15-day disabled list (July 12, 2003). ... Sent to Akron on rehab assignment (August 6, 2003). ... Recalled from Akron rehab assignment (August 8, 2003). ... Sent to Akron on rehab assignment (August 15, 2003). ... Recalled from Akron rehab assignment; removed from 15-day disabled list (August 18, 2003). ... Placed on 15-day disabled list (September 9, 2003).

2003 GAMES PLAYED BY POSITION (MLB): OF—74, DH—21.

Year	Team (League)	Pos.	G	AB	R	H	2B	3B	HR	RBI	BB	SO	HBP	GDP	SB-CS	Avg.	OBP	SLG	OPS	E	Pct.
1992— GC Twins (GCL)		2B	53	173	39	45	8	3	2	26	27	27	9	2	20-1	.260	.375	.376	.751	12	.958
1993— Fort Wayne (Midw.)		OF	111	340	50	97	21	3	9	38	65	42	8	8	23-15	.285	.410	.444	.854	3	.959
1994— Fort Myers (FSL)		OF	122	446	79	134	30	1	7	51	80	64	2	7	42-19	.300	*.407	.419	.826	6	.971
1995— New Britain (East.)		OF-DH	114	412	75	111	19	5	13	54	56	70	12	8	26-9	.269	.371	.434	.805	2	.991
— Minnesota (A.L.)		OF-DH	21	60	11	19	4	1	1	12	7	11	3	1	1-1	.317	.414	.467	.881	1	.972
1996— Minnesota (A.L.)		OF-DH	79	252	34	65	7	1	6	42	28	28	4	6	4-4	.258	.339	.365	.704	3	.985
— Salt Lake (PCL)		OF-DH	53	212	40	63	16	1	7	33	26	34	3	2	2-4	.297	.379	.481	.860	6	.936
1997— Minnesota (A.L.)		OF	142	460	74	114	29	3	14	60	76	81	10	7	7-4	.248	.366	.415	.781	4	.976
1998— Minnesota (A.L.)		OF	152	557	91	155	36	6	21	77	86	64	15	10	16-8	.278	.387	.478	.864	4	.990
1999— Minnesota (A.L.)		OF-DH	118	406	58	105	18	0	7	54	57	42	6	11	26-4	.259	.353	.355	.708	4	.982
— Fort Myers (FSL)		OF	4	14	3	8	1	0	0	2	3	1	0	0	1-0	.571	.647	.643	1.290	0	1.000
— GC Twins (GCL)		OF	1	4	0	1	0	0	0	1	0	2	0	0	0-0	.250	.250	.250	.500	0	1.000
2000— Minnesota (A.L.)		OF-DH	156	561	84	171	44	2	13	88	91	63	7	10	23-7	.305	.405	.460	.865	5	.983
2001— Minnesota (A.L.)		OF-DH	103	376	71	110	25	0	10	51	60	43	3	14	19-6	.293	.396	.439	.835	4	.980
— New York (N.L.)		OF	48	183	24	45	11	1	3	13	22	34	8	2	10-2	.246	.352	.366	.718	0	1.000
2002— Cleveland (A.L.)		OF-DH	114	416	71	98	19	2	15	57	59	34	8	13	8-9	.236	.342	.399	.741	6	.975
— Akron (East.)		OF	3	10	1	0	0	0	0	0	3	1	0	0	0-0	.000	.231	.000	.231	0	1.000
2003— Akron (East.)		DH	5	19	1	1	0	0	0	1	2	6	0	1	0-0	.053	.143	.053	.195	0	.000
— Cleveland (A.L.)		OF-DH	99	374	57	93	19	0	15	53	47	47	7	8	10-3	.249	.343	.420	.762	1	.993
American League totals (9 years)			984	3462	551	930	201	15	102	494	514	416	63	80	114-46	.269	.371	.424	.795	35	.983
National League totals (1 year)			48	183	24	45	11	1	3	13	22	34	8	2	10-2	.246	.352	.366	.718	0	1.000
Major League totals (9 years)			1032	3645	575	975	212	16	105	507	536	450	71	82	124-48	.267	.370	.421	.791	35	.984

LeCROY, MATTHEW — DH/C

PERSONAL: Born December 13, 1975, in Belton, S.C. ... 6-2/225. ... Bats right, throws right. ... Full name: Matthew Hanks LeCroy. ... Name pronounced: LEE-croy. ... High school: Belton-Honea Path (S.C.). ... College: Clemson.

TRANSACTIONS/CAREER NOTES: Selected by Minnesota Twins organization in supplemental round ("sandwich pick" between first and second round, 50th pick overall) of free-agent draft (June 3, 1997); pick received as compensation for failure to sign 1996 first-round pick Travis Lee. ... On Salt Lake disabled list (September 10, 1999-remainder of season). ... On Edmonton disabled list (May 25-June 4 and June 5-23, 2001).

2003 GAMES PLAYED BY POSITION (MLB): DH—64, C—22, 1B—17.

Year Team (League)	Pos.	G	AB	R	H	2B	3B	HR	RBI	BB	SO	HBP	GDP	SB-CS	Avg.	OBP	SLG	OPS	E	Pct.
1998— Fort Wayne (Midw.)	C	64	225	33	62	17	1	9	40	34	45	8	9	0-0	.276	.387	.480	.867	1	.997
— Fort Myers (FSL)	C	51	200	32	61	9	1	12	51	21	35	4	6	2-1	.305	.372	.540	.912	3	.991
— Salt Lake (PCL)	C	3	13	2	4	1	0	2	4	0	7	0	0	0-0	.308	.308	.846	1.154	0	1.000
1999— Fort Myers (FSL)	C	89	333	54	93	20	1	20	69	42	51	3	10	0-0	.279	.364	.526	.890	8	.983
— Salt Lake (PCL)	C	29	119	23	36	4	1	10	30	5	22	1	8	0-1	.303	.331	.605	.936	0	1.000
2000— Minnesota (A.L.)	C-DH-1B	56	167	18	29	10	0	5	17	17	38	2	6	0-0	.174	.254	.323	.577	4	.989
— New Britain (East.)	C	54	195	33	55	12	1	10	38	29	34	6	8	0-0	.282	.391	.508	.899	10	.970
— Salt Lake (PCL)	C-1B	16	65	15	20	5	0	5	15	4	11	0	4	0-0	.308	.348	.615	.963	0	1.000
2001— Edmonton (PCL)	C-1B	101	396	53	130	17	0	20	80	36	95	6	8	0-2	.328	.390	.523	.913	5	.980
— Minnesota (A.L.)	DH-C-1B	15	40	6	17	5	0	3	12	0	8	1	0	0-1	.425	.429	.775	1.204	0	1.000
2002— Edmonton (PCL)	C-1B	46	174	36	61	7	1	12	50	17	34	4	1	2-0	.351	.412	.609	1.021	1	.993
— Minnesota (A.L.)	DH-1B-C	63	181	19	47	11	1	7	27	13	38	0	5	0-2	.260	.306	.448	.754	1	.984
2003— Minnesota (A.L.)	DH-C-1B	107	345	39	99	19	0	17	64	25	82	4	8	0-1	.287	.342	.490	.832	3	.985
Major League totals (4 years)		241	733	82	192	45	1	32	120	55	166	7	19	0-4	.262	.317	.457	.774	8	.987

LEDEE, RICKY — OF

PERSONAL: Born November 22, 1973, in Ponce, Puerto Rico. ... 6-1/200. ... Bats left, throws left. ... Full name: Ricardo Alberto Ledee. ... Name pronounced: la-DAY. ... High school: Colonel Nuestra Sonora de Valvanera (Coano, Puerto Rico).

TRANSACTIONS/CAREER NOTES: Selected by New York Yankees organization in 16th round of free-agent draft (June 3, 1990). ... On Tampa disabled list (April 6-May 27, 1996). ... On Columbus disabled list (May 5-16 and May 22-August 4, 1997; and May 25-June 3, 1999). ... Traded by Yankees with two players to be named later to Cleveland Indians for OF David Justice (June 29, 2000); Indians acquired P Jake Westbrook and P Zach Day to complete deal (July 24, 2000). ... Traded by Indians to Texas Rangers for 1B/DH David Segui (July 28, 2000). ... On Texas disabled list (March 23-June 13, 2001); included rehabilitation assignment to Oklahoma (June 9-13). ... Granted free agency (December 21, 2001). ... Signed by Philadelphia Phillies (January 29, 2002).

2003 GAMES PLAYED BY POSITION (MLB): OF—71, DH—2.

Year Team (League)	Pos.	G	AB	R	H	2B	3B	HR	RBI	BB	SO	HBP	GDP	SB-CS	Avg.	OBP	SLG	OPS	E	Pct.
1990— GC Yankees (GCL)	OF	19	37	5	4	2	0	0	1	6	18	0	1	2-0	.108	.233	.162	.395	0	1.000
1991— GC Yankees (GCL)	OF	47	165	22	44	6	2	0	18	22	40	0	3	3-1	.267	.351	.327	.678	6	.934
1992— GC Yankees (GCL)	OF	52	179	25	41	9	2	2	23	24	47	1	2	1-4	.229	.322	.335	.657	2	.971
1993— Oneonta (NYP)	OF	52	192	32	49	7	6	8	20	25	46	2	2	7-5	.255	.347	.479	.826	3	.970
1994— Greensboro (S. Atl.)	OF	134	484	87	121	23	9	22	71	91	126	4	7	10-11	.250	.369	.471	.840	5	.973
1995— Greensboro (S. Atl.)	OF	89	335	65	90	16	6	14	49	51	66	2	3	10-4	.269	.368	.478	.845	3	.982
1996— Norwich (East.)	OF	39	137	27	50	11	1	8	37	16	25	1	4	2-2	.365	.421	.635	1.056	1	.980
— Columbus (Int'l)	OF	96	358	79	101	22	6	21	64	44	95	1	4	6-3	.282	.360	.553	.914	5	.952
1997— Columbus (Int'l)	OF-DH	43	170	38	52	12	1	10	39	21	49	1	5	4-0	.306	.385	.565	.950	2	.966
— GC Yankees (GCL)	DH-OF	7	21	3	7	1	0	0	2	2	4	1	1	0-0	.333	.417	.381	.798	0	1.000
1998— Columbus (Int'l)	OF-DH	96	360	70	102	21	1	19	41	54	108	4	7	7-2	.283	.378	.506	.884	4	.971
— New York (A.L.)	OF	42	79	13	19	5	2	1	12	7	29	0	1	3-1	.241	.299	.392	.691	1	.981
1999— New York (A.L.)	OF-DH	88	250	45	69	13	5	9	40	28	73	0	2	4-3	.276	.346	.476	.822	9	.942
— Columbus (Int'l)	OF	30	115	18	29	7	1	4	15	17	29	1	1	4-2	.252	.346	.435	.781	3	.953
2000— New York (A.L.)	OF-DH	62	191	23	46	11	1	7	31	26	39	1	7	7-3	.241	.332	.419	.751	2	.979
— Cleveland (A.L.)	OF	17	63	13	14	2	1	2	8	8	9	0	3	0-0	.222	.310	.381	.691	0	1.000
— Texas (A.L.)	OF	58	213	23	50	6	3	4	38	25	50	1	7	6-3	.235	.317	.347	.664	3	.977
2001— Oklahoma (PCL)	OF	4	16	4	8	1	0	1	3	1	1	0	1	0-0	.500	.529	.750	1.279	0	1.000
— Texas (A.L.)	OF	78	242	33	56	21	1	2	36	23	58	3	3	3-3	.231	.303	.351	.654	3	.979
2002— Philadelphia (N.L.)	OF	96	203	33	46	13	1	8	23	35	50	1	3	1-2	.227	.342	.419	.760	0	1.000
2003— Philadelphia (N.L.)	OF-DH	121	255	37	63	15	2	13	46	34	59	0	4	0-0	.247	.334	.475	.809	0	1.000
American League totals (4 years)		345	1038	150	254	58	13	25	165	117	258	5	23	23-13	.245	.322	.398	.720	18	.971
National League totals (2 years)		217	458	70	109	28	3	21	69	69	109	1	7	1-2	.238	.338	.450	.788	0	1.000
Major League totals (6 years)		562	1496	220	363	86	16	46	234	186	367	6	30	24-15	.243	.327	.414	.740	18	.978

LEDEZMA, WILFREDO — P

PERSONAL: Born January 21, 1981, in Guarico, Venezuela. ... 6-3/150. ... Throws left, bats left. ... Full name: Wilfredo J. Ledezma. ... College: Cuidad Jardin University.

TRANSACTIONS/CAREER NOTES: Signed as non-drafted free agent by Boston Red Sox organization (April 3, 1998). ... On disabled list (June 19, 2001-entire season). ... On Augusta disabled list (May 22-September 3, 2002). ... Selected by Detroit Tigers from Red Sox organization in Rule 5 major league draft (December 16, 2002).

CAREER HITTING: 0-for-0 (.000), 0 R, 0 2B, 0 3B, 0 HR, 0 RBI.

Year League	W	L	Pct.	ERA	WHIP	G	GS	CG	ShO	Hld.	Sv.-Opp.	IP	H	R	ER	HR	BB-IBB	SO	Avg.
1999— GC Red Sox (GCL)	5	1	.833	3.30	1.24	13	6	0	0	...	1-...	57.1	51	28	21	2	20-0	52	.233
2000— Augusta (S. Atl.)	2	4	.333	5.13	1.65	14	14	0	0	...	0-...	52.2	51	33	30	3	36-0	60	.256
2001—										Did not play.									
2002— Augusta (S. Atl.)	2	2	.500	3.80	1.31	5	5	0	0	...	0-...	23.2	23	10	10	0	8-0	38	.250
— GC Red Sox (GCL)	0	0	...	6.00	1.33	1	0	0	0	...	0-...	3.0	4	2	2	0	0-0	3	.308
2003— Detroit (A.L.)	3	7	.300	5.79	1.60	34	8	0	0	1	0-1	84.0	99	55	54	12	35-3	49	.297
Major League totals (1 year)	3	7	.300	5.79	1.60	34	8	0	0	1	0-1	84.0	99	55	54	12	35-3	49	.297

LEE, CARLOS — OF

PERSONAL: Born June 20, 1976, in Aguadulce, Panama. ... 6-2/235. ... Bats right, throws right. ... Full name: Carlos Noriel Lee.

TRANSACTIONS/CAREER NOTES: Signed as non-drafted free agent by Chicago White Sox organization (February 8, 1994). ... On suspended list (April 28-May 1, 2000).

2003 GAMES PLAYED BY POSITION (MLB): OF—156, DH—1.

L

Year	Team (League)	Pos.	G	AB	R	H	2B	3B	HR	RBI	BB	SO	HBP	GDP	SB-CS	Avg.	OBP	SLG	OPS	E	Pct.
1994—GC Whi. Sox (GCL)	3B	29	56	6	7	1	0	0	1	4	8	0	1	0-1	.125	.183	.143	.326	2	.959
1995—Hickory (S. Atl.)	3B	63	218	18	54	9	1	4	30	8	34	1	7	1-5	.248	.278	.353	.631	19	.848
—Bristol (Appal.)	3B-1B	•67	269	43	*93	17	1	7	45	8	34	2	6	17-7	.346	.365	.494	.860	18	.914
1996—Hickory (S. Atl.)	3B-1B	119	480	65	150	23	6	8	70	23	50	0	15	18-13	.313	.337	.435	.772	32	.923
1997—Win.-Salem (Car.)	3B-DH	*139	546	81	*173	*50	4	17	82	36	65	2	12	11-5	.317	.357	.516	.874	34	.906
1998—Birmingham (Sou.)	3B-DH	138	549	77	166	33	2	21	106	39	55	2	32	11-5	.302	.350	.485	.834	*35	.902
1999—Charlotte (Int'l)	3B-OF-1B	25	94	16	33	5	0	4	20	8	14	1	3	2-1	.351	.396	.532	.928	4	.951
—Chicago (A.L.)	OF-DH-1B	127	492	66	144	32	2	16	84	13	72	4	11	4-2	.293	.312	.463	.775	5	.979
2000—Chicago (A.L.)	OF-DH	152	572	107	172	29	2	24	92	38	94	3	17	13-4	.301	.345	.484	.829	3	.990
2001—Chicago (A.L.)	OF-DH	150	558	75	150	33	3	24	84	38	85	6	15	17-7	.269	.321	.468	.789	8	.969
2002—Chicago (A.L.)	OF-DH	140	492	82	130	26	2	26	80	75	73	2	5	1-4	.264	.359	.484	.843	1	.990
2003—Chicago (A.L.)	OF-DH	158	623	100	181	35	1	31	113	37	91	4	20	18-4	.291	.331	.499	.830	7	.978
Major League totals (5 years)		727	2737	430	777	155	10	121	453	201	415	19	68	53-21	.284	.334	.480	.814	24	.982

LEE, CLIFF   P

PERSONAL: Born August 30, 1978, in Benton, Ark. ... 6-3/190. ... Throws left, bats left. ... Full name: Clifton Phifer Lee. ... High school: Benton (Ark.). ... College: Arkansas.

TRANSACTIONS/CAREER NOTES: Selected by Montreal Expos organization in fourth round of free-agent draft (June 5, 2000). ... Traded by Expos with 1B Lee Stevens, SS Brandon Phillips and OF Grady Sizemore to Cleveland Indians for P Bartolo Colon and future considerations (June 27, 2002); Expos acquired P Tim Drew to complete deal (June 28, 2002). ... On disabled list (March 29, 2003). ... Optioned to Akron (May 30, 2003). ... Sent to Kinston for rehab assignment (May 29, 2003). ... Reinstated from the Emergency disabled list (May 30, 2003). ... Recalled from Buffalo (June 29, 2003). ... Optioned to Buffalo (June 30, 2003). ... Recalled from Buffalo (August 16, 2003).

CAREER HITTING: 0-for-6 (.000), 0 R, 0 2B, 0 3B, 0 HR, 0 RBI.

Year	League	W	L	Pct.	ERA	WHIP	G	GS	CG	ShO	Hld.	Sv.-Opp.	IP	H	R	ER	HR	BB-IBB	SO	Avg.
2000—Cape Fear (S. Atl.)	1	4	.200	5.24	1.93	11	11	0	0	...	0-...	44.2	50	39	26	1	36-0	63	.281
2001—Jupiter (FSL)	6	7	.462	2.79	1.13	21	20	0	0	...	0-...	109.2	78	43	34	13	46-0	129	.199
2002—Harrisburg (Eastern)	7	2	.778	3.23	0.97	15	15	0	0	...	0-...	86.1	61	31	31	12	23-0	105	.197
—Akron (East.)	2	1	.667	5.40	1.26	3	3	0	0	...	0-...	16.2	11	11	10	1	10-0	18	.180
—Buffalo (Int'l)	3	2	.600	3.77	1.35	8	8	0	0	...	0-...	43.0	36	18	18	7	22-0	30	.229
—Cleveland (A.L.)	0	1	.000	1.74	1.35	2	2	0	0	0	0-0	10.1	6	2	2	0	8-1	6	.171
2003—Kinston (Caro.)	0	0	...	0.00	0.69	1	1	0	0	...	0-...	4.1	0	1	0	0	3-0	4	.000
—Akron (East.)	1	0	1.000	1.50	0.92	2	2	0	0	...	0-...	12.0	7	2	2	1	4-0	13	.167
—Buffalo (Int'l)	6	1	.857	3.27	1.47	11	11	0	0	...	0-...	63.1	62	24	23	4	31-0	61	.261
—Cleveland (A.L.)	3	3	.500	3.61	1.17	9	9	0	0	0	0-0	52.1	41	28	21	7	20-1	44	.220
Major League totals (2 years)	3	4	.429	3.30	1.20	11	11	0	0	0	0-0	62.2	47	30	23	7	28-2	50	.213

LEE, DAVID   P

PERSONAL: Born March 12, 1973, in Pittsburgh, Pa. ... 6-1/202. ... Throws right, bats right. ... Full name: David Emmer Lee. ... High school: Langley (Pittsburgh). ... College: Mercyhurst (Pa.).

TRANSACTIONS/CAREER NOTES: Selected by Colorado Rockies organization in 23rd round of free-agent draft (June 1, 1995). ... On Colorado Springs disabled list (July 13-22, 2000). ... Traded by Rockies to New York Yankees for P Jay Tessmer and SS Seth Taylor (January 3, 2001). ... Traded by Yankees to San Diego Padres for P Carlos Almanzar (March 25, 2001). ... On San Diego disabled list (July 25-August 31, 2001); included rehabilitation assignment to Mobile (August 25-29). ... Signed by Minnesota Twins organization (January 29, 2002). ... Granted free agency (October 15, 2002). ... Signed by Los Angeles Dodgers organization (December 29, 2002). ... Traded by Dodgers to Cleveland Indians for OF Alex Requena (September 6, 2003).

CAREER HITTING: 1-for-6 (.167), 1 R, 0 2B, 0 3B, 0 HR, 0 RBI.

Year	League	W	L	Pct.	ERA	WHIP	G	GS	CG	ShO	Hld.	Sv.-Opp.	IP	H	R	ER	HR	BB-IBB	SO	Avg.
1996—Portland (NW)	5	1	.833	0.78	1.26	17	0	0	0	...	7-...	23.0	13	3	2	0	16-3	24	.171
—Salem (Caro.)	0	2	.000	2.25	1.67	8	0	0	0	...	1-...	12.0	14	6	3	1	6-0	10	.292
1997—Asheville (S. Atl.)	4	8	.333	4.08	1.58	51	0	0	0	...	22-...	53.0	61	30	24	5	23-0	59	.289
1998—Salem (Caro.)	3	5	.375	3.77	1.26	54	0	0	0	...	25-...	57.1	57	26	24	2	15-1	54	.261
1999—Carolina (Sou.)	0	0	...	1.04	0.63	16	0	0	0	...	10-...	17.1	8	3	2	1	3-0	16	.136
—Colorado (N.L.)	3	2	.600	3.67	1.47	36	0	0	0	2	0-...	49.0	43	21	20	4	29-1	38	.247
—Colo. Springs (PCL)	0	0	...	0.00	0.18	6	0	0	0	...	3-...	5.2	0	0	0	0	1-0	7	.000
2000—Colorado (N.L.)	0	0	...	11.12	2.82	7	0	0	0	1	1-1	5.2	10	9	7	3	6-0	6	.357
—Colo. Springs (PCL)	2	3	.400	5.96	1.61	47	0	0	0	...	12-...	48.1	50	38	32	9	28-1	44	.265
2001—Portland (PCL)	1	0	1.000	0.75	0.83	9	0	0	0	...	1-...	12.0	5	1	1	0	5-1	14	.132
—San Diego (N.L.)	1	0	1.000	3.70	1.62	41	0	0	0	4	0-0	48.2	52	20	20	6	27-1	42	.278
—Mobile (Sou.)	0	0	...	0.00	1.00	2	0	0	0	...	0-...	2.0	2	0	0	0	0-0	3	.286
2002—Edmonton (PCL)	9	1	.900	4.59	1.72	51	0	0	0	...	5-...	64.2	80	44	33	7	31-3	70	.296
2003—Las Vegas (PCL)	3	2	.600	3.13	1.38	56	0	0	0	...	9-...	60.1	47	22	21	4	36-3	61	.232
—Cleveland (A.L.)	1	0	1.000	4.70	1.30	8	0	0	0	1	0-0	7.2	4	4	4	1	6-1	7	.143
American League totals (1 year)	1	0	1.000	4.70	1.30	8	0	0	0	1	0-0	7.2	4	4	4	1	6-1	7	.143
National League totals (3 years)	4	2	.667	4.09	1.62	84	0	0	0	7	1-1	103.1	105	50	47	13	62-2	86	.270
Major League totals (4 years)	5	2	.714	4.14	1.59	92	0	0	0	8	1-1	111.0	109	54	51	14	68-3	93	.261

LEE, DEREK   1B

PERSONAL: Born September 6, 1975, in Sacramento, Calif. ... 6-5/248. ... Bats right, throws right. ... Full name: Derrek Leon Lee. ... High school: El Camino (Sacramento).

TRANSACTIONS/CAREER NOTES: Selected by San Diego Padres in first round (14th pick overall) of free-agent draft (June 1, 1993). ... Traded by Padres with P Rafael Medina and P Steve Hoff to Florida Marlins for P Kevin Brown (December 15, 1997).

2003 GAMES PLAYED BY POSITION (MLB): 1B—155.

Year	Team (League)	Pos.	G	AB	R	H	2B	3B	HR	RBI	BB	SO	HBP	GDP	SB-CS	Avg.	OBP	SLG	OPS	E	Pct.
1993—Ariz. Padres (Ariz.)	1B	15	52	11	17	1	1	2	5	6	7	0	1	4-0	.327	.397	.500	.897	2	.985
—Rancho Cuca. (Calif.)	DH-1B	20	73	13	20	5	1	1	10	10	20	1	0	0-2	.274	.369	.411	.780	5	.960
1994—Rancho Cuca. (Calif.)	DH-1B	126	442	66	118	19	2	8	53	42	95	7	11	18-14	.267	.336	.373	.709	4	.988
1995—Rancho Cuca. (Calif.)	1B	128	502	82	151	25	2	23	95	49	130	7	8	14-7	.301	.366	.496	.862	*18	.983
—Memphis (Sou.)	1B	2	9	0	1	0	0	0	1	0	2	0	0	0-0	.111	.111	.111	.222	0	1.000
1996—Memphis (Sou.) 1B-3B-DH	134	500	98	140	39	2	34	*104	65	170	2	8	13-6	.280	.360	.530	.930	11	.991
1997—Las Vegas (PCL)	1B	125	472	86	153	29	2	13	64	60	116	0	9	17-3	.324	.399	.477	.876	9	.992
—San Diego (N.L.)	1B	22	54	9	14	3	0	1	4	9	24	0	1	0-0	.259	.365	.370	.735	0	1.000

Year	Team (League)	Pos.	G	AB	R	H	2B	3B	HR	RBI	BB	SO	HBP	GDP	SB-CS	Avg.	OBP	SLG	OPS	E	Pct.
1998— Florida (N.L.)	1B	141	454	62	106	29	1	17	74	47	120	10	12	5-2	.233	.318	.414	.732	8	.993
1999— Florida (N.L.)	1B	70	218	21	45	9	1	5	20	17	70	0	3	2-1	.206	.263	.326	.588	3	.994
— Calgary (PCL)	1B-DH	89	339	60	96	20	1	19	73	30	90	4	7	3-4	.283	.345	.516	.861	14	.983
2000— Florida (N.L.)	1B	158	477	70	134	18	3	28	70	63	123	4	14	0-3	.281	.368	.507	.875	8	.993
2001— Florida (N.L.)	1B	158	561	83	158	37	4	21	75	50	126	8	18	4-2	.282	.346	.474	.820	8	.994
2002— Florida (N.L.)	1B	•162	581	95	157	35	7	27	86	98	164	5	14	19-9	.270	.378	.494	.872	12	.992
2003— Florida (N.L.)	1B	155	539	91	146	31	2	31	92	88	131	10	9	21-8	.271	.379	.508	.888	5	.996
Major League totals (7 years)		866	2884	431	760	162	18	130	421	372	758	37	71	51-25	.264	.353	.467	.820	44	.994

LEE, TRAVIS — 1B

PERSONAL: Born May 26, 1975, in San Diego, Calif. ... 6-3/225. ... Bats left, throws left. ... Full name: Travis Reynolds Lee. ... High school: Olympia (Wash.). ... College: San Diego State.

TRANSACTIONS/CAREER NOTES: Selected by Minnesota Twins organization in first round (second pick overall) of free-agent draft (June 4, 1996). ... Granted free agency (June 19, 1996). ... Signed by Arizona Diamondbacks organization (October 15, 1996). ... Loaned by Diamondbacks organization to Tucson, Milwaukee Brewers (June 5, 1997-remainder of season). ... On disabled list (July 25-August 9, 1998; and August 16-September 9, 1999). ... On Arizona disabled list (May 25-June 9, 2000); included rehabilitation assignment to El Paso (June 5-9). ... Traded by Diamondbacks with P Vicente Padilla, P Omar Daal and P Nelson Figueroa to Philadelphia Phillies for P Curt Schilling (July 26, 2000). ... Granted free agency (December 21, 2002). ... Signed by Tampa Bay Devil Rays (February 6, 2003). ... On disabled list (April 14-29, 2003). ... Reinstated from the 15-day disabled list (April 29, 2003).

2003 GAMES PLAYED BY POSITION (MLB): 1B—142, DH—2.

Year	Team (League)	Pos.	G	AB	R	H	2B	3B	HR	RBI	BB	SO	HBP	GDP	SB-CS	Avg.	OBP	SLG	OPS	E	Pct.
1997— High Desert (Calif.)	1B-DH	61	226	63	82	18	1	18	63	47	36	3	8	5-1	.363	.473	.690	1.163	1	.998
— Tucson (PCL)	1B-DH-OF	59	227	42	68	16	2	14	46	31	46	2	10	2-0	.300	.387	.573	.960	3	.993
1998— Arizona (N.L.)	1B	146	562	71	151	20	2	22	72	67	123	0	13	8-1	.269	.346	.429	.775	3	.998
1999— Arizona (N.L.)	1B-OF	120	375	57	89	16	2	9	50	58	50	0	10	17-3	.237	.337	.363	.700	3	.997
2000— Arizona (N.L.)	OF-1B	72	224	34	52	13	0	8	40	25	46	0	6	5-1	.232	.308	.397	.705	4	.983
— El Paso (Texas)	1B-OF	3	10	0	2	0	0	0	0	2	1	0	1	0-0	.200	.333	.200	.533	0	1.000
— Tucson (PCL)	1B-OF	7	30	4	11	4	0	0	3	1	6	0	1	1-0	.367	.387	.500	.887	0	1.000
— Philadelphia (N.L.)	1B-OF	56	180	19	43	11	1	1	14	40	33	2	6	3-0	.239	.381	.328	.709	0	1.000
2001— Philadelphia (N.L.)	1B	157	555	75	143	34	2	20	90	71	104	4	15	3-4	.258	.341	.434	.775	6	.996
2002— Philadelphia (N.L.)	1B	153	536	55	142	26	2	13	70	54	104	0	12	5-3	.265	.331	.394	.725	6	.996
2003— Tampa Bay (A.L.)	1B-DH	145	542	75	149	37	3	19	70	64	97	0	13	6-2	.275	.348	.459	.807	3	.998
American League totals (1 year)		145	542	75	149	37	3	19	70	64	97	0	13	6-2	.275	.348	.459	.807	3	.998
National League totals (5 years)		704	2432	311	620	120	9	73	336	315	465	6	62	41-12	.255	.340	.402	.741	22	.996
Major League totals (6 years)		849	2974	386	769	157	12	92	406	379	562	6	75	47-14	.259	.341	.412	.753	25	.996

LEITER, AL — P

PERSONAL: Born October 23, 1965, in Toms River, N.J. ... 6-3/220. ... Throws left, bats left. ... Full name: Alois Terry Leiter. ... Name pronounced: LIGH-ter. ... High school: Central Regional (Bayville, N.J.).

TRANSACTIONS/CAREER NOTES: Selected by New York Yankees organization in second round of free-agent draft (June 4, 1984). ... On New York disabled list (June 22-July 26, 1988; included rehabilitation assignment to Columbus (July 17-25). ... Traded by Yankees to Toronto Blue Jays for OF Jesse Barfield (April 30, 1989). ... On Toronto disabled list (May 11, 1989-remainder of season); included rehabilitation assignment to Dunedin (August 12-29). ... On Syracuse disabled list (May 20-June 13, 1990). ... On Toronto disabled list (April 27, 1991-remainder of season); included rehabilitation assignments to Dunedin (May 20-28 and July 19-August 7). ... On disabled list (April 24-May 9, 1993; and June 9-24, 1994). ... Granted free agency (November 6, 1995). ... Signed by Florida Marlins (December 14, 1995). ... On disabled list (May 1-20 and August 13-29, 1997). ... Traded by Marlins with 2B Ralph Milliard to New York Mets for P Jesus Sanchez, P A.J. Burnett and OF Robert Stratton (February 6, 1998). ... On disabled list (June 27-July 18, 1998; and April 21-May 18, 2001). ... Placed on the 15-day disabled list, retroactive to June 30 (July 7, 2003). ... Reinstated from 15-day disabled list (July 20, 2003).

CAREER HITTING: 40-for-458 (.087), 15 R, 6 2B, 1 3B, 0 HR, 16 RBI.

Year	League	W	L	Pct.	ERA	WHIP	G	GS	CG	ShO	Hld.	Sv.-Opp.	IP	H	R	ER	HR	BB-IBB	SO	Avg.
1984— Oneonta (N.Y.-Penn)	3	2	.600	3.63	1.37	10	10	0	0	...	0-...	57.0	52	32	23	1	26-0	48	.241
1985— Fort Lauderdale (FSL)	1	6	.143	6.48	1.76	17	17	1	0	...	0-...	82.0	87	70	59	3	57-1	44	.270
— Oneonta (N.Y.-Penn)	3	2	.600	2.37	1.37	6	6	2	0	...	0-...	38.0	27	14	10	0	25-0	34	.213
1986— Fort Lauderdale (FSL)	4	8	.333	4.05	1.58	22	21	1	1	...	0-...	117.2	96	64	53	2	90-1	101	.226
1987— Columbus (Int'l)	1	4	.200	6.17	1.54	5	5	0	0	...	0-...	23.1	21	18	16	1	15-0	23	.250
— Alb./Colon. (East.)	3	3	.500	3.35	1.29	15	14	2	0	...	0-...	78.0	64	34	29	4	37-0	71	.227
— New York (A.L.)	2	2	.500	6.35	1.72	4	4	0	0	0	0-0	22.2	24	16	16	2	15-0	28	.273
1988— New York (A.L.)	4	4	.500	3.92	1.43	14	14	0	0	0	0-0	57.1	49	27	25	7	33-0	60	.231
— Columbus (Int'l)	0	2	.000	3.46	1.46	4	4	0	0	...	0-...	13.0	5	7	5	0	14-0	12	.122
1989— New York (A.L.)	1	2	.333	6.08	1.65	4	4	0	0	0	0-0	26.2	23	20	18	1	21-0	22	.235
— Toronto (A.L.)	0	0	...	4.05	1.65	1	1	0	0	0	0-0	6.2	9	3	3	1	2-0	4	.310
— Dunedin (Fla. St.)	0	2	.000	5.63	2.00	3	3	0	0	...	0-...	8.0	11	5	5	0	5-0	4	.324
1990— Dunedin (Fla. St.)	0	0	...	2.63	1.25	6	6	0	0	...	0-...	24.0	18	8	7	1	12-0	14	.209
— Syracuse (Int'l)	3	8	.273	4.62	1.63	15	14	1	1	...	0-...	78.0	59	43	40	4	68-0	69	.215
— Toronto (A.L.)	0	0	...	0.00	0.47	4	0	0	0	0	0-0	6.1	1	0	0	0	2-0	5	.050
1991— Toronto (A.L.)	0	0	...	27.00	4.80	3	0	0	0	0	0-0	1.2	3	5	5	0	5-0	1	.429
— Dunedin (Fla. St.)	0	0	...	1.86	1.24	4	3	0	0	...	0-...	9.2	5	2	2	0	7-0	5	.161
1992— Syracuse (Int'l)	8	9	.471	3.86	1.37	27	27	2	0	...	0-...	163.1	159	82	70	9	64-0	108	.256
— Toronto (A.L.)	0	0	...	9.00	3.00	1	0	0	0	0	0-0	1.0	1	1	1	0	2-0	0	.200
1993— Toronto (A.L.)	9	6	.600	4.11	1.42	34	12	1	1	3	2-3	105.0	93	52	48	8	56-2	66	.240
1994— Toronto (A.L.)	6	7	.462	5.08	1.70	20	20	1	0	0	0-0	111.2	125	68	63	6	65-3	100	.285
1995— Toronto (A.L.)	11	11	.500	3.64	1.48	28	28	2	1	0	0-0	183.0	162	80	74	15	*108-1	153	.238
1996— Florida (N.L.)	16	12	.571	2.93	1.26	33	33	2	1	0	0-0	215.1	153	74	70	14	*119-3	200	*.202
1997— Florida (N.L.)	11	9	.550	4.34	1.48	27	27	0	0	0	0-0	151.1	133	78	73	13	91-4	132	.241
1998— New York (N.L.)	17	6	.739	2.47	1.15	28	28	4	2	0	0-0	193.0	151	55	53	8	71-2	174	.216
1999— New York (N.L.)	13	12	.520	4.23	1.42	32	32	1	1	0	0-0	213.0	209	107	100	19	93-8	162	.262
2000— New York (N.L.)	16	8	.667	3.20	1.21	31	31	2	1	0	0-0	208.0	176	84	74	19	76-1	200	.228
2001— New York (N.L.)	11	11	.500	3.31	1.20	29	29	0	0	0	0-0	187.1	178	81	69	18	46-3	142	.252
2002— New York (N.L.)	13	13	.500	3.48	1.29	33	33	2	2	0	0-0	204.1	194	99	79	23	69-5	172	.250
2003— New York (N.L.)	15	9	.625	3.99	1.49	30	30	1	1	0	0-0	180.2	176	88	80	15	94-11	139	.260
American League totals (9 years)	33	32	.508	4.36	1.53	113	83	4	2	3	2-3	522.0	490	272	253	40	309-6	439	.249
National League totals (8 years)	112	80	.583	3.47	1.31	243	243	12	8	0	0-0	1553.0	1370	661	598	129	659-37	1321	.239
Major League totals (17 years)	145	112	.564	3.69	1.36	356	326	16	10	3	2-3	2075.0	1860	933	851	169	968-43	1760	.241

L

LEON, JOSE — 3B

PERSONAL: Born December 8, 1976, in Caguas, Puerto Rico. ... 6-0/222. ... Bats right, throws right. ... Full name: Jose Geraldo Leon. ... Name pronounced: lee-OWN. ... High school: Tecnico de Portiro (Cayey, Puerto Rico).

TRANSACTIONS/CAREER NOTES: Selected by St. Louis Cardinals organization in 22nd round of free-agent draft (June 2, 1994). ... Traded by Cardinals to Baltimore Orioles for 1B Will Clark and cash (July 31, 2000). ... Recalled from Rochester (July 29, 2002). ... Optioned to Rochester (August 17, 2002). ... Recalled from Rochester (September 3, 2002). ... Recalled from Ottawa (April 23, 2003). ... Optioned to Ottawa (May 18, 2003). ... Recalled from Ottawa (July 29, 2003). ... Optioned to Ottawa (August 21, 2003). ... Recalled from Ottawa (September 29, 2003).

2003 GAMES PLAYED BY POSITION (MLB): 3B—10, 1B—7, DH—3.

Year— Team (League)	Pos.	G	AB	R	H	2B	3B	HR	RBI	BB	SO	HBP	GDP	SB-CS	Avg.	OBP	SLG	OPS	E	Pct.
1994— Ariz. Cardinals (Ariz.)	3B-2B	46	161	16	37	3	2	0	17	11	51	3	4	1-4	.230	.285	.273	.558	11	.922
1995— Savannah (S. Atl.)	3B-OF	41	133	15	22	4	1	0	11	10	46	1	6	0-1	.165	.229	.211	.440	8	.814
1996— Johnson City (App.)	3B-1B	59	222	29	55	9	3	10	36	17	92	2	1	5-3	.248	.306	.450	.756	11	.960
— New Jersey (NYP)	3B	7	28	4	8	3	1	1	3	0	7	2	0	0-0	.286	.333	.571	.905	3	.833
1997— Peoria (Midw.)	3B-OF-1B	118	399	50	92	21	2	20	54	32	122	9	10	6-5	.231	.301	.444	.745	25	.903
1998— Prince Will. (Car.)	3B-1B	124	436	77	127	31	3	21	74	53	137	9	6	5-3	.291	.376	.521	.897	25	.935
1999— Arkansas (Texas)	3B-OF	112	335	37	78	17	0	18	54	25	114	6	5	3-3	.233	.297	.445	.742	22	.900
2000— Arkansas (Texas)	3B-1B-OF	90	297	41	80	16	3	14	41	16	66	5	7	2-1	.269	.318	.485	.802	14	.951
— Bowie (East.)	3B	18	68	7	17	1	0	1	6	4	13	2	2	5-2	.250	.311	.309	.620	2	.955
2001— Bowie (East.)	3B	26	95	18	34	9	1	4	20	8	21	1	2	1-1	.358	.413	.600	1.013	7	.879
— Rochester (Int'l)	3B	109	416	54	116	20	4	12	53	25	96	4	14	7-3	.279	.325	.433	.758	21	.933
2002— Rochester (Int'l)	3B	83	312	39	87	16	1	8	40	18	54	2	9	0-0	.279	.319	.413	.733	10	.957
— Baltimore (A.L.)	1-3-D-OF	36	89	8	22	2	0	3	10	3	20	1	2	1-0	.247	.280	.371	.650	1	.994
2003— Baltimore (A.L.)	3B-1B-DH	21	54	6	13	1	0	0	0	3	18	2	1	0-0	.241	.305	.259	.564	2	.973
— Ottawa (Int'l)	3B-DH-1B	79	309	33	82	19	2	4	39	15	47	4	12	1-1	.265	.305	.379	.684	13	.944
Major League totals (2 years)		57	143	14	35	3	0	3	10	6	38	3	3	1-0	.245	.289	.329	.618	3	.988

LESKANIC, CURTIS — P

PERSONAL: Born April 2, 1968, in Homestead, Pa. ... 6-0/196. ... Throws right, bats right. ... Full name: Curtis John Leskanic. ... Name pronounced: les-CAN-ik. ... High school: Steel Valley (Munhall, Pa.). ... College: Louisiana State.

TRANSACTIONS/CAREER NOTES: Selected by Cleveland Indians organization in eighth round of free-agent draft (June 5, 1989). ... On disabled list (April 23-June 25, 1990). ... Traded by Indians with P Oscar Munoz to Minnesota Twins for 1B Paul Sorrento (March 28, 1992). ... Selected by Colorado Rockies in third round (66th pick overall) of expansion draft (November 17, 1992). ... Loaned by Rockies organization to Wichita, San Diego Padres organization (April 7-May 20, 1993). ... On Colorado disabled list (May 30-June 28, 1996); included rehabilitation assignment to Colorado Springs (June 22-27). ... On Colorado disabled list (March 23-April 12, 1997); included rehabilitation assignment to Salem (April 6-8). ... Traded by Rockies to Milwaukee Brewers for P Mike Myers (November 17, 1999). ... On disabled list (May 17-30, 2000). ... On Milwaukee disabled list (March 30, 2002-entire season); included rehabilitation assignments to Indianapolis (May 10-24) and Huntsville (May 25-29). ... Traded by Brewers to Kansas City Royals for P Wes Obermueller and IF Alejandro Machado (July 2, 2003).

CAREER HITTING: 7-for-39 (.179), 4 R, 3 2B, 0 3B, 1 HR, 7 RBI.

Year— League	W	L	Pct.	ERA	WHIP	G	GS	CG	ShO	Hld.	Sv.-Opp.	IP	H	R	ER	HR	BB-IBB	SO	Avg.
1990— Kinston (Caro.)	6	5	.545	3.68	1.24	14	14	2	0	...	0-...	73.1	61	34	30	6	30-1	71	.228
1991— Kinston (Caro.)	• 15	8	.652	2.79	1.34	28	28	0	0	...	0-...	174.1	143	63	54	10	91-0	* 163	.226
1992— Orlando (Sou.)	9	11	.450	4.30	1.45	26	23	3	0	...	0-...	152.2	158	84	73	15	64-0	126	.270
— Portland (PCL)	1	2	.333	9.98	1.57	5	3	0	0	...	0-...	15.1	16	17	17	1	8-0	14	.271
1993— Wichita (Texas)	3	2	.600	3.45	1.22	7	7	0	0	...	0-...	44.1	37	20	17	3	17-0	42	.230
— Colo. Springs (PCL)	4	3	.571	4.47	1.47	9	7	1	1	...	0-...	44.1	39	24	22	3	26-0	38	.239
— Colorado (N.L.)	1	5	.167	5.37	1.51	18	8	0	0	0	0-0	57.0	59	40	34	7	27-1	30	.266
1994— Colo. Springs (PCL)	5	7	.417	3.31	1.40	21	21	2	0	...	0-...	130.1	129	60	48	7	54-2	98	.263
— Colorado (N.L.)	1	1	.500	5.64	1.66	8	3	0	0	0	0-0	22.1	27	14	14	2	10-0	17	.314
1995— Colorado (N.L.)	6	3	.667	3.40	1.18	*76	0	0	0	19	10-16	98.0	83	38	37	7	33-1	107	.226
1996— Colorado (N.L.)	7	5	.583	6.23	1.63	70	0	0	0	9	6-10	73.2	82	51	51	12	38-1	76	.285
— Colo. Springs (PCL)	0	0	...	3.00	2.00	3	0	0	0	...	0-...	3.0	5	1	1	0	1-0	2	.385
1997— Salem (Caro.)	0	0	...	3.86	2.57	2	1	0	0	...	0-...	2.1	5	2	1	0	1-0	3	.455
— Colorado (N.L.)	4	0	1.000	5.55	1.42	55	0	0	0	6	2-4	58.1	59	36	36	8	24-0	53	.271
— Colo. Springs (PCL)	0	0	...	3.79	1.53	10	3	0	0	...	2-...	19.0	11	9	8	1	18-0	20	.175
1998— Colorado (N.L.)	6	4	.600	4.40	1.52	66	0	0	0	12	2-5	75.2	75	37	37	9	40-2	55	.259
1999— Colorado (N.L.)	6	2	.750	5.08	1.60	63	0	0	0	8	0-3	85.0	87	54	48	7	49-4	77	.272
2000— Milwaukee (N.L.)	9	3	.750	2.56	1.41	73	0	0	0	11	12-13	77.1	58	23	22	7	51-5	75	.212
2001— Milwaukee (N.L.)	2	6	.250	3.63	1.36	70	0	0	0	2	17-24	69.1	63	30	28	11	31-5	64	.241
2002— Indianapolis (Int'l)	0	0	...	1.35	0.90	5	1	0	0	...	0-...	6.2	5	1	1	0	1-0	7	.192
— Huntsville (Sou.)	0	0	...	3.00	2.00	3	0	0	0	...	0-...	3.0	4	2	1	0	2-0	2	.333
2003— Milwaukee (N.L.)	4	0	1.000	2.70	1.50	26	0	0	0	4	0-0	26.2	22	8	8	1	18-0	28	.227
— Kansas City (A.L.)	1	0	1.000	1.73	1.04	27	0	0	0	7	2-3	26.0	16	7	5	1	11-1	22	.180
American League totals (1 year)	1	0	1.000	1.73	1.04	27	0	0	0	7	2-3	26.0	16	7	5	1	11-1	22	.180
National League totals (10 years)	46	29	.613	4.41	1.45	525	11	0	0	71	49-75	643.1	615	331	315	71	321-19	582	.254
Major League totals (10 years)	47	29	.618	4.30	1.44	552	11	0	0	78	51-78	669.1	631	338	320	72	332-20	604	.251

LEVINE, AL — P

PERSONAL: Born May 22, 1968, in Park Ridge, Ill. ... 6-3/175. ... Throws right, bats left. ... Full name: Alan Brian Levine. ... Name pronounced: le-VINE. ... High school: Hoffman Estates (Ill.). ... College: Southern Illinois.

TRANSACTIONS/CAREER NOTES: Selected by Chicago White Sox in 11th round of free-agent draft (June 3, 1991). ... Traded by White Sox with P Larry Thomas to Texas Rangers for SS Benji Gil (December 19, 1997). ... Claimed on waivers by Anaheim Angels (April 2, 1999). ... On Anaheim disabled list (July 31-August 19, 2000); included rehabilitation assignment to Erie (August 17). ... On Anaheim disabled list (June 27-July 20, 2002); included rehabilitation assignment to Salt Lake (July 16-20). ... Granted free agency (December 21, 2002). ... Signed by St. Louis Cardinals (January 6, 2003). ... Released by Cardinals (March 26, 2003). ... Signed by Tampa Bay Devil Rays organization (April 2, 2003). ... Traded by Devil Rays to Kansas City Royals for cash (July, 31 2003).

CAREER HITTING: 0-for-0 (.000), 0 R, 0 2B, 0 3B, 0 HR, 0 RBI.

Year	League	W	L	Pct.	ERA	WHIP	G	GS	CG	ShO	Hld.	Sv.-Opp.	IP	H	R	ER	HR	BB-IBB	SO	Avg.
1991— Utica (N.Y.-Penn)	6	4	.600	3.18	1.19	16	12	2	1	...	1-...	85.0	75	45	30	2	26-0	83	.231
1992— South Bend (Mid.)	9	5	.643	2.81	1.19	23	23	2	0	...	0-...	156.2	151	67	49	6	36-1	131	.253
— Sarasota (Fla. St.)	0	2	.000	4.02	1.40	3	2	0	0	...	0-...	15.2	17	11	7	1	5-1	11	.293
1993— Sarasota (Fla. St.)	11	8	.579	3.68	1.36	27	26	5	1	...	0-...	161.1	169	87	66	6	50-3	* 129	.271
1994— Birmingham (Sou.)	5	9	.357	3.31	1.41	18	18	1	0	...	0-...	114.1	117	50	42	7	44-1	94	.267
— Nashville (A.A.)	0	2	.000	7.88	1.88	8	4	0	0	...	0-...	24.0	34	23	21	2	11-0	24	.343
1995— Nashville (A.A.)	0	2	.000	5.14	1.93	3	3	0	0	...	0-...	14.0	20	10	8	1	7-0	14	.323
— Birmingham (Sou.)	4	3	.571	2.34	1.18	43	1	0	0	...	7-...	73.0	61	22	19	2	25-5	68	.223
1996— Nashville (A.A.)	4	5	.444	3.65	1.33	43	0	0	0	...	12-...	61.2	58	27	25	4	24-6	45	.246
— Chicago (A.L.)	0	1	.000	5.40	1.58	16	0	0	0	0	0-1	18.1	22	14	11	1	7-1	12	.289
1997— Chicago (A.L.)	2	2	.500	6.91	1.87	25	0	0	0	3	0-1	27.1	35	22	21	4	16-1	22	.313
— Nashville (A.A.)	1	1	.500	7.13	1.95	26	0	0	0	...	2-...	35.1	58	32	28	3	11-1	29	.372
1998— Oklahoma (PCL)	1	3	.250	4.73	1.28	12	7	0	0	...	1-...	53.1	51	33	28	7	17-0	30	.252
— Texas (A.L.)	0	1	.000	4.50	1.45	30	0	0	0	0	0-0	58.0	68	30	29	6	16-1	19	.294
1999— Anaheim (A.L.)	1	1	.500	3.39	1.24	50	1	0	0	3	0-1	85.0	76	40	32	13	29-2	37	.247
2000— Anaheim (A.L.)	3	4	.429	3.87	1.54	51	5	0	0	5	2-2	95.1	98	44	41	10	49-5	42	.266
— Erie (East.)	0	0	...	0.00	1.50	1	1	0	0	...	0-...	2.0	3	2	0	0	0-0	0	.333
2001— Anaheim (A.L.)	8	10	.444	2.38	1.31	64	1	0	0	17	2-6	75.2	71	25	20	7	28-4	40	.257
2002— Anaheim (A.L.)	4	4	.500	4.24	1.49	52	0	0	0	10	5-7	63.2	61	35	30	8	34-3	40	.253
— Salt Lake (PCL)	0	0	...	3.00	1.67	2	0	0	0	...	0-...	3.0	5	1	1	0	0-0	3	.385
2003— Tampa Bay (A.L.)	3	5	.375	2.90	1.27	36	0	0	0	8	0-2	49.2	45	23	16	7	18-0	25	.243
— Kansas City (A.L.)	0	1	.000	2.53	1.55	18	0	0	0	2	1-2	21.1	22	6	6	2	11-1	5	.268
Major League totals (8 years)	21	29	.420	3.75	1.43	342	7	0	0	48	10-22	494.1	498	239	206	58	208-18	242	.265

LEVRAULT, ALLEN   P

PERSONAL: Born August 15, 1977, in Fall River, Mass. ... 6-3/241. ... Throws right, bats right. ... Full name: Allen Harry Levrault. ... Name pronounced: LEV-ralt. ... High school: Westport (Mass.). ... Junior college: Rhode Island Community College.
TRANSACTIONS/CAREER NOTES: Selected by Toronto Blue Jays organization in 11th round of free-agent draft (June 1, 1995); did not sign. ... Selected by Milwaukee Brewers organization in 13th round of free-agent draft (June 4, 1996). ... On Huntsville disabled list (June 20-July 10 and August 1-17, 1999). ... On Indianapolis disabled list (April 27-May 12 and September 12-19, 2000). ... Claimed on waivers by Oakland Athletics (February 1, 2002). ... On Sacramento disabled list (May 14-June 10, 2002). ... Granted free agency (October 15, 2002). ... Signed by Florida Marlins organization (November 25, 2002). ... Elected free agency (July 12, 2003).
CAREER HITTING: 2-for-38 (.053), 1 R, 0 2B, 0 3B, 0 HR, 1 RBI.

Year	League	W	L	Pct.	ERA	WHIP	G	GS	CG	ShO	Hld.	Sv.-Opp.	IP	H	R	ER	HR	BB-IBB	SO	Avg.
1996— Helena (Pio.)	4	3	.571	5.32	1.30	18	11	0	0	...	1-...	71.0	70	43	42	9	22-0	68	.257
1997— Beloit (Midw.)	3	10	.231	5.28	1.38	24	24	1	0	...	0-...	131.1	141	89	77	18	40-1	112	.275
1998— Stockton (Calif.)	9	3	.750	2.87	1.06	16	15	* 4	• 1	...	0-...	97.1	76	33	31	8	27-0	86	.216
— El Paso (Texas)	1	5	.167	5.89	1.50	11	11	0	0	...	0-...	62.2	77	51	41	7	17-0	46	.297
1999— Huntsville (Sou.)	9	2	.818	3.43	1.10	16	16	2	1	...	0-...	99.2	77	44	38	11	33-0	82	.213
— Louisville (Int'l)	1	3	.250	8.65	1.86	9	5	0	0	...	0-...	34.1	48	37	33	9	16-0	33	.327
2000— Indianapolis (Int'l)	6	8	.429	4.24	1.33	21	18	1	0	...	0-...	108.1	98	55	51	9	46-3	78	.248
— Milwaukee (N.L.)	0	1	.000	4.50	1.42	5	1	0	0	0	0-0	12.0	10	7	6	0	7-0	9	.238
2001— Indianapolis (Int'l)	2	1	.667	2.64	0.98	5	5	0	0	...	0-...	30.2	22	9	9	1	8-1	30	.200
— Milwaukee (N.L.)	6	10	.375	6.06	1.57	32	20	1	0	0	0-...	130.2	146	93	88	27	59-7	80	.281
2002— Sacramento (PCL)	7	8	.467	6.39	1.71	24	23	0	0	...	0-...	111.1	145	91	79	15	45-0	81	.315
2003— Florida (N.L.)	1	0	1.000	3.86	1.89	19	0	0	0	1	0-...	28.0	38	12	12	3	15-2	21	.333
— Albuquerque (PCL)	3	0	1.000	1.40	0.82	21	0	0	0	...	0-...	25.2	12	5	4	2	9-1	18	.143
Major League totals (3 years)	7	11	.389	5.59	1.61	56	21	1	0	1	0-0	170.2	194	112	106	30	81-9	110	.287

LEWIS, COLBY   P

PERSONAL: Born August 2, 1979, in Bakersfield, Calif. ... 6-4/230. ... Throws right, bats right. ... Full name: Colby Preston Lewis. ... High school: North (Bakersfield, Calif.). ... Junior college: Bakersfield College (Calif.).
TRANSACTIONS/CAREER NOTES: Selected by Texas Rangers organization in supplemental round ("sandwich pick" between first and second round, 38th pick overall) of free-agent draft (June 2, 1999); pick received as part of compensation for Arizona Diamondbacks signing Type A free agent P Todd Stottlemyre.
CAREER HITTING: 0-for-1 (.000), 0 R, 0 2B, 0 3B, 0 HR, 0 RBI.

Year	League	W	L	Pct.	ERA	WHIP	G	GS	CG	ShO	Hld.	Sv.-Opp.	IP	H	R	ER	HR	BB-IBB	SO	Avg.
1999— Pulaski (Appal.)	7	3	.700	1.95	1.13	14	11	1	1	...	0-...	64.2	46	24	14	3	27-0	84	.189
2000— Charlotte (Fla. St.)	11	10	.524	4.07	1.31	28	27	3	1	...	0-...	163.2	169	83	74	11	45-0	153	.270
2001— Charlotte (Fla. St.)	1	0	1.000	0.00	0.00	1	0	0	0	...	0-...	4.1	0	0	0	0	0-0	8	.000
— Tulsa (Texas)	10	10	.500	4.50	1.36	25	25	1	0	...	0-...	156.0	150	85	78	15	62-2	162	.253
2002— Texas (A.L.)	1	3	.250	6.29	1.98	15	4	0	0	1	0-2	34.1	42	26	24	4	26-2	28	.304
— Oklahoma (PCL)	5	6	.455	3.63	1.20	20	20	0	0	...	0-...	106.2	100	49	43	4	28-0	99	.245
2003— Oklahoma (PCL)	5	1	.833	3.02	1.15	7	7	0	0	...	0-...	47.2	36	16	16	6	19-0	43	.208
— Texas (A.L.)	10	9	.526	7.30	1.83	26	26	0	0	0	0-0	127.0	163	104	103	23	70-1	88	.317
Major League totals (2 years)	11	12	.478	7.08	1.87	41	30	0	0	1	0-2	161.1	205	130	127	27	96-3	116	.314

LIDGE, BRAD   P

PERSONAL: Born December 23, 1976, in Sacramento, Calif. ... 6-5/210. ... Throws right, bats right. ... Full name: Bradley Thomas Lidge. ... College: Notre Dame.
TRANSACTIONS/CAREER NOTES: Selected by Houston Astros in first round (17th pick overall) of free-agent draft (June 2, 1998); pick received from Colorado Rockies as part of compensation for signing Type A free agent Darryl Kile. ... On disabled list (August 18, 1998-remainder of season). ... On disabled list (April 1-June and July 10, 1999-remainder of season). ... On disabled list (April 24-June 13 and July 1, 2000-remainder of season). ... On disabled list (May 5, 2001-remainder of season).
CAREER HITTING: 2-for-6 (.333), 0 R, 1 2B, 0 3B, 0 HR, 2 RBI.

Year	League	W	L	Pct.	ERA	WHIP	G	GS	CG	ShO	Hld.	Sv.-Opp.	IP	H	R	ER	HR	BB-IBB	SO	Avg.
1998— Quad City (Midw.)	0	1	.000	3.27	1.36	4	4	0	0	...	0-...	11.0	10	5	4	0	5-0	5	.227
1999— Kissimmee (Fla. St.)	0	2	.000	3.38	1.13	6	6	0	0	...	0-...	21.1	13	8	8	0	11-0	19	.183
2000— Kissimmee (Fla. St.)	2	1	.667	2.81	1.03	8	8	0	0	...	0-...	41.2	28	14	13	3	15-0	46	.190
2001— Round Rock (Texas)	2	0	1.000	1.73	1.08	5	5	0	0	...	0-...	26.0	21	5	5	1	7-0	42	.219
2002— Round Rock (Texas)	1	1	.500	2.45	1.09	5	0	0	0	...	0-...	11.0	9	4	3	0	3-0	18	.220
— Houston (N.L.)	1	0	1.000	6.23	2.42	6	1	0	0	0	0-0	8.2	12	6	6	0	9-1	12	.333
— New Orleans (PCL)	5	5	.500	3.39	1.16	24	19	0	0	...	0-...	111.2	83	47	42	9	47-0	110	.206
2003— Houston (N.L.)	6	3	.667	3.60	1.20	78	0	0	0	28	1-6	85.0	60	36	34	6	42-7	97	.202
Major League totals (2 years)	7	3	.700	3.84	1.31	84	1	0	0	28	1-6	93.2	72	42	40	6	51-8	109	.216

L

LIDLE, CORY — P

PERSONAL: Born March 22, 1972, in Hollywood, Calif. ... 5-11/192. ... Throws right, bats right. ... Full name: Cory Fulton Lidle. ... Name pronounced: LIE-dell. ... High school: South Hills (Covina, Calif.).

TRANSACTIONS/CAREER NOTES: Signed as non-drafted free agent by Minnesota Twins organization (August 25, 1990). ... Released by Twins (April 1, 1993). ... Signed by Pocatello, Pioneer League (May 28, 1993). ... Contract sold by Pocatello to Milwaukee Brewers organization (September 17, 1993). ... Traded by Brewers to New York Mets for C Kelly Stinnett (January 17, 1996). ... Selected by Arizona Diamondbacks in first round (13th pick overall) of expansion draft (November 18, 1997). ... On Arizona disabled list (March 31, 1998-entire season); included rehabilitation assignments to High Desert (April 20-28) and Tucson (September 3-7). ... Claimed on waivers by Tampa Bay Devil Rays (October 7, 1998). ... On Tampa Bay disabled list (March 23-September 18, 1999); included rehabilitation assignments to St. Petersburg (August 20-28) and Durham (August 29-September 18). ... On suspended list (September 5-8, 2000). ... Traded by Devil Rays to Oakland Athletics as part of three-way deal in which Devil Rays received OF Ben Grieve and a player to be named later or cash from the A's, Royals received P Roberto Hernandez from Devil Rays, A's received OF Johnny Damon, IF Mark Ellis and a player to be named later from Royals and Royals received C A.J. Hinch, IF Angel Berroa and cash from A's (January 8, 2001). ... On Oakland disabled list (May 13-30, 2002); included rehabilitation assignment to Sacramento (May 26-30). ... Traded by A's to Toronto Blue Jays for IF Michael Rouse and P Christopher Mowday (November 16, 2002). ... Placed on 15-day disabled list (August 5, 2003). ... Sent on rehab assignment by Toronto (August 19, 2003). ... Recalled from minor league rehab assignment; removed from 15-day disabled list (August 25, 2003).

CAREER HITTING: 2-for-16 (.125), 2 R, 0 2B, 0 3B, 0 HR, 0 RBI.

Year League	W	L	Pct.	ERA	WHIP	G	GS	CG	ShO	Hld.	Sv.-Opp.	IP	H	R	ER	HR	BB-IBB	SO	Avg.
1991— GC Twins (GCL)	1	1	.500	5.79	1.07	4	0	0	0	...	0-...	4.2	5	3	3	0	0-0	5	.263
1992— Elizabethton (Appal.)	2	1	.667	3.71	1.40	19	2	0	0	...	6-...	43.2	40	29	18	2	21-0	32	.240
1993— Pocatello (Pio.)	•8	4	.667	4.13	1.48	17	16	3	0	...	1-...	106.2	104	59	49	6	54-0	91	.261
1994— Stockton (Calif.)	1	2	.333	4.43	1.71	25	1	0	0	...	4-...	42.2	60	32	21	2	13-1	38	.323
— Beloit (Midw.)	3	4	.429	2.61	1.10	13	9	1	1	...	0-...	69.0	65	24	20	4	11-0	62	.245
1995— El Paso (Texas)	5	4	.556	3.36	1.48	45	9	0	0	...	2-...	109.2	126	52	41	6	36-3	78	.292
1996— Binghamton (Eastern)	14	10	.583	3.31	1.23	27	27	•6	1	...	0-...	*190.1	186	78	70	13	49-4	141	.259
1997— Norfolk (Int'l)	4	2	.667	3.64	1.33	7	7	1	0	...	0-...	42.0	46	20	17	1	10-0	34	.279
— New York (N.L.)	7	2	.778	3.53	1.30	54	2	0	0	9	2-3	81.2	86	38	32	7	20-4	54	.274
1998— High Desert (Calif.)	0	0	...	0.00	1.50	1	1	0	0	...	0-...	2.2	2	1	0	0	2-0	6	.182
— Tucson (PCL)	0	0	...	0.00	0.86	1	1	0	0	...	0-...	4.2	2	0	0	0	2-0	2	.118
1999— St. Pete. (FSL)	0	0	...	0.00	0.80	2	2	0	0	...	0-...	5.0	2	0	0	0	2-0	0	.118
— Durham (Int'l)	0	0	...	4.76	1.76	3	2	0	0	...	0-...	5.2	9	3	3	0	1-0	6	.360
— Tampa Bay (A.L.)	1	0	1.000	7.20	2.00	5	1	0	0	0	0-0	5.0	8	4	4	0	2-0	4	.364
2000— Durham (Int'l)	6	2	.750	2.52	1.20	9	9	0	0	...	0-...	50.0	52	15	14	3	8-0	44	.267
— Tampa Bay (A.L.)	4	6	.400	5.03	1.48	31	11	0	0	2	0-0	96.2	114	61	54	13	29-3	62	.294
2001— Sacramento (PCL)	1	0	1.000	3.00	1.50	1	1	0	0	...	0-...	6.0	6	2	2	0	3-0	2	.261
— Oakland (A.L.)	13	6	.684	3.59	1.15	29	29	1	0	0	0-0	188.0	170	84	75	23	47-7	118	.242
2002— Oakland (A.L.)	8	10	.444	3.89	1.20	31	30	2	2	0	0-0	192.0	191	90	83	17	39-3	111	.258
— Sacramento (PCL)	0	0	...	2.25	1.25	1	1	0	0	...	0-...	4.0	2	1	1	0	3-0	3	.167
2003— Syracuse (Int'l)	0	0	...	0.00	1.25	1	1	0	0	...	0-...	4.0	5	0	0	0	0-0	3	.313
— Toronto (A.L.)	12	15	.444	5.75	1.43	31	31	2	0	0	0-0	192.2	216	*133	*123	24	60-3	112	.282
American League totals (5 years)	38	37	.507	4.52	1.30	127	102	5	2	2	0-0	674.1	699	372	339	77	177-16	407	.267
National League totals (1 year)	7	2	.778	3.53	1.30	54	2	0	0	9	2-3	81.2	86	38	32	7	20-4	54	.274
Major League totals (6 years)	45	39	.536	4.42	1.30	181	104	5	2	11	2-3	756.0	785	410	371	84	197-20	461	.268

LIEBER, JON — P

PERSONAL: Born April 2, 1970. ... 6-2/230. ... Throws right, bats left. ... Full name: Jonathan Ray Lieber. ... Name pronounced: LEE-ber. ... High school: Abraham Lincoln (Council Bluffs, Iowa.).

TRANSACTIONS/CAREER NOTES: Selected by Chicago Cubs organization in ninth round of free-agent draft (June 3, 1991); did not sign. ... Selected by Kansas City Royals organization in second round of free-agent draft (June 1, 1992); pick received as part of compensation for New York Yankees signing Type A free-agent OF Danny Tartabull. ... Traded by Royals with P Dan Miceli to Pittsburgh Pirates for P Stan Belinda (July 31, 1993). ... On disabled list (August 21-September 15, 1998). ... Traded by Pirates to Chicago Cubs for OF Brant Brown (December 14, 1998). ... On disabled list (April 21-May 8, 1999; and August 2, 2002-remainder of season). ... Granted free agency (November 1, 2002). ... Signed by New York Yankees (February 4, 2003). ... On disabled list (March 21-entire 2003 season).

CAREER HITTING: 71-for-461 (.154), 27 R, 15 2B, 0 3B, 0 HR, 20 RBI.

Year League	W	L	Pct.	ERA	WHIP	G	GS	CG	ShO	Hld.	Sv.-Opp.	IP	H	R	ER	HR	BB-IBB	SO	Avg.
1992— Eugene (NW)	3	0	1.000	1.16	0.90	5	5	0	0	...	0-...	31.0	26	6	4	1	2-0	23	.226
— Baseball City (FSL)	3	3	.500	4.65	1.71	7	6	0	0	...	0-...	31.0	45	20	16	2	8-0	19	.344
1993— Wilmington (Caro.)	9	3	.750	2.67	1.17	17	16	2	0	...	0-...	114.2	125	47	34	4	9-1	89	.272
— Memphis (Sou.)	2	1	.667	6.86	1.81	4	4	0	0	...	0-...	21.0	32	16	16	4	6-0	17	.340
— Carolina (Sou.)	4	2	.667	3.97	1.44	6	6	0	0	...	0-...	34.0	39	15	15	3	10-0	28	.298
1994— Carolina (Sou.)	2	0	1.000	1.29	0.71	3	3	1	1	...	0-...	21.0	13	4	3	0	2-0	21	.171
— Buffalo (A.A.)	1	1	.500	1.69	0.80	3	3	0	0	...	0-...	21.1	16	4	4	1	1-0	21	.208
— Pittsburgh (N.L.)	6	7	.462	3.73	1.30	17	17	1	0	0	0-0	108.2	116	62	45	12	25-3	71	.271
1995— Pittsburgh (N.L.)	4	7	.364	6.32	1.61	21	12	0	0	3	0-1	72.2	103	56	51	7	14-0	45	.346
— Calgary (PCL)	1	5	.167	7.01	1.83	14	14	0	0	...	0-...	77.0	122	69	60	6	19-0	34	.279
1996— Pittsburgh (N.L.)	9	5	.643	3.99	1.30	51	15	0	0	9	1-4	142.0	156	70	63	19	28-2	94	.279
1997— Pittsburgh (N.L.)	11	14	.440	4.49	1.30	33	32	1	0	0	0-0	188.1	193	102	94	23	51-8	160	.263
1998— Pittsburgh (N.L.)	8	14	.364	4.11	1.30	29	28	2	0	0	1-1	171.0	182	93	78	23	40-4	138	.269
1999— Chicago (N.L.)	10	11	.476	4.07	1.34	31	31	3	1	0	0-0	203.1	226	107	92	28	46-6	186	.279
2000— Chicago (N.L.)	12	11	.522	4.41	1.20	35	•35	0	0	0	0-0	*251.0	248	130	123	36	54-3	192	.257
2001— Chicago (N.L.)	20	6	.769	3.80	1.15	34	34	5	1	0	0-0	232.1	226	104	98	25	41-4	148	.255
2002— Chicago (N.L.)	6	8	.429	3.70	1.17	21	21	3	0	0	0-0	141.0	153	64	58	15	12-2	87	.277
2003— Tampa (Fla. St.)	0	0	...	13.50	2.50	1	1	0	0	...	0-...	2.0	5	3	3	0	0-0	4	.455
— Yankees (GCL)	0	0	...	4.50	1.30	2	2	0	0	...	0-0	6.0	8	3	3	0	0-0	6	.308
Major League totals (9 years)	86	83	.509	4.18	1.27	272	225	21	3	12	2-6	1510.1	1603	788	702	188	311-32	1121	.271

LIEBERTHAL, MIKE — C

PERSONAL: Born January 18, 1972, in Glendale, Calif. ... 6-0/195. ... Bats right, throws right. ... Full name: Michael Scott Lieberthal. ... Name pronounced: LEE-ber-thal. ... High school: Westlake (Westlake Village, Calif.).

TRANSACTIONS/CAREER NOTES: Selected by Philadelphia Phillies organization in first round (third pick overall) of free-agent draft (June 4, 1990). ... On Scranton/Wilkes-Barre disabled list (August 31, 1992-remainder of season). ... On disabled list (August 22, 1996-remainder of season; July 24-September 2, 1998; July 18-August 4 and September 11, 2000-remainder of season; and May 13, 2001-remainder of season).

2003 GAMES PLAYED BY POSITION (MLB): C—131.

Year — Team (League)	Pos.	G	AB	R	H	2B	3B	HR	RBI	BB	SO	HBP	GDP	SB-CS	Avg.	OBP	SLG	OPS	E	Pct.
1990— Martinsville (App.)	C	49	184	26	42	9	0	4	22	11	40	2	3	2-0	.228	.279	.342	.622	5	.990
1991— Spartanburg (SAL)	C	72	243	34	74	17	0	0	31	23	25	5	4	1-2	.305	.372	.374	.747	10	.984
— Clearwater (FSL)	C	16	52	7	15	2	0	0	7	3	12	1	2	0-0	.288	.333	.327	.660	1	.993
1992— Reading (East.)	C	86	309	30	88	16	1	2	37	19	26	10	15	4-1	.285	.342	.362	.705	7	.988
— Scran./W.B. (I.L.)	C	16	45	4	9	1	0	0	4	2	5	1	2	0-0	.200	.245	.222	.467	1	.989
1993— Scran./W.B. (I.L.)	C	112	382	35	100	17	0	7	40	24	32	6	15	2-0	.262	.313	.361	.674	•11	.985
1994— Scran./W.B. (I.L.)	C-DH	84	296	23	69	16	0	1	32	21	29	2	7	1-1	.233	.286	.297	.583	9	.983
— Philadelphia (N.L.)	C	24	79	6	21	3	1	1	5	3	5	1	4	0-0	.266	.301	.367	.668	4	.969
1995— Philadelphia (N.L.)	C	16	47	1	12	2	0	0	4	5	5	0	1	0-0	.255	.327	.298	.625	1	.991
— Scran./W.B. (I.L.)	C-DH-3B	85	278	44	78	20	2	6	42	44	26	9	14	1-4	.281	.388	.432	.819	5	.991
1996— Philadelphia (N.L.)	C	50	166	21	42	8	0	7	23	10	30	2	4	0-0	.253	.297	.428	.724	3	.990
1997— Philadelphia (N.L.)	C-DH	134	455	59	112	27	1	20	77	44	76	4	10	3-4	.246	.314	.442	.755	12	.988
1998— Philadelphia (N.L.)	C	86	313	39	80	15	3	8	45	17	44	7	4	2-1	.256	.304	.399	.703	8	.988
1999— Philadelphia (N.L.)	C	145	510	84	153	33	1	31	96	44	86	11	15	0-0	.300	.363	.551	.914	3	.997
2000— Philadelphia (N.L.)	C	108	389	55	108	30	0	15	71	40	53	6	12	2-0	.278	.352	.470	.822	5	.993
2001— Philadelphia (N.L.)	C	34	121	21	28	8	0	2	11	12	21	3	2	0-0	.231	.316	.347	.663	2	.992
2002— Philadelphia (N.L.)	C	130	476	46	133	29	2	15	52	38	58	14	16	0-1	.279	.349	.443	.792	6	.993
2003— Philadelphia (N.L.)	C	131	508	68	159	30	1	13	81	38	59	12	14	0-0	.313	.373	.453	.825	9	.990
Major League totals (10 years)		858	3064	400	848	185	9	112	465	251	437	60	82	7-6	.277	.340	.453	.793	53	.991

LIEFER, JEFF   3B/OF

PERSONAL: Born August 17, 1974, in Fontana, Calif. ... 6-3/210. ... Bats left, throws right. ... Full name: Jeffrey David Liefer. ... Name pronounced: LEAF-er. ... High school: Upland (Calif.). ... College: Long Beach State.

TRANSACTIONS/CAREER NOTES: Selected by Cleveland Indians organization in sixth round of free-agent draft (June 1, 1992); did not sign. ... Selected by Chicago White Sox organization in first round (25th pick overall) of free-agent draft (June 1, 1995). ... On Charlotte disabled list (August 30, 1999-remainder of season). ... On Chicago disabled list (March 25-April 17, 2000). ... Traded by White Sox with P Orlando Hernandez, P Rocky Biddle and cash to Montreal Expos for P Bartolo Colon and 2B/SS Jorge Nunez (January 15, 2003). ... Claimed off waivers by Tampa Bay (June 6, 2003). ... Elected free agency (September 29, 2003).

2003 GAMES PLAYED BY POSITION (MLB): 1B—21, 3B—6, DH—2, OF—1.

Year — Team (League)	Pos.	G	AB	R	H	2B	3B	HR	RBI	BB	SO	HBP	GDP	SB-CS	Avg.	OBP	SLG	OPS	E	Pct.
1996— South Bend (Mid.)	3B-DH	74	277	60	90	14	0	15	58	30	62	5	3	6-5	.325	.396	.538	.933	23	.802
— Prince Will. (Car.)	DH	37	147	17	33	6	0	1	13	11	27	0	6	0-0	.224	.277	.286	.562	0	...
1997— Birmingham (Sou.)	OF-DH	119	474	67	113	24	9	15	71	38	115	7	10	2-0	.238	.302	.422	.724	•8	.955
1998— Birmingham (Sou.)	1B-DH-OF	127	471	84	137	33	6	21	89	60	125	9	9	1-2	.291	.381	.520	.901	11	.987
— Calgary (PCL)	OF-DH-1B	8	31	3	8	3	0	1	10	2	12	0	1	0-0	.258	.303	.452	.755	0	1.000
1999— Chicago (A.L.)	OF-1B-3B	45	113	8	28	7	1	0	14	8	28	0	3	2-0	.248	.295	.327	.623	0	1.000
— Charlotte (Int'l)	1B-OF-3B	46	171	36	58	17	1	9	34	21	26	1	3	2-1	.339	.412	.608	1.021	3	.988
2000— Charlotte (Int'l)	1B-OF-3B	120	445	75	125	29	1	32	91	53	107	2	17	2-3	.281	.356	.566	.923	9	.987
— Chicago (A.L.)	OF-1B	5	11	0	2	0	0	0	0	0	4	0	0	0-0	.182	.182	.182	.364	1	.900
2001— Charlotte (Int'l)	1B-3B	32	119	23	34	7	0	6	21	15	41	4	1	3-1	.286	.381	.496	.877	3	.989
— Chicago (A.L.)	O-3-1-D	83	254	36	65	13	0	18	39	20	69	2	6	0-1	.256	.313	.520	.833	7	.964
2002— Chicago (A.L.)	OF-1B-DH	76	204	28	47	8	0	7	26	19	60	0	3	0-0	.230	.295	.373	.667	2	.992
2003— Montreal (N.L.)	1B	35	88	6	17	3	0	3	18	3	26	0	2	0-1	.193	.217	.330	.547	3	.980
— Tampa Bay (A.L.)	3B-DH-OF	9	25	4	3	1	0	1	3	3	13	0	0	0-0	.120	.214	.280	.494	1	.938
— Durham (Int'l)	O-D-1-3	44	157	20	41	10	3	7	24	14	49	1	2	0-0	.261	.326	.497	.822	1	.988
American League totals (5 years)		218	607	76	145	29	1	26	82	50	174	2	12	2-1	.239	.297	.418	.716	11	.982
National League totals (1 year)		35	88	6	17	3	0	3	18	3	26	0	2	0-1	.193	.217	.330	.547	3	.980
Major League totals (5 years)		253	695	82	162	32	1	29	100	53	200	2	14	2-2	.233	.287	.407	.695	14	.982

LIGTENBERG, KERRY   P

PERSONAL: Born May 11, 1971, in Rapid City, S.D. ... 6-2/222. ... Throws right, bats right. ... Full name: Kerry Dale Ligtenberg. ... Name pronounced: lite-en-berg. ... High school: Park (Cottage Grove, Minn.). ... College: Minnesota.

TRANSACTIONS/CAREER NOTES: Signed by Minneapolis, North Central League (1994). ... Contract sold by Minneapolis to Seattle Mariners organization (March 28, 1995). ... Released by Mariners (April 2, 1995). ... Signed by Minneapolis, Prairie League (1995). ... Contract sold by Minneapolis to Atlanta Braves organization (January 27, 1996). ... On disabled list (April 3, 1999-entire season). ... Granted free agency (December 21, 2002). ... Signed by Baltimore Orioles (January 16, 2003).

CAREER HITTING: 0-for-0 (.000), 0 R, 0 2B, 0 3B, 0 HR, 0 RBI.

Year — League	W	L	Pct.	ERA	WHIP	G	GS	CG	ShO	Hld.	Sv.-Opp.	IP	H	R	ER	HR	BB-IBB	SO	Avg.
1994— Minneapolis (NCL)	5	5	.500	3.31	1.29	19	19	2	...	...	0-...	114.1	103	47	42	11	44-4	94	.239
1995— Minneapolis (PRA)	11	2	.846	2.73	1.17	17	15	4	...	...	0-...	108.2	101	41	33		26-...	100	...
1996— Durham (Caro.)	7	4	.636	2.41	1.24	49	0	0	0	...	20-...	59.2	58	20	16	3	16-3	76	.251
1997— Greenville (Sou.)	3	1	.750	2.04	0.96	31	0	0	0	...	16-...	35.1	20	8	8	3	14-1	43	.160
— Richmond (Int'l)	0	3	.000	4.32	0.92	14	0	0	0	...	1-...	25.0	21	13	12	3	2-0	35	.236
— Atlanta (N.L.)	1	0	1.000	3.00	1.07	15	0	0	0	0	1-1	15.0	12	5	5	4	4-2	19	.211
1998— Atlanta (N.L.)	3	2	.600	2.71	1.03	75	0	0	0	11	30-34	73.0	51	24	22	6	24-1	79	.193
1999— Atlanta (N.L.)										Did not play.									
2000— Atlanta (N.L.)	2	3	.400	3.61	1.28	59	0	0	0	12	12-14	52.1	43	21	21	7	24-5	51	.226
— Richmond (Int'l)	0	0	...	0.00	0.71	5	0	0	0	...	1-...	5.2	0	0	0	0	4-0	7	.000
2001— Atlanta (N.L.)	3	3	.500	3.02	1.34	53	0	0	0	0	1-2	59.2	50	22	20	4	30-8	56	.226
— Richmond (Int'l)	0	0	...	0.00	1.00	1	0	0	0	...	0-...	1.0	0	0	0	0	1-0	2	.000
2002— Atlanta (N.L.)	3	4	.429	2.97	1.28	52	0	0	0	2	0-0	66.2	52	23	22	6	33-3	51	.213
2003— Baltimore (A.L.)	4	2	.667	3.34	1.25	68	0	0	0	14	1-4	59.1	60	23	22	9	14-3	47	.263
American League totals (1 year)	4	2	.667	3.34	1.25	68	0	0	0	14	1-4	59.1	60	23	22	9	14-3	47	.263
National League totals (5 years)	12	12	.500	3.04	1.21	254	0	0	0	25	44-51	266.2	208	95	90	27	115-19	256	.213
Major League totals (6 years)	16	14	.533	3.09	1.22	322	0	0	0	39	45-55	326.0	268	118	112	36	129-22	303	.223

LILLY, TED   P

PERSONAL: Born January 4, 1976, in Lamita, Calif. ... 6-1/190. ... Throws left, bats left. ... Full name: Theodore Roosevelt Lilly. ... Name pronounced: LILL-ee. ... High school: Yosemite (Oakhurst, Calif.). ... Junior college: Fresno City (Calif.) Community College.

TRANSACTIONS/CAREER NOTES: Selected by Los Angeles Dodgers in 23rd round of free-agent draft (June 4, 1996). ... Traded by Dodgers with 2B Wilton Guerrero, OF Peter Bergeron and 1B Jonathan Tucker to Montreal Expos for P Carlos Perez, SS Mark Grudzielanek and IF Hiram Bocachica (July 31, 1998). ... On Ottawa disabled list (June 21, 1999-remainder of season). ... Traded by Expos to New York Yankees (March 17, 2000), as part of deal in which Yankees traded P Hideki Irabu to Expos for P Jake Westbrook and two players to be named later (December 29, 1999); Yankees acquired P Christian Parker to complete deal (March 22, 2000). ... On New York disabled list (April 2-May 23, 2000); included rehabilitation assignments to Tampa (April 27-May 1) and Columbus (May 2-6 and May 20-23). ... On suspended list (August 11-17, 2001). ... Traded by Yankees with OF John-Ford Griffin and P Jason Arnold to Oakland Athletics as part of three-way deal in which Tigers acquired 1B Carlos Pena, P Franklyn German and a player to be named later from A's and Yankees acquired P Jeff Weaver from Tigers (July 5, 2002); Tigers acquired P Jeremy Bonderman to complete deal (August 22, 2002). ... On Oakland disabled list (July 23-September 10, 2002).

CAREER HITTING: 1-for-14 (.071), 0 R, 0 2B, 0 3B, 0 HR, 0 RBI.

Year League	W	L	Pct.	ERA	WHIP	G	GS	CG	ShO	Hld.	Sv.-Opp.	IP	H	R	ER	HR	BB-IBB	SO	Avg.
1996— Yakima (NW)	4	0	1.000	0.84	0.73	13	8	0	0	...	0-...	53.2	25	9	5	0	14-1	75	.135
1997— San Bernardino (Calif.)	7	8	.467	2.81	1.10	23	21	2	1	...	0-...	134.2	116	52	42	9	32-0	158	.234
1998— San Antonio (Texas)	8	4	.667	3.30	1.35	17	17	0	0	...	0-...	111.2	114	50	41	8	37-0	96	.266
— Albuquerque (PCL)	1	3	.250	4.94	1.55	5	5	0	0	...	0-...	31.0	39	20	17	3	9-0	25	.310
— Ottawa (Int'l)	2	2	.500	4.85	1.64	7	7	0	0	...	0-...	39.0	45	28	21	8	19-0	49	.280
1999— Ottawa (Int'l)	8	5	.615	3.84	1.17	16	16	0	0	...	0-...	89.0	81	40	38	12	23-0	78	.241
— Montreal (N.L.)	0	1	.000	7.61	1.65	9	3	0	0	0	0-0	23.2	30	20	20	7	9-0	28	.309
2000— Tampa (FSL)	0	0	...	1.35	0.90	1	1	0	0	...	0-...	6.2	5	3	1	0	1-0	6	.192
— Columbus (Int'l)	8	11	.421	4.19	1.49	22	22	3	1	...	0-...	137.1	157	77	64	14	48-0	127	.287
— New York (A.L.)	0	0	...	5.63	1.63	7	0	0	0	0	0-0	8.0	8	6	5	1	5-0	11	.235
2001— Columbus (Int'l)	0	0	...	2.84	0.95	5	5	0	0	...	0-...	25.1	16	10	8	2	8-0	30	.176
— New York (A.L.)	5	6	.455	5.37	1.47	26	21	0	0	0	0-0	120.2	126	81	72	20	51-1	112	.267
2002— New York (A.L.)	3	6	.333	3.40	1.06	16	11	2	1	0	0-0	76.2	57	31	29	10	24-3	59	.202
— Oakland (A.L.)	2	1	.667	4.63	1.29	6	5	0	0	0	0-0	23.1	23	12	12	5	7-0	18	.253
2003— Oakland (A.L.)	12	10	.545	4.34	1.33	32	31	0	0	0	0-0	178.1	179	92	86	24	58-3	147	.255
American League totals (4 years)	22	23	.489	4.51	1.32	87	68	2	1	0	0-0	407.0	393	222	204	60	145-7	347	.248
National League totals (1 year)	0	1	.000	7.61	1.65	9	3	0	0	0	0-0	23.2	30	20	20	7	9-0	28	.309
Major League totals (5 years)	22	24	.478	4.68	1.34	96	71	2	1	0	0-0	430.2	423	242	224	67	154-7	375	.252

LIMA, JOSE   P

PERSONAL: Born September 30, 1972, in Santiago, Dominican Republic. ... 6-2/205. ... Throws right, bats right. ... Full name: Jose Desiderio Lima. ... Name pronounced: LEE-mah. ... High school: Escuela Primaria Las Charcas (Santiago, Dominican Republic).

TRANSACTIONS/CAREER NOTES: Signed as non-drafted free agent by Detroit Tigers organization (July 5, 1989). ... Traded by Tigers with C Brad Ausmus, P C.J. Nitkowski, P Trever Miller and IF Daryle Ward to Houston Astros for OF Brian Hunter, IF Orlando Miller, P Doug Brocail, P Todd Jones and cash (December 10, 1996). ... On suspended list (May 9-15, 2001). ... Traded by Astros to Detroit Tigers for P Dave Mlicki (June 23, 2001). ... Released by Tigers (September 7, 2002). ... Contract purchased by Kansas City from Newark of the Atlantic League (June 4, 2003).

CAREER HITTING: 28-for-236 (.119), 17 R, 4 2B, 0 3B, 0 HR, 8 RBI.

Year League	W	L	Pct.	ERA	WHIP	G	GS	CG	ShO	Hld.	Sv.-Opp.	IP	H	R	ER	HR	BB-IBB	SO	Avg.
1990— Bristol (Appal.)	3	8	.273	5.02	1.47	14	12	1	0	...	1-...	75.1	89	49	42	9	22-3	64	.299
1991— Lakeland (Fla. St.)	0	1	.000	10.38	2.08	4	1	0	0	...	0-...	8.2	16	10	10	1	2-0	5	.421
— Fayetteville (S. Atl.)	1	3	.250	4.97	1.34	18	7	0	0	...	0-...	58.0	53	38	32	4	25-0	60	.241
1992— Lakeland (Fla. St.)	5	11	.313	3.16	1.01	25	25	5	2	...	0-...	151.0	132	57	53	* 14	21-2	137	.237
1993— London (East.)	8	•13	.381	4.07	1.24	27	27	2	0	...	0-...	177.0	160	96	80	19	59-4	138	.238
1994— Toledo (Int'l)	7	9	.438	3.60	1.21	23	22	3	2	...	0-...	142.1	124	70	57	16	48-1	117	.235
— Detroit (A.L.)	0	1	.000	13.50	2.10	3	1	0	0	0	0-0	6.2	11	10	10	2	3-1	7	.355
1995— Lakeland (Fla. St.)	3	1	.750	2.57	1.10	4	4	0	0	...	0-...	21.0	23	11	6	2	0-0	20	.271
— Toledo (Int'l)	5	3	.625	3.01	1.11	11	11	1	0	...	0-...	74.2	69	26	25	9	14-2	40	.247
— Detroit (A.L.)	3	9	.250	6.11	1.40	15	15	0	0	0	0-0	73.2	85	52	50	11	18-4	37	.288
1996— Toledo (Int'l)	5	4	.556	6.78	1.52	12	12	0	0	...	0-...	72.2	93	53	52	11	12-0	57	.322
— Detroit (A.L.)	5	6	.455	5.70	1.50	39	4	0	0	6	3-7	72.2	87	48	46	13	22-4	59	.296
1997— Houston (N.L.)	1	6	.143	5.28	1.27	52	1	0	0	3	2-2	75.0	79	45	44	9	16-2	63	.271
1998— Houston (N.L.)	16	8	.667	3.70	1.12	33	33	3	1	0	0-0	233.1	229	100	96	34	32-1	169	.256
1999— Houston (N.L.)	21	10	.677	3.58	1.22	35	•35	3	0	0	0-0	246.1	256	108	98	30	44-2	187	.265
2000— Houston (N.L.)	7	16	.304	6.65	1.62	33	33	0	0	0	0-0	196.1	251	* 152	* 145	* 48	68-3	124	.313
2001— Houston (N.L.)	1	2	.333	7.30	1.75	14	9	0	0	0	0-0	53.0	77	48	43	12	16-1	41	.339
— Detroit (A.L.)	5	10	.333	4.71	1.26	18	18	2	0	0	0-0	112.2	120	66	59	23	22-2	43	.274
2002— Detroit (A.L.)	4	6	.400	7.77	1.57	20	12	0	0	0	0-0	68.1	86	60	59	12	21-0	33	.314
2003— Kansas City (A.L.)	8	3	.727	4.91	1.45	14	14	0	0	0	0-0	73.1	80	40	40	7	26-0	32	.280
American League totals (6 years)	25	35	.417	5.83	1.43	109	64	2	0	6	3-7	407.1	469	276	264	67	112-11	211	.290
National League totals (5 years)	46	42	.523	4.77	1.33	167	111	6	1	3	2-2	804.0	892	453	426	133	176-9	584	.281
Major League totals (10 years)	71	77	.480	5.13	1.36	276	175	8	1	9	5-9	1211.1	1361	729	690	200	288-20	795	.284

LINCOLN, MIKE   P

PERSONAL: Born April 10, 1975, in Carmichael, Calif. ... 6-2/213. ... Throws right, bats right. ... Full name: Michael George Lincoln. ... High school: Casa Roble (Orangevale, Calif.). ... College: Tennessee.

TRANSACTIONS/CAREER NOTES: Selected by Minnesota Twins organization in 13th round of free-agent draft (June 4, 1996). ... On Minnesota disabled list (July 23, 2000-remainder of season). ... Released by Twins (January 15, 2001). ... Signed by Pittsburgh Pirates organization (February 17, 2001). ... On Pittsburgh disabled list (August 13-28, 2001). ... On disabled list (March 24, 2003). ... Sent to Nashville on rehab assignment (June 8, 2003). ... Recalled from Nashville rehab assignment; reinstated from Emergency disabled list (July 1, 2003).

CAREER HITTING: 1-for-10 (.100), 0 R, 0 2B, 0 3B, 0 HR, 0 RBI.

Year League	W	L	Pct.	ERA	WHIP	G	GS	CG	ShO	Hld.	Sv.-Opp.	IP	H	R	ER	HR	BB-IBB	SO	Avg.
1996— Fort Myers (Fla. St.)	5	2	.714	4.07	1.49	12	11	0	0	...	0-...	59.2	64	31	27	5	25-0	24	.279
1997— Fort Myers (Fla. St.)	13	4	.765	2.28	1.16	20	20	1	1	...	0-...	134.0	130	41	34	4	25-0	75	.252
1998— New Britain (East.)	* 15	7	.682	3.22	1.24	26	26	1	0	...	0-...	173.1	180	80	62	13	35-0	109	.270
1999— Minnesota (A.L.)	3	10	.231	6.84	1.68	18	15	0	0	1	0-0	76.1	102	59	58	11	26-0	27	.321
— Salt Lake (PCL)	5	2	.714	7.78	1.75	9	9	0	0	...	0-...	59.0	82	52	51	12	21-0	39	.335
2000— Salt Lake (PCL)	4	1	.800	3.87	1.18	12	12	2	1	...	0-...	74.1	72	35	32	4	16-1	37	.252
— Minnesota (A.L.)	0	3	.000	10.89	2.37	8	4	0	0	0	0-0	20.2	36	25	25	10	13-0	15	.383
2001— Nashville (PCL)	5	4	.556	3.44	1.25	18	13	1	0	...	0-...	91.2	90	39	35	10	25-0	71	.251
— Pittsburgh (N.L.)	2	1	.667	2.68	1.12	31	0	0	0	7	0-2	40.1	34	16	12	3	11-0	24	.225
2002— Pittsburgh (N.L.)	2	4	.333	3.11	1.48	55	0	0	0	11	0-3	72.1	80	28	25	7	27-8	50	.290
— Pittsburgh (N.L.)	0	0	...	1.23	1.09	10	0	0	0	...	2-...	14.2	14	2	2	0	2-0	15	.237
2003— Nashville (PCL)	1	1	.500	0.71	0.95	8	0	0	0	...	0-...	12.2	8	2	1	1	4-0	9	.174
— Pittsburgh (N.L.)	3	4	.429	5.20	1.40	36	0	0	0	5	5-8	36.1	38	22	21	5	13-0	28	.277
American League totals (2 years)	3	13	.188	7.70	1.82	26	19	0	0	1	0-0	97.0	138	84	83	21	39-0	42	.335
National League totals (3 years)	7	9	.438	3.50	1.36	122	0	0	0	23	5-13	149.0	152	66	58	15	51-8	102	.270
Major League totals (5 years)	10	22	.313	5.16	1.54	148	19	0	0	24	5-13	246.0	290	150	141	36	90-8	144	.297

LINDEN, TODD   OF

PERSONAL: Born June 30, 1980, in Edmonds, Wash. ... 6-3/210. ... Bats both, throws right. ... Full name: Todd A. Linden. ... High school: Central Kitsap (Silverdale, Wash.). ... College: Louisiana State.
TRANSACTIONS/CAREER NOTES: Selected by San Francisco Giants in first round (41st pick overall) of free-agent draft (June 5, 2001).
2003 GAMES PLAYED BY POSITION (MLB): OF—13.

Year Team (League)	Pos.	G	AB	R	H	2B	3B	HR	RBI	BB	SO	HBP	GDP	SB-CS	Avg.	OBP	SLG	OPS	E	Pct.
2002— Shreveport (Texas)	OF	111	392	64	123	26	2	12	52	61	101	12	12	9-5	.314	.419	.482	.901	3	.987
— Fresno (PCL)	OF	29	100	18	25	2	1	3	10	20	35	1	2	2-0	.250	.380	.380	.760	0	1.000
2003— Fresno (PCL)	OF-DH	125	471	75	131	24	3	11	56	40	105	17	9	14-4	.278	.356	.412	.768	4	.985
— San Francisco (N.L.)	OF	18	38	2	8	1	0	1	6	1	8	0	2	0-0	.211	.231	.316	.547	1	.929
Major League totals (1 year)		18	38	2	8	1	0	1	6	1	8	0	2	0-0	.211	.231	.316	.547	1	.929

LINEBRINK, SCOTT   P

PERSONAL: Born August 4, 1976, in Austin, Texas. ... 6-2/200. ... Throws right, bats right. ... Full name: Scott Cameron Linebrink. ... High school: McNeil (Austin, Texas). ... College: Southwest Texas State.
TRANSACTIONS/CAREER NOTES: Selected by San Francisco Giants organization in second round of free-agent draft (June 3, 1997). ... On disabled list (April 8-July 17, 1999). ... Traded by Giants to Houston Astros for P Doug Henry (July 30, 2000). ... On Houston disabled list (May 20-June 17, 2002); included rehabilitation assignment to New Orleans (June 11-14) and Round Rock (June 15-17). ... Contract purchased from New Orleans (April 18, 2003). ... Designated for assignment (May 26, 2003). ... Claimed off waivers by San Diego Padres (May 29, 2003).
CAREER HITTING: 3-for-13 (.231), 0 R, 1 2B, 0 3B, 0 HR, 0 RBI.

Year League	W	L	Pct.	ERA	WHIP	G	GS	CG	ShO	Hld.	Sv.-Opp.	IP	H	R	ER	HR	BB-IBB	SO	Avg.
1997— Salem-Keizer (NW)	0	0	...	4.50	1.30	3	3	0	0	...	0-...	10.0	7	5	5	1	6-0	6	.194
— San Jose (Calif.)	2	1	.667	3.18	1.38	6	6	0	0	...	0-...	28.1	29	11	10	2	10-0	40	.264
1998— Shreveport (Texas)	10	8	.556	5.02	1.41	21	21	0	0	...	0-...	113.0	101	66	63	12	58-1	128	.243
1999— Shreveport (Texas)	1	8	.111	6.44	1.43	10	10	0	0	...	0-...	43.1	48	31	31	7	14-0	33	.279
2000— Fresno (PCL)	1	4	.200	5.23	1.06	28	7	0	0	...	4-...	62.0	54	42	36	10	12-0	49	.225
— San Francisco (N.L.)	0	0	...	11.57	3.86	3	0	0	0	0	0-0	2.1	7	3	3	1	2-0	0	.500
— Houston (N.L.)	0	0	...	4.66	1.76	8	0	0	0	0	0-0	9.2	11	5	5	3	6-0	6	.289
— New Orleans (PCL)	2	0	1.000	1.80	1.47	11	0	0	0	...	1-...	15.0	15	4	3	0	7-0	22	.259
2001— Houston (N.L.)	0	0	...	2.61	1.16	9	0	0	0	0	0-0	10.1	6	4	3	0	6-0	9	.176
— New Orleans (PCL)	7	6	.538	3.50	1.06	50	0	0	0	...	8-...	72.0	52	28	28	4	24-6	72	.204
2002— Houston (N.L.)	0	0	...	7.03	1.81	22	0	0	0	1	0-...	24.1	31	21	19	2	13-4	24	.298
— New Orleans (PCL)	1	1	.500	6.00	1.87	13	0	0	0	...	0-...	15.0	17	11	10	1	11-3	16	.293
— Round Rock (Texas)	0	0	...	0.00	2.00	2	2	0	0	...	0-...	2.0	2	0	0	0	2-0	1	.286
2003— New Orleans (PCL)	0	2	.000	2.70	1.30	2	2	0	0	...	0-...	10.0	8	3	3	1	5-0	6	.222
— Houston (N.L.)	1	1	.500	4.26	1.64	18	0	0	0	0	0-0	31.2	38	15	15	4	14-1	17	.317
— San Diego (N.L.)	2	1	.667	2.82	1.27	43	6	0	0	6	0-0	60.2	55	22	19	5	22-3	51	.244
Major League totals (4 years)	3	2	.600	4.14	1.52	94	6	0	0	7	0-0	139.0	148	70	64	15	63-8	107	.277

LINTON, DOUG   P

PERSONAL: Born September 2, 1965, in Santa Ana, Calif. ... 6-1/190. ... Throws right, bats right. ... Full name: Douglas Warren Linton. ... High school: Canyon (Anaheim, Calif.). ... College: UC-Irvine.
TRANSACTIONS/CAREER NOTES: Selected by Toronto Blue Jays organization in 43rd round of free-agent draft (June 2, 1986). ... On disabled list (April 30-May 24 and July 29-September 2, 1987). ... On Knoxville disabled list (April 7-July 21, 1988). ... Claimed on waivers by California Angels (June 17, 1993). ... Released by Angels (September 14, 1993). ... Signed by New York Mets organization (December 17, 1993). ... On Norfolk suspended list (July 21-29, 1994). ... Granted free agency (October 15, 1994). ... Signed by Kansas City Royals organization (April 25, 1995). ... Granted free agency (October 11, 1995). ... Re-signed by Royals organization (October 22, 1995). ... Released by Royals (March 4, 1997). ... Signed by New York Yankees organization (January 26, 1998). ... Released by Yankees (March 14, 1998). ... Signed by Minnesota Twins organization (May 26, 1998). ... Granted free agency (October 16, 1998). ... Signed by Baltimore Orioles organization (December 17, 1998). ... Released by Orioles (December 7, 1999). ... Signed by Colorado Rockies organization (January 20, 2000). ... On Colorado Springs disabled list (June 13-24, 2000). ... Granted free agency (October 18, 2000). ... Signed by Los Angeles Dodgers organization (January 17, 2001). ... Released by Dodgers (2001). ... Signed by New York Mets as a free agent (May 9, 2001). ... On Norfolk disabled list (July 6-13, 2001). ... Contract sold by Mets to LG Twins of Korean League (July 16, 2001). ... Granted free agency (October 15, 2002). ... Signed by Toronto Blue Jays organization (October 30, 2002). ... Elected free agency (September 29, 2003).
CAREER HITTING: 0-for-7 (.000), 0 R, 0 2B, 0 3B, 0 HR, 0 RBI.

Year League	W	L	Pct.	ERA	WHIP	G	GS	CG	ShO	Hld.	Sv.-Opp.	IP	H	R	ER	HR	BB-IBB	SO	Avg.
1987— Myrtle Beach (SAL)	14	2	.875	1.55	0.98	20	19	2	0	...	1-...	122.0	94	34	21	9	25-0	155	.208
— Knoxville (Sou.)	0	0	...	9.00	2.00	1	1	0	0	...	0-...	3.0	5	3	3	0	1-0	1	.385
1988— Dunedin (Fla. St.)	2	1	.667	1.63	1.01	12	0	0	0	...	2-...	27.2	19	5	5	0	9-1	28	.190
1989— Dunedin (Fla. St.)	1	2	.333	2.96	1.32	9	1	0	0	...	2-...	27.1	27	12	9	1	9-0	35	.252
— Knoxville (Sou.)	5	4	.556	2.60	1.01	14	13	3	•2	...	0-...	90.0	68	28	26	2	23-2	93	.209
1990— Syracuse (Int'l)	10	10	.500	3.40	1.36	26	26	8	•3	...	0-...	*177.1	174	77	67	14	67-3	113	.261
1991— Syracuse (Int'l)	10	12	.455	5.01	1.47	30	26	3	1	...	0-...	161.2	181	108	90	*21	56-2	93	.288
1992— Syracuse (Int'l)	12	10	.545	3.74	1.44	25	25	7	1	...	0-...	170.2	176	83	71	17	70-3	126	.269
— Toronto (A.L.)	1	3	.250	8.63	2.00	8	3	0	0	...	0-0	24.0	31	23	23	5	17-0	16	.323
1993— Syracuse (Int'l)	2	6	.250	5.32	1.31	13	7	0	0	...	2-...	47.1	48	29	28	11	14-3	42	.258
— Toronto (A.L.)	0	1	.000	6.55	1.82	4	1	0	0	...	0-0	11.0	11	8	8	0	9-0	4	.256
— California (A.L.)	2	0	1.000	7.71	1.91	19	0	0	0	...	0-1	25.2	35	22	22	8	14-1	19	.324
1994— Norfolk (Int'l)	2	1	.667	2.00	0.67	3	0	0	0	...	0-...	18.0	11	6	4	1	1-0	15	.172
— New York (N.L.)	6	2	.750	4.47	1.87	32	3	0	0	...	0-0	50.1	74	27	25	4	20-3	29	.341
1995— Kansas City (A.L.)	0	1	.000	7.25	1.43	7	2	0	0	...	0-0	22.1	22	21	18	4	10-1	13	.256
— Omaha (Am. Assoc.)	7	7	.500	4.40	1.41	18	18	2	1	...	0-...	108.1	129	60	53	9	24-2	85	.298
1996— Omaha (Am. Assoc.)	1	1	.500	4.76	1.46	4	4	0	0	...	0-...	22.2	26	13	12	1	7-0	14	.292
— Kansas City (A.L.)	7	9	.438	5.02	1.32	21	18	0	0	...	1 0-0	104.0	111	65	58	13	26-1	87	.271
1997—										Did not play.									
1998— Salt Lake (PCL)	4	4	.500	5.99	1.51	18	14	0	0	...	0-...	79.2	106	57	53	19	14-1	60	.322
1999— Rochester (Int'l)	7	5	.583	3.65	1.24	18	18	1	0	...	0-...	118.1	120	58	48	13	27-1	97	.258
— Baltimore (A.L.)	1	4	.200	5.95	1.59	14	8	0	0	...	0-...	59.0	69	41	39	14	25-1	31	.296
2001— Norfolk (Int'l)	7	3	.700	3.21	1.11	12	12	0	0	...	0-...	75.2	74	28	27	8	10-0	67	.261
2002— Richmond (Int'l)	9	11	.450	2.53	1.11	28	28	1	1	...	0-...	174.0	167	63	49	14	26-0	*160	.250
2003— Toronto (A.L.)	0	0	...	3.00	1.22	7	0	0	0	...	0-0	9.0	7	3	3	2	4-0	7	.226
— Syracuse (Int'l)	2	10	.167	5.28	1.39	32	13	1	0	...	0-...	109.0	133	67	64	13	19-2	79	.304
American League totals (6 years)	11	18	.379	6.04	1.53	80	32	0	0	1	0-1	255.0	286	183	171	46	105-4	177	.284
National League totals (1 year)	6	2	.750	4.47	1.87	32	3	0	0		0-0	50.1	74	27	25	4	20-3	29	.341
Major League totals (7 years)	17	20	.459	5.78	1.59	112	35	0	0	1	0-1	305.1	360	210	196	50	125-7	206	.294

LLOYD, GRAEME — P

PERSONAL: Born April 9, 1967, in Geelong, Australia. ... 6-7/220. ... Throws left, bats left. ... Full name: Graeme John Lloyd. ... Name pronounced: gram. ... High school: Geelong Technical School (Victoria, Australia).

TRANSACTIONS/CAREER NOTES: Signed as non-drafted free agent by Toronto Blue Jays organization (January 26, 1988). ... On Myrtle Beach disabled list (June 29-September 1, 1989). ... Selected by Philadelphia Phillies from Blue Jays organization in Rule 5 major league draft (December 7, 1992). ... Traded by Phillies to Milwaukee Brewers for P John Trisler (December 8, 1992). ... On disabled list (August 20-September 4, 1993; and July 25-September 10, 1995). ... On suspended list (September 5-9, 1993). ... Traded by Brewers with OF Pat Listach to New York Yankees for OF Gerald Williams and P Bob Wickman (August 23, 1996). ... On disabled list (April 22-May 8, 1998). ... On suspended list (May 25-27, 1998). ... Traded by Yankees with P David Wells and 2B Homer Bush to Toronto Blue Jays for P Roger Clemens (February 18, 1999). ... Granted free agency (October 29, 1999). ... Signed by Montreal Expos (December 20, 1999). ... On disabled list (March 29, 2000-entire season). ... Traded by Expos with P Carl Pavano, IF Mike Mordecai and P Justin Wayne to Florida Marlins for OF Cliff Floyd, P Claudio Vargas, 2B/OF Wilton Guerrero, cash considerations and a player to be named later (July 11, 2002); Expos acquired P Don Levinski to complete deal (August 6, 2002). ... Granted free agency (October 30, 2002). ... Signed by New York Mets organization (January 24, 2003). ... Traded by Mets to Kansas City Royals for P Jeremy Hill (July 28, 2003).

CAREER HITTING: 0-for-6 (.000), 0 R, 0 2B, 0 3B, 0 HR, 0 RBI.

Year League	W	L	Pct.	ERA	WHIP	G	GS	CG	ShO	Hld.	Sv.-Opp.	IP	H	R	ER	HR	BB-IBB	SO	Avg.
1988— Myrtle Beach (SAL)	3	2	.600	3.62	1.69	41	0	0	0	...	2-...	59.2	71	33	24	2	30-5	43	.291
1989— Dunedin (Fla. St.)	0	0	...	10.13	2.63	2	0	0	0	...	0-...	2.2	6	3	3	0	1-0	0	.462
— Myrtle Beach (SAL)	0	0	...	5.40	1.00	1	1	0	0	...	0-...	5.0	5	4	3	1	0-0	3	.256
1990— Myrtle Beach (SAL)	5	2	.714	2.72	1.35	19	6	0	0	...	6-...	49.2	51	20	15	3	16-1	42	.256
1991— Dunedin (Fla. St.)	2	5	.286	2.24	1.31	50	0	0	0	...	24-...	60.1	54	17	15	1	25-2	39	.233
— Knoxville (Sou.)	0	0	...	0.00	1.20	2	0	0	0	...	0-...	1.2	1	0	0	0	1-0	2	.167
1992— Knoxville (Sou.)	4	8	.333	1.96	1.13	49	7	1	0	...	14-...	92.0	79	30	20	2	25-2	65	.229
1993— Milwaukee (A.L.)	3	4	.429	2.83	1.21	55	0	0	0	6	0-4	63.2	64	24	20	5	13-3	31	.256
1994— Milwaukee (A.L.)	2	3	.400	5.17	1.36	43	0	0	0	3	3-6	47.0	49	28	27	4	15-6	31	.269
1995— Milwaukee (A.L.)	0	5	.000	4.50	1.13	33	0	0	0	9	4-6	32.0	28	16	16	4	8-2	13	.246
1996— Milwaukee (A.L.)	2	4	.333	2.82	1.29	52	0	0	0	15	0-3	51.0	49	19	16	3	17-3	24	.254
— New York (A.L.)	0	2	.000	17.47	3.00	13	0	0	0	2	0-2	5.2	12	11	11	1	5-1	6	.429
1997— New York (A.L.)	1	1	.500	3.31	1.53	46	0	0	0	2	1-1	49.0	55	24	18	6	20-7	26	.293
1998— New York (A.L.)	3	0	1.000	1.67	0.85	50	0	0	0	9	0-2	37.2	26	10	7	3	6-2	20	.191
1999— Toronto (A.L.)	5	3	.625	3.63	1.26	74	0	0	0	22	3-9	72.0	68	36	29	11	23-4	47	.250
2000— Montreal (N.L.)											Did not play.								
2001— Montreal (N.L.)	9	5	.643	4.35	1.35	84	0	0	0	11	1-3	70.1	74	38	34	6	21-2	44	.272
2002— Montreal (N.L.)	2	3	.400	5.87	1.60	41	0	0	0	9	5-7	30.2	41	21	20	5	8-3	17	.325
— Florida (N.L.)	2	2	.500	4.44	1.41	25	0	0	0	2	0-1	26.1	26	13	13	1	11-1	20	.263
2003— New York (N.L.)	1	2	.333	3.31	1.30	36	0	0	0	6	0-0	35.1	39	16	13	2	7-2	17	.254
— Kansas City (A.L.)	0	2	.000	10.95	2.92	16	0	0	0	1	0-1	12.1	29	18	15	0	7-0	8	.453
American League totals (8 years)	16	24	.400	3.86	1.33	382	0	0	0	69	11-34	370.1	380	186	159	37	114-28	206	.266
National League totals (3 years)	14	12	.538	4.43	1.40	186	0	0	0	28	6-11	162.2	180	88	80	14	47-8	98	.283
Major League totals (10 years)	30	36	.455	4.04	1.35	568	0	0	0	97	17-45	533.0	560	274	239	51	161-36	304	.271

LOAIZA, ESTEBAN — P

PERSONAL: Born December 31, 1971, in Tijuana, Mexico. ... 6-3/215. ... Throws right, bats right. ... Full name: Esteban Antonio Veyna Loaiza. ... Name pronounced: s-TAY-bahn low-EYE-zah. ... High school: Mar Vista (Imperial Beach, Calif.).

TRANSACTIONS/CAREER NOTES: Signed as non-drafted free agent by Pittsburgh Pirates organization (March 21, 1991). ... Loaned by Pirates organization to Mexico City Red Devils of Mexican League (May 7-28, 1993). ... On disabled list (April 7-28 and July 7-14, 1996). ... Loaned to Red Devils of Mexican League (June 19-August 14, 1996). ... Traded by Pirates to Texas Rangers for P Todd Van Poppel and 2B Warren Morris (July 17, 1998). ... On Texas disabled list (May 12-July 5, 1999); included rehabilitation assignment to Oklahoma City (June 26-July 5). ... Traded by Rangers to Toronto Blue Jays for P Darwin Cubillan and 2B/SS Mike Young (July 19, 2000). ... On Toronto disabled list (March 22-May 14, 2002); included rehabilitation assignments to Dunedin (April 19-28), Syracuse (April 29-May 3) and Tennessee (May 4-14). ... Granted free agency (October 27, 2002). ... Signed by Chicago White Sox organization (January 27, 2003).

CAREER HITTING: 31-for-174 (.178), 12 R, 2 2B, 1 3B, 0 HR, 11 RBI.

Year League	W	L	Pct.	ERA	WHIP	G	GS	CG	ShO	Hld.	Sv.-Opp.	IP	H	R	ER	HR	BB-IBB	SO	Avg.
1991— GC Pirates (GCL)	5	1	.833	2.26	1.20	11	11	1	•1	...	0-...	51.2	48	17	13	0	14-0	41	.241
1992— Augusta (S. Atl.)	10	8	.556	3.89	1.35	26	25	3	0	...	0-...	143.1	134	72	62	7	60-0	123	.249
1993— Salem (Caro.)	6	7	.462	3.39	1.31	17	17	3	0	...	0-...	109.0	113	53	41	7	30-0	61	.268
— M.C. Red Devils (Mex.)	1	1	.500	5.18	1.48	4	3	0	0	...	0-...	24.1	32	18	14	...	4-...	15	...
— Carolina (Sou.)	2	1	.667	3.77	1.19	7	7	1	0	...	0-...	43.0	39	18	18	5	12-1	40	.241
1994— Carolina (Sou.)	10	5	.667	3.79	1.29	24	24	3	0	...	0-...	154.1	169	69	65	15	30-0	115	.280
1995— Pittsburgh (N.L.)	8	9	.471	5.16	1.51	32	•31	1	0	0	0-0	172.2	205	*115	*99	21	55-3	85	.300
1996— Calgary (PCL)	3	4	.429	4.02	1.24	12	11	1	0	...	0-...	69.1	61	34	31	5	25-2	38	.243
— Pittsburgh (N.L.)	2	3	.400	4.96	1.59	10	10	1	1	0	0-0	52.2	65	32	29	11	19-2	32	.308
— M.C. Red Devils (Mex.)	2	0	1.000	2.43	1.26	5	5	0	0	...	0-...	33.1	28	12	9	...	14-...	16	...
1997— Pittsburgh (N.L.)	11	11	.500	4.13	1.38	33	32	1	0	0	0-0	196.1	214	99	90	17	56-9	122	.279
1998— Pittsburgh (N.L.)	6	5	.545	4.52	1.37	21	14	0	0	0	0-1	91.2	96	50	46	13	30-1	53	.275
— Texas (A.L.)	3	6	.333	5.90	1.58	14	14	1	0	0	0-0	79.1	103	57	52	15	22-3	55	.316
1999— Texas (A.L.)	9	5	.643	4.56	1.40	30	15	0	0	0	0-0	120.1	128	65	61	10	40-2	77	.275
— Oklahoma (PCL)	0	0	...	0.00	1.38	2	2	0	0	...	0-...	4.1	3	0	0	0	3-0	6	.176
2000— Texas (A.L.)	5	6	.455	5.37	1.53	20	17	0	0	0	1-1	107.1	133	67	64	21	31-1	75	.302
— Toronto (A.L.)	5	7	.417	3.62	1.32	14	14	1	1	0	0-0	92.0	95	45	37	8	26-0	62	.270
2001— Toronto (A.L.)	11	11	.500	5.02	1.47	36	30	1	1	0	0-0	190.0	239	113	106	27	40-1	110	.307
2002— Toronto (A.L.)	9	10	.474	5.71	1.52	25	25	3	1	0	0-0	151.1	192	102	96	18	38-3	87	.309
— Dunedin (Fla. St.)	0	0	...	0.00	0.80	2	2	0	0	...	0-...	5.0	2	0	0	0	2-0	2	.125
— Syracuse (Int'l)	0	0	...	2.08	0.92	1	1	0	0	...	0-...	4.1	4	1	1	0	0-0	4	.222
— Tennessee (Sou.)	2	0	1.000	1.88	0.77	2	2	0	0	...	0-...	14.1	10	3	3	0	1-0	13	.208
2003— Chicago (A.L.)	21	9	.700	2.90	1.11	34	34	1	0	0	0-0	226.1	196	75	73	17	56-2	*207	.233
American League totals (6 years)	63	54	.538	4.55	1.39	173	149	7	3	0	1-1	966.2	1086	524	489	116	253-12	673	.284
National League totals (4 years)	27	28	.491	4.63	1.44	96	87	3	1	0	0-1	513.1	580	296	264	62	160-15	292	.289
Major League totals (9 years)	90	82	.523	4.58	1.40	269	236	10	4	0	1-2	1480.0	1666	820	753	178	413-27	965	.286

LOCKHART, KEITH — 2B

PERSONAL: Born November 10, 1964, in Whittier, Calif. ... 5-10/170. ... Bats left, throws right. ... Full name: Keith Virgil Lockhart. ... High school: Northview (Covina, Calif.). ... College: Oral Roberts.

TRANSACTIONS/CAREER NOTES: Selected by Cincinnati Reds organization in 11th round of free-agent draft (June 2, 1986). ... Contract sold by Reds to Oakland Athletics organization (February 4, 1992). ... Granted free agency (October 15, 1992). ... Signed by St. Louis Cardinals organization (December 12, 1992). ... Granted free agency

(October 15, 1993). ... Signed by San Diego Padres organization (January 7, 1994). ... Granted free agency (October 15, 1994). ... Signed by Kansas City Royals organization (November 14, 1994). ... Traded by Royals with OF Michael Tucker to Atlanta Braves for OF Jermaine Dye and P Jamie Walker (March 27, 1997). ... On disabled list (August 6-22, 1997). ... Granted free agency (November 5, 2001). ... Re-signed by Braves organization (January 8, 2002). ... Granted free agency (October 30, 2002). ... Signed by Padres organization (February 3, 2003). ... Placed on 15-day disabled list (June 30, 2003). ... Sent to Portland on rehab assignment (July 28, 2003). ... Recalled from Portland rehab assignment (August 6, 2003). ... Removed from 15-day disabled list (August 28, 2003). ... Given unconditional release (September 29, 2003).

2003 GAMES PLAYED BY POSITION (MLB): 2B—27, 3B—3.

Year Team (League)	Pos.	G	AB	R	H	2B	3B	HR	RBI	BB	SO	HBP	GDP	SB-CS	Avg.	OBP	SLG	OPS	E	Pct.
1986— Billings (Pio.)	2B-3B	53	202	51	70	11	3	7	31	35	22	4	0	4-2	.347	.447	.535	.981	17	.931
— Cedar Rap. (Midw.)	2B-3B	13	42	4	8	2	0	0	1	6	6	1	0	1-1	.190	.306	.238	.544	0	1.000
1987— Cedar Rap. (Midw.)	2B-3B	*140	511	101	160	37	5	23	84	86	70	13	6	20-8	.313	.420	.540	.961	28	.931
1988— Chattanooga (Sou.)	2B-3B	139	515	74	137	27	3	12	67	61	59	5	9	7-5	.266	.343	.400	.743	36	.922
1989— Nashville (A.A.)	2B	131	479	77	128	21	6	14	58	61	41	6	6	4-3	.267	.355	.424	.778	17	.973
1990— Nashville (A.A.)	2B-3B-OF	126	431	48	112	25	4	9	63	51	74	5	4	8-7	.260	.342	.399	.741	9	.979
1991— Nashville (A.A.)	2B-3B-OF	116	411	53	107	25	3	8	36	24	64	2	5	3-7	.260	.304	.394	.698	13	.968
1992— Tacoma (PCL)	2B-3B-SS	107	363	44	101	25	3	5	37	29	21	3	3	5-3	.278	.334	.405	.739	11	.976
1993— Louisville (A.A.)	2-3-1-OF	132	467	66	140	24	3	13	68	60	43	7	6	3-3	.300	.383	.448	.831	12	.971
1994— San Diego (N.L.)	3-2-S-OF	27	43	4	9	0	0	2	6	4	10	1	2	1-0	.209	.286	.349	.635	1	.969
— Las Vegas (PCL)	0-S-2-3-1-P-C	89	331	61	106	15	5	7	43	26	37	2	6	3-4	.320	.369	.459	.828	10	.962
1995— Omaha (A.A.)	3B-DH	44	148	24	56	7	1	5	19	16	10	1	0	1-3	.378	.442	.541	.983	8	.928
— Kansas City (A.L.)	2B-3B-DH	94	274	41	88	19	3	6	33	14	21	4	2	8-1	.321	.355	.478	.833	8	.973
1996— Kansas City (A.L.)	2B-3B-DH	138	433	49	118	33	3	7	55	30	40	2	7	11-6	.273	.319	.411	.730	13	.970
1997— Atlanta (N.L.)	2B-3B-DH	96	147	25	41	5	3	6	32	14	17	1	4	0-0	.279	.337	.476	.814	3	.960
1998— Atlanta (N.L.)	2B-DH-3B	109	366	50	94	21	0	9	37	29	37	1	2	2-2	.257	.311	.388	.699	6	.984
1999— Atlanta (N.L.)	2B-3B-DH	108	161	20	42	3	1	1	21	19	21	1	2	3-1	.261	.337	.311	.648	1	.989
2000— Atlanta (N.L.)	2B-3B	113	275	32	73	12	3	2	32	29	31	0	10	4-1	.265	.331	.353	.684	8	.975
2001— Atlanta (N.L.)	2B-3B	104	178	17	39	6	0	3	12	16	22	2	1	1-2	.219	.289	.303	.593	0	1.000
2002— Atlanta (N.L.)	2B-3B	128	296	34	64	13	3	5	32	27	50	1	4	0-1	.216	.282	.331	.613	8	.979
2003— Portland (PCL)	DH-2B	4	11	0	2	0	0	0	4	1	0	1	0	0-0	.182	.308	.182	.490	0	1.000
— San Diego (N.L.)	2B-3B	62	95	18	23	5	1	3	8	13	19	1	2	0-1	.242	.339	.411	.750	2	.975
American League totals (2 years)		232	707	90	206	52	6	13	88	44	61	6	9	19-7	.291	.333	.437	.770	21	.971
National League totals (8 years)		747	1561	200	385	65	11	31	180	151	207	8	27	11-8	.247	.313	.362	.675	29	.981
Major League totals (10 years)		979	2268	290	591	117	17	44	268	195	268	14	36	30-15	.261	.319	.385	.704	50	.978

LO DUCA, PAUL — C

PERSONAL: Born April 12, 1972, in Brooklyn, N.Y. ... 5-10/185. ... Bats right, throws right. ... Full name: Paul Anthony Lo Duca. ... Name pronounced: lah-duke-uh. ... High school: Apollo (Phoenix). ... College: Arizona State.
TRANSACTIONS/CAREER NOTES: Selected by Los Angeles Dodgers organization in 25th round of free-agent draft (June 3, 1993). ... On Albuquerque disabled list (June 4-July 20, 1999). ... On Los Angeles disabled list (April 29-May 21, 2001); included rehabilitation assignment to Las Vegas (May 18-21).

2003 GAMES PLAYED BY POSITION (MLB): C—123, 1B—22, OF—6.

Year Team (League)	Pos.	G	AB	R	H	2B	3B	HR	RBI	BB	SO	HBP	GDP	SB-CS	Avg.	OBP	SLG	OPS	E	Pct.
1993— Vero Beach (FSL)	C	39	134	17	42	6	0	0	13	13	22	2	2	0-0	.313	.380	.358	.738	2	.992
1994— Bakersfield (Calif.)	C-1B	123	455	65	144	32	1	6	68	52	49	3	5	16-9	.316	.387	.431	.818	5	.993
1995— San Antonio (Texas)	3B-C-1B	61	199	27	49	8	0	1	8	26	25	2	12	5-5	.246	.339	.302	.641	11	.973
1996— Vero Beach (FSL)	3B-C-1B	124	439	54	134	22	0	3	66	70	38	2	14	8-2	.305	.400	.376	.776	‡18	.980
1997— San Antonio (Texas)	C-1B	105	385	63	126	28	2	7	69	46	27	3	17	16-8	.327	.399	.465	.864	7	.990
1998— Albuquerque (PCL)	3B-C-1B	126	451	69	144	30	3	8	58	59	40	5	20	19-7	.319	.399	.452	.852	17	.980
— Los Angeles (N.L.)	C	6	14	2	4	1	0	0	1	0	1	0	0	0-0	.286	.286	.357	.643	0	1.000
1999— Los Angeles (N.L.)	C	36	95	11	22	1	0	3	11	10	9	2	3	1-2	.232	.337	.337	.649	2	.990
— Albuquerque (PCL)	C-DH-1B	26	76	17	28	9	0	1	8	10	1	6	0	1-1	.368	.478	.526	1.005	4	.978
2000— Albuquerque (PCL)	C-O-1-3-2	78	279	47	98	27	3	4	54	33	14	2	13	8-5	.351	.421	.513	.933	9	.979
— Los Angeles (N.L.)	C-OF-3B	34	65	6	16	2	0	2	8	6	8	0	2	0-2	.246	.301	.369	.671	1	.993
2001— Los Angeles (N.L.)	C-1-O-D	125	460	71	147	28	0	25	90	39	30	6	11	2-4	.320	.374	.543	.917	9	.990
— Las Vegas (PCL)	C-1B	3	9	3	3	2	0	0	3	1	0	0	0	0-0	.333	.400	.556	.956	1	.950
2002— Los Angeles (N.L.)	C-1B-OF	149	580	74	163	38	1	10	64	34	31	10	20	3-1	.281	.330	.402	.731	9	.992
2003— Los Angeles (N.L.)	C-1B-OF	147	568	64	155	34	2	7	52	44	54	10	21	0-2	.273	.335	.377	.712	16	.988
Major League totals (6 years)		497	1782	228	507	104	3	47	226	133	133	28	57	6-11	.285	.341	.425	.766	37	.990

LOEWER, CARLTON — P

PERSONAL: Born September 24, 1973, in Lafayette, La. ... 6-6/211. ... Throws right, bats right. ... Full name: Carlton Ernest Loewer. ... Name pronounced: LOE-er. ... High school: St. Edmund (Eunice, La.). ... College: Mississippi State.
TRANSACTIONS/CAREER NOTES: Selected by Toronto Blue Jays organization in seventh round of free-agent draft (June 3, 1991); did not sign. ... Selected by Philadelphia Phillies organization in first round (23rd pick overall) of free-agent draft (June 2, 1994). ... On Philadelphia disabled list (June 6-September 6, 1999); included rehabilitation assignments to Gulf Coast League Phillies (August 26-30) and Clearwater (August 31-September 6). ... Traded by Phillies with P Steve Montgomery and P Adam Eaton to San Diego Padres for P Andy Ashby (November 10, 1999). ... On San Diego disabled list (March 28, 2000-remainder of season); included rehabilitation assignments to Las Vegas (May 27-30) and Rancho Cucamonga (May 31-June 12). ... On San Diego disabled list (March 27-May 31, 2001); included rehabilitation assignments to Lake Elsinore (May 4-24) and Portland (May 25-31). ... On Portland disabled list (August 8-29, 2001). ... Granted free agency (October 16, 2001). ... Re-signed by Padres organization (December 9, 2002). ... Contract purchased from Portland (May 16, 2003). ... Sent outright to Portland (June 12, 2003).

CAREER HITTING: 8-for-62 (.129), 4 R, 0 2B, 0 3B, 0 HR, 3 RBI.

Year League	W	L	Pct.	ERA	WHIP	G	GS	CG	ShO	Hld.	Sv.-Opp.	IP	H	R	ER	HR	BB-IBB	SO	Avg.
1995— Clearwater (Fla. St.)	7	5	.583	3.30	1.40	20	20	1	0	...	0-...	114.2	124	59	42	6	36-0	83	.274
— Reading (East.)	4	1	.800	2.16	1.46	8	8	0	0	...	0-...	50.0	42	17	12	3	31-0	35	.235
1996— Reading (East.)	7	10	.412	5.26	1.45	27	27	3	1	...	0-...	171.0	*191	115	100	24	57-3	119	.282
1997— Scran./W.B. (I.L.)	5	13	.278	4.60	1.35	29	*29	4	0	...	0-...	184.0	*198	*120	94	20	50-6	152	.272
1998— Scran./W.B. (I.L.)	7	3	.700	2.87	1.18	12	12	*5	•2	...	0-...	94.0	89	34	30	5	22-0	69	.254
— Philadelphia (N.L.)	7	8	.467	6.09	1.57	21	21	1	0	0	0-0	122.2	154	86	83	18	39-1	58	.312
1999— Philadelphia (N.L.)	2	6	.250	5.12	1.41	20	13	2	1	1	0-...	89.2	100	54	51	9	26-0	48	.287
— GC Phillies (GCL)	0	0	...	0.00	1.00	1	1	0	0	...	0-...	2.0	2	0	0	0	0-0	2	.250
— Clearwater (Fla. St.)	0	2	.000	7.71	1.57	3	3	0	0	...	0-...	7.0	10	6	6	0	1-0	5	.333

– 223 –

Year League	W	L	Pct.	ERA	WHIP	G	GS	CG	ShO	Hld.	Sv.-Opp.	IP	H	R	ER	HR	BB-IBB	SO	Avg.
2000— Las Vegas (PCL)	0	0	...	0.00	0.64	1	1	0	0	...	0-...	4.2	3	0	0	0	0-0	4	.176
— Rancho Cuca. (Calif.)	0	0	...	2.57	1.00	1	1	0	0	...	0-...	7.0	7	3	2	2	0-0	4	.259
2001— Lake Elsinore (Calif.)	0	1	.000	1.59	0.88	4	4	0	0	...	0-...	11.1	6	7	2	0	4-0	14	.143
— Portland (PCL)	5	4	.556	3.87	1.38	14	12	0	0	...	0-...	81.1	97	42	35	7	15-0	64	.304
— San Diego (N.L.)	0	2	.000	24.92	3.69	2	2	0	0	0	0-0	4.1	13	12	12	2	3-0	1	.520
2002—										Did not play.									
2003— San Diego (N.L.)	1	2	.333	6.65	1.98	5	5	0	0	...	0-0	21.2	35	17	16	3	8-1	11	.368
— Portland (PCL)	7	8	.467	5.40	1.51	23	23	0	0	...	0-...	125.0	161	84	75	9	28-0	57	.320
Major League totals (4 years)	10	18	.357	6.12	1.59	48	41	3	1	1	0-0	238.1	302	169	162	32	76-2	118	.314

LOFTON, KENNY — OF

PERSONAL: Born May 31, 1967, in East Chicago, Ind. ... 6-0/180. ... Bats left, throws left. ... Full name: Kenneth Lofton. ... High school: Washington (East Chicago, Ind.). ... College: Arizona.

TRANSACTIONS/CAREER NOTES: Selected by Houston Astros organization in 17th round of free-agent draft (June 1, 1988). ... Traded by Astros with IF Dave Rohde to Cleveland Indians for P Willie Blair and C Eddie Taubensee (December 10, 1991). ... On disabled list (July 17-August 1, 1995). ... Traded by Indians with P Alan Embree to Atlanta Braves for OF Marquis Grissom and OF Dave Justice (March 25, 1997). ... On disabled list (June 18-July 5 and July 6-28, 1997). ... Granted free agency (October 28, 1997). ... Signed by Indians (December 8, 1997). ... On disabled list (July 28-August 14 and August 17-September 1, 1999; April 30-May 12, 2000; and May 16-June 1, 2001). ... Granted free agency (November 5, 2001). ... Signed by Chicago White Sox (February 1, 2002). ... Traded by White Sox to San Francisco Giants for P Felix Diaz and P Ryan Meaux (July 28, 2002). ... Granted free agency (November 4, 2002). ... Signed by Pittsburgh Pirates (March 14, 2003). ... Traded by Pirates with 3B Aramis Ramirez and cash to Chicago Cubs for IF Jose Hernandez, P Matt Brubeck and a player to be named (July 22, 2003).

2003 GAMES PLAYED BY POSITION (MLB): OF—136.

Year Team (League)	Pos.	G	AB	R	H	2B	3B	HR	RBI	BB	SO	HBP	GDP	SB-CS	Avg.	OBP	SLG	OPS	E	Pct.
1988— Auburn (NY-Penn)	OF	48	187	23	40	6	1	1	14	19	51	0	3	26-4	.214	.286	.273	.559	4	.961
1989— Auburn (NY-Penn)	OF	34	110	21	29	3	1	0	8	14	30	0	1	26-5	.264	.336	.309	.645	8	.837
— Asheville (S. Atl.)	OF	22	82	14	27	2	0	1	9	12	10	1	1	14-6	.329	.421	.390	.811	2	.951
1990— Osceola (Fla. St.)	OF	124	481	98	*159	15	5	2	35	61	77	3	4	62-16	.331	.407	.395	.802	7	.974
1991— Tucson (PCL)	OF	130	*545	93	*168	19	*17	2	50	52	95	0	2	40-23	.308	.367	.417	.784	9	.974
— Houston (N.L.)	OF	20	74	9	15	1	0	0	0	5	19	0	0	2-1	.203	.253	.216	.469	1	.977
1992— Cleveland (A.L.)	OF	148	576	96	164	15	8	5	42	68	54	2	7	*66-12	.285	.362	.365	.726	8	.982
1993— Cleveland (A.L.)	OF	148	569	116	185	28	8	1	42	81	83	1	8	*70-14	.325	.408	.408	.815	•9	.979
1994— Cleveland (A.L.)	OF	112	459	105	*160	32	9	12	57	52	56	2	5	*60-12	.349	.412	.536	.948	2	.993
1995— Cleveland (A.L.)	OF-DH	118	481	93	149	22	*13	7	53	40	49	1	6	*54-15	.310	.362	.453	.815	•8	.970
1996— Cleveland (A.L.)	OF	154	*662	132	210	35	4	14	67	61	82	0	7	*75-17	.317	.372	.446	.817	10	.975
1997— Atlanta (N.L.)	OF	122	493	90	164	20	6	5	48	64	83	2	10	27-20	.333	.409	.428	.837	5	.983
1998— Cleveland (A.L.)	OF	154	600	101	169	31	6	12	64	87	80	2	7	54-10	.282	.371	.413	.785	4	.983
1999— Cleveland (A.L.)	OF-DH	120	465	110	140	28	6	7	39	79	84	6	6	25-6	.301	.405	.432	.838	3	.989
2000— Cleveland (A.L.)	OF-DH	137	543	107	151	23	5	15	73	79	72	4	11	30-7	.278	.369	.422	.791	4	.989
2001— Cleveland (A.L.)	OF	133	517	91	135	21	4	14	66	47	69	2	8	16-8	.261	.322	.398	.721	6	.981
2002— Chicago (A.L.)	OF	93	352	68	91	20	6	8	42	49	51	0	0	22-8	.259	.348	.418	.766	0	1.000
— San Francisco (N.L.)	OF	46	180	30	48	10	3	3	9	23	22	1	1	7-3	.267	.353	.406	.758	0	1.000
2003— Pittsburgh (N.L.)	OF	84	339	58	94	19	4	9	26	28	29	2	2	18-5	.277	.333	.437	.770	0	1.000
— Chicago (N.L.)	OF	56	208	39	66	13	4	3	20	18	22	2	4	12-4	.327	.381	.471	.852	3	.974
American League totals (10 years)		1317	5224	1019	1554	255	69	95	545	643	680	20	65	472-109	.297	.374	.427	.801	58	.983
National League totals (4 years)		328	1294	226	389	63	17	20	103	138	175	7	17	66-33	.301	.369	.422	.791	9	.989
Major League totals (13 years)		1645	6518	1245	1943	318	86	115	648	781	855	27	82	538-142	.298	.373	.426	.799	67	.984

LOHSE, KYLE — P

PERSONAL: Born October 4, 1978, in Chico, Calif. ... 6-2/200. ... Throws right, bats right. ... Full name: Kyle Matthew Lohse. ... Name pronounced: lowshe. ... High school: Hamilton Union (Hamilton City, Calif.). ... Junior college: Butte (Calif.) Community College.

TRANSACTIONS/CAREER NOTES: Selected by Chicago Cubs organization in 29th round of free-agent draft (June 4, 1996). ... Traded with P Jason Ryan by Cubs to Minnesota Twins for P Rick Aguilera and P Scott Downs (May 21, 1999).

CAREER HITTING: 4-for-12 (.333), 0 R, 1 2B, 0 3B, 0 HR, 1 RBI.

Year League	W	L	Pct.	ERA	WHIP	G	GS	CG	ShO	Hld.	Sv.-Opp.	IP	H	R	ER	HR	BB-IBB	SO	Avg.
1997— Ariz. Cubs (Ariz.)	2	2	.500	3.02	1.43	12	11	0	0	...	0-...	47.2	46	22	16	0	22-0	49	.249
1998— Rockford (Midwest)	13	8	.619	3.22	1.19	28	26	3	1	...	0-...	170.2	158	76	61	8	45-1	121	.246
1999— Daytona (Fla. St.)	5	3	.625	2.89	1.21	9	9	1	1	...	0-...	53.0	48	21	17	4	16-0	41	.242
— Fort Myers (Fla. St.)	2	3	.400	5.18	1.34	7	7	0	0	...	0-...	41.2	47	28	24	5	9-0	33	.315
— New Britain (East.)	3	4	.429	5.89	1.56	11	11	1	0	...	0-...	70.1	87	49	46	9	23-0	41	.315
2000— New Britain (East.)	3	*18	.143	6.04	1.50	28	28	0	0	...	0-...	167.0	*196	*123	*112	23	55-0	124	.291
2001— New Britain (East.)	3	1	.750	2.37	0.95	6	6	0	0	...	0-...	38.0	32	10	10	5	4-0	32	.230
— Edmonton (PCL)	4	2	.667	3.12	1.29	8	8	1	1	...	0-...	49.0	50	21	17	3	13-0	48	.262
— Minnesota (A.L.)	4	7	.364	5.68	1.45	19	16	0	0	0	0-0	90.1	102	60	57	16	29-0	64	.284
2002— Minnesota (A.L.)	13	8	.619	4.23	1.39	32	31	1	1	0	0-1	180.2	181	92	85	26	70-2	124	.259
2003— Minnesota (A.L.)	14	11	.560	4.61	1.27	33	33	2	1	0	0-0	201.0	211	107	103	28	45-1	130	.268
Major League totals (3 years)	31	26	.544	4.67	1.35	84	80	3	2	0	0-1	472.0	494	259	245	70	144-3	318	.268

LOMBARD, GEORGE — OF

PERSONAL: Born September 14, 1975, in Atlanta, Ga. ... 6-0/215. ... Bats left, throws right. ... Full name: George Paul Lombard. ... High school: Lovett (Atlanta).

TRANSACTIONS/CAREER NOTES: Selected by Atlanta Braves organization in second round of free-agent draft (June 2, 1994). ... On disabled list (August 16, 1996-remainder of season). ... On Richmond disabled list (May 29-June 22 and July 2-August 11, 1999). ... On Atlanta disabled list (March 28, 2001-entire season); included rehabilitation assignments to Richmond (June 2-9 and June 11-19). ... On Atlanta disabled list (March 22-June 19, 2002); included rehabilitation assignment to Greenville (May 29-June 7) and Richmond (June 8-16). ... Traded by Braves to Detroit Tigers for P Kris Keller (June 19, 2002). ... Claimed on waivers by Tampa Bay (March 28, 2003).

2003 GAMES PLAYED BY POSITION (MLB): OF—13.

Year	Team (League)	Pos.	G	AB	R	H	2B	3B	HR	RBI	BB	SO	HBP	GDP	SB-CS	Avg.	OBP	SLG	OPS	E	Pct.
									BATTING											FIELDING	
1994— GC Braves (GCL)	OF	40	129	10	18	2	0	0	5	18	47	3	1	10-4	.140	.260	.155	.415	2	.944
1995— Macon (S. Atl.)	OF	49	180	32	37	6	1	3	16	27	44	5	4	16-4	.206	.325	.300	.625	2	.958
—Eugene (Northwest)	OF	68	262	38	66	5	3	5	19	23	91	5	0	35-13	.252	.323	.351	.674	3	.962
1996— Macon (S. Atl.)	OF-DH	116	444	76	109	16	8	15	51	36	122	7	4	24-17	.245	.311	.419	.730	7	.971
1997— Durham (Caro.)	OF-DH	131	462	65	122	25	7	14	72	66	145	9	4	35-7	.264	.365	.439	.805	9	.968
1998— Greenville (Sou.)	OF	122	422	84	130	25	4	22	65	71	140	5	2	35-5	.308	.410	.543	.953	10	.947
—Atlanta (N.L.)	OF	6	6	2	2	0	0	1	1	0	1	0	0	1-0	.333	.333	.833	1.167	0	1.000
1999— Richmond (Int'l)	OF	74	233	25	48	11	3	7	29	35	98	3	2	21-6	.206	.317	.369	.686	3	.974
—Atlanta (N.L.)	OF	6	6	1	2	0	0	0	0	1	2	0	0	2-0	.333	.429	.333	.762	0	1.000
2000— Richmond (Int'l)	OF	112	424	72	117	25	7	10	48	55	130	6	3	32-9	.276	.365	.439	.803	6	.972
—Atlanta (N.L.)	OF	27	39	8	4	0	0	0	2	1	14	1	2	4-0	.103	.146	.103	.249	0	1.000
2001— Richmond (Int'l)	OF	13	44	7	14	2	1	4	8	6	14	2	1	3-2	.318	.423	.682	1.105	0	1.000
2002— Greenville (Sou.)	OF	8	25	4	7	0	0	3	5	5	6	1	0	2-0	.280	.419	.640	1.059	0	1.000
—Richmond (Int'l)	OF	11	39	10	12	4	1	1	5	5	12	1	0	2-0	.308	.400	.538	.938	0	1.000
—Detroit (A.L.)	OF-DH	72	241	34	58	11	3	5	13	20	78	1	0	13-2	.241	.300	.373	.674	3	.982
2003— Tampa Bay (A.L.)	OF	13	37	8	8	1	0	1	4	0	6	1	0	1-0	.216	.237	.324	.561	1	.964
—Durham (Int'l)	OF-DH	112	438	57	117	25	4	17	64	45	143	6	6	23-6	.267	.342	.459	.801	3	.989
American League totals (2 years)		85	278	42	66	12	3	6	17	20	84	2	0	14-2	.237	.292	.367	.659	4	.979
National League totals (3 years)		39	51	11	8	0	0	1	3	2	17	1	2	7-0	.157	.204	.216	.419	0	1.000
Major League totals (5 years)		124	329	53	74	12	3	7	20	22	101	3	2	21-2	.225	.279	.343	.622	4	.981

LONG, TERRENCE — OF

PERSONAL: Born February 29, 1976, in Montgomery, Ala. ... 6-1/202. ... Bats left, throws left. ... Full name: Terrence Deon Long. ... High school: Stanhope Elmore (Millbrook, Ala.).

TRANSACTIONS/CAREER NOTES: Selected by New York Mets organization in first round (20th pick overall) of free-agent draft (June 2, 1994); pick received as compensation for Baltimore Orioles signing Type A free-agent P Sid Fernandez. ... On disabled list (May 15-27, 1996). ... Traded by Mets with P Leo Vasquez to Oakland Athletics for P Kenny Rogers (July 23, 1999). ... Given 3-game suspension by Major League Baseball (September 5, 2003). ... Reinstated (September 12, 2003).

2003 GAMES PLAYED BY POSITION (MLB): OF—137, DH—1.

Year	Team (League)	Pos.	G	AB	R	H	2B	3B	HR	RBI	BB	SO	HBP	GDP	SB-CS	Avg.	OBP	SLG	OPS	E	Pct.
									BATTING											FIELDING	
1994— Kingsport (Appal.)	1B-OF	60	215	39	50	9	2	12	39	32	52	4	2	9-3	.233	.340	.460	.800	5	.980
1995— Capital City (SAL)	OF	55	178	27	35	1	2	2	13	28	43	1	3	8-5	.197	.309	.258	.568	5	.937
—Pittsfield (NYP)	OF	51	187	24	48	9	4	4	31	18	36	1	2	11-4	.257	.324	.412	.735	1	.991
1996— Capital City (SAL)	DH-OF	123	473	66	136	26	9	12	78	36	120	5	9	32-7	.288	.342	.457	.798	5	.981
1997— St. Lucie (Fla. St.)	OF-DH	126	470	52	118	29	7	8	61	40	102	2	6	24-8	.251	.310	.394	.704	7	.972
1998— Binghamton (East.)	OF-DH	130	455	69	135	20 *	10	16	58	62	105	2	8	23-11	.297	.380	.490	.871	10	.958
1999— Norfolk (Int'l)	OF	78	304	41	99	20	4	7	47	23	41	1	6	14-6	.326	.374	.487	.861	4	.980
—New York (N.L.)		3	3	0	0	0	0	0	0	0	2	0	1	0-0	.000	.000	.000	.000	...	...
—Vancouver (PCL)	OF	40	154	16	38	6	2	2	21	10	29	1	4	7-5	.247	.297	.351	.648	6	.961
2000— Sacramento (PCL)	OF	15	60	11	24	6	0	3	15	4	4	0	2	0-3	.400	.431	.650	1.081	3	.903
—Oakland (A.L.)	OF	138	584	104	168	34	4	18	80	43	77	1	18	5-0	.288	.336	.452	.788	• 10	.971
2001— Oakland (A.L.)	OF	• 162	629	90	178	37	4	12	85	52	103	0	17	9-3	.283	.335	.412	.747	7	.980
2002— Oakland (A.L.)	OF	• 162	587	71	141	32	4	16	67	48	96	2	17	3-4	.240	.298	.390	.689	8	.980
2003— Oakland (A.L.)	OF-DH	140	486	64	119	22	2	14	61	31	67	3	9	4-1	.245	.293	.385	.678	4	.984
American League totals (4 years)		602	2286	329	606	125	14	60	293	174	343	6	61	21-10	.265	.317	.411	.728	29	.978
National League totals (1 year)		3	3	0	0	0	0	0	0	0	2	0	1	0-0	.000	.000	.000	.000	...	...
Major League totals (5 years)		605	2289	329	606	125	14	60	293	174	345	6	62	21-10	.265	.317	.410	.727	29	.978

LOOPER, AARON — P

PERSONAL: Born September 7, 1976, in Ada, Okla. ... 6-2/185. ... Throws right, bats right. ... Full name: Aaron Joseph Looper. ... Junior college: Indian Hills (Iowa) Community College.

TRANSACTIONS/CAREER NOTES: Selected by Seattle Mariners organization in 30th round of free-agent draft (June 3, 1997). ... Recalled by Seattle from Tacoma (August 2, 2003). ... Optioned to Tacoma by Seattle (August 8, 2003). ... Recalled by Seattle from Tacoma (September 2, 2003).

CAREER HITTING: 0-for-0 (.000), 0 R, 0 2B, 0 3B, 0 HR, 0 RBI.

Year	League	W	L	Pct.	ERA	WHIP	G	GS	CG	ShO	Hld.	Sv.-Opp.	IP	H	R	ER	HR	BB-IBB	SO	Avg.
1998— Everett (Northwest)	4	5	.444	6.86	1.75	14	14	0	0	...	0-...	59.0	72	52	45	8	31-0	40	.306
1999— Wisconsin (Midw.)	9	6	.600	4.10	1.28	38	7	0	0	...	3-...	90.0	89	47	41	8	26-0	73	.251
2000— Lancaster (Calif.)	5	3	.625	5.70	1.75	51	0	0	0	...	0-...	72.2	105	62	46	7	22-1	47	.329
2001— San Bernardino (Calif.)	6	11	.353	2.79	1.14	56	0	0	0	...	5-...	71.0	59	34	22	1	22-5	77	.224
2002— San Antonio (Texas)	6	1	.857	2.28	1.17	57	0	0	0	...	0-...	90.2	76	33	23	4	30-6	73	.230
2003— Tacoma (PCL)	5	2	.714	3.11	1.30	46	0	0	0	...	5-...	75.1	72	27	26	10	26-2	67	.247
—Seattle (A.L.)	0	0	...	5.14	1.29	6	0	0	0	0	0-0	7.0	7	4	4	1	2-0	6	.269
Major League totals (1 year)	0	0	...	5.14	1.29	6	0	0	0	0	0-0	7.0	7	4	4	1	2-0	6	.269

LOOPER, BRADEN — P

PERSONAL: Born October 28, 1974, in Weatherford, Okla. ... 6-3/220. ... Throws right, bats right. ... Full name: Braden LaVern Looper. ... High school: Mangum (Okla.). ... College: Wichita State.

TRANSACTIONS/CAREER NOTES: Selected by St. Louis Cardinals organization in first round (third pick overall) of free-agent draft (June 2, 1996). ... On Memphis disabled list (May 6-June 21, 1998). ... Traded by Cardinals with P Armando Almanza and SS Pablo Ozuna to Florida Marlins for SS Edgar Renteria (December 14, 1998).

CAREER HITTING: 1-for-6 (.167), 1 R, 0 2B, 0 3B, 0 HR, 0 RBI.

Year	League	W	L	Pct.	ERA	WHIP	G	GS	CG	ShO	Hld.	Sv.-Opp.	IP	H	R	ER	HR	BB-IBB	SO	Avg.
1997— Prince William (Caro.)	3	6	.333	4.48	1.49	12	12	0	0	...	0-...	64.1	71	38	32	6	25-0	58	.276
—Arkansas (Texas)	1	4	.200	5.91	1.45	19	0	0	0	...	5-...	21.1	24	14	14	2	7-2	20	.286
1998— St. Louis (N.L.)	0	1	.000	5.40	1.80	4	0	0	0	0	0-2	3.1	5	4	2	1	1-0	4	.357
—Memphis (PCL)	2	3	.400	3.10	1.38	40	0	0	0	...	20-...	40.2	43	16	14	3	13-1	43	.270
1999— Florida (N.L.)	3	3	.500	3.80	1.53	72	0	0	0	8	0-4	83.0	96	43	35	7	31-6	50	.293
2000— Florida (N.L.)	5	1	.833	4.41	1.59	73	0	0	0	18	2-5	67.1	71	41	33	6	36-6	29	.268
2001— Florida (N.L.)	3	3	.500	3.55	1.31	71	0	0	0	16	3-6	71.0	63	28	28	8	30-3	52	.242
2002— Florida (N.L.)	2	5	.286	3.14	1.17	78	0	0	0	16	13-16	86.0	73	31	30	8	28-3	55	.230
2003— Florida (N.L.)	6	4	.600	3.68	1.38	74	0	0	0	...	28-34	80.2	82	34	33	4	29-1	56	.264
Major League totals (6 years)	19	17	.528	3.70	1.39	372	0	0	0	58	46-67	391.1	390	181	161	31	155-19	246	.261

L

LOPEZ, ALBIE — P

PERSONAL: Born August 18, 1971, in Mesa, Ariz. ... 6-2/240. ... Throws right, bats right. ... Full name: Albert Anthony Lopez. ... Name pronounced: LOE-pezz. ... High school: Westwood (Mesa, Ariz.). ... Junior college: Mesa (Ari.) Community College.

TRANSACTIONS/CAREER NOTES: Selected by San Francisco Giants organization in 46th round of free-agent draft (June 5, 1989); did not sign. ... Selected by Seattle Mariners organization in 19th round of free-agent draft (June 4, 1990); did not sign. ... Selected by Cleveland Indians organization in 20th round of free-agent draft (June 3, 1991). ... On Cleveland disabled list (July 2-28 and August 13-September 1, 1997). ... Selected by Tampa Bay Devil Rays in second round (48th pick overall) of expansion draft (November 18, 1997). ... On Tampa Bay disabled list (August 1-26, 1998); included rehabilitation assignments to Durham (August 15-18) and St. Petersburg (August 25-26). ... On Tampa Bay disabled list (May 12-June 20, 1999); included rehabilitation assignment to St. Petersburg (June 14-20). ... Traded by Devil Rays with C Mike Difelice to Arizona Diamondbacks for OF Jason Conti and P Nick Bierbrodt (July 25, 2001). ... Granted free agency (November 6, 2001). ... Signed by Atlanta Braves (December 20, 2001). ... On Atlanta disabled list (April 9-28 and June 26-July 13, 2002); included rehabilitation assignments to Greenville (April 25-28) and Macon (July 13). ... Granted free agency (October 28, 2002). ... Signed by Kansas City Royals (January 7, 2003). ... Placed on 15-day disabled list (May 17, 2003). ... Activated by Royals from 15-day disabled list (July 5, 2003). ... Sent to Omaha (June 8, 2003). ... Recalled from Omaha; reinstated from 15-day disabled list (June 16, 2003). ... Given unconditional release (June 19, 2003).

CAREER HITTING: 2-for-46 (.043), 0 R, 0 2B, 0 3B, 0 HR, 0 RBI.

Year	League	W	L	Pct.	ERA	WHIP	G	GS	CG	ShO	Hld.	Sv.-Opp.	IP	H	R	ER	HR	BB-IBB	SO	Avg.
1991—	Burlington (Appal.)	4	5	.444	3.44	1.15	13	13	0	0	...	0-...	73.1	61	33	28	4	23-0	81	.224
1992—	Columbus (S. Atl.)	7	2	.778	2.88	1.16	16	16	1	0	...	0-...	97.0	80	41	31	4	33-0	117	.221
—	Kinston (Caro.)	5	2	.714	3.52	1.28	10	10	1	1	...	0-...	64.0	56	28	25	5	26-1	44	.235
1993—	Cant./Akr. (Eastern)	9	4	.692	3.11	1.15	16	16	2	0	...	0-...	110.0	79	44	38	10	47-0	80	.204
—	Cleveland (A.L.)	3	1	.750	5.98	1.63	9	9	0	0	...	0-0	49.2	49	34	33	7	32-1	25	.262
—	Charlotte (Int'l)	1	0	1.000	2.25	0.83	3	2	0	0	...	0-...	12.0	8	3	3	1	2-0	7	.186
1994—	Charlotte (Int'l)	13	3	.813	3.94	1.24	22	22	3	0	...	0-...	144.0	136	68	63	20	42-0	105	.250
—	Cleveland (A.L.)	1	2	.333	4.24	1.53	4	4	1	1	0	0-0	17.0	20	11	8	3	6-0	18	.290
1995—	Buffalo (A.A.)	5	10	.333	4.44	1.50	18	18	1	1	...	0-...	101.1	101	57	50	10	51-0	82	.259
—	Cleveland (A.L.)	0	0	...	3.13	1.04	6	2	0	0	0	0-0	23.0	17	8	8	4	7-1	22	.205
1996—	Buffalo (A.A.)	10	2	.833	3.87	1.24	17	17	2	0	...	0-...	104.2	90	54	45	13	40-0	89	.231
—	Cleveland (A.L.)	5	4	.556	6.39	1.65	13	10	0	0	...	0-0	62.0	80	47	44	14	22-1	45	.311
1997—	Cleveland (A.L.)	3	7	.300	6.93	1.84	37	6	0	0	4	0-1	76.2	101	61	59	11	40-9	63	.322
—	Akron (East.)	0	0	...	0.00	2.00	1	0	0	0	...	0-...	1.0	2	0	0	0	0-0	2	.500
—	Buffalo (A.A.)	1	0	1.000	0.00	0.71	7	0	0	0	...	1-...	11.1	6	0	0	0	2-0	13	.150
1998—	Tampa Bay (A.L.)	7	4	.636	2.60	1.32	54	0	0	0	4	1-5	79.2	73	31	23	7	32-4	62	.249
—	Durham (Int'l)	0	0	...	0.00	1.67	2	0	0	0	...	0-...	3.0	4	0	0	0	1-0	2	.333
—	St. Pete. (FSL)	0	1	.000	18.00	2.00	1	1	0	0	...	0-...	1.0	2	2	2	1	0-0	1	.400
1999—	Tampa Bay (A.L.)	3	2	.600	4.64	1.41	51	0	0	0	12	1-3	64.0	66	40	33	8	24-2	37	.263
—	St. Pete. (FSL)	0	0	...	5.40	2.10	2	1	0	0	...	0-...	3.1	7	5	2	0	0-0	3	.412
2000—	Tampa Bay (A.L.)	11	13	.458	4.13	1.45	45	24	4	1	1	2-4	185.1	199	95	85	24	70-3	96	.277
—	Princeton (Appal.)	0	0	...	0.00	0.00	1	0	0	0	...	0-...	.2	0	0	0	0	0-0	1	.000
2001—	Tampa Bay (A.L.)	5	12	.294	5.34	1.63	20	20	1	1	0	0-0	124.2	152	87	74	16	51-1	67	.302
—	Arizona (N.L.)	4	7	.364	4.00	1.21	13	13	2	2	0	0-0	81.0	74	36	36	10	24-2	69	.247
2002—	Atlanta (N.L.)	1	4	.200	4.37	1.51	30	4	0	0	1	0-0	55.2	66	29	27	1	18-3	39	.300
—	Greenville (Sou.)	0	0	...	4.50	1.50	1	1	0	0	...	0-...	4.0	2	2	2	0	4-0	4	.143
2003—	Omaha (PCL)	0	0	...	0.00	0.60	4	0	0	0	...	0-...	5.0	3	0	0	0	0-0	2	.167
—	Kansas City (A.L.)	4	2	.667	12.71	2.56	15	0	0	0	2	0-3	22.2	41	32	32	7	17-1	15	.383
American League totals (10 years)		42	47	.472	5.10	1.56	254	75	6	3	23	4-16	704.2	798	446	399	101	301-23	450	.287
National League totals (2 years)		5	11	.313	4.15	1.33	43	17	2	2	1	0-0	136.2	140	65	63	11	42-5	108	.269
Major League totals (11 years)		47	58	.448	4.94	1.52	297	92	8	5	24	4-16	841.1	938	511	462	112	343-28	558	.284

LOPEZ, AQUILINO — P

PERSONAL: Born April 21, 1975, in Villa Altagracia, Dominican Republic. ... 6-3/165. ... Throws right, bats right. ... Name pronounced: aquil-LEENO.

TRANSACTIONS/CAREER NOTES: Signed as non-drafted free agent by Seattle Mariners organization (July 3, 1997). ... Selected by Toronto Blue Jays from Mariners organization in Rule 5 major league draft (December 16, 2002).

CAREER HITTING: 0-for-0 (.000), 0 R, 0 2B, 0 3B, 0 HR, 0 RBI.

Year	League	W	L	Pct.	ERA	WHIP	G	GS	CG	ShO	Hld.	Sv.-Opp.	IP	H	R	ER	HR	BB-IBB	SO	Avg.
1999—	Everett (Northwest)	7	6	.538	3.80	1.21	15	15	1	0	...	0-...	87.2	76	44	37	8	30-2	93	.230
2000—	Wisconsin (Midw.)	6	1	.857	1.85	0.99	39	5	1	1	...	17-...	68.0	47	16	14	1	20-4	67	.193
2001—	San Antonio (Texas)	4	3	.571	3.02	1.16	42	0	0	0	...	2-...	62.2	48	24	21	4	25-2	79	.209
2002—	Tacoma (PCL)	4	4	.500	2.39	1.06	34	11	0	0	...	5-...	109.1	89	33	29	6	27-2	103	.221
2003—	Toronto (A.L.)	1	3	.250	3.42	1.25	72	0	0	0	16	14-16	73.2	58	31	28	5	34-5	64	.212
Major League totals (1 year)		1	3	.250	3.42	1.25	72	0	0	0	16	14-16	73.2	58	31	28	5	34-5	64	.212

LOPEZ, FELIPE — SS

PERSONAL: Born May 12, 1980, in Bayamon, Puerto Rico. ... 6-0/185. ... Bats both, throws right. ... Full name: Felipe Lopez Jr.. ... High school: Lake Brantley (Altamonte Springs, Fla.).

TRANSACTIONS/CAREER NOTES: Selected by Toronto Blue Jays organization in first round (eighth pick overall) of free-agent draft (June 2, 1998). ... Traded by Blue Jays to Cincinnati Reds as part of four-team trade in which Reds sent P Elmer Dessens and cash to Arizona Diamondbacks, Diamondbacks sent 1B Erubiel Durazo to Oakland Athletics and A's sent a player to be named later to Blue Jays (December 15, 2002); Blue Jays acquired P Jason Arnold to complete deal (December 16, 2002). ... Optioned to Louisville (June 16, 2003). ... Recalled from Louisville (September 15, 2003).

2003 GAMES PLAYED BY POSITION (MLB): SS—50, 3B—8, 2B—3.

									BATTING											FIELDING	
Year	Team (League)	Pos.	G	AB	R	H	2B	3B	HR	RBI	BB	SO	HBP	GDP	SB-CS	Avg.	OBP	SLG	OPS	E	Pct.
1998—	St. Catharines (NYP)	SS	19	83	14	31	5	2	1	11	3	14	0	1	4-2	.373	.395	.518	.913	9	.895
—	Dunedin (Fla. St.)	SS	4	13	3	5	0	1	1	1	0	3	0	0	0-0	.385	.385	.769	1.154	4	.692
1999—	Hagerstown (SAL)	SS	134	537	87	149	27	4	14	80	61	157	3	7	21-14	.277	.351	.421	.772	22	.960
2000—	Tennessee (Sou.)	SS	127	463	52	119	18	4	9	41	31	110	1	6	12-11	.257	.303	.371	.675	* 44	.923
2001—	Tennessee (Sou.)	SS-2B	19	72	12	16	2	1	2	4	9	23	0	1	4-4	.222	.309	.361	.670	8	.904
—	Syracuse (Int'l)	SS-2B-3B	89	358	65	100	19	7	16	44	30	94	3	5	13-5	.279	.337	.506	.842	19	.950
—	Toronto (A.L.)	3B-SS	49	177	21	46	4	4	5	23	12	39	0	0	4-3	.260	.304	.418	.722	9	.938
2002—	Toronto (A.L.)	SS-3B-DH	85	282	35	64	15	3	8	34	23	90	1	4	5-4	.227	.287	.387	.673	8	.975
—	Syracuse (Int'l)	SS	43	173	35	55	11	2	3	16	29	37	1	3	13-0	.318	.419	.457	.875	16	.934
2003—	Cincinnati (N.L.)	SS-3B-2B	59	197	28	42	7	2	2	18	28	59	1	2	8-5	.213	.313	.299	.612	16	.952
—	Louisville (Int'l)	SS-2B	35	143	22	40	11	0	2	18	12	38	0	0	2-5	.280	.333	.399	.732	9	.940
American League totals (2 years)			134	459	56	110	20	7	13	57	35	129	1	6	9-7	.240	.293	.399	.692	17	.964
National League totals (1 year)			59	197	28	42	7	2	2	18	28	59	1	2	8-5	.213	.313	.299	.612	16	.952
Major League totals (3 years)			193	656	84	152	27	9	15	70	63	188	2	8	17-12	.232	.299	.369	.668	33	.952

LOPEZ, JAVIER   P

PERSONAL: Born July 11, 1977, at San Juan, Puerto Rico. ... 6-4/200. ... Throws left, bats left. ... Full name: Javier Alfonso Lopez. ... College: Virginia.

TRANSACTIONS/CAREER NOTES: Selected by Arizona Diamondbacks in fourth round of free-agent draft (June 1998). ... Selected by Boston Red Sox from Diamondbacks in Rule 5 draft (December 16, 2002). ... Traded by Red Sox to Colorado Rockies for future considerations (March 18, 2003); Red Sox acquired P Ryan Cameron to complete deal (March 29, 2003).

CAREER HITTING: 1-for-5 (.200), 1 R, 0 2B, 0 3B, 0 HR, 1 RBI.

Year League	W	L	Pct.	ERA	WHIP	G	GS	CG	ShO	Hld.	Sv.-Opp.	IP	H	R	ER	HR	BB-IBB	SO	Avg.
1998— South Bend (Mid.)	2	4	.333	6.55	2.05	16	9	0	0	...	0-...	44.0	60	36	32	2	30-0	31	.328
1999— South Bend (Mid.)	4	6	.400	6.00	1.67	20	20	0	0	...	0-...	99.0	122	74	66	8	43-0	70	.300
2000— High Desert (Calif.)	4	8	.333	5.22	1.53	30	21	0	0	...	2-...	136.1	152	87	79	14	57-0	98	.288
2001— El Paso (Texas)	1	0	1.000	7.43	1.95	22	1	0	0	...	0-...	40.0	64	39	33	6	14-2	21	.370
— Lancaster (Calif.)	1	3	.250	2.63	1.46	17	0	0	0	...	1-...	24.0	30	9	7	2	5-0	18	.313
2002— El Paso (Texas)	2	2	.500	2.72	1.08	61	0	0	0	...	6-...	46.1	34	16	14	3	16-1	47	.204
2003— Colorado (N.L.)	4	1	.800	3.70	1.20	75	0	0	0	15	1-2	58.1	58	25	24	5	12-2	40	.258
Major League totals (1 year)	**4**	**1**	**.800**	**3.70**	**1.20**	**75**	**0**	**0**	**0**	**15**	**1-2**	**58.1**	**58**	**25**	**24**	**5**	**12-2**	**40**	**.258**

LOPEZ, JAVY   C

PERSONAL: Born November 5, 1970, in Ponce, Puerto Rico. ... 6-3/215. ... Bats right, throws right. ... Full name: Javier Torres Lopez. ... Name pronounced: HAH-vee LOE-pezz. ... High school: Academia Cristo Rey (Urb la Ramble Ponce, Puerto Rico).

TRANSACTIONS/CAREER NOTES: Signed as non-drafted free agent by Atlanta Braves organization (November 6, 1987). ... On Greenville disabled list (July 18-August 2, 1992). ... On Atlanta disabled list (July 6-22, 1997; and June 21-July 15 and July 25, 1999-remainder of season). ... Granted free agency (November 5, 2001). ... Re-signed by Braves (December 7, 2001). ... On disabled list (August 1-16, 2002).

2003 GAMES PLAYED BY POSITION (MLB): C—120, DH—3.

Year Team (League)	Pos.	G	AB	R	H	2B	3B	HR	RBI	BB	SO	HBP	GDP	SB-CS	Avg.	OBP	SLG	OPS	E	Pct.
1988— GC Braves (GCL)	C	31	94	8	18	4	0	1	9	3	19	0	0	1-0	.191	.214	.266	.480	7	.958
1989— Pulaski (Appal.)	C	51	153	27	40	8	1	3	27	5	35	1	8	3-2	.261	.284	.386	.670	5	.983
1990— Burlington (Midw.)	C	116	422	48	112	17	3	11	55	14	84	5	10	0-2	.265	.297	.398	.695	11	.986
1991— Durham (Caro.)	C	113	384	43	94	14	2	11	51	25	88	3	10	10-3	.245	.294	.378	.672	6	.991
1992— Greenville (Sou.)	C	115	442	63	142	28	3	16	60	24	47	5	8	7-3	.321	.362	.507	.868	8	.990
— Atlanta (N.L.)	C	9	16	3	6	2	0	0	2	0	1	0	0	0-0	.375	.375	.500	.875	0	1.000
1993— Richmond (Int'l)	C	100	380	56	116	23	2	17	74	12	53	6	8	1-6	.305	.334	.511	.845	10	.987
— Atlanta (N.L.)	C	8	16	1	6	1	1	1	2	0	2	1	0	0-0	.375	.412	.750	1.162	1	.975
1994— Atlanta (N.L.)	C	80	277	27	68	9	0	13	35	17	61	5	12	0-2	.245	.299	.419	.718	3	.995
1995— Atlanta (N.L.)	C	100	333	37	105	11	4	14	51	14	57	2	13	0-1	.315	.344	.498	.842	8	.988
1996— Atlanta (N.L.)	C	138	489	56	138	19	1	23	69	28	84	3	17	1-6	.282	.322	.466	.788	6	.994
1997— Atlanta (N.L.)	C	123	414	52	122	28	1	23	68	40	82	5	9	1-1	.295	.361	.534	.895	6	.993
1998— Atlanta (N.L.)	C-DH	133	489	73	139	21	1	34	106	30	85	6	22	5-3	.284	.328	.540	.868	5	.995
1999— Atlanta (N.L.)	C-DH	65	246	34	78	18	1	11	45	20	41	3	6	0-3	.317	.375	.533	.908	4	.991
2000— Atlanta (N.L.)	C	134	481	60	138	21	1	24	89	35	80	4	20	0-0	.287	.337	.484	.822	6	.993
2001— Atlanta (N.L.)	C	128	438	45	117	16	1	17	66	28	82	10	12	1-0	.267	.322	.425	.747	10	.989
2002— Atlanta (N.L.)	C	109	347	31	81	15	0	11	52	26	63	8	15	0-1	.233	.299	.372	.670	10	.986
2003— Atlanta (N.L.)	C-DH	129	457	89	150	29	3	43	109	33	90	4	10	0-1	.328	.378	.687	1.065	5	.994
Major League totals (12 years)		**1156**	**4003**	**508**	**1148**	**190**	**14**	**214**	**694**	**271**	**728**	**51**	**136**	**8-18**	**.287**	**.337**	**.502**	**.839**	**64**	**.992**

LOPEZ, MENDY   IF

PERSONAL: Born October 15, 1973, in Pimentel, Dominican Republic. ... 6-2/200. ... Bats right, throws right. ... Full name: Mendy Aupe Lopez. ... High school: Liceo Los Trinitanos (Santo Domingo, Dominican Republic).

TRANSACTIONS/CAREER NOTES: Signed by Kansas City Royals organization as a non-drafted free agent (February 26, 1992). ... On Omaha disabled list (May 28-July 7, 1999). ... Released by Royals (December 13, 1999). ... Signed by Florida Marlins organization (January 12, 2000). ... On Calgary disabled list (April 6-June 23, 2000). ... Granted free agency (October 2, 2000). ... Signed by Houston Astros organization (January 8, 2001). ... Claimed on waivers by Pittsburgh Pirates (August 13, 2001). ... Granted free agency (October 15, 2001). ... On Nashville disabled list (April 4-24, 2002). ... Released by Pirates (October 11, 2002). ... Signed by Kansas City Royals as a minor league free agent (November 30, 2002). ... Placed on 15-day disabled list (July 5, 2003). ... Sent to Arizona League on rehab assignment (August 2, 2003). ... Recalled from rehab assignment (August 12, 2003).

2003 GAMES PLAYED BY POSITION (MLB): 1B—17, 3B—13, 2B—11, SS—4, OF—3.

Year Team (League)	Pos.	G	AB	R	H	2B	3B	HR	RBI	BB	SO	HBP	GDP	SB-CS	Avg.	OBP	SLG	OPS	E	Pct.
1992— Dom. Royals (DSL)	SS	49	145	22	40	1	0	1	23	22	15	...	...	7-...	.276	...	.303	...	26	.901
1993— Dom. Royals (DSL)	IF	28	98	15	27	5	2	0	20	11	5	...	...	2-...	.276	...	.367	...	15	.894
1994— GC Royals (GCL)	2B-3B-SS	59	*235	56	85	*19	3	5	*50	22	27	3	5	10-2	.362	.415	.532	.947	12	.959
1995— Wilmington (Caro.)	3B-SS	130	428	42	116	29	3	2	36	28	73	5	12	18-10	.271	.322	.367	.689	25	.944
1996— Wichita (Texas)	3B-SS	93	327	47	92	20	5	6	32	26	67	4	6	14-4	.281	.341	.428	.769	24	.935
1997— Omaha (A.A.)	3B	17	52	6	12	2	0	1	6	8	21	0	0	0-0	.231	.333	.327	.660	6	.898
— Wichita (Texas)	SS	101	357	56	83	16	3	5	42	36	70	3	8	7-5	.232	.304	.336	.640	20	.961
1998— Omaha (PCL)	SS-3B	60	195	18	35	6	1	3	14	18	44	1	0	2-3	.179	.252	.267	.519	10	.960
— Kansas City (A.L.)	SS-3B	74	206	18	50	10	2	1	15	12	40	1	6	5-2	.243	.286	.325	.612	15	.956
1999— Omaha (PCL)	SS-2B-3B	61	222	41	69	8	0	12	40	18	41	0	5	2-2	.311	.361	.509	.870	8	.971
— GC Royals (GCL)	SS	3	5	0	1	1	0	0	2	3	1	1	0	0-0	.200	.500	.400	.900	0	1.000
— Kansas City (A.L.)	2B-SS	7	20	2	8	0	1	0	3	0	5	1	0	0-0	.400	.429	.500	.929	0	1.000
2000— Calgary (PCL)	SS-2B-3B	56	225	34	73	20	1	7	29	13	38	0	2	1-1	.324	.361	.516	.877	12	.955
— Florida (N.L.)		4	3	0	0	0	0	0	0	1	1	0	0	0-0	.000	.250	.000	.250	...	...
2001— New Orleans (PCL)	2-S-1-0-3	63	208	37	58	11	1	14	36	18	49	3	5	2-2	.279	.343	.543	.887	3	.990
— Houston (N.L.)	2B-3B	10	15	3	4	0	0	1	3	2	4	1	0	0-0	.267	.389	.467	.856	0	1.000
— Pittsburgh (N.L.)	2B-SS-3B	22	43	5	10	3	1	0	4	4	16	0	0	0-0	.233	.292	.349	.641	1	.983
2002— Nashville (PCL)	SS-3B-2B	101	385	60	97	26	0	11	72	34	99	2	10	4-1	.252	.309	.405	.714	9	.977
— Pittsburgh (N.L.)		3	3	0	0	0	0	0	0	0	3	0	0	0-0	.000	.000	.000	.000	0	...
2003— Ariz. Royals (Ariz.)	2B-3B-SS	7	20	9	5	1	0	3	6	4	5	1	0	0-0	.250	.400	.750	1.150	0	1.000
— Kansas City (A.L.)	1-3-2-S-O	52	94	13	26	5	1	3	11	4	28	0	3	2-0	.277	.306	.447	.753	1	.993
American League totals (3 years)		**133**	**320**	**33**	**84**	**15**	**4**	**4**	**29**	**16**	**73**	**2**	**9**	**7-2**	**.263**	**.301**	**.372**	**.673**	**16**	**.968**
National League totals (3 years)		**39**	**64**	**8**	**14**	**3**	**1**	**1**	**7**	**7**	**24**	**1**	**0**	**0-0**	**.219**	**.301**	**.344**	**.645**	**1**	**.985**
Major League totals (6 years)		**172**	**384**	**41**	**98**	**18**	**5**	**5**	**36**	**23**	**97**	**3**	**9**	**7-2**	**.255**	**.301**	**.367**	**.668**	**17**	**.970**

LOPEZ, RODRIGO   P

PERSONAL: Born December 14, 1975, in Tlalnepantla, Mexico. ... 6-1/187. ... Throws right, bats right. ... Full name: Rodrigo Munoz Lopez. ... Name pronounced: rod-REE-go.

TRANSACTIONS/CAREER NOTES: Signed by Aguila of Mexican League (1994). ... Contract sold by Aguila to San Diego Padres organization (March 21, 1995). ... Loaned by Padres to Mexico City Red Devils, Mexican League (March 13-August 19, 1998). ... On Portland disabled list (April 5-June 13, 2001). ... Granted free agency (October 15, 2001). ... Signed by Baltimore Orioles organization (February 4, 2002). ... Sent on rehab assignment to Bowie (June 9, 2003). ... Recalled from Bowie rehab assignment; reinstated from 15-day disabled list (June 15, 2003). ... Activated from 15-day disabled list (July 5, 2003).

CAREER HITTING: 1-for-14 (.071), 1 R, 0 2B, 0 3B, 0 HR, 0 RBI.

Year League	W	L	Pct.	ERA	WHIP	G	GS	CG	ShO	Hld.	Sv.-Opp.	IP	H	R	ER	HR	BB-IBB	SO	Avg.
1993— Aguila (Mex.)	0	0	...	36.00	6.00	2	0	0	0	...	0-...	1.0	3	4	4	0	3-...	0	...
1994— Aguila (Mex.)	0	0	...	4.97	1.42	10	0	0	0	...	0-...	12.2	15	7	7	2	3-...	5	...
1995— Ariz. Padres (Ariz.)	1	1	.500	5.45	1.59	11	7	0	0	...	1-...	34.2	41	29	21	0	14-0	33	.287
1996— Poza Rica (Mex.)	1	1	.500	3.54	1.52	7	3	0	0	...	1-...	20.1	15	8	8	2	16-...	22	...
— Idaho Falls (Pioneer)	4	4	.500	5.70	1.55	15	14	0	0	...	1-...	71.0	76	52	45	3	34-0	72	.283
1997— Clinton (Midw.)	6	8	.429	3.18	1.19	37	14	2	0	...	9-...	121.2	103	49	43	6	42-1	123	.228
1998— M.C. Red Devils (Mex.)	10	6	.625	3.35	1.49	26	26	1	0	...	0-...	163.2	165	73	61	9	79-...	95	...
— Mobile (Sou.)	3	0	1.000	1.40	0.97	4	4	2	1	...	0-...	25.2	21	11	4	1	4-0	20	.219
1999— Mobile (Sou.)	10	8	.556	4.41	1.45	28	•28	2	1	...	0-...	169.1	187	91	83	14	58-3	138	.286
2000— Las Vegas (PCL)	8	7	.533	4.69	1.54	20	20	1	0	...	0-...	109.1	123	66	57	9	45-1	100	.289
— San Diego (N.L.)	0	3	.000	8.76	2.15	6	6	0	0	0	0-0	24.2	40	24	24	5	13-0	17	.377
2001— Lake Elsinore (Calif.)	0	1	.000	0.69	1.46	9	0	0	0	...	0-...	13.0	15	7	1	1	4-0	9	.278
— Portland (PCL)	2	2	.500	3.44	1.15	11	8	0	0	...	0-...	52.1	45	22	20	7	15-0	37	.230
2002— Baltimore (A.L.)	15	9	.625	3.57	1.19	33	28	1	0	0	0-0	196.2	172	83	78	23	62-4	136	.234
2003— Bowie (East.)	1	0	1.000	0.00	0.47	1	1	0	0	...	0-...	6.1	3	0	0	0	0-0	13	.143
— Baltimore (A.L.)	7	10	.412	5.82	1.57	26	26	3	1	0	0-0	147.0	188	101	95	24	43-6	103	.313
American League totals (2 years)	22	19	.537	4.53	1.35	59	54	4	1	0	0-0	343.2	360	184	173	47	105-10	239	.270
National League totals (1 year)	0	3	.000	8.76	2.15	6	6	0	0	0	0-0	24.2	40	24	24	5	13-0	17	.377
Major League totals (3 years)	22	22	.500	4.81	1.41	65	60	4	1	0	0-0	368.1	400	208	197	52	118-10	256	.278

LORETTA, MARK   IF

PERSONAL: Born August 14, 1971, in Santa Monica, Calif. ... 6-0/186. ... Bats right, throws right. ... Full name: Mark David Loretta. ... High school: St. Francis (La Canada, Calif.). ... College: Northwestern.

TRANSACTIONS/CAREER NOTES: Selected by Milwaukee Brewers organization in seventh round of free-agent draft (June 3, 1993). ... On New Orleans suspended list (May 17-20, 1996). ... On Milwaukee disabled list (June 3-August 16, 2000); included rehabilitation assignment to Indianapolis (August 3-16). ... On Milwaukee disabled list (March 27-May 19, 2001); included rehabilitation assignment to Indianapolis (May 9-17). ... Traded by Brewers to Houston Astros from two players to be named later (August 31, 2002); Brewers acquired P Wayne Franklin (September 3, 2002) and 2B Keith Ginter (September 5, 2002) to complete deal. ... Granted free agency (October 28, 2002). ... Signed by San Diego Padres (December 16, 2002).

2003 GAMES PLAYED BY POSITION (MLB): 2B—150, SS—3.

Year Team (League)	Pos.	G	AB	R	H	2B	3B	HR	RBI	BB	SO	HBP	GDP	SB-CS	Avg.	OBP	SLG	OPS	E	Pct.
1993— Helena (Pio.)	SS	6	28	5	9	1	0	1	8	1	4	1	1	0-0	.321	.367	.464	.831	0	1.000
— Stockton (Calif.)	3B-SS	53	201	36	73	4	1	4	31	22	17	2	6	8-2	.363	.427	.453	.880	15	.943
1994— El Paso (Texas)	P	77	302	50	95	13	6	0	38	27	33	2	12	8-5	.315	.369	.397	.766	11	.973
— New Orleans (A.A.)	2B-SS	43	138	16	29	7	0	1	14	12	13	3	2	2-1	.210	.282	.283	.565	11	.945
1995— New Orleans (A.A.)	S-3-2-D	127	479	48	137	22	5	7	79	34	47	9	12	8-9	.286	.340	.397	.737	25	.959
— Milwaukee (A.L.)	SS-2B-DH	19	50	13	13	3	0	1	3	4	7	1	1	1-1	.260	.327	.380	.707	1	.984
1996— New Orleans (A.A.)	SS	19	71	10	18	5	1	0	11	9	8	2	1	1-1	.254	.345	.352	.697	5	.948
— Milwaukee (A.L.)	2B-3B-SS	73	154	20	43	3	0	1	13	14	15	0	7	2-1	.279	.339	.318	.657	2	.986
1997— Milwaukee (A.L.)	2-S-1-3	132	418	56	120	17	5	5	47	47	60	2	15	5-5	.287	.354	.388	.742	15	.976
1998— Milwaukee (N.L.)	1-S-3-2-D	140	434	55	137	29	0	6	54	42	47	7	14	9-6	.316	.382	.424	.806	6	.991
1999— Milwaukee (N.L.)	S-1-2-3	153	587	93	170	34	5	5	67	52	59	10	14	4-1	.290	.354	.390	.744	13	.986
2000— Milwaukee (N.L.)	SS-2B	91	352	49	99	21	1	7	40	37	38	1	9	0-3	.281	.350	.406	.757	2	.995
— Indianapolis (Int'l)	SS	10	25	6	6	1	0	0	5	2	4	1	1	0-0	.240	.310	.280	.590	0	1.000
2001— Indianapolis (Int'l)	SS-2B-3B	8	31	4	3	0	0	0	1	2	4	0	1	0-0	.097	.152	.097	.248	3	.850
— Milwaukee (N.L.)	2-3-S-D	102	384	40	111	14	2	2	29	28	46	7	6	1-2	.289	.346	.352	.698	8	.978
2002— Milwaukee (N.L.)	3-S-1-2-D	86	217	23	58	14	0	2	19	23	32	5	6	0-0	.267	.350	.359	.709	3	.982
— Houston (N.L.)	3B-SS-2B	21	66	10	28	4	0	2	8	9	5	0	1	1-1	.424	.481	.576	1.056	2	.964
2003— San Diego (N.L.)	2B-SS	154	589	74	185	28	4	13	72	54	62	3	17	5-4	.314	.372	.441	.814	7	.990
American League totals (3 years)		224	622	89	176	23	5	7	63	65	82	3	23	8-7	.283	.349	.370	.718	18	.979
National League totals (6 years)		747	2629	344	788	144	12	37	289	245	289	33	67	20-17	.300	.364	.406	.770	41	.987
Major League totals (9 years)		971	3251	433	964	167	17	44	352	310	371	36	90	28-24	.297	.361	.399	.760	59	.986

LOUX, SHANE   P

PERSONAL: Born August 31, 1979, in Rapid City, S.D. ... 6-2/235. ... Throws right, bats right. ... Full name: Shane A. Loux. ... Name pronounced: LEW-ks. ... High school: Highland (Gilbert, Ariz.).

TRANSACTIONS/CAREER NOTES: Selected by Detroit Tigers organization in second round of free-agent draft (June 3, 1997). ... On Toledo disabled list (July 18-26, 2002). ... Recalled from Toledo (July 29, 2003).

CAREER HITTING: 0-for-0 (.000), 0 R, 0 2B, 0 3B, 0 HR, 0 RBI.

Year League	W	L	Pct.	ERA	WHIP	G	GS	CG	ShO	Hld.	Sv.-Opp.	IP	H	R	ER	HR	BB-IBB	SO	Avg.
1997— GC Tigers (GCL)	4	1	.800	0.84	0.67	10	9	1	1	...	0-...	43.0	19	7	4	0	10-0	33	.129
1998— West. Mich. (Mid.)	7	13	.350	4.64	1.50	28	•28	2	1	...	0-...	157.0	184	96	81	13	52-0	88	.291
1999— West. Mich. (Mid.)	1	3	.250	6.27	1.50	8	8	0	0	...	0-...	47.1	55	39	33	5	16-1	43	.293
— Lakeland (Fla. St.)	6	5	.545	4.05	1.53	17	17	0	0	...	0-...	91.0	92	48	41	8	47-0	52	.264
2000— Lakeland (Fla. St.)	0	1	.000	1.80	1.00	1	1	0	0	...	0-...	5.0	2	1	1	0	3-0	6	.133
— Jacksonville (Sou.)	12	9	.571	3.82	1.30	26	26	2	0	...	0-...	157.2	150	78	67	12	55-0	130	.254
2001— Toledo (Int'l)	10	11	.476	5.78	1.83	28	27	2	0	...	0-...	151.0	203	111	*97	22	73-0	72	.325
2002— Toledo (Int'l)	11	10	.524	4.72	1.48	26	26	*5	*3	...	0-...	158.1	196	94	83	11	38-1	87	.307
2003— Detroit (A.L.)	0	3	.000	9.00	1.57	3	3	0	0	0	0-0	14.0	19	16	14	4	3-0	7	.317
— Toledo (Int'l)	11	6	.647	3.02	1.24	21	20	2	1	...	0-...	128.0	129	53	43	5	30-0	58	.265
— Detroit (A.L.)	1	1	.500	7.12	1.62	11	4	0	0	0	0-0	30.1	37	24	24	4	12-1	8	.303
Major League totals (2 years)	1	4	.200	7.71	1.60	14	7	0	0	0	0-0	44.1	56	40	38	8	15-1	15	.308

LOWE, DEREK   P

PERSONAL: Born June 1, 1973, in Dearborn, Mich. ... 6-6/214. ... Throws right, bats right. ... Full name: Derek Christopher Lowe. ... High school: Edsel Ford (Dearborn, Mich.).

TRANSACTIONS/CAREER NOTES: Selected by Seattle Mariners organization in eighth round of free-agent draft (June 3, 1991). ... Traded by Mariners with C Jason Varitek to Boston Red Sox for P Heathcliff Slocumb (July 31, 1997). ... On suspended list (September 15-20, 2002).

CAREER HITTING: 1-for-16 (.063), 0 R, 0 2B, 0 3B, 0 HR, 0 RBI.

Year League	W	L	Pct.	ERA	WHIP	G	GS	CG	ShO	Hld.	Sv.-Opp.	IP	H	R	ER	HR	BB-IBB	SO	Avg.
1991— Ariz. Mariners (Ariz.)	5	3	.625	2.41	1.11	12	12	0	0	...	0-...	71.0	58	26	19	2	21-0	60	.217
1992— Bellingham (N'west)	7	3	.700	2.42	1.06	14	13	2	•1	...	0-...	85.2	69	34	23	2	22-0	66	.216
1993— Riverside (Calif.)	12	9	.571	5.26	1.62	27	26	3	2	...	0-...	154.0	189	104	90	9	60-0	80	.304
1994— Jacksonville (Sou.)	7	10	.412	4.94	1.50	26	26	2	0	...	0-...	151.1	177	92	83	7	50-1	75	.291
1995— Ariz. Mariners (Ariz.)	1	0	1.000	0.93	0.72	2	2	0	0	...	0-...	9.2	5	1	1	0	2-0	11	.152
— Port City (Sou.)	1	6	.143	6.08	1.73	10	10	1	0	...	0-...	53.1	70	41	36	8	22-1	30	.327
1996— Port City (Sou.)	5	3	.625	3.05	1.12	10	10	0	0	...	0-...	65.0	56	27	22	7	17-0	33	.235
— Tacoma (PCL)	6	9	.400	4.54	1.48	17	16	1	1	...	0-...	105.0	118	64	53	7	37-1	54	.285
1997— Tacoma (PCL)	3	4	.429	3.45	1.27	10	9	1	0	...	0-...	57.1	53	26	22	3	20-0	49	.242
— Seattle (A.L.)	2	4	.333	6.96	1.49	12	9	0	0	0	0-0	53.0	59	43	41	11	20-2	39	.282
— Pawtucket (Int'l)	4	0	1.000	2.37	1.12	6	5	0	0	...	0-...	30.1	23	8	8	3	11-0	21	.213
— Boston (A.L.)	0	2	.000	3.38	1.13	8	0	0	0	1	0-2	16.0	15	6	6	0	3-1	13	.268
1998— Boston (A.L.)	3	9	.250	4.02	1.37	63	10	0	0	12	4-9	123.0	126	65	55	5	42-5	77	.267
1999— Boston (A.L.)	6	3	.667	2.63	0.00	74	0	0	0	22	15-20	109.1	84	35	32	7	25-1	80	.208
2000— Boston (A.L.)	4	4	.500	2.56	1.23	74	0	0	0	0	•42-47	91.1	90	27	26	6	22-5	79	.257
2001— Boston (A.L.)	5	10	.333	3.53	1.44	67	3	0	0	4	24-30	91.2	103	39	36	7	29-9	82	.283
2002— Boston (A.L.)	21	8	.724	2.58	0.97	32	32	1	1	0	0-0	219.2	166	65	63	12	48-0	127	.211
2003— Boston (A.L.)	17	7	.708	4.47	1.42	33	33	1	0	0	0-0	203.1	216	113	101	17	72-4	110	.272
Major League totals (7 years)	**58**	**47**	**.552**	**3.57**	**1.23**	**363**	**87**	**2**	**1**	**39**	**85-108**	**907.1**	**859**	**393**	**360**	**65**	**261-27**	**607**	**.250**

LOWE, SEAN   P

PERSONAL: Born March 29, 1971, in Dallas, Texas. ... 6-2/225. ... Throws right, bats right. ... Full name: Jonathan Sean Lowe. ... High school: Mesquite (Texas). ... College: Arizona State.

TRANSACTIONS/CAREER NOTES: Selected by Cincinnati Reds organization in 43rd round of free-agent draft (June 5, 1989); did not sign. ... Selected by Oakland Athletics organization in 43rd round of free-agent draft (June 4, 1990); did not sign. ... Selected by St. Louis Cardinals organization in first round (15th pick overall) of free-agent draft (June 1, 1992). ... On St. Petersburg disabled list (July 19-August 8, 1994). ... On Arkansas disabled list (May 28-June 4, 1996). ... On Louisville disabled list (April 9-18, 1997). ... Traded by Cardinals to Chicago White Sox for P John Ambrose (February 9, 1999). ... On Chicago disabled list (July 29-August 23, 2000); included rehabilitation assignment to Charlotte (August 8-23). ... Traded by White Sox with P Kip Wells and P Josh Fogg to Pittsburgh Pirates for P Todd Ritchie and C Lee Evans (December 13, 2001). ... Released by Pirates (September 8, 2002). ... Signed by Colorado Rockies (September 12, 2002). ... Released by Rockies (November 20, 2002). ... Signed by Kansas City Royals as a free agent (January 16, 2003). ... Released (September 4, 2003).

CAREER HITTING: 3-for-22 (.136), 0 R, 0 2B, 0 3B, 0 HR, 0 RBI.

Year League	W	L	Pct.	ERA	WHIP	G	GS	CG	ShO	Hld.	Sv.-Opp.	IP	H	R	ER	HR	BB-IBB	SO	Avg.
1992— Hamilton (NYP)	2	0	1.000	1.61	1.00	5	5	0	0	...	0-...	28.0	14	8	5	0	14-0	22	.149
1993— St. Pete. (FSL)	6	11	.353	4.27	1.61	25	25	0	0	...	0-...	132.2	152	80	63	6	62-1	81	.293
1994— St. Pete. (FSL)	5	6	.455	3.47	1.37	21	21	0	0	...	0-...	114.0	119	51	44	6	37-0	92	.270
— Arkansas (Texas)	2	1	.667	1.40	1.09	3	3	0	0	...	0-...	19.1	13	3	3	0	8-0	11	.197
1995— Arkansas (Texas)	9	8	.529	4.88	1.60	24	24	0	0	...	0-...	129.0	143	84	70	2	64-0	77	.287
1996— Louisville (A.A.)	8	9	.471	4.70	1.55	25	18	0	0	...	0-...	115.0	127	72	60	7	51-7	76	.284
— Arkansas (Texas)	2	3	.400	6.00	1.42	6	6	0	0	...	0-...	33.0	32	24	22	2	15-1	25	.244
1997— Louisville (A.A.)	6	10	.375	4.37	1.48	26	23	1	0	...	1-...	131.2	142	74	64	13	53-4	117	.277
— St. Louis (N.L.)	0	2	.000	9.35	2.13	6	4	0	0	0	0-0	17.1	27	21	18	2	10-0	8	.365
1998— Memphis (PCL)	12	8	.600	3.18	1.36	25	21	0	0	...	0-...	153.0	147	57	54	17	61-1	114	.260
— St. Louis (N.L.)	0	3	.000	15.19	3.00	4	1	0	0	0	0-0	5.1	11	9	9	1	5-0	2	.440
1999— Chicago (A.L.)	4	1	.800	3.67	1.42	64	0	0	0	6	0-3	95.2	90	39	39	10	46-1	62	.262
2000— Chicago (A.L.)	4	1	.800	5.48	1.66	50	5	0	0	6	0-0	70.2	78	47	43	10	39-3	53	.284
— Charlotte (Int'l)	0	0	...	3.00	2.00	2	1	0	0	...	0-...	3.0	5	1	1	1	1-0	1	.385
2001— Chicago (A.L.)	9	4	.692	3.61	1.22	45	11	0	0	3	3-3	127.0	123	55	51	12	32-2	71	.256
— Charlotte (Int'l)	1	1	.500	4.50	1.10	2	2	0	0	...	0-...	10.0	9	6	5	0	2-0	8	.231
2002— Pittsburgh (N.L.)	4	2	.667	5.35	1.72	43	1	0	0	9	0-2	69.0	85	45	41	8	34-6	57	.307
— Nashville (PCL)	1	1	.500	5.73	1.45	5	5	0	0	...	0-...	22.0	29	14	14	0	3-0	21	.319
— Colorado (N.L.)	1	1	.500	8.71	2.23	8	0	0	0	1	0-...	10.1	16	13	10	1	7-0	7	.348
2003— Kansas City (A.L.)	1	1	.500	6.25	1.70	28	0	0	0	7	0-1	44.2	55	32	31	7	21-5	28	.301
— Omaha (PCL)	4	0	1.000	3.25	1.39	14	7	0	0	...	0-...	52.2	54	22	19	3	19-0	27	.273
American League totals (4 years)	**18**	**7**	**.720**	**4.37**	**1.43**	**187**	**16**	**0**	**0**	**22**	**3-7**	**338.0**	**346**	**173**	**164**	**39**	**138-11**	**214**	**.270**
National League totals (3 years)	**5**	**8**	**.385**	**6.88**	**1.91**	**61**	**6**	**0**	**0**	**10**	**0-2**	**102.0**	**139**	**88**	**78**	**12**	**56-6**	**74**	**.329**
Major League totals (7 years)	**23**	**15**	**.605**	**4.95**	**1.54**	**248**	**22**	**0**	**0**	**32**	**3-9**	**440.0**	**485**	**261**	**242**	**51**	**194-17**	**288**	**.285**

LOWELL, MIKE   3B

PERSONAL: Born February 24, 1974, in San Juan, Puerto Rico. ... 6-3/215. ... Bats right, throws right. ... Full name: Michael Averett Lowell. ... High school: Coral Gables (Fla.). ... College: Florida International.

TRANSACTIONS/CAREER NOTES: Selected by New York Yankees organization in 20th round of free-agent draft (June 1, 1995). ... Traded by Yankees to Florida Marlins for P Ed Yarnall, P Mark Johnson and P Todd Noel (February 1, 1999). ... On Florida disabled list (March 26-May 29, 1999); included rehabilitation assignments to Calgary (April 8-13 and May 6-29). ... On disabled list (May 13-29, 2000). ... Placed on 15-day disabled list (August 31, 2003). ... Removed from 15-day disabled list (September 28, 2003).

2003 GAMES PLAYED BY POSITION (MLB): 3B—128, DH—2.

Year Team (League)	Pos.	G	AB	R	H	2B	3B	HR	RBI	BB	SO	HBP	GDP	SB-CS	Avg.	OBP	SLG	OPS	E	Pct.
1995— Oneonta (NYP)	3B	72	281	36	73	18	0	1	27	23	34	3	5	3-1	.260	.316	.335	.651	24	.911
1996— Greensboro (S. Atl.)	3B-SS	113	433	58	122	33	0	8	64	46	43	4	7	10-3	.282	.355	.413	.768	32	.925
— Tampa (Fla. St.)	3B	24	78	8	22	5	0	0	11	3	13	0	2	1-1	.282	.298	.346	.644	3	.954
1997— Norwich (East.)	3B-SS	78	285	60	98	17	0	15	47	48	30	4	11	2-1	.344	.439	.561	1.000	15	.927
— Columbus (Int'l)	3B-SS	57	210	36	58	13	1	15	45	23	34	4	6	2-4	.276	.347	.562	.909	5	.954
1998— Columbus (Int'l)	3B-SS-1B	126	510	79	155	34	3	26	99	37	85	6	10	4-0	.304	.355	.535	.890	§ 21	.950
— New York (A.L.)	3B-DH	8	15	1	4	0	0	0	0	0	1	0	0	0-0	.267	.267	.267	.533	0	1.000

L

Year Team (League)	Pos.	G	AB	R	H	2B	3B	HR	RBI	BB	SO	HBP	GDP	SB-CS	Avg.	OBP	SLG	OPS	E	Pct.
1999— Calgary (PCL)	3B	24	83	11	26	3	0	2	9	8	19	0	0	0-0	.313	.374	.422	.795	4	.939
— Florida (N.L.)	3B	97	308	32	78	15	0	12	47	26	69	5	8	0-0	.253	.317	.419	.736	4	.981
2000— Florida (N.L.)	3B	140	508	73	137	38	0	22	91	54	75	9	4	4-0	.270	.344	.474	.818	12	.968
2001— Florida (N.L.)	3B	146	551	65	156	37	0	18	100	43	79	10	9	1-2	.283	.340	.448	.789	9	.976
2002— Florida (N.L.)	3B	160	597	88	165	44	0	24	92	65	92	4	16	4-3	.276	.346	.471	.816	14	.969
2003— Florida (N.L.)	3B-DH	130	492	76	136	27	1	32	105	56	78	3	14	3-1	.276	.350	.530	.881	9	.973
American League totals (1 year)		8	15	1	4	0	0	0	0	0	0	1	0	0-0	.267	.267	.267	.533	0	1.000
National League totals (5 years)		673	2456	334	672	161	1	108	435	244	393	31	51	12-6	.274	.341	.472	.813	48	.972
Major League totals (6 years)		681	2471	335	676	161	1	108	435	244	394	31	51	12-6	.274	.341	.471	.812	48	.973

LOWRY, NOAH   P

PERSONAL: Born October 10, 1980, in Ventura, Calif. ... 6-2/190. ... Throws left, bats left. ... Full name: Noah Ryan Lowry. ... High school: Nordhoff (Ojai, Calif.). ... College: Pepperdine.

TRANSACTIONS/CAREER NOTES: Selected by San Francisco Giants organization in first round (30th pick overall) of free-agent draft (June 5, 2001).

CAREER HITTING: 1-for-2 (.500), 1 R, 0 2B, 0 3B, 0 HR, 0 RBI.

Year League	W	L	Pct.	ERA	WHIP	G	GS	CG	ShO	Hld.	Sv.-Opp.	IP	H	R	ER	HR	BB-IBB	SO	Avg.
2001— Salem-Keizer (NW)	1	1	.500	3.60	1.36	8	7	0	0	...	0-...	25.0	26	15	10	2	8-0	28	.265
2002— San Jose (Calif.)	6	5	.545	2.15	0.99	15	12	0	0	...	0-...	58.2	38	21	14	4	20-0	62	.186
2003— Norwich (East.)	9	6	.600	4.72	1.47	23	23	2	0	...	0-...	118.1	127	66	62	7	47-0	97	.285
— Fresno (PCL)	1	0	1.000	2.37	1.11	4	4	0	0	...	0-...	19.0	15	5	5	0	6-0	13	.227
— San Francisco (N.L.)	0	0	...	0.00	0.47	4	0	0	0	0	0-0	6.1	1	0	0	0	2-0	5	.048
Major League totals (1 year)	0	0	...	0.00	0.47	4	0	0	0	0	0-0	6.1	1	0	0	0	2-0	5	.048

LUDWICK, RYAN   OF

PERSONAL: Born July 13, 1978, in Satellite Beach, Fla. ... 6-3/203. ... Bats right, throws left. ... Full name: Ryan Andrew Ludwick. ... High school: Durango (Las Vegas, Nev.). ... College: UNLV.

TRANSACTIONS/CAREER NOTES: Selected by Oakland Athletics organization in second round of free-agent draft (June 2, 1999). ... Traded by A's with 1B Jason Hart, P Mario Ramos and C Gerald Laird to Texas Rangers for 1B Carlos Pena and P Mike Venafro (January 14, 2002). ... On Oklahoma disabled list (August 3, 2002-remainder of season). ... Recalled from Oklahoma (July 2, 2003). ... Traded by Rangers to Cleveland Indians for P Ricardo Rodriguez (July 18, 2003).

2003 GAMES PLAYED BY POSITION (MLB): OF—40, DH—4.

Year Team (League)	Pos.	G	AB	R	H	2B	3B	HR	RBI	BB	SO	HBP	GDP	SB-CS	Avg.	OBP	SLG	OPS	E	Pct.
1999— Modesto (Calif.)	OF	43	171	28	47	11	3	4	34	19	45	3	0	2-1	.275	.348	.444	.793	0	1.000
2000— Modesto (Calif.)	OF	129	493	86	130	26	3	29	102	68	128	9	6	10-6	.264	.359	.505	.864	5	.983
2001— Midland (Texas)	OF	119	443	82	119	23	3	25	96	53	113	7	6	9-10	.269	.352	.503	.856	6	.977
— Sacramento (PCL)	OF	17	57	10	13	3	0	1	7	2	16	0	0	2-0	.228	.246	.333	.579	1	.981
2002— Oklahoma (PCL)	OF	78	305	62	87	27	4	15	52	38	76	5	6	2-2	.285	.370	.548	.918	5	.973
— Texas (A.L.)	OF	23	81	10	19	6	0	1	9	7	24	0	4	2-1	.235	.295	.346	.641	0	1.000
2003— Oklahoma (PCL)	OF-DH	81	317	51	96	24	3	17	63	33	71	5	9	1-1	.303	.372	.558	.931	3	.975
— Texas (A.L.)	OF	8	26	3	4	1	0	0	0	4	9	0	0	0-0	.154	.267	.192	.459	0	1.000
— Cleveland (A.L.)	OF-DH	39	136	14	36	7	1	7	26	8	39	0	1	2-0	.265	.306	.485	.791	0	1.000
Major League totals (2 years)		70	243	27	59	14	1	8	35	19	72	0	5	4-1	.243	.298	.407	.705	0	1.000

LUGO, JULIO   SS

PERSONAL: Born November 16, 1975, in Barahona, Dominican Republic. ... 6-1/170. ... Bats right, throws right. ... Full name: Julio Cesar Lugo. ... Name pronounced: lou-GO. ... Junior college: Connors State College (Okla.).

TRANSACTIONS/CAREER NOTES: Selected by Houston Astros organization in 43rd round of free-agent draft (June 2, 1994). ... On disabled list (July 21-29, 1999). ... On disabled list (August 13, 2002-remainder of season). ... Designated for assignment (May 1, 2003). ... Given unconditional release (May 9, 2003). ... Signed by Tampa Bay Devil Rays as a free agent (May 15, 2003).

2003 GAMES PLAYED BY POSITION (MLB): SS—139.

Year Team (League)	Pos.	G	AB	R	H	2B	3B	HR	RBI	BB	SO	HBP	GDP	SB-CS	Avg.	OBP	SLG	OPS	E	Pct.
1995— Auburn (NY-Penn)	2B-SS-OF	59	230	36	67	6	3	1	16	26	31	2	7	17-7	.291	.368	.357	.725	12	.944
1996— Quad City (Midw.)	2B-3B-SS	101	393	60	116	18	2	10	50	32	75	3	7	24-11	.295	.350	.427	.777	29	.934
1997— Kissimmee (Fla. St.)	2B-3B-SS	125	505	89	135	22	*14	7	61	46	99	2	8	35-8	.267	.329	.408	.736	‡41	.938
1998— Kissimmee (Fla. St.)	SS	128	509	81	154	20	*14	7	62	49	72	4	13	51-18	.303	.367	.438	.805	42	.921
1999— Jackson (Texas)	SS-2B	116	445	77	142	24	5	10	42	44	53	3	6	25-11	.319	.381	.463	.844	29	.964
2000— New Orleans (PCL)	2B-SS	24	101	22	33	4	1	3	12	11	20	0	2	12-7	.327	.393	.475	.868	4	.964
— Houston (N.L.)	SS-2B-OF	116	420	78	119	22	5	10	40	37	93	4	9	22-9	.283	.346	.431	.777	17	.963
2001— Houston (N.L.)	SS-OF-2B	140	513	93	135	20	3	10	37	46	116	5	7	12-11	.263	.326	.372	.698	22	.964
2002— Houston (N.L.)	SS	88	322	45	84	15	1	8	35	28	74	2	6	9-3	.261	.322	.388	.710	8	.976
2003— Houston (N.L.)	SS	22	65	6	16	3	0	0	2	9	12	0	2	2-1	.246	.338	.292	.630	3	.966
— Tampa Bay (A.L.)	SS	117	433	58	119	13	4	15	53	35	88	4	5	10-3	.275	.333	.427	.760	17	.970
American League totals (1 year)		117	433	58	119	13	4	15	53	35	88	4	5	10-3	.275	.333	.427	.760	17	.970
National League totals (4 years)		366	1320	222	354	60	9	28	114	120	295	11	24	45-24	.268	.332	.391	.723	50	.966
Major League totals (4 years)		483	1753	280	473	73	13	43	167	155	383	15	29	55-27	.270	.332	.400	.732	67	.967

LUNSFORD, TREY   C

PERSONAL: Born May 25, 1979, in Odessa, Texas. ... 6-1/195. ... Bats right, throws right. ... Full name: James Lewis Lunsford. ... High school: Central (San Angelo, Texas). ... College: Texas Tech.

TRANSACTIONS/CAREER NOTES: Selected by San Francisco Giants organization in 33rd round of free-agent draft (June 5, 2000). ... On San Jose disabled list (April 4-28, 2002). ... Recalled from Fresno (June 17, 2003). ... Optioned to Fresno (June 22, 2003). ... Recalled from Fresno (September 29, 2003).

2003 GAMES PLAYED BY POSITION (MLB): C—1.

Year Team (League)	Pos.	G	AB	R	H	2B	3B	HR	RBI	BB	SO	HBP	GDP	SB-CS	Avg.	OBP	SLG	OPS	E	Pct.
2000— Salem-Keizer (NW)	C	59	215	23	58	9	0	3	30	30	40	8	6	1-0	.270	.378	.353	.731	7	.987
2001— Hagerstown (SAL)	C-1B	114	396	53	94	19	0	5	50	45	89	5	12	10-5	.237	.320	.323	.643	14	.986
2002— San Jose (Calif.)	C	16	51	7	13	3	0	1	5	3	5	2	2	2-0	.255	.321	.373	.694	1	.991
— Shreveport (Texas)	C-1B	66	210	26	59	13	0	1	20	29	42	4	3	5-2	.281	.379	.357	.736	5	.987
— Fresno (PCL)	C	19	57	3	10	0	0	2	9	6	15	1	2	0-0	.175	.258	.281	.538	2	.987
— San Francisco (N.L.)	C	3	3	0	2	1	0	0	0	1	0	1	0	0-0	.667	.667	1.000	1.667	1	.800
2003— San Francisco (N.L.)	C	1	1	0	0	0	0	0	0	0	0	0	0	0-0	.000	.000	.000	.000	0	...
— Ariz. Giants (Ariz.)	DH-C	5	13	5	6	0	1	0	3	7	3	0	0	1-1	.462	.619	.615	1.234	0	1.000
— Salem-Keizer (NW)	C	3	10	0	3	0	0	0	3	2	1	1	0	0-0	.300	.429	.300	.729	1	.960
— San Jose (Calif.)	DH-C	2	7	1	2	0	0	1	1	0	4	0	0	0-0	.286	.286	.714	1.000	0	1.000
— Fresno (PCL)	C-OF	69	206	20	59	10	1	2	20	17	33	1	4	0-1	.286	.341	.374	.714	4	.989
Major League totals (2 years)		4	4	0	2	1	0	0	1	0	1	0	0	0-0	.500	.500	.750	1.250	1	.800

LYON, BRANDON P

PERSONAL: Born August 10, 1979, in Salt Lake City, Utah. ... 6-1/185. ... Throws right, bats right. ... Full name: Brandon James Lyon. ... Name pronounced: lion. ... High school: Taylorsville (Salt Lake City). ... Junior college: Dixie College (Utah).

TRANSACTIONS/CAREER NOTES: Selected by Toronto Blue Jays organization in 14th round of free-agent draft (June 2, 1999). ... Claimed on waivers by Boston Red Sox (October 9, 2002). ... Traded by Red Sox with P Anastacio Martinez to Pittsburgh Pirates for P Scott Sauerbeck and P Mike Gonzalez (July 22, 2003). ... Traded by Pirates with P Jeff Suppan and P Anastacio Martinez to Red Sox for IF Freddy Sanchez, P Mike Gonzalez and cash (July 31, 2003).

CAREER HITTING: 0-for-0 (.000), 0 R, 0 2B, 0 3B, 0 HR, 0 RBI.

Year League	W	L	Pct.	ERA	WHIP	G	GS	CG	ShO	Hld.	Sv.-Opp.	IP	H	R	ER	HR	BB-IBB	SO	Avg.
2000— Queens (NY-P)	5	3	.625	2.39	0.81	15	13	0	0	...	0-...	60.1	43	20	16	1	6-0	55	.197
2001— Tennessee (Sou.)	5	0	1.000	3.68	1.13	9	9	0	0	...	0-...	58.2	57	25	24	7	9-0	45	.252
— Syracuse (Int'l)	5	3	.625	3.69	1.14	11	11	2	1	...	0-...	68.1	68	33	28	7	10-0	53	.257
— Toronto (A.L.)	5	4	.556	4.29	1.24	11	11	0	0	0	0-0	63.0	63	31	30	6	15-0	35	.266
2002— Toronto (A.L.)	1	4	.200	6.53	1.56	15	10	0	0	0	0-1	62.0	78	47	45	14	19-2	30	.308
— Syracuse (Int'l)	4	9	.308	5.11	1.56	14	14	0	0	...	0-...	75.2	99	54	43	4	19-0	35	.315
2003— Pawtucket (Int'l)	0	0	...	3.24	1.08	5	0	0	0	...	0-...	8.1	7	3	3	1	2-0	7	.219
— Boston (A.L.)	4	6	.400	4.12	1.56	49	0	0	0	2	9-12	59.0	73	33	27	6	19-5	50	.296
Major League totals (3 years)	10	14	.417	4.99	1.56	75	21	0	0	2	9-13	184.0	214	111	102	26	53-7	115	.290

MABRY, JOHN OF/1B

PERSONAL: Born October 17, 1970, in Wilmington, Del. ... 6-4/210. ... Bats left, throws right. ... Full name: John Steven Mabry. ... Name pronounced: MAY-bree. ... High school: Bohemia Manor (Chesapeake City, Md.). ... College: West Chester (Pa.).

TRANSACTIONS/CAREER NOTES: Selected by St. Louis Cardinals organization in sixth round of free-agent draft (June 3, 1991). ... On disabled list (April 22-30 and May 6-18, 1992). ... On disabled list (August 20-September 24, 1997). ... Granted free agency (December 21, 1998). ... Signed by Seattle Mariners (December 30, 1998). ... On disabled list (August 14, 1999-remainder of season). ... On Seattle disabled list (April 22-May 12, 2000); included rehabilitation assignment to Tacoma (May 8-12). ... Traded by Mariners with P Tom Davey to San Diego Padres for OF Al Martin (July 31, 2000). ... Granted free agency (October 30, 2000). ... Signed by Cardinals organization (January 5, 2001). ... Traded by Cardinals to Florida Marlins for cash considerations (April 9, 2001). ... On Florida disabled list (April 16-May 20, 2001); included rehabilitation assignment to Brevard County (May 16-20). ... Granted free agency (November 5, 2001). ... Signed by Philadelphia Phillies organization (January 28, 2002). ... Traded by Phillies to Oakland Athletics for 1B/OF Jeremy Giambi (May 22, 2002). ... Granted free agency (November 4, 2002). ... Signed by Seattle Mariners (January 15, 2003). ... Placed on 15-day disabled list (May 28, 2003). ... Sent to Tacoma on rehab assignment (June 17, 2003). ... Recalled from rehab assignment; reinstated from 15-day disabled list (June 20, 2003).

2003 GAMES PLAYED BY POSITION (MLB): OF—22, DH—12, 1B—9.

Year Team (League)	Pos.	G	AB	R	H	2B	3B	HR	RBI	BB	SO	HBP	GDP	SB-CS	Avg.	OBP	SLG	OPS	E	Pct.
1991— Hamilton (NYP)	OF	49	187	25	58	11	0	1	31	17	18	2	6	9-3	.310	.370	.385	.755	5	.943
— Savannah (S. Atl.)	OF	22	86	10	20	6	1	0	8	7	12	0	2	1-0	.233	.284	.326	.610	1	.974
1992— Springfield (Midw.)	OF	115	438	63	115	13	6	11	57	24	39	0	12	2-8	.263	.300	.395	.695	6	.969
1993— Arkansas (Texas)	OF *	136	528	68	153	32	2	16	72	27	68	4	17	7-15	.290	.326	.449	.775	3	.989
— Louisville (A.A.)	OF	4	7	0	1	0	0	0	1	0	1	0	1	0-0	.143	.143	.143	.286	0	1.000
1994— Louisville (A.A.)	OF	122	477	76	125	30	1	15	68	32	67	3	14	2-6	.262	.311	.423	.735	2	.992
— St. Louis (N.L.)	OF	6	23	2	7	3	0	0	3	2	4	0	0	0-0	.304	.360	.435	.795	0	1.000
1995— St. Louis (N.L.)	1B-OF	129	388	35	119	21	1	5	41	24	45	2	6	0-3	.307	.347	.405	.752	4	.994
— Louisville (A.A.)	OF	4	12	0	1	0	0	0	0	0	0	0	0	0-0	.083	.083	.083	.167	1	.889
1996— St. Louis (N.L.)	1B	151	543	63	161	30	2	13	74	37	84	3	21	3-2	.297	.342	.431	.773	8	.994
1997— St. Louis (N.L.)	OF-1B-3B	116	388	40	110	19	0	5	36	39	77	3	11	0-1	.284	.352	.371	.723	1	.998
1998— St. Louis (N.L.)	OF-3B-1B	142	377	41	94	22	0	9	46	30	76	1	6	0-2	.249	.305	.379	.684	9	.968
1999— Seattle (A.L.)	O-3-1-D	87	262	34	64	14	0	9	33	20	60	0	6	2-1	.244	.297	.401	.698	10	.964
2000— Seattle (A.L.)	3-O-D-1	48	103	18	25	5	0	1	7	10	31	2	1	0-1	.243	.322	.320	.642	4	.934
— Tacoma (PCL)	3B-1B	14	14	1	3	1	0	0	1	0	4	0	0	0-0	.214	.214	.286	.500	1	.800
— San Diego (N.L.)	OF-1B-P	48	123	17	28	8	0	7	25	5	38	0	3	0-0	.228	.256	.463	.719	1	.983
2001— St. Louis (N.L.)	1B-OF	5	7	0	0	0	0	0	0	0	2	0	0	0-0	.000	.000	.000	.000	0	1.000
— Florida (N.L.)	OF-DH-1B	82	147	14	32	7	0	6	20	13	44	5	6	1-0	.218	.299	.388	.687	2	.964
— Brevard County (FSL)	OF	4	13	0	2	0	0	0	4	2	1	0	0	0-0	.154	.250	.154	.404	0	1.000
2002— Philadelphia (N.L.)	1B-OF	21	21	1	6	0	0	0	3	1	5	0	0	0-0	.286	.304	.286	.590	1	1.000
— Oakland (A.L.)	OF-1B	89	193	27	53	13	1	11	40	14	37	1	7	1-1	.275	.322	.523	.846	2	.992
2003— Tacoma (PCL)	DH	3	11	1	4	0	0	0	0	0	2	1	0	0-0	.364	.462	.364	.825	0	.000
— Seattle (A.L.)	OF-DH-1B	64	104	12	22	6	0	3	16	15	21	3	3	0-0	.212	.328	.356	.684	1	.987
American League totals (4 years)		288	662	91	164	38	1	24	96	59	149	6	17	3-3	.248	.313	.417	.730	17	.974
National League totals (8 years)		700	2017	213	557	110	3	45	248	151	375	14	53	4-8	.276	.328	.401	.729	25	.991
Major League totals (10 years)		988	2679	304	721	148	4	69	344	210	524	20	70	7-11	.269	.325	.405	.729	42	.988

MacDOUGAL, MIKE P

PERSONAL: Born March 5, 1977, in Las Vegas, Nev. ... 6-4/195. ... Throws right, bats both. ... Full name: Robert Meiklejohn MacDougal. ... High school: Mesa (Ariz.). ... College: Wake Forest.

TRANSACTIONS/CAREER NOTES: Selected by Baltimore Orioles organization in 22nd round of free-agent draft (June 4, 1996); did not sign. ... Selected by Baltimore Orioles organization in 17th round of free-agent draft (June 2, 1998); did not sign. ... Selected by Kansas City Royals organization in first round (25th pick overall) of free-agent draft (June 2, 1999); pick received from Boston Red Sox as part of compensation for signing Type A free agent 2B Jose Offerman. ... On Wichita disabled list (July 1-August 20, 2002). ... Recalled by Royals (September 6, 2002).

CAREER HITTING: 0-for-0 (.000), 0 R, 0 2B, 0 3B, 0 HR, 0 RBI.

Year	League	W	L	Pct.	ERA	WHIP	G	GS	CG	ShO	Hld.	Sv.-Opp.	IP	H	R	ER	HR	BB-IBB	SO	Avg.
1999— Spokane (N'west)		2	2	.500	4.47	1.29	11	11	0	0	...	0-...	46.1	43	25	23	3	17-0	57	.251
2000— Wilmington (Caro.)		9	7	.563	3.92	1.32	26	25	0	0	...	1-...	144.2	115	79	63	5	76-0	129	.219
— Wichita (Texas)		0	1	.000	7.71	1.97	2	2	0	0	...	0-...	11.2	16	10	10	0	7-0	9	.356
2001— Omaha (PCL)		8	8	.500	4.68	1.52	28	27	1	0	...	0-...	144.1	144	90	75	13	76-0	110	.259
— Kansas City (A.L.)		1	1	.500	4.70	1.43	3	3	0	0	0	0-0	15.1	18	10	8	2	4-0	7	.290
2002— Omaha (PCL)		3	5	.375	5.60	2.02	12	10	0	0	...	0-...	53.0	52	42	33	4	55-0	30	.265
— Wichita (Texas)		1	1	.500	3.06	1.98	4	4	1	0	...	0-...	17.2	11	12	6	1	24-0	14	.193
— GC Royals (GCL)		0	0	...	3.00	1.00	1	1	0	0	...	0-...	3.0	3	1	1	0	0-0	3	.273
— Wilmington (Caro.)		0	1	.000	1.08	0.96	5	0	0	0	...	2-...	8.1	3	4	1	1	5-0	10	.107
— Kansas City (A.L.)		0	1	.000	5.00	1.33	6	0	0	0	0	0-0	9.0	5	5	5	0	7-1	10	.161
2003— Kansas City (A.L.)		3	5	.375	4.08	1.50	68	0	0	0	1	27-35	64.0	64	36	29	4	32-0	57	.267
Major League totals (3 years)		4	7	.364	4.28	1.47	77	3	0	0	1	27-35	88.1	87	51	42	6	43-1	74	.261

MACHADO, ANDY

PERSONAL: Born January 25, 1981, in Caracas, Venezuela. ... 5-11/165. ... Bats both, throws right. ... Full name: Anderson Javier Machado. ... Name pronounced: ma-CHAH-do.

TRANSACTIONS/CAREER NOTES: Signed by Philadelphia Phillies as a non-drafted free agent (January 14, 1998).

											BATTING										FIELDING	
Year	Team (League)	Pos.	G	AB	R	H	2B	3B	HR	RBI	BB	SO	HBP	GDP	SB-CS	Avg.	OBP	SLG	OPS	E	Pct.
1999— Clearwater (FSL)		SS	1	2	0	0	0	0	0	0	0	1	0	0	0-0	.000	.000	.000	.000	0	...
— Piedmont (S. Atl.)		SS	20	60	7	14	4	2	0	7	7	20	1	0	2-1	.233	.324	.367	.690	8	.910
— GC Phillies (GCL)		2B-SS-3B	43	143	26	37	6	3	2	12	15	38	2	5	6-3	.259	.335	.385	.720	8	.958
2000— Clearwater (FSL)		SS	117	417	55	102	19	7	1	35	54	103	0	7	32-18	.245	.330	.331	.661	43	.934
— Reading (East.)		SS	3	11	2	4	1	0	1	2	0	4	0	0	0-0	.364	.364	.727	1.091	1	.929
2001— Clearwater (FSL)		SS	82	272	49	71	5	8	5	36	31	66	4	3	23-9	.261	.342	.393	.735	16	.962
— Reading (East.)		SS	31	101	13	15	2	0	1	8	12	25	0	1	5-2	.149	.237	.198	.435	9	.941
2002— Reading (East.)		SS	126	450	71	113	24	3	12	77	72	118	2	5	40-11	.251	.353	.398	.751	28	.954
2003— Reading (East.)		SS	123	423	80	83	19	4	5	20	108	120	1	2	49-15	.196	.360	.296	.656	26	.951
— Philadelphia (N.L.)			1	0	0	0	0	0	0	0	0	0	0	0	1-0	...	...	...	...	0	...
Major League totals (1 year)			1	0	0	0	0	0	0	0	0	0	0	0	1-0	...	...	...	...	0	...

MACHADO, ROBERT   C

PERSONAL: Born June 3, 1973, in Puerto Cabello, Venezuela. ... 6-1/219. ... Bats right, throws right. ... Full name: Robert Alexis Machado. ... Name pronounced: muh-CHA-doh.

TRANSACTIONS/CAREER NOTES: Signed as non-drafted free agent by Chicago White Sox organization (August 10, 1989). ... Released by White Sox (May 19, 1999). ... Signed by Montreal Expos organization (May 21, 1999). ... Granted free agency (October 15, 1999). ... Signed by Seattle Mariners organization (November 17, 1999). ... Granted free agency (October 2, 2000). ... Signed by Chicago Cubs organization (December 13, 2000). ... Traded by Cubs to Milwaukee Brewers for OF Jackson Melian (June 8, 2002). ... Released by Brewers (March 26, 2003). ... Signed by Baltimore Orioles organization (May 8, 2003). ... Sent outright to Ottawa (May 13, 2003). ... Recalled by Baltimore (July 21, 2003). ... Elected free agency (October 15, 2003).

2003 GAMES PLAYED BY POSITION (MLB): C—18.

											BATTING										FIELDING	
Year	Team (League)	Pos.	G	AB	R	H	2B	3B	HR	RBI	BB	SO	HBP	GDP	SB-CS	Avg.	OBP	SLG	OPS	E	Pct.
1990— Dom. Orioles/W.S. (DSL)			55	191	28	53	9	0	5	20	14	32			2-...	.277	...	.403	...		
1991— GC Whi. Sox (GCL)		C	38	126	11	31	4	1	0	15	6	21	6	2	2-1	.246	.309	.294	.603	8	.977
1992— Utica (N.Y.-Penn)		C	45	161	16	44	13	1	2	20	5	26	0	3	1-5	.273	.293	.404	.697	12	.963
1993— South Bend (Mid.)		C	75	281	34	86	14	3	2	33	19	59	4	6	1-2	.306	.354	.399	.752	12	.979
1994— Prince Will. (Car.)		C	93	312	45	81	17	1	11	47	27	68	4	10	0-1	.260	.326	.426	.752	* 16	.975
1995— Nashville (A.A.)		C	16	49	7	7	3	0	1	5	7	12	0	1	0-1	.143	.250	.265	.515	3	.972
— Prince Will. (Car.)		C	83	272	37	69	14	0	6	31	40	47	7	6	0-0	.254	.363	.371	.734	5	.992
1996— Birmingham (Sou.)		C-DH	87	309	35	74	16	0	6	28	20	56	3	9	1-4	.239	.291	.350	.641	5	.991
— Chicago (A.L.)		C	4	6	1	4	1	0	0	2	0	0	0	0	0-0	.667	.667	.833	1.500	0	1.000
1997— Nashville (A.A.)		C-DH	84	308	43	83	18	0	8	30	12	61	1	6	5-0	.269	.297	.406	.703	6	.988
— Chicago (A.L.)		C	10	15	1	3	0	1	0	2	1	6	0	0	0-0	.200	.250	.333	.583	0	1.000
1998— Calgary (PCL)		C-DH	66	239	31	63	19	0	4	27	20	33	3	9	2-2	.264	.326	.393	.719	6	.981
— Chicago (A.L.)		C	34	111	14	23	6	0	3	15	7	22	0	3	0-0	.207	.254	.342	.597	4	.981
1999— Charlotte (Int'l)		C	16	54	4	11	3	0	2	7	4	13	2	3	0-0	.204	.283	.370	.654	3	.976
— Ottawa (Int'l)		C-DH	21	75	6	17	5	0	0	3	0	13	4	2	0-1	.227	.266	.293	.559	3	.981
— Montreal (N.L.)		C	17	22	3	4	1	0	0	0	2	6	0	0	0-0	.182	.250	.227	.477	0	1.000
2000— Tacoma (PCL)		C	92	330	41	99	20	0	9	58	28	43	3	10	1-5	.300	.357	.442	.800	• 11	.980
— Seattle (A.L.)		C	8	14	2	3	0	0	1	1	1	4	0	0	0-0	.214	.267	.429	.695	0	1.000
2001— Iowa (PCL)		C	53	180	20	51	11	0	8	30	11	36	2	5	0-0	.283	.332	.478	.809	5	.988
— Chicago (N.L.)		C	52	135	13	30	10	0	2	13	7	26	1	4	0-0	.222	.266	.341	.606	1	.997
2002— Chicago (N.L.)		C-1B	22	58	5	16	4	0	1	5	5	11	0	2	0-0	.276	.333	.397	.730	2	.985
— Milwaukee (N.L.)		C-1B	51	153	14	39	10	1	2	17	12	30	1	5	0-0	.255	.310	.373	.682	4	.988
2003— Ottawa (Int'l)		C-DH	59	221	30	74	17	0	8	38	17	36	3	6	0-0	.335	.390	.520	.910	2	.994
— Baltimore (A.L.)		C	18	49	8	13	1	0	1	3	6	12	0	0	0-0	.265	.345	.347	.692	1	.990
American League totals (5 years)			74	195	26	46	8	1	5	23	15	44	0	4	0-0	.236	.290	.364	.655	5	.987
National League totals (3 years)			142	368	35	89	25	1	5	35	26	73	2	11	0-0	.242	.294	.356	.650	7	.992
Major League totals (8 years)			216	563	61	135	33	2	10	58	41	117	2	15	0-0	.240	.293	.359	.652	12	.990

MACIAS, JOSE   OF/IF

PERSONAL: Born January 25, 1972, in Panama City, Panama. ... 5-8/190. ... Bats both, throws right. ... Full name: Jose Prade Macias. ... Name pronounced: muh-SEE-us. ... High school: Instituto Technologico (Panama City, Panama).

TRANSACTIONS/CAREER NOTES: Signed as non-drafted free agent by Montreal Expos organization (February 14, 1992). ... Selected by Detroit Tigers organization from Expos organization in Rule 5 minor league draft (December 9, 1996). ... Traded by Tigers to Montreal Expos for 3B Chris Truby (May 16, 2002). ... On Montreal disabled list (September 10, 2002-remainder of season). ... On suspended list (April 6-9, 2003).

2003 GAMES PLAYED BY POSITION (MLB): OF—62, 3B—25, 2B—4, DH—1.

Year	Team (League)	Pos.	G	AB	R	H	2B	3B	HR	RBI	BB	SO	HBP	GDP	SB-CS	Avg.	OBP	SLG	OPS	E	Pct.
1992— Dom. Expos (DSL)	OF	61	198	58	58	5	1	2	23	60	11	...	...	41-...	.293	...	.359	...	7	.942
1993— Dom. Expos (DSL)	OF	64	211	60	66	12	1	4	26	59	26	...	...	38-...	.313	...	.436	...	7	.954
1994— GC Expos (GCL)	2B-3B-OF	31	104	23	28	8	2	1	6	14	15	0	3	4-1	.269	.356	.413	.769	4	.937
1995— Vermont (NYP)	2B-3B-OF	53	176	24	42	4	2	0	9	19	19	2	3	11-7	.239	.320	.284	.604	9	.949
1996— Delmarva (S. Atl.)	2B-3B-OF	116	369	64	91	13	4	1	33	56	48	6	2	38-15	.247	.353	.312	.665	8	.970
1997— Lakeland (Fla. St.)	2B-OF	122	424	54	113	18	2	2	52	52	33	2	10	10-14	.267	.348	.333	.680	7	.989
1998— Jacksonville (Sou.)	2B	128	511	82	156	28	10	12	71	52	46	4	4	6-9	.305	.372	.470	.842	14	.977
1999— Toledo (Int'l)	2B-OF-SS	112	438	44	107	18	8	2	36	36	60	4	8	10-5	.244	.306	.336	.642	§18	.969
— Detroit (A.L.)	2B	5	4	2	1	0	0	1	2	0	1	0	0	0-0	.250	.250	1.000	1.250	0	1.000
2000— Toledo (Int'l)	OF-SS-2B	33	130	19	30	5	0	0	8	17	17	1	3	2-3	.231	.322	.269	.591	6	.940
— Detroit (A.L.)	2-3-O-S-D	73	173	25	44	3	5	2	24	18	24	1	3	2-0	.254	.328	.364	.692	4	.977
2001— Detroit (A.L.)	3-O-2-D	137	488	62	131	24	6	8	51	32	54	3	7	21-6	.268	.316	.391	.707	12	.970
2002— Detroit (A.L.)	2B-OF-3B	33	107	10	25	4	0	0	6	8	13	1	4	3-2	.234	.291	.271	.562	5	.959
— Montreal (N.L.)	0-3-2-S	90	231	33	59	17	1	7	33	13	44	1	2	5-6	.255	.294	.429	.723	6	.968
2003— Montreal (N.L.)	0-3-2-D	111	272	31	65	15	2	4	22	11	45	2	5	4-3	.239	.273	.353	.626	5	.964
American League totals (4 years)		248	772	99	201	31	11	11	83	58	92	5	14	26-8	.260	.315	.372	.686	21	.970
National League totals (2 years)		201	503	64	124	32	3	11	55	24	89	3	7	9-9	.247	.283	.388	.670	11	.966
Major League totals (5 years)		449	1275	163	325	63	14	22	138	82	181	8	21	35-17	.255	.302	.378	.680	32	.969

MACKOWIAK, ROB — IF/OF

PERSONAL: Born June 20, 1976, in Oak Lawn, Ill. ... 5-10/192. ... Bats left, throws right. ... Full name: Robert William Mackowiak. ... Name pronounced: mah-KOH-vee-ak. ... High school: Oak Lawn (Ill.), then Lake Central (Schererville, Ind.). ... Junior college: South Suburban College (Ill.).
TRANSACTIONS/CAREER NOTES: Selected by Pittsburgh Pirates organization in 53rd round of free-agent draft (June 4, 1996). ... On Pittsburgh disabled list (July 20-August 18, 2001); included rehabilitation assignment to Nashville (August 9-18).
2003 GAMES PLAYED BY POSITION (MLB): OF—30, 3B—19, 2B—15.

Year	Team (League)	Pos.	G	AB	R	H	2B	3B	HR	RBI	BB	SO	HBP	GDP	SB-CS	Avg.	OBP	SLG	OPS	E	Pct.
1996— GC Pirates (GCL)	SS-OF	27	86	8	23	6	1	0	14	13	11	1	3	3-1	.267	.366	.360	.727	10	.796
1997— Erie (N.Y.-Penn)	3-P-C-1-O	61	203	26	58	14	2	1	25	21	47	7	5	1-7	.286	.371	.389	.760	6	.949
1998— Augusta (S. Atl.)	1B-OF	25	70	16	17	4	0	1	8	13	19	1	2	4-2	.243	.369	.343	.712	2	.941
— Lynchburg (Caro.)	2B-3B-OF	86	292	30	80	24	6	3	31	17	65	4	4	6-3	.274	.321	.428	.749	18	.916
1999— Lynchburg (Caro.)	2B-OF	74	263	51	80	7	4	9	30	18	57	6	5	9-3	.304	.362	.441	.803	1	.996
— Altoona (East.)	1B-OF	53	195	21	51	15	3	3	27	8	34	7	6	0-2	.262	.308	.415	.724	8	.971
2000— Altoona (East.)	2-3-S-O	134	526	82	156	33	4	13	87	22	96	9	8	18-5	.297	.332	.449	.780	17	.965
2001— Nashville (PCL)	OF-2-3B	32	118	14	31	5	0	4	14	7	39	0	0	1-1	.263	.302	.407	.708	7	.940
— Pittsburgh (N.L.)	OF-2-3-1	83	214	30	57	15	2	4	21	15	52	3	3	4-3	.266	.319	.411	.730	6	.965
2002— Pittsburgh (N.L.)	OF-3B-2B	136	385	57	94	22	0	16	48	42	120	7	0	9-3	.244	.328	.426	.754	6	.974
2003— Nashville (PCL)	1-3-2-O	59	217	21	50	11	1	2	23	18	51	0	3	7-3	.230	.286	.318	.604	9	.978
— Pittsburgh (N.L.)	OF-3B-2B	77	174	20	47	4	4	6	19	15	53	4	1	6-0	.270	.342	.443	.784	2	.983
Major League totals (3 years)		296	773	107	198	41	6	26	88	72	225	14	4	19-6	.256	.329	.426	.754	14	.973

MADDUX, GREG — P

PERSONAL: Born April 14, 1966, in San Angelo, Texas. ... 6-0/185. ... Throws right, bats right. ... Full name: Gregory Alan Maddux. ... Name pronounced: MADD-ucks. ... High school: Valley (Las Vegas).
TRANSACTIONS/CAREER NOTES: Selected by Chicago Cubs organization in second round of free-agent draft (June 4, 1984). ... Granted free agency (October 26, 1992). ... Signed by Atlanta Braves (December 9, 1992). ... On disabled list (March 23-April 12, 2002). ... Granted free agency (October 29, 2002). ... Re-signed by Braves (February 17, 2003).
CAREER HITTING: 224-for-1261 (.178), 88 R, 31 2B, 2 3B, 4 HR, 64 RBI.

Year	League	W	L	Pct.	ERA	WHIP	G	GS	CG	ShO	Hld.	Sv.-Opp.	IP	H	R	ER	HR	BB-IBB	SO	Avg.
1984— Pikeville (Appal.)		6	2	.750	2.63	1.21	14	12	2	•2	...	0-...	85.2	63	35	25	2	41-2	62	.205
1985— Peoria (Midw.)		13	9	.591	3.19	1.23	27	27	6	0	...	0-...	186.0	176	86	66	9	52-0	125	.245
1986— Pittsfield (East.)		4	3	.571	2.73	1.02	8	8	4	2	...	0-...	62.2	49	22	19	1	15-0	35	.214
— Iowa (Am. Assoc.)		10	1	* .909	3.02	1.22	18	18	5	•2	...	0-...	128.1	127	49	43	3	30-3	65	.259
— Chicago (N.L.)		2	4	.333	5.52	1.77	6	5	1	0	0	0-0	31.0	44	20	19	3	11-2	20	.336
1987— Chicago (N.L.)		6	14	.300	5.61	1.64	30	27	1	1	0	0-0	155.2	181	111	97	17	74-13	101	.294
— Iowa (Am. Assoc.)		3	0	1.000	0.98	1.05	4	4	2	•2	...	0-...	27.2	17	3	3	1	12-0	22	.179
1988— Chicago (N.L.)		18	8	.692	3.18	1.25	34	34	9	3	0	0-0	249.0	230	97	88	13	81-16	140	.244
1989— Chicago (N.L.)		19	12	.613	2.95	1.28	35	35	7	1	0	0-0	238.1	222	90	78	13	82-13	135	.249
1990— Chicago (N.L.)		15	15	.500	3.46	1.32	35	• 35	8	2	0	0-0	237.0	* 242	* 116	91	11	71-6	144	.265
1991— Chicago (N.L.)		15	11	.577	3.35	1.13	37	* 37	7	2	0	0-0	* 263.0	232	113	98	18	66-9	198	.237
1992— Chicago (N.L.)		• 20	11	.645	2.18	1.01	35	• 35	9	4	0	0-0	* 268.0	201	68	65	7	70-7	199	.210
1993— Atlanta (N.L.)		20	10	.667	*2.36	1.05	36	• 36	• 8	1	0	0-0	* 267.0	228	85	70	14	52-7	197	.232
1994— Atlanta (N.L.)		• 16	6	.727	*1.56	0.90	25	25	* 10	•3	0	0-0	* 202.0	150	44	35	4	31-3	156	*.207
1995— Atlanta (N.L.)		* 19	2	*.905	*1.63	0.81	28	28	* 10	•3	0	0-0	• 209.2	147	39	38	8	23-3	181	.197
1996— Atlanta (N.L.)		15	11	.577	2.72	1.03	35	35	5	1	0	0-0	245.0	225	85	74	11	28-11	172	.241
1997— Atlanta (N.L.)		19	4	*.826	2.20	0.95	33	33	5	2	0	0-0	232.2	200	58	57	9	20-6	177	.236
1998— Atlanta (N.L.)		18	9	.667	*2.22	0.98	34	34	9	* 5	0	0-0	251.0	201	75	62	13	45-10	204	.220
1999— Atlanta (N.L.)		19	9	.679	3.57	1.34	33	33	4	0	0	0-0	219.1	258	103	87	16	37-8	136	.294
2000— Atlanta (N.L.)		19	9	.679	3.00	1.07	35	• 35	6	•3	0	0-0	249.1	225	91	83	19	42-12	190	.238
2001— Atlanta (N.L.)		17	11	.607	3.05	1.06	34	34	3	•3	0	0-0	233.0	220	86	79	20	27-10	173	.253
2002— Atlanta (N.L.)		16	6	.727	2.62	1.20	34	34	0	0	0	0-0	199.1	194	67	58	14	45-7	118	.257
2003— Atlanta (N.L.)		16	11	.593	3.96	1.18	36	*36	1	0	0	0-0	218.1	225	112	96	24	33-7	124	.268
Major League totals (18 years)		289	163	.639	2.89	1.12	575	571	103	34	0	0-0	3968.2	3625	1460	1275	234	838-154	2765	.244

MADSON, RYAN — P

PERSONAL: Born August 28, 1980, in Long Beach, Calif. ... 6-6/180. ... Throws right, bats left. ... Full name: Ryan Michael Madson. ... High school: Valley View High (Moreno County, Calif.).
TRANSACTIONS/CAREER NOTES: Selected by Philadelphia Phillies in ninth round of free-agent draft (June 1998).
CAREER HITTING: 0-for-0 (.000), 0 R, 0 2B, 0 3B, 0 HR, 0 RBI.

Year League	W	L	Pct.	ERA	WHIP	G	GS	CG	ShO	Hld.	Sv.-Opp.	IP	H	R	ER	HR	BB-IBB	SO	Avg.
1998— Martinsville (App.)	3	3	.500	4.83	1.43	12	10	0	0	...	0-...	54.0	57	38	29	5	20-0	52	.265
1999— Batavia (N.Y.-Penn)	5	5	.500	4.72	1.40	15	15	0	0	...	0-...	87.2	80	51	46	5	43-0	75	.247
2000— Piedmont (S. Atl.)	14	5	.737	2.59	1.16	21	21	2	1	...	0-...	135.2	113	50	39	5	45-0	123	.225
2001— Clearwater (Fla. St.)	9	9	.500	3.90	1.58	22	21	1	0	...	0-...	117.2	137	68	51	4	49-1	101	.291
2002— Reading (East.)	16	4	.800	3.20	1.18	26	26	2	0	...	0-...	171.1	150	68	61	11	53-0	132	.242
2003— Clearwater (Fla. St.)	0	0	...	5.63	1.63	2	2	0	0	...	0-...	8.0	11	5	5	0	2-0	9	.324
— Scran./W.B. (I.L.)	12	8	.600	3.50	1.27	26	26	0	0	...	0-...	157.0	157	70	61	9	42-2	138	.262
— Philadelphia (N.L.)	0	0	...	0.00	0.00	1	0	0	0	0	0-0	2.0	0	0	0	0	0-0	0	.000
Major League totals (1 year)	0	0	...	0.00	0.00	1	0	0	0	0	0-0	2.0	0	0	0	0	0-0	0	.000

MAGRUDER, CHRIS   OF

PERSONAL: Born April 26, 1977, in Tacoma, Wash. ... 5-11/200. ... Bats both, throws right. ... Full name: Christopher James Magruder. ... High school: West Valley (Yakima, Wash.). ... College: Washington.

TRANSACTIONS/CAREER NOTES: Selected by San Francisco Giants in second round of free agent draft (June 2, 1998); choice received from Tampa Bay Devil Rays as part of compensation for signing of Type A free agent P Wilson Alvarez. ... Traded with P Todd Ozias and P Erasmo Ramirez to Texas Rangers for 1B Andres Galarraga (July 24, 2001). ... Traded by Rangers to Cleveland Indians for OF Rashad Eldridge (April 4, 2002). ... Granted free agency (December 21, 2002). ... Re-signed by Indians (December 22, 2002).

2003 GAMES PLAYED BY POSITION (MLB): OF—8.

Year Team (League)	Pos.	G	AB	R	H	2B	3B	HR	RBI	BB	SO	HBP	GDP	SB-CS	Avg.	OBP	SLG	OPS	E	Pct.
1998— Salem-Keizer (NW)	OF	47	177	43	59	8	5	3	18	37	21	8	2	14-7	.333	.464	.486	.950	2	.976
— Bakersfield (Calif.)	OF	22	92	21	28	7	0	1	4	13	16	0	2	3-0	.304	.390	.413	.804	0	1.000
1999— Shreveport (Texas)	OF	133	476	78	122	21	4	6	60	69	85	8	15	17-12	.256	.358	.355	.713	3	.988
2000— Shreveport (Texas)	OF	134	496	85	140	33	3	4	39	67	75	8	11	18-10	.282	.375	.385	.760	5	.983
2001— Fresno (PCL)	OF	54	214	37	60	7	1	10	30	18	45	7	2	3-1	.280	.354	.463	.817	1	.992
— Shreveport (Texas)	OF	40	149	22	38	6	3	2	11	15	27	3	2	5-3	.255	.335	.376	.711	2	.979
— Oklahoma (PCL)	OF	33	127	28	46	14	4	5	21	21	19	4	3	1-2	.362	.464	.654	1.118	1	.986
— Texas (A.L.)	OF	17	29	3	5	0	0	0	1	1	5	1	1	0-0	.172	.226	.172	.398	0	1.000
2002— Cleveland (A.L.)	OF	87	258	34	56	15	1	6	29	15	55	1	7	2-0	.217	.261	.353	.614	2	.987
— Buffalo (Int'l)	OF	54	191	28	51	10	2	5	16	26	34	3	2	3-2	.267	.364	.419	.782	1	.991
2003— Mahoning Valley (NY-P)	OF-DH	3	11	5	2	2	0	0	0	2	1	1	0	2-0	.182	.357	.364	.721	0	1.000
— Akron (East.)	DH-OF	3	13	0	6	0	0	0	3	1	2	0	0	1-0	.462	.500	.462	.962	0	1.000
— Buffalo (Int'l)	OF	41	137	20	45	7	2	3	15	15	27	1	3	5-1	.328	.391	.474	.865	0	1.000
— Cleveland (A.L.)	OF	9	26	3	9	2	1	1	3	3	6	1	0	0-1	.346	.433	.615	1.049	0	1.000
Major League totals (3 years)		113	313	40	70	17	2	7	33	19	66	3	8	2-1	.224	.273	.358	.631	2	.989

MAHAY, RON   P

PERSONAL: Born June 28, 1971, in Crestwood, Ill. ... 6-2/190. ... Throws left, bats left. ... Full name: Ronald Matthew Mahay. ... High school: Alan B. Shepard (Palos Heights, Ill.). ... Junior college: South Suburban College (Ill.).

TRANSACTIONS/CAREER NOTES: Selected by Boston Red Sox organization in 18th round of free-agent draft (June 3, 1991). ... On disabled list (May 5, 1992-remainder of season). ... On Lynchburg disabled list (August 6-September 9, 1993). ... On disabled list (August 23-September 1, 1994). ... On Pawtucket temporarily inactive list (April 19-25, 1995). ... On Sarasota disabled list (April 4-25, 1996). ... Claimed on waivers by Oakland Athletics (March 30, 1999). ... Traded by Athletics to Florida Marlins for cash (May 11, 2000). ... Granted free agency (October 2, 2000). ... Signed by San Diego Padres organization (November 20, 2000). ... On Portland disabled list (April 12-24, 2001). ... Released by Padres (May 15, 2001). ... Signed by Chicago Cubs organization (May 19, 2001). ... On Chicago disabled list (May 24-June 13, 2002); included rehabilitation assignment to Iowa (June 7-13). ... Released by Cubs (September 30, 2002). ... Signed by Texas Rangers (November 13, 2002). ... Recalled from Oklahoma (June 26, 2003).

CAREER HITTING: 6-for-26 (.231), 3 R, 3 2B, 0 3B, 1 HR, 3 RBI.

Year League	W	L	Pct.	ERA	WHIP	G	GS	CG	ShO	Hld.	Sv.-Opp.	IP	H	R	ER	HR	BB-IBB	SO	Avg.
1996— Sarasota (Fla. St.)	2	2	.500	3.82	1.36	31	4	0	0	...	2-...	70.2	61	33	30	5	35-0	68	.236
— Trenton (East.)	0	1	.000	29.45	4.91	1	1	0	0	...	0-...	3.2	12	13	12	1	6-0	0	.522
1997— Trenton (East.)	3	3	.500	3.10	1.03	17	4	0	0	...	5-...	40.2	29	16	14	0	13-0	47	.193
— Pawtucket (Int'l)	1	0	1.000	0.00	0.86	2	0	0	0	...	0-...	4.2	3	0	0	0	1-0	6	.176
— Boston (A.L.)	3	0	1.000	2.52	1.20	28	0	0	0	6	0-2	25.0	19	7	7	3	11-0	22	.204
1998— Pawtucket (Int'l)	3	1	.750	4.17	1.37	23	1	0	0	...	3-...	41.0	37	20	19	8	19-2	41	.234
— Boston (A.L.)	1	1	.500	3.46	1.58	29	0	0	0	7	1-2	26.0	26	16	10	2	15-1	14	.263
1999— Vancouver (PCL)	7	2	.778	4.29	1.50	32	15	0	0	...	0-...	107.0	116	57	51	12	45-0	73	.280
— Oakland (A.L.)	2	0	1.000	1.86	0.57	6	1	0	0	0	1-1	19.1	8	4	4	2	3-0	15	.123
2000— Oakland (A.L.)	0	1	.000	9.00	2.19	5	2	0	0	0	0-0	16.0	26	18	16	4	9-0	5	.366
— Florida (N.L.)	1	0	1.000	6.04	1.86	18	0	0	0	2	0-0	25.1	31	17	17	6	16-1	27	.310
— Calgary (PCL)	0	1	.000	4.85	1.08	8	0	0	0	...	0-...	13.0	7	7	7	1	7-1	15	.175
2001— Portland (PCL)	1	2	.333	3.78	1.08	14	0	0	0	...	0-...	16.2	13	9	7	2	5-0	18	.210
— Iowa (PCL)	3	1	.750	2.31	0.84	36	0	0	0	...	14-...	46.2	29	12	12	5	10-1	52	.182
— Chicago (N.L.)	0	0	...	2.61	1.40	17	0	0	0	2	0-0	20.2	14	6	6	4	15-1	24	.197
2002— Iowa (PCL)	0	1	.000	1.93	1.01	39	1	0	0	...	2-...	46.2	32	11	10	3	15-1	50	.189
— Chicago (N.L.)	2	0	1.000	8.59	1.43	11	0	0	0	0	0-0	14.2	13	14	14	6	8-0	14	.228
2003— Oklahoma (PCL)	4	2	.667	4.22	1.08	26	0	0	0	...	3-...	42.2	36	21	20	5	10-1	51	.224
— Texas (A.L.)	3	3	.500	3.18	1.17	35	0	0	0	9	0-3	45.1	33	19	16	3	20-7	38	.195
American League totals (6 years)	9	5	.643	3.62	1.29	103	3	0	0	22	2-8	131.2	112	64	53	14	58-8	94	.235
National League totals (3 years)	3	0	1.000	5.49	1.60	46	0	0	0	4	0-0	60.2	58	37	37	16	39-2	65	.254
Major League totals (8 years)	12	5	.706	4.21	1.39	149	3	0	0	26	2-8	192.1	170	101	90	30	97-10	159	.234

MAHOMES, PAT   P

PERSONAL: Born August 9, 1970, in Bryan, Texas. ... 6-4/220. ... Throws right, bats right. ... Full name: Patrick Lavon Mahomes. ... Name pronounced: muh-HOMES. ... High school: Lindale (Texas).

TRANSACTIONS/CAREER NOTES: Selected by Minnesota Twins organization in eighth round of free-agent draft (June 1, 1988). ... On disabled list (July 6-23, 1994). ... Traded by Twins to Boston Red Sox for a player to be named later (August 26, 1996); Twins acquired P Brian Looney to complete deal (December 17, 1996). ... Contract sold by Red Sox to Yokohama BayStars of Japan Central League (1997). ... Signed by New York Mets (December 21, 1998). ... Granted free agency (December 21, 2000). ... Signed

M

by Texas Rangers organization (January 11, 2001). ... Granted free agency (November 5, 2001). ... Signed by Chicago Cubs organization (January 30, 2002). ... Granted free agency (October 30, 2002). ... Signed by Pittsburgh Pirates organization (January 27, 2003). ... Contract purchased by Pittsburgh from Nashville (May 16, 2003). ... Designated for assignment (August 27, 2003). ... Sent outright to Nashville (August 29, 2003). ... Elected free agency (September 29, 2003).

CAREER HITTING: 11-for-43 (.256), 6 R, 4 2B, 0 3B, 0 HR, 4 RBI.

Year League	W	L	Pct.	ERA	WHIP	G	GS	CG	ShO	Hld.	Sv.-Opp.	IP	H	R	ER	HR	BB-IBB	SO	Avg.
1988— Elizabethton (Appal.)	6	3	.667	3.69	1.50	13	13	3	0	...	0-...	78.0	66	45	32	4	51-0	93	.228
1989— Kenosha (Midw.)	13	7	.650	3.28	1.41	25	25	3	1	...	0-...	156.1	120	66	57	4	• 100-3	167	.215
1990— Visalia (Calif.)	11	11	.500	3.30	1.37	28	* 28	5	1	...	0-...	• 185.1	136	77	68	14	* 118-1	178	.208
1991— Orlando (Sou.)	8	5	.615	1.78	1.16	18	17	2	0	...	0-...	116.0	77	30	23	5	57-0	136	.193
— Portland (PCL)	3	5	.375	3.44	1.56	9	9	2	0	...	0-...	55.0	50	26	21	2	36-1	41	.246
1992— Minnesota (A.L.)	3	4	.429	5.04	1.58	14	13	0	0	0	0-0	69.2	73	41	39	5	37-0	44	.279
— Portland (PCL)	9	5	.643	3.41	1.26	17	16	3	* 3	...	1-...	111.0	97	43	42	7	43-1	87	.236
1993— Minnesota (A.L.)	1	5	.167	7.71	1.69	12	5	0	0	0	0-0	37.1	47	34	32	8	16-0	23	.309
— Portland (PCL)	11	4	.733	3.03	1.24	17	16	3	1	...	0-...	115.2	89	47	39	11	54-1	94	.219
1994— Minnesota (A.L.)	9	5	.643	4.73	1.53	21	21	0	0	0	0-0	120.0	121	68	63	22	62-1	53	.269
1995— Minnesota (A.L.)	4	10	.286	6.37	1.55	47	7	0	0	9	3-7	94.2	100	74	67	22	47-1	67	.271
1996— Minnesota (A.L.)	1	4	.200	7.20	2.00	20	5	0	0	3	0-0	45.0	63	38	36	10	27-0	30	.330
— Salt Lake (PCL)	3	1	.750	3.74	1.31	22	2	0	0	...	7-...	33.2	32	14	14	0	12-0	41	.250
— Boston (A.L.)	2	0	1.000	5.84	1.22	11	0	0	0	1	2-2	12.1	9	8	8	3	6-0	6	.209
1997— Boston (A.L.)	1	0	1.000	8.10	2.50	10	0	0	0	1	0-0	10.0	15	10	9	2	10-1	5	.366
— Pawtucket (Int'l)	5	1	.833	2.84	1.23	18	1	0	0	...	7-...	31.2	22	11	10	2	17-0	40	.198
— Yoko. Bay. (Jp. Cn.)	3	4	.429	4.82	1.51	11	9	0	0	...	0-...	52.1	54	30	28	...	25-...	42	...
1998— Yokohama (Jp. East.)	2	5	.286	4.68	1.48	19	5	0	0	...	5-...	50.0	38	30	26	...	36-...	50	...
— Yoko. Bay. (Jp. Cn.)	0	4	.000	5.98	2.06	10	8	0	0	...	0-...	43.2	61	30	29	...	29-...	24	...
1999— Norfolk (Int'l)	4	1	.800	3.49	1.29	6	6	0	0	...	0-...	38.2	38	17	15	6	12-1	24	.252
— New York (N.L.)	8	0	1.000	3.68	1.27	39	0	0	0	1	0-1	63.2	44	26	26	7	37-5	51	.198
2000— New York (N.L.)	5	3	.625	5.46	1.72	53	5	0	0	3	0-1	94.0	96	63	57	15	66-4	76	.263
2001— Texas (A.L.)	7	6	.538	5.70	1.58	56	4	0	0	6	0-1	107.1	115	71	68	17	55-9	61	.280
2002— Iowa (PCL)	4	5	.444	3.48	1.06	44	5	0	0	...	14-...	72.1	57	30	28	11	20-1	70	.214
— Chicago (N.L.)	1	1	.500	3.86	1.62	16	2	0	0	2	0-1	32.2	36	15	14	3	17-3	23	.286
2003— Pittsburgh (N.L.)	0	1	.000	4.84	1.39	9	1	0	0	0	0-0	22.1	19	13	12	2	12-1	13	.241
— Nashville (PCL)	8	4	.667	2.67	1.19	38	2	0	0	...	2-...	64.0	55	20	19	4	21-3	28	.235
American League totals (7 years)	**28**	**34**	**.452**	**5.84**	**1.62**	**191**	**55**	**0**	**0**	**20**	**5-10**	**496.1**	**543**	**344**	**322**	**89**	**260-12**	**289**	**.283**
National League totals (4 years)	**14**	**5**	**.737**	**4.61**	**1.54**	**117**	**8**	**0**	**0**	**6**	**0-3**	**212.2**	**195**	**117**	**109**	**27**	**132-13**	**163**	**.246**
Major League totals (11 years)	**42**	**39**	**.519**	**5.47**	**1.59**	**308**	**63**	**0**	**0**	**26**	**5-13**	**709.0**	**738**	**461**	**431**	**116**	**392-25**	**452**	**.272**

MALASKA, MARK — P

PERSONAL: Born January 17, 1978, in Youngstown, Ohio. ... 6-3/191. ... Throws left, bats left. ... Full name: Dennis Mark Malaska. ... High school: Cardinal Mooney (Youngstown, Ohio). ... College: Akron.

TRANSACTIONS/CAREER NOTES: Selected by Tampa Bay Devil Rays organization in eighth round of free-agent draft (June 5, 2000).

CAREER HITTING: 0-for-0 (.000), 0 R, 0 2B, 0 3B, 0 HR, 0 RBI.

Year League	W	L	Pct.	ERA	WHIP	G	GS	CG	ShO	Hld.	Sv.-Opp.	IP	H	R	ER	HR	BB-IBB	SO	Avg.
2000— Char., S.C. (SAL)	0	0	...	9.00	1.50	2	0	0	0	...	0-...	2.0	3	2	2	1	0-0	3	.375
— Hudson Valley (NYP)	0	2	.000	4.91	1.44	10	5	0	0	...	0-...	40.1	44	27	22	1	14-2	36	.273
2001— Char., S.C. (SAL)	7	12	.368	2.92	1.20	25	25	1	0	...	0-...	157.0	153	71	51	11	35-0	152	.249
— Bakersfield (Calif.)	2	1	.667	4.08	1.08	3	3	0	0	...	0-...	17.2	14	8	8	1	5-0	13	.219
2002— Bakersfield (Calif.)	7	4	.636	2.96	1.20	15	15	2	2	...	0-...	91.1	98	48	30	5	12-0	94	.263
— Orlando (Sou.)	4	5	.444	3.69	1.56	12	11	1	0	...	1-...	70.2	82	37	29	4	28-2	49	.292
2003— Orlando (Sou.)	1	1	.500	2.16	1.00	19	0	0	0	...	1-...	25.0	21	6	6	2	4-1	22	.236
— Durham (Int'l)	1	1	.500	4.30	1.39	15	0	0	0	...	0-...	23.0	24	12	11	1	8-0	22	.270
— Tampa Bay (A.L.)	2	1	.667	2.81	1.56	22	0	0	0	7	0-3	16.0	13	7	5	0	12-3	17	.232
Major League totals (1 year)	**2**	**1**	**.667**	**2.81**	**1.56**	**22**	**0**	**0**	**0**	**7**	**0-3**	**16.0**	**13**	**7**	**5**	**0**	**12-3**	**17**	**.232**

MANN, JIM — P

PERSONAL: Born November 17, 1974, in Brockton, Mass. ... 6-3/225. ... Throws right, bats right. ... Full name: James Joseph Mann. ... High school: Holbrook (Mass.). ... Junior college: Massasoit (Mass.) Community College.

TRANSACTIONS/CAREER NOTES: Selected by Toronto Blue Jays organization in 54th round of free-agent draft (June 3, 1993). ... Selected by New York Mets from Blue Jays organization in Rule 5 major league draft (December 13, 1999); Blue Jays acquired IF Jersen Perez as compensation for Mets keeping Mann (March 22, 2000). ... Granted free agency (October 18, 2000). ... Signed by Houston Astros organization (January 3, 2001). ... Claimed on waivers by Pittsburgh Pirates (October 10, 2002). ... Recalled from Nashville (July 28, 2003). ... Elected free agency (September 29, 2003).

CAREER HITTING: 0-for-1 (.000), 0 R, 0 2B, 0 3B, 0 HR, 0 RBI.

Year League	W	L	Pct.	ERA	WHIP	G	GS	CG	ShO	Hld.	Sv.-Opp.	IP	H	R	ER	HR	BB-IBB	SO	Avg.
1994— GC Blue Jays (GCL)	3	2	.600	3.74	1.51	11	9	0	0	...	0-...	53.0	54	28	22	1	26-1	41	.266
1995— Medicine Hat (Pio.)	5	4	.556	4.29	1.48	14	14	1	• 1	...	0-...	77.2	78	47	37	5	37-0	66	.262
1996— St. Catharines (N.Y.-P.)	2	1	.667	3.62	1.17	26	0	0	0	...	17-...	27.1	22	12	11	3	10-1	37	.220
1997— Hagerstown (S. Atl.)	0	1	.000	5.06	1.73	18	0	0	0	...	4-...	26.2	35	18	15	4	11-0	30	.321
— Dunedin (Fla. St.)	1	0	1.000	6.00	1.83	12	0	0	0	...	0-...	18.0	27	12	12	2	6-1	13	.338
1998— Dunedin (Fla. St.)	0	2	.000	3.04	1.09	51	0	0	0	...	25-...	50.1	31	19	17	4	24-1	59	.172
1999— Knoxville (Sou.)	1	2	.333	0.93	0.72	6	0	0	0	...	0-...	9.2	6	2	1	1	1-0	12	.188
— Syracuse (Int'l)	6	5	.545	4.64	1.39	47	0	0	0	...	5-...	66.0	53	35	34	11	39-1	72	.217
2000— Norfolk (Int'l)	3	4	.429	2.98	1.15	49	0	0	0	...	3-...	81.2	61	27	27	8	33-3	74	.213
— New York (N.L.)	0	0	...	10.13	2.63	2	0	0	0	0	0-0	2.2	6	3	3	1	1-0	0	.429
2001— New Orleans (PCL)	6	3	.667	2.51	1.01	53	0	0	0	...	27-...	68.0	52	21	19	7	17-2	81	.211
— Houston (N.L.)	0	0	...	3.38	1.31	4	0	0	0	0	0-0	5.1	3	2	2	0	4-0	5	.176
2002— New Orleans (PCL)	0	3	.000	4.15	1.18	33	0	0	0	...	22-...	34.2	33	20	16	6	8-1	29	.254
— Houston (N.L.)	0	1	.000	4.09	1.18	17	0	0	0	0	0-0	22.0	19	10	10	3	7-1	19	.235
— Round Rock (Texas)	0	0	...	4.50	0.50	1	0	0	0	...	0-...	2.0	1	1	1	1	0-0	2	.143
2003— Pittsburgh (N.L.)	0	0	...	10.80	3.60	2	0	0	0	0	0-0	1.2	5	4	2	1	1-0	1	.455
— Nashville (PCL)	3	2	.600	3.06	0.94	51	0	0	0	...	5-...	61.2	38	23	21	8	20-5	48	.175
Major League totals (4 years)	**0**	**1**	**.000**	**4.83**	**1.45**	**25**	**0**	**0**	**0**	**0**	**0-0**	**31.2**	**33**	**19**	**17**	**5**	**13-1**	**25**	**.268**

M

MANNING, DAVID   P

PERSONAL: Born August 14, 1972, in Buffalo, N.Y. ... 6-3/210. ... Throws right, bats right. ... Full name: David Anthony Manning. ... Junior college: Palm Beach College (Fla.).
TRANSACTIONS/CAREER NOTES: On Iowa disabled list (April 6-13, June 17-30 and July 24-September 5, 2000). ... Granted free agency (October 18, 2000). ... Selected by Milwaukee Brewers in Rule 5 draft (December 16, 2002). ... Released by Milwaukee (August 20, 2003).
CAREER HITTING: 0-for-1 (.000), 0 R, 0 2B, 0 3B, 0 HR, 0 RBI.

Year — League	W	L	Pct.	ERA	WHIP	G	GS	CG	ShO	Hld.	Sv.-Opp.	IP	H	R	ER	HR	BB-IBB	SO	Avg.
1992— Butte (Pio.)	0	4	.000	11.01	2.57	8	7	0	0	...	0-...	25.1	50	41	31	4	15-0	13	.403
— GC Rangers (GCL)	1	1	.500	6.06	1.59	5	3	0	0	...	0-...	16.1	22	13	11	0	4-0	9	.319
1993— Char., S.C. (SAL)	6	7	.462	3.03	1.30	37	10	0	0	...	2-...	116.0	112	54	39	3	39-4	83	.255
1994— Charlotte (Int'l)	4	11	.267	5.57	1.63	20	20	0	0	...	0-...	97.0	119	69	60	5	39-0	46	.308
1995— Charlotte (Int'l)	9	5	.643	3.50	1.34	26	20	0	0	...	0-...	128.2	127	56	50	7	46-0	66	.260
1996— Oklahoma City (A.A.)	0	0	...	5.40	1.60	1	1	0	0	...	0-...	5.0	6	3	3	0	2-0	1	.333
— Tulsa (Texas)	6	5	.545	3.26	1.47	39	5	0	0	...	3-...	91.0	89	36	33	5	45-6	48	.263
1997— Tulsa (Texas)	4	7	.364	4.88	1.37	13	12	1	0	...	0-...	75.2	77	46	41	8	27-0	55	.266
— Oklahoma City (A.A.)	1	3	.250	4.40	1.47	5	5	1	0	...	0-...	28.2	33	17	14	6	9-0	15	.277
— Charlotte (Int'l)	0	0	...	1.50	1.33	1	1	0	0	...	0-...	6.0	4	1	1	1	4-0	4	.182
1998— Tulsa (Texas)	2	0	1.000	4.85	1.85	6	0	0	0	...	0-...	13.0	13	7	7	2	11-0	15	.265
— GC Rangers (GCL)	0	0	...	5.40	1.40	3	3	0	0	...	0-...	5.0	6	3	3	0	1-0	2	.316
— Charlotte (Int'l)	0	0	...	0.00	1.20	7	0	0	0	...	0-...	8.1	4	4	0	1	6-0	11	.133
— Oklahoma (PCL)	0	0	...	1.00	1.22	6	0	0	0	...	1-...	9.0	11	1	1	1	0-0	9	.306
1999— Iowa (PCL)	0	0	...	4.66	1.76	7	0	0	0	...	0-...	9.2	9	6	5	2	8-0	7	.273
— West Tenn (Sou.)	8	5	.615	3.94	1.33	23	18	6	2	...	0-...	123.1	113	59	54	7	51-1	78	.248
2000— Iowa (PCL)	2	5	.286	6.35	1.61	19	11	0	0	...	0-...	66.2	82	52	47	11	25-1	40	.300
2001—											Did not play.								
2002— New Britain (East.)	3	3	.500	4.62	1.54	11	10	0	0	...	0-...	62.1	69	37	32	3	27-0	38	.296
2003— Milwaukee (N.L.)	0	2	.000	16.20	2.85	2	2	0	0	0	0-0	6.2	11	13	12	1	8-0	2	.393
— Indianapolis (Int'l)	6	8	.429	4.91	1.65	23	17	0	0	...	0-...	99.0	103	57	54	7	60-0	76	.268
Major League totals (1 year)	**0**	**2**	**.000**	**16.20**	**2.85**	**2**	**2**	**0**	**0**	**0**	**0-0**	**6.2**	**11**	**13**	**12**	**1**	**8-0**	**2**	**.393**

MANON, JULIO   P

PERSONAL: Born June 10, 1973, in Guerra Distrito, Dominican Republic. ... 6-0/200. ... Throws right, bats right. ... Full name: Julio Alberto Manon. ... Name pronounced: mah-YON.
TRANSACTIONS/CAREER NOTES: Signed as non-drafted free agent by St. Louis Cardinals organization (April 16, 1992). ... Loaned by Cardinals to River City, Appalachian League (June 13-September 7, 1995). ... Released by Cardinals (March 26, 1996). ... Signed by Tampa Bay Devil Rays organization (March 18, 1997). ... Loaned by Devil Rays to Orlando, Seattle Mariners organization (June 4-July 31, 1998). ... Released by Devil Rays (August 4, 1999). ... Signed by St. Paul, Northern League (August 1999). ... Signed by Milwaukee Brewers organization (December 17, 1999). ... Released by Brewers (March 28, 2000). ... Signed by Montreal Expos organization (June 20, 2000).
CAREER HITTING: 0-for-1 (.000), 0 R, 0 2B, 0 3B, 0 HR, 0 RBI.

Year — League	W	L	Pct.	ERA	WHIP	G	GS	CG	ShO	Hld.	Sv.-Opp.	IP	H	R	ER	HR	BB-IBB	SO	Avg.
1993— Ariz. Cardinals (Ariz.)	2	3	.400	5.13	1.68	15	4	0	0	...	0-...	33.1	44	21	19	2	12-0	22	.324
1994— Johnson City (App.)	1	2	.333	8.31	1.85	5	0	0	0	...	0-...	8.2	11	8	8	2	5-0	7	.289
— Ariz. Cardinals (Ariz.)	0	1	.000	5.06	1.31	14	0	0	0	...	1-...	16.0	20	9	9	0	1-0	18	.294
1995— River City (Appal.)	3	4	.429	3.65	1.42	16	8	2	0	...	1-...	74.0	75	34	30	4	30-2	77	.264
1996—											Did not play.								
1997— Char., S.C. (SAL)	3	5	.375	4.47	1.32	27	9	0	0	...	0-...	88.2	95	53	44	8	22-1	98	.265
1998— Orlando (Sou.)	0	2	.000	6.10	1.50	13	0	0	0	...	0-...	20.2	22	19	14	3	9-0	22	.256
— St. Pete. (FSL)	5	5	.500	3.72	1.08	38	0	0	0	...	1-...	55.2	41	25	23	7	19-1	73	.207
1999— Orlando (Sou.)	3	3	.500	5.10	1.54	30	5	0	0	...	0-...	67.0	80	43	38	9	23-0	53	.289
2000— GC Expos (GCL)	2	0	1.000	0.87	0.58	4	0	0	0	...	0-...	10.1	4	1	1	0	2-0	10	.114
— Harrisburg (Eastern)	2	1	.667	5.17	1.28	14	4	0	0	...	1-...	31.1	32	19	18	7	8-0	25	.260
2001— Harrisburg (Eastern)	4	3	.571	3.12	1.27	10	7	0	0	...	1-...	52.0	50	20	18	6	16-0	44	.265
— Ottawa (Int'l)	1	4	.200	3.11	1.25	15	14	0	0	...	0-...	84.0	71	31	29	11	34-0	67	.234
2002— Ottawa (Int'l)	8	6	.571	3.50	1.22	28	13	2	1	...	2-...	105.1	83	42	41	8	45-0	81	.217
— Harrisburg (Eastern)	5	1	.833	3.00	1.05	6	6	0	0	...	0-...	39.0	37	13	13	3	4-0	51	.245
2003— Montreal (N.L.)	1	2	.333	4.13	1.52	23	0	0	0	6	1-1	28.1	26	13	13	3	17-1	15	.252
— Edmonton (PCL)	3	1	.750	2.14	1.24	35	0	0	0	...	14-...	42.0	33	12	10	4	19-1	48	.205
Major League totals (1 year)	**1**	**2**	**.333**	**4.13**	**1.52**	**23**	**0**	**0**	**0**	**6**	**1-1**	**28.1**	**26**	**13**	**13**	**3**	**17-1**	**15**	**.252**

MANTEI, MATT   P

PERSONAL: Born July 7, 1973, in Tampa, Fla. ... 6-1/198. ... Throws right, bats right. ... Full name: Matthews Bruce Mantei. ... Name pronounced: MAN-tie. ... High school: River Valley (Three Oaks, Mich.).
TRANSACTIONS/CAREER NOTES: Selected by Seattle Mariners organization in 25th round of free-agent draft (June 3, 1991). ... Selected by Florida Marlins from Mariners organization in Rule 5 major league draft (December 5, 1994). ... On Florida disabled list (April 20-June 18 and July 29-September 1, 1995); included rehabilitation assignments to Portland and Charlotte (May 13-June 18). ... On Florida disabled list (June 19, 1996-remainder of season). ... On Florida disabled list (March 31, 1997-entire season). ... Granted free agency (December 21, 1997). ... Re-signed by Marlins organization (December 21, 1997). ... On Florida disabled list (August 19-September 4, 1998). ... Traded by Marlins to Arizona Diamondbacks for P Vladimir Nunez, P Brad Penny and a player to be named later (July 9, 1999); Marlins acquired OF Abraham Nunez to complete deal (December 13, 1999). ... On Arizona disabled list (April 2-21 and May 5-21, 2000); included rehabilitation assignment to Tucson (April 14-21). ... On disabled list (April 25, 2001-remainder of season). ... On Arizona disabled list (March 22-June 27, 2002); included rehabilitation assignments to El Paso (May 10-20) and Tucson (May 21-25 and June 14-27). ... Placed on the 15-day disabled list by Arizona (May 28, 2003). ... Sent on rehab assignment to Tucson (June 24, 2003). ... Recalled from Tucson rehab assignment (June 30, 2003).
CAREER HITTING: 1-for-5 (.200), 0 R, 0 2B, 0 3B, 0 HR, 0 RBI.

Year — League	W	L	Pct.	ERA	WHIP	G	GS	CG	ShO	Hld.	Sv.-Opp.	IP	H	R	ER	HR	BB-IBB	SO	Avg.
1991— Ariz. Mariners (Ariz.)	1	4	.200	6.69	2.03	17	5	0	0	...	0-...	40.1	54	40	30	0	28-2	29	.321
1992— Ariz. Mariners (Ariz.)	1	1	.500	5.63	1.44	3	3	0	0	...	0-...	16.0	18	10	10	1	5-0	19	.286
1993— Bellingham (N'west)	1	1	.500	5.96	1.60	26	0	0	0	...	* 12-...	25.2	26	19	17	2	15-0	34	.260
1994— Appleton (Midw.)	5	1	.833	2.06	1.31	48	0	0	0	...	26-...	48.0	42	14	11	2	21-3	70	.240
1995— Portland (East.)	1	0	1.000	2.38	1.32	8	0	0	0	...	1-...	11.1	10	3	3	0	5-0	15	.244
— Charlotte (Int'l)	0	0	...	2.57	0.86	6	0	0	0	...	0-...	7.0	1	3	2	0	5-0	10	.050
— Florida (N.L.)	0	1	.000	4.73	1.88	12	0	0	0	0	0-0	13.1	12	8	7	1	13-0	15	.245
1996— Florida (N.L.)	1	0	1.000	6.38	1.85	14	0	0	0	0	0-1	18.1	13	13	13	2	21-1	25	.197
— Charlotte (Int'l)	0	2	.000	4.70	1.70	7	0	0	0	...	2-...	7.2	6	4	4	1	7-0	8	.214

Year League	W	L	Pct.	ERA	WHIP	G	GS	CG	ShO	Hld.	Sv.-Opp.	IP	H	R	ER	HR	BB-IBB	SO	Avg.
1997— Brevard County (FSL)	0	0	...	6.00	1.67	4	0	0	0	...	0-...	6.0	4	4	4	1	6-0	11	.190
— Portland (East.)	1	0	1.000	6.75	2.25	5	0	0	0	...	0-...	4.0	1	3	3	0	8-0	7	.083
1998— Charlotte (Int'l)	1	2	.333	5.51	1.78	16	0	0	0	...	3-...	16.1	11	10	10	2	18-1	25	.196
— Florida (N.L.)	3	4	.429	2.96	1.12	42	0	0	0	2	9-12	54.2	38	19	18	1	23-3	63	.203
1999— Florida (N.L.)	1	2	.333	2.72	1.35	35	0	0	0	0	10-12	36.1	24	11	11	4	25-1	50	.186
— Arizona (N.L.)	0	1	.000	2.79	1.34	30	0	0	0	0	22-25	29.0	20	10	9	1	19-0	49	.192
2000— Tucson (PCL)	0	0	...	2.45	1.09	4	2	0	0	...	0-...	3.2	1	1	1	0	3-0	2	.100
— Arizona (N.L.)	1	1	.500	4.57	1.46	47	0	0	0	0	17-20	45.1	31	24	23	4	35-1	53	.193
2001— Arizona (N.L.)	0	0	...	2.57	1.43	8	0	0	0	1	2-2	7.0	6	2	2	2	4-0	12	.222
2002— El Paso (Texas)	0	1	.000	2.25	1.00	4	3	0	0	...	0-...	4.0	3	3	1	0	1-0	5	.200
— Tucson (PCL)	1	0	1.000	0.00	1.20	9	1	0	0	...	0-...	10.0	8	1	0	0	4-0	9	.211
— Arizona (N.L.)	2	2	.500	4.73	1.50	31	0	0	0	2	0-1	26.2	28	15	14	3	12-0	26	.257
2003— Tucson (PCL)	0	0	...	2.25	0.50	3	0	0	0	...	0-...	4.0	2	1	1	1	0-0	4	.154
— Arizona (N.L.)	5	4	.556	2.62	1.00	50	0	0	0	0	29-32	55.0	37	17	16	6	18-1	68	.191
Major League totals (8 years)	13	15	.464	3.56	1.33	269	0	0	0	5	89-105	285.2	209	119	113	24	170-7	361	.204

MANZANILLO, JOSIAS   P

PERSONAL: Born October 16, 1967, in San Pedro de Macoris, Dominican Republic. ... 6-0/200. ... Throws right, bats right. ... Name pronounced: hose-EYE-ess man-zah-NEE-oh.

TRANSACTIONS/CAREER NOTES: Signed as non-drafted free agent by Boston Red Sox organization (January 10, 1983). ... On disabled list (June 8, 1987-remainder of season; and April 8, 1988-entire season). ... Granted free agency (March 24, 1992). ... Signed by Kansas City Royals organization (April 3, 1992). ... Granted free agency (October 15, 1992). ... Signed by Milwaukee Brewers (November 20, 1992). ... Traded by Brewers to New York Mets for OF Wayne Housie (June 12, 1993). ... On New York disabled list (July 27, 1994-remainder of season). ... Claimed on waivers by New York Yankees (June 5, 1995). ... On New York disabled list (July 6, 1995-remainder of season). ... Granted free agency (October 16, 1995). ... Played in Taiwan for 1996 season. ... Signed by Seattle Mariners organization (December 21, 1996). ... On Seattle disabled list (April 9-May 6 and May 25-July 1, 1997; included rehabilitation assignments to Memphis (May 1-6) and Tacoma (May 25-July 1). ... Released by Mariners (July 17, 1997). ... Signed by Houston Astros organization (July 27, 1997). ... Granted free agency (October 15, 1997). ... Signed by Tampa Bay Devil Rays organization (December 18, 1997). ... Released by Devil Rays (July 1, 1998). ... Signed by Mets organization (July 3, 1998). ... Granted free agency (October 15, 1998). ... Re-signed by Mets organization (December 18, 1998). ... On Norfolk disabled list (June 21, 1999-remainder of season). ... Granted free agency (October 4, 1999). ... Signed by Pittsburgh Pirates organization (February 9, 2000). ... Granted free agency (November 5, 2001). ... Re-signed by Pirates organization (February 27, 2002). ... On Pittsburgh disabled list (May 4-July 13, 2002; included rehabilitation assignments to Nashville (June 25-July 10) and Hickory (July 11-13). ... Released by Pirates (August 15, 2002). ... Signed by Cincinnati Reds (January 7, 2003). ... Designated for assignment (April 20, 2003). ... Sent outright to Louisville (April 23, 2003).

CAREER HITTING: 1-for-11 (.091), 0 R, 0 2B, 0 3B, 0 HR, 0 RBI.

Year League	W	L	Pct.	ERA	WHIP	G	GS	CG	ShO	Hld.	Sv.-Opp.	IP	H	R	ER	HR	BB-IBB	SO	Avg.
1983— Elmira (N.Y.-Penn)	1	5	.167	7.98	1.88	12	4	0	0	...	0-...	38.1	52	44	34	7	20-1	19	...
1984— Elmira (N.Y.-Penn)	2	3	.400	5.26	2.06	14	0	0	0	...	1-...	25.2	27	24	15	1	26-1	15	.273
1985— Greensboro (S. Atl.)	1	1	.500	9.75	2.50	7	0	0	0	...	0-...	12.0	12	13	13	1	18-0	10	.273
— Elmira (N.Y.-Penn)	2	4	.333	3.86	1.82	19	4	0	0	...	1-...	39.2	36	19	17	1	36-4	43	.254
1986— Winter Haven (FSL)	13	5	.722	2.27	1.34	23	21	3	2	...	0-...	142.2	110	51	36	3	81-0	102	.217
1987— New Britain (East.)	2	0	1.000	4.50	1.60	2	2	0	0	...	0-...	10.0	8	5	5	1	8-0	12	.216
1988— New Britain (East.)										Did not play.									
1989— New Britain (East.)	9	10	.474	3.66	1.45	26	•26	3	1	...	0-...	147.2	129	78	60	11	85-7	93	.232
1990— New Britain (East.)	4	4	.500	3.41	1.39	12	12	2	1	...	0-...	74.0	66	34	28	3	37-1	51	.236
— Pawtucket (Int'l)	4	7	.364	5.55	1.45	15	15	5	0	...	0-...	82.2	75	57	51	9	45-0	77	.236
1991— Pawtucket (Int'l)	5	5	.500	5.61	1.58	20	16	0	0	...	0-...	102.2	109	69	64	12	53-0	65	.275
— New Britain (East.)	2	2	.500	2.90	1.31	7	7	0	0	...	0-...	49.2	37	25	16	0	28-1	35	.208
— Boston (A.L.)	0	0	...	18.00	5.00	1	0	0	0	0	0-0	1.0	2	2	2	0	3-0	1	.400
1992— Omaha (Am. Assoc.)	7	10	.412	4.36	1.53	26	21	0	0	...	0-...	136.1	138	76	66	12	71-0	114	.271
— Memphis (Sou.)	0	2	.000	7.36	1.64	2	0	0	0	...	0-...	7.1	6	6	6	0	6-0	8	.231
1993— Milwaukee (A.L.)	1	1	.500	9.53	1.88	10	1	0	0	0	1-2	17.0	22	20	18	1	10-3	10	.314
— New Orleans (A.A.)	0	1	.000	9.00	1.00	1	0	0	0	...	0-...	1.0	1	1	1	0	0-0	3	.250
— Norfolk (Int'l)	1	5	.167	3.11	1.27	14	12	2	1	...	0-...	84.0	82	40	29	3	25-1	79	.258
— New York (N.L.)	0	0	...	3.00	1.42	6	0	0	0	0	0-0	12.0	8	7	4	1	9-0	11	.186
1994— Norfolk (Int'l)	0	1	.000	4.38	1.46	8	0	0	0	...	3-...	12.1	12	6	6	1	6-1	10	.255
— New York (N.L.)	3	2	.600	2.66	0.99	37	0	0	0	11	2-5	47.1	34	15	14	4	13-2	48	.200
1995— New York (A.L.)	1	2	.333	7.88	1.50	12	0	0	0	0	0-0	16.0	18	15	14	3	6-2	14	.273
— New York (A.L.)	0	0	...	2.08	1.62	11	0	0	0	0	0-0	17.1	19	4	4	1	9-2	11	.279
1996—										Did not play.									
1997— Seattle (A.L.)	0	1	.000	5.40	1.96	16	0	0	0	1	0-1	18.1	19	13	11	3	17-1	18	.275
— Memphis (Sou.)	0	0	...	3.00	0.33	2	0	0	0	...	0-...	3.0	1	1	1	0	0-0	6	.100
— Tacoma (PCL)	0	0	...	6.43	1.71	11	0	0	0	...	1-...	14.0	16	10	10	4	8-0	15	.286
— New Orleans (A.A.)	0	0	...	4.40	1.60	11	0	0	0	...	0-...	14.1	17	7	7	3	6-0	11	.304
1998— Durham (Int'l)	7	6	.538	4.64	1.44	19	14	0	0	...	1-...	85.1	93	57	44	12	30-0	61	.272
— Norfolk (Int'l)	4	4	.500	3.24	1.39	13	12	1	0	...	1-...	77.2	77	35	28	5	31-0	72	.263
1999— New York (N.L.)	0	0	...	5.79	1.23	12	0	0	0	1	0-0	18.2	19	12	12	5	4-1	25	.264
2000— Nashville (PCL)	0	2	.000	2.70	1.07	15	0	0	0	...	3-...	23.1	19	8	7	0	6-1	23	.226
— Pittsburgh (N.L.)	2	2	.500	3.38	1.40	43	0	0	0	5	0-2	58.2	50	23	22	6	32-4	39	.240
2001— Pittsburgh (N.L.)	3	2	.600	3.39	1.08	71	0	0	0	9	2-7	79.2	60	32	30	4	26-3	80	.211
2002— Nashville (PCL)	1	0	1.000	2.66	0.98	15	1	0	0	...	1-...	20.1	18	6	6	3	2-1	14	.234
— Pittsburgh (N.L.)	0	0	...	7.62	1.92	13	0	0	0	0	0-1	13.0	20	11	11	5	5-0	4	.364
— Hickory (S. Atl.)	0	0	...	9.00	2.50	1	0	0	0	...	0-...	2.0	5	3	2	1	0-0	1	.417
2003— Cincinnati (N.L.)	0	2	.000	12.66	2.34	9	0	0	0	0	0-1	10.2	21	20	15	7	4-0	12	.389
— Louisville (Int'l)	1	1	.500	4.18	1.29	22	0	0	0	...	0-...	28.0	25	17	13	0	11-1	16	.250
American League totals (4 years)	1	2	.333	5.87	1.88	38	1	0	0	1	1-3	53.2	62	39	35	5	39-6	40	.292
National League totals (8 years)	9	10	.474	4.29	1.29	203	0	0	0	26	4-16	256.0	230	135	122	35	99-12	233	.241
Major League totals (10 years)	10	12	.455	4.56	1.39	241	1	0	0	27	5-19	309.2	292	174	157	40	138-18	273	.251

MAROTH, MIKE   P

PERSONAL: Born August 17, 1977, in Orlando, Fla. ... 6-0/190. ... Throws left, bats left. ... Full name: Michael Warren Maroth. ... Name pronounced: mah-ROTH. ... High school: William R. Boone (Orlando, Fla.). ... College: Central Florida.

TRANSACTIONS/CAREER NOTES: Selected by Boston Red Sox organization in third round of free-agent draft (June 2, 1998). ... Traded by Red Sox to Detroit Tigers for P Bryce Florie (July 31, 1999). ... On disabled list (July 31-August 22, 2001).

CAREER HITTING: 2-for-8 (.250), 1 R, 0 2B, 0 3B, 0 HR, 0 RBI.

M

Year — League	W	L	Pct.	ERA	WHIP	G	GS	CG	ShO	Hld.	Sv.-Opp.	IP	H	R	ER	HR	BB-IBB	SO	Avg.
1998— GC Red Sox (GCL)	1	1	.500	0.00	0.87	4	2	0	0	...	0-...	12.2	9	3	0	0	2-0	14	.191
— Lowell (NY-Penn)	2	3	.400	2.90	1.13	6	6	0	0	...	0-...	31.0	22	13	10	1	13-0	34	.200
1999— Sarasota (Fla. St.)	11	6	.647	4.04	1.43	20	19	0	0	...	0-...	111.1	124	65	50	3	35-1	64	.281
— Lakeland (Fla. St.)	2	1	.667	3.24	1.50	3	3	0	0	...	0-...	16.2	18	7	6	1	7-0	11	.286
— Jacksonville (Sou.)	1	2	.333	4.79	1.65	4	4	0	0	...	0-...	20.2	27	15	11	2	7-0	10	.310
2000— Jacksonville (Sou.)	9	14	.391	3.94	1.42	27	26	2	1	...	0-...	164.1	176	79	72	14	58-0	85	.289
2001— Toledo (Int'l)	7	10	.412	4.65	1.58	24	23	0	0	...	0-...	131.2	158	80	68	11	50-1	63	.302
2002— Toledo (Int'l)	8	1	.889	2.82	1.02	11	11	1	0	...	0-...	73.1	53	25	23	7	22-0	51	.201
— Detroit (A.L.)	6	10	.375	4.48	1.34	21	21	0	0	0	0-0	128.2	136	68	64	7	36-1	58	.276
2003— Detroit (A.L.)	9	*21	.300	5.73	1.45	33	33	1	0	0	0-0	193.1	231	131	123	•34	50-2	87	.299
Major League totals (2 years)	**15**	**31**	**.326**	**5.23**	**1.41**	**54**	**54**	**1**	**0**	**0**	**0-0**	**322.0**	**367**	**199**	**187**	**41**	**86-3**	**145**	**.290**

MARQUIS, JASON   P

PERSONAL: Born August 21, 1978, in Manhasset, N.Y. ... 6-1/210. ... Throws right, bats left. ... Full name: Jason Scott Marquis. ... Name pronounced: mar-KEE. ... High school: Tottenville (Staten Island, N.Y.).

TRANSACTIONS/CAREER NOTES: Selected by Atlanta Braves organization as "sandwich" pick between first and second round of free-agent draft (June 4, 1996); pick received as supplemental pick for failure to signed 1995 first-round choice. ... On Greenville disabled list (July 5-31, 1999). ... On disabled list (April 22-May 12, 2002). ... Optioned to Richmond by Atlanta (April 19, 2003). ... Recalled by Atlanta from Richmond (June 13, 2003). ... Optioned to Richmond (June 26, 2003). ... Recalled from Richmond (July 28, 2003).

CAREER HITTING: 7-for-73 (.096), 9 R, 1 2B, 0 3B, 1 HR, 2 RBI.

Year — League	W	L	Pct.	ERA	WHIP	G	GS	CG	ShO	Hld.	Sv.-Opp.	IP	H	R	ER	HR	BB-IBB	SO	Avg.
1996— Danville (Appal.)	1	1	.500	4.63	1.59	7	4	0	0	...	0-...	23.1	30	18	12	0	7-0	24	.286
1997— Macon (S. Atl.)	• 14	10	.583	4.38	1.49	28	28	0	0	...	0-...	141.2	156	78	69	10	55-1	121	.278
1998— Danville (Caro.)	2	12	.143	4.87	1.40	22	22	1	0	...	0-...	114.2	120	65	62	3	41-0	135	.269
1999— Myrtle Beach (Caro.)	3	0	1.000	0.28	1.22	6	6	0	0	...	0-...	32.0	22	2	1	0	17-0	41	.191
— Greenville (Sou.)	3	4	.429	4.58	1.47	12	12	1	0	...	0-...	55.0	52	33	28	7	29-0	35	.241
2000— Greenville (Sou.)	4	2	.667	3.57	1.34	11	11	0	0	...	0-...	68.0	68	35	27	10	23-0	49	.262
— Atlanta (N.L.)	1	0	1.000	5.01	1.50	15	0	0	0	1	0-1	23.1	23	16	13	4	12-1	17	.261
— Richmond (Int'l)	0	3	.000	9.00	1.95	6	6	0	0	...	0-...	20.0	26	21	20	2	13-0	18	.321
2001— Atlanta (N.L.)	5	6	.455	3.48	1.33	38	16	0	0	2	0-2	129.1	113	62	50	14	59-4	98	.234
2002— Richmond (Int'l)	0	1	.000	3.60	1.20	1	1	0	0	...	0-...	5.0	5	2	2	0	1-0	6	.263
— Atlanta (N.L.)	8	9	.471	5.04	1.54	22	22	0	0	0	0-0	114.1	127	66	64	19	49-3	84	.283
2003— Richmond (Int'l)	8	4	.667	3.35	1.35	15	15	3	1	...	0-...	94.0	93	40	35	5	34-0	75	.256
— Atlanta (N.L.)	0	0	...	5.53	1.50	21	2	0	0	0	1-1	40.2	43	27	25	3	18-2	19	.270
Major League totals (4 years)	**14**	**15**	**.483**	**4.45**	**1.44**	**96**	**40**	**0**	**0**	**3**	**1-4**	**307.2**	**306**	**171**	**152**	**40**	**138-10**	**218**	**.260**

MARRERO, ELI   OF/C

PERSONAL: Born November 17, 1973, in Havana, Cuba. ... 6-1/180. ... Bats right, throws right. ... Full name: Elieser Marrero. ... Name pronounced: muh-RARE-ro. ... High school: Coral Gables (Fla.).

TRANSACTIONS/CAREER NOTES: Selected by St. Louis Cardinals organization in third round of free-agent draft (June 3, 1993). ... On St. Louis disabled list (March 22-April 13, 1998). ... On St. Louis disabled list (July 2-September 1, 2000); included rehabilitation assignment to Memphis (August 24-September 1). ... Placed on 15-day disabled list (May 12, 2003). ... Sent to Memphis on rehab assignment (August 8, 2003). ... Recalled from Memphis rehab assignment (August 26, 2003). ... Removed from 15-day disabled list (September 1, 2003).

2003 GAMES PLAYED BY POSITION (MLB): OF—31, C—6, 1B—2.

M

Year — Team (League)	Pos.	G	AB	R	H	2B	3B	HR	RBI	BB	SO	HBP	GDP	SB-CS	Avg.	OBP	SLG	OPS	E	Pct.
1993— Johnson City (App.)	C	18	61	10	22	8	0	2	14	12	9	1	0	2-2	.361	.467	.590	1.057	1	.994
1994— Savannah (S. Atl.)	C	116	421	71	110	16	3	21	79	39	92	5	6	5-4	.261	.328	.463	.791	• 15	.984
1995— St. Pete. (FSL)	C	107	383	43	81	16	1	10	55	23	55	1	10	9-4	.211	.254	.337	.590	10	.984
1996— Arkansas (Texas)	C-DH	116	374	65	101	17	3	19	65	32	55	6	7	9-6	.270	.336	.484	.820	3	.996
1997— Louisville (A.A.)	C-DH	112	395	60	108	21	7	20	68	25	53	3	8	4-4	.273	.318	.514	.832	7	.991
— St. Louis (N.L.)	C	17	45	4	11	2	0	2	7	2	13	0	1	4-0	.244	.271	.422	.693	3	.969
1998— St. Louis (N.L.)	C-1B	84	254	28	62	18	1	4	20	28	42	0	5	6-2	.244	.318	.370	.688	4	.991
— Memphis (PCL)	C-DH	32	130	22	31	5	0	7	21	13	23	0	3	5-4	.238	.306	.438	.744	2	.991
1999— St. Louis (N.L.)	C-1B	114	317	32	61	13	1	6	34	18	56	1	14	11-2	.192	.236	.297	.533	7	.988
2000— St. Louis (N.L.)	C-1B	53	102	21	23	3	1	5	17	9	16	3	3	5-0	.225	.302	.422	.723	0	1.000
— Memphis (PCL)	C	6	15	1	1	0	0	0	0	0	2	0	1	0-0	.067	.067	.067	.133	0	1.000
2001— St. Louis (N.L.)	C-OF-1B	86	203	37	54	11	3	6	23	15	36	0	4	6-3	.266	.312	.438	.751	7	.983
2002— St. Louis (N.L.)	OF-C-1B	131	397	63	104	19	1	18	66	40	72	0	5	14-2	.262	.327	.451	.777	7	.981
2003— Memphis (PCL)	OF-DH	5	12	2	3	1	0	1	1	1	0	1	1	0-0	.250	.357	.583	.940	0	1.000
— St. Louis (N.L.)	OF-C-1B	41	107	10	24	4	2	2	20	7	18	0	0	0-1	.224	.267	.355	.622	1	.989
Major League totals (7 years)		**525**	**1425**	**195**	**339**	**70**	**9**	**43**	**187**	**119**	**253**	**4**	**32**	**46-10**	**.238**	**.295**	**.390**	**.686**	**29**	**.987**

MARTE, DAMASO   P

PERSONAL: Born February 14, 1975, in Santo Domingo, Dominican Republic. ... 6-2/200. ... Throws left, bats left. ... Full name: Damaso Savinon Marte. ... Name pronounced: da-muh-so mar-TAY.

TRANSACTIONS/CAREER NOTES: Signed as non-drafted free agent by Seattle Mariners organization (October 28, 1992). ... On disabled list (April 3-17, 1997). ... On disabled list (April 2-May 3 and September 2, 1998-remainder of season). ... On New Haven disabled list (April 7-August 22, 2000). ... Granted free agency (October 18, 2000). ... Signed by New York Yankees organization (November 16, 2000). ... Traded by Yankees to Pittsburgh Pirates for IF Enrique Wilson (June 13, 2001). ... Traded by Pirates with IF Edwin Yan to Chicago White Sox for P Matt Guerrier (March 27, 2002).

CAREER HITTING: 0-for-5 (.000), 0 R, 0 2B, 0 3B, 0 HR, 0 RBI.

Year — League	W	L	Pct.	ERA	WHIP	G	GS	CG	ShO	Hld.	Sv.-Opp.	IP	H	R	ER	HR	BB-IBB	SO	Avg.
1993— Dom. Mariners (DSL)	2	5	.286	6.55	1.99	17	15	2	0	...	0-...	56.1	62	48	41	...	50-...	29	...
1994— Dom. Mariners (DSL)	7	0	1.000	3.86	1.55	17	13	0	0	...	0-...	65.1	53	41	28	...	48-...	80	...
1995— Everett (Northwest)	2	2	.500	2.21	0.95	11	11	5	0	...	0-...	36.2	25	11	9	2	10-0	39	.195
1996— Wisconsin (Midw.)	8	6	.571	4.49	1.47	26	26	2	1	...	0-...	142.1	134	82	71	8	75-5	115	.254
1997— Lancaster (Calif.)	8	8	.500	4.13	1.48	25	25	2	1	...	0-...	139.1	144	75	64	15	62-1	127	.272
1998— Orlando (Sou.)	7	6	.538	5.27	1.51	22	20	0	0	...	0-...	121.1	136	82	71	14	47-0	99	.281
1999— Tacoma (PCL)	3	3	.500	5.13	1.62	31	11	0	0	...	0-...	73.2	79	43	42	13	40-1	59	.272
— Seattle (A.L.)	0	1	.000	9.35	2.54	5	0	0	0	0	0-0	8.2	16	9	9	3	6-0	5	.390

Year — League	W	L	Pct.	ERA	WHIP	G	GS	CG	ShO	Hld.	Sv.-Opp.	IP	H	R	ER	HR	BB-IBB	SO	Avg.
2000— Ariz. Mariners (Ariz.)	0	0	...	0.00	0.20	2	2	0	0	...	0-...	5.0	1	0	0	0	0-0	6	.063
— New Haven (East.)	0	0	...	1.59	1.41	4	0	0	0	...	0-...	5.2	6	1	1	1	2-0	4	.286
2001— Norwich (East.)	3	1	.750	3.50	1.00	23	0	0	0	...	1-...	36.0	29	16	14	3	7-0	36	.215
— Nashville (PCL)	0	0	...	3.38	0.56	4	0	0	0	...	0-...	5.1	3	2	2	2	0-0	4	.167
— Pittsburgh (N.L.)	0	1	.000	4.71	1.27	23	0	0	0	0	0-0	36.1	34	21	19	5	12-3	39	.250
2002— Chicago (A.L.)	1	1	.500	2.83	1.03	68	0	0	0	14	10-12	60.1	44	19	19	5	18-2	72	.204
2003— Chicago (A.L.)	4	2	.667	1.58	1.05	71	0	0	0	14	11-18	79.2	50	16	14	3	34-6	87	.185
American League totals (3 years)	5	4	.556	2.54	1.13	144	0	0	0	28	21-30	148.2	110	44	42	11	58-8	162	.208
National League totals (1 year)	0	1	.000	4.71	1.27	23	0	0	0	0	0-0	36.1	34	21	19	5	12-3	39	.250
Major League totals (4 years)	5	5	.500	2.97	1.16	167	0	0	0	28	21-30	185.0	144	65	61	16	70-11	201	.217

MARTIN, AL   OF

PERSONAL: Born November 24, 1967... 6-2/214. ... Bats left, throws left. ... Full name: Albert Lee Martin. ... High school: West Covina (Calif.).

TRANSACTIONS/CAREER NOTES: Selected by Atlanta Braves organization in eighth round of free-agent draft (June 3, 1985). ... Granted free agency (October 15, 1991). ... Signed by Pittsburgh Pirates organization (November 11, 1991). ... On suspended list (September 17-20, 1993). ... On disabled list (July 11, 1994-remainder of season). ... On Pittsburgh disabled list (May 22-June 24, 1997); included rehabilitation assignment to Carolina (June 21-23). ... Traded by Pirates with cash to San Diego Padres for OF John Vander Wal, P Geraldo Padua and P James Sak (February 23, 2000). ... Traded by Padres to Seattle Mariners for OF/3B John Mabry and P Tom Davey (July 31, 2000). ... Granted free agency (November 5, 2001). ... Signed by St. Louis Cardinals organization (February 8, 2002). ... Released by Cardinals (March 29, 2002). ... Signed by Florida Marlins organization (February 13, 2003). ... Released by Marlins (March 28, 2003). ... Signed by Tampa Bay Devil Rays (March 29, 2003).

2003 GAMES PLAYED BY POSITION (MLB): DH—57, OF—13, 1B—1.

									BATTING									FIELDING	
Year — Team (League)	Pos.	G	AB	R	H	2B	3B	HR	RBI	BB	SO	HBP	GDP	SB-CS	Avg.	OBP	SLG	OPS	E	Pct.
1985— GC Braves (GCL)	1B-OF	40	138	16	32	3	0	0	9	19	36	2	4	1-4	.232	.331	.254	.585	‡ 15	.945
1986— Sumter (S. Atl.)	1B	44	156	23	38	5	0	1	24	23	36	0	6	6-2	.244	.341	.295	.636	8	.975
— Idaho Falls (Pio.)	1B-OF	63	242	39	80	17	•6	4	44	20	53	2	1	11-2	.331	.386	.500	.886	8	.973
1987— Sumter (S. Atl.)	1B-OF	117	375	59	95	18	5	12	64	44	69	2	5	27-8	.253	.332	.424	.756	9	.941
1988— Burlington (Midw.)	OF	123	480	69	134	21	3	7	42	30	88	4	6	40-12	.279	.324	.379	.703	8	.966
1989— Durham (Caro.)	OF	128	457	* 84	124	26	3	9	48	34	107	3	6	27-14	.271	.324	.400	.724	7	.962
1990— Greenville (Sou.)	OF	133	455	64	110	17	4	11	50	43	102	3	9	20-7	.242	.310	.369	.679	7	.967
1991— Greenville (Sou.)	1B-OF	86	301	38	73	13	3	7	38	32	84	8	2	19-7	.243	.330	.375	.706	6	.959
— Richmond (Int'l)	OF	44	151	20	42	11	1	5	18	7	33	1	0	11-2	.278	.314	.464	.778	2	.975
1992— Buffalo (A.A.)	OF	125	420	85	128	16	* 15	20	59	35	93	6	1	20-5	.305	.363	.557	.920	8	.967
— Pittsburgh (N.L.)	OF	12	12	1	2	0	1	0	2	0	5	0	0	0-0	.167	.154	.333	.487	0	1.000
1993— Pittsburgh (N.L.)	OF	143	480	85	135	26	8	18	64	42	122	1	5	16-9	.281	.338	.481	.820	7	.975
1994— Pittsburgh (N.L.)	OF	82	276	48	79	12	4	9	33	34	56	2	3	15-6	.286	.367	.457	.824	3	.979
1995— Pittsburgh (N.L.)	OF	124	439	70	124	25	3	13	41	44	92	2	5	20-11	.282	.351	.442	.792	5	.977
1996— Pittsburgh (N.L.)	OF	155	630	101	189	40	1	18	72	54	116	2	9	38-12	.300	.354	.452	.806	6	.965
1997— Pittsburgh (N.L.)	OF	113	423	64	123	24	7	13	59	45	83	3	7	23-7	.291	.359	.473	.832	6	.957
— Carolina (Sou.)	OF	3	9	0	1	0	0	0	0	0	0	0	0	0-0	.111	.111	.111	.222	0	1.000
1998— Pittsburgh (N.L.)	OF-DH	125	440	57	105	15	2	12	47	32	91	5	13	20-3	.239	.296	.364	.660	3	.985
1999— Pittsburgh (N.L.)	OF	143	541	97	150	36	8	24	63	49	119	1	8	20-3	.277	.337	.506	.844	10	.952
2000— San Diego (N.L.)	OF	93	346	62	106	13	6	11	27	28	54	2	2	6-8	.306	.360	.474	.834	7	.950
— Seattle (A.L.)	OF-DH	42	134	19	31	2	4	4	9	8	31	2	1	4-1	.231	.283	.396	.678	3	.963
2001— Seattle (A.L.)	OF-DH	100	283	41	68	15	2	7	42	37	59	2	2	9-3	.240	.330	.382	.712	4	.971
2002—									Did not play.										
2003— Tampa Bay (A.L.)	DH-OF-1B	100	238	19	60	12	2	3	26	17	51	2	8	2-2	.252	.306	.357	.663	0	1.000
American League totals (3 years)		242	655	79	159	29	8	14	77	62	141	6	11	15-6	.243	.312	.376	.688	7	.972
National League totals (9 years)		990	3587	585	1013	191	40	118	408	328	738	18	52	158-59	.282	.344	.457	.800	49	.969
Major League totals (11 years)		1232	4242	664	1172	220	48	132	485	390	879	24	63	173-65	.276	.339	.444	.783	56	.969

MARTIN, TOM   P

PERSONAL: Born May 21, 1970, in Charleston, S.C. ... 6-1/206. ... Throws left, bats left. ... Full name: Thomas Edgar Martin. ... High school: Bay (Panama City, Fla.).

TRANSACTIONS/CAREER NOTES: Selected by Baltimore Orioles organization in sixth round of free-agent draft (June 1, 1988). ... Traded by Orioles with 3B Craig Worthington to San Diego Padres for P Jim Lewis and OF Steve Martin (February 17, 1992). ... Selected by Atlanta Braves organization from Padres organization in Rule 5 minor league draft (December 13, 1993). ... Loaned by Braves organization to Mexico City Tigres, Mexican League (May 1-7, 1995). ... Released by Braves (January 25, 1996). ... Signed by Houston Astros organization (February 21, 1996). ... On disabled list (May 30-June 15, 1997). ... Selected by Arizona Diamondbacks in second round (29th pick overall) of expansion draft (November 18, 1997). ... Traded by Diamondbacks with 3B Travis Fryman and cash to Cleveland Indians for 3B Matt Williams (December 1, 1997). ... On Cleveland disabled list (April 30-May 18 and August 31-September 19, 1998); included rehabilitation assignment to Buffalo (May 13-18 and September 3-19). ... On Cleveland disabled list (April 4-August 9, 1999); included rehabilitation assignment to Akron (July 27-August 9). ... On Cleveland disabled list (June 13-August 4, 2000); included rehabilitation assignment to Buffalo (July 28-August 4). ... Traded by Indians to New York Mets for C Javier Ochoa (January 11, 2001). ... On New York disabled list (May 13-August 16, 2001); included rehabilitation assignments to Brooklyn (July 27-30) and Norfolk (July 31-August 16). ... Released by Mets (October 11, 2001). ... Signed by Tampa Bay Devils Rays organization (January 29, 2002). ... On disabled list (April 23-September 30, 2002). ... Released by Devil Rays (September 30, 2002). ... Signed by Los Angeles Dodgers organization (February 26, 2003).

CAREER HITTING: 0-for-7 (.000), 0 R, 0 2B, 0 3B, 0 HR, 0 RBI.

Year — League	W	L	Pct.	ERA	WHIP	G	GS	CG	ShO	Hld.	Sv.-Opp.	IP	H	R	ER	HR	BB-IBB	SO	Avg.
1989— Bluefield (Appal.)	3	3	.500	4.62	1.56	8	8	0	0	...	0-...	39.0	36	28	20	3	25-0	31	.242
— Erie (N.Y.-Penn)	0	5	.000	6.64	1.65	7	7	0	0	...	0-...	40.2	42	39	30	2	25-0	44	.259
1990— Wausau (Midw.)	2	3	.400	2.48	1.45	9	9	0	0	...	0-...	40.0	31	25	11	1	27-0	45	.209
1991— Kane County (Midwest)	4	10	.286	3.64	1.49	38	10	0	0	...	6-...	99.0	92	50	40	4	56-3	106	.247
1992— High Desert (Calif.)	0	2	.000	9.37	2.39	11	0	0	0	...	0-...	16.1	23	19	17	4	16-0	10	.333
— Waterloo (Midw.)	2	6	.250	4.25	1.53	39	2	0	0	...	3-...	55.0	62	38	26	3	22-4	57	.287
1993— Rancho Cuca. (Calif.)	1	4	.200	5.61	1.87	47	1	0	0	...	3-...	59.1	72	41	37	4	39-2	53	.305
1994— Greenville (Sou.)	5	6	.455	4.62	1.47	36	6	0	0	...	0-...	74.0	82	40	38	6	27-3	51	.288
1995— Richmond (Int'l)	0	0	...	9.00	2.22	7	0	0	0	...	0-...	9.0	10	9	9	4	10-2	3	.286
— M.C. Tigers (Mex.)	0	1	.000	27.00	4.50	1	1	0	0	...	0-...	1.1	5	5	4	0	1-...	0	...
1996— Tucson (PCL)	0	0	...	0.00	1.33	5	0	0	0	...	0-...	6.0	6	0	0	0	2-2	1	.261
— Jackson (Texas)	6	2	.750	3.24	1.51	57	0	0	0	...	3-...	75.0	71	35	27	8	42-4	58	.250
1997— Houston (N.L.)	5	3	.625	2.09	1.34	55	0	0	0	7	2-3	56.0	52	13	13	2	23-2	36	.254
1998— Cleveland (A.L.)	1	1	.500	12.89	2.80	14	0	0	0	3	0-0	14.2	29	21	21	3	12-0	9	.408
— Buffalo (Int'l)	3	1	.750	6.00	1.64	41	0	0	0	...	0-...	36.0	46	25	24	4	13-0	35	.309

M

Year League	W	L	Pct.	ERA	WHIP	G	GS	CG	ShO	Hld.	Sv.-Opp.	IP	H	R	ER	HR	BB-IBB	SO	Avg.
1999— Akron (East.)	0	0	...	1.00	0.78	3	3	0	0	...	0-...	9.0	4	1	1	0	3-0	9	.138
— Cleveland (A.L.)	0	1	.000	8.68	1.71	6	0	0	0	0	0-0	9.1	13	9	9	2	3-1	8	.325
— Buffalo (Int'l)	1	0	1.000	3.00	1.00	5	0	0	0	0	0-...	6.0	5	2	2	1	1-0	6	.208
2000— Cleveland (A.L.)	1	0	1.000	4.05	1.41	31	0	0	0	0	0-0	33.1	32	16	15	3	15-2	21	.254
— Buffalo (Int'l)	0	1	.000	3.60	1.30	9	3	0	0	0	0-...	10.0	12	4	4	1	1-0	4	.300
2001— Norfolk (Int'l)	2	1	.667	6.26	1.78	23	0	0	0	0	1-...	23.0	31	17	16	4	10-0	24	.330
— New York (N.L.)	1	0	1.000	10.06	1.94	14	0	0	0	1	0-0	17.0	23	22	19	4	10-2	12	.319
— Brooklyn (NY-P)	0	0	...	0.00	2.00	1	1	0	0	0	0-...	1.0	2	0	0	0	0-0	0	.500
2002— Durham (Int'l)	0	0	...	0.00	1.20	4	0	0	0	0	2-...	3.1	3	0	0	0	1-0	6	.231
— Tampa Bay (A.L.)	0	0	...	16.20	3.60	2	0	0	0	0	0-0	1.2	5	3	3	0	1-0	1	.500
2003— Los Angeles (N.L.)	1	2	.333	3.53	1.18	80	0	0	0	28	0-1	51.0	36	21	20	6	24-4	51	.198
American League totals (4 years)	2	2	.500	7.32	1.86	53	0	0	0	3	0-0	59.0	79	49	48	8	31-3	39	.320
National League totals (3 years)	7	5	.583	3.77	1.35	149	0	0	0	36	2-4	124.0	111	56	52	12	57-8	99	.242
Major League totals (7 years)	9	7	.563	4.92	1.52	202	0	0	0	39	2-4	183.0	190	105	100	20	88-11	138	.269

MARTINEZ, EDGAR — DH

PERSONAL: Born January 2, 1963, in New York, N.Y. ... 5-11/204. ... Bats right, throws right. ... High school: Dorado (Puerto Rico). ... College: American College (P.R.).

TRANSACTIONS/CAREER NOTES: Signed as non-drafted free agent by Seattle Mariners organization (December 19, 1982). ... On Seattle disabled list (April 4-May 17, June 15-July 21 and August 17, 1993-remainder of season); included rehabilitation assignment to Jacksonville (July 17-21). ... On disabled list (April 16-May 6, 1994; July 21-August 12, 1996; and July 17-August 3, 2001). ... On suspended list (October 3-5, 2001). ... On disabled list (April 12-June 14, 2002).

2003 GAMES PLAYED BY POSITION (MLB): DH—140.

Year Team (League)	Pos.	G	AB	R	H	2B	3B	HR	RBI	BB	SO	HBP	GDP	SB-CS	Avg.	OBP	SLG	OPS	E	Pct.
1983— Bellingham (N'west)	3B	32	104	14	18	1	1	0	5	18	24	2	...	1-3	.173	.304	.202	.506	6	.930
1984— Wausau (Midw.)	3B	126	433	72	131	32	2	15	66	84	57	3	7	11-9	.303	.414	.490	.904	25	.930
1985— Chattanooga (Sou.)	3B	111	357	43	92	15	5	3	47	71	30	5	16	1-3	.258	.378	.353	.730	19 *	.947
— Calgary (PCL)	2B-3B	20	68	8	24	7	1	0	14	12	7	0	2	1-0	.353	.450	.485	.935	4	.937
1986— Chattanooga (Sou.)	2B-3B	132	451	71	119	29	5	6	74	89	35	2	8	2-5	.264	.383	.390	.773	15 ‡	.960
1987— Calgary (PCL)	3B	129	438	75	144	31	1	10	66	82	47	2	10	3-5	.329	.434	.473	.907	20	.949
— Seattle (A.L.)	3B-DH	13	43	6	16	5	2	0	5	2	5	1	0	0-0	.372	.413	.581	.994	0	1.000
1988— Calgary (PCL)	2B-3B	95	331	63	120	19	4	8	64	66	40	3	9	9-1	* .363	.467	.517	.983	20	.921
— Seattle (A.L.)	3B	14	32	0	9	4	0	0	5	4	7	0	0	0-0	.281	.351	.406	.758	1	.929
1989— Seattle (A.L.)	3B	65	171	20	41	5	0	2	20	17	26	3	3	2-1	.240	.314	.304	.619	6	.949
— Calgary (PCL)	2B-3B	32	113	30	39	11	0	3	23	22	13	3	1	2-2	.345	.457	.522	.979	12	.867
1990— Seattle (A.L.)	3B-DH	144	487	71	147	27	2	11	49	74	62	5	13	1-4	.302	.397	.433	.830	* 27	.928
1991— Seattle (A.L.)	3B-DH	150	544	98	167	35	1	14	52	84	72	8	19	0-3	.307	.405	.452	.857	15	.962
1992— Seattle (A.L.)	3B-DH-1B	135	528	100	181	• 46	3	18	73	54	61	4	15	14-4	* .343	.404	.544	.948	17	.946
1993— Seattle (A.L.)	DH-3B	42	135	20	32	7	0	4	13	28	19	0	4	0-0	.237	.366	.378	.744	2	.889
— Jacksonville (Sou.)	DH	4	14	2	5	0	0	1	3	2	0	0	1	0-0	.357	.438	.571	1.009	...	...
1994— Seattle (A.L.)	DH	89	326	47	93	23	1	13	51	53	42	3	2	6-2	.285	.387	.482	.869	9	.950
1995— Seattle (A.L.)	DH-3B-1B	• 145	511	• 121	182	• 52	0	29	113	116	87	8	11	4-3	* .356	* .479	.628	1.107	2	.944
1996— Seattle (A.L.)	DH-1B-3B	139	499	121	163	52	2	26	103	123	84	8	15	3-3	.327	.464	.595	1.059	1	.968
1997— Seattle (A.L.)	DH-1B-3B	155	542	104	179	35	1	28	108	119	86	11	21	2-4	.330	.456	.554	1.009	1	.985
1998— Seattle (A.L.)	DH-1B	154	556	86	179	46	1	29	102	106	96	6	13	1-1	.322	* .429	.565	.993	0	1.000
1999— Seattle (A.L.)	DH-1B	142	502	86	169	35	1	24	86	97	99	6	12	7-2	.337	* .447	.554	1.001	0	1.000
2000— Seattle (A.L.)	DH-1B	153	556	100	180	31	0	37	* 145	96	95	5	13	3-0	.324	.423	.579	1.002	0	1.000
2001— Seattle (A.L.)	DH-1B	132	470	80	144	40	1	23	116	93	90	9	11	4-1	.306	.423	.543	.966	0	1.000
2002— Seattle (A.L.)	DH	97	328	42	91	23	0	15	59	67	69	6	6	1-1	.277	.403	.485	.888	0	...
2003— Seattle (A.L.)	DH	145	497	72	146	25	0	24	98	92	95	7	17	0-1	.294	.406	.489	.895	0	...
Major League totals (17 years)		1914	6727	1174	2119	491	15	297	1198	1225	1095	87	175	48-30	.315	.423	.525	.948	81	.952

MARTINEZ, LUIS — P

PERSONAL: Born January 20, 1980, in Santo Domingo, Dominican Republic. ... 6-6/200. ... Throws left, bats left.

TRANSACTIONS/CAREER NOTES: Signed as non-drafted free agent by Milwaukee Brewers organization (October 15, 1996).

CAREER HITTING: 0-for-4 (.000), 0 R, 0 2B, 0 3B, 0 HR, 0 RBI.

Year League	W	L	Pct.	ERA	WHIP	G	GS	CG	ShO	Hld.	Sv.-Opp.	IP	H	R	ER	HR	BB-IBB	SO	Avg.
1998— Helena (Pio.)	0	9	.000	10.13	2.71	17	10	0	0	...	0-...	48.0	64	73	54	5	66-0	47	.318
1999— Ogden (Pio.)	0	7	.000	6.97	1.99	15	7	0	0	...	1-...	50.1	66	65	39	3	34-0	43	.303
2000— Beloit (Midw.)	5	7	.417	3.79	1.42	28	13	0	0	...	0-...	92.2	71	49	39	8	61-1	77	.224
2001— Huntsville (Sou.)	0	0	...	6.75	2.36	7	0	0	0	...	0-...	9.1	13	7	7	0	9-0	13	.333
— High Desert (Calif.)	8	9	.471	5.19	1.56	22	22	0	0	...	0-...	112.2	112	67	65	9	64-0	121	.263
2002— Huntsville (Sou.)	8	8	.500	5.20	1.64	29	18	0	0	...	1-...	109.0	114	70	63	6	65-0	106	.277
2003— Huntsville (Sou.)	8	5	.615	2.58	1.28	20	20	1	0	...	0-...	115.0	93	46	33	4	54-0	116	.224
— Indianapolis (Int'l)	4	0	1.000	0.99	1.23	7	7	0	0	...	0-...	45.2	37	5	5	0	19-0	46	.237
— Milwaukee (N.L.)	0	3	.000	9.92	2.45	4	4	0	0	...	0-0	16.1	25	18	18	3	15-2	10	.373
Major League totals (1 year)	0	3	.000	9.92	2.45	4	4	0	0	0	0-0	16.1	25	18	18	3	15-2	10	.373

MARTINEZ, PEDRO — P

PERSONAL: Born October 25, 1971, in Manoguayabo, Dominican Republic. ... 5-11/180. ... Throws right, bats right. ... Full name: Pedro Jaime Martinez. ... College: Ohio Dominican.

TRANSACTIONS/CAREER NOTES: Signed as non-drafted free agent by Los Angeles Dodgers organization (June 18, 1988). ... On Albuquerque disabled list (June 20-July 2 and July 13-August 25, 1992). ... Traded by Dodgers to Montreal Expos for 2B Delino DeShields (November 19, 1993). ... On suspended list (April 1-9, 1997). ... Traded by Expos to Boston Red Sox for P Carl Pavano and a player to be named later (November 18, 1997); Expos acquired P Tony Armas Jr. to complete deal (December 18, 1997). ... On disabled list (July 19-August 3, 1999; June 29-July 13, 2000; June 27-August 26 and September 8, 2001-remainder of season). ... Activated from the 15-day disabled list (June 11, 2003). ... Placed on the 15-day disabled list, retroactive to May 16 (May 26, 2003). ... Reinstated from 15-day disabled list (June 11, 2003).

CAREER HITTING: 25-for-263 (.095), 14 R, 3 2B, 2 3B, 0 HR, 11 RBI.

M

Year League	W	L	Pct.	ERA	WHIP	G	GS	CG	ShO	Hld.	Sv.-Opp.	IP	H	R	ER	HR	BB-IBB	SO	Avg.
1988—Dom. Dodgers (DSL)	5	1	.833	3.10	1.24	8	7	1	0	...	0-...	49.1	45	25	17	...	16-...	28	...
1989—Dom. Dodgers (DSL)	7	2	.778	2.73	0.98	13	7	2	3	...	1-...	85.2	59	30	26	...	25-...	63	...
1990—Great Falls (Pio.)	8	3	.727	3.62	1.48	14	•14	0	0	...	0-...	77.0	74	39	31	5	40-1	82	.253
1991—Bakersfield (Calif.)	8	0	1.000	2.05	0.98	10	10	0	0	...	0-...	61.1	41	17	14	3	19-0	83	.189
—San Antonio (Texas)	7	5	.583	1.76	1.15	12	12	4	•3	...	0-...	76.2	57	21	15	1	31-1	74	.210
—Albuquerque (PCL)	3	3	.500	3.66	1.12	6	6	0	0	...	0-...	39.1	28	17	16	3	16-0	35	.201
1992—Albuquerque (PCL)	7	6	.538	3.81	1.28	20	20	3	1	...	0-...	125.1	104	57	53	10	57-0	124	* .229
—Los Angeles (N.L.)	0	1	.000	2.25	0.88	2	1	0	0	0	0-0	8.0	6	2	2	0	1-0	8	.200
1993—Albuquerque (PCL)	0	0	...	3.00	0.67	1	1	0	0	...	0-...	3.0	1	1	1	0	1-0	4	.100
—Los Angeles (N.L.)	10	5	.667	2.61	1.24	65	2	0	0	14	2-3	107.0	76	34	31	5	57-4	119	.201
1994—Montreal (N.L.)	11	5	.688	3.42	1.11	24	23	1	1	0	1-1	144.2	115	58	55	11	45-3	142	.220
1995—Montreal (N.L.)	14	10	.583	3.51	1.15	30	30	2	2	0	0-0	194.2	158	79	76	21	66-1	174	.227
1996—Montreal (N.L.)	13	10	.565	3.70	1.20	33	33	4	1	0	0-0	216.2	189	100	89	19	70-3	222	.232
1997—Montreal (N.L.)	17	8	.680	*1.90	0.93	31	31	* 13	4	0	0-0	241.1	158	65	51	16	67-5	305	*.184
1998—Boston (A.L.)	19	7	.731	2.89	1.09	33	33	3	2	0	0-0	233.2	188	82	75	26	67-3	251	.217
1999—Boston (A.L.)	* 23	4	*.852	*2.07	0.92	31	29	5	1	0	0-0	213.1	160	56	49	9	37-1	* 313	*.205
2000—Boston (A.L.)	18	6	.750	*1.74	0.74	29	29	7	* 4	0	0-0	217.0	128	44	42	17	32-0	* 284	*.167
2001—Boston (A.L.)	7	3	.700	2.39	0.93	18	18	1	0	0	0-0	116.2	84	33	31	5	25-0	163	.199
2002—Boston (A.L.)	20	4	*.833	*2.26	0.92	30	30	2	0	0	0-0	199.1	144	62	50	13	40-1	* 239	*.198
2003—Boston (A.L.)	14	4	.778	*2.22	*1.04	29	29	3	0	0	0-0	186.2	147	52	46	7	47-0	206	*.215
American League totals (6 years)	101	28	.783	2.26	0.94	170	168	21	7	0	0-0	1166.2	851	329	293	77	248-5	1456	.200
National League totals (6 years)	65	39	.625	3.00	1.10	185	120	20	8	14	3-4	912.1	702	338	304	72	306-16	970	.213
Major League totals (12 years)	166	67	.712	2.58	1.01	355	288	41	15	14	3-4	2079.0	1553	667	597	149	554-21	2426	.206

MARTINEZ, RAMON   IF

PERSONAL: Born October 10, 1972, in Philadelphia, Pa. ... 6-1/195. ... Bats right, throws right. ... Full name: Ramon E. Martinez. ... High school: Escuela Superior Catholica (Bayamon, Puerto Rico). ... Junior college: Vernon Regional College (Texas).
TRANSACTIONS/CAREER NOTES: Signed as non-drafted free agent by Kansas City Royals organization (January 15, 1993). ... Traded by Royals to San Francisco Giants (December 9, 1996), completing deal in which Giants traded P Jamie Brewington to Royals for a player to be named later (November 26, 1996). ... On Fresno disabled list (June 10-23, 1999). ... On San Francisco disabled list (August 21-September 5, 1999). ... On disabled list (June 1-16, 2002). ... Granted free agency (December 21, 2002). ... Signed by Chicago Cubs (January 2, 2003).
2003 GAMES PLAYED BY POSITION (MLB): 2B—42, 3B—37, SS—32, 1B—2.

											BATTING									FIELDING	
Year Team (League)	Pos.	G	AB	R	H	2B	3B	HR	RBI	BB	SO	HBP	GDP	SB-CS	Avg.	OBP	SLG	OPS	E	Pct.
1993—GC Royals (GCL)	2B	37	97	16	23	5	0	0	9	8	6	2	5	3-0	.237	.303	.289	.591	5	.973
—Wilmington (Caro.)	2B-SS	24	75	8	19	4	0	0	6	11	9	1	2	1-4	.253	.352	.307	.659	6	.954
1994—Wilmington (Caro.)	2B	90	325	40	87	13	2	2	35	35	25	4	14	6-3	.268	.341	.338	.680	16	.964
—Rockford (Midwest)	2B	6	18	3	5	0	0	0	3	4	2	0	1	1-0	.278	.409	.278	.687	1	.955
1995—Wichita (Texas)	2B-SS	103	393	58	108	20	2	3	51	42	50	4	11	11-8	.275	.344	.359	.703	9	.982
1996—Omaha (A.A.)	2B	85	320	35	81	12	3	6	41	21	34	3	6	3-2	.253	.305	.366	.671	12	.969
—Wichita (Texas)	2B	26	93	16	32	4	1	1	8	7	8	0	4	4-1	.344	.390	.441	.831	6	.956
1997—Shreveport (Texas)	SS	105	404	72	129	32	4	5	54	40	48	3	6	4-5	.319	.382	.455	.838	18	.968
—Phoenix (PCL)	2B-SS	18	57	6	16	2	0	1	7	5	9	0	1	1-0	.281	.333	.368	.702	3	.959
1998—Fresno (PCL)	2B-SS	98	364	58	114	21	2	14	59	38	42	2	11	0-3	.313	.375	.497	.872	10	.980
—San Francisco (N.L.)	2B	19	19	4	6	1	0	0	4	2	0	0	0	0-0	.316	.435	.368	.803	0	1.000
1999—San Francisco (N.L.)	2-S-3-D	61	144	21	38	6	0	5	19	14	17	0	2	1-2	.264	.327	.410	.737	6	.966
—Fresno (PCL) SS-DH-3B	29	114	13	37	7	1	2	17	10	17	0	2	2-0	.325	.376	.456	.832	5	.951
2000—San Francisco (N.L.)	S-2-3-1	88	189	30	57	13	2	6	25	15	22	1	6	3-2	.302	.354	.487	.841	1	.995
2001—San Francisco (N.L.)	3B-2B-SS	128	391	48	99	18	3	5	37	38	52	5	11	1-2	.253	.323	.353	.676	8	.980
2002—San Francisco (N.L.)	S-2-1-0-3	72	181	26	49	10	2	4	25	14	26	4	1	2-0	.271	.335	.414	.749	6	.965
2003—Chicago (N.L.)	2-3-S-1	108	293	30	83	16	1	3	34	24	50	2	8	0-1	.283	.333	.375	.709	10	.966
Major League totals (6 years)		476	1217	159	332	64	8	23	140	109	169	12	28	7-7	.273	.334	.395	.730	33	.975

MARTINEZ, TINO   1B

PERSONAL: Born December 7, 1967, in Tampa, Fla. ... 6-2/230. ... Bats left, throws right. ... Full name: Constantino Martinez. ... High school: Tampa Catholic. ... College: Tampa.
TRANSACTIONS/CAREER NOTES: Selected by Boston Red Sox organization in third round of free-agent draft (June 3, 1985); did not sign. ... Selected by Seattle Mariners organization in first round (14th pick overall) of free-agent draft (June 1, 1988). ... On disabled list (August 10, 1993-remainder of season). ... Traded by Mariners with P Jeff Nelson and P Jim Mecir to New York Yankees for P Sterling Hitchcock and 3B Russ Davis (December 7, 1995). ... Granted free agency (November 5, 2001). ... Signed by St. Louis Cardinals (December 19, 2001).
2003 GAMES PLAYED BY POSITION (MLB): 1B—126, DH—5.

											BATTING									FIELDING	
Year Team (League)	Pos.	G	AB	R	H	2B	3B	HR	RBI	BB	SO	HBP	GDP	SB-CS	Avg.	OBP	SLG	OPS	E	Pct.
1989—Williamsport (East.)	1B	* 137	* 509	51	131	29	2	13	64	59	54	0	11	7-1	.257	.330	.399	.729	7	* .995
1990—Calgary (PCL)	3B-1B	128	453	83	145	28	1	17	93	74	37	3	9	8-5	.320	.413	.499	.912	10	‡ .991
—Seattle (A.L.)	1B	24	68	4	15	4	0	0	5	9	9	0	0	0-0	.221	.308	.279	.587	0	1.000
1991—Calgary (PCL)	3B-1B	122	442	94	144	34	5	18	86	82	44	3	5	3-3	.326	.428	.548	.976	9	.992
—Seattle (A.L.)	DH-1B	36	112	11	23	2	0	4	9	11	24	0	2	0-0	.205	.272	.330	.602	2	.993
1992—Seattle (A.L.)	1B-DH	136	460	53	118	19	2	16	66	42	77	2	24	2-1	.257	.316	.411	.727	4	.995
1993—Seattle (A.L.)	1B-DH	109	408	48	108	25	1	17	60	45	56	5	7	0-3	.265	.343	.456	.799	3	.997
1994—Seattle (A.L.)	1B-DH	97	329	42	86	21	0	20	61	29	52	1	9	1-2	.261	.320	.508	.828	2	.997
1995—Seattle (A.L.)	1B-DH	141	519	92	152	35	3	31	111	62	91	4	10	0-0	.293	.369	.551	.920	8	.993
1996—New York (A.L.)	1B-DH	155	595	82	174	28	0	25	117	68	85	2	18	2-1	.292	.364	.466	.830	5	.996
1997—New York (A.L.)	1B-DH	158	594	96	176	31	2	44	141	75	75	3	15	3-1	.296	.371	.577	.948	8	.994
1998—New York (A.L.)	1B	142	531	92	149	33	1	28	123	61	83	6	18	2-1	.281	.355	.505	.860	10	.992
1999—New York (A.L.)	1B	159	589	95	155	27	2	28	105	69	86	3	14	3-4	.263	.341	.458	.800	7	.995
2000—New York (A.L.)	1B	155	569	69	147	37	4	16	91	52	74	6	16	4-1	.258	.328	.422	.749	7	.994
2001—New York (A.L.)	1B-DH	154	589	89	165	24	2	34	113	42	89	2	12	1-2	.280	.329	.501	.830	5	.996
2002—St. Louis (N.L.)	1B	150	511	63	134	25	1	21	75	58	71	2	12	3-2	.262	.337	.438	.776	5	.996
2003—St. Louis (N.L.)	1B-DH	138	476	66	130	25	2	15	69	53	71	9	14	1-1	.273	.352	.429	.781	3	.997
American League totals (12 years)		1466	5363	773	1468	286	17	263	1002	565	801	36	145	18-16	.274	.343	.481	.824	61	.995
National League totals (2 years)		288	987	129	264	50	3	36	144	111	142	11	26	4-3	.267	.345	.434	.778	8	.997
Major League totals (14 years)		1754	6350	902	1732	336	20	299	1146	676	943	47	171	22-19	.273	.344	.473	.817	69	.995

M

MARTINEZ, VICTOR   C

PERSONAL: Born December 23, 1978, in Ciudad Bolivar, Venezuela. ... 6-2/190. ... Bats both, throws right. ... Full name: Victor Jesus Martinez.
TRANSACTIONS/CAREER NOTES: Signed as non-drafted free agent by Cleveland Indians organization (July 15, 1996). ... On Kinston disabled list (May 25-July 19, 2000). ... Recalled from Buffalo (June 27, 2003). ... Placed on 15-day disabled list (August 9, 2003). ... Sent on minor league rehab assignment (August 30, 2003). ... Recalled from minor league rehab assignment; removed from 15-day disabled list (September 2, 2003).
2003 GAMES PLAYED BY POSITION (MLB): C—40, DH—5.

Year — Team (League)	Pos.	G	AB	R	H	2B	3B	HR	RBI	BB	SO	HBP	GDP	SB-CS	Avg.	OBP	SLG	OPS	E	Pct.
1997— Maracay 1 (VSL)		53	122	21	42	12	0	0	26	32	11	...	...	6-...	.344	...	.443	...	...	...
1998— Guacara 2 (VSL)		55	160	28	43	13	0	1	27	32	14	...	...	8-...	.269	...	.369	...	...	...
1999— Mahoning Valley (NY-P)	C	64	235	37	65	9	0	4	36	27	31	1	4	0-1	.277	.346	.366	.712	8	.984
2000— Kinston (Caro.)	C	26	83	9	18	7	0	0	8	11	5	1	3	1-1	.217	.313	.301	.614	5	.980
— Columbus (S. Atl.)	C	21	70	11	26	9	1	2	12	11	6	1	1	0-0	.371	.452	.614	1.067	2	.988
2001— Kinston (Caro.)	C	114	420	59	138	33	2	10	57	39	60	8	12	3-3	.329	.394	.488	.882	* 16	.985
2002— Akron (East.)	C	121	443	* 84	149	40	0	22	85	58	62	8	10	3-3	.336	.417	.576	.993	10	.988
— Cleveland (A.L.)	C-DH	12	32	2	9	1	0	1	5	3	2	0	1	0-0	.281	.333	.406	.740	1	.983
2003— Buffalo (Int'l)	C-1B-DH	73	274	42	90	19	0	7	45	26	32	8	14	3-5	.328	.395	.474	.869	4	.993
— Akron (East.)	DH-C	3	12	1	4	2	0	0	2	0	1	0	1	0-0	.333	.333	.500	.833	0	1.000
— Cleveland (A.L.)	C-DH	49	159	15	46	4	0	1	16	13	21	1	8	1-1	.289	.345	.333	.678	1	.996
Major League totals (2 years)		61	191	17	55	5	0	2	21	16	23	1	9	1-1	.288	.343	.346	.688	2	.994

MATEO, HENRY   2B

PERSONAL: Born October 14, 1976, in Santo Domingo, Dominican Republic. ... 6-0/180. ... Bats both, throws right. ... Full name: Henry Antonio Valera Mateo. ... Name pronounced: MAH-ta-yo. ... High school: Centro Estudios Libres (Santurce, Puerto Rico).
TRANSACTIONS/CAREER NOTES: Selected by Montreal Expos organization in second round of free-agent draft (June 1, 1995).
2003 GAMES PLAYED BY POSITION (MLB): 2B—43, OF—10, DH—3, SS—2.

Year — Team (League)	Pos.	G	AB	R	H	2B	3B	HR	RBI	BB	SO	HBP	GDP	SB-CS	Avg.	OBP	SLG	OPS	E	Pct.
1995— GC Expos (GCL)	2B-SS	38	122	11	18	0	0	0	6	14	47	5	2	2-7	.148	.261	.148	.408	9	.951
1996— GC Expos (GCL)	2B	14	44	8	11	3	0	0	3	5	11	3	0	5-1	.250	.365	.318	.684	7	.901
1997— Vermont (NYP)	2B	67	228	32	56	9	3	1	31	30	44	7	4	21-11	.246	.348	.325	.673	14	.956
1998— Cape Fear (S. Atl.)	2B	114	416	72	115	20	5	4	41	40	111	13	5	22-16	.276	.355	.377	.733	15	.971
— Jupiter (FSL)	2B	12	43	11	12	3	1	0	6	2	6	2	0	3-0	.279	.333	.395	.729	0	1.000
1999— Jupiter (FSL)	2B	118	447	69	116	27	7	4	58	44	112	10	4	32-16	.260	.335	.378	.713	17	.962
2000— Harrisburg (East.)	2B	140	530	91	152	25	11	5	63	58	97	6	4	48-16	.287	.362	.404	.766	24	.962
2001— Ottawa (Int'l)	2B	118	500	71	134	14	* 12	5	43	33	89	7	2	* 47-14	.268	.322	.374	.696	22	.963
— Montreal (N.L.)	2B	5	9	1	3	1	0	0	0	0	1	0	0	0-0	.333	.333	.444	.778	2	.818
2002— Ottawa (Int'l)	2B-SS	74	285	35	73	10	6	5	25	18	53	3	6	15-6	.256	.306	.386	.692	12	.970
— Montreal (N.L.)	2B-SS	22	23	1	4	0	1	0	0	2	6	0	0	2-0	.174	.240	.261	.501	1	.950
2003— Montreal (N.L.)	2-0-D-S	100	154	29	37	3	1	0	7	11	38	3	0	11-1	.240	.304	.273	.576	4	.973
Major League totals (3 years)		127	186	31	44	4	2	0	7	13	45	3	0	13-1	.237	.297	.280	.577	7	.960

M

MATEO, JULIO   P

PERSONAL: Born August 2, 1977, in Bani, Dominican Republic. ... 6-0/177. ... Throws right, bats right. ... Full name: Julio Cesar Mateo.
TRANSACTIONS/CAREER NOTES: Signed as non-drafted free agent by Seattle Mariners organization (May 15, 1996).
CAREER HITTING: 0-for-0 (.000), 0 R, 0 2B, 0 3B, 0 HR, 0 RBI.

Year — League	W	L	Pct.	ERA	WHIP	G	GS	CG	ShO	Hld.	Sv.-Opp.	IP	H	R	ER	HR	BB-IBB	SO	Avg.
1996— Dom. Mariners (DSL)	4	2	.667	1.74	1.18	14	5	2	1	...	1-...	51.2	42	14	10		19-...	23	...
1997— Ariz. Mariners (Ariz.)	3	1	.750	3.30	1.13	13	6	0	0	...	1-...	60.0	45	32	22	1	23-0	54	.205
1998— Lancaster (Calif.)	0	0	...	6.75	1.50	1	0	0	0	...	0-...	1.1	1	1	1	1	1-0	1	.250
— Everett (Northwest)	3	3	.500	4.70	1.49	28	0	0	0	...	4-...	38.1	40	25	20	6	17-1	37	.274
1999— Wisconsin (Midw.)	1	3	.250	4.34	1.34	20	0	0	0	...	4-...	29.0	31	18	14	2	8-2	27	.261
2000— Wisconsin (Midw.)	4	8	.333	4.19	1.25	36	1	0	0	...	4-...	68.2	63	38	32	12	23-1	73	.241
2001— San Bernardino (Calif.) ...	5	4	.556	2.86	1.12	56	0	0	0	...	26-...	66.0	58	28	21	5	16-5	79	.230
2002— San Antonio (Texas)	1	0	1.000	0.52	0.58	12	0	0	0	...	0-...	17.1	7	3	1	2	3-0	18	.121
— Tacoma (PCL)	4	2	.667	4.06	1.48	20	0	0	0	...	6-...	31.0	39	15	14	2	7-1	23	.317
— Seattle (A.L.)	0	0	...	4.29	1.52	12	0	0	0	2	0-0	21.0	20	10	10	2	12-0	15	.247
2003— Seattle (A.L.)	4	0	1.000	3.15	0.96	50	0	0	0	2	1-1	85.2	69	32	30	14	13-1	71	.220
Major League totals (2 years)	4	0	1.000	3.38	1.07	62	0	0	0	4	1-1	106.2	89	42	40	16	25-1	86	.225

MATEO, RUBEN   OF

PERSONAL: Born February 10, 1978, in San Cristobal, Dominican Republic. ... 6-0/185. ... Bats right, throws right. ... Full name: Ruben Amaurys Mateo. ... Name pronounced: ma-TAY-oh. ... High school: Liceo Jose Manuel Maria Balance (San Cristobal, Dominican Republic).
TRANSACTIONS/CAREER NOTES: Signed as non-drafted free agent by Texas Rangers organization (October 24, 1994). ... On Tulsa disabled list (April 13-May 13, 1998). ... On Texas disabled list (June 23-July 9 and August 5, 1999-remainder of season); included rehabilitation assignment to Oklahoma (July 6-9). ... On disabled list (June 3, 2000-remainder of season). ... Traded by Rangers with 3B Edwin Encarnacion to Cincinnati Reds for P Rob Bell (June 15, 2001). ... On Louisville disabled list (September 11-13, 2001). ... On Louisville disabled list (July 4-24 and July 25-August 3, 2002). ... Designated for assignment (May 13, 2003). ... Sent outright to Louisville (May 15, 2003). ... Contract purchased from Louisville (July 18, 2003).
2003 GAMES PLAYED BY POSITION (MLB): OF—54.

Year — Team (League)	Pos.	G	AB	R	H	2B	3B	HR	RBI	BB	SO	HBP	GDP	SB-CS	Avg.	OBP	SLG	OPS	E	Pct.
1995— Dom. Rangers (DSL)	OF	48	176	30	53	9	3	4	42	20	23	...	...	1-2	.301	...	.455	...	1	.982
1996— Char., S.C. (SAL)	OF-DH	134	496	65	129	30	4	8	58	26	78	12	8	30-9	.260	.309	.401	.710	7	.970
1997— Charlotte (Fla. St.)	OF-DH	99	385	63	121	23	8	12	67	22	55	6	16	20-5	.314	.359	.509	.868	8	.958
1998— Tulsa (Texas)	OF	107	433	79	134	32	3	18	75	30	56	15	7	18-8	.309	.371	.522	.893	7	.970
— Charlotte (Fla. St.)	OF	1	4	0	0	0	0	0	1	0	1	0	0	0-0	.000	.000	.000	.000	0	1.000
1999— Texas (A.L.)	OF-DH	32	122	16	29	9	1	5	18	4	28	1	2	3-0	.238	.268	.451	.719	0	1.000
— Oklahoma (PCL)	OF	63	253	53	85	12	0	18	62	14	36	8	5	6-3	.336	.385	.597	.982	5	.963

– 242 –

Year	Team (League)	Pos.	G	AB	R	H	2B	3B	HR	RBI	BB	SO	HBP	GDP	SB-CS	Avg.	OBP	SLG	OPS	E	Pct.
2000— Texas (A.L.)		OF	52	206	32	60	11	0	7	19	10	34	5	5	6-0	.291	.339	.447	.786	3	.980
2001— Texas (A.L.)		OF	40	129	18	32	5	2	1	13	9	28	6	4	1-0	.248	.322	.341	.663	1	.986
— Oklahoma (PCL)		OF	14	51	3	11	3	0	1	8	2	8	0	1	1-2	.216	.241	.333	.574	1	.957
— Louisville (Int'l)		OF	65	251	35	63	16	4	2	25	13	45	8	7	2-0	.251	.307	.371	.677	5	.954
2002— Louisville (Int'l)		OF	52	209	37	63	14	0	9	23	11	40	3	2	6-2	.301	.342	.498	.840	3	.967
— Cincinnati (N.L.)		OF	46	86	11	22	6	0	2	7	6	20	2	1	0-0	.256	.319	.395	.714	0	1.000
2003— Louisville (Int'l)		OF	57	217	36	71	15	1	9	50	26	34	5	3	3-1	.327	.408	.530	.938	2	.984
— Cincinnati (N.L.)		OF	74	207	16	50	9	0	3	18	12	53	3	4	0-0	.242	.290	.329	.619	2	.982
American League totals (3 years)			124	457	66	121	25	3	13	50	23	90	12	11	10-0	.265	.316	.418	.734	4	.986
National League totals (2 years)			120	293	27	72	15	0	5	25	18	73	5	5	0-0	.246	.299	.348	.647	2	.986
Major League totals (5 years)			244	750	93	193	40	3	18	75	41	163	17	16	10-0	.257	.309	.391	.700	6	.986

MATHENY, MIKE — C

PERSONAL: Born September 22, 1970, in Reynoldsburg, Ohio. ... 6-3/220. ... Bats right, throws right. ... Full name: Michael Scott Matheny. ... Name pronounced: ma-THEE-nee. ... High school: Reynoldsburg (Ohio). ... College: Michigan.

TRANSACTIONS/CAREER NOTES: Selected by Toronto Blue Jays organization in 31st round of free-agent draft (June 1, 1988); did not sign. ... Selected by Milwaukee Brewers organization in eighth round of free-agent draft (June 3, 1991). ... On Milwaukee suspended list (June 20-23, 1996). ... On Milwaukee disabled list (June 15-July 12, 1998); included rehabilitation assignment to Beloit (July 11-13). ... Granted free agency (December 21, 1998). ... Signed by Blue Jays (December 23, 1998). ... Released by Blue Jays (November 16, 1999). ... Signed by St. Louis Cardinals (December 15, 1999). ... Suspended by Major League Baseball for two games (September 25, 2003). ... Reinstated (September 28, 2003).

2003 GAMES PLAYED BY POSITION (MLB): C—138, 1B—4.

Year	Team (League)	Pos.	G	AB	R	H	2B	3B	HR	RBI	BB	SO	HBP	GDP	SB-CS	Avg.	OBP	SLG	OPS	E	Pct.
1991— Helena (Pio.)		C	64	253	35	72	14	0	2	34	19	52	6	10	2-4	.285	.348	.364	.711	5	.991
1992— Stockton (Calif.)		C	106	333	42	73	13	2	6	46	35	81	3	11	2-2	.219	.297	.324	.621	8	.989
1993— El Paso (Texas)		C	107	339	39	86	21	2	2	28	17	73	2	6	1-4	.254	.292	.345	.638	9	.986
1994— Milwaukee (A.L.)		C	28	53	3	12	3	0	1	2	3	13	2	1	0-1	.226	.293	.340	.633	1	.989
— New Orleans (A.A.)		C-DH-1B	57	177	20	39	10	1	4	21	16	39	4	5	1-1	.220	.299	.356	.655	5	.987
1995— Milwaukee (A.L.)		C	80	166	13	41	9	1	0	21	12	28	2	3	2-1	.247	.306	.313	.619	4	.986
— New Orleans (A.A.)		C	6	17	3	6	2	0	3	4	0	5	3	0	0-0	.353	.450	1.000	1.450	0	1.000
1996— Milwaukee (A.L.)		C-DH	106	313	31	64	15	2	8	46	14	80	3	9	3-2	.204	.243	.342	.584	8	.985
— New Orleans (A.A.)		C-DH	20	66	3	15	4	0	1	6	2	17	0	1	1-0	.227	.246	.333	.580	0	1.000
1997— Milwaukee (A.L.)		C-1B	123	320	29	78	16	1	4	32	17	68	7	9	0-1	.244	.294	.338	.631	5	.993
1998— Milwaukee (N.L.)		C	108	320	24	76	13	0	6	27	11	63	7	6	1-0	.238	.278	.334	.612	8	.987
— Beloit (Midw.)		DH-C	2	8	1	2	1	0	0	2	1	3	0	0	0-0	.250	.333	.375	.708	0	1.000
1999— Toronto (A.L.)		C	57	163	16	35	6	0	3	17	12	37	1	3	0-0	.215	.271	.307	.578	2	.995
2000— St. Louis (N.L.)		C-1B	128	417	43	109	22	1	6	47	32	96	4	11	0-0	.261	.317	.362	.679	5	.994
2001— St. Louis (N.L.)		C-1B	121	381	40	83	12	0	7	42	28	76	4	11	0-1	.218	.276	.304	.581	4	.995
2002— St. Louis (N.L.)		C-1B	110	315	31	77	12	1	3	35	32	49	2	3	1-3	.244	.313	.317	.630	4	.994
2003— St. Louis (N.L.)		C-1B	141	441	43	111	18	2	8	47	44	81	2	11	1-1	.252	.320	.356	.676	0	1.000
American League totals (5 years)			394	1015	92	230	49	4	16	118	58	226	15	25	5-5	.227	.276	.330	.607	20	.990
National League totals (5 years)			608	1874	181	456	77	4	30	198	147	365	19	42	3-5	.243	.303	.337	.639	21	.995
Major League totals (10 years)			1002	2889	273	686	126	8	46	316	205	591	34	67	8-10	.237	.293	.334	.628	41	.993

MATOS, JULIUS — IF

PERSONAL: Born December 12, 1974, in New York, N.Y. ... 5-11/170. ... Bats right, throws right. ... High school: William Horlick (Wis.). ... Junior college: South Suburban College (Ill.).

TRANSACTIONS/CAREER NOTES: Selected by Cleveland Indians organization in 16th round of free-agent draft (June 2, 1994). ... Released by Indians (March 28, 1996). ... Signed by Thunder Bay of Northern League (May 1996). ... Signed by Sioux City of Northern League (May 1997). ... Contract purchased by Arizona Diamondbacks organization from Sioux City (September 8, 1997). ... Selected by San Diego Padres from Diamondbacks organization in Rule 5 minor league draft (December 13, 1999). ... Granted free agency (October 15, 2001). ... Re-signed by Padres organization (December 6, 2001). ... Granted free agency (October 15, 2002). ... Signed by Kansas City Royals (December 3, 2002).

2003 GAMES PLAYED BY POSITION (MLB): 3B—13, 2B—11, SS—2, DH—1, OF—1.

Year	Team (League)	Pos.	G	AB	R	H	2B	3B	HR	RBI	BB	SO	HBP	GDP	SB-CS	Avg.	OBP	SLG	OPS	E	Pct.
1994— Watertown (NYP)		SS-2B	43	138	13	34	2	2	0	18	13	33	0	6	3-2	.246	.307	.290	.597	19	.912
1995— Columbus (S. Atl.)		S-O-2-3	52	155	16	38	7	3	0	13	11	21	3	8	2-2	.245	.308	.329	.637	14	.929
1996— Thund. Bay (Nor.)			82	295	33	81	13	0	3	32	14	48	2	9	8-7	.275	.311	.349	.660	...	...
1997— Sioux City (Nor.)		SS	83	353	64	94	12	3	6	44	20	38	4	4	8-7	.266	.311	.368	.680	24	.943
1998— High Desert (Calif.)		SS	111	439	70	132	27	4	4	60	23	40	2	9	19-13	.301	.333	.408	.740	33	.941
1999— El Paso (Texas)		SS-2B	120	425	54	119	17	5	5	41	13	37	1	10	5-2	.280	.301	.379	.680	27	.954
2000— Mobile (Sou.)		SS-2B	135	546	61	144	30	4	5	35	31	57	2	13	11-9	.264	.306	.346	.652	29	.954
2001— Mobile (Sou.)		SS-2B	19	67	13	22	6	0	0	2	1	5	1	2	1-2	.328	.343	.418	.761	5	.941
— Portland (PCL)		SS-2B	106	383	40	107	12	2	7	34	15	48	6	6	6-8	.279	.314	.376	.690	14	.970
2002— Portland (PCL)		SS-2B	50	186	20	58	17	0	4	26	9	20	2	6	1-2	.312	.345	.468	.813	8	.961
— San Diego (N.L.)		2-3-S-O-1-D	76	185	19	44	3	0	2	19	9	33	2	5	1-1	.238	.279	.286	.566	9	.961
2003— Omaha (PCL)		SS-2B	92	370	44	107	19	0	7	48	13	31	8	7	10-5	.289	.325	.397	.722	19	.950
— Kansas City (A.L.)		3-2-S-D-O	28	57	7	15	1	0	2	7	1	12	0	2	1-0	.263	.276	.386	.662	1	.979
American League totals (1 year)			28	57	7	15	1	0	2	7	1	12	0	2	1-0	.263	.276	.386	.662	1	.979
National League totals (1 year)			76	185	19	44	3	0	2	19	9	33	2	5	1-1	.238	.279	.286	.566	9	.961
Major League totals (2 years)			104	242	26	59	4	0	4	26	10	45	2	7	2-1	.244	.278	.310	.588	10	.964

MATOS, LUIS — OF

PERSONAL: Born October 30, 1978, in Bayamon, Puerto Rico. ... 6-0/208. ... Bats right, throws right. ... Full name: Luis David Matos. ... Name pronounced: MAH-tose. ... High school: Disciple of Christ Academy (Bayamon, Puerto Rico).

TRANSACTIONS/CAREER NOTES: Selected by Baltimore Orioles organization in 10th round of free-agent draft (June 4, 1996). ... On Baltimore disabled list (March 30-August 24, 2001); included rehabilitation assignments to Gulf Coast Orioles (August 7-10), Frederick (August 11-13) and Bowie (August 14-24). ... On Baltimore disabled list (March 29-June 6, 2002); included rehabilitation assignment to Frederick (June 3-6).

2003 GAMES PLAYED BY POSITION (MLB): OF—107, DH—2.

Year	Team (League)	Pos.	G	AB	R	H	2B	3B	HR	RBI	BB	SO	HBP	GDP	SB-CS	Avg.	OBP	SLG	OPS	E	Pct.
1996—GC Orioles (GCL)	OF	43	130	21	38	2	0	0	13	15	18	2	3	12-7	.292	.374	.308	.682	1	.983
1997—Delmarva (S. Atl.)	OF	36	119	10	25	1	2	0	13	9	21	2	2	8-5	.210	.275	.252	.527	2	.972
—Bluefield (Appal.)	OF	61	240	37	66	7	3	2	35	20	36	4	5	26-4	.275	.340	.354	.694	3	.977
1998—Delmarva (S. Atl.)	OF	133	503	73	137	26	6	7	32	38	90	7	9	42-14	.272	.328	.390	.718	10	.964
—Bowie (East.)	OF	5	19	2	5	0	0	1	3	1	1	0	0	1-1	.263	.300	.421	.721	1	.833
1999—Frederick (Carolina)	OF	68	273	40	81	15	1	7	41	20	35	2	6	27-6	.297	.343	.436	.779	2	.987
—Bowie (East.)	OF	66	283	41	67	11	1	9	36	15	39	1	6	14-4	.237	.272	.378	.650	3	.982
2000—Rochester (Int'l)		11	35	2	6	1	0	0	0	3	8	1	0	2-0	.171	.256	.200	.456	0	1.000
—Bowie (East.)	OF	50	181	26	49	7	5	2	33	17	23	5	3	8-8	.271	.345	.398	.742	2	.984
—Baltimore (A.L.)	OF-DH	72	182	21	41	6	3	1	17	12	30	3	7	13-4	.225	.281	.308	.589	2	.988
2001—GC Orioles (GCL)	DH	3	14	1	4	2	0	0	2	0	3	0	0	0-0	.286	.286	.429	.714	...	...
—Frederick (Carolina)	DH	2	7	3	3	0	0	1	2	1	3	0	0	0-0	.429	.500	.857	1.357	...	...
—Bowie (East.)	OF	13	46	6	14	5	0	1	8	5	7	1	0	0-1	.304	.385	.478	.863	1	.955
—Baltimore (A.L.)	OF	31	98	16	21	7	0	4	12	11	30	1	1	7-0	.214	.300	.408	.708	1	.985
2002—Frederick (Carolina)	OF	3	12	2	4	1	0	0	1	2	3	0	0	0-0	.333	.429	.417	.845	0	1.000
—Bowie (East.)	OF	62	218	34	60	14	2	9	40	32	45	2	6	14-4	.275	.370	.482	.852	1	.992
—Baltimore (A.L.)	OF-DH	17	31	0	4	1	0	0	1	1	6	0	1	1-0	.129	.156	.161	.318	0	1.000
2003—Ottawa (Int'l)	OF	45	175	28	53	16	4	1	25	13	34	1	8	6-1	.303	.347	.457	.804	1	.990
—Baltimore (A.L.)	OF-DH	109	439	70	133	23	3	13	45	28	90	7	9	15-7	.303	.353	.458	.811	4	.987
Major League totals (4 years)		229	750	107	199	37	6	18	75	52	156	11	18	36-11	.265	.321	.403	.723	7	.988

MATRANGA, DAVE — 2B

PERSONAL: Born January 8, 1977, in Orange, Calif. ... 6-0/170. ... Bats right, throws right. ... Full name: David Michael Matranga. ... High school: Aliso Viejo (Calif.). ... College: Pepperdine.

TRANSACTIONS/CAREER NOTES: Selected by Houston Astros organization in sixth round of free-agent draft (June 2, 1998).

2003 GAMES PLAYED BY POSITION (MLB): 2B—2.

Year	Team (League)	Pos.	G	AB	R	H	2B	3B	HR	RBI	BB	SO	HBP	GDP	SB-CS	Avg.	OBP	SLG	OPS	E	Pct.
1998—Auburn (NY-Penn)	SS	40	144	34	44	13	1	4	24	25	38	5	0	16-3	.306	.423	.493	.916	10	.943
1999—Kissimmee (Fla. St.)	SS	124	472	70	109	20	4	6	48	48	118	12	3	17-10	.231	.341	.328	.670	28	.954
2000—Round Rock (Texas)	SS	120	373	50	87	14	3	6	44	48	99	17	1	5-5	.233	.346	.335	.681	27	.951
2001—New Orleans (PCL)	2B-SS	4	16	3	5	1	0	1	3	0	5	1	0	1-0	.313	.333	.563	.896	0	1.000
—Round Rock (Texas)	2B	103	387	78	117	34	2	10	60	45	91	14	2	17-7	.302	.391	.478	.869	6	.987
2002—New Orleans (PCL) 2B-SS-3B		101	300	47	82	15	3	7	40	27	79	6	4	7-2	.273	.342	.413	.756	6	.982
2003—Houston (N.L.)	2B	6	5	1	1	0	0	1	1	0	2	0	0	0-0	.200	.200	.800	1.000	0	1.000
—New Orleans (PCL) 2-S-3-D-O		102	315	34	76	16	4	3	25	21	71	4	3	3-3	.241	.296	.346	.642	8	.980
Major League totals (1 year)		6	5	1	1	0	0	1	1	0	2	0	0	0-0	.200	.200	.800	1.000	0	1.000

MATSUI, HIDEKI — OF

PERSONAL: Born June 12, 1974, in Kanazawa, Japan. ... 6-2/210. ... Bats left, throws right. ... Name pronounced: mat-SOO-ee.

TRANSACTIONS/CAREER NOTES: Signed as non-drafted free agent by New York Yankees (December 19, 2002).

2003 GAMES PLAYED BY POSITION (MLB): OF—159, DH—4.

Year	Team (League)	Pos.	G	AB	R	H	2B	3B	HR	RBI	BB	SO	HBP	GDP	SB-CS	Avg.	OBP	SLG	OPS	E	Pct.
1993—Yomiuri (Jp. Cen.)		57	184	26	41	9	0	11	27	17	50	2	...	1-0	.223	.296	.451	.747	1	...
1994—Yomiuri (Jp. Cen.)		130	503	70	148	23	4	20	66	57	101	4	...	6-3	.294	.368	.475	.843	5	...
1995—Yomiuri (Jp. Cen.)		131	501	76	142	31	1	22	80	62	93	2	...	9-7	.283	.363	.481	.844	3	...
1996—Yomiuri (Jp. Cen.)		130	487	*97	153	34	1	38	99	71	98	4	...	7-2	.314	.401	.622	1.023	6	...
1997—Yomiuri (Jp. Cen.)		135	484	93	144	18	0	37	103	100	84	6	...	9-3	.298	.419	.564	.984	7	...
1998—Yomiuri (Jp. Cen.)		135	487	*103	142	24	3	*34	*100	104	101	8	...	3-5	.292	.421	.563	.984	4	...
1999—Yomiuri (Jp. Cen.)		135	471	100	143	24	2	42	95	93	99	2	...	0-4	.304	.416	.631	1.047	1	...
2000—Yomiuri (Jp. Cen.)		135	474	*116	150	32	1	*42	*108	106	108	2	...	5-2	.316	.438	.654	1.092	2	...
2001—Yomiuri (Jp. Cen.)		140	481	*107	160	23	3	36	104	120	96	3	...	3-3	*.333	.463	.617	1.081	6	...
2002—Yomiuri (Jp. Cen.)		140	500	*112	167	27	1	*50	*107	114	104	6	...	3-4	.334	.461	.692	1.153	2	...
2003—New York (A.L.)	OF-DH	*163	623	82	179	42	1	16	106	63	86	3	25	2-2	.287	.353	.435	.788	8	.977
Major League totals (1 year)		163	623	82	179	42	1	16	106	63	86	3	25	2-2	.287	.353	.435	.788	8	.977

MATTHEWS JR., GARY — OF

PERSONAL: Born August 25, 1974, in San Francisco, Calif. ... 6-3/225. ... Bats both, throws right. ... Full name: Gary Nathaniel Matthews Jr.. ... High school: Granada Hills (Calif.). ... Junior college: Mission (Calif.) Community College.

TRANSACTIONS/CAREER NOTES: Selected by San Diego Padres organization in 13th round of free-agent draft (June 3, 1993). ... Traded by Padres to Chicago Cubs for P Rodney Myers (March 23, 2000). ... Claimed on waivers by Pittsburgh Pirates (August 10, 2001). ... Traded by Pirates to New York Mets for cash (December 28, 2001). ... Traded by Mets to Baltimore Orioles for P John Bale (April 3, 2002). ... On Baltimore disabled list (August 25-September 11, 2002). ... Claimed by San Diego off waivers from Baltimore (May 23, 2003). ... Contract purchased by San Diego (May 23, 2003).

2003 GAMES PLAYED BY POSITION (MLB): OF—132, DH—1.

Year	Team (League)	Pos.	G	AB	R	H	2B	3B	HR	RBI	BB	SO	HBP	GDP	SB-CS	Avg.	OBP	SLG	OPS	E	Pct.
1994—Spokane (N'west)	2B-OF	52	191	23	40	6	1	0	18	19	58	2	4	3-5	.209	.286	.251	.538	4	.961
1995—Clinton (Midw.)	OF	128	421	57	100	18	4	2	40	68	109	6	8	28-8	.238	.349	.344	.663	9	.966
1996—Rancho Cuca. (Calif.)	OF	123	435	65	118	21	11	4	54	60	102	6	11	7-8	.271	.366	.418	.784	16	.934
1997—Rancho Cuca. (Calif.)	OF	69	268	66	81	15	4	8	40	49	57	3	4	10-4	.302	.416	.478	.893	5	.959
—Mobile (Sou.)	OF	28	90	14	22	4	1	2	12	15	29	1	1	3-1	.244	.352	.378	.730	2	.960
1998—Mobile (Sou.)	OF	72	254	62	78	15	4	7	51	55	50	1	6	11-1	.307	.428	.480	.908	1	.995
1999—Las Vegas (PCL)	OF	121	422	57	108	23	3	9	52	58	104	7	13	17-6	.256	.352	.386	.739	7	.976
—San Diego (N.L.)	OF	23	36	4	8	0	0	0	7	9	9	0	1	2-0	.222	.378	.222	.600	0	1.000
2000—Iowa (PCL)	OF	60	211	27	51	11	3	5	22	18	41	0	4	6-1	.242	.300	.393	.693	4	.970
—Chicago (N.L.)	OF	80	158	24	30	1	2	4	14	15	28	1	2	3-0	.190	.264	.297	.562	2	.978

M

Year	Team (League)	Pos.	G	AB	R	H	2B	3B	HR	RBI	BB	SO	HBP	GDP	SB-CS	Avg.	OBP	SLG	OPS	E	Pct.
2001—Chicago (N.L.)	OF	106	258	41	56	9	1	9	30	38	55	1	4	5-3	.217	.320	.364	.684	4	.976
—Pittsburgh (N.L.)	OF	46	147	22	36	6	1	5	14	22	45	0	4	3-2	.245	.341	.401	.743	3	.971
2002—New York (N.L.)		2	1	0	0	0	0	0	0	0	0	0	0	0-0	.000	.000	.000	.000	...	...
—Baltimore (A.L.)	OF-DH	109	344	54	95	25	3	7	38	43	69	1	4	15-5	.276	.355	.427	.782	6	.969
2003—Baltimore (A.L.)	OF-DH	41	162	21	33	12	1	2	20	9	29	1	4	0-3	.204	.250	.327	.577	0	1.000
—San Diego (N.L.)	OF	103	306	50	83	19	1	4	22	34	66	1	4	12-5	.271	.346	.379	.725	1	.993
American League totals (2 years)		150	506	75	128	37	4	9	58	52	98	2	8	15-8	.253	.323	.395	.718	6	.979
National League totals (5 years)		360	906	141	213	35	5	22	87	118	203	3	15	25-10	.235	.325	.358	.683	10	.981
Major League totals (5 years)		510	1412	216	341	72	9	31	145	170	301	5	23	40-18	.242	.324	.371	.695	16	.981

MATTHEWS, MIKE — P

PERSONAL: Born October 24, 1973, in Fredericksburg, Va. ... 6-2/205. ... Throws left, bats left. ... Full name: Michael Scott Matthews. ... High school: Woodbridge Senior (Va.). ... Junior college: Montgomery (Md.) Community College.

TRANSACTIONS/CAREER NOTES: Selected by Cleveland Indians organization in second round of free-agent draft (June 1, 1992). ... On Watertown disabled list (June 17, 1993-entire season). ... On disabled list (June 7-28, 1995). ... On disabled list (June 8-July 1, 1998). ... Traded by Indians to Boston Red Sox for IF Jose Olmeda (August 4, 1999). ... Traded by Red Sox with C David Menham to St. Louis Cardinals for P Kent Mercker (August 24, 1999). ... On St. Louis disabled list (July 16, 2000-remainder of season). ... On St. Louis disabled list (August 21-September 11, 2002). ... Traded by Cardinals to Milwaukee Brewers (September 11, 2002), completing deal in which Brewers traded P Jamey Wright and cash to Cardinals for OF Chris Morris and a player to be named later (August 29, 2002). ... Claimed on waivers by San Diego Padres (March 26, 2003).

CAREER HITTING: 3-for-25 (.120), 2 R, 0 2B, 0 3B, 1 HR, 1 RBI.

Year	League	W	L	Pct.	ERA	WHIP	G	GS	CG	ShO	Hld.	Sv.-Opp.	IP	H	R	ER	HR	BB-IBB	SO	Avg.
1992—Burlington (Appal.)	7	0	1.000	1.01	0.96	10	10	0	0	...	0-...	62.1	33	13	7	1	27-0	55	.156
—Watertown (NYP)	1	0	1.000	3.27	1.64	2	2	2	0	...	0-...	11.0	10	4	4	0	8-0	5	.263
1993—											Did not play.								
1994—Columbus (S. Atl.)	6	8	.429	3.08	1.37	23	23	0	0	...	0-...	119.2	120	53	41	8	44-1	99	.270
1995—Cant./Akr. (Eastern)	5	8	.385	5.93	1.68	15	15	1	0	...	0-...	74.1	82	62	49	6	43-1	37	.283
1996—Cant./Akr. (Eastern)	9	11	.450	4.66	1.55	27	27	3	0	...	0-...	162.1	178	96	84	13	74-3	112	.287
1997—Buffalo (A.A.)	0	2	.000	7.71	2.00	5	5	0	0	...	0-...	21.0	32	19	18	7	10-0	17	.344
—Akron (East.)	6	8	.429	3.82	1.53	19	19	3	1	...	0-...	113.0	116	62	48	13	57-0	69	.273
1998—Buffalo (Int'l)	9	6	.600	4.63	1.57	24	23	0	0	...	0-...	130.1	137	79	67	19	68-1	86	.275
1999—Buffalo (Int'l)	1	2	.333	7.59	1.92	25	0	0	0	...	0-...	21.1	23	18	18	3	18-0	16	.303
—Akron (East.)	0	5	.000	8.77	1.99	6	6	0	0	...	0-...	25.2	36	30	25	7	15-0	10	.336
—Trenton (East.)	0	0	...	4.63	1.71	3	3	0	0	...	0-...	11.2	11	7	6	1	9-0	8	.268
—Arkansas (Texas)	2	0	1.000	0.00	0.33	2	2	1	1	...	0-...	12.0	3	0	0	0	1-0	10	.079
2000—Memphis (PCL)	3	1	.750	3.12	1.25	9	9	0	0	...	0-...	52.0	33	19	18	4	32-1	50	.182
—St. Louis (N.L.)	0	0	...	11.57	2.68	14	0	0	0	2	0-0	9.1	15	12	12	2	10-2	8	.349
2001—St. Louis (N.L.)	3	4	.429	3.24	1.20	51	10	0	0	3	1-3	89.0	74	32	32	11	33-4	72	.227
2002—St. Louis (N.L.)	2	1	.667	3.89	1.49	43	0	0	0	4	0-2	41.2	40	21	18	5	22-2	32	.260
—Milwaukee (N.L.)	0	0	...	4.50	2.50	4	0	0	0	0	0-0	4.0	3	2	2	0	7-1	2	.214
2003—San Diego (N.L.)	6	4	.600	4.45	1.45	77	0	0	0	16	0-3	64.2	65	34	32	4	29-5	44	.271
Major League totals (4 years)	11	9	.550	4.14	1.43	189	10	0	0	25	1-8	208.2	197	101	96	22	101-14	158	.254

MAY, DARRELL — P

PERSONAL: Born June 13, 1972, in San Bernardino, Calif. ... 6-2/185. ... Throws left, bats left. ... Full name: Darrell Kevin May. ... High school: Rogue River (Ore.). ... Junior college: Sacramento (Calif.) Community College.

TRANSACTIONS/CAREER NOTES: Selected by Atlanta Braves organization in 46th round of free-agent draft (June 1, 1992). ... Claimed on waivers by Pittsburgh Pirates (April 4, 1996). ... Claimed on waivers by California Angels (September 6, 1996). ... Angels franchise renamed Anaheim Angels for 1997 season. ... Released by Angels (March 27, 1998). ... Played with Hanshin Tigers of Japan Central League (1998-99). ... Played with Yomiuri Giants of Japan Central League (2000-01). ... Signed by Kansas City Royals organization (December 17, 2001). ... On Kansas City disabled list (March 27-April 13 and April 14-May 18, 2002) included rehabilitation assignments to Omaha (April 8-9 and May 14-18) and Wichita (May 8-13).

CAREER HITTING: 1-for-13 (.077), 1 R, 0 2B, 0 3B, 0 HR, 0 RBI.

Year	League	W	L	Pct.	ERA	WHIP	G	GS	CG	ShO	Hld.	Sv.-Opp.	IP	H	R	ER	HR	BB-IBB	SO	Avg.
1992—GC Braves (GCL)	4	3	.571	1.36	0.89	12	7	0	0	...	1-...	53.0	34	13	8	0	13-0	61	.182
1993—Macon (S. Atl.)	10	4	.714	2.24	0.99	17	17	0	0	...	0-...	104.1	81	29	26	6	22-1	111	.213
—Durham (Caro.)	5	2	.714	2.09	1.16	9	9	0	0	...	0-...	51.2	44	18	12	4	16-0	47	.232
1994—Durham (Caro.)	8	2	.800	3.01	1.22	12	12	1	0	...	0-...	74.2	74	29	25	6	17-1	73	.259
—Greenville (Sou.)	5	3	.625	3.11	1.23	11	11	1	0	...	0-...	63.2	61	25	22	4	17-0	42	.251
1995—Greenville (Sou.)	2	8	.200	3.55	1.11	15	15	0	0	...	0-...	91.1	81	44	36	18	20-0	79	.233
—Richmond (Int'l)	4	2	.667	3.71	1.35	9	9	0	0	...	0-...	51.0	53	21	21	1	16-1	42	.270
—Atlanta (N.L.)	0	0	...	11.25	2.50	2	0	0	0	0	0-0	4.0	10	5	5	0	0-0	1	.500
1996—Calgary (PCL)	7	6	.538	4.10	1.38	23	22	1	1	...	0-...	131.2	146	64	60	17	36-6	75	.284
—Pittsburgh (N.L.)	0	1	.000	9.35	2.19	5	2	0	0	1	0-0	8.2	15	10	9	5	4-0	5	.357
—California (A.L.)	0	0	...	10.13	1.88	5	0	0	0	0	0-0	2.2	3	3	3	1	2-0	1	.333
1997—Vancouver (PCL)	7	5	.583	3.26	1.20	13	12	2	2	...	0-...	80.0	65	31	29	10	31-0	62	.223
—Anaheim (A.L.)	2	1	.667	5.23	1.57	29	2	0	0	2	0-1	51.2	56	31	30	6	25-2	42	.277
1998—Hanshin (Jp. Cn.)	4	9	.308	3.47	1.37	21	21	1	1	...	0-...	129.2	122	55	50	...	55-...	94	...
—Hanshin (Jp. West.)	1	2	.333	5.82	1.24	5	3	0	0	...	0-...	17.0	19	11	11	...	2-...	11	...
1999—Hanshin (Jp. Cn.)	6	7	.462	4.25	1.24	18	18	0	0	...	0-...	112.1	101	56	53	...	38-...	113	...
—Hanshin (Jp. West.)	1	0	1.000	0.00	0.60	2	2	0	0	...	0-...	10.0	4	1	0	...	2-...	12	...
2000—Yomiuri (Jp. Cen.)	12	7	.632	2.95	1.05	24	24	3	3	...	0-...	155.1	123	52	51	...	40-...	165	...
—Yomiuri (Jp. East.)	0	0	...	0.75	1	0	0	0	0	...	0-...	4.0	2	0	0	...	1-...	4	...
2001—Yomiuri (Jp. Cen.)	10	8	.556	4.13	1.29	26	26	1	0	...	0-...	159.0	160	74	73	...	45-...	168	...
2002—Omaha (PCL)	1	0	1.000	0.75	0.67	2	2	0	0	...	0-...	12.0	8	1	1	0	0-0	9	.471
—Kansas City (A.L.)	4	10	.286	5.35	1.48	30	21	2	1	0	0-1	131.1	144	83	78	28	50-3	95	.277
—Wichita (Texas)	0	0	...	2.08	1.15	1	1	0	0	...	0-...	4.1	4	1	1	0	1-0	5	.235
2003—Kansas City (A.L.)	10	8	.556	3.77	1.19	35	32	2	1	0	0-1	210.0	197	98	88	31	53-1	115	.246
American League totals (4 years)	16	19	.457	5.34	1.34	99	55	4	2	2	0-3	395.2	400	215	199	66	130-6	253	.261
National League totals (2 years)	0	1	.000	9.95	2.29	7	2	0	0	1	0-0	12.2	25	15	14	5	4-0	6	.403
Major League totals (5 years)	16	20	.444	4.69	1.37	106	57	4	2	3	0-3	408.1	425	230	213	71	134-6	259	.266

M

MAYNE, BRENT — C

PERSONAL: Born April 19, 1968, in Loma Linda, Calif. ... 6-1/190. ... Bats left, throws right. ... Full name: Brent Danem Mayne. ... High school: Costa Mesa (Calif.). ... College: Cal State Fullerton.

TRANSACTIONS/CAREER NOTES: Selected by Kansas City Royals organization in first round (13th pick overall) of free-agent draft (June 5, 1989). ... On disabled list (July 24, 1989-remainder of season). ... Traded by Royals to New York Mets for OF Al Shirley (December 19, 1995). ... Granted free agency (December 7, 1996). ... Signed by Seattle Mariners organization (January 10, 1997). ... Released by Mariners (March 28, 1997). ... Signed by Oakland Athletics organization (April 8, 1997). ... Granted free agency (October 30, 1997). ... Signed by San Francisco Giants (November 21, 1997). ... Granted free agency (October 28, 1999). ... Signed by Colorado Rockies (December 9, 1999). ... Traded by Rockies to Royals for P Mac Suzuki and C Sal Fasano (June 24, 2001). ... On Kansas City disabled list (April 30-May 28, 2002); included rehabilitation assignment to Wichita (May 24-28). ... On suspended list (September 25-27, 2002).

2003 GAMES PLAYED BY POSITION (MLB): C—112.

Year	Team (League)	Pos.	G	AB	R	H	2B	3B	HR	RBI	BB	SO	HBP	GDP	SB-CS	Avg.	OBP	SLG	OPS	E	Pct.
1989—	Baseball City (FSL)	C	7	24	5	13	3	1	0	8	0	3	0	0	0-1	.542	.542	.750	1.292	0	1.000
1990—	Memphis (Sou.)	C	115	412	48	110	16	3	2	61	52	51	2	13	5-2	.267	.346	.335	.681	11	.983
—	Kansas City (A.L.)	C	5	13	2	3	0	0	0	1	3	3	0	0	0-1	.231	.375	.231	.606	1	.970
1991—	Kansas City (A.L.)	DH-C	85	231	22	58	8	0	3	31	23	42	0	6	2-4	.251	.315	.325	.640	6	.987
1992—	Kansas City (A.L.)	C-3B	82	213	16	48	10	0	0	18	11	26	0	5	0-4	.225	.260	.272	.532	3	.991
1993—	Kansas City (A.L.)	C-DH	71	205	22	52	9	1	2	22	18	31	1	6	3-2	.254	.317	.337	.654	2	.995
1994—	Kansas City (A.L.)	C-DH	46	144	19	37	5	1	2	20	14	27	0	3	1-0	.257	.323	.347	.670	1	.996
1995—	Kansas City (A.L.)	C	110	307	23	77	18	1	1	27	25	41	3	16	0-1	.251	.313	.326	.638	3	.995
1996—	New York (N.L.)	C	70	99	9	26	6	0	1	6	12	22	0	4	0-1	.263	.342	.354	.696	0	1.000
1997—	Edmonton (PCL)	C	2	3	0	0	0	0	0	0	0	1	0	0	0-0	.000	.000	.000	.000	1	1.000
—	Oakland (A.L.)	C	85	256	29	74	12	0	6	22	18	33	4	6	1-0	.289	.343	.406	.749	2	.996
1998—	San Francisco (N.L.)	C	94	275	26	75	15	0	3	32	37	47	1	8	2-1	.273	.359	.360	.719	5	.991
1999—	San Francisco (N.L.)	C	117	322	39	97	32	0	2	39	43	65	5	16	2-2	.301	.389	.419	.808	3	.995
2000—	Colorado (N.L.)	C-P	117	335	36	101	21	0	6	64	47	48	1	12	1-3	.301	.381	.418	.799	6	.990
2001—	Colorado (N.L.)	C-1B	49	160	15	53	7	0	0	20	16	24	0	4	0-0	.331	.385	.375	.760	1	.997
—	Kansas City (A.L.)	C	51	166	13	40	4	1	2	20	10	17	1	8	1-2	.241	.283	.313	.597	2	.993
2002—	Kansas City (A.L.)	C	101	326	35	77	8	2	4	30	34	54	2	8	4-4	.236	.309	.310	.619	4	.993
—	Wichita (Texas)	C	2	4	0	2	0	0	0	1	1	0	0	1	0-0	.500	.600	.500	1.100	0	1.000
2003—	Kansas City (A.L.)	C	113	372	39	91	17	1	6	36	32	59	3	10	0-2	.245	.307	.344	.651	4	.994
	American League totals (10 years)		749	2233	220	557	91	7	26	227	188	333	14	68	12-20	.249	.309	.331	.641	28	.993
	National League totals (5 years)		447	1191	125	352	81	0	12	161	155	206	7	44	5-7	.296	.375	.394	.769	15	.993
	Major League totals (14 years)		1196	3424	345	909	172	7	38	388	343	539	21	112	17-27	.265	.333	.353	.686	43	.993

MAYS, JOE — P

PERSONAL: Born December 10, 1975, in Flint, Mich. ... 6-1/192. ... Throws right, bats both. ... Full name: Joseph Emerson Mays. ... High school: Southeast (Bradenton, Fla.). ... Junior college: Manatee College (Fla.).

TRANSACTIONS/CAREER NOTES: Selected by Seattle Mariners organization in sixth round of free-agent draft (June 2, 1994). ... Traded by Mariners to Minnesota Twins (October 8, 1997), completing deal in which Twins traded OF Roberto Kelly to Mariners for P Jeromy Palki and a player to be named later (August 20, 1997). ... On Minnesota disabled list (April 15-July 20, 2002); included rehabilitation assignments to Fort Myers (July 2-14) and New Britain (July 15-17).

CAREER HITTING: 3-for-12 (.250), 1 R, 1 2B, 0 3B, 0 HR, 0 RBI.

Year	League	W	L	Pct.	ERA	WHIP	G	GS	CG	ShO	Hld.	Sv.-Opp.	IP	H	R	ER	HR	BB-IBB	SO	Avg.
1995—	Ariz. Mariners (Ariz.)	2	3	.400	3.25	1.33	10	10	0	0	...	0-...	44.1	41	24	16	0	18-0	44	.247
1996—	Everett (Northwest)	4	4	.500	3.08	1.20	13	10	0	0	...	0-...	64.1	55	33	22	3	22-0	56	.227
1997—	Wisconsin (Midw.)	9	3	.750	2.09	1.04	13	13	1	0	...	0-...	81.2	62	20	19	3	23-1	79	.214
—	Lancaster (Calif.)	7	4	.636	4.86	1.47	15	15	1	0	...	0-...	96.1	108	55	52	9	34-0	82	.290
1998—	Fort Myers (Fla. St.)	7	2	.778	3.04	1.31	16	15	0	0	...	0-...	94.2	101	45	32	7	23-0	83	.270
—	New Britain (East.)	5	3	.625	4.99	1.46	11	10	0	0	...	0-...	57.2	63	40	32	4	21-0	45	.273
1999—	Minnesota (A.L.)	6	11	.353	4.37	1.44	49	20	2	1	2	0-0	171.0	179	92	83	24	67-2	115	.270
2000—	Minnesota (A.L.)	7	15	.318	5.56	1.62	31	28	2	1	0	0-0	160.1	193	105	99	20	67-1	102	.299
—	Salt Lake (PCL)	2	0	1.000	1.72	1.15	3	3	0	0	...	0-...	15.2	16	4	3	0	2-0	18	.267
2001—	Minnesota (A.L.)	17	13	.567	3.16	1.15	34	34	4	2	0	0-0	233.2	205	87	82	25	64-2	123	.235
2002—	Minnesota (A.L.)	4	8	.333	5.38	1.45	17	17	1	1	0	0-0	95.1	113	60	57	14	25-0	38	.292
—	Fort Myers (Fla. St.)	0	1	.000	2.08	1.38	3	3	0	0	...	0-...	8.2	9	2	2	0	3-0	7	.273
—	New Britain (East.)	1	0	1.000	1.29	0.43	1	1	0	0	...	0-...	7.0	2	1	1	1	1-0	5	.087
2003—	Minnesota (A.L.)	8	8	.500	6.30	1.52	31	21	0	0	1	0-1	130.0	159	92	91	21	39-2	50	.302
	Major League totals (5 years)	42	55	.433	4.69	1.41	162	120	9	5	3	0-1	790.1	849	436	412	104	262-7	428	.274

McCARTY, DAVE — 1B/OF

PERSONAL: Born November 23, 1969, in Houston, Texas. ... 6-5/215. ... Bats right, throws left. ... Full name: David Andrew McCarty. ... High school: Sharpstown (Houston). ... College: Stanford.

TRANSACTIONS/CAREER NOTES: Selected by Minnesota Twins organization in first round (third pick overall) of free-agent draft (June 3, 1991). ... Traded by Twins to Cincinnati Reds for P John Courtright (June 8, 1995). ... Traded by Reds with OF Deion Sanders, P Ricky Pickett, P Scott Service and P John Roper to San Francisco Giants for OF Darren Lewis, P Mark Portugal and P Dave Burba (July 21, 1995). ... On San Francisco disabled list (June 6-27, 1996); included rehabilitation assignment to Phoenix (June 20-27). ... Traded by Giants to Seattle Mariners for OF Jay Leach and OF Scott Smith (January 30, 1998). ... Granted free agency (September 30, 1998). ... Signed by Detroit Tigers organization (December 18, 1998). ... Granted free agency (October 15, 1999). ... Signed by Oakland Athletics organization (November 23, 1999). ... Traded by A's to Kansas City Royals for cash (March 24, 2000). ... Released by Royals (May 15, 2002). ... Signed by Tampa Bay Devil Rays organization (May 21, 2002). ... Released by Devil Rays (August 7, 2002). ... Signed by A's organization (November 18, 2002). ... Designated for assignment (July 31, 2003). ... Claimed off waivers by Boston Red Sox (August 4, 2003).

2003 GAMES PLAYED BY POSITION (MLB): OF—13, 1B—8, DH—1.

Year	Team (League)	Pos.	G	AB	R	H	2B	3B	HR	RBI	BB	SO	HBP	GDP	SB-CS	Avg.	OBP	SLG	OPS	E	Pct.
1991—	Visalia (Calif.)	OF	15	50	16	19	3	0	3	8	13	7	3	0	3-1	.380	.530	.640	1.150	0	1.000
—	Orlando (South.)	OF	28	88	18	23	4	0	3	11	10	20	2	1	0-1	.261	.350	.409	.759	1	.977
1992—	Orlando (South.)	1B-OF	129	456	75	124	16	2	18	79	55	89	8	8	6-6	.272	.356	.434	.790	9	.977
—	Portland (PCL)	1B-OF	7	26	7	13	2	0	1	8	5	3	1	1	1-0	.500	.594	.692	1.286	1	.977
1993—	Portland (PCL)	OF-1B	40	143	42	55	11	0	8	31	27	25	1	3	5-2	.385	.477	.629	1.106	2	.990
—	Minnesota (A.L.)	OF-1B-DH	98	350	36	75	15	2	2	21	19	80	1	13	2-6	.214	.257	.286	.542	8	.983

| | | | | | | | | | BATTING | | | | | | | | | | | FIELDING | |
Year	Team (League)	Pos.	G	AB	R	H	2B	3B	HR	RBI	BB	SO	HBP	GDP	SB-CS	Avg.	OBP	SLG	OPS	E	Pct.
1994— Minnesota (A.L.)	1B-OF	44	131	21	34	8	2	1	12	7	32	5	3	2-1	.260	.322	.374	.696	5	.982
—Salt Lake (PCL)	OF-1B	55	186	32	47	9	3	3	19	35	34	4	9	1-3	.253	.379	.382	.761	5	.976
1995— Minnesota (A.L.)	1B-OF	25	55	10	12	3	1	0	4	4	18	1	1	0-1	.218	.279	.309	.588	1	.993
—Indianapolis (A.A.)	1B	37	140	31	47	10	1	8	32	15	30	1	5	0-0	.336	.401	.593	.994	2	.994
—Phoenix (PCL)	1B-OF-DH	37	151	31	53	19	2	4	19	17	27	6	6	1-1	.351	.434	.583	1.017	2	.995
—San Francisco (N.L.)	OF-1B	12	20	1	5	1	0	0	2	2	4	0	0	1-0	.250	.318	.300	.618	1	.950
1996— San Francisco (N.L.)	1B-OF	91	175	16	38	3	0	6	24	18	43	2	5	2-1	.217	.294	.337	.632	3	.990
—Phoenix (PCL)	OF-1B	6	25	4	10	1	1	1	7	2	4	0	0	0-0	.400	.429	.640	1.069	0	1.000
1997—Phoenix (PCL)	1B-OF-DH	121	434	85	153	27	5	22	92	49	75	2	18	9-4	.353	.419	.590	1.009	3	.995
1998—Tacoma (PCL)	OF-1B-DH	108	398	73	126	30	2	11	52	59	85	6	15	9-6	.317	.411	.485	.896	2	.996
—Seattle (A.L.)	OF-1B	8	18	1	5	0	0	1	2	5	4	0	0	1-0	.278	.435	.444	.879	0	1.000
1999—Toledo (Int'l)	1B-OF-DH	132	466	85	125	24	3	31	77	70	110	4	9	6-6	.268	.366	.532	.899	2	.998
2000—Kansas City (A.L.)	1B-OF-DH	103	270	34	75	14	2	12	53	22	68	0	6	0-0	.278	.329	.478	.807	5	.991
2001—Kansas City (A.L.)	1B-OF-DH	98	200	26	50	10	0	7	26	24	45	1	8	0-0	.250	.328	.405	.733	8	.984
2002—Kansas City (A.L.)	1B-DH	13	32	3	3	1	0	1	2	2	10	0	1	0-0	.094	.147	.219	.366	0	1.000
—Durham (Int'l)	1B-OF	29	114	25	37	7	1	8	22	14	33	0	1	0-1	.325	.398	.614	1.012	2	.992
—Tampa Bay (A.L.)	OF	12	34	2	6	0	0	1	2	4	9	2	0	0-0	.176	.300	.265	.565	0	1.000
2003—Sacramento (PCL)	1B-OF-DH	91	352	69	95	23	2	15	72	44	71	3	12	4-1	.270	.351	.474	.826	4	.993
—Oakland (A.L.)	OF-1B	8	26	2	7	2	0	0	2	1	7	0	0	0-0	.269	.286	.346	.632	1	.970
—Boston (A.L.)	OF-1B-DH	16	27	4	11	3	0	1	6	2	7	0	0	0-0	.407	.448	.630	1.078	1	.970
American League totals (8 years)		425	1143	139	278	56	7	26	130	90	280	10	32	5-8	.243	.302	.373	.675	29	.986
National League totals (2 years)		103	195	17	43	4	0	6	26	20	47	2	5	3-1	.221	.297	.333	.630	4	.988
Major League totals (9 years)		528	1338	156	321	60	7	32	156	110	327	12	37	8-9	.240	.301	.367	.668	33	.986

McCLUNG, SETH — P

PERSONAL: Born February 7, 1981, in Lewisburg, W.Va. ... 6-6/235. ... Throws right, bats left. ... Full name: Michael Seth McClung. ... High school: Greenbrier East (Lewisburg, W.Va.).

TRANSACTIONS/CAREER NOTES: Selected by Tampa Bay Devil Rays organization in fifth round of free-agent draft (June 2, 1999). ... Placed on the 15-day disabled list by Tampa Bay (May 23, 2003). ... Transferred to Emergency disabled list (June 6, 2003).

CAREER HITTING: 0-for-0 (.000), 0 R, 0 2B, 0 3B, 0 HR, 0 RBI.

Year	League	W	L	Pct.	ERA	WHIP	G	GS	CG	ShO	Hld.	Sv.-Opp.	IP	H	R	ER	HR	BB-IBB	SO	Avg.
1999— Princeton (Appal.)	2	4	.333	7.69	2.21	13	10	0	0	...	0-...	45.2	53	47	39	3	48-0	46	.285
2000— Char., S.C. (SAL)	2	1	.667	3.19	1.58	6	6	0	0	...	0-...	31.0	30	14	11	0	19-0	26	.246
—Hudson Valley (NYP)	2	2	.500	1.85	1.24	8	8	0	0	...	0-...	43.2	37	18	9	0	17-0	38	.227
2001—Char., S.C. (SAL)	10	11	.476	2.79	1.19	28	28	2	1	...	0-...	164.1	142	72	51	6	53-1	165	.231
2002—Bakersfield (Calif.)	3	2	.600	2.92	1.24	7	7	0	0	...	0-...	37.0	35	16	12	1	11-0	48	.243
—Orlando (Sou.)	5	7	.417	5.37	1.68	20	19	0	0	...	0-...	114.0	138	74	68	12	53-0	64	.299
2003—Tampa Bay (A.L.)	4	1	.800	5.35	1.50	12	5	0	0	1	0-0	38.2	33	23	23	6	25-1	25	.241
Major League totals (1 year)	4	1	.800	5.35	1.50	12	5	0	0	1	0-0	38.2	33	23	23	6	25-1	25	.241

McCRACKEN, QUINTON — OF

PERSONAL: Born March 16, 1970, in Wilmington, N.C. ... 5-7/188. ... Bats both, throws right. ... Full name: Quinton Antoine McCracken. ... High school: South Brunswick (Southport, N.C.). ... College: Duke.

TRANSACTIONS/CAREER NOTES: Selected by Colorado Rockies organization in 25th round of free-agent draft (June 1, 1992). ... Selected by Tampa Bay Devil Rays in first round (fourth pick overall) of expansion draft (November 18, 1997). ... On disabled list (May 25, 1999-remainder of season). ... Released by Devil Rays (November 27, 2000). ... Signed by St. Louis Cardinals (December 22, 2000). ... Released by Cardinals (March 28, 2001). ... Signed by Minnesota Twins organization (April 13, 2001). ... Granted free agency (October 8, 2001).

2003 GAMES PLAYED BY POSITION (MLB): OF—55, DH—1.

| | | | | | | | | | BATTING | | | | | | | | | | | FIELDING | |
Year	Team (League)	Pos.	G	AB	R	H	2B	3B	HR	RBI	BB	SO	HBP	GDP	SB-CS	Avg.	OBP	SLG	OPS	E	Pct.
1992— Bend (NW)	2B-OF	67	232	37	65	13	2	0	27	25	39	0	6	18-6	.280	.347	.353	.701	§ 17	.930
1993— Central Valley (Cal.)	2B-OF	127	483	94	141	17	7	2	58	78	90	2	15	60-19	.292	.390	.369	.758	13	.946
1994— New Haven (East.)	OF	136	544	94	151	27	4	5	39	48	72	4	6	36-19	.278	.338	.369	.708	8	.972
1995— New Haven (East.)	OF-DH	55	221	33	79	11	4	1	26	21	32	3	2	26-8	.357	.419	.457	.876	3	.971
—Colo. Springs (PCL)	OF-DH	61	244	55	88	14	6	3	28	23	30	1	4	17-6	.361	.418	.504	.922	1	.991
—Colorado (N.L.)	OF	3	1	0	0	0	0	0	0	0	1	0	0	0-0	.000	.000	.000	.000	0	...
1996—Colorado (N.L.)	OF	124	283	50	82	13	6	3	40	32	62	1	5	17-6	.290	.363	.410	.773	6	.957
1997—Colorado (N.L.)	OF	147	325	69	95	11	1	3	36	42	62	1	6	28-11	.292	.374	.360	.734	4	.980
1998—Tampa Bay (A.L.)	OF	155	614	77	179	38	7	7	59	41	107	3	12	19-10	.292	.335	.410	.745	3	.992
1999—Tampa Bay (A.L.)	OF	40	148	20	37	6	1	1	18	14	23	1	7	6-5	.250	.317	.324	.641	1	.988
2000—Tampa Bay (A.L.)	OF	15	31	5	4	0	0	0	2	6	4	0	3	0-1	.129	.270	.129	.399	0	1.000
—Durham (Int'l)	OF	85	334	54	87	18	2	2	28	34	57	2	10	13-7	.260	.332	.344	.676	4	.977
2001—Edmonton (PCL)	OF	81	361	53	122	27	4	4	45	21	54	1	5	8-10	.338	.374	.468	.842	5	.971
—Minnesota (A.L.)	OF-DH	24	64	7	14	2	2	0	3	5	13	0	2	0-1	.219	.275	.313	.588	1	1.000
2002—Arizona (N.L.)	OF	123	349	60	108	27	8	3	40	32	68	2	3	5-4	.309	.367	.458	.825	1	.995
2003—Arizona (N.L.)	OF-DH	115	203	17	46	5	2	0	18	15	34	0	4	5-1	.227	.276	.271	.547	1	.983
American League totals (4 years)		234	857	109	234	46	10	8	82	66	147	4	24	25-17	.273	.325	.378	.703	4	.992
National League totals (5 years)		512	1161	196	331	56	17	9	134	121	227	4	18	55-22	.285	.352	.386	.738	12	.980
Major League totals (9 years)		746	2018	305	565	102	27	17	216	187	374	8	42	80-39	.280	.341	.383	.723	16	.985

McDONALD, JOHN — IF

PERSONAL: Born September 24, 1974, in New London, Conn. ... 5-11/175. ... Bats right, throws right. ... Full name: John Joseph McDonald. ... High school: East Lyme (Conn.). ... College: Providence.

TRANSACTIONS/CAREER NOTES: Selected by Cleveland Indians organization in 12th round of free-agent draft (June 4, 1996). ... On Buffalo disabled list (April 27-May 9 and May 10-June 22, 2000). ... On Buffalo disabled list (May 10-17, 2001). ... Placed on 15-day disabled list (June 30, 2003). ... Sent to Lake Valley on rehab assignment by Cleveland (July 14, 2003). ... Recalled from Lake County rehab assignment; reinstated from 15-day disabled list (July 17, 2003). ... Placed on 15-day disabled list (August 27, 2003).

2003 GAMES PLAYED BY POSITION (MLB): 2B—37, SS—27, 3B—23.

M

Year Team (League)	Pos.	G	AB	R	H	2B	3B	HR	RBI	BB	SO	HBP	GDP	SB-CS	Avg.	OBP	SLG	OPS	E	Pct.
1996— Watertown (NYP)	SS	75	278	48	75	11	0	2	26	32	49	5	3	11-1	.270	.354	.331	.685	18	.946
1997— Kinston (Caro.)	SS	130	541	77	140	27	3	5	53	51	75	2	12	6-5	.259	.324	.348	.671	25	.961
1998— Akron (East.)	SS	132	514	68	118	18	2	2	43	43	61	6	7	17-6	.230	.293	.284	.578	23	.966
1999— Akron (East.)	SS-2B	55	226	31	67	12	0	1	26	19	26	2	5	7-3	.296	.351	.363	.713	8	.970
— Buffalo (Int'l)	SS-3B-2B	66	237	30	75	12	1	0	25	11	23	2	5	6-3	.316	.349	.376	.725	13	.956
— Cleveland (A.L.)	2B-SS	18	21	2	7	0	0	0	0	0	3	0	2	0-1	.333	.333	.333	.667	1	.967
2000— Akron (East.)	SS-2B	75	286	37	77	17	2	1	36	21	29	1	7	4-3	.269	.315	.353	.668	8	.975
— Mahoning Valley (NY-P)	SS	5	17	0	2	1	0	0	1	2	3	0	0	0-0	.118	.211	.176	.387	0	1.000
— Cleveland (A.L.)	SS-2B	9	9	0	4	0	0	0	0	0	1	0	0	0-0	.444	.444	.444	.889	0	1.000
— Kinston (Caro.)	SS	1	3	0	1	0	0	0	0	0	0	0	0	0-0	.333	.333	.333	.667	0	1.000
2001— Cleveland (A.L.)	SS-2B-3B	17	22	1	2	1	0	0	0	1	7	1	0	0-0	.091	.167	.136	.303	1	.964
— Buffalo (Int'l)	SS-2B-3B	116	410	52	100	17	1	2	33	33	72	6	11	17-10	.244	.305	.305	.610	23	.957
2002—	2-S-3-D	93	264	35	66	11	3	1	12	10	50	5	4	3-0	.250	.288	.284	.614	8	.979
2003— Mahoning Valley (NY-P)	SS	1	2	1	0	0	0	0	0	1	0	0	0	0-0	.000	.333	.000	.333	0	1.000
— Lake County (S. Atl.)	SS	1	3	0	0	0	0	0	0	0	0	0	0	0-0	.000	.000	.000	.000	0	1.000
— Cleveland (A.L.)	2B-SS-3B	82	214	21	46	9	1	1	14	11	31	2	4	3-3	.215	.258	.280	.538	10	.964
Major League totals (5 years)		219	530	59	125	21	4	2	26	22	92	8	10	6-4	.236	.275	.302	.577	20	.972

McEWING, JOE — OF/IF

PERSONAL: Born October 19, 1972, in Bristol, Pa. ... 5-11/170. ... Bats right, throws right. ... Full name: Joseph Earl McEwing. ... High school: Bishop Egan (Fairless Hills, Pa.). ... Junior college: Morris (N.J.) Community College.

TRANSACTIONS/CAREER NOTES: Selected by St. Louis Cardinals organization in 28th round of free-agent draft (June 1, 1992). ... Traded by Cardinals to New York Mets for P Jesse Orosco (March 18, 2000). ... On New York disabled list (July 14-31, 2002); included rehabilitation assignments to Brooklyn (July 29-30) and Binghamton (July 31). ... Optioned to Norfolk (April 17, 2003). ... Recalled from Norfolk (April 23, 2003).

2003 GAMES PLAYED BY POSITION (MLB): 2B—55, SS—42, OF—18, 1B—5, 3B—2.

Year Team (League)	Pos.	G	AB	R	H	2B	3B	HR	RBI	BB	SO	HBP	GDP	SB-CS	Avg.	OBP	SLG	OPS	E	Pct.
1992— Ariz. Cardinals (Ariz.)	SS-OF	55	211	* 55	71	4	2	0	13	24	18	5	1	23-7	.336	.415	.374	.789	1	.991
1993— Savannah (S. Atl.)	OF	138	511	* 94	127	35	1	0	43	89	73	4	7	22-9	.249	.362	.321	.683	5	.982
1994— Madison (Midw.)	OF	90	346	58	112	24	2	4	47	32	53	1	5	18-15	.324	.380	.439	.819	5	.974
— St. Pete. (FSL)	2B-OF	50	197	22	49	7	0	1	20	19	32	1	4	8-4	.249	.314	.299	.613	2	.985
1995— St. Pete. (FSL)	2B-OF	75	281	33	64	13	0	1	23	25	49	1	5	2-3	.228	.289	.285	.574	15	.955
— Arkansas (Texas)	2B-OF	42	121	16	30	4	0	2	12	9	13	1	4	3-2	.248	.305	.331	.636	0	1.000
1996— Arkansas (Texas)	2B-OF	106	216	27	45	7	3	2	14	13	32	0	8	2-4	.208	.252	.296	.548	2	.987
1997— Arkansas (Texas)	P	103	263	33	68	6	3	4	35	19	39	1	6	4-2	.259	.309	.350	.659	2	.988
1998— Arkansas (Texas)	P	60	223	45	79	21	4	9	46	21	18	1	2	4-2	.354	.409	.605	1.014	1	.994
— Memphis (PCL)	2-3-SS-OF	78	329	52	110	30	7	6	46	21	39	3	4	11-10	.334	.379	.523	.901	3	.982
— St. Louis (N.L.)	2B-OF	10	20	5	4	1	0	0	1	1	3	1	0	0-1	.200	.273	.250	.523	0	1.000
1999— St. Louis (N.L.) 2-0-3-S-1		152	513	65	141	28	4	9	44	41	87	6	3	7-4	.275	.333	.398	.730	11	.981
2000— Norfolk (Int'l)	0-2-3-S	43	171	28	44	10	2	5	18	16	34	0	3	7-3	.257	.319	.427	.746	4	.973
— New York (N.L.)	0-3-2-S	87	153	20	34	14	1	2	19	5	29	1	2	3-1	.222	.248	.366	.614	5	.957
2001— New York (N.L.) 0-3-S-2-1-D		116	283	41	80	17	3	8	30	17	57	10	2	8-5	.283	.342	.449	.791	3	.981
2002— New York (N.L.) 0-S-1-2-3		105	196	22	39	8	1	3	26	9	50	3	0	4-4	.199	.242	.296	.538	7	.967
— Brooklyn (NY-P)	DH	1	4	0	1	0	0	0	1	0	0	0	0	0-0	.250	.250	.250	.500	...	...
— Binghamton (East.)	2B-3B	1	5	0	0	0	0	0	0	0	1	0	0	0-0	.000	.000	.000	.000	0	1.000
2003— Norfolk (Int'l)	OF-2-3-1	5	19	3	6	0	0	1	3	2	2	2	0	3-0	.316	.435	.474	.908	0	1.000
— New York (N.L.) 2-S-0-1-3		119	278	31	67	11	0	1	16	25	57	3	6	3-0	.241	.309	.291	.601	6	.984
Major League totals (6 years)		589	1443	184	365	79	9	23	136	98	283	24	13	25-15	.253	.308	.368	.676	32	.978

McGRIFF, FRED — 1B

PERSONAL: Born October 31, 1963, in Tampa, Fla. ... 6-3/225. ... Bats left, throws left. ... Full name: Frederick Stanley McGriff. ... High school: Jefferson (Tampa).

TRANSACTIONS/CAREER NOTES: Selected by New York Yankees organization in ninth round of free-agent draft (June 8, 1981). ... Traded by Yankees with OF Dave Collins, P Mike Morgan and cash to Toronto Blue Jays for OF/C Tom Dodd and P Dale Murray (December 9, 1982). ... On disabled list (June 5-August 14, 1985). ... Traded by Blue Jays with SS Tony Fernandez to San Diego Padres for OF Joe Carter and 2B Roberto Alomar (December 5, 1990). ... On suspended list (June 23-26, 1992). ... Traded by Padres to Atlanta Braves for OF Melvin Nieves, P Donnie Elliott and OF Vince Moore (July 18, 1993). ... Granted free agency (November 6, 1995). ... Re-signed by Braves (December 2, 1995). ... Traded by Braves to Tampa Bay Devil Rays for a player to be named later or cash (November 18, 1997); Braves received an undisclosed amount of cash to complete deal (April 1, 1998). ... Traded by Devil Rays to Chicago Cubs for P Manny Aybar and a player to be named later (July 27, 2001); Devil Rays acquired SS Jason Smith to complete deal (August 5, 2001). ... Granted free agency (November 1, 2002). ... Signed by Los Angeles Dodgers (December 20, 2002).

2003 GAMES PLAYED BY POSITION (MLB): 1B—79.

Year Team (League)	Pos.	G	AB	R	H	2B	3B	HR	RBI	BB	SO	HBP	GDP	SB-CS	Avg.	OBP	SLG	OPS	E	Pct.
1981— GC Yankees (GCL)	1B	29	81	6	12	2	0	0	9	11	20	1	...	0-0	.148	.255	.173	.428	7	.963
1982— GC Yankees (GCL)	1B	62	217	38	59	11	1	* 9	• 41	* 48	63	5	...	6-6	.272	.413	.456	.870	8	.986
1983— Florence (S. Atl.)	1B	33	119	26	37	3	1	7	26	20	35	1	...	3-0	.311	.414	.529	.944	6	.978
— Kinston (Caro.)	1B	94	350	53	85	14	1	21	57	55	112	6	...	3-2	.243	.354	.469	.822	10	.988
1984— Knoxville (Sou.)	1B	56	189	29	47	13	2	9	25	29	55	1	2	0-2	.249	.347	.481	.828	10	.981
— Syracuse (Int'l)	1B	70	238	28	56	10	1	13	28	26	89	0	3	0-1	.235	.309	.450	.759	3	.996
1985— Syracuse (Int'l)	1B	51	176	19	40	8	2	5	20	23	53	4	2	0-0	.227	.330	.381	.711	5	.989
1986— Syracuse (Int'l)	1B-OF	133	468	69	121	23	4	19	74	83	119	4	16	0-3	.259	.369	.504	.816	10	‡ .992
— Toronto (A.L.)	DH-1B	3	5	1	1	0	0	0	0	0	2	0	0	0-0	.200	.200	.200	.400	0	1.000
1987— Toronto (A.L.)	DH-1B	107	295	58	73	16	0	20	43	60	104	1	3	3-2	.247	.376	.505	.881	2	.983
1988— Toronto (A.L.)	1B	154	536	100	151	35	4	34	82	79	149	4	15	6-1	.282	.376	.552	.928	5	* .997
1989— Toronto (A.L.)	DH-1B	161	551	98	148	27	3	* 36	92	119	132	4	14	7-4	.269	.399	.525	.924	* 17	.989
1990— Toronto (A.L.)	DH-1B	153	557	91	167	21	1	35	88	94	108	2	7	5-3	.300	.400	.530	.930	6	.996
1991— San Diego (N.L.)	1B	153	528	84	147	19	1	31	106	105	135	2	14	4-1	.278	.396	.494	.890	14	.991
1992— San Diego (N.L.)	1B	152	531	79	152	30	4	* 35	104	96	108	1	14	8-6	.286	.394	.556	.950	• 12	.991
1993— San Diego (N.L.)	1B	83	302	52	83	11	1	18	46	42	55	1	9	4-3	.275	.361	.497	.858	12	.983
— Atlanta (N.L.)	1B	68	255	59	79	18	1	19	55	34	51	1	5	1-0	.310	.392	.612	1.004	5	.992
1994— Atlanta (N.L.)	1B	113	424	81	135	25	1	34	94	50	76	1	7	7-3	.318	.389	.623	1.012	7	.994

Year	Team (League)	Pos.	G	AB	R	H	2B	3B	HR	RBI	BB	SO	HBP	GDP	SB-CS	Avg.	OBP	SLG	OPS	E	Pct.
1995—Atlanta (N.L.)		1B	•144	528	85	148	27	1	27	93	65	99	5	19	3-6	.280	.361	.489	.850	5	.996
1996—Atlanta (N.L.)		1B	159	617	81	182	37	1	28	107	68	116	2	20	7-3	.295	.365	.494	.859	12	.992
1997—Atlanta (N.L.)		1B	152	564	77	156	25	1	22	97	68	112	4	*22	5-0	.277	.356	.441	.797	13	.990
1998—Tampa Bay (A.L.)		1B-DH	151	564	73	160	33	0	19	81	79	118	2	14	7-2	.284	.371	.443	.815	6	.995
1999—Tampa Bay (A.L.)		1B-DH	144	529	75	164	30	1	32	104	86	107	1	12	1-0	.310	.405	.552	.957	13	.989
2000—Tampa Bay (A.L.)		1B-DH	158	566	82	157	18	0	27	106	91	120	0	16	2-0	.277	.373	.452	.826	10	.993
2001—Tampa Bay (A.L.)		1B-DH	97	343	40	109	18	0	19	61	40	69	0	7	1-1	.318	.387	.536	.923	9	.986
—Chicago (N.L.)		1B	49	170	27	48	7	2	12	41	26	37	3	6	0-1	.282	.383	.559	.942	4	.990
2002—Chicago (N.L.)		1B-DH	146	523	67	143	27	2	30	103	63	99	4	13	1-2	.273	.353	.505	.858	7	.993
2003—Vero Beach (FSL)		DH-1B	2	6	0	1	0	0	0	0	1	2	0	0	0-0	.167	.286	.167	.452	0	1.000
—GC Dodgers (GCL)		1B	1	3	1	2	1	0	0	0	0	0	0	0	0-0	.667	.667	1.000	1.667	0	1.000
—Los Angeles (N.L.)		1B	86	297	32	74	14	0	13	40	31	66	1	7	0-0	.249	.322	.428	.750	8	.989
American League totals (9 years)			1128	3946	618	1130	198	9	222	657	648	909	14	88	32-13	.286	.386	.510	.896	68	.992
National League totals (10 years)			1305	4739	724	1347	240	15	269	886	648	954	25	137	40-25	.284	.370	.512	.882	99	.991
Major League totals (18 years)			2433	8685	1342	2477	438	24	491	1543	1296	1863	39	225	72-38	.285	.378	.511	.889	167	.992

McLEMORE, MARK — OF/IF

PERSONAL: Born October 4, 1964, in San Diego, Calif. ... 5-11/207. ... Bats both, throws right. ... Full name: Mark Tremell McLemore. ... High school: Samuel F.B. Morse (San Diego).

TRANSACTIONS/CAREER NOTES: Selected by California Angels organization in ninth round of free-agent draft (June 7, 1982). ... On disabled list (May 15-27, 1985). ... On California disabled list (May 24-August 2, 1988); included rehabilitation assignments to Palm Springs (July 7-21) and Edmonton (July 22-27). ... On California disabled list (May 17-August 17, 1990); included rehabilitation assignments to Edmonton (May 24-June 6) and Palm Springs (August 9-13). ... Traded by Angels to Cleveland Indians (August 17, 1990), completing deal in which Indians traded C Ron Tingley to Angels for a player to be named later (September 6, 1989). ... Released by Indians (December 13, 1990). ... Signed by Houston Astros organization (March 6, 1991). ... On Houston disabled list (May 9-June 25, 1991); included rehabilitation assignments to Tucson (May 24-29) and Jackson (June 14-22). ... Released by Astros (June 25, 1991). ... Signed by Baltimore Orioles organization (July 5, 1991). ... Granted free agency (October 15, 1991). ... Re-signed by Orioles organization (February 5, 1992). ... Granted free agency (December 19, 1992). ... Re-signed by Orioles organization (January 6, 1993). ... Granted free agency (October 18, 1994). ... Signed by Texas Rangers (December 13, 1994). ... Granted free agency (December 7, 1996). ... Re-signed by Rangers (December 13, 1996). ... On Texas disabled list (May 15-June 12 and August 19-September 28, 1997); included rehabilitation assignments to Charlotte (June 7-8) and Oklahoma City (June 9-12). ... On disabled list (June 7-22, 1998). ... Granted free agency (October 29, 1999). ... Signed by Seattle Mariners (December 20, 1999). ... On suspended list (June 20-24, 2000). ... Granted free agency (November 5, 2001). ... Re-signed by Mariners (December 7, 2001).

2003 GAMES PLAYED BY POSITION (MLB): SS—38, 3B—29, OF—16, DH—11, 2B—6.

Year	Team (League)	Pos.	G	AB	R	H	2B	3B	HR	RBI	BB	SO	HBP	GDP	SB-CS	Avg.	OBP	SLG	OPS	E	Pct.
1982—Salem (NW)		2B-SS	55	165	42	49	6	2	0	25	39	38	2	...	14-6	.297	.431	.358	.789	11	.949
1983—Peoria (Midw.)		2B-SS	95	329	42	79	7	3	0	18	53	64	2	...	15-11	.240	.346	.280	.626	24	.946
1984—Redwood (Calif.)		2B-SS	134	482	102	142	8	3	0	45	106	75	1	2	59-15	.295	.421	.324	.744	25	.966
1985—Midland (Texas)		2B-SS	117	458	80	124	17	6	2	46	66	59	1	4	31-16	.271	.362	.347	.709	19	.971
1986—Midland (Texas)		2B	63	237	54	75	9	1	1	29	48	18	1	5	38-8	.316	.428	.376	.803	13	.964
—Edmonton (PCL)		2B	73	286	41	79	13	1	0	23	39	30	0	0	29-9	.276	.359	.329	.687	7	.982
—California (A.L.)		2B	5	4	0	0	0	0	0	0	1	2	0	0	0-1	.000	.200	.000	.200	0	1.000
1987—California (A.L.)		2B-SS-DH	138	433	61	102	13	3	3	41	48	72	0	7	25-8	.236	.310	.300	.610	17	.975
1988—California (A.L.)		2B-3B-DH	77	233	38	56	11	2	2	16	25	28	0	6	13-7	.240	.312	.330	.642	6	.979
—Palm Springs (Calif.)		2B	11	44	9	15	3	1	0	6	11	7	1	1	7-3	.341	.474	.455	.928	1	.977
—Edmonton (PCL)		2B	12	45	7	12	3	0	0	6	4	4	0	1	7-1	.267	.327	.333	.660	1	.935
1989—Edmonton (PCL)		2B	114	430	60	105	13	2	2	34	49	67	1	14	26-11	.244	.321	.298	.619	10	*.983
—California (A.L.)		2B-DH	32	103	12	25	3	1	0	14	7	19	1	2	6-1	.243	.295	.291	.586	5	.966
1990—California (A.L.)		2B	20	48	4	7	2	0	0	2	4	9	0	1	1-0	.146	.212	.188	.399	0	1.000
—Edmonton (PCL)		2B-SS	9	39	4	10	2	0	0	3	6	10	0	1	0-3	.256	.356	.308	.663	4	.933
—Palm Springs (Calif.)		2B	6	22	3	6	0	0	0	2	3	7	0	0	0-2	.273	.360	.273	.633	0	1.000
—Colo. Springs (PCL)		2B-3B-SS	14	54	11	15	2	0	1	7	11	8	0	2	5-0	.278	.400	.370	.770	2	.969
—Cleveland (A.L.)		2B-3B-SS	8	12	2	2	0	0	0	0	0	6	0	0	0-0	.167	.167	.167	.333	4	.922
1991—Houston (A.L.)		2B	21	61	6	9	1	0	0	2	6	13	0	1	0-1	.148	.221	.164	.385	2	.975
—Tucson (PCL)		2B	4	14	2	5	1	0	0	0	2	1	0	2	0-0	.357	.438	.429	.866	0	1.000
—Jackson (Texas)		2B	7	22	6	5	3	0	1	4	6	3	0	1	1-0	.227	.393	.500	.893	1	1.000
—Rochester (Int'l)		2B	57	228	32	64	11	4	1	28	27	29	0	5	12-5	.281	.354	.377	.731	5	.984
1992—Baltimore (A.L.)		2B-DH	101	228	40	56	7	2	0	27	21	26	0	6	11-5	.246	.308	.294	.602	7	.978
1993—Baltimore (A.L.)		O-2-3-D	148	581	81	165	27	5	4	72	64	92	1	21	21-15	.284	.353	.368	.721	6	.986
1994—Baltimore (A.L.)		2B-OF-DH	104	343	44	88	11	1	3	29	51	50	1	7	20-5	.257	.354	.321	.674	9	.982
1995—Texas (A.L.)		OF-2B-DH	129	467	73	122	20	5	5	41	59	71	3	10	21-11	.261	.346	.358	.703	4	.991
1996—Texas (A.L.)		2B-OF	147	517	84	150	23	4	5	46	87	69	0	8	27-10	.290	.389	.379	.768	12	.985
1997—Texas (A.L.)		2B-OF	89	349	47	91	17	2	1	25	40	54	2	5	7-5	.261	.338	.330	.668	8	.980
—Charlotte (Fla. St.)		2B	2	7	1	4	1	0	0	3	2	1	0	0	1-1	.571	.667	.714	1.381	0	1.000
—Okla. City (A.A.)		2B-DH	3	10	0	1	0	0	0	1	1	1	0	0	1-0	.100	.167	.100	.267	0	1.000
1998—Texas (A.L.)		2B-DH	126	461	79	114	15	1	5	53	89	64	2	15	12-4	.247	.369	.317	.686	15	.975
1999—Texas (A.L.)		2B-OF-DH	144	566	105	155	20	7	6	45	83	79	0	8	16-8	.274	.363	.366	.729	12	.983
2000—Seattle (A.L.)		2B-DH	138	481	72	118	23	1	3	46	81	78	1	12	30-14	.245	.353	.316	.669	8	.988
2001—Seattle (A.L.)		O-3-S-2-D	125	409	78	117	16	9	5	57	69	84	0	6	39-7	.286	.384	.406	.790	12	.963
2002—Seattle (A.L.)		O-3-D-2-S	104	337	54	91	17	2	7	41	61	63	1	3	18-10	.270	.380	.395	.774	7	.966
2003—Seattle (A.L.)		S-3-O-D-2	99	309	34	72	15	2	2	37	38	71	2	4	5-5	.233	.318	.314	.632	7	.973
American League totals (17 years)			1734	5881	908	1531	240	47	51	592	828	937	14	129	272-116	.260	.350	.343	.694	139	.980
National League totals (1 year)			21	61	6	9	1	0	0	2	6	13	0	1	0-1	.148	.221	.164	.385	2	.975
Major League totals (18 years)			1755	5942	914	1540	241	47	51	594	834	950	14	130	272-117	.259	.349	.341	.690	141	.980

McMILLON, BILLY — OF

PERSONAL: Born November 17, 1971, in Otero, N.M. ... 5-11/195. ... Bats left, throws left. ... Full name: William Edward McMillon. ... High school: Bishopville (S.C.). ... College: Clemson.

TRANSACTIONS/CAREER NOTES: Selected by Florida Marlins organization in eighth round of free-agent draft (June 3, 1993). ... On Charlotte disabled list (April 20-29, 1997). ... Traded by Marlins to Philadelphia Phillies for OF/1B Darren Daulton (July 21, 1997). ... On Scranton/Wilkes-Barre disabled list (May 20-July 13, 1998). ... Granted free agency (December 21, 1998). ... Re-signed by Phillies organization (January 25, 1999). ... Granted free agency (October 15, 1999). ... Signed by Detroit Tigers organization

M

(January 10, 2000). ... Claimed on waivers by Oakland Athletics (June 13, 2001). ... On Oakland disabled list (July 23, 2001-remainder of season). ... Released by A's (November 12, 2001). ... On Columbus disabled list (August 3-11, 2002). ... Granted free agency (October 15, 2002). ... Signed by A's organization (November 18, 2002). ... Contract purchased from Sacramento (May 29, 2003).

2003 GAMES PLAYED BY POSITION (MLB): OF—36, DH—9, 1B—3.

Year Team (League)	Pos.	G	AB	R	H	2B	3B	HR	RBI	BB	SO	HBP	GDP	SB-CS	Avg.	OBP	SLG	OPS	E	Pct.
1993— Elmira (N.Y.-Penn)	OF	57	226	38	69	14	2	6	35	31	43	4	3	5-4	.305	.398	.465	.863	5	.931
1994— Kane Co. (Midw.)	OF	•137	496	88	125	25	3	17	•101	•84	99	10	13	7-3	.252	.366	.417	.783	7	.966
1995— Portland (East.)	OF	141	518	92	162	29	3	14	93	96	90	7	10	15-9	.313	.423	.461	.885	4	.982
1996— Charlotte (Int'l)	OF-DH	97	347	72	122	32	2	17	70	36	76	5	8	5-3	.352	.418	.602	1.020	4	.973
— Florida (N.L.)	OF	28	51	4	11	0	0	0	4	5	14	0	1	0-0	.216	.286	.216	.501	0	1.000
1997— Charlotte (Int'l)	OF	57	204	34	57	18	0	8	26	32	51	1	3	8-0	.279	.378	.485	.863	2	.978
— Florida (N.L.)	OF	13	18	0	2	1	0	0	1	0	7	0	0	0-0	.111	.111	.167	.278	1	1.000
— Philadelphia (N.L.)	OF	24	72	10	21	4	1	2	13	6	17	0	1	2-1	.292	.333	.458	.792	2	.957
— Scran./W.B. (I.L.)	OF	26	92	18	27	8	1	4	21	12	24	0	1	2-0	.293	.375	.533	.908	0	1.000
1998— Scran./W.B. (I.L.)	OF-DH	77	267	42	69	16	1	13	38	34	59	3	6	6-3	.258	.345	.472	.817	2	.986
1999— Scran./W.B. (I.L.)	OF-DH	132	464	97	141	38	4	16	85	65	79	6	10	11-2	.304	.389	.506	.895	5	.979
2000— Toledo (Int'l)	OF	105	380	61	131	30	1	13	50	71	65	2	18	3-1	.345	.446	.532	.978	6	.973
— Detroit (A.L.)	DH-OF	46	123	20	37	7	1	4	24	19	19	1	2	1-0	.301	.388	.472	.859	1	.964
2001— Detroit (A.L.)	OF-DH	20	34	1	3	1	0	1	4	2	12	1	1	0-0	.088	.162	.206	.368	0	1.000
— Oakland (A.L.)	OF-DH	20	58	6	17	7	1	0	10	5	13	1	0	1-0	.293	.354	.448	.802	1	.950
2002— Columbus (Int'l)	OF-1B	115	442	72	133	32	3	8	46	59	71	6	6	2-5	.301	.388	.441	.829	1	.993
2003— Sacramento (PCL)	OF-DH	38	153	31	51	10	0	8	35	17	30	1	3	1-1	.333	.401	.556	.957	2	.966
— Oakland (A.L.)	OF-DH-1B	66	153	15	41	11	0	6	26	19	36	2	3	0-0	.268	.354	.458	.812	1	.981
American League totals (3 years)		152	368	42	98	26	2	11	64	45	80	5	6	2-0	.266	.349	.438	.787	3	.973
National League totals (2 years)		65	141	14	34	5	1	2	18	11	38	0	2	2-1	.241	.290	.333	.624	2	.970
Major League totals (5 years)		217	509	56	132	31	3	13	82	56	118	5	8	4-1	.259	.333	.409	.742	5	.972

MEADOWS, BRIAN   P

PERSONAL: Born November 21, 1975, in Montgomery, Ala. ... 6-3/236. ... Throws right, bats right. ... Full name: Matthew Brian Meadows. ... High school: Charles Henderson (Troy, Ala.).

TRANSACTIONS/CAREER NOTES: Selected by Florida Marlins organization in third round of free-agent draft (June 2, 1994); pick received as compensation for Colorado Rockies signing Type B free-agent SS Walt Weiss. ... On disabled list (July 28-August 13, 1998). ... Traded by Marlins to San Diego Padres for P Dan Miceli (November 15, 1999). ... Traded by Padres to Kansas City Royals for P Jay Witasick (July 31, 2000). ... Granted free agency (October 8, 2001). ... Signed by Minnesota Twins organization (January 15, 2002). ... Released by Twins (March 30, 2002). ... Signed by Pittsburgh Pirates organization (April 5, 2002). ... Recalled by Pittsburgh from Nashville (April 22, 2003). ... Optioned to Nashville (June 14, 2003). ... Recalled from Nashville (June 25, 2003). ... Optioned to Nashville (June 30, 2003). ... Recalled from Nashville (July 23, 2003).

CAREER HITTING: 21-for-176 (.119), 12 R, 3 2B, 0 3B, 0 HR, 7 RBI.

Year League	W	L	Pct.	ERA	WHIP	G	GS	CG	ShO	Hld.	Sv.-Opp.	IP	H	R	ER	HR	BB-IBB	SO	Avg.
1994— GC Marlins (GCL)	3	0	1.000	1.95	1.08	8	7	0	0	...	0-...	37.0	34	9	8	1	6-0	33	.236
1995— Kane County (Midwest)	9	9	.500	4.22	1.39	26	26	1	1	...	0-...	147.0	163	90	69	11	41-0	103	.281
1996— Brevard County (FSL)	8	7	.533	3.58	1.05	24	23	3	1	...	0-...	146.0	129	73	58	13	25-1	69	.231
— Portland (East.)	0	1	.000	4.33	1.11	4	4	1	0	...	0-...	27.0	26	15	13	1	4-0	13	.263
1997— Portland (East.)	9	7	.563	4.61	1.43	29	29	4	0	...	0-...	175.2	204	99	90	23	48-4	115	.292
1998— Florida (N.L.)	11	13	.458	5.21	1.54	31	31	1	0	0	0-0	174.1	222	106	101	20	46-3	88	.315
1999— Florida (N.L.)	11	15	.423	5.60	1.52	31	31	0	0	0	0-0	178.1	214	117	111	31	57-5	72	.302
2000— San Diego (N.L.)	7	8	.467	5.34	1.60	22	22	0	0	0	0-0	124.2	150	80	74	24	50-6	53	.301
— Kansas City (A.L.)	6	2	.750	4.77	1.37	11	10	2	0	0	0-0	71.2	84	39	38	8	14-0	26	.293
2001— Kansas City (A.L.)	1	6	.143	6.97	1.69	10	10	0	0	0	0-0	50.1	73	41	39	12	12-2	21	.351
— Omaha (PCL)	6	5	.545	6.17	1.55	18	18	0	0	...	0-...	105.0	143	73	72	21	20-1	74	.332
2002— Nashville (PCL)	9	8	.529	4.27	1.25	23	22	1	1	...	0-...	126.1	132	69	60	15	26-1	98	.267
— Pittsburgh (N.L.)	1	6	.143	3.88	1.21	11	11	0	0	0	0-0	62.2	62	29	27	7	14-8	31	.256
2003— Nashville (PCL)	7	0	1.000	1.41	0.63	9	8	1	1	...	0-...	51.0	32	11	8	2	0-0	40	.178
— Pittsburgh (N.L.)	2	1	.667	4.72	1.34	34	7	0	0	5	1-1	76.1	91	45	40	8	11-2	38	.290
American League totals (2 years)	7	8	.467	5.68	1.50	21	20	2	0	0	0-0	122.0	157	80	77	20	26-2	47	.317
National League totals (5 years)	32	43	.427	5.15	1.49	129	102	1	0	5	1-1	616.1	739	377	353	90	178-24	282	.299
Major League totals (6 years)	39	51	.433	5.24	1.49	150	122	3	0	5	1-1	738.1	896	457	430	110	204-26	329	.302

MEARS, CHRIS   P

PERSONAL: Born January 20, 1978, in Ottawa, Ontario. ... 6-4/190. ... Throws right, bats right. ... Full name: Christopher Peter Mears. ... High school: Lord Bing (Vancouver, B.C.).

TRANSACTIONS/CAREER NOTES: Selected by Seattle Mariners organization in fifth round of free agent draft (June 4, 1996). ... On Lancaster disabled list (August 20-29, 1999). ... On disabled list (May 24-31, 2001). ... Granted free agency (October 15, 2002). ... Signed by Detroit Tigers organization (December 19, 2002). ... Contract purchased by Detroit from Toledo (June 29, 2003). ... Optioned to Toledo by Detroit (August 17, 2003). ... Recalled by Detroit from Toledo (September 1, 2003).

CAREER HITTING: 0-for-0 (.000), 0 R, 0 2B, 0 3B, 0 HR, 0 RBI.

Year League	W	L	Pct.	ERA	WHIP	G	GS	CG	ShO	Hld.	Sv.-Opp.	IP	H	R	ER	HR	BB-IBB	SO	Avg.
1996— Ariz. Mariners (Ariz.)	1	2	.333	3.60	1.12	6	5	0	0	...	0-...	25.0	23	11	10	0	5-0	27	.240
1997— Everett (Northwest)	3	5	.375	5.34	1.64	12	12	0	0	...	0-...	62.1	82	47	37	5	20-0	47	.318
1998— Everett (Northwest)	9	1	.900	2.74	1.21	15	15	1	0	...	0-...	98.2	86	39	30	6	33-0	67	.234
— Orlando (Sou.)	0	1	.000	9.64	2.14	1	1	0	0	...	0-...	4.2	8	5	5	0	2-0	4	.364
1999— Wisconsin (Midw.)	10	1	.909	2.43	1.03	13	13	2	1	...	0-...	89.0	76	33	24	1	16-0	78	.228
— Lancaster (Calif.)	3	6	.333	7.08	1.63	10	10	0	0	...	0-...	54.2	71	44	43	12	18-0	45	.313
2000— Lancaster (Calif.)	11	8	.579	4.76	1.53	28	28	0	0	...	0-...	151.1	178	92	80	13	54-0	89	.300
2001— San Bernardino (Calif.)	7	6	.538	4.46	1.43	38	12	0	0	...	0-...	107.0	104	59	53	10	49-1	74	.260
2002— San Antonio (Texas)	6	9	.400	3.14	1.23	30	20	1	0	...	0-...	143.1	138	57	50	16	38-2	103	.253
2003— Toledo (Int'l)	5	1	.833	2.78	1.23	25	5	0	0	...	2-...	58.1	53	20	18	5	19-2	28	.245
— Detroit (A.L.)	1	3	.250	5.44	1.48	29	3	0	0	1	5-5	41.1	50	28	25	5	11-0	21	.307
Major League totals (1 year)	1	3	.250	5.44	1.48	29	3	0	0	1	5-5	41.1	50	28	25	5	11-0	21	.307

MECHE, GIL   P

PERSONAL: Born September 8, 1978, in Lafayette, La. ... 6-3/200. ... Throws right, bats right. ... Full name: Gilbert Allen Meche. ... Name pronounced: MESH. ... High school: Acadiana (Lafayette, La.).

TRANSACTIONS/CAREER NOTES: Selected by Seattle Mariners organization in first round (22nd pick overall) of free-agent draft (June 4, 1996). ... On Seattle disabled list (May 29-June 13 and July 31, 2000-remainder of season); included rehabilitation assignments to Tacoma (June 7-13), Wisconsin (August 22-27) and Everett (August 27-28). ... On disabled list (March 31, 2001-entire season). ... On San Antonio disabled list (June 21-July 20, 2002). ... Optioned to Tacoma by Seattle (August 31, 2003). ... Recalled from Tacoma (September 2, 2003).

CAREER HITTING: 1-for-5 (.200), 0 R, 0 2B, 0 3B, 0 HR, 0 RBI.

Year League	W	L	Pct.	ERA	WHIP	G	GS	CG	ShO	Hld.	Sv.-Opp.	IP	H	R	ER	HR	BB-IBB	SO	Avg.
1996— Ariz. Mariners (Ariz.)	0	1	.000	6.00	1.67	2	0	0	0	...	0-...	3.0	4	2	2	0	1-0	4	.333
1997— Everett (Northwest)	3	4	.429	3.98	1.33	12	12	•1	0	...	0-...	74.2	75	40	33	7	24-0	62	.264
— Wisconsin (Midw.)	0	2	.000	3.00	1.33	2	2	0	0	...	0-...	12.0	12	5	4	1	4-0	14	.261
1998— Wisconsin (Midw.)	8	7	.533	3.44	1.34	26	0	0	0	...	0-...	149.0	136	77	57	9	63-0	168	.238
1999— New Haven (East.)	3	4	.429	3.05	1.31	10	10	0	0	...	0-...	59.0	51	24	20	3	26-0	56	.231
— Tacoma (PCL)	2	2	.500	3.19	1.42	6	6	0	0	...	0-...	31.0	31	12	11	3	13-0	24	.261
— Seattle (A.L.)	8	4	.667	4.73	1.52	16	15	0	0	0	0-0	85.2	73	48	45	9	57-1	47	.237
2000— Seattle (A.L.)	4	4	.500	3.78	1.34	15	15	1	1	0	0-0	85.2	75	37	36	7	40-0	60	.240
— Tacoma (PCL)	1	1	.500	3.86	1.43	3	3	0	0	...	0-...	14.0	10	7	6	1	10-0	15	.200
— Wisconsin (Midw.)	0	0	...	0.00	0.60	1	1	0	0	...	0-...	5.0	1	0	0	0	2-0	6	.067
— Everett (Northwest)	0	1	.000	9.00	3.00	1	1	0	0	...	0-...	1.0	3	1	1	0	4-0	0	.600
2001— Seattle (A.L.)										Did not play.								
2002— San Antonio (Texas)	4	6	.400	6.51	1.54	25	13	0	0	...	0-...	65.0	68	49	47	8	32-0	56	.271
2003— Seattle (A.L.)	15	13	.536	4.59	1.34	32	32	1	0	0	0-0	186.1	187	97	95	30	63-2	130	.263
Major League totals (3 years)	**27**	**21**	**.563**	**4.43**	**1.38**	**63**	**62**	**2**	**1**	**0**	**0-0**	**357.2**	**335**	**182**	**176**	**46**	**160-3**	**237**	**.252**

MECIR, JIM   P

PERSONAL: Born May 16, 1970, in Queens, N.Y. ... 6-1/230. ... Throws right, bats both. ... Full name: James Jason Mecir. ... Name pronounced: mah-SEAR. ... High school: Smithtown East (St. James, N.Y.). ... College: Eckerd (Fla.).

TRANSACTIONS/CAREER NOTES: Selected by Seattle Mariners organization in third round of free-agent draft (June 3, 1991). ... On disabled list (June 25-August 25, 1992). ... Traded by Mariners with 1B Tino Martinez and P Jeff Nelson to New York Yankees for P Sterling Hitchcock and 3B Russ Davis (December 7, 1995). ... Traded by Yankees to Boston Red Sox (September 29, 1997), completing deal in which Yankees traded P Tony Armas Jr. and a player to be named later to Red Sox for C Mike Stanley and IF Randy Brown (August 13, 1997). ... Selected by Tampa Bay Devil Rays in second round (36th pick overall) of expansion draft (November 18, 1997). ... On disabled list (May 12, 1999-remainder of season). ... On Tampa Bay disabled list (April 27-May 23, 2000). ... Traded by Devil Rays with P Todd Belitz to Oakland Athletics for P Jesus Colome and a player to be named later (July 28, 2000). ... On Oakland disabled list (August 2-September 5, 2001); included rehabilitation assignment to Sacramento (September 3-5). ... On suspended list (September 2-7, 2002). ... On disabled list (March 21-April 23, 2003). ... Sent to Sacramento on rehab assignment (April 19, 2003). ... Reinstated from 15-day disabled list (April 23, 2003). ... Recalled from rehab assignment (April 24, 2003). ... Placed on 15-day disabled list (July 24, 2003). ... Reinstated from 15-day disabled list (August 13, 2003).

CAREER HITTING: 0-for-1 (.000), 0 R, 0 2B, 0 3B, 0 HR, 0 RBI.

Year League	W	L	Pct.	ERA	WHIP	G	GS	CG	ShO	Hld.	Sv.-Opp.	IP	H	R	ER	HR	BB-IBB	SO	Avg.
1991— San Bernardino (Calif.)	3	5	.375	4.22	1.55	14	12	0	0	...	1-...	70.1	72	40	33	3	37-0	48	.268
1992— San Bernardino (Calif.)	4	5	.444	4.67	1.59	14	11	0	0	...	0-...	61.2	72	40	32	8	26-0	53	.289
1993— Riverside (Calif.)	9	11	.450	4.33	1.50	26	26	1	0	...	0-...	145.1	160	89	70	3	58-2	85	.281
1994— Jacksonville (Sou.)	6	5	.545	2.69	1.34	46	0	0	0	...	13-...	80.1	73	28	24	5	35-3	53	.245
1995— Tacoma (PCL)	1	4	.200	3.10	1.31	40	0	0	0	...	8-...	69.2	63	29	24	3	28-7	46	.238
— Seattle (A.L.)	0	0	...	0.00	1.50	2	0	0	0	0	0-0	4.2	5	1	0	0	2-0	3	.263
1996— Columbus (Int'l)	3	3	.500	2.27	1.09	33	0	0	0	...	7-...	47.2	37	14	12	2	15-2	52	.214
— New York (A.L.)	1	1	.500	5.13	1.61	26	0	0	0	0	0-0	40.1	42	24	23	6	23-4	38	.275
1997— Columbus (Int'l)	1	1	.500	1.00	0.74	24	0	0	0	...	11-...	27.0	14	4	3	0	6-0	34	.157
— New York (A.L.)	0	4	.000	5.88	1.37	25	0	0	0	1	0-1	33.2	36	23	22	5	10-1	25	.279
1998— Tampa Bay (A.L.)	7	2	.778	3.11	1.20	68	0	0	0	14	0-3	84.0	68	30	29	6	33-5	77	.225
1999— Tampa Bay (A.L.)	0	1	.000	2.61	1.40	17	0	0	0	6	0-2	20.2	15	7	6	0	14-0	15	.205
2000— Tampa Bay (A.L.)	7	2	.778	3.08	1.15	38	0	0	0	11	1-4	49.2	35	17	17	2	22-0	33	.201
— Oakland (A.L.)	3	1	.750	2.80	1.39	25	0	0	0	10	4-9	35.1	35	14	11	2	14-2	37	.255
2001— Oakland (A.L.)	2	8	.200	3.43	1.27	54	0	0	0	17	3-8	63.0	54	25	24	4	26-7	61	.231
— Sacramento (PCL)	0	0	...	0.00	1.00	1	1	0	0	...	0-...	1.0	1	0	0	0	0-0	0	.250
2002— Oakland (A.L.)	6	4	.600	4.26	1.43	61	0	0	0	20	1-6	67.2	68	36	32	5	29-4	53	.259
2003— Sacramento (PCL)	0	0	...	5.40	2.10	3	2	0	0	...	0-...	3.1	5	4	2	0	2-0	3	.313
— Oakland (A.L.)	2	3	.400	5.59	1.51	41	0	0	0	12	1-2	37.0	40	25	23	4	16-1	25	.280
Major League totals (9 years)	**28**	**26**	**.519**	**3.86**	**1.35**	**357**	**0**	**0**	**0**	**91**	**10-35**	**436.0**	**398**	**202**	**187**	**34**	**189-24**	**367**	**.245**

MELHUSE, ADAM   C

PERSONAL: Born March 27, 1972, in Santa Clara, Calif. ... 6-2/200. ... Bats both, throws right. ... Full name: Adam Michael Melhuse. ... High school: Lincoln (Stockton, Calif.). ... College: UCLA.

TRANSACTIONS/CAREER NOTES: Selected by Toronto Blue Jays organization in 13th round of free-agent draft (June 3, 1993). ... Released by Blue Jays (April 2, 1999). ... Re-signed by Blue Jays (April 6, 1999). ... Granted free agency (October 15, 1999). ... Signed by Los Angeles Dodgers organization (December 15, 1999). ... Traded by Dodgers to Colorado Rockies for a player to be named later (June 17, 2000). ... Granted free agency (October 18, 2000). ... Re-signed by Rockies (May 29, 2001). ... Granted free agency (October 17, 2001). ... Granted free agency (October 15, 2002). ... Signed by Oakland A's (November 13, 2002).

2003 GAMES PLAYED BY POSITION (MLB): C—33, 3B—2, 1B—1.

										BATTING										FIELDING		
Year Team (League)	Pos.	G	AB	R	H	2B	3B	HR	RBI	BB	SO	HBP	GDP	SB-CS	Avg.	OBP	SLG	OPS		E	Pct.
1993— St. Catharines (NYP)	3B	73	266	40	68	14	2	5	32	45	61	0	4	4-0	.256	.360	.380	.740		14	.927
1994— Hagerstown (SAL)	C-1B	118	422	61	109	16	3	11	58	53	77	1	13	6-8	.258	.338	.389	.727		13	.983
1995— Dunedin (Fla. St.)	C-1B-OF	123	428	43	92	20	0	4	41	61	87	1	7	6-1	.215	.312	.290	.601		13	.980
1996— Dunedin (Fla. St.)	3-C-1-OF	97	315	50	78	23	2	13	51	69	68	3	5	3-1	.248	.384	.457	.841		15	.978
— Knoxville (Sou.)	C	32	94	13	20	3	0	1	6	14	29	0	3	0-1	.213	.312	.277	.589		2	.989
1997— Knoxville (Sou.)	C-1B-OF	31	87	14	20	3	0	3	10	19	19	0	1	0-0	.230	.364	.368	.732		2	.990
— Syracuse (Int'l)	2B-C-OF	118	118	7	28	5	1	2	9	12	18	1	2	1-1	.237	.311	.347	.658		2	.992
1998— Knoxville (Sou.)	C-1B-OF	76	240	56	72	22	0	15	43	70	39	0	6	4-4	.300	.458	.579	1.037		11	.977
— Syracuse (Int'l)	3B-C	12	38	4	11	3	0	1	7	7	6	0	0	0-0	.289	.391	.447	.839		2	.965

M

| | | | | | | | BATTING | | | | | | | | | | | | | FIELDING | |
Year	Team (League)	Pos.	G	AB	R	H	2B	3B	HR	RBI	BB	SO	HBP	GDP	SB-CS	Avg.	OBP	SLG	OPS	E	Pct.
1999— Knoxville (Sou.)	3B-C-1B	107	374	79	110	25	0	19	69	* 108	76	4	10	5-6	.294	.454	.513	.967	4	.986
— Syracuse (Int'l)	C	21	71	15	20	5	0	2	16	10	20	0	1	1-1	.282	.370	.437	.807	0	1.000
2000— San Antonio (Texas)	C-O-3-1	16	58	17	23	7	0	2	9	11	9	2	2	3-0	.397	.500	.621	1.121	2	.973
— Albuquerque (PCL)	C-1-3-O	36	108	21	37	9	0	1	19	22	21	0	2	4-2	.343	.454	.454	.908	0	1.000
— Los Angeles (N.L.)		1	1	0	0	0	0	0	0	0	1	0	0	0-0	.000	.000	.000	.000	...	...
— Colorado (N.L.)	1B-C-OF	23	23	3	4	0	1	0	4	3	5	0	1	0-0	.174	.269	.261	.530	0	1.000
— Colo. Springs (PCL)	OF-C-1B	42	140	23	39	5	1	3	18	21	35	0	4	2-3	.279	.373	.393	.766	2	.987
2001— Colo. Springs (PCL)	C-1B-OF	54	184	26	49	10	1	7	32	31	42	2	8	0-1	.266	.378	.446	.824	5	.986
— Colorado (N.L.)	C-1B	40	71	5	13	2	0	1	8	6	18	0	3	1-0	.183	.241	.254	.494	1	.991
2002— Iowa (PCL)	C-3-1-O-S	72	226	33	66	19	0	7	39	28	47	0	3	2-3	.292	.370	.469	.839	7	.983
— Colo. Springs (PCL)	C-1B	34	115	25	40	10	1	6	20	16	23	0	5	2-1	.348	.424	.609	1.033	4	.982
2003— Sacramento (PCL)	C-O-3-D	45	147	26	42	9	0	3	17	26	32	1	5	0-1	.286	.394	.408	.802	2	.992
— Oakland (A.L.)	C-3B-1B	40	77	13	23	7	0	5	14	9	19	0	2	0-0	.299	.372	.584	.957	2	.986
American League totals (1 year)		40	77	13	23	7	0	5	14	9	19	0	2	0-0	.299	.372	.584	.957	2	.986
National League totals (2 years)		64	95	8	17	2	1	1	12	9	24	0	4	1-0	.179	.245	.253	.498	1	.992
Major League totals (3 years)		104	172	21	40	9	1	6	26	18	43	0	6	1-0	.233	.302	.401	.703	3	.989

MELUSKEY, MITCH   C

PERSONAL: Born September 18, 1973, in Yakima, Wash. ... 6-0/200. ... Bats both, throws right. ... Full name: Mitchell Wade Meluskey. ... Name pronounced: mel-US-key. ... High school: Eisenhower (Yakima, Wash.).

TRANSACTIONS/CAREER NOTES: Selected by Cleveland Indians organization in 12th round of free-agent draft (June 1, 1992). ... Traded by Indians to Houston Astros for OF Buck McNabb (April 27, 1995). ... On disabled list (April 26, 1999-remainder of season; and July 31-August 18, 2000). ... Traded by Astros with P Chris Holt and OF Roger Cedeno to Detroit Tigers for C Brad Ausmus, P Doug Brocail and P Nelson Cruz (December 11, 2000). ... On disabled list (March 23, 2001-entire season; and April 21, 2002-remainder of season). ... Released by Tigers (October 2, 2002). ... Signed by Oakland Athletics organization (November 18, 2002). ... Released by A's (April 24, 2003). ... Signed by Houston Astros (August 10, 2003).

| | | | | | | | BATTING | | | | | | | | | | | | | FIELDING | |
Year	Team (League)	Pos.	G	AB	R	H	2B	3B	HR	RBI	BB	SO	HBP	GDP	SB-CS	Avg.	OBP	SLG	OPS	E	Pct.
1992— Burlington (Appal.)	C	43	126	23	29	7	0	3	16	29	36	0	0	3-0	.230	.369	.357	.727	4	.985
1993— Columbus (S. Atl.)	C	101	342	36	84	18	3	3	47	35	69	4	5	1-1	.246	.317	.342	.659	7	.990
1994— Kinston (Caro.)	C	100	319	36	77	16	1	3	41	49	62	2	4	3-4	.241	.342	.326	.668	6	.988
1995— Kinston (Caro.)	C	8	29	5	7	5	0	0	2	2	9	0	1	0-0	.241	.290	.414	.704	1	.985
— Kissimmee (Fla. St.)	C	78	261	23	56	18	1	3	31	27	33	1	12	3-0	.215	.287	.326	.612	10	.980
1996— Kissimmee (Fla. St.)	C	74	231	29	77	19	0	1	31	29	26	1	9	1-1	.333	.402	.429	.831	9	.974
— Jackson (Texas)	C	38	134	18	42	11	0	0	21	18	24	1	6	0-0	.313	.396	.396	.792	5	.978
1997— Jackson (Texas)	C	73	241	49	82	18	0	14	46	31	39	3	7	1-3	.340	.417	.589	1.006	6	.985
— New Orleans (A.A.)	C	51	172	22	43	7	0	3	21	25	38	1	6	0-0	.250	.347	.343	.690	4	.989
1998— New Orleans (PCL)	C-OF	121	397	76	140	41	0	17	71	85	59	3	15	2-0	.353	.465	.584	1.050	10	.987
— Houston (N.L.)	C	8	8	1	2	1	0	0	0	1	4	0	1	0-0	.250	.333	.375	.708	0	1.000
1999— Houston (N.L.)	C	10	33	4	7	1	0	1	3	5	6	0	1	0-0	.212	.316	.333	.649	0	1.000
2000— Houston (N.L.)	C-3B	117	337	47	101	21	0	14	69	55	74	4	7	1-0	.300	.401	.487	.888	13	.981
2001— Detroit (A.L.)										Did not play.										
2002— Detroit (A.L.)	C	8	27	3	6	0	0	0	1	5	3	1	0	0-0	.222	.353	.222	.575	0	1.000
2003— Sacramento (PCL)	DH-OF	4	14	0	2	2	0	0	4	1	3	0	0	0-0	.143	.188	.286	.473	0	1.000
— Round Rock (Texas)	C-DH-OF	13	49	5	13	2	0	1	6	5	9	0	1	1-0	.265	.327	.367	.695	1	.985
— Houston (N.L.)		12	9	1	1	1	0	0	2	2	2	0	0	0-0	.111	.250	.222	.472	0	...
American League totals (1 year)		8	27	3	6	0	0	0	1	5	3	1	0	0-0	.222	.353	.222	.575	0	1.000
National League totals (4 years)		147	387	53	111	24	0	15	74	63	86	4	9	2-0	.287	.389	.465	.854	13	.983
Major League totals (5 years)		155	414	56	117	24	0	15	75	68	89	5	9	2-0	.283	.386	.449	.835	13	.983

MENCH, KEVIN   OF

PERSONAL: Born January 7, 1978, in Wilmington, Del. ... 6-0/230. ... Bats right, throws right. ... Full name: Kevin Ford Mench. ... High school: St. Mark's (Wilmington, Del.). ... College: Delaware.

TRANSACTIONS/CAREER NOTES: Selected by Texas Rangers organization in fourth round of free-agent draft (June 2, 1999); pick received as part of compensation for Arizona Diamondbacks signing Type A free agent P Todd Stottlemyre. ... On disabled list (June 10-30, 2001). ... On Texas disabled list (March 21-April 17, 2003); included rehabilitation assignment to Frisco (April 14-17). ... Recalled from rehab assignment (April 17,2003). ... Optioned to Oklahoma (May 2, 2003). ... Recalled from 15-day disabled list (June 6, 2003). ... Placed on 15-day disabled list (July 9, 2003). ... Transferred to 60-day disabled list (September 6, 2003).

2003 GAMES PLAYED BY POSITION (MLB): OF—35.

| | | | | | | | BATTING | | | | | | | | | | | | | FIELDING | |
Year	Team (League)	Pos.	G	AB	R	H	2B	3B	HR	RBI	BB	SO	HBP	GDP	SB-CS	Avg.	OBP	SLG	OPS	E	Pct.
1999— Pulaski (Appal.)	OF	65	260	36	94	22	1	* 16	60	28	48	2	2	12-2	.362	.420	.638	1.059	1	.989
— Savannah (S. Atl.)	OF	6	23	4	7	1	1	2	8	2	4	0	1	0-0	.304	.360	.696	1.056	2	.900
2000— Charlotte (Fla. St.)	OF	132	491	* 118	* 164	* 39	2	27	* 121	78	72	7	9	19-7	.334	.427	.615	1.042	1	.996
2001— Tulsa (Texas)	OF	120	475	78	126	34	2	26	83	34	76	6	7	4-6	.265	.319	.509	.828	4	.983
2002— Oklahoma (PCL)	OF	26	98	17	21	8	0	6	15	17	33	2	7	0-0	.214	.342	.480	.821	2	.965
— Texas (A.L.)	OF-DH	110	366	52	95	20	2	15	60	31	83	8	4	1-1	.260	.327	.448	.775	2	.990
2003— Frisco (Texas)	OF	3	11	1	1	0	0	0	0	1	2	0	1	0-0	.091	.167	.091	.258	0	1.000
— Oklahoma (PCL)	OF	29	105	16	28	8	0	4	21	19	15	1	1	2-0	.267	.366	.457	.824	0	1.000
— Texas (A.L.)	OF	38	125	15	40	12	0	2	11	10	17	3	2	1-1	.320	.381	.464	.845	1	.984
Major League totals (2 years)		148	491	67	135	32	2	17	71	41	100	11	6	2-2	.275	.341	.452	.793	3	.989

MENDEZ, CARLOS   1B/DH

PERSONAL: Born June 18, 1974, in Caracas, Venezuela. ... 6-0/228. ... Bats right, throws right. ... Full name: Carlos Alberto Castillo Mendez. ... High school: Pedro E. Collegio (Venezuela).

TRANSACTIONS/CAREER NOTES: Signed by Kansas City Royals organization as a non-drafted free agent (January 10, 1991). ... Granted free agency (October 15, 1999). ... Signed by Detroit Tigers organization (November 17, 1999). ... Granted free agency (October 15, 2000). ... Re-signed by Tigers (November 17, 2000). ... Granted free agency (October 15, 2001). ... Signed by Oakland Athletics organization (January 29, 2002). ... Granted free agency (October 15, 2002). ... Signed by Baltimore Orioles as a minor league free agent (November 8, 2002).

2003 GAMES PLAYED BY POSITION (MLB): 1B—9, DH—8.

Year	Team (League)	Pos.	G	AB	R	H	2B	3B	HR	RBI	BB	SO	HBP	GDP	SB-CS	Avg.	OBP	SLG	OPS	E	Pct.
1992— GC Royals (GCL)	1B-C-3B	49	200	34	61	16	1	3	33	8	13	2	2	2-1	.305	.333	.440	.773	2	.995
1993— GC Royals (GCL)	C-1B	50	163	18	51	10	0	4	27	4	15	2	2	6-1	.313	.329	.448	.777	4	.983
1994— Rockford (Midwest)	C-1B	104	363	45	129	26	2	5	51	13	50	5	11	0-2	.355	.382	.479	.861	3	.991
1995— Wilmington (Caro.)	1B-C	107	396	46	108	19	2	7	61	18	36	0	17	0-4	.273	.301	.384	.685	6	.993
1996— Wilmington (Caro.)	C-1B	109	406	40	119	25	3	4	59	22	39	3	6	3-1	.293	.329	.399	.728	9	.981
1997— Wichita (Texas)	1B-C-OF	129	507	72	165	32	1	12	90	19	43	1	19	4-7	.325	.346	.464	.809	9	.990
1998— Omaha (PCL)	1B-C	50	173	23	47	13	0	2	18	10	24	1	4	3-0	.272	.312	.382	.693	0	1.000
— Wichita (Texas)	C-1B-SS	52	207	37	66	14	0	9	39	7	20	0	10	4-1	.319	.333	.517	.850	3	.989
1999— Omaha (PCL)	1B-OF-C	84	293	38	82	25	0	10	37	6	32	0	8	4-3	.280	.291	.468	.759	3	.992
2000— Toledo (Int'l)	C-1-OF-3	100	374	49	108	21	0	19	72	12	37	3	11	0-0	.289	.311	.497	.808	5	.990
2001— Toledo (Int'l)	1B-C	102	398	45	98	27	1	18	76	9	53	5	13	0-0	.246	.268	.455	.723	6	.992
2002— Sacramento (PCL)	C-1B-OF	103	404	58	131	26	1	12	74	12	52	3	11	3-1	.324	.348	.483	.830	5	.991
2003— Ottawa (Int'l)	1-D-3-C	61	248	32	86	18	4	4	42	11	28	1	7	1-2	.347	.375	.500	.875	3	.994
— Baltimore (A.L.)	1B-DH	26	45	3	10	2	0	0	5	0	12	0	0	0-0	.222	.217	.267	.484	2	.939
Major League totals (1 year)		26	45	3	10	2	0	0	5	0	12	0	0	0-0	.222	.217	.267	.484	2	.939

MENDEZ, DONALDO — SS

PERSONAL: Born June 7, 1978, in Barquisimeto, Venezuela. ... 6-1/155. ... Bats right, throws right. ... Full name: Donaldo Alfonso Mendez.
TRANSACTIONS/CAREER NOTES: Signed as non-drafted free agent by Houston Astros organization (November 16, 1995). ... On disabled list (June 19, 1998-entire season). ... Selected by San Diego Padres from Astros organization in Rule 5 major league draft (December 11, 2000). ... On disabled list (June 5-September 4, 2001). ... Recalled from Portland of the Pacific Coast League by San Diego (June 8, 2003). ... Optioned to Portland by San Diego (July 7, 2003). ... Recalled by San Diego from Portland (September 5, 2003).
2003 GAMES PLAYED BY POSITION (MLB): SS—26.

Year	Team (League)	Pos.	G	AB	R	H	2B	3B	HR	RBI	BB	SO	HBP	GDP	SB-CS	Avg.	OBP	SLG	OPS	E	Pct.
1996— Dom. Astros (DSL).		38	122	20	32	3	1	0	19	17	17	...	...	3-...	.262	...	.303	...	...	...
1997— Kissimmee (Fla. St.)	SS	5	16	0	3	0	0	0	0	1	4	0	0	1-1	.188	.235	.188	.423	1	.960
— GC Astros (GCL)	3B-SS	48	150	16	29	4	0	1	13	13	32	2	2	9-6	.193	.262	.240	.502	18	.924
1998—										Did not play.											
1999— Auburn (NY-Penn)	2B-SS	25	86	9	18	1	1	0	10	2	23	4	3	10-5	.209	.255	.244	.500	14	.877
2000— Michigan (Midw.)	SS	101	370	65	100	17	0	2	51	33	68	14	3	39-10	.270	.351	.332	.683	22	.957
2001— San Diego (N.L.)	SS	46	118	11	18	2	1	1	5	5	37	3	2	1-2	.153	.206	.212	.418	12	.920
2002— Mobile (Sou.)	SS	56	224	36	49	16	0	4	18	19	53	6	2	15-5	.219	.297	.344	.641	12	.952
— Portland (PCL)	SS	64	217	32	47	9	1	6	18	14	63	6	0	11-4	.217	.282	.350	.632	8	.969
2003— San Diego (N.L.)	SS	26	84	10	19	6	0	2	9	7	32	2	0	1-0	.226	.298	.369	.667	5	.951
— Portland (PCL)	SS-3B-2B	102	358	49	81	17	0	6	36	25	83	7	7	10-7	.226	.288	.324	.612	16	.959
Major League totals (2 years)		72	202	21	37	8	1	3	14	12	69	5	2	2-2	.183	.245	.277	.523	17	.933

MENDOZA, RAMIRO — P

PERSONAL: Born June 15, 1972, in Los Santos, Panama. ... 6-2/195. ... Throws right, bats right.
TRANSACTIONS/CAREER NOTES: Signed as non-drafted free agent by New York Yankees organization (November 13, 1991). ... On New York disabled list (June 28-July 28 and August 4, 2000-remainder of season); included rehabilitation assignment to Tampa (July 19-27). ... On disabled list (March 26-April 10, 2001). ... On disabled list (March 24-April 7, 2002). ... Granted free agency (October 28, 2002). ... Signed by Boston Red Sox (December 31, 2002). ... Sent on rehab assignment to Gulf Coast League (June 19, 2003). ... Recalled from Sarasota rehab assignment (July 1, 2003). ... Activated from 15-day disabled list; reinstated from 15-day disabled list (July 5, 2003). ... Placed on 15-day disabled list (August 3, 2003). ... Sent on rehab assignment (August 16, 2003). ... Removed from 15-day disabled list (September 3, 2003).
CAREER HITTING: 0-for-3 (.000), 0 R, 0 2B, 0 3B, 0 HR, 0 RBI.

Year	League	W	L	Pct.	ERA	WHIP	G	GS	CG	ShO	Hld.	Sv.-Opp.	IP	H	R	ER	HR	BB-IBB	SO	Avg.
1992— Dom. Yankees (DSL)		10	2	.833	2.13	1.10	15	15	5	0	...	0-...	109.2	93	37	26	...	28-...	79	...
1993— GC Yankees (GCL)		4	5	.444	2.79	0.98	15	9	0	0	...	1-...	67.2	59	26	21	3	7-0	61	.224
— Greensboro (S. Atl.)		0	1	.000	2.45	2.18	2	0	0	0	...	0-...	3.2	3	1	1	0	5-0	3	.231
1994— Tampa (FSL)		12	6	.667	3.01	1.25	22	21	1	0	...	0-...	134.1	133	54	45	7	35-1	110	.258
1995— Norwich (East.)		5	6	.455	3.21	1.34	19	19	2	1	...	0-...	89.2	87	39	32	4	33-0	68	.254
— Columbus (Int'l)		1	0	1.000	2.57	0.86	2	2	0	0	...	0-...	14.0	10	4	4	0	2-0	13	.208
1996— Columbus (Int'l)		6	2	.750	2.51	1.19	15	15	0	0	...	0-...	97.0	96	30	27	2	19-0	61	.266
— New York (A.L.)		4	5	.444	6.79	1.70	12	11	0	0	0	0-0	53.0	80	43	40	5	10-1	34	.343
1997— Columbus (Int'l)		0	0	...	5.68	1.26	1	1	0	0	...	0-...	6.1	7	6	4	1	1-0	4	.233
— New York (A.L.)		8	6	.571	4.24	1.38	39	15	0	0	4	2-4	133.2	157	67	63	15	28-2	82	.292
1998— New York (A.L.)		10	2	.833	3.25	1.24	41	14	1	1	5	1-4	130.1	131	50	47	9	30-6	56	.264
1999— New York (A.L.)		9	9	.500	4.29	1.36	53	6	0	0	4	3-6	123.2	141	68	59	13	27-3	80	.284
2000— New York (A.L.)		7	4	.636	4.25	1.31	14	9	1	1	0	0-1	65.2	66	32	31	9	20-1	30	.260
— Tampa (FSL)		0	2	.000	7.20	1.80	2	2	0	0	...	0-...	5.0	9	4	4	0	0-0	7	.409
2001— New York (A.L.)		8	4	.667	3.75	1.11	56	2	0	0	13	6-8	100.2	89	44	42	9	23-3	70	.241
2002— New York (A.L.)		8	4	.667	3.44	1.29	62	0	0	0	12	4-8	91.2	102	43	35	8	16-2	61	.275
2003— GC Red Sox (GCL)		0	0	...	0.00	0.43	2	2	0	0	...	0-...	7.0	3	0	0	0	0-0	4	.130
— Sarasota (Fla. St.)		1	0	1.000	0.00	0.60	1	1	0	0	...	0-...	5.0	2	0	0	0	1-0	4	.133
— Pawtucket (Int'l)		0	0	...	2.00	0.89	4	0	0	0	...	1-...	9.0	8	2	2	1	0-0	8	.242
— Boston (A.L.)		3	5	.375	6.75	1.77	37	5	0	0	3	0-1	66.2	98	51	50	10	20-4	36	.349
Major League totals (8 years)		57	39	.594	4.32	1.36	314	62	2	2	41	16-32	765.1	864	398	367	78	174-22	449	.284

MENECHINO, FRANK — IF

PERSONAL: Born January 7, 1971, in Staten Island, N.Y. ... 5-8/198. ... Bats right, throws right. ... Name pronounced: men-a-keen-o. ... High school: Susan E. Wagner (Staten Island, N.Y.). ... College: Alabama.
TRANSACTIONS/CAREER NOTES: Selected by Chicago White Sox organization in 45th round of free-agent draft (June 3, 1993). ... Selected by Oakland Athletics organization from White Sox organization in Rule 5 minor league draft (December 15, 1997). ... Placed on bereavement list (July 24, 2003). ... Removed from bereavement list (July 27, 2003).
2003 GAMES PLAYED BY POSITION (MLB): 2B—22, 3B—19, SS—3, DH—1.

M

Year	Team (League)	Pos.	G	AB	R	H	2B	3B	HR	RBI	BB	SO	HBP	GDP	SB-CS	Avg.	OBP	SLG	OPS	E	Pct.
1993—GC Whi. Sox (GCL)	2B	17	45	10	11	4	1	1	9	12	4	4	1	3-1	.244	.443	.444	.887	1	.979
— Hickory (S. Atl.)	2B	50	178	35	50	6	3	4	19	33	28	4	4	11-2	.281	.403	.416	.819	6	.977
1994—South Bend (Mid.)	2B	106	379	77	113	21	5	5	48	78	70	9	8	15-8	.298	.427	.420	.847	10	.979
1995—Prince Will. (Car.)	2B	* 137	476	65	124	31	3	6	58	96	75	11	17	6-2	.261	.391	.376	.767	15	.975
1996—Birmingham (Sou.)	2B	125	415	77	121	25	3	12	62	64	84	8	5	7-9	.292	.391	.453	.844	13	.978
1997—Nashville (A.A.)	2B-3B-OF	37	113	20	26	4	0	4	11	26	31	6	2	3-2	.230	.397	.372	.769	9	.948
— Birmingham (Sou.)	2B-3B	90	318	78	95	28	4	12	60	79	77	11	7	7-3	.299	.447	.525	.972	11	.974
1998—Edmonton (PCL)	2B	106	378	72	105	11	7	10	40	70	75	10	11	9-10	.278	.403	.423	.826	7	.979
1999—Vancouver (PCL)	3-S-2-D	130	501	103	155	31	•9	15	88	73	97	9	12	4-5	.309	.403	.497	.900	10	.980
— Oakland (A.L.)	SS-DH-3B	9	9	0	2	0	0	0	0	0	4	0	0	0-0	.222	.222	.222	.444	0	1.000
2000—Oakland (A.L.)	2-S-3-D	66	145	31	37	9	1	6	26	20	45	1	1	1-4	.255	.345	.455	.800	6	.974
— Sacramento (PCL)	SS-3B	9	38	8	12	2	0	2	2	5	4	0	0	1-0	.316	.395	.526	.922	0	1.000
2001—Oakland (A.L.)	2-S-3-D	139	471	82	114	22	2	12	60	79	97	19	13	2-3	.242	.369	.374	.742	16	.976
2002—Oakland (A.L.)	2-3-S-D	38	132	22	27	7	0	3	15	20	32	1	4	0-0	.205	.312	.326	.637	2	.986
— Sacramento (PCL)	SS-2B-3B	84	314	50	78	12	0	6	50	46	58	8	10	10-3	.248	.356	.344	.700	22	.941
2003—Oakland (A.L.)	2-3-S-D	43	83	10	16	0	0	2	9	19	16	4	2	0-0	.193	.364	.265	.630	4	.962
Major League totals (5 years)		295	840	145	196	38	3	23	110	138	194	25	20	3-7	.233	.354	.368	.722	28	.976

MERCADO, HECTOR — P

PERSONAL: Born April 29, 1974, in Catano, Puerto Rico. ... 6-3/235. ... Throws left, bats left. ... Full name: Hector Luis Mercado. ... Name pronounced: mur-CAH-do. ... High school: Jose S. Alegria (Dorado, Puerto Rico).

TRANSACTIONS/CAREER NOTES: Selected by Houston Astros organization in 13th round of free-agent draft (June 1, 1992). ... Selected by Florida Marlins organization from Astros organization in Rule 5 minor league draft (December 9, 1996). ... Selected by Philadelphia Phillies from Marlins organization in Rule 5 major league draft (December 15, 1997). ... Traded by Phillies to New York Mets for P Mike Welch (December 15, 1997). ... On disabled list (March 21, 1998-entire season). ... On disabled list (April 8-18 and April 24, 1999-remainder of season). ... Released by Mets (August 4, 1999). ... Signed by Cincinnati Reds organization (December 16, 1999). ... Traded by Reds to Philadelphia Phillies (March 30, 2002), completing deal in which Phillies traded OF Reggie Taylor to Reds for a player to be named (March 28, 2002). ... Placed on 15-day disabled list (April 16, 2003). ... Sent to Reading for rehab assignment (April 27, 2003). ... Activated from 15-day disabled list (May 26, 2003). ... Recalled from Scranton rehab assignment (May 24, 2003). ... Designated for assignment (July 21, 2003). ... Sent outright to Scranton (July 31, 2003). ... Recalled from Scranton (September 29, 2003).

CAREER HITTING: 1-for-9 (.111), 0 R, 0 2B, 0 3B, 0 HR, 0 RBI.

Year	League	W	L	Pct.	ERA	WHIP	G	GS	CG	ShO	Hld.	Sv.-Opp.	IP	H	R	ER	HR	BB-IBB	SO	Avg.
1992—GC Astros (GCL)		1	2	.333	4.20	1.57	13	3	0	0	...	0-...	30.0	22	17	14	0	25-0	36	.198
1993—GC Astros (GCL)		5	4	.556	2.42	1.16	11	11	1	1	...	0-...	67.0	49	26	18	1	29-0	59	.200
— Osceola (Florida St.)		1	1	.500	5.19	1.73	2	2	0	0	...	0-...	8.2	9	7	5	0	6-1	5	.273
1994—Osceola (Florida St.)		6	•13	.316	3.95	1.48	25	25	1	1	...	0-...	136.2	123	75	60	7	79-4	88	.243
1995—Jackson (Texas)		1	4	.200	7.80	2.27	8	7	0	0	...	0-...	30.0	36	33	26	5	32-1	20	.300
— Kissimmee (Fla. St.)		6	8	.429	3.46	1.28	19	17	2	0	...	0-...	104.0	96	50	40	2	37-0	68	.247
1996—Kissimmee (Fla. St.)		3	5	.375	4.16	1.58	56	0	0	0	...	3-...	80.0	78	43	37	4	48-1	68	.263
1997—Portland (East.)		11	3	.786	3.96	1.41	31	17	1	1	...	0-...	129.2	129	66	57	10	54-5	125	.257
— Charlotte (Int'l)		0	1	.000	9.00	2.00	1	1	0	0	...	0-...	5.0	5	5	5	2	5-0	1	.250
1998— New York (N.L.)											Did not play.									
1999—Norfolk (Int'l)		0	0	...	1.50	0.67	2	2	0	0	...	0-...	6.0	3	1	1	1	1-0	2	.150
2000—Cincinnati (N.L.)		0	0	...	4.50	1.43	12	0	0	0	...	1	0-0	14.0	12	7	7	2	8-0	13	.240
— Louisville (Int'l)		1	5	.167	3.04	1.52	47	5	0	0	...	2-...	77.0	69	26	26	2	48-2	67	.244
2001—Louisville (Int'l)		1	0	1.000	1.35	1.35	12	0	0	0	...	1-...	13.1	12	2	2	0	6-1	13	.250
— Cincinnati (N.L.)		3	2	.600	4.08	1.60	56	0	0	0	5	0-2	53.0	55	27	24	6	30-1	59	.267
2002—Scran./W.B. (I.L.)		3	1	.750	1.62	1.02	26	0	0	0	...	3-...	33.1	22	6	6	2	12-1	43	.186
— Philadelphia (N.L.)		2	2	.500	4.62	1.46	31	3	0	0	3	0-0	39.0	32	21	20	2	25-2	40	.224
2003—Reading (East.)		0	0	...	0.00	0.50	1	1	0	0	...	0-...	2.0	0	0	0	0	1-0	0	.000
— Philadelphia (N.L.)		0	0	...	5.79	1.61	13	0	0	0	0	1-2	18.2	18	12	12	5	12-0	15	.254
— Scran. (I.L.)		0	3	.000	1.41	1.41	14	2	0	0	...	0-...	32.0	34	12	5	2	11-0	20	.283
Major League totals (4 years)		5	4	.556	4.55	1.54	112	3	0	0	9	1-4	124.2	117	67	63	6	75-3	127	.249

MERCED, ORLANDO — OF/1B

PERSONAL: Born November 2, 1966... 6-1/195. ... Bats left, throws right. ... Full name: Orlando Luis Merced. ... Name pronounced: mer-SED. ... High school: University Garden (San Juan, Puerto Rico).

TRANSACTIONS/CAREER NOTES: Signed as non-drafted free agent by Pittsburgh Pirates organization (February 22, 1985). ... On Macon disabled list (April 18-28, 1987). ... On Watertown disabled list (June 23, 1987-remainder of season). ... On disabled list (May 1-18, August 1-16 and August 22-September 6, 1996). ... Traded by Pirates with IF Carlos Garcia and P Dan Plesac to Toronto Blue Jays for P Jose Silva, P Jose Pett, IF Brandon Cromer and three players to be named later (November 14, 1996); Pirates acquired P Mike Halperin, IF Abraham Nunez and C/OF Craig Wilson to complete deal (December 11, 1996). ... On disabled list (July 29-September 28, 1997). ... Granted free agency (October 27, 1997). ... Signed by Minnesota Twins organization (January 12, 1998). ... Traded by Twins with P Greg Swindell to Boston Red Sox for P Matt Kinney, P Joe Thomas and P John Barnes (July 31, 1998). ... Released by Red Sox (August 31, 1998). ... Signed by Chicago Cubs (September 5, 1998). ... Granted free agency (October 28, 1998). ... Signed by Montreal Expos organization (January 28, 1999). ... On disabled list (July 1-28, 1999). ... Granted free agency (October 15, 1999). ... Played with Orix Blue Wave of Japan Pacific League (2000). ... Signed by Houston Astros organization (August 16, 2000). ... Granted free agency (October 18, 2000). ... Re-signed by Astros organization (January 8, 2001). ... On disabled list (June 23-July 12, 2001). ... Granted free agency (November 5, 2001). ... Re-signed by Astros (December 7, 2001).

2003 GAMES PLAYED BY POSITION (MLB): OF—31, 1B—12, DH—7, 3B—2.

Year	Team (League)	Pos.	G	AB	R	H	2B	3B	HR	RBI	BB	SO	HBP	GDP	SB-CS	Avg.	OBP	SLG	OPS	E	Pct.
1985— GC Pirates (GCL)	3B-SS-1B	40	136	16	31	6	0	1	13	9	9	1	3	3-1	.228	.281	.294	.575	28	.816
1986— Macon (S. Atl.)	3B-OF	65	173	20	34	4	1	2	24	12	38	1	3	5-3	.197	.250	.266	.516	13	.840
— Watertown (NYP)	3B-1B-OF	27	89	12	16	0	1	3	9	14	21	2	2	6-2	.180	.302	.303	.605	10	.885
1987— Macon (S. Atl.)	OF	4	4	1	0	0	0	0	0	1	3	0	0	0-0	.000	.200	.000	.200	0	1.000
— Watertown (NYP)	2B	4	12	4	5	0	1	0	3	1	1	1	0	1-0	.417	.500	.583	1.083	2	.900
1988— Augusta (S. Atl.)	2B-3B-SS	37	136	19	36	6	3	1	17	7	20	2	2	2-0	.265	.308	.375	.683	7	.914
— Salem (Caro.)	2-3-S-O	80	298	47	87	12	7	7	42	27	64	1	7	13-3	.292	.347	.450	.797	31	.893
1989— Harrisburg (East.)	3B-1B-OF	95	341	43	82	16	4	6	48	32	66	2	6	13-3	.240	.306	.364	.670	10	.979
— Buffalo (A.A.)	3B-1B-OF	35	129	18	44	5	3	1	16	7	26	0	2	0-1	.341	.372	.450	.822	3	.984
1990— Buffalo (A.A.)	3B-1B-OF	101	378	52	99	12	6	9	55	46	63	0	8	14-5	.262	.341	.397	.738	20	.975
— Pittsburgh (N.L.)	C-OF	25	24	3	5	1	0	0	0	1	9	0	1	0-0	.208	.240	.250	.490	0	.000

M

Year Team (League)	Pos.	G	AB	R	H	2B	3B	HR	RBI	BB	SO	HBP	GDP	SB-CS	Avg.	OBP	SLG	OPS	E	Pct.
1991— Buffalo (A.A.)	1B	3	12	1	2	0	0	0	0	1	4	0	0	1-1	.167	.231	.167	.397	0	1.000
— Pittsburgh (N.L.)	1B-OF	120	411	83	113	17	2	10	50	64	81	1	6	8-4	.275	.373	.399	.772	12	.988
1992— Pittsburgh (N.L.)	1B-OF	134	405	50	100	28	5	6	60	52	63	2	6	5-4	.247	.332	.385	.717	5	.995
1993— Pittsburgh (N.L.)	OF-1B	137	447	68	140	26	4	8	70	77	64	1	9	3-3	.313	.414	.443	.857	10	.981
1994— Pittsburgh (N.L.)	OF-1B	108	386	48	105	21	3	9	51	42	58	1	17	4-1	.272	.343	.412	.755	5	.991
1995— Pittsburgh (N.L.)	OF-1B	132	487	75	146	29	4	15	83	52	74	1	9	7-2	.300	.365	.468	.833	6	.985
1996— Pittsburgh (N.L.)	OF-1B	120	453	69	130	24	1	17	80	51	74	0	9	8-4	.287	.357	.457	.814	3	.988
1997— Toronto (A.L.)	OF-DH-1B	98	368	45	98	23	2	9	40	47	62	3	6	7-3	.266	.352	.413	.765	3	.985
1998— Minnesota (A.L.)	1B-OF-DH	63	204	22	59	12	0	5	33	17	29	1	4	1-4	.289	.345	.422	.767	6	.983
— Boston (A.L.)	DH-OF	9	9	0	0	0	0	0	2	2	3	0	0	0-0	.000	.167	.000	.167	0	1.000
— Chicago (N.L.)	OF	12	10	2	3	0	0	1	5	1	2	0	2	0-0	.300	.333	.600	.933	0	1.000
1999— Montreal (N.L.)	OF-1B-DH	93	194	25	52	12	1	8	26	26	27	0	5	2-1	.268	.353	.464	.817	5	.952
2000— Orix (Jap. Pacific)		23	80	9	18	2	1	2	15	4	14	...	...	0-...	.225	...	.350	...	...	...
— New Orleans (PCL)	OF-3B-1B	17	67	8	18	4	0	1	14	2	4	0	2	0-1	.269	.290	.373	.663	1	.981
2001— Houston (N.L.)	OF-3B-1B	94	137	19	36	6	1	6	29	14	32	1	3	5-1	.263	.333	.453	.786	1	.976
2002— Houston (N.L.)	O-1-D-3	123	251	35	72	13	3	6	30	26	50	0	9	4-0	.287	.350	.434	.784	2	.987
2003— Houston (N.L.)	O-1-D-3	123	212	20	49	17	2	3	26	15	33	1	3	3-2	.231	.283	.373	.655	3	.971
American League totals (2 years)		170	581	67	157	35	2	14	75	66	94	4	10	8-7	.270	.347	.410	.756	9	.984
National League totals (12 years)		1221	3417	497	951	194	26	89	510	421	567	8	79	49-22	.278	.356	.428	.785	52	.987
Major League totals (13 years)		1391	3998	564	1108	229	28	103	585	487	661	12	89	57-29	.277	.355	.426	.781	61	.987

MERCEDES, JOSE — P

PERSONAL: Born March 5, 1971, in El Seibo, Dominican Republic. ... 6-1/180. ... Throws right, bats right. ... Full name: Jose Miguel Mercedes. ... Name pronounced: mer-SAY-deez.

TRANSACTIONS/CAREER NOTES: Signed as non-drafted free agent by Baltimore Orioles organization (August 10, 1989). ... Selected by Milwaukee Brewers from Orioles organization in Rule 5 major league draft (December 13, 1993). ... On Milwaukee disabled list (April 2-May 30, 1994); included rehabilitation assignments to El Paso (April 30-May 14) and New Orleans (May 14-28). ... On disabled list (May 14, 1995-remainder of season). ... On Milwaukee disabled list (May 5, 1998-remainder of season); included rehabilitation assignment to El Paso (June 15-16). ... Released by Brewers (December 16, 1998). ... Signed by San Diego Padres organization (March 19, 1999). ... Released by Padres (June 24, 1999). ... Signed by Florida Marlins organization (June 30, 1999). ... Released by Marlins (July 30, 1999). ... Signed by New York Mets organization (August 6, 1999). ... Granted free agency (October 15, 1999). ... Signed by Orioles organization (January 3, 2000). ... Granted free agency (November 5, 2001). ... Signed by Cleveland Indians organization (February 9, 2002). ... Elected free agency (May 1, 2002). ... Signed to minor league contract by Montreal Expos (September 2, 2003).

CAREER HITTING: 1-for-19 (.053), 0 R, 0 2B, 0 3B, 0 HR, 0 RBI.

Year League	W	L	Pct.	ERA	WHIP	G	GS	CG	ShO	Hld.	Sv.-Opp.	IP	H	R	ER	HR	BB-IBB	SO	Avg.
1990— Dom. Orioles/W.S. (DSL) ..	2	7	.222	5.96	1.72	15	12	3	...	...	1-...	68.0	81	51	45	...	36-...	42	...
1991— Dom. Orioles/W.S. (DSL) ..	5	2	.714	4.48	0.38	10	10	1	...	...	0-...	66.1	6	45	33	...	19-...	24	...
1992— GC Orioles (GCL)	2	3	.400	1.78	1.25	8	5	2	0	...	0-...	35.1	31	12	7	0	13-0	21	.242
— Kane County (Midwest)	3	2	.600	2.66	1.16	8	8	2	•2	...	0-...	47.1	40	26	14	1	15-0	45	.220
1993— Bowie (East.)	6	8	.429	4.78	1.60	26	23	3	0	...	0-...	147.0	170	86	78	13	65-0	75	.292
1994— El Paso (Texas)	2	0	1.000	4.66	1.76	3	0	0	0	...	0-...	9.2	13	6	5	1	4-0	8	.333
— New Orleans (A.A.)	0	0	...	4.91	1.47	3	3	0	0	...	0-...	18.1	19	10	10	1	8-0	7	.268
— Milwaukee (A.L.)	2	0	1.000	2.32	1.23	19	0	0	0	3	0-1	31.0	22	9	8	4	16-1	11	.216
1995— Milwaukee (A.L.)	0	1	.000	9.82	2.73	5	0	0	0	1	0-2	7.1	12	9	8	1	8-0	6	.375
1996— New Orleans (A.A.)	3	7	.300	3.56	1.36	25	15	0	0	...	1-...	101.0	109	58	40	14	28-1	47	.275
— Milwaukee (A.L.)	0	2	.000	9.18	1.50	11	0	0	0	2	0-1	16.2	20	18	17	6	5-0	6	.294
1997— Milwaukee (A.L.)	7	10	.412	3.79	1.25	29	23	2	1	1	0-0	159.0	146	76	67	24	53-2	80	.248
1998— Milwaukee (N.L.)	2	2	.500	6.75	1.59	7	5	0	0	0	0-0	32.0	42	25	24	5	9-1	11	.316
— El Paso (Texas)	0	0	...	10.80	2.70	1	1	0	0	...	0-...	3.1	9	4	4	2	0-0	0	.529
1999— Las Vegas (PCL)	2	6	.250	4.30	1.48	15	14	0	0	...	0-...	88.0	110	57	42	14	20-0	57	.300
— Calgary (PCL)	1	2	.333	3.12	1.27	4	4	0	0	...	0-...	26.0	30	13	9	2	3-0	13	.278
— Norfolk (Int'l)	2	1	.667	2.53	1.47	6	6	0	0	...	0-...	32.0	36	15	9	2	11-1	19	.283
2000— Baltimore (A.L.)	14	7	.667	4.02	1.47	36	20	1	0	0	0-0	145.2	150	71	65	15	64-1	70	.270
2001— Baltimore (A.L.)	8	* 17	.320	5.82	1.53	33	31	2	0	0	0-0	184.0	219	125	119	20	63-3	123	.294
2002— Buffalo (Int'l)	2	0	1.000	3.49	1.34	5	5	0	0	...	0-...	28.1	32	11	11	4	6-0	13	.283
2003— Montreal (N.L.)	0	0	...	0.00	1.50	5	0	0	0	0	0-0	7.1	6	3	0	0	5-0	3	.231
American League totals (6 years)	31	37	.456	4.70	1.43	133	74	5	1	7	0-4	543.2	569	308	284	70	209-7	296	.272
National League totals (2 years)	2	2	.500	5.49	1.58	12	5	0	0	0	0-0	39.1	48	28	24	5	14-1	14	.302
Major League totals (8 years)	33	39	.458	4.75	1.44	145	79	5	1	7	0-4	583.0	617	336	308	75	223-8	310	.274

M

MERCKER, KENT — P

PERSONAL: Born February 1, 1968, in Dublin, Ohio. ... 6-2/200. ... Throws left, bats left. ... Full name: Kent Franklin Mercker. ... High school: Dublin (Ohio).

TRANSACTIONS/CAREER NOTES: Selected by Atlanta Braves organization in first round (fifth pick overall) of free-agent draft (June 2, 1986). ... On Richmond disabled list (March 30-May 6, 1990). ... On disabled list (August 9-24, 1991). ... Traded by Braves to Baltimore Orioles for P Joe Borowski and P Rachaad Stewart (December 17, 1995). ... Traded by Orioles to Cleveland Indians for 1B Eddie Murray (July 21, 1996). ... Granted free agency (November 4, 1996). ... Signed by Cincinnati Reds (December 10, 1996). ... On disabled list (August 17-September 2, 1997). ... Granted free agency (October 27, 1997). ... Signed by St. Louis Cardinals (December 16, 1997). ... On disabled list (June 14-July 1, 1998). ... Traded by Cardinals to Boston Red Sox for P Mike Matthews and C David Benham (August 24, 1999). ... On Boston disabled list (September 7-23, 1999). ... Granted free agency (November 8, 1999). ... Signed by Anaheim Angels organization (January 26, 2000). ... On Anaheim disabled list (May 12-August 12, 2000); included rehabilitation assignment to Lake Elsinore (August 4-8). ... Granted free agency (November 8, 2000). ... Signed by Red Sox organization (January 5, 2001). ... Released by Red Sox (March 29, 2001). ... Signed by Colorado Rockies organization (January 31, 2002). ... On Colorado disabled list (June 6-July 30, 2002); included rehabilitation assignment to Colorado Springs (July 24-30). ... On suspended list (September 20-23, 2002). ... Granted free agency (November 1, 2002). ... Signed by Reds organization (January 7, 2003). ... On disabled list (June 25, 2003). ... Reinstated from 15-day disabled list (July 10, 2003). ... Claimed off waivers by Atlanta Braves (August 12, 2003).

CAREER HITTING: 28-for-246 (.114), 12 R, 5 2B, 2 3B, 1 HR, 18 RBI.

Year League	W	L	Pct.	ERA	WHIP	G	GS	CG	ShO	Hld.	Sv.-Opp.	IP	H	R	ER	HR	BB-IBB	SO	Avg.
1986— GC Braves (GCL)	4	3	.571	2.47	1.12	9	8	0	0	...	0-...	47.1	37	21	13	1	16-1	42	.200
1987— Durham (Caro.)	0	1	.000	5.40	1.46	3	3	0	0	...	0-...	11.2	11	8	7	1	6-0	14	.256
1988— Durham (Caro.)	11	4	.733	* 2.75	1.17	19	19	5	0	...	0-...	127.2	102	44	39	5	47-0	159	.214
— Greenville (Sou.)	3	1	.750	3.35	1.28	9	9	0	0	...	0-...	48.1	36	20	18	2	26-1	60	.201
1989— Richmond (Int'l)	9	12	.429	3.20	1.20	27	•27	4	0	...	0-...	168.2	107	66	60	17	* 95-4	* 144	.183
— Atlanta (N.L.)	0	0	...	12.46	3.23	2	1	0	0	0	0-0	4.1	8	6	6	0	6-0	4	.400

Year League	W	L	Pct.	ERA	WHIP	G	GS	CG	ShO	Hld.	Sv.-Opp.	IP	H	R	ER	HR	BB-IBB	SO	Avg.
1990— Richmond (Int'l)	5	4	.556	3.55	1.49	12	10	0	0	...	1-...	58.1	60	30	23	1	27-1	69	.260
— Atlanta (N.L.)	4	7	.364	3.17	1.39	36	0	0	0	0	7-10	48.1	43	22	17	6	24-3	39	.236
1991— Atlanta (N.L.)	5	3	.625	2.58	1.24	50	4	0	0	3	6-8	73.1	56	23	21	5	35-3	62	.211
1992— Atlanta (N.L.)	3	2	.600	3.42	1.26	53	0	0	0	6	6-9	68.1	51	27	26	4	35-1	49	.207
1993— Atlanta (N.L.)	3	1	.750	2.86	1.33	43	6	0	0	4	0-3	66.0	52	24	21	2	36-3	59	.214
1994— Atlanta (N.L.)	9	4	.692	3.45	1.20	20	17	2	1	0	0-0	112.1	90	46	43	16	45-3	111	.220
1995— Atlanta (N.L.)	7	8	.467	4.15	1.41	29	26	0	0	0	0-0	143.0	140	73	66	16	61-2	102	.258
1996— Baltimore (A.L.)	3	6	.333	7.76	1.86	14	12	0	0	0	0-0	58.0	73	56	50	12	35-1	22	.307
— Buffalo (A.A.)	0	2	.000	3.94	1.25	3	3	0	0	...	0-...	16.0	11	7	7	3	9-0	11	.193
— Cleveland (A.L.)	1	0	1.000	3.09	1.11	10	0	0	0	2	0-0	11.2	10	4	4	1	3-1	7	.244
1997— Cincinnati (N.L.)	8	11	.421	3.92	1.36	28	25	0	0	0	0-0	144.2	135	65	63	16	62-6	75	.250
1998— St. Louis (N.L.)	11	11	.500	5.07	1.56	30	29	0	0	0	0-0	161.2	199	99	91	11	53-4	72	.310
1999— St. Louis (N.L.)	6	5	.545	5.12	1.70	25	18	0	0	0	0-0	103.2	125	73	59	16	51-3	64	.303
— Boston (A.L.)	2	0	1.000	3.51	1.40	5	5	0	0	0	0-0	25.2	23	12	10	0	13-0	17	.235
2000— Anaheim (A.L.)	1	3	.250	6.52	1.78	21	7	0	0	1	0-0	48.1	57	35	35	12	29-3	30	.300
— Lake Elsinore (Calif.)	0	0	...	0.00	0.00	1	1	0	0	...	0-...	4.0	0	0	0	0	0-0	3	.000
2001—										Did not play.									
2002— Colorado (N.L.)	3	1	.750	6.14	1.75	58	0	0	0	9	0-3	44.0	55	33	30	12	22-2	37	.304
— Colo. Springs (PCL)	0	0	...	21.60	3.00	2	0	0	0	...	0-...	1.2	3	4	4	2	2-0	0	.429
2003— Cincinnati (N.L.)	0	2	.000	2.35	1.46	49	0	0	0	10	0-3	38.1	31	13	10	5	25-2	41	.225
— Atlanta (N.L.)	0	0	...	1.06	1.29	18	0	0	0	1	1-2	17.0	15	3	2	1	7-2	7	.231
American League totals (3 years)	7	9	.438	6.20	1.69	50	24	0	0	3	0-0	143.2	163	107	99	25	80-5	76	.287
National League totals (12 years)	59	55	.518	4.00	1.43	441	126	2	1	33	20-38	1025.0	1000	507	455	110	462-34	722	.257
Major League totals (14 years)	66	64	.508	4.27	1.46	491	150	2	1	36	20-38	1168.2	1163	614	554	135	542-39	798	.261

MERLONI, LOU — IF

PERSONAL: Born April 6, 1971, in Framingham, Mass. ... 5-10/201. ... Bats right, throws right. ... Full name: Louis William Merloni. ... Name pronounced: mer-LONE-ee. ... High school: Framingham (Mass.) South. ... College: Providence.

TRANSACTIONS/CAREER NOTES: Selected by Boston Red Sox organization in 10th round of free-agent draft (June 3, 1993). ... On Boston disabled list (June 29-September 12, 1998); included rehabilitation assignment to Gulf Coast Red Sox (August 8-20). ... Contract sold by Red Sox to Yokohama BayStars of Japan Central League (November 22, 1999). ... Re-signed by Red Sox organization (July 28, 2000). ... On Boston disabled list (June 6-21, 2001); included rehabilitation assignment to Pawtucket (June 10-21). ... Claimed on waivers by San Diego Padres (March 25, 2003). ... Placed on the 15-day disabled list by San Diego (June 9, 2003). ... Sent to Lake Elsinore on rehab assignment (June 27, 2003). ... Recalled from Lake Elsinore rehab assignment; reinstated from 15-day disabled list (July 4, 2003). ... Traded by San Diego to Boston Red Sox for P Rene Miniel (August 28, 2003).

2003 GAMES PLAYED BY POSITION (MLB): 3B—32, SS—23, 2B—17, OF—3, 1B—2.

									BATTING											FIELDING	
Year Team (League)	Pos.	G	AB	R	H	2B	3B	HR	RBI	BB	SO	HBP	GDP	SB-CS	Avg.	OBP	SLG	OPS	E	Pct.
1993— GC Red Sox (GCL)	SS	4	14	4	5	1	0	0	1	1	1	1	0	1-1	.357	.438	.429	.866	1	.952
— Fort Laud. (FSL)	3B-SS	44	156	14	38	1	1	2	21	13	26	1	6	1-1	.244	.299	.301	.600	8	.951
1994— Sarasota (Fla. St.)	2B-3B-SS	113	419	59	120	16	2	1	63	36	57	7	11	5-2	.286	.345	.341	.687	18	.965
1995— Trenton (East.)	2B-3B-SS	93	318	42	88	16	1	1	30	39	50	11	1	7-7	.277	.373	.343	.716	20	.951
1996— Trenton (East.)	2-3-S-1	28	95	11	22	6	1	3	16	9	18	5	2	0-2	.232	.330	.411	.741	8	.930
— GC Red Sox (GCL)	2B	1	4	1	1	0	0	0	1	0	0	0	0	0-0	.250	.200	.250	.450	0	1.000
— Pawtucket (Int'l)	2B-3B-SS	38	115	19	29	6	0	1	12	10	20	3	1	0-1	.252	.328	.330	.659	8	.945
1997— Trenton (East.)	2B-3B-SS	69	255	49	79	17	4	5	37	30	43	12	2	3-2	.310	.402	.467	.869	9	.951
— Pawtucket (Int'l)	2B-3B-SS	49	165	24	49	10	0	5	24	15	20	4	4	0-2	.297	.368	.448	.816	4	.979
1998— Pawtucket (Int'l)	2B-3B-SS	27	88	17	34	3	1	8	22	16	13	8	2	2-2	.386	.518	.716	1.234	2	.976
— Boston (A.L.)	2B-3B-SS	39	96	10	27	6	0	1	15	7	20	2	1	1-0	.281	.343	.375	.718	5	.962
— GC Red Sox (GCL)	2B	1	1	0	0	0	0	0	0	0	0	0	0	0-0	.000	.000	.000	.000	0	...
1999— Boston (A.L.)	S-3-2-D-1-O	43	126	18	32	7	0	1	13	8	16	2	6	0-0	.254	.307	.333	.640	10	.940
— Pawtucket (Int'l)	S-3-D-1-2	66	229	45	64	14	1	7	36	30	38	9	4	1-1	.279	.383	.441	.824	12	.945
2000— Yo. Bay. (Jp. Cn.)		42	94	10	20	4	0	1	3	7	15	...	...	0-...	.213	...	.287	...	...	...
— Pawtucket (Int'l)	S-2-3-1	11	39	6	16	2	0	1	5	3	3	0	2	0-1	.410	.452	.538	.991	4	.897
— Boston (A.L.)	3B	40	128	10	41	11	2	0	18	4	22	1	8	1-0	.320	.341	.438	.778	7	.954
2001— Pawtucket (Int'l)	S-2-3-1	52	195	30	51	12	0	4	20	15	37	5	6	2-0	.262	.330	.385	.715	10	.954
— Boston (A.L.)	SS-2B-3B	52	146	21	39	10	0	3	13	6	31	3	6	2-1	.267	.306	.397	.703	3	.983
2002— Boston (A.L.)	2-3-S-1-O	84	194	28	48	12	2	4	18	20	35	5	4	1-2	.247	.332	.392	.724	5	.983
— Pawtucket (Int'l)	3B-SS-OF	8	25	1	5	2	0	0	2	1	3	1	2	0-0	.200	.250	.280	.530	0	1.000
2003— Lake Elsinore (Calif.)	2B-3B-SS	5	19	3	9	3	0	1	7	1	0	0	0	0-0	.474	.476	.789	1.266	0	1.000
— San Diego (N.L.)	3-S-2-1-O	65	151	20	41	7	2	1	17	22	33	1	3	2-3	.272	.362	.364	.726	6	.962
— Boston (A.L.)	2B-3B-OF	15	30	4	7	1	0	0	1	4	8	0	0	0-0	.233	.324	.267	.590	0	1.000
American League totals (6 years)		273	720	91	194	47	4	9	78	49	132	13	25	5-3	.269	.325	.383	.708	30	.966
National League totals (1 year)		65	151	20	41	7	2	1	17	22	33	1	3	2-3	.272	.362	.364	.726	6	.962
Major League totals (6 years)		338	871	111	235	54	6	10	95	71	165	14	28	7-6	.270	.332	.380	.712	36	.965

MESA, JOSE — P

PERSONAL: Born May 22, 1966, in Azua, Dominican Republic. ... 6-3/230. ... Throws right, bats right. ... Full name: Jose Ramon Mesa. ... Name pronounced: MAY-sa. ... High school: Santa School (Azua, Dominican Republic).

TRANSACTIONS/CAREER NOTES: Signed as non-drafted free agent by Toronto Blue Jays organization (October 31, 1981). ... On Kinston disabled list (August 27, 1984-remainder of season). ... Traded by Blue Jays to Baltimore Orioles (September 4, 1987), completing deal in which Orioles traded P Mike Flanagan to Blue Jays for P Oswald Peraza and a player to be named later (August 31, 1987). ... On Rochester disabled list (April 18-May 16 and June 30, 1988-remainder of season; May 27, 1989-remainder of season; and August 21-September 5, 1991). ... Traded by Orioles to Cleveland Indians for OF Kyle Washington (July 14, 1992). ... On suspended list (April 5-8, 1993). ... Traded by Indians with IF Shawon Dunston and P Alvin Morman to San Francisco Giants for P Steve Reed and OF Jacob Cruz (July 23, 1998). ... Granted free agency (October 23, 1998). ... Signed by Seattle Mariners (November 13, 1998). ... Granted free agency (November 6, 2000). ... Signed by Philadelphia Phillies (November 17, 2000). ... On suspended list (August 28-30, 2001).

CAREER HITTING: 0-for-0 (.000), 1 R, 0 2B, 0 3B, 0 HR, 0 RBI.

M

Year	League	W	L	Pct.	ERA	WHIP	G	GS	CG	ShO	Hld.	Sv.-Opp.	IP	H	R	ER	HR	BB-IBB	SO	Avg.
1982—	GC Blue Jays (GCL)	6	4	.600	2.70	0.94	13	12	6	* 3	...	1-...	83.1	58	34	25	1	20-0	40	...
1983—	Florence (S. Atl.)	6	12	.333	5.48	1.74	28	27	1	0	...	0-...	141.1	153	* 116	86	14	93-0	91	...
1984—	Florence (S. Atl.)	4	3	.571	3.76	1.64	7	7	0	0	...	0-...	38.1	38	24	16	3	25-0	35	.255
—	Kinston (Caro.)	5	2	.714	3.91	1.56	10	9	0	0	...	0-...	50.2	51	23	22	2	28-0	24	.267
1985—	Kinston (Caro.)	5	10	.333	6.16	1.77	30	20	0	0	...	1-...	106.2	110	89	73	11	79-2	71	.269
1986—	Vent. County (Cal.)	10	6	.625	3.86	1.40	24	24	2	1	...	0-...	142.1	141	71	61	6	58-0	113	.256
—	Knoxville (Sou.)	2	2	.500	4.35	1.52	9	8	2	1	...	0-...	41.1	40	32	20	6	23-0	30	.242
1987—	Knoxville (Sou.)	10	• 13	.435	5.21	1.60	35	* 35	4	2	...	0-...	* 193.1	* 206	* 131	* 112	19	104-0	115	.273
—	Baltimore (A.L.)	1	3	.250	6.03	1.69	6	5	0	0	1	0-0	31.1	38	23	21	7	15-0	17	.297
1988—	Rochester (Int'l)	0	3	.000	8.62	2.23	11	2	0	0	...	0-...	15.2	21	20	15	2	14-0	15	.328
1989—	Rochester (Int'l)	0	2	.000	5.40	1.60	7	1	0	0	...	0-...	10.0	10	6	6	2	6-0	3	.263
—	Hagerstown (Eastern)	0	0	...	1.38	1.00	3	3	0	0	...	0-...	13.0	9	2	2	0	4-0	12	.191
1990—	Hagerstown (Eastern)	5	5	.500	3.42	1.35	15	15	3	1	...	0-...	79.0	77	35	30	4	30-0	72	.258
—	Rochester (Int'l)	1	2	.333	2.42	1.27	4	4	0	0	...	0-...	26.0	21	11	7	2	12-0	23	.223
—	Baltimore (A.L.)	3	2	.600	3.86	1.37	7	7	0	0	0	0-...	46.2	37	20	20	2	27-2	24	.218
1991—	Baltimore (A.L.)	6	11	.353	5.97	1.72	23	23	2	1	0	0-0	123.2	151	86	82	11	62-2	64	.307
—	Rochester (Int'l)	3	3	.500	3.86	1.31	8	8	1	1	...	0-...	51.1	37	25	22	4	30-0	48	.203
1992—	Baltimore (A.L.)	3	8	.273	5.19	1.54	13	12	0	0	0	0-0	67.2	77	41	39	9	27-1	22	.287
—	Cleveland (A.L.)	4	4	.500	4.16	1.45	15	15	1	1	0	0-0	93.0	92	45	43	5	43-0	40	.262
1993—	Cleveland (A.L.)	10	12	.455	4.92	1.41	34	33	3	0	0	0-0	208.2	232	122	114	21	62-2	118	.286
1994—	Cleveland (A.L.)	7	5	.583	3.82	1.33	51	0	0	0	8	2-6	73.0	71	33	31	3	26-7	63	.254
1995—	Cleveland (A.L.)	3	0	1.000	1.13	1.03	62	0	0	0	0	* 46-48	64.0	49	9	8	3	17-2	58	.216
1996—	Cleveland (A.L.)	2	7	.222	3.73	1.34	69	0	0	0	0	39-44	72.1	69	32	30	6	28-4	64	.257
1997—	Cleveland (A.L.)	4	4	.500	2.40	1.35	66	0	0	0	9	16-21	82.1	83	28	22	7	28-3	69	.259
1998—	Cleveland (A.L.)	3	4	.429	5.17	1.50	44	0	0	0	7	1-3	54.0	61	36	31	7	20-3	35	.282
—	San Francisco (N.L.)	5	3	.625	3.52	1.57	32	0	0	0	6	0-1	30.2	30	14	12	1	18-2	28	.256
1999—	Seattle (A.L.)	3	6	.333	4.98	1.81	68	0	0	0	1	33-38	68.2	84	42	38	11	40-4	42	.305
2000—	Seattle (A.L.)	4	6	.400	5.36	1.61	66	0	0	0	11	1-3	80.2	89	48	48	11	41-0	84	.280
2001—	Philadelphia (N.L.)	3	3	.500	2.34	1.23	71	0	0	0	1	42-46	69.1	65	26	18	4	20-2	59	.246
2002—	Philadelphia (N.L.)	4	6	.400	2.97	1.37	74	0	0	0	0	45-54	75.2	65	26	25	5	39-7	64	.231
2003—	Philadelphia (N.L.)	5	7	.417	6.52	1.76	61	0	0	0	2	24-28	58.0	71	44	42	7	31-2	45	.296
	American League totals (12 years)	53	72	.424	4.45	1.47	524	95	6	2	37	138-163	1066.0	1133	565	527	103	436-30	700	.255
	National League totals (4 years)	17	19	.472	3.74	1.45	238	0	0	0	9	111-129	233.2	231	110	97	17	108-13	196	.256
	Major League totals (15 years)	70	91	.435	4.32	1.47	762	95	6	2	46	249-292	1299.2	1364	675	624	120	544-43	896	.271

MEYERS, CHAD   2B/OF

PERSONAL: Born August 8, 1975, in Omaha, Neb. ... 5-11/185. ... Bats right, throws right. ... Full name: Chad William Meyers. ... High school: Daniel J. Gross (Omaha, Neb.). ... College: Creighton.

TRANSACTIONS/CAREER NOTES: Selected by Chicago Cubs organization in fifth round of free-agent draft (June 4, 1996). ... Released by Cubs (October 12, 2001). ... Signed by Oakland Athletics organization (November 7, 2001). ... Released by A's (April 29, 2002). ... Granted free agency (October 15, 2002). ... Signed by Seattle Mariners as a free agent (November 1, 2002).

2003 GAMES PLAYED BY POSITION (MLB): DH—6, OF—3.

Year	Team (League)	Pos.	G	AB	R	H	2B	3B	HR	RBI	BB	SO	HBP	GDP	SB-CS	Avg.	OBP	SLG	OPS	E	Pct.
1996—	Will. (NYP)	2B-OF	67	230	46	56	9	2	2	26	33	39	5	2	27-6	.243	.349	.326	.676	12	.956
1997—	Rockford (Midwest)		125	439	89	132	28	4	4	58	74	72	10	4	54-16	.301	.408	.410	.818	26	.948
1998—	Daytona (Fla. St.)	2B-OF	48	186	39	60	8	3	3	25	33	29	5	1	23-7	.323	.436	.446	.882	13	.941
—	West Tenn (Sou.)	2B	77	293	63	79	14	0	0	26	58	43	4	5	37-9	.270	.397	.317	.715	23	.934
1999—	West Tenn (Sou.)	2B	64	238	45	69	19	2	3	29	26	40	10	6	22-8	.290	.383	.424	.808	9	.966
—	Iowa (PCL)	2B-OF	44	175	39	62	13	2	0	16	29	20	3	1	17-7	.354	.454	.451	.906	4	.981
—	Chicago (N.L.)	2B-OF	43	142	17	33	9	0	0	4	9	27	3	5	4-2	.232	.292	.296	.588	2	.986
2000—	Iowa (PCL)	2-0-3-S	80	301	54	81	10	0	2	26	43	41	5	5	34-15	.269	.368	.322	.690	19	.943
—	Chicago (N.L.)	2B-3B	36	52	8	9	2	0	0	5	3	11	1	0	1-0	.173	.228	.212	.440	2	.938
2001—	Iowa (PCL)	2B-OF-3B	132	446	92	134	31	5	9	54	58	72	26	9	* 27-9	.300	.407	.453	.860	‡ 16	.966
—	Chicago (N.L.)	2B-OF-3B	18	17	1	2	0	0	0	0	2	5	4	0	0-1	.118	.348	.118	.465	0	1.000
2002—	Sacramento (PCL)	2-3-S-0	18	54	11	11	0	0	1	2	12	10	1	3	0-0	.204	.358	.259	.617	2	.959
—	Memphis (PCL)	0-2-S-3	100	358	56	96	19	1	8	35	51	54	20	4	* 43-9	.268	.387	.394	.780	6	.975
2003—	Tacoma (PCL)	0-2-D-1	97	377	50	113	20	3	4	34	30	46	7	7	37-12	.300	.361	.401	.762	10	.961
—	Seattle (A.L.)	DH-OF	9	1	1	0	0	0	0	0	0	0	0	0	1-0	.000	.000	.000	.000	0	...
	American League totals (1 year)		9	1	1	0	0	0	0	0	0	0	0	0	1-0	.000	.000	.000	.000	0	...
	National League totals (3 years)		97	211	26	44	11	0	0	9	14	43	8	5	5-3	.209	.282	.261	.543	4	.979
	Major League totals (4 years)		106	212	27	44	11	0	0	9	14	43	8	5	6-3	.208	.281	.259	.540	4	.979

MIADICH, BART   P

PERSONAL: Born February 3, 1976, in Torrance, Calif. ... 6-4/205. ... Throws right, bats right. ... Full name: John Barton Miadich. ... Name pronounced: me-AH-ditch. ... High school: Lakeridge (Lake Oswego, Ore.). ... College: San Diego.

TRANSACTIONS/CAREER NOTES: Selected by Colorado Rockies organization in 49th round of free-agent draft (June 2, 1994); did not sign. ... Signed as non-drafted free agent by Boston Red Sox organization (August 31, 1997). ... Traded by Red Sox to Arizona Diamondbacks organization (December 15, 1998), completing deal in which Diamondbacks traded P Bob Wolcott to Red Sox for a player to be named later (November 11, 1998). ... Released by Diamondbacks (March 30, 2000). ... Signed by Anaheim Angels organization (May 23, 2000).

CAREER HITTING: 0-for-0 (.000), 0 R, 0 2B, 0 3B, 0 HR, 0 RBI.

Year	League	W	L	Pct.	ERA	WHIP	G	GS	CG	ShO	Hld.	Sv.-Opp.	IP	H	R	ER	HR	BB-IBB	SO	Avg.
1998—	Sarasota (Fla. St.)	3	2	.600	3.14	1.13	22	0	0	0	...	7-...	48.2	40	20	17	1	15-4	64	.222
—	Trenton (East.)	1	6	.143	5.96	1.69	22	8	0	0	...	1-...	54.1	66	39	36	4	26-1	33	.301
1999—	El Paso (Texas)	0	2	.000	8.10	2.20	12	0	0	0	...	1-...	20.0	37	22	18	3	7-1	16	.398
—	High Desert (Calif.)	3	8	.273	5.42	1.68	21	16	0	0	...	0-...	98.0	125	71	59	9	40-0	85	.321
2000—	Erie (East.)	3	1	.750	3.35	1.19	28	0	0	0	...	2-...	40.1	27	16	15	2	21-0	38	.189
—	Edmonton (PCL)	2	1	.667	4.57	1.57	10	0	0	0	...	1-...	21.2	25	14	11	3	9-0	20	.275
2001—	Salt Lake (PCL)	4	4	.500	2.44	1.17	55	0	0	0	...	* 27-...	59.0	40	20	16	4	29-1	73	.190
—	Anaheim (A.L.)	0	0	...	4.50	1.40	11	0	0	0	0	0-...	10.0	6	5	5	2	8-0	11	.182
2002—	Salt Lake (PCL)	4	3	.571	3.68	1.54	59	0	0	0	...	14-...	80.2	60	43	33	5	64-2	92	.200
2003—	Anaheim (A.L.)	0	0	...	18.00	3.00	1	0	0	0	0	0-0	2.0	5	4	4	0	1-0	3	.500
—	Salt Lake (PCL)	5	5	.500	3.68	1.56	46	0	0	0	...	16-...	51.1	39	23	21	4	41-0	65	.210
	Major League totals (2 years)	0	0	...	6.75	1.67	12	0	0	0	0	0-0	12.0	11	9	9	2	9-0	14	.256

M

MICELI, DAN   P

PERSONAL: Born September 9, 1970, in Newark, N.J. ... 6-0/225. ... Throws right, bats right. ... Full name: Daniel Miceli. ... Name pronounced: muh-SELL-ee. ... High school: Dr. Phillips (Orlando).

TRANSACTIONS/CAREER NOTES: Signed as non-drafted free agent by Kansas City Royals organization (March 7, 1990). ... Traded by Royals with P Jon Lieber to Pittsburgh Pirates for P Stan Belinda (July 31, 1993). ... Traded by Pirates to Detroit Tigers for P Clint Sodowsky (November 1, 1996). ... Traded by Tigers with P Donne Wall and 3B Ryan Balfe to San Diego Padres for P Tim Worrell and OF Trey Beamon (November 19, 1997). ... Traded by Padres to Florida Marlins for P Brian Meadows (November 15, 1999). ... On Florida disabled list (May 30-July 19, 2000); included rehabilitation assignments to Gulf Coast Marlins (July 4-8) and Brevard County (July 9-19). ... Released by Marlins (June 25, 2001). ... Signed by Colorado Rockies organization (July 2, 2001). ... Granted free agency (November 5, 2001). ... Signed by Texas Rangers organization (January 29, 2002). ... Released by Rangers (May 6, 2002). ... Signed by Rockies organization (December 19, 2002). ... Designated for assignment by Colorado (May 12, 2003). ... Elected free agency (May 13, 2003). ... Contract purchased by Cleveland from Buffalo (May 27, 2003). ... Traded by Cleveland with OF Karim Garcia to New York Yankees for a player to be named (June 25, 2003). ... Designated for assignment (July 25, 2003). ... Traded by Yankees to Houston Astros for a player to be named or cash (July 29, 2003).

CAREER HITTING: 1-for-20 (.050), 0 R, 0 2B, 0 3B, 0 HR, 0 RBI.

Year— League	W	L	Pct.	ERA	WHIP	G	GS	CG	ShO	Hld.	Sv.-Opp.	IP	H	R	ER	HR	BB-IBB	SO	Avg.
1990— GC Royals (GCL)	3	4	.429	3.91	1.40	27	0	0	0	...	4-...	53.0	45	27	23	0	29-5	48	.234
1991— Eugene (NW)	0	1	.000	2.14	1.07	25	0	0	0	...	10-...	33.2	18	8	8	1	18-0	43	.158
1992— Appleton (Midw.)	1	1	.500	1.93	0.69	23	0	0	0	...	9-...	23.1	12	6	5	0	4-1	44	.145
— Memphis (Sou.)	3	0	1.000	1.91	0.88	32	0	0	0	...	4-...	37.2	20	10	8	5	13-0	46	.160
1993— Memphis (Sou.)	6	4	.600	4.60	1.59	40	0	0	0	...	7-...	58.2	54	30	30	7	39-3	68	.242
— Carolina (Sou.)	0	2	.000	5.11	1.22	13	0	0	0	...	10-...	12.1	11	8	7	2	4-1	19	.234
— Pittsburgh (N.L.)	0	0	...	5.06	1.69	9	0	0	0	0	0-0	5.1	6	3	3	0	3-0	4	.273
1994— Buffalo (A.A.)	1	1	.500	1.88	0.88	19	0	0	0	...	2-...	24.0	15	5	5	2	6-0	31	.185
— Pittsburgh (N.L.)	2	1	.667	5.93	1.43	28	0	0	0	4	2-3	27.1	28	19	18	5	11-2	27	.267
1995— Pittsburgh (N.L.)	4	4	.500	4.66	1.53	58	0	0	0	2	21-27	58.0	61	30	30	7	28-5	56	.270
1996— Pittsburgh (N.L.)	2	10	.167	5.78	1.68	44	9	0	0	4	1-1	85.2	99	65	55	15	45-5	66	.291
— Carolina (Sou.)	1	0	1.000	1.00	0.56	3	0	0	0	...	1-...	9.0	4	1	1	0	1-0	17	.125
1997— Detroit (A.L.)	3	2	.600	5.01	1.39	71	0	0	0	11	3-8	82.2	77	49	46	13	38-4	79	.248
1998— San Diego (N.L.)	10	5	.667	3.22	1.25	67	0	0	0	20	2-8	72.2	64	28	26	6	27-4	70	.238
1999— San Diego (N.L.)	4	5	.444	4.46	1.50	66	0	0	0	9	2-4	68.2	67	39	34	7	36-5	59	.266
2000— Florida (N.L.)	6	4	.600	4.25	1.29	45	0	0	0	11	0-3	48.2	45	23	23	4	18-2	40	.242
— GC Marlins (GCL)	0	0	...	0.00	0.33	2	2	0	0	...	0-...	3.0	0	0	0	0	1-0	3	.000
— Brevard County (FSL)	1	0	1.000	3.00	0.50	5	4	0	0	...	0-...	6.0	3	2	2	1	0-0	7	.143
2001— Florida (N.L.)	0	5	.000	6.93	1.62	29	0	0	0	8	0-3	24.2	29	21	19	5	11-2	31	.287
— Colo. Springs (PCL)	0	2	.000	6.00	1.00	4	0	0	0	...	0-...	3.0	2	2	2	0	1-1	4	.200
— Colorado (N.L.)	2	0	1.000	2.21	1.13	22	0	0	0	0	1-1	20.1	18	8	5	2	5-0	17	.231
2002— Texas (A.L.)	0	2	.000	8.64	1.92	9	0	0	0	0	0-1	8.1	13	8	8	1	3-0	5	.333
2003— Colorado (N.L.)	0	2	.000	5.66	1.60	14	0	0	0	1	0-0	20.2	24	13	13	7	9-1	18	.286
— Buffalo (Int'l)	0	1	.000	3.00	1.33	5	0	0	0	...	0-...	6.0	7	2	2	1	1-1	6	.280
— Cleveland (A.L.)	1	1	.500	1.20	1.00	10	0	0	0	0	0-1	15.0	9	4	2	1	6-1	19	.164
— New York (A.L.)	0	0	...	5.79	1.50	7	0	0	0	1	1-1	4.2	4	3	3	2	3-0	1	.211
— Houston (N.L.)	1	1	.500	2.10	0.97	23	0	0	0	3	0-0	30.0	22	7	7	3	7-1	20	.208
American League totals (3 years)	4	5	.444	4.80	1.38	100	0	0	0	12	4-11	110.2	103	64	59	17	50-5	104	.243
National League totals (9 years)	31	37	.456	4.54	1.44	405	9	0	0	62	29-50	462.0	463	256	233	61	200-27	408	.262
Major League totals (11 years)	35	42	.455	4.59	1.42	505	9	0	0	74	33-61	572.2	566	320	292	78	250-32	512	.258

M

MICHAELS, JASON   OF

PERSONAL: Born May 4, 1976, in Tampa, Fla. ... 6-0/204. ... Bats right, throws right. ... Full name: Jason Drew Michaels. ... High school: Jesuit (Tampa, Fla.). ... College: Miami (Fla.).

TRANSACTIONS/CAREER NOTES: Selected by San Diego Padres organization in 49th round of free-agent draft (June 2, 1994); did not sign. ... Selected by Tampa Bay Devil Rays organization in 44th round of free-agent draft (June 4, 1996); did not sign. ... Selected by St. Louis Cardinals organization in 15th round of free-agent draft (June 3, 1997); did not sign. ... Selected by Philadelphia Phillies organization in fourth round of free-agent draft (June 2, 1998). ... On Scranton/Wilkes-Barre disabled list (May 1-10, 2001). ... On Philadelphia disabled list (March 21-April 14, 2003); included rehabilitation assignment to Clearwater (April 10-14).

2003 GAMES PLAYED BY POSITION (MLB): OF—38.

									BATTING										FIELDING	
Year Team (League)	Pos.	G	AB	R	H	2B	3B	HR	RBI	BB	SO	HBP	GDP	SB-CS	Avg.	OBP	SLG	OPS	E	Pct.
1998— Batavia (NY-Penn)	OF	67	235	45	63	14	3	11	49	40	69	4	5	4-2	.268	.381	.494	.874	5	.949
1999— Clearwater (FSL)	OF	122	451	91	138	31	6	14	65	68	103	3	7	10-7	.306	.396	.494	.890	1	.996
2000— Reading (East.)	OF	113	437	71	129	30	4	10	74	28	87	3	9	7-4	.295	.337	.451	.788	6	.977
2001— Scran./W.B. (I.L.)	OF	109	418	58	109	19	3	17	69	37	126	8	7	11-3	.261	.332	.443	.774	0	1.000
— Philadelphia (N.L.)	OF	6	6	0	1	0	0	0	1	0	2	0	0	0-0	.167	.167	.167	.333	0	...
2002— Scran./W.B. (I.L.)	OF	9	32	3	9	2	0	0	7	5	5	0	0	1-3	.281	.359	.344	.703	0	1.000
— Philadelphia (N.L.)	OF-DH-3B	81	105	16	28	10	3	2	11	13	33	1	1	1-1	.267	.347	.476	.823	2	.923
2003— Clearwater (FSL)	OF	4	14	1	0	0	0	0	0	2	4	0	0	0-0	.000	.125	.000	.125	0	1.000
— Philadelphia (N.L.)	OF	76	109	20	36	11	0	5	17	15	22	1	3	0-0	.330	.416	.569	.985	1	.976
Major League totals (3 years)		163	220	36	65	21	3	7	29	28	57	2	4	1-1	.295	.377	.514	.891	3	.955

MIDDLEBROOK, JASON   P

PERSONAL: Born June 26, 1975, in Jackson, Mich. ... 6-3/215. ... Throws right, bats right. ... Full name: Jason Douglas Middlebrook. ... High school: Grass Lake (Mich.). ... College: Stanford.

TRANSACTIONS/CAREER NOTES: Selected by New York Mets organization in 18th round of free-agent draft (June 3, 1993); did not sign. ... Selected by San Diego Padres organization in ninth round of free-agent draft (June 4, 1996). ... On Rancho Cucamonga disabled list (April 8-June 25, 1999). ... On Mobile disabled list (May 8-June 2, 2000). ... Claimed on waivers by Mets (October 5, 2000). ... Claimed on waivers by Padres (November 22, 2000). ... On Mobile disabled list (May 22-June 1, 2001). ... On San Diego disabled list (July 1-31, 2002); included rehabilitation assignment to Portland (July 22-31). ... Traded by Padres with P Steve Reed to New York Mets for P Bobby M. Jones, P Josh Reynolds and OF Jay Bay (July 31, 2002). ... On New York disabled list (July 31-August 18, 2002); included rehabilitation assignment to Norfolk (August 6-18). ... Recalled by New York from Norfolk (April 17, 2003). ... Optioned to Norfolk (April 18, 2003). ... Recalled from Norfolk (April 30, 2003). ... Designated for assignment (September 2, 2003). ... Sent outright to Norfolk (September 11, 2003).

CAREER HITTING: 3-for-18 (.167), 2 R, 0 2B, 0 3B, 0 HR, 1 RBI.

Year League	W	L	Pct.	ERA	WHIP	G	GS	CG	ShO	Hld.	Sv.-Opp.	IP	H	R	ER	HR	BB-IBB	SO	Avg.
1997— Rancho Cuca. (Calif.)	0	2	.000	4.03	1.84	6	6	0	0	...	0-...	22.1	29	15	10	1	12-1	18	.326
— Clinton (Midw.)	6	4	.600	3.98	1.41	14	14	2	1	...	0-...	81.1	76	46	36	4	39-0	86	.246
1998— Rancho Cuca. (Calif.)	10	12	.455	4.92	1.50	28	•28	0	0	...	0-...	150.0	162	99	82	10	63-0	132	.276
1999— Ariz. Padres (Ariz.)	1	0	1.000	7.20	2.00	1	1	0	0	...	0-...	5.0	9	5	4	0	1-0	3	.375
— Mobile (Sou.)	4	6	.400	8.06	1.70	13	13	0	0	...	0-...	63.2	78	59	57	9	30-1	38	.302
2000— Mobile (Sou.)	5	13	.278	6.15	1.54	24	24	0	0	...	0-...	120.0	133	89	82	15	52-0	75	.284
— Las Vegas (PCL)	0	1	.000	99.99	24.00	1	1	0	0	...	0-...	.1	8	8	8	1	0-0	0	1.000
2001— Mobile (Sou.)	3	0	1.000	1.20	0.85	10	9	0	0	...	0-...	52.2	36	10	7	1	9-0	51	.191
— Portland (PCL)	7	4	.636	3.29	1.21	15	15	0	0	...	0-...	90.1	86	34	33	5	23-1	66	.250
— San Diego (N.L.)	2	1	.667	5.12	1.45	4	3	0	0	0	0-0	19.1	18	11	11	6	10-1	10	.247
2002— Portland (PCL)	2	5	.286	5.65	1.50	10	7	0	0	...	0-...	36.2	42	27	23	6	13-0	32	.278
— San Diego (N.L.)	1	3	.250	5.09	1.30	12	2	0	0	1	0-0	35.1	31	20	20	1	15-2	28	.244
— Norfolk (Int'l)	2	1	.667	2.66	0.59	5	5	0	0	...	0-...	23.2	13	7	7	1	1-0	22	.160
— New York (N.L.)	1	0	1.000	3.94	1.25	3	3	0	0	0	0-0	16.0	13	7	7	1	7-0	14	.220
2003— New York (N.L.)	0	0	...	10.29	2.43	5	0	0	0	0	0-0	7.0	13	8	8	0	4-0	3	.433
— Norfolk (Int'l)	7	10	.412	4.49	1.30	23	23	0	0	...	0-...	118.1	121	64	59	21	33-0	91	.267
Major League totals (3 years)	4	4	.500	5.33	1.43	24	8	0	0	1	0-0	77.2	75	46	46	8	36-3	55	.260

MIENTKIEWICZ, DOUG — 1B

PERSONAL: Born June 19, 1974, in Toledo, Ohio. ... 6-2/200. ... Bats left, throws right. ... Full name: Douglas Andrew Mientkiewicz. ... Name pronounced: mint-KAY-vich. ... High school: Westminster Christian (Miami). ... College: Florida State.

TRANSACTIONS/CAREER NOTES: Selected by Minnesota Twins organization in fifth round of free-agent draft (June 1, 1995).

2003 GAMES PLAYED BY POSITION (MLB): 1B—139, OF—3, 2B—1, 3B—1, DH—1.

Year Team (League)	Pos.	G	AB	R	H	2B	3B	HR	RBI	BB	SO	HBP	GDP	SB-CS	Avg.	OBP	SLG	OPS	E	Pct.
1995— Fort Myers (FSL)	1B	38	110	9	27	6	1	1	15	18	19	1	1	2-2	.245	.357	.345	.702	1	.994
1996— Fort Myers (FSL)	1B	133	492	69	143	•36	4	5	79	66	47	3	10	12-2	.291	.374	.411	.784	3	.998
1997— New Britain (East.)	1B-OF	132	467	87	119	28	2	15	61	*98	67	7	8	21-8	.255	.390	.420	.810	5	.995
1998— New Britain (East.)	1B-OF	139	502	*96	162	*45	4	16	88	96	58	6	6	11-4	.323	.432	.508	.940	12	.991
— Minnesota (A.L.)	1B	8	25	1	5	1	0	0	2	4	3	0	0	1-1	.200	.310	.240	.550	1	1.000
1999— Minnesota (A.L.)	1B	118	327	34	75	21	3	2	32	43	51	4	13	1-1	.229	.324	.330	.655	3	.997
2000— Salt Lake (PCL)	1-3-2-O	130	485	96	162	32	3	18	96	61	68	3	17	9-5	.334	.406	.524	.929	10	.989
— Minnesota (A.L.)	1B	3	14	0	6	0	0	0	4	0	0	0	1	0-0	.429	.400	.429	.829	1	1.000
2001— Minnesota (A.L.)	1B-DH	151	543	77	166	39	1	15	74	67	92	9	10	2-6	.306	.387	.464	.851	4	.997
2002— Minnesota (A.L.)	1B	143	467	60	122	29	1	10	64	74	69	6	7	1-2	.261	.365	.392	.756	5	.996
2003— Minnesota (A.L.)	1-O-2-3-D	142	487	67	146	38	1	11	65	74	55	5	9	4-1	.300	.393	.450	.843	4	.997
Major League totals (6 years)		565	1863	239	520	128	6	38	241	262	270	24	40	9-11	.279	.371	.415	.787	16	.997

MILES, AARON — 2B/DH

PERSONAL: Born December 15, 1976, in Pittsburg, Calif. ... 5-8/170. ... Bats both, throws right. ... Full name: Aaron Wade Miles. ... High school: Antioch High (Calif.).

TRANSACTIONS/CAREER NOTES: Selected by Houston Astros in 19th round of free-agent draft (June 1993). ... Selected by Chicago White Sox in Rule 5 draft (December 2000).

2003 GAMES PLAYED BY POSITION (MLB): 2B—3, DH—2.

Year Team (League)	Pos.	G	AB	R	H	2B	3B	HR	RBI	BB	SO	HBP	GDP	SB-CS	Avg.	OBP	SLG	OPS	E	Pct.
1995— GC Astros (GCL)	SS-2B	47	171	32	44	9	3	0	18	14	14	0	3	9-6	.257	.312	.345	.657	14	.916
1996— GC Astros (GCL)	2B	55	214	48	63	3	2	0	15	20	18	1	3	14-7	.294	.354	.327	.685	10	.947
1997— Quad City (Midw.)	2B	97	370	55	97	13	2	1	35	30	45	2	8	18-11	.262	.318	.316	.634	14	.961
1998— Quad City (Midw.)	2B-3B-OF	108	369	42	90	22	6	2	37	25	52	1	6	28-13	.244	.293	.352	.645	28	.945
1999— Michigan (Midw.)	2B-DH	112	470	72	149	28	8	10	71	28	33	2	8	17-12	.317	.353	.474	.828	11	.964
2000— Kissimmee (Fla. St.)	2B	75	295	40	86	20	1	2	36	28	29	0	7	11-6	.292	.352	.386	.738	17	.950
2001— Birmingham (Sou.)	3B-2B	84	343	53	89	16	3	8	42	26	35	2	10	3-5	.259	.313	.394	.706	6	.948
2002— Birmingham (Sou.)	2B-3B	138	531	67	171	39	1	9	68	40	45	2	4	25-16	.322	.369	.450	.819	26	.956
2003— Charlotte (Int'l)	2B-DH-3B	133	546	80	166	34	5	11	50	40	52	1	9	8-9	.304	.351	.445	.796	15	.973
— Chicago (A.L.)	2B-DH	8	12	3	4	3	0	0	2	0	0	0	0	0-0	.333	.333	.583	.917	0	1.000
Major League totals (1 year)		8	12	3	4	3	0	0	2	0	0	0	0	0-0	.333	.333	.583	.917	0	1.000

MILLAR, KEVIN — OF/1B

PERSONAL: Born September 24, 1971, in Los Angeles, Calif. ... 6-0/210. ... Bats right, throws right. ... Full name: Kevin Charles Millar. ... Name pronounced: mi-LAR. ... High school: University (Los Angeles). ... College: Lamar.

TRANSACTIONS/CAREER NOTES: Contract sold by St. Paul, Northern League to Florida Marlins organization (September 20, 1993). ... Granted free agency (December 21, 1997). ... Re-signed by Marlins (December 21, 1997). ... On Florida disabled list (April 19, 1998-remainder of season); included rehabilitation assignment to Charlotte (June 14-29). ... On Florida disabled list (May 4-28, 2002); included rehabilitation assignment to Portland (May 25-28). ... Contract sold by Marlins to Chunichi Dragons of the Japan Central League (January 8, 2003). ... Claimed on waivers by Boston Red Sox (January 14, 2003); Millar rejected claim as veteran. ... Traded by Marlins to Red Sox for cash considerations (February 15, 2003).

2003 GAMES PLAYED BY POSITION (MLB): 1B—101, OF—31, DH—19.

Year Team (League)	Pos.	G	AB	R	H	2B	3B	HR	RBI	BB	SO	HBP	GDP	SB-CS	Avg.	OBP	SLG	OPS	E	Pct.
1993— St. Paul (Nor.)		63	227	33	59	11	1	5	30	24	27	...		2-...	.260	...	.383		18	.911
1994— Kane Co. (Midw.)	1B	135	477	75	144	35	2	19	93	74	88	13	12	3-3	.302	.405	.503	.908	11	.990
1995— Brevard County (FSL)	1B	129	459	53	132	32	2	13	68	70	66	12	8	4-4	.288	.388	.451	.839	12	.991
1996— Portland (East.)	3B-1B	130	472	69	150	32	0	18	86	37	53	9	6	6-5	.318	.375	.500	.875	15	.983
1997— Portland (East.)	3B-1B	135	511	94	175	34	2	32	131	66	53	10	11	2-3	.342	.423	.605	1.027	17	.987
1998— Florida (N.L.)	3B	2	2	1	1	0	0	0	0	1	0	0	0	0-0	.500	.667	.500	1.167	1	.833
— Charlotte (Int'l)	3B-1B	14	46	14	15	3	0	4	15	9	7	2	3	1-0	.326	.448	.652	1.100	4	.930
1999— Calgary (PCL)	OF-3B	36	143	24	43	11	1	7	26	11	19	0	5	2-0	.301	.348	.538	.887	2	.973
— Florida (N.L.)	1B-3B-OF	105	351	48	100	17	4	9	67	40	64	7	7	1-0	.285	.364	.433	.795	4	.995
2000— Florida (N.L.)	1-O-3-D	123	259	36	67	14	3	14	42	36	47	8	5	0-0	.259	.364	.498	.862	5	.985
2001— Florida (N.L.)	O-1-3-D	144	449	62	141	39	5	20	85	39	70	5	8	0-0	.314	.374	.557	.931	2	.993

M

Year Team (League)	Pos.	G	AB	R	H	2B	3B	HR	RBI	BB	SO	HBP	GDP	SB-CS	Avg.	OBP	SLG	OPS	E	Pct.
2002—Florida (N.L.)	O-D-3-1	126	438	58	134	41	0	16	57	40	74	5	15	0-2	.306	.366	.509	.875	4	.981
—Portland (East.)	OF	3	12	1	1	0	0	1	3	0	5	0	0	0-0	.083	.077	.333	.410	0	1.000
2003—Boston (A.L.)	1B-OF-DH	148	544	83	150	30	1	25	96	60	108	5	14	3-2	.276	.348	.472	.820	5	.995
American League totals (1 year)		148	544	83	150	30	1	25	96	60	108	5	14	3-2	.276	.348	.472	.820	5	.995
National League totals (5 years)		500	1499	205	443	111	12	59	251	156	255	25	35	1-2	.296	.367	.504	.871	16	.990
Major League totals (6 years)		648	2043	288	593	141	13	84	347	216	363	30	49	4-4	.290	.362	.495	.858	21	.992

MILLER, CORKY   C

PERSONAL: Born March 18, 1976, in Yucaipa, Calif. ... 6-1/225. ... Bats right, throws right. ... Full name: Corky Abraham Philip Miller. ... High school: Yucaipa (Calif.). ... College: Nevada-Reno.

TRANSACTIONS/CAREER NOTES: Signed as non-drafted free agent by Cincinnati Reds organization (June 5, 1998).

2003 GAMES PLAYED BY POSITION (MLB): C—11.

Year Team (League)	Pos.	G	AB	R	H	2B	3B	HR	RBI	BB	SO	HBP	GDP	SB-CS	Avg.	OBP	SLG	OPS	E	Pct.
1998—Billings (Pio.)	C	45	129	28	35	8	0	5	24	24	24	21	2	1-4	.271	.455	.450	.904	* 14	.963
1999—Rockford (Midwest)	C	66	195	43	56	10	1	10	40	33	42	20	5	3-6	.287	.438	.503	.940	* 14	.975
—Chattanooga (Sou.)	C	33	104	20	23	10	0	4	16	11	30	11	3	0-0	.221	.354	.433	.787	3	.989
2000—Chattanooga (Sou.)	C	103	317	40	74	18	0	9	44	41	51	30	12	5-8	.233	.373	.375	.748	* 16	.981
2001—Chattanooga (Sou.)	C	59	170	25	47	12	0	9	42	25	32	19	1	1-2	.276	.425	.506	.931	7	.985
—Louisville (Int'l)	C	44	144	30	50	11	0	7	28	10	19	12	2	2-0	.347	.431	.569	1.001	2	.994
—Cincinnati (N.L.)	C	17	49	5	9	2	0	3	7	4	16	2	1	1-0	.184	.263	.408	.671	1	.991
2002—Louisville (Int'l)	C	43	134	14	31	5	0	6	21	16	21	6	6	1-2	.231	.340	.403	.743	2	.994
—Cincinnati (N.L.)	C	39	114	9	29	10	0	3	15	9	20	4	7	0-0	.254	.328	.421	.749	2	.992
2003—Louisville (Int'l)	C-DH	103	354	49	88	28	0	11	43	35	58	7	12	0-0	.249	.326	.421	.747	7	.989
—Cincinnati (N.L.)	C	14	30	4	8	0	0	0	1	5	7	2	1	0-0	.267	.395	.267	.661	0	1.000
Major League totals (3 years)		70	193	18	46	12	0	6	23	18	43	8	9	1-0	.238	.323	.394	.717	3	.993

MILLER, DAMIAN   C

PERSONAL: Born October 13, 1969, in La Crosse, Wis. ... 6-3/220. ... Bats right, throws right. ... Full name: Damian Donald Miller. ... High school: West Salem (Wis.). ... College: Viterbo (Wis.).

TRANSACTIONS/CAREER NOTES: Selected by Minnesota Twins organization in 20th round of free-agent draft (June 4, 1990). ... Selected by Arizona Diamondbacks in second round (47th pick overall) of expansion draft (November 18, 1997). ... On Arizona disabled list (July 24-August 14, 2002); included rehabilitation assignment to Tucson (August 9-14). ... Traded by Diamondbacks to Chicago Cubs for P David Noyce and OF Gary Johnson (November 13, 2002).

2003 GAMES PLAYED BY POSITION (MLB): C—114.

Year Team (League)	Pos.	G	AB	R	H	2B	3B	HR	RBI	BB	SO	HBP	GDP	SB-CS	Avg.	OBP	SLG	OPS	E	Pct.
1990—Elizabethton (App.)	C	14	45	7	10	1	0	1	6	9	3	0	2	1-0	.222	.352	.311	.663	2	.982
1991—Kenosha (Midw.)	C-1B-OF	80	267	28	62	11	1	3	34	24	53	2	4	3-2	.232	.297	.315	.612	4	.990
1992—Kenosha (Midw.)	C	115	377	53	110	27	2	5	56	53	66	7	13	6-1	.292	.385	.414	.799	9	.989
1993—Fort Myers (FSL)	C	87	325	31	69	12	1	1	26	31	44	0	5	6-3	.212	.281	.265	.546	8	.985
—Nashville (Sou.)	C	4	13	0	3	0	0	0	0	2	4	0	0	0-0	.231	.333	.231	.564	0	1.000
1994—Nashville (Sou.)	C	103	328	36	88	10	0	8	35	35	51	1	11	4-6	.268	.336	.372	.708	8	.989
1995—Salt Lake (PCL)	C-OF	83	295	39	84	23	1	3	41	15	39	3	11	2-4	.285	.324	.400	.724	1	.998
1996—Salt Lake (PCL)	C-1B	104	385	54	110	27	1	7	55	25	58	6	13	1-4	.286	.336	.416	.751	6	.992
1997—Salt Lake (PCL)	C-DH	85	314	48	106	19	3	11	82	29	62	3	7	6-1	.338	.395	.522	.918	6	.988
—Minnesota (A.L.)	C-DH	25	66	5	18	1	0	2	13	2	12	0	2	0-0	.273	.282	.379	.660	0	1.000
1998—Tucson (PCL)	C	18	63	14	22	7	1	0	11	9	9	2	2	0-0	.349	.434	.492	.926	3	.973
—Arizona (N.L.)	C-D-O-1	57	168	17	48	14	2	3	14	11	43	2	2	1-0	.286	.337	.446	.783	4	.986
1999—Arizona (N.L.)	C	86	296	35	80	19	0	11	47	19	78	2	6	0-0	.270	.316	.446	.762	6	.991
2000—Arizona (N.L.)	C-1B	100	324	43	89	24	0	10	44	36	74	1	6	2-2	.275	.347	.441	.788	7	.991
2001—Arizona (N.L.)	C	123	380	45	103	19	0	13	47	35	80	4	9	0-1	.271	.337	.424	.761	7	.993
2002—Arizona (N.L.)	C	101	297	40	74	22	0	11	42	38	88	3	14	0-0	.249	.340	.434	.775	2	.997
—Tucson (PCL)	C	3	9	1	3	1	0	0	0	0	1	0	1	0-0	.333	.333	.444	.778	0	1.000
2003—Chicago (N.L.)	C	114	352	34	82	19	1	9	36	39	91	1	15	1-0	.233	.310	.369	.680	3	.997
American League totals (1 year)		25	66	5	18	1	0	2	13	2	12	0	2	0-0	.273	.282	.379	.660	0	1.000
National League totals (6 years)		581	1817	214	476	117	3	57	230	178	454	13	52	4-3	.262	.331	.424	.755	29	.994
Major League totals (7 years)		606	1883	219	494	118	3	59	243	180	466	13	54	4-3	.262	.329	.422	.751	29	.994

MILLER, JUSTIN   P

PERSONAL: Born August 27, 1977... 6-2/195. ... Throws right, bats right. ... Full name: Justin Mark Miller. ... High school: Torrance (Calif.).

TRANSACTIONS/CAREER NOTES: Selected by San Francisco Giants organization in 34th round of free-agent draft (June 1, 1995); did not sign. ... Selected by Colorado Rockies organization in fifth round of free-agent draft (June 3, 1997). ... On Salem disabled list (May 5-June 18, 1999). ... Traded by Rockies with cash to Oakland Athletics as part of three-way deal in which Brewers received P Jimmy Haynes from A's, Rockies received 3B Jeff Cirillo, P Scott Karl and cash from Brewers and Brewers received P Jamey Wright and C Henry Blanco from Rockies (December 13, 1999). ... On Midland disabled list (June 8-17 and June 22-30, 2000). ... Traded by A's with 3B Eric Hinske to Toronto Blue Jays for P Billy Koch (December 7, 2001). ... Called up by Toronto from Syracuse (September 2, 2003).

CAREER HITTING: 0-for-2 (.000), 0 R, 0 2B, 0 3B, 0 HR, 0 RBI.

Year League	W	L	Pct.	ERA	WHIP	G	GS	CG	ShO	Hld.	Sv.-Opp.	IP	H	R	ER	HR	BB-IBB	SO	Avg.
1997—Portland (NW)	4	2	.667	2.14	1.31	14	11	0	0	...	0-...	67.1	68	26	16	3	20-0	54	.262
1998—Asheville (S. Atl.)	13	8	.619	3.69	1.33	27	27	3	1	...	0-...	163.1	177	89	67	14	40-0	142	.275
1999—Salem (Caro.)	1	2	.333	4.14	1.24	8	8	0	0	...	0-...	37.0	35	18	17	3	11-0	35	.245
2000—Midland (Texas)	5	4	.556	4.55	1.32	18	18	0	0	...	0-...	87.0	74	49	44	8	41-1	82	.230
—Sacramento (PCL)	4	1	.800	2.47	1.01	9	9	0	0	...	0-...	54.2	42	18	15	3	13-0	34	.210
2001—Sacramento (PCL)	7	10	.412	4.75	1.45	29	28	1	0	...	0-...	165.0	174	94	87	26	64-1	134	.276
2002—Syracuse (Int'l)	3	2	.600	1.61	1.12	8	8	0	0	...	0-...	44.2	34	11	8	0	16-0	29	.207
—Toronto (A.L.)	9	5	.643	5.54	1.65	25	18	0	0	1	0-0	102.1	103	70	63	12	66-2	68	.268
2003—Dunedin (Fla. St.)	0	1	.000	4.50	0.80	1	1	0	0	...	0-0	6.0	3	3	3	0	2-0	5	.167
Major League totals (1 year)	9	5	.643	5.54	1.65	25	18	0	0	1	0-0	102.1	103	70	63	12	66-2	68	.268

M

MILLER, MATT   P

PERSONAL: Born November 23, 1971, in Greenwood, Miss. ... 6-3/215. ... Throws right, bats right. ... Full name: Matt Jacob Miller. ... High school: Leland (Miss.). ... College: Delta State (Miss.).

TRANSACTIONS/CAREER NOTES: Signed by Greenville Bluesmen of the independent Big South League (June 1996). ... Signed by Texas Rangers organization (December 1, 1997). ... Released by Rangers (March 29, 1998). ... Signed by Greenville Bluesmen of the independent Texas-Louisiana League (May 1998). ... Contract purchased by Texas Rangers organization (June 27, 1998). ... Granted free agency (October 16, 1998). ... Re-signed by Texas organization (November 4, 1998). ... Granted free agency (October 15, 2000). ... Signed by San Diego Padres organization (November 5, 2000). ... Granted free agency (October 15, 2001), ... Signed by Oakland Athletics organization (November 15, 2001). ... Released by A's (2002). ... Signed by Colorado Rockies organization (November 20, 2002).

CAREER HITTING: 0-for-0 (.000), 0 R, 0 2B, 0 3B, 0 HR, 0 RBI.

Year League	W	L	Pct.	ERA	WHIP	G	GS	CG	ShO	Hld.	Sv.-Opp.	IP	H	R	ER	HR	BB-IBB	SO	Avg.
1996— Greenville (Big South)	5	2	.714	6.07	1.82	19	6	0	0	...	1-...	69.2	77	51	47	2	50-0	54	.286
1997— Greenville (Big South)	12	3	.800	2.26	1.16	15	15	5	3	...	0-...	107.1	76	34	27	0	49-0	129	.203
1998— Greenville (Tex.-La.)	1	7	.125	2.85	1.21	8	8	4	0	...	0-...	53.2	46	26	17	1	19-1	49	.230
— Savannah (S. Atl.)	3	1	.750	2.29	0.99	17	0	0	0	...	3-...	35.1	25	9	9	0	10-0	46	.203
1999— Charlotte (Int'l)	1	2	.333	3.03	1.35	22	0	0	0	...	8-...	29.2	27	12	10	0	13-1	39	.231
— Tulsa (Texas)	6	4	.600	3.40	1.26	34	0	0	0	...	7-...	55.2	42	24	21	2	28-2	83	.213
2000— Oklahoma (PCL)	3	3	.500	3.58	1.57	39	0	0	0	...	4-...	60.1	61	29	24	6	34-4	69	.264
— GC Rangers (GCL)	0	0	...	4.50	1.00	1	0	0	0	...	0-...	2.0	2	1	1	0	0-0	4	.250
— Tulsa (Texas)	0	0	...	14.73	3.00	3	0	0	0	...	0-...	3.2	7	7	6	0	4-0	4	.412
2001— Portland (East.)	1	7	.125	3.63	1.30	44	0	0	0	...	17-...	44.2	44	22	18	1	14-2	43	.254
2002— Sacramento (PCL)	3	7	.300	4.31	1.54	54	0	0	0	...	6-...	71.0	81	42	34	5	28-8	63	.286
2003— Colorado (N.L.)	0	0	...	2.08	1.62	4	0	0	0	0	0-0	4.1	5	1	1	0	2-0	5	.313
— Colo. Springs (PCL)	5	0	1.000	2.13	1.09	61	0	0	0	...	3-...	63.1	46	17	15	0	23-1	83	.204
Major League totals (1 year)	0	0	...	2.08	1.62	4	0	0	0	0	0-0	4.1	5	1	1	0	2-0	5	.313

MILLER, TREVER   P

PERSONAL: Born May 29, 1973, in Louisville, Ky. ... 6-4/195. ... Throws left, bats right. ... Full name: Trever Douglas Miller. ... High school: Trinity (Louisville, Ky.).

TRANSACTIONS/CAREER NOTES: Selected by Detroit Tigers organization in supplemental round ("sandwich pick" between first and second round, 41st pick overall) of free-agent draft (June 3, 1991); pick received as part of compensation for Atlanta Braves signing Type A free-agent C Mike Heath. ... Traded by Tigers with C Brad Ausmus, P Jose Lima, P C.J. Nitkowski and P Daryle Ward to Houston Astros for OF Brian Hunter, IF Orlando Miller, P Doug Brocail, P Todd Jones and cash (December 10, 1996). ... On disabled list (August 23-September 7, 1998). ... Traded by Astros to Philadelphia Phillies for P Yorkis Perez (March 29, 2000). ... Claimed on waivers by Los Angeles Dodgers (May 19, 2000). ... On Albuquerque disabled list (August 3-17 and August 31-September 11, 2000). ... Granted free agency (October 18, 2000). ... Signed by Boston Red Sox organization (January 22, 2001). ... Granted free agency (October 15, 2001). ... Signed by Cincinnati Reds organization (December 21, 2001). ... Released by Reds (2002). ... Signed by Toronto Blue Jays organization (October 30, 2002).

CAREER HITTING: 1-for-6 (.167), 1 R, 1 2B, 0 3B, 0 HR, 0 RBI.

Year League	W	L	Pct.	ERA	WHIP	G	GS	CG	ShO	Hld.	Sv.-Opp.	IP	H	R	ER	HR	BB-IBB	SO	Avg.
1991— Bristol (Appal.)	2	7	.222	5.67	1.65	13	13	0	0	...	0-...	54.0	60	44	34	7	29-0	46	.278
1992— Bristol (Appal.)	3	•8	.273	4.93	1.47	12	12	1	0	...	0-...	69.1	75	45	38	4	27-0	64	.271
1993— Fayetteville (S. Atl.)	8	13	.381	4.19	1.35	28	28	2	0	...	0-...	161.0	151	99	75	7	67-0	116	.245
1994— Trenton (East.)	7	16	.304	4.39	1.43	26	26	6	0	...	0-...	174.1	198	95	85	9	51-0	73	.290
1995— Jacksonville (Sou.)	8	2	.800	2.72	1.28	31	16	3	2	...	0-...	122.1	122	46	37	5	34-0	77	.261
1996— Toledo (Int'l)	13	6	.684	4.90	1.40	27	27	0	0	...	0-...	165.1	167	98	90	19	65-1	115	.260
— Detroit (A.L.)	0	4	.000	9.18	2.22	5	4	0	0	0	0-0	16.2	28	17	17	3	9-0	8	.384
1997— New Orleans (A.A.)	6	7	.462	3.30	1.41	29	27	2	0	...	0-...	163.2	177	71	60	15	54-1	99	.283
1998— Houston (N.L.)	2	0	1.000	3.04	1.44	37	1	0	0	1	1-2	53.1	57	21	18	4	20-1	30	.266
1999— Houston (N.L.)	3	2	.600	5.07	1.75	47	0	0	0	4	1-1	49.2	58	29	28	6	29-1	37	.299
2000— Philadelphia (N.L.)	0	0	...	8.36	2.00	14	0	0	0	0	0-0	14.0	19	16	13	3	9-1	10	.317
— Los Angeles (N.L.)	0	0	...	23.14	4.71	2	0	0	0	0	0-0	2.1	8	6	6	0	3-0	1	.571
— Albuquerque (PCL)	4	2	.667	3.41	1.38	12	9	1	1	...	0-...	58.0	60	29	22	5	20-0	39	.268
2001— Sarasota (Fla. St.)	0	0	...	2.25	0.50	3	2	0	0	...	0-...	8.0	3	2	2	0	1-0	6	.115
— Pawtucket (Int'l)	3	11	.214	5.20	1.52	33	15	0	0	...	0-...	116.0	142	79	67	16	34-2	93	.307
2002— Louisville (Int'l)	9	5	.643	3.18	1.21	65	1	0	0	...	0-...	82.0	76	30	29	6	23-4	80	.242
2003— Toronto (A.L.)	2	2	.500	4.61	1.41	*79	0	0	0	16	4-5	52.2	46	30	27	7	28-3	44	.231
American League totals (2 years)	2	6	.250	5.71	1.60	84	4	0	0	16	4-5	69.1	74	47	44	10	37-3	52	.272
National League totals (3 years)	5	2	.714	4.90	1.70	100	1	0	0	5	2-3	119.1	142	72	65	13	61-3	78	.295
Major League totals (5 years)	7	8	.467	5.20	1.66	184	5	0	0	21	6-8	188.2	216	119	109	23	98-6	130	.286

MILLER, WADE   P

PERSONAL: Born September 13, 1976, in Reading, Pa. ... 6-2/210. ... Throws right, bats right. ... Full name: Wade T. Miller. ... High school: Brandywine Heights (Pa.). ... College: Alvernia (Pa.).

TRANSACTIONS/CAREER NOTES: Selected by Houston Astros organization in 20th round of free-agent draft (June 4, 1996). ... On disabled list (June 1, 1998-remainder of season). ... On New Orleans disabled list (May 16-25, 2000). ... On Houston disabled list (April 15-May 29, 2002); included rehabilitation assignment to New Orleans (May 17-24). ... Optioned to New Orleans (August 28, 2003). ... Recalled from New Orleans (September 1, 2003).

CAREER HITTING: 36-for-232 (.155), 18 R, 9 2B, 0 3B, 0 HR, 14 RBI.

Year League	W	L	Pct.	ERA	WHIP	G	GS	CG	ShO	Hld.	Sv.-Opp.	IP	H	R	ER	HR	BB-IBB	SO	Avg.
1996— GC Astros (GCL)	3	4	.429	3.79	1.07	11	10	0	0	...	0-...	57.0	49	26	24	1	12-0	53	.233
— Auburn (N.Y.-Penn)	1	1	.500	5.00	1.33	2	2	0	0	...	0-...	9.0	8	9	5	0	4-0	11	.216
1997— Quad City (Midw.)	5	3	.625	3.36	0.93	10	8	2	0	...	0-...	59.0	45	27	22	7	10-0	50	.201
— Kissimmee (Fla. St.)	10	2	.833	1.80	0.93	14	14	4	1	...	0-...	100.0	79	28	20	3	14-1	76	.214
1998— Jackson (Texas)	5	0	1.000	2.32	1.23	10	10	0	0	...	0-...	62.0	49	23	16	7	27-2	48	.213
1999— New Orleans (PCL)	11	9	.550	4.38	1.36	26	26	2	0	...	0-...	162.1	156	85	79	16	64-0	135	.248
— Houston (N.L.)	0	1	.000	9.58	2.13	5	1	0	0	0	0-0	10.1	17	11	11	4	5-0	8	.362
2000— New Orleans (PCL)	4	5	.444	3.67	1.26	16	15	0	0	...	0-...	105.1	95	46	43	6	38-1	81	.245
— Houston (N.L.)	6	6	.500	5.14	1.39	16	16	2	0	0	0-0	105.0	104	66	60	14	42-1	89	.257
2001— Houston (N.L.)	16	8	.667	3.40	1.22	32	32	1	0	0	0-0	212.0	183	91	80	31	76-3	183	.234
2002— Houston (N.L.)	15	4	.789	3.28	1.29	26	26	1	1	0	0-0	164.2	151	63	60	14	62-9	144	.249
— New Orleans (PCL)	0	0	...	2.25	1.38	2	2	0	0	...	0-...	8.0	10	4	2	0	1-0	9	.323
2003— Houston (N.L.)	14	13	.519	4.13	1.31	33	33	1	0	0	0-0	187.1	168	96	86	17	77-1	161	.242
Major League totals (5 years)	51	32	.614	3.93	1.30	112	108	5	1	0	0-0	679.1	623	327	297	80	262-14	585	.246

M

MILLWOOD, KEVIN   P

PERSONAL: Born December 24, 1974, in Gastonia, N.C. ... 6-4/220. ... Throws right, bats right. ... Full name: Kevin Austin Millwood. ... High school: Bessemer City (N.C.).

TRANSACTIONS/CAREER NOTES: Selected by Atlanta Braves organization in 11th round of free-agent draft (June 3, 1993). ... On Atlanta disabled list (May 7-July 20, 2001); included rehabilitation assignments to Macon (July 4-9) and Greenville (July 10-20). ... Traded by Braves to Philadelphia Phillies for C Johnny Estrada (December 20, 2002).

CAREER HITTING: 45-for-380 (.118), 18 R, 12 2B, 0 3B, 2 HR, 23 RBI.

Year League	W	L	Pct.	ERA	WHIP	G	GS	CG	ShO	Hld.	Sv.-Opp.	IP	H	R	ER	HR	BB-IBB	SO	Avg.
1993—GC Braves (GCL)	3	3	.500	3.06	1.28	12	9	0	0	...	0-...	50.0	36	27	17	3	28-0	49	.196
1994—Danville (Appal.)	3	3	.500	3.72	1.65	13	5	0	0	...	1-...	46.0	42	25	19	4	34-2	56	.247
—Macon (S. Atl.)	0	5	.000	5.79	1.93	12	4	0	0	...	1-...	32.2	31	31	21	4	32-1	24	.242
1995—Macon (S. Atl.)	5	6	.455	4.63	1.39	29	12	0	0	...	0-...	103.0	86	65	53	10	57-0	89	.227
1996—Durham (Caro.)	6	9	.400	4.28	1.31	33	20	1	0	...	1-...	149.1	138	77	71	17	58-0	139	.248
1997—Greenville (Sou.)	3	5	.375	4.11	1.35	11	11	0	0	...	0-...	61.1	59	37	28	8	24-0	61	.250
—Richmond (Int'l)	7	0	1.000	1.93	0.89	9	9	1	0	...	0-...	60.2	38	13	13	2	16-0	46	.178
—Atlanta (N.L.)	5	3	.625	4.03	1.48	12	8	0	0	0	0-0	51.1	55	26	23	1	21-1	42	.282
1998—Atlanta (N.L.)	17	8	.680	4.08	1.33	31	29	3	1	1	0-0	174.1	175	86	79	18	56-3	163	.258
1999—Atlanta (N.L.)	18	7	.720	2.68	0.00	33	33	2	0	0	0-0	228.0	168	80	68	24	59-2	205	*.202
2000—Atlanta (N.L.)	10	13	.435	4.66	1.29	36	•35	0	0	0	0-0	212.2	213	115	110	26	62-2	168	.258
2001—Atlanta (N.L.)	7	7	.500	4.31	1.33	21	21	0	0	0	0-0	121.0	121	66	58	20	40-6	84	.260
—Macon (S. Atl.)	0	0	...	0.00	0.00	1	1	0	0	...	0-...	3.0	0	0	0	0	0-0	5	.000
—Greenville (Sou.)	0	1	.000	4.50	1.20	2	2	0	0	...	0-...	10.0	9	6	5	2	3-0	10	.243
2002—Atlanta (N.L.)	18	8	.692	3.24	1.16	35	34	1	1	0	0-0	217.0	186	83	78	16	65-7	178	.230
2003—Philadelphia (N.L.)	14	12	.538	4.01	1.25	35	35	5	•3	0	0-0	222.0	210	103	99	19	68-6	169	.250
Major League totals (7 years)	**89**	**58**	**.605**	**3.78**	**1.22**	**203**	**195**	**11**	**5**	**1**	**0-0**	**1226.1**	**1128**	**559**	**515**	**124**	**371-27**	**1009**	**.243**

MILTON, ERIC   P

PERSONAL: Born August 4, 1975, in State College, Pa. ... 6-3/225. ... Throws left, bats left. ... Full name: Eric Robert Milton. ... High school: Bellefonte (Pa.). ... College: Maryland.

TRANSACTIONS/CAREER NOTES: Selected by New York Yankees organization in first round (20th pick overall) of free-agent draft (June 2, 1996). ... Traded by Yankees with P Danny Mota, OF Brian Buchanan, SS Cristian Guzman and cash to Minnesota Twins for 2B Chuck Knoblauch (February 6, 1998). ... On disabled list (August 7-September 2, 2002). ... On disabled list (March 13, 2003). ... Sent on minor league rehab assignment (August 30, 2003). ... Recalled from minor league rehab assignment (September 8, 2003). ... Removed from 60-day disabled list (September 14, 2003).

CAREER HITTING: 6-for-20 (.300), 1 R, 0 2B, 0 3B, 0 HR, 2 RBI.

Year League	W	L	Pct.	ERA	WHIP	G	GS	CG	ShO	Hld.	Sv.-Opp.	IP	H	R	ER	HR	BB-IBB	SO	Avg.
1997—Tampa (FSL)	8	3	.727	3.09	0.99	14	14	1	0	...	0-...	93.1	78	35	32	8	14-0	95	.223
—Norwich (East.)	6	3	.667	3.13	1.22	14	14	1	0	...	0-...	77.2	59	29	27	2	36-0	67	.210
1998—Minnesota (A.L.)	8	14	.364	5.64	1.54	32	32	1	0	0	0-0	172.1	195	113	108	25	70-0	107	.282
1999—Minnesota (A.L.)	7	11	.389	4.49	1.23	34	34	5	2	0	0-0	206.1	190	111	103	28	63-2	163	.243
2000—Minnesota (A.L.)	13	10	.565	4.86	1.25	33	33	0	0	0	0-0	200.0	205	123	108	35	44-0	160	.260
2001—Minnesota (A.L.)	15	7	.682	4.32	1.28	35	34	2	1	0	0-0	220.2	222	109	106	35	61-0	157	.257
2002—Minnesota (A.L.)	13	9	.591	4.84	1.19	29	29	2	1	0	0-0	171.0	173	96	92	24	30-0	121	.258
2003—Fort Myers (Fla. St.)	0	0	...	0.00	1.50	1	1	0	0	...	0-...	2.0	1	0	0	0	2-0	2	.143
—Minnesota (A.L.)	1	0	1.000	2.65	0.94	3	3	0	0	0	0-0	17.0	15	5	5	2	1-0	7	.234
Major League totals (6 years)	**57**	**51**	**.528**	**4.76**	**1.29**	**166**	**165**	**10**	**4**	**0**	**0-0**	**987.1**	**1000**	**557**	**522**	**149**	**269-2**	**715**	**.259**

MIRABELLI, DOUG   C

PERSONAL: Born October 18, 1970, in Kingman, Ariz. ... 6-1/227. ... Bats right, throws right. ... Full name: Douglas Anthony Mirabelli. ... Name pronounced: mirr-uh-BEL-ee. ... High school: Valley (Las Vegas). ... College: Wichita State.

TRANSACTIONS/CAREER NOTES: Selected by Detroit Tigers organization in sixth round of free-agent draft (June 5, 1989); did not sign. ... Selected by San Francisco Giants organization in fifth round of free-agent draft (June 1, 1992). ... On Phoenix disabled list (May 16-23, 1995). ... Contract purchased by Texas Rangers from Giants (March 27, 2001). ... Traded by Rangers to Boston Red Sox for P Justin Duchscherer (June 12, 2001).

2003 GAMES PLAYED BY POSITION (MLB): C—55, DH—4, 1B—2.

Year Team (League)	Pos.	G	AB	R	H	2B	3B	HR	RBI	BB	SO	HBP	GDP	SB-CS	Avg.	OBP	SLG	OPS	E	Pct.
1992—San Jose (Calif.)	C	53	177	30	41	11	1	0	21	24	18	4	7	1-3	.232	.333	.305	.638	10	.973
1993—San Jose (Calif.)	C	113	371	58	100	19	2	1	48	72	55	4	7	0-4	.270	.390	.340	.730	9	.989
1994—Shreveport (Texas)	C-1B	85	255	23	56	8	0	4	24	36	48	0	6	3-1	.220	.316	.298	.614	3	.993
1995—Phoenix (PCL)	C	23	66	3	11	0	1	0	7	12	10	1	5	1-0	.167	.296	.197	.493	2	.985
—Shreveport (Texas)	C-1B	40	126	14	38	13	0	0	16	20	14	0	3	1-0	.302	.397	.405	.802	3	.986
1996—Shreveport (Texas)	C-DH-1B	115	380	60	112	23	0	21	70	76	49	6	9	0-1	.295 *	.419	.521	.940	7	.989
—Phoenix (PCL)	C	14	47	10	14	7	0	0	7	4	7	1	1	0-0	.298	.365	.447	.812	2	.982
—San Francisco (N.L.)	C	9	18	2	4	1	0	0	1	3	4	0	0	0-0	.222	.333	.278	.611	0	1.000
1997—Phoenix (PCL)	C-DH	100	332	49	88	23	2	8	48	58	69	7	9	1-2	.265	.384	.419	.803	4	.994
—San Francisco (N.L.)	C	6	7	0	1	0	0	0	0	1	3	0	0	0-0	.143	.250	.143	.393	0	1.000
1998—Fresno (PCL)	C-DH	85	265	45	69	12	2	13	53	52	55	3	9	2-0	.260	.386	.468	.854	3	.995
—San Francisco (N.L.)	C	10	17	2	4	2	0	1	4	2	6	0	0	0-0	.235	.316	.529	.845	1	.974
1999—Fresno (PCL)	C-1B-DH	86	320	63	100	24	1	14	51	48	56	1	6	8-2	.313	.398	.525	.923	5	.993
—San Francisco (N.L.)	C	33	87	10	22	6	0	1	10	9	25	1	1	0-0	.253	.327	.356	.683	0	1.000
2000—San Francisco (N.L.)	C	82	230	23	53	10	2	6	28	36	57	2	6	1-0	.230	.337	.370	.707	7	.985
2001—Texas (A.L.)	C-DH	23	49	4	5	2	0	2	3	10	21	0	1	0-0	.102	.254	.265	.520	1	.990
—Boston (A.L.)	C-DH	54	141	16	38	8	0	9	26	17	36	4	2	0-0	.270	.360	.518	.877	2	.995
2002—Boston (A.L.)	C	57	151	17	34	7	0	7	25	17	33	3	6	0-0	.225	.312	.411	.723	0	1.000
2003—Boston (A.L.)	C-DH-1B	62	163	23	42	13	0	6	18	11	36	1	3	0-0	.258	.307	.448	.755	5	.986
American League totals (3 years)		196	504	60	119	30	0	24	72	55	126	8	12	0-0	.236	.318	.438	.757	8	.993
National League totals (5 years)		140	359	37	84	19	2	8	43	51	95	3	7	1-0	.234	.332	.365	.697	8	.989
Major League totals (8 years)		336	863	97	203	49	2	32	115	106	221	11	19	1-0	.235	.324	.408	.732	16	.991

MITRE, SERGIO   P

PERSONAL: Born February 16, 1981, in Los Angeles, Calif. ... 6-4/210. ... Throws right, bats right. ... Full name: Sergio Armando Mitre. ... High school: Montgomery (Chula Vista, Calif.). ... Junior college: San Diego Community College.
TRANSACTIONS/CAREER NOTES: Selected by Chicago Cubs organization in seventh round of free-agent draft (June 2001).
CAREER HITTING: 1-for-2 (.500), 1 R, 0 2B, 0 3B, 0 HR, 0 RBI.

Year League	W	L	Pct.	ERA	WHIP	G	GS	CG	ShO	Hld.	Sv.-Opp.	IP	H	R	ER	HR	BB-IBB	SO	Avg.
2001— Boise (NW)	8	4	.667	3.07	1.13	15	15	1	1	...	0-...	91.0	85	37	31	2	18-1	71	.243
2002— Lansing (Midw.)	8	10	.444	2.83	1.14	27	27	2	0	...	0-...	168.2	166	72	53	7	27-1	96	.261
2003— West Tenn (Sou.)	7	9	.438	3.34	1.39	25	24	0	0	...	0-...	145.2	162	75	54	6	41-0	128	.282
— Chicago (N.L.)	0	1	.000	8.31	2.19	3	2	0	0	0	0-0	8.2	15	8	8	1	4-1	3	.395
Major League totals (1 year)	0	1	.000	8.31	2.19	3	2	0	0	0	0-0	8.2	15	8	8	1	4-1	3	.395

MOEHLER, BRIAN   P

PERSONAL: Born December 31, 1971, in Rockingham, N.C. ... 6-3/235. ... Throws right, bats right. ... Full name: Brian Merritt Moehler. ... Name pronounced: MOW-ler. ... High school: Richmond (N.C.) South. ... College: UNC-Greensboro.
TRANSACTIONS/CAREER NOTES: Selected by Detroit Tigers organization in sixth round of free-agent draft (June 3, 1993). ... On disabled list (August 9-22, 1997). ... On suspended list (May 3-13, 1999). ... On Detroit disabled list (April 17-May 19, 2000); included rehabilitation assignment to West Michigan (May 12-19). ... On Detroit disabled list (April 7, 2001-remainder of season); included rehabilitation assignment to Toledo (May 20-June 1). ... On Detroit disabled list (March 22-July 3, 2002); included rehabilitation assignment to Lakeland (June 1-10) and Toledo (June 11-27). ... Traded by Tigers with IF Matt Boone to Cincinnati Reds for SS David Espinosa and two players to be named later (July 23, 2002); Tigers acquired OF Gary Varner (August 30, 2002) and P Jorge Cordova (September 24, 2002) to complete deal. ... On Cincinnati disabled list (August 28-September 13, 2002). ... Granted free agency (October 28, 2002). ... Signed by Houston Astros (January 17, 2003). ... Placed on 15-day disabled list (April 17, 2003). ... Sent on rehab assignment to New Orleans (May 19, 2003). ... Recalled from rehab assignment (May 20, 2003). ... Transferred to Emergency disabled list (June 28, 2003).
CAREER HITTING: 0-for-30 (.000), 1 R, 0 2B, 0 3B, 0 HR, 0 RBI.

Year League	W	L	Pct.	ERA	WHIP	G	GS	CG	ShO	Hld.	Sv.-Opp.	IP	H	R	ER	HR	BB-IBB	SO	Avg.
1993— Niagara Falls (NYP)	6	5	.545	3.22	1.33	12	11	0	0	...	0-...	58.2	51	33	21	3	27-0	38	.225
1994— Lakeland (Fla. St.)	12	12	.500	3.01	1.32	26	25	5	2	...	0-...	164.2	153	66	55	3	65-0	92	.254
1995— Jacksonville (Sou.)	8	10	.444	4.82	1.40	28	27	0	0	...	0-...	162.1	176	94	87	14	52-1	89	.279
1996— Jacksonville (Sou.)	* 15	6	.714	3.48	1.36	28	28	1	0	...	0-...	173.1	186	80	67	9	50-2	120	.272
— Detroit (A.L.)	0	1	.000	4.35	1.84	2	2	0	0	0	0-0	10.1	11	10	5	1	8-1	2	.262
1997— Detroit (A.L.)	11	12	.478	4.67	1.48	31	31	2	1	0	0-0	175.1	198	97	91	22	61-1	97	.285
1998— Detroit (A.L.)	14	13	.519	3.90	1.25	33	33	4	3	0	0-0	221.1	220	103	96	30	56-1	123	.260
1999— Detroit (A.L.)	10	* 16	.385	5.04	1.47	32	32	2	2	0	0-0	196.1	229	116	110	22	59-5	106	.294
2000— Detroit (A.L.)	12	9	.571	4.50	1.47	29	29	2	0	0	0-0	178.0	222	99	89	20	40-0	103	.305
— West. Mich. (Mid.)	0	1	.000	4.26	0.95	1	1	0	0	...	0-...	6.1	5	3	3	1	1-0	4	.217
2001— Detroit (A.L.)	0	0	...	3.38	0.88	1	1	0	0	0	0-0	8.0	6	3	3	0	1-0	2	.207
— Toledo (Int'l)	0	2	.000	4.35	1.35	2	2	0	0	...	0-...	10.1	12	6	5	2	2-0	6	.279
2002— Lakeland (Fla. St.)	1	1	.500	2.92	0.89	2	2	0	0	...	0-...	12.1	10	9	4	2	1-0	7	.208
— Toledo (Int'l)	2	1	.667	4.88	1.29	4	4	0	0	...	0-...	24.0	28	15	13	3	3-0	7	.277
— Detroit (A.L.)	1	1	.500	2.29	0.97	3	3	0	0	0	0-0	19.2	17	5	5	3	2-0	13	.233
— Cincinnati (N.L.)	2	4	.333	6.02	1.66	10	9	0	0	0	0-0	43.1	61	34	29	8	11-0	18	.330
2003— Houston (N.L.)	0	0	...	7.90	2.05	3	3	0	0	0	0-0	13.2	22	12	12	4	6-0	5	.379
— New Orleans (PCL)	0	0	...	4.50	1.50	1	1	0	0	...	0-...	2.0	3	1	1	0	0-0	3	.375
American League totals (7 years)	48	52	.480	4.44	1.40	131	131	10	6	0	0-0	809.0	903	433	399	98	227-8	446	.283
National League totals (2 years)	2	4	.333	6.47	1.75	13	12	0	0	0	0-0	57.0	83	46	41	12	17-0	23	.342
Major League totals (8 years)	50	56	.472	4.57	1.42	144	143	10	6	0	0-0	866.0	986	479	440	110	244-8	469	.287

MOELLER, CHAD   C

PERSONAL: Born February 18, 1975, in Upland, Calif. ... 6-3/215. ... Bats right, throws right. ... Full name: Chad Edward Moeller. ... Name pronounced: MOE-ler. ... High school: Upland (Calif.). ... College: USC.
TRANSACTIONS/CAREER NOTES: Selected by New York Yankees organization in 25th round of free-agent draft (June 3, 1993); did not sign. ... Selected by Minnesota Twins organization in second round of free-agent draft (June 4, 1996). ... On disabled list (July 12, 1996-remainder of season). ... On Minnesota disabled list (August 12-30, 2000). ... Traded by Twins to Arizona Diamondbacks for SS Hanley Frias (March 28, 2001).
2003 GAMES PLAYED BY POSITION (MLB): C—76.

Year Team (League)	Pos.	G	AB	R	H	2B	3B	HR	RBI	BB	SO	HBP	GDP	SB-CS	Avg.	OBP	SLG	OPS	E	Pct.
1996— Elizabethton (App.)	C	17	59	17	21	4	0	4	13	18	9	2	3	1-2	.356	.519	.627	1.146	1	.991
1997— Fort Wayne (Midw.)	C	108	384	58	111	18	3	9	39	48	76	13	8	11-8	.289	.386	.422	.808	* 15	.984
1998— Fort Myers (FSL)	C	66	254	37	83	24	1	6	39	31	37	3	8	2-3	.327	.406	.500	.906	9	.980
— New Britain (East.)	C	58	187	21	44	10	0	6	23	24	41	3	4	2-1	.235	.332	.385	.717	6	.987
1999— New Britain (East.)	C	89	250	29	62	11	3	4	24	21	44	6	7	0-0	.248	.317	.364	.681	10	.984
2000— Salt Lake (PCL)	C	47	167	30	48	13	1	5	20	9	45	0	6	0-1	.287	.322	.467	.789	2	.993
— Minnesota (A.L.)	C	48	128	13	27	3	1	1	9	9	33	0	4	1-0	.211	.261	.273	.534	6	.979
2001— Tucson (PCL)	C	78	274	41	75	20	0	8	36	25	54	2	8	1-4	.274	.337	.434	.771	5	.989
— Arizona (N.L.)	C	25	56	8	13	0	1	1	2	6	12	0	2	0-0	.232	.306	.321	.628	0	1.000
2002— Tucson (PCL)	C	60	211	37	67	8	2	10	48	29	46	3	4	1-0	.318	.401	.517	.917	3	.994
— Arizona (N.L.)	C	37	105	10	30	11	1	2	16	17	23	0	6	0-1	.286	.385	.467	.852	1	.997
2003— Arizona (N.L.)	C	78	239	29	64	17	1	7	29	23	59	2	7	1-2	.268	.335	.435	.770	7	.987
American League totals (1 year)		48	128	13	27	3	1	1	9	9	33	0	4	1-0	.211	.261	.273	.534	6	.979
National League totals (3 years)		140	400	47	107	28	3	10	47	46	94	2	15	1-3	.268	.344	.428	.772	8	.992
Major League totals (4 years)		188	528	60	134	31	4	11	56	55	127	2	19	2-3	.254	.325	.390	.715	14	.989

MOHR, DUSTAN   OF

PERSONAL: Born June 19, 1976, in Hattiesburg, Miss. ... 6-1/210. ... Bats right, throws right. ... Full name: Dustan Kyle Mohr. ... High school: Oak Grove (Miss.). ... College: Alabama.
TRANSACTIONS/CAREER NOTES: Selected by California Angels organization in 20th round of free-agent draft (June 2, 1994); did not sign. ... Selected by Cleveland Indians organization in ninth round of free-agent draft (June 3, 1997). ... Released by Indians (March 31, 2000). ... Signed by Minnesota Twins organization (April 1, 2000). ... On disabled list (August 24-31, 2000).
2003 GAMES PLAYED BY POSITION (MLB): OF—110, DH—6.

M

Year	Team (League)	Pos.	G	AB	R	H	2B	3B	HR	RBI	BB	SO	HBP	GDP	SB-CS	Avg.	OBP	SLG	OPS	E	Pct.
1997—Watertown (NYP)		OF	74	275	52	80	20	2	7	53	31	76	4	1	3-6	.291	.366	.455	.821	1	.993
1998—Kinston (Caro.)		OF	134	491	60	119	23	9	19	65	39	146	9	7	8-4	.242	.309	.442	.751	6	.968
1999—Akron (East.)		OF	12	42	3	7	2	1	0	2	5	7	0	1	0-1	.167	.255	.262	.517	0	1.000
—Kinston (Caro.)		OF	112	429	46	120	29	3	8	60	26	104	1	13	6-6	.280	.322	.417	.739	6	.973
2000—Fort Myers (FSL)		OF	101	370	58	98	19	2	11	75	35	65	8	11	7-4	.265	.338	.416	.754	4	.978
2001—New Britain (East.)		OF	135	518	90	174	41	3	24	91	49	111	4	6	9-9	.336	.395	.566	.961	6	.978
—Minnesota (A.L.)		OF-DH	20	51	6	12	2	0	0	4	5	17	0	0	1-1	.235	.298	.275	.573	0	1.000
2002—Minnesota (A.L.)		OF-DH	120	383	55	103	23	2	12	45	31	86	1	5	6-3	.269	.325	.433	.759	2	.992
2003—Minnesota (A.L.)		OF-DH	121	348	50	87	22	0	10	36	33	106	1	10	5-2	.250	.314	.399	.714	6	.976
Major League totals (3 years)			261	782	111	202	47	2	22	85	69	209	2	15	12-6	.258	.319	.408	.726	8	.985

MOLINA, BENGIE   C

PERSONAL: Born July 20, 1974, in Rio Piedras, Puerto Rico. ... 5-11/220. ... Bats right, throws right. ... Full name: Benjamin Jose Molina. ... High school: Maestra Ladi (Puerto Rico). ... Junior college: Arizona Western Community College.

TRANSACTIONS/CAREER NOTES: Signed as non-drafted free agent by California Angels organization (May 23, 1993). ... Angels franchise renamed Anaheim Angels for 1997 season. ... On Vancouver disabled list (May 13-22, 1998). ... On Edmonton disabled list (June 4-14, 1999). ... On Anaheim disabled list (May 5-June 27, 2001); included rehabilitation assignments to Rancho Cucamonga (June 9-11, June 17-18 and June 26-27) and Salt Lake (June 19-26). ... On Anaheim disabled list (July 17-August 1, 2002); included rehabilitation assignment to Rancho Cucamonga (July 30-August 1). ... Placed on 60-day disabled list (September 5, 2003).

2003 GAMES PLAYED BY POSITION (MLB): C—117.

Year	Team (League)	Pos.	G	AB	R	H	2B	3B	HR	RBI	BB	SO	HBP	GDP	SB-CS	Avg.	OBP	SLG	OPS	E	Pct.
1993—Ariz. Angels (Ariz.)		C	27	80	9	21	6	2	0	10	10	4	1	1	0-2	.263	.348	.388	.735	0	1.000
1994—Cedar Rap. (Midw.)		C	48	171	14	48	8	0	3	16	8	12	3	3	1-2	.281	.324	.380	.704	10	.975
1995—Vancouver (PCL)		C	2	2	0	0	0	0	0	0	0	1	0	0	0-0	.000	.000	.000	.000	0	1.000
—Cedar Rap. (Midw.)		C	39	133	15	39	9	0	4	17	15	11	1	4	1-1	.293	.367	.451	.818	7	.989
—Lake Elsinore (Calif.)		C	27	96	21	37	7	2	2	12	8	7	4	2	0-0	.385	.450	.563	1.012	1	.995
1996—Midland (Texas)		C	108	365	45	100	21	2	8	54	25	25	6	16	0-1	.274	.327	.408	.735	7	.990
1997—Lake Elsinore (Calif.)		C	36	149	18	42	10	2	4	33	7	9	0	5	0-1	.282	.308	.456	.765	1	.996
—Midland (Texas)		C	29	106	18	35	8	0	6	30	10	7	0	2	0-0	.330	.381	.575	.957	2	.978
1998—Vancouver (PCL)		C	49	184	13	54	9	1	1	22	5	14	0	6	1-1	.293	.311	.370	.680	5	.986
—Midland (Texas)		C	41	154	28	55	8	0	9	39	14	7	3	7	0-1	.357	.419	.584	1.003	3	.988
—Anaheim (A.L.)		C	2	1	0	0	0	0	0	0	0	0	0	0	0-0	.000	.000	.000	.000	1	1.000
1999—Edmonton (PCL)		C-DH	65	241	28	69	16	0	7	41	15	17	6	7	1-2	.286	.338	.440	.778	3	.993
—Anaheim (A.L.)		C	31	101	8	26	5	0	1	10	6	6	2	5	0-1	.257	.312	.337	.649	2	.991
2000—Anaheim (A.L.)		C-DH	130	473	59	133	20	2	14	71	23	33	6	17	1-0	.281	.318	.421	.739	7	.991
2001—Anaheim (A.L.)		C-DH	96	325	31	85	11	0	6	40	16	51	8	8	0-1	.262	.309	.351	.660	5	.991
—Rancho Cuca. (Calif.)		C	3	11	1	6	1	0	0	2	0	1	0	0	0-0	.545	.545	.636	1.182	0	1.000
—Salt Lake (PCL)		C	5	18	2	5	1	0	0	3	2	3	0	2	0-0	.278	.350	.333	.683	0	1.000
2002—Anaheim (A.L.)		C	122	428	34	105	18	0	5	47	15	34	4	15	0-0	.245	.274	.322	.596	1	.999
—Rancho Cuca. (Calif.)		C	2	2	0	1	0	0	0	0	1	0	1	0	0-0	.500	.750	.500	1.250	0	1.000
2003—Anaheim (A.L.)		C	119	409	37	115	24	0	14	71	13	31	2	17	1-1	.281	.304	.443	.746	5	.993
Major League totals (6 years)			500	1737	169	464	78	2	40	239	73	155	22	62	2-3	.267	.302	.383	.685	20	.993

M

MOLINA, GABE   P

PERSONAL: Born May 3, 1975, in Denver, Colo. ... 5-11/204. ... Throws right, bats right. ... Full name: Cruz Gabriel Molina. ... Name pronounced: moe-LEE-nah. ... High school: John F. Kennedy (Denver). ... College: Arizona State.

TRANSACTIONS/CAREER NOTES: Selected by Baltimore Orioles organization in 21st round of free-agent draft (June 4, 1996). ... Traded by Orioles with OF B.J. Surhoff to Atlanta Braves for OF Trenidad Hubbard, C Fernando Lunar and P Luis Rivera (July 31, 2000). ... Granted free agency (December 21, 2000). ... Signed by Florida Marlins organization (January 10, 2001). ... Granted free agency (October 15, 2001). ... Signed by St. Louis Cardinals organization (November 21, 2001). ... Optioned to Memphis (May 27, 2003). ... Sent outright to Memphis; recalled from Memphis (August 7, 2003).

CAREER HITTING: 0-for-0 (.000), 0 R, 0 2B, 0 3B, 0 HR, 0 RBI.

Year	League	W	L	Pct.	ERA	WHIP	G	GS	CG	ShO	Hld.	Sv.-Opp.	IP	H	R	ER	HR	BB-IBB	SO	Avg.
1996—Bluefield (Appal.)		4	1	1.000	3.60	1.40	23	0	0	0	...	7-...	30.0	29	12	12	1	13-1	33	.252
1997—Delmarva (S. Atl.)		8	6	.571	2.18	1.00	46	0	0	0	...	7-...	91.0	59	24	22	3	32-5	119	.181
1998—Bowie (East.)		3	2	.600	3.36	1.22	47	0	0	0	...	24-...	61.2	48	24	23	5	27-0	75	.214
1999—Rochester (Int'l)		2	2	.500	3.14	1.19	45	0	0	0	...	18-...	57.1	45	22	20	3	23-1	58	.211
—Baltimore (A.L.)		1	2	.333	6.65	1.65	20	0	0	0	2	0-1	23.0	22	19	17	4	16-1	14	.256
2000—Baltimore (A.L.)		0	0	...	9.00	2.62	9	0	0	0	1	0-0	13.0	25	14	13	2	9-0	8	.397
—Rochester (Int'l)		1	2	.333	4.94	1.46	18	4	0	0	...	5-...	27.1	30	16	15	3	10-0	26	.278
—Richmond (Int'l)		1	0	1.000	3.60	1.00	9	0	0	0	...	3-...	10.0	7	5	4	2	3-0	9	.200
—Atlanta (N.L.)		0	0	...	9.00	2.00	2	0	0	0	0	0-0	2.0	3	4	2	1	1-0	1	.375
2001—Calgary (PCL)		5	9	.357	5.89	1.54	40	16	0	0	...	0-...	107.0	126	75	70	14	39-1	105	.289
2002—Memphis (PCL)		5	4	.556	2.15	1.17	56	0	0	0	...	12-...	71.0	59	21	17	7	24-1	54	.223
—St. Louis (N.L.)		1	0	1.000	1.59	1.06	12	0	0	0	2	0-0	11.1	6	2	2	1	6-0	4	.162
2003—St. Louis (N.L.)		0	0	...	13.50	2.25	3	0	0	0	0	0-0	2.2	5	4	4	1	1-0	1	.385
—Memphis (PCL)		2	9	.182	5.09	1.63	57	0	0	0	...	9-...	63.2	73	40	36	9	31-8	47	.292
American League totals (2 years)		1	2	.333	7.50	2.00	29	0	0	0	3	0-1	36.0	47	33	30	6	25-1	22	.315
National League totals (3 years)		1	0	1.000	4.50	1.38	17	0	0	0	2	0-0	16.0	14	10	8	3	8-0	6	.241
Major League totals (4 years)		2	2	.500	6.58	1.81	46	0	0	0	5	0-1	52.0	61	43	38	9	33-1	28	.295

MOLINA, JOSE   C

PERSONAL: Born June 3, 1975, in Bayamon, Puerto Rico. ... 6-2/220. ... Bats right, throws right. ... Full name: Jose Benjamin Molina. ... Name pronounced: mo-LEE-nah. ... High school: Maestro Ladi (Vega Alta, Puerto Rico).

TRANSACTIONS/CAREER NOTES: Selected by Chicago Cubs organization in 14th round of free-agent draft (June 3, 1993). ... On Iowa disabled list (July 31-August 10, 1999). ... On disabled list (August 4-September 5, 2000). ... Released by Cubs (November 27, 2000). ... Signed by Anaheim Angels organization (May 17, 2001). ... On Anaheim disabled list (May 21-July 1, 2001); included rehabilitation assignment to Salt Lake (June 26-July 1).

2003 GAMES PLAYED BY POSITION (MLB): C—53.

Year Team (League)	Pos.	G	AB	R	H	2B	3B	HR	RBI	BB	SO	HBP	GDP	SB-CS	Avg.	OBP	SLG	OPS	E	Pct.
1993— GC Cubs (GCL)	C-1B	33	78	5	17	2	0	0	4	12	12	0	2	3-2	.218	.322	.244	.566	7	.960
— Daytona (Fla. St.)	C	3	7	0	1	0	0	0	1	2	0	0	0	0-1	.143	.333	.143	.476	0	1.000
1994— Peoria (Midw.)	C	78	253	31	58	13	1	1	33	24	61	4	5	4-3	.229	.302	.300	.602	13	.980
1995— Daytona (Fla. St.)	C	82	233	27	55	9	1	1	19	29	53	7	7	1-0	.236	.336	.296	.632	8	.987
1996— Rockford (Midwest)	C	96	305	35	69	10	1	2	27	36	71	3	8	2-4	.226	.310	.285	.596	11	.985
1997— Daytona (Fla. St.)	C	55	179	17	45	9	1	0	23	14	25	1	5	4-0	.251	.306	.313	.619	8	.981
— Iowa (Am. Assoc.)	C	1	3	0	1	0	0	0	0	1	1	0	1	0-0	.333	.500	.333	.833	0	1.000
— Orlando (South.)	C	37	99	10	17	3	0	1	15	12	28	2	4	0-1	.172	.267	.232	.500	2	.993
1998— West Tenn (Sou.)	C-1B	109	320	33	71	10	1	2	28	32	74	3	10	1-5	.222	.296	.278	.574	8	.991
1999— West Tenn (Sou.)	C	14	35	2	6	3	0	0	5	2	14	0	1	0-0	.171	.211	.257	.468	2	.982
— Iowa (PCL)	C	74	240	24	63	11	1	4	26	20	54	4	3	0-1	.263	.327	.367	.694	7	.987
— Chicago (N.L.)	C	10	19	3	5	1	0	0	1	2	4	0	0	0-0	.263	.333	.316	.649	0	1.000
2000— Iowa (PCL)	C-1B	76	248	22	58	9	0	1	17	23	61	0	6	1-4	.234	.296	.282	.578	‡11	.981
2001— Salt Lake (PCL)	C	61	213	29	64	11	1	5	31	14	49	2	7	1-2	.300	.349	.432	.781	2	.996
— Anaheim (A.L.)	C	15	37	8	10	3	0	2	4	3	8	0	2	0-0	.270	.325	.514	.839	0	1.000
2002— Salt Lake (PCL)	C	79	290	30	89	14	2	4	43	12	60	4	4	0-3	.307	.341	.410	.751	4	.994
— Anaheim (A.L.)	C	29	70	5	19	3	0	0	5	5	15	0	2	0-2	.271	.312	.314	.626	3	.983
2003— Anaheim (A.L.)	C	53	114	12	21	4	0	0	6	1	26	3	1	0-0	.184	.210	.219	.429	1	.996
American League totals (3 years)		97	221	25	50	10	0	2	15	9	49	3	5	0-2	.226	.263	.299	.561	4	.992
National League totals (1 year)		10	19	3	5	1	0	0	1	2	4	0	0	0-0	.263	.333	.316	.649	0	1.000
Major League totals		107	240	28	55	11	0	2	16	11	53	3	5	0-2	.229	.268	.300	.568	4	.993

MONDESI, RAUL   OF

PERSONAL: Born March 12, 1971, in San Cristobal, Dominican Republic. ... 5-11/230. ... Bats right, throws right. ... Full name: Raul Ramon Mondesi. ... Name pronounced: MON-de-see. ... High school: Liceo Manuel Maria Valencia (Dominican Republic).

TRANSACTIONS/CAREER NOTES: Signed as non-drafted free agent by Los Angeles Dodgers organization (June 6, 1988). ... On Bakersfield disabled list (May 8-July 5, 1991). ... On Albuquerque disabled list (May 8-16, 1992). ... On San Antonio disabled list (June 2-16, June 24-August 10 and August 24, 1992-remainder of season). ... Traded by Dodgers with P Pedro Borbon to Toronto Blue Jays for OF Shawn Green and 2B Jorge Nunez (November 8, 1999). ... On disabled list (July 22-September 20, 2000). ... Traded by Blue Jays to New York Yankees for P Scott Wiggins (July 1, 2002). ... Traded by Yankees with cash to Arizona Diamondbacks for OF David Dellucci, P Bret Prinz and C John Prowl (July 29, 2003).

2003 GAMES PLAYED BY POSITION (MLB): OF—140, DH—1.

Year Team (League)	Pos.	G	AB	R	H	2B	3B	HR	RBI	BB	SO	HBP	GDP	SB-CS	Avg.	OBP	SLG	OPS	E	Pct.
1988— Dom. Dodgers (DSL)	OF	36	117	21	26	10	1	2	44	23	36	...	...	4-0	.222	...	.376	...	...	...
1989— Dom. Dodgers (DSL)	OF	46	156	32	43	15	3	2	27	16	26	...	...	8-0	.276	...	.449	...	...	...
1990— Great Falls (Pio.)	OF	44	175	35	53	10	4	8	31	11	30	2	0	30-6	.303	.349	.543	.892	1	.986
1991— Bakersfield (Calif.)	OF	28	106	23	30	7	2	3	13	5	21	3	1	9-4	.283	.330	.472	.802	3	.940
— San Antonio (Texas)	OF	53	213	32	58	11	5	5	26	8	47	4	1	8-3	.272	.307	.441	.748	4	.964
— Albuquerque (PCL)	OF	2	9	3	3	0	1	0	0	0	1	0	0	1-0	.333	.333	.556	.889	1	...
1992— Albuquerque (PCL)	OF	35	138	23	43	4	7	4	15	9	35	1	0	2-3	.312	.358	.529	.887	7	.933
— San Antonio (Texas)	OF	18	68	8	18	2	2	2	14	1	24	0	1	3-2	.265	.264	.441	.705	1	.974
1993— Albuquerque (PCL)	OF	110	425	65	119	22	7	12	65	18	85	2	4	13-10	.280	.309	.449	.758	10	.957
— Los Angeles (N.L.)	OF	42	86	13	25	3	1	4	10	4	16	0	1	4-1	.291	.322	.488	.811	3	.951
1994— Los Angeles (N.L.)	OF	112	434	63	133	27	8	16	56	16	78	2	9	11-8	.306	.333	.516	.849	8	.965
1995— Los Angeles (N.L.)	OF	139	536	91	153	23	6	26	88	33	96	4	7	27-4	.285	.328	.496	.824	6	.980
1996— Los Angeles (N.L.)	OF	157	634	98	188	40	7	24	88	32	122	5	6	14-7	.297	.334	.495	.830	• 12	.967
1997— Los Angeles (N.L.)	OF	159	616	95	191	42	5	30	87	44	105	6	11	32-15	.310	.360	.541	.901	4	.989
1998— Los Angeles (N.L.)	OF	148	580	85	162	26	5	30	90	30	112	3	4	16-10	.279	.316	.497	.813	6	.982
1999— Los Angeles (N.L.)	OF	159	601	98	152	29	5	33	99	71	134	3	3	36-9	.253	.332	.483	.815	6	.982
2000— Toronto (A.L.)	OF	96	388	78	105	22	2	24	67	32	73	3	8	22-6	.271	.329	.523	.852	7	.967
2001— Toronto (A.L.)	OF	149	572	88	144	26	4	27	84	73	128	6	13	30-11	.252	.342	.453	.794	8	.972
2002— Toronto (A.L.)	OF-DH	75	299	51	67	16	1	15	45	31	57	3	8	9-2	.224	.301	.435	.736	2	.984
— New York (A.L.)	OF-DH	71	270	39	65	18	0	11	43	28	46	2	3	6-4	.241	.315	.430	.744	4	.969
2003— New York (A.L.)	OF-DH	98	361	56	93	23	3	16	49	38	66	2	6	17-7	.258	.330	.471	.801	3	.986
— Arizona (N.L.)	OF	45	162	27	49	8	1	8	22	18	31	1	3	5-4	.302	.372	.512	.884	3	.965
American League totals (4 years)		489	1890	312	474	105	10	93	288	202	370	16	38	84-30	.251	.327	.465	.791	24	.975
National League totals (8 years)		961	3649	570	1053	198	38	171	540	248	694	24	48	145-58	.289	.336	.504	.840	48	.976
Major League totals (11 years)		1450	5539	882	1527	303	48	264	828	450	1064	40	86	229-88	.276	.333	.491	.823	72	.976

MONROE, CRAIG   OF

PERSONAL: Born February 27, 1977, in Texarkana, Texas. ... 6-1/215. ... Bats right, throws right. ... Full name: Craig Keystone Monroe. ... High school: Texas (Texarkana, Texas).

TRANSACTIONS/CAREER NOTES: Selected by Texas Rangers organization in eighth round of free-agent draft (June 1, 1995). ... Claimed on waivers by Detroit Tigers (February 1, 2002).

2003 GAMES PLAYED BY POSITION (MLB): OF—108, DH—13.

Year Team (League)	Pos.	G	AB	R	H	2B	3B	HR	RBI	BB	SO	HBP	GDP	SB-CS	Avg.	OBP	SLG	OPS	E	Pct.
1995— GC Rangers (GCL)	OF	54	193	22	48	6	2	0	33	18	25	2	1	13-2	.249	.316	.301	.617	4	.962
1996— Char., S.C. (SAL)	OF	49	153	11	23	11	1	0	9	18	48	3	3	2-2	.150	.253	.235	.488	4	.954
— Hudson Valley (NYP)	OF	67	268	53	74	16	6	5	29	23	63	2	4	21-7	.276	.336	.437	.772	6	.938
1997— Charlotte (Fla. St.)	OF	92	328	54	77	23	1	7	41	44	80	0	5	24-1	.235	.320	.375	.695	7	.959
1998— Charlotte (Fla. St.)	OF	132	472	73	114	26	7	17	76	66	102	3	15	50-13	.242	.334	.434	.768	11	.951
1999— Charlotte (Fla. St.)	OF	130	480	77	125	21	1	17	81	42	102	4	8	40-15	.260	.321	.415	.735	7	.980
— Oklahoma (PCL)	OF	6	16	2	4	1	0	0	1	1	4	0	0	0-0	.250	.429	.313	.741	0	1.000
2000— Tulsa (Texas)	OF	120	464	89	131	34	5	20	89	64	91	2	12	12-13	.282	.366	.506	.873	• 12	.948
2001— Oklahoma (PCL)	OF	114	410	60	115	25	5	20	75	46	85	5	11	10-8	.280	.358	.512	.870	5	.975
— Texas (A.L.)	OF-DH	27	52	8	11	1	0	2	5	6	18	0	1	2-0	.212	.293	.346	.639	0	1.000
2002— Toledo (Int'l)	OF	99	358	61	115	30	4	10	49	35	57	2	8	7-3	.321	.379	.511	.890	3	.983
— Detroit (A.L.)	OF-DH	13	25	3	3	1	0	1	1	0	5	1	1	0-2	.120	.154	.280	.434	1	.950
2003— Toledo (Int'l)	OF-DH	14	47	14	19	4	1	2	6	4	10	0	0	1-0	.404	.451	.660	1.111	0	1.000
— Detroit (A.L.)	OF-DH	128	425	51	102	18	1	23	70	27	89	2	10	4-2	.240	.287	.449	.736	7	.970
Major League totals (3 years)		168	502	62	116	20	1	26	76	33	112	3	12	6-4	.231	.281	.430	.711	8	.973

MORA, MELVIN — OF

PERSONAL: Born February 2, 1972, in Agua Negra, Venezuela. ... 5-11/198. ... Bats right, throws right. ... Name pronounced: MORE-a. ... High school: Libertador (Venezuela).
TRANSACTIONS/CAREER NOTES: Signed as non-drafted free agent by Houston Astros organization (March 30, 1991). ... Granted free agency (October 17, 1997). ... Played in Taiwan (1998). ... Signed by New York Mets organization (July 24, 1998). ... Granted free agency (October 16, 1998). ... Re-signed by Mets organization (February 5, 1999). ... On New York disabled list (May 13-30, 2000); included rehabilitation assignment to Norfolk (May 22-30). ... Traded by Mets with 3B Mike Kinkade, P Leslie Brea and P Pat Gorman to Baltimore Orioles for SS Mike Bordick (July 28, 2000). ... On suspended list (September 13-16, 2002). ... Placed on 15-day disabled list (August 1, 2003). ... Sent on minor league rehab assignment (August 26, 2003). ... Recalled from minor league rehab assignment; removed from 15-day disabled list (September 2, 2003).
2003 GAMES PLAYED BY POSITION (MLB): OF—79, SS—11, 2B—6, 1B—1.

									BATTING										FIELDING	
Year	Team (League)	Pos.	G	AB	R	H	2B	3B	HR	RBI	BB	SO	HBP	GDP	SB-CS	Avg.	OBP	SLG	OPS	E	Pct.
1991— Dom. Astros (DSL).	....		58	211	38	63	18	1	0	20	19	22	...	...	21-...	.299	...	.393	...	...	...
1992— GC Astros (GCL)	....	2B-3B-OF	49	144	28	32	3	0	0	8	18	16	5	2	16-3	.222	.327	.243	.570	4	.961
1993— Asheville (S. Atl.)	....		108	365	66	104	22	2	2	31	36	46	9	7	20-13	.285	.356	.373	.729	17	.936
1994— Osceola (Fla. St.)		3B-OF	118	425	57	120	29	4	8	46	37	60	10	8	24-16	.282	.352	.426	.777	15	.947
1995— Jackson (Texas)	....	2B-3B-OF	123	467	63	139	32	0	3	45	32	57	9	11	22-11	.298	.350	.385	.735	6	.977
— Tucson (PCL)	....	OF	2	5	3	3	0	1	0	1	2	0	0	0	1-0	.600	.714	1.000	1.714	0	1.000
1996— Jackson (Texas)	....	2-3-S-O	70	255	36	73	6	1	5	23	14	23	6	4	4-7	.286	.336	.376	.712	7	.959
— Tucson (PCL)	....	2B-3B-OF	62	228	35	64	11	2	3	26	17	27	1	7	3-5	.281	.328	.386	.714	14	.912
1997— New Orleans (A.A.)	....		119	370	55	95	15	3	2	38	47	52	11	7	7-7	.257	.356	.330	.686	11	.956
1998— Mercury (Taiwan)	....		...	164	34	55	11	2	3	11	...	...	...	...	...-...	.335	...	.482	...	...	...
— St. Lucie (Fla. St.)	....	2B-SS-OF	17	55	5	15	0	0	0	8	5	9	0	0	1-1	.273	.328	.273	.601	1	.985
— Norfolk (Int'l)	....	2B-3B-OF	11	28	5	5	1	0	0	2	5	7	0	0	0-0	.179	.303	.214	.517	2	.875
1999— Norfolk (Int'l)	....	S-O-2-3	82	304	55	92	17	2	8	36	41	54	7	8	18-8	.303	.393	.451	.844	16	.942
— New York (N.L.)	....	O-2-3-S	66	31	6	5	0	0	0	1	4	7	1	0	2-1	.161	.278	.161	.439	0	1.000
2000— New York (N.L.)	....	S-O-2-3	79	215	35	56	13	2	6	30	18	48	2	3	7-3	.260	.317	.423	.740	8	.962
— Norfolk (Int'l)	....	OF-2B-SS	8	27	7	9	2	0	0	7	7	3	0	0	2-0	.333	.471	.407	.878	0	1.000
— Baltimore (A.L.)	....	SS-2B	53	199	25	58	9	3	2	17	17	32	4	2	5-8	.291	.359	.397	.756	12	.953
2001— Baltimore (A.L.)	....	OF-SS-2B	128	436	49	109	28	0	7	48	41	91	14	6	11-4	.250	.329	.362	.692	11	.974
2002— Baltimore (A.L.)	....	O-S-2-D	149	557	86	130	30	4	19	64	70	108	20	7	16-10	.233	.338	.404	.742	12	.976
2003— Bowie (East.)	....	OF	6	21	3	6	0	0	2	5	2	4	0	0	0-0	.286	.348	.571	.919	0	1.000
— Baltimore (A.L.)	....	O-S-2-1	96	344	68	109	17	1	15	48	49	71	12	3	6-3	.317	.418	.503	.921	2	.992
American League totals (4 years)			426	1536	228	406	84	8	43	177	177	302	50	18	38-25	.264	.356	.413	.770	37	.974
National League totals (2 years)			145	246	41	61	13	2	6	31	22	55	3	3	9-4	.248	.312	.390	.702	8	.967
Major League totals (5 years)			571	1782	269	467	97	10	49	208	199	357	53	21	47-29	.262	.350	.410	.761	45	.973

MORBAN, JOSE — SS

PERSONAL: Born December 2, 1979, in Santiago, Dominican Republic. ... 6-1/170. ... Bats both, throws right. ... Name pronounced: more-bun.
TRANSACTIONS/CAREER NOTES: Signed as non-drafted free agent by Texas Rangers organization (December 15, 1996). ... Selected by Minnesota Twins from Rangers organization in Rule 5 major league draft (December 16, 2002). ... Claimed on waivers by Baltimore Orioles (March 28, 2003).
2003 GAMES PLAYED BY POSITION (MLB): SS—14, DH—14, 2B—12, 3B—1.

									BATTING										FIELDING	
Year	Team (League)	Pos.	G	AB	R	H	2B	3B	HR	RBI	BB	SO	HBP	GDP	SB-CS	Avg.	OBP	SLG	OPS	E	Pct.
1999— GC Rangers (GCL)	....	SS	54	205	45	58	10	5	4	18	31	70	2	1	19-14	.283	.378	.439	.817	12	.949
2000— Pulaski (Appal.)	....	SS	30	120	21	27	3	2	3	17	12	35	0	0	6-3	.225	.291	.358	.649	9	.937
— Savannah (S. Atl.)	....	SS	80	273	44	60	8	4	4	28	41	79	4	6	27-13	.220	.330	.322	.653	24	.934
2001— Savannah (S. Atl.)	....	SS	122	474	71	119	20	11	8	47	42	119	2	11	46-18	.251	.313	.390	.703	30	.942
2002— Charlotte (Int'l)	....	SS	126	485	75	126	27	12	8	66	46	111	3	2	21-9	.260	.326	.414	.740	34	.943
2003— Baltimore (A.L.)	....	S-D-2-3	61	71	14	10	0	0	2	5	3	21	1	0	8-0	.141	.187	.225	.412	1	.984
Major League totals (1 year)			61	71	14	10	0	0	2	5	3	21	1	0	8-0	.141	.187	.225	.412	1	.984

MORDECAI, MIKE — IF

PERSONAL: Born December 13, 1967, in Birmingham, Ala. ... 5-10/185. ... Bats right, throws right. ... Full name: Michael Howard Mordecai. ... Name pronounced: more-duh-KYE. ... High school: Hewitt Trussville (Ala.). ... College: South Alabama.
TRANSACTIONS/CAREER NOTES: Selected by Pittsburgh Pirates organization in 33rd round of free-agent draft (June 2, 1986); did not sign. ... Selected by Atlanta Braves organization in sixth round of free-agent draft (June 5, 1989). ... On disabled list (April 8-29, 1993). ... On Atlanta disabled list (April 19-May 11, 1996); included rehabilitation assignment to Richmond (May 8-11). ... Granted free agency (December 21, 1997). ... Signed by Montreal Expos organization (March 27, 1998). ... On Montreal disabled list (June 24-July 24, 1998); included rehabilitation assignments to Jupiter (July 16-19) and Ottawa (July 19-24). ... Traded by Expos with P Carl Pavano, P Graeme Lloyd and P Justin Wayne to Florida Marlins for OF Cliff Floyd, P Claudio Vargas, 2B/OF Wilton Guerrero, cash considerations and a player to be named later (July 11, 2002); Expos acquired P Don Levinski to complete deal (August 6, 2002).
2003 GAMES PLAYED BY POSITION (MLB): SS—14, 2B—12, 3B—12, 1B—1.

									BATTING										FIELDING	
Year	Team (League)	Pos.	G	AB	R	H	2B	3B	HR	RBI	BB	SO	HBP	GDP	SB-CS	Avg.	OBP	SLG	OPS	E	Pct.
1989— Burlington (Midw.)	....	3B-SS	65	241	39	61	11	1	1	22	33	43	5	2	12-5	.253	.352	.320	.672	21	.920
— Greenville (Sou.)	....	2B-3B	4	8	0	3	0	0	0	1	1	1	0	0	0-0	.375	.444	.375	.819	0	1.000
1990— Durham (Caro.)	....	SS	72	271	42	76	11	7	3	36	42	45	2	9	10-6	.280	.379	.406	.784	29	.920
1991— Durham (Caro.)	....	SS	109	397	52	104	15	2	4	42	40	58	2	7	30-16	.262	.330	.340	.670	27	.945
1992— Greenville (Sou.)	....	SS	65	222	31	58	13	1	4	31	29	31	0	6	9-6	.261	.344	.383	.727	11	.964
— Richmond (Int'l)	....	2B-3B-SS	36	118	12	29	3	0	1	6	5	19	0	1	0-4	.246	.272	.297	.569	10	.937
1993— Richmond (Int'l)	....	C	72	205	29	55	8	1	2	14	14	33	1	4	10-2	.268	.318	.346	.665	9	.964
1994— Richmond (Int'l)	....	S-1-3-D	99	382	67	107	25	1	14	57	35	50	2	5	14-7	.280	.340	.461	.800	22	.947
— Atlanta (N.L.)	....	SS	4	4	1	1	0	0	1	3	1	0	0	0	0-0	.250	.400	1.000	1.400	0	1.000
1995— Atlanta (N.L.)	....	2-1-3-S-O	69	75	10	21	6	0	3	11	9	16	0	0	0-0	.280	.353	.480	.833	0	1.000
1996— Atlanta (N.L.)	....	2-3-S-1	66	108	12	26	5	0	2	8	9	24	0	1	1-0	.241	.297	.343	.639	2	.977
— Richmond (Int'l)	....	SS	3	11	2	2	0	0	1	2	0	3	0	0	0-0	.182	.167	.455	.621	1	1.000
1997— Atlanta (N.L.)	....	3-2-S-1-D-0	61	81	8	14	2	1	0	3	6	16	0	4	0-1	.173	.227	.222	.449	0	1.000
— Richmond (Int'l)	....	2-3-D-S	31	122	23	38	10	0	3	15	9	17	1	0	0-1	.311	.361	.467	.828	1	.989
1998— Montreal (N.L.)	....	S-2-3-1	73	119	12	24	4	2	3	10	9	20	0	2	1-0	.202	.258	.345	.602	5	.960
— Jupiter (FSL)	....	2B-SS	2	8	0	0	0	0	0	0	1	3	0	1	0-0	.000	.111	.000	.111	0	1.000
— Ottawa (Int'l)	....	SS-2B	6	22	2	5	2	0	0	1	3	3	0	1	0-0	.227	.320	.318	.638	1	.969

Year Team (League)	Pos.	G	AB	R	H	2B	3B	HR	RBI	BB	SO	HBP	GDP	SB-CS	Avg.	OBP	SLG	OPS	E	Pct.
1999— Montreal (N.L.)	2-S-3-1	109	226	29	53	10	2	5	25	20	31	1	1	2-5	.235	.297	.363	.660	7	.970
2000— Montreal (N.L.)	3-S-2-1	86	169	20	48	16	0	4	16	12	34	1	1	2-2	.284	.335	.450	.785	8	.942
2001— Montreal (N.L.)	3-2-S-D-C-1-0	96	254	28	71	17	2	3	32	19	53	1	6	2-2	.280	.330	.398	.727	3	.985
2002— Montreal (N.L.)	3-2-S-1-0	55	74	9	15	4	0	0	4	8	14	1	2	1-1	.203	.289	.257	.546	4	.948
— Florida (N.L.)	SS-3B-1B	38	77	10	22	4	0	0	7	5	13	1	1	1-1	.286	.337	.338	.675	1	.989
2003— Florida (N.L.)	S-2-3-1	65	89	11	19	4	0	2	8	8	21	0	0	3-0	.213	.276	.326	.601	3	.961
Major League totals (10 years)		722	1276	150	314	72	7	23	127	106	242	5	18	13-12	.246	.305	.368	.672	33	.971

MORENO, ORBER — P

PERSONAL: Born April 27, 1977, in Caracas, Venezuela. ... 6-3/200. ... Throws right, bats right. ... Full name: Orber Aquiles Moreno. ... Name pronounced: MORE-a-no. ... High school: Luisa Caceres (Venezuela).

TRANSACTIONS/CAREER NOTES: Signed as non-drafted free agent by Kansas City Royals organization (November 10, 1993). ... On Kansas City disabled list (June 10, 1999-remainder of season); included rehabilitation assignment to Gulf Coast Royals (July 26-27). ... On disabled list (March 24, 2000-entire season). ... On Kansas City disabled list (March 31-May 28, 2001). ... On Omaha disabled list (April 4-16, 2002). ... On Wilmington disabled list (April 29-July 27, 2002). ... Signed by New York Mets as free agent; contract purchased by New York (September 1, 2003).

CAREER HITTING: 0-for-1 (.000), 0 R, 0 2B, 0 3B, 0 HR, 0 RBI.

Year League	W	L	Pct.	ERA	WHIP	G	GS	CG	ShO	Hld.	Sv.-Opp.	IP	H	R	ER	HR	BB-IBB	SO	Avg.
1994— Dom. Royals (DSL)	3	3	.500	3.19	1.15	16	11	0	0	...	1-...	67.2	51	33	24	...	27-...	44	...
1995— GC Royals (GCL)	1	1	.500	2.45	1.00	8	3	0	0	...	0-...	22.0	15	9	6	0	7-0	21	.188
1996— GC Royals (GCL)	5	1	.833	1.36	1.01	12	7	0	0	...	1-...	46.1	37	15	7	2	10-0	50	.214
1997— Lansing (Midw.)	4	8	.333	4.81	1.41	27	25	0	0	...	0-...	138.1	150	83	74	15	45-0	128	.278
1998— Wilmington (Caro.)	3	2	.600	0.82	0.55	23	0	0	0	...	7-...	33.0	8	3	3	1	10-1	50	.077
— Wichita (Texas)	0	1	.000	2.88	1.17	24	0	0	0	...	7-...	34.1	28	13	11	1	12-3	40	.215
1999— Omaha (PCL)	3	1	.750	2.10	0.82	16	0	0	0	...	4-...	25.2	17	6	6	2	4-0	30	.183
— Kansas City (A.L.)	0	0	...	5.63	1.25	7	0	0	0	1	0-1	8.0	4	5	5	1	6-0	7	.143
— GC Royals (GCL)	0	0	...	0.00	0.00	1	1	0	0	...	0-...	1.0	0	0	0	0	0-0	1	.000
2000— Kansas City (A.L.)										Did not play.									
2001— Wilmington (Caro.)	1	1	.500	2.53	1.22	8	1	0	0	...	0-...	10.2	12	5	3	1	1-0	16	.261
— Wichita (Texas)	0	0	...	0.00	0.58	5	0	0	0	...	1-...	8.2	3	0	0	0	2-0	10	.107
— Omaha (PCL)	1	1	.500	4.71	1.29	17	0	0	0	...	3-...	21.0	19	11	11	4	8-0	25	.232
2002— GC Royals (GCL)	0	0	...	0.00	0.50	2	2	0	0	...	0-...	2.0	1	0	0	0	0-0	3	.143
2003— Binghamton (Eastern)	2	0	1.000	1.69	0.94	4	0	0	0	...	1-...	5.1	4	1	1	1	1-0	7	.200
— Norfolk (Int'l)	5	1	.833	1.90	1.02	38	0	0	0	...	12-...	52.0	36	11	11	1	17-0	58	.191
— New York (N.L.)	0	0	...	7.88	1.63	7	0	0	0	0	0-0	8.0	10	7	7	1	3-0	5	.313
American League totals (1 year)	0	0	...	5.63	1.25	7	0	0	0	1	0-1	8.0	4	5	5	1	6-0	7	.143
National League totals (1 year)	0	0	...	7.88	1.63	7	0	0	0	0	0-0	8.0	10	7	7	1	3-0	5	.313
Major League totals (2 years)	0	0	...	6.75	1.44	14	0	0	0	1	0-1	16.0	14	12	12	2	9-0	12	.233

MORNEAU, JUSTIN — 1B

PERSONAL: Born May 15, 1981, in New Westminster, British Columbia. ... 6-4/205. ... Bats left, throws right. ... Full name: Justin Ernest Morneau. ... Name pronounced: more-no. ... High school: New Westminster Academy (B.C.).

TRANSACTIONS/CAREER NOTES: Selected by Minnesota Twins organization in third round of free-agent draft (June 2, 1999). ... Called up by Minnesota from Rochester (June 9, 2003). ... Optioned to Rochester of the International League by Minnesota (July 27, 2003). ... Recalled by Minnesota from Rochester (September 2, 2003).

2003 GAMES PLAYED BY POSITION (MLB): DH—23, 1B—7.

Year Team (League)	Pos.	G	AB	R	H	2B	3B	HR	RBI	BB	SO	HBP	GDP	SB-CS	Avg.	OBP	SLG	OPS	E	Pct.
1999— GC Twins (GCL)	DH	17	53	3	16	5	0	0	9	2	6	1	2	0-1	.302	.333	.396	.730	0	...
2000— GC Twins (GCL)	1B-C-OF	52	194	47	78	21	0	10	58	30	18	0	5	3-1	.402	.478	.665	1.143	3	.992
— Elizabethton (App.)	C	6	23	4	5	0	0	1	3	1	6	0	0	0-0	.217	.250	.348	.598	0	1.000
2001— Quad City (Midw.)	1B	64	236	50	84	17	2	12	53	26	38	3	4	0-0	.356	.420	.597	1.018	8	.985
— Fort Myers (FSL)	1B	53	197	25	58	10	3	4	40	24	41	8	4	0-0	.294	.385	.437	.821	3	.994
— New Britain (East.)	1B	10	38	3	6	1	0	0	4	3	8	0	1	0-0	.158	.214	.184	.398	0	1.000
2002— New Britain (East.)	1B	126	494	72	147	31	4	16	80	42	88	6	8	7-0	.298	.356	.474	.830	13	.989
2003— New Britain (East.)	1B	20	79	14	26	3	1	6	13	7	14	0	0	0-0	.329	.384	.620	1.004	0	1.000
— Rochester (Int'l)	1B-DH	71	265	39	71	11	1	16	42	28	56	4	2	0-2	.268	.344	.498	.843	4	.993
— Minnesota (A.L.)	DH-1B	40	106	14	24	4	0	4	16	9	30	0	4	0-0	.226	.287	.377	.664	1	.971
Major League totals (1 year)		40	106	14	24	4	0	4	16	9	30	0	4	0-0	.226	.287	.377	.664	1	.971

MORRIS, MATT — P

PERSONAL: Born August 9, 1974, in Middletown, N.Y. ... 6-5/220. ... Throws right, bats right. ... Full name: Matthew Christian Morris. ... High school: Valley Central (Montgomery, N.Y.). ... College: Seton Hall.

TRANSACTIONS/CAREER NOTES: Selected by Milwaukee Brewers organization in 25th round of free-agent draft (June 1, 1992); did not sign. ... Selected by St. Louis Cardinals organization in first round (12th pick overall) of free-agent draft (June 1, 1995). ... On St. Louis disabled list (March 24-April 11 and April 12-July 10, 1998); included rehabilitation assignments to Arkansas (April 6-11) and Memphis (June 21-July 10). ... On disabled list (March 26, 1999-entire season). ... On St. Louis disabled list (April 2-May 28, 2000); included rehabilitation assignments to Arkansas (May 2-11) and Memphis (May 12-May 28). ... On disabled list (August 24-September 10, 2002). ... Placed on 15-day disabled list (July 22, 2003). ... Removed from 15-day disabled list (August 23, 2003).

CAREER HITTING: 50-for-300 (.167), 19 R, 10 2B, 0 3B, 1 HR, 20 RBI.

Year League	W	L	Pct.	ERA	WHIP	G	GS	CG	ShO	Hld.	Sv.-Opp.	IP	H	R	ER	HR	BB-IBB	SO	Avg.
1995— New Jersey (NYP)	2	0	1.000	1.64	1.36	2	2	0	0	...	0-...	11.0	12	3	2	1	3-0	13	.286
— St. Pete. (FSL)	3	2	.600	2.38	0.97	6	6	1	1	...	0-...	34.0	22	16	9	1	11-0	31	.182
1996— Arkansas (Texas)	12	12	.500	3.88	1.35	27	27	4	* 4	...	0-...	167.0	178	79	72	14	48-1	120	.274
— Louisville (A.A.)	0	1	.000	3.38	1.13	1	1	0	0	...	0-...	8.0	8	3	3	0	1-0	9	.258
1997— St. Louis (N.L.)	12	9	.571	3.19	1.28	33	33	3	0	0	0-0	217.0	208	88	77	12	69-2	149	.258
1998— Arkansas (Texas)	0	0	...	0.00	1.00	1	0	0	0	...	1-...	4.0	4	0	0	0	0-0	2	.235
— St. Louis (N.L.)	7	5	.583	2.53	1.26	17	17	2	1	0	0-0	113.2	101	37	32	8	42-6	79	.243
— Memphis (PCL)	1	0	1.000	4.50	1.43	4	4	0	0	...	0-...	14.0	16	8	7	1	4-0	21	.286
1999— St. Louis (N.L.)										Did not play.									

Year League	W	L	Pct.	ERA	WHIP	G	GS	CG	ShO	Hld.	Sv.-Opp.	IP	H	R	ER	HR	BB-IBB	SO	Avg.
2000— Arkansas (Texas)	0	0	...	6.43	1.71	2	2	0	0	...	0-...	7.0	8	5	5	0	4-0	7	.296
— Memphis (PCL)	1	2	.333	7.98	1.77	3	3	0	0	...	0-...	14.2	20	13	13	2	6-1	8	.351
— St. Louis (N.L.)	3	3	.500	3.57	1.32	31	0	0	0	7	4-7	53.0	53	22	21	3	17-1	34	.261
2001— St. Louis (N.L.)	•22	8	.733	3.16	1.26	34	34	2	1	0	0-0	216.1	218	86	76	13	54-3	185	.265
2002— St. Louis (N.L.)	17	9	.654	3.42	1.30	32	32	1	1	0	0-0	210.1	210	86	80	16	64-3	171	.261
2003— St. Louis (N.L.)	11	8	.579	3.76	1.18	27	27	5	•3	0	0-0	172.1	164	76	72	20	39-1	120	.252
Major League totals (6 years)	72	42	.632	3.28	1.26	174	143	13	6	7	4-7	982.2	954	395	358	72	285-16	738	.257

MORRIS, WARREN   2B

PERSONAL: Born January 11, 1974, in Alexandria, La. ... 5-11/188. ... Bats left, throws right. ... Full name: Warren Randall Morris. ... High school: Bolton (Alexandria, La.). ... College: Louisiana State.

TRANSACTIONS/CAREER NOTES: Selected by Texas Rangers organization in fifth round of free-agent draft (June 2, 1996). ... Traded by Rangers with P Todd Van Poppel to Pittsburgh Pirates for P Esteban Loaiza (July 17, 1998). ... On Nashville disabled list (July 1-12, 2001). ... On Pittsburgh disabled list (August 14-September 1, 2001). ... Released by Pirates (March 13, 2002). ... Signed by Minnesota Twins organization (March 15, 2002). ... On Edmonton disabled list (May 22-June 10, 2002). ... Traded by Twins to St. Louis Cardinals for a player to be named later (June 11, 2002); Twins acquired SS Seth Davidson to complete deal (June 20). ... Claimed on waivers by Boston Red Sox (July 16, 2002). ... Granted free agency (October 15, 2002). ... Signed by Detroit Tigers organization (December 19, 2002). ... Contract purchased by Detroit from Toledo (June 5, 2003).

2003 GAMES PLAYED BY POSITION (MLB): 2B—89.

Year— Team (League)	Pos.	G	AB	R	H	2B	3B	HR	RBI	BB	SO	HBP	GDP	SB-CS	Avg.	OBP	SLG	OPS	E	Pct.
1997— Charlotte (Fla. St.)	2B-3B	128	494	78	151	27	9	12	75	62	100	7	6	16-5	.306	.390	.470	.860	18	.961
— Okla. City (A.A.)	2B	8	32	3	7	1	0	1	3	3	5	0	0	0-0	.219	.286	.344	.629	0	1.000
1998— Tulsa (Texas)	2B	95	390	59	129	22	5	14	73	43	63	4	11	12-7	.331	.401	.521	.921	17	.964
— Carolina (Sou.)	2B	44	151	28	50	8	3	5	30	24	34	1	2	5-2	.331	.419	.523	.942	7	.964
1999— Pittsburgh (N.L.)	2B	147	511	65	147	20	3	15	73	59	88	2	12	3-7	.288	.360	.427	.787	14	.979
2000— Pittsburgh (N.L.)	2B	144	528	68	137	31	2	3	43	65	78	2	7	7-10	.259	.341	.343	.684	15	.979
2001— Nashville (PCL)	2B-3B	57	223	26	68	16	2	5	40	12	21	2	5	3-4	.305	.342	.462	.804	9	.966
— Pittsburgh (N.L.)	2B-3B	48	103	6	21	6	0	2	11	3	9	2	2	2-3	.204	.239	.320	.559	4	.965
2002— Minnesota (A.L.)	2B	4	7	0	0	0	0	0	0	0	1	0	0	0-0	.000	.000	.000	.000	0	1.000
— Edmonton (PCL) 2B-3B-SS		27	92	15	24	6	2	2	10	3	16	0	3	2-1	.261	.281	.435	.716	6	.942
— Memphis (PCL)	2B-3B	29	100	16	26	4	1	2	14	8	12	0	5	0-1	.260	.306	.380	.686	4	.966
— Pawtucket (Int'l)	2B-OF	43	164	21	50	11	2	3	21	11	22	3	6	2-1	.305	.352	.451	.803	1	.991
2003— Toledo (Int'l)	2-3-D-1	56	206	26	57	13	4	2	19	16	26	1	4	4-1	.277	.330	.408	.738	6	.978
— Detroit (A.L.)	2B	97	346	37	94	13	2	6	37	23	42	1	6	4-2	.272	.316	.373	.689	6	.987
American League totals (2 years)		101	353	37	94	13	2	6	37	23	43	1	6	4-2	.266	.311	.365	.676	6	.987
National League totals (3 years)		339	1142	139	305	57	5	20	127	127	175	6	21	12-20	.267	.341	.378	.719	33	.978
Major League totals (5 years)		440	1495	176	399	70	7	26	164	150	218	7	27	16-22	.267	.334	.375	.709	39	.980

MOSS, DAMIAN   P

PERSONAL: Born November 24, 1976, in Darlinghurst, Australia. ... 6-0/187. ... Throws left, bats right. ... Full name: Damian Joseph Moss. ... High school: Liverpool Boys (Australia).

TRANSACTIONS/CAREER NOTES: Signed as non-drafted free agent by Atlanta Braves organization (July 1, 1993). ... On disabled list (March 27, 1998-entire season). ... On Atlanta disabled list (April 3-June 1, 1999). ... On Atlanta disabled list (May 11-June 18, 2001); included rehabilitation assignment to Greenville (June 8-18). ... On Richmond disabled list (August 3-12, 2001). ... Traded by Braves with P Manuel Mateo to San Francisco Giants for P Russ Ortiz (December 17, 2002). ... Traded by Giants with P Kurt Ainsworth and P Ryan Hannaman to Baltimore Orioles for P Sidney Ponson (July 31, 2003).

CAREER HITTING: 12-for-80 (.150), 3 R, 1 2B, 0 3B, 0 HR, 3 RBI.

Year League	W	L	Pct.	ERA	WHIP	G	GS	CG	ShO	Hld.	Sv.-Opp.	IP	H	R	ER	HR	BB-IBB	SO	Avg.
1994— Danville (Appal.)	2	5	.286	3.58	1.41	12	12	1	1	...	0-...	60.1	30	28	24	1	55-0	77	.154
1995— Macon (S. Atl.)	9	10	.474	3.56	1.37	27	27	0	0	...	0-...	149.1	134	73	59	13	70-0	•177	.236
1996— Durham (Caro.)	9	1	.900	2.25	1.10	14	14	0	0	...	0-...	84.0	52	25	21	9	40-0	89	.182
— Greenville (Sou.)	2	5	.286	4.97	1.59	11	10	0	0	...	0-...	58.0	57	41	32	5	35-0	48	.258
1997— Greenville (Sou.)	6	8	.429	5.35	1.50	21	19	1	0	...	0-...	112.2	111	73	67	13	58-0	116	.263
1998— Greenville (Sou.)										Did not play.									
1999— Macon (S. Atl.)	0	3	.000	4.32	1.15	12	12	0	0	...	0-...	41.2	33	20	20	8	15-0	49	.217
— Greenville (Sou.)	1	3	.250	8.54	2.17	7	7	0	0	...	0-...	32.2	50	33	31	6	21-0	22	.345
2000— Richmond (Int'l)	9	6	.600	3.14	1.47	29	•28	0	0	...	0-...	160.2	130	67	56	14	* 106-0	123	.222
2001— Richmond (Int'l)	5	4	.556	3.15	1.27	17	16	0	0	...	0-...	88.2	75	34	31	10	38-1	94	.231
— Atlanta (N.L.)	0	0	...	3.00	1.33	5	1	0	0	0	0-0	9.0	3	3	3	1	9-0	8	.097
— Greenville (Sou.)	0	1	.000	3.00	0.78	3	2	0	0	...	0-...	9.0	7	3	3	3	0-0	10	.200
2002— Atlanta (N.L.)	12	6	.667	3.42	1.28	33	29	0	0	0	0-0	179.0	140	80	68	20	89-5	111	.221
2003— San Francisco (N.L.)	9	7	.563	4.70	1.60	21	20	0	0	0	0-0	115.0	121	62	60	12	63-3	57	.273
— Baltimore (A.L.)	1	5	.167	6.22	1.82	10	9	0	0	0	0-0	50.2	63	40	35	12	29-2	22	.307
American League totals (1 year)	1	5	.167	6.22	1.82	10	9	0	0	0	0-0	50.2	63	40	35	12	29-2	22	.307
National League totals (3 years)	21	13	.618	3.89	1.40	59	50	0	0	0	0-0	303.0	264	145	131	33	161-8	176	.238
Major League totals (3 years)	22	18	.550	4.22	1.46	69	59	0	0	0	0-0	353.2	327	185	166	45	190-10	198	.249

MOTA, GUILLERMO   P

PERSONAL: Born July 25, 1973, in San Pedro de Macoris, Dominican Republic. ... 6-4/205. ... Throws right, bats right. ... Full name: Guillermo Reynoso Mota. ... Name pronounced: mo-TAH. ... High school: Jose Joaquin Perez (San Pedro de Macoris, Dominican Republic).

TRANSACTIONS/CAREER NOTES: Signed as non-drafted free agent by New York Mets organization (September 7, 1990). ... Selected by Montreal Expos organization from Mets organization in Rule 5 minor league draft (December 9, 1996). ... Re-signed by Expos organization (March 20, 1999). ... On Montreal disabled list (July 13-September 1, 2001); included rehabilitation assignment to Ottawa (August 24-31). ... Traded by Expos with OF Wilkin Ruan to Los Angeles Dodgers for P Matt Herges and IF Jorge Nunez (March 24, 2002). ... On suspended list (March 30-April 4, 2003).

CAREER HITTING: 5-for-18 (.278), 3 R, 0 2B, 0 3B, 2 HR, 5 RBI.

Year League	W	L	Pct.	ERA	WHIP	G	GS	CG	ShO	Hld.	Sv.-Opp.	IP	H	R	ER	HR	BB-IBB	SO	Avg.
1997— Cape Fear (S. Atl.)	5	10	.333	4.36	1.33	25	23	0	0	...	0-...	126.0	135	65	61	8	33-0	112	.278
1998— Jupiter (FSL)	3	2	.600	0.66	0.59	20	0	0	0	...	2-...	41.0	18	6	3	0	6-0	27	.130
— Harrisburg (Eastern)	2	0	1.000	1.06	0.71	12	0	0	0	...	4-...	17.0	10	2	2	0	2-0	19	.172
1999— Ottawa (Int'l)	2	0	1.000	1.89	1.11	14	0	0	0	...	5-...	19.0	16	6	4	0	5-0	17	.235
— Montreal (N.L.)	2	4	.333	2.93	1.43	51	0	0	0	3	0-1	55.1	54	24	18	5	25-3	27	.257

M

Year League	W	L	Pct.	ERA	WHIP	G	GS	CG	ShO	Hld.	Sv.-Opp.	IP	H	R	ER	HR	BB-IBB	SO	Avg.
2000— Ottawa (Int'l)	4	5	.444	2.29	1.27	35	0	0	0	...	7-...	63.0	49	16	16	4	31-3	35	.220
— Montreal (N.L.)	1	1	.500	6.00	1.30	29	0	0	0	5	0-0	30.0	27	21	20	3	12-0	24	.245
2001— Montreal (N.L.)	1	3	.250	5.26	1.39	53	0	0	0	12	0-3	49.2	51	30	29	9	18-1	31	.271
— Ottawa (Int'l)	0	0	...	2.25	0.25	4	0	0	0	...	0-...	4.0	1	1	1	1	0-0	4	.077
2002— Las Vegas (PCL)	1	3	.250	2.95	1.15	20	0	0	0	...	1-...	36.2	34	13	12	1	8-1	38	.260
— Los Angeles (N.L.)	1	3	.250	4.15	1.19	43	0	0	0	4	0-1	60.2	45	30	28	4	27-6	49	.202
2003— Los Angeles (N.L.)	6	3	.667	1.97	0.99	76	0	0	0	13	1-3	105.0	78	23	23	7	26-4	99	.206
Major League totals (5 years)	11	14	.440	3.53	1.21	252	0	0	0	37	1-8	300.2	255	128	118	28	108-14	230	.230

MOUNCE, TONY — P

PERSONAL: Born February 8, 1975, in Sacramento, Calif. ... 6-2/170. ... Throws left, bats left. ... Full name: Anthony David Mounce. ... High school: Kamaiken (Calif.).
TRANSACTIONS/CAREER NOTES: Selected by Houston Astros organization in seventh round of free-agent draft (June 1994). ... Released by Astros (1999); signed by Texas Rangers organization as a free agent (May 1, 2000).
CAREER HITTING: 0-for-2 (.000), 0 R, 0 2B, 0 3B, 0 HR, 0 RBI.

Year League	W	L	Pct.	ERA	WHIP	G	GS	CG	ShO	Hld.	Sv.-Opp.	IP	H	R	ER	HR	BB-IBB	SO	Avg.
1994— GC Astros (GCL)	4	2	.667	2.72	1.24	11	11	0	0	...	0-...	59.2	56	24	18	1	18-0	72	.250
1995— Quad City (Midw.)	16	8	.667	2.43	1.10	25	25	3	1	...	0-...	159.0	118	55	43	6	57-2	143	.205
1996— Kissimmee (Fla. St.)	9	9	.500	2.25	1.33	25	25	4	2	...	0-...	155.2	139	65	39	7	68-1	102	.236
1997— New Orleans (A.A.)	0	0	...	1.93	1.71	1	1	0	0	...	0-...	4.2	2	1	1	1	6-0	6	.133
— Jackson (Texas)	8	9	.471	5.03	1.59	25	25	1	0	...	0-...	145.0	165	91	81	18	66-3	116	.292
1998— Jackson (Texas)	6	6	.500	5.09	1.60	32	17	1	0	...	0-...	109.2	128	73	62	14	48-0	82	.292
— Kissimmee (Fla. St.)	1	2	.333	6.92	1.85	5	5	0	0	...	0-...	26.0	35	22	20	2	13-1	15	.333
1999— Jackson (Texas)	5	2	.714	3.69	1.38	31	6	0	0	...	0-...	68.1	64	33	28	6	30-0	80	.241
— New Orleans (A.A.)	0	1	.000	2.45	2.09	14	0	0	0	...	0-...	11.0	10	3	3	0	13-0	10	.244
2000— Oklahoma (PCL)	1	4	.200	5.66	1.68	32	4	0	0	...	0-...	62.0	74	49	39	4	30-1	48	.298
2001—										Did not play.									
2002— Savannah (S. Atl.)	2	0	1.000	0.82	0.82	4	1	0	0	...	1-...	11.0	7	1	1	0	2-0	16	.179
— Charlotte (Int'l)	3	0	1.000	2.06	1.09	11	5	0	0	...	0-...	39.1	32	12	9	1	11-0	31	.230
— Oklahoma (PCL)	0	1	.000	9.00	2.20	2	1	0	0	...	0-...	5.0	10	5	5	1	1-0	2	.455
— Tulsa (Texas)	5	3	.625	3.90	1.28	11	11	0	0	...	0-...	57.2	59	28	25	7	15-0	47	.271
2003— Frisco (Texas)	7	1	.875	1.43	1.05	9	7	0	0	...	0-...	50.1	41	13	8	2	12-0	31	.227
— Oklahoma (PCL)	2	4	.333	3.39	1.30	11	11	2	0	...	0-...	66.1	60	25	25	6	26-0	51	.243
— Texas (A.L.)	1	5	.167	7.11	1.78	11	11	0	0	0	0-0	50.2	65	42	40	9	25-0	30	.317
Major League totals (1 year)	1	5	.167	7.11	1.78	11	11	0	0	0	0-0	50.2	65	42	40	9	25-0	30	.317

MOYER, JAMIE — P

PERSONAL: Born November 18, 1962, in Sellersville, Pa. ... 6-0/175. ... Throws left, bats left. ... High school: Souderton (Pa.) Area. ... College: St. Joseph's (Pa.).
TRANSACTIONS/CAREER NOTES: Selected by Chicago Cubs organization in sixth round of free-agent draft (June 4, 1984). ... Traded by Cubs with OF Rafael Palmeiro and P Drew Hall to Texas Rangers for P Mitch Williams, P Paul Kilgus, P Steve Wilson, IF Curtis Wilkerson, IF Luis Benitez and OF Pablo Delgado (December 5, 1988). ... On Texas disabled list (May 31-September 1, 1989); included rehabilitation assignments to Gulf Coast Rangers (August 5-14) and Tulsa (August 15-24). ... Released by Rangers (November 13, 1990). ... Signed by St. Louis Cardinals organization (January 9, 1991). ... Released by Cardinals (October 14, 1991). ... Signed by Cubs organization (January 8, 1992). ... Released by Cubs (March 30, 1992). ... Signed by Detroit Tigers organization (May 24, 1992). ... Granted free agency (December 8, 1992). ... Signed by Baltimore Orioles organization (December 14, 1992). ... Granted free agency (November 1, 1995). ... Signed by Boston Red Sox (January 2, 1996). ... Traded by Red Sox to Seattle Mariners for OF Darren Bragg (July 30, 1996). ... Granted free agency (October 29, 1996). ... Re-signed by Mariners (November 20, 1996). ... On Seattle disabled list (March 23-April 29, 1997); included rehabilitation assignment to Tacoma (April 24-29). ... On disabled list (April 15-June 2, 2000). ... Granted free agency (October 28, 2002). ... Re-signed by Mariners (December 7, 2002).
CAREER HITTING: 26-for-171 (.152), 11 R, 2 2B, 0 3B, 0 HR, 4 RBI.

Year League	W	L	Pct.	ERA	WHIP	G	GS	CG	ShO	Hld.	Sv.-Opp.	IP	H	R	ER	HR	BB-IBB	SO	Avg.
1984— Geneva (N.Y.-Penn)	•9	3	.750	1.89	0.86	14	14	5	2	...	0-...	*104.2	59	27	22	5	31-0	*120	.160
1985— Winston-Salem (Caro.)	8	2	.800	2.30	1.11	12	12	6	2	...	0-...	94.0	82	36	24	1	22-3	94	.232
— Pittsfield (East.)	7	6	.538	3.72	1.36	15	15	3	0	...	0-...	96.2	99	49	40	4	32-1	51	.265
1986— Pittsfield (East.)	3	1	.750	0.88	1.05	6	6	0	0	...	0-...	41.0	27	10	4	2	16-0	42	.186
— Iowa (Am. Assoc.)	3	2	.600	2.55	0.85	6	6	2	0	...	0-...	42.1	25	14	12	2	11-0	25	.162
— Chicago (N.L.)	7	4	.636	5.05	1.71	16	16	1	1	0	0-0	87.1	107	52	49	10	42-1	45	.311
1987— Chicago (N.L.)	12	15	.444	5.10	1.53	35	33	1	0	0	0-0	201.0	210	127	*114	28	97-9	147	.271
1988— Chicago (N.L.)	9	15	.375	3.48	1.32	34	30	3	1	0	0-2	202.0	212	84	78	20	55-7	121	.272
1989— Texas (A.L.)	4	9	.308	4.86	1.54	15	15	1	0	0	0-0	76.0	84	51	41	10	33-0	44	.283
— GC Rangers (GCL)	1	0	1.000	1.64	0.82	3	3	0	0	...	0-...	11.0	8	4	2	0	1-0	18	.195
— Tulsa (Texas)	1	1	.500	5.11	1.54	2	2	1	1	...	0-...	12.1	16	8	7	1	3-0	9	.320
1990— Texas (A.L.)	2	6	.250	4.66	1.50	33	10	1	0	1	0-0	102.1	115	59	53	6	39-4	58	.290
1991— St. Louis (N.L.)	0	5	.000	5.74	1.72	8	7	0	0	0	0-0	31.1	38	21	20	5	16-0	20	.319
— Louisville (A.A.)	5	10	.333	3.80	1.34	20	20	1	0	...	0-...	125.2	125	64	53	*16	43-4	69	.260
1992— Toledo (Int'l)	10	8	.556	2.86	1.19	21	20	5	0	...	0-...	138.2	128	48	44	8	37-3	80	.246
1993— Rochester (Int'l)	6	0	1.000	1.67	1.02	8	8	1	1	...	0-...	54.0	42	13	10	2	13-0	41	.211
— Baltimore (A.L.)	12	9	.571	3.43	1.26	25	25	3	1	0	0-0	152.0	154	63	58	11	38-2	90	.265
1994— Baltimore (A.L.)	5	7	.417	4.77	1.32	23	23	0	0	0	0-0	149.0	158	81	79	23	38-3	87	.271
1995— Baltimore (A.L.)	8	6	.571	5.21	1.27	27	18	0	0	0	0-0	115.2	117	70	67	18	30-0	65	.265
1996— Boston (A.L.)	7	1	.875	4.50	1.53	23	10	0	0	1	0-0	90.0	111	50	45	14	27-2	50	.300
— Seattle (A.L.)	6	2	.750	3.31	1.20	11	11	0	0	0	0-0	70.2	66	36	26	9	19-3	29	.243
1997— Tacoma (PCL)	1	0	1.000	0.00	0.20	1	1	0	0	...	0-...	5.0	1	0	0	0	0-0	6	.063
— Seattle (A.L.)	17	5	.773	3.86	1.22	30	30	2	0	0	0-0	188.2	187	82	81	21	43-2	113	.256
1998— Seattle (A.L.)	15	9	.625	3.53	1.18	34	34	4	3	0	0-0	234.1	234	99	92	23	42-2	158	.256
1999— Seattle (A.L.)	14	8	.636	3.87	1.24	32	32	4	0	0	0-0	228.0	235	108	98	23	48-1	137	.267
2000— Seattle (A.L.)	13	10	.565	5.49	1.47	26	26	0	0	0	0-0	154.0	173	103	94	22	53-2	98	.281
2001— Seattle (A.L.)	20	6	.769	3.43	1.10	33	33	1	0	0	0-0	209.2	187	84	80	24	44-4	119	.239
2002— Seattle (A.L.)	13	8	.619	3.32	1.08	34	34	4	2	0	0-0	230.2	198	89	85	28	50-4	147	.230
2003— Seattle (A.L.)	21	7	.750	3.27	1.23	33	33	0	0	0	0-0	215.0	199	83	78	19	66-3	129	.246
American League totals (13 years)	157	93	.628	3.97	1.26	379	334	21	6	2	0-0	2216.0	2218	1058	977	251	570-32	1324	.260
National League totals (4 years)	28	39	.418	4.50	1.49	93	86	5	2	0	0-2	521.2	567	284	261	63	210-17	333	.281
Major League totals (17 years)	185	132	.584	4.07	1.30	472	420	26	8	2	0-2	2737.2	2785	1342	1238	314	780-49	1657	.264

M

MUELLER, BILL   3B

PERSONAL: Born March 17, 1971, in Maryland Heights, Mo. ... 5-10/180. ... Bats both, throws right. ... Full name: William Richard Mueller. ... Name pronounced: MILL-er. ... High school: DeSmet (Creve Coeur, Mo.). ... College: Southwest Missouri State.

TRANSACTIONS/CAREER NOTES: Selected by San Francisco Giants organization in 15th round of free-agent draft (June 3, 1993). ... On disabled list (July 1-16, 1997). ... On San Francisco disabled list (April 6-May 17, 1999); included rehabilitation assignment to Fresno (May 11-17). ... Traded by Giants to Chicago Cubs for P Tim Worrell (November 19, 2000). ... On Chicago disabled list (May 14-August 13, 2001); included rehabilitation assignment to Iowa (August 2-13). ... On Chicago disabled list (March 28-May 6, 2002); included rehabilitation assignment to Iowa (April 29-May 6). ... Traded by Cubs with cash to Giants for P Jeff Verplancke (September 3, 2002). ... Granted free agency (October 28, 2002). ... Signed by Boston Red Sox (January 14, 2003).

2003 GAMES PLAYED BY POSITION (MLB): 3B—135, 2B—10, DH—3, SS—1.

Year Team (League)	Pos.	G	AB	R	H	2B	3B	HR	RBI	BB	SO	HBP	GDP	SB-CS	Avg.	OBP	SLG	OPS	E	Pct.
1993— Everett (N'west)	2B	58	200	31	60	8	2	1	24	42	17	3	3	13-6	.300	.425	.375	.800	8	.966
1994— San Jose (Calif.)	2B-3B-SS	120	431	79	130	20	•9	5	72	*103	47	3	15	4-8	.302	.435	.425	.859	29	.925
1995— Shreveport (Texas)	2B-3B	88	330	56	102	16	2	1	39	53	36	4	9	6-5	.309	.406	.379	.784	5	.978
— Phoenix (PCL)	2B-3B	41	172	23	51	13	6	2	19	19	31	0	7	0-0	.297	.365	.477	.841	7	.941
1996— Phoenix (PCL)	3-S-2-3B	106	440	73	133	14	6	4	36	44	40	1	11	2-5	.302	.365	.389	.753	11	.969
— San Francisco (N.L.)	3B-2B	55	200	31	66	15	1	0	19	24	26	1	1	0-0	.330	.401	.415	.816	6	.962
1997— San Francisco (N.L.)	3B	128	390	51	114	26	3	7	44	48	71	3	10	4-3	.292	.369	.428	.797	14	.956
1998— San Francisco (N.L.)	3B-2B	145	534	93	157	27	0	9	59	79	83	1	12	3-3	.294	.383	.395	.778	19	.953
1999— San Francisco (N.L.)	3B-2B	116	414	61	120	24	0	2	36	65	52	3	11	4-2	.290	.388	.362	.751	12	.959
— Fresno (PCL)	3B	3	12	3	5	0	1	0	6	0	0	0	0	0-0	.417	.385	.583	.968	3	.800
2000— San Francisco (N.L.)	3B-2B	153	560	97	150	29	4	10	55	52	62	6	16	4-2	.268	.333	.388	.721	9	.975
2001— Chicago (N.L.)	3B-2B	70	210	38	62	12	1	6	23	37	19	3	4	1-1	.295	.403	.448	.851	8	.942
— Iowa (PCL)	3B	8	26	3	11	3	0	0	4	1	2	0	0	0-0	.423	.444	.538	.983	0	1.000
2002— Iowa (PCL)	3B	6	16	2	6	1	0	1	5	3	1	0	0	0-1	.375	.474	.625	1.099	1	.909
— Chicago (N.L.)	3B	103	353	51	94	19	4	7	37	51	41	0	8	0-0	.266	.355	.402	.757	6	.973
— San Francisco (N.L.)	3B	8	13	0	2	0	0	0	1	1	1	0	1	0-0	.154	.214	.154	.368	0	1.000
2003— Boston (A.L.)	3-2-D-S	146	524	85	171	45	5	19	85	59	77	7	11	1-4	*.326	.398	.540	.938	16	.956
American League totals (1 year)		146	524	85	171	45	5	19	85	59	77	7	11	1-4	.326	.398	.540	.938	16	.956
National League totals (7 years)		778	2674	422	765	152	13	41	274	357	355	17	63	16-11	.286	.370	.399	.769	74	.961
Major League totals (8 years)		924	3198	507	936	197	18	60	359	416	432	24	74	17-15	.293	.375	.422	.796	90	.960

MULDER, MARK   P

PERSONAL: Born August 5, 1977, in South Holland, Ill. ... 6-6/208. ... Throws left, bats left. ... Full name: Mark Alan Mulder. ... High school: Thornwood (South Holland, Ill.). ... College: Michigan State.

TRANSACTIONS/CAREER NOTES: Selected by Detroit Tigers organization in 55th round of free-agent draft (June 1, 1995); did not sign. ... Selected by Oakland Athletics organization in first round (second pick overall) of free-agent draft (June 2, 1998). ... On disabled list (April 12-May 10, 2002). ... Placed on 15-day disabled list (August 21, 2003).

CAREER HITTING: 1-for-18 (.056), 0 R, 0 2B, 0 3B, 0 HR, 1 RBI.

Year League	W	L	Pct.	ERA	WHIP	G	GS	CG	ShO	Hld.	Sv.-Opp.	IP	H	R	ER	HR	BB-IBB	SO	Avg.
1999— Vancouver (PCL)	6	7	.462	4.06	1.42	22	22	1	0	...	0-...	128.2	152	69	58	13	31-0	81	.300
2000— Sacramento (PCL)	1	1	.500	5.40	2.28	2	2	0	0	...	0-...	8.1	15	11	5	1	4-0	6	.375
— Oakland (A.L.)	9	10	.474	5.44	1.69	27	27	0	0	0	0-0	154.0	191	106	93	22	69-3	88	.308
2001— Oakland (A.L.)	*21	8	.724	3.45	1.16	34	34	6	*4	0	0-0	229.1	214	92	88	16	51-4	153	.249
2002— Oakland (A.L.)	19	7	.731	3.47	1.14	30	30	2	1	0	0-0	207.1	182	88	80	21	55-3	159	.232
2003— Oakland (A.L.)	15	9	.625	3.13	1.18	26	26	•9	•2	0	0-0	186.2	180	66	65	15	40-2	128	.259
Major League totals (4 years)	64	34	.653	3.77	1.26	117	117	17	7	0	0-0	777.1	767	352	326	74	215-12	528	.259

MULHOLLAND, TERRY   P

PERSONAL: Born March 9, 1963, in Uniontown, Pa. ... 6-3/220. ... Throws left, bats right. ... Full name: Terence John Mulholland. ... Name pronounced: mul-HOLLAND. ... High school: Laurel Highlands (Uniontown, Pa.). ... College: Marietta (Ohio).

TRANSACTIONS/CAREER NOTES: Selected by San Francisco Giants organization in first round (24th pick overall) of free-agent draft (June 4, 1984); pick received as compensation for Detroit Tigers signing free-agent IF Darrell Evans. ... On San Francisco disabled list (August 1, 1988-remainder of season). ... Traded by Giants with P Dennis Cook and 3B Charlie Hayes to Philadelphia Phillies for P Steve Bedrosian and a player to be named later (June 18, 1989); Giants acquired IF Rick Parker to complete deal (August 7, 1989). ... On Philadelphia disabled list (June 12-28, 1990); included rehabilitation assignment to Scranton/Wilkes-Barre (June 23-24). ... Traded by Phillies with a player to be named later to New York Yankees for P Bobby Munoz, 2B Kevin Jordan and P Ryan Karp (February 9, 1994); Yankees acquired P Jeff Patterson to complete deal (November 8, 1994). ... Granted free agency (October 17, 1994). ... Signed by Giants (April 8, 1995). ... On San Francisco disabled list (June 6-July 4, 1995); included rehabilitation assignment to Phoenix (June 23-July 4). ... Granted free agency (November 3, 1995). ... Signed by Phillies organization (February 17, 1996). ... Traded by Phillies to Seattle Mariners for IF Desi Relaford (July 31, 1996). ... Granted free agency (October 28, 1996). ... Signed by Chicago Cubs (December 10, 1996). ... Claimed on waivers by Giants (August 8, 1997). ... Granted free agency (October 27, 1997). ... Signed by Cubs (February 2, 1998). ... Granted free agency (October 28, 1998). ... Re-signed by Cubs (November 6, 1998). ... Traded by Cubs with IF Jose Hernandez to Atlanta Braves for P Micah Bowie, P Ruben Quevado and a player to be named later (July 31, 1999); Cubs acquired P Joey Nation to complete deal (August 24, 1999). ... Granted free agency (October 31, 2000). ... Signed by Pittsburgh Pirates (December 10, 2000). ... On Pittsburgh disabled list (April 6-20 and June 12-August 1, 2001); included rehabilitation assignment to Altoona (July 27-29). ... Traded by Pirates to Los Angeles Dodgers for P Mike Fetters and P Adrian Burnside (July 31, 2001). ... On Los Angeles disabled list (May 3-June 4, 2002). ... Traded by Dodgers with P Ricardo Rodriguez and P Francisco Cruceta to Cleveland Indians for P Paul Shuey (July 28, 2002). ... Granted free agency (October 31, 2002). ... Re-signed by Indians (January 8, 2003).

CAREER HITTING: 69-for-617 (.112), 26 R, 13 2B, 1 3B, 2 HR, 23 RBI.

Year League	W	L	Pct.	ERA	WHIP	G	GS	CG	ShO	Hld.	Sv.-Opp.	IP	H	R	ER	HR	BB-IBB	SO	Avg.
1984— Everett (Northwest)	1	0	1.000	0.00	0.74	3	3	0	0	...	0-...	19.0	10	2	0	0	4-0	15	...
— Fresno (Calif.)	5	2	.714	2.95	1.59	9	9	0	0	...	0-...	42.2	32	17	14	1	36-0	39	...
1985— Shreveport (Texas)	9	8	.529	2.90	1.43	26	26	8	*3	...	0-...	176.2	166	79	57	9	87-2	122	.250
1986— Phoenix (PCL)	8	5	.615	4.46	1.51	17	17	3	0	...	0-...	111.0	112	60	55	6	56-4	77	.269
— San Francisco (N.L.)	1	7	.125	4.94	1.57	15	10	0	0	0	0-0	54.2	51	33	30	3	35-2	27	.251
1987— Phoenix (PCL)	7	12	.368	5.07	1.68	37	*29	3	1	...	1-...	172.1	200	*124	*97	7	90-0	94	.289
1988— Phoenix (PCL)	7	3	.700	3.58	1.59	19	14	3	2	...	0-...	100.2	116	45	40	2	44-0	57	.291
— San Francisco (N.L.)	2	1	.667	3.72	1.24	9	6	2	1	1	0-0	46.0	50	20	19	3	7-0	18	.281
1989— Phoenix (PCL)	4	5	.444	2.99	1.19	13	10	3	0	...	0-...	78.1	67	30	26	3	26-2	61	.242
— San Francisco (N.L.)	0	0	...	4.09	1.73	5	1	0	0	1	0-0	11.0	15	5	5	0	4-0	6	.319
— Philadelphia (N.L.)	4	7	.364	5.00	1.48	20	17	2	1	0	0-0	104.1	122	61	58	8	32-3	60	.292
1990— Philadelphia (N.L.)	9	10	.474	3.34	1.18	33	26	6	1	0	0-1	180.2	172	78	67	15	42-7	75	.252
— Scran./W.B. (I.L.)	0	1	.000	3.00	1.83	1	1	0	0	...	0-...	6.0	9	4	2	0	2-0	2	.360

Year League	W	L	Pct.	ERA	WHIP	G	GS	CG	ShO	Hld.	Sv.-Opp.	IP	H	R	ER	HR	BB-IBB	SO	Avg.
1991— Philadelphia (N.L.)	16	13	.552	3.61	1.21	34	34	8	3	0	0-0	232.0	231	100	93	15	49-2	142	.260
1992— Philadelphia (N.L.)	13	11	.542	3.81	1.19	32	32	*12	2	0	0-0	229.0	227	101	97	14	46-3	125	.261
1993— Philadelphia (N.L.)	12	9	.571	3.25	1.14	29	28	7	2	0	0-0	191.0	177	80	69	20	40-2	116	.241
1994— New York (A.L.)	6	7	.462	6.49	1.55	24	19	2	0	0	0-0	120.2	150	94	87	24	37-1	72	.303
1995— San Francisco (N.L.)	5	13	.278	5.80	1.53	29	24	2	0	0	0-0	149.0	190	112	96	25	38-1	65	.313
— Phoenix (PCL)	0	0	...	2.25	1.25	1	1	0	0	0	0-...	4.0	4	3	1	0	1-0	4	.235
1996— Philadelphia (N.L.)	8	7	.533	4.66	1.34	21	21	3	0	0	0-0	133.1	157	74	69	17	21-1	52	.293
— Seattle (A.L.)	5	4	.556	4.67	1.49	12	12	0	0	0	0-0	69.1	75	38	36	5	28-3	34	.286
1997— Chicago (N.L.)	6	12	.333	4.07	1.32	25	25	1	0	0	0-0	157.0	162	79	71	20	45-2	74	.271
— San Francisco (N.L.)	0	1	.000	5.16	1.15	15	2	0	0	1	0-0	29.2	28	21	17	4	6-1	25	.248
1998— Chicago (N.L.)	6	5	.545	2.89	1.24	70	6	0	0	19	3-5	112.0	100	49	36	7	39-7	72	.235
1999— Chicago (N.L.)	6	6	.500	5.15	1.54	26	16	0	0	1	0-0	110.0	137	71	63	16	32-4	44	.309
— Atlanta (N.L.)	4	2	.667	2.98	1.28	16	8	0	0	3	1-1	60.1	64	24	20	5	13-2	39	.274
2000— Atlanta (N.L.)	9	9	.500	5.11	1.53	54	20	1	0	2	1-3	156.2	198	96	89	24	41-7	78	.308
2001— Pittsburgh (N.L.)	0	0	...	3.72	1.32	22	1	0	0	3	0-0	36.1	38	15	15	5	10-1	17	.277
— Altoona (East.)	0	2	.000	3.86	2.57	2	2	0	0	...	0-...	2.1	5	3	1	0	1-0	3	.417
— Los Angeles (N.L.)	1	1	.500	5.83	1.60	19	3	0	0	4	0-0	29.1	40	20	19	7	7-0	25	.315
2002— Los Angeles (N.L.)	0	0	...	7.31	1.63	21	0	0	0	0	0-0	32.0	45	29	26	10	7-0	17	.331
— Cleveland (A.L.)	3	2	.600	4.60	1.49	16	3	0	0	2	0-0	47.0	56	27	24	5	14-3	21	.301
2003— Cleveland (A.L.)	3	4	.429	4.91	1.56	45	3	0	0	2	0-2	99.0	117	60	54	17	37-6	42	.295
American League totals (4 years)	17	17	.500	5.38	1.53	97	37	2	0	4	0-2	336.0	398	219	201	51	116-13	169	.297
National League totals (15 years)	102	114	.472	4.20	1.32	495	280	44	10	35	5-10	2054.1	2204	1068	959	218	514-45	1077	.275
Major League totals (17 years)	119	131	.476	4.37	1.35	592	317	46	10	39	5-12	2390.1	2602	1287	1160	269	630-58	1246	.278

MULLEN, SCOTT   P

PERSONAL: Born January 17, 1975, in San Benito, Texas. ... 6-2/195. ... Throws left, bats right. ... Full name: Kenneth Scott Mullen. ... High school: Beaufort (S.C.). ... College: Dallas Baptist (Texas).

TRANSACTIONS/CAREER NOTES: Selected by Kansas City Royals organization in seventh round of free-agent draft (June 4, 1996). ... On Kansas City disabled list (March 31-May 4, 2001); included rehabilitation assignment to Omaha (April 5-May 4). ... On Omaha disabled list (April 4-11, 2002).

CAREER HITTING: 0-for-1 (.000), 0 R, 0 2B, 0 3B, 0 HR, 0 RBI.

Year League	W	L	Pct.	ERA	WHIP	G	GS	CG	ShO	Hld.	Sv.-Opp.	IP	H	R	ER	HR	BB-IBB	SO	Avg.
1996— Spokane (N'west)	5	6	.455	3.92	1.33	15	15	0	0	...	0-...	80.1	78	45	35	6	29-0	78	.250
1997— Lansing (Midw.)	5	2	.714	3.70	1.31	16	16	0	0	...	0-...	92.1	90	46	38	14	31-0	78	.255
— Wilmington (Caro.)	4	4	.500	4.55	1.52	11	11	0	0	...	0-...	59.1	64	35	30	5	26-4	43	.278
1998— Wilmington (Caro.)	8	4	.667	2.21	1.09	14	14	1	1	...	0-...	85.2	68	28	21	4	25-0	56	.221
— Wichita (Texas)	8	2	.800	4.11	1.31	12	12	0	0	...	0-...	70.0	66	34	32	7	26-0	42	.255
1999— Wichita (Texas)	4	3	.571	4.01	1.32	9	9	0	0	...	0-...	49.1	47	28	22	2	18-1	30	.245
— Omaha (PCL)	6	7	.462	6.26	1.70	20	20	0	0	...	0-...	119.1	150	91	83	24	53-2	87	.314
2000— Wichita (Texas)	3	2	.600	3.19	1.24	33	1	0	0	...	7-...	73.1	65	27	26	5	26-1	61	.243
— Omaha (PCL)	2	1	.667	3.05	1.11	16	0	0	0	...	0-...	20.2	15	10	7	1	8-0	21	.205
— Kansas City (A.L.)	0	0	...	4.35	1.26	11	0	0	0	2	0-0	10.1	10	5	5	2	3-0	7	.244
2001— Omaha (PCL)	5	4	.556	6.62	1.66	48	0	0	0	...	5-...	53.0	66	39	39	8	22-2	38	.316
— Kansas City (A.L.)	0	0	...	4.50	2.20	17	0	0	0	1	0-0	10.0	13	6	5	0	9-0	3	.310
2002— Omaha (PCL)	1	2	.333	2.61	1.32	19	1	0	0	...	0-...	31.0	32	12	9	0	9-3	21	.274
— Kansas City (A.L.)	4	5	.444	3.15	1.33	44	0	0	0	6	0-2	40.0	40	16	14	5	13-2	21	.267
2003— Kansas City (A.L.)	0	0	...	16.62	3.69	2	0	0	0	0	0-0	4.1	11	8	8	2	5-0	3	.458
— Omaha (PCL)	5	3	.625	3.88	1.39	20	9	0	0	...	1-...	69.2	75	35	30	3	22-1	50	.282
— Los Angeles (N.L.)	0	0	...	9.00	2.33	1	1	0	0	0	0-0	3.0	2	3	3	0	5-0	1	.200
— Las Vegas (PCL)	4	2	.667	3.95	1.56	7	7	0	0	...	0-...	41.0	50	22	18	4	14-0	23	.314
American League totals (4 years)	4	5	.444	4.45	1.61	74	0	0	0	9	0-2	64.2	74	35	32	9	30-2	34	.288
National League totals (1 year)	0	0	...	9.00	2.33	1	1	0	0	0	0-0	3.0	2	3	3	0	5-0	1	.200
Major League totals (4 years)	4	5	.444	4.66	1.64	75	1	0	0	9	0-2	67.2	76	38	35	9	35-2	35	.285

MUNRO, PETE   P

PERSONAL: Born June 14, 1975, in Flushing, N.Y. ... 6-3/210. ... Throws right, bats right. ... Full name: Peter Daniel Munro. ... Name pronounced: mun-ROW. ... High school: Benjamin Cardozo (Bayside, N.Y.). ... Junior college: Okaloosa-Walton (Fla.) Community College.

TRANSACTIONS/CAREER NOTES: Selected by Boston Red Sox organization in sixth round of free-agent draft (June 3, 1993). ... On disabled list (June 28, 1994-entire season). ... On Pawtucket disabled list (May 24-June 8, 1998). ... Traded by Red Sox with P Jay Yennaco to Toronto Blue Jays for 1B/DH Mike Stanley (July 30, 1998). ... On Toronto disabled list (June 4-July 3, 2000); included rehabilitation assignments to Dunedin (June 12-July 1) and Syracuse (July 2-3). ... Traded by Blue Jays to Texas Rangers (August 8, 2000); completing deal in which Rangers traded OF Dave Martinez to Blue Jays for a player to be named later (August 4, 2000). ... Granted free agency (December 21, 2000). ... Re-signed by Rangers organization (January 2, 2001). ... Granted free agency (October 15, 2001). ... Signed by Houston Astros organization (January 17, 2002). ... Designated for assignment (August 1, 2003). ... Sent outright to New Orleans (August 5, 2003).

CAREER HITTING: 3-for-24 (.125), 1 R, 0 2B, 0 3B, 0 HR, 2 RBI.

Year League	W	L	Pct.	ERA	WHIP	G	GS	CG	ShO	Hld.	Sv.-Opp.	IP	H	R	ER	HR	BB-IBB	SO	Avg.
1994—											Did not play.								
1995— Utica (N.Y.-Penn)	5	4	.556	2.60	1.24	14	14	0	0	...	0-...	90.0	79	38	26	3	33-1	74	.230
1996— Sarasota (Fla. St.)	11	6	.647	3.60	1.39	27	25	2	•2	...	1-...	155.0	153	76	62	4	62-1	115	.258
1997— Trenton (East.)	7	10	.412	4.95	1.38	22	22	1	0	...	0-...	116.1	113	76	64	12	47-0	109	.260
1998— Pawtucket (Int'l)	5	4	.556	4.05	1.37	18	17	0	0	...	0-...	106.2	111	49	48	10	35-2	75	.275
— Syracuse (Int'l)	2	5	.286	7.46	1.81	8	8	0	0	...	0-...	44.2	58	42	37	7	23-2	42	.312
1999— Toronto (A.L.)	0	2	.000	6.02	1.68	31	2	0	0	4	0-1	55.1	70	38	37	6	23-0	38	.318
— Syracuse (Int'l)	6	1	.857	3.10	1.48	18	11	0	0	...	0-...	69.2	70	29	24	6	33-1	68	.257
2000— Syracuse (Int'l)	4	3	.571	2.48	1.25	10	10	2	0	...	0-...	61.2	52	20	17	1	25-0	45	.235
— Dunedin (Fla. St.)	0	1	.000	5.56	1.32	3	3	0	0	...	0-...	11.1	11	7	7	0	4-0	12	.256
— Toronto (A.L.)	1	1	.500	5.96	2.10	9	3	0	0	0	0-0	25.2	38	22	17	1	16-0	16	.355
— Oklahoma (PCL)	1	2	.333	4.65	1.32	5	5	1	1	...	0-...	31.0	27	17	16	3	14-0	15	.229
2001— Oklahoma (PCL)	8	6	.571	4.67	1.49	33	8	0	0	...	0-...	88.2	89	50	46	12	43-1	73	.264
2002— New Orleans (PCL)	7	1	.875	2.39	0.88	19	13	1	1	...	0-...	94.1	68	30	25	3	15-1	73	.200
— Houston (N.L.)	5	5	.500	3.57	1.39	19	14	0	0	1	0-0	80.2	89	37	32	5	23-3	45	.283
2003— Houston (N.L.)	3	4	.429	4.67	1.65	40	2	0	0	3	0-1	54.0	63	30	28	7	26-2	27	.294
— New Orleans (PCL)	0	4	.000	6.04	1.79	5	4	0	0	...	0-...	22.1	28	16	15	1	12-1	12	.308
American League totals (2 years)	1	3	.250	6.00	1.81	40	5	0	0	4	0-1	81.0	108	60	54	7	39-0	54	.330
National League totals (2 years)	8	9	.471	4.01	1.49	59	16	0	0	4	0-1	134.2	152	67	60	12	49-5	72	.288
Major League totals (4 years)	9	12	.429	4.76	1.61	99	21	0	0	8	0-2	215.2	260	127	114	19	88-5	126	.304

M

MUNSON, ERIC — 3B/1B

PERSONAL: Born October 3, 1977, in San Diego, Calif. ... 6-3/230. ... Bats left, throws right. ... Full name: Eric Walter Munson. ... High school: Mount Carmel (San Diego). ... College: USC.

TRANSACTIONS/CAREER NOTES: Selected by Atlanta Braves organization in second round of free-agent draft (June 4, 1996); did not sign. ... Selected by Detroit Tigers organization in first round (third pick overall) of free-agent draft (June 2, 1999). ... On Jacksonville disabled list (August 28-September 18, 2000). ... Placed on 15-day disabled list (August 12, 2003). ... Reinstated from 15-day disabled list (September 29, 2003).

2003 GAMES PLAYED BY POSITION (MLB): 3B—91, DH—3.

											BATTING									FIELDING	
Year Team (League)	Pos.	G	AB	R	H	2B	3B	HR	RBI	BB	SO	HBP	GDP	SB-CS	Avg.	OBP	SLG	OPS		E	Pct.
1999—Lakeland (Fla. St.)	DH	2	6	0	2	0	0	0	1	1	1	0	0	0-0	.333	.429	.333	.762		...	...
— W. Mich. (Mid.)	1B-C	67	252	42	67	16	1	14	44	37	47	9	4	3-1	.266	.378	.504	.882		3	.991
2000—Jacksonville (Sou.)	1B	98	365	52	92	21	4	15	68	39	96	18	8	5-2	.252	.348	.455	.803		8	.989
— Detroit (A.L.)	1B	3	5	0	0	0	0	0	1	0	1	0	0	0-0	.000	.000	.000	.000		1	.941
2001—Erie (East.)	1B	* 142	519	88	135	35	1	26	* 102	* 84	141	11	6	0-3	.260	.371	.482	.853		* 17	.985
— Detroit (A.L.)	1B	17	66	4	10	3	1	1	6	3	21	0	2	0-1	.152	.188	.273	.461		1	.994
2002—Toledo (Int'l)	1B	136	477	77	125	30	4	24	84	77	114	7	9	1-3	.262	.367	.493	.860		• 12	.970
— Detroit (A.L.)	DH-1B	18	59	3	11	0	0	2	5	6	11	1	1	0-0	.186	.269	.288	.557		1	.970
2003—Detroit (A.L.)	3B-DH	99	313	28	75	9	0	18	50	35	61	1	4	3-0	.240	.312	.441	.753		19	.920
Major League totals (4 years)		137	443	35	96	12	1	21	62	44	94	2	7	3-1	.217	.286	.391	.676		22	.950

MUSSINA, MIKE — P

PERSONAL: Born December 8, 1968, in Williamsport, Pa. ... 6-2/185. ... Throws right, bats left. ... Full name: Michael Cole Mussina. ... Name pronounced: myoo-SEE-nuh. ... High school: Montoursville (Pa.). ... College: Stanford.

TRANSACTIONS/CAREER NOTES: Selected by Baltimore Orioles organization in 11th round of free-agent draft (June 2, 1987); did not sign. ... Selected by Orioles organization in first round (20th pick overall) of free-agent draft (June 4, 1990). ... On Rochester disabled list (May 5-12, 1991). ... On Baltimore disabled list (July 22-August 20, 1993); included rehabilitation assignment to Bowie (August 9-20). ... On disabled list (April 17-May 3 and May 15-June 6, 1998). ... Granted free agency (October 27, 2000). ... Signed by New York Yankees (November 30, 2000).

CAREER HITTING: 8-for-37 (.216), 3 R, 1 2B, 0 3B, 0 HR, 5 RBI.

Year League	W	L	Pct.	ERA	WHIP	G	GS	CG	ShO	Hld.	Sv.-Opp.	IP	H	R	ER	HR	BB-IBB	SO	Avg.
1990—Hagerstown (Eastern)	3	0	1.000	1.49	0.97	7	7	2	1	...	0-...	42.1	34	10	7	1	7-0	40	.214
—Rochester (Int'l)	0	0	...	1.35	0.90	2	2	0	0	...	0-...	13.1	8	2	2	2	4-0	15	.174
1991—Rochester (Int'l)	10	4	.714	2.87	1.14	19	19	3	1	...	0-...	122.1	108	42	39	9	31-0	107	.235
—Baltimore (A.L.)	4	5	.444	2.87	1.12	12	12	2	0	0	0-0	87.2	77	31	28	7	21-0	52	.239
1992—Baltimore (A.L.)	18	5	*.783	2.54	1.08	32	32	8	4	0	0-0	241.0	212	70	68	16	48-2	130	.239
1993—Baltimore (A.L.)	14	6	.700	4.46	1.23	25	25	3	2	0	0-0	167.2	163	84	83	20	44-2	117	.256
—Bowie (East.)	1	0	1.000	2.25	0.75	2	2	0	0	...	0-...	8.0	5	2	2	0	1-0	10	.172
1994—Baltimore (A.L.)	16	5	.762	3.06	1.16	24	24	3	0	0	0-0	176.1	163	63	60	19	42-1	99	.248
1995—Baltimore (A.L.)	* 19	9	.679	3.29	1.07	32	32	7	* 4	0	0-0	221.2	187	86	81	24	50-4	158	.226
1996—Baltimore (A.L.)	19	11	.633	4.81	1.37	36	* 36	4	1	0	0-0	243.1	264	137	130	31	69-0	204	.275
1997—Baltimore (A.L.)	15	8	.652	3.20	1.12	33	33	4	1	0	0-0	224.2	197	87	80	27	54-3	218	.234
1998—Baltimore (A.L.)	13	10	.565	3.49	1.11	29	29	4	2	0	0-0	206.1	189	85	80	22	41-3	175	.242
1999—Baltimore (A.L.)	18	7	.720	3.50	1.27	31	31	4	1	0	0-0	203.1	207	88	79	16	52-0	172	.268
2000—Baltimore (A.L.)	11	15	.423	3.79	1.19	34	34	6	1	0	* 237.2	236	105	100	28	46-0	210	.255
2001—New York (A.L.)	17	11	.607	3.15	1.07	34	34	4	3	0	0-0	228.2	202	87	80	20	42-2	214	.237
2002—New York (A.L.)	18	10	.643	4.05	1.19	33	33	2	2	0	0-0	215.2	208	103	97	27	48-1	182	.253
2003—New York (A.L.)	17	8	.680	3.40	1.08	31	31	2	1	0	0-0	214.2	192	86	81	21	40-4	195	.238
Major League totals (13 years)	199	110	.644	3.53	1.16	386	386	53	21	0	0-0	2668.2	2497	1112	1047	278	597-22	2126	.247

MYERS, BRETT — P

PERSONAL: Born August 17, 1980, in Jacksonville, Fla. ... 6-4/215. ... Throws right, bats right. ... Full name: Brett Allen Myers. ... High school: Englewood (Jacksonville, Fla.).

TRANSACTIONS/CAREER NOTES: Selected by Philadelphia Phillies organization in first round (12th pick overall) of free-agent draft (June 2, 1999).

CAREER HITTING: 12-for-85 (.141), 3 R, 2 2B, 0 3B, 0 HR, 2 RBI.

Year League	W	L	Pct.	ERA	WHIP	G	GS	CG	ShO	Hld.	Sv.-Opp.	IP	H	R	ER	HR	BB-IBB	SO	Avg.
1999—GC Phillies (GCL)	2	1	.667	2.33	0.89	7	5	0	0	...	0-...	27.0	17	8	7	0	7-0	30	.177
2000—Piedmont (S. Atl.)	13	7	.650	3.18	1.33	27	27	2	1	...	0-...	175.1	165	78	62	7	69-0	140	.252
2001—Reading (East.)	13	4	.765	3.87	1.28	26	23	1	1	...	0-...	156.0	156	71	67	21	43-1	130	.258
2002—Scran./W.B. (I.L.)	9	6	.600	3.59	1.10	19	19	4	1	...	0-...	128.0	121	54	51	9	20-0	97	.252
—Philadelphia (N.L.)	4	5	.444	4.25	1.42	12	12	1	0	0	0-0	72.0	73	38	34	11	29-1	34	.277
2003—Philadelphia (N.L.)	14	9	.609	4.43	1.46	32	32	1	1	0	0-0	193.0	205	99	95	20	76-8	143	.272
Major League totals (2 years)	18	14	.563	4.38	1.45	44	44	2	1	0	0-0	265.0	278	137	129	31	105-9	177	.273

MYERS, GREG — C

PERSONAL: Born April 14, 1966... 6-2/225. ... Bats left, throws right. ... Full name: Gregory Richard Myers. ... High school: Riverside (Calif.) Polytechnical.

TRANSACTIONS/CAREER NOTES: Selected by Toronto Blue Jays organization in third round of free-agent draft (June 4, 1984). ... On disabled list (June 17, 1988-remainder of season). ... On Toronto disabled list (March 26-June 5, 1989); included rehabilitation assignment to Knoxville (May 17-June 5). ... On Toronto disabled list (May 5-25, 1990); included rehabilitation assignment to Syracuse (May 21-24). ... Traded by Blue Jays with OF Rob Ducey to California Angels for P Mark Eichhorn (July 30, 1992). ... On California disabled list (August 27, 1992-remainder of season). ... On California disabled list (April 24-June 21, 1994); included rehabilitation assignments to Lake Elsinore (May 20-June 6 and June 13-21). ... On disabled list (April 21-May 6, June 1-21 and September 30, 1995-remainder of season). ... Granted free agency (November 3, 1995). ... Signed by Minnesota Twins (December 8, 1995). ... On disabled list (July 14-August 2, 1996). ... On Minnesota disabled list (August 9-24, 1997). ... Traded by Twins to Atlanta Braves for a player to be named later (September 5, 1997); Twins acquired 1B Steve Hacker to complete deal (December 18, 1997). ... Granted free agency (October 28, 1997). ... Signed by San Diego Padres (November 25, 1997). ... On San Diego disabled list (June 4-July 24, 1998); included rehabilitation assignments to Rancho Cucamonga (July 17-19) and Las Vegas (July 21-23). ... On San Diego disabled list (June 29-July 26, 1999); included rehabilitation assignment to Rancho Cucamonga (July 20-26). ... Traded by Padres to Braves for P Doug Dent (July 26, 1999). ... Granted free agency (November 1, 1999). ... Signed by Baltimore Orioles (December 17, 1999). ... On disabled list (April 2-17, 2000). ... Released by Orioles (June 14, 2001). ... Signed by Oakland Athletics (June 23, 2001). ... Granted free agency (November 5, 2001). ... Re-signed by A's (November 15, 2001). ... Granted free agency (October 29, 2002). ... Signed by Blue Jays (December 11, 2002).

2003 GAMES PLAYED BY POSITION (MLB): C—81, DH—22.

								BATTING												FIELDING	
Year	Team (League)	Pos.	G	AB	R	H	2B	3B	HR	RBI	BB	SO	HBP	GDP	SB-CS	Avg.	OBP	SLG	OPS	E	Pct.
1984— Medicine Hat (Pio.)		C	38	133	20	42	9	0	2	20	16	6	0	4	0-0	.316	.387	.429	.815	4	.984
1985— Florence (S. Atl.)		C	134	489	52	109	19	2	5	62	39	54	2	12	0-0	.223	.279	.301	.580	7 *	.989
1986— Ventura (Calif.)		C	124	451	65	133	23	4	20	79	43	46	2	10	9-4	.295	.355	.497	.852	19	.980
1987— Syracuse (Int'l)		C	107	342	35	84	19	1	10	47	22	46	1	5	3-3	.246	.292	.395	.686	11	.984
— Toronto (A.L.)		C	7	9	1	1	0	0	0	0	0	3	0	2	0-0	.111	.111	.111	.222	0	1.000
1988— Syracuse (Int'l)		C	34	120	18	34	7	1	7	21	8	24	0	1	1-0	.283	.328	.533	.861	1	.986
1989— Knoxville (Sou.)		C	29	90	11	30	10	0	5	19	3	16	0	2	1-0	.333	.351	.611	.962	1	.993
— Toronto (A.L.)		DH-C	17	44	0	5	2	0	0	1	2	9	0	2	0-1	.114	.152	.159	.311	0	1.000
— Syracuse (Int'l)		C	24	89	8	24	6	0	1	11	4	9	0	3	0-0	.270	.301	.371	.672	1	.985
1990— Toronto (A.L.)		C	87	250	33	59	7	1	5	22	22	33	0	12	0-1	.236	.293	.332	.625	3	.993
— Syracuse (Int'l)		C	3	11	0	2	1	0	0	2	1	1	0	0	0-0	.182	.231	.273	.503	0	1.000
1991— Toronto (A.L.)		C	107	309	25	81	22	0	8	36	21	45	0	13	0-0	.262	.306	.411	.717	11	.979
1992— Toronto (A.L.)		C	22	61	4	14	6	0	1	13	5	5	0	2	0-0	.230	.279	.377	.656	1	.991
— California (A.L.)		C-DH	8	17	0	4	1	0	0	0	0	6	0	0	0-0	.235	.235	.294	.529	0	1.000
1993— California (A.L.)		C-DH	108	290	27	74	10	0	7	40	17	47	2	8	3-3	.255	.298	.362	.660	6	.986
1994— California (A.L.)		C-DH	45	126	10	31	6	0	2	8	10	27	0	3	0-2	.246	.299	.341	.641	2	.991
— Lake Elsinore (Calif.)		C-DH	10	32	4	8	2	0	0	5	2	6	0	2	0-0	.250	.286	.313	.598	0	1.000
1995— California (A.L.)		C-DH	85	273	35	71	12	2	9	38	17	49	1	4	0-1	.260	.304	.418	.721	4	.989
1996— Minnesota (A.L.)		C	97	329	37	94	22	3	6	47	19	52	0	11	0-0	.286	.320	.426	.746	8	.985
1997— Minnesota (A.L.)		C-DH	62	165	24	44	11	1	5	28	16	29	0	4	0-0	.267	.328	.436	.764	3	.986
— Atlanta (N.L.)		C	9	9	0	1	0	0	0	1	1	3	0	0	0-0	.111	.200	.111	.311	0	1.000
1998— San Diego (N.L.)		C	69	171	19	42	10	0	4	20	17	36	0	6	0-1	.246	.312	.374	.686	4	.987
— Rancho Cuca. (Calif.)		C-DH	3	9	1	0	0	0	0	0	2	1	0	1	0-0	.000	.182	.000	.182	0	1.000
— Las Vegas (PCL)		C	3	9	0	5	0	0	1	0	0	0	0	0	0-0	.556	.556	.556	1.111	0	1.000
1999— San Diego (N.L.)		C	50	128	9	37	4	0	3	15	13	14	0	5	0-0	.289	.355	.391	.745	3	.986
— Rancho Cuca. (Calif.)		C-DH	3	3	0	0	0	0	0	0	1	1	0	0	0-0	.000	.250	.000	.250	0	1.000
— Atlanta (N.L.)		C	34	72	10	16	2	0	2	9	13	16	0	1	0-0	.222	.337	.333	.671	1	.994
2000— Baltimore (A.L.)		C-DH	43	125	9	28	6	0	3	12	8	29	0	7	0-0	.224	.271	.344	.615	0	1.000
2001— Baltimore (A.L.)		DH-C	25	74	11	20	2	0	4	18	8	17	0	3	0-0	.270	.341	.459	.801	0	1.000
— Sacramento (PCL)		C	2	5	0	0	0	0	0	1	3	2	0	1	0-0	.000	.375	.000	.375	0	1.000
— Oakland (A.L.)		C-DH	33	87	13	16	1	0	7	13	13	21	0	2	0-0	.184	.290	.437	.727	0	1.000
2002— Oakland (A.L.)		C-DH	65	144	15	32	5	0	6	21	26	36	0	4	0-0	.222	.341	.382	.723	1	.997
2003— Toronto (A.L.)		C	121	329	51	101	19	0	15	52	37	57	0	14	0-3	.307	.374	.502	.876	8	.982
American League totals (14 years)			932	2632	295	675	132	7	78	349	221	465	3	91	3-11	.256	.312	.401	.713	47	.988
National League totals (3 years)			162	380	38	96	16	0	9	45	44	69	0	12	0-1	.253	.329	.366	.694	8	.989
Major League totals (16 years)			1094	3012	333	771	148	7	87	394	265	534	3	103	3-12	.256	.314	.396	.711	55	.988

MYERS, MIKE — P

PERSONAL: Born June 26, 1969, in Arlington Heights, Ill. ... 6-3/219. ... Throws left, bats left. ... Full name: Michael Stanley Myers. ... High school: Crystal Lake (Ill.) Central. ... College: Iowa State.

TRANSACTIONS/CAREER NOTES: Selected by San Francisco Giants organization in fourth round of free-agent draft (June 4, 1990). ... On Clinton disabled list (June 3-September 16, 1991; April 9-June 2 and June 21-July 6, 1992). ... Selected by Florida Marlins from Giants organization in Rule 5 major league draft (December 7, 1992). ... On Edmonton disabled list (April 13-June 7, 1994). ... On Florida disabled list (June 7-August 5, 1994); included rehabilitation assignment to Brevard County (June 23-July 11). ... Traded by Marlins to Detroit Tigers (August 9, 1995), completing deal in which Marlins acquired P Buddy Groom for a player to be named later (August 1, 1995). ... Traded by Tigers with P Rick Greene and SS Santiago Perez to Milwaukee Brewers for P Bryce Florie and a player to be named later (November 20, 1997). ... Traded by Brewers to Colorado Rockies for P Curtis Leskanic (November 17, 1999). ... Traded by Rockies to Arizona Diamondbacks for OF Jack Cust and C J.D. Closser (January 7, 2002).

CAREER HITTING: 0-for-1 (.000), 0 R, 0 2B, 0 3B, 0 HR, 0 RBI.

Year	League	W	L	Pct.	ERA	WHIP	G	GS	CG	ShO	Hld.	Sv.-Opp.	IP	H	R	ER	HR	BB-IBB	SO	Avg.
1990— Everett (Northwest)		4	5	.444	3.90	1.42	15	14	1	0	...	0-...	85.1	91	43	37	9	30-0	73	.269
1991— Clinton (Midw.)		5	3	.625	2.62	1.21	11	11	1	0	...	0-...	65.1	61	23	19	3	18-0	59	.253
— Ariz. Giants (Ariz.)		0	1	.000	12.00	2.33	1	0	0	0	...	0-...	3.0	5	5	4	0	2-0	2	.357
1992— San Jose (Calif.)		5	1	.833	2.30	1.10	8	8	0	0	...	0-...	54.2	43	20	14	1	17-0	40	.221
— Clinton (Midw.)		1	2	.333	1.19	0.96	7	7	0	0	...	0-...	37.2	28	11	5	0	8-0	32	.207
1993— Edmonton (PCL)		7	14	.333	5.18	1.53	27	27	3	0	...	0-...	161.2	195	109	93	20	52-1	112	.296
1994— Edmonton (PCL)		1	5	.167	5.55	1.65	12	11	0	0	...	0-...	60.0	78	42	37	9	21-0	55	.307
— Brevard County (FSL)		0	0	...	0.79	0.97	3	2	0	0	...	0-...	11.1	7	1	1	1	4-0	15	.184
1995— Florida (N.L.)		0	0	...	0.00	2.00	2	0	0	0	0	0-0	2.0	1	0	0	0	3-0	0	.167
— Charlotte (Int'l)		0	5	.000	5.65	1.53	37	0	0	0	...	0-...	36.2	41	25	23	6	15-1	24	.283
— Toledo (Int'l)		0	0	...	4.32	1.08	6	0	0	0	...	0-...	8.1	6	4	4	1	3-0	8	.194
— Detroit (A.L.)		1	0	1.000	9.95	2.21	11	0	0	0	1	0-1	6.1	10	7	7	1	4-0	4	.385
1996— Detroit (A.L.)		1	5	.167	5.01	1.61	83	0	0	0	17	6-8	64.2	70	41	36	6	34-8	69	.272
1997— Detroit (A.L.)		0	4	.000	5.70	1.55	88	0	0	0	18	2-5	53.2	58	36	34	12	25-2	50	.274
1998— Milwaukee (N.L.)		2	2	.500	2.70	1.32	70	0	0	0	*23	1-3	50.0	44	19	15	5	22-1	40	.249
1999— Milwaukee (N.L.)		2	1	.667	5.23	1.43	71	0	0	0	14	0-3	41.1	46	24	24	7	13-1	35	.291
2000— Colorado (N.L.)		0	1	.000	1.99	1.06	78	0	0	0	15	1-2	45.1	24	10	10	2	24-3	41	.160
2001— Colorado (N.L.)		2	3	.400	3.60	1.40	73	0	0	0	10	0-2	40.0	32	17	16	2	24-7	36	.225
2002— Arizona (N.L.)		4	3	.571	4.38	1.51	69	0	0	0	17	4-9	37.0	39	18	18	2	17-0	31	.275
2003— Arizona (N.L.)		0	1	.000	5.70	1.62	64	0	0	0	6	0-3	36.1	38	23	23	4	21-1	21	.262
American League totals (3 years)		2	9	.182	5.56	1.61	182	0	0	0	36	8-14	124.2	138	84	77	19	63-10	123	.279
National League totals (7 years)		10	11	.476	3.79	1.38	427	0	0	0	85	6-22	252.0	224	111	106	22	124-13	204	.243
Major League totals (9 years)		12	20	.375	4.37	1.46	609	0	0	0	121	14-36	376.2	362	195	183	41	187-23	327	.256

MYERS, RODNEY — P

PERSONAL: Born June 26, 1969, in Rockford, Ill. ... 6-1/200. ... Throws right, bats right. ... Full name: Rodney Luther Myers. ... High school: Rockford (Ill.) East. ... College: Wisconsin.

TRANSACTIONS/CAREER NOTES: Selected by Kansas City Royals organization in 12th round of free-agent draft (June 4, 1990). ... On disabled list (May 17-June 3 and June 21-September 15, 1994; and June 30-July 21, 1995). ... Selected by Chicago Cubs from Royals organization in Rule 5 major league draft (December 4, 1995). ... On Iowa disabled list (June 7-15, 1998). ... Traded by Cubs to San Diego Padres for OF Gary Matthews Jr. (March 23, 2000). ... On San Diego disabled list (March 29-May 5 and May 12, 2000-remainder of season); included rehabilitation assignment to Rancho Cucamonga (April 30-May 5). ... On San Diego disabled list (May 20-June 19, 2001); included rehabilitation assignment to Portland (June 14-19). ... Granted free agency (October 8, 2001). ... Re-signed by Padres organization (March 11, 2002). ... Granted free agency (October 15, 2002). ... Signed by Los Angeles Dodgers (December 29, 2002).

CAREER HITTING: 3-for-18 (.167), 2 R, 1 2B, 0 3B, 0 HR, 1 RBI.

Year League	W	L	Pct.	ERA	WHIP	G	GS	CG	ShO	Hld.	Sv.-Opp.	IP	H	R	ER	HR	BB-IBB	SO	Avg.
1990— Eugene (NW)	0	2	.000	1.19	1.41	6	4	0	0	...	0-...	22.2	19	9	3	2	13-0	17	.226
1991— Appleton (Midw.)	1	1	.500	2.60	1.73	9	4	0	0	...	0-...	27.2	22	9	8	0	26-0	29	.224
1992— Lethbridge (Pio.)	5	•8	.385	4.01	1.49	15	15	*5	0	...	0-...	*103.1	93	57	46	3	61-1	76	.245
1993— Rockford (Midwest)	7	3	.700	1.79	0.97	12	12	5	2	...	0-...	85.1	65	22	17	3	18-0	65	.217
— Memphis (Sou.)	3	6	.333	5.62	1.60	12	12	1	1	...	0-...	65.2	73	46	41	8	32-0	42	.294
1994— Wilmington (Caro.)	1	1	.500	4.82	1.07	4	0	0	0	...	1-...	9.1	9	6	5	1	1-0	9	.250
— Memphis (Sou.)	5	1	.833	1.03	1.06	42	0	0	0	...	9-...	69.2	45	20	8	3	29-2	53	.184
1995— Omaha (Am. Assoc.)	4	5	.444	4.10	1.47	38	0	0	0	...	2-...	48.1	52	26	22	5	19-1	38	.277
1996— Chicago (N.L.)	2	1	.667	4.68	1.47	45	0	0	0	1	0-0	67.1	61	38	35	6	38-3	50	.243
1997— Iowa (Am. Assoc.)	7	8	.467	4.09	1.27	24	23	1	0	...	0-0	140.2	140	76	64	18	38-1	79	.261
— Chicago (N.L.)	0	0	...	6.00	2.11	5	1	0	0	0	0-0	9.0	12	6	6	1	7-1	6	.333
1998— Iowa (PCL)	7	5	.583	3.91	1.27	33	13	2	1	...	11-...	101.1	84	47	44	10	45-1	86	.226
— Chicago (N.L.)	0	0	...	7.00	1.78	12	0	0	0	0	0-1	18.0	26	14	14	3	6-0	15	.342
1999— Iowa (PCL)	2	4	.333	4.06	1.29	20	1	0	0	...	2-...	31.0	29	18	14	3	11-3	24	.248
— Chicago (N.L.)	3	1	.750	4.38	1.51	46	0	0	0	8	0-1	63.2	71	34	31	10	25-2	41	.289
2000— Rancho Cuca. (Calif.)	0	0	...	0.00	0.50	3	2	0	0	...	0-...	4.0	2	0	0	0	0-0	4	.154
— San Diego (N.L.)	0	0	...	4.50	1.00	3	0	0	0	0	0-0	2.0	2	1	1	0	0-0	3	.250
2001— San Diego (N.L.)	1	2	.333	5.32	1.54	37	0	0	0	3	1-2	47.1	53	31	28	6	20-0	29	.291
— Portland (PCL)	1	1	.500	3.00	1.20	8	1	0	0	...	0-...	15.0	13	5	5	1	5-0	14	.245
2002— Portland (PCL)	5	2	.714	3.70	1.25	42	0	0	0	...	4-...	48.2	48	23	20	2	13-1	35	.259
— San Diego (N.L.)	1	1	.500	5.91	1.83	14	0	0	0	2	0-...	21.1	29	20	14	1	10-0	11	.333
2003— Las Vegas (PCL)	9	1	.900	3.30	1.24	46	1	0	0	...	1-...	71.0	66	32	26	4	22-1	48	.246
— Los Angeles (N.L.)	0	0	...	6.00	1.56	4	0	0	0	0	0-0	9.0	10	7	6	1	4-0	5	.270
Major League totals (8 years)	**7**	**5**	**.583**	**5.11**	**1.57**	**166**	**1**	**0**	**0**	**14**	**1-4**	**237.2**	**264**	**151**	**135**	**28**	**110-6**	**160**	**.286**

MYETTE, AARON   P

PERSONAL: Born September 26, 1977, in New Westminster, British Columbia. ... 6-4/210. ... Throws right, bats right. ... Full name: Aaron Kenneth Myette. ... Name pronounced: MY-ett. ... High school: Johnston Heights Sectional (Surrey, B.C.). ... Junior college: Central Arizona College.

TRANSACTIONS/CAREER NOTES: Selected by Seattle Mariners organization in 17th round of free-agent draft (June 1, 1995); did not sign. ... Selected by Chicago White Sox organization in supplemental round ("sandwich pick" between first and second round, 43rd pick overall) of free-agent draft (June 3, 1997); pick received as part of compensation for Florida Marlins signing P Alex Fernandez. ... On Hickory disabled list (April 2-May 2, 1998). ... On Birmingham disabled list (July 25-August 2, 1999). ... On Chicago disabled list (March 25-May 9, 2000). ... Traded by White Sox with P Brian Schmack to Texas Rangers for SS Royce Clayton (December 14, 2000). ... Traded by Rangers with 1B Travis Hafner to Cleveland Indians for C Einar Diaz and P Ryan Drese (December 6, 2002). ... On Cleveland disabled list (March 26-April 20, 2003); included rehabilitation assignment to Buffalo. ... Traded by Indians to Philadelphia Phillies for OF Lyle Mouton (July 9, 2003). ... Recalled from rehab assignment from Buffalo (April 26, 2003). ... Sent outright to Buffalo (May 1, 2003).

CAREER HITTING: 0-for-0 (.000), 0 R, 0 2B, 0 3B, 0 HR, 0 RBI.

Year League	W	L	Pct.	ERA	WHIP	G	GS	CG	ShO	Hld.	Sv.-Opp.	IP	H	R	ER	HR	BB-IBB	SO	Avg.
1997— Bristol (Appal.)	4	3	.571	3.61	1.25	9	8	1	0	...	0-...	47.1	39	28	19	9	20-0	50	.207
— Hickory (S. Atl.)	3	1	.750	1.14	0.95	5	5	0	0	...	0-...	31.2	19	6	4	1	11-0	27	.178
1998— Hickory (S. Atl.)	9	4	.692	2.47	1.12	17	17	0	0	...	0-...	102.0	84	43	28	4	30-0	103	.223
— Winston-Salem (Caro.)	4	2	.667	2.01	1.03	6	6	1	1	...	0-...	44.2	32	14	10	4	14-0	54	.198
1999— Birmingham (Sou.)	12	7	.632	3.66	1.31	28	•28	0	0	...	0-...	164.2	138	76	67	19	77-0	135	.225
— Chicago (A.L.)	0	2	.000	6.32	1.98	4	3	0	0	0	0-0	15.2	17	11	11	2	14-1	11	.266
2000— Birmingham (Sou.)	2	0	1.000	3.52	1.24	3	3	0	0	...	0-...	15.1	11	7	6	1	8-0	21	.190
— Charlotte (Int'l)	5	5	.500	4.35	1.42	19	18	0	0	...	0-...	111.2	103	58	54	18	56-0	85	.245
— Chicago (A.L.)	0	0	...	0.00	1.50	2	0	0	0	0	0-0	2.2	0	0	0	0	4-0	1	.000
2001— Oklahoma (PCL)	4	3	.571	3.73	1.34	12	12	2	0	...	0-...	70.0	64	32	29	5	30-0	76	.241
— Texas (A.L.)	4	5	.444	7.14	1.62	19	15	0	0	0	0-0	80.2	94	65	64	12	37-0	67	.293
— Tulsa (Texas)	1	0	1.000	0.00	0.67	1	1	0	0	...	0-...	6.0	3	0	0	0	1-0	2	.143
2002— Oklahoma (PCL)	7	4	.636	3.14	1.23	16	16	2	1	...	0-...	106.0	86	41	37	5	44-0	106	.222
— Texas (A.L.)	2	5	.286	10.06	2.17	15	12	0	0	0	0-0	48.1	64	57	54	11	41-0	48	.325
2003— Akron (East.)	0	0	...	0.00	0.40	3	0	0	0	...	0-...	5.0	0	0	0	0	2-0	7	.000
— Cleveland (A.L.)	0	0	...	23.63	3.38	2	0	0	0	0	0-0	2.2	7	7	7	1	2-0	1	.467
— Buffalo (Int'l)	0	0	...	4.59	1.68	23	1	0	0	...	1-...	33.1	33	21	17	4	23-1	25	.262
— Scran./W.B. (I.L.)	5	4	.556	4.27	1.19	11	10	0	0	...	0-...	59.0	50	28	28	4	20-0	54	.229
Major League totals (5 years)	**6**	**12**	**.333**	**8.16**	**1.87**	**42**	**30**	**0**	**0**	**0**	**0-0**	**150.0**	**182**	**140**	**136**	**26**	**98-1**	**128**	**.301**

NADY, XAVIER   OF

PERSONAL: Born November 14, 1978, in Salinas, Calif. ... 6-0/180. ... Bats right, throws right. ... Full name: Xavier C. Nady. ... Name pronounced: ZAV-yer NAY-dee. ... High school: Salinas (Calif.). ... College: UC-Berkeley.

TRANSACTIONS/CAREER NOTES: Selected by San Diego Padres organization in second round of free-agent draft (June 5, 2000).

2003 GAMES PLAYED BY POSITION (MLB): OF—105.

Year Team (League)	Pos.	G	AB	R	H	2B	3B	HR	RBI	BB	SO	HBP	GDP	SB-CS	Avg.	OBP	SLG	OPS	E	Pct.
2000— San Diego (N.L.)		1	1	1	1	0	0	0	0	0	0	0	0	0-0	1.000	1.000	1.000	2.000	...	...
2001— Lake Elsinore (Calif.)	1B	137	524	96	158	38	1	26	100	62	109	10	14	6-0	.302	.381	.527	.908	10	.989
2002— Lake Elsinore (Calif.)	OF	45	169	41	47	6	3	13	37	28	40	1	2	2-0	.278	.382	.580	.962	0	1.000
— Portland (PCL)	OF	85	315	46	89	12	1	10	43	20	60	3	11	0-1	.283	.329	.422	.752	2	.981
2003— Portland (PCL)	OF-DH	37	136	19	36	7	0	7	23	12	28	2	2	0-0	.265	.329	.471	.800	3	.954
— San Diego (N.L.)	OF	110	371	50	99	17	1	9	39	24	74	6	14	6-2	.267	.321	.391	.712	6	.968
Major League totals (2 years)		**111**	**372**	**51**	**100**	**17**	**1**	**9**	**39**	**24**	**74**	**6**	**14**	**6-2**	**.269**	**.323**	**.392**	**.715**	**6**	**.968**

NAGY, CHARLES   P

PERSONAL: Born May 5, 1967, in Fairfield, Conn. ... 6-3/200. ... Throws right, bats left. ... Full name: Charles Harrison Nagy. ... Name pronounced: NAG-ee. ... High school: Roger Ludlowe (Fairfield, Conn.). ... College: Connecticut.

TRANSACTIONS/CAREER NOTES: Selected by Cleveland Indians organization in first round (17th pick overall) of free-agent draft (June 1, 1988); pick received as part of compensation for San Francisco Giants signing Type A free-agent OF Brett Butler. ... On Cleveland disabled list (May 16-October 1, 1993); included rehabilitation assignment to Canton/Akron (June 10-24). ... On Cleveland disabled list (May 17-September 14 and September 25, 2000-remainder of season); included rehabilitation assignments to Buffalo (June 19-July 12 and September 3-14) and Akron (July 13 and August 28-September 2). ... On Cleveland disabled list (March 31-June 1 and August 24, 2001-remainder of season); included rehabilitation assignment to Buffalo (April 30-May 29). ... On Cleveland disabled list (June 5-July 20, 2002); included rehabilitation assignment to Buffalo (June 19-July 18). ... Granted free agency (October 28, 2002). ... Signed by San Diego Padres organization (December 20, 2002). ... Contract purchased from Portland (May 16, 2003). ... Sent outright to Portland (June 1, 2003). ... Elected free agency (June 6, 2003). ... Signed by San Diego Padres (December 20, 2002).

CAREER HITTING: 2-for-19 (.105), 3 R, 0 2B, 0 3B, 0 HR, 0 RBI.

Year League	W	L	Pct.	ERA	WHIP	G	GS	CG	ShO	Hld.	Sv.-Opp.	IP	H	R	ER	HR	BB-IBB	SO	Avg.
1989— Kinston (Caro.)	8	4	.667	1.51	0.98	13	13	6	* 4	...	0-...	95.1	69	22	16	0	24-0	99	.202
—Cant./Akr. (Eastern)	4	5	.444	3.35	1.43	15	14	2	0	...	0-...	94.0	102	44	35	4	32-0	65	.283
1990—Cant./Akr. (Eastern)	13	8	.619	2.52	0.98	23	23	•9	0	...	0-...	175.0	132	62	49	9	39-0	99	.206
—Cleveland (A.L.)	2	4	.333	5.91	1.73	9	8	0	0	0	0-0	45.2	58	31	30	7	21-1	26	.315
1991—Cleveland (A.L.)	10	15	.400	4.13	1.39	33	33	6	1	0	0-0	211.1	228	103	97	15	66-7	109	.275
1992—Cleveland (A.L.)	17	10	.630	2.96	1.20	33	33	10	3	0	0-0	252.0	245	91	83	11	57-1	169	.260
1993—Cleveland (A.L.)	2	6	.250	6.29	1.62	9	9	1	0	0	0-0	48.2	66	38	34	6	13-1	30	.322
—Cant./Akr. (Eastern)	0	0	...	1.13	1.25	2	2	0	0	...	0-...	8.0	8	1	1	0	2-0	4	.267
1994—Cleveland (A.L.)	10	8	.556	3.45	1.32	23	23	3	0	0	0-0	169.1	175	76	65	15	48-1	108	.265
1995—Cleveland (A.L.)	16	6	.727	4.55	1.43	29	29	2	1	0	0-0	178.0	194	95	90	20	61-0	139	.278
1996—Cleveland (A.L.)	17	5	.773	3.41	1.25	32	32	5	0	0	0-0	222.0	217	89	84	21	61-2	167	.255
1997—Cleveland (A.L.)	15	11	.577	4.28	1.45	34	34	1	1	0	0-0	227.0	253	115	108	27	77-4	149	.283
1998—Cleveland (A.L.)	15	10	.600	5.22	1.50	33	33	2	0	0	0-0	210.1	250	* 139	122	34	66-12	120	.298
1999—Cleveland (A.L.)	17	11	.607	4.95	1.47	33	32	1	0	0	0-0	202.0	238	120	111	26	59-4	126	.293
2000—Cleveland (A.L.)	2	7	.222	8.21	1.61	11	11	0	0	0	0-0	57.0	71	53	52	15	21-2	41	.300
—Buffalo (Int'l)	1	1	.500	4.30	1.09	3	3	0	0	...	0-...	14.2	12	7	7	2	4-0	5	.214
—Akron (East.)	1	0	1.000	1.00	0.67	2	2	0	0	...	0-...	9.0	4	1	1	0	2-0	10	.129
2001—Buffalo (Int'l)	5	1	.833	2.56	1.27	6	6	0	0	...	0-...	38.2	40	12	11	0	9-0	18	.267
—Cleveland (A.L.)	5	6	.455	6.40	1.73	15	13	0	0	0	0-0	70.1	102	53	50	10	20-1	29	.342
2002—Cleveland (A.L.)	1	4	.200	8.88	1.83	19	7	0	0	0	0-0	48.2	76	51	48	10	13-1	22	.360
—Buffalo (Int'l)	1	2	.333	3.19	1.15	5	5	2	0	...	0-...	36.2	38	18	13	6	4-0	18	.268
2003—Portland (PCL)	1	0	1.000	1.23	1.09	3	1	0	0	...	1-...	7.1	8	1	1	1	0-0	5	.296
—San Diego (N.L.)	0	2	.000	4.38	1.46	5	0	0	0	0	0-0	12.1	15	7	6	0	3-0	7	.313
American League totals (13 years)	129	103	.556	4.51	1.42	313	297	31	6	0	0-0	1942.1	2173	1054	974	217	583-37	1235	.284
National League totals (1 year)	0	2	.000	4.38	1.46	5	0	0	0	0	0-0	12.1	15	7	6	0	3-0	7	.313
Major League totals (14 years)	129	105	.551	4.51	1.42	318	297	31	6	0	0-0	1954.2	2188	1061	980	217	586-37	1242	.284

NAKAMURA, MIKE   P

PERSONAL: Born September 6, 1976, in Nara, Japan. ... 5-10/178. ... Throws right, bats right. ... Full name: Micheal Yoshihide Nakamura. ... College: South Alabama.

TRANSACTIONS/CAREER NOTES: Signed by Minnesota Twins as a non-drafted free agent (December 24, 1997).

CAREER HITTING: 0-for-0 (.000), 0 R, 0 2B, 0 3B, 0 HR, 0 RBI.

Year League	W	L	Pct.	ERA	WHIP	G	GS	CG	ShO	Hld.	Sv.-Opp.	IP	H	R	ER	HR	BB-IBB	SO	Avg.
1998— Fort Wayne (Midw.)	2	5	.286	3.26	1.39	29	9	0	0	...	1-...	80.0	82	41	29	8	29-0	70	.266
—Fort Myers (Fla. St.)	1	3	.250	3.45	1.43	8	6	1	0	...	0-...	28.2	28	15	11	3	10-0	21	.257
1999—Fort Myers (Fla. St.)	2	0	1.000	1.83	0.71	14	0	0	0	...	2-...	19.2	9	5	4	1	5-0	18	.138
2000—Fort Myers (Fla. St.)	1	0	1.000	1.52	1.06	32	0	0	0	...	12-...	41.1	33	9	7	0	11-1	46	.228
2001—New Britain (East.)	5	1	.833	1.77	1.15	48	1	0	0	...	5-...	86.1	75	20	17	3	24-5	109	.229
2002—Edmonton (PCL)	4	3	.571	4.74	1.23	46	4	0	0	...	2-...	87.1	85	51	46	7	22-0	80	.254
2003—Minnesota (A.L.)	0	0	...	7.82	1.74	12	0	0	0	1	1-1	12.2	20	11	11	4	2-0	14	.339
—Rochester (Int'l)	6	6	.500	2.99	1.26	43	0	0	0	...	2-...	78.1	71	28	26	4	28-1	95	.244
Major League totals (1 year)	0	0	...	7.82	1.74	12	0	0	0	1	1-1	12.2	20	11	11	4	2-0	14	.339

NANCE, SHANE   P

PERSONAL: Born September 7, 1977, in Pasadena, Texas. ... 5-8/180. ... Throws left, bats left. ... Full name: Joseph Shane Nance. ... High school: Dobie (Texas). ... College: Houston.

TRANSACTIONS/CAREER NOTES: Selected by Los Angeles Dodgers organization in 11th round of free-agent draft (June 5, 2000). ... Traded by Dodgers with P Ben Diggins to Milwaukee Brewers for 3B Tyler Houston and a player to be named later (July 23, 2002); Dodgers acquired P Brian Mallette to complete deal (October 16, 2002). ... On Milwaukee disabled list (September 1, 2002-remainder of season).

CAREER HITTING: 1-for-3 (.333), 0 R, 0 2B, 0 3B, 0 HR, 1 RBI.

Year League	W	L	Pct.	ERA	WHIP	G	GS	CG	ShO	Hld.	Sv.-Opp.	IP	H	R	ER	HR	BB-IBB	SO	Avg.
2000— Yakima (NW)	2	4	.333	2.48	1.09	12	9	0	0	...	0-...	58.0	41	19	16	1	22-0	66	.203
2001—Vero Beach (FSL)	6	3	.667	2.63	1.02	21	0	0	0	...	4-...	48.0	28	15	14	3	21-1	63	.164
—Jacksonville (Sou.)	7	0	1.000	1.59	1.06	28	0	0	0	...	1-...	45.1	31	11	8	4	17-1	44	.195
2002—Las Vegas (PCL)	11	3	.786	4.17	1.44	37	0	0	0	...	1-...	58.1	58	32	27	5	26-1	53	.260
—Indianapolis (Int'l)	3	0	1.000	0.00	1.08	9	0	0	0	...	0-...	16.2	12	0	0	0	6-0	10	.207
—Milwaukee (N.L.)	0	0	...	4.26	1.20	4	0	0	0	0	0-0	6.1	4	3	3	1	4-0	5	.174
2003—Indianapolis (Int'l)	2	4	.333	1.38	0.90	35	1	0	0	...	3-...	52.1	34	10	8	4	13-1	53	.185
—Milwaukee (N.L.)	0	2	.000	4.81	1.81	26	0	0	0	1	0-1	24.1	34	16	13	5	10-1	25	.327
Major League totals (2 years)	0	2	.000	4.70	1.70	30	0	0	0	1	0-1	30.2	38	19	16	6	14-1	30	.299

NATHAN, JOE   P

PERSONAL: Born November 22, 1974, in Houston, Texas. ... 6-4/207. ... Throws right, bats right. ... Full name: Joseph Michael Nathan. ... High school: Pine Bush (N.Y.). ... College: SUNY-Stony Brook.

TRANSACTIONS/CAREER NOTES: Selected by San Francisco Giants organization in sixth round of free-agent draft (June 1, 1995). ... On San Francisco disabled list (May 13-June 6 and July 14-August 19, 2000); included rehabilitation assignments to San Jose (May 26-31), Bakersfield (May 31-June 6) and Fresno (August 2-19).

CAREER HITTING: 10-for-61 (.164), 4 R, 3 2B, 0 3B, 2 HR, 4 RBI.

N

Year League	W	L	Pct.	ERA	WHIP	G	GS	CG	ShO	Hld.	Sv.-Opp.	IP	H	R	ER	HR	BB-IBB	SO	Avg.
1996—											Did not play.								
1997—Salem-Keizer (NW)	2	1	.667	2.47	1.27	18	5	0	0	...	2-...	62.0	53	22	17	7	26-0	44	.243
1998—San Jose (Calif.)	8	6	.571	3.32	1.21	22	22	0	0	...	0-...	122.0	100	51	45	13	48-0	118	.224
—Shreveport (Texas)	1	3	.250	8.80	1.89	4	4	0	0	...	0-...	15.1	20	15	15	4	9-0	10	.317
1999—Shreveport (Texas)	0	1	.000	3.12	1.38	2	2	0	0	...	0-...	8.2	5	4	3	0	7-0	7	.179
—San Francisco (N.L.)	7	4	.636	4.18	1.44	19	14	0	0	0	1-1	90.1	84	45	42	17	46-0	54	.243
—Fresno (PCL)	6	4	.600	4.46	1.39	13	13	1	0	...	0-...	74.2	68	44	37	11	36-0	82	.244
2000—San Francisco (N.L.)	5	2	.714	5.21	1.63	20	15	0	0	0	0-1	93.1	89	63	54	12	63-4	61	.255
—San Jose (Calif.)	0	1	.000	3.60	1.00	1	1	0	0	...	0-...	5.0	4	2	2	1	1-0	2	.235
—Bakersfield (Calif.)	1	0	1.000	5.06	1.69	1	1	0	0	...	0-...	5.1	2	3	3	0	7-0	6	.118
—Fresno (PCL)	0	2	.000	4.40	1.53	3	3	0	0	...	0-...	14.1	15	8	7	4	7-0	9	.268
2001—Fresno (PCL)	0	5	.000	7.77	2.07	10	10	0	0	...	0-...	46.1	63	47	40	13	33-0	21	.333
—Shreveport (Texas)	3	6	.333	6.93	1.76	21	7	0	0	...	0-...	62.1	73	49	48	11	37-5	33	.299
2002—Fresno (PCL)	6	12	.333	5.60	1.65	31	25	1	0	...	0-...	146.1	167	97	91	20	74-0	117	.283
—San Francisco (N.L.)	0	0	...			0	0	0	0	0	0-0	3.2	1	0	0	0	0-0	2	.083
2003—San Francisco (N.L.)	12	4	.750	2.96	1.06	78	0	0	0	20	0-3	79.0	51	26	26	7	33-3	83	.186
Major League totals (4 years)	24	10	.706	4.12	1.38	121	29	0	0	20	1-5	266.1	225	134	122	36	142-7	200	.229

NEAGLE, DENNY P

PERSONAL: Born September 13, 1968, in Annapolis, Md. ... 6-3/225. ... Throws left, bats left. ... Full name: Dennis Edward Neagle. ... Name pronounced: NAY-gul. ... High school: Arundel (Gambrills, Md.). ... College: Minnesota.

TRANSACTIONS/CAREER NOTES: Selected by Minnesota Twins organization in third round of free-agent draft (June 5, 1989). ... On Portland disabled list (April 5-23, 1991). ... On Minnesota disabled list (July 28-August 12, 1991). ... Traded by Twins with OF Midre Cummings to Pittsburgh Pirates for P John Smiley (March 17, 1992). ... Traded by Pirates to Atlanta Braves for 1B Ron Wright and a player to be named later (August 28, 1996); Pirates acquired P Jason Schmidt to complete deal (August 30, 1996). ... Traded by Braves with OF Michael Tucker and P Rob Bell to Cincinnati Reds for 2B Bret Boone and P Mike Remlinger (November 10, 1998). ... On Cincinnati disabled list (March 24-April 21 and May 24-July 29, 1999); included rehabilitation assignment to Indianapolis (April 8-21 and July 23-29). ... Traded by Reds with OF Mike Frank to New York Yankees for 3B Drew Henson, OF Jackson Melian, P Brian Reith and P Ed Yarnall (July 12, 2000). ... Granted free agency (October 31, 2000). ... Signed by Colorado Rockies (December 4, 2000). ... On disabled list (June 9-24, 2001). ... On disabled list (March 27, 2003). ... Recalled from rehab assignment (May 19, 2003). ... Transferred to Emergency disabled list (May 23, 2003). ... Sent on rehab assignment to Colorado Springs (June 7, 2003). ... Reinstated from Emergency disabled list; optioned to Colorado Springs (June 17, 2003). ... Activated from 60-day disabled list (July 5, 2003). ... Placed on 15-day disabled list (July 21, 2003). ... Transferred to Emergency disabled list (July 30, 2003).

CAREER HITTING: 87-for-531 (.164), 31 R, 17 2B, 0 3B, 5 HR, 44 RBI.

Year League	W	L	Pct.	ERA	WHIP	G	GS	CG	ShO	Hld.	Sv.-Opp.	IP	H	R	ER	HR	BB-IBB	SO	Avg.
1989—Elizabethton (Appal.)	1	2	.333	4.50	1.27	6	3	0	0	...	1-...	22.0	20	11	11	1	8-0	32	.250
—Kenosha (Midw.)	2	1	.667	1.65	0.94	6	6	1	1	...	0-...	43.2	25	9	8	3	16-0	40	.175
1990—Visalia (Calif.)	8	0	1.000	1.43	0.87	10	10	0	0	...	0-...	63.0	39	13	10	2	16-0	92	.175
—Orlando (Sou.)	12	3	.800	2.45	1.03	17	17	4	1	...	0-...	121.1	94	40	33	11	31-0	94	.212
1991—Portland (PCL)	9	4	.692	3.27	1.27	19	17	1	1	...	0-...	104.2	101	41	38	6	32-1	94	.254
—Minnesota (A.L.)	0	1	.000	4.05	1.75	7	3	0	0	0	0-0	20.0	28	9	9	3	7-2	14	.329
1992—Pittsburgh (N.L.)	4	6	.400	4.48	1.44	55	6	0	0	5	2-4	86.1	81	46	43	9	43-8	77	.247
1993—Pittsburgh (N.L.)	3	5	.375	5.31	1.46	50	7	0	0	6	1-1	81.1	82	49	48	10	37-3	73	.258
—Buffalo (A.A.)	0	0	...	0.00	1.50	3	0	0	0	...	0-...	3.1	3	0	0	0	2-0	6	.250
1994—Pittsburgh (N.L.)	9	10	.474	5.12	1.34	24	24	2	0	0	0-0	137.0	135	80	78	18	49-3	122	.259
1995—Pittsburgh (N.L.)	13	8	.619	3.43	1.27	31	•31	5	1	0	0-0	•209.2	*221	91	80	20	45-3	150	.273
1996—Pittsburgh (N.L.)	14	6	.700	3.05	1.20	27	27	1	0	0	0-0	182.2	186	67	62	21	34-2	131	.267
—Atlanta (N.L.)	2	3	.400	5.59	1.40	6	6	1	0	0	0-0	38.2	40	26	24	5	14-0	18	.268
1997—Atlanta (N.L.)	*20	5	.800	2.97	1.08	34	34	4	4	0	0-0	233.1	204	87	77	18	49-5	172	.233
1998—Atlanta (N.L.)	16	11	.593	3.55	1.22	32	31	5	2	0	0-0	210.1	196	91	83	25	60-3	165	.250
1999—Indianapolis (Int'l)	2	0	1.000	4.67	0.75	3	3	0	0	...	0-...	17.1	11	9	9	2	2-0	9	.177
—Cincinnati (N.L.)	9	5	.643	4.27	1.21	20	19	0	0	0	0-0	111.2	95	54	53	23	40-3	76	.229
2000—Cincinnati (N.L.)	8	2	.800	3.52	1.37	18	18	0	0	0	0-0	117.2	111	48	46	15	50-3	88	.247
—New York (A.L.)	7	7	.500	5.81	1.42	16	15	1	0	0	0-0	91.1	99	61	59	16	31-1	58	.278
2001—Colorado (N.L.)	9	8	.529	5.38	1.48	30	30	0	0	0	0-0	170.2	192	107	102	29	60-3	139	.284
2002—Colorado (N.L.)	8	11	.421	5.26	1.42	35	28	1	0	2	0-0	164.1	170	101	96	26	63-5	111	.266
2003—Visalia (Calif.)	1	0	1.000	0.00	0.60	2	2	0	0	...	0-...	10.0	4	0	0	0	2-0	13	.118
—Colo. Springs (PCL)	3	0	1.000	3.38	1.33	4	4	0	0	...	0-...	24.0	28	10	9	2	4-0	16	.292
—Colorado (N.L.)	2	4	.333	7.90	1.67	7	7	0	0	0	0-0	35.1	47	31	31	12	12-0	21	.320
American League totals (2 years)	7	8	.467	5.50	1.48	23	18	1	0	0	0-0	111.1	127	70	68	19	38-3	72	.288
National League totals (12 years)	117	84	.582	4.16	1.30	369	268	19	7	13	3-5	1779.0	1760	878	823	231	556-41	1343	.258
Major League totals (13 years)	124	92	.574	4.24	1.31	392	286	20	7	13	3-5	1890.1	1887	948	891	250	594-44	1415	.260

NEAL, BLAINE P

PERSONAL: Born April 6, 1978, in Marlton, N.J. ... 6-5/240. ... Throws right, bats left. ... High school: Bishop Eustace Prep (Pennsauken, N.J.).

TRANSACTIONS/CAREER NOTES: Selected by Florida Marlins organization in fourth round of free-agent draft (June 4, 1996).

CAREER HITTING: 0-for-0 (.000), 0 R, 0 2B, 0 3B, 0 HR, 0 RBI.

Year League	W	L	Pct.	ERA	WHIP	G	GS	CG	ShO	Hld.	Sv.-Opp.	IP	H	R	ER	HR	BB-IBB	SO	Avg.
1996—GC Marlins (GCL)	1	1	.500	4.60	1.30	7	5	0	0	...	1-...	29.1	32	18	15	1	6-0	15	.274
1997—GC Marlins (GCL)	4	1	.800	3.63	1.57	10	0	0	0	...	1-...	22.1	24	11	9	1	11-0	19	.267
1999—Kane County (Midwest)	4	2	.667	2.32	1.00	26	0	0	0	...	6-...	31.0	21	8	8	2	10-0	31	.200
2000—Brevard County (FSL)	2	2	.500	2.15	1.18	41	0	0	0	...	11-...	54.1	40	27	13	1	24-3	65	.200
2001—Portland (East.)	2	3	.400	2.36	1.20	54	0	0	0	...	21-...	53.1	43	17	14	1	21-3	45	.218
—Florida (N.L.)	0	0	...	6.75	2.25	4	0	0	0	0	0-0	5.1	7	4	4	0	5-0	3	.304
2002—Calgary (PCL)	3	1	.750	2.90	1.35	29	0	0	0	...	11-...	31.0	27	11	10	2	15-1	26	.233
—Florida (N.L.)	3	0	1.000	2.73	1.39	32	0	0	0	2	0-0	33.0	32	12	10	1	14-2	33	.248
2003—Albuquerque (PCL)	3	2	.600	2.33	1.53	40	0	0	0	...	21-...	46.1	55	22	12	1	16-2	32	.304
—Florida (N.L.)	0	0	...	8.14	2.24	18	0	0	0	2	0-0	21.0	38	20	19	2	9-1	10	.413
Major League totals (3 years)	3	0	1.000	5.01	1.77	54	0	0	0	4	0-0	59.1	77	36	33	3	28-3	46	.316

NELSON, JEFF   P

PERSONAL: Born November 17, 1966, in Baltimore, Md. ... 6-8/225. ... Throws right, bats right. ... Full name: Jeffrey Allan Nelson. ... High school: Catonsville (Md.). ... Junior college: Cantonsville (Md.) Community College.

TRANSACTIONS/CAREER NOTES: Selected by Los Angeles Dodgers organization in 22nd round of free-agent draft (June 4, 1984). ... On Great Falls disabled list (April 10-June 4, 1986). ... Selected by Seattle Mariners organization from Dodgers organization in Rule 5 minor league draft (December 9, 1986). ... On disabled list (July 16, 1989-remainder of season). ... Traded by Mariners with 1B Tino Martinez and P Jim Mecir to New York Yankees for P Sterling Hitchcock and 3B Russ Davis (December 7, 1995). ... On suspended list (September 3-5, 1996). ... On suspended list (May 28-29, 1998). ... On New York disabled list (June 26-September 4, 1998); included rehabilitation assignment to Tampa (August 31-September 4). ... On New York disabled list (May 3-20 and June 3-August 11, 1999); included rehabilitation assignments to Gulf Coast Yankees (August 2-4 and August 9-10) and Tampa (August 5-8). ... Granted free agency (October 31, 2000). ... Signed by Mariners (December 4, 2000). ... On Seattle disabled list (May 8-June 27, 2002); included rehabilitation assignment to Everett (June 25-27). ... Traded by Mariners to New York Yankees for P Armando Benitez (August 6, 2003).

CAREER HITTING: 0-for-2 (.000), 0 R, 0 2B, 0 3B, 0 HR, 0 RBI.

Year League	W	L	Pct.	ERA	WHIP	G	GS	CG	ShO	Hld.	Sv.-Opp.	IP	H	R	ER	HR	BB-IBB	SO	Avg.
1984— Great Falls (Pio.)	0	0	...	54.00	9.00	1	0	0	0	...	0-...	.2	3	4	4	1	3-0	1	...
— GC Dodgers (GCL)	0	0	...	1.35	0.90	9	0	0	0	...	0-...	13.1	6	3	2	0	6-0	7	.122
1985— GC Dodgers (GCL)	0	5	.000	5.51	2.20	14	7	0	0	...	0-...	47.1	72	50	29	1	32-0	31	.344
1986— Bakersfield (Calif.)	0	7	.000	6.69	2.29	24	11	0	0	...	0-...	71.1	79	83	53	9	84-1	37	.252
— Great Falls (Pio.)	0	0	...	13.50	4.00	3	0	0	0	...	0-...	2.0	5	3	3	0	3-2	1	...
1987— Salinas (Calif.)	3	7	.300	5.74	1.89	17	16	1	0	...	0-...	80.0	80	61	51	2	71-0	43	.261
1988— San Bernardino (Calif.)	8	9	.471	5.54	1.70	27	27	1	1	...	0-...	149.1	163	115	92	9	91-2	94	.287
1989— Williamsport (Eastern)	7	5	.583	3.31	1.35	15	15	2	0	...	0-...	92.1	72	41	34	2	53-1	61	.217
1990— Williamsport (Eastern)	1	4	.200	6.44	1.92	10	10	0	0	...	0-...	43.1	65	35	31	2	18-1	14	.359
— Peninsula (Caro.)	2	2	.500	3.15	1.20	18	7	1	1	...	6-...	60.0	47	21	21	5	25-1	49	.214
1991— Jacksonville (Sou.)	4	0	1.000	1.27	1.13	21	0	0	0	...	12-...	28.1	23	5	4	0	9-0	34	.225
— Calgary (PCL)	3	4	.429	3.90	1.67	28	0	0	0	...	21-...	32.1	39	19	14	1	15-3	26	.310
1992— Calgary (PCL)	1	0	1.000	0.00	0.27	2	0	0	0	...	0-...	3.2	0	0	0	0	1-0	0	.000
— Seattle (A.L.)	1	7	.125	3.44	1.42	66	0	0	0	6	6-14	81.0	71	34	31	7	44-12	46	.245
1993— Calgary (PCL)	1	0	1.000	1.17	1.04	5	0	0	0	...	1-...	7.2	6	1	1	0	2-0	6	.222
— Seattle (A.L.)	5	3	.625	4.35	1.52	71	0	0	0	17	1-11	60.0	57	30	29	5	34-10	61	.258
1994— Seattle (A.L.)	0	0	...	2.76	1.30	28	0	0	0	2	0-0	42.1	35	18	13	3	20-4	44	.226
— Calgary (PCL)	1	4	.200	2.84	1.11	18	0	0	0	...	8-...	25.1	21	9	8	1	7-1	30	.236
1995— Seattle (A.L.)	7	3	.700	2.17	1.08	62	0	0	0	14	2-4	78.2	58	21	19	4	27-5	96	.209
1996— New York (A.L.)	4	4	.500	4.36	1.49	73	0	0	0	10	2-4	74.1	75	38	36	6	36-1	91	.262
1997— New York (A.L.)	3	7	.300	2.86	1.14	77	0	0	0	22	2-8	78.2	53	32	25	7	37-12	81	.191
1998— New York (A.L.)	5	3	.625	3.79	1.64	45	0	0	0	10	3-6	40.1	44	18	17	1	22-4	35	.278
— Tampa (FSL)	0	0	...	0.00	1.00	2	1	0	0	...	0-...	2.0	1	1	0	0	1-0	4	.143
1999— New York (A.L.)	2	1	.667	4.15	1.62	39	0	0	0	10	1-2	30.1	27	14	14	2	22-2	35	.245
— GC Yankees (GCL)	0	0	...	0.00	1.00	2	2	0	0	...	0-...	2.0	1	0	0	0	1-0	3	.143
— Tampa (FSL)	0	0	...	0.00	1.00	3	3	0	0	...	0-...	3.0	1	0	0	0	2-0	5	.100
2000— New York (A.L.)	8	4	.667	2.45	1.28	73	0	0	0	15	0-4	69.2	44	24	19	2	45-1	71	.183
2001— Seattle (A.L.)	4	3	.571	2.76	1.13	69	0	0	0	26	4-5	65.1	30	21	20	3	44-1	88	.136
2002— Seattle (A.L.)	3	2	.600	3.94	1.38	41	0	0	0	12	2-4	45.2	36	20	20	4	27-3	55	.221
— Everett (Northwest)	0	1	.000	0.00	0.75	1	1	0	0	...	0-...	1.1	1	1	0	0	0-0	4	.200
2003— Seattle (A.L.)	3	2	.600	3.35	1.27	46	0	0	0	6	7-11	37.2	34	16	14	3	14-1	47	.248
— New York (A.L.)	1	0	1.000	4.58	1.53	24	0	0	0	8	1-3	17.2	17	9	9	1	10-2	21	.246
Major League totals (12 years)	**46**	**39**	**.541**	**3.32**	**1.33**	**714**	**0**	**0**	**0**	**158**	**31-76**	**721.2**	**581**	**295**	**266**	**48**	**382-58**	**771**	**.223**

NEN, ROBB   P

PERSONAL: Born November 28, 1969... 6-5/222. ... Throws right, bats right. ... Full name: Robert Allen Nen. ... High school: Los Alamitos (Calif.).

TRANSACTIONS/CAREER NOTES: Selected by Texas Rangers organization in 32nd round of free-agent draft (June 2, 1987). ... On Charlotte disabled list (April 6-26 and May 6-24, 1990). ... On disabled list (April 23-June 10, June 28-July 8 and July 11-September 3, 1991; and May 7-September 9, 1992). ... On Texas disabled list (June 12-July 17, 1993); included rehabilitation assignment to Oklahoma City (June 21-July 17). ... Traded by Rangers with P Kurt Miller to Florida Marlins for P Cris Carpenter (July 17, 1993). ... Traded by Marlins to San Francisco Giants for P Mike Villano, P Joe Fontenot and P Mick Pageler (November 18, 1997). ... On disabled list (March 30-entire 2003 season).

CAREER HITTING: 1-for-15 (.067), 0 R, 0 2B, 0 3B, 0 HR, 0 RBI.

Year League	W	L	Pct.	ERA	WHIP	G	GS	CG	ShO	Hld.	Sv.-Opp.	IP	H	R	ER	HR	BB-IBB	SO	Avg.
1987— GC Rangers (GCL)	0	0	...	7.71	3.00	2	0	0	0	...	0-...	2.1	4	2	2	0	3-1	4	.400
1988— Gastonia (S. Atl.)	0	5	.000	7.45	2.36	14	10	0	0	...	0-...	48.1	69	57	40	5	45-0	36	.319
— Butte (Pio.)	4	5	.444	8.75	2.28	14	13	0	0	...	0-...	48.1	65	55	47	4	45-0	30	.311
1989— Gastonia (S. Atl.)	7	4	.636	2.41	1.24	24	24	1	1	...	0-...	138.1	96	47	37	7	76-0	146	.195
1990— Charlotte (Fla. St.)	1	4	.200	3.69	1.49	11	11	1	0	...	0-...	53.2	44	28	22	1	36-0	38	.230
— Tulsa (Texas)	0	5	.000	5.06	1.65	7	7	0	0	...	0-...	26.2	23	20	15	1	21-0	21	.240
1991— Tulsa (Texas)	0	2	.000	5.79	1.57	6	6	0	0	...	0-...	28.0	24	21	18	6	20-0	23	.242
1992— Tulsa (Texas)	1	1	.500	2.16	0.92	4	4	1	0	...	0-...	25.0	21	7	6	1	2-0	20	.223
1993— Texas (A.L.)	1	1	.500	6.35	2.38	9	3	0	0	0	0-0	22.2	28	17	16	1	26-0	12	.326
— Oklahoma City (A.A.)	0	2	.000	6.67	2.22	6	5	0	0	...	0-...	28.1	45	22	21	3	18-0	12	.381
— Florida (N.L.)	1	0	1.000	7.02	1.65	15	1	0	0	0	0-0	33.1	35	28	26	5	20-0	27	.255
1994— Florida (N.L.)	5	5	.500	2.95	1.09	44	0	0	0	1	15-15	58.0	46	20	19	6	17-2	60	.222
1995— Florida (N.L.)	0	7	.000	3.29	1.29	62	0	0	0	0	23-29	65.2	62	26	24	6	23-3	68	.244
1996— Florida (N.L.)	5	1	.833	1.95	1.06	75	0	0	0	0	35-42	83.0	67	21	18	2	21-6	92	.225
1997— Florida (N.L.)	9	3	.750	3.89	1.51	73	0	0	0	0	35-42	74.0	72	35	32	7	40-7	81	.250
1998— San Francisco (N.L.)	7	7	.500	1.52	0.95	78	0	0	0	0	40-45	88.2	59	21	15	4	25-5	110	.180
1999— San Francisco (N.L.)	3	8	.273	3.98	1.47	72	0	0	0	0	37-46	72.1	79	36	32	8	27-3	77	.275
2000— San Francisco (N.L.)	4	3	.571	1.50	0.85	68	0	0	0	0	41-46	66.0	37	15	11	4	19-1	92	.162
2001— San Francisco (N.L.)	4	5	.444	3.01	1.03	79	0	0	0	*	45-52	77.2	58	28	26	6	22-6	93	.203
2002— San Francisco (N.L.)	6	2	.750	2.20	1.14	68	0	0	0	0	43-51	73.2	64	19	18	2	20-8	81	.232
2003—											Did not play.								
American League totals (1 year)	**1**	**1**	**.500**	**6.35**	**2.38**	**9**	**3**	**0**	**0**	**0**	**0-0**	**22.2**	**28**	**17**	**16**	**1**	**26-0**	**12**	**.326**
National League totals (10 years)	**44**	**41**	**.518**	**2.87**	**1.17**	**634**	**1**	**0**	**0**	**1**	**314-368**	**692.1**	**579**	**249**	**221**	**50**	**234-41**	**781**	**.224**
Major League totals (10 years)	**45**	**42**	**.517**	**2.98**	**1.21**	**643**	**4**	**0**	**0**	**1**	**314-368**	**715.0**	**607**	**266**	**237**	**51**	**260-41**	**793**	**.227**

N

PERSONAL: Born March 9, 1978, in Napa, Calif. ... 5-10/175. ... Throws right, bats both. ... Full name: Michael Neu. ... Name pronounced: new. ... College: Miami (Fla.).
TRANSACTIONS/CAREER NOTES: Selected by Cincinnati Reds organization in 29th round of free-agent draft (June 2, 1999). ... Selected by Oakland Athletics in Rule 5 draft (December 16, 2002).
CAREER HITTING: 0-for-0 (.000), 0 R, 0 2B, 0 3B, 0 HR, 0 RBI.

Year League	W	L	Pct.	ERA	WHIP	G	GS	CG	ShO	Hld.	Sv.-Opp.	IP	H	R	ER	HR	BB-IBB	SO	Avg.
1999— Rockford (Midwest)	0	1	.000	4.50	1.61	9	0	0	0	...	1-...	18.0	17	10	9	1	12-1	23	.246
2000— Clinton (Midw.)	7	7	.500	3.13	1.43	58	0	0	0	...	24-...	69.0	47	27	24	5	52-8	95	.191
2001— Mudville (Calif.)	3	2	.600	2.37	1.24	53	0	0	0	...	21-...	64.2	50	21	17	3	30-4	102	.209
2002— Chattanooga (Sou.)	1	0	1.000	1.33	1.15	21	0	0	0	...	7-...	27.0	22	4	4	0	9-1	38	.218
— Louisville (Int'l)	2	3	.400	4.02	1.31	40	0	0	0	...	16-...	40.1	35	19	18	4	18-0	47	.232
2003— Oakland (A.L.)	0	0	...	3.64	1.64	32	0	0	0	0	1-1	42.0	43	18	17	2	26-2	20	.261
Major League totals (1 year)	0	0	...	3.64	1.64	32	0	0	0	0	1-1	42.0	43	18	17	2	26-2	20	.261

PERSONAL: Born July 15, 1980... 6-3/235. ... Throws right, bats right. ... Full name: Nickolas D. Neugebauer. ... High school: Arlington (Riverside, Calif.).
TRANSACTIONS/CAREER NOTES: Selected by Milwaukee Brewers organization in second round of free-agent draft (June 2, 1998). ... On Milwaukee disabled list (August 25, 2001-remainder of season). ... On Milwaukee disabled list (May 11-September 1, 2002); included rehabilitation assignment to Indianapolis (August 2-28). ... On disabled list (March 28-entire 2003 season).
CAREER HITTING: 2-for-22 (.091), 0 R, 1 2B, 0 3B, 0 HR, 1 RBI.

Year League	W	L	Pct.	ERA	WHIP	G	GS	CG	ShO	Hld.	Sv.-Opp.	IP	H	R	ER	HR	BB-IBB	SO	Avg.
1999— Beloit (Midw.)	7	5	.583	3.90	1.61	18	18	0	0	...	0-...	80.2	50	41	35	4	80-0	125	.178
2000— Mudville (Calif.)	4	4	.500	4.19	1.68	18	18	0	0	...	0-...	77.1	43	40	36	0	87-0	117	.168
— Huntsville (Sou.)	1	3	.250	3.73	1.62	10	10	0	0	...	0-...	50.2	35	28	21	2	47-0	57	.196
2001— Huntsville (Sou.)	5	6	.455	3.46	1.37	21	21	1	1	...	0-...	106.2	94	46	41	6	52-0	* 149	.240
— Indianapolis (Int'l)	2	1	.667	1.50	0.79	4	4	0	0	...	0-...	24.0	10	5	4	1	9-0	26	.128
— Milwaukee (N.L.)	1	1	.500	7.50	2.00	2	2	0	0	0	0-0	6.0	6	5	5	1	6-0	11	.250
2002— Milwaukee (N.L.)	1	7	.125	4.72	1.81	12	12	0	0	0	0-0	55.1	56	33	29	10	44-3	47	.264
— Indianapolis (Int'l)	0	3	.000	5.12	1.66	5	5	0	0	...	0-...	19.1	20	13	11	4	12-0	18	.263
2003—											Did not play.								
Major League totals (2 years)	2	8	.200	4.99	1.83	14	14	0	0	0	0-0	61.1	62	38	34	11	50-3	58	.263

PERSONAL: Born January 19, 1971, in Fullerton, Calif. ... 6-2/231. ... Bats right, throws right. ... Full name: Phillip Joseph Nevin. ... High school: El Dorado (Placentia, Calif.). ... College: Cal State Fullerton.
TRANSACTIONS/CAREER NOTES: Selected by Los Angeles Dodgers organization in third round of free-agent draft (June 5, 1989); did not sign. ... Selected by Houston Astros organization in first round (first pick overall) of free-agent draft (June 1, 1992). ... On Tucson disabled list (July 12-30, 1995). ... Traded by Astros to Detroit Tigers (August 15, 1995), completing deal in which Tigers traded P Mike Henneman to Astros for a player to be named later (August 10, 1995). ... On Detroit disabled list (March 21-April 16, 1997); included rehabilitation assignment to Lakeland (April 8-16). ... Traded by Tigers with C Matt Walbeck to Anaheim Angels for P Nick Skuse (November 20, 1997). ... On suspended list (June 12-15, 1998). ... Traded by Angels with P Keith Volkman to San Diego Padres for INF Andy Sheets and OF Gus Kennedy (March 29, 1999). ... On San Diego disabled list (April 1-16, 1999); included rehabilitaion assignment to Las Vegas (April 12-15). ... On San Diego disabled list (May 12-27 and May 30-July 12, 2002); included rehabilitation assignment to Lake Elsinore (July 9-12). ... On disabled list (March 25, 2003). ... Transferred to Emergency disabled list (May 9, 2003). ... Sent to Lake Elsinore on rehab assignment (July 12, 2003). ... Recalled from Portland rehab assignment; reinstated from Emergency disabled list (July 23, 2003).
2003 GAMES PLAYED BY POSITION (MLB): 1B—31, OF—29.

Year Team (League)	Pos.	G	AB	R	H	2B	3B	HR	RBI	BB	SO	HBP	GDP	SB-CS	Avg.	OBP	SLG	OPS	E	Pct.
																			FIELDING	
								BATTING												
1993— Tucson (PCL)	3B-OF	123	448	67	128	21	3	10	93	52	99	3	12	8-1	.286	.359	.413	.772	29	.898
1994— Tucson (PCL)	3B-OF	118	445	67	117	20	1	12	79	55	101	1	21	3-2	.263	.343	.393	.736	‡ 32	.907
1995— Tucson (PCL)	3B-DH	62	223	31	65	16	0	7	41	27	39	1	9	2-3	.291	.371	.457	.828	14	.923
— Houston (N.L.)	3B	18	60	4	7	1	0	0	1	7	13	1	2	1-0	.117	.221	.133	.354	3	.933
— Toledo (Int'l)	OF-DH	7	23	3	7	2	0	1	3	1	5	0	2	0-0	.304	.333	.522	.855	0	1.000
— Detroit (A.L.)	OF-DH	29	96	9	21	3	1	2	12	11	27	3	3	0-0	.219	.318	.333	.652	2	.963
1996— Jacksonville (Sou.)	C-D-3-0-1	98	344	77	101	18	1	24	69	60	83	3	9	6-2	.294	.397	.561	.958	11	.977
— Detroit (A.L.)	3-O-C-D	38	120	15	35	5	0	8	19	8	39	1	1	1-0	.292	.338	.533	.872	5	.950
1997— Lakeland (Fla. St.)	3B-DH-1B	3	9	3	5	1	0	1	4	3	2	0	0	0-0	.556	.667	1.000	1.667	1	.929
— Toledo (Int'l)	1B-3B-DH	5	19	1	3	0	0	1	3	2	9	0	1	0-0	.158	.238	.316	.554	0	1.000
— Detroit (A.L.)	0-D-3-1-C	93	251	32	59	16	1	9	35	25	68	1	5	0-1	.235	.306	.414	.720	2	.982
1998— Anaheim (A.L.)	C-DH-1B	75	237	27	54	8	1	8	27	17	67	5	6	0-0	.228	.291	.371	.662	5	.989
1999— Las Vegas (PCL)	C-3B-1B	3	10	2	2	0	0	2	2	0	2	0	1	0-0	.200	.200	.800	1.000	0	1.000
— San Diego (N.L.)	3-C-O-1-D	128	383	52	103	27	0	24	85	51	82	1	7	1-0	.269	.352	.527	.880	5	.989
2000— San Diego (N.L.)	3B	143	538	87	163	34	1	31	107	59	121	4	17	2-0	.303	.374	.543	.916	* 26	.929
2001— San Diego (N.L.)	3B-DH	149	546	97	167	31	0	41	126	71	147	4	13	4-4	.306	.388	.588	.976	27	.930
2002— San Diego (N.L.)	3B-1B	107	407	53	116	16	0	12	57	38	87	1	12	4-0	.285	.344	.413	.757	18	.973
— Lake Elsinore (Calif.)	3B	2	6	2	2	1	0	1	6	1	2	0	0	0-0	.333	.375	1.000	1.375	2	...
2003— Lake Elsinore (Calif.)	DH	5	15	1	4	1	0	0	5	2	2	0	1	0-0	.267	.300	.333	.633	0	.000
— Portland (PCL)	DH-1B-OF	6	18	0	2	0	0	0	1	1	1	0	2	0-0	.111	.158	.111	.269	1	1.000
— San Diego (N.L.)	1B-OF	59	226	30	63	8	0	13	46	21	44	0	9	2-0	.279	.339	.487	.825	2	.994
American League totals (4 years)		235	704	83	169	32	3	27	93	61	201	10	15	1-1	.240	.308	.409	.717	14	.980
National League totals (6 years)		604	2160	323	619	117	1	121	422	247	494	11	60	14-4	.287	.360	.510	.870	81	.960
Major League totals (9 years)		839	2864	406	788	149	4	148	515	308	695	21	75	15-5	.275	.348	.485	.833	95	.965

PERSONAL: Born January 29, 1979, in Winter Haven, Fla. ... 6-3/210. ... Bats right, throws right. ... Full name: Lance Joseph Niekro. ... High school: George Jenkins High (Lakeland, Florida). ... College: Florida Southern.
TRANSACTIONS/CAREER NOTES: Selected by San Francisco Giants organization in second round of free-agent draft (June 5, 2000). ... On disabled list (July 10, 2002-remainder of season). ... Called up by San Francisco from Fresno (September 2, 2003).
2003 GAMES PLAYED BY POSITION (MLB): 1B—3.

N

Year Team (League)	Pos.	G	AB	R	H	2B	3B	HR	RBI	BB	SO	HBP	GDP	SB-CS	Avg.	OBP	SLG	OPS	E	Pct.
2000— Salem-Keizer (NW)	3B	49	196	27	71	14	4	5	44	11	25	4	6	2-0	.362	.404	.551	.955	5	.939
2001— San Jose (Calif.)	3B	42	163	18	47	11	0	3	34	4	14	0	2	4-2	.288	.298	.411	.709	8	.927
2002— Shreveport (Texas)	1B-3B	79	297	33	92	20	1	4	34	7	32	1	11	0-2	.310	.327	.424	.751	11	.979
2003— Fresno (PCL)	3B-1B-DH	98	381	43	115	15	2	4	41	19	39	1	12	3-3	.302	.334	.383	.717	15	.954
— San Francisco (N.L.)	1B	5	5	2	1	1	0	0	2	0	1	0	0	0-0	.200	.200	.400	.600	0	1.000
Major League totals (1 year)		5	5	2	1	1	0	0	2	0	1	0	0	0-0	.200	.200	.400	.600	0	1.000

NITKOWSKI, C.J.   P

PERSONAL: Born March 9, 1973, in Suffern, N.Y. ... 6-3/205. ... Throws left, bats left. ... Full name: Christopher John Nitkowski. ... Name pronounced: nit-COW-ski. ... High school: Don Bosco (N.J.). ... College: St. John's.

TRANSACTIONS/CAREER NOTES: Selected by Cincinnati Reds organization in first round (ninth pick overall) of free-agent draft (June 2, 1994). ... Traded by Reds with P David Tuttle and a player to be named later to Detroit Tigers for P David Wells (July 31, 1995); Tigers acquired IF Mark Lewis to complete deal (November 16, 1995). ... On Detroit disabled list (August 11-29, 1996). ... Traded by Tigers with C Brad Ausmus, P Jose Lima, P Trever Miller and IF Daryle Ward to Houston Astros for OF Brian Hunter, IF Orlando Miller, P Doug Brocail, P Todd Jones and cash (December 10, 1996). ... Traded by Astros with C Brad Ausmus to Tigers for C Paul Bako, P Dean Crow, P Mark Persails, P Brian Powell and 3B Carlos Villalobos (January 14, 1999). ... On suspended list (May 28-30, 1999). ... Traded by Tigers with cash to New York Mets for a player to be named later (September 1, 2001); Tigers acquired P Kyle Kessel to complete deal (December 13, 2001). ... Granted free agency (October 15, 2001). ... Signed by Astros organization (December 21, 2001). ... Released by Astros (March 25, 2002). ... Re-signed by Astros organization (March 28, 2002). ... Released by Astros (June 6, 2002). ... Signed by St. Louis Cardinals organization (June 6, 2002). ... Released by Cardinals (July 21, 2002). ... Signed by Texas Rangers organization (July 29, 2002). ... Released by Rangers (September 30, 2002). ... Re-signed by Rangers organization (November 15, 2002). ... Designated for assignment (April 18, 2003). ... Sent outright to Oklahoma (April 22, 2003). ... Elected free agency (September 29, 2003).

CAREER HITTING: 2-for-15 (.133), 1 R, 0 2B, 0 3B, 0 HR, 1 RBI.

Year League	W	L	Pct.	ERA	WHIP	G	GS	CG	ShO	Hld.	Sv.-Opp.	IP	H	R	ER	HR	BB-IBB	SO	Avg.
1994— Chattanooga (Sou.)	6	3	.667	3.50	1.35	14	14	0	0	...	0-...	74.2	61	30	29	4	40-0	60	.227
1995— Chattanooga (Sou.)	4	2	.667	2.50	1.17	8	8	0	0	...	0-...	50.1	39	20	14	1	20-0	52	.217
— Indianapolis (A.A.)	0	2	.000	5.20	1.37	6	6	0	0	...	0-...	27.2	28	16	16	3	10-0	21	.262
— Cincinnati (N.L.)	1	3	.250	6.12	1.73	9	7	0	0	0	0-1	32.1	41	25	22	4	15-1	18	.306
— Detroit (A.L.)	1	4	.200	7.09	1.86	11	11	0	0	0	0-0	39.1	53	32	31	7	20-2	13	.335
1996— Toledo (Int'l)	4	6	.400	4.46	1.41	19	19	1	0	...	0-...	111.0	104	60	55	13	53-1	103	.254
— Detroit (A.L.)	2	3	.400	8.08	2.19	11	8	0	0	0	0-0	45.2	62	44	41	7	38-1	36	.332
1997— New Orleans (A.A.)	8	10	.444	3.98	1.37	28	28	1	0	...	0-...	174.1	183	82	77	10	56-2	* 141	.276
1998— Houston (N.L.)	3	3	.500	3.77	1.21	43	0	0	0	8	3-5	59.2	49	27	25	4	23-2	44	.228
— New Orleans (PCL)	0	1	.000	6.00	1.93	5	3	0	0	...	1-...	15.0	22	12	10	1	7-0	18	.338
1999— Detroit (A.L.)	4	5	.444	4.30	1.32	68	7	0	0	11	0-0	81.2	63	44	39	11	45-3	66	.213
2000— Detroit (A.L.)	4	9	.308	5.25	1.58	67	11	0	0	15	0-2	109.2	124	79	64	13	49-3	81	.286
2001— Detroit (A.L.)	0	3	.000	5.56	1.81	56	0	0	0	6	0-6	45.1	51	30	28	7	31-7	38	.285
— Toledo (Int'l)	0	0	...	0.00	1.00	1	0	0	0	...	0-...	1.0	1	0	0	0	0-0	1	.250
— New York (N.L.)	1	0	1.000	0.00	1.06	5	0	0	0	0	0-0	5.2	3	0	0	0	3-1	4	.167
2002— New Orleans (PCL)	1	2	.333	2.78	1.24	24	0	0	0	...	2-...	22.2	21	7	7	1	7-1	20	.244
— Memphis (PCL)	1	2	.333	9.82	2.25	16	1	0	0	...	0-...	14.2	24	18	16	3	9-0	12	.348
— Oklahoma (PCL)	1	1	.500	1.80	1.20	9	0	0	0	...	0-...	10.0	8	3	2	0	4-0	11	.211
— Texas (A.L.)	0	1	.000	2.63	1.76	12	0	0	0	1	0-0	13.2	11	4	4	0	13-0	14	.224
2003— Texas (A.L.)	0	0	...	7.45	2.59	6	0	0	0	1	0-0	9.2	17	8	8	0	8-1	5	.415
— Oklahoma (PCL)	5	4	.556	4.09	1.46	33	6	0	0	...	2-...	81.1	88	40	37	6	31-2	53	.281
American League totals (7 years)	11	25	.306	5.61	1.70	231	37	0	0	34	0-8	345.0	381	241	215	45	204-17	253	.284
National League totals (3 years)	5	6	.455	4.33	1.37	57	7	0	0	8	3-6	97.2	93	52	47	8	41-4	66	.253
Major League totals (8 years)	16	31	.340	5.33	1.62	288	44	0	0	42	3-14	442.2	474	293	262	53	245-21	319	.277

NIVAR, RAMON   OF/DH

PERSONAL: Born February 22, 1980, in San Cristobal, Dominican Republic. ... 5-10/170. ... Bats right, throws right. ... Full name: Ramon A. Nivar.

TRANSACTIONS/CAREER NOTES: Signed by Texas Rangers as a non-drafted free agent (January 25, 1998).

2003 GAMES PLAYED BY POSITION (MLB): OF—26, DH—1.

Year Team (League)	Pos.	G	AB	R	H	2B	3B	HR	RBI	BB	SO	HBP	GDP	SB-CS	Avg.	OBP	SLG	OPS	E	Pct.
2000— Charlotte (Int'l)	SS-3B	42	152	12	44	7	1	1	20	5	28	0	2	8-3	.289	.310	.368	.679	11	.947
— Savannah (S. Atl.)	SS	39	164	19	51	9	0	1	17	2	29	3	3	6-5	.311	.331	.384	.716	15	.917
2001— Charlotte (Int'l)	2B-SS	128	515	69	124	20	1	2	32	28	65	5	7	28-18	.241	.286	.295	.581	29	.955
2002— Charlotte (Int'l)	2B-SS	114	472	98	144	21	8	3	41	32	44	6	15	39-15	.305	.353	.403	.755	10	.983
2003— Frisco (Texas)	2B-SS-OF	79	317	53	110	17	4	4	37	20	23	2	5	9-9	.347	.387	.464	.851	12	.970
— Oklahoma (PCL)	OF-2B	23	89	11	30	2	2	2	12	5	5	0	4	6-1	.337	.368	.472	.840	1	.987
— Texas (A.L.)	OF-DH	28	90	9	19	1	2	0	7	4	10	1	1	4-2	.211	.253	.267	.519	3	.961
Major League totals (1 year)		28	90	9	19	1	2	0	7	4	10	1	1	4-2	.211	.253	.267	.519	3	.961

NIX, LAYNCE   OF

PERSONAL: Born October 30, 1980, in Houston, Texas. ... 6-0/190. ... Bats left, throws left. ... Full name: Layne Michael Nix. ... Name pronounced: nicks. ... High school: Midland High (Texas).

TRANSACTIONS/CAREER NOTES: Selected by Texas Rangers organization in fourth round of free-agent draft (June 5, 2000).

2003 GAMES PLAYED BY POSITION (MLB): OF—52, DH—1.

Year Team (League)	Pos.	G	AB	R	H	2B	3B	HR	RBI	BB	SO	HBP	GDP	SB-CS	Avg.	OBP	SLG	OPS	E	Pct.
2000— GC Rangers (GCL)	OF	51	199	34	45	7	1	2	25	23	37	2	3	4-2	.226	.307	.302	.609	1	.991
2001— Savannah (S. Atl.)	OF	104	407	50	113	26	8	8	59	37	94	2	7	9-6	.278	.337	.440	.777	5	.976
— Charlotte (Int'l)	OF	9	37	4	11	3	1	0	2	1	13	0	2	0-0	.297	.316	.432	.748	0	1.000
2002— Charlotte (Int'l)	OF	137	512	86	146	27	3	21	110	72	105	6	9	17-1	.285	.374	.473	.847	3	.988
2003— Frisco (Texas)	OF-DH	87	335	52	95	23	0	15	63	34	68	0	4	9-2	.284	.344	.487	.831	3	.984
— Texas (A.L.)	OF-DH	53	184	25	47	10	0	8	30	9	53	0	1	3-0	.255	.289	.440	.729	5	.963
Major League totals (1 year)		53	184	25	47	10	0	8	30	9	53	0	1	3-0	.255	.289	.440	.729	5	.963

N

NIXON, TROT — OF

PERSONAL: Born April 11, 1974, in Durham, N.C. ... 6-2/211. ... Bats left, throws left. ... Full name: Christopher Trotman Nixon. ... High school: New Hanover (Wilmington, N.C.).

TRANSACTIONS/CAREER NOTES: Selected by Boston Red Sox organization in first round (seventh pick overall) of free-agent draft (June 3, 1993). ... On disabled list (July 12, 1994-remainder of season). ... On Boston disabled list (June 27-July 25, 2000); included rehabilitation assignment to Gulf Coast Red Sox (July 8-9 and July 20-23).

2003 GAMES PLAYED BY POSITION (MLB): OF-130.

Year Team (League)	Pos.	G	AB	R	H	2B	3B	HR	RBI	BB	SO	HBP	GDP	SB-CS	Avg.	OBP	SLG	OPS	E	Pct.
1994— Lynchburg (Caro.)	OF	71	264	33	65	12	0	12	43	44	53	3	5	10-3	.246	.357	.428	.785	4	.974
1995— Sarasota (Fla. St.)	OF	73	264	43	80	11	4	5	39	45	46	1	5	7-5	.303	.404	.432	.836	2	.986
— Trenton (East.)	OF	25	94	9	15	3	1	2	8	7	20	0	0	2-1	.160	.214	.277	.490	0	1.000
1996— Trenton (East.)	OF-DH	123	438	55	110	11	4	11	63	50	65	3	6	7-9	.251	.329	.370	.698	5	.979
— Boston (A.L.)	OF	2	4	2	2	1	0	0	0	0	1	0	0	1-0	.500	.500	.750	1.250	0	1.000
1997— Pawtucket (Int'l)	OF	130	475	80	116	18	3	20	61	63	86	1	11	11-4	.244	.331	.421	.753	4	.986
1998— Pawtucket (Int'l)	OF-DH-1B	135	509	97	158	26	4	23	74	76	81	5	10	26-13	.310	.400	.513	.913	§ 11	.957
— Boston (A.L.)	OF-DH	13	27	3	7	1	0	0	0	1	3	0	0	0-0	.259	.286	.296	.582	0	1.000
1999— Boston (A.L.)	OF	124	381	67	103	22	5	15	52	53	75	3	7	3-1	.270	.357	.472	.830	7	.968
2000— Boston (A.L.)	OF-DH	123	427	66	118	27	8	12	60	63	85	2	11	8-1	.276	.368	.461	.830	2	.991
— GC Red Sox (GCL)	OF	3	10	3	4	0	0	1	5	2	0	1	0	0-0	.400	.538	.700	1.238	0	1.000
2001— Boston (A.L.)	OF-DH	148	535	100	150	31	4	27	88	79	113	7	8	7-4	.280	.376	.505	.881	8	.973
2002— Boston (A.L.)	OF	152	532	81	136	36	3	24	94	65	109	5	7	4-2	.256	.338	.470	.808	5	.984
2003— Boston (A.L.)	OF	134	441	81	135	24	6	28	87	65	96	3	3	4-2	.306	.396	.578	.975	4	.983
Major League totals (7 years)		696	2347	400	651	142	26	106	381	326	482	20	36	27-10	.277	.366	.496	.862	26	.980

NOMO, HIDEO — P

PERSONAL: Born August 31, 1968, in Osaka, Japan. ... 6-2/210. ... Throws right, bats right. ... Name pronounced: hih-DAY-oh NO-mo. ... High school: Seijyo Kogyo (Japan).

TRANSACTIONS/CAREER NOTES: Selected by Kintetsu Buffaloes in first round of 1989 Japanese free-agent draft. ... Signed as free agent by Los Angeles Dodgers organization (February 8, 1995). ... On Albuquerque temporarily inactive list (April 3-27, 1995). ... Traded by Dodgers with P Brad Clontz to New York Mets for P Dave Mlicki and P Greg McMichael (June 4, 1998). ... Released by Mets (March 26, 1999). ... Signed by Chicago Cubs organization (April 2, 1999). ... Released by Cubs (April 23, 1999). ... Signed by Milwaukee Brewers (April 29, 1999). ... Claimed on waivers by Philadelphia Phillies (October 28, 1999). ... Granted free agency (October 29, 1999). ... Signed by Detroit Tigers organization (January 21, 2000). ... On disabled list (July 30-August 18, 2000). ... Released by Tigers (November 2, 2000). ... Signed by Boston Red Sox (December 15, 2000). ... Granted free agency (November 5, 2001). ... Signed by Dodgers (December 21, 2001).

CAREER HITTING: 62-for-455 (.136), 20 R, 14 2B, 1 3B, 3 HR, 25 RBI.

Year League	W	L	Pct.	ERA	WHIP	G	GS	CG	ShO	Hld.	Sv.-Opp.	IP	H	R	ER	HR	BB-IBB	SO	Avg.
1990— Kintetsu (Jap. Pac.)	* 18	8	.692	2.91	1.17	29	27	21	2	...	0-...	235.0	167	...	76	...	* 109-...	* 287	...
1991— Kintetsu (Jap. Pac.)	* 17	11	.607	3.05	1.28	31	29	22	* 4	...	1-...	242.1	183	...	82	...	* 128-...	* 287	...
1992— Kintetsu (Jap. Pac.)	* 18	8	.692	2.66	1.23	30	29	17	* 5	...	0-...	216.2	150	...	64	...	* 117-...	* 228	...
1993— Kintetsu (Jap. Pac.)	* 17	12	.586	3.70	1.43	32	32	14	2	...	0-...	243.1	* 201	...	100	...	* 148-...	* 276	...
1994— Kintetsu (Jap. Pac.)	8	7	.533	3.63	0.75	17	17	6	0	...	0-...	114.0	...	...	46	...	86-...	126	...
1995— Bakersfield (Calif.)	0	1	.000	3.38	1.31	1	1	0	0	...	0-...	5.1	6	2	2	0	1-0	6	.273
— Los Angeles (N.L.)	13	6	.684	2.54	1.06	28	28	4	•3	0	0-0	191.1	124	63	54	14	78-2	* 236	*.182
1996— Los Angeles (N.L.)	16	11	.593	3.19	1.16	33	33	3	2	0	0-0	228.1	180	93	81	23	85-6	234	.218
1997— Los Angeles (N.L.)	14	12	.538	4.25	1.37	33	33	1	0	0	0-0	207.1	193	104	98	23	92-2	233	.243
1998— Los Angeles (N.L.)	2	7	.222	5.05	1.40	12	12	2	0	0	0-0	67.2	57	39	38	8	38-0	73	.228
— New York (N.L.)	4	5	.444	4.82	1.44	17	16	1	0	0	0-0	89.2	73	49	48	11	56-2	94	.224
1999— Iowa (PCL)	1	1	.500	3.71	1.41	3	3	0	0	...	0-...	17.0	12	7	7	1	12-0	18	.200
— Huntsville (Sou.)	1	0	1.000	0.00	0.86	1	1	0	0	...	0-...	7.0	5	0	0	0	1-0	7	.217
— Milwaukee (N.L.)	12	8	.600	4.54	1.42	28	28	0	0	0	0-0	176.1	173	96	89	27	78-2	161	.256
2000— Detroit (A.L.)	8	12	.400	4.74	1.47	32	31	1	0	0	0-0	190.0	191	102	100	31	89-1	181	.263
2001— Boston (A.L.)	13	10	.565	4.50	1.35	33	33	2	2	0	0-0	198.0	171	105	99	26	* 96-2	* 220	.231
2002— Los Angeles (N.L.)	16	6	.727	3.39	1.32	34	34	0	0	0	0-0	220.1	189	92	83	26	101-5	193	.228
2003— Los Angeles (N.L.)	16	13	.552	3.09	1.25	33	33	2	2	0	0-0	218.1	175	82	75	24	98-6	177	.223
American League totals (2 years)	21	22	.488	4.62	1.41	65	64	3	2	0	0-0	388.0	362	207	199	57	185-3	401	.247
National League totals (7 years)	93	68	.578	3.64	1.28	218	217	13	7	0	0-0	1399.1	1164	618	566	156	626-25	1401	.226
Major League totals (9 years)	114	90	.559	3.85	1.31	283	281	16	9	0	0-0	1787.1	1526	825	765	213	811-28	1802	.231

NORTON, GREG — IF

PERSONAL: Born July 6, 1972, in San Leandro, Calif. ... 6-1/200. ... Bats both, throws right. ... Full name: Gregory Blakemoor Norton. ... High school: Bishop O'Dowd (Oakland). ... College: Oklahoma.

TRANSACTIONS/CAREER NOTES: Selected by San Francisco Giants organization in seventh round of free-agent draft (June 4, 1990); did not sign. ... Selected by Chicago White Sox organization in second round of free-agent draft (June 3, 1993). ... Granted free agency (December 21, 2000). ... Signed by Colorado Rockies (January 5, 2001). ... On Colorado disabled list (June 30-July 18, 2002); included rehabilitation assignment to Colorado Springs (July 15-18).

2003 GAMES PLAYED BY POSITION (MLB): 3B—34, 1B—9, OF—3.

Year Team (League)	Pos.	G	AB	R	H	2B	3B	HR	RBI	BB	SO	HBP	GDP	SB-CS	Avg.	OBP	SLG	OPS	E	Pct.
1993— GC Whi. Sox (GCL)	3B	3	9	1	2	0	0	0	2	1	1	0	0	0-0	.222	.300	.222	.522	0	1.000
— Hickory (S. Atl.)	3B-SS	71	254	36	62	12	2	4	36	41	44	1	6	0-2	.244	.347	.354	.701	17	.928
1994— South Bend (Mid.)	3B	127	477	73	137	22	2	6	64	62	71	2	7	5-3	.287	.369	.379	.749	30	.922
1995— Birmingham (Sou.)	3B	133	469	65	117	23	2	6	60	64	90	5	10	19-12	.249	.339	.345	.685	25	.938
1996— Birmingham (Sou.)	SS	76	287	40	81	14	3	8	44	33	55	1	5	5-5	.282	.357	.436	.793	17	.949
— Nashville (A.A.)	SS-3B-DH	43	164	28	47	14	2	7	26	17	42	0	1	2-3	.287	.350	.524	.874	13	.914
— Chicago (A.L.)	SS-3B-DH	23	23	4	5	0	0	2	3	4	6	0	0	0-1	.217	.333	.478	.812	2	.867
1997— Nashville (A.A.)	3-S-2-D	114	414	82	114	27	1	26	76	57	101	4	9	3-5	.275	.366	.534	.900	‡ 38	.897
— Chicago (A.L.)	3B	18	34	5	9	2	2	0	1	2	8	0	0	0-0	.265	.306	.441	.747	3	.864
1998— Chicago (A.L.)	1-3-D-2	105	299	38	71	17	2	9	36	26	77	2	11	3-3	.237	.301	.398	.699	6	.991
1999— Chicago (A.L.)	3B-1B-DH	132	436	62	111	26	0	16	50	69	93	2	11	4-4	.255	.358	.424	.782	§ 27	.931
2000— Chicago (A.L.)	3B-1B-DH	71	201	25	49	6	1	6	28	26	47	2	2	1-0	.244	.333	.373	.706	4	.960
— Charlotte (Int'l)	3B-1B-SS	29	97	18	28	4	0	5	17	24	23	2	0	1-0	.289	.435	.485	.920	1	.991
2001— Colorado (N.L.)	O-3-1-D	117	225	30	60	13	2	13	40	19	65	0	6	1-0	.267	.321	.516	.837	4	.968
2002— Colorado (N.L.)	3-1-0-D	113	168	19	37	8	1	7	37	24	52	0	4	2-3	.220	.314	.405	.719	5	.955
— Colo. Springs (PCL)	1B-3B	3	12	2	1	0	0	0	0	3	5	0	0	0-0	.083	.267	.083	.350	0	1.000
2003— Colorado (N.L.)	3B-1B-OF	114	179	19	47	15	0	6	31	16	47	1	4	2-1	.263	.325	.447	.772	6	.955
American League totals (5 years)		337	993	134	245	51	5	33	118	127	231	6	24	8-8	.247	.334	.408	.742	46	.965
National League totals (3 years)		344	572	68	144	36	3	26	108	59	164	1	14	5-4	.252	.320	.462	.782	15	.955
Major League totals (8 years)		681	1565	202	389	87	8	59	226	186	395	7	38	13-12	.249	.329	.427	.756	61	.963

NORTON, PHIL — P

PERSONAL: Born February 1, 1976, in Texarkana, Texas. ... 6-1/190. ... Throws left, bats right. ... Full name: Phillip Douglas Norton. ... High school: Pleasant Grove (Texarkana, Texas). ... College: Texarkana (Texas).

TRANSACTIONS/CAREER NOTES: Selected by Chicago Cubs organization in 10th round of free-agent draft (June 4, 1996). ... Released by Cubs (January 14, 2002). ... Re-signed by Cubs (March 21, 2002). ... On Iowa disabled list (April 4, 2002-entire season). ... Contract purchased by Chicago from Iowa (May 17, 2003). ... Optioned to Iowa by Chicago (May 30, 2003). ... Designated for assignment by Chicago (August 19, 2003). ... Sent outright to Iowa (August 21, 2003). ... Traded by Chicago Cubs to Cincinnati Reds for P John Koronka (August 25, 2003). ... Contract purchased by Cincinnati from Louisville (August 26, 2003).

CAREER HITTING: 2-for-4 (.500), 1 R, 0 2B, 0 3B, 0 HR, 0 RBI.

Year League	W	L	Pct.	ERA	WHIP	G	GS	CG	ShO	Hld.	Sv.-Opp.	IP	H	R	ER	HR	BB-IBB	SO	Avg.
1996—GC Cubs (GCL)	0	0	...	0.00	0.33	1	0	0	0	...	0-...	3.0	1	0	0	0	0-0	6	.100
—Williamsport (NYP)	7	4	.636	2.54	1.19	15	13	2	1	...	0-...	85.0	68	33	24	1	33-2	77	.211
1997—Rockford (Midwest)	9	3	.750	3.22	1.25	18	18	3	0	...	0-...	109.0	92	51	39	4	44-1	114	.225
—Daytona (Fla. St.)	3	2	.600	2.34	1.23	7	6	3	0	...	0-...	42.1	40	11	11	5	12-0	44	.253
—Orlando (Sou.)	1	0	1.000	2.57	1.43	2	1	0	0	...	0-...	7.0	8	2	2	0	2-1	7	.308
1998—Daytona (Fla. St.)	4	3	.571	3.27	1.26	10	10	0	0	...	0-...	66.0	57	30	24	4	26-1	54	.233
—West Tenn (Sou.)	6	6	.500	3.52	1.40	19	19	1	1	...	0-...	120.1	118	60	47	11	50-1	119	.261
1999—West Tenn (Sou.)	7	4	.636	2.39	1.32	14	13	0	0	...	0-...	86.2	72	32	23	5	42-4	81	.230
—Iowa (PCL)	5	6	.455	6.67	1.64	14	14	0	0	...	0-...	79.2	98	63	59	20	33-0	61	.305
2000—Iowa (PCL)	8	•13	.381	4.96	1.69	28	26	2	1	...	0-...	159.2	166	100	88	16	*104-4	126	.271
—Chicago (N.L.)	0	1	.000	9.35	2.42	2	2	0	0	0	0-0	8.2	14	10	9	5	7-0	6	.350
2001—Iowa (PCL)	6	3	.667	2.69	1.44	46	3	0	0	...	2-...	73.2	65	27	22	3	41-7	75	.251
2002—										Did not play.									
2003—Chicago (N.L.)	0	0	...	5.40	1.50	4	0	0	0	0	0-0	3.1	2	2	2	0	3-0	0	.182
—Iowa (PCL)	4	2	.667	3.78	1.43	48	1	0	0	...	1-...	47.2	44	26	20	4	24-3	43	.242
—Cincinnati (N.L.)	0	0	...	2.45	0.89	17	0	0	0	5	0-0	14.2	7	4	4	0	6-0	7	.149
Major League totals (2 years)	0	1	.000	5.06	1.46	23	2	0	0	5	0-0	26.2	23	16	15	5	16-0	13	.235

NUNEZ, ABRAHAM O. — 2B/SS

PERSONAL: Born March 16, 1976, in Santo Domingo, Dominican Republic. ... 5-11/186. ... Bats both, throws right. ... Full name: Abraham Orlando Nunez. ... Name pronounced: NOON-yez. ... High school: Emmanuel (Santo Domingo, Dominican Republic).

TRANSACTIONS/CAREER NOTES: Signed as non-drafted free agent by Toronto Blue Jays organization (May 5, 1994). ... Traded by Blue Jays with P Mike Halperin and C/OF Craig Wilson to Pittsburgh Pirates (December 11, 1996), completing deal in which Blue Jays traded P Jose Silva, P Jose Pett, IF Brandon Cromer and three players to be named later to Pirates for OF/1B Orlando Merced, IF Carlos Garcia, and P Dan Plesac (November 14, 1996).

2003 GAMES PLAYED BY POSITION (MLB): 2B—71, SS—23, 3B—1.

Year Team (League)	Pos.	G	AB	R	H	2B	3B	HR	RBI	BB	SO	HBP	GDP	SB-CS	Avg.	OBP	SLG	OPS	E	Pct.
1994—Dom. B. Jays (DSL)	2B	59	188	31	47	5	0	0	15	42	37	...	...	22-...	.250	...	.277	...	12	.938
1995—Dom. B. Jays (DSL)	2B	54	186	49	56	10	3	4	25	30	27	...	...	24-...	.301	...	.452	...	7	.962
1996—St. Catharines (NYP)	2B-SS	75	*297	43	83	6	4	3	26	31	43	4	2	37-14	.279	.353	.357	.710	15	.962
1997—Lynchburg (Caro.)	SS	78	304	45	79	9	4	3	32	23	47	1	5	29-14	.260	.313	.345	.658	15	.955
—Carolina (Sou.)	SS	47	198	31	65	6	1	1	14	20	28	0	2	10-5	.328	.385	.384	.768	11	.949
—Pittsburgh (N.L.)	SS-2B	19	40	3	9	2	2	0	6	3	10	1	1	1-0	.225	.289	.375	.664	0	1.000
1998—Nashville (PCL)	SS	94	366	50	91	12	3	3	32	39	73	5	9	16-8	.249	.328	.322	.651	21	.953
—Lynchburg (Caro.)	SS-2B	5	18	2	4	1	0	0	2	3	1	0	2	1-0	.222	.333	.278	.611	1	.960
—Pittsburgh (N.L.)	SS	24	52	6	10	2	0	1	2	12	14	0	1	4-2	.192	.344	.288	.632	7	.930
1999—Pittsburgh (N.L.)	SS-2B	90	259	25	57	8	0	0	17	28	54	1	2	9-1	.220	.299	.251	.550	14	.959
—Nashville (PCL)	SS	15	58	12	18	0	0	0	3	5	8	0	2	1-0	.310	.365	.310	.675	2	.971
2000—Pittsburgh (N.L.)	SS-2B	40	91	10	20	1	0	1	8	8	14	0	3	0-0	.220	.283	.264	.547	2	.982
2001—Pittsburgh (N.L.)	2-S-3-OF	115	301	30	79	11	4	1	21	28	53	1	0	8-2	.262	.326	.336	.662	4	.990
2002—Pittsburgh (N.L.)	2B-SS-DH	112	253	28	59	14	1	2	15	27	44	2	2	3-4	.233	.311	.320	.631	7	.977
—Nashville (PCL)	SS-2B-OF	5	18	3	4	0	0	0	0	2	7	0	0	4-1	.222	.300	.222	.522	0	1.000
2003—Pittsburgh (N.L.)	2B-SS-3B	118	311	37	77	8	7	4	35	26	53	3	8	9-3	.248	.310	.357	.667	8	.980
Major League totals (7 years)		518	1307	139	311	46	14	9	104	132	242	8	17	34-12	.238	.311	.315	.626	42	.975

NUNEZ, VLADIMIR — P

PERSONAL: Born March 15, 1975, in Havana, Cuba. ... 6-4/240. ... Throws right, bats right. ... Full name: Vladimir Nunez Zarabaza. ... Name pronounced: NOON-yez.

TRANSACTIONS/CAREER NOTES: Signed as non-drafted free agent by Arizona Diamondbacks organization (February 1, 1996). ... On Tucson disabled list (April 7-24, 1998). ... Traded by Diamondbacks with P Brad Penny and a player to be named later to Florida Marlins for P Matt Mantei (July 9, 1999); Marlins acquired OF Abraham Nunez to complete deal (December 13, 1999). ... On Florida disabled list (July 19-August 3, 2001); included rehabilitation assignment to Kane County (August 1-2). ... Optioned to Albuquerque by Florida (April 25, 2003). ... Recalled by Florida from Albuquerque (June 5, 2003). ... Optioned to Albuquerque (June 10, 2003). ... Designated for assignment (September 8, 2003). ... Sent outright to Albuquerque by Florida (September 10, 2003).

CAREER HITTING: 8-for-59 (.136), 3 R, 0 2B, 0 3B, 1 HR, 5 RBI.

Year League	W	L	Pct.	ERA	WHIP	G	GS	CG	ShO	Hld.	Sv.-Opp.	IP	H	R	ER	HR	BB-IBB	SO	Avg.
1996—Visalia (Calif.)	1	6	.143	5.43	1.53	12	10	0	0	...	0-...	53.0	64	45	32	10	17-0	37	.306
—Lethbridge (Pio.)	*10	0	1.000	2.22	1.04	14	13	0	0	...	0-...	85.0	78	25	21	4	10-0	*93	.243
1997—High Desert (Calif.)	8	5	.615	5.17	1.32	28	28	1	1	...	0-...	158.1	169	102	91	36	40-1	142	.271
1998—Tucson (PCL)	4	4	.500	4.91	1.47	31	13	1	0	...	2-...	95.1	103	58	52	12	37-0	78	.277
—Arizona (N.L.)	0	0	...	10.13	1.69	4	0	0	0	0	0-0	5.1	7	6	6	0	2-0	2	.318
1999—Tucson (PCL)	1	0	1.000	6.75	1.88	3	0	0	0	...	0-...	2.2	5	2	2	0	0-0	3	.455
—Arizona (N.L.)	3	2	.600	2.91	1.44	27	0	0	0	3	1-2	34.0	29	15	11	2	20-5	28	.242
—Florida (N.L.)	4	8	.333	4.58	1.34	17	12	0	0	1	0-1	74.2	66	48	38	9	34-1	58	.243
2000—Florida (N.L.)	0	6	.000	7.90	1.79	17	12	0	0	1	0-0	68.1	88	63	60	12	34-2	45	.319
—Calgary (PCL)	6	7	.462	4.12	1.45	15	15	1	0	...	0-...	89.2	92	43	41	9	38-1	95	.272
2001—Florida (N.L.)	4	5	.444	2.74	1.18	52	3	0	0	4	0-1	92.0	79	33	28	9	30-5	64	.234
—Kane County (Midwest)	0	0	...	9.00	3.00	1	1	0	0	...	0-...	1.0	3	1	1	0	0-0	1	.600
2002—Florida (N.L.)	6	5	.545	3.41	1.20	77	0	0	0	11	20-28	97.2	80	38	37	8	37-1	73	.224
2003—Florida (N.L.)	0	3	.000	16.03	2.63	14	0	0	0	0	0-3	10.2	21	21	19	7	7-0	10	.396
—Albuquerque (PCL)	4	1	.800	4.76	1.28	46	3	0	0	...	5-...	68.0	67	36	36	13	20-0	54	.259
Major League totals (6 years)	17	29	.370	4.68	1.40	208	27	0	0	22	21-35	382.2	370	224	199	47	164-14	280	.257

N

OBERMUELLER, WES — P

PERSONAL: Born December 22, 1976, in Cedar Rapids, Iowa. ... 6-2/195. ... Throws right, bats right. ... Full name: Wesley Mitchell Obermueller. ... High school: Washington (Vinton, Iowa). ... College: Iowa.

TRANSACTIONS/CAREER NOTES: Selected by Kansas City Royals organization in second round of free-agent draft (June 2, 1999). ... Recalled from Omaha (July 2, 2003). ... Traded by Royals with IF Alejandro Machado to Milwaukee Brewers for P Curtis Leskanic (July 2, 2003). ... Optioned to Indianapolis (July 2, 2003). ... Recalled from Indianapolis (July 25, 2003).

CAREER HITTING: 3-for-23 (.130), 1 R, 0 2B, 0 3B, 0 HR, 1 RBI.

Year League	W	L	Pct.	ERA	WHIP	G	GS	CG	ShO	Hld.	Sv.-Opp.	IP	H	R	ER	HR	BB-IBB	SO	Avg.
1999— GC Royals (GCL)	2	1	.667	2.58	1.17	11	7	0	0	...	0-...	38.1	33	16	11	2	12-1	39	.228
2000— Char., W.Va. (SAL)	3	0	1.000	1.14	0.76	8	7	0	0	...	0-...	31.2	19	6	4	0	5-0	29	.174
2001— Wilmington (Caro.)	0	2	.000	3.08	1.42	20	6	0	0	...	0-...	38.0	38	15	13	3	16-1	28	.266
2002— Wilmington (Caro.)	5	0	1.000	2.76	1.14	8	4	0	0	...	0-...	45.2	38	14	14	1	14-0	44	.228
— Wichita (Texas)	9	5	.643	2.90	1.31	17	17	0	0	...	0-...	105.2	98	39	34	6	40-3	65	.250
— Kansas City (A.L.)	0	2	.000	11.74	2.09	2	2	0	0	0	0-0	7.2	14	10	10	3	2-0	5	.378
2003— Omaha (PCL)	10	5	.667	4.40	1.41	17	17	2	0	...	0-...	106.1	108	61	52	11	42-1	62	.262
— Indianapolis (Int'l)	0	2	.000	4.70	1.57	3	3	0	0	...	0-...	15.1	18	9	8	1	6-0	11	.300
— Milwaukee (N.L.)	2	5	.286	5.07	1.61	12	11	0	0	0	0-0	65.2	81	40	37	10	25-2	34	.301
American League totals (1 year)	0	2	.000	11.74	2.09	2	2	0	0	0	0-0	7.2	14	10	10	3	2-0	5	.378
National League totals (1 year)	2	5	.286	5.07	1.61	12	11	0	0	0	0-0	65.2	81	40	37	10	25-2	34	.301
Major League totals (2 years)	2	7	.222	5.77	1.66	14	13	0	0	0	0-0	73.1	95	50	47	13	27-2	39	.310

OHKA, TOMO — P

PERSONAL: Born March 18, 1976, in Kyoto, Japan. ... 6-1/180. ... Throws right, bats right. ... Full name: Tomokazu Ohka. ... Name pronounced: TOE-mo-KAH-zoo OH-kah. ... High school: Kyoto Siesio (Kyoto, Japan).

TRANSACTIONS/CAREER NOTES: Contract purchased by Boston Red Sox from Yokohama BayStars of Japan Central League (November 20, 1998). ... Traded by Red Sox with P Rich Rundles to Montreal Expos for P Ugueth Urbina (July 31, 2001). ... On suspended list (September 24-30, 2002).

CAREER HITTING: 20-for-128 (.156), 6 R, 1 2B, 0 3B, 0 HR, 6 RBI.

Year League	W	L	Pct.	ERA	WHIP	G	GS	CG	ShO	Hld.	Sv.-Opp.	IP	H	R	ER	HR	BB-IBB	SO	Avg.
1994— Yoko. Bay. (Jp. Cn.)	1	1	.500	4.18	1.68	15	2	0	0	...	0-...	28.0	29	13	13	...	18-...	18	...
1995— Yoko. Bay. (Jp. Cn.)	0	0	...	1.93	1.71	3	1	0	0	...	0-...	9.1	3	2	2	...	13-...	6	...
1996— Yoko. Bay. (Jp. Cn.)	0	1	.000	9.50	2.28	14	1	0	0	...	0-...	18.0	27	19	19	...	14-...	11	...
1997—											Did not play.								
1998— Yoko. Bay. (Jp. Cn.)	0	0	...	9.00	2.00	2	0	0	0	...	0-...	2.0	2	2	2	...	2-...	1	...
1999— Trenton (East.)	8	0	1.000	3.00	1.22	12	12	0	0	...	0-...	72.0	63	26	24	9	25-0	53	.233
— Pawtucket (Int'l)	7	0	1.000	1.58	1.04	12	12	1	1	...	0-...	68.1	60	17	12	5	11-0	63	.230
— Boston (A.L.)	1	2	.333	6.23	2.08	8	2	0	0	0	0-0	13.0	21	12	9	2	6-0	8	.362
2000— Pawtucket (Int'l)	9	6	.600	2.96	1.03	19	19	3	•2	...	0-...	130.2	111	52	43	15	23-1	78	.232
— Boston (A.L.)	3	6	.333	3.12	1.38	13	12	0	0	0	0-0	69.1	70	25	24	7	26-0	40	.263
2001— Boston (A.L.)	2	5	.286	6.19	1.68	12	11	0	0	0	0-0	52.1	69	40	36	7	19-0	37	.322
— Pawtucket (Int'l)	2	5	.286	5.57	1.52	8	8	1	0	...	0-...	42.0	55	35	26	5	9-0	33	.322
— Montreal (N.L.)	1	4	.200	4.77	1.37	10	10	0	0	0	0-0	54.2	65	30	29	8	10-0	31	.302
2002— Montreal (N.L.)	13	8	.619	3.18	1.24	32	31	2	0	0	0-0	192.2	194	83	68	19	45-7	118	.264
2003— Montreal (N.L.)	10	12	.455	4.16	1.40	34	34	2	0	0	0-0	199.0	233	106	92	24	45-11	118	.292
American League totals (3 years)	6	13	.316	4.61	1.57	33	25	0	0	0	0-0	134.2	160	77	69	16	51-0	85	.295
National League totals (3 years)	24	24	.500	3.81	1.33	76	75	4	0	0	0-0	446.1	492	219	189	51	100-18	267	.281
Major League totals (5 years)	30	37	.448	4.00	1.38	109	100	4	0	0	0-0	581.0	652	296	258	67	151-18	352	.285

OHME, KEVIN — P

PERSONAL: Born April 13, 1971, in Palm Beach, Fla. ... 6-1/180. ... Throws left, bats left. ... Full name: Kevin Arthur Ohme. ... College: North Florida.

TRANSACTIONS/CAREER NOTES: Selected by New York Yankees organization in 35th round of free-agent draft (June 1990); did not sign. ... Selected by Minnesota Twins organization in ninth round of free-agent draft (June 1993). ... Signed as a free agent by Nippon Ham Fighters of the Japanese Pacific League (2000). ... Signed as a free agent by St. Louis Cardinals organization (March 21, 2002).

CAREER HITTING: 1-for-1 (1.000), 0 R, 0 2B, 0 3B, 0 HR, 0 RBI.

Year League	W	L	Pct.	ERA	WHIP	G	GS	CG	ShO	Hld.	Sv.-Opp.	IP	H	R	ER	HR	BB-IBB	SO	Avg.
1993— Fort Wayne (Midw.)	3	2	.600	2.53	1.14	15	4	0	0	...	0-...	46.1	38	19	13	1	15-1	45	.232
1994— Fort Wayne (Midw.)	0	1	.000	2.57	1.00	2	2	0	0	...	0-...	7.0	7	2	2	0	0-0	8	.250
1995— Hardware City (East.)	3	4	.429	3.46	1.32	35	11	0	0	...	0-...	101.1	89	51	39	5	45-1	52	.244
1996— Hardware City (East.)	5	6	.455	4.33	1.43	51	0	0	0	...	3-...	81.0	83	49	39	7	33-5	42	.258
1997— Salt Lake (PCL)	2	5	.286	5.62	1.41	56	0	0	0	...	11-...	73.2	70	49	46	6	34-4	45	.252
1998— Salt Lake (PCL)	4	3	.571	5.01	1.46	51	0	0	0	...	6-...	82.2	90	48	46	5	31-3	47	.284
1999— Salt Lake (PCL)	5	3	.625	3.83	1.52	51	3	0	0	...	2-...	82.1	94	44	35	8	31-2	48	.292
2000—											Did not play.								
2001—											Did not play.								
2002— Memphis (PCL)	4	3	.571	4.52	1.41	56	5	0	0	...	2-...	87.2	103	44	44	10	21-1	56	.305
2003— St. Louis (N.L.)	0	0	...	0.00	0.92	2	0	0	0	1	0-0	4.1	3	0	0	0	1-1	2	.200
— Memphis (PCL)	5	5	.500	4.32	1.47	49	0	0	0	...	1-...	66.2	77	34	32	8	21-4	32	.285
Major League totals (1 year)	0	0	...	0.00	0.92	2	0	0	0	1	0-0	4.1	3	0	0	0	1-1	2	.200

OJEDA, AUGIE — IF

PERSONAL: Born December 20, 1974, in Los Angeles, Calif. ... 5-8/175. ... Bats both, throws right. ... Full name: Octavio Augie Ojeda. ... Name pronounced: oh-HAY-dah. ... High school: Pius X (Downey, Calif.). ... College: Tennessee.

TRANSACTIONS/CAREER NOTES: Selected by Baltimore Orioles organization in 13th round of free-agent draft (June 4, 1996). ... Traded by Orioles to Chicago Cubs for P Richard Negrette (December 13, 1999). ... Contract purchased from Iowa (August 3, 2003). ... Optioned to Iowa (August 19, 2003). ... Recalled from Iowa (September 1, 2003).

2003 GAMES PLAYED BY POSITION (MLB): SS—7, 2B—5, 3B—1.

Year	Team (League)	Pos.	G	AB	R	H	2B	3B	HR	RBI	BB	SO	HBP	GDP	SB-CS	Avg.	OBP	SLG	OPS	E	Pct.
1997— Bowie (East.)	SS	58	204	33	60	9	1	2	23	31	17	3	6	7-0	.294	.390	.377	.767	9	.967
— Frederick (Carolina)	SS	34	128	25	44	11	1	1	20	18	18	1	1	2-5	.344	.429	.469	.897	5	.966
— Rochester (Int'l)	SS	15	47	5	11	3	1	0	6	8	4	0	2	1-2	.234	.345	.340	.686	5	.922
1998— GC Orioles (GCL)	SS	4	15	6	6	2	0	0	2	3	1	2	0	3-0	.400	.550	.533	1.083	0	1.000
— Bowie (East.)	3B-SS	73	254	36	65	10	2	1	19	36	30	3	5	0-3	.256	.354	.323	.677	11	.964
1999— Rochester (Int'l)	SS	1	1	0	0	0	0	0	0	0	0	0	0	0-0	.000	.000	.000	.000	0	...
— Bowie (East.)	3B-SS	134	460	73	123	18	4	10	60	57	47	11	7	6-2	.267	.359	.389	.748	19	.969
2000— Iowa (PCL)	SS-2B	113	396	56	111	23	2	8	43	33	27	7	10	16-6	.280	.343	.409	.752	11	.976
— Chicago (N.L.)	SS-2B	28	77	10	17	3	1	2	8	10	9	0	1	0-1	.221	.307	.364	.670	1	.990
2001— Chicago (N.L.) 3B-SS-2B		78	144	16	29	5	1	1	12	12	20	2	2	1-0	.201	.269	.271	.540	6	.962
2002— Chicago (N.L.) SS-2B-3B		30	70	4	13	4	0	0	4	5	5	1	2	1-0	.186	.247	.243	.490	3	.969
— Iowa (PCL)	SS-3B	73	291	54	67	20	4	1	27	31	30	9	2	5-3	.230	.318	.337	.655	5	.984
2003— Iowa (PCL) SS-2B-3B		106	283	42	71	10	3	2	23	34	25	10	6	4-0	.251	.351	.329	.679	9	.978
— Chicago (N.L.) SS-2B-3B		12	25	2	3	0	0	0	0	1	5	1	1	0-0	.120	.185	.120	.305	0	1.000
Major League totals (4 years)		148	316	32	62	12	2	3	24	28	39	4	6	2-1	.196	.267	.275	.542	10	.974

OJEDA, MIGUEL   C

PERSONAL: Born January 29, 1975, in Sonora, Mexico. ... 6-2/190. ... Bats right, throws right. ... Full name: Miguel Arturo Ojeda.

TRANSACTIONS/CAREER NOTES: Mexican League contract purchased by Pittsburgh Pirates from Mexico City Red Devils (May 28, 1993). ... Re-acquired by Mexico City Red Devils in exchange for future considerations (December 14, 1998). ... Signed by San Diego Padres organization as a minor league free agent (January 12, 2002).

2003 GAMES PLAYED BY POSITION (MLB): C—48, 1B—2.

Year	Team (League)	Pos.	G	AB	R	H	2B	3B	HR	RBI	BB	SO	HBP	GDP	SB-CS	Avg.	OBP	SLG	OPS	E	Pct.
1993— GC Pirates (GCL)	C	27	97	9	27	3	1	3	11	10	18	0	1	2-0	.278	.339	.423	.762	3	.983
1994— Welland (NYP)	C-1B-P	48	142	11	27	6	0	2	8	5	30	2	0	1-0	.190	.228	.275	.503	0	1.000
1998— Carolina (Sou.)	C	18	58	4	9	2	0	1	4	3	12	1	0	0-0	.155	.210	.241	.451	1	.991
2003— San Diego (N.L.)	C-1B	61	141	13	33	6	0	4	22	18	26	3	2	1-1	.234	.331	.362	.693	6	.982
Major League totals (1 year)		61	141	13	33	6	0	4	22	18	26	3	2	1-1	.234	.331	.362	.693	6	.982

O'LEARY, TROY   OF

PERSONAL: Born August 4, 1969, in Compton, Calif. ... 6-0/205. ... Bats left, throws left. ... Full name: Troy Franklin O'Leary. ... High school: Cypress (Calif.). ... Junior college: Chaffey College (Calif.).

TRANSACTIONS/CAREER NOTES: Selected by Milwaukee Brewers organization in 13th round of free-agent draft (June 2, 1987). ... Claimed on waivers by Boston Red Sox (April 14, 1995). ... On Boston disabled list (June 19-July 3, 2000); included rehabilitation assignment to Gulf Coast Red Sox (June 30-July 3). ... Granted free agency (November 5, 2001). ... Signed by Tampa Bay Devil Rays organization (January 29, 2002). ... Released by Devil Rays (March 25, 2002). ... Signed by Montreal Expos organization (March 28, 2002). ... Granted free agency (October 29, 2002). ... Signed by Chicago Cubs (December 17, 2002).

2003 GAMES PLAYED BY POSITION (MLB): OF—51.

Year	Team (League)	Pos.	G	AB	R	H	2B	3B	HR	RBI	BB	SO	HBP	GDP	SB-CS	Avg.	OBP	SLG	OPS	E	Pct.
1987—Helena (Pio.)	OF	3	5	0	2	0	0	0	1	0	0	0	0	0-0	.400	.400	.400	.800	0	...
1988—Helena (Pio.)	OF	67	203	40	70	11	1	0	27	30	32	2	4	10-8	.345	.425	.394	.834	3	.958
1989—Beloit (Midw.)	OF	42	115	7	21	4	0	0	8	15	20	0	3	1-7	.183	.277	.217	.494	1	.982
—Helena (Pio.)	OF	• 68	263	54	* 89	16	3	11	* 56	28	43	2	6	9-8	.338	.402	.548	.950	3	.970
1990—Beloit (Midw.)	OF	118	436	73	130	29	1	6	62	41	90	0	4	12-12	.298	.356	.414	.767	8	.961
—Stockton (Calif.)	OF	2	6	1	3	1	0	0	0	2	1	0	0	0-0	.500	.625	.667	1.292	1	.750
1991—Stockton (Calif.)	OF	126	418	63	110	20	4	5	46	73	96	5	6	4-9	.263	.377	.366	.743	3	.982
1992—El Paso (Texas)	OF *	135	* 506	* 92	* 169	27	8	5	79	59	87	1	7	28-16	.334 *	.399	.449	.848	* 11	.955
1993—New Orleans (A.A.)	OF-1B	111	388	65	106	32	1	7	59	43	61	2	7	6-3	.273	.345	.415	.760	6	.970
—Milwaukee (A.L.)	OF	19	41	3	12	3	0	0	3	5	9	0	1	0-0	.293	.370	.366	.735	0	1.000
1994—New Orleans (A.A.) OF-DH-1B		63	225	44	74	18	5	8	43	32	37	2	10	10-2	.329	.411	.560	.971	2	.982
—Milwaukee (A.L.)	OF-DH	27	66	9	18	1	1	2	7	5	12	1	0	1-1	.273	.329	.409	.738	0	1.000
1995—Boston (A.L.)	OF-DH	112	399	60	123	31	6	10	49	29	64	1	8	5-3	.308	.355	.491	.846	5	.976
1996—Boston (A.L.)	OF	149	497	68	129	28	5	15	81	47	80	4	13	3-2	.260	.327	.427	.753	7	.971
1997—Boston (A.L.)	OF-DH	146	499	65	154	32	4	15	80	39	70	2	13	0-5	.309	.358	.479	.837	6	.979
1998—Boston (A.L.)	OF	156	611	95	165	36	8	23	83	36	108	5	17	2-2	.270	.314	.468	.782	3	.990
1999—Boston (A.L.)	OF	157	596	84	167	36	4	28	103	56	91	4	21	1-2	.280	.343	.495	.838	2	.993
2000—Boston (A.L.)	OF	138	513	68	134	30	4	13	70	44	76	2	12	0-2	.261	.320	.411	.731	3	.988
—GC Red Sox (GCL)	DH	3	8	3	6	1	0	0	1	3	1	0	0	0-0	.750	.818	.875	1.693	...	...
2001—Boston (A.L.)	OF-DH	104	341	50	82	16	6	13	50	25	73	5	9	1-3	.240	.298	.437	.735	1	.994
2002—Ottawa (Int'l)	OF	23	86	11	29	6	0	3	16	7	15	0	1	0-1	.337	.387	.512	.899	1	.974
—Montreal (N.L.)	OF-DH	97	273	27	78	12	2	3	37	34	47	3	6	1-2	.286	.371	.377	.748	3	.977
2003—Chicago (N.L.)	OF	93	174	18	38	9	0	5	28	14	31	1	8	3-0	.218	.275	.356	.631	0	1.000
American League totals (9 years)		1008	3563	502	984	213	38	119	526	286	583	24	94	13-20	.276	.332	.457	.789	27	.985
National League totals (2 years)		190	447	45	116	21	2	8	65	48	78	4	14	4-2	.260	.334	.369	.703	3	.984
Major League totals (11 years)		1198	4010	547	1100	234	40	127	591	334	661	28	108	17-22	.274	.332	.448	.780	30	.985

OLERUD, JOHN   1B

PERSONAL: Born August 5, 1968, in Seattle, Wash. ... 6-5/225. ... Bats left, throws left. ... Full name: John Garrett Olerud. ... Name pronounced: OLE-le-RUDE. ... High school: Interlake (Bellevue, Wash.). ... College: Washington State.

TRANSACTIONS/CAREER NOTES: Selected by New York Mets organization in 27th round of free-agent draft (June 2, 1986); did not sign. ... Selected by Toronto Blue Jays organization in third round of free-agent draft (June 5, 1989). ... Traded by Blue Jays with cash to Mets for P Robert Person (December 20, 1996). ... Granted free agency (October 27, 1997). ... Re-signed by Mets (November 24, 1997). ... Granted free agency (October 29, 1999). ... Signed by Seattle Mariners (December 15, 1999). ... Granted free agency (October 29, 2002). ... Re-signed by Mariners (December 6, 2002).

2003 GAMES PLAYED BY POSITION (MLB): 1B—152.

O

Year Team (League)	Pos.	G	AB	R	H	2B	3B	HR	RBI	BB	SO	HBP	GDP	SB-CS	Avg.	OBP	SLG	OPS	E	Pct.
1989—Toronto (A.L.)	DH-1B	6	8	2	3	0	0	0	0	0	1	0	0	0-0	.375	.375	.375	.750	0	1.000
1990—Toronto (A.L.)	DH-1B	111	358	43	95	15	1	14	48	57	75	1	5	0-2	.265	.364	.430	.794	2	.986
1991—Toronto (A.L.)	DH-1B	139	454	64	116	30	1	17	68	68	84	6	12	0-2	.256	.353	.438	.791	5	.996
1992—Toronto (A.L.)	1B-DH	138	458	68	130	28	0	16	66	70	61	1	15	1-0	.284	.375	.450	.825	7	.994
1993—Toronto (A.L.)	1B-DH	158	551	109	200	* 54	2	24	107	114	65	7	12	0-2	*.363	*.473	.599	1.072	10	.992
1994—Toronto (A.L.)	1B-DH	108	384	47	114	29	2	12	67	61	53	3	11	1-2	.297	.393	.404	.869	6	.993
1995—Toronto (A.L.)	1B	135	492	72	143	32	0	8	54	84	54	4	17	0-0	.291	.398	.404	.802	4	.997
1996—Toronto (A.L.)	1B-DH	125	398	59	109	25	0	18	61	60	37	10	10	1-0	.274	.382	.472	.854	2	.998
1997—New York (N.L.)	1B	154	524	90	154	34	1	22	102	85	67	13	19	0-0	.294	.400	.489	.889	7	.995
1998—New York (N.L.)	1B	160	557	91	197	36	4	22	93	96	73	4	15	2-2	.354	.447	.551	.998	5	.996
1999—New York (N.L.)	1B	• 162	581	107	173	39	0	19	96	125	66	11	22	3-0	.298	.427	.463	.890	9	.994
2000—Seattle (A.L.)	1B	159	565	84	161	45	0	14	103	102	96	4	17	0-2	.285	.392	.439	.831	5	.996
2001—Seattle (A.L.)	1B	159	572	91	173	32	1	21	95	94	70	5	*21	3-1	.302	.401	.472	.873	9	.993
2002—Seattle (A.L.)	1B-DH	154	553	85	166	39	0	22	102	98	66	5	19	0-0	.300	.403	.490	.893	5	.996
2003—Seattle (A.L.)	1B	152	539	64	145	35	0	10	83	84	67	6	20	0-1	.269	.372	.390	.761	3	.998
American League totals (12 years)		1544	5332	788	1555	364	7	176	854	892	729	52	159	6-12	.292	.394	.462	.856	58	.995
National League totals (3 years)		476	1662	288	524	109	5	63	291	306	206	28	56	5-2	.315	.425	.501	.926	21	.995
Major League totals (15 years)		2020	6994	1076	2079	473	12	239	1145	1198	935	80	215	11-14	.297	.402	.471	.872	79	.995

OLIVER, DARREN   P

PERSONAL: Born October 6, 1970, in Kansas City, Mo. ... 6-2/220. ... Throws left, bats right. ... Full name: Darren Christopher Oliver. ... High school: Rio Linda (Calif.) Senior.

TRANSACTIONS/CAREER NOTES: Selected by Texas Rangers organization in third round of free-agent draft (June 1, 1988). ... On Gulf Coast Rangers disabled list (April 6-August 9, 1990). ... On disabled list (May 1, 1991-remainder of season). ... On Tulsa disabled list (July 1, 1992-remainder of season). ... On disabled list (June 27, 1995-remainder of season). ... On Texas disabled list (June 11-26, 1998); included rehabilitation assignment to Oklahoma City (June 21-26). ... Traded by Rangers with 3B Fernando Tatis and a player to be named later to St. Louis Cardinals for P Todd Stottlemyre and SS Royce Clayton (July 31, 1998); Cardinals acquired OF Mark Little to complete deal (August 9, 1998). ... Granted free agency (October 29, 1999). ... Signed by Rangers (January 27, 2000). ... On Texas disabled list (June 21-July 20 and August 1-September 1, 2000); included rehabilitation assignments to Oklahoma (July 5-20 and August 12-26) and Tulsa (August 27-31). ... On Texas disabled list (May 8-June 6, 2001); included rehabilitation assignments to Oklahoma (May 27-31) and Tulsa (June 1-6). ... Traded by Rangers to Boston Red Sox for OF Carl Everett (December 13, 2001). ... Released by Red Sox (July 2, 2002). ... Signed by Cardinals organization (July 19, 2002). ... Released by Cardinals (August 13, 2002). ... Signed by Colorado Rockies organization (January 29, 2003).

CAREER HITTING: 43-for-180 (.239), 15 R, 10 2B, 0 3B, 1 HR, 17 RBI.

Year League	W	L	Pct.	ERA	WHIP	G	GS	CG	ShO	Hld.	Sv.-Opp.	IP	H	R	ER	HR	BB-IBB	SO	Avg.
1988—GC Rangers (GCL)	5	1	.833	2.15	1.05	12	9	0	0	...	0-...	54.1	39	16	13	0	18-0	59	.203
1989—Gastonia (S. Atl.)	8	7	.533	3.16	1.37	24	23	2	1	...	0-...	122.1	86	54	43	4	82-1	108	.199
1990—GC Rangers (GCL)	0	0	...	0.00	0.33	3	3	0	0	...	0-...	6.0	1	0	0	0	1-0	7	.053
—Gastonia (S. Atl.)	0	0	...	13.50	2.50	1	1	0	0	...	0-...	2.0	1	3	3	0	4-0	2	.143
1991—Charlotte (Fla. St.)	0	1	.000	4.50	1.13	2	2	0	0	...	0-...	8.0	6	4	4	1	3-0	12	.200
1992—Charlotte (Fla. St.)	1	0	1.000	0.72	0.84	8	2	1	1	...	2-...	25.0	11	2	2	0	10-2	33	.133
—Tulsa (Texas)	0	1	.000	3.14	1.33	3	3	0	0	...	0-...	14.1	15	9	5	1	4-0	14	.246
1993—Tulsa (Texas)	7	5	.583	1.96	1.25	46	0	0	0	...	6-...	73.1	51	18	16	1	41-5	77	.192
—Texas (A.L.)	0	0	...	2.70	0.90	2	0	0	0	0	0-0	3.1	2	1	1	1	1-1	4	.154
1994—Texas (A.L.)	4	0	1.000	3.42	1.50	43	0	0	0	9	2-3	50.0	40	24	19	4	35-4	50	.223
—Oklahoma City (A.A.)	0	0	...	0.00	0.55	6	0	0	0	...	1-...	7.1	1	0	0	0	3-2	6	.045
1995—Texas (A.L.)	4	2	.667	4.22	1.61	17	7	0	0	0	0-0	49.0	47	25	23	3	32-1	39	.257
1996—Charlotte (Fla. St.)	0	1	.000	3.00	0.92	2	1	0	0	...	0-...	12.0	8	4	4	1	0-0	9	.190
—Texas (A.L.)	14	6	.700	4.66	1.53	30	30	1	1	0	0-0	173.2	190	97	90	20	76-3	112	.279
1997—Texas (A.L.)	13	12	.520	4.20	1.47	32	32	3	1	0	0-0	201.1	213	111	94	29	82-3	104	.271
1998—Texas (A.L.)	6	7	.462	6.53	1.77	19	19	2	0	0	0-0	103.1	140	84	75	11	43-1	58	.325
—Oklahoma (PCL)	0	0	...	0.00	0.60	1	1	0	0	...	0-...	5.0	2	0	0	0	1-0	1	.118
—St. Louis (N.L.)	4	4	.500	4.26	1.53	10	10	0	0	0	0-0	57.0	64	31	27	7	23-1	29	.283
1999—St. Louis (N.L.)	9	9	.500	4.26	1.38	30	30	2	1	0	0-0	196.1	197	96	93	16	74-4	119	.265
2000—Texas (A.L.)	2	9	.182	7.42	1.79	21	21	0	0	0	0-0	108.0	151	95	89	16	42-3	49	.339
—Oklahoma (PCL)	2	1	.667	1.97	1.13	7	7	1	1	0	0-...	32.0	22	11	7	2	14-0	28	.196
—Tulsa (Texas)	0	1	.000	11.57	2.57	1	1	0	0	...	0-...	4.2	10	7	6	0	2-0	5	.417
2001—Texas (A.L.)	11	11	.500	6.02	1.65	28	28	1	0	0	0-0	154.0	189	109	103	23	65-0	104	.306
—Oklahoma (PCL)	0	0	...	0.00	1.00	1	1	0	0	...	0-...	3.0	3	0	0	0	0-0	3	.273
—Tulsa (Texas)	0	1	.000	5.40	1.20	1	1	0	0	...	0-...	5.0	4	3	3	1	2-0	5	.235
2002—Boston (A.L.)	4	5	.444	4.66	1.67	14	9	1	1	0	0-0	58.0	70	30	30	7	27-0	32	.317
—Memphis (PCL)	0	2	.000	7.88	2.13	5	5	0	0	...	0-...	16.0	17	16	14	1	17-0	9	.298
2003—Colorado (N.L.)	13	11	.542	5.04	1.45	33	32	1	0	0	0-0	180.1	201	108	101	21	61-3	88	.284
American League totals (9 years)	58	52	.527	5.24	1.60	206	146	8	3	9	2-3	900.2	1042	576	524	114	403-16	552	.291
National League totals (3 years)	26	24	.520	4.59	1.43	73	72	3	1	0	0-0	433.2	462	235	221	44	158-8	236	.276
Major League totals (11 years)	84	76	.525	5.02	1.55	279	218	11	4	9	2-3	1334.1	1504	811	745	158	561-24	788	.287

OLIVO, MIGUEL   C

PERSONAL: Born July 15, 1978, in Villa Vasquez, Dominican Republic. ... 6-0/220. ... Bats right, throws right. ... Full name: Miguel Eduardo Olivo.

TRANSACTIONS/CAREER NOTES: Signed as non-drafted free agent by Oakland Athletics organization (September 30, 1996). ... On Midland inactive list (July 8-10, 2000). ... On Modesto suspended list (July 13-23, 2000). ... On Modesto disabled list (August 8, 2000-remainder of season). ... Traded by A's to Chicago White Sox (December 12, 2000); completing deal in which White Sox traded P Chad Bradford to A's for player to be named later (December 7, 2000). ... On disabled list (April 22-May 2, 2001). ... On Birmingham disabled list (June 4-11, 2002).

2003 GAMES PLAYED BY POSITION (MLB): C—113.

Year Team (League)	Pos.	G	AB	R	H	2B	3B	HR	RBI	BB	SO	HBP	GDP	SB-CS	Avg.	OBP	SLG	OPS	E	Pct.
1997—Dom. Athletics (DSL)		63	221	37	60	11	4	6	57	34	36	...	...	6-...	.271	...	.439	...	...	...
1998—Ariz. A's (Ariz.)	C-OF	46	164	30	51	11	3	2	23	8	43	4	5	2-2	.311	.356	.451	.807	8	.977
1999—Modesto (Calif.)	C	73	243	46	74	13	6	9	42	21	60	2	5	4-5	.305	.363	.519	.882	15	.974
2000—Modesto (Calif.)	C	58	227	40	64	11	5	5	35	16	53	2	8	5-2	.282	.332	.441	.773	* 19	.959
—Midland (Texas)	C	19	59	8	14	2	0	1	9	5	15	0	3	0-0	.237	.297	.322	.619	2	.986
2001—Birmingham (Sou.)	C	93	316	45	82	23	1	14	55	37	62	7	4	6-3	.259	.347	.472	.819	9	.988
2002—Birmingham (Sou.)	C	106	359	51	110	24	* 10	6	49	40	66	5	11	29-13	.306	.381	.479	.860	13	.983
—Chicago (A.L.)	C	6	19	2	4	1	0	1	5	2	5	0	1	0-0	.211	.286	.421	.707	0	1.000
2003—Chicago (A.L.)	C	114	317	37	75	19	1	6	27	19	80	4	3	6-4	.237	.287	.360	.646	9	.988
Major League totals (2 years)		120	336	39	79	20	1	7	32	21	85	4	4	6-4	.235	.287	.363	.650	9	.988

O

OLMEDO, RAY — SS/2B

PERSONAL: Born May 31, 1981, in Maracay, Venezuela. ... 5-11/155. ... Bats both, throws right. ... Full name: Rainer Gustavo Olmedo. ... Name pronounced: ray-NEAR oh-MAY-doe.

TRANSACTIONS/CAREER NOTES: Signed by Cincinnati Reds organization as a non-drafted free agent (January 21, 1999).

2003 GAMES PLAYED BY POSITION (MLB): SS—51, 2B—18.

Year Team (League)	Pos.	G	AB	R	H	2B	3B	HR	RBI	BB	SO	HBP	GDP	SB-CS	Avg.	OBP	SLG	OPS	E	Pct.
1999— GC Reds (GCL)	2B-SS-3B	54	195	30	46	12	1	1	19	12	28	1	1	13-7	.236	.281	.323	.604	16	.936
2000— Dayton (Midw.)	SS-2B	111	369	50	94	19	1	4	41	30	70	1	11	17-11	.255	.309	.344	.654	29	.946
2001— Mudville California (Calif.)	SS	129	536	57	131	23	4	0	28	24	121	8	15	38-17	.244	.285	.302	.587	40	.930
2002— Chattanooga (Sou.)	SS-2B	132	478	62	118	21	1	3	30	53	86	7	4	15-16	.247	.331	.314	.645	25	.961
2003— Chattanooga (Sou.)	SS-2B	49	160	23	47	11	0	2	15	14	29	0	3	3-3	.294	.349	.400	.749	10	.951
— Louisville (Int'l)	SS-2B	9	25	4	6	1	0	1	4	2	6	0	0	0-0	.240	.296	.400	.696	1	.983
— Cincinnati (N.L.)	SS-2B	79	230	24	55	6	1	0	17	13	46	0	4	1-1	.239	.280	.274	.554	14	.948
Major League totals (1 year)		79	230	24	55	6	1	0	17	13	46	0	4	1-1	.239	.280	.274	.554	14	.948

OLSEN, KEVIN — P

PERSONAL: Born July 26, 1976, in Covina, Calif. ... 6-2/196. ... Throws right, bats right. ... Full name: Kevin Gary Olsen. ... High school: Norco (Calif.). ... College: Oklahoma.

TRANSACTIONS/CAREER NOTES: Selected by Florida Marlins organization in 26th round of free-agent draft (June 2, 1998). ... On Calgary disabled list (August 16, 2002-remainder of season). ... Recalled by Florida from Albuquerque of the Pacific Coast League (June 10, 2003). ... Placed on 15-day disabled list (June 28, 2003). ... Transferred to 60-day disabled list (August 22, 2003). ... Sent on minor league rehab assignment by Florida (August 29, 2003). ... Recalled from minor league rehab assignment; removed from 60-day disabled list (September 8, 2003).

CAREER HITTING: 1-for-15 (.067), 0 R, 0 2B, 0 3B, 0 HR, 0 RBI.

Year League	W	L	Pct.	ERA	WHIP	G	GS	CG	ShO	Hld.	Sv.-Opp.	IP	H	R	ER	HR	BB-IBB	SO	Avg.
1998— Utica (N.Y.-Penn)	4	3	.571	2.60	1.04	21	4	0	0	...	2-...	45.0	37	21	13	3	10-1	56	.219
1999— Brevard County (FSL)	2	5	.286	5.05	1.46	11	11	0	0	...	0-...	57.0	70	37	32	8	13-0	45	.295
— Kane County (Midwest)	5	2	.714	3.38	1.32	10	9	0	0	...	0-...	61.1	65	25	23	3	16-0	52	.275
2000— Brevard County (FSL)	4	8	.333	2.86	1.07	18	18	1	0	...	0-...	110.0	93	40	35	2	25-2	77	.233
— Portland (East.)	3	4	.429	4.83	1.39	9	9	0	0	...	0-...	54.0	54	30	29	8	21-0	47	.257
2001— Portland (East.)	10	3	.769	2.68	0.93	26	26	2	1	...	0-...	154.2	123	56	46	11	21-1	144	.214
— Florida (N.L.)	0	0	...	1.20	0.87	4	2	0	0	...	0-0	15.0	11	2	2	0	2-1	13	.204
2002— Florida (N.L.)	0	5	.000	4.53	1.58	17	8	0	0	1	0-0	55.2	57	31	28	5	31-1	38	.270
— Calgary (PCL)	2	5	.286	3.86	1.20	8	8	1	1	...	0-...	49.0	45	22	21	6	14-0	25	.245
2003— Albuquerque (PCL)	2	1	.667	2.11	1.12	7	7	0	0	...	0-...	38.1	36	12	9	1	7-1	28	.254
— Jupiter (FSL)	0	0	...	0.00	0.25	1	1	0	0	...	0-...	4.0	1	0	0	0	0-0	3	.083
— Florida (N.L.)	0	0	...	12.75	2.42	7	0	0	0	0	0-0	12.0	25	18	17	2	4-1	12	.431
Major League totals (3 years)	0	5	.000	5.12	1.57	28	10	0	0	1	0-0	82.2	93	51	47	7	37-3	63	.288

ORDONEZ, MAGGLIO — OF

PERSONAL: Born January 28, 1974, in Caracas, Venezuela. ... 6-0/210. ... Bats right, throws right. ... Name pronounced: or-DOAN-yez.

TRANSACTIONS/CAREER NOTES: Signed as non-drafted free agent by Chicago White Sox organization (May 18, 1991). ... On suspended list (May 1-6, 2000).

2003 GAMES PLAYED BY POSITION (MLB): OF—157, DH—2.

Year Team (League)	Pos.	G	AB	R	H	2B	3B	HR	RBI	BB	SO	HBP	GDP	SB-CS	Avg.	OBP	SLG	OPS	E	Pct.
1991— Dom. Orioles/W.S. (DSL)		25	94	17	28	3	1	0	8	6	12	...	...	4-...	.298	...	.351	...		...
1992— GC Whi. Sox (GCL)	OF	38	111	17	20	10	2	1	14	13	26	2	2	6-4	.180	.276	.324	.609	0	1.000
1993— Hickory (S. Atl.)	OF	84	273	32	59	14	4	3	20	26	66	0	6	5-5	.216	.284	.330	.614	6	.959
1994— Hickory (S. Atl.)	OF	132	490	86	144	24	5	11	69	45	57	1	11	16-7	.294	.353	.431	.783	6	.980
1995— Prince Will. (Car.)	OF	131	487	61	116	24	2	12	65	41	71	3	16	11-5	.238	.299	.370	.669	6	.978
1996— Birmingham (Sou.)	OF	130	479	66	126	41	0	18	67	39	74	9	16	9-10	.263	.330	.461	.792	6	.976
1997— Nashville (A.A.)	OF-DH	135	523	65	* 172	29	3	14	90	32	61	2	18	14-10	.329	.364	.476	.840	5	.983
— Chicago (A.L.)	OF	21	69	12	22	6	0	4	11	2	8	0	1	1-2	.319	.338	.580	.918	0	1.000
1998— Chicago (A.L.)	OF	145	535	70	151	25	2	14	65	28	53	9	19	9-7	.282	.326	.415	.741	5	.985
1999— Chicago (A.L.)	OF-DH	157	624	100	188	34	3	30	117	47	64	1	24	13-6	.301	.349	.510	.858	3	.991
2000— Chicago (A.L.)	OF	153	588	102	185	34	3	32	126	60	64	2	28	18-4	.315	.371	.546	.917	5	.983
2001— Chicago (A.L.)	OF-DH	160	593	97	181	40	1	31	113	70	70	5	14	25-7	.305	.382	.533	.914	5	.983
2002— Chicago (A.L.)	OF-DH	153	590	116	189	47	1	38	135	53	77	7	•21	7-5	.320	.381	.597	.978	4	.986
2003— Chicago (A.L.)	OF-DH	160	606	95	192	46	3	29	99	57	73	7	20	9-5	.317	.380	.546	.926	2	.994
Major League totals (7 years)		949	3605	592	1108	232	13	178	666	317	409	31	127	82-36	.307	.365	.527	.892	24	.988

ORDONEZ, REY — SS

PERSONAL: Born January 11, 1971, in Havana, Cuba. ... 5-9/159. ... Bats right, throws right. ... Full name: Reynaldo Ordonez. ... Name pronounced: RAY or-DOAN-yez. ... High school: Espa (Havana, Cuba). ... College: Fajardo (Cuba).

TRANSACTIONS/CAREER NOTES: Played with St. Paul Saints of Northern League (1993). ... Rights acquired by New York Mets organization in lottery of Cuban defectors (October 29, 1993). ... Signed by Mets organization (February 8, 1994). ... On disabled list (June 2-July 11, 1997; and May 30, 2000-remainder of season). ... Traded by Mets to Tampa Bay Devil Rays for two players to be named later (December 15, 2002). ... Transferred to 60-day disabled list (September 9, 2003).

2003 GAMES PLAYED BY POSITION (MLB): SS—34.

Year Team (League)	Pos.	G	AB	R	H	2B	3B	HR	RBI	BB	SO	HBP	GDP	SB-CS	Avg.	OBP	SLG	OPS	E	Pct.
1993— St. Paul (Nor.)		15	60	10	17	4	0	0	7	3	9	...	...	3-...	.283	...	.350	...	3	.971
1994— St. Lucie (Fla. St.)	SS	79	314	47	97	21	2	4	40	14	28	0	8	11-6	.309	.336	.408	.744	15	.966
— Binghamton (East.)	SS	48	191	22	50	10	2	1	20	4	18	1	2	4-3	.262	.279	.351	.630	8	.961
1995— Norfolk (Int'l)	SS	125	439	49	94	21	4	2	50	27	50	3	12	11-13	.214	.261	.294	.554	21	.967
1996— New York (N.L.)	SS	151	502	51	129	12	4	1	30	22	53	1	12	1-3	.257	.289	.303	.592	27	.962
1997— New York (N.L.)	SS	120	356	35	77	5	3	1	33	18	36	1	10	11-5	.216	.255	.256	.510	9	.983
1998— New York (N.L.)	SS	153	505	46	124	20	2	1	42	23	60	1	11	3-6	.246	.278	.299	.577	17	.975
1999— New York (N.L.)	SS	154	520	49	134	24	2	1	60	49	59	1	16	8-4	.258	.319	.317	.636	4	.994
2000— New York (N.L.)	SS	45	133	10	25	5	0	0	9	17	16	0	4	0-0	.188	.278	.226	.504	6	.965

Year Team (League)	Pos.	G	AB	R	H	2B	3B	HR	RBI	BB	SO	HBP	GDP	SB-CS	Avg.	OBP	SLG	OPS	E	Pct.
2001—New York (N.L.)	SS	149	461	31	114	24	4	3	44	34	43	1	17	3-2	.247	.299	.336	.635	12	.980
2002—New York (N.L.)	SS	144	460	53	117	25	2	1	42	24	46	2	19	2-2	.254	.292	.324	.616	19	.969
2003—Tampa Bay (A.L.)	SS	34	117	14	37	11	0	3	22	2	12	1	3	0-2	.316	.328	.487	.815	5	.970
American League totals (1 year)		34	117	14	37	11	0	3	22	2	12	1	3	0-2	.316	.328	.487	.815	5	.970
National League totals (7 years)		916	2937	275	720	115	17	8	260	187	313	7	89	28-22	.245	.290	.304	.594	94	.976
Major League totals (8 years)		950	3054	289	757	126	17	11	282	189	325	8	92	28-24	.248	.291	.311	.602	99	.976

OROPESA, EDDIE — P

PERSONAL: Born November 23, 1971, in Colen Matanzas, Cuba. ... 6-1/204. ... Throws left, bats left. ... Full name: Edilberto Oropesa. ... College: Matanzas (Cuba).

TRANSACTIONS/CAREER NOTES: Signed by St. Paul of Northern League (August 1993). ... Selected by Los Angeles Dodgers organization in 14th round of free-agent draft (June 2, 1994). ... Selected by San Francisco Giants organization from Dodgers organization in Rule 5 minor league draft (December 9, 1996). ... Loaned by Giants organization to Reynosa, Mexican League (July 8-August 5, 1999). ... Granted free agency (October 15, 2000). ... Signed by Philadelphia Phillies organization (November 15, 2000). ... On Philadelphia disabled list (June 13-July 5, 2001); included rehabilitation assignment to Scranton/Wilkes-Barre (June 29-July 5). ... Granted free agency (October 15, 2001). ... Signed by Arizona Diamondbacks organization (November 20, 2001). ... Contract purchased from Tucson (May 18, 2003). ... Optioned to Tucson (August 31, 2003). ... Recalled from Tucson (September 1, 2003).

CAREER HITTING: 0-for-0 (.000), 0 R, 0 2B, 0 3B, 0 HR, 0 RBI.

Year League	W	L	Pct.	ERA	WHIP	G	GS	CG	ShO	Hld.	Sv.-Opp.	IP	H	R	ER	HR	BB-IBB	SO	Avg.
1993—St. Paul (Nor.)	3	1	.750	1.93	0.80	4	3	0	0	...	0-...	18.2	6	4	4	...	9-...	19	...
1994—Vero Beach (FSL)	4	3	.571	2.13	1.10	19	10	1	1	...	0-...	72.0	54	24	17	2	25-2	67	.215
1995—San Antonio (Texas)	1	1	.500	3.12	1.96	16	0	0	0	...	1-...	17.1	22	8	6	2	12-1	16	.319
—Vero Beach (FSL)	3	1	.750	3.81	1.24	19	1	0	0	...	1-...	28.1	25	12	12	0	10-0	23	.240
—San Bernardino (Calif.)	0	0	...	0.00	0.00	1	0	0	0	...	0-...	1.0	0	0	0	0	0-0	0	.000
1996—San Bernardino (Calif.)	11	6	.647	3.34	1.34	33	19	0	0	...	1-...	156.1	133	74	58	8	77-1	133	.229
1997—Shreveport (Texas)	7	7	.500	3.92	1.50	43	9	1	0	...	0-...	124.0	122	58	54	7	64-0	65	.270
1998—Shreveport (Texas)	7	11	.389	3.78	1.47	32	20	2	0	...	0-...	143.0	143	71	60	6	67-3	104	.266
—Pres. Lions (Taiw.)	0	2	.000	6.43	0.79	8	0	0	0	...	1-...	14.0	...	...	10	...	11-...	6	...
1999—Fresno (PCL)	6	5	.545	4.85	1.59	21	18	1	0	...	0-...	102.0	113	69	55	15	49-0	61	.280
—Bakersfield (Calif.)	2	0	1.000	3.60	1.40	2	1	0	0	...	0-...	10.0	13	5	4	2	1-0	10	.325
—Reynosa (Mex.)	0	4	.000	7.06	2.22	7	3	0	0	...	0-...	21.2	32	19	17	3	16-...	8	...
2000—Shreveport (Texas)	2	4	.333	3.07	1.44	59	2	0	0	...	4-...	76.1	70	38	26	6	40-6	76	.238
2001—Philadelphia (N.L.)	1	0	1.000	4.74	1.74	30	0	0	0	6	0-1	19.0	16	10	10	1	17-6	15	.229
—Scran./W.B. (I.L.)	1	1	.500	2.35	1.17	14	1	0	0	...	0-...	15.1	14	5	4	1	4-1	11	.246
—Clearwater (Fla. St.)	0	0	...	0.00	1.50	2	0	0	0	...	0-...	2.0	2	0	0	0	1-0	3	.250
2002—Arizona (N.L.)	2	0	1.000	10.30	2.13	32	0	0	0	7	0-1	25.1	39	30	29	6	15-0	18	.348
—Tucson (PCL)	1	0	1.000	3.86	1.40	29	0	0	0	...	0-...	25.2	23	11	11	2	13-2	26	.242
2003—Tucson (PCL)	0	1	.000	2.35	1.17	15	0	0	0	...	0-...	15.1	14	4	4	0	4-1	9	.246
—Arizona (N.L.)	3	3	.500	5.82	1.68	47	0	0	0	10	0-0	38.2	38	27	25	3	27-2	39	.257
Major League totals (3 years)	6	3	.667	6.94	1.83	109	0	0	0	23	0-2	83.0	93	67	64	10	59-8	72	.283

OROSCO, JESSE — P

PERSONAL: Born April 21, 1957, in Santa Barbara, Calif. ... 6-2/200. ... Throws left, bats right. ... Full name: Jesse Russell Orosco. ... Name pronounced: ore-AHS-co. ... High school: Santa Barbara (Calif.). ... Junior college: Santa Barbara (Calif.) Community College.

TRANSACTIONS/CAREER NOTES: Selected by St. Louis Cardinals organization in seventh round of free-agent draft (January 11, 1977); did not sign. ... Selected by Minnesota Twins organization in second round of free-agent draft (January 10, 1978). ... Traded by Twins to New York Mets (February 7, 1979), completing deal in which Twins traded P Greg Field and a player to be named later to Mets for P Jerry Koosman (December 8, 1978). ... Traded by Mets as part of an eight-player, three-team deal in which Mets sent Orosco to Oakland Athletics (December 11, 1987); A's then traded Orosco, SS Alfredo Griffin and P Jay Howell to Los Angeles Dodgers for P Bob Welch, P Matt Young and P Jack Savage; A's then traded Savage, P Wally Whitehurst and P Kevin Tapani to Mets. ... Granted free agency (November 4, 1988). ... Signed by Cleveland Indians (December 3, 1988). ... Traded by Indians to Milwaukee Brewers for a player to be named later (December 6, 1991); deal settled in cash. ... Granted free agency (November 5, 1992). ... Re-signed by Brewers (December 4, 1992). ... Granted free agency (October 15, 1994). ... Signed by Baltimore Orioles (April 9, 1995). ... Granted free agency (October 27, 1996). ... Re-signed by Orioles (November 15, 1996). ... Traded by Orioles to Mets for P Chuck McElroy (December 10, 1999). ... Traded by Mets to Cardinals for 2B/OF Joe McEwing (March 18, 2000). ... On St. Louis disabled list (April 9-June 9 and June 22, 2000-remainder of season); included rehabilitation assignments to Peoria (May 30-June 5) and Memphis (June 6-9). ... Granted free agency (October 30, 2000). ... Signed by Los Angeles Dodgers organization (February 8, 2001). ... Released by Dodgers (March 30, 2001). ... Re-signed by Dodgers organization (April 24, 2001). ... On Los Angeles disabled list (August 13-September 1, 2001). ... Granted free agency (November 5, 2001). ... Re-signed by Dodgers organization (December 7, 2001). ... On disabled list (May 14-29, 2002). ... Granted free agency (October 28, 2002). ... Signed by San Diego Padres (November 19, 2002). ... Traded by Padres to New York Yankees for future considerations (July 22, 2003). ... Designated for assignment (August 26, 2003). ... Traded by Yankees to Minnesota Twins for P Juan Padilla (August 31, 2003).

CAREER HITTING: 10-for-59 (.169), 3 R, 0 2B, 0 3B, 0 HR, 4 RBI.

Year League	W	L	Pct.	ERA	WHIP	G	GS	CG	ShO	Hld.	Sv.-Opp.	IP	H	R	ER	HR	BB-IBB	SO	Avg.
1978—Elizabethton (Appal.)	4	4	.500	1.13	1.23	20	0	0	0	...	6-...	40.0	29	7	5	0	20-5	48	...
1979—Tidewater (Int'l)	4	4	.500	3.89	1.54	16	15	1	0	...	0-...	81.0	82	45	35	2	43-4	55	...
—New York (N.L.)	1	2	.333	4.89	1.57	18	2	0	0	0	0-0	35.0	33	20	19	4	22-0	22	.260
1980—Jackson (Texas)	4	4	.500	3.68	1.61	37	1	0	0	...	3-...	71.0	52	36	29	3	62-4	85	...
1981—Tidewater (Int'l)	9	5	.643	3.31	1.29	46	10	0	0	...	8-...	87.0	80	39	32	7	32-4	81	...
—New York (N.L.)	0	1	.000	1.56	1.10	8	0	0	0	0	1-1	17.1	13	4	3	2	6-2	18	.213
1982—New York (N.L.)	4	10	.286	2.72	1.21	54	2	0	0	5	4-5	109.1	92	37	33	7	40-2	89	.230
1983—New York (N.L.)	13	7	.650	1.47	1.04	62	0	0	0	1	17-22	110.0	76	27	18	3	38-7	84	.197
1984—New York (N.L.)	10	6	.625	2.59	1.06	60	0	0	0	0	31-39	87.0	58	29	25	7	34-6	85	.185
1985—New York (N.L.)	8	6	.571	2.73	1.27	54	0	0	0	1	17-25	79.0	66	26	24	6	34-7	68	.224
1986—New York (N.L.)	8	6	.571	2.33	1.22	58	0	0	0	1	21-29	81.0	64	23	21	6	35-3	62	.217
1987—New York (N.L.)	3	9	.250	4.44	1.42	58	0	0	0	4	16-22	77.0	78	41	38	5	31-9	78	.266
1988—Los Angeles (N.L.)	3	2	.600	2.72	1.34	55	0	0	0	11	9-15	53.0	41	18	16	4	30-3	43	.215
1989—Cleveland (A.L.)	3	4	.429	2.08	1.03	69	0	0	0	11	3-7	78.0	54	20	18	7	26-4	79	.194
1990—Cleveland (A.L.)	5	4	.556	3.90	1.48	55	0	0	0	2	2-3	64.2	58	35	28	9	38-7	55	.239
1991—Cleveland (A.L.)	2	0	1.000	3.74	1.47	47	0	0	0	3	0-0	45.2	52	20	19	4	15-8	36	.286
1992—Milwaukee (A.L.)	3	1	.750	3.23	1.18	59	0	0	0	11	1-2	39.0	33	15	14	5	13-1	40	.232
1993—Milwaukee (A.L.)	3	5	.375	3.18	1.13	57	0	0	0	11	8-13	56.2	47	25	20	2	17-3	67	.224
1994—Milwaukee (A.L.)	3	1	.750	5.08	1.49	40	0	0	0	8	0-4	39.0	32	26	22	4	26-2	36	.222
1995—Baltimore (A.L.)	2	4	.333	3.26	1.11	*65	0	0	0	15	3-6	49.2	28	19	18	4	27-7	58	.169
1996—Baltimore (A.L.)	3	1	.750	3.40	1.26	66	0	0	0	19	0-3	55.2	42	22	21	5	28-4	52	.207

O

Year — League	W	L	Pct.	ERA	WHIP	G	GS	CG	ShO	Hld.	Sv.-Opp.	IP	H	R	ER	HR	BB-IBB	SO	Avg.
1997— Baltimore (A.L.)	6	3	.667	2.32	1.17	71	0	0	0	21	0-4	50.1	29	13	13	6	30-0	46	.169
1998— Baltimore (A.L.)	4	1	.800	3.18	1.31	69	0	0	0	9	7-9	56.2	46	20	20	6	28-1	50	.221
1999— Baltimore (A.L.)	0	2	.000	5.34	1.50	65	0	0	0	12	1-4	32.0	28	21	19	5	20-3	35	.239
2000— St. Louis (N.L.)	0	0	...	3.86	2.57	6	0	0	0	3	0-0	2.1	3	3	1	1	3-2	4	.273
— Peoria (Midw.)	0	0	...	0.00	0.00	2	2	0	0	...	0-...	1.2	0	0	0	0	0-0	1	.000
— Memphis (PCL)	0	1	.000	9.00	1.00	2	1	0	0	...	0-...	1.0	1	1	1	0	0-0	0	.250
2001— Las Vegas (PCL)	1	0	1.000	0.00	0.82	10	0	0	0	...	0-...	7.1	4	0	0	0	2-0	11	.160
— Los Angeles (N.L.)	0	1	.000	3.94	1.50	35	0	0	0	10	0-2	16.0	17	7	7	3	7-1	21	.279
2002— Los Angeles (N.L.)	1	2	.333	3.00	1.33	56	0	0	0	17	1-1	27.0	24	10	9	4	12-1	22	.229
2003— San Diego (N.L.)	1	1	.500	7.56	1.72	42	0	0	0	7	2-3	25.0	33	22	21	4	10-0	22	.317
— New York (A.L.)	0	0	...	10.38	2.31	15	0	0	0	4	0-1	4.1	4	6	5	0	6-3	4	.250
— Minnesota (A.L.)	1	1	.500	5.79	1.93	8	0	0	0	0	0-0	4.2	4	3	3	0	5-0	3	.235
American League totals (12 years)	35	27	.565	3.44	1.28	686	0	0	0	126	25-56	576.1	457	245	220	57	279-43	561	.218
National League totals (13 years)	52	53	.495	2.94	1.25	566	4	0	0	60	119-164	719.0	598	267	235	56	302-43	618	.226
Major League totals (24 years)	87	80	.521	3.16	1.26	1252	4	0	0	186	144-220	1295.1	1055	512	455	113	581-86	1179	.223

ORTIZ, DAVID — DH/1B

PERSONAL: Born November 18, 1975, in Santo Domingo, Dominican Republic. ... 6-4/230. ... Bats left, throws left. ... Full name: David Americo Ortiz. ... Name pronounced: or-TEEZ. ... High school: Estudia Espallat (Dominican Republic).

TRANSACTIONS/CAREER NOTES: Signed as non-drafted free agent by Seattle Mariners organization (November 28, 1992). ... Traded by Mariners to Minnesota Twins (September 13, 1996), completing deal in which Twins traded 3B Dave Hollins to Mariners for a player to be named later (August 29, 1996). ... On Minnesota disabled list (May 10-July 9, 1998); included rehabilitation assignment to Salt Lake (June 25-July 9). ... On Minnesota disabled list (May 5-July 21, 2001); included rehabilitation assignments to Gulf Coast Twins (July 5-11), Fort Myers (July 11-12) and New Britain (July 12-21). ... On disabled list (April 19-May 12, 2002). ... Released by Twins (December 16, 2002). ... Signed by Boston Red Sox (January 22, 2003).

2003 GAMES PLAYED BY POSITION (MLB): DH—74, 1B—45.

							BATTING												FIELDING	
Year — Team (League)	Pos.	G	AB	R	H	2B	3B	HR	RBI	BB	SO	HBP	GDP	SB-CS	Avg.	OBP	SLG	OPS	E	Pct.
1993— Dom. Mariners (DSL)		61	201	61	53	17	1	7	31	34	44	...	...	1-...	.264		.463			
1994— Ariz. Mariners (Ariz.)	1B	53	167	14	41	10	1	2	20	14	46	2	2	1-4	.246	.305	.353	.658	6	.985
1995— Ariz. Mariners (Ariz.)	1B	48	184	30	61	* 18	4	4	• 37	23	52	1	2	2-0	.332	.403	.538	.941	5	.989
1996— Wisconsin (Midw.) 1B-DH-3B		129	485	89	156	34	2	18	93	52	108	5	5	3-4	.322	.390	.511	.901	13	.989
1997— Fort Myers (FSL)	1B-DH	61	239	45	79	15	0	13	58	22	53	1	3	2-1	.331	.385	.556	.941	9	.984
— New Britain (East.)	DH-1B	69	258	40	83	22	2	14	56	21	78	4	6	2-6	.322	.379	.585	.964	3	.990
— Salt Lake (PCL)	1B-DH	10	42	5	9	1	0	4	10	2	11	0	4	0-1	.214	.250	.524	.774	0	1.000
— Minnesota (A.L.)	1B	15	49	10	16	3	0	1	6	2	19	0	1	0-0	.327	.353	.449	.802	1	.989
1998— Minnesota (A.L.)	1B-DH	86	278	47	77	20	0	9	46	39	72	5	8	1-0	.277	.371	.446	.817	6	.989
— Salt Lake (PCL)	1B-DH	11	37	5	9	3	0	2	6	3	9	0	0	0-0	.243	.300	.486	.786	3	.966
1999— Salt Lake (PCL)	1B	130	476	85	150	35	3	30	* 110	79	105	3	8	2-2	.315	.412	.590	1.002	• 20	.980
— Minnesota (A.L.) DH-1B-OF		10	20	1	0	0	0	0	0	0	5	12	0	2	0-0	.000	.000	.200	.200	0	1.000
2000— Minnesota (A.L.)	DH-1B	130	415	59	117	36	1	10	63	57	81	0	13	0-0	.282	.364	.446	.810	1	.996
2001— Minnesota (A.L.)	DH-1B	89	303	46	71	17	1	18	48	40	68	1	6	1-0	.234	.324	.475	.799	0	1.000
— GC Twins (GCL)	DH	4	10	3	4	0	0	0	1	3	1	0	0	1-0	.400	.538	.400	.938	...	...
— Fort Myers (FSL)	1B	1	3	0	0	0	0	0	0	1	0	0	0	0-0	.000	.250	.000	.250	0	1.000
— New Britain (East.)	1B	9	37	3	9	4	0	0	1	3	9	0	1	0-0	.243	.293	.351	.644	0	1.000
2002— Minnesota (A.L.)	DH-1B	125	412	52	112	32	1	20	75	43	87	3	5	1-2	.272	.339	.500	.839	1	.990
2003— Boston (A.L.)	DH-1B	128	448	79	129	39	2	31	101	58	83	1	9	0-0	.288	.369	.592	.961	3	.992
Major League totals (7 years)		583	1925	294	522	147	5	89	339	244	422	10	44	4-2	.271	.353	.491	.844	12	.992

ORTIZ, RAMON — P

PERSONAL: Born March 23, 1973, in Cotui, Dominican Republic. ... 6-0/175. ... Throws right, bats right. ... Full name: Ramon Diogenes Ortiz. ... Name pronounced: or-TEEZ. ... High school: 8th Intermedian (Dominican Republic).

TRANSACTIONS/CAREER NOTES: Signed as non-drafted free agent by California Angels organization (June 20, 1995). ... Angels franchise renamed Anaheim Angels for 1997 season. ... On disabled list (May 9, 1998-remainder of season). ... On Anaheim disabled list (March 20-April 11, 2000); included rehabilitation assignment to Lake Elsinore (April 6).

CAREER HITTING: 0-for-19 (.000). 1 R, 0 2B, 0 3B, 0 HR, 0 RBI.

Year — League	W	L	Pct.	ERA	WHIP	G	GS	CG	ShO	Hld.	Sv.-Opp.	IP	H	R	ER	HR	BB-IBB	SO	Avg.
1995— Dom. Angels (DSL).	8	6	.571	2.23	1.37	16	16	7	0	...	0-...	97.0	79	44	24	...	54-...	100	
1996— Ariz. Angels (Ariz.)	5	4	.556	2.12	1.21	16	8	• 2	* 2	...	1-...	68.0	55	28	16	5	27-0	78	.216
— Boise (NW)	1	1	.500	3.66	1.37	3	3	0	0	...	0-...	19.2	21	10	8	3	6-0	18	.263
1997— Cedar Rapids (Midw.)	11	10	.524	3.58	1.15	27	• 27	* 8	* 4	...	0-...	181.0	156	78	72	22	53-0	* 225	.230
1998— Midland (Texas)	2	1	.667	5.55	1.40	7	7	0	0	...	0-...	47.0	50	31	29	10	16-0	53	.275
1999— Erie (East.)	9	4	.692	2.82	1.25	15	15	3	• 2	...	0-...	102.0	88	38	32	12	40-0	86	.237
— Edmonton (PCL)	5	3	.625	4.05	1.22	9	9	0	0	...	0-...	53.1	46	26	24	7	19-0	64	.227
— Anaheim (A.L.)	2	3	.400	6.52	1.55	9	9	0	0	...	0-0	48.1	50	35	35	7	25-0	44	.265
2000— Lake Elsinore (Calif.)	1	0	1.000	3.00	1.67	1	1	0	0	...	0-...	6.0	8	2	2	0	2-0	7	.333
— Anaheim (A.L.)	8	6	.571	5.09	1.36	18	18	2	0	0	0-0	111.1	96	69	63	18	55-0	73	.236
— Edmonton (PCL)	6	6	.500	4.55	1.25	15	15	1	0	...	0-...	89.0	74	49	45	7	37-0	76	.223
2001— Anaheim (A.L.)	13	11	.542	4.36	1.43	32	32	2	0	0	0-0	208.2	223	114	101	25	76-6	135	.274
2002— Anaheim (A.L.)	15	9	.625	3.77	1.18	32	32	4	1	0	0-0	217.1	188	97	91	* 40	68-0	162	.230
2003— Anaheim (A.L.)	16	13	.552	5.20	1.51	32	32	1	0	0	0-0	180.0	209	121	104	28	63-0	94	.287
Major League totals (5 years)	54	42	.563	4.63	1.38	123	123	9	1	0	0-0	765.2	766	436	394	118	287-6	508	.259

ORTIZ, RUSS — P

PERSONAL: Born June 5, 1974, in Encino, Calif. ... 6-1/208. ... Throws right, bats right. ... Full name: Russell Reid Ortiz. ... Name pronounced: OR-teez. ... High school: Montclair Prep (Van Nuys, Calif.). ... College: Oklahoma.

TRANSACTIONS/CAREER NOTES: Selected by San Francisco Giants organization in fourth round of free-agent draft (June 1, 1995). ... Traded by Giants to Atlanta Braves for P Damian Moss and P Manuel Mateo (December 17, 2002).

CAREER HITTING: 81-for-363 (.223). 40 R, 19 2B, 0 3B, 6 HR, 40 RBI.

0

Year League	W	L	Pct.	ERA	WHIP	G	GS	CG	ShO	Hld.	Sv.-Opp.	IP	H	R	ER	HR	BB-IBB	SO	Avg.
1995— Bellingham (N'west)	2	0	1.000	0.52	0.93	25	0	0	0	...	11-...	34.1	19	4	2	1	13-0	55	.162
— San Jose (Calif.)	0	1	.000	1.50	1.00	5	0	0	0	...	0-...	6.0	4	1	1	0	2-0	7	.190
1996— San Jose (Calif.)	0	0	...	0.25	0.98	34	0	0	0	...	23-...	36.2	16	2	1	0	20-0	63	.131
— Shreveport (Texas)	1	2	.333	4.05	1.61	26	0	0	0	...	13-...	26.2	22	14	12	0	21-3	29	.220
1997— Shreveport (Texas)	2	3	.400	4.13	1.57	12	12	0	0	...	0-...	56.2	52	28	26	3	37-0	50	.252
— Phoenix (PCL)	4	3	.571	5.51	1.53	14	14	0	0	...	0-...	85.0	96	57	52	11	34-0	70	.287
1998— San Francisco (N.L.)	4	4	.500	4.99	1.54	22	13	0	0	1	0-0	88.1	90	51	49	11	46-1	75	.269
— Fresno (PCL)	3	1	.750	1.60	1.13	10	10	0	0	...	0-...	50.2	35	10	9	3	22-0	59	.198
1999— San Francisco (N.L.)	18	9	.667	3.81	1.51	33	33	3	0	0	0-0	207.2	189	109	88	24	* 125-5	164	.244
2000— San Francisco (N.L.)	14	12	.538	5.01	1.55	33	32	0	0	0	0-0	195.2	192	117	109	28	112-1	167	.261
2001— San Francisco (N.L.)	17	9	.654	3.29	1.27	33	33	1	1	0	0-0	218.2	187	90	80	13	91-3	169	.232
2002— San Francisco (N.L.)	14	10	.583	3.61	1.33	33	33	2	0	0	0-0	214.1	191	89	86	15	94-5	137	.244
2003— Atlanta (N.L.)	*21	7	.750	3.81	1.31	34	34	1	1	0	0-0	212.1	177	101	90	17	*102-7	149	.223
Major League totals (6 years)	88	51	.633	3.97	1.40	188	178	7	2	1	0-0	1137.0	1026	557	502	108	570-22	861	.242

OSIK, KEITH — C

PERSONAL: Born October 22, 1968, in Port Jefferson, N.Y. ... 6-0/200. ... Bats right, throws right. ... Full name: Keith Richard Osik. ... Name pronounced: OH-sick. ... High school: Shoreham (N.Y.)-Wading River. ... College: Louisiana State.

TRANSACTIONS/CAREER NOTES: Selected by Texas Rangers organization in 47th round of free-agent draft (June 2, 1987); did not sign. ... Selected by Pittsburgh Pirates organization in 24th round of free-agent draft (June 4, 1990). ... On Pittsburgh disabled list (July 16-August 13, 1996); included rehabilitation assignment to Erie (August 10-13). ... On Pittsburgh disabled list (July 21-August 13, 1999); included rehabilitation assignment to Nashville (August 9-13). ... On disabled list (April 30-May 15, 2001). ... Granted free agency (October 28, 2002). ... Signed by Milwaukee Brewers organization (January 10, 2003).

2003 GAMES PLAYED BY POSITION (MLB): C—78.

Year Team (League)	Pos.	G	AB	R	H	2B	3B	HR	RBI	BB	SO	HBP	GDP	SB-CS	Avg.	OBP	SLG	OPS	E	Pct.
1990— Welland (NYP)	C	29	97	13	27	4	0	1	20	11	12	2	1	2-6	.278	.354	.351	.704	2	.978
1991— Salem (Caro.)	2B-3B-C	87	300	31	81	12	1	6	35	38	48	3	13	2-3	.270	.356	.377	.732	12	.970
— Carolina (Sou.)	3B-C	17	43	9	13	3	1	0	5	5	5	0	1	0-0	.302	.375	.419	.794	2	.980
1992— Carolina (Sou.)	P	129	425	41	110	17	1	5	45	52	69	15	12	2-9	.259	.357	.339	.696	19	.956
1993— Carolina (Sou.)	C	103	371	47	104	21	2	10	47	30	46	9	13	0-2	.280	.348	.429	.777	6	.992
1994— Buffalo (A.A.) C-0-1-D-2-P		83	260	27	55	16	0	5	33	28	41	3	5	0-1	.212	.294	.331	.624	8	.983
1995— Calgary (PCL) C-1-0-P-3		90	301	40	101	25	1	10	59	21	42	5	5	2-2	.336	.384	.525	.909	4	.992
1996— Pittsburgh (N.L.) C-3B-OF		48	140	18	41	14	1	1	14	14	22	1	3	1-0	.293	.361	.429	.790	1	.978
— Erie (N.Y.-Penn)	C	3	10	1	3	1	0	0	2	1	2	1	0	0-0	.300	.417	.400	.817	0	1.000
1997— Pittsburgh (N.L.) C-2-3-1		49	105	10	27	9	1	0	7	9	21	1	1	0-1	.257	.322	.362	.684	2	.989
1998— Pittsburgh (N.L.) C-3B		39	98	8	21	4	0	0	7	13	16	2	4	1-2	.214	.316	.255	.571	1	.995
1999— Pittsburgh (N.L.) .... C-P		66	167	12	31	3	1	2	13	11	30	1	8	0-0	.186	.239	.251	.490	1	.997
— Nashville (PCL)	C-OF	4	11	0	1	0	0	0	0	0	1	1	0	0-0	.091	.167	.091	.258	0	1.000
2000— Pittsburgh (N.L.) C-3-1-P-D		46	123	11	36	6	1	4	22	14	11	5	2	3-0	.293	.387	.455	.843	2	.989
2001— Pittsburgh (N.L.) C-1-3-2-O		56	120	9	25	4	0	2	13	13	24	3	1	1-0	.208	.299	.292	.591	1	.996
2002— Pittsburgh (N.L.) C-3-1-2-O		55	100	6	16	3	0	2	11	6	25	1	2	0-0	.160	.211	.250	.461	1	.994
2003— Milwaukee (N.L.)	C	80	241	22	60	12	0	2	21	31	44	3	7	0-1	.249	.342	.324	.665	5	.991
Major League totals (8 years)		439	1094	96	257	55	4	13	108	111	193	17	28	6-4	.235	.314	.328	.642	19	.991

OSUNA, ANTONIO — P

PERSONAL: Born April 12, 1973, in Sinaloa, Mexico. ... 5-11/200. ... Throws right, bats right. ... Full name: Antonio Pedro Osuna. ... Name pronounced: oh-SOON-a. ... High school: Secondaria Federal (Mexico).

TRANSACTIONS/CAREER NOTES: Signed as non-drafted free agent by Los Angeles Dodgers organization (June 12, 1991). ... Loaned by Dodgers to Mexico City Tigres, Mexican League (March 6-September 25, 1992). ... On suspended list (April 8-July 17, 1993). ... On San Antonio disabled list (April 8-June 6, 1994). ... On Los Angeles disabled list (May 19-June 16, 1995); included rehabilitation assignment to San Bernardino (June 6-16). ... On disabled list (September 9, 1998-remainder of season). ... On Los Angeles disabled list (March 25-April 16, April 18-May 3 and May 19, 1999-remainder of season); included rehabilitation assignments to San Bernardino (April 10-16, April 25-May 3, July 7-15 and September 1-29). ... On Los Angeles disabled list (March 31-May 5, 2000); included rehabilitation assignment to San Bernardino (April 8-May 5). ... Traded by Dodgers with P Carlos Ortega to Chicago White Sox for P Gary Majewski, P Andre Simpson and P Orlando Rodriguez (March 17, 2001). ... On disabled list (April 12, 2001-remainder of season). ... Traded by White Sox with P Delvis Lantigua to New York Yankees for P Orlando Hernandez and cash (January 15, 2003). ... On disabled list (April 23, 2003). ... Sent to Tampa for rehab assignment (May 12, 2003). ... Recalled from Tampa (May 14, 2003). ... Placed on 15-day disabled list (June 14, 2003). ... Sent to Gulf Coast League on rehab assignment (July 8, 2003). ... Recalled by New York from rehab assignment; reinstated from 15-day disabled list (July 8, 2003). ... Activated by New York from the 15-day disabled list (July 13, 2003). ... Placed on bereavement list (August 11, 2003). ... Removed from bereavement list (August 15, 2003).

CAREER HITTING: 1-for-9 (.111), 0 R, 0 2B, 0 3B, 0 HR, 1 RBI.

Year League	W	L	Pct.	ERA	WHIP	G	GS	CG	ShO	Hld.	Sv.-Opp.	IP	H	R	ER	HR	BB-IBB	SO	Avg.
1991— GC Dodgers (GCL)	0	0	...	0.82	0.73	8	0	0	0	...	4-...	11.0	8	5	1	0	0-0	13	.186
— Yakima (NW)	0	0	...	3.20	1.03	13	0	0	0	...	5-...	25.1	18	10	9	1	8-0	39	.205
1992— M.C. Tigers (Mex.)	13	7	.650	4.05	1.53	28	26	3	1	...	0-...	166.2	181	80	75	16	74-...	129	...
1993— Bakersfield (Calif.)	0	2	.000	4.91	1.31	14	2	0	0	...	2-...	18.1	19	10	10	2	5-0	20	.268
1994— San Antonio (Texas)	1	2	.333	0.98	0.80	35	0	0	0	...	19-...	46.0	19	6	5	0	18-1	53	.127
— Albuquerque (PCL)	0	0	...	0.00	1.00	6	0	0	0	...	4-...	6.0	5	1	0	0	1-0	8	.227
1995— Los Angeles (N.L.)	2	4	.333	4.43	1.32	39	0	0	0	11	0-2	44.2	39	22	22	5	20-2	46	.241
— San Bernardino (Calif.)	0	0	...	1.29	1.14	5	0	0	0	...	0-...	7.0	3	1	1	1	5-0	11	.130
— Albuquerque (PCL)	0	1	.000	4.42	1.31	19	0	0	0	...	11-...	18.1	15	9	9	2	9-0	19	.227
1996— Albuquerque (PCL)	0	0	...	0.00	2.00	1	0	0	0	...	0-...	1.0	2	0	0	0	0-0	1	.500
— Los Angeles (N.L.)	9	6	.600	3.00	1.15	73	0	0	0	16	4-9	84.0	65	33	28	6	32-12	85	.214
1997— Albuquerque (PCL)	1	1	.500	1.93	0.93	13	0	0	0	...	6-...	14.0	9	3	3	0	4-0	26	.176
— Los Angeles (N.L.)	3	4	.429	2.19	1.05	48	0	0	0	10	0-0	61.2	46	15	15	6	19-2	68	.209
1998— Los Angeles (N.L.)	7	1	.875	3.06	1.27	54	0	0	0	12	6-11	64.2	50	26	22	8	32-0	72	.214
1999— San Bernardino (Calif.)	0	0	...	2.33	1.29	13	4	0	0	...	0-...	19.1	19	6	5	0	6-0	27	.260
— Los Angeles (N.L.)	0	0	...	7.71	1.50	5	0	0	0	2	0-...	4.2	4	5	4	0	3-0	5	.222
2000— San Bernardino (Calif.)	0	2	.000	4.91	0.95	3	3	0	0	...	0-...	7.1	4	4	4	2	3-0	11	.095
— Albuquerque (PCL)	0	0	...	0.00	1.24	3	1	0	0	...	0-...	5.2	2	2	0	0	5-0	7	.095
— Los Angeles (N.L.)	3	6	.333	3.74	1.37	46	0	0	0	4	0-3	67.1	57	30	28	7	35-2	70	.229
2001— Chicago (A.L.)	0	0	...	20.77	2.31	4	0	0	0	...	0-1	4.1	8	10	10	3	2-1	6	.421

O

Year League	W	L	Pct.	ERA	WHIP	G	GS	CG	ShO	Hld.	Sv.-Opp.	IP	H	R	ER	HR	BB-IBB	SO	Avg.
2002— Chicago (A.L.)	8	2	.800	3.86	1.36	59	0	0	0	9	11-14	67.2	64	32	29	1	28-4	66	.250
2003— GC Yankees (GCL)	0	0	...	0.00	1.00	1	1	0	0	...	0-...	1.0	1	0	0	0	0-0	2	.250
—Tampa (FSL)	0	0	...	0.00	0.50	2	2	0	0	...	0-...	4.0	1	0	0	0	1-0	5	.083
—New York (A.L.)	2	5	.286	3.73	1.54	48	0	0	0	9	0-1	50.2	58	22	21	3	20-3	47	.282
American League totals (3 years)	10	7	.588	4.40	1.47	111	0	0	0	18	11-16	122.2	130	64	60	7	50-8	119	.270
National League totals (6 years)	24	21	.533	3.28	1.23	265	0	0	0	55	10-25	327.0	261	131	119	32	141-18	346	.221
Major League totals (9 years)	34	28	.548	3.58	1.29	376	0	0	0	73	21-41	449.2	391	195	179	39	191-26	465	.236

OSWALT, ROY   P

PERSONAL: Born August 29, 1977, in Weir, Miss. ... 6-0/175. ... Throws right, bats right. ... Full name: Roy Edward Oswalt. ... Name pronounced: OWES-walt. ... High school: Weir (Miss.). ... Junior college: Holmes College (Miss.).

TRANSACTIONS/CAREER NOTES: Selected by Houston Astros organization in 23rd round of free-agent draft (June 4, 1996). ... On suspended list (August 29-September 3, 2002). ... Placed on 15-day disabled list (May 16, 2003). ... Activated from 15-day disabled list (May 30, 2003). ... Placed on 15-day disabled list (June 12, 2003). ... Sent to New Orleans on rehab assignment (July 1, 2003). ... Recalled from New Orleans rehab assignment (July 3, 2003). ... Reinstated from 15-day disabled list (July 7, 2003). ... Placed on 15-day disabled list (July 30, 2003). ... Removed from 15-day disabled list (September 8, 2003).

CAREER HITTING: 26-for-163 (.160), 12 R, 4 2B, 0 3B, 0 HR, 7 RBI.

Year League	W	L	Pct.	ERA	WHIP	G	GS	CG	ShO	Hld.	Sv.-Opp.	IP	H	R	ER	HR	BB-IBB	SO	Avg.
1997— GC Astros (GCL)	1	1	.500	0.64	1.13	5	5	0	0	...	0-...	28.1	25	7	2	2	7-0	28	.227
—Auburn (N.Y.-Penn)	2	4	.333	4.53	1.26	9	9	1	1	...	0-...	51.2	50	29	26	1	15-1	44	.253
1998— GC Astros (GCL)	1	1	.500	2.25	0.69	4	4	0	0	...	0-...	16.0	10	6	4	2	1-0	27	.182
—Auburn (N.Y.-Penn)	4	5	.444	2.18	1.14	11	11	0	0	...	0-...	70.1	49	24	17	3	31-0	67	.194
1999— Michigan (Midw.)	13	4	.765	4.46	1.31	22	22	2	0	...	0-...	151.1	144	78	75	8	54-0	143	.250
2000— Kissimmee (Fla. St.)	4	3	.571	2.98	1.39	8	8	0	0	...	0-...	45.1	52	15	15	1	11-0	47	.294
—Round Rock (Texas)	11	4	.733	1.94	0.99	19	18	2	2	...	0-...	129.2	106	37	28	5	22-1	141	.216
2001— New Orleans (PCL)	2	3	.400	4.35	1.23	5	5	0	0	...	0-...	31.0	32	16	15	4	6-0	34	.267
—Houston (N.L.)	14	3	.824	2.73	1.06	28	20	3	1	0	0-0	141.2	126	48	43	13	24-2	144	.235
2002— Houston (N.L.)	19	9	.679	3.01	1.19	35	34	0	0	0	0-0	233.0	215	86	78	17	62-4	208	.247
2003— New Orleans (PCL)	0	0	...	3.00	1.00	1	1	0	0	...	0-...	3.0	3	1	1	0	0-0	2	.250
—Houston (N.L.)	10	5	.667	2.97	1.14	21	21	0	0	0	0-0	127.1	116	48	42	15	29-0	108	.246
Major League totals (3 years)	43	17	.717	2.92	1.14	84	75	3	1	0	0-0	502.0	457	182	163	45	115-6	460	.243

OVERBAY, LYLE   1B

PERSONAL: Born January 28, 1977, in Centralia, Wash. ... 6-2/222. ... Bats left, throws left. ... Full name: Lyle Stefan Overbay. ... College: Nevada.

TRANSACTIONS/CAREER NOTES: Selected by Arizona Diamondbacks organization in 18th round of free-agent draft (June 2, 1999).

2003 GAMES PLAYED BY POSITION (MLB): 1B—75.

Year Team (League)	Pos.	G	AB	R	H	2B	3B	HR	RBI	BB	SO	HBP	GDP	SB-CS	Avg.	OBP	SLG	OPS	E	Pct.
1999— Missoula (Pio.)	1B-OF	75	* 306	66	* 105	25	7	12	* 101	40	53	2	14	10-3	.343	.418	.588	1.006	10	.986
2000— South Bend (Mid.)	1B	71	259	47	86	19	3	6	47	27	36	2	2	9-2	.332	.397	.498	.895	11	.983
—El Paso (Texas)	1B	62	244	43	86	16	2	8	49	28	39	2	6	3-2	.352	.420	.533	.953	12	.979
2001— El Paso (Texas)	1B-OF	* 138	* 532	82	* 187	* 49	3	13	100	67	92	5	6	5-4	.352	.423	.528	.951	13	.987
—Arizona (N.L.)		2	2	0	1	0	0	0	0	0	1	0	0	0-0	.500	.500	.500	1.000	...	...
2002— Tucson (PCL)	1B	134	525	83	180	* 40	0	19	109	42	86	7	12	0-0	.343	.396	.528	.923	10	.991
—Arizona (N.L.)		10	10	0	1	0	0	0	1	0	5	0	0	0-0	.100	.100	.100	.200	0	...
2003— Tucson (PCL)	1B-DH	35	119	24	34	11	0	4	16	28	19	0	0	0-0	.286	.419	.479	.898	5	.985
—Arizona (N.L.)	1B	86	254	23	70	20	0	4	28	35	67	2	8	1-0	.276	.365	.402	.767	2	.997
Major League totals (3 years)		98	266	23	72	20	0	4	29	35	73	2	8	1-0	.271	.357	.391	.748	2	.997

OWENS, ERIC   OF

PERSONAL: Born February 3, 1971, in Danville, Va. ... 6-0/210. ... Bats right, throws right. ... Full name: Eric Blake Owens. ... High school: Tunstall (Dry Fork, Va.). ... Junior college: Ferrum College (Va.).

TRANSACTIONS/CAREER NOTES: Selected by Cincinnati Reds organization in fourth round of free-agent draft (June 1, 1992). ... On Indianapolis disabled list (August 20-September 11, 1995). ... Traded by Reds to Florida Marlins for a player to be named later (March 21, 1998); Reds acquired P Jesus Martinez to complete deal (March 26, 1998). ... Contract sold by Marlins to Milwaukee Brewers (March 25, 1998). ... Granted free agency (October 15, 1998). ... Signed by San Diego Padres organization (December 10, 1998). ... Traded by Padres with P Matt Clement and P Omar Ortiz to Marlins for OF Mark Kotsay and OF Cesar Crespo (March 28, 2001). ... On Florida disabled list (August 2-22, 2001); included rehabilitation assignment to Calgary (August 19-22). ... Granted free agency (December 21, 2002). ... Signed by Anaheim Angels (December 30, 2002).

2003 GAMES PLAYED BY POSITION (MLB): OF—97, DH—3.

Year Team (League)	Pos.	G	AB	R	H	2B	3B	HR	RBI	BB	SO	HBP	GDP	SB-CS	Avg.	OBP	SLG	OPS	E	Pct.
1992— Billings (Pio.)	3B-SS	67	239	41	72	10	3	3	26	23	22	0	1	15-4	.301	.363	.406	.768	§ 29	.895
1993— Win.-Salem (Car.)	SS	122	487	74	132	25	4	10	63	53	69	4	8	21-12	.271	.343	.400	.743	34	.943
1994— Chattanooga (Sou.)	2B-3B	134	523	73	133	17	3	3	36	54	86	2	10	38-14	.254	.325	.315	.641	40	.912
1995— Indianapolis (A.A.)	2B	108	427	* 86	134	24	• 8	12	63	52	61	1	7	* 33-12	.314	.388	.492	.880	* 17	.967
—Cincinnati (N.L.)	3B	2	2	0	2	0	0	0	1	0	0	0	0	0-0	1.000	1.000	1.000	2.000	0	...
1996— Cincinnati (N.L.)	OF-2B-3B	88	205	26	41	6	0	0	9	23	38	1	2	16-2	.200	.277	.229	.511	2	.978
—Indianapolis (A.A.)	S-3-2-O	33	128	24	41	8	2	4	14	11	16	1	3	6-3	.320	.379	.508	.886	6	.947
1997— Cincinnati (N.L.)	OF-2B	27	57	8	15	0	0	0	3	4	11	0	2	3-2	.263	.311	.263	.575	1	.938
—Indianapolis (A.A.)	2-S-O-3	104	391	56	112	15	4	11	44	42	55	3	8	23-10	.286	.357	.430	.786	§ 27	.940
1998— Milwaukee (N.L.)	OF-2B	34	40	5	5	2	0	1	4	2	6	0	3	0-0	.125	.167	.250	.417	1	.941
—Louisville (Int'l)	OF-3B-DH	77	254	48	85	11	4	5	40	34	30	0	7	21-6	.335	.408	.469	.876	8	.947
1999— San Diego (N.L.)	O-1-3-2	149	440	55	117	22	3	9	61	38	50	3	12	33-7	.266	.327	.391	.718	4	.986
2000— San Diego (N.L.)	OF-2B	145	583	87	171	19	7	6	51	45	63	4	16	29-14	.293	.346	.381	.727	0	1.000
2001— Florida (N.L.)	OF-DH	100	400	51	101	16	1	5	28	29	59	0	13	8-6	.253	.302	.335	.637	3	.984
—Calgary (PCL)	OF	3	15	2	4	2	0	0	2	0	2	0	1	1-0	.267	.267	.400	.667	1	.667
2002— Florida (N.L.)	OF	131	385	44	104	15	5	4	37	31	33	0	11	26-9	.270	.324	.366	.690	6	.975
2003— Anaheim (A.L.)	OF-DH	111	241	29	65	6	0	1	20	10	24	1	4	11-8	.270	.300	.307	.607	5	.971
American League totals (1 year)		111	241	29	65	6	0	1	20	10	24	1	4	11-8	.270	.300	.307	.607	5	.971
National League totals (8 years)		695	2112	276	556	80	16	25	194	172	260	8	59	115-40	.263	.320	.352	.672	17	.985
Major League totals (9 years)		806	2353	305	621	86	16	26	214	182	284	9	63	126-48	.264	.318	.347	.665	22	.984

O

OZUNA, PABLO   2B

PERSONAL: Born August 25, 1974, in Santo Domingo, Dominican Republic. ... 5-10/186. ... Bats right, throws right. ... Full name: Pablo Jose Ozuna. ... Name pronounced: oh-ZU-na.

TRANSACTIONS/CAREER NOTES: Signed as non-drafted free agent by St. Louis Cardinals orgnaization (April 8, 1996). ... Traded by Cardinals with P Braden Looper and P Armando Almanza to Florida Marlins for SS Edgar Renteria (December 14, 1998). ... On disabled list (March 23, 2001-entire season). ... Traded by Marlins with C Charles Johnson, P Vic Darensbourg and OF Preston Wilson to Colorado Rockies for P Mike Hampton, OF Juan Pierre and cash (November 16, 2002). ... Sent on rehab assignment to Visalia (May 31, 2003). ... Reinstated from 15-day disabled list (June 6, 2003). ... Optioned to Tulsa (June 6, 2003). ... Recalled from Colorado Springs (August 19, 2003).

2003 GAMES PLAYED BY POSITION (MLB): 2B—8, OF—5, SS—3.

										BATTING										FIELDING	
Year	Team (League)	Pos.	G	AB	R	H	2B	3B	HR	RBI	BB	SO	HBP	GDP	SB-CS	Avg.	OBP	SLG	OPS	E	Pct.
1996—	Dom. Cardinals (DSL)	SS	74	295	57	107	12	4	6	60	23	19	...	...	19-...	.363	...	.492	...	32	.915
1997—	Johnson City (App.)	SS	56	232	40	75	13	1	5	24	10	24	1	2	23-5	.323	.351	.453	.804	25	.898
1998—	Peoria (Midw.)	SS	133	538	* 122	* 192	27	10	9	62	29	56	11	6	62-26	.357	.400	.494	.894	45	.929
1999—	Portland (East.)	SS	117	502	62	141	25	7	7	46	13	50	13	8	31-15	.281	.315	.400	.715	28	.946
2000—	Portland (East.)	2B	118	464	74	143	25	6	7	59	40	55	7	9	35-24	.308	.368	.433	.801	* 25	.956
—	Florida (N.L.)	2B	14	24	2	8	1	0	0	0	0	2	0	0	1-0	.333	.333	.375	.708	1	.967
2001—	Florida (N.L.)									Did not play.											
2002—	Calgary (PCL)	2B-OF	77	261	37	85	16	1	7	33	17	37	3	5	16-3	.326	.371	.475	.846	9	.961
—	Florida (N.L.)	2B-OF	34	47	4	13	2	2	0	3	1	3	1	2	1-1	.277	.300	.404	.704	1	.967
2003—	Visalia (Calif.)	2B-SS	2	8	1	5	0	0	0	1	1	1	0	0	1-1	.625	.667	.625	1.292	0	1.000
—	Tulsa (Texas)	2B-SS-3B	12	59	4	15	3	0	0	4	2	5	0	0	4-2	.254	.279	.305	.584	3	.943
—	Colo. Springs (PCL)	2-O-S-3	56	219	30	59	13	7	1	17	9	23	1	3	12-6	.269	.300	.406	.706	6	.970
—	Colorado (N.L.)	2B-OF-SS	17	40	5	8	1	0	0	2	2	6	2	1	3-0	.200	.273	.225	.498	2	.969
Major League totals (3 years)			**65**	**111**	**11**	**29**	**4**	**2**	**0**	**5**	**3**	**11**	**3**	**3**	**5-1**	**.261**	**.297**	**.333**	**.630**	**4**	**.968**

PADILLA, VICENTE   P

PERSONAL: Born September 27, 1977, in Chinandega, Nicaragua. ... 6-2/215. ... Throws right, bats right. ... Full name: Vicente D. Padilla. ... Name pronounced: pa-DEE-ya. ... High school: Ruben Dario (Nicaragua).

TRANSACTIONS/CAREER NOTES: Signed as non-drafted free agent by Arizona Diamondbacks organization (August 31, 1998). ... Traded by Diamondbacks with OF Travis Lee, P Omar Daal and P Nelson Figueroa to Philadelphia Phillies for P Curt Schilling (July 26, 2000). ... On Philadelphia disabled list (May 4-30, 2001); included rehabilitation assignment to Scranton/Wilkes-Barre (May 22-30).

CAREER HITTING: 9-for-129 (.070), 3 R, 2 2B, 0 3B, 0 HR, 6 RBI.

Year	League	W	L	Pct.	ERA	WHIP	G	GS	CG	ShO	Hld.	Sv.-Opp.	IP	H	R	ER	HR	BB-IBB	SO	Avg.
1999—	High Desert (Calif.)	4	1	.800	3.73	1.32	9	9	0	0	...	0-...	50.2	50	27	21	3	17-0	55	.253
—	Tucson (PCL)	7	4	.636	3.75	1.40	18	14	0	0	...	0-...	93.2	107	47	39	6	24-7	58	.292
—	Arizona (N.L.)	0	1	.000	16.88	3.75	5	0	0	0	1	0-1	2.2	7	5	5	1	3-0	0	.467
2000—	Tucson (PCL)	0	1	.000	4.42	1.64	12	3	0	0	...	1-...	18.1	22	9	9	2	8-0	22	.306
—	Arizona (N.L.)	2	1	.667	2.31	1.20	27	0	0	0	7	0-1	35.0	32	10	9	0	10-2	30	.242
—	Philadelphia (N.L.)	2	6	.250	5.34	1.91	28	0	0	0	8	2-6	30.1	40	23	18	3	18-5	21	.328
2001—	Philadelphia (N.L.)	3	1	.750	4.24	1.41	23	0	0	0	1	0-3	34.0	36	18	16	1	12-0	29	.273
—	Scran./W.B. (I.L.)	7	0	1.000	2.42	0.92	16	16	0	0	...	0-...	81.2	64	24	22	8	11-0	75	.217
2002—	Philadelphia (N.L.)	14	11	.560	3.28	1.22	32	32	1	1	0	0-0	206.0	198	83	75	16	53-5	128	.254
2003—	Philadelphia (N.L.)	14	12	.538	3.62	1.24	32	32	1	1	0	0-0	208.2	196	94	84	22	62-4	133	.251
Major League totals (5 years)		**35**	**32**	**.522**	**3.61**	**1.29**	**147**	**64**	**2**	**2**	**17**	**2-11**	**516.2**	**509**	**233**	**207**	**43**	**158-16**	**341**	**.259**

PAINTER, LANCE   P

PERSONAL: Born July 21, 1967, in Bedford, England. ... 6-1/200. ... Throws left, bats left. ... Full name: Lance Telford Painter. ... High school: Nicolet (Glendale, Wis.). ... College: Wisconsin.

TRANSACTIONS/CAREER NOTES: Selected by San Diego Padres organization in 25th round of free-agent draft (June 4, 1990). ... Selected by Colorado Rockies in second round (34th pick overall) of expansion draft (November 17, 1992). ... On disabled list (April 17-May 6, 1995). ... On disabled list (August 6, 1996-remainder of season). ... Claimed on waivers by St. Louis Cardinals (December 2, 1996). ... On St. Louis disabled list (April 5-May 12 and May 20-June 20, 1997); included rehabilitation assignment to Louisville (May 1-12). ... On St. Louis disabled list (June 13-29, 1999); included rehabilitation assignment to Arkansas (June 28-29). ... Traded by Cardinals with C Alberto Castillo and P Matt DeWitt to Toronto Blue Jays for P Pat Hentgen and P Paul Spoljaric (November 11, 1999). ... On Toronto disabled list (May 17-June 6, 2000); included rehabilitation assignment to Dunedin (June 4). ... On Toronto disabled list (April 9-May 10, 2001); included rehabilitation assignment to Dunedin (April 26-May 7). ... Released by Blue Jays (June 29, 2001). ... Signed by Milwaukee Brewers organization (July 3, 2001). ... On Milwaukee disabled list (August 22, 2001-remainder of season). ... Granted free agency (November 9, 2001). ... Signed by St. Louis Cardinals organization (December 18, 2002). ... On disabled list (April 11, 2003). ... Sent to Palm Beach on rehab assignment (June 9, 2003). ... Recalled from rehab assignment; reinstated from 15-day disabled list (June 18, 2003). ... Placed on 15-day disabled list (July 28, 2003). ... Removed from 15-day disabled list (September 9, 2003).

CAREER HITTING: 10-for-65 (.154), 6 R, 2 2B, 1 3B, 0 HR, 5 RBI.

Year	League	W	L	Pct.	ERA	WHIP	G	GS	CG	ShO	Hld.	Sv.-Opp.	IP	H	R	ER	HR	BB-IBB	SO	Avg.
1990—	Spokane (N'west)	7	3	.700	1.51	0.84	23	1	0	0	...	3-...	71.2	45	18	12	4	15-0	104	.175
1991—	Waterloo (Midw.)	14	8	.636	2.30	1.10	28	28	7	* 4	...	0-...	200.0	162	64	51	14	57-7	201	.225
1992—	Wichita (Texas)	10	5	.667	3.53	1.18	27	• 27	1	1	...	0-...	163.1	138	74	64	11	55-1	137	.228
1993—	Colo. Springs (PCL)	9	7	.563	4.30	1.51	23	22	• 4	1	...	0-...	138.0	165	90	66	10	44-2	91	.302
—	Colorado (N.L.)	2	2	.500	6.00	1.56	10	6	1	0	0	0-0	39.0	52	26	26	5	9-0	16	.333
1994—	Colo. Springs (PCL)	4	3	.571	4.79	1.56	13	13	1	0	...	0-...	71.1	83	42	38	5	28-2	59	.291
—	Colorado (N.L.)	4	6	.400	6.11	1.59	15	14	0	0	0	0-0	73.2	91	51	50	9	26-2	41	.302
1995—	Colorado (N.L.)	3	0	1.000	4.37	1.43	33	1	0	0	4	1-1	45.1	55	23	22	9	10-0	36	.296
—	Colo. Springs (PCL)	0	3	.000	5.96	1.68	11	4	0	0	...	0-...	25.2	32	20	17	3	11-1	12	.305
1996—	Colorado (N.L.)	4	2	.667	5.86	1.60	34	1	0	0	4	0-1	50.2	56	37	33	12	25-3	48	.280
1997—	St. Louis (N.L.)	1	1	.500	4.76	1.24	14	0	0	0	3	0-...	17.0	13	9	9	1	8-2	11	.213
—	Louisville (A.A.)	1	0	1.000	5.23	1.06	18	2	1	0	...	0-...	20.2	18	14	12	2	4-0	22	.234
1998—	St. Louis (N.L.)	4	0	1.000	3.99	1.48	65	0	0	0	21	1-2	47.1	42	24	21	5	28-3	39	.249
1999—	St. Louis (N.L.)	4	5	.444	4.83	1.39	56	4	0	0	10	1-3	63.1	63	37	34	6	25-1	56	.265
—	Arkansas (Texas)	0	0	...	0.00	0.50	1	1	0	0	...	0-...	2.0	1	0	0	0	0-0	4	.143
2000—	Toronto (A.L.)	2	0	1.000	4.73	1.37	42	2	0	0	5	0-1	66.2	69	37	35	9	22-1	53	.271
—	Dunedin (Fla. St.)	0	0	...	0.00	0.00	1	1	0	0	...	0-...	1.0	0	0	0	0	0-0	0	.000

P

Year League	W	L	Pct.	ERA	WHIP	G	GS	CG	ShO	Hld.	Sv.-Opp.	IP	H	R	ER	HR	BB-IBB	SO	Avg.
2001— Toronto (A.L.)	0	1	.000	7.85	2.07	10	0	0	0	0	0-0	18.1	27	17	16	4	11-0	14	.342
— Dunedin (Fla. St.)	1	1	.500	0.96	1.18	5	1	0	0	...	0-...	9.1	10	1	1	0	1-0	10	.294
— Indianapolis (Int'l)	0	0	...	5.00	1.78	8	0	0	0	...	0-...	9.0	10	5	5	3	6-0	7	.294
— Milwaukee (N.L.)	1	0	1.000	4.22	1.69	13	0	0	0	0	0-0	10.2	11	5	5	3	7-2	6	.268
2002—										Did not play.									
2003— W.P. Beach (FSL)	0	0	...	0.00	0.00	1	1	0	0	...	0-...	1.0	0	0	0	0	0-0	1	.000
— Memphis (PCL)	0	0	...	0.00	0.67	3	0	0	0	...	0-...	3.0	2	0	0	0	0-0	1	.200
— St. Louis (N.L.)	0	1	.000	5.50	1.33	22	0	0	0	5	0-1	18.0	17	12	11	3	7-1	11	.246
American League totals (2 years)	2	1	.667	5.40	1.52	52	2	0	0	5	0-1	85.0	96	54	51	13	33-1	67	.287
National League totals (9 years)	23	17	.575	5.20	1.49	262	26	1	0	47	3-8	365.0	400	224	211	53	145-14	264	.281
Major League totals (10 years)	25	18	.581	5.24	1.50	314	28	1	0	52	3-9	450.0	496	278	262	66	178-15	331	.283

PALMEIRO, ORLANDO   OF

PERSONAL: Born January 19, 1969, in Hoboken, N.J. ... 5-11/180. ... Bats left, throws left. ... Name pronounced: pal-MAIR-oh. ... High school: Southridge (Miami). ... College: Miami (Fla.).

TRANSACTIONS/CAREER NOTES: Selected by California Angels organization in 33rd round of free-agent draft (June 3, 1991). ... On disabled list (September 1-26, 1994). ... Angels franchise renamed Anaheim Angels for 1997 season. ... On disabled list (August 23-September 7, 1997). ... Granted free agency (October 30, 2002). ... Signed by St. Louis Cardinals (February 2, 2003).

2003 GAMES PLAYED BY POSITION (MLB): OF—112.

									BATTING									FIELDING	
Year Team (League)	Pos.	G	AB	R	H	2B	3B	HR	RBI	BB	SO	HBP	GDP	SB-CS	Avg.	OBP	SLG	OPS	E	Pct.
1991— Boise (NW)	OF	70	277	56	77	11	2	1	24	33	22	3	8	8-8	.278	.358	.343	.701	2	.986
1992— Quad City (Midw.)	OF	127	451	83	143	22	4	0	41	56	41	5	5	31-13	.317	.393	.384	.777	6	.973
1993— Midland (Texas)	OF	131	* 535	85	163	19	5	0	64	42	35	2	13	18-14	.305	.356	.359	.715	9	.973
1994— Vancouver (PCL)	OF	117	458	79	150	28	4	1	47	58	46	1	7	21-16	.328	.402	.413	.815	1	.996
1995— Vancouver (PCL)	OF-DH	107	398	66	122	21	4	0	47	41	34	3	11	16-7	.307	.371	.379	.751	1	.995
— California (A.L.)	OF-DH	15	20	3	7	0	0	0	1	1	1	0	0	0-0	.350	.381	.350	.731	0	1.000
1996— Vancouver (PCL)	OF	62	245	40	75	13	4	0	33	30	19	4	4	7-3	.306	.384	.392	.776	5	.959
— California (A.L.)	OF-DH	50	87	6	25	6	1	0	6	8	13	2	1	0-1	.287	.361	.379	.740	0	1.000
1997— Anaheim (A.L.)	OF-DH	74	134	19	29	2	2	0	8	17	11	1	4	2-2	.216	.307	.261	.568	2	.975
1998— Vancouver (PCL)	OF	43	140	21	42	13	3	1	29	16	10	0	2	3-1	.300	.363	.457	.820	0	1.000
— Anaheim (A.L.)	OF-DH	75	165	28	53	7	2	0	21	20	11	0	2	5-4	.321	.395	.388	.782	0	1.000
1999— Anaheim (A.L.)	OF-DH	109	317	46	88	12	1	1	23	39	30	6	4	5-5	.278	.364	.331	.696	1	.994
2000— Anaheim (A.L.)	OF-DH	108	243	38	73	20	2	0	25	38	20	2	4	4-1	.300	.395	.399	.794	2	.984
2001— Anaheim (A.L.)	OF-DH	104	230	29	56	10	1	2	23	25	24	3	3	6-6	.243	.319	.322	.641	1	.989
2002— Anaheim (A.L.)	OF-DH	110	263	35	79	12	1	0	31	30	22	0	7	7-2	.300	.368	.354	.722	1	.993
2003— St. Louis (N.L.)	OF	141	317	37	86	13	1	3	33	32	31	2	1	3-3	.271	.336	.347	.683	0	1.000
American League totals (8 years)		645	1459	204	410	69	10	3	138	178	132	14	25	29-21	.281	.361	.348	.710	7	.991
National League totals (1 year)		141	317	37	86	13	1	3	33	32	31	2	1	3-3	.271	.336	.347	.683	0	1.000
Major League totals (9 years)		786	1776	241	496	82	11	6	171	210	163	16	26	32-24	.279	.357	.348	.705	7	.992

PALMEIRO, RAFAEL   1B

PERSONAL: Born September 24, 1964, in Havana, Cuba. ... 6-0/190. ... Bats left, throws left. ... Full name: Rafael Corrales Palmeiro. ... Name pronounced: pahl-MARE-oh. ... High school: Jackson (Miami). ... College: Mississippi State.

TRANSACTIONS/CAREER NOTES: Selected by New York Mets organization in eighth round of free-agent draft (June 7, 1982); did not sign. ... Selected by Chicago Cubs organization in first round (22nd pick overall) of free-agent draft (June 3, 1985); pick received as compensation for San Diego Padres signing Type A free-agent P Tim Stoddard. ... Traded by Cubs with P Jamie Moyer and P Drew Hall to Texas Rangers for P Mitch Williams, P Paul Kilgus, P Steve Wilson, IF Curtis Wilkerson, IF Luis Benitez and OF Pablo Delgado (December 5, 1988). ... Granted free agency (October 25, 1993). ... Signed by Baltimore Orioles (December 12, 1993). ... Granted free agency (October 23, 1998). ... Signed by Rangers (December 4, 1998).

2003 GAMES PLAYED BY POSITION (MLB): DH—97, 1B—55.

									BATTING									FIELDING	
Year Team (League)	Pos.	G	AB	R	H	2B	3B	HR	RBI	BB	SO	HBP	GDP	SB-CS	Avg.	OBP	SLG	OPS	E	Pct.
1985— Peoria (Midw.)	OF	73	279	34	83	22	4	5	51	31	34	2	4	9-3	.297	.369	.459	.828	1	.992
1986— Pittsfield (East.)	OF	• 140	509	66	* 156	29	2	12	* 95	54	32	2	8	15-7	.306	.367	.442	.809	3	* .988
— Chicago (N.L.)	OF	22	73	9	18	4	0	3	12	4	6	1	4	1-1	.247	.295	.425	.720	4	.900
1987— Iowa (Am. Assoc.)	1B-OF	57	214	36	64	14	3	11	41	22	22	3	2	4-3	.299	.366	.547	.913	2	.988
— Chicago (N.L.)	1B-OF	84	221	32	61	15	1	14	30	20	26	1	4	2-2	.276	.336	.543	.879	1	.995
1988— Chicago (N.L.)	1B-OF	152	580	75	178	41	5	8	53	38	34	3	11	12-2	.307	.349	.436	.785	5	.985
1989— Texas (A.L.)	DH-1B	156	559	76	154	23	4	8	64	63	48	6	18	4-3	.275	.354	.374	.728	12	.991
1990— Texas (A.L.)	DH-1B	154	598	72	* 191	35	6	14	89	40	59	2	24	3-3	.319	.361	.468	.829	7	.995
1991— Texas (A.L.)	DH-1B	159	631	115	203	* 49	3	26	88	68	72	6	17	4-3	.322	.389	.532	.922	* 12	.992
1992— Texas (A.L.)	1B-DH	159	608	84	163	27	4	22	85	72	83	10	10	2-3	.268	.352	.434	.786	7	.995
1993— Texas (A.L.)	1B	160	597	* 124	176	40	2	37	105	73	85	5	8	22-3	.295	.371	.554	.926	5	.997
1994— Baltimore (A.L.)	1B	111	436	82	139	32	0	23	76	54	63	2	11	7-3	.319	.392	.550	.942	4	.996
1995— Baltimore (A.L.)	1B	143	554	89	172	30	2	39	104	62	65	3	12	3-1	.310	.380	.583	.963	4	.997
1996— Baltimore (A.L.)	1B-DH	162	626	110	181	40	2	39	142	95	96	3	9	8-0	.289	.381	.546	.927	8	.995
1997— Baltimore (A.L.)	1B-DH	158	614	95	156	24	2	38	110	67	109	5	14	5-2	.254	.329	.485	.815	10	.993
1998— Baltimore (A.L.)	1B-DH	162	619	98	183	36	1	43	121	79	91	7	14	11-7	.296	.379	.565	.945	9	.994
1999— Texas (A.L.)	DH-1B	158	565	96	183	30	1	47	148	97	69	3	13	2-4	.324	.420	.630	1.050	1	.996
2000— Texas (A.L.)	1B-DH	158	565	102	163	29	3	39	120	103	77	3	14	2-1	.288	.397	.558	.954	4	.995
2001— Texas (A.L.)	1B-DH	160	600	98	164	33	0	47	123	101	91	7	8	1-1	.273	.381	.563	.944	8	.992
2002— Texas (A.L.)	1B-DH	155	546	99	149	34	0	43	105	104	94	6	10	2-0	.273	.391	.571	.962	5	.994
2003— Texas (A.L.)	DH-1B	154	561	92	146	21	2	38	112	84	77	5	7	2-0	.260	.359	.508	.867	2	.996
American League totals (15 years)		2309	8679	1432	2523	483	32	503	1592	1162	1178	74	189	78-34	.291	.376	.528	.903	98	.994
National League totals (3 years)		258	874	116	257	60	6	25	95	62	66	5	19	15-5	.294	.341	.462	.804	10	.982
Major League totals (18 years)		2567	9553	1548	2780	543	38	528	1687	1224	1244	79	208	93-39	.291	.373	.522	.894	108	.994

P

PALMER, DEAN — DH

PERSONAL: Born December 27, 1968, in Tallahassee, Fla. ... 6-1/210. ... Bats right, throws right. ... Full name: Dean William Palmer. ... High school: Florida (Tallahassee, Fla.).

TRANSACTIONS/CAREER NOTES: Selected by Texas Rangers organization in third round of free-agent draft (June 2, 1986). ... On disabled list (July 19, 1988-remainder of season; April 28-May 13, 1994; and June 4-September 22, 1995). ... Traded by Rangers to Kansas City Royals for OF Tom Goodwin (July 25, 1997). ... Granted free agency (October 27, 1997). ... Re-signed by Royals (December 15, 1997). ... Granted free agency (October 23, 1998). ... Signed by Detroit Tigers (November 13, 1998). ... On suspended list (April 28-May 5 and June 15-18, 2000). ... On Detroit disabled list (March 23-April 7, April 13-29 and July 3, 2001-remainder of season); included rehabilitation assignment to Toledo (April 28-29). ... On suspended list (June 15-18, 2001). ... On disabled list (March 22-April 7 and April 14, 2002-remainder of season). ... Placed on the 15-day disabled list (May 10, 2003). ... Transferred to Emergency disabled list (June 5, 2003).

2003 GAMES PLAYED BY POSITION (MLB): DH—22, 3B—1, 1B—1.

Year	Team (League)	Pos.	G	AB	R	H	2B	3B	HR	RBI	BB	SO	HBP	GDP	SB-CS	Avg.	OBP	SLG	OPS	E	Pct.
1986—	GC Rangers (GCL)	3B	50	163	19	34	7	1	0	12	22	34	5	3	6-3	.209	.318	.264	.582	13	.885
1987—	Gastonia (S. Atl.)	3B	128	484	51	104	16	0	9	54	36	126	6	16	5-4	.215	.277	.304	.581	*59	.819
1988—	Charlotte (Fla. St.)	3B	74	305	38	81	12	1	4	35	15	69	1	12	0-0	.266	.299	.351	.650	28	.873
1989—	Tulsa (Texas)	3B-SS	133	498	82	125	32	5	*25	90	41	152	4	6	15-5	.251	.311	.486	.797	‡31	.906
	— Texas (A.L.)	3-S-D-O	16	19	0	2	2	0	0	1	0	12	0	0	0-0	.105	.100	.211	.311	2	.778
1990—	Tulsa (Texas)	3B	7	24	4	7	0	1	3	9	4	10	1	0	0-1	.292	.414	.750	1.164	3	.833
	— Okla. City (A.A.)	3B-1B	88	316	33	69	17	4	12	39	20	106	4	2	1-1	.218	.271	.411	.683	21	.938
1991—	Okla. City (A.A.)	3B-OF	60	234	45	70	11	2	*22	59	20	61	2	2	4-5	.299	.357	.645	1.002	11	.933
	— Texas (A.L.)	3B-DH-OF	81	268	38	50	9	2	15	37	32	98	3	4	0-2	.187	.281	.403	.684	9	.941
1992—	Texas (A.L.)	3B	152	541	74	124	25	0	26	72	62	*154	4	9	10-4	.229	.311	.420	.731	22	.945
1993—	Texas (A.L.)	3B-SS	148	519	88	127	31	2	33	96	53	154	8	5	11-10	.245	.321	.503	.824	‡29	.922
1994—	Texas (A.L.)	3B	93	342	50	84	14	2	19	59	26	89	2	7	3-4	.246	.302	.465	.767	*22	.912
1995—	Texas (A.L.)	3B	36	119	30	40	6	0	9	24	21	21	4	2	1-1	.336	.448	.613	1.062	5	.948
1996—	Texas (A.L.)	3B-DH	154	582	98	163	26	2	38	107	59	145	5	15	2-0	.280	.348	.527	.876	16	.959
1997—	Texas (A.L.)	3B	94	355	47	87	21	0	14	55	26	84	1	4	1-0	.245	.296	.423	.719	10	.959
	— Kansas City (A.L.)	3B-DH	49	187	23	52	10	1	9	31	15	50	2	3	1-2	.278	.335	.487	.822	9	.924
1998—	Kansas City (A.L.)	3B-DH	152	572	84	159	27	2	34	119	48	134	6	18	8-2	.278	.333	.510	.844	22	.921
1999—	Detroit (A.L.)	3B	150	560	92	147	25	2	38	100	57	153	10	12	3-3	.263	.339	.518	.857	19	.945
2000—	Detroit (A.L.)	3B-1B-DH	145	524	73	134	22	2	29	102	66	146	4	9	4-2	.256	.338	.471	.809	25	.937
2001—	Toledo (Int'l)	DH	1	2	0	1	0	0	0	0	2	0	0	0	0-0	.500	.750	.500	1.250	...	...
	— Detroit (A.L.)	DH	57	216	34	48	11	0	11	40	27	59	3	3	4-1	.222	.317	.426	.743	...	...
2002—	Detroit (A.L.)	DH	4	12	0	0	0	0	0	0	1	5	0	1	0-0	.000	.077	.000	.077	...	...
2003—	Detroit (A.L.)	DH-3B-1B	26	86	3	12	2	0	0	6	9	28	2	2	0-0	.140	.235	.163	.397	0	1.000
	Major League totals (14 years)		1357	4902	734	1229	231	15	275	849	502	1332	54	94	48-31	.251	.324	.472	.796	190	.937

PANIAGUA, JOSE — P

PERSONAL: Born August 20, 1973, in San Jose de Ocoa, Dominican Republic. ... 6-2/195. ... Throws right, bats right. ... Full name: Jose Luis Paniagua. ... Name pronounced: pahn-ee-AH-gwah. ... High school: Liceo Nuestra Senora del Altagracia (Santo Domingo, Dominican Republic).

TRANSACTIONS/CAREER NOTES: Signed as non-drafted free agent by Montreal Expos organization (September 17, 1990). ... On Montreal disabled list (May 25-June 11, 1996). ... On Ottawa disabled list (July 16-August 2, 1996). ... Selected by Tampa Bay Devil Rays in second round (50th pick overall) of expansion draft (November 18, 1997). ... Claimed on waivers by Seattle Mariners (March 26, 1998). ... On suspended list (August 10-16, 1999; and August 22-24, 2001). ... Traded by Mariners with P Dennis Stark and P Brian Fuentes to Colorado Rockies for 3B Jeff Cirillo (December 15, 2001). ... Traded by Rockies to Detroit Tigers for P Victor Santos and IF Ronnie Merrill (March 25, 2002). ... Released by Tigers (September 7, 2002). ... Signed to minor league contract by Chicago White Sox (August 27, 2003). ... Contract purchased by Chicago (September 2, 2003). ... Released by Chicago (September 10, 2003).

CAREER HITTING: 0-for-18 (.000), 1 R, 0 2B, 0 3B, 0 HR, 0 RBI.

Year	League	W	L	Pct.	ERA	WHIP	G	GS	CG	ShO	Hld.	Sv.-Opp.	IP	H	R	ER	HR	BB-IBB	SO	Avg.
1991—	Dom. Expos (DSL)	2	2	.500	2.18	1.24	13	2	0	0	...	0-...	33.0	24	16	8	...	17-...	19	...
1992—	Dom. Expos (DSL)	3	7	.300	4.15	1.56	13	13	3	1	...	0-...	73.2	69	50	34	...	46-...	60	...
1993—	GC Expos (GCL)	3	0	1.000	0.67	0.67	4	4	1	0	...	0-...	27.0	13	2	2	0	5-0	25	.140
1994—	W.P. Beach (FSL)	9	9	.500	3.64	1.31	26	26	1	0	...	0-...	141.0	131	82	57	6	54-2	110	.244
1995—	Harrisburg (Eastern)	7	•12	.368	5.34	1.60	25	25	2	1	...	0-...	126.1	140	84	75	9	62-0	89	.285
1996—	Montreal (N.L.)	2	4	.333	3.53	1.53	13	11	0	0	0	0-0	51.0	55	24	20	7	23-0	27	.282
	— Harrisburg (Eastern)	3	0	1.000	0.00	0.78	3	3	0	0	...	0-...	18.0	12	1	0	0	2-0	16	.194
	— Ottawa (Int'l)	9	5	.643	3.18	1.12	15	14	2	1	...	0-...	85.0	72	39	30	7	23-0	61	.225
1997—	W.P. Beach (FSL)	1	0	1.000	0.00	0.70	2	2	0	0	...	0-...	10.0	5	0	0	0	2-0	11	.147
	— Ottawa (Int'l)	8	10	.444	4.64	1.51	22	22	1	0	...	0-...	137.2	164	79	71	13	44-1	87	.295
	— Montreal (N.L.)	1	2	.333	12.00	2.50	9	3	0	0	0	0-0	18.0	29	24	24	2	16-1	8	.372
1998—	Tacoma (PCL)	3	1	.750	2.77	1.29	44	0	0	0	...	5-...	68.1	66	25	21	2	22-1	61	.257
	— Seattle (A.L.)	2	0	1.000	2.05	0.91	18	0	0	0	6	1-2	22.0	15	5	5	3	5-0	16	.200
1999—	Seattle (A.L.)	6	11	.353	4.06	1.64	59	0	0	0	16	3-12	77.2	75	37	35	5	52-4	74	.264
2000—	Seattle (A.L.)	3	0	1.000	3.47	1.32	69	0	0	0	16	5-8	80.1	68	31	31	6	38-3	71	.234
2001—	Seattle (A.L.)	4	3	.571	4.36	1.47	60	0	0	0	16	3-4	66.0	59	35	32	7	38-2	46	.233
2002—	Detroit (A.L.)	0	1	.000	5.83	1.56	40	0	0	0	7	1-2	41.2	50	30	27	10	15-1	34	.294
	— Toledo (Int'l)	2	0	1.000	1.15	0.89	12	0	0	0	...	1-...	15.2	10	2	2	1	4-1	13	.189
2003—	Charlotte (Int'l)	0	0	...	7.71	2.57	3	0	0	0	...	0-...	2.1	4	2	2	0	2-0	2	.400
	— Chicago (A.L.)	0	0	...	99.99	12.00	1	0	0	0	...	0-0	.1	3	4	4	0	1-0	0	.750
	American League totals (6 years)	15	15	.500	4.19	1.45	248	0	0	0	59	13-28	288.0	270	142	134	31	149-10	241	.251
	National League totals (2 years)	3	6	.333	5.74	1.78	22	14	0	0	0	0-0	69.0	84	48	44	9	39-1	35	.308
	Major League totals (8 years)	18	21	.462	4.49	1.52	270	14	0	0	59	13-28	357.0	354	190	178	40	188-11	276	.262

PAQUETTE, CRAIG — 3B/OF

PERSONAL: Born March 28, 1969, in Long Beach, Calif. ... 6-0/210. ... Bats right, throws right. ... Full name: Craig Howard Paquette. ... Name pronounced: paw-KET. ... High school: Ranchos Alamitos (Garden Grove, Calif.). ... Junior college: Golden West College (Calif.).

TRANSACTIONS/CAREER NOTES: Selected by Minnesota Twins organization in 36th round of free-agent draft (June 2, 1987); did not sign. ... Selected by Oakland Athletics organization in eighth round of free-agent draft (June 5, 1989). ... On Modesto disabled list (April 10-May 5, 1991). ... On Huntsville disabled list (June 1-11, 1991). ... On Tacoma disabled list (July 18, 1994-remainder of season). ... Released by A's (March 26, 1996). ... Signed by Kansas City Royals organization (April 3, 1996). ... Granted free agency (October 15, 1997). ... Signed by New York Mets organization (December 23, 1997). ... On New York disabled list (May 7, 1998-remainder of season). ... Granted free agency (October 15, 1998). ... Re-signed by Mets organization (December 18, 1998). ... On Norfolk disabled list (April 22-May 1, 1999). ... Traded by Mets to St. Louis Cardinals for IF/OF Shawon Dunston (July 31, 1999). ... Granted free agency (November 5, 2001). ... Signed by Detroit Tigers (December 17, 2001). ... Released by Tigers (April 29, 2003).

2003 GAMES PLAYED BY POSITION (MLB): 1B—5, OF—5.

P

Year	Team (League)	Pos.	G	AB	R	H	2B	3B	HR	RBI	BB	SO	HBP	GDP	SB-CS	Avg.	OBP	SLG	OPS	E	Pct.
1989— S. Oregon (N'west)	2B-3B-SS	71	277	53	93	* 22	3	14	56	30	46	2	6	9-4	.336	.403	.588	.992	15	.935
1990— Modesto (Calif.)	3B	130	495	65	118	23	4	15	59	47	123	3	10	8-5	.238	.306	.392	.698	26	.922
1991— Huntsville (Sou.)	3B-1B	102	378	50	99	18	1	8	60	28	87	3	16	0-5	.262	.314	.378	.692	16	.920
1992— Huntsville (Sou.)	3B	115	450	59	116	25	4	17	71	29	118	2	12	13-10	.258	.304	.444	.748	* 32	.908
— Tacoma (PCL)	3B	17	66	10	18	7	0	2	11	2	16	0	3	3-1	.273	.294	.470	.764	3	.940
1993— Tacoma (PCL)	3B-SS	50	183	29	49	8	0	8	29	14	54	1	6	3-3	.268	.320	.443	.763	15	.908
— Oakland (A.L.)	3B-DH-OF	105	393	35	86	20	4	12	46	14	108	0	7	4-2	.219	.245	.382	.627	13	.950
1994— Tacoma (PCL)	3B	65	245	39	70	12	3	17	48	14	48	3	4	3-3	.286	.326	.567	.893	14	.936
— Oakland (A.L.)	3B	14	49	0	7	2	0	0	0	0	14	0	0	1-0	.143	.143	.184	.327	0	1.000
1995— Oakland (A.L.)	3-0-S-1	105	283	42	64	13	1	13	49	12	88	1	5	5-2	.226	.256	.417	.673	8	.958
1996— Omaha (A.A.)	D-3-1-0	18	63	9	21	3	0	4	13	8	14	0	3	1-0	.333	.403	.571	.974	3	.917
— Kansas City (A.L.)	3-0-1-S-D	118	429	61	111	15	1	22	67	23	101	2	11	5-3	.259	.296	.452	.749	14	.963
1997— Kansas City (A.L.)	3B-OF	77	252	26	58	15	1	8	33	10	57	2	13	2-2	.230	.263	.393	.656	12	.938
— Omaha (A.A.)	3B-DH	23	91	9	28	6	0	3	20	6	26	0	6	0-2	.308	.343	.473	.816	2	.953
1998— Norfolk (Int'l)	3B-SS-OF	15	61	11	17	1	1	3	14	1	13	0	2	2-1	.279	.286	.475	.761	4	.923
— New York (N.L.)	3B-1B-OF	7	19	3	5	2	0	0	0	0	6	0	3	1-0	.263	.263	.368	.632	0	1.000
1999— Norfolk (Int'l)	3-0-1-S	70	283	40	77	20	3	15	54	10	47	3	4	3-0	.272	.298	.523	.821	8	.969
— St. Louis (N.L.)	0-3-2-1	48	157	21	45	6	0	10	37	6	38	0	6	1-0	.287	.309	.516	.825	3	.975
2000— St. Louis (N.L.)	3-0-1-2	134	384	47	94	24	2	15	61	27	83	2	5	4-3	.245	.294	.435	.728	15	.958
2001— St. Louis (N.L.)	0-3-1-2	123	340	47	96	17	0	15	64	18	67	5	11	3-1	.282	.326	.465	.791	5	.982
2002— Detroit (A.L.)	3-1-0-D	72	252	20	49	14	1	4	20	10	53	0	7	1-0	.194	.223	.306	.528	9	.963
2003— Detroit (A.L.)	1B-OF	11	33	2	5	0	0	0	0	0	5	0	2	0-0	.152	.152	.152	.303	0	1.000
— Memphis (PCL)	3B-1B	11	49	3	13	1	0	0	4	2	12	0	1	0-0	.265	.288	.286	.574	3	.921
American League totals (7 years)		502	1691	186	380	79	8	59	215	69	426	5	45	18-9	.225	.255	.386	.640	56	.958
National League totals (4 years)		312	900	118	240	49	2	40	162	51	194	7	25	9-4	.267	.308	.459	.767	23	.970
Major League totals (11 years)		814	2591	304	620	128	10	99	377	120	620	12	70	27-13	.239	.274	.411	.685	79	.962

PARK, CHAN HO   P

PERSONAL: Born June 30, 1973, in Kong Ju City, South Korea. ... 6-2/204. ... Throws right, bats right. ... Full name: Chan Ho Park. ... High school: Kong Ju (Kong Ju City, Korea). ... College: Hanyang Univ. (South Korea).

TRANSACTIONS/CAREER NOTES: Signed as non-drafted free agent by Los Angeles Dodgers organization (January 14, 1994). ... On Albuquerque disabled list (July 16-29, 1995). ... On suspended list (June 8-17, 1999). ... Granted free agency (November 5, 2001). ... Signed by Texas Rangers (December 23, 2001). ... On Texas disabled list (April 2-May 12 and August 7-23, 2002); included rehabilitation assignment to Oklahoma (August 18-23). ... Placed on 15-day disabled list (April 28, 2003). ... Sent to Frisco on rehab assignment (May 12, 2003). ... Transferred rehab assignment from Frisco to Oklahoma (May 27, 2003). ... Recalled from Oklahoma rehab assignment (June 7, 2003). ... Placed on 15-day disabled list (June 8, 2003). ... Transferred to 60-day disabled list (September 1, 2003).

CAREER HITTING: 58-for-345 (.168), 24 R, 15 2B, 1 3B, 2 HR, 23 RBI.

Year	League	W	L	Pct.	ERA	WHIP	G	GS	CG	ShO	Hld.	Sv.-Opp.	IP	H	R	ER	HR	BB-IBB	SO	Avg.
1994— Los Angeles (N.L.)		0	0	...	11.25	2.50	2	0	0	0	...	0-0	4.0	5	5	5	1	5-0	6	.294
— San Antonio (Texas)		5	7	.417	3.55	1.46	20	20	0	0	...	0-...	101.1	91	52	40	4	57-0	100	.241
1995— Albuquerque (PCL)		6	7	.462	4.91	1.54	23	22	0	0	...	0-...	110.0	93	64	60	10	76-2	101	.233
— Los Angeles (N.L.)		0	0	...	4.50	1.00	2	1	0	0	0	0-0	4.0	2	2	2	1	2-0	7	.143
1996— Los Angeles (N.L.)		5	5	.500	3.64	1.41	48	10	0	0	4	0-0	108.2	82	48	44	7	71-3	119	.209
1997— Los Angeles (N.L.)		14	8	.636	3.38	1.14	32	29	2	0	0	0-0	192.0	149	80	72	24	70-1	166	.213
1998— Los Angeles (N.L.)		15	9	.625	3.71	1.34	34	34	2	0	0	0-0	220.2	199	101	91	16	97-1	191	.244
1999— Los Angeles (N.L.)		13	11	.542	5.23	1.58	33	33	0	0	0	0-0	194.1	208	120	113	31	100-4	174	.276
2000— Los Angeles (N.L.)		18	10	.643	3.27	1.31	34	34	3	1	0	0-0	226.0	173	92	82	21	124-4	217	.214
2001— Los Angeles (N.L.)		15	11	.577	3.50	1.17	36	• 35	2	1	0	0-0	234.0	183	98	91	23	91-1	218	.216
2002— Texas (A.L.)		9	8	.529	5.75	1.59	25	25	0	0	0	0-0	145.2	154	95	93	20	78-2	121	.273
— Oklahoma (PCL)		0	1	.000	27.00	4.00	1	1	0	0	...	0-...	2.0	9	9	9	0	3-0	3	.500
2003— Frisco (Texas)		1	0	1.000	2.45	1.27	2	2	0	0	...	0-...	11.0	10	5	3	0	4-0	6	.238
— Oklahoma (PCL)		1	0	1.000	5.89	1.91	3	3	0	0	...	0-...	18.1	27	12	12	4	8-0	12	.346
— Texas (A.L.)		1	3	.250	7.58	1.99	7	7	0	0	0	0-0	29.2	34	26	25	5	25-0	16	.306
American League totals (2 years)		10	11	.476	6.06	1.66	32	32	0	0	0	0-0	175.1	188	121	118	25	103-2	137	.279
National League totals (8 years)		80	54	.597	3.80	1.32	221	176	9	2	4	0-0	1183.2	1001	546	500	124	560-14	1098	.230
Major League totals (10 years)		90	65	.581	4.09	1.36	253	208	9	2	4	0-0	1359.0	1189	667	618	149	663-16	1235	.237

PARONTO, CHAD   P

PERSONAL: Born July 28, 1975, in Woodsville, N.H. ... 6-5/250. ... Throws right, bats right. ... Full name: Chad Michael Paronto. ... Name pronounced: pah-RON-toe. ... High school: Woodsville (N.H.). ... College: Massachusetts.

TRANSACTIONS/CAREER NOTES: Selected by Baltimore Orioles organization in eighth round of free-agent draft (June 4, 1996). ... On Bowie disabled list (April 7-June 2, 2000). ... Claimed on waivers by Cleveland Indians (November 19, 2001). ... On Cleveland disabled list (July 29, 2002-remainder of season); included rehabilitation assignment to Akron (August 12-30). ... Optioned to Buffalo (April 18, 2003). ... Recalled from Buffalo (April 30, 2003).

CAREER HITTING: 0-for-0 (.000), 0 R, 0 2B, 0 3B, 0 HR, 0 RBI.

Year	League	W	L	Pct.	ERA	WHIP	G	GS	CG	ShO	Hld.	Sv.-Opp.	IP	H	R	ER	HR	BB-IBB	SO	Avg.
1996— Bluefield (Appal.)		1	1	.500	1.69	0.98	9	2	0	0	...	1-...	21.1	16	4	4	0	5-0	24	.208
— Frederick (Caro.)		0	1	.000	4.80	1.27	8	1	0	0	...	0-...	15.0	11	9	8	0	8-0	6	.208
1997— Delmarva (S. Atl.)		6	9	.400	4.74	1.48	28	23	0	0	...	0-...	127.1	133	95	67	9	56-1	93	.265
1998— Frederick (Caro.)		7	6	.538	3.13	1.50	18	18	0	0	...	0-...	103.2	116	44	36	4	39-0	87	.287
— Bowie (East.)		1	3	.250	5.80	1.71	8	7	0	0	...	1-...	35.2	38	30	23	1	23-0	28	.275
1999— Bowie (East.)		0	4	.000	8.12	2.22	15	9	0	0	...	0-...	41.0	59	39	37	3	32-1	27	.345
— Frederick (Caro.)		3	5	.375	4.73	1.48	13	13	1	0	...	0-...	72.1	81	46	38	7	26-1	55	.280
2000— Rochester (Int'l)		1	1	.500	5.75	1.53	12	6	0	0	...	0-...	36.0	40	26	23	5	15-0	16	.286
— Bowie (East.)		4	2	.667	2.87	0.96	8	8	1	0	...	0-...	47.0	29	19	15	2	16-0	31	.180
2001— Rochester (Int'l)		3	3	.500	4.57	1.57	33	0	0	0	...	1-...	43.1	44	28	22	5	24-4	39	.263
— Baltimore (A.L.)		1	3	.250	5.00	1.63	24	0	0	0	5	0-1	27.0	33	24	15	5	11-0	16	.289
2002— Buffalo (Int'l)		0	0	...	0.00	0.85	8	0	0	0	...	1-...	13.0	10	0	0	0	1-1	7	.213
— Cleveland (A.L.)		0	2	.000	4.04	1.26	29	0	0	0	0	0-0	35.2	34	19	16	3	11-1	23	.248
— Akron (East.)		0	0	...	27.00	6.00	1	1	0	0	...	0-...	.1	1	1	1	0	1-0	0	.500
2003— Cleveland (A.L.)		0	2	.000	9.45	1.50	6	0	0	0	0	0-0	6.2	7	8	7	1	3-0	6	.292
— Buffalo (Int'l)		3	5	.375	4.34	1.54	49	0	0	0	...	18-...	56.0	64	36	27	2	22-7	48	.275
Major League totals (3 years)		1	7	.125	4.93	1.43	59	0	0	0	5	0-1	69.1	74	51	38	9	25-1	45	.269

P

PARQUE, JIM   P

PERSONAL: Born February 8, 1976, in Norwalk, Calif. ... 5-11/170. ... Throws left, bats left. ... Full name: James Vo Parque. ... Name pronounced: PAR-kay. ... High school: Crescenta Valley (Calif.). ... College: UCLA.
TRANSACTIONS/CAREER NOTES: Selected by Chicago White Sox organization in second round of free-agent draft (June 3, 1997). ... On suspended list (May 7-9, 2000). ... On disabled list (April 27, 2001-remainder of season). ... Granted free agency (December 21, 2002). ... Signed by Tampa Bay Devil Rays organization (January 20, 2003). ... On disabled list (April 9, 2003). ... Sent on rehab assignment to Durham (April 24, 2003). ... Recalled from Durham (May 8, 2003). ... Reinstated from 15-day disabled list (May 9, 2003). ... Optioned to Durham (May 22, 2003). ... Released by Tampa Bay (September 12, 2003).
CAREER HITTING: 2-for-10 (.200), 0 R, 0 2B, 0 3B, 0 HR, 0 RBI.

Year League	W	L	Pct.	ERA	WHIP	G	GS	CG	ShO	Hld.	Sv.-Opp.	IP	H	R	ER	HR	BB-IBB	SO	Avg.
1997— Winston-Salem (Caro.)	7	2	.778	2.77	0.84	11	11	0	0	...	0-...	61.2	29	19	19	3	23-0	76	.140
— Nashville (A.A.)	1	0	1.000	4.22	1.69	2	2	0	0	...	0-...	10.2	9	5	5	0	9-0	5	.231
1998— Calgary (PCL)	2	3	.400	3.94	1.54	8	8	0	0	...	0-...	48.0	49	26	21	7	25-0	31	.263
— Chicago (A.L.)	7	5	.583	5.10	1.63	21	21	0	0	0	0-0	113.0	135	72	64	14	49-0	77	.299
1999— Chicago (A.L.)	9	15	.375	5.13	1.66	31	30	1	0	0	0-0	173.2	210	111	99	23	79-2	111	.299
2000— Chicago (A.L.)	13	6	.684	4.28	1.49	33	32	0	0	0	0-0	187.0	208	105	89	21	71-1	111	.283
2001— Chicago (A.L.)	0	3	.000	8.04	1.64	5	5	1	0	0	0-0	28.0	36	26	25	7	10-1	15	.308
2002— Charlotte (Int'l)	7	9	.438	6.47	1.60	20	20	0	0	...	0-...	105.2	131	80	76	21	38-0	63	.310
— Chicago (A.L.)	1	4	.200	9.95	1.97	8	4	0	0	0	0-0	25.1	34	29	28	11	16-0	13	.318
2003— Tampa Bay (A.L.)	1	1	.500	11.94	2.48	5	5	0	0	0	0-0	17.1	27	23	23	2	16-0	8	.351
— Durham (Int'l)	5	7	.417	4.08	1.48	21	21	1	0	...	0-...	121.1	132	62	55	13	47-1	49	.286
Major League totals (6 years)	**31**	**34**	**.477**	**5.42**	**1.64**	**103**	**97**	**2**	**0**	**0**	**0-0**	**544.1**	**650**	**366**	**328**	**78**	**241-4**	**335**	**.297**

PARRIS, STEVE   P

PERSONAL: Born December 17, 1967, in Joliet, Ill. ... 6-0/195. ... Throws right, bats right. ... Full name: Steven Michael Parris. ... High school: Joliet (Ill.) West. ... College: St. Francis (Ill.).
TRANSACTIONS/CAREER NOTES: Selected by Philadelphia Phillies organization in fifth round of free-agent draft (June 5, 1989). ... Claimed on waivers by Los Angeles Dodgers (April 19, 1993). ... Claimed on waivers by Seattle Mariners (April 26, 1993). ... On Jacksonville disabled list (May 12-June 23 and July 17-31, 1993). ... Released by Mariners (July 31, 1993). ... Signed by Pittsburgh Pirates organization (June 24, 1994). ... On Pittsburgh disabled list (March 6-July 11 and August 18-September 10, 1996); included rehabilitation assignments to Augusta (June 12-13) and Carolina (June 13-July 11). ... Released by Pirates (March 13, 1997). ... Signed by Cincinnati Reds organization (May 6, 1997). ... Granted free agency (October 15, 1997). ... Re-signed by Reds organization (October 27, 1997). ... On Cincinnati disabled list (July 31-September 1, 1999); included rehabilitation assignment to Indianapolis (August 22-30). ... Traded by Reds to Toronto Blue Jays for P Clayton Andrews and P Leo Estrella (November 22, 2000). ... On Toronto disabled list (July 24, 2001-remainder of season); included rehabilitation assignments to Tennessee (August 24-29) and Syracuse (August 30-September 4). ... On Toronto disabled list (March 23-June 16, 2002); included rehabilitation assignment to Dunedin (May 16-31), Tennessee (June 1-6) and Syracuse (June 7-14). ... Granted free agency (October 28, 2002). ... Signed by Tampa Bay Devil Rays organization (January 16, 2003). ... Placed on 15-day disabled list (May 7, 2003). ... Reinstated from 15-day disabled list (June 3, 2003). ... Given unconditional release (June 18, 2003).
CAREER HITTING: 25-for-162 (.154), 8 R, 4 2B, 0 3B, 0 HR, 15 RBI.

Year League	W	L	Pct.	ERA	WHIP	G	GS	CG	ShO	Hld.	Sv.-Opp.	IP	H	R	ER	HR	BB-IBB	SO	Avg.
1989— Batavia (N.Y.-Penn)	3	5	.375	3.92	1.34	13	10	1	0	...	0-...	66.2	69	38	29	6	20-1	46	.263
1990— Batavia (N.Y.-Penn)	7	1	.875	2.64	1.13	14	14	0	0	...	0-...	81.2	70	34	24	1	22-2	50	.233
1991— Clearwater (Fla. St.)	7	5	.583	3.39	1.35	43	6	0	0	...	1-...	93.0	101	43	35	1	25-4	59	.285
1992— Reading (East.)	5	7	.417	4.64	1.35	18	14	0	0	...	0-...	85.1	94	55	44	9	21-1	60	.277
— Scran./W.B. (I.L.)	3	3	.500	4.03	1.44	11	6	0	0	...	1-...	51.1	57	25	23	1	17-1	29	.285
1993— Scran./W.B. (I.L.)	0	0	...	12.71	2.12	3	0	0	0	...	0-...	5.2	9	9	8	3	3-0	4	.346
— Jacksonville (Sou.)	0	1	.000	5.93	1.54	7	1	0	0	...	0-...	13.2	15	9	9	3	6-0	5	.273
1994— Salem (Caro.)	3	3	.500	3.63	1.39	17	7	0	0	...	0-...	57.0	58	24	23	7	21-1	48	.266
1995— Carolina (Sou.)	9	1	.900	2.51	0.86	14	14	2	2	...	0-...	89.2	61	25	25	2	16-1	86	.191
— Pittsburgh (N.L.)	6	6	.500	5.38	1.49	15	15	1	1	0	0-0	82.0	89	49	49	12	33-1	61	.283
1996— Augusta (S. Atl.)	0	0	...	0.00	0.40	1	1	0	0	...	0-...	5.0	1	0	0	0	1-0	6	.067
— Carolina (Sou.)	2	0	1.000	3.04	1.13	5	5	0	0	...	0-...	26.2	24	11	9	1	6-0	22	.245
— Pittsburgh (N.L.)	0	3	.000	7.18	1.75	8	4	0	0	0	0-0	26.1	35	22	21	4	11-0	27	.321
1997— Chattanooga (Sou.)	6	2	.750	4.13	1.33	14	14	0	0	...	0-...	80.2	78	44	37	9	29-0	68	.249
— Indianapolis (A.A.)	2	3	.400	3.57	1.05	5	5	1	1	...	0-...	35.1	26	15	14	4	11-1	27	.203
1998— Indianapolis (Int'l)	6	1	.857	3.84	1.19	13	13	1	1	...	0-...	84.1	74	38	36	8	26-1	102	.235
— Cincinnati (N.L.)	6	5	.545	3.73	1.22	18	16	1	1	0	0-0	99.0	89	44	41	9	32-3	77	.236
1999— Indianapolis (Int'l)	0	2	.000	4.04	1.35	6	6	0	0	...	0-...	35.2	39	16	16	5	9-1	31	.291
— Cincinnati (N.L.)	11	4	.733	3.50	1.37	22	21	2	1	0	0-0	128.2	124	59	50	16	52-4	86	.260
2000— Cincinnati (N.L.)	12	17	.414	4.81	1.55	33	33	0	0	0	0-0	192.2	227	109	103	30	71-5	117	.294
2001— Toronto (A.L.)	4	6	.400	4.60	1.58	19	19	1	0	0	0-0	105.2	126	60	54	18	41-4	49	.299
— Tennessee (Sou.)	0	0	...	0.00	1.00	1	1	0	0	...	0-...	3.0	2	0	0	0	1-0	2	.182
— Syracuse (Int'l)	0	0	...	4.70	1.04	2	2	0	0	...	0-...	7.2	6	4	4	1	2-0	8	.207
2002— Dunedin (Fla. St.)	0	1	.000	4.41	1.22	3	3	0	0	...	0-...	16.1	19	10	8	1	1-0	8	.292
— Tennessee (Sou.)	0	0	...	3.00	1.50	1	1	0	0	...	0-...	6.0	7	2	2	0	2-0	5	.269
— Syracuse (Int'l)	1	1	.500	1.29	0.86	2	2	0	0	...	0-...	14.0	10	6	2	0	2-0	5	.192
— Toronto (A.L.)	5	5	.500	5.97	1.74	14	14	0	0	0	0-0	75.1	96	50	50	13	35-5	48	.314
2003— Tampa Bay (A.L.)	0	3	.000	6.18	1.67	10	7	0	0	0	0-0	43.2	60	32	30	12	13-0	14	.338
American League totals (3 years)	**9**	**14**	**.391**	**5.37**	**1.65**	**43**	**40**	**1**	**0**	**0**	**0-0**	**224.2**	**282**	**142**	**134**	**43**	**89-9**	**111**	**.310**
National League totals (5 years)	**35**	**35**	**.500**	**4.49**	**1.44**	**96**	**89**	**4**	**3**	**0**	**0-0**	**528.2**	**564**	**283**	**264**	**71**	**199-13**	**368**	**.275**
Major League totals (8 years)	**44**	**49**	**.473**	**4.75**	**1.51**	**139**	**129**	**5**	**3**	**0**	**0-0**	**753.1**	**846**	**425**	**398**	**114**	**288-22**	**479**	**.286**

PARRISH, JOHN   P

PERSONAL: Born November 26, 1977, in Lancaster, Pa. ... 5-11/181. ... Throws left, bats left. ... Full name: John Henry Parrish Jr.. ... High school: J.P. McCaskey (Lancaster, Pa.).
TRANSACTIONS/CAREER NOTES: Selected by Baltimore Orioles organization in 25th round of free-agent draft (June 4, 1996). ... On disabled list (March 30, 2002-entire season). ... Signed by Baltimore Orioles (August 15, 2003).
CAREER HITTING: 0-for-0 (.000), 0 R, 0 2B, 0 3B, 0 HR, 0 RBI.

Year League	W	L	Pct.	ERA	WHIP	G	GS	CG	ShO	Hld.	Sv.-Opp.	IP	H	R	ER	HR	BB-IBB	SO	Avg.
1996— GC Orioles (GCL)	2	0	1.000	1.86	1.24	11	0	0	0	...	2-...	19.1	13	5	4	0	11-0	33	.186
— Bluefield (Appal.)	2	1	.667	2.70	1.50	8	0	0	0	...	1-...	13.1	11	6	4	0	9-1	18	.229
1997— Delmarva (S. Atl.)	3	3	.500	3.84	1.39	23	10	0	0	...	1-...	72.2	69	39	31	7	32-3	76	.250
— Bowie (East.)	1	0	1.000	1.80	1.00	1	1	0	0	...	0-...	5.0	3	1	1	0	2-0	3	.167
— Frederick (Caro.)	1	3	.250	6.04	1.75	5	5	0	0	...	0-...	22.1	23	18	15	3	16-0	17	.274

P

Year	League	W	L	Pct.	ERA	WHIP	G	GS	CG	ShO	Hld.	Sv.-Opp.	IP	H	R	ER	HR	BB-IBB	SO	Avg.
1998— Frederick (Caro.)		4	4	.500	3.27	1.26	16	16	1	0	...	0-...	82.2	77	39	30	5	27-1	81	.246
1999— Delmarva (S. Atl.)		0	1	.000	7.20	1.50	4	4	0	0	...	0-...	10.0	9	8	8	1	6-1	10	.225
— Frederick (Caro.)		2	2	.500	4.17	1.25	6	6	0	0	...	0-...	36.2	34	17	17	4	12-0	44	.250
— Bowie (East.)		0	2	.000	4.04	1.65	12	10	0	0	...	0-...	55.2	49	28	25	4	43-1	42	.258
2000— Bowie (East.)		2	0	1.000	1.69	1.19	3	3	0	0	...	0-...	16.0	12	3	3	0	7-0	16	.214
— Rochester (Int'l)		6	7	.462	4.24	1.36	18	18	0	0	...	0-...	104.0	85	54	49	10	56-1	87	.235
— Baltimore (A.L.)		2	4	.333	7.18	2.06	8	8	0	0	0	0-0	36.1	40	32	29	6	35-0	28	.288
2001— Rochester (Int'l)		7	7	.500	3.52	1.25	26	19	1	0	...	0-...	133.0	115	68	52	11	51-4	126	.231
— Baltimore (A.L.)		1	2	.333	6.14	1.77	16	1	0	0	2	0-0	22.0	22	17	15	5	17-1	20	.256
2002— Baltimore (A.L.)											Did not play.									
2003— Bowie (East.)		3	3	.500	2.00	1.19	49	0	0	0	...	6-...	76.1	58	22	17	5	33-0	85	.214
— Baltimore (A.L.)		0	1	.000	1.90	1.06	14	0	0	0	1	0-2	23.2	17	7	5	2	8-2	15	.205
Major League totals (3 years)		3	7	.300	5.38	1.70	38	9	0	0	3	0-2	82.0	79	56	49	13	60-3	63	.256

PATTERSON, COREY   OF

PERSONAL: Born August 13, 1979, in Atlanta, Ga. ... 5-9/180. ... Bats left, throws right. ... Full name: Donald Corey Patterson. ... High school: Harrison (Kennesaw, Ga.).

TRANSACTIONS/CAREER NOTES: Selected by Chicago Cubs organization in first round (third pick overall) of free-agent draft (June 2, 1998). ... On disabled list (May 27-June 11, 1999). ... Placed on the 15-day disabled list by Chicago (July 7, 2003). ... Transferred to Emergency disabled list (July 21, 2003).

2003 GAMES PLAYED BY POSITION (MLB): OF—82.

Year	Team (League)	Pos.	G	AB	R	H	2B	3B	HR	RBI	BB	SO	HBP	GDP	SB-CS	Avg.	OBP	SLG	OPS	E	Pct.
1999— Lansing (Midw.)	OF	112	475	94	152	35	*17	20	79	25	85	5	5	33-9	.320	.358	.592	.949	9	.965
2000— West Tenn (Sou.)	OF	118	444	73	116	26	5	22	82	45	115	10	7	27-15	.261	.338	.491	.829	3	.990
— Chicago (N.L.)	OF	11	42	9	7	1	0	2	2	3	14	1	0	1-1	.167	.239	.333	.572	1	.963
2001— Iowa (PCL)	OF	89	367	63	93	22	3	7	32	29	65	1	2	19-8	.253	.308	.387	.694	6	.968
— Chicago (N.L.)	OF	59	131	26	29	3	0	4	14	6	33	3	1	4-0	.221	.266	.336	.602	2	.976
2002— Chicago (N.L.)	OF	153	592	71	150	30	5	14	54	19	142	8	8	18-3	.253	.284	.392	.676	3	.990
2003— Chicago (N.L.)	OF	83	329	49	98	17	7	13	55	15	77	1	5	16-5	.298	.329	.511	.839	4	.975
Major League totals (4 years)		306	1094	155	284	51	12	33	125	43	266	13	14	39-9	.260	.293	.419	.712	10	.983

PATTERSON, DANNY   P

PERSONAL: Born February 17, 1971, in San Gabriel, Calif. ... 6-0/190. ... Throws right, bats right. ... Full name: Danny Shane Patterson. ... High school: San Gabriel (Calif.). ... Junior college: Cerritos College (Calif.).

TRANSACTIONS/CAREER NOTES: Selected by Texas Rangers organization in 47th round of free-agent draft (June 5, 1989). ... On Texas disabled list (May 22-June 14, 1997); included rehabilitation assignment to Tulsa (June 9-14). ... On Texas disabled list (March 22-April 17, 1998); included rehabilitation assignments to Tulsa (April 7-12) and Oklahoma (April 13-17). ... Traded by Rangers with OF Juan Gonzalez and C Gregg Zaun to Detroit Tigers for P Justin Thompson, P Francisco Cordero, OF Gabe Kapler, C Bill Haselman, 2B Frank Catalanotto and P Alan Webb (November 2, 1999). ... On disabled list (July 22-August 7, 2000). ... On Detroit disabled list (April 4-May 31 and June 9, 2002-remainder of season) included rehabilitation assignment to Toledo (May 22-31). ... On disabled list (March 29, 2003). ... Transferred to Emergency disabled list (May 27, 2003). ... Sent to Toledo on rehab assignment (June 22, 2003). ... Recalled from Toledo rehab assignment (July 12, 2003). ... Reinstated from Emergency disabled list (July 17, 2003).

CAREER HITTING: 0-for-1 (.000), 0 R, 0 2B, 0 3B, 0 HR, 0 RBI.

Year	League	W	L	Pct.	ERA	WHIP	G	GS	CG	ShO	Hld.	Sv.-Opp.	IP	H	R	ER	HR	BB-IBB	SO	Avg.
1990— Butte (Pio.)		0	3	.000	6.35	1.76	13	3	0	0	...	1-...	28.1	36	23	20	3	14-1	18	.308
1991— GC Rangers (GCL)		5	3	.625	3.24	1.10	11	9	0	0	...	0-...	50.0	43	21	18	1	12-0	46	.232
1992— Gastonia (S. Atl.)		4	6	.400	3.59	1.32	23	21	3	1	...	0-...	105.1	106	47	42	9	33-3	84	.261
1993— Charlotte (Fla. St.)		5	6	.455	2.51	1.22	47	0	0	0	...	7-...	68.0	55	22	19	2	28-4	41	.219
1994— Charlotte (Fla. St.)		1	0	1.000	4.61	1.32	7	0	0	0	...	0-...	13.2	13	7	7	1	5-0	9	.255
— Tulsa (Texas)		1	4	.200	1.64	1.18	30	1	0	0	...	6-...	44.0	35	13	8	2	17-1	33	.223
1995— Tulsa (Texas)		2	2	.500	6.19	1.60	26	0	0	0	...	5-...	36.1	45	27	25	2	13-2	24	.306
— Oklahoma City (A.A.)		1	0	1.000	1.65	1.17	14	0	0	0	...	2-...	27.1	23	8	5	0	9-2	9	.240
1996— Oklahoma City (A.A.)		6	2	.750	1.68	1.17	44	0	0	0	...	10-...	80.1	79	22	15	5	15-3	53	.256
— Texas (A.L.)		0	0	...	0.00	1.50	7	0	0	0	0	0-0	8.2	10	4	0	0	3-1	5	.286
1997— Texas (A.L.)		10	6	.625	3.42	1.31	54	0	0	0	9	1-8	71.0	70	29	27	3	23-4	69	.263
— Tulsa (Texas)		0	0	...	4.50	2.50	2	2	0	0	...	0-...	2.0	5	4	1	0	0-0	0	.417
1998— Tulsa (Texas)		0	0	...	4.50	0.75	2	1	0	0	...	0-...	4.0	3	2	2	1	0-0	4	.214
— Oklahoma (PCL)		0	0	...	4.50	2.50	1	0	0	0	...	0-...	2.0	4	1	1	0	1-0	2	.400
— Texas (A.L.)		2	5	.286	4.45	1.37	56	0	0	0	19	2-2	60.2	64	31	30	11	19-2	33	.274
1999— Texas (A.L.)		2	5	.286	5.67	1.59	53	0	0	0	4	0-1	60.1	77	38	38	5	19-3	43	.304
— Oklahoma (PCL)		1	0	1.000	0.00	0.67	2	0	0	0	...	0-...	3.0	1	0	0	0	1-0	4	.100
2000— Detroit (A.L.)		5	1	.833	3.97	1.46	58	0	0	0	12	0-2	56.2	69	26	25	4	14-2	29	.309
2001— Detroit (A.L.)		5	4	.556	3.06	1.18	60	0	0	0	16	1-5	64.2	64	24	22	4	12-5	27	.274
2002— Detroit (A.L.)		0	2	.000	15.00	2.33	6	0	0	0	0	0-1	3.0	5	5	5	0	2-0	1	.357
— Toledo (Int'l)		0	0	...	0.00	0.20	5	1	0	0	...	0-...	5.0	1	0	0	0	0-0	3	.067
2003— Toledo (Int'l)		1	0	1.000	2.45	1.18	10	0	0	0	...	0-...	11.0	8	3	3	0	5-1	6	.211
— Detroit (A.L.)		0	0	...	4.08	1.08	19	0	0	0	1	3-3	17.2	15	8	8	1	4-0	19	.227
Major League totals (8 years)		24	18	.571	4.07	1.37	313	0	0	0	61	7-22	342.2	374	165	155	28	96-17	226	.282

PATTERSON, JARROD   3B

PERSONAL: Born September 7, 1973, in Montgomery, Ala. ... 6-1/195. ... Bats left, throws right. ... Full name: Jarrod Lane Patterson. ... High school: Chilton County (Chilton, Ala.). ... Junior college: Jefferson Davis College (Ala.).

TRANSACTIONS/CAREER NOTES: Selected by New York Mets organization in 20th round of free-agent draft (June 3, 1993). ... Released by Mets (March 25, 1997). ... Signed by Regina, Prairie League (June 1997). ... Signed by Arizona Diamondbacks organization (June 24, 1998). ... Granted free agency (Ocotober 15, 1999). ... Signed by Pittsburgh Pirates organization (November 4, 1999). ... Released by Pirates (February 13, 1999). ... Re-signed by Pirates organization (February 14, 1999). ... Traded by Pirates to Montreal Expos for P Matt Skrmetta (August 12, 2000). ... Granted free agency (October 15, 2000). ... Signed by Detroit Tigers organization (November 21, 2000). ... Granted free agency (October 15, 2002). ... Signed by Kansas City Royals organization (November 16, 2002).

2003 GAMES PLAYED BY POSITION (MLB): 3B—4, DH—4, 1B—2.

P

Year Team (League)	Pos.	G	AB	R	H	2B	3B	HR	RBI	BB	SO	HBP	GDP	SB-CS	Avg.	OBP	SLG	OPS	E	Pct.
1993—GC Mets (GCL)	1B	46	166	27	40	9	1	2	25	24	28	0	5	1-3	.241	.330	.343	.673	...	.994
1994—Kingsport (Appal.)	1B	36	112	12	29	5	2	5	18	12	39	1	1	2-0	.259	.336	.473	.809	6	.975
—Pittsfield (NYP)	1B	29	106	8	19	6	1	1	15	10	34	0	1	0-1	.179	.246	.283	.529	5	.983
1995—Kingsport (Appal.)	1B	64	240	45	67	17	3	13	* 57	28	50	1	0	3-1	.279	.351	.538	.888	4	.992
1996—St. Lucie (Fla. St.)	1B	17	61	6	11	2	0	1	6	3	19	1	0	1-0	.180	.227	.262	.490	5	.968
—Capital City (SAL)	1B	70	213	26	49	9	1	3	37	33	65	2	3	1-1	.230	.333	.324	.657	1	.995
1997—Regina (PRA)		65	240	52	87	* 24	2	7	50	38	47	2	1	7-3	.363	.452	.567	1.019	...	...
1998—High Desert (Calif.)	2B-3B-1B	131	492	89	165	34	9	18	102	66	97	2	8	9-2	.335	.414	.551	.965	24	.959
1999—El Paso (Texas)	3B-1B-OF	67	249	63	95	27	3	8	51	51	45	1	3	3-2	.382	.484	.610	1.094	12	.939
—Tucson (PCL)	3B-C	75	274	46	92	25	3	11	47	36	37	3	9	4-1	.336	.415	.569	.984	13	.919
2000—Nashville (PCL)	3B-C-1B	70	198	25	55	10	0	5	30	13	40	2	2	0-2	.278	.326	.404	.730	9	.942
—Altoona (East.)	3B	11	36	1	5	1	0	0	4	3	11	1	1	0-...	.139	.220	.167	.387	6	.824
—Ottawa (Int'l)	3B	25	92	9	25	6	1	0	16	4	13	0	4	1-0	.272	.302	.359	.661	4	.940
2001—Toledo (Int'l)	3-1-2-0	69	213	41	63	15	2	7	25	30	47	1	9	2-1	.296	.381	.484	.864	7	.958
—Erie (East.)	3B	20	70	17	28	5	1	7	18	11	11	0	0	0-0	.400	.476	.800	1.276	4	.920
—Detroit (A.L.)	3B	13	41	6	11	1	1	2	4	0	4	2	2	0-1	.268	.302	.488	.790	2	.923
2002—Toledo (Int'l)	3B-2B	117	447	66	132	34	6	13	70	46	71	4	8	3-1	.295	.364	.485	.849	21	.945
2003—Omaha (PCL)	3-1-D-0	123	478	74	123	33	2	18	91	51	92	2	9	4-1	.257	.329	.448	.777	19	.960
—Kansas City (A.L.)	3B-DH-1B	13	22	3	4	0	0	0	0	3	6	0	0	0-0	.182	.280	.182	.462	1	.900
Major League totals (2 years)		26	63	9	15	1	1	2	4	3	10	2	2	0-1	.238	.294	.381	.675	3	.917

PATTERSON, JOHN   P

PERSONAL: Born January 30, 1978, in Orange, Texas. ... 6-5/208. ... Throws right, bats right. ... Full name: John Hollis Patterson. ... High school: West Orange-Stark (Orange, Texas).

TRANSACTIONS/CAREER NOTES: Signed as non-drafted free agent by Arizona Diamondbacks organization (November 7, 1996). ... On disabled list (April 6-24 and May 6-September 8, 2000). ... On El Paso disabled list (April 5-19 and April 25-May 13, 2001). ... On Tucson disabled list (April 4-May 5, 2002). ... Recalled from Tucson (May 28, 2003). ... Optioned to Tucson (July 9, 2003). ... Recalled from Tucson (September 1, 2003).

CAREER HITTING: 2-for-23 (.087), 2 R, 0 2B, 0 3B, 0 HR, 1 RBI.

Year League	W	L	Pct.	ERA	WHIP	G	GS	CG	ShO	Hld.	Sv.-Opp.	IP	H	R	ER	HR	BB-IBB	SO	Avg.
1997—South Bend (Mid.)	1	9	.100	3.23	1.24	18	18	0	0	...	0-...	78.0	63	32	28	3	34-0	95	.221
1998—High Desert (Calif.)	8	7	.533	2.83	1.13	25	25	0	0	...	0-...	127.0	102	54	40	12	42-0	148	.217
1999—El Paso (Texas)	8	6	.571	4.77	1.40	18	18	2	0	...	0-...	100.0	98	61	53	16	42-0	117	.256
—Tucson (PCL)	1	5	.167	7.04	1.99	7	6	0	0	...	0-...	30.2	43	26	24	3	18-0	29	.331
2000—Tucson (PCL)	0	2	.000	7.80	2.00	3	2	0	0	...	0-...	15.0	21	14	13	1	9-0	10	.323
2001—Lancaster (Calif.)	0	0	...	5.79	1.29	2	2	0	0	...	0-...	9.1	9	6	6	3	3-0	9	.243
—El Paso (Texas)	1	2	.333	4.26	1.54	5	5	0	0	...	0-...	25.1	30	15	12	7	9-0	19	.297
—Tucson (PCL)	2	7	.222	5.85	1.67	13	12	0	0	...	0-...	67.2	82	50	44	9	31-3	40	.301
2002—Tucson (PCL)	10	5	.667	4.23	1.44	19	18	0	0	...	0-...	112.2	117	59	53	14	45-1	104	.265
—Arizona (N.L.)	2	0	1.000	3.23	1.11	7	5	0	0	0	0-0	30.2	27	11	11	7	7-0	31	.235
2003—Tucson (PCL)	10	5	.667	2.63	1.31	18	18	2	2	...	0-...	109.1	100	48	32	6	43-0	74	.241
—Arizona (N.L.)	1	4	.200	6.05	1.65	16	8	0	0	0	1-1	55.0	61	39	37	7	30-5	43	.281
Major League totals (2 years)	3	4	.429	5.04	1.46	23	13	0	0	0	1-1	85.2	88	50	48	14	37-5	74	.265

PAUL, JOSH   C

PERSONAL: Born May 19, 1975, in Evanston, Ill. ... 6-1/200. ... Bats right, throws right. ... Full name: Joshua William Paul. ... High school: Buffalo Grove (Ill.). ... College: Vanderbilt.

TRANSACTIONS/CAREER NOTES: Selected by Chicago White Sox organization in second round of free-agent draft (June 4, 1996). ... On Birmingham disabled list (April 13-July 14, 1997; and July 9-27, 1999). ... On Charlotte disabled list (July 5-August 3, 2000). ... On Charlotte disabled list (July 25-August 9, 2001). ... Sent outright to Charlotte by Chicago White Sox (April 23, 2003). ... Contract purchased by Chicago from Charlotte (May 31, 2003). ... Elected free agency (June 25, 2003). ... Signed by Chicago Cubs (September 1, 2003).

2003 GAMES PLAYED BY POSITION (MLB): C—14, DH—1.

Year Team (League)	Pos.	G	AB	R	H	2B	3B	HR	RBI	BB	SO	HBP	GDP	SB-CS	Avg.	OBP	SLG	OPS	E	Pct.
1996—GC Whi. Sox (GCL)		1	0	0	0	0	0	0	0	1	0	0	0	0-0	...	1.000	...	1.000	...	...
—Hickory (S. Atl.)	C	59	226	41	74	16	0	8	37	21	53	1	2	13-4	.327	.386	.504	.890	2	.991
1997—Birmingham (Sou.)	C	34	115	18	34	5	0	1	16	12	25	1	4	6-2	.296	.367	.365	.732	3	.988
—GC Whi. Sox (GCL)	C	5	14	3	6	0	1	0	0	1	3	0	1	1-0	.429	.467	.571	1.038	3	.900
1998—Win.-Salem (Car.)	C	123	444	66	113	20	7	11	63	38	91	5	11	20-8	.255	.319	.405	.724	3	.997
1999—Birmingham (Sou.)	C-DH	93	319	47	89	19	3	4	42	29	68	5	6	6-6	.279	.345	.395	.740	5	.992
—Chicago (A.L.)	C	6	18	2	4	1	0	0	1	0	4	0	0	0-0	.222	.222	.278	.500	0	1.000
2000—Chicago (A.L.)	C-OF	36	71	15	20	3	2	1	8	5	17	1	3	1-0	.282	.338	.423	.760	4	.974
—Charlotte (Int'l)	C-OF	51	168	28	40	5	1	4	19	13	38	2	3	6-2	.238	.299	.351	.650	2	.994
2001—Chicago (A.L.)	C	57	139	20	37	11	0	3	18	13	25	0	3	6-2	.266	.327	.410	.737	6	.980
—Charlotte (Int'l)	C	22	75	11	21	4	0	4	14	7	18	0	0	0-0	.280	.337	.493	.831	1	1.000
2002—Charlotte (Int'l)	C-1B-OF	65	231	18	63	15	2	0	17	17	45	1	7	10-4	.273	.323	.355	.678	3	.993
—Chicago (A.L.)	C-DH	33	104	11	25	4	0	0	11	9	22	1	1	2-0	.240	.302	.279	.581	2	.991
2003—Charlotte (Int'l)	C-2B-DH	19	64	6	12	0	1	2	5	5	14	0	1	1-1	.188	.243	.313	.555	2	.982
—Chicago (A.L.)	C-DH	13	17	6	6	0	0	0	4	3	3	0	0	0-0	.353	.450	.353	.803	0	1.000
—Iowa (PCL)	C-O-D-1	47	146	12	37	4	0	2	15	8	30	1	5	0-2	.253	.297	.322	.619	1	.995
—Chicago (N.L.)	C	3	6	0	0	0	0	0	0	0	3	0	0	0-0	.000	.000	.000	.000	0	1.000
American League totals (5 years)		145	349	54	92	19	2	4	42	30	71	2	7	9-2	.264	.323	.364	.687	12	.984
National League totals (1 year)		3	6	0	0	0	0	0	0	0	3	0	0	0-0	.000	.000	.000	.000	0	1.000
Major League totals (5 years)		148	355	54	92	19	2	4	42	30	74	2	7	9-2	.259	.318	.358	.676	12	.984

PAVANO, CARL   P

PERSONAL: Born January 8, 1976, in New Britain, Conn. ... 6-5/235. ... Throws right, bats right. ... Full name: Carl Anthony Pavano. ... Name pronounced: pa-VAH-no. ... High school: Southington (Conn.).

TRANSACTIONS/CAREER NOTES: Selected by Boston Red Sox organization in 13th round of free-agent draft (June 2, 1994). ... Traded by Red Sox with a player to be named later to Montreal Expos for P Pedro Martinez (November 18, 1997); Expos acquired P Tony Armas Jr. to complete deal (December 18, 1997). ... On Montreal disabled list

(July 12-September 11, 1999); included rehabilitation assignments to Ottawa (July 29-30 and September 6-7). ... On disabled list (June 25, 2000-remainder of season). ... On Montreal disabled list (March 23-August 15, 2001); included rehabilitation assignments to Jupiter (July 14-29) and Ottawa (July 30-August 9). ... Traded by Expos with P Graeme Lloyd, IF Mike Mordecai and P Justin Wayne to Florida Marlins for OF Cliff Floyd, P Claudio Vargas, 2B/OF Wilton Guerrero, cash considerations and a player to be named later (July 11, 2002); Expos acquired P Don Levinski to complete deal (August 6, 2002).

CAREER HITTING: 28-for-220 (.127), 10 R, 5 2B, 2 3B, 0 HR, 8 RBI.

Year	League	W	L	Pct.	ERA	WHIP	G	GS	CG	ShO	Hld.	Sv.-Opp.	IP	H	R	ER	HR	BB-IBB	SO	Avg.
1994—	GC Red Sox (GCL)	4	3	.571	1.84	0.86	9	7	0	0	...	0-...	44.0	31	14	9	1	7-0	47	.186
1995—	Michigan (Midw.)	6	6	.500	3.45	1.21	22	22	1	0	...	0-...	141.0	118	63	54	7	52-0	138	.227
1996—	Trenton (East.)	16	5	.762	2.63	1.09	27	26	6	2	...	0-...	185.0	154	66	54	16	47-2	146	.230
1997—	Pawtucket (Int'l)	11	6	.647	3.12	1.13	23	23	3	0	...	0-...	161.2	148	62	56	13	34-2	147	.239
1998—	Jupiter (FSL)	0	0	...	6.60	1.53	4	4	0	0	...	0-...	15.0	20	11	11	1	3-0	14	.333
	— Ottawa (Int'l)	1	0	1.000	2.41	1.02	3	3	0	0	...	0-...	18.2	12	5	5	1	7-0	14	.190
	— Montreal (N.L.)	6	9	.400	4.21	1.28	24	23	0	0	0	0-0	134.2	130	70	63	18	43-1	83	.251
1999—	Montreal (N.L.)	6	8	.429	5.63	1.46	19	18	1	1	0	0-0	104.0	117	66	65	8	35-1	70	.285
	— Ottawa (Int'l)	0	1	.000	9.00	1.40	2	2	0	0	...	0-...	5.0	7	5	5	1	0-0	3	.318
2000—	Montreal (N.L.)	8	4	.667	3.06	1.27	15	15	0	0	0	0-0	97.0	89	40	33	8	34-1	64	.248
2001—	Jupiter (FSL)	1	1	.500	2.19	0.97	3	3	0	0	...	0-...	12.1	10	7	3	1	2-0	11	.213
	— Ottawa (Int'l)	2	1	.667	3.58	1.16	4	4	0	0	...	0-...	27.2	27	13	11	4	5-0	19	.248
	— Montreal (N.L.)	1	6	.143	6.33	1.76	8	8	0	0	0	0-0	42.2	59	33	30	7	16-1	36	.331
2002—	Montreal (N.L.)	3	8	.273	6.30	1.74	15	14	0	0	0	0-0	74.1	98	55	52	14	31-5	51	.318
	— Ottawa (Int'l)	3	0	1.000	3.10	1.23	3	3	0	0	...	0-...	20.1	23	8	7	2	2-0	9	.295
	— Florida (N.L.)	3	2	.600	3.79	1.46	22	8	0	0	3	0-0	61.2	76	33	26	5	14-3	41	.306
2003—	Florida (N.L.)	12	13	.480	4.30	1.26	33	32	2	0	0	0-0	201.0	204	99	96	19	49-10	133	.265
	Major League totals (6 years)	39	50	.438	4.59	1.39	136	118	3	1	3	0-0	715.1	773	396	365	79	222-22	478	.277

PAYTON, JAY   OF

PERSONAL: Born November 22, 1972, in Zanesville, Ohio. ... 5-10/185. ... Bats right, throws right. ... Full name: Jason Lee Payton. ... High school: Zanesville (Ohio). ... College: Georgia Tech.

TRANSACTIONS/CAREER NOTES: Selected by New York Mets organization in supplemental round ("sandwich pick" between first and second round, 29th pick overall) of free-agent draft (June 2, 1994); pick received as part of compensation for Baltimore Orioles signing Type A free-agent P Sid Fernandez. ... On Norfolk disabled list (April 29-July 3, 1996). ... On disabled list (April 3, 1997-entire season). ... On Norfolk disabled list (May 27-June 15 and June 24-July 20, 1998). ... On New York disabled list (March 21-June 8, 1999); included rehabilitation assignment to St. Lucie (May 30-June 8). ... On Norfolk disabled list (July 10-August 19, 1999). ... On New York disabled list (May 8-June 26, 2001); included rehabilitation assignment to St. Lucie (June 22-26). ... Traded by Mets with P Mark Corey and OF Robert Stratton to Colorado Rockies for P John Thomson and OF Mark Little (July 31, 2002).

2003 GAMES PLAYED BY POSITION (MLB): OF—151.

Year	Team (League)	Pos.	G	AB	R	H	2B	3B	HR	RBI	BB	SO	HBP	GDP	SB-CS	Avg.	OBP	SLG	OPS	E	Pct.
1994—	Pittsfield (NYP)	OF	58	219	47	80	16	2	3	37	23	19	9	1	10-2	.365	.439	.498	.937	5	.964
	— Binghamton (East.)	OF	8	25	3	7	1	0	0	1	2	3	1	1	1-1	.280	.357	.320	.677	1	.917
1995—	Binghamton (East.)	OF	85	357	59	123	20	3	14	54	29	32	2	11	16-7	.345	.395	.535	.930	3	.988
	— Norfolk (Int'l)	OF	50	196	33	47	11	4	4	30	11	22	2	5	11-3	.240	.284	.398	.682	2	.982
1996—	Norfolk (Int'l)	DH-OF	55	153	30	47	6	3	6	26	11	26	3	3	10-1	.307	.363	.503	.866	0	1.000
	— GC Mets (GCL)	DH	3	13	3	5	1	0	1	2	0	1	0	0	1-0	.385	.385	.692	1.077	...	...
	— St. Lucie (Fla. St.)	DH	9	26	4	8	2	0	0	1	4	5	0	1	2-1	.308	.400	.385	.785	...	...
	— Binghamton (East.)	DH	4	10	0	2	0	0	0	2	2	2	0	0	0-1	.200	.286	.200	.486	...	...
1997—											Did not play.										
1998—	Norfolk (Int'l)	OF-1B-DH	82	322	45	84	14	4	8	30	26	50	1	5	12-7	.261	.318	.404	.722	7	.980
	— St. Lucie (Fla. St.)	OF	3	7	0	1	0	0	0	0	3	1	0	0	0-0	.143	.400	.143	.543	0	1.000
	— New York (N.L.)	OF	15	22	2	7	1	0	0	0	1	4	0	0	0-0	.318	.348	.364	.711	0	1.000
1999—	St. Lucie (Fla. St.)	OF	7	26	3	9	1	1	0	3	4	5	0	1	0-1	.346	.433	.462	.895	1	.955
	— Norfolk (Int'l)	OF-DH	38	144	27	56	13	2	8	35	12	13	1	2	2-2	.389	.437	.674	1.110	1	.984
	— New York (N.L.)	OF	13	8	1	2	1	0	0	1	0	2	1	0	1-2	.250	.333	.375	.708	0	1.000
2000—	New York (N.L.)	OF	149	488	63	142	23	1	17	62	30	60	3	9	5-11	.291	.331	.447	.778	6	.981
2001—	New York (N.L.)	OF	104	361	44	92	16	1	8	34	18	52	5	11	4-3	.255	.298	.371	.669	4	.984
	— St. Lucie (Fla. St.)	OF	4	16	7	6	3	0	0	0	4	1	0	0	0-0	.375	.500	.563	1.063	0	1.000
2002—	New York (N.L.)	OF	87	275	33	78	6	3	8	31	21	34	1	8	4-1	.284	.336	.415	.750	1	.994
	— Colorado (N.L.)	OF	47	170	36	57	14	4	8	28	8	20	3	3	3-3	.335	.376	.606	.982	0	1.000
2003—	Colorado (N.L.)	OF	157	600	93	181	32	5	28	89	43	77	7	*27	6-4	.302	.354	.512	.865	4	.987
	Major League totals (6 years)		572	1924	272	559	93	14	69	245	121	249	20	58	23-24	.291	.337	.461	.798	15	.987

PEARCE, JOSH   P

PERSONAL: Born August 20, 1977, in Yakima, Wash. ... 6-3/220. ... Throws right, bats right. ... Full name: Joshua Ray Pearce. ... High school: West Valley (Yakima, Wash.). ... College: Arizona.

TRANSACTIONS/CAREER NOTES: Selected by New York Mets organization in 40th round of free-agent draft (June 4, 1996); did not sign. ... Selected by St. Louis Cardinals organization in supplemental round ("sandwich pick" between second and third round) of free-agent draft (June 2, 1999); pick received as compensation for Seattle Mariners signing Type C free agent C Tom Lampkin. ... On Memphis disabled list (May 11-August 30, 2002). ... On St. Louis disabled list (August 30, 2002-remainder of season). ... Recalled from Memphis (July 28, 2003). ... Optioned to Memphis (August 11, 2003). ... Recalled from Memphis (September 2, 2003).

CAREER HITTING: 1-for-4 (.250), 0 R, 0 2B, 0 3B, 0 HR, 1 RBI.

Year	League	W	L	Pct.	ERA	WHIP	G	GS	CG	ShO	Hld.	Sv.-Opp.	IP	H	R	ER	HR	BB-IBB	SO	Avg.
1999—	New Jersey (NYP)	3	7	.300	4.98	1.26	14	14	1	1	...	0-...	77.2	78	45	43	8	20-0	78	.257
2000—	Potomac (Caro.)	5	3	.625	3.45	1.28	10	10	1	0	...	0-...	62.2	70	25	24	5	10-0	42	.283
	— Arkansas (Texas)	5	6	.455	5.46	1.56	17	17	0	0	...	0-...	97.1	117	68	59	13	35-2	63	.298
2001—	New Haven (East.)	6	8	.429	2.34	0.78	18	18	0	0	...	0-...	185.0	111	55	48	11	34-1	96	.253
	— Memphis (PCL)	4	4	.500	2.58	0.73	10	10	0	0	...	0-...	115.1	72	43	33	11	12-1	36	.266
2002—	Memphis (PCL)	0	4	.000	7.65	1.55	4	4	0	0	...	0-...	20.0	28	18	17	8	3-0	17	.322
	— St. Louis (N.L.)	0	0	...	7.62	2.15	3	3	0	0	0	0-0	13.0	20	13	11	1	8-0	1	.377
2003—	W.P. Beach (FSL)	1	4	.200	3.21	1.07	6	5	0	0	...	0-...	28.0	28	10	10	2	2-0	15	.275
	— Tennessee (Sou.)	2	1	.667	4.09	1.12	5	5	0	0	...	0-...	33.0	34	15	15	3	3-0	20	.270
	— Memphis (PCL)	3	3	.500	4.08	1.27	10	9	0	0	...	0-...	46.1	51	22	21	8	8-1	27	.280
	— St. Louis (N.L.)	0	0	...	3.00	1.44	7	0	0	0	1	0-0	9.0	11	3	3	0	2-0	4	.306
	Major League totals (2 years)	0	0	...	5.73	1.86	10	3	0	0	1	0-0	22.0	31	16	14	1	10-0	5	.348

PEARSON, JASON   P

PERSONAL: Born December 29, 1975, in Freeport, Ill. ... 6-0/195. ... Throws left, bats left. ... Full name: Jason John Pearson. ... High school: Freeport (Ill.). ... College: Illinois State.

TRANSACTIONS/CAREER NOTES: Signed as non-drafted free agent by Florida Marlins organization (June 16, 1998). ... Released by Marlins (April 5, 1999). ... Signed by Sioux Falls, Northern League (May 1999). ... Signed by Fargo-Moorhead, Northern League (May 2000). ... Signed by Cincinnati Reds organization (October 10, 2000). ... Selected by San Diego Padres from Reds organization in Rule 5 minor league draft (December 11, 2000). ... Claimed on waivers by San Francisco Giants (June 10, 2002). ... Granted free agency (October 15, 2002). ... Signed by St. Louis Cardinals (March 31, 2003).

CAREER HITTING: 0-for-0 (.000), 0 R, 0 2B, 0 3B, 0 HR, 0 RBI.

Year	League	W	L	Pct.	ERA	WHIP	G	GS	CG	ShO	Hld.	Sv.-Opp.	IP	H	R	ER	HR	BB-IBB	SO	Avg.
1998—	GC Marlins (GCL)	4	0	1.000	1.57	0.96	11	3	0	0	...	2-...	34.1	28	8	6	0	5-0	36	.219
	— Kane County (Midwest)	0	0	...	3.38	1.50	2	0	0	0	...	0-...	2.2	3	3	1	0	1-0	1	.273
1999—	Sioux Falls (Nor.)	2	3	.400	3.00	1.35	27	2	0	0	...	0-...	63.0	57	29	21	6	28-...	48	....
2000—	Fargo-Moorhead (Nor.)	10	2	.833	3.00	1.29	18	16	1	...	...	0-...	108.0	90	45	36	6	49-...	82	....
2001—	Mobile (Sou.)	5	5	.500	4.17	1.37	54	5	0	0	...	1-...	86.1	88	40	40	5	30-3	67	.268
2002—	Portland (PCL)	3	0	1.000	1.50	1.13	23	0	0	0	...	0-...	30.0	25	5	5	3	9-0	18	.219
	— San Diego (N.L.)	0	0	...	0.00	0.60	2	0	0	0	0	0-0	1.2	1	0	0	0	0-0	3	.167
	— Fresno (PCL)	0	0	...	3.75	1.42	34	0	0	0	0	0-0	36.0	35	20	15	5	16-1	28	.261
2003—	Tennessee (Sou.)	0	0	...	0.00	0.82	9	0	0	0	...	0-...	11.0	7	0	0	0	2-0	11	.179
	— St. Louis (N.L.)	0	0	...	63.00	7.00	2	0	0	0	0	0-0	1.0	4	7	7	1	3-0	1	.571
	— Memphis (PCL)	4	4	.500	3.10	0.96	44	0	0	0	...	3-...	52.1	41	21	18	3	9-1	36	.211
Major League totals (2 years)		**0**	**0**	**...**	**23.63**	**3.00**	**4**	**0**	**0**	**0**	**0**	**0-0**	**2.2**	**5**	**7**	**7**	**1**	**3-0**	**4**	**.385**

PEAVY, JAKE   P

PERSONAL: Born May 31, 1981, in Mobile, Ala. ... 6-1/180. ... Throws right, bats right. ... Full name: Jacob Edward Peavy. ... Name pronounced: PEE-vee. ... High school: St. Paul (Mobile, Ala.).

TRANSACTIONS/CAREER NOTES: Selected by San Diego Padres organization in 15th round of free-agent draft (June 2, 1999).

CAREER HITTING: 11-for-88 (.125), 8 R, 3 2B, 0 3B, 0 HR, 3 RBI.

Year	League	W	L	Pct.	ERA	WHIP	G	GS	CG	ShO	Hld.	Sv.-Opp.	IP	H	R	ER	HR	BB-IBB	SO	Avg.
1999—	Ariz. Padres (Ariz.)	7	1	.875	1.34	1.02	13	11	1	0	...	0-...	73.2	52	16	11	4	23-0	90	.202
	— Idaho Falls (Pioneer)	2	0	1.000	0.00	0.55	2	2	0	0	...	0-...	11.0	5	0	0	0	1-0	13	.135
2000—	Fort Wayne (Midw.)	13	8	.619	2.90	1.20	26	25	0	0	...	0-...	133.2	107	61	43	6	53-0	164	.216
2001—	Lake Elsinore (Calif.)	7	5	.583	3.08	1.03	19	19	0	0	...	0-...	105.1	76	41	36	6	33-1	144	.200
	— Mobile (Sou.)	2	1	.667	2.57	1.11	5	5	0	0	...	0-...	28.0	19	8	8	3	12-1	44	.192
2002—	San Diego (N.L.)	4	5	.444	2.80	1.18	14	14	0	0	...	0-...	80.1	65	26	25	4	30-0	89	.220
	— San Diego (N.L.)	6	7	.462	4.52	1.42	17	17	0	0	0	0-0	97.2	106	54	49	11	33-4	90	.274
2003—	San Diego (N.L.)	12	11	.522	4.11	1.31	32	32	0	0	0	0-0	194.2	173	94	89	33	82-3	156	.238
Major League totals (2 years)		**18**	**18**	**.500**	**4.25**	**1.35**	**49**	**49**	**0**	**0**	**0**	**0-0**	**292.1**	**279**	**148**	**138**	**44**	**115-7**	**246**	**.250**

PELLOW, KIT   1B

PERSONAL: Born August 28, 1973, in Kansas City, Mo. ... 6-1/205. ... Bats right, throws right. ... Full name: Kit Donovan Pellow. ... High school: Olathe North (Kan.). ... College: Arkansas.

TRANSACTIONS/CAREER NOTES: Selected by Kansas City Royals organization in 22nd round of free-agent draft (June 4, 1996). ... Granted free agency (October 15, 2002). ... Signed by Colorado Rockies (November 24, 2002).

2003 GAMES PLAYED BY POSITION (MLB): C—7, 1B—1, OF—1.

											BATTING									FIELDING	
Year	Team (League)	Pos.	G	AB	R	H	2B	3B	HR	RBI	BB	SO	HBP	GDP	SB-CS	Avg.	OBP	SLG	OPS	E	Pct.
1996—	Spokane (N'west)	1-0-3-C	71	279	48	80	18	2	18	66	20	52	8	5	8-3	.287	.344	.559	.903	14	.971
1997—	Lansing (Midw.)	3B-1B	65	256	39	76	17	2	11	52	24	74	6	5	2-0	.297	.366	.508	.873	33	.890
	— Wichita (Texas)	3B	68	241	40	60	12	1	10	41	21	72	2	5	5-2	.249	.311	.432	.742	24	.898
1998—	Wichita (Texas)	3B	103	374	70	100	24	3	29	73	27	107	6	2	4-3	.267	.324	.580	.905	26	.904
	— Omaha (PCL)	3B	14	54	8	10	3	0	2	6	2	19	0	1	2-0	.185	.207	.352	.559	3	.919
1999—	Omaha (PCL)	3B-1B	131	475	88	136	28	4	35	99	20	117	18	11	6-5	.286	.335	.583	.918	33	.906
2000—	Omaha (PCL)	1B	117	421	61	105	17	3	22	75	38	89	16	5	6-4	.249	.331	.461	.792	8	.992
2001—	Omaha (PCL)	1B	129	484	81	141	15	0	20	81	37	101	13	3	4-3	.291	.353	.446	.799	8	.993
2002—	Omaha (PCL)	3B-1B	105	402	65	116	25	2	27	76	21	82	19	7	4-2	.289	.350	.562	.912	19	.950
	— Kansas City (A.L.)	3B-1B-DH	29	63	6	15	1	0	1	5	9	21	1	2	1-1	.238	.342	.302	.644	5	.929
2003—	Asheville (S. Atl.)	1B-3B-DH	6	20	3	9	2	0	1	8	5	5	2	0	0-0	.450	.571	.700	1.271	1	.967
	— Colo. Springs (PCL)	1-C-3-O-D	89	320	48	93	15	1	19	57	25	75	12	5	2-1	.291	.363	.522	.885	7	.989
	— Colorado (N.L.)	C-1B-OF	11	18	6	8	3	1	1	4	0	4	2	0	0-0	.444	.476	.889	1.365	0	1.000
American League totals (1 year)			29	63	6	15	1	0	1	5	9	21	1	2	1-1	.238	.342	.302	.644	5	.929
National League totals (1 year)			11	18	6	8	3	1	1	4	0	4	2	0	0-0	.444	.476	.889	1.365	0	1.000
Major League totals (2 years)			**40**	**81**	**12**	**23**	**4**	**1**	**2**	**9**	**9**	**25**	**3**	**2**	**1-1**	**.284**	**.372**	**.432**	**.804**	**5**	**.947**

PENA, CARLOS   1B

PERSONAL: Born May 17, 1978, in Santo Domingo, Dominican Republic. ... 6-2/215. ... Bats left, throws left. ... Full name: Carlos Felipe Pena. ... Name pronounced: PAIN-yuh. ... High school: Haverhill (Mass.). ... College: Northeastern (Mass.).

TRANSACTIONS/CAREER NOTES: Selected by Texas Rangers organization in first round (10th pick overall) of free-agent draft (June 2, 1998). ... Traded by Rangers with P Mike Venafro to Oakland Athletics for 1B Jason Hart, P Marion Ramos, C Gerald Laird and OF Ryan Ludwick (January 14, 2002). ... Traded by A's to Detroit Tigers with P Franklyn German and a player to be named later as part of three-way deal in which New York Yankees acquired P Jeff Weaver from Tigers and A's acquired P Ted Lilly, OF John-Ford Griffin and P Jason Arnold from Yankees (July 5, 2002); Tigers acquired P Jeremy Bonderman to complete deal (August 22, 2002). ... Placed on 15-day disabled list (June 2, 2003). ... Sent to Toledo on rehab assignment (June 20, 2003). ... Recalled from Toledo rehab assignment; reinstated from 15-day disabled list (June 27, 2003).

2003 GAMES PLAYED BY POSITION (MLB): 1B—128, DH—1.

											BATTING									FIELDING	
Year	Team (League)	Pos.	G	AB	R	H	2B	3B	HR	RBI	BB	SO	HBP	GDP	SB-CS	Avg.	OBP	SLG	OPS	E	Pct.
1998—	GC Rangers (GCL)	1B	2	5	1	2	0	0	0	0	3	1	0	0	1-1	.400	.625	.400	1.025	0	1.000
	— Savannah (S. Atl.)	1B-OF	30	117	22	38	14	0	6	20	28	26	4	0	3-2	.325	.385	.598	.983	3	.986
	— Charlotte (Fla. St.)	1B	7	22	1	6	1	0	0	3	2	8	1	0	0-1	.273	.360	.318	.678	1	.977
1999—	Charlotte (Fla. St.)	1B	136	501	85	128	31	8	18	103	74	135	16	7	2-5	.255	.365	.457	.822	16	.986

P

Year Team (League)	Pos.	G	AB	R	H	2B	3B	HR	RBI	BB	SO	HBP	GDP	SB-CS	Avg.	OBP	SLG	OPS	E	Pct.
2000— Tulsa (Texas)	1B	138	529	117	158	36	2	28	105	101	108	9	7	12-0	.299	.414	.533	.947	22	.982
2001— Oklahoma (PCL)	1B	119	431	71	124	38	3	23	74	80	127	8	6	11-3	.288	.408	.550	.958	11	.989
— Texas (A.L.)	1B-DH	22	62	6	16	4	1	3	12	10	17	0	1	0-0	.258	.361	.500	.861	2	.987
2002— Oakland (A.L.)	1B	40	124	12	27	4	0	7	16	15	38	1	2	0-0	.218	.305	.419	.724	1	.997
— Sacramento (PCL)	1B	44	175	30	42	10	1	10	33	24	49	4	3	3-0	.240	.340	.480	.820	3	.992
— Detroit (A.L.)	1B-DH	75	273	31	69	13	4	12	36	26	73	2	5	2-2	.253	.321	.462	.783	3	.996
2003— Toledo (Int'l)	1B-DH	8	30	4	10	4	1	0	5	4	7	1	0	0-0	.333	.429	.533	.962	1	.986
— Detroit (A.L.)	1B-DH	131	452	51	112	21	6	18	50	53	123	6	6	4-5	.248	.332	.440	.772	13	.990
Major League totals (3 years)		268	911	100	224	42	11	40	114	104	251	9	14	6-7	.246	.327	.448	.775	19	.992

PENA, WILY MO — OF

PERSONAL: Born January 23, 1982, in Laguna Salada, Dominican Republic. ... 6-3/215. ... Bats right, throws right. ... Full name: Wily Modesto Pena. ... Name pronounced: will-ee moe PAIN-ya.

TRANSACTIONS/CAREER NOTES: Signed by New York Mets organization (1998); contract nullified by Baseball Commissioner's Office. ... Declared a free agent (March 7, 1999). ... Signed by New York Yankees organization (April 1, 1999). ... On New York disabled list (July 13, 2000-remainder of season). ... Traded by Yankees to Cincinnati Reds for 3B Drew Henson and OF Michael Coleman (March 21, 2001). ... On Chattanooga disabled list (April 17-May 11, 2002). ... Placed on 15-day disabled list by Cincinnati (July 5, 2003). ... Sent on rehab assignment to Louisville (July 17, 2003). ... Recalled from Louisville rehab assignment; reinstated from 15-day disabled list (July 30, 2003).

2003 GAMES PLAYED BY POSITION (MLB): OF—47, 3B—1.

Year Team (League)	Pos.	G	AB	R	H	2B	3B	HR	RBI	BB	SO	HBP	GDP	SB-CS	Avg.	OBP	SLG	OPS	E	Pct.
1999— GC Yankees (GCL)	OF	45	166	21	41	10	1	7	26	12	54	7	2	3-2	.247	.323	.446	.768	2	.947
2000— Greensboro (S. Atl.)	OF	67	249	41	51	7	1	10	28	18	91	5	9	6-5	.205	.268	.361	.630	4	.964
— Staten Island (NY-P)	OF	20	73	7	22	1	2	0	10	2	23	4	1	2-0	.301	.354	.370	.724	0	1.000
2001— Dayton (Midw.)	OF *	135	511	87	135	25	5	26	* 113	33	177	17	6	26-10	.264	.327	.485	.813	9	.972
2002— Chattanooga (Sou.)	OF	105	388	47	99	23	1	11	47	36	126	9	9	0-0	.255	.330	.405	.735	4	.979
— Cincinnati (N.L.)	OF	13	18	1	4	0	0	1	1	0	11	0	0	0-0	.222	.222	.389	.611	0	1.000
2003— Louisville (Int'l)	OF	14	51	16	19	3	0	4	14	5	13	3	0	0-0	.373	.450	.667	1.117	2	.933
— Cincinnati (N.L.)	OF-3B	80	165	20	36	6	1	5	16	12	53	3	2	3-2	.218	.283	.358	.641	2	.978
Major League totals (2 years)		93	183	21	40	6	1	6	17	12	64	3	2	3-2	.219	.278	.361	.638	2	.978

PENNY, BRAD — P

PERSONAL: Born May 24, 1978, in Broken Arrow, Okla. ... 6-4/250. ... Throws right, bats right. ... Full name: Bradley Wayne Penny. ... High school: Broken Arrow (Okla.).

TRANSACTIONS/CAREER NOTES: Selected by Arizona Diamondbacks organization in fifth round of free-agent draft (June 4, 1996). ... On El Paso disabled list (April 20-30, 1999). ... Traded by Diamondbacks with P Vladimir Nunez and a player to be named later to Florida Marlins for P Matt Mantei (July 9, 1999); Marlins acquired OF Abraham Nunez to complete deal (December 13, 1999). ... On Florida disabled list (July 20-September 2, 2000); included rehabilitation assignments to Brevard County (August 5-15) and Calgary (August 16-September 2). ... On Florida disabled list (May 19-July 2, 2002); included rehabilitation assignment to Jupiter (June 23-July 2). ... On suspended list (March 30-April 6, 2003).

CAREER HITTING: 32-for-223 (.143), 11 R, 4 2B, 2 3B, 2 HR, 12 RBI.

Year League	W	L	Pct.	ERA	WHIP	G	GS	CG	ShO	Hld.	Sv.-Opp.	IP	H	R	ER	HR	BB-IBB	SO	Avg.
1996— Ariz. D'backs (Ariz.)	2	2	.500	2.36	1.01	11	8	0	0	...	0-...	49.2	36	18	13	1	14-0	52	.197
1997— South Bend (Mid.)	10	5	.667	2.73	1.13	25	25	0	0	...	0-...	118.2	91	44	36	4	43-2	116	.208
1998— High Desert (Calif.)	* 14	5	.737	2.96	1.05	28	* 28	1	0	...	0-...	164.0	138	65	54	15	35-0	* 207	.225
1999— El Paso (Texas)	2	7	.222	4.80	1.49	17	17	0	0	...	0-...	90.0	109	56	48	9	25-0	100	.303
— Portland (East.)	1	0	1.000	3.90	1.30	6	6	0	0	...	0-...	32.1	28	15	14	3	14-0	35	.231
2000— Florida (N.L.)	8	7	.533	4.81	1.50	23	22	0	0	0	0-0	119.2	120	70	64	13	60-4	80	.263
— Brevard County (FSL)	0	1	.000	1.13	1.13	2	2	0	0	...	0-...	8.0	5	2	1	0	4-0	11	.172
— Calgary (PCL)	2	0	1.000	1.80	1.20	3	3	0	0	...	0-...	15.0	8	3	3	1	10-0	16	.157
2001— Florida (N.L.)	10	10	.500	3.69	1.16	31	31	1	1	0	0-0	205.0	183	92	84	15	54-3	154	.240
2002— Florida (N.L.)	8	7	.533	4.66	1.53	24	24	1	1	0	0-0	129.1	148	76	67	18	50-7	93	.288
— Jupiter (FSL)	0	0	...	0.00	0.65	2	2	0	0	...	0-...	7.2	5	0	0	0	0-0	9	.179
2003— Florida (N.L.)	14	10	.583	4.13	1.28	32	32	0	0	0	0-0	196.1	195	96	90	21	56-6	138	.264
Major League totals (4 years)	40	34	.541	4.22	1.33	110	109	2	2	0	0-0	650.1	646	334	305	67	220-20	465	.261

PERALTA, JHONNY — SS/3B

PERSONAL: Born May 28, 1982, in Santiago, Dominican Republic. ... 6-1/180. ... Bats right, throws right. ... Full name: Jhonny Antonio Peralta. ... Name pronounced: pah-RALL-tah.

TRANSACTIONS/CAREER NOTES: Signed by Cleveland Indians organization as a non-drafted free agent (April 14, 1999).

2003 GAMES PLAYED BY POSITION (MLB): SS—72, 3B—6.

Year Team (League)	Pos.	G	AB	R	H	2B	3B	HR	RBI	BB	SO	HBP	GDP	SB-CS	Avg.	OBP	SLG	OPS	E	Pct.
2000— Columbus (S. Atl.)	SS-3B	106	349	52	84	13	1	3	34	59	102	2	13	7-6	.241	.352	.309	.661	26	.948
2001— Kinston (Caro.)	SS	125	441	57	106	24	2	7	47	58	148	1	9	4-8	.240	.328	.351	.680	27	.952
2002— Akron (East.)	SS	130	470	62	132	28	5	15	62	45	97	5	6	4-2	.281	.343	.457	.800	21	.965
2003— Buffalo (Int'l)	SS-3B	63	237	25	61	12	1	1	21	15	45	3	6	1-3	.257	.310	.329	.639	10	.969
— Cleveland (A.L.)	SS-3B	77	242	24	55	10	1	4	21	20	65	4	5	1-3	.227	.295	.326	.621	8	.977
Major League totals (1 year)		77	242	24	55	10	1	4	21	20	65	4	5	1-3	.227	.295	.326	.621	8	.977

PERCIVAL, TROY — P

PERSONAL: Born August 9, 1969, in Fontana, Calif. ... 6-3/235. ... Throws right, bats right. ... Full name: Troy Eugene Percival. ... Name pronounced: PURR-si-vul. ... High school: Moreno Valley (Calif.). ... College: UC-Riverside.

TRANSACTIONS/CAREER NOTES: Selected by California Angels organization in sixth round of free-agent draft (June 5, 1990). ... On Palm Springs disabled list (June 3-July 2, 1992). ... On disabled list (May 28, 1993-remainder of season). ... Angels franchise renamed Anaheim Angels for 1997 season. ... On disabled list (April 7-May 16, 1997); included rehabilitation assignment to Lake Elsinore (May 13-16). ... On Anaheim disabled list (August 5-26, 2000); included rehabilitation assignment to Lake Elsinore (August 22-26). ... On disabled list (April 3-18 and July 12-27, 2002). ... Placed on 15-day disabled list (May 23, 2003). ... Activated from the 15-day disabled list (June 8, 2003).

CAREER HITTING: 0-for-1 (.000), 0 R, 0 2B, 0 3B, 0 HR, 0 RBI.

Year	League	W	L	Pct.	ERA	WHIP	G	GS	CG	ShO	Hld.	Sv.-Opp.	IP	H	R	ER	HR	BB-IBB	SO	Avg.
1991— Boise (NW)		2	0	1.000	1.41	1.07	28	0	0	0	...	* 12-...	38.1	23	7	6	0	18-1	63	.172
1992— Palm Springs (Calif.)		1	1	.500	5.06	1.31	11	0	0	0	...	2-...	10.2	6	7	6	0	8-1	16	.188
— Midland (Texas)		3	0	1.000	2.37	1.53	20	0	0	0	...	5-...	19.0	18	5	5	1	11-1	21	.254
1993— Vancouver (PCL)		0	1	.000	6.27	1.98	18	0	0	0	...	4-...	18.2	24	14	13	0	13-1	19	.320
1994— Vancouver (PCL)		2	6	.250	4.13	1.51	49	0	0	0	...	15-...	61.0	63	31	28	4	29-5	73	.285
1995— California (A.L.)		3	2	.600	1.95	0.85	62	0	0	0	*29	3-6	74.0	37	19	16	6	26-2	94	.147
1996— California (A.L.)		0	2	.000	2.31	0.93	62	0	0	0	2	36-39	74.0	38	20	19	8	31-4	100	.149
1997— Anaheim (A.L.)		5	5	.500	3.46	1.19	55	0	0	0	0	27-31	52.0	40	20	20	6	22-2	72	.205
— Lake Elsinore (Calif.)		0	0	...	0.00	0.50	2	1	0	0	...	0-...	2.0	1	0	0	0	0-0	3	.143
1998— Anaheim (A.L.)		2	7	.222	3.65	1.23	67	0	0	0	0	42-48	66.2	45	31	27	5	37-4	87	.186
1999— Anaheim (A.L.)		4	6	.400	3.79	1.05	60	0	0	0	0	31-39	57.0	38	24	24	9	22-0	58	.186
2000— Anaheim (A.L.)		5	5	.500	4.50	1.44	54	0	0	0	0	32-42	50.0	42	27	25	7	30-4	49	.228
— Lake Elsinore (Calif.)		0	0	...	4.50	1.00	2	2	0	0	...	0-...	2.0	1	1	1	0	1-0	1	.143
2001— Anaheim (A.L.)		4	2	.667	2.65	0.99	57	0	0	0	0	39-42	57.2	39	19	17	3	18-1	71	.187
2002— Anaheim (A.L.)		4	1	.800	1.92	1.12	58	0	0	0	0	40-44	56.1	38	12	12	5	25-1	68	.188
2003— Anaheim (A.L.)		0	5	.000	3.47	1.14	52	0	0	0	0	33-37	49.1	33	22	19	7	23-1	48	.184
Major League totals (9 years)		27	35	.435	3.00	1.09	527	0	0	0	31	283-328	537.0	350	194	179	56	234-19	647	.182

PEREZ, ANTONIO — 2B/SS

PERSONAL: Born January 26, 1980, in Bani, Dominican Republic. ... 5-11/170. ... Bats right, throws right. ... Full name: Antonio Miguel Perez.

TRANSACTIONS/CAREER NOTES: Signed as non-drafted free agent by Cincinnati Reds organization (March 21, 1998). ... Traded by Reds with OF Mike Cameron, P Brett Tomko and P Jake Meyer to Seattle Mariners for OF Ken Griffey Jr. (February 10, 2000). ... On disabled list (May 2-June 5, 2000). ... On disabled list (April 5-June 1 and June 6, 2001-remainder of season). ... On San Antonio disabled list (May 3-July 5, 2002). ... Traded by Mariners to Tampa Bay Devil Rays for OF Randy Winn (October 28, 2002). ... Recalled by Tampa Bay from Durham (May 10, 2003). ... Optioned to Durham by Tampa Bay (May 16, 2003).

2003 GAMES PLAYED BY POSITION (MLB): 2B—31, 3B—6, SS—6, DH—3.

										BATTING									FIELDING	
Year	Team (League)	Pos.	G	AB	R	H	2B	3B	HR	RBI	BB	SO	HBP	GDP	SB-CS	Avg.	OBP	SLG	OPS	E	Pct.
1999— Rockford (Midwest)		SS-2B	119	385	69	111	20	3	7	41	43	80	13	3	35-24	.288	.376	.410	.787	36	.929
2000— Lancaster (Calif.)		SS	98	395	90	109	36	6	17	63	58	99	8	3	28-16	.276	.376	.527	.903	27	.939
2001— San Antonio (Texas)		SS	5	21	3	3	0	0	0	0	0	7	0	0	0-0	.143	.143	.143	.286	6	.818
2002— Ariz. Mariners (Ariz.)		2B-SS	6	15	3	5	1	0	1	3	4	2	1	0	4-0	.333	.476	.600	1.076	0	1.000
— San Antonio (Texas)		2B-SS	72	240	30	62	8	2	2	24	11	64	10	3	15-9	.258	.312	.333	.645	13	.955
2003— Orlando (South.)		2B-DH	24	81	16	22	5	1	2	10	18	18	4	0	3-1	.272	.423	.432	.855	3	.967
— Durham (Int'l)		2B-DH	34	134	27	38	12	2	6	20	10	38	3	2	3-1	.284	.345	.537	.882	8	.958
— Tampa Bay (A.L.)		2-3-S-D	48	125	19	31	6	1	2	12	18	34	1	1	4-1	.248	.345	.360	.705	2	.985
Major League totals (1 year)			48	125	19	31	6	1	2	12	18	34	1	1	4-1	.248	.345	.360	.705	2	.985

PEREZ, EDDIE — C

PERSONAL: Born May 4, 1968, in Ciudad Ojeda, Venezuela. ... 6-1/220. ... Bats right, throws right. ... Full name: Eduardo Rafael Perez. ... High school: Doctor Raul Cuenca (Cuidad Ojeda, Venezuela).

TRANSACTIONS/CAREER NOTES: Signed as non-drafted free agent by Atlanta Braves organization (September 27, 1986). ... On disabled list (August 30-September 14, 1996; and May 5, 2000-remainder of season). ... On Atlanta disabled list (March 28-September 1, 2001); included rehabilitation assignment to Greenville (August 21-September 1). ... Granted free agency (November 14, 2001). ... Re-signed by Braves organization (December 17, 2001). ... Traded by Braves to Cleveland Indians for a player to be named later (March 21, 2002). ... Granted free agency (November 1, 2002). ... Signed by Milwaukee Brewers organization (January 24, 2003).

2003 GAMES PLAYED BY POSITION (MLB): C—102.

										BATTING									FIELDING	
Year	Team (League)	Pos.	G	AB	R	H	2B	3B	HR	RBI	BB	SO	HBP	GDP	SB-CS	Avg.	OBP	SLG	OPS	E	Pct.
1987— GC Braves (GCL)		C	31	89	8	18	1	0	1	5	8	14	1	4	0-0	.202	.273	.247	.520	4	.980
1988— Burlington (Midw.)		C-1B	64	186	14	43	8	0	4	19	10	33	0	6	1-0	.231	.269	.339	.608	11	.963
1989— Sumter (S. Atl.)		C-1B	114	401	39	93	21	0	5	44	44	68	5	10	2-6	.232	.312	.322	.634	‡ 13	.985
1990— Sumter (S. Atl.)		C-1B	41	123	11	22	7	1	3	17	14	18	2	7	0-0	.179	.271	.325	.597	3	.991
— Durham (Caro.)		C-1B	31	93	9	22	1	0	3	10	1	12	1	3	0-0	.237	.250	.344	.594	3	.986
1991— Durham (Caro.)		C-1B	92	277	38	75	10	1	9	41	17	33	3	7	0-3	.271	.317	.412	.728	8	.986
— Greenville (Sou.)		1B	1	4	0	1	0	0	0	0	0	1	0	1	0-0	.250	.250	.250	.500	0	1.000
1992— Greenville (Sou.)		C-1B	91	275	28	63	16	0	6	41	24	41	2	11	3-3	.229	.292	.353	.645	14	.980
1993— Greenville (Sou.)		C-1B	28	84	15	28	6	0	6	17	2	8	0	4	1-0	.333	.341	.619	.960	3	.982
1994— Richmond (Int'l)		C-1B	113	388	37	101	16	2	9	49	18	47	3	4	1-1	.260	.294	.381	.675	§ 12	.985
1995— Richmond (Int'l)		C-DH-1B	92	324	31	86	19	0	5	40	12	58	2	12	1-2	.265	.294	.370	.664	7	.989
— Atlanta (N.L.)		C-1B	7	13	1	4	1	0	1	4	0	2	0	0	0-0	.308	.308	.615	.923	0	1.000
1996— Atlanta (N.L.)		C-1B	68	156	19	40	9	1	4	17	8	19	1	6	0-0	.256	.293	.404	.697	3	.990
1997— Atlanta (N.L.)		C	73	191	20	41	5	0	6	18	10	35	2	8	0-1	.215	.259	.335	.594	5	.989
1998— Atlanta (N.L.)		C-1B-DH	61	149	18	50	12	0	6	32	15	28	2	3	1-1	.336	.404	.537	.941	2	.994
1999— Atlanta (N.L.)		C-1B	104	309	30	77	17	0	7	30	17	40	6	9	0-1	.249	.299	.372	.671	5	.993
2000— Atlanta (N.L.)		C	7	22	0	4	1	0	0	3	0	2	0	0	0-0	.182	.182	.227	.409	1	.976
2001— Greenville (Sou.)		C-1B	10	38	7	13	2	0	4	5	0	9	1	0	0-0	.342	.359	.711	1.070	1	.984
— Atlanta (N.L.)		C	5	10	0	3	0	0	0	0	0	2	0	0	0-0	.300	.300	.300	.600	0	1.000
2002— Cleveland (A.L.)		C	42	117	6	25	9	0	4	5	5	25	1	6	0-0	.214	.252	.291	.543	3	.988
2003— Milwaukee (N.L.)		C	107	350	26	95	17	1	11	45	17	47	0	16	0-1	.271	.304	.420	.724	6	.991
American League totals (1 year)			42	117	6	25	9	0	4	5	5	25	1	6	0-0	.214	.252	.291	.543	3	.988
National League totals (8 years)			432	1200	114	314	62	2	35	149	67	175	11	42	1-4	.262	.305	.404	.709	22	.991
Major League totals (9 years)			474	1317	120	339	71	2	35	153	72	200	12	48	1-4	.257	.300	.394	.694	25	.991

PEREZ, EDUARDO — 1B/OF

PERSONAL: Born September 11, 1969... 6-4/215. ... Bats right, throws right. ... Full name: Eduardo Antanacio Perez. ... High school: Robinson (Santurce, Puerto Rico).

TRANSACTIONS/CAREER NOTES: Selected by California Angels organization in first round (17th pick overall) of free-agent draft (June 3, 1991). ... On Palm Springs disabled list (May 9-19, 1992). ... On Vancouver disabled list (June 26-July 7, 1994). ... Traded by Angels to Cincinnati Reds for P Will Pennyfeather (April 5, 1996). ... Released by Reds (December 14, 1998). ... Signed by St. Louis Cardinals organization (February 16, 1999). ... Granted free agency (October 15, 1999). ... Re-signed by Cardinals organization (February 3, 2000). ... On St. Louis disabled list (June 25-July 13 and August 13-September 1, 2000); included rehabilitation assignment to Memphis (August 24-September 1). ... Contract sold by Cardinals to Hanshin Tigers of Japan Central League (December 20, 2000). ... Re-signed by Cardinals organization (February 8, 2002).

2003 GAMES PLAYED BY POSITION (MLB): OF—71, 3B—12, 1B—5, DH—1.

P

Year— Team (League)	Pos.	G	AB	R	H	2B	3B	HR	RBI	BB	SO	HBP	GDP	SB-CS	Avg.	OBP	SLG	OPS	E	Pct.
1991— Boise (NW)	1B-OF	46	160	35	46	13	0	1	22	19	39	4	4	12-3	.288	.375	.388	.763	3	.969
1992— Palm Springs (Calif.)	3B-SS-OF	54	204	37	64	8	4	3	35	23	33	3	5	14-3	.314	.386	.436	.823	16	.882
— Midland (Texas)	3B-1B-OF	62	235	27	54	8	1	3	23	22	49	1	7	19-7	.230	.295	.311	.606	13	.920
1993— Vancouver (PCL)	3B-1B-OF	96	363	66	111	23	6	12	70	28	83	3	5	21-7	.306	.360	.501	.862	23	.922
— California (A.L.)	3B-DH	52	180	16	45	6	2	4	30	9	39	2	4	5-4	.250	.292	.372	.664	5	.962
1994— California (A.L.)	1B	38	129	10	27	7	0	5	16	12	29	0	5	3-0	.209	.275	.380	.654	1	.997
— Vancouver (PCL)	3B-DH	61	219	37	65	14	3	7	38	34	53	3	7	9-4	.297	.394	.484	.878	12	.926
— Ariz. Angels (Ariz.)	3B	1	3	0	0	0	0	0	0	1	1	0	0	0-0	.000	.250	.000	.250	0	1.000
1995— California (A.L.)	3B-DH	29	71	9	12	4	1	1	7	12	9	2	3	0-2	.169	.302	.296	.598	7	.883
— Vancouver (PCL)	3B-DH-1B	69	246	39	80	12	7	6	37	25	34	2	5	6-2	.325	.386	.504	.890	6	.968
1996— Indianapolis (A.A.)	3B-1B-OF	122	451	84	132	29	5	21	84	51	66	6	11	11-0	.293	.371	.519	.890	21	.939
— Cincinnati (N.L.)	1B-3B	18	36	8	8	0	0	3	5	5	9	0	2	0-0	.222	.317	.472	.789	0	1.000
1997— Cincinnati (N.L.)	1-0-3-D	106	297	44	75	18	0	16	52	29	76	2	6	5-1	.253	.321	.475	.796	2	.996
1998— Cincinnati (N.L.)	1B-3B-OF	84	172	20	41	4	0	4	30	21	45	2	2	0-1	.238	.325	.331	.656	5	.985
1999— Memphis (PCL)	1B-3B-DH	119	416	67	133	31	0	18	82	45	92	6	11	7-8	.320	.393	.524	.917	9	.989
— St. Louis (N.L.)	OF-1B	21	32	6	11	2	0	1	9	7	6	0	0	0-0	.344	.462	.500	.962	1	.970
2000— St. Louis (N.L.)	1B-OF-3B	35	91	9	27	4	0	3	10	5	19	3	2	1-0	.297	.350	.440	.790	0	1.000
— Memphis (PCL)	1B-3B-OF	77	277	57	80	12	3	19	66	43	48	1	9	10-4	.289	.383	.560	.942	8	.980
2001— Hanshin (Jp. Cn.)		52	167	20	37	11	0	3	19	21	48	...	...	3-...	.222	...	.341	...		
2002— St. Louis (N.L.)	0-1-3-D	96	154	22	31	9	0	10	26	17	36	3	7	0-0	.201	.290	.455	.744	2	.982
2003— St. Louis (N.L.)	0-3-1-D	105	253	47	72	16	0	11	41	29	53	4	7	5-2	.285	.365	.478	.843	7	.951
American League totals (3 years)		119	380	35	84	17	3	10	53	33	77	4	12	8-6	.221	.288	.361	.649	13	.975
National League totals (7 years)		465	1035	156	265	53	0	48	173	113	244	14	26	11-4	.256	.335	.446	.781	17	.988
Major League totals (10 years)		584	1415	191	349	70	3	58	226	146	321	18	38	19-10	.247	.322	.423	.746	30	.985

PEREZ, NEIFI — 2B/SS

PERSONAL: Born June 2, 1973, in Villa Mella, Dominican Republic. ... 6-0/175. ... Bats both, throws right. ... Full name: Neifi Neftali Perez. ... Name pronounced: NAY-fee.
TRANSACTIONS/CAREER NOTES: Signed as non-drafted free agent by Colorado Rockies organization (November 9, 1992). ... On Colorado disabled list (April 8-23, 2001). ... Traded by Rockies to Kansas City Royals for OF Jermaine Dye (July 25, 2001). ... Claimed on waivers by San Francisco Giants (November 20, 2002). ... Granted free agency (December 21, 2002). ... Re-signed by Giants (December 22, 2002).
2003 GAMES PLAYED BY POSITION (MLB): 2B—57, SS—45, 3B—2.

Year— Team (League)	Pos.	G	AB	R	H	2B	3B	HR	RBI	BB	SO	HBP	GDP	SB-CS	Avg.	OBP	SLG	OPS	E	Pct.
1993— Bend (NW)	2B-SS	75	296	35	77	11	4	3	32	19	43	2	3	19-14	.260	.306	.355	.661	25	.937
1994— Central Valley (Cal.)	SS	•134	506	64	121	16	7	1	35	32	79	2	6	9-7	.239	.284	.304	.589	*39	.940
1995— Colo. Springs (PCL)	SS	11	36	4	10	4	0	0	2	0	5	0	0	1-1	.278	.278	.389	.667	3	.936
— New Haven (East.)	SS	116	427	59	108	28	3	5	43	24	52	2	6	5-2	.253	.295	.368	.663	18	.967
1996— Colo. Springs (PCL)	SS	133	*570	77	180	28	12	7	72	21	48	2	13	16-13	.316	.337	.444	.781	*25	.963
— Colorado (N.L.)	SS-2B	17	45	4	7	2	0	0	3	0	8	0	2	2-2	.156	.156	.200	.356	2	.961
1997— Colo. Springs (PCL)	SS	68	303	68	110	24	3	8	46	17	27	0	3	8-2	.363	.393	.541	.934	8	.975
— Colorado (N.L.)	SS-2B-3B	83	313	46	91	13	10	5	31	21	43	1	3	4-3	.291	.333	.444	.777	9	.981
1998— Colorado (N.L.)	SS-C	•162	647	80	177	25	9	9	59	38	70	1	8	5-6	.274	.313	.382	.695	20	.975
1999— Colorado (N.L.)	SS	157	*690	108	193	27	•11	12	70	28	54	1	4	13-5	.280	.307	.403	.710	14	.981
2000— Colorado (N.L.)	SS	•162	651	90	187	39	11	10	71	30	63	0	9	3-6	.287	.314	.427	.741	18	.978
2001— Colorado (N.L.)	SS	87	382	65	114	19	8	7	47	16	49	0	8	6-2	.298	.326	.445	.771	10	.976
— Kansas City (A.L.)	SS-2B	49	199	18	48	7	1	1	12	10	19	1	2	3-4	.241	.277	.302	.579	5	.980
2002— Kansas City (A.L.)	SS	145	554	65	131	20	4	3	37	20	53	0	11	8-9	.236	.260	.303	.564	20	.971
2003— San Francisco (N.L.)	2B-SS-3B	120	328	27	84	19	4	1	31	14	23	0	9	3-2	.256	.285	.348	.632	5	.989
American League totals (2 years)		194	753	83	179	27	5	4	49	30	72	1	13	11-13	.238	.265	.303	.568	25	.974
National League totals (7 years)		788	3056	422	853	144	53	44	312	147	310	3	43	36-26	.279	.310	.404	.714	78	.979
Major League totals (8 years)		982	3809	505	1032	171	58	48	361	177	382	4	56	47-39	.271	.301	.384	.685	103	.978

PEREZ, ODALIS — P

PERSONAL: Born June 11, 1977, in Las Matas de Farfan, Dominican Republic. ... 6-0/150. ... Throws left, bats left. ... Full name: Odalis Amadol Perez. ... Name pronounced: oh-DALL-iss. ... High school: Damian Davis Ortiz (Las Matas de Farfan, Dominican Republic).
TRANSACTIONS/CAREER NOTES: Signed as non-drafted free agent by Atlanta Braves organization (July 2, 1994). ... On disabled list (July 23, 1999-remainder of season; and April 2, 2000-entire season). ... On Atlanta disabled list (July 22-September 1, 2001); included rehabilitation assignment to Richmond (August 9-September 1). ... Traded by Braves with OF Brian Jordan and P Andrew Brown to Los Angeles Dodgers for OF Gary Sheffield (January 15, 2002).
CAREER HITTING: 24-for-172 (.140), 10 R, 6 2B, 0 3B, 1 HR, 8 RBI.

Year— League	W	L	Pct.	ERA	WHIP	G	GS	CG	ShO	Hld.	Sv.-Opp.	IP	H	R	ER	HR	BB-IBB	SO	Avg.
1995— GC Braves (GCL)	3	5	.375	2.22	1.02	12	12	1	1	...	0-...	65.0	48	22	16	0	18-0	62	.200
1996— Eugene (NW)	2	1	.667	3.80	1.56	10	6	0	0	...	0-...	23.2	26	16	10	2	11-0	38	.268
1997— Macon (S. Atl.)	4	5	.444	1.65	1.08	36	0	0	0	...	5-...	87.1	67	31	16	4	27-1	100	.209
1998— Greenville (Sou.)	6	5	.545	4.02	1.36	23	21	0	0	...	0-...	132.0	127	67	59	15	53-2	143	.256
— Richmond (Int'l)	1	2	.333	2.96	1.36	13	0	0	0	...	3-...	24.1	26	10	8	4	7-1	22	.283
— Atlanta (N.L.)	0	1	.000	4.22	1.31	10	0	0	0	5	0-1	10.2	10	5	5	1	4-0	5	.244
1999— Atlanta (N.L.)	4	6	.400	6.00	1.65	18	17	0	0	0	0-0	93.0	100	65	62	12	53-2	82	.275
2000— Atlanta (N.L.)										Did not play.									
2001— Atlanta (N.L.)	7	8	.467	4.91	1.54	24	16	0	0	0	0-0	95.1	108	55	52	7	39-0	71	.290
— Richmond (Int'l)	1	0	1.000	2.74	1.09	5	5	0	0	0	0-...	23.0	23	7	7	1	2-0	22	.256
2002— Los Angeles (N.L.)	15	10	.600	3.00	0.99	32	32	4	2	0	0-0	222.1	182	76	74	21	38-5	155	.226
2003— Los Angeles (N.L.)	12	12	.500	4.52	1.28	30	30	0	0	0	0-0	185.1	191	98	93	28	46-4	141	.267
Major League totals (5 years)	38	37	.507	4.24	1.27	114	95	4	2	5	0-1	606.2	591	299	286	69	180-11	454	.257

PEREZ, OLIVER — P

PERSONAL: Born August 15, 1981, in Culiacan, Mexico. ... 6-3/160. ... Throws left, bats left.
TRANSACTIONS/CAREER NOTES: Signed as non-drafted free agent by San Diego Padres organization (March 4, 1999). ... Loaned by Padres to Yucatan of Mexican League (June 2-22 and July 18, 2000-remainder of season). ... On San Diego disabled list (August 7-September 2, 2002). ... Optioned to Portland (May 1, 2003). ... Recalled from Portland (June 13, 2003).
CAREER HITTING: 11-for-69 (.159), 1 R, 0 2B, 0 3B, 0 HR, 4 RBI.

P

Year League	W	L	Pct.	ERA	WHIP	G	GS	CG	ShO	Hld.	Sv.-Opp.	IP	H	R	ER	HR	BB-IBB	SO	Avg.
1999— Ariz. Padres (Ariz.)	1	2	.333	5.08	1.55	15	2	0	0	...	3-...	28.1	28	20	16	1	16-0	37	.243
2000— Yucatan (Mex.)	3	2	.600	4.40	1.30	11	6	0	0	...	1-...	43.0	39	24	21	...	17-...	37	...
— Idaho Falls (Pioneer)	3	1	.750	4.07	1.36	5	5	0	0	...	0-...	24.1	24	14	11	1	9-0	27	.270
2001— Fort Wayne (Midw.)	8	5	.615	3.46	1.25	19	19	0	0	...	0-...	101.1	84	46	39	9	43-0	98	.230
— Lake Elsinore (Calif.)	2	4	.333	2.72	1.32	9	9	0	0	...	0-...	53.0	45	22	16	4	25-0	62	.225
2002— Lake Elsinore (Calif.)	3	3	.500	1.85	1.23	9	8	0	0	...	0-...	48.2	36	13	10	0	24-0	66	.209
— Mobile (Sou.)	1	0	1.000	1.17	1.17	4	4	0	0	...	0-...	23.0	11	3	3	1	16-0	34	.147
— San Diego (N.L.)	4	5	.444	3.50	1.32	16	15	0	0	0	0-0	90.0	71	37	35	13	48-1	94	.218
2003— Portland (PCL)	3	3	.500	3.02	1.17	8	8	0	0	...	0-...	47.2	44	20	16	6	12-0	48	.246
— San Diego (N.L.)	4	7	.364	5.38	1.62	19	19	0	0	0	0-0	103.2	103	65	62	20	65-2	117	.258
— Pittsburgh (N.L.)	0	3	.000	5.87	1.65	5	5	0	0	0	0-0	23.0	26	15	15	2	12-1	24	.283
Major League totals (2 years)	8	15	.348	4.65	1.50	40	39	0	0	0	0-0	216.2	200	117	112	35	125-4	235	.245

PEREZ, TIMO — OF

PERSONAL: Born April 8, 1975, in Bani, Dominican Republic. ... 5-9/167. ... Bats left, throws left. ... Full name: Timoniel Perez.

TRANSACTIONS/CAREER NOTES: Played with Hiroshima Toyo Carp of Japan Central League (1996-99). ... Signed as non-drafted free agent by New York Mets organization (March 17, 2000). ... On New York disabled list (April 9-27, 2001); included rehabilitation assignment to Norfolk (April 20-27). ... Placed on 15-day disabled list (May 26, 2003). ... Sent to Norfolk on rehab assignment (June 7, 2003). ... Recalled from Norfolk rehab assignment; reinstated from 15-day disabled list (June 10, 2003).

2003 GAMES PLAYED BY POSITION (MLB): OF—104.

Year Team (League)	Pos.	G	AB	R	H	2B	3B	HR	RBI	BB	SO	HBP	GDP	SB-CS	Avg.	OBP	SLG	OPS	E	Pct.
1994— Hiroshima (DSL)		51	206	40	70	9	8	0	21	31	7			8-...	.340	...	.461	...	...	...
1995—										Did not play.										
1996— Hiroshima (Jp. Cn.)		31	54	8	15	1	0	1	7	2	7	...		3-...	.278	...	.352	...	...	...
1997— Hiroshima (Jap. West.)		19	69	9	21	3	1	2	12	10	3	...		9-...	.304	...	.464	...	...	...
— Hiroshima (Jp. Cn.)		86	139	17	34	4	2	3	15	10	16	...		4-...	.245	...	.367	...	...	...
1998— Hiroshima (Jap. West.)		2	7	0	2	0	0	0	0	0	0	...		0-...	.286	...	.286	...	...	...
— Hiroshima (Jp. Cn.)		98	230	22	68	8	1	5	35	20	21	...		2-...	.296	...	.404	...	...	...
1999— Hiroshima (Jap. West.)		60	160	19	58	13	4	1	24	34	13	...		6-...	.363	...	.513	...	...	...
— Hiroshima (Jp. Cn.)		12	23	2	4	0	0	0	2	3	3	...		0-...	.174	...	.174	...	...	...
2000— St. Lucie (Fla. St.)	OF	8	31	3	11	4	0	1	8	2	1	1	0	3-3	.355	.400	.581	.981	0	1.000
— Norfolk (Int'l)	OF	72	291	45	104	17	5	6	37	16	25	3	4	13-7	.357	.392	.512	.904	5	.976
— New York (N.L.)	OF	24	49	11	14	4	1	1	3	3	5	1	0	1-1	.286	.333	.469	.803	1	.976
2001— New York (N.L.)	OF	85	239	26	59	9	1	5	22	12	25	2	1	1-6	.247	.287	.356	.643	0	1.000
— Norfolk (Int'l)	OF	48	192	37	69	10	2	6	19	12	18	2	1	15-2	.359	.399	.526	.925	5	.951
2002— Norfolk (Int'l)	OF	5	21	5	12	2	1	1	5	2	2	0	1	3-1	.571	.609	.905	1.513	0	1.000
— New York (N.L.)	OF	136	444	52	131	27	6	8	47	23	36	2	10	10-6	.295	.331	.437	.768	6	.979
2003— Norfolk (Int'l)	OF	3	9	2	2	0	0	1	1	1	0	0	0	0-0	.222	.300	.556	.856	0	1.000
— New York (N.L.)	OF	127	346	32	93	21	0	4	42	18	29	2	5	5-6	.269	.301	.364	.665	2	.989
Major League totals (4 years)		372	1078	121	297	61	8	18	114	56	95	7	16	17-19	.276	.312	.397	.709	9	.986

PEREZ, TOMAS — IF

PERSONAL: Born December 29, 1973... 5-11/177. ... Bats both, throws right. ... Full name: Tomas Orlando Perez.

TRANSACTIONS/CAREER NOTES: Signed as non-drafted free agent by Montreal Expos organization (July 11, 1991). ... Selected by California Angels from Expos organization in Rule 5 major league draft (December 5, 1994). ... Contract sold by Angels to Toronto Blue Jays (December 5, 1994). ... On Toronto disabled list (June 25-July 25, 1997); included rehabilitation assignment to Syracuse (July 12-24). ... Traded by Blue Jays to Angels for IF Dave Hollins and cash (March 30, 1999). ... On Edmonton disabled list (April 21-June 10, 1999). ... Granted free agency (October 15, 1999). ... Signed by Philadelphia Phillies organization (December 15, 1999). ... On Philadelphia disabled list (March 26-April 16, 2002); included rehabilitation assignment to Reading (April 13-15).

2003 GAMES PLAYED BY POSITION (MLB): 3B—58, 2B—26, 1B—9, SS—4.

Year Team (League)	Pos.	G	AB	R	H	2B	3B	HR	RBI	BB	SO	HBP	GDP	SB-CS	Avg.	OBP	SLG	OPS	E	Pct.
1992— Dom. Expos (DSL)	IF	44	151	35	46	7	0	1	19	27	20			12-...	.305	...	.371	...	12	.954
1993— GC Expos (GCL)	SS	52	189	27	46	3	1	2	21	23	25	0	5	8-3	.243	.322	.302	.624	12	.964
1994— Burlington (Midw.)	2B-SS	119	465	76	122	22	1	8	47	48	78	1	2	8-10	.262	.329	.366	.695	34	.944
1995— Toronto (A.L.)	SS-2B-3B	41	98	12	24	3	1	1	8	7	18	0	6	0-1	.245	.292	.327	.619	5	.962
1996— Syracuse (Int'l)	SS-2B	40	123	15	34	10	1	1	13	7	19	0	2	8-1	.276	.313	.398	.711	7	.962
— Toronto (A.L.)	2B-3B-SS	91	295	24	74	13	4	1	19	25	29	1	10	1-2	.251	.311	.332	.643	15	.964
1997— Syracuse (Int'l)	SS	89	303	32	68	13	0	1	20	37	67	0	9	3-4	.224	.308	.277	.585	12	.973
— Toronto (A.L.)	SS-2B	40	123	9	24	3	2	0	9	11	28	1	2	1-1	.195	.267	.252	.519	3	.984
1998— Syracuse (Int'l)	SS-2B	116	404	40	102	15	4	3	37	18	67	0	10	4-7	.252	.284	.332	.616	15	.973
— Toronto (A.L.)	SS-2B	6	9	1	1	0	0	0	0	1	3	0	1	0-0	.111	.200	.111	.311	0	1.000
1999— Edmonton (PCL)	SS-2B	83	296	31	77	17	1	4	40	19	43	2	1	2-2	.260	.306	.365	.671	11	.973
2000— Philadelphia (N.L.)	SS	45	140	17	31	7	1	1	13	11	30	0	3	1-1	.221	.278	.307	.585	4	.976
— Scran./W.B. (I.L.)	3B-SS-2B	77	279	44	82	16	2	10	56	16	48	2	5	4-1	.294	.334	.473	.808	9	.962
2001— Philadelphia (N.L.)	2-3-S-O	62	135	11	41	7	1	3	19	7	22	2	2	0-1	.304	.347	.437	.784	1	.993
2002— Reading (East.)	2B-SS	2	9	2	4	0	0	0	1	0	1	0	0	0-0	.444	.444	.444	.889	0	1.000
— Philadelphia (N.L.)	2-3-S-1	92	212	22	53	13	1	5	20	21	40	1	5	1-0	.250	.319	.392	.711	4	.985
2003— Philadelphia (N.L.)	3-2-1-S	125	298	39	79	18	1	5	33	23	54	0	7	0-1	.265	.316	.383	.698	9	.969
American League totals (4 years)		178	525	46	123	19	7	2	36	44	78	2	19	2-4	.234	.295	.309	.604	23	.969
National League totals (4 years)		324	785	89	204	45	4	14	85	62	146	3	17	2-3	.260	.315	.381	.696	18	.979
Major League totals (8 years)		502	1310	135	327	64	11	16	121	106	224	5	36	4-7	.250	.307	.352	.659	41	.975

PERRY, HERBERT — 3B

PERSONAL: Born September 15, 1969, in Live Oak, Fla. ... 6-2/235. ... Bats right, throws right. ... Full name: Herbert Edward Perry. ... High school: Lafayette (Mayo, Fla.). ... College: Florida.

TRANSACTIONS/CAREER NOTES: Selected by Cleveland Indians organization in second round of free-agent draft (June 3, 1991). ... On disabled list (June 18-July 13, 1991; and July 23, 1993-remainder of season). ... On Buffalo disabled list (June 7-27, 1996). ... On Cleveland disabled list (September 11, 1996-remainder of season; and March 26, 1997-entire season). ... Selected by Tampa Bay Devil Rays in third round (68th pick overall) of expansion draft (November 18, 1997). ... On Tampa Bay disabled list (March 25, 1998-entire season); included rehabilitation assignments to Durham (June 1-7), Gulf Coast Devil Rays (August 17-25) and St. Petersburg (August 27-28). ... On Tampa

P

Bay disabled list (July 22-September 1, 1999); included rehabilitation assignment to Durham (August 25-31). ... Claimed on waivers by Chicago White Sox (April 21, 2000). ... On disabled list (June 8-22, 2001). ... Traded by White Sox to Texas Rangers for a player to be named later (November 27, 2001); White Sox acquired P Corey Lee to complete deal (December 17, 2001). ... On Texas disabled list (March 21, 2003); included rehabilitation assignment to Frisco (April 3-11). ... Sent to Frisco for rehab assignment (May 6, 2003). ... Recalled from Frisco rehab assignment; reinstated from 15-day disabled list (May 10, 2003). ... Placed on 15-day disabled list (May 29, 2003). ... Transferred to Emergency disabled list (June 26, 2003).

2003 GAMES PLAYED BY POSITION (MLB): 1B—5, 3B—2.

Year Team (League)	Pos.	G	AB	R	H	2B	3B	HR	RBI	BB	SO	HBP	GDP	SB-CS	Avg.	OBP	SLG	OPS	E	Pct.
1991— Watertown (NYP)	DH	14	52	3	11	2	0	0	5	8	7	2	3	0-0	.212	.339	.250	.589	...	...
1992— Kinston (Caro.)	3B-1B-OF	121	449	74	125	16	1	19	77	46	89	12	9	12-0	.278	.358	.445	.804	5	.985
1993— Cant./Akr. (Eastern)	1B-3B	89	327	52	88	21	1	9	55	37	47	15	5	7-4	.269	.364	.422	.786	10	.979
1994— Charlotte (Int'l)	1-3-D-O	102	376	67	123	20	4	13	70	41	55	5	10	9-4	.327	.397	.505	.902	6	.993
— Cleveland (A.L.)	3B-1B	4	9	1	1	0	0	0	1	3	1	1	0	0-0	.111	.357	.111	.468	1	.968
1995— Buffalo (A.A.)	1B-DH	49	180	27	57	14	1	2	17	15	18	3	4	1-0	.317	.375	.439	.814	3	.994
— Cleveland (A.L.)	1B-DH-3B	52	162	23	51	13	1	3	23	13	28	4	5	1-3	.315	.376	.463	.839	1	1.000
1996— Buffalo (A.A.)	1-3-D-O	40	151	21	51	7	1	5	30	7	19	2	0	4-0	.338	.375	.497	.872	4	.984
— Cleveland (A.L.)	1B-3B	7	12	1	1	1	0	0	0	1	2	0	0	1-0	.083	.154	.167	.321	0	1.000
1997— Cleveland (A.L.)							Did not play.													
1998— Durham (Int'l)	1B-DH	5	17	1	5	4	0	0	1	0	2	1	2	0-0	.294	.333	.529	.863	0	1.000
— GC Devil Rays (GCL)	3B-DH	8	26	1	3	0	0	0	1	3	5	1	0	0-0	.115	.233	.115	.349	1	.900
— St. Pete. (FSL)	3B	2	8	1	1	0	0	0	0	2	2	0	0	0-0	.125	.300	.125	.425	1	.875
1999— Durham (Int'l)	DH-1B-3B	27	103	21	32	8	0	5	20	6	21	2	3	0-0	.311	.360	.534	.894	2	.971
— Tampa Bay (A.L.)	3-1-O-D	66	209	29	53	10	1	6	32	16	42	10	13	0-0	.254	.331	.397	.728	5	.975
2000— Tampa Bay (A.L.)	3B-1B	7	28	2	6	1	0	0	1	2	7	0	0	0-0	.214	.267	.250	.517	1	.944
— Chicago (A.L.)	3B-DH-1B	109	383	69	118	29	1	12	61	22	68	9	13	4-1	.308	.356	.483	.839	9	.970
2001— Chicago (A.L.)	3B-1B-DH	92	285	38	73	21	1	7	32	23	55	7	11	2-2	.256	.326	.411	.736	10	.957
2002— Texas (A.L.)	3-1-D-O	132	450	64	124	24	1	22	77	34	66	6	17	4-2	.276	.333	.480	.813	14	.960
2003— Frisco (Texas)	DH-1B	9	34	5	11	2	0	1	6	3	3	2	2	0-0	.324	.410	.471	.881	0	1.000
— Texas (A.L.)	1B-3B	11	24	1	4	1	0	0	2	0	3	0	0	0-0	.167	.167	.208	.375	0	1.000
Major League totals (8 years)		480	1562	228	431	100	5	50	229	114	272	37	59	12-8	.276	.337	.442	.779	40	.975

PERSON, ROBERT   P

PERSONAL: Born October 6, 1969, in St. Louis, Mo. ... 6-0/193. ... Throws right, bats right. ... Full name: Robert Alan Person. ... High school: University City (Mo.). ... Junior college: Seminole College (Okla.).

TRANSACTIONS/CAREER NOTES: Selected by Cleveland Indians organization in 25th round of free-agent draft (June 5, 1989). ... Loaned by Indians organization to Bend, independent (June 12-25, 1991). ... Traded by Indians to Chicago White Sox for P Grady Hall (June 27, 1991). ... On disabled list (April 10-May 13, 1992). ... Selected by Florida Marlins in second round (47th pick overall) of expansion draft (November 17, 1992). ... Granted free agency (December 19, 1992). ... Re-signed by Marlins organization (January 8, 1993). ... Traded by Marlins to New York Mets for P Steve Long (March 30, 1994). ... Traded by Mets to Toronto Blue Jays for 1B John Olerud and cash (December 20, 1996). ... On Toronto disabled list (May 8-26 and September 9-28, 1997). ... On Syracuse disabled list (April 19-27, 1998). ... On Toronto disabled list (March 25-April 12, 1999); included rehabilitation assignment to Dunedin (April 9-10). ... Traded by Blue Jays to Philadelphia Phillies for P Paul Spoljaric (May 5, 1999). ... On Philadelphia disabled list (June 19-July 22, 2000); included rehabilitation assignments to Clearwater (July 12-16) and Reading (July 17-22). ... On suspended list (June 22-28, 2001). ... On Philadelphia disabled list (April 30-June 2 and July 23, 2002-remainder of season); included rehabilitation assignment to Scranton (May 21-June 2). ... Granted free agency (October 28, 2002). ... Signed by Boston Red Sox organization (February 22, 2003). ... On disabled list (March 26, 2003). ... Sent on rehab assignment to Sarasota (April 20, 2003). ... Recalled from Pawtucket rehab assignment (May 13, 2003). ... Placed on 15-day disabled list (June 8, 2003). ... Sent to Gulf Coast League on rehab assignment (August 2, 2003). ... Transferred to 60-day disabled list (August 28, 2003). ... Recalled from minor league rehab assignment (September 3, 2003).

CAREER HITTING: 25-for-214 (.117), 13 R, 5 2B, 0 3B, 4 HR, 16 RBI.

Year League	W	L	Pct.	ERA	WHIP	G	GS	CG	ShO	Hld.	Sv.-Opp.	IP	H	R	ER	HR	BB-IBB	SO	Avg.
1989— Burlington (Appal.)	0	1	.000	3.18	1.18	10	5	0	0	...	1-...	34.0	23	13	12	1	17-0	19	.189
1990— Watertown (NYP)	1	0	1.000	1.10	0.92	5	2	0	0	...	0-...	16.1	8	2	2	0	7-0	19	.145
— Kinston (Caro.)	1	0	1.000	2.70	1.56	4	3	0	0	...	0-...	16.2	17	6	5	0	9-0	7	.266
— GC Indians (GCL)	0	2	.000	7.36	1.91	24	0	0	0	...	2-...	7.1	10	7	6	0	4-1	8	.345
1991— Kinston (Caro.)	3	5	.375	4.67	1.88	11	11	0	0	...	0-...	52.0	56	37	27	2	42-0	45	.281
— Bend (NW)	1	1	.500	3.60	1.10	2	2	0	0	...	0-...	10.0	6	6	4	0	5-0	6	.171
— South Bend (Mid.)	4	3	.571	3.30	1.39	13	13	0	0	...	0-...	76.1	50	35	28	3	56-1	66	.192
1992— Sarasota (Fla. St.)	5	7	.417	3.59	1.44	19	18	1	0	...	0-...	105.1	90	48	42	7	62-1	85	.231
1993— High Desert (Calif.)	12	10	.545	4.69	1.37	28	26	4	0	...	0-...	169.0	184	* 115	88	13	48-0	107	.271
1994— Binghamton (Eastern)	9	6	.600	3.45	1.21	31	23	3	2	...	0-...	159.0	124	68	61	18	68-3	130	.219
1995— Binghamton (Eastern)	5	4	.556	3.11	1.07	26	7	1	0	...	7-...	66.2	46	27	23	4	25-0	65	.197
— Norfolk (Int'l)	2	1	.667	4.50	1.34	5	4	0	0	...	0-...	32.0	30	17	16	2	13-0	33	.244
— New York (N.L.)	1	0	1.000	0.75	0.58	3	1	0	0	0	0-0	12.0	5	1	1	1	2-0	10	.119
1996— New York (N.L.)	4	5	.444	4.52	1.35	27	13	0	0	1	0-0	89.2	86	50	45	16	35-3	76	.247
— Norfolk (Int'l)	5	0	1.000	3.35	1.26	8	8	0	0	...	0-0	43.0	33	16	16	7	21-0	32	.213
1997— Toronto (A.L.)	5	10	.333	5.61	1.44	23	22	0	0	0	0-0	128.1	125	86	80	19	60-2	99	.255
— Syracuse (Int'l)	1	0	1.000	0.00	0.86	1	1	0	0	...	0-0	7.0	4	1	0	0	2-0	5	.167
1998— Toronto (A.L.)	3	1	.750	7.04	1.75	27	0	0	0	6-8		38.1	45	31	30	9	22-1	31	.294
— Syracuse (Int'l)	3	3	.500	2.29	1.14	20	6	1	0	...	6-...	59.0	38	17	15	9	29-2	55	.184
1999— Dunedin (Fla. St.)	0	0	...	3.00	1.67	1	1	0	0	...	0-...	3.0	4	1	1	0	1-0	3	.400
— Toronto (A.L.)	0	2	.000	9.82	2.18	11	0	0	0	1	2-2	11.0	9	12	12	1	15-1	12	.231
— Philadelphia (N.L.)	10	5	.667	4.27	1.46	31	22	0	0	0	0-0	137.0	130	72	65	23	70-1	127	.252
2000— Philadelphia (N.L.)	9	7	.563	3.63	1.38	28	28	1	1	0	0-0	173.1	144	73	70	13	95-1	164	.229
— Clearwater (Fla. St.)	0	0	...	6.75	1.50	1	1	0	0	...	0-...	2.2	3	2	2	0	1-0	2	.273
— Reading (East.)	1	0	1.000	5.79	1.29	1	0	0	0	...	0-...	4.2	3	3	3	1	3-0	7	.176
2001— Philadelphia (N.L.)	15	7	.682	4.19	1.24	33	33	3	1	0	0-0	208.1	179	103	97	34	80-3	183	.234
2002— Philadelphia (N.L.)	4	5	.444	5.44	1.48	16	16	0	0	0	0-0	87.2	79	58	53	13	51-0	61	.241
— Scran./W.B. (I.L.)	0	1	.000	4.32	1.08	2	2	0	0	...	0-...	8.1	8	4	4	2	1-0	7	.267
2003— Pawtucket (Int'l)	0	0	...	4.70	1.30	6	1	0	0	...	1-...	7.2	5	4	4	0	5-0	6	.179
— Boston (A.L.)	0	0	...	7.71	1.63	7	0	0	0	1-1		11.2	11	10	10	0	8-0	10	.250
— GC Red Sox (GCL)	0	0	...	0.00	1.33	1	1	0	0	...	0-...	3.0	2	0	0	0	2-0	4	.222
— Sarasota (Fla. St.)	1	1	.500	2.92	1.34	7	7	0	0	...	0-...	24.2	27	12	8	1	6-0	17	.281
American League totals (4 years)	8	13	.381	6.27	1.56	68	22	0	0	1	9-11	189.1	190	139	132	29	105-4	152	.261
National League totals (6 years)	43	29	.597	4.21	1.35	138	113	4	2	1	0-0	708.0	623	357	331	100	333-8	621	.237
Major League totals (9 years)	51	42	.548	4.64	1.39	206	135	4	2	2	9-11	897.1	813	496	463	129	438-12	773	.242

P

PETRICK, BEN — OF/C

PERSONAL: Born April 7, 1977, in Salem, Ore. ... 6-0/200. ... Bats right, throws right. ... Full name: Benjamin Wayne Petrick. ... Name pronounced: PEET-rick. ... High school: Glencoe (Hillsboro, Ore.).

TRANSACTIONS/CAREER NOTES: Selected by Colorado Rockies organization in second round of free-agent draft (June 3, 1995). ... On Carolina disabled list (April 26-May 6, 1999). ... On Colorado disabled list (August 2-September 1, 2001); included rehabilitation assignment to Colorado Springs (August 9-29). ... Traded by Rockies to Detroit Tigers for P Adam Bernero (July 13, 2003).

2003 GAMES PLAYED BY POSITION (MLB): OF—34, C—7, 1B—2.

										BATTING									FIELDING	
Year	Team (League)	Pos.	G	AB	R	H	2B	3B	HR	RBI	BB	SO	HBP	GDP	SB-CS	Avg.	OBP	SLG	OPS	E	Pct.
1996— Asheville (S. Atl.)		C-DH	122	446	74	105	24	2	14	52	75	98	5	5	19-9	.235	.350	.392	.742	12	.986
1997— Salem (Caro.)		C-DH	121	412	68	102	23	3	15	56	62	100	2	6	30-11	.248	.347	.427	.774	10	.988
1998— New Haven (East.)		C-DH-OF	106	349	52	83	21	3	18	50	56	89	3	5	7-7	.238	.345	.470	.815	5	.991
1999— Carolina (Sou.)		C	20	68	18	21	5	1	4	22	9	15	1	0	3-1	.309	.388	.588	.976	1	.992
— Colo. Springs (PCL)		C-OF	84	282	56	88	16	5	19	64	44	58	3	4	9-6	.312	.403	.606	1.009	9	.980
— Colorado (N.L.)		C	19	62	13	20	3	0	4	12	10	13	0	1	1-0	.323	.417	.565	.981	2	.982
2000— Colorado (N.L.)		C	63	248	38	78	22	3	9	47	32	40	0	2	7-2	.315	.390	.536	.926	6	.985
— Colorado (N.L.)		C	52	146	32	47	10	1	3	20	20	33	2	1	1-2	.322	.401	.466	.867	4	.985
2001— Colorado (N.L.)		C-1B	85	244	41	58	15	3	11	39	31	67	3	5	3-3	.238	.327	.459	.786	8	.984
— Colo. Springs (PCL)		OF-C-1B	18	64	11	16	2	0	1	9	13	21	0	1	1-0	.250	.367	.328	.695	4	.957
2002— Colorado (N.L.)		OF-C	38	95	10	20	3	1	5	11	9	33	1	1	0-1	.211	.283	.421	.704	3	.974
— Colo. Springs (PCL)		OF-C-1B	79	265	51	85	18	4	16	54	40	77	1	4	10-6	.321	.406	.600	1.006	5	.969
2003— Colorado (N.L.)		C	3	2	0	0	0	0	0	0	0	1	0	0	0-0	.000	.000	.000	.000	0	1.000
— Colo. Springs (PCL)		O-1-C-D	80	228	38	59	16	3	11	40	26	53	1	8	4-4	.259	.333	.500	.833	8	.975
— Detroit (A.L.)		OF-C-1B	43	120	18	27	6	0	4	12	8	30	0	3	0-0	.225	.273	.375	.648	2	.978
American League totals (1 year)			43	120	18	27	6	0	4	12	8	30	0	3	0-0	.225	.273	.375	.648	2	.978
National League totals (5 years)			197	549	96	145	31	5	23	82	70	147	6	8	5-6	.264	.349	.464	.814	17	.983
Major League totals (5 years)			240	669	114	172	37	5	27	94	78	177	6	11	5-6	.257	.336	.448	.785	19	.983

PETTITTE, ANDY — P

PERSONAL: Born June 15, 1972, in Baton Rouge, La. ... 6-5/225. ... Throws left, bats left. ... Full name: Andrew Eugene Pettitte. ... Name pronounced: pet-it. ... High school: Deer Park (Texas). ... Junior college: San Jacinto College (Texas).

TRANSACTIONS/CAREER NOTES: Selected by New York Yankees organization in 22nd round of free-agent draft (June 4, 1990); did not sign. ... Signed as non-drafted free agent by Yankees organization (May 25, 1991). ... On Albany temporarily inactive list (June 5-10, 1994). ... On New York disabled list (March 26-April 17, 1999); included rehabilitation assignment to Tampa (April 13-26, 2000; and June 15-July 1, 2001). ... On New York disabled list (April 16-June 14, 2002); included rehabilitation assignments to Tampa (May 22-June 5) and Norwich (June 6-14).

CAREER HITTING: 3-for-28 (.107), 0 R, 1 2B, 0 3B, 0 HR, 2 RBI.

Year	League	W	L	Pct.	ERA	WHIP	G	GS	CG	ShO	Hld.	Sv.-Opp.	IP	H	R	ER	HR	BB-IBB	SO	Avg.
1991— GC Yankees (GCL)		4	1	.800	0.98	0.65	6	6	0	0	...	0-...	36.2	16	6	4	0	8-0	51	.127
— Oneonta (N.Y.-Penn)		2	2	.500	2.18	1.48	6	6	1	0	...	0-...	33.0	33	18	8	1	16-0	32	.252
1992— Greensboro (S. Atl.)		10	4	.714	2.20	1.17	27	27	2	1	...	0-...	168.0	141	53	41	4	55-0	130	.232
1993— Prince William (Caro.)		11	9	.550	3.04	1.21	26	26	2	1	...	0-...	159.2	146	68	54	7	47-0	129	.248
— Albany (East.)		1	0	1.000	3.60	1.40	1	1	0	0	...	0-...	5.0	5	4	2	0	2-0	6	.250
1994— Alb./Colon. (East.)		7	2	.778	2.71	1.07	11	11	0	0	...	0-...	73.0	60	32	22	5	18-1	50	.220
— Columbus (Int'l)		7	2	.778	2.98	1.26	16	16	3	0	...	0-...	96.2	101	40	32	3	21-0	61	.272
1995— New York (A.L.)		12	9	.571	4.17	1.41	31	26	3	0	0	0-0	175.0	183	86	81	15	63-3	114	.272
— Columbus (Int'l)		0	0	...	0.00	0.60	2	2	0	0	...	0-...	11.2	7	0	0	0	0-0	8	.184
1996— New York (A.L.)		* 21	8	.724	3.87	1.36	35	34	2	0	0	0-0	221.0	229	105	95	23	72-2	162	.271
1997— New York (A.L.)		18	7	.720	2.88	1.24	35	* 35	4	1	0	0-0	240.1	233	86	77	7	65-0	166	.256
1998— New York (A.L.)		16	11	.593	4.24	1.45	33	32	5	0	0	0-0	216.1	226	110	102	20	87-1	146	.272
1999— Tampa (FSL)		1	0	1.000	0.00	1.20	1	1	0	0	...	0-...	5.0	4	0	0	0	2-0	8	.222
— New York (A.L.)		14	11	.560	4.70	1.59	31	31	0	0	0	0-0	191.2	216	105	100	20	89-3	121	.289
2000— New York (A.L.)		19	9	.679	4.35	1.46	32	32	3	1	0	0-0	204.2	219	111	99	17	80-4	125	.271
2001— New York (A.L.)		15	10	.600	3.99	1.32	31	31	2	0	0	0-0	200.2	224	103	89	14	41-3	164	.281
2002— New York (A.L.)		13	5	.722	3.27	1.31	22	22	3	1	0	0-0	134.2	144	58	49	6	32-2	97	.272
— Tampa (FSL)		0	0	...	0.00	0.60	2	2	0	0	...	0-...	5.0	3	0	0	0	0-0	4	.167
— Norwich (East.)		0	0	...	1.42	0.32	1	1	0	0	...	0-...	6.1	2	1	1	0	0-0	5	.095
2003— New York (A.L.)		21	8	.724	4.02	1.33	33	33	1	0	0	0-0	208.1	227	109	93	21	50-3	180	.272
Major League totals (9 years)		149	78	.656	3.94	1.38	283	276	23	3	0	0-0	1792.2	1901	873	785	143	579-21	1275	.273

PHELPS, JOSH — DH/1B

PERSONAL: Born May 12, 1978, in Anchorage, Alaska. ... 6-3/220. ... Bats right, throws right. ... Full name: Joshua Lee Phelps. ... High school: Lakeland (Rathdrum, Idaho).

TRANSACTIONS/CAREER NOTES: Selected by Toronto Blue Jays organization in 10th round of free-agent draft (June 4, 1996). ... On Tennessee disabled list (April 6-May 1, 2000). ... Placed on 15-day disabled list (July 7, 2003). ... Sent to Syracuse on rehab assignment (July 21, 2003). ... Recalled from rehab assignment (July 25, 2003).

2003 GAMES PLAYED BY POSITION (MLB): DH—107, 1B—8.

										BATTING									FIELDING	
Year	Team (League)	Pos.	G	AB	R	H	2B	3B	HR	RBI	BB	SO	HBP	GDP	SB-CS	Avg.	OBP	SLG	OPS	E	Pct.
1996— Medicine Hat (Pio.)		C-OF	59	191	26	46	3	0	5	29	27	65	6	5	5-3	.241	.351	.335	.686	9	.964
1997— Hagerstown (SAL)		C	68	233	26	49	9	1	7	24	15	72	8	6	3-2	.210	.279	.348	.627	21	.965
1998— Hagerstown (SAL)		3B-C-OF	117	385	48	102	24	1	8	44	40	80	8	12	2-0	.265	.342	.395	.737	‡ 19	.975
1999— Dunedin (Fla. St.)		C	110	406	72	133	27	4	20	88	28	104	8	13	6-3	.328	.379	.562	.941	1	.994
2000— Tennessee (Sou.)		C	56	184	23	42	9	1	9	28	15	66	7	6	1-0	.228	.308	.435	.742	5	.983
— Toronto (A.L.)		C	1	1	0	0	0	0	0	0	0	1	0	0	0-0	.000	.000	.000	.000	0	1.000
— Dunedin (Fla. St.)		C	30	113	26	36	7	0	12	34	12	34	1	2	0-0	.319	.386	.699	1.085	1	.992
2001— Tennessee (Sou.)		C	• 136	486	95	142	* 36	1	* 31	97	80	127	17	5	3-3	.292	.406	.562	.968	2	.985
— Toronto (A.L.)		C	8	12	3	0	0	0	0	1	2	5	0	1	1-0	.000	.143	.000	.143	0	1.000
2002— Syracuse (Int'l)		C-1B	70	257	50	75	20	1	24	64	32	83	5	6	0-0	.292	.380	.658	1.037	4	.985
— Toronto (A.L.)		DH-1B	74	265	41	82	20	1	15	58	19	82	3	7	0-0	.309	.362	.562	.925	0	1.000
2003— Syracuse (Int'l)		DH	4	11	2	5	0	0	2	4	1	3	0	0	0-0	.455	.500	1.000	1.500	0	...
— Toronto (A.L.)		DH-1B	119	396	57	106	18	1	20	66	39	115	17	12	1-2	.268	.358	.470	.827	2	.967
Major League totals (4 years)			202	674	101	188	38	2	35	125	60	203	20	20	2-2	.279	.355	.497	.852	2	.980

P

PHELPS, TOMMY   P

PERSONAL: Born March 4, 1974, in Seoul, South Korea. ... 6-3/192. ... Throws left, bats left. ... Full name: Thomas Allen Phelps. ... High school: Robinson (Tampa, Fla.).
TRANSACTIONS/CAREER NOTES: Selected by Montreal Expos organization in eighth round of free-agent draft (June 1, 1992). ... On Harrisburg disabled list (June 24-July 13, 1997). ... On Harrisburg disabled list (April 9-May 18 and July 25-August 3, 1998). ... Released by Expos (June 20, 1999). ... Granted free agency (October 18, 2000). ... Signed by Detroit Tigers as a minor league free agent (November 23, 2999). ... On Toledo disabled list (July 25-August 2, 2001). ... Granted free agency (October 15, 2001). ... On Calgary disabled list (July 3-11, 2002). ... Granted free agency (October 15, 2002). ... Re-signed by Marlins organization (December 11, 2002). ... Recalled by Florida from Albuquerque (April 29, 2003). ... Placed on 15-day disabled list (August 2, 2003). ... Sent on minor league rehab assignment by Florida (August 29, 2003). ... Recalled from minor league rehab assignemnt; removed from 15-day disabled list (September 1, 2003).
CAREER HITTING: 1-for-11 (.091), 1 R, 0 2B, 0 3B, 0 RBI.

Year League	W	L	Pct.	ERA	WHIP	G	GS	CG	ShO	Hld.	Sv.-Opp.	IP	H	R	ER	HR	BB-IBB	SO	Avg.
1993— Burlington (Midw.)	2	4	.333	3.73	1.20	8	8	0	0	...	0-...	41.0	36	18	17	4	13-0	33	.229
— Jamestown (NYP)	3	8	.273	4.58	1.51	16	15	1	0	...	0-...	92.1	102	62	47	4	37-1	74	.278
1994— Burlington (Midw.)	8	8	.500	5.55	1.61	23	23	1	1	...	0-...	118.1	143	91	73	9	48-1	82	.307
1995— W.P. Beach (FSL)	0	2	.000	16.20	4.20	2	2	0	0	...	0-...	5.0	10	10	9	0	11-0	5	.455
— Albany (S. Atl.)	10	9	.526	3.33	1.38	24	24	1	0	...	0-...	135.1	142	76	50	6	45-0	119	.262
1996— W.P. Beach (FSL)	10	2	.833	2.89	1.25	18	18	1	1	...	0-...	112.0	105	42	36	5	35-0	71	.246
— Harrisburg (Eastern)	2	2	.500	2.47	1.31	8	8	2	2	...	0-...	47.1	43	16	13	3	19-2	23	.249
1997— Harrisburg (Eastern)	10	6	.625	4.71	1.52	18	18	0	0	...	0-...	101.1	115	68	53	14	39-1	86	.285
1998— Jupiter (FSL)	2	2	.500	4.39	1.39	7	7	0	0	...	0-...	41.0	42	21	20	3	15-0	21	.259
— Harrisburg (Eastern)	5	4	.556	3.62	1.39	12	10	0	0	...	0-...	59.2	57	29	24	5	26-0	26	.266
1999— Harrisburg (Eastern)	3	6	.333	5.71	1.58	13	13	1	0	...	0-...	64.2	76	53	41	13	26-0	36	.288
2000— Jacksonville (Sou.)	6	6	.500	4.94	1.34	38	11	0	0	...	0-...	102.0	111	59	56	17	26-2	62	.277
2001— Toledo (Int'l)	3	2	.600	3.62	1.56	29	0	0	0	...	1-...	59.2	74	30	24	4	19-3	53	.298
— Erie (East.)	1	1	.500	3.58	1.26	15	2	0	0	...	2-...	32.2	33	14	13	1	8-2	31	.268
2002— Calgary (PCL)	4	2	.667	3.15	1.30	51	0	0	0	...	5-...	74.1	76	27	26	8	21-3	62	.266
2003— Albuquerque (PCL)	0	0	...	1.17	1.04	5	0	0	0	...	0-...	7.2	5	1	1	1	3-0	13	.217
— Florida (N.L.)	3	2	.600	4.00	1.48	27	7	0	0	1	0-0	63.0	70	32	28	3	23-1	43	.282
— Jupiter (FSL)	0	0	...	6.00	1.67	2	1	0	0	...	0-...	3.0	5	2	2	0	0-0	3	.357
Major League totals (1 year)	**3**	**2**	**.600**	**4.00**	**1.48**	**27**	**7**	**0**	**0**	**1**	**0-0**	**63.0**	**70**	**32**	**28**	**3**	**23-1**	**43**	**.282**

PHILLIPS, BRANDON   2B/SS

PERSONAL: Born June 28, 1981, in Raleigh, N.C. ... 5-11/185. ... Bats right, throws right. ... Full name: Brandon Emil Phillips. ... High school: Redan (Stone Mountain, Ga.).
TRANSACTIONS/CAREER NOTES: Selected by Montreal Expos organization in second round of free-agent draft (June 2, 1999). ... Traded by Expos with 1B Lee Stevens, P Cliff Lee and OF Grady Sizemore to Cleveland Indians for P Bartolo Colon and future considerations (June 27, 2002); Expos acquired P Tim Drew to complete deal (June 28, 2002).
2003 GAMES PLAYED BY POSITION (MLB): 2B—109.

										BATTING							FIELDING	
Year Team (League)	Pos.	G	AB	R	H	2B	3B	HR	RBI	BB	SO	HBP	GDP	SB-CS	Avg.	OBP	SLG	OPS	E	Pct.
1999— GC Expos (GCL)	SS	47	169	23	49	11	3	1	21	15	35	3	6	12-3	.290	.358	.408	.767	17	.915
2000— Cape Fear (S. Atl.)	SS-2B	126	484	74	117	17	8	11	72	38	97	9	11	23-8	.242	.306	.378	.684	36	.940
2001— Jupiter (FSL)	SS	55	194	36	55	12	2	4	23	38	45	6	3	17-3	.284	.414	.428	.842	18	.930
— Harrisburg (East.)	SS-2B-3B	67	265	35	79	19	0	7	36	12	42	4	9	13-6	.298	.337	.449	.786	12	.958
2002— Harrisburg (East.)	SS	60	245	40	80	13	2	9	35	16	33	5	7	6-3	.327	.380	.506	.886	14	.936
— Ottawa (Int'l)	SS	10	35	1	9	4	0	1	5	2	6	0	0	0-0	.257	.297	.457	.754	0	1.000
— Buffalo (Int'l)	SS-2B	55	223	30	63	14	0	8	27	14	39	1	6	8-2	.283	.321	.453	.774	15	.952
— Cleveland (A.L.)	2B	11	31	5	8	3	1	0	4	3	6	1	0	0-0	.258	.343	.419	.762	2	.957
2003— Buffalo (Int'l)	2B	43	154	14	27	7	0	3	13	12	22	3	3	7-3	.175	.247	.279	.526	3	.985
— Cleveland (A.L.)	2B	112	370	36	77	18	1	6	33	14	77	3	12	4-5	.208	.242	.311	.553	11	.981
Major League totals (2 years)		**123**	**401**	**41**	**85**	**21**	**2**	**6**	**37**	**17**	**83**	**4**	**12**	**4-5**	**.212**	**.251**	**.319**	**.570**	**13**	**.979**

PHILLIPS, JASON   1B/C

PERSONAL: Born September 27, 1976, in La Mesa, Calif. ... 6-1/177. ... Bats right, throws right. ... Full name: Jason Lloyd Phillips. ... High school: El Capitan (Lakeside, Calif.). ... College: San Diego State.
TRANSACTIONS/CAREER NOTES: Selected by New York Mets organization in 24th round of free-agent draft (June 3, 1997). ... On Norfolk disabled list (July 25-August 12, 2002).
2003 GAMES PLAYED BY POSITION (MLB): 1B—84, C—29.

										BATTING							FIELDING	
Year Team (League)	Pos.	G	AB	R	H	2B	3B	HR	RBI	BB	SO	HBP	GDP	SB-CS	Avg.	OBP	SLG	OPS	E	Pct.
1997— Pittsfield (NYP)	C	48	155	15	32	9	0	2	17	13	24	4	2	4-0	.206	.282	.303	.585	4	.990
1998— Capital City (SAL)	C	69	251	36	68	15	1	5	37	23	35	5	3	5-2	.271	.343	.398	.741	4	.994
— St. Lucie (Fla. St.)	C	8	28	4	13	2	0	0	2	2	1	0	1	0-0	.464	.500	.536	1.036	0	1.000
1999— St. Lucie (Fla. St.)	C	81	283	36	73	12	1	9	48	43	28	8	10	0-1	.258	.367	.403	.770	4	.992
— Binghamton (East.)	C	39	141	13	32	5	0	7	23	13	20	3	4	0-0	.227	.304	.411	.715	5	.984
2000— St. Lucie (Fla. St.)	C	80	297	53	82	21	0	6	41	23	19	8	12	1-1	.276	.343	.407	.751	6	.989
— Binghamton (East.)	C	27	98	16	38	4	0	0	13	7	9	2	3	0-0	.388	.435	.429	.864	3	.983
2001— Binghamton (East.)	C	93	317	42	93	21	0	11	55	31	25	5	9	0-0	.293	.362	.464	.826	3	.995
— New York (N.L.)	C	6	7	2	1	1	0	0	0	0	1	0	0	0-0	.143	.143	.286	.429	0	1.000
— Norfolk (Int'l)	C	19	66	8	20	2	0	2	14	7	8	0	2	0-0	.303	.365	.424	.789	0	1.000
2002— Norfolk (Int'l)	C	88	323	35	91	22	1	13	65	24	29	2	10	1-0	.282	.327	.477	.804	4	.993
— New York (N.L.)	C	11	19	4	7	0	0	1	3	1	1	1	1	0-0	.368	.409	.526	.935	0	1.000
2003— Norfolk (Int'l)	C-1B-DH	22	78	13	27	5	0	4	20	11	9	2	4	0-0	.346	.435	.564	.999	0	1.000
— New York (N.L.)	1B-C	119	403	45	120	25	0	11	58	39	50	10	21	0-1	.298	.373	.442	.815	8	.991
Major League totals (3 years)		**136**	**429**	**51**	**128**	**26**	**0**	**12**	**61**	**40**	**52**	**11**	**22**	**0-1**	**.298**	**.371**	**.443**	**.814**	**8**	**.991**

PHILLIPS, JASON C.   P

PERSONAL: Born March 22, 1974, in Williamsport, Pa. ... 6-6/225. ... Throws right, bats right. ... Full name: Jason Charles Phillips. ... High school: Hughesville (Pa.).
TRANSACTIONS/CAREER NOTES: Selected by Pittsburgh Pirates organization in 14th round of free-agent draft (June 1, 1992). ... On Nashville disabled list (May 26, 1999-remainder of season). ... Granted free agency (October 15, 1999). ... Re-signed by Pirates organization (January 6, 1999). ... On Nashville disabled list (May 9-September 6, 2000). ... Granted free agency (October 18, 2000). ... Re-signed by Pirates organization (January 9, 2001). ... On Lynchburg disabled list (April 5-May 10, 2001). ... Released by Pirates (June 4, 2001). ... Signed by Cleveland Indians organization (June 7, 2001). ... On Buffalo disabled list (July 27-August 3, 2001). ... Granted free agency (October 15, 2001). ... Re-signed by Indians organization (October 26, 2001). ... On Cleveland disabled list (August 28, 2002-remainder of season).
CAREER HITTING: 0-for-0 (.000), 0 R, 0 2B, 0 3B, 0 HR, 0 RBI.

Year	League	W	L	Pct.	ERA	WHIP	G	GS	CG	ShO	Hld.	Sv.-Opp.	IP	H	R	ER	HR	BB-IBB	SO	Avg.
1992—GC Pirates (GCL)		1	2	.333	8.47	2.00	4	4	0	0	...	0-...	17.0	21	21	16	0	13-0	10	.288
1993—Welland (N.Y.-Penn)		4	6	.400	3.53	1.35	14	14	0	0	...	0-...	71.1	60	44	28	2	36-0	66	.218
1994—Augusta (S. Atl.)		6	12	.333	6.73	1.90	23	23	1	0	...	0-...	108.1	118	97	81	4	88-1	108	.278
1995—Augusta (S. Atl.)		4	3	.571	3.60	1.61	30	6	0	0	...	0-...	80.0	76	46	32	2	53-1	65	.256
1996—Augusta (S. Atl.)		5	4	.556	2.41	1.20	14	14	1	1	...	0-...	89.2	79	35	24	3	29-1	75	.242
—Lynchburg (Carolina)		5	6	.455	4.52	1.59	13	13	1	1	...	0-...	73.2	82	47	37	3	35-0	63	.274
1997—Lynchburg (Carolina)		11	6	.647	3.76	1.18	23	23	2	1	...	0-...	138.2	129	66	58	10	35-0	140	.243
—Carolina (Sou.)		1	2	.333	2.32	0.97	4	4	2	1	...	0-...	31.0	21	8	8	1	9-0	22	.189
1998—Carolina (Sou.)		7	•13	.350	4.71	1.41	25	25	1	1	...	0-...	151.0	161	89	79	14	52-3	114	.272
—Nashville (PCL)		2	0	1.000	2.59	1.60	5	5	0	0	...	0-...	31.1	38	10	9	3	12-0	21	.317
1999—Pittsburgh (N.L.)		0	0	...	11.57	2.43	6	0	0	0	0	0-0	7.0	11	9	9	2	6-1	7	.393
—Nashville (PCL)		0	0	...	15.00	3.67	1	1	0	0	...	0-...	3.0	6	6	5	0	5-1	5	.429
2000—Nashville (PCL)		2	4	.333	4.70	1.57	6	6	0	0	...	0-...	30.2	30	20	16	4	18-0	18	.261
2001—Altoona (East.)		0	1	.000	10.00	2.44	6	1	0	0	...	0-...	9.0	18	11	10	0	4-0	4	.419
—Akron (East.)		2	1	.667	4.13	1.38	10	3	0	0	...	0-...	24.0	18	11	11	2	15-0	20	.214
—Buffalo (Int'l)		2	2	.500	3.34	1.00	8	6	1	0	...	0-...	35.0	27	15	13	3	8-0	25	.213
2002—Buffalo (Int'l)		7	4	.636	3.39	1.07	16	16	1	0	...	0-...	98.1	88	37	37	8	17-0	71	.242
—Cleveland (A.L.)		1	3	.250	4.97	1.46	8	6	0	0	0	0-0	41.2	41	24	23	7	20-0	23	.259
2003—Cleveland (A.L.)		0	1	.000	9.00	2.20	3	0	0	0	0	0-0	5.0	9	5	5	1	2-0	2	.409
—Buffalo (Int'l)		10	1	.909	2.12	1.02	13	12	1	0	...	0-...	85.0	68	24	20	4	19-0	56	.222
American League totals (2 years)		1	4	.200	5.40	1.54	11	6	0	0	0	0-0	46.2	50	29	28	8	22-0	25	.278
National League totals (1 year)		0	0	...	11.57	2.43	6	0	0	0	0	0-0	7.0	11	9	9	2	6-1	7	.393
Major League totals (3 years)		1	4	.200	6.20	1.66	17	6	0	0	0	0-0	53.2	61	38	37	10	28-1	32	.293

PIATT, ADAM   OF/DH

PERSONAL: Born February 8, 1976, in Chicago, Ill. ... 6-2/205. ... Bats right, throws right. ... Full name: Adam David Piatt. ... Name pronounced: pie-at. ... High school: Bishop Verot (Fort Myers, Fla.). ... College: Mississippi State.

TRANSACTIONS/CAREER NOTES: Selected by Oakland Athletics organization in eighth round of free-agent draft (June 3, 1997). ... On Oakland disabled list (June 6-September 1, 2001); included rehabilitation assignments to Sacramento (July 12-28 and August 17-27) and Modesto (August 27-September 1). ... Designated for assignment (August 13, 2003). ... Claimed off waivers by Tampa Bay (August 19, 2003).

2003 GAMES PLAYED BY POSITION (MLB): OF—45, DH—6, 1B—1.

Year	Team (League)	Pos.	G	AB	R	H	2B	3B	HR	RBI	BB	SO	HBP	GDP	SB-CS	Avg.	OBP	SLG	OPS	E	Pct.
1997—S. Oregon (N'west)		3B-1B	57	216	63	63	9	1	13	35	35	58	1	4	19-4	.292	.391	.523	.914	21	.864
1998—Modesto (Calif.)		2B-3B	133	500	91	144	•40	3	20	*107	80	99	0	15	20-6	.288	.381	.500	.881	‡32	.892
1999—Midland (Texas)		3B-SS	129	476	*128	164	48	3	*39	*135	•93	101	7	11	7-3	.345	.451	.704	1.155	31	.917
—Vancouver (PCL)		3B-SS	6	18	1	4	1	0	0	3	3	6	2	0	0-0	.222	.417	.278	.694	2	.917
2000—Sacramento (PCL)		OF-3B-1B	65	254	36	72	15	0	8	42	26	57	4	3	3-2	.283	.355	.437	.792	9	.959
—Oakland (A.L.)		O-3-D-1	60	157	24	47	5	5	5	23	23	44	1	1	0-1	.299	.392	.490	.883	2	.967
2001—Oakland (A.L.)		OF-DH	36	95	9	20	5	1	0	6	13	26	0	5	0-0	.211	.300	.284	.584	2	.962
—Sacramento (PCL)		OF	35	109	14	28	9	0	1	15	11	27	3	5	2-0	.257	.339	.367	.706	3	.933
—Modesto (Calif.)		OF	4	15	4	7	2	0	1	2	1	5	1	0	0-0	.467	.529	.800	1.329	0	1.000
2002—Sacramento (PCL)		OF-1B	62	234	46	69	15	0	8	44	35	30	1	12	4-3	.295	.385	.462	.846	2	.981
—Oakland (A.L.)		OF-1B	55	137	18	32	8	0	5	18	12	33	2	1	2-1	.234	.303	.401	.704	0	1.000
2003—Oakland (A.L.)		OF-DH-1B	47	100	6	24	10	0	4	15	6	30	0	2	1-2	.240	.280	.460	.740	1	.981
—Tampa Bay (A.L.)		OF-DH	14	32	5	6	3	0	2	3	3	16	0	0	0-0	.188	.250	.469	.719	0	1.000
Major League totals (4 years)			212	521	62	129	31	6	16	65	57	149	3	9	3-4	.248	.323	.422	.745	5	.979

PIAZZA, MIKE   C

PERSONAL: Born September 4, 1968, in Norristown, Pa. ... 6-3/215. ... Bats right, throws right. ... Full name: Michael Joseph Piazza. ... Name pronounced: pee-AH-zuh. ... High school: Phoenixville (Pa.) Area. ... Junior college: Miami-Dade Community College.

TRANSACTIONS/CAREER NOTES: Selected by Los Angeles Dodgers organization in 62nd round of free-agent draft (June 1, 1988). ... On disabled list (May 11-June 4, 1995). ... Traded by Dodgers with 3B Todd Zeile to Florida Marlins for OF Gary Sheffield, 3B Bobby Bonilla, C Charles Johnson, OF Jim Eisenreich and P Manuel Barrios (May 15, 1998). ... Traded by Marlins to New York Mets for OF Preston Wilson, P Ed Yarnall and P Geoff Goetz (May 22, 1998). ... On disabled list (April 10-25, 1999). ... On suspended list (April 2-6, 2003). ... Placed on 15-day disabled list (May 17, 2003).

2003 GAMES PLAYED BY POSITION (MLB): C—64, 1B—1.

Year	Team (League)	Pos.	G	AB	R	H	2B	3B	HR	RBI	BB	SO	HBP	GDP	SB-CS	Avg.	OBP	SLG	OPS	E	Pct.
1989—Salem (NW)		C	57	198	22	53	11	0	8	25	13	51	2	11	0-1	.268	.318	.444	.762	6	.977
1990—Vero Beach (FSL)		C-1B	88	272	27	68	20	0	6	45	11	68	1	6	0-1	.250	.281	.390	.670	16	.967
1991—Bakersfield (Calif.)		C-1B	117	448	71	124	27	2	29	80	47	83	3	19	0-3	.277	.344	.540	.884	15	.981
1992—San Antonio (Texas)		C	31	114	18	43	11	0	7	21	13	18	0	2	0-0	.377	.441	.658	1.099	4	.981
—Albuquerque (PCL)		C-1B	94	358	54	122	22	5	16	69	37	57	2	9	1-3	.341	.405	.564	.969	9	.985
—Los Angeles (N.L.)		C	21	69	5	16	3	0	1	7	4	12	1	1	0-0	.232	.284	.319	.603	1	.990
1993—Los Angeles (N.L.)		C-1B	149	547	81	174	24	2	35	112	46	86	3	10	3-4	.318	.370	.561	.932	§11	.989
1994—Los Angeles (N.L.)		C	107	405	64	129	18	0	24	92	33	65	1	11	1-3	.319	.370	.541	.910	*10	.985
1995—Los Angeles (N.L.)		C	112	434	82	150	17	0	32	93	39	80	1	10	1-0	.346	.400	.606	1.006	9	.990
1996—Los Angeles (N.L.)		C	148	547	87	184	16	0	36	105	81	93	1	21	0-3	.336	.422	.563	.985	9	.992
1997—Los Angeles (N.L.)		C-DH	152	556	104	201	32	1	40	124	69	77	3	19	5-1	.362	.431	.638	1.070	*16	.986
1998—Los Angeles (N.L.)		C	37	149	20	42	5	0	9	30	11	27	0	3	0-0	.282	.329	.497	.826	2	.993
—Florida (N.L.)		C	5	18	1	5	0	1	0	5	0	0	0	0	0-0	.278	.263	.389	.652	1	.968
—New York (N.L.)		C-DH	109	394	67	137	33	0	23	76	47	53	2	12	1-0	.348	.417	.607	1.024	8	.989
1999—New York (N.L.)		C-DH	141	534	100	162	25	0	40	124	51	70	1	*27	2-2	.303	.361	.575	.936	11	.989
2000—New York (N.L.)		C-DH	136	482	90	156	26	0	38	113	58	69	3	15	4-2	.324	.398	.614	1.012	3	.997
2001—New York (N.L.)		C-DH	141	503	81	151	29	0	36	94	67	87	2	20	0-2	.300	.384	.573	.957	9	.991
2002—New York (N.L.)		C-DH	135	478	69	134	23	2	33	98	57	82	3	26	0-3	.280	.359	.544	.903	*12	.986
2003—Norfolk (Int'l)		C-DH-1B	5	17	2	3	0	0	1	2	1	3	0	0	0-0	.176	.222	.353	.575	0	1.000
—New York (N.L.)		C-1B	68	234	37	67	13	0	11	34	35	40	1	11	0-0	.286	.377	.483	.860	7	.982
Major League totals (12 years)			1461	5350	888	1708	264	6	358	1107	598	841	22	186	17-20	.319	.388	.572	.959	109	.989

P

PIERRE, JUAN — OF

PERSONAL: Born August 14, 1977, in Mobile, Ala. ... 6-0/180. ... Bats left, throws left. ... Full name: Juan D'Vaughn Pierre. ... Name pronounced: pee-AIR. ... High school: Alexandria (La.). ... College: South Alabama.

TRANSACTIONS/CAREER NOTES: Selected by Colorado Rockies organization in 13th round of free-agent draft (June 2, 1998). ... Traded by Rockies with P Mike Hampton and cash to Florida Marlins for C Charles Johnson, P Vic Darensbourg, OF Preston Wilson and 2B Pablo Ozuna (November 16, 2002).

2003 GAMES PLAYED BY POSITION (MLB): OF—161.

											BATTING									FIELDING	
Year	Team (League)	Pos.	G	AB	R	H	2B	3B	HR	RBI	BB	SO	HBP	GDP	SB-CS	Avg.	OBP	SLG	OPS	E	Pct.
1998—	Portland (NW)	OF	64	264	55	93	9	2	0	30	19	11	2	3	* 38-9	.352	.399	.402	.800	5	.955
1999—	Asheville (S. Atl.)	OF	* 140	* 585	93	* 187	28	5	1	55	38	37	8	12	66-19	.320	.366	.390	.756	4	.981
2000—	Carolina (Sou.)	OF	107	439	63	143	16	4	0	32	33	26	5	4	46-12	.326	.376	.380	.757	2	.992
	— Colo. Springs (PCL)	OF	4	17	3	8	0	1	0	1	0	0	0	0	1-1	.471	.471	.588	1.059	0	1.000
	— Colorado (N.L.)	OF	51	200	26	62	2	0	0	20	13	15	1	2	7-6	.310	.353	.320	.673	3	.975
2001—	Colorado (N.L.)	OF	156	617	108	202	26	11	2	55	41	29	10	6	• 46-17	.327	.378	.415	.793	8	.979
2002—	Colorado (N.L.)	OF	152	592	90	170	20	5	1	35	31	52	9	7	47-12	.287	.332	.343	.675	2	.995
2003—	Florida (N.L.)	OF	•162	•668	100	204	28	7	1	41	55	35	5	9	*65-*20	.305	.361	.373	.734	3	.993
Major League totals (4 years)			521	2077	324	638	76	23	4	151	140	131	25	24	165-55	.307	.357	.372	.729	16	.987

PIERZYNSKI, A.J. — C

PERSONAL: Born December 30, 1976, in Bridgehampton, N.Y. ... 6-3/220. ... Bats left, throws right. ... Full name: Anthony John Pierzynski. ... Name pronounced: PEER-zin-skee. ... High school: Dr. Phillips (Orlando).

TRANSACTIONS/CAREER NOTES: Selected by Minnesota Twins organization in third round of free-agent draft (June 2, 1994). ... On Salt Lake disabled list (August 24, 1999-remainder of season).

2003 GAMES PLAYED BY POSITION (MLB): C—135.

											BATTING									FIELDING	
Year	Team (League)	Pos.	G	AB	R	H	2B	3B	HR	RBI	BB	SO	HBP	GDP	SB-CS	Avg.	OBP	SLG	OPS	E	Pct.
1994—	GC Twins (GCL)	DH-C	43	152	21	44	8	1	1	19	12	19	0	3	0-2	.289	.337	.375	.712	8	.966
1995—	Fort Wayne (Midw.)	C	22	84	10	26	5	1	2	14	2	10	0	1	0-0	.310	.322	.464	.786	10	.939
	— Elizabethton (App.)	C-1B	56	205	29	68	13	1	7	45	14	23	0	6	0-2	.332	.373	.507	.880	§ 12	.974
1996—	Fort Wayne (Midw.)	C-DH-OF	114	431	48	118	30	3	7	70	22	53	2	10	0-4	.274	.308	.406	.714	‡ 21	.972
1997—	Fort Myers (FSL)	C-DH-1B	118	412	49	115	23	1	9	64	16	59	6	9	2-1	.279	.313	.405	.718	10	.987
1998—	New Britain (East.)	C-DH	59	212	30	63	11	0	3	17	10	25	2	4	0-2	.297	.333	.392	.725	2	.996
	— Salt Lake (PCL)	C	59	208	29	53	7	2	7	30	9	24	0	4	3-1	.255	.284	.409	.693	7	.983
	— Minnesota (A.L.)	C	7	10	1	3	0	0	0	1	1	2	1	0	0-0	.300	.385	.300	.685	0	1.000
1999—	Salt Lake (PCL)	C	67	228	29	59	10	0	1	25	16	29	1	11	0-0	.259	.307	.316	.623	7	.984
	— Minnesota (A.L.)	C	9	22	3	6	2	0	0	3	1	4	1	0	0-0	.273	.333	.364	.697	0	1.000
2000—	New Britain (East.)	C	62	228	36	68	17	2	4	34	8	22	9	13	0-0	.298	.341	.443	.784	6	.982
	— Salt Lake (PCL)	C	41	155	22	52	14	1	4	25	5	22	1	3	1-1	.335	.354	.516	.870	3	.990
	— Minnesota (A.L.)	C	33	88	12	27	5	1	2	11	5	14	2	1	0-0	.307	.354	.455	.809	0	1.000
2001—	Minnesota (A.L.)	C-DH	114	381	51	110	33	2	7	55	16	57	4	7	1-2	.289	.322	.441	.763	10	.985
2002—	Minnesota (A.L.)	C	130	440	54	132	31	6	6	49	13	61	11	14	1-2	.300	.334	.439	.773	3	.996
2003—	Minnesota (A.L.)	C	137	487	63	152	35	3	11	74	24	55	15	13	3-1	.312	.360	.464	.824	6	.993
Major League totals (6 years)			430	1428	184	430	106	12	26	193	60	193	34	35	6-10	.301	.341	.447	.788	19	.993

PINEIRO, JOEL — P

PERSONAL: Born September 25, 1978, in Rio Padres, Puerto Rico. ... 6-1/200. ... Throws right, bats right. ... Full name: Joel Alberto Pineiro. ... High school: Colonial (Orlando). ... Junior college: Edison (Fla.) Community College.

TRANSACTIONS/CAREER NOTES: Selected by Seattle Mariners organization in 12th round of free-agent draft (June 3, 1997). ... On suspended list (October 3-6, 2001).

CAREER HITTING: 1-for-11 (.091), 1 R, 0 2B, 0 3B, 0 HR, 2 RBI.

Year	League	W	L	Pct.	ERA	WHIP	G	GS	CG	ShO	Hld.	Sv.-Opp.	IP	H	R	ER	HR	BB-IBB	SO	Avg.
1997—	Ariz. Mariners (Ariz.)	1	0	1.000	0.00	0.33	1	0	0	0	...	0-...	3.0	1	0	0	0	0-0	4	.100
	— Everett (Northwest)	4	2	.667	5.33	1.47	18	6	0	0	...	2-...	49.0	54	33	29	2	18-1	59	.267
1998—	Wisconsin (Midw.)	8	4	.667	3.19	1.25	16	16	1	0	...	0-...	96.0	92	40	34	8	28-1	84	.252
	— Lancaster (Calif.)	2	0	1.000	7.80	1.87	9	9	1	• 1	...	0-...	45.0	58	40	39	6	22-0	48	.307
	— Orlando (Sou.)	1	0	1.000	5.40	1.80	1	1	0	0	...	0-...	5.0	7	4	3	0	2-0	2	.368
1999—	New Haven (East.)	10	* 15	.400	4.72	1.46	28	25	4	0	...	0-...	166.0	190	105	87	18	52-0	116	.290
2000—	New Haven (East.)	2	1	.667	4.13	1.03	9	9	0	0	...	0-...	52.1	42	25	24	6	12-0	43	.218
	— Tacoma (PCL)	7	1	.875	2.80	1.23	10	9	2	2	...	0-...	61.0	53	20	19	3	22-1	41	.232
	— Seattle (A.L.)	1	0	1.000	5.59	1.97	8	1	0	0	0	0-0	19.1	25	13	12	3	13-0	10	.316
2001—	Tacoma (PCL)	6	3	.667	3.62	1.31	18	10	0	0	...	0-...	77.0	68	31	31	8	33-0	64	.242
	— Seattle (A.L.)	6	2	.750	2.03	0.94	17	11	0	0	2	0-0	75.1	50	24	17	2	21-0	56	.191
2002—	Seattle (A.L.)	14	7	.667	3.24	1.25	37	28	2	1	3	0-0	194.1	189	75	70	24	54-1	136	.256
2003—	Seattle (A.L.)	16	11	.593	3.78	1.27	32	32	3	•2	0	0-0	211.2	192	94	89	19	76-3	151	.241
Major League totals (4 years)		37	20	.649	3.38	1.24	94	72	5	3	5	0-0	500.2	456	206	188	48	164-4	353	.243

PLESAC, DAN — P

PERSONAL: Born February 4, 1962, in Gary, Ind. ... 6-5/217. ... Throws left, bats left. ... Full name: Daniel Thomas Plesac. ... Name pronounced: PLEE-sack. ... High school: Crown Point (Ind.). ... College: North Carolina State.

TRANSACTIONS/CAREER NOTES: Selected by St. Louis Cardinals organization in second round of free-agent draft (June 3, 1980); did not sign. ... Selected by Milwaukee Brewers organization in first round (26th pick overall) of free-agent draft (June 6, 1983). ... Granted free agency (October 27, 1992). ... Signed by Chicago Cubs (December 8, 1992). ... Granted free agency (October 25, 1994). ... Signed by Pittsburgh Pirates (November 9, 1994). ... Traded by Pirates with OF Orlando Merced and IF Carlos Garcia to Toronto Blue Jays for P Jose Silva, P Jose Pett, IF Brandon Cromer and three players to be named later (November 14, 1996); Pirates acquired P Mike Halperin, IF Abraham Nunez and C/OF Craig Wilson to complete deal (December 11, 1996). ... Traded by Blue Jays to Arizona Diamondbacks for SS Tony Batista and P John Frascatore (June 12, 1999). ... Granted free agency (October 30, 2000). ... Signed by Blue Jays (December 8, 2000). ... Traded by Blue Jays to Philadelphia Phillies for P Cliff Politte (May 26, 2002). ... Granted free agency (October 29, 2002). ... Re-signed by Phillies (December 7, 2002).

CAREER HITTING: 1-for-15 (.067), 0 R, 0 2B, 0 3B, 0 HR, 0 RBI.

P

Year League	W	L	Pct.	ERA	WHIP	G	GS	CG	ShO	Hld.	Sv.-Opp.	IP	H	R	ER	HR	BB-IBB	SO	Avg.
1983— Paintsville (Appal.)	* 9	1	* .900	3.50	1.62	14	• 14	2	0	...	0-...	82.1	76	44	32	6	57-0	* 85	...
1984— Stockton (Calif.)	6	6	.500	3.32	1.44	16	16	2	0	...	0-...	108.1	106	51	40	7	50-0	101	...
— El Paso (Texas)	2	2	.500	3.46	1.51	7	7	0	0	...	0-...	39.0	43	19	15	2	16-0	24	.285
1985— El Paso (Texas)	12	5	.706	4.97	1.59	25	24	2	0	...	0-...	150.1	171	91	83	12	68-1	128	.295
1986— Milwaukee (A.L.)	10	7	.588	2.97	1.21	51	0	0	0	6	14-18	91.0	81	34	30	5	29-1	75	.240
1987— Milwaukee (A.L.)	5	6	.455	2.61	1.08	57	0	0	0	0	23-36	79.1	63	30	23	8	23-1	89	.213
1988— Milwaukee (A.L.)	1	2	.333	2.41	1.11	50	0	0	0	0	30-35	52.1	46	14	14	2	12-2	52	.234
1989— Milwaukee (A.L.)	3	4	.429	2.35	1.04	52	0	0	0	0	33-40	61.1	47	16	16	6	17-1	52	.213
1990— Milwaukee (A.L.)	3	7	.300	4.43	1.42	66	0	0	0	2	24-34	69.0	67	36	34	5	31-6	65	.257
1991— Milwaukee (A.L.)	2	7	.222	4.29	1.42	45	10	0	0	1	8-12	92.1	92	49	44	12	39-1	61	.263
1992— Milwaukee (A.L.)	5	4	.556	2.96	1.25	44	4	0	0	1	1-3	79.0	64	28	26	5	35-5	54	.229
1993— Chicago (N.L.)	2	1	.667	4.74	1.52	57	0	0	0	12	0-2	62.2	74	37	33	10	21-6	47	.298
1994— Chicago (N.L.)	2	3	.400	4.61	1.35	54	0	0	0	14	1-3	54.2	61	30	28	9	13-0	53	.279
1995— Pittsburgh (N.L.)	4	4	.500	3.58	1.33	58	0	0	0	11	3-5	60.1	53	26	24	3	27-7	57	.237
1996— Pittsburgh (N.L.)	6	5	.545	4.09	1.29	73	0	0	0	11	11-17	70.1	67	35	32	4	24-6	76	.247
1997— Toronto (A.L.)	2	4	.333	3.58	1.31	73	0	0	0	27	1-5	50.1	47	22	20	8	19-4	61	.244
1998— Toronto (A.L.)	4	3	.571	3.78	1.14	78	0	0	0	*27	4-5	50.0	41	23	21	4	16-1	55	.224
1999— Toronto (A.L.)	0	3	.000	8.34	1.63	30	0	0	0	9	0-2	22.2	28	21	21	4	9-1	26	.308
— Arizona (N.L.)	2	1	.667	3.32	1.38	34	0	0	0	6	1-1	21.2	22	9	8	3	8-1	27	.259
2000— Arizona (N.L.)	5	1	.833	3.15	1.50	62	0	0	0	9	0-4	40.0	34	21	14	4	26-2	45	.228
2001— Toronto (A.L.)	4	5	.444	3.57	1.28	62	0	0	0	16	1-2	45.1	34	18	18	4	24-5	68	.207
2002— Toronto (A.L.)	1	2	.333	3.38	1.28	19	0	0	0	5	0-1	13.1	11	5	5	1	6-0	14	.216
— Philadelphia (N.L.)	2	1	.667	4.70	1.22	41	0	0	0	13	1-3	23.0	16	12	12	5	12-3	27	.190
2003— Philadelphia (N.L.)	2	1	.667	2.70	1.20	58	0	0	0	10	2-4	33.1	29	12	10	3	11-1	37	.228
American League totals (12 years)	40	54	.426	3.47	1.25	627	14	0	0	94	139-193	706.0	621	296	272	64	260-28	672	.237
National League totals (8 years)	25	17	.595	3.96	1.36	437	0	0	0	86	19-39	366.0	356	182	161	41	142-26	369	.253
Major League totals (18 years)	65	71	.478	3.64	1.29	1064	14	0	0	180	158-232	1072.0	977	478	433	105	402-54	1041	.242

PODSEDNIK, SCOTT   OF

PERSONAL: Born March 18, 1976, in West, Texas. ... 6-0/170. ... Bats left, throws left. ... Full name: Scott Eric Podsednik. ... Name pronounced: puh-SED-nik. ... High school: West (Texas).

TRANSACTIONS/CAREER NOTES: Selected by Texas Rangers organization in third round of free-agent draft (June 2, 1994). ... Traded by Rangers to Florida Marlins (October 8, 1995), completing deal in which Marlins traded P Bobby Witt to Texas Rangers for two players to be named (August 8, 1995); Rangers also sent P Wilson Heredia to Marlins (August 11, 1995). ... Selected by Rangers from Marlins organization in Rule 5 minor league draft (December 15, 1997). ... On Charlotte disabled list (April 6-May 22, 2000). ... Granted free agency (October 15, 2000). ... Signed by Seattle Mariners organization (November 1, 2000). ... On Tacoma disabled list (May 4-June 12 and August 14-26, 2001). ... Claimed on waivers by Milwaukee Brewers (October 13, 2002).

2003 GAMES PLAYED BY POSITION (MLB): OF—139.

Year Team (League)	Pos.	G	AB	R	H	2B	3B	HR	RBI	BB	SO	HBP	GDP	SB-CS	Avg.	OBP	SLG	OPS	E	Pct.
1994— GC Rangers (GCL)	OF	60	211	34	48	7	1	1	17	• 41	34	3	1	18-5	.227	.357	.284	.641	0	1.000
1995— Hudson Valley (NYP)	OF	65	252	42	67	3	0	0	20	35	31	1	9	20-6	.266	.355	.278	.633	3	.978
1996— Brevard County (FSL)	OF	108	383	39	100	9	2	0	30	45	65	3	8	20-10	.261	.343	.295	.638	4	.984
1997— Kane Co. (Midw.)	OF *	135	* 531	80	147	23	4	3	49	60	72	3	5	28-11	.277	.352	.352	.704	5	.977
1998— Charlotte (Fla. St.)	OF	81	302	55	86	12	4	4	39	44	32	0	2	26-8	.285	.369	.391	.760	2	.986
— Tulsa (Texas)	OF	17	75	9	18	4	1	0	4	6	11	0	3	5-2	.240	.296	.320	.616	0	1.000
1999— GC Rangers (GCL)	OF	5	17	6	7	2	0	0	5	2	3	0	1	1-0	.412	.474	.529	1.003	0	1.000
— Tulsa (Texas)	OF	37	116	10	18	4	0	0	1	5	13	0	3	6-2	.155	.190	.190	.380	1	.987
2000— Tulsa (Texas)	OF	49	169	20	42	7	2	2	13	30	33	1	4	19-4	.249	.367	.349	.710	3	.968
2001— Tacoma (PCL)	OF	66	269	46	78	15	4	3	30	13	46	2	0	12-5	.290	.327	.409	.736	5	.967
— Seattle (A.L.)	OF	5	6	1	1	0	1	0	3	0	1	0	1	0-0	.167	.167	.500	.667	0	1.000
2002— Tacoma (PCL)	OF	125	438	63	122	25	6	9	61	43	70	9	18	35-13	.279	.347	.425	.772	5	.985
— Seattle (A.L.)	OF-DH	14	20	2	4	0	0	1	5	4	6	0	1	0-0	.200	.320	.350	.670	1	.938
2003— Milwaukee (N.L.)	OF	154	558	100	175	29	8	9	58	56	91	4	11	43-10	.314	.379	.443	.822	3	.992
American League totals (2 years)		19	26	3	5	0	1	1	8	4	7	0	2	0-0	.192	.290	.385	.675	1	.947
National League totals (1 year)		154	558	100	175	29	8	9	58	56	91	4	11	43-10	.314	.379	.443	.822	3	.992
Major League totals (3 years)		173	584	103	180	29	9	10	66	60	98	4	13	43-10	.308	.375	.440	.815	4	.989

POLANCO, PLACIDO   2B/3B

PERSONAL: Born October 10, 1975, in Santo Domingo, Dominican Republic. ... 5-10/185. ... Bats right, throws right. ... Full name: Placido Enrique Polanco. ... Name pronounced: PLAH-si-doh poh-LAHN-co. ... High school: Santa Clara (Santo Domingo, Dominican Republic). ... Junior college: Miami-Dade Community College.

TRANSACTIONS/CAREER NOTES: Selected by St. Louis Cardinals in 19th round of free-agent draft (June 3, 1994). ... On Memphis suspended list (August 28-29, 1999). ... On disabled list (July 1-16, 2000). ... Traded by Cardinals with P Bud Smith and P Mike Timlin to Philadelphia Phillies for 3B Scott Rolen and P Doug Nickle (July 29, 2002). ... Placed on 15-day disabled list (April 16, 2003). ... Reinstated from 15-day disabled list (May 1, 2003).

2003 GAMES PLAYED BY POSITION (MLB): 2B—99, 3B—21.

Year Team (League)	Pos.	G	AB	R	H	2B	3B	HR	RBI	BB	SO	HBP	GDP	SB-CS	Avg.	OBP	SLG	OPS	E	Pct.
1994— Ariz. Cardinals (Ariz.)	2B-SS	32	127	17	27	4	0	1	10	7	15	1	2	4-2	.213	.259	.268	.527	10	.932
1995— Peoria (Midw.)	2B-SS	103	361	43	96	7	4	2	41	18	30	2	8	7-6	.266	.303	.324	.627	21	.950
1996— St. Pete. (FSL)	2B *	137	* 540	65	* 157	29	5	0	51	24	34	5	31	4-4	.291	.323	.363	.686	4	.993
1997— Arkansas (Texas)	2B	129	508	71	148	16	3	2	51	29	51	3	11	19-5	.291	.331	.346	.678	14	.979
1998— Memphis (PCL)	2B-SS	70	246	36	69	19	1	1	21	16	15	3	8	6-3	.280	.331	.378	.709	5	.984
— St. Louis (N.L.)	SS-2B	45	114	10	29	3	2	1	11	5	9	1	1	2-0	.254	.292	.342	.634	7	.961
1999— St. Louis (N.L.)	2B-3B-SS	88	220	24	61	9	3	1	19	15	24	0	7	1-3	.277	.321	.359	.680	8	.972
— Memphis (PCL)	2B-SS-3B	29	120	18	33	4	1	0	10	3	11	1	7	2-0	.275	.296	.325	.621	2	.984
2000— St. Louis (N.L.)	2-3-S-1	118	323	50	102	12	3	5	39	16	26	1	8	4-4	.316	.347	.418	.765	3	.991
2001— St. Louis (N.L.)	3-S-2-D	144	564	87	173	26	4	3	38	25	43	6	22	12-3	.307	.342	.383	.725	4	.992
2002— St. Louis (N.L.)	3B-SS-2B	94	342	47	97	19	1	5	27	12	27	4	12	3-1	.284	.316	.389	.705	6	.978
— Philadelphia (N.L.)	3B	53	206	28	61	13	1	4	22	14	14	4	3	2-2	.296	.343	.427	.780	3	.983
2003— Philadelphia (N.L.)	2B-3B	122	492	87	142	30	3	14	63	42	38	8	16	14-2	.289	.352	.447	.799	6	.989
Major League totals (6 years)		664	2261	333	665	112	17	33	219	129	181	24	69	38-15	.294	.337	.402	.740	37	.984

P

POLITTE, CLIFF   P

PERSONAL: Born February 27, 1974, in St. Louis, Mo. ... 5-11/185. ... Throws right, bats right. ... Full name: Cliff Anthony Politte. ... Name pronounced: po-LEET. ... High school: Vianney (Kirkwood, Mo.). ... Junior college: Jefferson College (Mo.).

TRANSACTIONS/CAREER NOTES: Selected by St. Louis Cardinals organization in 54th round of free agent draft (June 1, 1995). ... Traded by Cardinals with OF Ron Gant and P Jeff Brantley to Philadelphia Phillies for P Ricky Bottalico and P Garrett Stephenson (November 19, 1998). ... On Scranton/Wilkes-Barre disabled list (April 30-May 9, 2000). ... On Philadelphia disabled list (March 31-July 6, 2001); included rehabilitation assignment to Clearwater (June 18-July 6). ... Traded by Phillies to Toronto Blue Jays for P Dan Plesac (May 26, 2002). ... Placed on 15-day disabled list (June 29, 2003). ... Sent to Syracuse on rehab assignment (July 21, 2003). ... Recalled from rehab assignment (July 25, 2003).

CAREER HITTING: 3-for-32 (.094), 2 R, 1 2B, 0 3B, 0 HR, 2 RBI.

Year League	W	L	Pct.	ERA	WHIP	G	GS	CG	ShO	Hld.	Sv.-Opp.	IP	H	R	ER	HR	BB-IBB	SO	Avg.
1996— Peoria (Midw.)	14	6	.700	2.59	1.04	25	25	0	0	...	0-...	149.2	108	50	43	8	47-0	151	.199
1997— Prince William (Caro.)	11	1	.917	2.24	0.00	19	19	0	0	...	0-...	120.1	89	37	30	11	31-0	118	.203
— Arkansas (Texas)	4	1	.800	2.15	1.17	6	6	0	0	...	0-...	37.2	35	15	9	3	9-1	26	.257
1998— St. Louis (N.L.)	2	3	.400	6.32	1.70	8	8	0	0	0	0-0	37.0	45	32	26	6	18-0	22	.304
— Memphis (PCL)	1	4	.200	7.64	1.88	10	10	0	0	...	0-...	50.2	71	46	43	10	24-0	42	.332
— Arkansas (Texas)	5	3	.625	2.96	1.07	10	10	1	• 1	...	0-...	67.0	56	25	22	6	16-0	61	.230
1999— Reading (East.)	9	8	.529	3.63	1.33	37	13	1	0	...	5-...	109.0	112	45	44	12	33-3	97	.270
— Philadelphia (N.L.)	1	0	1.000	7.13	1.92	13	0	0	0	1	0-0	17.2	19	14	14	2	15-0	15	.275
2000— Scran./W.B. (I.L.)	8	4	.667	3.12	1.20	21	20	1	0	...	0-...	112.2	94	45	39	8	41-2	106	.227
— Philadelphia (N.L.)	4	3	.571	3.66	1.39	12	8	0	0	0	0-0	59.0	55	24	24	8	27-1	50	.248
2001— Clearwater (Fla. St.)	0	1	.000	2.45	1.00	7	7	0	0	...	0-...	11.0	8	4	3	0	3-0	15	.200
— Philadelphia (N.L.)	2	3	.400	2.42	1.23	23	0	0	0	1	0-0	26.0	24	8	7	2	8-3	23	.250
2002— Philadelphia (N.L.)	2	0	1.000	3.86	1.71	13	0	0	0	0	0-1	16.1	19	10	7	0	9-1	15	.288
— Toronto (A.L.)	1	3	.250	3.61	0.99	55	0	0	0	25	1-3	57.1	38	23	23	5	19-1	57	.186
2003— Syracuse (Int'l)	0	0	...	0.00	0.00	1	0	0	0	...	0-...	1.0	0	0	0	0	0-0	1	.000
— Toronto (A.L.)	1	5	.167	5.66	1.40	54	0	0	0	8	12-18	49.1	52	32	31	11	17-4	40	.269
American League totals (2 years)	**2**	**8**	**.200**	**4.56**	**1.18**	**109**	**0**	**0**	**0**	**33**	**13-21**	**106.2**	**90**	**55**	**54**	**16**	**36-5**	**97**	**.227**
National League totals (5 years)	**11**	**9**	**.550**	**4.50**	**1.53**	**69**	**16**	**0**	**0**	**2**	**0-1**	**156.0**	**162**	**88**	**78**	**18**	**77-5**	**125**	**.270**
Major League totals (6 years)	**13**	**17**	**.433**	**4.52**	**1.39**	**178**	**16**	**0**	**0**	**35**	**13-22**	**262.2**	**252**	**143**	**132**	**34**	**113-10**	**222**	**.253**

PONSON, SIDNEY   P

PERSONAL: Born November 2, 1976, in Noord, Aruba. ... 6-1/249. ... Throws right, bats right. ... Full name: Sidney Alton Ponson. ... Name pronounced: pon-SONE. ... College: Maria College (Aruba).

TRANSACTIONS/CAREER NOTES: Signed as non-drafted free agent by Baltimore Orioles organization (August 17, 1993). ... On Bowie disabled list (June 13-July 15, 1997). ... On Baltimore disabled list (April 16-May 9, 2001); included rehabilitation assignment to Bowie (May 4-9). ... On disabled list (August 7-September 1, 2002). ... Traded by Orioles to San Francisco Giants for RHP Kurt Ainsworth, LHP Damian Moss and LHP Ryan Hannaman (July 31, 2003).

CAREER HITTING: 5-for-41 (.122), 3 R, 2 2B, 0 3B, 0 HR, 0 RBI.

Year League	W	L	Pct.	ERA	WHIP	G	GS	CG	ShO	Hld.	Sv.-Opp.	IP	H	R	ER	HR	BB-IBB	SO	Avg.
1994— GC Orioles (GCL)	4	3	.571	2.96	1.16	12	10	1	0	...	0-...	• 73.0	68	30	24	5	17-0	53	.245
1995— Bluefield (Appal.)	6	3	.667	4.17	1.22	13	13	0	0	...	0-...	77.2	79	44	36	7	16-0	56	.260
1996— Frederick (Caro.)	7	6	.538	3.45	1.18	18	16	3	0	...	0-...	107.0	98	56	41	6	28-0	110	.244
1997— Bowie (East.)	2	7	.222	5.42	1.46	13	13	1	1	...	0-...	74.2	77	51	45	11	32-2	56	.269
— GC Orioles (GCL)	1	0	1.000	0.00	0.00	1	0	0	0	...	0-...	2.0	0	0	0	0	0-0	1	.000
1998— Rochester (Int'l)	1	0	1.000	0.00	1.00	1	1	0	0	...	0-...	5.0	4	0	0	0	1-0	3	.211
— Baltimore (A.L.)	8	9	.471	5.27	1.47	31	20	0	0	0	1-2	135.0	157	82	79	19	42-2	85	.293
1999— Baltimore (A.L.)	12	12	.500	4.71	1.46	32	32	6	0	0	0-0	210.0	227	118	110	35	80-2	112	.282
2000— Baltimore (A.L.)	9	13	.409	4.82	1.38	32	32	6	1	0	0-0	222.0	223	125	119	30	83-0	152	.258
2001— Baltimore (A.L.)	5	10	.333	4.94	1.43	23	23	3	1	0	0-0	138.1	161	83	76	21	37-0	84	.289
— Bowie (East.)	0	0	...	0.00	1.00	1	1	0	0	...	0-...	4.0	3	0	0	0	1-0	2	.231
2002— Baltimore (A.L.)	7	9	.438	4.09	1.34	28	28	3	0	0	0-0	176.0	172	84	80	26	63-1	120	.258
2003— Baltimore (A.L.)	14	6	.700	3.77	1.28	21	21	4	0	0	0-0	148.0	147	65	62	10	43-2	100	.258
— San Francisco (N.L.)	3	6	.333	3.71	1.21	10	10	0	0	0	0-0	68.0	64	29	28	6	18-3	34	.255
American League totals (6 years)	**55**	**59**	**.482**	**4.60**	**1.39**	**167**	**156**	**22**	**2**	**0**	**1-2**	**1029.1**	**1087**	**557**	**526**	**141**	**348-7**	**653**	**.272**
National League totals (1 year)	**3**	**6**	**.333**	**3.71**	**1.21**	**10**	**10**	**0**	**0**	**0**	**0-0**	**68.0**	**64**	**29**	**28**	**6**	**18-3**	**34**	**.255**
Major League totals (6 years)	**58**	**65**	**.472**	**4.54**	**1.38**	**177**	**166**	**22**	**2**	**0**	**1-2**	**1097.1**	**1151**	**586**	**554**	**147**	**366-10**	**687**	**.271**

PORTER, COLIN   OF

PERSONAL: Born November 23, 1975, in Tucson, Ariz. ... 6-2/210. ... Bats left, throws left. ... Full name: Colin F. Porter. ... College: Arizona.

TRANSACTIONS/CAREER NOTES: Selected by Houston Astros organization in 17th round of free-agent draft (June 2, 1998).

2003 GAMES PLAYED BY POSITION (MLB): OF—14.

									BATTING								FIELDING	
Year Team (League)	Pos.	G	AB	R	H	2B	3B	HR	RBI	BB	SO	HBP	GDP	SB-CS	Avg.	OBP	SLG	OPS	E	Pct.
1998— Auburn (NY-Penn)	OF	67	240	40	68	18	4	4	30	19	61	5	3	14-11	.283	.347	.442	.789	4	.976
1999— Michigan (Midw.)	OF	127	453	91	132	28	9	18	68	53	123	7	4	23-13	.291	.369	.512	.881	4	.987
2000— Round Rock (Texas)	OF	124	435	76	119	25	5	14	57	56	130	6	6	17-9	.274	.363	.451	.814	4	.985
2001— Round Rock (Texas)	OF	25	100	14	32	5	5	2	12	5	25	1	0	1-3	.320	.358	.530	.888	1	.983
— New Orleans (PCL)	OF	101	312	48	74	14	1	7	33	34	105	3	2	11-6	.237	.314	.356	.670	0	1.000
2002— New Orleans (PCL)	OF	134	461	59	122	30	5	6	38	46	127	0	5	28-7	.265	.331	.390	.721	8	.965
2003— New Orleans (PCL)	OF-DH	102	356	52	114	23	6	11	50	22	80	3	3	22-6	.320	.361	.511	.872	3	.989
— Houston (N.L.)	OF	24	32	5	6	0	0	0	0	1	17	0	1	1-0	.188	.212	.188	.400	0	1.000
Major League totals (1 year)		**24**	**32**	**5**	**6**	**0**	**0**	**0**	**0**	**1**	**17**	**0**	**1**	**1-0**	**.188**	**.212**	**.188**	**.400**	**0**	**1.000**

PORZIO, MIKE   P

PERSONAL: Born August 20, 1972, in Waterbury, Conn. ... 6-3/205. ... Throws left, bats left. ... Full name: Lawrence Michael Porzio. ... High school: Fairfield Prep (Fairfield, Conn.). ... College: Villanova.

TRANSACTIONS/CAREER NOTES: Signed as non-drafted free agent by Chicago Cubs organization (June 30, 1993). ... Released by Cubs organization (July 19, 1994). ... Signed by Boston Red Sox organization (February 20, 1995). ... Released by Red Sox organization (April 1, 1995). ... Signed by Mobile, Texas-Louisiana League (May 1995). ... Signed by Ogden, Pioneer League (July 26, 1995). ... Signed by Tennessee, Big South League (June 1996). ... Signed by Baltimore Orioles organization (March 2, 1997). ... Released by Orioles organization (March 25, 1997). ... Signed by Sioux City, Northern League (May 1997). ... Signed by Atlanta Braves organization (March 8, 1998). ... Traded by Braves with P David Cortes and a player to be named later to Colorado Rockies for 1B Greg Colbrunn (July 30, 1998); Rockies acquired P Anthony Briggs to com-

P

plete deal (September 9, 1998). ... On Colorado Springs disabled list (June 6-25, 1999). ... Granted free agency (October 18, 2000). ... Signed by Chicago White Sox organization (January 31, 2001). ... Granted free agency (October 15, 2001). ... Re-signed by White Sox organization (January 22, 2002). ... Recalled by Chicago (July 12, 2003). ... Optioned to Charlotte (July 26, 2003). ... Designated for assignment (September 2, 2003). ... Sent outright to Charlotte (September 5, 2003). ... Elected free agency (September 29, 2003).

CAREER HITTING: 0-for-0 (.000), 0 R, 0 2B, 0 3B, 0 HR, 0 RBI.

Year League	W	L	Pct.	ERA	WHIP	G	GS	CG	ShO	Hld.	Sv.-Opp.	IP	H	R	ER	HR	BB-IBB	SO	Avg.
1993— GC Cubs (GCL)	1	3	.250	3.83	1.70	10	8	0	0	...	0-...	42.1	42	26	18	1	30-0	30	.259
1994— GC Cubs (GCL)	0	3	.000	5.93	1.83	7	0	0	0	...	1-...	13.2	19	10	9	0	6-0	5	.333
1995— Mobile (Tex.-La.)	0	3	.000	5.46	1.61	16	2	0	0	...	0-...	28.0	32	19	17	2	13-2	15	.291
— Ogden (Pio.)	4	3	.571	6.38	1.69	8	8	2	0	...	0-...	48.0	66	39	34	4	15-0	26	.330
1996— Tennessee (BSL)	7	4	.636	3.64	1.25	15	15	3	0	...	0-...	99.0	94	55	40	9	30-1	54	.245
1997— Sioux City (Nor.)	2	2	.500	4.28	1.67	27	5	1	1	...	0-...	61.0	75	32	29	6	27-1	63	...
1998— Danville (Caro.)	3	2	.600	2.51	1.07	26	11	1	0	...	2-...	97.0	74	34	27	7	30-5	95	.214
— Salem (Caro.)	2	3	.400	2.76	1.23	7	7	0	0	...	0-...	42.1	40	20	13	6	12-0	46	.253
1999— Colo. Springs (PCL)	5	1	.833	3.38	1.73	35	0	0	0	...	0-...	42.2	44	16	16	5	30-4	33	.272
— Colorado (N.L.)	0	0	...	8.59	2.11	16	0	0	0	0	0-0	14.2	21	14	14	5	10-0	10	.328
2000— Carolina (Sou.)	7	4	.636	3.41	1.17	20	18	1	1	...	0-...	121.1	111	53	46	11	31-0	90	.243
— Colo. Springs (PCL)	0	3	.000	10.04	2.27	6	6	0	0	...	0-...	26.0	39	30	29	7	20-0	26	.361
2001— Birmingham (Sou.)	1	0	1.000	1.38	0.62	2	2	0	0	...	0-...	13.0	3	2	2	1	5-0	10	.070
— Charlotte (Int'l)	6	6	.500	4.35	1.44	31	23	0	0	...	0-...	134.1	138	76	65	14	55-2	107	.267
2002— Chicago (A.L.)	2	2	.500	4.81	1.47	32	0	0	0	3	0-0	43.0	40	25	23	10	23-2	33	.248
— Charlotte (Int'l)	6	5	.545	4.52	1.48	14	13	0	0	...	0-...	75.2	83	43	38	9	29-0	59	.285
2003— Chicago (A.L.)	1	1	.500	6.43	1.36	3	3	0	0	...	0-...	14.0	18	10	10	2	1-0	9	.321
— Charlotte (Int'l)	8	6	.571	4.24	1.28	26	22	1	0	...	0-...	133.2	124	70	63	19	47-1	115	.248
American League totals (2 years)	3	3	.500	5.21	1.44	35	3	0	0	3	0-0	57.0	58	35	33	12	24-2	42	.267
National League totals (1 year)	0	0	...	8.59	2.11	16	0	0	0	0	0-0	14.2	21	14	14	5	10-0	10	.328
Major League totals (3 years)	3	3	.500	5.90	1.58	51	3	0	0	3	0-0	71.2	79	49	47	17	34-2	52	.281

POSADA, JORGE C

PERSONAL: Born August 17, 1971, in Santurce, Puerto Rico. ... 6-2/205. ... Bats both, throws right. ... Full name: Jorge Rafael Posada. ... Name pronounced: hor-hay po-sa-da. ... High school: Colegio Alejandrino (Puerto Rico). ... Junior college: Calhoun (Ala.) Community College.

TRANSACTIONS/CAREER NOTES: Selected by New York Yankees organization in 24th round of free-agent draft (June 4, 1990). ... On disabled list (July 26-September 4, 1994). ... On Columbus disabled list (May 3-12, 1995). ... On suspended list (July 17-18, 2000; and September 26-October 2, 2001).

2003 GAMES PLAYED BY POSITION (MLB): C—137, DH—2.

Year Team (League)	Pos.	G	AB	R	H	2B	3B	HR	RBI	BB	SO	HBP	GDP	SB-CS	Avg.	OBP	SLG	OPS	E	Pct.
1991— Oneonta (NYP)	2B-C	71	217	34	51	5	5	4	33	51	51	4	3	6-4	.235	.388	.359	.748	21	.947
1992— Greensboro (S. Atl.)	3B-C	101	339	60	94	22	4	12	58	58	87	6	8	11-6	.277	.389	.472	.861	11	.965
1993— Prince Will. (Car.)	3B-C	118	410	71	106	27	2	17	61	67	90	6	7	17-5	.259	.366	.459	.825	15	.958
— Albany (East.)	C	7	25	3	7	0	0	0	0	2	7	0	1	0-0	.280	.333	.280	.613	2	.958
1994— Columbus (Int'l)	C-OF	92	313	46	75	13	3	11	48	32	81	1	3	5-5	.240	.308	.406	.713	§ 11	.977
1995— Columbus (Int'l)	C-DH	108	368	60	94	32	5	8	51	54	101	1	14	4-4	.255	.350	.435	.785	4	.993
— New York (A.L.)	C	1	0	0	0	0	0	0	0	0	0	0	0	0-0	...	.000	...	...	0	1.000
1996— Columbus (Int'l)	C-DH-OF	106	354	76	96	22	6	11	62	* 79	86	3	13	3-3	.271	.405	.460	.866	10	.985
— New York (A.L.)	C-DH	8	14	1	1	0	0	0	0	1	6	0	1	0-0	.071	.133	.071	.205	0	1.000
1997— New York (A.L.)	C	60	188	29	47	12	0	6	25	30	33	3	2	1-2	.250	.359	.410	.768	3	.992
1998— New York (A.L.)	C-DH-1B	111	358	56	96	23	0	17	63	47	92	0	14	0-1	.268	.350	.475	.824	4	.994
1999— New York (A.L.)	C-DH-1B	112	379	50	93	19	2	12	57	53	91	3	9	1-0	.245	.341	.401	.742	5	.993
2000— New York (A.L.)	C-1B-DH	151	505	92	145	35	1	28	86	107	151	8	11	2-2	.287	.417	.527	.943	8	.992
2001— New York (A.L.)	C-DH-1B	138	484	59	134	28	1	22	95	62	132	6	10	2-6	.277	.363	.475	.838	11	.990
2002— New York (A.L.)	C-DH	143	511	79	137	40	1	20	99	81	143	3	23	1-0	.268	.370	.468	.837	12	.988
2003— New York (A.L.)	C-DH	142	481	83	135	24	0	30	101	93	110	10	13	2-4	.281	.405	.518	.922	6	.994
Major League totals (9 years)		866	2920	449	788	181	5	135	526	474	758	33	83	9-15	.270	.375	.474	.849	49	.992

POWELL, BRIAN P

PERSONAL: Born October 10, 1973, in Bainbridge, Ga. ... 6-2/215. ... Throws right, bats right. ... Full name: William Brian Powell. ... High school: Bainbridge (Ga.). ... College: Georgia.

TRANSACTIONS/CAREER NOTES: Selected by Detroit Tigers organization in second round of free-agent draft (June 1, 1995). ... Traded by Tigers with C Paul Bako, P Dean Crow, P Mark Persails and 3B Carlos Villalobos to Houston Astros for C Brad Ausmus and P C.J. Nitkowski (January 14, 1999). ... On disabled list (May 25, 1999-remainder of season). ... On New Orleans disabled list (April 6-22, 2000). ... Granted free agency (October 8, 2001). ... Signed by Tigers organization (December 19, 2001). ... Released by Tigers (October 2, 2002).

CAREER HITTING: 2-for-13 (.154), 2 R, 1 2B, 0 3B, 0 HR, 0 RBI.

Year League	W	L	Pct.	ERA	WHIP	G	GS	CG	ShO	Hld.	Sv.-Opp.	IP	H	R	ER	HR	BB-IBB	SO	Avg.
1995— Jamestown (NYP)	2	1	.667	3.08	1.03	5	5	0	0	...	0-...	26.1	19	12	9	1	8-0	15	.202
— Fayetteville (S. Atl.)	4	0	1.000	1.61	0.93	5	5	0	0	...	0-...	28.0	15	5	5	0	11-0	37	.156
1996— Lakeland (Fla. St.)	8	13	.381	4.90	1.39	29	27	* 5	0	...	0-...	• 174.1	* 195	106	* 95	12	47-0	84	.286
1997— Lakeland (Fla. St.)	13	9	.591	2.50	1.03	27	27	* 8	• 2	...	0-...	* 183.1	153	70	51	9	35-2	122	.224
1998— Jacksonville (Sou.)	10	2	.833	3.07	1.15	14	14	2	1	...	0-...	93.2	84	37	32	5	24-0	51	.242
— Toledo (Int'l)	0	0	...	0.00	0.71	1	1	0	0	...	0-...	7.0	5	0	0	0	0-0	7	.185
— Detroit (A.L.)	3	8	.273	6.35	1.64	18	16	0	0	0	0-0	83.2	101	67	59	17	36-2	46	.294
1999— New Orleans (PCL)	4	4	.500	6.19	1.56	9	9	0	0	...	0-...	48.0	54	39	33	5	21-0	36	.284
2000— New Orleans (PCL)	9	4	.692	4.95	1.39	18	18	1	0	...	0-...	103.2	103	63	57	9	41-1	57	.262
— Houston (N.L.)	2	1	.667	5.74	1.50	9	5	0	0	0	0-0	31.1	34	21	20	8	13-0	14	.279
2001— New Orleans (PCL)	9	8	.529	3.17	1.25	24	23	3	• 2	...	0-...	144.2	142	65	51	13	39-1	96	.260
— Houston (N.L.)	0	1	.000	18.00	2.67	1	1	0	0	0	0-0	3.0	5	6	6	1	3-0	3	.357
2002— Toledo (Int'l)	10	3	.769	3.92	1.28	20	20	0	0	...	0-...	119.1	127	54	52	8	26-0	82	.270
— Detroit (A.L.)	1	5	.167	4.84	1.47	13	9	0	0	0	0-0	57.2	64	34	31	11	21-0	30	.278
2003— San Francisco (N.L.)	0	1	.000	13.50	1.93	1	1	0	0	0	0-0	4.2	8	7	7	3	1-0	3	.381
— Fresno (PCL)	7	8	.467	4.19	1.49	23	15	0	0	...	0-...	101.0	118	57	47	10	32-2	59	.291
— Scran./W.B. (I.L.)	2	4	.333	4.61	1.31	8	7	2	1	...	0-...	52.2	57	33	27	1	12-2	36	.275
American League totals (2 years)	4	13	.235	5.73	1.57	31	25	0	0	0	0-0	141.1	165	101	90	28	57-2	76	.284
National League totals (3 years)	2	3	.400	7.62	1.64	11	7	0	0	0	0-0	39.0	47	34	33	12	17-0	20	.299
Major League totals (5 years)	6	16	.273	6.14	1.59	42	32	0	0	0	0-0	180.1	212	135	123	40	74-2	96	.290

P

POWELL, JAY   P

PERSONAL: Born January 9, 1972, in Meridian, Miss. ... 6-4/225. ... Throws right, bats right. ... Full name: James Willard Powell. ... High school: West Lauderdale (Collinsville, Miss.). ... College: Mississippi State.

TRANSACTIONS/CAREER NOTES: Selected by San Diego Padres organization in 11th round of free-agent draft (June 4, 1990); did not sign. ... Selected by Baltimore Orioles organization in first round (19th pick overall) of free-agent draft (June 3, 1993). ... On disabled list (April 7-26, 1994). ... Traded by Orioles to Florida Marlins for IF Bret Barberie (December 6, 1994). ... On Florida disabled list (April 20-May 10, 1996); included rehabilitation assignment to Brevard County (May 8-10). ... Traded by Marlins with C Scott Makarewicz to Houston Astros for C Ramon Castro (July 6, 1998). ... On Houston disabled list (May 17-June 3, June 19-August 6 and August 18, 2000-remainder of season); included rehabilitation assignments to New Orleans (May 30-June 3) and Round Rock (August 3). ... Traded by Astros to Colorado Rockies for P Ron Villone (June 27, 2001). ... Granted free agency (November 5, 2001). ... Signed by Texas Rangers (December 13, 2001). ... On Texas disabled list (March 31-June 10, 2002); included rehabilitation assignment to Tulsa (May 21-24) and Oklahoma (May 25-June 10). ... Placed on the 15-day disabled list (April 13, 2003). ... Sent to Frisco on rehab assignment by Texas (April 22, 2003). ... Recalled from Frisco rehab assignment (May 3, 2003).

CAREER HITTING: 2-for-12 (.167), 0 R, 0 2B, 0 3B, 0 HR, 1 RBI.

Year League	W	L	Pct.	ERA	WHIP	G	GS	CG	ShO	Hld.	Sv.-Opp.	IP	H	R	ER	HR	BB-IBB	SO	Avg.
1993— Albany (S. Atl.)	0	2	.000	4.55	1.52	6	6	0	0	...	0-...	27.2	29	19	14	0	13-0	29	.274
1994— Frederick (Caro.)	7	7	.500	4.96	1.51	26	20	0	0	...	1-...	123.1	132	79	68	13	54-0	87	.269
1995— Portland (East.)	5	4	.556	1.87	1.08	50	0	0	0	...	* 24-...	53.0	42	12	11	2	15-1	53	.219
— Florida (N.L.)	0	0	...	1.08	1.56	9	0	0	0	2	0-0	8.1	7	2	1	0	6-1	4	.241
1996— Florida (N.L.)	4	3	.571	4.54	1.50	67	0	0	0	10	2-5	71.1	71	41	36	5	36-1	52	.255
— Brevard County (FSL)	0	0	...	0.00	0.00	1	1	0	0	...	0-...	2.0	0	0	0	0	0-0	4	.000
1997— Florida (N.L.)	7	2	.778	3.28	1.27	74	0	0	0	24	2-4	79.2	71	35	29	3	30-3	65	.242
1998— Florida (N.L.)	4	4	.500	4.21	1.60	33	0	0	0	0	3-6	36.1	36	19	17	5	22-6	24	.263
— Houston (N.L.)	3	3	.500	2.38	1.09	29	0	0	0	3	4-5	34.0	22	9	9	1	15-3	38	.182
1999— Houston (N.L.)	5	4	.556	4.32	1.63	67	0	0	0	16	4-7	75.0	82	38	36	3	40-4	77	.282
2000— Houston (N.L.)	1	1	.500	5.67	1.78	29	0	0	0	5	0-0	27.0	29	18	17	1	19-1	16	.271
— New Orleans (PCL)	0	0	...	4.50	2.00	2	1	0	0	...	0-...	2.0	2	1	1	0	2-0	2	.286
— Round Rock (Texas)	0	0	...	0.00	0.50	1	1	0	0	...	0-...	2.0	0	0	0	0	1-0	1	.000
2001— Houston (N.L.)	2	2	.500	3.72	1.65	35	0	0	0	5	0-5	36.1	41	18	15	4	19-0	28	.275
— Colorado (N.L.)	3	1	.750	2.79	1.19	39	0	0	0	3	7-8	38.2	34	18	12	5	12-3	26	.245
2002— Tulsa (Texas)	0	0	...	0.00	0.50	2	0	0	0	...	0-...	2.0	0	0	0	0	1-0	0	.000
— Oklahoma (PCL)	2	0	1.000	12.38	2.13	8	0	0	0	...	0-...	8.0	14	11	11	2	3-1	8	.359
— Texas (A.L.)	3	2	.600	3.44	1.49	51	0	0	0	12	0-4	49.2	50	28	19	5	24-4	35	.253
2003— Frisco (Texas)	0	0	...	2.70	1.50	4	0	0	0	...	1-...	6.2	5	2	2	0	5-0	8	.208
— Texas (A.L.)	3	0	1.000	7.82	1.86	51	0	0	0	2	0-0	58.2	75	58	51	7	34-3	40	.319
American League totals (2 years)	6	2	.750	5.82	1.69	102	0	0	0	14	0-4	108.1	125	86	70	12	58-7	75	.289
National League totals (7 years)	29	20	.592	3.81	1.46	382	0	0	0	68	22-40	406.2	393	198	172	27	199-22	330	.255
Major League totals (9 years)	35	22	.614	4.23	1.50	484	0	0	0	82	22-44	515.0	518	284	242	39	257-29	405	.262

PRATT, TODD   C

PERSONAL: Born February 9, 1967, in Bellevue, Neb. ... 6-3/235. ... Bats right, throws right. ... Full name: Todd Alan Pratt. ... High school: Hilltop (Chula Vista, Calif.).

TRANSACTIONS/CAREER NOTES: Selected by Boston Red Sox organization in sixth round of free-agent draft (June 3, 1985). ... Selected by Cleveland Indians organization from Red Sox organization in Rule 5 minor league draft (December 7, 1987). ... Returned to Red Sox organization (March 28, 1988). ... Granted free agency (October 15, 1991). ... Signed by Baltimore Orioles organization (November 13, 1991). ... Selected by Philadelphia Phillies from Orioles organization in Rule 5 major league draft (December 9, 1991). ... On Philadelphia disabled list (April 28-May 27, 1993); included rehabilitation assignment to Scranton/Wilkes-Barre (May 23-27). ... Granted free agency (December 23, 1994). ... Signed by Chicago Cubs organization (April 8, 1995). ... Granted free agency (October 16, 1995). ... Signed by Seattle Mariners organization (January 25, 1996). ... Released by Mariners (March 27, 1996). ... Signed by New York Mets organization (December 23, 1996). ... On New York disabled list (May 7-June 23, 1998); included rehabilitation assignments to St. Lucie (June 14-18), Gulf Coast Mets (June 19-21) and Norfolk (June 22-23). ... Traded by Mets to Phillies for C Gary Bennett (July 23, 2001). ... Granted free agency (November 5, 2001). ... Re-signed by Phillies (December 15, 2001). ... Granted free agency (October 29, 2002). ... Re-signed by Phillies organization (December 19, 2002).

2003 GAMES PLAYED BY POSITION (MLB): C—35, 1B—6.

Year Team (League)	Pos.	G	AB	R	H	2B	3B	HR	RBI	BB	SO	HBP	GDP	SB-CS	Avg.	OBP	SLG	OPS	E	Pct.
1985— Elmira (N.Y.-Penn)	C	39	119	7	16	1	1	0	5	10	27	1	6	0-1	.134	.206	.160	.366	6	.979
1986— Greensboro (S. Atl.)	C-1B	107	348	63	84	16	0	12	56	75	114	5	10	0-1	.241	.380	.391	.770	§ 15	.983
1987— Winter Haven (FSL)	C-1B-OF	118	407	57	105	22	0	12	65	70	94	1	10	0-1	.258	.364	.400	.764	15	.980
1988— New Britain (East.)	C-1B	124	395	41	89	15	2	8	49	41	110	3	7	1-4	.225	.299	.334	.633	15	.975
1989— New Britain (East.)	C-1B	109	338	30	77	17	1	2	35	44	66	7	10	1-2	.228	.325	.302	.627	‡ 11	.977
1990— New Britain (East.)	C-1B	70	195	15	45	14	1	2	22	18	56	0	7	0-1	.231	.293	.344	.637	4	.978
1991— Pawtucket (Int'l)	C-1B	68	219	68	64	16	0	11	41	23	42	3	9	0-3	.292	.367	.516	.883	4	.985
1992— Reading (East.)	C	41	132	20	44	6	1	6	26	24	28	0	1	2-0	.333	.436	.530	.966	3	.970
— Scran./W.B. (I.L.)	C-1B	41	125	20	40	9	1	7	28	30	14	0	5	1-0	.320	.446	.576	1.022	4	.977
— Philadelphia (N.L.)	C	16	46	6	13	1	0	2	10	4	12	0	2	0-0	.283	.340	.435	.775	2	.979
1993— Philadelphia (N.L.)	C	33	87	8	25	6	0	5	13	5	19	1	2	0-0	.287	.330	.529	.859	2	.989
— Scran./W.B. (I.L.)	C	3	9	1	2	1	0	0	1	3	1	0	0	0-0	.222	.417	.333	.750	0	1.000
1994— Philadelphia (N.L.)	C	28	102	10	20	6	1	2	9	12	29	0	3	0-1	.196	.281	.333	.614	0	1.000
1995— Chicago (N.L.)	C	25	60	3	8	2	0	0	4	6	21	0	1	0-0	.133	.209	.167	.376	3	.981
— Iowa (Am. Assoc.)	C-1B-DH	23	58	3	19	1	0	0	5	4	17	0	0	0-0	.328	.371	.345	.716	2	.978
1996—										Did not play.										
1997— Norfolk (Int'l)	C-DH	59	206	42	62	8	3	9	34	26	48	2	8	1-2	.301	.383	.500	.883	4	.988
— New York (N.L.)	C	39	106	12	30	6	0	2	19	13	32	2	1	0-1	.283	.372	.396	.768	2	.990
1998— Norfolk (Int'l)	DH-C-OF-1B	35	118	16	42	6	0	7	30	15	19	4	4	2-0	.356	.442	.585	1.027	2	.984
— New York (N.L.)	C-1B	41	69	9	19	9	1	2	18	2	20	0	0	0-0	.275	.296	.522	.818	2	.976
— St. Lucie (Fla. St.)	C-1B-OF	5	20	2	9	1	0	1	3	1	5	2	0	1-0	.450	.522	.650	1.172	0	1.000
— GC Mets (GCL)	C-OF	2	4	1	1	0	0	0	0	4	1	0	0	0-0	.250	.625	.250	.875	0	1.000
1999— New York (N.L.)	C-1B-OF	71	140	18	41	4	0	3	21	15	32	3	1	2-0	.293	.369	.386	.754	1	.996
2000— New York (N.L.)	C-DH	80	160	33	44	6	0	8	25	22	31	5	5	0-0	.275	.378	.463	.840	1	.997
2001— New York (N.L.)	C	45	80	6	13	5	0	2	4	15	36	2	4	1-0	.163	.306	.300	.606	1	.994
— Philadelphia (N.L.)	C-1B	35	93	12	19	3	0	2	7	19	25	1	2	0-0	.204	.345	.301	.646	3	.986
2002— Philadelphia (N.L.)	C-1B	39	106	14	33	11	0	3	16	24	28	4	3	2-0	.311	.449	.500	.949	0	1.000
2003— Philadelphia (N.L.)	C-1B	43	125	16	34	10	1	4	20	22	38	6	3	0-0	.272	.400	.464	.864	1	.997
Major League totals (11 years)		495	1174	147	299	69	3	35	166	159	323	24	27	5-2	.255	.353	.408	.761	18	.993

P

PRIDE, CURTIS   OF

PERSONAL: Born December 17, 1968, in Washington, District of Columbia. ... 6-0/210. ... Bats left, throws right. ... Full name: Curtis John Pride. ... High school: John F. Kennedy (Silver Spring, Md.). ... College: William & Mary.

TRANSACTIONS/CAREER NOTES: Selected by New York Mets organization in 10th round of free-agent draft (June 2, 1986). ... Granted free agency (October 15, 1992). ... Signed by Montreal Expos organization (December 8, 1992). ... On Ottawa disabled list (April 7-May 13, July 6-15 and August 7-14, 1994). ... Granted free agency (October 16, 1995). ... Signed by Detroit Tigers (March 31, 1996). ... On Detroit disabled list (April 13-May 10, 1996); included rehabilitation assignment to Toledo (April 30-May 10). ... Granted free agency (August 21, 1997). ... Signed by Boston Red Sox organization (August 30, 1997). ... Granted free agency (October 15, 1997). ... Signed by Atlanta Braves organization (February 6, 1998). ... On suspended list (May 27-28, 1998). ... On Atlanta disabled list (June 28-July 14, 1998); included rehabilitation assignment to Richmond (July 13-14). ... Released by Braves (December 1, 1998). ... Signed by Kansas City Royals organization (February 24, 1999). ... Released by Royals (March 4, 1999). ... Signed by Mets organization (January 20, 2000). ... Traded by Mets to Red Sox for a player to be named later (April 26, 2000); Mets acquired SS Gavin Jackson to complete deal (July 9, 2000). ... Released by Red Sox (July 8, 2000). ... Signed by Los Angeles Dodgers organization (July 18, 2000). ... Granted free agency (October 18, 2000). ... Signed by Expos organization (December 21, 2000). ... On Ottawa disabled list (April 14-24, 2001). ... On Montreal disabled list (June 18-August 21, 2001); included rehabilitation assignments to Jupiter (August 6-13) and Ottawa (August 14-21). ... Granted free agency (October 11, 2001). ... Signed by Pittsburgh Pirates (March 5, 2002). ... Granted free agency (October 15, 2002). ... Signed by New York Yankees (May 23, 2003).

2003 GAMES PLAYED BY POSITION (MLB): OF—3.

										BATTING									FIELDING	
Year Team (League)	Pos.	G	AB	R	H	2B	3B	HR	RBI	BB	SO	HBP	GDP	SB-CS	Avg.	OBP	SLG	OPS	E	Pct.
1986— Kingsport (Appal.)	OF	27	46	5	5	0	0	1	4	6	24	1	0	5-0	.109	.226	.174	.400	0	1.000
1987— Kingsport (Appal.)	OF	31	104	22	25	4	0	1	9	16	34	1	0	14-5	.240	.347	.308	.655	5	.894
1988— Kingsport (Appal.)	OF	70	268	*59	76	13	1	8	27	50	48	1	2	23-7	.284	.397	.429	.826	5	.961
1989— Pittsfield (NYP)	OF	55	212	35	55	7	3	6	23	25	47	2	1	9-2	.259	.342	.406	.747	4	.964
1990— Columbia (S. Atl.)	OF	53	191	38	51	4	4	6	25	21	45	0	3	11-8	.267	.338	.424	.762	11	.874
1991— St. Lucie (Fla. St.)	OF	116	392	57	102	21	7	9	37	43	94	2	8	24-5	.260	.336	.418	.754	4	.981
1992— Binghamton (East.)	OF	118	388	54	88	15	3	10	42	47	110	4	5	14-11	.227	.316	.358	.674	8	.964
1993— Harrisburg (East.)	OF	50	180	51	64	6	3	15	39	12	36	4	2	21-6	.356	.404	.672	1.076	2	.972
— Ottawa (Int'l)	OF	69	262	55	79	11	4	6	22	34	61	3	3	29-12	.302	.388	.443	.831	2	.986
— Montreal (N.L.)	OF	10	9	3	4	1	1	1	5	0	3	0	0	1-0	.444	.444	1.111	1.556	0	1.000
1994— W.P. Beach (FSL)	OF	3	8	5	6	1	0	1	3	4	2	0	0	2-2	.750	.833	1.250	2.083	0	1.000
— Ottawa (Int'l)	OF-DH	82	300	56	77	16	4	9	32	39	81	2	3	22-6	.257	.345	.427	.772	3	.982
1995— Ottawa (Int'l)	OF-DH	42	154	25	43	8	3	4	24	12	35	2	2	8-4	.279	.339	.448	.787	2	.974
— Montreal (N.L.)	OF	48	63	10	11	1	0	0	2	5	16	0	2	3-2	.175	.235	.190	.426	2	.920
1996— Detroit (A.L.)	OF-DH	95	267	52	80	17	5	10	31	31	63	0	2	11-6	.300	.372	.513	.886	3	.967
— Toledo (Int'l)	DH-OF	9	26	4	6	1	0	1	2	9	7	1	1	4-1	.231	.444	.385	.829	0	1.000
1997— Detroit (A.L.)	OF-DH	79	162	21	34	4	4	2	19	24	45	1	4	6-4	.210	.314	.321	.635	1	.980
— Pawtucket (Int'l)	OF	1	3	0	0	0	0	0	0	0	2	0	0	0-0	.000	.000	.000	.000	0	1.000
— Boston (A.L.)		2	2	1	1	0	0	1	1	0	1	0	0	0-0	.500	.500	2.000	2.500	...	...
1998— Atlanta (N.L.)	OF-DH	70	107	19	27	6	1	3	9	9	29	3	2	4-0	.252	.325	.411	.736	0	1.000
— Richmond (Int'l)	OF-DH	21	78	11	19	2	1	2	6	15	17	0	3	8-0	.244	.366	.372	.737	2	.974
1999— Nashua (Atl.)	DH	14	32	0	2	0	0	0	2	7	11	...	...	0-0	.063	...	.063	...	...
2000— Norfolk (Int'l)	OF	15	31	9	9	2	2	1	4	11	7	1	0	3-2	.290	.488	.581	1.069	1	.929
— Pawtucket (Int'l)	OF	48	154	44	47	10	2	9	31	38	31	1	3	12-1	.305	.441	.571	1.012	1	.990
— Boston (A.L.)	OF-DH	9	20	4	5	1	0	0	0	1	7	0	0	0-0	.250	.286	.300	.586	0	1.000
— Albuquerque (PCL)	OF	38	133	30	39	7	3	6	17	20	37	0	2	7-5	.293	.383	.526	.909	3	.959
2001— Ottawa (Int'l)	OF	22	81	14	27	4	1	5	15	12	26	2	2	6-1	.333	.432	.593	1.024	1	.963
— Montreal (N.L.)	OF-DH	36	76	8	19	3	1	1	9	9	22	2	4	3-2	.250	.345	.355	.700	0	1.000
— Jupiter (FSL)	OF	6	21	3	4	1	0	0	0	3	3	0	0	0-1	.190	.292	.238	.530	0	1.000
2002— Nashville (PCL)	OF	110	385	71	114	22	1	10	46	33	75	7	7	22-8	.296	.362	.436	.798	6	.968
2003— New York (A.L.)	OF	4	12	1	1	0	0	1	1	0	2	0	1	0-0	.083	.083	.333	.417	0	1.000
— Columbus (Int'l)	OF-DH	55	225	44	65	11	4	7	34	20	48	4	7	7-7	.289	.357	.467	.824	1	.991
American League totals (4 years)		189	463	79	121	22	9	14	52	56	118	1	7	17-10	.261	.342	.438	.780	4	.975
National League totals (4 years)		164	255	40	61	11	3	5	25	23	70	5	8	11-4	.239	.313	.365	.678	2	.980
Major League totals (8 years)		353	718	119	182	33	12	19	77	79	188	6	15	28-14	.253	.332	.412	.744	6	.977

PRIETO, ALEX   SS

PERSONAL: Born June 19, 1976, in Caracas, Venezuela. ... 5-11/200. ... Bats right, throws right. ... Full name: Alejandro Antonio Prieto. ... High school: Juan Pablos II (Caracas, Venezuela).

TRANSACTIONS/CAREER NOTES: Signed by Kansas City Royals organization as a non-drafted free agent (November 12, 1992). ... Released by Royals (2001). ... Signed by Minnesota Twins organization as a free agent (January 23, 2002).

2003 GAMES PLAYED BY POSITION (MLB): 2B—5, SS—1.

										BATTING									FIELDING	
Year Team (League)	Pos.	G	AB	R	H	2B	3B	HR	RBI	BB	SO	HBP	GDP	SB-CS	Avg.	OBP	SLG	OPS	E	Pct.
1993— GC Royals (GCL)	SS-2B-OF	43	114	14	28	3	0	0	6	9	13	0	1	4-2	.246	.301	.272	.573	18	.879
1994— GC Royals (GCL)	SS-2B-3B	18	60	15	18	5	0	2	17	2	5	4	0	1-0	.300	.358	.483	.842	9	.885
1995— Springfield (Midw.)	SS	124	431	61	108	9	3	2	44	40	69	6	10	11-7	.251	.322	.299	.621	38	.936
1996— Wilmington (Caro.)	SS	119	447	65	127	19	6	1	40	31	66	3	7	26-15	.284	.331	.360	.691	40	.949
1997— Wilmington (Caro.)	SS	129	437	52	94	13	3	3	38	41	59	2	6	20-8	.215	.282	.279	.561	37	.940
1998— Wichita (Texas)	SS-2B-OF	113	384	61	101	18	7	2	35	31	54	2	13	4-8	.263	.321	.362	.683	35	.934
1999— Wichita (Texas)	S-2-3-O	114	360	56	106	23	4	6	41	35	47	1	10	12-6	.294	.356	.431	.786	25	.949
2000— Omaha (PCL)	S-2-3-O	118	384	54	101	19	0	7	37	26	40	6	12	14-6	.263	.318	.367	.685	15	.970
2001— Omaha (PCL)	3-2-S-O	105	376	45	106	21	3	8	44	36	59	1	12	9-2	.282	.344	.418	.762	7	.982
2002— Edmonton (PCL)	2B-SS-3B	80	276	38	73	14	1	7	29	19	47	2	5	4-4	.264	.315	.399	.714	12	.963
2003— Rochester (Int'l)	S-3-2-1-D	69	234	27	62	9	1	5	21	12	49	0	6	6-3	.265	.298	.376	.674	8	.974
— Minnesota (A.L.)	2B-SS	8	11	1	1	0	0	0	0	0	4	0	0	0-0	.091	.091	.091	.182	0	1.000
Major League totals (1 year)		8	11	1	1	0	0	0	0	0	4	0	0	0-0	.091	.091	.091	.182	0	1.000

PRINCE, TOM   C

PERSONAL: Born August 13, 1964, in Kankakee, Ill. ... 5-11/206. ... Bats right, throws right. ... Full name: Thomas Albert Prince. ... High school: Bradley-Bourbonnais (Bradley, Ill.). ... Junior college: Kankakee (Ill.) Community College.

TRANSACTIONS/CAREER NOTES: Selected by Atlanta Braves organization in eighth round of free-agent draft (January 11, 1983); did not sign. ... Selected by Braves organization in secondary phase of free-agent draft (June 6, 1983); did not sign. ... Selected by Pittsburgh Pirates organization in secondary phase of free-agent draft (January 17, 1984). ... On Pittsburgh disabled list (August 13-September 1, 1991); included rehabilitation assignment to Buffalo (August 28-September 1). ... Granted free agency (October 15, 1993). ... Signed by Los Angeles Dodgers organization (November 12, 1993). ... On Albuquerque disabled list (April 30-May 7, 1994). ... Released by Dodgers (December 5, 1994). ... Re-signed by Dodgers organization (January 5, 1995). ... On Los Angeles disabled list (June 4-July 10, 1995); included rehabilitation assignment to Albuquerque (June 26-July 10). ... Granted free agency (October 15, 1995). ... Re-signed by Dodgers organization (November 1, 1995). ... Granted free agency (October 22, 1998). ... Signed by Philadelphia Phillies (December 18, 1998). ... On Philadelphia disabled list (March 23-September 3, 1999); included rehabilitation assignments to Gulf Coast Phillies (July 21-28), Clearwater (July 29-August 9) and Scranton (August 10-29). ... Granted free agency (October 31, 2000). ... Signed by Minnesota Twins organization (December 19, 2000). ... Designated for assignment (July 8, 2003). ... Given unconditional release (July 16, 2003). ... Signed by Kansas City Royals (July 21, 2003).

2003 GAMES PLAYED BY POSITION (MLB): C—29, DH—3.

Year	Team (League)	Pos.	G	AB	R	H	2B	3B	HR	RBI	BB	SO	HBP	GDP	SB-CS	Avg.	OBP	SLG	OPS	E	Pct.
1984—	Watertown (NYP)	3B-C	23	69	6	14	3	0	2	13	9	13	1	1	0-0	.203	.304	.333	.637	2	.989
	— GC Pirates (GCL)	C-1B	18	48	4	11	0	0	1	6	8	10	1	0	1-0	.229	.351	.292	.643	4	.958
1985—	Macon (S. Atl.)	C	124	360	60	75	20	1	10	42	96	92	12	8	13-3	.208	.387	.353	.740	* 19	.980
1986—	Prince Will. (Car.)	C	121	395	59	100	34	1	10	47	50	74	7	5	4-5	.253	.346	.420	.766	20	.979
1987—	Harrisburg (East.)	C	113	365	41	112	23	2	6	54	51	46	8	16	6-3	.307	.401	.430	.832	• 11	.985
	— Pittsburgh (N.L.)	C	4	9	1	2	1	0	1	2	0	2	0	0	0-0	.222	.222	.667	.889	0	1.000
1988—	Buffalo (A.A.)	C	86	304	35	79	16	0	14	42	23	53	7	6	3-6	.260	.325	.451	.776	* 12	.977
	— Pittsburgh (N.L.)	C	29	74	3	13	2	0	0	6	4	15	0	5	0-0	.176	.218	.203	.421	2	.983
1989—	Buffalo (A.A.)	C	65	183	21	37	8	1	6	33	22	30	2	4	2-3	.202	.289	.355	.644	5	.985
	— Pittsburgh (N.L.)	C	21	52	1	7	4	0	0	5	6	12	0	1	1-1	.135	.220	.212	.432	4	.960
1990—	Pittsburgh (N.L.)	C	4	10	1	1	0	0	0	0	1	2	0	0	0-1	.100	.182	.100	.282	0	1.000
	— Buffalo (A.A.)	C-1B	94	284	38	64	13	0	7	37	39	46	5	6	4-7	.225	.326	.345	.671	8	.985
1991—	Pittsburgh (N.L.)	C-1B	26	34	4	9	3	0	1	2	7	3	1	3	0-0	.265	.405	.441	.846	1	.984
	— Buffalo (A.A.)	C	80	221	29	46	8	3	6	32	37	31	7	4	3-4	.208	.336	.353	.689	5	.989
1992—	Pittsburgh (N.L.)	C-3B	27	44	1	4	2	0	0	5	6	9	0	2	1-1	.091	.192	.136	.329	2	.977
	— Buffalo (A.A.)	C-OF	75	244	34	64	17	0	9	35	20	35	8	5	3-1	.262	.333	.443	.776	8	.978
1993—	Pittsburgh (N.L.)	C	66	179	14	35	14	0	2	24	13	38	7	5	1-1	.196	.272	.307	.580	5	.984
1994—	Albuquerque (PCL)	C-DH	103	330	61	94	31	2	20	54	51	67	12	9	2-2	.285	.396	.573	.969	9	.987
	— Los Angeles (N.L.)	C	3	6	2	2	0	0	0	1	1	3	0	0	0-0	.333	.429	.333	.762	0	1.000
1995—	Albuquerque (PCL)	C-DH	61	192	30	61	15	0	7	36	27	41	2	6	0-0	.318	.407	.505	.912	4	.989
	— Los Angeles (N.L.)	C	18	40	3	8	2	1	1	4	4	10	0	0	0-0	.200	.273	.375	.648	1	.988
1996—	Albuquerque (PCL)	C-D-3-O	32	95	24	39	5	1	7	22	15	14	2	1	0-2	.411	.500	.705	1.205	1	.991
	— Los Angeles (N.L.)	C	40	64	6	19	6	0	1	11	6	15	2	0	0-0	.297	.365	.438	.802	1	.994
1997—	Los Angeles (N.L.)	C	47	100	17	22	5	0	3	14	5	15	3	2	0-0	.220	.275	.360	.635	1	.996
1998—	Los Angeles (N.L.)	C	37	81	7	15	5	1	0	5	7	24	2	0	0-0	.185	.267	.272	.538	0	1.000
1999—	GC Phillies (GCL)	C-DH	7	21	3	5	3	0	0	3	4	0	1	0	0-0	.238	.385	.381	.766	0	1.000
	— Clearwater (FSL)	C	9	33	5	12	0	0	2	9	3	3	1	1	1-0	.364	.432	.545	.978	1	.981
	— Scran./W.B. (I.L.)	C-DH	7	22	2	2	0	0	1	1	3	5	1	1	1-0	.091	.231	.227	.458	0	1.000
	— Philadelphia (N.L.)	C	4	6	1	1	0	0	0	1	1	1	0	1	0-0	.167	.286	.167	.452	0	1.000
2000—	Philadelphia (N.L.)	C	46	122	14	29	9	0	2	16	13	31	2	6	1-0	.238	.321	.361	.682	1	.996
2001—	Minnesota (A.L.)	C	64	196	19	43	4	1	7	23	12	39	6	5	3-1	.219	.284	.357	.641	0	1.000
2002—	Minnesota (A.L.)	C	51	125	14	28	7	1	4	16	14	26	4	1	1-3	.224	.317	.392	.709	1	.997
2003—	Minnesota (A.L.)	C-DH	24	40	5	8	2	0	2	5	5	7	2	0	1-0	.200	.319	.400	.719	0	1.000
	— Omaha (PCL)	C	29	91	16	28	10	0	1	6	14	15	4	2	0-1	.308	.418	.451	.869	0	1.000
	— Kansas City (A.L.)	C-DH	8	8	0	2	0	0	0	1	0	0	0	2	0-0	.250	.250	.250	.500	0	1.000
	American League totals (3 years)		147	369	38	81	13	2	13	45	31	72	12	11	5-4	.220	.299	.371	.670	1	.999
	National League totals (14 years)		372	821	75	167	53	2	11	95	74	180	17	25	4-4	.203	.280	.313	.593	18	.989
	Major League totals (17 years)		519	1190	113	248	66	4	24	140	105	252	29	36	9-8	.208	.286	.331	.617	19	.992

PRINZ, BRET   P

PERSONAL: Born June 15, 1977, in Chicago Heights, Ill. ... 6-2/216. ... Throws right, bats right. ... Full name: Bret Randolph Prinz. ... High school: Centennial (Peoria, Ariz.). ... Junior college: Phoenix College (Ari.).

TRANSACTIONS/CAREER NOTES: Selected by Arizona Diamondbacks organization in 18th round of 1998 free-agent draft (June 3, 1998). ... On disabled list (April 1, 2003). ... Sent to Tucson on rehab assignment (June 26, 2003). ... Reinstated from Emergency disabled list; optioned to Tucson by Arizona (July 24, 2003). ... Traded by Diamondbacks with OF David Dellucci and C Jon Mark Sprowl to New York Yankees for OF Raul Mondesi (July 29, 2003).

CAREER HITTING: 0-for-0 (.000), 0 R, 0 2B, 0 3B, 0 HR, 0 RBI.

Year	League	W	L	Pct.	ERA	WHIP	G	GS	CG	ShO	Hld.	Sv.-Opp.	IP	H	R	ER	HR	BB-IBB	SO	Avg.
1998—	Ariz. D'backs (Ariz.)	0	0	...	3.38	1.31	4	0	0	0	...	0-...	5.1	7	3	2	0	0-0	3	.304
	— Lethbridge (Pio.)	4	2	.667	3.09	1.33	11	10	0	0	...	0-...	46.2	49	26	16	2	13-0	30	.262
1999—	South Bend (Mid.)	6	10	.375	4.48	1.31	30	23	0	0	...	0-...	138.2	129	82	69	16	52-0	98	.247
2000—	South Bend (Mid.)	1	0	1.000	0.00	0.41	6	0	0	0	...	1-...	7.1	2	2	0	0	1-0	10	.083
	— El Paso (Texas)	9	1	.900	3.56	1.43	53	0	0	0	...	26-...	60.2	71	24	24	6	16-3	69	.293
2001—	Tucson (PCL)	0	0	...	0.00	0.18	5	0	0	0	...	3-...	5.2	1	0	0	0	6	0	.056
	— Arizona (N.L.)	4	1	.800	2.63	1.27	46	0	0	0	6	9-12	41.0	33	13	12	4	19-1	27	.220
2002—	Arizona (N.L.)	0	2	.000	9.45	2.48	20	0	0	0	5	0-2	13.1	23	14	14	1	10-1	10	.404
	— Tucson (PCL)	1	0	1.000	2.97	1.30	37	0	0	0	...	18-...	39.1	42	14	13	4	9-1	34	.266
	— Lancaster (Calif.)	1	0	1.000	0.00	0.43	5	0	0	0	...	0-...	7.0	2	0	0	0	1-0	6	.083
2003—	Arizona (N.L.)	0	0	...	0.00	2.00	1	0	0	0	0	0-0	1.0	1	0	0	0	1-1	1	.250
	— Lancaster (Calif.)	0	0	...	0.00	0.00	1	1	0	0	...	0-...	1.0	0	0	0	0	1-0	2	.000
	— El Paso (Texas)	0	0	...	4.50	2.00	2	0	0	0	...	0-...	2.0	3	1	1	0	1-0	2	.333
	— Tucson (PCL)	0	1	.000	6.00	1.83	10	0	0	0	...	0-...	12.0	19	9	8	1	3-0	7	.345
	— New York (A.L.)	0	0	...	18.00	4.50	2	0	0	0	0	0-0	2.0	6	4	4	1	3-1	2	.500
	— Columbus (Int'l)	0	1	.000	8.03	1.70	10	0	0	0	...	0-...	12.1	20	11	11	2	1-0	13	.364
	American League totals (1 year)	0	0	...	18.00	4.50	2	0	0	0	0	0-0	2.0	6	4	4	1	3-1	2	.500
	National League totals (3 years)	4	3	.571	4.23	1.57	67	0	0	0	11	9-14	55.1	57	27	26	5	30-3	38	.270
	Major League totals (3 years)	4	3	.571	4.71	1.67	69	0	0	0	11	9-14	57.1	63	31	30	6	33-4	40	.283

P

PRIOR, MARK   P

PERSONAL: Born September 7, 1980, in San Diego, Calif. ... 6-5/230. ... Throws right, bats right. ... Full name: Mark William Prior. ... High school: University of San Diego High (Calif.). ... College: USC.

TRANSACTIONS/CAREER NOTES: Selected by New York Yankees organization in first round (43rd pick overall) of free-agent draft (June 2, 1998); did not sign. ... Selected by Chicago Cubs organization in first round (second pick overall) of free-agent draft (June 5, 2001). ... On Chicago disabled list (September 2-17, 2002). ... Placed on 15-day disabled list (July 12, 2003). ... Reinstated from 15-day disabled list (August 4, 2003).

CAREER HITTING: 24-for-107 (.224), 9 R, 8 2B, 0 3B, 1 HR, 10 RBI.

Year League	W	L	Pct.	ERA	WHIP	G	GS	CG	ShO	Hld.	Sv.-Opp.	IP	H	R	ER	HR	BB-IBB	SO	Avg.
2002—West Tenn (Sou.)	4	1	.800	2.60	1.04	6	6	0	0	...	0-...	34.2	26	16	10	0	10-0	55	.198
—Iowa (PCL)	1	1	.500	1.65	1.29	3	3	0	0	...	0-...	16.1	13	10	3	1	8-0	24	.203
—Chicago (N.L.)	6	6	.500	3.32	1.17	19	19	1	0	0	0-0	116.2	98	45	43	14	38-0	147	.226
2003—Chicago (N.L.)	18	6	.750	2.43	1.10	30	30	3	1	0	0-0	211.1	183	67	57	15	50-4	245	.231
Major League totals (2 years)	24	12	.667	2.74	1.13	49	49	4	1	0	0-0	328.0	281	112	100	29	88-4	392	.229

PROKOPEC, LUKE   P

PERSONAL: Born February 23, 1978... 5-11/175. ... Throws right, bats left. ... Full name: Kenneth Luke Prokopec. ... High school: Renmark (South Australia).

TRANSACTIONS/CAREER NOTES: Signed as non-drafted free agent by Los Angeles Dodgers organization (August 28, 1994). ... On San Antonio disabled list (April 29-May 12 and July 8-21, 2000). ... On Los Angeles disabled list (August 9-25, 2001). ... Traded by Dodgers with P Chad Ricketts to Toronto Blue Jays for P Paul Quantrill and 2B/SS Cesar Izturis (December 13, 2001). ... On Toronto disabled list (June 14-July 21 and August 24, 2002-remainder of season); included rehabilitation assignment to Syracuse (July 17-21). ... Granted free agency (October 15, 2002). ... Signed by Dodgers organization (November 4, 2002). ... Selected by Cincinnati Reds from Dodgers organization in Rule 5 major league draft (December 16, 2002). ... On disabled list (February 25, 2003-entire season).

CAREER HITTING: 7-for-41 (.171), 1 R, 1 2B, 0 3B, 0 HR, 0 RBI.

Year League	W	L	Pct.	ERA	WHIP	G	GS	CG	ShO	Hld.	Sv.-Opp.	IP	H	R	ER	HR	BB-IBB	SO	Avg.
1997—Savannah (S. Atl.)	3	1	.750	4.07	1.17	61	6	0	0	...	0-...	42.0	37	21	19	8	12-0	45	.234
1998—San Bernardino (Calif.)	8	5	.615	2.69	1.20	20	20	0	0	...	0-...	110.1	99	43	33	11	33-1	148	.234
—San Antonio (Texas)	3	0	1.000	1.38	1.12	5	5	0	0	...	0-...	26.0	16	5	4	0	13-0	25	.176
1999—San Antonio (Texas)	8	12	.400	5.42	1.38	27	27	0	0	...	0-...	157.2	172	113	95	18	46-0	128	.284
2000—San Antonio (Texas)	7	3	.700	2.45	1.10	22	22	1	0	...	0-...	128.2	118	40	35	8	23-1	124	.242
—Los Angeles (N.L.)	1	1	.500	3.00	1.33	5	3	0	0	0	0-0	21.0	19	10	7	2	9-0	12	.253
2001—Los Angeles (N.L.)	8	7	.533	4.88	1.34	29	22	0	0	0	0-0	138.1	146	80	75	27	40-1	91	.268
—Las Vegas (PCL)	1	0	1.000	3.00	0.83	1	1	0	0	...	0-...	6.0	3	2	2	1	2-0	8	.143
2002—Toronto (A.L.)	2	9	.182	6.78	1.60	22	12	0	0	0	0-0	71.2	90	57	54	19	25-2	41	.302
—Syracuse (Int'l)	0	0	...	0.00	0.00	2	0	0	0	...	0-...	2.0	0	0	0	0	0-0	2	.000
2003—										Did not play.									
American League totals (1 year)	2	9	.182	6.78	1.60	22	12	0	0	0	0-0	71.2	90	57	54	19	25-2	41	.302
National League totals (2 years)	9	8	.529	4.63	1.34	34	25	0	0	0	0-0	159.1	165	90	82	29	49-1	103	.266
Major League totals (3 years)	11	17	.393	5.30	1.42	56	37	0	0	0	0-0	231.0	255	147	136	48	74-3	144	.278

PUFFER, BRANDON   P

PERSONAL: Born October 5, 1975, in Downey, Calif. ... 6-3/190. ... Throws right, bats right. ... Full name: Brandon Duane Puffer. ... High school: Capistrano Valley (Mission Viejo, Calif.).

TRANSACTIONS/CAREER NOTES: Selected by Minnesota Twins organization in 27th round of free-agent draft (June 2, 1994). ... Released by Twins (May 6, 1996). ... Signed by California Angels organization (May 28, 1996). ... Released by Angels (December 15, 1997). ... Signed by Cincinnati Reds organization (January 14, 1998). ... Granted free agency (October 16, 1998). ... Re-signed by Reds organization (November 17, 1998). ... Granted free agency (October 15, 1999). ... Signed by Colorado Rockies organization (November 18, 1999). ... Released by Rockies (May 18, 2000). ... Signed by Somerset, Atlantic League (May 2000). ... Contract sold by Somerset to Houston Astros organization (July 17, 2000).

CAREER HITTING: 0-for-9 (.000), 0 R, 0 2B, 0 3B, 0 HR, 0 RBI.

Year League	W	L	Pct.	ERA	WHIP	G	GS	CG	ShO	Hld.	Sv.-Opp.	IP	H	R	ER	HR	BB-IBB	SO	Avg.
1994—GC Twins (GCL)	2	2	.500	3.06	1.47	18	0	0	0	...	2-...	35.1	33	18	12	1	19-0	40	.248
1995—GC Twins (GCL)	0	3	.000	2.88	1.23	14	5	0	0	...	1-...	40.2	29	21	13	0	21-0	35	.191
1996—Ariz. Angels (Ariz.)	0	1	.000	3.60	1.60	1	1	0	0	...	0-...	5.0	7	2	2	0	1-0	3	.318
—Boise (NW)	2	0	1.000	4.45	1.25	16	0	0	0	...	1-...	30.1	27	19	15	3	11-0	22	.239
1997—Boise (NW)	0	0	...	2.35	0.78	6	0	0	0	...	1-...	15.1	10	5	4	0	2-0	15	.169
—Cedar Rapids (Midw.)	0	0	...	2.60	1.04	10	0	0	0	...	0-...	17.1	8	6	5	0	10-0	11	.143
1998—Char., W.Va. (SAL)	2	7	.222	6.93	1.80	29	0	0	0	...	1-...	50.2	68	45	39	4	23-4	36	.325
—Chattanooga (Sou.)	0	0	...	3.12	0.58	7	0	0	0	...	0-...	8.2	3	3	3	2	3-0	6	.071
1999—Clinton (Midw.)	1	2	.333	1.99	1.22	59	0	0	0	...	* 34-...	63.1	53	20	14	2	24-3	60	.223
2000—Asheville (S. Atl.)	0	0	...	8.16	2.09	14	0	0	0	...	5-...	14.1	19	16	13	3	11-3	15	.322
—Somerset (Atl.)	0	2	.000	3.52	1.48	15	0	0	0	...	1-...	23.0	25	12	9	...	9-...	21	...
—Kissimmee (Fla. St.)	2	3	.400	1.27	1.36	18	0	0	0	...	9-...	21.1	18	6	3	0	11-4	26	.225
2001—Round Rock (Texas)	6	1	.857	2.07	1.05	56	0	0	0	...	8-...	82.2	52	19	19	4	35-2	91	.181
2002—New Orleans (PCL)	2	1	.667	1.80	0.80	11	0	0	0	...	0-...	15.0	8	3	3	1	4-0	13	.157
—Houston (N.L.)	3	3	.500	4.43	1.52	55	0	0	0	2	0-0	69.0	67	37	34	3	38-8	48	.258
2003—Houston (N.L.)	0	0	...	5.14	1.90	13	0	0	0	1	0-1	21.0	24	13	12	2	16-3	10	.300
—New Orleans (PCL)	7	3	.700	2.91	1.25	44	0	0	0	...	5-...	52.2	50	23	17	1	16-1	41	.253
Major League totals (2 years)	3	3	.500	4.60	1.61	68	0	0	0	3	0-1	90.0	91	50	46	5	54-11	58	.268

PUJOLS, ALBERT   OF/1B

PERSONAL: Born January 16, 1980, in Santo Domingo, Dominican Republic. ... 6-3/225. ... Bats right, throws right. ... Full name: Jose Albert Pujols. ... Name pronounced: POO-holes. ... High school: Fort Osage (Independence, Mo.). ... Junior college: Maple Woods (Mo.) Community College.

TRANSACTIONS/CAREER NOTES: Selected by St. Louis Cardinals organization in 13th round of free-agent draft (June 2, 1999). ... Suspended by Major League Baseball (August 19, 2003). ... Reinstated August 21, 2003).

2003 GAMES PLAYED BY POSITION (MLB): OF—113, 1B—62, DH—1.

Year Team (League)	Pos.	G	AB	R	H	2B	3B	HR	RBI	BB	SO	HBP	GDP	SB-CS	Avg.	OBP	SLG	OPS	E	Pct.
2000—Peoria (Midw.)	3B	109	395	62	128	32	6	17	84	38	37	5	10	2-4	.324	.389	.565	.953	19	.948
—Potomac Carolina (Caro.)	3B	21	81	11	23	8	1	2	10	7	8	0	3	1-1	.284	.341	.481	.822	3	.957
—Memphis (PCL)	3B-OF	3	14	1	3	1	0	0	2	1	2	0	0	1-0	.214	.267	.286	.552	0	1.000
2001—St. Louis (N.L.)	O-3-1-D	161	590	112	194	47	4	37	130	69	93	9	21	1-3	.329	.403	.610	1.013	20	.967
2002—St. Louis (N.L.)	O-3-1-D-S	157	590	118	185	40	2	34	127	72	69	9	20	2-4	.314	.394	.561	.955	11	.975
2003—St. Louis (N.L.)	O-1-D	157	591	*137	*212	*51	1	43	124	79	65	10	13	5-1	*.359	.439	.667	1.106	4	.993
Major League totals (3 years)		475	1771	367	591	138	7	114	381	220	227	28	54	8-8	.334	.412	.613	1.025	35	.978

PULIDO, CARLOS — P

PERSONAL: Born August 5, 1971, in Caracas, Venezuela. ... 6-0/200. ... Throws left, bats left. ... Full name: Juan Carlos Pulido. ... Name pronounced: puh-LEE-doe. ... High school: Liceo Andres Bello (Caracas, Venezuela).

TRANSACTIONS/CAREER NOTES: Signed as non-drafted free agent by Minnesota Twins organization (February 28, 1989). ... Granted free agency (October 16, 1995). ... Signed by Iowa, Chicago Cubs organization (February 18, 1996). ... Granted free agency (October 15, 1996). ... Signed by Montreal Expos organization (December 26, 1996). ... Granted free agency (October 15, 1997). ... Signed by Minnesota Twins (August 20, 2003). ... Optioned to Rochester (August 31, 2003). ... Recalled from Rochester (September 2, 2003).

CAREER HITTING: 0-for-0 (.000), 0 R, 0 2B, 0 3B, 0 HR, 0 RBI.

Year League	W	L	Pct.	ERA	WHIP	G	GS	CG	ShO	Hld.	Sv.-Opp.	IP	H	R	ER	HR	BB-IBB	SO	Avg.
1989— GC Twins (GCL)	3	0	1.000	2.25	1.00	22	0	0	0	...	2-...	36.0	22	9	9	0	14-0	46	.177
1990— Kenosha (Midw.)	5	5	.500	2.34	1.48	56	0	0	0	...	6-...	61.2	55	21	16	2	36-3	70	.242
1991— Visalia (Calif.)	1	5	.167	2.01	1.24	57	0	0	0	...	17-...	80.2	77	34	18	2	23-2	102	.253
— Portland (PCL)	0	0	...	16.20	3.00	2	0	0	0	...	0-...	1.2	4	3	3	1	1-0	2	.444
1992— Orlando (Sou.)	6	2	.750	4.40	1.36	52	5	0	0	...	1-...	100.1	99	52	49	7	37-0	87	.257
1993— Portland (PCL)	10	6	.625	4.19	1.47	33	22	1	0	...	0-...	146.0	169	74	68	8	45-1	79	.296
1994— Minnesota (A.L.)	3	7	.300	5.98	1.51	19	14	0	0	0	0-0	84.1	87	57	56	17	40-1	32	.273
1995— Salt Lake (PCL)	8	1	.889	4.67	1.50	43	3	0	0	...	3-...	71.1	87	42	37	10	20-4	38	.292
1996— Iowa (Am. Assoc.)	2	8	.200	5.31	1.66	28	17	0	0	...	0-...	101.2	133	64	60	17	36-3	48	.322
— Orlando (Sou.)	2	2	.500	7.45	2.07	6	0	0	0	...	0-...	9.2	17	9	8	0	3-0	12	.362
1997— Ottawa (Int'l)	5	2	.714	5.42	1.43	44	5	0	0	...	3-...	76.1	84	47	46	10	25-2	44	.276
1998— Somerset (Atl.)	2	2	.500	3.31	1.19	12	2	1	0	...	3-...	35.1	30	14	13	3	12-1	33	.234
— Norfolk (Int'l)	0	0	...	1.69	1.13	3	0	0	0	...	0-...	5.1	6	1	1	1	0-0	6	.300
1999— Somerset (Atl.)	9	4	.692	4.42	1.16	22	22	4	0	...	0-...	148.2	137	77	73	20	36-...	105	...
2003— Rochester (Int'l)	12	5	.706	3.56	1.24	25	25	1	0	...	0-...	149.1	145	65	59	13	40-0	87	.262
— Minnesota (A.L.)	0	1	.000	4.02	1.15	7	1	0	0	1	0-0	15.2	15	9	7	0	3-0	6	.254
Major League totals (2 years)	3	8	.273	5.67	1.45	26	15	0	0	1	0-0	100.0	102	66	63	17	43-1	38	.270

PUNTO, NICK — IF

PERSONAL: Born November 8, 1977, in San Diego, Calif. ... 5-9/175. ... Bats both, throws right. ... Full name: Nicholas Paul Punto. ... Name pronounced: POON-toh. ... High school: Trabuco Hills (Mission Vieh Vijo, Calif.). ... Junior college: Saddleback College (Calif.).

TRANSACTIONS/CAREER NOTES: Selected by Minnesota Twins organization in 33rd round of free-agent draft (June 3, 1997); did not sign. ... Selected by Philadelphia Phillies organization in 21st round of free-agent draft (June 2, 1998). ... On Scranton/Wilkes-Barre disabled list (June 8-16, 2001). ... On Scranton/Wilkes-Barre disabled list (June 19-July 2, 2002).

2003 GAMES PLAYED BY POSITION (MLB): 2B—16, 3B—9, SS—7.

Year Team (League)	Pos.	G	AB	R	H	2B	3B	HR	RBI	BB	SO	HBP	GDP	SB-CS	Avg.	OBP	SLG	OPS	E	Pct.
1998— Batavia (NY-Penn)	2B-SS	72	279	51	69	9	4	1	20	42	48	1	4	19-7	.247	.347	.319	.666	27	.924
1999— Clearwater (FSL)	SS	106	400	65	122	18	6	1	48	67	53	3	13	16-6	.305	.404	.388	.792	24	.958
2000— Reading (East.)	SS	121	456	77	116	15	4	5	47	69	71	2	5	33-10	.254	.351	.338	.689	20	.963
2001— Scran./W.B. (I.L.)	SS	123	463	57	106	19	5	1	39	68	114	0	15	33-9	.229	.327	.298	.625	21	.964
— Philadelphia (N.L.)	SS	4	5	0	2	0	0	0	0	0	0	0	0	0-0	.400	.400	.400	.800	0	1.000
2002— Philadelphia (N.L.)	2B-SS	9	6	0	1	0	0	0	0	0	3	0	0	0-0	.167	.167	.167	.333	1	.750
— Scran./W.B. (I.L.)	SS	115	443	74	120	12	5	1	29	76	84	2	5	•42-8	.271	.378	.327	.705	19	.967
2003— Scran./W.B. (I.L.)	SS	25	111	19	35	7	1	0	9	7	13	0	0	7-1	.315	.353	.396	.749	4	.969
— Philadelphia (N.L.)	2B-3B-SS	64	92	14	20	2	0	1	4	7	22	0	0	2-1	.217	.273	.272	.544	2	.980
Major League totals (3 years)		77	103	14	23	2	0	1	4	7	25	0	0	2-1	.223	.273	.272	.545	3	.972

PUTZ, J.J. — P

PERSONAL: Born February 22, 1977, in Trenton, Mich. ... 6-5/220. ... Throws right, bats right. ... Full name: Joseph Jason Putz. ... High school: Trenton (Mich.). ... College: Michigan.

TRANSACTIONS/CAREER NOTES: Selected by Seattle Mariners organization in sixth round of free-agent draft (June 2, 1999). ... On San Antonio disabled list (April 4-22, 2002).

CAREER HITTING: 0-for-0 (.000), 0 R, 0 2B, 0 3B, 0 HR, 0 RBI.

Year League	W	L	Pct.	ERA	WHIP	G	GS	CG	ShO	Hld.	Sv.-Opp.	IP	H	R	ER	HR	BB-IBB	SO	Avg.
1999— Everett (Northwest)	0	0	...	4.84	1.52	10	0	0	0	...	2-...	22.1	23	13	12	2	11-1	17	.284
2000— Wisconsin (Midw.)	12	6	.667	3.15	1.35	26	25	3	2	...	0-...	142.2	130	71	50	4	63-2	105	.247
2001— San Antonio (Texas)	7	9	.438	3.83	1.38	27	26	0	0	...	0-...	148.0	145	80	63	11	59-2	135	.259
2002— San Antonio (Texas)	3	10	.231	3.64	1.33	15	15	1	1	...	0-...	84.0	84	41	34	7	28-0	60	.264
— Tacoma (PCL)	2	4	.333	3.83	1.33	9	9	0	0	...	0-...	54.0	51	23	23	4	21-0	39	.258
2003— Tacoma (PCL)	0	3	.000	2.51	1.20	41	0	0	0	...	11-...	86.0	69	30	24	4	34-0	60	.225
— Seattle (A.L.)	0	0	...	4.91	1.91	3	0	0	0	0	0-0	3.2	4	2	2	0	3-0	3	.267
Major League totals (1 year)	0	0	...	4.91	1.91	3	0	0	0	0	0-0	3.2	4	2	2	0	3-0	3	.267

QUANTRILL, PAUL — P

PERSONAL: Born November 3, 1968, in London, Ontario. ... 6-1/195. ... Throws right, bats left. ... Full name: Paul John Quantrill. ... Name pronounced: KWAN-trill. ... High school: Okemos (Mich.). ... College: Wisconsin.

TRANSACTIONS/CAREER NOTES: Selected by Los Angeles Dodgers organization in 26th round of free-agent draft (June 2, 1986); did not sign. ... Selected by Boston Red Sox organization in sixth round of free-agent draft (June 5, 1989). ... Traded by Red Sox with OF Billy Hatcher to Philadelphia Phillies for OF Wes Chamberlain and P Mike Sullivan (May 31, 1994). ... Traded by Phillies to Toronto Blue Jays for 3B Howard Battle and P Ricardo Jordan (December 6, 1995). ... On Toronto disabled list (March 27-June 15, 1999); included rehabilitation assignments to Dunedin (June 4-10) and Syracuse (June 11-13). ... Traded by Blue Jays with 2B/SS Cesar Izturis to Los Angeles Dodgers for P Luke Prokopec and P Chad Ricketts (December 13, 2001).

CAREER HITTING: 7-for-65 (.108), 5 R, 0 2B, 0 3B, 0 HR, 0 RBI.

Year League	W	L	Pct.	ERA	WHIP	G	GS	CG	ShO	Hld.	Sv.-Opp.	IP	H	R	ER	HR	BB-IBB	SO	Avg.
1989— GC Red Sox (GCL)	0	0	...	0.00	0.40	2	0	0	0	...	2-...	5.0	2	0	0	0	0-0	5	.111
— Elmira (N.Y.-Penn)	5	4	.556	3.43	1.34	20	7	•5	0	...	2-...	76.0	90	37	29	5	12-2	57	.299
1990— Winter Haven (FSL)	2	5	.286	4.14	1.14	7	7	1	0	...	0-...	45.2	46	24	21	3	6-0	14	.264
— New Britain (East.)	7	11	.389	3.53	1.29	22	22	1	1	...	0-...	132.2	148	65	52	3	23-2	53	.290
1991— New Britain (East.)	2	1	.667	2.06	1.14	5	5	1	0	...	0-...	35.0	32	14	8	2	8-0	18	.248
— Pawtucket (Int'l)	10	7	.588	4.45	1.28	25	23	•6	2	...	0-...	155.2	169	81	77	14	30-1	75	.282

Year League	W	L	Pct.	ERA	WHIP	G	GS	CG	ShO	Hld.	Sv.-Opp.	IP	H	R	ER	HR	BB-IBB	SO	Avg.
1992—Pawtucket (Int'l)	6	8	.429	4.46	1.37	19	18	4	1	...	0-...	119.0	143	63	59	16	20-1	56	.300
—Boston (A.L.)	2	3	.400	2.19	1.42	27	0	0	0	3	1-5	49.1	55	18	12	1	15-5	24	.288
1993—Boston (A.L.)	6	12	.333	3.91	1.41	49	14	1	1	3	1-2	138.0	151	73	60	13	44-14	66	.279
1994—Boston (A.L.)	1	1	.500	3.52	1.30	17	0	0	0	2	0-2	23.0	25	10	9	4	5-1	15	.278
—Philadelphia (N.L.)	2	2	.500	6.00	1.63	18	1	0	0	1	1-2	30.0	39	21	20	3	10-3	13	.331
—Scran./W.B. (I.L.)	3	3	.500	3.47	1.07	8	8	1	1	...	0-...	57.0	55	25	22	5	6-0	36	.253
1995—Philadelphia (N.L.)	11	12	.478	4.67	1.43	33	29	0	0	0	0-0	179.1	212	102	93	20	44-3	103	.295
1996—Toronto (A.L.)	5	14	.263	5.43	1.66	38	20	0	0	1	0-2	134.1	172	90	81	27	51-3	86	.317
1997—Toronto (A.L.)	6	7	.462	1.94	1.36	77	0	0	0	16	5-10	88.0	103	25	19	5	17-3	56	.297
1998—Toronto (A.L.)	3	4	.429	2.59	1.38	82	0	0	0	*27	7-14	80.0	88	26	23	5	22-6	59	.285
1999—Dunedin (Fla. St.)	0	1	.000	4.50	1.00	5	4	0	0	...	0-...	6.0	5	3	3	1	1-0	2	.238
—Syracuse (Int'l)	0	0	...	0.00	0.50	2	0	0	0	...	0-...	2.0	1	0	0	0	0-0	1	.167
—Toronto (A.L.)	3	2	.600	3.33	1.44	41	0	0	0	8	0-4	48.2	53	19	18	5	17-1	28	.282
2000—Toronto (A.L.)	2	5	.286	4.52	1.49	68	0	0	0	13	1-3	83.2	100	45	42	7	25-1	47	.298
2001—Toronto (A.L.)	11	2	.846	3.04	1.18	80	0	0	0	21	2-9	83.0	86	29	28	6	12-7	58	.274
2002—Los Angeles (N.L.)	5	4	.556	2.70	1.37	86	0	0	0	*33	1-3	76.2	80	27	23	1	25-7	53	.267
2003—Los Angeles (N.L.)	2	5	.286	1.75	0.98	*89	0	0	0	28	1-5	77.1	61	18	15	2	15-2	44	.227
American League totals (9 years)	**39**	**50**	**.438**	**3.61**	**1.43**	**479**	**34**	**1**	**1**	**94**	**17-51**	**728.0**	**833**	**335**	**292**	**73**	**208-41**	**439**	**.291**
National League totals (4 years)	**20**	**23**	**.465**	**3.74**	**1.34**	**226**	**30**	**0**	**0**	**62**	**3-10**	**363.1**	**392**	**168**	**151**	**26**	**94-15**	**213**	**.279**
Major League totals (12 years)	**59**	**73**	**.447**	**3.65**	**1.40**	**705**	**64**	**1**	**1**	**156**	**20-61**	**1091.1**	**1225**	**503**	**443**	**99**	**302-56**	**652**	**.287**

QUEVEDO, RUBEN   P

PERSONAL: Born January 5, 1979, in Valencia Carabobo, Venezuela. ... 6-1/245. ... Throws right, bats right. ... Full name: Ruben Eduardo Quevedo. ... Name pronounced: keh-VAY-doh. ... High school: Don Bosco (Valencia, Venezuela).

TRANSACTIONS/CAREER NOTES: Signed as non-drafted free agent by Atlanta Braves organization (September 6, 1995). ... Traded by Braves with P Micah Bowie and a player to be named later to Chicago Cubs for P Terry Mulholland and SS Jose Hernandez (July 31, 1999); Cubs acquired P Joey Nation to complete deal (August 24, 1999). ... Traded by Cubs with OF Peter Zoccolillo to Milwaukee Brewers for P David Weathers and P Roberto Miniel (July 30, 2001). ... Recalled from Indianapolis (May 1, 2003). ... Placed on 15-day disabled list; sent outright to Indianapolis (June 27, 2003). ... Removed from 15-day disabled list (September 19, 2003).

CAREER HITTING: 15-for-98 (.153), 5 R, 0 2B, 0 3B, 0 HR, 5 RBI.

Year League	W	L	Pct.	ERA	WHIP	G	GS	CG	ShO	Hld.	Sv.-Opp.	IP	H	R	ER	HR	BB-IBB	SO	Avg.
1996—GC Braves (GCL)	2	6	.250	2.29	1.07	10	10	0	0	...	0-...	55.0	50	19	14	1	9-0	49	.243
1997—Danville (Appal.)	1	5	.167	3.56	1.07	13	11	0	0	...	0-...	68.1	46	37	27	6	27-0	78	.186
1998—Macon (S. Atl.)	11	3	.786	3.13	1.29	25	15	1	0	...	0-...	112.0	114	50	39	13	31-0	117	.265
—Danville (Caro.)	0	2	.000	3.58	1.26	6	6	0	0	...	0-...	32.2	28	22	13	2	13-1	35	.226
1999—Richmond (Int'l)	6	5	.545	5.37	1.38	21	21	0	0	...	0-...	105.2	112	65	63	26	34-0	98	.277
—Iowa (PCL)	3	1	.750	3.45	1.24	7	7	1	1	...	0-...	44.1	34	18	17	1	21-0	50	.214
2000—Iowa (PCL)	7	2	.778	4.22	1.33	13	13	0	0	...	0-...	74.2	68	37	35	7	31-0	77	.240
—Chicago (N.L.)	3	10	.231	7.47	1.70	21	15	1	0	0	0-0	88.0	96	81	73	21	54-4	65	.271
2001—Iowa (PCL)	9	5	.643	2.99	1.21	22	22	1	1	...	0-...	141.2	124	54	47	13	48-3	150	.237
—Milwaukee (N.L.)	4	5	.444	4.61	1.52	10	10	0	0	0	0-0	56.2	56	30	29	9	30-4	60	.257
2002—Milwaukee (N.L.)	6	11	.353	5.76	1.63	26	25	1	1	0	0-0	139.0	159	100	89	28	68-3	93	.288
2003—Indianapolis (Int'l)	0	0	...	0.00	1.00	1	1	0	0	...	0-...	2.0	1	0	0	0	1-0	3	.143
—Indianapolis (Int'l)	2	1	.667	2.10	1.25	5	5	0	0	...	0-...	25.2	24	7	6	1	8-1	23	.250
—Milwaukee (N.L.)	1	4	.200	6.75	1.78	9	8	0	0	0	0-0	42.2	53	32	32	12	23-1	19	.314
Major League totals (4 years)	**14**	**30**	**.318**	**6.15**	**1.65**	**66**	**58**	**2**	**1**	**0**	**0-0**	**326.1**	**364**	**243**	**223**	**70**	**175-12**	**237**	**.282**

QUINLAN, ROBB   1B

PERSONAL: Born March 17, 1977, in Maplewood, Minn. ... 6-1/195. ... Bats right, throws right. ... Full name: Robb William Quinlan. ... High school: Hill-Murray High (Maplewood, Minnesota).

TRANSACTIONS/CAREER NOTES: Selected by Anaheim Angels organization in 10th round of free-agent draft (June 2, 1999). ... Recalled by Anaheim from Salt Lake of the Pacific Coast League (July 28, 2003).

2003 GAMES PLAYED BY POSITION (MLB): 1B—33, DH—3, OF—1.

Year Team (League)	Pos.	G	AB	R	H	2B	3B	HR	RBI	BB	SO	HBP	GDP	SB-CS	Avg.	OBP	SLG	OPS	E	Pct.
1999—Boise (NW)	3B-2B-1B	73	295	51	95	20	1	9	77	35	52	4	5	5-3	.322	.400	.488	.888	27	.892
2000—Lake Elsinore (Calif.)	1B-OF	127	482	79	153	35	5	5	85	67	82	2	7	6-4	.317	.396	.442	.838	16	.986
2001—Arkansas (Texas)	1B-OF	129	492	82	145	33	7	14	79	53	84	6	12	0-4	.295	.366	.476	.841	8	.993
2002—Salt Lake (PCL)	OF-1B	136	528	95	176	31	13	20	112	41	93	4	16	8-2	.333	.376	.555	.931	3	.988
2003—Salt Lake (PCL) 1B-OF-DH		95	393	55	122	18	4	9	68	25	59	1	9	10-3	.310	.352	.445	.797	0	1.000
—Anaheim (A.L.) 1B-DH-OF		38	94	13	27	4	2	0	4	6	16	0	3	1-2	.287	.330	.372	.702	2	.988
Major League totals (1 year)		**38**	**94**	**13**	**27**	**4**	**2**	**0**	**4**	**6**	**16**	**0**	**3**	**1-2**	**.287**	**.330**	**.372**	**.702**	**2**	**.988**

QUINTERO, HUMBERTO   C

PERSONAL: Born August 8, 1979, in Maracaibo, Venezuela. ... 6-1/190. ... Bats right, throws right. ... High school: Andres Bello (Maracaibo, Venezuela).

TRANSACTIONS/CAREER NOTES: Signed by Chicago White Sox organization as a non-drafted free agent (January 16, 1997). ... Traded by the White Sox with OF Alex Fernandez to the San Diego Padres for INF D'Angelo Jimenez (July 12, 2002).

2003 GAMES PLAYED BY POSITION (MLB): C—11.

Year Team (League)	Pos.	G	AB	R	H	2B	3B	HR	RBI	BB	SO	HBP	GDP	SB-CS	Avg.	OBP	SLG	OPS	E	Pct.
1999—Bristol (Appal.)	C	48	155	30	43	5	2	0	15	9	19	6	8	11-1	.277	.341	.335	.677	6	.987
2000—Burlington (Appal.)	C	75	248	23	59	12	2	0	24	15	31	3	8	10-6	.238	.287	.302	.590	8	.986
—Ariz. White Sox (Ariz.)	C-OF	15	56	13	22	2	2	0	8	0	3	2	2	1-0	.393	.414	.500	.914	3	.976
2001—Kannapolis (S. Atl.)	C	60	197	32	53	7	1	1	20	8	20	7	5	7-3	.269	.321	.330	.651	7	.989
—Win.-Salem (Car.)	C	43	154	15	37	6	0	0	12	5	19	2	3	9-3	.240	.268	.279	.548	3	.992
—Birmingham (Sou.)	C	5	19	0	4	0	0	0	2	0	2	1	0	0-0	.211	.250	.211	.461	1	.971
2002—Win.-Salem (Car.)	C	52	160	15	31	1	1	0	12	8	23	4	4	2-3	.194	.247	.213	.460	4	.990
—Birmingham (Sou.)	C	4	12	1	6	0	0	0	3	1	1	0	1	1-0	.500	.538	.500	1.038	0	1.000
—Charlotte (Int'l)	C	15	41	2	9	1	0	0	5	3	8	0	3	0-0	.220	.273	.244	.517	3	.964
—Mobile (Sou.)	C	37	125	11	30	8	0	1	14	5	12	3	3	0-3	.240	.286	.328	.614	5	.983
2003—Mobile (Sou.)	C-DH	110	386	37	115	26	0	3	52	19	41	9	17	0-0	.298	.343	.389	.732	5	.995
—San Diego (N.L.)	C	12	23	1	5	0	0	0	2	1	6	0	0	0-0	.217	.250	.217	.467	1	.982
Major League totals (1 year)		**12**	**23**	**1**	**5**	**0**	**0**	**0**	**2**	**1**	**6**	**0**	**0**	**0-0**	**.217**	**.250**	**.217**	**.467**	**1**	**.982**

RADKE, BRAD   P

PERSONAL: Born October 27, 1972, in Eau Claire, Wis. ... 6-2/188. ... Throws right, bats right. ... Full name: Brad William Radke. ... Name pronounced: RAD-key. ... High school: Jesuit (Tampa).

TRANSACTIONS/CAREER NOTES: Selected by Minnesota Twins organization in eighth round of free-agent draft (June 3, 1991). ... On disabled list (August 4-21, 2001). ... On Minnesota disabled list (May 14-30 and May 31-August 3, 2002); included rehabilitation assignments to Gulf Coast Twins (July 19-24) and Fort Myers (July 25-30). ... Suspended by Major League Baseball (May 17, 2003). ... Reinstated (May 23, 2003).

CAREER HITTING: 3-for-21 (.143), 0 R, 0 2B, 0 3B, 0 HR, 0 RBI.

Year League	W	L	Pct.	ERA	WHIP	G	GS	CG	ShO	Hld.	Sv.-Opp.	IP	H	R	ER	HR	BB-IBB	SO	Avg.
1991—GC Twins (GCL)	3	4	.429	3.08	1.11	10	9	1	0	...	1-...	49.2	41	21	17	0	14-0	46	.220
1992—Kenosha (Midw.)	10	10	.500	2.93	1.18	26	25	4	1	...	0-...	165.2	149	70	54	8	47-1	127	.243
1993—Fort Myers (Fla. St.)	3	5	.375	3.82	1.15	14	14	0	0	...	0-...	92.0	85	42	39	3	21-1	69	.243
—Nashville (Sou.)	2	6	.250	4.62	1.28	13	13	1	0	...	0-...	76.0	81	42	39	6	16-0	76	.267
1994—Nashville (Sou.)	12	9	.571	2.66	1.08	29 *	28	5	1	...	0-...	186.1	167	66	55	9	34-0	123	.240
1995—Minnesota (A.L.)	11	14	.440	5.32	1.34	29	28	2	1	0	0-0	181.0	195	112	107 *	32	47-0	75	.275
1996—Minnesota (A.L.)	11	16	.407	4.46	1.24	35	35	3	0	0	0-0	232.0	231	125	115 *	40	57-2	148	.256
1997—Minnesota (A.L.)	20	10	.667	3.87	1.19	35 •	35	4	1	0	0-0	239.2	238	114	103	28	48-1	174	.257
1998—Minnesota (A.L.)	12	14	.462	4.30	1.32	32	32	5	1	0	0-0	213.2	238	109	102	23	43-1	146	.283
1999—Minnesota (A.L.)	12	14	.462	3.75	1.29	33	33	4	0	0	0-0	218.2	239	97	91	28	44-0	121	.280
2000—Minnesota (A.L.)	12 *	16	.429	4.45	1.38	34	34	4	1	0	0-0	226.2	261	119	112	27	51-1	141	.286
2001—Minnesota (A.L.)	15	11	.577	3.94	1.15	33	33	6	2	0	0-0	226.0	235	105	99	24	26-0	137	.271
2002—Minnesota (A.L.)	9	5	.643	4.72	1.22	21	21	2	1	0	0-0	118.1	124	64	62	12	20-0	62	.272
—GC Twins (GCL)	0	0	...	0.00	0.67	1	1	0	0	...	0-...	3.0	2	0	0	0	0-0	4	.182
—Fort Myers (Fla. St.)	0	1	.000	3.12	1.27	2	2	0	0	...	0-...	8.2	11	6	3	1	0-0	6	.289
2003—Minnesota (A.L.)	14	10	.583	4.49	1.27	33	33	3	1	0	0-0	212.1	242	111	106	32	28-2	120	.288
Major League totals (9 years)	**116**	**110**	**.513**	**4.32**	**1.27**	**285**	**284**	**33**	**8**	**0**	**0-0**	**1868.1**	**2003**	**956**	**897**	**246**	**364-7**	**1124**	**.274**

RAGGIO, BRADY   P

PERSONAL: Born September 17, 1972, in Los Angeles, Calif. ... 6-4/210. ... Throws right, bats right. ... Full name: Brady John Raggio. ... High school: San Ramon Valley (Los Angeles.). ... Junior college: Chabot College (Calif.).

TRANSACTIONS/CAREER NOTES: Selected by St. Louis Cardinals organization in 20th round of free-agent draft (June 1, 1992). ... Suffered non-baseball injury; missed entire 1993 season. ... Released by Cardinals (December 14, 1998). ... Signed by Texas Rangers organization (January 3, 1999). ... Granted free agency (October 15, 1999). ... Contract purchased by Arizona from Tucson (June 21, 2003). ... Sent outright to Tucson (July 20, 2003).

CAREER HITTING: 0-for-4 (.000), 0 R, 0 2B, 0 3B, 0 HR, 1 RBI.

Year League	W	L	Pct.	ERA	WHIP	G	GS	CG	ShO	Hld.	Sv.-Opp.	IP	H	R	ER	HR	BB-IBB	SO	Avg.
1992—Ariz. Cardinals (Ariz.)	4	3	.571	3.54	1.20	14	6	3	0	...	1-...	48.1	51	26	19	1	7-1	48	.264
1993—											Did not play.								
1994—New Jersey (NYP)	3	0	1.000	1.67	1.19	4	4	0	0	...	0-...	27.0	28	7	5	0	4-0	20	.255
—Madison (Midw.)	4	3	.571	3.21	1.14	11	11	1	0	...	0-...	67.1	63	31	24	8	14-1	66	.247
1995—Peoria (Midw.)	3	0	1.000	1.85	0.90	8	8	3	0	...	0-...	48.2	42	13	10	1	2-0	34	.237
—St. Pete. (FSL)	2	3	.400	3.80	1.18	20	3	0	0	...	0-...	47.1	43	24	20	2	13-2	25	.243
1996—Arkansas (Texas)	9	10	.474	3.22	1.23	26	24	4	1	...	0-...	162.1	160	68	58	17	40-2	123	.261
1997—Louisville (A.A.)	8	11	.421	4.17	1.28	22	22	2	0	...	0-...	138.0	145	68	64	18	32-0	91	.274
—St. Louis (N.L.)	1	2	.333	6.89	1.91	15	4	0	0	0	0-0	31.1	44	24	24	1	16-0	21	.336
1998—Memphis (PCL)	8	9	.471	3.07	1.23	24	23	2	1	...	0-...	152.1	156	57	52	11	31-0	100	.271
—St. Louis (N.L.)	1	1	.500	15.43	3.57	4	1	0	0	0	0-0	7.0	22	12	12	1	3-0	3	.579
1999—Oklahoma (PCL)	6	11	.353	5.14	1.44	30	24	4	2 *	...	1-...	168.0	193	100	96	16	49-1	114	.290
2002—											Did not play.								
2003—Arizona (N.L.)	0	0	...	6.48	1.80	10	0	0	0	3	1-1	8.1	9	6	6	1	6-1	8	.290
—Tucson (PCL)	4	4	.500	3.49	1.20	18	7	0	0	...	0-...	56.2	60	27	22	4	8-0	32	.268
Major League totals (3 years)	**2**	**3**	**.400**	**8.10**	**2.14**	**29**	**5**	**0**	**0**	**3**	**1-1**	**46.2**	**75**	**42**	**42**	**3**	**25-1**	**32**	**.375**

RAINES JR., TIM   OF

PERSONAL: Born August 31, 1979, in Memphis, Tenn. ... 5-10/183. ... Bats both, throws right. ... Full name: Timothy Raines Jr.. ... High school: Seminole (Sanford, Fla.).

TRANSACTIONS/CAREER NOTES: Selected by Baltimore Orioles organization in sixth round of free-agent draft (June 2, 1998). ... Contract purchased by Baltimore from Ottawa (August 22, 2003).

2003 GAMES PLAYED BY POSITION (MLB): OF—18, DH—1.

Year Team (League)	Pos.	G	AB	R	H	2B	3B	HR	RBI	BB	SO	HBP	GDP	SB-CS	Avg.	OBP	SLG	OPS	E	Pct.
1998—GC Orioles (GCL)	OF	56	197	40	48	7	4	1	13	30	53	12	0	37-4	.244	.377	.335	.712	3	.978
1999—Delmarva (S. Atl.)	OF	117	415	80	103	24	8	2	49	71	130	3	1	49-16	.248	.359	.359	.718	10	.961
2000—Frederick (Carolina)	OF	127	457	89	108	21	3	2	36	67	106	13	8	81-19	.236	.348	.309	.657	9	.972
2001—Frederick (Carolina)	OF	23	84	15	21	3	1	3	13	13	23	0	2	14-4	.250	.351	.417	.767	1	.976
—Bowie (East.)	OF	65	254	46	74	14	1	4	30	34	60	3	3	29-10	.291	.380	.402	.782	4	.976
—Rochester (Int'l)	OF	40	133	19	34	5	1	2	12	11	30	0	2	11-3	.256	.313	.353	.666	1	.986
—Baltimore (A.L.)	OF	7	23	6	4	2	0	0	0	3	8	0	0	3-0	.174	.269	.261	.530	0	1.000
2002—Bowie (East.)	OF	123	491	66	128	17	4	5	25	34	101	2	8	33-15	.261	.310	.342	.652	6	.978
2003—Bowie (East.)	OF-DH	66	247	44	76	15	4	4	26	21	40	5	3	28-6	.308	.371	.449	.820	3	.976
—Ottawa (Int'l)	OF	52	214	37	64	11	5	3	23	19	37	1	3	23-9	.299	.357	.439	.797	1	.993
—Baltimore (A.L.)	OF-DH	20	43	4	6	1	1	0	2	2	12	1	2	0-0	.140	.196	.209	.405	1	.974
Major League totals (2 years)		**27**	**66**	**10**	**10**	**3**	**1**	**0**	**2**	**5**	**20**	**1**	**2**	**3-0**	**.152**	**.222**	**.227**	**.449**	**1**	**.980**

RAMIREZ, ARAMIS   3B

PERSONAL: Born June 25, 1978, in Santo Domingo, Dominican Republic. ... 6-1/212. ... Bats right, throws right. ... Full name: Aramis Nin Ramirez. ... Name pronounced: ah-RAH-mis.

TRANSACTIONS/CAREER NOTES: Signed as non-drafted free agent by Pittsburgh Pirates organization (November 7, 1994). ... On suspended list (July 24-29, 1998). ... On Pittsburgh disabled list (August 10-September 4, 1998); included rehabilitation assignment to Nashville (August 27). ... On Pittsburgh disabled list (August 29, 2000-remainder of season). ... Traded by Pirates with OF Kenny Lofton and cash to Chicago Cubs for IF Jose Hernandez, P Matt Bruback and a player to be named (July 22, 2003).

2003 GAMES PLAYED BY POSITION (MLB): 3B—159.

R

| | | | BATTING | | | | | | | | | | | | | | | | FIELDING | |
Year	Team (League)	Pos.	G	AB	R	H	2B	3B	HR	RBI	BB	SO	HBP	GDP	SB-CS	Avg.	OBP	SLG	OPS	E	Pct.
1995—Dom. Pirates (DSL)	3B	64	214	41	63	13	0	11	54	42	26	...	...	2-...	.294	...	.509	...	19	.886
1996—Erie (N.Y.-Penn)	3B	61	223	37	68	14	4	9	42	31	41	7	7	0-0	.305	.403	.525	.928	17	.896
— Augusta (S. Atl.)	3B	6	20	3	4	1	0	1	2	1	7	2	0	0-2	.200	.304	.400	.704	2	.833
1997—Lynchburg (Caro.)	3B-DH	137	482	85	134	24	2	29	*114	80	103	12	12	5-3	.278	.390	.517	.907	*39	.897
1998—Nashville (PCL)	3B-SS-DH	47	168	19	46	10	0	5	18	24	28	4	3	0-2	.274	.374	.423	.796	8	.932
— Pittsburgh (N.L.)	3B	72	251	23	59	9	1	6	24	18	72	4	3	0-1	.235	.296	.351	.646	9	.941
1999—Nashville (PCL)	3B	131	460	92	151	35	1	21	74	73	56	9	11	5-3	.328	.425	.546	.971	*42	.884
— Pittsburgh (N.L.)	3B	18	56	2	10	2	1	0	7	6	9	0	0	0-0	.179	.254	.250	.504	3	.930
2000—Pittsburgh (N.L.)	3B	73	254	19	65	15	2	6	35	10	36	5	9	0-0	.256	.293	.402	.695	14	.917
— Nashville (PCL)	3B	44	167	28	59	12	2	4	23	11	26	4	5	2-1	.353	.407	.521	.928	9	.930
2001—Pittsburgh (N.L.)	3B	158	603	83	181	40	0	34	112	40	100	8	9	5-4	.300	.350	.536	.885	25	.945
2002—Pittsburgh (N.L.)	3B-DH	142	522	51	122	26	0	18	71	29	95	8	17	2-0	.234	.279	.387	.666	19	.946
2003—Pittsburgh (N.L.)	3B	96	375	44	105	25	1	12	67	25	68	7	17	1-1	.280	.330	.448	.778	23	.924
— Chicago (N.L.)	3B	63	232	31	60	7	1	15	39	17	31	3	4	1-1	.259	.314	.491	.805	10	.939
Major League totals (6 years)		622	2293	253	602	124	6	91	355	145	411	35	59	9-7	.263	.312	.441	.753	103	.937

RAMIREZ, ERASMO   P

PERSONAL: Born April 29, 1976, in Santa Ana, Calif. ... 6-0/180. ... Throws left, bats left. ... High school: Saddleback (Calif.). ... College: Cal State Fullerton.

TRANSACTIONS/CAREER NOTES: Selected by San Francisco Giants organization in 11th round of free-agent draft (June 2, 1998). ... Traded by Giants with P Todd Ozias and OF Chris Magruder to Texas Rangers for IF Andres Galarraga (July 24, 2001).

CAREER HITTING: 0-for-0 (.000), 0 R, 0 2B, 0 3B, 0 HR, 0 RBI.

Year	League	W	L	Pct.	ERA	WHIP	G	GS	CG	ShO	Hld.	Sv.-Opp.	IP	H	R	ER	HR	BB-IBB	SO	Avg.
1998—Bakersfield (Calif.)	1	1	.500	3.38	0.75	14	0	0	0	...	3-...	21.1	10	8	8	0	6-0	17	.143
— Salem-Keizer (NW)	0	1	.000	3.72	1.09	9	2	0	0	...	0-...	19.1	19	11	8	3	2-0	23	.247
1999—San Jose (Calif.)	2	0	1.000	2.67	0.87	31	0	0	0	...	5-...	57.1	42	18	17	2	8-0	52	.206
2000—Shreveport (Texas)	0	5	.000	6.44	1.72	39	2	0	0	...	1-...	58.2	80	45	42	7	21-5	46	.340
2001—San Jose (Calif.)	3	2	.600	3.41	0.88	17	0	0	0	...	1-...	31.2	23	14	12	2	5-0	33	.193
— Shreveport (Texas)	2	0	1.000	2.16	0.90	22	1	0	0	...	1-...	33.1	25	10	8	1	5-0	39	.205
— Tulsa (Texas)	2	1	.667	4.41	1.35	12	0	0	0	...	1-...	16.1	17	8	8	3	5-0	18	.270
2002—Tulsa (Texas)	4	2	.667	3.00	1.09	34	0	0	0	...	2-...	54.0	51	23	18	1	8-0	34	.254
— Oklahoma (PCL)	4	1	.800	1.29	0.90	25	0	0	0	...	1-...	21.0	15	5	3	0	4-1	17	.195
2003—Frisco (Texas)	1	0	1.000	6.00	1.67	3	0	0	0	...	0-...	3.0	4	2	2	1	1-0	4	.286
— Oklahoma (PCL)	2	1	.667	1.53	1.08	22	0	0	0	...	4-...	35.1	36	8	6	0	2-0	20	.257
— Texas (A.L.)	3	1	.750	3.86	1.12	34	0	0	0	2	0-1	49.0	46	21	21	4	9-0	28	.251
Major League totals (1 year)	3	1	.750	3.86	1.12	34	0	0	0	2	0-1	49.0	46	21	21	4	9-0	28	.251

RAMIREZ, HORACIO   P

PERSONAL: Born November 24, 1979, in Carson, Calif. ... 6-1/170. ... Throws left, bats left. ... High school: Inglewood (Calif.).

TRANSACTIONS/CAREER NOTES: Selected by Atlanta Braves organization in fifth round of free-agent draft (June 3, 1997). ... On disabled list (May 3, 2001-remainder of season). ... On Atlanta disabled list (March 22-June 18, 2002); included rehabilitation assignment to Macon (May 30) and Greenville (June 15).

CAREER HITTING: 6-for-61 (.098), 3 R, 0 2B, 1 3B, 0 HR, 2 RBI.

Year	League	W	L	Pct.	ERA	WHIP	G	GS	CG	ShO	Hld.	Sv.-Opp.	IP	H	R	ER	HR	BB-IBB	SO	Avg.
1997—GC Braves (GCL)	3	3	.500	2.25	1.09	8	8	0	0	...	0-...	44.0	30	13	11	1	18-0	61	.192
1998—Macon (S. Atl.)	1	7	.125	5.86	1.55	12	12	0	0	...	0-...	55.1	70	50	36	8	16-0	38	.310
— Eugene (NW)	2	7	.222	6.31	1.81	16	8	0	0	...	0-...	55.2	84	51	39	4	17-0	39	.346
1999—Macon (S. Atl.)	6	3	.667	2.67	1.22	17	14	1	1	...	0-...	77.2	70	30	23	6	25-0	43	.248
2000—Myrtle Beach (Caro.)	15	8	.652	3.22	1.20	27	26	3	2	...	0-...	148.1	136	57	53	14	42-0	125	.242
2001—Greenville (Sou.)	1	1	.500	4.91	1.70	3	3	0	0	...	0-...	14.2	17	8	8	2	8-0	17	.309
2002—Macon (S. Atl.)	0	2	.000	6.00	2.17	2	1	0	0	...	0-...	6.0	11	10	4	0	2-0	5	.355
— Greenville (Sou.)	9	5	.643	3.03	1.27	16	16	0	0	...	0-...	92.0	85	41	31	5	32-0	64	.253
2003—Atlanta (N.L.)	12	4	.750	4.00	1.39	29	29	1	0	0	0-0	182.1	181	91	81	21	72-10	100	.263
Major League totals (1 year)	12	4	.750	4.00	1.39	29	29	1	0	0	0-0	182.1	181	91	81	21	72-10	100	.263

RAMIREZ, JULIO   OF

PERSONAL: Born August 10, 1977, in San Juan de la Maguana, Dominican Republic. ... 5-11/170. ... Bats right, throws right. ... Full name: Julio Cesar Ramirez. ... High school: Escuela Otilia Pelaez (Santo Domingo, Dominican Republic).

TRANSACTIONS/CAREER NOTES: Signed as non-drafted free agent by Florida Marlins organization (December 6, 1993). ... On Calgary disabled list (April 15-May 2 and July 18-August 14, 2000). ... Traded by Marlins to Chicago White Sox for OF Jeff Abbott (December 10, 2000). ... On Charlotte disabled list (August 13-20, 2001). ... Released by White Sox (March 13, 2002). ... Signed by Anaheim Angels organization (March 16, 2002). ... On Anaheim disabled list (June 16-September 1, 2002); included rehabilitation assignment to Salt Lake (August 15-September 1). ... Released by Angels (November 6, 2002). ... Re-signed by Angels (2003). ... Sent outright to Salt Lake (April 23, 2003).

2003 GAMES PLAYED BY POSITION (MLB): OF—5, DH—1.

| | | | BATTING | | | | | | | | | | | | | | | | FIELDING | |
Year	Team (League)	Pos.	G	AB	R	H	2B	3B	HR	RBI	BB	SO	HBP	GDP	SB-CS	Avg.	OBP	SLG	OPS	E	Pct.
1994—Dom. Marlins (DSL)	OF	67	274	54	75	18	0	7	32	28	41	...	...	29-...	.274	...	.416	...	10	.936
1995—GC Marlins (GCL)	OF	48	204	35	58	9	4	2	13	13	42	1	2	17-6	.284	.330	.397	.727	2	.983
1996—GC Marlins (GCL)	OF	43	174	35	50	5	4	0	16	15	34	3	0	26-8	.287	.354	.362	.716	2	.980
— Brevard County (FSL)	OF	17	61	11	15	0	1	0	2	4	18	0	1	2-3	.246	.288	.279	.567	1	.933
1997—Kane Co. (Midw.)	OF	99	376	70	96	18	7	14	53	37	122	5	1	41-6	.255	.329	.452	.781	4	.979
1998—Brevard County (FSL)	OF	135	559	90	156	20	12	13	58	45	147	4	3	71-27	.279	.336	.428	.764	8	.979
1999—Portland (East.)	OF	138	*568	87	148	30	10	13	64	39	150	2	5	*64-14	.261	.308	.417	.725	•11	.969
— Florida (N.L.)	OF	15	21	3	3	1	0	0	2	1	6	0	0	0-1	.143	.182	.190	.372	1	.950
2000—Calgary (PCL)	OF	94	350	45	93	18	3	7	52	21	86	3	5	20-14	.266	.310	.394	.704	*11	.954
2001—Chicago (A.L.)	OF	22	37	2	3	0	0	0	1	2	15	0	0	0-0	.081	.128	.081	.209	1	.978
— Charlotte (Int'l)	OF	88	319	36	69	11	1	8	25	20	80	2	1	15-6	.216	.266	.332	.598	6	.962
2002—Salt Lake (PCL)	OF	39	139	17	38	3	5	2	10	4	31	1	2	8-3	.273	.299	.410	.709	2	.975
— Anaheim (A.L.)	OF-DH	29	32	6	9	1	1	1	7	2	14	1	0	0-2	.281	.343	.438	.780	0	1.000
2003—Anaheim (A.L.)	OF-DH	6	2	1	0	0	0	0	0	0	5	0	0	0-0	.000	.000	.000	.000	1	.750
— Salt Lake (PCL)	OF-DH	110	402	50	112	17	6	10	48	12	86	5	7	16-6	.279	.304	.425	.730	7	.975
American League totals (3 years)		57	71	9	12	1	1	1	8	4	29	1	0	0-2	.169	.224	.239	.463	2	.974
National League totals (1 year)		15	21	3	3	1	0	0	2	1	6	0	0	0-1	.143	.182	.190	.372	1	.950
Major League totals (4 years)		72	92	12	15	1	1	1	10	5	35	1	0	2-3	.163	.214	.228	.443	3	.969

RAMIREZ, MANNY — OF

PERSONAL: Born May 30, 1972, in Santo Domingo, Dominican Republic. ... 6-0/213. ... Bats right, throws right. ... Full name: Manuel Aristides Ramirez. ... Name pronounced: ruh-MEER-ez. ... High school: George Washington (New York).

TRANSACTIONS/CAREER NOTES: Selected by Cleveland Indians organization in first round (13th pick overall) of free-agent draft (June 3, 1991). ... On disabled list (July 10, 1992-remainder of season). ... On suspended list (June 8-11, 1999). ... On Cleveland disabled list (May 30-July 13, 2000); included rehabilitation assignments to Akron (June 16-23) and Buffalo (July 6-13). ... Granted free agency (October 27, 2000). ... Signed by Boston Red Sox (December 13, 2000). ... On Boston disabled list (May 14-June 25, 2002); included rehabilitation assignment to Pawtucket (June 13-25).

2003 GAMES PLAYED BY POSITION (MLB): OF—128, DH—26.

Year	Team (League)	Pos.	G	AB	R	H	2B	3B	HR	RBI	BB	SO	HBP	GDP	SB-CS	Avg.	OBP	SLG	OPS	E	Pct.
1991—Burlington (Appal.)		OF	59	215	44	70	11	4	* 19	* 63	34	41	6	4	7-8	.326	.426	.679	1.105	3	.966
1992—Kinston (Caro.)		OF	81	291	52	81	18	4	13	63	45	74	4	9	1-3	.278	.379	.502	.881	6	.956
1993—Cant./Akr. (Eastern)		OF	89	344	67	117	32	0	17	79	45	68	2	11	2-2	.340	.414	.581	.996	5	.967
—Charlotte (Int'l)		OF	40	145	38	46	12	0	14	36	27	35	2	1	1-1	.317	.424	.690	1.113	3	.961
—Cleveland (A.L.)		DH-OF	22	53	5	9	1	0	2	5	2	8	0	3	0-0	.170	.200	.302	.502	0	1.000
1994—Cleveland (A.L.)		OF-DH	91	290	51	78	22	0	17	60	42	72	0	6	4-2	.269	.357	.521	.878	1	.994
1995—Cleveland (A.L.)		OF-DH	137	484	85	149	26	1	31	107	75	112	5	13	6-6	.308	.402	.558	.960	5	.978
1996—Cleveland (A.L.)		OF-DH	152	550	94	170	45	3	33	112	85	104	3	18	8-5	.309	.399	.582	.981	9	.970
1997—Cleveland (A.L.)		OF-DH	150	561	99	184	40	0	26	88	79	115	7	19	2-3	.328	.415	.538	.953	7	.975
1998—Cleveland (A.L.)		OF-DH	150	571	108	168	35	2	45	145	76	121	6	18	5-3	.294	.377	.599	.976	7	.977
1999—Cleveland (A.L.)		OF-DH	147	522	131	174	34	3	44	* 165	96	131	13	12	2-4	.333	.442	*.663	1.105	7	.975
2000—Cleveland (A.L.)		OF-DH	118	439	92	154	34	2	38	122	86	117	3	9	1-1	.351	.457	*.697	1.154	2	.986
—Akron (East.)		DH	1	2	1	1	0	0	1	2	2	1	0	0	0-0	.500	.750	2.000	2.750	...	...
—Buffalo (Int'l)		DH	5	11	5	5	1	0	3	7	6	1	0	1	0-0	.455	.647	1.364	2.011	...	...
2001—Boston (A.L.)		DH-OF	142	529	93	162	33	2	41	125	81	147	8	9	0-1	.306	.405	.609	1.014	0	1.000
2002—Boston (A.L.)		OF-DH	120	436	84	152	31	0	33	107	73	85	8	13	0-0	*.349	*.450	.647	1.097	5	.959
—Pawtucket (Int'l)		OF	11	30	2	3	1	0	1	2	8	9	1	1	0-0	.100	.308	.233	.541	0	1.000
2003—Boston (A.L.)		OF-DH	154	569	117	185	36	1	37	104	97	94	8	22	3-1	.325	*.427	.587	1.014	4	.982
Major League totals (11 years)			1383	5004	959	1585	337	14	347	1140	792	1106	61	142	31-26	.317	.413	.598	1.010	47	.978

RAMOS, MARIO — P

PERSONAL: Born October 19, 1977, in Aurora, Ill. ... 5-11/180. ... Throws left, bats left. ... Full name: Mario Martin Ramos. ... High school: Pflugersville High (Texas). ... College: Rice.

TRANSACTIONS/CAREER NOTES: Selected by Oakland Athletics organization in sixth round of free-agent draft (June 2, 1999). ... Traded by A's with C Gerald Laird, 1B Jason Hart and OF Ryan Ludwick to Texas Rangers for P Mike Venafro and 1B Carlos Pena (January 14, 2002). ... Recalled by Texas from Oklahoma (June 19, 2003). ... Optioned to Oklahoma by Texas (June 30, 2003). ... Recalled by Texas from Frisco (September 30, 2003).

CAREER HITTING: 0-for-1 (.000), 0 R, 0 2B, 0 3B, 0 HR, 0 RBI.

Year	League	W	L	Pct.	ERA	WHIP	G	GS	CG	ShO	Hld.	Sv.-Opp.	IP	H	R	ER	HR	BB-IBB	SO	Avg.
2000—Modesto (Calif.)		12	5	.706	2.90	1.19	26	24	1	1	...	0-...	152.0	131	63	49	6	50-4	134	.234
—Midland (Texas)		2	0	1.000	1.32	1.10	4	4	0	0	...	0-...	27.1	24	6	4	0	6-0	19	.242
2001—Midland (Texas)		8	1	.889	3.07	1.06	15	15	0	0	...	0-...	93.2	71	37	32	7	28-0	68	.204
—Sacramento (PCL)		8	3	.727	3.14	1.26	13	13	1	1	...	0-...	80.1	74	32	28	5	27-0	82	.241
2002—Oklahoma (PCL)		3	8	.273	7.40	1.77	34	19	0	0	...	0-...	121.2	162	107	100	20	53-0	75	.321
2003—Texas (A.L.)		1	1	.500	6.23	1.85	3	3	0	0	0	0-0	13.0	11	9	9	3	13-0	8	.224
—Oklahoma (PCL)		0	3	.000	6.40	1.58	5	5	0	0	...	0-...	32.1	39	24	23	1	12-0	22	.305
—Frisco (Texas)		8	7	.533	3.86	1.30	19	19	0	0	...	0-...	121.1	130	59	52	9	28-1	103	.277
Major League totals (1 year)		1	1	.500	6.23	1.85	3	3	0	0	0	0-0	13.0	11	9	9	3	13-0	8	.224

RANDA, JOE — 3B

PERSONAL: Born December 18, 1969, in Milwaukee, Wis. ... 5-11/190. ... Bats right, throws right. ... Full name: Joseph Gregory Randa. ... High school: Kettle-Moraine (Wales, Wis.). ... College: Tennessee.

TRANSACTIONS/CAREER NOTES: Selected by California Angels organization in 30th round of free-agent draft (June 5, 1989); did not sign. ... Selected by Kansas City Royals organization in 11th round of free-agent draft (June 3, 1991). ... On Kansas City disabled list (May 5-27, 1996); included rehabilitation assignment to Omaha (May 23-27). ... Traded by Royals with P Jeff Granger, P Jeff Martin and P Jeff Wallace to Pittsburgh Pirates for SS Jay Bell and 1B Jeff King (December 13, 1996). ... On Pittsburgh disabled list (June 28-July 27, 1997); included rehabilitation assignment to Calgary (July 25-27). ... Selected by Arizona Diamondbacks in third round (57th pick overall) of expansion draft (November 18, 1997). ... Traded by Diamondbacks with P Matt Drews and 3B Gabe Alvarez to Detroit Tigers for 3B Travis Fryman (November 18, 1997). ... Traded by Tigers to New York Mets for P Willie Blair (December 4, 1998). ... Traded by Mets to Royals for OF Juan LeBron (December 10, 1998). ... Placed on 15-day disabled list by Kansas City (July 8, 2003). ... Reinstated from 15-day disabled list (July 23, 2003).

2003 GAMES PLAYED BY POSITION (MLB): 3B—129, DH—2.

Year	Team (League)	Pos.	G	AB	R	H	2B	3B	HR	RBI	BB	SO	HBP	GDP	SB-CS	Avg.	OBP	SLG	OPS	E	Pct.
1991—Eugene (Northwest)		3B	72	275	53	* 93	20	2	11	59	46	29	6	8	6-1	.338	* .438	.545	.984	14	.923
1992—Appleton (Midwest)		3B	72	266	55	80	13	0	5	43	34	37	6	6	6-2	.301	.385	.406	.791	12	.941
—Baseball City (FSL)		3B-SS	51	189	22	52	7	0	1	12	12	21	2	4	4-3	.275	.324	.328	.652	6	.961
1993—Memphis (Sou.)		3B	131	505	74	149	31	5	11	72	39	64	3	10	8-7	.295	.343	.442	.784	25	.942
1994—Omaha (A.A.)		3B	127	455	65	125	27	2	10	51	30	49	8	18	5-2	.275	.327	.409	.736	* 24	.945
1995—Kansas City (A.L.)		3B-2B	34	70	6	12	2	0	1	5	6	17	0	2	0-1	.171	.237	.243	.480	3	.952
—Omaha (A.A.)		3B	64	233	33	64	10	2	8	33	22	33	2	9	2-2	.275	.341	.438	.779	6	.958
1996—Kansas City (A.L.)		3-2-1-D	110	337	36	102	24	1	6	47	26	47	1	10	13-4	.303	.351	.433	.784	10	.960
—Omaha (A.A.)		3B	3	9	1	1	0	1	0	0	1	1	0	0	0-0	.111	.200	.333	.533	0	1.000
1997—Pittsburgh (N.L.)		3B-2B	126	443	58	134	27	9	7	60	41	64	6	10	4-2	.302	.366	.451	.817	21	.948
—Calgary (PCL)		3B	11	44	4	4	1	0	1	4	3	4	0	1	0-0	.364	.500	.727	1.227	1	.900
1998—Detroit (A.L.)		3-2-D-1	138	460	56	117	21	2	9	50	41	70	7	9	8-7	.254	.323	.367	.690	7	.981
1999—Kansas City (A.L.)		3B	156	628	92	197	36	8	16	84	50	80	3	15	5-4	.314	.363	.473	.836	22	.952
2000—Kansas City (A.L.)		3B	158	612	88	186	29	4	15	106	36	68	6	19	6-3	.304	.343	.438	.781	19	.957
2001—Kansas City (A.L.)		3B-DH-2B	151	581	59	147	34	2	13	83	42	80	6	15	3-2	.253	.307	.386	.693	13	.966
2002—Kansas City (A.L.)		3B-DH	151	549	63	155	36	5	11	80	46	69	9	13	2-1	.282	.341	.426	.768	10	.972
2003—Kansas City (A.L.)		3B-DH	131	502	80	146	31	1	16	72	41	61	7	12	1-0	.291	.348	.452	.800	7	.980
American League totals (8 years)			1029	3739	480	1062	213	23	87	527	288	490	39	95	38-22	.284	.338	.423	.761	91	.966
National League totals (1 year)			126	443	58	134	27	9	7	60	41	64	6	10	4-2	.302	.366	.451	.817	21	.948
Major League totals (9 years)			1155	4182	538	1196	240	32	94	587	329	554	45	105	42-24	.286	.341	.426	.767	112	.963

R

RANDALL, SCOTT   P

PERSONAL: Born October 29, 1975, in Fullerton, Calif. ... 6-3/225. ... Throws right, bats right. ... Full name: Scott Phillip Randall. ... High school: Dos Pueblos (Goleta, Calif.). ... College: UC-Santa Barbara.

TRANSACTIONS/CAREER NOTES: Selected by Colorado Rockies organization in 11th round of free-agent draft (June 1, 1995). ... Traded by Rockies to Minnesota Twins for OF Chris Latham (December 7, 1999). ... Claimed on waivers by Texas Rangers (June 14, 2000). ... Granted free agency (October 15, 2001). ... On Edmonton disabled list (June 19-July 1, 2002). ... Granted free agency (October 15, 2002). ... Signed by Cincinnati Reds (December 24, 2002).

CAREER HITTING: 1-for-4 (.250), 0 R, 0 2B, 0 3B, 0 HR, 0 RBI.

Year League	W	L	Pct.	ERA	WHIP	G	GS	CG	ShO	Hld.	Sv.-Opp.	IP	H	R	ER	HR	BB-IBB	SO	Avg.
1995— Portland (East.)	7	3	.700	1.99	1.09	15	15	1	0	...	0-...	95.0	76	35	21	2	28-1	78	.217
1996— Asheville (S. Atl.)	14	4	.778	2.74	1.11	24	24	1	1	...	0-...	154.1	121	53	47	11	50-3	136	.219
1997— Salem (Caro.)	9	10	.474	3.84	1.32	27	26	2	1	...	0-...	176.0	167	93	75	8	66-3	128	.249
1998— New Haven (East.)	10	14	.417	3.83	1.35	29	29	7	2	...	0-...	202.0	210	102	86	14	62-1	135	.272
1999— Colo. Springs (PCL)	1	4	.200	7.93	2.00	9	9	0	0	...	0-...	42.0	62	41	37	5	22-1	25	.348
— Carolina (Sou.)	5	8	.385	3.43	1.35	16	16	3	1	...	0-...	99.2	101	52	38	6	34-2	102	.264
2000— Salt Lake (PCL)	5	3	.625	5.47	1.68	14	14	0	0	...	0-...	75.2	105	52	46	9	22-0	54	.329
— Oklahoma (PCL)	2	3	.400	5.42	1.73	16	10	0	0	...	0-...	74.2	96	49	45	8	33-1	35	.330
2001— Salem (Caro.)	0	0	...	4.50	1.67	2	0	0	0	...	0-...	6.0	9	3	3	0	1-0	7	.346
— Carolina (Sou.)	0	0	...	0.00	0.83	1	1	0	0	...	0-...	6.0	5	0	0	0	0-0	3	.238
— Colo. Springs (PCL)	6	5	.545	5.48	1.53	19	12	0	0	...	0-...	70.2	74	48	43	11	34-3	47	.263
2002— New Britain (East.)	2	0	1.000	3.48	0.94	5	5	0	0	...	0-...	31.0	25	13	12	3	4-0	19	.216
— Edmonton (PCL)	12	0	1.000	3.25	1.27	19	15	2	0	...	0-...	105.1	110	47	38	6	24-0	54	.267
2003— Louisville (Int'l)	10	4	.714	4.63	1.54	30	20	0	0	...	3-...	136.0	170	76	70	9	39-0	86	.309
— Cincinnati (N.L.)	2	5	.286	6.51	1.63	15	2	0	0	2	0-1	27.2	34	20	20	1	11-3	25	.304
Major League totals (1 year)	**2**	**5**	**.286**	**6.51**	**1.63**	**15**	**2**	**0**	**0**	**2**	**0-1**	**27.2**	**34**	**20**	**20**	**1**	**11-3**	**25**	**.304**

RANDOLPH, STEPHEN   P

PERSONAL: Born May 1, 1974, in Okinawa, Japan. ... 6-3/185. ... Throws left, bats left. ... Full name: Stephen LeCharles Randolph. ... High school: James Bowie (Simms, Texas). ... College: Texas.

TRANSACTIONS/CAREER NOTES: Selected by New York Yankees organization in 18th round of free-agent draft (June 1, 1995). ... Selected by Arizona Diamondbacks from Yankees organization in Rule 5 major league draft (December 15, 1997). ... On Tucson disabled list (June 1-July 25, 1999); included rehabilitation assignment to Arizona League Diamondbacks (July 16-25). ... On El Paso disabled list (May 4-September 12, 2000). ... Granted free agency (October 15, 2001). ... Re-signed by Diamondbacks as a minor league free agent (December 10, 2001). ... Placed on 15-day disabled list by Arizona (May 4, 2003). ... Sent to Tucson on rehab assignment (May 17, 2003). ... Recalled by Arizona from Tucson (May 30, 2003).

CAREER HITTING: 0-for-3 (.000), 0 R, 0 2B, 0 3B, 0 HR, 0 RBI.

Year League	W	L	Pct.	ERA	WHIP	G	GS	CG	ShO	Hld.	Sv.-Opp.	IP	H	R	ER	HR	BB-IBB	SO	Avg.
1995— GC Yankees (GCL)	4	0	1.000	2.22	1.11	8	3	0	0	...	0-...	24.1	11	7	6	1	16-0	34	.145
— Oneonta (N.Y.-Penn)	0	3	.000	7.48	1.94	6	6	0	0	...	0-...	21.2	19	22	18	0	23-0	31	.229
1996— Greensboro (S. Atl.)	4	7	.364	3.77	1.59	32	17	0	0	...	0-...	100.1	64	46	42	8	96-1	111	.188
1997— Tampa (FSL)	4	7	.364	3.87	1.44	34	13	1	0	...	1-...	95.1	74	55	41	8	63-5	108	.217
1998— High Desert (Calif.)	4	4	.500	3.59	1.32	17	17	0	0	...	0-...	85.1	71	44	34	6	42-0	104	.231
— Tucson (PCL)	1	3	.250	3.18	1.54	17	1	0	0	...	0-...	22.2	16	11	8	1	19-2	23	.205
1999— El Paso (Texas)	2	2	.500	2.64	1.40	8	8	0	0	...	0-...	44.1	39	14	13	1	23-0	38	.244
— Tucson (PCL)	0	7	.000	6.91	1.90	11	10	1	0	...	0-...	41.2	47	37	32	7	32-1	26	.281
— Ariz. D'backs (Ariz.)	0	0	...	4.50	1.17	2	2	0	0	...	0-...	6.0	5	3	3	0	2-0	7	.217
2000— Tucson (PCL)	0	0	...	8.78	2.25	5	3	0	0	...	0-...	13.1	11	13	13	3	19-0	6	.229
2001— Tucson (PCL)	2	0	1.000	6.33	2.02	18	0	0	0	...	0-...	21.1	24	15	15	2	19-1	16	.282
— El Paso (Texas)	5	6	.455	5.16	1.63	18	14	1	1	...	0-...	75.0	69	50	43	11	53-1	66	.244
2002— Tucson (PCL)	15	7	.682	3.47	1.42	28	27	1	1	...	0-...	163.1	151	70	63	15	81-2	129	.250
2003— Tucson (PCL)	1	0	1.000	3.86	1.18	7	0	0	0	...	0-...	9.1	8	5	4	1	3-0	6	.229
— Arizona (N.L.)	8	1	.889	4.05	1.55	50	0	0	0	2	0-0	60.0	50	28	27	7	43-3	50	.226
Major League totals (1 year)	**8**	**1**	**.889**	**4.05**	**1.55**	**50**	**0**	**0**	**0**	**2**	**0-0**	**60.0**	**50**	**28**	**27**	**7**	**43-3**	**50**	**.226**

RANSOM, CODY   SS

PERSONAL: Born February 17, 1976, in Mesa, Ariz. ... 6-2/190. ... Bats right, throws right. ... Full name: Bryan Cody Ransom. ... High school: Chandler (Ariz.). ... College: Grand Canyon (Ari.).

TRANSACTIONS/CAREER NOTES: Selected by San Francisco Giants organization in ninth round of free-agent draft (June 2, 1998).

2003 GAMES PLAYED BY POSITION (MLB): SS—12.

Year Team (League)	Pos.	G	AB	R	H	2B	3B	HR	RBI	BB	SO	HBP	GDP	SB-CS	Avg.	OBP	SLG	OPS	E	Pct.
1998— Salem-Keizer (NW)	SS	71	236	52	55	12	7	6	27	43	56	2	4	19-6	.233	.351	.419	.770	* 24	.928
1999— Bakersfield (Calif.)	SS	99	356	69	98	12	6	11	47	54	108	8	2	15-8	.275	.382	.435	.817	30	.938
— Shreveport (Texas)	SS	14	41	6	5	0	0	2	4	4	22	1	0	0-0	.122	.208	.268	.477	3	.953
2000— Shreveport (Texas)	SS	130	459	58	92	21	3	7	47	40	141	0	9	9-3	.200	.263	.305	.568	25	.958
2001— Fresno (PCL)	SS	134	469	77	113	21	6	23	78	44	137	0	10	17-2	.241	.303	.458	.762	12	.980
— San Francisco (N.L.)	SS	9	7	1	0	0	0	0	0	0	5	0	0	0-0	.000	.000	.000	.000	0	1.000
2002— Fresno (PCL)	SS	135	449	53	93	18	4	13	46	47	151	3	5	6-4	.207	.283	.352	.635	15	.973
— San Francisco (N.L.)	SS	7	3	2	2	0	0	0	1	1	1	0	0	0-0	.667	.750	.667	1.417	0	1.000
2003— Fresno (PCL)	SS	112	396	56	100	16	4	12	50	45	91	3	14	14-4	.253	.331	.404	.735	20	.959
— San Francisco (N.L.)	SS	20	27	7	6	1	0	1	1	1	11	0	0	0-0	.222	.250	.370	.620	1	.963
Major League totals (3 years)		36	37	10	8	1	0	1	2	2	17	0	0	0-0	.216	.256	.324	.581	1	.973

REAMES, BRITT   P

PERSONAL: Born August 19, 1973, in Seneca, S.C. ... 5-10/180. ... Throws right, bats right. ... Full name: William Britt Reames. ... Name pronounced: REEMS. ... High school: Seneca (S.C.). ... College: The Citadel.

TRANSACTIONS/CAREER NOTES: Selected by St. Louis Cardinals organization in 17th round of free-agent draft (June 1, 1995). ... On disabled list (April 4, 1997-entire season; and April 10, 1998-entire season). ... On Potomac disabled list (April 23-June 10 and June 14-August 10, 1999). ... On Arkansas disabled list (April 19-29, 2000). ... On Memphis disabled list (July 7-14 and July 20-August 3, 2000). ... Traded by Cardinals with 3B Fernando Tatis to Montreal Expos for P Dustin Hermanson and P Steve Kline (December 14, 2000).

CAREER HITTING: 5-for-39 (.128), 3 R, 0 2B, 0 3B, 1 HR, 3 RBI.

Year	League	W	L	Pct.	ERA	WHIP	G	GS	CG	ShO	Hld.	Sv.-Opp.	IP	H	R	ER	HR	BB-IBB	SO	Avg.
1995— New Jersey (NYP)		2	1	.667	1.52	1.04	5	5	0	0	...	0-...	29.2	19	7	5	1	12-0	42	.181
— Savannah (S. Atl.)		3	5	.375	3.46	1.02	10	10	1	0	...	0-...	54.2	41	23	21	7	15-0	63	.198
1996— Peoria (Midw.)		15	7	.682	1.90	0.86	25	25	2	• 1	...	0-...	161.0	97	43	34	5	41-0	* 167	.170
1997—											Did not play.									
1998—											Did not play.									
1999— Potomac (Caro.)		3	2	.600	3.19	1.50	10	8	0	0	...	0-...	36.2	34	21	13	2	21-0	22	.250
2000— Arkansas (Texas)		2	3	.400	6.13	1.61	8	8	0	0	...	0-...	39.2	46	28	27	4	18-0	39	.291
— Memphis (PCL)		6	2	.750	2.28	1.00	13	13	2	1	...	0-...	75.0	55	20	19	2	20-0	77	.212
— St. Louis (N.L.)		2	1	.667	2.88	1.30	8	7	0	0	0	0-0	40.2	30	17	13	4	23-1	31	.207
2001— Montreal (N.L.)		4	8	.333	5.59	1.57	41	13	0	0	6	0-1	95.0	101	68	59	16	48-3	86	.273
— Ottawa (Int'l)		4	3	.571	3.50	1.11	8	8	1	0	...	0-...	54.0	47	24	21	4	13-0	38	.242
2002— Montreal (N.L.)		1	4	.200	5.03	1.59	42	6	0	0	6	0-1	68.0	70	42	38	8	38-6	76	.266
— Ottawa (Int'l)		3	2	.600	2.79	1.07	7	7	0	0	...	0-...	42.0	31	16	13	3	14-0	26	.207
2003— Montreal (N.L.)		0	0	...	27.00	4.50	2	0	0	0	0	0-0	1.1	4	4	4	0	2-0	1	.500
— Edmonton (PCL)		5	13	.278	5.42	1.63	25	20	0	0	...	0-...	118.0	146	80	71	8	46-1	86	.299
Major League totals (4 years)		**7**	**13**	**.350**	**5.00**	**1.54**	**93**	**26**	**0**	**0**	**12**	**0-2**	**205.0**	**205**	**131**	**114**	**28**	**111-10**	**194**	**.261**

REBOULET, JEFF   IF

PERSONAL: Born April 30, 1964, in Dayton, Ohio. ... 6-0/174. ... Bats right, throws right. ... Full name: Jeffrey Allen Reboulet. ... Name pronounced: REB-uh-lay. ... High school: Alter (Kettering, Ohio). ... College: Louisiana State.

TRANSACTIONS/CAREER NOTES: Selected by Houston Astros organization in 26th round of free-agent draft (June 3, 1985); did not sign. ... Selected by Minnesota Twins organization in 10th round of free-agent draft (June 2, 1986). ... Granted free agency (October 4, 1996). ... Signed by Baltimore Orioles organization (January 30, 1997). ... Traded by Orioles to Kansas City Royals for a player to be named later (December 12, 1999). ... Granted free agency (October 31, 2000). ... Signed by Los Angeles Dodgers organization (February 20, 2001). ... On Los Angeles disabled list (July 21-September 1, 2002); included rehabilitation assignment to Las Vegas (August 10-August 29). ... Granted free agency (October 29, 2002). ... Signed by Orioles organization (January 29, 2003). ... Released by Orioles (March 28, 2003). ... Signed by Pittsburgh Pirates (April 18, 2003).

2003 GAMES PLAYED BY POSITION (MLB): 2B—76, 3B—7.

Year	Team (League)	Pos.	G	AB	R	H	2B	3B	HR	RBI	BB	SO	HBP	GDP	SB-CS	Avg.	OBP	SLG	OPS	E	Pct.
1986— Visalia (Calif.)		SS	72	254	54	73	13	1	0	29	54	33	1	4	14-11	.287	.412	.346	.758	20	.939
1987— Orlando (South.)	...............2B-3B-SS		129	422	52	108	15	1	1	35	58	56	1	9	9-5	.256	.347	.303	.651	26	.958
1988— Orlando (South.)	....	SS	125	439	57	112	24	2	4	41	53	55	3	9	18-8	.255	.338	.346	.684	30	.950
— Portland (PCL)		2B-SS	4	12	0	1	0	0	0	1	3	2	0	1	0-0	.083	.267	.083	.350	1	.955
1989— Portland (PCL)	....	2-3-S-O	26	65	9	16	1	0	0	3	12	11	0	2	2-1	.246	.354	.262	.616	7	.935
— Orlando (South.)	............2B-SS-OF		81	291	43	63	5	1	0	26	49	33	1	7	11-6	.216	.328	.271	.569	22	.942
1990— Orlando (South.)	....	SS	97	287	43	66	12	2	2	28	57	37	2	5	10-5	.230	.357	.307	.664	12	.968
1991— Portland (PCL)	....	SS	134	391	50	97	27	3	3	46	57	52	2	9	5-2	.248	.345	.355	.701	* 32	.951
1992— Portland (PCL)	....	SS	48	161	21	46	11	1	2	21	35	18	1	7	3-3	.286	.414	.404	.818	7	.968
— Minnesota (A.L.)	..........S-3-2-0-D		73	137	15	26	7	1	1	16	23	26	1	0	3-2	.190	.311	.277	.588	5	.979
1993— Minnesota (A.L.)	..........S-3-2-0-D		109	240	33	62	8	0	1	15	35	37	2	6	5-5	.258	.356	.304	.660	6	.983
1994— Minnesota (A.L.)	........S-2-1-3-0-D		74	189	28	49	11	1	3	23	18	23	1	6	0-0	.259	.327	.376	.703	7	.976
1995— Minnesota (A.L.)	..........S-3-1-2-C		87	216	39	63	11	0	4	23	27	34	1	3	1-2	.292	.373	.398	.771	4	.988
1996— Minnesota (A.L.)	........S-3-2-1-0-D		107	234	20	52	9	0	0	23	25	34	1	10	4-2	.222	.298	.261	.558	2	.992
1997— Baltimore (A.L.)		2-S-3-O	99	228	26	54	9	0	4	27	23	44	1	3	3-0	.237	.307	.329	.636	7	.975
1998— Baltimore (A.L.)	..........2B-SS-3B		79	126	20	31	6	0	1	8	19	34	2	3	0-1	.246	.351	.317	.669	6	.966
1999— Baltimore (A.L.)	..........3B-2B-SS		99	154	25	25	4	0	0	4	33	29	2	1	1-0	.162	.317	.188	.506	2	.991
2000— Kansas City (A.L.)		2-3-S-D	66	182	29	44	7	0	0	14	23	32	0	8	3-1	.242	.325	.280	.605	9	.965
2001— Los Angeles (N.L.)		S-2-3-O	94	214	35	57	15	2	3	22	33	48	1	3	0-1	.266	.367	.397	.764	10	.960
2002— Los Angeles (N.L.)		2-S-3-O	38	48	3	10	3	0	0	2	6	13	0	1	0-0	.208	.291	.271	.562	4	.892
— Las Vegas (PCL)		2B-3B-SS	18	63	10	16	2	0	1	3	6	9	0	1	2-0	.254	.314	.333	.648	2	.966
2003— Nashville (PCL)	....	S-2-3-D	17	49	6	11	1	0	0	2	10	11	0	1	0-3	.224	.356	.245	.601	1	.977
— Pittsburgh (N.L.)		2B-3B	83	261	37	63	10	2	3	25	27	47	4	6	2-1	.241	.321	.330	.650	4	.989
American League totals (9 years)			**793**	**1706**	**235**	**406**	**72**	**2**	**14**	**153**	**226**	**293**	**11**	**40**	**20-13**	**.238**	**.330**	**.307**	**.637**	**48**	**.980**
National League totals (3 years)			**225**	**523**	**75**	**130**	**28**	**4**	**6**	**49**	**66**	**108**	**5**	**10**	**2-2**	**.249**	**.337**	**.352**	**.689**	**18**	**.972**
Major League totals (12 years)			**1018**	**2229**	**310**	**536**	**100**	**6**	**20**	**202**	**292**	**401**	**16**	**50**	**22-15**	**.240**	**.332**	**.318**	**.649**	**66**	**.978**

REDDING, TIM   P

PERSONAL: Born February 12, 1978, in Rochester, N.Y. ... 6-0/195. ... Throws right, bats right. ... Full name: Timothy J. Redding. ... Junior college: Monroe (N.Y.) Community College.

TRANSACTIONS/CAREER NOTES: Selected by Houston Astros organization in 20th round of free-agent draft (June 3, 1997). ... On New Orleans disabled list (August 20-28, 2002).

CAREER HITTING: 15-for-84 (.179), 4 R, 3 2B, 0 3B, 0 HR, 5 RBI.

Year	League	W	L	Pct.	ERA	WHIP	G	GS	CG	ShO	Hld.	Sv.-Opp.	IP	H	R	ER	HR	BB-IBB	SO	Avg.
1998— Auburn (N.Y.-Penn)		7	3	.700	4.52	1.34	16	15	0	0	...	0-...	73.2	49	44	37	2	* 50-0	98	.188
1999— Michigan (Midw.)		8	6	.571	4.97	1.52	43	11	0	0	...	14-...	105.0	84	69	58	4	76-1	144	.221
2000— Kissimmee (Fla. St.)		12	5	.706	2.68	1.18	24	24	0	0	...	0-...	154.2	125	62	46	5	57-1	* 170	.219
— Round Rock (Texas)		2	0	1.000	3.46	1.38	5	5	0	0	...	0-...	26.0	14	12	10	4	22-0	22	.167
2001— Round Rock (Texas)		10	2	.833	2.18	0.98	14	14	1	1	...	0-...	90.2	64	26	22	5	25-0	113	.192
— New Orleans (PCL)		4	1	.800	4.54	1.09	6	6	0	0	...	0-...	37.2	22	21	19	4	19-0	42	.172
— Houston (N.L.)		3	1	.750	5.50	1.54	13	9	0	0	0	0-0	55.2	62	38	34	11	24-0	55	.286
2002— New Orleans (PCL)		3	3	.500	5.21	1.18	11	7	0	0	...	0-...	38.0	32	22	22	6	13-1	50	.232
— Houston (N.L.)		3	6	.333	5.40	1.54	18	14	0	0	0	0-0	73.1	78	49	44	10	35-3	63	.276
2003— Houston (N.L.)		10	14	.417	3.68	1.39	33	32	0	0	0	0-0	176.0	179	85	72	16	65-4	116	.261
Major League totals (3 years)		**16**	**21**	**.432**	**4.43**	**1.45**	**64**	**55**	**0**	**0**	**0**	**0-0**	**305.0**	**319**	**172**	**150**	**37**	**124-7**	**234**	**.269**

REDMAN, MARK   P

PERSONAL: Born January 5, 1974, in San Diego, Calif. ... 6-5/245. ... Throws left, bats left. ... Full name: Mark Allen Redman. ... High school: Escondido (Calif.). ... College: Oklahoma.

TRANSACTIONS/CAREER NOTES: Selected by Detroit Tigers organization in 41st round of free-agent draft (June 1, 1992); did not sign. ... Selected by Minnesota Twins organization in first round (13th pick overall) of free-agent draft (June 1, 1995). ... On Salt Lake disabled list (August 1-8, 1998). ... On Minnesota disabled list (July 25-August

10, 1999). ... On Minnesota disabled list (May 21-July 28, 2001); included rehabilitation assignment to Edmonton (June 15-27). ... Traded by Twins to Tigers for P Todd Jones (July 28, 2001). ... On Detroit disabled list (July 28-August 22, 2001); included rehabilitation assignment to Toledo (August 6-22). ... Traded by Tigers with P Jerrod Fuell to Florida Marlins for P Gary Knotts, P Nate Robertson and P Rob Henkel (January 11, 2003). ... Placed on 15-day disabled list by Florida (April 30, 2003). ... Reinstated from 15-day disabled list (May 30, 2003).

CAREER HITTING: 2-for-70 (.029), 1 R, 0 2B, 0 3B, 0 HR, 1 RBI.

Year — League	W	L	Pct.	ERA	WHIP	G	GS	CG	ShO	Hld.	Sv.-Opp.	IP	H	R	ER	HR	BB-IBB	SO	Avg.
1995— Fort Myers (Fla. St.)	2	1	.667	2.76	1.26	8	5	0	0	...	0-...	32.2	28	13	10	4	13-0	26	.239
1996— Fort Myers (Fla. St.)	3	4	.429	1.85	1.17	13	13	0	0	...	0-...	82.2	63	24	17	1	34-0	75	.220
— New Britain (East.)	7	7	.500	3.81	1.42	16	16	3	0	...	0-...	106.1	101	51	45	5	50-1	96	.251
— Salt Lake (PCL)	0	0	...	9.00	2.25	1	1	0	0	...	0-...	4.0	7	4	4	1	2-0	4	.389
1997— Salt Lake (PCL)	8	* 15	.348	6.31	1.79	29	28	0	0	...	1-...	158.1	204	* 123	111	19	80-3	125	.316
1998— New Britain (East.)	4	2	.667	1.52	1.20	8	8	0	0	...	0-...	47.1	40	11	8	3	17-0	51	.237
— Salt Lake (PCL)	6	7	.462	5.53	1.53	19	18	0	0	...	0-...	99.1	111	75	61	13	41-1	88	.282
1999— Salt Lake (PCL)	9	9	.500	5.05	1.44	24	24	1	0	...	0-...	133.2	141	87	75	12	51-1	114	.272
— Minnesota (A.L.)	1	0	1.000	8.53	1.89	5	1	0	0	0	0-0	12.2	17	13	12	3	7-0	11	.298
2000— Minnesota (A.L.)	12	9	.571	4.76	1.41	32	24	0	0	0	0-0	151.1	168	81	80	22	45-0	117	.281
2001— Minnesota (A.L.)	2	4	.333	4.22	1.55	9	9	0	0	0	0-0	49.0	57	26	23	6	19-0	29	.286
— Edmonton (PCL)	0	0	...	13.50	3.00	1	1	0	0	...	0-...	1.1	3	2	2	0	1-0	0	.500
— Toledo (Int'l)	0	1	.000	5.27	1.10	3	3	0	0	...	0-...	13.2	14	10	8	3	1-0	12	.259
— Detroit (A.L.)	0	2	.000	6.00	1.67	2	2	0	0	0	0-0	9.0	11	6	6	1	4-0	4	.306
2002— Detroit (A.L.)	8	15	.348	4.21	1.29	30	30	3	0	0	0-0	203.0	211	107	95	15	51-2	109	.268
2003— Florida (N.L.)	14	9	.609	3.59	1.22	29	29	3	0	0	0-0	190.2	172	82	76	16	61-3	151	.239
American League totals (4 years)	23	30	.434	4.57	1.39	78	66	3	0	0	0-0	425.0	464	233	216	47	126-2	270	.277
National League totals (1 year)	14	9	.609	3.59	1.22	29	29	3	0	0	0-0	190.2	172	82	76	16	61-3	151	.239
Major League totals (5 years)	37	39	.487	4.27	1.34	107	95	6	0	0	0-0	615.2	636	315	292	63	187-5	421	.265

REDMAN, PRENTICE   OF

PERSONAL: Born August 23, 1979, in Tuscaloosa, Ala. ... 6-3/185. ... Bats right, throws right. ... Full name: Prentice Montezz Redman. ... High school: Tuscaloosa Academy.
TRANSACTIONS/CAREER NOTES: Selected by New York Mets organization in 10th round of free-agent draft (June 1999).
2003 GAMES PLAYED BY POSITION (MLB): OF—10.

											BATTING									FIELDING	
Year — Team (League)	Pos.	G	AB	R	H	2B	3B	HR	RBI	BB	SO	HBP	GDP	SB-CS	Avg.	OBP	SLG	OPS		E	Pct.
1999— Kingsport (Appal.)	OF-1B	58	200	40	59	14	1	6	29	24	42	2	0	16-11	.295	.373	.465	.838		4	.938
2000— Capital City (SAL)	OF	131	497	60	129	19	1	3	46	52	90	3	5	26-10	.260	.332	.320	.652		7	.963
2001— St. Lucie (Fla. St.)	OF	132	495	70	129	18	1	9	65	42	91	6	7	29-8	.261	.322	.356	.678		5	.977
2002— Binghamton (East.)	OF	135	491	79	139	35	2	11	63	59	112	9	0	43-9	.283	.367	.430	.797		5	.979
2003— Norfolk (Int'l)	OF-DH	128	433	60	110	29	2	11	48	40	96	7	5	24-8	.254	.326	.406	.733		5	.978
— New York (N.L.)	OF	15	24	3	3	1	0	1	2	1	9	1	1	2-0	.125	.192	.292	.484		0	1.000
Major League totals (1 year)		15	24	3	3	1	0	1	2	1	9	1	1	2-0	.125	.192	.292	.484		0	1.000

REDMAN, TIKE   OF

PERSONAL: Born March 10, 1977, in Tuscaloosa, Ala. ... 5-11/166. ... Bats left, throws left. ... Full name: Julian Jawonn Redman. ... High school: Tuscaloosa (Ala.) Academy.
TRANSACTIONS/CAREER NOTES: Selected by Pittsburgh Pirates organization in fifth round of free-agent draft (June 4, 1996). ... On Nashville disabled list (April 14-June 20, 2002). ... Released by Pirates (December 18, 2002).
2003 GAMES PLAYED BY POSITION (MLB): OF—54.

											BATTING									FIELDING	
Year — Team (League)	Pos.	G	AB	R	H	2B	3B	HR	RBI	BB	SO	HBP	GDP	SB-CS	Avg.	OBP	SLG	OPS		E	Pct.
1996— GC Pirates (GCL)	OF	26	104	20	31	4	1	1	16	12	12	0	0	15-3	.298	.368	.385	.752		1	.978
— Erie (N.Y.-Penn)	OF	43	170	31	50	4	6	2	21	17	30	0	2	7-3	.294	.353	.424	.776		7	.920
1997— Lynchburg (Caro.)	1B-OF	125	415	55	104	18	5	4	45	45	82	7	8	21-8	.251	.333	.347	.680		6	.975
1998— Lynchburg (Caro.)	OF	131	525	70	135	26	10	6	46	32	73	1	5	36-16	.257	.298	.379	.677		8	.971
1999— Altoona (East.)	OF	136	532	84	143	20	* 12	3	60	52	52	3	6	29-16	.269	.332	.368	.700		9	.972
2000— Nashville (PCL)	OF	121	506	62	132	24	11	4	51	32	73	3	4	24-18	.261	.306	.375	.682		5	.981
— Pittsburgh (N.L.)	OF	9	18	2	6	1	0	1	1	1	7	0	0	1-0	.333	.368	.556	.924		0	1.000
2001— Nashville (PCL)	OF	95	398	53	121	18	10	3	42	24	37	4	6	21-7	.304	.347	.422	.769		7	.970
— Pittsburgh (N.L.)	OF	37	125	8	28	4	1	1	4	4	25	0	2	3-5	.224	.246	.296	.542		2	.980
2002— Nashville (PCL)	OF	76	311	40	84	9	4	2	20	21	24	1	3	16-7	.270	.315	.344	.660		3	.982
2003— Nashville (PCL)	OF-DH	100	360	60	106	12	7	4	29	36	32	0	5	42-9	.294	.357	.400	.757		3	.987
— Pittsburgh (N.L.)	OF	56	230	36	76	16	5	3	19	14	18	2	1	7-3	.330	.374	.483	.857		2	.985
Major League totals (3 years)		102	373	46	110	21	6	5	24	19	50	2	3	11-8	.295	.332	.424	.755		4	.983

REDMOND, MIKE   C

PERSONAL: Born May 5, 1971, in Seattle, Wash. ... 5-11/210. ... Bats right, throws right. ... Full name: Michael Patrick Redmond. ... High school: Gonzaga Prep (Spokane, Wash.). ... College: Gonzaga.
TRANSACTIONS/CAREER NOTES: Signed as a non-drafted free agent by Florida Marlins organization (August 18, 1992). ... On Florida disabled list (August 24-September 8, 1998).
2003 GAMES PLAYED BY POSITION (MLB): C—37, 3B—1, 1B—1.

											BATTING									FIELDING	
Year — Team (League)	Pos.	G	AB	R	H	2B	3B	HR	RBI	BB	SO	HBP	GDP	SB-CS	Avg.	OBP	SLG	OPS		E	Pct.
1993— Kane Co. (Midw.)	C	43	100	10	20	2	0	0	10	6	17	4	1	2-0	.200	.273	.220	.493		1	.996
1994— Kane Co. (Midw.)	C	92	306	39	83	10	0	1	24	26	31	9	10	3-4	.271	.344	.314	.658		6	.992
— Brevard County (FSL)	C	12	42	4	11	4	0	0	2	3	4	1	1	0-0	.262	.326	.357	.683		0	1.000
1995— Portland (East.)	3B-C	105	333	37	85	11	1	3	39	22	27	3	9	2-2	.255	.305	.321	.626		6	.992
1996— Portland (East.)	C	120	394	43	113	22	0	4	44	26	45	5	12	3-4	.287	.335	.373	.708		4	.996
1997— Charlotte (Int'l)	C	22	61	8	13	5	1	1	2	1	10	3	1	0-1	.213	.262	.377	.639		2	.985
— GC Marlins (GCL)	DH	16	55	7	19	3	0	0	5	9	5	3	1	2-0	.345	.463	.400	.863		...	...
— Brevard County (FSL)	1B	5	17	2	0	0	0	0	0	2	2	0	2	0-0	.000	.105	.000	.105		0	1.000
1998— Portland (East.)	C	8	28	7	9	4	0	1	7	2	2	2	2	0-0	.321	.406	.571	.978		1	.983
— Charlotte (Int'l)	C	18	58	4	14	2	0	2	7	0	3	1	3	0-0	.241	.246	.379	.625		0	1.000
— Florida (N.L.)	C	37	118	10	39	9	0	2	12	5	16	2	6	0-0	.331	.368	.458	.826		2	.992

Year Team (League)	Pos.	G	AB	R	H	2B	3B	HR	RBI	BB	SO	HBP	GDP	SB-CS	Avg.	OBP	SLG	OPS	E	Pct.
1999—Florida (N.L.)	C	84	242	22	73	9	0	1	27	26	34	5	8	0-0	.302	.381	.351	.732	4	.992
2000—Florida (N.L.)	C	87	210	17	53	8	1	0	15	13	19	8	5	0-0	.252	.316	.300	.616	2	.996
2001—Florida (N.L.)	C	48	141	19	44	4	0	4	14	13	13	2	6	0-0	.312	.376	.426	.801	2	.994
2002—Florida (N.L.)	C-1B	89	256	19	78	15	0	2	28	21	34	8	4	0-2	.305	.372	.387	.758	4	.993
2003—Florida (N.L.)	C-3B-1B	59	125	12	30	7	1	0	11	7	16	5	2	0-0	.240	.302	.312	.614	1	.995
Major League totals (6 years)		**404**	**1092**	**99**	**317**	**52**	**2**	**9**	**107**	**85**	**132**	**30**	**31**	**0-2**	**.290**	**.355**	**.366**	**.722**	**15**	**.993**

REED, RICK — P

PERSONAL: Born August 16, 1965, in Huntington, W.Va. ... 6-1/195. ... Throws right, bats right. ... Full name: Richard Allen Reed. ... High school: Huntington (W.Va.). ... College: Marshall.

TRANSACTIONS/CAREER NOTES: Selected by Pittsburgh Pirates organization in 26th round of free-agent draft (June 2, 1986). ... On Buffalo disabled list (May 2-13, 1991). ... Granted free agency (April 3, 1992). ... Signed by Kansas City Royals organization (April 4, 1992). ... Granted free agency (August 5, 1993). ... Signed by Texas Rangers organization (August 11, 1993). ... Claimed on waivers by Cincinnati Reds (May 13, 1994). ... On Indianapolis disabled list (May 29-June 9, 1995). ... Granted free agency (October 16, 1995). ... Signed by New York Mets organization (November 7, 1995). ... On New York disabled list (April 12-May 3 and August 9-September 4, 1999); included rehabilitation assignments to Norfolk (August 27-31) and Binghamton (September 1-4). ... On disabled list (June 30-July 17, 2000). ... Granted free agency (November 8, 2000). ... Re-signed by Mets (December 6, 2000). ... Traded by Mets to Minnesota Twins for OF Matt Lawton (July 30, 2001). ... Placed on 15-day disabled list (June 1, 2003). ... Reinstated from 15-day disabled list (June 18, 2003). ... Placed on 15-day disabled list (August 20, 2003). ... Removed from 15-day disabled list (September 7, 2003).

CAREER HITTING: 51-for-297 (.172), 23 R, 9 2B, 0 3B, 2 HR, 24 RBI.

Year League	W	L	Pct.	ERA	WHIP	G	GS	CG	ShO	Hld.	Sv.-Opp.	IP	H	R	ER	HR	BB-IBB	SO	Avg.
1986—GC Pirates (GCL)	0	2	.000	3.75	1.08	8	3	0	0	...	0-...	24.0	20	12	10	0	6-0	15	.233
— Macon (S. Atl.)	0	0	...	2.84	1.11	1	1	0	0	...	0-...	6.1	5	3	2	0	2-0	1	.217
1987—Macon (S. Atl.)	8	4	.667	2.50	1.16	46	0	0	0	...	7-...	93.2	80	38	26	6	29-3	92	.233
1988—Salem (Caro.)	6	2	.750	2.74	1.01	15	8	4	1	...	0-...	72.1	56	28	22	6	17-1	73	.207
— Harrisburg (Eastern)	1	0	1.000	1.13	0.81	2	2	0	0	...	0-...	16.0	11	2	2	0	2-0	17	.190
— Buffalo (A.A.)	5	2	.714	1.64	0.96	10	9	3	2	...	0-...	77.0	62	15	14	0	12-2	50	.221
— Pittsburgh (N.L.)	1	0	1.000	3.00	1.00	2	2	0	0	0	0-0	12.0	10	4	4	1	2-0	6	.233
1989—Buffalo (A.A.)	9	8	.529	3.72	1.26	20	20	3	0	...	0-...	125.2	130	58	52	9	28-0	75	.269
— Pittsburgh (N.L.)	1	4	.200	5.60	1.34	15	7	0	0	0	0-0	54.2	62	35	34	5	11-3	34	.290
1990—Buffalo (A.A.)	7	4	.636	3.46	1.13	15	15	2	2	...	0-...	91.0	82	37	35	4	21-0	63	.244
— Pittsburgh (N.L.)	2	3	.400	4.36	1.38	13	8	1	1	1	1-1	53.2	62	32	26	6	12-6	27	.279
1991—Buffalo (A.A.)	* 14	4	.778	2.15	1.06	25	25	•5	2	...	0-...	167.2	151	45	40	3	26-3	102	.245
— Pittsburgh (N.L.)	0	0	...	10.38	2.08	1	1	0	0	0	0-0	4.1	8	6	5	1	1-0	2	.400
1992—Omaha (Am. Assoc.)	5	4	.556	4.35	1.27	11	10	3	0	...	1-...	62.0	67	33	30	8	12-0	35	.280
— Kansas City (A.L.)	3	7	.300	3.68	1.25	19	18	1	1	0	0-0	100.1	105	47	41	10	20-3	49	.271
1993—Omaha (Am. Assoc.)	11	4	.733	3.09	1.01	19	19	3	* 2	...	0-...	128.1	116	48	44	19	14-1	58	.242
— Kansas City (A.L.)	0	0	...	9.82	1.91	1	0	0	0	0	0-0	3.2	6	4	4	0	1-0	3	.375
— Oklahoma City (A.A.)	1	3	.250	4.19	1.31	5	5	1	0	...	0-...	34.1	43	20	16	2	2-0	21	.309
— Texas (A.L.)	1	0	1.000	2.25	1.75	2	0	0	0	0	0-0	4.0	6	1	1	1	1-0	2	.375
1994—Oklahoma City (A.A.)	1	1	.500	3.86	0.86	2	2	0	0	...	0-...	11.2	10	5	5	0	0-0	8	.222
— Texas (A.L.)	1	1	.500	5.94	1.44	4	3	0	0	0	0-...	16.2	17	13	11	3	7-0	12	.254
— Indianapolis (A.A.)	9	5	.643	4.68	1.29	21	21	3	1	...	0-...	140.1	162	80	73	20	19-0	79	.268
1995—Indianapolis (A.A.)	11	4	.733	3.33	1.13	22	21	3	1	...	0-...	135.0	127	60	50	16	26-2	92	.246
— Cincinnati (N.L.)	0	0	...	5.82	1.24	4	3	0	0	0	0-...	17.0	18	12	11	5	3-0	10	.273
1996—Norfolk (Int'l)	8	10	.444	3.16	1.08	28	28	1	0	...	0-...	182.0	164	72	64	13	33-2	128	.243
1997—New York (N.L.)	13	9	.591	2.89	1.04	33	31	2	0	0	0-0	208.1	186	76	67	19	31-4	113	.239
1998—New York (N.L.)	16	11	.593	3.48	1.12	31	31	2	1	0	0-0	212.1	208	84	82	30	29-2	153	.261
1999—New York (N.L.)	11	5	.688	4.58	1.41	26	26	1	1	0	0-0	149.1	163	77	76	23	47-2	104	.281
— Norfolk (Int'l)	0	1	.000	27.00	4.00	1	1	0	0	...	0-...	3.0	10	9	9	1	2-0	2	.556
— Binghamton (Eastern)	0	0	...	1.80	0.40	1	1	0	0	...	0-...	5.0	1	1	1	1	1-0	5	.063
2000—New York (N.L.)	11	5	.688	4.11	1.23	30	30	0	0	0	0-0	184.0	192	90	84	28	34-3	121	.266
2001—New York (N.L.)	8	6	.571	3.48	1.01	20	20	3	1	0	0-0	134.2	119	53	52	16	17-3	99	.236
— Minnesota (A.L.)	4	6	.400	5.19	1.57	12	12	0	0	0	0-0	67.2	92	45	39	12	14-0	43	.329
2002—Minnesota (A.L.)	15	7	.682	3.78	1.16	33	32	2	1	1	0-0	188.0	192	89	79	32	26-0	121	.259
2003—Minnesota (A.L.)	6	12	.333	5.07	1.36	27	21	2	1	0	0-1	135.0	155	80	76	21	29-2	71	.285
American League totals (6 years)	**30**	**33**	**.476**	**4.38**	**1.30**	**98**	**86**	**5**	**3**	**1**	**0-1**	**515.1**	**573**	**279**	**251**	**79**	**98-5**	**301**	**.279**
National League totals (10 years)	**63**	**43**	**.594**	**3.85**	**1.18**	**175**	**159**	**9**	**4**	**1**	**1-1**	**1030.1**	**1028**	**469**	**441**	**134**	**187-23**	**669**	**.261**
Major League totals (15 years)	**93**	**76**	**.550**	**4.03**	**1.22**	**273**	**245**	**14**	**7**	**2**	**1-2**	**1545.2**	**1601**	**748**	**692**	**213**	**285-28**	**970**	**.267**

REED, STEVE — P

PERSONAL: Born March 11, 1966, in Los Angeles, Calif. ... 6-2/212. ... Throws right, bats right. ... Full name: Steven Vincent Reed. ... High school: Chatsworth (Calif.). ... College: Lewis-Clark (Idaho) State.

TRANSACTIONS/CAREER NOTES: Signed as non-drafted free agent by San Francisco Giants organization (June 24, 1988). ... On disabled list (July 17-August 13, 1990). ... Selected by Colorado Rockies in third round (60th pick overall) of expansion draft (November 17, 1992). ... Granted free agency (December 21, 1997). ... Signed by Giants (December 24, 1997). ... Traded by Giants with OF Jacob Cruz to Cleveland Indians for P Jose Mesa, IF Shawon Dunston and P Alvin Morman (July 23, 1998). ... Traded by Indians with P Steve Karsay to Atlanta Braves for P John Rocker and 3B Troy Cameron (June 22, 2001). ... Granted free agency (November 5, 2001). ... Signed by San Diego Padres organization (January 23, 2002). ... Traded by Padres with P Jason Middlebrook to New York Mets for P Bobby M. Jones, P Josh Reynolds and OF Jay Bay (July 31, 2002). ... Granted free agency (October 28, 2002). ... Signed by Colorado Rockies (January 24, 2003).

CAREER HITTING: 3-for-23 (.130), 0 R, 0 2B, 0 3B, 0 HR, 1 RBI.

Year League	W	L	Pct.	ERA	WHIP	G	GS	CG	ShO	Hld.	Sv.-Opp.	IP	H	R	ER	HR	BB-IBB	SO	Avg.
1988—Pocatello (Pio.)	4	1	.800	2.54	1.09	31	0	0	0	...	* 13-...	46.0	42	20	13	3	8-1	49	.237
1989—Clinton (Midw.)	5	3	.625	1.05	0.97	60	0	0	0	...	26-...	94.2	54	16	11	1	38-10	104	.171
— San Jose (Calif.)	0	0	...	0.00	0.50	2	0	0	0	...	0-...	2.0	0	0	0	0	1-0	3	.000
1990—Shreveport (Texas)	3	1	.750	1.64	1.21	45	1	0	0	...	8-...	60.1	53	20	11	2	20-6	59	.230
1991—Shreveport (Texas)	2	0	1.000	0.83	0.92	15	0	0	0	...	7-...	21.2	17	2	2	1	3-0	26	.218
— Phoenix (PCL)	2	3	.400	4.31	1.31	41	0	0	0	...	6-...	56.1	62	33	27	5	12-0	46	.279
1992—Shreveport (Texas)	1	0	1.000	0.62	0.62	27	0	0	0	...	23-...	29.0	18	3	2	1	4-0	33	.175
— Phoenix (PCL)	0	1	.000	3.48	1.19	29	0	0	0	...	20-...	31.0	27	13	12	2	10-3	30	.237
— San Francisco (N.L.)	1	0	1.000	2.30	1.02	18	0	0	0	1	0-0	15.2	13	5	4	2	3-0	11	.220
1993—Colorado (N.L.)	9	5	.643	4.48	1.30	64	0	0	0	9	3-6	84.1	80	47	42	13	30-5	51	.259
— Colo. Springs (PCL)	0	0	...	0.00	0.89	11	0	0	0	...	7-...	12.1	8	1	0	0	3-1	10	.182

R

Year League	W	L	Pct.	ERA	WHIP	G	GS	CG	ShO	Hld.	Sv.-Opp.	IP	H	R	ER	HR	BB-IBB	SO	Avg.
1994— Colorado (N.L.)	3	2	.600	3.94	1.64	61	0	0	0	14	3-10	64.0	79	33	28	9	26-3	51	.306
1995— Colorado (N.L.)	5	2	.714	2.14	0.98	71	0	0	0	11	3-6	84.0	61	24	20	8	21-3	79	.203
1996— Colorado (N.L.)	4	3	.571	3.96	1.13	70	0	0	0	*22	0-6	75.0	66	38	33	11	19-0	51	.239
1997— Colorado (N.L.)	4	6	.400	4.04	1.22	63	0	0	0	10	6-13	62.1	49	28	28	10	27-1	43	.219
1998— San Francisco (N.L.)	2	1	.667	1.48	0.90	50	0	0	0	13	1-5	54.2	30	10	9	4	19-5	50	.160
— Cleveland (A.L.)	2	2	.500	6.66	1.32	20	0	0	0	8	0-1	25.2	26	19	19	4	8-0	23	.260
1999— Cleveland (A.L.)	3	2	.600	4.23	1.44	63	0	0	0	8	0-3	61.2	69	33	29	10	20-5	44	.285
2000— Cleveland (A.L.)	2	0	1.000	4.34	1.41	57	0	0	0	9	0-1	56.0	58	30	27	7	21-4	39	.269
2001— Cleveland (A.L.)	1	1	.500	3.62	1.17	31	0	0	0	6	0-1	27.1	22	11	11	3	10-2	21	.212
— Atlanta (N.L.)	2	2	.500	3.48	1.39	39	0	0	0	5	1-1	31.0	30	14	12	3	13-3	25	.259
2002— San Diego (N.L.)	2	4	.333	1.98	1.05	40	0	0	0	11	1-3	41.0	33	9	9	2	10-2	36	.228
— New York (N.L.)	0	1	.000	2.08	1.04	24	0	0	0	6	0-1	26.0	23	6	6	0	4-1	14	.240
2003— Colorado (N.L.)	5	3	.625	3.27	1.34	67	0	0	0	14	0-2	63.1	59	24	23	9	26-3	39	.254
American League totals (4 years)	8	5	.615	4.54	1.37	171	0	0	0	31	0-6	170.2	175	93	86	24	59-11	127	.264
National League totals (10 years)	37	29	.561	3.20	1.20	567	0	0	0	116	18-53	601.1	523	238	214	71	198-26	450	.237
Major League totals (12 years)	45	34	.570	3.50	1.24	738	0	0	0	147	18-59	772.0	698	331	300	95	257-37	577	.244

REESE, POKEY   2B

PERSONAL: Born June 10, 1973, in Columbia, S.C. ... 5-11/180. ... Bats right, throws right. ... Full name: Calvin Reese Jr.. ... High school: Lower Richland (Hopkins, S.C.).

TRANSACTIONS/CAREER NOTES: Selected by Cincinnati Reds organization in first round (20th pick overall) of free-agent draft (June 3, 1991). ... On disabled list (June 23-July 25, 1995; September 17, 1996-remainder of season; and July 31, 1998-remainder of season). ... Traded by Reds with P Dennys Reyes to Colorado Rockies for P Gabe White and P Luke Hudson (December 18, 2001). ... Traded by Rockies to Boston Red Sox for C Scott Hatteberg (December 19, 2001). ... Granted free agency (December 21, 2001). ... Signed by Pittsburgh Pirates organization (January 30, 2002). ... On disabled list (April 20-May 5, 2002). ... Placed on Emergency disabled list (May 14, 2003).

2003 GAMES PLAYED BY POSITION (MLB): 2B—33.

Year Team (League)	Pos.	G	AB	R	H	2B	3B	HR	RBI	BB	SO	HBP	GDP	SB-CS	Avg.	OBP	SLG	OPS	FIELDING E	Pct.
1991— Princeton (Appal.)	SS	62	231	30	55	8	3	3	27	23	44	0	4	10-8	.238	.305	.338	.642	* 31	.885
1992— Char., W.Va. (SAL)	SS	106	380	50	102	19	3	6	53	24	75	5	2	19-8	.268	.315	.382	.696	34	.932
1993— Chattanooga (Sou.)	SS	102	345	35	73	17	4	3	37	23	77	1	2	8-5	.212	.258	.310	.568	25	.951
1994— Chattanooga (Sou.)	SS	134	484	77	130	23	4	12	49	43	75	7	6	21-4	.269	.336	.407	.743	38	.939
1995— Indianapolis (A.A.)	SS	89	343	51	82	21	1	10	46	36	81	4	3	8-5	.239	.316	.394	.710	27	.935
1996— Indianapolis (A.A.)	SS-3B	79	280	26	65	16	0	1	23	21	46	5	10	5-2	.232	.294	.300	.594	22	.944
1997— Cincinnati (N.L.)	SS-2B-3B	128	397	48	87	15	0	4	26	31	82	5	1	25-7	.219	.284	.287	.571	15	.969
— Indianapolis (A.A.)	SS-2B	17	72	12	17	2	0	4	11	9	12	0	2	4-0	.236	.321	.431	.752	3	.966
1998— Cincinnati (N.L.)	3B-SS-2B	59	133	20	34	2	2	1	16	14	28	0	3	3-2	.256	.322	.323	.645	8	.941
1999— Cincinnati (N.L.)	2B-SS	149	585	85	167	37	5	10	52	35	81	6	9	38-7	.285	.330	.417	.747	7	.991
2000— Cincinnati (N.L.)	2B	135	518	76	132	20	6	12	46	45	86	6	8	29-3	.255	.319	.386	.705	14	.980
2001— Cincinnati (N.L.)	SS-2B	133	428	50	96	20	2	9	40	34	82	3	7	25-4	.224	.284	.343	.627	15	.975
2002— Pittsburgh (N.L.)	2B	119	421	46	111	25	0	4	50	41	81	3	4	12-1	.264	.330	.352	.681	8	.988
2003— Pittsburgh (N.L.)	2B	37	107	9	23	2	0	1	12	9	31	0	2	6-0	.215	.271	.262	.533	6	.969
Major League totals (7 years)		760	2589	334	650	121	15	41	242	209	471	23	34	138-24	.251	.310	.357	.667	73	.979

REICHERT, DAN   P

PERSONAL: Born July 12, 1976, in Monterey, Calif. ... 6-3/170. ... Throws right, bats right. ... Full name: Daniel Robert Reichert. ... Name pronounced: RIE-curt. ... High school: Turlock (Calif.). ... College: Pacific.

TRANSACTIONS/CAREER NOTES: Selected by Kansas City Royals organization in first round (seventh pick overall) of free-agent draft (June 3, 1997). ... On Kansas City disabled list (August 25, 1999-remainder of season). ... Claimed on waivers by Tampa Bay Devil Rays (September 20, 2002). ... Released by Devil Rays (March 12, 2003). ... Signed by Toronto Blue Jays organization (July 11, 2003).

CAREER HITTING: 1-for-9 (.111), 0 R, 0 2B, 0 3B, 0 HR, 0 RBI.

Year League	W	L	Pct.	ERA	WHIP	G	GS	CG	ShO	Hld.	Sv.-Opp.	IP	H	R	ER	HR	BB-IBB	SO	Avg.
1997— Spokane (N'west)	3	4	.429	2.84	1.47	9	9	0	0	...	0-...	38.0	40	25	12	2	16-0	39	.255
1998— Wichita (Texas)	1	4	.200	9.75	2.25	8	8	0	0	...	0-...	36.0	52	40	39	7	29-1	24	.344
— Lansing (Midw.)	1	1	.500	3.28	1.26	13	6	0	0	...	0-...	35.2	25	16	13	0	20-0	35	.198
— Wilmington (Caro.)	2	0	1.000	3.21	1.21	2	2	0	0	...	0-...	14.0	13	5	5	0	4-0	10	.255
— Omaha (PCL)	1	1	.500	4.67	0.92	3	3	0	0	...	0-...	17.1	14	10	9	2	2-0	11	.222
1999— Omaha (PCL)	9	2	.818	3.71	1.27	17	17	1	0	...	0-...	111.2	92	51	46	9	50-0	123	.228
— Kansas City (A.L.)	2	2	.500	9.08	2.18	8	8	0	0	0	0-0	36.2	48	38	37	2	32-1	20	.327
2000— Kansas City (A.L.)	8	10	.444	4.70	1.62	44	18	1	1	4	2-6	153.1	157	92	80	15	91-1	94	.271
2001— Kansas City (A.L.)	8	8	.500	5.63	1.61	27	19	0	0	1	0-0	123.0	131	83	77	14	67-2	77	.278
— Omaha (PCL)	1	5	.167	8.27	1.87	10	5	1	0	...	0-...	32.2	45	30	30	4	16-0	30	.333
2002— Kansas City (A.L.)	3	5	.375	5.32	1.55	30	6	0	0	6	0-0	66.0	77	48	39	10	25-2	36	.306
— Omaha (PCL)	0	0	...	5.40	2.00	5	0	0	0	...	0-...	5.0	6	3	3	0	4-1	3	.353
— Wichita (Texas)	0	1	.000	11.45	2.27	8	0	0	0	...	0-...	11.0	16	15	14	0	9-0	11	.340
2003— Syracuse (Int'l)	4	3	.571	3.57	1.55	41	0	0	0	...	0-...	58.0	55	26	23	2	35-1	60	.255
— Toronto (A.L.)	0	0	...	6.06	2.20	15	0	0	0	2	0-1	16.1	28	12	11	2	8-3	13	.389
Major League totals (5 years)	21	25	.457	5.55	1.68	124	51	1	1	13	2-7	395.1	441	273	244	43	223-9	240	.290

REITH, BRIAN   P

PERSONAL: Born February 28, 1978, in Fort Wayne, Ind. ... 6-5/220. ... Throws right, bats right. ... Full name: Brian Eric Reith. ... Name pronounced: REETH. ... High school: Concordia Lutheran (Fort Wayne, Ind.).

TRANSACTIONS/CAREER NOTES: Selected by New York Yankees organization in sixth round of free-agent draft (June 4, 1996). ... Traded by Yankees with 3B Drew Henson, OF Jackson Melian and P Ed Yarnall to Cincinnati Reds for P Denny Neagle and OF Mike Frank (July 12, 2000). ... On Louisville disabled list (June 8-16, 2001). ... On Louisville disabled list (May 13-20, 2002). ... Claimed on waivers by Philadelphia Phillies (July 11, 2002). ... Claimed on waivers by Reds (August 6, 2002).

CAREER HITTING: 3-for-19 (.158), 0 R, 0 2B, 0 3B, 0 HR, 2 RBI.

Year— League	W	L	Pct.	ERA	WHIP	G	GS	CG	ShO	Hld.	Sv.-Opp.	IP	H	R	ER	HR	BB-IBB	SO	Avg.
1996— GC Yankees (GCL)	2	3	.400	4.13	1.44	10	4	0	0	...	0-...	32.2	31	16	15	1	16-0	21	.254
1997— GC Yankees (GCL)	4	2	.667	2.86	1.33	12	11	1	0	...	0-...	63.0	70	28	20	1	14-0	40	.281
1998— Greensboro (S. Atl.)	6	7	.462	2.28	0.00	20	20	3	1	...	0-...	118.1	86	42	30	7	32-0	116	.196
1999— Tampa (FSL)	9	9	.500	4.70	1.50	26	23	0	0	...	0-...	139.2	174	87	73	12	35-1	101	.307
2000— Tampa (FSL)	9	4	.692	2.18	1.12	18	18	1	1	...	0-...	119.2	101	39	29	4	33-0	100	.227
— Dayton (Midw.)	2	1	.667	2.88	1.19	5	5	0	0	...	0-...	34.1	33	12	11	2	8-0	30	.252
— Chattanooga (Sou.)	1	3	.250	3.90	1.40	5	5	0	0	...	0-...	30.0	31	14	13	3	11-0	29	.277
2001— Chattanooga (Sou.)	6	4	.600	3.97	1.39	18	18	1	1	...	0-...	104.1	103	63	46	10	42-1	89	.259
— Cincinnati (N.L.)	0	7	.000	7.81	1.79	9	8	0	0	0	0-0	40.1	56	37	35	13	16-0	22	.333
— Louisville (Int'l)	0	0	...	3.60	1.60	1	1	0	0	...	0-...	5.0	7	2	2	0	1-0	6	.368
2002— Scran./W.B. (I.L.)	0	4	.000	7.00	2.06	4	4	0	0	...	0-...	18.0	26	18	14	1	11-0	13	.329
— Louisville (Int'l)	8	9	.471	4.75	1.38	23	22	0	0	...	0-...	132.2	137	76	70	15	46-3	99	.267
2003— Louisville (Int'l)	3	1	.750	1.96	0.91	16	0	0	0	...	1-...	23.0	12	9	5	1	9-2	28	.152
— Cincinnati (N.L.)	2	3	.400	4.11	1.58	42	1	0	0	4	1-1	61.1	61	32	28	8	36-6	39	.263
Major League totals (2 years)	2	10	.167	5.58	1.66	51	9	0	0	4	1-1	101.2	117	69	63	21	52-6	61	.293

REITSMA, CHRIS — P

PERSONAL: Born December 31, 1977, in Minneapolis, Minn. ... 6-5/235. ... Throws right, bats right. ... Full name: Christopher Michael Reitsma. ... Name pronounced: REETS-muh. ... High school: Calgary (Alta.) Christian.

TRANSACTIONS/CAREER NOTES: Selected by Boston Red Sox organization as "sandwich pick" between first and second round of free-agent draft (June 4, 1996); pick received as compensation for Toronto Blue Jays signing P Erik Hanson. ... On disabled list (June 5-September 8, 1997). ... On disabled list (April 8-May 3, 1999). ... Selected by Tampa Bay Devil Rays from Red Sox organization in Rule 5 major league draft (December 13, 1999). ... Returned to Red Sox (March 28, 2000). ... Traded by Tampa Bay Devil Rays with P John Curtice to Cincinnati Reds for OF Dante Bichette (August 31, 2000).

CAREER HITTING: 9-for-86 (.105), 3 R, 1 2B, 0 HR, 5 RBI.

Year— League	W	L	Pct.	ERA	WHIP	G	GS	CG	ShO	Hld.	Sv.-Opp.	IP	H	R	ER	HR	BB-IBB	SO	Avg.
1996— GC Red Sox (GCL)	3	1	.750	1.35	0.94	7	6	0	0	...	0-...	26.2	24	7	4	0	1-0	32	.229
1997— Michigan (Midw.)	4	1	.800	2.90	1.41	9	9	0	0	...	0-...	49.2	57	23	16	4	13-0	41	.285
1998— Sarasota (Fla. St.)	0	0	...	2.84	1.34	8	8	0	0	...	0-...	12.2	12	6	4	0	5-0	9	.245
1999— Sarasota (Fla. St.)	4	10	.286	5.61	1.53	19	19	0	0	...	0-...	96.1	116	71	60	11	31-1	79	.294
2000— Sarasota (Fla. St.)	3	4	.429	3.66	1.16	11	11	0	0	...	0-...	64.0	57	29	26	3	17-0	47	.238
— Trenton (East.)	7	2	.778	2.58	1.09	14	14	1	0	...	0-...	90.2	78	28	26	7	21-1	58	.232
2001— Cincinnati (N.L.)	7	15	.318	5.29	1.42	36	29	0	0	1	0-0	182.0	209	121	107	23	49-6	96	.288
2002— Cincinnati (N.L.)	6	12	.333	3.64	1.37	32	21	1	1	0	0-0	138.1	144	73	56	17	45-5	84	.267
— Louisville (Int'l)	2	0	1.000	3.86	1.19	3	3	1	0	...	0-...	21.0	17	10	9	2	8-1	13	.224
2003— Louisville (Int'l)	1	2	.333	4.00	1.50	4	4	0	0	...	0-...	18.0	22	10	8	1	5-0	11	.293
— Cincinnati (N.L.)	9	5	.643	4.29	1.32	57	3	0	0	3	12-18	84.0	92	41	40	14	19-6	53	.281
Major League totals (3 years)	22	32	.407	4.52	1.38	125	53	1	1	4	12-18	404.1	445	235	203	54	113-17	233	.280

RELAFORD, DESI — IF

PERSONAL: Born September 16, 1973, in Valdosta, Ga. ... 5-9/180. ... Bats both, throws right. ... Full name: Desmond Lamont Relaford. ... High school: Sandalwood (Jacksonville).

TRANSACTIONS/CAREER NOTES: Selected by Seattle Mariners organization in fourth round of free-agent draft (June 3, 1991). ... Traded by Mariners to Philadelphia Phillies for P Terry Mulholland (July 31, 1996). ... On Philadelphia disabled list (June 17-September 13, 1999); included rehabilitation assignment to Clearwater (September 4-13). ... Traded by Phillies to San Diego Padres for a player to be named later (August 4, 2000); Phillies acquired IF David Newhan to complete deal (August 7, 2000). ... Claimed on waivers by New York Mets (October 12, 2000). ... Traded by Mets with OF Tsuyoshi Shinjo to San Francisco Giants for P Shawn Estes (December 16, 2001). ... Traded by Giants with cash to Mariners for 3B David Bell (January 25, 2002). ... Granted free agency (December 21, 2002). ... Signed by Kansas City Royals (January 10, 2003).

2003 GAMES PLAYED BY POSITION (MLB): 2B—89, 3B—33, OF—20, SS—6, DH—5.

Year— Team (League)	Pos.	G	AB	R	H	2B	3B	HR	RBI	BB	SO	HBP	GDP	SB-CS	Avg.	OBP	SLG	OPS	E	Pct.
1991— Ariz. Mariners (Ariz.)	2B-SS	46	163	36	44	7	3	0	18	22	24	1	0	17-3	.270	.351	.350	.700	24	.885
1992— Peninsula (Caro.)	SS	130	445	53	96	18	1	3	34	39	88	1	7	27-7	.216	.277	.281	.558	* 52	.913
1993— Jacksonville (Sou.) 2B-3B-SS	133	472	49	115	16	4	8	47	50	103	7	4	16-12	.244	.323	.345	.668	§ 38	.935
1994— Jacksonville (Sou.)	SS	37	143	24	29	7	3	3	11	22	28	0	2	10-1	.203	.305	.357	.662	4	.979
— Riverside (Calif.)	SS	99	374	95	116	27	5	5	59	78	78	4	7	27-6	.310	.429	.449	.878	36	.921
1995— Port City (Sou.) SS-2B-DH	90	352	51	101	11	2	7	27	41	58	2	4	25-9	.287	.365	.389	.754	31	.930
— Tacoma (PCL)	2B-SS	30	113	20	27	5	1	2	7	13	24	0	2	6-0	.239	.313	.354	.666	6	.960
1996— Tacoma (PCL) 2B-SS-DH	93	317	27	65	12	0	4	32	23	58	1	7	10-6	.205	.259	.281	.539	20	.960
— Philadelphia (N.L.)	SS-2B	15	40	2	7	2	0	0	1	3	9	0	1	1-0	.175	.233	.225	.458	2	.959
— Scran./W.B. (I.L.)	SS	21	85	12	20	4	1	1	11	8	19	1	0	7-1	.235	.305	.341	.646	6	.938
1997— Scran./W.B. (I.L.)	SS	131	517	82	138	34	4	9	53	43	77	7	12	29-8	.267	.329	.400	.729	34	.942
— Philadelphia (N.L.)	SS	15	38	3	7	1	2	0	6	5	6	0	0	3-0	.184	.279	.316	.595	1	.977
1998— Philadelphia (N.L.)	SS	142	494	45	121	25	3	5	41	33	87	3	9	9-5	.245	.293	.338	.631	24	.960
1999— Philadelphia (N.L.)	SS	65	211	31	51	11	2	1	26	19	34	6	5	4-3	.242	.322	.327	.649	14	.952
— Clearwater (FSL)	SS	2	7	1	2	0	0	0	1	1	1	0	0	0-0	.286	.375	.286	.661	1	.800
2000— Philadelphia (N.L.)	SS	83	253	29	56	12	3	3	30	48	45	9	7	5-0	.221	.363	.328	.691	24	.930
— San Diego (N.L.)	SS	45	157	26	32	2	0	2	16	27	26	3	3	8-0	.204	.330	.255	.585	† 7	.965
2001— New York (N.L.) 2B-SS-3B	120	301	43	91	27	0	8	36	27	65	5	4	13-5	.302	.364	.472	.836	11	.963
2002— Seattle (A.L.) S-3-O-2-D	112	329	55	88	13	2	6	43	33	51	6	6	10-3	.267	.339	.374	.713	10	.965
2003— Kansas City (A.L.) 2-3-O-S-D	141	500	70	127	27	5	8	59	40	70	6	10	20-4	.254	.315	.376	.691	16	.971
American League totals (2 years)		253	829	125	215	40	7	14	102	73	121	12	16	30-7	.259	.325	.375	.700	26	.969
National League totals (6 years)		485	1494	179	365	80	10	19	156	162	272	26	29	43-13	.244	.326	.349	.676	83	.954
Major League totals (8 years)		738	2323	304	580	120	17	33	258	235	393	38	45	73-20	.250	.326	.359	.684	109	.959

REMLINGER, MIKE — P

PERSONAL: Born March 23, 1966, in Middletown, N.Y. ... 6-1/215. ... Throws left, bats left. ... Full name: Michael John Remlinger. ... Name pronounced: REM-lin-jurr. ... High school: Carver (Plymouth, Mass.). ... College: Dartmouth.

TRANSACTIONS/CAREER NOTES: Selected by San Francisco Giants organization in first round (16th pick overall) of free-agent draft (June 2, 1987). ... On disabled list (April 30, 1988-remainder of season). ... Traded by Giants with OF Kevin Mitchell to Seattle Mariners for P Bill Swift, P Mike Jackson and P Dave Burba (December 11, 1991). ... On Jacksonville disabled list (July 30, 1992-remainder of season). ... Granted free agency (October 15, 1993). ... Signed by New York Mets organization (November 22, 1993).

... Traded by Mets to Cincinnati Reds for OF Cobi Cradle (May 11, 1995). ... Granted free agency (October 6, 1995). ... Re-signed by Reds (October 22, 1995). ... Traded by Reds to Kansas City Royals as part of a three-team deal in which Reds sent SS Luis Ordaz to St. Louis Cardinals for OF Andre King. Royals then sent OF Miguel Mejia to Cardinals to complete deal (December 4, 1995). ... Claimed on waivers by Reds (April 4, 1996). ... Traded by Reds with 2B Bret Boone to Atlanta Braves for P Denny Neagle, OF Michael Tucker and P Rob Bell (November 10, 1998). ... On disabled list (April 3-18, 1999; June 23-July 13, 2000; and August 8-24, 2002). ... Granted free agency (October 28, 2002). ... Signed by Chicago Cubs (December 3, 2002).

CAREER HITTING: 8-for-109 (.073), 5 R, 3 2B, 0 3B, 0 HR, 8 RBI.

Year League	W	L	Pct.	ERA	WHIP	G	GS	CG	ShO	Hld.	Sv.-Opp.	IP	H	R	ER	HR	BB-IBB	SO	Avg.
1987— Everett (Northwest)	0	0	...	3.60	1.20	2	1	0	0	...	0-...	5.0	1	2	2	0	5-0	11	.071
— Clinton (Midw.)	2	1	.667	3.30	1.17	6	5	0	0	...	0-...	30.0	21	12	11	2	14-0	43	.196
— Shreveport (Texas)	4	2	.667	2.36	1.05	6	6	0	0	...	0-...	34.1	14	11	9	2	22-0	51	.120
1988— Shreveport (Texas)	1	0	1.000	0.69	0.85	3	3	0	0	...	0-...	13.0	7	4	1	0	4-0	18	.163
1989— Shreveport (Texas)	4	6	.400	2.98	1.56	16	16	0	0	...	0-...	90.2	68	43	30	2	73-0	92	.212
— Phoenix (PCL)	1	6	.143	9.21	2.40	11	10	0	0	...	0-...	43.0	51	47	44	8	52-0	28	.290
1990— Shreveport (Texas)	9	11	.450	3.90	1.50	25	25	2	1	...	0-...	147.2	149	82	64	9	72-1	75	.270
1991— Phoenix (PCL)	5	5	.500	6.38	1.78	19	19	1	1	...	0-...	108.2	134	86	77	15	59-0	68	.305
— San Francisco (N.L.)	2	1	.667	4.37	1.60	8	6	1	1	0	0-0	35.0	36	17	17	5	20-1	19	.271
1992— Calgary (PCL)	1	7	.125	6.65	2.06	21	11	0	0	...	0-...	70.1	97	65	52	7	48-1	24	.342
— Jacksonville (Sou.)	1	1	.500	3.46	1.38	5	5	0	0	...	0-...	26.0	25	15	10	1	11-0	21	.250
1993— Calgary (PCL)	4	3	.571	5.53	1.80	19	18	0	0	...	0-...	84.2	100	57	52	8	52-0	51	.300
— Jacksonville (Sou.)	1	3	.250	6.58	1.49	7	7	0	0	...	0-...	39.2	40	30	29	7	19-0	23	.261
1994— Norfolk (Int'l)	2	4	.333	3.14	1.30	12	9	0	0	...	0-...	63.0	57	29	22	5	25-0	45	.242
— New York (N.L.)	1	5	.167	4.61	1.65	10	9	0	0	1	0-0	54.2	55	30	28	9	35-4	33	.261
1995— New York (N.L.)	0	1	.000	6.35	1.59	5	0	0	0	0	0-1	5.2	7	5	4	1	2-0	6	.292
— Cincinnati (N.L.)	0	0	...	9.00	5.00	2	0	0	0	0	0-0	1.0	2	1	1	0	3-0	1	.500
— Indianapolis (A.A.)	5	3	.625	4.05	1.54	41	1	0	0	...	0-...	46.2	40	24	21	4	32-4	58	.231
1996— Indianapolis (A.A.)	4	3	.571	2.52	1.21	28	13	0	0	...	0-...	89.1	64	29	25	4	44-0	97	.203
— Cincinnati (N.L.)	0	1	.000	5.60	1.57	19	4	0	0	1	0-0	27.1	24	17	17	4	19-2	19	.242
1997— Cincinnati (N.L.)	8	8	.500	4.14	1.29	69	12	2	0	14	2-2	124.0	100	61	57	11	60-6	145	.223
1998— Cincinnati (N.L.)	8	15	.348	4.82	1.53	35	28	1	1	0	0-0	164.1	164	96	88	23	87-1	144	.266
1999— Atlanta (N.L.)	10	1	.909	2.37	1.21	73	0	0	0	21	3-5	83.2	66	24	22	9	35-5	81	.215
2000— Atlanta (N.L.)	5	3	.625	3.47	1.27	71	0	0	0	23	12-16	72.2	55	29	28	6	37-1	72	.207
2001— Atlanta (N.L.)	3	3	.500	2.76	1.20	74	0	0	0	31	1-5	75.0	67	25	23	9	23-4	93	.234
2002— Atlanta (N.L.)	7	3	.700	1.99	1.12	73	0	0	0	30	0-5	68.0	48	17	15	3	28-3	69	.198
2003— Chicago (N.L.)	6	5	.545	3.65	1.35	73	0	0	0	17	0-1	69.0	54	30	28	11	39-4	83	.211
Major League totals (11 years)	50	46	.521	3.78	1.37	512	59	4	2	138	16-33	780.1	678	352	328	91	388-31	765	.235

RENTERIA, EDGAR   SS

PERSONAL: Born August 7, 1975, in Barranquilla, Colombia. ... 6-1/200. ... Bats right, throws right. ... Full name: Edgar Enrique Renteria. ... Name pronounced: ren-ter-ee-AH. ... High school: Instituto Los Alpes (Barranquilla, Colombia).

TRANSACTIONS/CAREER NOTES: Signed as non-drafted free agent by Florida Marlins organization (February 14, 1992). ... On Florida disabled list (June 24-July 11, 1996); included rehabilitation assignment to Charlotte (July 3-11). ... On disabled list (August 25-September 9, 1998). ... Traded by Marlins to St. Louis Cardinals for P Braden Looper, P Armando Almanza and SS Pablo Ozuna (December 14, 1998).

2003 GAMES PLAYED BY POSITION (MLB): SS—156.

Year Team (League)	Pos.	G	AB	R	H	2B	3B	HR	RBI	BB	SO	HBP	GDP	SB-CS	Avg.	OBP	SLG	OPS	E	Pct.
1992— GC Marlins (GCL)	SS	43	163	25	47	8	1	0	9	8	29	2	1	10-6	.288	.329	.350	.679	* 24	.897
1993— Kane Co. (Midw.)	SS	116	384	40	78	8	0	1	35	35	94	0	3	7-8	.203	.268	.232	.500	34	.934
1994— Brevard County (FSL)	SS	128	439	46	111	15	1	0	36	35	56	0	14	6-11	.253	.307	.292	.598	23	.959
1995— Portland (East.)	SS	135	508	70	147	15	7	7	68	32	85	2	10	30-11	.289	.329	.388	.717	33	.944
1996— Charlotte (Int'l)	SS	35	132	17	37	8	0	2	16	9	17	0	5	10-4	.280	.326	.386	.713	7	.959
— Florida (N.L.)	SS	106	431	68	133	18	3	5	31	33	68	2	12	16-2	.309	.358	.399	.757	11	.979
1997— Florida (N.L.)	SS	154	617	90	171	21	3	4	52	45	108	4	17	32-15	.277	.327	.340	.668	17	.975
1998— Florida (N.L.)	SS	133	517	79	146	18	2	3	31	48	78	4	13	41-22	.282	.347	.342	.689	20	.966
1999— St. Louis (N.L.)	SS	154	585	92	161	36	2	11	63	53	82	2	16	37-8	.275	.334	.400	.734	26	.959
2000— St. Louis (N.L.)	SS	150	562	94	156	32	1	16	76	63	77	1	19	21-13	.278	.346	.423	.770	27	.958
2001— St. Louis (N.L.)	SS-DH-1B	141	493	54	128	19	3	10	57	39	73	3	15	17-4	.260	.314	.371	.685	24	.961
2002— St. Louis (N.L.)	SS	152	544	77	166	36	2	11	83	49	57	4	17	22-7	.305	.364	.439	.803	19	.970
2003— St. Louis (N.L.)	SS	157	587	96	194	47	3	13	100	65	54	1	21	34-7	.330	.394	.480	.874	16	.975
Major League totals (8 years)		1147	4336	650	1255	227	17	73	493	395	597	21	130	220-78	.289	.348	.400	.748	160	.968

RESTOVICH, MICHAEL   OF

PERSONAL: Born January 3, 1979, in Rochester, Minn. ... 6-4/245. ... Bats right, throws right. ... Full name: Michael Jerome Restovich. ... High school: Mayo (Rochester, Minn.).

TRANSACTIONS/CAREER NOTES: Selected by Minnesota Twins organization in second round of free-agent draft (June 3, 1997). ... Recalled from Rochester (July 28, 2003). ... Optioned to Rochester (August 19, 2003). ... Recalled from Rochester (September 2, 2003).

2003 GAMES PLAYED BY POSITION (MLB): OF—17, DH—7.

Year Team (League)	Pos.	G	AB	R	H	2B	3B	HR	RBI	BB	SO	HBP	GDP	SB-CS	Avg.	OBP	SLG	OPS	E	Pct.
1998— Elizabethton (App.)	OF	65	242	* 68	86	20	1	13	* 64	* 54	58	9	10	5-2	.355	.489	.607	1.096	9	.912
— Fort Wayne (Midw.)	OF	11	45	9	20	5	2	0	6	4	12	0	1	0-0	.444	.490	.644	1.134	0	1.000
1999— Quad City (Midw.)	3B-OF	131	493	91	154	30	6	19	107	74	100	13	9	7-9	.312	.412	.513	.925	9	.958
2000— Fort Myers (FSL)	OF	135	475	73	125	27	9	8	64	61	100	4	11	19-7	.263	.350	.408	.758	6	.975
2001— New Britain (East.)	1B-OF	140	501	69	135	33	4	23	84	54	125	6	8	15-7	.269	.345	.489	.834	3	.989
2002— Edmonton (PCL)	OF	138	518	95	148	32	7	29	98	53	151	4	10	11-7	.286	.353	.542	.896	6	.976
— Minnesota (A.L.)	OF-DH	8	13	3	4	0	0	1	1	1	4	0	2	1-0	.308	.357	.538	.896	0	1.000
2003— Rochester (Int'l)	OF-DH	119	454	75	125	34	2	16	72	47	117	4	10	10-3	.275	.346	.465	.811	3	.989
— Minnesota (A.L.)	OF-DH	24	53	10	15	3	2	0	4	10	12	1	0	0-0	.283	.406	.415	.821	0	1.000
Major League totals (2 years)		32	66	13	19	3	2	1	5	11	16	1	5	1-0	.288	.397	.439	.837	0	1.000

REYES, AL   P

PERSONAL: Born April 10, 1971, in San Cristobal, Dominican Republic. ... 6-1/212. ... Throws right, bats right. ... Full name: Rafael Alberto Reyes. ... Name pronounced: RAY-ess. ... High school: Francisco del Rosario Sanche (Santo Domingo, Dominican Republic).

TRANSACTIONS/CAREER NOTES: Signed as non-drafted free agent by Montreal Expos organization (February 17, 1988). ... On disabled list (May 23, 1991-remainder of season). ... Selected by Milwaukee Brewers from Expos organization in Rule 5 major league draft (December 5, 1994). ... On disabled list (July 19, 1995-remainder of season). ... On New Orleans disabled list (April 4-August 2, 1996). ... On Milwaukee disabled list (July 25-September 8, 1998); included rehabilitation assignment to Louisville (September 1-8). ... Traded by Brewers to Baltimore Orioles (July 21, 1999), completing deal in which Orioles traded P Rocky Coppinger to Brewers for a player to be named later (July 16, 1999). ... Traded by Orioles to Los Angeles Dodgers for P Alan Mills and cash considerations (June 13, 2000). ... On Las Vegas disabled list (April 5-May 8, 2001). ... Granted free agency (October 17, 2001). ... Signed by Pittsburgh Pirates organization (January 25, 2002). ... Released by Pirates (March 10, 2003). ... Signed by New York Yankees organization (March 24, 2003). ... Contract purchased from Columbus (April 23, 2003). ... Designated for assignment (July 17, 2003). ... Given unconditional release (July 25, 2003).

CAREER HITTING: 2-for-10 (.200), 2 R, 0 2B, 0 3B, 0 HR, 0 RBI.

Year	League	W	L	Pct.	ERA	WHIP	G	GS	CG	ShO	Hld.	Sv.-Opp.	IP	H	R	ER	HR	BB-IBB	SO	Avg.
1989— DSL Expos (DSL)		3	4	.429	2.79	1.42	12	10	1	0	...	0-...	71.0	68	36	22		33-...	49	...
1990— W.P. Beach (FSL)		5	4	.556	4.74	1.58	16	10	0	0	...	1-...	57.0	58	32	30	4	32-2	47	.272
1991— Rockford (Midwest)		0	1	.000	5.56	1.41	3	3	0	0	...	0-...	11.1	14	8	7	1	2-0	10	.304
1992— Albany (S. Atl.)		0	2	.000	3.95	1.35	27	0	0	0	...	4-...	27.1	24	14	12	0	13-0	29	.226
1993— Burlington (Midw.)		7	6	.538	2.68	1.05	53	0	0	0	...	11-...	74.0	52	33	22	7	26-3	80	.193
1994— Harrisburg (Eastern)		2	2	.500	3.25	1.17	60	0	0	0	...	* 35-...	69.1	68	26	25	4	13-0	60	.257
1995— Milwaukee (A.L.)		1	1	.500	2.43	1.11	27	0	0	0	4	1-1	33.1	19	9	9	3	18-2	29	.167
1996— Beloit (Midw.)		1	0	1.000	1.83	1.17	13	0	0	0	...	0-...	19.2	17	7	4	1	6-0	22	.227
— Milwaukee (A.L.)		1	0	1.000	7.94	1.76	5	0	0	0	0	0-0	5.2	8	5	5	1	2-0	2	.320
1997— Tucson (PCL)		2	4	.333	5.02	1.50	38	0	0	0	...	7-...	57.1	52	39	32	12	34-2	70	.243
— Milwaukee (A.L.)		1	2	.333	5.40	1.38	19	0	0	0	1	1-1	29.2	32	19	18	4	9-0	28	.274
1998— Milwaukee (N.L.)		5	1	.833	3.95	1.51	50	0	0	0	10	0-1	57.0	55	26	25	9	31-1	58	.255
— Louisville (Int'l)		0	1	.000	8.31	1.62	3	2	0	0	...	0-...	4.1	5	5	4	1	2-0	5	.294
1999— Louisville (Int'l)		0	2	.000	8.38	1.97	6	0	0	0	...	0-...	9.2	12	9	9	0	7-2	8	.343
— Milwaukee (N.L.)		2	0	1.000	4.25	1.44	26	0	0	0	2	0-1	36.0	27	17	17	5	25-1	39	.206
— Baltimore (A.L.)		2	3	.400	4.85	1.31	27	0	0	0	4	0-3	29.2	23	16	16	4	16-2	28	.225
2000— Rochester (Int'l)		0	1	.000	7.71	1.89	9	0	0	0	...	2-...	11.2	13	11	10	2	9-1	17	.271
— Baltimore (A.L.)		1	0	1.000	6.92	1.85	13	0	0	0	2	0-1	13.0	13	10	10	2	11-1	10	.271
— Albuquerque (PCL)		3	2	.600	3.72	1.40	30	0	0	0	...	8-...	38.2	33	20	16	5	21-0	39	.226
— Los Angeles (N.L.)		0	0	...	0.00	0.45	6	0	0	0	1	0-0	6.2	2	0	0	0	1-0	8	.087
2001— Las Vegas (PCL)		0	1	.000	3.38	1.16	19	0	0	0	...	0-...	29.1	24	11	11	3	10-1	37	.218
— Los Angeles (N.L.)		2	1	.667	3.86	1.60	19	0	0	0	0	1-2	25.2	28	13	11	3	13-1	23	.269
2002— Nashville (PCL)		7	3	.700	2.70	0.93	43	0	0	0	...	1-...	66.2	40	21	20	5	22-2	90	.167
— Pittsburgh (N.L.)		0	0	...	2.65	0.94	15	0	0	0	3	0-1	17.0	9	5	5	1	7-0	21	.161
2003— Columbus (Int'l)		1	1	.500	3.71	1.24	15	0	0	0	...	2-...	17.0	16	7	7	1	5-0	21	.239
— New York (A.L.)		0	0	...	3.18	1.29	13	0	0	0	0	0-1	17.0	13	7	6	1	9-1	9	.203
American League totals (6 years)		6	6	.500	4.49	1.35	104	0	0	0	11	2-7	128.1	108	66	64	15	65-6	106	.230
National League totals (5 years)		9	2	.818	3.67	1.39	116	0	0	0	16	1-5	142.1	121	61	58	18	77-3	149	.228
Major League totals (9 years)		15	8	.652	4.06	1.37	220	0	0	0	27	3-12	270.2	229	127	122	33	142-9	255	.229

REYES, CARLOS   P

PERSONAL: Born April 4, 1969, in Miami, Fla. ... 6-0/190. ... Throws right, bats both. ... Full name: Carlos Alberto Reyes. ... Name pronounced: RAY-ess. ... High school: Tampa Catholic. ... College: Florida Southern.

TRANSACTIONS/CAREER NOTES: Signed as non-drafted free agent by Atlanta Braves organization (June 21, 1991). ... Selected by Oakland Athletics from Braves organization in Rule 5 major league draft (December 13, 1993). ... On Oakland disabled list (July 18-August 4, 1994); included rehabilitation assignment to Modesto (July 25-30). ... Granted free agency (December 20, 1996). ... Signed by New York Yankees organization (February 6, 1997). ... Released by Yankees (April 8, 1997). ... Signed by A's (April 10, 1997). ... On Oakland disabled list (August 21-September 12, 1997); included rehabilitation assignment to Edmonton (September 3-12). ... Granted free agency (October 15, 1997). ... Signed by San Diego Padres (November 7, 1997). ... Traded by Padres with P Dario Veras and C Mandy Romero to Boston Red Sox for C Jim Leyritz and OF Ethan Faggett (June 21, 1998). ... Released by Red Sox (December 14, 1998). ... Signed by Padres organization (February 4, 1999). ... Claimed on waivers by Philadelphia Phillies (October 6, 1999). ... On Philadelphia disabled list (March 29-April 13, 2000); included rehabilitation assignment to Reading (April 10-13). ... Released by Phillies (May 11, 2000). ... Signed by Padres organization (May 22, 2000). ... Released by Padres (2001). ... Signed by Tampa Bay (January 3, 2003).

CAREER HITTING: 0-for-3 (.000), 0 R, 0 2B, 0 3B, 0 HR, 0 RBI.

Year	League	W	L	Pct.	ERA	WHIP	G	GS	CG	ShO	Hld.	Sv.-Opp.	IP	H	R	ER	HR	BB-IBB	SO	Avg.
1991— GC Braves (GCL)		3	2	.600	1.77	1.16	20	0	0	0	...	5-...	45.2	44	15	9	0	9-1	37	.239
1992— Macon (S. Atl.)		2	3	.400	2.10	1.13	23	0	0	0	...	2-...	60.0	57	16	14	2	11-1	57	.256
— Durham (Caro.)		2	1	.667	2.43	1.01	21	0	0	0	...	5-...	40.2	31	11	11	1	10-0	33	.214
1993— Greenville (Sou.)		8	1	.889	2.06	1.26	33	2	0	0	...	2-...	70.0	64	22	16	5	24-1	57	.247
— Richmond (Int'l)		1	0	1.000	3.77	1.43	18	1	0	0	...	1-...	28.2	30	12	12	2	11-3	30	.263
1994— Oakland (A.L.)		0	3	.000	4.15	1.47	27	9	0	0	0	1-1	78.0	71	38	36	10	44-1	57	.242
— Modesto (Calif.)		0	0	...	0.00	0.40	3	3	0	0	...	0-...	5.0	2	0	0	0	0-0	3	.118
1995— Oakland (A.L.)		4	6	.400	5.09	1.43	40	1	0	0	4	0-1	69.0	71	43	39	10	28-4	48	.264
1996— Oakland (A.L.)		7	10	.412	4.78	1.59	46	10	0	0	1	0-0	122.1	134	71	65	19	61-8	78	.282
1997— Columbus (Int'l)		0	0	...	18.00	2.50	1	1	0	0	...	0-...	2.0	5	4	4	0	0-0	2	.455
— Edmonton (PCL)		2	0	1.000	3.48	1.06	5	4	1	0	...	0-...	31.0	30	14	12	2	3-1	23	.254
— Oakland (A.L.)		3	4	.429	5.82	1.63	37	6	0	0	1	0-1	77.1	101	52	50	13	25-2	43	.316
1998— Las Vegas (PCL)		0	0	...	0.00	0.60	1	0	0	0	...	0-...	1.2	1	0	0	0	0-0	2	.167
— San Diego (N.L.)		2	2	.500	3.58	1.05	22	0	0	0	1	1-2	27.2	23	11	11	4	6-0	24	.235
— Boston (A.L.)		1	1	.500	3.52	1.28	24	0	0	0	2	0-0	38.1	35	15	15	2	14-2	23	.246
1999— San Diego (N.L.)		2	4	.333	3.72	1.29	65	0	0	0	6	1-2	77.1	76	38	32	11	24-4	57	.254
2000— Reading (East.)		0	0	...	0.00	0.33	2	0	0	0	...	0-...	3.0	1	0	0	0	0-0	3	.111
— Philadelphia (N.L.)		0	2	.000	5.23	1.45	10	0	0	0	0	0-0	10.1	10	6	6	2	5-0	4	.270
— Las Vegas (PCL)		0	2	.000	2.86	1.31	16	0	0	0	...	1-...	28.1	28	13	9	5	9-1	24	.248
— San Diego (N.L.)		1	1	.500	6.00	1.28	12	0	0	0	2	1-3	18.0	15	12	12	5	8-0	13	.221
2001— Sacramento (PCL)		2	0	1.000	6.23	1.48	17	0	0	0	...	0-...	30.1	31	21	21	5	14-1	26	.265
— Tucson (PCL)		0	1	.000	8.68	1.93	8	0	0	0	...	0-...	9.1	13	10	9	1	5-1	7	.333
2002—												Did not play.								
2003— Durham (Int'l)		10	3	.769	2.86	1.04	22	21	1	0	...	0-...	132.1	124	47	42	9	14-1	78	.246
— Tampa Bay (A.L.)		0	3	.000	5.22	1.13	10	3	0	0	0	0-0	39.2	40	23	23	10	5-0	13	.265
American League totals (6 years)		15	27	.357	4.83	1.48	184	29	0	0	8	1-3	424.2	452	242	228	64	177-17	262	.274
National League totals (3 years)		5	9	.357	4.12	1.25	109	0	0	0	9	3-7	133.1	124	67	61	22	43-4	98	.247
Major League totals (8 years)		20	36	.357	4.66	1.43	293	29	0	0	17	4-10	558.0	576	309	289	86	220-21	360	.268

R

– 327 –

REYES, DENNYS   P

PERSONAL: Born April 19, 1977, in Higuera de Zaragoza, Mexico. ... 6-3/245. ... Throws left, bats right. ... Name pronounced: RAY-us. ... High school: Ignacio Zaragoza (Higuera de Zaragoza, Mexico).

TRANSACTIONS/CAREER NOTES: Signed as non-drafted free agent by Los Angeles Dodgers organization (July 5, 1993). ... Loaned by Dodgers organization to Mexico City Red Devils, Mexican League (March 28-August 22, 1995). ... Traded by Dodgers with 1B/3B Paul Konerko to Cincinnati Reds for P Jeff Shaw (July 4, 1998). ... On Cincinnati disabled list (May 30-July 2, 2001). ... Traded by Reds with 2B Pokey Reese to Colorado Rockies for P Gabe White and P Luke Hudson (December 18, 2001). ... Traded by Rockies with OF Todd Hollandsworth to Texas Rangers for OF Gabe Kapler and 2B Jason Romano (July 31, 2002). ... Granted free agency (December 21, 2002). ... Signed by Pittsburgh Pirates organization (January 24, 2003). ... Elected free agency (May 19, 2003). ... Signed by Arizona Diamondbacks as free agent (September 1, 2003).

CAREER HITTING: 3-for-43 (.070), 2 R, 1 2B, 0 3B, 0 HR, 0 RBI.

Year	League	W	L	Pct.	ERA	WHIP	G	GS	CG	ShO	Hld.	Sv.-Opp.	IP	H	R	ER	HR	BB-IBB	SO	Avg.
1993—	M.C. Red Devils (Mex.)	0	1	.000	5.06	2.44	7	1	0	0	...	0-...	5.1	4	4	3	1	9-...	5	...
1994—	Vero Beach (FSL)	2	4	.333	6.70	1.82	9	9	0	0	...	0-...	41.2	58	37	31	6	18-0	25	.324
	— Great Falls (Pio.)	7	1	.875	3.78	1.44	14	9	0	0	...	0-...	66.2	71	37	28	0	25-0	70	.267
1995—	M.C. Red Devils (Mex.)	5	5	.500	6.60	1.99	17	15	1	0	...	0-...	58.2	76	49	43	4	41-...	44	...
	— Vero Beach (FSL)	1	0	1.000	1.80	1.40	3	2	0	0	...	0-...	10.0	8	2	2	0	6-0	9	.222
1996—	San Bernardino (Calif.)	11	12	.478	4.17	1.46	29	•28	0	0	...	0-...	166.0	166	106	77	11	77-0	176	.259
1997—	San Antonio (Texas)	8	1	.889	3.02	1.33	12	12	1	0	...	0-...	80.1	79	33	27	6	28-1	66	.262
	— Albuquerque (PCL)	6	3	.667	5.65	1.80	10	10	1	0	...	0-...	57.1	70	40	36	4	33-0	45	.303
	— Los Angeles (N.L.)	2	3	.400	3.83	1.47	14	5	0	0	0	0-0	47.0	51	21	20	4	18-3	36	.280
1998—	Albuquerque (PCL)	1	4	.200	1.44	1.12	7	7	1	1	...	0-...	43.2	31	13	7	5	18-0	58	.197
	— Los Angeles (N.L.)	0	4	.000	4.71	1.64	11	3	0	0	0	0-0	28.2	27	17	15	1	20-4	33	.255
	— Indianapolis (Int'l)	2	0	1.000	3.00	1.42	4	4	0	0	...	0-...	24.0	20	10	8	1	14-0	27	.233
	— Cincinnati (N.L.)	3	1	.750	4.42	1.60	8	7	0	0	0	0-0	38.2	35	19	19	2	27-1	44	.255
1999—	Cincinnati (N.L.)	2	2	.500	3.79	1.49	65	1	0	0	14	2-3	61.2	53	30	26	5	39-1	72	.232
2000—	Cincinnati (N.L.)	2	1	.667	4.53	1.65	62	0	0	0	10	0-1	43.2	43	31	22	5	29-0	36	.262
2001—	Cincinnati (N.L.)	2	6	.250	4.92	1.62	35	6	0	0	6	0-0	53.0	51	35	29	5	35-1	52	.248
	— Louisville (Int'l)	4	2	.667	3.67	1.46	7	6	0	0	...	0-...	34.1	34	15	14	3	16-0	34	.260
2002—	Colorado (N.L.)	0	1	.000	4.24	1.66	43	0	0	0	4	0-0	40.1	43	19	19	1	24-3	30	.279
	— Texas (A.L.)	4	3	.571	6.38	1.80	15	5	0	0	0	0-0	42.1	55	33	30	9	21-1	29	.316
2003—	Pittsburgh (N.L.)	0	0	...	10.45	1.84	12	0	0	0	2	0-0	10.1	10	13	12	1	9-1	11	.263
	— Tucson (PCL)	2	1	.667	2.84	1.45	33	0	0	0	...	2-...	31.2	24	16	10	0	22-2	30	.207
	— Arizona (N.L.)	0	0	...	11.57	2.57	3	0	0	0	0	0-0	2.1	5	3	3	1	1-0	5	.417
American League totals (1 year)		4	3	.571	6.38	1.80	15	5	0	0	0	0-0	42.1	55	33	30	9	21-1	29	.316
National League totals (7 years)		11	18	.379	4.56	1.60	253	22	0	0	36	2-4	325.2	318	188	165	25	202-14	319	.259
Major League totals (7 years)		15	21	.417	4.77	1.62	268	27	0	0	36	2-4	368.0	373	221	195	34	223-15	348	.266

REYES, JOSE   SS

PERSONAL: Born June 11, 1983, in Villa Gonzalez, Dominican Republic. ... 6-0/160. ... Bats both, throws right. ... Full name: Jose Bernabe Reyes.

TRANSACTIONS/CAREER NOTES: Signed as non-drafted free agent by New York Mets organization (August 16, 1999).

2003 GAMES PLAYED BY POSITION (MLB): SS—69.

Year	Team (League)	Pos.	G	AB	R	H	2B	3B	HR	RBI	BB	SO	HBP	GDP	SB-CS	Avg.	OBP	SLG	OPS	E	Pct.
2000—Kingsport (Appal.)		S-3-2-O	49	132	22	33	3	3	0	8	20	37	3	1	10-4	.250	.359	.318	.677	11	.942
2001—Capital City (SAL)		SS	108	407	71	125	22	15	5	48	18	71	2	4	30-10	.307	.337	.472	.809	18	.964
2002—St. Lucie (Fla. St.)		SS	69	288	58	83	10	11	6	38	30	35	1	5	31-13	.288	.353	.462	.815	12	.967
—Binghamton (East.)		SS	65	275	46	79	16	8	2	24	16	42	2	2	27-11	.287	.331	.425	.757	17	.940
2003—Norfolk (Int'l)		SS-DH	42	160	28	43	6	4	0	13	15	25	1	2	26-5	.269	.333	.356	.690	5	.969
—New York (N.L.)		SS	69	274	47	84	12	4	5	32	13	36	0	1	13-3	.307	.334	.434	.769	9	.973
Major League totals (1 year)			69	274	47	84	12	4	5	32	13	36	0	1	13-3	.307	.334	.434	.769	9	.973

REYES, RENE   OF/1B

PERSONAL: Born February 21, 1978, in Margarita, Venezuela. ... 5-11/213. ... Bats both, throws right. ... Name pronounced: RAY-es. ... High school: Nueva Esparata (Margarita, Venezuela).

TRANSACTIONS/CAREER NOTES: Signed as non-drafted free agent by Colorado Rockies organization (August 29, 1996). ... On Asheville disabled list (April 8-June 23, 1999). ... On disabled list (April 6, 2000-entire season). ... On disabled list (August 30, 2001-remainder of season).

2003 GAMES PLAYED BY POSITION (MLB): OF—36.

Year	Team (League)	Pos.	G	AB	R	H	2B	3B	HR	RBI	BB	SO	HBP	GDP	SB-CS	Avg.	OBP	SLG	OPS	E	Pct.
1998—Ariz. Rockies (Ariz.)		1B-C	49	177	40	76	9	4	5	39	8	15	15	5	16-7	.429	.493	.610	1.103	17	.961
1999—Ariz. Rockies (Ariz.)		1B	22	97	21	35	4	4	1	20	4	14	2	2	6-1	.361	.398	.515	.914	2	.989
—Asheville (S. Atl.)		1B-DH	40	160	26	56	6	1	3	19	6	22	1	1	1-0	.350	.377	.456	.833	0	1.000
2000—										Did not play.											
2001—Asheville (S. Atl.)		OF-1B	128	484	71	156	27	2	11	61	28	80	12	9	53-12	.322	.371	.455	.826	11	.983
2002—Carolina (Sou.)		OF-1B	123	455	64	133	33	4	14	54	29	69	5	10	10-11	.292	.339	.475	.813	11	.979
2003—Colo. Springs (PCL)		OF-DH	98	370	60	127	23	3	6	50	22	56	2	11	12-8	.343	.380	.470	.851	5	.970
—Colorado (N.L.)		OF	53	116	13	30	7	1	2	7	5	19	0	3	2-1	.259	.287	.388	.675	2	.964
Major League totals (1 year)			53	116	13	30	7	1	2	7	5	19	0	3	2-1	.259	.287	.388	.675	2	.964

REYNOLDS, SHANE   P

PERSONAL: Born March 26, 1968, in Bastrop, La. ... 6-3/215. ... Throws right, bats right. ... Full name: Richard Shane Reynolds. ... High school: Ouachita Christian (Monroe, La.). ... College: Texas.

TRANSACTIONS/CAREER NOTES: Selected by Houston Astros organization in third round of free-agent draft (June 5, 1989). ... On Houston disabled list (June 10-July 14, 1997); included rehabilitation assignment to New Orleans (July 10-14). ... On disabled list (August 2, 2000-remainder of season). ... On Houston disabled list (March 31-April 18 and August 14-September 1, 2001); included rehabilitation assignments to Round Rock (April 3-5) and New Orleans (April 5-18). ... On disabled list (June 14, 2002-remainder of season). ... Granted free agency (October 28, 2002). ... Re-signed by Astros (December 7, 2002). ... Released by Astros (March 27, 2003). ... Signed by Atlanta Braves (April 10, 2003).

CAREER HITTING: 77-for-546 (.141), 34 R, 15 2B, 0 3B, 5 HR, 43 RBI.

Year	League	W	L	Pct.	ERA	WHIP	G	GS	CG	ShO	Hld.	Sv.-Opp.	IP	H	R	ER	HR	BB-IBB	SO	Avg.
1989— Auburn (N.Y.-Penn)	3	2	.600	2.31	1.43	6	6	1	0	...	0-...	35.0	36	16	9	1	14-0	23	.275
— Asheville (S. Atl.)	5	3	.625	3.68	1.44	8	8	2	1	...	0-...	51.1	53	25	21	2	21-0	33	.268
1990— Columbus (Sou.)	9	10	.474	4.81	1.62	29	27	2	1	...	0-...	155.1	•181	104	83	14	70-1	92	.293
1991— Jackson (Texas)	8	9	.471	4.47	1.50	27	•27	2	0	...	0-...	151.0	165	93	75	8	62-1	116	.278
1992— Tucson (PCL)	9	8	.529	3.68	1.34	25	22	2	0	...	1-...	142.0	156	73	58	4	34-2	106	.279
— Houston (N.L.)	1	3	.250	7.11	1.89	8	5	0	0	0	0-0	25.1	42	22	20	2	6-1	10	.385
1993— Tucson (PCL)	10	6	.625	3.62	1.21	25	20	2	0	...	1-...	139.1	147	74	56	4	21-0	106	.268
— Houston (N.L.)	0	0	...	0.82	1.55	5	1	0	0	0	0-0	11.0	11	4	1	0	6-1	10	.256
1994— Houston (N.L.)	8	5	.615	3.05	1.20	33	14	1	1	5	0-0	124.0	128	46	42	10	21-3	110	.263
1995— Houston (N.L.)	10	11	.476	3.47	1.23	30	30	3	2	0	0-0	189.1	196	87	73	15	37-6	175	.263
1996— Houston (N.L.)	16	10	.615	3.65	1.13	35	35	4	1	0	0-0	239.0	227	103	97	20	44-3	204	.249
1997— Houston (N.L.)	9	10	.474	4.23	1.30	30	30	2	0	0	0-0	181.0	189	92	85	19	47-5	152	.267
— New Orleans (A.A.)	1	0	1.000	0.00	0.80	1	1	0	0	0	0-...	5.0	3	0	0	0	1-0	6	.176
1998— Houston (N.L.)	19	8	.704	3.51	1.33	35	•35	3	1	0	0-0	233.1	257	99	91	25	53-2	209	.280
1999— Houston (N.L.)	16	14	.533	3.85	1.24	35	•35	4	2	0	0-0	231.2	250	108	99	23	37-0	197	.275
2000— Houston (N.L.)	7	8	.467	5.22	1.49	22	22	0	0	0	0-0	131.0	150	86	76	20	45-2	93	.287
2001— Round Rock (Texas)	1	0	1.000	1.29	1.00	1	1	0	0	0	0-...	7.0	5	1	1	0	2-0	5	.200
— New Orleans (PCL)	1	0	1.000	0.00	1.14	1	1	0	0	0	0-...	7.0	8	0	0	0	0-0	7	.276
— Houston (N.L.)	14	11	.560	4.34	1.34	28	28	3	0	0	0-0	182.2	208	95	88	24	36-2	102	.290
2002— Houston (N.L.)	3	6	.333	4.86	1.43	13	13	0	0	0	0-0	74.0	80	43	40	13	26-2	47	.274
2003— Atlanta (N.L.)	11	9	.550	5.43	1.49	30	29	0	0	0	0-0	167.1	191	104	101	20	59-6	94	.293
Major League totals (12 years)	**114**	**95**	**.545**	**4.09**	**1.31**	**304**	**277**	**20**	**7**	**5**	**0-0**	**1789.2**	**1929**	**889**	**813**	**191**	**417-33**	**1403**	**.275**

RHODES, ARTHUR — P

PERSONAL: Born October 24, 1969, in Waco, Texas. ... 6-2/212. ... Throws left, bats left. ... Full name: Arthur Lee Rhodes. ... High school: LaVega (Waco, Texas).

TRANSACTIONS/CAREER NOTES: Selected by Baltimore Orioles organization in second round of free-agent draft (June 1, 1988). ... On Hagerstown disabled list (May 13-June 5, 1991). ... On Baltimore disabled list (May 16-August 2, 1993); included rehabilitation assignment to Rochester (July 4-August 2). ... On Baltimore disabled list (May 2-20, 1994); included rehabilitation assignment to Frederick (May 16-20). ... On Baltimore disabled list (August 25, 1995-remainder of season). ... On disabled list (July 14-August 2 and August 6-September 27, 1996). ... On Baltimore disabled list (July 5-August 17, 1998); included rehabilitation assignment to Rochester (August 15-17). ... Granted free agency (November 1, 1999). ... Signed by Seattle Mariners (December 21, 1999).

CAREER HITTING: 1-for-4 (.250), 0 R, 0 2B, 0 3B, 0 HR, 0 RBI.

Year	League	W	L	Pct.	ERA	WHIP	G	GS	CG	ShO	Hld.	Sv.-Opp.	IP	H	R	ER	HR	BB-IBB	SO	Avg.
1988— Bluefield (Appal.)	3	4	.429	3.31	1.25	11	7	0	0	...	0-...	35.1	29	17	13	1	15-0	44	.210
1989— Erie (N.Y.-Penn)	2	0	1.000	1.16	0.74	5	5	1	0	...	0-...	31.0	13	7	4	1	10-0	45	.124
— Frederick (Caro.)	2	2	.500	5.18	1.56	7	6	0	0	...	0-...	24.1	19	16	14	2	19-0	28	.213
1990— Frederick (Caro.)	4	6	.400	2.12	1.03	13	13	3	0	...	0-...	80.2	62	25	19	6	21-0	103	.207
— Hagerstown (Eastern)	3	4	.429	3.73	1.40	12	12	0	0	...	0-...	72.1	62	32	30	3	39-0	60	.238
1991— Hagerstown (Eastern)	7	4	.636	2.70	1.13	19	19	2	2	...	0-...	106.2	73	37	32	2	47-1	115	.194
— Baltimore (A.L.)	0	3	.000	8.00	1.94	8	8	0	0	0	0-0	36.0	47	35	32	4	23-0	23	.320
1992— Rochester (Int'l)	6	6	.500	3.72	1.28	17	17	1	0	...	0-...	101.2	84	48	42	7	46-0	115	.220
— Baltimore (A.L.)	7	5	.583	3.63	1.33	15	15	2	1	0	0-0	94.1	87	39	38	6	38-2	77	.250
1993— Baltimore (A.L.)	5	6	.455	6.51	1.63	17	17	0	0	0	0-0	85.2	91	62	62	16	49-1	49	.274
— Rochester (Int'l)	1	1	.500	4.05	1.54	6	6	0	0	...	0-...	26.2	26	12	12	5	15-0	33	.260
1994— Baltimore (A.L.)	3	5	.375	5.81	1.54	10	10	3	2	0	0-0	52.2	51	34	34	8	30-1	47	.254
— Frederick (Caro.)	0	0	...	0.00	0.60	1	1	0	0	...	0-...	5.0	3	0	0	0	0-0	7	.176
— Rochester (Int'l)	7	5	.583	2.79	1.15	15	15	0	0	...	0-...	90.1	70	41	28	7	34-1	86	.208
1995— Baltimore (A.L.)	2	5	.286	6.21	1.54	19	9	0	0	0	0-1	75.1	68	53	52	13	48-1	77	.239
— Rochester (Int'l)	2	1	.667	2.70	1.17	4	4	1	0	...	0-...	30.0	27	12	9	2	8-0	33	.239
1996— Baltimore (A.L.)	9	1	.900	4.08	1.34	28	2	0	0	2	1-1	53.0	48	28	24	6	23-3	62	.241
1997— Baltimore (A.L.)	10	3	.769	3.02	1.06	53	0	0	0	9	1-2	95.1	75	32	32	9	26-5	102	.218
1998— Baltimore (A.L.)	4	4	.500	3.51	1.29	45	0	0	0	10	4-8	77.0	65	30	30	8	34-2	83	.233
— Rochester (Int'l)	0	0	...	4.50	2.00	1	1	0	0	...	0-...	2.0	3	1	1	0	1-0	1	.333
1999— Baltimore (A.L.)	3	4	.429	5.43	1.66	43	0	0	0	5	3-5	53.0	43	37	32	9	45-6	59	.221
2000— Seattle (A.L.)	5	8	.385	4.28	1.15	72	0	0	0	24	0-7	69.1	51	34	33	6	29-3	77	.205
2001— Seattle (A.L.)	8	0	1.000	1.72	0.85	71	0	0	0	*32	3-7	68.0	46	14	13	5	12-0	83	.189
2002— Seattle (A.L.)	10	4	.714	2.33	0.83	66	0	0	0	27	2-7	69.2	45	18	18	4	13-1	81	.187
2003— Seattle (A.L.)	3	3	.500	4.17	1.31	67	0	0	0	18	3-6	54.0	53	25	25	4	18-2	48	.256
Major League totals (13 years)	**69**	**51**	**.575**	**4.33**	**1.31**	**514**	**61**	**5**	**3**	**127**	**17-44**	**883.1**	**770**	**441**	**425**	**98**	**388-27**	**868**	**.235**

RICHARD, CHRIS — OF/1B

PERSONAL: Born June 7, 1974, in San Diego, Calif. ... 6-2/208. ... Bats left, throws left. ... Full name: Christopher Robert Richard. ... High school: University City (San Diego). ... College: Oklahoma State.

TRANSACTIONS/CAREER NOTES: Selected by St. Louis Cardinals organization in 19th round of free-agent draft (June 1, 1995). ... On Arkansas disabled list (April 2-June 16, 1998 and July 31-August 11, 1998). ... On Prince William disabled list (June 28-July 16, 1998). ... Traded by Cardinals with P Mark Nussbeck to Baltimore Orioles for P Mike Timlin and cash (July 29, 2000). ... On disabled list (June 20-July 5, 2001). ... On Baltimore disabled list (March 30-July 31, 2002); included rehabilitation assignments to Gulf Coast Orioles (July 2-4), Bowie (July 5-8), Aberdeen (July 9-10) and Rochester (July 15-31). ... Traded by Orioles to Colorado Rockies for OF Jack Cust (March 11, 2003). ... Placed on 15-day disabled list (May 1, 2003). ... Transferred to Emergency disabled list (May 9, 2003).

2003 GAMES PLAYED BY POSITION (MLB): OF—3, 1B—1.

									BATTING										FIELDING	
Year	Team (League)	Pos.	G	AB	R	H	2B	3B	HR	RBI	BB	SO	HBP	GDP	SB-CS	Avg.	OBP	SLG	OPS	E	Pct.
1995— New Jersey (NYP)	1B	75	284	36	80	14	3	3	43	47	31	6	3	6-6	.282	.392	.384	.776	11	.984
1996— St. Pete. (FSL)	1B-OF	129	460	65	130	28	6	14	82	57	50	9	11	7-3	.283	.369	.461	.830	7	.994
1997— Arkansas (Texas)	1B-OF	113	390	62	105	24	3	11	58	60	59	5	8	6-4	.269	.371	.431	.802	10	.990
1998— Prince Will. (Car.)	DH	8	30	5	8	2	0	0	1	1	5	0	2	1-0	.267	.290	.333	.624	...	...
— Arkansas (Texas)	1B	28	89	7	18	5	1	2	17	9	10	1	1	0-1	.202	.280	.348	.628	3	.986
1999— Arkansas (Texas)	1B-OF	133	442	78	130	26	3	29	94	43	75	8	14	7-7	.294	.363	.563	.926	13	.989
— Memphis (PCL)	1B	4	17	3	7	2	0	1	4	1	2	0	1	0-0	.412	.444	.706	1.150	0	1.000
2000— Memphis (PCL)	OF-1B	95	375	64	104	24	0	16	75	50	70	4	5	9-3	.277	.366	.469	.835	2	.993
— St. Louis (N.L.)	OF-1B	6	16	1	2	0	0	1	1	2	2	0	0	0-0	.125	.222	.313	.535	0	1.000
— Baltimore (A.L.) 1B-DH-OF	56	199	38	55	14	2	13	36	15	38	4	5	7-5	.276	.335	.563	.898	5	.989

Year	Team (League)	Pos.	G	AB	R	H	2B	3B	HR	RBI	BB	SO	HBP	GDP	SB-CS	Avg.	OBP	SLG	OPS	E	Pct.
2001—Baltimore (A.L.)	OF-DH-1B	136	483	74	128	31	3	15	61	45	100	8	15	11-9	.265	.335	.435	.770	0	1.000	
2002—GC Orioles (GCL)	DH	1	1	1	1	0	0	0	0	1	0	0	0	0-0	1.000	1.000	1.000	2.000	...	...	
— Bowie (East.)	DH	2	6	0	2	1	0	0	1	1	2	0	0	0-0	.333	.375	.500	.875	...	...	
— Aberdeen (NY-P)	DH	1	5	2	3	1	0	1	3	0	1	0	0	0-0	.600	.600	1.400	2.000	...	...	
— Rochester (Int'l)	DH	14	53	10	17	6	0	6	18	6	14	2	2	0-0	.321	.397	.774	1.170	...	...	
— Baltimore (A.L.)	DH-1B	50	155	15	36	11	0	4	21	12	30	2	2	0-3	.232	.292	.381	.673	0	1.000	
2003—Colorado (N.L.)	OF-1B	19	27	3	6	1	1	1	3	3	6	0	1	0-1	.222	.300	.444	.744	0	1.000	
American League totals (3 years)		242	837	127	219	56	5	32	118	72	168	14	22	18-17	.262	.327	.455	.782	5	.994	
National League totals (2 years)		25	43	4	8	1	1	2	4	5	8	0	1	0-1	.186	.271	.395	.666	0	1.000	
Major League totals (4 years)		267	880	131	227	57	6	34	122	77	176	14	23	18-18	.258	.324	.452	.777	5	.995	

RIEDLING, JOHN — P

PERSONAL: Born August 29, 1975, in Fort Lauderdale, Fla. ... 5-11/190. ... Throws right, bats right. ... Full name: John Richard Riedling. ... Name pronounced: READ-ling. ... High school: Ely (Pompano Beach, Fla.).

TRANSACTIONS/CAREER NOTES: Selected by Cincinnati Reds organization in 22nd round of free-agent draft (June 2, 1994). ... Released by Reds (December 14, 1998). ... Re-signed by Reds organization (January 5, 1999). ... On Cincinnati disabled list (May 27-August 12 and August 31, 2001-remainder of season); included rehabilitation assignment to Louisville (August 10-12). ... On Cincinnati disabled list (March 26-May 1 and August 20-September 4, 2002). ... Placed on 15-day disabled list (June 12, 2003). ... Reinstated from 15-day disabled list (June 27, 2003). ... Placed on the 15-day disabled list, retroactive to June 12 (July 3, 2003).

CAREER HITTING: 4-for-22 (.182), 2 R, 0 2B, 0 3B, 0 HR, 2 RBI.

Year	League	W	L	Pct.	ERA	WHIP	G	GS	CG	ShO	Hld.	Sv.-Opp.	IP	H	R	ER	HR	BB-IBB	SO	Avg.
1994—Billings (Pio.)		4	1	.800	5.48	2.03	15	15	0	0	...	0-...	44.1	62	36	27	0	28-0	27	.333
1995—Billings (Pio.)		2	2	.500	7.04	1.88	13	7	0	0	...	1-...	38.1	51	38	30	4	21-2	28	.305
1996—Char., W.Va. (SAL)		6	10	.375	3.99	1.44	26	26	0	0	...	0-...	140.0	135	85	62	2	66-6	90	.258
1997—Burlington (Midw.)		4	6	.400	5.26	1.44	35	16	0	0	...	0-...	102.2	101	70	60	8	47-0	104	.253
1998—Chattanooga (Sou.)		3	10	.231	5.00	1.68	24	20	0	0	...	0-...	102.2	112	70	57	10	60-5	86	.277
1999—Chattanooga (Sou.)		9	5	.643	3.43	1.45	40	0	0	0	...	5-...	42.0	41	23	16	2	20-3	38	.253
— Indianapolis (Int'l)		1	0	1.000	1.54	1.06	24	0	0	0	...	1-...	35.0	19	9	6	1	18-2	26	.160
2000—Louisville (Int'l)		6	3	.667	2.52	1.24	53	0	0	0	...	5-...	75.0	63	24	21	7	30-3	75	.226
— Cincinnati (N.L.)		3	1	.750	2.35	1.24	13	0	0	0	2	1-2	15.1	11	7	4	1	8-0	18	.208
2001—Cincinnati (N.L.)		1	1	.500	2.41	1.07	29	0	0	0	5	1-3	33.2	22	9	9	1	14-0	23	.186
— Louisville (Int'l)		0	0	...	0.00	1.00	1	0	0	0	...	0-...	1.0	0	0	0	0	1-0	1	.000
2002—Chattanooga (Sou.)		1	1	.500	11.05	2.45	6	0	0	0	...	0-...	7.1	13	11	9	0	5-2	5	.382
— Louisville (Int'l)		1	0	1.000	4.66	1.45	7	0	0	0	...	0-...	9.2	10	6	5	0	4-0	10	.256
— Cincinnati (N.L.)		2	4	.333	2.70	1.39	33	0	0	0	8	0-0	46.2	39	16	14	2	26-6	30	.234
2003—Cincinnati (N.L.)		2	3	.400	4.90	1.52	55	8	0	0	6	1-4	101.0	107	61	55	7	47-0	65	.270
Major League totals (4 years)		8	9	.471	3.75	1.39	130	8	0	0	21	3-9	196.2	179	93	82	11	95-6	136	.244

RIGGAN, JERROD — P

PERSONAL: Born May 16, 1974, in Brewster, Wash. ... 6-3/197. ... Throws right, bats right. ... Full name: Jerrod Ashley Riggan. ... Name pronounced: RIG-gan. ... High school: Brewster (Wash.). ... College: San Diego State.

TRANSACTIONS/CAREER NOTES: Selected by California Angels organization in eighth round of free-agent draft (June 4, 1996). ... Angels franchise renamed Anaheim Angels for 1997 season. ... Released by Angels (April 17, 1998). ... Signed by New York Mets organization (July 9, 1998). ... Traded by Mets with OF Matt Lawton, OF Alex Escobar and two players to be named later to Cleveland Indians for 2B Roberto Alomar, P Mike Bacsik and OF Danny Peoples (December 11, 2001); Indians acquired P Billy Traber and 1B Earl Snyder to complete deal (December 13, 2001). ... Contract purchased from Buffalo (May 13, 2003). ... Sent outright to Buffalo (May 21, 2003). ... Elected free agency (May 21, 2003). ... Signed by New York Mets and optioned to Norfolk (May 26, 2003).

CAREER HITTING: 0-for-2 (.000), 0 R, 0 2B, 0 3B, 0 HR, 0 RBI.

Year	League	W	L	Pct.	ERA	WHIP	G	GS	CG	ShO	Hld.	Sv.-Opp.	IP	H	R	ER	HR	BB-IBB	SO	Avg.
1996—Boise (NW)		3	5	.375	4.63	1.43	15	15	•1	0	...	0-...	89.1	90	62	46	10	38-5	80	.262
1997—Cedar Rapids (Midw.)		9	8	.529	4.89	1.45	19	19	3	1	...	0-...	116.0	132	70	63	15	36-2	65	.288
— Lake Elsinore (Calif.)		2	5	.286	6.07	1.77	8	8	0	0	...	0-...	43.0	60	36	29	1	16-0	31	.341
1998—Capital City (S. Atl.)		4	1	.800	3.70	1.26	14	0	0	0	...	1-...	41.1	38	21	17	5	14-1	40	.241
1999—St. Lucie (Fla. St.)		5	5	.500	3.33	1.27	44	0	0	0	...	12-...	73.0	69	33	27	4	24-5	66	.257
2000—Binghamton (Eastern)		2	0	1.000	1.11	0.94	52	0	0	0	...	•28-...	65.0	43	9	8	2	18-0	79	.189
— New York (N.L.)		0	0	...	0.00	1.50	1	0	0	0	0	0-0	2.0	3	2	0	0	0-0	1	.300
2001—Norfolk (Int'l)		2	0	1.000	1.95	0.93	28	0	0	0	0	13-...	32.1	26	7	7	4	4-1	37	.222
— New York (N.L.)		3	3	.500	3.40	1.38	35	0	0	0	4	0-1	47.2	42	19	18	5	24-7	41	.243
2002—Cleveland (A.L.)		2	1	.667	7.64	2.15	29	0	0	0	0	0-0	33.0	53	28	28	3	18-4	22	.373
— Buffalo (Int'l)		4	1	.800	2.38	1.13	27	0	0	0	0	3-...	45.1	40	12	12	3	11-2	37	.247
2003—Buffalo (Int'l)		2	1	.667	2.20	1.16	9	0	0	0	0	0-1	16.1	14	5	4	0	5-1	14	.237
— Cleveland (A.L.)		0	0	...	9.00	2.00	2	0	0	0	0	0-0	4.0	7	4	4	0	1-0	2	.412
— Norfolk (Int'l)		0	0	...	2.84	1.26	5	0	0	0	...	1-...	6.1	7	2	2	0	1-0	11	.280
American League totals (2 years)		2	1	.667	7.78	2.14	31	0	0	0	0	0-0	37.0	60	32	32	3	19-4	24	.377
National League totals (2 years)		3	3	.500	3.26	1.39	36	0	0	0	4	0-1	49.2	45	21	18	5	24-7	42	.246
Major League totals (4 years)		5	4	.556	5.19	1.71	67	0	0	0	4	0-1	86.2	105	53	50	8	43-11	66	.307

RIGGS, ADAM — OF/IF

PERSONAL: Born October 4, 1972, in Steubenville, Ohio. ... 6-0/190. ... Bats right, throws right. ... Full name: Adam David Riggs. ... High school: Lenape Valley (Stanhope, N.J.). ... College: South Carolina-Aiken.

TRANSACTIONS/CAREER NOTES: Selected by Los Angeles Dodgers organization in 22nd round of free-agent draft (June 2, 1994). ... On Albuquerque disabled list (April 4-June 9, 1997; and May 28-June 5, 1998). ... On Los Angeles disabled list (June 5, 1998-remainder of season). ... Granted free agency (October 18, 2000). ... Signed by San Diego Padres organization (December 15, 2000). ... Signed by Detroit Tigers organization (December 19, 2001). ... Granted free agency (October 15, 2002). ... Signed by Anaheim Angels organization (January 23, 2003).

2003 GAMES PLAYED BY POSITION (MLB): 1B—10, OF—8, 2B—3, DH—3.

Year	Team (League)	Pos.	G	AB	R	H	2B	3B	HR	RBI	BB	SO	HBP	GDP	SB-CS	Avg.	OBP	SLG	OPS	E	Pct.
1994—Great Falls (Pio.)	2B	62	234	55	73	20	3	5	44	31	38	4	2	19-8	.312	.399	.487	.886	23	.908	
— Yakima (N'west)	2B	4	7	1	2	1	0	0	0	0	1	0	0	0-0	.286	.286	.429	.714	...	...	
1995—San Bern. (Calif.)	2B	134	*542	*111	*196	*39	5	24	106	59	93	10	9	31-10	.362	.431	.585	1.016	*41	.928	
1996—San Antonio (Texas)	2B	134	506	68	143	31	6	14	66	37	82	9	13	16-6	.283	.339	.451	.790	27	.962	
1997—Albuquerque (PCL)	2B-3B-OF	57	227	59	69	8	3	13	38	29	39	3	2	12-2	.304	.390	.537	.927	8	.973	
— Los Angeles (N.L.)	2B	9	20	3	4	1	0	0	1	4	3	0	0	1-0	.200	.333	.250	.583	0	1.000	
1998—Albuquerque (PCL)	2B	44	170	30	63	13	3	4	25	21	29	3	1	12-6	.371	.446	.553	.999	10	.954	

Year Team (League)	Pos.	G	AB	R	H	2B	3B	HR	RBI	BB	SO	HBP	GDP	SB-CS	Avg.	OBP	SLG	OPS	E	Pct.
1999—Albuquerque (PCL) 2B-3B-DH		133	513	87	150	29	7	13	81	54	114	10	8	25-17	.292	.368	.452	.820	‡ 23	.963
2000—Albuquerque (PCL) 3B-2B-OF		124	348	71	109	24	4	12	57	35	67	2	11	11-7	.313	.376	.509	.885	19	.939
2001—Portland (PCL) 2B-3B-OF		110	394	42	103	18	2	21	65	12	78	0	9	8-3	.261	.282	.477	.759	16	.961
—San Diego (N.L.)	2B-3B	12	36	2	7	1	0	0	1	2	8	0	1	1-1	.194	.237	.222	.459	0	1.000
2002—Memphis (PCL)	O-3-2-1	43	122	26	28	9	0	2	11	23	27	0	3	5-1	.230	.347	.352	.699	7	.929
2003—Salt Lake (PCL)	D-0-1-2	103	394	59	116	35	0	14	82	37	67	5	13	8-2	.294	.354	.490	.844	7	.974
—Anaheim (A.L.)	1-O-2-D	24	61	11	15	4	1	3	5	9	9	0	2	3-1	.246	.343	.492	.835	2	.981
American League totals (1 year)		24	61	11	15	4	1	3	5	9	9	0	2	3-1	.246	.343	.492	.835	2	.981
National League totals (2 years)		21	56	5	11	2	0	0	2	6	11	0	1	2-1	.196	.274	.232	.506	0	1.000
Major League totals (3 years)		45	117	16	26	6	1	3	7	15	20	0	3	5-2	.222	.311	.368	.678	2	.988

RILEY, MATT   P

PERSONAL: Born August 2, 1979, in Antioch, Calif. ... 6-1/201. ... Throws left, bats left. ... Full name: Matthew Paul Riley. ... High school: Linerty Union (Oakley, Calif.). ... Junior college: Sacramento (Calif.) Community College.

TRANSACTIONS/CAREER NOTES: Selected by Baltimore Orioles organization in third round of free-agent draft (June 3, 1997). ... On Bowie disabled list (June 30-July 8, 1999). ... On Rochester disabled list (April 16-May 28, 2000). ... On Baltimore disabled list (September 29, 2000-remainder of season). ... On disabled list (April 1, 2001-entire season). ... On Bowie disabled list (April 22-May 15, 2002).

CAREER HITTING: 0-for-0 (.000), 0 R, 0 2B, 0 3B, 0 HR, 0 RBI.

Year League	W	L	Pct.	ERA	WHIP	G	GS	CG	ShO	Hld.	Sv.-Opp.	IP	H	R	ER	HR	BB-IBB	SO	Avg.
1998—Delmarva (S. Atl.)	5	4	.556	1.19	1.04	16	14	0	0	...	0-...	83.0	42	19	11	0	44-0	136	.152
1999—Frederick (Caro.)	3	2	.600	2.61	0.93	8	8	0	0	...	0-...	51.2	34	19	15	5	14-0	58	.188
—Bowie (East.)	10	6	.625	3.22	1.23	20	20	3	0	...	0-...	125.2	113	53	45	13	42-0	131	.241
—Baltimore (A.L.)	0	0	...	7.36	2.73	3	3	0	0	0	0-0	11.0	17	9	9	4	13-0	6	.378
2000—Rochester (Int'l)	0	2	.000	14.14	2.71	2	2	0	0	...	0-...	7.0	15	12	11	3	4-0	8	.417
—Bowie (East.)	5	7	.417	6.08	1.66	19	14	2	0	...	1-...	74.0	74	56	50	9	49-0	66	.262
2001—Baltimore (A.L.)										Did not play.									
2002—Bowie (East.)	4	10	.286	6.34	1.68	22	22	0	0	...	0-...	109.1	136	84	77	12	48-1	105	.306
2003—Bowie (East.)	5	2	.714	3.11	1.09	14	14	1	1	...	0-...	72.1	56	27	25	4	23-1	73	.210
—Ottawa (Int'l)	4	2	.667	3.58	1.39	13	13	0	0	...	0-...	70.1	70	30	28	4	28-1	77	.261
—Baltimore (A.L.)	1	0	1.000	1.80	1.20	2	2	0	0	0	0-0	10.0	7	2	2	1	5-0	8	.194
Major League totals (2 years)	1	0	1.000	4.71	2.00	5	5	0	0	0	0-0	21.0	24	11	11	5	18-0	14	.296

RINCON, JUAN   P

PERSONAL: Born January 23, 1979, in Maracaibo, Venezuela. ... 5-11/192. ... Throws right, bats right. ... Full name: Juan Manuel Rincon. ... Name pronounced: rin-CONE. ... High school: Instituto Cervantes (Maracaibo, Venezuela).

TRANSACTIONS/CAREER NOTES: Signed as non-drafted free agent by Minnesota Twins organization (November 15, 1996). ... Optioned to Rochester by Minnesota Twins (April 19, 2003). ... Recalled by Minnesota from Rochester (May 2, 2003).

CAREER HITTING: 1-for-1 (1.000), 0 R, 0 2B, 0 3B, 0 HR, 0 RBI.

Year League	W	L	Pct.	ERA	WHIP	G	GS	CG	ShO	Hld.	Sv.-Opp.	IP	H	R	ER	HR	BB-IBB	SO	Avg.
1997—GC Twins (GCL)	3	3	.500	2.95	1.36	11	10	1	0	...	0-...	58.0	55	21	19	0	24-0	46	.259
—Elizabethton (Appal.)	0	1	.000	3.86	1.50	2	1	0	0	...	0-...	9.1	11	4	4	0	3-0	7	.289
1998—Fort Wayne (Midw.)	6	4	.600	3.83	1.43	37	13	0	0	...	6-...	96.1	84	51	41	6	54-1	74	.232
1999—Quad City (Midw.)	14	8	.636	2.92	1.30	28	•28	0	0	...	0-...	163.1	146	67	53	8	66-3	*153	.239
2000—Fort Myers (Fla. St.)	5	3	.625	2.13	1.18	13	13	0	0	...	0-...	76.0	67	26	18	3	23-2	55	.238
—New Britain (East.)	3	9	.250	4.65	1.52	15	15	2	0	...	0-...	89.0	96	55	46	9	39-0	79	.267
2001—New Britain (East.)	14	6	.700	2.88	1.22	29	23	2	1	...	0-...	153.1	130	60	49	9	57-5	133	.226
—Minnesota (A.L.)	0	0	...	6.35	2.12	4	0	0	0	0	0-0	5.2	7	5	4	1	5-0	4	.318
2002—Edmonton (PCL)	7	4	.636	4.78	1.44	19	16	•3	0	...	0-...	101.2	111	56	54	12	35-0	75	.278
—Minnesota (A.L.)	0	2	.000	6.28	1.85	10	3	0	0	0	0-1	28.2	44	23	20	5	9-0	21	.352
2003—Rochester (Int'l)	0	2	.000	7.56	2.04	2	2	0	0	...	0-...	8.1	12	7	7	0	5-0	8	.364
—Minnesota (A.L.)	5	6	.455	3.68	1.31	58	0	0	0	...	0-1	85.2	74	38	35	5	38-7	63	.231
Major League totals (3 years)	5	8	.385	4.43	1.48	72	3	0	0	5	0-2	120.0	125	66	59	11	52-7	88	.267

RINCON, RICARDO   P

PERSONAL: Born April 13, 1970, in Veracruz, Mexico. ... 5-9/190. ... Throws left, bats left. ... Full name: Ricardo Rincon Espinoza. ... Name pronounced: rin-CONE.

TRANSACTIONS/CAREER NOTES: Signed as non-drafted free agent by Pittsburgh Pirates organization (March 30, 1997). ... On Pittsburgh disabled list (March 22-April 14, 1998); included rehabilitation assignments to Carolina (April 6) and Nashville (April 11-April 14). ... Traded by Pirates to Cleveland Indians for OF Brian Giles (November 18, 1998). ... On Cleveland disabled list (April 12-May 14, 1999); included rehabilitation assignment to Akron (May 11-14). ... On Cleveland disabled list (May 17-August 23, 2000); included rehabilitation assignment to Buffalo (August 20-23). ... Traded by Indians to Oakland Athletics for IF Marshall McDougall (July 30, 2002).

CAREER HITTING: 0-for-4 (.000), 0 R, 0 2B, 0 3B, 0 HR, 0 RBI.

Year League	W	L	Pct.	ERA	WHIP	G	GS	CG	ShO	Hld.	Sv.-Opp.	IP	H	R	ER	HR	BB-IBB	SO	Avg.
1990—Union Laguna (Mex.)	3	0	1.000	3.78	1.78	19	4	0	0	...	0-...	47.2	53	22	20	6	32-...	29	...
1991—Union Laguna (Mex.)	2	8	.200	6.54	1.98	32	9	0	0	...	1-...	74.1	99	60	54	12	48-...	66	...
1992—Union Laguna (Mex.)	6	5	.545	3.91	1.48	49	9	0	0	...	4-...	89.2	87	45	39	4	46-...	91	...
1993—Torreon (Mex.)	7	3	.700	3.17	1.41	57	4	0	0	...	8-...	82.1	80	33	29	8	36-...	81	...
1994—M.C. Red Devils (Mex.)	2	4	.333	3.21	1.44	20	9	0	0	...	1-...	53.1	57	23	19	4	20-...	38	...
1995—M.C. Red Devils (Mex.)	6	6	.500	5.16	1.69	27	11	0	0	...	3-...	75.0	86	45	43	7	41-...	41	...
1996—M.C. Red Devils (Mex.)	5	3	.625	2.97	1.08	50	0	0	0	...	10-...	78.2	58	28	26	2	27-...	60	...
1997—Pittsburgh (N.L.)	4	8	.333	3.45	1.25	62	0	0	0	18	4-6	60.0	51	26	23	5	24-6	71	.230
1998—Carolina (Sou.)	0	0	...	6.00	2.33	2	0	0	0	...	0-...	3.0	5	2	2	1	2-0	1	.385
—Nashville (PCL)	0	0	...	0.00	0.00	1	0	0	0	...	0-...	1.0	0	0	0	0	0-0	1	.000
—Pittsburgh (N.L.)	0	2	.000	2.91	1.22	60	0	0	0	11	14-17	65.0	50	31	21	6	29-2	64	.208
1999—Cleveland (A.L.)	2	3	.400	4.43	1.46	59	0	0	0	11	0-2	44.2	41	22	22	6	24-5	30	.248
—Akron (East.)	0	0	...	5.40	1.20	2	2	0	0	...	0-...	1.2	2	1	1	1	0-0	2	.250
2000—Cleveland (A.L.)	2	0	1.000	2.70	1.50	35	0	0	0	10	0-...	20.0	17	7	6	1	13-1	20	.224
—Buffalo (Int'l)	0	0	...	0.00	0.50	2	0	0	0	...	0-...	2.0	1	1	0	0	0-0	2	.111
2001—Cleveland (A.L.)	2	1	.667	2.83	1.20	67	0	0	0	12	2-4	54.0	44	18	17	3	21-5	50	.223
2002—Cleveland (A.L.)	1	4	.200	4.79	1.23	46	0	0	0	11	0-3	35.2	36	21	19	3	8-1	30	.263
—Oakland (A.L.)	0	0	...	3.10	0.69	25	0	0	0	16	1-2	20.1	11	7	7	1	3-0	19	.164
2003—Oakland (A.L.)	6	4	.600	3.25	1.39	64	0	0	0	13	0-3	55.1	45	21	20	4	32-4	40	.230
American League totals (5 years)	15	12	.556	3.56	1.28	296	0	0	0	73	3-14	230.0	194	96	91	18	101-16	189	.232
National League totals (2 years)	4	10	.286	3.17	1.23	122	0	0	0	29	18-23	125.0	101	57	44	11	53-8	135	.219
Major League totals (7 years)	19	22	.463	3.42	1.26	418	0	0	0	102	21-37	355.0	295	153	135	29	154-24	324	.227

RIOS, ARMANDO   OF

PERSONAL: Born September 13, 1971, in Santurce, Puerto Rico. ... 5-9/190. ... Bats left, throws left. ... High school: Villa Fontana (Carolina, Puerto Rico). ... College: Louisiana State.

TRANSACTIONS/CAREER NOTES: Signed as non-drafted free agent by San Francisco Giants organization (January 6, 1994). ... On disabled list (May 15-29, 1996). ... On San Francisco disabled list (June 22-September 2, 1999); included rehabilitation assignment to Fresno (July 23-30 and August 12-31). ... Traded by Giants with P Ryan Vogelsong to Pittsburgh Pirates for P Jason Schmidt and OF John Vander Wal (July 30, 2001). ... On Pittsburgh disabled list (August 2, 2001-remainder of season). ... On Pittsburgh disabled list (May 17-August 2, 2002); included rehabilitation assignments to Altoona (June 9-10) and Nashville (July 15-August 2). ... Released by Pirates (November 20, 2002). ... Signed by Chicago White Sox (January 15, 2003). ... Designated for assignment (July 2, 2003). ... Sent outright to Charlotte (July 10, 2003). ... Contract purchased from Charlotte (September 2, 2003).

2003 GAMES PLAYED BY POSITION (MLB): OF—32, DH—4.

Year — Team (League)	Pos.	G	AB	R	H	2B	3B	HR	RBI	BB	SO	HBP	GDP	SB-CS	Avg.	OBP	SLG	OPS	E	Pct.
1994— Clinton (Midw.)	OF	119	407	67	120	23	4	8	60	59	69	4	7	16-12	.295	.384	.430	.814	12	.951
1995— San Jose (Calif.)	OF	128	488	76	143	34	3	8	75	74	75	1	8	51-10	.293	.382	.424	.807	9	.963
1996— Shreveport (Texas)	OF	92	329	62	93	22	2	12	49	44	42	1	2	9-9	.283	.365	.471	.836	7	.963
1997— Shreveport (Texas)	OF-DH	127	461	86	133	30	6	14	79	63	85	0	11	17-7	.289	.370	.471	.841	6	.972
1998— Fresno (PCL)	OF-DH-1B	125	445	85	134	23	1	26	103	55	73	3	9	17-5	.301	.378	.533	.911	7	.972
— San Francisco (N.L.)	OF	12	7	3	4	0	0	2	3	3	2	0	0	0-0	.571	.700	1.429	2.129	0	1.000
1999— Fresno (PCL)	OF-1B	31	109	24	30	3	0	4	21	11	22	4	2	3-1	.275	.363	.413	.776	0	1.000
— San Francisco (N.L.)	OF	72	150	32	49	9	0	7	29	24	35	1	3	7-4	.327	.420	.527	.947	2	.978
2000— San Francisco (N.L.)	OF-1B	115	233	38	62	15	5	10	50	31	43	0	9	3-2	.266	.347	.502	.849	6	.959
2001— San Francisco (N.L.)	OF	93	316	38	82	17	3	14	49	34	73	0	2	3-2	.259	.330	.465	.795	6	.971
— Pittsburgh (N.L.)	OF	2	3	0	1	0	0	0	1	2	1	0	1	0-0	.333	.500	.333	.833	0	...
2002— Pittsburgh (N.L.)	OF	76	208	20	55	11	0	1	24	16	39	1	8	1-1	.264	.319	.332	.650	0	1.000
— Altoona (East.)	OF	1	2	0	0	0	0	0	0	1	0	0	0	0-0	.000	.333	.000	.333	1	.000
— Nashville (PCL)	OF	15	52	6	13	2	0	0	6	5	10	1	1	1-2	.250	.322	.288	.610	1	.923
2003— Charlotte (Int'l)	OF-DH	45	155	23	50	9	1	6	30	14	30	4	4	5-6	.323	.389	.510	.898	2	.976
— Chicago (A.L.)	OF-DH	49	104	4	22	3	0	2	11	5	13	0	6	0-1	.212	.245	.298	.544	1	.981
American League totals (1 year)		49	104	4	22	3	0	2	11	5	13	0	6	0-1	.212	.245	.298	.544	1	.981
National League totals (5 years)		370	917	131	253	52	8	34	156	110	193	2	23	14-9	.276	.352	.461	.813	14	.974
Major League totals (6 years)		419	1021	135	275	55	8	36	167	115	206	2	29	14-10	.269	.341	.445	.786	15	.975

RISKE, DAVID   P

PERSONAL: Born October 23, 1976, in Renton, Wash. ... 6-2/190. ... Throws right, bats right. ... Full name: David R. Riske. ... Name pronounced: RISK-ee. ... High school: Lindbergh (Renton, Wash.). ... Junior college: Green River (Wash.) Community College.

TRANSACTIONS/CAREER NOTES: Selected by Cleveland Indians organization in 56th round of free-agent draft (June 4, 1996). ... On Cleveland disabled list (March 25-April 28 and May 29-September 4 and September 14, 2000-remainder of season); included rehabilitation assignment to Akron (April 22-26 and August 28-September 4). ... On Cleveland disabled list (June 19-July 17, 2002); included rehabilitation assignment to Akron (July 4-17).

CAREER HITTING: 0-for-0 (.000), 0 R, 0 2B, 0 3B, 0 HR, 0 RBI.

Year — League	W	L	Pct.	ERA	WHIP	G	GS	CG	ShO	Hld.	Sv.-Opp.	IP	H	R	ER	HR	BB-IBB	SO	Avg.
1997— Kinston (Caro.)	4	4	.500	2.25	1.26	39	0	0	0	...	2-...	72.0	58	22	18	3	33-4	90	.227
1998— Kinston (Caro.)	1	1	.500	2.33	1.17	53	0	0	0	...	* 33-...	54.0	48	15	14	4	15-0	67	.241
— Akron (East.)	0	0	...	0.00	0.67	2	0	0	0	...	1-...	3.0	1	0	0	0	1-0	5	.100
1999— Akron (East.)	0	0	...	1.90	0.76	23	0	0	0	...	12-...	23.2	5	6	5	1	13-0	33	.067
— Buffalo (Int'l)	3	0	1.000	0.65	0.76	23	0	0	0	...	6-...	27.2	14	3	2	0	7-0	22	.151
— Cleveland (A.L.)	1	1	.500	8.36	1.86	12	0	0	0	0	0-1	14.0	20	15	13	2	6-0	16	.333
2000— Cleveland (A.L.)	0	0	...	0.00	0.50	3	1	0	0	...	1-...	4.0	2	0	0	0	0-0	4	.143
— Buffalo (Int'l)	0	0	...	3.00	1.33	2	0	0	0	...	1-...	3.0	2	1	1	0	2-0	1	.182
2001— Buffalo (Int'l)	1	2	.333	2.36	1.16	38	0	0	0	...	15-...	53.1	45	16	14	2	17-0	72	.232
— Cleveland (A.L.)	2	0	1.000	1.98	1.39	26	0	0	0	3	1-1	27.1	20	7	6	3	18-3	29	.206
2002— Cleveland (A.L.)	2	2	.500	5.26	1.64	51	0	0	0	5	1-1	51.1	49	32	30	8	35-4	65	.257
— Akron (East.)	0	0	...	3.00	1.00	4	0	0	0	...	0-...	6.0	5	2	2	1	1-0	10	.217
— Buffalo (Int'l)	0	1	.000	3.72	1.03	9	0	0	0	...	3-...	9.2	6	4	4	2	4-0	17	.182
2003— Cleveland (A.L.)	2	2	.500	2.29	0.96	68	0	0	0	17	8-13	74.2	52	21	19	9	20-3	82	.196
Major League totals (4 years)	7	5	.583	3.66	1.31	157	0	0	0	25	10-16	167.1	141	75	68	22	79-10	192	.230

RITCHIE, TODD   P

PERSONAL: Born November 7, 1971, in Portsmouth, Va. ... 6-3/210. ... Throws right, bats right. ... Full name: Todd Everett Ritchie. ... High school: Duncanville (Texas).

TRANSACTIONS/CAREER NOTES: Selected by Minnesota Twins organization in first round (12th pick overall) of free-agent draft (June 4, 1990). ... On disabled list (August 19, 1991-remainder of season; June 24-July 9, 1993; and April 28, 1994-remainder of season). ... Released by Twins (October 3, 1998). ... Signed by Pittsburgh Pirates organization (December 22, 1998). ... On Pittsburgh disabled list (August 21-September 6, 1999). ... On disabled list (July 24-August 11, 2000). ... Traded by Pirates with C Lee Evans to Chicago White Sox for P Kip Wells, P Sean Lowe and P Josh Fogg (December 13, 2001). ... On disabled list (August 4-September 10, 2002). ... Granted free agency (December 21, 2002). ... Signed by Milwaukee Brewers (January 14, 2003). ... Placed on 15-day disabled list (April 25, 2003). ... Reinstated from Emergency disabled list (September 29, 2003).

CAREER HITTING: 33-for-187 (.176), 9 R, 5 2B, 0 3B, 0 HR, 6 RBI.

Year — League	W	L	Pct.	ERA	WHIP	G	GS	CG	ShO	Hld.	Sv.-Opp.	IP	H	R	ER	HR	BB-IBB	SO	Avg.
1990— Elizabethton (Appal.)	5	2	.714	1.94	1.06	11	11	1	0	...	0-...	65.0	45	22	14	5	24-0	49	.198
1991— Kenosha (Midw.)	7	6	.538	3.55	1.40	21	21	0	0	...	0-...	116.2	113	53	46	3	50-0	101	.259
1992— Visalia (Calif.)	11	9	.550	5.06	1.49	28	•28	3	1	...	0-...	172.2	193	113	97	13	65-2	129	.284
1993— Nashville (Sou.)	3	2	.600	3.66	1.31	12	10	0	0	...	0-...	46.2	46	21	19	2	15-0	41	.260
1994— Nashville (Sou.)	0	2	.000	4.24	1.82	4	4	0	0	...	0-...	17.0	24	10	8	1	7-0	9	.364
1995— New Britain (East.)	4	9	.308	5.73	1.67	24	21	0	0	...	0-...	113.0	135	78	72	12	54-0	60	.303
1996— New Britain (East.)	3	7	.300	5.44	1.58	29	10	0	0	...	4-...	82.2	101	55	50	6	30-1	53	.302
— Salt Lake (PCL)	0	4	.000	5.47	1.54	16	0	0	0	...	0-...	24.2	27	15	15	1	11-0	19	.270
1997— Minnesota (A.L.)	2	3	.400	4.58	1.54	42	0	0	0	3	0-2	74.2	87	41	38	11	28-0	44	.290
1998— Minnesota (A.L.)	0	0	...	5.63	1.63	15	0	0	0	...	0-0	24.0	30	17	15	1	9-0	21	.288
— Salt Lake (PCL)	1	3	.250	4.15	1.42	36	0	0	0	...	4-...	60.2	55	38	28	5	31-3	62	.259
1999— Nashville (PCL)	0	0	...	1.80	1.40	1	1	0	0	...	0-...	5.0	6	1	1	0	1-0	2	.300
— Pittsburgh (N.L.)	15	9	.625	3.50	1.29	28	26	2	0	1	0-0	172.1	169	79	67	17	54-3	107	.259

Year League	W	L	Pct.	ERA	WHIP	G	GS	CG	ShO	Hld.	Sv.-Opp.	IP	H	R	ER	HR	BB-IBB	SO	Avg.
2000— Pittsburgh (N.L.)	9	8	.529	4.81	1.39	31	31	1	1	0	0-0	187.0	208	111	100	26	51-1	124	.282
2001— Pittsburgh (N.L.)	11	15	.423	4.47	1.27	33	33	4	2	0	0-0	207.1	211	118	103	23	52-7	124	.259
2002— Chicago (A.L.)	5	15	.250	6.06	1.71	26	23	0	0	0	0-0	133.2	176	104	90	18	52-2	77	.318
2003— Milwaukee (N.L.)	1	2	.333	5.08	1.62	5	5	0	0	0	0-0	28.1	36	17	16	4	10-0	15	.319
American League totals (3 years)	7	18	.280	5.54	1.64	83	23	0	0	3	0-2	232.1	293	162	143	30	89-2	142	.306
National League totals (4 years)	36	34	.514	4.33	1.33	97	95	7	3	1	0-0	595.0	624	325	286	70	167-11	370	.269
Major League totals (7 years)	43	52	.453	4.67	1.42	180	118	7	3	4	0-2	827.1	917	487	429	100	256-13	512	.280

RIVAS, LUIS — 2B

PERSONAL: Born August 30, 1979, in La Guaira, Venezuela. ... 5-11/175. ... Bats right, throws right. ... Full name: Luis Wilfredo Rivas. ... Name pronounced: REE-vas. ... High school: Riceniado Le Guaria (La Guaria, Venezuela).
TRANSACTIONS/CAREER NOTES: Signed as non-drafted free agent by Minnesota Twins organization (October 9, 1995). ... On New Britain disabled list (July 7-21, 2000). ... On Minnesota disabled list (April 7-June 4, 2002); included rehabilitation assignment to Fort Myers (May 28-June 4).
2003 GAMES PLAYED BY POSITION (MLB): 2B—134, DH—1.

											BATTING							FIELDING	
Year Team (League)	Pos.	G	AB	R	H	2B	3B	HR	RBI	BB	SO	HBP	GDP	SB-CS	Avg.	OBP	SLG	OPS	E	Pct.
1996— GC Twins (GCL)	SS	53	201	29	52	12	1	1	13	18	37	0	2	• 35-10	.259	.320	.343	.663	21	.922
1997— Fort Wayne (Midw.)	SS	121	419	61	100	20	6	1	30	33	90	5	5	28-18	.239	.301	.322	.623	* 58	.907
1998— Fort Myers (FSL)	SS	126	463	58	130	21	5	4	51	14	75	3	11	34-8	.281	.302	.374	.676	55	.913
1999— New Britain (East.)	SS-2B	132	527	78	134	30	7	7	49	41	92	2	16	31-14	.254	.309	.378	.687	‡ 39	.934
2000— New Britain (East.)	2B-SS	82	328	56	82	23	6	3	40	36	41	4	3	11-4	.250	.329	.384	.713	11	.971
— Salt Lake (PCL)	2B-SS	41	157	33	50	14	1	3	25	13	21	2	3	7-4	.318	.376	.478	.853	2	.989
— Minnesota (A.L.)	2B-SS	16	58	8	18	4	1	0	6	2	4	0	2	2-0	.310	.323	.414	.736	1	.984
2001— Minnesota (A.L.)	2B	153	563	70	150	21	6	7	47	40	99	6	15	31-11	.266	.319	.362	.682	15	.974
2002— Minnesota (A.L.)	2B	93	316	46	81	23	4	4	35	19	51	3	12	9-4	.256	.305	.392	.697	5	.986
— Fort Myers (FSL)	2B	6	22	1	2	0	1	0	3	2	2	0	0	1-0	.091	.167	.182	.348	2	.900
2003— Minnesota (A.L.)	2B-DH	135	475	69	123	16	9	8	43	30	65	5	20	17-7	.259	.308	.381	.689	10	.982
Major League totals (4 years)		397	1412	193	372	64	20	19	131	91	219	14	49	59-22	.263	.312	.377	.690	31	.980

RIVERA, CARLOS — 1B

PERSONAL: Born June 10, 1978, in Fajardo, Puerto Rico. ... 6-1/245. ... Bats left, throws left. ... Full name: Carlos Alberto Rivera. ... High school: Rio Grande (Puerto Rico).
TRANSACTIONS/CAREER NOTES: Selected by Pittsburgh Pirates organization in 10th round of free-agent draft (June 4, 1996).
2003 GAMES PLAYED BY POSITION (MLB): 1B—60.

											BATTING							FIELDING	
Year Team (League)	Pos.	G	AB	R	H	2B	3B	HR	RBI	BB	SO	HBP	GDP	SB-CS	Avg.	OBP	SLG	OPS	E	Pct.
1996— GC Pirates (GCL)	1B	48	183	24	52	8	3	3	26	15	22	1	8	1-1	.284	.338	.410	.748	6	.982
1997— Augusta (S. Atl.)	1B-OF	120	415	52	113	16	5	9	65	19	82	10	9	4-1	.272	.316	.400	.716	6	.993
1998— Lynchburg (Caro.)	1B	29	113	11	26	4	0	4	16	0	19	1	3	0-1	.230	.235	.372	.606	2	.989
— Augusta (S. Atl.)	1B-OF	87	316	38	90	17	1	5	53	11	46	6	9	3-5	.285	.318	.392	.711	6	.989
1999— Hickory (S. Atl.)	1B	119	457	63	147	30	1	13	86	15	45	11	13	2-1	.322	.355	.477	.832	15	.985
2000— GC Pirates (GCL)	1B	6	24	2	7	0	0	0	1	0	2	0	1	0-0	.292	.320	.292	.612	0	1.000
— Lynchburg (Caro.)	1B	64	233	20	63	17	0	5	47	6	34	2	7	0-1	.270	.284	.408	.692	1	.998
2001— Altoona (East.)	1B-OF	111	389	44	91	30	0	10	50	13	71	1	11	0-2	.234	.258	.388	.646	10	.989
2002— Altoona (East.)	1B	128	494	67	149	28	2	22	84	27	75	8	18	1-1	.302	.345	.500	.845	7	.993
2003— Nashville (PCL)	1B-DH	72	262	28	69	18	0	9	31	13	38	1	2	3-1	.263	.300	.435	.735	2	.997
— Pittsburgh (N.L.)	1B	78	95	12	21	5	0	3	10	8	28	1	2	0-0	.221	.283	.368	.651	4	.984
Major League totals (1 year)		78	95	12	21	5	0	3	10	8	28	1	2	0-0	.221	.283	.368	.651	4	.984

RIVERA, JUAN — OF

PERSONAL: Born July 3, 1978, in Caracas, Venezuela. ... 6-2/170. ... Bats right, throws right. ... Full name: Juan Luis Rivera.
TRANSACTIONS/CAREER NOTES: Signed as non-drafted free agent by New York Yankees organization (April 12, 1996). ... On Columbus disabled list (April 16-27, 2002). ... On New York disabled list (June 9-August 19, 2002); included rehabilitation assignments to Gulf Coast Yankees (July 31-August 7) and Columbus (August 8-19).
2003 GAMES PLAYED BY POSITION (MLB): OF—56.

											BATTING							FIELDING	
Year Team (League)	Pos.	G	AB	R	H	2B	3B	HR	RBI	BB	SO	HBP	GDP	SB-CS	Avg.	OBP	SLG	OPS	E	Pct.
1996— Dom. Yankees (DSL)	OF	10	18	0	3	0	0	0	2	0	1	...	...	0-...	.167	...	.167	...	0	1.000
1997— Maracay 1 (VSL)		52	142	25	40	9	0	0	14	12	16	...	...	12-...	.282	...	.345	...		...
1998— GC Yankees (GCL)	OF	57	210	43	70	9	1	* 12	* 45	26	27	1	10	8-5	.333	.408	.557	.965	2	.979
— Oneonta (NYP)	OF	6	18	2	5	0	0	1	3	1	4	0	0	1-1	.278	.316	.444	.760	0	1.000
1999— Tampa (Fla. St.)	OF	109	426	50	112	20	2	14	77	26	67	5	13	5-3	.263	.308	.418	.725	4	.979
— GC Yankees (GCL)	OF	5	18	7	6	0	0	1	4	4	1	0	1	0-0	.333	.455	.500	.955	0	1.000
2000— Norwich (East.)	OF	17	62	9	14	5	0	2	12	6	15	0	2	0-0	.226	.294	.403	.697	1	.955
— Tampa (Fla. St.)	1B-OF	115	409	62	113	26	1	14	69	33	56	6	9	11-7	.276	.336	.447	.783	5	.978
2001— Norwich (East.)	OF	77	316	50	101	18	3	14	58	15	50	3	10	5-7	.320	.353	.528	.882	6	.963
— Columbus (Int'l)	OF	55	199	39	65	11	1	14	40	15	31	1	7	4-5	.327	.372	.603	.975	4	.970
— New York (A.L.)	OF	3	4	0	0	0	0	0	0	0	0	0	0	0-0	.000	.000	.000	.000	0	1.000
2002— Columbus (Int'l)	OF	65	265	40	86	21	1	8	47	13	39	1	4	5-1	.325	.355	.502	.856	6	.955
— New York (A.L.)	OF	28	83	9	22	5	0	1	6	6	10	0	4	1-1	.265	.311	.361	.673	2	.966
— GC Yankees (GCL)	OF	4	13	1	4	2	0	0	4	2	3	1	1	0-0	.308	.438	.462	.899	0	1.000
2003— Columbus (Int'l)	OF	79	308	47	100	21	0	7	37	26	37	0	8	1-3	.325	.374	.461	.835	3	.982
— New York (A.L.)	OF	57	173	22	46	14	0	7	26	10	27	0	8	0-0	.266	.304	.468	.773	2	.979
Major League totals (3 years)		88	260	31	68	19	0	8	32	16	37	0	12	1-1	.262	.302	.427	.729	4	.974

RIVERA, MARIANO — P

PERSONAL: Born November 29, 1969, in Panama City, Panama. ... 6-2/170. ... Throws right, bats right.
TRANSACTIONS/CAREER NOTES: Signed as non-drafted free agent by New York Yankees organization (February 17, 1990). ... On disabled list (April 10-May 19, July 11-28 and August 12-September 8, 1992). ... On Albany/Colonie disabled list (April 9-June 28, 1993). ... On Greensboro disabled list (September 6, 1993-remainder of season). ...

On Tampa disabled list (April 23-May 9, 1994). ... On Columbus disabled list (August 4-14, 1994). ... On disabled list (April 6-24, 1998). ... On New York disabled list (June 10-25, July 21-August 8 and August 18-September 21, 2002); included rehabilitation assignment to Gulf Coast Yankees (August 6-8). ... On disabled list (March 25-April 29, 2003). ... Reinstated from the 15-day disabled list (April 29, 2003).

CAREER HITTING: 0-for-0 (.000), 0 R, 0 2B, 0 3B, 0 HR, 0 RBI.

Year	League	W	L	Pct.	ERA	WHIP	G	GS	CG	ShO	Hld.	Sv.-Opp.	IP	H	R	ER	HR	BB-IBB	SO	Avg.
1990— GC Yankees (GCL)		5	1	.833	0.17	0.46	22	1	1	1	...	1-...	52.0	17	3	1	0	7-0	58	.102
1991— Greensboro (S. Atl.)		4	9	.308	2.75	1.21	29	15	1	0	...	0-...	114.2	103	48	35	2	36-0	123	.237
1992— Fort Lauderdale (FSL)		5	3	.625	2.28	0.76	10	10	3	1	...	0-...	59.1	40	17	15	5	5-0	42	.191
1993— Greensboro (S. Atl.)		1	0	1.000	2.06	1.17	10	10	0	0	...	0-...	39.1	31	12	9	0	15-0	32	.214
— GC Yankees (GCL)		0	1	.000	2.25	0.75	2	2	0	0	...	0-...	4.0	2	1	1	0	1-0	6	.143
1994— Tampa (FSL)		3	0	1.000	2.21	1.25	7	7	0	0	...	0-...	36.2	34	12	9	2	12-0	27	.258
— Alb./Colon. (East.)		3	0	1.000	2.27	1.04	9	9	0	0	...	0-...	63.1	58	20	16	5	8-0	39	.242
— Columbus (Int'l)		4	2	.667	5.81	1.42	6	6	1	0	...	0-...	31.0	34	22	20	5	10-0	23	.268
1995— New York (A.L.)		2	2	.500	2.10	0.93	7	7	1	1	...	0-...	30.0	25	10	7	2	3-0	30	.227
— New York (A.L.)		5	3	.625	5.51	1.51	19	10	0	0	0	0-1	67.0	71	43	41	11	30-0	51	.266
1996— New York (A.L.)		8	3	.727	2.09	0.99	61	0	0	0	*27	5-8	107.2	73	25	25	1	34-3	130	.189
1997— New York (A.L.)		6	4	.600	1.88	1.19	66	0	0	0	0	43-52	71.2	65	17	15	5	20-6	68	.237
1998— New York (A.L.)		3	0	1.000	1.91	1.06	54	0	0	0	0	36-41	61.1	48	13	13	3	17-1	36	.215
1999— New York (A.L.)		4	3	.571	1.83	0.88	66	0	0	0	0	* 45-49	69.0	43	15	14	2	18-3	52	.176
2000— New York (A.L.)		7	4	.636	2.85	1.10	66	0	0	0	0	36-41	75.2	58	26	24	4	25-3	58	.208
2001— New York (A.L.)		4	6	.400	2.34	0.90	71	0	0	0	0	* 50-57	80.2	61	24	21	5	12-2	83	.209
2002— New York (A.L.)		1	4	.200	2.74	1.00	45	0	0	0	2	28-32	46.0	35	16	14	3	11-2	41	.203
— GC Yankees (GCL)		0	0	...	0.00	1.50	1	1	0	0	0	0-...	2.0	2	0	0	0	1-0	2	.286
2003— New York (A.L.)		5	2	.714	1.66	1.00	64	0	0	0	0	40-46	70.2	61	15	13	3	10-1	63	.235
Major League totals (9 years)		**43**	**29**	**.597**	**2.49**	**1.07**	**512**	**10**	**0**	**0**	**29**	**283-327**	**649.2**	**515**	**194**	**180**	**37**	**177-21**	**582**	**.215**

RIVERA, MICHAEL   C

PERSONAL: Born September 8, 1976, in Rio Piedras, Puerto Rico. ... 6-0/210. ... Bats right, throws right. ... Full name: Michael R. Rivera. ... High school: Dr. Augustin Stahl (Bayamon, Puerto Rico). ... College: Troy State.

TRANSACTIONS/CAREER NOTES: Signed as non-drafted free agent by Detroit Tigers organization (January 20, 1997). ... On Toledo disabled list (July 24-August 2, 2002). ... Traded by Tigers to San Diego Padres for OF Gene Kingsale (November 15, 2002). ... Claimed off waivers by Chicago White Sox and optioned to Charlotte (June 9, 2003).

2003 GAMES PLAYED BY POSITION (MLB): C—19, 1B—1.

Year	Team (League)	Pos.	G	AB	R	H	2B	3B	HR	RBI	BB	SO	HBP	GDP	SB-CS	Avg.	OBP	SLG	OPS	E	Pct.
1997— GC Tigers (GCL)		C-1B	47	154	34	44	9	2	* 10	36	18	25	3	2	0-0	.286	.367	.565	.932	1	.996
1998— W. Mich. (Mid.)		C	108	403	40	111	34	3	9	67	15	68	2	8	0-0	.275	.301	.442	.743	10	.990
1999— Lakeland (Fla. St.)		C	104	370	44	103	20	2	14	72	20	59	3	10	1-1	.278	.314	.457	.771	8	.989
— Jacksonville (Sou.)		C	7	23	3	4	1	0	2	6	2	5	0	0	0-0	.174	.240	.478	.718	0	1.000
2000— Lakeland (Fla. St.)		C	64	243	30	71	19	4	11	53	16	45	1	8	2-0	.292	.336	.539	.875	5	.988
— Toledo (Int'l)		C	4	13	0	3	3	0	0	1	0	2	0	0	0-0	.231	.231	.462	.692	1	.968
— Jacksonville (Sou.)		C	39	150	10	29	8	1	2	9	7	30	0	4	0-0	.193	.228	.300	.528	8	.969
2001— Erie (East.)		C	112	415	76	120	19	1	* 33	101	44	96	10	9	2-2	.289	.368	.578	.946	10	.989
— Detroit (A.L.)		C	4	12	2	4	2	0	0	1	0	2	0	0	0-0	.333	.333	.500	.833	2	.929
2002— Detroit (A.L.)		C-DH	39	132	11	30	8	1	1	11	4	35	1	5	0-0	.227	.254	.326	.579	2	.990
— Toledo (Int'l)		C	74	265	43	66	11	1	20	53	35	64	3	6	0-1	.249	.341	.525	.866	3	.993
2003— San Diego (N.L.)		C-1B	19	53	2	9	1	0	1	2	5	11	0	4	0-0	.170	.241	.245	.487	2	.986
— Portland (PCL)		C	13	50	0	8	1	0	0	2	1	21	0	1	0-1	.160	.176	.180	.356	1	.990
— Charlotte (Int'l)		C-DH-1B	68	245	38	76	11	0	12	52	16	50	9	4	0-1	.310	.373	.502	.875	2	.992
American League totals (2 years)			43	144	13	34	10	1	1	12	4	37	1	5	0-0	.236	.254	.340	.600	4	.983
National League totals (1 year)			19	53	2	9	1	0	1	2	5	11	0	4	0-0	.170	.241	.245	.487	2	.986
Major League totals (3 years)			62	197	15	43	11	1	2	14	9	48	1	9	0-0	.218	.255	.315	.570	6	.984

RIVERA, RUBEN   OF

PERSONAL: Born November 14, 1973, in La Chorrera, Panama. ... 6-3/200. ... Bats right, throws right. ... Full name: Ruben Moreno Rivera.

TRANSACTIONS/CAREER NOTES: Signed as non-drafted free agent by New York Yankees organization (November 21, 1990). ... On New York disabled list (March 27-May 30, 1997). ... Traded by Yankees with P Rafael Medina and $3 million to San Diego Padres for the rights to P Hideki Irabu, 2B Homer Bush, OF Gordon Amerson and a player to be named later (April 22, 1997); Yankees acquired OF Vernon Maxwell to complete deal (June 9, 1997). ... On San Diego disabled list (May 30-August 13, 1997); included rehabilitation assignments to Rancho Cucamonga (May 30-July 22) and Las Vegas (July 23-August 4). ... On San Diego disabled list (April 12-May 5, 2000); included rehabilitation assignment to Las Vegas (May 3-5). ... Released by Padres (March 14, 2001). ... Signed by Cincinnati Reds (March 21, 2001). ... Claimed on waivers by San Francisco Giants (November 16, 2001). ... Granted free agency (December 21, 2001). ... Signed by Yankees (February 14, 2002). ... Released by Yankees (March 11, 2002). ... Signed by Texas Rangers (March 31, 2002). ... Released by Rangers (September 30, 2002). ... Signed by San Francisco Giants organization (January 24, 2003). ... Given unconditional release (June 3, 2003).

2003 GAMES PLAYED BY POSITION (MLB): OF—27.

Year	Team (League)	Pos.	G	AB	R	H	2B	3B	HR	RBI	BB	SO	HBP	GDP	SB-CS	Avg.	OBP	SLG	OPS	E	Pct.
1991— Dom. Yankees (DSL)			51	170	27	34	3	2	2	16	23	37	...	...	14-...	.200		.276	...	...	...
1992— GC Yankees (GCL)		OF	53	194	37	53	10	3	1	20	42	49	6	2	21-6	.273	.417	.371	.788	4	.951
1993— Oneonta (NYP)		OF	55	199	45	55	7	6	13	47	32	66	5	2	12-5	.276	.385	.568	.953	3	.976
1994— Greensboro (S. Atl.)		OF	105	400	83	115	24	3	* 28	81	47	125	8	6	36-5	.288	.372	.573	.944	5	.979
— Tampa (Fla. St.)		OF	34	134	18	35	4	3	5	20	8	38	1	7	12-5	.261	.308	.448	.755	2	.976
1995— Norwich (East.)		OF	71	256	49	75	16	8	9	39	37	77	11	4	16-8	.293	.402	.523	.925	3	.984
— Columbus (Int'l)		OF	48	174	37	47	8	2	15	35	26	62	3	5	8-4	.270	.373	.598	.970	3	.975
— New York (A.L.)		OF	5	1	0	0	0	0	0	0	0	1	0	0	0-0	.000	.000	.000	.000	0	1.000
1996— Columbus (Int'l)		OF	101	362	59	85	20	4	10	46	40	96	8	4	15-10	.235	.324	.395	.719	7	.972
— New York (A.L.)		OF	46	88	17	25	6	1	2	16	13	26	2	1	6-2	.284	.381	.443	.824	0	1.000
1997— Rancho Cuca. (Calif.)		OF	6	23	6	4	1	0	1	3	3	9	0	0	1-0	.174	.259	.348	.607	...	...
— Las Vegas (PCL)		DH-1B	12	48	6	12	5	1	1	6	1	20	1	0	1-0	.250	.280	.458	.738	0	1.000
— San Diego (N.L.)		OF	17	20	2	5	1	0	0	1	2	9	0	0	2-1	.250	.318	.300	.618	0	1.000
1998— Las Vegas (PCL)		OF	30	104	9	15	3	0	3	11	11	42	0	4	4-4	.144	.222	.260	.482	0	1.000
— San Diego (N.L.)		OF	95	172	31	36	7	2	6	29	28	52	2	1	5-1	.209	.325	.378	.703	3	.973
1999— San Diego (N.L.)		OF	147	411	65	80	16	1	23	48	55	143	5	9	18-7	.195	.295	.406	.701	8	.976

Year Team (League)	Pos.	G	AB	R	H	2B	3B	HR	RBI	BB	SO	HBP	GDP	SB-CS	Avg.	OBP	SLG	OPS	E	Pct.
2000— San Diego (N.L.)	OF	135	423	62	88	18	6	17	57	44	137	10	8	8-4	.208	.296	.400	.696	5	.984
— Las Vegas (PCL)	OF	2	10	1	2	0	0	0	1	0	3	0	0	0-0	.200	.200	.200	.400	0	1.000
2001— Cincinnati (N.L.)	OF	117	263	37	67	13	1	10	34	21	83	5	7	6-3	.255	.321	.426	.747	3	.983
2002— Tulsa (Texas)	OF	59	205	38	64	17	4	10	43	23	46	5	5	4-3	.312	.388	.580	.969	2	.986
— Oklahoma (PCL)	OF	27	98	19	27	2	4	7	23	13	23	1	2	2-0	.276	.366	.592	.958	3	.955
— Texas (A.L.)	OF-DH	69	158	17	33	4	0	4	14	17	45	5	2	4-2	.209	.302	.310	.612	3	.983
2003— San Francisco (N.L.)	OF	31	50	6	9	2	0	2	4	5	14	0	0	1-0	.180	.255	.340	.595	0	1.000
— Bowie (East.)	OF-DH	41	128	17	25	5	1	6	20	12	35	2	4	0-1	.195	.273	.391	.663	0	1.000
— Ottawa (Int'l)	OF	14	48	12	20	3	2	2	7	4	12	2	1	2-0	.417	.481	.688	1.169	2	.950
American League totals (3 years)		120	247	34	58	10	1	6	30	30	72	7	3	10-4	.235	.330	.356	.686	3	.988
National League totals (6 years)		542	1339	203	285	57	10	58	173	155	438	22	25	40-16	.213	.303	.400	.703	19	.981
Major League totals (9 years)		662	1586	237	343	67	11	64	203	185	510	29	28	50-20	.216	.307	.393	.701	22	.982

ROA, JOE — P

PERSONAL: Born October 11, 1971, in Southfield, Mich. ... 6-2/206. ... Throws right, bats right. ... Full name: Joseph Rodger Roa. ... Name pronounced: ROH-ah. ... High school: Hazel Park (Mich.).

TRANSACTIONS/CAREER NOTES: Selected by Atlanta Braves organization in 18th round of free-agent draft (June 5, 1989). ... Traded by Braves to New York Mets organization (August 29, 1991), completing deal in which Mets traded P Alejandro Pena to Braves for P Tony Castillo and a player to be named (August 28, 1991). ... On Norfolk suspended list (July 31-August 2, 1994). ... Traded by Mets organization with OF Jeromy Burnitz to Cleveland Indians organization for P Dave Mlicki, P Paul Byrd, P Jerry DiPoto and a player to be named (November 18, 1994); Mets acquired 2B Jesus Azuaje to complete deal (December 6, 1994). ... Traded by Indians to San Francisco Giants for OF Trenidad Hubbard (December 16, 1996), completing deal in which Giants traded 3B Matt Williams and a player to be named later to Indians for IF Jeff Kent, IF Jose Vizcaino, P Julian Tavarez and a player to be named later (November 13, 1996). ... On Fresno disabled list (June 29-July 11, 1998). ... Granted free agency (October 15, 1998). ... Signed by Kansas City Royals organization (December 17, 1998). ... Released by Royals (March 29, 1999). ... Signed by Cleveland Indians organization (March 28, 2000). ... On Buffalo disabled list (April 6-May 19, 2000). ... Granted free agency (October 18, 2000). ... Signed by Florida Marlins organization (December 28, 2000). ... Granted free agency (October 15, 2001). ... Re-signed by Marlins organization (November 20, 2001). ... On Portland disabled list (April 15-May 2, 2001). ... Released by Marlins (March 19, 2002). ... Signed by Pittsburgh Pirates organization (March 22, 2002). ... Traded by Pirates to Philadelphia Phillies for future considerations (March 28, 2002). ... Elected free agency (June 3, 2003). ... Signed by Colorado Rockies (July 4, 2003). ... Claimed off waivers by San Diego (July 23, 2003).

CAREER HITTING: 10-for-47 (.213), 1 R, 1 2B, 0 3B, 0 HR, 3 RBI.

Year League	W	L	Pct.	ERA	WHIP	G	GS	CG	ShO	Hld.	Sv.-Opp.	IP	H	R	ER	HR	BB-IBB	SO	Avg.
1989— GC Braves (GCL)	2	2	.500	2.89	1.34	13	4	0	0	...	0-...	37.1	40	18	12	2	10-1	21	.276
1990— Pulaski (Appal.)	4	2	.667	2.97	1.07	14	11	3	1	...	0-...	75.2	55	29	25	3	26-0	49	.195
1991— Macon (S. Atl.)	13	3	.813	2.17	0.99	30	18	4	2	...	1-...	141.0	106	46	34	6	33-4	96	.206
1992— St. Lucie (Fla. St.)	9	7	.563	3.63	1.22	26	24	2	1	...	0-...	156.1	176	80	63	9	15-1	61	.287
1993— Binghamton (Eastern)	12	7	.632	3.87	1.28	32	23	2	1	...	0-...	167.1	190	80	72	9	24-0	73	.291
1994— Binghamton (Eastern)	2	1	.667	1.80	0.95	3	3	0	0	...	0-...	20.0	18	6	4	0	1-0	11	.240
— Norfolk (Int'l)	8	8	.500	3.49	1.30	25	25	5	0	...	0-...	167.2	184	82	65	16	34-1	74	.283
1995— Buffalo (A.A.)	* 17	3	.850	3.50	1.19	25	24	3	0	...	0-...	164.2	168	71	64	9	28-1	93	.264
— Cleveland (A.L.)	0	1	.000	6.00	1.83	1	1	0	0	0	0-0	6.0	9	4	4	1	2-0	0	.360
1996— Buffalo (A.A.)	11	8	.579	3.27	1.19	26	24	5	0	...	0-...	165.1	161	66	60	19	36-0	82	.257
— Cleveland (A.L.)	0	0	...	10.80	4.20	1	0	0	0	0	0-0	1.2	4	2	2	0	3-0	0	.500
1997— San Francisco (N.L.)	2	5	.286	5.21	1.61	28	3	0	0	2	0-0	65.2	86	40	38	8	20-5	34	.333
— Phoenix (PCL)	3	1	.750	4.75	1.50	6	5	0	0	...	0-...	36.0	43	21	19	4	11-0	16	.297
1998— Fresno (PCL)	12	9	.571	5.17	1.38	27	27	2	1	...	0-...	162.0	192	102	93	26	32-0	97	.293
1999—										Did not play.									
2000— Akron (East.)	6	5	.545	3.41	1.25	19	14	1	0	...	0-...	103.0	91	48	39	7	38-0	59	.235
2001— Portland (East.)	0	2	.000	3.00	1.08	7	7	0	0	...	0-...	36.0	36	15	12	2	3-1	26	.267
— Calgary (PCL)	6	6	.500	3.92	1.18	19	19	1	0	...	0-...	124.0	134	58	54	16	12-2	81	.276
2002— Scran./W.B. (I.L.)	14	0	1.000	1.86	0.89	17	17	1	0	...	0-...	111.0	83	24	23	4	16-2	74	.209
— Philadelphia (N.L.)	4	4	.500	4.04	1.28	14	11	0	0	0	0-0	71.1	78	33	32	11	13-2	35	.279
2003— Philadelphia (N.L.)	0	2	.000	6.05	1.66	6	3	0	0	0	0-0	19.1	28	13	13	3	4-0	16	.341
— Indianapolis (Int'l)	2	2	.500	4.74	1.42	5	4	0	0	...	0-...	24.2	32	15	13	3	3-0	18	.323
— Colorado (N.L.)	0	0	...	4.05	1.05	4	0	0	0	0	0-0	6.2	7	3	3	2	0-0	4	.269
— San Diego (N.L.)	1	1	.500	6.75	1.58	18	1	0	0	0	0-0	25.1	34	20	19	5	6-0	18	.315
American League totals (2 years)	0	1	.000	7.04	2.35	2	1	0	0	0	0-0	7.2	13	6	6	1	5-0	0	.394
National League totals (3 years)	7	12	.368	5.02	1.47	70	18	0	0	2	0-0	188.1	233	109	105	29	43-7	107	.309
Major League totals (5 years)	7	13	.350	5.10	1.50	72	19	0	0	2	0-0	196.0	246	115	111	30	48-7	107	.313

ROACH, JASON — P

PERSONAL: Born April 20, 1976, in Kinston, N.C. ... 6-4/205. ... Throws right, bats right. ... Full name: Jason Glenn Roach. ... High school: North Lenoir (N.C.). ... College: UNC-Wilmington.

TRANSACTIONS/CAREER NOTES: Selected by New York Mets organization in 20th round of free-agent draft (June 1997).

CAREER HITTING: 2-for-2 (1.000), 0 R, 0 2B, 0 3B, 0 HR, 0 RBI.

Year League	W	L	Pct.	ERA	WHIP	G	GS	CG	ShO	Hld.	Sv.-Opp.	IP	H	R	ER	HR	BB-IBB	SO	Avg.
1998— Capital City (S. Atl.)	0	0	...	0.00	2.00	1	0	0	0	...	0-...	1.0	1	0	0	0	1-0	1	.250
1999— St. Lucie (Fla. St.)	0	0	...	0.00	0.50	2	0	0	0	...	0-...	2.0	1	0	0	0	0-0	3	.143
2000— St. Lucie (Fla. St.)	5	3	.625	2.59	1.11	9	9	0	0	...	0-...	48.2	42	15	14	2	12-0	22	.239
— Binghamton (Eastern)	0	0	...	3.60	2.00	1	1	0	0	...	0-...	5.0	7	3	2	0	3-0	3	.350
— Pittsfield (NYP)	1	1	.500	2.36	0.94	5	5	0	0	...	0-...	26.2	18	11	7	0	7-0	26	.182
2001— Binghamton (Eastern)	8	7	.533	3.26	1.35	22	21	0	0	...	0-...	116.0	129	54	42	7	28-1	70	.282
— Norfolk (Int'l)	1	2	.333	7.16	1.71	4	4	0	0	...	0-...	16.1	21	13	13	1	7-1	7	.318
2002— Binghamton (Eastern)	3	4	.429	3.65	1.17	8	8	0	0	...	0-...	44.1	40	19	18	3	12-0	23	.252
— Norfolk (Int'l)	6	6	.500	2.79	1.39	19	17	0	0	...	0-...	106.1	117	41	33	9	31-2	64	.278
2003— New York (N.L.)	0	2	.000	12.00	2.00	2	2	0	0	0	0-0	9.0	14	12	12	3	4-0	2	.350
— Norfolk (Int'l)	5	11	.313	5.07	1.46	31	20	2	0	...	0-...	120.2	140	74	68	12	36-1	98	.292
Major League totals (1 year)	0	2	.000	12.00	2.00	2	2	0	0	0	0-0	9.0	14	12	12	3	4-0	2	.350

ROBERTS, BRIAN   SS

PERSONAL: Born October 9, 1977, in Durham, N.C. ... 5-9/172. ... Bats both, throws right. ... Full name: Brian Michael Roberts. ... High school: Chapel Hill (N.C.). ... College: South Carolina.

TRANSACTIONS/CAREER NOTES: Selected by Baltimore Orioles organization in supplemental round ("sandwich pick" between first and second round, 50th pick overall) of free-agent draft (June 2, 1999); pick received as part of compensation for Texas Rangers signing Type A free agent 1B Rafael Palmeiro. ... On Frederick disabled list (April 19-July 13, 2000); included rehabilitation assignment to Gulf Coast Orioles (July 2-13). ... Recalled from Ottawa (May 21, 2003).

2003 GAMES PLAYED BY POSITION (MLB): 2B—107, DH—4, SS—2.

Year	Team (League)	Pos.	G	AB	R	H	2B	3B	HR	RBI	BB	SO	HBP	GDP	SB-CS	Avg.	OBP	SLG	OPS	E	Pct.
1999— Delmarva (S. Atl.)		SS	47	167	22	40	12	1	0	21	27	42	1	0	17-5	.240	.347	.323	.670	8	.964
2000— Frederick (Carolina)		SS	48	163	27	49	6	3	0	16	27	24	1	4	13-10	.301	.403	.374	.777	8	.952
— GC Orioles (GCL)		SS	9	29	8	9	1	2	1	3	7	4	0	0	7-1	.310	.432	.586	1.019	2	.905
2001— Bowie (East.)		2B-SS	22	81	12	24	7	0	1	7	9	12	1	2	10-0	.296	.366	.420	.785	3	.968
— Rochester (Int'l)		SS	44	161	16	43	4	1	1	12	28	22	0	0	23-3	.267	.376	.323	.699	13	.927
— Baltimore (A.L.)		SS-2B-DH	75	273	42	69	12	3	2	17	13	36	0	3	12-3	.253	.284	.341	.624	16	.941
2002— Rochester (Int'l)		2B	78	313	49	86	9	7	3	30	40	46	3	3	22-4	.275	.361	.377	.738	7	.978
— Baltimore (A.L.)		2B-DH	38	128	18	29	6	0	1	11	15	21	1	3	9-2	.227	.308	.297	.605	3	.977
2003— Ottawa (Int'l)		2B-SS	44	178	36	56	13	1	0	15	27	12	0	3	19-6	.315	.401	.399	.800	4	.979
— Baltimore (A.L.)		2B-DH-SS	112	460	65	124	22	4	5	41	46	58	1	9	23-6	.270	.337	.367	.704	9	.983
Major League totals (3 years)			225	861	125	222	40	7	8	69	74	115	2	15	44-11	.258	.316	.348	.664	28	.970

ROBERTS, DAVE   OF

PERSONAL: Born May 31, 1972, in Okinawa, Japan. ... 5-10/180. ... Bats left, throws left. ... Full name: David Ray Roberts. ... High school: Rancho Buena Vista (Oceanside, Calif.). ... College: UCLA.

TRANSACTIONS/CAREER NOTES: Selected by Detroit Tigers organization in 28th round of free-agent draft (June 2, 1994). ... Loaned by Tigers to Visalia, Oakland Athletics organization (March 30-August 30, 1996). ... Traded by Tigers with P Tim Worrell to Cleveland Indians for OF Geronimo Berroa (June 24, 1998). ... On Akron disabled list (August 10-18, 1998). ... On Cleveland disabled list (March 31-June 24, 2001); included rehabilitation assignment to Akron (June 4-24). ... Traded by Indians to Los Angeles Dodgers for P Christian Bridenbaugh and P Nial Hughes (December 21, 2001). ... Placed on the 15-day diasbled list (May 17, 2003). ... Sent on rehab assignment to Las Vegas (May 29, 2003). ... Recalled from Las Vegas rehab assignment (May 29, 2003). ... Reinstated from 15-day disabled list (June 1, 2003). ... Placed on 15-day disabled list (July 2, 2003). ... Sent to Ogden on rehab assignment (July 22, 2003). ... Recalled from Ogden rehab assignment (July 25, 2003). ... Reinstated from 15-day disabled list (July 26, 2003).

2003 GAMES PLAYED BY POSITION (MLB): OF—105.

Year	Team (League)	Pos.	G	AB	R	H	2B	3B	HR	RBI	BB	SO	HBP	GDP	SB-CS	Avg.	OBP	SLG	OPS	E	Pct.
1994— Jamestown (NYP)		OF	54	178	33	52	7	2	0	12	29	27	1	0	12-8	.292	.392	.354	.746	0	1.000
1995— Lakeland (Fla. St.)		OF	92	357	67	108	10	5	3	30	39	43	1	7	30-8	.303	.371	.384	.755	1	.985
1996— Visalia (Calif.)		OF	126	482	* 112	131	24	7	5	37	98	105	1	6	* 65-21	.272	.391	.382	.773	5	.977
— Jacksonville (Sou.)		OF	3	9	0	2	0	0	0	0	1	0	0	0	0-1	.222	.300	.222	.522	0	1.000
1997— Jacksonville (Sou.)		OF	105	415	76	123	24	2	4	41	45	62	2	5	23-5	.296	.366	.393	.759	4	.954
1998— Jacksonville (Sou.)		OF	69	279	71	91	14	5	5	42	53	59	3	4	21-9	.326	.434	.466	.900	1	.992
— Akron (East.)		OF	56	227	49	82	10	5	7	33	35	30	1	3	28-6	.361	.447	.542	.989	1	.992
— Buffalo (Int'l)		OF	5	15	2	2	0	0	0	2	0	3	0	0	2-0	.133	.133	.133	.258	0	1.000
1999— Buffalo (Int'l)		OF-DH	89	350	65	95	17	* 10	0	38	43	52	2	1	39-3	.271	.351	.377	.728	1	.996
— Cleveland (A.L.)		OF	41	143	26	34	4	0	2	12	9	16	0	0	11-3	.238	.281	.308	.589	0	1.000
2000— Buffalo (Int'l)		OF	120	462	93	135	16	3	13	55	59	68	2	3	39-11	.292	.373	.424	.798	1	.997
— Cleveland (A.L.)		OF	19	10	1	2	0	0	0	0	2	2	0	0	1-1	.200	.333	.200	.533	0	1.000
2001— Akron (East.)		OF	17	64	9	13	5	0	0	2	9	8	1	1	4-0	.203	.307	.281	.588	1	.969
— Buffalo (Int'l)		OF	62	241	34	73	12	4	0	22	18	44	2	2	17-6	.303	.352	.386	.738	3	.978
— Cleveland (A.L.)		OF-DH	15	12	3	4	1	0	0	2	1	2	0	0	0-1	.333	.385	.417	.801	0	1.000
2002— Los Angeles (N.L.)		OF	127	422	63	117	14	7	3	34	48	51	2	1	45-10	.277	.353	.365	.718	0	1.000
2003— Las Vegas (PCL)		OF	2	5	2	0	0	0	0	0	1	0	0	0	0-0	.000	.167	.000	.167	0	.000
— Ogden (Pio.)		OF	3	10	4	4	0	0	0	0	1	0	0	0	1-0	.400	.455	.400	.855	0	1.000
— Los Angeles (N.L.)		OF	107	388	56	97	6	5	2	16	43	39	4	0	40-14	.250	.331	.307	.638	5	.976
American League totals (3 years)			75	165	30	40	5	0	2	14	12	20	0	0	12-5	.242	.292	.309	.601	0	1.000
National League totals (2 years)			234	810	119	214	20	12	5	50	91	90	6	1	85-24	.264	.343	.337	.680	5	.989
Major League totals (5 years)			309	975	149	254	25	12	7	64	103	110	6	1	97-29	.261	.334	.332	.667	5	.991

ROBERTS, GRANT   P

PERSONAL: Born September 13, 1977, in El Cajon, Calif. ... 6-3/205. ... Throws right, bats right. ... Full name: Grant William Roberts. ... High school: Grossmont (La Mesa, Calif.).

TRANSACTIONS/CAREER NOTES: Selected by New York Mets organization in 11th round of free-agent draft (June 1, 1995). ... On New York disabled list (June 9-30 and July 13-September 10, 2002); included rehabilitation assignment to Binghamton (June 28-30). ... On disabled list (March 28-April 30, 2003). ... Recalled from New York from St. Lucie rehab assignment (April 24, 2003). ... Transferred to Emergency disabled list (May 15, 2003). ... Sent to St. Lucie on rehab assignment (July 7, 2003).

CAREER HITTING: 1-for-4 (.250), 1 R, 0 2B, 0 3B, 0 HR, 0 RBI.

Year	League	W	L	Pct.	ERA	WHIP	G	GS	CG	ShO	Hld.	Sv.-Opp.	IP	H	R	ER	HR	BB-IBB	SO	Avg.
1995— GC Mets (GCL)		2	1	.667	2.15	1.13	11	3	0	0	...	0-...	29.1	19	13	7	1	14-1	24	.186
1996— Kingsport (Appal.)		* 9	1	.900	2.10	1.17	13	13	2	* 2	...	0-...	68.2	43	18	16	3	37-1	* 92	.179
1997— Capital City (S. Atl.)		11	3	.786	2.36	1.10	22	22	2	1	...	0-...	129.2	98	37	34	1	44-0	122	.208
1998— St. Lucie (Fla. St.)		4	5	.444	4.23	1.51	17	17	0	0	...	0-...	72.1	72	37	34	11	37-0	70	.258
1999— Binghamton (Eastern)		7	6	.538	4.87	1.40	23	23	0	0	...	0-...	131.1	135	81	71	9	49-0	94	.267
— Norfolk (Int'l)		2	1	.667	4.50	1.54	5	5	0	0	...	0-...	28.0	32	15	14	1	11-2	30	.291
2000— Norfolk (Int'l)		7	8	.467	3.38	1.38	25	25	5	0	...	0-...	157.1	154	67	59	6	63-5	115	.254
— New York (N.L.)		0	0	...	11.57	2.14	4	1	0	0	0	0-0	7.0	11	10	9	0	4-1	6	.344
2001— Norfolk (Int'l)		3	5	.375	4.52	1.46	30	6	0	0	...	2-...	67.2	80	38	34	4	19-1	54	.297
— New York (N.L.)		1	0	1.000	3.81	1.23	16	0	0	0	1	0-1	26.0	24	11	11	2	8-1	29	.240
2002— New York (N.L.)		3	1	.750	2.20	1.31	34	0	0	0	4	0-0	45.0	43	12	11	3	16-7	31	.253
— Binghamton (Eastern)		0	0	...	0.00	0.00	1	1	0	0	...	0-...	1.0	0	0	0	0	0-0	1	.000
2003— St. Lucie (Fla. St.)		1	0	1.000	0.00	0.89	5	2	0	0	...	0-...	9.0	5	4	0	0	3-0	5	.156
— Norfolk (Int'l)		0	0	...	3.52	1.57	8	0	0	0	...	0-...	7.2	7	3	3	0	5-0	6	.233
— New York (N.L.)		0	3	.000	3.79	1.16	18	0	0	0	4	1-1	19.0	19	9	8	0	3-1	10	.257
Major League totals (4 years)		4	4	.500	3.62	1.32	72	1	0	0	5	1-2	97.0	97	42	39	5	31-10	76	.258

ROBERTS, WILLIS   P

PERSONAL: Born June 19, 1975, in San Cristobal, Dominican Republic. ... 6-3/240. ... Throws right, bats right. ... Full name: Willis Augusto Roberts.

TRANSACTIONS/CAREER NOTES: Signed as non-drafted free agent by Detroit Tigers organization (February 18, 1992). ... On disabled list (July 14-August 1 and August 1-September 13, 1994). ... On Toledo disabled list (May 3-20, 1999). ... Released by Tigers (February 1, 2000). ... Signed by Cincinnati Reds organization (February 1, 2000). ... Granted free agency (October 18, 2000). ... Signed by Baltimore Orioles organization (November 16, 2000). ... On suspended list (September 13-18, 2002). ... Placed on 15-day disabled list (June 29, 2003). ... Transferred to emergency disabled list (July 31, 2003).

CAREER HITTING: 1-for-4 (.250), 0 R, 0 2B, 0 3B, 0 HR, 0 RBI.

Year League	W	L	Pct.	ERA	WHIP	G	GS	CG	ShO	Hld.	Sv.-Opp.	IP	H	R	ER	HR	BB-IBB	SO	Avg.
1992— Dominican Tigers (DSL)	0	6	.000	8.23	2.54	12	7	1	0	...	0-...	35.0	43	49	32	...	46-...	17	...
1993— Bristol (Appal.)	2	3	.400	1.38	1.35	10	2	0	0	...	1-...	26.0	24	16	4	0	11-0	23	.235
1994— Bristol (Appal.)	1	2	.333	3.92	0.82	4	4	0	0	...	0-...	20.2	9	9	9	1	8-0	17	.129
1995— Fayetteville (S. Atl.)	6	3	.667	2.70	1.40	17	15	0	0	...	0-...	80.0	72	33	24	2	40-0	52	.248
1996— Lakeland (Fla. St.)	9	7	.563	2.89	1.35	23	22	2	0	...	0-...	149.1	133	60	48	5	69-0	105	.244
1997— Jacksonville (Sou.)	6	* 15	.286	6.28	1.64	26	26	2	0	...	0-...	149.0	181	* 120	* 104	18	64-0	86	.301
1998— Jacksonville (Sou.)	3	1	.750	2.19	1.26	12	2	0	0	...	0-...	24.2	21	10	6	0	10-1	15	.233
— Toledo (Int'l)	3	3	.500	4.61	1.66	39	0	0	0	...	2-...	54.2	63	33	28	4	28-2	40	.294
1999— Toledo (Int'l)	5	8	.385	6.26	1.86	31	12	2	0	...	0-...	92.0	112	68	64	10	59-3	52	.307
— Detroit (A.L.)	0	0	...	13.50	2.25	1	0	0	0	0	0-0	1.1	3	4	2	0	0-0	0	.500
2000— Chattanooga (Sou.)	4	0	1.000	3.06	1.42	5	5	0	0	...	0-...	32.1	33	12	11	0	13-1	28	.280
— Louisville (Int'l)	7	8	.467	5.66	1.56	25	20	2	1	...	0-...	124.0	138	80	78	19	55-0	66	.288
2001— Baltimore (A.L.)	9	10	.474	4.91	1.49	46	18	1	0	1	6-10	132.0	142	75	72	15	55-1	95	.274
2002— Baltimore (A.L.)	5	4	.556	3.36	1.48	66	0	0	0	13	1-3	75.0	79	34	28	5	32-3	51	.270
2003— Baltimore (A.L.)	3	1	.750	5.72	1.45	26	0	0	0	1	0-0	39.1	41	26	25	7	16-2	26	.273
Major League totals (4 years)	17	15	.531	4.62	1.49	139	18	1	0	15	7-13	247.2	265	139	127	27	103-6	172	.274

ROBERTSON, JERIOME   P

PERSONAL: Born March 30, 1977, in San Jose, Calif. ... 6-1/200. ... Throws left, bats left. ... Full name: Jeriome Paul Robertson. ... Name pronounced: JER-oh-mee. ... High school: Exeter (Calif.) Union. ... College: Washington.

TRANSACTIONS/CAREER NOTES: Selected by Houston Astros organization in 24th round of free-agent draft (June 1, 1995). ... On Round Rock disabled list (April 6-24, 2000). ... Optioned to New Orleans (May 2, 2003). ... Recalled from New Orleans (May 12, 2003).

CAREER HITTING: 8-for-52 (.154), 4 R, 0 2B, 1 3B, 0 HR, 3 RBI.

Year League	W	L	Pct.	ERA	WHIP	G	GS	CG	ShO	Hld.	Sv.-Opp.	IP	H	R	ER	HR	BB-IBB	SO	Avg.
1996— GC Astros (GCL)	5	3	.625	1.72	0.84	13	• 13	1	1	...	0-...	78.1	51	20	15	2	15-0	* 98	.181
— Kissimmee (Fla. St.)	0	0	...	2.57	0.71	1	1	0	0	...	0-...	7.0	4	4	2	0	1-0	2	.154
1997— Quad City (Midw.)	11	8	.579	4.07	1.42	26	25	2	1	...	1-...	146.0	151	86	66	12	56-1	135	.261
1998— Kissimmee (Fla. St.)	10	10	.500	3.70	1.36	28	• 28	2	0	...	0-...	* 175.0	185	83	72	13	53-3	131	.276
1999— Jackson (Texas)	* 15	7	.682	3.06	1.20	28	• 28	1	0	...	0-...	* 191.0	184	81	65	22	45-2	133	.253
2000— Kissimmee (Fla. St.)	2	1	.667	4.66	1.14	5	5	1	1	...	0-...	29.0	28	19	15	1	5-0	13	.248
— Round Rock (Texas)	2	2	.500	4.13	1.31	11	10	0	0	...	0-...	61.0	62	36	28	8	18-1	30	.257
— New Orleans (PCL)	1	7	.125	7.07	1.75	9	9	0	0	...	0-...	49.2	64	42	39	10	23-1	27	.323
2001— Round Rock (Texas)	5	1	.833	3.91	1.49	57	0	0	0	...	3-...	73.2	89	33	32	10	21-0	72	.296
2002— New Orleans (PCL)	12	8	.600	2.55	1.14	27	27	2	1	...	0-...	* 180.0	160	59	51	13	45-0	114	.238
— Houston (N.L.)	0	2	.000	6.52	1.86	11	1	0	0	0	0-0	9.2	13	8	7	4	5-3	6	.394
2003— New Orleans (PCL)	1	0	1.000	6.75	1.35	1	1	0	0	...	0-...	6.2	7	5	5	2	2-0	6	.269
— Houston (N.L.)	15	9	.625	5.10	1.52	32	31	0	0	0	0-0	160.2	180	98	91	23	64-8	99	.287
Major League totals (2 years)	15	11	.577	5.18	1.54	43	32	0	0	0	0-0	170.1	193	106	98	27	69-11	105	.292

ROBERTSON, NATE   P

PERSONAL: Born September 3, 1977, in Wichita, Kan. ... 6-2/215. ... Throws left, bats right. ... Full name: Nathan D. Robertson. ... College: Wichita State.

TRANSACTIONS/CAREER NOTES: Selected by Florida Marlins organization in fifth round of free-agent draft (June 2, 1999). ... Traded by Marlins with P Gary Knotts and P Rob Henkel to Detroit Tigers for P Mark Redman and P Jerrod Fuell (January 11, 2003).

CAREER HITTING: 0-for-2 (.000), 0 R, 0 2B, 0 3B, 0 HR, 0 RBI.

Year League	W	L	Pct.	ERA	WHIP	G	GS	CG	ShO	Hld.	Sv.-Opp.	IP	H	R	ER	HR	BB-IBB	SO	Avg.
1999— Utica (N.Y.-Penn)	2	0	1.000	2.77	1.15	5	5	0	0	...	0-...	26.0	22	9	8	0	8-0	26	.244
— Kane County (Midwest)	6	1	.857	2.29	1.06	8	8	1	1	...	0-...	51.0	42	14	13	1	12-0	33	.230
2000— Kane County (Midwest)	0	2	.000	5.09	1.70	6	6	0	0	...	0-...	17.2	24	13	10	0	6-0	15	.324
2001— Brevard County (FSL)	11	4	.733	2.88	1.30	19	19	2	0	...	0-...	106.1	95	44	34	3	43-1	67	.244
2002— Portland (East.)	10	9	.526	3.42	1.26	27	27	3	0	...	0-...	163.0	156	77	62	12	50-2	109	.260
— Florida (N.L.)	0	1	.000	11.88	2.28	6	1	0	0	0	0-0	8.1	15	11	11	3	4-1	3	.375
2003— Toledo (Int'l)	9	7	.563	3.14	1.24	24	23	3	1	...	0-...	155.0	145	62	54	14	47-2	102	.250
— Detroit (A.L.)	1	2	.333	5.44	1.75	8	8	0	0	0	0-0	44.2	55	27	27	6	23-2	33	.306
American League totals (1 year)	1	2	.333	5.44	1.75	8	8	0	0	0	0-0	44.2	55	27	27	6	23-2	33	.306
National League totals (1 year)	0	1	.000	11.88	2.28	6	1	0	0	0	0-0	8.1	15	11	11	3	4-1	3	.375
Major League totals (2 years)	1	3	.250	6.45	1.83	14	9	0	0	0	0-0	53.0	70	38	38	9	27-3	36	.318

ROBINSON, KERRY   OF

PERSONAL: Born October 3, 1973, in St. Louis, Mo. ... 6-0/175. ... Bats left, throws left. ... Full name: Kerry Keith Robinson. ... High school: Hazelwood East (St. Louis). ... College: Southeast Missouri State.

TRANSACTIONS/CAREER NOTES: Selected by St. Louis Cardinals organization in 34th round of free-agent draft (June 1, 1995). ... Selected by Tampa Bay Devil Rays in second round (44th pick overall) of expansion draft (November 18, 1997). ... Claimed on waivers by Seattle Mariners (November 19, 1998). ... Traded by Mariners to Cincinnati Reds for P Todd Williams (July 22, 1999). ... Granted free agency (October 18, 2000). ... Signed by Cardinals organization (May 17, 2001).

2003 GAMES PLAYED BY POSITION (MLB): OF—88.

Year Team (League)	Pos.	G	AB	R	H	2B	3B	HR	RBI	BB	SO	HBP	GDP	SB-CS	Avg.	OBP	SLG	OPS	E	Pct.
1995— Johnson City (App.)	OF	60	250	44	74	12	8	1	26	16	30	0	3	14-10	.296	.336	.420	.756	6	.938
1996— Peoria (Midw.)	OF	123	440	98	158	17	4	2	47	51	51	3	2	•50-26	.359	.422	.430	.852	7	.962
1997— Arkansas (Texas)	OF	135	*523	80	168	16	3	2	62	54	64	2	7	40-23	.321	.386	.375	.760	7	.966
— Louisville (A.A.)	OF	2	9	0	1	0	0	0	0	0	1	0	0	0-0	.111	.111	.111	.222	0	1.000
1998— Orlando (South.)	OF	72	309	45	83	7	5	2	26	27	28	0	6	28-9	.269	.325	.343	.668	0	1.000
— Durham (Int'l)	OF	58	242	28	73	7	4	1	28	23	30	0	1	18-11	.302	.361	.376	.737	2	.987
— Tampa Bay (A.L.)	OF	2	3	0	0	0	0	0	0	0	1	0	0	0-0	.000	.000	.000	.000	0	1.000
1999— Tacoma (PCL)	OF-DH	79	335	53	108	16	•9	0	34	14	44	0	4	30-7	.322	.348	.424	.771	4	.974
— Indianapolis (Int'l)	OF	34	129	24	34	3	2	1	14	4	12	1	2	14-4	.264	.285	.341	.626	2	.977
— Cincinnati (N.L.)	OF	9	1	4	0	0	0	0	0	0	1	0	0	0-1	.000	.000	.000	.000	0	...
2000— Columbus (Int'l)	OF	119	437	71	139	17	9	0	32	41	40	2	5	37-18	.318	.378	.384	.777	3	.988
2001— Memphis (PCL)	OF	10	40	4	13	1	0	0	3	4	10	0	1	4-1	.325	.386	.350	.736	0	1.000
— St. Louis (N.L.)	OF	114	186	34	53	6	1	1	15	12	20	2	1	11-2	.285	.330	.344	.674	2	.981
2002— St. Louis (N.L.)	OF-DH	124	181	27	47	7	4	1	15	11	29	0	1	7-4	.260	.301	.359	.660	2	.977
2003— Memphis (PCL)	OF	16	61	14	21	2	1	0	3	1	7	0	0	5-0	.344	.355	.410	.765	1	.979
— St. Louis (N.L.)	OF	116	208	19	52	6	3	1	16	8	27	1	3	6-1	.250	.281	.322	.603	0	1.000
American League totals (1 year)		2	3	0	0	0	0	0	0	0	1	0	0	0-0	.000	.000	.000	.000	0	1.000
National League totals (4 years)		363	576	84	152	19	8	3	46	31	77	3	5	24-8	.264	.303	.340	.643	4	.986
Major League totals (5 years)		365	579	84	152	19	8	3	46	31	78	3	5	24-8	.263	.301	.339	.640	4	.986

ROCKER, JOHN — P

PERSONAL: Born October 17, 1974, in Statesboro, Ga. ... 6-4/225. ... Throws left, bats right. ... Full name: John Loy Rocker. ... High school: First Presbyterian Day School (Macon, Ga.). ... College: Mercer.

TRANSACTIONS/CAREER NOTES: Selected by Atlanta Braves organization in 18th round of free-agent draft (June 3, 1993). ... On suspended list (April 3-18, 2000). ... Traded by Braves with 3B Troy Cameron to Cleveland Indians for P Steve Karsay and P Steve Reed (June 22, 2001). ... Traded by Indians to Texas Rangers for P David Elder (December 18, 2001). ... On Texas disabled list (July 4, 2002-remainder of season); included rehabilitation assignment to Tulsa (August 8-21). ... Released by Rangers (October 3, 2002). ... Signed by Tampa Bay Devil Rays organization (April 10, 2003). ... Assigned to Orlando (May 1, 2003). ... Contract purchased by Tampa Bay (May 9, 2003). ... Optioned to Durham (May 16, 2003). ... Designated for assignment (May 27, 2003). ... Sent outright to Durham; elected free agency (May 29, 2003).

CAREER HITTING: 0-for-0 (.000), 0 R, 0 2B, 0 3B, 0 HR, 0 RBI.

Year League	W	L	Pct.	ERA	WHIP	G	GS	CG	ShO	Hld.	Sv.-Opp.	IP	H	R	ER	HR	BB-IBB	SO	Avg.
1994— Danville (Appal.)	1	5	.167	3.53	1.38	12	12	1	0	...	0-...	63.2	50	36	25	4	38-1	72	.214
1995— Macon (S. Atl.)	4	4	.500	4.50	1.60	16	16	0	0	...	0-...	86.0	86	50	43	5	52-0	61	.271
— Eugene (NW)	1	5	.167	5.16	1.37	12	12	0	0	...	0-...	59.1	45	40	34	4	36-0	74	.206
1996— Macon (S. Atl.)	5	3	.625	3.89	1.39	20	19	2	2	...	0-...	106.1	85	60	46	7	63-1	107	.224
— Durham (Caro.)	4	3	.571	3.39	1.51	9	9	0	0	...	0-...	58.1	63	24	22	4	25-0	43	.288
1997— Durham (Caro.)	1	1	.500	4.33	1.56	11	11	0	0	...	0-...	35.1	33	21	17	3	22-0	39	.254
— Greenville (Sou.)	5	6	.455	4.86	1.59	22	18	0	0	...	0-...	113.0	119	69	61	12	61-0	96	.269
1998— Richmond (Int'l)	1	1	.500	1.42	1.21	9	0	0	0	...	1-...	19.0	13	4	3	1	10-0	22	.186
— Atlanta (N.L.)	1	3	.250	2.13	1.16	47	0	0	0	15	24-9	38.0	22	10	9	4	22-4	42	.172
1999— Atlanta (N.L.)	4	5	.444	2.49	1.16	74	0	0	0	0	38-45	72.1	47	24	20	5	37-4	104	.180
2000— Atlanta (N.L.)	1	2	.333	2.89	1.70	59	0	0	0	4	24-27	53.0	42	25	17	7	48-4	77	.210
— Richmond (Int'l)	0	0	...	3.00	1.33	3	0	0	0	...	1-...	3.0	3	1	1	0	1-0	6	.273
2001— Atlanta (N.L.)	2	2	.500	3.09	1.28	30	0	0	0	0	19-23	32.0	25	13	11	2	16-1	36	.216
— Cleveland (A.L.)	3	7	.300	5.45	1.67	38	0	0	0	7	4-7	34.2	33	23	21	2	25-3	43	.250
2002— Texas (A.L.)	2	3	.400	6.66	1.73	30	0	0	0	10	1-4	24.1	29	19	18	5	13-1	30	.299
— Oklahoma (PCL)	1	0	1.000	0.00	0.69	6	0	0	0	...	0-...	8.2	4	0	0	0	2-0	14	.133
— Tulsa (Texas)	0	1	.000	13.50	1.88	3	0	0	0	...	0-...	2.2	3	4	4	0	2-0	5	.300
2003— Tampa Bay (A.L.)	0	0	...	9.00	5.00	2	0	0	0	...	0-0	1.0	2	1	1	0	3-0	0	.500
— Orlando (Sou.)	0	1	.000	9.15	2.49	17	0	0	0	...	0-...	19.2	23	23	20	4	26-0	20	.295
American League totals (3 years)	5	10	.333	6.00	1.75	70	0	0	0	17	5-11	60.0	64	43	40	7	41-4	73	.275
National League totals (4 years)	8	12	.400	2.63	1.33	210	0	0	0	19	83-99	195.1	136	72	57	16	123-13	259	.193
Major League totals (6 years)	13	22	.371	3.42	1.43	280	0	0	0	36	88-110	255.1	200	115	97	23	164-17	332	.213

RODNEY, FERNANDO — P

PERSONAL: Born March 18, 1977, in Samana, Dominican Republic. ... 5-11/208. ... Throws right, bats right.

TRANSACTIONS/CAREER NOTES: Signed as non-drafted free agent by Detroit Tigers organization (November 1, 1997). ... On disabled list (August 14, 2000-remainder of season). ... On Lakeland disabled list (May 22-June 30 and July 13-18, 2001).

CAREER HITTING: 0-for-0 (.000), 0 R, 0 2B, 0 3B, 0 HR, 0 RBI.

Year League	W	L	Pct.	ERA	WHIP	G	GS	CG	ShO	Hld.	Sv.-Opp.	IP	H	R	ER	HR	BB-IBB	SO	Avg.
1998— Dominican Tigers (DSL)	1	3	.250	3.38	1.38	11	5	0	0	...	1-...	32.0	25	16	12	...	19-...	37	...
1999— GC Tigers (GCL)	3	3	.500	2.40	1.37	22	0	0	0	...	9-...	30.0	20	8	8	1	21-0	39	.200
— Lakeland (Fla. St.)	1	0	1.000	1.42	1.26	4	0	0	0	...	2-...	6.1	7	1	1	0	1-0	5	.304
2000— West. Mich. (Mid.)	6	4	.600	2.94	1.32	22	10	0	0	...	0-...	82.2	74	34	27	2	35-0	56	.238
2001— Lakeland (Fla. St.)	4	2	.667	3.42	1.30	16	9	0	0	...	0-...	55.1	53	26	21	2	19-1	44	.249
— GC Tigers (GCL)	0	0	...	0.00	1.00	1	1	0	0	...	0-...	1.0	0	0	0	0	1-0	1	.000
— Erie (East.)	0	0	...	4.26	1.58	4	0	0	0	...	1-...	6.1	7	3	3	1	3-0	8	.292
2002— Erie (East.)	1	0	1.000	1.33	0.93	21	0	0	0	...	11-...	20.1	14	4	3	0	5-0	18	.194
— Detroit (A.L.)	1	3	.250	6.00	1.94	20	0	0	0	0	0-4	18.0	25	15	12	2	10-2	10	.329
— Toledo (Int'l)	1	1	.500	0.81	0.99	20	0	0	0	0	4-...	22.1	13	4	2	1	9-0	25	.171
2003— Toledo (Int'l)	1	1	.500	1.33	0.86	38	0	0	0	0	23-...	40.2	22	6	6	0	13-0	58	.163
— Detroit (A.L.)	1	3	.250	6.07	1.75	27	0	0	0	3	3-6	29.2	35	20	20	2	17-1	33	.294
Major League totals (2 years)	2	6	.250	6.04	1.83	47	0	0	0	3	3-10	47.2	60	35	32	4	27-3	43	.308

RODRIGUEZ, ALEX — SS

PERSONAL: Born July 27, 1975, in New York, N.Y. ... 6-3/210. ... Bats right, throws right. ... Full name: Alexander Emmanuel Rodriguez. ... Name pronounced: rod-RI-guez. ... High school: Westminster Christian (Miami).

TRANSACTIONS/CAREER NOTES: Selected by Seattle Mariners organization in first round (first pick overall) of free-agent draft (June 3, 1993). ... On Seattle disabled list (April 22-May 7, 1996); included rehabilitation assignment to Tacoma (May 5-7). ... On disabled list (June 12-27, 1997; April 7-May 14, 1999; and July 8-24, 2000). ... Granted free agency (October 30, 2000). ... Signed by Texas Rangers (December 11, 2000).

2003 GAMES PLAYED BY POSITION (MLB): SS—158, DH—1.

Year	Team (League)	Pos.	G	AB	R	H	2B	3B	HR	RBI	BB	SO	HBP	GDP	SB-CS	Avg.	OBP	SLG	OPS	E	Pct.
1994— Appleton (Midwest)		SS-DH	65	248	49	79	17	6	14	55	24	44	2	7	16-5	.319	.379	.605	.984	19	.934
— Jacksonville (Sou.)		SS	17	59	7	17	4	1	1	8	10	13	0	1	2-1	.288	.391	.441	.832	3	.964
— Seattle (A.L.)		SS	17	54	4	11	0	0	0	2	3	20	0	0	3-0	.204	.241	.204	.445	6	.915
— Calgary (PCL)		SS	32	119	22	37	7	4	6	21	8	25	1	1	2-4	.311	.359	.588	.948	3	.980
1995— Tacoma (PCL)		SS-DH	54	214	37	77	12	3	15	45	18	44	2	2	2-4	.360	.411	.654	1.065	10	.961
— Seattle (A.L.)		SS-DH	48	142	15	33	6	2	5	19	6	42	0	0	4-2	.232	.264	.408	.672	8	.953
1996— Seattle (A.L.)		SS	146	601	* 141	215	* 54	1	36	123	59	104	4	15	15-4	*.358	.414	.631	1.045	15	.977
— Tacoma (PCL)		SS	2	5	0	1	0	0	0	0	2	1	0	0	0-0	.200	.429	.200	.629	1	.833
1997— Seattle (A.L.)		SS-DH	141	587	100	176	40	3	23	84	41	99	5	14	29-6	.300	.350	.496	.846	* 24	.962
1998— Seattle (A.L.)		SS-DH	161	* 686	123	* 213	35	5	42	124	45	121	10	12	46-13	.310	.360	.560	.919	18	.975
1999— Seattle (A.L.)		SS	129	502	110	143	25	0	42	111	56	109	5	12	21-7	.285	.357	.586	.943	14	.977
2000— Seattle (A.L.)		SS	148	554	134	175	34	2	41	132	100	121	7	10	15-4	.316	.420	.606	1.026	10	.986
2001— Texas (A.L.)		SS-DH	• 162	632	* 133	201	34	1	* 52	135	75	131	16	17	18-3	.318	.399	.622	1.021	18	.976
2002— Texas (A.L.)		SS	• 162	624	125	187	27	2	* 57	* 142	87	122	10	14	9-4	.300	.392	.623	1.015	10	.987
2003— Texas (A.L.)		SS-DH	161	607	*124	181	30	6	* 47	118	87	126	15	16	17-3	.298	.396	*.600	.995	8	.989
Major League totals (10 years)			1275	4989	1009	1535	285	22	345	990	559	995	72	110	177-46	.308	.382	.581	.963	131	.977

RODRIGUEZ, FELIX   P

PERSONAL: Born September 9, 1972, in Montecristi, Dominican Republic. ... 6-1/198. ... Throws right, bats right. ... Full name: Felix Antonio Rodriguez. ... High school: Liceo Bijiador (Monte Cristi, Dominican Republic).

TRANSACTIONS/CAREER NOTES: Signed as non-drafted free agent by Los Angeles Dodgers organization (October 17, 1989). ... On disabled list (August 11, 1992-remainder of season). ... On Albuquerque disabled list (July 5-18, 1995). ... On disabled list (April 20-May 2 and May 12-27, 1996). ... Claimed on waivers by Cincinnati Reds (December 18, 1996). ... Traded by Reds to Arizona Diamondbacks for a player to be named later (November 11, 1997); Reds acquired P Scott Winchester to complete deal (November 18, 1997). ... On Arizona disabled list (June 21-July 30, 1998); included rehabilitation assignments to Arizona League Diamondbacks (July 20-27) and Tucson (July 28-30). ... Traded by Diamondbacks to San Francisco Giants for future considerations (December 8, 1998); Diamondbacks acquired P Troy Brohawn and OF Chris Van Rossum to complete deal (December 21, 1998). ... Placed on 15-day disabled list (August 26, 2003). ... Removed from 15-day disabled list (August 18, 2003).

CAREER HITTING: 4-for-15 (.267), 4 R, 1 2B, 0 3B, 1 HR, 3 RBI.

Year	League	W	L	Pct.	ERA	WHIP	G	GS	CG	ShO	Hld.	Sv.-Opp.	IP	H	R	ER	HR	BB-IBB	SO	Avg.
1993— Vero Beach (FSL)		8	8	.500	3.75	1.36	32	20	2	1	...	0-...	132.0	109	71	55	15	71-1	80	.225
1994— San Antonio (Texas)		6	8	.429	4.03	1.42	26	26	0	0	...	0-...	136.1	106	70	61	8	* 88-3	126	.219
1995— Albuquerque (PCL)		3	2	.600	4.24	1.53	14	11	0	0	...	0-...	51.0	52	29	24	5	26-0	46	.269
— Los Angeles (N.L.)		1	1	.500	2.53	1.50	11	0	0	0	0	0-1	10.2	11	3	3	2	5-0	5	.275
1996— Albuquerque (PCL)		3	9	.250	5.53	1.59	27	19	0	0	...	0-...	107.1	111	70	66	17	60-1	65	.280
1997— Indianapolis (A.A.)		3	3	.500	1.01	1.43	23	0	0	0	...	1-...	26.2	22	10	3	0	16-1	26	.212
— Cincinnati (N.L.)		0	0	...	4.30	1.65	26	1	0	0	0	0-0	46.0	48	23	22	2	28-2	34	.271
1998— Arizona (N.L.)		0	2	.000	6.14	1.66	43	0	0	0	0	5-8	44.0	44	31	30	5	29-1	36	.259
— Ariz. D'backs (Ariz.)		0	0	...	4.15	1.15	3	2	0	0	...	0-...	4.1	3	4	2	0	2-0	5	.200
— Tucson (PCL)		0	0	...	9.00	3.00	1	0	0	0	...	0-...	1.0	1	1	1	0	2-0	0	.250
1999— San Francisco (N.L.)		2	3	.400	3.80	1.45	47	0	0	0	3	0-1	66.1	67	32	28	6	29-2	55	.262
2000— San Francisco (N.L.)		4	2	.667	2.64	1.31	76	0	0	0	*30	3-8	81.2	65	29	24	6	42-2	95	.220
2001— San Francisco (N.L.)		9	1	.900	1.68	0.00	80	0	0	0	*32	0-3	80.1	53	16	15	5	27-2	91	.188
2002— San Francisco (N.L.)		8	6	.571	4.17	1.19	71	0	0	0	24	0-6	69.0	53	33	32	5	29-1	58	.212
2003— San Francisco (N.L.)		8	2	.800	3.10	1.44	68	0	0	0	19	2-3	61.0	59	21	21	5	29-2	46	.259
Major League totals (8 years)		32	17	.653	3.43	1.35	422	1	0	0	108	10-30	459.0	400	188	175	35	218-12	420	.235

RODRIGUEZ, FRANCISCO   P

PERSONAL: Born January 7, 1982, in Caracas, Venezuela. ... 6-0/185. ... Throws right, bats right. ... Full name: Francisco Jose Rodriguez.

TRANSACTIONS/CAREER NOTES: Signed as non-drafted free agent by Anaheim Angels organization (September 24, 1998).

CAREER HITTING: 0-for-0 (.000), 0 R, 0 2B, 0 3B, 0 HR, 0 RBI.

Year	League	W	L	Pct.	ERA	WHIP	G	GS	CG	ShO	Hld.	Sv.-Opp.	IP	H	R	ER	HR	BB-IBB	SO	Avg.
1999— Boise (NW)		1	0	1.000	5.40	0.80	1	1	0	0	...	0-...	5.0	3	4	3	0	1-0	6	.150
— Butte (Pio.)		1	1	.500	3.31	1.05	12	9	1	0	...	0-...	51.2	33	21	19	1	21-1	69	.179
2000— Lake Elsinore (Calif.)		4	4	.500	2.81	1.17	13	12	0	0	...	0-...	64.0	43	29	20	2	32-0	79	.189
2001— Rancho Cuca. (Calif.)		5	7	.417	5.38	1.60	20	20	1	1	...	0-...	113.2	127	72	68	13	55-1	147	.277
2002— Arkansas (Texas)		3	3	.500	1.96	1.14	23	0	0	0	9	9-...	41.1	32	13	9	2	15-0	61	.206
— Salt Lake (PCL)		2	3	.400	2.57	1.02	27	0	0	0	6	6-...	42.0	30	13	12	1	13-0	59	.204
— Anaheim (A.L.)		0	0	...	0.00	0.88	5	0	0	0	0	0-0	5.2	3	0	0	0	2-1	13	.167
2003— Anaheim (A.L.)		8	3	.727	3.03	0.99	59	0	0	0	7	2-6	86.0	50	30	29	12	35-5	95	.172
Major League totals (2 years)		8	3	.727	2.85	0.98	64	0	0	0	7	2-6	91.2	53	30	29	12	37-6	108	.172

RODRIGUEZ, IVAN   C

PERSONAL: Born November 30, 1971, in Vega Baja, Puerto Rico. ... 5-9/218. ... Bats right, throws right. ... Name pronounced: rod-RI-gez. ... High school: Lina Padron Rivera (Vega Baja, Puerto Rico).

TRANSACTIONS/CAREER NOTES: Signed as non-drafted free agent by Texas Rangers organization (July 27, 1988). ... On disabled list (June 6-27, 1992; July 25, 2000-remainder of season; May 2-17 and August 31, 2001-remainder of season). ... On Texas disabled list (April 15-June 7, 2002); included rehabilitation assignment to Charlotte (June 2-7). ... On suspended list (September 28-29, 2002). ... Granted free agency (October 28, 2002). ... Signed by Florida Marlins (January 22, 2003).

2003 GAMES PLAYED BY POSITION (MLB): C—138, DH—1.

Year	Team (League)	Pos.	G	AB	R	H	2B	3B	HR	RBI	BB	SO	HBP	GDP	SB-CS	Avg.	OBP	SLG	OPS	E	Pct.
1989—Gastonia (S. Atl.)		C	112	386	38	92	22	1	7	42	21	58	2	6	2-5	.238	.278	.355	.633	11	.986
1990—Charlotte (Fla. St.)		C	109	408	48	117	17	7	2	55	12	50	7	6	1-0	.287	.316	.377	.693	14	.983
1991—Tulsa (Texas)		C	50	175	16	48	7	2	3	28	6	27	1	5	1-2	.274	.294	.389	.683	3	.988
—Texas (A.L.)		C	88	280	24	74	16	0	3	27	5	42	0	10	0-1	.264	.276	.354	.630	10	.983
1992—Texas (A.L.)		C-DH	123	420	39	109	16	1	8	37	24	73	1	15	0-0	.260	.300	.360	.659	* 15	.983
1993—Texas (A.L.)		C-DH	137	473	56	129	28	4	10	66	29	70	4	16	8-7	.273	.315	.412	.727	8	.991
1994—Texas (A.L.)		C	99	363	56	108	19	1	16	57	31	42	7	10	6-3	.298	.360	.488	.848	5	.992
1995—Texas (A.L.)		C-DH	130	492	56	149	32	2	12	67	16	48	4	11	0-2	.303	.327	.449	.776	8	.990
1996—Texas (A.L.)		C-DH	153	639	116	192	47	3	19	86	38	55	4	15	5-0	.300	.342	.473	.814	• 10	.989
1997—Texas (A.L.)		C-DH	150	597	98	187	34	4	20	77	38	89	8	18	7-3	.313	.360	.484	.844	7	.992
1998—Texas (A.L.)		C-DH	145	579	88	186	40	4	21	91	32	88	3	18	9-0	.321	.358	.513	.871	6	.994
1999—Texas (A.L.)		C-DH	144	600	116	199	29	1	35	113	24	64	1	*31	25-12	.332	.356	.558	.914	7	.993
2000—Texas (A.L.)		C-DH	91	363	66	126	27	4	27	83	19	48	1	17	5-5	.347	.375	.667	1.042	2	.996
2001—Texas (A.L.)		C-DH	111	442	70	136	24	2	25	65	23	73	4	13	10-3	.308	.347	.541	.888	7	.990
2002—Texas (A.L.)		C-DH	108	408	67	128	32	2	19	60	25	71	2	13	5-4	.314	.353	.542	.895	7	.990
—Charlotte (Fla. St.)		C	3	9	1	3	0	0	0	0	0	3	0	0	0-0	.333	.333	.333	.667	0	1.000
2003—Florida (N.L.)		C-DH	144	511	90	152	36	3	16	85	55	92	6	18	10-6	.297	.369	.474	.843	8	.992
American League totals (12 years)			1479	5656	852	1723	344	28	215	829	304	763	39	187	80-40	.305	.342	.489	.831	92	.990
National League totals (1 year)			144	511	90	152	36	3	16	85	55	92	6	18	10-6	.297	.369	.474	.843	8	.992
Major League totals (13 years)			1623	6167	942	1875	380	31	231	914	359	855	45	205	90-46	.304	.344	.488	.832	100	.990

RODRIGUEZ, RICARDO   P

PERSONAL: Born May 21, 1978, in Manga, Dominican Republic. ... 6-3/190. ... Throws right, bats right. ... Full name: Ricardo Antonio Rodriguez.

TRANSACTIONS/CAREER NOTES: Signed as non-drafted free agent by Los Angeles Dodgers organization (September 2, 1996). ... On Jacksonville disabled list (April 4-May 17, 2002). ... Traded by Dodgers with P Terry Mulholland and P Francisco Cruceta to Cleveland Indians for P Paul Shuey (July 28, 2002). ... Placed on 15-day disabled list (June 9, 2003). ... Sent to Buffalo on rehab assignment (June 20, 2003). ... Recalled from rehab assignment; reinstated from 15-day disabled list (June 26, 2003). ... Placed on 15-day disabled list, retroactive to July 2 (July 9, 2003). ... Traded by Indians with OF Shane Spencer to Texas Rangers for OF Ryan Ludwick (July 18, 2003). ... Transferred to Emergency disabled list (August 12, 2003).

CAREER HITTING: 0-for-3 (.000), 0 R, 0 2B, 0 3B, 0 HR, 0 RBI.

Year	League	W	L	Pct.	ERA	WHIP	G	GS	CG	ShO	Hld.	Sv.-Opp.	IP	H	R	ER	HR	BB-IBB	SO	Avg.
1997—San. Dom. (In.-Am.)		1	2	.333	6.40	2.10	12	10	0	0	...	0-...	32.1	42	39	23	6	26-...	20	...
1998—Dom. Dodgers (DSL)		1	1	.500	3.55	1.88	13	9	1	1	...	0-...	33.0	28	19	13	1	34-...	36	...
1999—San. Dom. (In.-Am.)		3	2	.600	3.43	1.24	9	9	0	0	...	0-...	42.0	34	22	16	2	18-...	51	...
2000—Great Falls (Pio.)		* 10	3	.769	1.88	0.93	15	15	* 2	0	...	0-...	* 95.2	66	32	20	2	23-0	* 129	.192
2001—Vero Beach (FSL)		* 14	6	.700	3.21	1.25	26	26	2	0	...	0-...	154.1	133	67	55	13	60-0	* 154	.232
2002—Jacksonville (Sou.)		5	4	.556	1.99	1.01	11	11	2	0	...	0-...	68.0	56	21	15	4	13-0	44	.224
—Las Vegas (PCL)		1	0	1.000	3.86	1.54	2	2	0	0	...	0-...	11.2	13	5	5	1	5-0	7	.295
—Buffalo (Int'l)		3	1	.750	3.60	1.32	4	4	0	0	...	0-...	25.0	26	10	10	1	7-0	14	.271
—Cleveland (A.L.)		2	2	.500	5.66	1.40	7	7	0	0	0	0-0	41.1	40	27	26	5	18-3	24	.255
2003—Cleveland (A.L.)		3	9	.250	5.73	1.43	15	15	0	0	0	0-0	81.2	89	57	52	16	28-1	41	.275
—Buffalo (Int'l)		0	1	.000	4.32	1.08	2	2	0	0	...	0-...	8.1	6	4	4	2	3-0	7	.200
Major League totals (2 years)		5	11	.313	5.71	1.42	22	22	0	0	0	0-0	123.0	129	84	78	21	46-4	65	.268

RODRIGUEZ, RICH   P

PERSONAL: Born March 1, 1963, in Downey, Calif. ... 6-0/200. ... Throws left, bats left. ... Full name: Richard Anthony Rodriguez. ... High school: Mountain View (El Monte, Calif.). ... College: Tennessee.

TRANSACTIONS/CAREER NOTES: Selected by Kansas City Royals organization in 17th round of free-agent draft (June 8, 1981); did not sign. ... Selected by New York Mets organization in ninth round of free-agent draft (June 4, 1984). ... Traded by Mets to San Diego Padres for 1B Brad Pounders and 1B Bill Stevenson (January 13, 1989). ... Traded by Padres with 3B Gary Sheffield to Florida Marlins for P Trevor Hoffman, P Jose Martinez and P Andres Berumen (June 24, 1993). ... Released by Marlins (March 29, 1994). ... Signed by St. Louis Cardinals (April 1, 1994). ... On disabled list (April 27, 1995-remainder of season). ... Released by Cardinals (November 20, 1995). ... Signed by Cincinnati Reds organization (January 2, 1996). ... Released by Reds (March 24, 1996). ... Signed by Kansas City Royals organization (April 9, 1996). ... On disabled list (May 18-29, 1996). ... Granted free agency (October 15, 1996). ... Signed by San Francisco Giants organization (November 25, 1996). ... Granted free agency (October 30, 1997). ... Re-signed by Giants (December 7, 1997). ... Granted free agency (October 28, 1999). ... Signed by Mets (February 8, 2000). ... Released by Mets (March 29, 2001). ... Signed by Cleveland Indians organization (April 8, 2001). ... Granted free agency (November 6, 2001). ... Signed by Atlanta Braves organization (February 1, 2002). ... Traded by Braves to Texas Rangers for a player to be named (March 25, 2002). ... On Texas disabled list (April 6-July 11, 2002); included rehabilitation assignments to Tulsa (June 27-July 4) and Oklahoma (July 5-11). ... Granted free agency (October 30, 2002). ... Signed by Anaheim Angels organization (January 23, 2003). ... Contract purchased by Anaheim (April 28, 2003). ... Designated for assignment (May 7, 2003). ... Sent outright to Salt Lake (May 9, 2003).

CAREER HITTING: 3-for-28 (.107), 3 R, 0 2B, 0 3B, 0 HR, 1 RBI.

Year	League	W	L	Pct.	ERA	WHIP	G	GS	CG	ShO	Hld.	Sv.-Opp.	IP	H	R	ER	HR	BB-IBB	SO	Avg.
1984—Little Falls (NYP)		2	1	.667	2.80	1.81	25	1	0	0	...	0-...	35.1	28	21	11	0	36-7	27	.219
1985—Columbia (S. Atl.)		6	3	.667	4.03	1.56	49	3	0	0	...	6-...	80.1	89	41	36	4	36-2	71	.277
1986—Lynchburg (Carolina)		2	1	.667	3.57	1.24	36	0	0	0	...	3-...	45.1	37	20	18	2	19-0	38	.228
—Jackson (Texas)		3	4	.429	9.00	2.00	13	5	1	0	...	0-...	33.0	51	33	33	5	15-2	15	.359
1987—Lynchburg (Carolina)		3	1	.750	2.78	1.40	69	0	0	0	...	5-...	68.0	69	23	21	3	26-6	59	.263
1988—Jackson (Texas)		2	7	.222	2.87	1.38	47	1	0	0	...	6-...	78.1	66	35	25	3	42-6	68	.237
1989—Wichita (Texas)		8	3	.727	3.63	1.49	54	0	0	0	...	8-...	74.1	74	30	30	3	37-11	40	.268
1990—Las Vegas (PCL)		3	4	.429	3.51	1.22	27	2	0	0	...	8-...	59.0	50	24	23	5	22-1	46	.231
—San Diego (N.L.)		1	1	.500	2.83	1.43	32	0	0	0	3	1-1	47.2	52	17	15	2	16-4	22	.287
1991—San Diego (N.L.)		3	1	.750	3.26	1.38	64	1	0	0	8	0-2	80.0	66	31	29	8	44-8	40	.234
1992—San Diego (N.L.)		6	3	.667	2.37	1.16	61	1	0	0	5	0-1	91.0	77	28	24	4	29-4	64	.229
1993—San Diego (N.L.)		2	3	.400	3.30	1.43	34	0	0	0	8	2-5	30.0	34	15	11	2	9-3	22	.281
—Florida (N.L.)		0	1	.000	4.11	1.37	36	0	0	0	2	1-2	46.0	39	23	21	6	24-5	21	.229
1994—St. Louis (N.L.)		3	5	.375	4.03	1.46	56	0	0	0	15	0-3	60.1	62	30	27	6	26-4	43	.270
1995—St. Louis (N.L.)		0	0	...	0.00	0.00	1	0	0	0	0	0-0	1.2	0	0	0	0	0-0	0	.000
1996—Omaha (Am. Assoc.)		2	3	.400	3.99	1.36	47	0	0	0	...	3-...	70.0	75	40	31	11	20-1	68	.269
1997—San Francisco (N.L.)		4	3	.571	3.17	1.32	71	0	0	0	14	1-5	65.1	65	24	23	7	21-4	32	.264
1998—San Francisco (N.L.)		4	0	1.000	3.70	1.36	68	0	0	0	22	2-6	65.2	69	28	27	7	20-5	44	.272
1999—San Francisco (N.L.)		3	0	1.000	5.24	1.55	62	0	0	0	11	0-2	56.2	60	33	33	8	28-5	44	.274

R

Year League	W	L	Pct.	ERA	WHIP	G	GS	CG	ShO	Hld.	Sv.-Opp.	IP	H	R	ER	HR	BB-IBB	SO	Avg.
2000— New York (N.L.)	0	1	.000	7.78	2.00	32	0	0	0	0	0-0	37.0	59	40	32	7	15-0	18	.364
— Norfolk (Int'l)	0	0	.000	3.05	1.11	14	3	0	0	...	1-...	20.2	17	7	7	2	6-3	16	.221
2001— Akron (East.)	0	0	...	0.00	0.40	4	0	0	0	...	1-...	5.0	2	0	0	0	0-0	4	.118
— Cleveland (A.L.)	2	2	.500	4.15	1.49	53	0	0	0	8	0-2	39.0	41	24	18	2	17-3	31	.270
2002— Texas (A.L.)	3	2	.600	5.40	1.50	36	0	0	0	4	1-3	16.2	14	10	10	1	11-1	12	.237
— Tulsa (Texas)	0	0	...	6.75	2.25	3	0	0	0	...	0-...	2.2	4	2	2	0	2-0	3	.333
— Oklahoma (PCL)	0	0	...	13.50	2.25	3	0	0	0	...	0-...	2.2	6	4	4	0	0-0	1	...
2003— Anaheim (A.L.)	0	0	...	2.45	1.36	3	0	0	0	0	0-0	3.2	4	1	1	0	1-0	3	.308
— Salt Lake (PCL)	3	2	.600	2.47	1.35	34	0	0	0	...	1-...	43.2	47	14	12	3	12-0	18	.283
American League totals (3 years)	5	4	.556	4.40	1.48	92	0	0	0	12	1-5	59.1	59	35	29	3	29-4	46	.263
National League totals (10 years)	26	18	.591	3.75	1.40	517	2	0	0	88	7-27	581.1	583	269	242	59	232-42	350	.264
Major League totals (13 years)	31	22	.585	3.81	1.41	609	2	0	0	100	8-32	640.2	642	304	271	62	261-46	396	.264

ROGERS, KENNY — P

R

PERSONAL: Born November 10, 1964, in Savannah, Ga. ... 6-1/217. ... Throws left, bats left. ... Full name: Kenneth Scott Rogers. ... High school: Plant City (Fla.).

TRANSACTIONS/CAREER NOTES: Selected by Texas Rangers organization in 39th round of free-agent draft (June 7, 1982). ... On Tulsa disabled list (April 12-30, 1986). ... Granted free agency (October 31, 1995). ... Signed by New York Yankees (December 30, 1995). ... Traded by Yankees with IF Mariano Duncan and P Kevin Henthorne to San Diego Padres for OF Greg Vaughn, P Kerry Taylor and P Chris Clark (July 4, 1997); trade later voided because Vaughn failed physical (July 6). ... Traded by Yankees with cash to Oakland Athletics for a player to be named later (November 7, 1997); Yankees acquired 3B Scott Brosius to complete deal (November 18, 1997). ... Traded by A's to New York Mets for OF Terrance Long and P Leo Vasquez (July 23, 1999). ... Granted free agency (October 29, 1999). ... Signed by Rangers (December 29, 1999). ... On disabled list (July 24, 2001-remainder of season). ... Granted free agency (October 29, 2002). ... Signed by Minnesota Twins (March 17, 2003). ... Suspended by Major League Baseball (July 11, 2003). ... Reinstated (July 19, 2003).

CAREER HITTING: 7-for-48 (.146), 4 R, 0 2B, 0 3B, 0 HR, 3 RBI.

Year League	W	L	Pct.	ERA	WHIP	G	GS	CG	ShO	Hld.	Sv.-Opp.	IP	H	R	ER	HR	BB-IBB	SO	Avg.
1982— GC Rangers (GCL)	0	0	...	0.00	0.00	2	0	0	0	...	0-...	3.0	0	0	0	0	0-0	4	...
1983— GC Rangers (GCL)	4	1	.800	2.36	1.13	15	6	0	0	...	1-...	53.1	40	21	14	0	20-0	36	...
1984— Burlington (Midw.)	4	7	.364	3.98	1.29	39	4	1	0	...	3-...	92.2	87	52	41	9	33-3	93	.246
1985— Daytona Beach (FSL)	0	1	.000	7.20	2.30	6	0	0	0	...	0-...	10.0	12	9	8	0	11-1	9	.300
— Burlington (Midw.)	2	5	.286	2.84	1.36	33	4	2	1	...	4-...	95.0	67	34	30	3	62-9	96	.202
1986— Tulsa (Texas)	0	3	.000	9.91	2.16	10	4	0	0	...	0-...	26.1	39	30	29	4	18-1	23	.333
— Salem (Caro.)	2	7	.222	6.27	1.53	12	12	0	0	...	0-...	66.0	75	54	46	9	26-0	46	.282
1987— Charlotte (Fla. St.)	0	3	.000	4.76	1.47	5	3	0	0	...	0-...	17.0	17	13	9	1	8-0	14	.258
— Tulsa (Texas)	1	5	.167	5.35	1.67	28	6	0	0	...	2-...	69.0	80	51	41	5	35-3	59	.291
1988— Charlotte (Fla. St.)	2	0	1.000	1.27	0.93	8	6	0	0	...	1-...	35.1	22	8	5	1	11-0	26	.179
— Tulsa (Texas)	4	6	.400	4.00	1.28	13	13	2	0	...	0-...	83.1	73	43	37	6	34-0	76	.233
1989— Texas (A.L.)	3	4	.429	2.93	1.38	73	0	0	0	15	2-5	73.2	60	28	24	2	42-9	63	.232
1990— Texas (A.L.)	10	6	.625	3.13	1.38	69	3	0	0	6	15-23	97.2	93	40	34	6	42-5	74	.249
1991— Texas (A.L.)	10	10	.500	5.42	1.66	63	9	0	0	11	5-6	109.2	121	80	66	14	61-7	73	.281
1992— Texas (A.L.)	3	6	.333	3.09	1.35	81	0	0	0	16	6-10	78.2	80	32	27	7	26-8	70	.261
1993— Texas (A.L.)	16	10	.615	4.10	1.35	35	33	5	0	1	0-0	208.1	210	108	95	18	71-2	140	.263
1994— Texas (A.L.)	11	8	.579	4.46	1.32	24	24	6	2	0	0-0	167.1	169	93	83	24	52-1	120	.260
1995— Texas (A.L.)	17	7	.708	3.38	1.29	31	31	3	1	0	0-0	208.0	192	87	78	26	76-1	140	.243
1996— New York (A.L.)	12	8	.600	4.68	1.46	30	30	2	1	0	0-0	179.0	179	97	93	16	83-2	92	.261
1997— New York (A.L.)	6	7	.462	5.65	1.54	31	22	1	0	1	0-0	145.0	161	100	91	18	62-1	78	.280
1998— Oakland (A.L.)	16	8	.667	3.17	1.18	34	34	7	1	0	0-0	238.2	215	96	84	19	67-0	138	.242
1999— Oakland (A.L.)	5	3	.625	4.30	1.47	19	19	3	0	0	0-0	119.1	135	66	57	8	41-0	68	.288
— New York (N.L.)	5	1	.833	4.03	1.30	12	12	2	1	0	0-0	76.0	71	35	34	8	28-1	58	.253
2000— Texas (A.L.)	13	13	.500	4.55	1.47	34	34	2	0	0	0-0	227.1	257	126	115	20	78-2	127	.285
2001— Texas (A.L.)	5	7	.417	6.19	1.65	20	20	0	0	0	0-0	120.2	150	88	83	18	49-2	74	.307
2002— Texas (A.L.)	13	8	.619	3.84	1.34	33	33	2	1	0	0-0	210.2	212	101	90	21	70-1	107	.261
2003— Minnesota (A.L.)	13	8	.619	4.57	1.42	33	31	0	0	0	0-0	195.0	227	108	99	22	50-5	116	.292
American League totals (15 years)	153	113	.575	4.23	1.40	610	323	31	6	50	28-44	2379.0	2461	1250	1119	239	870-46	1480	.267
National League totals (1 year)	5	1	.833	4.03	1.30	12	12	2	1	0	0-0	76.0	71	35	34	8	28-1	58	.253
Major League totals (15 years)	158	114	.581	4.23	1.40	622	335	33	7	50	28-44	2455.0	2532	1285	1153	247	898-47	1538	.267

ROLEN, SCOTT — 3B

PERSONAL: Born April 4, 1975, in Jasper, Ind. ... 6-4/240. ... Bats right, throws right. ... Full name: Scott Bruce Rolen. ... Name pronounced: ROH-len. ... High school: Jasper (Ind.).

TRANSACTIONS/CAREER NOTES: Selected by Philadelphia Phillies organization in second round of free-agent draft (June 3, 1993). ... On disabled list (May 24-June 8, 2000). ... Traded by Phillies with P Doug Nickle to St. Louis Cardinals for IF/OF Placido Polanco, P Bud Smith and P Mike Timlin (July 29, 2002).

2003 GAMES PLAYED BY POSITION (MLB): 3B—153.

Year Team (League)	Pos.	G	AB	R	H	2B	3B	HR	RBI	BB	SO	HBP	GDP	SB-CS	Avg.	OBP	SLG	OPS	E	Pct.
1993— Martinsville (App.)	3B	25	80	8	25	5	0	0	12	10	15	7	3	3-4	.313	.429	.375	.804	10	.889
1994— Spartanburg (SAL)	3B	138	513	83	151	34	5	14	72	55	90	4	8	6-8	.294	.363	.462	.825	38	.917
1995— Clearwater (FSL)	3B	66	238	45	69	13	2	10	39	37	46	5	4	4-0	.290	.392	.487	.880	20	.899
— Reading (East.)	3B	20	76	16	22	3	0	3	15	7	14	1	2	1-0	.289	.353	.447	.800	4	.934
1996— Reading (East.)	3B	61	230	44	83	22	2	9	42	34	32	5	5	8-3	.361	.445	.591	1.037	9	.949
— Scran./W.B. (I.L.)	3B	45	168	23	46	17	0	2	19	28	28	0	9	4-5	.274	.376	.411	.786	6	.952
— Philadelphia (N.L.)	3B	37	130	10	33	7	0	4	18	13	27	1	4	0-2	.254	.322	.400	.722	4	.954
1997— Philadelphia (N.L.)	3B	156	561	93	159	35	3	21	92	76	138	13	6	16-6	.283	.377	.469	.846	24	.948
1998— Philadelphia (N.L.)	3B	160	601	120	174	45	4	31	110	93	141	11	10	14-7	.290	.391	.532	.923	14	.970
1999— Philadelphia (N.L.)	3B	112	421	74	113	28	1	26	77	67	114	9	3	12-2	.268	.368	.525	.893	14	.960
2000— Philadelphia (N.L.)	3B	128	483	88	144	32	6	26	89	51	99	5	4	8-1	.298	.370	.551	.920	10	.971
2001— Philadelphia (N.L.)	3B	151	554	96	160	39	1	25	107	74	127	13	6	16-5	.289	.378	.498	.876	12	.973
2002— Philadelphia (N.L.)	3B	100	375	52	97	21	4	17	66	52	68	8	12	5-2	.259	.358	.472	.830	8	.973
— St. Louis (N.L.)	3B	55	205	37	57	8	4	14	44	20	34	4	10	3-2	.278	.354	.561	.915	8	.958
2003— St. Louis (N.L.)	3B	154	559	98	160	49	1	28	104	82	104	9	19	13-3	.286	.382	.528	.910	13	.969
Major League totals (8 years)		1053	3889	668	1097	264	24	192	707	528	852	67	79	87-30	.282	.374	.510	.884	107	.965

ROLLINS, JIMMY — SS

PERSONAL: Born November 27, 1978, in Oakland, Calif. ... 5-8/165. ... Bats both, throws right. ... Full name: James Calvin Rollins. ... High school: Encinal (Alameda, Calif.).
TRANSACTIONS/CAREER NOTES: Selected by Philadelphia Phillies organization in second round of free-agent draft (June 4, 1996).
2003 GAMES PLAYED BY POSITION (MLB): SS—154.

Year Team (League)	Pos.	G	AB	R	H	2B	3B	HR	RBI	BB	SO	HBP	GDP	SB-CS	Avg.	OBP	SLG	OPS	E	Pct.
1996— Martinsville (App.)	SS	49	172	22	41	3	1	1	16	28	20	2	2	11-5	.238	.351	.285	.636	20	.906
1997— Piedmont (S. Atl.)	SS	139	560	94	151	22	8	6	59	52	80	0	4	46-6	.270	.330	.370	.700	26	.960
1998— Clearwater (FSL)	SS	119	495	72	121	18	9	6	35	41	62	4	9	23-9	.244	.306	.354	.659	29	.952
1999— Reading (East.)	SS	133	532	81	145	21	8	11	56	51	47	1	8	24-12	.273	.336	.404	.740	22	.965
— Scran./W.B. (I.L.)	SS	4	13	0	1	1	0	0	0	1	1	0	0	1-0	.077	.143	.154	.297	1	.960
2000— Scran./W.B. (I.L.)	SS	133	470	67	129	28	• 11	12	69	49	55	2	4	24-7	.274	.341	.457	.798	26	.958
— Philadelphia (N.L.)	SS	14	53	5	17	1	1	0	5	2	7	0	0	3-0	.321	.345	.377	.723	1	.978
2001— Philadelphia (N.L.)	SS	158	656	97	180	29	* 12	14	54	48	108	2	5	• 46-8	.274	.323	.419	.743	14	.979
2002— Philadelphia (N.L.)	SS-2B	154	* 637	82	156	33	* 10	11	60	54	103	4	14	31-13	.245	.306	.380	.686	14	.980
2003— Philadelphia (N.L.)	SS	156	628	85	165	42	6	8	62	54	113	0	9	20-12	.263	.320	.387	.707	14	.979
Major League totals (4 years)		482	1974	269	518	105	29	33	181	158	331	6	28	100-33	.262	.317	.395	.712	43	.979

ROLLS, DAMIAN — 3B/OF

PERSONAL: Born September 15, 1977, in Manhattan, Kan. ... 6-2/215. ... Bats right, throws right. ... Full name: Damian Michael Rolls. ... High school: F.L. Schlagle (Kansas City, Kan.).
TRANSACTIONS/CAREER NOTES: Selected by Los Angeles Dodgers organization in first round (23rd pick overall) of free-agent draft (June 4, 1996). ... Selected by Kansas City Royals from Dodgers organization in Rule 5 major league draft (December 13, 1999). ... Traded by Royals to Tampa Bay Devil Rays for a player to be named later and cash (December 13, 1999). ... On Tampa Bay disabled list (March 25-September 1, 2000); included rehabilitation assignments to St. Petersburg (August 12-18) and Orlando (August 19-September 1). ... On Durham disabled list (May 30-August 13, 2002). ... On disabled list (April 23, 2003). ... Activated from 15-day disabled list and optioned to Durham (May 27, 2003). ... Recalled from Durham (June 13, 2003).
2003 GAMES PLAYED BY POSITION (MLB): 3B—73, OF—37, 2B—2.

Year Team (League)	Pos.	G	AB	R	H	2B	3B	HR	RBI	BB	SO	HBP	GDP	SB-CS	Avg.	OBP	SLG	OPS	E	Pct.
1996— Yakima (N'west)	3B	66	257	31	68	11	1	4	27	7	46	3	5	8-3	.265	.291	.362	.653	• 23	.893
1997— Savannah (S. Atl.)	3B	130	475	57	100	17	5	5	47	38	83	5	9	11-3	.211	.274	.299	.573	31	.920
1998— Vero Beach (FSL)	3B	73	266	28	65	9	0	0	30	23	43	2	6	13-3	.244	.307	.278	.585	13	.951
— San Antonio (Texas)	3B	50	160	18	35	6	0	1	9	6	28	0	9	2-0	.219	.246	.275	.521	9	.947
1999— Vero Beach (FSL)	3B-2B	127	474	68	141	26	2	9	54	36	66	14	6	24-13	.297	.361	.418	.779	25	.924
2000— St. Pete. (FSL)	3B	5	16	2	3	2	0	0	2	2	3	1	0	1-0	.188	.316	.313	.628	0	1.000
— Orlando (South.)	3B	14	51	6	13	5	0	0	3	7	6	1	0	1-1	.255	.350	.353	.703	3	.906
— Tampa Bay (A.L.)	3B-DH	4	3	0	1	0	0	0	0	0	1	0	0	0-0	.333	.333	.333	.667	0	...
2001— Tampa Bay (A.L.)	2-0-D-3	81	237	33	62	11	1	2	12	10	47	0	5	12-4	.262	.291	.342	.633	6	.974
2002— Orlando (South.)	OF	2	7	1	3	0	1	0	0	1	0	0	0	0-1	.429	.500	.714	1.214	0	1.000
— Durham (Int'l)	OF-3B	67	244	41	65	6	4	6	35	21	43	5	4	15-0	.266	.332	.398	.730	6	.962
— Tampa Bay (A.L.)	OF	21	89	15	26	6	1	0	6	3	16	2	1	2-5	.292	.330	.382	.712	3	.947
2003— Durham (Int'l)	OF-DH	18	77	11	19	4	1	0	9	4	15	0	0	4-2	.247	.284	.325	.609	2	.913
— Tampa Bay (A.L.)	3B-OF-2B	107	373	43	95	20	0	7	46	19	84	7	5	11-3	.255	.301	.365	.666	7	.975
Major League totals (4 years)		213	702	91	184	37	2	9	64	32	148	9	11	25-12	.262	.302	.359	.661	16	.972

ROMANO, JASON — OF/2B

PERSONAL: Born June 24, 1979, in Tampa, Fla. ... 6-0/185. ... Bats right, throws right. ... Full name: Jason Anthony Romano. ... Name pronounced: ROW-maun-oh. ... High school: Hillsborough (Tampa, Fla.).
TRANSACTIONS/CAREER NOTES: Selected by Texas Rangers organization in supplemental round ("sandwich pick" between first and second round, 39th pick overall) of free-agent draft (June 3, 1997); pick received as part of compensation of New York Yankees signed Type-A free agent P Mike Stanton. ... On Oklahoma disabled list (June 17-August 9, 2001). ... Traded by Rangers with OF Gabe Kapler to Colorado Rockies for OF Todd Hollandsworth and P Dennys Reyes (July 31, 2002). ... Traded by Rockies to Los Angeles Dodgers for OF Luke Allen (January 27, 2003).
2003 GAMES PLAYED BY POSITION (MLB): OF—28, 2B—1, DH—1.

Year Team (League)	Pos.	G	AB	R	H	2B	3B	HR	RBI	BB	SO	HBP	GDP	SB-CS	Avg.	OBP	SLG	OPS	E	Pct.
1997— GC Rangers (GCL)	3B	34	109	27	28	5	3	2	11	13	19	3	1	13-4	.257	.349	.413	.762	15	.810
1998— Savannah (S. Atl.)	2B	134	524	72	142	19	4	7	52	46	94	8	6	40-17	.271	.336	.363	.699	• 32	.952
— Charlotte (Fla. St.)	2B	7	24	3	5	1	0	0	1	2	2	0	0	1-2	.208	.259	.250	.509	1	.978
1999— Charlotte (Fla. St.)	2B	120	459	84	143	27	* 14	13	71	39	72	13	4	34-15	.312	.376	.516	.893	23	.952
2000— Tulsa (Texas)	2B	131	535	87	145	35	2	8	70	56	84	6	13	25-10	.271	.343	.389	.732	24	.963
2001— Tulsa (Texas)	2B	46	186	19	45	9	1	1	19	16	31	1	8	8-3	.242	.304	.317	.621	8	.962
— Oklahoma (PCL)	2B-OF	41	149	32	47	6	1	4	13	20	28	0	4	3-4	.315	.394	.450	.844	2	.951
— GC Rangers (GCL)	2B-OF	5	21	2	3	0	0	0	0	1	8	0	0	1-0	.143	.182	.143	.325	5	.808
— Charlotte (Fla. St.)	OF	3	10	3	4	2	0	0	1	4	1	0	0	1-0	.400	.571	.600	1.171	0	1.000
2002— Oklahoma (PCL)	OF-2B-SS	48	196	28	53	8	1	4	28	19	41	0	5	10-3	.270	.329	.383	.711	5	.977
— Texas (A.L.)	O-2-D-3	29	54	8	11	4	0	0	4	4	13	0	0	2-0	.204	.254	.278	.532	1	.981
— Colo. Springs (PCL)	OF-2B-SS	31	129	20	40	7	2	0	9	6	27	0	1	8-3	.310	.338	.395	.734	3	.973
— Colorado (N.L.)	2-S-O-3	18	37	9	12	0	1	0	1	3	11	0	0	4-1	.324	.375	.378	.753	4	.981
2003— Las Vegas (PCL)	O-2-3-S	57	216	45	66	18	4	4	23	11	32	0	3	10-6	.306	.336	.481	.818	4	.977
— Los Angeles (N.L.)	OF-2B-DH	37	36	3	3	0	0	0	0	1	8	0	0	2-0	.083	.108	.083	.191	0	1.000
American League totals (1 year)		29	54	8	11	4	0	0	4	4	13	0	0	2-0	.204	.254	.278	.532	1	.981
National League totals (2 years)		55	73	12	15	0	1	0	1	4	19	0	0	6-1	.205	.247	.233	.480	4	.934
Major League totals (2 years)		84	127	20	26	4	1	0	5	8	32	0	2	8-1	.205	.250	.252	.502	5	.956

ROMERO, J.C. — P

PERSONAL: Born June 4, 1976, in Rio Piedras, Puerto Rico. ... 5-11/195. ... Throws left, bats both. ... Full name: Juan Carlos Romero. ... High school: Berwing (San Juan, Puerto Rico). ... College: Mobile (Ala.).

TRANSACTIONS/CAREER NOTES: Selected by Minnesota Twins organization in 21st round of free-agent draft (June 3, 1997). ... On Minnesota disabled list (March 25-May 10, 2000); included rehabilitation assignment to Fort Myers (May 3-10).

CAREER HITTING: 1-for-3 (.333), 1 R, 1 2B, 0 3B, 0 HR, 0 RBI.

Year	League	W	L	Pct.	ERA	WHIP	G	GS	CG	ShO	Hld.	Sv.-Opp.	IP	H	R	ER	HR	BB-IBB	SO	Avg.
1997—	Elizabethton (Appal.)	3	2	.600	4.88	1.42	18	0	0	0	...	3-...	24.0	27	16	13	4	7-0	29	.276
—	Fort Myers (Fla. St.)	1	1	.500	4.38	1.22	7	1	0	0	...	0-...	12.1	11	6	6	1	4-0	9	.244
1998—	New Britain (East.)	6	3	.667	2.19	1.17	51	1	0	0	...	2-...	78.0	48	28	19	3	43-3	79	.178
1999—	New Britain (East.)	4	4	.500	3.40	1.60	36	1	0	0	...	7-...	53.0	51	25	20	6	34-0	53	.254
—	Salt Lake (PCL)	4	1	.800	3.20	1.63	15	0	0	0	...	1-...	19.2	18	11	7	1	14-0	20	.250
—	Minnesota (A.L.)	0	0	...	3.72	1.34	5	0	0	0	0	0-0	9.2	13	4	4	0	0-0	4	.333
2000—	Fort Myers (Fla. St.)	0	0	...	1.93	1.07	2	0	0	0	...	0-...	4.2	4	1	1	0	1-0	3	.222
—	Salt Lake (PCL)	4	2	.667	3.44	1.30	17	11	1	0	...	4-...	65.1	60	40	25	6	25-0	38	.244
—	Minnesota (A.L.)	2	7	.222	7.02	1.77	12	11	0	0	0	0-0	57.2	72	51	45	8	30-0	50	.312
2001—	Minnesota (A.L.)	1	4	.200	6.23	1.46	14	11	0	0	0	0-0	65.0	71	48	45	10	24-1	39	.277
—	Edmonton (PCL)	3	3	.500	3.68	1.43	12	10	0	0	...	0-...	63.2	67	33	26	4	24-0	55	.276
2002—	Minnesota (A.L.)	9	2	.818	1.89	1.21	81	0	0	0	*33	1-5	81.0	62	17	17	3	36-4	76	.213
2003—	Minnesota (A.L.)	2	0	1.000	5.00	1.71	73	0	0	0	22	0-4	63.0	66	37	35	7	42-7	50	.272
Major League totals (5 years)		**14**	**13**	**.519**	**4.76**	**1.51**	**185**	**22**	**0**	**0**	**55**	**1-9**	**276.1**	**284**	**157**	**146**	**28**	**132-12**	**219**	**.268**

ROMERO, MANDY   C

PERSONAL: Born October 29, 1967, in Miami, Fla. ... 5-11/196. ... Bats both, throws right. ... Full name: Armando Romero. ... High school: Miami Senior. ... Junior college: Brevard (Fla.) Community College.

TRANSACTIONS/CAREER NOTES: Selected by Pittsburgh Pirates in 19th round of free-agent draft (June 1, 1988). ... On disabled list (April 11-29 and June 20-28, 1991; July 13-August 7, 1992; and June 28-July 8 and August 23, 1993-remainder of season). ... Released by Pirates (May 6, 1994). ... Signed by Kansas City Royals organization (January 30, 1995). ... Granted free agency (October 16, 1995). ... Signed by San Diego Padres organization (November 25, 1995). ... Granted free agency (October 15, 1996). ... Re-signed by Padres (October 27, 1996). ... Traded by Padres with P Carlos Reyes and P Dario Veras to Boston Red Sox for C Jim Leyritz and OF Ethan Faggett (June 21, 1998). ... On Pawtucket disabled list (July 29-August 5, 1998). ... Traded by Red Sox to New York Mets for a player to be named later (July 30, 1999). ... Granted free agency (October 5, 1999). ... Signed by Cleveland Indians organization (December 22, 1999). ... On Buffalo disabled list (August 6-September 6, 2000). ... Granted free agency (October 18, 2000). ... Signed by Florida Marlins organization (November 21, 2000). ... Released by Marlins (April 13, 2001). ... On Sacramento disabled list (July 6, 2001-remainder of season). ... Granted free agency (October 15, 2001). ... Signed by Colorado Rockies (August 15, 2003).

2003 GAMES PLAYED BY POSITION (MLB): C—2.

Year	Team (League)	Pos.	G	AB	R	H	2B	3B	HR	RBI	BB	SO	HBP	GDP	SB-CS	Avg.	OBP	SLG	OPS	E	Pct.
1988—	Princeton (Appal.)	C	30	71	7	22	6	0	2	11	13	15	1	0	1-0	.310	.424	.479	.902	2	.987
1989—	Augusta (S. Atl.)	3B-C	121	388	58	87	26	3	4	55	67	74	6	10	8-5	.224	.343	.338	.680	9	.987
1990—	Salem (Caro.)	C	124	460	62	134	31	3	17	*90	55	68	5	10	0-2	.291	.370	.483	.853	7	.989
1991—	Carolina (Sou.)	C	98	323	29	70	12	0	3	31	45	53	1	9	1-2	.217	.313	.282	.594	4	.994
1992—	Carolina (Sou.)	C-3B	80	269	28	58	16	0	3	27	29	39	1	10	0-3	.216	.292	.309	.601	§ 14	.976
1993—	Buffalo (A.A.)	C	42	136	11	31	6	1	2	14	6	12	0	5	0-0	.228	.259	.331	.590	5	.973
1994—	Buffalo (A.A.)	C	7	23	3	3	0	0	0	1	2	1	0	2	0-0	.130	.200	.130	.330	0	1.000
1995—	Wichita (Texas)	DH-C-1B	121	440	73	133	32	1	21	82	69	60	5	15	1-3	.302	.402	.523	.925	4	.978
1996—	Memphis (Sou.)	C-DH	88	297	40	80	15	0	10	46	41	52	1	15	3-1	.269	.358	.421	.779	12	.983
1997—	Mobile (Sou.)	C-DH	61	222	50	71	22	0	13	52	38	31	2	4	0-1	.320	.422	.595	1.017	6	.987
—	Las Vegas (PCL)	C-3-D-1	33	91	19	28	4	1	3	13	11	19	1	4	0-0	.308	.385	.473	.857	3	.981
—	San Diego (N.L.)	C	21	48	7	10	0	0	2	4	2	18	0	1	1-0	.208	.240	.333	.573	0	1.000
1998—	Las Vegas (PCL)	C-1B-DH	40	131	25	38	8	0	8	22	20	25	1	9	0-1	.290	.388	.534	.923	7	.980
—	San Diego (N.L.)	C	6	9	1	0	0	0	0	0	1	3	0	0	0-0	.000	.100	.000	.100	1	.963
—	Pawtucket (Int'l)	C-DH	45	139	20	46	5	0	8	27	24	15	0	1	0-0	.331	.419	.540	.959	3	.991
—	Boston (A.L.)	C-DH	12	13	2	3	1	0	0	1	3	3	0	1	0-0	.231	.375	.308	.683	0	1.000
1999—	Pawtucket (Int'l)	C	46	143	8	31	7	0	3	22	13	26	1	6	0-0	.217	.283	.329	.612	2	.994
—	Norfolk (Int'l)	C-DH	28	97	7	25	6	0	1	9	9	18	0	5	0-0	.258	.321	.351	.671	3	.983
2000—	Akron (East.)	C	79	280	55	87	19	2	12	46	43	34	2	6	1-1	.311	.401	.521	.923	2	.996
—	Buffalo (Int'l)	C	4	17	1	7	2	0	0	4	0	2	0	0	0-0	.412	.412	.529	.941	0	1.000
2001—	Calgary (PCL)	C	3	6	0	0	0	0	0	0	3	3	0	0	0-0	.000	.333	.000	.333	0	1.000
—	Midland (Texas)	C	29	103	12	32	8	0	1	12	11	10	1	1	0-0	.311	.379	.417	.797	2	.991
—	Sacramento (PCL)	C	19	60	4	11	4	0	1	5	5	13	0	2	0-0	.183	.246	.300	.546	2	.987
2002—	Nashville (PCL)	C-1B	88	283	40	84	25	0	17	51	24	47	4	7	1-1	.297	.354	.565	.920	3	.995
2003—	Colorado (N.L.)	C	3	7	2	3	1	0	0	0	0	1	2	1	0-0	.429	.556	.571	1.127	1	.938
—	Colo. Springs (PCL)	C-1B-DH	81	250	30	74	11	1	4	31	18	38	2	7	0-0	.296	.341	.396	.737	7	.985
American League totals (1 year)			12	13	2	3	1	0	0	1	3	3	0	1	0-0	.231	.375	.308	.683	0	1.000
National League totals (3 years)			30	64	10	13	1	0	2	4	3	22	2	2	1-0	.203	.261	.313	.573	2	.986
Major League totals (3 years)			**42**	**77**	**12**	**16**	**2**	**0**	**2**	**5**	**6**	**25**	**2**	**3**	**1-0**	**.208**	**.282**	**.312**	**.594**	**2**	**.987**

RONEY, MATT   P

PERSONAL: Born January 10, 1980, in Tulsa, Okla. ... 6-3/230. ... Throws right, bats right. ... Full name: Matthew S. Roney. ... High school: Edmond North (Edmond, Okla.).

TRANSACTIONS/CAREER NOTES: Selected by Colorado Rockies organization in first round (28th pick overall) of free-agent draft (June 2, 1998). ... On disabled list (June 23, 1999-entire season). ... Selected by Pittsburgh Pirates from Rockies organization in Rule 5 major league draft (December 16, 2002). ... Traded by Pirates to Detroit Tigers for cash (December 16, 2002).

CAREER HITTING: 1-for-2 (.500), 0 R, 0 2B, 0 3B, 0 HR, 0 RBI.

Year	League	W	L	Pct.	ERA	WHIP	G	GS	CG	ShO	Hld.	Sv.-Opp.	IP	H	R	ER	HR	BB-IBB	SO	Avg.
1998—	Ariz. Rockies (Ariz.)	1	1	.500	5.80	1.51	9	9	1	1	...	0-...	40.1	50	31	26	1	11-0	49	.291
1999—	....										Did not play.									
2000—	Portland (East.)	7	5	.583	3.14	1.48	15	15	0	0	...	0-...	80.1	75	35	28	6	44-0	85	.244
2001—	Asheville (S. Atl.)	8	10	.444	4.98	1.44	23	23	1	0	...	0-...	121.0	131	74	67	16	43-0	115	.275
2002—	Asheville (S. Atl.)	4	6	.400	3.48	1.29	14	14	1	1	...	0-...	82.2	82	39	32	7	25-1	88	.261
—	Carolina (Sou.)	3	6	.333	6.11	1.50	13	13	0	0	...	0-...	70.2	73	52	48	6	33-0	61	.265
2003—	Detroit (A.L.)	1	9	.100	5.45	1.49	45	11	0	0	6	0-2	100.2	102	67	61	17	48-4	47	.262
Major League totals (1 year)		**1**	**9**	**.100**	**5.45**	**1.49**	**45**	**11**	**0**	**0**	**6**	**0-2**	**100.2**	**102**	**67**	**61**	**17**	**48-4**	**47**	**.262**

R

ROSARIO, RODRIGO — P

PERSONAL: Born December 14, 1977, in La Romana, Dominican Republic. ... 6-2/165. ... Throws right, bats right. ... Name pronounced: ROD-ree-go RO-zar-ee-oh.

TRANSACTIONS/CAREER NOTES: Signed as non-drafted free agent by Houston Astros organization (July 6, 1996). ... Placed on 15-day disabled list (June 28, 2003). ... Transferred to Emergency disabled list (August 14, 2003).

CAREER HITTING: 0-for-0 (.000), 0 R, 0 2B, 0 3B, 0 HR, 0 RBI.

Year League	W	L	Pct.	ERA	WHIP	G	GS	CG	ShO	Hld.	Sv.-Opp.	IP	H	R	ER	HR	BB-IBB	SO	Avg.
1998— GC Astros (GCL)	2	2	.500	4.12	1.34	13	12	0	0	...	0-...	67.2	61	36	31	6	30-0	65	.245
—Auburn (N.Y.-Penn)	0	0	...	0.00	1.50	2	0	0	0	...	0-...	2.0	0	0	0	0	3-0	2	.000
1999— Martinsville (App.)	5	5	.500	4.69	1.40	14	14	0	0	...	0-...	78.2	78	46	41	9	32-0	86	.267
2000— Auburn (N.Y.-Penn)	5	6	.455	3.45	1.31	14	14	0	0	...	0-...	75.2	67	36	29	3	32-1	67	.232
2001— Lexington (S. Atl.)	13	4	.765	2.14	0.96	30	21	1	0	...	2-...	147.0	105	46	35	8	36-1	131	.198
2002— Round Rock (Texas)	11	6	.647	3.11	1.27	26	23	0	0	...	0-...	130.1	106	56	45	5	59-1	94	.222
2003— New Orleans (PCL)	5	7	.417	4.03	1.18	15	15	1	1	...	0-...	87.0	71	40	39	7	32-0	68	.222
—Houston (N.L.)	1	0	1.000	1.13	1.00	2	2	0	0	0	0-0	8.0	5	2	1	0	3-1	6	.172
Major League totals (1 year)	**1**	**0**	**1.000**	**1.13**	**1.00**	**2**	**2**	**0**	**0**	**0**	**0-0**	**8.0**	**5**	**2**	**1**	**0**	**3-1**	**6**	**.172**

ROSS, CODY — OF

PERSONAL: Born December 23, 1980, in Portales, N.M. ... 5-11/180. ... Bats right, throws left. ... Full name: Cody J. Ross. ... High school: Carlsbad (N.M.).

TRANSACTIONS/CAREER NOTES: Selected by Detroit Tigers organization in fourth round of free-agent draft (June 2, 1999).

2003 GAMES PLAYED BY POSITION (MLB): OF—6.

Year Team (League)	Pos.	G	AB	R	H	2B	3B	HR	RBI	BB	SO	HBP	GDP	SB-CS	Avg.	OBP	SLG	OPS	E	Pct.
1999— GC Tigers (GCL)	OF	42	142	19	31	8	3	4	18	16	28	2	3	3-1	.218	.304	.401	.706	2	.980
2000— W. Mich. (Mid.)	OF	122	434	71	116	17	9	7	68	55	83	9	14	11-3	.267	.356	.396	.753	6	.978
2001— Lakeland (Fla. St.)	OF	127	482	84	133	34	5	15	80	44	96	5	9	28-5	.276	.337	.461	.798	4	.975
2002— Erie (East.)	OF	105	400	73	112	28	3	19	72	44	86	3	11	16-2	.280	.352	.508	.859	6	.975
2003— Toledo (Int'l)	OF-DH	124	470	74	135	35	6	20	61	32	86	5	12	15-6	.287	.333	.515	.848	6	.977
—Detroit (A.L.)	OF	6	19	1	4	1	0	1	5	1	3	1	0	0-0	.211	.286	.421	.707	2	.882
Major League totals (1 year)		**6**	**19**	**1**	**4**	**1**	**0**	**1**	**5**	**1**	**3**	**1**	**0**	**0-0**	**.211**	**.286**	**.421**	**.707**	**2**	**.882**

ROSS, DAVE — C

PERSONAL: Born March 19, 1977, in Bainbridge, Ga. ... 6-2/205. ... Bats right, throws right. ... Full name: David Wade Ross. ... College: Florida.

TRANSACTIONS/CAREER NOTES: Selected by Los Angeles Dodgers organization in seventh round of free-agent draft (June 2, 1998).

2003 GAMES PLAYED BY POSITION (MLB): C—38.

Year Team (League)	Pos.	G	AB	R	H	2B	3B	HR	RBI	BB	SO	HBP	GDP	SB-CS	Avg.	OBP	SLG	OPS	E	Pct.
1998— Yakima (N'west)	C	59	191	31	59	14	1	6	25	34	49	1	5	2-2	.309	.412	.487	.899	10	.979
1999— Vero Beach (FSL)	C-1B-OF	114	375	47	85	19	1	7	39	46	111	7	10	5-9	.227	.318	.339	.657	16	.979
2000— San Bern. (Calif.)	C	51	191	27	49	11	1	7	21	17	43	1	3	3-2	.257	.319	.435	.754	3	.992
—San Antonio (Texas)	C	24	67	11	14	2	1	3	12	9	17	1	0	1-0	.209	.308	.403	.711	1	.994
2001— Jacksonville (Sou.)	C	74	246	35	65	13	1	11	45	34	72	10	5	1-1	.264	.372	.459	.831	9	.985
2002— Las Vegas (PCL)	C	92	293	48	87	16	2	15	68	35	86	9	4	1-1	.297	.384	.519	.903	7	.989
—Los Angeles (N.L.)	C	8	10	2	2	1	0	1	2	2	4	1	0	0-0	.200	.385	.600	.985	0	1.000
2003— Las Vegas (PCL)	C	24	86	12	19	4	0	5	16	11	27	1	0	0-2	.221	.313	.442	.755	2	.985
—Los Angeles (N.L.)	C	40	124	19	32	7	0	10	18	13	42	2	4	0-0	.258	.336	.556	.892	4	.986
Major League totals (2 years)		**48**	**134**	**21**	**34**	**8**	**0**	**11**	**20**	**15**	**46**	**3**	**4**	**0-0**	**.254**	**.340**	**.560**	**.900**	**4**	**.987**

ROWAND, AARON — OF

PERSONAL: Born August 29, 1977, in Portland, Ore. ... 6-1/210. ... Bats right, throws right. ... Full name: Aaron Ryan Rowand. ... High school: Glendora (Calif.). ... College: Cal State Fullerton.

TRANSACTIONS/CAREER NOTES: Selected by New York Mets organization in 40th round of free-agent draft (June 1, 1995); did not sign. ... Selected by Chicago White Sox organization in supplemental round ("sandwich pick" between first and second round, 35th pick overall) of free-agent draft (June 2, 1998); pick received as part of compensation for Tampa Bay Devil Rays signing Type A free agent OF Dave Martinez.

2003 GAMES PLAYED BY POSITION (MLB): OF—87, DH—1.

Year Team (League)	Pos.	G	AB	R	H	2B	3B	HR	RBI	BB	SO	HBP	GDP	SB-CS	Avg.	OBP	SLG	OPS	E	Pct.
1998— Hickory (S. Atl.)	OF	61	222	42	76	13	3	5	32	21	36	6	5	7-3	.342	.410	.495	.906	3	.966
1999— Win.-Salem (Car.)	OF	133	512	•96	143	37	3	24	88	33	94	13	13	15-9	.279	.336	.504	.840	5	.973
2000— Birmingham (Sou.)	OF	139	532	80	137	26	5	20	98	38	117	14	12	22-7	.258	.321	.438	.759	8	.975
2001— Charlotte (Int'l)	OF	82	329	54	97	28	0	16	48	21	47	9	9	8-2	.295	.353	.526	.879	6	.966
—Chicago (A.L.)	OF	63	123	21	36	5	0	4	20	15	28	4	2	5-1	.293	.385	.431	.816	1	.991
2002— Chicago (A.L.)	OF	126	302	41	78	16	2	7	29	12	54	6	8	0-1	.258	.298	.394	.692	4	.983
2003— Charlotte (Int'l)	OF	32	120	15	29	9	0	3	13	11	12	2	3	0-0	.242	.316	.392	.707	5	.950
—Chicago (A.L.)	OF-DH	93	157	22	45	8	0	6	24	7	21	3	1	0-0	.287	.327	.452	.780	0	1.000
Major League totals (3 years)		**282**	**582**	**84**	**159**	**29**	**2**	**17**	**73**	**34**	**103**	**13**	**11**	**5-2**	**.273**	**.325**	**.418**	**.743**	**5**	**.989**

RUAN, WILKIN — OF

PERSONAL: Born September 18, 1978, in Ramon Santana, Dominican Republic. ... 6-0/170. ... Bats right, throws right. ... Full name: Wilkin Chal Ruan. ... Name pronounced: ROO-ahn.

TRANSACTIONS/CAREER NOTES: Signed as non-drafted free agent by Montreal Expos organization (November 15, 1996). ... On Harrisburg disabled list (July 12-August 11, 2001). ... Traded by Expos with P Guillermo Mota to Los Angeles Dodgers for P Matt Herges and IF Jorge Nunez (March 24, 2002). ... On Jacksonville disabled list (July 19-August 10, 2002).

2003 GAMES PLAYED BY POSITION (MLB): OF—20.

Year— Team (League)	Pos.	G	AB	R	H	2B	3B	HR	RBI	BB	SO	HBP	GDP	SB-CS	Avg.	OBP	SLG	OPS	E	Pct.
1997— Dom. Expos (DSL)	OF	69	293	53	102	16	5	4	46	31	34	...	...	33-...	.348	...	.478	...	...	...
1998— Jupiter (FSL)	OF	5	18	2	3	0	0	0	0	1	3	0	0	2-0	.167	.211	.167	.377	0	1.000
— GC Expos (GCL)	OF	54	201	22	48	9	3	1	19	5	43	2	1	13-13	.239	.262	.328	.590	1	.991
1999— Cape Fear (S. Atl.)	OF	112	397	43	89	16	4	1	47	18	79	6	5	29-17	.224	.268	.292	.561	4	.986
2000— Cape Fear (S. Atl.)	OF	134	574	95	165	29	10	0	51	24	75	8	4	64-10	.287	.323	.373	.696	3	.990
2001— Jupiter (FSL)	OF	72	293	41	83	8	2	2	26	10	35	3	3	25-14	.283	.313	.345	.657	7	.964
— Harrisburg (East.)	OF	30	117	14	29	7	0	0	6	3	18	2	1	6-0	.248	.279	.308	.586	2	.976
2002— Jacksonville (Sou.)	OF	78	324	44	82	16	6	3	34	17	33	8	4	23-3	.253	.306	.367	.673	4	.979
— Las Vegas (PCL)	OF	40	153	18	50	7	3	0	29	2	17	0	7	12-0	.327	.335	.412	.747	0	1.000
— Los Angeles (N.L.)	OF	12	11	2	3	1	0	0	3	0	2	0	0	0-0	.273	.273	.364	.636	0	1.000
2003— Las Vegas (PCL)	OF-DH	108	403	58	124	6	3	0	40	10	38	7	6	41-7	.308	.334	.337	.672	2	.992
— Los Angeles (N.L.)	OF	21	41	2	9	2	1	0	2	0	7	0	0	1-0	.220	.220	.317	.537	0	1.000
Major League totals (2 years)		33	52	4	12	3	1	0	5	0	9	0	0	1-0	.231	.231	.327	.558	0	1.000

RUETER, KIRK   P

PERSONAL: Born December 1, 1970, in Centralia, Ill. ... 6-3/212. ... Throws left, bats left. ... Full name: Kirk Wesley Rueter. ... Name pronounced: REE-ter. ... High school: Nashville (Ill.) Community. ... College: Murray State.

TRANSACTIONS/CAREER NOTES: Selected by Montreal Expos organization in 18th round of free-agent draft (June 3, 1991). ... On Montreal disabled list (May 10-26, 1996); included rehabilitation assignment to Ottawa (May 20-24). ... Traded by Expos with P Tim Scott to San Francisco Giants for P Mark Leiter (July 30, 1996). ... Placed on 15-day disabled list (July 9, 2003). ... Reinstated from 15-day disabled list (July 25, 2003). ... Sent on rehab assignment (August 19, 2003). ... Recalled from minor league rehab assignment; removed from 15-day disabled list (August 24, 2003).

CAREER HITTING: 82-for-531 (.154), 39 R, 6 2B, 0 3B, 0 HR, 37 RBI.

Year League	W	L	Pct.	ERA	WHIP	G	GS	CG	ShO	Hld.	Sv.-Opp.	IP	H	R	ER	HR	BB-IBB	SO	Avg.
1991— GC Expos (GCL)	1	1	.500	0.95	1.05	5	4	0	0	...	0-...	19.0	16	5	2	0	4-0	19	.232
— Sumter (S. Atl.)	3	1	.750	1.33	1.03	8	5	0	0	...	0-...	40.2	32	8	6	3	10-0	27	.215
1992— Rockford (Midwest)	11	9	.550	2.58	1.07	26	26	6	•2	...	0-...	174.1	150	68	50	5	36-2	153	.232
1993— Harrisburg (Eastern)	5	0	1.000	1.36	0.91	9	8	1	1	...	0-...	59.2	47	10	9	4	7-0	36	.218
— Ottawa (Int'l)	4	2	.667	2.70	1.13	7	7	1	0	...	0-...	43.1	46	20	13	7	3-0	27	.277
— Montreal (N.L.)	8	0	1.000	2.73	1.20	14	14	1	0	0	0-0	85.2	85	33	26	5	18-1	31	.264
1994— Montreal (N.L.)	7	3	.700	5.17	1.40	20	20	0	0	0	0-0	92.1	106	60	53	11	23-1	50	.294
— Ottawa (Int'l)	0	0	...	4.50	0.50	1	1	0	0	0	0-...	2.0	1	1	1	1	0-0	1	.143
1995— Montreal (N.L.)	5	3	.625	3.23	0.99	9	9	1	1	0	0-0	47.1	38	17	17	3	9-0	28	.224
— Ottawa (Int'l)	9	7	.563	3.06	1.20	20	20	3	1	...	0-0	120.2	120	50	41	7	25-0	67	.260
1996— Ottawa (Int'l)	1	2	.333	4.20	1.60	3	3	1	0	...	0-...	15.0	21	7	7	3	3-0	3	.333
— Montreal (N.L.)	5	6	.455	4.58	1.44	16	16	0	0	0	0-0	78.2	91	44	40	12	22-0	30	.294
— San Francisco (N.L.)	1	2	.333	1.93	0.99	4	3	0	0	0	0-0	23.1	18	6	5	0	5-0	16	.207
— Phoenix (PCL)	1	2	.333	3.51	1.44	5	5	0	0	...	0-...	25.2	25	12	10	2	12-0	15	.253
1997— San Francisco (N.L.)	13	6	.684	3.45	1.28	32	32	0	0	0	0-0	190.2	194	83	73	17	51-8	115	.264
1998— San Francisco (N.L.)	16	9	.640	4.36	1.33	33	33	1	0	0	0-0	187.2	193	100	91	27	57-3	102	.265
1999— San Francisco (N.L.)	15	10	.600	5.41	1.48	33	33	1	0	0	0-0	184.2	219	118	111	28	55-2	94	.297
2000— San Francisco (N.L.)	11	9	.550	3.96	1.38	32	31	0	0	0	0-0	184.0	205	92	81	23	62-5	71	.290
2001— San Francisco (N.L.)	14	12	.538	4.42	1.43	34	34	0	0	0	0-0	195.1	213	105	96	25	66-4	83	.283
2002— San Francisco (N.L.)	14	8	.636	3.23	1.27	33	33	0	0	0	0-0	203.2	204	83	73	22	54-7	76	.262
2003— Fresno (PCL)	0	0	...	0.00	0.64	1	1	0	0	...	0-...	4.2	1	0	0	0	2-0	6	.071
— San Francisco (N.L.)	10	5	.667	4.53	1.48	27	27	0	0	0	0-0	147.0	170	77	74	14	47-2	41	.297
Major League totals (11 years)	119	73	.620	4.11	1.36	287	285	4	1	0	0-0	1620.1	1736	818	740	187	469-33	737	.277

RUPE, RYAN   P

PERSONAL: Born March 31, 1975, in Houston, Texas. ... 6-5/248. ... Throws right, bats right. ... Full name: Ryan Kittman Rupe. ... Name pronounced: ROOP. ... High school: Northbrook (Houston). ... College: Texas A&M.

TRANSACTIONS/CAREER NOTES: Selected by New York Mets organization in 19th round of free-agent draft (June 3, 1993); did not sign. ... Selected by Kansas City Royals organization in 36th round of free-agent draft (June 4, 1996); did not sign. ... Selected by Tampa Bay Devil Rays organization in sixth round of free-agent draft (June 2, 1998). ... On Durham disabled list (May 9-June 16, 2000). ... On Tampa Bay disabled list (September 11, 2000-remainder of season). ... On disabled list (June 20-July 11 and July 16, 2002-remainder of season). ... Claimed on waivers by Boston Red Sox (November 27, 2002). ... Recalled from Pawtucket (July 3, 2003). ... Optioned to Pawtucket (July 5, 2003). ... Recalled from Pawtucket (September 19, 2003).

CAREER HITTING: 1-for-9 (.111), 1 R, 1 2B, 0 3B, 0 HR, 0 RBI.

Year League	W	L	Pct.	ERA	WHIP	G	GS	CG	ShO	Hld.	Sv.-Opp.	IP	H	R	ER	HR	BB-IBB	SO	Avg.
1998— Hudson Valley (NYP)	1	0	1.000	0.68	0.75	3	3	0	0	...	0-...	13.1	8	1	1	0	2-0	18	.170
— Char., S.C. (SAL)	6	1	.857	2.40	0.75	10	10	0	0	...	0-...	56.1	33	18	15	3	9-0	62	.166
1999— Orlando (Sou.)	2	2	.500	2.73	0.91	5	5	0	0	...	0-...	26.1	18	13	8	1	6-0	22	.180
— Tampa Bay (A.L.)	8	9	.471	4.55	1.36	24	24	0	0	0	0-0	142.1	136	81	72	17	57-2	97	.253
2000— Tampa Bay (A.L.)	5	6	.455	6.92	1.67	18	18	0	0	0	0-0	91.0	121	75	70	19	31-3	61	.321
— Durham (Int'l)	0	1	.000	6.52	1.60	5	5	0	0	...	0-...	19.1	24	16	14	3	7-0	18	.304
2001— Tampa Bay (A.L.)	5	12	.294	6.59	1.46	28	26	0	0	0	0-1	143.1	161	111	105	30	48-0	123	.283
— Durham (Int'l)	0	1	.000	0.82	0.36	2	2	0	0	...	0-...	11.0	3	1	1	0	1-0	17	.088
2002— Tampa Bay (A.L.)	5	10	.333	5.60	1.20	15	15	2	0	...	0-...	90.0	83	60	56	11	25-0	67	.243
2003— Boston (A.L.)	1	1	.500	6.30	1.40	4	1	0	0	0	0-1	10.0	13	9	7	4	1-0	7	.302
— Pawtucket (Int'l)	8	4	.667	3.26	1.10	20	18	0	0	...	0-...	102.0	93	50	37	11	19-1	77	.237
Major League totals (5 years)	24	38	.387	5.85	1.42	89	84	2	0	0	0-2	476.2	514	336	310	81	162-5	355	.275

RUSCH, GLENDON   P

PERSONAL: Born November 7, 1974, in Seattle, Wash. ... 6-1/223. ... Throws left, bats left. ... Full name: Glendon James Rusch. ... Name pronounced: RUSH. ... High school: Shorecrest (Seattle).

TRANSACTIONS/CAREER NOTES: Selected by Kansas City Royals organization in 17th round of free-agent draft (June 3, 1993). ... On Kansas City disabled list (June 16-July 1, 1997); included rehabilitation assignment to Omaha (June 26-July 1). ... On Kansas City disabled list (August 9-September 4, 1998); included rehabilitation assignment to Omaha (August 24-September 4). ... On Omaha disabled list (May 31-July 1, 1999). ... Traded by Royals to New York Mets for P Dan Murray (September 14, 1999). ... Traded by Mets to Milwaukee Brewers as part of three-way deal in which Brewers traded P Jeff D'Amico, OF Jeromy Burnitz, IF Lou Collier, OF/1B Mark Sweeney and cash to Mets, Colorado Rockies traded OF Alex Ochoa to Brewers, Mets traded 1B/3B Todd Zeile, OF Benny Agbayani, IF/OF Lenny Harris and cash to Rockies and Rockies traded 1B/OF Ross Gload and P Craig House to Mets (January 21, 2002). ... Optioned to Indianapolis (June 20, 2003). ... Recalled from Indianapolis (July 6, 2003). ... Placed on 15-day disabled list (July 29, 2003). ... Removed from 15-day disabled list (August 22, 2003).

CAREER HITTING: 32-for-210 (.152), 10 R, 0 2B, 0 3B, 1 HR, 16 RBI.

Year	League	W	L	Pct.	ERA	WHIP	G	GS	CG	ShO	Hld.	Sv.-Opp.	IP	H	R	ER	HR	BB-IBB	SO	Avg.
1993— GC Royals (GCL)		4	2	.667	1.60	0.87	11	10	0	0	...	0-...	62.0	43	14	11	0	11-0	48	.197
— Rockford (Midwest)		0	1	.000	3.38	2.13	2	2	0	0	...	0-...	8.0	10	6	3	0	7-0	8	.313
1994— Rockford (Midwest)		8	5	.615	4.66	1.27	28	17	1	1	...	1-...	114.0	111	61	59	5	34-2	122	.256
1995— Wilmington (Caro.)	* 14	6	.700	1.74	0.87	26	26	1	1	...	0-...	165.2	110	41	32	5	34-3	147	.188
1996— Omaha (Am. Assoc.)		11	9	.550	3.98	1.28	28	28	1	0	...	0-...	169.2	177	88	75	15	40-3	117	.267
1997— Kansas City (A.L.)		6	9	.400	5.50	1.51	30	27	1	0	0	0-0	170.1	206	111	104	28	52-0	116	.301
— Omaha (Am. Assoc.)		0	1	.000	4.50	1.33	1	1	0	0	...	0-...	6.0	7	3	3	3	1-0	2	.292
1998— Kansas City (A.L.)		6	15	.286	5.88	1.56	29	24	1	1	0	1-1	154.2	191	104	101	22	50-0	94	.304
— Omaha (PCL)		1	1	.500	7.98	1.77	3	3	0	0	...	0-...	14.2	20	18	13	4	6-0	14	.317
1999— Omaha (PCL)		4	7	.364	4.42	1.54	20	20	1	0	...	0-...	114.0	143	68	56	10	33-0	102	.307
— GC Royals (GCL)		0	0	...	1.50	1.00	2	2	0	0	...	0-...	6.0	3	1	1	0	3-0	9	.136
— Kansas City (A.L.)		0	1	.000	15.75	2.50	3	0	0	0	0	0-0	4.0	7	7	7	1	3-0	4	.368
— New York (N.L.)		0	0	...	0.00	1.00	1	0	0	0	0	0-0	1.0	1	0	0	0	0-0	0	.333
2000— New York (N.L.)		11	11	.500	4.01	1.26	31	30	2	0	0	0-0	190.2	196	91	85	18	44-2	157	.267
2001— New York (N.L.)		8	12	.400	4.63	1.45	33	33	1	0	0	0-0	179.0	216	101	92	23	43-2	156	.301
2002— Milwaukee (N.L.)		10	• 16	.385	4.70	1.44	34	34	4	1	0	0-0	210.2	227	118	110	30	76-1	140	.279
2003— Indianapolis (Int'l)		1	1	.500	3.86	1.00	4	3	1	0	...	0-...	21.0	17	9	9	4	4-0	20	.218
— Milwaukee (N.L.)		1	12	.077	6.42	1.75	32	19	1	0	7	1-1	123.1	171	93	88	11	45-3	93	.331
American League totals (3 years)		**12**	**25**	**.324**	**5.80**	**1.55**	**62**	**51**	**2**	**1**	**0**	**1-1**	**329.0**	**404**	**222**	**212**	**51**	**105-0**	**214**	**.303**
National League totals (5 years)		**30**	**51**	**.370**	**4.79**	**1.45**	**131**	**116**	**8**	**1**	**7**	**1-1**	**704.2**	**811**	**403**	**375**	**82**	**208-8**	**546**	**.291**
Major League totals (7 years)		**42**	**76**	**.356**	**5.11**	**1.48**	**193**	**167**	**10**	**2**	**7**	**2-2**	**1033.2**	**1215**	**625**	**587**	**133**	**313-8**	**760**	**.295**

RYAN, B.J.   P

PERSONAL: Born December 28, 1975, in Bossier City, La. ... 6-6/247. ... Throws left, bats left. ... Full name: Robert Victor Ryan. ... High school: Airline (Bossier City, La.). ... College: Southwestern Louisiana.

TRANSACTIONS/CAREER NOTES: Selected by Cincinnati Reds organization in 17th round of free-agent draft (June 2, 1998). ... Traded by Reds with P Jacobo Sequea to Baltimore Orioles for P Juan Guzman (July 31, 1999).

CAREER HITTING: 0-for-2 (.000), 0 R, 0 2B, 0 3B, 0 HR, 0 RBI.

Year	League	W	L	Pct.	ERA	WHIP	G	GS	CG	ShO	Hld.	Sv.-Opp.	IP	H	R	ER	HR	BB-IBB	SO	Avg.
1998— Billings (Pio.)		2	1	.667	1.93	1.07	14	0	0	0	...	4-...	18.2	15	4	4	0	5-0	25	.211
— Char., W.Va. (SAL)		0	0	...	2.08	0.46	3	0	0	0	...	2-...	4.1	1	1	1	0	1-0	5	.077
— Chattanooga (Sou.)		1	0	1.000	2.20	1.16	16	0	0	0	...	4-...	16.1	13	4	4	0	6-0	21	.220
1999— Chattanooga (Sou.)		2	1	.667	2.59	1.20	35	0	0	0	...	6-...	41.2	33	13	12	1	17-0	46	.217
— Indianapolis (Int'l)		1	0	1.000	4.00	1.33	11	0	0	0	...	0-...	9.0	9	4	4	0	3-1	12	.265
— Cincinnati (N.L.)		0	0	...	4.50	2.50	1	0	0	0	0	0-0	2.0	4	1	1	0	1-0	1	.500
— Rochester (Int'l)		0	0	...	2.51	0.84	11	0	0	0	...	1-...	14.1	8	4	4	2	4-1	20	.160
— Baltimore (A.L.)		1	0	1.000	2.95	1.15	13	0	0	0	0	0-0	18.1	9	6	6	0	12-1	28	.150
2000— Baltimore (A.L.)		2	3	.400	5.91	1.57	42	0	0	0	7	0-3	42.2	36	29	28	7	31-1	41	.225
— Rochester (Int'l)		0	1	.000	4.74	1.30	14	4	0	0	...	0-...	24.2	23	13	13	4	9-0	28	.247
2001— Baltimore (A.L.)		2	4	.333	4.25	1.45	61	0	0	0	14	2-4	53.0	47	31	25	6	30-4	54	.233
2002— Baltimore (A.L.)		2	1	.667	4.68	1.46	67	0	0	0	12	1-2	57.2	51	31	30	7	33-4	56	.241
2003— Baltimore (A.L.)		4	1	.800	3.40	1.37	76	0	0	0	19	0-2	50.1	42	19	19	1	27-0	43	.227
American League totals (5 years)		**11**	**9**	**.550**	**4.38**	**1.43**	**259**	**0**	**0**	**0**	**52**	**3-11**	**222.0**	**185**	**116**	**108**	**21**	**133-10**	**242**	**.226**
National League totals (1 year)		**0**	**0**	**...**	**4.50**	**2.50**	**1**	**0**	**0**	**0**	**0**	**0-0**	**2.0**	**4**	**1**	**1**	**0**	**1-0**	**1**	**.500**
Major League totals (5 years)		**11**	**9**	**.550**	**4.38**	**1.44**	**260**	**0**	**0**	**0**	**52**	**3-11**	**224.0**	**189**	**117**	**109**	**21**	**134-10**	**243**	**.229**

RYAN, MICHAEL   OF

PERSONAL: Born July 6, 1977, in Indiana, Pa. ... 6-0/185. ... Bats left, throws right. ... Full name: Michael Sean Ryan. ... High school: Indiana (Pa.).

TRANSACTIONS/CAREER NOTES: Selected by Minnesota Twins organization in fifth round of free-agent draft (June 4, 1996).

2003 GAMES PLAYED BY POSITION (MLB): OF—16, DH—4.

Year	Team (League)	Pos.	G	AB	R	H	2B	3B	HR	RBI	BB	SO	HBP	GDP	SB-CS	Avg.	OBP	SLG	OPS	E	Pct.
1996— GC Twins (GCL)		3B	43	157	12	31	8	2	0	13	13	20	1	3	3-0	.197	.260	.274	.534	10	.910
1997— Elizabethton (App.)		3B	62	220	44	66	10	0	3	29	38	39	3	8	2-2	.300	.404	.386	.790	28	.825
1998— Fort Wayne (Midw.)		3B-1B	113	412	68	131	24	6	9	72	44	92	2	8	7-3	.318	.382	.471	.853	33	.906
1999— Fort Myers (FSL)		2B	131	507	85	139	26	5	8	71	63	60	5	11	3-4	.274	.356	.393	.749	35	.949
2000— New Britain (East.)		OF-2B	122	481	64	133	23	8	11	69	34	79	2	13	4-3	.277	.323	.426	.749	9	.965
— Salt Lake (PCL)		OF	3	9	1	2	0	0	0	2	3	2	0	1	0-0	.222	.417	.222	.639	0	1.000
2001— Edmonton (PCL)		OF-2B	135	527	89	152	36	7	18	73	52	121	2	17	1-6	.288	.353	.486	.839	11	.966
2002— Edmonton (PCL)		OF	131	540	92	141	36	6	31	101	55	124	2	9	4-5	.261	.330	.522	.852	3	.987
— Minnesota (A.L.)		OF-DH	7	11	3	1	0	0	0	0	0	2	0	0	0-0	.091	.091	.091	.182	0	1.000
2003— Rochester (Int'l)		OF-DH	115	408	56	92	20	4	15	60	38	89	1	8	6-1	.225	.289	.404	.694	2	.988
— Minnesota (A.L.)		OF-DH	27	61	13	24	7	0	5	13	6	12	0	4	2-1	.393	.441	.754	1.195	0	1.000
Major League totals (2 years)			**34**	**72**	**16**	**25**	**7**	**0**	**5**	**13**	**6**	**14**	**0**	**4**	**2-1**	**.347**	**.392**	**.653**	**1.045**	**0**	**1.000**

SAARLOOS, KIRK   P

PERSONAL: Born May 23, 1979, in Long Beach, Calif. ... 6-0/180. ... Throws right, bats right. ... Full name: Kirk Craig Saarloos. ... Name pronounced: sar-LOHS. ... College: Cal State Fullerton.

TRANSACTIONS/CAREER NOTES: Selected by Houston Astros organization in third round of free-agent draft (June 1, 2001).

CAREER HITTING: 2-for-35 (.057), 0 R, 1 2B, 0 3B, 0 HR, 3 RBI.

Year	League	W	L	Pct.	ERA	WHIP	G	GS	CG	ShO	Hld.	Sv.-Opp.	IP	H	R	ER	HR	BB-IBB	SO	Avg.
2001— Lexington (S. Atl.)		1	1	.500	1.17	0.82	22	0	0	0	...	11-...	30.2	18	5	4	1	7-0	40	.165
2002— Round Rock (Texas)		10	1	.909	1.40	0.83	13	13	1	1	...	0-...	83.1	48	17	13	1	21-0	82	.168
— New Orleans (PCL)		2	0	1.000	2.25	0.88	4	2	0	0	...	0-...	16.0	12	4	4	1	2-0	19	.211
— Houston (N.L.)		6	7	.462	6.01	1.49	17	11	1	1	0	0-0	85.1	100	59	57	12	27-5	54	.301
2003— New Orleans (PCL)		5	0	1.000	3.08	1.06	13	7	2	1	...	0-...	61.1	54	22	21	4	11-1	34	.242
— Houston (N.L.)		2	1	.667	4.93	1.46	36	4	0	0	4	0-0	49.1	55	31	27	4	17-3	43	.281
Major League totals (2 years)		**8**	**8**	**.500**	**5.61**	**1.48**	**53**	**21**	**1**	**1**	**4**	**0-0**	**134.2**	**155**	**90**	**84**	**16**	**44-8**	**97**	**.294**

SABATHIA, C.C.　　　　　　　　　P

PERSONAL: Born July 21, 1980, in Vallejo, Calif. ... 6-7/290. ... Throws left, bats left. ... Full name: Carsten Charles Sabathia. ... Name pronounced: sa-BATH-ee-a. ... High school: Vallejo (Calif.).
TRANSACTIONS/CAREER NOTES: Selected by Cleveland Indians organization in first round (20th pick overall) of free-agent draft (June 2, 1998).
CAREER HITTING: 4-for-15 (.267), 1 R, 0 2B, 0 3B, 0 HR, 0 RBI.

Year League	W	L	Pct.	ERA	WHIP	G	GS	CG	ShO	Hld.	Sv.-Opp.	IP	H	R	ER	HR	BB-IBB	SO	Avg.
1998— Burlington (Appal.)	1	0	1.000	4.50	1.56	5	5	0	0	...	0-...	18.0	20	14	9	1	8-0	35	.274
1999— Mahoning Valley (NY-P)	0	0	...	1.83	1.07	6	6	0	0	...	0-...	19.2	9	5	4	0	12-0	27	.143
— Columbus (S. Atl.)	2	0	1.000	1.08	0.78	3	3	0	0	...	0-...	16.2	8	2	2	1	5-0	20	.140
— Kinston (Caro.)	3	3	.500	5.34	1.53	7	7	0	0	...	0-...	32.0	30	22	19	3	19-0	29	.256
2000— Kinston (Caro.)	3	2	.600	3.54	1.29	10	10	2	2	...	0-...	56.0	48	23	22	4	24-0	69	.234
— Akron (East.)	3	7	.300	3.59	1.36	17	17	0	0	...	0-...	90.1	75	41	36	6	48-0	90	.223
2001— Cleveland (A.L.)	17	5	.773	4.39	1.35	33	33	0	0	0	0-0	180.1	149	93	88	19	95-1	171	.228
2002— Cleveland (A.L.)	13	11	.542	4.37	1.36	33	33	2	0	0	0-0	210.0	198	109	102	17	88-2	149	.252
2003— Cleveland (A.L.)	13	9	.591	3.60	1.30	30	30	2	1	0	0-0	197.2	190	85	79	19	66-3	141	.255
Major League totals (3 years)	**43**	**25**	**.632**	**4.12**	**1.34**	**96**	**96**	**4**	**1**	**0**	**0-0**	**588.0**	**537**	**287**	**269**	**55**	**249-6**	**461**	**.246**

SADLER, CARL　　　　　　　　　P

PERSONAL: Born October 11, 1976, in Gainesville, Fla. ... 6-2/180. ... Throws left, bats left. ... Full name: William Carl Sadler. ... Name pronounced: sad-LER. ... High school: Taylor County (Perry, Fla.).
TRANSACTIONS/CAREER NOTES: Selected by Montreal Expos organization in 34th round of free-agent draft (June 4, 1996). ... Released by Expos (April 1, 1998). ... Signed by Cleveland Indians organization (April 3, 1998). ... On disabled list (June 16, 1998-entire season).
CAREER HITTING: 0-for-0 (.000), 0 R, 0 2B, 0 3B, 0 HR, 0 RBI.

Year League	W	L	Pct.	ERA	WHIP	G	GS	CG	ShO	Hld.	Sv.-Opp.	IP	H	R	ER	HR	BB-IBB	SO	Avg.
1996— GC Expos (GCL)	2	2	.500	3.89	1.43	17	3	0	0	...	1-...	37.0	41	24	16	2	12-0	24	.268
1997— GC Expos (GCL)	0	2	.000	4.35	1.50	9	3	0	0	...	0-...	20.2	26	11	10	0	5-0	14	.313
— Vermont (NY-P)	2	2	.500	4.21	1.54	7	6	0	0	...	0-...	36.1	33	20	17	2	23-0	27	.239
1998—										Did not play.									
1999— Burlington (Appal.)	1	0	1.000	3.13	1.22	5	5	0	0	...	0-...	23.0	18	10	8	0	10-0	22	.220
— Mahoning Valley (NY-P)	0	1	.000	31.50	5.50	1	1	0	0	...	0-...	2.0	8	7	7	0	3-0	3	.571
2000— Mahoning Valley (NY-P)	0	0	...	3.00	1.33	5	0	0	0	...	0-...	6.0	5	2	2	0	3-0	3	.238
— Columbus (S. Atl.)	1	3	.250	6.61	1.65	10	0	0	0	...	0-...	16.1	20	13	12	0	7-0	21	.303
2001— Kinston (Caro.)	6	0	1.000	1.88	1.11	27	2	0	0	...	2-...	62.1	51	19	13	2	18-1	78	.216
— Akron (East.)	2	3	.400	6.50	1.78	11	0	0	0	...	0-...	18.0	23	16	13	1	9-0	14	.303
2002— Akron (East.)	4	1	.800	2.33	1.10	21	0	0	0	...	0-...	46.1	39	12	12	0	12-1	37	.229
— Buffalo (Int'l)	1	1	.500	1.93	1.45	12	0	0	0	...	1-...	18.2	19	7	4	1	8-1	13	.268
— Cleveland (A.L.)	1	2	.333	4.43	1.28	24	0	0	0	5	0-1	20.1	15	10	10	2	11-0	23	.211
2003— Cleveland (A.L.)	0	0	...	1.86	1.66	18	0	0	0	3	0-0	9.2	11	2	2	0	5-0	10	.306
— Buffalo (Int'l)	2	1	.667	6.28	1.75	31	0	0	0	...	3-...	53.0	62	41	37	4	31-3	32	.298
Major League totals (2 years)	**1**	**2**	**.333**	**3.60**	**1.40**	**42**	**0**	**0**	**0**	**8**	**0-1**	**30.0**	**26**	**12**	**12**	**2**	**16-0**	**33**	**.243**

SADLER, DONNIE　　　　　　　OF/IF

PERSONAL: Born June 17, 1975, in Gohlson, Texas. ... 5-6/175. ... Bats right, throws right. ... Full name: Donnie Lamont Sadler. ... High school: Valley Mills (Texas).
TRANSACTIONS/CAREER NOTES: Selected by Boston Red Sox organization in 11th round of free-agent draft (June 2, 1994). ... On Pawtucket disabled list (May 4-June 4 and June 23-30, 1998; and June 25-July 18, 1999). ... Traded by Red Sox with OF Michael Coleman to Cincinnati Reds for IF Chris Stynes (November 16, 2000). ... Traded by Reds to Kansas City Royals for P Cary Ammons (June 20, 2001). ... Granted free agency (December 21, 2001). ... Re-signed by Royals (January 7, 2002). ... On Kansas City disabled list (June 14-July 8, 2002); included rehabilitation assignment to Omaha (July 3-8). ... Claimed on waivers by Texas Rangers (July 8, 2002). ... Released by Rangers (September 30, 2002). ... Re-signed by Rangers (November 13, 2002). ... Contract purchased by Texas from Oklahoma (April 29, 2003).
2003 GAMES PLAYED BY POSITION (MLB): OF—41, 3B—23, SS—19, 2B—1.

Year Team (League)	Pos.	G	AB	R	H	2B	3B	HR	RBI	BB	SO	HBP	GDP	SB-CS	Avg.	OBP	SLG	OPS	E	Pct.
1994— GC Red Sox (GCL)	2B-3B-SS	53	206	52	56	8	6	1	16	23	27	3	1	32-8	.272	.349	.383	.732	18	.928
1995— Michigan (Midw.)	SS	118	438	* 103	124	25	8	9	55	79	85	6	5	41-13	.283	.397	.438	.836	28	.944
1996— Trenton (East.)	SS-OF	115	454	68	121	20	8	6	46	38	75	6	4	34-8	.267	.329	.385	.715	27	.940
1997— Pawtucket (Int'l)	2B-SS-OF	125	481	74	102	18	2	11	36	57	121	2	11	20-14	.212	.295	.326	.621	§ 15	.976
1998— Boston (A.L.)	2B-SS-DH	58	124	21	28	4	4	3	15	6	28	3	1	4-0	.226	.276	.395	.671	5	.973
— Pawtucket (Int'l)	2B-SS	36	131	25	29	5	1	2	10	26	23	1	1	11-1	.221	.348	.321	.669	4	.978
1999— Boston (A.L.)	S-2-3-O-D	49	107	18	30	5	1	0	4	5	20	0	1	2-1	.280	.313	.346	.658	9	.916
— Pawtucket (Int'l)	SS-DH	43	172	23	50	12	4	1	17	16	36	3	3	4-2	.291	.361	.424	.786	10	.944
— GC Red Sox (GCL)	SS	4	13	2	5	2	0	0	1	2	1	0	0	0-0	.385	.467	.538	1.005	1	.950
2000— Pawtucket (Int'l)	OF-SS-2B	91	313	45	63	6	5	5	23	45	60	4	8	10-1	.201	.306	.300	.606	7	.979
— Boston (A.L.)	S-0-2-3-D	49	99	14	22	5	0	1	10	5	18	1	1	3-1	.222	.262	.303	.565	3	.976
2001— Cincinnati (N.L.)	2-S-O-D	39	84	9	17	3	0	1	3	9	20	0	3	3-3	.202	.280	.274	.553	3	.965
— Kansas City (A.L.)	O-3-2-S-D	54	101	19	13	3	0	0	2	9	17	2	0	4-1	.129	.212	.158	.371	2	.987
2002— Kansas City (A.L.)	O-3-2-S-D	35	68	10	13	1	1	0	5	4	12	0	0	3-1	.191	.233	.235	.468	3	.943
— Omaha (PCL)	3B-SS-2B	5	21	6	7	0	0	0	2	2	3	1	0	0-2	.333	.417	.333	.750	0	1.000
— Texas (A.L.)	O-S-3-2-D	38	30	6	3	1	0	0	2	3	7	2	1	2-2	.100	.229	.133	.362	0	1.000
— Oklahoma (PCL)	OF-2B	12	43	7	10	3	1	0	4	6	7	1	0	2-1	.233	.340	.349	.689	1	.978
2003— Oklahoma (PCL)	S-2-D-O	19	66	14	20	4	1	1	9	10	9	2	1	6-1	.303	.405	.439	.844	4	.956
— Texas (A.L.)	O-3-S-2	77	131	27	26	5	2	1	5	13	34	2	1	4-3	.198	.277	.290	.567	4	.966
American League totals (6 years)		**360**	**660**	**115**	**135**	**24**	**8**	**5**	**43**	**45**	**136**	**10**	**5**	**22-9**	**.205**	**.263**	**.288**	**.551**	**26**	**.967**
National League totals (1 year)		**39**	**84**	**9**	**17**	**3**	**0**	**1**	**3**	**9**	**20**	**0**	**3**	**3-3**	**.202**	**.280**	**.274**	**.553**	**3**	**.965**
Major League totals (6 years)		**399**	**744**	**124**	**152**	**27**	**8**	**6**	**46**	**54**	**156**	**10**	**8**	**25-12**	**.204**	**.265**	**.286**	**.551**	**29**	**.967**

SAENZ, OLMEDO　　　　　　　3B/1B

PERSONAL: Born October 8, 1970... 5-11/221. ... Bats right, throws right. ... Full name: Olmedo Sanchez Saenz. ... Name pronounced: SIGNS.
TRANSACTIONS/CAREER NOTES: Signed as non-drafted free agent by Chicago White Sox organization (May 11, 1990). ... Granted free agency (October 15, 1997). ... Re-signed by White Sox organization (January 25, 1998). ... Granted free agency (October 15, 1998). ... Signed by Oakland Athletics (November 13, 1998). ... On Oakland dis-

S

abled list (July 26-August 16, 1999); included rehabilitation assignment to Vancouver (August 13-16). ... On Oakland disabled list (August 1-September 19, 2000); included rehabilitation assignment to Sacramento (August 29-30). ... Granted free agency (November 1, 2002).

Year	Team (League)	Pos.	G	AB	R	H	2B	3B	HR	RBI	BB	SO	HBP	GDP	SB-CS	Avg.	OBP	SLG	OPS	E	Pct.
1991— Sarasota (Fla. St.)	3B	5	19	1	2	0	1	0	2	2	0	0	1		0-1	.105	.190	.211	.401	3	.842
— South Bend (Mid.)	3B	56	192	23	47	10	1	2	22	21	48	5	3	5-3	.245	.332	.339	.670	12	.890
1992— South Bend (Mid.)	3B-1B	132	493	66	121	26	4	7	59	36	52	11	16	16-13	.245	.309	.357	.666	48	.895
1993— Sarasota (Fla. St.)	3B	33	121	13	31	9	4	0	27	9	18	2	1	3-1	.256	.316	.397	.712	5	.933
— South Bend (Mid.)	3B	13	50	3	18	4	1	0	7	7	7	0	1	1-1	.360	.439	.480	.919	4	.913
— Birmingham (Sou.)	3B	49	173	30	60	17	2	6	29	20	21	5	7	2-1	.347	.427	.572	.999	14	.899
1994— Nashville (A.A.)	3B-DH	107	383	48	100	27	2	12	59	30	57	9	5	3-2	.261	.326	.436	.762	22	.917
— Chicago (A.L.)	3B	5	14	2	2	0	1	0	0	0	5	0	1	0-0	.143	.143	.286	.429	0	1.000
1995— Nashville (A.A.)	3B	111	415	60	126	26	1	13	74	45	60	12	11	0-2	.304	.385	.465	.850	* 24	.939
1996— Nashville (A.A.)	3B-DH	134	476	86	124	29	1	18	63	53	80	13	5	4-2	.261	.350	.439	.789	22	.939
1997— GC Whi. Sox (GCL)	DH	2	1	0	1	1	0	0	0	0	0	0	1	0-0	1.000	1.000	2.000	3.000	...	...
1998— Calgary (PCL)	3B-DH	124	466	89	146	29	0	29	102	45	49	22	16	3-3	.313	.394	.562	.957	21	.937
1999— Oakland (A.L.)	3B-1B-DH	97	255	41	70	18	0	11	41	22	47	15	6	1-1	.275	.363	.475	.837	8	.971
— Vancouver (PCL)	3B	2	5	1	3	1	0	0	2	0	0	1	0	0-0	.600	.571	.800	1.371	0	1.000
2000— Oakland (A.L.)	DH-3B-1B	76	214	40	67	12	2	9	33	25	40	7	6	1-0	.313	.401	.514	.915	4	.977
— Sacramento (PCL)		1	4	1	2	0	0	0	1	0	0	0	0	0-0	.500	.500	.500	1.000	...	...
2001— Oakland (A.L.)	DH-1B-3B	106	305	33	67	21	1	9	32	19	64	13	9	0-1	.220	.291	.384	.675	5	.979
2002— Oakland (A.L.)	1B-DH	68	156	15	43	10	1	6	18	13	31	7	2	1-1	.276	.354	.468	.822	5	.980
2003— Athletics (Ariz..)	1B-3B-DH	13	45	13	15	2	0	2	8	8	6	2	1	1-0	.333	.455	.511	.966	1	.974
— Modesto (Calif.)	DH	1	4	0	0	0	0	0	1	0	1	1	0	0-0	.000	.200	.000	.200	0	.000
Major League totals (5 years)		352	944	131	249	61	5	35	124	79	187	42	24	3-3	.264	.345	.450	.795	22	.977

S

SALMON, TIM — OF

PERSONAL: Born August 24, 1968, in Long Beach, Calif. ... 6-3/235. ... Bats right, throws right. ... Full name: Timothy James Salmon. ... Name pronounced: SAM-en. ... High school: Greenway (Phoenix). ... College: Grand Canyon (Ari.).

TRANSACTIONS/CAREER NOTES: Selected by Atlanta Braves organization in 18th round of free-agent draft (June 2, 1986); did not sign. ... Selected by California Angels organization in third round of free-agent draft (June 5, 1989). ... On disabled list (May 12-23 and May 27-August 7, 1990; and July 18-August 3, 1994). ... Angels franchise renamed Anaheim Angels for 1997 season. ... On disabled list (April 23-May 9, 1998). ... On Anaheim disabled list (May 4-July 17, 1999); included rehabilitation assignment to Lake Elsinore (July 16-17). ... On Anaheim disabled list (July 1-19, 2001); included rehabilitation assignment to Rancho Cucamonga (July 17-19). ... On disabled list (August 14-September 1, 2002).

2003 GAMES PLAYED BY POSITION (MLB): OF—78, DH—68.

Year	Team (League)	Pos.	G	AB	R	H	2B	3B	HR	RBI	BB	SO	HBP	GDP	SB-CS	Avg.	OBP	SLG	OPS	E	Pct.
1989— Bend (NW)	OF	55	196	37	48	6	5	6	31	33	60	6	2	2-4	.245	.367	.418	.785	4	.958
1990— Palm Springs (Calif.)	OF	36	118	19	34	6	0	2	21	21	44	4	1	11-1	.288	.413	.390	.802	1	.985
— Midland (Texas)	OF	27	97	17	26	3	1	3	16	18	38	1	1	1-0	.268	.385	.412	.797	3	.950
1991— Midland (Texas)	OF	131	465	100	114	26	4	23	94	* 89	166	6	6	12-6	.245	.372	.467	.839	10	.966
1992— Edmonton (PCL)	OF	118	409	• 101	142	38	4	* 29	* 105	91	103	6	9	9-7	.347	* .469	.672	1.141	3	.988
— California (A.L.)	OF	23	79	8	14	1	0	2	6	11	23	1	1	1-1	.177	.283	.266	.548	2	.953
1993— California (A.L.)	OF-DH	142	515	93	146	35	1	31	95	82	135	5	6	5-6	.283	.382	.536	.918	7	.980
1994— California (A.L.)	OF	100	373	67	107	19	2	23	70	54	102	5	3	1-3	.287	.382	.531	.912	8	.966
1995— California (A.L.)	OF-DH	143	537	111	177	34	3	34	105	91	111	6	9	5-5	.330	.429	.594	1.024	4	.981
1996— California (A.L.)	OF-DH	156	581	90	166	27	4	30	98	93	125	9	8	4-2	.286	.386	.501	.887	8	.975
1997— Anaheim (A.L.)	OF-DH	157	582	95	172	28	1	33	129	95	142	7	7	9-12	.296	.394	.517	.911	11	.971
1998— Anaheim (A.L.)	DH-OF	136	463	84	139	28	1	26	88	90	100	3	4	0-1	.300	.410	.533	.943	2	.959
1999— Anaheim (A.L.)	OF	98	353	60	94	24	2	17	69	63	80	0	7	4-1	.266	.372	.490	.862	4	.981
— Lake Elsinore (Calif.)	DH	1	5	0	3	2	0	0	2	0	1	0	0	0-0	.600	.600	1.000	1.600	...	...
2000— Anaheim (A.L.)	OF-DH	158	568	108	165	36	2	34	97	104	149	6	14	0-2	.290	.404	.540	.945	6	.979
2001— Anaheim (A.L.)	OF-DH	137	475	63	108	21	1	17	49	96	121	8	11	9-3	.227	.365	.383	.748	3	.989
— Rancho Cuca. (Calif.)	OF	2	7	1	1	1	0	0	0	1	4	0	0	0-0	.143	.250	.286	.536	1	.667
2002— Anaheim (A.L.)	OF-DH	138	483	84	138	37	1	22	88	71	102	7	6	6-3	.286	.380	.503	.883	3	.986
2003— Anaheim (A.L.)	OF-DH	148	528	78	145	35	4	19	72	77	93	10	12	3-1	.275	.374	.464	.838	6	.958
Major League totals (12 years)		1536	5537	941	1571	324	22	288	966	927	1275	62	88	47-40	.284	.389	.506	.895	64	.977

SANCHEZ, ALEX — OF

PERSONAL: Born August 26, 1976, in Havana, Cuba. ... 5-10/159. ... Bats left, throws left. ... Full name: Alexis Sanchez. ... Junior college: Miami-Dade Community College.

TRANSACTIONS/CAREER NOTES: Selected by Tampa Bay Devil Rays organization in fifth round of free-agent draft (June 4, 1996). ... Claimed on waivers by Milwaukee Brewers (April 6, 2001). ... On Milwaukee disabled list (July 16-31, 2001). ... On disabled list (September 2, 2002-remainder of season). ... Traded by Brewers to Detroit Tigers for P Chad Petty and OF Gary Varner (May 27, 2003).

2003 GAMES PLAYED BY POSITION (MLB): OF—135.

Year	Team (League)	Pos.	G	AB	R	H	2B	3B	HR	RBI	BB	SO	HBP	GDP	SB-CS	Avg.	OBP	SLG	OPS	E	Pct.
1996— GC Devil Rays (GCL)	OF	56	227	36	64	7	6	1	22	10	35	6	2	20-12	.282	.328	.379	.707	3	.968
1997— Char., S.C. (SAL)	OF	131	537	73	155	15	6	0	34	37	72	3	7	92-40	.289	.336	.339	.675	11	.963
1998— St. Pete. (FSL)	OF	128	545	77	* 180	17	9	1	50	31	70	1	5	66-33	.330	.360	.400	.760	• 12	.965
1999— Orlando (South.)	OF	121	500	68	127	12	4	2	29	26	88	0	8	48-26	.254	.290	.306	.596	* 14	.958
— Durham (Int'l)	OF	3	10	2	2	1	0	0	0	1	0	0	0	0-0	.200	.273	.300	.573	0	1.000
2000— Durham (Int'l)	OF	107	446	76	130	18	3	2	33	30	66	5	6	* 52-20	.291	.342	.359	.700	6	.977
— Orlando (South.)	OF	20	86	12	25	2	1	0	4	1	13	1	1	2-6	.291	.307	.337	.644	1	.972
2001— Indianapolis (Int'l)	OF	83	335	52	105	14	5	1	26	22	44	2	2	27-8	.313	.359	.394	.753	6	.968
— Milwaukee (N.L.)	OF	30	68	7	14	3	2	0	4	5	13	0	0	6-2	.206	.260	.309	.569	1	.963
2002— Milwaukee (N.L.)	OF	112	394	55	114	10	7	1	33	31	62	2	4	37-14	.289	.343	.358	.701	5	.990
2003— Milwaukee (N.L.)	OF	43	163	15	46	10	3	0	10	7	28	2	1	8-6	.282	.316	.380	.696	1	.990
— Detroit (A.L.)	OF	101	394	43	114	13	5	1	22	18	46	1	4	44-*18	.289	.320	.355	.675	2	.979
American League totals (1 year)		101	394	43	114	13	5	1	22	18	46	1	4	44-18	.289	.320	.355	.675	6	.979
National League totals (3 years)		185	625	77	174	23	12	1	47	43	103	4	5	51-22	.278	.327	.358	.685	7	.983
Major League totals (3 years)		286	1019	120	288	36	17	2	69	61	149	5	9	95-40	.283	.324	.357	.681	13	.981

SANCHEZ, DUANER　　　　　　　　　　P

PERSONAL: Born October 14, 1979, in Cotui, Dominican Republic. ... 6-0/180. ... Throws right, bats right. ... High school: Francisco H. Carvajal (Cotui, Dominican Repblic).
TRANSACTIONS/CAREER NOTES: Signed as non-drafted free agent by Arizona Diamondbacks organization (October 16, 1996). ... On El Paso disabled list (June 12-July 16, 2001). ... Traded by Diamondbacks to Pittsburgh Pirates for P Mike Fetters (July 6, 2002). ... Recalled from Nashville (June 23, 2003). ... Optioned to Nashville (June 24, 2003). ... Recalled from Nashville (July 26, 2003).
CAREER HITTING: 0-for-0 (.000), 0 R, 0 2B, 0 3B, 0 HR, 0 RBI.

Year　League	W	L	Pct.	ERA	WHIP	G	GS	CG	ShO	Hld.	Sv.-Opp.	IP	H	R	ER	HR	BB-IBB	SO	Avg.
1997— Dom. D'backs (DSL)	4	4	.500	5.13	1.76	21	6	0	0	...	1-...	59.2	57	50	34	...	48-...	44	...
1998— Dom. D'backs (DSL)	2	3	.400	1.79	1.19	14	8	1	0	...	1-...	50.1	36	19	10	...	24-...	44	...
1999— High Desert (Calif.)	0	0	...	7.53	1.67	3	3	0	0	...	0-...	14.1	15	13	12	2	9-0	9	.288
— Missoula (Pio.)	5	3	.625	3.13	1.22	13	11	0	0	...	0-...	63.1	54	34	22	3	23-0	51	.224
2000— South Bend (Mid.)	8	9	.471	3.65	1.25	28	28	4	0	...	0-...	165.1	152	80	67	6	54-1	121	.243
2001— El Paso (Texas)	3	7	.300	6.78	1.66	13	13	0	0	...	0-...	70.1	92	56	53	5	25-1	41	.324
— Lancaster (Calif.)	2	4	.333	4.58	1.41	10	10	1	0	...	0-...	59.0	65	44	30	7	18-0	49	.274
2002— El Paso (Texas)	4	3	.571	3.03	1.23	31	0	0	0	...	13-...	35.2	31	16	12	1	13-1	37	.223
— Arizona (N.L.)	0	0	...	4.91	2.18	6	0	0	0	1	0-1	3.2	3	2	2	1	5-0	4	.214
— Tucson (PCL)	1	1	.500	6.75	1.31	4	0	0	0	...	1-...	5.1	6	4	4	1	1-0	9	.261
— Nashville (PCL)	0	3	.000	4.76	1.50	20	0	0	0	...	6-...	22.2	23	12	12	2	11-2	20	.274
— Pittsburgh (N.L.)	0	0	...	15.43	2.14	3	0	0	0	0	0-0	2.1	3	4	4	1	2-0	2	.300
2003— Nashville (PCL)	4	4	.500	3.69	1.48	41	1	0	0	...	1-...	61.0	63	28	25	3	27-5	34	.265
— Pittsburgh (N.L.)	1	0	1.000	16.50	2.67	6	0	0	0	0	0-0	6.0	15	11	11	2	1-0	3	.500
Major League totals (2 years)	1	0	1.000	12.75	2.42	15	0	0	0	1	0-1	12.0	21	17	17	4	8-0	9	.389

SANCHEZ, FELIX　　　　　　　　　　P

PERSONAL: Born August 3, 1981, in Puerto Plata, Dominican Republic. ... 6-3/180. ... Throws left, bats right. ... Full name: Felix Antonio Sanchez.
TRANSACTIONS/CAREER NOTES: Signed as non-drafted free agent by Chicago Cubs organization (September 15, 1998).
CAREER HITTING: 0-for-0 (.000), 0 R, 0 2B, 0 3B, 0 HR, 0 RBI.

Year　League	W	L	Pct.	ERA	WHIP	G	GS	CG	ShO	Hld.	Sv.-Opp.	IP	H	R	ER	HR	BB-IBB	SO	Avg.
2001— Ariz. Cubs (Ariz.)	2	5	.286	4.01	1.30	12	9	0	0	...	0-...	60.2	57	38	27	2	22-0	55	.250
— Boise (NW)	2	0	1.000	1.56	1.21	3	3	0	0	...	0-...	17.1	11	4	3	0	10-0	16	.180
2002— Lansing (Midw.)	6	6	.500	4.15	1.46	26	21	0	0	...	2-...	119.1	130	67	55	7	44-0	101	.286
2003— Ariz. Cubs (Ariz.)	0	0	...	0.00	1.00	1	1	0	0	...	0-...	2.0	2	0	0	0	0-0	3	.250
— West Tenn. (Sou.)	2	2	.500	3.23	1.38	30	8	0	0	...	0-...	64.0	57	30	23	3	31-0	55	.235
— Chicago (N.L.)	0	0	...	10.80	3.00	3	0	0	0	0	0-0	1.2	2	2	2	1	3-0	2	.333
Major League totals (1 year)	0	0	...	10.80	3.00	3	0	0	0	0	0-0	1.2	2	2	2	1	3-0	2	.333

SANCHEZ, FREDDY　　　　　　　　　　IF

PERSONAL: Born December 21, 1977, in Hollywood, Calif. ... 5-11/185. ... Bats right, throws right. ... Full name: Frederick P. Sanchez. ... Junior college: Oklahoma City Community College.
TRANSACTIONS/CAREER NOTES: Selected by Boston Red Sox oragnization in 11th round of free-agent draft (June 5, 2000). ... Traded by Red Sox with P Mike Gonzalez and cash to Pittsburgh Pirates for P Jeff Suppan, P Brandon Lyon and P Anastacio Martinez (July 31, 2003).
2003 GAMES PLAYED BY POSITION (MLB): 3B—7, SS—6, 2B—3.

Year　Team (League)	Pos.	G	AB	R	H	2B	3B	HR	RBI	BB	SO	HBP	GDP	SB-CS	Avg.	OBP	SLG	OPS	E	Pct.
2000— Lowell (NY-Penn)	SS	34	132	24	38	13	2	1	14	9	16	3	1	2-4	.288	.347	.439	.787	4	.974
— Augusta (S. Atl.)	SS	30	109	17	33	7	0	0	15	11	19	1	1	4-0	.303	.372	.367	.739	3	.976
2001— Sarasota (Fla. St.)	SS	69	280	40	95	19	4	1	24	22	30	2	3	5-3	.339	.388	.446	.834	17	.944
— Trenton (East.)	SS	44	178	25	58	20	0	2	19	9	21	2	6	3-1	.326	.361	.472	.835	9	.948
2002— Trenton (East.)	SS-2B	80	311	60	102	23	1	3	38	37	45	5	9	19-3	.328	.403	.437	.841	16	.955
— Pawtucket (Int'l)	SS-2B	45	183	25	55	10	1	4	28	12	21	3	5	5-3	.301	.350	.432	.782	13	.942
— Boston (A.L.) 2B-SS-DH		12	16	3	3	0	0	0	2	2	3	0	0	0-0	.188	.278	.188	.465	0	1.000
2003— Boston (A.L.) 3B-SS-2B		20	34	6	8	2	0	0	2	0	8	0	0	0-0	.235	.235	.294	.529	0	1.000
— Pawtucket (Int'l)	S-2-3-D	58	211	46	72	17	0	5	25	31	36	2	7	8-0	.341	.430	.493	.923	4	.983
— Nashville (PCL)	2B	1	5	1	2	1	0	0	0	0	1	0	0	0-0	.400	.400	.600	1.000	0	1.000
Major League totals (2 years)		32	50	9	11	2	0	0	4	2	11	0	0	0-0	.220	.250	.260	.510	0	1.000

SANCHEZ, JESUS　　　　　　　　　　P

PERSONAL: Born October 11, 1974, in Nizao Bani, Dominican Republic. ... 5-10/165. ... Throws left, bats left. ... Full name: Jesus Paulino Sanchez. ... Name pronounced: HAY-soos.
TRANSACTIONS/CAREER NOTES: Signed as non-drafted free agent by New York Mets organization (June 7, 1992). ... On disabled list (April 4-May 26, 1996). ... Traded by Mets with P A.J. Burnett and OF Robert Stratton to Florida Marlins for P Al Leiter and 2B Ralph Milliard (February 6, 1998). ... Traded by Marlins to Chicago Cubs for P Nate Teut (December 11, 2001). ... Released by Cubs (October 1, 2002). ... Signed by Houston Astros organization (December 10, 2002). ... Released by Astros (March 30, 2003). ... Signed by Colorado Rockies (August 24, 2003). ... Elected free agency (September 30, 2003).
CAREER HITTING: 25-for-138 (.181), 10 R, 0 2B, 1 3B, 0 HR, 6 RBI.

Year　League	W	L	Pct.	ERA	WHIP	G	GS	CG	ShO	Hld.	Sv.-Opp.	IP	H	R	ER	HR	BB-IBB	SO	Avg.
1992— Dom. Mets (DSL)	5	5	.500	4.19	1.52	15	15	1	0	...	0-...	81.2	86	52	38	...	38-...	72	...
1993— Dom. Mets (DSL)	7	3	.700	2.40	1.20	16	13	2	• 2	...	0-...	82.1	63	30	22	...	36-...	94	...
1994— Kingsport (Appal.)	7	4	.636	1.96	1.01	13	12	• 3	0	...	0-...	87.1	61	27	19	2	27-0	71	.193
1995— Capital City (S. Atl.)	9	7	.563	3.13	1.25	27	27	4	0	...	0-...	169.2	154	76	59	9	58-0	• 177	.243
1996— St. Lucie (Fla. St.)	9	3	.750	1.96	0.84	16	16	2	1	...	0-...	92.0	53	22	20	6	24-0	81	.168
1997— Binghamton (Eastern)	* 13	10	.565	4.30	1.25	26	26	3	0	...	0-...	165.1	146	87	79	* 25	61-2	* 176	.237
1998— Florida (N.L.)	7	9	.438	4.47	1.55	35	29	0	0	0	0-1	173.0	178	98	86	18	91-2	137	.272
1999— Florida (N.L.)	5	7	.417	6.01	1.89	59	10	0	0	11	0-2	76.1	84	53	51	16	60-11	62	.291
— Calgary (PCL)	0	0	...	5.79	1.39	4	1	0	0	...	1-...	9.1	9	6	6	0	5-0	14	.242
2000— Florida (N.L.)	9	12	.429	5.34	1.50	32	32	2	2	0	0-0	182.0	197	118	108	32	76-4	123	.280
2001— Calgary (PCL)	6	1	.857	3.21	1.24	16	11	0	0	...	0-...	75.2	61	32	27	4	33-0	58	.216
— Florida (N.L.)	2	4	.333	4.74	1.47	16	9	0	0	0	0-0	62.2	61	33	33	7	31-2	46	.256
2002— Chicago (N.L.)	0	0	...	12.96	3.00	8	0	0	0	0	0-0	8.1	15	12	12	4	10-1	6	.395
— Iowa (PCL)	8	9	.471	5.90	1.67	26	24	0	0	...	0-...	125.0	144	90	82	27	65-3	94	.294
2003— Colo. Springs (PCL)	2	0	1.000	3.98	1.37	46	3	0	0	...	2-...	63.1	61	28	28	6	26-1	52	.257
— Colorado (N.L.)	0	0	...	9.00	1.88	9	0	0	0	1	0-0	8.0	11	8	8	1	4-2	2	.324
Major League totals (6 years)	23	32	.418	5.26	1.60	159	80	2	2	12	0-3	510.1	546	322	298	78	272-22	376	.279

S

SANCHEZ, REY — SS/2B

PERSONAL: Born October 5, 1967, in Rio Piedras, Puerto Rico. ... 5-9/170. ... Bats right, throws right. ... Full name: Rey Francisco Sanchez. ... Name pronounced: RAY SAN-chezz. ... High school: Live Oak (Morgan Hill, Calif.).

TRANSACTIONS/CAREER NOTES: Selected by Texas Rangers organization in 13th round of free-agent draft (June 2, 1986). ... Traded by Rangers to Chicago Cubs for IF Bryan House (January 3, 1990). ... On disabled list (April 6, 1990-entire season). ... On Chicago disabled list (May 6-21, 1992); included rehabilitation assignment to Iowa (May 13-21). ... On disabled list (July 24-August 9, 1995). ... On Chicago disabled list (June 5-July 20 and August 11-September 1, 1996); included rehabilitation assignment to Iowa (July 16-20). ... Traded by Cubs to New York Yankees for P Frisco Parotte (August 16, 1997). ... Granted free agency (November 3, 1997). ... Signed by San Francisco Giants (January 22, 1998). ... Granted free agency (November 5, 1998). ... Signed by Kansas City Royals (December 11, 1998). ... Granted free agency (October 29, 1999). ... Re-signed by Royals (December 7, 1999). ... Traded by Royals to Atlanta Braves for P Brad Voyles and 2B Alejandro Machado (July 31, 2001). ... Granted free agency (November 5, 2001). ... Signed by Boston Red Sox organization (February 27, 2002). ... On disabled list (June 13-July 11, 2002). ... On suspended list (September 15-16, 2002). ... Granted free agency (October 30, 2002). ... Signed by New York Mets (December 27, 2002). ... Placed on 15-day disabled list (May 10, 2003). ... Activated from 15-day disabled list (May 27, 2003). ... Placed on 15-day disabled list, retroactive to June 6 (June 10, 2003). ... Sent on rehab assignment to Binghamton (June 27, 2003). ... Recalled from rehab assignment; reinstated from 15-day disabled list (July 1, 2003). ... Traded by Mets with cash to Seattle for OF Kenny Kelly (July 29, 2003).

2003 GAMES PLAYED BY POSITION (MLB): SS—88, 2B—12.

									BATTING								FIELDING	
Year Team (League)	Pos.	G	AB	R	H	2B	3B	HR	RBI	BB	SO	HBP	GDP	SB-CS	Avg.	OBP	SLG	OPS	E	Pct.
1986— GC Rangers (GCL)	2B-SS	52	169	27	49	3	1	0	23	41	18	3	3	10-10	.290	.435	.320	.754	15	.938
1987— Gastonia (S. Atl.)	SS	50	160	19	35	1	2	1	10	22	17	2	9	6-3	.219	.321	.269	.589	18	.933
— Butte (Pio.)	SS	49	189	36	69	10	6	0	25	21	12	2	6	22-6	.365	.430	.481	.911	12	.953
1988— Charlotte (Fla. St.)	SS	128	418	60	128	6	5	0	38	35	24	5	14	29-11	.306	.364	.344	.709	35	.948
1989— Okla. City (A.A.)	SS	134	464	38	104	10	4	1	39	21	50	2	14	4-4	.224	.259	.269	.529	29	.958
1990— Iowa (Am. Assoc.)										Did not play.									
1991— Iowa (Am. Assoc.)	SS	126	417	60	121	16	5	2	46	37	27	7	11	13-7	.290	.356	.367	.723	17	.971
— Chicago (N.L.)	2B-SS	13	23	1	6	0	0	0	2	4	3	0	0	0-0	.261	.370	.261	.631	0	1.000
1992— Iowa (Am. Assoc.)	SS-2B	20	76	12	26	3	0	0	3	4	1	0	3	6-3	.342	.375	.382	.757	5	.956
— Chicago (N.L.)	SS-2B	74	255	24	64	14	3	1	19	10	17	3	7	2-1	.251	.285	.341	.626	9	.975
1993— Chicago (N.L.)	SS	105	344	35	97	11	2	0	28	15	22	3	8	1-1	.282	.316	.326	.642	15	.969
1994— Chicago (N.L.)	2B-SS-3B	96	291	26	83	13	1	0	24	20	29	7	9	2-5	.285	.345	.337	.682	9	.979
1995— Chicago (N.L.)	2B-SS	114	428	57	119	22	2	3	27	14	48	1	9	6-4	.278	.301	.360	.661	7	.987
1996— Chicago (N.L.)	2B-SS	95	289	28	61	9	0	1	12	22	42	3	6	7-1	.211	.272	.253	.525	11	.977
— Iowa (Am. Assoc.)	SS	3	12	2	2	0	0	0	1	1	2	0	0	2-0	.167	.231	.167	.397	1	.933
1997— Chicago (N.L.)	SS-2B-3B	97	205	14	51	9	0	1	12	11	26	0	7	4-2	.249	.287	.307	.594	6	.977
— New York (A.L.)	2B-SS	38	138	21	43	12	0	1	15	5	21	1	1	0-4	.312	.338	.420	.758	4	.978
1998— San Francisco (N.L.)	SS-2B	109	316	44	90	14	2	2	30	16	47	1	11	0-0	.285	.325	.361	.686	8	.981
1999— Kansas City (A.L.)	SS	134	479	66	141	18	6	2	56	22	48	4	14	11-5	.294	.329	.370	.698	13	.982
2000— Kansas City (A.L.)	SS	143	509	68	139	18	2	1	38	28	55	4	17	7-3	.273	.314	.322	.637	4	.994
2001— Kansas City (A.L.)	SS	100	390	46	118	14	5	0	28	11	34	2	11	9-1	.303	.322	.364	.686	3	.994
— Atlanta (N.L.)	SS	49	154	10	35	4	1	0	9	4	15	0	9	2-0	.227	.245	.266	.512	3	.986
2002— Boston (A.L.)	2B-SS	107	357	46	102	12	3	1	38	17	31	2	9	2-2	.286	.318	.345	.662	5	.989
2003— Binghamton (East.)	SS	3	9	1	1	0	0	0	0	1	1	0	3	0-0	.111	.200	.111	.311	1	.900
— New York (N.L.)	SS-2B	56	174	11	36	3	1	0	12	8	18	0	7	1-1	.207	.240	.236	.476	4	.981
— Seattle (A.L.)	SS	46	170	22	50	5	1	0	11	8	21	2	3	1-0	.294	.330	.335	.665	4	.979
American League totals (6 years)		568	2043	269	593	79	17	5	186	91	210	15	55	30-15	.290	.323	.353	.675	33	.988
National League totals (10 years)		808	2479	250	642	99	12	8	175	124	267	21	73	25-15	.259	.298	.318	.617	72	.979
Major League totals (13 years)		1376	4522	519	1235	178	29	13	361	215	477	36	128	55-30	.273	.309	.334	.643	105	.983

SANDBERG, JARED — 3B

PERSONAL: Born March 2, 1978, in Olympia, Wash. ... 6-3/226. ... Bats right, throws right. ... Full name: Jared Lawrence Sandberg. ... High school: Capital (Olympia, Wash.).

TRANSACTIONS/CAREER NOTES: Selected by Tampa Bay Devil Rays organization in 16th round of free-agent draft (June 4, 1996). ... On Orlando disabled list (April 13-25 and May 9-June 30, 2000).

2003 GAMES PLAYED BY POSITION (MLB): 3B—50, SS—1, 1B—1.

									BATTING								FIELDING	
Year Team (League)	Pos.	G	AB	R	H	2B	3B	HR	RBI	BB	SO	HBP	GDP	SB-CS	Avg.	OBP	SLG	OPS	E	Pct.
1996— GC Devil Rays (GCL)	2B	22	77	6	13	2	1	0	7	9	26	0	1	1-0	.169	.256	.221	.477	3	.969
1997— St. Pete. (FSL)	2B	2	3	1	1	0	0	0	2	2	2	0	0	0-0	.333	.600	.333	.933	0	1.000
— Princeton (Appal.)	2B-3B	• 67	* 268	61	81	15	5	17	* 68	42	94	2	4	12-3	.302	.401	.586	.986	13	.949
1998— Char., S.C. (SAL)	3B	56	191	31	35	11	0	3	15	27	76	3	6	4-0	.183	.293	.288	.581	22	.862
— Hudson Valley (NYP)	3B	73	271	49	78	15	2	• 12	54	42	76	5	6	13-3	.288	.388	.491	.879	20	.915
1999— St. Pete. (FSL)	3B	136	504	73	139	24	1	22	96	51	133	9	12	8-2	.276	.350	.458	.808	* 37	.913
2000— Orlando (South.)	3B	67	244	30	63	15	1	5	35	33	55	2	6	5-3	.258	.348	.389	.737	10	.946
— Durham (Int'l)	3B	3	15	2	6	3	0	2	7	0	6	0	1	0-0	.400	.400	1.000	1.400	1	.933
2001— Orlando (South.)	3B-1B	8	28	4	8	2	0	1	4	6	10	0	1	0-0	.286	.412	.464	.876	0	1.000
— Durham (Int'l)	3B	93	322	39	77	16	0	16	50	38	81	6	13	0-1	.239	.331	.438	.768	13	.944
— Tampa Bay (A.L.)	3B-1B	39	136	13	28	7	0	1	15	10	45	1	2	1-0	.206	.265	.279	.545	4	.933
2002— Tampa Bay (A.L.)	3B	30	114	20	32	9	0	4	21	14	42	2	2	1-0	.281	.369	.465	.834	5	.933
— Tampa Bay (A.L.)	3B-1B-DH	102	358	55	82	21	1	18	54	39	139	1	7	3-2	.229	.305	.444	.749	15	.949
2003— Durham (Int'l)	3-1-2-D-O	74	272	40	63	17	1	12	37	30	95	2	4	1-0	.232	.313	.434	.746	8	.971
— Tampa Bay (A.L.)	3B-SS-1B	55	136	15	29	10	1	6	23	16	52	2	3	0-0	.213	.305	.434	.739	5	.959
Major League totals (3 years)		196	630	83	139	38	2	25	92	65	236	4	12	4-2	.221	.297	.406	.703	26	.950

SANDERS, DAVID — P

PERSONAL: Born August 29, 1979, in Oklahoma City, Okla. ... 6-0/200. ... Throws left, bats left. ... Full name: David Andrew Sanders. ... High school: Derby (Kan.). ... Junior college: Barton County Community College.

TRANSACTIONS/CAREER NOTES: Selected by Chicago White Sox organization in sixth round of free-agent draft (June 2, 1999).

CAREER HITTING: 0-for-0 (.000), 0 R, 0 2B, 0 3B, 0 HR, 0 RBI.

Year League	W	L	Pct.	ERA	WHIP	G	GS	CG	ShO	Hld.	Sv.-Opp.	IP	H	R	ER	HR	BB-IBB	SO	Avg.
1999— Ariz. White Sox (Ariz.)	1	0	1.000	1.10	1.10	7	1	0	0	...	1-...	16.1	12	3	2	0	6-3	26	.207
2000— Winston-Salem (Caro.)	3	2	.600	5.21	1.61	51	0	0	0	...	6-...	48.1	39	35	28	4	39-1	50	.215
2001— Birmingham (Sou.)	3	0	1.000	2.65	1.53	36	0	0	0	...	0-...	34.0	27	12	10	1	25-1	25	.227
2002— Birmingham (Sou.)	3	1	.750	1.84	1.32	47	0	0	0	...	0-...	63.2	56	17	13	3	28-7	61	.234
2003— Chicago (A.L.)	0	0	...	6.14	1.64	20	0	0	0	0	0-0	22.0	25	16	15	5	11-0	14	.281
— Charlotte (Int'l)	1	1	.500	3.68	1.32	19	0	0	0	0	4-...	22.0	23	9	9	3	6-0	25	.264
Major League totals (1 year)	0	0	...	6.14	1.64	20	0	0	0	0	0-0	22.0	25	16	15	5	11-0	14	.281

SANDERS, REGGIE — OF

PERSONAL: Born December 1, 1967, in Florence, S.C. ... 6-1/205. ... Bats right, throws right. ... Full name: Reginald Laverne Sanders. ... High school: Wilson (Florence, S.C.). ... College: Spartanburg Methodist (S.C.).

TRANSACTIONS/CAREER NOTES: Selected by Cincinnati Reds organization in seventh round of free-agent draft (June 2, 1987). ... On disabled list (July 11-September 15, 1988; and July 15-September 5, 1989). ... On Chattanooga disabled list (June 30-July 26, 1991). ... On Cincinnati disabled list (August 24-September 20, 1991; and May 13-29 and July 17-August 2, 1992). ... On suspended list (June 3-9, 1994). ... On Cincinnati disabled list (April 20-May 22, May 31-June 15 and September 17, 1996-remainder of season); included rehabilitation assignment to Indianapolis (May 17-22). ... On Cincinnati disabled list (April 19-May 6 and May 24-July 23, 1997); included rehabilitation assignments to Chattanooga (May 3-5) and Indianapolis (July 15-22). ... Traded by Reds with SS Damian Jackson and P Josh Harris to San Diego Padres for OF Greg Vaughn and OF/1B Mark Sweeney (February 2, 1999). ... On disabled list (June 3-18, 1999). ... Traded by Padres with 2B Quilvio Veras and 1B Wally Joyner to Atlanta Braves for OF/1B Ryan Klesko, 2B Bret Boone and P Jason Shiell (December 22, 1999). ... On disabled list (April 30-May 23 and July 28-August 15, 2000). ... Granted free agency (October 31, 2000). ... Signed by Arizona Diamondbacks (January 5, 2001). ... On Arizona disabled list (March 23-April 8, 2001); included rehabilitation assignment to Tucson (April 5-8). ... Granted free agency (November 6, 2001). ... Signed by San Francisco Giants (January 8, 2002). ... Granted free agency (October 31, 2002). ... Signed by Pittsburgh Pirates (February 25, 2003).

2003 GAMES PLAYED BY POSITION (MLB): OF—120, DH—2.

												BATTING									FIELDING	
Year Team (League)	Pos.	G	AB	R	H	2B	3B	HR	RBI	BB	SO	HBP	GDP	SB-CS	Avg.	OBP	SLG	OPS			E	Pct.
1988— Billings (Pio.)	SS	17	64	11	15	1	1	0	3	6	4	0	1	10-2	.234	.296	.281	.577			3	.944
1989— Greensboro (S. Atl.)	SS	81	315	53	91	18	5	9	53	29	63	3	3	21-7	.289	.353	.463	.817			42	.875
1990— Cedar Rap. (Midw.)	OF	127	466	89	133	21	4	17	63	59	97	4	8	40-15	.285	.370	.457	.827			10	.962
1991— Chattanooga (Sou.)	OF	86	302	50	95	15	•8	8	49	41	67	1	5	15-2	.315	.394	.497	.890			3	.982
— Cincinnati (N.L.)	OF	9	40	6	8	0	0	1	3	0	9	0	1	1-1	.200	.200	.275	.475			0	1.000
1992— Cincinnati (N.L.)	OF	116	385	62	104	26	6	12	36	48	98	4	6	16-7	.270	.356	.462	.819			6	.978
1993— Cincinnati (N.L.)	OF	138	496	90	136	16	4	20	83	51	118	5	10	27-10	.274	.343	.444	.786			8	.975
1994— Cincinnati (N.L.)	OF	107	400	66	105	20	8	17	62	41	*114	2	2	21-9	.263	.332	.480	.812			6	.975
1995— Cincinnati (N.L.)	OF	133	484	91	148	36	6	28	99	69	122	8	9	36-12	.306	.397	.579	.975			5	.982
1996— Cincinnati (N.L.)	OF	81	287	49	72	17	1	14	33	44	86	2	8	24-8	.251	.353	.463	.817			2	.988
— Indianapolis (A.A.)	OF-DH	4	12	3	5	2	0	0	1	1	4	1	0	0-1	.417	.500	.583	1.083			0	1.000
1997— Cincinnati (N.L.)	OF	86	312	52	79	19	2	19	56	42	93	3	9	13-7	.253	.347	.510	.857			5	.974
— Chattanooga (Sou.)	OF	3	11	3	6	1	1	1	3	1	2	1	0	0-0	.545	.615	1.091	1.706			0	1.000
— Indianapolis (A.A.)	OF	5	19	1	4	0	0	0	1	1	6	0	0	0-0	.211	.250	.211	.461			2	.750
1998— Cincinnati (N.L.)	OF	135	481	83	129	18	6	14	59	51	137	7	10	20-9	.268	.346	.418	.764			6	.978
1999— San Diego (N.L.)	OF-DH	133	478	92	136	24	7	26	72	65	108	6	10	36-13	.285	.376	.527	.904			6	.975
2000— Atlanta (N.L.)	OF	103	340	43	79	23	1	11	37	32	78	2	9	21-4	.232	.302	.403	.705			6	.964
2001— Tucson (PCL)	OF	2	6	0	2	1	0	0	1	2	0	0	2	1-0	.333	.500	.500	1.000			0	1.000
— Arizona (N.L.)	OF	126	441	84	116	21	3	33	90	46	126	5	2	14-10	.263	.337	.549	.886			1	.996
2002— San Francisco (N.L.)	OF	140	505	75	126	23	6	23	85	47	121	12	10	18-6	.250	.324	.455	.779			5	.984
2003— Pittsburgh (N.L.)	OF-DH	130	453	74	129	27	4	31	87	38	110	5	10	15-5	.285	.345	.567	.913			4	.983
Major League totals (13 years)		1437	5102	867	1367	270	54	249	802	574	1320	61	96	262-101	.268	.347	.488	.835			60	.980

SANTANA, JOHAN — P

PERSONAL: Born March 13, 1979, in Tovar Merida, Venezuela. ... 6-0/195. ... Throws left, bats left. ... Full name: Johan Alexander Santana. ... High school: Liceo Nucete Sardi (Venezuela).

TRANSACTIONS/CAREER NOTES: Signed as non-drafted free agent by Houston Astros organization (July 2, 1995). ... Selected by Florida Marlins from Astros organization in Rule 5 major league draft (December 13, 1999). ... Traded by Marlins with cash to Minnesota Twins for P Jared Camp (December 13, 1999). ... On disabled list (July 7-September 21, 2001).

CAREER HITTING: 2-for-8 (.250), 0 R, 0 2B, 0 3B, 0 HR, 0 RBI.

Year League	W	L	Pct.	ERA	WHIP	G	GS	CG	ShO	Hld.	Sv.-Opp.	IP	H	R	ER	HR	BB-IBB	SO	Avg.
1996— Dom. Astros (DSL)	4	3	.571	2.70	1.20	23	1	0	0	...	3-...	40.0	26	16	12	0	22-...	51	...
1997— GC Astros (GCL)	0	4	.000	7.93	1.84	9	5	1	0	...	0-...	36.1	49	36	32	2	18-0	25	.322
— Auburn (N.Y.-Penn)	0	0	...	2.25	1.75	1	1	0	0	...	0-...	4.0	1	1	1	0	6-0	5	.083
1998— Quad City (Midw.)	0	1	.000	9.45	2.55	2	1	0	0	...	0-...	6.2	14	7	7	1	3-0	6	.452
— Auburn (N.Y.-Penn)	7	5	.583	4.36	1.18	15	15	1	•1	...	0-...	86.2	81	52	42	9	21-0	88	.243
1999— Michigan (Midw.)	8	8	.500	4.66	1.35	27	26	1	0	...	0-...	160.1	162	94	83	14	55-0	150	.263
2000— Minnesota (A.L.)	2	3	.400	6.49	1.81	30	5	0	0	0	0-0	86.0	102	64	62	11	54-0	64	.302
2001— Minnesota (A.L.)	1	0	1.000	4.74	1.51	15	4	0	0	0	0-0	43.2	50	25	23	6	16-0	28	.292
2002— Edmonton (PCL)	5	2	.714	3.14	1.32	11	9	0	0	...	0-...	48.2	37	24	17	7	27-0	75	.202
— Minnesota (A.L.)	8	6	.571	2.99	1.23	27	14	0	0	3	1-1	108.1	84	41	36	7	49-0	137	.212
2003— Minnesota (A.L.)	12	3	*.800	3.07	1.10	45	18	0	0	5	0-0	158.1	127	56	54	17	47-1	169	.216
Major League totals (4 years)	23	12	.657	3.97	1.33	117	41	0	0	8	1-1	396.1	363	186	175	41	166-1	398	.243

SANTIAGO, BENITO — C

PERSONAL: Born March 9, 1965, in Ponce, Puerto Rico. ... 6-1/200. ... Bats right, throws right. ... Full name: Benito Rivera Santiago. ... Name pronounced: sahn-tee-AH-go. ... High school: John F. Kennedy (Ponce, Puerto Rico).

TRANSACTIONS/CAREER NOTES: Signed as non-drafted free agent by San Diego Padres organization (September 1, 1982). ... On disabled list (June 21-July 2, 1985). ... On San Diego disabled list (June 15-August 10, 1990); included rehabilitation assignment to Las Vegas (August 2-9). ... On San Diego disabled list (May 31-July 11, 1992); included rehabilitation assignment to Las Vegas (July 7-11). ... Granted free agency (October 26, 1992). ... Signed by Florida Marlins (December 16, 1992). ... On suspended list (May 5-9, 1994). ... Granted free agency (October 20, 1994). ... Signed by Cincinnati Reds (April 17, 1995). ... On disabled list (May 8-July 4, 1995). ... Granted free agency (October 31, 1995). ... Signed by Philadelphia Phillies (January 30, 1996). ... Granted free agency (November 18, 1996). ... Signed by Toronto Blue Jays (December 9, 1996). ... On disabled list (April 14-29, 1997). ... On Toronto disabled list (March 18-September 3, 1998); included rehabilitation assignments to Dunedin (August 15-26) and Syracuse (August 28-September 3). ... Granted free agency (October 23, 1998). ... Signed by Chicago Cubs (December 10, 1998). ... Granted free agency (October 29, 1999). ... Signed by Reds organization (February 24, 2000). ... Granted free agency (November 3, 2000). ... Signed by San Francisco Giants organization (March 17, 2001). ... Granted free agency (November 7, 2001). ... Re-signed by Giants (December 7, 2001). ... On suspended list (September 20-22, 2002). ... Placed on 15-day disabled list (July 14, 2003). ... Reinstated from 15-day disabled list (July 29, 2003).

2003 GAMES PLAYED BY POSITION (MLB): C—106.

Year Team (League)	Pos.	G	AB	R	H	2B	3B	HR	RBI	BB	SO	HBP	GDP	SB-CS	Avg.	OBP	SLG	OPS	E	Pct.
1983— Miami (Fla. St.)	C	122	429	34	106	25	3	5	56	11	79	7	...	3-7	.247	.276	.354	.630	* 21	.963
1984— Reno (Calif.)	C	114	416	64	116	20	6	16	83	36	75	4	11	5-2	.279	.338	.471	.809	25	.969
1985— Beaumont (Texas)	3B-C-1B	101	372	55	111	16	6	5	52	16	59	2	6	12-2	.298	.328	.414	.742	15	.976
1986— Las Vegas (PCL)	C	117	437	55	125	26	3	17	71	17	81	1	12	19-7	.286	.312	.476	.788	* 21	.968
— San Diego (N.L.)	C	17	62	10	18	2	0	3	6	2	12	0	0	0-1	.290	.308	.468	.775	5	.946
1987— San Diego (N.L.)	C	146	546	64	164	33	2	18	79	16	112	5	12	21-12	.300	.324	.467	.791	* 22	.976
1988— San Diego (N.L.)	C	139	492	49	122	22	2	10	46	24	82	1	18	15-7	.248	.282	.362	.643	* 12	.985
1989— San Diego (N.L.)	C	129	462	50	109	16	3	16	62	26	89	1	9	11-6	.236	.277	.387	.664	* 20	.975
1990— San Diego (N.L.)	C	100	344	42	93	8	5	11	53	27	55	3	4	5-5	.270	.323	.419	.741	12	.980
— Las Vegas (PCL)	C	6	20	5	6	2	0	1	8	3	1	0	1	0-0	.300	.375	.550	.925	0	1.000
1991— San Diego (N.L.)	C-OF	152	580	60	155	22	3	17	87	23	114	4	*21	8-10	.267	.296	.403	.700	‡ 14	.985
1992— San Diego (N.L.)	C	106	386	37	97	21	0	10	42	21	52	0	14	2-5	.251	.287	.383	.671	* 12	.982
— Las Vegas (PCL)	C	4	13	3	4	0	0	1	2	1	1	0	0	0-0	.308	.357	.538	.896	0	1.000
1993— Florida (N.L.)	C-OF	139	469	49	108	19	6	13	50	37	88	5	9	10-7	.230	.291	.380	.671	• 11	.987
1994— Florida (N.L.)	C	101	337	35	92	14	2	11	41	25	57	1	11	1-2	.273	.322	.424	.746	5	.991
1995— Cincinnati (N.L.)	C-1B	81	266	40	76	20	0	11	44	24	48	4	7	2-2	.286	.351	.485	.836	2	.996
1996— Philadelphia (N.L.)	C-1B	136	481	71	127	21	2	30	85	49	104	1	8	2-0	.264	.332	.503	.835	11	.988
1997— Toronto (A.L.)	C-DH	97	341	31	83	10	0	13	42	17	80	2	10	1-0	.243	.279	.387	.667	2	.997
1998— Dunedin (Fla. St.)	DH-C	11	37	4	6	1	0	1	5	3	9	0	1	3-0	.162	.225	.270	.495	0	1.000
— Syracuse (Int'l)	C-DH	5	22	0	5	2	0	0	2	1	3	0	1	0-0	.227	.261	.318	.579	0	1.000
— Toronto (A.L.)	C	15	29	3	9	5	0	0	4	1	6	0	1	0-0	.310	.333	.483	.816	0	1.000
1999— Chicago (N.L.)	C-1B	109	350	28	87	18	3	7	36	32	71	2	12	1-1	.249	.313	.377	.691	6	.990
2000— Cincinnati (N.L.)	C	89	252	22	66	11	1	8	45	19	45	1	7	2-2	.262	.310	.409	.719	3	.994
2001— San Francisco (N.L.)	C-1B	133	477	39	125	25	4	6	45	23	78	2	19	5-4	.262	.295	.369	.664	5	.994
2002— San Francisco (N.L.)	C	126	478	56	133	24	5	16	74	27	73	2	19	4-2	.278	.315	.450	.765	4	.995
2003— San Francisco (N.L.)	C	108	401	33	112	21	2	11	56	29	69	2	13	0-1	.279	.329	.424	.753	5	.993
American League totals (2 years)		112	370	34	92	15	0	13	46	18	86	2	11	1-0	.249	.284	.395	.678	2	.997
National League totals (16 years)		1811	6383	705	1684	297	40	198	851	404	1149	34	183	89-67	.264	.308	.416	.724	149	.987
Major League totals (18 years)		1923	6753	739	1776	312	40	211	897	422	1235	36	194	90-67	.263	.307	.415	.722	151	.987

SANTIAGO, JOSE   P

PERSONAL: Born November 5, 1974, in Fajardo, Puerto Rico. ... 6-3/225. ... Throws right, bats right. ... Full name: Jose Rafael Santiago. ... Name pronounced: SAWN-tea-ah-go. ... High school: Carlos Escobar Lopez (Loiza, Puerto Rico).

TRANSACTIONS/CAREER NOTES: Selected by Kansas City Royals organization in 70th round of free agent draft (June 3, 1994). ... On Kansas City disabled list (June 26-July 9, 1997). ... On Kansas City disabled list (June 20-September 13, 1999); included rehabilitation assignments to Gulf Coast Royals (July 3-9), Wichita (July 10-11 and August 30-September 5) and Omaha (July 18-19 and September 6-12). ... Traded by Royals to Philadelphia Phillies for P Paul Byrd (June 5, 2001). ... Released by Phillies (October 11, 2002). ... Signed by Cleveland Indians organization (November 2, 2002).

CAREER HITTING: 0-for-5 (.000), 0 R, 0 2B, 0 3B, 0 HR, 0 RBI.

Year League	W	L	Pct.	ERA	WHIP	G	GS	CG	ShO	Hld.	Sv.-Opp.	IP	H	R	ER	HR	BB-IBB	SO	Avg.
1994— GC Royals (GCL)	1	0	1.000	2.37	1.26	10	1	0	0	...	2-...	19.0	17	7	5	1	7-0	10	.224
1995— Spokane (N'west)	2	4	.333	3.14	1.64	22	0	0	0	...	1-...	48.2	60	26	17	1	20-4	32	.302
1996— Lansing (Midw.)	7	6	.538	3.74	1.29	54	0	0	0	...	19-...	77.0	78	34	32	4	21-3	55	.263
1997— Wilmington (Caro.)	1	1	.500	4.91	1.09	4	0	0	0	...	2-...	3.2	3	3	2	0	1-0	1	.200
— Lansing (Midw.)	1	0	1.000	2.08	1.23	9	0	0	0	...	1-...	13.0	10	6	3	0	6-1	8	.200
— Kansas City (A.L.)	0	0	...	1.93	1.93	4	0	0	0	0	0-0	4.2	7	2	1	0	2-1	1	.333
— Wichita (Texas)	2	1	.667	4.00	1.48	22	0	0	0	...	3-...	27.0	32	13	12	1	8-1	12	.299
1998— Wichita (Texas)	3	4	.429	3.61	1.47	52	0	0	0	...	22-...	72.1	79	36	29	9	27-7	31	.281
— Kansas City (A.L.)	0	0	...	9.00	2.00	2	0	0	0	0	0-0	2.0	4	2	2	0	0-0	2	.444
— Omaha (PCL)	0	0	...	7.04	1.96	4	0	0	0	...	1-...	7.2	10	9	6	0	5-2	4	.303
1999— Kansas City (A.L.)	3	4	.429	3.42	1.27	34	0	0	0	4	2-3	47.1	46	23	18	7	14-2	15	.251
— GC Royals (GCL)	0	0	...	1.80	0.20	3	3	0	0	...	0-...	5.0	1	1	1	0	0-0	4	.063
— Wichita (Texas)	0	1	.000	2.00	0.89	4	2	0	0	...	0-...	9.0	8	2	2	0	0-0	6	.258
— Omaha (PCL)	0	0	...	0.00	1.80	1	0	0	0	...	0-...	1.2	3	0	0	0	0-0	0	.429
2000— Kansas City (A.L.)	8	6	.571	3.91	1.39	45	0	0	0	5	2-8	69.0	70	33	30	7	26-3	44	.260
— Omaha (PCL)	0	1	.000	3.18	1.29	11	0	0	0	...	4-...	17.0	19	7	6	2	3-1	14	.279
2001— Kansas City (A.L.)	2	2	.500	6.75	1.67	20	0	0	0	0	0-1	29.1	40	22	22	2	9-1	15	.333
— Philadelphia (N.L.)	2	4	.333	3.61	1.27	53	0	0	0	9	0-1	62.1	66	25	25	3	13-1	28	.272
2002— Philadelphia (N.L.)	1	3	.250	6.70	1.51	42	0	0	0	9	0-1	47.0	56	35	35	7	15-1	30	.290
— Scran./W.B. (I.L.)	3	2	.600	1.29	1.25	22	0	0	0	...	7-...	28.0	28	6	4	0	7-1	21	.264
2003— Buffalo (Int'l)	3	3	.500	2.43	1.52	25	4	0	0	...	2-...	66.2	79	25	18	1	22-1	33	.298
— Cleveland (A.L.)	1	3	.250	2.84	1.61	25	0	0	0	4	0-2	31.2	37	11	10	2	14-3	15	.298
American League totals (6 years)	14	15	.483	4.06	1.46	130	0	0	0	13	4-14	184.0	204	93	83	18	65-10	92	.281
National League totals (2 years)	3	7	.300	4.94	1.37	95	0	0	0	18	0-2	109.1	122	60	60	10	28-2	58	.281
Major League totals (7 years)	17	22	.436	4.39	1.43	225	0	0	0	31	4-16	293.1	326	153	143	28	93-12	150	.281

SANTIAGO, RAMON   SS

PERSONAL: Born August 31, 1979, in Las Matas de Farfan, Dominican Republic. ... 5-11/167. ... Bats both, throws right. ... Full name: Ramon D. Santiago.

TRANSACTIONS/CAREER NOTES: Signed as non-drafted free agent by Detroit Tigers organization (July 29, 1998). ... On Detroit disabled list (July 24-September 1, 2002).

2003 GAMES PLAYED BY POSITION (MLB): SS—85, 2B—53.

Year Team (League)	Pos.	G	AB	R	H	2B	3B	HR	RBI	BB	SO	HBP	GDP	SB-CS	Avg.	OBP	SLG	OPS	E	Pct.
1999— GC Tigers (GCL)	SS	35	134	25	43	9	2	0	11	9	17	1	3	20-7	.321	.361	.418	.778	4	.974
— Oneonta (NYP)	SS	12	50	9	17	1	2	1	8	2	12	1	0	5-0	.340	.377	.500	.877	1	.979
2000— W. Mich. (Mid.)	SS	98	379	69	103	15	1	1	42	34	60	12	10	39-12	.272	.346	.325	.670	8	.976
2001— Lakeland (Fla. St.)	DH	120	429	64	115	15	3	2	46	54	60	11	7	34-8	.268	.361	.331	.692	...	...
2002— Erie (East.)	SS	22	75	9	21	0	2	1	7	3	12	3	2	6-0	.280	.329	.373	.703	3	.966
— Toledo (Int'l)	SS	9	28	8	12	1	0	2	6	3	4	2	0	0-2	.429	.515	.679	1.194	2	.957
— Detroit (A.L.)	SS-DH	65	222	33	54	5	5	4	20	13	48	8	2	8-5	.243	.306	.365	.671	7	.955
2003— Detroit (A.L.)	SS-2B	141	444	41	100	18	1	2	29	33	66	10	9	10-4	.225	.292	.284	.576	20	.970
Major League totals (2 years)		206	666	74	154	23	6	6	49	46	114	18	11	18-9	.231	.297	.311	.608	27	.972

SANTOS, ANGEL — 2B

PERSONAL: Born August 14, 1979, in Rio Piedras, Puerto Rico. ... 5-11/178. ... Bats both, throws right. ... Full name: Angel Ramon Santos. ... High school: Miguel Melendez Munoz (Cayey, Puerto Rico).
TRANSACTIONS/CAREER NOTES: Selected by Boston Red Sox organization in fourth round of free-agent draft (June 3, 1997). ... On disabled list (July 19, 2000-remainder of season). ... On Pawtucket disabled list (August 14-September 5, 2002). ... Released by Boston (2003). ... Signed by Cleveland Indians (July 2, 2003).
2003 GAMES PLAYED BY POSITION (MLB): 2B—28, 3B—4.

Year Team (League)	Pos.	G	AB	R	H	2B	3B	HR	RBI	BB	SO	HBP	GDP	SB-CS	Avg.	OBP	SLG	OPS	E	Pct.
1997— GC Red Sox (GCL)	SS	17	60	8	11	1	0	0	7	7	11	0	0	8-3	.183	.261	.200	.461	1	.964
1998— GC Red Sox (GCL)	2B-3B-SS	23	77	14	27	5	1	0	13	13	10	0	1	7-3	.351	.435	.442	.876	9	.900
— Lowell (NY-Penn)	2B-3B-SS	28	102	19	25	4	1	1	12	9	12	0	4	2-1	.245	.306	.333	.640	12	.903
1999— Augusta (S. Atl.)	2B-3B-SS	130	466	83	126	30	2	15	55	62	88	5	12	25-10	.270	.360	.440	.800	34	.933
2000— Trenton (East.)	2B	80	275	32	71	17	2	3	32	32	60	2	7	18-8	.258	.335	.367	.703	12	.968
2001— Trenton (East.)	2B	129	510	75	138	32	0	14	52	54	106	5	4	26-9	.271	.343	.416	.759	•19	.966
— Pawtucket (Int'l)	2B	4	15	1	3	1	0	0	2	1	4	0	0	1-0	.200	.235	.267	.502	0	1.000
— Boston (A.L.)	2B	9	16	2	2	1	0	0	1	2	7	0	2	0-0	.125	.211	.188	.398	2	.905
2002— Pawtucket (Int'l)	2B-SS-3B	102	350	40	91	15	2	10	50	38	70	2	8	12-8	.260	.332	.400	.732	18	.964
2003— Pawtucket (Int'l)	2-S-3-D	70	214	25	51	8	0	5	20	32	50	1	6	9-4	.238	.339	.346	.685	11	.962
— Buffalo (Int'l)	2B-SS-3B	13	46	10	11	2	0	2	8	5	8	0	0	5-0	.239	.314	.413	.727	2	.961
— Cleveland (A.L.)	2B-3B	32	76	9	17	3	1	3	6	3	18	0	0	1-1	.224	.253	.408	.661	2	.981
Major League totals (2 years)		41	92	11	19	4	1	3	7	5	25	0	2	1-1	.207	.245	.370	.614	4	.969

SANTOS, FRANCISCO — 1B

PERSONAL: Born March 9, 1974, in Santo Domingo, Dominican Republic. ... 6-1/175. ... Bats left, throws left. ... Full name: Francisco Alejandro Santos.
TRANSACTIONS/CAREER NOTES: Signed as non-drafted free agent by San Francisco Giants organization (May 30, 1997). ... On Arizona Giants disabled list (July 10-August 27, 2000).
2003 GAMES PLAYED BY POSITION (MLB): OF—3, 1B—1.

Year Team (League)	Pos.	G	AB	R	H	2B	3B	HR	RBI	BB	SO	HBP	GDP	SB-CS	Avg.	OBP	SLG	OPS	E	Pct.
2000— Ariz. Giants (Ariz.)	1B	12	43	13	16	2	1	2	10	7	6	0	0	4-1	.372	.460	.605	1.065	0	1.000
— Salem-Keizer (NW)	1B	2	7	0	0	0	0	0	0	0	0	0	0	0-0	.000	.000	.000	.000	0	1.000
2001— Hagerstown (SAL)	1B-OF	131	520	64	151	27	3	12	80	25	91	4	15	16-10	.290	.325	.423	.748	14	.988
2002— Shreveport (Texas)	OF-1B	109	407	54	127	33	5	3	56	18	42	5	9	4-4	.312	.349	.440	.789	6	.988
— Fresno (PCL)	1B	23	88	8	25	3	1	3	14	2	14	0	2	4-0	.284	.297	.443	.740	3	.985
2003— San Francisco (N.L.)	OF-1B	8	15	2	3	2	0	1	1	0	3	0	0	0-0	.200	.200	.533	.733	0	1.000
— Fresno (PCL)	OF-1B-DH	87	301	23	72	15	5	6	42	10	38	0	3	1-0	.239	.261	.382	.643	4	.986
Major League totals (1 year)		8	15	2	3	2	0	1	1	0	3	0	0	0-0	.200	.200	.533	.733	0	1.000

SANTOS, VICTOR — P

PERSONAL: Born October 2, 1976, in San Pedro de Macoris, Dominican Republic. ... 6-3/190. ... Throws right, bats right. ... Full name: Victor Irving Santos. ... High school: Passaic (N.J.).
TRANSACTIONS/CAREER NOTES: Signed as non-drafted free agent by Detroit Tigers organization (June 11, 1995). ... On Toledo disabled list (April 6-July 1, July 7-14 and July 19-September 18, 2000). ... Traded by Tigers with IF Ronnie Merrill to Colorado Rockies for P Jose Paniagua (March 25, 2002). ... On Colorado Springs disabled list (April 14-24, 2002). ... Released by Rockies (October 9, 2002). ... Signed by Texas Rangers organization (November 13, 2002). ... Contract purchased from Oklahoma (June 5, 2003). ... Sent outright to Oklahoma (July 16, 2003).
CAREER HITTING: 1-for-4 (.250), 0 R, 0 2B, 0 3B, 0 HR, 0 RBI.

Year League	W	L	Pct.	ERA	WHIP	G	GS	CG	ShO	Hld.	Sv.-Opp.	IP	H	R	ER	HR	BB-IBB	SO	Avg.
1995— Dominican Tigers (DSL)	7	5	.583	3.72	1.37	15	12	3		...	0-...	77.1	88	46	32	...	18-...	75	...
1996— Lakeland (Fla. St.)	2	2	.500	2.22	0.99	5	4	0	0	...	0-...	28.1	19	11	7	2	9-0	25	.194
— GC Tigers (GCL)	3	2	.600	1.98	1.14	9	9	0	0	...	0-...	50.0	44	12	11	1	13-0	39	.251
1997— Lakeland (Fla. St.)	10	5	.667	3.23	1.34	26	26	4	•2	...	0-...	145.0	136	74	52	10	59-1	108	.248
1998— Lakeland (Fla. St.)	5	2	.714	2.51	1.12	16	15	0	0	...	1-...	100.1	88	38	28	9	24-1	74	.235
— Toledo (Int'l)	1	2	.333	11.05	2.32	5	3	0	0	...	0-...	14.2	24	22	18	5	10-0	12	.353
— Jacksonville (Sou.)	4	2	.667	4.17	1.50	6	6	0	0	...	0-...	36.2	40	20	17	2	15-1	37	.288
1999— Jacksonville (Sou.)	12	6	.667	3.49	1.20	28	•28	2	1	...	0-...	173.0	150	86	67	16	58-2	*146	.230
2000— GC Tigers (GCL)	0	0	...	0.00	1.33	1	1	0	0	...	0-...	3.0	2	1	0	0	2-0	5	.182
— Lakeland (Fla. St.)	1	0	1.000	0.00	1.20	1	1	0	0	...	0-...	5.0	5	0	0	0	1-0	4	.263
— Toledo (Int'l)	0	1	.000	11.37	2.05	2	2	0	0	...	0-...	6.1	7	8	8	4	6-0	2	.280
2001— Detroit (A.L.)	2	2	.500	3.30	1.45	33	7	0	0	2	0-0	76.1	62	33	28	9	49-4	52	.222
— Toledo (Int'l)	2	1	.667	6.37	1.75	6	6	0	0	...	0-...	35.1	50	27	25	6	12-0	22	.340
2002— Colo. Springs (PCL)	4	9	.308	5.72	1.61	21	21	1	1	...	0-...	118.0	147	81	75	17	43-0	134	.307
— Colorado (N.L.)	0	4	.000	10.38	2.42	24	2	0	0	1	0-0	26.0	41	30	30	3	22-3	25	.360
2003— Texas (A.L.)	0	2	.000	7.01	1.75	8	4	0	0	0	0-0	25.2	29	21	20	5	16-1	15	.299
— Oklahoma (PCL)	5	4	.556	3.41	1.36	20	16	1	1	...	1-...	108.1	112	54	41	6	35-0	65	.264
American League totals (2 years)	2	4	.333	4.24	1.53	41	11	0	0	2	0-0	102.0	91	54	48	14	65-5	67	.242
National League totals (1 year)	0	4	.000	10.38	2.42	24	2	0	0	1	0-0	26.0	41	30	30	3	22-3	25	.360
Major League totals (3 years)	2	8	.200	5.48	1.71	65	13	0	0	3	0-0	128.0	132	84	78	17	87-8	92	.269

SARDINHA, DANE — C

PERSONAL: Born April 8, 1979, in Honolulu, Hawaii. ... 6-0/215. ... Bats right, throws right. ... Full name: Dane K.A.A. Sardinha. ... Name pronounced: sar-DEEN-uh. ... High school: Kamehameha High (Honolulu). ... College: Pepperdine.
TRANSACTIONS/CAREER NOTES: Selected by Cincinnati Reds organization in second round of free-agent draft (June 5, 2000).
2003 GAMES PLAYED BY POSITION (MLB): C—1.

Year Team (League)	Pos.	G	AB	R	H	2B	3B	HR	RBI	BB	SO	HBP	GDP	SB-CS	Avg.	OBP	SLG	OPS	E	Pct.
2001— Mudville California (Calif.)	C	109	422	45	99	24	2	9	55	12	97	3	12	0-1	.235	.259	.365	.623	10	.991
2002— Chattanooga (Sou.)	C	106	394	34	81	20	0	4	40	14	114	2	6	0-2	.206	.234	.287	.521	9	.990
2003— Chattanooga (Sou.)	C	72	246	21	63	15	0	3	32	22	61	1	1	5-3	.256	.313	.354	.666	8	.985
— Cincinnati (N.L.)	C	1	2	0	0	0	0	0	0	0	1	0	0	0-0	.000	.000	.000	.000	0	1.000
Major League totals (1 year)		1	2	0	0	0	0	0	0	0	1	0	0	0-0	.000	.000	.000	.000	0	1.000

S

SASAKI, KAZUHIRO   P

PERSONAL: Born February 22, 1968, in Sendai, Japan. ... 6-4/220. ... Throws right, bats right. ... Name pronounced: kaz-oo-hero sa-sa-key. ... College: Tohoku Fukushi Univ. (Japan).

TRANSACTIONS/CAREER NOTES: Signed as non-drafted free agent by Seattle Mariners (December 18, 1999). ... Placed on the 15-day disabled list (April 23, 2003). ... Sent to Inland Empire on rehab assignment by Seattle (May 6, 2003). ... Reinstated from 15-day disabled list (May 8, 2003). ... Placed on the 15-day disabled list, retroactive to June 6 (June 11, 2003). ... Sent on rehab assignment to Tacoma by Seattle (July 26, 2003). ... Recalled from Tacoma rehab assignment; reinstated from 15-day disabled list (August 12, 2003).

CAREER HITTING: 0-for-0 (.000), 0 R, 0 2B, 0 3B, 0 HR, 0 RBI.

Year League	W	L	Pct.	ERA	WHIP	G	GS	CG	ShO	Hld.	Sv.-Opp.	IP	H	R	ER	HR	BB-IBB	SO	Avg.
1990— Yoko. Tai. (Jp. Cn.)	2	4	.333	5.85	1.66	16	...	...	...	...	2-...	47.2	49	31	31	10	30-...	44	...
1991— Yoko. Tai. (Jp. Cn.)	6	9	.400	2.00	1.09	58	...	...	...	...	17-...	117.0	72	33	26	7	55-...	137	...
1992— Yoko. Tai. (Jp. Cn.)	12	6	.667	2.46	0.99	53	...	...	...	...	21-...	87.2	47	32	24	6	40-...	135	...
1993— Yoko. Bay. (Jp. Cn.)	3	6	.333	3.27	1.05	38	...	...	...	...	20-...	55.0	35	24	20	6	23-...	84	...
1994— Yoko. Bay. (Jp. Cn.)	3	1	.750	2.15	0.91	31	...	...	...	...	10-...	46.0	27	11	11	5	15-...	59	...
1995— Yoko. Bay. (Jp. Cn.)	7	2	.778	1.75	0.83	47	...	...	...	...	32-...	56.2	30	12	11	5	17-...	78	...
1996— Yoko. Bay. (Jp. Cn.)	4	3	.571	2.90	1.09	39	...	...	...	...	25-...	49.2	37	17	16	6	17-...	80	...
1997— Yoko. Bay. (Jp. Cn.)	3	0	1.000	0.90	0.72	49	...	...	...	...	38-...	60.0	25	6	6	6	18-...	99	...
1998— Yoko. Bay. (Jp. Cn.)	1	1	.500	0.64	0.82	51	...	...	...	...	45-...	56.0	32	7	4	1	14-...	78	...
1999— Yoko. Bay. (Jp. Cn.)	1	1	.500	1.93	1.50	23	...	...	...	...	19-...	23.1	19	5	5	1	16-...	34	...
2000— Seattle (A.L.)	2	5	.286	3.16	1.16	63	0	0	0	0	37-40	62.2	42	25	22	10	31-5	78	.184
2001— Seattle (A.L.)	0	4	.000	3.24	0.89	69	0	0	0	0	45-52	66.2	48	24	24	6	11-2	62	.195
2002— Seattle (A.L.)	4	5	.444	2.52	1.05	61	0	0	0	0	37-45	60.2	44	24	17	6	20-4	73	.201
2003— Inland Empire (Calif.)	0	0	...	0.00	1.00	1	1	0	0	0	0-...	1.0	0	0	0	0	0-0	2	.000
— Everett (Northwest)	0	1	.000	22.50	2.50	2	2	0	0	0	0-...	2.0	5	5	5	3	0-0	5	.455
— Tacoma (PCL)	0	1	.000	9.82	1.64	3	2	0	0	0	1-...	3.2	5	4	4	0	1-0	5	.313
— Seattle (A.L.)	1	2	.333	4.05	1.38	35	0	0	0	0	10-14	33.1	31	17	15	2	15-2	29	.238
Major League totals (4 years)	**7**	**16**	**.304**	**3.14**	**1.08**	**228**	**0**	**0**	**0**	**0**	**129-151**	**223.1**	**165**	**90**	**78**	**24**	**77-13**	**242**	**.200**

SAUERBECK, SCOTT   P

PERSONAL: Born November 9, 1971, in Cincinnati, Ohio. ... 6-3/200. ... Throws left, bats right. ... Full name: Scott William Sauerbeck. ... Name pronounced: SOW-er-beck. ... High school: Northwest (Cincinnati, Ohio). ... College: Miami (Ohio).

TRANSACTIONS/CAREER NOTES: Selected by New York Mets organization in 23rd round of free-agent draft (June 2, 1994). ... Selected by Pittsburgh Pirates from Mets organization in Rule 5 major league draft (December 14, 1998). ... On Pittsburgh disabled list (June 14-July 3, 2000); included rehabilitation assignment to Nashville (June 29-July 3). ... Traded by Pirates with P Mike Gonzalez to Boston Red Sox for P Brandon Lyon and P Anastacio Martinez (July 22, 2003).

CAREER HITTING: 0-for-7 (.000), 0 R, 0 2B, 0 3B, 0 HR, 0 RBI.

Year League	W	L	Pct.	ERA	WHIP	G	GS	CG	ShO	Hld.	Sv.-Opp.	IP	H	R	ER	HR	BB-IBB	SO	Avg.
1994— Pittsfield (NYP)	3	1	.750	2.05	1.20	21	0	0	0	...	1-...	48.1	39	16	11	0	19-2	39	.222
1995— St. Lucie (Fla. St.)	0	1	.000	2.03	1.50	20	1	0	0	...	0-...	26.2	26	10	6	0	14-1	25	.260
— Capital City (S. Atl.)	5	4	.556	3.27	1.27	19	0	0	0	...	2-...	33.0	28	14	12	2	14-1	33	.230
1996— St. Lucie (Fla. St.)	6	6	.500	2.27	1.29	17	16	2	• 2	...	0-...	99.1	101	37	25	1	27-0	62	.269
— Binghamton (Eastern)	3	3	.500	3.47	1.29	8	8	2	0	...	0-...	46.2	48	24	18	4	12-0	30	.274
1997— Binghamton (Eastern)	8	9	.471	4.93	1.48	27	20	2	0	...	0-...	131.1	144	89	72	15	50-0	88	.280
— Norfolk (Int'l)	1	0	1.000	3.60	1.40	1	1	0	0	...	0-...	5.0	3	2	2	0	4-0	4	.200
1998— Norfolk (Int'l)	7	13	.350	3.93	1.54	27	27	2	0	...	0-...	160.1	178	82	70	8	69-1	119	.287
1999— Pittsburgh (N.L.)	4	1	.800	2.00	1.34	65	0	0	0	10	2-5	67.2	53	19	15	6	38-5	55	.220
2000— Pittsburgh (N.L.)	5	4	.556	4.04	1.81	75	0	0	0	13	1-4	75.2	76	36	34	4	61-8	83	.270
— Nashville (PCL)	0	0	...	0.00	0.50	2	0	0	0	...	0-...	2.0	1	0	0	0	0-0	0	.167
2001— Pittsburgh (N.L.)	2	2	.500	5.60	1.61	70	0	0	0	19	2-4	62.2	61	41	39	4	40-6	79	.257
2002— Pittsburgh (N.L.)	5	4	.556	2.30	1.23	78	0	0	0	28	0-0	62.2	50	18	16	4	27-4	70	.220
2003— Pittsburgh (N.L.)	3	4	.429	4.05	1.38	53	0	0	0	16	0-4	40.0	30	20	18	5	25-2	32	.207
— Boston (A.L.)	0	1	.000	6.48	2.10	26	0	0	0	2	0-1	16.2	17	14	12	1	18-3	18	.266
American League totals (1 year)	**0**	**1**	**.000**	**6.48**	**2.10**	**26**	**0**	**0**	**0**	**2**	**0-1**	**16.2**	**17**	**14**	**12**	**1**	**18-3**	**18**	**.266**
National League totals (5 years)	**19**	**15**	**.559**	**3.56**	**1.49**	**341**	**0**	**0**	**0**	**86**	**5-17**	**308.2**	**270**	**134**	**122**	**23**	**191-25**	**319**	**.239**
Major League totals (5 years)	**19**	**16**	**.543**	**3.71**	**1.52**	**367**	**0**	**0**	**0**	**88**	**5-18**	**325.1**	**287**	**148**	**134**	**24**	**209-28**	**337**	**.240**

SCHILLING, CURT   P

PERSONAL: Born November 14, 1966, in Anchorage, Alaska. ... 6-5/235. ... Throws right, bats right. ... Full name: Curtis Montague Schilling. ... Name pronounced: SHILL-ing. ... High school: Shadow Mountain (Phoenix). ... Junior college: Yavapai College (Ari.).

TRANSACTIONS/CAREER NOTES: Selected by Boston Red Sox organization in second round of free-agent draft (January 14, 1986). ... Traded by Red Sox with OF Brady Anderson to Baltimore Orioles for P Mike Boddicker (July 29, 1988). ... Traded by Orioles with P Pete Harnisch and OF Steve Finley to Houston Astros for 1B Glenn Davis (January 10, 1991). ... Traded by Astros to Philadelphia Phillies for P Jason Grimsley (April 2, 1992). ... On Philadelphia disabled list (May 17-July 25, 1994); included rehabilitation assignments to Scranton/Wilkes-Barre (July 10-15) and Reading (July 15-20). ... On disabled list (July 19, 1995-remainder of season). ... On Philadelphia disabled list (March 23-May 14, 1996); included rehabilitation assignments to Clearwater (April 23-May 3) and Scranton/Wilkes-Barre (May 3-14). ... On disabled list (August 8-September 3, 1999). ... On Philadelphia disabled list (March 25-April 30, 2000); included rehabilitation assignments to Clearwater (April 6-29) and Scranton/Wilkes-Barre (April 30). ... Traded by Phillies to Arizona Diamondbacks for OF Travis Lee, P Omar Daal, P Vicente Padilla and P Nelson Figueroa (July 26, 2000). ... Placed on 15-day disabled list (April 18, 2003). ... Reinstated from 15-day disabled list (May 3, 2003). ... Fined by MLB for actions in a May 24 game against San Diego (June 1, 2003). ... Sent to Tucson on rehab assignment (July 2, 2003). ... Recalled from Tucson rehab assignment; reinstated from 15-day disabled list (July 12, 2003). ... Activated from bereavement list (July 13, 2003).

CAREER HITTING: 114-for-762 (.150), 39 R, 13 2B, 1 3B, 0 HR, 29 RBI.

Year League	W	L	Pct.	ERA	WHIP	G	GS	CG	ShO	Hld.	Sv.-Opp.	IP	H	R	ER	HR	BB-IBB	SO	Avg.
1986— Elmira (N.Y.-Penn)	7	3	.700	2.59	1.30	16	15	2	1	...	0-...	93.2	92	34	27	3	30-1	75	.254
1987— Greensboro (S. Atl.)	8	* 15	.348	3.82	1.33	29	28	7	3	...	0-...	184.0	179	96	78	10	65-8	* 189	.255
1988— New Britain (East.)	8	5	.615	2.97	1.24	21	17	4	1	...	0-...	106.0	91	44	35	3	40-0	62	.232
— Charlotte (Sou.)	5	2	.714	3.18	1.30	7	7	2	1	...	0-...	45.1	36	19	16	3	23-0	32	.217
— Baltimore (A.L.)	0	3	.000	9.82	2.18	4	4	0	0	...	0-0	14.2	22	19	16	3	10-1	4	.355
1989— Rochester (Int'l)	• 13	11	.542	3.21	1.27	27	• 27	• 9	• 3	...	0-...	* 185.1	176	76	66	11	59-0	109	.254
— Baltimore (A.L.)	0	1	.000	6.23	1.50	5	1	0	0	0	0-0	8.2	10	6	6	2	3-0	6	.286
1990— Rochester (Int'l)	4	4	.500	3.92	1.37	15	14	1	0	...	0-...	87.1	95	46	38	10	25-1	83	.277
— Baltimore (A.L.)	1	2	.333	2.54	1.24	35	0	0	0	5	3-9	46.0	38	13	13	1	19-0	32	.229

Year	League	W	L	Pct.	ERA	WHIP	G	GS	CG	ShO	Hld.	Sv.-Opp.	IP	H	R	ER	HR	BB-IBB	SO	Avg.
1991— Houston (N.L.)		3	5	.375	3.81	1.56	56	0	0	0	5	8-11	75.2	79	35	32	2	39-7	71	.271
— Tucson (PCL)		0	1	.000	3.42	1.18	13	0	0	0	...	3-...	23.2	16	9	9	0	12-1	21	.186
1992— Philadelphia (N.L.)		14	11	.560	2.35	0.99	42	26	10	4	0	2-3	226.1	165	67	59	11	59-4	147	* .201
1993— Philadelphia (N.L.)		16	7	.696	4.02	1.24	34	34	7	2	0	0-0	235.1	234	114	105	23	57-6	186	.259
1994— Philadelphia (N.L.)		2	8	.200	4.48	1.40	13	13	1	0	0	0-0	82.1	87	42	41	10	28-3	58	.270
— Scran./W.B. (I.L.)		0	0	...	1.80	1.10	2	2	0	0	...	0-...	10.0	6	2	2	0	5-0	6	.171
— Reading (East.)		0	0	...	0.00	1.75	1	1	0	0	...	0-...	4.0	6	0	0	0	1-0	4	.375
1995— Philadelphia (N.L.)		7	5	.583	3.57	1.05	17	17	1	0	0	0-0	116.0	96	52	46	12	26-2	114	.220
1996— Clearwater (Fla. St.)		2	0	1.000	1.29	0.71	2	2	0	0	...	0-...	14.0	9	2	2	0	1-0	17	.173
— Scran./W.B. (I.L.)		1	0	1.000	1.38	1.08	2	2	0	0	...	0-...	13.0	9	2	2	0	5-0	10	.200
— Philadelphia (N.L.)		9	10	.474	3.19	1.09	26	26	* 8	2	0	0-0	183.1	149	69	65	16	50-5	182	.223
1997— Philadelphia (N.L.)		17	11	.607	2.97	1.05	35	• 35	7	2	0	0-0	254.1	208	96	84	25	58-3	* 319	.224
1998— Philadelphia (N.L.)		15	14	.517	3.25	1.11	35	• 35	* 15	2	0	0-0	* 268.2	236	101	97	23	61-3	* 300	.236
1999— Philadelphia (N.L.)		15	6	.714	3.54	1.13	24	24	8	1	0	0-0	180.1	159	74	71	25	44-0	152	.237
2000— Clearwater (Fla. St.)		1	0	1.000	1.31	0.58	4	4	0	0	...	0-...	20.2	10	3	3	0	2-0	23	.137
— Scran./W.B. (I.L.)		0	0	...	3.60	2.00	1	1	0	0	...	0-...	5.0	9	2	2	0	1-0	7	.375
— Philadelphia (N.L.)		6	6	.500	3.91	1.26	16	16	4	, 1	0	0-0	112.2	110	49	49	17	32-4	96	.253
— Arizona (N.L.)		5	6	.455	3.69	1.10	13	13	† 4	1	0	0-0	97.2	94	41	40	10	13-0	72	.257
2001— Arizona (N.L.)		• 22	6	.786	2.98	1.08	35	• 35	* 6	1	0	0-0	* 256.2	237	86	85	• 37	39-0	293	.245
2002— Arizona (N.L.)		23	7	.767	3.23	0.97	36	35	5	1	0	0-0	259.1	218	95	93	29	33-1	316	.224
2003— Tucson (PCL)		1	0	1.000	4.50	1.30	2	2	0	0	...	0-...	10.0	10	5	5	3	3-0	5	.256
— Arizona (N.L.)		8	9	.471	2.95	1.05	24	24	3	2	0	0-0	168.0	144	58	55	17	32-2	194	.230
American League totals (3 years)		**1**	**6**	**.143**	**4.54**	**1.47**	**44**	**5**	**0**	**0**	**5**	**3-9**	**69.1**	**70**	**38**	**35**	**6**	**32-1**	**42**	**.266**
National League totals (13 years)		**162**	**111**	**.593**	**3.30**	**1.11**	**406**	**333**	**79**	**19**	**5**	**10-14**	**2516.2**	**2216**	**979**	**922**	**257**	**571-40**	**2500**	**.235**
Major League totals (16 years)		**163**	**117**	**.582**	**3.33**	**1.12**	**450**	**338**	**79**	**19**	**10**	**13-23**	**2586.0**	**2286**	**1017**	**957**	**263**	**603-41**	**2542**	**.236**

SCHMACK, BRIAN P

PERSONAL: Born December 7, 1973, in Chicago, Ill. ... 6-2/190. ... Throws right, bats right. ... Full name: Brian Robert Schmack. ... College: Northern Illinois.
TRANSACTIONS/CAREER NOTES: Signed by Chicago White Sox organization as a non-drafted free agent (March 9, 1996). ... Signed by Detroit Tigers organization as a six-year free agent (November 19, 2002).
CAREER HITTING: 0-for-0 (.000), 0 R, 0 2B, 0 3B, 0 HR, 0 RBI.

Year	League	W	L	Pct.	ERA	WHIP	G	GS	CG	ShO	Hld.	Sv.-Opp.	IP	H	R	ER	HR	BB-IBB	SO	Avg.
1996— Hickory (S. Atl.)		6	4	.600	2.31	1.24	43	0	0	0	...	5-...	62.1	61	24	16	4	16-5	56	.260
1997— Winston-Salem (Caro.)		2	5	.286	2.75	1.34	42	0	0	0	...	6-...	75.1	65	32	23	0	36-4	71	.233
1998— Winston-Salem (Caro.)		5	5	.500	2.20	1.06	42	0	0	0	...	10-...	61.1	48	23	15	3	17-0	52	.213
1999— Birmingham (Sou.)		4	4	.500	3.43	1.24	43	0	0	0	...	6-...	63.0	60	31	24	3	18-0	56	.249
2000— Charlotte (Int'l)		11	7	.611	2.78	1.22	51	0	0	0	...	1-...	90.2	82	32	28	10	29-5	84	.238
2001— Oklahoma (PCL)		2	2	.500	4.08	1.32	40	0	0	0	...	1-...	53.0	56	31	24	5	14-1	34	.262
2002— Tulsa (Texas)		1	3	.250	5.79	1.39	12	7	0	0	...	0-...	37.1	45	26	24	1	7-0	20	.302
— Oklahoma (PCL)		0	4	.000	4.94	1.54	29	1	0	0	...	1-...	54.2	66	35	30	6	18-0	45	.307
2003— Erie (East.)		3	3	.500	2.05	1.11	53	0	0	0	...	29-...	57.0	53	15	13	2	10-2	47	.252
— Detroit (A.L.)		1	0	1.000	3.46	1.38	11	0	0	0	2	0-0	13.0	14	6	5	1	4-0	4	.292
Major League totals (1 year)		**1**	**0**	**1.000**	**3.46**	**1.38**	**11**	**0**	**0**	**0**	**2**	**0-0**	**13.0**	**14**	**6**	**5**	**1**	**4-0**	**4**	**.292**

SCHMIDT, JASON P

PERSONAL: Born January 29, 1973, in Lewiston, Idaho. ... 6-5/205. ... Throws right, bats right. ... Full name: Jason David Schmidt. ... High school: Kelso (Wash.).
TRANSACTIONS/CAREER NOTES: Selected by Atlanta Braves organization in eighth round of free-agent draft (June 3, 1991). ... On Atlanta disabled list (July 15-August 30, 1996); included rehabilitation assignment to Greenville (August 11-30). ... Traded by Braves to Pittsburgh Pirates (August 30, 1996), completing deal in which Pirates traded P Denny Neagle to Braves for a player to be named later (August 28, 1996). ... On Pittsburgh disabled list (April 15-May 1 and June 10, 2000-remainder of season); included rehabilitation assignment to Gulf Coast Pirates (July 29-August 23). ... On Pittsburgh disabled list (March 31-May 10, 2001); included rehabilitation assignments to Altoona (April 13-May 5) and Nashville (May 5-7). ... Traded by Pirates with OF John Vander Wal to San Francisco Giants for OF Armando Rios and P Ryan Vogelsong (July 30, 2001). ... Granted free agency (November 5, 2001). ... Re-signed by Giants (December 18, 2001). ... On San Francisco disabled list (March 21-April 24, 2002); included rehabilitation assignment to Fresno (April 13-24).
CAREER HITTING: 38-for-399 (.095), 17 R, 6 2B, 0 3B, 2 HR, 14 RBI.

Year	League	W	L	Pct.	ERA	WHIP	G	GS	CG	ShO	Hld.	Sv.-Opp.	IP	H	R	ER	HR	BB-IBB	SO	Avg.
1991— GC Braves (GCL)		3	4	.429	2.38	1.21	11	11	0	0	...	0-...	45.1	32	21	12	0	23-0	44	.189
1992— Pulaski (Appal.)		3	4	.429	4.01	1.18	11	11	0	0	...	0-...	58.1	38	36	26	4	31-0	56	.170
— Macon (S. Atl.)		0	3	.000	4.01	2.03	7	7	0	0	...	0-...	24.2	31	18	11	2	19-0	33	.316
1993— Durham (Caro.)		7	11	.389	4.94	1.50	22	22	0	0	...	0-...	116.2	128	69	64	12	47-3	110	.286
1994— Greenville (Sou.)		8	7	.533	3.65	1.34	24	24	1	0	...	0-...	140.2	135	64	57	9	54-1	131	.255
1995— Atlanta (N.L.)		2	2	.500	5.76	1.80	9	2	0	0	0	0-1	25.0	27	17	16	2	18-3	19	.287
— Richmond (Int'l)		8	6	.571	2.25	1.25	19	19	0	0	...	0-...	116.0	97	40	29	2	48-3	95	.233
1996— Atlanta (N.L.)		3	4	.429	6.75	1.72	13	11	0	0	0	0-0	58.2	69	48	44	8	32-0	48	.296
— Richmond (Int'l)		3	0	1.000	2.56	1.20	7	7	0	0	...	0-...	45.2	36	17	13	2	19-1	41	.220
— Greenville (Sou.)		0	0	...	9.00	2.00	1	1	0	0	...	0-...	2.0	4	2	2	0	0-0	2	.444
— Pittsburgh (N.L.)		2	2	.500	4.06	1.59	6	6	1	0	0	0-0	37.2	39	19	17	2	21-0	26	.271
1997— Pittsburgh (N.L.)		10	9	.526	4.60	1.43	32	32	2	0	0	0-0	187.2	193	106	96	16	76-2	136	.265
1998— Pittsburgh (N.L.)		11	14	.440	4.07	1.40	33	33	0	0	0	0-0	214.1	228	106	97	24	71-3	158	.275
1999— Pittsburgh (N.L.)		13	11	.542	4.19	1.43	33	33	2	0	0	0-0	212.2	219	110	99	24	85-4	148	.262
2000— Pittsburgh (N.L.)		2	5	.286	5.40	1.77	11	11	0	0	0	0-0	63.1	71	43	38	6	41-2	51	.284
— GC Pirates (GCL)		0	0	...	2.25	1.25	1	1	0	0	...	0-...	4.0	4	2	1	0	1-0	1	.267
2001— Altoona (East.)		0	1	.000	0.96	0.86	3	3	0	0	...	0-...	9.1	7	1	1	0	1-0	17	.200
— Nashville (PCL)		1	0	1.000	0.00	0.57	1	1	0	0	...	0-...	7.0	4	0	0	0	0-0	6	.160
— Pittsburgh (N.L.)		6	6	.500	4.61	1.30	14	14	1	0	0	0-0	84.0	81	46	43	11	28-2	77	.256
— San Francisco (N.L.)		7	1	.875	3.39	1.36	11	11	0	0	0	0-0	66.1	57	29	25	2	33-1	65	.230
2002— Fresno (PCL)		2	0	1.000	3.00	1.08	2	2	0	0	...	0-...	12.0	11	4	4	0	2-0	12	.262
— San Francisco (N.L.)		13	8	.619	3.45	1.19	29	29	2	2	0	0-0	185.1	148	78	71	15	73-1	196	.220
2003— San Francisco (N.L.)		17	5	*.773	*2.34	*0.95	29	29	5	•3	0	0-0	207.2	152	56	54	14	46-1	208	*.200
Major League totals (9 years)		**86**	**67**	**.562**	**4.02**	**1.35**	**220**	**211**	**13**	**5**	**0**	**0-1**	**1342.2**	**1284**	**658**	**600**	**124**	**524-19**	**1132**	**.251**

S

SCHNEIDER, BRIAN   C

PERSONAL: Born November 26, 1976, in Jacksonville, Fla. ... 6-1/200. ... Bats left, throws right. ... Full name: Brian Duncan Schneider. ... High school: Northampton (Pa.).
TRANSACTIONS/CAREER NOTES: Selected by Montreal Expos organization in fifth round of free-agent draft (June 1, 1995).
2003 GAMES PLAYED BY POSITION (MLB): C—98, DH—2.

Year Team (League)	Pos.	G	AB	R	H	2B	3B	HR	RBI	BB	SO	HBP	GDP	SB-CS	Avg.	OBP	SLG	OPS	E	Pct.
1995—GC Expos (GCL)	C	30	97	7	22	3	0	0	4	14	23	1	1	2-4	.227	.330	.258	.588	3	.982
1996—GC Expos (GCL)	C	52	144	26	44	5	2	0	23	24	15	3	3	2-3	.306	.415	.368	.783	3	.988
—Delmarva (S. Atl.)	C	5	9	0	3	0	0	0	1	1	1	1	1	0-0	.333	.455	.333	.788	0	1.000
1997—Cape Fear (S. Atl.)	C	113	381	46	96	20	1	4	49	53	45	4	9	3-6	.252	.345	.341	.687	10	.988
1998—Cape Fear (S. Atl.)	C	38	134	33	40	7	2	7	30	16	9	3	3	6-3	.299	.381	.537	.918	6	.980
—Jupiter (FSL)	C	82	302	32	82	12	1	3	30	22	38	1	9	4-4	.272	.321	.348	.669	11	.981
1999—Harrisburg (East.)	C-1B	121	421	48	111	19	1	17	66	32	56	2	6	2-2	.264	.318	.435	.753	6	.992
2000—Ottawa (Int'l)	C-1B	67	238	22	59	22	3	4	31	16	42	0	5	1-0	.248	.285	.416	.701	8	.982
—Montreal (N.L.)	C	45	115	6	27	6	0	0	11	7	24	0	1	0-1	.235	.276	.287	.563	6	.974
2001—Ottawa (Int'l)	C	97	338	33	93	27	1	6	43	27	55	4	5	2-0	.275	.336	.414	.750	4	.994
—Montreal (N.L.)	C	27	41	4	13	3	0	1	6	6	3	0	0	0-0	.317	.396	.463	.859	0	1.000
2002—Montreal (N.L.)	C-OF	73	207	21	57	19	2	5	29	21	41	0	7	1-2	.275	.339	.459	.798	3	.993
2003—Montreal (N.L.)	C-DH	108	335	34	77	26	1	9	46	37	75	2	12	0-2	.230	.309	.394	.703	3	.996
Major League totals (4 years)		253	698	65	174	54	3	15	92	71	143	2	20	1-5	.249	.318	.400	.718	12	.992

SCHOENEWEIS, SCOTT   P

S

PERSONAL: Born October 2, 1973, in Long Branch, N.J. ... 6-0/190. ... Throws left, bats left. ... Full name: Scott David Schoeneweis. ... Name pronounced: show-en-weiss. ... High school: Lenape (Medford, N.J.). ... College: Duke.
TRANSACTIONS/CAREER NOTES: Selected by California Angels organization in third round of free-agent draft (June 4, 1996). ... Angels franchise renamed Anaheim Angels for 1997 season. ... On Anaheim disabled list (June 17-July 26, 2000); included rehabilitation assignments to Lake Elsinore (July 14-17) and Edmonton (July 18-24). ... Traded by Anaheim Angels with P Doug Nickle to Chicago White Sox for P Gary Glover, P Scott Dunn and P Tim Bittner (July 29, 2003).
CAREER HITTING: 1-for-5 (.200), 0 R, 0 2B, 0 3B, 0 HR, 1 RBI.

Year League	W	L	Pct.	ERA	WHIP	G	GS	CG	ShO	Hld.	Sv.-Opp.	IP	H	R	ER	HR	BB-IBB	SO	Avg.
1996—Lake Elsinore (Calif.)	8	3	.727	3.94	1.21	14	12	0	0	...	0-...	93.2	86	47	41	6	27-0	83	.244
1997—Midland (Texas)	7	5	.583	5.96	1.62	20	20	3	0	...	0-...	113.1	145	84	75	7	39-0	84	.313
1998—Vancouver (PCL)	11	8	.579	4.50	1.37	27	27	2	0	...	0-...	180.0	188	102	90	18	59-0	133	.266
1999—Anaheim (A.L.)	1	1	.500	5.49	1.55	31	0	0	0	3	0-0	39.1	47	27	24	4	14-1	22	.294
—Edmonton (PCL)	2	4	.333	7.64	1.98	9	7	0	0	...	0-...	35.1	58	35	30	6	12-0	29	.360
2000—Anaheim (A.L.)	7	10	.412	5.45	1.47	27	27	1	1	0	0-0	170.0	183	112	103	21	67-2	78	.276
—Lake Elsinore (Calif.)	0	0	...	1.93	1.29	1	1	0	0	...	0-...	4.2	3	1	1	0	3-0	3	.200
—Edmonton (PCL)	0	0	...	0.00	0.43	1	1	0	0	...	0-...	7.0	2	1	0	0	1-0	6	.083
2001—Anaheim (A.L.)	10	11	.476	5.08	1.48	32	32	1	0	0	0-0	205.1	227	122	116	21	77-2	104	.281
2002—Anaheim (A.L.)	9	8	.529	4.88	1.42	54	15	0	0	11	1-4	118.0	119	68	64	17	49-4	65	.264
2003—Anaheim (A.L.)	1	1	.500	3.96	1.22	39	0	0	0	4	0-1	38.2	37	19	17	2	10-3	29	.255
—Chicago (A.L.)	2	1	.667	4.50	1.35	20	0	0	0	0	0-1	26.0	26	16	13	1	9-2	27	.255
Major League totals (5 years)	30	32	.484	5.08	1.45	203	74	2	1	18	1-6	597.1	639	364	337	66	226-14	325	.274

SCUTARO, MARCO   IF

PERSONAL: Born October 30, 1975, in San Felipe, Venezuela. ... 5-10/170. ... Bats right, throws right. ... Full name: Marcos Scutaro. ... Name pronounced: scoo-TAHR-oh.
TRANSACTIONS/CAREER NOTES: Signed as non-drafted free agent by Cleveland Indians organization (July 26, 1994). ... Traded by Indians to Milwaukee Brewers (August 30, 2000); completed trade in which Indians traded OF Richie Sexson, P Paul Rigdon, P Kane Davis and a player to be named to Brewers for P Bob Wickman, P Jason Bere and P Steve Woodard (July 28, 2000). ... Claimed on waivers by New York Mets (April 5, 2002).
2003 GAMES PLAYED BY POSITION (MLB): 2B—39, SS—1.

Year Team (League)	Pos.	G	AB	R	H	2B	3B	HR	RBI	BB	SO	HBP	GDP	SB-CS	Avg.	OBP	SLG	OPS	E	Pct.
1995—Dom. Inds. (DSL)	3B	66	262	71	103	18	6	0	38	20	11	...	...	32-...	.393	...	.508	...	17	.931
1996—Columbus (S. Atl.)	2B-3B-SS	85	315	66	79	12	3	10	45	38	86	4	6	6-3	.251	.334	.403	.737	17	.959
1997—Kinston (Caro.)	2B-3B	97	378	58	103	17	6	10	59	35	72	9	3	23-7	.272	.346	.429	.774	11	.972
—Buffalo (A.A.)	2B-3B-SS	21	57	8	15	3	0	1	6	6	8	0	4	0-1	.263	.328	.368	.697	3	.959
1998—Akron (East.)	2B-SS	124	462	68	146	27	6	11	62	47	71	10	8	33-16	.316	.387	.472	.859	15	.976
—Buffalo (Int'l)	2B-3B	8	26	3	6	3	0	0	4	0	2	0	0	0-0	.231	.231	.346	.577	2	.939
1999—Buffalo (Int'l)	2B-SS	129	462	76	126	24	2	8	51	61	69	6	5	21-6	.273	.362	.385	.747	16	.974
2000—Buffalo (Int'l)	2B-SS	124	425	67	117	20	5	5	54	61	53	9	8	9-6	.275	.373	.381	.754	15	.976
—Indianapolis (Int'l)		4	13	5	7	1	1	1	3	1	2	0	1	1-0	.538	.571	1.000	1.571	0	1.000
2001—Indianapolis (Int'l)	2B-3B-SS	132	495	87	146	29	3	11	50	62	83	10	9	11-11	.295	.382	.432	.815	19	.968
2002—Norfolk (Int'l)	2-S-O-3	97	354	48	113	22	6	7	28	30	61	2	7	7-8	.319	.375	.475	.849	10	.974
—New York (N.L.)	2-S-3-O	27	36	2	8	0	1	1	6	0	11	0	1	0-1	.222	.216	.361	.577	1	.968
2003—Norfolk (Int'l)	3-2-S-O-D	70	244	42	76	18	3	9	32	33	34	6	6	11-6	.311	.401	.520	.921	7	.970
—New York (N.L.)	2B-SS	48	75	10	16	4	0	2	6	13	14	1	1	2-0	.213	.333	.347	.680	2	.981
Major League totals (2 years)		75	111	12	24	4	1	3	12	13	25	1	2	2-1	.216	.299	.351	.651	3	.978

SEANEZ, RUDY   P

PERSONAL: Born October 20, 1968, in Brawley, Calif. ... 5-11/205. ... Throws right, bats right. ... Full name: Rudy Caballero Seanez. ... Name pronounced: see-AHN-ez. ... High school: Brawley (Calif.) Union.
TRANSACTIONS/CAREER NOTES: Selected by Cleveland Indians organization in fourth round of free-agent draft (June 10, 1986). ... On disabled list (May 4-July 11 and August 9-29, 1987). ... On Cleveland disabled list (April 1-16 and July 30-September 2, 1991); included rehabilitation assignment to Colorado Springs (August 14-September 2). ... Traded by Indians to Los Angeles Dodgers for P Dennis Cook and P Mike Christopher (December 10, 1991). ... On disabled list (March 29, 1992-entire season). ... Traded by Dodgers to Colorado Rockies for 2B Jody Reed (November 17, 1992). ... On Colorado disabled list (April 4-July 16, 1993); included rehabilitation assignments to Central Valley (June 16-July 4) and Colorado Springs (July 4-15). ... Granted free agency (July 16, 1993). ... Signed by San Diego Padres organization (July 22, 1993). ... Released by Padres (November 18, 1993). ... Signed by Dodgers organization (January 12, 1994). ... On Los Angeles disabled list (May 28-June 16, 1995); included rehabilitation assignment to San Bernardino (June 9-16). ... Granted free agency (October 15, 1996). ... Signed by New York Mets organization (January 15, 1997). ... Traded by Mets to Kansas City Royals for future considerations (May 30, 1997). ... Granted free agency (October 15, 1997). ... Signed by Atlanta Braves organization (December 9,

1997). ... On disabled list (August 21, 1999-remainder of season). ... Granted free agency (November 2, 1999). ... Re-signed by Braves (December 12, 1999). ... On Atlanta disabled list (March 23-April 27, 2000 and June 14-remainder of season); included rehabilitation assignment to Greenville (April 22-27). ... Granted free agency (October 30, 2000). ... Signed by Padres organization (February 14, 2001). ... On Portland disabled list (April 5-May 6, 2001). ... On San Diego disabled list (June 6-21, 2001). ... Traded by Padres to Braves for a player to be named later (August 31, 2001); Padres acquired P Winston Abreu to complete deal (September 6, 2001). ... Granted free agency (November 5, 2001). ... Signed by Texas Rangers (January 28, 2002). ... On Texas disabled list (May 30-September 2, 2002); included rehabilitation assignments to Oklahoma (June 24-26 and August 24-September 2). ... Granted free agency (October 28, 2002). ... Re-signed by Rangers organization (December 6, 2002). ... Released by Rangers (May 3, 2003). ... Signed by Boston Red Sox (May 9, 2003).

CAREER HITTING: 0-for-4 (.000), 1 R, 0 2B, 0 3B, 0 HR, 0 RBI.

Year League	W	L	Pct.	ERA	WHIP	G	GS	CG	ShO	Hld.	Sv.-Opp.	IP	H	R	ER	HR	BB-IBB	SO	Avg.
1986— Burlington (Appal.)	5	2	.714	3.20	1.20	13	12	1	1	...	0-...	76.0	59	37	27	5	32-0	56	.212
1987— Waterloo (Midw.)	0	4	.000	6.75	1.67	10	10	0	0	...	0-...	34.2	35	29	26	6	23-0	23	.263
1988— Waterloo (Midw.)	6	6	.500	4.69	1.46	22	22	1	1	...	0-...	113.1	98	69	59	10	68-0	93	.230
1989— Kinston (Caro.)	8	10	.444	4.14	1.81	25	25	1	0	...	0-...	113.0	94	66	52	0	* 111-1	149	.223
— Colo. Springs (PCL)	0	0	...	0.00	1.00	1	0	0	0	...	0-...	1.0	1	0	0	0	0-0	0	.250
— Cleveland (A.L.)	0	0	...	3.60	1.00	5	0	0	0	0	0-0	5.0	1	2	2	0	4-1	7	.071
1990— Cant./Akr. (Eastern)	1	0	1.000	2.16	1.26	15	0	0	0	...	5-...	16.2	9	4	4	0	12-0	27	.170
— Cleveland (A.L.)	2	1	.667	5.60	1.72	24	0	0	0	3	0-0	27.1	22	17	17	2	25-1	24	.220
— Colo. Springs (PCL)	1	4	.200	6.75	2.08	12	0	0	0	...	1-...	12.0	15	10	9	2	10-0	7	.313
1991— Colo. Springs (PCL)	0	0	...	7.27	2.25	16	0	0	0	...	0-...	17.1	17	14	14	2	22-0	19	.274
— Cant./Akr. (Eastern)	4	2	.667	2.58	1.23	25	0	0	0	...	7-...	38.1	17	12	11	2	30-1	73	.132
— Cleveland (A.L.)	0	0	...	16.20	3.40	5	0	0	0	0	0-1	5.0	10	12	9	2	7-0	7	.385
1992— Los Angeles (N.L.)										Did not play.									
1993— Central Valley (Cal.)	0	2	.000	9.72	2.40	5	1	0	0	...	0-...	8.1	9	9	9	0	11-0	7	.265
— Colo. Springs (PCL)	0	0	...	9.00	1.33	3	0	0	0	...	0-...	3.0	3	3	3	1	1-0	5	.250
— Las Vegas (PCL)	0	1	.000	6.41	1.78	14	0	0	0	...	0-...	19.2	24	15	14	2	11-0	14	.308
— San Diego (N.L.)	0	0	...	13.50	3.00	3	0	0	0	0	0-...	3.1	8	6	5	1	2-0	1	.471
1994— Albuquerque (PCL)	2	1	.667	5.32	1.86	20	0	0	0	...	9-...	22.0	28	14	13	3	13-1	26	.308
— Los Angeles (N.L.)	1	1	.500	2.66	1.39	17	0	0	0	1	0-1	23.2	24	7	7	2	9-1	18	.273
1995— Los Angeles (N.L.)	1	3	.250	6.75	1.64	37	0	0	0	6	3-4	34.2	39	27	26	5	18-3	29	.285
— San Bernardino (Calif.)	2	0	1.000	0.00	0.83	4	0	0	0	...	1-...	6.0	2	0	0	0	3-0	5	.100
1996— Albuquerque (PCL)	0	2	.000	6.52	1.97	21	0	0	0	...	6-...	19.1	27	18	14	0	11-1	20	.325
1997— Norfolk (Int'l)	1	0	1.000	4.05	1.73	9	0	0	0	...	0-...	13.1	12	8	6	1	11-0	17	.231
— Omaha (Am. Assoc.)	2	5	.286	6.51	1.66	28	3	0	0	...	0-...	47.0	53	42	34	13	25-0	46	.270
1998— Richmond (Int'l)	2	0	1.000	1.29	0.95	16	0	0	0	...	7-...	21.0	13	9	3	1	7-1	33	.169
— Atlanta (N.L.)	4	1	.800	2.75	1.14	34	0	0	0	8	2-4	36.0	25	13	11	2	16-0	50	.195
1999— Atlanta (N.L.)	6	1	.857	3.35	1.27	56	0	0	0	18	3-8	53.2	47	21	20	3	21-1	41	.234
2000— Greenville (Sou.)	0	0	...	0.00	1.00	2	1	0	0	...	0-...	2.0	2	0	0	0	0-0	3	.250
— Atlanta (N.L.)	2	4	.333	4.29	1.14	23	0	0	0	6	2-3	21.0	15	11	10	3	9-1	20	.192
2001— Lake Elsinore (Calif.)	2	0	1.000	2.08	1.04	7	0	0	0	...	0-...	8.2	7	3	2	1	2-0	8	.219
— San Diego (N.L.)	0	2	.000	2.63	1.25	26	0	0	0	5	1-3	24.0	15	8	7	3	15-0	24	.176
— Atlanta (N.L.)	0	0	...	3.00	1.00	12	0	0	0	4	0-0	12.0	8	4	4	1	4-0	17	.182
2002— Texas (A.L.)	1	3	.250	5.73	1.58	33	0	0	0	10	0-4	33.0	28	25	21	5	24-1	40	.230
— Oklahoma (PCL)	0	0	...	4.50	1.00	4	0	0	0	...	0-...	4.0	4	2	2	0	0-0	3	.267
2003— Oklahoma (PCL)	0	1	.000	2.08	1.85	5	0	0	0	...	0-...	4.1	3	4	1	0	5-0	7	.176
— Boston (A.L.)	0	1	.000	6.23	1.96	9	0	0	0	0	0-1	8.2	11	7	6	2	6-1	9	.297
— Pawtucket (Int'l)	2	2	.500	6.10	1.45	17	0	0	0	...	3-...	20.2	20	14	14	5	10-1	24	.253
— Iowa (PCL)	1	2	.333	3.46	1.62	13	0	0	0	...	2-...	13.0	12	10	5	1	9-2	13	.235
American League totals (5 years)	3	5	.375	6.27	1.75	76	0	0	0	13	0-6	79.0	72	63	55	11	66-4	87	.241
National League totals (7 years)	14	12	.538	3.89	1.32	208	0	0	0	48	11-23	208.1	181	97	90	20	94-6	200	.233
Major League totals (12 years)	17	17	.500	4.54	1.44	284	0	0	0	61	11-29	287.1	253	160	145	31	160-10	287	.235

SEARS, TODD — 1B

PERSONAL: Born October 23, 1975, in Des Moines, Iowa. ... 6-5/215. ... Bats left, throws right. ... Full name: Todd Andrew Sears. ... High school: Ankeny (Iowa). ... College: Nebraska.

TRANSACTIONS/CAREER NOTES: Selected by California Angels organization in 19th round of free-agent draft (June 2, 1994); did not sign. ... Selected by Colorado Rockies organization in third round of free-agent draft (June 3, 1997). ... Traded by Rockies with cash to Minnesota Twins for 2B Todd Walker and OF Butch Huskey (July 16, 2000). ... Traded by Twins to San Diego Padres for IF Alex Garcia (September 9, 2003).

2003 GAMES PLAYED BY POSITION (MLB): 1B—15, DH—6.

Year Team (League)	Pos.	G	AB	R	H	2B	3B	HR	RBI	BB	SO	HBP	GDP	SB-CS	Avg.	OBP	SLG	OPS	E	Pct.
1997— Portland (NW)	1B	55	200	37	54	13	1	2	29	41	49	0	4	2-0	.270	.393	.375	.768	6	.989
1998— Asheville (S. Atl.)	3B	130	459	71	133	26	2	11	82	72	89	5	9	10-4	.290	.387	.427	.814	• 31	.888
1999— Salem (Caro.)	3B-1B	109	385	58	108	21	0	14	59	58	99	4	9	11-2	.281	.379	.444	.824	26	.950
2000— Carolina (Sou.)	1B	86	299	54	90	21	0	12	72	72	76	2	7	12-3	.301	.434	.492	.926	12	.982
— New Britain (East.)	1B	40	140	15	44	8	1	3	15	18	40	1	5	1-0	.314	.396	.450	.846	2	.993
— Salt Lake (PCL)	1B	3	11	2	4	1	0	1	4	1	2	0	1	0-0	.364	.417	.727	1.144	0	1.000
2001— Edmonton (PCL)	1B-3B	118	408	61	127	25	2	13	50	41	71	3	16	2-1	.311	.376	.478	.854	6	.993
2002— Edmonton (PCL)	1B	129	484	88	150	36	4	20	100	59	142	5	6	2-1	.310	.388	.525	.912	3	.997
— Minnesota (A.L.)	1B	7	12	2	4	2	0	0	0	1	0	0	0	0-0	.333	.333	.500	.833	0	1.000
2003— Minnesota (A.L.)	1B-DH	24	65	7	16	2	0	2	11	7	15	1	4	0-0	.246	.324	.369	.694	1	.990
— Rochester (Int'l)	1B-DH	80	283	35	72	12	1	7	41	37	90	4	6	6-1	.254	.347	.378	.725	5	.989
— San Diego (N.L.)	1B	9	8	2	2	1	0	0	0	0	3	0	0	0-0	.250	.250	.375	.625	0	1.000
American League totals (2 years)		31	77	9	20	4	0	2	11	7	16	1	4	0-0	.260	.326	.390	.715	1	.992
National League totals (1 year)		9	8	2	2	1	0	0	0	0	3	0	0	0-0	.250	.250	.375	.625	0	1.000
Major League totals (2 years)		40	85	11	22	5	0	2	11	7	19	1	4	0-0	.259	.319	.388	.707	1	.992

SEAY, BOBBY — P

PERSONAL: Born June 20, 1978, in Sarasota, Fla. ... 6-2/235. ... Throws left, bats left. ... Full name: Robert Michael Seay. ... Name pronounced: see. ... High school: Sarasota (Fla.).

TRANSACTIONS/CAREER NOTES: Selected by Chicago White Sox organization in first round (12th pick overall) of free-agent draft (June 4, 1996). ... Rights relinquished by White Sox (August 15, 1996). ... Signed by Tampa Bay Devil Rays organization (November 8, 1996). ... On disabled list (June 9, 1997-remainder of season). ... On Orlando disabled list (May 8-June 30, 2001). ... On Tampa Bay disabled list (March 22-June 3, 2002); included rehabilitation assignment to Orlando (May 7-June 3). ... On Orlando disabled list (June 9-July 7, 2002). ... Placed on 15-day disabled list by Tampa Bay (April 24, 2003). ... Reinstated from 15-day disabled list; optioned to Durham (June 3, 2003). ... Recalled from Durham (July 6, 2003). ... Optioned to Durham (July 13, 2003). ... Recalled from Durham (September 19, 2003).

CAREER HITTING: 0-for-0 (.000), 0 R, 0 2B, 0 3B, 0 HR, 0 RBI.

Year	League	W	L	Pct.	ERA	WHIP	G	GS	CG	ShO	Hld.	Sv.-Opp.	IP	H	R	ER	HR	BB-IBB	SO	Avg.
1997—Char., S.C. (SAL)		3	4	.429	4.55	1.52	13	13	0	0	...	0-...	61.1	56	35	31	2	37-0	64	.249
1998—Char., S.C. (SAL)		1	7	.125	4.30	1.28	15	15	0	0	...	0-...	69.0	59	40	33	10	29-0	74	.236
1999—St. Pete. (FSL)		2	6	.250	3.00	1.39	12	11	0	0	...	0-...	57.0	56	25	19	0	23-0	45	.271
— Orlando (Sou.)		1	2	.333	7.94	2.18	6	6	0	0	...	0-...	17.0	22	15	15	2	15-0	16	.319
2000—Orlando (Sou.)		8	7	.533	3.88	1.40	24	24	0	0	...	0-...	132.1	132	64	57	13	53-1	106	.265
2001—Orlando (Sou.)		2	5	.286	5.98	1.65	15	13	0	0	...	0-...	64.2	81	48	43	9	26-0	49	.310
— Tampa Bay (A.L.)		1	1	.500	6.23	1.38	12	0	0	0	0	0-0	13.0	13	11	9	3	5-1	12	.260
2002—Orlando (Sou.)		2	0	1.000	3.28	1.29	15	3	0	0	...	0-...	35.2	31	16	13	2	15-0	24	.237
— Durham (Int'l)		0	0	...	6.00	1.13	10	0	0	0	...	0-...	15.0	15	10	10	1	2-0	14	.254
2003—Tampa Bay (A.L.)		0	0	...	3.00	1.44	12	0	0	0	0	0-1	9.0	7	3	3	0	6-0	5	.226
— Durham (Int'l)		3	0	1.000	2.10	1.27	25	0	0	0	...	0-...	30.0	23	10	7	1	15-0	29	.205
Major League totals (2 years)		1	1	.500	4.91	1.41	24	0	0	0	0	0-1	22.0	20	14	12	3	11-1	17	.247

SEGUI, DAVID   1B/DH

PERSONAL: Born July 19, 1966, in Kansas City, Kan. ... 6-1/216. ... Bats both, throws left. ... Full name: David Vincent Segui. ... Name pronounced: seh-GHEE. ... High school: Bishop Ward (Kansas City, Kan.). ... College: Louisiana Tech.

TRANSACTIONS/CAREER NOTES: Selected by Baltimore Orioles organization in 18th round of free-agent draft (June 2, 1987). ... On Rochester disabled list (April 19-26, 1991). ... On suspended list (August 16-19, 1993). ... Traded by Orioles to New York Mets for SS Kevin Baez and P Tom Wegmann (March 27, 1994). ... On disabled list (June 20-July 5, 1994). ... Traded by Mets to Montreal Expos for P Reid Cornelius (June 8, 1995). ... On disabled list (July 4-August 16, 1996). ... On disabled list (June 4-21, 1997). ... On suspended list (July 26, 1997). ... Granted free agency (October 28, 1997). ... Signed by Seattle Mariners (December 12, 1997). ... Traded by Mariners to Toronto Blue Jays for P Tom Davey and P Steve Sinclair (July 28, 1999). ... On suspended list (July 30-31, 1999). ... On Toronto disabled list (August 8-September 2, 1999). ... Granted free agency (October 29, 1999). ... Re-signed by Blue Jays (January 18, 2000). ... Traded by Blue Jays with cash to Texas Rangers as part of three-way deal in which Rangers sent 1B Lee Stevens to Montreal Expos and Expos sent 1B Brad Fullmer to Blue Jays (March 16, 2000). ... Traded by Rangers to Cleveland Indians for OF Ricky Ledee (July 28, 2000). ... Granted free agency (October 30, 2000). ... Signed by Orioles (December 21, 2000). ... On disabled list (April 28-May 15 and July 16-August 4, 2001; and May 18, 2002-remainder of season). ... On disabled list (May 18, 2002-remainder of season). ... On Baltimore disabled list; included rehabilitation assignment to Frederick (April 4-5). ... Placed on 15-day disabled list (April 18, 2003). ... Reinstated from 15-day disabled list (May 3, 2003). ... Placed on 15-day disabled list (July 26, 2003). ... Transferred to 60-day disabled list (September 15, 2003).

2003 GAMES PLAYED BY POSITION (MLB): DH—53, 1B—8.

Year	Team (League)	Pos.	G	AB	R	H	2B	3B	HR	RBI	BB	SO	HBP	GDP	SB-CS	Avg.	OBP	SLG	OPS	E	Pct.
1988—Hagerstown (Car.)		1B-OF	60	190	35	51	12	4	3	31	22	23	3	7	0-0	.268	.347	.421	.768	9	.976
1989—Frederick (Carolina)		1B	83	284	43	90	19	0	10	50	41	32	4	4	2-1	.317	.407	.489	.896	4	.995
—Hagerstown (East.)		1B	44	173	22	56	14	1	1	27	16	16	2	6	0-0	.324	.383	.434	.817	1	.998
1990—Rochester (Int'l)		1B-OF	86	307	55	103	28	0	2	51	45	28	0	15	5-4	.336	.415	.446	.861	3	.996
—Baltimore (A.L.)		DH-1B	40	123	14	30	7	0	2	15	11	15	1	12	0-0	.244	.311	.350	.661	3	.990
1991—Rochester (Int'l)		1B	28	96	9	26	2	0	1	10	15	6	1	6	1-1	.271	.365	.323	.688	0	1.000
—Baltimore (A.L.) DH-1B-OF			86	212	15	59	7	0	2	22	12	19	0	7	1-1	.278	.316	.340	.655	3	.990
1992—Baltimore (A.L.)		1B-OF	115	189	21	44	9	0	1	17	20	23	0	4	1-0	.233	.306	.296	.603	1	.998
1993—Baltimore (A.L.)		1B-DH	146	450	54	123	27	0	10	60	58	53	0	18	2-1	.273	.351	.400	.751	5	.996
1994—New York (N.L.)		1B-OF	92	336	46	81	17	1	10	43	33	43	1	6	0-0	.241	.308	.387	.695	5	.993
1995—New York (N.L.)		OF-1B	33	73	9	24	3	1	2	11	12	9	1	2	1-3	.329	.420	.479	.900	0	1.000
—Montreal (N.L.)		1B-OF	97	383	59	117	22	3	10	57	28	38	2	8	1-4	.305	.355	.457	.812	3	.997
1996—Montreal (N.L.)		1B	115	416	69	119	30	1	11	58	60	54	0	8	4-4	.286	.375	.442	.818	7	.993
1997—Montreal (N.L.)		1B	125	459	75	141	22	3	21	68	57	66	1	9	1-0	.307	.380	.505	.886	6	.995
1998—Seattle (A.L.)		1B-OF	143	522	79	159	36	1	19	84	49	80	0	12	3-1	.305	.359	.487	.845	1	.999
1999—Seattle (A.L.)		1B	90	345	43	101	22	3	9	39	32	43	1	9	1-2	.293	.352	.452	.804	3	.996
—Toronto (A.L.)		DH-1B	31	95	14	30	5	0	5	13	8	17	0	1	0-0	.316	.365	.526	.892	1	.955
2000—Texas (A.L.)		DH-1B	93	351	52	118	29	1	11	57	34	51	0	12	0-1	.336	.391	.519	.909	0	1.000
—Cleveland (A.L.) 1B-DH-OF			57	223	41	74	13	0	8	46	19	33	1	8	0-0	.332	.384	.498	.881	0	1.000
2001—Baltimore (A.L.)		1B-DH	82	292	48	88	18	1	10	46	49	61	4	4	1-1	.301	.406	.473	.879	9	.983
2002—Baltimore (A.L.)		DH-1B	26	95	10	25	4	0	2	16	11	22	0	0	0-0	.263	.336	.368	.705	0	1.000
2003—Frederick (Carolina)		DH	1	4	0	1	0	0	0	0	0	1	0	0	0-0	.250	.250	.250	.500	0	.000
—Baltimore (A.L.)		DH-1B	67	224	26	59	10	1	5	25	26	47	1	8	1-0	.263	.341	.384	.725	0	1.000
American League totals (10 years)			976	3121	417	910	187	7	84	440	329	464	8	95	10-7	.292	.357	.437	.794	26	.995
National League totals (4 years)			462	1667	258	482	94	9	54	237	190	210	5	33	7-11	.289	.361	.454	.815	21	.995
Major League totals (14 years)			1438	4788	675	1392	281	16	138	677	519	674	13	128	17-18	.291	.359	.443	.801	47	.995

SEGUIGNOL, FERNANDO   1B/OF

PERSONAL: Born January 19, 1975, in Bocas del Toro, Panama. ... 6-5/230. ... Bats both, throws right. ... Full name: Fernando Alfredo Seguignol. ... Name pronounced: SEG-ee-nol. ... High school: Almirante de Bocas del Toro (Bocas del Toro, Panama).

TRANSACTIONS/CAREER NOTES: Signed as non-drafted free agent by New York Yankees organization (January 29, 1993). ... Traded by Yankees with and cash to Montreal Expos for P John Wetteland (April 5, 1995). ... On Harrisburg disabled list (June 24-July 17, 1998). ... On Montreal disabled list (July 11-September 7, 1999); included rehabilitation assignment to Ottawa (August 9-September 7). ... On Ottawa disabled list (May 1-12, 2000). ... Granted free agency (October 8, 2001). ... Signed by New York Yankees (January 21, 2003).

2003 GAMES PLAYED BY POSITION (MLB): 1B—3, DH—1.

Year	Team (League)	Pos.	G	AB	R	H	2B	3B	HR	RBI	BB	SO	HBP	GDP	SB-CS	Avg.	OBP	SLG	OPS	E	Pct.
1993—GC Yankees (GCL)		1B-OF	45	161	16	35	3	3	2	20	9	37	5	2	2-0	.217	.280	.311	.591	2	.979
1994—Oneonta (NYP)		OF	73	266	36	77	14	* 9	2	32	16	61	2	6	4-6	.289	.335	.432	.767	4	.952
1995—Albany (S. Atl.)		OF	121	457	59	95	22	2	12	66	28	141	6	6	12-8	.208	.260	.344	.603	8	.964
1996—Delmarva (S. Atl.)		OF	118	410	59	98	14	5	8	55	48	126	6	5	12-13	.239	.327	.356	.683	4	.978
1997—W.P. Beach (FSL)		1B-OF	124	456	70	116	27	5	18	83	30	129	5	1	5-5	.254	.299	.454	.753	15	.986
1998—Harrisburg (East.)		1B-OF	80	281	54	81	13	0	25	69	29	77	6	6	6-1	.288	.366	.601	.967	9	.984
—Ottawa (Int'l)		1B-OF	32	109	16	28	8	0	6	16	12	43	1	1	0-0	.257	.333	.495	.829	1	.979
—Montreal (N.L.)		OF-1B	16	42	6	11	4	0	2	3	3	15	0	1	0-0	.262	.304	.500	.804	0	1.000
1999—Ottawa (Int'l) 1B-DH-OF			87	312	54	89	17	3	23	74	40	96	11	9	3-7	.285	.381	.580	.962	10	.978
—Montreal (N.L.)		1B-OF	35	105	14	27	9	0	5	10	5	33	7	1	0-0	.257	.328	.486	.813	2	.990

									BATTING												FIELDING	
Year	Team (League)	Pos.	G	AB	R	H	2B	3B	HR	RBI	BB	SO	HBP	GDP	SB-CS	Avg.	OBP	SLG	OPS	E	Pct.
2000—Ottawa (Int'l)	1B-OF	41	141	20	39	16	0	8	31	13	26	5	8	1-1	.277	.352	.560	.912	5	.979
—Montreal (N.L.)	OF-1B-DH	76	162	22	45	8	0	10	22	9	46	3	5	0-1	.278	.326	.512	.838	5	.972
2001—Montreal (N.L.)	OF-1B	46	50	0	7	2	0	0	5	2	17	1	4	0-0	.140	.185	.180	.365	2	.941
—Ottawa (Int'l)	1B-OF	60	242	36	75	12	0	14	45	15	49	5	6	0-1	.310	.363	.533	.896	4	.992
2002—						Did not play.															
2003—Tampa (Fla. St.)	1B-DH	3	13	1	5	0	0	0	1	0	2	0	1	0-0	.385	.385	.385	.769	0	1.000
—Columbus (Int'l)	DH-1B	106	402	78	137	28	1	28	87	34	81	8	19	0-0	.341	.401	.624	1.026	2	.992
—New York (A.L.)	1B-DH	5	7	0	1	0	0	0	0	1	3	0	0	0-0	.143	.250	.143	.393	0	1.000
American League totals (1 year)		5	7	0	1	0	0	0	0	1	3	0	0	0-0	.143	.250	.143	.393	0	1.000
National League totals (4 years)		173	359	42	90	23	0	17	40	19	111	11	11	0-1	.251	.305	.457	.761	9	.981
Major League totals (5 years)		178	366	42	91	23	0	17	40	20	114	11	11	0-1	.249	.303	.451	.754	9	.982

SELBY, BILL — OF/IF

PERSONAL: Born June 11, 1970, in Monroeville, Ala. ... 5-10/195. ... Bats left, throws right. ... Full name: William Frank Selby. ... High school: Horn Lake (Mich.). ... College: Southern Mississippi.

TRANSACTIONS/CAREER NOTES: Selected by Boston Red Sox organization in 13th round of free-agent draft (June 1, 1992). ... Contract sold by Red Sox to Yokohama BayStars of Japan Central League (October 22, 1996). ... Signed by Cleveland Indians organization (February 1, 1998). ... Granted free agency (October 16, 1998). ... Re-signed by Indians organization (February 3, 1999). ... Granted free agency (October 15, 1999). ... Re-signed by Indians organization (December 23, 1999). ... Released by Indians (October 20, 2000). ... Signed by Cincinnati Reds organization (May 29, 2001). ... On Louisville disabled list (August 28, 2001-remainder of season). ... Granted free agency (October 15, 2001). ... Signed by Cleveland Indians organization (December 18, 2001). ... Elected free agency (September 30, 2003).

2003 GAMES PLAYED BY POSITION (MLB): 3B—10, DH—2, 2B—1, 1B—1, OF—1.

									BATTING												FIELDING	
Year	Team (League)	Pos.	G	AB	R	H	2B	3B	HR	RBI	BB	SO	HBP	GDP	SB-CS	Avg.	OBP	SLG	OPS	E	Pct.
1992—Elmira (N.Y.-Penn)	2B-3B	73	275	38	72	16	1	10	41	31	53	2	3	4-4	.262	.339	.436	.775	16	.930
1993—Lynchburg (Caro.)	3B-1B	113	394	57	99	22	1	7	38	24	66	3	6	1-2	.251	.294	.365	.660	8	.954
1994—Lynchburg (Caro.)	2B-3B-1B	97	352	58	109	20	2	19	69	28	62	5	7	3-1	.310	.367	.540	.907	23	.924
—New Britain (East.)	3B	35	107	15	28	5	0	1	18	15	16	0	2	0-1	.262	.336	.336	.672	6	.930
1995—Trenton (East.) 3B-2B-DH	117	451	64	129	29	2	13	68	46	52	3	14	4-6	.286	.350	.446	.796	29	.918
1996—Pawtucket (Int'l)	2B-3B-OF	71	260	39	66	14	5	11	47	22	39	2	5	0-3	.254	.313	.473	.786	16	.936
—Boston (A.L.)	2B-3B-OF	40	95	12	26	4	0	3	6	9	11	0	3	1-1	.274	.337	.411	.747	4	.948
1997—Yo. Bay. (Jp. Cn.)		90	171	19	39	4	1	5	17	21	37	...	...	3-...	.228	...	.351	...	...	...
1998—Buffalo (Int'l)	2B-3B-OF	97	334	45	85	23	0	14	52	38	50	0	6	3-0	.254	.328	.449	.777	4	.967
—Akron (East.)	2B-3B-OF	20	77	15	30	7	1	3	10	3	11	1	0	0-0	.390	.415	.623	1.038	1	.977
1999—Buffalo (Int'l)	2B-3B-OF	122	447	75	132	32	5	20	85	57	63	2	11	4-3	.295	.372	.523	.895	5	.967
2000—Buffalo (Int'l)	3B-OF-2B	100	384	69	106	21	6	21	86	48	61	3	9	1-1	.276	.355	.526	.881	15	.949
—Cleveland (A.L.)	O-2-D-3	30	46	8	11	1	0	0	4	1	9	1	1	0-0	.239	.271	.261	.532	0	1.000
2001—Louisville (Int'l)	2-1-3-O	88	330	47	85	19	1	14	56	25	47	2	6	1-0	.258	.310	.448	.759	10	.975
—Cincinnati (N.L.)	2B-3B-1B	36	92	7	21	7	1	2	12	5	13	1	1	0-0	.228	.273	.391	.664	2	.981
2002—Buffalo (Int'l)	OF-2B-3B	51	184	28	55	14	2	5	22	20	33	0	0	4-1	.299	.364	.478	.842	5	.962
—Cleveland (A.L.)	3B-OF-2B	65	159	15	34	7	2	6	21	15	27	0	4	0-1	.214	.278	.396	.675	5	.952
2003—Cleveland (A.L.) 3-D-2-1-O	27	39	3	4	1	0	0	5	3	11	0	0	0-0	.103	.163	.128	.291	2	.931
—Memphis (PCL)	O-2-3-D	76	279	33	73	12	6	9	41	24	32	0	5	5-1	.262	.319	.444	.764	4	.981
American League totals (4 years)		162	339	38	75	13	2	9	36	28	58	1	8	1-2	.221	.280	.351	.631	11	.953
National League totals (1 year)		36	92	7	21	7	1	2	12	5	13	1	1	0-0	.228	.273	.391	.664	2	.981
Major League totals (5 years)		198	431	45	96	20	3	11	48	33	71	2	9	1-2	.223	.279	.360	.638	13	.962

SELE, AARON — P

PERSONAL: Born June 25, 1970, in Golden Valley, Minn. ... 6-5/230. ... Throws right, bats right. ... Full name: Aaron Helmer Sele. ... Name pronounced: SEE-lee. ... High school: North Kitsap (Poulsbo, Wash.). ... College: Washington State.

TRANSACTIONS/CAREER NOTES: Selected by Minnesota Twins organization in 37th round of free-agent draft (June 1, 1988); did not sign. ... Selected by Boston Red Sox organization in first round (23rd pick overall) of free-agent draft (June 3, 1991). ... On Boston disabled list (May 24, 1995-remainder of season); included rehabilitation assignments to Trenton (June 19-22), Sarasota (July 10-21 and August 7-16) and Pawtucket (August 16-23). ... On Boston disabled list (August 14-September 1, 1996); included rehabilitation assignment to Pawtucket (August 26-27). ... Traded by Red Sox with P Mark Brandenburg and C Bill Haselman to Texas Rangers for C Jim Leyritz and OF Damon Buford (November 6, 1997). ... Granted free agency (November 5, 1999). ... Signed by Seattle Mariners (January 10, 2000). ... Granted free agency (November 5, 2001). ... Signed by Anaheim Angels (January 4, 2002). ... On disabled list (August 21-September 29, 2002). ... On Anaheim disabled list (March 21, 2003); included rehabilitation assignment to Rancho Cucamonga. ... Recalled from Salt Lake (May 5, 2003). ... Reinstated from 15-day disabled list (May 9, 2003).

CAREER HITTING: 4-for-24 (.167), 2 R, 1 2B, 0 3B, 0 HR, 1 RBI.

Year	League	W	L	Pct.	ERA	WHIP	G	GS	CG	ShO	Hld.	Sv.-Opp.	IP	H	R	ER	HR	BB-IBB	SO	Avg.
1991—Winter Haven (FSL)	3	6	.333	4.96	1.41	13	11	4	0	...	1-...	69.0	65	42	38	2	32-2	51	.247
1992—Lynchburg (Carolina)	13	5	.722	2.91	1.18	20	19	2	1	...	0-...	127.0	104	51	41	5	46-0	112	.222
—New Britain (East.)	2	1	.667	6.27	1.76	7	6	1	0	...	0-...	33.0	43	29	23	2	15-0	29	.305
1993—Pawtucket (Int'l)	8	2	.800	2.19	1.03	14	14	2	1	...	0-...	94.1	74	30	23	8	23-0	87	.216
—Boston (A.L.)	7	2	.778	2.74	1.33	18	18	0	0	0	0-0	111.2	100	42	34	5	48-2	93	.237
1994—Boston (A.L.)	8	7	.533	3.83	1.40	22	22	2	0	0	0-0	143.1	140	68	61	13	60-2	105	.261
1995—Boston (A.L.)	3	1	.750	3.06	1.42	6	6	0	0	0	0-0	32.1	32	14	11	3	14-0	21	.252
—Trenton (East.)	0	1	.000	3.38	1.25	2	2	0	0	...	0-...	8.0	8	3	3	0	2-0	9	.286
—Sarasota (Fla. St.)	0	0	...	0.00	1.00	2	2	0	0	...	0-...	7.0	6	0	0	0	1-0	8	.231
—Pawtucket (Int'l)	0	0	...	9.00	2.20	2	2	0	0	...	0-...	5.0	9	5	5	3	2-0	1	.409
1996—Boston (A.L.)	7	11	.389	5.32	1.65	29	29	1	0	0	0-0	157.1	192	110	93	14	67-2	137	.303
—Pawtucket (Int'l)	0	0	...	6.00	1.33	1	1	0	0	...	0-...	3.0	3	2	2	0	1-0	4	.250
1997—Boston (A.L.)	13	12	.520	5.38	1.56	33	33	1	0	0	0-0	177.1	196	115	106	25	80-4	122	.279
1998—Texas (A.L.)	19	11	.633	4.23	1.42	33	33	3	2	0	0-0	212.2	239	116	100	14	84-6	167	.283
1999—Texas (A.L.)	18	9	.667	4.79	1.53	33	33	2	2	0	0-0	205.0	244	115	109	21	70-3	186	.293
2000—Seattle (A.L.)	17	10	.630	4.51	1.39	34	34	2	2	0	0-0	211.2	221	110	106	17	74-7	137	.271
2001—Seattle (A.L.)	15	5	.750	3.60	1.24	34	33	2	1	0	0-0	215.0	216	93	86	25	51-2	114	.261
2002—Anaheim (A.L.)	8	9	.471	4.89	1.49	26	26	1	1	0	0-0	160.0	190	92	87	21	49-2	82	.299
2003—Rancho Cuca. (Calif.)	0	0	...	4.50	1.88	3	2	0	0	...	0-...	8.0	12	4	4	0	3-0	7	.375
—Salt Lake (PCL)	1	2	.333	6.43	1.79	3	3	0	0	...	0-...	14.0	16	10	10	2	9-0	8	.296
—Anaheim (A.L.)	7	11	.389	5.77	1.59	25	25	0	0	0	0-0	121.2	135	82	78	17	58-1	53	.284
Major League totals (11 years)	122	88	.581	4.48	1.46	293	292	14	8	0	0-0	1748.0	1905	957	871	175	655-31	1217	.278

SEO, JAE WEONG   P

PERSONAL: Born May 24, 1977, in Kwanju, South Korea. ... 6-1/210. ... Throws right, bats right. ... Full name: Jae Weong Seo. ... Name pronounced: jay wong sew. ... High school: First (Kwanju, South Korea). ... College: Inha (South Korea).

TRANSACTIONS/CAREER NOTES: Signed as non-drafted free agent by New York Mets organization (December 17, 1997). ... On Binghamton disabled list (May 4, 1999-remainder of season). ... On disabled list (April 6, 2000-entire season).

CAREER HITTING: 5-for-51 (.098), 3 R, 1 2B, 0 HR, 0 RBI.

Year	League	W	L	Pct.	ERA	WHIP	G	GS	CG	ShO	Hld.	Sv.-Opp.	IP	H	R	ER	HR	BB-IBB	SO	Avg.
1998—St. Lucie (Fla. St.)		3	1	.750	2.27	1.01	8	7	0	0	...	0-...	35.2	26	13	9	2	10-0	37	.206
—GC Mets (GCL)		0	0	...	0.00	0.80	2	0	0	0	...	0-...	5.0	4	0	0	0	0-0	0	.235
1999—St. Lucie (Fla. St.)		2	0	1.000	1.84	0.68	3	3	0	0	...	0-...	14.2	8	3	3	0	2-0	14	.154
2000—St. Lucie (Fla. St.)												Did not play.								
2001—St. Lucie (Fla. St.)		2	3	.400	3.55	1.07	6	5	0	0	...	0-...	25.1	21	11	10	2	6-0	19	.221
—Binghamton (Eastern)		5	1	.833	1.94	0.91	12	10	0	0	...	0-...	60.1	44	14	13	3	11-1	47	.206
—Norfolk (Int'l)		2	2	.500	3.42	1.25	9	9	0	0	...	0-...	47.1	53	18	18	4	6-1	25	.296
2002—Binghamton (Eastern)		0	0	...	5.40	1.20	1	0	0	0	...	0-...	5.0	5	3	3	1	1-0	6	.250
—Norfolk (Int'l)		6	9	.400	3.99	1.30	26	24	1	0	...	0-...	128.2	145	66	57	14	22-1	87	.284
—New York (N.L.)		0	0	...	0.00	0.00	1	0	0	0	0	0-0	1.0	0	0	0	0	0-0	1	.000
2003—New York (N.L.)		9	12	.429	3.82	1.27	32	31	0	0	0	0-0	188.1	193	94	80	18	46-11	110	.260
Major League totals (2 years)		**9**	**12**	**.429**	**3.80**	**1.26**	**33**	**31**	**0**	**0**	**0**	**0-0**	**189.1**	**193**	**94**	**80**	**18**	**46-11**	**111**	**.259**

SERAFINI, DAN   P

PERSONAL: Born January 25, 1974, in San Francisco, Calif. ... 6-1/195. ... Throws left, bats both. ... Full name: Daniel Joseph Serafini. ... Name pronounced: sair-uh-FEE-nee. ... High school: Serra (San Mateo, Calif.). ... College: Stanford.

TRANSACTIONS/CAREER NOTES: Selected by Minnesota Twins organization in first round (26th pick overall) of free-agent draft (June 1, 1992). ... On Salt Lake disabled list (May 11-31, 1996). ... Traded by Twins to Chicago Cubs for cash (March 31, 1999). ... Traded by Cubs to San Diego Padres for OF Brandon Pernell (December 22, 1999). ... Traded by Padres to Pittsburgh Pirates for a player to be named later (June 28, 2000). ... Released by Pirates (March 20, 2001). ... Signed by San Francisco Giants organization (April 4, 2001). ... Released by Giants (2001). ... Signed by New York Mets organization (May 8, 2001). ... Released by Mets (2001). ... Signed by Milwaukee Brewers organization (August 7, 2001). ... Released by Brewers (2001). ... Signed by Anaheim Angels organization (November 3, 2001). ... Granted free agency (October 15, 2001). ... Signed by St. Louis Cardinals organization (December 3, 2002). ... Released by Cardinals (2003). ... Signed to minor league contract by Cincinnati (August 25, 2003). ... Elected free agency (October 9, 2003).

CAREER HITTING: 3-for-43 (.070), 2 R, 0 2B, 0 3B, 0 HR, 2 RBI.

Year	League	W	L	Pct.	ERA	WHIP	G	GS	CG	ShO	Hld.	Sv.-Opp.	IP	H	R	ER	HR	BB-IBB	SO	Avg.
1992—GC Twins (GCL)		1	0	1.000	3.64	1.42	8	6	0	0	...	0-...	29.2	27	16	12	0	15-0	33	.241
1993—Fort Wayne (Midw.)		10	8	.556	3.65	1.42	27	27	1	1	...	0-...	140.2	117	72	57	5	83-0	147	.228
1994—Fort Myers (Fla. St.)		9	9	.500	4.61	1.51	23	23	2	1	...	0-...	136.2	149	84	70	11	57-1	130	.284
1995—New Britain (East.)		12	9	.571	3.38	1.40	27	27	1	1	...	0-...	162.2	155	74	61	7	72-0	123	.258
—Salt Lake (PCL)		0	0	...	6.75	1.25	1	0	0	0	...	1-...	4.0	4	3	3	2	1-0	4	.250
1996—Salt Lake (PCL)		7	7	.500	5.58	1.70	25	23	1	0	...	0-...	130.2	164	84	81	20	58-1	109	.317
—Minnesota (A.L.)		0	1	.000	10.38	2.08	1	1	0	0	0	0-0	4.1	7	5	5	1	2-0	1	.368
1997—Salt Lake (PCL)		9	7	.563	4.97	1.45	28	24	2	0	...	0-...	152.0	166	87	84	18	55-0	118	.282
—Minnesota (A.L.)		2	1	.667	3.42	1.44	6	4	1	0	0	0-0	26.1	27	11	10	1	11-0	15	.273
1998—Salt Lake (PCL)		2	4	.333	3.71	1.44	9	8	0	0	...	0-...	53.1	56	29	22	4	21-0	39	.268
—Minnesota (A.L.)		7	4	.636	6.48	1.65	28	9	0	0	2	0-0	75.0	95	58	54	10	29-1	46	.310
1999—Chicago (N.L.)		3	2	.600	6.93	1.89	42	4	0	0	5	1-1	62.1	86	51	48	9	32-3	17	.333
—Iowa (PCL)		0	0	...	2.77	1.31	2	2	0	0	...	0-...	13.0	12	6	4	1	5-0	11	.240
2000—San Diego (N.L.)		0	0	...	18.00	3.67	3	0	0	0	0	0-0	3.0	9	6	6	2	2-0	3	.500
—Las Vegas (PCL)		2	4	.333	6.88	1.90	26	4	0	0	...	0-...	51.0	74	44	39	6	23-1	45	.338
—Nashville (PCL)		4	3	.571	2.68	1.21	7	7	0	0	...	0-...	47.0	39	17	14	4	18-1	22	.228
—Pittsburgh (N.L.)		2	5	.286	4.91	1.54	11	11	0	0	0	0-0	62.1	70	35	34	9	26-1	32	.292
2001—Fresno (PCL)		1	1	.500	10.32	2.29	7	0	0	0	...	0-...	11.1	17	14	13	2	9-1	9	.370
—Norfolk (Int'l)		5	2	.714	3.31	1.31	31	2	0	0	...	1-...	49.0	48	18	18	3	16-3	38	.257
—Indianapolis (Int'l)		2	2	.500	5.96	1.41	9	4	0	0	...	0-...	22.2	30	17	15	2	2-0	18	.309
2002—												Did not play.								
2003—Memphis (PCL)		0	1	.000	9.00	2.63	3	2	0	0	...	0-...	8.0	19	9	8	0	2-0	2	.475
—Cincinnati (N.L.)		1	3	.250	5.40	1.83	10	4	0	0	0	0-0	30.0	41	23	18	5	14-1	13	.336
American League totals (3 years)		**9**	**6**	**.600**	**5.88**	**1.62**	**35**	**14**	**1**	**0**	**2**	**0-0**	**105.2**	**129**	**74**	**69**	**12**	**42-1**	**62**	**.304**
National League totals (3 years)		**6**	**10**	**.375**	**6.05**	**1.78**	**66**	**19**	**0**	**0**	**5**	**1-1**	**157.2**	**206**	**115**	**106**	**25**	**74-5**	**65**	**.323**
Major League totals (6 years)		**15**	**16**	**.484**	**5.98**	**1.71**	**101**	**33**	**1**	**0**	**7**	**1-1**	**263.1**	**335**	**189**	**175**	**37**	**116-6**	**127**	**.315**

SERVICE, SCOTT   P

PERSONAL: Born February 26, 1967, in Cincinnati, Ohio. ... 6-6/240. ... Throws right, bats right. ... Full name: Scott David Service. ... High school: Aiken (Cincinnati).

TRANSACTIONS/CAREER NOTES: Signed as non-drafted free agent by Philadelphia Phillies organization (August 24, 1985). ... Granted free agency (October 11, 1990). ... Signed by Montreal Expos organization (November 15, 1990). ... Contract sold by Expos to Chunichi Dragons of Japan Central League (August 1991). ... Re-signed by Expos organization (January 10, 1992). ... Granted free agency (June 8, 1992). ... Signed by Cincinnati Reds organization (June 9, 1992). ... On Indianapolis disabled list (May 15-22, 1993). ... Claimed on waivers by Colorado Rockies (June 28, 1993). ... Claimed on waivers by Reds (July 7, 1993). ... On Indianapolis disabled list (April 17-24, 1994). ... Released by Reds (November 17, 1994). ... Re-signed by Reds organization (February 24, 1995). ... Traded by Reds with OF Deion Sanders, P John Roper, P Ricky Pickett and IF Dave McCarty to San Francisco Giants for OF Darren Lewis, P Mark Portugal and P Dave Burba (July 21, 1995). ... Signed by Reds organization (April 2, 1996). ... Claimed on waivers by Oakland Athletics (March 27, 1997). ... Claimed on waivers by Reds (April 4, 1997). ... Traded by Reds with P Hector Carrasco to Kansas City Royals for OF Jon Nunnally and IF/OF Chris Stynes (July 15, 1997). ... On suspended list (June 15-16, 1998). ... Released by Royals (December 17, 1999). ... Signed by Oakland Athletics (December 30, 1999). ... Granted free agency (October 18, 2000). ... Signed by Cincinnati Reds organization (June 23, 2001). ... On Louisville disabled list (August 28, 2001-remainder of season). ... Granted free agency (October 15, 2001). ... Signed by Pittsburgh Pirates organization (January 16, 2002). ... Granted free agency (October 15, 2002). ... Signed by Arizona Diamondbacks organization (February 12, 2003). ... Claimed off waivers by Toronto (June 16, 2003). ... Given unconditional release (August 10, 2003). ... Signed by Cincinnati Reds organization (August 26, 2003).

CAREER HITTING: 1-for-16 (.063), 0 R, 0 2B, 0 3B, 0 HR, 1 RBI.

Year	League	W	L	Pct.	ERA	WHIP	G	GS	CG	ShO	Hld.	Sv.-Opp.	IP	H	R	ER	HR	BB-IBB	SO	Avg.
1986—	Spartanburg (SAL)	1	6	.143	5.83	1.74	14	9	1	0	...	0-...	58.2	68	44	38	3	34-0	49	.287
—	Utica (N.Y.-Penn)	5	4	.556	2.67	1.17	10	10	2	0	...	0-...	70.2	65	30	21	1	18-0	43	.240
—	Clearwater (Fla. St.)	1	2	.333	3.20	1.38	4	4	1	1	...	0-...	25.1	20	10	9	2	15-0	19	.225
1987—	Reading (East.)	0	3	.000	7.78	1.93	5	4	0	0	...	0-...	19.2	22	19	17	5	16-1	12	.278
—	Clearwater (Fla. St.)	13	4	.765	2.48	1.15	21	21	5	2	...	0-...	137.2	127	46	38	8	32-0	73	.247
1988—	Reading (East.)	3	4	.429	2.86	1.31	10	9	1	1	...	0-...	56.2	52	25	18	4	22-2	39	.241
—	Maine (Int'l)	8	8	.500	3.67	1.27	19	18	1	0	...	0-...	110.1	109	51	45	10	31-3	87	.256
—	Philadelphia (N.L.)	0	0	...	1.69	1.50	5	0	0	0	0	0-0	5.1	7	1	1	0	1-0	6	.333
1989—	Scran./W.B. (I.L.)	3	1	.750	2.16	1.50	23	0	0	0	...	6-...	33.1	27	8	8	2	23-6	23	.227
—	Reading (East.)	6	6	.500	3.26	1.10	23	10	1	1	...	1-...	85.2	71	36	31	8	23-0	82	.226
1990—	Scran./W.B. (I.L.)	5	4	.556	4.76	1.45	45	9	0	0	...	2-...	96.1	96	56	51	10	44-1	94	.258
1991—	Indianapolis (A.A.)	6	7	.462	2.97	1.01	18	17	3	1	...	0-...	121.1	83	42	40	7	39-0	91	.194
—	Chunichi (Jp. Cn.)	0	0	...	9.00	0.00	1	...	...	...	...	0-...	1.0	...	1	1	0	0-...	0	...
1992—	Indianapolis (A.A.)	2	0	1.000	0.74	0.86	13	0	0	0	...	2-...	24.1	12	3	2	0	9-0	25	.148
—	Montreal (N.L.)	0	0	...	14.14	2.86	5	0	0	0	1	0-0	7.0	15	11	11	1	5-0	11	.417
—	Nashville (A.A.)	6	2	.750	2.29	1.26	39	2	0	0	...	4-...	70.2	54	22	18	2	35-3	87	.209
1993—	Indianapolis (A.A.)	4	2	.667	4.45	1.38	21	1	0	0	...	2-...	30.1	25	16	15	5	17-3	28	.223
—	Colorado (N.L.)	0	0	...	9.64	1.93	3	0	0	0	0	0-0	4.2	8	5	5	1	1-0	3	.400
—	Cincinnati (N.L.)	2	2	.500	3.70	1.23	26	0	0	0	3	2-2	41.1	36	19	17	5	15-4	40	.235
1994—	Indianapolis (A.A.)	5	5	.500	2.31	1.06	40	0	0	0	...	13-...	58.1	35	16	15	1	27-9	67	.172
—	Cincinnati (N.L.)	1	2	.333	7.36	1.50	6	0	0	0	0	0-0	7.1	8	9	6	2	3-0	5	.267
1995—	Indianapolis (A.A.)	4	1	.800	2.18	1.16	36	0	0	0	...	18-...	41.1	33	13	10	4	15-2	48	.214
—	San Francisco (N.L.)	3	1	.750	3.19	1.23	28	0	0	0	7	0-0	31.0	18	11	11	4	20-4	30	.176
1996—	Indianapolis (A.A.)	1	4	.200	3.00	0.92	35	1	0	0	...	15-...	48.0	34	18	16	5	10-2	58	.190
—	Cincinnati (N.L.)	1	0	1.000	3.94	1.44	34	1	0	0	3	0-0	48.0	51	21	21	7	18-4	46	.277
1997—	Cincinnati (N.L.)	0	0	...	11.81	2.25	4	0	0	0	1	0-0	5.1	11	7	7	1	1-0	3	.458
—	Indianapolis (A.A.)	3	2	.600	3.71	1.24	33	0	0	0	...	15-...	34.0	30	15	14	5	12-1	53	.231
—	Omaha (Am. Assoc.)	0	0	...	0.00	0.89	16	0	0	0	...	† 9-...	14.2	9	0	0	0	4-0	16	.170
—	Kansas City (A.L.)	0	3	.000	4.76	1.29	12	0	0	0	2	0-1	17.0	17	9	9	1	5-0	19	.274
1998—	Kansas City (A.L.)	6	4	.600	3.48	1.26	73	0	0	0	18	4-8	82.2	70	35	32	7	34-4	95	.231
1999—	Kansas City (A.L.)	5	5	.500	6.09	1.71	68	0	0	0	8	8-15	75.1	87	51	51	13	42-8	68	.294
2000—	Oakland (A.L.)	1	2	.333	6.38	1.75	20	0	0	0	1	1-1	36.2	45	31	26	5	19-1	35	.302
—	Sacramento (PCL)	6	2	.750	1.30	0.91	33	0	0	0	...	13-...	41.2	27	8	6	1	11-4	50	.175
2001—	Dayton (Midw.)	0	0	...	0.00	0.35	4	0	0	0	...	2-...	5.2	2	0	0	0	0-0	6	.095
—	Louisville (Int'l)	2	0	1.000	4.74	1.30	20	0	0	0	...	5-...	24.2	22	13	13	6	10-1	27	.242
2002—	Nashville (PCL)	4	4	.500	3.36	1.15	47	0	0	0	...	6-...	61.2	47	25	23	8	24-3	70	.209
2003—	Tucson (PCL)	0	0	...	0.00	0.65	9	0	0	0	...	3-...	12.1	6	2	0	0	2-0	13	.133
—	Arizona (N.L.)	0	2	.000	4.91	1.25	18	0	0	0	0	1-1	18.1	21	10	10	1	2-1	18	.288
—	Toronto (A.L.)	0	0	...	4.50	1.44	15	0	0	0	3	0-1	16.0	17	8	8	3	6-0	17	.274
—	Louisville (Int'l)	0	0	...	2.45	0.82	4	0	0	0	...	0-...	3.2	3	1	1	0	0-0	7	.214
	American League totals (5 years)	12	14	.462	4.98	1.50	188	0	0	0	32	13-26	227.2	236	134	126	29	106-13	234	.271
	National League totals (8 years)	7	7	.500	4.76	1.43	129	1	0	0	15	3-3	168.1	175	94	89	22	66-13	162	.272
	Major League totals (11 years)	19	21	.475	4.89	1.47	317	1	0	0	47	16-29	396.0	411	228	215	51	172-26	396	.271

SEXSON, RICHIE — 1B

PERSONAL: Born December 29, 1974, in Portland, Ore. ... 6-8/236. ... Bats right, throws right. ... Full name: Richmond Lockwood Sexson. ... Name pronounced: SECKS-un. ... High school: Prairie (Brush Prairie, Wash.).

TRANSACTIONS/CAREER NOTES: Selected by Cleveland Indians organization in 24th round of free-agent draft (June 2, 1993). ... Traded by Indians with P Paul Rigdon, P Kane Davis and a player to be named later to Milwaukee Brewers for P Bob Wickman, P Steve Woodard and P Jason Bere (July 28, 2000); Brewers acquired 2B Marcos Scutaro to complete deal (August 30).

2003 GAMES PLAYED BY POSITION (MLB): 1B—162.

Year	Team (League)	Pos.	G	AB	R	H	2B	3B	HR	RBI	BB	SO	HBP	GDP	SB-CS	Avg.	OBP	SLG	OPS	E	Pct.
1993—	Burlington (Appal.)	1B	40	97	11	18	3	0	1	5	18	21	1	1	1-1	.186	.213	.247	.564	4	.988
1994—	Columbus (S. Atl.)	1B	130	488	88	133	25	2	14	77	37	87	14	5	7-3	.273	.338	.418	.756	10	.990
1995—	Kinston (Caro.)	1B	131	494	80	* 151	* 34	0	22	* 85	43	115	10	8	4-6	.306	.368	.508	.876	12	.990
1996—	Cant./Akr. (Eastern)	1B	133	518	85	143	33	3	16	76	39	118	6	13	2-1	.276	.331	.444	.775	11	.989
1997—	Buffalo (A.A.)	1B-DH	115	434	57	113	20	2	* 31	88	27	87	4	11	5-1	.260	.307	.530	.837	4	.996
—	Cleveland (A.L.)	1B-DH	5	11	1	3	0	0	0	0	0	2	0	2	0-0	.273	.273	.273	.545	0	1.000
1998—	Buffalo (Int'l) OF-1B-DH		89	344	58	102	20	1	21	74	25	50	3	11	1-2	.297	.386	.544	.929	3	.990
—	Cleveland (A.L.) 1B-OF-DH		49	174	28	54	14	1	11	35	6	42	3	3	1-1	.310	.344	.592	.936	6	.984
1999—	Cleveland (A.L.)	OF-1B-DH	134	479	72	122	17	7	31	116	34	117	4	19	3-3	.255	.305	.514	.818	7	.989
2000—	Cleveland (A.L.)	OF-1B-DH	91	324	45	83	16	1	16	44	25	96	4	8	1-0	.256	.315	.460	.774	1	.997
—	Milwaukee (N.L.)	1B	57	213	44	63	14	0	14	47	34	63	3	3	1-0	.296	.398	.559	.957	5	.991
2001—	Milwaukee (N.L.)	1B	158	598	94	162	24	3	45	125	60	178	6	20	2-4	.271	.342	.547	.889	8	.995
2002—	Milwaukee (N.L.)	1B-DH	157	570	86	159	37	2	29	102	70	136	8	17	0-0	.279	.363	.504	.867	7	.995
2003—	Milwaukee (N.L.)	1B	•162	606	97	165	28	2	45	124	98	151	9	18	2-3	.272	.379	.548	.927	11	.993
	American League totals (4 years)		279	988	146	262	47	9	58	195	65	257	11	32	5-4	.265	.314	.507	.822	14	.989
	National League totals (4 years)		534	1987	321	549	103	7	133	398	262	528	26	58	5-7	.276	.366	.536	.902	31	.994
	Major League totals (7 years)		813	2975	467	811	150	16	191	593	327	785	37	90	10-11	.273	.349	.526	.876	45	.993

SHEETS, BEN — P

PERSONAL: Born July 18, 1978, in Baton Rouge, La. ... 6-1/200. ... Throws right, bats right. ... Full name: Ben M. Sheets. ... High school: St. Amant (La.). ... College: Northeast Louisiana.

TRANSACTIONS/CAREER NOTES: Selected by Milwaukee Brewers organization in first round (10th pick overall) of free-agent draft (June 2, 1999). ... On Milwaukee disabled list (August 6-September 21, 2001).

CAREER HITTING: 14-for-176 (.080), 6 R, 1 2B, 0 3B, 0 HR, 6 RBI.

S

Year League	W	L	Pct.	ERA	WHIP	G	GS	CG	ShO	Hld.	Sv.-Opp.	IP	H	R	ER	HR	BB-IBB	SO	Avg.
1999— Ogden (Pio.)	0	1	.000	5.63	1.25	2	2	0	0	...	0-...	8.0	8	5	5	2	2-0	12	.267
— Stockton (Calif.)	1	0	1.000	3.58	1.34	5	5	0	0	...	0-...	27.2	23	11	11	1	14-0	28	.232
2000— Huntsville (Sou.)	5	3	.625	1.88	1.11	13	13	0	0	...	0-...	72.0	55	17	15	4	25-0	60	.215
— Indianapolis (Int'l)	3	5	.375	2.87	1.32	14	13	1	0	...	0-...	81.2	77	31	26	4	31-0	59	.251
2001— Milwaukee (N.L.)	11	10	.524	4.76	1.41	25	25	1	1	0	0-0	151.1	166	89	80	23	48-6	94	.283
— Indianapolis (Int'l)	1	1	.500	3.38	1.59	2	2	0	0	...	0-...	10.2	14	5	4	0	3-0	6	.318
2002— Milwaukee (N.L.)	11	•16	.407	4.15	1.42	34	34	1	0	0	0-0	216.2	237	105	100	21	70-10	170	.281
2003— Milwaukee (N.L.)	11	13	.458	4.45	1.25	34	34	1	0	0	0-0	220.2	232	122	109	29	43-2	157	.268
Major League totals (3 years)	33	39	.458	4.42	1.35	93	93	3	1	0	0-0	588.2	635	316	289	73	161-18	421	.277

SHEFFIELD, GARY   OF

PERSONAL: Born November 18, 1968, in Tampa, Fla. ... 6-0/205. ... Bats right, throws right. ... Full name: Gary Antonian Sheffield. ... High school: Hillsborough (Tampa).

TRANSACTIONS/CAREER NOTES: Selected by Milwaukee Brewers organization in first round (sixth pick overall) of free-agent draft (June 2, 1986). ... On Milwaukee disabled list (July 14-September 9, 1989). ... On suspended list (August 31-September 3, 1990). ... On disabled list (June 15-July 3 and July 25, 1991-remainder of season). ... Traded by Brewers with P Geoff Kellogg to San Diego Padres for P Ricky Bones, SS Jose Valentin and OF Matt Mieske (March 27, 1992). ... Traded by Padres with P Rich Rodriguez to Florida Marlins for P Trevor Hoffman, P Jose Martinez and P Andres Berumen (June 24, 1993). ... On Florida suspended list (July 9-12, 1993). ... On Florida disabled list (May 10-25 and May 28-June 12, 1994); included rehabilitation assignment to Portland (June 10-12). ... On disabled list (June 11-September 1, 1995; and May 14-29, 1997). ... Traded by Marlins with 3B Bobby Bonilla, C Charles Johnson, OF Jim Eisenreich and P Manuel Barrios to Los Angeles Dodgers for C Mike Piazza and 3B Todd Zeile (May 15, 1998). ... On suspended list (August 4-6, 1998). ... On suspended list (August 23-27, 2000). ... On disabled list (May 24-June 8, 2001). ... Traded by Dodgers to Atlanta Braves for OF Brian Jordan, P Odalis Perez and P Andrew Brown (January 15, 2002).

2003 GAMES PLAYED BY POSITION (MLB): OF—153.

Year Team (League)	Pos.	G	AB	R	H	2B	3B	HR	RBI	BB	SO	HBP	GDP	SB-CS	Avg.	OBP	SLG	OPS	E	Pct.
1986— Helena (Pio.)	SS	57	222	53	81	12	2	15	* 71	20	14	3	3	14-4	.365	.413	.640	1.052	24	.911
1987— Stockton (Calif.)	SS	129	469	84	130	23	3	17	* 103	81	49	8	7	25-15	.277	.388	.448	.836	39	.937
1988— El Paso (Texas)	3B-SS-OF	77	296	70	93	19	3	19	65	35	41	3	9	5-4	.314	.386	.591	.978	23	.936
— Denver (A.A.)	3B-SS	57	212	42	73	9	5	9	54	21	22	5	3	8-4	.344	.407	.561	.969	8	.950
— Milwaukee (A.L.)	SS	24	80	12	19	1	0	4	12	7	7	0	5	3-1	.238	.295	.400	.695	3	.967
1989— Milwaukee (A.L.)	3B-SS-DH	95	368	34	91	18	0	5	32	27	33	4	4	10-6	.247	.303	.337	.640	16	.955
— Denver (A.A.)	SS	7	29	3	4	1	1	0	0	2	0	0	1	0-0	.138	.194	.241	.435	0	1.000
1990— Milwaukee (A.L.)	3B	125	487	67	143	30	1	10	67	44	41	3	11	25-10	.294	.350	.421	.771	25	.934
1991— Milwaukee (A.L.)	3B-DH	50	175	25	34	12	2	2	22	19	15	3	3	5-5	.194	.277	.320	.597	8	.922
1992— San Diego (N.L.)	3B	146	557	87	184	34	3	33	100	48	40	6	19	5-6	*.330	.385	.580	.965	16	.961
1993— San Diego (N.L.)	3B	68	258	34	76	12	2	10	36	18	30	3	9	5-1	.295	.344	.473	.817	15	.905
— Florida (N.L.)	3B	72	236	33	69	8	3	10	37	29	34	6	2	12-4	.292	.378	.479	.857	19	.894
1994— Florida (N.L.)	OF	87	322	61	89	16	1	27	78	51	50	6	10	12-6	.276	.380	.584	.964	5	.970
— Portland (East.)	OF	2	7	1	2	1	0	0	0	1	3	0	0	0-0	.286	.375	.429	.804	0	1.000
1995— Florida (N.L.)	OF	63	213	46	69	8	0	16	46	55	45	4	3	19-4	.324	.467	.587	1.054	7	.942
1996— Florida (N.L.)	OF	161	519	118	163	33	1	42	120	142	66	10	16	16-9	.314	* .465	.624	1.090	6	.976
1997— Florida (N.L.)	OF-DH	135	444	86	111	22	1	21	71	121	79	15	7	11-7	.250	.424	.446	.870	5	.980
1998— Florida (N.L.)	OF	40	136	21	37	11	1	6	28	26	16	2	3	4-2	.272	.392	.500	.892	1	.986
— Los Angeles (N.L.)	OF	90	301	52	95	16	1	16	57	69	30	6	4	18-5	.316	.444	.535	.979	1	.994
1999— Los Angeles (N.L.)	OF-DH	152	549	103	165	20	0	34	101	101	64	4	10	11-5	.301	.407	.523	.930	7	.972
2000— Los Angeles (N.L.)	OF-DH	141	501	105	163	24	3	43	109	101	71	4	13	4-6	.325	.438	.643	1.081	• 10	.954
2001— Los Angeles (N.L.)	OF-DH	143	515	98	160	28	2	36	100	94	67	4	12	10-4	.311	.417	.583	1.000	6	.972
2002— Atlanta (N.L.)	OF-DH	135	492	82	151	26	0	25	84	72	53	11	16	12-2	.307	.404	.512	.916	4	.984
2003— Atlanta (N.L.)	OF	155	576	126	190	37	2	39	132	86	55	8	16	18-4	.330	.419	.604	1.023	4	.986
American League totals (4 years)		294	1110	138	287	61	3	21	133	97	96	10	23	43-22	.259	.319	.376	.695	52	.944
National League totals (12 years)		1588	5619	1052	1722	295	20	358	1099	1013	700	89	140	157-65	.306	.416	.557	.973	106	.965
Major League totals (16 years)		1882	6729	1190	2009	356	23	379	1232	1110	796	99	163	200-87	.299	.401	.527	.928	158	.960

SHIELDS, SCOT   P

PERSONAL: Born July 22, 1975, in Fort Lauderdale, Fla. ... 6-1/170. ... Throws right, bats right. ... Full name: Robert Scot Shields. ... High school: Fort Lauderdale (Fla.). ... College: Lincoln Memorial (Tenn.).

TRANSACTIONS/CAREER NOTES: Selected by Anaheim Angels organization in 38th round of free-agent draft (June 3, 1997).

CAREER HITTING: 0-for-0 (.000), 0 R, 0 2B, 0 3B, 0 HR, 0 RBI.

Year League	W	L	Pct.	ERA	WHIP	G	GS	CG	ShO	Hld.	Sv.-Opp.	IP	H	R	ER	HR	BB-IBB	SO	Avg.
1997— Boise (NW)	7	2	.778	2.94	1.33	30	0	0	0	...	2-...	52.0	45	20	17	1	24-4	61	.233
1998— Cedar Rapids (Midw.)	6	5	.545	3.65	1.23	58	0	0	0	...	7-...	74.0	62	33	30	5	29-0	81	.232
1999— Lake Elsinore (Calif.)	10	3	.769	2.52	1.21	24	9	2	1	...	1-...	107.1	91	37	30	1	39-4	113	.233
— Erie (East.)	4	4	.500	2.89	1.11	10	10	1	1	...	0-...	74.2	57	26	24	10	26-0	81	.216
2000— Edmonton (PCL)	7	• 13	.350	5.41	1.47	27	27	4	1	...	0-...	163.0	158	114	98	16	82-0	* 156	.250
2001— Salt Lake (PCL)	6	11	.353	4.97	1.25	21	21	4	0	...	0-...	137.2	141	84	76	24	31-0	104	.267
— Anaheim (A.L.)	0	0	...	0.00	1.36	8	0	0	0	0	0-0	11.0	8	1	0	0	7-0	7	.200
2002— Salt Lake (PCL)	2	2	.500	3.06	0.96	28	1	0	0	...	1-...	47.0	39	18	16	5	6-0	50	.223
— Anaheim (A.L.)	5	3	.625	2.20	1.06	29	1	0	0	3	0-0	49.0	31	13	12	4	21-1	30	.188
2003— Anaheim (A.L.)	5	6	.455	2.85	1.19	44	13	0	0	3	1-1	148.1	138	56	47	12	38-6	111	.247
Major League totals (3 years)	10	9	.526	2.55	1.17	81	14	0	0	6	1-1	208.1	177	70	59	16	66-7	148	.232

SHIELL, JASON   P

PERSONAL: Born October 19, 1976, in Savannah, Ga. ... 6-0/180. ... Throws right, bats right. ... Full name: Jason Alexander Shiell. ... High school: Windsor-Forest (Savannah, Ga.).

TRANSACTIONS/CAREER NOTES: Selected by Atlanta Braves organization in 48th round of free-agent draft (June 1, 1995). ... On Myrtle Beach disabled list (September 3-20, 1999). ... Traded by Braves with OF/1B Ryan Klesko and 2B Bret Boone to San Diego Padres for 2B Quilvio Veras, 1B Wally Joyner and OF Reggie Sanders (December 22, 1999). ... On Rancho Cucamonga disabled list (July 8-September 13, 2000). ... Claimed on waivers by Boston Red Sox (October 2, 2002). ... Optioned to Pawtucket (May 20, 2003). ... Recalled from Pawtucket (June 11, 2003). ... Optioned to Pawtucket (July 17, 2003). ... Recalled from Pawtucket (July 30, 2003). ... Optioned to Pawtucket (August 1, 2003). ... Recalled from Pawtucket (September 19, 2003).

CAREER HITTING: 0-for-0 (.000), 0 R, 0 2B, 0 3B, 0 HR, 0 RBI.

Year— League	W	L	Pct.	ERA	WHIP	G	GS	CG	ShO	Hld.	Sv.-Opp.	IP	H	R	ER	HR	BB-IBB	SO	Avg.
1995— GC Braves (GCL)	1	3	.250	4.43	1.48	12	0	0	0	...	2-...	22.1	23	16	11	0	10-1	13	.258
1996— Danville (Appal.)	3	1	.750	1.97	1.06	12	12	0	0	...	0-...	59.1	44	14	13	1	19-0	57	.210
1997— Macon (S. Atl.)	10	5	.667	2.86	1.12	27	24	0	0	...	0-...	129.0	113	53	41	12	32-0	101	.238
1998— Macon (S. Atl.)	0	1	.000	4.50	1.00	4	3	0	0	...	0-...	8.0	7	4	4	2	1-0	8	.226
1999— Myrtle Beach (Caro.)	6	7	.462	3.77	1.34	26	17	0	0	...	0-...	114.2	118	51	48	5	36-0	90	.268
2000— Rancho Cuca. (Calif.)	7	5	.583	5.33	1.41	16	14	0	0	...	0-...	81.0	73	54	48	9	41-0	80	.239
2001— Mobile (Sou.)	2	3	.400	4.44	1.52	45	2	0	0	...	0-...	81.0	91	46	40	5	32-2	60	.295
2002— Portland (PCL)	4	3	.571	2.78	1.22	56	0	0	0	...	6-...	74.1	62	26	23	6	29-0	74	.219
— San Diego (N.L.)	0	0	...	27.00	7.50	3	0	0	0	0	0-0	1.1	7	4	4	0	3-0	1	.700
2003— Boston (A.L.)	2	0	1.000	4.63	1.71	17	0	0	0	0	1-2	23.1	23	13	12	4	17-2	23	.253
— Pawtucket (Int'l)	3	2	.600	2.42	1.23	20	0	0	0	...	2-...	26.0	26	11	7	0	6-0	22	.263
American League totals (1 year)	2	0	1.000	4.63	1.71	17	0	0	0	0	1-2	23.1	23	13	12	4	17-2	23	.253
National League totals (1 year)	0	0	...	27.00	7.50	3	0	0	0	0	0-0	1.1	7	4	4	0	3-0	1	.700
Major League totals (2 years)	2	0	1.000	5.84	2.03	20	0	0	0	0	1-2	24.2	30	17	16	4	20-2	24	.297

SHINJO, TSUYOSHI   OF

PERSONAL: Born January 28, 1972, in Fukuoka, Japan. ... 6-1/185. ... Bats right, throws right. ... Name pronounced: su-yo-she shin-joe. ... High school: Nishinihon Tandai Fuzoku (Fukuoka, Japan).

TRANSACTIONS/CAREER NOTES: Signed by Hanshin Tigers of Japan Central League (1991). ... Signed as non-drafted free agent by New York Mets (December 11, 2000). ... On New York disabled list (June 18-July 16, 2001); included rehabilitation assignment to Brooklyn (July 14-16). ... Traded by Mets with SS Desi Relaford to San Francisco Giants for P Shawn Estes (December 16, 2001). ... On San Francisco disabled list (July 26-August 13, 2002); included rehabilitation assignment to Fresno (August 9-13). ... Released by Giants (November 15, 2002). ... Signed by New York Mets (January 11, 2003).

2003 GAMES PLAYED BY POSITION (MLB): OF—54.

										BATTING								FIELDING	
Year— Team (League)	Pos.	G	AB	R	H	2B	3B	HR	RBI	BB	SO	HBP	GDP	SB-CS	Avg.	OBP	SLG	OPS	E	Pct.
1991— Hanshin (Jp. Cn.)		13	17	...	2	...	...	0	1	...	...	...	...	0-...	.118	...	...	...	...	...
1992— Hanshin (Jp. Cn.)		95	353	...	98	...	...	11	46	...	...	...	...	5-...	.278	...	...	...	...	...
1993— Hanshin (Jp. Cn.)		102	408	50	105	13	1	23	62	...	...	...	...	13-...	.257	...	.463	...	...	...
1994— Hanshin (Jp. Cn.)		122	466	...	117	...	...	17	68	...	...	...	...	7-...	.251	...	...	...	...	...
1995— Hanshin (Jp. Cn.)		87	311	...	70	...	...	7	37	...	...	...	...	6-...	.225	...	...	...	...	...
1996— Hanshin (Jp. Cn.)		113	408	97	97	...	...	19	66	...	...	...	...	2-...	.238	...	...	...	...	...
1997— Hanshin (Jp. Cn.)		136	482	...	112	...	...	20	68	...	...	...	...	8-...	.232	...	...	...	...	...
1998— Hanshin (Jp. Cn.)		132	414	...	92	...	...	6	27	...	...	...	...	1-...	.222	...	...	...	...	...
1999— Hanshin (Jp. Cn.)		123	471	53	120	21	7	14	58	...	...	...	...	8-...	.255	...	.418	...	...	...
2000— Hanshin (Jp. Cn.)		131	511	71	142	23	1	28	85	32	93	...	...	15-...	.278	...	.491	...	...	...
2001— New York (N.L.)	OF	123	400	46	107	23	1	10	56	25	70	7	8	4-5	.268	.320	.405	.725	3	.989
— Brooklyn (NY-P)	OF	2	7	0	2	0	0	0	1	1	2	0	1	0-0	.286	.375	.286	.661	0	1.000
2002— San Francisco (N.L.)	OF	118	362	42	86	15	3	9	37	24	46	6	5	5-0	.238	.294	.370	.664	6	.980
— Fresno (PCL)	OF	2	7	0	0	0	0	0	0	1	1	0	0	0-0	.000	.125	.000	.125	0	1.000
2003— New York (N.L.)	OF	62	114	10	22	3	0	1	7	6	12	1	0	0-1	.193	.238	.246	.483	3	.972
— Norfolk (Int'l)	OF-DH	36	111	12	36	5	2	3	9	9	17	1	2	0-1	.324	.377	.486	.864	1	.983
Major League totals (3 years)		303	876	98	215	41	4	20	100	55	128	14	13	9-6	.245	.299	.370	.668	12	.982

SHOUSE, BRIAN   P

PERSONAL: Born September 26, 1968, in Effingham, Ill. ... 5-11/180. ... Throws left, bats left. ... Full name: Brian Douglas Shouse. ... High school: Effingham (Ill.). ... College: Bradley.

TRANSACTIONS/CAREER NOTES: Selected by Pittsburgh Pirates organization in 13th round of free-agent draft (June 4, 1990). ... Released by Pirates (May 16, 1996). ... Signed by Baltimore Orioles organization (May 22, 1996). ... Granted free agency (October 15, 1997). ... Signed by Boston Red Sox organization (October 28, 1997). ... Contract sold by Red Sox to Kintetsu Buffaloes of Japan Pacific League (June 25, 1998). ... Signed by Arizona Diamondbacks organization (November 19, 1998). ... On Tucson disabled list (April 24-May 28 and August 11-September 7, 1999). ... On Arizona disabled list (September 18, 1999-remainder of season). ... Granted free agency (October 15, 1999). ... Signed by New York Mets organization (December 2, 1999). ... Released by Mets (April 14, 2000). ... Signed by Baltimore Orioles organization (May 13, 2000). ... Granted free agency (October 18, 2000). ... Signed by Houston Astros organization (December 22, 2000). ... Granted free agency (October 15, 2001). ... Signed by Kansas City Royals organization (December 7, 2001). ... On Kansas City disabled list (April 28-May 13, 2002). ... Released by Royals (June 27, 2002). ... Signed by Astros organization (July 22, 2002). ... Granted free agency (October 15, 2002). ... Signed by Texas Rangers organization (November 13, 2002). ... Contract purchased by Texas Rangers (April 28, 2003).

CAREER HITTING: 0-for-0 (.000), 0 R, 0 2B, 0 3B, 0 HR, 0 RBI.

Year— League	W	L	Pct.	ERA	WHIP	G	GS	CG	ShO	Hld.	Sv.-Opp.	IP	H	R	ER	HR	BB-IBB	SO	Avg.
1990— Welland (N.Y.-Penn)	4	3	.571	5.22	1.44	17	1	0	0	...	2-...	39.2	50	27	23	2	7-0	39	.309
1991— Augusta (S. Atl.)	2	3	.400	3.19	1.00	26	0	0	0	...	8-...	31.0	22	13	11	1	9-1	32	.200
— Salem (Caro.)	2	1	.667	2.94	1.49	17	0	0	0	...	3-...	33.2	35	12	11	2	15-2	25	.269
1992— Carolina (Sou.)	5	6	.455	2.44	1.28	59	0	0	0	...	4-...	77.1	71	31	21	3	28-4	79	.252
1993— Buffalo (A.A.)	1	0	1.000	3.83	1.37	48	0	0	0	...	2-...	51.2	54	24	22	7	17-2	25	.276
— Pittsburgh (N.L.)	0	0	...	9.00	2.25	6	0	0	0	0	0-0	4.0	7	4	4	1	2-0	3	.368
1994— Buffalo (A.A.)	3	4	.429	3.63	1.13	43	0	0	0	...	0-...	52.0	44	22	21	6	15-4	31	.232
1995— Carolina (Sou.)	7	6	.538	4.47	1.26	21	20	0	0	...	0-...	114.2	126	64	57	14	19-2	76	.281
— Calgary (PCL)	4	4	.500	6.18	1.75	8	8	1	0	...	0-...	39.1	62	35	27	2	7-0	17	.354
1996— Calgary (PCL)	1	0	1.000	10.66	2.05	12	1	0	0	...	0-...	12.2	22	15	15	4	4-1	12	.367
— Rochester (Int'l)	1	2	.333	4.50	1.38	32	0	0	0	...	2-...	50.0	53	27	25	6	16-1	45	.270
1997— Rochester (Int'l)	6	2	.750	2.27	0.97	54	0	0	0	...	9-...	71.1	48	21	18	6	21-4	81	.191
1998— Pawtucket (Int'l)	2	0	1.000	2.90	0.90	22	1	0	0	...	6-...	31.0	21	11	10	7	7-0	25	.188
— Boston (A.L.)	0	1	.000	5.63	1.63	7	0	0	0	1	0-0	8.0	9	5	5	2	4-0	5	.281
— Kintetsu (Jap. Pac.)	2	0	.000	6.58	2.04	13	3	0	0	...	0-...	26.0	40	20	19	...	13-...	20	...
— Kintetsu (Jp. West.)	1	0	1.000	1.38	1.23	5	2	0	0	...	0-...	13.0	9	2	2	0	7-...	9	...
1999— Tucson (PCL)	3	4	.429	6.25	1.81	30	0	0	0	...	0-...	44.2	63	35	31	4	18-3	32	.339
— Norfolk (Int'l)	0	1	.000	15.00	2.67	4	0	0	0	...	0-...	3.0	6	5	5	2	2-0	1	.429
— Rochester (Int'l)	4	4	.500	2.79	1.33	43	0	0	0	...	2-...	58.0	63	20	18	4	14-1	52	.279
2001— New Orleans (PCL)	2	2	.500	2.89	1.25	56	1	0	0	...	1-...	53.0	51	21	17	4	15-0	56	.249
2002— Kansas City (A.L.)	0	0	...	6.14	1.64	23	0	0	0	2	0-0	14.2	15	10	10	3	9-1	11	.259
— Omaha (PCL)	0	0	...	11.57	3.43	5	0	0	0	...	0-...	2.1	7	3	3	0	1-0	2	.538
— New Orleans (PCL)	1	0	1.000	3.43	0.95	19	0	0	0	...	0-...	21.0	17	10	8	2	3-0	20	.215
2003— Oklahoma (PCL)	0	1	.000	3.68	1.50	6	0	0	0	...	1-...	7.1	8	3	3	0	3-0	2	.286
— Texas (A.L.)	0	1	.000	3.10	1.25	62	0	0	0	10	1-1	61.0	62	24	21	1	14-6	40	.267
American League totals (3 years)	0	2	.000	3.87	1.35	92	0	0	0	13	1-1	83.2	86	39	36	6	27-7	56	.267
National League totals (1 year)	0	0	...	9.00	2.25	6	0	0	0	0	0-0	4.0	7	4	4	1	2-0	3	.368
Major League totals (4 years)	0	2	.000	4.11	1.39	98	0	0	0	13	1-1	87.2	93	43	40	7	29-7	59	.273

PERSONAL: Born September 16, 1970, in Lima, Ohio. ... 6-3/215. ... Throws right, bats right. ... Full name: Paul Kenneth Shuey. ... Name pronounced: SHOE-ee. ... High school: Millbrook (Raleigh, N.C.). ... College: North Carolina.

TRANSACTIONS/CAREER NOTES: Selected by Cleveland Indians organization in first round (second pick overall) of free-agent draft (June 1, 1992). ... On Cleveland disabled list (June 27-July 21, 1994); included rehabilitation assignment to Charlotte (July 5-21). ... On Cleveland disabled list (May 4-22, 1995). ... On Buffalo disabled list (June 2-July 10, 1995). ... On Cleveland disabled list (April 25-May 18, June 19-July 4 and July 11-August 1, 1997); included rehabilitation assignments to Buffalo (May 5-10) and Akron (May 1-18). ... On Cleveland disabled list (April 11-June 15, 1998); included rehabilitation assignments to Akron (April 24) and Buffalo (May 23-June 14). ... On Cleveland disabled list (April 26-May 11, 1999); included rehabilitation assignment to Buffalo (May 9-11). ... On Cleveland disabled list (May 21-June 27, 2000); included rehabilitation assignment to Akron (June 24-27). ... On Cleveland disabled list (June 13-29 and July 22-September 18, 2001); included rehabilitation assignment to Akron (June 27). ... On Cleveland disabled list (June 10-25, 2002); included rehabilitation assignment to Akron (June 22-25). ... Traded by Indians to Los Angeles Dodgers for P Terry Mulholland, P Ricardo Rodriguez and P Francisco Cruceta (July 28, 2002). ... Placed on 15-day disabled list (April 25, 2003). ... Sent on rehab assignment to Las Vegas (May 15, 2003). ... Recalled from rehab assignment; reinstated from 15-day disabled list (May 17, 2003).

CAREER HITTING: 1-for-7 (.143), 0 R, 0 2B, 0 3B, 0 HR, 0 RBI.

Year	League	W	L	Pct.	ERA	WHIP	G	GS	CG	ShO	Hld.	Sv.-Opp.	IP	H	R	ER	HR	BB-IBB	SO	Avg.
1992—	Columbus (S. Atl.)	5	5	.500	3.35	1.40	14	14	0	0	...	0-...	78.0	62	35	29	2	47-2	73	.221
1993—	Cant./Akr. (Eastern)	4	8	.333	7.30	1.82	27	7	0	0	...	0-...	61.2	76	50	50	13	36-3	41	.308
	— Kinston (Caro.)	1	0	1.000	4.84	1.66	15	0	0	0	...	0-...	22.1	29	12	12	1	8-0	27	.326
1994—	Kinston (Caro.)	1	0	1.000	3.75	1.08	13	0	0	0	...	8-...	12.0	10	5	5	1	3-0	16	.227
	— Cleveland (A.L.)	0	1	.000	8.49	2.23	14	0	0	0	1	5-5	11.2	14	11	11	1	12-1	16	.280
	— Charlotte (Int'l)	2	1	.667	1.93	1.07	20	0	0	0	...	10-...	23.1	15	9	5	1	10-0	25	.181
1995—	Cleveland (A.L.)	0	2	.000	4.26	1.58	7	0	0	0	0	0-0	6.1	5	4	3	0	5-0	5	.238
	— Buffalo (A.A.)	1	2	.333	2.63	1.02	25	0	0	0	...	11-...	27.1	21	9	8	2	7-0	27	.214
1996—	Buffalo (A.A.)	3	2	.600	0.81	0.69	19	0	0	0	...	4-...	33.1	14	4	3	1	9-2	57	.126
	— Cleveland (A.L.)	5	2	.714	2.85	1.32	42	0	0	0	7	4-7	53.2	45	19	17	6	26-3	44	.231
1997—	Cleveland (A.L.)	4	2	.667	6.20	1.78	40	0	0	0	4	2-3	45.0	52	31	31	5	28-3	46	.294
	— Buffalo (A.A.)	0	0	...	3.60	1.60	2	0	0	0	...	0-...	5.0	4	2	2	0	4-0	6	.222
	— Akron (East.)	0	0	...	3.38	1.25	3	0	0	0	...	0-...	8.0	10	3	3	1	0-0	9	.313
1998—	Cleveland (A.L.)	5	4	.556	3.00	1.35	43	0	0	0	12	2-5	51.0	44	19	17	6	25-5	58	.229
	— Akron (East.)	0	0	...	54.00	12.00	1	0	0	0	...	0-...	.1	3	2	2	0	1-0	0	.750
	— Buffalo (Int'l)	0	0	...	2.51	1.19	11	0	0	0	...	2-...	14.1	11	4	4	0	6-0	22	.204
1999—	Cleveland (A.L.)	8	5	.615	3.53	1.32	72	0	0	0	19	6-12	81.2	68	37	32	8	40-7	103	.223
	— Buffalo (Int'l)	0	0	...	0.00	1.00	1	0	0	0	...	0-...	1.0	0	0	0	0	1-0	1	.000
2000—	Cleveland (A.L.)	4	2	.667	3.39	1.27	57	0	0	0	*28	0-5	63.2	51	25	24	4	30-3	69	.219
	— Akron (East.)	0	0	...	4.50	1.00	2	1	0	0	...	0-...	2.0	1	1	1	0	1-0	1	.143
2001—	Cleveland (A.L.)	5	3	.625	2.82	1.45	47	0	0	0	9	2-5	54.1	53	25	17	1	26-5	70	.251
	— Akron (East.)	0	0	...	0.00	1.00	1	1	0	0	...	0-...	1.0	0	0	0	0	1-0	2	.000
2002—	Cleveland (A.L.)	3	0	1.000	2.41	1.10	39	0	0	0	12	0-2	37.1	31	11	10	1	10-1	39	.225
	— Akron (East.)	0	0	...	4.50	1.00	2	2	0	0	...	0-...	2.0	2	1	1	0	0-0	3	.250
	— Los Angeles (N.L.)	5	2	.714	4.40	1.50	28	0	0	0	7	1-3	30.2	25	18	15	2	21-1	24	.217
2003—	Las Vegas (PCL)	0	1	.000	27.00	3.00	1	1	0	0	...	0-...	1.0	2	3	3	1	1-0	1	.400
	— Los Angeles (N.L.)	6	4	.600	3.00	1.20	62	0	0	0	10	0-1	69.0	50	24	23	6	33-3	60	.207
American League totals (9 years)		**34**	**21**	**.618**	**3.60**	**1.40**	**361**	**0**	**0**	**0**	**92**	**21-44**	**404.2**	**363**	**182**	**162**	**32**	**202-28**	**450**	**.239**
National League totals (2 years)		**11**	**6**	**.647**	**3.43**	**1.29**	**90**	**0**	**0**	**0**	**17**	**1-4**	**99.2**	**75**	**42**	**38**	**8**	**54-4**	**84**	**.210**
Major League totals (10 years)		**45**	**27**	**.625**	**3.57**	**1.38**	**451**	**0**	**0**	**0**	**109**	**22-48**	**504.1**	**438**	**224**	**200**	**40**	**256-32**	**534**	**.233**

PERSONAL: Born August 16, 1966, in Paducah, Ky. ... 6-0/198. ... Bats right, throws right. ... Full name: Terrance Darnell Shumpert. ... High school: Paducah (Ky.) Tilghman. ... College: Kentucky.

TRANSACTIONS/CAREER NOTES: Selected by Kansas City Royals organization in second round of free-agent draft (June 2, 1987). ... On disabled list (July 19-August 13, 1989). ... On Kansas City disabled list (June 3-September 10, 1990); included rehabilitation assignment to Omaha (August 7-25). ... On Kansas City disabled list (August 7-September 7, 1992). ... Traded by Royals to Boston Red Sox for a player to be named later (December 13, 1994). ... Granted free agency (October 6, 1995). ... Signed by Chicago Cubs organization (March 12, 1996). ... On Chicago disabled list (August 19-September 3, 1996). ... Granted free agency (October 15, 1996). ... Signed by San Diego Padres (November 4, 1996). ... On San Diego disabled list (May 27-August 5, 1997). ... Released by Padres (August 5, 1997). ... Signed by Colorado Rockies organization (August 13, 1997). ... Granted free agency (October 15, 1998). ... Re-signed by Rockies organization (December 18, 1998). ... On Colorado Springs disabled list (May 13-23, 1999). ... Granted free agency (October 29, 1999). ... Re-signed by Rockies (January 1, 1999). ... Granted free agency (October 28, 2002). ... Signed by Los Angeles Dodgers organization (January 17, 2003). ... Released by Dodgers (March 29, 2003). ... Signed by Tampa Bay Devil Rays (March 30, 2003). ... Placed on 15-day disabled list (July 31, 2003). ... Sent on minor league rehab assignment (September 1, 2003). ... Recalled from minor league rehab assignment; removed from 15-day disabled list (September 2, 2003).

2003 GAMES PLAYED BY POSITION (MLB): DH—17, 2B—14, OF—14, 3B—11, SS—1.

											BATTING										FIELDING	
Year	Team (League)	Pos.	G	AB	R	H	2B	3B	HR	RBI	BB	SO	HBP	GDP	SB-CS	Avg.	OBP	SLG	OPS	E	Pct.
1987—	Eugene (Northwest)	2B	48	186	38	54	16	1	4	22	27	41	3	0	16-4	.290	.385	.452	.837	11	.945
1988—	Appleton (Midwest)	2B-OF	114	422	64	102	* 37	2	7	38	56	90	3	1	36-3	.242	.331	.389	.720	20	.960
1989—	Omaha (A.A.)	2B	113	355	54	88	29	2	4	22	25	63	10	5	23-7	.248	.315	.375	.689	* 22	.959
1990—	Omaha (A.A.)	2B	39	153	24	39	6	4	2	12	14	28	3	4	18-0	.255	.327	.386	.713	7	.960
	— Kansas City (A.L.)	2B-DH	32	91	7	25	6	1	0	8	2	17	1	4	3-3	.275	.292	.363	.654	3	.977
1991—	Kansas City (A.L.)	2B	144	369	45	80	16	4	5	34	30	75	5	10	17-11	.217	.283	.322	.605	16	.975
1992—	Kansas City (A.L.)	2B-SS-DH	36	94	6	14	5	1	1	11	3	17	0	2	2-2	.149	.175	.255	.431	4	.969
	— Omaha (A.A.)	2B-SS	56	210	23	42	12	0	1	14	13	33	4	1	3-5	.200	.259	.271	.530	9	.967
1993—	Omaha (A.A.)	2B	111	413	70	124	29	1	14	59	41	62	6	7	* 36-8	.300	.367	.477	.844	14	.972
	— Kansas City (A.L.)	2B	8	10	0	1	0	0	0	0	2	2	0	0	1-0	.100	.250	.100	.350	0	1.000
1994—	Kansas City (A.L.)	2-3-D-S	64	183	28	44	6	2	8	24	13	39	0	0	18-3	.240	.289	.426	.716	8	.961
1995—	Boston (A.L.)	2-3-S-D	21	47	6	11	3	0	0	3	4	13	0	0	3-1	.234	.294	.298	.592	2	.966
	— Pawtucket (Int'l)	3-2-D-O	37	133	17	36	7	0	2	11	14	27	1	3	10-3	.271	.345	.368	.713	11	.899
1996—	Iowa (Am. Assoc.)	2-3-S-D-1	72	246	45	68	13	4	5	32	24	44	2	5	13-3	.276	.342	.423	.765	7	.976
	— Chicago (N.L.)	3B-2B-SS	27	31	5	7	1	0	2	6	2	11	1	0	0-1	.226	.286	.452	.737	1	.952
1997—	Las Vegas (PCL)	3-2-S-D	32	109	18	31	8	1	1	16	9	20	3	1	3-0	.284	.350	.404	.753	4	.960
	— San Diego (N.L.)	2B-OF-3B	13	33	4	9	3	0	1	6	3	4	0	1	0-0	.273	.324	.455	.779	2	.952
	— New Haven (East.)	2B	5	17	2	4	0	0	1	1	0	2	0	1	0-0	.235	.235	.412	.647	0	1.000
	— Colo. Springs (PCL)	S-2-3-O	10	37	8	11	3	0	1	2	2	7	0	1	0-0	.297	.333	.459	.793	5	.848
1998—	Colo. Springs (PCL)	2-0-3-D-S	97	376	66	115	29	8	12	50	35	59	4	11	11-11	.306	.370	.521	.891	4	.986
	— Colorado (N.L.)	2B	23	26	3	6	1	0	1	2	2	8	0	0	0-0	.231	.286	.385	.670	0	1.000

														BATTING					FIELDING	
Year	Team (League)	Pos.	G	AB	R	H	2B	3B	HR	RBI	BB	SO	HBP	GDP	SB-CS	Avg.	OBP	SLG	OPS	E	Pct.
1999—Colo. Springs (PCL)	3-2-S-O	29	79	15	30	8	1	6	17	4	9	0	1	3-1	.380	.410	.734	1.144	5	.922
—Colorado (N.L.)	2-O-3-S	92	262	58	91	26	3	10	37	31	41	2	2	14-0	.347	.413	.584	.997	5	.983
2000—Colorado (N.L.) ...	O-2-3-S-1-D	115	263	52	68	11	7	9	40	28	40	6	3	8-4	.259	.340	.456	.796	4	.977
2001—Colorado (N.L.)	2-O-3-S	114	242	37	70	14	5	4	24	15	44	3	2	14-3	.289	.337	.438	.775	8	.959
2002—Colorado (N.L.) ...	2-O-3-S	106	234	30	55	12	1	6	21	21	41	4	9	4-1	.235	.304	.372	.676	6	.975
2003—Orlando (South.)	2B-DH	2	9	1	2	0	0	0	1	0	2	1	0	0-0	.222	.300	.222	.522	0	1.000
—Tampa Bay (A.L.)	D-2-O-3-S	59	84	14	16	5	2	2	7	10	17	2	0	1-0	.190	.289	.369	.658	2	.971
American League totals (7 years)		364	878	106	191	41	10	16	87	64	180	8	16	45-20	.218	.275	.342	.617	35	.972
National League totals (7 years)		490	1091	189	306	68	16	33	136	102	189	16	17	40-9	.280	.346	.463	.809	26	.974
Major League totals (14 years)		854	1969	295	497	109	26	49	223	166	369	24	33	85-29	.252	.315	.409	.724	61	.973

SIERRA, RUBEN   DH/OF

PERSONAL: Born October 6, 1965, in Rio Piedras, Puerto Rico. ... 6-1/215. ... Bats both, throws right. ... Full name: Ruben Angel Sierra. ... High school: Dr. Secario Rosario (Rio Piedras, Puerto Rico).

TRANSACTIONS/CAREER NOTES: Signed as non-drafted free agent by Texas Rangers organization (November 21, 1982). ... Traded by Rangers with P Jeff Russell, P Bobby Witt and cash to Oakland Athletics for OF Jose Canseco (August 31, 1992). ... Granted free agency (October 26, 1992). ... Re-signed by A's (December 21, 1992). ... On Oakland disabled list (July 7-22, 1995). ... Traded by A's with P Jason Beverlin to New York Yankees for OF/DH Danny Tartabull (July 28, 1995). ... Traded by Yankees with P Matt Drews to Detroit Tigers for 1B/DH Cecil Fielder (July 31, 1996). ... Traded by Tigers to Cincinnati Reds for OF Decomba Conner and P Ben Bailey (October 28, 1996). ... Released by Reds (May 9, 1997). ... Signed by Toronto Blue Jays organization (May 11, 1997). ... Released by Blue Jays (June 16, 1997). ... Signed by Chicago White Sox organization (January 9, 1998). ... Released by White Sox (May 29, 1998). ... Signed by New York Mets organization (June 20, 1998). ... Granted free agency (October 16, 1998). ... Signed by Atlantic City, Atlantic League (May 1, 1999). ... Signed by Cleveland Indians organization (December 23, 1999). ... Released by Indians (March 20, 2000). ... Signed by Rangers organization (May 1, 2000). ... Granted free agency (October 30, 2000). ... Re-signed by Rangers organization (December 13, 2000). ... On Texas disabled list (July 27-August 11, 2001). ... Granted free agency (November 5, 2001). ... Signed by Seattle Mariners (January 3, 2002). ... Granted free agency (October 31, 2002). ... Signed by Rangers organization (January 27, 2003). ... Traded by Rangers to New York Yankees for OF Marcus Thames (June 6, 2003).

2003 GAMES PLAYED BY POSITION (MLB): DH—47, OF—40.

														BATTING					FIELDING	
Year	Team (League)	Pos.	G	AB	R	H	2B	3B	HR	RBI	BB	SO	HBP	GDP	SB-CS	Avg.	OBP	SLG	OPS	E	Pct.
1983—GC Rangers (GCL)	OF	48	182	26	44	7	3	1	26	16	38	1	...	3-4	.242	.300	.330	.630	4	.948
1984—Burlington (Midw.)	OF	•138	482	55	127	33	5	6	75	49	97	1	9	13-9	.263	.331	.390	.721	* 20	.928
1985—Tulsa (Texas)	OF	* 137	* 545	63	138	34	* 8	13	74	35	111	1	8	22-7	.253	.297	.417	.713	* 15	.943
1986—Okla. City (A.A.)	OF	46	189	31	56	11	2	9	41	15	27	0	5	8-2	.296	.341	.519	.860	2	.983
—Texas (A.L.)	DH-OF	113	382	50	101	13	10	16	55	22	65	1	8	7-8	.264	.302	.470	.779	6	.972
1987—Texas (A.L.)	OF	158	* 643	97	169	35	4	30	109	39	114	2	18	16-11	.263	.302	.470	.779	11	.963
1988—Texas (A.L.)	DH-OF	156	615	77	156	32	2	23	91	44	91	1	15	18-4	.254	.301	.424	.725	7	.979
1989—Texas (A.L.)	OF	•162	634	101	194	35	* 14	29	* 119	43	82	2	7	8-2	.306	.347	*.543	.889	9	.973
1990—Texas (A.L.)	DH-OF	159	608	70	170	37	2	16	96	49	86	1	15	9-0	.280	.330	.426	.756	10	.967
1991—Texas (A.L.)	OF	161	661	110	203	44	5	25	116	56	91	0	17	16-4	.307	.357	.502	.859	7	.979
1992—Texas (A.L.)	OF-DH	124	500	66	139	30	6	14	70	31	59	0	9	12-4	.278	.315	.446	.761	7	.970
—Oakland (A.L.)	OF-DH	27	101	17	28	4	1	3	17	14	9	0	2	2-0	.277	.359	.426	.785	0	1.000
1993—Oakland (A.L.)	OF-DH	158	630	77	147	23	5	22	101	52	97	0	17	25-5	.233	.288	.390	.678	7	.977
1994—Oakland (A.L.)	OF-DH	110	426	71	114	21	1	23	92	23	64	0	15	8-5	.268	.298	.484	.781	* 9	.948
1995—Oakland (A.L.)	OF-DH	70	264	40	70	17	0	12	42	24	42	0	2	4-4	.265	.323	.466	.789	4	.957
—New York (A.L.)	DH-OF	56	215	33	56	15	0	7	44	22	34	0	6	1-0	.260	.322	.428	.750	1	.950
1996—Campeche (Mex.)	DH	1	1	1	0	0	0	0	0	0	0	...	...	0-0	.000	...	.000	...	...	...
—New York (A.L.)	DH-OF	96	360	39	93	17	1	11	52	40	58	0	10	1-3	.258	.327	.403	.730	1	.984
—Detroit (A.L.)	OF-DH	46	158	22	35	9	1	1	20	20	25	0	2	3-1	.222	.306	.310	.616	5	.914
1997—Cincinnati (N.L.)	OF	25	90	6	22	5	1	2	7	6	21	0	1	0-0	.244	.292	.389	.681	0	1.000
—Syracuse (Int'l)	OF	8	32	5	7	2	0	1	5	2	6	0	0	0-0	.219	.265	.375	.640	1	.923
—Toronto (A.L.)	OF-DH	14	48	4	10	0	2	1	5	3	13	0	0	0-0	.208	.250	.354	.604	1	.929
1998—Chicago (A.L.)	OF-DH	27	74	7	16	4	1	4	11	3	11	0	2	2-0	.216	.247	.459	.706	0	1.000
—Norfolk (Int'l)	OF-DH	28	108	16	28	5	0	3	19	13	18	0	4	3-0	.259	.331	.389	.720	1	1.000
1999—Atlantic City (Atl.)	DH-OF	112	422	76	124	22	2	28	82	59	63	...	...	3-2	.294	...	.555	...	3	.960
2000—Cancun (Mex.)	OF	16	62	8	22	2	1	3	12	10	10	0	0	0-1	.355	...	.565	...	0	1.000
—Oklahoma (PCL)	OF	112	439	70	143	26	3	18	82	55	63	0	24	5-2	.326	.398	.522	.919	6	.962
—Texas (A.L.)	DH	20	60	5	14	0	0	1	7	4	9	0	1	1-0	.233	.281	.283	.565	...	...
2001—Oklahoma (PCL)	OF	24	94	14	25	2	1	3	12	10	14	0	5	2-0	.266	.337	.404	.741	0	1.000
—Texas (A.L.)	DH-OF	94	344	55	100	22	1	23	67	19	52	0	13	2-0	.291	.322	.561	.884	4	.937
2002—Seattle (A.L.)	DH-OF	122	419	47	113	23	0	13	60	31	66	0	17	4-0	.270	.319	.418	.736	2	.979
2003—Texas (A.L.)	OF-DH	43	133	14	35	9	0	3	12	14	27	0	2	1-1	.263	.333	.398	.732	1	.962
—New York (A.L.)	DH-OF	63	174	19	48	8	1	6	31	13	20	0	7	1-0	.276	.323	.437	.760	1	1.000
American League totals (17 years)		1979	7449	1021	2011	398	57	283	1217	566	1115	7	185	141-52	.270	.318	.453	.770	92	.970
National League totals (1 year)		25	90	6	22	5	1	2	7	6	21	0	1	0-0	.244	.292	.389	.681	0	1.000
Major League totals (17 years)		2004	7539	1027	2033	403	58	285	1224	572	1136	7	186	141-52	.270	.317	.452	.769	92	.970

SILVA, CARLOS   P

PERSONAL: Born April 23, 1979, in Bolivar, Venezuela. ... 6-4/240. ... Throws right, bats right. ... High school: U.E. General Ezequiel Zamora Bolivar.

TRANSACTIONS/CAREER NOTES: Signed as non-drafted free agent by Philadelphia Phillies organization (March 22, 1996). ... On Philadelphia disabled list (May 27-June 14, 2002); included rehabilitation assignment to Reading (June 11-14). ... Suspended by Major League Baseball (July 17, 2003). ... Reinstated (July 22, 2003).

CAREER HITTING: 2-for-11 (.182), 0 R, 1 2B, 0 3B, 0 HR, 1 RBI.

Year	League	W	L	Pct.	ERA	WHIP	G	GS	CG	ShO	Hld.	Sv.-Opp.	IP	H	R	ER	HR	BB-IBB	SO	Avg.
1996—Martinsville (App.)		0	0	...	4.00	1.39	7	1	0	0	...	0-...	18.0	20	11	8	1	5-0	16	.299
1997—Martinsville (App.)		2	2	.500	5.15	1.39	11	11	0	0	...	0-...	57.2	66	46	33	9	14-0	31	.284
1998—Martinsville (App.)		1	4	.200	5.05	1.27	7	7	1	0	...	0-...	41.0	48	24	23	2	4-0	21	.284
—Batavia (N.Y.-Penn)		2	3	.400	6.35	1.54	9	7	0	0	...	0-...	45.1	61	37	32	4	9-0	27	.314
1999—Piedmont (S. Atl.)		11	8	.579	3.12	1.32	26	26	3	1	...	0-...	164.1	176	79	57	6	41-2	99	.273
2000—Clearwater (Fla. St.)		8	* 13	.381	3.57	1.45	26	24	* 4	0	...	0-...	176.1	* 229	99	70	7	26-1	82	.314
2001—Reading (East.)		15	8	.652	3.90	1.24	28	28	4	1	...	0-...	180.0	* 197	85	78	20	27-0	100	.284
2002—Philadelphia (N.L.)		5	0	1.000	3.21	1.31	68	0	0	0	8	1-5	84.0	88	34	30	4	22-6	41	.282
—Reading (East.)		0	0	...	0.00	0.00	2	0	0	0	0	1-...	3.0	0	0	0	0	0-0	1	.000
2003—Philadelphia (N.L.)		3	1	.750	4.43	1.48	62	1	0	0	4	1-3	87.1	92	43	43	7	37-5	48	.280
Major League totals (2 years)		8	1	.889	3.83	1.39	130	1	0	0	12	2-8	171.1	180	77	73	11	59-11	89	.281

S

SIMON, RANDALL — 1B

PERSONAL: Born May 26, 1975, in Willemstad, Curacao. ... 6-0/240. ... Bats left, throws left. ... Full name: Randall Carlito Simon. ... High school: Juan Pablo Duarte Tech (Willemstad, Curacao).

TRANSACTIONS/CAREER NOTES: Signed as non-drafted free agent by Atlanta Braves organization (July 17, 1992). ... Released by Braves (March 31, 2000). ... Signed by Florida Marlins organization (April 5, 2000). ... Released by Marlins (May 8, 2000). ... Signed by New York Yankees organization (May 14, 2000). ... On Columbus disabled list (July 6-13, 2000). ... Granted free agency (October 18, 2000). ... Signed by Detroit Tigers organization (January 18, 2001). ... Traded by Tigers to Pittsburgh Pirates for P Adrian Burnside and two players to be named later (November 25, 2002); Tigers acquired P Roberto Novoa as partial completion (December 16, 2002). ... Placed on 15-day disabled list (June 21, 2003). ... Sent to Nashville on rehab assignment (July 7, 2003). ... Activated from 15-day disabled list by Pittsburgh (July 7, 2003). ... Suspended by Major League Baseball (July 10, 2003). ... Reinstated (July 13, 2003). ... Traded by Pirates to Chicago Cubs for OF Ray Sadler (August 17, 2003).

2003 GAMES PLAYED BY POSITION (MLB): 1B—109.

Year	Team (League)	Pos.	G	AB	R	H	2B	3B	HR	RBI	BB	SO	HBP	GDP	SB-CS	Avg.	OBP	SLG	OPS	E	Pct.
1992— Dominican Braves (DSL) ...		C	11	43	7	12	4	2	0	7	5	6	...		1-...	.279		.465	...	4	.979
1993— Danville (Appal.)		1B	61	232	28	59	17	1	3	31	10	34	2	4	1-1	.254	.289	.375	.664	10	.980
1994— Macon (S. Atl.)		1B	106	358	48	105	23	1	0	54	6	56	1	7	7-6	.293	.305	.447	.752	9	.986
1995— Durham (Caro.)		1B	122	420	56	111	18	1	18	79	36	63	5	15	6-5	.264	.326	.440	.767	10	.989
1996— Greenville (Sou.)		1B-OF	134	498	74	139	26	2	18	77	37	61	4	13	4-9	.279	.331	.448	.779	16	.989
1997— Richmond (Int'l)		1B-DH	133	519	62	160	* 45	1	14	* 102	17	76	4	18	1-6	.308	.335	.480	.814	• 14	.988
—Atlanta (N.L.)		1B	13	14	2	6	1	0	0	1	1	2	0	1	0-0	.429	.467	.500	.967	0	1.000
1998— Richmond (Int'l)		1B-DH	126	484	52	124	20	1	13	70	24	62	2	22	4-4	.256	.292	.382	.674	* 11	.989
—Atlanta (N.L.)		1B	7	16	2	3	0	0	0	4	0	1	0	0	0-0	.188	.176	.188	.364	0	1.000
1999— Atlanta (N.L.)		1B	90	218	26	69	16	0	5	25	17	25	1	10	2-2	.317	.367	.459	.826	3	.994
—Richmond (Int'l)		1B-DH	15	59	7	16	4	0	1	8	3	10	0	0	0-1	.271	.302	.390	.691	0	1.000
2000— Calgary (PCL)		1B	22	68	5	20	3	0	1	11	0	3	0	1	0-0	.294	.290	.382	.672	4	.966
—Columbus (Int'l)		1B-OF	94	364	52	97	20	4	17	74	35	42	0	17	6-5	.266	.325	.484	.809	9	.987
2001— Toledo (Int'l)		1B	59	222	27	75	13	0	10	31	21	21	2	8	0-3	.338	.400	.532	.932	7	.986
—Detroit (A.L.)		1B-DH	81	256	28	78	14	2	6	37	15	28	0	9	0-1	.305	.341	.445	.786	3	.992
2002— Detroit (A.L.)		DH-1B	130	482	51	145	17	1	19	82	13	30	4	13	0-1	.301	.320	.459	.779	7	.988
2003— Nashville (PCL)		1B	2	8	3	3	1	0	1	2	0	0	0	1	0-0	.375	.375	.875	1.250	0	1.000
—Pittsburgh (N.L.)		1B	91	307	34	84	14	0	10	51	12	30	2	6	0-0	.274	.305	.417	.722	4	.994
—Chicago (N.L.)		1B	33	103	13	29	3	0	6	21	4	7	2	1	0-0	.282	.318	.485	.804	2	.991
American League totals (2 years)			211	738	79	223	31	3	25	119	28	58	4	22	0-2	.302	.327	.454	.781	10	.990
National League totals (4 years)			234	658	77	191	34	0	21	102	34	65	5	18	2-2	.290	.329	.438	.766	9	.994
Major League totals (6 years)			445	1396	156	414	65	3	46	221	62	123	9	40	2-4	.297	.328	.446	.774	19	.992

SIMONTACCHI, JASON — P

PERSONAL: Born November 13, 1973, in Mountain View, Calif. ... 6-2/190. ... Throws right, bats right. ... Full name: Jason William Simontacchi. ... Name pronounced: cy-mun-TACH-ee. ... High school: Fremont (Sunnyvale, Calif.). ... College: San Jose State, then Albertson (Idaho).

TRANSACTIONS/CAREER NOTES: Selected by Kansas City Royals organization in 21st round of free-agent draft (June 4, 1996). ... Released by Royals (July 30, 1997). ... Signed by Springfield of the Frontier League (June 1998). ... Signed by Pittsburgh Pirates organization (January 6, 1999). ... Released by Pirates (September 29, 1999). ... Signed by Minnesota Twins organization (September 27, 2000). ... Granted free agency (October 15, 2001). ... Signed by St. Louis Cardinals organization (December 21, 2001).

CAREER HITTING: 17-for-88 (.193), 8 R, 1 2B, 0 3B, 0 HR, 2 RBI.

Year	League	W	L	Pct.	ERA	WHIP	G	GS	CG	ShO	Hld.	Sv.-Opp.	IP	H	R	ER	HR	BB-IBB	SO	Avg.
1996— Spokane (N'west)		2	5	.286	5.17	1.57	14	6	0	0	...	2-...	47.0	59	37	27	8	15-0	43	.312
1997— Lansing (Midw.)		3	7	.300	6.97	1.78	29	1	0	0	...	2-...	60.2	93	56	47	7	15-1	38	.346
1998— Springfield (Fron.)		10	2	.833	2.95	1.13	16	16	3		...	0-...	110.0	103	43	36	14	21-3	92	.247
1999— Hickory (S. Atl.)		4	6	.400	4.02	1.30	23	7	0	0	...	1-...	69.1	71	34	31	8	19-1	66	.264
2000—												Did not play.								
2001— Edmonton (PCL)		7	13	.350	5.34	1.50	32	18	2	0	...	0-...	143.1	192	97	85	21	23-1	83	.327
2002— Memphis (PCL)		5	1	.833	2.34	1.16	6	6	0	0	...	0-...	42.1	44	12	11	2	5-1	28	.273
—St. Louis (N.L.)		11	5	.688	4.02	1.31	24	24	0	0	0	0-0	143.1	134	68	64	18	54-4	72	.253
2003— St. Louis (N.L.)		9	5	.643	5.56	1.54	46	16	1	0	7	1-3	126.1	153	82	78	21	41-0	74	.299
Major League totals (2 years)		20	10	.667	4.74	1.42	70	40	1	0	7	1-3	269.2	287	150	142	39	95-4	146	.276

SINGLETON, CHRIS — OF

PERSONAL: Born August 15, 1972, in Martinez, Calif. ... 6-2/217. ... Bats left, throws left. ... Full name: Christopher Verdell Singleton. ... High school: Pinole (Calif.) Valley. ... College: Nevada.

TRANSACTIONS/CAREER NOTES: Selected by San Francisco Giants organization in second round of free-agent draft (June 3, 1993). ... Traded by Giants with P Alberto Castillo to New York Yankees for 3B Charlie Hayes and cash (November 11, 1997). ... Traded by Yankees to Chicago White Sox for a player to be named later (December 8, 1998); Yankees acquired P Rich Pratt to complete deal (January 10, 1999). ... Traded by White Sox to Baltimore Orioles for 2B/OF Willie Harris (January 29, 2002). ... Granted free agency (December 21, 2002). ... Signed by Oakland Athletics (December 23, 2002).

2003 GAMES PLAYED BY POSITION (MLB): OF—113.

Year	Team (League)	Pos.	G	AB	R	H	2B	3B	HR	RBI	BB	SO	HBP	GDP	SB-CS	Avg.	OBP	SLG	OPS	E	Pct.
1993— Everett (N'west)		OF	58	219	39	58	14	4	3	18	18	46	1	3	14-3	.265	.322	.406	.729	3	.974
1994— San Jose (Calif.)		OF	113	425	51	106	17	5	2	49	27	62	3	9	19-6	.249	.297	.327	.624	13	.952
1995— San Jose (Calif.)		OF	94	405	55	112	13	5	2	31	17	49	5	5	33-13	.277	.313	.348	.661	7	.955
1996— Shreveport (Texas)		OF	129	500	68	149	31	9	5	72	24	58	6	12	27-12	.298	.333	.426	.759	4	.986
—Phoenix (PCL)		OF	9	32	3	4	0	0	0	0	1	2	0	0	0-0	.125	.152	.125	.277	0	1.000
1997— Shreveport (Texas)		OF	126	464	85	147	26	10	9	61	22	50	1	7	27-11	.317	.343	.474	.817	7	.974
1998— Columbus (Int'l)		OF	121	413	55	105	17	10	6	45	27	78	4	7	9-3	.254	.304	.387	.691	7	.974
1999— Chicago (A.L.)		OF-DH	133	496	72	149	31	6	17	72	22	45	1	10	20-5	.300	.328	.490	.818	4	.990
2000— Chicago (A.L.)		OF-DH	147	511	83	130	22	5	11	62	35	85	1	6	22-7	.254	.301	.382	.683	3	.992
2001— Chicago (A.L.)		OF-DH	140	392	57	117	21	5	7	45	20	61	1	6	12-11	.298	.331	.431	.762	3	.991
2002— Baltimore (A.L.)		OF-DH	136	466	67	122	30	6	9	50	21	83	4	8	20-2	.262	.296	.410	.706	4	.986
2003— Oakland (A.L.)		OF	120	306	38	75	24	1	1	36	26	55	1	2	7-2	.245	.301	.340	.641	6	.969
Major League totals (5 years)			676	2171	317	593	128	23	45	265	124	329	8	31	81-27	.273	.311	.415	.727	20	.987

SMITH, DAN   P

PERSONAL: Born September 15, 1975, in Flemington, N.J. ... 6-3/225. ... Throws right, bats right. ... Full name: Daniel Charles Smith. ... High school: Girard (Kan.).

TRANSACTIONS/CAREER NOTES: Selected by Texas Rangers organization in seventh round of free-agent draft (June 3, 1993). ... On Charlotte disabled list (June 12-July 7, 1995). ... Claimed on waivers by Montreal Expos (December 14, 1998). ... Granted free agency (December 21, 1999). ... Signed by Boston Red Sox organization (June 2, 2000). ... Granted free agency (October 18, 2000). ... Signed by Cleveland Indians organization (November 15, 2000). ... On disabled list (April 16-May 19, 2001). ... Granted free agency (October 15, 2001). ... Signed by Expos organization (January 11, 2002). ... Placed on 15-day disabled list (June 26, 2003). ... Transferred to 60-day disabled list (August 20, 2003).

CAREER HITTING: 2-for-29 (.069), 3 R, 0 2B, 0 3B, 0 HR, 1 RBI.

Year	League	W	L	Pct.	ERA	WHIP	G	GS	CG	ShO	Hld.	Sv.-Opp.	IP	H	R	ER	HR	BB-IBB	SO	Avg.
1993—	GC Rangers (GCL)	3	2	.600	2.87	1.09	12	10	1	0	...	0-...	53.1	50	19	17	1	8-0	27	.253
1994—	Char., S.C. (SAL)	7	10	.412	4.92	1.44	27	27	4	0	...	0-...	157.1	171	*111	86	12	55-0	86	.270
1995—	GC Rangers (GCL)	0	3	.000	4.26	1.26	4	3	0	0	...	0-...	19.0	19	9	9	0	5-0	12	.260
—	Charlotte (Fla. St.)	5	1	.833	2.95	1.19	9	9	1	1	...	0-...	58.0	53	23	19	4	16-0	34	.241
1996—	Charlotte (Fla. St.)	3	7	.300	5.07	1.59	18	18	1	0	...	0-...	87.0	100	61	49	6	38-0	55	.286
1997—	Charlotte (Fla. St.)	8	10	.444	4.43	1.46	26	25	2	0	...	0-...	160.2	169	93	79	17	66-1	113	.273
1998—	Tulsa (Texas)	13	9	.591	5.81	1.43	26	25	1	0	...	0-...	153.1	162	101	99	27	58-1	105	.271
—	Oklahoma (PCL)	0	0	...	6.00	1.17	1	1	0	0	...	0-...	6.0	6	4	4	2	1-0	3	.273
1999—	Ottawa (Int'l)	5	4	.556	3.68	1.24	11	11	0	0	...	0-...	71.0	61	31	29	7	27-0	59	.234
—	Montreal (N.L.)	4	9	.308	6.02	1.59	20	17	0	0	0	0-1	89.2	104	64	60	12	39-0	72	.293
2000—	Pawtucket (Int'l)	7	10	.412	4.84	1.40	24	21	2	1	...	0-...	124.2	134	72	67	15	41-1	70	.273
—	Boston (A.L.)	0	0	...	8.10	1.50	2	0	0	0	0	0-0	3.1	3	3	3	0	3-0	1	.250
2001—	Buffalo (Int'l)	6	4	.600	4.50	1.45	21	16	1	0	...	0-...	106.0	110	58	53	17	44-0	68	.274
2002—	Ottawa (Int'l)	5	4	.556	3.24	1.07	14	14	1	0	...	0-...	83.1	71	30	30	10	18-1	61	.231
—	Montreal (N.L.)	1	1	.500	3.47	1.18	33	0	0	0	2	2-2	46.2	34	18	18	6	21-0	34	.210
2003—	Montreal (N.L.)	2	2	.500	5.26	1.59	32	0	0	0	2	0-1	37.2	42	23	22	11	18-2	35	.280
American League totals (1 year)		0	0	...	8.10	1.50	2	0	0	0	0	0-0	3.1	3	3	3	0	3-0	1	.250
National League totals (3 years)		7	12	.368	5.17	1.48	85	17	0	0	4	2-4	174.0	180	105	100	29	78-2	141	.270
Major League totals (4 years)		7	12	.368	5.23	1.48	87	17	0	0	4	2-4	177.1	182	108	103	29	81-2	142	.270

SMITH, JASON   SS

PERSONAL: Born July 24, 1977, in Meridian, Miss. ... 6-3/199. ... Bats left, throws right. ... Full name: Jason William Smith. ... High school: Demopolis (Ala.). ... Junior college: Meridian College (Miss.).

TRANSACTIONS/CAREER NOTES: Selected by Chicago Cubs organization in 23rd round free-agent draft (June 4, 1996). ... On Iowa disabled list (July 9-August 2, 2001). ... Traded by Cubs to Tampa Bay Devil Rays (August 5, 2001), completing deal in which Devil Rays traded 1B Fred McGriff to Cubs for P Manny Aybar and a player to be named later (July 27, 2001). ... Contract purchased by Tampa Bay from Durham (June 4, 2003). ... Optioned to Durham by Tampa Bay (June 7, 2003). ... Recalled by Tampa Bay from Durham (September 19, 2003).

2003 GAMES PLAYED BY POSITION (MLB): 3B—1.

Year	Team (League)	Pos.	G	AB	R	H	2B	3B	HR	RBI	BB	SO	HBP	GDP	SB-CS	Avg.	OBP	SLG	OPS	E	Pct.
1997—	Will. (NYP)	SS	51	205	25	59	5	2	0	11	10	44	0	0	9-2	.288	.321	.332	.653	19	.930
—	Rockford (Midwest)	SS	9	33	4	6	0	1	0	3	2	11	0	1	1-0	.182	.229	.242	.471	5	.884
1998—	Rockford (Midwest)	SS	126	464	67	111	15	9	7	60	31	122	1	2	23-6	.239	.286	.356	.642	38	.939
1999—	Daytona (Fla. St.)	SS	39	142	22	37	5	2	5	26	12	29	3	2	9-3	.261	.329	.430	.759	7	.953
2000—	West Tenn (Sou.)	SS	119	481	55	114	22	7	12	60	22	130	2	7	16-10	.237	.273	.387	.659	37	.927
2001—	Iowa (PCL)	SS	70	240	31	56	8	6	4	15	12	71	1	4	6-3	.233	.271	.367	.637	19	.942
—	Chicago (N.L.)	SS	2	1	0	0	0	0	0	0	0	1	0	0	0-0	.000	.000	.000	.000	0	1.000
—	Durham (Int'l)	SS	8	31	2	6	1	0	0	3	0	11	0	0	0-0	.194	.194	.226	.419	3	.917
2002—	Tampa Bay (A.L.)	3-S-2-D	26	65	9	13	1	2	1	6	2	24	0	0	3-0	.200	.224	.323	.547	6	.905
—	Durham (Int'l)	SS-3B	54	206	29	57	11	2	4	28	10	44	1	2	5-1	.277	.312	.408	.720	16	.936
2003—	Tampa Bay (A.L.)	3B	1	4	0	1	0	0	0	0	0	0	0	0	0-0	.250	.250	.250	.500	2	.500
—	Durham (Int'l)	S-2-3-D	130	515	76	147	20	14	15	71	11	128	5	1	14-9	.285	.304	.466	.770	23	.959
American League totals (2 years)			27	69	9	14	1	2	1	6	2	24	0	0	3-0	.203	.225	.319	.544	8	.881
National League totals (1 year)			2	1	0	0	0	0	0	0	0	1	0	0	0-0	.000	.000	.000	.000	0	1.000
Major League totals (3 years)			29	70	9	14	1	2	1	6	2	25	0	0	3-0	.200	.222	.314	.537	8	.884

SMITH, MARK   OF

PERSONAL: Born May 7, 1970, in Pasadena, Calif. ... 6-3/225. ... Bats right, throws right. ... Full name: Mark Edward Smith. ... High school: Arcadia (Calif.). ... College: USC.

TRANSACTIONS/CAREER NOTES: Selected by Baltimore Orioles organization in first round (ninth pick overall) of free-agent draft (June 3, 1991). ... On Baltimore disabled list (July 23, 1996-remainder of season); included rehabilitation assignments to Frederick (August 12-13), Bowie (August 21-23) and Rochester (September 3-13). ... Traded by Orioles to San Diego Padres for C Leroy McKinnis (January 9, 1997). ... Traded by Padres with P Hal Garrett to Pittsburgh Pirates for OF Trey Beamon and OF Angelo Encarnacion (March 29, 1997). ... On Pittsburgh disabled list (May 23-June 14, 1997); included rehabilitation assignment to Carolina (June 12-14). ... On Pittsburgh disabled list (May 4-19, 1998); included rehabilitation assignment to Nashville (May 9-19). ... Granted free agency (September 29, 1998). ... Signed by Florida Marlins organization (December 22, 1999). ... On disabled list (May 11-June 5, 2000). ... Granted free agency (October 5, 2000). ... Signed by Montreal Expos organization (November 17, 2000). ... Granted free agency (October 12, 2001). ... Re-signed by Expos organization (December 21, 2001). ... Released by Expos (2002). ... Signed by Florida Marlins organization (February 18, 2002). ... Granted free agency (October 15, 2002). ... Signed by Milwaukee Brewers organization (January 24, 2003).

2003 GAMES PLAYED BY POSITION (MLB): OF—15.

Year	Team (League)	Pos.	G	AB	R	H	2B	3B	HR	RBI	BB	SO	HBP	GDP	SB-CS	Avg.	OBP	SLG	OPS	E	Pct.
1991—	Frederick (Carolina)	OF	38	148	20	37	5	1	4	29	9	24	2	4	1-3	.250	.296	.378	.675	1	.980
1992—	Hagerstown (East.)	OF	128	472	51	136	*32	6	4	62	45	55	4	17	15-5	.288	.351	.407	.758	4	.983
1993—	Rochester (Int'l)	OF	129	485	69	136	27	1	12	68	37	90	9	9	4-6	.280	.341	.414	.756	7	.975
1994—	Rochester (Int'l)	OF-DH	114	437	69	108	27	1	19	66	35	88	7	13	4-3	.247	.311	.444	.755	5	.977
—	Baltimore (A.L.)	OF	3	7	0	1	0	0	0	2	0	2	0	0	0-0	.143	.143	.143	.286	0	1.000
1995—	Rochester (Int'l)	OF-DH	96	364	55	101	25	3	12	66	24	69	7	8	7-3	.277	.328	.462	.790	7	.961
—	Baltimore (A.L.)	OF-DH	37	104	11	24	5	0	3	15	12	22	1	4	3-0	.231	.314	.365	.679	1	1.000
1996—	Rochester (Int'l)	OF-DH	39	132	24	46	14	1	8	32	14	22	4	0	10-1	.348	.424	.652	1.075	2	.966
—	Baltimore (A.L.)	OF-DH	27	78	9	19	2	0	4	10	3	20	3	0	0-2	.244	.298	.423	.721	1	.980
—	Frederick (Carolina)	DH	1	1	0	0	0	0	0	0	0	0	0	1	0-0	.000	.000	.000	.000	...	...
—	Bowie (East.)	DH	6	22	1	2	0	0	1	2	1	6	2	1	0-0	.091	.200	.227	.427	...	...

Year	Team (League)	Pos.	G	AB	R	H	2B	3B	HR	RBI	BB	SO	HBP	GDP	SB-CS	Avg.	OBP	SLG	OPS	E	Pct.
1997—Calgary (PCL)	OF-DH	39	137	37	51	14	1	14	42	21	15	2	5	2-1	.372	.463	.796	1.258	1	.982
—Pittsburgh (N.L.)	OF-1B-DH	71	193	29	55	13	1	9	35	28	36	0	3	3-1	.285	.374	.503	.876	0	1.000
—Carolina (Sou.)	OF	3	12	5	5	1	0	3	4	0	1	0	0	0-0	.417	.417	1.250	1.667	1	.800
1998—Pittsburgh (N.L.)	OF-1B-DH	59	128	18	25	6	0	2	13	10	26	3	1	7-0	.195	.264	.289	.553	1	.987
—Nashville (PCL)	O-1-3-D	24	93	18	33	10	1	8	30	11	20	3	1	3-1	.355	.435	.742	1.177	2	.980
1999—Yakult (Jp. East.)		6	14	2	5	1	0	2	5	4	1	...	...	0-...	.357	...	.857	...	...	...
—Yakult (Jp. Cen.)		98	293	38	76	11	1	20	55	22	83	...	...	3-...	.259	...	.509	...	...	...
2000—Florida (N.L.)	OF-DH	104	192	22	47	8	1	5	27	17	54	2	2	2-0	.245	.310	.375	.685	0	1.000
2001—Ottawa (Int'l)	OF	40	145	20	30	8	0	6	17	15	38	2	1	4-2	.207	.290	.386	.676	2	.974
—Montreal (N.L.)	OF-1B	80	194	28	47	13	1	6	18	23	38	2	3	0-2	.242	.326	.412	.738	0	1.000
2002—Calgary (PCL)	OF	115	389	60	113	30	0	12	55	41	79	9	10	5-2	.290	.369	.460	.829	3	.980
2003—Indianapolis (Int'l)	OF-DH-1B	103	388	46	114	25	2	15	62	21	58	5	14	3-2	.294	.337	.485	.821	2	.986
—Milwaukee (N.L.)	OF	33	63	8	15	4	0	3	10	4	13	0	5	0-0	.238	.275	.444	.720	1	.960
American League totals (3 years)		67	189	20	44	7	0	7	27	15	44	4	4	3-2	.233	.301	.381	.682	1	.992
National League totals (5 years)		347	770	105	189	44	3	25	103	82	167	7	14	12-3	.245	.320	.408	.728	2	.995
Major League totals (8 years)		414	959	125	233	51	3	32	130	97	211	11	18	15-5	.243	.316	.403	.719	3	.994

SMITHERMAN, STEPHEN — OF

PERSONAL: Born September 1, 1978, in McAlester, Okla. ... 6-4/235. ... Bats right, throws right. ... Full name: Stephen Lydell Smitherman. ... High school: Hartshorne High (Oklahoma). ... College: Eastern Oklahoma State.

TRANSACTIONS/CAREER NOTES: Selected by Cincinnati Reds organization in 23rd round of free-agent draft (June 5, 2000).

2003 GAMES PLAYED BY POSITION (MLB): OF—14.

Year	Team (League)	Pos.	G	AB	R	H	2B	3B	HR	RBI	BB	SO	HBP	GDP	SB-CS	Avg.	OBP	SLG	OPS	E	Pct.
2000—Billings (Pio.)	OF-1B	70	301	61	95	16	5	15	65	23	67	6	10	14-1	.316	.373	.551	.925	3	.968
2001—Dayton (Midw.)	OF	134	497	89	139	45	2	20	73	43	113	10	9	16-7	.280	.348	.499	.847	7	.969
2002—Stockton (Calif.)	OF	128	482	78	151	36	1	19	99	39	126	6	14	17-2	.313	.362	.510	.873	5	.975
2003—Louisville (Int'l)	OF-DH-1B	17	63	1	8	0	0	0	5	4	19	1	2	0-0	.127	.188	.127	.315	1	.971
—Chattanooga (Sou.)	OF-1B-DH	105	365	60	113	21	2	19	73	54	95	6	7	11-3	.310	.402	.534	.937	2	.991
—Cincinnati (N.L.)	OF	21	44	3	7	2	0	1	6	3	9	0	0	1-0	.159	.213	.273	.485	0	1.000
Major League totals (1 year)		21	44	3	7	2	0	1	6	3	9	0	0	1-0	.159	.213	.273	.485	0	1.000

SMOLTZ, JOHN — P

PERSONAL: Born May 15, 1967, in Warren, Mich. ... 6-3/220. ... Throws right, bats right. ... Full name: John Andrew Smoltz. ... High school: Waverly (Lansing, Mich.).

TRANSACTIONS/CAREER NOTES: Selected by Detroit Tigers organization in 22nd round of free-agent draft (June 3, 1985). ... Traded by Tigers to Atlanta Braves for P Doyle Alexander (August 12, 1987). ... On suspended list (June 20-29, 1994). ... Granted free agency (October 31, 1996). ... Re-signed by Braves (November 20, 1996). ... On Atlanta disabled list (March 29-April 15, and May 24-June 20, 1998); included rehabilitation assignments to Greenville (April 2-10 and June 10-14) and Macon (April 10-14 and June 14-16). ... On Atlanta disabled list (May 17-June 1 and July 5-24, 1999); included rehabilitation assignment to Greenville (July 15-18). ... On disabled list (April 2, 2000-entire season). ... On Atlanta disabled list (March 23-May 17 and June 10-July 22, 2001); included rehabilitation assignments to Macon (May 9-17) and Greenville (May 5-8 and July 17-22). ... Granted free agency (November 5, 2001). ... Re-signed by Braves (December 4, 2001). ... Placed on 15-day disabled list (August 27, 2003). ... Removed from 15-day disabled list (September 20, 2003).

CAREER HITTING: 127-for-737 (.172), 69 R, 20 2B, 1 3B, 5 HR, 51 RBI.

Year	League	W	L	Pct.	ERA	WHIP	G	GS	CG	ShO	Hld.	Sv.-Opp.	IP	H	R	ER	HR	BB-IBB	SO	Avg.
1986—Lakeland (Fla. St.)	7	8	.467	3.56	1.22	17	14	2	1	...	0-...	96.0	86	44	38	7	31-0	47	.242
1987—Glens Falls (East.)	4	10	.286	5.68	1.63	21	21	0	0	...	0-...	130.0	131	89	82	17	81-2	86	.268
—Richmond (Int'l)	0	1	.000	6.19	1.75	3	3	0	0	...	0-...	16.0	17	11	11	2	11-0	5	.266
1988—Richmond (Int'l)	10	5	.667	2.79	1.15	20	20	3	0	...	0-...	135.1	118	49	42	5	37-1	115	.233
—Atlanta (N.L.)	2	7	.222	5.48	1.67	12	12	0	0	0	0-0	64.0	74	40	39	10	33-4	37	.285
1989—Atlanta (N.L.)	12	11	.522	2.94	1.12	29	29	5	0	0	0-0	208.0	160	79	68	15	72-2	168	.212
1990—Atlanta (N.L.)	14	11	.560	3.85	1.28	34	34	6	2	0	0-0	231.1	206	109	99	20	* 90-3	170	.240
1991—Atlanta (N.L.)	14	13	.519	3.80	1.23	36	36	5	0	0	0-0	229.2	206	101	97	16	77-1	148	.243
1992—Atlanta (N.L.)	15	12	.556	2.85	1.16	35	• 35	9	3	0	0-0	246.2	206	90	78	17	80-5	* 215	.224
1993—Atlanta (N.L.)	15	11	.577	3.62	1.26	35	35	3	1	0	0-0	243.2	208	104	98	23	100-12	208	.230
1994—Atlanta (N.L.)	6	10	.375	4.14	1.25	21	21	1	0	0	0-0	134.2	120	69	62	15	48-4	113	.239
1995—Atlanta (N.L.)	12	7	.632	3.18	1.24	29	29	2	1	0	0-0	192.2	166	76	68	15	72-8	193	.232
1996—Atlanta (N.L.)	* 24	8	*.750	2.94	1.00	35	35	6	2	0	0-0	* 253.2	199	93	83	19	55-3	* 276	.216
1997—Atlanta (N.L.)	15	12	.556	3.02	1.16	35	• 35	7	2	0	0-0	* 256.0	* 234	97	86	21	63-9	241	.242
1998—Greenville (Sou.)	0	1	.000	2.57	1.00	3	3	0	0	...	0-...	14.0	11	4	4	2	3-0	16	.216
—Macon (S. Atl.)	0	0	...	3.60	0.80	2	2	0	0	...	0-...	10.0	7	4	4	1	1-0	14	.179
—Atlanta (N.L.)	17	3	*.850	2.90	1.13	26	26	2	2	0	0-0	167.2	145	58	54	10	44-2	173	.231
1999—Atlanta (N.L.)	11	8	.579	3.19	1.12	29	29	1	1	0	0-0	186.1	168	70	66	14	40-2	156	.245
—Greenville (Sou.)	0	0	...	4.50	1.50	2	1	0	0	...	0-...	4.0	5	2	2	0	1-0	7	.294
2000—Atlanta (N.L.)											Did not play.								
2001—Atlanta (N.L.)	0	0	...	0.00	0.50	3	1	0	0	...	0-...	6.0	3	0	0	0	0-0	6	.150
—Macon (S. Atl.)	0	0	...	1.80	0.80	1	1	0	0	...	0-...	5.0	4	1	1	0	0-0	5	.235
—Atlanta (N.L.)	3	3	.500	3.36	1.07	36	5	0	0	5	10-11	59.0	53	24	22	7	10-2	57	.238
2002—Atlanta (N.L.)	3	2	.600	3.25	1.03	75	0	0	0	0	* 55-59	80.1	59	30	29	4	24-1	85	.206
2003—Atlanta (N.L.)	0	2	.000	1.12	0.87	62	0	0	0	0	45-49	64.1	48	9	8	2	8-1	73	.204
Major League totals (15 years)	163	120	.576	3.29	1.17	529	361	47	14	5	110-119	2618.0	2252	1049	957	208	816-59	2313	.232

SNELLING, CHRIS — OF

PERSONAL: Born December 3, 1981... 5-10/165. ... Bats left, throws left. ... Full name: Christopher Doyle Snelling. ... High school: Corpus Christi College Tuggerah (Australia).

TRANSACTIONS/CAREER NOTES: Signed as non-drafted free agent by Seattle Mariners organization (March 2, 1999). ... On San Antonio disabled list (April 4-May 1, 2002). ... On Seattle disabled list (June 5, 2002-remainder of season). ... On disabled list (March 21-entire 2003 season).

Year Team (League)	Pos.	G	AB	R	H	2B	3B	HR	RBI	BB	SO	HBP	GDP	SB-CS	Avg.	OBP	SLG	OPS	E	Pct.
1999— Everett (N'west)	OF	69	265	46	81	15	3	10	50	33	24	6	4	8-9	.306	.388	.498	.886	1	.993
2000— Wisconsin (Midw.)	OF	72	259	44	79	9	5	9	56	34	34	6	2	7-4	.305	.386	.483	.869	2	.983
2001— San Bern. (Calif.)	OF	114	450	90	151	29	10	7	73	45	63	21	7	12-5	.336	.418	.491	.909	4	.978
2002— San Antonio (Texas)	OF	23	89	10	29	9	2	1	12	12	11	4	1	5-1	.326	.429	.506	.934	0	1.000
— Seattle (A.L.)	OF	8	27	2	4	0	0	1	3	2	4	0	2	0-0	.148	.207	.259	.466	0	1.000
2003— Tacoma (PCL)	OF-DH	18	67	11	18	2	0	3	10	5	12	2	0	1-0	.269	.333	.433	.766	0	1.000
— San Antonio (Texas)	OF-DH	47	186	24	62	12	2	3	25	8	30	5	0	1-7	.333	.371	.468	.839	0	1.000
Major League totals (1 year)		8	27	2	4	0	0	1	3	2	4	0	2	0-0	.148	.207	.259	.466	0	1.000

SNOW, J.T.   1B

PERSONAL: Born February 26, 1968, in Long Beach, Calif. ... 6-2/209. ... Bats left, throws left. ... Full name: Jack Thomas Snow. ... High school: Los Alamitos (Calif.). ... College: Arizona.

TRANSACTIONS/CAREER NOTES: Selected by New York Yankees organization in fifth round of free-agent draft (June 5, 1989). ... Traded by Yankees with P Jerry Nielsen and P Russ Springer to California Angels for P Jim Abbott (December 6, 1992). ... Traded by Angels to San Francisco Giants for P Allen Watson and P Fausto Macey (November 27, 1996). ... On San Francisco disabled list (May 27-June 14, June 24-July 15 and July 27-August 7, 2001); included rehabilitation assignments to Fresno (June 12-14 and July 12-15). ... Placed on 15-day disabled list (June 18, 2003). ... Reinstated from 15-day disabled list (July 3, 2003). ... Placed on 15-day disabled list (August 17, 2003). ... Removed from 15-day disabled list (September 1, 2003).

2003 GAMES PLAYED BY POSITION (MLB): 1B—97.

Year Team (League)	Pos.	G	AB	R	H	2B	3B	HR	RBI	BB	SO	HBP	GDP	SB-CS	Avg.	OBP	SLG	OPS	E	Pct.
1989— Oneonta (NYP)	1B	73	274	41	80	18	2	8	51	29	35	2	9	4-1	.292	.359	.460	.819	6	.991
1990— Prince Will. (Car.)	1B	* 138	520	57	133	25	1	8	72	46	65	5	20	2-0	.256	.318	.354	.672	12	.991
1991— Alb./Colon. (East.)	1B	132	477	78	133	33	3	13	76	67	78	3	10	5-1	.279	.364	.442	.807	8	.993
1992— Columbus (Int'l)	1B-OF	135	492	81	154	26	4	15	78	70	65	1	9	3-3	.313	.395	.474	.869	8	.993
— New York (A.L.)	1B-DH	7	14	1	2	1	0	0	2	5	5	0	0	0-0	.143	.368	.214	.583	0	1.000
1993— California (A.L.)	1B	129	419	60	101	18	2	16	57	55	88	2	10	3-0	.241	.328	.408	.736	6	.995
— Vancouver (PCL)	1B	23	94	19	32	9	1	5	24	10	13	1	2	0-0	.340	.410	.617	1.027	2	.991
1994— Vancouver (PCL)	1B-DH	53	189	35	56	13	2	8	43	22	32	0	5	1-2	.296	.364	.513	.878	1	.998
— California (A.L.)	1B	61	223	22	49	4	0	8	30	19	48	3	2	0-1	.220	.289	.345	.634	2	.996
1995— California (A.L.)	1B	143	544	80	157	22	1	24	102	52	91	3	16	2-1	.289	.353	.465	.818	4	.997
1996— California (A.L.)	1B	155	575	69	148	20	1	17	67	56	96	5	19	1-6	.257	.327	.384	.711	10	.993
1997— San Francisco (N.L.)	1B	157	531	81	149	36	1	28	104	96	124	1	8	6-4	.281	.387	.510	.898	7	.995
1998— San Francisco (N.L.)	1B	138	435	65	108	29	1	15	79	58	84	0	12	1-2	.248	.332	.423	.755	1	.999
1999— San Francisco (N.L.)	1B	161	570	93	156	25	2	24	98	86	121	5	16	0-4	.274	.370	.451	.821	6	.996
2000— San Francisco (N.L.)	1B	155	536	82	152	33	2	19	96	66	129	11	20	1-3	.284	.365	.459	.824	6	.995
2001— San Francisco (N.L.)	1B	101	285	43	70	12	1	8	34	55	81	4	2	0-0	.246	.371	.379	.750	1	.999
— Fresno (PCL)	1B	4	12	1	0	0	0	0	0	2	7	0	0	0-0	.000	.143	.000	.143	0	1.000
2002— San Francisco (N.L.)	1B	143	422	47	104	26	2	6	53	59	90	7	11	0-0	.246	.344	.360	.704	7	.993
2003— San Francisco (N.L.)	1B	103	330	48	90	18	3	8	51	55	55	8	7	1-2	.273	.387	.418	.806	5	.994
American League totals (5 years)		495	1775	232	457	65	4	65	258	187	328	13	47	6-8	.257	.331	.408	.739	22	.995
National League totals (7 years)		958	3109	459	829	179	12	108	515	475	684	36	76	9-15	.267	.366	.436	.802	33	.996
Major League totals (12 years)		1453	4884	691	1286	244	16	173	773	662	1012	49	123	15-23	.263	.353	.426	.779	55	.995

SNYDER, KYLE   P

PERSONAL: Born September 9, 1977, in Houston, Texas. ... 6-8/220. ... Throws right, bats both. ... Full name: Kyle Ehren Snyder. ... High school: Riverview (Sarasota, Fla.). ... College: North Carolina.

TRANSACTIONS/CAREER NOTES: Selected by Tampa Bay Devil Rays organization in 27th round of free-agent draft (June 4, 1996); did not sign. ... Selected by Kansas City Royals organization in first round (seventh pick overall) of free-agent draft (June 2, 1999). ... On disabled list (June 19-August 25 and August 28, 2000-remainder of season). ... On Spokane disabled list (June 19-July 16, 2001). ... On Burlington disabled list (July 16, 2001-remainder of season). ... Called up by Kansas City from Omaha of the Pacific Coast League (May 1, 2003). ... Placed on 15-day disabled list (July 1, 2003). ... Sent to Arizona League on rehab assignment (July 10, 2003). ... Recalled from Wichita rehab assignment; reinstated from 15-day disabled list (July 21, 2003). ... Placed on 15-day disabled list (August 6, 2003). ... Transferred to 60-day disabled list (September 2, 2003).

CAREER HITTING: 0-for-2 (.000), 0 R, 0 2B, 0 3B, 0 HR, 0 RBI.

Year League	W	L	Pct.	ERA	WHIP	G	GS	CG	ShO	Hld.	Sv.-Opp.	IP	H	R	ER	HR	BB-IBB	SO	Avg.
1999— Spokane (N'west)	1	0	1.000	4.13	1.13	7	7	0	0	...	0-...	24.0	20	13	11	1	7-0	25	.220
2000— GC Royals (GCL)	0	0	...	0.00	0.50	1	1	0	0	...	0-...	2.0	1	0	0	0	0-0	4	.143
— Wilmington (Caro.)	0	0	...	...	...	1	1	0	0	...	0-...	.0	0	1	0	0	1-0	0	...
2001—										Did not play.									
2002— Wilmington (Caro.)	0	2	.000	2.98	1.24	15	15	0	0	...	0-...	48.1	49	19	16	1	11-0	48	.261
— Wichita (Texas)	2	2	.500	4.21	1.09	6	6	0	0	...	0-...	25.2	21	12	12	4	7-1	18	.226
2003— Omaha (PCL)	3	1	1.000	2.79	1.17	5	5	0	0	...	0-...	29.0	28	9	9	3	6-0	15	.259
— Ariz. Royals (Ariz.)	0	0	...	4.50	1.50	1	1	0	0	...	0-...	2.0	3	1	1	0	0-0	1	.375
— Wichita (Texas)	0	0	...	0.00	0.40	1	1	0	0	...	0-...	5.0	2	0	0	0	0-0	2	.125
— Kansas City (A.L.)	1	6	.143	5.17	1.35	15	15	0	0	0	0-0	85.1	94	52	49	11	21-3	39	.283
Major League totals (1 year)	1	6	.143	5.17	1.35	15	15	0	0	0	0-0	85.1	94	52	49	11	21-3	39	.283

SOJO, LUIS   IF

PERSONAL: Born January 3, 1966, in Barquisimeto, Venezuela. ... 5-11/185. ... Bats right, throws right. ... Full name: Luis Beltran Sojo. ... Name pronounced: SO-ho.

TRANSACTIONS/CAREER NOTES: Signed as non-drafted free agent by Toronto Blue Jays organization (January 3, 1986). ... Traded by Blue Jays with OF Junior Felix and a player to be named later to California Angels for OF Devon White, P Willie Fraser and a player to be named later (December 2, 1990); Blue Jays acquired P Marcus Moore and Angels acquired C Ken Rivers to complete deal (December 4, 1990). ... Traded by Angels to Blue Jays for 3B Kelly Gruber and cash (December 8, 1992). ... On Toronto disabled list (May 10-30, 1993). ... Granted free agency (October 15, 1993). ... Signed by Seattle Mariners organization (January 10, 1994). ... On Seattle disabled list (June 7-23, 1995); included rehabilitation assignment to Tacoma (June 19-23). ... Claimed on waivers by New York Yankees (August 22, 1996). ... Granted free agency (December 20, 1996). ... Re-signed by Yankees (January 9, 1997). ... On disabled list (August 15, 1997-remainder of season). ... Granted free agency (October 31, 1997). ... Re-signed by Yankees (November 12, 1997). ... On New York disabled list (March 22-April 27, 1998); included rehabilitation assignments to Tampa (April 17-20) and Columbus (April 20-27). ... Granted free agency (November 10, 1999). ... Signed by Pittsburgh Pirates organization (January 19, 2000). ... On Pittsburgh disabled list (July 6-24, 2000). ... Traded by Pirates to Yankees for P Chris Spurling (August 7, 2000). ... Granted free agency (November 7, 2000). ... Re-signed by Yankees (December 7, 2000). ... Granted free agency (November 6, 2001). ... Re-signed by Yankees organization (January 8, 2002). ... Released by Yankees (October 27, 2003).

2003 GAMES PLAYED BY POSITION (MLB): 2B—1, DH—1, 1B—1.

Year	Team (League)	Pos.	G	AB	R	H	2B	3B	HR	RBI	BB	SO	HBP	GDP	SB-CS	Avg.	OBP	SLG	OPS	E	Pct.
1986—	....										Did not play.										
1987—Myrtle Beach (SAL)		2-3-S-O	72	223	23	47	5	4	2	15	17	18	0	9	5-1	.211	.266	.296	.562	14	.942
1988—Myrtle Beach (SAL)		SS	135	*536	83	*155	22	5	5	56	35	35	2	18	14-9	.289	.332	.377	.708	28	.955
1989—Syracuse (Int'l)		2B-SS	121	482	54	133	20	5	3	54	21	42	1	9	9-14	.276	.305	.357	.661	23 ‡	.957
1990—Syracuse (Int'l)		2B-SS	75	297	39	88	12	3	6	25	14	23	1	8	10-2	.296	.321	.418	.738	10	.972
—Toronto (A.L.)		DH	33	80	14	18	3	0	1	9	5	5	0	1	1-1	.225	.271	.300	.571	5	.929
1991—California (A.L.)		DH	113	364	38	94	14	1	3	20	14	26	5	12	4-2	.258	.295	.327	.622	11	.981
1992—Edmonton (PCL)		3B-2B-SS	37	145	22	43	9	1	1	24	9	17	1	5	4-2	.297	.338	.393	.731	4	.972
—California (A.L.)		2B-3B-SS	106	368	37	100	12	3	7	43	14	24	1	14	7-11	.272	.299	.378	.677	9	.982
1993—Toronto (A.L.)		2B-SS-3B	19	47	5	8	2	0	0	6	4	2	0	3	0-0	.170	.231	.213	.444	2	.967
—Syracuse (Int'l)		2-0-3-S	43	142	17	31	7	2	1	12	8	12	0	6	2-1	.218	.260	.317	.577	4	.964
1994—Calgary (PCL)		SS-2B-3-D	24	102	19	33	9	3	1	18	10	7	0	3	5-0	.324	.377	.500	.877	2	.983
—Seattle (A.L.)		2-S-D-3	63	213	32	59	9	2	6	22	8	25	2	2	2-1	.277	.308	.423	.731	7	.976
1995—Seattle (A.L.)		SS-2B-OF	102	339	50	98	18	2	7	39	23	19	1	9	4-2	.289	.335	.416	.751	9	.976
—Tacoma (PCL)		2B-SS-DH	4	17	1	3	0	0	1	1	0	2	0	0	0-0	.176	.176	.353	.529	0	1.000
1996—Seattle (A.L.)		3B-2B-SS	77	247	20	52	8	1	1	16	10	13	1	8	2-2	.211	.244	.263	.507	8	.970
—New York (A.L.)		2B-SS-3B	18	40	3	11	2	0	0	5	1	4	0	2	0-0	.275	.286	.325	.611	0	1.000
1997—New York (A.L.)		2-S-3-1	77	215	27	66	6	1	2	25	16	14	1	5	3-1	.307	.355	.372	.727	5	.986
1998—Tampa (Fla. St.)		SS	3	9	1	2	0	0	0	0	2	0	0	0	0-0	.222	.364	.222	.586	1	.923
—Columbus (Int'l)		SS-2B-DH	6	23	1	5	2	0	0	2	1	1	0	1	1-0	.217	.250	.304	.554	1	.962
—New York (A.L.)		S-1-2-3-D	54	147	16	34	3	1	0	14	4	15	0	5	1-0	.231	.250	.265	.515	3	.987
1999—New York (A.L.)		3-2-S-1-D	49	127	20	32	6	0	2	16	4	17	0	4	1-0	.252	.275	.346	.621	2	.986
2000—Pittsburgh (N.L.)		3B-2B	61	176	14	50	11	0	5	20	11	16	1	6	1-0	.284	.328	.432	.760	5	.960
—New York (A.L.)		2-3-1-S	34	125	19	36	7	1	2	17	6	6	0	5	1-0	.288	.321	.408	.729	2	.986
2001—New York (A.L.)		3-1-2-S-D	39	79	5	13	2	0	0	9	4	12	1	0	1-0	.165	.214	.190	.404	2	.979
2002—	....										Did not play.										
2003—New York (A.L.)		2B-DH-1B	3	4	0	0	0	0	0	0	0	0	0	0	0-0	.000	.000	.000	.000	0	1.000
American League totals (13 years)			787	2395	286	621	92	12	31	241	113	182	12	70	27-20	.259	.295	.347	.642	65	.979
National League totals (1 year)			61	176	14	50	11	0	5	20	11	16	1	6	1-0	.284	.328	.432	.760	5	.960
Major League totals (13 years)			848	2571	300	671	103	12	36	261	124	198	13	76	28-20	.261	.297	.352	.650	70	.978

SORENSEN, ZACH   2B/SS/3B

PERSONAL: Born January 3, 1977, in Salt Lake City, Utah. ... 6-0/190. ... Bats both, throws right. ... Full name: Zach Hart Sorensen. ... High school: Highland (Salt Lake City, Utah). ... College: Wichita State.

TRANSACTIONS/CAREER NOTES: Selected by Cleveland Indians organization in second round of free-agent draft (June 2, 1998).

2003 GAMES PLAYED BY POSITION (MLB): 2B—14, SS—3, 3B—1, DH—1, OF—1.

Year	Team (League)	Pos.	G	AB	R	H	2B	3B	HR	RBI	BB	SO	HBP	GDP	SB-CS	Avg.	OBP	SLG	OPS	E	Pct.
1998—Watertown (NYP)		SS	53	200	38	60	7	8	4	26	35	35	0	2	14-4	.300	.404	.475	.879	12	.951
1999—Kinston (Caro.)		SS	130	508	79	121	16	7	7	59	62	126	2	6	24-12	.238	.322	.339	.661	22	.963
2000—Buffalo (Int'l)		SS	12	38	5	10	1	1	0	2	3	9	0	2	1-0	.263	.310	.342	.652	2	.961
—Akron (East.)		SS	96	382	62	99	17	4	6	38	42	62	2	8	16-6	.259	.333	.372	.705	18	.972
2001—Mahoning Valley (NY-P)		SS	14	53	10	13	0	1	1	11	2	8	0	2	2-0	.245	.263	.340	.603	1	.970
—Akron (East.)		SS	46	194	24	45	6	1	5	16	11	30	0	3	10-8	.232	.273	.351	.624	10	.956
—Buffalo (Int'l)		2B	2	7	2	2	0	0	0	1	0	0	0	0	0-0	.286	.286	.286	.571	0	1.000
2002—Buffalo (Int'l)		2B-SS	120	455	55	120	12	12	7	54	24	72	1	9	13-6	.264	.300	.389	.689	13	.978
2003—Buffalo (Int'l)		2-0-S-3	61	238	39	57	12	3	3	29	22	42	0	3	12-5	.239	.299	.353	.652	10	.957
—Cleveland (A.L.)		2-S-3-D-O	36	37	2	5	1	0	1	2	7	13	0	0	0-3	.135	.273	.243	.516	2	.955
Major League totals (1 year)			36	37	2	5	1	0	1	2	7	13	0	0	0-3	.135	.273	.243	.516	2	.955

SORIANO, ALFONSO   2B

PERSONAL: Born January 7, 1978, in San Pedro de Macoris, Dominican Republic. ... 6-1/160. ... Bats right, throws right. ... Full name: Alfonso Guilleard Soriano. ... Name pronounced: soar-ee-ah-no. ... High school: Eugenio Maria de Osto (Dominican Republic).

TRANSACTIONS/CAREER NOTES: Signed by Hiroshima Toyo Carp of Japan Central League (November 1994). ... Played in Toyo Carp organization (1995-97). ... Retired from Japan Central League and declared free agent by Major League Baseball (1998). ... Signed by New York Yankees (September 29, 1998). ... On Norwich disabled list (July 15-August 15, 1999).

2003 GAMES PLAYED BY POSITION (MLB): 2B—155.

Year	Team (League)	Pos.	G	AB	R	H	2B	3B	HR	RBI	BB	SO	HBP	GDP	SB-CS	Avg.	OBP	SLG	OPS	E	Pct.
1995—	....										Did not play.										
—Hiroshima (DSL)			63	227	52	83	12	3	4	55	30	19	...	...	8-...	.366	...	.498	...	...	...
1996—Hiroshima (Jap. West.)			57	131	11	28	...	...	0	13	...	...	...	...	...-...	.214	...	...	...	...	...
—	....										Did not play.										
1997—Hiroshima (Jap. West.)			68	242	28	61	13	2	8	34	13	35	...	...	14-...	.252	...	.421	...	...	...
—Hiroshima (Jp. Cn.)		OF	9	17	2	2	0	0	0	0	2	4	...	...	0-...	.118	...	.118	...	...	...
1998—	....										Did not play.										
1999—Norwich (East.)		SS-DH	89	361	57	110	20	3	15	68	32	67	4	9	24-16	.305	.363	.501	.865	27	.937
—GC Yankees (GCL)		SS-DH	5	19	7	5	2	0	1	5	1	3	1	1	0-0	.263	.318	.526	.844	1	.929
—Columbus (Int'l)		SS-3B-2B	20	82	8	15	5	1	2	11	5	18	0	1	1-1	.183	.225	.341	.566	3	.955
—New York (A.L.)		DH-SS	9	8	2	1	0	0	1	1	0	3	0	0	0-1	.125	.125	.500	.625	1	.500
2000—Columbus (Int'l)		SS-2B	111	459	90	133	32	6	12	66	25	85	3	8	14-7	.290	.327	.464	.791	21	.952
—New York (A.L.)		3-S-2-D	22	50	5	9	3	0	2	3	1	15	0	0	2-0	.180	.196	.360	.556	7	.837
2001—New York (A.L.)		2B-DH	158	574	77	154	34	3	18	73	29	125	3	7	43-14	.268	.304	.432	.736	19	.973
2002—New York (A.L.)		2B-DH	156	*696	*128	*209	51	2	39	102	23	157	14	8	*41-13	.300	.332	.547	.880	*23	.968
2003—New York (A.L.)		2B	156	*682	114	198	36	5	38	91	38	130	12	8	35-8	.290	.338	.525	.863	19	.975
Major League totals (5 years)			501	2010	326	571	124	10	98	270	91	430	29	23	121-36	.284	.322	.502	.824	69	.969

SORIANO, RAFAEL — P

PERSONAL: Born December 19, 1979, in San Jose, Dominican Republic. ... 6-1/175. ... Throws right, bats right.
TRANSACTIONS/CAREER NOTES: Signed as non-drafted free agent by Seattle Mariners organization (August 30, 1996). ... On Wisconsin disabled list (April 6-May 5, 2000). ... On San Bernardino disabled list (April 26-May 6, 2001). ... On San Antonio disabled list (July 4-12 and August 31, 2001-remainder of season). ... On disabled list (July 3-August 2, 2002). ... Optioned to Tacoma (May 8, 2003). ... Recalled from Tacoma (July 5, 2003).
CAREER HITTING: 0-for-4 (.000), 0 R, 0 2B, 0 3B, 0 HR, 0 RBI.

Year League	W	L	Pct.	ERA	WHIP	G	GS	CG	ShO	Hld.	Sv.-Opp.	IP	H	R	ER	HR	BB-IBB	SO	Avg.
1999— Everett (Northwest)	5	4	.556	3.11	1.39	14	14	0	0	...	0-...	75.1	56	34	26	8	49-0	83	.208
2000— Wisconsin (Midw.)	8	4	.667	2.87	1.20	21	21	1	0	...	0-...	122.1	97	41	39	3	50-0	90	.225
2001— San Bernardino (Calif.)	6	3	.667	2.53	0.99	15	15	* 2	1	...	0-...	89.0	49	28	25	4	39-0	98	.164
— San Antonio (Texas)	2	2	.500	3.35	0.99	8	8	0	0	...	0-...	48.1	34	18	18	5	14-0	53	.192
2002— San Antonio (Texas)	2	3	.400	2.31	1.01	10	8	0	0	...	0-...	46.2	32	13	12	6	15-0	52	.190
— Seattle (A.L.)	0	3	.000	4.56	1.29	10	8	0	0	0	1-1	47.1	45	25	24	8	16-1	32	.243
2003— Tacoma (PCL)	4	3	.571	3.19	0.89	11	10	0	0	...	0-...	62.0	43	24	22	2	12-0	63	.192
— Seattle (A.L.)	3	0	1.000	1.53	0.79	40	0	0	0	5	1-2	53.0	30	9	9	2	12-1	68	.162
Major League totals (2 years)	**3**	**3**	**.500**	**2.96**	**1.03**	**50**	**8**	**0**	**0**	**5**	**2-3**	**100.1**	**75**	**34**	**33**	**10**	**28-2**	**100**	**.203**

SOSA, JORGE — P

PERSONAL: Born April 28, 1977, in Santo Domingo, Dominican Republic. ... 6-2/170. ... Throws right, bats both. ... Full name: Jorge Bolivar Sosa. ... Name pronounced: hor-hey.
TRANSACTIONS/CAREER NOTES: Signed as non-drafted free agent by Colorado Rockies organization (June 23, 1995). ... Selected by Seattle Mariners from Rockies organization in Rule 5 minor league draft (December 11, 2000). ... Selected by Milwaukee Brewers from Mariners organization in Rule 5 major league draft (December 13, 2001). ... Claimed on waivers by Tampa Bay Devil Rays (March 18, 2002). ... On Tampa Bay disabled list (May 26-June 25, 2002); included rehabilitation assignment to Orlando (June 14-25).
CAREER HITTING: 0-for-0 (.000), 0 R, 0 2B, 0 3B, 0 HR, 0 RBI.

Year League	W	L	Pct.	ERA	WHIP	G	GS	CG	ShO	Hld.	Sv.-Opp.	IP	H	R	ER	HR	BB-IBB	SO	Avg.
2001— Everett (Northwest)	3	1	.750	1.69	1.09	21	7	0	0	...	7-...	58.2	45	22	11	2	19-0	57	.204
— Wisconsin (Midw.)	0	0	...	9.00	1.50	2	0	0	0	...	0-...	2.0	3	2	2	1	0-0	4	.333
2002— Tampa Bay (A.L.)	2	7	.222	5.53	1.43	31	14	0	0	1	0-0	99.1	88	63	61	16	54-0	48	.236
— Orlando (Sou.)	0	0	...	0.00	0.71	2	2	0	0	...	0-...	7.0	4	2	0	1	1-0	3	.167
2003— Durham (Int'l)	1	1	.500	5.47	1.66	4	4	0	0	...	0-...	24.2	32	15	15	3	9-0	17	.314
— Tampa Bay (A.L.)	5	12	.294	4.62	1.53	29	19	1	1	0	0-0	128.2	137	71	66	14	60-4	72	.278
Major League totals (2 years)	**7**	**19**	**.269**	**5.01**	**1.49**	**60**	**33**	**1**	**1**	**1**	**0-0**	**228.0**	**225**	**134**	**127**	**30**	**114-4**	**120**	**.260**

SOSA, SAMMY — OF

PERSONAL: Born November 12, 1968, in San Pedro de Macoris, Dominican Republic. ... 6-0/220. ... Bats right, throws right. ... Full name: Samuel Peralta Sosa.
TRANSACTIONS/CAREER NOTES: Signed as non-drafted free agent by Texas Rangers organization (July 30, 1985). ... Traded by Rangers with SS Scott Fletcher and P Wilson Alvarez to Chicago White Sox for OF Harold Baines and IF Fred Manrique (July 29, 1989). ... Traded by White Sox with P Ken Patterson to Chicago Cubs for OF George Bell (March 30, 1992). ... On Chicago disabled list (June 13-July 27, and August 7-September 16, 1992); included rehabilitation assignment to Iowa (July 21-27). ... On disabled list (August 21, 1996-remainder of season). ... Placed on 15-day disabled list (May 10, 2003). ... Reinstated from 15-day disabled list (May 30, 2003). ... Suspended by Major League Baseball (June 11, 2003). ... Reinstated (June 18, 2003).
2003 GAMES PLAYED BY POSITION (MLB): OF—137.

Year Team (League)	Pos.	G	AB	R	H	2B	3B	HR	RBI	BB	SO	HBP	GDP	SB-CS	Avg.	OBP	SLG	OPS	E	Pct.
1986— GC Rangers (GCL)	OF	61	229	38	63	* 19	1	4	28	22	51	0	4	11-3	.275	.336	.419	.755	• 6	.944
1987— Gastonia (S. Atl.)	OF	129	519	73	145	27	4	11	59	21	123	5	7	22-8	.279	.312	.410	.722	17	.920
1988— Charlotte (Fla. St.)	OF	131	507	70	116	13 *	12	9	51	35	106	4	14	42-24	.229	.282	.355	.637	7	.971
1989— Tulsa (Texas)	OF	66	273	45	81	15	4	7	31	15	52	3	4	16-11	.297	.338	.458	.796	4	.967
— Texas (A.L.)	DH-OF	25	84	8	20	3	0	1	3	0	20	0	3	0-2	.238	.238	.310	.548	2	.944
— Okla. City (A.A.)	OF	10	39	2	4	2	0	0	3	2	8	0	2	4-2	.103	.146	.154	.300	2	.917
— Vancouver (PCL)	OF	13	49	7	18	3	0	1	5	0	20	0	1	0-1	.367	.367	.490	.857	0	1.000
— Chicago (A.L.)	OF	33	99	19	27	5	0	3	10	11	27	2	3	7-3	.273	.351	.414	.765	2	.969
1990— Chicago (A.L.)	OF	153	532	72	124	26	10	15	70	33	150	6	10	32-16	.233	.282	.404	.687	* 13	.962
1991— Chicago (A.L.)	DH-OF	116	316	39	64	10	1	10	33	14	98	2	5	13-6	.203	.240	.335	.576	6	.973
— Vancouver (PCL)	OF	32	116	19	31	7	2	3	19	17	32	1	2	9-2	.267	.358	.440	.797	3	.970
1992— Chicago (N.L.)	OF	67	262	41	68	7	2	8	25	19	63	4	4	15-7	.260	.317	.393	.710	6	.961
— Iowa (Am. Assoc.)	OF	5	19	3	6	2	0	0	1	1	2	0	0	5-0	.316	.350	.421	.771	0	1.000
1993— Chicago (N.L.)	OF	159	598	92	156	25	5	33	93	38	135	4	14	36-11	.261	.309	.485	.794	9	.976
1994— Chicago (N.L.)	OF	105	426	59	128	17	6	25	70	25	92	2	7	22-13	.300	.339	.545	.884	7	.973
1995— Chicago (N.L.)	OF • 144	564	89	151	17	3	36	119	58	134	5	8	34-7	.268	.340	.500	.840	* 13	.962
1996— Chicago (N.L.)	OF	124	498	84	136	21	2	40	100	34	134	5	5	18-5	.273	.323	.564	.888	10	.964
1997— Chicago (N.L.)	OF • 162	642	90	161	31	4	36	119	45	*174	2	16	22-12	.251	.300	.480	.779	8	.977
1998— Chicago (N.L.)	OF	159	643	* 134	198	20	0	66	* 158	73	*171	1	20	18-9	.308	.377	.647	1.024	9	.975
1999— Chicago (N.L.)	OF • 162	625	114	180	24	2	63	141	78	*171	3	17	7-8	.288	.367	.635	1.002	9	.978
2000— Chicago (N.L.)	OF	156	604	106	193	38	1	* 50	138	91	168	2	12	7-4	.320	.406	.634	1.040	• 10	.970
2001— Chicago (N.L.)	OF	160	577	* 146	189	34	5	64	* 160	116	153	6	6	0-2	.328	.437	.737	1.174	6	.982
2002— Chicago (N.L.)	OF	150	556	* 122	160	19	2	* 49	108	103	144	3	14	2-0	.288	.399	.594	.993	6	.980
2003— Chicago (N.L.)	OF	137	517	99	144	22	0	40	103	62	143	5	14	0-1	.279	.358	.553	.911	5	.977
American League totals (3 years)		327	1031	138	235	44	11	29	116	58	295	10	21	52-27	.228	.273	.376	.650	23	.966
National League totals (12 years)		1685	6512	1176	1864	275	32	510	1334	742	1682	42	146	181-79	.286	.360	.573	.933	98	.974
Major League totals (15 years)		2012	7543	1314	2099	319	43	539	1450	800	1977	52	167	233-106	.278	.349	.546	.895	121	.972

SPARKS, STEVE — P

PERSONAL: Born July 2, 1965, in Tulsa, Okla. ... 6-0/195. ... Throws right, bats right. ... Full name: Steven William Sparks. ... High school: Holland Hall (Tulsa, Okla.). ... College: Sam Houston State.
TRANSACTIONS/CAREER NOTES: Selected by Milwaukee Brewers organization in fifth round of free-agent draft (June 2, 1987). ... On disabled list (March 24, 1997-entire season). ... Granted free agency (October 15, 1997). ... Signed by Anaheim Angels (February 23, 1998). ... On Cedar Rapids disabled list (April 9-19, 1998). ... Granted free agency (October 15, 1999). ... Signed by Philadelphia Phillies organization (February 1, 2000). ... Released by Phillies (February 28, 2000). ... Signed by Detroit Tigers organization (March 2, 2000). ... Released by Tigers (August 27, 2003). ... Signed to minor league contract by Oakland Athletics (August 30, 2003).
CAREER HITTING: 1-for-10 (.100), 1 R, 1 2B, 0 3B, 0 HR, 2 RBI.

Year	League	W	L	Pct.	ERA	WHIP	G	GS	CG	ShO	Hld.	Sv.-Opp.	IP	H	R	ER	HR	BB-IBB	SO	Avg.
1987— Helena (Pio.)		6	3	.667	4.68	1.53	10	9	2	0		0-...	57.2	68	44	30	8	20-1	47	.298
1988— Beloit (Midw.)		9	13	.409	3.79	1.30	25	24	5	1		0-...	164.0	162	80	69	8	51-2	96	.260
1989— Stockton (Calif.)		• 13	5	.722	2.41	1.09	23	22	3	2		0-...	164.0	125	55	44	6	53-0	126	.210
1990— Stockton (Calif.)		10	7	.588	3.69	1.29	19	19	5	1		0-...	129.1	136	63	53	4	31-0	77	.270
— El Paso (Texas)		1	2	.333	6.53	1.91	7	6	1	0		0-...	30.1	43	24	22	4	15-0	17	.341
1991— Stockton (Calif.)		9	10	.474	3.06	1.44	24	24	• 8	2		0-...	179.2	160	70	61	4	98-2	139	.246
— El Paso (Texas)		1	2	.333	9.53	2.29	4	4	0	0		0-...	17.0	30	22	18	1	9-0	10	.370
1992— El Paso (Texas)		9	8	.529	5.37	1.49	28	22	3	0		1-...	140.2	159	99	84	11	50-1	79	.295
1993— New Orleans (A.A.)		9	13	.409	3.84	1.41	29	• 28	* 7	1		0-...	* 180.1	174	89	77	17	* 80-1	104	.260
1994— New Orleans (A.A.)		10	12	.455	4.46	1.37	28	27	5	1		0-...	* 183.2	183	101	91	23	68-0	105	.261
1995— Milwaukee (A.L.)		9	11	.450	4.63	1.47	33	27	3	0	0	0-...	202.0	210	111	104	17	86-1	96	.274
1996— Milwaukee (A.L.)		4	7	.364	6.60	1.75	20	13	1	0	0	0-...	88.2	103	66	65	19	52-0	21	.297
— New Orleans (A.A.)		2	6	.250	4.99	1.72	11	10	3	2	...	0-...	57.2	64	43	32	8	35-0	27	.284
1997— Milwaukee (A.L.)											Did not play.									
1998— Midland (Texas)		0	4	.000	7.08	1.57	7	7	0	0		0-...	40.2	49	38	32	3	15-0	34	.295
— Vancouver (PCL)		0	4	.000	2.89	1.04	4	4	2	0	...	0-...	28.0	23	11	9	2	6-0	19	.223
— Anaheim (A.L.)		9	4	.692	4.34	1.46	22	20	0	0	0	0-0	128.2	130	66	62	14	58-0	90	.263
1999— Anaheim (A.L.)		5	11	.313	5.42	1.67	28	26	0	0	0	0-...	147.2	165	101	89	21	82-0	73	.281
2000— Toledo (Int'l)		5	7	.417	3.77	1.40	16	14	1	0	...	0-...	90.2	86	53	38	8	41-0	44	.250
— Detroit (A.L.)		7	5	.583	4.07	1.32	20	15	1	1	0	1-1	104.0	108	55	47	7	29-0	53	.263
2001— Detroit (A.L.)		14	9	.609	3.65	1.33	35	33	* 8	1	0	0-0	232.0	244	110	94	22	64-1	116	.271
2002— Detroit (A.L.)		8	16	.333	5.52	1.61	32	30	3	0	0	0-0	189.0	238	134	116	23	67-3	98	.306
2003— Detroit (A.L.)		0	6	.000	4.72	1.44	42	0	0	0	0	2-4	89.2	95	57	47	11	34-4	49	.278
— Oakland (A.L.)		0	0	...	5.71	1.27	9	0	0	0	0	0-0	17.1	19	11	11	2	3-0	5	.271
Major League totals (8 years)		**56**	**69**	**.448**	**4.77**	**1.49**	**241**	**164**	**16**	**2**	**0**	**3-5**	**1199.0**	**1312**	**711**	**635**	**136**	**475-9**	**601**	**.279**

SPEIER, JUSTIN   P

PERSONAL: Born November 6, 1973, in Walnut Creek, Calif. ... 6-4/205. ... Throws right, bats right. ... Full name: Justin James Speier. ... Name pronounced: SPY-er. ... High school: Brophy College Prep (Phoenix). ... College: Nicholls State.

TRANSACTIONS/CAREER NOTES: Selected by Chicago Cubs organization in 55th round of free-agent draft (June 1, 1995). ... Traded by Cubs with 3B Kevin Orie and P Todd Noel to Florida Marlins for P Felix Heredia and P Steve Hoff (July 31, 1998). ... Traded by Marlins to Atlanta Braves for a player to be named (April 1, 1999); Marlins acquired P Matthew Targac to complete deal (June 11, 1999). ... Claimed on waivers by Cleveland Indians (November 23, 1999). ... Traded by Indians to New York Mets for OF Brian Jenkins (May 19, 2001). ... Claimed on waivers by Colorado Rockies (May 29, 2001). ... On Colorado disabled list (March 31-May 6, 2002); included rehabilitation assignment to Colorado Springs (April 8-May 6).

CAREER HITTING: 3-for-16 (.188), 0 R, 0 2B, 0 3B, 0 HR, 0 RBI.

Year	League	W	L	Pct.	ERA	WHIP	G	GS	CG	ShO	Hld.	Sv.-Opp.	IP	H	R	ER	HR	BB-IBB	SO	Avg.
1995— Williamsport (NYP)		2	1	.667	1.49	0.85	30	0	0	0		12-...	36.1	27	6	6	1	4-0	39	.203
1996— Daytona (Fla. St.)		2	4	.333	3.76	1.33	33	0	0	0		13-...	38.1	32	19	16	3	19-3	34	.225
— Orlando (Sou.)		4	1	.800	2.05	1.06	24	0	0	0		6-...	26.1	23	7	6	2	5-1	14	.228
1997— Orlando (Sou.)		6	5	.545	4.48	1.28	50	0	0	0		6-...	78.1	77	46	39	8	23-0	63	.260
— Iowa (Am. Assoc.)		2	0	1.000	0.00	0.49	8	0	0	0		1-...	12.1	5	0	0	0	1-0	9	.128
1998— Iowa (PCL)		3	3	.500	5.05	1.37	45	0	0	0	0	12-...	51.2	52	31	29	10	19-1	49	.261
— Chicago (N.L.)		0	0	...	13.50	2.25	1	0	0	0	0	0-0	1.1	2	2	2	0	1-0	2	.333
— Florida (N.L.)		0	3	.000	8.38	1.91	18	0	0	0	1	0-1	19.1	25	18	18	7	12-1	15	.325
1999— Richmond (Int'l)		2	4	.333	5.62	1.75	27	0	0	0	0	3-...	41.2	51	28	26	4	22-4	39	.293
— Atlanta (N.L.)		0	0	...	5.65	1.43	19	0	0	0	0	0-0	28.2	28	18	18	8	13-1	22	.248
2000— Buffalo (Int'l)		0	0	...	4.15	1.23	13	0	0	0	0	9-...	13.0	13	6	6	0	3-0	12	.255
— Cleveland (A.L.)		5	2	.714	3.29	1.24	47	0	0	0	6	0-1	68.1	57	27	25	9	28-3	69	.226
2001— Cleveland (A.L.)		2	0	1.000	6.97	1.55	12	0	0	0	0	0-0	20.2	24	16	16	5	8-0	15	.293
— Colorado (N.L.)		4	3	.571	3.70	1.05	42	0	0	0	4	0-1	56.0	47	24	23	8	12-3	47	.229
— Colo. Springs (PCL)		1	0	1.000	1.46	1.38	11	0	0	0	0	2-...	12.1	10	2	2	0	7-0	16	.227
2002— Colo. Springs (PCL)		2	0	1.000	3.86	1.64	12	0	0	0	0	2-...	14.0	20	7	6	2	3-1	14	.333
— Colorado (N.L.)		5	1	.833	4.33	1.12	63	0	0	0	18	1-4	62.1	51	31	30	9	19-4	47	.216
2003— Colorado (N.L.)		3	1	.750	4.05	1.31	72	0	0	0	12	9-12	73.1	73	37	33	11	23-6	66	.257
American League totals (2 years)		**7**	**2**	**.778**	**4.15**	**1.31**	**59**	**0**	**0**	**0**	**6**	**0-1**	**89.0**	**81**	**43**	**41**	**14**	**36-3**	**84**	**.243**
National League totals (5 years)		**12**	**8**	**.600**	**4.63**	**1.27**	**215**	**0**	**0**	**0**	**35**	**10-18**	**241.0**	**226**	**130**	**124**	**43**	**80-15**	**199**	**.245**
Major League totals (6 years)		**19**	**10**	**.655**	**4.50**	**1.28**	**274**	**0**	**0**	**0**	**41**	**10-19**	**330.0**	**307**	**173**	**165**	**57**	**116-18**	**283**	**.245**

SPENCER, SHANE   OF

PERSONAL: Born February 20, 1972, in Key West, Fla. ... 6-0/225. ... Bats right, throws right. ... Full name: Michael Shane Spencer. ... High school: Granite Hills (El Cajon, Calif.).

TRANSACTIONS/CAREER NOTES: Selected by New York Yankees organization in 28th round of free-agent draft (June 4, 1990). ... On disabled list (April 10-May 9, 1994). ... On New York disabled list (July 3-27, 1999); included rehabilitation assignment to Columbus (July 21-27). ... On disabled list (July 12, 2000-remainder of season). ... On New York disabled list (March 31-April 29, 2001); included rehabilitation assignment to Columbus (April 14-29). ... Granted free agency (December 21, 2002). ... Signed by Cleveland Indians (January 14, 2003). ... Traded by Indians with P Ricardo Rodriguez to Texas Rangers for OF Ryan Ludwick (July 18, 2003).

2003 GAMES PLAYED BY POSITION (MLB): OF—97, 1B—11, DH—8.

Year	Team (League)	Pos.	G	AB	R	H	2B	3B	HR	RBI	BB	SO	HBP	GDP	SB-CS	Avg.	OBP	SLG	OPS	E	Pct.
1990— GC Yankees (GCL)	OF	42	147	20	27	4	0	0	7	20	23	1	3	11-2	.184	.284	.211	.495	3	.965
1991— GC Yankees (GCL)	OF	44	160	25	49	7	0	0	30	14	19	2	6	9-2	.306	.361	.350	.711	3	.959
— Oneonta (NYP)	OF	18	53	10	13	2	1	0	3	10	9	1	1	2-2	.245	.375	.321	.696	1	.917
1992— Greensboro (S. Atl.)	P	83	258	43	74	10	2	3	27	33	37	3	12	8-2	.287	.372	.376	.748	0	1.000
1993— Greensboro (S. Atl.)	P	122	431	89	116	35	2	12	80	52	62	3	8	14-2	.269	.346	.443	.789	5	.967
1994— Tampa (Fla. St.)	OF	90	334	44	97	22	3	8	53	30	53	1	8	5-3	.290	.350	.446	.796	4	.962
1995— Tampa (Fla. St.)	OF	• 134	500	87	* 150	31	3	16	* 88	61	60	7	7	14-8	.300	.382	.470	.852	6	.966
1996— Norwich (East.)	3B-1B-OF	126	450	70	114	19	0	29	89	68	99	4	6	4-2	.253	.353	.489	.842	3	.988
— Columbus (Int'l)	OF	9	31	7	11	4	0	3	6	5	5	1	0	0-1	.355	.459	.774	1.234	1	.963
1997— Columbus (Int'l)	OF-DH-3B	125	452	78	109	34	4	30	86	71	105	4	8	0-2	.241	.346	.533	.879	4	.980
1998— New York (A.L.)	OF-DH-1B	27	67	18	25	6	0	10	27	5	12	0	0	0-1	.373	.411	.910	1.321	0	1.000
— Columbus (Int'l)	OF-DH-1B	87	342	66	110	29	1	18	67	41	59	3	1	1-3	.322	.397	.570	.967	5	.979

Year	Team (League)	Pos.	G	AB	R	H	2B	3B	HR	RBI	BB	SO	HBP	GDP	SB-CS	Avg.	OBP	SLG	OPS	E	Pct.
1999— New York (A.L.)	OF-DH	71	205	25	48	8	0	8	20	18	51	2	1	0-4	.234	.301	.390	.691	0	1.000
— Columbus (Int'l)	OF-DH	14	50	17	18	2	0	2	10	9	8	0	3	0-0	.360	.458	.520	.978	1	.958
2000— New York (A.L.)	OF-DH	73	248	33	70	11	3	9	40	19	45	2	4	1-2	.282	.330	.460	.789	1	.989
2001— Columbus (Int'l)	OF	49	173	17	40	10	1	3	14	23	21	2	9	4-1	.231	.323	.353	.676	1	.985
— New York (A.L.)	OF-DH	80	283	40	73	14	2	10	46	21	58	4	4	4-1	.258	.315	.428	.743	1	.993
2002— New York (A.L.)	OF-DH	94	288	32	71	15	2	6	34	31	62	4	5	0-3	.247	.324	.375	.699	4	.975
2003— Cleveland (A.L.) OF-1B-DH		64	210	23	57	10	0	8	26	18	52	1	6	2-0	.271	.328	.433	.761	1	.993
— Texas (A.L.)	OF-DH	55	185	16	42	10	0	4	23	27	40	2	2	0-0	.227	.329	.346	.675	2	.982
Major League totals (6 years)		464	1486	187	386	74	7	55	216	139	320	15	22	7-11	.260	.325	.430	.755	9	.989

PERSONAL: Born September 21, 1972, in Joliet, Ill. ... 6-2/225. ... Bats both, throws right. ... Full name: Scott Edward Spiezio. ... Name pronounced: SPEE-zio. ... High school: Morris (Ill.). ... College: Illinois.
TRANSACTIONS/CAREER NOTES: Selected by Oakland Athletics organization in sixth round of free-agent draft (June 3, 1993). ... On Oakland disabled list (June 8-25, 1997); included rehabilitation assignment to Southern Oregon (June 23-25). ... On Oakland disabled list (June 15-July 31, 1998); included rehabilitation assignment to Edmonton (July 26-31). ... Granted free agency (December 21, 1999). ... Signed by Anaheim Angels (January 11, 2000).
2003 GAMES PLAYED BY POSITION (MLB): 1B—114, 3B—52, OF—10.

Year	Team (League)	Pos.	G	AB	R	H	2B	3B	HR	RBI	BB	SO	HBP	GDP	SB-CS	Avg.	OBP	SLG	OPS	E	Pct.
1993— S. Oregon (N'west)	3B-1B	31	125	32	41	10	2	3	19	16	18	0	1	0-1	.328	.404	.512	.916	9	.928
— Modesto (Calif.)	3B-1B	32	110	12	28	9	1	1	13	23	19	1	4	1-5	.255	.388	.382	.770	5	.949
1994— Modesto (Calif.)	3B-SS-1B	127	453	84	127	32	5	14	68	88	72	7	15	5-0	.280	.399	.466	.864	18	.951
1995— Huntsville (Sou.)	2B-3B-1B	141	528	78	149	33	8	13	86	67	78	4	10	10-3	.282	.359	.449	.808	‡ 29	.935
1996— Edmonton (PCL) 3B-1B-DH	*	140	523	87	137	30	4	20	91	56	66	4	7	6-5	.262	.335	.449	.784	15	.970
— Oakland (A.L.)	3B-DH	9	29	6	9	2	0	2	8	4	4	0	0	0-1	.310	.394	.586	.980	2	.846
1997— Oakland (A.L.)	2B-3B	147	538	58	131	28	4	14	65	44	75	1	13	9-3	.243	.300	.388	.688	7	.990
— S. Oregon (N'west)	2B-DH	2	9	1	5	0	0	0	2	2	1	0	0	0-0	.556	.583	.556	1.139	1	.875
1998— Oakland (A.L.)	2B-DH	114	406	54	105	19	1	9	50	44	56	2	10	1-3	.259	.333	.377	.709	13	.975
— Edmonton (PCL)	2B-DH	5	13	3	3	1	0	1	4	3	2	0	0	0-0	.231	.375	.538	.913	1	.889
1999— Oakland (A.L.)	2-3-1-D	89	247	31	60	24	0	8	33	29	36	2	5	0-0	.243	.324	.437	.761	7	.976
— Vancouver (PCL)	2B-3B-DH	28	105	27	41	7	1	6	27	15	16	2	3	0-0	.390	.475	.648	1.123	4	.969
2000— Anaheim (A.L.) D-1-3-0-2		123	297	47	72	11	2	17	49	40	56	3	5	1-2	.242	.334	.465	.799	3	.984
2001— Anaheim (A.L.)	1-D-0-3	139	457	57	124	29	4	13	54	34	65	5	6	5-2	.271	.326	.438	.764	2	.998
2002— Anaheim (A.L.)	1-3-0-2	153	491	80	140	34	2	12	82	67	52	4	12	6-7	.285	.371	.436	.807	5	.996
2003— Anaheim (A.L.)	1B-3B-OF	158	521	69	138	36	7	16	83	46	66	5	12	6-3	.265	.326	.453	.779	11	.988
Major League totals (8 years)		932	2986	402	779	183	20	91	424	308	410	22	63	28-21	.261	.331	.427	.758	50	.989

PERSONAL: Born January 28, 1975, in Oklahoma City, Okla. ... 6-0/201. ... Bats right, throws right. ... Full name: Ernest Lee Spivey. ... Name pronounced: spy-VEE. ... High school: Douglass (Oklahoma City). ... Junior college: Cowley County College (Kan.).
TRANSACTIONS/CAREER NOTES: Selected by Arizona Diamondbacks organization in 36th round of free-agent draft (June 4, 1996). ... Loaned by Diamondbacks to Tulsa, Texas Rangers organization (July 18-August 29, 1998). ... On El Paso disabled list (April 8-May 15 and July 4-August 19, 1999). ... On Arizona disabled list (August 19, 1999-remainder of season). ... On Tucson disabled list (May 8-June 14, 2000). ... On El Paso disabled list (June 25-August 17, 2000). ... On Arizona disabled list (August 31, 2000-remainder of season). ... On disabled list (June 14-26, 2002). ... Placed on 15-day disabled list (June 15, 2003). ... Placed on the 15-day disabled list by Arizona (July 4, 2003). ... Sent to El Paso on rehab assignment by Arizona (July 10, 2003). ... Reinstated from 15-day disabled list (July 21, 2003).
2003 GAMES PLAYED BY POSITION (MLB): 2B—98, OF—1.

Year	Team (League)	Pos.	G	AB	R	H	2B	3B	HR	RBI	BB	SO	HBP	GDP	SB-CS	Avg.	OBP	SLG	OPS	E	Pct.
1996— Ariz. D'backs (Ariz.) 2B-3B-SS		20	69	13	23	0	0	0	3	12	16	4	0	11-2	.333	.453	.333	.787	3	.970
— Lethbridge (Pio.)	2B-SS	31	107	30	36	3	4	2	25	23	24	3	2	8-3	.336	.459	.495	.955	10	.930
1997— High Desert (Calif.)	2B	136	491	88	134	24	6	6	53	69	115	11	9	14-9	.273	.373	.383	.756	* 33	.949
1998— High Desert (Calif.) 2B-3B-SS		79	285	64	80	14	5	5	35	64	61	3	4	34-12	.281	.416	.418	.834	§ 20	.949
— Tulsa (Texas)	2B	34	119	26	37	10	1	3	16	28	25	3	1	8-4	.311	.450	.487	.938	3	.980
1999— El Paso (Texas)	2B-SS	44	164	40	48	10	4	3	19	36	27	2	5	14-10	.293	.424	.457	.881	9	.963
2000— Tucson (PCL) 2B-SS-3B		28	117	21	33	8	4	3	16	11	17	0	4	3-1	.282	.341	.496	.837	6	.958
— El Paso (Texas)	2B	6	19	5	8	5	0	1	2	0	5	0	1	0-0	.421	.421	.842	1.263	0	1.000
2001— Tucson (PCL)	2B-SS	54	194	25	45	6	0	6	27	27	32	0	4	9-6	.232	.326	.356	.681	3	.990
— Arizona (N.L.)	2B-SS	72	163	33	42	6	3	5	21	23	47	2	3	3-0	.258	.354	.423	.778	3	.985
2002— Arizona (N.L.)	2B	143	538	103	162	34	6	16	78	65	100	16	10	11-6	.301	.389	.476	.865	15	.977
2003— El Paso (Texas)	2B	4	11	2	5	1	0	0	1	2	1	1	1	2-0	.455	.533	.545	1.079	1	.909
— Tucson (PCL)	2B	5	15	3	4	2	0	0	1	1	1	0	0	0-0	.267	.313	.400	.713	0	1.000
— Arizona (N.L.)	2B-OF	106	365	52	93	22	2	13	50	33	95	7	7	4-3	.255	.326	.433	.759	8	.982
Major League totals (3 years)		321	1066	188	297	62	11	34	149	121	242	25	20	18-9	.279	.363	.453	.816	26	.980

PERSONAL: Born October 21, 1979, in San Diego, Calif. ... 6-3/190. ... Throws right, bats right. ... Full name: Timothy Floyd Spooneybarger. ... High school: Pine Forest (Pensacola, Fla.). ... Junior college: Okaloosa-Walton (Fla.) Community College.
TRANSACTIONS/CAREER NOTES: Selected by Atlanta Braves organization in 29th round of free-agent draft (June 2, 1998). ... On disabled list (May 21-July 22, 2000). ... Traded by Braves with P Ryan Baker to Florida Marlins for P Mike Hampton and cash (November 18, 2002). ... Placed on the 15-day disabled list by Florida (July 5, 2003). ... Transferred to 60-day disabled list (August 22, 2003).
CAREER HITTING: 0-for-4 (.000), 0 R, 0 2B, 0 3B, 0 HR, 0 RBI.

Year	League	W	L	Pct.	ERA	WHIP	G	GS	CG	ShO	Hld.	Sv.-Opp.	IP	H	R	ER	HR	BB-IBB	SO	Avg.
1999— Danville (Appal.)		3	1	1.000	2.22	1.19	12	0	0	0	...	0-...	24.1	15	11	6	0	14-0	36	.172
— Macon (S. Atl.)		0	1	.000	3.60	1.70	7	0	0	0	...	0-...	10.0	7	4	4	1	10-1	17	.194
2000— Myrtle Beach (Caro.)		3	0	1.000	0.91	0.74	19	6	0	0	...	0-...	49.2	18	7	5	0	19-0	57	.110
2001— Greenville (Sou.)		1	1	.500	5.14	1.14	15	0	0	0	...	0-...	21.0	20	12	12	1	4-0	24	.247
— Richmond (Int'l)		3	0	1.000	0.71	1.07	42	0	0	0	...	5-...	50.2	33	5	4	1	21-1	58	.185
— Atlanta (N.L.)		0	1	.000	2.25	1.75	4	0	0	0	0	0-0	4.0	5	1	1	0	2-1	3	.313
2002— Atlanta (N.L.)		1	0	1.000	2.63	1.25	51	0	0	0	11	1-1	51.1	38	16	15	4	26-5	33	.207
— Richmond (Int'l)		1	0	1.000	0.90	1.05	18	0	0	0	...	11-...	20.0	13	2	2	1	8-0	21	.178
2003— Florida (N.L.)		1	2	.333	4.07	0.90	33	0	0	0	6	0-1	42.0	27	21	19	1	11-0	32	.190
Major League totals (3 years)		2	3	.400	3.24	1.12	88	0	0	0	17	1-2	97.1	70	38	35	5	39-6	68	.205

S

SPRINGER, RUSS — P

PERSONAL: Born November 7, 1968, in Alexandria, La. ... 6-4/211. ... Throws right, bats right. ... Full name: Russell Paul Springer. ... High school: Grant (Dry Prong, La.). ... College: Louisiana State.

TRANSACTIONS/CAREER NOTES: Selected by New York Yankees organization in seventh round of free-agent draft (June 5, 1989). ... Traded by Yankees with 1B J.T. Snow and P Jerry Nielsen to California Angels for P Jim Abbott (December 6, 1992). ... On California disabled list (August 2, 1993-remainder of season). ... Traded by Angels to Philadelphia Phillies (August 15, 1995), completing deal in which Phillies traded OF Dave Gallagher to Angels for 2B Kevin Flora and a player to be named later (August 9, 1995). ... Released by Phillies (December 20, 1996). ... Signed by Houston Astros organization (December 30, 1996). ... On Houston disabled list (June 17-July 10, 1997); included rehabilitation assignment to Jackson (July 8-10). ... Selected by Arizona Diamondbacks in third round (61st pick overall) of expansion draft (November 18, 1997). ... Traded by Diamondbacks to Atlanta Braves for P Alan Embree (June 23, 1998). ... On Atlanta disabled list (August 6-21, 1998). ... On Atlanta disabled list (April 3-May 17, 1999); included rehabilitation assignment to Richmond (April 20-May 16). ... Granted free agency (November 2, 1999). ... Signed by Diamondbacks (December 3, 1999). ... On Arizona disabled list (May 23, 2001-remainder of season); included rehabilitation assignment to Tucson (July 16-31). ... Granted free agency (November 7, 2001). ... Signed by St. Louis Cardinals (December 19, 2002). ... Placed on 15-day disabled list (May 1, 2003). ... Recalled from Memphis rehab assignment; transferred to Emergency disabled list (July 9, 2003). ... Sent on rehab assignment (August 21, 2003). ... Recalled from rehab assignment (August 30, 2003). ... Removed from 60-day disabled list (August 30, 2003).

CAREER HITTING: 2-for-26 (.077), 1 R, 0 2B, 0 3B, 0 HR, 0 RBI.

Year League	W	L	Pct.	ERA	WHIP	G	GS	CG	ShO	Hld.	Sv.-Opp.	IP	H	R	ER	HR	BB-IBB	SO	Avg.
1989— GC Yankees (GCL)	3	0	1.000	1.50	1.00	6	6	0	0	...	0-...	24.0	14	8	4	0	10-0	34	.167
1990— GC Yankees (GCL)	0	2	.000	1.20	0.93	4	4	0	0	...	0-...	15.0	10	6	2	0	4-0	17	.172
— Greensboro (S. Atl.)	2	3	.400	3.67	1.46	10	10	0	0	...	0-...	56.1	51	33	23	3	31-0	51	.236
1991— Fort Lauderdale (FSL)	5	9	.357	3.49	1.18	25	25	2	0	...	0-...	152.1	118	68	59	9	62-1	139	.213
— Alb./Colon. (East.)	1	0	1.000	1.80	1.00	2	2	0	0	...	0-...	15.0	9	4	3	0	6-1	16	.167
1992— Columbus (Int'l)	8	5	.615	2.69	1.16	20	20	1	0	...	0-...	123.2	89	46	37	11	54-0	95	.204
— New York (A.L.)	0	0	...	6.19	1.75	14	0	0	0	2	0-0	16.0	18	11	11	0	10-0	12	.281
1993— Vancouver (PCL)	5	4	.556	4.27	1.54	11	9	1	0	...	0-...	59.0	58	37	28	5	33-1	40	.256
— California (A.L.)	1	6	.143	7.20	1.75	14	9	1	0	0	0-0	60.0	73	48	48	11	32-1	31	.303
1994— Vancouver (PCL)	7	4	.636	3.04	1.16	12	12	• 4	0	...	0-...	83.0	77	35	28	7	19-0	58	.242
— California (A.L.)	2	2	.500	5.52	1.47	18	5	0	0	1	2-3	45.2	53	28	28	9	14-0	28	.291
1995— California (A.L.)	1	2	.333	6.10	1.65	19	6	0	0	0	1-2	51.2	60	37	35	11	25-1	38	.290
— Vancouver (PCL)	2	0	1.000	3.44	1.38	6	6	0	0	...	0-...	34.0	24	16	13	3	23-0	23	.200
— Philadelphia (N.L.)	0	0	...	3.71	1.20	14	0	0	0	0	0-0	26.2	22	11	11	5	10-3	32	.227
1996— Philadelphia (N.L.)	3	10	.231	4.66	1.49	51	7	0	0	6	0-3	96.2	106	60	50	12	38-6	94	.272
1997— Houston (N.L.)	3	3	.500	4.23	1.36	54	0	0	0	9	3-7	55.1	48	28	26	4	27-2	74	.232
— Jackson (Texas)	0	0	...	9.00	2.00	1	0	0	0	...	0-...	1.0	2	1	1	0	0-0	2	.400
1998— Arizona (N.L.)	4	3	.571	4.13	1.32	26	0	0	0	1	0-3	32.2	29	16	15	4	14-1	37	.232
— Atlanta (N.L.)	1	1	.500	4.05	1.90	22	0	0	0	6	0-1	20.0	22	10	9	0	16-3	19	.301
1999— Richmond (Int'l)	1	0	1.000	1.17	0.65	11	0	0	0	...	2-...	15.1	9	2	2	0	1-0	13	.170
— Atlanta (N.L.)	2	1	.667	3.42	1.12	49	0	0	0	8	1-1	47.1	31	20	18	5	22-2	49	.185
2000— Arizona (N.L.)	2	4	.333	5.08	1.56	52	0	0	0	3	0-2	62.0	63	36	35	11	34-6	59	.261
2001— Arizona (N.L.)	0	0	...	7.13	1.36	18	0	0	0	2	1-1	17.2	20	16	14	5	4-0	12	.274
— Tucson (PCL)	0	0	...	4.91	1.36	7	3	0	0	...	0-...	7.1	7	4	4	1	3-0	6	.250
2002—										Did not play.									
2003— Memphis (PCL)	0	0	...	1.42	0.95	7	0	0	0	...	0-...	6.1	2	1	1	1	4-0	5	.105
— St. Louis (N.L.)	1	1	.500	8.31	1.44	17	0	0	0	5	0-1	17.1	19	16	16	8	6-0	11	.271
American League totals (4 years)	4	10	.286	6.33	1.64	65	20	1	0	3	3-5	173.1	204	124	122	31	81-2	109	.294
National League totals (8 years)	16	23	.410	4.65	1.41	303	7	0	0	40	5-19	375.2	360	213	194	54	171-23	387	.249
Major League totals (11 years)	20	33	.377	5.18	1.49	368	27	1	0	43	8-24	549.0	564	337	316	85	252-25	496	.264

SPURLING, CHRIS — P

PERSONAL: Born June 28, 1977, in Dayton, Ohio. ... 6-5/228. ... Throws right, bats right. ... Full name: Christopher Michael Spurling. ... High school: Northridge (Johnstown, Ohio). ... Junior college: Sinclair (Ohio) Community College.

TRANSACTIONS/CAREER NOTES: Selected by New York Yankees organization in 41st round of free-agent draft (June 3, 1997). ... Traded by Yankees to Pittsburgh Pirates for IF Luis Sojo (August 7, 2000). ... On Altoona disabled list (May 11-20 and June 25-July 6, 2001). ... Selected by Atlanta Braves from Pirates organization in Rule 5 major league draft (December 16, 2002). ... Traded by Braves to Detroit Tigers for P Matt Coenen (March 25, 2003).

CAREER HITTING: 0-for-0 (.000), 0 R, 0 2B, 0 3B, 0 HR, 0 RBI.

Year League	W	L	Pct.	ERA	WHIP	G	GS	CG	ShO	Hld.	Sv.-Opp.	IP	H	R	ER	HR	BB-IBB	SO	Avg.
1998— GC Yankees (GCL)	2	1	.667	2.28	1.32	13	6	0	0	...	1-...	51.1	57	21	13	3	11-0	44	.279
— Greensboro (S. Atl.)	1	0	1.000	3.00	1.33	1	1	0	0	...	0-...	6.0	7	2	2	1	1-0	5	.292
1999— Greensboro (S. Atl.)	4	6	.400	3.66	1.32	49	0	0	0	...	4-...	76.1	78	34	31	8	23-3	68	.265
2000— Lynchburg (Carolina)	1	0	1.000	0.98	0.60	9	0	0	0	...	5-...	18.1	8	2	2	1	3-0	17	.129
— Tampa (FSL)	4	6	.400	3.79	1.26	34	0	0	0	...	1-...	57.0	50	27	24	1	22-5	55	.237
2001— Altoona (East.)	5	7	.417	3.11	1.32	34	15	0	0	...	1-...	121.2	133	48	42	9	28-1	63	.279
2002— Altoona (East.)	4	3	.571	2.19	0.94	51	0	0	0	...	20-...	70.0	54	18	17	8	12-1	60	.210
2003— Detroit (A.L.)	1	3	.250	4.68	1.30	66	0	0	0	5	3-6	77.0	78	42	40	9	22-1	38	.266
Major League totals (1 year)	1	3	.250	4.68	1.30	66	0	0	0	5	3-6	77.0	78	42	40	9	22-1	38	.266

STAIRS, MATT — OF/1B

PERSONAL: Born February 27, 1968, in Saint John, New Brunswick. ... 5-9/210. ... Bats left, throws right. ... Full name: Matthew Wade Stairs. ... High school: Fredericton (N.B.).

TRANSACTIONS/CAREER NOTES: Signed as non-drafted free agent by Montreal Expos organization (January 17, 1989). ... On disabled list (May 16-23, 1991). ... On Ottawa disabled list (May 7-18, 1993). ... Contract sold by Expos to Chunichi Dragons of Japan Central League (June 8, 1993). ... Signed by Expos organization (December 15, 1993). ... Traded by Expos with P Pete Young to Boston Red Sox for cash (February 18, 1994). ... Granted free agency (October 14, 1995). ... Signed by Oakland Athletics organization (December 1, 1995). ... Traded by A's to Chicago Cubs for P Eric Ireland (November 20, 2000). ... Granted free agency (November 5, 2001). ... Signed by Milwaukee Brewers (January 25, 2002). ... On disabled list (May 16-June 3, 2002). ... Granted free agency (October 28, 2002). ... Signed by Pittsburgh Pirates (December 18, 2002). ... Placed on 15-day disabled list (May 19, 2003). ... Sent to Nashville for rehab assignment (June 1, 2003). ... Activated from the 15-day disabled list (June 10, 2003).

2003 GAMES PLAYED BY POSITION (MLB): OF—55, 1B—31, DH—2.

Year	Team (League)	Pos.	G	AB	R	H	2B	3B	HR	RBI	BB	SO	HBP	GDP	SB-CS	Avg.	OBP	SLG	OPS	E	Pct.
1989—	W.P. Beach (FSL)	2B-3B-SS	36	111	12	21	3	1	1	9	9	18	0	3	0-0	.189	.248	.261	.509	4	.956
	—Jamestown (NYP)	2B-3B	14	43	8	11	1	0	1	5	3	5	0	0	1-2	.256	.304	.349	.653	6	.893
	—Rockford (Midwest)	3B	44	141	20	40	9	2	2	14	15	29	2	4	5-4	.284	.358	.418	.777	7	.929
1990—	W.P. Beach (FSL)	2B-3B	55	183	30	62	9	3	3	30	41	19	5	5	15-2	.339	.468	.470	.937	17	.899
	—Jacksonville (Sou.)	2-3-S-O	79	280	26	71	17	0	3	34	22	43	3	6	5-3	.254	.310	.346	.656	22	.893
1991—	Harrisburg (East.)	2B-3B-OF	129	505	87	*168	30	•10	13	78	66	47	3	14	23-11	.333	.411	.509	.920	22	.958
1992—	Indianapolis (A.A.)	OF	110	401	57	107	23	4	11	56	49	61	4	10	11-11	.267	.351	.426	.777	3	.985
	—Montreal (N.L.)	OF	13	30	2	5	2	0	0	5	7	7	0	0	0-0	.167	.316	.233	.549	1	.933
1993—	Ottawa (Int'l)	OF	34	125	18	35	4	2	3	20	11	15	2	3	4-1	.280	.348	.416	.764	0	1.000
	—Montreal (N.L.)	OF	6	8	1	3	1	0	0	2	0	1	0	1	0-0	.375	.375	.500	.875	0	1.000
	—Chunichi (Jp. Cn.)		60	132	10	33	6	0	6	23	7	34	...	...	1-...	.250	...	.432	...	...	...
1994—	New Britain (East.)	OF-DH-1B	93	317	44	98	25	2	9	61	54	38	3	10	10-7	.309	.407	.486	.893	3	.975
1995—	Pawtucket (Int'l)	OF-DH	75	271	40	77	17	0	13	56	29	41	1	10	3-3	.284	.352	.491	.843	0	1.000
	—Boston (A.L.)	OF-DH	39	88	8	23	7	1	1	17	4	14	1	4	0-1	.261	.298	.398	.696	2	.913
1996—	Oakland (A.L.)	OF-DH-1B	61	137	21	38	5	1	10	23	19	23	1	2	1-1	.277	.367	.547	.915	1	.987
	—Edmonton (PCL)	DH-OF-1B	51	180	35	62	16	1	8	41	21	34	0	4	0-0	.344	.401	.578	.979	3	.944
1997—	Oakland (A.L.)	OF-DH-1B	133	352	62	105	19	0	27	73	50	60	3	6	3-2	.298	.386	.582	.969	4	.974
1998—	Oakland (A.L.)	DH-OF-1B	149	523	88	154	33	1	26	106	59	93	6	13	8-3	.294	.370	.511	.880	0	1.000
1999—	Oakland (A.L.)	OF-DH-1B	146	531	94	137	26	3	38	102	89	124	2	8	2-7	.258	.366	.533	.899	5	.981
2000—	Oakland (A.L.)	OF-DH-1B	143	476	74	108	26	0	21	81	78	122	1	7	5-2	.227	.333	.414	.747	4	.980
2001—	Chicago (N.L.)	1-O-D-2	128	340	48	85	21	0	17	61	52	76	7	4	2-3	.250	.358	.462	.820	4	.993
2002—	Milwaukee (N.L.)	OF	107	270	41	66	15	0	16	41	36	50	8	7	2-0	.244	.349	.478	.827	1	.993
2003—	Nashville (PCL)	OF-1B-DH	7	18	4	3	0	0	2	3	7	2	2	1	0-0	.167	.444	.500	.944	0	1.000
	—Pittsburgh (N.L.)	OF-1B-DH	121	305	49	89	20	1	20	57	45	64	5	7	0-1	.292	.389	.561	.950	3	.990
American League totals (6 years)			671	2107	347	565	116	6	123	402	299	436	14	40	19-16	.268	.360	.504	.864	16	.980
National League totals (5 years)			375	953	141	248	59	1	53	166	140	198	20	19	4-4	.260	.364	.491	.855	9	.991
Major League totals (11 years)			1046	3060	488	813	175	7	176	568	439	634	34	59	23-20	.266	.362	.500	.862	25	.986

STANDRIDGE, JASON — P

PERSONAL: Born November 9, 1978, in Birmingham, Ala. ... 6-4/230. ... Throws right, bats right. ... Full name: Jason Wayne Standridge. ... High school: Hewitt-Trussville (Ala.).

TRANSACTIONS/CAREER NOTES: Selected by Tampa Bay Devil Rays organization in first round (31st pick overall) of free-agent draft (June 3, 1997).

CAREER HITTING: 0-for-0 (.000), 0 R, 0 2B, 0 3B, 0 HR, 0 RBI.

Year	League	W	L	Pct.	ERA	WHIP	G	GS	CG	ShO	Hld.	Sv.-Opp.	IP	H	R	ER	HR	BB-IBB	SO	Avg.
1997—	GC Devil Rays (GCL)	0	6	.000	3.59	1.20	13	13	0	0	...	0-...	57.2	56	30	23	3	13-1	55	.250
1998—	Princeton (Appal.)	4	4	.500	7.00	1.75	12	12	0	0	...	0-...	63.0	82	61	49	4	28-0	47	.314
1999—	Char., S.C. (SAL)	9	1	.900	2.02	0.96	18	18	3	3	...	0-...	116.0	80	35	26	5	31-1	84	.197
	—St. Pete. (FSL)	4	4	.500	3.91	1.43	8	8	0	0	...	0-...	48.1	49	21	21	0	20-0	26	.268
2000—	St. Pete. (FSL)	2	4	.333	3.38	1.36	10	10	1	0	...	0-...	56.0	45	28	21	4	31-0	41	.214
	—Orlando (Sou.)	6	8	.429	3.62	1.32	17	17	2	0	...	0-...	97.0	85	46	39	4	43-0	55	.237
2001—	Durham (Int'l)	5	10	.333	5.28	1.76	20	20	0	0	...	0-...	102.1	130	73	60	13	50-0	48	.315
	—Tampa Bay (A.L.)	0	0	...	4.66	1.71	9	1	0	0	0	0-0	19.1	19	10	10	5	14-1	9	.260
	—Orlando (Sou.)	0	2	.000	5.59	1.66	2	2	0	0	...	0-...	9.2	12	6	6	0	4-0	7	.300
2002—	Durham (Int'l)	10	9	.526	3.12	1.34	29	•29	0	0	...	0-...	173.0	168	71	60	12	64-1	111	.259
	—Tampa Bay (A.L.)	0	0	...	9.00	3.67	1	0	0	0	0	0-0	3.0	7	3	3	1	4-0	1	.500
2003—	Tampa Bay (A.L.)	0	5	.000	6.37	1.53	18	8	1	0	0	0-0	35.1	38	25	25	7	16-0	20	.275
	—Durham (Int'l)	2	4	.333	4.50	1.50	12	10	0	0	...	1-...	60.0	62	32	30	5	28-0	37	.270
Major League totals (3 years)		0	5	.000	5.93	1.70	18	8	1	0	0	0-0	57.2	64	38	38	13	34-1	30	.284

STANFORD, JASON — P

PERSONAL: Born January 27, 1977, in Tucson, Ariz. ... 6-2/200. ... Throws left, bats left. ... Full name: Jason John Stanford. ... High school: Canyon Del Oro (Tucson, Ariz.). ... College: Charlotte.

TRANSACTIONS/CAREER NOTES: Signed by Cleveland Indians organization as a non-drafted free agent (November 16, 1999).

CAREER HITTING: 0-for-0 (.000), 0 R, 0 2B, 0 3B, 0 HR, 0 RBI.

Year	League	W	L	Pct.	ERA	WHIP	G	GS	CG	ShO	Hld.	Sv.-Opp.	IP	H	R	ER	HR	BB-IBB	SO	Avg.
2000—	Columbus (Int'l)	7	4	.636	2.73	1.29	14	14	0	0	...	0-...	79.0	82	32	24	3	20-0	72	.265
	—Kinston (Caro.)	4	3	.571	2.57	1.21	11	11	1	0	...	0-...	70.0	68	22	20	2	17-0	58	.250
	—Akron (East.)	1	0	1.000	1.59	1.06	1	1	0	0	...	0-...	5.2	5	1	1	0	1-0	5	.238
2001—	Akron (East.)	6	11	.353	4.07	1.30	24	24	1	0	...	0-...	141.2	152	71	64	11	32-4	108	.276
	—Buffalo (Int'l)	1	0	1.000	0.00	0.33	1	1	1	1	...	0-...	9.0	3	0	0	0	0-0	10	.103
2002—	Buffalo (Int'l)	3	1	.750	2.78	1.23	6	5	0	0	...	0-...	35.2	33	12	11	5	11-0	23	.244
	—Akron (East.)	7	6	.538	3.43	1.38	18	18	1	1	...	0-...	102.1	108	44	39	3	33-0	86	.276
2003—	Buffalo (Int'l)	10	4	.714	3.43	1.18	20	20	1	0	...	0-...	126.0	124	57	48	13	25-1	108	.261
	—Cleveland (A.L.)	1	3	.250	3.60	1.28	13	8	0	0	0	0-0	50.0	48	20	20	5	16-1	30	.246
Major League totals (1 year)		1	3	.250	3.60	1.28	13	8	0	0	0	0-0	50.0	48	20	20	5	16-1	30	.246

STANTON, MIKE — P

PERSONAL: Born June 2, 1967, in Houston, Texas. ... 6-1/215. ... Throws left, bats left. ... Full name: William Michael Stanton. ... High school: Midland (Texas). ... Junior college: Alvin (Texas) Community College.

TRANSACTIONS/CAREER NOTES: Selected by Atlanta Braves organization in 13th round of free-agent draft (June 2, 1987). ... On Atlanta disabled list (April 27, 1990-remainder of season); included rehabilitation assignments to Greenville (May 31-June 5 and August 21-29). ... Granted free agency (December 23, 1994). ... Re-signed by Braves (April 12, 1995). ... Traded by Braves with a player to be named later to Boston Red Sox for two players to be named later (July 31, 1995); Red Sox acquired P Matt Murray and Braves acquired OF Marc Lewis and P Mike Jacobs to complete deal (August 31, 1995). ... Traded by Red Sox to Texas Rangers for P Mark Brandenburg and P Kerry Lacy (July 31, 1996). ... Granted free agency (October 27, 1996). ... Signed by New York Yankees (December 11, 1996). ... On suspended list (July 3-10, 1998). ... Granted free agency (November 5, 1999). ... Re-signed by Yankees (November 29, 1999). ... Granted free agency (October 30, 2002). ... Signed by New York Mets (December 16, 2002). ... Placed on 15-day disabled list, retroactive to May 22 (May 30, 2003). ... Reinstated from 15-day disabled list (June 6, 2003). ... Placed on 15-day disabled list (June 11, 2003). ... Sent on rehab assignment to Binghamton (July 8, 2003). ... Recalled from rehab assignment; activated from 15-day disabled list (July 13, 2003).

CAREER HITTING: 7-for-17 (.412), 2 R, 1 2B, 0 3B, 0 HR, 2 RBI.

S

Year	League	W	L	Pct.	ERA	WHIP	G	GS	CG	ShO	Hld.	Sv.-Opp.	IP	H	R	ER	HR	BB-IBB	SO	Avg.
1987— Pulaski (Appal.)		4	8	.333	3.24	1.27	15	13	3	2	...	0-...	83.1	64	37	30	7	42-0	82	.212
1988— Burlington (Midw.)		11	5	.688	3.62	1.45	30	23	1	1	...	0-...	154.0	154	86	62	7	69-2	160	.258
— Durham (Caro.)		1	0	1.000	1.46	1.54	2	2	1	1	...	0-...	12.1	14	3	2	0	5-0	14	.280
1989— Greenville (Sou.)		4	1	.800	1.58	1.23	47	0	0	0	...	19-...	51.1	32	10	9	1	31-3	58	.189
— Richmond (Int'l)		2	0	1.000	0.00	0.95	13	0	0	0	...	8-...	20.0	6	0	0	0	13-2	20	.097
— Atlanta (N.L.)		0	1	.000	1.50	1.04	20	0	0	0	2	7-8	24.0	17	4	4	0	8-1	27	.207
1990— Atlanta (N.L.)		0	3	.000	18.00	2.86	7	0	0	0	0	2-3	7.0	16	16	14	1	4-2	7	.444
— Greenville (Sou.)		0	1	.000	1.59	1.76	4	4	0	0	...	0-...	5.2	7	1	1	1	3-0	4	.292
1991— Atlanta (N.L.)		5	5	.500	2.88	1.06	74	0	0	0	15	7-10	78.0	62	27	25	6	21-6	54	.217
1992— Atlanta (N.L.)		5	4	.556	4.10	1.24	65	0	0	0	15	8-11	63.2	59	32	29	6	20-2	44	.247
1993— Atlanta (N.L.)		4	6	.400	4.67	1.54	63	0	0	0	5	27-33	52.0	51	35	27	4	29-7	43	.255
1994— Atlanta (N.L.)		3	1	.750	3.55	1.47	49	0	0	0	10	3-4	45.2	41	18	18	2	26-3	35	.248
1995— Atlanta (N.L.)		1	1	.500	5.59	1.91	26	0	0	0	4	1-2	19.1	31	14	12	3	6-2	13	.369
— Boston (A.L.)		1	0	1.000	3.00	1.19	22	0	0	0	4	0-1	21.0	17	9	7	3	8-0	10	.224
1996— Boston (A.L.)		4	3	.571	3.83	1.44	59	0	0	0	15	1-5	56.1	58	24	24	9	23-4	46	.275
— Texas (A.L.)		0	1	.000	3.22	1.07	22	0	0	0	7	0-1	22.1	20	8	8	2	4-1	14	.241
1997— New York (A.L.)		6	1	.857	2.57	1.26	64	0	0	0	26	3-5	66.2	50	19	19	3	34-2	70	.205
1998— New York (A.L.)		4	1	.800	5.47	1.23	67	0	0	0	18	6-10	79.0	71	51	48	13	26-1	69	.239
1999— New York (A.L.)		2	2	.500	4.33	1.43	73	1	0	0	21	0-5	62.1	71	30	30	5	18-4	59	.289
2000— New York (A.L.)		2	3	.400	4.10	1.35	69	0	0	0	15	0-4	68.0	68	32	31	5	24-2	75	.263
2001— New York (A.L.)		9	4	.692	2.58	1.36	76	0	0	0	23	0-1	80.1	80	25	23	4	29-9	78	.263
2002— New York (A.L.)		7	1	.875	3.00	1.29	79	0	0	0	17	6-9	78.0	73	29	26	4	28-3	44	.256
2003— Binghamton (Eastern)		0	1	.000	9.00	6.00	1	1	0	0	...	0-...	1.0	6	3	1	0	0-0	1	.750
— Brooklyn (NY-P)		0	0	...	0.00	0.50	1	1	0	0	...	0-...	2.0	1	0	0	0	0-0	1	.167
— New York (N.L.)		2	7	.222	4.57	1.24	50	0	0	0	10	5-7	45.1	37	25	23	6	19-4	34	.219
American League totals (8 years)		35	16	.686	3.64	1.31	531	1	0	0	146	16-41	534.0	508	227	216	48	194-26	465	.253
National League totals (8 years)		20	28	.417	4.08	1.33	354	0	0	0	61	60-78	335.0	314	171	152	28	133-27	257	.249
Major League totals (15 years)		55	44	.556	3.81	1.32	885	1	0	0	207	76-119	869.0	822	398	368	76	327-53	722	.252

STARK, DENNY — P

PERSONAL: Born October 27, 1974, in Edgerton, Ohio. ... 6-2/210. ... Throws right, bats right. ... Full name: Dennis Stark. ... High school: Edgerton (Ohio). ... College: Toledo.

TRANSACTIONS/CAREER NOTES: Selected by Seattle Mariners organization in fourth round of free-agent draft (June 4, 1996). ... On Lancaster disabled list (April 26, 1998-remainder of season); included rehabilitation assignment to Arizona League Mariners (July 30-August 11). ... On New Haven disabled list (May 20-August 30, 2000). ... On Seattle disabled list (August 31, 2000-remainder of season). ... Traded by Mariners with P Jose Paniagua and P Brian Fuentes to Colorado Rockies for 3B Jeff Cirillo (December 15, 2001). ... On disabled list (March 21, 2003). ... Transferred from 15-day to 60-day disabled list by Colorado (May 1, 2003). ... Sent on rehab assignment to Visalia (June 1, 2003). ... Recalled from Colorado Springs rehab assignment (June 30, 2003). ... Reinstated from Emergency disabled list (July 1, 2003).

CAREER HITTING: 7-for-63 (.111), 5 R, 3 2B, 0 3B, 1 HR, 8 RBI.

Year	League	W	L	Pct.	ERA	WHIP	G	GS	CG	ShO	Hld.	Sv.-Opp.	IP	H	R	ER	HR	BB-IBB	SO	Avg.
1996— Everett (Northwest)		1	3	.250	4.45	1.38	12	4	0	0	...	0-...	30.1	25	19	15	2	17-0	49	.225
1997— Wisconsin (Midw.)		6	3	.667	1.97	0.93	16	15	1	0	...	0-...	91.1	52	27	20	3	33-0	105	.162
— Lancaster (Calif.)		1	1	.500	3.24	1.38	3	3	0	0	...	0-...	16.2	13	7	6	1	10-0	17	.224
1998— Lancaster (Calif.)		1	2	.333	4.29	1.67	5	5	0	0	...	0-...	21.0	18	12	10	1	17-0	21	.222
— Ariz. Mariners (Ariz.)		0	0	...	2.16	1.32	3	1	0	0	...	0-...	8.1	9	2	2	0	2-0	13	.265
1999— New Haven (East.)		9	11	.450	4.40	1.45	26	26	2	1	...	0-...	147.1	151	82	72	14	62-0	103	.268
— Seattle (A.L.)		0	0	...	9.95	2.21	5	0	0	0	0	0-0	6.1	10	8	7	0	4-0	4	.370
2000— New Haven (East.)		4	3	.571	2.19	0.97	8	8	1	0	...	0-...	49.1	31	13	12	1	17-0	42	.181
2001— Tacoma (PCL)		* 14	2	.875	2.37	1.09	24	24	0	0	...	0-...	151.2	124	52	40	12	41-0	130	.225
— Seattle (A.L.)		1	1	.500	9.20	1.70	4	3	0	0	0	0-0	14.2	21	15	15	5	4-0	12	.333
— San Antonio (Texas)		1	0	1.000	0.00	0.83	1	1	0	0	...	0-...	6.0	2	0	0	0	3-0	7	.095
2002— Colo. Springs (PCL)		1	2	.333	3.82	1.30	7	7	0	0	...	0-...	37.2	35	20	16	4	14-0	38	.246
— Colorado (N.L.)		11	4	.733	4.00	1.34	32	20	0	0	1	0-1	128.1	108	69	57	25	64-4	64	.225
2003— Visalia (Calif.)		0	0	...	0.00	0.75	1	1	0	0	...	0-...	4.0	2	0	0	0	1-0	5	.143
— Tulsa (Texas)		0	1	.000	6.23	1.85	1	1	0	0	...	0-...	4.1	4	5	3	0	4-0	3	.250
— Colo. Springs (PCL)		0	2	.000	5.95	1.58	4	4	0	0	...	0-...	19.2	22	14	13	1	9-0	10	.275
— Colorado (N.L.)		3	3	.500	5.83	1.67	17	13	0	0	0	0-0	78.2	98	57	51	12	33-2	30	.305
American League totals (2 years)		1	1	.500	9.43	1.86	9	3	0	0	0	0-0	21.0	31	23	22	5	8-0	16	.344
National League totals (2 years)		14	7	.667	4.70	1.46	49	33	0	0	1	0-1	207.0	206	126	108	37	97-6	94	.258
Major League totals (4 years)		15	8	.652	5.13	1.50	58	36	0	0	1	0-1	228.0	237	149	130	42	105-6	110	.266

STENSON, DERNELL — OF

PERSONAL: Born June 17, 1978, in LaGrange, Ga. Died November 5, 2003, in Chandler, Ariz. ... 6-1/230. ... Batted left, threw left. ... Full name: Dernell Renuald Stenson. ... High school: La Grange (Ga.).

TRANSACTIONS/CAREER NOTES: Selected by Boston Red Sox organization in third round of free-agent draft (June 2, 1996). ... On Pawtucket disabled list (June 24-July 15, 1999). ... On disabled list (April 17-May 10 and June 1-18, 2000; and May 8-17, 2001). ... Claimed on waivers by Cincinnati Reds (February 25, 2003).

2003 GAMES PLAYED BY POSITION (MLB): OF—22, 1B—1.

Year	Team (League)	Pos.	G	AB	R	H	2B	3B	HR	RBI	BB	SO	HBP	GDP	SB-CS	Avg.	OBP	SLG	OPS	E	Pct.
1996— GC Red Sox (GCL)	OF	32	97	16	21	3	1	2	15	16	26	7	0	4-3	.216	.358	.330	.688	0	1.000
1997— Michigan (Midw.)	OF	131	471	79	137	35	2	15	80	72	105	19	10	6-4	.291	.400	.469	.869	14	.918
1998— Trenton (East.)	OF	138	505	90	130	21	1	24	71	84	135	14	6	5-3	.257	.376	.446	.821	6	.975
1999— Pawtucket (Int'l)	1B	121	440	64	119	28	2	18	82	55	119	6	7	2-1	.270	.356	.466	.822	34	.966
— GC Red Sox (GCL)	1B	6	23	2	5	0	0	2	7	3	5	0	0	0-0	.217	.308	.478	.786	1	.947
2000— Pawtucket (Int'l)	1B-OF	98	380	59	102	14	0	23	71	45	99	4	8	0-0	.268	.349	.487	.836	12	.980
2001— Pawtucket (Int'l)	OF	122	464	53	110	18	1	16	69	43	116	2	6	0-0	.237	.302	.384	.685	8	.964
2002— Pawtucket (Int'l)	OF	107	368	44	92	20	1	9	36	37	96	2	6	4-3	.250	.321	.383	.704	9	.957
2003— Chattanooga (Sou.) 1B-OF-DH		101	356	51	109	28	0	14	76	39	74	2	10	4-5	.306	.371	.503	.874	12	.981
— Louisville (Int'l)	OF	17	59	9	14	3	0	5	14	5	10	0	1	0-0	.237	.292	.542	.835	1	.960
— Cincinnati (N.L.)	OF-1B	37	81	14	20	5	0	3	13	11	24	0	0	0-0	.247	.333	.420	.753	1	.979
Major League totals (1 year)		37	81	14	20	5	0	3	13	11	24	0	0	0-0	.247	.333	.420	.753	1	.979

STEPHENSON, GARRETT　　　　　P

PERSONAL: Born January 2, 1972, in Takoma Park, Md. ... 6-5/215. ... Throws right, bats right. ... Full name: Garrett Charles Stephenson. ... High school: Boonsboro (Md.). ... College: Idaho State.

TRANSACTIONS/CAREER NOTES: Selected by Baltimore Orioles organization in 18th round of free-agent draft (June 1, 1992). ... Traded by Orioles with P Calvin Maduro to Philadelphia Phillies (September 4, 1996), completing deal in which Phillies traded 3B Todd Zeile and OF Pete Incaviglia to Orioles for two players to be named later (August 29, 1996). ... On Philadelphia disabled list (June 5-22 and August 18-September 2, 1997). ... On Scranton/Wilkes-Barre disabled list (July 8-August 3, 1998). ... Traded by Phillies with P Ricky Bottalico to St. Louis Cardinals for OF Ron Gant, P Jeff Brantley and P Cliff Politte (November 19, 1998). ... On Memphis disabled list (April 8-June 13, 1999). ... On St. Louis disabled list (March 28, 2001-entire season); included rehabilitation assignment to Memphis (April 5-9). ... On St. Louis disabled list (April 15-May 14 and May 30-August 28, 2002); included rehabilitation assignments to Peoria (May 8-14 and July 31-August 4) and Memphis (August 5-28).

CAREER HITTING: 18-for-180 (.100), 1 R, 2 2B, 0 3B, 0 HR, 7 RBI.

Year　League	W	L	Pct.	ERA	WHIP	G	GS	CG	ShO	Hld.	Sv.-Opp.	IP	H	R	ER	HR	BB-IBB	SO	Avg.
1992— Bluefield (Appal.)	3	1	.750	4.73	1.30	12	3	0	0	...	0-...	32.1	35	22	17	4	7-0	30	.265
1993— Albany (S. Atl.)	16	7	.696	2.84	1.09	30	24	3	•2	...	1-...	171.1	142	65	54	6	44-0	147	.221
1994— Frederick (Caro.)	7	5	.583	4.02	1.18	18	17	1	0	...	0-...	107.1	91	62	48	13	36-2	133	.226
— Bowie (East.)	3	2	.600	5.15	1.58	7	7	1	1	...	0-...	36.2	47	22	21	2	11-1	32	.315
1995— Bowie (East.)	7	10	.412	3.64	1.15	29	*29	1	0	...	0-...	175.1	154	87	71	*23	47-0	139	.232
1996— Rochester (Int'l)	7	6	.538	4.81	1.37	23	21	3	1	...	0-...	121.2	123	66	65	13	44-0	86	.271
— Baltimore (A.L.)	0	1	.000	12.79	2.53	3	0	0	0	0	0-0	6.1	13	9	9	1	3-1	3	.433
1997— Scran./W.B. (I.L.)	3	1	.750	5.90	1.34	7	3	0	0	...	0-...	29.0	27	19	19	6	12-0	27	.241
— Philadelphia (N.L.)	8	6	.571	3.15	1.21	20	18	2	0	0	0-0	117.0	104	45	41	11	38-0	81	.244
1998— Philadelphia (N.L.)	0	2	.000	9.00	2.17	6	6	0	0	0	0-0	23.0	31	24	23	3	19-0	17	.316
— Scran./W.B. (I.L.)	1	8	.111	5.25	1.32	13	11	2	0	...	0-...	73.2	81	49	43	15	16-0	48	.278
1999— Memphis (PCL)	1	1	.500	3.16	1.13	4	4	0	0	...	0-...	25.2	22	9	9	2	7-0	19	.234
— Arkansas (Texas)	0	0	...	3.38	1.69	1	1	0	0	...	0-...	5.1	8	3	2	1	1-0	2	.381
— St. Louis (N.L.)	6	3	.667	4.22	1.39	18	12	0	0	0	0-0	85.1	90	43	40	11	29-1	59	.275
2000— St. Louis (N.L.)	16	9	.640	4.49	1.36	32	31	3	2	1	0-0	200.1	209	105	100	31	63-0	123	.270
2001— Memphis (PCL)	0	0	...	0.00	0.00	1	1	0	0	...	0-...	2.0	2	0	0	0	0-0	2	.250
2002— St. Louis (N.L.)	2	5	.286	5.40	1.62	12	10	0	0	0	0-0	45.0	48	27	27	4	25-0	34	.282
— Peoria (Midw.)	0	0	...	0.00	0.00	2	2	0	0	...	0-...	8.2	0	0	0	0	0-0	11	.000
— Memphis (PCL)	0	1	.000	3.55	1.11	3	3	0	0	...	0-...	12.2	12	5	5	0	2-0	12	.261
2003— St. Louis (N.L.)	7	13	.350	4.59	1.30	32	27	1	0	0	0-0	174.1	167	94	89	30	60-3	91	.255
American League totals (1 year)	0	1	.000	12.79	2.53	3	0	0	0	0	0-0	6.1	13	9	9	1	3-1	3	.433
National League totals (6 years)	39	38	.506	4.47	1.37	120	104	6	2	1	0-0	645.0	649	338	320	90	234-4	405	.265
Major League totals (7 years)	39	39	.500	4.55	1.38	123	104	6	2	1	0-0	651.1	662	347	329	91	237-5	408	.267

STEWART, JOSH　　　　　P

PERSONAL: Born December 5, 1978, in Paducah, Ky. ... 6-3/205. ... Throws left, bats left. ... Full name: Joshua Craig Stewart. ... High school: Livingston Central (Ky.). ... College: Memphis.

TRANSACTIONS/CAREER NOTES: Selected by Boston Red Sox organization in free-agent draft (June 1996), but did not sign. ... Selected by Chicago White Sox organization in fifth round of free-agent draft (June 2, 1999).

CAREER HITTING: 0-for-0 (.000), 0 R, 0 2B, 0 3B, 0 HR, 0 RBI.

Year　League	W	L	Pct.	ERA	WHIP	G	GS	CG	ShO	Hld.	Sv.-Opp.	IP	H	R	ER	HR	BB-IBB	SO	Avg.
1999— Burlington (Midw.)	2	0	1.000	7.28	1.79	16	0	0	0	...	1-...	29.2	32	25	24	6	21-0	35	.283
— Bristol (Appal.)	1	0	1.000	1.50	1.00	5	0	0	0	...	1-...	18.0	13	5	3	0	5-0	25	.206
2000— Burlington (Midw.)	9	9	.500	4.57	1.56	25	25	1	1	...	0-...	138.0	157	84	70	14	58-2	82	.290
2001— Winston-Salem (Caro.)	4	6	.400	3.82	1.45	12	12	1	0	...	0-...	63.2	64	41	27	6	28-1	38	.258
— Birmingham (Sou.)	3	4	.429	6.67	1.85	16	16	0	0	...	0-...	82.1	110	68	61	7	42-0	47	.330
2002— Birmingham (Sou.)	11	7	.611	3.53	1.34	26	26	1	1	...	0-...	150.1	145	65	59	11	56-1	92	.255
2003— Chicago (A.L.)	1	2	.333	5.96	1.71	5	5	0	0	0	0-0	25.2	28	18	17	4	16-0	13	.272
— Bristol (Appal.)	0	0	...	0.00	1.17	2	2	0	0	...	0-...	6.0	5	0	0	0	2-0	5	.227
— Charlotte (Int'l)	0	3	.000	6.15	1.67	5	5	0	0	...	0-...	26.1	38	18	18	4	6-0	10	.345
Major League totals (1 year)	1	2	.333	5.96	1.71	5	5	0	0	0	0-0	25.2	28	18	17	4	16-0	13	.272

STEWART, SCOTT　　　　　P

PERSONAL: Born August 14, 1975, in Stoughton, Mass. ... 6-2/225. ... Throws left, bats right. ... Full name: Scott Edward Stewart. ... High school: East Gaston (Mount Holly, N.C.).

TRANSACTIONS/CAREER NOTES: Selected by Texas Rangers organization in 20th round of free-agent draft (June 2, 1994). ... Released by Rangers (May 30, 1995). ... Signed by Minnesota Twins organization (June 13, 1995). ... Released by Twins (July 13, 1995). ... Signed by St. Paul, Northern League (June 1996). ... Sold by St. Paul to New York Mets organization (February 25, 1997). ... Granted free agency (October 15, 2000). ... Signed by Montreal Expos organization (November 17, 2000). ... On Montreal disabled list (May 11-June 2, 2001); included rehabilitation assignment to Ottawa (May 19-June 2). ... Placed on 15-day disabled list (July 10, 2003). ... Sent on minor league rehab assignment (August 28, 2003). ... Recalled from minor league rehab assignment (August 31, 2003). ... Removed from 15-day disabled list (September 1, 2003).

CAREER HITTING: 0-for-4 (.000), 0 R, 0 2B, 0 3B, 0 HR, 0 RBI.

Year　League	W	L	Pct.	ERA	WHIP	G	GS	CG	ShO	Hld.	Sv.-Opp.	IP	H	R	ER	HR	BB-IBB	SO	Avg.
1994— GC Rangers (GCL)	4	1	.800	2.82	1.09	14	8	0	0	...	1-...	54.1	47	22	17	1	12-0	62	.228
1995— Char., S.C. (SAL)	1	7	.125	3.69	1.19	11	11	1	0	...	0-...	75.2	76	38	31	6	14-1	47	.269
— GC Twins (GCL)	0	0	...	6.35	1.94	3	1	0	0	...	0-...	5.2	7	4	4	0	4-0	9	.292
1996— St. Paul (Nor.)	6	8	.429	5.84	1.89	19	18	0	0	...	0-...	86.1	121	70	56	13	42-2	54	...
1997— St. Lucie (Fla. St.)	5	10	.333	4.01	1.07	22	18	4	0	...	0-...	123.1	114	62	55	8	18-1	64	.246
1998— Binghamton (Eastern)	8	5	.615	3.70	1.33	24	13	0	0	...	2-...	90.0	91	44	37	12	29-2	65	.263
— Norfolk (Int'l)	0	6	.000	6.66	1.60	9	9	0	0	...	0-...	51.1	60	43	38	12	22-0	32	.290
1999— Norfolk (Int'l)	6	4	.600	4.42	1.45	35	14	0	0	...	0-...	99.2	109	55	49	9	36-1	85	.275
— Binghamton (Eastern)	1	0	1.000	0.00	0.60	1	1	0	0	...	0-...	5.0	3	0	0	0	0-0	5	.167
2000— Norfolk (Int'l)	3	5	.375	3.50	1.36	53	1	0	0	...	5-...	72.0	80	32	28	3	18-2	57	.281
2001— Montreal (N.L.)	3	1	.750	3.78	1.17	62	0	0	0	8	3-4	47.2	43	20	20	5	13-0	39	.243
— Ottawa (Int'l)	0	0	...	1.80	1.20	4	0	0	0	...	0-...	5.0	5	1	1	0	1-0	4	.278
2002— Montreal (N.L.)	4	2	.667	3.09	1.11	60	0	0	0	14	17-19	64.0	49	29	22	4	22-5	67	.207
2003— Brevard County (FSL)	0	0	...	0.00	0.55	2	2	0	0	...	0-...	3.2	1	0	0	0	1-0	4	.083
— Montreal (N.L.)	3	1	.750	3.98	1.51	51	0	0	0	13	0-1	43.0	52	22	19	5	13-4	29	.306
Major League totals (3 years)	10	4	.714	3.55	1.24	180	0	0	0	35	20-24	154.2	144	71	61	14	48-9	135	.247

S

STEWART, SHANNON — OF

PERSONAL: Born February 25, 1974, in Cincinnati, Ohio. ... 6-1/210. ... Bats right, throws right. ... Full name: Shannon Harold Stewart. ... High school: Southridge Senior (Miami).

TRANSACTIONS/CAREER NOTES: Selected by Toronto Blue Jays organization in first round (19th pick overall) of free-agent draft (June 1, 1992); pick received as part of compensation for Los Angeles Dodgers signing Type A free-agent P Tom Candiotti. ... On disabled list (June 13, 1994-remainder of season). ... On Syracuse disabled list (May 13-31, 1996). ... On Toronto disabled list (May 1-14, 2000); included rehabilitation assignment to Dunedin (May 12-14). ... On disabled list (May 1-16, 2002). ... Placed on 15-day disabled list (May 29, 2003). ... Sent on rehab assignment to Syracuse by Toronto (June 20, 2003). ... Recalled from Syracuse rehab assignment (June 23, 2003). ... Traded by Toronto Blue Jays to Minnesota Twins for OF Bobby Kielty (July 16, 2003).

2003 GAMES PLAYED BY POSITION (MLB): OF—127, DH—8.

											BATTING									FIELDING	
Year	Team (League)	Pos.	G	AB	R	H	2B	3B	HR	RBI	BB	SO	HBP	GDP	SB-CS	Avg.	OBP	SLG	OPS	E	Pct.
1992— GC Jays (GCL)		OF	50	172	44	40	1	0	1	11	24	27	3	3	*32-5	.233	.333	.256	.589	1	.988
1993— St. Catharines (NYP)		OF	75	*301	•53	84	15	2	3	29	33	43	2	7	25-10	.279	.351	.372	.723	0	1.000
1994— Hagerstown (SAL)		OF	56	225	39	73	10	5	4	25	23	39	1	3	15-11	.324	.386	.467	.853	1	.990
1995— Knoxville (Sou.)		OF-DH	138	498	89	143	24	6	5	55	*89	61	6	13	42-16	.287	.398	.390	.788	6	.980
— Toronto (A.L.)		OF	12	38	2	8	0	0	0	1	5	5	1	0	2-0	.211	.318	.211	.529	1	.955
1996— Syracuse (Int'l)		OF	112	420	77	125	26	8	6	42	54	61	2	6	*35-8	.298	.377	.440	.818	5	.983
— Toronto (A.L.)		OF	7	17	2	3	1	0	0	2	1	4	0	1	1-0	.176	.222	.235	.458	1	.800
1997— Toronto (A.L.)		OF-DH	44	168	25	48	13	7	0	22	19	24	4	3	10-3	.286	.368	.446	.814	2	.980
— Syracuse (Int'l)		OF	58	208	41	72	13	1	5	24	36	26	4	1	9-6	.346	.452	.490	.942	2	.983
1998— Toronto (A.L.)		OF	144	516	90	144	29	3	12	55	67	77	15	5	51-18	.279	.377	.417	.794	6	.980
1999— Toronto (A.L.)		OF-DH	145	608	102	185	28	2	11	67	59	83	8	12	37-14	.304	.371	.411	.782	5	.981
2000— Toronto (A.L.)		OF	136	583	107	186	43	5	21	69	37	79	6	12	20-5	.319	.363	.518	.882	2	.993
— Dunedin (Fla. St.)		OF	1	3	2	3	1	0	0	1	2	0	0	0	0-1	1.000	1.000	1.333	2.333	0	...
2001— Toronto (A.L.)		OF-DH	155	640	103	202	44	7	12	60	46	72	11	9	27-10	.316	.371	.463	.834	5	.981
2002— Toronto (A.L.)		OF-DH	141	577	103	175	38	6	10	45	54	60	9	17	14-2	.303	.371	.442	.813	2	.990
2003— Syracuse (Int'l)		OF	1	3	0	0	0	0	0	0	1	0	0	0	0-0	.000	.250	.000	.250	0	1.000
— Toronto (A.L.)		OF-DH	71	303	47	89	22	2	7	35	27	30	2	6	1-2	.294	.347	.449	.796	4	.974
— Minnesota (A.L.)		OF-DH	65	270	43	87	22	0	6	38	25	36	4	4	3-4	.322	.384	.470	.854	1	.993
Major League totals (9 years)			920	3720	624	1127	240	32	79	394	340	470	60	69	166-58	.303	.368	.448	.817	29	.984

STINNETT, KELLY — C

PERSONAL: Born February 4, 1970, in Lawton, Okla. ... 5-11/225. ... Bats right, throws right. ... Full name: Kelly Lee Stinnett. ... Name pronounced: sti-NETT. ... High school: Lawton (Okla.). ... Junior college: Seminole College (Okla.).

TRANSACTIONS/CAREER NOTES: Selected by Cleveland Indians organization in 11th round of free-agent draft (June 5, 1989). ... Selected by New York Mets from Indians organization in Rule 5 major league draft (December 13, 1993). ... Traded by Mets to Milwaukee Brewers for P Cory Lidle (January 17, 1996). ... On Milwaukee disabled list (July 27-September 2, 1997). ... Selected by Arizona Diamondbacks in third round (65th pick overall) of expansion draft (November 18, 1997). ... Granted free agency (December 21, 2000). ... Signed by Cincinnati Reds (January 9, 2001). ... On disabled list (September 4, 2001-remainder of season). ... On Cincinnati disabled list (April 6-July 15, 2002); included rehabilitation assignments to Louisville (May 24-June 11 and June 26-July 15). ... Traded by Reds to Philadelphia Phillies for OF Eric Valent (August 31, 2003).

2003 GAMES PLAYED BY POSITION (MLB): C—51.

											BATTING									FIELDING	
Year	Team (League)	Pos.	G	AB	R	H	2B	3B	HR	RBI	BB	SO	HBP	GDP	SB-CS	Avg.	OBP	SLG	OPS	E	Pct.
1990— Watertown (NYP)		C-1B	60	192	29	46	10	2	2	21	40	43	4	8	3-7	.240	.378	.344	.722	‡18	.957
1991— Columbus (S. Atl.)		C-1B	102	384	49	101	15	1	14	74	26	70	9	17	4-1	.263	.321	.417	.737	‡28	.966
1992— Cant./Akr. (Eastern)		C	91	296	37	84	10	0	6	32	16	43	4	8	7-6	.284	.326	.378	.704	*13	.979
1993— Charlotte (Int'l)		C	98	288	42	79	10	3	6	33	17	52	2	4	0-0	.274	.318	.392	.711	8	.985
1994— New York (N.L.)		C	47	150	20	38	6	2	2	14	11	28	5	3	2-0	.253	.323	.360	.683	5	.979
1995— New York (N.L.)		C	77	196	23	43	8	1	4	18	29	65	6	3	2-0	.219	.338	.332	.669	7	.983
1996— Milwaukee (A.L.)		C-DH	14	26	1	2	0	0	0	0	2	11	1	0	0-0	.077	.172	.077	.249	2	.960
— New Orleans (A.A.)		C-DH-3B	95	334	63	96	21	1	27	70	31	83	13	6	3-3	.287	.366	.599	.965	‡11	.980
1997— Tucson (PCL)		C-DH-1B	64	209	50	67	15	3	10	43	42	46	6	2	1-1	.321	.444	.565	1.009	2	.993
— Milwaukee (A.L.)		C-DH	30	36	2	9	4	0	0	3	3	9	0	0	0-0	.250	.308	.361	.669	1	.993
1998— Arizona (N.L.)		C-DH	92	274	35	71	14	1	11	34	35	74	6	9	0-1	.259	.353	.438	.791	8	.984
1999— Arizona (N.L.)		C	88	284	36	66	13	0	14	38	24	83	5	4	2-1	.232	.302	.426	.728	6	.990
2000— Arizona (N.L.)		C	76	240	22	52	7	0	8	33	19	56	6	5	0-1	.217	.291	.346	.636	6	.990
2001— Cincinnati (N.L.)		C-DH	63	187	27	48	11	0	9	25	17	61	5	5	2-2	.257	.333	.460	.793	12	.966
2002— Cincinnati (N.L.)		C	34	93	10	21	5	0	3	13	15	25	0	1	2-0	.226	.333	.376	.710	2	.990
— Louisville (Int'l)		C	30	86	6	17	6	0	0	5	3	24	0	1	0-0	.198	.225	.267	.492	2	.988
2003— Cincinnati (N.L.)		C	60	179	14	41	13	0	3	19	13	51	4	3	0-0	.229	.294	.352	.646	2	.990
— Philadelphia (N.L.)		C	7	7	0	3	0	0	0	1	1	1	0	0	0-0	.429	.500	.429	.929	0	1.000
American League totals (2 years)			44	62	3	11	4	0	0	3	5	20	1	0	0-0	.177	.250	.242	.492	3	.978
National League totals (8 years)			544	1610	187	383	77	4	54	194	164	444	37	33	10-5	.238	.321	.391	.713	48	.985
Major League totals (10 years)			588	1672	190	394	81	4	54	197	169	464	38	33	10-5	.236	.319	.386	.704	51	.985

STONE, RICKY — P

PERSONAL: Born February 28, 1975, in Hamilton, Ohio. ... 6-1/170. ... Throws right, bats right. ... Full name: Ricky L. Stone. ... High school: Hamilton (Ohio).

TRANSACTIONS/CAREER NOTES: Selected by Los Angeles Dodgers organization in fourth round of free-agent draft (June 2, 1994). ... Granted free agency (October 18, 2000). ... Signed by Houston Astros organization (January 8, 2001).

CAREER HITTING: 0-for-7 (.000), 0 R, 0 2B, 0 3B, 0 HR, 0 RBI.

Year	League	W	L	Pct.	ERA	WHIP	G	GS	CG	ShO	Hld.	Sv.-Opp.	IP	H	R	ER	HR	BB-IBB	SO	Avg.
1994— Great Falls (Pio.)		2	2	.500	4.44	1.56	13	7	0	0	...	2-...	50.2	55	40	25	5	24-0	48	.268
1995— San Bernardino (Calif.)		3	5	.375	6.52	1.79	12	12	0	0	...	0-...	58.0	79	50	42	7	25-0	31	.333
— Yakima (NW)		4	4	.500	5.25	1.54	16	6	0	0	...	2-...	48.0	54	31	28	5	20-0	28	.289
1996— Savannah (S. Atl.)		2	1	.667	3.98	1.36	5	5	0	0	...	0-...	31.2	34	15	14	2	9-0	31	.288
— Vero Beach (FSL)		8	6	.571	3.83	1.43	21	21	1	0	...	0-...	112.2	115	58	48	9	46-0	74	.267
1997— San Antonio (Texas)		0	3	.000	5.47	1.77	25	5	0	0	...	3-...	52.2	63	33	32	4	30-0	46	.304
— San Bernardino (Calif.)		3	3	.500	3.35	0.93	8	8	0	0	...	0-...	53.2	40	22	20	4	10-0	40	.209
1998— San Antonio (Texas)		7	2	.778	3.84	1.24	13	13	1	1	...	0-...	82.0	76	40	35	7	26-0	69	.251
— Albuquerque (PCL)		5	5	.500	5.38	1.53	18	16	0	0	...	0-...	105.1	120	69	63	13	41-0	85	.287

Year League	W	L	Pct.	ERA	WHIP	G	GS	CG	ShO	Hld.	Sv.-Opp.	IP	H	R	ER	HR	BB-IBB	SO	Avg.
1999— Albuquerque (PCL)	6	10	.375	5.50	1.65	27	27	2	0	...	0-...	167.0	205	*123	•102	23	71-4	132	.306
2000— Albuquerque (PCL)	9	5	.643	4.94	1.56	48	7	0	0	...	5-...	120.1	146	79	66	9	42-3	75	.309
2001— New Orleans (PCL)	6	3	.667	3.59	1.31	51	8	0	0	...	2-...	95.1	98	42	38	8	27-4	78	.269
— Houston (N.L.)	0	0	...	2.35	1.30	6	0	0	0	0	0-0	7.2	8	3	2	1	2-1	4	.258
2002— Houston (N.L.)	3	3	.500	3.61	1.45	78	0	0	0	12	1-2	77.1	78	36	31	9	34-3	63	.266
2003— Houston (N.L.)	6	4	.600	3.69	1.29	65	0	0	0	7	1-1	83.0	76	36	34	11	31-4	47	.247
Major League totals (3 years)	**9**	**7**	**.563**	**3.59**	**1.36**	**149**	**0**	**0**	**0**	**19**	**2-3**	**168.0**	**162**	**75**	**67**	**21**	**67-8**	**114**	**.256**

STRANGE, PAT   P

PERSONAL: Born August 23, 1980, in Springfield, Mass. ... 6-5/243. ... Throws right, bats right. ... Full name: Patrick Martin Strange. ... High school: Springfield Central (Springfield, Mass.).

TRANSACTIONS/CAREER NOTES: Selected by New York Mets organization in second round of free-agent draft (June 2, 1998).

CAREER HITTING: 0-for-1 (.000), 0 R, 0 2B, 0 3B, 0 HR, 0 RBI.

Year League	W	L	Pct.	ERA	WHIP	G	GS	CG	ShO	Hld.	Sv.-Opp.	IP	H	R	ER	HR	BB-IBB	SO	Avg.
1998— GC Mets (GCL)	1	1	.500	1.42	1.32	4	4	0	0	...	0-...	19.0	18	3	3	0	7-0	19	.254
1999— Capital City (S. Atl.)	12	5	.706	2.63	1.08	28	21	2	0	...	1-...	154.0	138	57	45	4	29-1	113	.238
2000— St. Lucie (Fla. St.)	10	1	.909	3.58	1.25	19	13	2	0	...	0-...	88.0	78	48	35	4	32-0	77	.240
— Binghamton (Eastern)	4	3	.571	4.55	1.66	10	10	0	0	...	0-...	55.1	62	30	28	2	30-0	36	.287
2001— Binghamton (Eastern)	11	6	.647	4.87	1.45	26	24	1	0	...	0-...	153.1	171	94	83	18	52-1	106	.288
— Norfolk (Int'l)	1	0	1.000	0.00	0.83	1	1	0	0	...	0-...	6.0	4	0	0	0	1-0	6	.182
2002— Norfolk (Int'l)	10	10	.500	3.82	1.36	29	25	2	0	...	0-...	165.0	165	77	70	12	59-2	109	.265
— New York (N.L.)	0	0	...	1.13	0.88	5	0	0	0	0	0-0	8.0	6	1	1	0	1-1	4	.207
2003— New York (N.L.)	0	0	...	11.00	2.67	6	0	0	0	1	0-0	9.0	13	11	11	4	11-0	5	.351
— Norfolk (Int'l)	5	4	.556	5.74	1.74	31	10	0	0	...	1-...	89.1	111	61	57	8	44-1	64	.313
Major League totals (2 years)	**0**	**0**	**...**	**6.35**	**1.82**	**11**	**0**	**0**	**0**	**1**	**0-0**	**17.0**	**19**	**12**	**12**	**4**	**12-1**	**9**	**.288**

STRICKLAND, SCOTT   P

PERSONAL: Born April 26, 1976, in Houston, Texas. ... 5-11/180. ... Throws right, bats right. ... Full name: Scott Michael Strickland. ... High school: Klein Oak (Spring, Texas). ... College: New Mexico.

TRANSACTIONS/CAREER NOTES: Selected by Montreal Expos organization in 10th round of free-agent draft (June 3, 1997). ... On Montreal disabled list (May 3-July 3, 2000); included rehabilitation assignment to Ottawa (June 25-July 1). ... Traded by Expos with OF Matt Watson and P Philip Seibel to New York Mets for P Bruce Chen, P Dicky Gonzalez and SS/2B Luis Figueroa (April 5, 2002). ... Placed on 15-day disabled list by New York (May 11, 2003). ... Transferred to Emergency disabled list (June 18, 2003).

CAREER HITTING: 0-for-6 (.000), 0 R, 0 2B, 0 3B, 0 HR, 0 RBI.

Year League	W	L	Pct.	ERA	WHIP	G	GS	CG	ShO	Hld.	Sv.-Opp.	IP	H	R	ER	HR	BB-IBB	SO	Avg.
1997— Vermont (NY-P)	5	2	.714	3.82	1.24	15	9	1	0	...	0-...	61.1	56	27	26	5	20-0	69	.250
— Cape Fear (S. Atl.)	0	1	.000	6.35	1.59	3	1	0	0	...	1-...	5.2	8	7	4	0	1-0	8	.320
1998— Cape Fear (S. Atl.)	0	3	.000	4.46	1.32	15	2	0	0	...	4-...	36.1	36	19	18	3	12-0	53	.254
— Jupiter (FSL)	4	3	.571	3.39	1.22	22	11	0	0	...	2-...	69.0	64	28	26	5	20-0	51	.251
1999— Jupiter (FSL)	1	1	.500	3.51	0.97	12	1	0	0	...	2-...	25.2	21	11	10	1	4-1	33	.221
— Harrisburg (Eastern)	1	1	.500	2.48	1.21	14	1	0	0	...	3-...	29.0	25	8	8	1	10-0	36	.238
— Ottawa (Int'l)	3	0	1.000	1.63	1.23	19	0	0	0	...	5-...	27.2	23	5	5	0	11-2	34	.223
— Montreal (N.L.)	0	1	.000	4.50	1.44	17	0	0	0	2	0-0	18.0	15	10	9	3	11-0	23	.231
2000— Montreal (N.L.)	4	3	.571	3.00	1.13	49	0	0	0	6	9-13	48.0	38	18	16	3	16-2	48	.215
— Ottawa (Int'l)	0	0	...	0.00	0.25	3	0	0	0	...	0-0	4.0	1	0	0	0	0-0	4	.077
2001— Montreal (N.L.)	2	6	.250	3.21	1.33	77	0	0	0	12	9-12	81.1	67	36	29	9	41-5	85	.222
2002— Montreal (N.L.)	0	0	...	0.00	0.00	1	0	0	0	0	0-0	1.0	0	0	0	0	0-0	2	.000
— New York (N.L.)	6	9	.400	3.59	1.39	68	0	0	0	15	2-6	67.2	61	29	27	7	33-9	67	.236
2003— New York (N.L.)	0	2	.000	2.25	1.30	19	0	0	0	4	0-1	20.0	16	6	5	1	10-1	16	.219
Major League totals (5 years)	**12**	**21**	**.364**	**3.28**	**1.31**	**231**	**0**	**0**	**0**	**39**	**20-32**	**236.0**	**197**	**99**	**86**	**23**	**111-17**	**241**	**.224**

STRONG, JAMAL   OF

PERSONAL: Born August 5, 1978, in Pasadena, Calif. ... 5-10/180. ... Bats right, throws right. ... Full name: Jamal Najar Strong. ... High school: Pasadena High (Calif.). ... College: Nebraska.

TRANSACTIONS/CAREER NOTES: Selected by Seattle Mariners organization in sixth round of free-agent draft (June 5, 2000). ... On San Antonio disabled list (May 17-24, 2002). ... Called up by Seattle from San Antonio (September 2, 2003).

2003 GAMES PLAYED BY POSITION (MLB): DH—7, OF—2.

										BATTING						**FIELDING**	
Year Team (League)	Pos.	G	AB	R	H	2B	3B	HR	RBI	BB	SO	HBP	GDP	SB-CS	Avg.	OBP	SLG	OPS	E	Pct.
---	---	---	---	---	---	---	---	---	---	---	---	---	---	---	---	---	---	---	---	---
2000— Everett (N'west)	OF	75	296	63	93	7	3	1	28	52	29	4	0	60-14	.314	.422	.368	.790	2	.988
2001— Wisconsin (Midw.)	OF	51	184	41	65	12	1	0	19	40	27	5	2	35-4	.353	.478	.429	.908	1	.988
— San Bern. (Calif.)	OF	81	331	74	103	11	2	0	32	51	60	5	4	47-8	.311	.411	.356	.767	4	.977
2002— San Antonio (Texas)	OF	127	503	63	140	16	5	1	31	62	87	10	7	46-16	.278	.366	.336	.702	6	.980
2003— Ariz. Mariners (Ariz.)	OF	2	7	5	5	0	1	0	4	3	1	1	0	3-0	.714	.692	1.000	1.692	1	.889
— Tacoma (PCL)	OF	56	210	38	64	6	1	2	19	25	38	5	3	26-11	.305	.390	.371	.761	6	.958
— Seattle (A.L.)	DH-OF	12	2	2	0	0	0	0	0	0	0	0	0	0-0	.000	.000	.000	.000	0	...
Major League totals (1 year)		**12**	**2**	**2**	**0**	**0**	**0**	**0**	**0**	**0**	**0**	**0**	**0**	**0-0**	**.000**	**.000**	**.000**	**.000**	**0**	**...**

STURTZE, TANYON   P

PERSONAL: Born October 12, 1970, in Worcester, Mass. ... 6-5/221. ... Throws right, bats right. ... Full name: Tanyon James Sturtze. ... Name pronounced: sturts. ... High school: St. Peter-Marian (Worcester, Mass.). ... Junior college: Quinsigamond (Mass.) Community College.

TRANSACTIONS/CAREER NOTES: Selected by Oakland Athletics organization in 23rd round of free-agent draft (June 4, 1990). ... On Huntsville disabled list (April 7-16, 1994). ... Selected by Chicago Cubs from A's organization in Rule 5 major league draft (December 5, 1994). ... Granted free agency (October 15, 1996). ... Signed by Texas Rangers (November 20, 1996). ... Released by Rangers (March 6, 1998). ... Re-signed by Rangers organization (March 11, 1998). ... Granted free agency (October 15, 1998). ... Signed by Florida Marlins organization (November 23, 1998). ... Signed by Chicago White Sox organization (November 23, 1998). ... On suspended list (May 1-3, 2000). ... Traded by White Sox to Tampa Bay Devil Rays for 2B/SS Tony Graffanino (May 31, 2000). ... On Tampa Bay disabled list (August 27, 2000-remainder of season). ... Granted free agency (December 21, 2002). ... Signed by Toronto Blue Jays (December 22, 2002). ... Suspended by Major League Baseball for two games; started serving suspension (September 26, 2003). ... Reinstated (September 28, 2003).

CAREER HITTING: 1-for-13 (.077), 0 R, 0 2B, 0 3B, 0 HR, 0 RBI.

Year League	W	L	Pct.	ERA	WHIP	G	GS	CG	ShO	Hld.	Sv.-Opp.	IP	H	R	ER	HR	BB-IBB	SO	Avg.
1990— Ariz. A's (Ariz.)	2	5	.286	5.44	1.71	12	10	0	0	...	0-...	48.0	55	41	29	3	27-0	30	.276
1991— Madison (Midw.)	10	5	.667	3.09	1.19	27	27	0	0	...	0-...	163.0	136	77	56	5	58-5	88	.223
1992— Modesto (Calif.)	7	11	.389	3.75	1.46	25	25	1	0	...	0-...	151.0	143	72	63	6	78-1	126	.254
1993— Huntsville (Sou.)	5	12	.294	4.78	1.53	28	• 28	1	1	...	0-...	165.2	169	102	* 88	16	85-2	112	.269
1994— Huntsville (Sou.)	6	3	.667	3.22	1.35	17	17	1	0	...	0-...	103.1	100	40	37	5	39-1	63	.259
— Tacoma (PCL)	4	5	.444	4.04	1.65	11	9	0	0	...	0-...	64.2	73	36	29	5	34-2	28	.284
1995— Chicago (N.L.)	0	0	...	9.00	1.50	2	0	0	0	0	0-0	2.0	2	2	2	1	1-0	0	.250
— Iowa (Am. Assoc.)	4	7	.364	6.80	1.74	23	17	1	1	...	0-...	86.0	108	66	65	18	42-1	48	.314
1996— Iowa (Am. Assoc.)	6	4	.600	4.85	1.56	51	1	0	0	...	4-...	72.1	80	42	39	7	33-2	51	.290
— Chicago (N.L.)	1	0	1.000	9.00	1.91	6	0	0	0	0	0-0	11.0	16	11	11	3	5-0	7	.348
1997— Oklahoma City (A.A.)	8	6	.571	5.10	1.57	25	19	1	0	...	0-...	114.2	133	76	65	10	47-1	79	.295
— Texas (A.L.)	1	1	.500	8.27	1.93	9	5	0	0	0	0-0	32.2	45	30	30	6	18-0	18	.338
1998— GC Rangers (GCL)	0	1	.000	7.71	2.29	3	3	0	0	...	0-...	7.0	12	7	6	1	4-0	10	.364
— Charlotte (Fla. St.)	0	1	.000	6.00	1.00	1	0	0	0	...	0-...	3.0	2	3	2	0	1-0	3	.200
— Tulsa (Texas)	1	0	1.000	5.40	2.40	1	0	0	0	...	0-...	1.2	2	1	1	0	2-0	3	.400
— Oklahoma (PCL)	3	1	.750	3.34	1.46	13	3	0	0	...	0-...	35.0	33	13	13	3	18-0	31	.252
1999— Charlotte (Int'l)	9	4	.692	4.05	1.19	33	14	2	1	...	3-...	104.1	83	53	47	7	41-1	107	.214
— Chicago (A.L.)	0	0	...	0.00	1.00	1	1	0	0	0	0-0	6.0	4	0	0	0	2-0	2	.200
2000— Chicago (A.L.)	1	2	.333	12.06	2.55	10	1	0	0	0	0-0	15.2	25	23	21	4	15-0	6	.379
— Tampa Bay (A.L.)	4	0	1.000	2.56	1.16	19	5	0	0	0	0-0	52.2	47	16	15	4	14-1	38	.236
2001— Tampa Bay (A.L.)	11	12	.478	4.42	1.43	39	27	0	0	3	1-3	195.1	200	98	96	23	79-0	110	.271
2002— Tampa Bay (A.L.)	4	* 18	.182	5.18	1.61	33	33	4	0	0	0-0	224.0	* 271	* 141	* 129	33	* 89-2	137	.302
2003— Toronto (A.L.)	7	6	.538	5.94	1.68	40	8	0	0	1	0-0	89.1	107	67	59	14	43-3	54	.296
American League totals (6 years)	28	39	.418	5.12	1.56	151	80	4	0	4	1-3	615.2	699	375	350	84	260-6	365	.290
National League totals (2 years)	1	0	1.000	9.00	1.85	8	0	0	0	0	0-0	13.0	18	13	13	4	6-0	7	.333
Major League totals (8 years)	29	39	.426	5.20	1.56	159	80	4	0	4	1-3	628.2	717	388	363	88	266-6	372	.291

S

STYNES, CHRIS — 3B/2B

PERSONAL: Born January 19, 1973, in Queens, N.Y. ... 5-10/205. ... Bats right, throws right. ... Full name: Christopher Desmond Stynes. ... High school: Boca Raton (Fla.).
TRANSACTIONS/CAREER NOTES: Selected by Toronto Blue Jays in third round of free-agent draft (June 3, 1991). ... Traded by Blue Jays with P David Sinnes and IF Tony Medrano to Kansas City Royals for P David Cone (April 6, 1995). ... Traded by Royals with OF Jon Nunnally to Cincinnati Reds for P Hector Carrasco and P Scott Service (July 15, 1997). ... Traded by Reds to Boston Red Sox for OF Michael Coleman and IF Donnie Sadler (November 16, 2000). ... On Boston disabled list (April 6-24 and May 10-June 7, 2001); included rehabilitation assignment to Pawtucket (June 3-7). ... Granted free agency (December 21, 2001). ... Signed by Chicago Cubs (January 2, 2002). ... Released by Cubs (December 4, 2002). ... Signed by Colorado Rockies (January 7, 2003).
2003 GAMES PLAYED BY POSITION (MLB): 3B—119, 2B—5.

Year Team (League)	Pos.	G	AB	R	H	2B	3B	HR	RBI	BB	SO	HBP	GDP	SB-CS	Avg.	OBP	SLG	OPS	FIELDING E	Pct.
1991— GC Jays (GCL)	3B	57	219	29	67	15	1	4	39	9	39	1	1	10-3	.306	.336	.438	.775	8	.957
1992— Myrtle Beach (SAL)	3B	127	489	67	139	36	4	9	46	16	43	8	8	28-14	.284	.315	.401	.716	26	.919
1993— Dunedin (Fla. St.)	3B	123	496	72	151	28	5	7	48	25	40	3	12	19-9	.304	.339	.423	.762	21	.938
1994— Knoxville (Sou.)	2B	136	* 545	79	* 173	32	4	8	79	23	36	7	12	28-12	.317	.351	.435	.785	20	.968
1995— Omaha (A.A.)	2B-3B	83	306	51	84	12	5	9	42	27	24	5	7	4-5	.275	.338	.435	.773	13	.964
— Kansas City (A.L.)	2B-DH	22	35	7	6	1	0	0	2	4	3	0	3	0-0	.171	.256	.200	.456	1	.982
1996— Omaha (A.A.)	0-3-2-D	72	284	50	101	22	2	10	40	18	17	4	7	7-3	.356	.398	.553	.951	9	.951
— Kansas City (A.L.)	0-2-D-3	36	92	8	27	6	0	0	6	2	5	0	1	5-2	.293	.309	.359	.667	3	.939
1997— Omaha (A.A.)	2-0-D-3	82	332	53	88	18	1	8	44	19	25	0	7	3-1	.265	.303	.398	.701	10	.948
— Indianapolis (A.A.)	2B	21	86	14	31	8	0	1	17	2	5	1	3	4-1	.360	.374	.488	.862	2	.982
— Cincinnati (N.L.) OF-2B-3B	49	198	31	69	7	1	6	28	11	13	4	5	11-2	.348	.394	.485	.879	2	.984
1998— Cincinnati (N.L.)	0-3-2-S	123	347	52	88	10	1	6	27	32	36	4	5	15-1	.254	.323	.340	.663	2	.990
1999— Cincinnati (N.L.) 2B-3B-OF	73	113	18	27	1	0	2	14	12	13	0	2	5-2	.239	.310	.301	.610	6	.953
2000— Cincinnati (N.L.) ... 3B-2B-OF	119	380	71	127	24	1	12	40	32	54	2	5	5-2	.334	.386	.497	.883	7	.970
2001— Boston (A.L.) 3B-2B-OF	96	361	52	101	19	2	8	33	20	56	3	12	4-5	.280	.322	.410	.732	5	.980
— Pawtucket (Int'l)	2B-3B	4	15	1	5	1	0	0	1	1	2	1	0	0-0	.333	.412	.400	.812	0	1.000
2002— Chicago (N.L.)	3B-2B	98	195	25	47	9	1	5	26	21	29	1	5	1-1	.241	.314	.374	.688	5	.957
2003— Colorado (N.L.)	3B-2B	138	443	71	113	31	3	11	73	48	76	6	8	3-1	.255	.335	.413	.748	9	.974
American League totals (3 years)		154	488	67	134	26	2	8	41	26	64	3	16	9-7	.275	.315	.385	.700	10	.975
National League totals (6 years)		600	1676	268	471	82	7	42	208	156	221	17	30	40-9	.281	.346	.413	.760	31	.973
Major League totals (9 years)		754	2164	335	605	108	9	50	249	182	285	20	46	49-16	.280	.340	.407	.747	41	.974

SULLIVAN, SCOTT — P

PERSONAL: Born March 13, 1971, in Carrollton, Ala. ... 6-3/210. ... Throws right, bats right. ... Full name: William Scott Sullivan. ... High school: Pickens Academy (Carrollton, Ala.). ... College: Auburn.
TRANSACTIONS/CAREER NOTES: Selected by Cincinnati Reds organization in second round of free-agent draft (June 3, 1993). ... On Indianapolis disabled list (August 21, 1995-remainder of season). ... On disabled list (August 10-25, 2002). ... Placed on 15-day disabled list (July 14, 2003). ... Reinstated from 15-day disabled list (August 7, 2003). ... Traded by Reds to Chicago White Sox for IF Tim Hummel and cash (August 21, 2003).
CAREER HITTING: 4-for-48 (.083), 1 R, 0 2B, 0 3B, 0 HR, 1 RBI.

Year League	W	L	Pct.	ERA	WHIP	G	GS	CG	ShO	Hld.	Sv.-Opp.	IP	H	R	ER	HR	BB-IBB	SO	Avg.
1993— Billings (Pio.)	5	0	1.000	1.67	1.07	18	7	2	2	...	3-...	54.0	33	13	10	1	25-0	79	.174
1994— Chattanooga (Sou.)	11	7	.611	3.41	1.16	34	13	2	0	...	7-...	121.1	101	60	46	8	40-1	111	.220
1995— Indianapolis (A.A.)	4	3	.571	3.53	1.28	44	0	0	0	...	1-...	58.2	51	31	23	2	24-4	54	.232
— Cincinnati (N.L.)	0	0	...	4.91	1.64	3	0	0	0	0	0-0	3.2	4	2	2	0	2-0	2	.286
1996— Indianapolis (A.A.)	5	2	.714	2.73	1.21	53	3	0	0	...	1-...	108.2	95	38	33	10	37-3	77	.233
— Cincinnati (N.L.)	0	0	...	2.25	1.50	7	0	0	0	0	0-0	8.0	7	2	2	0	5-0	3	.241
1997— Cincinnati (N.L.)	5	3	.625	3.24	1.12	59	0	0	0	13	1-2	97.1	79	36	35	12	30-8	96	.220
— Indianapolis (A.A.)	3	1	.750	1.30	0.72	19	0	0	0	...	2-...	27.2	16	4	4	0	4-1	23	.186
1998— Cincinnati (N.L.)	5	5	.500	5.21	1.31	67	0	0	0	5	1-4	102.0	98	62	59	14	36-4	86	.253
1999— Cincinnati (N.L.)	5	4	.556	3.01	1.19	79	0	0	0	13	3-5	113.2	88	41	38	10	47-4	78	.217
2000— Cincinnati (N.L.)	3	6	.333	3.47	1.18	79	0	0	0	22	3-6	106.1	87	44	41	14	38-8	96	.226
2001— Cincinnati (N.L.)	7	1	.875	3.31	1.26	79	0	0	0	20	0-3	103.1	94	44	38	10	36-8	82	.243
2002— Cincinnati (N.L.)	6	5	.545	6.06	1.58	71	0	0	0	19	1-3	78.2	93	60	53	15	31-11	78	.294
2003— Cincinnati (N.L.)	6	0	1.000	3.62	1.31	50	0	0	0	10	0-1	49.2	39	22	20	4	26-4	43	.213
— Chicago (A.L.)	0	0	...	3.77	1.05	15	0	0	0	2	0-0	14.1	9	6	6	2	6-0	13	.184
American League totals (1 year)	0	0	...	3.77	1.05	15	0	0	0	2	0-0	14.1	9	6	6	2	6-0	13	.184
National League totals (9 years)	37	24	.607	3.91	1.27	494	0	0	0	102	9-24	662.2	589	313	288	79	251-47	564	.239
Major League totals (9 years)	37	24	.607	3.91	1.26	509	0	0	0	104	9-24	677.0	598	319	294	81	257-47	577	.238

SUPPAN, JEFF   P

PERSONAL: Born January 2, 1975, in Oklahoma City, Okla. ... 6-2/220. ... Throws right, bats right. ... Full name: Jeffrey Scot Suppan. ... Name pronounced: SOO-pahn. ... High school: Crespi (Encino, Calif.).

TRANSACTIONS/CAREER NOTES: Selected by Boston Red Sox organization in second round of free-agent draft (June 3, 1993). ... On Trenton disabled list (April 9-29, 1995). ... On Boston disabled list (August 25, 1996-remainder of season). ... Selected by Arizona Diamondbacks in first round (third pick overall) of expansion draft (November 18, 1997). ... Contract purchased by Kansas City Royals from Diamondbacks (September 3, 1998). ... Granted free agency (December 21, 2002). ... Signed by Pittsburgh Pirates (January 31, 2003). ... Traded by Pirates with P Brandon Lyon and P Anastacio Martinez to Boston Red Sox for 2B Freddy Sanchez, P Mike Gonzalez and cash (July 31, 2003).

CAREER HITTING: 21-for-81 (.259), 4 R, 1 2B, 0 3B, 0 HR, 4 RBI.

Year	League	W	L	Pct.	ERA	WHIP	G	GS	CG	ShO	Hld.	Sv.-Opp.	IP	H	R	ER	HR	BB-IBB	SO	Avg.
1993— GC Red Sox (GCL)		4	3	.571	2.18	1.18	10	9	2	1	...	0-...	57.2	52	20	14	0	16-0	64	.237
1994— Sarasota (Fla. St.)		• 13	7	.650	3.26	1.17	27	27	4	2	...	0-...	174.0	153	74	63	10	50-0	* 173	.236
1995— Trenton (East.)		6	2	.750	2.36	1.13	15	15	1	1	...	0-...	99.0	86	35	26	5	26-1	88	.232
— Boston (A.L.)		1	2	.333	5.96	1.50	8	3	0	0	1	0-0	22.2	29	15	15	4	5-1	19	.312
— Pawtucket (Int'l)		2	3	.400	5.32	1.29	7	7	0	0	...	0-...	45.2	50	29	27	9	9-0	32	.278
1996— Boston (A.L.)		1	1	.500	7.54	1.85	8	4	0	0	0	0-0	22.2	29	19	19	3	13-0	13	.330
— Pawtucket (Int'l)		10	6	.625	3.22	1.07	22	22	7	1	0	0-0	145.1	130	66	52	16	25-1	142	.233
1997— Pawtucket (Int'l)		5	1	.833	3.71	1.09	9	9	2	1	...	0-...	60.2	51	26	25	7	15-0	40	.233
— Boston (A.L.)		7	3	.700	5.69	1.57	23	22	0	0	0	0-0	112.1	140	75	71	12	36-1	67	.305
1998— Arizona (N.L.)		1	7	.125	6.68	1.56	13	13	1	0	0	0-0	66.0	82	55	49	12	21-1	39	.301
— Tucson (PCL)		4	3	.571	3.63	1.37	13	12	0	0	...	0-...	67.0	75	29	27	4	17-1	62	.277
— Kansas City (A.L.)		0	0	...	0.71	0.79	4	1	0	0	0	0-0	12.2	9	1	1	1	1-0	12	.200
1999— Kansas City (A.L.)		10	12	.455	4.53	1.36	32	32	4	1	0	0-0	208.2	222	113	105	28	62-4	103	.274
2000— Kansas City (A.L.)		10	9	.526	4.94	1.49	35	33	3	1	0	0-0	217.0	240	121	119	*36	84-3	128	.284
2001— Kansas City (A.L.)		10	14	.417	4.37	1.38	34	34	1	0	0	0-0	218.1	227	120	106	26	74-3	120	.267
2002— Kansas City (A.L.)		9	16	.360	5.32	1.43	33	33	3	1	0	0-0	208.0	229	134	123	32	68-3	109	.279
2003— Pittsburgh (N.L.)		10	7	.588	3.57	1.26	21	21	3	2	0	0-0	141.0	147	57	56	11	31-5	78	.268
— Boston (A.L.)		3	4	.429	5.57	1.43	11	10	0	0	0	0-0	63.0	70	41	39	12	20-0	32	.281
American League totals (9 years)		**51**	**61**	**.455**	**4.96**	**1.44**	**188**	**172**	**11**	**3**	**1**	**0-0**	**1085.1**	**1195**	**639**	**598**	**154**	**363-15**	**603**	**.280**
National League totals (2 years)		**11**	**14**	**.440**	**4.57**	**1.36**	**34**	**34**	**4**	**2**	**0**	**0-0**	**207.0**	**229**	**112**	**105**	**23**	**52-6**	**117**	**.279**
Major League totals (9 years)		**62**	**75**	**.453**	**4.90**	**1.42**	**222**	**206**	**15**	**5**	**1**	**0-0**	**1292.1**	**1424**	**751**	**703**	**177**	**415-21**	**720**	**.280**

SURHOFF, B.J.   1B/OF

PERSONAL: Born August 4, 1964, in Bronx, N.Y. ... 6-1/215. ... Bats left, throws right. ... Full name: William James Surhoff. ... High school: Rye (N.Y.). ... College: North Carolina.

TRANSACTIONS/CAREER NOTES: Selected by New York Yankees organization in fifth round of free-agent draft (June 7, 1982); did not sign. ... Selected by Milwaukee Brewers organization in first round (first pick overall) of free-agent draft (June 3, 1985). ... On suspended list (August 23-25, 1990). ... On Milwaukee disabled list (March 25-April 16, April 20-May 23 and July 7, 1994-remainder of season); included rehabilitation assignments to El Paso (April 12-16) and New Orleans (May 17-23). ... Granted free agency (October 20, 1994). ... Re-signed by Brewers organization (April 7, 1995). ... Granted free agency (November 6, 1995). ... Signed by Baltimore Orioles (December 20, 1995). ... On disabled list (May 18-June 2, 1996). ... Granted free agency (October 26, 1998). ... Re-signed by Orioles (December 7, 1998). ... Traded by Orioles with P Gabe Molina to Atlanta Braves for OF Trenidad Hubbard, C Fernando Lunar and P Luis Rivera (July 31, 2000). ... On disabled list (April 28, 2002-remainder of season). ... Granted free agency (October 28, 2002). ... Signed by Orioles organization (February 12, 2002). ... Reinstated from the 15-day disabled list (May 4, 2003). ... Activated from the 15-day disabled list (May 28, 2003). ... Placed on 15-day disabled list (July 25, 2003). ... Reinstated from 15-day disabled list (August 12, 2003).

2003 GAMES PLAYED BY POSITION (MLB): DH—39, OF—27, 1B—22.

Year	Team (League)	Pos.	G	AB	R	H	2B	3B	HR	RBI	BB	SO	HBP	GDP	SB-CS	Avg.	OBP	SLG	OPS	E	Pct.
1985— Beloit (Midw.)		C	76	289	39	96	13	4	7	58	22	35	0	3	10-9	.332	.373	.478	.851	3	.994
1986— Vancouver (PCL)		C	116	458	71	141	19	3	5	59	29	30	8	16	21-8	.308	.356	.395	.751	7 *	.989
1987— Milwaukee (A.L.)		DH-C	115	395	50	118	22	3	7	68	36	30	0	13	11-10	.299	.350	.423	.773	11	.985
1988— Milwaukee (A.L.)		C	139	493	47	121	21	0	5	38	31	49	3	12	21-6	.245	.292	.318	.611	8	.988
1989— Milwaukee (A.L.)		3B-DH-C	126	436	42	108	17	4	5	55	25	29	3	8	14-12	.248	.287	.339	.626	10	.983
1990— Milwaukee (A.L.)		3B-C	135	474	55	131	21	4	6	59	41	37	1	8	18-7	.276	.331	.376	.706	12	.983
1991— Milwaukee (A.L.)		DH-C	143	505	57	146	19	4	5	68	26	33	0	*21	5-8	.289	.319	.372	.691	4	.995
1992— Milwaukee (A.L.)		C-1-D-O-3	139	480	63	121	19	1	4	62	46	41	2	9	14-8	.252	.314	.321	.635	6	.992
1993— Milwaukee (A.L.)		3-0-1-C-D	148	552	66	151	38	3	7	79	36	47	2	9	12-9	.274	.318	.391	.709	18	.956
1994— El Paso (Texas)		OF	3	12	2	3	1	0	0	0	0	2	0	0	0-0	.250	.250	.333	.583	0	1.000
— Milwaukee (A.L.)		3-C-1-0-D	40	134	20	35	11	2	5	22	16	14	0	5	0-1	.261	.336	.485	.821	4	.974
— New Orleans (A.A.)		3-0-C-1	5	19	3	6	2	0	0	1	1	2	0	0	0-0	.316	.350	.421	.771	0	1.000
1995— Milwaukee (A.L.)		0-1-C-D	117	415	72	133	26	3	13	73	37	43	4	7	7-3	.320	.378	.492	.870	5	.991
1996— Baltimore (A.L.)		3-0-D-1	143	537	74	157	27	6	21	82	47	79	3	7	0-1	.292	.352	.482	.834	15	.955
1997— Baltimore (A.L.)		0-D-3-1	147	528	80	150	30	4	18	88	49	60	5	7	1-1	.284	.345	.458	.803	2	.993
1998— Baltimore (A.L.)		OF-1B	162	573	79	160	34	1	22	92	49	81	1	13	9-7	.279	.332	.457	.789	3	.989
1999— Baltimore (A.L.)		OF-DH-3B	* 162	104	207	38	1	28	107	43	78	2	15	5-1	.308	.347	.492	.839	0	1.000
2000— Baltimore (A.L.)		OF-DH	103	411	56	120	27	0	13	57	29	46	2	5	7-2	.292	.341	.453	.793	3	.987
— Atlanta (N.L.)		OF	44	128	13	37	9	2	1	11	12	12	1	5	3-0	.289	.352	.414	.766	0	1.000
2001— Atlanta (N.L.)		OF-DH	141	484	68	131	33	1	10	58	38	48	1	5	9-3	.271	.321	.405	.726	3	.986
2002— Atlanta (N.L.)		1B-OF	25	75	5	22	5	0	0	9	9	5	0	1	1-3	.293	.369	.360	.729	0	1.000
2003— Baltimore (A.L.)		DH-OF-1B	93	319	32	94	20	0	5	41	29	29	1	4	2-2	.295	.353	.404	.758	2	.991
American League totals (15 years)			1912	6925	897	1952	370	36	164	991	540	696	29	143	126-78	.282	.332	.417	.749	103	.985
National League totals (3 years)			210	687	86	190	47	3	11	78	59	65	2	11	13-6	.277	.332	.402	.734	3	.992
Major League totals (17 years)			2122	7612	983	2142	417	39	175	1069	599	761	31	154	139-84	.281	.332	.415	.748	106	.986

SUZUKI, ICHIRO   OF

PERSONAL: Born October 22, 1973, in Kasugai, Japan. ... 5-9/172. ... Bats left, throws right. ... Name pronounced: ee-chee-row. ... High school: Aikoudai Meiden (Kasugai, Japan).

TRANSACTIONS/CAREER NOTES: Signed as non-drafted free agent by Seattle Mariners organization (November 18, 2000).

2003 GAMES PLAYED BY POSITION (MLB): OF—159.

Year Team (League)	Pos.	G	AB	R	H	2B	3B	HR	RBI	BB	SO	HBP	GDP	SB-CS	Avg.	OBP	SLG	OPS	E	Pct.
1992— Orix (Jap. Pacific)		40	95	9	24	5	0	0	5	3	11	...	...	3-2	.253	...	.305	...	...	...
1993— Orix (Jap. Pacific)		43	64	4	12	2	0	1	3	2	7	...	...	0-2	.188	...	.266	...	...	...
1994— Orix (Jap. Pacific)		130	546	111	210	41	5	13	54	51	53	...	...	29-7	.385	...	.549	...	...	...
1995— Orix (Jap. Pacific)		130	524	104	179	23	4	25	80	68	52	...	...	49-9	.342	...	.544	...	...	...
1996— Orix (Jap. Pacific)		130	542	104	193	24	4	16	84	56	52	...	...	35-3	.356	...	.504	...	...	...
1997— Orix (Jap. Pacific)		135	536	94	185	31	4	17	91	62	36	...	...	39-4	.345	...	.513	...	...	...
1998— Orix (Jap. Pacific)		135	506	79	181	36	3	13	71	43	35	...	...	11-4	.358	...	.518	...	...	...
1999— Orix (Jap. Pacific)		103	411	80	141	27	2	21	68	45	46	...	...	12-1	.343	...	.572	...	...	...
2000— Orix (Jap. Pacific)		105	395	73	153	22	1	12	74	54	36	...	...	21-..	.387	...	.539	...	...	...
2001— Seattle (A.L.)	OF-DH	157	* 692	127	* 242	34	8	8	69	30	53	8	3	* 56-14	*.350	.381	.457	.838	1	.997
2002— Seattle (A.L.)	OF-DH	157	647	111	208	27	8	8	51	68	62	5	8	31-15	.321	.388	.425	.813	3	.991
2003— Seattle (A.L.)	OF	159	679	111	212	29	8	13	62	36	69	6	3	34-8	.312	.352	.436	.788	2	.994
Major League totals (3 years)		473	2018	349	662	90	24	29	182	134	184	19	14	121-37	.328	.374	.440	.813	6	.994

SWANN, PEDRO — OF

PERSONAL: Born October 27, 1970, in Wilmington, Del. ... 6-0/200. ... Bats left, throws right. ... Full name: Pedro Maurice Swann. ... High school: St. Mark's (Wilmington, Del.). ... College: Delaware State.

TRANSACTIONS/CAREER NOTES: Selected by Atlanta Braves organization in 26th round of free-agent draft (June 3, 1991). ... Granted free agency (October 17, 1997). ... Signed by Detroit Tigers organization (December 8, 1997). ... Granted free agency (October 16, 1998). ... Re-signed by Tigers organization (December 17, 1998). ... Granted free agency (October 15, 1999). ... Signed by Braves organization (December 18, 1999). ... On Richmond disabled list (July 9-24, 2000). ... Granted free agency (October 18, 2000). ... Re-signed by Braves organization (January 22, 2001). ... Granted free agency (October 15, 2001). ... Signed by Toronto Blue Jays organization (February 15, 2002). ... Granted free agency (October 15, 2002). ... Signed by Baltimore Orioles (February 3, 2003).

2003 GAMES PLAYED BY POSITION (MLB): OF—6, DH—1.

Year Team (League)	Pos.	G	AB	R	H	2B	3B	HR	RBI	BB	SO	HBP	GDP	SB-CS	Avg.	OBP	SLG	OPS	E	Pct.
1991— Idaho Falls (Pio.)	OF	55	174	35	48	6	1	3	28	33	45	2	4	8-5	.276	.393	.374	.767	5	.935
1992— Pulaski (Appal.)	OF	59	203	36	61	* 18	4	5	34	32	33	7	6	13-6	.300	.412	.473	.884	8	.912
1993— Durham (Caro.)	1B-OF	61	182	27	63	8	2	6	27	19	38	1	2	6-12	.346	.411	.511	.922	2	.958
— Greenville (Sou.)	OF	44	157	19	48	9	2	3	21	9	23	1	5	2-2	.306	.347	.446	.793	3	.932
1994— Greenville (Sou.)	OF	126	428	55	121	25	2	10	49	46	85	4	14	16-9	.283	.356	.421	.777	6	.943
1995— Richmond (Int'l)	OF	15	38	2	8	1	0	0	3	1	2	1	0	0-2	.211	.250	.237	.487	0	1.000
— Greenville (Sou.)	1B-OF	102	339	57	110	24	2	11	64	45	63	3	8	14-11	.324	.405	.504	.910	6	.961
1996— Greenville (Sou.)	OF	35	129	15	40	5	0	3	20	18	23	3	3	4-4	.310	.404	.419	.823	3	.949
— Richmond (Int'l)	OF	93	296	42	74	11	4	4	35	22	56	4	5	7-7	.250	.308	.355	.662	3	.983
1997— Greenville (Sou.)	OF	124	465	78	133	29	2	24	83	49	75	4	14	5-5	.286	.358	.512	.870	7	.957
1998— Toledo (Int'l)	OF	120	419	56	122	28	2	15	66	41	74	3	11	6-3	.291	.355	.475	.830	2	.985
1999— Toledo (Int'l)	OF	103	332	51	86	14	2	10	37	36	67	6	7	3-1	.259	.338	.404	.741	1	.993
2000— Richmond (Int'l)	OF-1B	125	442	70	135	22	2	9	57	54	68	5	10	6-5	.305	.386	.425	.812	3	.987
— Atlanta (N.L.)	OF	4	2	0	0	0	0	0	0	0	2	0	0	0-0	.000	.000	.000	.000	0	...
2001— Richmond (Int'l)	OF	139	488	68	142	33	5	8	72	52	95	8	14	12-6	.291	.362	.428	.790	4	.985
2002— Syracuse (Int'l)	OF	97	368	52	102	17	4	14	62	37	77	8	14	1-3	.277	.353	.459	.813	1	.994
— Toronto (A.L.)	DH-OF	13	12	3	1	0	0	0	1	1	6	0	0	0-0	.083	.154	.083	.237	0	...
2003— Ottawa (Int'l) OF-DH-1B	121	418	62	117	21	2	10	53	35	73	2	17	4-6	.280	.338	.411	.749	4	.980
— Baltimore (A.L.)	OF-DH	8	14	3	3	1	0	1	2	1	4	0	1	0-0	.214	.267	.500	.767	0	1.000
American League totals (2 years)		21	26	6	4	1	0	1	3	2	10	0	1	0-0	.154	.214	.308	.522	0	1.000
National League totals (1 year)		4	2	0	0	0	0	0	0	0	2	0	0	0-0	.000	.000	.000	.000	0	...
Major League totals (3 years)		25	28	6	4	1	0	1	3	2	12	0	1	0-0	.143	.200	.286	.486	0	1.000

SWEENEY, BRIAN — P

PERSONAL: Born June 13, 1974, in Yonkers, N.Y. ... 6-2/185. ... Throws right, bats right. ... Full name: Brian Edward Sweeney. ... High school: Yonkers (N.Y.). ... College: Mercy (N.Y.).

TRANSACTIONS/CAREER NOTES: Signed by Seattle Mariners organization as a non-drafted free agent (September 17, 1996).

CAREER HITTING: 0-for-0 (.000), 0 R, 0 2B, 0 3B, 0 HR, 0 RBI.

Year League	W	L	Pct.	ERA	WHIP	G	GS	CG	ShO	Hld.	Sv.-Opp.	IP	H	R	ER	HR	BB-IBB	SO	Avg.
1997— Lancaster (Calif.)	6	3	.667	3.80	1.22	40	0	0	0	...	1-...	85.1	83	39	36	11	21-1	73	.252
1998— Lancaster (Calif.)	6	0	1.000	3.63	1.19	17	4	0	0	...	0-...	52.0	41	26	21	6	21-1	48	.218
1999— Tacoma (PCL)	0	2	.000	6.75	1.75	5	1	0	0	...	0-...	16.0	26	17	12	5	2-0	10	.366
— New Haven (East.)	4	6	.400	4.69	1.40	23	18	0	0	...	1-...	111.1	125	65	58	18	31-1	83	.285
— Lancaster (Calif.)	0	0	...	6.75	1.82	5	0	0	0	...	0-...	9.1	14	7	7	4	3-0	14	.341
2000— Tacoma (PCL)	0	1	.000	6.00	1.67	2	1	0	0	...	0-...	6.0	9	4	4	2	1-0	1	.360
— New Haven (East.)	4	3	.571	3.40	1.43	19	7	0	0	...	1-...	47.2	49	20	18	3	19-0	27	.268
2001— San Antonio (Texas)	7	4	.636	3.80	1.34	37	9	0	0	...	1-...	104.1	117	47	44	8	23-1	96	.283
2002— Tacoma (PCL)	9	5	.643	3.80	1.30	30	23	1	1	...	2-...	142.0	157	67	60	16	28-0	113	.275
2003— Tacoma (PCL)	11	10	.524	4.28	1.40	29	21	0	0	...	0-...	141.0	165	80	67	17	32-0	115	.288
— Seattle (A.L.)	0	0	...	1.93	0.86	5	0	0	0	0	0-0	9.1	7	2	2	0	1-0	7	.212
Major League totals (1 year)	0	0	...	1.93	0.86	5	0	0	0	0	0-0	9.1	7	2	2	0	1-0	7	.212

SWEENEY, MARK — OF/1B

PERSONAL: Born October 26, 1969, in Framingham, Mass. ... 6-1/215. ... Bats left, throws left. ... Full name: Mark Patrick Sweeney. ... High school: Holliston (Mass.). ... College: Maine.

TRANSACTIONS/CAREER NOTES: Selected by Los Angeles Dodgers organization in 39th round of free-agent draft (June 4, 1990); did not sign. ... Selected by California Angels organization in ninth round of free-agent draft (June 3, 1991). ... Traded by Angels with a player to be named later to St. Louis Cardinals for P John Habyan (July 8, 1995); Cardinals acquired IF Rod Correia to complete deal (January 31, 1996). ... Traded by Cardinals with P Danny Jackson and P Rich Batchelor to San Diego Padres for P Fernando Valenzuela, 3B Scott Livingstone and OF Phil Plantier (June 13, 1997). ... Traded by Padres with OF Greg Vaughn to Cincinnati Reds for OF Reggie Sanders, SS Damian Jackson and P Josh Harris (February 2, 1999). ... Traded by Reds with a player to be named later to Milwaukee Brewers for OF Alex Ochoa (January 14, 2000); Brewers acquired P Gene Altman to complete deal (May 15, 2000). ... On Milwaukee disabled list (March 31-May 7 and July 18-August 14, 2000); included rehabilitation assignments to Indianapolis (July 21-26 and August 3-14). ... Granted free agency (October 5, 2000). ... Re-signed by Brewers organization (January 3, 2001). ... Traded by Brewers to New York Mets as part of three-way deal in which Mets traded P Glendon Rusch to Brewers, Colorado Rockies traded 1B/OF Ross Gload and P Craig House to

S

Mets, Brewers traded P Jeff D'Amico, OF Jeromy Burnitz, IF Lou Collier and cash to Mets, Mets traded 1B/3B Todd Zeile, OF Benny Agbayani, IF/OF Lenny Harris and cash to Rockies and Rockies traded OF Alex Ochoa to Brewers (January 21, 2002). ... Released by Mets (March 13, 2002). ... Signed by Padres organization (March 16, 2002). ... On San Diego disabled list (June 6-26, 2002). ... Released by Padres (July 15, 2002). ... Signed by Colorado Rockies (January 21, 2003).

2003 GAMES PLAYED BY POSITION (MLB): OF—17, 1B—8, DH—1.

Year Team (League)	Pos.	G	AB	R	H	2B	3B	HR	RBI	BB	SO	HBP	GDP	SB-CS	Avg.	OBP	SLG	OPS	E	Pct.
1991— Boise (NW)	OF	70	234	45	66	10	3	4	34	* 51	42	5	7	9-5	.282	.416	.402	.818	2	.954
1992— Quad City (Midw.)	OF	120	424	65	115	20	5	14	76	47	85	4	6	15-11	.271	.346	.441	.787	4	.981
1993— Palm Springs (Calif.)	OF-1B	66	245	41	87	18	3	3	47	42	29	2	4	9-6	.355	.449	.490	.938	7	.955
— Midland (Texas)	OF	51	188	41	67	13	2	9	32	27	22	6	5	1-1	.356	.444	.590	1.035	1	.989
1994— Vancouver (PCL)	DH-1B-OF	103	344	59	98	12	3	8	49	59	50	5	5	3-3	.285	.394	.407	.801	2	.994
— Midland (Texas)	OF-1B-DH	14	50	13	15	3	0	3	18	10	10	0	3	1-1	.300	.403	.540	.943	2	.973
1995— Vancouver (PCL)	OF-DH-1B	69	226	48	78	14	2	7	59	43	33	2	6	3-1	.345	.452	.518	.970	2	.981
— Louisville (A.A.)	1B	22	76	15	28	8	0	2	22	14	8	2	0	2-0	.368	.468	.553	1.021	2	.990
— St. Louis (N.L.)	1B-OF	37	77	5	21	2	0	2	13	10	15	0	3	1-1	.273	.348	.377	.725	2	.988
1996— St. Louis (N.L.)	OF-1B	98	170	32	45	9	0	3	22	33	29	1	4	3-0	.265	.387	.371	.758	3	.977
1997— St. Louis (N.L.)	OF-1B	44	61	5	13	3	0	0	4	9	14	1	2	0-1	.213	.319	.262	.582	0	1.000
— San Diego (N.L.)	OF-1B	71	103	11	33	4	0	2	19	11	18	0	1	2-2	.320	.383	.417	.800	2	.957
1998— San Diego (N.L.)	OF-1B-DH	122	192	17	45	8	3	2	15	26	37	1	5	1-2	.234	.324	.339	.663	1	.994
1999— Cincinnati (N.L.)	1B-OF	37	31	6	11	3	0	2	7	4	9	0	2	0-0	.355	.429	.645	1.074	0	1.000
— Indianapolis (Int'l)	OF-DH-1B	86	311	66	100	17	1	12	51	59	40	4	7	3-2	.322	.432	.498	.931	5	.982
2000— Milwaukee (N.L.)	DH-OF-1B	71	73	9	16	6	0	1	6	12	18	1	1	0-0	.219	.337	.342	.680	0	1.000
— Indianapolis (Int'l)	1B-OF	18	55	13	28	8	0	2	14	10	8	0	3	0-0	.509	.585	.764	1.348	0	1.000
2001— Indianapolis (Int'l)	OF-1B	109	404	65	116	34	1	6	69	56	71	2	6	3-1	.287	.373	.421	.793	1	.994
— Milwaukee (N.L.)	OF-1B	48	89	9	23	3	1	3	11	12	23	0	0	2-1	.258	.347	.416	.762	1	.971
2002— San Diego (N.L.)	1B-OF-DH	48	65	3	11	3	0	1	4	4	19	0	1	0-0	.169	.217	.262	.479	2	.956
— Portland (PCL)	1B	1	1	0	1	0	0	0	0	0	0	0	0	0-0	1.000	1.000	1.000	2.000	0	...
2003— Colo. Springs (PCL)	OF-1B-DH	51	165	24	49	10	1	5	35	34	32	0	5	1-4	.297	.407	.461	.867	2	.985
— Colorado (N.L.)	OF-1B-DH	67	97	13	25	9	0	2	14	9	27	0	2	0-1	.258	.321	.412	.733	0	1.000
Major League totals (9 years)		643	958	110	243	50	4	18	115	130	209	4	21	9-8	.254	.343	.371	.714	11	.984

SWEENEY, MIKE — 1B

PERSONAL: Born July 22, 1973, in Orange, Calif. ... 6-3/225. ... Bats right, throws right. ... Full name: Michael John Sweeney. ... High school: Ontario (Calif.).

TRANSACTIONS/CAREER NOTES: Selected by Kansas City Royals organization in 10th round of free-agent draft (June 3, 1991). ... On disabled list (May 24-July 5, 1994). ... On suspended list (August 17-27, 2001). ... On Kansas City disabled list (July 14-August 13, 2002); included rehabilitation assignment to Omaha (August 9-13). ... Placed on 15-day disabled list (June 21, 2003). ... Sent to Omaha on rehab assignment by Kansas City (August 2, 2003). ... Recalled from Omaha rehab assignment (August 4, 2003). ... Reinstated from 15-day disabled list (August 8, 2003).

2003 GAMES PLAYED BY POSITION (MLB): DH—62, 1B—45.

Year Team (League)	Pos.	G	AB	R	H	2B	3B	HR	RBI	BB	SO	HBP	GDP	SB-CS	Avg.	OBP	SLG	OPS	E	Pct.
1991— GC Royals (GCL)	C-1B	38	102	8	22	3	0	1	11	11	9	0	2	1-0	.216	.287	.275	.561	4	.972
1992— Eugene (Northwest)	C	59	199	17	44	12	1	4	28	13	54	4	0	3-3	.221	.280	.352	.632	14	.967
1993— Eugene (Northwest)	C	53	175	32	42	10	2	6	29	30	41	3	2	1-0	.240	.359	.423	.782	7	.983
1994— Rockford (Midwest)	C	86	276	47	83	20	3	10	52	55	43	9	8	0-1	.301	.427	.504	.931	6	.988
1995— Wilmington (Caro.)	C-DH-3B	99	332	61	103	23	1	18	53	60	39	9	4	6-1	.310	.424	.548	.972	7	.989
— Kansas City (A.L.)	C	4	4	1	1	0	0	0	0	0	0	0	0	0-0	.250	.250	.250	.500	1	.875
1996— Wichita (Texas)	DH-C	66	235	45	75	18	1	14	51	32	29	2	5	3-2	.319	.399	.583	.982	1	.995
— Omaha (A.A.)	C-DH	25	101	14	26	9	0	3	16	6	13	3	0	0-0	.257	.318	.436	.754	0	1.000
— Kansas City (A.L.)	C-DH	50	165	23	46	10	0	4	24	18	21	4	7	1-2	.279	.358	.412	.770	1	.994
1997— Kansas City (A.L.)	C-DH	84	240	30	58	8	0	7	31	17	33	6	8	3-2	.242	.306	.363	.668	3	.993
— Omaha (A.A.)	C-DH	40	144	22	34	8	1	10	29	18	20	2	3	0-2	.236	.323	.514	.837	1	.996
1998— Kansas City (A.L.)	C	92	282	32	73	18	0	8	35	24	38	2	7	2-3	.259	.320	.408	.728	• 9	.984
1999— Kansas City (A.L.)	1B-DH-C	150	575	101	185	44	2	22	102	54	48	10	21	6-1	.322	.387	.520	.907	12	.981
2000— Kansas City (A.L.)	1B-DH	159	618	105	206	30	0	29	144	71	67	•15	15	8-3	.333	.407	.523	.930	9	.991
2001— Kansas City (A.L.)	1B-DH	147	559	97	170	46	0	29	99	64	64	2	13	10-3	.304	.374	.542	.916	12	.989
2002— Kansas City (A.L.)	1B-DH	126	471	81	160	31	1	24	86	61	46	6	9	9-7	.340	.417	.563	.979	9	.991
— Omaha (PCL)	1B	3	12	2	3	1	0	1	4	1	2	0	1	0-0	.250	.286	.583	.869	0	1.000
2003— Omaha (PCL)	DH	2	8	3	2	1	0	1	1	1	1	0	0	0-0	.250	.333	.750	1.083	0	.000
— Kansas City (A.L.)	DH-1B	108	392	62	115	18	1	16	83	64	56	2	13	3-2	.293	.391	.467	.858	4	.990
Major League totals (9 years)		920	3306	532	1014	205	4	139	604	373	373	47	93	42-23	.307	.381	.497	.878	60	.989

SWITZER, JON — P

PERSONAL: Born August 13, 1979, in Houston, Texas. ... 6-3/191. ... Throws left, bats left. ... Full name: Jon Michael Switzer. ... High school: Clear Lake (Texas). ... College: Arizona State.

TRANSACTIONS/CAREER NOTES: Selected by Pittsburgh Pirates organization in 26th round of free-agent draft (June 2, 1998); did not sign. ... Selected by Tampa Bay Devil Rays organization in second round of free-agent draft (June 5, 2001).

CAREER HITTING: 0-for-0 (.000), 0 R, 0 2B, 0 3B, 0 HR, 0 RBI.

Year League	W	L	Pct.	ERA	WHIP	G	GS	CG	ShO	Hld.	Sv.-Opp.	IP	H	R	ER	HR	BB-IBB	SO	Avg.
2001— Hudson Valley (NYP)	2	0	1.000	0.63	0.77	5	0	0	0	...	0-...	14.1	9	3	1	0	2-0	20	.173
2002— Bakersfield (Calif.)	7	5	.583	4.27	1.30	20	20	0	0	...	0-...	103.1	108	55	49	8	26-0	129	.269
2003— Orlando (Sou.)	8	8	.500	3.43	1.18	22	22	2	0	...	0-...	126.0	117	63	48	10	32-1	100	.246
— Durham (Int'l)	1	0	1.000	1.80	1.20	1	1	0	0	...	0-...	5.0	6	1	1	1	0-0	3	.316
— Tampa Bay (A.L.)	0	0	...	7.45	1.66	5	0	0	0	...	0-0	9.2	13	8	8	2	3-0	7	.342
Major League totals (1 year)	0	0	...	7.45	1.66	5	0	0	0	...	0-0	9.2	13	8	8	2	3-0	7	.342

TAGUCHI, SO — OF

PERSONAL: Born July 2, 1969, in Hyogo Prefecture, Japan. ... 5-10/163. ... Bats right, throws right. ... Name pronounced: tah-gu-chee. ... College: Kansai Gakuin (Japan).

TRANSACTIONS/CAREER NOTES: Played with Orix Blue Wave of Japan Pacific League (1992-2001). ... Signed as non-drafted free agent by St. Louis Cardinals (January 9, 2002).

2003 GAMES PLAYED BY POSITION (MLB): OF—38, 2B—1.

T

Year Team (League)	Pos.	G	AB	R	H	2B	3B	HR	RBI	BB	SO	HBP	GDP	SB-CS	Avg.	OBP	SLG	OPS	E	Pct.
1992—Orix (Jap. Pacific)	OF	47	123	...	33	...	...	1	7	...	...	...	...	5-...	.268	...	...	...	...	...
1993—Orix (Jap. Pacific)	OF	31	83	...	23	...	...	0	5	...	...	...	...	3-...	.277	...	...	...	...	...
1994—Orix (Jap. Pacific)	OF	108	329	...	101	...	...	6	43	...	...	...	...	10-...	.307	...	...	...	...	...
1995—Orix (Jap. Pacific)	OF	130	495	...	122	...	...	9	61	...	...	...	...	14-...	.246	...	...	...	...	...
1996—Orix (Jap. Pacific)	OF	128	509	...	142	...	...	7	44	...	...	...	...	10-...	.279	...	...	...	...	...
1997—Orix (Jap. Pacific)	OF	135	572	...	168	...	...	10	56	...	...	...	...	7-...	.294	...	...	...	...	...
1998—Orix (Jap. Pacific)	OF	132	497	...	135	...	...	9	41	...	...	...	...	8-...	.272	...	...	...	...	...
1999—Orix (Jap. Pacific)	OF	133	524	...	141	...	...	9	56	...	...	...	...	11-...	.269	...	...	...	...	...
2000—Orix (Jap. Pacific)	OF	129	509	...	142	...	...	8	49	...	...	...	...	9-...	.279	...	...	...	...	...
2001—Orix (Jap. Pacific)	OF	134	453	70	127	21	6	8	42	43	88	...	...	6-...	.280	...	.406	...	...	...
2002—Memphis (PCL)	OF	91	304	37	75	17	0	5	36	13	44	5	5	6-3	.247	.286	.352	.638	2	.990
—St. Louis (N.L.)	OF	19	15	4	6	0	0	0	2	2	1	0	0	1-0	.400	.471	.400	.871	1	.929
—New Haven (East.)	OF	26	107	21	33	10	0	1	15	9	15	3	1	3-1	.308	.375	.430	.805	2	.970
2003—Memphis (PCL)	OF-DH	90	258	31	66	8	2	2	24	22	36	2	5	14-5	.256	.318	.326	.644	1	.994
—St. Louis (N.L.)	OF-2B	43	54	9	14	3	1	3	13	4	11	0	2	0-0	.259	.310	.519	.829	0	1.000
Major League totals (2 years)		62	69	13	20	3	1	3	15	6	12	0	2	1-0	.290	.347	.493	.839	1	.978

TALLET, BRIAN — P

PERSONAL: Born September 21, 1977, in Midwest City, Okla. ... 6-7/208. ... Throws left, bats left. ... Full name: Brian Curtis Tallet. ... Name pronounced: tal-ETT. ... College: Louisiana State.

TRANSACTIONS/CAREER NOTES: Selected by Cleveland Indians organization in second round of free-agent draft (June 5, 2000).

CAREER HITTING: 0-for-2 (.000), 0 R, 0 2B, 0 3B, 0 HR, 0 RBI.

Year League	W	L	Pct.	ERA	WHIP	G	GS	CG	ShO	Hld.	Sv.-Opp.	IP	H	R	ER	HR	BB-IBB	SO	Avg.
2000—Mahoning Valley (NY-P)	0	0	...	1.15	0.83	6	6	0	0	...	0-...	15.2	10	2	2	0	3-0	20	.172
2001—Kinston (Caro.)	9	7	.563	3.04	1.08	27	27	2	0	...	0-...	160.0	134	62	54	12	38-0	164	.224
2002—Akron (East.)	10	1	.909	3.08	1.22	18	16	1	0	...	0-...	102.1	93	41	35	9	32-0	73	.243
—Buffalo (Int'l)	2	3	.400	3.07	1.43	8	7	0	0	...	0-...	44.0	47	17	15	1	16-0	25	.281
—Cleveland (A.L.)	1	0	1.000	1.50	1.08	2	2	0	0	0	0-0	12.0	9	3	2	0	4-0	5	.214
2003—Cleveland (A.L.)	0	2	.000	4.74	1.63	5	3	0	0	0	0-0	19.0	23	14	10	2	8-0	9	.303
—Buffalo (Int'l)	4	4	.500	5.14	1.46	15	15	0	0	...	0-...	84.0	89	50	48	10	34-1	67	.270
Major League totals (2 years)	1	2	.333	3.48	1.42	7	5	0	0	0	0-0	31.0	32	17	12	2	12-0	14	.271

TAM, JEFF — P

PERSONAL: Born August 19, 1970, in Fullerton, Calif. ... 6-1/219. ... Throws right, bats right. ... Full name: Jeffrey Eugene Tam. ... High school: Eau Gaille (Melbourne, Fla.). ... College: Florida State.

TRANSACTIONS/CAREER NOTES: Signed as a non-drafted free agent by New York Mets organization (June 27, 1993). ... On New York disabled list (March 21-May 16, 1999); included rehabilitation assignment to St. Lucie (May 2-16). ... Claimed on waivers by Cleveland Indians (June 18, 1999). ... On Buffalo disabled list (July 23-August 1, 1999). ... Claimed on waivers by Mets (August 11, 1999). ... Granted free agency (October 15, 1999). ... Signed by Oakland Athletics organization (November 23, 1999). ... Released by A's (October 15, 2002). ... Signed by Toronto Blue Jays organization (November 1, 2002). ... Sent outright to Syracuse by Toronto (July 10, 2003). ... Released by Toronto (September 7, 2003).

CAREER HITTING: 1-for-2 (.500), 0 R, 1 2B, 0 3B, 0 HR, 1 RBI.

Year League	W	L	Pct.	ERA	WHIP	G	GS	CG	ShO	Hld.	Sv.-Opp.	IP	H	R	ER	HR	BB-IBB	SO	Avg.
1993—Pittsfield (NYP)	3	3	.500	3.35	1.41	21	1	0	0	...	0-...	40.1	50	21	15	0	7-0	31	.292
1994—Capital City (S. Atl.)	1	1	.500	1.29	1.04	26	0	0	0	...	18-...	28.0	23	14	4	0	6-0	22	.217
—St. Lucie (Fla. St.)	0	0	...	0.00	0.71	24	0	0	0	...	16-...	26.2	13	0	0	0	6-1	15	.144
—Binghamton (Eastern)	0	0	...	8.10	2.10	4	0	0	0	...	0-...	6.2	9	6	6	0	5-0	7	.321
1995—Binghamton (Eastern)	0	2	.000	4.50	1.33	14	0	0	0	...	3-...	18.0	20	11	9	1	4-2	9	.278
—GC Mets (GCL)	0	0	...	3.00	1.00	2	1	0	0	...	0-...	3.0	2	1	1	0	1-0	2	.200
1996—Binghamton (Eastern)	6	2	.750	2.44	1.07	49	0	0	0	...	2-...	62.2	51	19	17	6	16-3	48	.233
1997—Norfolk (Int'l)	7	5	.583	4.67	1.35	40	11	0	0	...	6-...	111.2	137	72	58	9	14-4	67	.305
1998—Norfolk (Int'l)	3	3	.500	1.83	0.75	45	0	0	0	...	11-...	64.0	42	14	13	3	6-0	54	.187
—New York (N.L.)	1	1	.500	6.28	1.19	15	0	0	0	1	0-1	14.1	13	10	10	2	4-1	8	.241
1999—St. Lucie (Fla. St.)	0	0	...	3.38	1.50	2	0	0	0	...	0-...	2.2	4	1	1	0	0-0	3	.308
—Norfolk (Int'l)	0	1	.000	3.10	1.33	16	0	0	0	...	3-...	20.1	24	7	7	1	3-1	10	.289
—Buffalo (Int'l)	2	2	.500	2.08	1.19	16	0	0	0	...	0-...	26.0	23	9	6	2	8-1	13	.237
—Cleveland (A.L.)	0	0	...	81.00	9.00	1	0	0	0	0	0-0	.1	2	3	3	0	1-1	0	.500
—New York (N.L.)	0	0	...	3.18	0.79	9	0	0	0	0	0-0	11.1	6	4	4	3	3-0	8	.150
2000—Oakland (A.L.)	3	3	.500	2.63	1.27	72	0	0	0	19	3-6	85.2	86	30	25	3	23-8	46	.268
2001—Oakland (A.L.)	2	4	.333	3.01	1.30	70	0	0	0	25	3-6	74.2	68	27	25	3	29-9	44	.250
2002—Oakland (A.L.)	1	2	.333	5.13	1.71	40	0	0	0	3	0-4	40.1	56	26	23	2	13-5	14	.333
—Sacramento (PCL)	1	3	.250	5.59	1.24	20	0	0	0	...	2-...	29.0	31	20	18	2	5-0	26	.277
2003—Toronto (A.L.)	0	4	.000	5.64	1.86	44	0	0	0	6	1-2	44.2	58	30	28	5	25-7	26	.314
—Syracuse (Int'l)	1	0	1.000	1.53	1.08	17	0	0	0	...	4-...	17.2	16	3	3	1	3-0	11	.232
American League totals (5 years)	6	13	.316	3.81	1.47	227	0	0	0	53	7-18	245.2	270	116	104	13	91-30	130	.285
National League totals (2 years)	1	1	.500	4.91	1.01	24	0	0	0	1	0-1	25.2	19	14	14	5	7-1	16	.202
Major League totals (6 years)	7	14	.333	3.91	1.43	251	0	0	0	54	7-19	271.1	289	130	118	18	98-31	146	.277

TANKERSLEY, DENNIS — P

PERSONAL: Born February 24, 1979, in Troy, Mo. ... 6-2/185. ... Throws right, bats right. ... Full name: Dennis Lee Tankersley. ... Name pronounced: TANK-ers-lee. ... High school: St. Charles (Mo.). ... Junior college: Meramec College (Mo.).

TRANSACTIONS/CAREER NOTES: Selected by Boston Red Sox organization in 38th round of free-agent draft (June 2, 1998). ... Traded by Red Sox with IF Cesar Saba to San Diego Padres for 3B Ed Sprague (June 30, 2000). ... Called up by San Diego from Portland (September 5, 2003).

CAREER HITTING: 4-for-13 (.308), 2 R, 1 2B, 0 3B, 1 HR, 1 RBI.

Year League	W	L	Pct.	ERA	WHIP	G	GS	CG	ShO	Hld.	Sv.-Opp.	IP	H	R	ER	HR	BB-IBB	SO	Avg.
1999— GC Red Sox (GCL)	1	0	1.000	0.76	0.64	11	6	0	0	...	1-...	35.2	14	7	3	2	9-1	57	.116
2000— Augusta (S. Atl.)	5	3	.625	4.06	1.39	15	15	1	1	...	0-...	75.1	73	41	34	4	32-0	74	.252
— Fort Wayne (Midw.)	5	2	.714	2.85	1.10	12	12	0	0	...	0-...	66.1	48	25	21	5	25-0	87	.205
2001— Lake Elsinore (Calif.)	5	1	.833	0.52	0.78	9	8	0	0	...	0-...	52.1	29	5	3	1	12-0	68	.158
— Mobile (Sou.)	4	1	.800	2.07	0.98	13	13	0	0	...	0-...	69.2	44	23	16	6	24-1	89	.174
— Portland (PCL)	1	2	.333	6.91	1.67	3	3	0	0	...	0-...	14.1	16	13	11	2	8-0	16	.286
2002— Mobile (Sou.)	3	3	.500	3.02	1.34	10	10	0	0	...	0-...	50.2	47	20	17	1	21-0	56	.245
— San Diego (N.L.)	1	4	.200	8.06	1.93	17	9	0	0	0	0-0	51.1	59	46	46	10	40-3	39	.304
— Portland (PCL)	3	4	.429	3.88	1.43	9	9	0	0	0	0-0	51.0	43	29	22	6	30-0	51	.229
2003— San Diego (N.L.)	0	1	.000	...	...	1	1	0	0	0	0-0	.0	3	7	7	0	4-0	0	1.000
— Portland (PCL)	8	11	.421	4.65	1.43	27	27	0	0	0	0-...	151.0	149	82	78	15	67-0	148	.257
Major League totals (2 years)	1	5	.167	9.29	2.06	18	10	0	0	0	0-0	51.1	62	53	53	10	44-3	39	.315

TATIS, FERNANDO   3B

PERSONAL: Born January 1, 1975, in San Pedro de Macoris, Dominican Republic. ... 5-10/180. ... Bats right, throws right. ... Full name: Fernando Tatis Jr.. ... Name pronounced: TAH-tece.

TRANSACTIONS/CAREER NOTES: Signed as non-drafted free agent by Texas Rangers organization (August 25, 1992). ... Traded by Rangers with P Darren Oliver and a player to be named later to St. Louis Cardinals for P Todd Stottlemyre and SS Royce Clayton (July 31, 1998); Cardinals acquired OF Mark Little to complete deal (August 9, 1998). ... On St. Louis disabled list (April 30-June 30, 2000); included rehabilitation assignment to Memphis (June 26-30). ... Traded by Cardinals with P Britt Reames to Montreal Expos for P Dustin Hermanson and P Steve Kline (December 14, 2000). ... On disabled list (May 11-26 and June 3, 2001-remainder of season). ... On suspended list (July 8-9, 2001). ... On Montreal disabled list (March 22-April 28, 2002); included rehabilitation assignment to Brevard County (April 22-29). ... On suspended list (August 31-September 3, 2002). ... Placed on 15-day disabled list (June 16, 2003). ... Transferred to 60-day disabled list (August 30, 2003).

2003 GAMES PLAYED BY POSITION (MLB): 3B—49.

Year Team (League)	Pos.	G	AB	R	H	2B	3B	HR	RBI	BB	SO	HBP	GDP	SB-CS	Avg.	OBP	SLG	OPS	E	Pct.
1993— Dom. Rangers (DSL)	IF	59	198	22	54	5	1	4	34	27	12	...		7-...	.273	...	.369	...	11	.940
1994— GC Rangers (GCL)	2B-3B	•60	212	34	70	10	2	6	32	25	33	3	4	21-4	.330	.405	.481	.886	17	.927
1995— Char., S.C. (SAL)	3B	131	499	74	•151	*43	4	15	84	45	95	7	5	22-19	.303	.366	.495	.861	37	.900
1996— Charlotte (Fla. St.)	3B	85	325	46	93	25	0	12	53	30	48	6	9	9-3	.286	.353	.474	.827	24	.893
— Okla. City (A.A.)	3B	2	4	0	2	1	0	0	0	0	1	0	0	0-0	.500	.500	.750	1.250	0	1.000
1997— Tulsa (Texas)	3B-DH	102	382	73	120	26	1	24	61	46	72	3	15	17-8	.314	.390	.576	.966	21	.921
— Texas (A.L.)	3B	60	223	29	57	9	0	8	29	14	42	0	6	3-0	.256	.297	.404	.701	7	.951
1998— Texas (A.L.)	3B	95	330	41	89	17	2	3	32	12	66	4	10	6-2	.270	.303	.361	.664	15	.945
— St. Louis (N.L.)	3B-SS	55	202	28	58	16	2	8	26	24	57	2	6	7-3	.287	.367	.505	.872	12	.930
1999— St. Louis (N.L.)	3B	149	537	104	160	31	2	34	107	82	128	16	11	21-9	.298	.404	.553	.957	16	.958
2000— St. Louis (N.L.) 3B-DH-1B		96	324	59	82	21	1	18	64	57	94	10	13	2-3	.253	.379	.491	.870	8	.955
— Memphis (PCL)	3B	3	9	0	0	0	0	0	0	1	3	0	0	0-0	.000	.100	.000	.100	0	1.000
2001— Montreal (N.L.)	3B	41	145	20	37	9	0	2	11	16	43	4	5	0-0	.255	.339	.359	.698	9	.889
2002— Brevard County (FSL)	3B	6	17	2	4	1	0	0	2	3	4	2	1	0-0	.235	.391	.294	.685	1	.929
— Montreal (N.L.)	3B-DH	114	381	43	87	18	1	15	55	35	90	8	15	2-2	.228	.303	.399	.702	13	.948
2003— Montreal (N.L.)	3B	53	175	15	34	6	0	2	15	18	40	3	7	2-1	.194	.281	.263	.543	4	.968
American League totals (2 years)		155	553	70	146	26	2	11	61	26	108	4	16	9-2	.264	.301	.378	.679	22	.947
National League totals (6 years)		508	1764	269	458	101	6	79	278	232	452	43	57	34-18	.260	.357	.458	.815	62	.948
Major League totals (7 years)		663	2317	339	604	127	8	90	339	258	560	47	73	43-20	.261	.344	.439	.783	84	.948

TAVAREZ, JULIAN   P

PERSONAL: Born May 22, 1973, in Santiago, Dominican Republic. ... 6-2/195. ... Throws right, bats left. ... Name pronounced: JOOL-ee-en tah-VAR-rez. ... High school: Santiago (Dominican Republic) Public School.

TRANSACTIONS/CAREER NOTES: Signed as non-drafted free agent by Cleveland Indians organization (March 16, 1990). ... On Cleveland suspended list (June 18-21, 1996). ... Traded by Indians with IF Jeff Kent, IF Jose Vizcaino and a player to be named later to San Francisco Giants for 3B Matt Williams and a player to be named later (November 13, 1996); Indians traded P Joe Roa to Giants for OF Trenidad Hubbard to complete deal (December 16, 1996). ... On San Francisco disabled list (July 13-August 7, 1998); included rehabilitation assignment to Fresno (August 5-7). ... On suspended list (September 14-16, 1998). ... On San Francisco disabled list (May 1-June 1, 1999); included rehabilitation assignment to Fresno (May 25-June 1). ... Claimed on waivers by Colorado Rockies (November 21, 1999). ... Granted free agency (October 31, 2000). ... Signed by Chicago Cubs (November 16, 2000). ... On suspended list (April 29-May 5, 2001). ... Traded by Cubs with P Jose Cueto, P Dontrelle Willis and C Ryan Jorgensen to Florida Marlins for P Antonio Alfonseca and P Matt Clement (March 27, 2002). ... On disabled list (April 17-May 12, 2002). ... Granted free agency (October 28, 2002). ... Signed by Pittsburgh Pirates organization (January 28, 2003). ... Suspended by Major League Baseball (June 22, 2003). ... Reinstated (June 25, 2003).

CAREER HITTING: 15-for-135 (.111), 8 R, 0 2B, 0 3B, 0 HR, 9 RBI.

Year League	W	L	Pct.	ERA	WHIP	G	GS	CG	ShO	Hld.	Sv.-Opp.	IP	H	R	ER	HR	BB-IBB	SO	Avg.
1990— DSL Indians (DSL)	5	5	.500	3.29	1.62	14	12	3	0	...	0-...	82.0	85	53	30	...	48-...	33	...
1991— DSL Indians (DSL)	8	2	.800	2.67	1.01	19	18	1	0	...	0-...	121.1	95	41	36	...	28-...	75	...
1992— Burlington (Appal.)	6	3	.667	2.68	1.12	14	•14	2	•2	...	0-...	87.1	86	41	26	3	12-0	69	.250
1993— Kinston (Caro.)	11	5	.688	2.42	1.09	18	18	2	0	...	0-...	119.0	102	48	32	6	28-0	107	.228
— Cant./Akr. (Eastern)	2	1	.667	0.95	0.79	3	2	1	1	...	0-...	19.0	14	2	2	0	1-0	11	.212
— Cleveland (A.L.)	2	2	.500	6.57	1.78	8	7	0	0	0	0-0	37.0	53	29	27	7	13-2	19	.340
1994— Charlotte (Int'l)	•15	6	.714	3.48	1.19	26	26	2	2	...	0-...	176.0	167	79	68	15	43-0	102	.247
— Cleveland (A.L.)	0	1	.000	21.60	4.20	1	1	0	0	0	0-0	1.2	6	8	4	1	1-1	0	.500
1995— Cleveland (A.L.)	10	2	.833	2.44	1.14	57	0	0	0	19	0-4	85.0	76	36	23	7	21-0	68	.235
1996— Cleveland (A.L.)	4	7	.364	5.36	1.52	51	4	0	0	13	0-0	80.2	101	49	48	9	22-5	46	.315
— Buffalo (A.A.)	1	0	1.000	1.29	0.93	2	2	0	0	...	0-...	14.0	10	2	2	0	3-0	10	.200
1997— San Francisco (N.L.)	6	4	.600	3.87	1.42	*89	0	0	0	26	0-3	88.1	91	43	38	6	34-5	38	.277
1998— San Francisco (N.L.)	5	3	.625	3.80	1.55	60	0	0	0	10	1-6	85.1	96	41	36	5	36-11	52	.298
— Fresno (PCL)	0	0	...	19.29	2.57	1	0	0	0	...	0-...	2.1	6	5	5	0	0-0	1	.500
1999— San Francisco (N.L.)	2	0	1.000	5.93	1.65	47	0	0	0	5	0-2	54.2	65	38	36	7	25-3	33	.295
— Fresno (PCL)	0	0	...	2.25	0.75	4	1	0	0	...	0-...	8.0	3	2	2	1	3-0	9	.115
— San Jose (Calif.)	0	0	...	0.00	0.50	1	1	0	0	...	0-...	4.0	1	0	0	0	1-0	9	.091
2000— Colorado (N.L.)	11	5	.688	4.43	1.48	51	12	1	0	6	1-1	120.0	124	68	59	11	53-9	62	.268
2001— Chicago (N.L.)	10	9	.526	4.52	1.49	34	28	0	0	2	0-0	161.1	172	98	81	13	69-4	107	.277
2002— Florida (N.L.)	10	12	.455	5.39	1.70	29	27	0	0	0	0-1	153.2	188	100	92	9	74-7	67	.308
2003— Pittsburgh (N.L.)	3	3	.500	3.66	1.22	64	0	0	0	0	11-14	83.2	75	37	34	1	27-8	39	.244
American League totals (4 years)	16	12	.571	4.49	1.43	117	12	0	0	32	0-4	204.1	236	122	102	24	57-8	133	.290
National League totals (7 years)	47	36	.566	4.53	1.51	374	67	1	0	58	13-27	747.0	811	425	376	52	318-47	398	.282
Major League totals (11 years)	63	48	.568	4.52	1.49	491	79	1	0	90	13-31	951.1	1047	547	478	76	375-55	531	.284

T

TAYLOR, AARON   P

PERSONAL: Born August 20, 1977, in Valdosta, Ga. ... 6-8/245. ... Throws right, bats right. ... Full name: Aaron Wade Taylor. ... High school: Lowndes (Valdosta, Ga.).

TRANSACTIONS/CAREER NOTES: Selected by Atlanta Braves organization in 11th round of free-agent draft (June 4, 1996). ... Selected by Seattle Mariners organization from Braves organization in Rule 5 minor league draft (December 13, 1999). ... Recalled by Seattle from Tacoma (June 30, 2003). ... Optioned to Tacoma by Seattle (August 2, 2003). ... Recalled by Seattle from Tacoma (September 26, 2003).

CAREER HITTING: 0-for-0 (.000), 0 R, 0 2B, 0 3B, 0 HR, 0 RBI.

Year League	W	L	Pct.	ERA	WHIP	G	GS	CG	ShO	Hld.	Sv.-Opp.	IP	H	R	ER	HR	BB-IBB	SO	Avg.
1996— GC Braves (GCL)	0	*9	.000	7.74	1.83	13	9	0	0	...	0-...	52.1	68	*54	45	0	28-0	33	.315
1997— Danville (Appal.)	1	•8	.111	5.53	1.73	15	7	0	0	...	0-...	55.1	65	49	34	4	31-0	38	.288
1998— Danville (Appal.)	3	6	.333	6.25	1.71	14	•14	1	0	...	0-...	72.0	87	60	*50	2	36-0	55	.300
1999— Macon (S. Atl.)	6	7	.462	4.88	1.42	27	8	0	0	...	1-...	79.1	86	56	43	9	27-2	78	.270
2000— Everett (Northwest)	1	4	.200	7.43	1.79	15	14	0	0	...	0-...	63.0	76	54	52	1	37-0	57	.304
2001— Wisconsin (Midw.)	3	1	.750	2.45	1.02	28	0	0	0	...	9-...	29.1	19	9	8	1	11-2	50	.184
2002— San Antonio (Texas)	4	3	.571	2.34	1.10	61	0	0	0	0	24-...	77.0	51	28	20	5	34-0	93	.184
— Seattle (A.L.)	0	0	...	9.00	1.60	5	0	0	0	0	0-1	5.0	8	5	5	2	0-0	6	.348
2003— Tacoma (PCL)	1	3	.250	2.45	1.07	33	0	0	0	0	16-...	40.1	30	11	11	3	13-1	34	.208
— Seattle (A.L.)	0	0	...	8.53	1.82	10	0	0	0	0	0-0	12.2	17	12	12	0	6-0	9	.315
Major League totals (2 years)	0	0	...	8.66	1.75	15	0	0	0	0	0-1	17.2	25	17	17	2	6-0	15	.325

TAYLOR, REGGIE   OF

PERSONAL: Born January 12, 1977, in Newberry, S.C. ... 6-1/178. ... Bats left, throws right. ... Full name: Reginald Tremain Taylor. ... High school: Newberry (S.C.).

TRANSACTIONS/CAREER NOTES: Selected by Philadelphia Phillies organization in first round (14th pick overall) of free-agent draft (June 1, 1995). ... On disabled list (July 23, 1998-remainder of season). ... On Scranton/Wilkes-Barre disabled list (April 6-May 26, 2000; and April 6-May 1, 2001). ... Traded by Phillies to Cincinnati Reds for a player to be named (March 28, 2002); Phillies acquired P Hector Mercado to complete deal (March 30, 2002). ... Placed on 60-day disabled list (August 26, 2003).

2003 GAMES PLAYED BY POSITION (MLB): OF—60.

Year Team (League)	Pos.	G	AB	R	H	2B	3B	HR	RBI	BB	SO	HBP	GDP	SB-CS	Avg.	OBP	SLG	OPS	E	Pct.
1995— Martinsville (App.)	OF	64	239	36	53	4	6	2	32	23	58	6	5	18-7	.222	.301	.314	.615	8	.940
1996— Piedmont (S. Atl.)	OF	128	499	68	131	20	6	0	31	29	136	3	10	36-17	.263	.305	.327	.632	•12	.961
1997— Clearwater (FSL)	OF	134	545	73	133	18	6	12	47	30	130	4	3	40-23	.244	.285	.365	.651	11	.969
1998— Reading (East.)	OF	79	337	49	92	14	6	5	22	12	73	2	2	22-10	.273	.300	.395	.695	10	.944
1999— Reading (East.)	OF	127	526	75	140	17	10	15	61	18	79	3	11	38-20	.266	.293	.422	.715	9	.971
2000— Scran./W.B. (I.L.)	OF	98	422	60	116	10	8	15	43	21	87	2	4	23-13	.275	.310	.443	.753	5	.980
— Philadelphia (N.L.)	OF	9	11	1	1	0	0	0	0	0	8	0	0	1-0	.091	.091	.091	.182	1	.750
2001— Scran./W.B. (I.L.)	OF	111	464	56	122	20	9	7	50	24	94	3	10	31-15	.263	.301	.390	.691	5	.980
— Philadelphia (N.L.)	OF	5	7	1	0	0	0	0	0	1	1	0	0	0-0	.000	.125	.000	.125	0	1.000
2002— Cincinnati (N.L.)	OF	135	287	41	73	15	4	9	38	14	79	2	6	11-8	.254	.291	.429	.719	5	.973
2003— Cincinnati (N.L.)	OF	100	180	17	39	5	2	5	19	11	68	1	4	7-0	.217	.266	.350	.616	1	.990
Major League totals (4 years)		249	485	60	113	20	6	14	57	26	156	3	10	19-8	.233	.275	.386	.660	7	.976

TEIXEIRA, MARK   1B/3B

PERSONAL: Born April 11, 1980, in Severna Park, Md. ... 6-2/215. ... Bats both, throws right. ... Full name: Mark Charles Teixeira. ... Name pronounced: tuh-SHARE-uh. ... High school: Mount St. Joseph (Baltimore). ... College: Georgia Tech.

TRANSACTIONS/CAREER NOTES: Selected by Boston Red Sox organization in ninth round of free-agent draft (June 2, 1998); did not sign. ... Selected by Texas Rangers organization in first round (fifth pick overall) of free-agent draft (June 5, 2001).

2003 GAMES PLAYED BY POSITION (MLB): 1B—116, OF—25, 3B—16, DH—5.

Year Team (League)	Pos.	G	AB	R	H	2B	3B	HR	RBI	BB	SO	HBP	GDP	SB-CS	Avg.	OBP	SLG	OPS	E	Pct.
2001—										Did not play.										
2002— Charlotte (Int'l)	3B	38	150	32	48	10	2	9	41	21	24	3	4	2-0	.320	.411	.593	1.005	9	.902
— Tulsa (Texas)	3B	48	171	31	54	11	3	10	28	25	36	4	2	3-2	.316	.415	.591	1.006	12	.925
2003— Texas (A.L.)	1-0-3-D	146	529	66	137	29	5	26	84	44	120	14	14	1-2	.259	.331	.480	.811	12	.989
Major League totals (1 year)		146	529	66	137	29	5	26	84	44	120	14	14	1-2	.259	.331	.480	.811	12	.989

TEJADA, MIGUEL   SS

PERSONAL: Born May 25, 1976, in Bani, Dominican Republic. ... 5-9/200. ... Bats right, throws right. ... Full name: Miguel Odalis Tejada. ... Name pronounced: mee-GHEL tay-HA-duh.

TRANSACTIONS/CAREER NOTES: Signed as non-drafted free agent by Oakland Athletics organization (July 17, 1993). ... On suspended list (July 4-7, 1996). ... On disabled list (July 20-August 10, 1996). ... On Oakland disabled list (March 22-May 20, 1998); included rehabilitation assignments to Edmonton (May 11-12) and Huntsville (May 12-20).

2003 GAMES PLAYED BY POSITION (MLB): SS—162.

Year Team (League)	Pos.	G	AB	R	H	2B	3B	HR	RBI	BB	SO	HBP	GDP	SB-CS	Avg.	OBP	SLG	OPS	E	Pct.
1994— Dom. Athletics (DSL)	2B	74	218	51	64	9	1	18	62	37	36	...		13-...	.294		.592		16	.927
1995— S. Oregon (N'west)	SS	74	269	45	66	15	5	8	44	41	54	1	3	19-2	.245	.346	.428	.774	26	.930
1996— Modesto (Calif.)	SS-DH-3B	114	458	97	128	12	5	20	72	51	93	4	9	27-16	.279	.352	.459	.810	‡45	.925
1997— Huntsville (Sou.)	SS	128	502	85	138	20	3	22	97	50	99	7	9	15-11	.275	.344	.458	.802	*36	.948
— Oakland (A.L.)	SS	26	99	10	20	3	2	2	10	2	22	3	3	2-0	.202	.240	.333	.574	4	.969
1998— Edmonton (PCL)	SS	1	3	0	0	0	0	0	0	1	1	0	1	0-0	.000	.250	.000	.250	0	1.000
— Huntsville (Sou.)	SS-DH	15	52	9	17	6	0	2	7	4	8	0	2	1-0	.327	.362	.538	.920	5	.922
— Oakland (A.L.)	SS	105	365	53	85	20	1	11	45	28	86	7	8	5-6	.233	.298	.384	.681	26	.951
1999— Oakland (A.L.)	SS	159	593	93	149	33	4	21	84	57	94	10	11	8-7	.251	.325	.427	.751	21	.973
2000— Oakland (A.L.)	SS	160	607	105	167	32	1	30	115	66	102	4	15	6-0	.275	.349	.479	.828	21	.972
2001— Oakland (A.L.)	SS	•162	622	107	166	31	3	31	113	43	89	13	14	11-5	.267	.326	.476	.801	20	.973
2002— Oakland (A.L.)	SS	*162	662	108	204	30	0	34	131	38	84	11	•21	7-2	.308	.354	.508	.861	19	.975
2003— Oakland (A.L.)	SS	162	636	98	177	42	0	27	106	53	65	6	12	10-0	.278	.336	.472	.807	21	.972
Major League totals (7 years)		936	3584	574	968	191	11	156	604	287	542	54	84	49-20	.270	.331	.460	.791	132	.970

TEJERA, MICHAEL　　　　　　　P

PERSONAL: Born October 18, 1976, in Havana, Cuba. ... 5-9/190. ... Throws left, bats left. ... Name pronounced: te-HAIR-ah. ... High school: Southwest (Miami).
TRANSACTIONS/CAREER NOTES: Selected by Florida Marlins organization in sixth round of free-agent draft (June 1, 1995). ... On disabled list (April 2, 2000-entire season).
CAREER HITTING: 8-for-52 (.154), 5 R, 0 2B, 0 3B, 1 HR, 5 RBI.

Year League	W	L	Pct.	ERA	WHIP	G	GS	CG	ShO	Hld.	Sv.-Opp.	IP	H	R	ER	HR	BB-IBB	SO	Avg.
1995— GC Marlins (GCL)	3	1	.750	2.65	1.29	11	3	0	0	...	2-...	34.0	28	13	10	2	16-1	28	.235
1996— GC Marlins (GCL)	1	0	1.000	3.60	1.20	2	0	0	0	...	0-...	5.0	6	2	2	0	0-0	2	.286
1997— Utica (N.Y.-Penn)	3	3	.500	3.76	1.10	12	12	0	0	...	0-...	69.1	65	36	29	8	11-0	67	.248
1998— Kane County (Midwest)	6	1	.857	2.77	1.03	10	10	0	0	...	0-...	55.1	44	20	17	3	13-0	47	.221
— Portland (East.)	9	5	.643	4.11	1.39	18	18	2	2	...	0-...	107.1	113	55	49	15	36-2	97	.268
1999— Portland (East.)	13	4	.765	2.62	1.18	25	25	0	0	...	0-...	154.2	137	55	45	13	45-1	152	.238
— Calgary (PCL)	0	2	.000	12.00	2.56	2	2	0	0	...	0-...	9.0	19	14	12	2	4-0	5	.452
— Florida (N.L.)	0	0	...	11.37	2.37	3	1	0	0	0	0-0	6.1	10	8	8	1	5-0	7	.385
2000— Florida (N.L.)										Did not play.									
2001— Portland (East.)	9	8	.529	3.57	1.30	25	25	0	0	...	0-...	141.0	143	61	56	17	41-0	131	.266
2002— Florida (N.L.)	8	8	.500	4.45	1.46	47	18	0	0	8	1-3	139.2	144	71	69	17	60-3	95	.269
2003— Florida (N.L.)	3	4	.429	4.67	1.46	50	6	0	0	5	2-2	81.0	82	44	42	6	36-3	58	.267
Major League totals (3 years)	**11**	**12**	**.478**	**4.72**	**1.48**	**100**	**25**	**0**	**0**	**13**	**3-5**	**227.0**	**236**	**123**	**119**	**24**	**101-6**	**160**	**.272**

TELEMACO, AMAURY　　　　　　P

PERSONAL: Born January 19, 1974, in Higuey, Dominican Republic. ... 6-3/222. ... Throws right, bats right. ... Full name: Amaury Regalado Telemaco. ... Name pronounced: ah-MARR-ee tel-ah-MAH-ko. ... High school: Cristo Rey (La Romana, Dominican Republic).
TRANSACTIONS/CAREER NOTES: Signed as non-drafted free agent by Chicago Cubs organization (May 23, 1991). ... On temporarily inactive list (August 17, 1993-remainder of season). ... On Orlando disabled list (August 23-September 8, 1994). ... On Chicago disabled list (August 20-September 4, 1996); included rehabilitation assignment to Iowa (September 2-4). ... Claimed on waivers by Arizona Diamondbacks (May 15, 1998). ... On Arizona disabled list (March 26-May 8, 1999); included rehabilitation assignment to Tucson (April 8-May 7). ... Claimed on waivers by Philadelphia Phillies (June 8, 1999). ... On Scranton/Wilkes-Barre disabled list (July 19-August 5, 2000; and August 22, 2001). ... Granted free agency (October 8, 2001). ... On Scranton/Wilkes-Barre disabled list (April 4-May 4 and May 12-July 1, 2002). ... On Reading disabled list (July 3-August 14, 2002). ... Granted free agency (October 15, 2002). ... Signed by Philadelphia Phillies to a minor league contract (November 24, 2002).
CAREER HITTING: 14-for-112 (.125), 6 R, 4 2B, 1 3B, 0 HR, 3 RBI.

Year League	W	L	Pct.	ERA	WHIP	G	GS	CG	ShO	Hld.	Sv.-Opp.	IP	H	R	ER	HR	BB-IBB	SO	Avg.
1991— Puerta Plata (DSL)	3	3	.500	3.55	1.71	15	13	0	0	...	0-...	66.0	81	43	26	...	32-...	43	...
1992— Huntington (Appal.)	3	5	.375	4.01	1.15	12	12	2	0	...	0-...	76.1	71	45	34	6	17-0	* 93	.240
— Peoria (Midw.)	0	1	.000	7.94	2.47	2	1	0	0	...	0-...	5.2	9	5	5	0	5-0	5	.360
1993— Peoria (Midw.)	8	11	.421	3.45	1.27	23	23	3	0	...	0-...	143.2	129	69	55	9	54-0	133	.241
1994— Daytona (Fla. St.)	7	3	.700	3.40	1.11	11	11	2	0	...	0-...	76.2	62	35	29	4	23-0	59	.221
— Orlando (Sou.)	3	5	.375	3.45	1.21	12	12	2	0	...	0-...	62.2	56	29	24	6	20-0	49	.239
1995— Orlando (Sou.)	8	8	.500	3.29	1.04	22	22	3	1	...	0-...	147.2	112	60	54	13	42-3	151	.211
1996— Iowa (Am. Assoc.)	3	1	.750	3.06	1.12	8	8	1	0	...	0-...	50.0	38	19	17	5	18-2	42	.210
— Chicago (N.L.)	5	7	.417	5.46	1.43	25	17	0	0	0	0-0	97.1	108	67	59	20	31-2	64	.281
1997— Iowa (Am. Assoc.)	5	9	.357	4.51	1.40	18	18	3	• 2	...	0-...	113.2	121	70	57	20	38-1	75	.267
— Chicago (N.L.)	0	3	.000	6.16	1.53	10	5	0	0	0	0-0	38.0	47	26	26	4	11-0	29	.303
— Orlando (Sou.)	1	0	1.000	2.25	1.38	1	1	0	0	0	0-0	8.0	9	2	2	0	2-0	6	.281
1998— Chicago (N.L.)	1	1	.500	3.90	1.30	14	0	0	0	1	0-0	27.2	23	12	12	5	13-0	18	.219
— Arizona (N.L.)	6	9	.400	3.94	1.32	27	18	0	0	0	0-0	121.0	127	63	53	13	33-2	60	.271
1999— Tucson (PCL)	0	3	.000	5.09	1.53	13	12	0	0	...	0-...	17.2	21	11	10	1	6-0	17	.304
— Arizona (N.L.)	1	0	1.000	7.50	2.17	5	0	0	0	0	0-0	6.0	7	5	5	2	6-1	2	.333
— Philadelphia (N.L.)	3	0	1.000	5.55	1.38	44	0	0	0	3	0-1	47.0	45	29	29	8	20-3	41	.250
2000— Philadelphia (N.L.)	1	3	.250	6.66	1.60	13	2	0	0	0	0-1	24.1	25	22	18	6	14-0	22	.275
— Scran./W.B. (I.L.)	8	3	.727	3.87	1.27	21	21	0	0	...	0-...	123.1	115	60	53	15	42-0	88	.248
2001— Philadelphia (N.L.)	5	5	.500	5.54	1.40	24	14	1	0	1	0-...	89.1	93	59	55	15	32-3	59	.274
— Scran./W.B. (I.L.)	1	2	.333	4.01	1.50	4	4	0	0	...	0-...	24.2	31	11	11	4	6-0	25	.307
2002— Scran./W.B. (I.L.)	1	0	1.000	1.80	1.00	1	1	0	0	...	0-...	5.0	3	1	1	1	0-0	3	.263
— GC Phillies (GCL)	1	0	1.000	1.64	0.55	2	2	0	0	...	0-...	11.0	4	2	2	0	2-0	5	.105
— Reading (East.)	0	0	...	9.00	1.00	1	1	0	0	...	0-...	1.0	1	1	1	1	0-0	1	.333
— Clearwater (Fla. St.)	0	1	.000	1.50	1.50	3	3	0	0	...	0-...	12.0	15	5	2	0	3-0	10	.300
2003— Scran./W.B. (I.L.)	10	9	.526	3.24	0.95	25	24	3	2	...	0-...	155.1	125	59	56	15	22-1	116	.222
— Philadelphia (N.L.)	1	4	.200	3.97	1.15	8	8	0	0	0	0-0	45.1	41	22	20	5	11-2	29	.238
Major League totals (7 years)	**23**	**32**	**.418**	**5.03**	**1.39**	**170**	**64**	**1**	**0**	**5**	**0-2**	**496.0**	**516**	**305**	**277**	**78**	**171-13**	**324**	**.269**

TERRERO, LUIS　　　　　　　OF

PERSONAL: Born May 18, 1980, in Barahona, Dominican Republic. ... 6-2/206. ... Bats right, throws right. ... Full name: Luis Enrique Terrero. ... Name pronounced: LOU-eese tuh-RARE-oh. ... High school: Barney Morgan (Barahona, Dominican Republic).
TRANSACTIONS/CAREER NOTES: Signed as non-drafted free agent by Arizona Diamondbacks organization (October 15, 1997). ... On South Bend disabled list (May 8-June 15, 2001). ... On El Paso disabled list (May 9-21, 2002). ... Recalled from Tucson by Arizona (July 9, 2003). ... Optioned to Tucson by Arizona (July 21, 2003). ... Recalled by Arizona from Tucson (September 23, 2003).
2003 GAMES PLAYED BY POSITION (MLB): OF—3.

Year Team (League)	Pos.	G	AB	R	H	2B	3B	HR	RBI	BB	SO	HBP	GDP	SB-CS	Avg.	OBP	SLG	OPS	E	Pct.
1999— Missoula (Pio.)	OF	71	272	74	78	13	7	8	40	32	91	5	2	27-10	.287	.365	.474	.839	11	.928
2000— Missoula (Pio.)	OF	68	276	48	72	10	0	8	44	10	75	8	5	23-11	.261	.305	.384	.689	5	.941
— High Desert (Calif.)	OF	19	79	10	15	3	1	0	1	3	16	1	2	5-5	.190	.229	.253	.482	3	.949
2001— South Bend (Mid.)	OF	24	89	4	14	2	0	1	8	0	29	2	2	3-0	.157	.176	.213	.389	0	1.000
— Yakima (N'west)	OF	11	41	7	13	2	1	0	0	2	8	0	0	0-3	.317	.349	.415	.763	0	1.000
— Lancaster (Calif.)	OF	19	71	16	32	9	1	4	11	1	14	1	3	5-0	.451	.466	.775	1.240	1	.971
— El Paso (Texas)	OF	34	147	29	44	13	3	3	8	4	45	3	2	9-2	.299	.331	.490	.821	5	.943
2002— El Paso (Texas)	OF	104	360	49	103	20	6	8	54	23	89	8	9	18-22	.286	.342	.442	.784	7	.973
2003— Arizona (N.L.)	OF	5	4	0	1	0	0	0	0	0	1	1	0	0-0	.250	.400	.250	.650	0	1.000
— Tucson (PCL)	OF-DH	118	467	83	134	20	15	3	46	31	103	11	6	23-19	.287	.345	.413	.758	10	.968
Major League totals (1 year)		**5**	**4**	**0**	**1**	**0**	**0**	**0**	**0**	**0**	**1**	**1**	**0**	**0-0**	**.250**	**.400**	**.250**	**.650**	**0**	**1.000**

THAMES, MARCUS — OF

PERSONAL: Born March 6, 1977, in Louisville, Miss. ... 6-2/200. ... Bats right, throws right. ... Full name: Marcus Markey Thames. ... Name pronounced: timms. ... Junior college: East Central College (Miss.).

TRANSACTIONS/CAREER NOTES: Selected by New York Yankees organization in 30th round of free-agent draft (June 4, 1996). ... On Columbus disabled list (May 2-18, 2002). ... Traded by Yankees to Texas Rangers for OF Ruben Sierra (June 6, 2003).

2003 GAMES PLAYED BY POSITION (MLB): OF—24, DH—4.

Year	Team (League)	Pos.	G	AB	R	H	2B	3B	HR	RBI	BB	SO	HBP	GDP	SB-CS	Avg.	OBP	SLG	OPS	E	Pct.
1997—	GC Yankees (GCL)	OF	57	195	* 51	67	* 17	4	7	36	16	26	3	3	6-4	.344	.394	.579	.974	2	.978
—	Greensboro (S. Atl.)	OF	4	16	2	5	1	0	0	2	0	3	0	0	1-0	.313	.313	.375	.688	0	1.000
1998—	Tampa (Fla. St.)	OF	122	457	62	130	18	3	11	59	24	78	8	5	13-6	.284	.328	.409	.737	9	.970
1999—	Norwich (East.)	OF	51	182	25	41	6	2	4	26	22	40	3	2	0-1	.225	.316	.346	.662	7	.929
—	Tampa (Fla. St.)	OF	69	266	47	65	12	4	11	38	33	58	3	1	3-0	.244	.332	.444	.776	3	.974
2000—	Norwich (East.)	OF	131	474	72	114	30	2	15	79	50	89	4	13	1-5	.241	.313	.407	.721	• 9	.959
2001—	Norwich (East.)	OF	139	520	* 114	167	* 43	4	31	97	73	101	7	6	10-4	.321	.410	.598	1.008	8	.973
2002—	Columbus (Int'l.)	OF	107	386	51	80	21	3	13	45	43	71	7	8	5-4	.207	.297	.378	.675	5	.983
—	New York (A.L.)	OF	7	13	2	3	1	0	1	2	0	4	0	0	0-0	.231	.231	.538	.769	0	1.000
2003—	Columbus (Int'l.)	OF	52	194	26	54	15	2	2	28	17	48	1	4	3-4	.278	.332	.407	.739	3	.975
—	Oklahoma (PCL)	OF-DH	18	66	9	17	4	0	2	7	8	12	0	2	1-0	.258	.338	.409	.747	1	.968
—	Texas (A.L.)	OF-DH	30	73	12	15	2	0	1	4	8	18	2	2	0-1	.205	.298	.274	.572	0	1.000
Major League totals (2 years)			37	86	14	18	3	0	2	6	8	22	2	2	0-1	.209	.289	.314	.603	0	1.000

THOMAS, BRAD — P

PERSONAL: Born October 22, 1977, in Sydney, Australia. ... 6-4/220. ... Throws left, bats left. ... Full name: Bradley Richard Thomas. ... High school: Mitchell (Australia).

TRANSACTIONS/CAREER NOTES: Signed as non-drafted free agent by Los Angeles Dodgers organization (July 2, 1995). ... Released by Dodgers (May 9, 1997). ... Signed by Minnesota Twins organization (May 12, 1997). ... On New Britain disabled list (August 20-September 2, 2001). ... Recalled by Minnesota from New Britain (September 2, 2003).

CAREER HITTING: 0-for-0 (.000), 0 R, 0 2B, 0 3B, 0 HR, 0 RBI.

Year	League	W	L	Pct.	ERA	WHIP	G	GS	CG	ShO	Hld.	Sv.-Opp.	IP	H	R	ER	HR	BB-IBB	SO	Avg.
1996—	Great Falls (Pio.)	3	2	.600	6.31	1.65	11	5	0	0	...	0-...	35.2	48	27	25	2	11-0	28	.320
1997—	Elizabethton (Appal.)	3	4	.429	4.48	1.41	14	13	0	0	...	0-...	70.1	78	43	35	5	21-0	53	.279
1998—	Fort Wayne (Midw.)	11	8	.579	2.95	1.25	27	26	1	0	...	0-...	152.1	146	68	50	9	45-1	126	.248
1999—	Fort Myers (Fla. St.)	8	11	.421	4.78	1.49	27	* 27	1	1	...	0-...	152.2	182	99	81	11	46-0	108	.303
2000—	Fort Myers (Fla. St.)	6	2	.750	1.66	1.20	12	12	0	0	...	0-...	65.0	62	33	12	3	16-0	57	.239
—	New Britain (East.)	6	6	.500	4.06	1.67	14	13	1	1	...	0-...	75.1	80	47	34	3	46-1	66	.277
2001—	New Britain (East.)	10	3	.769	1.96	0.98	19	19	1	0	...	0-...	119.1	91	37	26	4	26-0	97	.206
—	Minnesota (A.L.)	0	2	.000	9.37	2.08	5	5	0	0	0	0-0	16.1	20	17	17	6	14-0	6	.303
2002—	Edmonton (PCL)	6	12	.333	5.74	1.51	28	27	1	0	...	0-...	152.0	175	* 112	97	20	54-0	97	.291
2003—	GC Twins (GCL)	0	0	...	0.00	0.70	2	2	0	0	...	0-...	10.0	6	0	0	0	1-0	12	.167
—	Rochester (Int'l.)	0	3	.000	3.53	1.33	15	11	0	0	...	0-...	58.2	68	23	23	3	10-0	50	.292
—	Minnesota (A.L.)	0	1	.000	7.71	1.93	3	0	0	0	0	0-0	4.2	6	4	4	1	3-1	2	.316
Major League totals (2 years)		0	3	.000	9.00	2.05	8	5	0	0	0	0-0	21.0	26	21	21	7	17-1	8	.306

THOMAS, FRANK — DH/1B

PERSONAL: Born May 27, 1968, in Columbus, Ga. ... 6-5/275. ... Bats right, throws right. ... Full name: Frank Edward Thomas. ... High school: Columbus (Ga.). ... College: Auburn.

TRANSACTIONS/CAREER NOTES: Selected by Chicago White Sox organization in first round (seventh pick overall) of free-agent draft (June 5, 1989). ... On disabled list (July 11-30, 1996; June 7-22, 1997; and May 10, 2001-remainder of season). ... Granted free agency (October 31, 2002). ... Re-signed by White Sox (December 6, 2002).

2003 GAMES PLAYED BY POSITION (MLB): DH—124, 1B—27.

Year	Team (League)	Pos.	G	AB	R	H	2B	3B	HR	RBI	BB	SO	HBP	GDP	SB-CS	Avg.	OBP	SLG	OPS	E	Pct.
1989—	GC Whi. Sox (GCL)	1B	17	52	8	19	5	0	1	11	11	3	1	0	4-0	.365	.470	.519	.989	2	.986
—	Sarasota (Fla. St.)	1B	55	188	27	52	9	1	4	30	31	33	3	6	0-1	.277	.386	.399	.785	7	.985
1990—	Birmingham (Sou.)	1B	109	353	85	114	27	5	18	71	* 112	74	5	13	7-5	.323	* .487	.581	1.068	14	.987
—	Chicago (A.L.)	DH-1B	60	191	39	63	11	3	7	31	44	54	2	5	0-1	.330	.454	.529	.983	5	.989
1991—	Chicago (A.L.)	DH-1B	158	559	104	178	31	2	32	109	* 138	112	1	20	1-2	.318	* .453	.553	1.006	2	.996
1992—	Chicago (A.L.)	1B-DH	160	573	108	185	• 46	2	24	115	• 122	88	5	19	6-3	.323	* .439	.536	.975	13	.992
1993—	Chicago (A.L.)	1B-DH	153	549	106	174	36	0	41	128	112	54	2	10	4-2	.317	.426	.607	1.033	15	.989
1994—	Chicago (A.L.)	1B-DH	113	399	* 106	141	34	1	38	101	* 109	61	2	15	2-3	.353	* .487	* .729	1.217	7	.991
1995—	Chicago (A.L.)	1B-DH	• 145	493	102	152	27	0	40	111	* 136	74	6	14	3-2	.308	.454	.606	1.061	7	.991
1996—	Chicago (A.L.)	1B	141	527	110	184	26	0	40	134	109	70	5	25	1-1	.349	.459	.626	1.085	9	.992
1997—	Chicago (A.L.)	DH-1B	146	530	110	184	35	0	35	125	109	69	3	15	1-1	* .347	* .456	.611	1.067	11	.986
1998—	Chicago (A.L.)	DH-1B	160	585	109	155	35	2	29	109	110	93	6	14	7-0	.265	.381	.480	.861	2	.984
1999—	Chicago (A.L.)	DH-1B	135	486	74	148	36	0	15	77	87	66	9	15	3-3	.305	.414	.471	.885	4	.990
2000—	Chicago (A.L.)	DH-1B	159	582	115	191	44	0	43	143	112	94	5	13	1-3	.328	.436	.625	1.061	1	.996
2001—	Chicago (A.L.)	DH-1B	20	68	8	15	3	0	4	10	10	12	0	0	0-0	.221	.316	.441	.758	1	.955
2002—	Chicago (A.L.)	DH-1B	148	523	77	132	29	1	28	92	88	115	7	10	3-0	.252	.361	.472	.834	2	.955
2003—	Chicago (A.L.)	DH-1B	153	546	87	146	35	0	42	105	100	115	12	11	0-0	.267	.390	.562	.952	1	.995
Major League totals (14 years)			1851	6611	1255	2048	428	11	418	1390	1386	1077	65	186	32-21	.310	.428	.568	.996	80	.991

THOME, JIM — 1B

PERSONAL: Born August 27, 1970, in Peoria, Ill. ... 6-4/240. ... Bats left, throws right. ... Full name: James Howard Thome. ... Name pronounced: TOE-mee. ... High school: Limestone (Bartonville, Ill.). ... College: Illinois Central.

TRANSACTIONS/CAREER NOTES: Selected by Cleveland Indians organization in 13th round of free-agent draft (June 5, 1989). ... On Cleveland disabled list (March 28-May 18, 1992); included rehabilitation assignment to Canton/Akron (May 9-18). ... On Cleveland disabled list (May 20-June 15, 1992); included rehabilitation assignment to Canton/Akron (June 1-15). ... On disabled list (August 8-September 16, 1998). ... Granted free agency (October 28, 2002). ... Signed by Philadelphia Phillies (December 3, 2002).

2003 GAMES PLAYED BY POSITION (MLB): 1B—156, DH—2.

Year Team (League)	Pos.	G	AB	R	H	2B	3B	HR	RBI	BB	SO	HBP	GDP	SB-CS	Avg.	OBP	SLG	OPS	FIELDING E	Pct.
1989— GC Indians (GCL)	3B-SS	55	186	22	44	5	3	0	22	21	33	1	5	6-4	.237	.314	.296	.610	21	.909
1990— Burlington (Appal.)	3B	34	118	31	44	7	1	12	34	27	18	4	2	6-3	.373	.503	.754	1.258	11	.907
— Kinston (Caro.)	3B	33	117	19	36	4	1	4	16	24	26	1	4	4-1	.308	.427	.462	.888	8	.905
1991— Cant./Akr. (Eastern)	3B	84	294	47	99	20	2	5	45	44	58	4	7	8-2	.337	.426	.469	.895	17	.924
— Colo. Springs (PCL)	3B	41	151	20	43	7	3	2	28	12	29	0	4	0-0	.285	.331	.411	.742	6	.949
— Cleveland (A.L.)	3B	27	98	7	25	4	2	1	9	5	16	1	4	1-1	.255	.298	.367	.665	8	.900
1992— Colo. Springs (PCL)	3B	12	48	11	15	4	1	2	14	6	16	1	0	0-0	.313	.400	.563	.963	8	.784
— Cleveland (A.L.)	3B	40	117	8	24	3	1	2	12	10	34	2	3	2-0	.205	.275	.299	.574	11	.882
— Cant./Akr. (Eastern)	3B	30	107	16	36	9	2	1	14	24	30	1	3	0-2	.336	.462	.486	.948	4	.920
1993— Charlotte (Int'l)	3B	115	410	85	136	21	4	25	*102	76	94	7	9	1-3	.332	*.441	.585	1.026	15	.951
— Cleveland (A.L.)	3B	47	154	28	41	11	0	7	22	29	36	4	3	2-1	.266	.385	.474	.859	6	.950
1994— Cleveland (A.L.)	3B	98	321	58	86	20	1	20	52	46	84	0	11	3-3	.268	.359	.523	.882	15	.940
1995— Cleveland (A.L.)	3B-DH	137	452	92	142	29	3	25	73	97	113	5	8	4-3	.314	.438	.558	.996	16	.948
1996— Cleveland (A.L.)	3B-DH	151	505	122	157	28	5	38	116	123	141	6	13	2-2	.311	.450	.612	1.062	17	.953
1997— Cleveland (A.L.)	1B	147	496	104	142	25	0	40	102	*120	146	3	9	1-1	.286	.423	.579	1.001	10	.993
1998— Cleveland (A.L.)	1B-DH	123	440	89	129	34	2	30	85	89	141	4	7	1-0	.293	.413	.584	.997	10	.991
1999— Cleveland (A.L.)	1B-DH	146	494	101	137	27	2	33	108	*127	*171	4	6	0-0	.277	.426	.540	.967	6	.994
2000— Cleveland (A.L.)	1B-DH	158	557	106	150	33	1	37	106	118	171	4	8	1-0	.269	.398	.531	.929	5	.995
2001— Cleveland (A.L.)	1B-DH	156	526	101	153	26	1	49	124	111	*185	4	9	0-1	.291	.416	.624	1.040	10	.992
2002— Cleveland (A.L.)	1B-DH	147	480	101	146	19	2	52	118	*122	139	5	5	1-2	.304	.445	*.677	1.122	10	.991
2003— Philadelphia (N.L.)	1B-DH	159	578	111	154	30	3	*47	131	111	*182	4	5	0-3	.266	.385	.573	.958	5	.997
American League totals (12 years)		1377	4640	917	1332	259	20	334	927	997	1377	42	86	18-14	.287	.414	.567	.982	124	.985
National League totals (1 year)		159	578	111	154	30	3	47	131	111	182	4	5	0-3	.266	.385	.573	.958	5	.997
Major League totals (13 years)		1536	5218	1028	1486	289	23	381	1058	1108	1559	46	91	18-17	.285	.411	.568	.979	129	.986

THOMSON, JOHN   P

PERSONAL: Born October 1, 1973, in Vicksburg, Miss. ... 6-3/190. ... Throws right, bats right. ... Full name: John Carl Thomson. ... Name pronounced: TOM-son. ... High school: Sulphur (La.). ... Junior college: Blinn College (Texas).

TRANSACTIONS/CAREER NOTES: Selected by Colorado Rockies organization in seventh round of free-agent draft (June 3, 1993). ... On Colorado disabled list (June 16-July 26, 1998); included rehabilitation assignment to Asheville (July 16-22). ... On Colorado Springs disabled list (May 19-July 19, 1999); included rehabilitation assignment to Salem (July 17-19). ... On Colorado disabled list (March 23, 2000-remainder of season); included rehabilitation assignments to Arizona League Rockies (August 16-September 1) and Portland (September 2-4). ... On Colorado disabled list (March 23-May 12 and May 26-August 2, 2001); included rehabilitation assignments to Colorado Springs (April 1-6, April 17-May 12 and June 24-July 23). ... Traded by Rockies with OF Mark Little to New York Mets for OF Jay Payton, P Mark Corey and OF Robert Stratton (July 31, 2002). ... Granted free agency (December 21, 2002). ... Signed by Texas Rangers (January 3, 2002).

CAREER HITTING: 37-for-197 (.188), 14 R, 1 2B, 1 3B, 0 HR, 12 RBI.

Year League	W	L	Pct.	ERA	WHIP	G	GS	CG	ShO	Hld.	Sv.-Opp.	IP	H	R	ER	HR	BB-IBB	SO	Avg.
1993— Ariz. Rockies (Ariz.)	3	5	.375	4.62	1.46	11	11	0	0	...	0-...	50.2	43	40	26	0	31-0	36	.225
1994— Asheville (S. Atl.)	6	6	.500	2.85	1.17	19	15	1	1	...	0-...	88.1	70	34	28	3	33-1	79	.219
— Central Valley (Cal.)	3	1	.750	3.28	1.24	9	8	0	0	...	0-...	49.1	43	20	18	0	18-1	41	.239
1995— New Haven (East.)	7	8	.467	4.18	1.43	26	24	0	0	...	0-...	131.1	132	69	61	8	56-0	82	.261
1996— New Haven (East.)	9	4	.692	2.86	1.12	16	16	1	0	...	0-...	97.2	82	35	31	8	27-1	86	.230
— Colo. Springs (PCL)	4	7	.364	5.04	1.46	11	11	0	0	...	0-...	69.2	76	45	39	6	26-2	62	.280
1997— Colo. Springs (PCL)	4	2	.667	3.43	1.19	7	7	0	0	...	0-...	42.0	36	18	16	4	14-1	49	.235
— Colorado (N.L.)	7	9	.438	4.71	1.47	27	27	2	1	0	0-0	166.1	193	94	87	15	51-0	106	.296
1998— Colorado (N.L.)	8	11	.421	4.81	1.39	26	26	2	0	0	0-0	161.0	174	86	86	21	49-0	106	.280
— Asheville (S. Atl.)	1	0	1.000	0.00	0.67	2	2	0	0	0	0-0	9.0	5	1	0	0	1-0	12	.161
1999— Colorado (N.L.)	1	10	.091	8.04	1.93	14	13	1	0	0	0-0	62.2	85	62	56	11	36-1	34	.324
— Colo. Springs (PCL)	0	2	.000	9.45	2.20	5	5	1	0	...	0-...	20.0	36	25	21	3	8-0	19	.414
— Salem (Caro.)	0	1	.000	9.00	2.00	1	1	0	0	...	0-...	2.0	4	2	2	0	0-0	2	.400
2000— Ariz. Rockies (Ariz.)	0	1	.000	13.50	2.25	3	3	0	0	...	0-...	5.1	8	8	8	0	4-0	7	.333
— Portland (NW)	0	0	...	2.25	1.25	1	1	0	0	...	0-...	4.0	4	1	1	0	1-0	3	.250
2001— Colo. Springs (PCL)	5	3	.625	3.31	1.28	12	12	0	0	...	0-...	68.0	74	29	25	6	13-0	52	.274
— Colorado (N.L.)	4	5	.444	4.04	1.16	14	14	1	1	0	0-0	93.2	84	46	42	15	25-3	68	.239
2002— Colorado (N.L.)	7	8	.467	4.88	1.28	21	21	0	0	0	0-0	127.1	136	77	69	21	27-6	76	.268
— New York (N.L.)	2	6	.250	4.31	1.51	9	9	0	0	0	0-0	54.1	65	39	26	7	17-3	31	.290
2003— Texas (A.L.)	13	14	.481	4.85	1.30	35	35	3	1	0	0-0	217.0	234	125	117	27	49-2	136	.276
American League totals (1 year)	13	14	.481	4.85	1.30	35	35	3	1	0	0-0	217.0	234	125	117	27	49-2	136	.276
National League totals (5 years)	29	49	.372	4.95	1.42	111	110	6	2	0	0-0	665.1	737	404	366	90	205-13	421	.282
Major League totals (6 years)	42	63	.400	4.93	1.39	146	145	9	3	0	0-0	882.1	971	529	483	117	254-15	557	.281

THURMAN, COREY   P

PERSONAL: Born November 5, 1978, in Augusta, Ga. ... 6-1/215. ... Throws right, bats right. ... Full name: Corey Lamar Thurman. ... High school: Texas (Texarkana, Texas).

TRANSACTIONS/CAREER NOTES: Selected by Kansas City Royals organization in fourth round of free-agent draft (June 4, 1996). ... Selected by Toronto Blue Jays from Royals organization in Rule 5 major league draft (December 13, 2001).

CAREER HITTING: 0-for-1 (.000), 0 R, 0 2B, 0 3B, 0 HR, 0 RBI.

Year League	W	L	Pct.	ERA	WHIP	G	GS	CG	ShO	Hld.	Sv.-Opp.	IP	H	R	ER	HR	BB-IBB	SO	Avg.
1996— GC Royals (GCL)	1	6	.143	6.08	1.71	11	11	0	0	...	0-...	47.1	53	32	32	2	28-0	52	.282
1997— GC Royals (GCL)	2	1	.667	2.38	1.47	8	8	1	0	...	0-...	34.0	28	12	9	1	22-0	42	.226
— Spokane (N'west)	1	2	.333	5.16	1.59	5	5	0	0	...	0-...	22.2	23	19	13	2	13-0	24	.258
1998— Lansing (Midw.)	5	6	.455	3.61	1.24	14	11	0	0	...	0-...	62.1	47	31	25	6	30-0	61	.208
— Spokane (N'west)	3	3	.500	4.05	1.72	12	12	0	0	...	0-...	60.0	72	35	27	3	31-0	49	.303
1999— Wilmington (Caro.)	8	11	.421	4.88	1.50	27	27	0	0	...	0-...	149.1	160	89	81	11	64-0	131	.274
2000— Wilmington (Caro.)	10	5	.667	2.26	1.24	19	19	1	0	...	0-...	115.2	97	33	29	6	46-0	96	.235
— Wichita (Texas)	4	5	.444	4.83	1.39	9	9	0	0	...	0-...	50.1	46	34	27	10	24-0	47	.240
2001— Wichita (Texas)	13	5	.722	3.37	1.17	25	25	0	0	...	0-...	155.0	117	66	58	16	65-1	148	.207
— Omaha (PCL)	0	0	...	5.40	1.60	1	1	0	0	...	0-...	5.0	6	4	3	0	2-0	4	.273
2002— Toronto (A.L.)	2	3	.400	4.37	1.62	43	1	0	0	4	0-2	68.0	65	34	33	11	45-2	56	.248
2003— Toronto (A.L.)	1	1	.500	6.46	1.96	6	3	0	0	0	0-0	15.1	21	11	11	3	9-1	11	.313
— Syracuse (Int'l)	6	6	.600	4.27	1.34	17	16	0	0	...	0-...	86.1	90	45	41	8	26-0	72	.268
Major League totals (2 years)	3	4	.429	4.75	1.68	49	4	0	0	4	0-2	83.1	86	45	44	14	54-3	67	.261

T

THURSTON, JOE — 2B

PERSONAL: Born September 29, 1979, in Fairfield, Calif. ... 5-11/175. ... Bats left, throws right. ... Full name: Joseph William Thurston. ... High school: Vallejo (Calif.). ... Junior college: Sacramento (Calif.) Community College.

TRANSACTIONS/CAREER NOTES: Selected by Los Angeles Dodgers organization in fourth round of free-agent draft (June 2, 1999). ... Called up by Los Angeles from Las Vegas (September 2, 2003).

2003 GAMES PLAYED BY POSITION (MLB): 2B—3.

Year	Team (League)	Pos.	G	AB	R	H	2B	3B	HR	RBI	BB	SO	HBP	GDP	SB-CS	Avg.	OBP	SLG	OPS	E	Pct.
1999—	Yakima (N'west)	SS-1B	71	277	48	79	10	3	0	32	27	34	21	3	27-17	.285	.387	.343	.730	‡ 29	.899
	—San Bern. (Calif.)	SS	2	3	0	0	0	0	0	0	0	1	1	0	0-0	.000	.250	.000	.250	0	1.000
2000—	San Bern. (Calif.)	2B-SS	• 138	551	97	* 167	31	8	4	70	56	61	17	8	43-25	.303	.380	.410	.790	34	.953
2001—	Jacksonville (Sou.)	2B-SS	134	544	80	145	25	7	7	46	48	65	12	5	20-18	.267	.338	.377	.715	17	.973
2002—	Las Vegas (PCL)	2B-SS	136	* 587	* 106	* 196	39	13	12	55	25	60	12	10	22-9	.334	.372	.506	.878	21	.973
	—Los Angeles (N.L.)	2B	8	13	1	6	1	0	0	1	0	1	0	0	0-0	.462	.429	.538	.967	0	1.000
2003—	Las Vegas (PCL)	2B-SS	132	538	77	156	27	6	7	68	31	48	18	10	1-12	.290	.345	.401	.746	15	.978
	—Los Angeles (N.L.)	2B	12	10	2	2	0	0	0	0	1	1	0	0	0-0	.200	.273	.200	.473	1	.857
	Major League totals (2 years)		20	23	3	8	1	0	0	1	1	2	0	0	0-0	.348	.360	.391	.751	1	.941

TIMLIN, MIKE — P

PERSONAL: Born March 10, 1966, in Midland, Texas. ... 6-4/210. ... Throws right, bats right. ... Full name: Michael August Timlin. ... Name pronounced: TIM-lin. ... High school: Midland (Texas). ... College: Southwestern (Texas).

TRANSACTIONS/CAREER NOTES: Selected by Toronto Blue Jays organization in fifth round of free-agent draft (June 2, 1987). ... On disabled list (April 4-May 2, 1989 and August 2-17, 1991). ... On Toronto disabled list (March 27-June 12, 1992); included rehabilitation assignments to Dunedin (April 11-15 and May 24-June 5) and Syracuse (June 5-12). ... On disabled list (May 25-June 9, 1994). ... On Toronto disabled list (June 22-August 18, 1995); included rehabilitation assignment to Syracuse (July 31-August 18). ... Traded by Blue Jays with P Paul Spoljaric to Seattle Mariners for OF Jose Cruz Jr. (July 31, 1997). ... Granted free agency (October 22, 1998). ... Signed by Baltimore Orioles (November 16, 1998). ... On Baltimore disabled list (April 2-17, 2000). ... Traded by Orioles with cash to St. Louis Cardinals for 1B Chris Richard and P Mark Nussbeck (July 29, 2000). ... On disabled list (July 26-August 17, 2001). ... Traded by Cardinals with IF/OF Placido Polanco and P Bud Smith to Philadelphia Phillies for 3B Scott Rolen and P Doug Nickle (July 29, 2002). ... Granted free agency (October 28, 2002). ... Signed by Boston Red Sox (December 18, 2002).

CAREER HITTING: 0-for-7 (.000), 0 R, 0 2B, 0 3B, 0 HR, 0 RBI.

Year	League	W	L	Pct.	ERA	WHIP	G	GS	CG	ShO	Hld.	Sv.-Opp.	IP	H	R	ER	HR	BB-IBB	SO	Avg.
1987—	Medicine Hat (Pio.)	4	8	.333	5.14	1.39	13	12	2	0	...	0-...	75.1	79	50	43	4	26-0	66	.271
1988—	Myrtle Beach (SAL)	10	6	.625	2.86	1.30	35	22	0	0	...	0-...	151.0	119	68	48	4	77-2	106	.215
1989—	Dunedin (Fla. St.)	5	8	.385	3.25	1.42	33	7	1	0	...	7-...	88.2	90	44	32	2	36-2	64	.262
1990—	Dunedin (Fla. St.)	7	2	.778	1.43	1.03	42	0	0	0	...	22-...	50.1	36	11	8	0	16-2	46	.197
	—Knoxville (Sou.)	1	2	.333	1.73	1.04	17	0	0	0	...	8-...	26.0	20	6	5	0	7-1	21	.206
1991—	Toronto (A.L.)	11	6	.647	3.16	1.33	63	3	0	0	9	3-8	108.1	94	43	38	6	50-11	85	.233
1992—	Dunedin (Fla. St.)	0	0	...	0.90	1.10	6	1	0	0	...	1-...	10.0	9	2	1	0	2-0	7	.243
	—Syracuse (Int'l)	0	1	.000	8.74	1.76	7	1	0	0	...	3-...	11.1	15	11	11	3	5-1	7	.333
	—Toronto (A.L.)	0	2	.000	4.12	1.49	26	0	0	0	1	1-1	43.2	45	23	20	0	20-5	35	.271
1993—	Toronto (A.L.)	4	2	.667	4.69	1.62	54	0	0	0	9	1-4	55.2	63	32	29	7	27-3	49	.284
	—Dunedin (Fla. St.)	0	0	...	1.00	0.44	4	0	0	0	...	1-...	9.0	4	1	1	0	0-0	8	.133
1994—	Toronto (A.L.)	0	1	.000	5.18	1.53	34	0	0	0	5	2-4	40.0	41	25	23	5	20-0	38	.261
1995—	Toronto (A.L.)	4	3	.571	2.14	1.31	31	0	0	0	4	5-9	42.0	38	13	10	1	17-5	36	.242
	—Syracuse (Int'l)	1	1	.500	1.04	0.98	8	0	0	0	...	1-...	17.1	13	6	2	2	4-0	13	.197
1996—	Toronto (A.L.)	1	6	.143	3.65	1.15	59	0	0	0	2	31-38	56.2	47	25	23	4	18-4	52	.229
1997—	Toronto (A.L.)	3	2	.600	2.87	1.19	38	0	0	0	2	9-13	47.0	41	17	15	6	15-4	36	.243
	—Seattle (A.L.)	3	2	.600	3.86	1.29	26	0	0	0	7	1-5	25.2	28	13	11	2	5-1	9	.280
1998—	Seattle (A.L.)	3	3	.500	2.95	1.18	70	0	0	0	6	19-24	79.1	78	26	26	5	16-2	60	.264
1999—	Baltimore (A.L.)	3	9	.250	3.57	1.17	62	0	0	0	0	27-36	63.0	51	30	25	9	23-3	50	.221
2000—	Baltimore (A.L.)	2	3	.400	4.89	1.49	37	0	0	0	1	11-15	35.0	37	22	19	6	15-3	26	.271
	—St. Louis (N.L.)	3	1	.750	3.34	1.69	25	0	0	0	5	1-3	29.2	30	11	11	2	20-3	26	.265
2001—	St. Louis (N.L.)	4	5	.444	4.09	1.33	67	0	0	0	12	3-7	72.2	78	35	33	6	19-4	47	.277
2002—	St. Louis (N.L.)	1	3	.250	2.51	0.90	42	1	0	0	12	0-2	61.0	48	19	17	9	7-2	35	.215
	—Philadelphia (N.L.)	3	3	.500	3.79	0.95	30	0	0	0	8	0-2	35.2	27	16	15	6	7-0	15	.206
2003—	Boston (A.L.)	6	4	.600	3.55	1.03	72	0	0	0	17	2-6	83.2	77	37	33	11	9-3	65	.239
	American League totals (11 years)	40	43	.482	3.60	1.29	572	3	0	0	63	112-163	680.0	640	306	272	62	235-44	541	.250
	National League totals (3 years)	11	12	.478	3.44	1.19	164	1	0	0	37	4-14	199.0	183	81	76	23	53-9	123	.244
	Major League totals (13 years)	51	55	.481	3.56	1.26	736	4	0	0	100	116-177	879.0	823	387	348	85	288-53	664	.248

TOLAR, KEVIN — P

PERSONAL: Born January 28, 1971, in Panama City, Fla. ... 6-3/230. ... Throws left, bats right. ... Full name: Kevin Anthony Tolar. ... High school: A. Crawford Mosley (Panama City, Fla.).

TRANSACTIONS/CAREER NOTES: Selected by Chicago White Sox organization in ninth round of free-agent draft (June 5, 1989). ... Loaned by White Sox organization to Salinas, California League (April 9-June 9, 1994). ... Released by White Sox (April 4, 1994). ... Signed by Pittsburgh Pirates organization (March 28, 1995). ... Granted free agency (October 16, 1995). ... Signed by Cleveland Indians organization (November 17, 1995). ... Granted free agency (October 15, 1996). ... Signed by Chicago Cubs organization (November 30, 1996). ... Released by Cubs (March 28, 1997). ... Signed by New York Mets organization (April 18, 1997). ... Granted free agency (October 17, 1997). ... Signed by Pirates organization (December 27, 1997). ... Traded by Pirates organization to Cincinnati Reds for future considerations (July 31, 1998). ... Granted free agency (October 15, 1999). ... Signed by Detroit Tigers organization (December 17, 1999). ... On Toledo disabled list (June 20-July 3, 2000). ... Granted free agency (October 15, 2001). ... Signed by Pirates organization (January 8, 2002). ... Granted free agency (October 15, 2002). ... Signed by Boston Red Sox organization (November 22, 2002). ... Contract purchased by Boston Red Sox (April 16, 2003). ... Optioned to Pawtucket by Boston (May 5, 2003). ... Recalled by Boston from Pawtucket (September 19, 2003).

CAREER HITTING: 0-for-0 (.000), 0 R, 0 2B, 0 3B, 0 HR, 0 RBI.

Year	League	W	L	Pct.	ERA	WHIP	G	GS	CG	ShO	Hld.	Sv.-Opp.	IP	H	R	ER	HR	BB-IBB	SO	Avg.
1989—	GC White Sox (GCL)	6	2	.750	1.65	1.38	13	12	1	0	...	0-...	60.0	29	16	11	0	* 54-0	58	.146
1990—	Utica (N.Y.-Penn)	4	6	.400	3.29	1.56	15	15	1	0	...	0-...	90.1	80	44	33	2	61-1	69	.237
1991—	South Bend (Mid.)	8	5	.615	2.83	1.50	30	19	0	0	...	1-...	114.2	87	54	36	3	85-0	87	.214
1992—	Salinas (Calif.)	1	8	.111	6.08	1.89	14	8	3	0	...	0-...	53.1	55	43	36	4	46-0	24	.281
	—South Bend (Mid.)	6	5	.545	2.88	1.23	18	10	0	0	...	0-...	81.1	59	34	26	5	41-0	81	.207
1993—	Sarasota (Fla. St.)	2	6	.250	5.35	1.63	23	11	0	0	...	1-...	77.1	75	55	46	1	51-1	60	.260
1994—	....											Did not play.								

Year	League	W	L	Pct.	ERA	WHIP	G	GS	CG	ShO	Hld.	Sv.-Opp.	IP	H	R	ER	HR	BB-IBB	SO	Avg.
1995—	Lynchburg (Carolina)	2	0	1.000	2.79	0.98	18	0	0	0	...	0-...	19.1	13	7	6	1	6-0	19	.188
	— Carolina (Sou.)	1	0	1.000	3.65	1.86	12	0	0	0	...	0-...	12.1	16	5	5	0	7-0	9	.320
1996—	Cant./Akr. (Eastern)	1	3	.250	2.62	1.52	50	0	0	0	...	1-...	44.2	42	19	13	1	26-2	39	.253
1997—	Binghamton (Eastern)	1	1	.500	5.12	1.89	22	0	0	0	...	0-...	31.2	38	20	18	3	22-1	26	.297
	— St. Lucie (Fla. St.)	0	0	...	2.03	1.13	9	0	0	0	...	1-...	13.1	9	3	3	0	6-0	8	.188
1998—	Carolina (Sou.)	1	2	.333	2.22	1.40	42	0	0	0	...	1-...	48.2	35	12	12	1	33-0	48	.205
	— Nashville (PCL)	0	0	...	6.00	2.00	1	0	0	0	...	0-...	3.0	2	2	2	0	4-0	1	.200
	— Indianapolis (Int'l)	0	1	.000	10.43	2.59	19	0	0	0	...	0-...	14.2	21	18	17	3	17-1	19	.328
1999—	Chattanooga (Sou.)	4	4	.500	4.97	1.95	47	1	0	0	...	1-...	54.1	61	32	30	2	45-4	60	.286
	— Indianapolis (Int'l)	1	0	1.000	2.08	1.15	8	1	0	0	...	0-...	13.0	8	4	3	1	7-1	18	.178
2000—	Jacksonville (Sou.)	2	0	1.000	0.52	0.87	9	0	0	0	...	0-...	17.1	7	3	1	0	8-0	19	.121
	— Toledo (Int'l)	4	2	.667	3.30	1.36	33	0	0	0	...	2-...	46.1	37	23	17	4	26-1	42	.213
	— Detroit (A.L.)	0	0	...	3.00	0.67	5	0	0	0	0	0-0	3.0	1	1	1	0	1-0	3	.091
2001—	Toledo (Int'l)	3	4	.429	2.73	1.25	44	0	0	0	...	7-...	56.0	49	18	17	3	21-2	73	.237
	— Detroit (A.L.)	0	0	...	6.75	1.88	9	0	0	0	0	0-0	10.2	7	8	8	0	13-1	11	.189
2002—	Nashville (PCL)	6	1	.857	2.54	1.19	44	7	1	1	...	1-...	78.0	66	23	22	5	27-0	82	.224
2003—	Boston (A.L.)	0	0	...	9.00	1.75	6	0	0	0	1	0-0	4.0	5	5	4	1	2-0	3	.313
	— Pawtucket (Int'l)	5	1	.833	2.27	1.14	47	0	0	0	...	4-...	31.2	19	9	8	3	17-2	34	.178
	Major League totals (3 years)	0	0	...	6.62	1.64	20	0	0	0	1	0-0	17.2	13	14	13	1	16-1	17	.203

TOLLBERG, BRIAN   P

PERSONAL: Born September 16, 1972, in Tampa, Fla. ... 6-3/195. ... Throws right, bats right. ... Full name: Brian Patrick Tollberg. ... High school: Manatee (Bradenton, Fla.). ... College: North Florida.

TRANSACTIONS/CAREER NOTES: Signed by Chillicothe, Frontier League (1994). ... Signed as non-drafted free agent by Milwaukee Brewers organization (January 31, 1995). ... Traded by Brewers to San Diego Padres for 3B Antonio Fernandez (March 13, 1997). ... On Las Vegas disabled list (May 6, 1999-remainder of season). ... On San Diego disabled list (May 7-July 16, 2001); included rehabilitation assignments to Lake Elsinore (July 2-6 and July 11-16) and Portland (June 27-July 1 and July 7-10). ... On disabled list (May 30, 2002-remainder of season). ... Released by Padres (December 14, 2002). ... Re-signed by Padres organization (January 10, 2003). ... Contract purchased from Portland (May 30, 2003). ... Optioned to Portland (June 12, 2003).

CAREER HITTING: 14-for-93 (.151), 5 R, 1 2B, 0 3B, 0 HR, 2 RBI.

Year	League	W	L	Pct.	ERA	WHIP	G	GS	CG	ShO	Hld.	Sv.-Opp.	IP	H	R	ER	HR	BB-IBB	SO	Avg.
1994—	Chillicothe (Fron.)	7	4	.636	2.85	1.24	13	13	4	0	...	0-...	94.2	90	34	30	5	27-2	69	.248
1995—	Beloit (Midw.)	13	4	.765	3.41	1.11	22	22	1	1	...	0-...	132.0	119	59	50	10	27-0	110	.243
1996—	El Paso (Texas)	7	5	.583	4.90	1.33	26	26	0	0	...	0-...	154.1	183	90	84	15	23-0	109	.293
1997—	Mobile (Sou.)	6	3	.667	3.72	1.19	31	13	1	0	...	0-...	123.1	123	60	51	15	24-2	108	.256
1998—	Mobile (Sou.)	3	2	.600	2.41	0.85	6	6	1	0	...	0-...	41.0	31	11	11	3	4-0	45	.212
	— Las Vegas (PCL)	6	6	.500	6.38	1.50	33	15	1	0	...	3-...	110.0	138	85	78	21	27-2	109	.307
1999—	Las Vegas (PCL)	1	2	.333	4.85	1.35	5	5	0	0	...	0-...	29.2	34	17	16	3	6-0	23	.298
	— Ariz. Padres (Ariz.)	0	0	...	4.50	1.00	2	2	0	0	...	0-...	4.0	4	2	2	0	0-0	6	.250
2000—	Las Vegas (PCL)	6	0	1.000	2.83	1.09	13	13	0	0	...	0-...	76.1	72	28	24	5	11-0	60	.244
	— San Diego (N.L.)	4	5	.444	3.58	1.36	19	19	0	0	0	0-0	118.0	126	58	47	13	35-4	76	.274
2001—	San Diego (N.L.)	10	4	.714	4.30	1.35	19	19	0	0	0	0-0	117.1	133	58	56	15	25-3	71	.287
	— Portland (PCL)	1	0	1.000	5.40	1.40	4	4	0	0	...	0-...	20.0	24	11	10	3	4-0	10	.293
	— Lake Elsinore (Calif.)	0	2	.000	6.30	1.90	2	2	0	0	...	0-...	10.0	18	11	7	1	1-0	9	.391
2002—	San Diego (N.L.)	1	5	.167	6.13	1.74	12	11	0	0	0	0-0	61.2	88	47	42	11	19-2	33	.342
2003—	San Diego (N.L.)	0	2	.000	6.97	1.26	3	3	0	0	0	0-0	10.1	9	11	8	1	4-0	2	.231
	— Portland (PCL)	5	3	.625	5.25	1.30	20	12	0	0	...	0-...	82.1	94	52	48	12	13-0	45	.283
	Major League totals (4 years)	15	16	.484	4.48	1.43	53	52	1	0	0	0-0	307.1	356	174	153	40	83-9	182	.292

TOMKO, BRETT   P

PERSONAL: Born April 7, 1973, in Euclid, Ohio. ... 6-4/215. ... Throws right, bats right. ... Full name: Brett Daniel Tomko. ... Name pronounced: TOM-koh. ... High school: El Dorado (Placentia, Calif.). ... College: Florida Southern.

TRANSACTIONS/CAREER NOTES: Selected by Los Angeles Dodgers organization in 20th round of free-agent draft (June 2, 1994); did not sign. ... Selected by Cincinnati Reds organization in second round of free-agent draft (June 1, 1995). ... Traded by Reds with OF Mike Cameron, IF Antonio Perez and P Jake Meyer to Seattle Mariners for OF Ken Griffey Jr. (February 10, 2000). ... On disabled list (June 7-24, 2000). ... Traded by Mariners with C Tom Lampkin and SS Ramon Vazquez to San Diego Padres for C Ben Davis, P Wascar Serrano and SS Alex Arias (December 11, 2001). ... Traded by Padres to St. Louis Cardinals for P Luther Hackman and a player to be named later (December 15, 2002); Padres acquired P Mike Wodnicki to complete deal (December 16, 2002).

CAREER HITTING: 52-for-277 (.188), 15 R, 7 2B, 0 3B, 0 HR, 23 RBI.

Year	League	W	L	Pct.	ERA	WHIP	G	GS	CG	ShO	Hld.	Sv.-Opp.	IP	H	R	ER	HR	BB-IBB	SO	Avg.
1995—	Char., W.Va. (SAL)	4	2	.667	1.84	1.02	9	7	0	0	...	0-...	49.0	41	12	10	1	9-1	46	.228
1996—	Chattanooga (Sou.)	11	7	.611	3.88	1.17	27	27	0	0	...	0-...	157.2	131	73	68	20	54-4	164	.226
1997—	Indianapolis (A.A.)	6	3	.667	2.95	1.02	10	10	0	0	...	0-...	61.0	53	21	20	7	9-0	60	.232
	— Cincinnati (N.L.)	11	7	.611	3.43	1.21	22	19	0	0	0	0-0	126.0	106	50	48	14	47-4	95	.234
1998—	Cincinnati (N.L.)	13	12	.520	4.44	1.24	34	34	1	0	0	0-0	210.2	198	111	104	22	64-3	162	.247
1999—	Cincinnati (N.L.)	5	7	.417	4.92	1.37	33	26	1	0	1	0-0	172.0	175	103	94	31	60-10	132	.263
	— Indianapolis (Int'l)	2	0	1.000	4.97	1.26	2	2	0	0	...	0-...	12.2	15	7	7	1	1-0	9	.288
2000—	Tacoma (PCL)	1	0	1.000	2.84	1.42	2	2	0	0	...	0-...	12.2	13	4	4	1	5-1	8	.271
	— Seattle (A.L.)	7	5	.583	4.68	1.43	32	8	0	0	3	1-2	92.1	92	53	48	12	40-4	59	.264
2001—	Seattle (A.L.)	3	1	.750	5.19	1.64	11	4	0	0	0	0-1	34.2	42	24	20	9	15-2	22	.288
	— Tacoma (PCL)	10	6	.625	4.04	1.17	19	18	3	•2	...	0-...	127.0	124	64	57	12	25-1	117	.254
2002—	San Diego (N.L.)	10	10	.500	4.49	1.33	32	32	3	0	0	0-0	204.1	212	107	102	31	60-9	126	.267
2003—	St. Louis (N.L.)	13	9	.591	5.28	1.52	33	32	2	0	0	0-0	202.2	*252	126	•119	35	57-2	114	.305
	American League totals (2 years)	10	6	.625	4.82	1.49	43	12	0	0	3	1-3	127.0	134	77	68	21	55-6	81	.271
	National League totals (5 years)	52	45	.536	4.59	1.34	154	143	7	0	1	0-0	915.2	943	497	467	133	288-28	629	.266
	Major League totals (7 years)	62	51	.549	4.62	1.36	197	155	7	0	4	1-3	1042.2	1077	574	535	154	343-34	710	.267

TORCATO, TONY   OF

PERSONAL: Born October 25, 1979, in Woodland, Calif. ... 6-1/195. ... Bats left, throws right. ... Full name: Anthony Dale Torcato. ... Name pronounced: tor-ka-TO. ... High school: Woodland (Calif.).

TRANSACTIONS/CAREER NOTES: Selected by San Francisco Giants organization in first round (19th pick overall) of free-agent draft (June 2, 1998); pick received from Houston Astros as part of compensation for signing Type B free agent P Doug Henry.

2003 GAMES PLAYED BY POSITION (MLB): OF—6.

T

Year	Team (League)	Pos.	G	AB	R	H	2B	3B	HR	RBI	BB	SO	HBP	GDP	SB-CS	Avg.	OBP	SLG	OPS	E	Pct.
1998— Salem-Keizer (NW)	3B	59	220	31	64	15	2	3	43	14	38	3	0	4-2	.291	.333	.418	.752	17	.886
1999— Bakersfield (Calif.)	3B	110	422	50	123	25	0	4	58	30	67	3	6	2-1	.291	.338	.379	.717	28	.886
2000— San Jose (Calif.)	3B	119	490	77	159	37	2	7	88	41	62	6	2	19-4	.324	.379	.451	.830	40	.882
— Shreveport (Texas)	3B	2	8	1	4	0	0	0	2	0	1	0	0	0-0	.500	.500	.500	1.000	0	1.000
2001— San Jose (Calif.)	OF	67	258	38	88	21	2	2	47	17	40	4	5	9-3	.341	.381	.461	.842	1	.952
— Shreveport (Texas)	OF	36	147	13	43	9	1	1	23	9	15	4	6	0-1	.293	.344	.388	.731	2	.975
— Fresno (PCL)	OF	35	150	20	48	8	1	2	8	2	20	0	5	0-1	.320	.329	.427	.756	1	.985
2002— Fresno (PCL)	OF	130	490	64	142	23	3	13	64	29	65	2	6	4-6	.290	.330	.429	.758	8	.964
— San Francisco (N.L.)	OF	5	11	0	3	1	0	0	0	0	2	0	0	0-0	.273	.273	.364	.636	0	1.000
2003— Fresno (PCL)	1-0-3-D	106	423	36	125	18	2	3	48	6	33	2	18	4-0	.296	.304	.369	.672	12	.981
— San Francisco (N.L.)	OF	14	16	0	3	1	0	0	1	0	4	1	0	0-0	.188	.235	.250	.485	1	.833
Major League totals (2 years)		19	27	0	6	2	0	0	1	0	6	1	0	0-0	.222	.250	.296	.546	1	.875

TORREALBA, YORVIT — C

PERSONAL: Born July 19, 1978, in Caracas, Venezuela. ... 5-11/180. ... Bats right, throws right. ... Full name: Yorvit Adolfo Torrealba. ... Name pronounced: yor-VEET tor-EE-all-buh. ... High school: Vincente Emilio Sojo (Venezuela).

TRANSACTIONS/CAREER NOTES: Signed as non-drafted free agent by San Francisco Giants organization (September 14, 1994).

2003 GAMES PLAYED BY POSITION (MLB): C—66, OF—1.

Year	Team (League)	Pos.	G	AB	R	H	2B	3B	HR	RBI	BB	SO	HBP	GDP	SB-CS	Avg.	OBP	SLG	OPS	E	Pct.
1995— Bellingham (N'west)	C	26	71	2	11	3	0	0	8	2	14	1	1	0-1	.155	.187	.197	.384	5	.973
1996— San Jose (Calif.)	C	2	5	0	0	0	0	0	0	1	1	0	0	0-0	.000	.167	.000	.167	0	1.000
— Burlington (Midw.)	C	1	4	0	0	0	0	0	0	0	1	0	1	0-0	.000	.000	.000	.000	1	1.000
— Bellingham (N'west)	C	48	150	23	40	4	0	1	10	9	27	0	7	4-1	.267	.304	.313	.618	2	.994
1997— Bakersfield (Calif.)	C	119	446	52	122	15	3	4	40	31	58	5	8	4-2	.274	.326	.348	.673	6	.993
1998— Shreveport (Texas)	C	59	196	18	46	7	0	0	13	18	30	4	3	0-5	.235	.311	.270	.581	2	.996
— San Jose (Calif.)	C	21	70	10	20	2	0	0	10	1	6	0	2	2-2	.286	.292	.314	.606	2	.989
— Fresno (PCL)	C	4	11	1	2	1	0	0	1	1	4	0	0	0-0	.182	.250	.273	.523	0	1.000
1999— Shreveport (Texas)	C	65	217	25	53	10	1	4	19	9	34	2	6	0-1	.244	.278	.355	.633	2	.994
— Fresno (PCL)	C	17	63	9	16	2	0	2	10	4	11	2	2	0-1	.254	.319	.381	.700	2	.988
— San Jose (Calif.)	C	19	73	10	23	3	0	2	14	6	15	1	2	0-0	.315	.370	.438	.809	5	.975
2000— Shreveport (Texas)	C	108	398	50	114	21	1	4	32	34	55	6	17	2-3	.286	.350	.374	.724	8	.990
2001— Fresno (PCL)	C	115	394	56	108	23	3	8	36	19	65	4	11	2-3	.274	.313	.409	.721	9	.989
— San Francisco (N.L.)	C	3	4	0	2	0	1	0	2	0	0	0	0	0-0	.500	.500	1.000	1.500	0	1.000
2002— San Francisco (N.L.)	C	53	136	17	38	10	0	2	14	14	20	2	11	0-0	.279	.355	.397	.752	2	.993
2003— San Francisco (N.L.)	C-OF	66	200	22	52	10	2	4	29	14	39	2	3	1-0	.260	.312	.390	.702	1	.997
Major League totals (3 years)		122	340	39	92	20	3	6	45	28	59	4	14	1-0	.271	.332	.400	.732	3	.996

TORRES, ANDRES — OF

PERSONAL: Born January 26, 1978, in Aguada, Puerto Rico. ... 5-10/190. ... Bats both, throws right. ... Full name: Andres Vungo Torres. ... Junior college: Miami-Dade Community College.

TRANSACTIONS/CAREER NOTES: Selected by Florida Marlins organization in 23rd round of free-agent draft (June 3, 1997); did not sign. ... Selected by Detroit Tigers organization in fourth round of free-agent draft (June 2, 1998). ... On disabled list (July 2, 2001-remainder of season).

2003 GAMES PLAYED BY POSITION (MLB): OF—50, DH—3.

Year	Team (League)	Pos.	G	AB	R	H	2B	3B	HR	RBI	BB	SO	HBP	GDP	SB-CS	Avg.	OBP	SLG	OPS	E	Pct.
1998— Jamestown (NYP)	OF	48	192	28	45	2	6	1	21	25	50	1	1	13-2	.234	.323	.323	.646	5	.944
1999— W. Mich. (Mid.)	OF	117	407	72	96	20	5	2	34	92	116	10	2	39-18	.236	.385	.324	.710	7	.972
2000— Lakeland (Fla. St.)	OF	108	398	82	118	11	11	3	33	63	82	5	10	65-16	.296	.399	.402	.801	6	.979
— Jacksonville (Sou.)	OF	14	54	3	8	0	0	0	0	5	14	0	1	2-0	.148	.220	.148	.368	1	.971
2001— Erie (East.)	OF	64	252	54	74	16	3	1	23	36	50	5	1	19-11	.294	.391	.393	.784	1	.993
2002— Toledo (Int'l)	OF	115	462	80	123	17	8	4	42	53	116	5	3	• 42-12	.266	.345	.364	.709	10	.967
— Detroit (A.L.)	OF	19	70	7	14	1	1	0	3	6	16	1	2	2-2	.200	.266	.243	.509	1	.981
2003— Toledo (Int'l)	OF	70	271	36	69	13	3	2	16	18	61	0	1	27-11	.255	.301	.347	.648	5	.973
— Detroit (A.L.)	OF-DH	59	168	23	37	4	3	1	9	10	35	0	5	5-5	.220	.263	.298	.560	1	.991
Major League totals (2 years)		78	238	30	51	5	4	1	12	16	51	1	7	7-7	.214	.264	.282	.545	2	.987

TORRES, SALOMON — P

PERSONAL: Born March 11, 1972, in San Pedro de Macoris, Dominican Republic. ... 5-11/210. ... Throws right, bats right. ... Full name: Salomon Ramirez Torres. ... High school: Centro Academico Rogus (San Pedro de Macoris, Dominican Republic).

TRANSACTIONS/CAREER NOTES: Signed as non-drafted free agent by San Francisco Giants organization (September 15, 1989). ... Traded by Giants to Seattle Mariners for P Shawn Estes and IF Wilson Delgado (May 21, 1995). ... Claimed on waivers by Montreal Expos (April 18, 1997). ... On voluntarily retired list (August 1, 1997-January 29, 2001). ... Released by Expos (January 29, 2001). ... Signed by Samsung, Korean League (2001). ... Signed by Pittsburgh Pirates organization (January 8, 2002). ... On Nashville disabled list (July 2-15, 2002). ... Placed on 15-day disabled list by Pittsburgh (August 6, 2003). ... Sent on rehab assignment by Pittsburgh (August 24, 2003). ... Recalled from minor league rehab assignment; removed from 15-day disabled list (August 29, 2003).

CAREER HITTING: 11-for-91 (.121), 5 R, 0 2B, 1 3B, 0 HR, 1 RBI.

Year	League	W	L	Pct.	ERA	WHIP	G	GS	CG	ShO	Hld.	Sv.-Opp.	IP	H	R	ER	HR	BB-IBB	SO	Avg.
1990— San Pedro (DSL)	11	1	.917	0.50	0.82	13	13	6	0	...	0-...	90.0	44	15	5	0	30-...	101	...
1991— Clinton (Midw.)	• 16	5	.762	1.41	0.93	28	28	* 8	3	...	0-...	* 210.1	148	48	33	4	47-2	* 214	.195
1992— Shreveport (Texas)	6	10	.375	4.21	1.24	25	25	4	2	...	0-...	162.1	167	93	76	10	34-2	151	.263
1993— Shreveport (Texas)	7	4	.636	2.70	0.95	12	12	2	1	...	0-...	83.1	67	27	25	6	12-0	67	.218
— Phoenix (PCL)	7	4	.636	3.50	1.25	14	14	• 4	1	...	0-...	105.1	105	43	41	5	27-0	99	.261
— San Francisco (N.L.)	3	5	.375	4.03	1.43	8	8	0	0	0	0-0	44.2	37	21	20	5	27-3	23	.231
1994— San Francisco (N.L.)	2	8	.200	5.44	1.53	16	14	1	0	0	0-0	84.1	95	55	51	10	34-2	42	.292
— Phoenix (PCL)	5	6	.455	4.22	1.47	13	13	0	0	...	0-...	79.0	85	49	37	7	31-0	64	.278
1995— San Francisco (N.L.)	0	1	.000	9.00	2.50	4	1	0	0	0	0-0	8.0	13	8	8	4	7-0	2	.394
— Phoenix (PCL)	0	0	...	0.00	1.00	1	0	0	0	...	0-...	2.0	2	0	0	0	0-0	5	.286
— Tacoma (PCL)	1	1	.500	3.21	1.18	5	4	0	0	...	0-...	28.0	20	10	10	2	13-1	19	.206
— Seattle (A.L.)	3	8	.273	6.00	1.79	16	13	1	0	0	0-0	72.0	87	53	48	12	42-3	45	.291

Year	League	W	L	Pct.	ERA	WHIP	G	GS	CG	ShO	Hld.	Sv.-Opp.	IP	H	R	ER	HR	BB-IBB	SO	Avg.
1996—Tacoma (PCL)		7	10	.412	5.29	1.50	22	21	3	1	...	0-...	134.1	150	87	79	16	52-1	121	.279
—Seattle (A.L.)		3	3	.500	4.59	1.37	10	7	1	1	0	0-0	49.0	44	27	25	5	23-2	36	.242
1997—Seattle (A.L.)		0	0	...	27.00	3.00	2	0	0	0	0	0-0	3.1	7	10	10	0	3-0	0	.412
—Montreal (N.L.)		0	0	...	7.25	1.66	12	0	0	0	0	0-0	22.1	25	19	18	2	12-0	11	.284
—Ottawa (Int'l)		0	0	...	5.40	1.80	2	1	0	0	...	0-...	5.0	7	5	3	0	2-0	2	.318
2001—Samsung (Korean)		0	2	.000	0.00	2.00	2	...	...	...	...	0-...	5.0	...	...	...	...	10-...	5	...
2002—Nashville (PCL)		8	5	.615	3.83	1.28	26	24	2	1	...	0-...	162.1	169	78	69	12	39-2	136	.270
—Pittsburgh (N.L.)		2	1	.667	2.70	1.37	5	5	0	0	0	0-0	30.0	28	10	9	2	13-1	12	.257
2003—Nashville (PCL)		1	0	1.000	1.80	0.60	1	1	0	0	...	0-...	5.0	2	1	1	0	1-0	4	.118
—Pittsburgh (N.L.)		7	5	.583	4.76	1.40	41	16	0	0	6	2-3	121.0	128	65	64	19	42-5	84	.276
American League totals (3 years)		6	11	.353	6.01	1.66	28	20	2	1	0	0-0	124.1	138	90	83	17	68-5	81	.277
National League totals (6 years)		14	20	.412	4.93	1.49	86	44	1	0	6	2-3	310.1	326	178	170	42	135-11	174	.277
Major League totals (7 years)		20	31	.392	5.24	1.53	114	64	3	1	6	2-3	434.2	464	268	253	59	203-16	255	.277

TOWERS, JOSH   P

PERSONAL: Born February 26, 1977, in Port Hueneme, Calif. ... 6-1/188. ... Throws right, bats right. ... Full name: Joshua Eric Towers. ... High school: Hueneme (Oxnard, Calif.). ... Junior college: Oxnard College (Calif.).
TRANSACTIONS/CAREER NOTES: Selected by Baltimore Orioles organization in 15th round of free-agent draft (June 4, 1996). ... On Rochester disabled list (May 30-June 13 and August 5-24, 2000). ... On disabled list (October 1, 2001-remainder of season). ... On Rochester disabled list (June 12-July 5 and August 18-30, 2002). ... Granted free agency (October 15, 2002). ... Signed by Toronto Blue Jays organization (November 8, 2002).
CAREER HITTING: 0-for-3 (.000), 0 R, 0 2B, 0 3B, 0 HR, 0 RBI.

Year	League	W	L	Pct.	ERA	WHIP	G	GS	CG	ShO	Hld.	Sv.-Opp.	IP	H	R	ER	HR	BB-IBB	SO	Avg.
1996—Bluefield (Appal.)		4	1	.800	5.24	1.24	14	9	0	0	...	0-...	55.0	63	35	32	9	5-0	61	.278
1997—Delmarva (S. Atl.)		0	0	...	3.44	1.09	9	1	0	0	...	1-...	18.1	18	8	7	1	2-0	16	.261
—Frederick (Caro.)		6	2	.750	4.86	1.71	25	3	0	0	...	1-...	53.2	74	36	29	4	18-0	64	.323
1998—Frederick (Caro.)		8	7	.533	3.34	1.00	25	20	3	0	...	1-...	145.1	137	58	54	11	9-0	122	.247
—Bowie (East.)		2	1	.667	3.50	1.33	5	2	0	0	...	0-...	18.0	20	9	7	1	4-0	7	.270
1999—Bowie (East.)		12	7	.632	3.76	1.22	29	•28	5	•2	...	0-...	*189.0	*204	86	79	*26	26-1	106	.276
2000—Rochester (Int'l)		8	6	.571	3.47	1.20	24	24	5	1	...	0-...	148.0	157	63	57	17	21-0	102	.269
2001—Rochester (Int'l)		3	1	.750	3.51	1.17	6	6	1	1	...	0-...	41.0	40	18	16	2	8-2	27	.255
—Baltimore (A.L.)		8	10	.444	4.49	1.29	24	20	1	1	0	0-0	140.1	165	74	70	21	16-0	58	.297
2002—Baltimore (A.L.)		0	3	.000	7.90	1.72	5	3	0	0	0	0-0	27.1	42	24	24	11	5-0	13	.362
—Rochester (Int'l)		0	9	.000	7.57	1.78	15	13	1	0	...	0-...	69.0	109	65	58	16	14-0	43	.353
2003—Syracuse (Int'l)		5	7	.417	3.32	1.15	21	20	1	1	...	0-...	132.2	133	55	49	10	20-1	76	.259
—Toronto (A.L.)		8	1	.889	4.48	1.15	14	8	1	0	0	1-1	64.1	67	34	32	15	7-1	42	.266
Major League totals (3 years)		16	14	.533	4.89	1.30	43	31	2	1	0	1-1	232.0	274	132	126	47	28-1	113	.297

TRABER, BILLY   P

PERSONAL: Born September 18, 1979, in Torrance, Calif. ... 6-5/205. ... Throws left, bats left. ... Full name: William Henry Traber Jr.. ... High school: El Segundo (Calif.). ... College: Loyola Marymount.
TRANSACTIONS/CAREER NOTES: Selected by the New York Mets organization in first round (16th pick overall) of free-agent draft (June 5, 2000). ... Traded by Mets with OF Matt Lawton, P Jerrod Riggan, OF Alex Escobar and 1B Earl Snyder to Cleveland Indians for 2B Roberto Alomar, P Mike Bascik and OF Danny Peoples (December 11, 2001).
CAREER HITTING: 0-for-4 (.000), 0 R, 0 2B, 0 3B, 0 HR, 0 RBI.

Year	League	W	L	Pct.	ERA	WHIP	G	GS	CG	ShO	Hld.	Sv.-Opp.	IP	H	R	ER	HR	BB-IBB	SO	Avg.
2001—St. Lucie (Fla. St.)		6	5	.545	2.66	1.06	18	18	0	0	...	0-...	101.2	85	36	30	2	23-0	79	.223
—Binghamton (Eastern)		4	3	.571	4.43	1.48	8	8	0	0	...	0-...	42.2	50	25	21	4	13-1	45	.296
—Norfolk (Int'l)		0	1	.000	1.29	0.71	1	1	0	0	...	0-...	7.0	5	3	1	0	0-0	0	.192
2002—Akron (East.)		13	2	.867	2.76	1.11	18	17	2	2	...	0-...	107.2	99	38	33	8	20-0	82	.243
—Buffalo (Int'l)		4	3	.571	3.29	1.28	9	9	0	0	...	0-...	54.2	58	22	20	3	12-0	33	.276
2003—Cleveland (A.L.)		6	9	.400	5.24	1.54	33	18	1	1	1	0-0	111.2	132	67	65	15	40-4	88	.293
Major League totals (1 year)		6	9	.400	5.24	1.54	33	18	1	1	1	0-0	111.2	132	67	65	15	40-4	88	.293

TRACHSEL, STEVE   P

PERSONAL: Born October 31, 1970, in Oxnard, Calif. ... 6-4/205. ... Throws right, bats right. ... Full name: Stephen Christopher Trachsel. ... Name pronounced: track-s'l. ... High school: Troy (Fullerton, Calif.). ... College: Long Beach State.
TRANSACTIONS/CAREER NOTES: Selected by Chicago Cubs organization in eighth round of free-agent draft (June 3, 1991). ... On Chicago disabled list (July 20-August 4, 1994). ... Granted free agency (October 28, 1999). ... Signed by Tampa Bay Devil Rays (January 28, 2000). ... Traded by Devil Rays with P Mark Guthrie to Toronto Blue Jays for 2B Brent Abernathy and a player to be named later (July 31, 2000). ... Granted free agency (October 31, 2000). ... Signed by New York Mets (December 11, 2000). ... On New York disabled list (July 1-22, 2002; included rehabilitation assignment to Binghamton (July 16-18). ... Granted free agency (October 28, 2002). ... Re-signed by Mets (December 7, 2002).
CAREER HITTING: 86-for-515 (.167), 39 R, 15 2B, 1 3B, 2 HR, 33 RBI.

Year	League	W	L	Pct.	ERA	WHIP	G	GS	CG	ShO	Hld.	Sv.-Opp.	IP	H	R	ER	HR	BB-IBB	SO	Avg.
1991—Geneva (N.Y.-Penn)		1	0	1.000	1.26	1.12	2	2	0	0	...	0-...	14.1	10	2	2	0	6-0	7	.217
—Winston-Salem (Caro.)		4	4	.500	3.67	1.21	12	12	1	0	...	0-...	73.2	70	38	30	3	19-0	69	.245
1992—Charlotte (Sou.)		•13	8	.619	3.06	1.13	29	•29	5	2	...	0-...	*191.0	180	76	65	19	35-3	135	.250
1993—Iowa (Am. Assoc.)		13	6	.684	3.96	1.26	27	26	1	1	...	0-...	170.2	170	78	75	20	45-0	135	.264
—Chicago (N.L.)		0	2	.000	4.58	0.97	3	3	0	0	0	0-0	19.2	16	10	10	4	3-0	14	.219
1994—Chicago (N.L.)		9	7	.563	3.21	1.28	22	22	1	0	0	0-0	146.0	133	57	52	19	54-4	108	.242
—Iowa (Am. Assoc.)		0	2	.000	10.00	2.00	2	2	0	0	...	0-...	9.0	11	10	10	1	7-0	8	.289
1995—Chicago (N.L.)		7	13	.350	5.15	1.56	30	29	2	0	0	0-0	160.2	174	104	92	25	76-8	117	.277
1996—Orlando (Sou.)		0	1	.000	2.77	0.85	2	2	0	0	...	0-...	13.0	11	6	4	0	0-0	12	.220
—Chicago (N.L.)		13	9	.591	3.03	1.19	31	31	3	2	0	0-0	205.0	181	82	69	30	62-3	132	.235
1997—Chicago (N.L.)		8	12	.400	4.51	1.46	34	34	0	0	0	0-0	201.1	225	110	101	*32	69-6	160	.287
1998—Chicago (N.L.)		15	8	.652	4.46	1.38	33	33	1	0	0	0-0	208.0	204	107	103	27	84-5	149	.260
1999—Chicago (N.L.)		8	*18	.308	5.56	1.41	34	34	4	0	0	0-0	205.2	226	133	127	32	64-4	149	.280
2000—Tampa Bay (A.L.)		6	10	.375	4.58	1.52	23	23	3	1	0	0-0	137.2	160	76	70	16	49-1	78	.294
—Toronto (A.L.)		2	5	.286	5.29	1.54	11	11	0	0	0	0-0	63.0	72	40	37	10	25-1	32	.293
2001—New York (N.L.)		11	13	.458	4.46	1.24	28	28	1	1	0	0-0	173.2	168	90	86	28	47-7	144	.254
—Norfolk (Int'l)		2	0	1.000	2.79	0.98	3	3	1	0	...	0-...	19.1	13	6	6	0	6-0	12	.188

Year — League	W	L	Pct.	ERA	WHIP	G	GS	CG	ShO	Hld.	Sv.-Opp.	IP	H	R	ER	HR	BB-IBB	SO	Avg.
2002— New York (N.L.)	11	11	.500	3.37	1.38	30	30	1	1	0	0-0	173.2	170	80	65	16	69-4	105	.258
— Binghamton (Eastern)	1	0	1.000	0.00	1.24	1	1	0	0	...	0-...	5.2	3	1	0	0	4-0	5	.150
2003— New York (N.L.)	16	10	.615	3.78	1.31	33	33	2	2	0	0-0	204.2	204	90	86	26	65-9	111	.264
American League totals (1 year)	8	15	.348	4.80	1.52	34	34	3	1	0	0-0	200.2	232	116	107	26	74-2	110	.294
National League totals (10 years)	98	103	.488	4.19	1.35	278	277	15	6	0	0-0	1698.1	1701	863	791	239	593-50	1189	.262
Major League totals (11 years)	106	118	.473	4.26	1.37	312	311	18	7	0	0-0	1899.0	1933	979	898	265	667-52	1299	.265

TRAMMELL, BUBBA   OF

PERSONAL: Born November 6, 1971, in Knoxville, Tenn. ... 6-2/220. ... Bats right, throws right. ... Full name: Thomas Bubba Trammell. ... Name pronounced: TRAM-mull. ... High school: Knoxville (Tenn.) Central. ... College: Tennessee.

TRANSACTIONS/CAREER NOTES: Selected by Detroit Tigers organization in 11th round of free-agent draft (June 2, 1994). ... Selected by Tampa Bay Devil Rays in first round (22nd pick overall) of expansion draft (November 18, 1997). ... On Durham disabled list (May 17-25, 1999). ... Traded by Devil Rays with P Rick White to New York Mets for OF Jason Tyner and P Paul Wilson (July 28, 2000). ... Traded by Mets to San Diego Padres for P Donne Wall (December 11, 2000). ... Traded by Padres with P Mark Phillips and cash considerations to New York Yankees for OF Rondell White (March 19, 2003).

2003 GAMES PLAYED BY POSITION (MLB): DH—15, OF—3.

								BATTING										FIELDING	
Year — Team (League)	Pos.	G	AB	R	H	2B	3B	HR	RBI	BB	SO	HBP	GDP	SB-CS	Avg.	OBP	SLG	OPS	E	Pct.
1994— Jamestown (NYP)	OF	65	235	37	70	18	6	5	41	23	32	4	1	9-7	.298	.365	.489	.854	5	.941
1995— Lakeland (Fla. St.)	OF	122	454	61	129	32	6	16	72	48	80	4	9	13-3	.284	.355	.487	.842	5	.973
1996— Jacksonville (Sou.)	OF	83	311	63	102	23	2	27	75	32	61	8	11	3-2	.328	.403	.675	1.079	5	.955
— Toledo (Int'l)	OF	51	180	32	53	14	1	6	24	22	44	0	1	5-1	.294	.369	.483	.853	1	.987
1997— Detroit (A.L.)	OF-DH	44	123	14	28	5	0	4	13	15	35	0	2	3-1	.228	.307	.366	.673	0	1.000
— Toledo (Int'l)	OF-DH	90	319	56	80	15	1	28	75	38	91	5	1	2-2	.251	.336	.567	.903	3	.972
1998— Tampa Bay (A.L.)	OF-DH	59	199	28	57	18	1	12	35	16	45	0	4	0-2	.286	.338	.568	.906	0	1.000
— Durham (Int'l)	OF	57	217	46	63	12	0	16	48	38	42	0	2	6-1	.290	.395	.567	.961	2	.983
1999— Durham (Int'l) OF-DH-3B		47	186	25	50	12	0	7	31	15	36	0	1	0-0	.269	.317	.446	.763	3	.961
— Tampa Bay (A.L.)	OF-DH	82	283	49	82	19	0	14	39	43	37	1	7	0-2	.290	.384	.505	.889	1	.993
2000— Tampa Bay (A.L.)	OF-DH	66	189	19	52	11	2	7	33	21	30	2	5	3-0	.275	.352	.466	.818	0	1.000
— New York (N.L.)	OF	36	56	9	13	2	0	3	12	8	19	0	1	1-0	.232	.323	.429	.752	1	.963
2001— San Diego (N.L.)	OF-DH	142	490	66	128	20	3	25	92	48	78	4	10	2-2	.261	.330	.467	.797	4	.985
2002— San Diego (N.L.)	OF-DH	133	403	54	98	16	1	17	56	53	71	3	6	1-3	.243	.333	.414	.748	5	.973
2003— New York (A.L.)	DH-OF	22	55	4	11	5	0	0	5	6	10	0	1	0-0	.200	.279	.291	.570	0	1.000
American League totals (5 years)		273	849	114	230	58	3	37	125	101	157	3	19	6-5	.271	.349	.477	.826	1	.997
National League totals (3 years)		311	949	129	239	38	4	45	160	109	168	7	19	4-5	.252	.331	.443	.773	10	.979
Major League totals (7 years)		584	1798	243	469	96	7	82	285	210	325	10	38	10-10	.261	.339	.459	.798	11	.986

TRUBY, CHRIS   3B

PERSONAL: Born December 9, 1973, in Palm Springs, Calif. ... 6-2/210. ... Bats right, throws right. ... Full name: Christopher John Truby. ... High school: Damien (Hawaii).

TRANSACTIONS/CAREER NOTES: Signed as non-drafted free agent by Houston Astros organization (August 25, 1992). ... On disabled list (April 26-May 11, 1999). ... Traded by Astros to Montreal Expos for 3B/OF Geoff Blum (March 12, 2002). ... Traded by Expos to Detroit Tigers for 2B Jose Macias (May 16, 2002). ... On Detroit disabled list (July 4-29, 2002); included rehabilitation assignment to Toledo (July 26-29). ... Granted free agency (October 15, 2002). ... Signed by Tampa Bay Devil Rays organization (January 6, 2003). ... Contract purchased by Tampa Bay from Durham (April 28, 2003). ... Designated for assignment by Tampa Bay (May 9, 2003). ... Sent outright to Durham by Tampa Bay (May 13, 2003).

2003 GAMES PLAYED BY POSITION (MLB): 3B—13.

								BATTING										FIELDING	
Year — Team (League)	Pos.	G	AB	R	H	2B	3B	HR	RBI	BB	SO	HBP	GDP	SB-CS	Avg.	OBP	SLG	OPS	E	Pct.
1993— GC Astros (GCL)	3B-SS	57	215	30	49	10	2	1	24	22	30	1	5	16-1	.228	.301	.307	.608	§ 26	.885
— Osceola (Fla. St.)	3B	3	13	0	0	0	0	0	0	0	2	0	0	0-0	.000	.000	.000	.000	2	.857
1994— Quad City (Midw.)	3B-1B	36	111	12	24	4	1	2	19	3	29	2	3	1-1	.216	.246	.324	.570	6	.933
— Auburn (NY-Penn)	3B	73	282	* 56	* 91	17	6	7	* 61	23	48	3	8	20-4	.323	.370	.500	.870	• 27	.882
1995— Quad City (Midw.)	3B-OF	118	400	68	93	23	4	9	64	41	66	3	11	27-8	.233	.306	.378	.684	38	.903
1996— Quad City (Midw.)	3B-1B	109	362	45	91	15	3	8	37	28	74	2	8	6-10	.251	.305	.376	.680	17	.975
1997— Quad City (Midw.)	3B	68	268	34	75	14	1	7	46	22	32	1	8	13-4	.280	.334	.418	.752	15	.926
— Kissimmee (Fla. St.)	2-3-S-1	57	199	23	49	11	0	2	29	8	40	2	4	8-3	.246	.278	.332	.610	16	.916
1998— Kissimmee (Fla. St.)	3B	52	212	36	66	16	1	14	48	19	30	3	2	6-1	.311	.373	.594	.967	9	.951
— Jackson (Texas)	3B-1B	80	308	46	89	20	5	16	63	20	50	4	5	8-3	.289	.335	.542	.878	15	.944
— New Orleans (PCL)	3B	5	17	6	7	1	1	1	1	1	3	0	0	1-0	.412	.444	.765	1.209	1	.917
1999— Jackson (Texas)	3B-SS	124	465	78	131	21	3	28	87	36	88	3	11	20-8	.282	.329	.520	.850	20	.949
2000— New Orleans (PCL)	3B	64	268	31	76	11	3	2	30	17	32	0	7	6-2	.284	.318	.369	.688	12	.943
— Houston (N.L.)	3B	78	258	28	67	15	4	11	59	10	56	5	4	2-1	.260	.295	.477	.772	14	.926
2001— Houston (N.L.)	3B-1B	48	136	11	28	6	1	8	23	13	38	1	1	1-2	.206	.276	.441	.717	6	.924
— New Orleans (PCL)	3B-1B	81	321	53	100	25	6	12	71	24	66	4	11	10-5	.312	.365	.539	.904	11	.973
2002— Montreal (N.L.) 3B-1B-OF		35	105	12	27	5	2	2	7	5	27	1	2	1-1	.257	.297	.400	.697	5	.934
— Detroit (A.L.)	3B	89	277	23	55	13	2	2	15	5	71	2	5	1-1	.199	.215	.282	.496	11	.958
— Toledo (Int'l)	3B	3	12	2	4	0	2	1	1	2	1	0	1	0-0	.333	.429	.917	1.345	2	.818
2003— Tampa Bay (A.L.)	3B	13	43	4	12	3	0	0	3	5	13	0	1	0-0	.279	.354	.349	.703	1	.976
— Durham (Int'l)	3-1-D-P	112	430	57	113	27	0	16	68	44	77	7	11	4-6	.263	.339	.437	.776	11	.977
American League totals (2 years)		102	320	27	67	16	2	2	18	10	84	2	6	1-1	.209	.234	.291	.525	12	.961
National League totals (3 years)		161	499	51	122	26	7	21	89	28	121	7	7	4-4	.244	.290	.451	.741	25	.928
Major League totals (4 years)		263	819	78	189	42	9	23	107	38	205	9	13	5-5	.231	.269	.388	.657	37	.943

TSAO, CHIN-HUI   P

PERSONAL: Born June 2, 1981, in Hua-Lien, Taiwan. ... 6-2/177. ... Throws right, bats right. ... Full name: Chin-Hui Tsao.

TRANSACTIONS/CAREER NOTES: Signed by Colorado Rockies organization as a non-drafted free agent (October 7, 1999).

CAREER HITTING: 2-for-13 (.154), 2 R, 1 2B, 0 3B, 0 HR, 0 RBI.

Year League	W	L	Pct.	ERA	WHIP	G	GS	CG	ShO	Hld.	Sv.-Opp.	IP	H	R	ER	HR	BB-IBB	SO	Avg.
2000— Asheville (S. Atl.)	11	8	.579	2.73	1.10	24	24	0	0	...	0-...	145.0	119	54	44	8	40-0	187	.220
2001— Salem (Caro.)	0	4	.000	4.67	1.62	4	4	0	0	...	0-...	17.1	23	11	9	1	5-0	18	.333
2002— Tri-Cities (N'west)	0	0	...	0.00	0.73	3	3	0	0	...	0-...	11.0	6	2	0	0	2-0	16	.150
— Salem (Caro.)	4	2	.667	2.09	0.97	9	9	0	0	...	0-...	47.1	34	13	11	3	12-0	45	.204
2003— Tulsa (Texas)	11	4	.733	2.46	1.01	18	18	0	0	...	0-...	113.1	88	34	31	7	26-0	125	.214
— Colorado (N.L.)	3	3	.500	6.02	1.57	9	8	0	0	0	0-0	43.1	48	30	29	11	20-1	29	.284
Major League totals (1 year)	**3**	**3**	**.500**	**6.02**	**1.57**	**9**	**8**	**0**	**0**	**0**	**0-0**	**43.1**	**48**	**30**	**29**	**11**	**20-1**	**29**	**.284**

TUCKER, MICHAEL — OF

PERSONAL: Born June 25, 1971, in South Boston, Va. ... 6-2/195. ... Bats left, throws right. ... Full name: Michael Anthony Tucker. ... High school: Bluestone (Skipwith, Va.). ... College: Longwood College (Va.).

TRANSACTIONS/CAREER NOTES: Selected by Kansas City Royals organization in first round (10th pick overall) of free-agent draft (June 1, 1992). ... On Kansas City disabled list (June 4-21 and August 28, 1996-remainder of season); included rehabilitation assignment to Wichita (June 15-21). ... Traded by Royals to Atlanta Braves for OF Jermaine Dye and P Jamie Walker (March 27, 1997). ... Traded by Braves with P Denny Neagle and P Rob Bell to Cincinnati Reds for 2B Bret Boone and P Mike Remlinger (November 10, 1998). ... Traded by Reds to Chicago Cubs for P Chris Booker and P Ben Shaffar (July 20, 2001). ... Traded by Cubs to Royals for a player to be named later (December 19, 2001); Cubs acquired P Shawn Sonnier to complete deal (March 15, 2002). ... Placed on 15-day disabled list (August 5, 2003). ... Removed from 15-day disabled list (September 24, 2003).

2003 GAMES PLAYED BY POSITION (MLB): OF—85, DH—15.

Year Team (League)	Pos.	G	AB	R	H	2B	3B	HR	RBI	BB	SO	HBP	GDP	SB-CS	Avg.	OBP	SLG	OPS	FIELDING E	Pct.
1993— Wilmington (Caro.)	2B	61	239	42	73	14	2	6	44	34	49	2	0	12-2	.305	.391	.456	.847	10	.965
— Memphis (Sou.)	2B	72	244	38	68	7	4	9	35	42	51	6	1	12-5	.279	.392	.451	.843	13	.962
1994— Omaha (A.A.)	OF	132	485	75	134	16	7	21	77	69	111	3	6	11-3	.276	.366	.468	.834	•7	.967
1995— Kansas City (A.L.)	OF-DH	62	177	23	46	10	0	4	17	18	51	1	3	2-3	.260	.332	.384	.716	1	.986
— Omaha (A.A.)	OF	71	275	37	84	18	4	4	28	24	39	4	3	11-4	.305	.367	.444	.811	2	.986
1996— Kansas City (A.L.)	OF-1B-DH	108	339	55	88	18	4	12	53	40	69	7	7	10-4	.260	.346	.442	.789	2	.992
— Wichita (Texas)	OF-1B	6	20	4	9	1	3	0	7	5	4	0	0	0-2	.450	.538	.800	1.338	0	1.000
1997— Atlanta (N.L.)	OF	138	499	80	141	25	7	14	56	44	116	6	7	12-7	.283	.347	.445	.792	5	.980
1998— Atlanta (N.L.)	OF	130	414	54	101	27	3	13	46	49	112	3	4	8-3	.244	.327	.418	.745	1	.995
1999— Cincinnati (N.L.)	OF	133	296	55	75	8	5	11	44	37	81	3	5	11-4	.253	.338	.426	.764	2	.990
2000— Cincinnati (N.L.)	OF-2B	148	270	55	72	13	4	15	36	44	64	7	6	13-6	.267	.381	.511	.892	5	.969
2001— Cincinnati (N.L.)	OF	86	231	31	56	10	1	7	30	23	55	1	4	12-5	.242	.308	.385	.693	3	.978
— Chicago (N.L.)	OF-1B	63	205	31	54	9	7	5	31	23	47	1	4	4-3	.263	.339	.449	.788	3	.978
2002— Kansas City (A.L.)	O-D-1-2	144	475	65	118	27	6	12	56	56	105	3	5	23-9	.248	.330	.406	.737	4	.985
2003— Kansas City (A.L.)	OF-DH	104	389	61	102	20	5	13	55	39	88	2	8	8-10	.262	.331	.440	.771	2	.989
American League totals (4 years)		418	1380	204	354	75	15	41	181	153	313	13	23	43-26	.257	.335	.422	.756	9	.988
National League totals (5 years)		698	1915	306	499	92	27	65	243	220	475	21	30	60-28	.261	.341	.439	.779	19	.982
Major League totals (9 years)		1116	3295	510	853	167	42	106	424	373	788	34	53	103-54	.259	.338	.432	.770	28	.985

TUCKER, T.J. — P

PERSONAL: Born August 20, 1978, in Clearwater, Fla. ... 6-3/265. ... Throws right, bats right. ... Full name: Thomas John Tucker. ... High school: River Ridge (New Port Richey, Fla.).

TRANSACTIONS/CAREER NOTES: Selected by Montreal Expos organization in supplemental round ("sandwich pick" between first and second round, 47th pick overall) of free-agent draft (June 3, 1997); pick received as compensation for Chicago Cubs signing P Mel Rojas. ... On Harrisburg disabled list (April 6-23, 2000). ... On Montreal disabled list (June 10, 2000-remainder of season). ... On Harrisburg disabled list (May 25-June 6, 2001). ... On disabled list (August 18-September 6, 2002). ... Optioned to Edmonton (July 9, 2003). ... Recalled from Edmonton (July 31, 2003).

CAREER HITTING: 9-for-24 (.375), 3 R, 1 2B, 0 3B, 0 HR, 0 RBI.

Year League	W	L	Pct.	ERA	WHIP	G	GS	CG	ShO	Hld.	Sv.-Opp.	IP	H	R	ER	HR	BB-IBB	SO	Avg.
1997— GC Expos (GCL)	1	0	1.000	1.93	1.29	3	2	0	0	...	0-...	4.2	5	1	1	0	1-0	11	.278
1998— GC Expos (GCL)	1	0	1.000	0.75	0.78	7	7	0	0	...	0-...	36.0	23	5	3	1	5-0	40	.178
— Vermont (NY-P)	3	1	.750	2.18	1.18	6	6	0	0	...	0-...	33.0	24	9	8	0	15-0	34	.205
— Jupiter (FSL)	1	1	.500	1.00	0.56	2	1	0	0	...	0-...	9.0	5	1	1	0	0-0	10	.167
1999— Jupiter (FSL)	5	1	.833	1.23	0.91	7	7	0	0	...	0-...	44.0	24	7	6	2	16-0	35	.156
— Harrisburg (Eastern)	8	5	.615	4.10	1.27	19	19	1	1	...	0-...	116.1	110	55	53	12	38-0	85	.249
2000— Harrisburg (Eastern)	2	1	.667	3.60	1.11	8	8	0	0	...	0-...	45.0	33	19	18	7	17-0	24	.208
— Montreal (N.L.)	0	1	.000	11.57	2.00	2	2	0	0	0	0-0	7.0	11	9	9	5	3-0	2	.344
2001— Harrisburg (Eastern)	5	5	.500	3.73	1.39	13	13	0	0	...	0-...	82.0	77	38	34	10	37-0	57	.255
— Ottawa (Int'l)	3	5	.375	3.11	1.20	14	14	1	0	...	0-...	84.0	68	42	29	11	33-0	63	.220
2002— Montreal (N.L.)	6	3	.667	4.11	1.63	57	0	0	0	17	4-7	61.1	69	32	28	5	31-9	42	.290
2003— Edmonton (PCL)	1	0	1.000	2.76	1.41	3	3	0	0	...	0-...	16.1	16	5	5	2	7-0	6	.262
— Montreal (N.L.)	2	3	.400	4.73	1.38	45	7	0	0	3	0-2	80.0	90	49	42	8	20-1	47	.278
Major League totals (3 years)	**8**	**7**	**.533**	**4.79**	**1.51**	**104**	**9**	**0**	**0**	**20**	**4-9**	**148.1**	**170**	**90**	**79**	**18**	**54-10**	**91**	**.286**

TURNBOW, DERRICK — P

PERSONAL: Born January 25, 1978, in Union City, Tenn. ... 6-3/200. ... Throws right, bats right. ... Full name: Thomas Derrick Turnbow. ... High school: Franklin (Tenn.).

TRANSACTIONS/CAREER NOTES: Selected by Philadelphia Phillies organization in fifth round of free-agent draft (June 3, 1997). ... Selected by Anaheim Angels from Phillies organization in Rule 5 major league draft (December 13, 1999). ... On disabled list (April 20, 2001-remainder of season). ... On Arkansas disabled list (April 4-June 28 and July 18, 2002-remainder of season). ... Recalled from Salt Lake by Anaheim (April 23, 2003). ... Optioned to Salt Lake by Anaheim (April 28, 2003). ... Recalled by Anaheim from Salt Lake (September 1, 2003).

CAREER HITTING: 0-for-0 (.000), 0 R, 0 2B, 0 3B, 0 HR, 0 RBI.

Year League	W	L	Pct.	ERA	WHIP	G	GS	CG	ShO	Hld.	Sv.-Opp.	IP	H	R	ER	HR	BB-IBB	SO	Avg.
1997— Martinsville (App.)	1	3	.250	7.40	2.05	7	7	0	0	...	0-...	24.1	34	29	20	5	16-1	7	.354
1998— Martinsville (App.)	2	6	.250	5.01	1.31	13	13	1	0	...	0-...	70.0	66	44	39	7	26-1	45	.249
1999— Piedmont (S. Atl.)	12	8	.600	3.35	1.14	26	26	•4	1	...	0-...	161.0	130	67	60	10	53-0	149	.221
2000— Anaheim (A.L.)	0	0	...	4.74	1.89	24	1	0	0	1	0-0	38.0	36	21	20	7	36-0	25	.254
2001— Arkansas (Texas)	0	0	...	2.57	1.21	3	3	0	0	...	0-...	14.0	12	4	4	0	5-0	11	.240
2002— Ariz. Angels (Ariz.)	0	1	.000	4.50	1.00	3	3	0	0	...	0-...	8.0	5	5	4	0	3-0	12	.161
— Rancho Cuca. (Calif.)	0	0	...	5.25	2.08	13	0	0	0	...	0-...	12.0	16	11	7	1	9-0	14	.320
2003— Arkansas (Texas)	1	0	1.000	0.64	1.14	7	0	0	0	...	3-...	14.0	4	0	0	0	5-0	19	.087
— Salt Lake (PCL)	1	2	.333	5.73	1.67	35	0	0	0	...	2-...	55.0	68	36	35	5	24-0	63	.300
— Anaheim (A.L.)	2	0	1.000	0.59	0.65	11	0	0	0	0	0-0	15.1	7	1	1	0	3-0	15	.140
Major League totals (2 years)	**2**	**0**	**1.000**	**3.54**	**1.54**	**35**	**1**	**0**	**0**	**1**	**0-0**	**53.1**	**43**	**22**	**21**	**7**	**39-0**	**40**	**.224**

TYNER, JASON   OF

PERSONAL: Born April 23, 1977, in Beaumont, Texas. ... 6-1/168. ... Bats left, throws left. ... Full name: Jason Renyt Tyner. ... Name pronounced: tie-ner. ... High school: Westbrook (Beaumont, Texas). ... College: Texas A&M.

TRANSACTIONS/CAREER NOTES: Selected by New York Mets organization in first round (21st pick overall) of free-agent draft (June 2, 1998). ... Traded by Mets with P Paul Wilson to Tampa Bay Devil Rays for P Rick White and OF Bubba Trammell (July 28, 2000).

2003 GAMES PLAYED BY POSITION (MLB): OF—32, DH—4.

Year	Team (League)	Pos.	G	AB	R	H	2B	3B	HR	RBI	BB	SO	HBP	GDP	SB-CS	Avg.	OBP	SLG	OPS	E	Pct.
1998—St. Lucie (Fla. St.)		OF	50	201	30	61	2	3	0	16	17	20	1	3	15-11	.303	.361	.343	.704	2	.976
1999—Binghamton (East.)		OF	129	518	91	162	19	5	0	33	62	46	1	8	49-15	.313	.387	.369	.755	2	.993
—Norfolk (Int'l)		OF	3	8	0	0	0	0	0	0	0	5	0	0	0-0	.000	.000	.000	.000	0	1.000
2000—Norfolk (Int'l)		OF	84	327	54	105	5	2	0	28	30	32	2	3	33-14	.321	.380	.349	.728	1	.995
—New York (N.L.)		OF	13	41	3	8	2	0	0	5	1	4	1	1	1-1	.195	.222	.244	.466	2	.920
—Tampa Bay (A.L.)		OF-DH	37	83	6	20	2	0	0	8	4	12	1	1	6-1	.241	.281	.265	.546	1	1.000
2001—Durham (Int'l)		OF	39	157	25	49	2	1	0	12	15	10	2	1	11-5	.312	.371	.338	.708	0	1.000
—Tampa Bay (A.L.)		OF	105	396	51	111	8	5	0	21	15	42	3	6	31-6	.280	.311	.326	.637	5	.978
2002—Tampa Bay (A.L.)		OF-DH	44	168	17	36	2	1	0	9	7	19	1	1	7-1	.214	.249	.238	.487	1	.990
—Durham (Int'l)		OF	88	351	59	102	12	4	0	27	34	27	6	3	20-7	.291	.362	.348	.710	1	.994
2003—Tampa Bay (A.L.)		OF-DH	46	90	12	25	7	0	0	6	10	12	0	1	2-1	.278	.350	.356	.706	2	.962
—Durham (Int'l)		OF-DH	65	275	34	89	11	5	0	24	22	25	1	5	10-7	.324	.372	.400	.772	1	.993
American League totals (4 years)			232	737	86	192	19	6	0	44	36	85	5	9	46-9	.261	.298	.303	.601	8	.982
National League totals (1 year)			13	41	3	8	2	0	0	5	1	4	1	1	1-1	.195	.222	.244	.466	2	.920
Major League totals (4 years)			245	778	89	200	21	6	0	49	37	89	6	10	47-10	.257	.294	.299	.594	10	.978

UGUETO, LUIS   SS

PERSONAL: Born February 15, 1979, in Caracas, Venezuela. ... 5-11/170. ... Bats both, throws right. ... Full name: Luis Enrique Ugueto. ... High school: Liceo Juan Pablo II (Macaracuay, Venezuela).

TRANSACTIONS/CAREER NOTES: Signed as non-drafted free agent by Florida Marlins organization (April 28, 1996). ... Selected by Pittsburgh Pirates from Marlins organization in Rule 5 major league draft (December 13, 2001). ... Traded by Pirates to Seattle Mariners for cash considerations (December 13, 2001). ... On Seattle disabled list (August 8-September 1, 2002); included rehabilitation assignment to Tacoma (August 19-September 1). ... Recalled by Seattle from San Antonio (June 15, 2003). ... Optioned to San Antonio by Seattle (June 28, 2003). ... Called up by Seattle from San Antonio (July 4, 2003). ... Recalled from San Antonio of the Texas League (July 9, 2003). ... Optioned to Tacoma by Seattle (August 1, 2003). ... Recalled by Seattle from Tacoma (September 15, 2003).

2003 GAMES PLAYED BY POSITION (MLB): 2B—4, DH—3, 3B—1, SS—1.

Year	Team (League)	Pos.	G	AB	R	H	2B	3B	HR	RBI	BB	SO	HBP	GDP	SB-CS	Avg.	OBP	SLG	OPS	E	Pct.
1996—Dom. Marlins (DSL)		SS	70	240	37	61	4	2	0	12	41	33	...		14-...	.254	...	.288	...	34	.912
1997—Venez. Marlins (VSL)			50	111	17	20	3	2	0	17	18	16	...		7-...	.180	...	.243	...		
1998—Brevard County (FSL)		SS	3	11	0	2	0	0	0	0	0	5	0	0	0-0	.182	.182	.182	.364	2	.857
—GC Marlins (GCL)		SS	50	166	20	38	8	2	0	15	8	37	2	2	7-1	.229	.270	.301	.571	15	.925
1999—Brevard County (FSL)		SS	12	30	1	4	0	0	0	3	7	5	0	3	1-0	.133	.297	.133	.431	2	.958
—GC Marlins (GCL)		DH	1	3	0	0	0	0	0	2	1	0	0	0	0-0	.000	.200	.000	.200	...	...
—Utica (N.Y.-Penn)		SS	56	217	33	60	11	2	1	26	18	46	1	4	9-4	.276	.335	.359	.694	17	.940
2000—Kane Co. (Midw.)		SS	114	393	43	92	13	2	1	32	28	83	5	10	12-14	.234	.291	.285	.576	33	.941
2001—Brevard County (FSL)		2B-SS	121	392	53	103	12	5	3	43	38	96	2	7	22-7	.263	.330	.342	.672	30	.950
2002—Seattle (A.L.)		D-2-S-3	62	23	19	5	0	0	1	1	2	8	0	0	8-4	.217	.280	.348	.628	3	.923
—Tacoma (PCL)		SS	12	51	5	13	1	0	0	5	3	13	0	0	2-1	.255	.291	.275	.565	0	1.000
2003—Tacoma (PCL)		SS	8	26	9	8	3	0	2	4	5	4	0	0	2-0	.308	.419	.654	1.073	3	.936
—San Antonio (Texas)		2-S-3-D	89	350	53	91	12	2	1	40	27	75	1	7	25-10	.260	.312	.314	.627	19	.953
—Seattle (A.L.)		2-D-3-S	12	5	4	1	0	0	0	1	1	0	0	0	2-0	.200	.333	.200	.533	0	1.000
Major League totals (2 years)			74	28	23	6	0	0	1	2	3	8	0	0	10-4	.214	.290	.321	.612	3	.932

URBINA, UGUETH   P

PERSONAL: Born February 15, 1974, in Caracas, Venezuela. ... 6-0/205. ... Throws right, bats right. ... Full name: Ugueth Urtain Urbina. ... Name pronounced: oo-get oor-bee-NAH. ... High school: Liceo Peres Bonalde de Miranda (Miranda, Venezuela).

TRANSACTIONS/CAREER NOTES: Signed as non-drafted free agent by Montreal Expos organization (July 2, 1990). ... On disabled list (April 8-17, 1994). ... On temporarily inactive list (May 9-June 6, 1994). ... On Ottawa disabled list (August 10-September 14, 1995). ... On disabled list (May 9, 2000-remainder of season). ... Traded by Expos to Boston Red Sox for P Tomo Ohka and P Rich Rundles (July 31, 2001). ... Granted free agency (October 28, 2002). ... Signed by Texas Rangers (December 20, 2002). ... Traded by Rangers to Florida Marlins for 1B Adriana Gonzalez, P Ryan Snare and OF Will Smith (July 11, 2003).

CAREER HITTING: 5-for-53 (.094), 3 R, 0 2B, 0 3B, 0 HR, 1 RBI.

Year	League	W	L	Pct.	ERA	WHIP	G	GS	CG	ShO	Hld.	Sv.-Opp.	IP	H	R	ER	HR	BB-IBB	SO	Avg.
1991—GC Expos (GCL)		3	3	.500	2.29	1.08	10	10	3	1	...	0-...	63.0	58	24	16	2	10-0	51	.244
1992—Albany (S. Atl.)		7	•13	.350	3.22	1.16	24	24	5	2	...	0-...	142.1	111	68	51	14	54-0	100	.215
1993—Burlington (Midw.)		2	3	.400	4.50	1.37	10	8	0	0	...	0-...	46.0	41	31	23	7	22-1	30	.105
—Harrisburg (Eastern)		4	5	.444	3.99	1.40	11	11	3	1	...	0-...	70.0	66	32	31	5	32-1	45	.259
1994—Harrisburg (Eastern)		9	3	.750	3.28	1.14	21	21	0	0	...	0-...	120.2	95	49	44	11	43-0	86	.216
1995—W.P. Beach (FSL)		1	0	1.000	0.00	0.56	2	2	0	0	...	0-...	9.0	4	0	0	0	1-0	11	.143
—Ottawa (Int'l)		6	2	.750	3.04	1.06	13	11	2	1	...	0-...	68.0	46	26	23	1	26-0	55	.191
—Montreal (N.L.)		2	2	.500	6.17	1.71	7	4	0	0	0	0-0	23.1	26	17	16	6	14-1	15	.280
1996—W.P. Beach (FSL)		1	1	.500	1.29	1.14	3	3	0	0	...	0-...	14.0	13	3	2	0	3-0	21	.255
—Ottawa (Int'l)		2	0	1.000	2.66	0.97	5	5	0	0	...	0-...	23.2	17	9	7	2	6-0	28	.195
—Montreal (N.L.)		10	5	.667	3.71	1.28	33	17	0	0	6	0-1	114.0	102	54	47	18	44-4	108	.234
1997—Montreal (N.L.)		5	8	.385	3.78	1.26	63	0	0	0	1	27-32	64.1	52	29	27	9	29-2	84	.215
1998—Montreal (N.L.)		6	3	.667	1.30	1.01	64	0	0	0	0	34-38	69.1	37	11	10	2	33-2	94	.157
1999—Montreal (N.L.)		6	6	.500	3.69	1.26	71	0	0	0	0	*41-50	75.2	59	35	31	6	36-6	100	.208
2000—Montreal (N.L.)		0	1	.000	4.05	1.20	13	0	0	0	0	8-10	13.1	11	6	6	1	5-0	22	.224
2001—Montreal (N.L.)		2	1	.667	4.24	1.35	45	0	0	0	1	15-18	46.2	42	24	22	8	21-1	57	.236
—Boston (A.L.)		0	1	.000	2.25	0.95	19	0	0	0	2	9-10	20.0	16	5	5	1	3-0	32	.219
2002—Boston (A.L.)		1	6	.143	3.00	1.07	61	0	0	0	0	40-46	60.0	44	21	20	8	20-5	71	.202
2003—Texas (A.L.)		0	4	.000	4.19	1.32	39	0	0	0	0	26-30	38.2	33	19	18	6	18-2	41	.232
—Florida (N.L.)		3	0	1.000	1.41	0.94	33	0	0	0	11	6-8	38.1	23	6	6	2	13-0	37	.174
American League totals (3 years)		1	11	.083	3.26	1.13	119	0	0	0	2	75-86	118.2	93	45	43	15	41-7	144	.215
National League totals (8 years)		34	26	.567	3.34	1.23	329	21	0	0	19	131-157	445.0	352	182	165	52	195-16	517	.213
Major League totals (9 years)		35	37	.486	3.32	1.21	448	21	0	0	21	206-243	563.2	445	227	208	67	236-23	661	.214

URIBE, JUAN — SS

PERSONAL: Born July 22, 1979, in Bani, Dominican Republic. ... 5-11/173. ... Bats right, throws right. ... Full name: Juan C. Uribe. ... Name pronounced: ohh-ree-bay. ... High school: Abel Uribe (Dominican Republic).

TRANSACTIONS/CAREER NOTES: Signed as non-drafted free agent by Colorado Rockies organization (January 15, 1997). ... On disabled list (March 18, 2003). ... Sent to Visalia on rehab assignment (May 26, 2003). ... Recalled by Colorado from Tulsa rehab assignment (June 3, 2003). ... Reinstated from 15-day disabled list (June 3, 2003).

2003 GAMES PLAYED BY POSITION (MLB): SS—74, 2B—11, OF—1.

									BATTING									FIELDING	
Year Team (League)	Pos.	G	AB	R	H	2B	3B	HR	RBI	BB	SO	HBP	GDP	SB-CS	Avg.	OBP	SLG	OPS	E	Pct.
1997— DSL Rockies (DSL)		65	234	32	63	12	0	0	29	31	22	...	...	7-...	.269	...	.321	...	...	...
1998— Ariz. Rockies (Ariz.)	SS	40	148	25	41	5	3	0	17	12	25	3	1	8-1	.277	.339	.351	.691	14	.927
1999— Asheville (S. Atl.)	SS	125	430	57	115	28	3	9	46	20	79	6	12	11-7	.267	.307	.409	.716	38	.938
2000— Salem (Caro.)	SS	134	485	64	124	22	7	13	65	38	100	4	11	22-5	.256	.314	.410	.724	26	.961
2001— Carolina (Sou.)	SS	3	13	1	3	1	0	0	1	0	4	0	1	1-0	.231	.231	.308	.538	2	.833
— Colorado (N.L.)	SS	72	273	32	82	15	11	8	53	8	55	2	6	3-0	.300	.325	.524	.849	5	.983
— Colo. Springs (PCL)	SS	74	281	40	87	27	7	7	48	12	43	2	8	11-8	.310	.340	.530	.870	16	.960
2002— Colorado (N.L.)	SS	155	566	69	136	25	7	6	49	34	120	5	17	9-2	.240	.286	.341	.627	27	.966
2003— Visalia (Calif.)	2B-SS	2	9	4	5	1	0	0	1	1	0	0	1	0-0	.556	.600	.667	1.267	0	1.000
— Tulsa (Texas)	2-3-S-OF	5	20	3	5	2	0	1	4	0	2	0	0	0-0	.250	.238	.500	.738	0	1.000
— Colorado (N.L.) SS-2B-OF		87	316	45	80	19	3	10	33	17	60	3	3	7-2	.253	.297	.427	.724	12	.974
Major League totals (3 years)		314	1155	146	298	59	21	24	135	59	235	10	26	19-4	.258	.298	.408	.706	44	.972

UTLEY, CHASE — 2B/3B

PERSONAL: Born December 17, 1978, in Pasadena, Calif. ... 6-1/170. ... Bats left, throws right. ... Full name: Chase Cameron Utley. ... High school: Long Beach Poly (Calif.). ... College: UCLA.

TRANSACTIONS/CAREER NOTES: Selected by Philadelphia Phillies organization in first round (15th pick overall) of free-agent draft (June 5, 2000).

2003 GAMES PLAYED BY POSITION (MLB): 2B—37.

									BATTING									FIELDING	
Year Team (League)	Pos.	G	AB	R	H	2B	3B	HR	RBI	BB	SO	HBP	GDP	SB-CS	Avg.	OBP	SLG	OPS	E	Pct.
2000— Batavia (NY-Penn)	2B	40	153	21	47	13	1	2	22	18	23	2	3	5-3	.307	.383	.444	.827	3	.983
2001— Clearwater (FSL)	2B	122	467	65	120	25	2	16	59	37	88	12	6	19-8	.257	.324	.422	.746	17	.970
2002— Scran./W.B. (I.L.)	3B	125	464	73	122	39	1	17	70	46	89	20	5	8-3	.263	.352	.461	.813	28	.918
2003— Scran./W.B. (I.L.)	2B	113	431	80	139	26	2	18	77	41	75	11	3	10-4	.323	.390	.517	.907	13	.978
— Philadelphia (N.L.)	2B	43	134	13	32	10	1	2	21	11	22	6	3	2-0	.239	.322	.373	.696	3	.983
Major League totals (1 year)		43	134	13	32	10	1	2	21	11	22	6	3	2-0	.239	.322	.373	.696	3	.983

VALDERRAMA, CARLOS — OF

PERSONAL: Born November 30, 1977, in Bachaquero, Venezuela. ... 5-11/175. ... Bats right, throws right. ... Full name: Carlos Alberto Valderrama. ... Name pronounced: val-der-RAH-ma.

TRANSACTIONS/CAREER NOTES: Signed as non-drafted free agent by San Francisco Giants organization (February 23, 1995). ... On disabled list (May 23-September 3, 2001). ... On Shreveport disabled list (April 4-25, 2002). ... Recalled by San Francisco from Fresno (June 21, 2003). ... Optioned to Fresno by San Francisco (July 2, 2003). ... Recalled by San Francisco from Fresno (September 29, 2003).

2003 GAMES PLAYED BY POSITION (MLB): OF—5, DH—1.

									BATTING									FIELDING	
Year Team (League)	Pos.	G	AB	R	H	2B	3B	HR	RBI	BB	SO	HBP	GDP	SB-CS	Avg.	OBP	SLG	OPS	E	Pct.
1997— Salem-Keizer (NW)	OF	41	138	21	44	7	3	3	28	12	29	0	2	22-0	.319	.368	.478	.847	1	.963
1998— Salem-Keizer (NW)	OF	7	29	5	10	1	0	0	4	1	7	0	2	4-0	.345	.367	.379	.746	0	1.000
1999— Salem-Keizer (NW)	OF	40	134	27	39	3	1	2	18	12	34	0	0	17-2	.291	.349	.373	.722	2	.971
— San Jose (Calif.)	OF	26	90	12	23	2	0	0	12	4	19	0	1	8-4	.256	.287	.278	.565	0	1.000
2000— Bakersfield (Calif.)	OF	121	435	78	137	21	5	13	81	39	96	4	4	54-12	.315	.370	.476	.846	6	.972
2001— Shreveport (Texas)	OF	41	159	29	49	12	2	1	8	18	29	0	1	11-5	.308	.379	.428	.806	0	1.000
2002— Shreveport (Texas)		37	135	13	33	3	1	4	15	10	23	2	3	4-0	.244	.304	.370	.674	0	...
— San Jose (Calif.)		74	299	65	94	19	6	15	45	34	60	0	5	14-5	.314	.384	.569	.953	0	...
2003— Norwich (East.)	OF	65	240	37	74	15	3	1	18	25	34	1	7	13-6	.308	.375	.408	.783	2	.983
— San Francisco (N.L.)	OF-DH	7	7	0	1	0	0	0	0	0	3	0	0	1-0	.143	.143	.143	.286	0	1.000
— Fresno (PCL)	OF-DH	54	202	20	56	5	0	3	10	12	28	2	3	7-8	.277	.324	.347	.671	3	.969
Major League totals (1 year)		7	7	0	1	0	0	0	0	0	3	0	0	1-0	.143	.143	.143	.286	0	1.000

VALDES, ISMAEL — P

PERSONAL: Born August 21, 1973, in Ciudad Victoria, Mexico. ... 6-4/225. ... Throws right, bats right. ... Name pronounced: ees-mah-ALE val-DEZ. ... High school: Mexico (Ciudad Victoria).

TRANSACTIONS/CAREER NOTES: Signed as non-drafted free agent by Los Angeles Dodgers (June 14, 1991). ... Loaned by Dodgers organization to Mexico City Tigers of Mexican League (April 21-June 26, 1992; and March 17-August 19, 1993). ... On disabled list (July 6-28, 1997). ... On Los Angeles disabled list (July 26-September 1, 1998); included rehabilitation assignments to Vero Beach (August 22) and San Bernardino (August 27). ... Traded by Dodgers with 2B Eric Young to Chicago Cubs for P Terry Adams, P Chad Ricketts and a player to be named later (December 12, 1999); Dodgers acquired P Brian Stephenson to complete deal (December 16, 1999). ... On Chicago disabled list (March 20-May 4, 2000); included rehabilitation assignment to Daytona (April 29-May 1). ... Traded by Cubs to Dodgers for P Jamie Arnold, OF Jorge Piedra and cash (July 26, 2000). ... On suspended list (September 12-18, 2000). ... Granted free agency (October 30, 2000). ... Signed by Anaheim Angels (January 4, 2001). ... On disabled list (March 29-April 14 and June 15-July 4, 2001). ... Granted free agency (November 5, 2001). ... Signed by Texas Rangers (January 28, 2002). ... Traded by Rangers to Seattle Mariners for 2B Jermaine Clark and P Derrick Van Dusen (August 18, 2002). ... Granted free agency (October 29, 2002). ... Signed by Rangers (January 15, 2003). ... Placed on 15-day disabled list (April 20, 2003). ... Sent to Frisco by Texas on rehab assignment (May 11, 2003). ... Recalled by Texas from Frisco; reinstated from 15-day disabled list (May 17, 2003). ... Placed on 15-day disabled list (July 24, 2003). ... Sent to Frisco on rehab assignment by Texas (August 8, 2003). ... Recalled from Oklahoma rehab assignment; removed from 15-day disabled list (August 18, 2003).

CAREER HITTING: 40-for-334 (.120), 14 R, 5 2B, 0 3B, 1 HR, 12 RBI.

V

Year	League	W	L	Pct.	ERA	WHIP	G	GS	CG	ShO	Hld.	Sv.-Opp.	IP	H	R	ER	HR	BB-IBB	SO	Avg.
1991— GC Dodgers (GCL)		2	2	.500	2.32	1.13	10	10	0	0	...	0-...	50.1	44	15	13	0	13-0	44	.233
1992— M.C. Tigers (Mex.)		0	0	...	19.64	4.36	5	0	0	0	...	0-...	3.2	15	9	8	1	1-...	2	...
— La Vega (DSL)		3	0	1.000	1.42	1.16	6	0	0	0	...	0-...	38.0	27	9	6	6	17-...	34	...
1993— M.C. Tigers (Mex.)		16	7	.696	3.94	1.42	26	25	11	1	...	0-...	173.2	192	87	76	16	55-...	113	...
— San Antonio (Texas)		1	0	1.000	1.38	0.92	3	2	0	0	...	0-...	13.0	12	2	2	0	0-0	11	.240
1994— San Antonio (Texas)		2	3	.400	3.38	1.18	8	8	0	0	...	0-...	53.1	54	22	20	4	9-1	55	.263
— Albuquerque (PCL)		4	1	.800	3.40	1.27	8	8	0	0	...	0-...	45.0	44	21	17	1	13-0	39	.256
— Los Angeles (N.L.)		3	1	.750	3.18	1.09	21	1	0	0	4	0-0	28.1	21	10	10	2	10-2	28	.206
1995— Los Angeles (N.L.)		13	11	.542	3.05	1.11	33	27	6	2	2	1-1	197.2	168	76	67	17	51-5	150	.228
1996— Los Angeles (N.L.)		15	7	.682	3.32	1.21	33	33	0	0	0	0-0	225.0	219	94	83	20	54-10	173	.251
1997— Los Angeles (N.L.)		10	11	.476	2.65	1.11	30	30	0	0	0	0-0	196.2	171	68	58	16	47-1	140	.234
1998— Los Angeles (N.L.)		11	10	.524	3.98	1.36	27	27	2	2	0	0-0	174.0	171	82	77	17	66-4	122	.256
— Vero Beach (FSL)		0	0	...	0.00	1.00	1	1	0	0	...	0-...	3.0	2	0	0	0	1-0	3	.200
— San Bernardino (Calif.)		1	0	1.000	2.84	1.26	1	1	0	0	...	0-...	6.1	7	2	2	0	1-0	4	.280
1999— Los Angeles (N.L.)		9	14	.391	3.98	1.33	32	32	2	1	0	0-0	203.1	213	97	90	32	58-2	143	.270
2000— Daytona (Fla. St.)		1	0	1.000	1.80	1.20	1	1	0	0	...	0-...	5.0	3	2	1	0	3-0	5	.176
— Chicago (N.L.)		2	4	.333	5.37	1.46	12	12	0	0	0	0-0	67.0	71	40	40	17	27-2	45	.270
— Los Angeles (N.L.)		0	3	.000	6.08	1.65	9	8	0	0	0	0-0	40.0	53	29	27	5	13-0	29	.327
2001— Anaheim (A.L.)		9	13	.409	4.45	1.39	27	27	1	0	0	0-0	163.2	177	82	81	20	50-3	100	.277
2002— Texas (A.L.)		6	9	.400	3.93	1.17	23	23	0	0	0	0-0	146.2	135	65	64	19	36-1	75	.242
— Seattle (A.L.)		2	3	.400	4.93	1.42	8	8	1	0	0	0-0	49.1	59	29	27	7	11-0	27	.299
2003— Frisco (Texas)		1	2	.333	2.03	1.05	3	3	0	0	...	0-...	13.1	12	5	3	0	2-0	6	.235
— Texas (A.L.)		8	8	.500	6.10	1.54	22	22	0	0	0	0-...	115.0	148	83	78	23	29-0	47	.318
American League totals (3 years)		**25**	**33**	**.431**	**4.74**	**1.36**	**80**	**80**	**2**	**0**	**0**	**0-0**	**474.2**	**519**	**259**	**250**	**69**	**126-4**	**249**	**.279**
National League totals (7 years)		**63**	**61**	**.508**	**3.59**	**1.25**	**197**	**170**	**10**	**5**	**6**	**1-1**	**1132.0**	**1087**	**496**	**452**	**126**	**326-26**	**830**	**.251**
Major League totals (10 years)		**88**	**94**	**.484**	**3.93**	**1.28**	**277**	**250**	**12**	**5**	**6**	**1-1**	**1606.2**	**1606**	**755**	**702**	**195**	**452-30**	**1079**	**.260**

VALENT, ERIC — OF

PERSONAL: Born April 4, 1977, in La Mirada, Calif. ... 5-11/198. ... Bats left, throws left. ... Full name: Eric Christian Valent. ... Name pronounced: va-LENT. ... High school: Canyon (Anaheim, Calif.). ... College: UCLA.

TRANSACTIONS/CAREER NOTES: Selected by Detroit Tigers organization in 26th round of free-agent draft (June 1, 1995); did not sign. ... Selected by Philadelphia Phillies organization in supplemental round ('sandwich pick' between first and second round, 42nd pick overall) of free-agent draft (June 2, 1998); pick received for failure to sign 1997 first-round pick J.D. Drew. ... Traded by Phillies to Cincinnati Reds to complete an earlier trade for C Kelly Stinnett(September 2, 2003).

2003 GAMES PLAYED BY POSITION (MLB): OF—8.

									BATTING										FIELDING	
Year	Team (League)	Pos.	G	AB	R	H	2B	3B	HR	RBI	BB	SO	HBP	GDP	SB-CS	Avg.	OBP	SLG	OPS	E	Pct.
1998— Piedmont (S. Atl.)		OF	22	89	24	38	12	0	8	28	14	19	0	0	0-0	.427	.500	.831	1.331	2	.952
— Clearwater (FSL)		OF	34	125	24	33	8	1	5	25	16	29	3	4	1-2	.264	.359	.464	.823	0	1.000
1999— Clearwater (FSL)		OF	134	520	91	150	31	9	20	*106	58	110	5	10	5-3	.288	.359	.498	.857	9	.969
2000— Reading (East.)		OF	128	469	81	121	22	5	22	90	70	89	5	7	2-3	.258	.356	.467	.823	4	.984
2001— Scran./W.B. (I.L.)		OF-1B	117	448	65	122	30	2	21	78	49	105	8	13	0-1	.272	.352	.489	.841	3	.992
— Philadelphia (N.L.)		OF-DH	22	41	3	4	2	0	0	1	4	11	1	0	0-0	.098	.196	.146	.342	0	1.000
2002— Scran./W.B. (I.L.)		OF-1B	140	546	69	137	34	2	9	84	49	94	1	13	0-2	.251	.311	.370	.681	10	.980
— Philadelphia (N.L.)		OF-1B	7	10	1	2	0	0	0	0	3	3	0	1	0-0	.200	.200	.200	.400	1	.750
2003— Scran./W.B. (I.L.)		OF-1B	134	450	62	98	27	2	12	51	60	102	1	5	0-0	.218	.308	.367	.675	8	.974
— Cincinnati (N.L.)		OF	18	42	3	9	0	0	0	1	2	9	0	0	0-0	.214	.250	.214	.464	0	1.000
Major League totals (3 years)			**47**	**93**	**7**	**15**	**2**	**0**	**0**	**2**	**6**	**23**	**1**	**1**	**0-0**	**.161**	**.220**	**.183**	**.403**	**1**	**.979**

VALENTIN, JAVIER — C

PERSONAL: Born September 19, 1975, in Manati, Puerto Rico. ... 5-10/192. ... Bats both, throws right. ... Full name: Jose Javier Valentin. ... Name pronounced: val-en-TEEN. ... High school: Fernando Callejo (Manati, Puerto Rico).

TRANSACTIONS/CAREER NOTES: Selected by Minnesota Twins organization in third round of free-agent draft (June 3, 1993). ... On disabled list (May 25-July 5 and September 4-20, 2000). ... Traded by Twins with P Matt Kinney to Milwaukee Brewers for P Matt Yeatman and P Gerard Oakes (November 15, 2002). ... Traded by Brewers to Tampa Bay Devil Rays for OF Jason Conti (March 24, 2003).

2003 GAMES PLAYED BY POSITION (MLB): C—42, DH—6.

									BATTING										FIELDING	
Year	Team (League)	Pos.	G	AB	R	H	2B	3B	HR	RBI	BB	SO	HBP	GDP	SB-CS	Avg.	OBP	SLG	OPS	E	Pct.
1993— GC Twins (GCL)		3B-DH-C	32	103	18	27	6	1	1	19	14	19	1	1	0-2	.262	.344	.369	.713	5	.966
— Elizabethton (App.)		C	9	24	3	5	1	0	0	3	4	2	1	0	0-0	.208	.345	.250	.595	2	.977
1994— Elizabethton (App.)		3B-C	54	210	23	44	5	0	9	27	15	44	2	9	0-1	.210	.263	.362	.625	12	.966
1995— Fort Wayne (Midw.)		3B-C	112	383	59	124	26	5	19	65	47	75	2	7	0-5	.324	.400	.567	.967	‡23	.974
1996— Fort Myers (FSL)		C-DH-3B	87	338	34	89	26	1	7	54	32	65	4	5	1-0	.263	.330	.408	.738	4	.991
— New Britain (East.)		C-DH-3B	48	165	22	39	8	0	3	14	16	35	1	2	0-3	.236	.308	.339	.647	5	.978
1997— New Britain (East.)		C-DH-3B	102	370	41	90	17	0	8	50	30	61	1	5	2-3	.243	.297	.354	.651	6	.990
— Minnesota (A.L.)		C	4	7	1	2	0	0	0	0	0	3	0	0	0-0	.286	.286	.286	.571	0	1.000
1998— Minnesota (A.L.)		C-DH	55	162	11	32	7	1	3	18	11	30	0	7	0-0	.198	.247	.309	.556	5	.983
1999— Minnesota (A.L.)		C	78	218	22	54	12	1	5	28	22	39	1	2	0-0	.248	.313	.381	.694	1	.998
2000— Salt Lake (PCL)		C	39	140	25	50	16	2	7	35	9	27	1	1	1-0	.357	.397	.650	1.047	1	.994
2001— Edmonton (PCL)		C-3B-1B	121	431	53	121	29	2	17	71	47	108	4	14	0-1	.281	.352	.476	.827	14	.977
2002— Edmonton (PCL)		C-3B-1B	127	455	69	130	33	1	21	80	41	96	5	15	0-1	.286	.346	.501	.847	9	.984
— Minnesota (A.L.)		C	4	4	0	2	0	0	0	0	0	0	0	0	0-0	.500	.500	.500	1.000	0	1.000
2003— Tampa Bay (A.L.)		C-DH	49	135	13	30	7	1	3	15	5	31	1	7	0-0	.222	.254	.356	.609	1	1.000
Major League totals (5 years)			**190**	**526**	**47**	**120**	**26**	**3**	**11**	**61**	**38**	**103**	**2**	**16**	**0-0**	**.228**	**.279**	**.352**	**.631**	**6**	**.994**

VALENTIN, JOSE — SS

PERSONAL: Born October 12, 1969, in Manati, Puerto Rico. ... 5-10/185. ... Bats both, throws right. ... Full name: Jose Antonio Valentin. ... Name pronounced: val-en-TEEN. ... High school: Fernando Callejo (Manati, Puerto Rico).

TRANSACTIONS/CAREER NOTES: Signed as non-drafted free agent by San Diego Padres organization (October 12, 1986). ... On disabled list (April 16-May 1 and May 18-July 11, 1990). ... Traded by Padres with P Ricky Bones and OF Matt Mieske to Milwaukee Brewers for 3B Gary Sheffield and P Geoff Kellogg (March 27, 1992). ... On

V

Milwaukee disabled list (April 14-May 5, 1997); included rehabilitation assignment to Beloit (May 3-5). ... On Milwaukee disabled list (April 13-June 16, 1999); included rehabilitation assignment to Louisville (June 9-16). ... Traded by Brewers with P Cal Eldred to Chicago White Sox for P Jaime Navarro and P John Snyder (January 12, 2000). ... Granted free agency (October 30, 2000). ... Re-signed by White Sox (November 22, 2000). ... On disabled list (June 8-24, 2001).

2003 GAMES PLAYED BY POSITION (MLB): SS—143.

Year	Team (League)	Pos.	G	AB	R	H	2B	3B	HR	RBI	BB	SO	HBP	GDP	SB-CS	Avg.	OBP	SLG	OPS	E	Pct.
1987— Spokane (N'west)		SS	70	244	52	61	8	2	2	24	35	38	1	4	8-5	.250	.346	.324	.670	26	.914
1988— Char., S.C. (SAL)		SS	133	444	56	103	20	1	6	44	45	83	3	10	11-4	.232	.304	.322	.627	60	.911
1989— Riverside (Calif.)		SS	114	381	40	74	10	5	10	41	37	93	5	4	8-7	.194	.273	.325	.598	* 46	.924
— Wichita (Texas)		3B-SS	18	49	8	12	1	0	2	5	5	12	0	1	1-0	.245	.315	.388	.703	8	.899
1990— Wichita (Texas)		SS	11	36	4	10	2	0	0	2	5	7	0	1	2-1	.278	.366	.333	.699	2	.959
1991— Wichita (Texas)		SS	129	447	73	112	22	5	17	68	55	115	4	5	8-6	.251	.335	.436	.771	40	.939
1992— Denver (A.A.)		SS	* 139	492	78	118	19	11	3	45	53	99	5	8	9-4	.240	.317	.341	.658	* 38	.941
— Milwaukee (A.L.)		2B-SS	4	3	1	0	0	0	0	1	0	0	0	0	0-0	.000	.000	.000	.000	1	.667
1993— New Orleans (A.A.)		SS-1B	122	389	56	96	22	5	9	53	47	87	8	3	9-10	.247	.337	.398	.736	29	.951
— Milwaukee (A.L.)		SS	19	53	10	13	1	2	1	7	7	16	1	1	1-0	.245	.344	.396	.740	6	.922
1994— Milwaukee (A.L.)		S-2-3-D	97	285	47	68	19	0	11	46	38	75	2	1	12-3	.239	.330	.421	.751	‡ 20	.961
1995— Milwaukee (A.L.)		SS-DH-3B	112	338	62	74	23	3	11	49	37	83	0	0	16-8	.219	.293	.402	.695	15	.971
1996— Milwaukee (A.L.)		SS	154	552	90	143	33	7	24	95	66	145	0	4	17-4	.259	.336	.475	.811	* 37	.950
1997— Milwaukee (A.L.)		SS-DH	136	494	58	125	23	1	17	58	39	109	4	5	19-8	.253	.310	.407	.717	20	.967
— Beloit (Midw.)		SS	2	6	3	3	1	0	0	1	2	1	0	0	0-0	.500	.625	.667	1.292	0	1.000
1998— Milwaukee (N.L.)		SS-DH	151	428	65	96	24	0	16	49	63	105	1	2	10-7	.224	.323	.393	.716	21	.963
1999— Milwaukee (N.L.)		SS	89	256	45	58	9	5	10	38	48	52	2	3	3-2	.227	.347	.418	.765	22	.937
— Louisville (Int'l)		SS	6	20	6	5	0	0	3	3	4	3	0	0	0-1	.250	.375	.700	1.075	0	1.000
2000— Chicago (A.L.)		SS	144	568	107	155	37	6	25	92	59	106	4	11	19-2	.273	.343	.491	.835	‡ 36	.950
2001— Chicago (A.L.)		3B-SS-OF	124	438	74	113	22	2	28	68	50	114	3	7	9-6	.258	.336	.509	.845	22	.947
2002— Chicago (A.L.)		3B-SS-DH	135	474	70	118	26	4	25	75	43	99	2	9	3-3	.249	.311	.479	.790	19	.957
2003— Chicago (A.L.)		SS	144	503	79	119	26	2	28	74	54	114	3	6	8-3	.237	.313	.463	.776	20	.969
American League totals (10 years)			1069	3708	598	928	210	27	170	565	393	861	19	44	104-37	.250	.323	.459	.782	196	.958
National League totals (2 years)			240	684	110	154	33	5	26	87	111	157	3	5	13-9	.225	.333	.402	.735	43	.953
Major League totals (12 years)			1309	4392	708	1082	243	32	196	652	504	1018	22	49	117-46	.246	.324	.450	.775	239	.957

VALENTINE, JOE — P

PERSONAL: Born December 24, 1979, in Las Vegas, Nev. ... 6-2/195. ... Throws right, bats right. ... Full name: Joseph John Valentine. ... Junior college: Jefferson Davis College (Ala.).

TRANSACTIONS/CAREER NOTES: Selected by Chicago White Sox organization in 26th round of free-agent draft (June 2, 1999). ... Selected by Montreal Expos from White Sox organization in Rule 5 major league draft (December 13, 2001). ... Traded by Expos to Detroit Tigers for cash considerations (December 13, 2001). ... Returned to White Sox organization (April 1, 2002). ... Traded by White Sox with P Keith Foulke, C Mark Johnson and cash to Oakland Athletics for P Billy Koch and two players to be named later (December 3, 2002); White Sox acquired P Neal Cotts and OF Daylon Holt to complete deal (December 16, 2002). ... Traded by A's with P Aaron Harang and P Jeff Bruksch to Cincinnati Reds for OF Jose Guillen (July 30, 2003).

CAREER HITTING: 0-for-0 (.000), 0 R, 0 2B, 0 3B, 0 HR, 0 RBI.

Year	League	W	L	Pct.	ERA	WHIP	G	GS	CG	ShO	Hld.	Sv.-Opp.	IP	H	R	ER	HR	BB-IBB	SO	Avg.
1999— Ariz. White Sox (Ariz.)		0	0	...	0.00	0.69	3	0	0	0	...	0-...	4.1	2	0	0	0	1-0	2	.154
— Bristol (Appal.)		0	0	...	7.02	2.16	11	0	0	0	...	0-...	16.2	27	17	13	2	9-0	14	.360
2000— Bristol (Appal.)		2	1	.667	2.88	1.04	19	0	0	0	...	7-...	25.0	14	10	8	1	12-1	30	.163
2001— Kannapolis (S. Atl.)		2	2	.500	2.93	1.01	30	0	0	0	...	14-...	30.2	21	10	10	0	10-1	33	.194
— Winston-Salem (Caro.)		5	1	.833	1.01	1.01	27	0	0	0	...	8-...	44.2	18	7	5	0	27-3	50	.122
2002— Birmingham (Sou.)		4	1	.800	1.97	1.11	55	0	0	0	...	36-...	59.1	36	16	13	1	30-3	63	.173
2003— Sacramento (PCL)		1	3	.250	4.82	1.55	40	0	0	0	...	4-...	52.1	44	33	28	5	37-3	53	.222
— Cincinnati (N.L.)		0	0	...	18.00	3.00	2	0	0	0	0	0-...	2.0	5	4	4	1	1-0	1	.455
— Louisville (Int'l)		1	0	1.000	0.79	0.71	9	0	0	0	0	1-...	11.1	5	1	1	0	3-0	8	.132
Major League totals (1 year)		0	0	...	18.00	3.00	2	0	0	0	0	0-0	2.0	5	4	4	1	1-0	1	.455

VALVERDE, JOSE — P

PERSONAL: Born July 24, 1979, in San Pedro de Macoris, Dominican Republic. ... 6-4/254. ... Throws right, bats right. ... Full name: Jose Rafael Valverde. ... Name pronounced: val-VARE-day. ... High school: Wscuela San Lorenzo (El Seybo, Dominican Republic).

TRANSACTIONS/CAREER NOTES: Signed as non-drafted free agent by Arizona Diamondbacks organization (February 6, 1997). ... On disabled list (July 10-29, 2000). ... On disabled list (July 23, 2001-remainder of season). ... On Tucson disabled list (May 4-24, 2002). ... Recalled by Arizona from Tucson of the Pacific Coast League (May 30, 2003).

CAREER HITTING: 1-for-1 (1.000), 1 R, 1 2B, 0 3B, 0 HR, 0 RBI.

Year	League	W	L	Pct.	ERA	WHIP	G	GS	CG	ShO	Hld.	Sv.-Opp.	IP	H	R	ER	HR	BB-IBB	SO	Avg.
1999— Ariz. D'backs (Ariz.)		1	2	.333	4.08	1.53	20	0	0	0	...	8-...	28.2	34	21	13	1	10-0	47	.274
— South Bend (Mid.)		0	0	...	0.00	1.50	2	0	0	0	...	0-...	2.2	2	0	0	0	2-0	3	.250
2000— Missoula (Pio.)		1	0	1.000	0.00	0.60	12	0	0	0	...	4-...	11.2	3	0	0	0	4-0	24	.075
— South Bend (Mid.)		0	5	.000	5.40	1.77	31	0	0	0	...	14-...	31.2	31	20	19	1	25-0	39	.254
2001— El Paso (Texas)		2	2	.500	3.92	1.52	39	0	0	0	...	13-...	41.1	36	19	18	1	27-0	72	.225
2002— Tucson (PCL)		2	4	.333	5.85	1.43	49	0	0	0	...	5-...	47.2	45	33	31	8	23-1	65	.250
2003— Tucson (PCL)		1	1	.500	3.10	1.38	22	0	0	0	...	5-...	29.0	26	11	10	1	14-1	26	.236
— Arizona (N.L.)		2	1	.667	2.15	0.99	54	0	0	0	8	10-11	50.1	24	16	12	4	26-2	71	.137
Major League totals (1 year)		2	1	.667	2.15	0.99	54	0	0	0	8	10-11	50.1	24	16	12	4	26-2	71	.137

VANCE, CORY — P

PERSONAL: Born June 20, 1979, in Dayton, Ohio. ... 6-1/195. ... Throws left, bats left. ... Full name: Cory Wade Vance. ... High school: Butler (Vandalia, Ohio). ... College: Georgia Tech.

TRANSACTIONS/CAREER NOTES: Selected by Colorado Rockies organization in fourth round of free-agent draft (June 5, 2000). ... Recalled from Colorado Springs by Colorado (August 19, 2003).

CAREER HITTING: 2-for-8 (.250), 2 R, 1 2B, 0 3B, 0 HR, 0 RBI.

Year	League	W	L	Pct.	ERA	WHIP	G	GS	CG	ShO	Hld.	Sv.-Opp.	IP	H	R	ER	HR	BB-IBB	SO	Avg.
2000—Portland (NW)		0	2	.000	1.11	0.78	7	3	0	0	...	0-...	24.1	11	5	3	1	8-0	26	.138
2001—Salem (Caro.)		10	8	.556	3.10	1.26	26	26	1	0	...	0-...	154.0	129	65	53	9	65-0	142	.232
2002—Carolina (Sou.)		10	8	.556	3.77	1.45	25	25	1	0	...	0-...	150.1	142	73	63	8	76-1	114	.256
—Colorado (N.L.)		0	0	...	6.75	2.00	2	1	0	0	0	0-0	4.0	4	3	3	2	4-0	1	.267
2003—Colo. Springs (PCL)		9	11	.450	4.63	1.46	24	24	3	2	...	0-...	157.1	179	89	81	18	50-2	96	.294
—Colorado (N.L.)		1	3	.250	5.60	1.50	9	3	0	0	1	0-1	27.1	31	19	17	6	10-0	12	.287
Major League totals (2 years)		1	3	.250	5.74	1.56	11	4	0	0	1	0-1	31.1	35	22	20	8	14-0	13	.285

VANDER WAL, JOHN — OF/1B

PERSONAL: Born April 29, 1966, in Grand Rapids, Mich. ... 6-1/210. ... Bats left, throws left. ... Full name: John Henry Vander Wal. ... High school: Hudsonville (Mich.). ... College: Western Michigan.

TRANSACTIONS/CAREER NOTES: Selected by Houston Astros organization in eighth round of free-agent draft (June 4, 1984); did not sign. ... Selected by Montreal Expos organization in third round of free-agent draft (June 2, 1987). ... Contract purchased by Rockies with OF Ronnie Hall from Expos (March 31, 1994). ... Traded by Rockies to San Diego Padres for a player to be named later (August 31, 1998). ... Granted free agency (October 26, 1998). ... Re-signed by Padres (November 13, 1998). ... Traded by Padres with P Geraldo Padua and P James Sak to Pittsburgh Pirates for OF Al Martin and cash (February 23, 2000). ... Traded by Pirates with P Jason Schmidt to San Francisco Giants for OF Armando Rios and P Ryan Vogelsong (July 30, 2001). ... Traded by Giants to New York Yankees for P Jay Witasick (December 13, 2001). ... Granted free agency (October 28, 2002). ... Signed by Milwaukee Brewers organization (January 28, 2003).

2003 GAMES PLAYED BY POSITION (MLB): OF—89.

Year	Team (League)	Pos.	G	AB	R	H	2B	3B	HR	RBI	BB	SO	HBP	GDP	SB-CS	Avg.	OBP	SLG	OPS	E	Pct.
1987—Jamestown (NYP)		OF	18	69	24	33	12	3	3	15	3	14	0	2	3-2	.478	.493	.870	1.363	0	1.000
—W.P. Beach (FSL)		OF	50	189	29	54	11	2	2	22	30	25	0	2	8-3	.286	.378	.397	.775	3	.972
1988—W.P. Beach (FSL)		OF	62	231	50	64	15	2	10	33	32	40	3	0	11-4	.277	.368	.489	.857	1	.991
—Jacksonville (Sou.)		OF	58	208	22	54	14	0	3	14	17	49	1	3	3-4	.260	.317	.370	.687	0	1.000
1989—Jacksonville (Sou.)		OF	71	217	30	55	9	2	6	24	22	51	1	5	2-3	.253	.322	.396	.719	1	.987
1990—Jacksonville (Sou.)		OF	77	277	45	84	25	3	8	40	39	46	3	7	6-3	.303	.393	.502	.894	1	.991
—Indianapolis (A.A.)		OF	51	135	16	40	6	0	2	14	13	28	0	3	0-1	.296	.358	.385	.743	2	.963
1991—Indianapolis (A.A.)		OF	133	478	84	140	36	8	15	71	79	118	2	10	8-1	.293	.393	.496	.888	1	.995
—Montreal (N.L.)		OF	21	61	4	13	4	1	1	8	1	18	0	2	0-0	.213	.222	.361	.583	0	1.000
1992—Montreal (N.L.)		OF-1B	105	213	21	51	8	2	4	20	24	36	0	2	3-0	.239	.316	.352	.669	2	.985
1993—Montreal (N.L.)		1B-OF	106	215	34	50	7	4	5	30	27	30	1	4	6-3	.233	.320	.372	.692	4	.986
1994—Colorado (N.L.)		1B-OF	91	110	12	27	3	1	5	15	16	31	0	4	2-1	.245	.339	.427	.766	0	1.000
1995—Colorado (N.L.)		1B-OF	105	101	15	35	8	1	5	21	16	23	0	1	1-1	.347	.432	.594	1.026	2	.965
1996—Colorado (N.L.)		OF-1B	104	151	20	38	6	2	5	31	19	38	1	1	2-2	.252	.335	.417	.752	1	.987
1997—Colorado (N.L.)		OF-1B-DH	76	92	7	16	2	0	1	11	10	33	0	2	1-1	.174	.255	.228	.483	1	.974
—Colo. Springs (PCL)		1B-OF-DH	25	103	29	42	12	1	3	19	11	17	0	1	1-1	.408	.465	.631	1.096	4	.977
1998—Colorado (N.L.)		OF-1B-DH	89	104	18	30	10	1	5	20	16	29	0	1	0-0	.288	.380	.548	.928	0	1.000
—San Diego (N.L.)		OF-1B	20	25	3	6	3	0	0	0	6	5	0	1	0-0	.240	.387	.360	.747	0	1.000
1999—San Diego (N.L.)		OF-1B-DH	132	246	26	67	18	0	6	41	37	59	2	5	2-1	.272	.368	.419	.787	1	.996
2000—Pittsburgh (N.L.)		OF-1B-DH	134	384	74	115	29	0	24	94	72	92	2	7	11-2	.299	.410	.563	.972	6	.985
2001—Pittsburgh (N.L.)		OF-1B-DH	97	313	39	87	22	3	11	50	42	84	1	7	7-4	.278	.361	.473	.834	4	.982
—San Francisco (N.L.)		OF-1B	49	139	19	35	6	1	3	20	26	38	0	3	1-2	.252	.370	.374	.744	0	1.000
2002—New York (A.L.)		OF-DH-1B	84	219	30	57	17	1	6	20	23	58	0	7	1-1	.260	.327	.429	.756	2	.983
2003—Milwaukee (N.L.)		OF	117	327	50	84	25	1	14	45	46	104	1	5	1-2	.257	.350	.468	.818	3	.984
American League totals (1 year)			84	219	30	57	17	1	6	20	23	58	0	7	1-1	.260	.327	.429	.756	2	.983
National League totals (12 years)			1246	2481	342	654	151	17	89	406	358	620	8	46	37-19	.264	.356	.446	.802	24	.987
Major League totals (13 years)			1330	2700	372	711	168	18	95	426	381	678	8	53	38-20	.263	.354	.444	.798	26	.987

VAN POPPEL, TODD — P

PERSONAL: Born December 9, 1971, in Hinsdale, Ill. ... 6-5/240. ... Throws right, bats right. ... Full name: Todd Matthew Van Poppel. ... Name pronounced: VAN-pop-pell. ... High school: St. Martin (Arlington, Texas).

TRANSACTIONS/CAREER NOTES: Selected by Oakland Athletics organization in first round (14th pick overall) of free-agent draft (June 4, 1990); pick received as part of compensation for Milwaukee Brewers signing Type A free-agent DH Dave Parker. ... On disabled list (May 28-September 11, 1992). ... Claimed on waivers by Detroit Tigers (August 6, 1996). ... Claimed on waivers by California Angels (November 12, 1996). ... Released by Angels (March 26, 1997). ... Signed by Kansas City Royals organization (April 17, 1997). ... Released by Royals (June 6, 1997). ... Signed by Texas Rangers organization (June 20, 1997). ... Traded by Rangers with 2B Warren Morris to Pittsburgh Pirates for P Esteban Loaiza (July 17, 1998). ... Granted free agency (October 15, 1998). ... Re-signed by Pirates (January 18, 1999). ... Granted free agency (October 15, 1999). ... Signed by Chicago Cubs organization (November 22, 1999). ... Granted free agency (November 5, 2001). ... Signed by Texas Rangers (November 26, 2001). ... On disabled list (March 21, 2003). ... Sent on rehab assignment to Frisco (April 23, 2003). ... Reinstated from 15-day disabled list; recalled from Frisco rehab assignment (May 3, 2003). ... Given unconditional release (June 4, 2003). ... Accepted a non-guaranteed contract from Cincinnati Reds (June 12, 2003). ... Contract purchased from Louisville (July 2, 2003). ... Designated for assignment (July 10, 2003). ... Sent outright to Louisville (July 12, 2003). ... Contract purchased from Louisville (September 3, 2003).

CAREER HITTING: 6-for-40 (.150), 4 R, 1 2B, 0 3B, 0 HR, 1 RBI.

Year	League	W	L	Pct.	ERA	WHIP	G	GS	CG	ShO	Hld.	Sv.-Opp.	IP	H	R	ER	HR	BB-IBB	SO	Avg.
1990—S. Oregon (N'west)		1	1	.500	1.13	0.79	5	5	0	0	...	0-...	24.0	10	5	3	1	9-0	32	.125
—Madison (Midw.)		2	1	.667	3.95	1.32	3	3	0	0	...	0-...	13.2	8	11	6	0	10-0	17	.163
1991—Huntsville (Sou.)		6	* 13	.316	3.47	1.57	24	24	1	1	...	0-...	132.1	118	69	51	2	90-0	115	.236
—Oakland (A.L.)		0	0	...	9.64	1.93	1	1	0	0	...	0-0	4.2	7	5	5	1	2-0	6	.368
1992—Tacoma (PCL)		4	2	.667	3.97	1.74	9	9	0	0	...	0-...	45.1	44	22	20	1	35-0	29	.277
1993—Tacoma (PCL)		4	8	.333	5.83	1.54	16	16	0	0	...	0-...	78.2	67	53	51	5	54-0	71	.230
—Oakland (A.L.)		6	6	.500	5.04	1.64	16	16	0	0	...	0-...	84.0	76	50	47	10	62-0	47	.243
1994—Oakland (A.L.)		7	10	.412	6.09	1.69	23	23	0	0	...	0-...	116.2	108	80	79	20	•89-2	83	.250
1995—Oakland (A.L.)		4	8	.333	4.88	1.31	36	14	1	0	...	0-0	138.1	125	77	75	16	56-1	122	.244
1996—Oakland (A.L.)		1	5	.167	7.71	1.89	28	6	0	0	...	1-2	63.0	86	56	54	13	33-3	37	.333
—Detroit (A.L.)		2	4	.333	11.39	2.26	9	9	1	1	...	0-0	36.1	53	51	46	11	29-0	16	.338
1997—Omaha (Am. Assoc.)		1	5	.167	8.03	2.00	11	6	0	0	...	0-...	37.0	50	36	33	10	24-0	27	.321
—Charlotte (Fla. St.)		0	0	.000	4.04	1.29	6	6	2	0	...	0-...	35.2	36	19	16	3	10-0	33	.263
—Tulsa (Texas)		3	3	.500	5.06	1.59	7	7	0	0	...	0-...	42.2	53	27	24	2	15-0	26	.303
1998—Tulsa (Texas)		0	0	...	4.50	1.50	1	1	0	0	...	0-...	4.0	2	2	2	1	4-0	2	.154
—Oklahoma (PCL)		5	5	.500	3.72	1.30	15	13	2	0	...	0-...	87.0	88	44	36	11	25-0	69	.257
—Texas (A.L.)		1	2	.333	8.84	1.86	4	4	0	0	...	0-0	19.1	26	20	19	5	10-0	10	.313
—Pittsburgh (N.L.)		1	2	.333	5.36	1.51	18	7	0	0	...	0-0	47.0	53	32	28	4	18-3	32	.286

V

Year	League	W	L	Pct.	ERA	WHIP	G	GS	CG	ShO	Hld.	Sv.-Opp.	IP	H	R	ER	HR	BB-IBB	SO	Avg.
1999— Nashville (PCL)	10	6	.625	4.95	1.44	27	27	2	0	...	0-...	163.2	173	95	90	23	62-1	*157	.271
2000— Iowa (PCL)	3	4	.429	3.10	1.16	10	6	0	0	...	0-...	40.2	37	18	14	2	10-0	52	.237
— Chicago (N.L.)	4	5	.444	3.75	1.48	51	2	0	0	7	2-5	86.1	80	38	36	10	48-2	77	.249
2001— Chicago (N.L.)	4	1	.800	2.52	1.35	59	0	0	0	5	0-0	75.0	63	22	21	9	38-4	90	.223
2002— Texas (A.L.)	3	2	.600	5.45	1.50	50	0	0	0	3	1-2	72.2	80	44	44	14	29-1	85	.275
2003— Frisco (Texas)	0	0	...	2.00	1.11	2	2	0	0	...	0-...	9.0	8	2	2	0	2-0	7	.235
— Texas (A.L.)	1	0	1.000	8.53	2.29	7	1	0	0	0	0-0	12.2	20	14	12	1	9-2	9	.345
— Louisville (Int'l)	4	3	.571	3.17	1.11	20	5	0	0	...	1-...	54.0	49	23	19	4	11-1	45	.247
— Cincinnati (N.L.)	2	1	.667	4.54	1.04	9	4	0	0	1	0-0	35.2	31	18	18	7	6-0	25	.228
American League totals (8 years)	25	37	.403	6.26	1.64	174	74	2	1	4	2-4	547.2	581	397	381	91	319-9	415	.274
National League totals (4 years)	11	9	.550	3.80	1.38	137	13	0	0	13	2-5	244.0	227	110	103	30	110-9	224	.246
Major League totals (10 years)	36	46	.439	5.50	1.56	311	87	2	1	17	4-9	791.2	808	507	484	121	429-18	639	.265

VARGAS, CLAUDIO — P

PERSONAL: Born May 19, 1979, in Valverde Mao, Dominican Republic. ... 6-3/225. ... Throws right, bats right. ... Full name: Claudio Almonte Vargas.

TRANSACTIONS/CAREER NOTES: Signed as non-drafted free agent by Florida Marlins organization (August 25, 1995). ... On Kane County disabled list (July 22-August 13, 1999). ... Granted free agency (December 21, 1999). ... Re-signed by Marlins organization (December 21, 1999). ... Traded by Marlins with OF Cliff Floyd, OF/2B Wilton Guerrero and cash considerations to Montreal Expos for P Carl Pavano, P Graeme Lloyd, IF Mike Mordecai and P Justin Wayne (July 11, 2002); Expos acquired P Don Levinski to complete deal (August 6, 2002). ... On Harrisburg disabled list (July 26-August 9, 2002). ... Recalled by Montreal from Edmonton (April 25, 2003). ... Removed from 15-day disabled list (September 15, 2003).

CAREER HITTING: 0-for-30 (.000), 1 R, 0 2B, 0 3B, 0 HR, 0 RBI.

Year	League	W	L	Pct.	ERA	WHIP	G	GS	CG	ShO	Hld.	Sv.-Opp.	IP	H	R	ER	HR	BB-IBB	SO	Avg.
1998— Brevard County (FSL)	0	1	.000	4.66	1.97	2	2	0	0	...	0-...	9.2	5	5	5	1	4-0	9	.366
— GC Marlins (GCL)	0	4	.000	4.08	1.08	5	4	0	0	...	0-...	28.2	24	15	13	1	7-0	27	.226
1999— Kane County (Midwest)	5	5	.500	3.88	1.38	19	19	1	0	...	0-...	99.2	97	47	43	8	41-0	88	.255
2000— Brevard County (FSL)	10	5	.667	3.28	1.17	24	23	0	0	...	0-...	145.1	126	64	53	.10	44-3	143	.234
— Portland (East.)	1	1	.500	3.60	1.47	3	2	0	0	...	0-...	15.0	16	9	6	1	6-0	13	.276
2001— Portland (East.)	8	9	.471	4.19	1.19	27	27	0	0	...	0-...	159.0	122	77	74	25	67-1	151	.211
2002— Calgary (PCL)	4	11	.267	6.72	1.61	17	16	1	0	...	0-...	76.1	88	63	57	18	35-0	61	.291
— Harrisburg (Eastern)	2	2	.500	4.64	1.42	8	8	0	0	...	0-...	33.0	38	17	17	2	9-0	34	.286
2003— Edmonton (PCL)	0	0	...	2.79	1.24	2	2	0	0	...	0-...	9.2	7	3	3	1	5-2	12	.189
— Harrisburg (Eastern)	1	0	1.000	0.75	0.83	2	2	0	0	...	0-...	12.0	7	1	1	0	3-0	13	.171
— Montreal (N.L.)	6	8	.429	4.34	1.33	23	20	0	0	0	0-0	114.0	111	59	55	16	41-5	62	.255
Major League totals (1 year)	6	8	.429	4.34	1.33	23	20	0	0	0	0-0	114.0	111	59	55	16	41-5	62	.255

VARITEK, JASON — C

PERSONAL: Born April 11, 1972, in Rochester, Mich. ... 6-2/237. ... Bats both, throws right. ... Full name: Jason Andrew Varitek. ... Name pronounced: VAIR-eh-teck. ... High school: Lake Brantley (Longwood, Fla.). ... College: Georgia Tech.

TRANSACTIONS/CAREER NOTES: Selected by Minnesota Twins organization first round (21st pick overall) of free-agent draft (June 3, 1993); did not sign. ... Selected by Seattle Mariners organization in first round (14th pick overall) of free-agent draft (June 2, 1994). ... Traded by Mariners with P Derek Lowe to Boston Red Sox for P Heathcliff Slocumb (July 31, 1997). ... On disabled list (June 8, 2001-remainder of season). ... On suspended list (September 16-20, 2002).

2003 GAMES PLAYED BY POSITION (MLB): C—137, DH—4.

Year	Team (League)	Pos.	G	AB	R	H	2B	3B	HR	RBI	BB	SO	HBP	GDP	SB-CS	Avg.	OBP	SLG	OPS	E	Pct.
1995— Port City (Sou.)	C	104	352	42	79	14	3	10	44	61	126	2	8	0-1	.224	.340	.366	.706	8	.988
1996— Port City (Sou.)	C-D-3-0	134	503	63	132	34	1	12	67	66	93	4	14	7-6	.262	.350	.406	.756	5	.993
1997— Tacoma (PCL)	C-DH	87	307	54	78	13	0	15	48	34	71	2	13	0-1	.254	.329	.443	.772	3	.995
— Pawtucket (Int'l)	C	20	66	6	13	5	0	1	5	8	12	0	4	0-0	.197	.284	.318	.602	1	.993
— Boston (A.L.)	C	1	1	0	1	0	0	0	0	0	0	0	0	0-0	1.000	1.000	1.000	2.000	0	1.000
1998— Boston (A.L.)	C-DH	86	221	31	56	13	0	7	33	17	45	2	8	2-2	.253	.309	.407	.716	5	.988
1999— Boston (A.L.)	C-DH	144	483	70	130	39	2	20	76	46	85	2	13	1-2	.269	.330	.482	.813	*11	.990
2000— Boston (A.L.)	C-DH	139	448	55	111	31	1	10	65	60	84	6	16	1-1	.248	.342	.388	.730	7	.992
2001— Boston (A.L.)	C	51	174	19	51	11	1	7	25	21	35	1	6	0-0	.293	.371	.489	.859	2	.996
2002— Boston (A.L.)	C-DH	132	467	58	124	27	1	10	61	41	95	7	13	4-3	.266	.332	.392	.724	4	.996
2003— Boston (A.L.)	C-DH	142	451	63	123	31	1	25	85	51	106	7	10	3-2	.273	.351	.512	.863	9	.990
Major League totals (7 years)		695	2245	296	596	152	6	79	345	236	450	25	66	11-10	.265	.338	.444	.783	38	.992

VAUGHN, GREG — OF/DH

PERSONAL: Born July 3, 1965, in Sacramento, Calif. ... 6-0/206. ... Bats right, throws right. ... Full name: Gregory Lamont Vaughn. ... Name pronounced: von. ... High school: John F. Kennedy (Sacramento). ... College: Miami (Fla.).

TRANSACTIONS/CAREER NOTES: Selected by St. Louis Cardinals organization in fifth round of free-agent draft (January 17, 1984); did not sign. ... Selected by Milwaukee Brewers organization in secondary phase of free-agent draft (June 4, 1984); did not sign. ... Selected by Pittsburgh Pirates organization in secondary phase of free-agent draft (January 9, 1985); did not sign. ... Selected by California Angels organization in secondary phase of free-agent draft (June 3, 1985); did not sign. ... Selected by Brewers organization in secondary phase of free-agent draft (June 2, 1986). ... On disabled list (May 26-June 10, 1990). ... On Milwaukee disabled list (April 8-27, 1994); included rehabilitation assignment to Beloit (April 25-27). ... Traded by Brewers with a player to be named later to San Diego Padres for P Bryce Florie, P Ron Villone and OF Marc Newfield (July 31, 1996); Padres acquired OF Gerald Parent to complete deal (September 16, 1996). ... Granted free agency (October 28, 1996). ... Re-signed by Padres (December 19, 1996). ... Traded by Padres with P Kerry Taylor and P Chris Clark to New York Yankees for P Kenny Rogers, IF Mariano Duncan and P Kevin Henthorne (July 4, 1997); trade later voided because Vaughn failed physical (July 6, 1997). ... Traded by Padres with OF/1B Mark Sweeney to Cincinnati Reds for OF Reggie Sanders, SS Damian Jackson and P Josh Harris (February 2, 1999). ... Granted free agency (October 28, 1999). ... Signed by Tampa Bay Devil Rays (December 13, 1999). ... On disabled list (June 18-July 7, 2000; and June 23-September 1, 2002). ... Released by Devil Rays (March 22, 2003). ... Signed by Colorado Rockies organization (April 9, 2003). ... Contract purchased from Colorado Springs (June 4, 2003). ... Refused minor league assignment, becoming a free agent (July 13, 2003).

2003 GAMES PLAYED BY POSITION (MLB): OF—7, DH—3.

Year	Team (League)	Pos.	G	AB	R	H	2B	3B	HR	RBI	BB	SO	HBP	GDP	SB-CS	Avg.	OBP	SLG	OPS	E	Pct.
1986— Helena (Pio.)	OF	66	258	64	75	13	2	16	54	30	69	2	1	23-5	.291	.363	.543	.905	3	.972
1987— Beloit (Midw.)	OF	139	492	* 120	150	31	6	* 33	105	102	115	5	8	36-9	.305	.425	.593	1.018	10	.963
1988— El Paso (Texas)	OF	131	505	* 104	152	* 39	2	* 28	* 105	63	120	3	11	22-5	.301	.379	.552	.932	7	.970
1989— Denver (A.A.)	OF	110	387	74	107	17	5	* 26	* 92	62	94	0	10	20-3	.276	.376	.548	.923	3	.980
— Milwaukee (A.L.)	DH-OF	38	113	18	30	3	0	5	23	13	23	0	0	4-1	.265	.336	.425	.761	2	.943
1990— Milwaukee (A.L.)	DH-OF	120	382	51	84	26	2	17	61	33	91	1	11	7-4	.220	.280	.432	.712	7	.967
1991— Milwaukee (A.L.)	DH-OF	145	542	81	132	24	5	27	98	62	125	1	5	2-2	.244	.319	.456	.774	2	.994
1992— Milwaukee (A.L.)	OF-DH	141	501	77	114	18	2	23	78	60	123	5	8	15-15	.228	.313	.409	.723	3	.990
1993— Milwaukee (A.L.)	OF-DH	154	569	97	152	28	2	30	97	89	118	5	6	10-7	.267	.369	.482	.850	3	.986
1994— Milwaukee (A.L.)	OF-DH	95	370	59	94	24	1	19	55	51	93	1	6	9-5	.254	.345	.478	.824	3	.982
— Beloit (Midw.)	DH	2	6	1	1	0	0	0	0	4	1	0	0	0-0	.167	.500	.167	.667	...	...
1995— Milwaukee (A.L.)	DH	108	392	67	88	19	1	17	59	55	89	0	10	10-4	.224	.317	.408	.725	...	...
1996— Milwaukee (A.L.)	OF-DH	102	375	78	105	16	0	31	95	58	99	4	6	5-2	.280	.378	.571	.948	4	.980
— San Diego (N.L.)	OF	43	141	20	29	3	1	10	22	24	31	2	1	4-1	.206	.329	.454	.783	2	.974
1997— San Diego (N.L.)	OF-DH	120	361	60	78	10	0	18	57	56	110	2	7	7-4	.216	.322	.393	.716	1	.994
1998— San Diego (N.L.)	OF-DH	158	573	112	156	28	4	50	119	79	121	5	7	11-4	.272	.363	.597	.960	2	.993
1999— Cincinnati (N.L.)	OF-DH	153	550	104	135	20	2	45	118	85	137	3	9	15-2	.245	.347	.535	.881	4	.986
2000— Tampa Bay (A.L.)	OF-DH	127	461	83	117	27	1	28	74	80	128	2	10	8-1	.254	.365	.499	.864	1	.993
2001— Tampa Bay (A.L.)	DH-OF	136	485	74	113	25	0	24	82	71	130	3	10	11-5	.233	.333	.433	.766	3	.978
2002— Tampa Bay (A.L.)	DH-OF	69	251	28	41	10	2	8	29	41	82	3	5	3-2	.163	.286	.315	.601	1	.987
2003— Colo. Springs (PCL)	OF-1B-DH	35	116	26	35	7	1	12	35	16	28	1	2	1-0	.302	.388	.690	1.078	5	.947
— Colorado (N.L.)	OF-DH	22	37	8	7	3	0	3	5	8	13	0	0	0-0	.189	.326	.514	.840	0	1.000
American League totals (11 years)		1235	4441	713	1070	220	16	229	751	613	1101	25	77	84-48	.241	.334	.452	.786	29	.984
National League totals (5 years)		496	1662	304	405	64	7	126	321	252	412	12	24	37-11	.244	.345	.518	.863	9	.989
Major League totals (15 years)		1731	6103	1017	1475	284	23	355	1072	865	1513	37	101	121-59	.242	.337	.470	.807	38	.986

VAUGHN, MO   1B

PERSONAL: Born December 15, 1967, in Norwalk, Conn. ... 6-1/275. ... Bats left, throws right. ... Full name: Maurice Samuel Vaughn. ... High school: Trinity Pawling Prep (Pawling, N.Y.). ... College: Seton Hall.

TRANSACTIONS/CAREER NOTES: Selected by Boston Red Sox organization in first round (23rd pick overall) of free-agent draft (June 9, 1989). ... On disabled list (June 17-July 10, 1997). ... Granted free agency (October 23, 1998). ... Signed by Anaheim Angels (December 11, 1998). ... On disabled list (April 7-22, 1999; and March 23, 2001-entire season). ... Traded by Angels to New York Mets for P Kevin Appier (December 27, 2001). ... On disabled list (April 6-21, 2002). ... Placed on 15-day disabled list (May 3, 2003). ... Transferred to Emergency disabled list (May 22, 2003).

2003 GAMES PLAYED BY POSITION (MLB): 1B—24.

Year	Team (League)	Pos.	G	AB	R	H	2B	3B	HR	RBI	BB	SO	HBP	GDP	SB-CS	Avg.	OBP	SLG	OPS	E	Pct.
1989— New Britain (East.)	1B	73	245	28	68	15	0	8	38	25	47	3	7	1-3	.278	.350	.437	.787	• 10	.983
1990— Pawtucket (Int'l)	1B	108	386	62	114	26	1	22	72	44	87	6	10	3-2	.295	.374	.539	.913	11	.988
1991— Pawtucket (Int'l)	1B	69	234	35	64	10	0	14	50	60	44	3	6	2-1	.274	.422	.496	.918	3	.993
— Boston (A.L.)	DH-1B	74	219	21	57	12	0	4	32	26	43	2	7	2-1	.260	.339	.370	.709	6	.985
1992— Boston (A.L.)	1B-DH	113	355	42	83	16	2	13	57	47	67	3	8	3-3	.234	.326	.400	.726	* 15	.982
— Pawtucket (Int'l)	1B	39	149	15	42	6	0	6	28	18	35	0	5	1-0	.282	.357	.443	.800	8	.980
1993— Boston (A.L.)	1B-DH	152	539	86	160	34	1	29	101	79	130	8	14	4-3	.297	.390	.525	.915	* 16	.987
1994— Boston (A.L.)	1B-DH	111	394	65	122	25	1	26	82	57	112	10	7	4-4	.310	.408	.576	.984	• 10	.989
1995— Boston (A.L.)	1B-DH	140	550	98	165	28	3	39	• 126	68	150	14	17	11-4	.300	.388	.575	.963	11	.992
1996— Boston (A.L.)	1B-DH	161	635	118	207	29	1	44	143	95	154	14	17	2-0	.326	.420	.583	1.003	* 15	.988
1997— Boston (A.L.)	1B-DH	141	527	91	166	24	0	35	96	86	154	12	10	2-2	.315	.420	.560	.980	* 14	.991
1998— Boston (A.L.)	1B-DH	154	609	107	205	31	2	40	115	61	144	8	13	0-0	.337	.402	.591	.993	12	.991
1999— Anaheim (A.L.)	1B-DH	139	524	63	147	20	0	33	108	54	127	11	11	0-0	.281	.358	.508	.866	3	.995
2000— Anaheim (A.L.)	1B-DH-OF	161	614	93	167	31	0	36	117	79	181	14	14	2-0	.272	.365	.498	.864	‡ 14	.990
2001— Anaheim (A.L.)						Did not play.															
2002— New York (N.L.)	1B	139	487	67	126	18	0	26	72	59	145	10	15	0-1	.259	.349	.456	.805	18	.984
2003— New York (N.L.)	1B	27	79	10	15	2	0	3	15	14	22	2	2	0-0	.190	.323	.329	.652	5	.974
American League totals (10 years)		1346	4966	784	1479	250	10	299	977	652	1262	96	118	30-17	.298	.387	.533	.920	116	.989
National League totals (2 years)		166	566	77	141	20	0	29	87	73	167	12	17	0-1	.249	.346	.438	.784	23	.983
Major League totals (12 years)		1512	5532	861	1620	270	10	328	1064	725	1429	108	135	30-18	.293	.383	.523	.906	139	.988

VAZQUEZ, JAVIER   P

PERSONAL: Born July 25, 1976, in Ponce, Puerto Rico. ... 6-2/205. ... Throws right, bats right. ... Full name: Javier Carlos Vazquez. ... Name pronounced: VAS-kez. ... High school: Colegio de Ponce (Ponce, Puerto Rico).

TRANSACTIONS/CAREER NOTES: Selected by Montreal Expos organization in fifth round of free-agent draft (June 2, 1994). ... On suspended list (July 23-27, 1998).

CAREER HITTING: 75-for-359 (.209), 28 R, 8 2B, 2 3B, 0 HR, 22 RBI.

Year	League	W	L	Pct.	ERA	WHIP	G	GS	CG	ShO	Hld.	Sv.-Opp.	IP	H	R	ER	HR	BB-IBB	SO	Avg.
1994— GC Expos (GCL)	5	2	.714	2.53	0.77	15	11	1	1	...	0-...	67.2	37	25	19	0	15-0	56	.155
1995— Albany (S. Atl.)	6	6	.500	5.08	1.52	21	21	1	0	...	0-...	102.2	109	67	58	8	47-0	87	.273
1996— Delmarva (S. Atl.)	14	3	.824	2.68	1.19	27	27	1	0	...	0-...	164.1	138	64	49	12	57-0	173	.229
1997— W.P. Beach (FSL)	6	3	.667	2.16	1.12	19	19	1	0	...	0-...	112.2	98	40	27	8	28-0	100	.231
— Harrisburg (Eastern)	4	0	1.000	1.07	0.64	6	6	1	0	...	0-...	42.0	15	5	5	2	12-0	47	.107
1998— Montreal (N.L.)	5	15	.250	6.06	1.53	33	32	0	0	0	0-0	172.1	196	121	116	31	68-2	139	.292
1999— Montreal (N.L.)	9	8	.529	5.00	1.33	26	26	3	1	0	0-0	154.2	154	98	86	20	52-4	113	.255
— Ottawa (Int'l)	4	2	.667	4.85	1.43	7	7	0	0	...	0-...	42.2	45	24	23	7	16-0	46	.280
2000— Montreal (N.L.)	11	9	.550	4.05	1.42	33	33	2	1	0	0-0	217.2	247	104	98	24	61-10	196	.290
2001— Montreal (N.L.)	16	11	.593	3.42	1.08	32	32	5	• 3	0	0-0	223.2	197	92	85	24	44-4	208	.235
2002— Montreal (N.L.)	10	13	.435	3.91	1.27	34	34	2	0	0	0-0	230.1	* 243	111	100	28	49-6	179	.271
2003— Montreal (N.L.)	13	12	.520	3.24	1.11	34	34	4	1	0	0-0	230.2	198	93	83	28	57-5	241	.229
Major League totals (6 years)	64	68	.485	4.16	1.27	192	191	16	6	0	0-0	1229.1	1235	619	568	155	331-31	1076	.260

V

VAZQUEZ, RAMON — SS

PERSONAL: Born August 21, 1976, in Aibonito, Puerto Rico. ... 5-11/170. ... Bats left, throws right. ... Full name: Ramon Luis Vazquez. ... Junior college: Indian Hills (Iowa) Community College.

TRANSACTIONS/CAREER NOTES: Selected by Seattle Mariners organization in 27th round of free-agent draft (June 1, 1995). ... On disabled list (June 29-July 11, 2000). ... On Tacoma disabled list (June 20-29, 2001). ... Traded by Mariners with P Brett Tomko and C Tom Lampkin to San Diego Padres for C Ben Davis, P Wascar Serrano and SS Alex Arias (December 11, 2001). ... Placed on 15-day disabled list, retroactive to June 1 (June 8, 2003). ... Sent to Lake Elsinore on rehab assignment (July 1, 2003). ... Recalled from Lake Elsinore rehab assignment; reinstated from 15-day disabled list (July 7, 2003).

2003 GAMES PLAYED BY POSITION (MLB): SS—108, 3B—4, 2B—3.

| | | | | | | | BATTING | | | | | | | | | | | FIELDING | |
Year Team (League)	Pos.	G	AB	R	H	2B	3B	HR	RBI	BB	SO	HBP	GDP	SB-CS	Avg.	OBP	SLG	OPS	E	Pct.
1995— Ariz. Mariners (Ariz.)	2B-3B-SS	39	141	20	29	3	1	0	11	19	27	2	2	4-3	.206	.309	.241	.550	11	.941
1996— Everett (N'west)	SS	33	126	25	35	5	2	1	18	26	26	1	3	7-2	.278	.392	.373	.765	20	.873
— Tacoma (PCL)	2B-SS	18	49	7	11	2	1	0	4	4	12	1	2	0-0	.224	.296	.306	.602	1	.985
— Wisconsin (Midw.)	3B	3	10	1	3	1	0	0	1	2	2	0	1	0-0	.300	.417	.400	.817	2	.818
1997— Wisconsin (Midw.)	SS	131	479	79	129	25	5	8	49	78	93	3	8	16-10	.269	.373	.392	.765	35	.935
1998— Lancaster (Calif.)	SS	121	468	77	129	26	4	2	72	81	66	2	6	15-11	.276	.384	.361	.745	31	.944
1999— New Haven (East.)	2B-3B-SS	127	438	58	113	27	3	5	45	62	77	5	11	8-1	.258	.354	.368	.722	31	.942
2000— New Haven (East.)	SS	124	405	58	116	25	4	8	59	52	76	2	6	1-6	.286	.367	.427	.794	22	.961
2001— Tacoma (PCL)	SS	127	466	85	140	28	1	10	79	76	84	1	13	9-7	.300	.397	.429	.827	12	.979
— Seattle (A.L.)	S-2-3-D	17	35	5	8	0	0	0	4	0	3	0	0	0-0	.229	.222	.229	.451	1	.969
2002— San Diego (N.L.)	2B-SS-3B	128	423	50	116	21	5	2	32	45	79	1	6	7-2	.274	.344	.362	.706	7	.986
2003— Lake Elsinore (Calif.)	SS	5	16	3	3	0	0	1	4	3	3	1	1	0-1	.188	.350	.375	.725	1	.950
— San Diego (N.L.)	SS-3B-2B	116	422	56	110	17	4	3	30	52	88	2	4	10-3	.261	.342	.341	.684	14	.968
American League totals (1 year)		17	35	5	8	0	0	0	4	0	3	0	0	0-0	.229	.222	.229	.451	1	.969
National League totals (2 years)		244	845	106	226	38	9	5	62	97	167	3	10	17-5	.267	.343	.351	.695	21	.977
Major League totals (3 years)		261	880	111	234	38	9	5	66	97	170	3	10	17-5	.266	.339	.347	.685	22	.977

VELANDIA, JORGE — SS

PERSONAL: Born January 12, 1975, in Caracas, Venezuela. ... 5-9/185. ... Bats right, throws right. ... Full name: Jorge Luis Velandia. ... Name pronounced: vuh-LAHN-dee-uh.

TRANSACTIONS/CAREER NOTES: Signed as non-drafted free agent by Detroit Tigers organization (January 15, 1992). ... Traded by Tigers with 3B Scott Livingstone to San Diego Padres for P Gene Harris (May 11, 1994). ... Traded by Padres with P Doug Bochtler to Oakland Athletics for P Don Wengert and IF David Newhan (November 26, 1997). ... On disabled list (August 7, 1999-remainder of season). ... Traded by A's to New York Mets for OF Nelson Cruz (August 30, 2000). ... Granted free agency (December 21, 2000). ... Re-signed by Mets (January 5, 2001). ... On New York disabled list (June 29-September 8, 2001; included rehabilitation assignment to Norfolk (August 27-September 8). ... Granted free agency (October 15, 2001). ... On Norfolk disabled list (April 4-15 and May 13-22, 2002). ... Granted free agency (October 15, 2002). ... Re-signed by Mets (July 17, 2003).

2003 GAMES PLAYED BY POSITION (MLB): SS—23.

| | | | | | | | BATTING | | | | | | | | | | | FIELDING | |
Year Team (League)	Pos.	G	AB	R	H	2B	3B	HR	RBI	BB	SO	HBP	GDP	SB-CS	Avg.	OBP	SLG	OPS	E	Pct.
1992— Bristol (Appal.)	2B-SS	45	119	20	24	6	1	0	9	15	16	0	1	3-2	.202	.291	.269	.560	12	.922
1993— Niagara Falls (NYP)	SS	72	212	30	41	11	0	1	22	19	48	0	2	22-4	.193	.258	.259	.517	24	.918
— Fayetteville (SAL)	2B-3B-SS	37	106	15	17	4	0	0	11	13	21	3	3	5-0	.160	.266	.198	.464	9	.940
1994— Lakeland (Fla. St.)	2B-3B-SS	22	60	8	14	4	0	0	3	6	14	0	0	0-2	.233	.299	.300	.599	4	.960
— Springfield (Midw.)	2B-SS	98	290	42	71	14	0	4	36	21	46	4	8	5-6	.245	.302	.334	.636	26	.942
1995— Memphis (Sou.)	SS	63	186	23	38	10	2	4	17	14	37	1	4	0-2	.204	.262	.344	.606	12	.952
— Las Vegas (PCL)	SS	66	206	25	54	12	3	0	25	13	37	2	5	0-0	.262	.309	.350	.659	* 31	.903
1996— Memphis (Sou.)	SS	122	392	42	94	19	0	9	48	31	65	3	10	3-7	.240	.295	.357	.652	33	.943
1997— Las Vegas (PCL)	SS	114	405	46	110	15	2	3	35	29	62	4	5	13-3	.272	.326	.341	.666	21	.961
— San Diego (N.L.)	SS-2B-3B	14	29	0	3	2	0	0	1	1	7	0	0	0-0	.103	.133	.172	.306	3	.919
1998— Oakland (A.L.)	SS-2B	8	4	0	1	0	0	0	0	0	1	0	0	0-0	.250	.250	.250	.500	1	.933
— Edmonton (PCL)	SS-DH	128	488	64	140	35	1	6	57	37	52	6	19	8-6	.287	.341	.400	.741	17	.974
1999— Oakland (A.L.)	2-S-3-D	63	48	4	9	1	0	0	2	2	13	1	0	2-0	.188	.235	.208	.444	3	.977
2000— Oakland (A.L.)	SS	18	24	1	3	1	0	0	2	0	6	1	0	0-0	.125	.160	.167	.327	0	1.000
— Sacramento (PCL)	SS	83	302	56	84	20	1	9	57	34	52	5	8	4-3	.278	.359	.440	.799	11	.973
— Norfolk (Int'l)	SS	4	10	0	1	0	0	0	0	1	1	0	0	1-0	.100	.182	.100	.282	0	1.000
— New York (N.L.)	2B-SS-3B	15	7	1	0	0	0	0	0	2	2	0	0	0-0	.000	.222	.000	.222	1	.929
2001— Norfolk (Int'l)	SS-2B	67	260	25	65	21	0	5	37	16	47	5	7	9-4	.250	.303	.388	.691	7	.978
— New York (N.L.)	SS-3B	9	9	1	0	0	0	0	0	0	2	1	0	0-0	.000	.182	.000	.182	0	1.000
2002— Norfolk (Int'l)	SS-2B-3B	115	407	43	82	20	1	6	37	30	79	2	6	5-2	.201	.257	.300	.557	10	.981
2003— Norfolk (Int'l)	SS-2B-3B	111	374	45	88	22	2	11	48	37	90	4	9	2-5	.235	.306	.393	.699	18	.961
— New York (N.L.)	SS	23	58	6	11	3	1	0	8	10	15	0	1	0-0	.190	.304	.276	.580	3	.972
American League totals (3 years)		89	76	5	13	2	0	0	4	2	20	2	0	2-0	.171	.213	.197	.410	4	.978
National League totals (4 years)		61	103	8	14	5	1	0	8	15	25	0	1	0-0	.136	.244	.204	.448	7	.959
Major League totals (6 years)		150	179	13	27	7	1	0	12	17	45	2	1	2-0	.151	.231	.201	.432	11	.969

VENAFRO, MIKE — P

PERSONAL: Born August 2, 1973, in Takoma Park, Md. ... 5-10/180. ... Throws left, bats left. ... Full name: Michael Robert Venafro. ... Name pronounced: VEN-a-fro. ... High school: Paul VI (Fairfax, Va.). ... College: James Madison (Va.).

TRANSACTIONS/CAREER NOTES: Selected by Texas Rangers organization in 29th round of free-agent draft (June 1, 1995). ... Traded by Rangers with 1B Carlos Pena to Oakland Athletics for 1B Jason Hart, P Marion Ramos, C Gerald Laird and OF Ryan Ludwick (January 14, 2002). ... On Sacramento disabled list (August 17-31, 2002). ... Granted free agency (December 21, 2002). ... Signed by Atlanta Braves (January 13, 2003). ... Released by Braves (March 26, 2003). ... Signed by Tampa Bay Devil Rays (March 28, 2003). ... Designated for assignment by Tampa Bay (June 26, 2003). ... Given unconditional release (June 30, 2003).

CAREER HITTING: 0-for-0 (.000), 0 R, 0 2B, 0 3B, 0 HR, 0 RBI.

Year League	W	L	Pct.	ERA	WHIP	G	GS	CG	ShO	Hld.	Sv.-Opp.	IP	H	R	ER	HR	BB-IBB	SO	Avg.
1995— Hudson Valley (NYP)	9	1	.900	2.13	1.14	32	0	0	0	...	2-...	50.2	37	13	12	0	21-0	32	.216
1996— Char., S.C. (SAL)	1	3	.250	3.51	1.32	50	0	0	0	...	19-...	59.0	57	27	23	0	21-3	62	.250
1997— Charlotte (Fla. St.)	4	2	.667	3.43	1.61	35	0	0	0	...	10-...	44.2	51	17	17	2	21-1	35	.305
— Tulsa (Texas)	0	1	.000	3.45	1.60	11	0	0	0	...	1-...	15.2	13	12	6	1	12-0	13	.220
1998— Tulsa (Texas)	3	4	.429	3.10	1.30	46	0	0	0	...	14-...	52.1	42	21	18	5	26-0	45	.219
— Okla. City (PCL)	0	0	...	6.35	1.71	13	0	0	0	...	0-...	17.0	19	12	12	3	10-0	15	.271

Year	League	W	L	Pct.	ERA	WHIP	G	GS	CG	ShO	Hld.	Sv.-Opp.	IP	H	R	ER	HR	BB-IBB	SO	Avg.
1999— Oklahoma (PCL)	0	0	...	5.40	1.37	6	0	0	0	...	1-...	11.2	16	7	7	2	0-0	7	.348
— Texas (A.L.)	3	2	.600	3.29	1.24	65	0	0	0	19	0-1	68.1	63	29	25	4	22-0	37	.251
2000— Texas (A.L.)	3	1	.750	3.83	1.51	77	0	0	0	17	1-2	56.1	64	27	24	2	21-4	32	.295
2001— Texas (A.L.)	5	5	.500	4.80	1.37	70	0	0	0	21	4-8	60.0	54	35	32	2	28-4	29	.240
2002— Oakland (A.L.)	2	2	.500	4.62	1.59	47	0	0	0	15	0-0	37.0	45	22	19	5	14-2	16	.308
— Sacramento (PCL)	0	1	.000	6.97	1.26	8	0	0	0	...	0-...	10.1	12	8	8	2	1-0	14	.293
2003— Tampa Bay (A.L.)	1	0	1.000	4.74	1.42	24	0	0	0	4	0-0	19.0	24	10	10	1	3-0	9	.308
— New Orleans (PCL)	2	1	.667	3.54	1.43	23	0	0	0	...	0-...	28.0	35	11	11	0	5-1	11	.310
Major League totals (5 years)	14	10	.583	4.11	1.40	283	0	0	0	76	5-11	240.2	250	123	110	14	88-10	123	.273

VENTURA, ROBIN — 3B

PERSONAL: Born July 14, 1967, in Santa Maria, Calif. ... 6-1/190. ... Bats left, throws right. ... Full name: Robin Mark Ventura. ... High school: Righetti (Santa Maria, Calif.). ... College: Oklahoma State.

TRANSACTIONS/CAREER NOTES: Selected by Chicago White Sox organization in first round (10th pick overall) of free-agent draft (June 1, 1988). ... On suspended list (August 23-25, 1993). ... On disabled list (March 31-July 24, 1997; included rehabilitation assignments to Nashville (July 13-17) and Birmingham (July 18-22). ... Granted free agency (October 23, 1998). ... Signed by New York Mets (December 1, 1998). ... On disabled list (July 14-29, 2000). ... Traded by Mets to New York Yankees for OF David Justice (December 7, 2001). ... Granted free agency (October 29, 2002). ... Re-signed by Yankees (December 5, 2002). ... Traded by New York Yankees to Los Angeles Dodgers for OF Bubba Crosby and P Scott Proctor (July 31, 2003).

2003 GAMES PLAYED BY POSITION (MLB): 3B—83, 1B—42, DH—4, 2B—1.

Year	Team (League)	Pos.	G	AB	R	H	2B	3B	HR	RBI	BB	SO	HBP	GDP	SB-CS	Avg.	OBP	SLG	OPS	E	Pct.
1989— Birmingham (Sou.)	2B-3B-1B	129	454	75	126	25	2	3	67	93	51	6	9	9-7	.278	.403	.361	.764	27 ‡	.930
— Chicago (A.L.)	3B	16	45	5	8	3	0	0	7	8	6	1	1	0-0	.178	.298	.244	.543	2	.962
1990— Chicago (A.L.)	3B-1B	150	493	48	123	17	1	5	54	55	53	1	5	1-4	.249	.324	.318	.643	25	.939
1991— Chicago (A.L.)	3B-1B	157	606	92	172	25	1	23	100	80	67	4	22	2-4	.284	.367	.442	.810	‡ 18	.966
1992— Chicago (A.L.)	3B-1B	157	592	85	167	38	1	16	93	93	71	0	14	2-4	.282	.375	.431	.806	23	.957
1993— Chicago (A.L.)	3B-1B	157	554	85	145	27	1	22	94	105	82	3	18	1-6	.262	.379	.433	.812	14	.966
1994— Chicago (A.L.)	3B-1B-SS	109	401	57	113	15	1	18	78	61	69	2	8	3-1	.282	.373	.459	.832	20	.931
1995— Chicago (A.L.)	3B-1B-DH	135	492	79	145	22	0	26	93	75	98	1	8	4-3	.295	.384	.498	.882	19	.956
1996— Chicago (A.L.)	3B-1B	158	586	96	168	31	2	34	105	78	81	2	18	1-3	.287	.368	.520	.888	11	.975
1997— Nashville (A.A.)	3B-DH	5	15	3	6	1	0	2	5	2	1	0	0	0-1	.400	.471	.867	1.337	0	1.000
— Birmingham (Sou.)	3B	4	17	3	5	1	0	1	2	1	1	0	2	0-0	.294	.333	.529	.863	2	.714
— Chicago (A.L.)	3B	54	183	27	48	10	1	6	26	34	21	0	3	0-0	.262	.373	.426	.799	7	.956
1998— Chicago (A.L.)	3B	161	590	84	155	31	4	21	91	79	111	1	10	1-1	.263	.349	.436	.785	15	.966
1999— New York (N.L.)	3B-1B	161	588	88	177	38	0	32	120	74	109	3	14	1-1	.301	.379	.529	.908	9	.980
2000— New York (N.L.)	3B-1B	141	469	61	109	23	1	24	84	75	91	2	14	3-5	.232	.338	.439	.777	17	.955
2001— New York (N.L.)	3B	142	456	70	108	20	0	21	61	88	101	1	13	2-5	.237	.359	.419	.778	16	.957
2002— New York (A.L.)	3B-1B	141	465	68	115	17	0	27	93	90	101	2	14	3-1	.247	.368	.458	.826	* 23	.944
2003— New York (A.L.)	3B-DH-2B	89	283	31	71	13	0	9	42	40	62	0	8	0-0	.251	.344	.392	.736	5	.975
— Los Angeles (N.L.)	1B-3B	49	109	11	24	5	1	5	13	18	25	0	3	0-0	.220	.331	.422	.753	3	.989
American League totals (12 years)		1484	5290	757	1430	249	12	207	876	798	822	17	129	18-27	.270	.364	.439	.803	182	.958
National League totals (4 years)		493	1622	230	418	86	2	82	278	255	326	6	44	6-11	.258	.358	.465	.823	45	.969
Major League totals (15 years)		1977	6912	987	1848	335	14	289	1154	1053	1148	23	173	24-38	.267	.363	.445	.808	227	.961

VERES, DAVE — P

PERSONAL: Born October 19, 1966, in Montgomery, Ala. ... 6-2/225. ... Throws right, bats right. ... Full name: David Scott Veres. ... Name pronounced: VEERZ. ... High school: Gresham (Ore.). ... Junior college: Mt. Hood (Ore.) Community College.

TRANSACTIONS/CAREER NOTES: Selected by Oakland Athletics organization in fourth round of free-agent draft (January 14, 1986). ... Traded by A's to Los Angeles Dodgers for P Kevin Campbell (January 15, 1991). ... Loaned by Dodgers organization to Mexico City Tigers, Mexican League (April 3-May 15, 1992). ... Released by Dodgers (May 15, 1992). ... Signed by Houston Astros organization (May 28, 1992). ... Traded by Astros with C Raul Chavez to Montreal Expos for 3B Sean Berry (December 20, 1995). ... On disabled list (August 21-September 17, 1997). ... Traded by Expos with a player to be named later to Colorado Rockies for OF Terry Jones and a player to be named later (December 10, 1997). ... Traded by Rockies with P Darryl Kile and P Luther Hackman to St. Louis Cardinals for P Jose Jimenez, P Manny Aybar, P Rick Croushore and SS Brent Butler (November 16, 1999). ... Granted free agency (October 30, 2002). ... Signed by Chicago Cubs (January 3, 2003). ... Placed on 15-day disabled list (April 15, 2003). ... Sent to Iowa on rehab assignment (May 19, 2003). ... Recalled from rehab assignment from Iowa (May 24, 2003). ... Sent on rehab assignment to Iowa by Chicago (June 10, 2003). ... Recalled from Iowa rehab assignment by Chicago; reinstated from 15-day disabled list (July 4, 2003). ... Placed on 15-day disabled list (August 27, 2003). ... Removed from 15-day disabled list (September 6, 2003).

CAREER HITTING: 7-for-27 (.259), 1 R, 1 2B, 0 3B, 0 HR, 1 RBI.

Year	League	W	L	Pct.	ERA	WHIP	G	GS	CG	ShO	Hld.	Sv.-Opp.	IP	H	R	ER	HR	BB-IBB	SO	Avg.
1986— Medford (N'west)	5	2	.714	3.26	1.49	15	•15	0	0	...	0-...	77.1	58	38	28	5	57-0	60	
1987— Modesto (Calif.)	8	9	.471	4.79	1.56	26	26	2	0	...	0-...	148.1	124	90	79	9	108-3	124	.231
1988— Modesto (Calif.)	4	11	.267	3.31	1.42	19	19	3	0	...	0-...	125.0	100	61	46	7	78-1	91	.224
— Huntsville (Sou.)	3	4	.429	4.15	1.67	8	8	0	0	...	0-...	39.0	50	20	18	1	15-2	17	.311
1989— Huntsville (Sou.)	8	11	.421	4.86	1.53	29	28	2	1	...	0-...	159.1	160	93	86	15	83-1	105	.261
1990— Tacoma (PCL)	11	8	.579	4.69	1.48	32	23	0	0	...	1-...	151.2	136	90	79	13	88-1	88	.249
1991— Albuquerque (PCL)	7	6	.538	4.47	1.40	57	3	0	0	...	5-...	100.2	89	52	50	8	52-5	81	.237
1992— M.C. Tigers (Mex.)	1	5	.167	8.10	1.76	14	1	0	0	...	1-...	23.1	29	21	21	5	12-...	12	
— Tucson (PCL)	2	3	.400	5.30	1.46	29	1	0	0	...	0-...	52.2	60	36	31	1	17-1	46	.296
1993— Tucson (PCL)	6	10	.375	4.90	1.44	43	15	1	0	...	5-...	130.1	156	88	71	7	32-1	122	.292
1994— Tucson (PCL)	1	1	.500	1.88	1.13	16	0	0	0	...	1-...	24.0	17	8	5	0	10-2	19	.186
— Houston (N.L.)	3	3	.500	2.41	1.12	32	0	0	0	3	1-1	41.0	39	13	11	4	7-3	28	.247
1995— Houston (N.L.)	5	1	.833	2.26	1.15	72	0	0	0	19	1-3	103.1	89	29	26	5	30-6	94	.241
1996— Montreal (N.L.)	6	3	.667	4.17	1.51	68	0	0	0	15	4-6	77.2	85	39	36	10	32-2	81	.277
1997— Montreal (N.L.)	2	3	.400	3.48	1.53	53	0	0	0	10	1-4	62.0	68	28	24	5	27-3	47	.278
1998— Colorado (N.L.)	3	1	.750	2.83	1.23	63	0	0	0	8	8-13	76.1	67	26	24	6	27-2	74	.233
1999— Colorado (N.L.)	4	8	.333	5.14	1.62	73	0	0	0	...	31-39	77.0	88	46	44	14	37-7	71	.290
2000— St. Louis (N.L.)	3	5	.375	2.85	1.19	71	0	0	0	1	29-36	75.2	65	26	24	8	25-2	67	.239
2001— St. Louis (N.L.)	3	2	.600	3.70	1.29	71	0	0	0	8	15-19	65.2	57	29	27	12	28-1	61	.232
2002— St. Louis (N.L.)	5	8	.385	3.48	1.28	71	0	0	0	16	4-8	82.2	67	34	32	12	39-4	68	.224
2003— Iowa (PCL)	0	1	.000	2.81	1.00	11	4	0	0	...	0-...	16.0	15	5	5	2	1-0	13	.242
— Chicago (N.L.)	2	1	.667	4.68	1.26	31	0	0	0	4	1-2	32.2	36	17	17	4	5-0	26	.290
Major League totals (10 years)	36	35	.507	3.44	1.32	605	0	0	0	84	95-131	694.0	661	287	265	78	257-30	617	.253

V

VICTORINO, SHANE — OF

PERSONAL: Born November 30, 1980, in Wailuku, Hawaii. ... 5-9/160. ... Bats both, throws right. ... Full name: Shane Patrick Victorino. ... High school: St. Anthony (Wailuku, Hawaii).

TRANSACTIONS/CAREER NOTES: Selected by Los Angeles Dodgers organization in sixth round of free-agent draft (June 2, 1999). ... Selected by San Diego Padres from Dodgers organization in Rule 5 major league draft (December 16, 2002). ... Claimed off waivers by Los Angeles from San Diego and assigned to Jacksonville of the Southern League (May 28, 2003). ... Designated for assignment by San Diego (May 23, 2003). ... Optioned to Las Vegas by San Diego (May 28, 2003).

2003 GAMES PLAYED BY POSITION (MLB): OF—32.

										BATTING									FIELDING	
Year — Team (League)	Pos.	G	AB	R	H	2B	3B	HR	RBI	BB	SO	HBP	GDP	SB-CS	Avg.	OBP	SLG	OPS	E	Pct.
1999— Great Falls (Pio.)	OF	55	225	53	63	7	6	2	25	20	31	0	3	20-5	.280	.335	.391	.726	2	.986
2000— Yakima (N'west)	2B-SS	61	236	32	58	7	2	2	20	20	44	3	3	21-9	.246	.310	.318	.628	11	.964
2001— Wilmington (Caro.)	OF	112	435	71	123	21	9	4	32	36	61	5	3	47-13	.283	.344	.400	.744	6	.976
— Vero Beach (FSL)	OF	2	6	2	1	0	0	0	0	3	1	0	0	0-0	.167	.444	.167	.611	0	1.000
2002— Jacksonville (Sou.)	OF	122	481	61	124	15	1	4	34	47	49	4	6	45-16	.258	.328	.318	.646	4	.986
2003— San Diego (N.L.)	OF	36	73	8	11	2	0	0	4	7	17	1	5	7-2	.151	.232	.178	.410	0	1.000
— Jacksonville (Sou.)	OF	66	266	37	75	9	4	2	15	21	41	3	3	16-7	.282	.340	.368	.709	4	.978
— Las Vegas (PCL)	OF	11	41	6	16	1	2	1	9	1	5	0	1	0-1	.390	.395	.585	.981	1	.966
Major League totals (1 year)		36	73	8	11	2	0	0	4	7	17	1	5	7-2	.151	.232	.178	.410	0	1.000

VIDRO, JOSE — 2B

PERSONAL: Born August 27, 1974, in Mayaguez, Puerto Rico. ... 5-11/195. ... Bats both, throws right. ... Full name: Jose Angel Vidro. ... Name pronounced: VEE-droe. ... High school: Blanco Morales (Sabana Grande, Puerto Rico).

TRANSACTIONS/CAREER NOTES: Selected by Montreal Expos organization in sixth round of free agent draft (June 1, 1992). ... On disabled list (June 1-15 and July 26, 1993-remainder of season). ... On disabled list (May 20-June 12, 2001).

2003 GAMES PLAYED BY POSITION (MLB): 2B—137.

										BATTING									FIELDING	
Year — Team (League)	Pos.	G	AB	R	H	2B	3B	HR	RBI	BB	SO	HBP	GDP	SB-CS	Avg.	OBP	SLG	OPS	E	Pct.
1992— GC Expos (GCL)	2B	54	200	29	66	6	2	4	31	16	31	0	5	10-1	.330	.376	.440	.816	4	.982
1993— Burlington (Midw.)	2B	76	287	39	69	19	0	2	34	28	54	5	7	3-2	.240	.317	.328	.644	7	.974
1994— W.P. Beach (FSL)	2B	125	465	57	124	30	2	4	49	51	56	5	5	8-2	.267	.344	.366	.709	20	.964
1995— W.P. Beach (FSL)	IF	44	163	20	53	15	2	3	24	8	21	2	5	0-1	.325	.360	.497	.857	4	.981
— Harrisburg (East.)	IF	64	246	33	64	16	2	4	38	20	37	1	5	7-7	.260	.315	.390	.705	9	.966
1996— Harrisburg (East.)	IF	126	452	57	117	25	3	18	82	29	71	2	6	3-1	.259	.300	.447	.747	15	.964
1997— Ottawa (Int'l)	3B-2B-DH	73	279	40	90	17	0	13	47	22	40	1	6	2-0	.323	.370	.523	.894	8	.967
— Montreal (N.L.)	3B-2B-DH	67	169	19	42	12	1	2	17	11	20	2	1	1-0	.249	.297	.367	.664	4	.955
1998— Montreal (N.L.)	2B-3B	83	205	24	45	12	0	0	18	27	33	4	5	2-2	.220	.318	.278	.596	6	.972
— Ottawa (Int'l)	2B-3B-DH	63	235	35	68	14	2	2	32	24	25	4	4	5-2	.289	.361	.391	.752	6	.973
1999— Montreal (N.L.)	2-1-0-3	140	494	67	150	45	2	12	59	29	51	4	12	0-4	.304	.346	.476	.822	11	.981
2000— Montreal (N.L.)	2B	153	606	101	200	51	2	24	97	49	69	2	17	5-4	.330	.379	.540	.918	10	.986
2001— Montreal (N.L.)	2B-DH	124	486	82	155	34	1	15	59	31	49	10	18	4-1	.319	.371	.486	.856	9	.983
2002— Montreal (N.L.)	2B	152	604	103	190	43	3	19	96	60	70	3	12	2-1	.315	.378	.490	.868	11	.986
2003— Montreal (N.L.)	2B	144	509	77	158	36	0	15	65	69	50	7	16	3-2	.310	.397	.470	.866	10	.983
Major League totals (7 years)		863	3073	473	940	233	9	87	411	276	342	32	81	17-14	.306	.367	.473	.839	61	.983

VILLAFUERTE, BRANDON — P

PERSONAL: Born December 17, 1975, in Hilo, Hawaii. ... 5-11/165. ... Throws right, bats right. ... Full name: Brandon Paul Villafuerte. ... Name pronounced: vila-FERT-tee. ... High school: Live Oak (Morgan Hill, Calif.). ... College: West Valley (Calif.).

TRANSACTIONS/CAREER NOTES: Selected by New York Mets organization 66th round of free-agent draft (June 2, 1994). ... Traded by Mets with a player to be named later to Florida Marlins for OF Robert Stratton (March 20,1998); Marlins acquired 2B Cesar Crespo to complete deal (September 14, 1998). ... Traded by Marlins to Detroit Tigers for P Mike Drumright (July 31, 1999). ... Traded by Tigers with P Kevin Mobley to Texas Rangers for P Matt Perisho (December 15, 2000). ... Granted free agency (October 11, 2001). ... Signed by San Diego Padres organization (December 6, 2001).

CAREER HITTING: 0-for-1 (.000), 0 R, 0 2B, 0 3B, 0 HR, 0 RBI.

Year — League	W	L	Pct.	ERA	WHIP	G	GS	CG	ShO	Hld.	Sv.-Opp.	IP	H	R	ER	HR	BB-IBB	SO	Avg.
1995— Kingsport (Appal.)	5	1	.833	5.63	1.69	20	0	0	0	...	0-...	32.0	28	21	20	0	26-0	42	.243
1996— Pittsfield (NYP)	8	3	.727	3.02	1.28	18	7	1	0	...	1-...	62.2	53	21	21	5	27-0	59	.231
1997— Capital City (S. Atl.)	3	1	.750	2.38	1.20	47	3	0	0	...	7-...	75.2	58	23	20	6	33-0	88	.216
1998— Brevard County (FSL)	1	0	1.000	0.93	0.83	3	0	0	0	...	0-...	9.2	7	3	1	0	1-0	6	.212
— Portland (East.)	0	2	.000	4.97	1.86	30	0	0	0	...	1-...	54.1	68	35	30	3	33-2	52	.311
— Charlotte (Int'l)	1	0	1.000	6.35	2.03	10	0	0	0	...	1-...	11.1	15	8	8	2	8-0	9	.333
1999— Portland (East.)	6	8	.429	3.50	1.37	22	12	0	0	...	0-...	100.1	97	45	39	11	40-3	85	.261
— Jacksonville (Sou.)	0	2	.000	1.88	1.21	15	0	0	0	...	5-...	24.0	17	6	5	0	12-0	20	.200
2000— Toledo (Int'l)	4	9	.308	6.67	1.84	46	6	0	0	...	4-...	87.2	112	70	65	7	49-1	85	.309
— Detroit (A.L.)	0	0	...	10.38	1.85	3	0	0	0	0	0-0	4.1	4	5	5	0	4-0	1	.250
2001— Oklahoma (PCL)	5	5	.500	2.83	1.40	38	0	0	0	...	10-...	63.2	63	21	20	4	26-1	65	.267
— Texas (A.L.)	0	0	...	14.29	2.82	6	0	0	0	0	0-0	5.2	12	9	9	3	4-0	4	.414
2002— Portland (PCL)	8	4	.667	2.02	1.12	47	0	0	0	...	1-...	58.0	43	17	13	2	22-1	54	.207
— San Diego (N.L.)	1	2	.333	1.41	1.28	31	0	0	0	8	1-1	32.0	29	5	5	2	12-2	25	.248
2003— Lake Elsinore (Calif.)	0	0	...	0.00	1.00	2	0	0	0	...	2-...	2.0	1	0	0	0	1-0	2	.143
— Portland (PCL)	3	1	.750	1.84	1.27	37	0	0	0	...	12-...	44.0	42	10	9	1	14-1	40	.258
— San Diego (N.L.)	0	2	.000	4.20	1.60	31	0	0	0	2	2-5	40.2	39	20	19	7	26-2	34	.252
American League totals (2 years)	0	0	...	12.60	2.40	9	0	0	0	0	0-0	10.0	16	14	14	3	8-0	5	.356
National League totals (2 years)	1	4	.200	2.97	1.46	62	0	0	0	10	3-6	72.2	68	25	24	9	38-4	59	.250
Major League totals (4 years)	1	4	.200	4.14	1.57	71	0	0	0	10	3-6	82.2	84	39	38	12	46-4	64	.265

V

VILLARREAL, OSCAR — P

PERSONAL: Born November 22, 1981, in Nuevo Leon, Mexico. ... 6-0/177. ... Throws right, bats left. ... Full name: Oscar Eduardo Villarreal. ... Name pronounced: VEE-yuh-ray-al.

TRANSACTIONS/CAREER NOTES: Signed by Arizona Diamondbacks as a non-drafted free agent (November 6, 1998). ... On disabled list (August 31, 2001-remainder of season). ... On disabled list (May 14-June 7, 2002).

CAREER HITTING: 0-for-3 (.000), 0 R, 0 2B, 0 3B, 0 HR, 0 RBI.

Year League	W	L	Pct.	ERA	WHIP	G	GS	CG	ShO	Hld.	Sv.-Opp.	IP	H	R	ER	HR	BB-IBB	SO	Avg.
1999— Ariz. D'backs (Ariz.)	1	5	.167	3.78	1.38	14	11	0	0	...	0-...	64.1	64	39	27	1	25-0	51	.260
2000— Tucson (PCL)	1	0	1.000	2.08	1.85	2	0	0	0	...	0-...	4.1	6	1	1	0	2-0	4	.353
— South Bend (Mid.)	1	3	.250	4.41	1.65	13	5	0	0	...	0-...	32.2	37	19	16	0	17-3	30	.274
—Ariz. D'backs (Ariz.)	0	0	...	9.00	2.00	1	0	0	0	...	0-...	1.0	2	1	1	0	0-0	1	.400
— High Desert (Calif.)	0	2	.000	3.65	1.54	9	4	0	0	...	0-...	24.2	24	20	10	4	14-0	18	.253
2001— El Paso (Texas)	6	9	.400	4.41	1.54	27	27	0	0	...	0-...	140.2	154	96	69	10	63-1	108	.274
2002— El Paso (Texas)	6	3	.667	3.74	1.17	14	12	1	0	...	0-...	84.1	73	36	35	2	26-0	85	.233
—Tucson (PCL)	3	3	.500	4.36	1.41	10	10	0	0	...	0-...	64.0	68	33	31	8	22-0	40	.278
2003— Arizona (N.L.)	10	7	.588	2.57	1.29	86	1	0	0	10	0-4	98.0	80	40	28	6	46-10	80	.222
Major League totals (1 year)	**10**	**7**	**.588**	**2.57**	**1.29**	**86**	**1**	**0**	**0**	**10**	**0-4**	**98.0**	**80**	**40**	**28**	**6**	**46-10**	**80**	**.222**

VILLONE, RON — P

PERSONAL: Born January 16, 1970, in Englewood, N.J. ... 6-3/243. ... Throws left, bats left. ... Full name: Ronald Thomas Villone. ... Name pronounced: vill-OWN. ... High school: South Bergenfield (Bergenfield, N.J.). ... College: Massachusetts.

TRANSACTIONS/CAREER NOTES: Selected by Seattle Mariners in first round (14th pick overall) of free-agent draft (June 1, 1992). ... On disabled list (April 19-26, 1994). ... Traded by Mariners with OF Marc Newfield to San Diego Padres for P Andy Benes and a player to be named later (July 31, 1995); Mariners acquired P Greg Keagle to complete deal (September 16, 1995). ... Traded by Padres with P Bryce Florie and OF Marc Newfield to Milwaukee Brewers for OF Greg Vaughn and a player to be named later (July 31, 1996); Padres acquired OF Gerald Parent to complete deal (September 16, 1996). ... Traded by Brewers with P Ben McDonald and P Mike Fetters to Cleveland Indians for OF Marquis Grissom and P Jeff Juden (December 8, 1997). ... On Cleveland disabled list (August 15-September 1, 1998); included rehabilitation assignment to Buffalo (August 22-September 1). ... Released by Indians (April 2, 1999). ... Signed by Cincinnati Reds organization (April 5, 1999). ... Traded by Reds to Colorado Rockies for two players to be named later (November 8, 2000); Reds acquired P Jeff Taglienti and P Justin Carter to complete deal (December 20, 2000). ... Traded by Rockies to Houston Astros for P Jay Powell (June 27, 2001). ... Granted free agency (November 5, 2001). ... Signed by Pittsburgh Pirates organization (February 12, 2002). ... On disabled list (August 15-September 1, 2002). ... Granted free agency (October 29, 2002). ... Signed by Arizona Diamondbacks organization (January 29, 2003). ... Contract purchased by Houston from New Orleans (June 17, 2003).

CAREER HITTING: 22-for-168 (.131), 7 R, 3 2B, 1 3B, 1 HR, 7 RBI.

Year League	W	L	Pct.	ERA	WHIP	G	GS	CG	ShO	Hld.	Sv.-Opp.	IP	H	R	ER	HR	BB-IBB	SO	Avg.
1993— Riverside (Calif.)	7	4	.636	4.21	1.63	16	16	0	0	...	0-...	83.1	74	47	39	5	62-0	82	.241
— Jacksonville (Sou.)	3	4	.429	4.38	1.41	11	11	0	0	...	0-...	63.2	49	34	31	6	41-3	66	.219
1994— Jacksonville (Sou.)	6	7	.462	3.86	1.56	41	5	0	0	...	8-...	79.1	56	37	34	7	68-3	94	.199
1995— Seattle (A.L.)	0	2	.000	7.91	2.22	19	0	0	0	3	0-3	19.1	20	19	17	6	23-0	26	.270
—Tacoma (PCL)	1	0	1.000	0.61	0.94	22	0	0	0	...	13-...	29.2	9	6	2	1	19-0	43	.095
— San Diego (N.L.)	2	1	.667	4.21	1.36	19	0	0	0	3	1-2	25.2	24	12	12	5	11-0	37	.242
1996— Las Vegas (PCL)	2	1	.667	1.64	1.00	23	0	0	0	...	3-...	22.0	13	5	4	0	9-0	29	.169
— San Diego (N.L.)	1	1	.500	2.95	1.31	21	0	0	0	4	0-1	18.1	17	6	6	2	7-0	19	.243
— Milwaukee (A.L.)	0	0	...	3.28	1.30	23	0	0	0	5	2-2	24.2	14	9	9	4	18-0	19	.155
1997— Milwaukee (A.L.)	1	0	1.000	3.42	1.71	50	0	0	0	8	0-2	52.2	54	23	20	4	36-2	40	.271
1998— Buffalo (Int'l)	2	2	.500	2.01	1.39	23	0	0	0	...	7-...	22.1	20	11	5	2	11-1	28	.235
— Cleveland (A.L.)	0	0	...	6.00	1.93	25	0	0	0	1	0-0	27.0	30	18	18	3	22-0	15	.297
1999— Indianapolis (Int'l)	2	0	1.000	1.42	1.16	18	0	0	0	...	1-...	19.0	9	3	3	1	13-1	23	.155
— Cincinnati (N.L.)	9	7	.563	4.23	1.31	29	22	0	0	0	2-2	142.2	114	70	67	8	73-2	97	.219
2000— Cincinnati (N.L.)	10	10	.500	5.43	1.65	35	23	2	0	1	0-0	141.0	154	95	85	22	78-3	77	.286
2001— Colorado (N.L.)	1	3	.250	6.36	1.82	22	6	0	0	2	0-0	46.2	56	35	33	6	29-4	48	.295
— Houston (N.L.)	5	7	.417	5.56	1.49	31	6	0	0	4	0-0	68.0	77	46	42	12	24-1	65	.282
2002— Pittsburgh (N.L.)	4	6	.400	5.81	1.39	45	7	0	0	0	0-1	93.0	95	63	60	8	34-3	55	.270
2003— Tucson (PCL)	1	1	.500	3.55	1.26	15	0	0	0	...	1-...	25.1	20	14	10	2	12-1	22	.233
— New Orleans (PCL)	3	1	.750	1.23	1.16	5	5	0	0	...	0-...	29.1	24	5	4	0	10-0	18	.233
— Houston (N.L.)	6	6	.500	4.13	1.30	19	19	0	0	0	0-0	106.2	91	51	49	16	48-1	91	.233
American League totals (4 years)	**1**	**2**	**.333**	**4.66**	**1.75**	**117**	**0**	**0**	**0**	**17**	**2-7**	**123.2**	**118**	**69**	**64**	**17**	**99-2**	**100**	**.260**
National League totals (7 years)	**38**	**41**	**.481**	**4.96**	**1.45**	**221**	**83**	**2**	**0**	**14**	**3-6**	**642.0**	**628**	**378**	**354**	**79**	**304-14**	**489**	**.258**
Major League totals (9 years)	**39**	**43**	**.476**	**4.91**	**1.50**	**338**	**83**	**2**	**0**	**31**	**5-13**	**765.2**	**746**	**447**	**418**	**96**	**403-16**	**589**	**.258**

VINA, FERNANDO — 2B

PERSONAL: Born April 16, 1969, in Sacramento, Calif. ... 5-9/180. ... Bats left, throws right. ... Name pronounced: VEEN-yah. ... High school: Valley (Sacramento). ... College: Arizona State.

TRANSACTIONS/CAREER NOTES: Selected by New York Yankees organization in 51st round of free-agent draft (June 1, 1988); did not sign. ... Selected by New York Mets organization in ninth round of free-agent draft (June 4, 1990). ... Selected by Seattle Mariners from Mets organization in Rule 5 major league draft (December 7, 1992). ... Returned to Mets organization (June 15, 1993). ... On New York disabled list (May 22-June 6, 1994). ... On Norfolk disabled list (August 30-September 6, 1994). ... Traded by Mets to Milwaukee Brewers (December 22, 1994), completing deal in which Brewers traded P Doug Henry for two players to be named later (November 30, 1994); Brewers acquired C Javier Gonzalez as partial completion of deal (December 6, 1994). ... On Milwaukee disabled list (April 20-July 17, 1997); included rehabilitation assignments to Stockton (July 9-11) and Tucson (July 12-17). ... On suspended list (May 11-13 and May 25-27, 1999). ... On Milwaukee disabled list (May 10-25 and June 4, 1999-remainder of season); included rehabilitation assignment to Beloit (August 6-8). ... Traded by Brewers to St. Louis Cardinals for P Juan Acevedo and two players to be named later (December 20, 1999); Brewers acquired P Matt Parker and C Eliezer Alfonzo to complete deal (June 13, 2000). ... On disabled list (June 20-July 4, 2000). ... Placed on 15-day disabled list (May 26, 2003). ... Sent on minor league rehab assignment (August 23, 2003). ... Recalled from minor league rehab assignment; removed from 15-day disabled list (August 30, 2003).

2003 GAMES PLAYED BY POSITION (MLB): 2B—60.

Year	Team (League)	Pos.	G	AB	R	H	2B	3B	HR	RBI	BB	SO	HBP	GDP	SB-CS	Avg.	OBP	SLG	OPS	E	Pct.
1991— Columbia (S. Atl.)	2B	129	498	77	135	23	6	6	50	46	27	13	5	42-•22	.271	.344	.378	.721	21	.965
1992— St. Lucie (Fla. St.)	2B	111	421	61	124	15	5	1	42	32	26	3	7	36-17	.295	.347	.361	.708	17	.971
— Tidewater (Int'l)	2B	11	30	3	6	0	0	0	2	0	2	0	1	0-0	.200	.194	.200	.394	1	.978
1993— Seattle (A.L.) 2B-SS-DH	24	45	5	10	2	0	0	2	4	3	3	0	6-0	.222	.327	.267	.594	0	1.000
— Norfolk (Int'l) SS-2B-OF	73	287	24	66	6	4	4	27	7	17	4	12	16-11	.230	.258	.321	.578	14	.964
1994— New York (N.L.) 2-3-S-O	79	124	20	31	6	0	0	6	12	11	*12	4	3-1	.250	.372	.298	.670	4	.963
— Norfolk (Int'l) SS-2B	6	17	2	3	0	0	0	1	1	1	1	0	1-1	.176	.250	.176	.426	1	.952
1995— Milwaukee (A.L.) 2B-SS-3B	113	288	46	74	7	7	3	29	22	28	9	6	6-3	.257	.327	.361	.688	8	.982
1996— Milwaukee (A.L.)	2B	140	554	94	157	19	10	7	46	38	35	13	15	16-7	.283	.342	.392	.733	* 16	.979
1997— Milwaukee (A.L.) 2B-DH	79	324	37	89	12	2	4	28	12	23	7	4	8-7	.275	.312	.361	.673	7	.982
— Stockton (Calif.)	2B	3	9	2	4	0	1	0	3	0	0	0	0	0-2	.444	.444	.667	1.111	0	1.000
— Tucson (PCL)	2B	6	19	3	9	3	0	1	5	3	1	2	0	0-1	.474	.583	.789	1.373	2	.923
1998— Milwaukee (N.L.)	2B	159	637	101	198	39	7	7	45	54	46	25	7	22-16	.311	.386	.427	.813	12	.986
1999— Milwaukee (N.L.)	2B	37	154	17	41	7	0	1	16	14	6	4	1	5-2	.266	.339	.331	.670	1	.995
— Beloit (Midw.)	2B-DH	2	10	1	2	1	0	0	0	0	2	0	0	0-1	.200	.200	.300	.500	2	.500
2000— St. Louis (N.L.)	2B	123	487	81	146	24	6	4	31	36	36	*28	5	10-8	.300	.380	.398	.779	7	.988
2001— St. Louis (N.L.)	2B	154	631	95	191	30	8	9	56	32	35	22	7	17-7	.303	.357	.418	.775	9	.987
2002— St. Louis (N.L.)	2B	150	622	75	168	29	5	1	54	44	36	18	11	17-11	.270	.333	.338	.670	13	.981
2003— Memphis (PCL) 2B-DH	5	17	1	3	0	0	0	1	2	2	0	1	0-0	.176	.250	.176	.426	0	1.000
— St. Louis (N.L.)	2B	61	259	35	65	14	4	4	23	11	24	11	5	4-4	.251	.309	.382	.691	8	.974
American League totals (4 years)		356	1211	182	330	40	19	14	105	76	89	32	25	36-17	.273	.330	.372	.701	31	.981
National League totals (7 years)		763	2914	424	840	149	30	26	231	203	194	120	40	78-49	.288	.358	.387	.744	54	.985
Major League totals (11 years)		1119	4125	606	1170	189	49	40	336	279	283	152	65	114-66	.284	.350	.382	.732	85	.984

VITIELLO, JOE   1B/OF

PERSONAL: Born April 11, 1970, in Cambridge, Mass. ... 6-3/230. ... Bats right, throws right. ... Full name: Joseph David Vitiello. ... Name pronounced: vit-ee-ELL-o. ... High school: Stoneham (Mass.). ... College: Alabama.

TRANSACTIONS/CAREER NOTES: Selected by New York Yankees organization in 31st round of free-agent draft (June 1, 1988); did not sign. ... Selected by Kansas City Royals organization in first round (seventh pick overall) of free-agent draft (June 3, 1991). ... On disabled list (April 12-23, 1992; June 2-11, 1993; and May 23-June 16, 1994). ... On disabled list (June 17-July 28 and August 13, 1997-remainder of season); included rehabilitation assignment to Omaha (July 15-28). ... On Kansas City disabled list (April 8-May 18, 1998); included rehabilitation assignment to Omaha (April 21-May 9). ... On Omaha disabled list (August 4-12, 1998). ... Granted free agency (October 15, 1998). ... Re-signed by Royals organization (December 17, 1998). ... Granted free agency (October 8, 1999). ... Signed by San Diego Padres organization (November 22, 1999). ... Granted free agency (October 18, 2000). ... On Ottawa disabled list (August 3-18, 2002). ... Granted free agency (October 15, 2002). ... Signed by San Francisco Giants as a minor league free agent (January 13, 2003). ... Traded by Giants to Montreal Expos for P Ben Washburn (May 3, 2003). ... Elected free agency (October 8, 2003).

2003 GAMES PLAYED BY POSITION (MLB): OF—15, 1B—12, DH—1.

Year	Team (League)	Pos.	G	AB	R	H	2B	3B	HR	RBI	BB	SO	HBP	GDP	SB-CS	Avg.	OBP	SLG	OPS	E	Pct.
1991— Eugene (Northwest)	1B-OF	19	64	16	21	2	0	6	21	11	18	1	0	1-1	.328	.423	.641	1.064	1	.981
— Memphis (Sou.)	1B-OF	36	128	15	28	4	1	0	18	23	36	1	2	0-0	.219	.340	.266	.605	1	.988
1992— Baseball City (FSL)	1B	115	400	52	113	16	1	8	65	46	101	7	11	0-5	.283	.360	.388	.748	13	.986
1993— Memphis (Sou.)	1B	117	413	62	119	25	2	15	66	57	95	5	8	2-0	.288	.377	.467	.844	• 17	.981
1994— Omaha (A.A.)	1B-DH	98	352	46	121	28	3	10	61	56	63	7	15	3-2	.344	.440	.526	.966	8	.988
1995— Kansas City (A.L.)	DH-1B	53	130	13	33	4	0	7	21	8	25	4	4	0-0	.254	.317	.446	.763	1	.982
— Omaha (A.A.) DH-1B-OF	59	229	33	64	14	2	12	42	12	50	6	9	0-1	.279	.329	.515	.845	4	.984
1996— Kansas City (A.L.) DH-1B-OF	85	257	29	62	15	1	8	40	38	69	3	12	2-0	.241	.342	.401	.743	0	1.000
— Omaha (A.A.)	1B	36	132	26	37	7	0	9	31	16	32	3	0	1-0	.280	.368	.538	.906	3	.990
1997— Kansas City (A.L.) OF-DH-1B	51	130	11	31	6	0	5	18	14	37	2	2	0-0	.238	.322	.400	.722	1	.982
— Omaha (A.A.)	DH-OF	13	42	5	9	1	0	3	9	5	16	0	0	0-0	.214	.298	.452	.750	0	1.000
1998— Kansas City (A.L.)	DH	3	7	0	1	0	0	0	0	1	2	0	0	0-0	.143	.250	.143	.393	...	...
— Omaha (PCL) 1B-DH-3B	103	376	44	107	20	2	18	71	39	68	6	19	0-0	.285	.355	.492	.847	8	.990
1999— Omaha (PCL)	DH-1B	122	447	70	142	33	0	28	98	66	84	4	16	3-4	.318	.407	.579	.986	6	.981
— Kansas City (A.L.)	1B-DH	13	41	4	6	1	0	1	4	2	9	2	2	0-0	.146	.222	.244	.466	0	1.000
2000— Las Vegas (PCL)	1B	77	274	43	96	31	0	11	46	27	59	2	11	2-0	.350	.411	.584	.995	5	.991
— San Diego (N.L.)	1B-OF	39	52	7	13	3	0	2	8	10	9	0	1	0-0	.250	.365	.423	.788	3	.966
2002— Ottawa (Int'l)	1B	119	431	57	142	34	0	16	82	39	58	7	16	1-0	.329	.390	.520	.910	4	.996
2003— Fresno (PCL) 1B-OF-DH	23	75	9	16	5	0	0	3	8	9	0	3	0-0	.213	.289	.280	.569	2	.987
— Edmonton (PCL)	1B-DH	27	96	11	26	7	0	2	14	10	17	0	3	0-0	.271	.333	.406	.740	1	.995
— Montreal (N.L.) OF-1B-DH	38	76	12	26	6	0	3	13	7	14	2	1	0-0	.342	.407	.539	.946	2	.980
American League totals (5 years)		205	565	57	133	26	1	21	83	63	142	11	20	2-0	.235	.322	.396	.719	2	.991
National League totals (2 years)		77	128	19	39	9	0	5	21	17	23	2	2	0-0	.305	.389	.492	.881	5	.973
Major League totals (7 years)		282	693	76	172	35	1	26	104	80	165	13	22	2-0	.248	.335	.414	.749	7	.983

VIZCAINO, JOSE   IF

PERSONAL: Born March 26, 1968, in San Cristobal, Dominican Republic. ... 6-1/185. ... Bats both, throws right. ... Full name: Jose Luis Vizcaino. ... Name pronounced: vis-kie-ee-no. ... High school: Americo Tolentino (Palenque de San Cristobal, Dominican Republic).

TRANSACTIONS/CAREER NOTES: Signed as non-drafted free agent by Los Angeles Dodgers organization (February 18, 1986). ... Traded by Dodgers to Chicago Cubs for IF Greg Smith (December 14, 1990). ... On disabled list (April 20-May 6 and August 26-September 16, 1992). ... Traded by Cubs to New York Mets for P Anthony Young and P Ottis Smith (March 30, 1994). ... Traded by Mets with IF Jeff Kent to Cleveland Indians for 2B Carlos Baerga and IF Alvaro Espinoza (July 29, 1996). ... Traded by Indians with IF Jeff Kent, P Julian Tavarez and a player to be named later to San Francisco Giants for 3B Matt Williams and a player to be named later (November 13, 1996); Indians traded P Joe Roa to Giants for OF Trenidad Hubbard to complete deal (December 16, 1996). ... Granted free agency (October 29, 1997). ... Signed by Dodgers (December 8, 1997). ... On disabled list (June 22-September 9, 1998; and May 19-June 4, 1999). ... Traded by Dodgers to New York Yankees for IF/DH Jim Leyritz (June 20, 2000). ... Granted free agency (November 1, 2000). ... Signed by Houston Astros (November 20, 2000). ... Granted free agency (November 5, 2001). ... Re-signed by Astros (December 3, 2001). ... Placed on 15-day disabled list by Houston (June 25, 2003). ... Sent on rehab assignment by Houston (August 19, 2003). ... Recalled from rehab assignment (August 21, 2003). ... Removed from 15-day disabled list (August 21, 2003).

2003 GAMES PLAYED BY POSITION (MLB): SS—32, 2B—20, 3B—2, 1B—1.

Year	Team (League)	Pos.	G	AB	R	H	2B	3B	HR	RBI	BB	SO	HBP	GDP	SB-CS	Avg.	OBP	SLG	OPS	E	Pct.
1987— GC Dodgers (GCL)	SS-1B	49	150	26	38	5	1	0	12	22	24	0	1	8-5	.253	.347	.300	.647	13	.933
1988— Bakersfield (Calif.)	SS	122	433	77	126	11	4	0	38	50	54	7	6	13-14	.291	.372	.335	.707	30	.946
1989— Albuquerque (PCL)	SS	129	434	60	123	10	4	1	44	33	41	1	10	16-14	.283	.333	.332	.665	* 30	.951
— Los Angeles (N.L.)	SS	7	10	2	2	0	0	0	0	0	1	0	0	0-0	.200	.200	.200	.400	2	.882
1990— Albuquerque (PCL)	2B-SS	81	276	46	77	10	2	2	38	30	33	0	6	13-6	.279	.346	.351	.698	14	.964
— Los Angeles (N.L.)	SS	37	51	3	14	1	1	0	2	4	8	0	1	1-1	.275	.327	.333	.661	2	.962
1991— Chicago (N.L.)	2B-3B-SS	93	145	7	38	5	0	0	10	5	18	0	1	2-1	.262	.283	.297	.579	7	.960
1992— Chicago (N.L.)	SS-3B-2B	86	285	25	64	10	4	1	17	14	35	0	4	3-0	.225	.260	.298	.558	9	.970
1993— Chicago (N.L.)	SS-3B-2B	151	551	74	158	19	4	4	54	46	71	3	9	12-9	.287	.340	.358	.697	17	.974
1994— New York (N.L.)	SS	103	410	47	105	13	3	3	33	33	62	2	5	1-11	.256	.310	.324	.635	13	.970
1995— New York (N.L.)	SS-2B	135	509	66	146	21	5	3	56	35	76	1	14	8-3	.287	.332	.365	.698	10	.984
1996— New York (N.L.)	2B	96	363	47	110	12	6	1	32	28	58	3	6	9-5	.303	.356	.377	.733	6	.986
— Cleveland (A.L.)	2B-SS-DH	48	179	23	51	5	2	0	13	7	24	0	2	6-2	.285	.310	.335	.645	4	.982
1997— San Francisco (N.L.)	SS-2B	151	568	77	151	19	7	5	50	48	87	0	13	8-8	.266	.323	.350	.673	16	.976
1998— Los Angeles (N.L.)	SS	67	237	30	62	9	0	3	29	17	35	1	4	7-3	.262	.311	.338	.649	4	.985
1999— Los Angeles (N.L.)	S-2-3-0	94	266	27	67	9	0	1	29	20	23	1	9	2-1	.252	.304	.297	.601	7	.976
2000— Los Angeles (N.L.)	S-3-2-D-1	40	93	9	19	2	1	0	4	10	15	1	3	1-0	.204	.288	.247	.536	2	.978
— New York (N.L.)	2-3-D-S	73	174	23	48	8	1	0	10	12	28	0	3	5-7	.276	.319	.333	.652	2	.991
2001— Houston (N.L.)	SS-2B-3B	107	256	38	71	8	3	1	14	15	33	2	6	3-2	.277	.322	.344	.666	14	.939
2002— Houston (N.L.)	S-3-2-1	125	406	53	123	19	2	5	37	24	40	1	5	3-5	.303	.342	.397	.738	4	.989
2003— New Orleans (PCL)	2B-SS	2	8	1	2	0	0	1	1	1	0	0	0	0-0	.250	.333	.625	.958	1	.889
— Houston (N.L.)	S-2-3-1	91	189	14	47	7	3	3	26	8	22	1	5	0-1	.249	.281	.365	.646	5	.970
American League totals (2 years)		121	353	46	99	13	3	0	23	19	52	0	5	11-9	.280	.315	.334	.649	6	.986
National League totals (15 years)		1383	4339	519	1177	154	39	30	393	307	584	16	85	60-50	.271	.320	.345	.665	118	.975
Major League totals (15 years)		1504	4692	565	1276	167	42	30	416	326	636	16	90	71-59	.272	.319	.345	.664	124	.976

VIZCAINO, LUIS — P

PERSONAL: Born August 6, 1974, in Bani, Dominican Republic. ... 5-11/180. ... Throws right, bats right. ... Full name: Luis Viczaino Arias Vizcaino. ... Name pronounced: vis-ki-ee-no.

TRANSACTIONS/CAREER NOTES: Signed as non-drafted free agent by Oakland Athletics organization (December 9, 1994). ... Traded by A's to Texas Rangers for P Justin Duchscherer (March 18, 2002). ... Traded by Rangers to Milwaukee Brewers for P Jesus Pena (March 24, 2002).

CAREER HITTING: 0-for-2 (.000), 0 R, 0 2B, 0 3B, 0 HR, 0 RBI.

Year	League	W	L	Pct.	ERA	WHIP	G	GS	CG	ShO	Hld.	Sv.-Opp.	IP	H	R	ER	HR	BB-IBB	SO	Avg.
1995— Dominican Athletics (DSL)	10	2	.833	2.27	1.06	16	15	5	1	...	0-...	* 115.0	93	41	29	...	29-...	89	...
1996— Ariz. A's (Ariz.)	6	3	.667	4.07	1.37	15	10	0	0	...	1-...	59.2	58	36	27	1	24-1	52	.247
1997— Modesto (Calif.)	0	3	.000	13.19	2.58	7	0	0	0	...	0-...	14.1	24	24	21	4	13-4	15	.387
— S. Oregon (N'west)	1	6	.143	7.93	1.87	22	5	0	0	...	0-...	47.2	62	51	42	5	27-0	42	.308
1998— Modesto (Calif.)	6	3	.667	2.74	1.13	23	16	0	0	...	0-...	102.0	72	39	31	5	43-1	108	.196
— Huntsville (Sou.)	3	2	.600	4.66	1.68	7	7	0	0	...	0-...	38.2	43	27	20	8	22-0	26	.279
1999— Midland (Texas)	8	7	.533	5.85	1.61	25	19	0	0	...	0-...	104.2	120	74	68	18	48-2	88	.287
— Oakland (A.L.)	0	0	...	5.40	1.80	1	0	0	0	0	0-0	3.1	3	2	2	1	3-0	2	.231
— Vancouver (PCL)	0	1	.000	1.38	1.46	7	0	0	0	0	0-...	13.0	13	4	2	0	6-0	7	.260
2000— Oakland (A.L.)	0	1	.000	7.45	1.86	12	0	0	0	0	0-0	19.1	25	17	16	2	11-0	18	.305
— Sacramento (PCL)	6	2	.750	5.03	1.43	33	2	0	0	...	5-...	48.1	48	27	27	4	21-0	41	.276
2001— Sacramento (PCL)	2	2	.500	2.14	1.07	27	0	0	0	...	7-...	42.0	35	10	10	5	10-4	56	.220
— Oakland (A.L.)	2	1	.667	4.66	1.36	36	0	0	0	3	1-1	36.2	38	19	19	8	12-1	31	.266
2002— Milwaukee (N.L.)	5	3	.625	2.99	1.05	76	0	0	0	19	5-6	81.1	55	27	27	6	30-4	79	.192
2003— Milwaukee (N.L.)	4	3	.571	6.39	1.44	75	0	0	0	9	0-6	62.0	64	45	44	16	25-3	61	.263
American League totals (3 years)	2	2	.500	5.61	1.55	49	0	0	0	3	1-1	59.1	66	38	37	11	26-1	51	.277
National League totals (2 years)	9	6	.600	4.46	1.21	151	0	0	0	28	5-12	143.1	119	72	71	22	55-7	140	.225
Major League totals (5 years)	11	8	.579	4.80	1.31	200	0	0	0	31	6-13	202.2	185	110	108	33	81-8	191	.241

VIZQUEL, OMAR — SS

PERSONAL: Born April 24, 1967, in Caracas, Venezuela. ... 5-9/175. ... Bats both, throws right. ... Full name: Omar Enrique Vizquel. ... Name pronounced: viz-KELL. ... High school: Francisco Espejo (Caracas, Venezuela).

TRANSACTIONS/CAREER NOTES: Signed as non-drafted free agent by Seattle Mariners organization (April 1, 1984). ... On Seattle disabled list (April 7-May 13, 1990); included rehabilitation assignments to Calgary (May 3-7) and San Bernardino (May 8-12). ... On Seattle disabled list (April 13-May 11, 1992); included rehabilitation assignment to Calgary (May 5-11). ... Traded by Mariners to Cleveland Indians for SS Felix Fermin, 1B Reggie Jefferson and cash (December 20, 1993). ... On Cleveland disabled list (April 23-June 13, 1994); included rehabilitation assignment to Charlotte (June 6-13). ... On suspended list (September 17-18, 1998). ... Placed on 15-day disabled list (June 12, 2003). ... Sent on rehab assignment by Cleveland (August 21, 2003). ... Recalled from minor league rehab assignment; removed from 15-day disabled list (August 26, 2003). ... Placed on 60-day disabled list (September 6, 2003).

2003 GAMES PLAYED BY POSITION (MLB): SS—64.

Year	Team (League)	Pos.	G	AB	R	H	2B	3B	HR	RBI	BB	SO	HBP	GDP	SB-CS	Avg.	OBP	SLG	OPS	E	Pct.
1984— Butte (Pio.)	2B-SS	15	45	7	14	2	0	0	4	3	8	0	0	2-0	.311	.347	.356	.702	5	.894
1985— Bellingham (N'west)	2B-SS	50	187	24	42	9	0	5	17	12	27	0	0	4-3	.225	.270	.353	.623	19	.932
1986— Wausau (Midw.)	2B-SS	105	352	60	75	13	2	4	28	64	56	2	6	19-6	.213	.333	.295	.629	16 ‡	.968
1987— Salinas (Calif.)	2B-SS	114	407	61	107	12	8	0	38	57	55	0	5	25-19	.263	.350	.332	.682	25	.938
1988— Vermont (East.)	SS	103	374	54	95	18	2	2	35	42	44	3	6	30-11	.254	.328	.329	.657	19	* .959
— Calgary (PCL)	SS	33	107	10	24	2	3	1	12	5	14	0	1	2-4	.224	.259	.327	.586	6	.957
1989— Seattle (A.L.)	SS	143	387	45	85	7	3	1	20	28	40	1	6	1-4	.220	.273	.261	.534	18	.971
— Calgary (PCL)	SS	7	28	3	6	2	0	0	3	3	4	1	1	0-2	.214	.313	.286	.598	0	1.000
1990— Calgary (PCL)	SS	48	150	18	35	6	2	0	8	13	10	2	3	4-3	.233	.299	.300	.599	6	.972
— San Bern. (Calif.)	SS	6	20	5	7	0	0	0	3	3	1	0	0	1-2	.250	.333	.250	.583	3	.914
— Seattle (A.L.)	SS	81	255	19	63	3	2	2	18	18	22	0	4	4-1	.247	.295	.298	.593	7	.980
1991— Seattle (A.L.)	2B-SS	142	426	42	98	16	4	1	41	45	37	0	8	7-2	.230	.302	.293	.595	13	.980
1992— Seattle (A.L.)	SS	136	483	49	142	20	4	0	21	32	38	2	14	15-13	.294	.340	.352	.692	7	.989
— Calgary (PCL)	SS	6	22	0	6	1	0	0	2	1	3	1	3	0-1	.273	.333	.318	.652	1	.972
1993— Seattle (A.L.)	SS-DH	158	560	68	143	14	2	2	31	50	71	4	7	12-14	.255	.319	.298	.618	15	.980

Year	Team (League)	Pos.	G	AB	R	H	2B	3B	HR	RBI	BB	SO	HBP	GDP	SB-CS	Avg.	OBP	SLG	OPS	E	Pct.
1994— Cleveland (A.L.)		SS	69	286	39	78	10	1	1	33	23	23	0	4	13-4	.273	.325	.325	.650	6	.981
— Charlotte (Int'l)		SS	7	26	3	7	1	0	0	1	2	1	0	0	1-0	.269	.321	.308	.629	1	.967
1995— Cleveland (A.L.)		SS	136	542	87	144	28	0	6	56	59	59	1	4	29-11	.266	.333	.351	.684	9	.986
1996— Cleveland (A.L.)		SS	151	542	98	161	36	1	9	64	56	42	4	10	35-9	.297	.362	.417	.779	20	.971
1997— Cleveland (A.L.)		SS	153	565	89	158	23	6	5	49	57	58	2	16	43-12	.280	.347	.368	.715	10	.985
1998— Cleveland (A.L.)		SS	151	576	86	166	30	6	2	50	62	64	4	10	37-12	.288	.358	.372	.730	5	.993
1999— Cleveland (A.L.)		SS-OF	144	574	112	191	36	4	5	66	65	50	1	8	42-9	.333	.397	.436	.833	15	.976
2000— Cleveland (A.L.)		SS	156	613	101	176	27	3	7	66	87	72	5	13	22-10	.287	.377	.375	.753	3	.995
2001— Cleveland (A.L.)		SS	155	611	84	156	26	8	2	50	61	72	2	14	13-9	.255	.323	.334	.657	7	.989
2002— Cleveland (A.L.)		SS	151	582	85	160	31	5	14	72	56	64	8	7	18-10	.275	.341	.418	.759	7	.990
2003— Lake County (S. Atl.)		SS	4	14	0	1	0	0	0	0	1	2	0	0	1-0	.071	.133	.071	.205	0	1.000
— Cleveland (A.L.)		SS	64	250	43	61	13	2	2	19	29	20	0	11	8-3	.244	.321	.336	.657	7	.978
Major League totals (15 years)				1990	7252	1047	1982	320	51	59	656	728	732	34	139	299-123	.273	.340	.356	.695	149	.983

VOGELSONG, RYAN   P

PERSONAL: Born July 22, 1977, in Charlotte, N.C. ... 6-3/205. ... Throws right, bats right. ... Full name: Ryan Andrew Vogelsong. ... High school: Octorara Area (Atglen, Pa.). ... College: Kutztown State (Pa.).

TRANSACTIONS/CAREER NOTES: Selected by San Francisco Giants organization in fifth round of free agent draft (June 2, 1998). ... Traded by Giants with OF Armando Rios to Pittsburgh Pirates for P Jason Schmidt (July 30, 2001). ... On Pittsburgh disabled list (March 30-August 1, 2002); included rehabilitation assignments to Lynchburg (July 3-23) and Altoona (July 24-August 1). ... Recalled by Pittsburgh from Nashville (June 14, 2003). ... Optioned to Nashville by Pittsburgh (June 22, 2003). ... Recalled by Pittsburgh from Nashville (September 14, 2003).

CAREER HITTING: 2-for-16 (.125), 0 R, 1 2B, 0 3B, 0 HR, 0 RBI.

Year	League	W	L	Pct.	ERA	WHIP	G	GS	CG	ShO	Hld.	Sv.-Opp.	IP	H	R	ER	HR	BB-IBB	SO	Avg.
1998— Salem-Keizer (NW)		6	1	.857	1.77	0.95	10	10	0	0	...	0-...	56.0	37	15	11	5	16-0	66	.186
— San Jose (Calif.)		0	0	...	7.58	1.42	4	4	0	0	...	0-...	19.0	23	16	16	3	4-0	26	.307
1999— San Jose (Calif.)		4	4	.500	2.45	0.92	13	13	0	0	...	0-...	69.2	37	26	19	3	27-0	86	.154
— Shreveport (Texas)		0	2	.000	7.31	1.94	6	6	0	0	...	0-...	28.1	40	25	23	7	15-0	23	.336
2000— Shreveport (Texas)		6	10	.375	4.23	1.43	27	27	1	0	...	0-...	155.1	153	82	73	15	69-2	* 147	.260
— San Francisco (N.L.)		0	0	...	0.00	1.00	4	0	0	0	0	0-0	6.0	4	0	0	0	2-0	6	.182
2001— Fresno (PCL)		3	3	.500	2.79	0.91	10	10	0	0	...	0-...	58.0	35	18	18	6	18-0	53	.170
— San Francisco (N.L.)		0	3	.000	5.65	1.50	13	0	0	0	1	0-0	28.2	29	21	18	5	14-0	17	.257
— Nashville (PCL)		2	3	.400	3.98	1.29	6	6	0	0	...	0-...	31.2	26	15	14	2	15-0	33	.230
— Pittsburgh (N.L.)		0	2	.000	12.00	2.67	2	2	0	0	0	0-0	6.0	10	10	8	1	6-1	7	.357
2002— Lynchburg (Carolina)		1	1	.500	8.04	1.66	4	4	0	0	...	0-...	15.2	19	14	14	0	7-0	20	.297
— Altoona (East.)		1	5	.167	5.56	1.31	8	8	0	0	...	0-...	43.2	47	27	27	5	10-0	35	.278
2003— Nashville (PCL)		12	8	.600	4.29	1.32	26	26	1	1	...	0-...	149.0	142	75	71	12	54-5	146	.250
— Pittsburgh (N.L.)		2	2	.500	6.55	1.77	6	5	0	0	0	0-0	22.0	30	19	16	1	9-3	15	.323
Major League totals (3 years)		2	7	.222	6.03	1.66	25	7	0	0	1	0-0	62.2	73	50	42	7	31-4	45	.285

VOYLES, BRAD   P

PERSONAL: Born December 30, 1976, in Green Bay, Wis. ... 6-0/195. ... Throws right, bats right. ... Full name: Bradley Roy Voyles. ... High school: Luxemburg-Casco (Luxemburg, Wis.). ... College: Lincoln Memorial (Tenn.).

TRANSACTIONS/CAREER NOTES: Selected by Atlanta Braves organization in 45th round of free-agent draft (June 2, 1998). ... On Atlanta disabled list (March 28-June 8, 2001); included rehabilitation assignment to Myrtle Beach (June 3-8). ... Traded by Braves with 2B Alejandro Machado to Kansas City Royals for SS Rey Sanchez (July 31, 2001).

CAREER HITTING: 0-for-1 (.000), 0 R, 0 2B, 0 3B, 0 HR, 0 RBI.

Year	League	W	L	Pct.	ERA	WHIP	G	GS	CG	ShO	Hld.	Sv.-Opp.	IP	H	R	ER	HR	BB-IBB	SO	Avg.
1998— Eugene (NW)		0	0	...	3.09	1.63	11	7	0	0	...	0-...	11.2	9	5	4	0	10-1	22	.209
1999— Macon (S. Atl.)		3	3	.500	2.98	1.29	38	0	0	0	...	14-...	51.1	27	21	17	0	39-2	65	.151
— Myrtle Beach (Caro.)		1	1	.500	2.25	1.33	5	0	0	0	...	0-...	12.0	7	3	3	1	9-1	13	.175
2000— Myrtle Beach (Caro.)		5	2	.714	1.11	0.81	39	0	0	0	...	19-...	56.2	21	8	7	1	25-2	70	.115
2001— Myrtle Beach (Caro.)		0	0	...	0.00	0.60	2	0	0	0	...	1-...	1.2	0	0	0	0	1-0	3	.000
— Greenville (Sou.)		0	0	...	1.08	1.26	15	0	0	0	...	6-...	16.2	11	3	2	0	10-1	25	.193
— Wichita (Texas)		1	0	1.000	0.00	1.17	11	0	0	0	...	4-...	15.1	8	0	0	0	10-1	19	.163
— Kansas City (A.L.)		0	0	...	3.86	1.39	7	0	0	0	1	0-0	9.1	5	4	4	1	8-0	6	.161
2002— Omaha (PCL)		3	4	.429	4.18	1.58	26	0	0	0	...	5-...	32.1	29	15	15	2	22-1	34	.248
— Kansas City (A.L.)		0	2	.000	6.51	1.77	22	0	0	0	1	1-2	27.2	31	21	20	5	18-1	26	.284
2003— Omaha (PCL)		2	2	.500	2.99	1.13	29	9	1	0	...	2-...	81.1	68	27	27	5	24-0	69	.231
— Kansas City (A.L.)		0	2	.000	7.18	2.07	11	3	0	0	0	0-0	31.1	47	29	25	6	18-1	24	.348
Major League totals (3 years)		0	4	.000	6.45	1.86	40	3	0	0	2	1-2	68.1	83	54	49	12	44-2	56	.302

WAECHTER, DOUG   P

PERSONAL: Born January 28, 1981, in St. Petersburg, Fla. ... 6-4/209. ... Throws right, bats right. ... Full name: Douglas Michael Waechter. ... High school: Northeast Senior High (St. Petersburg, Florida).

TRANSACTIONS/CAREER NOTES: Selected by Tampa Bay Devil Rays in third round of free-agent draft (June 1999).

CAREER HITTING: 0-for-0 (.000), 0 R, 0 2B, 0 3B, 0 HR, 0 RBI.

Year	League	W	L	Pct.	ERA	WHIP	G	GS	CG	ShO	Hld.	Sv.-Opp.	IP	H	R	ER	HR	BB-IBB	SO	Avg.
1999— Princeton (Appal.)		0	5	.000	9.77	2.31	11	7	0	0	...	0-...	35.0	46	45	38	2	35-0	38	.317
2000— Hudson Valley (NYP)		4	4	.500	2.35	1.24	14	14	2	2	...	0-...	72.2	53	23	19	2	37-0	58	.205
2001— Char., S.C. (SAL)		8	11	.421	4.34	1.42	26	26	1	0	...	0-...	153.1	179	97	74	14	38-1	107	.285
2002— Char., S.C. (SAL)		3	3	.500	3.47	1.41	7	7	0	0	...	0-...	36.1	39	20	14	2	16-3	36	.277
— Bakersfield (Calif.)		6	3	.667	2.66	1.32	17	17	0	0	...	0-...	108.1	114	43	32	9	29-0	101	.267
— Orlando (Sou.)		1	3	.250	9.00	2.22	4	4	1	0	...	0-...	18.0	27	20	18	4	13-0	18	.338
2003— Orlando (Sou.)		5	3	.625	4.13	1.22	13	12	0	0	...	0-...	76.1	74	39	35	6	19-0	45	.257
— Durham (Int'l)		3	3	.500	3.33	1.23	10	10	0	0	...	0-...	51.1	51	25	19	9	12-0	35	.262
— Tampa Bay (A.L.)		3	2	.600	3.31	1.25	6	5	1	1	0	0-0	35.1	29	13	13	4	15-0	29	.225
Major League totals (1 year)		3	2	.600	3.31	1.25	6	5	1	1	0	0-0	35.1	29	13	13	4	15-0	29	.225

W

WAGNER, BILLY — P

PERSONAL: Born July 25, 1971, in Tannersville, Va. ... 5-11/195. ... Throws left, bats left. ... Full name: William Edward Wagner. ... High school: Tazewell (Va.). ... Junior college: Ferrum College (Va.).

TRANSACTIONS/CAREER NOTES: Selected by Houston Astros organization in first round (12th pick overall) of free-agent draft (June 3, 1993). ... On Houston disabled list (August 23-September 7, 1996). ... On Houston disabled list (July 16-August 7, 1998); included rehabilitation assignment to Jackson (August 1-7). ... On disabled list (June 21, 2000-remainder of season). ... On Houston disabled list (June 5-June 19, 2001); included rehabilitation assignment to Round Rock (June 16-17). ... Traded by Astros to Philadelphia Phillies for P Brandon Duckworth, P Taylor Buchholz and P Ezequiel Astacio (November 3, 2003).

CAREER HITTING: 1-for-15 (.067), 1 R, 0 2B, 0 3B, 0 HR, 1 RBI.

Year League	W	L	Pct.	ERA	WHIP	G	GS	CG	ShO	Hld.	Sv.-Opp.	IP	H	R	ER	HR	BB-IBB	SO	Avg.
1993— Auburn (N.Y.-Penn)	1	3	.250	4.08	1.74	7	7	0	0	...	0-...	28.2	25	19	13	2	25-0	31	.231
1994— Quad City (Midw.)	8	9	.471	3.29	1.24	26	26	2	0	...	0-...	153.0	99	71	56	9	* 91-0	* 204	.188
1995— Jackson (Texas)	2	2	.500	2.57	1.21	12	12	0	0	...	0-...	70.0	49	25	20	7	36-1	77	.199
— Tucson (PCL)	5	3	.625	3.18	1.34	13	13	0	0	...	0-...	76.1	70	28	27	3	32-0	80	.245
— Houston (N.L.)	0	0	...	0.00	0.00	1	0	0	0	0	0-0	.1	0	0	0	0	0-0	0	.000
1996— Tucson (PCL)	6	2	.750	3.28	1.28	12	12	1	1	...	0-...	74.0	62	32	27	2	33-0	86	.225
— Houston (N.L.)	2	2	.500	2.44	1.12	37	0	0	0	3	9-13	51.2	28	16	14	6	30-2	67	.165
1997— Houston (N.L.)	7	8	.467	2.85	1.19	62	0	0	0	1	23-29	66.1	49	23	21	5	30-1	106	.204
1998— Houston (N.L.)	4	3	.571	2.70	1.18	58	0	0	0	1	30-35	60.0	46	19	18	6	25-1	97	.211
— Jackson (Texas)	0	0	...	0.00	0.33	3	1	0	0	...	0-...	3.0	1	0	0	0	0-0	7	.100
1999— Houston (N.L.)	4	1	.800	1.57	0.78	66	0	0	0	1	39-42	74.2	35	14	13	5	23-1	124	.135
2000— Houston (N.L.)	2	4	.333	6.18	1.66	28	0	0	0	0	6-15	27.2	28	19	19	6	18-0	28	.255
2001— Houston (N.L.)	2	5	.286	2.73	1.02	64	0	0	0	0	39-41	62.2	44	19	19	5	20-0	79	.198
— Round Rock (Texas)	0	0	...	0.00	0.00	1	1	0	0	...	0-...	1.0	0	0	0	0	0-0	2	.000
2002— Houston (N.L.)	4	2	.667	2.52	0.97	70	0	0	0	0	35-41	75.0	51	21	21	7	22-5	88	.196
2003— Houston (N.L.)	1	4	.200	1.78	0.87	78	0	0	0	0	44-47	86.0	52	18	17	8	23-5	105	.169
Major League totals (9 years)	**26**	**29**	**.473**	**2.53**	**1.04**	**464**	**0**	**0**	**0**	**6**	**225-263**	**504.1**	**333**	**149**	**142**	**48**	**191-15**	**694**	**.186**

WAGNER, RYAN — P

PERSONAL: Born July 15, 1982, in Yoakum, Texas. ... 6-4/210. ... Throws right, bats right. ... Full name: Ryan S. Wagner. ... High school: Yoakum (Texas). ... College: Houston.

TRANSACTIONS/CAREER NOTES: Selected by Cincinnati Reds organization in first round (14th pick overall) of free-agent draft (June 3, 2003).

CAREER HITTING: 0-for-0 (.000), 0 R, 0 2B, 0 3B, 0 HR, 0 RBI.

Year League	W	L	Pct.	ERA	WHIP	G	GS	CG	ShO	Hld.	Sv.-Opp.	IP	H	R	ER	HR	BB-IBB	SO	Avg.
2003— Chattanooga (Sou.)	1	0	1.000	0.00	0.80	5	0	0	0	...	0-...	5.0	2	1	0	0	2-0	6	.125
— Louisville (Int'l)	0	1	.000	4.50	1.25	4	0	0	0	...	0-...	4.0	5	2	2	0	0-0	4	.313
— Cincinnati (N.L.)	2	0	1.000	1.66	1.15	17	0	0	0	6	0-1	21.2	13	4	4	2	12-1	25	.173
Major League totals (1 year)	**2**	**0**	**1.000**	**1.66**	**1.15**	**17**	**0**	**0**	**0**	**6**	**0-1**	**21.2**	**13**	**4**	**4**	**2**	**12-1**	**25**	**.173**

WAKEFIELD, TIM — P

PERSONAL: Born August 2, 1966, in Melbourne, Fla. ... 6-2/214. ... Throws right, bats right. ... Full name: Timothy Stephen Wakefield. ... High school: Eau Gallie (Melbourne, Fla.). ... College: Florida Tech.

TRANSACTIONS/CAREER NOTES: Selected by Pittsburgh Pirates organization in eighth round of free-agent draft (June 1, 1988). ... Released by Pirates (April 20, 1995). ... Signed by Boston Red Sox organization (April 26, 1995). ... On disabled list (April 15-May 6, 1997). ... Granted free agency (November 1, 2000). ... Re-signed by Red Sox (December 7, 2000).

CAREER HITTING: 10-for-82 (.122), 3 R, 2 2B, 0 3B, 1 HR, 3 RBI.

Year League	W	L	Pct.	ERA	WHIP	G	GS	CG	ShO	Hld.	Sv.-Opp.	IP	H	R	ER	HR	BB-IBB	SO	Avg.
1989— Welland (N.Y.-Penn)	1	1	.500	3.40	1.29	36	1	0	0	...	2-...	39.2	30	17	15	1	21-0	42	.211
1990— Salem (Caro.)	10	• 14	.417	4.73	1.43	28	• 28	2	0	...	0-...	* 190.1	* 187	109	* 100	* 24	* 85-2	127	.261
1991— Carolina (Sou.)	15	8	.652	2.90	1.13	26	25	• 8	1	...	0-...	183.0	155	68	59	13	51-6	120	.231
— Buffalo (A.A.)	0	1	.000	11.57	1.93	1	1	0	0	...	0-...	4.2	8	6	6	3	1-0	4	.364
1992— Buffalo (A.A.)	10	3	.769	3.06	1.28	20	20	* 6	1	...	0-...	135.1	122	52	46	10	51-1	71	.246
— Pittsburgh (N.L.)	8	1	.889	2.15	1.21	13	13	4	1	0	0-0	92.0	76	26	22	3	35-1	51	.232
1993— Pittsburgh (N.L.)	6	11	.353	5.61	1.71	24	20	3	2	0	0-0	128.1	145	83	80	14	75-2	59	.291
— Carolina (Sou.)	3	5	.375	6.99	1.59	9	9	1	0	...	0-...	56.2	68	48	44	5	22-0	36	.293
1994— Buffalo (A.A.)	5	* 15	.250	5.84	1.68	30	• 29	4	1	...	0-...	175.2	* 197	* 127	* 114	* 27	* 98-0	83	.290
1995— Pawtucket (Int'l)	2	1	.667	2.52	1.28	4	4	0	0	...	0-...	25.0	23	10	7	1	9-0	14	.253
— Boston (A.L.)	16	8	.667	2.95	1.18	27	27	6	1	0	0-0	195.1	163	76	64	22	68-0	119	.227
1996— Boston (A.L.)	14	13	.519	5.14	1.55	32	32	6	0	0	0-0	211.2	238	* 151	121	38	90-0	140	.280
1997— Boston (A.L.)	12	• 15	.444	4.25	1.39	35	29	4	2	1	0-0	201.1	193	109	95	24	87-5	151	.256
1998— Boston (A.L.)	17	8	.680	4.58	1.34	36	33	2	0	0	0-0	216.0	211	123	110	30	79-1	146	.252
1999— Boston (A.L.)	6	11	.353	5.08	1.56	49	17	0	0	0	15-18	140.0	146	93	79	19	72-2	104	.266
2000— Boston (A.L.)	6	10	.375	5.48	1.47	51	17	0	0	3	0-1	159.1	170	107	97	31	65-3	102	.272
2001— Boston (A.L.)	9	12	.429	3.90	1.36	45	17	0	0	3	3-5	168.2	156	84	73	13	73-5	148	.248
2002— Boston (A.L.)	11	5	.688	2.81	1.05	45	15	0	0	5	3-5	163.1	121	57	51	15	51-2	134	.204
2003— Boston (A.L.)	11	7	.611	4.09	1.30	35	33	0	0	0	1-1	202.1	193	106	92	23	71-0	169	.246
American League totals (9 years)	**102**	**89**	**.534**	**4.24**	**1.36**	**355**	**220**	**18**	**3**	**12**	**22-30**	**1658.0**	**1591**	**906**	**782**	**215**	**656-18**	**1213**	**.251**
National League totals (2 years)	**14**	**12**	**.538**	**4.17**	**1.50**	**37**	**33**	**7**	**3**	**0**	**0-0**	**220.1**	**221**	**109**	**102**	**17**	**110-3**	**110**	**.268**
Major League totals (11 years)	**116**	**101**	**.535**	**4.24**	**1.37**	**392**	**253**	**25**	**6**	**12**	**22-30**	**1878.1**	**1812**	**1015**	**884**	**232**	**766-21**	**1323**	**.253**

WALBECK, MATT — C

PERSONAL: Born October 2, 1969, in Fair Oaks, Calif. ... 5-11/190. ... Bats both, throws right. ... Full name: Matthew Lovick Walbeck. ... High school: Sacramento High.

TRANSACTIONS/CAREER NOTES: Selected by Chicago Cubs organization in eighth round of free-agent draft (June 2, 1987). ... On Winston-Salem disabled list (April 12-July 11, 1990). ... On Charleston, W.Va. disabled list (September 5, 1992-remainder of season). ... Traded by Cubs with P Dave Stevens to Minnesota Twins for P Willie Banks

W

(November 24, 1993). ... On Minnesota disabled list (March 31-June 17, 1996); included rehabilitation assignments to Fort Myers (May 31-June 11) and New Britain (June 12-17). ... Traded by Twins to Detroit Tigers for P Brent Stentz (December 11, 1996). ... On Detroit disabled list (April 19-July 9, 1997); included rehabilitation assignments to Lakeland (June 12-15) and Toledo (June 16-July 9). ... Traded by Tigers with 3B Phil Nevin to Anaheim Angels for P Nick Skuse (November 20, 1997). ... On disabled list (August 17-September 1, 2000). ... Granted free agency (November 1, 2000). ... Signed by Cincinnati Reds organization (February 9, 2001). ... Contract purchased Philadelphia Phillies organization from Reds (July 11, 2001). ... Granted free agency (October 8, 2001). ... Signed by San Diego Padres organization (January 2, 2002). ... Traded by Padres with IF Damian Jackson to Detroit Tigers for C Javier Cardona and OF Rich Gomez (March 24, 2002). ... Granted free agency (October 30, 2002). ... Re-signed by Tigers organization (November 18, 2002). ... Optioned to Toledo by Detroit (August 24, 2003). ... Recalled by Detroit from Toledo (September 2, 2003).
2003 GAMES PLAYED BY POSITION (MLB): C—55, DH—1.

Year — Team (League)	Pos.	G	AB	R	H	2B	3B	HR	RBI	BB	SO	HBP	GDP	SB-CS	Avg.	OBP	SLG	OPS	E	Pct.
1987— Wytheville (App.)	C	51	169	24	53	9	3	1	28	22	39	0	4	0-1	.314	.387	.420	.807	1	.997
1988— Char., W.Va. (SAL)	C	104	312	28	68	9	0	2	24	30	44	3	8	7-5	.218	.292	.266	.558	14	.978
1989— Peoria (Midw.)	C	94	341	38	86	19	0	4	47	20	47	3	7	5-2	.252	.297	.343	.640	11	.984
1990— Peoria (Midw.)	C	25	66	2	15	1	0	0	5	5	7	2	1	1-0	.227	.301	.242	.544	2	.987
1991— Win.-Salem (Car.)	C	91	260	25	70	11	0	3	41	20	23	2	7	3-2	.269	.315	.346	.661	12	.978
1992— Charlotte (Sou.)	C-1B	105	385	48	116	22	1	7	42	33	56	2	6	0-7	.301	.358	.418	.776	10	.984
1993— Chicago (N.L.)	C	11	30	2	6	2	0	1	6	1	6	0	0	0-0	.200	.226	.367	.592	0	1.000
— Iowa (Am. Assoc.)	C	87	331	31	93	18	2	6	43	18	47	2	6	1-2	.281	.320	.402	.722	1	.998
1994— Minnesota (A.L.)	C-DH	97	338	31	69	12	0	5	35	17	37	2	7	1-1	.204	.246	.284	.530	4	.993
1995— Minnesota (A.L.)	C	115	393	40	101	18	1	1	44	25	71	1	11	3-1	.257	.302	.316	.617	6	.991
1996— Fort Myers (FSL)	C-DH	9	33	4	9	1	1	0	9	4	2	1	0	0-1	.273	.350	.364	.714	0	1.000
— New Britain (East.)	DH-C	7	24	1	5	0	0	0	0	1	1	0	1	0-0	.208	.240	.208	.448	0	1.000
— Minnesota (A.L.)	C	63	215	25	48	10	0	2	24	9	34	0	6	3-1	.223	.252	.298	.550	2	.994
1997— Detroit (A.L.)	C	47	137	18	38	3	0	3	10	12	19	0	4	3-3	.277	.331	.365	.696	3	.988
— Lakeland (Fla. St.)	C-DH	4	10	4	5	1	0	0	3	4	1	0	0	0-1	.500	.643	.600	1.243	1	.933
— Toledo (Int'l)	C-DH	17	59	6	18	2	1	1	8	4	15	0	1	0-0	.305	.338	.424	.762	3	.955
1998— Anaheim (A.L.)	C-DH	108	338	41	87	15	2	6	46	30	68	2	9	1-1	.257	.317	.367	.684	7	.990
1999— Anaheim (A.L.)	C-DH	107	288	26	69	8	1	3	22	26	46	3	12	2-3	.240	.308	.306	.614	5	.989
2000— Anaheim (A.L.)	C-1B-DH	47	146	17	29	5	0	6	12	7	22	1	2	0-1	.199	.240	.356	.596	2	.991
2001— Louisville (Int'l)	C	67	197	20	45	7	0	3	25	23	26	0	6	1-0	.228	.309	.310	.619	0	1.000
— Scran./W.B. (I.L.)	C-1B	40	141	18	42	11	0	2	21	11	20	2	2	0-2	.298	.355	.418	.773	0	1.000
— Philadelphia (N.L.)		1	1	0	1	0	0	0	0	0	0	0	0	0-0	1.000	1.000	1.000	2.000	...	...
2002— Toledo (Int'l)	C-1B	21	75	4	16	3	0	1	6	4	10	0	6	0-0	.213	.250	.293	.543	3	.980
— Detroit (A.L.)	C	27	85	4	20	2	0	0	3	3	14	0	2	0-0	.235	.258	.259	.517	1	.993
2003— Toledo (Int'l)	DH-C	4	12	2	5	0	0	0	1	3	2	0	0	0-0	.417	.533	.417	.950	0	1.000
— Detroit (A.L.)	C-DH	59	138	11	24	4	1	1	6	3	26	1	3	0-1	.174	.197	.239	.436	4	.979
American League totals (9 years)		670	2078	213	485	77	5	27	202	132	337	10	56	13-12	.233	.281	.314	.595	34	.990
National League totals (2 years)		12	31	2	7	2	0	1	6	1	6	0	0	0-0	.226	.250	.387	.637	0	1.000
Major League totals (11 years)		682	2109	215	492	79	5	28	208	133	343	10	56	13-12	.233	.280	.315	.596	34	.991

WALKER, JAMIE   P

PERSONAL: Born July 1, 1971, in McMinnville, Tenn. ... 6-2/190. ... Throws left, bats left. ... Full name: Jamie Ross Walker. ... High school: Warren County (McMinnville, Tenn.). ... College: Austin Peay.
TRANSACTIONS/CAREER NOTES: Selected by Houston Astros organization in 10th round of free-agent draft (June 1, 1992). ... Selected by Atlanta Braves organization from Astros organization in Rule 5 major league draft (December 9, 1996). ... Traded by Braves with OF Jermaine Dye to Kansas City Royals for OF Michael Tucker and IF Keith Lockhart (March 27, 1997). ... On Kansas City disabled list (June 5-24, 1997); included rehabilitation assignment to Wichita (June 11-24). ... On Kansas City disabled list (June 1, 1998-remainder of season). ... Granted free agency (December 21, 1998). ... Re-signed by Royals organization (December 21, 1998). ... On Omaha disabled list (April 8-May 17 and May 25-August 27, 1999). ... Released by Royals (July 27, 2000). ... Signed by Cleveland Indians organization (February 9, 2001). ... Granted free agency (October 15, 2001). ... Signed by Detroit Tigers organization (December 19, 2001).
CAREER HITTING: 0-for-0 (.000), 0 R, 0 2B, 0 3B, 0 HR, 0 RBI.

Year — League	W	L	Pct.	ERA	WHIP	G	GS	CG	ShO	Hld.	Sv.-Opp.	IP	H	R	ER	HR	BB-IBB	SO	Avg.
1992— Auburn (N.Y.-Penn)	4	6	.400	3.13	1.15	15	14	0	0	...	0-...	83.1	75	35	29	4	21-0	67	.243
1993— Quad City (Midw.)	3	11	.214	5.13	1.43	25	24	1	1	...	0-...	131.2	140	92	75	12	48-1	121	.271
1994— Quad City (Midw.)	8	10	.444	4.18	1.40	32	18	0	0	...	1-...	125.0	133	80	58	10	42-2	104	.269
1995— Jackson (Texas)	4	2	.667	4.50	1.43	50	0	0	0	...	2-...	58.0	59	29	29	6	24-5	38	.269
1996— Jackson (Texas)	5	1	.833	2.50	1.28	45	7	0	0	...	2-...	101.0	94	34	28	7	35-2	79	.249
1997— Kansas City (A.L.)	3	3	.500	5.44	1.53	50	0	0	0	3	0-1	43.0	46	28	26	6	20-3	24	.271
— Wichita (Texas)	0	1	.000	9.45	1.65	5	0	0	0	...	0-...	6.2	6	8	7	1	5-0	6	.261
1998— Omaha (PCL)	5	1	.833	2.70	1.46	7	7	0	0	...	0-...	46.2	57	15	14	3	11-1	21	.313
— Kansas City (A.L.)	0	1	.000	9.87	1.90	6	2	0	0	1	0-0	17.1	30	20	19	5	15-0	15	.380
1999— Omaha (PCL)	0	1	.000	4.67	1.50	4	4	0	0	...	0-...	17.1	22	12	9	1	4-0	11	.314
— GC Royals (GCL)	1	0	1.000	3.38	1.25	2	2	0	0	...	0-...	8.0	10	3	3	1	0-0	9	.286
2000— Omaha (PCL)	3	10	.231	5.22	1.60	24	15	0	0	...	0-...	101.2	138	65	59	25	25-1	52	.306
2001— Buffalo (Int'l)	7	2	.778	3.87	1.41	38	8	0	0	...	2-...	93.0	104	44	40	12	27-1	51	.282
2002— Toledo (Int'l)	0	1	.000	1.98	0.73	10	0	0	0	...	1-...	13.2	7	3	3	2	3-0	9	.156
— Detroit (A.L.)	1	1	.500	3.71	0.94	57	0	0	0	5	1-4	43.2	32	19	18	9	9-1	40	.199
2003— Detroit (A.L.)	4	3	.571	3.32	1.20	78	0	0	0	12	3-7	65.0	61	30	24	8	17-1	45	.247
Major League totals (4 years)	8	8	.500	4.63	1.29	191	2	0	0	21	4-12	169.0	169	97	87	29	49-5	124	.257

WALKER, KEVIN   P

PERSONAL: Born September 20, 1976, in Irving, Texas. ... 6-4/190. ... Throws left, bats left. ... Full name: Kevin Michael Walker. ... High school: Grand Prairie (Texas).
TRANSACTIONS/CAREER NOTES: Selected by San Diego Padres organization in sixth round of free-agent draft (June 1, 1995). ... On Mobile disabled list (April 8-24, 1999). ... On Rancho Cucamonga disabled list (June 19-July 30, 1999). ... On disabled list (April 20-May 8 and May 23, 2001-remainder of season). ... On San Diego disabled list (March 27-August 8 and August 12-September 1, 2002); included rehabilitation assignments to Lake Elsinore (July 18-August 2) and Portland (August 3-8). ... On disabled list (March 26, 2003). ... Transferred to Emergency disabled list (May 16, 2003). ... Transferred to Lake Elsinore on rehab assignment (May 18, 2003). ... Optioned to Portland (June 9, 2003). ... Recalled from Portland (August 29, 2003).
CAREER HITTING: 1-for-4 (.250), 0 R, 0 2B, 0 3B, 0 HR, 0 RBI.

W

Year League	W	L	Pct.	ERA	WHIP	G	GS	CG	ShO	Hld.	Sv.-Opp.	IP	H	R	ER	HR	BB-IBB	SO	Avg.
1995— Ariz. Padres (Ariz.)	5	5	.500	3.01	1.20	13	12	0	0	...	0-...	71.2	74	34	24	1	12-0	69	.267
1996— Idaho Falls (Pioneer)	1	0	1.000	3.00	1.00	1	1	0	0	...	0-...	6.0	4	3	2	1	2-0	4	.182
— Clinton (Midw.)	4	6	.400	4.74	1.49	13	13	0	0	...	0-...	76.0	80	46	40	9	33-0	43	.276
1997— Clinton (Midw.)	6	10	.375	4.88	1.54	19	19	3	1	...	0-...	110.2	133	80	60	9	37-0	80	.298
1998— Clinton (Midw.)	2	0	1.000	1.23	1.23	2	2	0	0	...	0-...	14.2	11	2	2	0	7-0	10	.216
— Rancho Cuca. (Calif.)	11	7	.611	4.15	1.40	22	22	0	0	...	0-...	121.1	122	62	56	10	48-0	94	.267
1999— Rancho Cuca. (Calif.)	1	1	.500	3.46	1.38	27	1	0	0	...	4-...	39.0	35	19	15	2	19-3	35	.243
2000— Mobile (Sou.)	0	1	.000	2.25	0.50	4	0	0	0	...	0-...	4.0	1	1	1	1	1-0	6	.077
— San Diego (N.L.)	7	1	.875	4.19	1.31	70	0	0	0	19	0-0	66.2	49	35	31	5	38-6	56	.206
2001— San Diego (N.L.)	0	0	...	3.00	1.08	16	0	0	0	4	0-1	12.0	5	4	4	0	8-2	17	.122
2002— Lake Elsinore (Calif.)	0	0	...	0.00	0.43	5	1	0	0	...	0-...	7.0	3	0	0	0	1-0	10	.136
— Portland (PCL)	0	0	...	3.00	0.33	3	0	0	0	...	0-...	3.0	1	1	1	1	0-0	4	.100
— San Diego (N.L.)	0	1	.000	5.63	2.13	11	0	0	0	1	0-1	8.0	12	6	5	2	5-1	11	.333
2003— Lake Elsinore (Calif.)	0	0	...	13.50	2.00	4	0	0	0	...	0-...	4.0	6	6	6	1	2-0	3	.333
— Portland (PCL)	3	1	.750	4.08	1.36	34	1	0	0	...	0-...	46.1	53	24	21	5	10-1	43	.291
— San Diego (N.L.)	0	0	...	5.40	1.50	11	0	0	0	0	0-0	6.2	5	4	4	1	5-0	5	.200
Major League totals (4 years)	7	2	.778	4.24	1.36	108	0	0	0	24	0-2	93.1	71	49	44	8	56-9	89	.209

WALKER, LARRY   OF

PERSONAL: Born December 1, 1966, in Maple Ridge, British Columbia. ... 6-3/235. ... Bats left, throws right. ... Full name: Larry Kenneth Robert Walker. ... High school: Maple Ridge (B.C.) Senior Secondary School.

TRANSACTIONS/CAREER NOTES: Signed as non-drafted free agent by Montreal Expos organization (November 14, 1984). ... On disabled list (April 4, 1988-entire season; June 28-July 13, 1991; and May 26-June 10, 1993). ... On suspended list (June 24-28, 1994). ... Granted free agency (October 24, 1994). ... Signed by Colorado Rockies (April 8, 1995). ... On Colorado disabled list (June 10-August 15, 1996); included rehabilitation assignments to Salem (August 6-9) and Colorado Springs (August 9-15). ... On disabled list (June 18-July 3, 1998; March 29-April 14, 1999; May 11-June 9 and August 20, 2000-remainder of season).

2003 GAMES PLAYED BY POSITION (MLB): OF—131, DH—2.

									BATTING											FIELDING	
Year Team (League)	Pos.	G	AB	R	H	2B	3B	HR	RBI	BB	SO	HBP	GDP	SB-CS	Avg.	OBP	SLG	OPS		E	Pct.
1985— Utica (N.Y.-Penn)	3B-1B	62	215	24	48	8	2	2	26	18	57	5	1	12-6	.223	.297	.307	.604		8	.981
1986— Burlington (Midw.)	3B-OF	95	332	67	96	12	6	29	74	46	112	9	4	16-8	.289	.387	.623	1.011		10	.940
— W.P. Beach (FSL)	OF	38	113	20	32	7	5	4	16	26	32	2	2	2-2	.283	.423	.540	.962		0	1.000
1987— Jacksonville (Sou.)	OF	128	474	91	136	25	7	26	83	67	120	9	6	24-3	.287	.383	.534	.917		9	.968
1988— Montreal (N.L.)								Did not play.													
1989— Indianapolis (A.A.)	OF	114	385	68	104	18	2	12	59	50	87	9	8	36-6	.270	.361	.421	.782		* 11	.959
— Montreal (N.L.)	OF	20	47	4	8	0	0	0	4	5	13	1	0	1-1	.170	.264	.170	.434		0	1.000
1990— Montreal (N.L.)	OF	133	419	59	101	18	3	19	51	49	112	5	8	21-7	.241	.326	.434	.761		4	.985
1991— Montreal (N.L.)	1B-OF	137	487	59	141	30	2	16	64	42	102	5	7	14-9	.290	.349	.458	.807		6	.990
1992— Montreal (N.L.)	OF	143	528	85	159	31	4	23	93	41	97	6	9	18-6	.301	.353	.506	.859		2	.993
1993— Montreal (N.L.)	OF-1B	138	490	85	130	24	5	22	86	80	76	6	8	29-7	.265	.371	.469	.841		6	.982
1994— Montreal (N.L.)	OF-1B	103	395	76	127	* 44	2	19	86	47	74	4	8	15-5	.322	.394	.587	.981		9	.980
1995— Colorado (N.L.)	OF	131	494	96	151	31	5	36	101	49	72	14	13	16-3	.306	.381	.607	.988		3	.988
1996— Colorado (N.L.)	OF	83	272	58	75	18	4	18	58	20	58	9	7	18-2	.276	.342	.570	.912		1	.994
— Salem (Caro.)	DH	2	8	3	4	3	0	1	1	0	1	0	1	0-0	.500	.500	1.250	1.750		...	...
— Colo. Springs (PCL)	OF	3	11	2	4	0	0	2	8	1	4	0	0	0-0	.364	.385	.909	1.294		0	1.000
1997— Colorado (N.L.)	OF-1B-DH	153	568	143	208	46	4	* 49	130	78	90	14	15	33-8	.366	*.452	*.720	1.172		2	.993
1998— Colorado (N.L.)	O-2-3-D	130	454	113	165	46	3	23	67	64	61	4	11	14-4	*.363	.445	.630	1.075		4	.984
1999— Colorado (N.L.)	OF-DH	127	438	108	166	26	4	37	115	57	52	12	12	11-4	*.379	*.458	*.710	1.168		4	.982
2000— Colorado (N.L.)	OF-DH	87	314	64	97	21	7	9	51	46	40	9	12	5-5	.309	.409	.506	.915		1	.994
2001— Colorado (N.L.)	OF-DH	142	497	107	174	35	3	38	123	82	103	14	9	14-5	*.350	.449	.662	1.111		4	.984
2002— Colorado (N.L.)	OF-DH	136	477	95	161	40	4	26	104	65	73	7	8	6-5	.338	.421	.602	1.023		4	.984
2003— Colorado (N.L.)	OF-DH	143	454	86	129	25	7	16	79	98	87	11	9	7-4	.284	.422	.476	.898		4	.983
Major League totals (15 years)		1806	6334	1238	1992	435	57	351	1212	823	1110	121	136	222-75	.314	.400	.567	.967		54	.987

WALKER, PETE   P

PERSONAL: Born April 8, 1969, in Beverly, Mass. ... 6-2/195. ... Throws right, bats right. ... Full name: Peter Brian Walker. ... High school: East Lyme (Conn.). ... College: Connecticut.

TRANSACTIONS/CAREER NOTES: Selected by New York Mets organization in seventh round of free-agent draft (June 4, 1990). ... On disabled list (June 6-18, 1992; and April 25-May 9, 1993). ... On Norfolk disabled list (April 7-May 16, 1994). ... On Norfolk suspended list (August 5-6, 1994). ... Traded by Mets with P Luis Arroyo to San Diego Padres for 1B Roberto Petagine and P Scott Adair (March 17, 1996). ... On Las Vegas disabled list (May 4-July 11, 1996). ... Granted free agency (October 15, 1996). ... Signed by Boston Red Sox organization (June 30, 1997). ... Granted free agency (October 17, 1997). ... Re-signed by Red Sox organization (January 14, 1998). ... On Pawtucket disabled list (June 11-22 and June 26-September 8, 1998). ... Granted free agency (October 16, 1998). ... Signed by Colorado Rockies organization (February 8, 1999). ... On Colorado Springs disabled list (July 16-August 6, 1999). ... Granted free agency (October 15, 1999). ... Re-signed by Rockies organization (November 17, 1999). ... Released by Rockies (November 13, 2000). ... Signed by Mets organization (December 26, 2000). ... Granted free agency (October 15, 2001). ... Re-signed by Mets organization (December 10, 2001). ... Claimed on waivers by Toronto Blue Jays (May 3, 2002).

CAREER HITTING: 0-for-1 (.000), 0 R, 0 2B, 0 3B, 0 HR, 0 RBI.

Year League	W	L	Pct.	ERA	WHIP	G	GS	CG	ShO	Hld.	Sv.-Opp.	IP	H	R	ER	HR	BB-IBB	SO	Avg.
1990— Pittsfield (NYP)	5	7	.417	4.16	1.50	16	13	1	0	...	0-...	80.0	74	43	37	2	46-0	73	.253
1991— St. Lucie (Fla. St.)	10	12	.455	3.21	1.30	26	25	1	0	...	0-...	151.1	145	77	54	9	52-2	95	.254
1992— Binghamton (Eastern)	7	12	.368	4.12	1.47	24	23	4	0	...	0-...	139.2	159	77	64	9	46-0	72	.289
1993— Binghamton (Eastern)	4	9	.308	3.44	1.36	45	10	0	0	19	0-...	99.1	89	45	38	6	46-1	89	.244
1994— St. Lucie (Fla. St.)	0	0	...	2.25	1.00	3	0	0	0	...	0-...	4.0	3	2	1	1	1-0	5	.200
— Norfolk (Int'l)	2	4	.333	3.97	1.51	37	0	0	0	...	3-...	47.2	48	22	21	3	24-2	42	.269
1995— Norfolk (Int'l)	5	2	.714	3.91	1.39	34	1	0	0	...	8-...	48.1	51	24	21	4	16-1	39	.274
— New York (N.L.)	1	0	1.000	4.58	1.64	13	0	0	0	1	0-0	17.2	24	9	9	3	5-0	5	.329
1996— Las Vegas (PCL)	5	1	.833	6.83	1.84	26	0	0	0	...	0-...	27.2	37	22	21	7	14-2	23	.336
— Ariz. Padres (Ariz.)	0	1	.000	2.25	1.00	2	2	0	0	...	0-...	4.0	4	1	1	0	0-0	5	.250
— San Diego (N.L.)	0	0	...	0.00	4.50	1	0	0	0	0	0-...	.2	0	0	0	0	3-0	1	.000
1997— GC Red Sox (GCL)	0	0	...	0.96	0.64	4	3	0	0	...	0-...	9.1	5	1	1	0	1-0	14	.147
— Trenton (East.)	0	0	...	4.05	1.58	8	0	0	0	...	3-...	13.1	14	6	6	1	7-0	13	.275
— Pawtucket (Int'l)	0	0	...	5.40	1.80	7	0	0	0	...	0-...	11.2	14	8	7	2	7-1	8	.280

W

Year League	W	L	Pct.	ERA	WHIP	G	GS	CG	ShO	Hld.	Sv.-Opp.	IP	H	R	ER	HR	BB-IBB	SO	Avg.
1998—Pawtucket (Int'l)	1	4	.200	5.94	1.53	22	0	0	0	...	0-...	33.1	34	26	22	8	17-1	19	.272
1999—Colo. Springs (PCL)	8	4	.667	4.48	1.48	48	0	0	0	...	5-...	62.1	64	37	31	9	28-3	57	.268
2000—Colo. Springs (PCL)	7	3	.700	3.07	1.28	58	0	0	0	...	5-...	73.1	64	29	25	3	30-1	61	.231
—Colorado (N.L.)	0	0	...	17.36	3.00	3	0	0	0	0	0-0	4.2	10	9	9	1	4-0	2	.435
2001—Norfolk (Int'l)	13	4	.765	2.99	1.13	26	26	0	0	...	0-...	168.1	145	64	56	12	46-5	106	.234
—New York (N.L.)	0	0	...	2.70	0.90	2	0	0	0	0	0-0	6.2	6	2	2	0	0-0	4	.240
2002—Norfolk (Int'l)	0	0	...	3.00	1.11	2	1	0	0	...	0-...	9.0	9	3	3	1	1-0	6	.243
—New York (N.L.)	0	0	...	9.00	2.00	1	0	0	0	0	0-0	1.0	2	1	1	0	0-0	0	.400
—Toronto (A.L.)	10	5	.667	4.33	1.39	37	20	0	0	3	1-1	139.1	143	72	67	18	51-5	80	.270
2003—New Haven (East.)	0	1	.000	9.00	1.50	2	2	0	0	...	0-...	2.0	3	2	2	0	0-0	1	.375
—Syracuse (Int'l)	0	1	.000	6.75	1.35	5	5	0	0	...	0-...	13.1	15	10	10	2	3-0	8	.278
—Toronto (A.L.)	2	2	.500	4.88	1.50	23	7	0	0	2	0-0	55.1	59	31	30	11	24-2	29	.277
American League totals (2 years)	12	7	.632	4.48	1.42	60	27	0	0	5	1-1	194.2	202	103	97	29	75-7	109	.272
National League totals (5 years)	1	0	1.000	6.16	1.76	20	0	0	0	1	0-0	30.2	42	21	21	4	12-0	12	.328
Major League totals (6 years)	13	7	.650	4.71	1.47	80	27	0	0	6	1-1	225.1	244	124	118	33	87-7	121	.280

WALKER, TODD — 2B

PERSONAL: Born May 25, 1973, in Bakersfield, Calif. ... 6-0/190. ... Bats left, throws right. ... Full name: Todd Arthur Walker. ... High school: Airline (Bossier City, La.). ... College: Louisiana State.

TRANSACTIONS/CAREER NOTES: Selected by Texas Rangers organization in 51st round of free-agent draft (June 3, 1991); did not sign. ... Selected by Minnesota Twins organization in first round (eighth pick overall) of free-agent draft (June 2, 1994). ... Traded by Twins with OF/1B Butch Huskey to Colorado Rockies for 2B Todd Sears and cash considerations (July 16, 2000). ... Traded by Rockies with OF Robin Jennings to Cincinnati Reds for OF Alex Ochoa (July 19, 2001). ... Traded by Reds to Boston Red Sox for two players to be named later (December 12, 2002); Reds acquired P Josh Thigpen and 3B Tony Blanco to complete deal (December 16, 2002).

2003 GAMES PLAYED BY POSITION (MLB): 2B—139, DH—2.

Year Team (League)	Pos.	G	AB	R	H	2B	3B	HR	RBI	BB	SO	HBP	GDP	SB-CS	Avg.	OBP	SLG	OPS	E	Pct.
1994—Fort Myers (FSL)	2B	46	171	29	52	5	2	10	34	32	15	0	4	6-3	.304	.406	.532	.938	9	.959
1995—New Britain (East.)	2B-3B	137	513	83	149	27	3	21	85	63	101	2	13	23-9	.290	.365	.478	.843	27	.955
1996—Salt Lake (PCL)	3B-2B-DH	135	551	94	*187	*41	9	*28	*111	57	91	5	17	13-8	.339	.400	.599	.999	19	.955
—Minnesota (A.L.)	3B-2B-DH	25	82	8	21	6	0	0	6	4	13	0	4	2-0	.256	.281	.329	.610	2	.965
1997—Minnesota (A.L.)	3B-2B-DH	52	156	15	37	7	1	3	16	11	30	1	5	7-0	.237	.288	.353	.641	4	.968
—Salt Lake (PCL)	3B-DH	83	322	69	111	20	1	11	53	46	49	1	10	5-5	.345	.420	.516	.936	*24	.901
1998—Minnesota (A.L.)	2B-DH	143	528	85	167	41	3	12	62	47	65	2	13	19-7	.316	.372	.473	.845	13	.978
1999—Minnesota (A.L.)	2B-DH	143	531	62	148	37	4	6	46	52	83	1	15	18-10	.279	.343	.397	.740	7	.984
2000—Minnesota (A.L.)	2B-DH	23	77	14	18	1	0	2	8	7	10	0	3	3-0	.234	.287	.325	.612	4	.946
—Salt Lake (PCL)	2B	63	249	51	81	14	1	2	37	32	32	0	6	8-3	.325	.398	.414	.812	11	.964
—Colorado (N.L.)	2B	57	171	28	54	10	4	7	36	20	19	1	2	4-1	.316	.385	.544	.928	5	.975
2001—Colorado (N.L.)	2B	85	290	52	86	18	2	12	43	25	40	0	8	1-3	.297	.349	.497	.846	7	.981
—Cincinnati (N.L.)	2B-SS	66	261	41	77	17	0	5	32	26	42	1	6	0-5	.295	.361	.418	.779	4	.987
2002—Cincinnati (N.L.)	2B	155	612	79	183	42	3	11	64	50	81	3	9	8-5	.299	.353	.431	.785	8	.989
2003—Boston (A.L.)	2B-DH	144	587	92	166	38	4	13	85	48	54	1	17	1-1	.283	.333	.428	.760	16	.975
American League totals (6 years)		530	1961	276	557	130	12	36	223	169	255	5	57	50-18	.284	.339	.418	.756	46	.976
National League totals (3 years)		363	1334	200	400	87	9	35	175	121	182	5	25	13-14	.300	.358	.457	.815	24	.985
Major League totals (8 years)		893	3295	476	957	217	21	71	398	290	437	10	82	63-32	.290	.346	.434	.780	70	.980

WALROND, LES — P

PERSONAL: Born November 7, 1976, in Muskogee, Okla. ... 6-0/210. ... Throws left, bats left. ... Full name: Leslie Dale Walrond. ... Name pronounced: WALL-run. ... High school: Union (Tulsa, Okla.). ... College: Kansas.

TRANSACTIONS/CAREER NOTES: Selected by St. Louis Cardinals organization in 13th round of free-agent draft (June 2, 1998). ... On disabled list (May 12-July 20, 2001). ... Claimed off waivers by Kansas City Royals (May 29, 2003).

CAREER HITTING: 0-for-0 (.000), 0 R, 0 2B, 0 3B, 0 HR, 0 RBI.

Year League	W	L	Pct.	ERA	WHIP	G	GS	CG	ShO	Hld.	Sv.-Opp.	IP	H	R	ER	HR	BB-IBB	SO	Avg.
1998—New Jersey (NYP)	2	4	.333	4.01	1.47	13	10	0	0	...	0-...	51.2	52	31	23	1	24-0	52	.259
1999—Peoria (Midw.)	7	10	.412	5.70	1.60	21	20	0	0	...	0-...	109.0	115	77	69	12	59-0	78	.274
2000—Potomac (Caro.)	10	5	.667	3.34	1.25	27	27	0	0	...	0-...	151.0	134	66	56	9	54-0	153	.234
2001—New Haven (East.)	2	8	.200	3.87	1.40	16	16	1	0	...	0-...	81.1	68	41	35	5	46-0	67	.227
2002—New Haven (East.)	2	1	.667	2.42	1.30	4	4	0	0	...	0-...	22.1	19	8	6	2	10-0	31	.221
—Memphis (PCL)	8	7	.533	4.98	1.54	28	18	0	0	...	0-...	123.0	127	75	68	20	63-2	111	.270
2003—Memphis (PCL)	0	0	...	1.04	1.10	10	1	0	0	...	0-...	17.1	12	2	2	0	7-1	14	.194
—Tennessee (Sou.)	0	0	...	2.70	1.20	4	0	0	0	...	0-...	6.2	4	2	2	1	4-0	7	.167
—Kansas City (A.L.)	0	2	.000	10.13	2.25	7	0	0	0	1	0-0	8.0	11	9	9	2	7-1	6	.324
—Omaha (PCL)	3	1	.750	2.45	1.09	18	0	0	0	...	2-...	25.2	19	9	7	1	9-0	20	.196
—Wichita (Texas)	2	0	1.000	3.27	0.82	2	2	0	0	...	0-...	11.0	7	4	4	2	2-0	9	.171
Major League totals (1 year)	0	2	.000	10.13	2.25	7	0	0	0	1	0-0	8.0	11	9	9	2	7-1	6	.324

WARD, DARYLE — OF/1B

PERSONAL: Born June 27, 1975, in Lynwood, Calif. ... 6-2/230. ... Bats left, throws left. ... Full name: Daryle Lamar Ward. ... High school: Brethren Christian (Riverside, Calif.). ... College: Rancho Santiago (Calif.).

TRANSACTIONS/CAREER NOTES: Selected by Detroit Tigers organization in 15th round of free-agent draft (June 2, 1994). ... Traded by Tigers with C Brad Ausmus, P Jose Lima, P C.J. Nitkowski and P Trever Miller to Houston Astros for OF Brian Hunter, IF Orlando Miller, P Doug Brocail, P Todd Jones and cash (December 10, 1996). ... Traded by Astros to Los Angeles Dodgers for P Ruddy Lugo (January 25, 2003).

2003 GAMES PLAYED BY POSITION (MLB): 1B—13, OF—11.

W

Year Team (League)	Pos.	G	AB	R	H	2B	3B	HR	RBI	BB	SO	HBP	GDP	SB-CS	Avg.	OBP	SLG	OPS	E	Pct.
1994— Bristol (Appal.)	1B	48	161	17	43	6	0	5	30	19	33	0	3	5-1	.267	.343	.398	.740	11	.968
1995— Fayetteville (SAL)	1B	137	524	75	149	32	0	14	106	46	111	5	13	1-2	.284	.344	.426	.769	14	.987
1996— Lakeland (Fla. St.)	1B-DH	128	464	65	135	29	4	10	68	57	77	6	9	1-1	.291	.373	.435	.808	8	.993
— Toledo (Int'l)	1B	6	23	1	4	0	0	0	1	0	3	0	2	0-0	.174	.174	.174	.348	1	.979
1997— Jackson (Texas)	1B-DH	114	422	72	139	25	0	19	90	46	68	3	11	4-2	.329	.398	.524	.922	12	.988
— New Orleans (A.A.)	1B-DH	14	48	4	18	1	0	2	8	7	7	0	0	0-0	.375	.455	.521	.975	2	.976
1998— New Orleans (PCL) OF-1B-DH		116	463	78	141	31	1	23	96	41	78	2	17	2-0	.305	.361	.525	.886	13	.976
— Houston (N.L.)		4	3	1	1	0	0	0	0	1	2	0	0	0-0	.333	.500	.333	.833	...	...
1999— New Orleans (PCL)	1B-OF	61	241	56	85	15	1	28	65	23	43	3	3	1-1	.353	.416	.772	1.188	5	.991
— Houston (N.L.) OF-1B-DH		64	150	11	41	6	0	8	30	9	31	0	3	0-0	.273	.311	.473	.784	2	.973
2000— Houston (N.L.) OF-1B-DH		119	264	36	68	10	2	20	47	15	61	0	6	0-0	.258	.295	.538	.833	1	.992
2001— Houston (N.L.) OF-1B-DH		95	213	21	56	15	0	9	39	19	48	1	3	0-0	.263	.323	.460	.783	1	.988
2002— Houston (N.L.)	OF-DH	136	453	41	125	31	0	12	72	33	82	1	9	1-3	.276	.324	.424	.748	3	.981
2003— Jacksonville (Sou.)	1B-OF	4	16	0	2	0	0	0	1	0	3	0	0	0-0	.125	.125	.125	.250	1	.950
— Los Angeles (N.L.)	1B-OF	52	109	6	20	1	0	9	9	3	19	1	4	0-0	.183	.211	.193	.403	1	.992
— Las Vegas (PCL)	1B-DH	34	128	16	38	9	0	4	24	10	22	0	3	0-0	.297	.343	.461	.804	2	.992
Major League totals (6 years)		470	1192	116	311	63	2	49	197	80	243	3	25	1-3	.261	.306	.440	.747	8	.986

WASDIN, JOHN — P

PERSONAL: Born August 5, 1972, in Fort Belvoir, Va. ... 6-2/196. ... Throws right, bats right. ... Full name: John Truman Wasdin. ... Name pronounced: WAAZ-din. ... High school: Amos P. Godby (Tallahassee, Fla.). ... College: Florida State.

TRANSACTIONS/CAREER NOTES: Selected by New York Yankees organization in 41st round of free-agent draft (June 4, 1990); did not sign. ... Selected by Oakland Athletics organization in first round (25th pick overall) of free-agent draft (June 3, 1993). ... Traded by A's with cash to Boston Red Sox for OF Jose Canseco (January 27, 1997). ... On Boston disabled list (July 18-August 5, 1999); included rehabilitation assignment to Gulf Coast Red Sox (July 30-31). ... Traded by Red Sox with P Brian Rose, P Jeff Taglienti and 2B Jeff Frye to Colorado Rockies for P Rolando Arrojo, P Rick Croushore, 2B Mike Lansing and cash (July 27, 2000). ... On suspended list (September 8-10, 2000). ... Released by Rockies (June 7, 2001). ... Signed by Baltimore Orioles organization (July 18, 2001). ... Traded by Orioles to Philadelphia Phillies for P Chris Brock (December 13, 2001). ... Granted free agency (December 21, 2001). ... Signed by Yomiuri Giants of Japan Central League (January 9, 2002). ... Traded by Pittsburgh Pirates to Toronto Blue Jays for OF Rich Thompson (July 8, 2003). ... Optioned to Syracuse (July 31, 2003). ... Elected free agency (September 29, 2003).

CAREER HITTING: 3-for-11 (.273), 2 R, 1 2B, 0 HR, 1 RBI.

Year League	W	L	Pct.	ERA	WHIP	G	GS	CG	ShO	Hld.	Sv.-Opp.	IP	H	R	ER	HR	BB-IBB	SO	Avg.
1993— Ariz. A's (Ariz.)	0	0	...	3.00	1.00	1	1	0	0	...	0-...	3.0	3	1	1	0	0-0	1	.250
— Madison (Midw.)	2	3	.400	1.86	0.85	9	9	0	0	...	0-...	48.1	32	11	10	1	9-1	40	.186
— Modesto (Calif.)	0	3	.000	3.86	1.29	3	3	0	0	...	0-...	16.1	17	9	7	0	4-0	11	.266
1994— Modesto (Calif.)	3	1	.750	1.69	0.83	6	4	0	0	...	0-...	26.2	17	6	5	2	5-0	30	.179
— Huntsville (Sou.)	12	3	.800	3.43	1.09	21	21	0	0	...	0-...	141.2	126	61	54	13	29-2	108	.236
1995— Edmonton (PCL)	12	8	.600	5.52	1.33	29	•28	2	1	...	0-...	174.1	193	117	107	26	38-3	111	.281
— Oakland (A.L.)	1	1	.500	4.67	0.98	5	2	0	0	...	0-0	17.1	14	9	9	4	3-0	6	.215
1996— Edmonton (PCL)	2	1	.667	4.14	1.38	9	9	0	0	...	0-...	50.0	52	23	23	6	17-2	30	.267
— Oakland (A.L.)	8	7	.533	5.96	1.48	25	21	1	0	0	0-1	131.1	145	96	87	24	50-5	75	.284
1997— Boston (A.L.)	4	6	.400	4.40	1.28	53	7	0	0	11	0-2	124.2	121	68	61	18	38-4	84	.251
1998— Boston (A.L.)	6	4	.600	5.25	1.44	47	8	0	0	4	0-1	96.0	111	57	56	14	27-8	59	.288
— Pawtucket (Int'l)	1	0	1.000	3.00	1.33	4	2	0	0	...	0-...	12.0	11	6	4	0	5-0	10	.239
1999— Pawtucket (Int'l)	1	1	.500	2.12	0.88	5	5	0	0	...	0-...	29.2	19	9	7	1	7-0	28	.184
— Boston (A.L.)	8	3	.727	4.12	1.13	45	0	0	0	2	2-5	74.1	66	38	34	14	18-0	57	.236
— GC Red Sox (GCL)	0	0	...	0.00	0.50	1	1	0	0	...	0-...	2.0	1	0	0	0	0-0	4	.143
2000— Boston (A.L.)	1	3	.250	5.04	1.41	25	1	0	0	0	1-2	44.2	48	25	25	8	15-1	36	.273
— Pawtucket (Int'l)	1	0	1.000	2.25	0.56	5	3	0	0	...	1-...	16.0	7	4	4	0	2-0	11	.130
— Colorado (N.L.)	0	3	.000	5.80	1.43	14	3	1	0	0	0-0	35.2	42	23	23	6	9-2	35	.302
2001— Colorado (N.L.)	2	1	.667	7.03	1.64	18	0	0	0	0	0-3	24.1	32	19	19	7	8-2	17	.320
— Rochester (Int'l)	2	1	.667	3.98	1.57	5	3	0	0	...	0-...	20.1	27	9	9	3	5-0	20	.321
— Baltimore (A.L.)	1	1	.500	4.17	1.41	26	0	0	0	4	0-2	49.2	54	25	23	4	16-4	47	.277
2003— Nashville (PCL)	8	4	.667	3.04	1.11	18	18	3	1	...	0-...	112.1	101	46	38	4	24-4	116	.238
— Toronto (A.L.)	0	1	.000	23.40	4.00	3	2	0	0	0	0-0	5.0	16	13	13	2	4-0	5	.533
— Syracuse (Int'l)	2	1	.667	5.23	1.40	10	1	0	0	...	0-...	20.2	28	13	12	1	1-0	21	.318
American League totals (8 years)	29	26	.527	5.10	1.37	229	41	1	0	21	3-13	543.0	575	331	308	88	171-22	369	.270
National League totals (2 years)	2	4	.333	6.30	1.52	32	3	1	0	0	0-3	60.0	74	42	42	13	17-4	52	.310
Major League totals (8 years)	31	30	.508	5.22	1.39	261	44	2	0	21	3-16	603.0	649	373	350	101	188-26	421	.274

WASHBURN, JARROD — P

PERSONAL: Born August 13, 1974, in La Crosse, Wis. ... 6-1/195. ... Throws left, bats left. ... Full name: Jarrod Michael Washburn. ... High school: Webster (Wis.). ... College: Wisconsin-Oshkosh.

TRANSACTIONS/CAREER NOTES: Selected by California Angels organizaiton in second round of free-agent draft (June 1, 1995). ... Angels franchise renamed Anaheim Angels for 1997 season. ... On Edmonton disabled list (April 26-June 17, 1999). ... On Anaheim disabled list (March 25-April 9, July 22-August 7 and August 8, 2000-remainder of season); included rehabilitation assignment to Lake Elsinore (April 7). ... On Anaheim disabled list (March 23-April 16, 2001); included rehabilitation assignment to Salt Lake (April 8-16).

CAREER HITTING: 6-for-19 (.316), 1 R, 0 2B, 0 3B, 0 HR, 2 RBI.

Year League	W	L	Pct.	ERA	WHIP	G	GS	CG	ShO	Hld.	Sv.-Opp.	IP	H	R	ER	HR	BB-IBB	SO	Avg.
1995— Boise (NW)	3	2	.600	3.33	1.07	8	8	0	0	...	0-...	46.0	35	17	17	1	14-0	54	.208
— Cedar Rapids (Midw.)	0	1	.000	3.44	1.31	3	3	0	0	...	0-...	18.1	17	7	7	1	7-0	20	.258
1996— Lake Elsinore (Calif.)	6	3	.667	3.30	1.21	14	14	3	0	...	0-...	92.2	79	38	34	5	33-0	93	.229
— Midland (Texas)	5	6	.455	4.40	1.16	13	13	1	0	...	0-...	88.0	77	44	43	11	25-0	58	.235
— Vancouver (PCL)	0	2	.000	10.80	2.88	2	2	0	0	...	0-...	8.1	12	16	10	1	12-0	5	.333
1997— Midland (Texas)	15	•12	.556	4.80	1.46	29	*29	5	•1	...	0-...	*189.1	*211	*115	*101	*23	65-0	*146	.288
— Vancouver (PCL)	0	0	...	3.60	1.20	1	1	0	0	...	0-...	5.0	4	2	2	0	2-0	6	.211
1998— Vancouver (PCL)	4	5	.444	4.32	1.46	14	14	2	0	...	0-...	91.2	91	44	44	7	43-0	66	.254
— Anaheim (A.L.)	6	3	.667	4.62	1.31	15	11	0	0	1	0-0	74.0	70	40	38	11	27-1	48	.248
— Midland (Texas)	0	1	.000	6.23	1.73	1	1	0	0	...	0-...	8.2	13	8	6	2	2-0	8	.351
1999— Edmonton (PCL)	1	5	.167	4.73	1.14	11	11	1	0	...	0-...	59.0	50	31	31	6	17-0	55	.226
— Anaheim (A.L.)	4	5	.444	5.25	1.41	16	10	0	0	1	0-0	61.2	61	36	36	6	26-0	39	.261

W

Year League	W	L	Pct.	ERA	WHIP	G	GS	CG	ShO	Hld.	Sv.-Opp.	IP	H	R	ER	HR	BB-IBB	SO	Avg.
2000— Lake Elsinore (Calif.)	0	0	...	6.00	1.67	1	1	0	0	...	0-...	3.0	3	2	2	0	2-0	7	.250
— Edmonton (PCL)	3	0	1.000	3.52	1.57	5	5	0	0	...	0-...	30.2	35	13	12	2	13-0	20	.299
— Anaheim (A.L.)	7	2	.778	3.74	1.20	14	14	0	0	0	0-0	84.1	64	38	35	16	37-0	49	.215
2001— Salt Lake (PCL)	0	1	.000	5.87	1.30	1	1	0	0	...	0-...	7.2	9	5	5	1	1-0	5	.300
— Anaheim (A.L.)	11	10	.524	3.77	1.29	30	30	1	0	0	0-0	193.1	196	89	81	25	54-4	126	.263
2002— Anaheim (A.L.)	18	6	.750	3.15	1.17	32	32	1	0	0	0-0	206.0	183	75	72	19	59-1	139	.235
2003— Anaheim (A.L.)	10	15	.400	4.43	1.25	32	32	2	0	0	0-0	207.1	205	106	102	•34	54-4	118	.256
Major League totals (6 years)	56	41	.577	3.96	1.25	139	129	4	0	2	0-0	826.2	779	384	364	111	257-10	519	.248

WATSON, MARK   P

PERSONAL: Born January 23, 1974, in Atlanta, Ga. ... 6-3/238. ... Throws left, bats right. ... Full name: Mark Bradford Watson. ... High school: Marist (Atlanta). ... College: Georgia.

TRANSACTIONS/CAREER NOTES: Signed as non-drafted free agent by Milwaukee Brewers organization (June 16, 1996). ... Traded by Brewers to Cleveland Indians for P Ben McDonald (March 11, 1998); traded arranged as compensation for McDonald, who was injured and had been acquired by Indians (December 8, 1997). ... Claimed on waivers by Seattle Mariners (June 23, 2000). ... On Tacoma disabled list (August 27-September 21, 2000). ... Released by Mariners (May 4, 2001). ... Signed by Indians organization (May 24, 2001). ... Granted free agency (October 15, 2001). ... Signed by Chicago Cubs organization (December 14, 2001). ... Claimed on waivers by Colorado Rockies (July 26, 2002). ... On Colorado Springs disabled list (August 23-September 1, 2002). ... Released by Rockies, elected free agency (October 15, 2002). ... Signed by Cincinnati Reds organization (November 19, 2002). ... Contract purchased from Louisville (August 12, 2003). ... Placed on 15-day disabled list (August 26, 2003). ... Transferred to 60-day disabled list (September 8, 2003).

CAREER HITTING: 0-for-0 (.000), 0 R, 0 2B, 0 3B, 0 HR, 0 RBI.

Year League	W	L	Pct.	ERA	WHIP	G	GS	CG	ShO	Hld.	Sv.-Opp.	IP	H	R	ER	HR	BB-IBB	SO	Avg.
1996— Helena (Pio.)	5	2	.714	4.77	1.44	13	13	0	0	...	0-...	60.1	59	43	32	2	28-0	68	.257
1997— Beloit (Midw.)	0	3	.000	6.68	1.86	8	7	0	0	...	0-...	32.1	40	33	24	3	20-0	33	.310
— Ogden (Pio.)	4	3	.571	4.15	1.32	10	10	1	0	...	0-...	47.2	44	26	22	4	19-0	49	.244
1998— Columbus (S. Atl.)	3	4	.429	4.05	1.30	31	12	1	0	...	0-...	97.2	95	53	44	10	32-0	77	.259
— Kinston (Caro.)	0	1	.000	0.00	0.79	1	1	0	0	...	0-...	6.1	3	4	0	0	2-0	8	.130
1999— Kinston (Caro.)	6	0	1.000	1.04	0.88	11	4	0	0	...	0-...	43.1	28	7	5	1	10-0	40	.183
— Akron (East.)	9	8	.529	4.34	1.65	19	17	0	0	...	0-...	110.0	143	64	53	9	38-0	57	.323
2000— Buffalo (Int'l)	1	2	.333	4.43	1.48	16	0	0	0	...	1-...	20.1	18	11	10	1	12-6	16	.237
— Cleveland (A.L.)	0	1	.000	8.53	2.21	6	0	0	0	0	0-0	6.1	12	7	6	0	2-0	4	.400
— Tacoma (PCL)	2	1	.667	3.96	1.44	16	0	0	0	...	0-...	25.0	30	16	11	3	6-0	17	.294
2001— Tacoma (PCL)	0	1	.000	2.25	1.50	3	0	0	0	...	1-...	4.0	4	2	1	1	2-0	1	.222
— Akron (East.)	3	1	.750	4.12	1.19	30	0	0	0	...	4-...	39.1	34	19	18	2	13-0	34	.227
— Buffalo (Int'l)	0	1	.000	13.50	3.00	3	0	0	0	...	0-...	4.0	9	7	6	1	3-1	3	.409
2002— Iowa (PCL)	4	0	1.000	4.30	1.43	28	0	0	0	...	1-...	37.2	35	22	18	3	19-3	25	.255
— Seattle (A.L.)	1	0	1.000	18.00	3.00	3	0	0	0	0	0-0	4.0	8	8	8	1	4-0	1	.421
— Tacoma (PCL)	2	0	1.000	0.73	1.05	6	0	0	0	...	2-...	12.1	10	2	1	0	3-0	8	.213
— Colo. Springs (PCL)	0	0	...	16.03	3.09	10	0	0	0	...	0-...	10.2	22	19	19	3	11-1	10	.423
2003— Louisville (Int'l)	4	4	.500	4.36	1.25	44	0	0	0	...	4-...	53.2	53	30	26	1	14-1	46	.268
— Cincinnati (N.L.)	0	0	...	4.50	1.50	2	0	0	0	0	0-0	2.0	2	1	1	0	1-0	2	.250
American League totals (2 years)	1	1	.500	12.19	2.52	9	0	0	0	0	0-0	10.1	20	15	14	1	6-0	5	.408
National League totals (1 year)	0	0	...	4.50	1.50	2	0	0	0	0	0-0	2.0	2	1	1	0	1-0	2	.250
Major League totals (3 years)	1	1	.500	10.95	2.35	11	0	0	0	0	0-0	12.1	22	16	15	1	7-0	7	.386

WATSON, MATT   OF

PERSONAL: Born November 5, 1978, in Lancaster, Pa. ... 5-11/200. ... Bats left, throws right. ... Full name: Matthew Kyle Watson. ... High school: McCaskey (Pa.). ... College: Xavier.

TRANSACTIONS/CAREER NOTES: Selected by Montreal Expos organization in 16th round of free-agent draft (June 1999). ... Traded by Expos with P Scott Strickland and P Phil Seibel to New York Mets for P Bruce Chen, P Dicky Gonzalez, INF Luis Figueroa and a player to be named later (April 5, 2002). P Saul Rivers later sent to Montreal to complete deal (July 14, 2002).

2003 GAMES PLAYED BY POSITION (MLB): OF—5.

Year Team (League)	Pos.	G	AB	R	H	2B	3B	HR	RBI	BB	SO	HBP	GDP	SB-CS	Avg.	OBP	SLG	OPS	E	Pct.
1999— Vermont (NYP)	OF	70	284	55	108	12	3	7	47	30	27	3	6	17-7	.380	.439	.518	.957	6	.959
2000— Jupiter (FSL)	OF	40	137	10	24	5	2	0	8	18	23	1	6	4-3	.175	.276	.241	.517	2	.951
2001— Jupiter (FSL)	OF	124	446	70	147	33	4	5	74	63	45	6	11	17-9	.330	.417	.455	.872	4	.982
2002— Harrisburg (East.)	OF	1	4	1	1	0	0	0	0	0	0	0	0	0-0	.250	.250	.250	.500	0	1.000
— Binghamton (East.)	OF	127	437	55	122	26	2	10	67	39	52	3	14	12-8	.279	.339	.416	.755	4	.979
2003— St. Lucie (Fla. St.)	OF	2	7	2	2	0	1	0	2	1	2	0	0	1-0	.286	.333	.571	.905	0	1.000
— Binghamton (East.)	OF-DH	8	28	6	11	3	0	1	1	2	2	1	0	1-1	.393	.452	.607	1.059	1	1.000
— Norfolk (Int'l)	OF-DH	74	254	40	75	18	1	11	55	23	23	8	4	2-2	.295	.366	.504	.869	8	.939
— Brooklyn (NY-P)	OF-DH	4	14	0	2	1	0	0	0	2	3	1	0	2-1	.143	.294	.214	.508	0	1.000
— New York (N.L.)	OF	15	23	0	4	2	0	0	2	1	5	0	1	0-0	.174	.208	.261	.469	2	.846
Major League totals (1 year)		15	23	0	4	2	0	0	2	1	5	0	1	0-0	.174	.208	.261	.469	2	.846

WAYNE, JUSTIN   P

PERSONAL: Born April 16, 1979, in Honolulu, Hawaii. ... 6-3/205. ... Throws right, bats right. ... Full name: Justin Morgan Wayne. ... 0-for-9 (.000), 0 R, 0 RBI.

TRANSACTIONS/CAREER NOTES: Selected by Montreal Expos organization in first round (fifth pick overall) of free-agent draft (June 5, 2000). ... Traded by Expos with P Carl Pavano, P Graeme Lloyd and IF Mike Mordecai to Florida Marlins for P Claudio Vargas, OF/2B Wilton Guerrero, OF Cliff Floyd, cash considerations and a player to be named later (July 11, 2002); Expos acquired P Don Levinski to complete deal (August 5, 2002). ... On Florida disabled list (March 25-April 12, 2003); included rehabilitation assignment to Jupiter (April 12).

CAREER HITTING: 0-for-9 (.000), 0 R, 0 2B, 0 3B, 0 HR, 0 RBI.

Year League	W	L	Pct.	ERA	WHIP	G	GS	CG	ShO	Hld.	Sv.-Opp.	IP	H	R	ER	HR	BB-IBB	SO	Avg.
2000— Jupiter (FSL)	0	3	.000	5.81	1.41	5	5	0	0	...	0-...	26.1	26	22	17	2	11-0	24	.263
2001— Jupiter (FSL)	2	3	.400	3.02	0.96	8	7	0	0	...	0-...	41.2	31	16	14	0	9-0	35	.204
— Harrisburg (Eastern)	9	2	.818	2.62	1.31	14	14	2	0	...	0-...	92.0	87	28	27	4	34-0	70	.248
2002— Harrisburg (Eastern)	5	2	.714	2.37	1.07	17	17	0	0	...	0-...	98.2	74	41	26	7	32-0	47	.213
— Florida (N.L.)	2	3	.400	5.32	1.48	5	5	0	0	0	0-...	23.2	22	16	14	3	13-0	16	.244
— Portland (East.)	3	3	.500	4.85	1.31	7	7	1	1	...	0-...	42.2	43	26	23	3	13-0	30	.269
— Calgary (PCL)	0	1	.000	6.35	1.24	2	2	0	0	...	0-...	11.1	8	8	8	3	6-0	10	.195
2003— Jupiter (FSL)	0	0	...	0.00	1.00	1	1	0	0	...	0-...	6.0	6	0	0	0	0-0	5	.250
— Florida (N.L.)	0	2	.000	11.81	2.63	2	2	0	0	0	0-0	5.1	9	7	7	1	5-0	1	.375
— Albuquerque (PCL)	4	12	.250	4.24	1.31	23	23	2	0	...	0-...	136.0	138	81	64	10	40-0	82	.266
Major League totals (2 years)	2	5	.286	6.52	1.69	7	7	0	0	0	0-0	29.0	31	23	21	4	18-0	17	.272

W

WEATHERS, DAVE   P

PERSONAL: Born September 25, 1969, in Lawrenceburg, Tenn. ... 6-3/230. ... Throws right, bats right. ... Full name: John David Weathers. ... High school: Loretto (Tenn.). ... Junior college: Motlow State (Tenn.) Community College.

TRANSACTIONS/CAREER NOTES: Selected by Toronto Blue Jays organization in third round of free-agent draft (June 1, 1988). ... On Syracuse disabled list (May 11-July 31, 1992). ... Selected by Florida Marlins in second round (29th pick overall) of expansion draft (November 17, 1992). ... On Florida disabled list (June 26-July 13, 1995); included rehabilitation assignments to Brevard County (July 4-10) and Charlotte (July 11-13). ... Traded by Marlins to New York Yankees for P Mark Hutton (July 31, 1996). ... Traded by Yankees to Cleveland Indians for OF Chad Curtis (June 9, 1997). ... Claimed on waivers by Cincinnati Reds (December 20, 1997). ... Claimed on waivers by Milwaukee Brewers (June 24, 1998). ... Granted free agency (October 29, 1999). ... Re-signed by Brewers (December 2, 1999). ... On disabled list (August 2-22, 2000). ... Traded by Brewers with P Roberto Miniel to Chicago Cubs for P Ruben Quevedo and OF Peter Zoccolillo (July 30, 2001). ... Granted free agency (November 5, 2001). ... Signed by New York Mets (December 13, 2001). ... On suspended list (September 20-22, 2002).

CAREER HITTING: 14-for-135 (.104), 7 R, 0 2B, 0 3B, 2 HR, 4 RBI.

Year — League	W	L	Pct.	ERA	WHIP	G	GS	CG	ShO	Hld.	Sv.-Opp.	IP	H	R	ER	HR	BB-IBB	SO	Avg.
1988— St. Catharines (NYP)	4	4	.500	3.02	1.34	15	12	0	0	...	0-...	62.2	58	30	21	3	26-0	36	.245
1989— Myrtle Beach (SAL)	11	• 13	.458	3.86	1.44	31	* 31	2	0	...	0-...	172.2	163	99	74	3	86-2	111	.247
1990— Dunedin (Fla. St.)	10	7	.588	3.70	1.37	27	• 27	2	0	...	0-...	158.0	158	82	65	2	59-0	96	.266
1991— Knoxville (Sou.)	10	7	.588	2.45	1.22	24	22	5	2	...	0-...	139.1	121	51	38	3	49-1	114	.236
— Toronto (A.L.)	1	0	1.000	4.91	2.18	15	0	0	0	1	0-0	14.2	15	9	8	1	17-3	13	.263
1992— Syracuse (Int'l)	1	4	.200	4.66	1.43	12	10	0	0	...	0-...	48.1	48	29	25	3	21-2	30	.254
— Toronto (A.L.)	0	0	...	8.10	2.10	2	0	0	0	0	0-0	3.1	5	3	3	1	2-0	3	.385
1993— Edmonton (PCL)	11	4	.733	3.83	1.40	22	22	3	1	...	0-...	141.0	150	77	60	12	47-2	117	.271
— Florida (N.L.)	2	3	.400	5.12	1.53	14	6	0	0	0	0-0	45.2	57	26	26	3	13-1	34	.306
1994— Florida (N.L.)	8	12	.400	5.27	1.67	24	24	0	0	0	0-0	135.0	166	87	79	13	59-9	72	.306
1995— Florida (N.L.)	4	5	.444	5.98	1.73	28	15	0	0	1	0-0	90.1	104	68	60	8	52-3	60	.295
— Brevard County (FSL)	0	0	...	0.00	1.25	1	1	0	0	...	0-...	4.0	4	0	0	0	1-0	3	.286
— Charlotte (Int'l)	0	1	.000	9.00	3.00	1	1	0	0	...	0-...	5.0	10	5	5	0	5-0	0	.455
1996— Florida (N.L.)	2	2	.500	4.54	1.58	31	8	0	0	3	0-0	71.1	85	41	36	7	28-4	40	.302
— Charlotte (Int'l)	0	0	...	7.71	3.43	1	1	0	0	...	0-...	2.1	5	2	2	0	3-0	0	.500
— New York (A.L.)	0	2	.000	9.35	2.13	11	4	0	0	0	0-0	17.1	23	19	18	1	14-1	13	.315
— Columbus (Int'l)	0	2	.000	5.40	1.50	3	3	0	0	...	0-...	16.2	20	13	10	1	5-0	7	.299
1997— New York (A.L.)	0	1	.000	10.00	2.44	10	0	0	0	0	0-1	9.0	15	10	10	1	7-0	4	.375
— Columbus (Int'l)	2	2	.500	3.19	1.15	5	5	1	0	...	0-...	36.2	35	18	13	3	7-0	35	.250
— Buffalo (A.A.)	4	3	.571	3.15	1.28	11	11	2	1	...	0-...	68.2	71	37	24	7	17-0	51	.266
— Cleveland (A.L.)	1	2	.333	7.56	1.86	9	1	0	0	0	0-0	16.2	23	14	14	2	8-0	14	.343
1998— Cincinnati (N.L.)	2	4	.333	6.21	1.81	16	9	0	0	0	0-0	62.1	86	47	43	3	27-2	51	.330
— Milwaukee (N.L.)	4	1	.800	3.21	1.22	28	0	0	0	3	0-1	47.2	44	22	17	3	14-1	43	.246
1999— Milwaukee (N.L.)	7	4	.636	4.65	1.51	63	0	0	0	9	2-6	93.0	102	49	48	14	38-3	74	.279
2000— Milwaukee (N.L.)	3	5	.375	3.07	1.38	69	0	0	0	14	1-7	76.1	73	29	26	7	32-8	50	.260
2001— Milwaukee (N.L.)	3	4	.429	2.03	1.08	52	0	0	0	10	4-7	57.2	37	14	13	3	25-7	46	.188
— Chicago (N.L.)	1	1	.500	3.18	1.31	28	0	0	0	6	0-3	28.1	28	10	10	3	9-1	20	.269
2002— New York (N.L.)	6	3	.667	2.91	1.36	71	0	0	0	18	0-5	77.1	69	30	25	6	36-7	61	.245
2003— New York (N.L.)	1	6	.143	3.08	1.45	77	0	0	0	26	7-9	87.2	87	33	30	6	40-6	75	.264
American League totals (4 years)	2	5	.286	7.82	2.11	47	5	0	0	1	0-1	61.0	81	55	53	6	48-4	47	.324
National League totals (10 years)	43	50	.462	4.26	1.50	501	62	0	0	90	14-38	872.2	938	456	413	76	373-52	626	.279
Major League totals (13 years)	45	55	.450	4.49	1.54	548	67	0	0	91	14-39	933.2	1019	511	466	82	421-56	673	.282

WEAVER, JEFF   P

PERSONAL: Born August 22, 1976, in Northridge, Calif. ... 6-5/200. ... Throws right, bats right. ... Full name: Jeffrey Charles Weaver. ... High school: Simi Valley (Calif.). ... College: Fresno State.

TRANSACTIONS/CAREER NOTES: Selected by Chicago White Sox organziation in second-round of free-agent draft (June 3, 1997); did not sign. ... Selected by Detroit Tigers organization in first round (14th pick overall) of free-agent draft (June 2, 1998). ... Traded by Tigers to New York Yankees as part of three-way deal in which Oakland Athletics acquired P Ted Lilly, OF John-Ford Griffin and P Jason Arnold from Yankees and Tigers acquired 1B Carlos Pena, P Franklyn German and a player to be named later from A's (July 5, 2002); Tigers acquired P Jeremy Bonderman to complete deal (August 22, 2002). ... Optioned to Columbus by New York (August 25, 2003). ... Recalled from Columbus by New York (August 28, 2003).

CAREER HITTING: 4-for-19 (.211), 2 R, 1 2B, 0 3B, 0 HR, 1 RBI.

Year — League	W	L	Pct.	ERA	WHIP	G	GS	CG	ShO	Hld.	Sv.-Opp.	IP	H	R	ER	HR	BB-IBB	SO	Avg.
1998— Jamestown (NYP)	1	0	1.000	1.50	0.58	3	3	0	0	...	0-...	12.0	6	4	2	0	1-0	12	.143
— West. Mich. (Mid.)	1	0	1.000	1.38	0.62	2	2	0	0	...	0-...	13.0	8	3	2	1	0-0	21	.182
1999— Jacksonville (Sou.)	0	0	...	3.00	0.83	1	1	0	0	...	0-...	6.0	5	2	2	0	0-0	6	.227
— Detroit (A.L.)	9	12	.429	5.55	1.42	30	29	0	0	0	0-0	163.2	176	104	101	27	56-2	114	.278
2000— Toledo (Int'l)	0	1	.000	3.38	1.13	1	1	0	0	...	0-...	5.1	5	2	2	1	1-0	10	.250
— Detroit (A.L.)	11	15	.423	4.32	1.29	31	30	2	0	0	0-0	200.0	205	102	96	26	52-2	136	.267
2001— Detroit (A.L.)	13	16	.448	4.08	1.32	33	33	5	0	0	0-0	229.1	235	116	104	19	68-4	152	.265
2002— Detroit (A.L.)	6	8	.429	3.18	1.19	17	17	3	† 3	0	0-0	121.2	112	50	43	4	33-1	75	.243
— New York (A.L.)	5	3	.625	4.04	1.23	15	8	0	† 0	0	2-2	78.0	81	38	35	12	15-3	57	.260
2003— New York (A.L.)	7	9	.438	5.99	1.62	32	24	0	0	1	0-0	159.1	211	113	106	16	47-2	93	.320
Major League totals (5 years)	51	63	.447	4.59	1.36	158	141	10	3	1	2-2	952.0	1020	523	485	104	271-14	627	.274

WEBB, BRANDON   P

PERSONAL: Born May 9, 1979, in Ashland, Ky. ... 6-2/228. ... Throws right, bats right. ... Full name: Brandon T. Webb. ... High school: Ashland (Ky.). ... College: Kentucky.

TRANSACTIONS/CAREER NOTES: Selected by Arizona Diamondbacks organization in eighth round of free-agent draft (June 5, 2000). ... On disabled list (August 9 through remainder of 2000 season).

CAREER HITTING: 5-for-50 (.100), 2 R, 1 2B, 0 3B, 0 HR, 0 RBI.

Year — League	W	L	Pct.	ERA	WHIP	G	GS	CG	ShO	Hld.	Sv.-Opp.	IP	H	R	ER	HR	BB-IBB	SO	Avg.
2000— Ariz. D'backs (Ariz.)	0	0	...	9.00	2.00	1	1	0	0	...	0-...	1.0	2	1	1	0	0-0	3	.400
— South Bend (Mid.)	0	0	...	3.24	1.14	12	0	0	0	...	2-...	16.2	10	7	6	0	9-1	18	.172
2001— Lancaster (Calif.)	6	10	.375	3.99	1.34	29	28	0	0	...	0-...	162.1	174	90	72	9	44-0	158	.276
2002— El Paso (Texas)	10	6	.625	3.14	1.32	26	25	1	0	...	0-...	152.0	141	66	53	4	59-1	122	.247
— Tucson (PCL)	0	1	.000	3.86	1.29	1	1	0	0	...	0-...	7.0	5	3	3	0	4-0	5	.200
2003— Tucson (PCL)	1	1	.500	6.00	1.50	3	3	0	0	...	0-...	18.0	18	17	12	0	9-0	17	.257
— Arizona (N.L.)	10	9	.526	2.84	1.15	29	28	1	1	0	0-0	180.2	140	65	57	12	68-4	172	.212
Major League totals (1 year)	10	9	.526	2.84	1.15	29	28	1	1	0	0-0	180.2	140	65	57	12	68-4	172	.212

W

WEBER, BEN — P

PERSONAL: Born November 17, 1969, in Port Arthur, Texas. ... 6-4/205. ... Throws right, bats right. ... Full name: Benjamin Edward Weber. ... Name pronounced: webb-er. ... High school: Port Neches-Groves (Port Neches, Texas). ... College: Houston.

TRANSACTIONS/CAREER NOTES: Selected by Toronto Blue Jays organization in 20th round of free-agent draft (June 3, 1991). ... Released by Blue Jays (March 24, 1996). ... Signed by Salinas, Western League (May 1996). ... Signed by Taipei, Taiwan League (1997). ... Signed by San Francisco Giants organization (October 30, 1998). ... Claimed on waivers by Anaheim Angels (August 30, 2000).

CAREER HITTING: 0-for-0 (.000), 0 R, 0 2B, 0 3B, 0 HR, 0 RBI.

Year — League	W	L	Pct.	ERA	WHIP	G	GS	CG	ShO	Hld.	Sv.-Opp.	IP	H	R	ER	HR	BB-IBB	SO	Avg.
1991— St. Catharines (NYP)	6	3	.667	3.24	1.33	16	14	1	0	...	0-...	97.1	•105	43	35	3	24-2	60	.274
1992— Myrtle Beach (SAL)	4	7	.364	1.64	1.14	41	1	0	0	...	6-...	98.2	83	27	18	1	29-3	65	.227
1993— Dunedin (Fla. St.)	8	3	.727	2.92	1.34	55	0	0	0	...	12-...	83.1	87	36	27	4	25-5	45	.278
1994— Dunedin (Fla. St.)	3	2	.600	2.73	1.14	18	0	0	0	...	3-...	26.1	25	8	8	1	5-3	19	.255
— Knoxville (Sou.)	4	3	.571	3.76	1.24	25	10	0	0	...	0-...	95.2	103	49	40	8	16-0	55	.272
1995— Syracuse (Int'l)	4	5	.444	5.40	1.51	25	15	0	0	...	1-...	91.2	111	62	55	10	27-1	38	.300
— Knoxville (Sou.)	4	1	.800	3.91	1.26	12	1	0	0	...	0-...	25.1	26	12	11	3	6-0	16	.268
1996— Salinas (West.)	•12	6	.667	3.47	1.22	22	22	2	...	...	0-...	148.0	138	68	57	11	42-1	102	.248
1997— Taipei (Taiwan)	7	3	.700	0.00	1.19	40	...	...	...	...	5-...	99.0	85	...	...	...	33-...	78	...
1998— Taipei (Taiwan)	12	7	.632	0.00	1.40	56	...	...	...	...	7-...	144.0	150	...	...	...	52-...	122	...
1999— Fresno (PCL)	2	4	.333	3.34	1.23	51	0	0	0	...	8-...	86.1	78	34	32	6	28-2	67	.245
2000— San Francisco (N.L.)	0	1	.000	14.63	2.50	9	0	0	0	1	0-2	8.0	16	13	13	0	4-0	6	.400
— Fresno (PCL)	4	8	.333	2.42	1.18	38	3	0	0	...	7-...	78.0	72	31	21	7	20-0	66	.245
— Erie (East.)	0	1	.000	16.20	3.00	2	0	0	0	...	0-...	1.2	3	5	3	1	2-0	2	.333
— Anaheim (A.L.)	1	0	1.000	1.84	0.95	10	0	0	0	1	0-0	14.2	12	6	3	0	2-1	8	.214
2001— Anaheim (A.L.)	6	2	.750	3.42	1.42	56	0	0	0	6	0-1	68.1	66	28	26	4	31-8	40	.251
2002— Anaheim (A.L.)	7	2	.778	2.54	1.18	63	0	0	0	18	7-11	78.0	70	25	22	4	22-3	43	.249
2003— Anaheim (A.L.)	5	1	.833	2.69	1.32	62	0	0	0	11	0-2	80.1	84	26	24	7	22-7	46	.275
American League totals (4 years)	19	5	.792	2.80	1.28	191	0	0	0	36	7-14	241.1	232	85	75	15	77-19	137	.256
National League totals (1 year)	0	1	.000	14.63	2.50	9	0	0	0	1	0-2	8.0	16	13	13	0	4-0	6	.400
Major League totals (4 years)	19	6	.760	3.18	1.32	200	0	0	0	37	7-16	249.1	248	98	88	15	81-19	143	.262

WEEKS, RICKIE — 2B

PERSONAL: Born September 13, 1982, in Daytona Beach, Fla. ... 6-0/195. ... Bats right, throws right. ... Full name: Rickie Darnell Weeks. ... High school: Lake Brantley (Altamonte Springs, Fla.). ... College: Southern University.

TRANSACTIONS/CAREER NOTES: Selected by Milwaukee Brewers organization in first round (second pick overall) of free-agent draft (June 3, 2003).

2003 GAMES PLAYED BY POSITION (MLB): 2B—4.

Year — Team (League)	Pos.	G	AB	R	H	2B	3B	HR	RBI	BB	SO	HBP	GDP	SB-CS	Avg.	OBP	SLG	OPS	E	Pct.
2003—Ariz. Brewers (Ariz.)	DH	1	4	0	2	0	0	4	0	2	1	0	1-0	.500	.600	.500	1.100	0	.000
— Beloit (Midw.)	2B-DH	20	63	13	22	8	1	1	16	15	9	6	1	2-0	.349	.494	.556	1.050	7	.923
— Milwaukee (N.L.)	2B	7	12	1	2	1	0	0	0	1	6	1	0	0-0	.167	.286	.250	.536	1	.667
Major League totals (1 year)		7	12	1	2	1	0	0	0	1	6	1	0	0-0	.167	.286	.250	.536	1	.667

WELLEMEYER, TODD — P

PERSONAL: Born August 30, 1978, in Louisville, Ky. ... 6-3/195. ... Throws right, bats right. ... Full name: Todd Allen Wellemeyer. ... Name pronounced: WELL-my-er. ... High school: Eastern (Louisville, Ky.). ... College: Bellarmine (Ky.) College.

TRANSACTIONS/CAREER NOTES: Selected by Chicago Cubs organization in fourth round of free-agent draft (June 5, 2000). ... On disabled list (June 8-July 10, 2002).

CAREER HITTING: 0-for-1 (.000), 0 R, 0 2B, 0 3B, 0 HR, 0 RBI.

Year — League	W	L	Pct.	ERA	WHIP	G	GS	CG	ShO	Hld.	Sv.-Opp.	IP	H	R	ER	HR	BB-IBB	SO	Avg.
2000— Eugene (NW)	4	4	.500	3.67	1.25	15	15	0	0	...	0-...	76.0	62	35	31	3	33-2	85	.225
2001— Lansing (Midw.)	13	9	.591	4.16	1.63	27	27	1	0	...	0-...	147.0	165	85	68	14	74-0	167	.288
2002— Daytona (Fla. St.)	2	4	.333	3.79	1.11	14	14	0	0	...	0-...	73.2	63	33	31	7	19-1	87	.230
— West Tenn (Sou.)	3	3	.500	4.70	1.11	8	8	1	1	...	0-...	46.0	33	25	24	2	18-0	37	.204
2003— West Tenn (Sou.)	1	1	.500	5.48	1.36	4	4	0	0	...	0-...	21.1	19	13	13	1	10-0	34	.238
— Iowa (PCL)	5	5	.500	5.18	1.53	13	12	0	0	...	0-...	66.0	68	39	38	7	33-4	56	.272
— Chicago (N.L.)	1	1	.500	6.51	1.59	15	0	0	0	1	1-1	27.2	25	22	20	5	19-1	30	.245
Major League totals (1 year)	1	1	.500	6.51	1.59	15	0	0	0	1	1-1	27.2	25	22	20	5	19-1	30	.245

WELLS, DAVID — P

PERSONAL: Born May 20, 1963, in Torrance, Calif. ... 6-4/230. ... Throws left, bats left. ... Full name: David Lee Wells. ... High school: Point Loma (San Diego).

TRANSACTIONS/CAREER NOTES: Selected by Toronto Blue Jays organization in second round of free-agent draft (June 7, 1982). ... On Knoxville disabled list (June 28, 1984-remainder of season). ... On disabled list (April 10, 1985-entire season). ... On Knoxville disabled list (July 7-August 20, 1986). ... Released by Blue Jays (March 30, 1993). ... Signed by Detroit Tigers (April 3, 1993). ... On disabled list (August 1-20, 1993). ... Granted free agency (October 28, 1993). ... Re-signed by Tigers (December 13, 1993). ... On Detroit disabled list (April 19-June 6, 1994); included rehabilitation assignment to Lakeland (May 27-June 6). ... Traded by Tigers to Cincinnati Reds for P C.J. Nitkowski, P David Tuttle and a player to be named later (July 31, 1995); Tigers acquired IF Mark Lewis to complete deal (November 16, 1995). ... Traded by Reds to Baltimore Orioles for OF Curtis Goodwin and OF Trovin Valdez (December 26, 1995). ... Granted free agency (October 29, 1996). ... Signed by New York Yankees (December 24, 1996). ... Traded by Yankees with P Graeme Lloyd and 2B Homer Bush to Blue Jays for P Roger Clemens (February 18, 1999). ... Traded by Blue Jays with P Matt DeWitt to Chicago White Sox for P Mike Sirotka, P Kevin Beirne, OF Brian Simmons and P Mike Williams (January 14, 2001). ... On disabled list (July 2, 2001-remainder of season). ... Granted free agency (November 5, 2001). ... Signed by Yankees (January 17, 2002). ... Placed on bereavement list by New York (July 13, 2003).

CAREER HITTING: 7-for-56 (.125), 2 R, 1 2B, 0 3B, 0 HR, 0 RBI.

Year — League	W	L	Pct.	ERA	WHIP	G	GS	CG	ShO	Hld.	Sv.-Opp.	IP	H	R	ER	HR	BB-IBB	SO	Avg.
1982— Medicine Hat (Pio.)	4	3	.571	5.18	1.60	12	12	1	0	...	0-...	64.1	71	42	37	5	32-1	53	...
1983— Kinston (Caro.)	6	5	.545	3.73	1.35	25	25	5	0	...	0-...	157.0	141	81	65	13	71-2	115	.238
1984— Kinston (Caro.)	1	6	.143	4.71	1.67	7	7	0	0	...	0-...	42.0	51	29	22	1	19-1	44	.302
— Knoxville (Sou.)	3	2	.600	2.59	1.27	8	8	3	1	...	0-...	59.0	58	22	17	3	17-0	34	.262
1985— Syracuse (Int'l)										Did not play.									
1986— Florence (S. Atl.)	0	0	...	3.55	1.26	4	1	0	0	...	0-...	12.2	7	6	5	1	9-0	14	.159
— Ventura (Calif.)	2	1	.667	1.89	0.89	5	2	0	0	...	0-...	19.0	13	5	4	0	4-0	26	.200
— Knoxville (Sou.)	1	3	.250	4.05	1.50	10	7	1	0	...	0-...	40.0	42	24	18	1	18-0	32	.280
— Syracuse (Int'l)	0	1	.000	9.82	1.91	3	0	0	0	...	0-...	3.2	6	4	4	0	4-0	4	.400

W

Year League	W	L	Pct.	ERA	WHIP	G	GS	CG	ShO	Hld.	Sv.-Opp.	IP	H	R	ER	HR	BB-IBB	SO	Avg.
1987— Syracuse (Int'l)	4	6	.400	3.87	1.23	43	12	0	0	...	6-...	109.1	102	49	47	9	32-0	106	.248
— Toronto (A.L.)	4	3	.571	3.99	1.67	18	2	0	0	2	1-2	29.1	37	14	13	0	12-0	32	.311
1988— Toronto (A.L.)	3	5	.375	4.62	1.49	41	0	0	0	8	4-6	64.1	65	36	33	12	31-9	56	.269
— Syracuse (Int'l)	0	0	...	0.00	1.59	6	0	0	0	...	3-...	5.2	7	1	0	0	2-1	8	.269
1989— Toronto (A.L.)	7	4	.636	2.40	1.09	54	0	0	0	8	2-9	86.1	66	25	23	5	28-7	78	.207
1990— Toronto (A.L.)	11	6	.647	3.14	1.11	43	25	0	0	3	3-3	189.0	165	72	66	14	45-3	115	.235
1991— Toronto (A.L.)	15	10	.600	3.72	1.19	40	28	2	0	3	1-2	198.1	188	88	82	24	49-1	106	.252
1992— Toronto (A.L.)	7	9	.438	5.40	1.45	41	14	0	0	3	2-4	120.0	138	84	72	16	36-6	62	.289
1993— Detroit (A.L.)	11	9	.550	4.19	1.20	32	30	0	0	1	0-0	187.0	183	93	87	26	42-6	139	.254
1994— Detroit (A.L.)	5	7	.417	3.96	1.23	16	16	5	1	0	0-0	111.1	113	54	49	13	24-6	71	.260
— Lakeland (Fla. St.)	0	0	...	0.00	0.83	2	2	0	0	...	0-...	6.0	5	1	0	0	0-0	3	.217
1995— Detroit (A.L.)	10	3	.769	3.04	1.20	18	18	3	0	0	0-0	130.1	120	54	44	17	37-5	83	.242
— Cincinnati (N.L.)	6	5	.545	3.59	1.24	11	11	3	0	0	0-0	72.2	74	34	29	6	16-4	50	.265
1996— Baltimore (A.L.)	11	14	.440	5.14	1.33	34	34	3	0	0	0-0	224.1	247	132	128	32	51-7	130	.285
1997— New York (A.L.)	16	10	.615	4.21	1.30	32	32	5	2	0	0-0	218.0	239	109	102	24	45-0	156	.278
1998— New York (A.L.)	18	4	.818	3.49	1.05	30	30	8	* 5	0	0-0	214.1	195	86	83	29	29-0	163	.239
1999— Toronto (A.L.)	17	10	.630	4.82	1.33	34	34	* 7	1	0	0-0	* 231.2	* 246	132	124	32	62-2	169	.271
2000— Toronto (A.L.)	• 20	8	.714	4.11	1.29	35	• 35	* 9	1	0	0-0	229.2	* 266	115	105	23	31-0	166	.289
2001— Chicago (A.L.)	5	7	.417	4.47	1.40	16	16	1	0	0	0-0	100.2	120	55	50	12	21-1	59	.297
2002— Chicago (A.L.)	19	7	.731	3.75	1.24	31	31	2	1	0	0-0	206.1	210	100	86	21	45-2	137	.259
2003— New York (A.L.)	15	7	.682	4.14	1.23	31	30	4	1	0	0-0	213.0	242	101	98	24	20-0	101	.286
American League totals (17 years)	194	123	.612	4.07	1.25	546	375	49	12	28	13-26	2754.0	2840	1350	1245	324	608-55	1823	.266
National League totals (1 year)	6	5	.545	3.59	1.24	11	11	3	0	0	0-0	72.2	74	34	29	6	16-4	50	.265
Major League totals (17 years)	200	128	.610	4.06	1.25	557	386	52	12	28	13-26	2826.2	2914	1384	1274	330	624-59	1873	.266

WELLS, KIP   P

PERSONAL: Born April 21, 1977, in Houston, Texas. ... 6-3/205. ... Throws right, bats right. ... Full name: Robert Kip Wells. ... High school: Elkins (Fort Bend, Texas). ... College: Baylor.

TRANSACTIONS/CAREER NOTES: Selected by Milwaukee Brewers organization in 58th round of free-agent draft (June 1, 1995); did not sign. ... Selected by Chicago White Sox organization in first round (16th pick overall) of free-agent draft (June 2, 1998). ... Traded by White Sox with P Sean Lowe and P Josh Fogg to Pittsburgh Pirates for P Todd Ritchie and C Lee Evans (December 13, 2001).

CAREER HITTING: 26-for-139 (.187), 13 R, 5 2B, 0 3B, 2 HR, 10 RBI.

Year League	W	L	Pct.	ERA	WHIP	G	GS	CG	ShO	Hld.	Sv.-Opp.	IP	H	R	ER	HR	BB-IBB	SO	Avg.
1999— Winston-Salem (Caro.)	5	6	.455	3.57	1.31	14	14	0	0	...	0-...	85.2	78	39	34	4	34-1	95	.252
— Birmingham (Sou.)	8	2	.800	2.94	1.14	11	11	0	0	...	0-...	70.1	49	24	23	5	31-0	44	.198
— Chicago (A.L.)	4	1	.800	4.04	1.35	7	7	0	0	0	0-0	35.2	33	17	16	2	15-0	29	.248
2000— Chicago (A.L.)	6	9	.400	6.02	1.86	20	20	0	0	0	0-0	98.2	126	76	66	15	58-4	71	.312
— Charlotte (Int'l)	5	3	.625	5.37	1.52	12	12	2	1	...	0-...	62.0	67	38	37	10	27-1	38	.272
2001— Charlotte (Int'l)	2	1	.667	3.55	1.34	4	4	0	0	...	0-...	25.1	26	11	10	2	8-0	24	.260
— Chicago (A.L.)	10	11	.476	4.79	1.55	40	20	0	0	6	0-2	133.1	145	80	71	14	61-5	99	.281
2002— Pittsburgh (N.L.)	12	14	.462	3.58	1.35	33	33	1	1	0	0-0	198.1	197	92	79	21	71-11	134	.261
2003— Pittsburgh (N.L.)	10	9	.526	3.28	1.25	31	31	1	0	0	0-0	197.1	171	77	72	24	76-7	147	.233
American League totals (3 years)	20	21	.488	5.14	1.64	67	47	0	0	6	0-2	267.2	304	173	153	31	134-9	199	.289
National League totals (2 years)	22	23	.489	3.43	1.30	64	64	2	1	0	0-0	395.2	368	169	151	45	147-18	281	.247
Major League totals (5 years)	42	44	.488	4.12	1.44	131	111	2	1	6	0-2	663.1	672	342	304	76	281-27	480	.264

WELLS, VERNON   OF

PERSONAL: Born December 8, 1978, in Shreveport, La. ... 6-1/225. ... Bats right, throws right. ... Full name: Vernon III Wells. ... High school: Bowie (Arlington, Texas).

TRANSACTIONS/CAREER NOTES: Selected by Toronto Blue Jays organization in first round (fifth pick overall) of free-agent draft (June 3, 1997). ... On Syracuse disabled list (April 14-24, 2001).

2003 GAMES PLAYED BY POSITION (MLB): OF—161.

Year Team (League)	Pos.	G	AB	R	H	2B	3B	HR	RBI	BB	SO	HBP	GDP	SB-CS	Avg.	OBP	SLG	OPS	E	Pct.
1997— St. Catharines (NYP)	OF	66	264	52	81	20	1	10	31	30	44	1	2	8-6	.307	.377	.504	.881	7	.953
1998— Hagerstown (SAL)	OF	134	509	86	145	35	2	11	65	49	84	1	8	13-8	.285	.348	.426	.774	5	.980
1999— Dunedin (Fla. St.)	OF-DH	70	265	43	91	16	2	11	43	26	34	1	6	13-2	.343	.403	.543	.946	1	.993
— Knoxville (Sou.)	OF	26	106	18	36	6	2	3	17	12	15	0	0	6-2	.340	.400	.519	.919	0	1.000
— Syracuse (Int'l)	OF	33	129	20	40	8	1	4	21	10	22	1	3	5-1	.310	.357	.481	.837	2	.976
— Toronto (A.L.)	OF	24	88	8	23	5	0	1	8	4	18	0	6	1-1	.261	.293	.352	.646	0	1.000
2000— Syracuse (Int'l)	OF	127	493	76	120	31	7	16	66	48	88	4	8	23-4	.243	.313	.432	.745	3	.990
— Toronto (A.L.)	OF	3	2	0	0	0	0	0	0	0	0	0	0	0-0	.000	.000	.000	.000	0	1.000
2001— Syracuse (Int'l)	OF	107	413	57	116	27	4	12	52	29	68	4	3	15-11	.281	.333	.453	.785	5	.978
— Toronto (A.L.)	OF	30	96	14	30	8	0	1	6	5	15	1	0	5-0	.313	.350	.427	.777	2	.969
2002— Toronto (A.L.)	OF	159	608	87	167	34	4	23	100	27	85	3	15	9-4	.275	.305	.457	.762	3	.990
2003— Toronto (A.L.)	OF	161	678	118	*215	•49	5	33	117	42	80	7	21	4-1	.317	.359	.550	.909	4	.990
Major League totals (5 years)		377	1472	227	435	96	9	58	231	78	198	11	42	19-6	.296	.332	.491	.823	9	.990

WENDELL, TURK   P

PERSONAL: Born May 19, 1967, in Pittsfield, Mass. ... 6-2/205. ... Throws right, bats left. ... Full name: Steven John Wendell. ... Name pronounced: WEN-del. ... High school: Wahconah Regional (Dalton, Mass.). ... College: Quinnipiac.

TRANSACTIONS/CAREER NOTES: Selected by Atlanta Braves organization in fifth round of free-agent draft (June 1, 1988). ... Traded by Braves with P Yorkis Perez to Chicago Cubs for P Mike Bielecki and C Damon Berryhill (September 29, 1991). ... On disabled list (May 4, 1992-remainder of season). ... On Chicago disabled list (April 16-May 27, 1995); included rehabilitation assignments to Daytona (May 5-15) and Orlando (May 15-27). ... Traded by Cubs with OF Brian McRae and P Mel Rojas to New York Mets for OF Lance Johnson and two players to be named later (August 8, 1997); Cubs acquired P Mark Clark (August 11, 1997) and IF Manny Alexander (August 14, 1997) to complete deal. ... Granted free agency (November 3, 2000). ... Re-signed by Mets (December 1, 2000). ... Traded by Mets with P Dennis Cook to Philadelphia Phillies for P Bruce Chen and P Adam Walker (July 27, 2001). ... On disabled list (March 30, 2002-entire season). ... On Philadelphia disabled list (March 21-April 14, 2003); included rehabilitation assignment to Clearwater (April 3-14).

CAREER HITTING: 3-for-41 (.073), 1 R, 0 2B, 0 3B, 0 HR, 0 RBI.

W

Year	League	W	L	Pct.	ERA	WHIP	G	GS	CG	ShO	Hld.	Sv.-Opp.	IP	H	R	ER	HR	BB-IBB	SO	Avg.
1988— Pulaski (Appal.)		3	• 8	.273	3.83	1.14	14	14	* 6	1	...	0-...	* 101.0	85	50	43	3	30-0	87	.228
1989— Burlington (Midw.)		9	11	.450	2.21	1.06	22	22	• 9	* 5	...	0-...	159.0	127	63	39	7	41-1	153	.213
— Greenville (Sou.)		0	0	...	9.82	2.18	1	1	0	0	...	0-...	3.2	7	5	4	3	1-0	3	.389
— Durham (Caro.)		2	0	1.000	1.13	0.79	3	3	1	0	...	0-...	24.0	13	4	3	0	6-0	27	.157
1990— Greenville (Sou.)		4	9	.308	5.74	1.68	36	13	1	1	...	2-...	91.0	105	70	58	5	48-2	85	.288
— Durham (Caro.)		1	3	.250	1.86	1.01	6	5	1	0	...	0-...	38.2	24	10	8	3	15-1	26	.175
1991— Greenville (Sou.)		11	3	.786	2.56	1.23	25	20	1	1	...	0-...	147.2	130	47	42	4	51-5	122	.236
— Richmond (Int'l)		0	2	.000	3.43	1.71	3	3	1	0	...	0-...	21.0	20	9	8	3	16-0	18	.260
1992— Iowa (Am. Assoc.)		2	0	1.000	1.44	1.28	4	4	0	0	...	0-...	25.0	17	7	4	3	15-0	12	.191
1993— Iowa (Am. Assoc.)		10	8	.556	4.60	1.31	25	25	3	0	...	0-...	148.2	148	88	76	9	47-0	110	.257
— Chicago (N.L.)		1	2	.333	4.37	1.41	7	4	0	0	0	0-0	22.2	24	13	11	0	8-1	15	.273
1994— Iowa (Am. Assoc.)		11	6	.647	2.95	1.01	23	23	6	• 3	...	0-...	168.0	141	58	55	12	28-1	118	.230
— Chicago (N.L.)		0	1	.000	11.93	2.23	6	2	0	0	0	0-0	14.1	22	20	19	3	10-1	9	.349
1995— Daytona (Fla. St.)		0	0	...	1.17	0.78	4	2	0	0	...	0-...	7.2	5	2	1	0	1-0	8	.179
— Orlando (Sou.)		1	0	1.000	3.86	1.43	5	0	0	0	...	1-...	7.0	6	3	3	0	4-0	7	.250
— Chicago (N.L.)		3	1	.750	4.92	1.57	43	0	0	0	3	0-0	60.1	71	35	33	11	24-4	50	.298
1996— Chicago (N.L.)		4	5	.444	2.84	1.29	70	0	0	0	6	18-21	79.1	58	26	25	8	44-4	75	.201
1997— Chicago (N.L.)		3	5	.375	4.20	1.53	52	0	0	0	2	4-5	60.0	53	32	28	4	39-5	54	.238
— New York (N.L.)		0	0	...	4.96	1.78	13	0	0	0	0	1-2	16.1	15	10	9	3	14-1	10	.250
1998— New York (N.L.)		5	1	.833	2.93	1.24	66	0	0	0	11	4-8	76.2	62	25	25	4	33-9	58	.221
1999— New York (N.L.)		5	4	.556	3.05	1.37	80	0	0	0	21	3-6	85.2	80	31	29	9	37-8	77	.245
2000— New York (N.L.)		8	6	.571	3.59	1.22	77	0	0	0	16	1-5	82.2	60	36	33	9	41-7	73	.206
2001— New York (N.L.)		4	3	.571	3.51	1.25	49	0	0	0	6	1-3	51.1	42	23	20	8	22-6	41	.223
— Philadelphia (N.L.)		0	2	.000	7.47	2.11	21	0	0	0	2	0-0	15.2	21	13	13	4	12-3	15	.323
2002— Philadelphia (N.L.)										Did not play.										
2003— Clearwater (Fla. St.)		0	0	...	0.00	0.50	5	5	0	0	...	0-...	6.0	3	0	0	0	0-0	5	.143
— Philadelphia (N.L.)		3	3	.500	3.38	1.28	56	0	0	0	8	1-5	64.0	54	24	24	6	28-5	27	.235
Major League totals (10 years)		**36**	**33**	**.522**	**3.85**	**1.39**	**540**	**6**	**0**	**0**	**75**	**33-55**	**629.0**	**562**	**288**	**269**	**69**	**312-54**	**504**	**.240**

PERSONAL: Born May 20, 1979, in Springfield, Ill. ... 6-5/215. ... Bats right, throws right. ... Full name: Jayson Richard Werth. ... High school: Chatham Glenwood (Chatham, Ill.).

TRANSACTIONS/CAREER NOTES: Selected by Baltimore Orioles organization in first round (22nd pick overall) of free-agent draft (June 3, 1997). ... Traded by Orioles to Toronto Blue Jays for P John Bale (December 11, 2000). ... On Tennessee disabled list (April 5-14, 2001). ... On Toronto disabled list (March 21-April 13, 2003); included rehabilitation assignment to Dunedin (April 3-11).

2003 GAMES PLAYED BY POSITION (MLB): OF—20, DH—3.

Year	Team (League)	Pos.	G	AB	R	H	2B	3B	HR	RBI	BB	SO	HBP	GDP	SB-CS	Avg.	OBP	SLG	OPS	E	Pct.
1997— GC Orioles (GCL)		C-1B	32	88	16	26	6	0	1	8	22	22	0	0	7-1	.295	.432	.398	.830	9	.958
1998— Delmarva (S. Atl.)		C	120	408	71	108	20	3	8	53	50	92	15	14	21-6	.265	.364	.364	.751	9	.991
— Bowie (East.)		C	5	19	2	3	2	0	0	1	2	6	0	0	1-0	.158	.238	.263	.501	1	1.000
1999— Frederick (Carolina)		C	66	236	41	72	10	1	3	30	37	37	3	4	16-3	.305	.403	.394	.797	10	.981
— Bowie (East.)		C-OF	35	121	18	33	5	1	1	11	17	26	2	1	7-1	.273	.364	.355	.719	1	.996
2000— Bowie (East.)		C-OF	85	276	47	63	16	2	5	26	54	50	4	10	9-3	.228	.361	.355	.716	7	.988
— Frederick (Carolina)		C	24	83	16	23	3	0	2	18	10	15	0	3	5-1	.277	.347	.386	.733	2	.985
2001— Dunedin (Fla. St.)		C	21	70	9	14	3	0	2	14	17	19	0	2	1-1	.200	.356	.329	.685	0	1.000
— Tennessee (Sou.)		C-1B	104	369	51	105	23	1	18	69	63	93	3	5	12-3	.285	.387	.499	.886	7	.988
2002— Syracuse (Int'l)		OF-C	127	443	65	114	25	2	18	82	67	125	4	7	24-7	.257	.354	.445	.798	5	.985
— Toronto (A.L.)		OF	15	46	4	12	2	1	0	6	6	11	0	4	1-0	.261	.340	.348	.688	0	1.000
2003— Dunedin (Fla. St.)		OF-DH	18	62	10	23	5	0	4	18	3	14	0	2	1-0	.371	.388	.645	1.033	0	1.000
— Toronto (A.L.)		OF-DH	26	48	7	10	4	0	2	10	3	22	0	0	1-0	.208	.255	.417	.672	0	1.000
— Syracuse (Int'l)		OF-DH	64	236	37	56	19	1	9	34	15	68	2	7	11-1	.237	.285	.441	.726	7	.954
Major League totals (2 years)			**41**	**94**	**11**	**22**	**6**	**1**	**2**	**16**	**9**	**33**	**0**	**4**	**2-0**	**.234**	**.298**	**.383**	**.681**	**0**	**1.000**

PERSONAL: Born April 6, 1977, in Tupelo, Miss. ... 6-2/210. ... Bats right, throws right. ... Full name: Barry Jarvis Wesson. ... High school: Brandon (Miss.).

TRANSACTIONS/CAREER NOTES: Selected by Houston Astros organization in 14th round of free-agent draft (June 1, 1995). ... Granted free agency (October 15, 2001). ... Re-signed by Astros organization (December 4, 2001). ... Claimed on waivers by Anaheim Angels (September 3, 2002). ... Contract purchased by Anaheim from Salt Lake (September 2, 2003).

2003 GAMES PLAYED BY POSITION (MLB): OF—9, DH—1.

Year	Team (League)	Pos.	G	AB	R	H	2B	3B	HR	RBI	BB	SO	HBP	GDP	SB-CS	Avg.	OBP	SLG	OPS	E	Pct.
1995— GC Astros (GCL)		OF	45	138	14	26	2	2	2	18	19	40	1	2	4-0	.188	.289	.275	.565	0	1.000
— Jackson (Texas)		OF	4	3	2	2	0	1	0	1	0	0	0	0	0-0	.667	.667	1.333	2.000	1	1.000
1996— Auburn (NY-Penn)		OF	55	176	11	28	7	0	0	12	12	46	1	5	5-3	.159	.214	.199	.412	5	.943
1997— Auburn (NY-Penn)		OF	58	208	24	54	7	3	3	26	10	45	1	1	8-4	.260	.295	.365	.661	5	.956
1998— Quad City (Midw.)		OF	138	493	71	124	21	2	7	43	32	90	5	10	22-12	.252	.304	.345	.649	4	.986
1999— Kissimmee (Fla. St.)		OF	115	352	32	76	15	1	4	34	26	84	4	3	8-7	.216	.276	.298	.574	2	.992
2000— Round Rock (Texas)		OF-1B	39	110	12	26	1	2	2	15	10	32	0	2	6-2	.236	.295	.336	.631	0	1.000
— Kissimmee (Fla. St.)		OF	81	308	50	84	21	3	5	35	33	66	2	2	24-5	.273	.346	.409	.755	2	.988
2001— Round Rock (Texas)		OF	133	472	67	119	23	7	16	54	41	135	6	4	20-10	.252	.317	.432	.750	3	.990
2002— New Orleans (PCL)		OF	111	413	43	121	25	5	11	61	16	100	5	9	4-7	.293	.325	.458	.783	1	.996
— Houston (N.L.)		OF	15	20	1	4	0	1	0	1	1	5	0	2	0-0	.200	.238	.300	.538	0	1.000
2003— Salt Lake (PCL)		OF-DH	123	475	62	133	27	6	8	53	38	86	3	10	17-3	.280	.334	.413	.747	9	.968
— Anaheim (A.L.)		OF-DH	10	11	2	2	0	0	1	3	0	4	0	0	1-0	.182	.182	.455	.636	0	1.000
American League totals (1 year)			**10**	**11**	**2**	**2**	**0**	**0**	**1**	**3**	**0**	**4**	**0**	**0**	**1-0**	**.182**	**.182**	**.455**	**.636**	**0**	**1.000**
National League totals (1 year)			**15**	**20**	**1**	**4**	**0**	**1**	**0**	**1**	**1**	**5**	**0**	**2**	**0-0**	**.200**	**.238**	**.300**	**.538**	**0**	**1.000**
Major League totals (2 years)			**25**	**31**	**3**	**6**	**0**	**1**	**1**	**4**	**1**	**9**	**0**	**2**	**1-0**	**.194**	**.219**	**.355**	**.574**	**0**	**1.000**

W

WESTBROOK, JAKE · P

PERSONAL: Born September 29, 1977, in Athens, Ga. ... 6-3/185. ... Throws right, bats right. ... Full name: Jacob Cauthen Westbrook. ... High school: Madison County (Danielsville, Ga.).

TRANSACTIONS/CAREER NOTES: Selected by Colorado Rockies organization in first round (21st pick overall) of free-agent draft (June 4, 1996). ... Traded by Rockies with P John Nicholson and OF Mark Hamlin to Montreal Expos for 2B Mike Lansing (December 16, 1997). ... Traded by Expos with two players to be named later to New York Yankees for P Hideki Irabu (December 22, 1999); Yankees acquired P Ted Lilly (March 17, 2000) and P Christian Parker (March 22, 2000) to complete deal. ... On Columbus disabled list (July 5-23, 2000). ... Traded by Yankees with P Zach Day to Cleveland Indians (July 25, 2000), completing deal in which Indians traded OF Dave Justice to Yankees for OF Ricky Ledee and two players to be named later (June 29, 2000). ... On Buffalo disabled list (July 25-September 1, 2000). ... On Cleveland disabled list (September 1, 2000-remainder of season). ... On Cleveland disabled list (March 30-July 11 and August 26, 2002-remainder of season); included rehabilitation assignments to Akron (June 16-July 6) and Buffalo (July 7-11). ... Optioned to Buffalo by Cleveland (June 29, 2003). ... Recalled by Cleveland from Buffalo of the International League (July 12, 2003).

CAREER HITTING: 0-for-1 (.000), 0 R, 0 2B, 0 3B, 0 HR, 0 RBI.

Year	League	W	L	Pct.	ERA	WHIP	G	GS	CG	ShO	Hld.	Sv.-Opp.	IP	H	R	ER	HR	BB-IBB	SO	Avg.
1996—	Ariz. Rockies (Ariz.)	4	2	.667	2.87	1.28	11	11	0	0	...	0-...	62.2	66	33	20	0	14-0	57	.269
—	Portland (NW)	1	1	.500	2.55	1.09	4	4	0	0	...	0-...	24.2	22	8	7	1	5-0	19	.237
1997—	Asheville (S. Atl.)	* 14	11	.560	4.82	1.36	28	27	3	2	...	0-...	170.0	176	93	91	16	55-0	92	.269
1998—	Jupiter (FSL)	11	6	.647	3.26	1.34	27	27	2	0	...	0-...	171.0	169	70	62	11	60-0	79	.264
1999—	Harrisburg (Eastern)	11	5	.688	3.92	1.39	27	27	2	•2	...	0-...	174.2	180	88	76	14	63-1	90	.274
2000—	Columbus (Int'l)	5	7	.417	4.65	1.48	16	15	2	0	...	0-...	89.0	94	53	46	3	38-0	61	.272
—	New York (A.L.)	0	2	.000	13.50	2.85	3	2	0	0	0	0-0	6.2	15	10	10	1	4-1	1	.469
2001—	Buffalo (Int'l)	8	1	.889	3.20	1.28	12	12	0	0	...	0-...	64.2	60	27	23	2	23-0	45	.249
—	Cleveland (A.L.)	4	4	.500	5.85	1.56	23	6	0	0	5	0-0	64.2	79	43	42	6	22-4	48	.306
2002—	Akron (East.)	0	1	.000	4.80	0.93	3	3	0	0	...	0-...	15.0	13	8	8	0	1-0	8	.228
—	Buffalo (Int'l)	1	0	1.000	6.00	1.33	1	1	0	0	...	0-...	6.0	8	4	4	1	0-0	2	.333
—	Cleveland (A.L.)	1	3	.250	5.83	1.49	11	4	0	0	1	0-2	41.2	50	30	27	6	12-1	20	.296
2003—	Buffalo (Int'l)	1	0	1.000	0.00	0.40	2	2	0	0	...	0-...	10.0	0	0	0	0	4-0	7	.000
—	Cleveland (A.L.)	7	10	.412	4.33	1.49	34	22	1	0	1	0-0	133.0	142	70	64	9	56-1	58	.281
Major League totals (4 years)		12	19	.387	5.23	1.54	71	34	1	0	7	0-2	246.0	286	153	143	22	94-7	127	.297

WHEELER, DAN · P

PERSONAL: Born December 10, 1977, in Providence, R.I. ... 6-3/222. ... Throws right, bats right. ... Full name: Daniel Michael Wheeler. ... High school: Pilgrim (Warwick, R.I.). ... Junior college: Central Arizona College.

TRANSACTIONS/CAREER NOTES: Selected by Tampa Bay Devil Rays organization in 34th round of free-agent draft (June 4, 1996). ... On Durham disabled list (July 7-16, 2001). ... Released by Devil Rays (December 13, 2001). ... Signed by Atlanta Braves organization (January 10, 2002). ... On Richmond disabled list (August 7-22, 2002). ... Granted free agency (October 15, 2002). ... Signed by New York Mets organization (January 27, 2003). ... Contract purchased by New York Mets from Norfolk (June 18, 2003).

CAREER HITTING: 0-for-2 (.000), 0 R, 0 2B, 0 3B, 0 HR, 0 RBI.

Year	League	W	L	Pct.	ERA	WHIP	G	GS	CG	ShO	Hld.	Sv.-Opp.	IP	H	R	ER	HR	BB-IBB	SO	Avg.
1997—	Hudson Valley (NYP)	6	7	.462	3.00	1.10	15	15	0	0	...	0-...	84.0	75	38	28	2	17-0	81	.228
1998—	Char., S.C. (SAL)	12	14	.462	4.43	1.30	29	•29	3	1	...	0-...	181.0	206	96	•89	16	29-0	136	.290
1999—	Orlando (Sou.)	3	0	1.000	3.26	1.10	9	9	0	0	...	0-...	58.0	56	27	21	7	8-0	53	.252
—	Durham (Int'l)	7	5	.583	4.92	1.55	14	14	2	1	...	0-...	82.1	103	59	45	16	25-0	58	.307
—	Tampa Bay (A.L.)	0	4	.000	5.87	1.57	6	6	0	0	0	0-0	30.2	35	20	20	7	13-1	32	.287
2000—	Tampa Bay (A.L.)	1	1	.500	5.48	1.74	11	2	0	0	1	0-1	23.0	29	14	14	2	11-2	17	.302
—	Durham (Int'l)	5	11	.313	5.63	1.50	26	26	0	0	...	0-...	150.1	183	* 109	94	35	42-1	91	.300
2001—	Durham (Int'l)	3	5	.375	5.23	1.27	18	10	0	0	...	0-...	65.1	72	51	38	11	11-0	39	.271
—	Tampa Bay (A.L.)	1	0	1.000	8.66	1.98	13	0	0	0	0	0-0	17.2	30	17	17	3	5-0	12	.375
—	Orlando (Sou.)	0	2	.000	2.81	1.31	3	3	0	0	...	0-...	16.0	15	5	5	2	6-1	12	.242
2002—	Richmond (Int'l)	9	6	.600	4.65	1.32	27	25	0	0	...	0-...	155.0	163	87	80	23	42-0	110	.268
2003—	Norfolk (Int'l)	4	2	.667	3.94	1.40	22	5	0	0	...	4-...	45.2	48	20	20	4	16-3	44	.265
—	New York (N.L.)	1	3	.250	3.71	1.29	35	0	0	0	0	2-3	51.0	49	23	21	6	17-4	35	.253
American League totals (3 years)		2	5	.286	6.43	1.72	30	8	0	0	1	0-1	71.1	94	51	51	12	29-3	61	.315
National League totals (1 year)		1	3	.250	3.71	1.29	35	0	0	0	0	2-3	51.0	49	23	21	6	17-4	35	.253
Major League totals (4 years)		3	8	.273	5.30	1.54	65	8	0	0	1	2-4	122.1	143	74	72	18	46-7	96	.291

WHITE, GABE · P

PERSONAL: Born November 20, 1971, in Sebring, Fla. ... 6-2/204. ... Throws left, bats left. ... Full name: Gabriel Allen White. ... High school: Sebring (Fla.).

TRANSACTIONS/CAREER NOTES: Selected by Montreal Expos organization in supplemental round ("sandwich pick" between first and second round, 28th pick overall) of free-agent draft (June 4, 1990); pick received as part of compensation for California Angels signing Type A free-agent P Mark Langston. ... On Harrisburg disabled list (July 2-27, 1993). ... On Ottawa disabled list (April 7-May 6, 1994). ... Traded by Expos to Cincinnati Reds for 2B Jhonny Carvajal (December 15, 1995). ... On disabled list (September 17, 1996-remainder of season). ... Traded by Reds to Colorado Rockies for P Manny Aybar (April 7, 2000). ... Traded by Rockies with P Luke Hudson to Reds for 2B Pokey Reese and P Dennys Reyes (December 18, 2001). ... On disabled list (July 12-31 and August 29, 2002-remainder of season). ... Placed on 15-day disabled list (June 21, 2003). ... Sent on rehab assignment to Louisville (July 8, 2003). ... Traded by Reds to New York Yankees for a player to be named (August 1, 2003). ... Sent on rehab assignment by Yankees (August 18, 2003). ... Recalled from minor league rehab assignment (August 25, 2003). ... Removed from 15-day disabled list (August 26, 2003).

CAREER HITTING: 4-for-38 (.105), 1 R, 0 2B, 0 3B, 1 HR, 3 RBI.

Year	League	W	L	Pct.	ERA	WHIP	G	GS	CG	ShO	Hld.	Sv.-Opp.	IP	H	R	ER	HR	BB-IBB	SO	Avg.
1990—	GC Expos (GCL)	4	2	.667	3.14	1.08	11	11	1	0	...	0-...	57.1	50	21	20	3	12-0	41	.231
1991—	Sumter (S. Atl.)	6	9	.400	3.26	1.21	24	24	5	0	...	0-...	149.0	127	73	54	7	53-0	140	.229
1992—	Rockford (Midwest)	14	8	.636	2.84	1.12	27	27	7	0	...	0-...	187.0	148	73	59	10	61-0	* 176	.215
1993—	Harrisburg (Eastern)	7	2	.778	2.16	1.08	16	16	2	1	...	0-...	100.0	80	30	24	4	28-0	80	.221
—	Ottawa (Int'l)	2	1	.667	3.12	1.09	6	6	1	1	...	0-...	40.1	38	15	14	3	6-0	28	.243
1994—	W.P. Beach (FSL)	1	0	1.000	1.50	0.50	1	1	0	0	...	0-...	6.0	2	2	1	0	1-0	4	.105
—	Ottawa (Int'l)	8	3	.727	5.05	1.44	14	14	0	0	...	0-...	73.0	77	49	41	11	28-2	63	.270
—	Montreal (N.L.)	1	1	.500	6.08	1.48	7	5	0	0	0	1-1	23.2	24	16	16	4	11-0	17	.261
1995—	Ottawa (Int'l)	2	3	.400	3.90	1.20	12	12	0	0	...	0-...	62.1	58	31	27	10	17-0	37	.244
—	Montreal (N.L.)	1	2	.333	7.01	1.36	19	1	0	0	0	0-0	25.2	26	21	20	7	9-0	25	.260
1996—	Indianapolis (A.A.)	6	3	.667	2.77	1.14	11	11	0	0	...	0-...	68.1	69	25	21	6	9-3	51	.257
1997—	Indianapolis (A.A.)	7	4	.636	2.82	1.16	20	19	0	0	...	0-...	118.0	119	46	37	10	18-0	62	.257
—	Cincinnati (N.L.)	2	2	.500	4.39	1.15	12	6	0	0	3	1-1	41.0	39	20	20	8	8-1	25	.253

W

Year	League	W	L	Pct.	ERA	WHIP	G	GS	CG	ShO	Hld.	Sv.-Opp.	IP	H	R	ER	HR	BB-IBB	SO	Avg.
1998— Cincinnati (N.L.)		5	5	.500	4.01	1.15	69	3	0	0	6	9-13	98.2	86	46	44	17	27-6	83	.231
1999— Cincinnati (N.L.)		1	2	.333	4.43	1.34	50	0	0	0	3	0-1	61.0	68	31	30	13	14-1	61	.281
2000— Cincinnati (N.L.)		0	0	...	18.00	3.00	1	0	0	0	0	0-0	1.0	2	2	2	1	1-0	2	.400
— Colorado (N.L.)		11	2	.846	2.17	0.92	67	0	0	0	19	5-9	83.0	62	21	20	5	14-2	82	.208
2001— Colorado (N.L.)		1	7	.125	6.25	1.42	69	0	0	0	8	0-2	67.2	70	47	47	18	26-5	47	.270
2002— Cincinnati (N.L.)		6	1	.857	2.98	1.09	62	0	0	0	19	0-1	54.1	49	19	18	3	10-2	41	.239
2003— Cincinnati (N.L.)		3	0	1.000	3.93	1.22	34	0	0	0	6	0-1	34.1	36	15	15	5	6-3	23	.275
— Louisville (Int'l)		0	0	...	9.00	3.00	1	1	0	0	...	0-...	1.0	2	1	1	0	1-0	0	.400
— GC Yankees (GCL)		0	0	...	0.00	1.00	1	1	0	0	...	0-...	1.0	0	0	0	0	1-0	1	.000
— Tampa (FSL)		0	0	...	0.00	1.50	1	1	0	0	...	0-...	.2	1	0	0	0	0-0	0	.333
— Trenton (East.)		0	0	...	7.71	1.29	2	2	0	0	...	0-...	2.1	3	2	2	1	0-0	2	.300
— New York (A.L.)		2	1	.667	4.38	0.81	12	0	0	0	6	0-1	12.1	8	7	6	2	2-1	6	.182
American League totals (1 year)		2	1	.667	4.38	0.81	12	0	0	0	6	0-1	12.1	8	7	6	2	2-1	6	.182
National League totals (9 years)		31	22	.585	4.26	1.20	390	15	0	0	64	16-29	490.1	462	238	232	79	126-20	406	.249
Major League totals (9 years)		33	23	.589	4.26	1.19	402	15	0	0	70	16-30	502.2	470	245	238	81	128-21	412	.247

WHITE, MATT — P

PERSONAL: Born August 19, 1977, in Pittsfield, Mass. ... 6-1/180. ... Throws left, bats right. ... Full name: Matthew J. White. ... College: Clemson.

TRANSACTIONS/CAREER NOTES: Selected by Cleveland Indians in 15th round of free-agent draft (June 2, 1998). ... Selected by Boston Red Sox in Rule 5 draft (December 16, 2002). ... Traded by Red Sox to Seattle Mariners for OF Shelton Fulse (June 6, 2003).

CAREER HITTING: 0-for-0 (.000), 0 R, 0 2B, 0 3B, 0 HR, 0 RBI.

Year	League	W	L	Pct.	ERA	WHIP	G	GS	CG	ShO	Hld.	Sv.-Opp.	IP	H	R	ER	HR	BB-IBB	SO	Avg.
1998— Burlington (Midw.)		4	1	.800	1.94	1.25	8	8	0	0	...	0-...	46.1	34	14	10	0	24-0	47	.210
— Watertown (NYP)		3	2	.600	4.28	1.54	6	6	0	0	...	0-...	27.1	31	19	13	4	11-1	24	.295
1999— Columbus (Int'l)		3	10	.231	5.29	1.36	19	18	1	0	...	0-...	95.1	99	67	56	12	31-0	75	.266
2000— Kinston (Caro.)		11	9	.550	4.07	1.39	28	26	2	0	...	0-...	143.2	136	76	65	14	63-0	115	.257
2001— Akron (East.)		8	10	.444	4.81	1.47	25	25	0	0	...	0-...	144.0	151	84	77	18	60-1	72	.277
2002— Akron (East.)		6	2	.750	3.93	1.52	27	11	0	0	...	1-...	89.1	97	42	39	9	39-0	63	.280
— Buffalo (Int'l)		0	0	...	4.76	1.71	7	1	0	0	...	0-...	17.0	23	13	9	1	6-0	12	.319
2003— Sarasota (Fla. St.)		0	0	...	0.00	1.40	2	2	0	0	...	0-...	5.0	6	1	0	0	1-0	2	.286
— Portland (East.)		0	0	...	0.00	1.00	2	1	0	0	...	0-...	3.0	1	1	0	0	2-0	3	.111
— Pawtucket (Int'l)		0	0	...	0.00	0.30	2	0	0	0	...	0-...	3.1	1	1	0	0	0-0	5	.083
— Boston (A.L.)		0	1	.000	27.00	3.55	3	0	0	0	0	0-0	3.2	10	11	11	1	3-0	0	.526
— Seattle (A.L.)		0	0	...	13.50	2.50	3	0	0	0	0	0-0	2.0	3	3	3	2	2-0	0	.375
— Buffalo (Int'l)		2	3	.400	2.13	1.23	19	1	0	0	...	0-...	42.1	36	12	10	3	16-0	34	.231
Major League totals (1 year)		0	1	.000	22.24	3.18	6	0	0	0	0	0-0	5.2	13	14	14	3	5-0	0	.481

WHITE, RICK — P

PERSONAL: Born December 23, 1968, in Springfield, Ohio. ... 6-4/230. ... Throws right, bats right. ... Full name: Richard Allen White. ... High school: Kenton Ridge (Springfield, Ohio). ... Junior college: Paducah (Ky.) Community College.

TRANSACTIONS/CAREER NOTES: Selected by Pittsburgh Pirates organization in 15th round of free-agent draft (June 4, 1990). ... On Carolina disabled list (May 15-July 6, 1993). ... On Buffalo disabled list (August 28-September 4, 1993). ... On Pittsburgh disabled list (April 14-May 17, 1995); included rehabilitation assignment to Gulf Coast Pirates (April 26-May 17). ... Granted free agency (December 21, 1995). ... Re-signed by Pirates organization (December 21, 1995). ... On Calgary disabled list (April 4-August 7, 1996). ... On Carolina disabled list (August 7-23, 1996). ... Granted free agency (October 15, 1996). ... Signed by Tampa Bay Devil Rays organization (February 4, 1997). ... Loaned by Devil Rays to Orlando, Chicago Cubs organization (April 3-September 11, 1997). ... Traded by Devil Rays with OF Bubba Trammell to New York Mets for OF Jason Tyner and P Paul Wilson (July 28, 2000). ... On disabled list (March 31-April 21, 2001 and May 1-17, 2001). ... Granted free agency (December 21, 2001). ... Signed by Colorado Rockies (January 10, 2002). ... On disabled list (May 27-June 18, 2002); included rehabilitation assignment to Colorado Springs (June 14-18). ... Released by Rockies (August 12, 2002). ... Signed by St. Louis Cardinals organization (August 17, 2002). ... Granted free agency (October 29, 2002). ... Signed by Chicago White Sox (January 22, 2003). ... Designated for assignment by Chicago (August 2, 2003). ... Given unconditional release (August 11, 2003). ... Signed by Houston Astros as free agent (August 14, 2003).

CAREER HITTING: 4-for-40 (.100), 1 R, 1 2B, 0 3B, 0 HR, 1 RBI.

Year	League	W	L	Pct.	ERA	WHIP	G	GS	CG	ShO	Hld.	Sv.-Opp.	IP	H	R	ER	HR	BB-IBB	SO	Avg.
1990— GC Pirates (GCL)		3	1	.750	0.76	0.84	7	6	0	0	...	0-...	35.2	26	11	3	0	4-0	27	.194
— Welland (N.Y.-Penn)		1	4	.200	3.26	1.37	9	5	1	0	...	0-...	38.2	39	19	14	2	14-2	43	.265
1991— Augusta (S. Atl.)		4	4	.500	3.00	1.37	34	0	0	0	...	6-...	63.0	68	26	21	2	18-2	52	.264
— Salem (Caro.)		2	3	.400	4.66	1.08	13	5	1	0	...	1-...	46.1	41	27	24	2	9-3	36	.233
1992— Salem (Caro.)		7	9	.438	3.80	1.16	18	18	• 5	0	...	0-...	120.2	116	58	51	15	24-1	70	.255
— Carolina (Sou.)		1	7	.125	4.21	1.34	10	10	1	0	...	0-...	57.2	59	32	27	8	18-1	45	.265
1993— Carolina (Sou.)		4	3	.571	3.50	1.02	12	12	1	0	...	0-...	69.1	59	29	27	5	12-0	52	.231
— Buffalo (A.A.)		0	3	.000	3.54	1.18	7	3	0	0	...	0-...	28.0	25	13	11	1	8-0	16	.238
1994— Pittsburgh (N.L.)		4	5	.444	3.82	1.27	43	5	0	0	3	6-9	75.1	79	35	32	9	17-3	38	.280
1995— Pittsburgh (N.L.)		2	3	.400	4.75	1.53	15	9	0	0	0	0-0	55.0	66	33	29	3	18-0	29	.299
— Calgary (PCL)		6	4	.600	4.20	1.35	14	11	1	0	...	0-...	79.1	97	40	37	13	10-0	56	.302
1996— GC Pirates (GCL)		0	0	...	2.25	0.92	3	3	0	0	...	0-...	12.0	8	4	3	0	3-0	8	.205
— Carolina (Sou.)		0	1	.000	11.37	1.58	2	1	0	0	...	0-...	6.1	9	8	8	2	1-0	7	.321
1997— Orlando (Sou.)		5	7	.417	4.71	1.34	39	8	0	0	...	12-...	86.0	93	55	45	7	22-2	65	.275
1998— Durham (Int'l)		4	2	.667	4.22	1.39	9	9	1	0	...	0-...	53.1	63	29	25	3	11-0	31	.294
— Tampa Bay (A.L.)		2	6	.250	3.80	1.30	38	3	0	0	2	0-0	68.2	66	32	29	8	23-2	39	.253
1999— Tampa Bay (A.L.)		5	3	.625	4.08	1.57	63	1	0	0	4	0-2	108.0	132	56	49	8	38-5	81	.304
2000— Tampa Bay (A.L.)		3	6	.333	3.41	1.16	44	0	0	0	2	2-5	71.1	57	30	27	7	26-3	47	.220
— New York (N.L.)		2	3	.400	3.81	1.34	22	0	0	0	2	1-2	28.1	26	14	12	2	12-2	20	.232
2001— New York (N.L.)		4	5	.444	3.88	1.26	55	0	0	0	10	2-4	69.2	71	38	30	7	17-4	51	.257
2002— Colorado (N.L.)		2	6	.250	6.20	1.65	41	0	0	0	9	0-1	40.2	49	30	28	4	18-4	27	.310
— Memphis (PCL)		0	0	...	2.45	1.91	3	0	0	0	...	0-...	3.2	4	1	1	0	3-0	4	.286
— St. Louis (N.L.)		3	1	.750	0.82	0.73	20	0	0	0	7	0-0	22.0	13	3	2	0	3-1	14	.169
2003— Chicago (A.L.)		1	2	.333	6.61	1.45	34	0	0	0	3	1-1	47.2	56	39	35	11	13-2	37	.295
— Houston (N.L.)		0	0	...	3.72	1.34	15	0	0	0	1	0-0	19.1	18	9	8	2	8-0	17	.243
American League totals (4 years)		11	17	.393	4.26	1.39	179	4	0	0	11	3-8	295.2	311	157	140	34	100-12	204	.272
National League totals (6 years)		17	23	.425	4.09	1.34	211	14	0	0	32	9-16	310.1	322	162	141	27	93-14	196	.268
Major League totals (8 years)		28	40	.412	4.17	1.36	390	18	0	0	43	12-24	606.0	633	319	281	61	193-26	400	.270

W

WHITE, RONDELL — OF

PERSONAL: Born February 23, 1972, in Milledgeville, Ga. ... 6-1/220. ... Bats right, throws right. ... Full name: Rondell Bernard White. ... High school: Jones County (Gray, Ga.).

TRANSACTIONS/CAREER NOTES: Selected by Montreal Expos organization in first round (24th pick overall) of free-agent draft (June 4, 1990); pick received as part of compensation for California Angels signing Type A free-agent P Mark Langston. ... On Montreal disabled list (April 28-July 16, 1996); included rehabilitation assignments to West Palm Beach (July 5-10), Gulf Coast Expos (July 5-10) and Harrisburg (July 10-16). ... On disabled list (July 21, 1998-remainder of season; June 14-29 and July 2-17, 1999). ... On Montreal disabled list (July 8-August 31, 2000). ... Traded by Expos to Chicago Cubs for P Scott Downs (July 31, 2000). ... On Chicago disabled list (August 1-6 and August 27, 2000-remainder of season). ... On Chicago disabled list (June 26-July 12 and July 14-September 1, 2001); included rehabilitation assignment to West Tenn (August 15-September 1). ... Granted free agency (November 5, 2001). ... Signed by New York Yankees (December 21, 2001). ... Traded by Yankees to San Diego Padres for OF Bubba Trammell, P Mark Phillips and cash considerations (March 19, 2003). ... Traded by Padres to Kansas City Royals for P Chris Tierney and P Brian Sanches (August 26, 2003).

2003 GAMES PLAYED BY POSITION (MLB): OF—121, DH—7.

Year Team (League)	Pos.	G	AB	R	H	2B	3B	HR	RBI	BB	SO	HBP	GDP	SB-CS	Avg.	OBP	SLG	OPS	E	Pct.
1990— GC Expos (GCL)	OF	57	221	33	66	7	4	5	34	17	33	5	4	10-7	.299	.362	.434	.797	2	.973
1991— Sumter (S. Atl.)	OF	123	465	80	122	23	6	13	68	57	109	8	7	50-17	.262	.351	.422	.772	3	.987
1992— W.P. Beach (FSL)	OF	111	450	80	142	10 * 12	4	41	46	78	5	7	42-16	.316	.384	.418	.802	3	.984
— Harrisburg (East.)	OF	21	89	22	27	7	1	2	7	6	14	4	3	6-1	.303	.374	.472	.846	2	.938
1993— Harrisburg (East.)	OF	90	372	72	122	16	10	12	52	22	72	5	3	21-6	.328	.371	.522	.892	1	.995
— Ottawa (Int'l)	OF	37	150	28	57	8	2	7	32	12	20	3	4	10-1	.380	.436	.600	1.036	1	.988
— Montreal (N.L.)	OF	23	73	9	19	3	1	2	15	7	16	0	2	1-2	.260	.321	.411	.732	0	1.000
1994— Montreal (N.L.)	OF	40	97	16	27	10	1	2	13	9	18	3	1	1-1	.278	.358	.464	.822	2	.946
— Ottawa (Int'l)	OF	42	169	23	46	7	0	7	18	15	17	4	5	9-2	.272	.344	.438	.782	2	.979
1995— Montreal (N.L.)	OF	130	474	87	140	33	4	13	57	41	87	6	11	25-5	.295	.356	.464	.820	4	.986
1996— Montreal (N.L.)	OF	88	334	35	98	19	4	6	41	22	53	2	11	14-6	.293	.340	.428	.768	2	.990
— W.P. Beach (FSL)	DH-OF	3	10	0	2	1	0	0	2	0	4	0	0	0-1	.200	.200	.300	.500	0	1.000
— GC Expos (GCL)	OF	3	12	3	3	0	0	2	4	0	1	0	1	1-0	.250	.250	.750	1.000	0	1.000
— Harrisburg (East.)	OF	5	20	5	7	1	0	3	6	1	1	0	1	1-1	.350	.381	.850	1.231	0	1.000
1997— Montreal (N.L.)	OF	151	592	84	160	29	5	28	82	31	111	10	18	16-8	.270	.316	.478	.794	3	.992
1998— Montreal (N.L.)	OF-DH	97	357	54	107	21	2	17	58	30	57	7	7	16-7	.300	.363	.513	.875	1	.996
1999— Montreal (N.L.)	OF	138	539	83	168	26	6	22	64	32	85	11	17	10-6	.312	.359	.505	.863	11	.964
2000— Montreal (N.L.)	OF	75	290	52	89	24	0	11	54	28	67	2	4	5-1	.307	.370	.503	.873	1	.994
— Chicago (N.L.)	OF	19	67	7	22	2	0	2	7	5	12	2	0	0-2	.328	.392	.448	.840	0	1.000
2001— Chicago (N.L.)	OF	95	323	43	99	19	1	17	50	26	56	7	14	1-0	.307	.371	.529	.900	3	.979
— West Tenn (Sou.)	OF	9	28	2	4	1	0	2	4	1	7	2	1	0-0	.143	.226	.393	.619	0	1.000
2002— New York (A.L.)	OF-DH	126	455	59	109	21	0	14	62	25	86	8	11	1-2	.240	.288	.378	.666	1	1.000
2003— San Diego (N.L.)	OF-DH	115	413	49	115	17	3	18	66	25	71	8	11	1-4	.278	.330	.465	.795	4	.978
— Kansas City (A.L.)	OF-DH	22	75	13	26	6	1	4	21	6	8	2	2	0-0	.347	.400	.613	1.013	1	.978
American League totals (2 years)		148	530	72	135	27	1	18	83	31	94	10	13	1-2	.255	.304	.411	.716	1	.997
National League totals (10 years)		971	3559	519	1044	203	27	138	507	256	633	58	96	90-42	.293	.348	.482	.830	31	.985
Major League totals (11 years)		1119	4089	591	1179	230	28	156	590	287	727	68	109	91-44	.288	.343	.473	.816	32	.986

WICKMAN, BOB — P

PERSONAL: Born February 6, 1969... 6-1/240. ... Throws right, bats right. ... Full name: Robert Joe Wickman. ... High school: Oconto Falls (Wis.).

TRANSACTIONS/CAREER NOTES: Selected by Chicago White Sox organization in second round of free-agent draft (June 4, 1990). ... Traded by White Sox with P Melido Perez and P Domingo Jean to New York Yankees for 2B Steve Sax and cash (January 10, 1992). ... Traded by Yankees with OF Gerald Williams to Milwaukee Brewers for P Graeme Lloyd and OF Pat Listach (August 23, 1996). ... Traded by Brewers with P Steve Woodard and P Jason Bere to Cleveland Indians for 1B/OF Richie Sexson, P Paul Rigdon, P Kane Davis and a player to be named later (July 28, 2000); Brewers acquired 2B Marcos Scutaro to complete deal (August 30). ... On disabled list (July 22-August 10 and August 11, 2002-remainder of season). ... On disabled list (March 29, 2003). ... Sent on rehab assignment by Cleveland (August 16, 2003). ... Recalled from minor league rehab assignment (September 2, 2003).

CAREER HITTING: 0-for-2 (.000), 0 R, 0 2B, 0 3B, 0 HR, 0 RBI.

Year League	W	L	Pct.	ERA	WHIP	G	GS	CG	ShO	Hld.	Sv.-Opp.	IP	H	R	ER	HR	BB-IBB	SO	Avg.
1990— GC White Sox (GCL)	2	0	1.000	2.45	0.73	2	2	0	0	...	0-...	11.0	7	4	3	0	1-0	15	.175
— Sarasota (Fla. St.)	0	1	.000	1.98	1.54	2	2	0	0	...	0-...	13.2	17	7	3	0	4-0	8	.304
— South Bend (Mid.)	7	2	.778	1.38	1.01	9	9	3	0	...	0-...	65.1	50	16	10	1	16-0	50	.212
1991— Sarasota (Fla. St.)	5	1	.833	2.05	1.23	7	7	1	1	...	0-...	44.0	43	16	10	2	11-0	32	.247
— Birmingham (Sou.)	6	10	.375	3.56	1.35	20	20	4	1	...	0-...	131.1	127	68	52	5	50-0	81	.250
1992— Columbus (Int'l)	12	5	.706	2.92	1.18	23	23	2	1	...	0-...	157.0	131	61	51	12	55-0	108	.227
— New York (A.L.)	6	1	.857	4.11	1.41	8	8	0	0	0	0-0	50.1	51	25	23	2	20-0	21	.273
1993— New York (A.L.)	14	4	.778	4.63	1.61	41	19	1	1	2	4-8	140.0	156	82	72	13	69-7	70	.284
1994— New York (A.L.)	5	4	.556	3.09	1.16	53	0	0	0	11	6-10	70.0	54	26	24	3	27-3	56	.213
1995— New York (A.L.)	2	4	.333	4.05	1.38	63	1	0	0	21	1-10	80.0	77	38	36	6	33-3	51	.253
1996— New York (A.L.)	4	1	.800	4.67	1.62	58	0	0	0	6	0-3	79.0	94	41	41	7	34-1	61	.299
— Milwaukee (A.L.)	3	0	1.000	3.24	1.32	12	0	0	0	4	0-1	16.2	12	9	6	3	10-2	14	.200
1997— Milwaukee (A.L.)	7	6	.538	2.73	1.36	74	0	0	0	*28	1-5	95.2	89	32	29	8	41-7	78	.252
1998— Milwaukee (N.L.)	6	9	.400	3.72	1.43	72	0	0	0	9	25-32	82.1	79	38	34	5	39-2	71	.262
1999— Milwaukee (N.L.)	3	8	.273	3.39	1.52	71	0	0	0	9	37-45	74.1	75	31	28	0	38-6	60	.262
2000— Milwaukee (N.L.)	2	2	.500	2.93	1.24	43	0	0	0	9	16-20	46.0	37	18	15	1	20-2	44	.215
— Cleveland (A.L.)	1	3	.250	3.38	1.46	26	0	0	0	0	14-17	26.2	27	12	10	0	12-3	11	.270
2001— Cleveland (A.L.)	5	0	1.000	2.39	1.11	70	0	0	0	4	32-35	67.2	61	18	18	4	14-2	66	.240
2002— Cleveland (A.L.)	1	3	.250	4.46	1.51	36	0	0	0	0	20-22	34.1	42	22	17	3	10-0	36	.284
2003— Akron (East.)	0	0	...	16.20	2.40	2	2	0	0	...	0-0	1.2	3	3	3	0	1-0	2	.429
— Lake County (S. Atl.)	0	0	...	0.00	0.50	2	2	0	0	...	0-0	2.0	1	0	0	0	0-0	4	.143
American League totals (9 years)	48	26	.649	3.76	1.41	441	28	1	1	76	78-111	660.1	663	305	276	49	270-28	464	.263
National League totals (3 years)	11	19	.367	3.42	1.42	186	0	0	0	9	78-97	202.2	191	87	77	12	97-10	175	.252
Major League totals (11 years)	59	45	.567	3.68	1.41	627	28	1	1	85	156-208	863.0	854	392	353	61	367-38	639	.260

WIDGER, CHRIS — C

PERSONAL: Born May 21, 1971, in Wilmington, Del. ... 6-2/210. ... Bats right, throws right. ... Full name: Christopher Jon Widger. ... High school: Pennsville (N.J.). ... College: George Mason.

TRANSACTIONS/CAREER NOTES: Selected by Seattle Mariners organization in third round of free-agent draft (June 1, 1992). ... On disabled list (June 6-16, 1993). ... Traded by Mariners with P Trey Moore and P Matt Wagner to Montreal Expos for P Jeff Fassero and P Alex Pacheco (October 29, 1996). ... On Montreal disabled list (May 25-June 9, 2000). ... Traded by Expos to Mariners for two players to be named later (August 8, 2000); Expos acquired OF Terrmel Sledge (September 28) and Sean Spencer (August 10) to complete deal. ... On Seattle disabled list (March 31, 2001-entire season); included rehabilitation assignment to Everett (June 24-July 6). ... Granted free agency (November 6, 2001). ... Signed by New York Yankees organization (February 1, 2002). ... Granted free agency (November 8, 2002). ... Re-signed by Yankees (December 7, 2002). ... Released by Yankees (April 7, 2003). ... Signed by St. Louis Cardinals (April 12, 2003).

2003 GAMES PLAYED BY POSITION (MLB): C—41, 1B—1, OF—1.

Year	Team (League)	Pos.	G	AB	R	H	2B	3B	HR	RBI	BB	SO	HBP	GDP	SB-CS	Avg.	OBP	SLG	OPS	E	Pct.
1992— Bellingham (N'west)	C	51	166	28	43	7	2	5	30	22	36	1	4	8-1	.259	.340	.416	.756	4	.987
1993— Riverside (Calif.)	C-OF	97	360	44	95	28	2	9	58	19	64	3	8	5-4	.264	.303	.428	.731	14	.974
1994— Jacksonville (Sou.)	C-1B-OF	116	388	58	101	15	3	16	59	39	69	5	7	8-7	.260	.334	.438	.772	13	.980
1995— Tacoma (PCL)	C-DH-OF	50	174	29	48	11	1	9	21	9	29	0	4	0-0	.276	.311	.506	.817	4	.981
— Seattle (A.L.)	C-OF-DH	23	45	2	9	0	0	1	2	3	11	0	0	0-0	.200	.245	.267	.512	0	1.000
1996— Tacoma (PCL)	C-DH	97	352	42	107	20	2	13	48	27	62	2	13	7-1	.304	.355	.483	.838	8	.988
— Seattle (A.L.)	C	8	11	1	2	0	0	0	0	0	5	1	0	0-0	.182	.250	.182	.432	2	.905
1997— Montreal (N.L.)	C	91	278	30	65	20	3	7	37	22	59	1	7	2-0	.234	.290	.403	.693	11	.981
1998— Montreal (N.L.)	C	125	417	36	97	18	1	15	53	29	85	0	5	6-1	.233	.281	.388	.670	* 14	.983
1999— Montreal (N.L.)	C	124	383	42	101	24	1	14	56	28	86	7	5	1-4	.264	.325	.441	.766	6	.992
2000— Montreal (N.L.)	C	86	281	31	67	17	2	12	34	29	61	1	5	1-2	.238	.311	.441	.752	8	.985
— Seattle (A.L.)	C-D-1-O	10	11	1	1	0	0	1	1	1	2	0	0	0-0	.091	.167	.364	.530	0	1.000
2001— Everett (N'west)	1B	5	13	2	1	0	0	0	0	6	1	0	0	0-0	.077	.368	.077	.445	0	1.000
2002— Columbus (Int'l)	C-OF	61	217	26	53	14	1	10	39	17	31	1	3	0-3	.244	.300	.456	.756	4	.990
— New York (A.L.)	C	21	64	4	19	5	0	0	5	2	9	2	0	0-0	.297	.338	.375	.713	2	.983
2003— Memphis (PCL)	C-OF-1B	23	71	8	17	7	0	2	10	7	12	0	0	1-0	.239	.304	.423	.726	4	.970
— St. Louis (N.L.)	C-1B-OF	44	102	9	24	9	0	0	14	6	20	1	5	0-0	.235	.279	.324	.603	1	.995
American League totals (4 years)		62	131	8	31	5	0	2	8	6	27	3	0	0-0	.237	.284	.321	.604	4	.982
National League totals (5 years)		470	1461	148	354	88	7	48	194	114	311	10	27	10-7	.242	.300	.411	.711	40	.986
Major League totals (8 years)		532	1592	156	385	93	7	50	202	120	338	13	27	10-7	.242	.299	.403	.702	44	.986

WIGGINTON, TY — 3B

PERSONAL: Born October 11, 1977, in San Diego, Calif. ... 6-0/200. ... Bats right, throws right. ... Full name: Ty Allen Wigginton. ... College: UNC-Asheville.

TRANSACTIONS/CAREER NOTES: Selected by New York Mets organization in 17th round of free-agent draft (June 2, 1998).

2003 GAMES PLAYED BY POSITION (MLB): 3B—155.

Year	Team (League)	Pos.	G	AB	R	H	2B	3B	HR	RBI	BB	SO	HBP	GDP	SB-CS	Avg.	OBP	SLG	OPS	E	Pct.
1998— Pittsfield (NYP)	2B-3B-OF	70	272	39	65	14	4	8	29	16	72	1	4	11-2	.239	.284	.408	.692	14	.949
1999— St. Lucie (Fla. St.)	2B	123	456	69	133	23	5	21	73	56	82	4	5	9-12	.292	.373	.502	.875	16	.974
2000— Binghamton (East.)	2B-3B	122	453	64	129	27	3	20	77	24	107	2	4	5-5	.285	.319	.490	.809	23	.943
2001— Norfolk (Int'l)	3-2-1-C-O	78	260	29	65	12	0	7	24	27	66	2	4	3-3	.250	.323	.377	.700	17	.924
— St. Lucie (Fla. St.)	2B	3	9	1	3	1	0	0	1	4	2	1	0	0-0	.333	.571	.444	1.016	0	1.000
— Binghamton (East.)	2B-3B	8	28	5	8	3	0	0	0	5	5	0	0	1-0	.286	.394	.393	.787	3	.870
2002— Norfolk (Int'l)	3-2-0-1	104	383	49	115	26	3	6	48	43	50	1	7	5-3	.300	.366	.431	.796	11	.967
— New York (N.L.)	3-1-2-0	46	116	18	35	8	0	6	18	8	19	2	4	2-1	.302	.354	.526	.880	5	.966
2003— New York (N.L.)	3B	156	573	73	146	36	6	11	71	46	124	9	15	12-2	.255	.318	.396	.714	16	.962
Major League totals (2 years)		202	689	91	181	44	6	17	89	54	143	11	19	14-3	.263	.324	.418	.742	21	.963

WILKERSON, BRAD — OF/1B

PERSONAL: Born June 1, 1977, in Daviess, Ky. ... 6-0/205. ... Bats left, throws left. ... Full name: Stephen Bradley Wilkerson. ... High school: Apollo (Owensboro, Ky.). ... College: Florida.

TRANSACTIONS/CAREER NOTES: Selected by Montreal Expos organization in supplemental round ("sandwich pick" between first and second round, 33rd pick overall) of free-agent draft (June 2, 1998); pick received as part of compensation for Toronto Blue Jays signing Type A free agent C Darrin Fletcher. ... On Ottawa disabled list (April 5-May 5, 2001).

2003 GAMES PLAYED BY POSITION (MLB): OF—135, 1B—27.

Year	Team (League)	Pos.	G	AB	R	H	2B	3B	HR	RBI	BB	SO	HBP	GDP	SB-CS	Avg.	OBP	SLG	OPS	E	Pct.
1999— Harrisburg (East.)	1B-OF	138	422	66	99	21	3	8	49	88	100	7	3	3-5	.235	.372	.355	.727	7	.972
2000— Harrisburg (East.)	1B-OF	66	229	53	77	36	2	6	44	42	38	4	4	8-4	.336	.442	.590	1.032	3	.983
— Ottawa (Int'l)	OF	63	212	40	53	11	1	12	35	45	60	3	0	5-4	.250	.387	.481	.868	6	.956
2001— Jupiter (FSL)	DH	6	26	3	6	3	0	0	1	3	10	0	0	0-0	.231	.310	.346	.656	...	...
— Ottawa (Int'l)	OF	69	233	43	63	10	0	12	48	60	68	3	2	12-5	.270	.423	.468	.891	3	.973
— Montreal (N.L.)	OF	47	117	11	24	7	2	1	5	17	41	0	2	2-1	.205	.304	.325	.628	2	.970
2002— Montreal (N.L.)	OF-1B	153	507	92	135	27	8	20	59	81	161	5	5	7-8	.266	.370	.469	.840	7	.984
2003— Montreal (N.L.)	OF-1B	146	504	78	135	34	4	19	77	89	155	4	5	13-10	.268	.380	.464	.844	5	.988
Major League totals (3 years)		346	1128	181	294	68	14	40	141	187	357	9	12	22-19	.261	.368	.452	.820	14	.985

W

PERSONAL: Born September 13, 1968, in San Juan, Puerto Rico. ... 6-2/205. ... Bats both, throws right. ... Full name: Bernabe Figueroa Williams. ... High school: Escuela Libre de Musica (San Juan, Puerto Rico). ... College: University of Puerto Rico.

TRANSACTIONS/CAREER NOTES: Signed as non-drafted free agent by New York Yankees organization (September 13, 1985). ... On disabled list (July 15, 1988-remainder of seasonl; and May 13-June 7, 1993). ... On disabled list (May 11-May 26, 1996; June 16-July 2 and July 15-August 1, 1997). ... On New York disabled list (June 11-July 18, 1998); included rehabilitation assignments to Tampa (July 6-7) and Norwich (July 14-16). ... Granted free agency (October 26, 1998). ... Re-signed by Yankees (November 25, 1998). ... Placed on 15-day disabled list (May 23, 2003). ... Sent to Trenton on rehab assignment (July 4, 2003). ... Recalled by New York from Trenton rehab assignment ; reinstated from the 15-day disabled list (July 9, 2003).

2003 GAMES PLAYED BY POSITION (MLB): OF—115, DH—4.

											BATTING							FIELDING	
Year	Team (League)	Pos.	G	AB	R	H	2B	3B	HR	RBI	BB	SO	HBP	GDP	SB-CS	Avg.	OBP	SLG	OPS	E	Pct.
1986— GC Yankees (GCL)		OF	61	230	* 45	62	5	3	2	25	39	40	1	3	33-• 12	.270	.374	.343	.717	3	.976
1987— Fort Laud. (FSL)		OF	25	71	11	11	3	0	0	4	18	23	3	1	9-1	.155	.348	.197	.545	0	1.000
— Oneonta (NYP)		OF	25	93	13	32	4	0	0	15	10	14	1	0	9-3	.344	.410	.387	.797	2	.952
1988— Prince Will. (Car.)		OF	92	337	72	113	16	7	7	45	65	65	4	5	29-11	* .335	.447	.487	.934	5	.975
1989— Columbus (Int'l)		OF	50	162	21	35	8	1	2	16	25	38	2	3	11-5	.216	.325	.315	.639	1	.991
— Alb./Colon. (East.)		OF	91	314	63	79	11	8	11	42	60	72	6	9	26-13	.252	.381	.443	.823	5	.974
1990— Alb./Colon. (East.)		OF	134	466	* 91	131	28	5	8	54	* 98	97	4	12	* 39-18	.281	.409	.414	.823	4	.987
1991— Columbus (Int'l)		OF	78	306	52	90	14	6	8	37	38	43	2	5	9-8	.294	.372	.458	.830	1	.994
— New York (A.L.)		OF	85	320	43	76	19	4	3	34	48	57	1	4	10-5	.238	.336	.350	.686	5	.979
1992— New York (A.L.)		OF	62	261	39	73	14	2	5	26	29	36	1	5	7-6	.280	.354	.406	.760	1	.995
— Columbus (Int'l)		OF	95	363	68	111	23	• 9	8	50	52	61	1	8	20-8	.306	.389	.485	.873	2	.990
1993— New York (A.L.)		OF	139	567	67	152	31	4	12	68	53	106	4	17	9-9	.268	.333	.400	.734	4	.989
1994— New York (A.L.)		OF	108	408	80	118	29	1	12	57	61	54	3	11	16-9	.289	.384	.453	.837	3	.990
1995— New York (A.L.)		OF	144	563	93	173	29	9	18	82	75	98	5	12	8-6	.307	.392	.487	.878	• 8	.982
1996— New York (A.L.)		OF-DH	143	551	108	168	26	7	29	102	82	72	0	15	17-4	.305	.391	.535	.926	5	.986
1997— New York (A.L.)		OF	129	509	107	167	35	6	21	100	73	80	1	10	15-8	.328	.408	.544	.952	2	.993
1998— New York (A.L.)		OF-DH	128	499	101	169	30	5	26	97	74	81	1	19	15-9	.339	.422	.575	.997	3	.990
— Tampa (Fla. St.)		OF	1	2	0	1	1	0	0	0	1	0	0	0	0-0	.500	.667	1.000	1.667	0	1.000
— Norwich (East.)		OF	3	11	6	6	2	0	2	5	2	1	0	1	0-0	.545	.571	1.273	1.844	0	1.000
1999— New York (A.L.)		OF-DH	158	591	116	202	28	6	25	115	100	95	1	11	9-10	.342	.435	.536	.971	5	.987
2000— New York (A.L.)		OF-DH	141	537	108	165	37	6	30	121	71	84	5	15	13-5	.307	.391	.566	.957	0	1.000
2001— New York (A.L.)		OF-DH	146	540	102	166	38	0	26	94	78	67	6	15	11-5	.307	.395	.522	.917	2	.994
2002— New York (A.L.)		OF-DH	154	612	102	204	37	2	19	102	83	97	3	19	8-4	.333	.415	.493	.908	5	.986
2003— Trenton (East.)		OF-DH	5	15	4	5	2	0	0	4	4	1	1	1	0-1	.333	.476	.467	.943	0	1.000
— New York (A.L.)		OF-DH	119	445	77	117	19	1	15	64	71	61	3	21	5-0	.263	.367	.411	.778	1	.997
Major League totals (13 years)			1656	6403	1143	1950	372	53	241	1062	898	988	34	174	143-80	.305	.390	.492	.882	44	.990

PERSONAL: Born August 10, 1966, in New Orleans, La. ... 6-2/187. ... Bats right, throws right. ... Full name: Gerald Floyd Williams. ... High school: East St. John (Reserve, La.). ... College: Grambling State.

TRANSACTIONS/CAREER NOTES: Selected by New York Yankees organization in 14th round of free-agent draft (June 2, 1987). ... Traded by Yankees with P Bob Wickman to Milwaukee Brewers for P Graeme Lloyd and OF Pat Listach (August 23, 1996). ... Traded by Brewers to Atlanta Braves for P Chad Fox (December 11, 1997). ... Granted free agency (November 3, 1999). ... Signed by Tampa Bay Devil Rays (December 19, 1999). ... On suspended list (September 22-25, 2000). ... Released by Devil Rays (June 24, 2001). ... Signed by New York Yankees (June 28, 2001). ... Released by Yankees (June 5, 2002). ... Signed by St. Louis Cardinals organization (June 12, 2002). ... Contract purchased by Cincinnati Reds organization from Cardinals (July 12, 2002). ... Granted free agency (October 15, 2002). ... Signed by Florida Marlins (January 10, 2003). ... Sent outright to Albuquerque by Florida (May 8, 2003). ... Contract purchased by Florida from Albuquerque (September 1, 2003).

2003 GAMES PLAYED BY POSITION (MLB): OF—16.

											BATTING							FIELDING	
Year	Team (League)	Pos.	G	AB	R	H	2B	3B	HR	RBI	BB	SO	HBP	GDP	SB-CS	Avg.	OBP	SLG	OPS	E	Pct.
1987— Oneonta (NYP)		OF	29	115	26	42	6	2	2	29	16	18	1	3	6-2	.365	.447	.504	.951	3	.959
1988— Prince Will. (Car.)		OF	54	159	20	29	3	0	2	18	15	47	0	4	6-1	.182	.251	.239	.490	3	.961
— Fort Laud. (FSL)		OF	63	212	21	40	7	2	2	17	16	56	3	4	4-3	.189	.255	.269	.524	6	.965
1989— Prince Will. (Car.)		OF	134	454	63	104	19	6	13	69	51	120	7	7	15-10	.229	.316	.383	.699	8	.974
1990— Fort Laud. (FSL)		OF	50	204	25	59	4	5	7	43	16	52	2	1	19-5	.289	.344	.461	.805	3	.975
— Alb./Colon. (East.)		OF	96	324	54	81	17	2	13	58	35	74	2	7	18-8	.250	.324	.435	.759	7	.969
1991— Alb./Colon. (East.)		OF	45	175	28	50	15	0	5	32	18	26	0	5	18-3	.286	.347	.457	.804	3	.974
— Columbus (Int'l)		OF	61	198	20	51	8	3	2	27	16	39	1	3	9-12	.258	.309	.359	.668	3	.977
1992— Columbus (Int'l)		OF	* 142	547	92	* 156	31	6	16	86	38	98	5	12	36-14	.285	.334	.452	.786	8	.977
— New York (A.L.)		OF	15	27	7	8	2	0	3	6	0	3	0	0	2-0	.296	.296	.704	1.000	2	.913
1993— Columbus (Int'l)		OF	87	336	53	95	19	6	8	38	20	64	2	7	29-12	.283	.321	.446	.768	3	.985
— New York (A.L.)		OF-DH	42	67	11	10	2	3	0	6	1	14	2	2	2-0	.149	.183	.269	.452	2	.956
1994— New York (A.L.)		OF-DH	57	86	19	25	8	0	4	13	4	17	0	6	1-3	.291	.319	.523	.842	2	.957
1995— New York (A.L.)		OF-DH	100	182	33	45	18	2	6	28	22	34	1	4	4-2	.247	.327	.467	.794	1	.993
1996— New York (A.L.)		OF-DH	99	233	37	63	15	4	5	30	15	39	4	7	7-8	.270	.319	.433	.753	3	.978
— Milwaukee (A.L.)		OF	26	92	6	19	4	0	0	4	4	18	1	1	3-1	.207	.247	.250	.497	1	.987
1997— Milwaukee (A.L.)		OF-DH	155	566	73	143	32	2	10	41	19	90	6	9	23-9	.253	.282	.369	.651	3	.992
1998— Atlanta (N.L.)		OF	129	266	46	81	19	2	10	44	17	48	3	5	11-5	.305	.352	.504	.856	5	.970
1999— Atlanta (N.L.)		OF	143	422	76	116	24	1	17	68	33	67	6	8	19-11	.275	.335	.457	.792	3	.985
2000— Tampa Bay (A.L.)		OF-DH	146	632	87	173	30	2	21	89	34	103	3	5	12-12	.274	.312	.427	.739	6	.983

W

Year Team (League)	Pos.	G	AB	R	H	2B	3B	HR	RBI	BB	SO	HBP	GDP	SB-CS	Avg.	OBP	SLG	OPS	E	Pct.
2001— Tampa Bay (A.L.)	OF	62	232	30	48	17	0	4	17	13	42	4	8	10-4	.207	.261	.332	.593	2	.989
— New York (A.L.)	OF-DH	38	47	12	8	1	0	0	2	5	13	1	1	3-1	.170	.264	.191	.456	1	.967
2002— New York (A.L.)	OF-DH	33	17	6	0	0	0	0	0	2	4	0	1	2-0	.000	.105	.000	.105	0	1.000
— Memphis (PCL)	OF	21	73	11	11	3	0	1	3	3	8	1	2	2-0	.151	.195	.233	.428	1	1.000
— Louisville (Int'l)	OF	48	205	29	54	10	3	2	12	11	36	2	4	6-4	.263	.307	.371	.678	1	.992
2003— Albuquerque (PCL)	OF	85	327	59	99	22	5	14	50	24	45	4	2	15-11	.303	.356	.529	.885	6	.972
— Florida (N.L.)	OF	27	31	5	4	1	0	0	3	2	5	0	0	3-0	.129	.182	.161	.343	1	.941
American League totals (9 years)		773	2181	321	542	129	13	53	236	119	377	22	44	69-40	.249	.292	.392	.684	23	.984
National League totals (3 years)		299	719	127	201	44	3	27	115	52	120	9	13	33-16	.280	.335	.462	.796	9	.976
Major League totals (12 years)		1072	2900	448	743	173	16	80	351	171	497	31	57	102-56	.256	.302	.410	.712	32	.982

WILLIAMS, JEROME — P

PERSONAL: Born December 4, 1981, in Honolulu, Hawaii. ... 6-3/180. ... Throws right, bats right. ... Full name: Jerome Lee Williams. ... High school: Waipahu (Hawaii).

TRANSACTIONS/CAREER NOTES: Selected by San Francisco Giants organization in first round (39th pick overall) of free-agent draft (June 2, 1999).

CAREER HITTING: 4-for-37 (.108), 1 R, 1 2B, 0 3B, 0 HR, 1 RBI.

Year League	W	L	Pct.	ERA	WHIP	G	GS	CG	ShO	Hld.	Sv.-Opp.	IP	H	R	ER	HR	BB-IBB	SO	Avg.
1999— Salem-Keizer (NW)	1	1	.500	2.19	1.08	7	7	1	1	...	0-...	37.0	29	13	9	1	11-0	34	.213
2000— San Jose (Calif.)	7	6	.538	2.94	1.09	23	19	0	0	...	0-...	125.2	89	53	41	6	48-3	115	.201
2001— Shreveport (Texas)	9	7	.563	3.95	1.15	23	23	2	1	...	0-...	130.0	116	69	57	14	34-0	84	.235
2002— Fresno (PCL)	6	11	.353	3.59	1.18	28	28	0	0	...	0-...	160.2	140	76	64	16	50-1	130	.234
2003— Fresno (PCL)	4	2	.667	2.68	1.19	10	10	1	0	...	0-...	57.0	52	19	17	3	16-0	40	.237
— San Francisco (N.L.)	7	5	.583	3.30	1.26	21	21	2	1	0	0-0	131.0	116	54	48	10	49-3	88	.242
Major League totals (1 year)	7	5	.583	3.30	1.26	21	21	2	1	0	0-0	131.0	116	54	48	10	49-3	88	.242

WILLIAMS, MATT — 3B

PERSONAL: Born November 28, 1965, in Bishop, Calif. ... 6-2/223. ... Bats right, throws right. ... Full name: Matthew Derrick Williams. ... High school: Carson (Nev.). ... College: UNLV.

TRANSACTIONS/CAREER NOTES: Selected by New York Mets organization in 27th round of free-agent draft (June 6, 1983); did not sign. ... Selected by San Francisco Giants organization in first round (third pick overall) of free-agent draft (June 2, 1986). ... On disabled list (June 28-July 14, 1993). ... On San Francisco disabled list (June 4-August 19, 1995); included rehabilitation assignments to San Jose (July 24-25 and August 13-19). ... On disabled list (August 5, 1996-remainder of season). ... Traded by Giants with a player to be named later to Cleveland Indians for IF Jeff Kent, IF Jose Vizcaino, P Julian Tavarez and a player to be named later (November 13, 1996); Giants traded OF Trenidad Hubbard to Indians for P Joe Roa to complete deal (December 16, 1996). ... Traded by Indians to Arizona Diamondbacks for 3B Travis Fryman, P Tom Martin and cash (December 1, 1997). ... On Arizona disabled list (July 18-August 3, 1998); included rehabilitation assignment to Tucson (July 31-August 3). ... On Arizona disabled list (March 29-May 23 and June 25-July 13, 2000); included rehabilitation assignments to El Paso (May 16-23) and High Desert (July 8-10). ... On Arizona disabled list (May 18-July 12, 2001); included rehabilitation assignment to Tucson (July 4-12). ... On Arizona disabled list (March 22-July 11, 2002); included rehabilitation assignments to Tucson (June 26-July 4) and Lancaster (July 4-11). ... Designated for assignment by Arizona (May 30, 2003). ... Given unconditional release by Arizona (June 9, 2003).

2003 GAMES PLAYED BY POSITION (MLB): 3B—42.

Year Team (League)	Pos.	G	AB	R	H	2B	3B	HR	RBI	BB	SO	HBP	GDP	SB-CS	Avg.	OBP	SLG	OPS	E	Pct.
1986— Everett (N'west)	SS	4	17	3	4	0	1	1	10	1	4	0	0	0-0	.235	.263	.529	.793	2	.882
— Clinton (Midw.)	SS	68	250	32	60	14	3	7	29	23	62	3	6	3-3	.240	.308	.404	.712	10	.960
1987— Phoenix (PCL)	2B-3B-SS	56	211	36	61	15	2	6	37	19	53	0	2	6-2	.289	.345	.464	.809	14	.931
— San Francisco (N.L.)	3B-SS	84	245	28	46	9	2	8	21	16	68	1	5	4-3	.188	.240	.339	.578	9	.975
1988— Phoenix (PCL)	2-3-S-O	82	306	45	83	19	1	12	51	13	56	1	9	6-5	.271	.299	.458	.757	13	.946
— San Francisco (N.L.)	3B-SS	52	156	17	32	6	1	8	19	8	41	2	7	0-1	.205	.251	.410	.662	7	.957
1989— San Francisco (N.L.)	3B-SS	84	292	31	59	18	1	18	50	14	72	2	5	1-2	.202	.242	.455	.697	10	.963
— Phoenix (PCL) 3B-SS-OF		76	284	61	91	20	2	26	61	32	51	3	8	9-3	.320	.394	.680	1.073	11	.958
1990— San Francisco (N.L.)	3B	159	617	87	171	27	2	33	*122	33	138	7	13	7-4	.277	.319	.488	.807	19	.959
1991— San Francisco (N.L.)	3B-SS	157	589	72	158	24	5	34	98	33	128	6	11	5-5	.268	.310	.499	.809	16	.964
1992— San Francisco (N.L.)	3B	146	529	58	120	13	5	20	66	39	109	6	15	7-7	.227	.286	.384	.670	* 23	.945
1993— San Francisco (N.L.)	3B	145	579	105	170	33	4	38	110	27	80	4	12	1-3	.294	.325	.561	.886	12	.970
1994— San Francisco (N.L.)	3B	112	445	74	119	16	3	* 43	96	33	87	2	11	1-0	.267	.319	.607	.926	12	.963
1995— San Francisco (N.L.)	3B	76	283	53	95	17	1	23	65	30	58	2	8	2-0	.336	.399	.647	1.046	10	.958
— San Jose (Calif.)	3B	4	11	2	2	0	0	1	2	0	3	1	0	0-0	.182	.250	.455	.705	0	1.000
1996— San Francisco (N.L.) 3B-1B-SS		105	404	69	122	16	1	22	85	39	91	6	10	1-2	.302	.367	.510	.877	14	.962
1997— Cleveland (A.L.)	3B	151	596	86	157	32	3	32	105	34	108	4	14	12-4	.263	.307	.488	.795	12	.970
1998— Arizona (N.L.)	3B	135	510	72	136	26	1	20	71	43	102	3	19	5-1	.267	.327	.439	.766	11	.972
— Tucson (PCL)	3B	2	5	0	1	0	0	0	0	0	0	0	0	0-0	.200	.200	.200	.400	0	1.000
1999— Arizona (N.L.)	3B	154	627	98	190	37	2	35	142	41	93	2	17	2-0	.303	.344	.536	.880	10	.977
2000— El Paso (Texas)	3B	5	13	3	6	2	0	0	1	2	1	0	0	0-0	.462	.533	.615	1.149	0	1.000
— Arizona (N.L.)	3B-DH	96	371	43	102	18	2	12	47	20	51	3	11	1-2	.275	.315	.431	.746	9	.964
— High Desert (Calif.)	3B	2	8	1	3	0	0	1	1	0	1	0	0	0-0	.375	.375	.750	1.125	0	1.000
2001— Arizona (N.L.)	3B-SS	106	408	58	112	30	0	16	65	22	70	3	15	1-0	.275	.314	.466	.780	9	.964
— Tucson (PCL)	3B	5	17	4	6	2	0	2	5	2	2	0	0	1-0	.353	.421	.824	1.245	1	.833
2002— Tucson (PCL)	3B	5	15	1	3	0	0	1	3	0	0	0	...	0-0	.200	.200	.400	.600	1	.875
— Arizona (N.L.)	3B	60	215	29	56	7	2	12	40	21	41	0	8	3-1	.260	.324	.479	.803	4	.969
— Lancaster (Calif.)	3B	4	12	2	4	1	0	1	5	2	1	0	0	0-0	.333	.429	.667	1.095	1	.889
2003— Arizona (N.L.)	3B	44	134	17	33	9	0	4	16	16	26	2	1	0-0	.246	.327	.403	.730	4	.959
American League totals (1 year)		151	596	86	157	32	3	32	105	34	108	4	14	12-4	.263	.307	.488	.795	12	.970
National League totals (16 years)		1715	6404	911	1721	306	32	346	1113	435	1255	51	168	41-31	.269	.318	.489	.806	179	.964
Major League totals (17 years)		1866	7000	997	1878	338	35	378	1218	469	1363	55	182	53-35	.268	.317	.489	.805	191	.965

W

WILLIAMS, MIKE — P

PERSONAL: Born July 29, 1968, in Radford, Va. ... 6-2/200. ... Throws right, bats right. ... Full name: Michael Darren Williams. ... High school: Giles (Pearisburg, Va.). ... College: Virginia Tech.

TRANSACTIONS/CAREER NOTES: Selected by Philadelphia Phillies organization in 14th round of free-agent draft (June 4, 1990). ... On suspended list (September 26, 1996-remainder of season). ... Granted free agency (December 20, 1996). ... Signed by Boston Red Sox organization (February 15, 1997). ... Released by Red Sox (March 14, 1997). ... Signed by Kansas City Royals organization (April 30, 1997). ... On suspended list (May 16-18, 1997). ... Granted free agency (October 15, 1997). ... Signed by Pittsburgh Pirates organization (December 18, 1997). ... On disabled list (June 24-July 9, 1999). ... Traded by Pirates to Houston Astros for P Tony McKnight (July 31, 2001). ... Granted free agency (November 5, 2001). ... Signed by Pirates (January 7, 2002). ... Traded by Pirates to Philadelphia Phillies for P Frank Brooks (July 21, 2003).

CAREER HITTING: 17-for-108 (.157), 7 R, 2 2B, 0 3B, 0 HR, 7 RBI.

Year League	W	L	Pct.	ERA	WHIP	G	GS	CG	ShO	Hld.	Sv.-Opp.	IP	H	R	ER	HR	BB-IBB	SO	Avg.
1990—Batavia (N.Y.-Penn)	2	3	.400	2.30	1.11	27	0	0	0	...	11-...	47.0	39	17	12	0	13-4	42	.223
1991—Clearwater (Fla. St.)	7	3	.700	1.74	0.85	14	14	2	1	...	0-...	93.1	65	23	18	5	14-0	76	.199
—Reading (East.)	7	5	.583	3.69	1.26	16	15	2	1	...	0-...	102.1	93	44	42	1	36-0	51	.250
1992—Reading (East.)	1	2	.333	5.17	1.53	3	3	0	0	...	0-...	15.2	17	10	9	1	7-0	12	.283
—Scran./W.B. (I.L.)	9	1	.900	2.43	1.23	16	16	3	1	...	0-...	92.2	84	26	25	4	30-2	59	.242
—Philadelphia (N.L.)	1	1	.500	5.34	1.26	5	5	1	0	0	0-0	28.2	29	20	17	3	7-0	5	.259
1993—Scran./W.B. (I.L.)	9	2	.818	2.87	1.12	14	13	1	1	...	0-...	97.1	93	34	31	7	16-0	53	.258
—Philadelphia (N.L.)	1	3	.250	5.29	1.41	17	4	0	0	0	0-0	51.0	50	32	30	5	22-2	33	.253
1994—Philadelphia (N.L.)	2	4	.333	5.01	1.61	12	8	0	0	0	0-0	50.1	61	31	28	7	20-3	29	.310
—Scran./W.B. (I.L.)	2	7	.222	5.79	1.51	14	14	1	0	...	0-...	84.0	91	55	54	14	36-0	53	.276
1995—Philadelphia (N.L.)	3	3	.500	3.29	1.22	33	8	0	0	1	0-0	87.2	78	37	32	10	29-2	57	.239
—Scran./W.B. (I.L.)	0	1	.000	4.66	1.03	3	3	1	0	...	0-...	9.2	8	5	5	0	2-0	8	.216
1996—Philadelphia (N.L.)	6	14	.300	5.44	1.53	32	29	0	0	0	0-0	167.0	188	107	101	25	67-6	103	.290
1997—Omaha (Am. Assoc.)	3	6	.333	4.22	1.38	20	11	1	0	...	5-...	79.0	71	41	37	10	38-0	68	.243
—Kansas City (A.L.)	0	2	.000	6.43	2.00	10	0	0	0	1	1-1	14.0	20	11	10	1	8-1	10	.333
1998—Pittsburgh (N.L.)	4	2	.667	1.94	1.08	37	1	0	0	7	0-1	51.0	39	12	11	1	16-4	59	.211
—Nashville (PCL)	0	2	.000	5.59	1.35	16	4	0	0	...	1-...	37.0	36	25	23	11	14-2	34	.250
1999—Pittsburgh (N.L.)	3	4	.429	5.09	1.71	58	0	0	0	1	23-28	58.1	63	36	33	9	37-7	76	.276
2000—Pittsburgh (N.L.)	3	4	.429	3.50	1.33	72	0	0	0	0	24-29	72.0	56	34	28	8	40-3	71	.214
2001—Pittsburgh (N.L.)	2	4	.333	3.67	1.44	40	0	0	0	0	22-24	41.2	39	18	17	6	21-2	43	.244
—Houston (N.L.)	4	0	1.000	4.03	1.57	25	0	0	0	3	0-1	22.1	21	10	10	3	14-1	16	.244
2002—Pittsburgh (N.L.)	2	6	.250	2.93	1.22	59	0	0	0	0	46-50	61.1	54	24	20	6	21-3	43	.233
2003—Pittsburgh (N.L.)	1	3	.250	6.27	1.71	40	0	0	0	0	25-30	37.1	42	26	26	5	22-1	20	.282
—Philadelphia (N.L.)	0	4	.000	5.96	1.68	28	0	0	0	2	3-5	25.2	24	18	17	0	19-5	19	.247
American League totals (1 year)	0	2	.000	6.43	2.00	10	0	0	0	1	1-1	14.0	20	11	10	1	8-1	10	.333
National League totals (11 years)	32	52	.381	4.41	1.43	458	55	1	0	14	143-168	754.1	744	405	370	88	335-39	574	.259
Major League totals (12 years)	32	54	.372	4.45	1.44	468	55	1	0	15	144-169	768.1	764	416	380	89	343-40	584	.260

WILLIAMS, WOODY — P

PERSONAL: Born August 19, 1966, in Houston, Texas. ... 6-0/200. ... Throws right, bats right. ... Full name: Gregory Scott Williams. ... High school: Cypress-Fairbanks (Houston). ... College: Houston.

TRANSACTIONS/CAREER NOTES: Selected by Toronto Blue Jays organization in 28th round of free-agent draft (June 1, 1988). ... On disabled list (April 9-May 17, 1992). ... On Toronto disabled list (July 17, 1995-remainder of season); included rehabilitation assignment to Syracuse (August 15-25). ... On Toronto disabled list (March 22-May 31 and June 11-July 26, 1996); included rehabilitation assignments to Dunedin (May 2-10), Syracuse (May 10-28 and July 13-20) and St. Catharines (July 20-26). ... Traded by Blue Jays with P Carlos Almanzar and OF Peter Tucci to San Diego Padres for P Joey Hamilton (December 13, 1998). ... On San Diego disabled list (May 2-July 2, 2000); included rehabilitation assignment to Rancho Cucamonga (June 22-27) and Las Vegas (June 28). ... Traded by Padres to St. Louis Cardinals for OF Ray Lankford and cash (August 2, 2001). ... On St. Louis disabled list (April 6-May 15 and July 7-August 29, 2002); included rehabilitation assignment to Memphis (August 24-26). ... Granted free agency (October 30, 2002). ... Re-signed by Cardinals (November 25, 2002).

CAREER HITTING: 70-for-320 (.219), 40 R, 20 2B, 1 3B, 3 HR, 32 RBI.

Year League	W	L	Pct.	ERA	WHIP	G	GS	CG	ShO	Hld.	Sv.-Opp.	IP	H	R	ER	HR	BB-IBB	SO	Avg.
1988—St. Catharines (NYP)	8	2	.800	1.54	0.91	12	12	2	0	...	0-...	76.0	48	22	13	1	21-0	58	.178
—Knoxville (Sou.)	2	2	.500	3.81	1.38	6	4	0	0	...	0-...	28.1	27	13	12	1	12-0	25	.250
1989—Dunedin (Fla. St.)	3	5	.375	2.32	1.11	20	9	0	0	...	3-...	81.1	63	26	21	3	27-1	60	.217
—Knoxville (Sou.)	3	5	.375	3.55	1.32	14	12	2	•2	...	1-...	71.0	61	32	28	6	33-2	51	.235
1990—Knoxville (Sou.)	7	9	.438	3.14	1.19	42	12	0	0	...	5-...	126.0	111	55	44	7	39-3	74	.236
—Syracuse (Int'l)	0	1	.000	10.00	2.11	3	0	0	0	...	0-...	9.0	15	10	10	1	4-0	8	.375
1991—Knoxville (Sou.)	3	2	.600	3.59	1.31	18	1	0	0	...	3-...	42.2	42	18	17	1	14-0	37	.261
—Syracuse (Int'l)	3	4	.429	4.12	1.45	31	0	0	0	...	6-...	54.2	52	27	25	2	27-3	37	.250
1992—Syracuse (Int'l)	6	8	.429	3.13	1.29	25	16	1	0	...	1-...	120.2	115	46	42	4	41-0	81	.253
1993—Syracuse (Int'l)	1	1	.500	2.20	1.22	12	0	0	0	...	3-...	16.1	15	5	4	2	5-3	16	.246
—Toronto (A.L.)	3	1	.750	4.38	1.68	30	0	0	0	4	0-2	37.0	40	18	18	2	22-3	24	.274
—Dunedin (Fla. St.)	0	0	...	0.00	0.50	2	0	0	0	...	0-...	4.0	0	0	0	0	2-0	2	.000
1994—Toronto (A.L.)	1	3	.250	3.64	1.30	38	0	0	0	5	0-0	59.1	44	24	24	5	33-1	56	.205
—Syracuse (Int'l)	0	0	...	0.00	0.00	1	0	0	0	...	1-...	1.2	0	0	0	0	0-0	1	.000
1995—Toronto (A.L.)	1	2	.333	3.69	1.34	23	3	0	0	1	0-1	53.2	44	23	22	6	28-1	41	.220
—Syracuse (Int'l)	0	0	...	3.52	1.30	5	1	0	0	...	1-...	7.2	5	3	3	0	5-0	13	.172
1996—Dunedin (Fla. St.)	0	2	.000	8.22	1.43	2	2	0	0	...	0-...	7.2	9	7	7	1	2-0	11	.281
—Syracuse (Int'l)	3	1	.750	1.41	0.91	7	7	1	1	...	0-...	32.0	22	5	5	3	7-0	33	.191
—Toronto (A.L.)	4	5	.444	4.73	1.44	12	10	1	0	0	0-0	59.0	64	33	31	8	21-1	43	.278
—St. Catharines (NYP)	0	0	...	3.68	1.50	2	2	0	0	...	0-...	7.1	7	3	3	0	4-0	12	.269
1997—Toronto (A.L.)	9	14	.391	4.35	1.37	31	31	0	0	0	0-0	194.2	201	98	94	31	66-3	124	.269
1998—Toronto (A.L.)	10	9	.526	4.46	1.32	32	32	1	1	0	0-0	209.2	196	112	104	36	81-3	151	.245
1999—San Diego (N.L.)	12	12	.500	4.41	1.37	33	33	0	0	0	0-0	208.1	213	106	102	33	73-5	137	.268
2000—San Diego (N.L.)	10	8	.556	3.75	1.23	23	23	4	0	0	0-0	168.0	152	74	70	23	54-2	111	.239
—Rancho Cuca. (Calif.)	0	0	...	0.00	0.60	1	1	0	0	...	0-...	5.0	3	0	0	0	0-0	10	.167
—Las Vegas (PCL)	0	0	...	1.50	1.17	1	1	0	0	...	0-...	6.0	7	2	1	1	0-0	5	.292

W

Year League	W	L	Pct.	ERA	WHIP	G	GS	CG	ShO	Hld.	Sv.-Opp.	IP	H	R	ER	HR	BB-IBB	SO	Avg.
2001—San Diego (N.L.)	8	8	.500	4.97	1.43	23	23	0	0	0	0-0	145.0	170	88	80	28	37-4	102	.296
—St. Louis (N.L.)	7	1	.875	2.28	0.97	11	11	3	1	0	0-0	75.0	54	22	19	7	19-1	52	.205
2002—St. Louis (N.L.)	9	4	.692	2.53	1.05	17	17	1	0	0	0-0	103.1	84	30	29	10	25-2	76	.222
—Memphis (PCL)	1	0	1.000	1.80	0.40	1	1	0	0	...	0-...	5.0	1	1	1	0	1-0	7	.067
2003—St. Louis (N.L.)	18	9	.667	3.87	1.25	34	33	0	0	0	0-1	220.2	220	101	95	20	55-2	153	.256
American League totals (6 years)	28	34	.452	4.30	1.37	166	76	2	1	10	0-3	613.1	589	308	293	88	251-12	439	.252
National League totals (5 years)	64	42	.604	3.86	1.26	141	140	8	1	0	0-1	920.1	893	421	395	121	263-16	631	.255
Major League totals (11 years)	92	76	.548	4.04	1.30	307	216	10	2	10	0-4	1533.2	1482	729	688	209	514-28	1070	.254

WILLIAMSON, SCOTT — P

PERSONAL: Born February 17, 1976, in Fort Polk, La. ... 6-0/185. ... Throws right, bats right. ... Full name: Scott Ryan Williamson. ... High school: Friendswood (Texas). ... College: Oklahoma State.

TRANSACTIONS/CAREER NOTES: Selected by Cincinnati Reds organization in ninth round of free-agent draft (June 3, 1997). ... On disabled list (August 24-September 8, 2000; and April 4, 2001-remainder of season). ... Traded by Reds to Boston Red Sox for P Phil Dumatrait, a player to be named and cash (July 30, 2003).

CAREER HITTING: 1-for-23 (.043), 1 R, 0 2B, 0 3B, 0 HR, 0 RBI.

Year League	W	L	Pct.	ERA	WHIP	G	GS	CG	ShO	Hld.	Sv.-Opp.	IP	H	R	ER	HR	BB-IBB	SO	Avg.
1997—Billings (Pio.)	•8	2	.800	1.78	1.03	13	13	2	•1	...	0-...	86.0	66	25	17	5	23-0	*101	.209
1998—Chattanooga (Sou.)	4	5	.444	3.78	1.31	18	18	0	0	...	0-...	100.0	85	49	42	4	46-4	105	.234
—Indianapolis (Int'l)	0	0	...	3.48	1.40	5	5	0	0	...	0-...	20.2	20	9	8	2	9-0	17	.260
1999—Cincinnati (N.L.)	12	7	.632	2.41	1.04	62	0	0	0	5	19-26	93.1	54	29	25	8	43-6	107	.171
2000—Cincinnati (N.L.)	5	8	.385	3.29	1.49	48	10	0	0	6	6-8	112.0	92	45	41	7	75-7	136	.224
2001—Cincinnati (N.L.)	0	0	...	0.00	4.50	2	0	0	0	1	0-0	.2	1	0	0	0	2-0	0	.333
2002—Cincinnati (N.L.)	3	4	.429	2.92	1.11	63	0	0	0	8	8-12	74.0	46	27	24	5	36-5	84	.181
2003—Cincinnati (N.L.)	5	3	.625	3.19	1.39	42	0	0	0	8	21-26	42.1	34	15	15	6	25-4	53	.214
—Boston (A.L.)	0	1	.000	6.20	1.43	24	0	0	0	5	0-2	20.1	20	15	14	1	9-2	21	.253
American League totals (1 year)	0	1	.000	6.20	1.43	24	0	0	0	5	0-2	20.1	20	15	14	1	9-2	21	.253
National League totals (5 years)	25	22	.532	2.93	1.27	217	10	0	0	20	54-72	322.1	227	116	105	26	181-22	380	.199
Major League totals (5 years)	25	23	.521	3.13	1.28	241	10	0	0	25	54-74	342.2	247	131	119	27	190-24	401	.202

WILLIS, DONTRELLE — P

PERSONAL: Born January 12, 1982, in Oakland, Calif. ... 6-4/195. ... Throws left, bats left. ... Full name: Dontrelle Wayne Willis. ... High school: Encinal (Alameda, Calif.).

TRANSACTIONS/CAREER NOTES: Selected by Chicago Cubs organization in eighth round of free-agent draft (June 5, 2000). ... Traded by Cubs with P Julian Tavarez, P Jose Cueto and C Ryan Jorgensen to Florida Marlins for P Antonio Alfonseca and P Matt Clement (March 27, 2002).

CAREER HITTING: 14-for-58 (.241), 2 R, 2 2B, 0 3B, 1 HR, 4 RBI.

Year League	W	L	Pct.	ERA	WHIP	G	GS	CG	ShO	Hld.	Sv.-Opp.	IP	H	R	ER	HR	BB-IBB	SO	Avg.
2000—Ariz. Cubs (Ariz.)	3	1	.750	3.86	1.21	9	1	0	0	...	0-...	28.0	26	15	12	0	8-1	22	.245
2001—Boise (NW)	8	2	.800	2.98	1.01	15	15	0	0	...	0-...	93.2	76	36	31	1	19-0	77	.217
2002—Kane County (Midwest)	10	2	.833	1.83	0.88	19	19	3	2	...	0-...	127.2	91	29	26	3	21-0	101	.200
—Jupiter (FSL)	2	0	1.000	1.80	0.90	5	5	0	0	...	0-...	30.0	24	7	6	2	3-0	27	.216
2003—Carolina (Sou.)	4	0	1.000	1.49	0.91	6	6	0	0	...	0-...	36.1	24	6	6	2	9-0	32	.194
—Florida (N.L.)	14	6	.700	3.30	1.28	27	27	2	2	0	0-0	160.2	148	61	59	13	58-0	142	.245
Major League totals (1 year)	14	6	.700	3.30	1.28	27	27	2	2	0	0-0	160.2	148	61	59	13	58-0	142	.245

WILSON, CRAIG — OF/1B

PERSONAL: Born November 30, 1976, in Fountain Valley, Calif. ... 6-2/218. ... Bats right, throws right. ... Full name: Craig Alan Wilson. ... High school: Marina (Huntington Beach, Calif.).

TRANSACTIONS/CAREER NOTES: Selected by Toronto Blue Jays organization in second round of free-agent draft (June 1, 1995). ... Traded by Blue Jays to Pittsburgh Pirates (December 11, 1996), completing deal in which Pirates traded 2B Carlos Garcia, 1B Orlando Merced and P Dan Plesac to Blue Jays for P Mike Halperin, SS Abraham Nunez, P Jose Pett, P Jose Silva, SS Brandon Cromer and a player to be named later (November 14, 1996).

2003 GAMES PLAYED BY POSITION (MLB): OF—46, 1B—36, C—21, DH—3.

Year Team (League)	Pos.	G	AB	R	H	2B	3B	HR	RBI	BB	SO	HBP	GDP	SB-CS	Avg.	OBP	SLG	OPS	E	Pct.
1995—Medicine Hat (Pio.)	C	49	184	33	52	14	1	7	35	24	44	3	1	8-2	.283	.367	.484	.851	5	.982
1996—Hagerstown (SAL)	C-OF	131	495	66	129	27	5	11	70	32	120	10	12	17-11	.261	.316	.402	.718	9	.986
1997—Lynchburg (Caro.)	C	117	401	54	106	26	1	19	69	39	98	15	3	6-5	.264	.350	.476	.826	12	.985
1998—Lynchburg (Caro.)	C-1B	61	219	26	59	12	2	12	45	22	53	5	3	2-1	.269	.348	.507	.855	6	.986
—Carolina (Sou.)	C	45	148	20	49	11	0	5	21	14	32	4	2	4-1	.331	.399	.507	.906	1	.995
1999—Altoona (East.)	C-1B-OF	111	362	57	97	21	3	20	69	40	104	19	8	1-3	.268	.367	.508	.875	9	.978
2000—Nashville (PCL)	C-1B	124	396	83	112	24	1	33	86	44	121	25	7	1-2	.283	.383	.598	.982	13	.982
2001—Nashville (PCL)	1B-C	11	45	4	13	2	1	1	3	2	14	1	1	0-0	.289	.333	.444	.778	2	.976
—Pittsburgh (N.L.)	1-O-C-D	88	158	27	49	3	1	13	32	15	53	7	4	3-1	.310	.390	.589	.979	3	.987
2002—Pittsburgh (N.L.)	O-1-C-D	131	368	48	97	16	1	16	57	32	116	*21	10	2-3	.264	.355	.443	.798	5	.988
2003—Pittsburgh (N.L.)	O-1-C-D	116	309	49	81	15	4	18	48	35	89	13	6	3-1	.262	.360	.511	.872	6	.986
Major League totals (3 years)		335	835	124	227	34	6	47	137	82	258	41	20	8-5	.272	.363	.496	.859	14	.987

WILSON, DAN — C

PERSONAL: Born March 25, 1969, in Barrington, Ill. ... 6-3/215. ... Bats right, throws right. ... Full name: Daniel Allen Wilson. ... High school: Barrington (Ill.). ... College: Minnesota.

TRANSACTIONS/CAREER NOTES: Selected by New York Mets organization in 26th round of free-agent draft (June 2, 1987); did not sign. ... Selected by Cincinnati Reds organization in first round (seventh pick overall) of free-agent draft (June 4, 1990). ... Traded by Reds with P Bobby Ayala to Seattle Mariners for P Erik Hanson and 2B Bret Boone (November 2, 1993). ... On disabled list (July 21-September 1, 1998). ... On Seattle disabled list (June 15-July 14, 2000); included rehabilitation assignments to Everett (July 12-13) and Tacoma (July 14). ... On Seattle disabled list (March 19-April 6, 2003); included rehabilitation assignment to San Antonio (April 3-6).

2003 GAMES PLAYED BY POSITION (MLB): C—96.

W

Year	Team (League)	Pos.	G	AB	R	H	2B	3B	HR	RBI	BB	SO	HBP	GDP	SB-CS	Avg.	OBP	SLG	OPS	E	Pct.
1990— Char., W.Va. (SAL)		C	32	113	16	28	9	1	2	17	13	17	0	1	0-0	.248	.323	.398	.721	1	.995
1991— Char., W.Va. (SAL)		C	52	197	25	62	11	1	3	29	25	21	2	6	1-1	.315	.396	.426	.822	3	.992
—Chattanooga (Sou.)		C	81	292	32	75	19	2	2	38	21	39	0	10	2-2	.257	.303	.356	.659	4	.993
1992— Nashville (A.A.)		C	106	366	27	92	16	1	4	34	31	58	2	7	1-4	.251	.310	.333	.644	* 8	.990
—Cincinnati (N.L.)		C	12	25	2	9	1	0	0	3	3	8	0	2	0-0	.360	.429	.400	.829	0	1.000
1993— Cincinnati (N.L.)		C	36	76	6	17	3	0	0	8	9	16	0	2	0-0	.224	.302	.263	.565	1	.994
—Indianapolis (A.A.)		C	51	191	18	50	11	1	1	17	19	31	1	4	1-0	.262	.330	.346	.676	2	.994
1994— Seattle (A.L.)		C	91	282	24	61	14	2	3	27	10	57	1	11	1-2	.216	.244	.312	.556	* 9	.986
1995— Seattle (A.L.)		C	119	399	40	111	22	3	9	51	33	63	2	12	2-1	.278	.336	.416	.752	5	.995
1996— Seattle (A.L.)		C	138	491	51	140	24	0	18	83	32	88	3	15	1-2	.285	.330	.444	.774	4	.996
1997— Seattle (A.L.)		C	146	508	66	137	31	1	15	74	39	72	5	12	7-2	.270	.326	.423	.749	6	.995
1998— Seattle (A.L.)		C	96	325	39	82	17	1	9	44	24	56	5	6	2-1	.252	.308	.394	.702	4	.994
1999— Seattle (A.L.)		C-1B	123	414	46	110	23	2	7	38	29	83	2	10	5-0	.266	.315	.382	.697	4	.995
2000— Seattle (A.L.)		C-3B-1B	90	268	31	63	12	0	5	27	22	51	0	8	1-2	.235	.291	.336	.627	5	.990
—Everett (N'west)		C	1	2	2	1	0	0	1	1	1	0	0	0	0-0	.500	.667	2.000	2.667	0	1.000
—Tacoma (PCL)		DH	1	4	0	1	1	0	0	0	0	1	0	0	0-0	.250	.250	.500	.750		
2001— Seattle (A.L.)		C-1B	123	377	44	100	20	1	10	42	20	69	2	6	3-2	.265	.305	.403	.708	1	.999
2002— Seattle (A.L.)		C-1B	115	359	35	106	16	1	6	44	18	81	2	8	1-0	.295	.326	.396	.721	2	.997
2003— San Antonio (Texas)		C	2	7	0	0	0	0	0	0	0	3	0	0	0-0	.000	.000	.000	.000	1	.941
—Seattle (A.L.)		C	96	316	32	76	15	2	4	43	15	52	0	8	0-0	.241	.272	.339	.611	1	.998
American League totals (10 years)			1137	3739	408	986	194	13	86	473	242	672	22	96	23-12	.264	.310	.392	.701	41	.995
National League totals (2 years)			48	101	8	26	4	0	0	11	12	24	0	4	0-0	.257	.333	.297	.630	1	.995
Major League totals (12 years)			1185	3840	416	1012	198	13	86	484	254	696	22	100	23-12	.264	.310	.389	.699	42	.995

WILSON, ENRIQUE — IF

PERSONAL: Born July 27, 1973, in Santo Domingo, Dominican Republic. ... 5-11/195. ... Bats both, throws right. ... Full name: Enrique Martes Wilson. ... High school: Liceo Ramon Amelio Jiminez (Santo Domingo, Dominican Republic).

TRANSACTIONS/CAREER NOTES: Signed as non-drafted free agent by Minnesota Twins organization (April 15, 1992). ... Traded by Twins to Cleveland Indians (February 21, 1994), completing deal in which Twins acquired P Shawn Bryant for a player to be named later (February 21, 1994). ... On Cleveland disabled list (April 4-June 15, 1998); included rehabilitation assignment to Buffalo (June 2-15). ... On Cleveland disabled list (July 14-July 28, 2000). ... Traded by Indians with OF Alex Ramirez to Pittsburgh Pirates for 1B/OF Wil Cordero (July 28, 2000). ... On Pittsburgh disabled list (July 29-August 1, 2000); included rehabilitation assignment to Nashville (July 31-August 1). ... Traded by Pirates to New York Yankees for P Damaso Marte (June 13, 2001).

2003 GAMES PLAYED BY POSITION (MLB): SS—33, 3B—17, 2B—10, DH—1.

Year	Team (League)	Pos.	G	AB	R	H	2B	3B	HR	RBI	BB	SO	HBP	GDP	SB-CS	Avg.	OBP	SLG	OPS	E	Pct.
1992— GC Twins (GCL)		SS	13	44	12	15	1	0	0	8	4	4	4	0	3-0	.341	.434	.364	.798	4	.897
1993— Elizabethton (App.)		3B-SS	58	197	42	57	8	4	13	50	14	18	6	1	5-4	.289	.352	.569	.920	19	.909
1994— Columbus (S. Atl.)		SS	133	512	82	143	28	12	10	72	44	34	6	7	21-13	.279	.341	.439	.780	33	.947
1995— Kinston (Caro.)		2B-SS	117	464	55	124	24	•7	6	52	25	38	2	10	18-19	.267	.301	.388	.689	21	.964
1996— Cant./Akr. (Eastern)		SS-2B	117	484	70	147	17	5	5	50	31	46	4	9	23-16	.304	.346	.390	.737	28	.949
—Buffalo (A.A.)		3B-SS	3	8	1	4	1	0	0	0	1	1	0	1	0-2	.500	.556	.625	1.181	1	.750
1997— Buffalo (A.A.)		SS-2B-3B	118	451	78	138	20	3	11	39	42	41	5	7	9-8	.306	.369	.437	.805	20	.965
—Cleveland (A.L.)		SS-2B	5	15	2	5	0	0	0	1	0	2	0	0	0-0	.333	.333	.333	.667	1	.952
1998— Cleveland (A.L.)		2B-SS-3B	32	90	13	29	6	0	2	12	4	8	1	1	2-4	.322	.354	.456	.810	2	.983
—Buffalo (Int'l)		2B-SS	56	221	40	62	13	0	4	23	19	21	0	6	8-3	.281	.335	.394	.728	6	.976
1999— Cleveland (A.L.)		3-S-2-D	113	332	41	87	22	1	2	24	25	41	1	12	5-4	.262	.310	.352	.663	8	.968
2000— Cleveland (A.L.)		3-D-2-S	40	117	16	38	9	0	2	12	7	11	0	2	2-1	.325	.360	.453	.813	1	.985
—Nashville (PCL)		2B-SS	2	7	0	2	0	0	0	1	0	0	0	2	0-0	.286	.286	.286	.571	1	.889
—Pittsburgh (N.L.)		3B-2B-SS	40	122	11	32	6	1	3	15	11	13	0	4	0-1	.262	.321	.402	.723	6	.942
2001— Pittsburgh (N.L.)		SS-2B-3B	46	129	7	24	3	0	1	8	3	23	0	7	0-3	.186	.203	.233	.436	4	.974
—New York (A.L.)		S-3-2-D	48	99	10	24	5	1	1	12	6	14	0	3	0-2	.242	.283	.343	.626	2	.981
2002— New York (A.L.)		3-S-2-D-O	60	105	17	19	2	2	2	11	8	22	0	2	1-1	.181	.239	.295	.534	5	.955
2003— New York (A.L.)		S-3-2-D	63	135	18	31	9	0	3	15	7	14	2	3	3-1	.230	.276	.363	.639	3	.979
American League totals (7 years)			361	893	117	233	53	4	12	87	57	112	4	23	13-13	.261	.305	.370	.675	22	.973
National League totals (2 years)			86	251	18	56	9	1	4	23	14	36	0	11	0-4	.223	.262	.315	.577	10	.961
Major League totals (7 years)			447	1144	135	289	62	5	16	110	71	148	4	34	13-17	.253	.296	.358	.653	32	.970

WILSON, JACK — SS

PERSONAL: Born December 29, 1977, in Westlake Village, Calif. ... 6-0/193. ... Bats right, throws right. ... Full name: Jack Eugene Wilson. ... High school: Thousand Oaks (Calif.). ... Junior college: Oxnard College (Calif.).

TRANSACTIONS/CAREER NOTES: Selected by St. Louis Cardinals organization in ninth round of free-agent draft (June 2, 1998). ... Traded by Cardinals to Pittsburgh Pirates for P Jason Christiansen (July 30, 2000).

2003 GAMES PLAYED BY POSITION (MLB): SS—149.

W

Year	Team (League)	Pos.	G	AB	R	H	2B	3B	HR	RBI	BB	SO	HBP	GDP	SB-CS	Avg.	OBP	SLG	OPS	E	Pct.
1998— Johnson City (App.)		SS	61	241	50	90	18	4	4	29	18	30	3	4	22-6	.373	.424	.531	.955	16	.940
1999— Peoria (Midw.)		SS	64	251	47	86	22	4	3	28	15	23	2	2	11-5	.343	.384	.498	.882	16	.943
—Potomac Carolina (Caro.)		SS	64	257	44	76	10	1	2	18	19	31	1	2	7-4	.296	.345	.366	.711	18	.941
2000— Potomac Carolina (Caro.)		SS	13	47	7	13	0	1	2	7	5	10	0	1	2-3	.277	.340	.447	.786	2	.967
—Arkansas (Texas)		SS	88	343	65	101	20	8	6	34	36	59	5	5	2-3	.294	.368	.452	.820	12	.971
—Altoona (East.)		SS	33	139	17	35	7	2	1	16	14	17	2	3	1-3	.252	.325	.353	.677	5	.966
2001— Pittsburgh (N.L.)		SS	108	390	44	87	17	1	3	25	16	70	1	4	1-3	.223	.255	.295	.550	16	.968
—Nashville (PCL)		SS	27	103	20	38	6	1	1	6	9	13	2	1	2-2	.369	.430	.476	.906	3	.974
2002— Pittsburgh (N.L.)		SS	147	527	77	133	22	4	4	47	37	74	4	7	5-2	.252	.306	.332	.638	15	.977
2003— Pittsburgh (N.L.)		SS	150	558	58	143	21	3	9	62	36	74	4	11	5-5	.256	.303	.353	.656	17	.975
Major League totals (3 years)			405	1475	179	363	60	8	16	134	89	218	9	22	11-10	.246	.292	.330	.622	48	.974

WILSON, KRIS   P

PERSONAL: Born August 6, 1976, in Washington, District of Columbia. ... 6-4/225. ... Throws right, bats right. ... Full name: Kristopher Kyle Wilson. ... High school: Tarpon Springs (Fla.). ... College: Georgia Tech.

TRANSACTIONS/CAREER NOTES: Selected by Kansas City Royals organization in ninth round of free-agent draft (June 3, 1997). ... On Kansas City disabled list (March 22-May 26, 2002); included rehabilitation assignment to Omaha (May 25-26).

CAREER HITTING: 1-for-3 (.333), 1 R, 0 2B, 0 3B, 0 HR, 0 RBI.

Year League	W	L	Pct.	ERA	WHIP	G	GS	CG	ShO	Hld.	Sv.-Opp.	IP	H	R	ER	HR	BB-IBB	SO	Avg.
1997— Spokane (N'west)	5	3	.625	4.52	1.66	15	15	0	0	...	0-...	73.2	101	50	37	6	21-1	72	.320
1998— Wilmington (Caro.)	0	3	.000	3.75	1.04	10	2	0	0	...	1-...	24.0	19	10	10	0	6-1	20	.229
— Lansing (Midw.)	10	5	.667	3.53	1.14	18	18	1	0	...	0-...	117.1	119	50	46	7	15-0	74	.267
1999— Wilmington (Caro.)	8	1	.889	1.13	0.75	14	4	0	0	...	0-...	48.0	25	7	6	0	11-0	45	.158
— Omaha (PCL)	0	1	.000	8.44	1.50	1	1	0	0	...	0-...	5.1	8	5	5	3	0-0	3	.348
— Wichita (Texas)	5	7	.417	5.45	1.41	23	10	0	0	...	0-...	74.1	91	51	45	11	14-0	45	.301
2000— Wichita (Texas)	7	3	.700	3.51	1.17	21	15	1	0	...	0-...	102.2	99	52	40	12	21-0	69	.252
— Kansas City (A.L.)	0	1	.000	4.19	1.43	20	0	0	0	0	0-1	34.1	38	16	16	3	11-3	17	.288
2001— Kansas City (A.L.)	6	5	.545	5.19	1.50	29	15	0	0	0	1-1	109.1	132	78	63	26	32-0	67	.297
— Omaha (PCL)	2	2	.500	2.79	1.28	6	5	0	0	...	0-...	29.0	31	9	9	2	6-0	18	.279
2002— Wilmington (Caro.)	0	0	...	0.00	0.50	4	3	0	0	...	0-...	8.0	3	0	0	0	1-0	10	.107
— Omaha (PCL)	2	0	1.000	3.08	1.48	8	3	0	0	...	1-...	26.1	38	9	9	0	1-0	17	.342
— Wichita (Texas)	3	3	.500	1.88	1.06	13	7	1	0	...	0-...	48.0	47	17	10	4	4-1	33	.260
— Kansas City (A.L.)	2	0	1.000	8.20	1.82	12	0	0	0	0	0-2	18.2	29	18	17	7	5-0	10	.354
2003— Omaha (PCL)	0	2	.000	8.03	1.95	5	0	0	0	...	0-...	12.1	21	12	11	2	3-0	9	.382
— Kansas City (A.L.)	6	3	.667	5.33	1.49	29	4	0	0	1	0-1	72.2	92	49	43	13	16-3	42	.305
Major League totals (4 years)	**14**	**9**	**.609**	**5.32**	**1.51**	**90**	**19**	**0**	**0**	**1**	**1-5**	**235.0**	**291**	**161**	**139**	**49**	**64-6**	**136**	**.303**

WILSON, PAUL   P

PERSONAL: Born March 28, 1973, in Orlando, Fla. ... 6-5/215. ... Throws right, bats right. ... Full name: Paul Anthony Wilson. ... High school: William R. Boone (Orlando). ... College: Florida State.

TRANSACTIONS/CAREER NOTES: Selected by New York Mets organization in first round (first pick overall) of free-agent draft (June 2, 1994). ... On New York disabled list (June 5-July 15, 1996); included rehabilitation assignments to St. Lucie (June 28-July 10) and Binghamton (July 10-15). ... On New York disabled list (March 27, 1997-entire season); included rehabilitation assignments to Gulf Coast Mets (August 2-23) and St. Lucie (August 28-September 8). ... On New York disabled list (March 13-August 4, 1998); included rehabilitation assignment to St. Lucie (July 9-August 1). ... On disabled list (April 8, 1999-entire season). ... Traded by Mets with OF Jason Tyner to Tampa Bay Devil Rays for OF Bubba Trammell and P Rick White (July 28, 2000). ... Granted free agency (December 21, 2002). ... Signed by Cincinnati Reds (January 11, 2003).

CAREER HITTING: 10-for-107 (.093), 4 R, 1 2B, 0 3B, 1 HR, 5 RBI.

Year League	W	L	Pct.	ERA	WHIP	G	GS	CG	ShO	Hld.	Sv.-Opp.	IP	H	R	ER	HR	BB-IBB	SO	Avg.
1994— GC Mets (GCL)	0	2	.000	3.00	1.00	3	3	0	0	...	0-...	12.0	8	4	4	0	4-0	13	.190
— St. Lucie (Fla. St.)	0	5	.000	5.06	1.31	8	8	0	0	...	0-...	37.1	32	23	21	3	17-1	37	.230
1995— Binghamton (Eastern)	6	3	.667	2.17	0.94	16	16	4	1	...	0-...	120.1	89	34	29	5	24-2	127	.208
— Norfolk (Int'l)	5	3	.625	2.85	1.19	10	10	•4	2	...	0-...	66.1	59	25	21	3	20-0	67	.242
1996— New York (N.L.)	5	12	.294	5.38	1.53	26	26	1	0	0	0-0	149.0	157	102	89	15	71-11	109	.268
— St. Lucie (Fla. St.)	0	1	.000	3.38	1.25	2	2	0	0	...	0-...	8.0	6	5	3	0	4-0	5	.194
— Binghamton (Eastern)	0	1	.000	7.20	2.20	1	1	0	0	...	0-...	5.0	6	4	4	0	5-0	5	.316
1997— GC Mets (GCL)	1	0	1.000	1.45	0.96	4	3	0	0	...	1-...	18.2	14	7	3	0	4-0	18	.203
— St. Lucie (Fla. St.)	0	0	...	2.57	0.86	1	1	0	0	...	0-...	7.0	6	2	2	1	0-0	6	.231
1998— St. Lucie (Fla. St.)	0	1	.000	6.38	1.47	5	5	0	0	...	0-...	18.1	23	13	13	2	4-0	16	.315
— Norfolk (Int'l)	4	1	.800	4.42	1.32	7	7	0	0	...	0-...	38.2	42	19	19	2	9-0	30	.273
1999— Norfolk (Int'l)										Did not play.									
2000— St. Lucie (Fla. St.)	2	0	1.000	1.40	1.01	5	5	0	0	...	0-...	25.2	22	9	4	0	4-0	19	.234
— Norfolk (Int'l)	5	5	.500	4.23	1.33	15	13	0	0	...	0-...	83.0	85	40	39	7	25-1	56	.266
— Tampa Bay (A.L.)	1	4	.200	3.35	1.06	11	7	0	0	1	0-0	51.0	38	20	19	1	16-2	40	.209
2001— Tampa Bay (A.L.)	8	9	.471	4.88	1.43	37	24	0	0	0	0-1	151.1	165	94	82	21	52-2	119	.278
2002— Tampa Bay (A.L.)	6	12	.333	4.83	1.48	30	30	1	0	0	0-0	193.2	219	113	104	29	67-2	111	.287
2003— Cincinnati (N.L.)	8	10	.444	4.64	1.44	28	28	0	0	0	0-0	166.2	190	97	86	24	50-5	93	.285
American League totals (3 years)	**15**	**25**	**.375**	**4.66**	**1.41**	**78**	**61**	**1**	**0**	**1**	**0-1**	**396.0**	**422**	**227**	**205**	**51**	**135-6**	**270**	**.274**
National League totals (2 years)	**13**	**22**	**.371**	**4.99**	**1.48**	**54**	**54**	**1**	**0**	**0**	**0-0**	**315.2**	**347**	**199**	**175**	**39**	**121-16**	**202**	**.277**
Major League totals (5 years)	**28**	**47**	**.373**	**4.81**	**1.44**	**132**	**115**	**2**	**0**	**1**	**0-1**	**711.2**	**769**	**426**	**380**	**90**	**256-22**	**472**	**.276**

WILSON, PRESTON   OF

PERSONAL: Born July 19, 1974, in Bamberg, S.C. ... 6-2/213. ... Bats right, throws right. ... Full name: Preston James Richard Wilson. ... High school: Bamberg Erhardt (Bamberg, S.C.).

TRANSACTIONS/CAREER NOTES: Selected by New York Mets organization in first round (ninth pick overall) of free-agent draft (June 1, 1992). ... On disabled list (April 4-29, May 21-July 13 and July 29-September 8, 1996). ... On Norfolk disabled list (April 20-May 2, 1998). ... Traded by Mets with P Ed Yarnall and P Geoff Goetz to Florida Marlins for C Mike Piazza (May 22, 1998). ... On Florida disabled list (July 2-August 10, 2001); included rehabilitation assignment to Calgary (August 7-10). ... Traded by Marlins with C Charles Johnson, P Vic Darensbourg and 2B Pablo Ozuna to Colorado Rockies for P Mike Hampton, OF Juan Pierre and cash (November 16, 2002).

2003 GAMES PLAYED BY POSITION (MLB): OF—155.

									BATTING											FIELDING	
Year— Team (League)	Pos.	G	AB	R	H	2B	3B	HR	RBI	BB	SO	HBP	GDP	SB-CS	Avg.	OBP	SLG	OPS	E	Pct.
1993— Kingsport (Appal.)	3B	66	259	44	60	10	0	* 16	48	24	75	3	6	6-2	.232	.303	.456	.759	* 25	.873
— Pittsfield (NYP)	3B	8	29	6	16	5	1	1	12	2	7	1	0	1-0	.552	.576	.897	1.472	6	.700
1994— Capital City (SAL)	3B	131	474	55	108	17	4	14	58	20	135	3	4	10-10	.228	.262	.369	.631	47	.884
1995— Capital City (SAL)	OF	111	442	70	119	26	5	20	61	19	114	9	4	20-6	.269	.311	.486	.797	8	.961
1996— St. Lucie (Fla. St.)	OF	23	85	6	15	3	0	1	7	8	21	2	3	1-1	.176	.263	.247	.510	2	.956

W

Year	Team (League)	Pos.	G	AB	R	H	2B	3B	HR	RBI	BB	SO	HBP	GDP	SB-CS	Avg.	OBP	SLG	OPS	E	Pct.
1997— St. Lucie (Fla. St.)	....	OF-DH	63	245	32	60	12	1	11	48	8	66	1	4	3-4	.245	.267	.437	.704	3	.973
— Binghamton (East.)	.........OF-DH-3B	70	259	37	74	12	1	19	47	21	71	2	5	7-1	.286	.340	.560	.900	6	.952
1998— Norfolk (Int'l)	....	OF	18	73	9	18	5	1	1	9	2	22	1	2	1-1	.247	.273	.384	.656	2	.958
— New York (N.L.)	....	OF	8	20	3	6	2	0	0	2	2	8	0	0	1-1	.300	.364	.400	.764	1	.909
— Charlotte (Int'l)	....	OF-DH	94	356	71	99	25	3	25	77	34	121	2	6	14-6	.278	.341	.576	.917	4	.979
— Florida (N.L.)	....	OF	14	31	4	2	0	0	1	1	4	13	1	0	0-0	.065	.194	.161	.356	0	1.000
1999— Florida (N.L.)	....	OF	149	482	67	135	21	4	26	71	46	156	9	15	11-4	.280	.350	.502	.852	9	.973
2000— Florida (N.L.)	....	OF	161	605	94	160	35	3	31	121	55	*187	8	11	36-14	.264	.331	.486	.817	5	.988
2001— Florida (N.L.)	....	OF	123	468	70	128	30	2	23	71	36	107	6	14	20-8	.274	.331	.494	.825	2	.993
— Calgary (PCL)	....	OF	4	10	3	5	2	0	0	1	5	1	0	0	2-0	.500	.667	.700	1.367	0	1.000
2002— Florida (N.L.)	....	OF	141	510	80	124	22	2	23	65	58	140	9	17	20-11	.243	.329	.429	.759	6	.981
2003— Colorado (N.L.)	....	OF	155	600	94	169	43	1	36	*141	54	139	4	23	14-7	.282	.343	.537	.880	7	.980
Major League totals (6 years)			751	2716	412	724	153	12	140	472	255	750	37	80	102-45	.267	.335	.486	.822	30	.983

WILSON, TOM   C

PERSONAL: Born December 19, 1970, in Fullerton, Calif. ... 6-3/220. ... Bats right, throws right. ... Full name: Thomas Leroy Wilson. ... High school: Troy (Fullerton, Calif.). ... Junior college: Fullerton College (Calif.).

TRANSACTIONS/CAREER NOTES: Selected by New York Yankees organization in 23rd round of free-agent draft (June 4, 1990). ... Traded by Yankees to Cleveland Indians for C Ryan Martindale and OF Marc Marini (April 6, 1996). ... Released by Indians (October 15, 1996). ... Signed by Yankees organization (February 1, 1997). ... Granted free agency (October 17, 1997). ... Signed by Arizona Diamondbacks organization (December 15, 1997). ... Granted free agency (October 16, 1998). ... Signed by Tampa Bay Devil Rays organization (November 23, 1998). ... Granted free agency (October 15, 1999). ... Signed by Yankees organization (November 9, 1999). ... Granted free agency (October 15, 2000). ... Signed by Oakland Athletics organization (November 7, 2000). ... Traded by A's to Toronto Blue Jays for C Mike Kremblas (January 2, 2002).

2003 GAMES PLAYED BY POSITION (MLB): C—76, 1B—14, OF—2, DH—1.

Year	Team (League)	Pos.	G	AB	R	H	2B	3B	HR	RBI	BB	SO	HBP	GDP	SB-CS	Avg.	OBP	SLG	OPS	E	Pct.
1991— Oneonta (NYP)	....	C-OF	70	243	38	59	12	2	4	42	34	72	3	6	4-4	.243	.337	.358	.695	17	.950
1992— Greensboro (S. Atl.)	....	C-OF	117	395	50	83	22	0	6	48	68	128	3	8	2-1	.210	.325	.311	.636	10	.984
1993— Greensboro (S. Atl.)	....	C	120	394	55	98	20	1	10	63	•91	112	4	5	2-5	.249	.388	.381	.769	13	.986
1994— Albany (East.)	....	3B-C	123	408	54	100	20	1	7	42	58	100	6	6	4-6	.245	.345	.350	.695	8	.990
1995— Columbus (Int'l)	....	C	22	62	11	16	3	1	0	9	9	10	0	0	0-0	.258	.352	.339	.691	5	.962
— Norwich (East.)	....	3B-C	28	84	6	12	4	0	0	4	17	22	0	3	0-0	.143	.287	.190	.478	6	.964
— Tampa (Fla. St.)	....	C	17	48	3	8	0	0	0	2	11	13	0	0	1-0	.167	.317	.167	.483	0	1.000
1996— Columbus (Int'l)	....	DH	1	1	0	0	0	0	0	0	1	0	0	0	0-0	.000	.500	.000	.500	....	....
— Buffalo (A.A.)	....	SS-C	72	208	28	56	14	2	9	30	35	66	6	4	0-1	.269	.390	.486	.875	5	.988
1997— Norwich (East.)	....	3B-C-1B	124	419	88	124	21	4	21	80	86	126	4	8	1-4	.296	.416	.516	.932	8	.990
— Columbus (Int'l)	....	C	1	3	0	0	0	0	0	0	1	0	0	0	0-0	.000	.250	.000	.250	0	1.000
1998— Tucson (PCL)	....	3-C-1-O	111	370	59	112	17	3	12	54	41	81	7	10	3-1	.303	.380	.462	.842	§ 16	.978
1999— Durham (Int'l)	....	C-1B-OF	67	215	41	60	19	0	16	44	49	59	0	9	0-2	.279	.411	.591	1.002	6	.987
— Orlando (South.)	....	C	30	104	12	30	2	0	7	23	18	34	3	2	0-0	.288	.405	.510	.914	4	.971
2000— Columbus (Int'l)	....	3B-C-OF	104	330	63	91	20	0	20	71	73	114	3	9	2-2	.276	.410	.518	.929	8	.987
2001— Sacramento (PCL)	....	C-3-0-1	77	259	43	73	15	1	8	48	49	62	4	5	0-1	.282	.394	.440	.834	5	.988
— Oakland (A.L.)	....	C	9	21	4	4	0	0	2	4	1	5	1	1	0-0	.190	.250	.476	.726	1	.974
2002— Toronto (A.L.)	....	C-DH-1B	96	265	33	68	10	0	8	37	28	79	5	6	0-0	.257	.334	.385	.719	4	.991
2003— Toronto (A.L.)	....	C-1-O-D	96	256	37	66	19	0	5	35	28	80	1	4	0-0	.258	.331	.391	.722	5	.990
Major League totals (3 years)			201	542	74	138	29	0	15	76	57	164	7	11	0-0	.255	.330	.391	.721	10	.989

WILSON, VANCE   C

PERSONAL: Born March 17, 1973, in Mesa, Ariz. ... 5-11/190. ... Bats right, throws right. ... Full name: Vance Allen Wilson. ... High school: Red Mountain (Mesa, Ariz.). ... Junior college: Mesa (Ari.) Community College.

TRANSACTIONS/CAREER NOTES: Selected by New York Mets organization in 44th round of free-agent draft (June 3, 1993). ... On Norfolk disabled list (May 2-July 18, 1998). ... On New York disabled list (September 8, 1998-remainder of season). ... On Norfolk disabled list (May 13-August 28, 1999). ... On New York disabled list (August 28, 1999-remainder of season).

2003 GAMES PLAYED BY POSITION (MLB): C—89.

Year	Team (League)	Pos.	G	AB	R	H	2B	3B	HR	RBI	BB	SO	HBP	GDP	SB-CS	Avg.	OBP	SLG	OPS	E	Pct.
1994— Pittsfield (NYP)	....	C	44	166	22	51	12	0	2	20	5	27	5	1	4-1	.307	.343	.416	.758	5	.977
1995— Capital City (SAL)	....	C	91	324	34	81	11	0	6	32	19	45	8	6	4-3	.250	.306	.340	.645	* 14	.981
1996— St. Lucie (Fla. St.)	....	C	93	311	29	76	14	2	6	44	31	41	6	7	2-4	.244	.321	.360	.681	8	.987
1997— Binghamton (East.)	....	C	92	322	46	89	17	0	15	40	20	46	5	6	2-5	.276	.328	.469	.797	11	.984
1998— Norfolk (Int'l)	....	C	46	154	18	40	3	0	4	16	9	29	1	5	0-3	.260	.305	.357	.662	4	.990
— GC Mets (GCL)	....	C	10	28	5	10	5	0	2	9	0	0	1	2	0-1	.357	.367	.750	1.117	2	.957
— St. Lucie (Fla. St.)	....	C	4	16	0	1	0	0	0	0	0	5	0	0	0-0	.063	.063	.063	.125	0	1.000
1999— Norfolk (Int'l)	....	C	15	53	10	14	3	0	3	5	4	8	1	4	1-0	.264	.328	.491	.818	1	.991
— New York (N.L.)	....	C	1	0	0	0	0	0	0	0	0	0	0	0	0-0	....	....	....	....	0	....
2000— Norfolk (Int'l)	....	C	111	400	47	104	23	1	16	62	24	65	12	12	11-6	.260	.319	.443	.761	3	.990
— New York (N.L.)	....	C	4	4	0	0	0	0	0	0	0	2	0	0	0-0	.000	.000	.000	.000	0	1.000
2001— Norfolk (Int'l)	....	C	65	228	24	56	14	0	6	31	12	34	9	7	0-1	.246	.306	.386	.692	8	.984
— New York (N.L.)	....	C	32	57	3	17	3	0	0	6	2	16	2	1	0-1	.298	.339	.351	.690	1	.993
2002— New York (N.L.)	....	C-1B	74	163	19	40	7	0	5	26	5	32	8	4	0-1	.245	.301	.380	.682	6	.983
2003— New York (N.L.)	....	C	96	268	28	65	9	1	8	39	15	56	5	6	1-2	.243	.293	.373	.666	5	.990
Major League totals (5 years)			207	492	50	122	19	1	13	71	22	106	15	11	1-4	.248	.299	.370	.669	12	.988

WINN, RANDY — OF

PERSONAL: Born June 9, 1974, in Los Angeles, Calif. ... 6-2/197. ... Bats both, throws right. ... Full name: Dwight Randolph Winn. ... High school: San Ramon Valley (Danville, Calif.). ... College: Santa Clara.

TRANSACTIONS/CAREER NOTES: Selected by Florida Marlins organization in third round of free-agent draft (June 1, 1995). ... On disabled list (August 22-September 11, 1995). ... Selected by Tampa Bay Devil Rays in third round (58th pick overall) of expansion draft (November 18, 1997). ... Traded by Devil Rays to Seattle Mariners for SS Antonio Perez (October 28, 2002).

2003 GAMES PLAYED BY POSITION (MLB): OF—157.

Year Team (League)	Pos.	G	AB	R	H	2B	3B	HR	RBI	BB	SO	HBP	GDP	SB-CS	Avg.	OBP	SLG	OPS	E	Pct.
1995— Elmira (N.Y.-Penn)	OF	51	213	38	67	7	4	0	22	15	31	3	1	19-7	.315	.365	.385	.750	5	.954
1996— Kane Co. (Midw.)	OF	130	514	90	139	16	3	0	35	47	115	8	3	30-18	.270	.340	.313	.654	8	.970
1997— Brevard County (FSL)	OF	36	143	26	45	8	2	0	15	16	28	5	3	16-8	.315	.400	.399	.799	0	1.000
—Portland (East.)	OF	96	384	66	112	15	6	8	36	42	92	7	4	35-20	.292	.371	.424	.795	4	.979
1998— Durham (Int'l)	OF	29	123	25	35	5	2	1	16	15	24	0	1	10-4	.285	.362	.382	.744	2	.966
—Tampa Bay (A.L.)	OF-DH	109	338	51	94	9	9	1	17	29	69	1	2	26-12	.278	.337	.367	.704	4	.980
1999— Durham (Int'l)	OF	46	207	38	73	20	3	3	30	16	27	1	2	9-6	.353	.402	.522	.924	4	.966
—Tampa Bay (A.L.)	OF	79	303	44	81	16	4	2	24	17	63	1	3	9-9	.267	.307	.366	.673	1	.995
2000— Durham (Int'l)	OF	79	303	67	100	24	5	7	40	48	53	3	5	18-5	.330	.425	.512	.937	7	.960
—Tampa Bay (A.L.)	OF-DH	51	159	28	40	5	0	1	16	26	25	2	2	6-7	.252	.362	.302	.664	1	.990
2001— Tampa Bay (A.L.)	OF-DH	128	429	54	117	25	6	6	50	38	81	6	10	12-10	.273	.339	.401	.740	5	.981
2002— Tampa Bay (A.L.)	OF-DH	152	607	87	181	39	6	14	75	55	109	6	9	27-8	.298	.360	.461	.821	3	.993
2003— Seattle (A.L.)	OF	157	600	103	177	37	4	11	75	41	108	8	9	23-5	.295	.346	.425	.771	3	.992
Major League totals (6 years)		676	2436	367	690	131	32	35	257	206	455	24	35	103-51	.283	.343	.406	.750	17	.989

WITASICK, JAY — P

PERSONAL: Born August 28, 1972, in Baltimore, Md. ... 6-4/235. ... Throws right, bats right. ... Full name: Gerald Alphonse Witasick. ... Name pronounced: wi-TASS-ik. ... High school: C. Milton Wright (Bel Air, Md.). ... College: Maryland-Baltimore County.

TRANSACTIONS/CAREER NOTES: Selected by St. Louis Cardinals organization in second round of free-agent draft (June 3, 1993). ... On disabled list (July 17, 1995-remainder of season). ... Traded by Cardinals with OF Allen Battle, P Bret Wagner and P Carl Dale to Oakland Athletics for P Todd Stottlemyre (January 9, 1996). ... On Oakland disabled list (March 31-June 14, 1997); included rehabilitation assignment to Modesto (June 11-14). ... Traded by A's to Kansas City Royals for a player to be named later and cash (March 30, 1999); A's acquired P Scott Chiasson to complete deal (June 10, 1999). ... Traded by Royals to San Diego Padres for P Brian Meadows (July 31, 2000). ... Traded by Padres to New York Yankees for IF D'Angelo Jimenez (June 23, 2001). ... Traded by Yankees to San Francisco Giants for OF John Vander Wal (December 13, 2001). ... On San Francisco disabled list (July 27-August 15, 2002); included rehabilitation assignment to Fresno (August 10-15). ... Granted free agency (December 21, 2002). ... Signed by Padres (December 24, 2002). ... On disabled list (March 21, 2003). ... Transferred to Emergency disabled list (May 16, 2003). ... Contract purchased by San Diego (May 18, 2003). ... Activated from the 60-day disabled list by San Diego; recalled from Portland rehab assignment (June 9, 2003).

CAREER HITTING: 3-for-37 (.081), 0 R, 0 2B, 0 3B, 0 HR, 3 RBI.

Year League	W	L	Pct.	ERA	WHIP	G	GS	CG	ShO	Hld.	Sv.-Opp.	IP	H	R	ER	HR	BB-IBB	SO	Avg.
1993— Johnson City (App.)	4	3	.571	4.12	1.24	12	12	0	0	...	0-...	67.2	65	42	31	8	19-0	74	.246
—Savannah (S. Atl.)	1	0	1.000	4.50	1.50	1	1	0	0	...	0-...	6.0	7	3	3	0	2-0	8	.280
1994— Madison (Midw.)	10	4	.714	2.32	1.03	18	18	2	0	...	0-...	112.1	74	36	29	5	42-0	141	.189
1995— St. Pete. (FSL)	7	7	.500	2.74	1.10	18	18	1	1	...	0-...	105.0	80	39	32	4	36-1	109	.208
—Arkansas (Texas)	2	4	.333	6.88	1.82	7	7	0	0	...	0-...	34.0	46	29	26	4	16-1	26	.317
1996— Huntsville (Sou.)	0	3	.000	2.30	1.10	25	6	0	0	...	4-...	66.2	47	21	17	3	26-2	63	.195
—Oakland (A.L.)	1	1	.500	6.23	1.31	12	0	0	0	0	0-1	13.0	12	9	9	5	5-0	12	.245
—Edmonton (PCL)	0	0	...	4.15	1.73	6	0	0	0	0	2-...	8.2	9	4	4	1	6-0	9	.300
1997— Modesto (Calif.)	0	1	.000	4.15	1.21	9	2	0	0	...	1-...	17.1	16	9	8	1	5-0	29	.232
—Edmonton (PCL)	3	2	.600	4.28	1.46	13	1	0	0	...	0-...	27.1	25	13	13	3	15-3	17	.243
—Oakland (A.L.)	0	0	...	5.73	1.82	8	0	0	0	1	0-0	11.0	14	7	7	2	6-0	8	.304
1998— Edmonton (PCL)	11	7	.611	3.87	1.17	27	26	2	1	...	0-...	149.0	126	74	64	19	49-0	155	.226
—Oakland (A.L.)	1	3	.250	6.33	1.89	7	3	0	0	0	0-0	27.0	36	24	19	9	15-1	29	.310
1999— Kansas City (A.L.)	9	12	.429	5.57	1.73	32	28	1	1	0	0-0	158.1	191	108	98	23	83-1	102	.304
2000— Kansas City (A.L.)	3	8	.273	5.94	1.65	22	14	2	0	0	0-0	89.1	109	65	59	15	38-0	67	.301
—San Diego (N.L.)	3	2	.600	5.64	1.71	11	11	0	0	0	0-0	60.2	69	42	38	9	35-5	54	.284
2001— San Diego (N.L.)	5	2	.714	1.86	1.19	31	0	0	0	5	1-3	38.2	31	14	8	3	15-3	53	.218
—New York (A.L.)	3	0	1.000	4.69	1.61	32	0	0	0	5	0-1	40.1	47	27	21	5	18-1	53	.283
2002— San Francisco (N.L.)	1	0	1.000	2.37	1.16	44	0	0	0	4	0-0	68.1	58	19	18	3	21-3	54	.234
—Fresno (PCL)	0	0	...	4.50	1.00	2	2	0	0	...	0-...	2.0	1	1	1	0	1-0	2	.143
2003— Lake Elsinore (Calif.)	0	0	...	5.79	1.29	4	0	0	0	...	0-...	4.2	6	4	3	0	0-0	7	.300
—Portland (PCL)	0	0	...	3.00	0.83	5	0	0	0	...	1-...	6.0	4	2	2	0	1-0	8	.182
—San Diego (N.L.)	3	7	.300	4.53	1.47	46	0	0	0	12	2-7	45.2	42	24	23	6	25-4	42	.244
American League totals (6 years)	17	24	.415	5.65	1.69	113	45	3	1	6	0-2	339.0	409	240	213	59	165-3	271	.299
National League totals (4 years)	12	11	.522	3.67	1.39	132	11	0	0	21	3-10	213.1	200	99	87	21	96-15	203	.248
Major League totals (8 years)	29	35	.453	4.89	1.58	245	56	3	1	27	3-12	552.1	609	339	300	80	261-18	474	.280

WITT, KEVIN — 1B/OF

PERSONAL: Born January 5, 1976, in High Point, N.C. ... 6-4/220. ... Bats left, throws right. ... Full name: Kevin Joseph Witt. ... High school: Bishop Kenny (Jacksonville, Fla.).

TRANSACTIONS/CAREER NOTES: Selected by Toronto Blue Jays organization in first round (28th pick overall) of free-agent draft (June 2, 1994). ... Granted free agency (October 18, 2000). ... Signed by San Diego Padres organization (December 15, 2000). ... Granted free agency (October 15, 2001). ... Signed by Cincinnati Reds organization (December 21, 2001). ... Granted free agency (October 15, 2002). ... Signed by Detroit Tigers organization (January 29, 2003). ... Contract purchased by Detroit Tigers (May 16, 2003).

2003 GAMES PLAYED BY POSITION (MLB): DH—36, 1B—27, OF—13, 3B—5.

								BATTING												FIELDING	
Year	Team (League)	Pos.	G	AB	R	H	2B	3B	HR	RBI	BB	SO	HBP	GDP	SB-CS	Avg.	OBP	SLG	OPS	E	Pct.
1994—Medicine Hat (Pio.)	SS	60	243	37	62	10	4	7	36	15	52	1	3	4-1	.255	.300	.416	.716	25	.914	
1995—Hagerstown (SAL)	SS	119	479	58	111	35	1	14	50	28	148	4	5	1-5	.232	.280	.397	.677	48	.919	
1996—Dunedin (Fla. St.)	SS	124	446	63	121	18	6	13	70	39	96	6	9	9-4	.271	.335	.426	.761	48	.917	
1997—Knoxville (Sou.) 1-3-D-O-S	127	501	76	145	27	4	•30	91	44	109	3	13	1-0	.289	.349	.539	.888	15	.978		
1998—Syracuse (Int'l) 1B-OF-DH	126	455	71	124	20	3	23	67	53	124	7	5	3-3	.273	.354	.481	.835	4	.996		
—Toronto (A.L.)	1B	5	7	0	1	0	0	0	0	0	3	0	0	0-0	.143	.143	.143	.286	0	1.000	
1999—Syracuse (Int'l)	1B-OF	114	421	72	117	24	3	24	71	64	109	3	11	0-0	.278	.376	.520	.896	4	.994	
—Toronto (A.L.)	DH	15	34	3	7	1	0	1	5	2	9	0	0	0-0	.206	.250	.324	.574	0	...	
2000—Syracuse (Int'l)	1B-OF	135	489	58	121	24	5	26	72	45	132	4	9	1-1	.247	.316	.476	.792	‡ 14	.986	
2001—Portland (PCL) 1B-OF-3B	129	456	66	132	28	5	27	87	22	127	3	13	1-1	.289	.322	.550	.873	12	.984		
—San Diego (N.L.)	1B	14	27	5	5	0	0	2	5	2	7	0	0	0-0	.185	.233	.407	.641	0	1.000	
2002—Louisville (Int'l) 1B-OF-3B	131	509	77	134	32	1	24	*107	34	140	6	18	0-1	.263	.314	.472	.786	9	.987		
2003—Toledo (Int'l) 1B-3B-DH	39	133	22	42	10	0	9	28	16	36	1	2	0-0	.316	.391	.594	.985	9	.967		
—Detroit (A.L.)	D-1-O-3	93	270	25	71	9	0	10	26	15	68	1	5	1-1	.263	.301	.407	.708	0	1.000	
American League totals (3 years)		113	311	28	79	10	0	11	31	17	80	1	5	1-1	.254	.292	.392	.684	0	1.000	
National League totals (1 year)		14	27	5	5	0	0	2	5	2	7	0	0	0-0	.185	.233	.407	.641	0	1.000	
Major League totals (4 years)		127	338	33	84	10	0	13	36	19	87	1	5	1-1	.249	.287	.393	.681	0	1.000	

WOHLERS, MARK — P

PERSONAL: Born January 23, 1970... 6-4/207. ... Throws right, bats right. ... Full name: Mark Edward Wohlers. ... High school: Holyoke (Mass.).

TRANSACTIONS/CAREER NOTES: Selected by Atlanta Braves organization in eighth round of free-agent draft (June 1, 1988). ... On Atlanta disabled list (May 3-24 and August 21, 1998-remainder of season); included rehabilitation assignments to Greenville (May 23) and Richmond (August 25-September 8). ... Traded by Braves with cash to Cincinnati Reds for P John Hudek (April 16, 1999). ... On Cincinnati disabled list (April 17, 1999-remainder of season); included rehabilitation assignments to Indianapolis (May 2-3), Rockford (June 17-21) and Chattanooga (June 22-July 1). ... Granted free agency (November 5, 1999). ... Re-signed by Reds organization (January 28, 2000). ... On Louisville disabled list (April 6-May 29, 2000). ... Granted free agency (October 31, 2000). ... Re-signed by Reds (December 15, 2000). ... Traded by Reds to New York Yankees for P Ricardo Aromboles (June 30, 2001). ... Granted free agency (November 5, 2001). ... Signed by Cleveland Indians (January 10, 2002). ... On disabled list (March 29-entire 2003 season).

CAREER HITTING: 1-for-12 (.083), 1 R, 0 2B, 0 3B, 0 HR, 0 RBI.

Year	League	W	L	Pct.	ERA	WHIP	G	GS	CG	ShO	Hld.	Sv.-Opp.	IP	H	R	ER	HR	BB-IBB	SO	Avg.
1988—Pulaski (Appal.)	5	3	.625	3.32	1.63	13	9	1	0	...	0-...	59.2	47	37	22	0	50-0	49	.215
1989—Sumter (S. Atl.)	2	7	.222	6.49	1.96	14	14	0	0	...	0-...	68.0	74	55	49	3	59-0	51	.288
—Pulaski (Appal.)	1	1	.500	5.48	1.65	14	8	0	0	...	0-...	46.0	48	36	28	5	28-0	50	.255
1990—Sumter (S. Atl.)	5	4	.556	1.88	0.89	37	2	0	0	...	5-...	52.2	27	13	11	1	20-0	85	.149
—Greenville (Sou.)	0	1	.000	4.02	1.79	14	0	0	0	...	6-...	15.2	14	7	7	0	14-0	20	.250
1991—Greenville (Sou.)	0	0	...	0.57	0.70	28	0	0	0	...	21-...	31.1	9	4	2	0	13-0	44	.092
—Richmond (Int'l)	1	0	1.000	1.03	1.33	23	0	0	0	...	11-...	26.1	23	4	3	1	12-1	22	.245
—Atlanta (N.L.)	3	1	.750	3.20	1.53	17	0	0	0	2	2-4	19.2	17	7	7	1	13-3	13	.239
1992—Richmond (Int'l)	0	2	.000	3.93	1.43	27	2	0	0	...	9-...	34.1	32	16	15	5	17-3	33	.248
—Atlanta (N.L.)	1	2	.333	2.55	1.19	32	0	0	0	2	4-6	35.1	28	11	10	0	14-4	17	.235
1993—Richmond (Int'l)	1	3	.250	1.84	1.09	25	0	0	0	...	4-...	29.1	21	7	6	0	11-0	39	.194
—Atlanta (N.L.)	6	2	.750	4.50	1.23	46	0	0	0	12	0-0	48.0	37	25	24	2	22-3	45	.218
1994—Atlanta (N.L.)	7	2	.778	4.59	1.65	51	0	0	0	7	1-2	51.0	51	35	26	1	33-9	58	.264
1995—Atlanta (N.L.)	7	3	.700	2.09	1.16	65	0	0	0	2	25-29	64.2	51	16	15	2	24-3	90	.211
1996—Atlanta (N.L.)	2	4	.333	3.03	1.19	77	0	0	0	0	39-44	77.1	71	30	26	8	21-3	100	.240
1997—Atlanta (N.L.)	5	7	.417	3.50	1.37	71	0	0	0	1	33-40	69.1	57	29	27	4	38-0	92	.224
1998—Atlanta (N.L.)	0	1	.000	10.18	2.51	27	0	0	0	0	8-8	20.1	18	23	23	2	33-0	22	.331
—Greenville (Sou.)	0	0	...	0.00	2.00	1	1	0	0	...	0-...	1.0	1	1	0	0	1-0	1	.333
—Richmond (Int'l)	0	3	.000	20.43	4.62	16	0	0	0	...	0-...	12.1	21	28	28	5	36-0	16	.382
1999—Atlanta (N.L.)	0	0	...	27.00	10.50	2	0	0	0	0	0-0	.2	1	2	2	0	6-0	0	.333
—Indianapolis (Int'l)	0	0	...	99.99	18.00	1	0	0	0	...	0-...	.1	1	4	4	0	5-0	1	.500
—Rockford (Midwest)	0	0	...	4.50	1.50	2	0	0	0	...	0-...	2.0	1	1	1	0	2-0	4	.143
—Chattanooga (Sou.)	0	0	...	16.20	2.40	2	0	0	0	...	0-...	1.2	1	3	3	1	3-0	3	.167
2000—Dayton (Midw.)	0	0	...	3.00	0.67	3	3	0	0	...	0-...	3.0	1	1	1	0	1-0	1	.100
—Louisville (Int'l)	1	2	.333	6.10	1.89	17	2	0	0	...	0-...	20.2	30	21	14	4	9-0	16	.330
—Cincinnati (N.L.)	1	2	.333	4.50	1.29	20	0	0	0	0	0-0	28.0	19	14	14	3	17-0	20	.192
2001—Cincinnati (N.L.)	3	1	.750	3.94	1.34	30	0	0	0	8	0-1	32.0	36	20	14	5	7-2	21	.286
—New York (A.L.)	1	0	1.000	4.54	1.43	31	0	0	0	5	0-0	35.2	33	20	18	3	18-0	33	.241
2002—Cleveland (A.L.)	3	4	.429	4.79	1.36	64	0	0	0	10	7-11	71.1	71	44	38	6	26-3	46	.261
2003—Akron (East.)	0	0	...	5.40	4.20	2	1	0	0	...	0-...	1.2	5	1	1	0	2-0	1	.625
American League totals (2 years)	4	4	.500	4.71	1.38	95	0	0	0	15	7-11	107.0	104	61	56	9	44-3	79	.254
National League totals (11 years)	35	25	.583	3.79	1.38	438	0	0	0	34	112-134	446.1	386	212	188	28	228-27	478	.234
Major League totals (12 years)	39	29	.574	3.97	1.38	533	0	0	0	49	119-145	553.1	490	273	244	37	272-30	557	.238

WOLF, RANDY — P

PERSONAL: Born August 22, 1976, in Canoga Park, Calif. ... 6-0/194. ... Throws left, bats left. ... Full name: Randall Christopher Wolf. ... High school: El Camino Real (Woodland Hills, Calif.). ... College: Pepperdine.

TRANSACTIONS/CAREER NOTES: Selected by Los Angeles Dodgers organization in 25th round of free-agent draft (June 2, 1994); did not sign. ... Selected by Philadelphia Phillies organization in second round of free-agent draft (June 3, 1997). ... On Philadelphia disabled list (August 2-September 1, 2001); included rehabilitation assignments to Scranton/Wilkes-Barre (August 17-28) and Reading (August 29-September 1). ... On Philadelphia disabled list (March 25-April 12, 2002); included rehabilitation assignment to Clearwater (April 6-12).

CAREER HITTING: 48-for-261 (.184), 24 R, 13 2B, 0 3B, 1 HR, 21 RBI.

Year	League	W	L	Pct.	ERA	WHIP	G	GS	CG	ShO	Hld.	Sv.-Opp.	IP	H	R	ER	HR	BB-IBB	SO	Avg.
1997—Batavia (N.Y.-Penn)	4	0	1.000	1.58	0.93	7	7	0	0	...	0-...	40.0	29	8	7	1	8-0	53	.204
1998—Reading (East.)	2	0	1.000	1.44	0.76	4	4	0	0	...	0-...	25.0	15	4	4	0	4-0	33	.172
—Scran./W.B. (I.L.)	9	7	.563	4.62	1.45	24	23	1	0	...	0-...	148.0	167	88	76	16	48-4	118	.285
1999—Scran./W.B. (I.L.)	4	5	.444	3.61	1.32	12	12	0	0	...	0-...	77.1	73	36	31	8	29-1	72	.247
—Philadelphia (N.L.)	6	9	.400	5.55	1.59	22	21	0	0	...	0-0	121.2	126	78	75	20	67-0	116	.266

W

Year League	W	L	Pct.	ERA	WHIP	G	GS	CG	ShO	Hld.	Sv.-Opp.	IP	H	R	ER	HR	BB-IBB	SO	Avg.
2000— Philadelphia (N.L.)	11	9	.550	4.36	1.42	32	32	1	0	0	0-0	206.1	210	107	100	25	83-2	160	.269
2001— Philadelphia (N.L.)	10	11	.476	3.70	1.23	28	25	4	2	0	0-0	163.0	150	74	67	15	51-4	152	.248
— Scran./W.B. (I.L.)	0	1	.000	5.00	1.67	2	2	0	0	...	0-...	9.0	10	6	5	2	5-0	7	.286
— Reading (East.)	0	0	...	4.50	1.17	1	1	0	0	...	0-...	6.0	5	3	3	0	2-0	7	.208
2002— Clearwater (Fla. St.)	0	0	...	0.00	0.40	1	1	0	0	...	0-...	5.0	1	0	0	0	1-0	8	.071
— Philadelphia (N.L.)	11	9	.550	3.20	1.12	31	31	3	2	0	0-0	210.2	172	77	75	23	63-5	172	.223
2003— Philadelphia (N.L.)	16	10	.615	4.23	1.27	33	33	2	2	0	0-0	200.0	176	101	94	27	78-4	177	.233
Major League totals (5 years)	54	48	.529	4.10	1.30	146	142	10	6	0	0-0	901.2	834	437	411	110	342-15	777	.246

WOMACK, TONY   SS

PERSONAL: Born September 25, 1969, in Danville, Va. ... 5-9/168. ... Bats left, throws right. ... Full name: Anthony Darrell Womack. ... Name pronounced: WO-mack. ... High school: Gretna (Va.). ... College: Guilford (N.C.).

TRANSACTIONS/CAREER NOTES: Selected by Pittsburgh Pirates organization in seventh round of free-agent draft (June 3, 1991). ... On disabled list (April 17-26 and August 28, 1992-remainder of season). ... Traded by Pirates to Arizona Diamondbacks for OF Paul Weichard and a player to be named later (February 26, 1999); Pirates acquired P Jason Boyd to complete deal (August 25, 1999). ... On Arizona disabled list (March 26-April 12, 1999); included rehabilitation assignment to Tucson (April 8-12). ... On Arizona disabled list (July 23-August 6, 2001); included rehabilitation assignment to Tucson (August 2-6). ... Placed on 15-day disabled list (June 29, 2003). ... Sent to El Paso on rehab assignment (July 10, 2003). ... Traded by Diamondbacks to Colorado Rockies for P Mike Watson (July 18, 2003). ... Traded by Rockies to Chicago Cubs for P Enmanuel Ramires (August 19, 2003).

2003 GAMES PLAYED BY POSITION (MLB): SS—73, 2B—21, OF—1.

									BATTING										FIELDING	
Year Team (League)	Pos.	G	AB	R	H	2B	3B	HR	RBI	BB	SO	HBP	GDP	SB-CS	Avg.	OBP	SLG	OPS	E	Pct.
1991— Welland (NYP)	2B-SS	45	166	30	46	3	0	1	8	17	39	0	1	26-5	.277	.344	.313	.658	16	.921
1992— Augusta (S. Atl.)	2B-SS	102	380	62	93	8	3	0	18	41	59	5	2	50-25	.245	.325	.282	.606	40	.923
1993— Salem (Caro.)	SS	72	304	41	91	11	3	2	18	13	34	2	2	28-14	.299	.331	.375	.706	28	.927
— Carolina (Sou.)	SS	60	247	41	75	7	2	0	23	17	34	1	3	21-6	.304	.346	.348	.694	11	.961
— Pittsburgh (N.L.)	SS	15	24	5	2	0	0	0	0	3	3	0	0	2-0	.083	.185	.083	.269	1	.971
1994— Buffalo (A.A.)	SS-2B	106	421	40	93	9	2	0	18	19	76	0	2	41-10	.221	.253	.252	.505	22	.957
— Pittsburgh (N.L.)	2B-SS	5	12	4	4	0	0	0	1	2	3	0	0	0-0	.333	.429	.333	.762	2	.818
1995— Calgary (PCL)	2B-SS	30	107	12	30	3	1	0	6	12	11	0	1	7-5	.280	.353	.327	.680	5	.963
— Carolina (Sou.)	SS-2B	82	332	52	85	9	4	1	19	19	36	2	2	27-10	.256	.300	.316	.617	18	.953
1996— Calgary (PCL)	S-2-O-D	131	506	75	151	19	11	1	47	31	79	3	3	37-12	.298	.339	.385	.725	24	.961
— Pittsburgh (N.L.)	OF-2B	17	30	11	10	3	1	0	7	6	1	1	0	2-0	.333	.459	.500	.959	2	.905
1997— Pittsburgh (N.L.)	2B-SS	155	641	85	178	26	9	6	50	43	109	3	6	* 60-7	.278	.326	.374	.700	‡ 20	.975
1998— Pittsburgh (N.L.)	2B-OF-SS	159	655	85	185	26	7	3	45	38	94	0	4	* 58-8	.282	.319	.357	.677	17	.978
1999— Tucson (PCL)	OF	4	16	1	4	1	0	1	3	2	3	0	2	0-1	.250	.333	.500	.833	0	1.000
— Arizona (N.L.)	OF-2B-SS	144	614	111	170	25	10	4	41	52	68	2	4	* 72-13	.277	.332	.370	.702	5	.987
2000— Arizona (N.L.)	SS-OF	146	617	95	167	21	* 14	7	57	30	74	5	6	45-11	.271	.307	.384	.692	18	.970
2001— Arizona (N.L.)	SS-OF	125	481	66	128	19	5	3	30	23	54	6	4	28-7	.266	.307	.345	.652	22	.955
— Tucson (PCL)	SS	4	13	1	5	0	1	0	2	0	1	0	0	0-1	.385	.385	.538	.923	2	.846
2002— Arizona (N.L.)	SS-OF	153	590	90	160	23	5	5	57	46	80	4	9	29-12	.271	.325	.353	.678	20	.964
2003— Arizona (N.L.)	SS	61	219	30	52	10	3	2	15	8	27	2	6	8-3	.237	.270	.338	.607	7	.966
— El Paso (Texas)	SS	4	17	3	5	0	0	0	2	2	2	0	0	3-0	.294	.368	.294	.663	1	.923
— Colorado (N.L.)	SS-2B-OF	21	79	9	15	2	0	0	5	0	9	1	1	3-1	.190	.200	.215	.415	2	.974
— Chicago (N.L.)	2B-SS	21	51	4	12	2	1	0	2	1	11	0	0	2-1	.235	.250	.314	.564	0	1.000
Major League totals (10 years)		1022	4013	595	1083	157	55	30	310	252	533	24	40	309-63	.270	.315	.359	.674	116	.971

WOOD, KERRY   P

PERSONAL: Born June 16, 1977, in Irving, Texas. ... 6-5/225. ... Throws right, bats right. ... Full name: Kerry Lee Wood. ... High school: Grand Prairie (Texas).

TRANSACTIONS/CAREER NOTES: Selected by Chicago Cubs organization in first round (fourth pick overall) of free-agent draft (June 1, 1995). ... On disabled list (May 24-June 19, 1996). ... On disabled list (March 31, 1999-entire season). ... On Chicago disabled list (March 25-May 2 and July 30-August 22, 2000); included rehabilitation assignments to Daytona (April 13-23) and Iowa (April 23-April 28). ... On suspended list (September 8-11, 2000). ... On disabled list (August 4-September 7, 2001).

CAREER HITTING: 48-for-275 (.175), 21 R, 2 2B, 0 3B, 6 HR, 25 RBI.

Year League	W	L	Pct.	ERA	WHIP	G	GS	CG	ShO	Hld.	Sv.-Opp.	IP	H	R	ER	HR	BB-IBB	SO	Avg.
1995— GC Cubs (GCL)	0	0	...	0.00	0.33	1	1	0	0	...	0-...	3.0	0	0	0	0	1-0	2	.000
— Williamsport (NYP)	0	0	...	10.38	2.31	2	2	0	0	...	0-...	4.1	5	8	5	0	5-0	5	.278
1996— Daytona (Fla. St.)	10	2	.833	2.91	1.24	22	22	0	0	...	0-...	114.1	72	51	37	6	70-0	136	.179
1997— Orlando (Sou.)	6	7	.462	4.50	1.46	19	19	0	0	...	0-...	94.0	58	49	47	2	79-2	106	.181
— Iowa (Am. Assoc.)	4	2	.667	4.68	1.51	10	10	0	0	...	0-...	57.2	35	35	30	2	52-0	80	.181
1998— Iowa (PCL)	1	0	1.000	0.00	0.60	1	1	0	0	...	0-...	5.0	1	0	0	0	2-0	11	.067
— Chicago (N.L.)	13	6	.684	3.40	1.21	26	26	1	1	0	0-0	166.2	117	69	63	14	85-1	233	*.196
1999— Chicago (N.L.)											Did not play.								
2000— Daytona (Fla. St.)	2	0	1.000	1.50	0.67	2	2	0	0	...	0-...	12.0	3	2	2	0	5-0	17	.081
— Iowa (PCL)	0	0	...	2.57	1.14	1	1	0	0	...	0-...	7.0	4	2	2	1	4-0	7	.174
— Chicago (N.L.)	8	7	.533	4.80	1.45	23	23	1	0	0	0-0	137.0	112	77	73	17	87-0	132	.226
2001— Chicago (N.L.)	12	6	.667	3.36	1.26	28	28	1	1	0	0-0	174.1	127	70	65	16	92-3	217	*.202
2002— Chicago (N.L.)	12	11	.522	3.66	1.24	33	33	4	1	0	0-0	213.2	169	92	87	22	97-5	217	.221
2003— Chicago (N.L.)	14	11	.560	3.20	1.19	32	32	4	2	0	0-0	211.0	152	77	75	24	100-2	*266	.203
Major League totals (5 years)	59	41	.590	3.62	1.26	142	142	11	5	0	0-0	902.2	677	385	363	93	461-11	1065	.209

WOOD, MIKE   P

PERSONAL: Born April 26, 1980, in West Palm Beach, Fla. ... 6-3/180. ... Throws right, bats right. ... Full name: Michael Burton Wood. ... High school: Forest Hill Community (West Palm Beach, Fla.). ... College: North Florida.

TRANSACTIONS/CAREER NOTES: Selected by Oakland A's organization in 10th round of free-agent draft (June 5, 2001).

CAREER HITTING: 0-for-0 (.000), 0 R, 0 2B, 0 3B, 0 HR, 0 RBI.

W

Year League	W	L	Pct.	ERA	WHIP	G	GS	CG	ShO	Hld.	Sv.-Opp.	IP	H	R	ER	HR	BB-IBB	SO	Avg.
2001— Vancouver (NW)	2	0	1.000	1.25	0.97	5	2	0	0	...	0-...	21.2	17	4	3	0	4-0	24	.210
— Modesto (Calif.)	4	3	.571	3.09	0.96	10	9	0	0	...	0-...	58.1	46	22	20	6	10-3	52	.211
2002— Modesto (Calif.)	3	3	.500	3.48	1.14	7	7	0	0	...	0-...	41.1	41	17	16	4	6-0	50	.265
— Midland (Texas)	11	3	.786	3.15	1.25	17	17	0	0	...	0-...	105.2	103	41	37	8	29-0	63	.259
2003— Sacramento (PCL)	9	3	.750	3.05	1.20	16	16	0	0	...	0-...	91.1	87	34	31	5	23-1	59	.257
— Oakland (A.L.)	2	1	.667	10.54	2.27	7	1	0	0	0	0-0	13.2	24	17	16	1	7-2	15	.387
Major League totals (1 year)	2	1	.667	10.54	2.27	7	1	0	0	0	0-0	13.2	24	17	16	1	7-2	15	.387

WOODARD, STEVE — P

PERSONAL: Born May 15, 1975, in Hartselle, Ala. ... 6-4/210. ... Throws right, bats left. ... Full name: Steve Larry Woodard. ... High school: Hartselle (Ala.).

TRANSACTIONS/CAREER NOTES: Selected by Milwaukee Brewers organization in fifth round of free-agent draft (June 2, 1994). ... On disabled list (August 14-September 11, 1999). ... Traded by Brewers with P Bob Wickman and P Jason Bere to Cleveland Indians for 1B/OF Richie Sexson, P Paul Rigdon, P Kane Davis and a player to be named later (July 28, 2000); Brewers acquired 2B Marcos Scutaro to complete deal (August 30). ... On Cleveland disabled list (April 10-30, 2001); included rehabilitation assignment to Akron (April 30). ... Released by Indians (December 12, 2001). ... Signed by Texas Rangers organization (January 14, 2002). ... Released by Rangers (June 3, 2002). ... Signed by Philadelphia Phillies organization (June 4, 2002). ... Released by Phillies (July 24, 2002). ... Signed by St. Louis Cardinals organization (July 25, 2002). ... Granted free agency (October 15, 2002). ... Signed by Boston Red Sox organization (November 22, 2002). ... Optioned to Pawtucket by Boston (May 13, 2003). ... Designated for assignment (September 12, 2003). ... Sent outright to Pawtucket by Boston (September 17, 2003).

CAREER HITTING: 15-for-126 (.119), 6 R, 3 2B, 0 3B, 0 HR, 6 RBI.

Year League	W	L	Pct.	ERA	WHIP	G	GS	CG	ShO	Hld.	Sv.-Opp.	IP	H	R	ER	HR	BB-IBB	SO	Avg.
1994— Ariz. Brewers (Ariz.)	•8	0	1.000	2.40	0.98	15	12	2	0	...	0-...	82.2	68	29	22	3	13-1	85	.217
1995— Beloit (Midw.)	7	4	.636	4.54	1.25	21	21	0	0	...	0-...	115.0	113	68	58	12	31-0	94	.253
1996— Stockton (Calif.)	12	9	.571	4.02	1.29	28	•28	0	0	...	0-...	* 181.1	201	89	81	14	33-1	142	.261
1997— El Paso (Texas)	14	3	.824	3.17	1.18	19	19	* 6	• 1	...	0-...	136.1	136	56	48	8	25-2	97	.259
— Tucson (PCL)	1	0	1.000	0.00	0.57	1	1	0	0	...	0-...	7.0	3	0	0	0	1-0	6	.125
— Milwaukee (A.L.)	3	3	.500	5.15	1.23	7	7	0	0	0	0-0	36.2	39	25	21	5	6-0	32	.269
1998— Milwaukee (N.L.)	10	12	.455	4.18	1.23	34	26	0	0	0	0-0	165.2	170	83	77	19	33-4	135	.264
1999— Milwaukee (N.L.)	11	8	.579	4.52	1.38	31	29	2	0	0	0-0	185.0	219	101	93	23	36-7	119	.294
2000— Milwaukee (N.L.)	1	7	.125	5.96	1.69	27	11	1	0	0	0-0	93.2	125	70	62	16	33-4	65	.325
— Cleveland (A.L.)	3	3	.500	5.67	1.26	13	11	0	0	0	0-0	54.0	57	35	34	10	11-1	35	.269
2001— Cleveland (A.L.)	3	3	.500	5.20	1.51	29	10	0	0	1	0-0	97.0	129	60	56	10	17-1	52	.325
— Akron (East.)	0	0	...	3.00	1.33	1	1	0	0	...	0-...	3.0	3	1	1	0	1-0	2	.273
— Buffalo (Int'l)	4	2	.667	2.39	0.98	6	6	1	0	...	0-...	37.2	36	11	10	2	1-1	32	.248
2002— Texas (A.L.)	0	0	...	6.62	1.58	14	0	0	0	1	0-1	17.2	20	13	13	4	8-1	14	.274
— Scran./W.B. (I.L.)	3	1	.750	2.16	0.92	15	1	0	0	...	5-...	25.0	17	6	6	1	6-1	13	.191
— Memphis (PCL)	2	3	.400	6.30	1.40	7	6	1	0	...	0-...	40.0	53	28	28	7	3-0	42	.319
2003— Boston (A.L.)	1	0	1.000	5.09	1.58	7	0	0	0	0	0-0	17.2	23	10	10	3	5-2	12	.311
— Pawtucket (Int'l)	6	7	.462	4.69	1.22	31	11	0	0	...	2-...	94.0	103	55	49	9	12-1	58	.280
American League totals (5 years)	10	9	.526	5.41	1.41	70	28	0	0	2	0-1	223.0	268	143	134	32	47-5	145	.297
National League totals (3 years)	22	27	.449	4.70	1.39	92	66	3	0	0	0-0	444.1	514	254	232	58	102-15	319	.290
Major League totals (7 years)	32	36	.471	4.94	1.40	162	94	3	0	2	0-1	667.1	782	397	366	90	149-20	464	.292

WOODWARD, CHRIS — SS

PERSONAL: Born June 27, 1976, in Covina, Calif. ... 6-0/185. ... Bats right, throws right. ... Full name: Christopher Michael Woodward. ... High school: Northview (Covina, Calif.). ... College: Mt. San Antonio (Calif.).

TRANSACTIONS/CAREER NOTES: Selected by Toronto Blue Jays organization in 54th round of free-agent draft (June 2, 1994). ... On Syracuse disabled list (May 2-17 and May 21-June 6, 1999). ... On Toronto disabled list (July 1-26, 2001); included rehabilitation assignment to Syracuse (July 20-26). ... On Toronto disabled list (June 21-July 11, 2002); included rehabilitation assignment to Dunedin (July 8-11).

2003 GAMES PLAYED BY POSITION (MLB): SS—103.

Year Team (League)	Pos.	G	AB	R	H	2B	3B	HR	RBI	BB	SO	HBP	GDP	SB-CS	Avg.	OBP	SLG	OPS	E	Pct.
1995— Medicine Hat (Pio.)	SS	•72	241	44	56	8	0	3	21	33	41	6	1	9-4	.232	.336	.303	.639	30	.911
1996— Hagerstown (SAL)	SS	123	424	41	95	24	2	1	48	43	70	5	3	11-3	.224	.300	.297	.597	30	.951
1997— Dunedin (Fla. St.)	SS	91	314	38	92	13	4	1	38	52	52	5	3	4-8	.293	.397	.369	.767	12	.972
1998— Knoxville (Sou.)	SS	73	253	36	62	12	0	3	27	26	47	3	4	3-5	.245	.319	.328	.647	11	.971
— Syracuse (Int'l)	SS	25	85	9	17	6	0	2	6	7	20	0	4	1-1	.200	.261	.341	.602	4	.961
1999— Syracuse (Int'l)	SS-2B	75	281	46	82	20	3	1	20	38	49	1	5	4-1	.292	.378	.395	.773	11	.966
— Toronto (A.L.)	SS-3B	14	26	1	6	1	0	0	2	2	6	0	1	0-0	.231	.276	.269	.545	2	.944
2000— Toronto (A.L.)	S-3-2-1	37	104	16	19	7	0	3	14	10	28	0	1	1-0	.183	.254	.337	.591	5	.963
— Syracuse (Int'l)	2B-3B-SS	37	143	23	46	13	2	5	25	11	30	0	2	2-0	.322	.370	.545	.916	2	.988
2001— Toronto (A.L.)	2-3-S-1-D	37	63	9	12	3	2	2	5	1	14	0	1	0-1	.190	.203	.397	.600	8	.933
— Syracuse (Int'l)	3-S-2-1	51	193	29	59	14	3	11	31	16	40	1	4	0-0	.306	.360	.580	.941	9	.950
2002— Dunedin (Fla. St.)	SS	2	6	1	2	0	0	0	0	0	1	0	0	0-0	.333	.429	.333	.762	0	1.000
— Toronto (A.L.)	S-2-1-3-D	90	312	48	86	13	4	13	45	26	72	3	8	3-0	.276	.330	.468	.797	15	.964
2003— Toronto (A.L.)	SS	104	349	49	91	22	2	7	45	28	72	3	6	1-2	.261	.316	.395	.711	17	.964
Major League totals (5 years)		282	854	123	214	46	8	25	111	67	192	6	17	5-3	.251	.305	.411	.716	47	.960

W

WOOTEN, SHAWN — 1B/C

PERSONAL: Born July 24, 1972, in Glendora, Calif. ... 5-10/230. ... Bats right, throws right. ... Full name: William Shawn Wooten. ... High school: South Hills (Covina, Calif.). ... College: Mt. San Antonio (Calif.).

TRANSACTIONS/CAREER NOTES: Selected by Detroit Tigers organization in 18th round of free-agent draft (June 3, 1993). ... Released by Tigers (June 19, 1995). ... Signed by Moose Jaw, Prairie League (1995). ... Signed by California Angels organization (February 26, 1997). ... Angels franchise renamed Anaheim Angels for 1997 season. ... On Anaheim disabled list (March 21-July 11, 2002); included rehabilitation assignment to Salt Lake (May 28-June 1) and Rancho Cucamonga (June 28-July 11).

2003 GAMES PLAYED BY POSITION (MLB): 1B—32, DH—28, C—19, 3B—17.

Year	Team (League)	Pos.	G	AB	R	H	2B	3B	HR	RBI	BB	SO	HBP	GDP	SB-CS	Avg.	OBP	SLG	OPS	E	Pct.
1993—	Bristol (Appal.)	3B-1B-OF	52	177	26	62	12	2	8	39	24	20	3	7	1-2	.350	.432	.576	1.008	10	.956
—	Fayetteville (SAL)	3B-1B	5	16	2	4	0	0	1	5	3	3	0	1	0-0	.250	.368	.438	.806	0	1.000
1994—	Fayetteville (SAL)	3B-1B	121	439	45	118	25	4	3	61	27	84	11	11	1-3	.269	.324	.364	.689	24	.938
1995—	Jacksonville (Sou.)	3B	20	70	4	9	1	0	2	7	1	17	1	3	0-0	.129	.151	.229	.379	5	.921
—	Lakeland (Fla. St.)	3B	38	135	11	31	10	1	2	11	10	28	2	2	0-1	.230	.291	.363	.654	7	.942
—	Moose Jaw (PRA)		52	201	38	75	12	2	11	55	18	26	...	...	3-...	.373	...	.617	...	...	...
1996—	Moose Jaw (PRA)		77	292	44	89	17	0	12	57	18	46	2	8	2-0	.305	.348	.486	.835	...	...
1997—	Cedar Rap. (Midw.)	C-1B	108	353	43	102	23	1	15	75	49	71	6	8	0-1	.289	.379	.487	.866	0	1.000
1998—	Lake Elsinore (Calif.)	2B-3B-1B	105	395	56	116	31	0	16	74	38	82	3	9	0-2	.294	.357	.494	.850	1	.999
—	Midland (Texas)	1B	8	28	3	9	4	0	1	6	3	4	0	0	0-0	.321	.387	.571	.959	1	.967
1999—	Erie (East.)	3B-C-1B	137	518	70	151	27	1	19	88	50	102	10	12	3-1	.292	.360	.458	.818	22	.940
2000—	Erie (East.)	C-3B	51	191	32	56	12	2	9	35	17	30	2	3	4-1	.293	.350	.518	.869	9	.970
—	Edmonton (PCL)	C-3B-1B	66	252	43	89	21	3	11	42	18	38	3	4	0-0	.353	.401	.591	.993	7	.982
—	Anaheim (A.L.)	C-1B	7	9	2	5	1	0	0	1	0	0	0	0	0-0	.556	.556	.667	1.222	0	1.000
2001—	Anaheim (A.L.)	D-C-1-3	79	221	24	69	8	1	8	32	5	42	3	5	2-0	.312	.332	.466	.798	2	.992
2002—	Anaheim (A.L.)	D-1-C-3	49	113	13	33	8	0	3	19	6	24	1	3	2-0	.292	.331	.442	.773	0	1.000
—	Salt Lake (PCL)	1B-3B-C	10	42	2	11	2	0	0	7	0	11	1	1	0-0	.262	.279	.310	.589	1	.976
—	Rancho Cuca. (Calif.)	1B	6	18	2	4	3	0	0	3	4	4	0	1	0-0	.222	.348	.389	.737	0	1.000
2003—	Anaheim (A.L.)	1-D-C-3	98	272	25	66	8	0	7	32	24	45	1	7	0-4	.243	.303	.349	.653	2	.994
	Major League totals (4 years)		233	615	64	173	25	1	18	84	35	111	5	15	4-4	.281	.322	.413	.735	4	.994

WORRELL, TIM — P

PERSONAL: Born July 5, 1967, in Pasadena, Calif. ... 6-4/230. ... Throws right, bats right. ... Full name: Timothy Howard Worrell. ... Name pronounced: wor-RELL. ... High school: Maranatha (Sierra Madre, Calif.). ... College: Biola (Calif.).

TRANSACTIONS/CAREER NOTES: Selected by San Diego Padres organization in 20th round of free-agent draft (June 5, 1989). ... On disabled list (April 19, 1994-remainder of season). ... On San Diego disabled list (April 24-September 1, 1995); included rehabilitation assignments to Rancho Cucamonga (May 3-17 and August 1-10) and Las Vegas (May 17-June 1 and August 10-30). ... Traded by Padres with OF Trey Beamon to Detroit Tigers for P Dan Miceli, P Donne Wall and 3B Ryan Balfe (November 19, 1997). ... Traded by Tigers with OF David Roberts to Cleveland Indians for OF Geronimo Berroa (June 24, 1998). ... Traded by Indians to Oakland Athletics for a player to be named later (July 12, 1998); Indians acquired SS Adam Robinson to complete deal (July 27, 1998). ... On Oakland disabled list (July 20-August 8, 1999); included rehabilitation assignment to Modesto (August 5-8). ... Granted free agency (October 29, 1999). ... Signed by Baltimore Orioles organization (February 4, 2000). ... Released by Orioles (May 1, 2000). ... Signed by Chicago Cubs organization (May 8, 2000). ... Traded by Cubs to San Francisco Giants for 3B Bill Mueller (November 19, 2000). ... On San Francisco disabled list (July 9-26, 2001); included rehabilitation assignment to Arizona League Giants (July 22-26).

CAREER HITTING: 8-for-79 (.101), 6 R, 1 2B, 0 3B, 0 HR, 4 RBI.

Year	League	W	L	Pct.	ERA	WHIP	G	GS	CG	ShO	Hld.	Sv.-Opp.	IP	H	R	ER	HR	BB-IBB	SO	Avg.
1990—	Char., S.C. (SAL)	5	5	.385	4.64	1.34	20	19	3	0	...	0-...	110.2	120	65	57	6	28-2	68	.272
1991—	Waterloo (Midw.)	8	4	.667	3.34	1.19	14	14	3	2	...	0-...	86.1	70	36	32	5	33-0	83	.217
—	High Desert (Calif.)	5	2	.714	4.24	1.54	11	11	2	0	...	0-...	63.2	65	32	30	2	33-0	70	.267
1992—	Wichita (Texas)	8	6	.571	2.86	1.17	19	19	1	1	...	0-...	125.2	115	46	40	8	32-0	109	.245
—	Las Vegas (PCL)	4	2	.667	4.26	1.26	10	10	1	1	...	0-...	63.1	61	32	30	4	19-0	32	.253
1993—	Las Vegas (PCL)	5	6	.455	5.48	1.47	15	14	2	0	...	0-...	87.0	102	61	53	13	26-1	89	.294
—	San Diego (N.L.)	2	7	.222	4.92	1.46	21	16	0	0	1	0-0	100.2	104	63	55	11	43-5	52	.269
1994—	San Diego (N.L.)	0	1	.000	3.68	0.95	3	3	0	0	0	0-0	14.2	9	7	6	0	5-0	14	.170
1995—	Rancho Cuca. (Calif.)	0	2	.000	5.16	1.37	9	3	0	0	...	1-...	22.2	25	17	13	2	6-1	17	.266
—	Las Vegas (PCL)	0	2	.000	6.00	1.83	10	3	0	0	...	0-...	24.0	27	21	16	1	17-0	18	.273
—	San Diego (N.L.)	1	0	1.000	4.73	1.65	9	0	0	0	0	0-0	13.1	16	7	7	2	6-0	13	.291
1996—	San Diego (N.L.)	9	7	.563	3.05	1.22	50	11	0	0	10	1-2	121.0	109	45	41	9	39-1	99	.236
1997—	San Diego (N.L.)	4	8	.333	5.16	1.56	60	10	0	0	16	3-7	106.1	116	67	61	14	50-2	81	.280
1998—	Detroit (A.L.)	2	6	.250	5.98	1.38	15	9	0	0	0	0-1	61.2	66	42	41	11	19-2	47	.270
—	Cleveland (A.L.)	0	0	...	5.06	1.50	3	0	0	0	0	0-0	5.1	6	3	3	0	2-0	2	.305
—	Oakland (A.L.)	0	1	.000	4.00	1.17	25	0	0	0	6	0-2	36.0	34	17	16	5	8-1	33	.241
1999—	Oakland (A.L.)	2	2	.500	4.15	1.49	53	0	0	0	5	0-5	69.1	69	38	32	6	34-1	62	.256
—	Modesto (Calif.)	0	0	...	0.00	0.00	1	1	0	0	...	0-...	2.0	0	0	0	0	0-0	5	.000
2000—	Baltimore (A.L.)	2	2	.500	7.36	2.32	5	0	0	0	0	0-0	7.1	12	6	6	3	5-3	5	.353
—	Iowa (PCL)	2	0	1.000	5.06	1.31	6	0	0	0	...	0-...	10.2	9	6	6	0	5-1	7	.237
—	Chicago (N.L.)	3	4	.429	2.47	1.35	54	0	0	0	12	3-6	62.0	60	20	17	7	24-8	52	.252
2001—	San Francisco (N.L.)	2	5	.286	3.45	1.33	73	0	0	0	13	0-3	78.1	71	33	30	4	33-4	63	.240
—	Ariz. Giants (Ariz.)	0	0	...	0.00	0.67	1	1	0	0	...	0-...	3.0	1	0	0	0	1-0	2	.125
2002—	San Francisco (N.L.)	8	2	.800	2.25	1.18	80	0	0	0	23	0-1	72.0	55	21	18	3	30-2	55	.212
2003—	San Francisco (N.L.)	4	4	.500	2.87	1.30	76	0	0	0	1	38-45	78.1	74	35	25	5	28-6	65	.246
	American League totals (3 years)	6	11	.353	4.91	1.42	101	9	0	0	11	0-8	179.2	187	106	98	25	68-7	149	.264
	National League totals (9 years)	33	38	.465	3.62	1.35	426	40	0	0	76	45-64	646.2	614	298	260	55	258-28	494	.249
	Major League totals (11 years)	39	49	.443	3.90	1.36	527	49	0	0	87	45-72	826.1	801	404	358	80	326-35	643	.252

W

WRIGHT, DAN　　　　　　　　　　　　　P

PERSONAL: Born December 14, 1977, in Longview, Texas. ... 6-5/225. ... Throws right, bats right. ... Full name: Jonathan Daniel Wright. ... High school: Sullivan South (Kingsport, Tenn.). ... College: Arkansas.

TRANSACTIONS/CAREER NOTES: Selected by Cleveland Indians organization in 19th round of free-agent draft (June 4, 1996); did not sign. ... Selected by Chicago White Sox organization in second round of free-agent draft (June 2, 1999); choice received from Baltimore Orioles as part of compensation for signing of Type A free-agent OF Albert Belle. ... On disabled list (March 25, 2003). ... Sent on rehab assignment to Charlotte (April 17, 2003). ... Recalled by from Charlotte rehab assignment; reinstated from 15-day disabled list (May 5, 2003). ... Optioned to Charlotte (July 11, 2003). ... Recalled from Charlotte (August 2, 2003).

CAREER HITTING: 0-for-6 (.000), 0 R, 0 2B, 0 3B, 0 HR, 0 RBI.

Year	League	W	L	Pct.	ERA	WHIP	G	GS	CG	ShO	Hld.	Sv.-Opp.	IP	H	R	ER	HR	BB-IBB	SO	Avg.
1999—	Bristol (Appal.)	2	0	1.000	1.00	1.28	10	0	0	0	...	1-...	18.0	14	8	2	1	9-1	18	.203
	Burlington (Midw.)	0	0	...	6.00	1.33	2	0	0	0	...	0-...	6.0	5	4	4	1	3-0	3	.227
2000—	Winston-Salem (Caro.)	9	8	.529	3.74	1.40	21	21	1	0	...	0-...	132.1	135	64	55	4	50-0	106	.266
	Birmingham (Sou.)	2	4	.333	2.49	1.20	7	7	0	0	...	0-...	43.1	28	15	12	3	24-0	31	.187
2001—	Birmingham (Sou.)	7	7	.500	2.82	1.14	20	20	0	0	...	0-...	134.0	112	54	42	6	41-0	128	.229
	Chicago (A.L.)	5	3	.625	5.70	1.76	13	12	0	0	0	0-0	66.1	78	45	42	12	39-1	36	.300
2002—	Chicago (A.L.)	14	12	.538	5.18	1.38	33	33	1	1	0	0-0	196.1	200	124	113	32	71-1	136	.263
2003—	Charlotte (Int'l)	1	3	.250	4.64	1.06	8	7	1	0	...	0-...	33.0	25	18	17	5	10-0	25	.212
	Chicago (A.L.)	1	7	.125	6.15	1.59	20	15	0	0	...	1-1	86.1	91	63	59	16	46-2	47	.277
Major League totals (3 years)		**20**	**22**	**.476**	**5.52**	**1.50**	**66**	**60**	**1**	**1**	**0**	**1-1**	**349.0**	**369**	**232**	**214**	**60**	**156-4**	**219**	**.273**

WRIGHT, JAMEY　　　　　　　　　　　　P

PERSONAL: Born December 24, 1974, in Oklahoma City, Okla. ... 6-5/234. ... Throws right, bats right. ... Full name: Jamey Alan Wright. ... High school: Westmoore (Moore, Okla.).

TRANSACTIONS/CAREER NOTES: Selected by Colorado Rockies organization in first round (28th pick overall) of free-agent draft (June 3, 1993). ... On Colorado disabled list (May 15-June 8, 1997); included rehabilitation assignment to Salem (June 1-8). ... Traded by Rockies with C Henry Blanco to Milwaukee Brewers as part of three-way deal in which Rockies received 3B Jeff Cirillo, P Scott Karl and cash from Brewers, Oakland Athletics received P Justin Miller and cash from Rockies and Brewers received P Jimmy Haynes to A's (December 13, 1999). ... On Milwaukee disabled list (March 28-May 23, 2000); included rehabilitation assignments to Huntsville (May 6-13) and Indianapolis (May 14-20). ... On disabled list (May 25-June 10, 2001). ... On Milwaukee disabled list (April 11-May 24, 2002); included rehabilitation assignment to Indianapolis (May 9-20). ... Traded by Brewers with cash to St. Louis Cardinals for OF Chris Morris and a player to be named later (August 29, 2002); Brewers acquired P Mike Matthews to complete deal (September 11, 2002). ... Granted free agency (November 1, 2002). ... Signed by Seattle Mariners organization (January 24, 2003). ... Released by Mariners (March 18, 2003). ... Signed by Milwaukee Brewers organization (March 23, 2003). ... Released by Brewers (April 28, 2003). ... Signed by Kansas City as free agent (September 4, 2003).

CAREER HITTING: 43-for-314 (.137), 19 R, 11 2B, 1 3B, 1 HR, 13 RBI.

Year	League	W	L	Pct.	ERA	WHIP	G	GS	CG	ShO	Hld.	Sv.-Opp.	IP	H	R	ER	HR	BB-IBB	SO	Avg.
1993—	Ariz. Rockies (Ariz.)	1	3	.250	4.00	1.22	8	8	0	0	...	0-...	36.0	35	19	16	1	9-0	26	.243
1994—	Asheville (S. Atl.)	7	•14	.333	5.97	1.72	28	27	2	0	...	0-...	143.1	*188	107	*95	6	59-1	103	.329
1995—	Salem (Caro.)	10	8	.556	2.47	1.36	26	26	1	1	...	0-...	•171.0	160	74	47	7	72-3	95	.251
	New Haven (East.)	0	1	.000	9.00	3.00	1	1	0	0	...	0-...	3.0	6	6	3	0	3-0	3	.375
1996—	New Haven (East.)	5	1	.833	0.81	0.87	7	7	1	1	...	0-...	44.2	27	7	4	0	12-0	54	.180
	Colo. Springs (PCL)	4	2	.667	2.72	1.26	9	9	0	0	...	0-...	59.2	53	20	18	3	22-0	40	.240
	Colorado (N.L.)	4	4	.500	4.93	1.60	16	15	0	0	1	0-0	91.1	105	60	50	8	41-1	45	.298
1997—	Colorado (N.L.)	8	12	.400	6.25	1.80	26	26	1	0	0	0-0	149.2	198	113	104	19	71-3	59	.327
	Salem (Caro.)	0	1	.000	9.00	2.00	1	1	0	0	...	0-...	1.0	1	1	1	0	1-0	1	.250
	Colo. Springs (PCL)	1	0	1.000	1.64	1.27	2	2	0	0	...	0-...	11.0	9	3	2	1	5-0	11	.231
1998—	Colorado (N.L.)	9	14	.391	5.67	1.60	34	34	1	0	0	0-0	206.1	235	143	130	24	95-3	86	.294
1999—	Colorado (N.L.)	4	3	.571	4.87	1.74	16	16	0	0	0	0-0	94.1	110	52	51	10	54-3	49	.308
	Colo. Springs (PCL)	5	7	.417	6.46	1.70	17	16	2	0	...	0-...	100.1	133	87	72	13	38-2	75	.324
2000—	Huntsville (Sou.)	2	0	1.000	0.00	0.97	2	2	0	0	...	0-...	12.1	7	0	0	0	5-0	10	.175
	Indianapolis (Int'l)	0	0	...	1.80	2.20	1	1	0	0	...	0-...	5.0	8	5	1	0	3-0	7	.364
	Milwaukee (N.L.)	7	9	.438	4.10	1.49	26	25	0	0	0	0-0	164.2	157	81	75	12	88-5	96	.261
2001—	Milwaukee (N.L.)	11	12	.478	4.90	1.54	33	33	1	1	0	0-0	194.2	201	115	106	26	98-10	129	.272
2002—	Indianapolis (Int'l)	1	1	.500	4.11	1.37	3	3	0	0	...	0-...	15.1	16	7	7	3	5-0	13	.271
	Milwaukee (N.L.)	5	13	.278	5.35	1.56	19	19	1	1	0	0-0	114.1	115	72	68	15	63-8	69	.270
	St. Louis (N.L.)	2	0	1.000	4.80	1.80	4	3	0	0	0	0-0	15.0	15	8	8	2	12-1	8	.259
2003—	Indianapolis (Int'l)	1	3	.250	7.36	1.91	7	4	0	0	...	0-...	22.0	32	21	18	5	10-0	17	.344
	Oklahoma (PCL)	2	1	.667	4.12	1.50	7	7	2	1	...	0-...	39.1	38	18	18	1	21-0	40	.260
	Omaha (PCL)	3	5	.375	3.64	1.41	13	12	1	0	...	0-...	76.2	70	35	31	10	38-0	65	.246
	Kansas City (A.L.)	1	2	.333	4.26	1.34	4	4	2	1	0	0-0	25.1	23	14	12	1	11-0	19	.245
American League totals (1 year)		**1**	**2**	**.333**	**4.26**	**1.34**	**4**	**4**	**2**	**1**	**0**	**0-0**	**25.1**	**23**	**14**	**12**	**1**	**11-0**	**19**	**.245**
National League totals (7 years)		**50**	**67**	**.427**	**5.17**	**1.61**	**174**	**171**	**4**	**2**	**1**	**0-0**	**1030.1**	**1136**	**644**	**592**	**116**	**522-34**	**541**	**.289**
Major League totals (8 years)		**51**	**69**	**.425**	**5.15**	**1.60**	**178**	**175**	**6**	**3**	**1**	**0-0**	**1055.2**	**1159**	**658**	**604**	**117**	**533-34**	**560**	**.288**

WRIGHT, JARET　　　　　　　　　　　　P

PERSONAL: Born December 29, 1975, in Anaheim, Calif. ... 6-2/230. ... Throws right, bats right. ... Full name: Jaret Samuel Wright. ... High school: Katella (Anaheim, Calif.).

TRANSACTIONS/CAREER NOTES: Selected by Cleveland Indians organization in first round (10th pick overall) of free-agent draft (June 2, 1994). ... On disabled list (June 19-September 23, 1996). ... On suspended list (May 10-16, 1999). ... On disabled list (July 19-August 3 and August 9-September 10, 1999); included rehabilitation assignments to Buffalo (September 2) and Akron (September 6). ... On Cleveland disabled list (May 12-27 and June 3, 2000-remainder of season); included rehabilitation assignments to Buffalo (July 29-August 2) and Akron (August 3-10). ... On Cleveland disabled list (March 31-May 19 and September 1, 2001-remainder of season); included rehabilitation assignments to Buffalo (April 30-May 12) and Akron (May 13-19). ... On Buffalo disabled list (July 4-August 9 and August 19-Septmeber 1, 2001) ... On Cleveland disabled list (March 30-July 20, 2002); included rehabilitation assignment to Buffalo (June 17-July 7 and July 11-19). ... Granted free agency (October 15, 2002). ... Signed

W

by San Diego Padres (December 10, 2002). ... Optioned to Portland by San Diego (June 5, 2003). ... Designated for Assignment by San Diego (June 5, 2003). ... Recalled from Portland by San Diego (July 16, 2003). ... Claimed off waivers by Atlanta from San Diego (August 29, 2003).

CAREER HITTING: 5-for-18 (.278), 2 R, 1 2B, 0 3B, 0 HR, 1 RBI.

Year League	W	L	Pct.	ERA	WHIP	G	GS	CG	ShO	Hld.	Sv.-Opp.	IP	H	R	ER	HR	BB-IBB	SO	Avg.
1994— Burlington (Appal.)	0	1	.000	5.40	1.65	4	4	0	0	...	0-...	13.1	13	10	8	1	9-0	16	.260
1995— Columbus (S. Atl.)	5	6	.455	3.00	1.33	24	24	0	0	...	0-...	129.0	93	55	43	9	79-0	113	.205
1996— Kinston (Caro.)	7	4	.636	2.50	1.19	19	19	0	0	...	0-...	101.0	65	32	28	1	55-0	109	.190
1997— Akron (East.)	3	3	.500	3.67	1.22	8	8	1	0	...	0-...	54.0	43	26	22	4	23-2	59	.223
— Buffalo (A.A.)	4	1	.800	1.80	1.09	7	7	1	1	...	0-...	45.0	30	16	9	4	19-0	47	.185
— Cleveland (A.L.)	8	3	.727	4.38	1.28	16	16	0	0	0	0-0	90.1	81	45	44	9	35-0	63	.238
1998— Cleveland (A.L.)	12	10	.545	4.72	1.53	32	32	1	1	0	0-0	192.2	207	109	101	22	87-4	140	.277
1999— Cleveland (A.L.)	8	10	.444	6.06	1.65	26	26	0	0	0	0-0	133.2	144	99	90	18	77-1	91	.277
— Buffalo (Int'l)	0	0	...	0.00	0.00	1	1	0	0	...	0-...	3.0	0	0	0	0	0-0	4	.000
— Akron (East.)	1	0	1.000	0.00	0.80	1	1	0	0	...	0-...	5.0	3	0	0	0	1-0	6	.167
2000— Cleveland (A.L.)	3	4	.429	4.70	1.39	9	9	1	1	0	0-0	51.2	44	27	27	6	28-0	36	.235
— Buffalo (Int'l)	0	0	...	0.00	0.50	1	1	0	0	...	0-...	2.0	0	0	0	0	1-0	1	.000
— Akron (East.)	0	0	...	3.38	0.88	2	2	0	0	...	0-...	8.0	4	3	3	0	3-0	5	.133
2001— Buffalo (Int'l)	3	1	.750	4.71	1.33	7	7	0	0	...	0-...	28.2	25	18	15	3	13-0	28	.234
— Akron (East.)	0	0	...	1.29	0.29	1	1	0	0	...	0-...	7.0	2	1	1	1	0-0	4	.087
— Cleveland (A.L.)	2	2	.500	6.52	2.00	7	7	0	0	0	0-0	29.0	36	22	21	2	22-0	18	.313
2002— Cleveland (A.L.)	2	3	.400	15.71	3.22	8	6	0	0	0	0-0	18.1	40	34	32	3	19-0	12	.435
— Buffalo (Int'l)	5	3	.625	3.88	1.46	10	10	1	0	...	0-...	55.2	57	27	24	5	24-0	43	.268
2003— Portland (PCL)	2	1	.667	1.42	1.21	12	1	0	0	...	0-...	19.0	16	7	3	0	7-0	21	.222
— San Diego (N.L.)	1	5	.167	8.37	2.05	39	0	0	0	1	2-4	47.1	69	44	44	9	28-2	41	.348
— Atlanta (N.L.)	1	0	1.000	2.00	1.11	11	0	0	0	3	0-1	9.0	7	2	2	0	3-0	9	.226
American League totals (6 years)	35	32	.522	5.50	1.59	98	96	2	2	0	0-0	515.2	552	336	315	60	268-5	360	.276
National League totals (1 year)	2	5	.286	7.35	1.90	50	0	0	0	4	2-5	56.1	76	46	46	9	31-2	50	.332
Major League totals (7 years)	37	37	.500	5.68	1.62	148	96	2	2	4	2-5	572.0	628	382	361	69	299-7	410	.282

WUNSCH, KELLY   P

PERSONAL: Born July 12, 1972, in Houston, Texas. ... 6-5/225. ... Throws left, bats left. ... Full name: Kelly Douglas Wunsch. ... Name pronounced: wunch. ... High school: Bellaire (Texas). ... College: Texas A&M.

TRANSACTIONS/CAREER NOTES: Selected by Atlanta Braves organization in 54th round of free-agent draft (June 4, 1990); did not sign. ... Selected by Milwaukee Brewers organization in first round (26th pick overall) of free-agent draft (June 3, 1993); pick received as compensation for Toronto Blue Jays signing Type-A free agent Paul Molitor. ... On El Paso disabled list (April 4-May 13, 1996; and April 8-May 7, 1998). ... On Stockton disabled list (June 19-September 10, 1996). ... On Louisville disabled list (July 10-17, 1999). ... Granted free agency (October 15, 1999). ... Signed by Chicago White Sox organization (November 15, 1999). ... On disabled list (June 18, 2001-remainder of season). ... On Chicago disabled list (March 27-May 18, 2002); included rehabilitation assignments to Charlotte (April 4-11 and April 21-May 18).

CAREER HITTING: 0-for-0 (.000), 0 R, 0 2B, 0 3B, 0 HR, 0 RBI.

Year League	W	L	Pct.	ERA	WHIP	G	GS	CG	ShO	Hld.	Sv.-Opp.	IP	H	R	ER	HR	BB-IBB	SO	Avg.
1993— Beloit (Midw.)	1	5	.167	4.83	1.53	12	12	0	0	...	0-...	63.1	58	39	34	5	39-1	61	.245
1994— Beloit (Midw.)	3	10	.231	6.16	1.62	17	17	0	0	...	0-...	83.1	88	69	57	11	47-1	77	.264
— Helena (Pio.)	4	2	.667	5.12	1.61	9	9	1	0	...	0-...	51.0	52	39	29	7	30-0	57	.267
1995— Beloit (Midw.)	4	7	.364	4.20	1.48	14	14	3	1	...	0-...	85.2	90	47	40	7	37-0	66	.280
— Stockton (Calif.)	5	6	.455	5.33	1.72	14	13	1	1	...	0-...	74.1	89	51	44	4	39-0	62	.303
1996—										Did not play.									
1997— Stockton (Calif.)	7	9	.438	3.46	1.42	24	22	2	2	...	0-...	143.0	141	65	55	11	62-0	98	.263
1998— El Paso (Texas)	5	6	.455	5.95	1.56	17	17	1	1	...	0-...	101.1	127	81	67	11	31-0	70	.301
— Louisville (Int'l)	3	1	.750	3.83	1.32	9	8	0	0	...	0-...	51.2	53	23	22	6	15-0	36	.264
1999— Huntsville (Sou.)	4	1	.800	1.95	1.24	22	3	0	0	...	1-...	50.2	40	13	11	1	23-1	35	.229
— Louisville (Int'l)	2	1	.667	4.75	1.58	16	2	0	0	...	0-...	41.2	52	23	22	4	14-0	20	.311
2000— Chicago (A.L.)	6	3	.667	2.93	1.29	83	0	0	0	25	1-5	61.1	50	22	20	4	29-1	51	.221
2001— Chicago (A.L.)	2	1	.667	7.66	1.34	33	0	0	0	3	0-2	22.1	21	19	19	4	9-1	16	.247
2002— Charlotte (Int'l)	1	0	1.000	2.25	1.50	10	2	0	0	...	0-...	12.0	13	3	3	0	5-0	9	.295
— Chicago (A.L.)	2	1	.667	3.41	1.42	50	0	0	0	9	0-1	31.2	26	12	12	3	19-1	22	.230
2003— Charlotte (Int'l)	0	1	.000	5.40	1.80	3	0	0	0	...	0-...	3.1	6	3	2	1	0-0	4	.429
— Chicago (A.L.)	0	0	...	2.75	1.17	43	0	0	0	5	0-0	36.0	17	13	11	1	25-4	33	.139
Major League totals (4 years)	10	5	.667	3.69	1.30	209	0	0	0	42	1-8	151.1	114	66	62	12	82-7	122	.209

YAN, ESTEBAN   P

PERSONAL: Born June 22, 1975, in Campina del Seibo, Dominican Republic. ... 6-4/255. ... Throws right, bats right. ... Full name: Esteban Luis Yan. ... Name pronounced: YAHN. ... High school: Escuela Hicayagua (Dominican Republic).

TRANSACTIONS/CAREER NOTES: Signed as non-drafted free agent by Atlanta Braves organization (November 21, 1990). ... Traded by Braves with OF Roberto Kelly and OF Tony Tarasco to Montreal Expos for OF Marquis Grissom (April 6, 1995). ... Contract sold by Expos to Baltimore Orioles organization (April 6, 1996). ... Selected by Tampa Bay Devil Rays in first round (18th pick overall) of expansion draft (November 18, 1997). ... On Tampa Bay disabled list (June 17-July 15, 1999); included rehabilitation assignment to St. Petersburg (July 10-15). ... On Tampa Bay disabled list (June 22-July 21, 2001); included rehabilitation assignment to Orlando (July 5-12). ... Granted free agency (December 21, 2002). ... Signed by Texas Rangers (December 26, 2002). ... Designated for assignment by Texas (May 17, 2003). ... Traded by Texas Rangers to St. Louis Cardinals for OF Rick Asadoorian (May 27, 2003). ... Released by St. Louis (August 23, 2003).

CAREER HITTING: 2-for-2 (1.000), 1 R, 0 2B, 0 3B, 1 HR, 1 RBI.

Y

Year League	W	L	Pct.	ERA	WHIP	G	GS	CG	ShO	Hld.	Sv.-Opp.	IP	H	R	ER	HR	BB-IBB	SO	Avg.
1991—San Pedro (DSL)	4	1	.800	3.63	1.21	18	11	0	0	...	0-...	72.0	61	36	29	...	26-...	34	...
1992—San Pedro (DSL)	12	3	.800	1.32	0.93	16	16	7	4	...	0-...	115.2	85	37	17	1	23-...	86	...
1993—Danville (Appal.)	4	7	.364	3.03	1.36	14	•14	0	0	...	0-...	71.1	73	46	24	4	24-1	50	.253
1994—Macon (S. Atl.)	11	12	.478	3.27	1.11	28	•28	4	•3	...	0-...	170.2	155	85	62	15	34-1	121	.242
1995—W.P. Beach (FSL)	6	8	.429	3.07	1.25	24	21	1	0	...	1-...	137.2	139	63	47	3	33-0	89	.265
1996—Bowie (East.)	0	2	.000	5.63	1.63	9	1	0	0	...	0-...	16.0	18	12	10	2	8-0	15	.277
—Baltimore (A.L.)	0	0	...	5.79	1.71	4	0	0	0	0	0-...	9.1	13	7	6	3	3-1	7	.333
—Rochester (Int'l)	5	4	.556	4.27	1.30	22	10	0	0	...	1-...	71.2	75	37	34	6	18-0	61	.269
1997—Rochester (Int'l)	11	5	.688	3.10	1.21	34	12	0	0	...	2-...	119.0	107	54	41	13	37-0	131	.243
—Baltimore (A.L.)	0	1	.000	15.83	2.79	3	2	0	0	0	0-0	9.2	20	18	17	3	7-0	4	.417
1998—Tampa Bay (A.L.)	5	4	.556	3.86	1.34	64	0	0	0	8	1-5	88.2	78	41	38	11	41-2	77	.236
1999—Tampa Bay (A.L.)	3	4	.429	5.90	1.79	50	1	0	0	7	0-3	61.0	77	41	40	8	32-4	46	.326
—St. Pete. (FSL)	0	0	...	0.00	1.00	2	2	0	0	...	0-...	4.0	3	1	0	0	1-0	0	.214
2000—Tampa Bay (A.L.)	7	8	.467	6.21	1.45	43	20	0	0	3	0-2	137.2	158	98	95	26	42-0	111	.285
2001—Tampa Bay (A.L.)	4	6	.400	3.90	1.20	54	0	0	0	0	22-31	62.1	64	34	27	7	11-1	64	.262
—Orlando (Sou.)	0	0	...	3.00	1.00	2	2	0	0	...	0-...	3.0	3	1	1	0	0-0	4	.250
2002—Tampa Bay (A.L.)	7	8	.467	4.30	1.43	55	0	0	0	0	19-27	69.0	70	35	33	10	29-1	53	.259
2003—Texas (A.L.)	0	1	.000	6.94	1.63	15	0	0	0	1	0-0	23.1	31	19	18	5	7-1	25	.307
—St. Louis (N.L.)	2	0	1.000	6.02	1.59	39	0	0	0	3	1-1	43.1	53	29	29	8	16-4	28	.308
American League totals (8 years)	26	32	.448	5.35	1.48	288	23	0	0	19	42-68	461.0	511	293	274	73	172-10	387	.280
National League totals (1 year)	2	0	1.000	6.02	1.59	39	0	0	0	3	1-1	43.1	53	29	29	8	16-4	28	.308
Major League totals (8 years)	28	32	.467	5.41	1.49	327	23	0	0	22	43-69	504.1	564	322	303	81	188-14	415	.283

YOUNG, DMITRI   OF/3B/1B

PERSONAL: Born October 11, 1973, in Vicksburg, Miss. ... 6-2/245. ... Bats both, throws right. ... Full name: Dmitri Dell Young. ... High school: Rio Mesa (Oxnard, Calif.).

TRANSACTIONS/CAREER NOTES: Selected by St. Louis Cardinals organization in first round (fourth pick overall) of free-agent draft (June 3, 1991). ... On disabled list (June 2-9, 1994). ... On Arkansas suspended list (August 1-11 and August 17-27, 1995). ... On Louisville disabled list (July 14-24, 1996). ... On St. Louis disabled list (May 11-29, 1997); included rehabilitation assignment to Louisville (May 25-29). ... Traded by Cardinals to Cincinnati Reds for P Jeff Brantley (November 10, 1997). ... Selected by Tampa Bay Devil Rays in first round (16th pick overall) of expansion draft (November 18, 1997). ... Traded by Devil Rays to Reds (November 18, 1997), completing deal in which Reds traded OF Mike Kelly to Devil Rays for a player to be named later (November 11, 1997). ... Traded by Reds to Detroit Tigers for OF Juan Encarnacion and P Luis Pineda (December 11, 2001). ... On disabled list (April 23-May 14 and July 6, 2002-remainder of season).

2003 GAMES PLAYED BY POSITION (MLB): DH—75, OF—61, 3B—16, 1B—1.

										BATTING									FIELDING	
Year Team (League)	Pos.	G	AB	R	H	2B	3B	HR	RBI	BB	SO	HBP	GDP	SB-CS	Avg.	OBP	SLG	OPS	E	Pct.
1991— Johnson City (App.)	3B	37	129	22	33	10	0	2	22	21	28	2	1	2-1	.256	.364	.380	.743	5	.932
1992— Springfield (Midw.)	3B	135	493	74	153	* 36	6	14	72	51	94	5	9	14-13	.310	.378	.493	.871	42	.879
1993— St. Pete. (FSL)	3B-1B	69	270	31	85	13	3	5	43	24	28	2	7	3-4	.315	.369	.441	.810	10	.972
—Arkansas (Texas)	3B-1B	45	166	13	41	11	2	3	21	9	29	2	5	4-4	.247	.294	.392	.685	7	.982
1994— Arkansas (Texas)	1B-OF	125	453	53	123	33	2	8	54	36	60	5	6	0-3	.272	.330	.406	.736	‡ 16	.971
1995— Arkansas (Texas)	OF-DH	97	367	54	107	18	6	10	62	30	46	3	11	2-4	.292	.347	.455	.802	9	.931
—Louisville (A.A.)	OF	2	7	3	2	0	0	0	0	1	1	0	0	0-0	.286	.375	.286	.661	1	.750
1996— Louisville (A.A.)	1B	122	459	* 90	153	31	8	15	64	34	67	1	5	16-5	.333	.378	.534	.912	8	.993
—St. Louis (N.L.)	1B	16	29	3	7	0	0	0	2	4	5	1	1	0-1	.241	.353	.241	.594	1	.976
1997— St. Louis (N.L.)	1B-OF-DH	110	333	38	86	14	3	5	34	38	63	2	8	6-5	.258	.335	.453	.698	13	.985
—Louisville (A.A.)	OF-1B	24	84	10	23	7	0	4	14	13	15	0	1	1-1	.274	.371	.500	.871	1	.985
1998— Cincinnati (N.L.)	OF-1B	144	536	81	166	48	1	14	83	47	94	2	16	2-4	.310	.364	.481	.846	12	.976
1999— Cincinnati (N.L.) OF-1B-DH		127	373	63	112	30	2	14	56	30	71	2	11	3-1	.300	.352	.504	.856	4	.982
2000— Cincinnati (N.L.) OF-1B-DH		152	548	68	166	37	6	18	88	36	80	3	16	0-3	.303	.346	.481	.837	8	.981
2001— Cincinnati (N.L.) OF-1B-3B		142	540	68	163	28	3	21	69	37	77	5	22	8-5	.302	.350	.481	.832	16	.967
2002— Detroit (A.L.)	D-1-3-O	54	201	25	57	14	0	7	27	12	39	2	12	2-0	.284	.329	.458	.786	4	.972
2003— Detroit (A.L.)	D-O-3-1	155	562	78	167	34	7	29	85	58	130	11	16	2-1	.297	.372	.537	.909	10	.947
American League totals (2 years)		209	763	103	224	48	7	36	112	70	169	13	28	4-1	.294	.361	.516	.877	14	.958
National League totals (6 years)		691	2359	321	700	157	15	72	332	192	390	15	74	19-19	.297	.351	.468	.818	54	.977
Major League totals (8 years)		900	3122	424	924	205	22	108	444	262	559	28	102	23-20	.296	.353	.480	.833	68	.975

YOUNG, ERIC   2B

PERSONAL: Born May 18, 1967, in New Brunswick, N.J. ... 5-8/186. ... Bats right, throws right. ... Full name: Eric Orlando Young. ... High school: New Brunswick (N.J.). ... College: Rutgers.

TRANSACTIONS/CAREER NOTES: Selected by Los Angeles Dodgers organization in 43rd round of free-agent draft (June 5, 1989). ... Selected by Colorado Rockies organization in first round (11th pick overall) of expansion draft (November 17, 1992). ... On Colorado disabled list (March 22-April 22, 1996); included rehabilitation assignments to New Haven (April 5-10), Salem (April 10-13) and Colorado Springs (April 13-22). ... Traded by Rockies to Dodgers for P Pedro Astacio (August 19, 1997). ... On disabled list (July 13-31, 1998). ... On Los Angeles disabled list (July 24-August 13, 1999); included rehabilitation assignment to San Bernardino (August 8-13). ... Traded by Dodgers with P Ismael Valdes to Chicago Cubs for P Terry Adams, P Chad Ricketts and a player to be named later (December 12, 1999); Dodgers acquired P Brian Stephenson to complete deal (December 16, 1999). ... Granted free agency (November 7, 2001). ... Signed by Milwaukee Brewers (January 17, 2002). ... Traded by Brewers to San Francisco Giants for P Greg Bruso (August 19, 2003).

2003 GAMES PLAYED BY POSITION (MLB): 2B—117, OF—2, DH—1.

Year	Team (League)	Pos.	G	AB	R	H	2B	3B	HR	RBI	BB	SO	HBP	GDP	SB-CS	Avg.	OBP	SLG	OPS	E	Pct.
1989— GC Dodgers (GCL)	2B	56	197	53	65	11	5	2	22	33	16	3	1	* 41-10	.330	.432	.467	.899	* 15	.939
1990— Vero Beach (FSL)	2B-OF	127	460	* 101	132	23	7	2	50	69	35	6	4	* 76-16	.287	.384	.380	.764	‡ 25	.937
1991— San Antonio (Texas)	2B-OF	127	461	82	129	17	4	3	35	67	36	2	13	* 70-26	.280	.373	.354	.726	13	.974
— Albuquerque (PCL)	2B	1	5	0	2	0	0	0	0	0	0	0	0	0-0	.400	.400	.400	.800	0	1.000
1992— Albuquerque (PCL)	2B	94	350	61	118	16	5	3	49	33	18	4	10	28-11	.337	.393	.437	.831	• 20	.961
— Los Angeles (N.L.)	2B	49	132	9	34	1	0	1	11	8	9	0	3	6-1	.258	.300	.288	.588	9	.957
1993— Colorado (N.L.)	2B-OF	144	490	82	132	16	8	3	42	63	41	4	9	42-19	.269	.355	.353	.708	18	.964
1994— Colorado (N.L.)	OF-2B	90	228	37	62	13	1	7	30	38	17	2	3	18-7	.272	.378	.430	.808	2	.981
1995— Colorado (N.L.)	2B-OF	120	366	68	116	21	• 9	6	36	49	29	5	4	35-12	.317	.404	.473	.876	§ 11	.974
1996— New Haven (East.)	2B	3	15	0	1	0	0	0	0	0	3	0	0	0-0	.067	.067	.067	.133	0	1.000
— Salem (Caro.)	2B	3	10	2	3	3	0	0	0	3	1	0	0	2-0	.300	.462	.600	1.062	2	.875
— Colo. Springs (PCL)	2B	7	23	4	6	1	1	0	3	5	1	0	1	0-0	.261	.393	.391	.784	3	.917
— Colorado (N.L.)	2B	141	568	113	184	23	4	8	74	47	31	21	9	* 53-19	.324	.380	.421	.814	12	.985
1997— Colorado (N.L.)	2B	118	468	78	132	29	6	6	45	57	37	5	16	32-12	.282	.363	.408	.771	15	.978
— Los Angeles (N.L.)	2B	37	154	28	42	4	2	2	16	14	17	4	2	13-2	.273	.347	.364	.710	3	.979
1998— Los Angeles (N.L.)	2B-DH	117	452	78	129	24	1	8	43	45	32	5	4	42-13	.285	.355	.396	.751	13	.976
1999— Los Angeles (N.L.)	2B	119	456	73	128	24	2	2	41	63	26	5	12	51-22	.281	.371	.355	.726	9	.984
— San Bern. (Calif.)	2B	3	12	0	3	0	0	0	0	0	2	0	0	0-0	.250	.250	.250	.500	2	.833
2000— Chicago (N.L.)	2B	153	607	98	180	40	2	6	47	63	39	8	12	54-7	.297	.367	.399	.766	15	.979
2001— Chicago (N.L.)	2B	149	603	98	168	43	4	6	42	42	45	9	15	31-14	.279	.333	.393	.726	12	.981
2002— Milwaukee (N.L.)	2B-DH-OF	138	496	57	139	29	3	3	28	39	38	6	14	31-11	.280	.338	.369	.707	12	.979
2003— Milwaukee (N.L.)	2B-DH	109	404	71	105	18	1	15	31	48	34	4	9	25-7	.260	.344	.421	.764	15	.967
— San Francisco (N.L.)	2B-OF	26	71	9	14	2	0	0	3	9	10	1	3	3-5	.197	.293	.225	.518	1	.989
Major League totals (12 years)		1510	5495	899	1565	287	43	73	489	585	405	79	115	436-151	.285	.360	.393	.752	147	.977

YOUNG, ERNIE   OF

PERSONAL: Born July 8, 1969, in Chicago, Ill. ... 6-1/234. ... Bats right, throws right. ... Full name: Ernest Wesley Young. ... High school: Mendel Catholic (Chicago). ... College: Lewis (Ill.) University.

TRANSACTIONS/CAREER NOTES: Selected by Oakland Athletics organization in 10th round of free-agent draft (June 4, 1990). ... On disabled list (July 11, 1992-remainder of season). ... Traded by A's to Kansas City Royals for cash (March 17, 1998). ... On Kansas City disabled list (May 22-June 15, 1998); included rehabilitation assignment to Omaha (June 5-15). ... Granted free agency (October 15, 1998). ... Signed by Arizona Diamondbacks organization (December 17, 1998). ... Released by Diamondbacks (November 22, 1999). ... Signed by St. Louis Cardinals organization (January 19, 2000). ... Granted free agency (October 18, 2000). ... Signed by San Diego Padres organization (November 20, 2000). ... Granted free agency (October 15, 2001). ... Signed by Cardinals organization (November 21, 2001). ... Traded by Cardinals to Arizona Diamondbacks for a player to be named later (March 24, 2002). ... Released by Diamondbacks (2002). ... Signed by Detroit Tigers organization (December 19, 2002).

2003 GAMES PLAYED BY POSITION (MLB): DH—4.

Year	Team (League)	Pos.	G	AB	R	H	2B	3B	HR	RBI	BB	SO	HBP	GDP	SB-CS	Avg.	OBP	SLG	OPS	E	Pct.
1990— S. Oregon (N'west)	OF	50	168	34	47	6	2	6	23	29	53	3	2	4-4	.280	.391	.446	.838	2	.971
1991— Madison (Midw.)	OF	114	362	75	92	19	2	15	71	58	115	9	4	20-9	.254	.366	.442	.808	7	.968
1992— Modesto (Calif.)	OF	74	253	55	63	12	4	11	33	47	74	6	5	11-3	.249	.378	.458	.836	6	.958
1993— Modesto (Calif.)	OF	85	301	83	92	18	6	23	71	72	92	4	2	23-7	.306	.442	.635	1.077	3	.984
— Huntsville (Sou.)	OF	45	120	26	25	5	0	5	15	24	36	2	1	8-5	.208	.345	.375	.720	4	.963
1994— Huntsville (Sou.)	OF-DH	72	257	45	89	19	4	14	55	37	45	2	6	5-6	.346	.427	.615	1.041	2	.982
— Oakland (A.L.)	OF-DH	11	30	2	2	1	0	0	3	1	8	0	1	0-0	.067	.100	.100	.197	1	.958
— Tacoma (PCL)	OF-DH	29	102	19	29	4	0	6	16	13	27	2	3	0-5	.284	.370	.500	.870	2	.965
1995— Edmonton (PCL)	OF-DH	95	347	70	96	21	4	15	72	49	73	3	5	2-2	.277	.365	.490	.854	6	.971
— Oakland (A.L.)	OF	26	50	9	10	3	0	2	5	8	12	0	1	0-0	.200	.310	.380	.690	2	.946
1996— Oakland (A.L.)	OF	141	462	72	112	19	4	19	64	52	118	7	13	7-5	.242	.326	.424	.750	1	.997
1997— Oakland (A.L.)	OF	71	175	22	39	7	0	5	15	19	57	2	6	1-3	.223	.303	.349	.652	4	.972
— Edmonton (PCL)	OF-DH	54	195	39	63	10	0	9	45	37	46	6	7	5-2	.323	.442	.513	.954	1	.991
1998— Kansas City (A.L.)	OF	25	53	2	10	3	0	1	3	2	9	1	3	2-1	.189	.232	.302	.534	0	1.000
— Omaha (PCL)	OF-DH	79	297	58	97	13	1	22	55	29	68	5	8	6-4	.327	.395	.599	.994	2	.989
1999— Arizona (N.L.)	OF	6	11	1	2	0	0	0	0	3	2	1	0	0-0	.182	.400	.182	.582	0	1.000
— Tucson (PCL)	OF-DH	126	453	78	133	25	1	30	95	57	129	5	9	4-1	.294	.374	.552	.926	2	.987
2000— Memphis (PCL)	OF	124	453	76	119	16	0	35	98	66	117	4	17	11-1	.263	.359	.530	.888	2	.990
2001— Portland (PCL)	OF	116	409	66	112	21	2	20	67	38	115	14	13	0-3	.274	.355	.482	.837	4	.974
2003— Detroit (A.L.)	DH	5	11	0	2	0	0	0	0	4	5	0	1	0-2	.182	.400	.182	.582	0	...
— Toledo (Int'l) DH-OF-1B	128	454	56	120	22	0	21	84	50	119	6	10	10-6	.264	.342	.452	.793	3	.979
American League totals (6 years)		279	781	107	175	33	4	27	90	86	209	10	25	10-11	.224	.307	.380	.687	8	.987
National League totals (1 year)		6	11	1	2	0	0	0	0	3	2	1	0	0-0	.182	.400	.182	.582	0	1.000
Major League totals (7 years)		285	792	108	177	33	4	27	90	89	211	11	25	10-11	.223	.308	.378	.686	8	.987

YOUNG, JASON   P

PERSONAL: Born September 28, 1979, in Oakland, Calif. ... 6-5/210. ... Throws right, bats right. ... Full name: Jason Kariya Young. ... High school: Berkeley (Calif.). ... College: Stanford.

TRANSACTIONS/CAREER NOTES: Selected by Colorado Rockies organization in second round of free-agent draft (June 5, 2000).

CAREER HITTING: 2-for-7 (.286), 1 R, 1 2B, 0 3B, 0 HR, 0 RBI.

Year League	W	L	Pct.	ERA	WHIP	G	GS	CG	ShO	Hld.	Sv.-Opp.	IP	H	R	ER	HR	BB-IBB	SO	Avg.
2001— Salem (Caro.)	6	7	.462	3.44	1.26	17	17	2	1	...	0-...	104.2	104	47	40	8	28-0	91	.259
2002— Carolina (Sou.)	7	4	.636	2.64	1.14	14	14	1	1	...	0-...	88.2	71	30	26	1	30-0	76	.219
— Colo. Springs (PCL)	6	5	.545	4.97	1.57	13	13	0	0	...	0-...	79.2	87	52	44	10	38-0	74	.272
2003— Colo. Springs (PCL)	6	7	.462	3.95	1.42	23	21	2	1	...	0-...	116.1	128	63	51	10	37-0	99	.271
— Colorado (N.L.)	0	2	.000	8.44	2.02	8	3	0	0	0	0-0	21.1	34	22	20	8	9-0	18	.354
Major League totals (1 year)	0	2	.000	8.44	2.02	8	3	0	0	0	0-0	21.1	34	22	20	8	9-0	18	.354

YOUNG, KEVIN   1B

PERSONAL: Born June 16, 1969, in Alpena, Mich. ... 6-3/230. ... Bats right, throws right. ... Full name: Kevin Stacey Young. ... High school: Washington (Kansas City, Kan.). ... College: Southern Mississippi.

TRANSACTIONS/CAREER NOTES: Selected by Pittsburgh Pirates organization in seventh round of free-agent draft (June 4, 1990). ... On Pittsburgh disabled list (July 24-August 8, 1995). ... Released by Pirates (March 26, 1996). ... Signed by Kansas City Royals organization (April 1, 1996). ... Released by Royals (December 5, 1996). ... Signed by Pirates (March 31, 1997). ... On suspended list (September 28-30, 2000). ... Given unconditional release (June 29, 2003).

2003 GAMES PLAYED BY POSITION (MLB): 1B—44, OF—1.

Year Team (League)	Pos.	G	AB	R	H	2B	3B	HR	RBI	BB	SO	HBP	GDP	SB-CS	Avg.	OBP	SLG	OPS	E	Pct.
1990— Welland (NYP)	SS	72	238	46	58	16	2	5	30	31	36	7	4	10-2	.244	.342	.391	.732	26	.883
1991— Salem (Caro.)	3B	56	201	38	63	12	4	6	28	20	34	7	5	3-2	.313	.390	.502	.892	12	.925
— Carolina (Sou.)	3B-1B	75	263	36	90	19	6	3	33	15	38	8	7	9-3	.342	.394	.494	.888	§ 28	.907
— Buffalo (A.A.)	3B-1B	4	9	1	2	1	0	0	2	0	0	1	0	1-0	.222	.273	.333	.606	2	.857
1992— Buffalo (A.A.)	3B-1B	137	490	* 91	154	29	6	8	65	67	67	11	11	18-12	.314	.406	.447	.853	‡ 32	.932
— Pittsburgh (N.L.)	3B-1B	10	7	2	4	0	0	0	4	2	0	0	0	1-0	.571	.667	.571	1.238	1	.800
1993— Pittsburgh (N.L.)	1B-3B	141	449	38	106	24	3	6	47	36	82	9	10	2-2	.236	.300	.343	.643	3	.998
1994— Pittsburgh (N.L.) 1B-3B-OF		59	122	15	25	7	2	1	11	8	34	1	3	0-2	.205	.258	.320	.577	3	.987
— Buffalo (A.A.)	3B-1B	60	228	26	63	14	5	5	27	15	45	3	5	6-2	.276	.327	.447	.774	4	.982
1995— Calgary (PCL) 3B-1B-DH		45	163	24	58	23	1	8	34	15	21	0	4	6-3	.356	.403	.656	1.060	12	.950
— Pittsburgh (N.L.)	1B	56	181	13	42	9	0	6	22	8	53	2	5	1-3	.232	.268	.381	.649	12	.933
1996— Omaha (A.A.) 1B-3B-DH		50	186	29	57	11	1	13	46	12	41	4	2	3-0	.306	.358	.586	.944	5	.985
— Kansas City (A.L.)	1-0-3-D	55	132	20	32	6	0	8	23	11	32	0	2	3-3	.242	.301	.470	.770	1	.995
1997— Pittsburgh (N.L.) 1B-3B-OF		97	333	59	100	18	3	18	74	16	89	4	6	11-2	.300	.332	.535	.867	5	.993
1998— Pittsburgh (N.L.)	1B	159	592	88	160	40	2	27	108	44	127	11	20	15-7	.270	.328	.481	.809	8	.994
1999— Pittsburgh (N.L.)	1B	156	584	103	174	41	6	26	106	75	124	12	13	22-10	.298	.387	.522	.909	* 23	.985
2000— Pittsburgh (N.L.)	1B-DH	132	496	77	128	27	0	20	88	32	96	8	15	8-3	.258	.311	.433	.744	* 17	.986
2001— Pittsburgh (N.L.)	1B	142	449	53	104	33	0	14	65	42	119	11	17	15-11	.232	.310	.399	.708	7	.994
2002— Pittsburgh (N.L.)	1B	146	468	60	115	26	1	16	51	50	101	4	13	4-6	.246	.322	.408	.730	13	.991
2003— Pittsburgh (N.L.)	1B-OF	52	84	8	17	4	0	2	7	12	25	0	1	1-0	.202	.302	.321	.624	2	.991
— Rochester (Int'l)	DH	4	7	0	1	1	0	0	1	3	3	0	1	0-0	.143	.400	.286	.686	0	.000
American League totals (1 year)		55	132	20	32	6	0	8	23	11	32	0	2	3-3	.242	.301	.470	.770	1	.995
National League totals (11 years)		1150	3765	516	975	229	17	136	583	325	850	62	103	80-46	.259	.324	.437	.762	94	.990
Major League totals (12 years)		1205	3897	536	1007	235	17	144	606	336	882	62	105	83-49	.258	.324	.438	.762	95	.990

YOUNG, MICHAEL   2B

PERSONAL: Born October 19, 1976, in Covina, Calif. ... 6-1/190. ... Bats right, throws right. ... Full name: Michael Brian Young. ... High school: Bishop Amat (La Puente, Calif.). ... College: UC-Santa Barbara.

TRANSACTIONS/CAREER NOTES: Selected by Toronto Blue Jays organization in fifth round of free-agent draft (June 3, 1997). ... Traded by Blue Jays with P Darwin Cubillan to Texas Rangers for P Esteban Loaiza (July 19, 2000).

2003 GAMES PLAYED BY POSITION (MLB): 2B—159, SS—7.

Year Team (League)	Pos.	G	AB	R	H	2B	3B	HR	RBI	BB	SO	HBP	GDP	SB-CS	Avg.	OBP	SLG	OPS	E	Pct.
1997— St. Catharines (NYP)	2B-SS	74	276	49	85	18	3	9	48	33	59	7	6	9-5	.308	.392	.493	.885	18	.946
1998— Hagerstown (SAL) 2B-SS-OF		* 140	522	86	147	33	5	16	87	55	96	7	12	16-8	.282	.354	.456	.810	13	.949
1999— Dunedin (Fla. St.)	2B-SS	129	495	86	155	• 36	3	5	83	61	78	4	10	30-6	.313	.389	.428	.818	22	.961
2000— Tennessee (Sou.)	2B-SS	91	345	51	95	24	5	6	47	36	72	1	5	16-5	.275	.340	.426	.766	16	.965
— Tulsa (Texas)	SS	43	188	30	60	13	5	1	32	17	28	0	4	9-3	.319	.368	.457	.826	7	.965
— Texas (A.L.)	2B	2	2	0	0	0	0	0	0	0	1	0	0	0-0	.000	.000	.000	.000	0	...
2001— Oklahoma (PCL)	2B-SS	47	189	28	55	8	0	8	28	20	34	1	6	3-3	.291	.358	.460	.819	6	.968
— Texas (A.L.)	2B	106	386	57	96	18	4	11	49	26	91	3	9	3-1	.249	.298	.402	.699	8	.984
2002— Texas (A.L.)	2-S-3-D	156	573	77	150	26	8	9	62	41	112	0	14	6-7	.262	.308	.382	.690	9	.987
2003— Texas (A.L.)	2B-SS	160	666	106	204	33	9	14	72	36	103	1	14	13-2	.306	.339	.446	.785	10	.987
Major League totals (4 years)		424	1627	240	450	77	21	34	183	103	307	4	37	22-10	.277	.318	.412	.730	27	.987

ZAMBRANO, CARLOS   P

PERSONAL: Born June 1, 1981, in Puerto Cabello, Venezuela. ... 6-5/245. ... Throws right, bats both. ... Full name: Carlos Alberto Zambrano. ... Name pronounced: zam-BRAH-no.

TRANSACTIONS/CAREER NOTES: Signed as non-drafted free agent by Chicago Cubs organization (July 12, 1997). ... On Chicago disabled list (May 10-June 7, 2002); included rehabilitation assignment to Iowa (May 30-June 6). ... On suspended list (August 3-9, 2002).

CAREER HITTING: 19-for-107 (.178), 9 R, 6 2B, 0 3B, 2 HR, 6 RBI.

Year League	W	L	Pct.	ERA	WHIP	G	GS	CG	ShO	Hld.	Sv.-Opp.	IP	H	R	ER	HR	BB-IBB	SO	Avg.
1998—Ariz. Cubs (Ariz.)	0	1	.000	3.15	1.60	14	2	0	0	...	1-...	40.0	39	17	14	0	25-3	36	.257
1999—Lansing (Midw.)	13	7	.650	4.17	1.38	27	24	2	1	...	0-...	153.1	150	87	71	9	62-1	98	.258
2000—West Tenn (Sou.)	3	1	.750	1.34	0.99	9	9	0	0	...	0-...	60.1	39	14	9	2	21-0	43	.181
—Iowa (PCL)	2	5	.286	3.97	1.66	34	0	0	0	...	6-...	56.2	54	30	25	3	40-2	46	.260
2001—Iowa (PCL)	10	5	.667	3.88	1.27	26	25	1	0	...	0-...	150.2	124	73	65	9	68-1	155	.226
—Chicago (N.L.)	1	2	.333	15.26	2.48	6	1	0	0	0	0-1	7.2	11	13	13	2	8-0	4	.355
2002—Iowa (PCL)	0	0	...	0.00	0.89	3	3	0	0	0	0-...	9.0	2	0	0	0	6-0	11	.069
—Chicago (N.L.)	4	8	.333	3.66	1.45	32	16	0	0	0	0-0	108.1	94	53	44	9	63-2	93	.235
2003—Chicago (N.L.)	13	11	.542	3.11	1.32	32	32	3	1	0	0-0	214.0	188	88	74	9	94-12*	168	.239
Major League totals (3 years)	18	21	.462	3.57	1.39	70	49	3	1	0	0-1	330.0	293	154	131	20	165-14	265	.241

ZAMBRANO, VICTOR   P

PERSONAL: Born August 6, 1975, in Los Teques, Venezuela. ... 6-0/203. ... Throws right, bats right. ... Full name: Victor Manuel Zambrano. ... High school: Manve Maria Billolobo (Los Teques, Venezuela).

TRANSACTIONS/CAREER NOTES: Signed as non-drafted free agent by New York Yankees organization (August 19, 1993). ... Released by Yankees organization (February 7, 1996). ... Signed by Tampa Bay Devil Rays organization (March 14, 1996). ... Optioned to Durham by Tampa Bay (May 9, 2003). ... Recalled by Tampa Bay from Durham (May 23, 2003).

CAREER HITTING: 0-for-4 (.000), 0 R, 0 2B, 0 3B, 0 HR, 0 RBI.

Year League	W	L	Pct.	ERA	WHIP	G	GS	CG	ShO	Hld.	Sv.-Opp.	IP	H	R	ER	HR	BB-IBB	SO	Avg.
1996—GC Devil Rays (GCL)	0	0	...	8.10	1.20	1	0	0	0	...	0-...	3.1	4	4	3	0	0-0	6	.250
1997—GC Devil Rays (GCL)	0	0	...	0.00	0.33	2	0	0	0	...	0-...	3.0	1	0	0	0	0-0	2	.100
—Princeton (Appal.)	0	2	.000	1.82	0.91	20	0	0	0	...	0-...	29.2	18	13	6	1	9-1	36	.159
1998—Char., S.C. (SAL)	6	4	.600	3.38	1.19	48	2	0	0	...	0-...	77.1	72	32	29	5	20-1	89	.246
1999—St. Pete. (FSL)	0	2	.000	4.00	1.67	7	0	0	0	...	0-...	9.0	10	6	4	1	5-0	15	.278
—Orlando (Sou.)	7	2	.778	4.59	1.58	40	4	0	0	...	1-...	82.1	92	55	42	5	38-2	81	.280
2000—Durham (Int'l)	0	6	.000	5.03	1.61	53	0	0	0	...	8-...	62.2	72	38	35	9	29-2	55	.285
2001—Durham (Int'l)	1	2	.333	2.08	1.25	29	0	0	0	...	12-...	30.1	26	10	7	2	12-1	29	.232
—Tampa Bay (A.L.)	6	2	.750	3.16	1.09	36	0	0	0	5	2-6	51.1	38	21	18	6	18-0	58	.201
2002—Tampa Bay (A.L.)	8	8	.500	5.53	1.65	42	11	0	0	6	1-3	114.0	120	77	70	15	68-5	73	.278
—Durham (Int'l)	0	1	.000	1.93	0.93	10	0	0	0	...	1-...	14.0	9	4	3	2	4-0	15	.180
2003—Durham (Int'l)	0	1	.000	4.50	1.50	1	1	0	0	...	0-...	4.0	4	6	2	0	2-0	6	.222
—Tampa Bay (A.L.)	12	10	.545	4.21	1.44	34	28	1	0	2	0-0	188.1	165	97	88	21	*106-2	132	.237
Major League totals (3 years)	26	20	.565	4.48	1.46	112	39	1	0	13	3-9	353.2	323	195	176	42	192-7	263	.245

ZAUN, GREGG   C

PERSONAL: Born April 14, 1971, in Glendale, Calif. ... 5-10/190. ... Bats both, throws right. ... Full name: Gregory Owen Zaun. ... Name pronounced: ZAHN. ... High school: St. Francis (La Canada, Calif.).

TRANSACTIONS/CAREER NOTES: Selected by Baltimore Orioles organization in 17th round of free-agent draft (June 5, 1989). ... On Bowie disabled list (June 17-July 15, 1993). ... Traded by Orioles to Florida Marlins (August 23, 1996), completing deal in which Marlins traded P Terry Mathews to Orioles for a player to be named later (August 21, 1996). ... Traded by Marlins to Texas Rangers for a player to be named later or cash (November 23, 1998); Marlins received cash to complete deal (April 15, 1999). ... Traded by Rangers with OF Juan Gonzalez and P Danny Patterson to Detroit Tigers for P Justin Thompson, P Francisco Cordero, OF Gabe Kapler, C Bill Haselman, 2B Frank Catalanotto and P Alan Webb (November 2, 1999). ... Traded by Tigers to Kansas City Royals for a player to be named later or cash (March 7, 2000). ... On Kansas City disabled list (April 15-May 29, 2000); included rehabilitation assignment to Omaha (May 16-29). ... On Kansas City disabled list (March 31-July 23, 2001); included rehabilitation assignments to Gulf Coast Royals (July 3-12) and Omaha (July 13-23). ... Granted free agency (November 5, 2001). ... Signed by Houston Astros (December 11, 2001).

2003 GAMES PLAYED BY POSITION (MLB): C—45.

Year Team (League)	Pos.	G	AB	R	H	2B	3B	HR	RBI	BB	SO	HBP	GDP	SB-CS	Avg.	OBP	SLG	OPS	E	Pct.
1990—Wausau (Midw.)	C	37	100	3	13	0	1	1	7	7	17	1	2	0-0	.130	.194	.180	.374	3	.990
—Bluefield (Appal.)	P	61	184	29	55	5	2	2	21	23	15	1	2	5-5	.299	.378	.380	.758	10	.980
1991—Kane Co. (Midw.)	C	113	409	67	112	17	5	4	51	50	41	2	10	4-4	.274	.353	.369	.722	16	.980
1992—Frederick (Carolina)	2B-C	108	383	54	96	18	6	6	52	42	45	3	10	3-5	.251	.324	.376	.700	‡18	.979
1993—Bowie (East.)	C-P	79	258	25	79	10	0	3	38	27	26	1	7	4-7	.306	.373	.380	.753	10	.979
—Rochester (Int'l)	C	21	78	10	20	4	2	1	11	6	11	0	1	0-0	.256	.302	.397	.700	4	.975
1994—Rochester (Int'l)	C	123	388	61	92	16	4	7	43	56	72	4	5	4-2	.237	.337	.353	.690	9	.989
1995—Rochester (Int'l)	C-DH	42	140	26	41	13	1	6	18	14	21	3	0	0-3	.293	.367	.529	.896	3	.989
—Baltimore (A.L.)	C	40	104	18	27	8	1	3	14	16	14	0	2	1-1	.260	.358	.394	.753	3	.987
1996—Baltimore (A.L.)	C	50	108	16	25	8	1	1	13	11	15	2	3	0-0	.231	.309	.352	.661	3	.987
—Rochester (Int'l)	C-DH	14	47	11	15	2	0	0	4	11	6	0	0	0-2	.319	.441	.362	.802	2	.965
—Florida (N.L.)	C	10	31	4	9	1	0	1	2	3	5	0	2	1-0	.290	.353	.419	.772	0	1.000
1997—Florida (N.L.)	C-1B	58	143	21	43	10	2	2	20	26	18	2	3	1-0	.301	.415	.441	.856	8	.978
1998—Florida (N.L.)	C-2B	106	298	19	56	12	2	5	29	35	52	1	7	5-2	.188	.274	.292	.566	8	.986
1999—Texas (A.L.)	C-DH	43	93	12	23	2	1	1	12	10	7	0	2	1-0	.247	.314	.323	.637	3	.984
2000—Kansas City (A.L.)	C-2B-1B	83	234	36	64	11	0	7	33	43	34	3	4	7-3	.274	.390	.410	.800	5	.988
—Omaha (PCL)	C	9	25	7	7	3	0	0	3	4	3	0	1	1-1	.280	.379	.400	.779	0	1.000
2001—GC Royals (GCL)	C	6	18	3	1	0	0	0	1	7	5	0	1	0-0	.056	.360	.056	.376	0	1.000
—Omaha (PCL)	C	11	43	5	12	4	0	1	8	3	3	1	2	0-0	.279	.333	.442	.775	1	.985
—Kansas City (A.L.)	C-DH	39	125	15	40	9	0	6	18	12	16	0	2	1-2	.320	.377	.536	.913	5	.975
2002—Houston (N.L.)	C	76	185	18	41	7	1	3	24	12	36	2	4	1-0	.222	.275	.319	.594	5	.985
2003—Houston (N.L.)	C	59	120	9	26	7	0	1	13	14	14	1	5	1-0	.217	.299	.300	.599	4	.976
—Colorado (N.L.)	C	15	46	6	12	1	0	3	8	5	7	0	0	0-1	.261	.333	.478	.812	2	.973
American League totals (5 years)		255	664	97	179	35	2	18	90	92	86	5	13	10-6	.270	.359	.410	.769	19	.985
National League totals (5 years)		324	823	77	187	38	5	15	96	95	132	6	21	9-3	.227	.310	.340	.650	27	.983
Major League totals (9 years)		579	1487	174	366	73	7	33	186	187	218	11	34	19-9	.246	.332	.371	.704	46	.984

Z

Z

ZEILE, TODD — 3B/1B

PERSONAL: Born September 9, 1965, in Van Nuys, Calif. ... 6-1/200. ... Bats right, throws right. ... Full name: Todd Edward Zeile. ... Name pronounced: ZEAL. ... High school: Hart (Newhall, Calif.). ... College: UCLA.

TRANSACTIONS/CAREER NOTES: Selected by Kansas City Royals organization in 30th round of free-agent draft (June 6, 1983); did not sign. ... Selected by St. Louis Cardinals organization in supplemental round ("sandwich pick" between second and third round 55th pick overall) of free-agent draft (June 2, 1986); pick received as compensation for New York Yankees signing Type C free-agent IF Ivan DeJesus. ... On St. Louis disabled list (April 23-May 9, 1995); included rehabilitation assignment to Louisville (May 6-9). ... Traded by Cardinals with cash to Chicago Cubs for P Mike Morgan, 3B/OF Paul Torres and C Francisco Morales (June 16, 1995). ... Granted free agency (December 21, 1995). ... Signed by Philadelphia Phillies (December 22, 1995). ... Traded by Phillies with OF Pete Incaviglia to Baltimore Orioles for two players to be named later (August 29, 1996); Phillies acquired P Calvin Maduro and P Garrett Stephenson to complete deal (September 4, 1996). ... Granted free agency (October 27, 1996). ... Signed by Los Angeles Dodgers (December 8, 1996). ... Traded by Dodgers with C Mike Piazza to Florida Marlins for OF Gary Sheffield, 3B Bobby Bonilla, C Charles Johnson, OF Jim Eisenreich and P Manuel Barrios (May 15, 1998). ... Traded by Marlins to Texas Rangers for 3B Jose Santo and P Dan DeYoung (July 31, 1998). ... Granted free agency (October 28, 1999). ... Signed by New York Mets (December 11, 1999). ... Traded by Mets to Colorado Rockies as part of three-way deal in which Mets traded P Glendon Rusch to Milwaukee Brewers, Rockies traded 1B/OF Ross Gload and P Craig House to Mets, Brewers traded P Jeff D'Amico, OF Jeromy Burnitz, IF Lou Collier, OF/1B Mark Sweeney and cash to Mets, Mets traded OF Benny Agbayani, IF/OF Lenny Harris and cash to Rockies and Rockies traded OF Alex Ochoa to Brewers (January 21, 2002). ... Granted free agency (October 28, 2002). ... Signed by New York Yankees (December 18, 2002). ... Released by Yankees (August 18, 2003). ... Signed by Montreal Expos (August 20, 2003).

2003 GAMES PLAYED BY POSITION (MLB): 3B—64, 1B—23, DH—8.

Year	Team (League)	Pos.	G	AB	R	H	2B	3B	HR	RBI	BB	SO	HBP	GDP	SB-CS	Avg.	OBP	SLG	OPS	E	Pct.
1986— Erie (N.Y.-Penn)		C	70	248	40	64	14	1	14	* 63	37	52	2	3	5-1	.258	.352	.492	.843	8	.983
1987— Springfield (Midw.)		3B-C	130	487	94	142	24	4	25	* 106	70	85	1	10	1-3	.292	.380	.511	.891	14	.985
1988— Arkansas (Texas)		C-1B-OF	129	430	95	117	33	2	19	75	83	64	1	11	6-5	.272	.388	.491	.879	10	.987
1989— Louisville (A.A.)		3B-C-1B	118	453	71	131	26	3	19	85	45	78	1	10	0-1	.289	.350	.486	.835	6 ‡	.991
— St. Louis (N.L.)		C	28	82	7	21	3	1	1	8	9	14	0	1	0-0	.256	.326	.354	.680	4	.971
1990— St. Louis (N.L.)		3-C-1-O	144	495	62	121	25	3	15	57	67	77	2	11	2-4	.244	.333	.398	.731	15	.980
1991— St. Louis (N.L.)		3B	155	565	76	158	36	3	11	81	62	94	5	15	17-11	.280	.353	.412	.765	* 25	.943
1992— St. Louis (N.L.)		3B	126	439	51	113	18	4	7	48	68	70	0	11	7-10	.257	.352	.364	.717	13	.960
— Louisville (A.A.)		3B	21	74	11	23	4	1	5	13	9	13	0	4	0-0	.311	.381	.595	.976	5	.918
1993— St. Louis (N.L.)		3B	157	571	82	158	36	1	17	103	70	76	0	15	5-4	.277	.352	.433	.785	33	.923
1994— St. Louis (N.L.)		3B	113	415	62	111	25	1	19	75	52	56	3	13	1-3	.267	.348	.470	.818	12	.960
1995— Louisville (A.A.)		1B	2	8	0	1	0	0	0	0	0	2	0	0	0-0	.125	.125	.125	.250	1	.923
— St. Louis (N.L.)		1B	34	127	16	37	6	0	5	22	18	23	1	2	1-0	.291	.378	.457	.835	7	.980
— Chicago (N.L.)		3B-OF-1B	79	299	34	68	16	0	9	30	16	53	3	11	0-0	.227	.271	.371	.642	12	.939
1996— Philadelphia (N.L.)		3B-1B	134	500	61	134	24	0	20	80	67	88	1	16	1-1	.268	.353	.436	.789	14	.972
— Baltimore (A.L.)		3B	29	117	17	28	8	0	5	19	15	16	0	2	0-0	.239	.326	.436	.762	3	.964
1997— Los Angeles (N.L.)		3B	160	575	89	154	17	0	31	90	85	112	6	18	8-7	.268	.365	.459	.824	* 26	.931
1998— Los Angeles (N.L.)		3B-1B	40	158	22	40	6	1	7	27	10	24	1	5	1-1	.253	.300	.437	.737	6	.930
— Florida (N.L.)		3B	66	234	37	68	12	1	6	39	31	34	2	4	2-3	.291	.374	.427	.801	5	.971
— Texas (A.L.)		3B	52	180	26	47	14	1	6	28	28	32	1	3	1-0	.261	.358	.450	.808	12	.915
1999— Texas (A.L.)		3B-DH-1B	156	588	80	172	41	1	24	98	56	94	4	20	1-2	.293	.354	.488	.842	§ 25	.941
2000— New York (N.L.)		1B	153	544	67	146	36	3	22	79	74	85	2	15	3-4	.268	.356	.467	.823	10	.992
2001— New York (N.L.)		1B	151	531	66	141	25	1	10	62	73	102	6	15	1-0	.266	.359	.373	.732	11	.992
2002— Colorado (N.L.)		3B	144	506	61	138	23	0	18	87	66	92	1	27	1-1	.273	.353	.425	.778	* 21	.942
2003— New York (A.L.)		3B-1B-DH	66	186	29	39	8	0	6	23	24	36	0	3	0-0	.210	.294	.349	.644	7	.974
— Montreal (N.L.)		3B	34	113	11	29	2	2	5	10	11	18	3	3	1-0	.257	.331	.442	.773	5	.947
American League totals (4 years)			303	1071	152	286	71	2	41	168	123	178	5	28	2-2	.267	.341	.452	.793	47	.949
National League totals (14 years)			1718	6154	804	1637	310	21	203	907	778	1018	36	182	51-49	.266	.348	.422	.771	219	.969
Major League totals (15 years)			2021	7225	956	1923	381	23	244	1075	901	1196	41	210	53-51	.266	.347	.427	.774	266	.967

ZERBE, CHAD — P

PERSONAL: Born April 27, 1972, in Findlay, Ohio. ... 6-0/200. ... Throws left, bats left. ... Full name: William Chad Zerbe. ... Name pronounced: ZER-bee. ... High school: Vivian Gaither (Tampa). ... Junior college: Hillsborough (Fla.) Community College.

TRANSACTIONS/CAREER NOTES: Selected by Los Angeles Dodgers organization in 17th round of free-agent draft (June 3, 1991). ... Released by Dodgers (December 10, 1996). ... Signed by Arizona Diamondbacks organization (January 28, 1997). ... Released by Diamondbacks (May 20, 1997). ... Signed by Sonoma County, Western League (1997). ... Signed by San Francisco Giants organization (November 26, 1997). ... Granted free agency (October 16, 1998). ... Re-signed by Giants organization (March 4, 1999). ... Granted free agency (October 15, 1999). ... Re-signed by Giants organization (October 22, 1999).

CAREER HITTING: 3-for-20 (.150), 1 R, 0 2B, 0 3B, 0 HR, 2 RBI.

Year	League	W	L	Pct.	ERA	WHIP	G	GS	CG	ShO	Hld.	Sv.-Opp.	IP	H	R	ER	HR	BB-IBB	SO	Avg.
1991— GC Dodgers (GCL)		0	2	.000	2.20	1.41	16	1	0	0	...	0-...	32.2	31	19	8	1	15-0	23	.246
1992— Great Falls (Pio.)		8	3	.727	2.14	1.09	15	15	1	1	...	0-...	92.1	75	27	22	2	26-0	70	.218
1993— Bakersfield (Calif.)		0	10	.000	5.91	1.94	14	12	1	0	...	0-...	67.0	83	60	44	2	47-0	41	.303
— Vero Beach (FSL)		1	0	1.000	6.57	2.03	10	0	0	0	...	0-...	12.1	12	10	9	0	13-1	11	.255
1994— Vero Beach (FSL)		5	5	.500	3.39	1.22	18	18	1	0	...	0-...	98.1	88	50	37	6	32-0	68	.235
1995— San Bernardino (Calif.)		11	7	.611	4.57	1.42	28	27	1	0	...	0-...	163.1	168	103	83	15	64-0	94	.265
1996— San Antonio (Texas)		4	6	.400	4.50	1.57	17	11	1	0	...	1-...	86.0	98	52	43	9	37-0	38	.290
1997— High Desert (Calif.)		1	6	.143	7.43	2.09	9	8	0	0	...	0-...	36.1	61	49	30	7	15-0	26	.353
— Sonoma County (West.)		4	5	.444	5.40	1.70	14	13	2	0	...	0-...	90.0	117	70	54	7	36-1	52	.317
1998— San Jose (Calif.)		2	0	1.000	3.35	1.30	23	0	0	0	...	1-...	37.2	37	16	14	3	12-0	28	.259
1999— Bakersfield (Calif.)		7	7	.500	3.64	1.25	21	21	0	0	...	0-...	126.0	124	66	51	4	33-0	81	.252
— Shreveport (Texas)		1	3	.250	1.96	1.02	7	6	0	0	...	0-...	41.1	32	13	9	2	10-0	16	.216
2000— Shreveport (Texas)		2	1	.667	2.33	1.19	9	9	0	0	...	0-...	38.2	37	11	10	1	9-0	34	.257
— Fresno (PCL)		7	3	.700	4.32	1.36	17	11	0	0	...	0-...	81.1	94	46	39	5	17-0	41	.294
— San Francisco (N.L.)		0	0	...	4.50	1.17	4	0	0	0	0	0-0	6.0	6	3	3	1	1-0	5	.273
2001— Fresno (PCL)		3	4	.429	3.55	1.46	17	0	0	0	...	5-...	25.1	28	13	10	2	9-0	17	.272
— San Francisco (N.L.)		3	0	1.000	3.92	1.31	27	1	0	0	0	0-0	39.0	41	21	17	3	10-0	22	.281

Year League	W	L	Pct.	ERA	WHIP	G	GS	CG	ShO	Hld.	Sv.-Opp.	IP	H	R	ER	HR	BB-IBB	SO	Avg.
2002—Fresno (PCL)	0	0	...	0.00	1.06	3	3	0	0	...	0-...	10.1	8	0	0	0	3-0	5	.216
—San Francisco (N.L.)	2	0	1.000	3.04	1.30	50	0	0	0	5	0-1	56.1	52	22	19	3	21-2	26	.248
2003—San Jose (Calif.)	0	0	...	0.00	1.67	2	2	0	0	...	0-...	3.0	3	2	0	0	2-0	1	.250
—Fresno (PCL)	1	1	.500	2.61	1.16	7	0	0	0	...	2-...	10.1	11	6	3	3	1-0	7	.275
—San Francisco (N.L.)	1	1	.500	4.71	1.49	33	1	0	0	2	0-1	49.2	60	26	26	3	14-2	17	.311
Major League totals (4 years)	6	1	.857	3.87	1.36	114	2	0	0	7	0-2	151.0	159	72	65	10	46-4	70	.278

ZITO, BARRY   P

PERSONAL: Born May 13, 1978, in Las Vegas, Nev. ... 6-4/215. ... Throws left, bats left. ... Full name: Barry William Zito. ... Name pronounced: ZEE-toe. ... High school: University (San Diego). ... College: USC.

TRANSACTIONS/CAREER NOTES: Selected by Texas Rangers organization in third round of free-agent draft (June 2, 1998); did not sign. ... Selected by Oakland Athletics organization in first round (ninth pick overall) of free-agent draft (June 2, 1999).

CAREER HITTING: 0-for-15 (.000), 0 R, 0 2B, 0 3B, 0 HR, 0 RBI.

Year League	W	L	Pct.	ERA	WHIP	G	GS	CG	ShO	Hld.	Sv.-Opp.	IP	H	R	ER	HR	BB-IBB	SO	Avg.
1999—Visalia (Calif.)	3	0	1.000	2.45	1.07	8	8	0	0	...	0-...	40.1	21	13	11	3	22-0	62	.157
—Midland (Texas)	2	1	.667	4.91	1.50	4	4	0	0	...	0-...	22.0	22	15	12	1	11-0	29	.253
—Vancouver (PCL)	1	0	1.000	1.50	1.17	1	1	0	0	...	0-...	6.0	5	1	1	0	2-0	6	.227
2000—Sacramento (PCL)	8	5	.615	3.19	1.31	18	18	0	0	...	0-...	101.2	88	44	36	4	45-0	91	.230
—Oakland (A.L.)	7	4	.636	2.72	1.18	14	14	1	1	0	0-0	92.2	64	30	28	6	45-2	78	.195
2001—Oakland (A.L.)	17	8	.680	3.49	1.23	35	•35	3	2	0	0-0	214.1	184	92	83	18	80-0	205	.230
2002—Oakland (A.L.)	*23	5	.821	2.75	1.13	35	*35	1	0	0	0-0	229.1	182	79	70	24	78-2	182	.218
2003—Oakland (A.L.)	14	12	.538	3.30	1.18	35	35	4	1	0	0-0	231.2	186	98	85	19	88-3	146	.219
Major League totals (4 years)	61	29	.678	3.12	1.18	119	119	9	4	0	0-0	768.0	616	299	266	67	291-7	611	.219

ZOCCOLILLO, PETE   OF

PERSONAL: Born February 6, 1977, in Bronx, N.Y. ... 6-2/200. ... Bats left, throws right. ... Full name: Peter G. Zoccolillo. ... High school: Pelham (N.Y.). ... College: Rutgers.

TRANSACTIONS/CAREER NOTES: Selected by Chicago Cubs organization in 23rd round of free-agent draft (June 2, 1999). ... Traded by Cubs with P Ruben Quevedo to Milwaukee Brewers for P David Weathers and P Roberto Miniel (July 30, 2001).

2003 GAMES PLAYED BY POSITION (MLB): OF—7.

Year Team (League)	Pos.	G	AB	R	H	2B	3B	HR	RBI	BB	SO	HBP	GDP	SB-CS	Avg.	OBP	SLG	OPS	E	Pct.
1999—Eugene (Northwest)	1B-OF	64	183	20	43	7	1	1	15	22	26	2	2	3-2	.235	.321	.301	.621	5	.988
2000—Lansing (Midw.)	OF-1B	109	358	58	104	22	2	8	56	46	47	8	4	5-2	.291	.380	.430	.810	7	.977
2001—Daytona (Fla. St.)	OF-1B	96	326	42	86	18	4	2	35	35	57	1	4	7-5	.264	.332	.362	.693	8	.962
—Beloit (Midw.)	OF	31	123	16	41	8	0	6	23	10	19	1	3	0-2	.333	.385	.545	.930	1	.984
2002—High Desert (Calif.)	OF	44	161	31	55	10	0	8	37	28	24	2	3	2-1	.342	.436	.553	.989	1	.986
—Huntsville (Sou.)	OF-1B	75	227	43	67	12	1	12	45	40	50	1	7	6-7	.295	.399	.515	.914	1	.990
2003—Indianapolis (Int'l)	OF-DH	132	443	57	124	36	1	12	73	51	70	10	14	3-5	.280	.360	.447	.807	3	.986
—Milwaukee (N.L.)	OF	20	37	0	4	1	0	0	3	2	13	0	1	0-0	.108	.154	.135	.289	0	1.000
Major League totals (1 year)		20	37	0	4	1	0	0	3	2	13	0	1	0-0	.108	.154	.135	.289	0	1.000

Z

MAJOR LEAGUE MANAGERS

PERSONAL: Born May 12, 1935, in Haina, Dominican Republic. ... 6-1/195. ... Batted right, threw right. ... Full name: Felipe Rojas Alou. ... College: University of Santo Domingo (Dominican Republic).

TRANSACTIONS/CAREER NOTES: Signed as free agent by New York Giants organization (November 14, 1955). ... Giants franchise moved from New York to San Francisco (1958). ... Traded by Giants with P Billy Hoeft, C Ed Bailey and a player to be named later to Milwaukee Braves for P Bob Hendley, P Bob Shaw and C Del Crandall (December 3, 1963); Braves acquired IF Ernie Bowman to complete deal (January 8, 1964). ... On disabled list (June 24-July 25, 1964). ... Braves franchise moved from Milwaukee to Atlanta (1966). ... Traded by Braves to Oakland Athletics for P Jim Nash (December 3, 1969). ... Traded by A's to New York Yankees for P Rob Gardner and P Ron Klimkowski (April 9, 1971). ... Contract sold by Yankees to Montreal Expos (September 5, 1973). ... Contract sold by Expos to Milwaukee Brewers (December 7, 1973). ... Released by Brewers (April 29, 1974).

						BATTING									FIELDING			
Year Team (League)	Pos.	G	AB	R	H	2B	3B	HR	RBI	Avg.	BB	SO	SB	PO	A	E	Avg.
1956— Lake Char. (Evan.)	OF	5	9	1	2	0	0	0	1	.222	0	0	0	6	1	0	1.000
— Cocoa (FSL)	3B-OF	119	445	111	169	15	6	21	99	.380	68	40	48	199	60	23	.918
1957— Minneapolis (A.A.)	OF	24	57	7	12	2	0	0	3	.211	5	8	1	32	1	1	.971
— Springfield (East.)	3B-OF	106	359	45	110	14	3	12	71	.306	27	29	18	215	26	9	.964
1958— Phoenix (PCL)	OF	55	216	61	69	16	2	13	42	.319	17	24	10	150	3	3	.981
— San Francisco (N.L.)	OF	75	182	21	46	9	2	4	16	.253	19	34	4	126	2	2	.985
1959— San Francisco (N.L.)	OF	95	247	38	68	13	2	10	33	.275	17	38	5	111	2	3	.974
1960— San Francisco (N.L.)	OF	106	322	48	85	17	3	8	44	.264	16	42	10	156	5	7	.958
1961— San Francisco (N.L.)	OF	132	415	59	120	19	0	18	52	.289	26	41	11	196	10	2	.990
1962— San Francisco (N.L.)	OF	154	561	96	177	30	3	25	98	.316	33	66	10	262	7	8	.971
1963— San Francisco (N.L.)	OF	157	565	75	159	31	9	20	82	.281	27	87	11	279	9	4	.986
1964— Milwaukee (N.L.)	1B-OF	121	415	60	105	26	3	9	51	.253	30	41	5	329	12	5	.986
1965— Milwaukee (N.L.)	3-S-1-O	143	555	80	165	29	2	23	78	.297	31	63	8	626	43	6	.991
1966— Atlanta (N.L.)	3-S-1-O	154	666	122	218	32	6	31	74	.327	24	51	5	935	64	13	.987
1967— Atlanta (N.L.)	1B-OF	140	574	76	157	26	3	15	43	.274	32	50	6	864	34	9	.990
1968— Atlanta (N.L.)	OF	160	662	72	210	37	5	11	57	.317	48	56	12	379	8	8	.980
1969— Atlanta (N.L.)	OF	123	476	54	134	13	1	5	32	.282	23	23	4	260	4	3	.989
1970— Oakland (A.L.)	1B-OF	154	575	70	156	25	3	8	55	.271	32	31	10	290	11	7	.977
1971— Oakland (A.L.)	OF	2	8	0	2	1	0	0	0	.250	0	1	0	7	0	0	1.000
— New York (A.L.)	1B-OF	131	461	52	133	20	6	8	69	.289	32	24	5	506	23	4	.992
1972— New York (A.L.)	1B-OF	120	324	33	90	18	1	6	37	.278	22	27	1	669	54	7	.990
1973— New York (A.L.)	1B-OF	93	280	25	66	12	0	4	27	.236	9	25	0	512	31	7	.987
— Montreal (N.L.)	1B-OF	19	48	4	10	1	0	1	4	.208	2	4	0	30	3	0	1.000
1974— Milwaukee (A.L.)	OF	3	3	0	0	0	0	0	0	.000	0	2	0	0	0	1	...
American League totals (5 years)		503	1651	180	447	76	10	26	188	.271	95	110	16	1984	119	26	.988
National League totals (13 years)		1579	5688	805	1654	283	39	180	664	.291	328	596	91	4553	203	70	.985
Major League totals (17 years)		2082	7339	985	2101	359	49	206	852	.286	423	706	107	6537	322	96	.986

RECORD AS MANAGER

BACKGROUND: Spring training instructor, Montreal Expos (1976). ... Coach, Expos (1979-80, 1984 and October 8, 1991-May 22, 1992).

HONORS: Named Florida State League Manager of the Year (1990). ... Named N.L. Manager of the Year by The Sporting News (1994). ... Named N.L. Manager of the Year by Baseball Writers' Association of America (1994).

		REGULAR SEASON			POSTSEASON								
					Playoffs		Champ. Series		World Series		All-Star Game	
Year Team (League)	W	L	Pct.	Pos	W	L	W	L	W	L	W	L
1977— West Palm Beach (FSL)	77	65	.542	1st	1	2	—	—	—	—	—	—
1978— Memphis (Sou.)	71	73	.493	2nd	—	—	—	—	—	—	—	—
1981— Denver (A.A.)	76	60	.558	2nd	4	0	—	—	—	—	—	—
1982— Wichita (A.A.)	70	67	.510	2nd	—	—	—	—	—	—	—	—
1983— Wichita (A.A.)	65	71	.477	3rd	—	—	—	—	—	—	—	—
1985— Indianapolis (A.A.)	61	81	.429	4th	—	—	—	—	—	—	—	—
1986— West Palm Beach (FSL)	80	55	.592	1st	3	3	—	—	—	—	—	—
1987— West Palm Beach (FSL)	75	63	.543	2nd	—	—	—	—	—	—	—	—
1988— West Palm Beach (FSL)	41	27	.602	2nd	—	—	—	—	—	—	—	—
— Second half	30	36	.455	3rd	2	2	—	—	—	—	—	—
1989— West Palm Beach (FSL)	39	31	.557	2nd	—	—	—	—	—	—	—	—
— Second half	35	33	.515	2nd	—	—	—	—	—	—	—	—
1990— West Palm Beach (FSL)	49	19	.720	1st	—	—	—	—	—	—	—	—
— Second half	43	21	.672	1st	3	3	—	—	—	—	—	—
1991— West Palm Beach (FSL)	33	31	.515	4th	—	—	—	—	—	—	—	—
— Second half	39	28	.582	2nd	6	1	—	—	—	—	—	—
1992— Montreal (N.L.)	70	55	.560	2nd	—	—	—	—	—	—	—	—
1993— Montreal (N.L.)	94	68	.580	2nd	—	—	—	—	—	—	—	—
1994— Montreal (N.L.)	74	40	.649	—	—	—	—	—	—	—	—	—
1995— Montreal (N.L.)	66	78	.458	5th	—	—	—	—	—	—	1	0
1996— Montreal (N.L.)	88	74	.543	2nd	—	—	—	—	—	—	—	—
1997— Montreal (N.L.)	78	84	.481	4th	—	—	—	—	—	—	—	—
1998— Montreal (N.L.)	65	97	.401	4th	—	—	—	—	—	—	—	—
1999— Montreal (N.L.)	68	94	.419	4th	—	—	—	—	—	—	—	—
2000— Montreal (N.L.)	67	95	.413	4th	—	—	—	—	—	—	—	—
2001— Montreal (N.L.)	21	32	.396	—	—	—	—	—	—	—	—	—
2003— San Francisco (N.L.)	100	61	.621	1st	1	3	—	—	—	—	—	—
Major League totals (11 years)	791	778	.504		1	3	—	—	—	—	1	0

NOTES:
1977—Lost to St. Petersburg in semifinals.
1978—Memphis tied one game.
1981—Defeated Omaha in league championship.

1986—Defeated Winter Haven, two games to none, in semifinals; lost to St. Petersburg, three games to one, in league championship.
1988—Defeated Vero Beach, two games to none, in first round; lost to Osceola, two games to none, in semifinals.
1990—Defeated Lakeland, two games to one, in semifinals; lost to Vero Beach, two games to one, in league championship.
1991—Defeated Vero Beach, two games to one, in first round; defeated Lakeland, two games to none, in semifinals; defeated Clearwater, two games to none, in league championship.
1992—Replaced Montreal manager Tom Runnells with club in fourth place and record of 17-20 (May 22).
1994—Montreal was in first place in N.L. East at time of season-ending strike (August 12).
2003—Lost to Florida in N.L. divisional playoff.

BAKER, DUSTY — CUBS

PERSONAL: Born June 15, 1949, in Riverside, Calif. ... 6-2/200. ... Batted right, threw right. ... Full name: Johnnie B. Baker Jr.. ... High school: Del Campo (Fair Oaks, Calif.). ... College: American River College (Calif.).
TRANSACTIONS/CAREER NOTES: Selected by Atlanta Braves organization in 26th round of free-agent draft (June 6, 1967). ... On West Palm Beach restricted list (April 5-June 13, 1968). ... On Atlanta military list (January 24-April 3, 1969 and June 17-July 3, 1972). ... Traded by Braves with 1B/3B Ed Goodson to Los Angeles Dodgers for OF Jimmy Wynn, 2B Lee Lacy, 1B/OF Tom Paciorek and IF Jerry Royster (November 17, 1975). ... Released on waivers by Dodgers (February 10, 1984); San Francisco Giants claim rejected (February 16, 1984). ... Granted free agency (February 21, 1984). ... Signed by Giants (April 1, 1984). ... On restricted list (April 2-11, 1984). ... Traded by Giants to Oakland Athletics for P Ed Puikunas and C Dan Winters (March 24, 1985). ... Granted free agency (November 10, 1986).

							BATTING								FIELDING			
Year Team (League)	Pos.	G	AB	R	H	2B	3B	HR	RBI	Avg.	BB	SO	SB	PO	A	E	Avg.
1967— Austin (Texas)	OF	9	39	6	9	1	0	0	1	.231	2	7	0	17	0	1	.944
1968— W.P. Beach (FSL)	OF	6	21	2	4	0	0	0	2	.190	1	4	0	6	2	0	1.000
— Greenw. (W. Car.)	OF	52	199	45	68	11	3	6	39	.342	23	39	6	82	1	3	.965
— Atlanta (N.L.)	OF	6	5	0	2	0	0	0	0	.400	0	1	0	0	0	0	...
1969— Shreveport (Texas)	OF	73	265	40	68	5	1	9	31	.257	36	41	2	135	10	3	.980
— Richmond (Int'l)	3B-OF	25	89	7	22	4	0	0	8	.247	11	22	3	40	9	4	.925
— Atlanta (N.L.)	OF	3	7	0	0	0	0	0	0	.000	0	3	0	2	0	0	1.000
1970— Richmond (Int'l)	OF	118	461	97	150	29	3	11	51	.325	53	45	10	236	10	7	.972
— Atlanta (N.L.)	OF	13	24	3	7	0	0	0	4	.292	2	4	0	11	1	3	.800
1971— Richmond (Int'l)	3B-OF	80	341	62	106	23	2	11	41	.311	25	37	10	136	13	4	.974
— Atlanta (N.L.)	OF	29	62	2	14	2	0	0	4	.226	1	14	0	29	1	0	1.000
1972— Atlanta (N.L.)	OF	127	446	62	143	27	2	17	76	.321	45	68	4	344	8	4	.989
1973— Atlanta (N.L.)	OF	159	604	101	174	29	4	21	99	.288	67	72	24	390	10	7	.983
1974— Atlanta (N.L.)	OF	149	574	80	147	35	0	20	69	.256	71	87	18	359	10	7	.981
1975— Atlanta (N.L.)	OF	142	494	63	129	18	2	19	72	.261	67	57	12	287	10	3	.990
1976— Los Angeles (N.L.)	OF	112	384	36	93	13	0	4	39	.242	31	54	2	254	3	1	.996
1977— Los Angeles (N.L.)	OF	153	533	86	155	26	1	30	86	.291	58	89	2	227	8	3	.987
1978— Los Angeles (N.L.)	OF	149	522	62	137	24	1	11	66	.262	47	66	12	250	13	4	.985
1979— Los Angeles (N.L.)	OF	151	554	86	152	29	1	23	88	.274	56	70	11	289	14	3	.990
1980— Los Angeles (N.L.)	OF	153	579	80	170	26	4	29	97	.294	43	66	12	308	5	3	.991
1981— Los Angeles (N.L.)	OF	103	400	48	128	17	3	9	49	.320	29	43	10	181	8	2	.990
1982— Los Angeles (N.L.)	OF	147	570	80	171	19	1	23	88	.300	56	62	17	226	7	6	.975
1983— Los Angeles (N.L.)	OF	149	531	71	138	25	1	15	73	.260	72	59	7	249	4	5	.981
1984— San Francisco (N.L.)	OF	100	243	31	71	7	2	3	32	.292	40	27	4	112	1	3	.974
1985— Oakland (A.L.)	DH-1B-OF	111	343	48	92	15	1	14	52	.268	50	47	2	465	29	5	.990
1986— Oakland (A.L.)	DH-1B-OF	83	242	25	58	8	0	4	19	.240	27	37	0	90	4	0	1.000
American League totals (2 years)		194	585	73	150	23	1	18	71	.256	77	84	2	555	33	5	.992
National League totals (17 years)		1845	6532	891	1831	297	22	224	942	.280	685	842	135	3518	103	54	.985
Major League totals (19 years)		2039	7117	964	1981	320	23	242	1013	.278	762	926	137	4073	136	59	.986

RECORD AS MANAGER
BACKGROUND: Coach, San Francisco Giants (1988-92). ... Manager, Scottsdale Scorpions, Arizona Fall League (1992, record: 20-22, second place/Northern Division).
HONORS: Named N.L. Manager of the Year by the Baseball Writers' Association of America (1993, 1997 and 2000). ... Named N.L. Manager of the Year by THE SPORTING NEWS (1997 and 2000).

		REGULAR SEASON					POSTSEASON								
						Playoffs		Champ. Series		World Series		All-Star Game			
Year Team (League)	W	L	Pct.	Pos	W	L	W	L	W	L	W	L			
1993— San Francisco (N.L.)	103	59	.635	2nd	—	—	—	—	—	—	—	—			
1994— San Francisco (N.L.)	55	60	.478	—	—	—	—	—	—	—	—	—			
1995— San Francisco (N.L.)	67	77	.465	4th	—	—	—	—	—	—	—	—			
1996— San Francisco (N.L.)	68	94	.419	4th	—	—	—	—	—	—	—	—			
1997— San Francisco (N.L.)	90	72	.555	1st	0	3	—	—	—	—	—	—			
1998— San Francisco (N.L.)	89	74	.546	2nd	—	—	—	—	—	—	—	—			
1999— San Francisco (N.L.)	86	76	.530	2nd	—	—	—	—	—	—	—	—			
2000— San Francisco (N.L.)	97	65	.598	1st	1	3	—	—	—	—	—	—			
2001— San Francisco (N.L.)	90	72	.555	2nd	—	—	—	—	—	—	—	—			
2002— San Francisco (N.L.)	95	66	.590	2nd	3	2	4	1	3	4	—	—			
2003— Chicago (N.L.)	88	74	.543	1st	3	2	3	4	—	—	0	1			
Major League totals (11 years)	928	789	.540		7	10	7	5	3	4	0	1			

NOTES:
1994—San Francisco was in second place in N.L. West at time of season-ending strike (August 12).
1997—Lost to Florida in N.L. divisional playoff.
2000—Lost to New York Mets in N.L. divisional playoff.
2002—Defeated Atlanta in N.L. divisional playoff; defeated St. Louis in N.L. Championship Series; lost to Anaheim in World Series.
2003—Defeated Atlanta in N.L. divisional playoff; lost to Florida in N.L. Championship Series.

BOCHY, BRUCE — PADRES

PERSONAL: Born April 16, 1955, in Landes de Boussac, France. ... 6-4/225. ... Batted right, threw right. ... Full name: Bruce Douglas Bochy. ... Name pronounced: BO-chee. ... High school: Melbourne (Fla.). ... Junior college: Brevard Community College (Fla.). ... College: Florida State.
TRANSACTIONS/CAREER NOTES: Selected by Chicago White Sox organization in eighth round of free-agent draft (January 9, 1975); did not sign. ... Selected by Houston Astros organization in secondary phase of free-agent draft (June 4, 1975). ... Traded by Astros to New York Mets for two players to be named later (February 11, 1981); Astros acquired IF Randy Rodgers and C Stan Hough to complete deal (April 3, 1981). ... Released by Mets (January 21, 1983). ... Signed by Las Vegas, San Diego Padres organization (February 23, 1983). ... On disabled list (April 13-May 6, 1987). ... Granted free agency (November 9, 1987).

Year	Team (League)	Pos.	G	AB	R	H	2B	3B	HR	RBI	Avg.	BB	SO	SB	PO	A	E	Avg.
1975—	Covington (Appal.)	C	37	145	31	49	9	0	4	34	.338	11	18	0	231	36	4	.985
1976—	Columbus (Southern)	C	69	230	9	53	6	0	0	16	.230	14	30	0	266	45	6	.981
	— Dubuque (Midw.)	C-1B	30	103	9	25	4	0	1	8	.243	12	11	1	165	25	5	.974
1977—	Cocoa (Flor. St.)	C	128	430	40	109	18	2	3	35	.253	35	50	0	492	67	12	.979
1978—	Columbus (Southern)	C	79	261	25	70	10	2	7	34	.268	13	30	0	419	49	7	.985
	— Houston (N.L.)	C	54	154	8	41	8	0	3	15	.266	11	35	0	268	35	8	.974
1979—	Houston (N.L.)	C	56	129	11	28	4	0	1	6	.217	17	25	0	198	29	7	.970
1980—	Houston (N.L.)	C-1B	22	22	0	4	1	0	0	0	.182	0	7	0	19	1	0	1.000
1981—	Tidewater (Int'l)	C	85	269	23	61	11	2	8	38	.227	22	47	0	253	35	3	.990
1982—	Tidewater (Int'l)	C	81	251	32	57	11	0	15	52	.227	19	47	2	427	57	5	.990
	— New York (N.L.)	C-1B	17	49	4	15	4	0	2	8	.306	4	6	0	92	8	4	.962
1983—	Las Vegas (PCL)	C	42	145	28	44	8	1	11	33	.303	15	25	3	157	21	3	.983
	— San Diego (N.L.)	C	23	42	2	9	1	1	0	3	.214	0	9	0	51	5	0	1.000
1984—	Las Vegas (PCL)	C	34	121	18	32	7	0	7	22	.264	17	13	0	189	17	2	.990
	— San Diego (N.L.)	C	37	92	10	21	5	1	4	15	.228	3	21	0	147	12	2	.988
1985—	San Diego (N.L.)	C	48	112	16	30	2	0	6	13	.268	6	30	0	148	11	2	.988
1986—	San Diego (N.L.)	C	63	127	16	32	9	0	8	22	.252	14	23	1	202	22	2	.991
1987—	San Diego (N.L.)	C	38	75	8	12	3	0	2	11	.160	11	21	0	95	7	4	.962
1988—	Las Vegas (PCL)	C	53	147	17	34	5	0	5	13	.231	17	28	1	207	19	3	.987
	Major League totals (9 years)		358	802	75	192	37	2	26	93	.239	66	177	1	1220	130	29	.979

RECORD AS MANAGER

BACKGROUND: Player/coach, Las Vegas, San Diego Padres organization (1988). ... Coach, Padres (1993-94).

HONORS: Named N.L. Manager of the Year by The Sporting News (1996 and 1998). ... Named N.L. Manager of the Year by Baseball Writers' Association of America (1996).

		REGULAR SEASON				Playoffs		Champ. Series		World Series		All-Star Game	
Year	Team (League)	W	L	Pct.	Pos	W	L	W	L	W	L	W	L
1989—	Spokane (NW)	41	34	.546	1st	2	1	—	—	—	—	—	—
1990—	Riverside (Calif.)	35	36	.492	4th	—	—	—	—	—	—	—	—
	— Second half	29	42	.408	5th	—	—	—	—	—	—	—	—
1991—	High Desert (Calif.)	31	37	.455	3rd	—	—	—	—	—	—	—	—
	— Second half	42	26	.618	1st	6	2	—	—	—	—	—	—
1992—	Wichita (Texas)	39	29	.573	1st	—	—	—	—	—	—	—	—
	— Second half	31	37	.456	4th	6	1	—	—	—	—	—	—
1995—	San Diego (N.L.)	70	74	.486	3rd	—	—	—	—	—	—	—	—
1996—	San Diego (N.L.)	91	71	.561	1st	0	3	—	—	—	—	—	—
1997—	San Diego (N.L.)	76	86	.469	4th	—	—	—	—	—	—	—	—
1998—	San Diego (N.L.)	98	64	.604	1st	3	1	4	2	0	4	—	—
1999—	San Diego (N.L.)	74	88	.456	4th	—	—	—	—	—	—	0	1
2000—	San Diego (N.L.)	76	86	.469	5th	—	—	—	—	—	—	—	—
2001—	San Diego (N.L.)	79	83	.487	4th	—	—	—	—	—	—	—	—
2002—	San Diego (N.L.)	66	96	.407	5th	—	—	—	—	—	—	—	—
2003—	San Diego (N.L.)	64	98	.395	5th	—	—	—	—	—	—	—	—
	Major League totals (9 years)	694	746	.481		3	4	4	2	0	4	0	1

NOTES:
1989—Defeated Southern Oregon in league championship.
1991—Defeated Bakersfield, three games to none, in semifinals; defeated Stockton, three games to two, in league championship.
1992—Defeated El Paso, two games to one, in semifinals; defeated Shreveport, four games to none, in league championship.
1996—Lost to St. Louis in N.L. divisional playoff.
1998—Defeated Houston in N.L. divisional playoff; defeated Atlanta in N.L. Championship Series; lost to New York Yankees in World Series.

BOWA, LARRY   PHILLIES

PERSONAL: Born December 6, 1945, in Sacramento. ... 5-10/155. ... Batted both, threw right. ... Full name: Lawrence Robert Bowa. ... High school: McClatchy (Sacramento) ... Junior college: Sacramento City College.

TRANSACTIONS/CAREER NOTES: Signed as non-drafted free agent by Philadelphia Phillies organization (October 12, 1965). ... On military list (March 7-July 18, 1967). ... On disabled list (July 26-September 1, 1973). ... On disabled list (May 27-June 23, 1975). ... On disabled list (May 25-June 9, 1979). ... Traded with 2B Ryne Sandberg to Chicago Cubs for SS Ivan DeJesus (January 27, 1982). ... Released by Cubs (August 13, 1985). ... Signed by New York Mets (August 20, 1985). ... Granted free agency (November 12, 1985).

Year	Team (League)	Pos.	G	AB	R	H	2B	3B	HR	RBI	Avg.	BB	SO	SB	PO	A	E	Avg.
1966—	Spartan. (W. Car.)	SS	97	429	70	134	14	4	2	36	.312	36	44	24	138	284	12	.972
	— San Diego (PCL)	SS	5	19	0	6	0	1	0	1	.316	1	3	0	13	20	2	.943
1967—	Bakersfield (Calif.)	2B-SS	7	32	4	6	2	0	0	3	.188	1	6	2	15	12	1	.964
	— Reading (East.)	SS	22	89	11	25	4	0	0	9	.281	3	17	0	35	79	9	.961
1968—	Reading (East.)	SS	133	480	47	116	14	2	3	36	.242	24	27	14	192	395	24	.961
1969—	Eugene (PCL)	2B-SS	135	568	80	163	11	6	1	26	.287	31	56	48	215	469	18	.974
1970—	Philadelphia (N.L.)	2B-SS	145	547	50	137	17	6	0	34	.250	21	48	24	202	418	13	.979
1971—	Philadelphia (N.L.)	SS	159	650	74	162	18	5	0	25	.249	36	61	28	272	560	11	.987
1972—	Philadelphia (N.L.)	SS	152	579	67	145	11	13	1	31	.250	32	51	17	212	494	9	.987
1973—	Philadelphia (N.L.)	SS	122	446	42	94	11	3	0	23	.211	24	31	10	191	361	12	.979
1974—	Philadelphia (N.L.)	SS	162	669	97	184	19	10	1	36	.275	23	52	39	256	462	12	.984
1975—	Philadelphia (N.L.)	SS	136	583	79	178	18	9	2	38	.305	24	32	24	227	403	25	.962
1976—	Philadelphia (N.L.)	SS	156	624	71	155	15	9	0	49	.248	32	31	30	180	492	17	.975
1977—	Philadelphia (N.L.)	SS	154	624	93	175	19	3	4	41	.280	32	32	32	222	518	13	.982
1978—	Philadelphia (N.L.)	SS	156	654	78	192	31	5	3	43	.294	24	40	27	224	548	10	.987
1979—	Philadelphia (N.L.)	SS	147	539	74	130	17	11	0	31	.241	61	32	20	229	448	6	.991
1980—	Philadelphia (N.L.)	SS	147	540	57	144	16	4	2	39	.267	24	28	21	225	449	17	.975
1981—	Philadelphia (N.L.)	SS	103	360	34	102	14	3	0	31	.283	26	17	16	117	309	11	.975
1982—	Chicago (N.L.)	SS	142	499	50	123	15	7	0	29	.246	39	38	8	210	396	17	.973
1983—	Chicago (N.L.)	SS	147	499	73	133	20	5	2	43	.267	35	30	7	230	464	11	.984
1984—	Chicago (N.L.)	SS	133	391	33	87	14	2	0	17	.223	28	24	10	217	378	16	.974
1985—	Chicago (N.L.)	2B-SS	72	195	13	48	6	4	0	13	.246	11	20	5	91	197	9	.970
	— New York (N.L.)	2B-SS	14	19	2	2	1	0	0	2	.105	2	2	0	9	6	2	.882
	Major League totals (16 years)		2247	8418	987	2191	262	99	15	525	.260	474	569	318	3314	6857	211	.980

RECORD AS MANAGER

BACKGROUND: Coach, Phillies (May 11, 1989-96). ... Coach, Anaheim Angels (1997-99). ... Coach, Seattle Mariners (2000).
HONORS: Named N.L. Manager of the Year by The Sporting News (2001). ... Named N.L. Manager of the Year by Baseball Writers' Association of America (2001).

| | | REGULAR SEASON | | | | POSTSEASON | | | | | | | |
| | | | | | | Playoffs | | Champ. Series | | World Series | | All-Star Game | |
Year Team (League)	W	L	Pct.	Pos	W	L	W	L	W	L	W	L	
1986— Las Vegas (PCL)	36	34	.514	3rd	—	—	—	—	—	—	—	—	
— Second half	44	28	.611	1st	6	4	—	—	—	—	—	—	
1987— San Diego (N.L.)	65	97	.401	6th	—	—	—	—	—	—	—	—	
1988— San Diego (N.L.)	16	30	.347	—	—	—	—	—	—	—	—	—	
2001— Philadelphia (N.L.)	86	76	.530	2nd	—	—	—	—	—	—	—	—	
2002— Philadelphia (N.L.)	80	81	.496	3rd	—	—	—	—	—	—	—	—	
2003— Philadelphia (N.L.)	86	76	.530	3rd	—	—	—	—	—	—	—	—	
Major League totals (5 years)	333	360	.480		—	—	—	—	—	—	—	—	

NOTES:
1986—Defeated Phoenix, three games to two, in league semifinals; defeated Vancouver, three games to two, to win league championship.
1988—Replaced as Padres manager by Jack McKeon, with club in fifth place (May 28).

BRENLY, BOB — DIAMONDBACKS

PERSONAL: Born February 25, 1954, in Coshocton, Ohio. ... 6-2/205. ... Batted right, threw right. ... Full name: Robert Earl Brenly. ... College: Ohio University
TRANSACTIONS/CAREER NOTES: Signed as a free agent by San Francisco Giants organization (June 21, 1976). ... On disabled list (March 25-May 13, 1982). ... Released by Giants (December 21, 1988). ... Signed by Toronto Blue Jays (January 18, 1989). ... Released by Blue Jays (July 14, 1989). ... Signed by Giants organization (August 2, 1989). ... Granted free agency (November 13, 1989).

| | | | | | BATTING | | | | | | | | | FIELDING | | |
Year Team (League)	Pos.	G	AB	R	H	2B	3B	HR	RBI	Avg.	BB	SO	SB	PO	A	E	Avg.
1976— Great Falls (Pio.)	3B	25	86	16	27	5	1	1	17	.314	12	9	1	10	16	2	.929
— Fresno (Calif.)	3B	17	60	16	22	3	1	1	9	.367	12	17	1	2	6	1	.889
1977— Cedar Rap. (Midw.)	3B-OF	136	499	85	135	16	1	22	73	.271	90	108	6	90	263	31	.919
1978— Fresno (Calif.)	3B	135	489	102	139	34	5	17	89	.284	81	90	12	118	247	27	.931
1979— Fresno (Calif.)	3B	56	212	49	65	11	2	9	37	.307	28	31	6	39	133	17	.910
— Shreveport (Texas)	3-C-1-O	64	193	33	57	8	1	9	30	.295	38	19	0	199	55	7	.973
1980— Shreveport (Texas)	3B	2	10	2	3	0	0	1	3	.300	0	3	1	1	2	0	1.000
— Phoenix (PCL)	3-S-C-O	84	287	34	74	9	6	7	56	.258	24	51	2	183	110	20	.936
1981— Phoenix (PCL)	3B-C-OF	76	257	42	75	11	3	7	41	.292	29	37	2	177	41	9	.960
— San Francisco (N.L.)	3B-C-OF	19	45	5	15	2	1	1	4	.333	6	4	0	52	6	4	.935
1982— San Francisco (N.L.)	3B-C	65	180	26	51	4	1	4	15	.283	18	26	6	265	32	12	.961
1983— San Francisco (N.L.)	C-1B-OF	104	281	36	63	12	2	7	34	.224	37	48	10	465	73	9	.984
1984— San Francisco (N.L.)	C-1B-OF	145	506	74	147	28	0	20	80	.291	48	52	6	807	76	13	.985
1985— San Francisco (N.L.)	3B-C-1B	133	440	41	97	16	1	19	56	.220	57	62	1	719	85	17	.979
1986— San Francisco (N.L.)	3B-C-1B	149	472	60	116	26	0	16	62	.246	74	97	10	688	118	16	.981
1987— San Francisco (N.L.)	3B-C-1B	123	375	55	100	19	1	18	51	.267	47	85	10	685	86	9	.988
1988— San Francisco (N.L.)	C	73	206	13	39	7	0	5	22	.189	20	40	1	334	27	6	.984
1989— Toronto (A.L.)	C-1B	48	88	9	15	3	1	1	6	.170	10	17	1	61	5	1	.985
— Phoenix (PCL)	3B-C-1B	27	98	11	25	3	0	2	11	.255	8	12	3	78	16	4	.959
— San Francisco (N.L.)	C	12	22	2	4	2	0	0	3	.182	1	7	0	31	5	0	1.000
American League totals (1 year)		48	88	9	15	3	1	1	6	.170	10	17	1	61	5	1	.985
National League totals (9 years)		823	2527	312	632	116	6	90	327	.250	308	421	44	4046	508	86	.981
Major League totals (9 years)		871	2615	321	647	119	7	91	333	.247	318	438	45	4107	513	87	.982

RECORD AS MANAGER

BACKGROUND: Coach, Giants (1992-95).

| | | REGULAR SEASON | | | | POSTSEASON | | | | | | | |
| | | | | | | Playoffs | | Champ. Series | | World Series | | All-Star Game | |
Year Team (League)	W	L	Pct.	Pos	W	L	W	L	W	L	W	L	
2001— Arizona (N.L.)	92	70	.567	1st	3	2	4	1	4	3	—	—	
2002— Arizona (N.L.)	98	64	.604	1st	0	3	—	—	—	—	0	0	
2003— Arizona (N.L.)	84	78	.518	3rd	—	—	—	—	—	—	—	—	
Major League totals (3 years)	274	212	.563		3	5	4	1	4	3	0	0	

NOTES:
2001—Defeated St. Louis in N.L. divisional playoff; defeated Atlanta in N.L. Championship Series; defeated New York Yankees in World Series.
2002—All-Star Game ended in tie. Lost to St. Louis in N.L. divisional playoff.

COX, BOBBY — BRAVES

PERSONAL: Born May 21, 1941, in Tulsa, Okla. ... 6-0/185. ... Batted right, threw right. ... Full name: Robert Joseph Cox. ... High school: Selma (Calif.). ... Junior college: Reedley Junior College (Calif.).
TRANSACTIONS/CAREER NOTES: Signed by Los Angeles Dodgers organization (1959). ... Selected by Chicago Cubs organization from Dodgers organization in Rule 5 minor league draft (November 30, 1964). ... Acquired by Atlanta Braves organization (1966). ... On Austin disabled list (May 8-18 and May 30-June 9, 1966). ... On disabled list (May 1-June 12, 1967). ... Traded by Braves to New York Yankees for C Bob Tillman and P Dale Roberts (December 7, 1967); Roberts later was transferred to Richmond. ... On disabled list (May 28-June 18, 1970). ... Released by Yankees organization (September 22, 1970). ... Signed by Yankees organization (July 17, 1971). ... Released as player by Fort Lauderdale (August 28, 1971).

| | | | | | BATTING | | | | | | | | | FIELDING | | |
Year Team (League)	Pos.	G	AB	R	H	2B	3B	HR	RBI	Avg.	BB	SO	SB	PO	A	E	Avg.
1960— Reno (California)	2B	125	440	99	112	20	5	13	75	.255	95	129	28	282	*385	*39	.945
1961— Salem (NW)	2B	14	44	3	9	2	0	0	2	.205	0	14	0	25	25	2	.962
— Pan. City (Al.-Fla.)	2B	92	335	66	102	27	4	17	73	.304	48	72	17	220	247	8	.983
1962— Salem (Northwest)	3B-2B	*141	514	83	143	26	7	16	82	.278	63	119	7	174	296	28	.944
1963— Albuquerque (Tex.)	3B	17	53	5	15	2	0	2	5	.283	3	12	1	8	27	1	.972
— Great Falls (Pio.)	3B	109	407	103	137	31	4	19	85	.337	73	84	7	82	211	21	.933

Year	Team (League)	Pos.	BATTING												FIELDING			
			G	AB	R	H	2B	3B	HR	RBI	Avg.	BB	SO	SB	PO	A	E	Avg.
1964—	Albuquerque (Tex.)	2B	138	523	98	152	29	13	16	91	.291	52	84	8	322	415	28	.963
1965—	Salt Lake (PCL)	2B-3B	136	473	58	125	32	1	12	55	.264	35	96	1	133	337	22	.955
1966—	Tacoma (PCL)	2B-3B	10	34	2	4	1	0	0	4	.118	6	9	0	23	15	0	1.000
	Austin (Texas)	2B-3B	92	339	35	77	11	1	7	30	.227	25	55	7	140	216	12	.967
1967—	Richmond (Int'l)	3B-1B	99	350	52	104	17	4	14	51	.297	34	73	3	84	136	8	.965
1968—	New York (A.L.)	3B	135	437	33	100	15	1	7	41	.229	41	85	3	98	279	17	.957
1969—	New York (A.L.)	2B-3B	85	191	17	41	7	1	2	17	.215	34	41	0	50	147	11	.947
1970—	Syracuse (Int'l)	2B-3B-SS	90	251	34	55	15	0	9	30	.219	49	40	0	86	163	13	.950
1971—	Fort Laud. (FSL)	P	4	9	1	1	0	0	0	0	.111	1	0	0	4	5	0	1.000
	Major League totals (2 years)		220	628	50	141	22	2	9	58	.225	75	126	3	148	426	28	.953

RECORD AS MANAGER

BACKGROUND: Minor league instructor, New York Yankees (October 28, 1970-March 24, 1971). ... Player/manager, Fort Lauderdale, Yankees organization (1971). ... Coach, Yankees (1977). ... General manager, Atlanta (October 1986-1989).

HONORS: Named Major League Manager of the Year by THE SPORTING NEWS (1985). ... Named A.L. Manager of the Year by Baseball Writers' Association of America (1985). ... Named N.L. Manager of the Year by THE SPORTING NEWS (1991, 1993, 1999 and 2003). ... Named N.L. Manager of the Year by Baseball Writers' Association of America (1991).

			REGULAR SEASON				POSTSEASON								
							Playoffs		Champ. Series		World Series		All-Star Game		
Year	Team (League)	W	L	Pct.	Pos	W	L	W	L	W	L	W	L		
1971—	Fort Lauderdale (FSL)	71	70	.503	4th	—	—	—	—	—	—	—	—		
1972—	West Haven (East.)	84	56	.600	1st	3	0	—	—	—	—	—	—		
1973—	Syracuse (I.L.)	76	70	.520	3rd	—	—	—	—	—	—	—	—		
1974—	Syracuse (I.L.)	74	70	.513	2nd	—	—	—	—	—	—	—	—		
1975—	Syracuse (I.L.)	72	64	.529	3rd	—	—	—	—	—	—	—	—		
1976—	Syracuse (I.L.)	82	57	.589	2nd	6	1	—	—	—	—	—	—		
1978—	Atlanta (N.L.)	69	93	.425	6th	—	—	—	—	—	—	—	—		
1979—	Atlanta (N.L.)	66	94	.412	6th	—	—	—	—	—	—	—	—		
1980—	Atlanta (N.L.)	81	80	.503	4th	—	—	—	—	—	—	—	—		
1981—	Atlanta (N.L.)	25	29	.462	4th	—	—	—	—	—	—	—	—		
	Second half	25	27	.481	5th	—	—	—	—	—	—	—	—		
1982—	Toronto (A.L.)	78	84	.481	6th	—	—	—	—	—	—	—	—		
1983—	Toronto (A.L.)	89	73	.549	4th	—	—	—	—	—	—	—	—		
1984—	Toronto (A.L.)	89	73	.549	2nd	—	—	—	—	—	—	—	—		
1985—	Toronto (A.L.)	99	62	.614	1st	—	—	3	4	—	—	—	—		
1990—	Atlanta (N.L.)	40	57	.412	6th	—	—	—	—	—	—	—	—		
1991—	Atlanta (N.L.)	94	68	.580	1st	—	—	4	3	3	4	—	—		
1992—	Atlanta (N.L.)	98	64	.604	1st	—	—	4	3	2	4	0	1		
1993—	Atlanta (N.L.)	104	58	.641	1st	—	—	2	4	—	—	0	1		
1994—	Atlanta (N.L.)	68	46	.596	—	—	—	—	—	—	—	—	—		
1995—	Atlanta (N.L.)	90	54	.625	1st	3	1	4	0	4	2	—	—		
1996—	Atlanta (N.L.)	96	66	.592	1st	3	0	4	3	2	4	1	0		
1997—	Atlanta (N.L.)	101	61	.623	1st	3	0	2	4	—	—	0	1		
1998—	Atlanta (N.L.)	106	56	.654	1st	3	0	2	4	—	—	—	—		
1999—	Atlanta (N.L.)	103	59	.635	1st	3	1	4	2	0	4	—	—		
2000—	Atlanta (N.L.)	95	67	.586	1st	0	3	—	—	—	—	0	1		
2001—	Atlanta (N.L.)	88	74	.543	1st	3	0	1	4	—	—	—	—		
2002—	Atlanta (N.L.)	101	59	.631	1st	2	3	—	—	—	—	—	—		
2003—	Atlanta (N.L.)	101	61	.623	1st	2	3	—	—	—	—	—	—		
American League totals (4 years)		355	292	.549		—	—	3	4	—	—	—	—		
National League totals (18 years)		1551	1173	.570		22	11	27	27	11	18	1	4		
Major League totals (22 years)		1906	1465	.565		22	11	30	31	11	18	1	4		

NOTES:
1972—Defeated Three Rivers in playoff.
1976—Defeated Memphis, three games to none, in playoffs; defeated Richmond, three games to one, in league championship.
1985—Lost to Kansas City in A.L. Championship Series.
1990—Replaced Atlanta manager Russ Nixon with club in sixth place and record of 25-40 (June 22).
1991—Defeated Pittsburgh in N.L. Championship Series; lost to Minnesota in World Series.
1992—Defeated Pittsburgh in N.L. Championship Series; lost to Toronto in World Series.
1993—Lost to Philadelphia in N.L. Championship Series.
1994—Atlanta was in second place in N.L. East at time of season-ending strike (August 12).
1995—Defeated Colorado in N.L. divisional playoff; defeated Cincinnati in N.L. Championship Series; defeated Cleveland in World Series.
1996—Defeated Los Angeles in N.L. divisional playoff; defeated St. Louis in N.L. Championship Series; lost to New York Yankees in World Series.
1997—Defeated Houston in N.L. divisional playoff; lost to Florida in N.L. Championship Series.
1998—Defeated Chicago Cubs in N.L. divisional playoff; lost to San Diego in N.L. Championship Series.
1999—Defeated Houston in N.L. divisional playoff; defeated New York Mets in N.L. Championship Series; lost to New York Yankees in World Series.
2000—Lost to St. Louis in N.L. divisional playoff.
2001—Defeated Houston in N.L. divisional playoff; lost to Arizona in N.L. Championship Series.
2002—Lost to San Francisco in N.L. divisional playoff.
2003—Lost to Chicago in N.L. divisional playoff.

GARDENHIRE, RON   TWINS

PERSONAL: Born October 24, 1957, in Butzbach, West Germany. ... 6-0/180. ... Batted right, threw right. ... Full name: Ronald Clyde Gardenhire. ... High school: Okmulgee (Okla.) High School ... Junior college: Paris (Texas) ... College: Texas.

TRANSACTIONS/CAREER NOTES: Selected by New York Mets organization in sixth round of free-agent draft (June 5, 1979). ... On Tidewater disabled list (July 21-31, 1983). ... On disabled list (July 20-August 9 and August 20-September 10, 1984). ... On disabled list (May 2-17, May 25-July 19 and August 16-September 1, 1985); included rehabilitation assignment to Tidewater (June 24-July 13). ... Traded by Mets to Minnesota Twins for P Don Iasparro (November 12, 1986).

Year — Team (League)	Pos.	G	AB	R	H	2B	3B	HR	RBI	Avg.	BB	SO	SB	PO	A	E	Avg.
1979— Lynchburg (Caro.)	SS	70	277	36	82	13	3	4	27	.296	21	45	9	120	252	21	.947
1980— Jackson (Texas)	2B-SS	127	458	58	118	16	6	6	64	.258	45	68	13	168	411	41	.934
1981— Tidewater (Int'l)	2B-3B-SS	125	414	52	105	17	8	2	40	.254	28	61	28	206	373	33	.946
— New York (N.L.)	2B-3B-SS	27	48	2	13	1	0	0	3	.271	5	9	2	28	50	2	.975
1982— New York (N.L.)	2B-3B-SS	141	384	29	92	17	1	3	33	.240	23	55	5	235	399	29	.956
1983— New York (N.L.)	SS	17	32	1	2	0	0	0	1	.063	1	4	0	13	30	0	1.000
— Tidewater (Int'l)	SS	102	387	63	111	20	6	4	39	.287	34	54	9	202	321	27	.951
1984— New York (N.L.)	2B-3B-SS	74	207	20	51	7	1	1	10	.246	9	43	6	98	154	12	.955
1985— New York (N.L.)	2B-3B-SS	26	39	5	7	2	1	0	2	.179	8	11	0	21	32	4	.930
— Tidewater (Int'l)	2B-3B-SS	22	71	3	15	2	0	1	10	.211	6	13	0	20	36	5	.918
1986— Tidewater (Int'l)	2B-SS	96	323	41	89	10	4	4	33	.276	44	48	11	161	288	19	.959
1987— Portland (PCL)	2-3-S-1	117	389	49	106	16	4	6	50	.272	45	70	1	384	126	5	.990
Major League totals (5 years)		285	710	57	165	27	3	4	49	.232	46	122	13	395	665	47	.958

RECORD AS MANAGER

BACKGROUND: Coach, Minnesota Twins (1991-2001).

		REGULAR SEASON				Playoffs		Champ. Series		World Series		All-Star Game	
Year — Team (League)	W	L	Pct.	Pos	W	L	W	L	W	L	W	L	
1988— Kenosha (Midw.)	41	27	.602	1st	—	—	—	—	—	—	—	—	
— Second half	40	32	.556	2nd	3	3	—	—	—	—	—	—	
1989— Orlando (Sou.)	40	31	.563	1st	—	—	—	—	—	—	—	—	
— Second half	39	34	.534	4th	1	3	—	—	—	—	—	—	
1990— Orlando (Sou.)	42	30	.583	1st	—	—	—	—	—	—	—	—	
— Second half	43	29	.597	2nd	5	4	—	—	—	—	—	—	
2002— Minnesota (A.L.)	94	67	.583	1st	3	2	1	4	—	—	—	—	
2003— Minnesota (A.L.)	90	72	.555	1st	1	3	—	—	—	—	—	—	
Major League totals (2 years)	184	139	.569		4	5	1	4	—	—	—	—	

NOTES:
1988—Defeated Rockford, two games to none, in playoffs; lost to Cedar Rapids, three games to one, in league championship.
1989—Lost to Greenville in playoffs.
1990—Defeated Jacksonville, three games to one, in playoffs; lost to Memphis, three games to two, in league championship.
2002—Defeated Oakland in A.L. divisional playoff; lost to Anaheim in A.L. Championship Series.
2003—Lost to New York in A.L. divisional playoff.

GUILLEN, OZZIE — WHITE SOX

PERSONAL: Born January 20, 1964, in Oculare del Tuy, Venezuela. ... 5-11/165. ... Batted left, threw right. ... Full name: Oswaldo Jose Barrios Guillen. ... Name pronounced: GHEE-un.

TRANSACTIONS/CAREER NOTES: Signed as non-drafted free agent by San Diego Padres organization (December 17, 1980). ... Traded by Padres with P Tim Lollar, P Bill Long and 3B Luis Salazar to Chicago White Sox for P LaMarr Hoyt, P Kevin Kristan and P Todd Simmons (December 6, 1984). ... On disabled list (April 22, 1992-remainder of season). ... Granted free agency (October 31, 1997). ... Signed by Baltimore Orioles organization (January 29, 1998). ... Released by Orioles (May 1, 1998). ... Signed by Atlanta Braves (May 6, 1998). ... Granted free agency (November 2, 1998). ... Re-signed by Braves (December 2, 1998). ... Released by Braves (April 5, 2000). ... Signed by Tampa Bay Devil Rays (April 5, 2000). ... Granted free agency (November 9, 2000). ... Re-signed by Devil Rays organization (December 6, 2000). ... Released by Devil Rays (March 31, 2001).

Year — Team (League)	Pos.	G	AB	R	H	2B	3B	HR	RBI	Avg.	BB	SO	SB	PO	A	E	Avg.
1981— GC Padres (GCL)	2B-SS	55	189	26	49	4	1	0	16	.259	13	24	8	105	135	14	.941
1982— Reno (Calif.)	SS	130	528	* 103	* 183	33	1	2	54	.347	16	53	25	* 240	399	41	.940
1983— Beaumont (Texas)	SS	114	427	62	126	20	4	2	48	.295	15	29	7	185	327	* 38	.931
1984— Las Vegas (PCL)	2B-SS	122	463	81	137	26	6	5	53	.296	13	40	9	172	‡ 364	17	.969
1985— Chicago (A.L.)	SS	150	491	71	134	21	9	1	33	.273	12	36	7	220	382	12	* .980
1986— Chicago (A.L.)	SS-DH	159	547	58	137	19	4	2	47	.250	12	52	8	261	459	22	.970
1987— Chicago (A.L.)	SS	149	560	64	156	22	7	2	51	.279	22	52	25	266	475	19	.975
1988— Chicago (A.L.)	SS	156	566	58	148	16	7	0	39	.261	25	40	25	273	* 570	20	.977
1989— Chicago (A.L.)	SS	155	597	63	151	20	8	1	54	.253	15	48	36	272	512	22	.973
1990— Chicago (A.L.)	SS	160	516	61	144	21	4	1	58	.279	26	37	13	252	474	17	.977
1991— Chicago (A.L.)	SS	154	524	52	143	20	3	3	49	.273	11	38	21	249	439	21	.970
1992— Chicago (A.L.)	SS	12	40	5	8	4	0	0	7	.200	1	5	1	20	39	0	1.000
1993— Chicago (A.L.)	SS	134	457	44	128	23	4	4	50	.280	10	41	5	189	361	16	.972
1994— Chicago (A.L.)	SS	100	365	46	105	9	5	1	39	.288	14	35	5	139	237	16	.959
1995— Chicago (A.L.)	SS-DH	122	415	50	103	20	3	1	41	.248	13	25	6	167	319	12	.976
1996— Chicago (A.L.)	SS-OF	150	499	62	131	24	8	4	45	.263	10	27	6	222	348	11	.981
1997— Chicago (A.L.)	SS	142	490	59	120	21	6	4	52	.245	22	24	5	207	348	15	.974
1998— Baltimore (A.L.)	SS-3B	12	16	2	1	0	0	0	0	.063	1	2	0	3	11	1	.933
— Atlanta (N.L.)	S-2-3-1	83	264	35	73	15	1	1	22	.277	24	25	1	97	166	6	.978
1999— Atlanta (N.L.)	SS-3B-2B	92	232	21	56	16	0	1	20	.241	15	17	4	58	146	7	.967
2000— Tampa Bay (A.L.)	S-3-1-2	63	107	22	26	4	0	2	12	.243	6	7	1	40	90	5	.963
American League totals (15 years)		1818	6190	717	1635	244	68	26	577	.264	200	469	164	2780	5264	209	.974
National League totals (2 years)		175	496	56	129	31	1	2	42	.260	39	42	5	155	312	13	.973
Major League totals (16 years)		1993	6686	773	1635	275	69	28	619	.264	239	511	169	2935	5376	222	.974

RECORD AS MANAGER

BACKGROUND: Coach, Montreal Expos (2001). ... Coach, Florida Marlins (2002-03).

HOWE, ART — METS

PERSONAL: Born December 15, 1946, in Pittsburgh. ... 6-1/185. ... Batted right, threw right. ... Full name: Arthur Henry Howe Jr.. ... High school: Shaler (Glenshaw, Pa.). ... College: Wyoming.

TRANSACTIONS/CAREER NOTES: Signed as free agent by Pittsburgh Pirates organization (June, 1971). ... On disabled list (August 17-September 2, 1972 and April 13-May 6, 1973). ... Traded by Pirates to Houston Astros (January 6, 1976), completing deal in which Astros traded 2B Tommy Helms to Pirates for a player to be named later (December 12, 1975). ... On disabled list (May 12-June 19, 1982 and March 27, 1983-entire season). ... Granted free agency (November 7, 1983). ... Signed by St. Louis Cardinals (March 21, 1984). ... Released by Cardinals (April 22, 1985).

Year — Team (League)	Pos.	G	AB	R	H	2B	3B	HR	RBI	Avg.	BB	SO	SB	PO	A	E	Avg.
1971— Salem (Caro.)	3B-SS	114	382	77	133	27	7	12	79	.348	82	74	11	110	221	21	.940
1972— Char., W.Va. (Int'l)	2B-3B-SS	109	365	68	99	21	3	14	53	.271	63	69	8	105	248	24	.936
1973— Char., W.Va. (Int'l)	2B-3B-SS	119	372	50	85	20	1	8	44	.228	54	70	6	141	229	21	.946
1974— Char., W.Va. (Int'l)	3B	60	207	26	70	17	4	8	36	.338	31	27	4	35	90	9	.933
— Pittsburgh (N.L.)	3B-SS	29	74	10	18	4	1	1	5	.243	9	13	0	11	49	4	.938
1975— Char., W.Va. (Int'l)	2B-3B	11	42	4	15	1	3	0	3	.357	2	4	0	15	23	1	.974
— Pittsburgh (N.L.)	3B-SS	63	146	13	25	9	0	1	10	.171	15	15	1	19	89	7	.939
1976— Memphis (Int'l)	3B-1B	74	259	50	92	21	3	12	59	.355	34	31	1	93	120	14	.938
— Houston (N.L.)	2B-3B	21	29	0	4	1	0	0	0	.138	6	6	0	17	16	1	.971
1977— Houston (N.L.)	2B-3B-SS	125	413	44	109	23	7	8	58	.264	41	60	0	213	333	8	.986
1978— Houston (N.L.)	2B-3B-1B	119	420	46	123	33	3	7	55	.293	34	41	2	240	302	13	.977
1979— Houston (N.L.)	2B-3B-1B	118	355	32	88	15	2	6	33	.248	36	37	3	188	261	7	.985
1980— Houston (N.L.)	2B-3B-SS-1B	110	321	34	91	12	5	10	46	.283	34	29	1	598	86	10	.986
1981— Houston (N.L.)	3B-1B	103	361	43	107	22	4	3	36	.296	41	23	1	67	206	9	.968
1982— Houston (N.L.)	3B-1B	110	365	29	87	15	1	5	38	.238	41	45	2	344	174	7	.987
1983—								Did not play.									
1984— St. Louis (N.L.)	2-3-S-1	89	139	17	30	5	0	2	12	.216	18	18	0	71	80	3	.981
1985— St. Louis (N.L.)	3B-1B	4	3	0	0	0	0	0	0	.000	0	0	0	5	1	0	1.000
Major League totals (11 years)		891	2626	268	682	139	23	43	293	.260	275	287	10	1773	1597	69	.980

RECORD AS MANAGER

BACKGROUND: Coach, Texas Rangers (May 21, 1985-88). ... Scout, Los Angeles Dodgers organization (1994). ... Coach, Colorado Rockies (1995).

	REGULAR SEASON				Playoffs		Champ. Series		World Series		All-Star Game	
Year — Team (League)	W	L	Pct.	Pos	W	L	W	L	W	L	W	L
1989— Houston (N.L.)	86	76	.530	3rd	—	—	—	—	—	—	—	—
1990— Houston (N.L.)	75	87	.462	4th	—	—	—	—	—	—	—	—
1991— Houston (N.L.)	65	97	.401	6th	—	—	—	—	—	—	—	—
1992— Houston (N.L.)	81	81	.500	4th	—	—	—	—	—	—	—	—
1993— Houston (N.L.)	85	77	.524	3rd	—	—	—	—	—	—	—	—
1996— Oakland (A.L.)	78	84	.481	3rd	—	—	—	—	—	—	—	—
1997— Oakland (A.L.)	65	97	.401	4th	—	—	—	—	—	—	—	—
1998— Oakland (A.L.)	74	88	.456	4th	—	—	—	—	—	—	—	—
1999— Oakland (A.L.)	87	75	.537	2nd	—	—	—	—	—	—	—	—
2000— Oakland (A.L.)	91	70	.565	1st	2	3	—	—	—	—	—	—
2001— Oakland (A.L.)	102	60	.629	2nd	2	3	—	—	—	—	—	—
2002— Oakland (A.L.)	103	59	.635	1st	2	3	—	—	—	—	—	—
2003— New York (N.L.)	66	95	.409	5th	—	—	—	—	—	—	—	—
American League totals (7 years)	600	533	.529		6	9	—	—	—	—	—	—
National League totals (6 years)	458	513	.471		—	—	—	—	—	—	—	—
Major League totals (13 years)	1058	1046	.502		6	9	—	—	—	—	—	—

NOTES:
2000—Lost to New York Yankees in A.L. divisional playoff.
2001—Lost to New York Yankees in A.L. divisional playoff.
2002—Lost to Minnesota in A.L. divisional playoff.

HURDLE, CLINT — ROCKIES

PERSONAL: Born July 30, 1957, in Big Rapids, Mich. ... 6-3/210. ... Batted right, threw right. ... Full name: Clinton Merrick Hurdle. ... High school: Merritt Island (Fla.).
TRANSACTIONS/CAREER NOTES: Selected by Kansas City Royals organization in first round (ninth pick overall) of free-agent draft (June 4, 1975). ... On disabled list (April 20-May 30 and August 9-September 13, 1981). ... Traded by Royals to Cincinnati Reds for P Scott Brown (December 11, 1981). ... Released by Reds (November 15, 1982). ... Signed by New York Mets organization (April 7, 1983). ... Selected by St. Louis Cardinals (December 10, 1985). ... Granted free agency (November 12, 1986). ... Signed by Mets organization (February 9, 1987).

Year — Team (League)	Pos.	G	AB	R	H	2B	3B	HR	RBI	Avg.	BB	SO	SB	PO	A	E	Avg.
1975— Sarasota Royals (GCL)	OF	49	175	34	48	4	4	1	31	.274	...	...	...	94	5	2	.980
1976— Waterloo (Midw.)	OF	127	429	89	101	22	5	19	89	.235	...	...	...	179	12	7	.965
1977— Omaha (A.A.)	OF	129	442	85	145	35	3	16	66	.328	...	...	...	198	17	6	.973
— Kansas City (A.L.)	OF	9	26	5	8	0	0	2	7	.308	...	...	...	17	0	0	1.000
1978— Kansas City (A.L.)	3B-1B-OF	133	417	48	110	25	5	7	56	.264	...	...	...	544	30	12	.980
1979— Omaha (A.A.)	OF	68	220	30	52	13	0	6	29	.236	...	...	...	124	14	4	.972
— Kansas City (A.L.)	3B-OF	59	171	16	41	10	3	3	30	.240	...	...	...	89	2	3	.968
1980— Kansas City (A.L.)	OF	130	395	50	116	31	2	10	60	.294	...	...	...	233	8	10	.960
1981— Kansas City (A.L.)	OF	28	76	12	25	3	1	4	15	.329	...	...	...	59	1	0	1.000
1982— Cincinnati (N.L.)	OF	19	34	2	7	1	0	0	1	.206	...	...	...	17	2	1	.950
— Indianapolis (A.A.)	1B-OF	88	261	38	64	18	0	12	58	.245	...	...	...	113	7	4	.968
1983— Tidewater (Int'l)	3B-1B-OF	139	477	82	136	33	4	22	105	.285	...	...	...	130	149	22	.927
— New York (N.L.)	3B-OF	13	33	3	6	2	0	0	2	.182	...	...	...	1	15	4	.800
1984— Tidewater (Int'l)	C	128	412	60	100	15	1	21	64	.243	...	...	...	1036	60	9	.992
1985— New York (N.L.)	C-OF	43	82	7	16	4	0	3	7	.195	...	...	...	89	7	1	.990
1986— St. Louis (N.L.)	C	78	154	18	30	5	1	3	15	.195	...	...	...	334	31	3	.992
1987— New York (N.L.)	1B	3	3	1	1	0	0	0	0	.333	...	...	...	1	0	0	1.000
— Tidewater (Int'l)	C-1B-OF	97	288	38	74	27	0	7	45	.257	...	...	...	275	16	3	.990
American League totals (5 years)		359	1085	131	300	69	11	26	168	.276	...	...	...	942	41	25	.975
National League totals (5 years)		156	306	31	60	12	1	6	25	.196	...	...	...	442	55	9	.982
Major League totals (10 years)		515	1391	162	360	81	12	32	193	.259	...	...	...	1384	96	34	.978

RECORD AS MANAGER

BACKGROUND: Roving hitting instructor, Colorado Rockies (1994-96). ... Third base coach, Rockies (1997-98). ... Hitting coach, Rockies (1997-April 26, 2002).
HONORS: Named Texas League Manager of the Year (1990).

Year	Team (League)	W	L	Pct.	Pos	Playoffs W	Playoffs L	Champ. Series W	Champ. Series L	World Series W	World Series L	All-Star Game W	All-Star Game L
1988—	St. Lucie (FSL)	36	34	.514	4th	—	—	—	—	—	—	—	—
	—Second half	38	31	.551	1st	6	1	—	—	—	—	—	—
1989—	St. Lucie (FSL)	42	28	.600	1st	—	—	—	—	—	—	—	—
	—Second half	37	27	.578	1st	1	2	—	—	—	—	—	—
1990—	Jackson (Texas)	35	32	.522	2nd	—	—	—	—	—	—	—	—
	—Second half	38	30	.559	1st	0	2	—	—	—	—	—	—
1991—	Williamsport (East.)	60	79	.431	7th	—	—	—	—	—	—	—	—
1992—	Tidewater (I.L.)	56	86	.394	4th	—	—	—	—	—	—	—	—
1993—	Norfolk (I.L.)	70	71	.496	4th	—	—	—	—	—	—	—	—
2002—	Colorado (N.L.)	67	73	.478	4th	—	—	—	—	—	—	—	—
2003—	Colorado (N.L.)	74	88	.456	4th	—	—	—	—	—	—	—	—
Major League totals (2 years)		**141**	**161**	**.466**		—	—	—	—	—	—	—	—

NOTES:

1988—Defeated Lakeland, two games to one, in playoffs; defeated Tampa, two games to none, in playoffs; defeated Osceola, two games to none, to win league championship.

1989—Lost to Port Charlotte in playoffs.

1990—Lost to Shreveport in playoffs.

2002—Replaced Colorado manager Buddy Bell, with club in fifth place and record of 6-16 (April 26).

LA RUSSA, TONY — CARDINALS

PERSONAL: Born October 4, 1944, in Tampa. ... 6-0/185. ... Batted right, threw right. ... Full name: Anthony La Russa Jr. ... High school: Jefferson (Tampa). ... College: Tampa, then South Florida.

TRANSACTIONS/CAREER NOTES: Signed by Kansas City Athletics organization (June 6, 1962). ... On disabled list (May 9-September 8, 1964; June 3-July 15, 1965; and April 12-May 6 and July 3-September 5, 1967). ... A's franchise moved from Kansas City to Oakland (October 1967). ... Contract sold by A's to Atlanta Braves (August 14, 1971). ... Traded by Braves to Chicago Cubs for P Tom Phoebus (October 20, 1972). ... Contract sold by Cubs to Pittsburgh Pirates organization (March 23, 1974). ... Released by Pirates organization (April 4, 1975). ... Signed by Chicago White Sox organization (April 7, 1975). ... On disabled list (August 8-18, 1976). ... Contract sold by White Sox to St. Louis Cardinals organization (December 13, 1976). ... Released by Cardinals organization (September 29, 1977).

Year	Team (League)	Pos.	G	AB	R	H	2B	3B	HR	RBI	Avg.	BB	SO	SB	PO	A	E	Avg.
1962—	Daytona Beach (FSL)	SS	64	225	37	58	7	0	1	32	.258	42	47	11	135	173	38	.890
	—Binghamton (East.)	2B-SS	12	43	3	8	0	0	0	4	.186	5	9	2	20	27	8	.855
1963—	Kansas City (A.L.)	2B-SS	34	44	4	11	1	1	0	1	.250	7	12	1	29	25	2	.964
1964—	Lewiston (N'west)	2B-SS	90	329	50	77	22	1	1	25	.234	53	56	10	188	218	18	.958
1965—	Birmingham (Sou.)	2B	75	259	24	50	11	2	1	18	.193	26	37	5	202	161	21	.945
1966—	Modesto (California)	2B	81	316	67	92	20	1	7	54	.291	44	37	18	201	212	20	.954
	—Mobile (Sou.)	2B	51	170	20	50	9	4	4	26	.294	23	24	4	117	130	10	.962
1967—	Birmingham (Sou.)	2B	41	139	12	32	6	1	5	22	.230	10	11	3	88	120	5	.977
1968—	Oakland (A.L.)		5	3	0	1	0	0	0	0	.333	0	0	0	...	...	...	...
	—Vancouver (PCL)	2B	122	455	55	109	16	8	5	29	.240	52	58	4	249	321	14	.976
1969—	Iowa (Am. Assoc.)	2B	67	235	37	72	11	1	4	27	.306	42	30	5	177	222	15	.964
	—Oakland (A.L.)		8	8	0	0	0	0	0	0	.000	0	1	0	...	...	...	...
1970—	Iowa (Am. Assoc.)	2B	22	88	13	22	5	0	2	5	.250	9	14	0	52	59	3	.974
	—Oakland (A.L.)	2B	52	106	6	21	4	1	0	6	.198	15	19	0	67	89	5	.969
1971—	Iowa (Am. Assoc.)	2-3-S-O	28	107	21	31	5	1	2	11	.290	10	11	0	70	85	2	.987
	—Oakland (A.L.)	2B-3B-SS	23	8	3	0	0	0	0	0	.000	0	4	0	8	7	2	.882
	—Atlanta (N.L.)	2B	9	7	1	2	0	0	0	0	.286	1	1	0	8	6	1	.933
1972—	Richmond (Int'l)	2B	122	389	68	120	13	2	10	42	.308	72	41	0	305	289	20	.967
1973—	Wichita (A.A.)	2B-3B-1B	106	392	82	123	16	0	5	75	.314	60	46	10	423	213	26	.961
	—Chicago (N.L.)		1	0	1	0	0	0	0	0	.000	0	0	0	...	...	...	...
1974—	Char., W.Va. (Int'l)	2B	139	457	50	119	17	1	8	35	.260	51	50	4	262	378	17	.974
1975—	Denver (A.A.)	2-3-S-O	118	354	87	99	23	2	7	46	.280	70	46	13	95	91	10	.949
1976—	Iowa (Am. Assoc.)	P	107	332	53	86	11	0	4	34	.259	40	43	10	132	160	22	.930
1977—	New Orleans (A.A.)	2B-3B	50	128	17	24	2	2	3	6	.188	20	21	0	66	87	7	.956
American League totals (5 years)			122	169	13	33	5	2	0	7	.195	22	36	1	104	121	9	.961
National League totals (2 years)			10	7	2	2	0	0	0	0	.286	1	1	0	8	6	1	.933
Major League totals (6 years)			132	176	15	35	5	2	0	7	.199	23	37	0	112	127	10	.960

RECORD AS MANAGER

BACKGROUND: Coach, St. Louis Cardinals organization (June 20-September 29, 1977). ... Coach, Chicago White Sox (July 3, 1978-remainder of season).

HONORS: Named Major League Manager of the Year by THE SPORTING NEWS (1983). ... Named A.L. Manager of the Year by the Baseball Writers' Association of America (1983, 1988 and 1992). ... Named A.L. Manager of the Year by THE SPORTING NEWS (1988 and 1992). ... Named N.L. Manager of the Year by Baseball Writers' Association of America (2002).

Year	Team (League)	W	L	Pct.	Pos	Playoffs W	Playoffs L	Champ. Series W	Champ. Series L	World Series W	World Series L	All-Star Game W	All-Star Game L
1978—	Knoxville (Sou.)	49	21	.700	1st	—	—	—	—	—	—	—	—
	—Second half	4	4	.500	—	—	—	—	—	—	—	—	—
1979—	Iowa (A.A.)	54	52	.509	—	—	—	—	—	—	—	—	—
	—Chicago (A.L.)	27	27	.500	5th	—	—	—	—	—	—	—	—
1980—	Chicago (A.L.)	70	90	.437	5th	—	—	—	—	—	—	—	—
1981—	Chicago (A.L.)	31	22	.584	3rd	—	—	—	—	—	—	—	—
	—Second half	23	30	.434	6th	—	—	—	—	—	—	—	—
1982—	Chicago (A.L.)	87	75	.537	3rd	—	—	—	—	—	—	—	—
1983—	Chicago (A.L.)	99	63	.611	1st	—	—	1	3	—	—	—	—
1984—	Chicago (A.L.)	74	88	.456	5th	—	—	—	—	—	—	—	—
1985—	Chicago (A.L.)	85	77	.524	3rd	—	—	—	—	—	—	—	—
1986—	Chicago (A.L.)	26	38	.406	—	—	—	—	—	—	—	—	—
	—Oakland (A.L.)	45	34	.569	3rd	—	—	—	—	—	—	—	—
1987—	Oakland (A.L.)	81	81	.500	3rd	—	—	—	—	—	—	—	—

– 451 –

Year—Team (League)	W	L	Pct.	Pos	Playoffs W	L	Champ. Series W	L	World Series W	L	All-Star Game W	L
1988— Oakland (A.L.)	104	58	.641	1st	—	—	4	0	1	4	—	—
1989— Oakland (A.L.)	99	63	.611	1st	—	—	4	1	4	0	1	0
1990— Oakland (A.L.)	103	59	.635	1st	—	—	4	0	0	4	1	0
1991— Oakland (A.L.)	84	78	.518	4th	—	—	—	—	—	—	1	0
1992— Oakland (A.L.)	96	66	.592	1st	—	—	2	4	—	—	—	—
1993— Oakland (A.L.)	68	94	.419	7th	—	—	—	—	—	—	—	—
1994— Oakland (A.L.)	51	63	.447	—	—	—	—	—	—	—	—	—
1995— Oakland (A.L.)	67	77	.465	4th	—	—	—	—	—	—	—	—
1996— St. Louis (N.L.)	88	74	.543	1st	3	0	3	4	—	—	—	—
1997— St. Louis (N.L.)	73	89	.450	4th	—	—	—	—	—	—	—	—
1998— St. Louis (N.L.)	83	79	.512	3rd	—	—	—	—	—	—	—	—
1999— St. Louis (N.L.)	75	86	.465	4th	—	—	—	—	—	—	—	—
2000— St. Louis (N.L.)	95	67	.586	1st	3	0	1	4	—	—	—	—
2001— St. Louis (N.L.)	93	69	.574	2nd	2	3	—	—	—	—	—	—
2002— St. Louis (N.L.)	97	65	.598	1st	3	0	1	4	—	—	—	—
2003— St. Louis (N.L.)	85	77	.524	3rd	—	—	—	—	—	—	—	—
American League totals (17 years)	1320	1183	.527		—	—	15	8	5	8	3	0
National League totals (8 years)	689	606	.532		11	3	5	12	—	—	—	—
Major League totals (25 years)	2009	1789	.529		11	3	20	20	5	8	3	0

NOTES:
1978—Became Chicago White Sox coach and replace as Knoxville manager by Joe JOnes, with club in third place (July 3).
1979—Replaced as Iowa manager by Joe Sparks, with club in second place (August 3); replaced Chicago manager Don Kessinger with club in fifth place and record of 46-60 (August 3).
1983—Lost to Baltimore in A.L. Championship Series.
1985—On suspended list (August 10-11).
1986—Replaced as White Sox manager by interim manager Doug Rader, with club in sixth place (June 20); replaced Oakland manager Jackie Moore (record of 29-44) and interim manager Jeff Newman (record of 2-8) with club in seventh place and record of 31-52 (July 7).
1988—Defeated Boston in A.L. Championship Series; lost to Los Angeles in World Series.
1989—Defeated Toronto in A.L. Championship Series; defeated San Francisco in World Series.
1990—Defeated Boston in A.L. Championship Series; lost to Cincinnati in World Series.
1992—Lost to Toronto in A.L. Championship Series.
1993—On suspended list (October 1-remainder of season).
1994—Oakland was in second place in A.L. West at time of season-ending strike (August 12).
1996—Defeated San Diego in N.L. divisional playoff; lost to Atlanta in N.L. Championship Series.
2000—Defeated Atlanta in N.L. divisional playoff; lost to New York Mets in N.L. Championship Series.
2001—Lost to Arizona in N.L. divisional playoff.
2002—Defeated Arizona in N.L. divisional playoff; lost to San Francisco in N.L. Championship Series.

MACHA, KEN — ATHLETICS

PERSONAL: Born September 29, 1950, in Monroeville, Pa. ... 6-2/200. ... Batted right, threw right. ... Full name: Kenneth Edward Macha. ... High school: Gateway (Pittsburgh) ... College: Pittsburgh.

TRANSACTIONS/CAREER NOTES: Selected by Pittsburgh Pirates organization in sixth round of free-agent draft (June 6, 1972). ... Drafted by Montreal Expos (December 4, 1978). ... Contract sold by Expos to Toronto Blue Jays (January 15, 1981). ... Played in Japan (1982-85).

Year—Team (League)	Pos.	G	AB	R	H	2B	3B	HR	RBI	Avg.	BB	SO	SB	PO	A	E	Avg.
1972— Salem (Caro.)	3B-C	62	197	20	50	7	2	8	33	.254	...	...	...	386	36	13	.970
1973— Sherbrooke (East.)	C	106	322	40	86	15	0	12	52	.267	...	...	...	551	53	17	.973
1974— Char., W.Va. (Int'l)	3B-C	21	65	6	12	3	0	2	10	.185	...	...	...	100	13	4	.966
— Thet. Mines (Ea.)	C	117	386	87	133	22	2	21	100	.345	...	...	...	531	70	6	.990
— Pittsburgh (N.L.)	C	5	5	1	3	1	0	0	1	.600	0	0	0	1	0	0	1.000
1975— Char., W.Va. (Int'l)		138	478	63	128	21	1	14	63	.268	...	...	...	1051	88	22	.981
1976— Char., W.Va. (Int'l)	C	126	458	68	138	29	1	14	77	.301	...	...	...	232	116	26	.930
1977— Columbus (Int'l)	C	76	254	51	85	18	2	11	64	.335	...	...	...	187	25	9	.959
— Pittsburgh (N.L.)	OF	35	95	2	26	4	0	0	11	.274	6	17	1	72	25	1	.990
1978— Columbus (Int'l)	3B-C-OF	65	233	34	61	10	1	6	34	.262	...	...	...	62	114	18	.907
— Pittsburgh (N.L.)	3B	29	52	5	11	1	1	0	5	.212	12	10	2	11	21	1	.970
1979— Denver (A.A.)	C	31	102	12	27	1	0	1	10	.265	...	...	...	92	17	8	.932
— Montreal (N.L.)	C	25	36	8	10	3	1	0	4	.278	2	9	0	24	18	0	1.000
1980— Montreal (N.L.)	C	49	107	10	31	5	1	1	8	.290	11	17	0	30	43	6	.924
1981— Toronto (A.L.)	3B-C-1B	37	85	4	17	2	0	0	6	.200	8	15	1	99	36	5	.964
American League totals (1 year)		37	85	4	17	2	0	0	6	.200	8	15	1	99	36	5	.964
National League totals (5 years)		143	295	26	81	14	3	1	29	.275	31	53	3	138	107	8	.968
Major League totals (6 years)		180	380	30	98	16	3	1	35	.258	39	68	4	237	143	13	.967

RECORD AS MANAGER

BACKGROUND: Coach, Montreal Expos (1986). ... Third base coach, Expos (1987-91). ... Bullpen coach/third base coach, California Angels (1992-94). ... Bench coach, Oakland Athletics (1999-2002).

HONORS: Named International League Manager of the Year (1998).

Year—Team (League)	W	L	Pct.	Pos	Playoffs W	L	Champ. Series W	L	World Series W	L	All-Star Game W	L
1995— Trenton (East.)	73	69	.514	1st	0	3	—	—	—	—	—	—
1996— Trenton (East.)	86	56	.605	1st	2	3	—	—	—	—	—	—
1997— Pawtucket (I.L.)	81	60	.574	2nd	1	3	—	—	—	—	—	—
1998— Pawtucket (I.L.)	77	64	.546	3rd	—	—	—	—	—	—	—	—
2003— Oakland (A.L.)	96	66	.592	1st	2	3	—	—	—	—	—	—
Major League totals (1 year)	96	66	.592		2	3	—	—	—	—	—	—

NOTES:
1995—Lost to Reading in playoffs.
1996—Lost to Harrisburg in playoffs.
1997—Lost to Rochester in playoffs.
2003—Lost to Boston in A.L. divisional playoff.

MAZZILLI, LEE — ORIOLES

PERSONAL: Born March 25, 1955, in Brooklyn, N.Y. ... 6-1/195. ... Batted both, threw right. ... Full name: Lee Louis Mazzilli. ... High school: Lincoln (Brooklyn, N.Y.).

TRANSACTIONS/CAREER NOTES: Selected by New York Mets organization in first round (14th overall) of free-agent draft (June 5, 1973). ... Traded to Texas Rangers for P Ron Darling and P Walt Terrell (April 8, 1982). ... On disabled list (May 20-June 29, 1982). ... Traded to New York Yankees for SS Bucky Dent (August 8, 1982). ... Traded to Pittsburgh Pirates for OF Don Aubin, P Tim Burke, C John Holland and IF Jose Rivera (December 22, 1982). ... On disabled list (August 28-September 11, 1984). ... Released by Pirates (July 23, 1986). ... Signed by Mets (August 3, 1986). ... Granted free agency (November 9, 1987). ... Re-signed by Mets (December 17, 1987). ... Claimed on waivers by Toronto Blue Jays (July 31, 1989). ... Granted free agency (November 13, 1989).

							BATTING									FIELDING			
Year Team (League)	Pos.	G	AB	R	H	2B	3B	HR	RBI	Avg.	BB	SO	SB		PO	A	E	Avg.
1974—Anderson (W. Car.)	OF	132	472	82	127	24	3	11	48	.269	76	89	46		227	9	9	.963
1975—Visalia (Calif.)	OF-1B	125	430	103	121	10	4	13	52	.281	88	72	49		185	9	9	.956
1976—Jackson (Texas)	OF	131	439	91	128	21	5	13	43	.292	111	69	28		55	2	1	.971
—New York (N.L.)	OF	24	77	9	15	2	0	2	7	.195	14	10	5		55	2	1	.983
1977—New York (N.L.)	OF	159	537	66	134	24	3	6	46	.250	72	72	22		386	9	3	.992
1978—New York (N.L.)	OF	148	542	78	148	28	5	16	61	.273	69	82	20		386	8	5	.987
1979—New York (N.L.)	OF-1B	158	597	78	181	34	4	15	79	.303	93	74	34		480	24	5	.990
1980—New York (N.L.)	1B-OF	152	578	82	162	31	4	16	76	.280	82	92	41		874	53	14	.985
1981—New York (N.L.)	OF	95	324	36	74	14	5	6	34	.228	46	53	17		192	5	6	.970
1982—Texas (A.L.)/N.Y. (A.L.)	OF-1B	95	323	43	81	10	0	10	34	.251	43	41	13		234	8	4	.984
1983—Pittsburgh (N.L.)	OF-1B	109	246	37	59	9	0	5	24	.240	49	43	15		173	3	4	.978
1984—Pittsburgh (N.L.)	OF-1B	111	266	37	63	11	1	4	21	.237	40	42	8		103	2	1	.991
1985—Pittsburgh (N.L.)	1B-OF	92	117	20	33	8	0	1	9	.282	29	17	4		152	6	3	.981
1986—Pitt. (N.L.)/N.Y. (N.L.)	OF-1B	100	151	28	37	5	1	3	15	.245	38	36	4		128	7	0	1.000
1986—Tidewater (Int'l)	1B-OF	6	20	3	6	1	0	1	1	.300	3	2	2		28	1	0	1.000
1987—New York (N.L.)	1B-OF	88	124	26	38	8	1	3	24	.306	21	14	5		82	3	0	1.000
1988—New York (N.L.)	OF-1B	68	116	9	17	2	0	0	12	.147	12	16	4		114	4	3	.975
1989—N.Y. (N.L.)/Tor. (A.L.)	OF-1B	76	126	22	26	5	0	6	18	.206	34	35	5		66	2	2	.971
Major League totals (14 years)		1475	4124	571	1068	191	24	93	460	.259	642	627	197		3425	131	51	.986

RECORD AS MANAGER

BACKGROUND: First base/outfield coach, New York Yankees (2000-03).

		REGULAR SEASON						POSTSEASON						
									Champ.		World		All-Star	
						Playoffs			Series		Series		Game	
Year Team (League)	W	L	Pct.	Pos	W	L	W	L	W	L	W	L		
1997—Tampa (FSL)	41	26	.612	2nd	—	—	—	—	—	—	—	—		
—(Second half)	29	40	.420	6th	—	—	—	—	—	—	—	—		
1998—Tampa (FSL)	26	44	.371	8th	—	—	—	—	—	—	—	—		
—(Second half)	46	23	.667	1st	2	0	2	3	—	—	—	—		
1999—Norwich (East.)	78	64	.549	2nd	3	1	2	3	—	—	—	—		

NOTES:
1998—Defeated Charlotte, two games to none, in league semifinals; lost to St. Lucie, three games to two, in league championship series.
1999—Defeated Trenton, three games to one, in league semifinals; lost to Harrisburg in playoffs, three games to two.

McCLENDON, LLOYD — PIRATES

PERSONAL: Born January 11, 1959, in Gary, Ind. ... 6-0/208. ... Batted right, threw right. ... Full name: Lloyd Glenn McClendon. ... High school: Roosevelt (Gary, Ind.). ... College: Valparaiso.

TRANSACTIONS/CAREER NOTES: Selected by New York Mets organization in eighth round of free-agent draft (June 3, 1980). ... On disabled list (April 4-27, 1982). ... Traded by Mets organization with P Charlie Puleo and OF Jason Felice to Cincinnati Reds for P Tom Seaver (December 16, 1982). ... Traded by Reds organization to Chicago Cubs for OF Rolando Roomes (December 9, 1988). ... Traded by Cubs to Pittsburgh Pirates for a player to be named later (September 7, 1990); Cubs acquired P Mike Pomeranz to complete deal (September 28, 1990). ... Granted free agency (October 25, 1994). ... Signed by Buffalo, Cleveland Indians organization (May 5, 1995). ... Granted free agency (October 16, 1995).

							BATTING									FIELDING			
Year Team (League)	Pos.	G	AB	R	H	2B	3B	HR	RBI	Avg.	BB	SO	SB		PO	A	E	Avg.
1980—Kingsport (Appalachian)	C	14	46	7	15	2	0	1	9	.326	5	7	0		19	5	3	.889
—Little Falls (NYP)	C	40	117	25	32	9	1	3	20	.274	32	20	2		203	20	7	.970
1981—Lynchburg (Caro.)	3B-C	103	363	55	91	12	6	7	57	.251	60	68	3		437	74	17	.968
1982—Lynchburg (Caro.)	3B-C	108	384	61	105	25	1	18	78	.273	55	65	4		492	87	15	.975
1983—Waterbury (East.)	3B-C-1B	123	434	58	114	19	2	15	57	.263	42	64	4		466	99	8	.986
1984—Vermont (East.)	3-C-1-O	60	202	36	56	16	0	7	27	.277	28	28	2		174	24	3	.985
—Wichita (A.A.)	3B-C-1B	48	152	28	45	13	1	6	28	.296	21	33	2		143	45	4	.979
1985—Denver (A.A.)	3-C-1-O	114	379	57	105	18	5	16	79	.277	51	56	4		470	104	17	.971
1986—Denver (A.A.)	3-C-1-O	132	433	75	112	30	1	24	88	.259	70	75	2		656	45	11	.985
1987—Cincinnati (N.L.)	3-C-1-O	45	72	8	15	5	0	2	13	.208	4	15	1		80	5	2	.977
—Nashville (A.A.)	C-1B	26	84	11	24	6	0	3	14	.286	17	15	1		72	3	1	.987
1988—Cincinnati (N.L.)	3-C-1-O	72	137	9	30	4	0	3	14	.219	15	22	4		197	13	4	.981
—Nashville (A.A.)	C-OF	2	7	0	1	0	0	0	0	.143	1	1	0		12	2	0	1.000
1989—Iowa (Am. Assoc.)	C-1B-OF	34	109	18	35	10	0	4	13	.321	21	19	4		115	6	6	.953
—Chicago (N.L.)	3-C-1-O	92	259	47	74	12	1	12	40	.286	37	31	6		310	18	6	.982
1990—Chicago (N.L.)	C-1B-OF	49	107	5	17	3	0	1	10	.159	14	21	1		120	9	1	.992
—Iowa (Am. Assoc.)	3-C-1-O	25	91	14	26	2	0	2	10	.286	8	19	3		125	12	2	.986
—Pittsburgh (N.L.)	OF	4	3	1	1	0	0	1	2	.333	0	1	0		0	0	0	...
1991—Pittsburgh (N.L.)	C-1B-OF	85	163	24	47	7	0	7	24	.288	18	23	2		163	12	3	.983
1992—Pittsburgh (N.L.)	OF-1B	84	190	26	48	8	1	3	20	.253	28	24	1		136	9	3	.980
1993—Pittsburgh (N.L.)	OF-1B	88	181	21	40	11	1	2	19	.221	23	17	0		98	5	3	.972
1994—Pittsburgh (N.L.)	OF-1B	51	92	9	22	4	0	4	12	.239	4	11	0		46	2	1	.980
1995—Buffalo (A.A.)	OF-DH-3B	37	108	19	30	6	0	5	19	.278	20	20	0		32	1	2	.943
Major League totals (8 years)		570	1204	150	294	54	3	35	154	.244	143	165	15		1150	73	23	.982

MAJOR LEAGUE MANAGERS

RECORD AS MANAGER

BACKGROUND: Minor league hitting instructor, Pittsburgh Pirates (1996). ... Hitting coach, Pirates (1997-2000).

Year Team (League)	W	L	Pct.	Pos	Playoffs W	L	Champ. Series W	L	World Series W	L	All-Star Game W	L
2001— Pittsburgh (N.L.)	62	100	.382	6th	—	—	—	—	—	—	—	—
2002— Pittsburgh (N.L.)	72	89	.447	4th	—	—	—	—	—	—	—	—
2003— Pittsburgh (N.L.)	75	87	.462	4th	—	—	—	—	—	—	—	—
Major League totals (3 years)	209	276	.430		—	—	—	—	—	—	—	—

McKEON, JACK   MARLINS

PERSONAL: Born November 23, 1930, in South Amboy, NJ. ... 5-8/205. ... Batted right, threw right. ... Full name: John Aloysius McKeon. ... High school: St. Mary's (South Amboy, N.J.). ... College: Holy Cross, then Seton Hall, then Elon (N.C.) College.
TRANSACTIONS/CAREER NOTES: Signed by Pittsburgh Pirates organization (1951). ... Released by Pirates organization (September 28, 1954). ... Played 10 games with Fayetteville, five games with Greensboro and was player/manager with Fayetteville for 44 games during 1955 season. ... Player/manager, Missoula, Pioneer League (1956-58).

Year Team (League)	Pos.	G	AB	R	H	2B	3B	HR	RBI	Avg.	BB	SO	SB	PO	A	E	Avg.
1949— Greenville (Alabama St.)	C	116	390	34	98	12	1	1	49	.251	41	34	8	*.806	65	13	*.985
1950— York (Inter-state)	C	1	3	0	1	0	0	0	0	.333	0	0	0	0	0	0	...
— Gloverton (Can.-Amer.)	C	72	209	18	45	5	0	0	14	.215	19	28	2	281	30	15	.954
1951—								In military service.									
1952— Hutchinson (W. Assn.)	C	116	358	42	78	10	1	4	40	.218	69	54	0	756	68	11	.987
1953— Burlington (Caro.)	C	140	474	46	86	19	2	6	52	.181	60	110	3	836	*82	21	.978
1954— Burlington (Caro.)	C	17	30	1	4	0	0	0	2	.133	1	5	0	60	9	0	1.000
— Hutchinson (W. Assn.)	C	46	140	18	29	5	0	1	13	.207	27	31	1	273	33	4	.987
1955— Fayette.-Greens. (Caro.)	C	59	172	20	29	3	0	1	17	.169	29	28	1	292	20	6	.981
1956— Missoula (Pio.)	P-C	113	370	44	63	8	0	0	29	.170	53	62	3	630	78	9	.987
1957— Missoula (Pio.)	P-C	102	299	37	65	7	0	4	40	.217	60	44	6	645	55	10	.986
1958— Missoula (Pio.)	P-C	108	354	49	93	16	0	8	51	.263	51	55	2	739	64	12	.985
1959— Fox Cities (I.I.I.)	C	11	20	1	2	0	0	0	1	.100	8	3	0	0	0	0	...

RECORD AS MANAGER

BACKGROUND: Scout, Minnesota Twins (1965-67). ... Coach, Oakland Athletics (April 7-May 22, 1978). ... Scout/assistant to general manager, San Diego Padres (1980). ... Vice-president of baseball operations, Padres (1980-90). ... Senior adviser/player personnel, Cincinnati Reds (Janury 6, 1993-July 25, 1997).
HONORS: Named N.L. Manager of the Year by Baseball Writers' Association of America (1999 and 2003).

Year Team (League)	W	L	Pct.	Pos	Playoffs W	L	Champ. Series W	L	World Series W	L	All-Star Game W	L
1955— Fayetteville (Caro.)	70	67	.510	3rd	—	—	—	—	—	—	—	—
1956— Missoula (Pio.)	61	71	.462	7th	—	—	—	—	—	—	—	—
1957— Missoula (Pio.)	26	35	.426	6th	—	—	—	—	—	—	—	—
— Second half	36	29	.554	3rd	—	—	—	—	—	—	—	—
1958— Missoula (Pio.)	34	29	.539	4th	—	—	—	—	—	—	—	—
— Second half	36	30	.545	3rd	—	—	—	—	—	—	—	—
1959— Fox Cities (I.I.I.)	26	39	.400	7th	—	—	—	—	—	—	—	—
— Second half	33	28	.541	4th	—	—	—	—	—	—	—	—
1960— Wilson (Caro.)	36	34	.514	3rd	—	—	—	—	—	—	—	—
— Second half	37	31	.544	2nd	—	—	—	—	—	—	—	—
1961— Wilson (Caro.)	41	28	.594	1st	—	—	—	—	—	—	—	—
— Second half	42	28	.600	1st	—	—	—	—	—	—	—	—
1962— Vancouver (PCL)	72	79	.476	7th	—	—	—	—	—	—	—	—
1963— Dallas/Fort Worth (PCL.)	79	79	.500	3rd	—	—	—	—	—	—	—	—
1964— Atlanta (I.L.)	19	42	.311	—	—	—	—	—	—	—	—	—
1968— High Point-Thomasville (Caro.)	69	71	.492	2nd	3	0	2	1	—	—	—	—
1969— Omaha (A.A.)	85	55	.607	1st	—	—	—	—	—	—	—	—
1970— Omaha (A.A.)	73	65	.528	1st	4	1	1	4	—	—	—	—
1971— Omaha (A.A.)	69	70	.496	3rd	—	—	—	—	—	—	—	—
1972— Omaha (A.A.)	71	69	.507	2nd	—	—	—	—	—	—	—	—
1973— Kansas City (A.L.)	88	74	.543	2nd	—	—	—	—	—	—	—	—
1974— Kansas City (A.L.)	77	85	.475	5th	—	—	—	—	—	—	—	—
1975— Kansas City (A.L.)	50	46	.520	—	—	—	—	—	—	—	—	—
1976— Richmond (I.L.)	69	71	.492	4th	—	—	—	—	—	—	—	—
1977— Oakland (A.L.)	26	27	.490	—	—	—	—	—	—	—	—	—
1978— Oakland (A.L.)	45	78	.365	4th	—	—	—	—	—	—	—	—
1980— Denver (A.A.)	62	73	.459	3rd	—	—	—	—	—	—	—	—
1988— San Diego (N.L.)	67	48	.582	3rd	—	—	—	—	—	—	—	—
1989— San Diego (N.L.)	89	73	.549	2nd	—	—	—	—	—	—	—	—
1990— San Diego (N.L.)	37	43	.462	—	—	—	—	—	—	—	—	—
1997— Cincinnati (N.L.)	33	30	.523	3rd	—	—	—	—	—	—	—	—
1998— Cincinnati (N.L.)	77	85	.475	4th	—	—	—	—	—	—	—	—
1999— Cincinnati (N.L.)	96	67	.588	2nd	—	—	—	—	—	—	—	—
2000— Cincinnati (N.L.)	85	77	.524	2nd	—	—	—	—	—	—	—	—
2003— Florida (N.L.)	75	49	.604	2nd	3	1	4	3	4	2	—	—
American League totals (5 years)	286	310	.479		—	—	—	—	—	—	—	—
National League totals (8 years)	559	472	.542		3	1	4	3	4	2	—	—
Major League totals (13 years)	845	782	.519		3	1	4	3	4	2	—	—

NOTES:

1955—Replaced Fayetteville manager Aaron Robinson (June 11). Replaced as Fayetteville manager by John Sanford (August 6) because of hand injury with team tied for first place (record is for full season).

1964—Replaced as Atlanta manager by Peter Appleton, with club in eighth place (June 21).

1968—Defeated Greensboro, one game to one, in quarterfinals; defeated Lynchburg, two games to none in semifinals; defeated Raleigh-Durham, two games to none, in championship.

1970—Defeated Denver, four games to one, in championship; lost to Syracuse, four games to one, in Junior World Series.

1975—Replaced as Kansas City manager by Whitey Herzog, with club in second place (July 24).

1977—Replaced as Oakland manager by Bobby Winkles, with club tied for fifth place (June 10).

1978—Replaced Oakland manager Bobby Winkles, with club in first place and record of 24-15 (May 23).

1988—Replaced San Diego manager Larry Bowa, with club in fifth place and record of 16-30 (May 28).

1997—Replaced Cincinnati manager Ray Knight, with club in fourth place and record of 43-56 (July 25).

2003—Replaced Florida manager Jeff Torborg, with club in fourth place and record of 16-22 (May 11); defeated San Francisco in N.L. divisional playoff, defeated Chicago in N.L. Championship Series, defeated New York Yankees in World Series.

MELVIN, BOB — MARINERS

PERSONAL: Born October 28, 1961, in Palo Alto, Calif. ... 6-4/210. ... Batted right, threw right. ... Full name: Robert Paul Melvin. ... High school: Menlo-Atherton (Menlo Park, Calif.). ... Junior college: Canada College (Calif.). ... College: California.

TRANSACTIONS/CAREER NOTES: Selected by Baltimore Orioles organization in third round of free-agent draft (June 5, 1979); did not sign. ... Selected by Detroit Tigers organization in secondary phase of free-agent draft (January 13, 1981). ... On disabled list (May 1-25, 1982). ... Traded by Tigers with P Juan Berenguer and a player to be named later to San Francisco Giants for P Dave LaPoint, P Eric King and C Matt Nokes (October 7, 1985); Giants acquired P Scott Medvin to complete deal (December 11, 1985). ... On disabled list (July 11-26, 1987). ... Traded by Giants to Baltimore Orioles for C Terry Kennedy (January 24, 1989). ... On disabled list (April 22-May 7, 1989). ... Traded by Orioles to Kansas City Royals for P Storm Davis (December 11, 1991). ... Granted free agency (October 26, 1992). ... Signed by Boston Red Sox (December 1, 1992). ... On disabled list (July 16-31, 1993). ... Released by Red Sox (April 12, 1994). ... Signed by New York Yankees organization (April 26, 1994). ... On New York disabled list (June 23-July 22, 1994); included rehabilitation assignment to Columbus (July 8-22). ... Claimed on waivers by California Angels (July 22, 1994). ... Traded by Angels to Chicago White Sox for P Jeff Schwarz (July 22, 1994). ... Granted free agency (October 25, 1994). ... Signed by Yankees organization (May 6, 1995). ... On suspended list (June 3, 1995-remainder of season). ... Released by Yankees (November 1, 1995).

							BATTING								FIELDING		
Year Team (League)	Pos.	G	AB	R	H	2B	3B	HR	RBI	Avg.	BB	SO	SB	PO	A	E	Avg.
1981—Macon (S. Atl.)	C	114	412	56	112	19	1	14	64	.272	35	71	5	456	67	2	.996
1982—Birmingham (Sou.)	3B-C-1B	98	364	33	86	12	1	13	52	.236	24	70	1	638	54	9	.987
1983—Birmingham (Sou.)	2B-C-1B	78	285	43	82	14	2	10	56	.288	18	54	0	404	30	2	.995
—Evansville (A.A.)	C-1B	45	142	10	27	6	0	2	11	.190	7	41	0	213	16	1	.996
1984—Evansville (A.A.)	C-1B	44	141	12	35	13	0	0	11	.248	3	32	0	214	21	1	.996
—Birmingham (Sou.)	3B-C-1B	69	271	34	73	14	1	2	33	.269	18	47	1	341	38	4	.990
1985—Nashville (A.A.)	C-1B-OF	53	177	27	48	7	1	9	24	.271	16	38	3	276	28	2	.993
—Detroit (A.L.)	C	41	82	10	18	4	1	0	4	.220	3	21	0	175	13	2	.989
1986—San Francisco (N.L.)	3B-C	89	268	24	60	14	2	5	25	.224	15	69	3	443	60	6	.988
1987—San Francisco (N.L.)	C-1B	84	246	31	49	8	0	11	31	.199	17	44	0	414	44	1	.998
1988—San Francisco (N.L.)	C-1B	92	273	23	64	13	1	8	27	.234	13	46	0	406	31	7	.984
—Phoenix (PCL)	C	21	75	11	23	5	0	2	9	.307	8	13	0	123	6	1	.992
1989—Baltimore (A.L.)	DH-C	85	278	22	67	10	1	1	32	.241	15	53	1	303	20	3	.991
1990—Baltimore (A.L.)	DH-C-1B	93	301	30	73	14	1	5	37	.243	11	53	0	365	26	1	.997
1991—Baltimore (A.L.)	DH-C	79	228	11	57	10	0	1	23	.250	11	46	0	383	31	1	.998
1992—Kansas City (A.L.)	C-1B	32	70	5	22	5	0	0	6	.314	5	13	0	99	9	1	.991
1993—Boston (A.L.)	C-1B	77	176	13	39	7	0	3	23	.222	7	44	0	309	19	2	.994
1994—Columbus (Int'l)	1B-C-DH	17	62	5	17	5	0	1	15	.274	1	9	0	122	12	3	.978
—New York (A.L.)	C-1B-DH	9	14	2	4	0	0	1	3	.286	0	3	0	16	0	0	1.000
—Chicago (A.L.)	C	11	19	3	3	0	0	0	1	.158	1	4	0	48	0	0	1.000
1995—Columbus (Int'l)	C-DH-1B	19	66	7	19	5	0	1	4	.288	3	12	0	77	3	2	.976
American League totals (7 years)		427	1168	96	283	50	3	11	129	.242	53	237	1	1698	118	10	.995
National League totals (3 years)		265	787	78	173	35	3	24	83	.220	45	159	3	1263	135	14	.990
Major League totals (10 years)		692	1955	174	456	85	6	35	212	.233	98	396	4	2961	253	24	.993

RECORD AS MANAGER

BACKGROUND: Scout, Milwaukee Brewers (1996). ... Roving fielding instructor, Brewers (1997). ... Assistant to general manager, Brewers (1998). ... Bench coach, Brewers (1999). ... Bench coach, Detroit Tigers (2000). ... Bench coach, Arizona Diamondbacks (2001-02).

	REGULAR SEASON				POSTSEASON							
					Playoffs		Champ. Series		World Series		All-Star Game	
Year Team (League)	W	L	Pct.	Pos	W	L	W	L	W	L	W	L
2003—Seattle (A.L.)	93	69	.574	2nd	—	—	—	—	—	—	—	—
Major League totals (1 year)	93	69	.574		—	—	—	—	—	—	—	—

MILEY, DAVE — REDS

PERSONAL: Born April 3, 1962, in Tampa, Fla. ... 6-3/220. ... Batted left, threw right. ... Full name: David Allen Miley. ... High school: Chamberlain (Tampa).

TRANSACTIONS/CAREER NOTES: Drafted by Cincinnati Reds organization in second round of free-agent draft (June 1980).

							BATTING								FIELDING		
Year Team (League)	Pos.	G	AB	R	H	2B	3B	HR	RBI	Avg.	BB	SO	SB	PO	A	E	Avg.
1980—Billings (Pio.)	C-1B	58	194	33	56	8	0	2	38	.289	35	21	10	368	39	4	.990
1981—Eugene (N'west)	C-3B	40	136	24	40	2	0	2	29	.294	26	8	0	273	30	10	.968
—Cedar Rapids (Midw.)	C	38	118	9	23	5	0	1	11	.195	14	16	0	228	27	7	.973
1982—Tampa (FSL.)	C	30	93	11	19	8	3	0	10	.204	11	9	1	207	23	3	.987
1983—Waterbury (East.)	C	65	186	19	45	11	0	4	24	.242	36	7	1	346	48	7	.983
1984—Wichita (A.A.)	C	78	205	24	50	6	0	5	26	.244	28	20	0	335	44	4	.990
1985—Cedar Rapids (Midw.)	C	12	39	2	8	0	0	1	6	.205	2	1	0	97	8	0	1.000
—Denver (A.A.)	C-1B	63	167	9	30	6	0	0	19	.180	14	15	1	279	36	2	.994
1986—Tampa (FSL.)		2	1	0	0	0	0	0	0	.000	0	1	0	0	0	0	.000
—Denver (A.A.)	1B-C	17	46	3	11	0	1	1	9	.239	4	6	0	86	3	2	.978

BACKGROUND: Bench coach, Cincinnati Reds (1993).

HONORS: Named International League Manager of the Year (1997). ... Named Southern League Manager of the Year (1995). ... Named Class AA Manager of the Year (1995).

Year	Team (League)	W	L	Pct.	Pos.	Playoff W	Playoff L	Champ. Series W	Champ. Series L	World Series W	World Series L	All-Star Game W	All-Star Game L
1988	Greensboro (S. Atl.)	37	33	.529	2nd	—	—	—	—	—	—	—	—
	— (Second half)	42	27	.609	1st	0	2	—	—	—	—	—	—
1989	Cedar Rapids (Midw.)	41	27	.603	1st	—	—	—	—	—	—	—	—
	— (Second half)	39	30	.565	3rd	0	2	—	—	—	—	—	—
1990	Cedar Rapids (Midw.)	45	21	.682	1st	—	—	—	—	—	—	—	—
	— (Second half)	43	25	.632	2nd	0	2	—	—	—	—	—	—
1991	Charleston (WV) (S. Atl.)	29	19	.604	1st	—	—	—	—	—	—	—	—
	— (Second half)	46	24	.657	1st	0	3	—	—	—	—	—	—
1992	Chattanooga (Sou.)	46	25	.648	1st	—	—	—	—	—	—	—	—
	— (Second half)	5	1	.833	—	—	—	—	—	—	—	—	—
	— Nashville (A.A.)	—	—	—	—	—	—	—	—	—	—	—	—
	— (Second half)	32	36	.471	4th	—	—	—	—	—	—	—	—
1995	Chattanooga (Sou.)	36	36	.500	2nd	—	—	—	—	—	—	—	—
	— (Second half)	47	24	.662	1st	5	5	—	—	—	—	—	—
1996	Indianapolis (A.A.)	78	66	.542	2nd	4	5	—	—	—	—	—	—
1997	Indianapolis (A.A.)	85	59	.590	2nd	2	3	—	—	—	—	—	—
1998	Indianapolis (A.A.)	76	67	.531	2nd	—	—	—	—	—	—	—	—
1999	Indianapolis (A.A.)	75	69	.521	—	—	—	—	—	—	—	—	—
2000	Louisville (I.L.)	71	73	.493	3rd	—	—	—	—	—	—	—	—
2001	Louisville (I.L.)	84	60	.583	1st	4	2	—	—	—	—	—	—
2002	Louisville (I.L.)	79	65	.549	2nd	—	—	—	—	—	—	—	—
2003	Louisville (I.L.)	62	47	.569	—	—	—	—	—	—	—	—	—
	— Cincinnati (N.L.)	22	35	.386	5th	—	—	—	—	—	—	—	—

NOTES:
1988—Lost to Spartanburg in playoffs.
1989—Lost to Springfield in playoffs.
1990—Lost to Quad City in playoffs.
1991—Lost to Columbia in playoffs.
1995—Lost to Carolina in championship series.
1996—Lost to Oklahoma City in championship series.
1997—Lost to Buffalo in playoffs.
2001—Louisville was leading final series, one game to none, and declared I.L. champion due to stoppage of play in professional ball.
2003—Replaced Cincinnati manager Bob Boone, with club in fifth place and record of 46-58 (July 28).

PENA, TONY   ROYALS

PERSONAL: Born June 4, 1957, in Monte Cristi, Dominican Republic. ... 6-0/190. ... Batted right, threw right. ... Full name: Antonio Francisco Padilla Pena. ... High school: Liceo Marti (Monte Cristi, Dominican Republic).

TRANSACTIONS/CAREER NOTES: Signed as non-drafted free agent by Pittsburgh Pirates organization (July 22, 1975). ... Traded by Pirates to St. Louis Cardinals for OF Andy Van Slyke, C Mike LaValliere and P Mike Dunne (April 1, 1987). ... On St. Louis disabled list (April 11-May 22, 1987); included rehabilitation assignment to Louisville (May 19-22). ... Granted free agency (November 13, 1989). ... Signed by Boston Red Sox (November 27, 1989). ... Granted free agency (October 29, 1993). ... Signed by Cleveland Indians organization (February 7, 1994). ... Re-signed by Indians organization (October 25, 1994). ... Re-signed by Indians organization (December 13, 1994). ... Granted free agency (November 2, 1995). ... Re-signed by Indians (December 6, 1995). ... Granted free agency (November 18, 1996). ... Signed by Chicago White Sox organization (January 10, 1997). ... On Chicago disabled list (June 10-20, 1997). ... Traded by White Sox to Houston Astros for P Julien Tucker (August 15, 1997). ... Granted free agency (October 30, 1997).

Year	Team (League)	Pos.	G	AB	R	H	2B	3B	HR	RBI	Avg.	BB	SO	SB	PO	A	E	Avg.
1976	GC Pirates (GCL)	3-C-1-O	33	110	10	23	2	2	1	11	.209	4	17	5	108	14	4	.968
	— Char., S.C. (W. Car.)	C	14	49	4	11	2	0	1	8	.224	4	7	0	64	7	2	.973
1977	Char., S.C. (W. Car.)	C	29	101	10	24	4	0	3	16	.238	7	21	2	172	19	6	.970
	— Salem (Caro.)	C	84	319	36	88	15	3	7	46	.276	14	60	3	470	66	17	.969
1978	Shreveport (Texas)	C	104	348	34	80	14	0	8	42	.230	15	96	3	637	54	25	.965
1979	Buffalo (East.)	C	134	515	89	161	16	4	34	97	.313	39	83	5	768	120	26	.972
1980	Portland (PCL)	C	124	452	57	148	24	13	9	77	.327	29	75	5	639	85	23	.969
	— Pittsburgh (N.L.)	C	8	21	1	9	1	1	0	1	.429	0	4	0	38	2	2	.952
1981	Pittsburgh (N.L.)	C	66	210	16	63	9	1	2	17	.300	8	23	1	286	41	5	.985
1982	Pittsburgh (N.L.)	C	138	497	53	147	28	4	11	63	.296	17	57	2	763	89	16	.982
1983	Pittsburgh (N.L.)	C	151	542	51	163	22	3	15	70	.301	31	73	6	976	90	9	.992
1984	Pittsburgh (N.L.)	C	147	546	77	156	27	2	15	78	.286	36	79	12	895	95	9	.991
1985	Pittsburgh (N.L.)	C-1B	147	546	53	136	27	2	10	59	.249	29	67	12	925	102	12	.988
1986	Pittsburgh (N.L.)	C-1B	144	510	56	147	26	2	10	52	.288	53	69	9	824	99	18	.981
1987	St. Louis (N.L.)	C-1B-OF	116	384	40	82	13	4	5	44	.214	36	54	6	624	51	8	.988
	— Louisville (A.A.)	C	2	8	0	3	0	0	0	0	.375	0	2	0	7	1	0	1.000
1988	St. Louis (N.L.)	C-1B	149	505	55	133	23	1	10	51	.263	33	60	6	796	72	6	.993
1989	St. Louis (N.L.)	C-OF	141	424	36	110	17	2	4	37	.259	35	33	5	675	70	2	.997
1990	Boston (A.L.)	C-1B	143	491	62	129	19	1	7	56	.263	43	71	8	866	74	5	.995
1991	Boston (A.L.)	C	141	464	45	107	23	2	5	48	.231	37	53	8	864	60	5	.995
1992	Boston (A.L.)	C	133	410	39	99	21	1	1	38	.241	24	61	3	786	57	6	.993
1993	Boston (A.L.)	C-DH	126	304	20	55	11	0	4	19	.181	25	46	1	698	53	4	.995
1994	Cleveland (A.L.)	C	40	112	18	33	8	1	2	10	.295	9	11	0	209	17	1	.996
1995	Cleveland (A.L.)	C	91	263	25	69	15	0	5	28	.262	14	44	1	508	36	7	.987
1996	Cleveland (A.L.)	C	67	174	14	34	4	0	1	27	.195	15	25	0	336	27	3	.992
1997	Chicago (A.L.)	C-3B	31	67	4	11	1	0	0	8	.164	8	13	0	143	8	0	1.000
	— Houston (N.L.)	C	9	19	2	4	3	0	0	2	.211	2	3	0	48	6	0	1.000
	American League totals (8 years)		772	2285	227	537	102	5	25	234	.235	175	324	21	4410	332	31	.994
	National League totals (11 years)		1216	4204	440	1150	196	22	82	474	.274	280	522	59	6850	717	87	.989
	Major League totals (18 years)		1988	6489	667	1687	298	27	107	708	.260	455	846	80	11260	1049	118	.991

BACKGROUND: Bench coach, Houston Astros (2002).
HONORS: Named A.L. Manager of the Year by THE SPORTING NEWS (2003). ... Named A.L. Manager of the Year by Baseball Writers' Association of America (2003).

			REGULAR SEASON				Playoffs		POSTSEASON Champ. Series		World Series		All-Star Game	
Year	Team (League)	W	L	Pct.	Pos	W	L	W	L	W	L	W	L
1999— New Orleans (PCL)		55	85	.392	4th	—	—	—	—	—	—	—	—
2000— New Orleans (PCL)		68	74	.478	3rd	—	—	—	—	—	—	—	—
2001— New Orleans (PCL)		82	57	.589	1st	3	0	—	—	—	—	—	—
2002— Kansas City (A.L.)		49	77	.388	4th	—	—	—	—	—	—	—	—
2003— Kansas City (A.L.)		83	79	.512	3rd	—	—	—	—	—	—	—	—
Major League totals (2 years)		**132**	**156**	**.458**		—	—	—	—	—	—	—	—

NOTES:
2001—Defeated Iowa in playoffs. Shared League Championship due to stoppage of play in professional baseball.
2002—Replaced Kansas City manager Tony Muser (record of 8-15) and interim manager John Mizerock (record of 5-8) with club in fourth place and record of 13-23 (May 15).

PINIELLA, LOU   DEVIL RAYS

PERSONAL: Born August 28, 1943, in Tampa. ... 6-2/199. ... Batted right, threw right. ... Full name: Louis Victor Piniella. ... Name pronounced: pin-ELL-uh. ... High school: Jesuit (Tampa). ... College: Tampa.
TRANSACTIONS/CAREER NOTES: Signed as free agent by Cleveland Indians organization (June 9, 1962). ... Selected by Washington Senators organization from Jacksonville, Indians organization, in Rule 5 major league draft (November 26, 1962). ... On military list (March 9-July 20, 1964). ... Traded by Senators organization to Baltimore Orioles organization (August 4, 1964), completing deal in which Orioles traded P Lester (Buster) Narum to Senators for cash and a player to be named later (March 31, 1964). ... On suspended list (June 27-29, 1965). ... Traded by Orioles organization to Indians organization for C Camilo Carreon (March 10, 1966). ... On temporarily inactive list (May 19-22, 1967). ... On disabled list (May 22-June 6, 1968). ... On temporarily inactive list (June 6-25, 1968). ... Selected by Seattle Pilots in expansion draft (October 15, 1968). ... Traded by Pilots to Kansas City Royals for OF Steve Whitaker and P John Gelnar (April 1, 1969). ... On military list (August 7-22, 1969). ... On disabled list (May 5-June 8, 1971). ... Traded by Royals with P Ken Wright to New York Yankees for P Lindy McDaniel (December 7, 1973). ... On disabled list (June 17-July 6, 1975; August 23-September 7, 1981; and March 30-April 22, 1983). ... Placed on voluntarily retired list (June 17, 1984).

							BATTING										FIELDING		
Year	Team (League)	Pos.	G	AB	R	H	2B	3B	HR	RBI	Avg.	BB	SO	SB	PO	A	E	Avg.
1962— Selma (Ala.-Fla.)		OF	70	278	40	75	10	5	8	44	.270	10	57	4	94	6	9	.917
1963— Peninsula (Caro.)		OF	143	548	71	170	29	4	16	77	.310	34	70	8	271	23	8	.974
1964— Aberdeen (North.)		OF	20	74	8	20	8	3	0	12	.270	6	9	1	37	1	1	.974
— Baltimore (A.L.)			4	1	0	0	0	0	0	0	.000	0	0	0	...	...	...	.000
1965— Elmira (East.)		OF	126	490	64	122	29	6	11	64	.249	22	57	5	176	5	7	.963
1966— Portland (PCL)		OF	133	457	47	132	22	3	7	52	.289	20	52	6	177	11	11	.945
1967— Portland (PCL)		OF	113	396	46	122	20	1	8	56	.308	23	47	2	199	7	6	.972
1968— Portland (PCL)		OF	88	331	49	105	15	3	13	62	.317	19	31	0	167	6	7	.961
— Cleveland (A.L.)		OF	6	5	1	0	0	0	0	1	.000	0	0	0	1	0	0	1.000
1969— Kansas City (A.L.)		OF	135	493	43	139	21	6	11	68	.282	33	56	2	278	13	7	.977
1970— Kansas City (A.L.)		1B-OF	144	542	54	163	24	5	11	88	.301	35	42	3	250	6	4	.985
1971— Kansas City (A.L.)		OF	126	448	43	125	21	5	3	51	.279	21	43	5	201	6	3	.986
1972— Kansas City (A.L.)		OF	151	574	65	179	33	4	11	72	.312	34	59	7	275	8	7	.976
1973— Kansas City (A.L.)		DH-OF	144	513	53	128	28	1	9	69	.250	30	65	5	196	9	3	.986
1974— New York (A.L.)		DH-1B-OF	140	518	71	158	26	0	9	70	.305	32	58	1	270	16	3	.990
1975— New York (A.L.)		DH-OF	74	199	7	39	4	1	0	22	.196	16	22	0	65	5	1	.986
1976— New York (A.L.)		DH-OF	100	327	36	92	16	6	3	38	.281	18	34	0	199	10	4	.981
1977— New York (A.L.)		DH-1B-OF	103	339	47	112	19	3	12	45	.330	20	31	2	86	3	2	.978
1978— New York (A.L.)		DH-OF	130	472	67	148	34	5	6	69	.314	34	36	3	213	4	7	.969
1979— New York (A.L.)		DH-OF	130	461	49	137	22	2	11	69	.297	17	31	3	204	13	4	.982
1980— New York (A.L.)		DH-OF	116	321	39	92	18	0	2	27	.287	29	20	0	157	8	5	.971
1981— New York (A.L.)		DH-OF	60	159	16	44	9	0	5	18	.277	13	9	0	69	2	1	.986
1982— New York (A.L.)		DH-OF	102	261	33	80	17	1	6	37	.307	18	18	0	68	2	0	1.000
1983— New York (A.L.)		DH-OF	53	148	19	43	9	1	2	16	.291	11	12	1	67	4	3	.959
1984— New York (A.L.)		DH-OF	29	86	8	26	4	1	1	6	.302	7	5	0	40	3	0	1.000
Major League totals (18 years)			**1747**	**5867**	**651**	**1705**	**305**	**41**	**102**	**766**	**.291**	**368**	**541**	**32**	**2639**	**112**	**54**	**.981**

RECORD AS MANAGER

BACKGROUND: Coach, New York Yankees (June 25, 1984-85). ... Vice-president/general manager, Yankees (beginning of 1988 season-June 22, 1988). ... Special adviser, Yankees (1989).
HONORS: Named A.L. Manager of the Year by Baseball Writers' Association of America (1995 and 2001). ... Named A.L. Manager of the Year by THE SPORTING NEWS (2001).

			REGULAR SEASON				Playoffs		POSTSEASON Champ. Series		World Series		All-Star Game	
Year	Team (League)	W	L	Pct.	Pos	W	L	W	L	W	L	W	L
1986— New York (A.L.)		90	72	.555	2nd	—	—	—	—	—	—	—	—
1987— New York (A.L.)		89	73	.549	4th	—	—	—	—	—	—	—	—
1988— New York (A.L.)		45	48	.483	5th	—	—	—	—	—	—	—	—
1990— Cincinnati (N.L.)		91	71	.561	1st	—	—	4	2	4	0	—	—
1991— Cincinnati (N.L.)		74	88	.456	5th	—	—	—	—	—	—	0	1
1992— Cincinnati (N.L.)		90	72	.555	2nd	—	—	—	—	—	—	—	—
1993— Seattle (A.L.)		82	80	.506	4th	—	—	—	—	—	—	—	—
1994— Seattle (A.L.)		49	63	.437	—	—	—	—	—	—	—	—	—
1995— Seattle (A.L.)		79	66	.544	1st	3	2	2	4	—	—	—	—
1996— Seattle (A.L.)		85	76	.527	2nd	—	—	—	—	—	—	—	—
1997— Seattle (A.L.)		90	72	.555	1st	1	3	—	—	—	—	—	—
1998— Seattle (A.L.)		76	85	.472	3rd	—	—	—	—	—	—	—	—
1999— Seattle (A.L.)		79	83	.487	3rd	—	—	—	—	—	—	—	—
2000— Seattle (A.L.)		91	71	.561	2nd	3	0	2	4	—	—	—	—
2001— Seattle (A.L.)		116	46	.716	1st	3	2	1	4	—	—	—	—
2002— Seattle (A.L.)		93	69	.574	3rd	—	—	—	—	—	—	—	—
2003— Tampa Bay (A.L.)		63	99	.388	5th	—	—	—	—	—	—	—	—
American League totals (14 years)		**1127**	**1003**	**.529**		10	7	5	12	—	—	—	—
National League totals (3 years)		**255**	**231**	**.524**		—	—	4	2	4	0	0	1
Major League totals (17 years)		**1382**	**1234**	**.528**		10	7	9	14	4	0	0	1

MAJOR LEAGUE MANAGERS

NOTES:
1988—Replaced New York manager Billy Martin with club in second place and record of 40-28 (June 23).
1990—Defeated Pittsburgh in N.L. Championship Series; defeated Oakland in World Series.
1994—Seattle was in third place in A.L. West at time of season-ending strike (August 12).
1995—Defeated New York in A.L. divisional playoff; lost to Cleveland in A.L. Championship Series.
1997—Lost to Baltimore in A.L. divisional playoff.
2000—Defeated Chicago White Sox in A.L. divisional playoff; lost to New York Yankees in A.L. Championship Series.
2001—Defeated Cleveland in A.L. divisional playoff; lost to New York Yankees in A.L. Championship Series.

ROBINSON, FRANK — EXPOS

PERSONAL: Born August 31, 1935, in Beaumont, Tex. ... 6-1/194. ... Batted right, threw right. ... High school: McClymonds (Oakland). ... College: Xavier.
TRANSACTIONS/CAREER NOTES: Signed by Tulsa, Cincinnati Reds organization (June 19, 1953). ... On temporarily inactive list (April 7-April 18, 1955). ... Traded by Reds to Baltimore Orioles for OF Dick Simpson, P Milt Pappas and P Jack Baldschun (December 9, 1965). ... Traded by Orioles with P Pete Richert to Los Angeles Dodgers for P Doyle Alexander, P Bob O'Brien, C Sergio Robles and 1B//OF Royle Stillman (December 2, 1971). ... Traded by Dodgers with IF Billy Grabarkewitz, IF Bob Valentine, P Bill Singer and P Mike Strahler to California Angels for 3B Ken McMullen and P Andy Messersmith (November 28, 1972). ... Released by Angels on waivers to Cleveland Indians (September 12, 1974); Indians assigned OF Rusty Torres and C Ken Suarez to Angels to complete deal (December 4, 1974). ... On disabled list (July 4-23, 1975; April 4-26, 1976). ... Released by Indians (October 5, 1976). ... Served as player//manager (1975).

							BATTING									FIELDING			
Year	Team (League)	Pos.	G	AB	R	H	2B	3B	HR	RBI	Avg.	BB	SO	SB	PO	A	E	Avg.
1953—Ogden (Pio.)	3B-1B-OF	72	270	70	94	20	6	17	83	.348	53	69	3	105	28	18	.881
1954—Tulsa (Texas)	2B-3B	8	30	4	8	0	0	0	1	.267	...	...	0	17	15	1	.970
—Columbia (S. Atl.)	2B-3B-OF	132	491	112	165	32	9	25	110	.336	88	65	6	258	63	18	.947
1955—Columbia (S. Atl.)	1B-OF	80	243	50	64	15	7	12	52	.263	41	44	3	203	3	4	.981
1956—Cincinnati (N.L.)	OF	152	572	122	166	27	6	38	83	.290	64	95	8	323	5	8	.976
1957—Cincinnati (N.L.)	1B-OF	150	611	97	197	29	5	29	75	.322	44	92	10	487	36	6	.989
1958—Cincinnati (N.L.)	3B-OF	148	554	90	149	25	6	31	83	.269	62	80	10	314	24	6	.983
1959—Cincinnati (N.L.)	1B-OF	146	540	106	168	31	4	36	125	.311	69	93	18	1049	78	18	.984
1960—Cincinnati (N.L.)	3B-1B-OF	139	464	86	138	33	6	31	83	.297	82	67	13	775	62	10	.988
1961—Cincinnati (N.L.)	3B-OF	153	545	117	176	32	7	37	124	.323	71	64	22	284	15	3	.990
1962—Cincinnati (N.L.)	OF	162	609	134	208	51	2	39	136	.342	76	62	18	315	10	2	.994
1963—Cincinnati (N.L.)	1B-OF	140	482	79	125	19	3	21	91	.259	81	69	26	238	13	4	.984
1964—Cincinnati (N.L.)	OF	156	568	103	174	38	6	29	96	.306	79	67	23	279	7	4	.986
1965—Cincinnati (N.L.)	OF	156	582	109	172	33	5	33	113	.296	70	100	13	282	5	3	.990
1966—Baltimore (A.L.)	1B-OF	155	576	122	182	34	2	49	122	.316	87	90	8	282	6	5	.983
1967—Baltimore (A.L.)	1B-OF	129	479	83	149	23	7	30	94	.311	71	84	2	207	8	2	.991
1968—Baltimore (A.L.)	1B-OF	130	421	69	113	27	1	15	52	.268	73	84	11	193	5	7	.966
1969—Baltimore (A.L.)	1B-OF	148	539	111	166	19	5	32	100	.308	88	62	9	367	19	5	.987
1970—Baltimore (A.L.)	1B-OF	132	471	88	144	24	1	25	78	.306	69	70	1	262	11	4	.986
1971—Baltimore (A.L.)	1B-OF	133	455	82	128	16	2	28	99	.281	72	62	3	449	20	11	.977
1972—Los Angeles (N.L.)	OF	103	342	41	86	6	1	19	59	.251	55	76	2	168	6	6	.967
1973—California (A.L.)	DH-OF	147	534	85	142	29	0	30	97	.266	82	93	1	38	3	1	.976
1974—California (A.L.)	DH-OF	129	427	75	107	26	2	20	63	.251	75	85	5	0	0	0	...
—Cleveland (A.L.)	DH-1B	15	50	6	10	1	1	2	5	.200	10	10	0	23	0	1	.958
1975—Cleveland (A.L.)	DH	49	118	19	28	5	0	9	24	.237	29	15	0	...	...	...	...
1976—Cleveland (A.L.)	1B-OF	36	67	5	15	0	0	3	10	.224	11	12	0	11	0	0	1.000
American League totals (10 years)		1203	4137	745	1184	204	21	243	744	.286	667	667	40	1832	72	36	.981
National League totals (11 years)		1605	5869	1084	1759	324	51	343	1068	.300	753	865	163	4514	261	70	.986
Major League totals (21 years)		2808	10006	1829	2943	528	72	586	1812	.294	1420	1532	203	6346	333	106	.984

RECORD AS MANAGER

BACKGROUND: Player/manager, Indians (1975). ... Coach, California Angels (July 11, 1997-remainder of season). ... Coach, Baltimore Orioles (1978-May 8, 1978, 1979-80 and 1985-87). ... Coach, Milwaukee Brewers (1984). ... Special assistant to president, Orioles (1988-April 11, 1988).
HONORS: Named A.L. Manager of the Year by THE SPORTING NEWS (1989).

		REGULAR SEASON				POSTSEASON								
						Playoffs		Champ. Series		World Series		All-Star Game		
Year	Team (League)	W	L	Pct.	Pos	W	L	W	L	W	L	W	L	
1975—Cleveland (A.L.)		79	80	.496	4th	—	—	—	—	—	—	—	—	
1976—Cleveland (A.L.)		81	78	.509	4th	—	—	—	—	—	—	—	—	
1977—Cleveland (A.L.)		26	31	.368		—	—	—	—	—	—	—	—	
1978—Rochester (I.L.)		58	64	.475	6th	—	—	—	—	—	—	—	—	
1981—San Francisco (N.L.)		27	32	.457	5th	—	—	—	—	—	—	—	—	
—Second half		29	23	.558	3rd	—	—	—	—	—	—	—	—	
1982—San Francisco (N.L.)		87	75	.537	3rd	—	—	—	—	—	—	—	—	
1983—San Francisco (N.L.)		79	83	.487	5th	—	—	—	—	—	—	—	—	
1984—San Francisco (N.L.)		42	64	.396	6th	—	—	—	—	—	—	—	—	
1988—Baltimore (A.L.)		54	101	.348	7th	—	—	—	—	—	—	—	—	
1989—Baltimore (A.L.)		87	75	.537	2nd	—	—	—	—	—	—	—	—	
1990—Baltimore (A.L.)		76	85	.472	5th	—	—	—	—	—	—	—	—	
1991—Baltimore (A.L.)		13	24	.351	—	—	—	—	—	—	—	—	—	
2002—Montreal (N.L.)		83	79	.512	2nd	—	—	—	—	—	—	—	—	
2003—Montreal (N.L.)		83	79	.512	4th	—	—	—	—	—	—	—	—	
American League totals (7 years)		416	474	.467		—	—	—	—	—	—	—	—	
National League totals (6 years)		430	435	.497		—	—	—	—	—	—	—	—	
Major League totals (13 years)		846	909	.482		—	—	—	—	—	—	—	—	

SCIOSCIA, MIKE — ANGELS

PERSONAL: Born November 27, 1958, in Upper Darby, Pa. ... 6-2/220. ... Batted left, threw right. ... Full name: Michael Lorri Scioscia. ... Name pronounced: SO-sha. ... High school: Springfield (Pa.). ... College: Penn State.
TRANSACTIONS/CAREER NOTES: Selected by Los Angeles Dodgers organization in first round (19th pick overall) of free-agent draft (June 8, 1976). ... On disabled list (May 19-August 4, 1978; April 10-20, 1980; May 15, 1983-remainder of season; May 6-21, 1984; June 10-July 15, 1986; June 1-16, 1987; and July 5-20, 1991). ... Granted free agency (November 4, 1992). ... Signed by San Diego Padres (February 11, 1993). ... On San Diego disabled list (March 29, 1993-entire season). ... Released by Padres (October 15, 1993). ... Signed by Texas Rangers organization (December 14, 1993). ... Placed on voluntary retired list (August 2, 1994).

Year	Team (League)	Pos.	G	AB	R	H	2B	3B	HR	RBI	Avg.	BB	SO	SB	PO	A	E	Avg.
1976—Bellingham (N'west)		C	46	151	25	42	6	0	7	26	.278	36	22	2	202	35	14	.944
1977—Clinton (Midw.)		C-1B	121	364	58	92	20	1	7	44	.253	79	25	9	764	95	22	.975
1978—San Antonio (Texas)		C	58	204	29	61	16	0	2	34	.299	31	20	3	214	17	4	.983
1979—Albuquerque (PCL)		C	143	461	80	155	34	0	3	68	.336	73	33	5	690	86	15	.981
1980—Albuquerque (PCL)		C	52	160	33	53	11	1	3	33	.331	36	13	3	207	19	5	.978
—Los Angeles (N.L.)		C	54	134	8	34	5	1	1	8	.254	12	9	1	226	26	2	.992
1981—Los Angeles (N.L.)		C	93	290	27	80	10	0	2	29	.276	36	18	0	493	48	7	.987
1982—Los Angeles (N.L.)		C	129	365	31	80	11	1	5	38	.219	44	31	2	631	57	10	.986
1983—Los Angeles (N.L.)		C	12	35	3	11	3	0	1	7	.314	5	2	0	55	4	0	1.000
1984—Los Angeles (N.L.)		C	114	341	29	93	18	0	5	38	.273	52	26	2	701	64	12	.985
1985—Los Angeles (N.L.)		C	141	429	47	127	26	3	7	53	.296	77	21	3	818	66	13	.986
1986—Los Angeles (N.L.)		C	122	374	36	94	18	1	5	26	.251	62	23	3	756	64	15	.982
1987—Los Angeles (N.L.)		C	142	461	44	122	26	1	6	38	.265	55	23	7	925	80	11	.989
1988—Los Angeles (N.L.)		C	130	408	29	105	18	0	3	35	.257	38	31	0	748	63	7	.991
1989—Los Angeles (N.L.)		C	133	408	40	102	16	0	10	44	.250	52	29	0	822	82	11	.988
1990—Los Angeles (N.L.)		C	135	435	46	115	25	0	12	66	.264	55	31	4	842	58	10	.989
1991—Los Angeles (N.L.)		C	119	345	39	91	16	2	8	40	.264	47	32	4	677	51	7	.990
1992—Los Angeles (N.L.)		C	117	348	19	77	6	3	3	24	.221	32	31	3	641	74	9	.988
1993—San Diego (N.L.)									Did not play.									
1994—Charlotte (Fla. St.)		C	1	2	0	1	0	0	0	0	.500	0	0	0	3	1	0	1.000
Major League totals (13 years)			1441	4373	398	1131	198	12	68	446	.259	567	307	29	8335	737	114	.988

RECORD AS MANAGER

BACKGROUND: Minor league catching coordinator, Dodgers organization (1995-96). ... Bench coach, Dodgers (1997-98). ... Manager, Peoria Javelinas, Arizona fall league (1997).

HONORS: Named A.L. Manager of the Year by THE SPORTING NEWS (2002). ... Named A.L. Manager of the Year by Baseball Writers' Association of America (2002).

		REGULAR SEASON				Playoffs		Champ. Series		World Series		All-Star Game	
Year	Team (League)	W	L	Pct.	Pos	W	L	W	L	W	L	W	L
1999—Albuquerque (PCL)		65	74	.467	3rd	—	—	—	—	—	—	—	—
2000—Anaheim (A.L.)		82	80	.506	3rd	—	—	—	—	—	—	—	—
2001—Anaheim (A.L.)		75	87	.462	3rd	—	—	—	—	—	—	—	—
2002—Anaheim (A.L.)		99	63	.611	2nd	3	1	4	1	4	3	—	—
2003—Anaheim (A.L.)		77	85	.475	3rd	—	—	—	—	—	—	1	0
Major League totals (4 years)		333	315	.513		3	1	4	1	4	3	1	0

NOTES:

2002—Defeated New York Yankees in A.L. divisional playoff; defeated Minnesota in A.L. Championship Series; defeated San Francisco in World Series.

SHOWALTER, BUCK   RANGERS

PERSONAL: Born May 23, 1956, in DeFuniak Springs, Fla. ... 5-9/195. ... Batted left, threw left. ... Full name: William Nathaniel Showalter III. ... High school: Century (Fla.). ... Junior college: Chipola Junior College (Fla.). ... College: Mississippi State.

TRANSACTIONS/CAREER NOTES: Selected by New York Yankees organization in fifth round of free-agent draft (June 7, 1977). ... On disabled list (July 1-11 and July 19-August 4, 1981).

Year	Team (League)	Pos.	G	AB	R	H	2B	3B	HR	RBI	Avg.	BB	SO	SB	PO	A	E	Avg.
1977—Fort Laud. (FSL)		OF	56	196	32	71	8	1	1	25	.362	36	13	4	96	2	2	.980
1978—West Haven (East.)		OF	123	429	52	124	13	2	3	46	.289	55	34	19	192	15	7	.967
1979—West Haven (East.)		1B-OF	129	469	71	131	7	3	6	51	.279	36	30	8	575	52	7	.989
1980—Nashville (Southern)		1B-OF	142	550	84	178	19	3	1	82	.324	53	23	6	71	2	1	.986
1981—Columbus (Int'l)		OF	14	37	6	7	1	0	1	3	.189	3	0	0	11	0	1	.917
—Nashville (Southern)		1B-OF	90	307	46	81	17	6	0	38	.264	46	16	3	201	14	7	.968
1982—Nashville (Southern)		1B-OF	132	517	66	152	29	3	3	46	.294	61	42	2	1282	51	13	.990
1983—Nashville (Southern)		IB-OF	89	297	35	82	13	4	1	37	.276	39	22	1	127	6	2	.985
—Columbus (Int'l)		IB	18	63	9	15	3	0	1	8	.238	7	3	1	139	14	1	.994

RECORD AS MANAGER

BACKGROUND: Minor league coach, New York Yankees organization (1984). ... Coach, Yankees (1990-91). ... Manager/scout, Arizona Diamondbacks (1996-97). ... Broadcaster (2001-02).

HONORS: Named New York-Pennsylvania League Manager of the Year (1985). ... Named Eastern League Manager of the Year (1989). ... Coach, A.L. All-Star team (1992). ... Named A.L. Manager of the Year by THE SPORTING NEWS (1994). ... Named A.L. Manager of the Year by Baseball Writers' Association of America (1994).

		REGULAR SEASON				Playoffs		Champ. Series		World Series		All-Star Game	
Year	Team (League)	W	L	Pct.	Pos	W	L	W	L	W	L	W	L
1985—Oneonta (NY-P)		55	23	.705	1st	3	0	—	—	—	—	—	—
1986—Oneonta (NY-P)		59	18	.766	1st	0	1	—	—	—	—	—	—
1987—Fort Lauderdale (FSL)		85	53	.615	1st	5	1	—	—	—	—	—	—
1988—Fort Lauderdale (FSL)		39	29	.573	3rd	—	—	—	—	—	—	—	—
—Second half		30	36	.455	3rd	—	—	—	—	—	—	—	—
1989—Albany (East.)		92	48	.657	1st	6	2	—	—	—	—	—	—
1992—New York (A.L.)		76	86	.469	4th	—	—	—	—	—	—	—	—
1993—New York (A.L.)		88	74	.543	2nd	—	—	—	—	—	—	—	—
1994—New York (A.L.)		70	43	.619	—	—	—	—	—	—	—	—	—
1995—New York (A.L.)		79	65	.548	2nd	2	3	—	—	—	—	—	—
1998—Arizona (N.L.)		65	97	.401	5th	—	—	—	—	—	—	—	—
1999—Arizona (N.L.)		100	62	.617	1st	1	3	—	—	—	—	—	—
2000—Arizona (N.L.)		85	77	.524	3rd	—	—	—	—	—	—	—	—
2003—Texas (A.L.)		71	91	.438	4th	—	—	—	—	—	—	—	—
American League totals (5 years)		384	359	.516		2	3	—	—	—	—	—	—
National League totals (3 years)		250	236	.514		1	3	—	—	—	—	—	—
Major League totals (8 years)		634	595	.515		3	6	—	—	—	—	—	—

NOTES:
1985—Defeated Geneva in one-game semifinal playoff; defeated Auburn, two games to none, in league championship.
1986—Lost to Newark in playoffs.
1987—Defeated Lakeland, two games to none, in playoffs; defeated Osceola, three games to one, in league championship.
1989—Defeated Reading, three games to one, in playoffs; defeated Harrisburg, three games to one, in league championship.
1994—New York was in first place in A.L. East at time of season-ending strike (August 12).
1995—Lost to Seattle in A.L. divisional playoff. Named Arizona Diamondbacks manager (November 15).
1999—Lost to New York Mets in N.L. divisional playoff.

TORRE, JOE — YANKEES

PERSONAL: Born July 18, 1940, in Brooklyn, NY. ...6-1/210. ... Batted right, threw right. ... Full name: Joseph Paul Torre. ... Name pronounced: TORE-ee. ... High school: St. Francis Prep (Brooklyn, N.Y.).
TRANSACTIONS/CAREER NOTES: Signed by Jacksonville, Milwaukee Braves organization (August 24, 1959). ... On military list (September 30, 1962-March 26, 1963). ... Braves franchise moved from Milwaukee to Atlanta (1966). ... On disabled list (April 18-May 9, 1968). ... Traded by Braves to St. Louis Cardinals for 1B Orlando Cepeda (March 17, 1969). ... Traded by Cardinals to New York Mets for P Tommy Moore and P Ray Sadecki (October 13, 1974). ... Released as player by Mets (June 18, 1977).

							BATTING							FIELDING		
Year	Team (League)	Pos.	G	AB	R	H	2B	3B	HR	RBI	Avg.	BB	SO	SB	PO	A	E	Avg.
1960—	Eau Claire (North.)	C	117	369	63	127	23	3	16	74	.344	70	45	7	636	64	9	.987
—	Milwaukee (N.L.)		2	2	0	1	0	0	0	0	.500	0	1	0	...	...	...	.000
1961—	Louisville (A.A.)	C	27	111	18	38	8	2	3	24	.342	6	9	0	185	14	2	.990
—	Milwaukee (N.L.)	C	113	406	40	113	21	4	10	42	.278	28	60	3	494	50	10	.982
1962—	Milwaukee (N.L.)	C	80	220	23	62	8	1	5	26	.282	24	24	1	325	39	5	.986
1963—	Milwaukee (N.L.)	C-1B-OF	142	501	57	147	19	4	14	71	.293	42	79	1	919	76	6	.994
1964—	Milwaukee (N.L.)	C-1B	154	601	87	193	36	5	20	109	.321	36	67	4	1081	94	7	.994
1965—	Milwaukee (N.L.)	C-1B	148	523	68	152	21	1	27	80	.291	61	79	0	1022	73	8	.993
1966—	Atlanta (N.L.)	C-1B	148	546	83	172	20	3	36	101	.315	60	61	0	874	87	12	.988
1967—	Atlanta (N.L.)	C-1B	135	477	67	132	18	1	20	68	.277	49	75	2	785	81	8	.991
1968—	Atlanta (N.L.)	C-1B	115	424	45	115	11	2	10	55	.271	34	72	1	733	48	2	.995
1969—	St. Louis (N.L.)		159	602	72	174	29	6	18	101	.289	66	85	0	1360	91	7	.995
1970—	St. Louis (N.L.)	3B-C-1B	161	624	89	203	27	9	21	100	.325	70	91	2	651	162	13	.984
1971—	St. Louis (N.L.)	3B	161	634	97	230	34	8	24	137	.363	63	70	4	136	271	21	.951
1972—	St. Louis (N.L.)	3B-1B	149	544	71	157	26	6	11	81	.289	54	64	3	336	198	15	.973
1973—	St. Louis (N.L.)	3B-1B	141	519	67	149	17	2	13	69	.287	65	78	2	881	128	12	.988
1974—	St. Louis (N.L.)	3B-1B	147	529	59	149	28	1	11	70	.282	69	88	1	1173	121	14	.989
1975—	New York (N.L.)	3B-1B	114	361	33	89	16	3	6	35	.247	35	55	0	172	157	15	.956
1976—	New York (N.L.)	3B-1B	114	310	36	95	10	3	5	31	.306	21	35	1	593	52	7	.989
1977—	New York (N.L.)	3B-1B	26	51	2	9	3	0	1	9	.176	2	10	0	83	3	1	.989
	Major League totals (18 years)		2209	7874	996	2342	344	59	252	1185	.297	779	1094	23	11618	1731	163	.988

RECORD AS MANAGER

BACKGROUND: Player/manager, New York Mets (May 31-June 18, 1977).
HONORS: Named Sportsman of the Year by THE SPORTING NEWS (1996). ... Named co-A.L. Manager of the Year by Baseball Writers' Association of America (1996). ... Named A.L. Manager of the Year by THE SPORTING NEWS (1998). ... Named A.L. Manager of the Year by Baseball Writers' Association of America (1998).

		REGULAR SEASON				POSTSEASON								
						Playoffs		Champ. Series		World Series		All-Star Game	
Year	Team (League)	W	L	Pct.	Pos	W	L	W	L	W	L	W	L
1977—	New York (N.L.)	49	68	.418	6th	—	—	—	—	—	—	—	—
1978—	New York (N.L.)	66	96	.407	6th	—	—	—	—	—	—	—	—
1979—	New York (N.L.)	63	99	.388	6th	—	—	—	—	—	—	—	—
1980—	New York (N.L.)	67	95	.413	5th	—	—	—	—	—	—	—	—
1981—	New York (N.L.)	17	34	.333	5th	—	—	—	—	—	—	—	—
—	Second half	24	28	.462	4th	—	—	—	—	—	—	—	—
1982—	Atlanta (N.L.)	89	73	.549	1st	—	—	0	3	—	—	—	—
1983—	Atlanta (N.L.)	88	74	.543	2nd	—	—	—	—	—	—	—	—
1984—	Atlanta (N.L.)	80	82	.493	2nd	—	—	—	—	—	—	—	—
1990—	St. Louis (N.L.)	24	34	.413	6th	—	—	—	—	—	—	—	—
1991—	St. Louis (N.L.)	84	78	.518	2nd	—	—	—	—	—	—	—	—
1992—	St. Louis (N.L.)	83	79	.512	3rd	—	—	—	—	—	—	—	—
1993—	St. Louis (N.L.)	87	75	.537	3rd	—	—	—	—	—	—	—	—
1994—	St. Louis (N.L.)	53	61	.464	—	—	—	—	—	—	—	—	—
1995—	St. Louis (N.L.)	20	27	.425	4th	—	—	—	—	—	—	—	—
1996—	New York (A.L.)	92	70	.567	1st	3	1	4	1	4	2	—	—
1997—	New York (A.L.)	96	66	.592	2nd	2	3	—	—	—	—	1	0
1998—	New York (A.L.)	114	48	.703	1st	3	0	4	2	4	0	—	—
1999—	New York (A.L.)	98	64	.604	1st	3	0	4	1	4	0	1	0
2000—	New York (A.L.)	87	74	.540	1st	3	2	4	2	4	1	1	0
2001—	New York (A.L.)	95	65	.593	1st	3	2	4	1	3	4	1	0
2002—	New York (A.L.)	103	58	.639	1st	1	3	—	—	—	—	0	0
2003—	New York (A.L.)	101	61	.623	1st	3	1	4	3	2	4	—	—
	American League totals (8 years)	786	506	.608		21	12	24	10	21	11	4	0
	National League totals (14 years)	894	1003	.471		—	—	0	3	—	—	—	—
	Major League totals (22 years)	1680	1509	.527		21	12	24	13	21	11	4	0

NOTES:
1977—Replaced New York manager Joe Frazier with club in sixth place and record of 15-30 (May 31); served as player/manager (May 31-June 18, when released as player).
1982—Lost to St. Louis in N.L. Championship Series.
1990—Replaced St. Louis manager Whitey Herzog (33-47) and interim manager Red Schoendienst (13-11) with club in sixth place and record of 46-58 (August 1).
1994—St. Louis was tied for third place in N.L. Central at time of season-ending strike (August 12).
1995—Replaced as Cardinals manager by interim manager Mike Jorgensen, with club in fourth place (June 16).
1996—Defeated Texas in A.L. divisional playoff; defeated Baltimore in A.L. Championship Series; defeated Atlanta in World Series.
1997—Lost to Cleveland in A.L. divisional playoff.
1998—Defeated Texas in A.L. divisional playoff; defeated Cleveland in A.L. Championship Series; defeated San Diego in World Series.
1999—Defeated Texas in A.L. divisional playoff; defeated Boston in A.L. Championship Series; defeated Atlanta in World Series.

2000—Defeated Oakland in A.L. divisional playoff; defeated Seattle in A.L. Championship Series; defeated New York Mets in World Series.
2001—Defeated Oakland in A.L. divisional playoff; defeated Seattle in A.L. Championship Series; lost to Arizona in World Series.
2002—All-Star Game ended in tie. Lost to Anaheim in A.L. divisional playoff.
2003—Defeated Minnesota in A.L. divisional playoff; defeated Boston in A.L. Championship Series; lost to Florida in World Series.

TOSCA, CARLOS — BLUE JAYS

PERSONAL: Born September 29, 1953, in Pinar Del Rio, Cuba. ... 5-7/158. ... Batted left, threw left. ... College: South Florida.

RECORD AS MANAGER

BACKGROUND: Bench coach, Arizona Diamondbacks (1998-2000). ... Third base coach, Toronto Blue Jays (December 10, 2001-June 3, 2002).
HONORS: Named Gulf Coast League Manager of the Year (1988). ... Named Eastern League Manager of the Year (1996).

| | | | | | | | POSTSEASON | | | | | |
| | REGULAR SEASON | | | | Playoffs | | Champ. Series | | World Series | | All-Star Game | |
Year Team (League)	W	L	Pct.	Pos	W	L	W	L	W	L	W	L
1980— Gulf Coast Yankees (GCL)	27	35	.435	7th	—	—	—	—	—	—	—	—
1981— Gulf Coast Yankees (GCL)	30	29	.508	7th	—	—	—	—	—	—	—	—
1982— Gulf Coast Yankees (GCL)	42	21	.666	1st	—	—	—	—	—	—	—	—
1983— Greensboro (S.Atl.)	39	33	.541	2nd	—	—	—	—	—	—	—	—
— Second half	34	38	.472	3rd	—	—	—	—	—	—	—	—
1984— Greensboro (S.Atl.)	44	28	.611	1st	—	—	—	—	—	—	—	—
— Second half	31	41	.431	4th	1	2	—	—	—	—	—	—
1985— Gulf Coast Yankees (GCL)	43	18	.704	1st	—	—	—	—	—	—	—	—
1988— Gulf Coast Royals (GCL)	39	24	.619	1st	0	1	—	—	—	—	—	—
1989— Gulf Coast Royals (GCL)	35	28	.555	3rd	—	—	—	—	—	—	—	—
1990— Gulf Coast Royals (GCL)	25	38	.396	5th	—	—	—	—	—	—	—	—
1991— Baseball City (FSL)	27	39	.409	3rd	—	—	—	—	—	—	—	—
— Second half	35	30	.538	2nd	—	—	—	—	—	—	—	—
1992— Gulf Coast Marlins (GCL)	33	27	.550	2nd	—	—	—	—	—	—	—	—
1993— Kane County (Midw.)	39	29	.573	3rd	—	—	—	—	—	—	—	—
— Second half	36	33	.522	4th	—	—	—	—	—	—	—	—
1994— Portland (East.)	60	81	.425	4th	—	—	—	—	—	—	—	—
1995— Portland (East.)	86	56	.605	1st	1	3	—	—	—	—	—	—
1996— Portland (East.)	83	58	.588	1st	3	2	1	3	—	—	—	—
1997— Charlotte (I.L.)	76	65	.539	2nd	1	3	—	—	—	—	—	—
2001— Richmond (I.L.)	68	76	.472	3rd	—	—	—	—	—	—	—	—
2002— Toronto (A.L.)	58	51	.532	3rd	—	—	—	—	—	—	—	—
2003— Toronto (A.L.)	86	76	.530	3rd	—	—	—	—	—	—	—	—
Major League totals (2 years)	144	127	.531		—	—	—	—	—	—	—	—

NOTES:
1984—Lost to Asheville in playoffs.
1985—Championship game rained out.
1988—Lost to Gulf Coast Yankees in championship game.
1995—Lost to New Haven in playoffs.
1996—Defeated Binghamton, three games to two, in playoffs; lost to Harrisburg, three games to one, in league championship.
1997—Lost to Columbus in playoffs.
2002—Replaced Toronto manager Buck Martinez with club in fourth place and record of 20-33 (June 3).

TRACY, JIM — DODGERS

PERSONAL: Born December 31, 1955, in Hamilton, Ohio. ... 6-3/205. ... Batted left, threw right. ... Full name: James Edwin Tracy. ... High school: Badin (Hamilton, Ohio) ... College: Marietta College (Ohio).
TRANSACTIONS/CAREER NOTES: Selected by Chicago Cubs organization in fourth round of free-agent draft (January 11, 1977). ... Traded by Cubs to Houston Astros for OF Gary Woods (December 9, 1981).

| | | | | | BATTING | | | | | | | | FIELDING | | | |
Year Team (League)	Pos.	G	AB	R	H	2B	3B	HR	RBI	Avg.	BB	SO	SB	PO	A	E	Avg.
1977— Pomp. Bea. (FSL)	1B-OF	93	261	27	59	13	2	4	34	.226	41	66	1	147	6	4	.975
1978— Pomp. Bea. (FSL)	1B-OF	78	225	42	55	7	5	6	43	.244	58	34	2	329	27	4	.989
— Midland (Texas)	1B-OF	54	189	34	49	9	2	8	29	.259	20	50	2	174	10	2	.989
1979— Midland (Texas)	1B	86	301	75	107	16	1	15	67	.355	63	41	7	799	31	6	.993
— Wichita (A.A.)	1B-OF	44	150	26	41	9	1	4	18	.273	21	36	0	364	20	11	.972
1980— Wichita (A.A.)	3B-1B-OF	112	406	66	130	17	6	16	63	.320	67	68	4	428	33	5	.989
— Chicago (N.L.)	1B-OF	42	122	12	31	3	3	3	9	.254	13	37	2	44	0	2	.957
1981— Midland (Texas)	1B-OF	22	73	8	20	3	0	2	7	.274	13	22	0	73	2	0	1.000
— Chicago (N.L.)	OF	45	63	6	15	2	1	0	5	.238	12	14	1	16	0	0	1.000
1982— Tucson (PCL)	1B-OF	133	481	85	153	35	3	12	100	.318	81	83	5	294	14	4	.987
1983— Taiyo (Jap. Cen.)		125	469	61	142	29	2	19	66	.303	32	74	3	...	...	...	...
1984— Taiyo (Jap. Cen.)		3	9	1	2	0	0	1	5	.222	2	1	0	...	...	...	...
— Tucson (PCL)	1B-OF	52	156	22	38	12	3	1	21	.244	31	39	2	67	0	2	.971
Major League totals (2 years)		87	185	18	46	5	4	3	14	.249	25	51	3	60	0	2	.968

RECORD AS MANAGER

BACKGROUND: Minor league field coordinator, Cincinnati Reds (1992). ... Coach, Montreal Expos (1995-98). ... Coach, Los Angeles Dodgers (1999 and 2000).
HONORS: Named Minor League Manager of the Year by THE SPORTING NEWS (1993).

| | | | | | | | POSTSEASON | | | | | |
| | REGULAR SEASON | | | | Playoffs | | Champ. Series | | World Series | | All-Star Game | |
Year Team (League)	W	L	Pct.	Pos	W	L	W	L	W	L	W	L
1987— Peoria (Midw.)	71	69	.507	2nd	—	—	—	—	—	—	—	—
1988— Peoria (Midw.)	29	40	.420	6th	—	—	—	—	—	—	—	—
— Second half	41	30	.577	3rd	—	—	—	—	—	—	—	—
1989— Chattanooga (Sou.)	33	38	.464	4th	—	—	—	—	—	—	—	—
— Second half	25	43	.368	5th	—	—	—	—	—	—	—	—
1990— Chattanooga (Sou.)	35	36	.492	4th	—	—	—	—	—	—	—	—
— Second half	31	42	.425	4th	—	—	—	—	—	—	—	—

Year Team (League)	REGULAR SEASON				POSTSEASON							
					Playoffs		Champ. Series		World Series		All-Star Game	
	W	L	Pct.	Pos	W	L	W	L	W	L	W	L
1991— Chattanooga (Sou.)	35	32	.522	2nd	—	—	—	—	—	—	—	—
— Second half	38	39	.494	3rd	—	—	—	—	—	—	—	—
1993— Harrisburg (East.)	94	44	.681	1st	3	1	3	2	—	—	—	—
1994— Ottawa (I.L.)	70	72	.492	3rd	—	—	—	—	—	—	—	—
2001— Los Angeles (N.L.)	86	76	.530	3rd	—	—	—	—	—	—	—	—
2002— Los Angeles (N.L.)	92	70	.567	3rd	—	—	—	—	—	—	—	—
2003— Los Angeles (N.L.)	85	77	.524	2nd	—	—	—	—	—	—	—	—
Major League totals (3 years)	263	223	.541		—	—	—	—	—	—	—	—

NOTES:

1993—Defeated Albany, three games to one, in playoff; defeated Canton-Akron, three games to two, in championship playoff.

TRAMMELL, ALAN   TIGERS

PERSONAL: Born February 21, 1958, in Garden Grove, Calif. ... 6-0/185. ... Batted right, threw right. ... Full name: Alan Stuart Trammell. ... Name pronounced: TRAM-ull. ... High school: Kearney (San Diego).

TRANSACTIONS/CAREER NOTES: Selected by Detroit Tigers organization in second round of free-agent draft (June 8, 1976). ... On disabled list (July 9-31, 1984; June 29-July 17, 1988; June 4-23, 1989; July 18-August 13, 1991; and May 16, 1992-remainder of season). ... Granted free agency (November 6, 1992). ... Re-signed by Tigers (December 2, 1992). ... On disabled list (April 2-17, 1993). ... Granted free agency (October 28, 1993). ... Re-signed by Tigers (November 3, 1993). ... Granted free agency (October 25, 1994). ... Re-signed by Tigers (April 8, 1995). ... On disabled list (April 21-May 6, 1995). ... Granted free agency (December 21, 1995). ... Re-signed by Tigers (January 24, 1996). ... On disabled list (July 6-July 25 and July 27-September 1, 1996). ... Announced retirement (September 30, 1996).

Year Team (League)	Pos.	BATTING												FIELDING			
		G	AB	R	H	2B	3B	HR	RBI	Avg.	BB	SO	SB	PO	A	E	Avg.
1976— Bristol (Appal.)	SS	41	140	27	38	2	2	0	7	.271	26	20	8	59	131	12	.941
— Montgom. (Sou.)	SS	21	56	4	10	0	0	0	2	.179	7	12	3	40	64	2	.981
1977— Montgom. (Sou.)	SS	134	454	78	132	9	19	3	50	.291	56	92	4	188	397	27	.956
— Detroit (A.L.)	SS	19	43	6	8	0	0	0	0	.186	4	12	0	15	34	2	.961
1978— Detroit (A.L.)	SS	139	448	49	120	14	6	2	34	.268	45	56	3	239	421	14	.979
1979— Detroit (A.L.)	SS	142	460	68	127	11	4	6	50	.276	43	55	17	245	388	26	.961
1980— Detroit (A.L.)	SS	146	560	107	168	21	5	9	65	.300	69	63	12	225	412	13	.980
1981— Detroit (A.L.)	SS	105	392	52	101	15	3	2	31	.258	49	31	10	181	347	9	.983
1982— Detroit (A.L.)	SS	157	489	66	126	34	3	9	57	.258	52	47	19	259	459	16	.978
1983— Detroit (A.L.)	SS	142	505	83	161	31	2	14	66	.319	57	64	30	236	367	13	.979
1984— Detroit (A.L.) .... SS-DH		139	555	85	174	34	5	14	69	.314	60	63	19	180	314	10	.980
1985— Detroit (A.L.)	SS	149	605	79	156	21	7	13	57	.258	50	71	14	225	400	15	.977
1986— Detroit (A.L.) .... SS-DH		151	574	107	159	33	7	21	75	.277	59	57	25	238	445	22	.969
1987— Detroit (A.L.)	SS	151	597	109	205	34	3	28	105	.343	60	47	21	222	421	19	.971
1988— Detroit (A.L.)	SS	128	466	73	145	24	1	15	69	.311	46	46	7	195	355	11	.980
1989— Detroit (A.L.) .... SS-DH		121	449	54	109	20	3	5	43	.243	45	45	10	188	396	9	.985
1990— Detroit (A.L.) .... SS-DH		146	559	71	170	37	1	14	89	.304	68	55	12	232	409	14	.979
1991— Detroit (A.L.) .... SS-DH		101	375	57	93	20	0	9	55	.248	37	39	11	131	296	9	.979
1992— Detroit (A.L.)	SS	29	102	11	28	7	1	1	11	.275	15	4	2	46	80	3	.977
1993— Detroit (A.L.) S-3-O-D		112	401	72	132	25	3	12	60	.329	38	38	12	113	238	9	.975
1994— Detroit (A.L.) .... SS-DH		76	292	38	78	17	1	8	28	.267	16	35	3	117	181	10	.968
1995— Detroit (A.L.) .... SS-DH		74	223	28	60	12	0	2	23	.269	27	19	3	86	158	5	.980
1996— Detroit (A.L.) S-2-3-O		66	193	16	45	2	0	1	16	.233	10	27	6	75	144	6	.973
Major League totals (20 years)		2293	8288	1231	2365	412	55	185	1003	.285	850	874	236	3448	6215	235	.976

RECORD AS MANAGER

BACKGROUND: Assistant Director of Baseball Operations, Detroit Tigers (1997-98). ... Hitting coach, Tigers (1999). ... First base coach, San Diego Padres (2000-02).

Year Team (League)	REGULAR SEASON				POSTSEASON							
					Playoffs		Champ. Series		World Series		All-Star Game	
	W	L	Pct.	Pos	W	L	W	L	W	L	W	L
2003— Detroit (A.L.)	43	119	.265	5th	—	—	—	—	—	—	—	—
Major League totals (1 year)	43	119	.265		—	—	—	—	—	—	—	—

WEDGE, ERIC   INDIANS

PERSONAL: Born January 27, 1968, in Fort Wayne, Ind. ... 6-3/215. ... Batted right, threw right. ... Full name: Eric Michael Wedge. ... High school: Northrop (Fort Wayne, Ind.). ... College: Wichita State.

TRANSACTIONS/CAREER NOTES: Selected by Boston Red Sox organization in third round of free-agent draft (June 5, 1989). ... On Pawtucket disabled list (May 15-22 and May 24-July 10, 1991; and June 3-10 and June 25-July 28, 1992). ... Selected by Colorado Rockies in second round (48th pick overall) of expansion draft (November 17, 1992). ... On Colorado disabled list (March 27-June 17, 1993); included rehabilitation assignments to Central Valley (May 28-June 3) and Colorado Springs (June 3-16). ... On Colorado disabled list (June 17-July 26, 1993). ... Released by Rockies (March 29, 1994). ... Signed by Red Sox organization (May 2, 1994). ... On Pawtucket disabled list (June 21-28, 1994). ... Granted free agency (October 16, 1995). ... Signed by Detroit Tigers organization (1996). ... Granted free agency (October 15, 1996). ... Signed by Philadelphia Phillies organization (1997). ... Granted free agency (October 15, 1997).

Year Team (League)	Pos.	BATTING												FIELDING			
		G	AB	R	H	2B	3B	HR	RBI	Avg.	BB	SO	SB	PO	A	E	Avg.
1989— Elmira (N.Y.-Penn)	C	41	145	20	34	6	2	7	22	.234	15	21	1	283	30	2	.994
— New Britain (East.)	C	14	40	3	8	2	0	0	2	.200	5	10	0	83	9	0	1.000
1990— New Britain (East.)	C	103	339	36	77	13	1	5	47	.227	50	54	1	583	62	9	.986
1991— Pawtucket (Int'l)	C	53	163	24	38	14	1	5	18	.233	25	26	0	282	36	6	.981
— New Britain (East.)	C	2	8	0	2	0	0	0	2	.250	0	2	0	6	1	0	1.000
— Winter Haven (FSL)	C	8	21	2	5	0	0	1	1	.238	3	7	1	17	2	0	1.000
— Boston (A.L.)	DH	1	1	0	1	0	0	0	0	1.000	0	0	0	...	...	...	...
1992— Pawtucket (Int'l)	C	65	211	28	63	9	0	11	40	.299	32	40	0	209	20	3	.987
— Boston (A.L.) .... DH-C		27	68	11	17	2	0	5	11	.250	13	18	0	19	2	0	1.000

Year—Team (League)	Pos.	G	AB	R	H	2B	3B	HR	RBI	Avg.	BB	SO	SB	PO	A	E	Avg.
1993—Central Valley (Cal.)	C	6	23	6	7	0	0	3	11	.304	2	6	0	30	0	0	1.000
—Colo. Springs (PCL)	1B	38	90	17	24	6	0	3	13	.267	16	22	0	134	22	3	.981
—Colorado (N.L.)	C	9	11	2	2	0	0	0	1	.182	0	4	0	6	1	0	1.000
1994—Pawtucket (Int'l)	DH-C-1B	77	255	44	73	14	0	19	59	.286	51	48	0	47	4	1	.981
—Boston (A.L.)	DH	2	6	0	0	0	0	0	0	.000	1	3	0	...	...	...	...
1995—Pawtucket (Int'l)	1B-DH-C	108	376	52	88	17	1	20	68	.234	63	96	1	596	46	3	.995
1996—Toledo (Int'l)	DH-C-1B	96	332	61	78	25	0	15	57	.235	43	81	2	209	15	2	.991
1997—Scran./W.B. (I.L.)	C-DH-1B	47	129	25	33	8	1	7	36	.256	22	40	0	137	9	4	.973
American League totals (3 years)		30	75	11	18	2	0	5	11	.240	14	21	0	19	2	0	1.000
National League totals (1 year)		9	11	2	2	0	0	0	1	.182	0	4	0	6	1	0	1.000
Major League totals (4 years)		39	86	13	20	2	0	5	12	.233	14	25	0	25	3	0	1.000

RECORD AS MANAGER

HONORS: Named Carolina League Manager of the Year (1999). ... Named International League Manager of the Year (2001).

Year—Team (League)	REGULAR SEASON				Playoffs		Champ. Series		World Series		All-Star Game	
	W	L	Pct.	Pos	W	L	W	L	W	L	W	L
1998—Columbus (S.Atl.)	28	42	.400	4th	—	—	—	—	—	—	—	—
—Second half	31	39	.443	3rd	—	—	—	—	—	—	—	—
1999—Kinston (Caro.)	37	32	.536	1st	—	—	—	—	—	—	—	—
—Second half	42	26	.618	2nd	1	2	—	—	—	—	—	—
2000—Akron (East.)	75	68	.524	3rd	—	—	—	—	—	—	—	—
2001—Buffalo (I.L.)	91	51	.640	1st	2	3	—	—	—	—	—	—
2002—Buffalo (I.L.)	87	57	.604	2nd	3	3	3	3	—	—	—	—
2003—Cleveland (A.L.)	68	94	.419	4th	—	—	—	—	—	—	—	—
Major League totals (1 year)	68	94	.419		—	—	—	—	—	—	—	—

NOTES:
1999—Lost to Myrtle Beach in playoffs.
2001—Lost to Scranton/Wilkes-Barre in playoffs.
2002—Defeated Scranton/Wilkes-Barre, three games to none, in playoffs; lost to Durham, three games to none, in league championship.

WILLIAMS, JIMY — ASTROS

PERSONAL: Born October 4, 1943, in Arroyo Grande, Calif. ... 5-11/170. ... Batted right, threw right.... Full name: James Francis Williams. ... High school: Arroyo Grande (Calif.). ... College: Fresno State.

TRANSACTIONS/CAREER NOTES: Selected by St. Louis Cardinals organization from Toronto, Boston Red Sox organization (November 29, 1965). ... In military service (July 24, 1966-remainder of season). ... Traded by Cardinals with C Pat Corrales to Cincinnati Reds for C John Edwards (February 8, 1968). ... Selected by Montreal Expos in expansion draft (October 14, 1968). ... On disabled list (May 13-30 and June 24-September 2, 1969). ... On suspended list (June 7-16, 1971). ... Sold to New York Mets organization (June 16, 1971). ... On temporary inactive list (August 12-16, 1971). ... On disabled list (May 15-July 17 and July 29-August 20, 1975).

Year—Team (League)	Pos.	G	AB	R	H	2B	3B	HR	RBI	Avg.	BB	SO	SB	PO	A	E	Avg.
1965—Waterloo (Midw.)	SS	115	435	64	125	19	3	2	31	.287	...	...	...	173	312	26	.949
1966—St. Louis (N.L.)	2B-SS	13	11	1	3	0	0	0	1	.273	1	5	0	2	5	0	1.000
1967—Arkansas (Texas)	SS	28	101	8	21	1	1	0	8	.208	...	...	...	49	80	2	.985
—Tulsa (PCL)	SS	61	164	18	37	2	0	1	21	.226	...	...	...	87	156	26	.903
—St. Louis (N.L.)	SS	1	2	0	0	0	0	0	0	.000	0	1	0	6	1	0	1.000
1968—Indianapolis (PCL)	2B-SS	120	403	38	91	19	5	2	34	.226	...	...	...	198	323	27	.951
1969—Vancouver (PCL)	3B-SS-OF	35	66	7	17	1	1	0	9	.258	...	...	...	17	23	2	.952
1970—Winnipeg (Int'l)	2B-3B-SS	109	361	49	83	15	0	3	18	.230	...	...	...	178	244	30	.934
1971—Win./Tide. (Int'l)	2B-3B-SS	105	327	40	84	7	4	5	31	.257	...	...	...	120	219	22	.939
1972—							Did not play.										
1973—							Did not play.										
1974—							Did not play.										
1975—El Paso (Texas)	DH	6	17	3	2	0	0	0	2	.118	...	...	...	0	0	0	...
Major League totals (2 years)		14	13	1	3	0	0	0	1	.231	1	6	0	8	6	0	1.000

RECORD AS MANAGER

BACKGROUND: Coach, Toronto Blue Jays (1980-85). ... Minor league instructor, Atlanta Braves (October 4, 1989-June 25, 1990). ... Coach, Braves (1990-96).

HONORS: Named Pacific Coast League Manager of the Year (1976 and 1979). ... Named A.L. Manager of the Year by THE SPORTING NEWS (1999). ... Named A.L. Manager of the Year by Baseball Writers' Association of America (1999).

Year—Team (League)	REGULAR SEASON				Playoffs		Champ. Series		World Series		All-Star Game	
	W	L	Pct.	Pos	W	L	W	L	W	L	W	L
1974—Quad Cities (Midw.)	33	26	.559	1st	—	—	—	—	—	—	—	—
—Second half	32	32	.500	3rd	1	2	—	—	—	—	—	—
1975—El Paso (Texas)	62	71	.466	3rd	—	—	—	—	—	—	—	—
1976—Salt Lake (PCL)	90	54	.625	1st	2	3	—	—	—	—	—	—
1977—Salt Lake (PCL)	74	65	.532	2nd	—	—	—	—	—	—	—	—
1978—Springfield (A.A.)	70	66	.514	3rd	—	—	—	—	—	—	—	—
1979—Salt Lake (PCL)	34	40	.459	4th	—	—	—	—	—	—	—	—
—Second half	46	28	.622	1st	2	0	3	0	—	—	—	—
1986—Toronto (A.L.)	86	76	.530	4th	—	—	—	—	—	—	—	—
1987—Toronto (A.L.)	96	66	.592	2nd	—	—	—	—	—	—	—	—
1988—Toronto (A.L.)	87	75	.537	3rd	—	—	—	—	—	—	—	—
1989—Toronto (A.L.)	12	24	.333	—	—	—	—	—	—	—	—	—
1997—Boston (A.L.)	78	84	.481	4th	—	—	—	—	—	—	—	—
1998—Boston (A.L.)	92	70	.567	2nd	1	3	—	—	—	—	—	—
1999—Boston (A.L.)	94	68	.580	2nd	3	2	1	4	—	—	—	—
2000—Boston (A.L.)	85	77	.524	2nd	—	—	—	—	—	—	—	—
2001—Boston (A.L.)	65	53	.550	—	—	—	—	—	—	—	—	—
2002—Houston (N.L.)	84	78	.518	2nd	—	—	—	—	—	—	—	—
2003—Houston (N.L.)	87	75	.537	2nd	—	—	—	—	—	—	—	—
American League totals (9 years)	695	593	.539		4	5	1	4	—	—	—	—
National League totals (2 years)	171	153	.527		—	—	—	—	—	—	—	—
Major League totals (11 years)	866	746	.537		4	5	1	4	—	—	—	—

NOTES:
1974—Lost to Danville in playoffs.
1976—Lost to Hawaii in championship playoff.
1979—Defeated Albuquerque, two games to none, in playoff; defeated Hawaii, three games to none, in championship series.
1989—Replaced as Toronto manager by Cito Gaston, with club tied for sixth place (May 15).
1998—Lost to Cleveland in A.L. divisional playoff.
1999—Defeated Cleveland in A.L. divisional playoff; lost to New York Yankees in A.L. Championship Series.
2001—Replaced as manager by Joe Kerrigan with club in second place (August 16).

YOST, NED   BREWERS

PERSONAL: Born August 19, 1955, in Eureka, Calif. ... 6-1/185. ... Batted right, threw right. ... Full name: Edgar Frederick Yost. ... Junior college: Chabot Junior College.
TRANSACTIONS/CAREER NOTES: Signed as non-drafted free agent by New York Mets organization (June 11, 1974). ... Drafted by Milwaukee Brewers (December 5, 1977). ... On disabled list (July 10-28, 1978). ... On disabled list (July 11-August 15, 1983). ... Traded by Brewers with P Dan Scarpetta to Texas Rangers for C Jim Sundberg (December 8, 1983). ... Released by Rangers (April 1, 1985). ... Signed by Montreal Expos (April 28, 1985). ... Released by Expos (December 19, 1985).

| | | | | | | | BATTING | | | | | | | | FIELDING | | | |
Year Team (League)	Pos.	G	AB	R	H	2B	3B	HR	RBI	Avg.	BB	SO	SB	PO	A	E	Avg.
1974— Batavia (NY-Penn)	C	44	123	14	31	2	2	2	11	.252	...	...	...	199	21	11	.952
1975— Wausau (Midw.)	C	79	265	26	51	7	0	6	27	.192	...	...	...	450	42	19	.963
1976— Jackson (Texas)	C	83	266	25	53	5	0	3	25	.199	...	...	...	390	42	7	.984
1977— Jackson (Texas)	C	30	94	7	29	9	0	1	8	.309	...	...	...	145	21	4	.976
— Tidewater (Int'l)	C	60	165	27	48	8	1	12	31	.291	...	...	...	171	29	3	.985
1979— Vancouver (PCL)	C	130	419	43	110	12	2	3	53	.263	...	...	...	604	64	10	.985
1980— Vancouver (PCL)	C-1B	80	259	32	80	20	4	2	41	.309	...	...	...	312	34	8	.977
— Milwaukee (A.L.)	C	15	31	0	5	0	0	0	0	.161	0	6	0	41	5	0	1.000
1981— Milwaukee (A.L.)	C	18	27	4	6	0	0	3	3	.222	3	6	0	37	6	2	.956
1982— Milwaukee (A.L.)	C	40	98	13	27	6	3	1	8	.276	7	20	3	121	6	3	.977
1983— Milwaukee (A.L.)	C	61	196	21	44	5	1	6	28	.224	5	36	1	252	16	8	.971
1984— Texas (A.L.)	C	80	242	15	44	4	0	6	25	.182	6	47	1	368	20	2	.995
1985— Indianapolis (A.A.)	C-1B	95	267	17	70	15	0	2	24	.262	...	...	...	375	48	12	.972
— Montreal (N.L.)	C	5	11	1	2	0	0	0	0	.182	0	2	0	24	1	1	.962
1986— Greenville (Sou.)		80	254	35	63	13	0	7	30	.248	...	...	...	...	...	...	...
— Richmond (Int'l)		8	17	0	5	0	0	0	0	.294	...	...	...	...	...	...	...
1987— Greenville (Sou.)		40	115	6	19	1	0	1	1	.165	...	...	...	...	...	...	...
— Richmond (Int'l)		9	23	3	7	1	0	1	8	.304	...	...	...	...	...	...	...
American League totals (5 years)		214	594	53	126	15	4	16	64	.212	21	115	5	819	53	15	.984
National League totals (1 year)		5	11	1	2	0	0	0	0	.182	0	2	0	24	1	1	.962
Major League totals (6 years)		219	605	54	128	15	4	16	64	.212	21	117	5	843	54	16	.982

RECORD AS MANAGER

BACKGROUND: Bullpen coach, Atlanta Braves (1991-98). ... Third base coach, Braves (1999-2002).

| | REGULAR SEASON | | | | POSTSEASON | | | | | | | |
| | | | | | Playoffs | | Champ. Series | | World Series | | All-Star Game | |
Year Team (League)	W	L	Pct.	Pos	W	L	W	L	W	L	W	L
1988— Sumter (S.Atl.)	29	40	.420	6th	—	—	—	—	—	—	—	—
— Second half	35	33	.515	4th	—	—	—	—	—	—	—	—
1989— Sumter (S.Atl.)	30	40	.428	5th	—	—	—	—	—	—	—	—
— Second half	30	41	.423	6th	—	—	—	—	—	—	—	—
1990— Sumter (S.Atl.)	38	34	.527	4th	—	—	—	—	—	—	—	—
— Second half	35	35	.500	4th	—	—	—	—	—	—	—	—
2003— Milwaukee (N.L.)	68	94	.419	6th	—	—	—	—	—	—	—	—
Major League totals (1 year)	68	94	.419		—	—	—	—	—	—	—	—

2003 MANAGERIAL TENDENCIES

OFFENSE

					STOLEN BASES							SACRIFICE BUNTS				HIT & RUN	
			Pitchout	2nd	3rd	Home	Dbl	— Out Percentage —					Suc.	Fav.			Suc.
	G	Att.	SB%	Rn Mv	SB-CS	SB-CS	SB-CS	Stls	0	1	2	Att.	%	Inn.	Sqz.	Att.	%
A.L. Managers																	
Gardenhire, Ron, Min	162	138	68.1	4	79-35	15-7	0-2	3	16.7	39.1	44.2	61	77.0	7	8	87	29.9
Hargrove, Mike, Bal	163	125	71.2	3	79-30	10-4	0-2	3	16.0	37.6	46.4	68	85.3	8	0	57	42.1
Little, Grady, Bos	162	123	71.5	4	83-31	5-3	0-1	1	22.0	32.5	45.5	34	73.5	8	3	40	42.5
Macha, Ken, Oak	162	62	77.4	1	39-14	9-0	0-0	2	14.5	33.9	51.6	32	71.9	9	2	39	46.2
Manuel, Jerry, CWS	162	106	72.6	1	69-25	7-4	1-0	2	23.6	44.3	32.1	66	83.3	7	2	58	19.0
Melvin, Bob, Sea	162	145	74.5	8	89-34	19-3	0-0	6	25.5	36.6	37.9	47	80.9	4	2	58	50.0
Pena, Tony, KC	162	162	74.1	2	101-35	17-5	2-2	6	18.5	34.0	47.5	81	85.2	2	2	81	35.8
Piniella, Lou, TB	162	184	77.2	14	122-36	19-4	1-2	4	19.6	37.0	43.5	55	70.9	7	4	92	47.8
Scioscia, Mike, Ana	162	190	67.9	1	113-54	14-3	2-4	7	16.3	32.1	51.6	70	81.4	3	6	109	35.8
Showalter, Buck, Tex	162	90	72.2	2	61-24	4-1	0-0	2	15.6	33.3	51.1	36	80.6	7	0	64	28.1
Torre, Joe, NYY	163	131	74.8	4	84-26	14-6	0-1	3	22.1	28.2	49.6	40	87.5	1	3	79	38.0
Tosca, Carlos, Tor	162	62	59.7	1	30-20	7-3	0-2	1	14.5	38.7	46.8	14	85.7	8	4	49	42.9
Trammell, Alan, Det	162	161	60.9	10	86-60	12-2	0-1	3	16.8	37.9	45.3	96	85.4	3	6	119	31.1
Wedge, Eric, Cle	162	147	58.5	9	73-53	12-7	1-1	6	15.6	32.0	52.4	68	75.0	3	1	75	36.0
N.L. Managers																	
Alou, Felipe, SF	161	90	58.9	0	48-33	5-2	0-2	1	34.4	23.3	42.2	96	83.3	4	9	55	36.4
Baker, Dusty, ChC	162	104	70.2	3	66-30	7-1	0-0	2	22.1	37.5	40.4	97	85.6	5	1	63	31.7
Bochy, Bruce, SD	162	115	66.1	2	66-36	10-2	0-1	0	14.8	40.0	45.2	67	77.6	3	3	77	27.3
Boone, Bob, Cin	104	86	73.3	5	53-18	9-1	1-4	5	10.5	36.0	53.5	70	74.3	2	6	35	22.9
Bowa, Larry, Phi	162	101	71.3	1	64-24	8-3	0-2	1	14.9	22.8	62.4	71	69.0	2	5	46	45.7
Brenly, Bob, Ari	162	114	66.7	2	74-32	2-4	0-2	0	19.3	34.2	46.5	92	73.9	2	5	65	32.3
Cox, Bobby, Atl	162	90	75.6	1	60-17	8-4	0-1	3	15.6	41.1	43.3	87	75.9	4	3	36	33.3
Howe, Art, NYM	161	101	69.3	6	62-29	8-2	0-0	2	16.8	42.6	40.6	108	83.3	7	3	84	26.2
Hurdle, Clint, Col	162	100	63.0	3	57-34	6-3	0-0	1	20.0	27.0	53.0	86	73.3	5	4	48	22.9
Knight, Ray, Cin	1	1	0.0	0	0-1	0-0	0-0	0	0.0	100.0	0.0	1	0.0	2	0	0	-
La Russa, Tony, StL	162	114	71.9	1	65-24	17-6	0-2	10	18.4	41.2	40.4	116	82.8	5	9	91	37.4
McClendon, Lloyd, Pit	162	123	69.9	4	70-33	16-2	0-2	5	22.8	28.5	48.8	104	79.8	5	8	102	39.2
McKeon, Jack, Fla	124	150	62.7	10	85-49	9-6	0-1	6	29.3	35.3	35.3	92	83.7	1	6	69	42.0
Miley, Dave, Cin	57	27	63.0	5	16-8	1-2	0-0	0	22.2	48.1	29.6	25	68.0	8	4	14	35.7
Robinson, Frank, Mon	162	139	71.9	9	81-37	19-1	0-1	2	23.0	32.4	44.6	90	82.2	7	5	95	30.5
Torborg, Jeff, Fla	38	74	75.7	2	48-14	8-3	0-1	2	18.9	29.7	51.4	18	83.3	7	2	24	20.8
Tracy, Jim, LA	162	116	69.0	5	73-29	7-5	0-2	3	19.0	34.5	46.6	98	76.5	3	4	62	33.9
Williams, Jimy, Hou	162	96	68.8	1	59-26	7-2	0-2	2	14.6	46.9	38.5	77	80.5	2	5	69	23.2
Yost, Ned, Mil	162	138	71.7	12	89-34	9-5	1-0	0	20.3	38.4	41.3	86	79.1	3	9	63	38.1

DEFENSE

		PITCHOUT			Non-PO	INTENTIAL BB			DEFENSIVE SUBS				
			Runners				Pct. of	Fav. Score		Favorite			
	G	Total	Moving	CS%	CS%	IBB	Situations	Diff.	Total	Inning	Pos. 1	Pos. 2	Pos. 3
A.L. Managers													
Gardenhire, Ron, Min	162	15	5	60.0	26.1	28	4.5	0	19	9	rf-6	c-3	1b-3
Hargrove, Mike, Bal	163	17	7	28.6	23.2	35	5.2	0	6	9	ss-3	2b-2	cf-1
Little, Grady, Bos	162	30	6	83.3	23.1	29	4.3	0	27	9	2b-8	3b-5	lf-5
Macha, Ken, Oak	162	10	2	0.0	32.6	31	4.9	-1	17	8	lf-7	cf-4	rf-3
Manuel, Jerry, CWS	162	20	7	85.7	28.8	20	3.3	-2	64	9	cf-31	lf-18	1b-10
Melvin, Bob, Sea	162	6	2	100.0	32.6	18	4.0	2	28	7	3b-9	ss-7	1b-6
Pena, Tony, KC	162	6	1	100.0	30.1	21	3.4	-1	13	9	1b-6	2b-2	lf-2
Piniella, Lou, TB	162	27	2	0.0	39.4	30	4.6	1	15	9	rf-7	3b-5	ss-1
Scioscia, Mike, Ana	162	27	12	66.7	34.5	27	4.8	-1	36	8	rf-13	1b-11	2b-4
Showalter, Buck, Tex	162	13	3	33.3	31.9	33	5.3	-1	33	9	cf-14	lf-13	3b-5
Torre, Joe, NYY	163	31	6	16.7	29.3	24	3.8	-1	10	8	3b-2	ss-2	rf-2
Tosca, Carlos, Tor	162	49	12	50.0	17.8	28	4.4	-2	22	9	rf-9	c-4	1b-3
Trammell, Alan, Det	162	27	3	66.7	29.1	29	4.1	-2	13	8	3b-4	ss-3	cf-3
Wedge, Eric, Cle	162	12	3	33.3	33.9	27	3.9	-1	23	8	1b-10	3b-5	rf-3

N.L. Managers	G	PITCHOUT Total	Runners Moving	CS%	Non-PO CS%	IBB	Pct. of Situations	Fav. Score Diff.	DEFENSIVE SUBS Total	Favorite Inning	Pos. 1	Pos. 2	Pos. 3
Alou, Felipe, SF	161	11	3	66.7	29.0	29	5.0	-1	19	6	1b-3	2b-3	lf-3
Baker, Dusty, ChC	162	28	5	60.0	36.4	25	4.5	-1	18	9	3b-5	2b-4	ss-3
Bochy, Bruce, SD	162	7	0	-	20.8	36	6.2	-1	11	8	lf-6	3b-2	rf-2
Boone, Bob, Cin	104	5	1	100.0	32.7	27	6.4	-2	5	7	ss-2	c-1	2b-1
Bowa, Larry, Phi	162	33	9	33.3	16.5	36	5.3	0	14	7	3b-9	2b-5	ph-0
Brenly, Bob, Ari	162	47	9	55.6	29.2	43	6.5	-2	10	8	3b-3	ss-3	rf-2
Cox, Bobby, Atl	162	47	5	60.0	25.8	43	6.9	-1	18	8	1b-5	lf-5	cf-5
Howe, Art, NYM	161	14	1	0.0	34.9	56	8.6	0	39	8	rf-10	1b-6	2b-6
Hurdle, Clint, Col	162	19	3	66.7	35.7	37	6.7	-2	10	7	3b-6	lf-2	c-1
Knight, Ray, Cin	1	0	0	-	0.0	0	0.0	0	0	0	ph-0	ph-0	ph-0
La Russa, Tony, StL	162	8	1	100.0	29.5	23	3.9	0	17	9	lf-5	rf-5	3b-3
McClendon, Lloyd, Pit	162	79	6	50.0	25.8	37	6.0	-2	26	8	1b-14	3b-4	cf-3
McKeon, Jack, Fla	124	17	2	50.0	26.0	17	4.1	-2	8	4	c-2	1b-2	2b-1
Miley, Dave, Cin	57	7	1	0.0	20.8	15	7.4	-1	6	8	3b-2	2b-1	ss-1
Robinson, Frank, Mon	162	7	2	50.0	48.7	40	6.8	-2	20	7	cf-5	3b-4	lf-4
Torborg, Jeff, Fla	38	4	0	-	25.0	7	3.9	-1	2	7	c-1	rf-1	ph-0
Tracy, Jim, LA	162	8	1	0.0	39.3	27	4.4	0	51	7	lf-12	1b-11	cf-11
Williams, Jimy, Hou	162	42	10	70.0	33.1	35	6.2	-2	8	8	c-4	ss-2	1b-1
Yost, Ned, Mil	162	26	6	66.7	25.2	22	3.6	-2	16	9	rf-8	ss-3	lf-2

LINEUPS

	G	STARTING LINEUP Lineups Used	%LHB vs. RHSP	%RHB vs. LHSP	#PH	SUBSTITUTIONS Percent PH Platoon	PH BA	PH HR	#PR	PR SB-CS
A.L. Managers										
Gardenhire, Ron, Min	162	126	60.3	67.7	122	69.7	.324	5	41	1-1
Hargrove, Mike, Bal	163	119	40.6	81.1	70	74.3	.267	1	31	2-0
Little, Grady, Bos	162	117	60.2	71.9	110	78.2	.242	4	63	15-7
Macha, Ken, Oak	162	111	54.4	62.7	117	73.5	.225	2	25	1-0
Manuel, Jerry, CWS	162	105	37.4	98.3	126	81.0	.190	3	33	4-0
Melvin, Bob, Sea	162	111	54.1	81.0	73	69.9	.167	2	48	6-0
Pena, Tony, KC	162	125	55.2	72.7	86	67.4	.274	3	26	1-0
Piniella, Lou, TB	162	124	58.5	64.0	159	83.6	.226	3	29	4-1
Scioscia, Mike, Ana	162	130	57.0	77.8	114	70.2	.313	1	47	3-5
Showalter, Buck, Tex	162	133	48.5	84.7	81	69.1	.191	0	40	2-2
Torre, Joe, NYY	163	103	62.7	73.0	100	78.0	.205	1	40	2-1
Tosca, Carlos, Tor	162	126	52.7	79.8	128	75.0	.231	0	25	1-0
Trammell, Alan, Det	162	129	72.4	71.9	125	83.2	.301	2	24	3-0
Wedge, Eric, Cle	162	145	62.3	77.8	104	83.7	.159	0	32	0-2
N.L. Managers										
Alou, Felipe, SF	161	127	42.7	87.4	195	56.9	.254	5	26	3-0
Baker, Dusty, ChC	162	114	34.9	89.5	239	74.5	.155	2	20	2-1
Bochy, Bruce, SD	162	135	49.5	72.3	307	80.1	.222	4	17	2-2
Boone, Bob, Cin	104	82	38.5	74.6	177	69.5	.216	8	24	1-0
Bowa, Larry, Phi	162	119	48.4	77.8	244	80.7	.244	5	17	3-0
Brenly, Bob, Ari	162	145	58.2	71.1	269	89.2	.263	6	28	0-1
Cox, Bobby, Atl	162	70	36.2	93.1	248	69.4	.222	6	37	0-1
Howe, Art, NYM	161	133	50.9	80.6	269	71.7	.153	3	54	1-1
Hurdle, Clint, Col	162	108	33.0	79.0	287	79.8	.260	5	13	0-0
Knight, Ray, Cin	1	1	-	77.8	2	100.0	.000	0	0	0-0
La Russa, Tony, StL	162	126	37.5	79.3	296	72.0	.232	2	20	0-0
McClendon, Lloyd, Pit	162	114	42.9	83.5	284	68.7	.218	9	21	1-0
McKeon, Jack, Fla	124	56	32.3	83.5	160	78.1	.239	3	23	2-0
Miley, Dave, Cin	57	52	50.1	81.9	94	67.0	.214	2	9	0-0
Robinson, Frank, Mon	162	133	51.2	81.0	227	85.0	.272	4	46	4-1
Torborg, Jeff, Fla	38	23	37.9	80.8	68	82.4	.274	0	6	1-0
Tracy, Jim, LA	162	103	59.5	68.9	242	62.4	.223	3	18	2-0
Williams, Jimy, Hou	162	85	28.8	94.1	291	79.7	.210	6	19	1-0
Yost, Ned, Mil	162	97	34.0	77.8	286	56.3	.220	6	15	0-0

PITCHING

		STARTERS					RELIEVERS					
	G	Slow Hooks	Quick Hooks	> 120 Pitches	> 140 Pitches	3 Days Rest	Relief App	Mid-Inning Change	Save > 1 IP	1st Batter Platoon Pct	1-Batter App	3 Pit. (<=2run)
A.L. Managers												
Gardenhire, Ron, Min	162	20	15	2	0	1	399	147	2	53.6	19	29
Hargrove, Mike, Bal	163	18	15	12	0	0	425	200	5	62.0	55	22
Little, Grady, Bos	162	14	21	4	0	2	437	131	8	55.8	20	22
Macha, Ken, Oak	162	11	20	4	0	0	364	128	12	61.0	26	35
Manuel, Jerry, CWS	162	14	8	5	0	6	361	170	10	72.3	20	21
Melvin, Bob, Sea	162	11	10	7	0	2	366	131	6	57.4	23	36
Pena, Tony, KC	162	13	36	1	0	1	407	117	6	48.9	16	30
Piniella, Lou, TB	162	19	23	9	0	3	372	171	5	60.6	20	18
Scioscia, Mike, Ana	162	16	26	1	0	0	375	114	4	53.3	15	32
Showalter, Buck, Tex	162	16	26	4	0	3	494	237	7	65.8	34	18
Torre, Joe, NYY	163	17	6	15	0	1	367	165	10	56.9	27	26
Tosca, Carlos, Tor	162	24	20	4	0	4	444	237	14	64.8	46	14
Trammell, Alan, Det	162	16	13	2	0	1	451	221	14	61.9	33	17
Wedge, Eric, Cle	162	13	24	1	0	0	428	148	5	57.2	22	32
N.L. Managers												
Alou, Felipe, SF	161	7	26	8	0	0	461	181	5	62.5	57	42
Baker, Dusty, ChC	162	16	10	26	1	0	420	151	3	68.5	37	40
Bochy, Bruce, SD	162	16	17	2	0	0	473	199	3	65.5	51	30
Boone, Bob, Cin	104	16	9	2	0	11	303	110	1	66.7	23	14
Bowa, Larry, Phi	162	6	17	5	0	0	437	146	2	64.8	39	29
Brenly, Bob, Ari	162	6	19	7	0	1	452	146	7	61.5	49	32
Cox, Bobby, Atl	162	13	19	5	0	7	489	144	10	58.9	48	36
Howe, Art, NYM	161	16	16	6	0	3	412	132	11	56.1	33	34
Hurdle, Clint, Col	162	20	21	0	0	1	500	160	4	57.6	27	23
Knight, Ray, Cin	1	0	0	0	0	0	4	2	0	75.0	1	0
La Russa, Tony, StL	162	9	14	12	0	0	461	185	9	63.7	42	23
McClendon, Lloyd, Pit	162	14	26	4	0	0	457	166	10	62.9	46	26
McKeon, Jack, Fla	124	8	12	7	0	0	280	76	6	57.5	11	29
Miley, Dave, Cin	57	2	14	0	0	0	168	52	3	62.5	9	14
Robinson, Frank, Mon	162	10	16	25	0	2	437	158	4	60.6	41	30
Torborg, Jeff, Fla	38	1	7	1	0	0	115	32	1	56.5	8	4
Tracy, Jim, LA	162	8	20	5	0	2	438	125	11	61.8	49	49
Williams, Jimy, Hou	162	5	40	1	0	1	502	148	9	59.6	28	43
Yost, Ned, Mil	162	21	17	5	0	2	460	127	6	55.7	23	17

One of the things about baseball which appeals to many of us is the game's endless opportunity for analysis. . . and few things are analyzed more than managerial decisions. Major league skippers may not have batting averages and slugging percentages to point to at the end of the season, but when it comes time to judge their performance and production, there's no reason we can't take a look at their statistics.

Which manager posted the best stolen-base success rate?

Which skippers were constantly tinkering with their lineups?

Which managers wore out a path to the pitching mound?

It's questions like these that get our second-guessing juices going, and it's questions like these that inspired the following pages, which look at managerial tendencies in a number of situations. Once again, the skippers are compared based on offense, defense, lineups and pitching use. We don't rank the managers; there is plenty of room for argument on whether certain moves are good or bad. We are simply providing fodder for the discussion.

Offensively, managers have control over bunting, stealing and the timing of hit-and-runs. This section looks at the quantity, timing and success of these moves.

Defensively, this section looks at the success of pitchouts, the frequency of intentional walks, and the pattern of defensive substitutions.

Most managers spend large amounts of their time devising lineups. Here you'll find the number of lineups used, as well as the platoon percentage. The use of pinch-hitters and pinch-runners also is explored.

Finally, how does the manager use pitchers? For starters, this section shows slow and quick hooks, along with the number of times a starter was allowed to throw more than 120 and 140 pitches. For relievers, we look at the number of relief appearances, mid-inning changes and how often a pitcher gets a save going more than one inning (a rare occurrence these days).

For the purposes of this section, it is assumed that a coach filling in for his manager will make his decisions based on what the manager would do in a given situation.

The categories include:

Stolen Base Success Percentage: Stolen bases divided by attempts.

Pitchout Runners Moving: The number of times the opposition is running when a manager calls a pitchout.

Double Steals: The number of double steals attempted in 2003.

Out Percentage: The proportion of stolen bases with that number of outs.

Sacrifice Bunt Attempts: A bunt is considered a sac attempt if no runner is on third, there are no outs, or the pitcher attempts a bunt.

Sacrifice Bunt Success %: A bunt that results in a sacrifice or a hit, divided by the number of attempts.

Favorite Inning: The most common inning in which an event occurred.

Hit-and-Run Success: The hit-and-run results in baserunner advancement with no double play.

Intentional Walk Situation: Runners on base, first base open, and anyone but the pitcher up. The teams must be within two runs of each other, or the tying run must be on base, at bat or on deck.

Defensive Substitutions: Straight defensive substitutions, with the team leading by four runs or less.

Number of Lineups: Based on batting order, 1-8 for National Leaguers, 1-9 for American Leaguers.

Percent LHB vs. RHSP and RHB vs. LHSP: A measure of platooning. A batter is considered to always have the platoon advantage if he is a switch-hitter.

Percent PH platoon: Frequency the manager gets his pinch-hitter the platoon advantage. Switch-hitters always have the advantage.

Score Diff: The most common score differential on which an intentional walk is called for.

Slow and Quick Hooks: A quick hook is the removal of a pitcher who has pitched fewer than six innings and given up three runs or less. A slow hook occurs when a pitcher pitches more than nine innings, or allows seven or more runs, or whose combined innings pitched and runs allowed totals 13 or more.

Mid-Inning Change: The number of times a manager changed pitchers in the middle of an inning.

1-Batter Appearances: The number of times a pitcher was brought in to face only one batter. Called the "Tony La Russa special" because of his penchant for trying to orchestrate specific matchups for specific situations.

3 Pitchers (2 runs or less): The club gives up two runs or less in a game, but uses at least three pitchers.

2003 STATISTICAL LEADERS

American League leaders

National League leaders

Active career leaders

2003 AMERICAN LEAGUE LEADERS

BATTING

Batting Average
(minimum 502 PA)

Player, Team	AB	H	Avg.
B Mueller, Bos.	524	171	.326
M Ramirez, Bos.	569	185	.325
D Jeter, N.Y.	482	156	.324
V Wells, Tor.	678	215	.317
M Ordonez, Chi.	606	192	.317
G Anderson, Ana.	638	201	.315
I Suzuki, Sea.	679	212	.312
A Pierzynski, Min.	487	152	.312
A Huff, T.B.	636	198	.311
S Stewart, Tor.-Min.	573	176	.307

On-Base Percentage
(minimum 502 PA; *AB+BB+HBP+SF)

Player, Team	*PA	OB	OBP
M Ramirez, Bos.	679	290	.427
C Delgado, Tor.	705	300	.426
J Giambi, N.Y.	690	284	.412
E Martinez, Sea.	603	245	.406
J Posada, N.Y.	588	238	.405
B Mueller, Bos.	596	237	.398
T Nixon, Bos.	512	203	.396
A Rodriguez, Tex.	715	283	.396
D Mientkiewicz, Min.	572	225	.393
D Jeter, N.Y.	539	212	.393

Slugging Percentage
(minimum 502 PA)

Player, Team	AB	TB	Slg.
A Rodriguez, Tex.	607	364	.600
C Delgado, Tor.	570	338	.593
D Ortiz, Bos.	448	265	.592
M Ramirez, Bos.	569	334	.587
T Nixon, Bos.	441	255	.578
F Thomas, Chi.	546	307	.562
A Huff, T.B.	636	353	.555
V Wells, Tor.	678	373	.550
M Ordonez, Chi.	606	331	.546
G Anderson, Ana.	638	345	.541

Games

H Matsui, N.Y.	163
A Huff, T.B.	162
M Tejada, Oak.	162
4 tied with	161

Plate Appearances

V Wells, Tor.	735
A Soriano, N.Y.	734
I Suzuki, Sea.	725
N Garciaparra, Bos.	719
A Rodriguez, Tex.	715

At-Bats

A Soriano, N.Y.	682
I Suzuki, Sea.	679
V Wells, Tor.	678
M Young, Tex.	666
N Garciaparra, Bos.	658

Hits

V Wells, Tor.	215
I Suzuki, Sea.	212
M Young, Tex.	204
G Anderson, Ana.	201
3 tied with	198

Singles

I Suzuki, Sea.	162
M Young, Tex.	148
C Crawford, T.B.	145
R Baldelli, T.B.	133
V Wells, Tor.	128

Doubles

G Anderson, Ana.	49
V Wells, Tor.	49
A Huff, T.B.	47
M Ordonez, Chi.	46
2 tied with	45

Triples

C Guzman, Min.	14
N Garciaparra, Bos.	13
C Beltran, K.C.	10
4 tied with	9

Home Runs

A Rodriguez, Tex.	47
C Delgado, Tor.	42
F Thomas, Chi.	42
J Giambi, N.Y.	41
2 tied with	38

Total Bases

V Wells, Tor.	373
A Rodriguez, Tex.	364
A Soriano, N.Y.	358
A Huff, T.B.	353
2 tied with	345

Runs Scored

A Rodriguez, Tex.	124
N Garciaparra, Bos.	120
V Wells, Tor.	118
C Delgado, Tor.	117
M Ramirez, Bos.	117

Runs Batted In

C Delgado, Tor.	145
A Rodriguez, Tex.	118
B Boone, Sea.	117
V Wells, Tor.	117
G Anderson, Ana.	116

GDP

P Konerko, Chi.	28
H Matsui, N.Y.	25
M Ramirez, Bos.	22
V Wells, Tor.	21
B Williams, N.Y.	21

Sacrifice Hits

R Santiago, Det.	18
A Berroa, K.C.	13
C Guzman, Min.	12
3 tied with	10

Sacrifice Flies

J Conine, Bal.	12
S Stewart, Tor.-Min.	11
N Garciaparra, Bos.	10
R Ibanez, K.C.	10
T Walker, Bos.	10

Stolen Bases

C Crawford, T.B.	55
A Sanchez, Det.	44
C Beltran, K.C.	41
A Soriano, N.Y.	35
I Suzuki, Sea.	34

Caught Stealing

A Sanchez, Det.	18
R Baldelli, T.B.	10
C Crawford, T.B.	10
M Tucker, K.C.	10
4 tied with	9

Walks

J Giambi, N.Y.	129
C Delgado, Tor.	109
E Durazo, Oak.	100
F Thomas, Chi.	100
M Ramirez, Bos.	97

Intentional Walks

M Ramirez, Bos.	28
C Delgado, Tor.	23
A Huff, T.B.	17
D Young, Det.	16
2 tied with	12

Hit by Pitch

J Giambi, N.Y.	21
R Johnson, Tor.	20
C Delgado, Tor.	19
A Berroa, K.C.	18
J Phelps, Tor.	17

Strikeouts

J Giambi, N.Y.	140
M Cameron, Sea.	137
C Delgado, Tor.	137
A Soriano, N.Y.	130
D Young, Det.	130

2003 NATIONAL LEAGUE LEADERS

BATTING

Batting Average
(minimum 502 PA)

Player, Team	AB	H	Avg.
A Pujols, St.L.	591	212	.359
T Helton, Col.	583	209	.358
B Bonds, S.F.	390	133	.341
E Renteria, St.L.	587	194	.330
G Sheffield, Atl.	576	190	.330
J Kendall, Pit.	587	191	.325
M Giles, Atl.	551	174	.316
L Castillo, Fla.	595	187	.314
M Loretta, S.D.	589	185	.314
M Grudzielanek, Chi.	481	151	.314

On-Base Percentage
(minimum 502 PA; *AB+BB+HBP+SF)

Player, Team	*PA	OB	OBP
B Bonds, S.F.	550	291	.529
T Helton, Col.	703	322	.458
A Pujols, St.L.	685	301	.439
B Giles, Pit.-S.D.	609	260	.427
L Walker, Col.	564	238	.422
G Sheffield, Atl.	678	284	.419
L Berkman, Hou.	657	271	.412
B Abreu, Phi.	695	284	.409
C Jones, Atl.	656	264	.402
L Gonzalez, Ari.	679	273	.402

Slugging Percentage
(minimum 502 PA)

Player, Team	AB	TB	Slg.
B Bonds, S.F.	390	292	.749
A Pujols, St.L.	591	394	.667
T Helton, Col.	583	367	.630
J Edmonds, St.L.	447	276	.617
G Sheffield, Atl.	576	348	.604
J Thome, Phi.	578	331	.573
R Hidalgo, Hou.	514	294	.572
S Sosa, Chi.	517	286	.553
R Sexson, Mil.	606	332	.548
G Jenkins, Mil.	487	262	.538

Games
- O Cabrera, Mon. 162
- J Pierre, Fla. 162
- R Sexson, Mil. 162
- 3 tied with 160

Plate Appearances
- J Pierre, Fla. 747
- R Furcal, Atl. 734
- R Sexson, Mil. 718
- C Biggio, Hou. 717
- T Helton, Col. 703

At-Bats
- J Pierre, Fla. 668
- R Furcal, Atl. 664
- C Biggio, Hou. 628
- J Rollins, Phi. 628
- O Cabrera, Mon. 626

Hits
- A Pujols, St.L. 212
- T Helton, Col. 209
- J Pierre, Fla. 204
- R Furcal, Atl. 194
- E Renteria, St.L. 194

Singles
- J Pierre, Fla. 168
- L Castillo, Fla. 156
- J Kendall, Pit. 153
- M Loretta, S.D. 140
- R Furcal, Atl. 134

Doubles
- A Pujols, St.L. 51
- M Giles, Atl. 49
- S Green, L.A. 49
- T Helton, Col. 49
- S Rolen, St.L. 49

Triples
- S Finley, Ari. 10
- R Furcal, Atl. 10
- K Lofton, Pit.-Chi. 8
- S Podsednik, Mil. 8
- 4 tied with 7

Home Runs
- J Thome, Phi. 47
- B Bonds, S.F. 45
- R Sexson, Mil. 45
- J Lopez, Atl. 43
- A Pujols, St.L. 43

Total Bases
- A Pujols, St.L. 394
- T Helton, Col. 367
- G Sheffield, Atl. 348
- R Sexson, Mil. 332
- J Thome, Phi. 331

Runs Scored
- A Pujols, St.L. 137
- T Helton, Col. 135
- R Furcal, Atl. 130
- G Sheffield, Atl. 126
- 2 tied with 111

Runs Batted In
- P Wilson, Col. 141
- G Sheffield, Atl. 132
- J Thome, Phi. 131
- A Pujols, St.L. 124
- R Sexson, Mil. 124

GDP
- J Payton, Col. 27
- J Bagwell, Hou. 25
- R Clayton, Mil. 25
- P Wilson, Col. 23
- V Castilla, Atl. 22

Sacrifice Hits
- L Castillo, Fla. 15
- J Pierre, Fla. 15
- J Schmidt, S.F. 15
- 3 tied with 12

Sacrifice Flies
- A Ramirez, Pit.-Chi. 11
- O Cabrera, Mon. 9
- R Klesko, S.D. 9
- T Perez, N.Y. 9
- 2 tied with 8

Stolen Bases
- J Pierre, Fla. 65
- S Podsednik, Mil. 43
- D Roberts, L.A. 40
- E Renteria, St.L. 34
- K Lofton, Pit.-Chi. 30

Caught Stealing
- J Pierre, Fla. 20
- L Castillo, Fla. 19
- D Roberts, L.A. 14
- J Rollins, Phi. 12
- E Young, Mil.-S.F. 12

Walks
- B Bonds, S.F. 148
- T Helton, Col. 111
- J Thome, Phi. 111
- B Abreu, Phi. 109
- L Berkman, Hou. 107

Intentional Walks
- B Bonds, S.F. 61
- V Guerrero, Mon. 22
- T Helton, Col. 21
- L Gonzalez, Ari. 17
- M Matheny, St.L. 16

Hit by Pitch
- C Biggio, Hou. 27
- J Kendall, Pit. 25
- J LaRue, Cin. 20
- K Ginter, Mil. 17
- M Kinkade, L.A. 16

Strikeouts
- J Thome, Phi. 182
- J Hernandez, Col.-Chi.-Pit. 177
- B Wilkerson, Mon. 155
- R Sexson, Mil. 151
- S Sosa, Chi. 143

Earned Run Average
(minimum 162 IP)

Pitcher, Team	IP	ER	ERA
P Martinez, Bos.	186.2	46	2.22
T Hudson, Oak.	240.0	72	2.70
E Loaiza, Chi.	226.1	73	2.90
M Mulder, Oak.	186.2	65	3.13
R Halladay, Tor.	266.0	96	3.25
J Moyer, Sea.	215.0	78	3.27
B Zito, Oak.	231.2	85	3.30
M Mussina, N.Y.	214.2	81	3.40
R Franklin, Sea.	212.0	84	3.57
C Sabathia, Cle.	197.2	79	3.60

Won-Lost Percentage
(minimum 15 decisions)

Pitcher, Team	W	L	Pct.
J Santana, Min.	12	3	.800
P Martinez, Bos.	14	4	.778
R Halladay, Tor.	22	7	.759
J Moyer, Sea.	21	7	.750
A Pettitte, N.Y.	21	8	.724
D Lowe, Bos.	17	7	.708
E Loaiza, Chi.	21	9	.700
S Ponson, Bal.	14	6	.700
T Hudson, Oak.	16	7	.696
D Wells, N.Y.	15	7	.682

Opponents' Batting Average
(minimum 162 IP)

Pitcher, Team	AB	H	Avg.
P Martinez, Bos.	685	147	.215
B Zito, Oak.	849	186	.219
T Hudson, Oak.	883	197	.223
E Loaiza, Chi.	843	196	.233
V Zambrano, T.B.	697	165	.237
M Mussina, N.Y.	807	192	.238
J Pineiro, Sea.	796	192	.241
D May, K.C.	802	197	.246
J Moyer, Sea.	810	199	.246
T Wakefield, Bos.	783	193	.246

Games

T Miller, Tor.	79
J Walker, Det.	78
J Grimsley, K.C.	76
B Ryan, Bal.	76
L Hawkins, Min.	74

Games Started

R Halladay, Tor.	36
M Buehrle, Chi.	35
J Thomson, Tex.	35
B Zito, Oak.	35
3 tied with	34

Complete Games

B Colon, Chi.	9
R Halladay, Tor.	9
M Mulder, Oak.	9
3 tied with	4

Games Finished

K Foulke, Oak.	67
M MacDougal, K.C.	61
E Guardado, Min.	60
M Rivera, N.Y.	57
L Carter, T.B.	55

Wins

R Halladay, Tor.	22
E Loaiza, Chi.	21
J Moyer, Sea.	21
A Pettitte, N.Y.	21
3 tied with	17

Losses

M Maroth, Det.	21
J Bonderman, Det.	19
N Cornejo, Det.	17
J Lackey, Ana.	16
2 tied with	15

Saves

K Foulke, Oak.	43
E Guardado, Min.	41
M Rivera, N.Y.	40
J Julio, Bal.	36
T Percival, Ana.	33

Shutouts

R Halladay, Tor.	2
T Hudson, Oak.	2
J Lackey, Ana.	2
M Mulder, Oak.	2
J Pineiro, Sea.	2

Hits Allowed

R Halladay, Tor.	253
M Buehrle, Chi.	250
B Radke, Min.	242
D Wells, N.Y.	242
N Cornejo, Det.	236

Doubles Allowed

R Halladay, Tor.	54
D Wells, N.Y.	54
J Burkett, Bos.	53
J Thomson, Tex.	51
M Buehrle, Chi.	48

Triples Allowed

C Lidle, Tor.	11
M Maroth, Det.	9
B Anderson, Cle.-K.C.	8
J Benoit, Tex.	8
5 tied with	7

Home Runs Allowed

R Franklin, Sea.	34
M Maroth, Det.	34
J Washburn, Ana.	34
B Radke, Min.	32
3 tied with	31

Batters Faced

R Halladay, Tor.	1071
B Colon, Chi.	984
M Buehrle, Chi.	978
T Hudson, Oak.	967
B Zito, Oak.	957

Innings Pitched

R Halladay, Tor.	266.0
B Colon, Chi.	242.0
T Hudson, Oak.	240.0
B Zito, Oak.	231.2
M Buehrle, Chi.	230.1

Runs Allowed

C Lidle, Tor.	133
M Maroth, Det.	131
J Thomson, Tex.	125
M Buehrle, Chi.	124
R Ortiz, Ana.	121

Strikeouts

E Loaiza, Chi.	207
P Martinez, Bos.	206
R Halladay, Tor.	204
M Mussina, N.Y.	195
R Clemens, N.Y.	190

Walks Allowed

V Zambrano, T.B.	106
B Zito, Oak.	88
J Johnson, Bal.	80
K Escobar, Tor.	78
J Pineiro, Sea.	76

Hit Batsmen

V Zambrano, T.B.	20
6 tied with	12

Wild Pitches

V Zambrano, T.B.	15
J Bonderman, Det.	12
F Garcia, Sea.	11
J Lackey, Ana.	11
K Lohse, Min.	10

Balks

T Lilly, Oak.	4
K Rogers, Min.	4
4 tied with	3

Earned Run Average

(minimum 162 IP)

Pitcher, Team	IP	ER	ERA
J Schmidt, S.F.	207.2	54	2.34
K Brown, L.A.	211.0	56	2.39
M Prior, Chi.	211.1	57	2.43
B Webb, Ari.	180.2	57	2.84
C Schilling, Ari.	168.0	55	2.95
H Nomo, L.A.	218.1	75	3.09
C Zambrano, Chi.	214.0	74	3.11
K Wood, Chi.	211.0	75	3.20
L Hernandez, Mon.	233.1	83	3.20
J Vazquez, Mon.	230.2	83	3.24

Won-Lost Percentage

(minimum 15 decisions)

Pitcher, Team	W	L	Pct.
J Schmidt, S.F.	17	5	.773
R Ortiz, Atl.	21	7	.750
M Prior, Chi.	18	6	.750
J Nathan, S.F.	12	4	.750
H Ramirez, Atl.	12	4	.750
D Willis, Fla.	14	6	.700
W Williams, St.L.	18	9	.667
R Oswalt, Hou.	10	5	.667
K Rueter, S.F.	10	5	.667
M Hampton, Atl.	14	8	.636

Opponents' Batting Average

(minimum 162 IP)

Pitcher, Team	AB	H	Avg.
J Schmidt, S.F.	759	152	.200
K Wood, Chi.	749	152	.203
B Webb, Ari.	659	140	.212
R Ortiz, Atl.	793	177	.223
H Nomo, L.A.	784	175	.223
M Clement, Chi.	746	169	.227
J Vazquez, Mon.	865	198	.229
C Schilling, Ari.	626	144	.230
M Prior, Chi.	793	183	.231
K Wells, Pit.	735	171	.233

Games

P Quantrill, L.A.	89
O Villarreal, Ari.	86
R King, Atl.	80
T Martin, L.A.	80
4 tied with	78

Games Started

G Maddux, Atl.	36
K Millwood, Phi.	35
5 tied with	34

Complete Games

L Hernandez, Mon.	8
K Millwood, Phi.	5
M Morris, St.L.	5
J Schmidt, S.F.	5
2 tied with	4

Games Finished

E Gagne, L.A.	67
B Wagner, Hou.	67
B Looper, Fla.	64
T Worrell, S.F.	64
J Borowski, Chi.	59

Wins

R Ortiz, Atl.	21
M Prior, Chi.	18
W Williams, St.L.	18
J Schmidt, S.F.	17
4 tied with	16

Losses

J D'Amico, Pit.	16
D Graves, Cin.	15
B Lawrence, S.D.	15
T Glavine, N.Y.	14
T Redding, Hou.	14

Saves

E Gagne, L.A.	55
J Smoltz, Atl.	45
B Wagner, Hou.	44
T Worrell, S.F.	38
R Biddle, Mon.	34

Shutouts

K Millwood, Phi.	3
M Morris, St.L.	3
J Schmidt, S.F.	3
7 tied with	2

Hits Allowed

B Tomko, St.L.	252
T Ohka, Mon.	233
B Sheets, Mil.	232
L Hernandez, Mon.	225
G Maddux, Atl.	225

Doubles Allowed

J Seo, N.Y.	61
D Graves, Cin.	56
C Pavano, Fla.	54
B Tomko, St.L.	54
2 tied with	52

Triples Allowed

T Glavine, N.Y.	10
W Franklin, Mil.	8
8 tied with	7

Home Runs Allowed

W Franklin, Mil.	36
B Tomko, St.L.	35
J Peavy, S.D.	33
D Graves, Cin.	30
G Stephenson, St.L.	30

Batters Faced

L Hernandez, Mon.	967
W Williams, St.L.	944
J Vazquez, Mon.	938
B Sheets, Mil.	931
K Millwood, Phi.	930

Innings Pitched

L Hernandez, Mon.	233.1
J Vazquez, Mon.	230.2
K Millwood, Phi.	222.0
B Sheets, Mil.	220.2
W Williams, St.L.	220.2

Runs Allowed

W Franklin, Mil.	129
B Tomko, St.L.	126
B Sheets, Mil.	122
M Kinney, Mil.	121
J Jennings, Col.	115

Strikeouts

K Wood, Chi.	266
M Prior, Chi.	245
J Vazquez, Mon.	241
J Schmidt, S.F.	208
C Schilling, Ari.	194

Walks Allowed

R Ortiz, Atl.	102
K Ishii, L.A.	101
K Wood, Chi.	100
H Nomo, L.A.	98
3 tied with	94

Hit Batsmen

K Wood, Chi.	21
V Padilla, Phi.	16
M Clement, Chi.	14
G Stephenson, St.L.	13
B Webb, Ari.	13

Wild Pitches

M Clement, Chi.	13
Z Day, Mon.	13
J Foppert, S.F.	12
C Silva, Phi.	12
J Wright, S.D.-Atl.	12

Balks

W Franklin, Mil.	4
B Penny, Fla.	4
J Lopez, Col.	3
D Moss, S.F.	3
11 tied with	2

Scoring-Position Average†
(minimum 100 PA)

Player, Team	AB	H	Avg.
M Sweeney, K.C.	108	43	.398
C Delgado, Tor.	157	56	.357
E Martinez, Sea.	142	50	.352
R Winn, Sea.	169	59	.349
C Beltran, K.C.	150	52	.347
C Lee, Chi.	153	53	.346
F Catalanotto, Tor.	96	33	.344
I Suzuki, Sea.	105	36	.343
M Anderson, T.B.	126	43	.341

Leadoff OBP†
(minimum 150 PA; *AB+BB+HBP+SF)

Player, Team	*PA	OB	OBP
J Hairston Jr., Bal.	203	79	.389
A Guiel, K.C.	282	109	.387
S Stewart, Tor.-Min.	641	233	.363
R Johnson, Tor.	365	129	.353
I Suzuki, Sea.	718	253	.352
T Graffanino, Chi.	165	58	.352
C Figgins, Ana.	151	53	.351
D Jimenez, Chi.	244	84	.344
A Soriano, N.Y.	675	231	.342
M Lawton, Cle.	181	61	.337

Cleanup Slugging†
(minimum 150 PA)

Player, Team	AB	TB	Slg.
C Delgado, Tor.	570	338	.593
M Ramirez, Bos.	569	334	.587
G Anderson, Ana.	456	266	.583
M Bradley, Cle.	179	101	.564
M Tejada, Oak.	305	166	.544
M Ordonez, Chi.	563	306	.544
D Young, Det.	448	240	.536
J Giambi, N.Y.	152	80	.526
E Chavez, Oak.	154	79	.513
M LeCroy, Min.	212	108	.509

Avg. vs. LHP
(minimum 125 PA)

M Bradley, Cle.	.402
M Ramirez, Bos.	.385
I Suzuki, Sea.	.359
N Garciaparra, Bos.	.357
V Wells, Tor.	.347

Avg. vs. RHP
(minimum 377 PA)

B Mueller, Bos.	.342
T Nixon, Bos.	.330
H Blalock, Tex.	.329
A Pierzynski, Min.	.324
R Ibanez, K.C.	.319

Avg. at Home
(minimum 251 PA)

N Garciaparra, Bos.	.359
M Young, Tex.	.353
L Matos, Bal.	.350
H Blalock, Tex.	.342
B Mueller, Bos.	.342

Avg. on Road
(minimum 251 PA)

E Martinez, Sea.	.339
G Anderson, Ana.	.339
D Jeter, N.Y.	.330
V Wells, Tor.	.329
A Pierzynski, Min.	.328

OBP vs. LHP
(minimum 125 PA)

M Bradley, Cle.	.500
M Ramirez, Bos.	.476
E Martinez, Sea.	.457
F Thomas, Chi.	.446
B Kielty, Min.-Tor.	.417

OBP vs. RHP
(minimum 377 PA)

C Delgado, Tor.	.439
J Giambi, N.Y.	.430
T Nixon, Bos.	.423
M Ramirez, Bos.	.411
B Mueller, Bos.	.409

Late & Close Avg.†
(minimum 50 PA)

L Bigbie, Bal.	.426
M Ordonez, Chi.	.425
D Mientkiewicz, Min.	.397
G Anderson, Ana.	.370
S Hatteberg, Oak.	.361

Bases Loaded Avg.
(minimum 10 PA)

M Sweeney, K.C.	.667
R Baldelli, T.B.	.600
M Bordick, Tor.	.600
C Delgado, Tor.	.588
D Jeter, N.Y.	.533

Slg. vs. LHP
(minimum 125 PA)

F Thomas, Chi.	.732
A Rodriguez, Tex.	.652
M Bradley, Cle.	.634
C Monroe, Det.	.631
M Ramirez, Bos.	.629

Slg. vs. RHP
(minimum 377 PA)

D Ortiz, Bos.	.654
C Delgado, Tor.	.649
T Nixon, Bos.	.635
A Huff, T.B.	.596
H Blalock, Tex.	.596

AB per Home Run
(minimum 502 PA)

A Rodriguez, Tex.	12.9
F Thomas, Chi.	13.0
J Giambi, N.Y.	13.0
C Delgado, Tor.	13.6
D Ortiz, Bos.	14.5

Times on Base*
(*H+BB+HBP)

C Delgado, Tor.	300
M Ramirez, Bos.	290
J Giambi, N.Y.	284
A Rodriguez, Tex.	283
V Wells, Tor.	264

Pitches Seen

J Giambi, N.Y.	2916
J Damon, Bos.	2850
F Thomas, Chi.	2824
C Delgado, Tor.	2807
M Young, Tex.	2788

Pitches per PA
(minimum 502 PA)

E Martinez, Sea.	4.32
F Thomas, Chi.	4.27
J Giambi, N.Y.	4.23
J Damon, Bos.	4.13
E Hinske, Tor.	4.08

Pct. of Pitches Taken
(minimum 1500 pitches)

S Hatteberg, Oak.	67.1
E Martinez, Sea.	65.0
N Johnson, N.Y.	64.3
J Olerud, Sea.	64.2
F Thomas, Chi.	63.4

Ground/Fly Ratio†
(minimum 502 PA)

J Jones, Min.	2.58
K Harvey, K.C.	2.49
D Jeter, N.Y.	2.41
H Matsui, N.Y.	2.17
L Rivas, Min.	2.16

GDP/GDP Opp.†
(minimum 50 PA)

C Singleton, Oak.	0.03
I Suzuki, Sea.	0.03
T Nixon, Bos.	0.03
L Bigbie, Bal.	0.04
M Mora, Bal.	0.04

SB Success Pct.
(minimum 20 SB attempts)

C Beltran, K.C.	91.1
M Anderson, T.B.	86.4
A Rodriguez, Tex.	85.0
C Crawford, T.B.	84.6
2 tied with	83.3

Steals of Third

I Suzuki, Sea.	12
C Crawford, T.B.	9
A Sanchez, Det.	7
C Beltran, K.C.	6
A Berroa, K.C.	6

Pct. CS by Catchers
(minimum 50 SB attempts)

T Hall, T.B.	41.3
B Molina, Ana.	40.8
M Olivo, Chi.	35.8
J Bard, Cle.	31.7
E Diaz, Tex.	31.0

†**Scoring-Position Average** denotes batting average when a runner is at second and/or third base. **Leadoff OBP** denotes OBP for a player batting in the first position of the batting order. **Cleanup Slugging** denotes slugging percentage for a player batting in the fourth position of the batting order. **Late & Close Avg.** refers to batting average when the game is in the seventh inning or later and the batting team is either leading by one run, tied, or has the potential tying run on base, at bat or on deck (a batting situation coming close to a pitcher's save situation). **Ground/Fly Ratio** denotes ground balls hit divided by fly balls hit. All batted balls except line drives and bunts are included. **GDP/GDP Opp.** denotes the ratio of times grounding into double plays per opportunities to do so (any situation with a runner on first and less than two out).

Scoring-Position Average†
(minimum 100 PA)

Player, Team	AB	H	Avg.
T Helton, Col.	133	55	.414
S Podsednik, Mil.	105	40	.381
G Sheffield, Atl.	153	58	.379
I Rodriguez, Fla.	144	54	.375
M Cabrera, Fla.	96	36	.375
A Pujols, St.L.	131	49	.374
B Abreu, Phi.	155	56	.361
J Kent, Hou.	134	48	.358
M Loretta, S.D.	136	47	.346
2 tied with			.342

Leadoff OBP†
(minimum 150 PA; *AB+BB+HBP+SF)

Player, Team	*PA	OB	OBP
M Grissom, S.F.	170	70	.412
S Podsednik, Mil.	276	110	.399
M Byrd, Phi.	356	133	.374
T Redman, Pit.	218	80	.367
C Counsell, Ari.	225	81	.360
R Durham, S.F.	370	133	.359
J Pierre, Fla.	675	242	.359
M Grudzielanek, Chi.	321	115	.358
K Lofton, Pit.-Chi.	593	210	.354
R Furcal, Atl.	729	257	.353

Cleanup Slugging†
(minimum 150 PA)

Player, Team	AB	TB	Slg.
B Bonds, S.F.	324	249	.769
R Sanders, Pit.	140	95	.679
J Thome, Phi.	220	144	.655
J Edmonds, St.L.	250	156	.624
V Guerrero, Mon.	262	159	.607
B Abreu, Phi.	165	98	.594
S Rolen, St.L.	133	77	.579
C Floyd, N.Y.	244	140	.574
L Gonzalez, Ari.	184	105	.571
R Sexson, Mil.	336	191	.568

Avg. vs. LHP
(minimum 125 PA)

E Renteria, St.L.	.391
A Pujols, St.L.	.387
T Helton, Col.	.387
I Rodriguez, Fla.	.376
E Karros, Chi.	.366

Avg. vs. RHP
(minimum 377 PA)

L Gonzalez, Ari.	.354
A Pujols, St.L.	.350
T Helton, Col.	.344
J Kendall, Pit.	.331
B Bonds, S.F.	.331

Avg. at Home
(minimum 251 PA)

T Helton, Col.	.391
A Pujols, St.L.	.388
B Bonds, S.F.	.369
E Renteria, St.L.	.356
B Abreu, Phi.	.349

Avg. on Road
(minimum 251 PA)

G Sheffield, Atl.	.343
L Gonzalez, Ari.	.342
M Giles, Atl.	.342
J Kendall, Pit.	.336
A Pujols, St.L.	.331

OBP vs. LHP
(minimum 125 PA)

B Bonds, S.F.	.509
E Renteria, St.L.	.503
T Helton, Col.	.470
D Lee, Fla.	.462
I Rodriguez, Fla.	.460

OBP vs. RHP
(minimum 377 PA)

B Bonds, S.F.	.537
L Gonzalez, Ari.	.459
T Helton, Col.	.452
B Abreu, Phi.	.440
A Pujols, St.L.	.434

Late & Close Avg.†
(minimum 50 PA)

C Baerga, Ari.	.407
S Podsednik, Mil.	.398
A Pujols, St.L.	.390
D Jimenez, Cin.	.377
J Kendall, Pit.	.374

Bases Loaded Avg.
(minimum 10 PA)

R Belliard, Col.	.625
C Stynes, Col.	.615
J Kent, Hou.	.600
M Lieberthal, Phi.	.563
3 tied with	.556

Slg. vs. LHP
(minimum 125 PA)

B Bonds, S.F.	.790
A Pujols, St.L.	.732
C Wilson, Pit.	.692
G Sheffield, Atl.	.675
E Renteria, St.L.	.670

Slg. vs. RHP
(minimum 377 PA)

B Bonds, S.F.	.729
J Lopez, Atl.	.677
A Pujols, St.L.	.646
J Edmonds, St.L.	.631
J Thome, Phi.	.623

AB per Home Run
(minimum 502 PA)

B Bonds, S.F.	8.7
J Edmonds, St.L.	11.5
J Thome, Phi.	12.3
S Sosa, Chi.	12.9
R Sexson, Mil.	13.5

Times on Base*
(*H+BB+HBP)

T Helton, Col.	322
A Pujols, St.L.	301
B Bonds, S.F.	291
B Abreu, Phi.	284
G Sheffield, Atl.	284

Pitches Seen

B Abreu, Phi.	2994
J Thome, Phi.	2870
R Furcal, Atl.	2845
R Sexson, Mil.	2838
T Helton, Col.	2830

Pitches per PA
(minimum 502 PA)

B Wilkerson, Mon.	4.37
B Abreu, Phi.	4.31
S Rolen, St.L.	4.15
P Burrell, Phi.	4.14
J Edmonds, St.L.	4.13

Pct. of Pitches Taken
(minimum 1500 pitches)

B Bonds, S.F.	65.9
B Abreu, Phi.	65.6
C Counsell, Ari.	64.3
D Roberts, L.A.	64.1
J Kendall, Pit.	63.0

Ground/Fly Ratio†
(minimum 502 PA)

L Castillo, Fla.	2.81
J Pierre, Fla.	2.67
E Chavez, Mon.	2.17
R Cedeno, N.Y.	2.10
C Izturis, L.A.	1.98

GDP/GDP Opp.†
(minimum 50 PA)

R Furcal, Atl.	0.01
O Palmeiro, St.L.	0.02
J Reyes, N.Y.	0.02
J Thome, Phi.	0.03
J Burnitz, N.Y.-L.A.	0.05

SB Success Pct.
(minimum 20 SB attempts)

R Furcal, Atl.	92.6
O Cabrera, Mon.	92.3
E Renteria, St.L.	82.9
G Sheffield, Atl.	81.8
S Podsednik, Mil.	81.1

Steals of Third

J Pierre, Fla.	11
E Renteria, St.L.	8
R Sanders, Pit.	7
O Cabrera, Mon.	6
2 tied with	5

Pct. CS by Catchers
(minimum 50 SB attempts)

D Miller, Chi.	38.2
P Lo Duca, L.A.	34.1
I Rodriguez, Fla.	32.2
B Ausmus, Hou.	31.3
C Johnson, Col.	29.4

†**Scoring-Position Average** denotes batting average when a runner is at second and/or third base. **Leadoff OBP** denotes OBP for a player batting in the first position of the batting order. **Cleanup Slugging** denotes slugging percentage for a player batting in the fourth position of the batting order. **Late & Close Avg.** refers to batting average when the game is in the seventh inning or later and the batting team is either leading by one run, tied, or has the potential tying run on base, at bat or on deck (a batting situation coming close to a pitcher's save situation). **Ground/Fly Ratio** denotes ground balls hit divided by fly balls hit. All batted balls except line drives and bunts are included. **GDP/GDP Opp.** denotes the ratio of times grounding into double plays per opportunities to do so (any situation with a runner on first and less than two out).

Baserunners per 9 IP
(minimum 162 IP)

Pitcher, Team	IP	BR	BR/9
P Martinez, Bos.	186.2	203	9.79
M Mussina, N.Y.	214.2	235	9.85
R Halladay, Tor.	266.0	294	9.95
T Hudson, Oak.	240.0	268	10.05
E Loaiza, Chi.	226.1	262	10.42
M Mulder, Oak.	186.2	222	10.70
D May, K.C.	210.0	252	10.80
B Zito, Oak.	231.2	280	10.88
B Colon, Chi.	242.0	295	10.97
R Clemens, N.Y.	211.2	262	11.14

Strikeouts per 9 IP
(minimum 162 IP)

Pitcher, Team	IP	SO	SO/9
P Martinez, Bos.	186.2	206	9.93
E Loaiza, Chi.	226.1	207	8.23
M Mussina, N.Y.	214.2	195	8.18
R Clemens, N.Y.	211.2	190	8.08
K Escobar, Tor.	180.1	159	7.94
A Pettitte, N.Y.	208.1	180	7.78
T Wakefield, Bos.	202.1	169	7.52
T Lilly, Oak.	178.1	147	7.42
R Halladay, Tor.	266.0	204	6.90
J Lackey, Ana.	204.0	151	6.66

Run Support per 9 IP†
(minimum 162 IP)

Pitcher, Team	IP	R	RS/9
D Lowe, Bos.	203.1	164	7.26
A Pettitte, N.Y.	208.1	163	7.04
B Anderson, Cle.-K.C.	197.2	141	6.42
R Ortiz, Ana.	180.0	127	6.35
D Wells, N.Y.	213.0	150	6.34
J Garland, Chi.	191.2	129	6.06
R Halladay, Tor.	266.0	179	6.06
P Martinez, Bos.	186.2	125	6.03
J Pineiro, Sea.	211.2	141	6.00
G Meche, Sea.	186.1	124	5.99

Opposition OBP
(minimum 162 IP)

P Martinez, Bos.	.272
M Mussina, N.Y.	.275
R Halladay, Tor.	.275
T Hudson, Oak.	.280
E Loaiza, Chi.	.286

Opposition SLG
(minimum 162 IP)

T Hudson, Oak.	.308
P Martinez, Bos.	.314
B Zito, Oak.	.324
E Loaiza, Chi.	.350
J Pineiro, Sea.	.359

Hits per 9 IP
(minimum 162 IP)

P Martinez, Bos.	7.09
B Zito, Oak.	7.23
T Hudson, Oak.	7.39
E Loaiza, Chi.	7.79
V Zambrano, T.B.	7.88

Home Runs per 9 IP
(minimum 162 IP)

P Martinez, Bos.	0.34
T Hudson, Oak.	0.56
E Loaiza, Chi.	0.68
M Mulder, Oak.	0.72
B Zito, Oak.	0.74

Avg. vs. LHB
(minimum 125 BFP)

D Riske, Cle.	.145
K Foulke, Oak.	.158
D Marte, Chi.	.168
F Rodriguez, Ana.	.186
J Santana, Min.	.191

Avg. vs. RHB
(minimum 225 BFP)

P Martinez, Bos.	.179
E Loaiza, Chi.	.191
V Zambrano, T.B.	.206
T Hudson, Oak.	.214
B Zito, Oak.	.218

Avg. Allowed Sc. Pos.†
(minimum 125 BFP)

J Santana, Min.	.165
R Clemens, N.Y.	.186
E Loaiza, Chi.	.192
P Martinez, Bos.	.200
J Gonzalez, T.B.	.209

OBP Leading off Inn.
(minimum 150 BFP)

R Clemens, N.Y.	.243
P Martinez, Bos.	.245
B Zito, Oak.	.253
R Halladay, Tor.	.261
M Mussina, N.Y.	.264

SO/BB Ratio
(minimum 162 IP)

R Halladay, Tor.	6.38
D Wells, N.Y.	5.05
M Mussina, N.Y.	4.88
P Martinez, Bos.	4.38
B Radke, Min.	4.29

Grd/Fly Ratio Off†
(minimum 162 IP)

D Lowe, Bos.	3.92
R Halladay, Tor.	2.70
T Hudson, Oak.	2.26
M Mulder, Oak.	2.01
A Pettitte, N.Y.	1.76

Pitches per Start
(minimum 30 games started)

J Pineiro, Sea.	109.3
B Zito, Oak.	107.1
C Sabathia, Cle.	104.9
R Clemens, N.Y.	104.8
M Mussina, N.Y.	104.6

Pitches per Batter
(minimum 162 IP)

D Wells, N.Y.	3.39
R Halladay, Tor.	3.39
M Mulder, Oak.	3.51
C Lidle, Tor.	3.52
B Radke, Min.	3.52

Stolen Bases Allowed

J Johnson, Bal.	32
J Bonderman, Det.	25
K Escobar, Tor.	24
T Lilly, Oak.	24
2 tied with	23

Caught Stealing Off

M Maroth, Det.	11
M Mulder, Oak.	10
M Mussina, N.Y.	10
3 tied with	9

SB Pct. Allowed
(minimum 162 IP)

B Anderson, Cle.-K.C.	11.1
B Colon, Chi.	14.3
M Buehrle, Chi.	20.0
J Davis, Cle.	27.3
C Sabathia, Cle.	35.7

Pickoffs

M Maroth, Det.	8
M Mulder, Oak.	7
B Anderson, Cle.-K.C.	6
N Cornejo, Det.	6
R Franklin, Sea.	6

PkOf Throw/Runner†
(minimum 162 IP)

M Maroth, Det.	0.87
B Colon, Chi.	0.84
R Clemens, N.Y.	0.82
A Pettitte, N.Y.	0.76
T Lilly, Oak.	0.63

GDP Induced

B Colon, Chi.	31
N Cornejo, Det.	30
J Westbrook, Cle.	26
B Anderson, Cle.-K.C.	25
2 tied with	24

GDP per 9 IP
(minimum 162 IP)

N Cornejo, Det.	1.4
B Colon, Chi.	1.2
B Anderson, Cle.-K.C.	1.1
J Thomson, Tex.	1.0
J Davis, Cle.	1.0

Quality Starts†

T Hudson, Oak.	27
E Loaiza, Chi.	27
M Buehrle, Chi.	24
R Halladay, Tor.	23
B Zito, Oak.	23

†**Run Support per 9 IP** denotes the number of runs scored by a pitcher's team while he was still in the game times nine divided by his innings pitched. **Avg. Allowed Sc. Pos.** denotes batting average allowed when a runner is at second and/or third base. **Grd/Fly Ratio Off** denotes ground balls allowed divided by fly balls allowed. All batted balls except line drives and bunts are included. **PkOf Throw/Runner** denotes the number of pickoff throws made by a pitcher divided by the number of runners on first base. **Quality Starts** denote the number of outings in which a starting pitcher works at least six innings and allows three or fewer earned runs.

Baserunners per 9 IP
(minimum 162 IP)

Pitcher, Team	IP	BR	BR/9
J Schmidt, S.F.	207.2	203	8.80
C Schilling, Ari.	168.0	179	9.59
J Vazquez, Mon.	230.2	259	10.11
M Prior, Chi.	211.1	242	10.31
K Brown, L.A.	211.0	245	10.45
M Morris, St.L.	172.1	207	10.81
G Maddux, Atl.	218.1	266	10.96
B Webb, Ari.	180.2	221	11.01
M Redman, Fla.	190.2	238	11.23
L Hernandez, Mon.	233.1	292	11.26

Strikeouts per 9 IP
(minimum 162 IP)

Pitcher, Team	IP	SO	SO/9
K Wood, Chi.	211.0	266	11.35
M Prior, Chi.	211.1	245	10.43
C Schilling, Ari.	168.0	194	10.39
J Vazquez, Mon.	230.2	241	9.40
J Schmidt, S.F.	207.2	208	9.01
B Webb, Ari.	180.2	172	8.57
R Wolf, Phi.	200.0	177	7.97
K Brown, L.A.	211.0	185	7.89
W Miller, Hou.	187.1	161	7.73
M Clement, Chi.	201.2	171	7.63

Run Support per 9 IP†
(minimum 162 IP)

Pitcher, Team	IP	R	RS/9
W Williams, St.L.	220.2	171	6.97
B Tomko, St.L.	202.2	152	6.75
R Wolf, Phi.	200.0	149	6.70
R Ortiz, Atl.	212.1	153	6.49
S Reynolds, Atl.	167.1	120	6.45
D Oliver, Col.	180.1	123	6.14
B Penny, Fla.	196.1	132	6.05
H Ramirez, Atl.	182.1	121	5.97
M Hampton, Atl.	190.0	118	5.59
W Miller, Hou.	187.1	114	5.48

Opposition OBP
(minimum 162 IP)

J Schmidt, S.F.	.250
C Schilling, Ari.	.270
J Vazquez, Mon.	.278
M Prior, Chi.	.283
K Brown, L.A.	.290

Opposition SLG
(minimum 162 IP)

B Webb, Ari.	.307
J Schmidt, S.F.	.316
K Brown, L.A.	.318
C Zambrano, Chi.	.331
K Wood, Chi.	.344

Hits per 9 IP
(minimum 162 IP)

K Wood, Chi.	6.48
J Schmidt, S.F.	6.59
B Webb, Ari.	6.97
H Nomo, L.A.	7.21
R Ortiz, Atl.	7.50

Home Runs per 9 IP
(minimum 162 IP)

C Zambrano, Chi.	0.38
K Brown, L.A.	0.47
B Webb, Ari.	0.60
M Batista, Ari.	0.61
J Schmidt, S.F.	0.61

Avg. vs. LHB
(minimum 125 BFP)

E Gagne, L.A.	.130
O Dotel, Hou.	.152
M Hampton, Atl.	.164
G Mota, L.A.	.181
K Ishii, L.A.	.192

Avg. vs. RHB
(minimum 225 BFP)

B Wagner, Hou.	.154
B Webb, Ari.	.167
R Ortiz, Atl.	.187
O Villarreal, Ari.	.204
J Schmidt, S.F.	.204

Avg. Allowed Sc. Pos.†
(minimum 125 BFP)

K Wood, Chi.	.157
K Ishii, L.A.	.166
K Wells, Pit.	.169
K Brown, L.A.	.178
M Prior, Chi.	.183

OBP Leading off Inn.
(minimum 150 BFP)

J Seo, N.Y.	.227
D Willis, Fla.	.251
C Schilling, Ari.	.254
J Schmidt, S.F.	.258
W Williams, St.L.	.272

SO/BB Ratio
(minimum 162 IP)

C Schilling, Ari.	6.06
M Prior, Chi.	4.90
J Schmidt, S.F.	4.52
J Vazquez, Mon.	4.23
G Maddux, Atl.	3.76

Grd/Fly Ratio Off†
(minimum 162 IP)

B Webb, Ari.	3.44
K Brown, L.A.	3.37
C Zambrano, Chi.	2.28
M Clement, Chi.	2.04
M Batista, Ari.	2.04

Pitches per Start
(minimum 30 games started)

M Prior, Chi.	113.4
K Wood, Chi.	110.8
W Williams, St.L.	110.2
J Vazquez, Mon.	110.0
L Hernandez, Mon.	108.5

Pitches per Batter
(minimum 162 IP)

G Maddux, Atl.	3.26
D Graves, Cin.	3.35
T Ohka, Mon.	3.44
J D'Amico, Pit.	3.47
D Oliver, Col.	3.50

Stolen Bases Allowed

K Millwood, Phi.	41
G Maddux, Atl.	26
O Perez, L.A.	25
M Kinney, Mil.	24
R Ortiz, Atl.	22

Caught Stealing Off

H Nomo, L.A.	14
K Ishii, L.A.	13
A Leiter, N.Y.	11
3 tied with	9

SB Pct. Allowed
(minimum 162 IP)

T Ohka, Mon.	20.0
M Hampton, Atl.	33.3
J Seo, N.Y.	36.4
C Zambrano, Chi.	37.5
K Wood, Chi.	38.5

Pickoffs

J Beimel, Pit.	7
O Perez, L.A.	7
J Robertson, Hou.	7
3 tied with	5

PkOf Throw/Runner†
(minimum 162 IP)

S Trachsel, N.Y.	0.99
G Maddux, Atl.	0.85
J Seo, N.Y.	0.82
A Leiter, N.Y.	0.80
D Oliver, Col.	0.64

GDP Induced

H Ramirez, Atl.	29
S Estes, Chi.	27
B Penny, Fla.	26
K Rueter, S.F.	24
C Zambrano, Chi.	24

GDP per 9 IP
(minimum 162 IP)

H Ramirez, Atl.	1.4
B Penny, Fla.	1.2
T Glavine, N.Y.	1.1
D Oliver, Col.	1.1
J Jennings, Col.	1.1

Quality Starts†

K Brown, L.A.	25
K Millwood, Phi.	23
M Prior, Chi.	23
4 tied with	22

†**Run Support per 9 IP** denotes the number of runs scored by a pitcher's team while he was still in the game times nine divided by his innings pitched. **Avg. Allowed Sc. Pos.** denotes batting average allowed when a runner is at second and/or third base. **Grd/Fly Ratio Off** denotes ground balls allowed divided by fly balls allowed. All batted balls except line drives and bunts are included. **PkOf Throw/Runner** denotes the number of pickoff throws made by a pitcher divided by the number of runners on first base. **Quality Starts** denote the number of outings in which a starting pitcher works at least six innings and allows three or fewer earned runs.

Saves

Pitcher, Team	Saves
K Foulke, Oak.	43
E Guardado, Min.	41
M Rivera, N.Y.	40
J Julio, Bal.	36
T Percival, Ana.	33
M MacDougal, K.C.	27
L Carter, T.B.	26
U Urbina, Tex.	26
D Baez, Cle.	25
2 tied with	16

Save Percentage
(minimum 20 save opportunities)

Pitcher, Team	Opp.	Sv.	Pct.
E Guardado, Min.	45	41	91.1
K Foulke, Oak.	48	43	89.6
T Percival, Ana.	37	33	89.2
M Rivera, N.Y.	46	40	87.0
U Urbina, Tex.	30	26	86.7
J Julio, Bal.	44	36	81.8
L Carter, T.B.	33	26	78.8
M MacDougal, K.C.	35	27	77.1
D Baez, Cle.	35	25	71.4
F Cordero, Tex.	25	15	60.0

Relief ERA
(minimum 50 relief IP)

Pitcher, Team	IP	ER	ERA
S Hasegawa, Sea.	73.0	12	1.48
R Soriano, Sea.	53.0	9	1.53
B Donnelly, Ana.	74.0	13	1.58
D Marte, Chi.	79.2	14	1.58
M Rivera, N.Y.	70.2	13	1.66
S Shields, Ana.	69.2	13	1.68
L Hawkins, Min.	77.1	16	1.86
K Foulke, Oak.	86.2	20	2.08
D Riske, Cle.	74.2	19	2.29
B Weber, Ana.	80.1	24	2.69

Relief Wins

K Foulke, Oak.	9
L Hawkins, Min.	9
R Rincon, Oak.	8
F Rodriguez, Ana.	8
3 tied with	7

Relief Losses

D Baez, Cle.	9
F Cordero, Tex.	8
T Harper, T.B.	8
J Colome, T.B.	7
J Julio, Bal.	7

Holds†

B Donnelly, Ana.	29
J Grimsley, K.C.	28
L Hawkins, Min.	28
C Bradford, Oak.	23
J Romero, Min.	22

Blown Saves†

D Baez, Cle.	10
F Cordero, Tex.	10
J Julio, Bal.	8
M MacDougal, K.C.	8
3 tied with	7

Relief Games

T Miller, Tor.	79
J Walker, Det.	78
J Grimsley, K.C.	76
B Ryan, Bal.	76
L Hawkins, Min.	74

Games Finished

K Foulke, Oak.	67
M MacDougal, K.C.	61
E Guardado, Min.	60
M Rivera, N.Y.	57
L Carter, T.B.	55

Relief Innings

S Sparks, Det.-Oak.	107.0
T Harper, T.B.	93.0
K Foulke, Oak.	86.2
F Rodriguez, Ana.	86.0
2 tied with	85.2

Pct. Inherited Scored†
(minimum 30 inherited runners)

B Groom, Bal.	14.6
C Bradford, Oak.	16.4
S Hasegawa, Sea.	16.7
T Gordon, Chi.	18.9
R Rincon, Oak.	20.0

Opposition Avg.
(minimum 50 relief IP)

R Soriano, Sea.	.162
F Rodriguez, Ana.	.172
K Foulke, Oak.	.184
D Marte, Chi.	.185
D Riske, Cle.	.196

Opposition OBP
(minimum 50 relief IP)

R Soriano, Sea.	.224
E Guardado, Min.	.249
K Foulke, Oak.	.249
J Mateo, Sea.	.259
D Riske, Cle.	.260

Opposition SLG
(minimum 50 relief IP)

R Soriano, Sea.	.238
D Marte, Chi.	.266
B Ryan, Bal.	.286
B Donnelly, Ana.	.287
T Gordon, Chi.	.291

First Batter Avg.
(minimum 40 first BFP)

J Kershner, Tor.	.114
T Gordon, Chi.	.133
E Guardado, Min.	.136
R Soriano, Sea.	.139
S Sparks, Det.-Oak.	.143

Avg. vs. LHB
(minimum 50 relief IP)

D Riske, Cle.	.145
K Foulke, Oak.	.158
D Marte, Chi.	.168
E Guardado, Min.	.175
J Kershner, Tor.	.178

Avg. vs. RHB
(minimum 50 relief IP)

R Soriano, Sea.	.132
F Rodriguez, Ana.	.156
D Baez, Cle.	.165
J Boyd, Cle.	.176
A Lopez, Tor.	.186

Avg., Runners On†
(minimum 50 relief IP)

S Hasegawa, Sea.	.134
K Foulke, Oak.	.138
A Lopez, Tor.	.162
R Soriano, Sea.	.164
B Donnelly, Ana.	.176

Avg., Scoring Pos.†
(minimum 50 relief IP)

R Soriano, Sea.	.111
M Roney, Det.	.114
B Donnelly, Ana.	.134
T Miller, Tor.	.150
A Lopez, Tor.	.164

Easy Saves†

K Foulke, Oak.	28
E Guardado, Min.	28
T Percival, Ana.	24
M Rivera, N.Y.	23
2 tied with	19

Regular Saves†

J Julio, Bal.	16
E Guardado, Min.	13
M Rivera, N.Y.	12
K Foulke, Oak.	11
4 tied with	9

Tough Saves†

M Rivera, N.Y.	5
K Foulke, Oak.	4
D Marte, Chi.	4
7 tied with	2

Pitches per Batter
(minimum 50 relief IP)

C Hammond, N.Y.	3.47
J Kershner, Tor.	3.50
K Wilson, K.C.	3.50
M Timlin, Bos.	3.51
B Lyon, Bos.	3.53

†**Holds** denote the number of times a relief pitcher enters the game in a save situation, records at least one out and leaves the game never having relinquished the lead. A pitcher cannot finish the game and receive credit for a hold, nor can he earn a hold and a save in the same game. **Blown Saves** denote the number of times a relief pitcher enters a game in a save situation and allows the tying or go-ahead run to score. **Pct. Inherited Scored** denotes the percent of inherited runners (those on base when a reliever enters the game) that score. **Avg., Runners On** denotes batting average allowed when runners are on base. **Avg., Scoring Pos.** denotes batting average allowed when a runner is at second and/or third base. **Easy Saves** denote saves in which the first batter faced doesn't represent the tying run and the reliever pitches one inning or less. **Regular Saves** denote those saves that are not Easy Saves or Tough Saves. **Tough Saves** denote saves which occur after the reliever enters with the tying run anywhere on base.

NATIONAL LEAGUE RELIEF PITCHING LEADERS

Saves

Pitcher, Team	Saves
E Gagne, L.A.	55
J Smoltz, Atl.	45
B Wagner, Hou.	44
T Worrell, S.F.	38
R Biddle, Mon.	34
J Borowski, Chi.	33
M Mantei, Ari.	29
B Looper, Fla.	28
M Williams, Pit.-Phi.	28
J Mesa, Phi.	24

Save Percentage
(minimum 20 save opportunities)

Pitcher, Team	Opp.	Sv.	Pct.
R Beck, S.D.	20	20	100.0
E Gagne, L.A.	55	55	100.0
B Wagner, Hou.	47	44	93.6
J Smoltz, Atl.	49	45	91.8
D Kolb, Mil.	23	21	91.3
M Mantei, Ari.	32	29	90.6
J Borowski, Chi.	37	33	89.2
J Isringhausen, St.L.	25	22	88.0
J Jimenez, Col.	23	20	87.0
J Mesa, Phi.	28	24	85.7

Relief ERA
(minimum 50 relief IP)

Pitcher, Team	IP	ER	ERA
J Smoltz, Atl.	64.1	8	1.12
E Gagne, L.A.	82.1	11	1.20
R Cormier, Phi.	84.2	16	1.70
P Quantrill, L.A.	77.1	15	1.75
B Wagner, Hou.	86.0	17	1.78
K Mercker, Cin.-Atl.	55.1	12	1.95
G Mota, L.A.	105.0	23	1.97
J Valverde, Ari.	50.1	12	2.15
O Villarreal, Ari.	95.0	26	2.46
O Dotel, Hou.	87.0	24	2.48

Relief Wins

J Nathan, S.F.	12
L Ayala, Mon.	10
O Villarreal, Ari.	10
4 tied with	8

Relief Losses

R Biddle, Mon.	8
M DeJean, Mil.-St.L.	8
5 tied with	7

Holds†

O Dotel, Hou.	33
B Lidge, Hou.	28
T Martin, L.A.	28
P Quantrill, L.A.	28
D Weathers, N.Y.	26

Blown Saves†

M DeJean, Mil.-St.L.	8
A Benitez, N.Y.	7
R Biddle, Mon.	7
M Williams, Pit.-Phi.	7
T Worrell, S.F.	7

Relief Games

P Quantrill, L.A.	89
O Villarreal, Ari.	85
R King, Atl.	80
T Martin, L.A.	80
4 tied with	78

Games Finished

E Gagne, L.A.	67
B Wagner, Hou.	67
B Looper, Fla.	64
T Worrell, S.F.	64
J Borowski, Chi.	59

Relief Innings

G Mota, L.A.	105.0
O Villarreal, Ari.	95.0
D Weathers, N.Y.	87.2
O Dotel, Hou.	87.0
B Wagner, Hou.	86.0

Pct. Inherited Scored†
(minimum 30 inherited runners)

T Martin, L.A.	11.9
R Cormier, Phi.	13.9
L Ayala, Mon.	16.7
J Lopez, Col.	18.6
S Reed, Col.	20.5

Opposition Avg.
(minimum 50 relief IP)

E Gagne, L.A.	.133
J Valverde, Ari.	.137
B Wagner, Hou.	.169
O Dotel, Hou.	.172
R Cormier, Phi.	.182

Opposition OBP
(minimum 50 relief IP)

E Gagne, L.A.	.199
J Smoltz, Atl.	.230
B Wagner, Hou.	.234
R Cormier, Phi.	.248
O Dotel, Hou.	.253

Opposition SLG
(minimum 50 relief IP)

E Gagne, L.A.	.176
J Valverde, Ari.	.234
B Wagner, Hou.	.266
R Cormier, Phi.	.269
J Smoltz, Atl.	.281

First Batter Avg.
(minimum 40 first BFP)

T Martin, L.A.	.100
J Valverde, Ari.	.114
L Hackman, S.D.	.143
R Cormier, Phi.	.145
J Riedling, Cin.	.163

Avg. vs. LHB
(minimum 50 relief IP)

R Cormier, Phi.	.119
E Gagne, L.A.	.130
O Dotel, Hou.	.152
M Mantei, Ari.	.155
J Valverde, Ari.	.169

Avg. vs. RHB
(minimum 50 relief IP)

J Valverde, Ari.	.112
E Gagne, L.A.	.135
J Nathan, S.F.	.136
B Wagner, Hou.	.154
S Reed, Col.	.165

Avg., Runners On†
(minimum 50 relief IP)

E Gagne, L.A.	.121
M Mantei, Ari.	.132
K Mercker, Cin.-Atl.	.157
B Wagner, Hou.	.167
J Smoltz, Atl.	.169

Avg., Scoring Pos.†
(minimum 50 relief IP)

M Mantei, Ari.	.088
B Wagner, Hou.	.094
E Gagne, L.A.	.118
P Shuey, L.A.	.149
J Smoltz, Atl.	.152

Easy Saves†

E Gagne, L.A.	28
J Smoltz, Atl.	27
B Wagner, Hou.	24
T Worrell, S.F.	22
R Biddle, Mon.	21

Regular Saves†

E Gagne, L.A.	25
B Wagner, Hou.	16
J Borowski, Chi.	15
J Smoltz, Atl.	15
T Worrell, S.F.	14

Tough Saves†

J Tavarez, Pit.	4
B Wagner, Hou.	4
J Smoltz, Atl.	3
7 tied with	2

Pitches per Batter
(minimum 50 relief IP)

L Estrella, Mil.	3.38
F Heredia, Cin.	3.39
D Wheeler, N.Y.	3.41
J Tavarez, Pit.	3.42
B Kieschnick, Mil.	3.43

†**Holds** denote the number of times a relief pitcher enters the game in a save situation, records at least one out and leaves the game never having relinquished the lead. A pitcher cannot finish the game and receive credit for a hold, nor can he earn a hold and a save in the same game. **Blown Saves** denote the number of times a relief pitcher enters a game in a save situation and allows the tying or go-ahead run to score. **Pct. Inherited Scored** denotes the percent of inherited runners (those on base when a reliever enters the game) that score. **Avg., Runners On** denotes batting average allowed when runners are on base. **Avg., Scoring Pos.** denotes the batting average allowed when a runner is at second and/or third base. **Easy Saves** denote saves in which the first batter faced doesn't represent the tying run and the reliever pitches one inning or less. **Regular Saves** denote those saves that are not Easy Saves or Tough Saves. **Tough Saves** denote saves which occur after the reliever enters with the tying run anywhere on base.

BATTING

Batting Average

(minimum 1000 PA)

Rk.	Player	AB	H	Avg.
1.	Todd Helton	3504	1182	.337
2.	Albert Pujols	1771	591	.334
3.	Ichiro Suzuki	2018	662	.328
4.	Nomar Garciaparra	3812	1231	.323
5.	Vladimir Guerrero	3763	1215	.323
6.	Mike Piazza	5350	1708	.319
7.	Derek Jeter	4870	1546	.317
8.	Manny Ramirez	5004	1585	.317
9.	Edgar Martinez	6727	2119	.315
10.	Larry Walker	6334	1992	.314
11.	Frank Thomas	6611	2048	.310
12.	Chipper Jones	5144	1588	.309
13.	Alex Rodriguez	4989	1535	.308
14.	Magglio Ordonez	3605	1108	.307
15.	Juan Pierre	2077	638	.307
16.	Mike Sweeney	3306	1014	.307
17.	Bobby Abreu	3566	1091	.306
18.	Jose Vidro	3073	940	.306
19.	Bernie Williams	6403	1950	.305
20.	Jason Kendall	4032	1226	.304
21.	Ivan Rodriguez	6167	1875	.304
22.	Mark Grace	8065	2445	.303
23.	Shannon Stewart	3720	1127	.303
24.	Jason Giambi	4493	1358	.302
25.	Brian Giles	3502	1056	.302

On-Base Percentage

(minimum 1000 PA; *AB+BB+HBP+SF)

Rk.	Player	*PA	OB	OBP
1.	Barry Bonds	10963	4749	.433
2.	Frank Thomas	8167	3499	.428
3.	Todd Helton	4113	1750	.425
4.	Edgar Martinez	8113	3431	.423
5.	Brian Giles	4271	1783	.417
6.	Jason Giambi	5460	2266	.415
7.	Manny Ramirez	5910	2438	.413
8.	Albert Pujols	2035	839	.412
9.	Jim Thome	6420	2640	.411
10.	Jeff Bagwell	8626	3543	.411
11.	Bobby Abreu	4245	1737	.409
12.	Lance Berkman	2560	1043	.407
13.	Chipper Jones	6064	2451	.404
14.	John Olerud	8360	3357	.402
15.	Rickey Henderson	13316	5343	.401
16.	Gary Sheffield	8026	3218	.401
17.	Larry Walker	7340	2936	.400
18.	Carlos Delgado	5467	2157	.395
19.	Bernie Williams	7385	2882	.390
20.	Vladimir Guerrero	4220	1646	.390
21.	Derek Jeter	5489	2137	.389
22.	Tim Salmon	6589	2560	.389
23.	Mike Piazza	6007	2328	.388
24.	Jason Kendall	4616	1778	.385
25.	Mark Grace	9273	3554	.383

Slugging Percentage

(minimum 1000 PA)

Rk.	Player	AB	TB	Slg.
1.	Todd Helton	3504	2158	.616
2.	Albert Pujols	1771	1085	.613
3.	Barry Bonds	8725	5253	.602
4.	Manny Ramirez	5004	2991	.598
5.	Vladimir Guerrero	3763	2211	.588
6.	Alex Rodriguez	4989	2899	.581
7.	Mike Piazza	5350	3058	.572
8.	Jim Thome	5218	2964	.568
9.	Frank Thomas	6611	3752	.568
10.	Larry Walker	6334	3594	.567
11.	Juan Gonzalez	6428	3620	.563
12.	Brian Giles	3502	1970	.563
13.	Lance Berkman	2139	1203	.562
14.	Ken Griffey Jr.	7079	3977	.562
15.	Carlos Delgado	4550	2541	.558
16.	Nomar Garciaparra	3812	2116	.555
17.	Jason Giambi	4493	2468	.549
18.	Jeff Bagwell	7125	3909	.549
19.	Sammy Sosa	7543	4121	.546
20.	Chipper Jones	5144	2785	.541
21.	Jim Edmonds	4592	2447	.533
22.	Gary Sheffield	6729	3548	.527
23.	Magglio Ordonez	3605	1900	.527
24.	Richie Sexson	2975	1566	.526
25.	Edgar Martinez	6727	3531	.525

Hits

Rickey Henderson	3055
Rafael Palmeiro	2780
Roberto Alomar	2679
Barry Bonds	2595
Fred McGriff	2477
Craig Biggio	2461
Mark Grace	2445
Julio Franco	2358
Andres Galarraga	2330
Barry Larkin	2240
Steve Finley	2166
B.J. Surhoff	2142
Jeff Bagwell	2137
Edgar Martinez	2119
Ellis Burks	2101
Sammy Sosa	2099
Ken Griffey Jr.	2080
John Olerud	2079
Marquis Grissom	2065
Frank Thomas	2048

Home Runs

Barry Bonds	658
Sammy Sosa	539
Rafael Palmeiro	528
Fred McGriff	491
Ken Griffey Jr.	481
Juan Gonzalez	429
Jeff Bagwell	419
Frank Thomas	418
Andres Galarraga	398
Jim Thome	381
Gary Sheffield	379
Matt Williams	378
Mike Piazza	358
Greg Vaughn	355
Ellis Burks	351
Larry Walker	351
Manny Ramirez	347
Alex Rodriguez	345
Mo Vaughn	328
Ron Gant	321

Runs Batted In

Barry Bonds	1742
Rafael Palmeiro	1687
Fred McGriff	1543
Sammy Sosa	1450
Andres Galarraga	1423
Jeff Bagwell	1421
Frank Thomas	1390
Juan Gonzalez	1387
Ken Griffey Jr.	1384
Gary Sheffield	1232
Ruben Sierra	1224
Matt Williams	1218
Larry Walker	1212
Ellis Burks	1205
Edgar Martinez	1198
Robin Ventura	1154
Mark Grace	1146
Tino Martinez	1146
John Olerud	1145
Manny Ramirez	1140

Stolen Bases

Rickey Henderson	1406
Kenny Lofton	538
Barry Bonds	500
Roberto Alomar	474
Eric Young	436
Marquis Grissom	425
Craig Biggio	389
Barry Larkin	377
Tom Goodwin	364
Tony Womack	309
Omar Vizquel	299
Steve Finley	296
Mark McLemore	272
Julio Franco	265
Reggie Sanders	262
Brian L. Hunter	260
Luis Castillo	250
Johnny Damon	244
Ron Gant	243
Sammy Sosa	233

Seasons Played

Rickey Henderson	25
Jesse Orosco	24
Roger Clemens	20
Julio Franco	19
John Franco	19
Fred McGriff	18
Mark McLemore	18
Andres Galarraga	18
Dan Plesac	18
Rafael Palmeiro	18

Games

Rickey Henderson	3081
Barry Bonds	2569
Rafael Palmeiro	2567
Fred McGriff	2433
Roberto Alomar	2323
Craig Biggio	2253
Andres Galarraga	2250
Mark Grace	2245
Julio Franco	2144
Steve Finley	2127

At-Bats

Rickey Henderson	10961
Rafael Palmeiro	9553
Roberto Alomar	8902
Barry Bonds	8725
Fred McGriff	8685
Craig Biggio	8588
Andres Galarraga	8086
Mark Grace	8065
Julio Franco	7869
Steve Finley	7843

Runs Scored

Rickey Henderson	2295
Barry Bonds	1941
Rafael Palmeiro	1548
Craig Biggio	1503
Roberto Alomar	1490
Jeff Bagwell	1402
Fred McGriff	1342
Sammy Sosa	1314
Barry Larkin	1274
Ken Griffey Jr.	1271

Doubles

Rafael Palmeiro	543
Barry Bonds	536
Craig Biggio	517
Mark Grace	511
Rickey Henderson	510
Roberto Alomar	498
Edgar Martinez	491
John Olerud	473
Jeff Bagwell	455
Andres Galarraga	444

Triples

Steve Finley	108
Kenny Lofton	86
Roberto Alomar	78
Barry Bonds	74
Barry Larkin	73
Johnny Damon	68
Jay Bell	67
Rickey Henderson	66
Ellis Burks	63
Ray Durham	62

AB per HR
(minimum 1000 AB)

Barry Bonds	13.3
Jim Thome	13.7
Sammy Sosa	14.0
Manny Ramirez	14.4
Alex Rodriguez	14.5
Ken Griffey Jr.	14.7
Mike Piazza	14.9
Carlos Delgado	15.0
Juan Gonzalez	15.0
Albert Pujols	15.5

AB per RBI
(minimum 1000 AB)

Manny Ramirez	4.4
Juan Gonzalez	4.6
Albert Pujols	4.6
Todd Helton	4.7
Carlos Delgado	4.7
Frank Thomas	4.8
Mike Piazza	4.8
Jim Thome	4.9
Jason Giambi	5.0
Lance Berkman	5.0

Total Bases

Barry Bonds	5253
Rafael Palmeiro	4983
Rickey Henderson	4588
Fred McGriff	4436
Sammy Sosa	4121
Andres Galarraga	4032
Ken Griffey Jr.	3977
Roberto Alomar	3951
Jeff Bagwell	3909
Frank Thomas	3752

Walks

Rickey Henderson	2190
Barry Bonds	2070
Frank Thomas	1386
Fred McGriff	1296
Jeff Bagwell	1287
Edgar Martinez	1225
Rafael Palmeiro	1224
John Olerud	1198
Gary Sheffield	1110
Jim Thome	1108

Intentional Walks

Barry Bonds	484
Ken Griffey Jr.	204
Fred McGriff	169
Frank Thomas	159
Rafael Palmeiro	153
John Olerud	151
Jeff Bagwell	148
Sammy Sosa	144
Mo Vaughn	144
Robin Ventura	131

Hit by Pitch

Craig Biggio	241
Andres Galarraga	177
Jason Kendall	158
Fernando Vina	152
Larry Walker	121
Jeff Bagwell	119
Carlos Delgado	109
Mo Vaughn	108
Damion Easley	103
Gary Sheffield	99

Strikeouts

Andres Galarraga	2000
Sammy Sosa	1977
Fred McGriff	1863
Rickey Henderson	1694
Jim Thome	1559
Greg Vaughn	1513
Jay Bell	1443
Mo Vaughn	1429
Ron Gant	1411
Jeff Bagwell	1406

SO/BB Ratio
(minimum 1000 AB)

Mark Grace	.597
Barry Bonds	.670
Eric Young	.692
Brian Giles	.702
Gary Sheffield	.717
Rickey Henderson	.774
Orlando Palmeiro	.776
Frank Thomas	.777
John Olerud	.780
Matt Lawton	.840

Sacrifice Hits

Tom Glavine	178
Omar Vizquel	165
Jay Bell	159
Roberto Alomar	145
Greg Maddux	143
Mark McLemore	103
Curt Schilling	102
Jose Vizcaino	99
Mike Bordick	97
Shane Reynolds	97

Sacrifice Flies

Ruben Sierra	111
Frank Thomas	105
Rafael Palmeiro	102
Mark Grace	99
B.J. Surhoff	99
Roberto Alomar	96
Jeff Bagwell	95
John Olerud	88
Gary Sheffield	88
Barry Bonds	84

SB Success Pct.
(minimum 100 SB attempts)

Carlos Beltran	88.2
Pokey Reese	85.2
Tony Womack	83.1
Barry Larkin	83.0
Doug Glanville	81.6
Brian L. Hunter	81.0
Roberto Alomar	80.9
Rickey Henderson	80.8
Aaron Boone	80.5
Alex Rodriguez	79.4

Caught Stealing

Rickey Henderson	335
Eric Young	151
Kenny Lofton	142
Barry Bonds	140
Omar Vizquel	123
Tom Goodwin	118
Mark McLemore	117
Craig Biggio	116
Marquis Grissom	114
Roberto Alomar	112

GDP

Julio Franco	279
Fred McGriff	225
John Olerud	215
Todd Zeile	210
Rafael Palmeiro	208
Jeff Bagwell	207
Ivan Rodriguez	205
Roberto Alomar	202
Benito Santiago	194
Mark Grace	192

AB per GDP
(minimum 1000 AB)

Greg Maddux	180.1
Ichiro Suzuki	144.1
Rafael Furcal	129.9
Alex Sanchez	113.2
Joe McEwing	111.0
Russell Branyan	110.4
Tom Glavine	107.7
Johnny Damon	100.7
Tony Womack	100.3
Brad Wilkerson	94.0

Wins

Roger Clemens	310
Greg Maddux	289
Tom Glavine	251
Randy Johnson	230
David Wells	200
Mike Mussina	199
Kevin Brown	197
David Cone	194
Jamie Moyer	185
Kevin Appier	169

Losses

Greg Maddux	163
Roger Clemens	160
Tom Glavine	157
Kevin Appier	136
John Burkett	136
Jamie Moyer	132
Kevin Brown	131
Terry Mulholland	131
David Wells	128
David Cone	126

Won-Lost Percentage
(minimum 100 decisions)

Pedro Martinez	.712
Tim Hudson	.708
Randy Johnson	.669
Roger Clemens	.660
Andy Pettitte	.656
Mike Mussina	.644
Greg Maddux	.639
Russ Ortiz	.633
Matt Morris	.632
Freddy Garcia	.626

ERA
(minimum 750 IP)

Pedro Martinez	2.58
John Franco	2.74
Greg Maddux	2.89
Randy Johnson	3.10
Barry Zito	3.12
Jesse Orosco	3.16
Kevin Brown	3.16
Roger Clemens	3.19
Tim Hudson	3.26
Matt Morris	3.28

Games

Jesse Orosco	1252
Dan Plesac	1064
John Franco	1036
Mike Stanton	885
Mark Guthrie	765
Roberto Hernandez	762
Jose Mesa	762
Steve Reed	738
Mike Timlin	736
Jeff Nelson	714

Games Started

Roger Clemens	606
Greg Maddux	571
Tom Glavine	537
Randy Johnson	444
Kevin Brown	441
John Burkett	423
Jamie Moyer	420
David Cone	419
Kevin Appier	400
2 tied with	386

Innings Pitched

Roger Clemens	4278.2
Greg Maddux	3968.2
Tom Glavine	3528.0
Randy Johnson	3122.1
Kevin Brown	3051.0
David Cone	2898.2
David Wells	2826.2
Jamie Moyer	2737.2
Mike Mussina	2668.2
John Burkett	2648.1

Batters Faced

Roger Clemens	17653
Greg Maddux	16117
Tom Glavine	14821
Randy Johnson	12900
Kevin Brown	12645
David Cone	12184
David Wells	11811
Jamie Moyer	11585
John Burkett	11324
Kevin Appier	10936

Complete Games

Roger Clemens	117
Greg Maddux	103
Randy Johnson	88
Curt Schilling	79
Kevin Brown	72
David Cone	56
Mike Mussina	53
Tom Glavine	52
David Wells	52
John Smoltz	47

Complete Game Pct.
(minimum 100 games started)

Curt Schilling	0.23
Randy Johnson	0.20
Roger Clemens	0.19
Greg Maddux	0.18
Kevin Brown	0.16
Livan Hernandez	0.15
Mark Mulder	0.15
Terry Mulholland	0.15
Pedro Martinez	0.14
Mike Mussina	0.14

Shutouts

Roger Clemens	46
Randy Johnson	35
Greg Maddux	34
David Cone	22
Tom Glavine	22
Mike Mussina	21
Curt Schilling	19
Kevin Brown	17
Pedro Martinez	15
John Smoltz	14

Quality Start Pct.†
(minimum 100 games started)

Barry Zito	71.4
Pedro Martinez	70.8
Randy Johnson	70.0
Greg Maddux	68.3
Curt Schilling	68.0
Tim Hudson	67.9
Kevin Brown	67.8
Kerry Wood	66.9
Matt Morris	65.7
Mark Buehrle	65.4

Strikeouts

Roger Clemens	4099
Randy Johnson	3871
Greg Maddux	2765
David Cone	2668
Curt Schilling	2542
Pedro Martinez	2426
John Smoltz	2313
Kevin Brown	2264
Tom Glavine	2136
Mike Mussina	2126

Walks Allowed

Roger Clemens	1379
Randy Johnson	1258
Tom Glavine	1206
David Cone	1137
Al Leiter	968
Kevin Appier	930
Kenny Rogers	898
Tom Gordon	870
Kevin Brown	847
Greg Maddux	838

Strikeouts per 9 IP
(minimum 750 IP)

Randy Johnson	11.16
Kerry Wood	10.62
Pedro Martinez	10.50
Hideo Nomo	9.07
Curt Schilling	8.85
Arthur Rhodes	8.84
Mike Remlinger	8.82
Dan Plesac	8.74
Roger Clemens	8.62
David Cone	8.28

Walks per 9 IP
(minimum 750 IP)

Rick Reed	1.66
Brad Radke	1.75
Brian Anderson	1.87
Greg Maddux	1.90
David Wells	1.99
Mike Mussina	2.01
Ramiro Mendoza	2.05
Shane Reynolds	2.10
Curt Schilling	2.10
Jose Lima	2.14

†**Quality Starts** denote the number of outings in which a starting pitcher works at least six innings and allows three or fewer earned runs.

SO/BB Ratio
(minimum 750 IP)

Pedro Martinez..................4.38
Curt Schilling 4.22
Mike Mussina...................3.56
Rick Reed........................3.40
Shane Reynolds 3.36
Greg Maddux 3.30
Javier Vazquez.................3.25
Brad Radke 3.09
Randy Johnson 3.08
David Wells 3.00

Hits per 9 IP
(minimum 750 IP)

Pedro Martinez...................6.72
Kerry Wood 6.75
Randy Johnson 7.02
Barry Zito.........................7.22
Jesse Orosco....................7.33
Hideo Nomo......................7.68
Roger Clemens 7.73
John Smoltz......................7.74
David Cone.......................7.77
Mike Remlinger 7.82

Baserunners per 9 IP
(minimum 750 IP)

Pedro Martinez...................9.55
Curt Schilling 10.19
Greg Maddux 10.37
Mike Mussina...................10.55
John Smoltz.....................10.68
Roger Clemens 10.93
Barry Zito........................10.98
Randy Johnson 11.07
Kevin Millwood 11.18
Tim Hudson 11.23

Home Runs per 9 IP
(minimum 750 IP)

Greg Maddux 0.53
Kevin Brown 0.56
John Franco 0.57
Terry Adams.....................0.57
Derek Lowe 0.64
Pedro Martinez..................0.65
Matt Morris 0.66
Roger Clemens 0.68
Tom Glavine 0.68
John Smoltz......................0.72

Opposition Avg.
(minimum 750 IP)

Pedro Martinez.................. .206
Kerry Wood .... .209
Randy Johnson .... .215
Barry Zito........................ .219
Jesse Orosco................... .223
Roger Clemens .... .231
Hideo Nomo...................... .231
John Smoltz...................... .232
David Cone....................... .232
Mike Remlinger .... .235

Opposition OBP
(minimum 750 IP)

Pedro Martinez.................. .268
Curt Schilling .... .282
Greg Maddux .... .287
Mike Mussina.................... .290
John Smoltz...................... .292
Roger Clemens .... .296
Barry Zito........................ .297
Randy Johnson .... .300
Kevin Millwood .... .301
Rick Reed........................ .303

Opposition Slg.
(minimum 750 IP)

Pedro Martinez.................. .315
Barry Zito........................ .333
Jesse Orosco................... .335
Randy Johnson .... .338
John Franco .... .339
Greg Maddux .... .339
Kevin Brown .... .343
Roger Clemens .... .344
Kerry Wood .... .345
John Smoltz...................... .351

Home Runs Allowed

David Wells 330
Roger Clemens 321
Jamie Moyer.....................314
Randy Johnson 283
Mike Mussina...................278
Terry Mulholland 269
Tom Glavine 268
Steve Trachsel.................265
Curt Schilling 263
2 tied with 258

Hit Batsmen

Randy Johnson 146
Roger Clemens 141
Kevin Brown 129
Greg Maddux 109
Tim Wakefield 109
Pedro Astacio 108
David Cone.......................106
Pedro Martinez...................99
Aaron Sele........................98
Al Leiter............................94

Wild Pitches

David Cone 149
Roger Clemens 125
John Smoltz......................122
Kevin Appier 104
Hideo Nomo......................102
Tom Gordon 98
Kevin Brown 96
David Wells 94
Randy Johnson 92
Jason Grimsley 88

GDP Induced

Greg Maddux 338
Tom Glavine 336
Kevin Brown 309
Roger Clemens 283
Kenny Rogers 248
Terry Mulholland 239
Mike Hampton...................231
Jamie Moyer.....................227
John Burkett 224
Andy Pettitte 212

GDP per 9 IP
(minimum 750 IP)

Shawn Estes 1.24
Jamey Wright 1.23
Julian Tavarez 1.20
Mike Hampton 1.13
Andy Pettitte 1.06
Paul Quantrill 1.03
Jason Grimsley 1.03
Kirk Rueter........................1.02
Derek Lowe 1.01
Terry Adams......................1.01

Saves

John Franco 424
Trevor Hoffman 352
Roberto Hernandez 320
Rod Beck..........................286
Troy Percival 283
Mariano Rivera 283
Jose Mesa 249
Billy Wagner 225
Ugueth Urbina...................206
Armando Benitez...............197

Save Percentage
(minimum 50 save opportunities)

Eric Gagne 96.4
John Smoltz......................92.4
Trevor Hoffman 88.9
Mariano Rivera..................86.5
Troy Percival 86.3
Keith Foulke 85.6
Billy Wagner 85.6
Kazuhiro Sasaki 85.4
Jose Mesa 85.3
Mike Williams 85.2

Games Finished

John Franco 754
Roberto Hernandez 597
Trevor Hoffman 527
Rod Beck..........................509
Jesse Orosco 501
Jose Mesa 473
Dan Plesac 422
Troy Percival 418
Mariano Rivera 405
Todd Jones 401

SB Pct. Allowed
(minimum 750 IP)

Kirk Rueter........................35.6
Terry Mulholland 42.1
Omar Daal 42.2
Kenny Rogers 42.5
Jeff Weaver.......................48.4
Chan Ho Park 49.5
Wilson Alvarez 49.7
Brian Anderson 50.5
Chris Hammond..................50.8
Ryan Dempster 51.9

2003 LEFTY/RIGHTY STATISTICS

Batters versus lefthanded and righthanded pitchers

Pitchers versus lefthanded and righthanded batters

Batter	vs.	Avg.	AB	H	2B	3B	HR	RBI	BB	SO	OBP	Slg.
Abad, Andy	L	.000	2	0	0	0	0	0	0	1	.000	.000
Bats Left	R	.133	15	2	0	0	0	0	2	4	.235	.133
Abernathy, B	L	.000	13	0	0	0	0	0	0	3	.000	.000
Bats Right	R	.095	21	2	0	0	0	0	1	0	.136	.095
Abreu, Bobby	L	.272	180	49	10	0	3	31	17	41	.330	.378
Bats Left	R	.312	397	124	25	1	17	70	92	85	.440	.509
Alfonzo, E	L	.236	106	25	3	0	4	13	17	6	.339	.377
Bats Right	R	.265	408	108	22	2	9	68	41	35	.333	.395
Allen, Chad	L	.250	12	3	1	0	0	0	0	5	.250	.333
Bats Right	R	.167	12	2	0	0	0	0	0	0	.231	.333
Allen, Luke	L	.000	0	0	0	0	0	0	0	0	.000	.000
Bats Left	R	.000	2	0	0	0	0	0	0	0	.000	.000
Almonte, Erick	L	.280	25	7	1	0	0	3	4	8	.379	.320
Bats Right	R	.253	75	19	5	0	1	8	4	16	.300	.360
Alomar, R	L	.189	148	28	5	1	2	10	10	21	.250	.277
Bats Both	R	.285	368	105	23	1	3	29	49	56	.364	.378
Alomar Jr., S	L	.233	60	14	4	0	0	6	1	4	.242	.300
Bats Right	R	.284	134	38	8	0	5	20	3	13	.299	.455
Alou, Moises	L	.346	127	44	8	1	6	28	10	11	.399	.567
Bats Right	R	.260	438	114	27	0	16	63	53	56	.346	.432
Amezaga, A	L	.214	28	6	0	0	0	1	1	7	.241	.214
Bats Both	R	.208	77	16	3	2	2	6	8	16	.291	.377
Anderson, G	L	.310	232	72	19	1	8	39	8	34	.329	.504
Bats Left	R	.318	406	129	30	3	21	77	23	49	.353	.562
Anderson, M	L	.315	73	23	7	0	2	15	5	7	.370	.493
Bats Left	R	.262	409	107	20	3	4	52	36	53	.320	.355
Atkins, G	L	.063	16	1	1	0	0	2	2	7	.167	.125
Bats Right	R	.189	53	10	1	0	0	2	1	7	.218	.208
Aurilia, Rich	L	.277	112	31	8	1	8	21	12	15	.347	.580
Bats Right	R	.277	393	109	18	0	5	37	24	67	.318	.361
Ausmus, Brad	L	.237	76	18	5	1	1	11	17	14	.383	.368
Bats Right	R	.227	374	85	7	1	3	36	29	52	.285	.275
Baerga, Carlos	L	.302	43	13	4	0	1	6	1	4	.340	.465
Bats Both	R	.354	164	58	9	0	3	33	17	16	.410	.463
Bagwell, Jeff	L	.327	107	35	5	0	7	20	24	16	.450	.570
Bats Right	R	.267	498	133	23	2	32	80	64	103	.356	.514
Bako, Paul	L	.200	25	5	2	0	0	0	2	5	.259	.280
Bats Left	R	.233	163	38	11	3	0	17	20	42	.319	.337
Baldelli, R	L	.298	188	56	11	4	4	21	9	24	.333	.463
Bats Right	R	.285	449	128	21	4	7	57	21	104	.323	.396
Banks, Brian	L	.196	51	10	2	0	2	9	9	11	.311	.353
Bats Both	R	.255	98	25	4	2	2	14	16	27	.368	.398
Barajas, Rod	L	.244	41	10	4	0	1	6	5	7	.326	.415
Bats Right	R	.212	179	38	11	0	2	22	9	36	.250	.307
Bard, Josh	L	.289	83	24	3	0	2	13	3	9	.310	.398
Bats Both	R	.227	220	50	10	1	6	23	19	44	.286	.364
Barmes, Clint	L	.429	14	6	2	0	0	1	0	4	.429	.571
Bats Right	R	.182	11	2	0	0	0	1	0	6	.286	.182
Barnes, Larry	L	.000	2	0	0	0	0	0	0	1	.000	.000
Bats Left	R	.222	36	8	2	0	0	2	1	8	.243	.278
Barrett, M	L	.205	78	16	4	1	3	11	11	15	.303	.397
Bats Right	R	.209	148	31	5	1	7	19	10	22	.267	.399
Batista, Tony	L	.193	161	31	2	0	9	22	8	28	.238	.373
Bats Right	R	.249	470	117	18	1	17	77	20	74	.281	.400
Bautista, D	L	.267	101	27	10	0	1	11	10	17	.339	.396
Bats Right	R	.279	183	51	6	3	3	25	11	33	.325	.393
Bay, Jason	L	.281	32	9	4	0	1	1	5	7	.378	.500
Bats Right	R	.291	55	16	3	1	3	13	14	22	.443	.545
Bell, David	L	.169	71	12	2	0	3	10	3	11	.213	.324
Bats Right	R	.204	226	46	12	0	1	27	38	29	.319	.270
Bell, Jay	L	.139	36	5	0	0	0	0	9	12	.326	.139
Bats Right	R	.200	80	16	1	0	0	3	13	26	.316	.213
Bellhorn, Mark	L	.211	71	15	3	1	1	11	10	20	.310	.324
Bats Both	R	.225	178	40	7	0	1	15	40	58	.369	.281
Belliard, R	L	.345	113	39	15	0	4	20	15	18	.426	.584
Bats Right	R	.254	334	85	16	2	4	30	34	53	.324	.350
Beltran, C	L	.325	151	49	4	4	7	25	25	19	.416	.543
Bats Both	R	.300	370	111	10	6	19	75	47	62	.377	.514
Beltre, Adrian	L	.232	138	32	5	1	7	21	16	23	.312	.435
Bats Right	R	.242	421	102	25	1	16	59	21	80	.283	.420
Benard, Marvin	L	.000	6	0	0	0	0	0	0	0	.000	.000
Bats Left	R	.215	65	14	3	1	0	4	4	9	.257	.292
Bennett, Gary	L	.218	101	22	6	0	1	15	7	11	.266	.307
Bats Right	R	.248	206	51	9	0	1	27	17	37	.310	.306
Berg, Dave	L	.304	79	24	5	1	3	14	6	15	.353	.506
Bats Right	R	.207	82	17	1	0	1	4	5	19	.250	.256
Berger, B	L	.045	22	1	0	0	0	0	5	1	.222	.045
Bats Right	R	.600	10	6	0	0	0	3	0	3	.600	.600
Berkman, Lance	L	.282	117	33	5	1	4	26	22	18	.403	.444
Bats Both	R	.290	421	122	30	5	21	67	85	90	.415	.534
Berroa, Angel	L	.313	179	56	12	1	9	26	8	24	.339	.542
Bats Right	R	.276	388	107	16	6	8	47	21	76	.337	.410
Bigbie, Larry	L	.324	71	23	2	0	1	7	8	11	.388	.394
Bats Left	R	.296	216	64	13	1	8	24	21	49	.357	.477
Biggio, Craig	L	.267	120	32	11	0	2	10	16	18	.367	.408
Bats Right	R	.264	508	134	33	2	13	52	41	98	.346	.413
Blake, Casey	L	.245	159	39	12	0	7	21	12	25	.307	.453
Bats Right	R	.261	398	104	23	0	10	46	26	84	.314	.394
Blalock, Hank	L	.209	139	29	3	0	3	11	7	32	.245	.295
Bats Left	R	.329	428	141	30	3	26	79	37	65	.382	.596
Blanco, Henry	L	.281	32	9	2	0	0	4	3	3	.343	.344
Bats Right	R	.176	119	21	6	0	1	9	7	18	.227	.252
Bloomquist, W	L	.242	91	22	6	1	0	3	9	15	.307	.330
Bats Right	R	.257	105	27	1	1	1	11	10	24	.325	.314
Blum, Geoff	L	.135	37	5	1	0	0	6	3	11	.200	.162
Bats Both	R	.274	383	105	18	0	10	46	17	39	.305	.399
Bocachica, H	L	.143	7	1	1	0	0	0	0	4	.143	.286
Bats Right	R	.000	15	0	0	0	0	0	0	3	.000	.000
Bonds, Barry	L	.363	124	45	5	0	16	30	36	22	.509	.790
Bats Left	R	.331	266	88	17	1	29	60	112	36	.537	.729
Boone, Aaron	L	.216	153	33	7	1	5	16	18	22	.306	.373
Bats Right	R	.285	439	125	25	2	19	80	28	82	.335	.481
Boone, Bret	L	.257	167	43	11	1	8	35	26	26	.352	.479
Bats Right	R	.308	455	140	24	4	27	82	42	99	.372	.556
Borchard, Joe	L	.176	17	3	0	0	0	1	0	9	.176	.176
Bats Both	R	.188	32	6	1	0	1	4	5	9	.275	.313
Borders, Pat	L	.333	3	1	1	0	0	1	0	0	.333	.667
Bats Right	R	.091	11	1	0	0	0	0	1	5	.167	.091
Bordick, Mike	L	.347	95	33	8	2	2	23	15	16	.441	.537
Bats Right	R	.246	248	61	10	0	3	31	18	44	.299	.323
Bowen, Rob	L	.500	2	1	0	0	0	0	0	0	.500	.500
Bats Both	R	.000	8	0	0	0	0	1	0	4	.000	.000

Batter	vs.	Avg.	AB	H	2B	3B	HR	RBI	BB	SO	OBP	Slg.
Bradley, M	L	.402	112	45	14	0	4	19	20	20	.500	.634
Bats Both	R	.287	265	76	20	2	6	37	44	53	.387	.445
Bragg, Darren	L	.292	48	14	2	1	0	3	5	9	.382	.375
Bats Left	R	.219	114	25	3	0	0	6	8	29	.270	.246
Branyan, R	L	.250	44	11	4	0	2	9	4	18	.306	.477
Bats Left	R	.205	132	27	8	0	7	17	23	51	.327	.424
Broussard, Ben	L	.175	103	18	2	1	2	12	10	22	.250	.272
Bats Left	R	.276	283	78	19	2	14	43	22	53	.335	.505
Brown, Adrian	L	.000	1	0	0	0	0	0	0	0	.000	.000
Bats Both	R	.214	14	3	0	0	0	1	1	4	.267	.214
Brown, Dee	L	.259	27	7	2	0	1	5	1	6	.310	.444
Bats Left	R	.219	105	23	5	0	1	9	7	31	.272	.295
Bruntlett, E	L	.190	21	4	0	0	0	1	0	5	.182	.190
Bats Right	R	.303	33	10	3	0	1	3	0	5	.303	.485
Buchanan, B	L	.302	106	32	6	0	6	18	21	27	.415	.528
Bats Right	R	.217	92	20	4	2	2	11	3	24	.255	.370
Budzinski, M	L	.000	0	0	0	0	0	0	0	0	.000	.000
Bats Left	R	.000	7	0	0	0	0	0	0	4	.000	.000
Burke, Jamie	L	.333	6	2	0	0	0	1	0	0	.333	.333
Bats Right	R	.500	2	1	0	0	0	1	0	0	.500	.500
Burkhart, M	L	.111	9	1	0	0	0	0	0	2	.111	.111
Bats Both	R	.333	6	2	0	0	0	1	1	0	.429	.333
Burks, Ellis	L	.322	59	19	4	1	3	11	13	8	.444	.576
Bats Right	R	.237	139	33	7	0	3	17	14	38	.321	.353
Burnitz, J	L	.250	136	34	3	0	8	24	7	39	.299	.449
Bats Left	R	.235	328	77	19	0	23	53	28	73	.299	.503
Burrell, Pat	L	.198	111	22	5	1	4	6	16	30	.305	.369
Bats Right	R	.212	411	87	26	3	17	58	56	112	.310	.414
Burroughs, S	L	.260	146	38	7	2	3	23	12	17	.335	.397
Bats Left	R	.296	371	110	20	4	4	35	32	58	.359	.404
Butler, Brent	L	.154	26	4	0	0	0	0	0	2	.154	.154
Bats Right	R	.234	64	15	3	1	1	4	7	11	.319	.359
Byrd, Marlon	L	.315	111	35	6	1	1	10	11	25	.381	.414
Bats Right	R	.299	384	115	22	3	6	35	33	69	.362	.419
Byrnes, Eric	L	.286	147	42	9	4	6	18	11	22	.340	.524
Bats Right	R	.251	267	67	18	5	6	33	31	49	.329	.423
Cabrera, J	L	.307	137	42	17	1	2	12	5	16	.336	.489
Bats Right	R	.267	210	56	15	1	4	25	12	46	.329	.405
Cabrera, M	L	.364	55	20	5	1	3	11	3	10	.397	.655
Bats Right	R	.247	259	64	16	2	9	51	22	74	.310	.429
Cabrera, O	L	.311	148	46	15	0	2	20	17	18	.376	.453
Bats Right	R	.293	478	140	32	2	15	60	35	46	.338	.462
Cairo, Miguel	L	.244	78	19	4	1	2	11	2	7	.253	.397
Bats Right	R	.246	183	45	11	1	3	21	11	23	.304	.366
Calloway, Ron	L	.169	59	10	1	0	1	7	4	27	.219	.237
Bats Left	R	.253	281	71	16	1	8	45	16	53	.296	.402
Cameron, Mike	L	.286	147	42	7	2	4	22	17	26	.365	.442
Bats Right	R	.240	387	93	24	3	14	54	53	111	.336	.426
Carroll, Jamey	L	.268	82	22	5	0	1	3	7	18	.326	.366
Bats Right	R	.255	145	37	5	1	0	7	12	21	.321	.303
Casey, Sean	L	.320	181	58	4	1	4	22	13	22	.367	.420
Bats Left	R	.278	392	109	15	2	10	58	38	36	.342	.403
Cash, Kevin	L	.100	30	3	1	0	1	3	1	7	.125	.233
Bats Right	R	.158	76	12	2	0	0	5	3	15	.200	.184
Castilla, V	L	.290	124	36	5	0	5	17	9	14	.333	.452
Bats Right	R	.273	418	114	23	3	17	59	17	72	.303	.464
Castillo, A	L	.500	2	1	0	0	1	4	0	0	.500	2.000
Bats Right	R	.154	13	2	1	0	0	0	0	5	.154	.231

Batter	vs.	Avg.	AB	H	2B	3B	HR	RBI	BB	SO	OBP	Slg.
Castillo, Luis	L	.320	172	55	8	2	6	13	19	13	.391	.494
Bats Both	R	.312	423	132	11	4	0	26	44	47	.377	.357
Castro, Juan	L	.193	88	17	4	0	0	2	11	17	.283	.239
Bats Right	R	.276	232	64	10	1	9	31	7	41	.293	.444
Castro, Ramon	L	.409	22	9	1	0	3	3	1	4	.435	.864
Bats Right	R	.194	31	6	1	0	2	5	3	7	.265	.419
Catalanotto, F	L	.176	68	12	3	1	1	6	7	13	.250	.294
Bats Left	R	.318	421	134	31	5	12	53	28	49	.368	.501
Cedeno, Roger	L	.241	108	26	4	2	3	12	9	23	.299	.398
Bats Both	R	.274	376	103	21	2	4	25	29	63	.326	.372
Cepicky, Matt	L	.000	0	0	0	0	0	0	0	0	.000	.000
Bats Left	R	.250	8	2	1	0	0	0	0	2	.250	.375
Chamblee, Jim	L	.000	1	0	0	0	0	0	0	1	.000	.000
Bats Right	R	.000	1	0	0	0	0	0	0	1	.000	.000
Chapman, T	L	.000	1	0	0	0	0	0	0	0	.000	.000
Bats Right	R	.000	0	0	0	0	0	0	0	0	.000	.000
Chavez, Endy	L	.304	92	28	8	0	0	13	10	7	.373	.391
Bats Left	R	.238	391	93	17	5	5	34	21	52	.275	.345
Chavez, Eric	L	.220	191	42	6	1	9	29	14	36	.271	.403
Bats Left	R	.312	397	124	33	4	20	72	48	53	.387	.567
Chavez, Raul	L	.429	14	6	1	1	0	2	1	3	.467	.643
Bats Right	R	.174	23	4	0	0	1	2	0	3	.174	.304
Chen, C	L	.000	0	0	0	0	0	0	0	0	.000	.000
Bats Right	R	.000	1	0	0	0	0	0	0	0	.000	.000
Choi, Hee Seop	L	.059	17	1	1	0	0	1	7	9	.360	.118
Bats Left	R	.232	185	43	16	0	8	27	30	62	.349	.449
Christenson, R	L	.109	55	6	2	0	0	5	5	15	.197	.145
Bats Right	R	.209	110	23	5	0	2	11	10	29	.285	.309
Cintron, Alex	L	.365	137	50	8	3	5	19	12	7	.418	.577
Bats Both	R	.296	311	92	18	3	8	32	17	26	.331	.450
Cirillo, Jeff	L	.227	88	20	3	0	1	6	9	7	.313	.295
Bats Right	R	.194	170	33	8	0	1	17	15	25	.268	.259
Clark, Brady	L	.263	114	30	7	1	3	14	7	11	.320	.421
Bats Right	R	.279	201	56	14	0	3	26	14	29	.335	.393
Clark, Howie	L	.000	1	0	0	0	0	0	0	1	.000	.000
Bats Left	R	.362	69	25	3	1	0	7	3	5	.405	.435
Clark, J	L	.000	0	0	0	0	0	0	0	0	.000	.000
Bats Left	R	.167	48	8	2	0	0	7	6	5	.250	.208
Clark, Tony	L	.279	68	19	3	0	4	10	7	19	.355	.500
Bats Both	R	.215	186	40	10	0	12	33	17	54	.279	.462
Clayton, Royce	L	.240	96	23	4	0	1	8	16	15	.348	.313
Bats Right	R	.225	387	87	12	1	10	31	33	77	.288	.339
Colbrunn, Greg	L	.250	48	12	1	1	3	6	3	13	.294	.500
Bats Right	R	.400	10	4	0	0	0	1	1	3	.455	.400
Collier, Lou	L	.000	1	0	0	0	0	0	0	0	.000	.000
Bats Right	R	.000	0	0	0	0	0	0	0	0	.000	.000
Conine, Jeff	L	.288	125	36	7	0	3	13	17	23	.368	.416
Bats Right	R	.281	452	127	29	3	17	82	33	47	.329	.471
Conti, Jason	L	.000	4	0	0	0	0	0	1	4	.200	.000
Bats Left	R	.250	44	11	2	0	2	7	1	14	.261	.432
Coomer, Ron	L	.355	62	22	4	0	4	11	3	5	.379	.613
Bats Right	R	.127	63	8	0	0	0	4	7	14	.225	.127
Cora, Alex	L	.308	65	20	3	2	0	5	2	7	.348	.415
Bats Left	R	.240	412	99	21	1	4	29	14	52	.278	.325
Cordero, Wil	L	.324	108	35	10	0	4	19	17	19	.421	.528
Bats Right	R	.262	328	86	17	0	12	52	32	71	.331	.424
Cordova, Marty	L	.375	8	3	1	0	0	0	3	0	.545	.500
Bats Right	R	.182	22	4	0	0	1	4	5	5	.357	.318

Batter	vs.	Avg.	AB	H	2B	3B	HR	RBI	BB	SO	OBP	Slg.
Cota, Humberto	L	.250	4	1	1	0	0	0	1	1	.400	.500
Bats Right	R	.250	12	3	0	0	0	1	0	4	.250	.250
Counsell, C	L	.219	73	16	1	0	1	8	7	10	.301	.274
Bats Left	R	.239	230	55	5	3	2	13	34	22	.336	.313
Crawford, Carl	L	.263	179	47	5	1	0	12	5	30	.283	.302
Bats Left	R	.288	451	130	13	8	5	42	21	72	.319	.386
Crede, Joe	L	.300	150	45	9	2	6	23	10	21	.344	.507
Bats Right	R	.246	386	95	22	0	13	52	22	54	.294	.404
Crisp, Coco	L	.321	112	36	4	2	0	8	5	15	.347	.393
Bats Both	R	.245	302	74	11	4	3	19	18	36	.286	.338
Cromer, Tripp	L	.000	0	0	0	0	0	0	0	0	.000	.000
Bats Right	R	.250	4	1	0	1	0	1	0	0	.250	.750
Crosby, Bobby	L	.000	6	0	0	0	0	0	0	2	.000	.000
Bats Right	R	.000	6	0	0	0	0	0	1	3	.250	.000
Crosby, Bubba	L	.000	0	0	0	0	0	0	0	0	.000	.000
Bats Left	R	.083	12	1	0	0	0	1	0	3	.083	.083
Cruz, Deivi	L	.286	140	40	5	0	7	23	6	11	.320	.471
Bats Right	R	.238	408	97	19	2	7	42	7	38	.251	.346
Cruz, Enrique	L	.000	11	0	0	0	0	0	1	3	.083	.000
Bats Right	R	.100	60	6	1	0	0	2	3	27	.156	.117
Cruz, Jose	L	.304	135	41	8	0	7	17	23	20	.405	.519
Bats Both	R	.233	404	94	18	1	13	51	79	101	.353	.379
Cuddyer, M	L	.220	41	9	0	0	1	2	6	6	.319	.293
Bats Right	R	.262	61	16	1	3	3	6	6	13	.328	.525
Cust, Jack	L	.364	11	4	1	0	0	0	0	2	.364	.455
Bats Left	R	.242	62	15	6	0	4	11	10	23	.356	.532
Damon, Johnny	L	.275	193	53	7	4	3	23	18	26	.333	.399
Bats Left	R	.272	415	113	25	2	9	44	50	48	.350	.407
Daubach, Brian	L	.188	16	3	1	0	1	3	0	6	.188	.438
Bats Left	R	.234	167	39	10	0	5	18	34	48	.365	.383
DaVanon, Jeff	L	.342	38	13	3	0	2	7	8	12	.457	.579
Bats Both	R	.274	292	80	13	1	10	36	34	47	.346	.428
Davis, Ben	L	.281	57	16	7	0	3	12	5	13	.333	.561
Bats Both	R	.222	189	42	11	0	3	30	13	48	.268	.328
Davis, J.J.	L	.211	19	4	0	0	1	2	3	8	.318	.368
Bats Right	R	.188	16	3	0	0	0	2	0	5	.188	.188
Dawkins, G	L	.000	0	0	0	0	0	0	1	0	1.000	.000
Bats Right	R	.000	2	0	0	0	0	0	0	2	.000	.000
DeJesus, David	L	.000	0	0	0	0	0	0	0	0	.000	.000
Bats Left	R	.286	7	2	0	1	0	0	1	2	.444	.571
Delgado, C	L	.284	183	52	14	0	7	46	29	48	.395	.475
Bats Left	R	.310	387	120	24	1	35	99	80	89	.439	.649
Delgado, W	L	.195	41	8	1	0	0	0	2	7	.233	.220
Bats Both	R	.244	86	21	2	0	0	7	9	11	.320	.267
Dellucci, D	L	.132	38	5	1	0	1	6	4	18	.227	.237
Bats Left	R	.247	178	44	11	3	2	17	19	40	.332	.376
DePastino, Joe	L	.000	0	0	0	0	0	0	0	0	.000	.000
Bats Right	R	.000	2	0	0	0	0	0	0	1	.000	.000
DeRosa, Mark	L	.277	83	23	4	0	3	12	5	10	.322	.434
Bats Right	R	.257	183	47	10	0	3	10	11	39	.313	.361
Diaz, Einar	L	.253	79	20	3	0	1	11	2	9	.274	.329
Bats Right	R	.259	255	66	11	1	3	24	7	23	.300	.345
Diaz, Matt	L	.000	3	0	0	0	0	0	1	2	.250	.000
Bats Right	R	.167	6	1	0	0	0	0	0	1	.167	.167
DiFelice, Mike	L	.313	64	20	7	1	1	7	5	9	.371	.500
Bats Right	R	.224	125	28	9	0	2	18	4	21	.261	.344
Drew, J.D.	L	.218	55	12	2	0	3	7	6	15	.306	.418
Bats Left	R	.306	232	71	11	3	12	35	30	33	.390	.534
Duncan, Jeff	L	.067	15	1	0	0	0	3	5	5	.333	.067
Bats Left	R	.210	124	26	0	2	1	7	12	36	.285	.266
Dunn, Adam	L	.202	119	24	3	0	9	25	19	41	.333	.454
Bats Left	R	.221	262	58	9	1	18	32	55	85	.363	.469
Durazo, E	L	.283	173	49	9	0	7	27	28	39	.380	.457
Bats Left	R	.247	364	90	20	0	14	50	72	66	.370	.418
Durham, Ray	L	.370	100	37	9	2	1	10	12	16	.439	.530
Bats Both	R	.258	310	80	21	3	7	23	38	66	.342	.413
Durrington, T	L	.000	2	0	0	0	0	1	3	0	.600	.000
Bats Right	R	.167	12	2	0	0	0	0	0	0	.167	.167
Dye, Jermaine	L	.260	50	13	1	0	2	5	9	9	.377	.400
Bats Right	R	.146	171	25	5	0	2	15	16	33	.224	.211
Easley, Damion	L	.184	38	7	1	1	0	1	0	5	.184	.263
Bats Right	R	.188	69	13	2	0	1	6	2	13	.211	.261
Eckstein, D	L	.256	133	34	6	0	2	12	8	13	.324	.346
Bats Right	R	.251	319	80	16	1	1	19	28	32	.326	.317
Edmonds, Jim	L	.225	111	25	6	0	11	22	15	39	.320	.577
Bats Left	R	.292	336	98	26	2	28	67	62	88	.405	.631
Edwards, Mike	L	.333	3	1	0	0	0	0	0	1	.333	.333
Bats Right	R	.000	1	0	0	0	0	0	2	0	.667	.000
Ellis, Mark	L	.217	152	33	11	1	2	13	13	20	.279	.342
Bats Right	R	.259	401	104	20	4	7	39	35	74	.326	.382
Ellison, Jason	L	.000	8	0	0	0	0	0	0	0	.000	.000
Bats Right	R	.500	2	1	0	0	0	0	0	1	.500	.500
Encarnacion, J	L	.267	116	31	8	1	2	19	11	13	.331	.456
Bats Right	R	.270	485	131	29	5	17	75	26	69	.309	.456
Ensberg, M	L	.316	98	31	6	0	7	20	19	15	.429	.592
Bats Right	R	.282	287	81	9	1	18	40	29	45	.358	.509
Erstad, Darin	L	.302	86	26	1	0	2	7	6	12	.362	.384
Bats Left	R	.227	172	39	6	1	2	10	12	28	.282	.308
Escalona, F	L	.250	4	1	0	0	0	0	0	1	.250	.250
Bats Right	R	.174	23	4	2	0	0	2	2	5	.240	.261
Escobar, Alex	L	.350	40	14	2	0	3	8	4	14	.413	.625
Bats Right	R	.220	59	13	0	0	2	6	3	19	.258	.322
Estalella, B	L	.294	17	5	1	0	3	8	1	6	.316	.882
Bats Right	R	.187	123	23	6	0	4	13	18	49	.292	.333
Estrada, J	L	.167	6	1	0	0	0	0	0	1	.167	.167
Bats Both	R	.333	30	10	0	0	0	2	0	2	.394	.333
Everett, Adam	L	.324	74	24	3	0	3	16	11	12	.425	.486
Bats Right	R	.240	313	75	15	3	5	35	17	54	.293	.355
Everett, Carl	L	.254	138	35	5	0	4	19	9	28	.320	.377
Bats Both	R	.299	388	116	22	3	24	73	44	56	.382	.557
Febles, Carlos	L	.333	63	21	3	0	0	6	6	7	.391	.381
Bats Right	R	.188	133	25	2	0	0	5	7	23	.255	.203
Feliz, Pedro	L	.231	52	12	2	0	4	14	3	12	.273	.365
Bats Right	R	.251	183	46	7	3	12	34	7	41	.280	.519
Fick, Robert	L	.135	52	7	1	0	2	8	3	12	.182	.269
Bats Left	R	.289	357	103	25	1	9	72	39	35	.356	.440
Figgins, Chone	L	.284	88	25	4	2	0	13	8	9	.340	.375
Bats Both	R	.303	152	46	5	2	0	14	12	29	.347	.362
Finley, Steve	L	.245	163	40	8	3	7	25	14	28	.309	.460
Bats Left	R	.306	353	108	16	7	15	45	43	66	.387	.518
Flaherty, John	L	.297	37	11	2	0	2	6	1	7	.316	.514
Bats Right	R	.250	68	17	6	0	2	8	3	12	.288	.426
Floyd, Cliff	L	.262	122	32	6	0	7	19	14	27	.340	.484
Bats Left	R	.305	243	74	19	2	11	49	37	39	.394	.535
Ford, Lew	L	.297	37	11	4	1	1	5	4	3	.366	.541
Bats Right	R	.361	36	13	3	0	2	10	4	6	.439	.611

Batter	vs.	Avg.	AB	H	2B	3B	HR	RBI	BB	SO	OBP	Slg.
Fordyce, Brook	L	.345	84	29	4	1	3	8	4	7	.371	.524
Bats Right	R	.250	264	66	8	1	3	23	15	37	.292	.322
Fox, Andy	L	.364	11	4	0	0	0	2	0	4	.364	.364
Bats Left	R	.175	97	17	5	1	0	6	7	25	.259	.247
Franco, Julio	L	.351	94	33	6	1	3	19	17	16	.446	.532
Bats Right	R	.243	103	25	6	1	2	12	8	27	.297	.379
Franco, Matt	L	.333	9	3	0	0	1	1	3	2	.500	.667
Bats Left	R	.240	125	30	5	0	2	14	8	24	.281	.328
Freel, Ryan	L	.326	43	14	2	0	4	5	3	2	.370	.651
Bats Right	R	.266	94	25	4	1	0	7	6	11	.333	.330
Fullmer, Brad	L	.267	30	8	1	0	1	6	2	4	.324	.400
Bats Left	R	.313	176	55	8	2	8	29	24	27	.398	.517
Furcal, Rafael	L	.247	154	38	14	0	5	18	19	21	.328	.435
Bats Both	R	.306	510	156	21	10	10	43	41	55	.359	.445
Galarraga, A	L	.309	94	29	4	0	7	17	8	15	.369	.574
Bats Right	R	.298	178	53	11	0	5	25	11	46	.342	.444
Gant, Ron	L	.185	27	5	0	0	1	2	1	3	.214	.296
Bats Right	R	.071	14	1	0	0	0	2	1	6	.125	.071
Garcia, Danny	L	.333	18	6	1	0	1	1	0	3	.333	.556
Bats Right	R	.158	38	6	1	0	1	5	2	8	.250	.263
Garcia, Jesse	L	.000	1	0	0	0	0	0	0	0	.000	.000
Bats Right	R	.444	9	4	0	1	0	2	0	1	.444	.667
Garcia, Karim	L	.164	55	9	1	0	1	3	1	15	.179	.236
Bats Left	R	.291	189	55	5	0	10	32	13	37	.335	.476
Garciaparra, N	L	.357	171	61	7	3	7	29	8	14	.390	.556
Bats Right	R	.281	487	137	30	10	21	76	31	47	.330	.513
German, E	L	.000	1	0	0	0	0	0	0	0	.000	.000
Bats Right	R	.333	3	1	0	0	0	1	0	1	.333	.333
Gerut, Jody	L	.209	134	28	5	0	3	14	7	30	.274	.313
Bats Left	R	.306	346	106	28	2	19	61	28	40	.360	.564
Giambi, Jason	L	.192	146	28	6	0	6	30	30	46	.362	.356
Bats Left	R	.272	389	106	19	0	35	77	99	94	.430	.591
Giambi, Jeremy	L	.125	24	3	1	0	0	2	2	12	.192	.167
Bats Left	R	.214	103	22	4	0	5	13	24	30	.372	.398
Gibbons, Jay	L	.273	187	51	10	0	5	19	12	34	.320	.406
Bats Left	R	.279	438	122	29	2	18	81	37	55	.334	.477
Gil, Benji	L	.177	79	14	5	1	0	5	3	17	.202	.266
Bats Right	R	.217	46	10	0	0	1	4	1	16	.234	.283
Gil, Geronimo	L	.293	41	12	1	0	0	6	3	6	.341	.317
Bats Right	R	.219	128	28	3	0	3	10	9	28	.286	.313
Giles, Brian	L	.286	161	46	11	4	3	31	33	21	.416	.460
Bats Left	R	.305	331	101	23	2	17	57	72	37	.432	.541
Giles, Marcus	L	.283	127	36	4	0	8	20	15	17	.361	.504
Bats Right	R	.325	424	138	45	2	13	49	44	63	.399	.533
Ginter, Keith	L	.224	85	19	3	0	4	6	13	23	.340	.400
Bats Right	R	.267	273	73	12	2	10	38	24	64	.356	.436
Gipson, C	L	.000	3	0	0	0	0	1	1	1	.250	.000
Bats Right	R	.286	7	2	0	0	0	1	0	1	.286	.286
Girardi, Joe	L	.000	4	0	0	0	0	0	1	1	.200	.000
Bats Right	R	.158	19	3	0	0	0	1	2	3	.238	.158
Glanville, D	L	.280	93	26	3	0	1	7	4	8	.306	.344
Bats Right	R	.255	153	39	2	0	4	9	4	21	.274	.346
Glaus, Troy	L	.303	89	27	6	1	2	10	16	18	.410	.461
Bats Right	R	.226	230	52	11	1	14	40	30	55	.317	.465
Glavine, Mike	L	.000	0	0	0	0	0	0	0	0	.000	.000
Bats Left	R	.143	7	1	0	0	0	0	0	2	.143	.143
Gomes, Jonny	L	.250	8	2	1	0	0	0	0	2	.333	.375
Bats Right	R	.000	7	0	0	0	0	0	0	4	.000	.000

Batter	vs.	Avg.	AB	H	2B	3B	HR	RBI	BB	SO	OBP	Slg.
Gomez, Chris	L	.250	56	14	4	1	1	7	2	4	.276	.411
Bats Right	R	.252	119	30	5	2	0	8	5	9	.280	.328
Gonzalez, Alex	L	.274	113	31	9	2	4	18	8	19	.333	.496
Bats Right	R	.251	415	104	24	4	14	59	25	87	.307	.429
Gonzalez, Alex S.	L	.228	123	28	10	0	3	11	13	27	.301	.382
Bats Right	R	.228	413	94	27	0	17	48	34	96	.293	.416
Gonzalez, Juan	L	.273	99	27	4	0	4	8	7	16	.321	.434
Bats Right	R	.303	228	69	13	1	20	62	7	57	.333	.632
Gonzalez, Luis	L	.223	220	49	9	3	8	30	24	36	.302	.400
Bats Left	R	.354	359	127	37	1	18	74	70	31	.459	.613
Gonzalez, Raul	L	.240	96	23	6	0	0	7	7	12	.291	.302
Bats Right	R	.223	121	27	6	2	2	14	20	22	.336	.355
Gonzalez, Wiki	L	.214	14	3	1	0	0	4	3	2	.333	.286
Bats Right	R	.196	51	10	4	0	0	6	2	11	.241	.275
Goodwin, Tom	L	.238	42	10	1	0	1	3	2	12	.273	.333
Bats Left	R	.302	129	39	9	0	0	9	9	21	.345	.372
Grabowski, J	L	.000	0	0	0	0	0	0	0	0	.000	.000
Bats Left	R	.000	8	0	0	0	0	0	1	5	.111	.000
Grace, Mark	L	.217	23	5	2	0	0	0	6	1	.379	.304
Bats Left	R	.196	112	22	3	0	3	16	10	14	.256	.304
Graffanino, T	L	.303	165	50	14	3	6	21	14	20	.356	.533
Bats Right	R	.176	85	15	1	0	1	2	10	17	.286	.224
Green, Shawn	L	.252	214	54	17	1	8	41	18	43	.319	.453
Bats Left	R	.295	397	117	32	1	11	44	50	69	.373	.463
Greene, Khalil	L	.318	22	7	1	1	0	1	2	5	.375	.455
Bats Right	R	.163	43	7	3	0	2	5	2	14	.217	.372
Greene, Todd	L	.211	76	16	2	1	3	6	1	10	.231	.382
Bats Right	R	.240	129	31	8	0	7	14	1	37	.250	.465
Gregorio, Tom	L	.000	1	0	0	0	0	0	0	0	.500	.000
Bats Right	R	.167	18	3	0	0	0	2	1	8	.211	.167
Grieve, Ben	L	.208	53	11	3	0	0	7	8	13	.348	.264
Bats Left	R	.241	112	27	4	0	4	10	24	28	.381	.384
Griffey Jr., K	L	.250	56	14	4	0	4	7	11	14	.400	.536
Bats Left	R	.245	110	27	8	1	9	19	16	30	.354	.582
Grissom, M	L	.364	140	51	12	1	9	25	8	12	.399	.657
Bats Right	R	.280	447	125	21	2	11	54	12	70	.298	.409
Grudzielanek, M	L	.360	100	36	11	0	0	4	15	14	.444	.470
Bats Right	R	.302	381	115	27	1	3	34	15	50	.344	.402
Guerrero, V	L	.393	84	33	6	1	9	22	15	9	.485	.810
Bats Right	R	.313	310	97	14	2	16	57	48	44	.410	.526
Guiel, Aaron	L	.275	102	28	9	0	2	15	10	25	.358	.422
Bats Right	R	.278	252	70	21	0	13	37	17	38	.341	.516
Guillen, C	L	.265	113	30	4	1	2	15	10	18	.323	.372
Bats Both	R	.280	275	77	15	2	5	37	42	46	.373	.404
Guillen, Jose	L	.315	130	41	10	0	7	20	8	26	.371	.554
Bats Right	R	.310	355	110	18	2	24	66	16	69	.355	.575
Gutierrez, R	L	.313	16	5	0	0	0	0	0	0	.313	.313
Bats Right	R	.235	34	8	3	0	0	3	3	5	.308	.324
Guzman, C	L	.250	164	41	9	2	1	14	12	23	.302	.348
Bats Both	R	.276	370	102	6	12	2	39	18	56	.315	.373
Guzman, E	L	.200	25	5	0	0	0	3	1	4	.231	.200
Bats Left	R	.248	121	30	5	0	1	11	4	13	.270	.314
Hafner, Travis	L	.190	84	16	7	0	2	12	8	29	.284	.345
Bats Left	R	.280	207	58	12	3	12	28	14	52	.345	.541
Hairston Jr., J	L	.255	55	14	5	0	0	7	5	3	.311	.345
Bats Right	R	.276	163	45	7	2	2	14	18	22	.367	.380
Hall, Bill	L	.185	27	5	1	0	0	1	4	9	.290	.222
Bats Right	R	.278	115	32	8	2	5	19	3	19	.300	.513

Batter	vs.	Avg.	AB	H	2B	3B	HR	RBI	BB	SO	OBP	Slg.
Hall, Toby	L	.253	150	38	9	0	3	11	12	8	.307	.373
Bats Right	R	.252	313	79	14	0	9	36	11	32	.290	.383
Halter, Shane	L	.243	152	37	3	1	6	15	15	30	.310	.395
Bats Right	R	.197	208	41	2	1	6	15	12	47	.239	.303
Hammock, R	L	.308	78	24	4	2	2	10	5	10	.345	.487
Bats Right	R	.265	117	31	6	0	6	18	12	34	.341	.470
Hammonds, J	L	.360	25	9	1	0	0	0	3	5	.429	.400
Bats Right	R	.215	107	23	11	0	4	13	13	23	.306	.430
Hansen, Dave	L	.500	6	3	0	0	1	2	3	1	.667	1.000
Bats Left	R	.233	129	30	4	1	1	13	20	24	.340	.302
Harris, Lenny	L	.050	20	1	0	0	0	1	2	5	.130	.050
Bats Left	R	.216	125	27	3	0	1	7	14	16	.295	.264
Harris, Willie	L	.105	19	2	0	0	0	0	1	8	.150	.105
Bats Left	R	.220	118	26	3	1	0	5	9	20	.276	.263
Hart, Bo	L	.300	90	27	6	3	0	8	6	19	.344	.433
Bats Right	R	.267	206	55	7	2	4	20	6	45	.306	.379
Harvey, Ken	L	.333	156	52	15	0	7	27	10	22	.377	.564
Bats Right	R	.234	329	77	15	0	6	37	19	72	.282	.334
Haselman, Bill	L	.000	0	0	0	0	0	0	0	0	.000	.000
Bats Right	R	.000	3	0	0	0	0	0	0	1	.000	.000
Hatteberg, S	L	.255	149	38	10	0	2	15	15	18	.351	.362
Bats Left	R	.253	392	99	24	0	10	46	51	35	.339	.390
Helms, Wes	L	.314	86	27	5	0	6	18	16	24	.425	.581
Bats Right	R	.249	390	97	16	0	17	49	27	107	.307	.421
Helton, Todd	L	.387	199	77	17	2	10	49	34	24	.470	.643
Bats Left	R	.344	384	132	32	3	23	68	77	48	.452	.622
Henderson, R	L	.167	36	6	1	0	0	1	8	8	.333	.194
Bats Right	R	.250	36	9	0	0	2	4	3	8	.308	.417
Henson, Drew	L	.250	4	1	0	0	0	0	0	1	.250	.250
Bats Right	R	.000	4	0	0	0	0	0	0	1	.000	.000
Hermansen, C	L	.000	3	0	0	0	0	0	1	3	.250	.000
Bats Right	R	.182	22	4	1	0	0	2	1	6	.217	.227
Hernandez, J	L	.235	153	36	4	2	9	29	14	54	.299	.464
Bats Right	R	.221	366	81	14	1	4	28	32	123	.282	.298
Hernandez, M	L	.000	0	0	0	0	0	0	1	0	1.000	.000
Bats Right	R	.250	4	1	0	0	0	0	0	1	.250	.250
Hernandez, R	L	.208	149	31	5	1	6	13	8	20	.255	.376
Bats Right	R	.302	334	101	19	0	15	65	25	59	.365	.494
Hessman, Mike	L	.333	12	4	2	0	1	1	3	2	.467	.750
Bats Right	R	.222	9	2	0	0	1	2	2	4	.364	.556
Hidalgo, R	L	.307	88	27	4	0	7	14	14	26	.394	.591
Bats Right	R	.310	426	132	39	4	21	74	44	78	.383	.568
Higginson, B	L	.227	154	35	6	1	3	19	18	29	.305	.338
Bats Left	R	.238	315	75	7	3	11	33	41	44	.328	.384
Hill, Bobby	L	.250	4	1	0	0	0	0	2	1	.500	.250
Bats Both	R	.333	3	1	0	0	0	0	0	1	.333	.333
Hill, Koyie	L	.000	1	0	0	0	0	0	0	1	.000	.000
Bats Both	R	.500	2	1	1	0	0	0	0	1	.500	1.000
Hillenbrand, S	L	.298	161	48	12	1	6	32	9	22	.331	.497
Bats Right	R	.271	354	96	23	0	14	65	15	48	.306	.455
Hinch, A.J.	L	.190	21	4	1	0	0	2	0	3	.217	.238
Bats Right	R	.208	53	11	2	1	3	9	3	15	.259	.453
Hinske, Eric	L	.256	133	34	18	0	2	26	11	36	.309	.436
Bats Left	R	.237	316	75	27	3	10	37	48	68	.337	.437
Hocking, Denny	L	.172	64	11	4	0	1	4	2	16	.197	.281
Bats Both	R	.274	124	34	6	2	2	18	13	21	.336	.403
Hollandsworth, T	L	.250	32	8	2	1	0	1	2	14	.294	.375
Bats Left	R	.255	196	50	21	2	3	19	20	41	.321	.429

Batter	vs.	Avg.	AB	H	2B	3B	HR	RBI	BB	SO	OBP	Slg.
House, J.R.	L	.000	0	0	0	0	0	0	0	0	.000	.000
Bats Right	R	1.000	1	1	0	0	0	0	0	0	1.000	1.000
Houston, Tyler	L	.333	3	1	0	0	0	1	0	2	.333	.333
Bats Left	R	.277	94	26	6	0	2	13	6	17	.320	.404
Hubbard, T	L	.333	12	4	1	0	0	2	3	1	.467	.417
Bats Right	R	.000	4	0	0	0	0	0	1	2	.333	.000
Huckaby, Ken	L	.333	3	1	0	0	0	0	0	0	.333	.333
Bats Right	R	.125	8	1	1	0	0	2	0	2	.125	.250
Hudson, O	L	.160	100	16	3	0	0	4	8	19	.222	.190
Bats Both	R	.297	374	111	18	6	9	53	31	68	.356	.449
Huff, Aubrey	L	.318	220	70	12	1	7	29	11	30	.353	.477
Bats Left	R	.308	416	128	35	2	27	78	42	50	.374	.596
Hummel, Tim	L	.259	27	7	1	0	2	4	5	4	.375	.519
Bats Right	R	.211	57	12	4	0	0	6	3	9	.246	.281
Hundley, Todd	L	.000	6	0	0	0	0	0	1	3	.143	.000
Bats Both	R	.222	27	6	1	0	2	11	7	10	.382	.481
Hunter, B	L	.263	38	10	0	0	0	5	2	9	.310	.263
Bats Right	R	.217	60	13	6	1	0	8	4	12	.258	.350
Hunter, Torii	L	.251	167	42	6	2	9	35	21	28	.330	.473
Bats Right	R	.249	414	103	25	2	17	67	29	78	.304	.442
Hyzdu, Adam	L	.188	32	6	2	0	1	5	6	9	.308	.344
Bats Right	R	.226	31	7	3	0	0	3	4	12	.333	.323
Ibanez, Raul	L	.245	204	50	7	1	7	29	11	33	.291	.392
Bats Left	R	.319	404	129	26	4	11	61	38	48	.371	.485
Infante, Omar	L	.155	71	11	2	1	0	3	5	10	.208	.211
Bats Right	R	.253	150	38	4	0	0	5	13	27	.311	.280
Inge, Brandon	L	.245	110	27	6	1	5	12	10	24	.306	.455
Bats Right	R	.182	220	40	9	2	3	18	14	55	.245	.282
Izturis, Cesar	L	.263	156	41	8	3	0	12	3	14	.275	.353
Bats Both	R	.246	402	99	13	3	1	28	22	56	.284	.301
Jackson, D	L	.241	87	21	4	0	0	7	3	14	.264	.287
Bats Right	R	.284	74	21	3	0	1	6	5	14	.329	.365
Jenkins, Geoff	L	.270	159	43	8	0	4	22	10	48	.322	.396
Bats Left	R	.308	328	101	22	2	24	73	48	72	.400	.607
Jeter, Derek	L	.370	100	37	4	0	3	13	10	14	.442	.500
Bats Right	R	.312	382	119	21	3	7	39	33	74	.380	.437
Jimenez, D	L	.273	154	42	6	1	2	12	18	15	.345	.364
Bats Both	R	.273	407	111	18	6	12	45	48	74	.351	.435
Johnson, C	L	.250	96	24	5	0	2	10	20	19	.381	.365
Bats Right	R	.223	260	58	15	0	18	51	29	65	.295	.488
Johnson, Gary	L	.000	0	0	0	0	0	0	0	0	.000	.000
Bats Left	R	.375	8	3	1	0	0	0	1	1	.444	.500
Johnson, Mark	L	.500	2	1	0	0	0	0	0	1	.667	.500
Bats Left	R	.080	25	2	1	0	0	3	2	3	.172	.120
Johnson, Nick	L	.282	71	20	5	0	2	9	10	15	.393	.437
Bats Left	R	.285	253	72	14	0	12	38	60	42	.429	.482
Johnson, Reed	L	.328	122	40	10	0	5	17	6	14	.366	.533
Bats Right	R	.279	290	81	11	2	5	35	14	53	.348	.383
Johnson, Ron.	L	.000	1	0	0	0	0	0	0	1	.000	.000
Bats Right	R	.500	2	1	0	0	0	0	0	1	.500	.500
Jones, Andruw	L	.260	131	34	7	0	11	27	13	24	.329	.565
Bats Right	R	.282	464	131	21	2	25	89	40	101	.341	.498
Jones, Chipper	L	.306	121	37	3	0	2	18	25	17	.425	.380
Bats Both	R	.304	434	132	30	2	25	88	69	66	.396	.555
Jones, Jacque	L	.269	145	39	12	0	2	14	6	41	.310	.393
Bats Left	R	.317	372	118	21	1	14	55	15	64	.342	.492
Jones, Jason	L	.182	22	4	1	0	1	2	2	2	.240	.364
Bats Both	R	.224	85	19	5	0	2	9	8	19	.313	.353

Batter	vs.	Avg.	AB	H	2B	3B	HR	RBI	BB	SO	OBP	Slg.
Jordan, Brian	L	.397	58	23	2	0	4	12	12	5	.493	.638
Bats Right	R	.265	166	44	7	0	2	16	11	25	.324	.343
Jose, Felix	L	.400	5	2	1	0	0	3	2	1	.571	.600
Bats Both	R	.308	13	4	0	0	1	3	4	2	.471	.538
Kapler, Gabe	L	.326	92	30	9	1	0	6	9	13	.386	.446
Bats Right	R	.233	133	31	4	0	4	21	13	28	.301	.353
Karros, Eric	L	.366	112	41	9	1	3	10	15	11	.441	.545
Bats Right	R	.246	224	55	7	0	9	30	13	35	.286	.397
Kata, Matt	L	.299	97	29	7	1	4	15	6	15	.333	.515
Bats Both	R	.236	191	45	9	4	3	14	19	38	.307	.372
Kearns, Austin	L	.266	79	21	2	0	1	8	11	17	.356	.329
Bats Right	R	.263	213	56	9	0	14	50	30	51	.367	.502
Kelton, David	L	.125	8	1	0	0	0	0	0	4	.125	.125
Bats Right	R	.250	4	1	1	0	0	1	0	1	.250	.500
Kendall, Jason	L	.310	158	49	11	0	1	14	12	11	.376	.399
Bats Right	R	.331	429	142	18	3	5	44	37	29	.407	.422
Kennedy, Adam	L	.235	115	27	3	0	2	13	5	23	.268	.313
Bats Left	R	.281	334	94	14	1	11	36	40	50	.369	.428
Kent, Jeff	L	.361	97	35	12	1	2	17	11	12	.422	.567
Bats Right	R	.282	408	115	27	0	20	76	28	73	.334	.495
Kielty, Bobby	L	.300	140	42	11	0	8	27	24	20	.417	.550
Bats Both	R	.216	287	62	15	1	5	30	47	72	.328	.328
Kingsale, Gene	L	.270	37	10	3	0	0	3	2	6	.293	.351
Bats Both	R	.181	83	15	0	1	1	5	8	11	.253	.241
Kinkade, Mike	L	.370	54	20	6	0	3	10	5	11	.507	.648
Bats Right	R	.139	108	15	1	0	2	4	8	27	.238	.204
Klassen, Danny	L	.281	32	9	1	0	1	5	2	12	.324	.406
Bats Right	R	.220	41	9	2	1	0	2	2	14	.256	.317
Klesko, Ryan	L	.194	103	20	3	0	4	11	10	28	.270	.340
Bats Left	R	.272	294	80	15	0	17	56	55	55	.382	.497
Konerko, Paul	L	.327	150	49	10	0	10	28	11	10	.373	.593
Bats Right	R	.187	294	55	9	0	8	37	32	40	.272	.299
Koonce, Graham	L	.000	3	0	0	0	0	0	0	2	.000	.000
Bats Left	R	.200	5	1	1	0	0	0	0	4	.200	.400
Koskie, Corey	L	.224	170	38	9	0	3	20	17	46	.306	.329
Bats Left	R	.331	299	99	20	2	11	49	60	67	.440	.522
Kotsay, Mark	L	.236	140	33	6	2	1	9	16	20	.316	.329
Bats Left	R	.278	342	95	22	2	6	29	40	62	.353	.406
Kreuter, Chad	L	.000	1	0	0	0	0	0	0	0	.000	.000
Bats Both	R	.118	17	2	1	0	0	0	3	2	.250	.176
LaForest, Pete	L	.000	0	0	0	0	0	0	0	0	.000	.000
Bats Left	R	.167	48	8	2	0	0	6	1	14	.196	.208
Laird, Gerald	L	.294	17	5	1	1	0	2	1	4	.333	.471
Bats Right	R	.259	27	7	1	0	1	2	4	7	.375	.407
Laker, Tim	L	.189	53	10	1	0	1	6	4	12	.246	.264
Bats Right	R	.266	109	29	10	0	2	15	5	26	.298	.413
Lamb, Mike	L	.000	2	0	0	0	0	0	0	0	.000	.000
Bats Left	R	.139	36	5	0	0	0	2	2	6	.200	.139
Lane, Jason	L	.273	11	3	1	0	1	4	0	1	.273	.636
Bats Right	R	.313	16	5	1	0	3	6	0	1	.313	.938
Langerhans, R	L	.400	5	2	0	0	0	0	0	2	.400	.400
Bats Left	R	.200	10	2	0	0	0	0	0	4	.200	.200
Larkin, Barry	L	.200	60	12	4	1	0	3	10	6	.314	.300
Bats Right	R	.309	181	56	12	0	2	15	12	26	.356	.409
LaRocca, Greg	L	.200	5	1	1	0	0	0	1	1	.333	.400
Bats Right	R	.500	4	2	0	0	0	0	0	0	.500	.500
Larson, B	L	.143	28	4	1	0	0	3	4	7	.242	.179
Bats Right	R	.082	61	5	0	0	1	6	9	24	.197	.131

Batter	vs.	Avg.	AB	H	2B	3B	HR	RBI	BB	SO	OBP	Slg.
LaRue, Jason	L	.210	105	22	6	0	4	16	12	31	.288	.381
Bats Right	R	.237	274	65	17	1	12	34	21	80	.333	.438
Latham, Chris	L	.000	0	0	0	0	0	0	0	0	.000	.000
Bats Both	R	1.000	2	2	0	0	0	0	0	0	1.000	1.000
Lawton, Matt	L	.183	93	17	3	0	3	15	8	8	.269	.312
Bats Left	R	.270	281	76	16	0	12	38	39	39	.366	.456
LeCroy, M	L	.298	131	39	6	0	7	20	14	35	.370	.504
Bats Right	R	.280	214	60	13	0	10	44	11	47	.325	.481
Ledee, Ricky	L	.250	20	5	1	0	0	4	3	5	.348	.300
Bats Left	R	.247	235	58	14	2	13	42	31	54	.333	.489
Lee, Carlos	L	.218	165	36	8	0	5	20	11	25	.274	.358
Bats Right	R	.317	458	145	27	1	26	93	26	66	.352	.550
Lee, Derrek	L	.333	105	35	8	1	6	23	25	24	.462	.600
Bats Right	R	.256	434	111	23	1	25	69	63	107	.358	.486
Lee, Travis	L	.285	193	55	15	2	3	25	10	42	.316	.430
Bats Left	R	.269	349	94	22	1	16	45	54	55	.365	.476
Leon, Jose	L	.286	35	10	1	0	0	0	2	8	.342	.314
Bats Right	R	.158	19	3	0	0	0	0	1	10	.238	.158
Lieberthal, M	L	.319	116	37	7	0	1	12	10	9	.378	.405
Bats Right	R	.311	392	122	23	1	12	69	28	50	.371	.467
Liefer, Jeff	L	.125	16	2	1	0	0	4	0	4	.125	.188
Bats Left	R	.186	97	18	3	0	4	17	6	35	.231	.340
Linden, Todd	L	.667	3	2	0	0	1	3	1	0	.750	1.667
Bats Both	R	.171	35	6	1	0	0	3	0	8	.171	.200
Lockhart, K	L	.100	10	1	0	1	0	0	3	2	.308	.300
Bats Left	R	.259	85	22	5	0	3	8	10	17	.344	.424
Lo Duca, Paul	L	.281	153	43	9	1	3	13	15	12	.357	.412
Bats Right	R	.270	415	112	25	1	4	39	29	42	.327	.364
Lofton, Kenny	L	.244	135	33	7	3	1	11	5	17	.283	.363
Bats Left	R	.313	412	129	25	5	11	35	41	34	.373	.478
Lombard, G	L	.000	4	0	0	0	0	0	0	2	.000	.000
Bats Left	R	.242	33	8	1	0	1	4	0	4	.265	.364
Long, Terrence	L	.236	140	33	7	0	2	16	5	29	.270	.329
Bats Left	R	.249	346	86	15	2	12	45	26	38	.302	.408
Lopez, Felipe	L	.196	51	10	0	1	0	0	8	17	.305	.235
Bats Both	R	.219	146	32	7	1	2	13	20	42	.315	.322
Lopez, Javy	L	.336	110	37	9	0	11	30	6	22	.373	.718
Bats Right	R	.326	347	113	20	3	32	79	27	68	.379	.677
Lopez, Mendy	L	.316	38	12	1	1	0	4	3	9	.366	.395
Bats Right	R	.250	56	14	4	0	3	7	1	19	.263	.482
Loretta, Mark	L	.307	189	58	9	3	4	20	27	14	.394	.450
Bats Right	R	.318	400	127	19	1	9	52	27	48	.361	.438
Lowell, Mike	L	.295	112	33	8	0	12	35	12	14	.363	.688
Bats Right	R	.271	380	103	19	1	20	70	44	64	.346	.484
Ludwick, Ryan	L	.220	59	13	3	0	4	8	4	21	.270	.475
Bats Right	R	.262	103	27	5	1	3	18	8	27	.315	.417
Lugo, Julio	L	.240	146	35	4	2	5	12	11	33	.304	.397
Bats Right	R	.284	352	100	12	2	10	43	33	67	.345	.415
Lunsford, Trey	L	.000	1	0	0	0	0	0	0	0	.000	.000
Bats Right	R	.000	0	0	0	0	0	0	0	0	.000	.000
Mabry, John	L	.000	6	0	0	0	0	0	0	1	.143	.000
Bats Left	R	.224	98	22	6	0	3	16	15	20	.339	.378
Machado, Andy	L	.000	0	0	0	0	0	0	0	0	.000	.000
Bats Both	R	.000	0	0	0	0	0	0	0	0	.000	.000
Machado, R	L	.600	10	6	0	0	1	3	2	1	.667	.900
Bats Right	R	.179	39	7	1	0	0	0	4	11	.256	.205
Macias, Jose	L	.250	112	28	7	0	2	11	2	15	.270	.366
Bats Both	R	.231	160	37	8	2	2	11	9	30	.275	.344

Batter	vs.	Avg.	AB	H	2B	3B	HR	RBI	BB	SO	OBP	Slg.
Mackowiak, Rob	L	.257	35	9	0	2	1	2	0	7	.257	.457
Bats Left	R	.273	139	38	4	2	5	17	15	46	.361	.439
Magruder, C	L	.400	5	2	0	1	1	1	0	1	.400	1.400
Bats Both	R	.333	21	7	2	0	0	2	3	5	.440	.429
Marrero, Eli	L	.231	26	6	1	1	0	4	3	3	.310	.346
Bats Right	R	.222	81	18	3	1	2	16	4	15	.253	.358
Martin, Al	L	.333	6	2	0	0	0	0	2	3	.500	.333
Bats Left	R	.250	232	58	12	2	3	26	15	48	.300	.358
Martinez, E	L	.301	123	37	10	0	8	32	37	19	.457	.577
Bats Right	R	.291	374	109	15	0	16	66	55	76	.388	.460
Martinez, R	L	.346	81	28	6	0	2	14	8	16	.391	.494
Bats Right	R	.259	212	55	10	1	1	20	16	34	.311	.330
Martinez, Tino	L	.235	81	19	3	0	2	12	10	15	.323	.346
Bats Left	R	.281	395	111	22	2	13	57	43	56	.358	.446
Martinez, V	L	.271	59	16	1	0	1	8	6	9	.333	.339
Bats Both	R	.300	100	30	3	0	0	8	7	12	.352	.330
Mateo, Henry	L	.241	58	14	3	1	0	3	0	10	.254	.328
Bats Both	R	.240	96	23	0	0	0	4	11	28	.330	.240
Mateo, Ruben	L	.257	74	19	2	0	1	9	5	24	.296	.324
Bats Right	R	.233	133	31	7	0	2	9	7	29	.287	.331
Matheny, Mike	L	.340	100	34	5	0	3	15	9	13	.384	.480
Bats Right	R	.226	341	77	13	2	5	32	35	68	.302	.320
Matos, Julius	L	.421	19	8	0	0	1	4	0	1	.421	.579
Bats Right	R	.184	38	7	1	0	1	3	1	11	.205	.289
Matos, Luis	L	.269	108	29	5	1	1	9	10	21	.336	.361
Bats Right	R	.314	331	104	18	2	12	36	18	69	.359	.489
Matranga, Dave	L	.000	1	0	0	0	0	0	0	1	.000	.000
Bats Right	R	.250	4	1	0	0	1	1	0	1	.250	1.000
Matsui, Hideki	L	.287	195	56	9	0	3	24	13	31	.335	.379
Bats Left	R	.287	428	123	33	1	13	82	50	55	.360	.460
Matthews Jr., G	L	.287	129	37	14	1	1	9	9	28	.343	.434
Bats Both	R	.233	339	79	17	1	5	33	34	67	.303	.333
Mayne, Brent	L	.236	106	25	2	0	3	13	8	26	.291	.340
Bats Left	R	.248	266	66	15	1	3	23	24	33	.314	.346
McCarty, Dave	L	.400	25	10	3	0	1	5	2	6	.444	.640
Bats Right	R	.286	28	8	2	0	0	3	1	8	.300	.357
McCracken, Q	L	.215	79	17	2	0	0	5	4	17	.247	.241
Bats Both	R	.234	124	29	3	2	0	13	11	17	.294	.290
McDonald, John	L	.215	65	14	1	0	0	4	2	7	.246	.231
Bats Right	R	.215	149	32	8	1	1	10	9	24	.263	.302
McEwing, Joe	L	.247	77	19	3	0	0	8	10	17	.330	.286
Bats Right	R	.239	201	48	8	0	1	8	15	40	.301	.294
McGriff, Fred	L	.194	93	18	4	0	5	11	3	22	.219	.398
Bats Left	R	.275	204	56	10	0	8	29	28	44	.365	.441
McLemore, M	L	.433	30	13	3	0	0	8	6	5	.541	.533
Bats Both	R	.211	279	59	12	2	2	29	32	66	.292	.290
McMillon, B	L	.118	17	2	0	0	1	1	0	8	.118	.294
Bats Left	R	.287	136	39	11	0	5	25	19	28	.380	.478
Melhuse, Adam	L	.333	24	8	3	0	2	3	0	6	.333	.708
Bats Both	R	.283	53	15	4	0	3	11	9	13	.387	.528
Meluskey, M	L	1.000	1	1	1	0	0	1	0	0	1.000	2.000
Bats Both	R	.000	8	0	0	0	0	1	2	2	.182	.000
Mench, Kevin	L	.346	52	18	4	0	1	2	2	3	.370	.481
Bats Right	R	.301	73	22	8	0	1	9	8	14	.388	.452
Mendez, Carlos	L	.350	20	7	0	0	0	5	0	3	.333	.350
Bats Right	R	.120	25	3	2	0	0	0	0	9	.120	.200
Mendez, D	L	.176	17	3	2	0	0	1	2	5	.300	.294
Bats Right	R	.239	67	16	4	0	2	8	5	27	.297	.388
Menechino, F	L	.250	36	9	0	0	2	3	7	6	.386	.417
Bats Right	R	.149	47	7	0	0	0	6	12	10	.349	.149
Merced, O	L	.296	27	8	2	0	1	6	0	7	.296	.481
Bats Left	R	.222	185	41	15	2	2	20	15	26	.281	.357
Merloni, Lou	L	.196	92	18	2	1	1	8	15	20	.308	.272
Bats Right	R	.337	89	30	6	1	0	10	11	21	.404	.427
Meyers, Chad	L	.000	0	0	0	0	0	0	0	0	.000	.000
Bats Right	R	.000	1	0	0	0	0	0	0	0	.000	.000
Michaels, J	L	.382	55	21	6	0	3	12	10	11	.477	.655
Bats Right	R	.278	54	15	5	0	2	5	5	11	.350	.481
Mientkiewicz, D	L	.280	168	47	10	0	8	26	20	20	.363	.482
Bats Left	R	.310	319	99	28	1	3	39	54	35	.408	.433
Miles, Aaron	L	.667	3	2	1	0	0	0	0	0	.667	1.000
Bats Both	R	.222	9	2	2	0	0	2	0	0	.222	.444
Millar, Kevin	L	.289	149	43	9	0	5	25	20	24	.370	.450
Bats Right	R	.271	395	107	21	1	20	71	40	84	.339	.481
Miller, Corky	L	.250	4	1	0	0	0	0	1	1	.400	.250
Bats Right	R	.269	26	7	0	0	0	1	4	6	.394	.269
Miller, Damian	L	.248	109	27	8	0	0	9	14	17	.333	.321
Bats Right	R	.226	243	55	11	1	9	27	25	74	.300	.391
Mirabelli, D	L	.250	52	13	2	0	0	4	4	8	.298	.288
Bats Right	R	.261	111	29	11	0	6	14	7	28	.311	.523
Moeller, Chad	L	.284	81	23	2	0	2	14	8	15	.348	.383
Bats Right	R	.259	158	41	15	1	5	15	15	44	.328	.462
Mohr, Dustan	L	.265	117	31	10	0	4	12	15	35	.348	.453
Bats Right	R	.242	231	56	12	0	6	24	18	71	.296	.372
Molina, Bengie	L	.289	114	33	8	0	7	19	6	7	.322	.544
Bats Right	R	.278	295	82	16	0	7	52	7	24	.296	.403
Molina, Jose	L	.240	50	12	2	0	0	3	1	10	.269	.280
Bats Right	R	.141	64	9	2	0	0	3	0	16	.164	.172
Mondesi, Raul	L	.262	122	32	9	4	5	18	11	22	.319	.525
Bats Right	R	.274	401	110	22	0	19	53	45	75	.350	.471
Monroe, Craig	L	.293	157	46	9	1	14	34	11	28	.337	.631
Bats Right	R	.209	268	56	9	0	9	36	16	61	.257	.343
Mora, Melvin	L	.324	74	24	3	0	5	12	13	10	.440	.568
Bats Right	R	.315	270	85	14	1	10	36	36	61	.411	.485
Morban, Jose	L	.100	20	2	0	0	1	1	0	5	.100	.250
Bats Both	R	.157	51	8	0	0	1	4	3	16	.218	.216
Mordecai, Mike	L	.263	38	10	1	0	1	2	4	6	.333	.368
Bats Right	R	.176	51	9	3	0	1	6	4	15	.232	.294
Morneau, J	L	.154	26	4	1	0	0	1	1	7	.185	.192
Bats Left	R	.250	80	20	3	0	4	15	8	23	.318	.438
Morris, Warren	L	.286	77	22	3	0	0	7	4	17	.329	.325
Bats Left	R	.268	269	72	10	2	6	30	19	25	.313	.387
Mueller, Bill	L	.295	173	51	15	0	8	27	21	21	.375	.520
Bats Both	R	.342	351	120	30	5	11	58	38	56	.409	.550
Munson, Eric	L	.208	77	16	4	0	3	8	10	17	.299	.377
Bats Left	R	.250	236	59	5	0	15	42	25	44	.316	.462
Myers, Greg	L	.333	42	14	5	0	0	6	3	9	.370	.452
Bats Left	R	.303	287	87	14	0	15	46	34	48	.375	.509
Nady, Xavier	L	.311	106	33	8	0	1	8	8	24	.365	.481
Bats Right	R	.249	265	66	9	1	8	31	16	50	.303	.381
Nevin, Phil	L	.349	63	22	3	0	9	27	5	12	.397	.825
Bats Right	R	.252	163	41	5	0	4	19	16	32	.317	.356
Niekro, Lance	L	.000	0	0	0	0	0	0	0	0	.000	.000
Bats Right	R	.200	5	1	1	0	0	2	0	1	.200	.400
Nivar, Ramon	L	.147	34	5	0	0	1	1	1	4	.171	.147
Bats Right	R	.250	56	14	1	2	0	6	3	6	.300	.339

Batter	vs.	Avg.	AB	H	2B	3B	HR	RBI	BB	SO	OBP	Slg.
Nix, Laynce	L	.150	20	3	0	0	1	3	2	7	.227	.300
Bats Left	R	.268	164	44	10	0	7	27	7	46	.297	.457
Nixon, Trot	L	.219	96	21	4	1	3	10	9	21	.296	.375
Bats Left	R	.330	345	114	20	5	25	77	56	75	.423	.635
Norton, Greg	L	.273	22	6	2	0	0	5	2	8	.333	.364
Bats Both	R	.261	157	41	13	0	6	26	14	39	.324	.459
Nunez, A	L	.163	43	7	1	0	0	3	6	12	.302	.186
Bats Both	R	.261	268	70	7	7	4	32	20	41	.311	.384
Ojeda, Augie	L	.200	5	1	0	0	0	0	0	1	.200	.200
Bats Both	R	.100	20	2	0	0	0	0	1	4	.182	.100
Ojeda, Miguel	L	.233	43	10	2	0	2	6	4	5	.292	.419
Bats Right	R	.235	98	23	4	0	2	16	14	21	.348	.337
O'Leary, Troy	L	.214	28	6	0	0	1	2	4	8	.313	.321
Bats Left	R	.219	146	32	9	0	4	26	10	23	.267	.363
Olerud, John	L	.239	155	37	11	0	0	23	15	30	.318	.310
Bats Left	R	.281	384	108	24	0	10	60	69	37	.392	.422
Olivo, Miguel	L	.302	86	26	9	0	4	12	2	17	.315	.547
Bats Right	R	.212	231	49	10	1	2	15	17	63	.277	.290
Olmedo, Ray	L	.215	65	14	2	0	0	5	3	15	.250	.246
Bats Both	R	.248	165	41	4	1	0	12	10	31	.291	.285
Ordonez, M	L	.317	164	52	12	1	12	35	11	14	.358	.622
Bats Right	R	.317	442	140	34	2	17	64	46	59	.388	.518
Ordonez, Rey	L	.308	26	8	4	0	0	6	0	1	.296	.462
Bats Right	R	.319	91	29	7	0	3	16	2	11	.337	.495
Ortiz, David	L	.216	116	25	9	1	4	22	7	26	.260	.414
Bats Left	R	.313	332	104	30	1	27	79	51	57	.404	.654
Osik, Keith	L	.378	37	14	5	0	0	7	6	3	.465	.514
Bats Right	R	.225	204	46	7	0	2	14	25	41	.319	.289
Overbay, Lyle	L	.291	86	25	10	0	0	9	4	29	.326	.407
Bats Left	R	.268	168	45	10	0	4	19	31	38	.383	.399
Owens, Eric	L	.308	143	44	4	0	1	18	5	12	.329	.357
Bats Right	R	.214	98	21	2	0	0	2	5	12	.260	.235
Ozuna, Pablo	L	.125	8	1	0	0	0	0	0	2	.125	.125
Bats Right	R	.219	32	7	1	0	0	2	2	4	.306	.250
Palmeiro, O	L	.182	55	10	1	0	0	3	2	4	.224	.200
Bats Left	R	.290	262	76	12	1	3	30	30	27	.358	.378
Palmeiro, R	L	.282	170	48	5	1	15	43	24	18	.374	.588
Bats Left	R	.251	391	98	16	1	23	69	60	59	.353	.473
Palmer, Dean	L	.189	37	7	1	0	0	0	4	9	.268	.216
Bats Right	R	.102	49	5	1	0	0	6	5	19	.211	.122
Paquette, C	L	.000	16	0	0	0	0	0	0	2	.000	.000
Bats Right	R	.294	17	5	0	0	0	0	0	3	.294	.294
Patterson, C	L	.289	90	26	2	1	4	22	3	25	.316	.467
Bats Left	R	.301	239	72	15	6	9	33	12	52	.333	.527
Patterson, J	L	.000	5	0	0	0	0	0	2	1	.286	.000
Bats Left	R	.235	17	4	0	0	0	0	1	5	.278	.235
Paul, Josh	L	.333	9	3	0	0	0	0	0	2	.333	.333
Bats Right	R	.214	14	3	0	0	0	4	3	4	.353	.214
Payton, Jay	L	.288	160	46	9	1	11	27	16	23	.354	.563
Bats Right	R	.307	440	135	23	4	17	62	27	54	.354	.493
Pellow, Kit	L	.250	8	2	0	0	1	1	0	2	.333	.625
Bats Right	R	.600	10	6	3	1	0	3	0	2	.583	1.100
Pena, Carlos	L	.208	149	31	5	1	5	18	14	49	.284	.356
Bats Left	R	.267	303	81	16	5	13	32	39	74	.355	.482
Pena, Wily Mo	L	.204	54	11	2	0	2	5	5	19	.283	.352
Bats Right	R	.225	111	25	4	1	3	11	7	34	.283	.360
Peralta, J	L	.260	73	19	3	1	3	9	4	21	.316	.452
Bats Right	R	.213	169	36	7	0	1	12	16	44	.286	.272
Perez, Antonio	L	.237	59	14	3	1	0	2	15	18	.392	.322
Bats Right	R	.258	66	17	3	0	2	10	3	16	.296	.394
Perez, Eddie	L	.342	76	26	6	0	2	11	6	11	.386	.500
Bats Right	R	.252	274	69	11	1	9	34	11	36	.280	.398
Perez, Eduardo	L	.353	102	36	8	0	8	17	18	20	.459	.667
Bats Right	R	.238	151	36	8	0	3	24	11	33	.295	.351
Perez, Neifi	L	.253	75	19	6	0	1	14	3	6	.278	.373
Bats Both	R	.257	253	65	13	4	0	17	11	17	.287	.340
Perez, Timo	L	.172	29	5	2	0	0	3	1	4	.200	.241
Bats Left	R	.278	317	88	19	0	4	39	17	25	.310	.375
Perez, Tomas	L	.266	79	21	6	0	3	9	4	12	.301	.456
Bats Both	R	.265	219	58	12	1	2	24	19	42	.321	.356
Perry, Herbert	L	.154	13	2	0	0	0	1	0	1	.154	.154
Bats Right	R	.182	11	2	1	0	0	1	0	2	.182	.273
Petrick, Ben	L	.259	58	15	4	0	1	7	4	11	.306	.379
Bats Right	R	.188	64	12	2	0	3	5	4	20	.235	.359
Phelps, Josh	L	.317	145	46	3	0	7	20	15	34	.393	.483
Bats Right	R	.239	251	60	15	1	13	46	24	81	.338	.462
Phillips, B	L	.179	95	17	3	0	2	8	6	20	.228	.274
Bats Right	R	.218	275	60	15	1	4	25	8	57	.247	.324
Phillips, J	L	.308	117	36	8	0	2	18	20	12	.406	.427
Bats Right	R	.294	286	84	17	0	9	40	19	38	.359	.448
Piatt, Adam	L	.263	95	25	10	0	4	13	6	26	.301	.495
Bats Right	R	.135	37	5	3	0	2	5	3	20	.200	.378
Piazza, Mike	L	.265	49	13	6	0	1	7	10	8	.390	.449
Bats Right	R	.292	185	54	7	0	10	27	25	32	.374	.492
Pierre, Juan	L	.311	206	64	7	2	0	8	10	9	.346	.364
Bats Left	R	.303	462	140	21	5	1	33	45	26	.368	.377
Pierzynski, A	L	.281	135	38	9	1	4	22	2	22	.333	.452
Bats Left	R	.324	352	114	26	2	7	52	22	33	.370	.469
Podsednik, S	L	.270	148	40	3	4	4	22	13	26	.333	.426
Bats Left	R	.329	410	135	26	4	5	36	43	65	.395	.449
Polanco, P	L	.292	96	28	5	1	5	14	12	8	.364	.521
Bats Right	R	.288	396	114	25	2	9	49	30	30	.349	.429
Porter, Colin	L	.111	9	1	0	0	0	0	0	5	.111	.111
Bats Left	R	.217	23	5	0	0	0	0	1	12	.250	.217
Posada, Jorge	L	.295	122	36	6	0	8	27	19	23	.403	.541
Bats Both	R	.276	359	99	18	0	22	74	74	87	.405	.510
Pratt, Todd	L	.267	30	8	3	0	1	4	6	8	.378	.467
Bats Right	R	.274	95	26	7	1	3	16	16	30	.407	.463
Pride, Curtis	L	.000	0	0	0	0	0	0	0	0	.000	.000
Bats Left	R	.083	12	1	0	0	1	1	0	2	.083	.333
Prieto, Alex	L	.200	5	1	0	0	0	0	0	1	.200	.200
Bats Right	R	.000	0	0	0	0	0	0	0	3	.000	.000
Prince, Tom	L	.316	19	6	0	0	1	1	0	4	.316	.474
Bats Right	R	.138	29	4	2	0	1	5	5	3	.306	.310
Pujols, Albert	L	.387	142	55	16	0	11	32	21	8	.458	.732
Bats Right	R	.350	449	157	35	1	32	92	58	57	.434	.646
Punto, Nick	L	.278	36	10	2	0	0	1	2	6	.316	.333
Bats Both	R	.179	56	10	0	0	1	3	5	16	.246	.232
Quinlan, Robb	L	.286	35	10	1	1	0	2	3	3	.342	.371
Bats Right	R	.288	59	17	3	1	0	2	3	13	.323	.373
Quintero, H	L	.286	7	2	0	0	0	0	0	2	.286	.286
Bats Right	R	.188	16	3	0	0	0	2	1	4	.235	.188
Raines Jr., T	L	.143	21	3	1	0	0	1	1	6	.182	.190
Bats Both	R	.136	22	3	0	1	0	1	1	6	.208	.227
Ramirez, A	L	.285	137	39	8	0	10	28	7	17	.322	.562
Bats Right	R	.268	470	126	24	2	17	78	35	82	.324	.436

Batter	vs.	Avg.	AB	H	2B	3B	HR	RBI	BB	SO	OBP	Slg.
Ramirez, Julio	L	.000	0	0	0	0	0	0	0	0	.000	.000
Bats Right	R	.000	2	0	0	0	0	0	0	0	.000	.000
Ramirez, Manny	L	.385	143	55	11	0	8	23	25	16	.476	.629
Bats Right	R	.305	426	130	25	1	29	81	72	78	.411	.573
Randa, Joe	L	.311	151	47	10	0	6	21	10	18	.356	.497
Bats Right	R	.282	351	99	21	1	10	51	31	43	.345	.433
Ransom, Cody	L	.250	4	1	1	0	0	0	0	1	.250	.500
Bats Right	R	.217	23	5	0	0	1	1	1	10	.250	.348
Reboulet, Jeff	L	.220	100	22	3	1	2	4	10	11	.297	.330
Bats Right	R	.255	161	41	7	1	1	21	17	36	.335	.329
Redman, P	L	.167	12	2	1	0	0	1	1	4	.231	.250
Bats Right	R	.083	12	1	0	0	1	1	0	5	.154	.333
Redman, Tike	L	.329	73	24	5	1	0	6	3	6	.372	.425
Bats Left	R	.331	157	52	11	4	3	13	11	12	.375	.510
Redmond, Mike	L	.314	35	11	3	1	0	4	0	5	.324	.457
Bats Right	R	.211	90	19	4	0	0	7	7	11	.294	.256
Reese, Pokey	L	.161	31	5	0	0	1	4	4	6	.257	.258
Bats Right	R	.237	76	18	2	0	0	8	5	25	.277	.263
Relaford, Desi	L	.300	130	39	7	1	3	19	22	19	.409	.438
Bats Both	R	.238	370	88	20	4	5	40	18	51	.278	.354
Renteria, E	L	.391	115	45	17	0	5	34	27	8	.503	.670
Bats Right	R	.316	472	149	30	1	8	66	38	46	.364	.434
Restovich, M	L	.227	22	5	0	1	0	1	1	2	.261	.318
Bats Right	R	.323	31	10	3	1	0	3	9	10	.488	.484
Reyes, Jose	L	.225	80	18	5	0	3	17	5	13	.267	.400
Bats Both	R	.340	194	66	7	4	2	15	8	23	.363	.448
Reyes, Rene	L	.289	38	11	3	0	1	3	3	7	.341	.447
Bats Both	R	.244	78	19	4	1	1	4	2	12	.259	.359
Richard, Chris	L	.500	2	1	0	0	0	0	0	0	.500	.500
Bats Left	R	.200	25	5	1	1	1	3	3	6	.286	.440
Riggs, Adam	L	.350	20	7	3	0	0	1	5	2	.480	.500
Bats Right	R	.195	41	8	1	1	3	4	4	7	.267	.488
Rios, Armando	L	.214	14	3	0	0	0	0	0	2	.214	.214
Bats Left	R	.211	90	19	3	0	2	11	5	11	.250	.311
Rivas, Luis	L	.200	130	26	1	1	1	9	10	18	.259	.246
Bats Right	R	.281	345	97	15	8	7	34	20	47	.327	.432
Rivera, Carlos	L	.188	16	3	1	0	1	2	0	6	.188	.438
Bats Left	R	.228	79	18	4	0	2	8	8	22	.300	.354
Rivera, Juan	L	.340	50	17	4	0	4	10	2	5	.358	.660
Bats Right	R	.236	123	29	10	0	3	16	8	22	.282	.390
Rivera, M	L	.000	9	0	0	0	0	0	2	3	.182	.000
Bats Right	R	.205	44	9	1	0	1	2	3	8	.255	.295
Rivera, Ruben	L	.182	11	2	1	0	1	1	1	1	.250	.545
Bats Right	R	.179	39	7	1	0	1	3	4	13	.256	.282
Roberts, Brian	L	.264	129	34	7	0	2	8	6	16	.296	.364
Bats Both	R	.272	331	90	15	4	3	33	40	42	.351	.369
Roberts, Dave	L	.265	83	22	3	0	0	3	14	6	.378	.301
Bats Left	R	.246	305	75	3	5	2	13	29	33	.318	.308
Robinson, K	L	.238	21	5	0	1	1	1	0	2	.238	.476
Bats Left	R	.251	187	47	6	2	0	15	8	25	.286	.305
Rodriguez, A	L	.305	187	57	11	3	16	37	31	40	.404	.652
Bats Right	R	.295	420	124	19	3	31	81	56	86	.392	.576
Rodriguez, I	L	.376	117	44	12	1	3	18	19	18	.460	.573
Bats Right	R	.274	394	108	24	2	13	67	36	74	.340	.444
Rolen, Scott	L	.283	113	32	12	0	7	27	28	24	.427	.575
Bats Right	R	.287	446	128	37	1	21	77	54	80	.370	.516
Rollins, Jimmy	L	.262	145	38	9	0	2	11	10	24	.308	.366
Bats Both	R	.263	483	127	33	6	6	51	44	89	.324	.393

Batter	vs.	Avg.	AB	H	2B	3B	HR	RBI	BB	SO	OBP	Slg.
Rolls, Damian	L	.273	121	33	3	0	3	11	4	25	.294	.372
Bats Right	R	.246	252	62	17	0	4	35	15	59	.304	.361
Romano, Jason	L	.050	20	1	0	0	0	0	0	3	.050	.050
Bats Right	R	.125	16	2	0	0	0	0	1	5	.176	.125
Romero, Mandy	L	1.000	1	1	0	0	0	0	0	0	1.000	1.000
Bats Both	R	.333	6	2	1	0	0	0	0	1	.333	.500
Ross, Cody	L	.286	7	2	0	0	1	4	0	1	.286	.714
Bats Right	R	.167	12	2	1	0	0	1	1	2	.286	.250
Ross, Dave	L	.258	31	8	0	0	3	6	4	10	.333	.548
Bats Right	R	.258	93	24	7	0	7	12	9	32	.337	.559
Rowand, Aaron	L	.338	65	22	4	0	1	7	2	9	.380	.446
Bats Right	R	.250	92	23	4	0	5	17	5	12	.289	.457
Ruan, Wilkin	L	.100	10	1	0	1	0	0	0	4	.100	.300
Bats Right	R	.258	31	8	2	0	0	2	0	3	.258	.323
Ryan, Michael	L	.438	16	7	4	0	0	2	1	4	.471	.688
Bats Left	R	.378	45	17	3	0	5	11	5	8	.431	.778
Sadler, Donnie	L	.203	59	12	1	0	1	4	7	13	.290	.271
Bats Right	R	.194	72	14	4	2	0	1	6	21	.266	.306
Salmon, Tim	L	.274	157	43	10	1	7	26	33	20	.400	.484
Bats Right	R	.275	371	102	25	3	12	46	44	73	.362	.456
Sanchez, Alex	L	.309	152	47	6	2	0	9	7	16	.335	.375
Bats Left	R	.279	405	113	17	6	1	23	18	58	.312	.358
Sanchez, F	L	.462	13	6	0	0	0	1	0	1	.462	.462
Bats Right	R	.095	21	2	2	0	0	1	0	7	.095	.190
Sanchez, Rey	L	.292	89	26	2	1	0	5	8	9	.347	.337
Bats Right	R	.235	255	60	6	1	0	18	8	30	.262	.267
Sandberg, J	L	.209	67	14	4	1	2	8	7	28	.284	.388
Bats Right	R	.217	69	15	6	0	4	15	9	24	.325	.478
Sanders, R	L	.301	136	41	7	2	12	33	15	26	.368	.647
Bats Right	R	.278	317	88	20	2	19	54	23	84	.335	.533
Santiago, B	L	.290	100	29	5	0	4	12	7	22	.336	.460
Bats Right	R	.276	301	83	16	2	7	44	22	47	.327	.412
Santiago, R	L	.187	134	25	5	0	1	4	7	10	.232	.246
Bats Both	R	.242	310	75	13	1	1	25	26	56	.317	.300
Santos, Angel	L	.231	13	3	0	0	1	1	1	7	.286	.462
Bats Both	R	.222	63	14	3	1	2	5	2	11	.246	.397
Santos, F	L	.000	2	0	0	0	0	0	0	0	.000	.000
Bats Left	R	.231	13	3	2	0	1	1	0	3	.231	.615
Sardinha, Dane	L	.000	1	0	0	0	0	0	0	0	.000	.000
Bats Right	R	.000	1	0	0	0	0	0	0	1	.000	.000
Schneider, B	L	.179	67	12	3	0	3	9	10	20	.282	.358
Bats Left	R	.243	268	65	23	1	6	37	27	55	.315	.403
Scutaro, Marco	L	.095	21	2	1	0	0	0	2	3	.174	.143
Bats Right	R	.259	54	14	3	0	2	6	11	11	.388	.426
Sears, Todd	L	.167	6	1	0	0	0	1	0	2	.167	.167
Bats Left	R	.254	67	17	3	0	2	10	7	16	.329	.388
Segui, David	L	.200	50	10	2	0	0	4	3	7	.259	.240
Bats Both	R	.282	174	49	8	1	5	21	23	40	.364	.425
Seguignol, F	L	.000	3	0	0	0	0	0	0	0	.000	.000
Bats Both	R	.250	4	1	0	0	0	0	1	1	.400	.250
Selby, Bill	L	.000	2	0	0	0	0	0	0	0	.000	.000
Bats Left	R	.108	37	4	1	0	0	5	3	11	.171	.135
Sexson, Richie	L	.279	122	34	2	1	10	23	38	25	.448	.557
Bats Right	R	.271	484	131	26	1	35	101	60	126	.359	.545
Sheffield, G	L	.341	123	42	9	1	10	32	25	10	.450	.675
Bats Right	R	.327	453	148	28	1	29	100	61	45	.410	.585
Shinjo, T	L	.247	81	20	3	0	1	6	5	10	.295	.321
Bats Right	R	.061	33	2	0	0	0	1	1	2	.088	.061

Batter	vs.	Avg.	AB	H	2B	3B	HR	RBI	BB	SO	OBP	Slg.
Shumpert, T	L	.203	69	14	4	2	2	6	7	14	.282	.406
Bats Right	R	.133	15	2	1	0	0	1	3	3	.316	.200
Sierra, Ruben	L	.236	89	21	6	0	3	13	6	14	.281	.404
Bats Both	R	.284	218	62	11	1	6	30	21	33	.346	.427
Simon, Randall	L	.269	52	14	0	0	2	10	2	6	.296	.385
Bats Left	R	.277	358	99	17	0	14	62	14	31	.310	.441
Singleton, C	L	.167	48	8	4	0	0	6	7	12	.276	.250
Bats Left	R	.260	258	67	20	1	1	30	19	43	.306	.357
Smith, Jason	L	.000	0	0	0	0	0	0	0	0	.000	.000
Bats Left	R	.250	4	1	0	0	0	0	0	0	.250	.250
Smith, Mark	L	.241	29	7	2	0	0	1	2	5	.290	.310
Bats Right	R	.235	34	8	2	0	3	9	2	8	.263	.559
Smitherman, S	L	.190	21	4	2	0	0	2	1	3	.227	.286
Bats Right	R	.130	23	3	0	0	1	4	2	6	.200	.261
Snow, J.T.	L	.208	48	10	1	0	0	6	10	12	.387	.229
Bats Left	R	.284	282	80	17	3	8	45	45	43	.387	.450
Sojo, Luis	L	.000	1	0	0	0	0	0	0	0	.000	.000
Bats Right	R	.000	3	0	0	0	0	0	0	0	.000	.000
Sorensen, Zach	L	.111	9	1	1	0	0	0	3	1	.333	.222
Bats Both	R	.143	28	4	0	0	1	2	4	12	.250	.250
Soriano, A	L	.312	138	43	10	2	7	16	14	25	.379	.565
Bats Right	R	.285	544	155	26	3	31	75	24	105	.327	.515
Sosa, Sammy	L	.333	105	35	4	0	7	14	20	23	.440	.571
Bats Right	R	.265	412	109	18	0	33	89	42	120	.336	.549
Spencer, Shane	L	.277	166	46	7	0	7	26	15	33	.335	.446
Bats Right	R	.231	229	53	13	0	5	23	30	59	.323	.354
Spiezio, Scott	L	.223	148	33	6	1	3	22	11	22	.282	.338
Bats Both	R	.282	373	105	30	6	13	61	35	44	.344	.499
Spivey, Junior	L	.288	125	36	11	1	5	19	15	21	.366	.512
Bats Right	R	.238	240	57	11	1	8	31	18	74	.305	.392
Stairs, Matt	L	.188	32	6	0	0	2	4	3	7	.278	.375
Bats Left	R	.304	273	83	20	1	18	53	42	57	.402	.582
Stenson, D	L	.200	5	1	0	0	0	0	1	4	.333	.200
Bats Left	R	.250	76	19	5	0	3	13	10	20	.333	.434
Stewart, S	L	.331	139	46	10	1	4	16	14	19	.389	.504
Bats Right	R	.300	434	130	34	1	9	57	38	47	.357	.445
Stinnett, K	L	.193	57	11	6	0	0	2	5	16	.270	.298
Bats Right	R	.256	129	33	7	0	3	17	9	36	.317	.380
Strong, Jamal	L	.000	1	0	0	0	0	0	0	0	.000	.000
Bats Right	R	.000	1	0	0	0	0	0	0	0	.000	.000
Stynes, Chris	L	.284	134	38	11	3	2	22	17	26	.373	.455
Bats Right	R	.243	309	75	20	0	9	51	31	50	.318	.395
Surhoff, B.J.	L	.284	74	21	2	0	0	9	8	11	.357	.311
Bats Left	R	.298	245	73	18	0	5	32	21	18	.352	.433
Suzuki, Ichiro	L	.359	209	75	13	2	0	17	9	19	.391	.440
Bats Left	R	.291	470	137	16	6	13	45	27	50	.335	.434
Swann, Pedro	L	1.000	1	1	0	0	0	1	0	0	1.000	1.000
Bats Left	R	.154	13	2	1	0	1	1	1	4	.214	.462
Sweeney, Mark	L	.000	6	0	0	0	0	0	0	4	.000	.000
Bats Left	R	.275	91	25	9	0	2	14	9	23	.340	.440
Sweeney, Mike	L	.277	112	31	6	0	5	20	18	14	.374	.464
Bats Right	R	.300	280	84	12	1	11	63	46	42	.398	.468
Taguchi, So	L	.259	27	7	0	0	2	6	3	2	.333	.481
Bats Right	R	.259	27	7	3	1	1	7	1	9	.286	.556
Tatis, F	L	.240	50	12	0	0	2	6	2	9	.296	.360
Bats Right	R	.176	125	22	6	0	0	9	16	31	.275	.224
Taylor, Reggie	L	.167	30	5	0	0	2	5	1	9	.194	.367
Bats Left	R	.227	150	34	5	2	3	14	10	59	.280	.347

Batter	vs.	Avg.	AB	H	2B	3B	HR	RBI	BB	SO	OBP	Slg.
Teixeira, Mark	L	.295	173	51	8	2	11	32	17	38	.368	.555
Bats Both	R	.242	356	86	21	3	15	52	27	82	.313	.444
Tejada, Miguel	L	.269	167	45	9	0	8	25	24	7	.361	.467
Bats Right	R	.281	469	132	33	0	19	81	29	58	.326	.473
Terrero, Luis	L	.000	2	0	0	0	0	0	0	0	.000	.000
Bats Right	R	.500	2	1	0	0	0	0	0	1	.667	.500
Thames, M	L	.250	52	13	1	0	1	3	3	10	.304	.327
Bats Right	R	.095	21	2	1	0	0	1	5	8	.286	.143
Thomas, Frank	L	.315	149	47	11	0	17	35	34	22	.446	.732
Bats Right	R	.249	397	99	24	0	25	70	66	93	.368	.499
Thome, Jim	L	.254	177	45	6	0	10	34	24	62	.338	.458
Bats Left	R	.272	401	109	24	3	37	97	87	120	.405	.623
Thurston, Joe	L	.000	0	0	0	0	0	0	0	0	.000	.000
Bats Left	R	.200	10	2	0	0	0	0	1	1	.273	.200
Torcato, Tony	L	.000	2	0	0	0	0	0	0	0	.000	.000
Bats Left	R	.214	14	3	1	0	0	1	0	4	.267	.286
Torrealba, Y	L	.212	33	7	2	2	0	2	5	5	.333	.394
Bats Right	R	.269	167	45	8	0	4	27	9	34	.307	.389
Torres, Andres	L	.258	62	16	3	1	1	5	3	5	.288	.387
Bats Both	R	.198	106	21	1	2	0	4	7	30	.248	.245
Trammell, B	L	.188	32	6	2	0	0	4	4	5	.278	.250
Bats Right	R	.217	23	5	3	0	0	1	2	5	.280	.348
Truby, Chris	L	.385	13	5	0	0	0	1	2	4	.467	.385
Bats Right	R	.233	30	7	3	0	0	2	3	9	.303	.333
Tucker, M	L	.236	123	29	6	2	2	11	11	29	.307	.366
Bats Left	R	.274	266	73	14	3	11	44	28	59	.342	.474
Tyner, Jason	L	.167	12	2	0	0	0	0	1	2	.231	.167
Bats Left	R	.295	78	23	7	0	0	6	9	10	.368	.385
Ugueto, Luis	L	.250	4	1	0	0	0	0	0	0	.250	.250
Bats Both	R	.000	1	0	0	0	0	1	1	0	.500	.000
Uribe, Juan	L	.301	83	25	5	1	2	7	4	14	.341	.458
Bats Right	R	.236	233	55	14	2	8	26	13	46	.281	.416
Utley, Chase	L	.333	12	4	2	0	0	2	1	2	.500	.500
Bats Left	R	.230	122	28	8	1	2	19	10	20	.301	.361
Valderrama, C	L	.000	3	0	0	0	0	0	0	1	.000	.000
Bats Right	R	.250	4	1	0	0	0	0	0	2	.250	.250
Valent, Eric	L	.286	7	2	0	0	0	0	0	1	.286	.286
Bats Left	R	.200	35	7	0	0	0	1	2	8	.243	.200
Valentin, J	L	.231	13	3	0	0	0	0	1	2	.286	.231
Bats Both	R	.221	122	27	7	1	3	15	4	29	.250	.369
Valentin, Jose	L	.131	107	14	1	0	2	6	8	28	.190	.196
Bats Both	R	.265	396	105	25	2	26	60	46	86	.345	.535
Vander Wal, J	L	.158	38	6	2	0	0	2	4	18	.256	.211
Bats Left	R	.270	289	78	23	1	14	43	42	86	.363	.502
Varitek, Jason	L	.309	136	42	9	1	10	33	17	24	.387	.610
Bats Both	R	.257	315	81	22	0	15	52	34	82	.335	.470
Vaughn, Greg	L	.250	12	3	1	0	2	3	4	3	.438	.833
Bats Right	R	.160	25	4	2	0	1	2	4	10	.267	.360
Vaughn, Mo	L	.133	15	2	0	0	0	4	1	6	.235	.133
Bats Left	R	.203	64	13	2	0	3	11	13	16	.342	.375
Vazquez, R	L	.224	116	26	5	0	0	7	11	24	.292	.267
Bats Left	R	.275	306	84	12	4	3	23	41	64	.361	.369
Velandia, J	L	.250	8	2	0	0	0	5	2	3	.364	.250
Bats Right	R	.180	50	9	3	1	0	3	8	12	.293	.280
Ventura, Robin	L	.216	51	11	3	0	3	5	6	16	.298	.451
Bats Left	R	.246	341	84	15	1	11	50	52	71	.346	.393
Victorino, S	L	.133	15	2	0	0	0	0	2	2	.235	.133
Bats Both	R	.155	58	9	2	0	0	4	5	15	.231	.190

Batter	vs.	Avg.	AB	H	2B	3B	HR	RBI	BB	SO	OBP	Slg.
Vidro, Jose	L	.315	127	40	7	0	7	22	15	14	.389	.535
Bats Both	R	.309	382	118	29	0	8	43	54	36	.399	.448
Vina, Fernando	L	.163	49	8	2	1	0	5	2	10	.236	.245
Bats Left	R	.271	210	57	12	3	4	18	9	14	.326	.414
Vitiello, Joe	L	.375	56	21	6	0	2	10	6	9	.435	.589
Bats Right	R	.250	20	5	0	0	1	3	1	5	.333	.400
Vizcaino, Jose	L	.222	36	8	0	0	0	0	0	5	.243	.222
Bats Both	R	.255	153	39	7	3	3	26	8	17	.290	.399
Vizquel, Omar	L	.224	67	15	5	0	0	3	8	5	.303	.299
Bats Both	R	.251	183	46	8	2	2	16	21	15	.328	.350
Walbeck, Matt	L	.269	26	7	1	0	1	4	1	5	.296	.423
Bats Both	R	.152	112	17	3	1	0	2	2	21	.174	.196
Walker, Larry	L	.321	156	50	9	3	4	32	23	26	.422	.494
Bats Left	R	.265	298	79	16	4	12	47	75	61	.422	.466
Walker, Todd	L	.234	158	37	10	0	4	25	12	10	.282	.373
Bats Left	R	.301	429	129	28	4	9	60	36	44	.352	.448
Ward, Daryle	L	.400	5	2	0	0	0	0	0	1	.500	.400
Bats Left	R	.173	104	18	1	0	0	9	3	18	.194	.183
Watson, Matt	L	.000	2	0	0	0	0	0	0	1	.000	.000
Bats Left	R	.190	21	4	2	0	0	2	1	4	.227	.286
Weeks, Rickie	L	.000	2	0	0	0	0	0	1	2	.333	.000
Bats Right	R	.200	10	2	1	0	0	0	0	4	.273	.300
Wells, Vernon	L	.347	173	60	18	3	4	26	17	12	.402	.555
Bats Right	R	.307	505	155	31	2	29	91	25	68	.344	.549
Werth, Jayson	L	.056	18	1	1	0	0	4	2	7	.150	.111
Bats Right	R	.300	30	9	3	0	2	6	1	15	.323	.600
Wesson, Barry	L	.000	4	0	0	0	0	0	0	2	.000	.000
Bats Right	R	.286	7	2	0	0	1	3	0	2	.286	.714
White, Rondell	L	.299	137	41	7	1	4	20	8	19	.351	.453
Bats Right	R	.285	351	100	16	3	18	67	23	60	.337	.501
Widger, Chris	L	.227	22	5	2	0	0	5	1	6	.250	.318
Bats Right	R	.238	80	19	7	0	0	9	5	14	.287	.325
Wigginton, Ty	L	.297	155	46	11	1	4	17	20	34	.377	.458
Bats Right	R	.239	418	100	25	5	7	54	26	90	.295	.373
Wilkerson, B	L	.281	128	36	11	1	3	19	27	44	.405	.453
Bats Left	R	.263	376	99	23	3	16	58	62	111	.371	.468
Williams, B	L	.280	132	37	5	1	4	18	28	17	.414	.424
Bats Both	R	.256	313	80	14	0	11	46	43	44	.345	.406
Williams, G	L	.167	18	3	1	0	0	3	0	2	.167	.222
Bats Right	R	.077	13	1	0	0	0	0	2	3	.200	.077
Williams, Matt	L	.302	43	13	3	0	3	8	7	5	.396	.581
Bats Right	R	.220	91	20	6	0	1	8	9	21	.291	.319
Wilson, Craig	L	.308	107	33	6	1	11	26	21	24	.431	.692
Bats Right	R	.238	202	48	9	3	7	22	14	65	.320	.416

Batter	vs.	Avg.	AB	H	2B	3B	HR	RBI	BB	SO	OBP	Slg.
Wilson, Dan	L	.264	106	28	7	0	2	20	6	16	.304	.387
Bats Right	R	.229	210	48	8	2	2	23	9	36	.257	.314
Wilson, E	L	.133	30	4	0	0	1	2	4	3	.235	.233
Bats Both	R	.257	105	27	9	0	2	13	3	11	.288	.400
Wilson, Jack	L	.261	134	35	4	1	2	11	13	9	.324	.351
Bats Right	R	.255	424	108	17	2	7	51	23	65	.296	.354
Wilson, P	L	.274	179	49	7	0	5	25	25	43	.361	.397
Bats Right	R	.285	421	120	36	1	31	116	29	96	.336	.596
Wilson, Tom	L	.299	107	32	10	0	1	9	16	22	.387	.421
Bats Right	R	.228	149	34	9	0	4	26	12	58	.288	.369
Wilson, Vance	L	.243	74	18	2	0	2	8	3	15	.273	.351
Bats Right	R	.242	194	47	7	1	6	31	12	41	.300	.381
Winn, Randy	L	.314	169	53	15	3	3	16	13	22	.368	.491
Bats Both	R	.288	431	124	22	1	8	59	28	86	.337	.399
Witt, Kevin	L	.241	29	7	1	0	0	2	2	11	.290	.276
Bats Left	R	.266	241	64	8	0	10	24	13	57	.302	.423
Womack, Tony	L	.268	56	15	4	1	0	6	1	7	.293	.375
Bats Left	R	.218	293	64	10	3	2	16	8	40	.243	.294
Woodward, C	L	.307	101	31	10	1	2	16	10	19	.360	.485
Bats Right	R	.242	248	60	12	1	5	29	18	53	.298	.359
Wooten, Shawn	L	.238	151	36	6	0	5	21	14	20	.304	.377
Bats Right	R	.248	121	30	2	0	2	11	10	25	.303	.314
Young, Dmitri	L	.293	191	56	11	1	9	27	24	45	.382	.503
Bats Both	R	.299	371	111	23	6	20	58	34	85	.366	.555
Young, Eric	L	.246	114	28	4	0	6	8	19	10	.356	.439
Bats Right	R	.252	361	91	16	1	9	26	38	34	.329	.377
Young, Ernie	L	.167	6	1	0	0	0	0	2	4	.375	.167
Bats Right	R	.200	5	1	0	0	0	0	2	1	.429	.200
Young, Kevin	L	.167	48	8	1	0	1	4	4	12	.231	.250
Bats Right	R	.250	36	9	3	0	1	3	8	13	.386	.417
Young, Michael	L	.308	198	61	13	2	5	23	8	33	.332	.470
Bats Right	R	.306	468	143	20	7	9	49	28	70	.343	.436
Zaun, Gregg	L	.308	39	12	2	0	0	3	5	5	.378	.359
Bats Both	R	.205	127	26	6	0	4	18	14	16	.287	.346
Zeile, Todd	L	.235	98	23	4	1	7	21	14	14	.319	.510
Bats Right	R	.224	201	45	6	1	4	21	20	40	.302	.323
Zoccolillo, P	L	.000	1	0	0	0	0	0	0	0	.000	.000
Bats Left	R	.111	36	4	1	0	0	3	2	13	.158	.139
A.L.	L	.268	...	...	...	...	...	...	...	...	.331	.423
	R	.267	...	...	...	...	...	...	...	...	.334	.429
N.L.	L	.266	...	...	...	...	...	...	...	...	.341	.429
	R	.260	...	...	...	...	...	...	...	...	.329	.413
MLB	L	.267	...	...	...	...	...	...	...	...	.336	.426
	R	.263	...	...	...	...	...	...	...	...	.331	.420

Pitcher	vs.	Avg.	AB	H	2B	3B	HR	RBI	BB	SO	OBP	Slg.
Abbott, Paul	L	.305	105	32	5	0	5	16	18	17	.413	.495
Throws Right	R	.192	78	15	4	0	3	6	8	15	.267	.359
Acevedo, Jose	L	.136	44	6	3	0	2	3	4	8	.204	.341
Throws Right	R	.224	49	11	3	1	1	5	2	15	.264	.388
Acevedo, Juan	L	.292	72	21	8	0	2	12	8	16	.370	.486
Throws Right	R	.341	91	31	5	1	4	18	10	12	.400	.549
Adams, Terry	L	.264	110	29	7	0	0	9	10	23	.331	.327
Throws Right	R	.271	144	39	6	1	1	15	13	28	.331	.347
Adkins, Jon	L	.176	17	3	3	0	0	2	2	2	.250	.353
Throws Right	R	.333	15	5	0	0	1	3	5	1	.524	.533
Affeldt, J	L	.223	112	25	5	1	2	16	13	24	.302	.339
Throws Left	R	.272	371	101	23	1	10	37	25	74	.323	.420
Ainsworth, K	L	.286	105	30	7	1	2	9	15	19	.372	.429
Throws Right	R	.261	161	42	8	0	6	19	12	33	.314	.422
Alfonseca, A	L	.340	100	34	1	1	3	16	14	11	.417	.460
Throws Right	R	.259	162	42	7	1	4	38	13	40	.322	.389
Almanza, A	L	.277	65	18	2	0	3	12	11	24	.385	.446
Throws Left	R	.306	134	41	8	0	7	21	14	25	.371	.522
Almonte, Edwin	L	.357	14	5	0	0	1	2	2	2	.438	.571
Throws Right	R	.432	37	16	5	1	2	10	3	5	.475	.784
Almonte, H	L	.326	46	15	3	1	1	7	12	12	.466	.500
Throws Right	R	.280	100	28	4	0	4	19	12	20	.362	.440
Alvarez, Juan	L	.222	9	2	0	0	1	2	2	2	.417	.556
Throws Left	R	.214	28	6	1	0	1	2	6	4	.353	.357
Alvarez, V	L	.500	4	2	0	0	0	1	0	1	.500	.500
Throws Left	R	.368	19	7	3	0	1	7	6	2	.538	.684
Alvarez, W	L	.235	68	16	3	0	1	7	4	9	.288	.324
Throws Left	R	.230	278	64	7	1	4	17	19	73	.288	.306
Anderson, B	L	.258	182	47	10	0	9	20	9	27	.293	.462
Throws Left	R	.286	577	165	29	8	18	80	34	60	.324	.458
Anderson, Ja.	L	.354	48	17	3	0	4	9	10	2	.467	.667
Throws Right	R	.219	73	16	3	0	1	9	9	14	.310	.301
Anderson, Ji.	L	.357	42	15	6	1	2	11	1	4	.372	.690
Throws Left	R	.360	125	45	9	1	6	26	13	9	.411	.592
Anderson, Matt	L	.286	35	10	2	0	2	7	1	3	.297	.514
Throws Right	R	.263	57	15	1	0	3	10	8	10	.364	.439
Appier, Kevin	L	.253	249	63	13	1	14	34	26	26	.336	.482
Throws Right	R	.289	197	57	10	3	7	31	17	29	.353	.477
Armas, Tony	L	.250	44	11	3	1	0	4	2	7	.271	.364
Throws Right	R	.209	67	14	1	0	4	5	6	16	.284	.403
Arroyo, B	L	.161	31	5	1	1	0	1	4	3	.257	.258
Throws Right	R	.167	30	5	3	0	0	2	0	11	.194	.267
Asencio, M	L	.344	96	33	7	2	2	18	11	15	.396	.521
Throws Right	R	.241	87	21	2	1	2	9	10	12	.337	.356
Ashby, Andy	L	.336	131	44	4	1	6	22	9	13	.389	.519
Throws Right	R	.291	158	46	7	3	2	17	8	28	.323	.411
Astacio, Pedro	L	.324	71	23	7	1	4	10	14	7	.442	.620
Throws Right	R	.300	80	24	4	0	4	18	4	13	.345	.500
Austin, Jeff	L	.205	39	8	1	0	2	5	10	7	.367	.385
Throws Right	R	.282	71	20	3	0	7	16	11	15	.378	.620
Avery, Steve	L	.348	23	8	0	1	1	7	3	2	.423	.565
Throws Left	R	.275	40	11	2	0	4	8	4	4	.341	.625
Ayala, Luis	L	.337	101	34	2	3	5	14	9	14	.398	.564
Throws Right	R	.188	165	31	4	0	3	14	4	32	.221	.267
Aybar, Manny	L	.000	0	0	0	0	0	0	2	0	1.000	.000
Throws Right	R	.333	12	4	1	0	1	3	1	2	.357	.667
Backe, Brandon	L	.302	53	16	1	1	2	7	14	6	.456	.472
Throws Right	R	.220	109	24	4	0	4	18	11	30	.295	.367
Bacsik, Mike	L	.500	20	10	1	1	2	7	2	6	.545	.950
Throws Left	R	.321	56	18	5	1	3	13	6	6	.381	.607
Baez, Danys	L	.285	151	43	11	0	4	16	12	32	.341	.437
Throws Right	R	.165	133	22	6	0	5	18	11	34	.243	.323
Baldwin, James	L	.361	36	13	1	1	3	8	2	1	.385	.694
Throws Right	R	.296	27	8	1	0	3	5	2	6	.333	.667
Bale, John	L	.103	29	3	1	0	0	0	1	8	.133	.138
Throws Left	R	.315	149	47	10	4	7	22	11	29	.366	.577
Balfour, Grant	L	.229	48	11	2	0	1	6	11	14	.367	.333
Throws Right	R	.240	50	12	3	0	3	8	3	16	.283	.480
Batista, M	L	.297	347	103	12	5	6	40	29	60	.355	.412
Throws Right	R	.241	390	94	20	2	7	42	31	82	.301	.356
Bauer, Rick	L	.247	93	23	6	0	2	12	17	21	.375	.376
Throws Right	R	.261	134	35	7	1	3	33	7	22	.301	.396
Beck, Rod	L	.159	69	11	1	0	2	4	10	18	.275	.261
Throws Right	R	.241	58	14	2	0	2	6	1	14	.254	.379
Beckett, Josh	L	.220	241	53	14	0	3	15	32	89	.310	.315
Throws Right	R	.267	296	79	12	2	6	29	24	63	.326	.382
Beimel, Joe	L	.311	106	33	5	1	3	22	16	27	.408	.462
Throws Left	R	.288	125	36	6	2	4	23	17	15	.372	.464
Belisle, Matt	L	.250	12	3	1	0	0	1	1	1	.286	.333
Throws Right	R	.333	21	7	1	0	1	4	1	5	.391	.524
Bell, Rob	L	.247	215	53	16	1	9	28	23	24	.318	.456
Throws Right	R	.282	177	50	14	2	6	30	16	20	.357	.486
Benes, Alan	L	.438	48	21	6	1	2	10	9	10	.526	.729
Throws Right	R	.308	52	16	3	1	0	9	5	10	.362	.404
Benitez, A	L	.214	140	30	4	0	5	23	28	38	.345	.350
Throws Right	R	.221	131	29	7	0	1	8	13	37	.290	.298
Benoit, J	L	.222	212	47	6	6	13	34	30	48	.314	.491
Throws Right	R	.272	191	52	15	2	10	30	21	39	.352	.529
Benson, Kris	L	.339	189	64	14	0	9	37	19	22	.396	.556
Throws Right	R	.260	242	63	13	1	5	26	17	46	.308	.384
Bere, Jason	L	.294	17	5	2	0	0	1	2	0	.350	.412
Throws Right	R	.000	7	0	0	0	0	0	0	1	.000	.000
Bernero, Adam	L	.306	265	81	16	6	10	42	31	28	.377	.525
Throws Right	R	.225	249	56	10	3	9	38	23	52	.301	.398
Betancourt, R	L	.270	63	17	4	1	3	14	11	17	.373	.508
Throws Right	R	.133	75	10	1	1	2	3	2	19	.167	.253
Biddle, Rocky	L	.242	120	29	5	0	3	15	19	23	.355	.358
Throws Right	R	.264	159	42	10	1	7	29	21	31	.362	.472
Bierbrodt, N	L	.393	56	22	7	1	3	15	6	13	.439	.714
Throws Left	R	.328	128	42	9	0	6	31	21	16	.432	.539
Bland, Nate	L	.273	44	12	1	0	0	7	5	13	.340	.295
Throws Left	R	.303	33	10	2	1	3	6	7	5	.452	.697
Boehringer, B	L	.193	88	17	3	0	3	11	17	24	.330	.330
Throws Right	R	.309	152	47	10	1	8	29	13	23	.367	.546
Bonderman, J	L	.306	382	117	28	2	14	60	38	46	.369	.500
Throws Right	R	.277	274	76	16	3	9	39	20	62	.329	.456
Bong, Jung	L	.264	72	19	3	1	4	15	7	22	.341	.500
Throws Left	R	.268	138	37	8	1	4	20	24	25	.377	.428
Bootcheck, C	L	.286	21	6	1	0	1	3	4	3	.400	.476
Throws Right	R	.385	26	10	2	0	4	8	2	4	.429	.923
Borbon, Pedro	L	.556	9	5	0	0	1	4	1	0	.636	.889
Throws Left	R	.563	16	9	4	0	1	8	1	0	.588	1.000
Borland, Toby	L	.077	13	1	0	0	0	1	6	1	.368	.077
Throws Right	R	.111	18	2	0	0	0	2	2	3	.190	.111
Borowski, Joe	L	.212	104	22	4	0	4	12	4	35	.248	.365
Throws Right	R	.204	152	31	3	0	1	13	15	31	.275	.243

Pitcher	vs.	Avg.	AB	H	2B	3B	HR	RBI	BB	SO	OBP	Slg.
Bottalico, R	L	.000	2	0	0	0	0	0	2	0	.500	.000
Throws Right	R	.500	6	3	1	0	0	0	0	2	.500	.667
Bowie, Micah	L	.364	11	4	2	0	0	3	1	0	.417	.545
Throws Left	R	.360	25	9	1	1	1	4	1	4	.385	.600
Bowles, Brian	L	.200	10	2	1	0	0	0	2	1	.333	.300
Throws Right	R	.300	20	6	1	0	1	3	0	1	.364	.500
Boyd, Jason	L	.232	82	19	1	0	2	14	18	12	.370	.317
Throws Right	R	.176	108	19	9	0	2	14	8	19	.248	.315
Bradford, Chad	L	.326	95	31	9	0	5	17	19	11	.458	.579
Throws Right	R	.190	189	36	2	2	2	16	11	51	.246	.254
Brazelton, D	L	.287	108	31	7	2	5	26	11	14	.347	.528
Throws Right	R	.299	87	26	8	1	4	14	12	10	.402	.552
Brohawn, Troy	L	.000	15	0	0	0	0	0	2	6	.118	.000
Throws Left	R	.345	29	10	3	0	2	8	2	7	.387	.655
Brower, Jim	L	.291	148	43	8	2	4	18	23	16	.384	.453
Throws Right	R	.220	214	47	11	1	4	28	16	49	.274	.336
Brown, Kevin	L	.254	374	95	10	4	0	23	36	76	.319	.302
Throws Right	R	.219	407	89	11	1	11	37	20	109	.263	.332
Buehrle, Mark	L	.263	274	72	13	0	7	38	8	39	.291	.387
Throws Left	R	.285	624	178	35	3	15	75	53	80	.340	.423
Bukvich, Ryan	L	.235	17	4	1	0	1	4	4	5	.364	.471
Throws Right	R	.333	24	8	2	0	1	6	5	3	.448	.542
Bullinger, K	L	.300	10	3	0	0	1	2	1	1	.364	.600
Throws Right	R	.182	22	4	1	2	1	5	0	4	.182	.545
Bump, Nate	L	.229	48	11	3	0	2	6	10	8	.362	.417
Throws Right	R	.258	89	23	5	1	1	18	10	9	.374	.371
Burba, Dave	L	.219	64	14	5	0	1	1	8	12	.315	.344
Throws Right	R	.269	104	28	5	0	4	16	11	23	.356	.433
Burkett, John	L	.273	384	105	30	0	9	51	29	56	.327	.422
Throws Right	R	.290	335	97	23	0	11	53	18	51	.334	.457
Burnett, A.J.	L	.234	47	11	2	2	1	5	8	14	.345	.426
Throws Right	R	.194	36	7	1	0	1	8	10	7	.388	.306
Bynum, Mike	L	.278	36	10	0	1	1	5	4	9	.350	.417
Throws Left	R	.304	112	34	4	0	13	33	11	26	.371	.688
Calero, Kiko	L	.222	54	12	2	0	1	3	7	17	.323	.315
Throws Right	R	.205	83	17	4	1	4	14	13	34	.303	.422
Callaway, M	L	.358	137	49	10	1	4	26	12	16	.412	.533
Throws Right	R	.307	114	35	4	0	3	15	12	25	.364	.421
Capuano, Chris	L	.129	31	4	0	0	0	4	1	7	.229	.129
Throws Left	R	.271	85	23	6	0	3	12	10	16	.364	.447
Carrara, G	L	.387	62	24	3	1	5	16	9	5	.472	.710
Throws Right	R	.276	58	16	2	0	1	5	5	8	.344	.362
Carrasco, D.J.	L	.290	138	40	5	0	5	22	28	24	.415	.435
Throws Right	R	.255	165	42	8	0	3	25	12	33	.317	.358
Carrasco, H	L	.288	66	19	1	1	5	10	7	13	.356	.561
Throws Right	R	.256	82	21	4	1	0	7	13	14	.371	.329
Carter, Lance	L	.222	162	36	10	2	5	23	10	29	.272	.401
Throws Right	R	.265	136	36	8	0	7	18	9	18	.313	.463
Cerda, Jaime	L	.242	33	8	3	0	1	8	8	4	.390	.424
Throws Left	R	.276	87	24	4	1	3	14	12	15	.356	.448
Cerros, Juan	L	.250	16	4	0	0	1	4	4	1	.400	.438
Throws Right	R	.212	33	7	1	1	0	6	1	8	.270	.303
Chacon, Shawn	L	.254	272	69	17	3	6	29	32	42	.330	.404
Throws Right	R	.230	239	55	14	1	6	36	26	51	.332	.372
Chen, Bruce	L	.323	31	10	2	1	2	11	2	6	.368	.645
Throws Left	R	.262	61	16	3	0	4	9	8	14	.348	.508
Choate, Randy	L	.600	5	3	1	0	0	1	0	0	.600	.800
Throws Left	R	.400	10	4	1	0	0	3	1	0	.455	.500
Christiansen, J	L	.208	48	10	2	1	0	8	3	10	.255	.292
Throws Left	R	.273	55	15	4	1	3	4	8	12	.375	.545
Chulk, Vinnie	L	.231	13	3	0	1	0	3	1	2	.286	.385
Throws Right	R	.333	9	3	0	0	0	1	2	0	.455	.333

Pitcher	vs.	Avg.	AB	H	2B	3B	HR	RBI	BB	SO	OBP	Slg.
Claussen, B	L	.250	4	1	0	0	0	0	0	2	.250	.250
Throws Left	R	.304	23	7	0	0	1	2	1	3	.333	.435
Clemens, Roger	L	.215	455	98	14	2	12	44	37	106	.276	.334
Throws Right	R	.288	351	101	28	1	12	39	21	84	.330	.476
Clement, Matt	L	.246	358	88	19	1	12	45	45	84	.337	.405
Throws Right	R	.209	388	81	14	0	10	41	34	87	.288	.322
Colome, Jesus	L	.218	119	26	7	0	4	14	27	24	.367	.378
Throws Right	R	.269	160	43	8	0	5	31	19	45	.346	.413
Colon, Bartolo	L	.250	509	127	30	2	16	54	33	111	.294	.411
Throws Right	R	.246	390	96	14	0	14	45	34	62	.311	.390
Colyer, Steve	L	.364	22	8	1	0	0	1	4	4	.462	.409
Throws Left	R	.269	52	14	2	0	0	5	5	12	.333	.308
Condrey, Clay	L	.309	55	17	7	1	3	16	9	6	.415	.636
Throws Right	R	.302	86	26	3	0	4	13	12	19	.400	.477
Cone, David	L	.281	32	9	3	0	2	7	8	3	.425	.563
Throws Right	R	.282	39	11	1	0	2	5	5	10	.364	.462
Contreras, J	L	.203	143	29	7	0	2	15	19	44	.299	.294
Throws Right	R	.202	114	23	6	0	2	7	11	28	.295	.307
Cook, Aaron	L	.342	219	75	13	2	6	44	34	16	.424	.502
Throws Right	R	.298	285	85	16	0	2	32	23	27	.365	.375
Corcoran, Roy	L	.083	12	1	1	0	0	0	2	1	.214	.167
Throws Right	R	.375	16	6	1	1	0	2	1	1	.412	.563
Cordero, Chad	L	.111	9	1	0	0	0	0	2	4	.273	.111
Throws Right	R	.111	27	3	0	0	1	2	1	8	.143	.222
Cordero, F	L	.236	148	35	4	0	1	13	24	43	.343	.284
Throws Right	R	.223	157	35	4	1	3	26	14	47	.287	.318
Corey, Mark	L	.316	38	12	2	2	2	13	4	8	.372	.632
Throws Right	R	.221	77	17	6	0	0	9	7	19	.287	.299
Cormier, Rheal	L	.119	84	10	3	0	0	5	11	22	.229	.155
Throws Left	R	.207	213	44	9	1	4	15	14	45	.256	.315
Cornejo, Nate	L	.309	375	116	25	4	12	53	41	20	.374	.493
Throws Right	R	.305	393	120	22	1	6	42	17	26	.337	.412
Correia, Kevin	L	.280	75	21	2	0	4	10	9	11	.353	.467
Throws Right	R	.270	74	20	4	0	2	8	9	17	.379	.405
Cortes, David	L	.667	9	6	3	0	0	2	0	1	.667	1.000
Throws Right	R	.250	8	2	0	0	1	3	0	0	.222	.625
Cotts, Neal	L	.250	4	1	0	0	0	0	4	1	.625	.250
Throws Left	R	.298	47	14	5	0	1	10	13	9	.450	.468
Creek, Doug	L	.269	26	7	1	0	1	7	5	2	.375	.423
Throws Left	R	.259	27	7	2	0	1	4	7	9	.432	.444
Cressend, Jack	L	.253	75	19	8	0	1	3	5	12	.300	.400
Throws Right	R	.250	84	21	6	0	0	9	4	16	.300	.321
Crudale, Mike	L	.105	19	2	2	0	0	3	11	4	.419	.211
Throws Right	R	.189	53	10	2	1	1	6	7	9	.295	.321
Cruz, Juan	L	.292	89	26	3	1	2	13	12	28	.382	.416
Throws Right	R	.265	151	40	9	1	5	24	16	37	.354	.437
Cruz, Nelson	L	.308	104	32	5	2	8	25	7	15	.360	.625
Throws Right	R	.295	112	33	4	0	7	21	4	23	.322	.518
Cunnane, Will	L	.200	30	6	2	0	1	2	2	5	.250	.367
Throws Right	R	.182	44	8	1	0	1	4	4	15	.250	.273
Daal, Omar	L	.312	77	24	4	0	1	12	7	13	.372	.403
Throws Left	R	.350	314	110	33	2	10	48	23	40	.394	.564
D'Amico, Jeff	L	.293	311	91	21	3	7	33	27	40	.348	.447
Throws Right	R	.290	389	113	26	1	16	56	15	60	.325	.486
Darensbourg, V	L	.545	11	6	0	0	1	1	0	0	.545	.818
Throws Left	R	.333	33	11	4	0	1	8	1	4	.353	.545
Davis, Doug	L	.293	92	27	8	1	5	11	13	18	.381	.565
Throws Left	R	.283	339	96	10	1	11	34	38	44	.355	.416
Davis, Jason	L	.259	344	89	16	2	14	49	30	47	.320	.439
Throws Right	R	.289	287	83	16	1	11	38	17	38	.341	.467
Dawley, Joe	L	.444	18	8	3	0	3	9	1	2	.500	1.111
Throws Right	R	.368	19	7	2	1	0	4	2	6	.429	.579

Pitcher	vs.	Avg.	AB	H	2B	3B	HR	RBI	BB	SO	OBP	Slg.
Day, Zach	L	.282	234	66	14	0	4	24	22	22	.347	.393
Throws R	R	.244	270	66	18	2	4	32	37	39	.348	.370
Deago, Roger	L	.000	5	0	0	0	0	1	0	3	.000	.000
Throws Left	R	.324	34	11	3	1	0	6	8	7	.452	.471
DeHart, Rick	L	.444	9	4	2	0	1	3	0	0	.444	1.000
Throws Left	R	.400	10	4	2	0	0	2	2	1	.500	.600
DeJean, Mike	L	.329	149	49	7	2	9	28	19	22	.400	.584
Throws Right	R	.216	171	37	8	0	4	20	20	49	.304	.333
de los Santos, V	L	.267	60	16	1	0	2	8	4	15	.324	.383
Throws Left	R	.228	127	29	4	1	6	17	21	24	.346	.417
Dempster, Ryan	L	.300	207	62	17	1	7	36	41	42	.415	.493
Throws Right	R	.288	250	72	14	1	7	46	29	42	.368	.436
DePaula, Jorge	L	.056	18	1	0	0	0	0	1	2	.105	.056
Throws Right	R	.111	18	2	1	0	1	1	0	5	.158	.333
Dessens, Elmer	L	.364	332	121	25	2	12	50	29	41	.414	.560
Throws Right	R	.242	376	91	18	0	10	49	28	72	.300	.370
Dickey, R.A.	L	.279	251	70	11	2	11	31	20	52	.333	.470
Throws Right	R	.307	212	65	16	1	5	34	18	42	.369	.462
Dominguez, J	L	.346	26	9	2	0	2	6	6	8	.455	.654
Throws Right	R	.212	33	7	1	0	3	6	6	5	.333	.515
Donnelly, B	L	.199	146	29	2	2	2	11	14	32	.272	.281
Throws Right	R	.202	129	26	10	1	0	5	10	47	.275	.295
Dotel, Octavio	L	.152	132	20	4	0	3	10	23	33	.287	.250
Throws Right	R	.186	177	33	5	2	6	20	8	64	.225	.339
Douglass, Sean	L	.421	19	8	2	0	1	8	4	1	.522	.684
Throws Right	R	.333	18	6	0	0	1	3	2	2	.429	.500
Downs, Scott	L	.000	1	0	0	0	0	0	0	1	.000	.000
Throws Left	R	.385	13	5	2	0	2	4	3	3	.500	1.000
Dreifort, D	L	.306	108	33	8	0	3	14	18	27	.402	.463
Throws Right	R	.202	124	25	6	0	3	11	7	40	.244	.323
Drese, Ryan	L	.438	89	39	9	0	4	18	13	8	.519	.674
Throws Right	R	.210	105	22	3	0	4	13	11	18	.303	.352
Drew, Tim	L	.429	14	6	4	0	1	3	2	2	.500	.929
Throws Right	R	.286	21	6	1	0	2	10	6	1	.414	.619
Driskill, T	L	.313	96	30	6	0	5	20	4	15	.340	.531
Throws Right	R	.308	104	32	8	0	3	19	5	18	.339	.471
DuBose, Eric	L	.305	82	25	5	0	1	7	9	16	.383	.402
Throws Left	R	.186	188	35	8	2	5	18	16	28	.258	.330
Duchscherer, J	L	.225	40	9	1	0	1	5	3	9	.279	.325
Throws Right	R	.320	25	8	2	0	2	0	6	3	.370	.400
Duckworth, B	L	.246	175	43	11	0	4	20	15	39	.311	.377
Throws Right	R	.297	185	55	17	3	8	30	29	29	.414	.551
Durbin, Chad	L	.368	19	7	0	0	1	3	2	6	.429	.526
Throws Right	R	.478	23	11	5	1	1	8	1	2	.500	.913
Durocher, J	L	.333	9	3	0	0	2	5	2	3	.455	1.000
Throws Right	R	.286	21	6	3	0	2	6	0	4	.318	.714
Eaton, Adam	L	.276	315	87	20	3	10	40	45	48	.364	.454
Throws Right	R	.222	388	86	24	1	10	41	23	98	.275	.366
Eckenstahler, E	L	.185	27	5	2	0	0	3	7	6	.389	.259
Throws Left	R	.148	27	4	1	0	0	2	8	6	.343	.185
Eischen, Joey	L	.255	98	25	4	2	3	12	5	25	.305	.429
Throws Left	R	.308	104	32	4	0	4	24	8	15	.363	.462
Elarton, Scott	L	.318	129	41	4	3	9	26	13	9	.378	.605
Throws Right	R	.344	93	32	5	4	4	16	7	11	.402	.613
Elder, Dave	L	.400	5	2	1	0	1	4	2	2	.571	1.200
Throws Right	R	.429	7	3	1	0	1	2	2	1	.556	1.000
Eldred, Cal	L	.295	78	23	2	1	2	11	9	25	.378	.423
Throws Right	R	.227	172	39	8	1	7	21	22	42	.318	.407
Ellis, Robert	L	.450	40	18	5	0	2	5	8	2	.531	.725
Throws Right	R	.222	36	8	1	0	5	10	2	6	.275	.667
Embree, Alan	L	.263	99	26	4	0	4	20	2	20	.272	.424
Throws Left	R	.221	104	23	5	1	1	7	14	25	.314	.317

Pitcher	vs.	Avg.	AB	H	2B	3B	HR	RBI	BB	SO	OBP	Slg.
Escobar, K	L	.233	356	83	17	1	8	45	38	86	.311	.354
Throws Right	R	.308	344	106	16	0	7	39	40	73	.387	.416
Estes, Shawn	L	.276	116	32	4	0	4	19	12	24	.346	.414
Throws Left	R	.312	481	150	28	0	16	80	71	79	.396	.470
Estrella, Leo	L	.290	107	31	10	0	5	20	12	8	.358	.523
Throws Right	R	.289	152	44	9	0	5	16	9	17	.337	.447
Etherton, Seth	L	.452	42	19	5	1	3	11	3	7	.500	.833
Throws Right	R	.253	79	20	8	0	1	9	12	10	.354	.392
Eyre, Scott	L	.219	96	21	2	0	1	13	9	15	.283	.271
Throws Left	R	.305	128	39	6	0	3	13	17	20	.385	.422
Farnsworth, K	L	.189	90	17	3	0	1	8	14	28	.298	.256
Throws Right	R	.199	181	36	4	1	5	19	22	64	.284	.315
Fassero, Jeff	L	.337	98	33	8	0	3	11	8	20	.398	.510
Throws Left	R	.278	216	60	11	0	14	31	26	35	.354	.523
Feliciano, P	L	.304	46	14	1	0	1	5	7	14	.407	.391
Throws Left	R	.259	147	38	7	0	4	19	14	29	.329	.388
Fernandez, J	L	.311	61	19	2	0	0	5	5	6	.377	.344
Throws Right	R	.220	82	18	5	0	2	10	7	13	.281	.354
Ferrari, A	L	.143	7	1	0	0	0	0	3	1	.455	.143
Throws Left	R	.375	8	3	1	0	1	2	2	0	.500	.875
Fetters, Mike	L	.100	10	1	0	0	0	0	1	0	.182	.100
Throws Right	R	.100	10	1	0	0	0	0	0	1	.182	.100
Field, Nate	L	.214	42	9	0	0	1	2	8	6	.340	.286
Throws Right	R	.256	39	10	2	0	2	8	6	13	.362	.462
Figueroa, N	L	.190	42	8	0	0	2	2	4	7	.277	.381
Throws Right	R	.235	85	20	2	0	6	12	9	16	.309	.471
Fikac, Jeremy	L	.227	22	5	2	0	0	6	5	4	.370	.318
Throws Right	R	.257	35	9	0	0	4	6	6	5	.409	.600
Fiore, Tony	L	.237	59	14	1	1	2	11	15	11	.387	.390
Throws Right	R	.247	73	18	4	0	3	16	6	12	.321	.425
Fogg, Josh	L	.320	247	79	16	3	8	38	17	30	.367	.506
Throws Right	R	.273	319	87	23	0	14	44	23	41	.332	.476
Foppert, Jesse	L	.267	206	55	7	3	9	27	31	46	.363	.461
Throws Right	R	.231	208	48	11	0	7	35	38	55	.345	.385
Ford, Matt	L	.304	46	14	4	1	0	3	7	3	.396	.435
Throws Left	R	.250	128	32	5	0	5	19	14	23	.326	.406
Fossum, Casey	L	.230	87	20	4	1	1	11	7	22	.299	.333
Throws Left	R	.286	217	62	21	3	8	35	27	41	.367	.521
Foster, John	L	.391	23	9	1	1	4	11	1	3	.440	1.043
Throws Left	R	.323	65	21	3	0	1	7	7	13	.384	.415
Foulke, Keith	L	.158	152	24	4	1	5	12	14	50	.243	.296
Throws Right	R	.210	157	33	7	1	5	13	6	38	.256	.363
Fox, Chad	L	.205	73	15	4	0	2	7	16	23	.352	.342
Throws Right	R	.241	83	20	3	0	1	19	15	23	.343	.313
Franco, John	L	.267	45	12	3	0	2	7	2	9	.298	.467
Throws Left	R	.264	87	23	3	0	3	6	11	7	.350	.402
Franklin, Ryan	L	.267	408	109	12	2	23	57	44	52	.341	.475
Throws Right	R	.233	386	90	13	0	11	33	17	47	.274	.352
Franklin, W	L	.255	145	37	7	1	8	32	11	31	.317	.483
Throws Left	R	.271	606	164	43	7	28	87	83	85	.364	.503
Fuentes, Brian	L	.238	105	25	2	2	1	7	9	34	.319	.324
Throws Left	R	.227	172	39	8	0	6	24	25	48	.328	.378
Fultz, Aaron	L	.218	119	26	5	0	2	13	13	28	.295	.311
Throws Left	R	.345	142	49	13	1	7	28	14	25	.406	.599
Gagne, Eric	L	.130	138	18	2	0	1	2	13	55	.216	.167
Throws Right	R	.135	141	19	4	0	1	8	7	82	.181	.184
Gallo, Mike	L	.227	44	10	1	0	1	3	3	6	.265	.318
Throws Left	R	.295	61	18	2	0	3	10	10	10	.371	.426
Garcia, Freddy	L	.281	420	118	20	1	23	69	43	61	.352	.498
Throws Right	R	.223	350	78	17	1	8	27	28	83	.288	.346
Garcia, R	L	.333	30	10	1	0	5	15	7	7	.474	.867
Throws Right	R	.231	39	9	0	0	1	3	7	8	.354	.308

Pitcher	vs.	Avg.	AB	H	2B	3B	HR	RBI	BB	SO	OBP	Slg.
Garcia, Rosman	L	.333	72	24	6	0	1	10	13	6	.435	.458
Throws Right	R	.312	125	39	10	0	3	23	10	19	.370	.464
Garland, Jon	L	.278	432	120	21	2	16	51	48	56	.351	.447
Throws Right	R	.234	290	68	14	1	12	41	26	52	.296	.414
Gaudin, Chad	L	.269	67	18	5	0	0	5	7	8	.329	.343
Throws Right	R	.218	87	19	3	0	4	11	9	15	.299	.391
Geary, Geoff	L	.273	11	3	1	0	0	3	2	3	.385	.364
Throws Right	R	.385	13	5	2	1	0	2	1	0	.429	.692
George, Chris	L	.280	100	28	3	1	7	22	6	9	.333	.540
Throws Left	R	.319	288	92	15	0	15	44	38	30	.396	.528
German, F	L	.238	80	19	6	1	2	13	27	20	.430	.413
Throws Right	R	.304	92	28	3	1	3	12	18	21	.425	.457
Gilfillan, J	L	.370	27	10	4	0	1	6	4	5	.469	.630
Throws Right	R	.273	44	12	3	0	2	8	6	7	.360	.477
Ginter, Matt	L	.333	6	2	0	0	1	4	0	0	.500	.833
Throws Right	R	.000	5	0	0	0	0	0	1	0	.167	.000
Glavine, Tom	L	.285	144	41	6	3	0	16	14	14	.348	.368
Throws Left	R	.289	567	164	31	7	21	71	52	68	.349	.480
Glover, Gary	L	.360	125	45	11	1	4	22	15	20	.430	.560
Throws Right	R	.258	124	32	5	1	2	18	7	17	.299	.363
Gobble, Jimmy	L	.263	57	15	2	0	1	6	3	7	.333	.351
Throws Left	R	.273	150	41	10	1	7	26	12	24	.325	.493
Gonzalez, E	L	.407	27	11	4	0	1	2	5	6	.500	.667
Throws Right	R	.347	49	17	3	0	2	10	2	8	.365	.531
Gonzalez, J	L	.235	293	69	17	3	9	31	37	51	.322	.406
Throws Right	R	.220	282	62	17	1	9	31	32	46	.316	.383
Gonzalez, Mike	L	.222	9	2	0	1	1	5	4	4	.429	.778
Throws Left	R	.238	21	5	0	0	3	6	2	2	.304	.667
Good, Andrew	L	.337	104	35	6	0	5	17	8	16	.395	.538
Throws Right	R	.245	159	39	10	1	10	21	8	26	.279	.509
Gordon, Tom	L	.231	130	30	4	0	3	17	17	41	.315	.331
Throws Right	R	.196	138	27	5	0	1	6	14	50	.287	.254
Grabow, John	L	.444	9	4	0	0	0	3	0	3	.444	.444
Throws Left	R	.154	13	2	0	0	0	0	0	6	.154	.154
Graves, Danny	L	.297	293	87	23	4	11	43	27	27	.358	.515
Throws Right	R	.299	391	117	33	2	19	57	14	33	.331	.540
Gregg, Kevin	L	.205	44	9	2	2	1	6	3	7	.271	.409
Throws Right	R	.205	44	9	2	0	2	2	5	7	.286	.386
Griffiths, J	L	.346	81	28	4	2	3	21	8	13	.411	.556
Throws Right	R	.312	93	29	5	1	2	11	11	12	.390	.452
Grimsley, J	L	.316	152	48	11	3	2	33	21	23	.403	.467
Throws Right	R	.282	142	40	4	2	4	33	15	35	.354	.423
Groom, Buddy	L	.270	89	24	4	1	2	13	5	17	.320	.404
Throws Left	R	.343	99	34	4	2	5	12	9	17	.404	.576
Gryboski, K	L	.227	44	10	3	1	0	5	10	7	.370	.341
Throws Right	R	.288	118	34	5	1	3	24	13	25	.368	.424
Guardado, E	L	.175	63	11	3	0	0	5	2	21	.197	.222
Throws Left	R	.219	178	39	8	0	7	19	12	39	.267	.382
Guthrie, Mark	L	.280	75	21	4	1	3	15	12	14	.393	.480
Throws Left	R	.241	79	19	4	0	3	9	10	10	.326	.405
Hackman, L	L	.238	122	29	4	1	4	12	19	19	.340	.385
Throws Right	R	.277	177	49	11	1	3	34	17	29	.363	.401
Halama, John	L	.214	112	24	4	0	4	14	11	18	.285	.357
Throws Left	R	.287	324	93	19	0	14	44	25	33	.339	.475
Hall, Josh	L	.317	41	13	2	1	1	6	8	5	.429	.488
Throws Right	R	.313	64	20	3	0	3	12	7	13	.375	.500
Halladay, Roy	L	.262	610	160	30	3	17	69	22	105	.291	.405
Throws Right	R	.224	415	93	24	4	9	35	10	99	.252	.366
Hamilton, Joey	L	.529	17	9	5	0	1	2	5	3	.636	1.000
Throws Right	R	.343	35	12	5	0	2	10	0	4	.343	.657
Hammond, Chris	L	.292	89	26	4	1	3	13	7	12	.340	.461
Throws Left	R	.257	152	39	12	0	2	16	4	33	.280	.375

Pitcher	vs.	Avg.	AB	H	2B	3B	HR	RBI	BB	SO	OBP	Slg.
Hampton, Mike	L	.164	146	24	2	0	3	9	16	32	.248	.240
Throws Left	R	.278	583	162	35	2	11	65	62	78	.346	.401
Hancock, Josh	L	.200	5	1	0	0	0	1	0	2	.200	.200
Throws Right	R	.167	6	1	0	0	0	0	0	2	.167	.167
Harang, Aaron	L	.272	158	43	8	0	7	27	13	23	.329	.456
Throws Right	R	.322	143	46	10	0	4	17	6	19	.349	.476
Harden, Rich	L	.271	166	45	6	0	4	24	26	37	.367	.380
Throws Right	R	.241	112	27	6	1	1	9	14	30	.325	.339
Haren, Danny	L	.278	126	35	10	1	7	16	14	18	.348	.540
Throws Right	R	.304	161	49	8	2	2	18	8	25	.354	.416
Harper, Travis	L	.287	157	45	7	1	4	23	18	32	.370	.420
Throws Right	R	.223	184	41	5	0	5	19	13	32	.280	.332
Harville, Chad	L	.303	33	10	3	1	1	5	10	5	.465	.545
Throws Right	R	.288	52	15	3	0	2	9	7	13	.377	.462
Hasegawa, S	L	.246	142	35	4	0	2	10	11	13	.301	.317
Throws Right	R	.221	122	27	8	0	3	6	7	19	.264	.361
Hawkins, L	L	.205	122	25	2	0	4	12	10	33	.263	.320
Throws Right	R	.263	167	44	10	0	0	11	5	42	.289	.323
Haynes, Jimmy	L	.299	154	46	12	1	4	33	25	16	.392	.468
Throws Right	R	.320	225	72	9	1	10	32	32	33	.412	.502
Hebson, Bryan	L	.500	2	1	1	0	0	1	0	0	.333	1.000
Throws Left	R	.429	7	3	0	0	1	2	1	1	.556	.857
Heilman, Aaron	L	.299	117	35	7	1	8	23	14	27	.376	.581
Throws Right	R	.301	146	44	8	1	5	27	27	24	.412	.473
Helling, Rick	L	.281	302	85	20	2	16	49	27	59	.353	.520
Throws Right	R	.273	300	82	13	1	15	32	18	39	.324	.473
Hendrickson, M	L	.269	167	45	14	0	1	18	11	21	.311	.371
Throws Left	R	.333	487	162	33	2	23	83	29	55	.366	.550
Hentgen, Pat	L	.237	333	79	14	3	15	41	33	59	.315	.432
Throws Right	R	.258	275	71	13	2	10	29	25	41	.319	.429
Heredia, Felix	L	.233	133	31	7	1	7	21	9	25	.290	.459
Throws Left	R	.225	191	43	10	1	3	14	24	20	.310	.335
Herges, Matt	L	.209	115	24	3	0	1	9	11	30	.277	.261
Throws Right	R	.249	177	44	8	0	2	23	18	38	.320	.328
Hermanson, D	L	.282	110	31	9	0	2	13	9	18	.331	.418
Throws Right	R	.264	148	39	6	0	7	21	15	21	.343	.446
Hernandez, L	L	.278	388	108	17	1	11	37	28	73	.333	.412
Throws Right	R	.233	502	117	17	2	16	49	29	105	.281	.371
Hernandez, R	L	.248	105	26	5	2	5	20	23	17	.383	.476
Throws Right	R	.276	127	35	8	0	5	21	20	28	.387	.457
Hernandez, R	L	.267	180	48	14	3	5	27	22	26	.346	.461
Throws Right	R	.231	169	39	9	0	4	18	15	22	.309	.355
Herrera, Alex	L	.167	12	2	1	0	1	1	3	4	.333	.500
Throws Left	R	.313	16	5	1	0	2	5	5	2	.476	.750
Hill, Jeremy	L	.333	3	1	0	0	0	1	0	0	.333	.333
Throws Right	R	.000	1	0	0	0	0	0	0	0	.000	.000
Hitchcock, S	L	.202	99	20	5	0	1	13	9	17	.269	.283
Throws Left	R	.291	244	71	11	0	13	29	23	51	.351	.496
Hodges, Trey	L	.269	104	28	8	0	6	22	16	25	.374	.519
Throws Right	R	.268	153	41	11	0	5	26	15	41	.333	.438
Hoffman, T	L	.182	22	4	1	0	1	1	2	9	.250	.364
Throws Right	R	.273	11	3	3	0	0	1	1	2	.333	.545
Holmes, Darren	L	.355	62	22	3	0	2	10	7	8	.420	.500
Throws Right	R	.236	106	25	6	0	3	12	4	38	.261	.377
Howard, Ben	L	.227	66	15	1	1	3	4	9	11	.320	.409
Throws Right	R	.242	66	16	5	0	7	11	6	13	.306	.636
Howry, Bob	L	.500	10	5	0	0	0	3	2	1	.583	.500
Throws Right	R	.462	13	6	1	0	1	3	1	3	.467	.769
Hudson, Tim	L	.229	524	120	17	1	9	45	35	91	.286	.317
Throws Right	R	.214	359	77	9	1	6	31	26	71	.272	.295
Ishii, K	L	.192	125	24	3	1	4	12	17	41	.299	.328
Throws Left	R	.252	416	105	23	4	12	45	84	99	.381	.413

Pitcher	vs.	Avg.	AB	H	2B	3B	HR	RBI	BB	SO	OBP	Slg.
Isringhausen, J	L	.254	67	17	2	0	2	6	6	12	.315	.373
Throws Right	R	.159	88	14	4	0	0	5	12	29	.260	.205
Jackson, Edwin	L	.143	35	5	0	0	2	2	7	7	.302	.314
Throws Right	R	.286	42	12	2	1	0	3	4	12	.340	.381
Jarvis, Kevin	L	.288	163	47	7	1	5	18	17	15	.355	.436
Throws Right	R	.316	209	66	14	0	10	40	15	34	.360	.526
Jennings, J	L	.323	378	122	30	2	9	58	48	41	.399	.484
Throws Right	R	.271	332	90	21	2	11	49	40	78	.353	.446
Jensen, Ryan	L	.438	16	7	2	0	2	5	4	2	.524	.938
Throws Right	R	.389	36	14	0	1	4	10	1	1	.410	.778
Jimenez, Jose	L	.382	204	78	18	1	3	34	22	19	.439	.525
Throws Right	R	.266	222	59	14	3	4	30	10	26	.314	.410
Johnson, Adam	L	.600	5	3	1	0	0	2	0	0	.600	.800
Throws Right	R	.714	7	5	0	0	1	3	1	0	.750	1.143
Johnson, Jason	L	.283	407	115	24	2	12	48	51	58	.366	.440
Throws Right	R	.283	357	101	9	0	10	39	29	60	.349	.392
Johnson, Jon.	L	.241	29	7	3	0	0	2	9	4	.410	.345
Throws Right	R	.394	33	13	1	1	2	6	6	3	.487	.667
Johnson, Randy	L	.303	66	20	5	1	3	9	6	13	.382	.545
Throws Left	R	.276	380	105	24	0	13	47	21	112	.321	.442
Jones, Greg	L	.283	53	15	4	0	2	14	6	15	.367	.472
Throws Right	R	.241	58	14	2	0	1	5	8	13	.343	.328
Jones, Todd	L	.323	130	42	8	1	3	21	15	22	.388	.469
Throws Right	R	.323	158	51	9	2	7	33	16	37	.386	.538
Journell, J	L	.357	14	5	0	0	0	2	5	2	.526	.357
Throws Right	R	.227	22	5	1	0	0	5	6	6	.379	.273
Julio, Jorge	L	.273	121	33	6	1	5	17	19	26	.371	.463
Throws Right	R	.239	113	27	2	0	5	19	15	26	.336	.389
Junge, Eric	L	.111	9	1	0	0	1	1	0	2	.111	.444
Throws Right	R	.222	18	4	1	0	0	1	1	3	.263	.278
Keisler, Randy	L	.600	5	3	1	0	2	6	2	1	.625	2.000
Throws Left	R	.211	19	4	2	0	1	3	5	4	.400	.474
Kennedy, Joe	L	.230	126	29	7	0	3	19	15	21	.329	.357
Throws Left	R	.324	426	138	28	6	16	78	32	56	.375	.531
Kershner, J	L	.178	90	16	2	0	2	5	6	21	.229	.267
Throws Left	R	.250	108	27	6	0	3	14	9	11	.311	.389
Kida, Masao	L	.300	20	6	1	1	0	1	0	5	.300	.450
Throws Right	R	.300	30	9	2	0	0	3	3	3	.364	.367
Kieschnick, B	L	.239	88	21	5	1	3	12	7	11	.302	.420
Throws Right	R	.338	133	45	15	0	2	21	6	28	.389	.496
Kim, B	L	.221	222	49	9	0	6	28	20	54	.319	.342
Throws Right	R	.227	242	55	9	0	6	25	13	48	.265	.339
Kim, Sun-Woo	L	.400	30	12	1	1	5	9	6	1	.500	1.000
Throws Right	R	.414	29	12	0	0	1	4	2	4	.500	.517
King, Ray	L	.200	95	19	1	1	1	11	8	17	.260	.263
Throws Left	R	.223	121	27	7	0	2	25	19	26	.331	.331
Kinney, Matt	L	.284	359	102	19	4	12	47	40	64	.355	.460
Throws Right	R	.260	381	99	14	3	15	63	40	88	.332	.430
Kline, Steve	L	.243	107	26	5	1	1	12	10	17	.314	.336
Throws Left	R	.233	129	30	6	2	4	15	20	14	.340	.403
Knott, Eric	L	.286	21	6	1	0	0	1	3	4	.375	.333
Throws Right	R	.298	57	17	5	0	2	7	3	13	.328	.491
Knotts, Gary	L	.323	201	65	13	2	12	43	29	19	.410	.587
Throws Right	R	.249	185	46	8	1	2	17	18	32	.319	.335
Koch, Billy	L	.294	109	32	7	0	5	17	16	26	.386	.495
Throws Right	R	.267	101	27	8	1	5	22	12	16	.339	.515
Kolb, Danny	L	.209	67	14	4	0	1	3	10	15	.312	.313
Throws Right	R	.230	87	20	2	1	1	7	9	24	.309	.310
Koplove, Mike	L	.224	58	13	2	1	2	4	5	17	.288	.397
Throws Right	R	.225	80	18	2	0	1	6	5	10	.303	.288
Lackey, John	L	.286	448	128	26	1	15	61	40	85	.346	.449
Throws Right	R	.269	353	95	17	0	16	45	26	66	.329	.453
Lawrence, B	L	.275	360	99	19	2	12	35	33	38	.341	.439
Throws Right	R	.244	439	107	16	2	15	60	24	78	.291	.392
Ledezma, W	L	.309	97	30	5	0	4	22	14	15	.393	.485
Throws Left	R	.292	236	69	13	4	8	39	21	34	.354	.483
Lee, Cliff	L	.278	54	15	2	0	4	11	1	12	.304	.537
Throws Left	R	.197	132	26	3	1	3	13	19	32	.301	.303
Lee, David	L	.000	8	0	0	0	0	0	3	2	.273	.000
Throws Right	R	.200	20	4	0	0	1	4	3	5	.304	.350
Leiter, Al	L	.299	117	35	3	2	3	11	13	29	.376	.436
Throws Left	R	.252	560	141	38	1	12	61	81	110	.351	.388
Leskanic, C	L	.176	85	15	6	0	0	5	16	23	.307	.247
Throws Right	R	.228	101	23	7	0	2	13	13	27	.319	.356
Levine, Al	L	.218	133	29	5	0	5	19	20	10	.329	.368
Throws Right	R	.284	134	38	8	0	4	13	9	20	.333	.433
Levrault, A	L	.383	47	18	4	0	2	10	12	10	.500	.596
Throws Right	R	.299	67	20	3	2	1	8	3	11	.333	.448
Lewis, Colby	L	.319	285	91	19	4	12	41	44	43	.411	.540
Throws Right	R	.313	230	72	22	1	11	48	26	45	.391	.561
Lidge, Brad	L	.230	135	31	8	2	3	18	20	34	.335	.385
Throws Right	R	.179	162	29	6	0	3	14	22	63	.286	.272
Lidle, Cory	L	.265	427	113	30	6	11	61	31	53	.317	.440
Throws Right	R	.305	338	103	17	5	13	55	29	59	.361	.500
Ligtenberg, K	L	.356	87	31	3	0	4	13	11	12	.424	.529
Throws Right	R	.206	141	29	7	0	5	21	3	35	.233	.362
Lilly, Ted	L	.235	162	38	9	0	2	11	8	33	.277	.327
Throws Left	R	.261	541	141	31	2	22	71	50	114	.325	.447
Lima, Jose	L	.329	167	55	11	1	6	27	24	16	.418	.515
Throws Right	R	.210	119	25	5	2	1	10	2	16	.238	.311
Lincoln, Mike	L	.333	45	15	3	0	0	2	9	10	.444	.400
Throws Right	R	.250	92	23	5	0	5	15	4	18	.286	.467
Linebrink, S	L	.275	149	41	3	0	3	13	18	27	.359	.356
Throws Right	R	.265	196	52	14	1	6	28	18	41	.332	.439
Linton, Doug	L	.231	13	3	1	0	0	3	2	1	.333	.308
Throws Right	R	.222	18	4	0	0	2	5	2	6	.300	.556
Lloyd, Graeme	L	.338	68	23	4	0	0	12	1	5	.347	.397
Throws Left	R	.333	135	45	12	0	2	25	13	20	.387	.467
Loaiza, E	L	.259	514	133	26	1	11	46	42	135	.322	.377
Throws Right	R	.191	329	63	14	3	6	22	14	72	.229	.307
Loewer, C	L	.432	44	19	2	0	2	7	3	5	.479	.614
Throws Right	R	.314	51	16	1	0	1	8	5	6	.368	.392
Lohse, Kyle	L	.283	446	126	27	0	16	64	26	61	.323	.451
Throws Right	R	.249	341	85	17	0	12	33	19	69	.293	.405
Looper, Aaron	L	.286	14	4	0	0	1	3	2	4	.375	.500
Throws Right	R	.250	12	3	0	0	0	1	0	2	.308	.250
Looper, Braden	L	.280	143	40	8	2	3	22	12	28	.331	.427
Throws Right	R	.250	168	42	3	2	1	16	17	28	.321	.310
Lopez, Albie	L	.411	56	23	6	0	4	16	9	8	.492	.732
Throws Right	R	.353	51	18	6	0	3	9	8	7	.441	.647
Lopez, A	L	.250	112	28	6	0	4	16	18	12	.359	.411
Throws Right	R	.186	161	30	7	0	1	15	16	52	.273	.248
Lopez, Javier	L	.250	116	29	6	0	2	15	3	30	.269	.353
Throws Left	R	.266	109	29	3	0	3	6	9	10	.344	.376
Lopez, Rodrigo	L	.308	318	98	20	0	16	45	27	54	.364	.522
Throws Right	R	.319	282	90	20	2	8	48	16	49	.367	.489
Loux, Shane	L	.352	71	25	8	3	2	18	4	4	.403	.634
Throws Right	R	.235	51	12	3	0	2	9	8	4	.355	.412
Lowe, Derek	L	.276	431	119	17	4	13	52	42	52	.345	.425
Throws Right	R	.266	364	97	18	3	4	43	30	58	.331	.365
Lowe, Sean	L	.267	90	24	5	0	4	11	16	12	.377	.456
Throws Right	R	.333	93	31	8	0	3	22	5	16	.376	.516
Lowry, Noah	L	.000	5	0	0	0	0	0	2	1	.286	.000
Throws Left	R	.063	16	1	0	0	0	0	0	4	.118	.063

Pitcher	vs.	Avg.	AB	H	2B	3B	HR	RBI	BB	SO	OBP	Slg.
Lyon, Brandon	L	.317	120	38	9	2	5	21	11	21	.381	.550
Throws Right	R	.276	127	35	10	0	1	15	8	29	.312	.378
MacDougal, M	L	.230	135	31	4	1	2	16	20	32	.333	.319
Throws Right	R	.314	105	33	7	0	2	17	12	25	.413	.438
Maddux, Greg	L	.271	391	106	23	5	9	40	21	56	.311	.425
Throws Right	R	.264	450	119	21	1	15	64	12	68	.287	.416
Madson, Ryan	L	.000	2	0	0	0	0	0	0	0	.000	.000
Throws Right	R	.000	4	0	0	0	0	0	0	0	.000	.000
Mahay, Ron	L	.208	53	11	4	0	1	8	6	13	.288	.340
Throws Left	R	.190	116	22	10	0	2	11	14	25	.277	.328
Mahomes, Pat	L	.192	26	5	1	1	0	4	8	5	.361	.308
Throws Right	R	.264	53	14	2	1	2	11	4	8	.305	.453
Malaska, Mark	L	.219	32	7	0	0	0	4	5	12	.342	.219
Throws Left	R	.250	24	6	1	0	0	5	7	5	.419	.292
Mann, Jim	L	.500	4	2	0	0	0	0	1	0	.600	.500
Throws Right	R	.429	7	3	0	0	1	3	0	1	.429	.857
Manning, David	L	.300	10	3	0	1	0	4	6	1	.563	.500
Throws Right	R	.444	18	8	1	0	1	8	2	1	.476	.667
Manon, Julio	L	.195	41	8	1	1	0	4	8	5	.320	.268
Throws Right	R	.290	62	18	3	0	3	14	9	10	.384	.484
Mantei, Matt	L	.155	84	13	1	0	4	6	8	28	.237	.310
Throws Right	R	.218	110	24	2	1	2	8	10	40	.285	.309
Manzanillo, J	L	.455	22	10	2	1	2	8	2	5	.500	.909
Throws Right	R	.344	32	11	1	0	5	13	2	7	.382	.844
Maroth, Mike	L	.257	171	44	11	1	5	22	10	24	.303	.421
Throws Left	R	.311	602	187	26	8	29	93	40	63	.356	.525
Marquis, Jason	L	.250	72	18	3	0	0	11	6	6	.309	.292
Throws Right	R	.287	87	25	5	1	3	12	12	13	.376	.471
Marte, Damaso	L	.168	125	21	6	0	1	12	11	42	.245	.240
Throws Left	R	.199	146	29	5	1	2	16	23	45	.308	.288
Martin, Tom	L	.189	106	20	3	0	3	7	9	32	.248	.302
Throws Right	R	.211	76	16	3	0	3	9	15	19	.355	.368
Martinez, Luis	L	.231	13	3	0	0	0	0	1	2	.286	.231
Throws Left	R	.407	54	22	8	0	3	17	14	8	.529	.722
Martinez, P	L	.238	412	98	24	3	7	38	25	114	.289	.362
Throws Right	R	.179	273	49	13	2	0	10	22	92	.248	.242
Mateo, Julio	L	.220	168	37	5	0	8	22	5	28	.237	.393
Throws Right	R	.219	146	32	4	0	6	12	8	43	.283	.370
Matthews, Mike	L	.294	102	30	5	1	2	25	10	22	.362	.422
Throws Left	R	.254	138	35	8	3	2	15	19	22	.346	.399
May, Darrell	L	.217	203	44	9	0	6	18	9	28	.252	.350
Throws Left	R	.255	599	153	36	7	25	68	44	87	.305	.464
Mays, Joe	L	.346	295	102	21	5	16	62	22	25	.393	.614
Throws Right	R	.246	232	57	9	0	5	29	17	25	.302	.349
McClung, Seth	L	.281	64	18	3	0	2	8	14	14	.418	.422
Throws Right	R	.205	73	15	2	1	4	10	11	11	.322	.425
Meadows, Brian	L	.276	127	35	5	1	4	20	7	21	.311	.425
Throws Right	R	.299	187	56	7	0	4	20	4	17	.318	.401
Mears, Chris	L	.395	76	30	5	1	4	18	5	10	.432	.645
Throws Right	R	.230	87	20	4	0	1	10	6	11	.299	.310
Meche, Gil	L	.275	385	106	14	4	17	38	44	67	.350	.465
Throws Right	R	.248	326	81	11	1	13	41	19	63	.291	.408
Mecir, Jim	L	.311	61	19	3	0	3	11	7	9	.380	.508
Throws Right	R	.256	82	21	4	1	1	7	9	16	.330	.366
Mendoza, R	L	.320	125	40	10	1	5	17	13	15	.387	.536
Throws Right	R	.372	156	58	9	1	5	29	7	21	.405	.538
Mercado, H	L	.158	19	3	0	0	0	2	6	4	.346	.158
Throws Left	R	.288	52	15	2	1	5	12	6	11	.367	.654
Mercedes, Jose	L	.222	9	2	0	0	0	1	2	0	.364	.222
Throws Right	R	.235	17	4	0	0	0	2	3	3	.350	.235
Mercker, Kent	L	.222	81	18	6	1	1	14	17	20	.354	.358
Throws Left	R	.230	122	28	5	0	5	12	15	28	.314	.393
Mesa, Jose	L	.213	94	20	6	1	1	9	15	17	.327	.330
Throws Right	R	.349	146	51	3	2	6	29	16	28	.414	.521
Miadich, Bart	L	.250	4	1	0	0	0	0	0	2	.400	.250
Throws Right	R	.667	6	4	2	0	0	4	1	1	.714	1.000
Miceli, Dan	L	.194	108	21	6	1	7	9	11	16	.275	.463
Throws Right	R	.244	156	38	5	1	6	21	14	42	.310	.404
Middlebrook, J	L	.375	8	3	1	0	0	2	1	0	.400	.500
Throws Right	R	.455	22	10	3	0	0	5	3	3	.520	.591
Miller, Matt	L	.400	5	2	0	0	0	0	2	0	.571	.400
Throws Right	R	.273	11	3	0	0	0	1	0	5	.273	.273
Miller, Trever	L	.226	106	24	3	0	6	16	12	28	.328	.425
Throws Left	R	.237	93	22	1	1	1	9	16	16	.355	.301
Miller, Wade	L	.258	329	85	23	2	10	39	40	71	.343	.432
Throws Right	R	.227	366	83	11	2	7	41	37	90	.305	.325
Millwood, K	L	.246	362	89	17	3	6	40	36	79	.315	.359
Throws Right	R	.253	479	121	28	4	13	55	32	90	.301	.409
Milton, Eric	L	.389	18	7	2	0	1	3	1	0	.400	.667
Throws Left	R	.174	46	8	0	0	1	2	0	7	.174	.239
Mitre, Sergio	L	.467	15	7	2	1	0	3	2	1	.529	.733
Throws Right	R	.348	23	8	2	0	1	5	2	2	.385	.565
Moehler, Brian	L	.600	20	12	4	1	3	8	4	2	.667	1.350
Throws Right	R	.263	38	10	1	0	1	4	2	3	.293	.368
Molina, Gabe	L	.333	6	2	1	0	1	3	0	1	.333	1.000
Throws Right	R	.429	7	3	1	0	0	1	1	0	.500	.571
Moreno, Orber	L	.333	15	5	1	1	0	4	0	0	.333	.533
Throws Right	R	.294	17	5	3	0	1	6	3	5	.400	.647
Morris, Matt	L	.255	271	69	17	0	4	22	19	45	.306	.362
Throws Right	R	.249	381	95	21	2	16	48	20	75	.290	.441
Moss, Damian	L	.342	184	63	15	1	7	27	24	25	.433	.549
Throws Left	R	.261	464	121	26	0	17	63	68	54	.358	.427
Mota, G	L	.181	138	25	1	1	3	18	19	37	.278	.268
Throws Right	R	.220	241	53	8	1	4	17	7	62	.245	.311
Mounce, Tony	L	.310	58	18	4	0	2	8	7	4	.429	.483
Throws Left	R	.320	147	47	8	1	7	29	18	26	.392	.531
Moyer, Jamie	L	.275	247	68	14	0	7	29	23	25	.343	.417
Throws Left	R	.233	563	131	25	1	12	49	43	104	.290	.345
Mulder, Mark	L	.252	119	30	5	0	3	7	9	22	.305	.370
Throws Left	R	.260	577	150	31	4	12	57	31	106	.299	.390
Mulholland, T	L	.252	131	33	4	0	3	13	14	17	.329	.351
Throws Left	R	.317	265	84	18	1	14	47	23	25	.375	.551
Mullen, Scott	L	.429	7	3	0	0	0	2	1	1	.556	.429
Throws Left	R	.370	27	10	2	0	2	11	9	3	.514	.667
Munro, Pete	L	.293	82	24	4	1	3	15	8	9	.370	.476
Throws Right	R	.295	132	39	4	1	4	19	18	18	.390	.432
Mussina, Mike	L	.229	419	96	19	1	10	37	28	110	.278	.351
Throws Right	R	.247	388	96	22	1	11	43	12	85	.272	.394
Myers, Brett	L	.270	333	90	22	1	10	40	48	64	.363	.432
Throws Right	R	.273	421	115	21	5	10	48	28	79	.329	.418
Myers, Mike	L	.237	76	18	5	0	3	15	8	14	.318	.421
Throws Left	R	.290	69	20	3	0	1	15	13	7	.430	.377
Myers, Rodney	L	.200	15	3	1	0	0	1	1	2	.294	.267
Throws Right	R	.318	22	7	0	0	1	7	3	3	.400	.455
Myette, Aaron	L	.800	5	4	1	1	0	3	2	0	.875	1.400
Throws Right	R	.300	10	3	2	0	1	4	0	1	.300	.800
Nagy, Charles	L	.368	19	7	3	0	0	5	1	2	.400	.526
Throws Right	R	.276	29	8	1	0	0	2	2	5	.323	.310
Nakamura, Mike	L	.385	26	10	1	1	1	4	2	6	.429	.615
Throws Right	R	.303	33	10	3	0	3	10	0	8	.324	.667
Nance, Shane	L	.256	39	10	0	1	2	9	3	9	.318	.462
Throws Left	R	.369	65	24	2	0	3	9	7	16	.425	.538
Nathan, Joe	L	.276	98	27	4	0	2	14	17	31	.385	.378
Throws Right	R	.136	176	24	6	0	5	22	16	52	.213	.256

Pitcher	vs.	Avg.	AB	H	2B	3B	HR	RBI	BB	SO	OBP	Slg.
Neagle, Denny	L	.415	41	17	4	0	5	12	0	3	.415	.878
Throws Left	R	.283	106	30	7	2	7	19	12	18	.361	.585
Neal, Blaine	L	.447	38	17	3	0	1	12	4	4	.478	.605
Throws Right	R	.389	54	21	5	1	1	14	5	6	.426	.574
Nelson, Jeff	L	.273	77	21	4	0	2	16	14	23	.404	.403
Throws Right	R	.233	129	30	3	1	2	21	10	45	.289	.318
Neu, Mike	L	.214	70	15	5	0	0	8	12	11	.337	.286
Throws Right	R	.295	95	28	6	2	2	14	14	9	.391	.463
Nitkowski, C	L	.550	20	11	1	0	0	4	1	4	.545	.600
Throws Left	R	.286	21	6	1	0	0	2	7	1	.448	.333
Nomo, Hideo	L	.213	357	76	12	0	10	27	54	79	.316	.331
Throws Right	R	.232	427	99	19	1	14	43	44	98	.304	.379
Norton, Phil	L	.214	28	6	0	0	0	1	1	3	.241	.214
Throws Left	R	.100	30	3	0	0	0	0	8	4	.289	.100
Nunez, V	L	.368	19	7	1	1	1	9	3	5	.417	.684
Throws Right	R	.412	34	14	3	0	6	12	4	5	.474	1.029
Obermueller, W	L	.301	103	31	5	2	3	11	15	13	.398	.476
Throws Right	R	.301	166	50	7	2	7	24	10	21	.352	.494
Ohka, Tomo	L	.311	318	99	22	2	6	26	18	44	.356	.450
Throws Right	R	.279	481	134	30	0	18	57	27	74	.322	.453
Ohme, Kevin	L	.000	5	0	0	0	0	1	0	1	.000	.000
Throws Left	R	.300	10	3	1	0	0	1	1	1	.364	.400
Oliver, Darren	L	.256	156	40	14	3	5	26	15	21	.331	.481
Throws Left	R	.292	552	161	30	4	16	70	46	67	.349	.447
Olsen, Kevin	L	.560	25	14	2	1	1	10	3	4	.607	.840
Throws Right	R	.333	33	11	3	0	1	6	1	8	.353	.515
Oropesa, Eddie	L	.206	63	13	3	1	1	6	11	21	.333	.333
Throws Left	R	.294	85	25	0	0	2	19	16	18	.412	.388
Orosco, Jesse	L	.231	78	18	3	1	2	14	10	20	.330	.372
Throws Left	R	.390	59	23	5	0	2	11	11	9	.473	.576
Ortiz, Ramon	L	.291	378	110	21	4	16	54	42	32	.366	.495
Throws Right	R	.282	351	99	14	0	12	57	21	62	.332	.425
Ortiz, Russ	L	.265	366	97	25	1	7	41	54	54	.355	.396
Throws Right	R	.187	427	80	16	2	10	45	48	95	.274	.304
Osuna, Antonio	L	.305	82	25	9	0	0	15	12	24	.389	.415
Throws Right	R	.266	124	33	11	0	3	14	8	23	.319	.427
Oswalt, Roy	L	.263	198	52	4	1	3	13	15	43	.315	.338
Throws Right	R	.234	274	64	10	0	12	33	14	65	.282	.401
Padilla, V	L	.267	344	92	26	4	7	40	34	51	.333	.427
Throws Right	R	.239	436	104	26	0	15	45	28	82	.303	.401
Painter, Lance	L	.290	31	9	3	0	2	7	3	4	.353	.581
Throws Left	R	.211	38	8	2	0	1	4	4	7	.286	.342
Paniagua, Jose	L	1.000	2	2	0	1	0	2	1	0	1.000	2.000
Throws Right	R	.500	2	1	1	0	0	0	0	0	.500	1.000
Park, Chan Ho	L	.367	60	22	2	0	3	15	17	8	.494	.550
Throws Right	R	.235	51	12	2	0	2	7	8	8	.391	.392
Paronto, Chad	L	.429	7	3	0	0	0	2	1	1	.500	.429
Throws Right	R	.235	17	4	0	0	1	3	2	5	.300	.412
Parque, Jim	L	.294	17	5	1	0	0	3	3	2	.429	.353
Throws Left	R	.367	60	22	4	2	2	17	13	6	.479	.600
Parris, Steve	L	.290	93	27	4	0	5	14	7	5	.333	.495
Throws Right	R	.367	90	33	11	1	7	18	6	9	.406	.744
Parrish, John	L	.194	31	6	3	0	0	5	3	6	.278	.290
Throws Left	R	.212	52	11	1	0	2	2	5	9	.281	.346
Patterson, D	L	.176	34	6	2	0	1	4	3	12	.243	.324
Throws Right	R	.281	32	9	1	1	0	4	1	7	.324	.375
Patterson, J	L	.281	89	25	3	3	2	7	20	20	.409	.449
Throws Right	R	.281	128	36	15	0	5	28	10	23	.340	.516
Pavano, Carl	L	.267	341	91	26	2	7	31	27	53	.322	.416
Throws Right	R	.263	430	113	28	1	12	56	22	80	.302	.416
Pearce, Josh	L	.333	15	5	1	0	0	2	1	0	.375	.400
Throws Right	R	.286	21	6	3	0	0	1	1	4	.348	.429

Pitcher	vs.	Avg.	AB	H	2B	3B	HR	RBI	BB	SO	OBP	Slg.
Pearson, Jason	L	.500	4	2	0	0	0	2	1	0	.600	.500
Throws Left	R	.667	3	2	0	0	1	2	2	1	.800	1.667
Peavy, Jake	L	.246	362	89	16	4	16	40	42	70	.327	.445
Throws Right	R	.230	365	84	9	1	17	46	40	86	.310	.400
Penny, Brad	L	.269	360	97	15	6	8	40	32	72	.334	.411
Throws Right	R	.258	380	98	28	1	13	52	24	66	.298	.439
Percival, Troy	L	.165	91	15	0	0	3	11	19	27	.313	.264
Throws Right	R	.205	88	18	2	1	4	9	4	21	.255	.386
Perez, Odalis	L	.201	149	30	7	1	3	12	9	35	.261	.322
Throws Left	R	.284	566	161	26	3	25	81	37	106	.327	.473
Perez, Oliver	L	.292	72	21	4	0	3	8	8	21	.370	.472
Throws Left	R	.258	419	108	21	4	19	65	69	120	.365	.463
Person, Robert	L	.200	15	3	2	1	0	4	5	2	.429	.467
Throws Right	R	.276	29	8	2	0	0	5	3	8	.324	.345
Pettitte, Andy	L	.321	224	72	7	1	5	25	11	46	.356	.429
Throws Left	R	.254	611	155	27	5	16	66	39	134	.296	.393
Phelps, Tommy	L	.233	60	14	2	0	1	6	7	13	.333	.317
Throws Left	R	.298	188	56	13	1	2	23	16	30	.350	.410
Phillips, J	L	.308	13	4	0	0	0	2	0	1	.286	.308
Throws Right	R	.556	9	5	1	0	1	3	2	1	.636	1.000
Pineiro, Joel	L	.234	441	103	23	0	11	53	49	85	.310	.361
Throws Right	R	.251	355	89	12	1	8	35	27	66	.308	.358
Plesac, Dan	L	.224	76	17	3	0	2	9	6	21	.289	.342
Throws Left	R	.235	51	12	1	0	1	4	5	16	.304	.314
Politte, Cliff	L	.287	101	29	5	0	3	17	12	19	.360	.426
Throws Right	R	.250	92	23	6	1	8	21	5	21	.290	.598
Ponson, Sidney	L	.271	410	111	19	4	5	40	35	61	.328	.373
Throws Right	R	.243	411	100	33	0	11	42	26	73	.293	.404
Porzio, Mike	L	.538	13	7	4	0	0	4	0	0	.571	.846
Throws Left	R	.256	43	11	2	0	2	6	1	9	.283	.442
Powell, Brian	L	.143	7	1	0	0	0	0	1	1	.250	.143
Throws Left	R	.500	14	7	2	0	3	7	0	2	.500	1.286
Powell, Jay	L	.255	94	24	11	0	3	28	18	20	.365	.468
Throws Right	R	.362	141	51	12	1	4	33	16	20	.426	.546
Prinz, Bret	L	.200	5	1	0	0	0	0	3	2	.500	.200
Throws Right	R	.545	11	6	4	0	1	8	1	1	.583	1.182
Prior, Mark	L	.240	362	87	12	3	6	29	31	103	.307	.340
Throws Right	R	.223	431	96	27	3	9	35	19	142	.263	.362
Puffer, B	L	.313	32	10	3	0	2	5	9	4	.463	.594
Throws Right	R	.292	48	14	3	0	0	9	7	6	.393	.354
Pulido, Carlos	L	.250	16	4	0	0	0	2	0	1	.250	.250
Throws Left	R	.256	43	11	5	0	0	5	3	5	.292	.372
Putz, J.J.	L	.444	9	4	2	0	0	2	2	1	.545	.667
Throws Right	R	.000	6	0	0	0	0	0	1	2	.143	.000
Quantrill, P	L	.198	96	19	3	0	1	6	11	21	.287	.260
Throws Right	R	.243	173	42	8	0	1	19	4	23	.268	.306
Quevedo, Ruben	L	.297	74	22	4	1	7	15	10	4	.376	.662
Throws Right	R	.326	95	31	4	2	5	13	13	15	.400	.568
Radke, Brad	L	.297	465	138	20	4	18	53	17	68	.326	.473
Throws Right	R	.278	374	104	23	0	14	46	11	52	.299	.452
Raggio, Brady	L	.333	9	3	1	0	0	3	4	2	.538	.444
Throws Right	R	.273	22	6	0	0	1	6	2	6	.333	.409
Ramirez, E	L	.250	64	16	2	0	2	11	3	10	.300	.375
Throws Left	R	.252	119	30	4	0	2	9	6	18	.297	.336
Ramirez, H	L	.206	141	29	7	1	2	12	12	25	.282	.312
Throws Left	R	.278	547	152	40	2	19	66	60	75	.351	.463
Ramos, Mario	L	.211	19	4	0	0	1	1	4	5	.375	.368
Throws Left	R	.233	30	7	2	0	2	7	9	3	.425	.500
Randall, Scott	L	.375	32	12	2	0	0	6	3	6	.429	.438
Throws Right	R	.275	80	22	3	0	1	9	8	19	.356	.350
Randolph, S	L	.222	90	20	3	1	3	14	13	20	.327	.378
Throws Left	R	.229	131	30	8	1	4	14	30	30	.377	.397

Pitcher	vs.	Avg.	AB	H	2B	3B	HR	RBI	BB	SO	OBP	Slg.
Reames, Britt	L	.000	1	0	0	0	0	0	0	2	.667	.000
Throws Right	R	.571	7	4	2	0	0	3	0	1	.571	.857
Redding, Tim	L	.297	316	94	23	3	8	41	38	51	.375	.465
Throws Right	R	.229	371	85	17	2	8	34	27	65	.289	.350
Redman, Mark	L	.200	140	28	4	1	4	13	9	42	.257	.329
Throws Left	R	.248	581	144	32	2	12	64	52	109	.311	.372
Reed, Rick	L	.264	295	78	13	1	8	34	20	44	.309	.397
Throws Right	R	.310	248	77	18	1	13	39	9	27	.345	.548
Reed, Steve	L	.374	99	37	5	0	7	19	14	15	.456	.636
Throws Right	R	.165	133	22	4	0	2	10	12	24	.268	.241
Reichert, Dan	L	.436	39	17	1	1	1	9	5	4	.511	.590
Throws Right	R	.333	33	11	3	0	1	10	3	9	.405	.515
Reith, Brian	L	.206	68	14	6	0	2	12	17	13	.360	.382
Throws Right	R	.287	164	47	13	1	6	20	19	26	.356	.488
Reitsma, Chris	L	.298	131	39	5	1	9	19	14	25	.363	.557
Throws Right	R	.270	196	53	10	0	5	20	5	28	.289	.398
Remlinger, M	L	.263	95	25	2	0	5	16	11	27	.343	.442
Throws Left	R	.180	161	29	3	1	6	17	28	56	.304	.323
Reyes, Al	L	.192	26	5	2	0	1	5	5	2	.323	.385
Throws Right	R	.211	38	8	3	0	0	6	4	7	.286	.289
Reyes, Carlos	L	.243	70	17	1	0	6	13	3	5	.286	.514
Throws Right	R	.284	81	23	6	0	4	10	2	8	.301	.506
Reyes, Dennys	L	.118	17	2	0	0	1	2	1	7	.167	.294
Throws Left	R	.394	33	13	3	0	1	11	9	9	.500	.576
Reynolds, S	L	.254	264	67	15	1	4	28	34	37	.342	.364
Throws Right	R	.320	387	124	24	1	16	63	25	57	.369	.512
Rhodes, Arthur	L	.269	104	28	2	0	2	9	7	25	.321	.346
Throws Left	R	.243	103	25	8	1	2	19	11	23	.316	.398
Riedling, John	L	.245	159	39	8	3	2	27	17	23	.320	.371
Throws Right	R	.286	238	68	11	0	5	34	30	42	.364	.395
Riggan, Jerrod	L	.444	9	4	0	0	1	0	1	1	.444	.444
Throws Right	R	.375	8	3	2	0	0	2	1	1	.400	.625
Riley, Matt	L	.143	7	1	0	0	0	0	2	3	.333	.143
Throws Left	R	.207	29	6	1	0	1	2	3	5	.281	.345
Rincon, Juan	L	.222	158	35	6	0	2	15	24	27	.332	.297
Throws Right	R	.239	163	39	9	0	3	20	14	36	.299	.350
Rincon, R	L	.200	80	16	3	0	1	6	7	20	.273	.275
Throws Left	R	.250	116	29	7	0	3	16	25	20	.386	.388
Riske, David	L	.145	124	18	5	0	5	12	12	44	.225	.306
Throws Right	R	.241	141	34	5	0	4	14	8	38	.291	.362
Ritchie, Todd	L	.409	44	18	3	0	2	8	5	4	.471	.614
Throws Right	R	.261	69	18	1	1	2	6	5	11	.333	.391
Rivera, M	L	.197	147	29	1	0	1	12	2	39	.217	.224
Throws Right	R	.283	113	32	5	1	2	18	8	24	.339	.398
Roa, Joe	L	.434	76	33	3	2	3	18	7	12	.488	.645
Throws Right	R	.257	140	36	10	1	7	20	3	26	.273	.493
Roach, Jason	L	.389	18	7	1	0	2	7	2	0	.450	.778
Throws Right	R	.318	22	7	1	0	1	5	2	2	.400	.500
Roberts, Grant	L	.231	26	6	1	0	0	1	2	4	.286	.269
Throws Right	R	.271	48	13	2	2	0	4	1	6	.300	.396
Roberts, W	L	.298	57	17	1	0	5	13	7	11	.375	.579
Throws Right	R	.258	93	24	1	2	2	18	9	15	.367	.376
Robertson, J	L	.243	152	37	5	2	3	19	16	30	.335	.362
Throws Left	R	.300	476	143	37	0	20	64	48	69	.362	.504
Robertson, N	L	.300	30	9	3	0	0	2	5	11	.400	.400
Throws Left	R	.307	150	46	5	0	6	19	18	22	.381	.460
Rocker, John	L	.333	3	1	0	0	0	1	2	0	.600	.333
Throws Right	R	1.000	1	1	0	0	0	0	1	0	1.000	1.000
Rodney, F	L	.345	58	20	3	0	1	15	10	14	.423	.448
Throws Right	R	.246	61	15	3	0	1	9	7	19	.333	.344
Rodriguez, Felix	L	.264	91	24	3	1	1	4	15	28	.374	.352
Throws Right	R	.255	137	35	7	1	4	21	14	18	.335	.409
Rodriguez, Fran.	L	.186	156	29	1	0	8	29	24	35	.293	.346
Throws Right	R	.156	135	21	5	0	4	12	11	60	.225	.281
Rodriguez, Rica.	L	.300	160	48	10	1	9	31	13	13	.354	.544
Throws Right	R	.250	164	41	9	0	7	22	15	28	.319	.433
Rodriguez, Rich	L	.143	7	1	0	0	0	1	0	2	.125	.143
Throws Left	R	.500	6	3	0	0	0	1	1	1	.571	.500
Rogers, Kenny	L	.251	215	54	12	1	6	22	18	55	.311	.400
Throws Left	R	.307	563	173	34	5	16	74	32	61	.354	.471
Romero, J.C.	L	.214	103	22	3	1	1	13	15	24	.336	.291
Throws Left	R	.314	140	44	8	0	6	25	27	26	.432	.500
Roney, Matt	L	.297	182	54	6	1	10	32	32	28	.402	.505
Throws Right	R	.232	207	48	8	1	7	21	16	19	.292	.382
Rosario, R	L	.286	14	4	3	0	0	0	1	3	.333	.500
Throws Right	R	.067	15	1	0	0	0	1	2	3	.222	.067
Rueter, Kirk	L	.212	146	31	8	0	1	13	9	13	.256	.288
Throws Left	R	.326	427	139	25	2	13	51	38	28	.381	.485
Rupe, Ryan	L	.231	13	3	1	0	1	3	1	2	.286	.538
Throws Right	R	.333	30	10	1	0	3	6	0	5	.333	.667
Rusch, Glendon	L	.307	127	39	10	1	2	21	6	23	.348	.449
Throws Left	R	.338	390	132	25	2	9	57	39	70	.400	.482
Ryan, B.J.	L	.186	97	18	3	0	0	14	13	45	.283	.216
Throws Left	R	.273	88	24	3	1	1	14	14	18	.381	.364
Saarloos, Kirk	L	.270	74	20	7	2	1	11	10	17	.357	.459
Throws Right	R	.287	122	35	6	0	3	18	7	26	.338	.410
Sabathia, C.C.	L	.275	178	49	8	2	1	17	13	34	.330	.360
Throws Left	R	.248	568	141	30	5	18	59	53	107	.315	.414
Sadler, Carl	L	.333	18	6	1	0	0	2	2	5	.435	.389
Throws Left	R	.278	18	5	1	0	0	5	3	5	.381	.333
Sanchez, D	L	.500	10	5	0	0	1	3	1	1	.500	.800
Throws Left	R	.500	20	10	2	0	1	8	0	2	.545	.750
Sanchez, Felix	L	.333	3	1	0	0	1	4	2	0	.600	1.333
Throws Left	R	.333	3	1	1	0	0	1	2	1	.500	.667
Sanchez, Jesus	L	.250	8	2	1	0	0	0	2	0	.400	.375
Throws Left	R	.346	26	9	5	0	1	7	2	2	.393	.654
Sanders, David	L	.375	40	15	1	1	3	12	5	4	.444	.675
Throws Left	R	.204	49	10	2	0	2	9	6	10	.298	.367
Santana, Johan	L	.191	178	34	6	0	5	14	14	57	.256	.309
Throws Left	R	.227	410	93	26	3	12	37	33	112	.284	.393
Santiago, Jose	L	.353	34	12	0	0	0	1	6	4	.450	.353
Throws Right	R	.278	90	25	4	0	2	13	8	11	.337	.389
Santos, Victor	L	.346	52	18	4	0	2	16	10	7	.444	.538
Throws Right	R	.244	45	11	3	0	3	10	6	8	.346	.511
Sasaki, K	L	.235	68	16	4	0	1	8	10	19	.325	.338
Throws Right	R	.242	62	15	2	0	1	8	5	10	.309	.323
Sauerbeck, S	L	.192	104	20	1	1	3	14	18	28	.325	.308
Throws Left	R	.257	105	27	2	1	3	18	25	22	.409	.381
Schilling, C	L	.255	278	71	9	1	7	26	16	75	.303	.371
Throws Right	R	.210	348	73	18	0	10	28	16	119	.244	.348
Schmack, Brian	L	.296	27	8	2	0	1	6	4	0	.375	.481
Throws Right	R	.286	21	6	0	0	0	5	0	4	.304	.286
Schmidt, Jason	L	.197	401	79	14	3	7	27	31	95	.256	.299
Throws Right	R	.204	358	73	18	4	7	23	15	113	.243	.335
Schoeneweis, S	L	.227	119	27	6	0	0	20	8	28	.295	.277
Throws Left	R	.275	131	36	4	0	3	16	11	28	.331	.374
Seanez, Rudy	L	.200	15	3	1	0	0	1	5	3	.400	.267
Throws Right	R	.364	22	8	1	0	2	7	1	6	.375	.682
Seay, Bobby	L	.250	16	4	2	1	0	2	4	1	.364	.500
Throws Left	R	.200	15	3	1	0	0	2	2	4	.294	.267
Sele, Aaron	L	.252	262	66	11	3	7	41	34	28	.350	.397
Throws Right	R	.322	214	69	13	1	10	34	24	25	.399	.533
Seo, Jae Weong	L	.223	336	75	23	3	6	37	30	60	.287	.363
Throws Right	R	.291	406	118	38	2	12	51	16	50	.324	.483

Pitcher	vs.	Avg.	AB	H	2B	3B	HR	RBI	BB	SO	OBP	Slg.
Serafini, Dan	L	.423	26	11	2	0	1	4	1	2	.429	.615
Throws Left	R	.313	96	30	5	3	4	17	13	11	.391	.552
Service, Scott	L	.327	55	18	2	3	1	9	6	12	.387	.527
Throws Right	R	.250	80	20	3	0	3	14	2	23	.265	.400
Sheets, Ben	L	.247	396	98	18	4	9	40	20	72	.286	.381
Throws Right	R	.286	469	134	25	1	20	76	23	85	.321	.471
Shields, Scot	L	.229	271	62	15	0	9	27	28	61	.307	.384
Throws Right	R	.264	288	76	16	1	3	25	10	50	.290	.358
Shiell, Jason	L	.195	41	8	1	1	2	5	7	10	.327	.415
Throws Right	R	.300	50	15	4	0	2	12	10	13	.426	.500
Shouse, Brian	L	.195	133	26	7	0	1	18	2	31	.230	.271
Throws Left	R	.364	99	36	9	2	0	10	12	9	.432	.495
Shuey, Paul	L	.224	107	24	5	1	2	9	20	23	.352	.346
Throws Right	R	.193	135	26	6	2	4	14	13	37	.278	.356
Silva, Carlos	L	.300	130	39	8	2	2	22	17	16	.381	.438
Throws Right	R	.266	199	53	11	1	5	32	20	32	.355	.407
Simontacchi, J	L	.307	215	66	15	1	11	36	20	30	.367	.540
Throws Right	R	.294	296	87	22	2	10	42	21	44	.346	.483
Smith, Dan	L	.273	55	15	4	0	4	7	11	10	.394	.564
Throws Right	R	.284	95	27	1	0	7	18	7	25	.346	.516
Smoltz, John	L	.189	111	21	5	0	0	6	4	37	.217	.234
Throws Right	R	.218	124	27	7	0	2	10	4	36	.240	.323
Snyder, Kyle	L	.273	194	53	8	3	5	23	16	21	.324	.423
Throws Right	R	.297	138	41	9	0	6	25	5	18	.318	.493
Soriano, R	L	.191	94	18	6	0	1	6	6	32	.248	.287
Throws Right	R	.132	91	12	2	0	1	3	6	36	.200	.187
Sosa, Jorge	L	.315	248	78	17	2	7	38	39	29	.402	.484
Throws Right	R	.241	245	59	10	0	7	34	21	43	.310	.367
Sparks, Steve	L	.286	175	50	13	0	5	37	21	33	.359	.446
Throws Right	R	.270	237	64	13	1	8	42	16	21	.318	.435
Speier, Justin	L	.273	121	33	12	0	3	10	9	31	.338	.446
Throws Right	R	.245	163	40	5	1	8	27	14	35	.313	.436
Spooneybarger, T	L	.152	66	10	0	1	1	7	4	13	.197	.227
Throws Right	R	.224	76	17	2	1	0	9	7	19	.291	.276
Springer, Russ	L	.240	25	6	1	0	2	7	2	2	.296	.520
Throws Right	R	.289	45	13	2	0	6	13	4	9	.360	.733
Spurling, C	L	.352	128	45	9	3	4	29	14	10	.413	.563
Throws Right	R	.200	165	33	8	0	5	22	8	28	.244	.339
Standridge, J	L	.250	64	16	5	0	1	5	11	9	.368	.375
Throws Right	R	.297	74	22	5	1	6	15	5	11	.338	.635
Stanford, J	L	.260	50	13	5	0	0	5	1	12	.269	.360
Throws Left	R	.241	145	35	6	1	5	14	15	18	.317	.400
Stanton, Mike	L	.206	63	13	3	0	0	4	7	15	.296	.254
Throws Left	R	.226	106	24	4	0	6	19	12	19	.303	.434
Stark, Denny	L	.346	153	53	9	2	8	28	24	8	.433	.588
Throws Right	R	.268	168	45	6	2	4	29	9	22	.306	.399
Stephenson, G	L	.280	268	75	19	2	12	38	25	33	.348	.500
Throws Right	R	.238	386	92	21	1	18	49	35	58	.311	.438
Stewart, Josh	L	.333	18	6	3	0	0	1	4	0	.455	.500
Throws Left	R	.259	85	22	4	2	4	13	12	13	.347	.494
Stewart, Scott	L	.283	60	17	2	0	2	7	4	13	.328	.417
Throws Left	R	.318	110	35	9	0	3	16	9	16	.372	.482
Stone, Ricky	L	.290	124	36	5	1	6	24	10	14	.343	.492
Throws Right	R	.217	184	40	6	0	5	26	21	33	.316	.332
Strange, Pat	L	.500	12	6	0	0	2	10	5	3	.647	1.000
Throws Right	R	.280	25	7	0	0	2	4	6	2	.419	.520
Strickland, S	L	.222	27	6	1	0	1	4	3	5	.323	.370
Throws Right	R	.217	46	10	0	0	0	3	7	11	.321	.217
Sturtze, T	L	.271	177	48	10	1	5	28	30	23	.385	.424
Throws Right	R	.321	184	59	10	1	9	31	13	31	.375	.533
Sullivan, S	L	.238	84	20	8	0	2	11	10	17	.333	.405
Throws Right	R	.187	150	28	7	0	4	18	22	39	.302	.313
Suppan, Jeff	L	.310	374	116	29	4	12	54	28	52	.364	.505
Throws Right	R	.239	423	101	24	5	11	38	23	58	.281	.397
Sweeney, Brian	L	.250	20	5	0	0	0	1	0	4	.250	.250
Throws Right	R	.154	13	2	0	0	1	1	1	3	.267	.154
Switzer, Jon	L	.176	17	3	0	0	0	1	0	6	.250	.176
Throws Left	R	.476	21	10	2	0	2	10	3	1	.577	.857
Tallet, Brian	L	.143	14	2	1	1	0	1	1	3	.250	.357
Throws Left	R	.339	62	21	8	1	2	13	7	6	.406	.597
Tam, Jeff	L	.303	66	20	5	0	2	8	16	12	.439	.470
Throws Right	R	.319	119	38	4	2	3	24	9	14	.369	.462
Tankersley, D	L	.000	0	0	0	0	0	0	2	4	1.000	.000
Throws Right	R	1.000	3	3	1	0	0	3	0	0	1.000	1.333
Tavarez, J	L	.292	113	33	7	0	0	12	19	14	.398	.354
Throws Right	R	.215	195	42	10	0	1	26	8	25	.260	.282
Taylor, Aaron	L	.320	25	8	2	0	0	4	4	5	.400	.400
Throws Right	R	.310	29	9	0	1	0	4	2	4	.375	.379
Tejera, M	L	.392	79	31	8	1	2	21	11	10	.467	.595
Throws Left	R	.224	228	51	12	0	4	24	25	48	.302	.329
Telemaco, A	L	.288	73	21	9	0	2	5	3	10	.325	.493
Throws Right	R	.202	99	20	4	0	3	12	8	19	.298	.333
Thomas, Brad	L	.167	6	1	0	0	0	0	0	0	.167	.167
Throws Left	R	.385	13	5	3	0	1	4	3	2	.500	.846
Thomson, John	L	.281	455	128	27	3	13	54	29	69	.326	.440
Throws Right	R	.270	393	106	24	2	14	56	20	67	.305	.448
Thurman, Corey	L	.389	36	14	3	1	3	6	6	5	.476	.778
Throws Right	R	.226	31	7	2	0	0	3	3	6	.294	.290
Timlin, Mike	L	.287	150	43	9	1	7	25	4	24	.308	.500
Throws Right	R	.198	172	34	4	0	4	18	5	41	.233	.291
Tolar, Kevin	L	.222	9	2	0	0	1	3	1	3	.300	.556
Throws Left	R	.429	7	3	1	0	0	1	1	0	.500	.571
Tollberg, B	L	.192	26	5	0	0	1	3	4	0	.300	.308
Throws Right	R	.308	13	4	1	0	0	3	0	2	.286	.385
Tomko, Brett	L	.325	329	107	24	3	14	47	24	41	.372	.544
Throws Right	R	.292	496	145	30	3	21	72	33	73	.340	.492
Torres, S	L	.307	202	62	11	0	10	36	20	32	.368	.510
Throws Right	R	.252	262	66	14	0	9	25	22	52	.326	.408
Towers, Josh	L	.281	128	36	3	4	6	18	5	20	.316	.508
Throws Right	R	.250	124	31	5	1	9	20	2	22	.271	.524
Traber, Billy	L	.219	114	25	6	0	1	14	15	29	.318	.298
Throws Left	R	.318	337	107	20	0	14	46	25	59	.368	.501
Trachsel, S	L	.199	327	65	13	2	6	18	29	46	.266	.306
Throws Right	R	.312	446	139	35	5	20	65	36	65	.361	.547
Tsao, Chin-hui	L	.309	68	21	2	0	3	9	11	9	.413	.471
Throws Right	R	.267	101	27	4	0	8	18	9	20	.345	.545
Tucker, T.J.	L	.254	130	33	9	0	5	22	5	11	.285	.438
Throws Right	R	.294	194	57	13	0	3	24	15	36	.354	.407
Turnbow, D	L	.167	24	4	0	0	0	1	1	6	.200	.167
Throws Right	R	.115	26	3	0	0	0	0	2	9	.179	.115
Urbina, Ugueth	L	.182	143	26	10	0	2	15	21	32	.280	.294
Throws Right	R	.229	131	30	7	1	6	21	10	46	.282	.435
Valdes, Ismael	L	.283	223	63	11	3	8	33	16	27	.331	.466
Throws Right	R	.350	243	85	10	1	15	46	13	20	.385	.584
Valentine, Joe	L	1.000	1	1	1	0	0	0	0	0	1.000	2.000
Throws Right	R	.400	10	4	0	1	1	4	1	1	.455	.900
Valverde, Jose	L	.169	77	13	2	0	2	7	8	22	.247	.273
Throws Right	R	.112	98	11	3	0	2	11	18	49	.261	.204
Vance, Cory	L	.161	31	5	2	0	0	2	4	4	.250	.226
Throws Left	R	.338	77	26	8	1	6	18	6	8	.388	.701
Van Poppel, T	L	.225	80	18	2	1	5	16	11	13	.319	.463
Throws Right	R	.289	114	33	6	2	3	15	4	21	.319	.456
Vargas, C	L	.270	196	53	14	2	4	16	22	24	.348	.423
Throws Right	R	.242	240	58	18	0	12	37	19	38	.307	.467

Pitcher	vs.	Avg.	AB	H	2B	3B	HR	RBI	BB	SO	OBP	Slg.
Vazquez, J	L	.233	377	88	20	4	10	35	29	100	.290	.387
Throws Right	R	.225	488	110	19	0	18	53	28	141	.269	.375
Venafro, Mike	L	.265	34	9	2	0	0	4	2	6	.342	.324
Throws Left	R	.341	44	15	3	0	1	8	1	3	.362	.477
Veres, Dave	L	.174	46	8	4	0	1	6	1	13	.188	.326
Throws Right	R	.359	78	28	5	0	3	17	4	13	.384	.538
Villafuerte, B	L	.200	60	12	2	1	3	9	7	10	.290	.417
Throws Right	R	.284	95	27	1	0	4	15	19	24	.414	.421
Villarreal, O	L	.252	135	34	7	0	4	16	19	24	.340	.393
Throws Right	R	.204	226	46	7	0	2	22	27	56	.296	.261
Villone, Ron	L	.267	101	27	4	1	5	9	10	26	.345	.475
Throws Left	R	.221	289	64	13	1	11	30	38	65	.315	.388
Vizcaino, Luis	L	.253	83	21	4	2	5	16	11	21	.340	.530
Throws Right	R	.269	160	43	6	1	11	30	14	40	.330	.525
Vogelsong, R	L	.295	44	13	0	0	0	6	7	6	.392	.295
Throws Right	R	.347	49	17	2	0	1	8	2	9	.389	.449
Voyles, Brad	L	.357	84	30	9	0	5	17	13	16	.439	.643
Throws Right	R	.333	51	17	6	1	1	8	5	8	.397	.549
Waechter, Doug	L	.182	66	12	2	0	1	1	10	14	.289	.258
Throws Right	R	.270	63	17	4	0	3	10	5	15	.333	.476
Wagner, Billy	L	.216	74	16	1	0	1	1	2	27	.247	.270
Throws Left	R	.154	234	36	3	1	7	16	21	78	.230	.265
Wagner, Ryan	L	.240	25	6	1	0	0	1	6	9	.387	.280
Throws Right	R	.140	50	7	0	0	2	4	6	16	.228	.260
Wakefield, Tim	L	.266	379	101	25	2	7	39	44	70	.344	.398
Throws Right	R	.228	404	92	11	3	16	53	27	99	.291	.389
Walker, Jamie	L	.212	113	24	6	1	6	14	7	29	.262	.442
Throws Left	R	.276	134	37	6	0	3	27	10	16	.329	.388
Walker, Kevin	L	.300	10	3	1	0	0	1	3	1	.462	.400
Throws Left	R	.133	15	2	1	0	1	2	2	4	.235	.400
Walker, Pete	L	.278	115	32	9	2	3	13	15	16	.364	.470
Throws Right	R	.276	98	27	3	0	8	14	9	13	.343	.551
Walrond, Les	L	.250	8	2	1	0	1	2	3	1	.455	.750
Throws Left	R	.346	26	9	3	0	1	4	4	5	.433	.577
Wasdin, John	L	.533	15	8	3	2	0	4	2	3	.588	1.000
Throws Right	R	.533	15	8	3	0	2	8	2	2	.556	1.133
Washburn, J	L	.230	191	44	12	1	6	23	12	41	.284	.398
Throws Left	R	.264	609	161	28	3	28	78	42	77	.318	.458
Watson, Mark	L	.000	1	0	0	0	0	0	1	0	.500	.000
Throws Right	R	.286	7	2	1	0	0	1	0	2	.286	.429
Wayne, Justin	L	.182	11	2	1	0	0	2	2	1	.357	.273
Throws Right	R	.538	13	7	2	0	1	5	3	0	.588	.923
Weathers, Dave	L	.239	109	26	3	1	2	10	21	36	.366	.339
Throws Right	R	.276	221	61	11	1	4	23	19	39	.347	.389
Weaver, Jeff	L	.342	383	131	33	4	11	62	27	48	.389	.535
Throws Right	R	.290	276	80	13	2	5	38	20	45	.344	.406
Webb, Brandon	L	.257	335	86	17	2	10	35	38	71	.338	.409
Throws Right	R	.167	324	54	5	0	2	20	30	101	.258	.201
Weber, Ben	L	.268	149	40	8	0	1	9	16	15	.339	.342
Throws Right	R	.282	156	44	4	2	6	22	6	31	.307	.449
Wellemeyer, T	L	.219	32	7	1	0	3	8	6	10	.342	.531
Throws Right	R	.257	70	18	6	1	2	13	13	20	.373	.457
Wells, David	L	.274	201	55	14	1	8	25	5	30	.307	.473
Throws Left	R	.290	645	187	40	2	16	72	15	71	.306	.433
Wells, Kip	L	.252	314	79	9	2	10	34	48	51	.350	.389
Throws Right	R	.219	421	92	18	1	14	36	28	96	.278	.366
Wendell, Turk	L	.302	86	26	6	0	3	11	10	9	.381	.477
Throws Right	R	.194	144	28	5	0	3	19	18	18	.300	.292
Westbrook, J	L	.276	275	76	16	1	5	28	46	26	.387	.396
Throws Right	R	.287	230	66	12	0	4	33	10	32	.335	.391

Pitcher	vs.	Avg.	AB	H	2B	3B	HR	RBI	BB	SO	OBP	Slg.
Wheeler, Dan	L	.208	72	15	4	1	1	10	7	12	.284	.333
Throws Right	R	.279	122	34	3	0	5	20	10	23	.328	.426
White, Gabe	L	.247	77	19	5	0	2	15	3	9	.268	.390
Throws Left	R	.255	98	25	8	0	5	16	5	20	.302	.490
White, Matt	L	.700	10	7	4	0	1	6	1	0	.727	1.400
Throws Left	R	.353	17	6	2	1	2	6	4	0	.455	.941
White, Rick	L	.223	112	25	8	3	1	18	10	28	.285	.375
Throws Right	R	.322	152	49	7	0	12	32	11	26	.381	.605
Williams, J	L	.215	228	49	7	1	1	13	31	40	.309	.268
Throws Right	R	.266	252	67	10	2	9	28	18	48	.329	.429
Williams, Mike	L	.277	112	31	8	0	3	19	23	17	.394	.429
Throws Right	R	.261	134	35	10	0	2	26	18	22	.365	.381
Williams, W	L	.268	385	103	22	2	8	36	25	64	.316	.397
Throws Right	R	.246	476	117	25	4	12	55	30	89	.299	.391
Williamson, S	L	.200	95	19	2	0	4	8	19	27	.336	.347
Throws Right	R	.245	143	35	7	0	3	25	15	47	.316	.357
Willis, D	L	.216	88	19	3	1	1	6	10	28	.296	.307
Throws Left	R	.250	515	129	30	5	12	49	48	114	.317	.398
Wilson, Kris	L	.355	152	54	13	1	7	24	12	20	.411	.592
Throws Right	R	.253	150	38	5	1	6	25	4	22	.281	.420
Wilson, Paul	L	.290	269	78	13	1	12	36	29	46	.361	.480
Throws Right	R	.282	397	112	27	2	12	54	21	47	.328	.451
Witasick, Jay	L	.292	65	19	5	2	1	11	15	18	.420	.477
Throws Right	R	.215	107	23	2	0	5	20	10	24	.288	.374
Wolf, Randy	L	.232	125	29	6	0	7	13	13	39	.304	.448
Throws Left	R	.234	629	147	40	2	20	74	65	138	.310	.399
Wood, Kerry	L	.198	313	62	12	1	10	30	53	109	.328	.339
Throws Right	R	.206	436	90	18	1	14	38	47	157	.299	.349
Wood, Mike	L	.344	32	11	4	0	0	7	5	6	.432	.469
Throws Right	R	.433	30	13	3	0	1	8	2	9	.500	.633
Woodard, Steve	L	.355	31	11	6	0	2	7	2	4	.394	.742
Throws Right	R	.279	43	12	2	1	1	6	3	8	.333	.442
Worrell, Tim	L	.241	145	35	5	0	2	22	15	30	.313	.317
Throws Right	R	.250	156	39	6	0	3	23	13	35	.302	.346
Wright, Dan	L	.280	189	53	10	3	10	37	25	26	.367	.524
Throws Right	R	.271	140	38	9	0	6	15	21	21	.366	.464
Wright, Jamey	L	.296	54	16	1	1	1	7	6	11	.367	.407
Throws Right	R	.175	40	7	3	0	0	6	5	8	.283	.250
Wright, Jaret	L	.365	85	31	3	3	4	21	14	14	.462	.612
Throws Right	R	.313	144	45	9	1	5	33	17	36	.380	.493
Wunsch, Kelly	L	.127	63	8	2	0	1	11	14	18	.301	.206
Throws Left	R	.153	59	9	3	0	0	7	11	15	.316	.203
Yan, Esteban	L	.309	94	29	11	0	2	21	12	12	.376	.489
Throws Right	R	.307	179	55	9	0	11	35	11	41	.369	.542
Young, Jason	L	.366	41	15	4	1	3	8	5	9	.438	.732
Throws Right	R	.345	55	19	0	0	5	10	4	9	.390	.618
Zambrano, C	L	.245	314	77	19	1	5	28	41	75	.335	.309
Throws Right	R	.235	472	111	24	0	4	44	53	93	.320	.311
Zambrano, V	L	.263	372	98	15	2	11	49	64	61	.371	.403
Throws Right	R	.206	325	67	24	1	10	40	42	71	.324	.378
Zerbe, Chad	L	.365	74	27	9	2	1	17	6	6	.395	.581
Throws Left	R	.277	119	33	8	1	2	11	8	11	.318	.412
Zito, Barry	L	.223	197	44	7	1	5	29	19	37	.291	.345
Throws Left	R	.218	652	142	21	1	14	62	69	109	.296	.317
A.L.	L	.269	...	...	...	...	...	...	...	...	.341	.430
	R	.266	...	...	...	...	...	...	...	...	.325	.424
N.L.	L	.266	...	...	...	...	...	...	...	...	.342	.419
	R	.259	...	...	...	...	...	...	...	...	.326	.417
MLB	L	.267	...	...	...	...	...	...	...	...	.341	.425
	R	.262	...	...	...	...	...	...	...	...	.326	.420

FANTASY BASEBALL DOLLAR VALUES

These dollar values are based on the Sporting News Ultimate Fantasy Baseball salary cap game. To learn more about Sporting News games, go to http://fantasygames.sportingnews.com. To see a different ranking system for a traditional league style game, check out STATS Fantasy Baseball at http://www.stats.com.

PITCHERS

Rank		Team	$ Value	Points
1.	Eric Gagne	LA	7,020,000	2947
2.	Roy Halladay	TOR	6,820,000	2814
3.	Jason Schmidt	SF	6,670,000	2721
4.	Mark Prior	CHC	5,090,000	2693
5.	Esteban Loaiza	CHW	3,240,000	2603
6.	Tim Hudson	OAK	6,340,000	2543
7.	Keith Foulke	OAK	4,950,000	2543
8.	Pedro Martinez	BOS	8,870,000	2415
9.	Javier Vazquez	MON	5,480,000	2390
10.	Billy Wagner	HOU	4,980,000	2387
11.	Kerry Wood	CHC	6,440,000	2345
12.	Kevin Brown	LA	5,350,000	2342
13.	Mike Mussina	NYY	6,380,000	2296
14.	Livan Hernandez	MON	3,010,000	2178
15.	Hideo Nomo	LA	6,080,000	2169
16.	John Smoltz	ATL	6,020,000	2160
17.	Jamie Moyer	SEA	5,600,000	2140
18.	Mariano Rivera	NYY	5,370,000	2092
19.	Barry Zito	OAK	7,630,000	2091
20.	Russ Ortiz	ATL	4,750,000	2054
21.	Roger Clemens	NYY	4,950,000	2041
22.	Bartolo Colon	CHW	6,560,000	2033
23.	Andy Pettitte	NYY	4,580,000	1957
24.	Carlos Zambrano	CHC	3,250,000	1947
25.	Woody Williams	STL	4,450,000	1926
26.	Eddie Guardado	MIN	4,840,000	1903
27.	Brandon Webb	ARI	1,550,000	1878
28.	Johan Santana	MIN	3,240,000	1872
29.	Tim Worrell	SF	2,490,000	1866
30.	Joel Pineiro	SEA	4,690,000	1847
31.	Curt Schilling	ARI	8,560,000	1837
32.	Mark Mulder	OAK	6,700,000	1823
33.	Sidney Ponson	SF	2,910,000	1822
34.	Kevin Millwood	PHI	6,450,000	1821
35.	Randy Wolf	PHI	5,760,000	1789
36.	Mark Redman	FLA	2,670,000	1780
37.	Ugueth Urbina	FLA	2,360,000	1766
38.	Greg Maddux	ATL	5,560,000	1754
39.	Kip Wells	PIT	1,590,000	1742
40.	Matt Clement	CHC	4,360,000	1734
41.	Joe Borowski	CHC	2,250,000	1718
42.	Vicente Padilla	PHI	4,030,000	1715
43.	C.C. Sabathia	CLE	3,910,000	1697
44.	Tim Wakefield	BOS	3,250,000	1663
45.	Dontrelle Willis	FLA	830,000	1653
46.	Steve Trachsel	NYM	1,430,000	1649
47.	Darrell May	KC	570,000	1645
48.	Byung-Hyun Kim	BOS	3,590,000	1636
49.	Matt Mantei	ARI	1,540,000	1584
50.	Brad Penny	FLA	1,700,000	1577
51.	Wade Miller	HOU	3,790,000	1572
52.	David Wells	NYY	5,770,000	1569
53.	Ryan Franklin	SEA	2,130,000	1567
54.	Jake Peavy	SD	2,530,000	1564
55.	Miguel Batista	ARI	2,150,000	1547
56.	Ben Sheets	MIL	2,580,000	1519
57.	Mark Buehrle	CHW	4,740,000	1514
58.	Braden Looper	FLA	1,400,000	1508
59.	Mike Hampton	ATL	3,180,000	1503
60.	Kelvim Escobar	TOR	1,740,000	1491
61.	Matt Morris	STL	5,470,000	1486
62.	Derek Lowe	BOS	5,630,000	1456
63.	Al Leiter	NYM	3,280,000	1453
64.	Brian Anderson	KC	520,000	1450
65.	Brad Radke	MIN	2,290,000	1446
66.	Carl Pavano	FLA	1,330,000	1436
67.	Lance Carter	TB	700,000	1432
68.	Kyle Lohse	MIN	4,020,000	1425
69.	Rocky Biddle	MON	1,490,000	1424
70.	Josh Beckett	FLA	2,610,000	1422
71.	Jeff Suppan	BOS	2,500,000	1403
72.	Horacio Ramirez	ATL	610,000	1386
73.	Ted Lilly	OAK	2,580,000	1382
74.	Brett Myers	PHI	1,900,000	1379
75.	Damaso Marte	CHW	500,000	1375
76.	Brian Lawrence	SD	1,620,000	1369
77.	Troy Percival	ANA	3,940,000	1366
78.	Freddy Garcia	SEA	3,810,000	1366
79.	Scot Shields	ANA	520,000	1359
80.	Adam Eaton	SD	560,000	1358
81.	Roy Oswalt	HOU	5,930,000	1357
82.	Gil Meche	SEA	580,000	1357
83.	Odalis Perez	LA	2,920,000	1351
84.	Armando Benitez	SEA	1,610,000	1351
85.	Jorge Julio	BAL	1,560,000	1348
86.	Victor Zambrano	TB	500,000	1348
87.	John Thomson	TEX	500,000	1344
88.	Guillermo Mota	LA	500,000	1336
89.	Jae Weong Seo	NYM	620,000	1329
90.	Jarrod Washburn	ANA	3,410,000	1299
91.	Danys Baez	CLE	500,000	1282
92.	Francisco Cordero	TEX	500,000	1250
93.	Tim Redding	HOU	860,000	1247
94.	Jon Garland	CHW	970,000	1230
95.	Mike MacDougal	KC	1,240,000	1226
96.	Kenny Rogers	MIN	1,500,000	1225
97.	Octavio Dotel	HOU	500,000	1219
98.	Rheal Cormier	PHI	500,000	1218
99.	Scott Williamson	BOS	2,420,000	1217
100.	Tom Gordon	CHW	500,000	1213
101.	Tomo Ohka	MON	1,460,000	1212
102.	Kazuhisa Ishii	LA	3,610,000	1194
103.	S. Hasegawa	SEA	600,000	1187
104.	John Lackey	ANA	540,000	1180
105.	Francisco Rodriguez	ANA	1,360,000	1179
106.	Pat Hentgen	BAL	500,000	1161
107.	Jerome Williams	SF	510,000	1136
108.	Jason Johnson	BAL	2,070,000	1119
109.	Wilson Alvarez	LA	780,000	1117
110.	David Riske	CLE	500,000	1117
111.	LaTroy Hawkins	MIN	500,000	1117
112.	Jeremy Affeldt	KC	500,000	1115
113.	Joe Nathan	SF	500,000	1111
114.	Jason Isringhausen	STL	2,650,000	1079
115.	Jeremi Gonzalez	TB	500,000	1073
116.	Mike DeJean	STL	500,000	1070
117.	Oscar Villarreal	ARI	500,000	1063
118.	Matt Kinney	MIL	550,000	1058
119.	Chris Reitsma	CIN	500,000	1057
120.	Rod Beck	SD	560,000	1055
121.	John Burkett	BOS	1,710,000	1053
122.	Danny Kolb	MIL	500,000	1047
123.	Shawn Chacon	COL	1,370,000	1014
124.	Aquilino Lopez	TOR	500,000	1005
125.	Jeriome Robertson	HOU	560,000	1002
126.	Brett Tomko	STL	890,000	1001
127.	Luis Ayala	MON	500,000	999
128.	Jose Valverde	ARI	500,000	989
129.	Brendan Donnelly	ANA	500,000	978
130.	Darren Oliver	COL	500,000	972
131.	Garrett Stephenson	STL	500,000	964
132.	Brad Lidge	HOU	500,000	950
133.	Julio Mateo	SEA	500,000	949
134.	Ramon Ortiz	ANA	3,090,000	947
135.	Julian Tavarez	PIT	500,000	936
136.	Mike Williams	PHI	1,560,000	932
137.	Jason Davis	CLE	500,000	925
138.	Jim Brower	SF	500,000	910
139.	Tom Glavine	NYM	3,980,000	907
140.	Cal Eldred	STL	500,000	906
141.	Jose Mesa	PHI	1,600,000	899
142.	Paul Wilson	CIN	500,000	888
143.	Zach Day	MON	1,450,000	876
144.	Mike Timlin	BOS	500,000	876
145.	Randy Johnson	ARI	8,350,000	875
146.	Jason Jennings	COL	800,000	873
147.	Matt Herges	SF	500,000	873
148.	Brian Fuentes	COL	500,000	871
149.	Elmer Dessens	ARI	720,000	866
150.	Wayne Franklin	MIL	500,000	866
151.	Jeff D'Amico	PIT	500,000	863
152.	Ron Villone	HOU	510,000	859
153.	Justin Speier	COL	500,000	858
154.	Cory Lidle	TOR	3,200,000	856
155.	Chad Bradford	OAK	500,000	845
156.	Rick Helling	FLA	500,000	843
157.	Felix Heredia	NYY	500,000	840
158.	Jose Contreras	NYY	860,000	836
159.	Salomon Torres	PIT	500,000	835
160.	Rafael Soriano	SEA	500,000	834
161.	Kyle Farnsworth	CHC	500,000	828
162.	Shane Reynolds	ATL	1,220,000	821
163.	Kirk Rueter	SF	2,430,000	819

Rank	Team	$ Value	Points	Rank	Team	$ Value	Points	Rank	Team	$ Value	Points
164. Dave Weathers	NYM	500,000	817	228. Turk Wendell	PHI	500,000	504	292. Rick White	HOU	500,000	327
165. Paul Quantrill	LA	500,000	798	229. Chad Fox	FLA	500,000	502	293. Antonio Alfonseca	CHC	500,000	326
166. Jeff Nelson	NYY	500,000	795	230. Kurt Ainsworth	BAL	500,000	502	294. Scott Stewart	MON	500,000	325
167. Jose Jimenez	COL	550,000	781	231. Jesus Colome	TB	500,000	500	295. Mark Guthrie	CHC	500,000	322
168. R.A. Dickey	TEX	500,000	748	232. Ray King	ATL	500,000	500	296. Jimmy Gobble	KC	530,000	321
169. Ben Weber	ANA	500,000	747	233. Jose Lima	KC	720,000	498	297. Dave Burba	MIL	500,000	321
170. Paul Shuey	LA	500,000	744	234. Jeremy Bonderman	DET	500,000	498	298. Gary Glover	ANA	500,000	321
171. Curtis Leskanic	KC	500,000	740	235. Kevin Appier	KC	880,000	497	299. Antonio Osuna	NYY	500,000	320
172. Jesse Foppert	SF	500,000	722	236. Jason Kershner	TOR	500,000	495	300. Adam Bernero	COL	500,000	319
173. Felix Rodriguez	SF	500,000	719	237. Cliff Lee	CLE	570,000	481	301. Ryan Wagner	CIN	500,000	319
174. Scott Linebrink	SD	500,000	718	238. Dustin Hermanson	SF	500,000	481	302. Kirk Saarloos	HOU	500,000	309
175. Mike Remlinger	CHC	500,000	716	239. Chris Spurling	DET	500,000	479	303. Kyle Snyder	KC	500,000	308
176. Claudio Vargas	MON	500,000	707	240. Jung Bong	ATL	500,000	477	304. Aaron Fultz	TEX	500,000	302
177. Ricky Stone	HOU	500,000	705	241. Mike Matthews	SD	500,000	477	305. Darren Holmes	ATL	500,000	300
178. Joaquin Benoit	TEX	500,000	704	242. Brian Shouse	TEX	500,000	476	306. Todd Van Poppel	CIN	500,000	299
179. Josh Fogg	PIT	500,000	701	243. Trever Miller	TOR	500,000	472	307. Danny Haren	STL	500,000	293
180. Scott Sullivan	CHW	500,000	694	244. Rob Bell	TB	500,000	470	308. Jason Grimsley	KC	500,000	286
181. Juan Rincon	MIN	500,000	687	245. Kris Benson	PIT	3,440,000	468	309. John Bale	CIN	500,000	284
182. Travis Harper	TB	500,000	686	246. Steve Sparks	OAK	500,000	462	310. Jeff Fassero	STL	500,000	282
183. Jake Westbrook	CLE	500,000	675	247. Joey Eischen	MON	500,000	462	311. Seth McClung	TB	500,000	281
184. Jamie Walker	DET	500,000	673	248. Gabe White	NYY	500,000	462	312. Derrick Turnbow	ANA	500,000	281
185. Damian Moss	BAL	2,780,000	663	249. Tom Martin	LA	500,000	459	313. Jared Fernandez	HOU	500,000	280
186. Jason Simontacchi	STL	500,000	659	250. Jeff Weaver	NYY	2,360,000	455	314. Amaury Telemaco	PHI	500,000	278
187. Josh Towers	TOR	530,000	658	251. Ron Mahay	TEX	500,000	454	315. Chris Mears	DET	500,000	276
188. Doug Davis	MIL	500,000	655	252. Brandon Duckworth	PHI	500,000	452	316. Dave Veres	CHC	500,000	275
189. Brandon Lyon	BOS	500,000	637	253. Mike Koplove	ARI	500,000	446	317. Nate Bump	FLA	500,000	275
190. Oliver Perez	PIT	500,000	635	254. Kiko Calero	STL	500,000	445	318. Pete Walker	TOR	500,000	274
191. Sterling Hitchcock	STL	500,000	625	255. Scott Eyre	SF	500,000	443	319. Brandon Villafuerte	SD	500,000	270
192. Dan Miceli	HOU	500,000	623	256. Brian Meadows	PIT	500,000	443	320. Matt Roney	DET	500,000	270
193. Runelvys Hernandez	KC	800,000	620	257. Trey Hodges	ATL	500,000	441	321. Franklyn German	DET	500,000	267
194. Nate Cornejo	DET	500,000	620	258. Dan Plesac	PHI	500,000	435	322. Colby Lewis	TEX	500,000	264
195. Mark Hendrickson	TOR	500,000	613	259. Tommy Phelps	FLA	500,000	429	323. John Franco	NYM	500,000	261
196. Chris Hammond	NYY	500,000	606	260. V. de los Santos	PHI	500,000	427	324. Kevin Jarvis	SD	500,000	260
197. Billy Koch	CHW	2,500,000	604	261. Jason Boyd	PIT	500,000	426	325. Brooks Kieschnick	MIL	500,000	257
198. Rick Reed	MIN	1,560,000	601	262. T.J. Tucker	MON	500,000	424	326. Joe Kennedy	TB	500,000	257
199. Ricardo Rincon	OAK	500,000	600	263. Jack Cressend	CLE	500,000	421	327. Esteban Yan	STL	500,000	254
200. John Halama	OAK	500,000	589	264. Mike Stanton	NYM	500,000	409	328. Mike Neu	OAK	500,000	251
201. Kerry Ligtenberg	BAL	500,000	583	265. Roberto Hernandez	ATL	500,000	407	329. Ricardo Rodriguez	TEX	800,000	250
202. Jorge Sosa	TB	500,000	579	266. Dan Wheeler	NYM	500,000	406	330. Wilfredo Ledezma	DET	500,000	243
203. Carlos Silva	PHI	500,000	569	267. Kevin Gryboski	ATL	500,000	396	331. Brandon Backe	TB	500,000	242
204. Steve Kline	STL	500,000	563	268. Kris Wilson	KC	500,000	395	332. Danny Patterson	DET	500,000	242
205. D.J. Carrasco	KC	500,000	560	269. Andrew Good	ARI	500,000	394	333. Joe Beimel	PIT	500,000	240
206. Rich Harden	OAK	3,440,000	558	270. Terry Mulholland	CLE	500,000	387	334. Ryan Dempster	CIN	800,000	237
207. B.J. Ryan	BAL	500,000	558	271. Joe Mays	MIN	500,000	386	335. Ben Howard	SD	500,000	237
208. Mike Maroth	DET	500,000	557	272. Brian Reith	CIN	500,000	386	336. Grant Balfour	MIN	500,000	233
209. Cliff Politte	TOR	500,000	556	273. Aaron Harang	CIN	500,000	376	337. Pete Munro	HOU	500,000	233
210. Javier Lopez	COL	500,000	552	274. Ismael Valdes	TEX	500,000	374	338. Armando Almanza	FLA	500,000	231
211. Eric DuBose	BAL	500,000	547	275. Brian Boehringer	PIT	500,000	367	339. Miguel Asencio	KC	500,000	229
212. Steve Reed	COL	500,000	545	276. Mike Lincoln	PIT	500,000	367	340. Andy Ashby	LA	500,000	228
213. Michael Tejera	FLA	500,000	543	277. Tim Spooneybarger	FLA	500,000	365	341. Bronson Arroyo	BOS	500,000	227
214. Alan Embree	BOS	500,000	542	278. Rick Bauer	BAL	500,000	365	342. John Parrish	BAL	500,000	223
215. Billy Traber	CLE	500,000	539	279. Aaron Sele	ANA	500,000	364	343. Chris George	KC	500,000	221
216. Shawn Estes	CHC	500,000	537	280. Luther Hackman	SD	500,000	362	344. Juan Cruz	CHC	500,000	220
217. Kazuhiro Sasaki	SEA	1,360,000	534	281. Luis Vizcaino	MIL	500,000	350	345. Eddie Oropesa	ARI	500,000	220
218. Al Levine	KC	500,000	534	282. Jose Acevedo	CIN	500,000	348	346. Willis Roberts	BAL	500,000	219
219. Darren Dreifort	LA	500,000	531	283. Tanyon Sturtze	TOR	500,000	347	347. Jason Shiell	BOS	500,000	217
220. Terry Adams	PHI	500,000	528	284. Kelly Wunsch	CHW	500,000	343	348. Paul Abbott	KC	500,000	212
221. Rodrigo Lopez	BAL	1,850,000	525	285. Jay Witasick	SD	500,000	338	349. Dan Smith	MON	500,000	210
222. John Riedling	CIN	500,000	520	286. Tony Armas	MON	620,000	337	350. Aaron Cook	COL	500,000	209
223. Kent Mercker	ATL	500,000	518	287. Scott Sauerbeck	BOS	500,000	336	351. Denny Stark	COL	500,000	207
224. Arthur Rhodes	SEA	500,000	517	288. Chad Gaudin	TB	500,000	333	352. Chad Zerbe	SF	500,000	206
225. Scott Schoeneweis	CHW	500,000	509	289. Will Cunnane	ATL	500,000	332	353. Gary Knotts	DET	500,000	205
226. Danny Graves	CIN	1,030,000	506	290. J.C. Romero	MIN	500,000	331	354. Travis Driskill	BAL	500,000	204
227. Casey Fossum	BOS	2,270,000	505	291. Nelson Figueroa	PIT	500,000	329	355. Wes Obermueller	MIL	500,000	204

Rank	Team	$ Value	Points	Rank	Team	$ Value	Points	Rank	Team	$ Value	Points
356. Dan Wright	CHW	500,000	199	421. Shane Nance	MIL	500,000	77	486. Alex Herrera	COL	500,000	-6
357. Juan Acevedo	TOR	500,000	194	422. Mike Fetters	MIN	500,000	77	487. Brian Tollberg	SD	500,000	-6
358. Jim Mecir	OAK	500,000	194	423. Doug Creek	TOR	500,000	76	488. Reynaldo Garcia	TEX	500,000	-8
359. Fernando Rodney	DET	500,000	190	424. Jose Mercedes	MON	500,000	74	489. Jeremy Griffiths	NYM	500,000	-8
360. Buddy Groom	BAL	500,000	186	425. Cory Vance	COL	500,000	73	490. Jonathan Johnson	HOU	500,000	-9
361. John Patterson	ARI	500,000	183	426. Eric Junge	PHI	500,000	72	491. Aaron Taylor	SEA	500,000	-9
362. Matt Ford	MIL	500,000	182	427. Lance Painter	STL	500,000	72	492. Tony Mounce	TEX	500,000	-10
363. Mark Malaska	TB	500,000	182	428. Pedro Astacio	NYM	500,000	72	493. Jerrod Riggan	NYM	500,000	-12
364. Chin-hui Tsao	COL	500,000	180	429. Aaron Heilman	NYM	500,000	71	494. Randy Choate	NYY	500,000	-13
365. Hector Carrasco	BAL	500,000	180	430. Jeff Tam	TOR	500,000	70	495. John Rocker	TB	500,000	-17
366. Eric Milton	MIN	760,000	178	431. Ramiro Mendoza	BOS	500,000	68	496. Dennys Reyes	ARI	500,000	-17
367. Jose Santiago	CLE	500,000	178	432. Bobby Seay	TB	500,000	67	497. Brad Thomas	MIN	500,000	-18
368. Mark Corey	PIT	500,000	175	433. Giovanni Carrara	SEA	500,000	66	498. Micah Bowie	OAK	500,000	-19
369. Jason Marquis	ATL	500,000	172	434. Josh Stewart	CHW	500,000	66	499. Matt Ginter	CHW	500,000	-19
370. Tony Fiore	MIN	500,000	172	435. Masao Kida	LA	500,000	65	500. Robert Ellis	TEX	500,000	-19
371. Matt Anderson	DET	500,000	169	436. Hector Almonte	MON	500,000	63	501. Jim Mann	PIT	500,000	-20
372. Todd Wellemeyer	CHC	500,000	168	437. Ryan Vogelsong	PIT	500,000	62	502. Jesus Sanchez	COL	500,000	-21
373. Jamey Wright	KC	500,000	166	438. Jeremy Fikac	OAK	500,000	60	503. Vic Darensbourg	MON	500,000	-21
374. Troy Brohawn	LA	500,000	162	439. Brandon Puffer	HOU	500,000	54	504. Clay Condrey	SD	500,000	-22
375. Jorge DePaula	NYY	500,000	160	440. James Baldwin	MIN	500,000	54	505. Gabe Molina	STL	500,000	-25
376. Nate Field	KC	500,000	157	441. Mike Porzio	CHW	500,000	53	506. Chad Paronto	CLE	500,000	-26
377. Mike Crudale	MIL	500,000	157	442. Robert Person	BOS	500,000	53	507. Brian Moehler	HOU	500,000	-28
378. Scott Strickland	NYM	500,000	155	443. Josh Pearce	STL	500,000	53	508. C.J. Nitkowski	TEX	500,000	-29
379. Nate Robertson	DET	500,000	155	444. Ryan Rupe	BOS	500,000	48	509. Chad Durbin	CLE	500,000	-30
380. Allen Levrault	FLA	500,000	155	445. Jayson Durocher	MIL	500,000	47	510. Bart Miadich	ANA	500,000	-32
381. Jason Anderson	NYM	500,000	147	446. Mario Ramos	TEX	500,000	44	511. Bret Prinz	NYY	500,000	-33
382. Jason Christiansen	SF	500,000	145	447. Jason Bere	CLE	500,000	42	512. Joe Valentine	CIN	500,000	-35
383. Justin Duchscherer	OAK	500,000	145	448. Brian Tallet	CLE	500,000	40	513. Chan Ho Park	TEX	500,000	-35
384. Joe Roa	SD	500,000	143	449. Brian Bowles	TOR	500,000	39	514. Brad Voyles	KC	500,000	-40
385. Nelson Cruz	COL	500,000	137	450. Josh Hancock	PHI	500,000	37	515. Alan Benes	CHC	500,000	-42
386. John Foster	MIL	500,000	136	451. Corey Thurman	TOR	500,000	36	516. Scott Downs	MON	500,000	-42
387. Matt Riley	BAL	500,000	134	452. Kevin Walker	SD	500,000	35	517. Jason Middlebrook	NYM	500,000	-43
388. Al Reyes	NYY	500,000	130	453. Jeff Austin	CIN	500,000	33	518. Britt Reames	MON	500,000	-43
389. Jaime Cerda	NYM	500,000	127	454. Charles Nagy	SD	500,000	32	519. Bob Howry	BOS	500,000	-47
390. Glendon Rusch	MIL	500,000	127	455. Russ Springer	STL	500,000	32	520. Randy Keisler	HOU	500,000	-49
391. Eric Eckenstahler	DET	500,000	125	456. Rich Rodriguez	ANA	500,000	31	521. Brian Powell	PHI	500,000	-49
392. Rodrigo Rosario	HOU	500,000	121	457. Ricky Bottalico	ARI	500,000	30	522. Jose Paniagua	CHW	500,000	-53
393. Todd Jones	BOS	500,000	121	458. Ryan Madson	PHI	500,000	30	523. Jason Young	COL	500,000	-56
394. Chad Harville	OAK	500,000	120	459. Ryan Drese	TEX	500,000	26	524. Pat Strange	NYM	500,000	-58
395. Sean Lowe	KC	500,000	115	460. David Cone	NYM	500,000	25	525. Mike Bacsik	NYM	500,000	-63
396. Jesse Orosco	MIN	500,000	114	461. Rodney Myers	LA	500,000	25	526. Blaine Neal	FLA	500,000	-65
397. Grant Roberts	NYM	500,000	113	462. Mickey Callaway	TEX	500,000	25	527. Duaner Sanchez	PIT	500,000	-65
398. A.J. Burnett	FLA	2,600,000	108	463. Jason Standridge	TB	500,000	24	528. Victor Alvarez	LA	500,000	-67
399. Pat Mahomes	PIT	500,000	108	464. Seth Etherton	CIN	500,000	22	529. Aaron Myette	PHI	500,000	-71
400. Hector Mercado	PHI	500,000	106	465. Shane Loux	DET	500,000	21	530. Ryan Jensen	SF	500,000	-74
401. Trevor Hoffman	SD	710,000	104	466. Geoff Geary	PHI	500,000	20	531. Sun-Woo Kim	MON	500,000	-76
402. Mike Venafro	HOU	500,000	104	467. Vinnie Chulk	TOR	500,000	17	532. Justin Wayne	FLA	500,000	-80
403. Steve Avery	DET	500,000	102	468. Jimmy Journell	STL	500,000	16	533. Sean Douglass	MIN	500,000	-82
404. Edgar Gonzalez	ARI	500,000	101	469. J.J. Putz	SEA	500,000	15	534. Scott Mullen	LA	500,000	-86
405. Steve Woodard	BOS	500,000	98	470. Ruben Quevedo	MIL	500,000	13	535. Joey Hamilton	CIN	500,000	-89
406. Eric Knott	MON	500,000	98	471. Steve Parris	TB	500,000	13	536. Kevin Olsen	FLA	500,000	-91
407. Scott Elarton	COL	500,000	98	472. Jimmy Haynes	CIN	500,000	12	537. Tim Drew	MON	500,000	-95
408. Toby Borland	FLA	500,000	98	473. Ryan Bukvich	KC	500,000	12	538. Joe Dawley	ATL	500,000	-98
409. Jaret Wright	ATL	500,000	98	474. Jeremy Hill	NYM	500,000	10	539. Albie Lopez	KC	500,000	-101
410. Jay Powell	TEX	500,000	97	475. Denny Neagle	COL	500,000	9	540. Josias Manzanillo	CIN	500,000	-101
411. Graeme Lloyd	KC	500,000	95	476. Rudy Seanez	CHC	500,000	9	541. Adam Johnson	MIN	500,000	-108
412. Mike Myers	ARI	500,000	95	477. Juan Dominguez	TEX	500,000	8	542. Dennis Tankersley	SD	500,000	-112
413. Bruce Chen	BOS	500,000	94	478. Orber Moreno	NYM	520,000	6	543. Jim Parque	TB	500,000	-117
414. Omar Daal	BAL	500,000	93	479. Dan Reichert	TOR	500,000	4	544. Pedro Borbon	STL	500,000	-124
415. David Lee	CLE	500,000	88	480. Victor Santos	TEX	500,000	4	545. John Wasdin	TOR	500,000	-147
416. Todd Ritchie	MIL	500,000	88	481. Dewon Brazelton	TB	500,000	4	546. Jimmy Anderson	SF	500,000	-148
417. Brandon Claussen	CIN	500,000	87	482. Manny Aybar	SF	500,000	2	547. Nick Bierbrodt	CLE	500,000	-149
418. Juan Alvarez	FLA	500,000	86	483. Kevin Tolar	BOS	500,000	-2	548. Matt White	CLE	500,000	-150
419. Carl Sadler	CLE	500,000	79	484. Mike Bynum	SD	500,000	-3	549. Vladimir Nunez	FLA	500,000	-171
420. Nate Bland	HOU	500,000	77	485. Carlton Loewer	SD	500,000	-4				

HITTERS

Rank		Team	$ Value	Points
1.	Albert Pujols	STL	7,490,000	2764
2.	Gary Sheffield	ATL	6,050,000	2645
3.	Todd Helton	COL	7,000,000	2594
4.	Alex Rodriguez	TEX	7,860,000	2506
5.	Carlos Delgado	TOR	6,230,000	2451
6.	Barry Bonds	SF	8,780,000	2437
7.	Manny Ramirez	BOS	7,210,000	2253
8.	Vernon Wells	TOR	4,910,000	2216
9.	Nomar Garciaparra	BOS	5,890,000	2184
10.	Carlos Beltran	KC	5,450,000	2179
11.	Alfonso Soriano	NYY	6,820,000	2177
12.	Bret Boone	SEA	4,870,000	2172
13.	Jim Thome	PHI	6,430,000	2165
14.	Preston Wilson	COL	4,580,000	2063
15.	Richie Sexson	MIL	4,700,000	2058
16.	Edgar Renteria	STL	4,410,000	2053
17.	Jeff Bagwell	HOU	5,790,000	2009
18.	Aubrey Huff	TB	4,290,000	1987
19.	Magglio Ordonez	CHW	5,840,000	1981
20.	Luis Gonzalez	ARI	5,600,000	1973
21.	Scott Rolen	STL	5,090,000	1971
22.	Javy Lopez	ATL	2,870,000	1962
23.	Jason Giambi	NYY	6,680,000	1941
24.	Carlos Lee	CHW	2,630,000	1928
25.	Bobby Abreu	PHI	4,190,000	1924
26.	Chipper Jones	ATL	4,530,000	1920
27.	Frank Thomas	CHW	3,990,000	1916
28.	Lance Berkman	HOU	6,010,000	1909
29.	Garret Anderson	ANA	5,330,000	1881
30.	Rafael Furcal	ATL	3,580,000	1838
31.	Derrek Lee	FLA	3,370,000	1832
32.	Rafael Palmeiro	TEX	3,780,000	1825
33.	Andruw Jones	ATL	5,210,000	1824
34.	Eric Chavez	OAK	4,560,000	1806
35.	Miguel Tejada	OAK	5,520,000	1804
36.	Richard Hidalgo	HOU	3,280,000	1804
37.	Marcus Giles	ATL	2,140,000	1796
38.	Brian Giles	SD	5,410,000	1786
39.	Ichiro Suzuki	SEA	4,570,000	1768
40.	Orlando Cabrera	MON	3,360,000	1750
41.	Sammy Sosa	CHC	6,750,000	1747
42.	Jim Edmonds	STL	5,160,000	1733
43.	Scott Podsednik	MIL	1,060,000	1721
44.	Jay Payton	COL	3,540,000	1720
45.	Juan Pierre	FLA	3,600,000	1717
46.	Carl Everett	CHW	4,080,000	1695
47.	David Ortiz	BOS	2,070,000	1681
48.	Aaron Boone	NYY	4,360,000	1678
49.	Bill Mueller	BOS	2,210,000	1670
50.	Jorge Posada	NYY	4,360,000	1657
51.	Trot Nixon	BOS	2,680,000	1641
52.	Dmitri Young	DET	1,590,000	1627
53.	Hank Blalock	TEX	1,480,000	1624
54.	Mike Lowell	FLA	4,370,000	1622
55.	Johnny Damon	BOS	3,070,000	1602
56.	Vladimir Guerrero	MON	6,730,000	1596
57.	Raul Ibanez	KC	3,170,000	1589
58.	Reggie Sanders	PIT	2,440,000	1586
59.	Michael Young	TEX	2,480,000	1584
60.	Randy Winn	SEA	1,520,000	1563
61.	Geoff Jenkins	MIL	3,270,000	1562
62.	Edgar Martinez	SEA	4,420,000	1560
63.	Jeff Conine	FLA	2,510,000	1557
64.	Larry Walker	COL	3,710,000	1545
65.	Jose Guillen	OAK	1,080,000	1541
66.	Shawn Green	LA	4,130,000	1530
67.	Angel Berroa	KC	800,000	1530
68.	Hideki Matsui	NYY	4,660,000	1529
69.	Moises Alou	CHC	3,000,000	1529
70.	Ivan Rodriguez	FLA	3,620,000	1528
71.	Juan Encarnacion	FLA	1,840,000	1523
72.	Jeff Kent	HOU	5,560,000	1522
73.	Kenny Lofton	CHC	1,480,000	1522
74.	Steve Finley	ARI	2,680,000	1519
75.	Raul Mondesi	ARI	4,160,000	1518
76.	Kevin Millar	BOS	4,210,000	1499
77.	Aramis Ramirez	CHC	2,870,000	1498
78.	Jay Gibbons	BAL	3,220,000	1483
79.	Rocco Baldelli	TB	2,580,000	1467
80.	Shannon Stewart	MIN	2,360,000	1454
81.	Torii Hunter	MIN	2,850,000	1450
82.	Marquis Grissom	SF	1,860,000	1437
83.	Brad Wilkerson	MON	1,720,000	1411
84.	Erubiel Durazo	OAK	4,510,000	1410
85.	Tim Salmon	ANA	2,190,000	1407
86.	Jose Vidro	MON	3,660,000	1401
87.	Todd Walker	BOS	3,370,000	1396
88.	Placido Polanco	PHI	1,500,000	1392
89.	Craig Biggio	HOU	3,470,000	1387
90.	Carl Crawford	TB	1,500,000	1383
91.	Mark Loretta	SD	1,110,000	1373
92.	Jason Kendall	PIT	2,650,000	1365
93.	Corey Koskie	MIN	2,430,000	1345
94.	Travis Lee	TB	560,000	1329
95.	Jason Varitek	BOS	2,660,000	1327
96.	Mike Cameron	SEA	1,290,000	1325
97.	Scott Spiezio	ANA	560,000	1306
98.	Luis Castillo	FLA	3,240,000	1304
99.	Jacque Jones	MIN	1,840,000	1300
100.	Derek Jeter	NYY	4,320,000	1293
101.	Jose Cruz	SF	4,120,000	1292
102.	Doug Mientkiewicz	MIN	1,030,000	1290
103.	Mike Lieberthal	PHI	2,760,000	1288
104.	Mark Teixeira	TEX	1,730,000	1288
105.	Milton Bradley	CLE	2,530,000	1287
106.	Jose Valentin	CHW	3,070,000	1284
107.	Morgan Ensberg	HOU	620,000	1281
108.	Shea Hillenbrand	ARI	3,750,000	1278
109.	Joe Randa	KC	980,000	1276
110.	Rondell White	KC	2,340,000	1268
111.	Jody Gerut	CLE	560,000	1264
112.	Sean Casey	CIN	1,630,000	1254
113.	Frank Catalanotto	TOR	3,100,000	1250
114.	Mike Sweeney	KC	4,250,000	1248
115.	A.J. Pierzynski	MIN	2,540,000	1232
116.	Jimmy Rollins	PHI	3,370,000	1213
117.	Ramon Hernandez	OAK	1,860,000	1206
118.	John Olerud	SEA	1,710,000	1195
119.	Cliff Floyd	NYM	1,820,000	1178
120.	Bernie Williams	NYY	4,630,000	1175
121.	Vinny Castilla	ATL	1,400,000	1172
122.	Eric Hinske	TOR	1,440,000	1171
123.	Tony Batista	BAL	1,200,000	1171
124.	D'Angelo Jimenez	CIN	2,360,000	1169
125.	Marlon Byrd	PHI	550,000	1164
126.	Jeromy Burnitz	LA	1,250,000	1162
127.	Alex Cintron	ARI	710,000	1153
128.	Ty Wigginton	NYM	1,760,000	1152
129.	Eric Young	SF	2,570,000	1150
130.	Melvin Mora	BAL	2,360,000	1132
131.	Joe Crede	CHW	1,360,000	1127
132.	Tino Martinez	STL	1,560,000	1123
133.	Adam Dunn	CIN	3,640,000	1118
134.	Edgardo Alfonzo	SF	1,210,000	1113
135.	Casey Blake	CLE	540,000	1112
136.	Adam Kennedy	ANA	500,000	1103
137.	Luis Matos	BAL	650,000	1098
138.	Desi Relaford	KC	1,950,000	1087
139.	Chris Stynes	COL	1,300,000	1086
140.	Marlon Anderson	TB	500,000	1078
141.	Alex Sanchez	DET	500,000	1076
142.	Eric Byrnes	OAK	760,000	1066
143.	Wil Cordero	MON	500,000	1064
144.	Bobby Kielty	TOR	500,000	1056
145.	Juan Gonzalez	TEX	3,410,000	1054
146.	Nick Johnson	NYY	1,940,000	1053
147.	Sean Burroughs	SD	540,000	1052
148.	Alex Gonzalez	FLA	1,450,000	1041
149.	Reed Johnson	TOR	500,000	1041
150.	Matt Stairs	PIT	500,000	1034
151.	Julio Lugo	TB	500,000	1033
152.	Ronnie Belliard	COL	500,000	1026
153.	Josh Phelps	TOR	1,140,000	1018
154.	Adrian Beltre	LA	500,000	1018
155.	Corey Patterson	CHC	2,820,000	1014
156.	Scott Hatteberg	OAK	500,000	1014
157.	Robert Fick	ATL	1,110,000	1012
158.	Mark Grudzielanek	CHC	510,000	1004
159.	Wes Helms	MIL	500,000	1004
160.	Cristian Guzman	MIN	500,000	1002
161.	Ryan Klesko	SD	1,770,000	997
162.	Aaron Guiel	KC	500,000	990
163.	Brian Roberts	BAL	500,000	986
164.	Alex S. Gonzalez	CHC	1,030,000	973
165.	Matt Lawton	CLE	500,000	973
166.	Jeff DaVanon	ANA	500,000	971
167.	Mark Ellis	OAK	2,300,000	964
168.	Rich Aurilia	SF	2,120,000	959
169.	Craig Monroe	DET	500,000	942
170.	Luis Rivas	MIN	500,000	936
171.	Jason Phillips	NYM	610,000	931
172.	Roberto Alomar	CHW	1,810,000	928
173.	Michael Tucker	KC	500,000	924
174.	Greg Myers	TOR	590,000	923
175.	Paul Lo Duca	LA	3,200,000	922
176.	Pat Burrell	PHI	2,570,000	920
177.	J.D. Drew	STL	1,080,000	916
178.	Randall Simon	CHC	500,000	914
179.	Troy Glaus	ANA	2,610,000	903
180.	Ray Durham	SF	2,190,000	901
181.	Craig Wilson	PIT	550,000	899
182.	Terrence Long	OAK	700,000	896
183.	Carlos Guillen	SEA	500,000	893
184.	Ben Broussard	CLE	500,000	891
185.	Carlos Pena	DET	500,000	889
186.	Bengie Molina	ANA	500,000	876
187.	Endy Chavez	MON	580,000	875
188.	Charles Johnson	COL	730,000	873
189.	Orlando Hudson	TOR	500,000	871
190.	Matthew LeCroy	MIN	500,000	868

Rank	Team	$ Value	Points	Rank	Team	$ Value	Points	Rank	Team	$ Value	Points
191. Roger Cedeno	NYM	500,000	866	255. Timo Perez	NYM	500,000	545	319. Yorvit Torrealba	SF	500,000	368
192. Bobby Higginson	DET	500,000	865	256. Bo Hart	STL	1,100,000	542	320. Russell Branyan	CIN	500,000	364
193. Paul Konerko	CHW	2,850,000	861	257. Brad Ausmus	HOU	500,000	530	321. Billy McMillon	OAK	500,000	358
194. Mark Kotsay	SD	610,000	861	258. Brian Buchanan	SD	500,000	528	322. Shawn Wooten	ANA	500,000	358
195. Ken Harvey	KC	500,000	861	259. Chone Figgins	ANA	500,000	524	323. Raul Gonzalez	NYM	500,000	351
196. J.T. Snow	SF	2,090,000	839	260. Orlando Palmeiro	STL	500,000	524	324. Jose Macias	MON	500,000	350
197. Deivi Cruz	BAL	500,000	839	261. Miguel Cairo	STL	500,000	523	325. Dave Ross	LA	500,000	349
198. Benito Santiago	SF	1,500,000	836	262. Danny Bautista	ARI	500,000	518	326. Sandy Alomar Jr.	CHW	500,000	346
199. Austin Kearns	CIN	4,960,000	830	263. Gabe Kapler	BOS	500,000	517	327. Mark Bellhorn	COL	850,000	343
200. Gary Matthews Jr.	SD	500,000	826	264. Chris Singleton	OAK	500,000	514	328. Eric Owens	ANA	500,000	336
201. Jack Wilson	PIT	500,000	819	265. Robby Hammock	ARI	500,000	508	329. Orlando Merced	HOU	500,000	334
202. Junior Spivey	ARI	1,450,000	806	266. Alex Cora	LA	500,000	503	330. Ryan Ludwick	CLE	500,000	334
203. Dave Roberts	LA	780,000	805	267. Tomas Perez	PHI	500,000	502	331. Todd Pratt	PHI	500,000	334
204. John Vander Wal	MIL	500,000	791	268. Damian Miller	CHC	500,000	499	332. Ben Grieve	TB	500,000	329
205. Adam Everett	HOU	500,000	789	269. Jerry Hairston Jr.	BAL	500,000	494	333. Doug Mirabelli	BOS	500,000	328
206. Jason LaRue	CIN	500,000	789	270. Brian Jordan	LA	920,000	492	334. Bill Hall	MIL	500,000	326
207. Keith Ginter	MIL	500,000	788	271. Brent Mayne	KC	500,000	489	335. Brandon Phillips	CLE	500,000	323
208. Eduardo Perez	STL	500,000	769	272. Julio Franco	ATL	500,000	489	336. Todd Greene	TEX	500,000	319
209. Miguel Cabrera	FLA	500,000	767	273. Craig Counsell	ARI	500,000	488	337. Troy O'Leary	CHC	500,000	312
210. Robin Ventura	LA	1,160,000	763	274. Tom Wilson	TOR	500,000	487	338. Al Martin	TB	500,000	310
211. David Eckstein	ANA	950,000	752	275. Omar Vizquel	CLE	790,000	484	339. Jason Bay	PIT	500,000	307
212. Jose Reyes	NYM	500,000	728	276. Chad Moeller	ARI	500,000	476	340. Michael Ryan	MIN	500,000	307
213. Jolbert Cabrera	LA	500,000	721	277. Ramon Martinez	CHC	500,000	473	341. Lou Merloni	BOS	500,000	304
214. Toby Hall	TB	500,000	718	278. Hee Seop Choi	CHC	1,820,000	461	342. Lew Ford	MIN	500,000	302
215. Larry Bigbie	BAL	500,000	717	279. Fernando Vina	STL	500,000	459	343. Brian Banks	FLA	500,000	300
216. Brady Clark	MIL	500,000	712	280. Barry Larkin	CIN	500,000	456	344. Jamey Carroll	MON	500,000	299
217. Geoff Blum	HOU	500,000	706	281. Mark DeRosa	ATL	500,000	452	345. Willie Bloomquist	SEA	500,000	297
218. Shane Spencer	TEX	500,000	700	282. Lyle Overbay	ARI	500,000	451	346. Keith Osik	MIL	500,000	296
219. Eric Karros	CHC	500,000	698	283. Einar Diaz	TEX	500,000	449	347. Rey Ordonez	TB	500,000	292
220. Ramon Vazquez	SD	500,000	697	284. Brook Fordyce	BAL	500,000	448	348. Jeffrey Hammonds	SF	500,000	288
221. Mike Bordick	TOR	500,000	692	285. Juan Castro	CIN	500,000	441	349. Doug Glanville	CHC	500,000	286
222. Xavier Nady	SD	500,000	687	286. Mark McLemore	SEA	500,000	440	350. Rey Sanchez	SEA	500,000	284
223. Eric Munson	DET	500,000	681	287. Michael Barrett	MON	500,000	439	351. Dave Berg	TOR	500,000	279
224. Ricky Ledee	PHI	500,000	679	288. Karim Garcia	NYY	500,000	438	352. Denny Hocking	MIN	500,000	277
225. Travis Hafner	CLE	500,000	676	289. David Dellucci	NYY	500,000	437	353. Kevin Mench	TEX	500,000	277
226. Andres Galarraga	SF	500,000	672	290. Miguel Olivo	CHW	500,000	435	354. Joe McEwing	NYM	500,000	275
227. Chris Woodward	TOR	500,000	665	291. Ramon Santiago	DET	500,000	435	355. Felipe Lopez	CIN	500,000	273
228. Tony Graffanino	CHW	500,000	659	292. Ellis Burks	CLE	1,180,000	433	356. Bobby Estalella	COL	500,000	271
229. Damian Rolls	TB	500,000	658	293. Vance Wilson	NYM	500,000	433	357. Mike Kinkade	LA	500,000	270
230. Coco Crisp	CLE	500,000	655	294. Dan Wilson	SEA	500,000	423	358. Jared Sandberg	TB	500,000	268
231. Mike Piazza	NYM	2,980,000	654	295. Ben Davis	SEA	500,000	422	359. Chase Utley	PHI	500,000	265
232. Juan Uribe	COL	500,000	653	296. Tom Goodwin	CHC	500,000	421	360. Henry Mateo	MON	500,000	265
233. Jose Hernandez	PIT	2,270,000	650	297. Todd Hollandsworth	FLA	500,000	416	361. Jose Vizcaino	HOU	500,000	261
234. Brad Fullmer	ANA	1,780,000	647	298. Darin Erstad	ANA	960,000	415	362. Matt Williams	ARI	500,000	261
235. Phil Nevin	SD	2,210,000	643	299. Josh Bard	CLE	500,000	415	363. Adam Melhuse	OAK	500,000	260
236. Dustan Mohr	MIN	500,000	639	300. Tony Womack	CHC	500,000	414	364. Carlos Febles	KC	500,000	259
237. Mike Matheny	STL	1,310,000	637	301. Neifi Perez	SF	500,000	411	365. Gregg Zaun	COL	500,000	258
238. Pedro Feliz	SF	500,000	636	302. Laynce Nix	TEX	1,020,000	410	366. Kerry Robinson	STL	500,000	253
239. B.J. Surhoff	BAL	500,000	631	303. Greg Norton	COL	500,000	405	367. Rod Barajas	ARI	500,000	253
240. Ruben Sierra	NYY	500,000	626	304. Jeff Reboulet	PIT	500,000	405	368. Reggie Taylor	CIN	500,000	251
241. Ron Calloway	MON	500,000	623	305. Gary Bennett	SD	500,000	402	369. Antonio Perez	TB	500,000	250
242. Carlos Baerga	ARI	500,000	608	306. David Segui	BAL	500,000	399	370. Jhonny Peralta	CLE	500,000	248
243. Royce Clayton	MIL	500,000	603	307. Juan Rivera	NYY	500,000	394	371. Joe Vitiello	MON	500,000	243
244. Tike Redman	PIT	500,000	595	308. Kevin Witt	DET	500,000	392	372. Enrique Wilson	NYY	500,000	240
245. Ken Griffey Jr.	CIN	3,690,000	585	309. Rob Mackowiak	PIT	500,000	390	373. Tim Laker	CLE	500,000	238
246. Fred McGriff	LA	970,000	579	310. David Bell	PHI	710,000	382	374. Jeff Cirillo	SEA	500,000	235
247. Eddie Perez	MIL	500,000	579	311. Mike DiFelice	KC	500,000	382	375. John Flaherty	NYY	500,000	232
248. Matt Kata	ARI	500,000	577	312. Jason Michaels	PHI	500,000	375	376. Wily Mo Pena	CIN	500,000	229
249. Brian Schneider	MON	500,000	576	313. Shane Halter	DET	500,000	375	377. Adam Piatt	TB	500,000	227
250. Tony Clark	NYM	500,000	572	314. Damian Jackson	BOS	500,000	373	378. Alex Escobar	CLE	500,000	227
251. Warren Morris	DET	500,000	571	315. Brandon Inge	DET	500,000	372	379. Jeremy Giambi	BOS	500,000	223
252. Todd Zeile	MON	500,000	563	316. Aaron Rowand	CHW	500,000	370	380. Victor Martinez	CLE	500,000	220
253. Cesar Izturis	LA	500,000	559	317. Ryan Freel	CIN	500,000	370	381. Dave Hansen	SD	500,000	218
254. Abraham O. Nunez	PIT	500,000	556	318. Brian Daubach	CHW	500,000	369	382. Paul Bako	CHC	500,000	217

Rank	Team	$ Value	Points	Rank	Team	$ Value	Points	Rank	Team	$ Value	Points
383. Chris Gomez	MIN	500,000	216	443. Greg Colbrunn	SEA	500,000	117	503. Wilkin Ruan	LA	500,000	24
384. Kelly Stinnett	PHI	500,000	213	444. A.J. Hinch	DET	500,000	114	504. Felix Escalona	BAL	500,000	21
385. Geronimo Gil	BAL	500,000	208	445. Greg Vaughn	COL	500,000	111	505. Dave Matranga	HOU	500,000	20
386. Jermaine Dye	OAK	710,000	206	446. Angel Santos	CLE	500,000	108	506. Carlos Mendez	BAL	500,000	18
387. Keith Lockhart	SD	500,000	199	447. Jeff Duncan	NYM	500,000	107	507. Jose Leon	BAL	500,000	15
388. Mendy Lopez	KC	500,000	198	448. Jayson Werth	TOR	500,000	106	508. Jose Molina	ANA	500,000	15
389. Michael Cuddyer	MIN	500,000	198	449. Rickey Henderson	LA	500,000	106	509. Rontrez Johnson	ATL	500,000	14
390. John Mabry	SEA	500,000	194	450. Gerald Laird	TEX	500,000	103	510. Ron Gant	OAK	500,000	12
391. Quinton McCracken	ARI	500,000	194	451. Brent Butler	COL	500,000	99	511. Chad Allen	FLA	500,000	10
392. Ruben Mateo	CIN	500,000	188	452. Benji Gil	CLE	500,000	97	512. J.J. Davis	PIT	500,000	10
393. Mark Sweeney	COL	500,000	186	453. Julius Matos	KC	500,000	97	513. Ken Huckaby	TOR	500,000	10
394. Ron Coomer	LA	500,000	184	454. Kevin Young	MIN	500,000	97	514. Mark Johnson	OAK	500,000	10
395. Justin Morneau	MIN	500,000	183	455. Henry Blanco	ATL	500,000	95	515. Bobby Hill	PIT	500,000	9
396. Adam Riggs	ANA	500,000	181	456. Ramon Nivar	TEX	500,000	93	516. Humberto Cota	PIT	500,000	9
397. Erick Almonte	NYY	500,000	180	457. Tom Prince	KC	500,000	93	517. Jamal Strong	SEA	520,000	6
398. Jack Cust	BAL	500,000	180	458. Khalil Greene	SD	1,520,000	89	518. Curtis Pride	NYY	500,000	6
399. Willie Harris	CHW	500,000	179	459. Marty Cordova	BAL	500,000	86	519. Joe Thurston	LA	500,000	6
400. Ben Petrick	DET	500,000	178	460. Nick Punto	PHI	500,000	85	520. Kevin Cash	TOR	500,000	6
401. Donnie Sadler	TEX	500,000	176	461. Lenny Harris	FLA	500,000	83	521. Esteban German	OAK	500,000	3
402. Eli Marrero	STL	500,000	172	462. Todd Hundley	LA	500,000	82	522. Matt Walbeck	DET	500,000	3
403. So Taguchi	STL	500,000	171	463. Danny Klassen	DET	500,000	81	523. Morgan Burkhart	KC	500,000	2
404. Andres Torres	DET	500,000	168	464. Gene Kingsale	DET	500,000	78	524. Ryan Langerhans	ATL	500,000	2
405. Ray Olmedo	CIN	500,000	168	465. Chris Magruder	CLE	500,000	77	525. Julio Ramirez	ANA	500,000	1
406. Mark Grace	ARI	500,000	167	466. Wilson Delgado	ANA	500,000	77	526. Matt Cepicky	MON	500,000	1
407. Matt Franco	ATL	500,000	165	467. Robert Machado	BAL	500,000	74	527. Michael Rivera	CHW	500,000	1
408. Rene Reyes	COL	500,000	164	468. Marcus Thames	TEX	500,000	71	528. Chad Hermansen	LA	500,000	0
409. Omar Infante	DET	500,000	163	469. Andy Fox	FLA	500,000	70	529. David Kelton	CHC	500,000	0
410. John McDonald	CLE	500,000	162	470. George Lombard	TB	500,000	69	530. Colin Porter	HOU	500,000	-1
411. Dee Brown	KC	500,000	159	471. Raul Chavez	HOU	500,000	68	531. Drew Henson	NYY	500,000	-1
412. Tyler Houston	PHI	500,000	159	472. Shane Victorino	LA	500,000	68	532. Jason Smith	TB	500,000	-1
413. Javier Valentin	TB	500,000	157	473. Ruben Rivera	BAL	500,000	64	533. Pat Borders	SEA	500,000	-1
414. Darren Bragg	ATL	500,000	156	474. Armando Rios	CHW	500,000	63	534. Brandon Larson	CIN	500,000	-2
415. Ramon Castro	FLA	500,000	155	475. Jason Conti	MIL	500,000	54	535. Travis Chapman	PHI	500,000	-2
416. Mo Vaughn	NYM	1,070,000	153	476. Jesse Garcia	ATL	500,000	52	536. Trey Lunsford	SF	500,000	-2
417. Jason Tyner	TB	500,000	153	477. Pablo Ozuna	COL	500,000	52	537. Gookie Dawkins	KC	500,000	-3
418. Terry Shumpert	TB	500,000	153	478. Chris Truby	TB	500,000	50	538. Herbert Perry	TEX	500,000	-3
419. Jason Jones	TEX	500,000	152	479. Josh Paul	CHC	500,000	49	539. Eric Valent	CIN	500,000	-4
420. Ryan Christenson	TEX	500,000	148	480. Chris Richard	COL	500,000	46	540. Mike Lamb	TEX	500,000	-4
421. Jason Lane	HOU	500,000	145	481. Wiki Gonzalez	SD	500,000	46	541. Dane Sardinha	CIN	500,000	-5
422. Howie Clark	TOR	500,000	144	482. Bubba Trammell	NYY	500,000	45	542. Daryle Ward	LA	500,000	-5
423. Marco Scutaro	OAK	500,000	140	483. Eric Bruntlett	HOU	500,000	45	543. Zach Sorensen	CLE	500,000	-6
424. Mike Redmond	FLA	500,000	140	484. Luis Ugueto	SEA	500,000	45	544. Bill Haselman	BOS	500,000	-7
425. Adam Hyzdu	PIT	500,000	137	485. Tsuyoshi Shinjo	NYM	500,000	45	545. Bill Selby	STL	500,000	-7
426. Alfredo Amezaga	ANA	500,000	136	486. Trenidad Hubbard	CHC	500,000	43	546. Lou Collier	BOS	500,000	-7
427. Carlos Rivera	PIT	500,000	136	487. Gerald Williams	FLA	500,000	42	547. Chad Kreuter	TEX	500,000	-10
428. Fernando Tatis	MON	500,000	136	488. Cody Ransom	SF	500,000	40	548. Joe Girardi	STL	500,000	-10
429. Brian L. Hunter	HOU	500,000	135	489. Marvin Benard	SF	500,000	39	549. Ernie Young	DET	500,000	-11
430. Mike Mordecai	FLA	500,000	133	490. Ricky Gutierrez	CLE	500,000	38	550. Alex Prieto	MIN	500,000	-14
431. Pokey Reese	PIT	500,000	133	491. Alberto Castillo	SF	500,000	36	551. Bubba Crosby	NYY	500,000	-15
432. Todd Sears	SD	500,000	131	492. Charles Gipson	NYY	500,000	35	552. Bobby Crosby	OAK	1,520,000	-18
433. Edwards Guzman	MON	500,000	129	493. Corky Miller	CIN	500,000	35	553. Augie Ojeda	CHC	500,000	-18
434. Robb Quinlan	ANA	500,000	128	494. Todd Linden	SF	500,000	35	554. Jason Grabowski	OAK	500,000	-18
435. Tim Hummel	CIN	500,000	126	495. Johnny Estrada	ATL	500,000	31	555. Jason Romano	LA	500,000	-21
436. Chris Widger	STL	500,000	125	496. Freddy Sanchez	PIT	500,000	30	556. Craig Paquette	STL	500,000	-26
437. Dave McCarty	BOS	500,000	125	497. Damion Easley	TB	500,000	29	557. Dean Palmer	DET	500,000	-28
438. Donaldo Mendez	SD	500,000	125	498. Joe Borchard	CHW	500,000	27	558. Brent Abernathy	KC	500,000	-29
439. Michael Restovich	MIN	500,000	125	499. Brandon Berger	KC	500,000	26	559. Hiram Bocachica	DET	500,000	-34
440. Frank Menechino	OAK	500,000	124	500. Adrian Brown	BOS	500,000	25	560. Enrique Cruz	MIL	500,000	-70
441. Jose Morban	BAL	500,000	124	501. Chris Latham	NYY	500,000	25				
442. Jeff Liefer	TB	500,000	123	502. Jay Bell	NYM	500,000	24				